International Financial Statistics on CD-ROM

The IMF's *International Financial Statistics (IFS)* is available on CD-ROM. The *IFS* CD-ROM includes historical data not found in the monthly printed issues, and the data are presented with a greater degree of precision than in our magnetic tapes. Software included on the CD-ROM supports data extraction and downloading, and provides multilingual (English, French, and Spanish) instructions and help screens.

Hardware and Software Requirements

IBM compatible personal computer with minimum 640K RAM memory–(500K for program)

Hard disk drive

CD-ROM disc drive

DOS 3.0 or higher

Microsoft CD-ROM extensions

IMPORTANT NOTE

A subscription to *IFS* on CD-ROM requires adherence to a license agreement that accompanies each disc. Information retrieved from the *IFS* disc may be used only for the Licensee's own internal purposes. It may not be sold, rented, or otherwise provided to any third party. Subscription rates are available upon request for additional services such as networking or timesharing use of the product.

— Order Now —

International Financial Statistics on CD-ROM

ORDER FORM

❑ Please enter ________ annual single-user PC subscription(s) for the *IFS* CD-ROM which includes 12 monthly issues (discs), software to access the data, documentation, and priority mail delivery for US$1,000.

❑ A special single-user PC subscription which includes 4 quarterly issues (discs) is available only to full-time university professors and full-time students for US$350. (Libraries must order the regular subscription option.)

XF110

IMF Account # ________________ *(if known)*

Name ________________

Institution ________________

Address ________________

____

Country ________________ Postal Code ________________

Telephone ________________ Fax ________________

Payment Options

❑ Payment enclosed. ❑ Please send pro-forma invoice.
(All subscriptions will commence with receipt of payment.)

Please debit my credit card account US$________________

❑ American Express ❑ MasterCard ❑ VISA

Account # ________ - ________ - ________ - ________

Expiry Date ________________

Signature ________________
(required on all orders)

Return completed order form to:

International Monetary Fund
Publication Services
700 19th Street, N.W., Suite 10-540
Washington, D.C. 20431 U.S.A.

Or call:

Telephone: (202) 623-7430 Telefax: (202) 623-7201
Cable Address: INTERFUND

For further price information:

❑ MULTIPLE COPIES ❑ PC NETWORK
❑ TIME-SHARING

Please
affix
postage

Publication Services
International Monetary Fund
700 19th Street, N.W., Suite 10-540
Washington, D.C. 20431 U.S.A.

BALANCE OF PAYMENTS STATISTICS YEARBOOK

Part 1: Country Tables

EXPANDED COVERAGE

In the previous (1995) *Yearbook*, balance of payments data were published for the first time according to the methodology and format of the fifth edition of the *Balance of Payments Manual (BPM5)*. The conversion of the historical series to the format of the *BPM5* was undertaken by the Fund's Statistics Department in consultation with its member countries. In 1996, a similar conversion was completed for data on stocks of external financial assets and liabilities. These stock data, for those countries that report them, are presented in Part 1 of this *Yearbook* under the standard components of the international investment position (IIP), as set forth in the *BPM5*.

Part 3 of this *Yearbook* also includes, for the first time, technical reviews describing, for most countries, the methodologies, compilation practices, and data sources used by the countries in compiling their balance of payments statistics; this information was reported to the Fund by the countries.

Other Statistical Publications of the International Monetary Fund

International Financial Statistics (IFS)
Acknowledged as a standard source of statistics on all aspects of international and domestic finance, *IFS* publishes, for most countries of the world, current data on exchange rates, international liquidity, international banking, money and banking, interest rates, prices, production, international transactions (including balance of payments), government finance, and national accounts. Information is presented in tables for specific countries and in tables for area and world aggregates. *IFS* is published monthly and annually in English, French, and Spanish. *Price:* Subscription price is US$230 a year (US$115 to university faculty and students) for twelve monthly issues and the yearbook. Single copy price is US$27 for a monthly issue and US$60 for a yearbook issue.

Direction of Trade Statistics (DOTS)
Quarterly issues of this publication provide, for about 152 countries, tables with current data (or estimates) on the value of imports from and exports to their most important trading partners. In addition, similar summary tables for the world, industrial countries, and developing countries are included. The yearbook provides, for the most recent seven years, detailed trade data by country for approximately 184 countries, the world, and major areas. *Price*: Subscription price is US$104 a year (US$52 to university faculty and students) for the quarterly issues and the yearbook. Price for a quarterly issue only is US$22, the yearbook only is US$34, and a guide only is US$12.50.

Government Finance Statistics Yearbook (GFSY)
This annual publication provides detailed data on revenue, grants, expenditure, lending, financing, and debt of central governments and indicates the amounts represented by social security funds and extrabudgetary operations. Also provided are data for state and local governments, information on the institutional units of government, and lists of sources of information. *Price*: US$58.

A Manual on Government Finance Statistics
Issued in 1986, this manual covers concepts, definitions, and procedures for the compilation of government finance statistics. Emphasis is placed on summarizing and organizing statistics appropriately for analysis, planning, and policy formulation. The text focuses on transactions (taxes, expenditures, borrowing, and lending) and on debt. *Price*: US$10.

Balance of Payments Manual
Revised in 1993, the fifth edition of the manual addresses significant changes that have occurred in international transactions since the fourth edition was published in 1977 and presents salient revisions in the structure and classification of international accounts. The new edition also reflects a major shift in orientation that accords prominence to stocks of external financial assets and liabilities (the international investment position) as well as to balance of payments transactions. *Price*: US$27.50.

CD-ROM and Tape Subscriptions

International Financial Statistics (IFS) is available on CD-ROM disk and 9-track computer tape. *GFSY, BOPSY,* and *DOTS* are available monthly on 9-track computer tape. *Price of the CD-ROM*: US$1,000 a year for single users (US$350 to university faculty and students); multiple user options are available. *Price of a tape subscription per publication (includes corresponding printed publication)*: US$1,850 a year to single users (US$950 to university faculty and students) and US$7,500 a year to time sharers.

Subscription Packages

Combined Subscription Package
The combined subscription package includes all issues of *IFS, DOTS, BOPSY, GFSY,* and *Staff Papers*, the Fund's economic journal. *Combined subscription price:* US$360 a year (US$180 to university faculty and students). Airspeed delivery available at additional cost; please inquire.

Combined Statistical Yearbook Subscription
This subscription comprises the *BOPSY,* the *GFSY*, and the yearbooks to *IFS* and *DOTS* at a combined rate of US$150. Because of different publication dates of the four yearbooks, it may take up to one year to service an order. Airspeed delivery available at additional cost; please inquire.

Address orders to
Publication Services, IMF, Washington, DC, USA 20431
Telephone (202) 623-7430 Telefax (202) 623-7201

Note: Prices include the cost of delivery by surface mail. Enhanced delivery is available for an additional charge.

Balance of Payments Statistics Yearbook

Part 1: Country Tables

1996

INTERNATIONAL MONETARY FUND

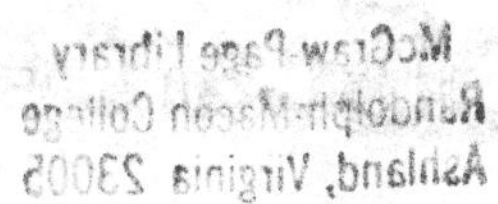

Balance of Payments Statistics Yearbook
Volume 47, Part 1: Country Tables, 1996

Prepared by Balance of Payments and
External Debt Divisions I and II, IMF Statistics Department
John B. McLenaghan, Director, Statistics Department
Mahinder S. Gill, Assistant Director for
Balance of Payments and External Debt Division I
Richard T. Stillson, Chief,
Balance of Payments and External Debt Division II

For information related to this publication, please:
fax the Public Affairs Division at (202) 623-6278,
or write Public Affairs Division
International Monetary Fund
Washington, D.C. 20431
or telephone the Statistics Department at (202) 623-6180.
For copyright inquiries, please fax the Editorial Division at (202) 623-6579.
For purchases only, please contact Publication Services (see information below).

Balance of Payments Statistics Yearbook (BOPSY): Issued in three parts, this annual publication contains balance of payments and international investment position data. Part 1 provides detailed tables on balance of payments statistics for approximately 160 countries and international investment position data for 35 countries. Part 2 presents tables of regional and world totals of major balance of payments components. Part 3 contains descriptions of methodologies, compilation practices, and data sources used by reporting countries.

Cutoff date: September 30, 1996

Price: US$64, which includes the cost of delivery by surface mail, for the three-part yearbook. Enhanced delivery is available for an additional charge.

Address orders to:
International Monetary Fund
Attention: Publication Services
Washington, D.C. 20431
U.S.A.
Telephone (202) 623-7430
Telefax (202) 623-7201

ISSN 0252-3035
ISBN 1-55775-592-2
Recycled paper

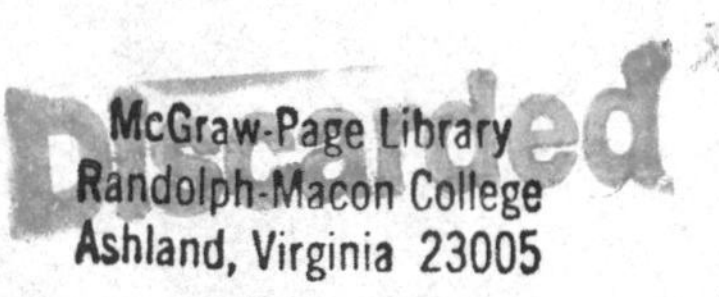

Table of Contents

Country Tables

Table of Contents *(concluded)*

INTRODUCTION[1]

Volume 47 of the *Balance of Payments Statistics Yearbook (Yearbook)*, published by the International Monetary Fund (the Fund), contains balance of payments data that member countries have reported to the Fund. The Fund is indebted to these countries for their cooperation in providing these data. For some of these countries, some data have been supplemented by details Fund economists have derived from other sources. This volume of the *Yearbook* continues the features introduced in Volume 46 and offers some new ones. Specifically, for the first time, Volume 47 contains international investment position (IIP) data in the format set forth in the fifth edition of the Fund's *Balance of Payments Manual (BPM5)* for those countries that compile such data. Also, in a new Part 3 of the *Yearbook*, Volume 47 breaks new ground by publishing detailed reviews of the methodologies, compilation practices, and sources of data for most of the countries included in the volume.

As in Volume 46, balance of payments data are presented in this *Yearbook* in accordance with the standard components of the *BPM5*.[2] The *BPM5*, which the Fund published in September 1993,[3] introduced a number of methodological changes in the compilation of balance of payments data. These changes are described in detail in chapter I of the *BPM5* and are summarized in a text box on page ix in this volume. In addition, following Volume 46, data presented in this *Yearbook* under the standard components of the *BPM5* are accompanied by a set of data codes developed jointly by the Fund, the Organization for Economic Cooperation and Development (OECD), and the Statistical Office of the European Union (Eurostat). The structure of these codes is explained in an annex to this introduction. This volume, however, unlike its predecessors, no longer presents quarterly balance of payments data for those countries that report quarterly balance of payments statistics to the Fund. Such quarterly data will continue to be published in the monthly Fund publication *International Financial Statistics (IFS)*.

Data conversion work undertaken by the Fund staff has made possible the presentation in the *BPM5* format of both historical data from the Fund's database and more recent statistics reported by those member countries who are still compiling their data in the format of the fourth edition of the *Balance of Payments Manual (BPM4)*. In 1995, the Fund staff developed formulas to transform reported balance of payments data for each country in the Fund's database to approximate the *BPM5* methodology and presentation. Converted data for each reporting country were sent to the respective authorities for review, and their comments were incorporated in the new *BPM5* database. In 1996, the Fund staff, in collaboration with country authorities, completed a similar conversion of the *BPM4* international investment position (IIP) data into the *BPM5* presentation. The IIP of a country is a balance sheet of its stock of external financial assets and liabilities. These stock data for reporting countries are presented, for the first time, in this volume under the standard components for IIP, as set forth in the *BPM5*. For certain countries the converted IIP data do not contain sufficient detail to warrant publication. As the authorities of member countries and the Fund staff continue to refine the data conversion, and as more detailed stock data are collected and reported to the Fund, the database will be revised, and an expanded presentation of IIP data will be published in subsequent volumes of the *Yearbook*.

Also presented for the first time in this volume are technical descriptions of reporting countries' methodologies, compiling practices, and data sources. These descriptions are largely based on information provided to the Fund by the countries. They are intended to enhance users' understanding of the coverage, as well as of the limitations, of individual country's data published in this *Yearbook*. They are also designed to inform compilers of data sources and practices used by their counterparts in other countries. As this is a new initiative, it is expected that these reviews will be expanded and improved in subsequent editions of the *Yearbook*, particularly with respect to the more uniform standardization of contents across countries. Future changes in sources and compilation practices will also be reflected in subsequent versions of these descriptions.

This *Yearbook* consists of three parts. Part 1 presents balance of payments and IIP data of individual countries. Part 2 contains regional and world totals for major components of the balance of payments. Part 3 provides technical descriptions of selected reporting countries. Part 1 is separately bound, and Parts 2 and 3 are published together.

The balance of this introduction is organized as follows:

- Section I describes essential features of the tables published in Part 1 of this volume of the *Yearbook*. (Details on coverage for Parts 2 and 3 can be found in the separately bound publication.)
- Section II offers information on the accessibility of the Fund's balance of payments data on computer tapes.
- There are six annexes. Annex I shows an analytic presentation of balance of payments components (and related data codes) arranged in a summary form. Annex II presents the standard components of the *BPM5* (and related

[1]French and Spanish translations of this introduction appear after the annexes; data on individual countries follow immediately thereafter.

[2]Volume 1 of the *Yearbook*, published in 1949, was based on the first edition of the Fund's *Balance of Payments Manual*, issued in 1948; Volumes 2-12 were compiled pursuant to the second edition of the manual, issued in 1950; Volumes 13-23 were based on the third edition of the manual, issued in 1961; and Volumes 24-29 were associated with that edition as well as the *Balance of Payments Manual: Supplement to Third Edition*, issued in 1973. Volumes 30-45 followed the guidance of the fourth edition of the manual, published in 1977.

[3]International Monetary Fund, *Balance of Payments Manual*, fifth edition, Washington, D.C., September 1993.

data codes). Annex III explains the data coding scheme. Annex IV presents the standard components for IIP as shown in the *BPM5*. Annex V provides the conceptual framework of the balance of payments. Annex VI explains the coverage of major components of the balance of payments accounts, as set forth in the *BPM5*.

I. Part 1 of the Yearbook: Individual Country Data

Part 1 of the *Yearbook* presents country pages alphabetically. Note, however, the term "country," as used in this publication, does not in all cases refer to a territorial entity that is a state as understood by international law and practice; the term also covers some nonsovereign territorial entities for which statistical data are maintained and provided internationally on a separate and independent basis.

For most countries, balance of payments data are presented in two tables. Table 1 is an analytical summary of the more detailed data of Table 2. Balance of payments components in Table 1 are arrayed to highlight the financing items (the reserves and related items). (See also Annex I.) Table 2 presents data displayed in the standard components described in the *BPM5*. (See also Annex II.) For countries for which IIP statistics are available, the data are presented in Table 3. Tables 1, 2, and 3 present data for the years 1988–95 for each country. Countries are only represented if at least two years of data are available within this time period. Unless otherwise indicated, figures are reported for calendar years.

Analytic Presentation

In the analytic presentation, balance of payment components are classified into five major data categories (groups A through E), which the Fund regards as useful for analyzing balance of payments developments in a uniform manner. The selected groups, however, should not be considered to reflect the Fund's recommendation about the analytic approach appropriate for every country. Other analytical presentations could be arrayed by regrouping the standard components of Table 2 in other ways to take account of the special circumstances of a specific country or to serve particular analytical requirements.

Note that the figures shown in Tables 1 and 2 for balances of the current account, the capital account, and the financial account for some countries differ. This is because in Table 1 certain transactions under these accounts are excluded and reclassified as "exceptional financing" or "liabilities constituting foreign authorities' reserves" (LCFARs). The excluded transactions are grouped under reserves and related items. "Exceptional financing" refers to transactions undertaken by the authorities to finance balance of payments needs, including such items as external borrowing, payment arrears, and debt forgiveness. Exceptional financing does not include reserves and LCFARs. LCFARs are liabilities that are considered reserve assets by the creditor economy.

Standard Presentation

The standard components of *BPM5*, as shown in Table 2, list a more detailed classification of goods and services than appears in *BPM4*. The designated "capital and financial account" has separate components for the "capital" and the "financial account." Under the "financial account," components are classified by types of investment (i.e., direct investment, portfolio investment, other investment, and reserve assets), assets/liabilities, domestic sectors (monetary authorities, general government, banks, and other sectors), and by maturity (long-term and short-term).

International Investment Position

IIP data, as shown in Table 3, are arrayed in accordance with the standard components for IIP, as set forth in the *BPM5*. (See also Annex IV.)

Although the classification of the IIP components in Table 3 is consistent with that of the financial account of the balance of payments as shown in Table 2, there are a number of differences between the two tables. As mentioned earlier, IIP data reflect a country's external financial assets and liabilities at a specific point in time. In Table 3, therefore, the basic presentation of the IIP components is provided under two general categories, namely, assets and liabilities, as opposed to the functional types of investment (direct investment, portfolio investment, other investment, and reserve assets) shown in Table 2. Also, the data in Table 3 reflect a country's IIP at the end of the reporting period, as opposed to transactions during the period shown in Table 2. Furthermore, unlike Table 2, which shows the value of financial transactions over a period, the valuation of a country's IIP, as shown in Table 3, reflects the value of financial transactions, valuation changes, and other adjustments during the period. The net IIP shown in Table 3 is derived by taking the difference between the value of external financial assets and that of external financial liabilities.

Readers may refer to Chapter XXIII of the *BPM5* for a full discussion of the concept of international investment position.

Data Codes

In both Tables 1 and 2, codes are shown for each data category and component. As mentioned earlier, these codes were developed jointly by the Fund, OECD, and the Eurostat. They are intended to facilitate international data reporting. The codes are designed for the standard components of balance of payments and international investment position data as defined in the *BPM5*, as well as for the OECD/Eurostat components for trade in services.

Box. Salient Features of the *BPM5* Compared to *BPM4*

The *BPM5* incorporates major changes to take account of developments in international trade and finance over the past decade. In addition, the concepts in *BPM5*, to the extent possible, have been harmonized with the methodology of the 1993 *System of National Accounts (1993 SNA)* and the Fund's methodologies pertaining to financial and government finance statistics. The major changes in the *BPM5* methodology that significantly affect the meaning and presentation of the balance of payments data presented in the *Yearbook* are:

(1) The *BPM5* coverage of the "current account" differs from that of *BPM4*. *BPM5* defines the "current account" as encompassing transactions with nonresidents in goods, services, income, and the receipts/payments of current transfers; in *BPM4*, the "current account" was defined to include goods, services, and all transfers. In *BPM5*, capital transfers are covered under an expanded and redesignated "capital and financial account." The distinction between current and capital transfers is based on guidelines established in the *1993 SNA*, which characterize capital transfers as follows: (a) a transfer in kind is a capital transfer when it consists of the transfer of ownership of a fixed asset, or of the forgiveness of a liability by a creditor when no counterpart is received in return; and (b) a transfer of cash is a capital transfer when it is linked to, or conditional on, the acquisition or disposal of a fixed asset (for example, an investment grant) by one or both parties to the transaction.

(2) The coverage of goods in *BPM5* has been expanded to include (a) the value of goods (on a gross basis) received/sent for processing and their subsequent export/import in the form of processed goods; (b) the value of repairs on goods; and (c) the value of goods procured in ports by carriers. In *BPM4*, the net value between goods imported for processing and subsequently re-exported was included in processing services; repairs of goods and goods procured in ports by carriers were also included under services.

(3) The *BPM5* classifies income and services separately; in *BPM4*, income was a subcomponent of services. *BPM5* also reclassifies certain income and services transactions. In *BPM4*, labor income included nonresident workers' expenditures as well as workers' earnings; in *BPM5*, workers' earnings are classified under compensation of employees in the income category, and their expenditures appear under travel services. In *BPM4*, compensation of resident staff of foreign embassies and military bases and of international organizations was included under government services; this compensation is classified as a credit item of compensation of employees in *BPM5*. *BPM4* treated payments for the use of patents, copyrights, and similar nonfinancial intangible assets as property income; these are regarded as subcomponents of other services in *BPM5*. In general, the *BPM5* concept of income covers investment income plus all forms of compensation of employees; whereas, in *BPM4* the concept included investment income, most forms of labor income (including workers' expenditures abroad), and property income.

(4) The *BPM4* "capital account" was expanded and redesignated as the "capital and financial account" in *BPM5*, and it comprises two major categories. The first is the capital account, which covers all transactions that involve (a) the receipt or payment of capital transfers, and (b) the acquisition/disposal of nonproduced, nonfinancial assets. The second is the financial account, roughly equivalent to the capital account under *BPM4*, which covers all transactions associated with changes in ownership with nonresidents of foreign financial assets and liabilities of an economy. Such changes involve the creation, exchange, and liquidation of claims on, or by, the rest of the world.

(5) As in *BPM4*, direct investment in *BPM5* is classified primarily on a directional basis—resident direct investment abroad and nonresident direct investment in the reporting economy. In *BPM5*, all transactions between nonfinancial direct investment enterprises and their parents are included in direct investment. Transactions between affiliated banks and between other affiliated financial intermediaries are limited to those in equities and loan capital representing a permanent interest; other transactions between banks and affiliated financial institutions are classified under portfolio or other investment. (In *BPM4*, only short-term transactions of these types were excluded from direct investment.)

(6) The coverage of portfolio investment was expanded in *BPM5* to reflect the growth in recent years of new financial instruments. The major change is that money market debt instruments and tradable financial derivatives are now included in portfolio investment; such instruments were treated as "other capital" in *BPM4*.

There are many other changes in the *BPM5* presentation of balance of payments data as compared to the *BPM4* one. (For a detailed description of the new methodology, see the *BPM5*).

There are six digits/characters for each code shown in the *Yearbook*. The first digit designates credit/debit/net, with the number "2" assigned to credit, "3" to debit, and "4" to net (the difference between credit and debit). The next three digits are used to classify balance of payments components. For example the current account is coded 993, the capital account, 994, and the financial account, 995. Readers may refer to Annex III for details of the coding scheme.

The fifth and sixth digits/characters of the code shown in the *Yearbook* denote special features pertaining to specific data components. For example, in Table 1, the fifth character Y indicates that exceptional financing and LCFARs are excluded from the component; X is used to show where exceptional financing, LCFARs, and use of Fund credit and loans from the Fund are excluded. Letters A, B, C, and D in Table 1 are used to differentiate the various domestic sectors. In Table 2, the letters A, B, and C are used to indicate nonstandard subcomponents, such as those for transportation (viz., passenger, freight, and other).

Credits and Debits

In Tables 1 and 2, the transactions data are shown as gross credit or gross debit entries in the current and capital accounts, and as net credit or net debit entries (to reflect net changes in liabilities and net changes in assets) in the financial account. Credit entries, gross or net, are positive (but without a plus sign), and debit entries, gross or net, are negative (with a minus sign). Thus, decreases in assets and increases in liabilities (credits) are shown as positive, and increases in assets and decreases in liabilities (debits) are shown as negative.

Nil or Unavailable Entries

It is frequently difficult to discern in data reported by countries whether missing numbers are not available or are zero or insignificant. In the *Yearbook* tables, dots (...) indicate that data are either not available, zero, or insignificant.

Rounding of Figures

Most data in the tables are expressed in units of one million; it should not be assumed that any table showing smaller units necessarily contains more accurate figures. The unit is chosen to present the figures conveniently. Because of the calculation routines used, there may be rounding differences between an aggregate and the sum of its components.

Currency Conversion

Most of the balance of payments data reported to the Fund are expressed in national currencies or in U.S. dollars, although some countries report certain data in SDRs. To facilitate comparisons among countries, all balance of payments statements published in the *Yearbook* are expressed in U.S. dollars. In addition, all countries' reported data on transactions with the Fund and transactions in SDRs are replaced with data obtained from the Fund records, which are kept in SDRs. This information is, in turn, converted to U.S. dollars.

For countries that do not report in U.S. dollars, data are converted using the country conversion rates shown at the bottom of Table 1. These rates are normally the average exchange rates for a country for the relevant period taken from the *IFS*. For example, the *IFS* pages for the Netherlands contain line "rf," giving average rates for guilders per U.S. dollar. Conversions of transactions data from SDRs into U.S. dollars are made at the rates shown in line "sb" of the *IFS* pages for the United States. For countries reporting quarterly data in national currencies, annual U.S. dollar totals are obtained by aggregating the quarterly U.S. dollar figures.

More information on the exchange rates used may be found in the introduction to *IFS*, Section 1.

II. Tape Subscription

Statistics published in the *Yearbook* are also available on computer tape.[1] The number of countries and time series covered in the tape version is slightly larger than that appearing in the printed version of the *Yearbook*, as is the number of periods for which data observations of time series are given. Quarterly data reported by countries are also available on the tape. Tape subscribers receive Part 1 of the printed version of the *Yearbook* and twelve monthly magnetic tapes; the tapes include updates and revisions of the data as they become available. Inquiries about the tapes should be addressed to:

Publication Services
International Monetary Fund
Washington, D.C. 20431, U.S.A.
Telephone (202) 623-7430
Telefax (202) 623-7201

[1]In addition, data will be available in CD-ROMs in the future.

Annex I. Analytic Presentation

	Data Codes
A. CURRENT ACCOUNT[1]	4 993 Y .
Goods: exports f.o.b.	2 100 . .
Goods: imports f.o.b.	3 100 . .
Balance on Goods	4 100 . .
Services: credit	2 200 . .
Services: debit	3 200 . .
Balance on Goods and Services	4 991 . .
Income: credit	2 300 . .
Income: debit	3 300 . .
Balance on Goods, Services, and Income	4 992 . .
Current transfers: credit	2 379 Y .
Current transfers: debit	3 379 . .
B. CAPITAL ACCOUNT[1]	4 994 Y .
Capital account: credit	2 994 Y .
Capital account: debit	3 994 . .
Total, Groups A plus B	4 010 . .
C. FINANCIAL ACCOUNT[1]	4 995 X .
Direct investment abroad	4 505 . .
Direct investment in reporting economy	4 555 Y .
Portfolio investment assets	4 602 . .
Equity securities	4 610 . .
Debt securities	4 619 . .
Portfolio investment liabilities	4 652 Y .
Equity securities	4 660 Y .
Debt securities	4 669 Y .
Other investment assets	4 703 . .
Monetary authorities	4 703 .A
General government	4 703 .B
Banks	4 703 .C
Other sectors	4 703 .D
Other investment liabilities	4 753 X .
Monetary authorities	4 753 XA
General government	4 753 YB
Banks	4 753 YC
Other sectors	4 753 YD
Total, Groups A through C	4 020 . .
D. NET ERRORS AND OMISSIONS	4 998 . .
Total, Groups A through D	4 030 . .
E. RESERVES AND RELATED ITEMS	4 040 . .
Reserve assets	4 800 . .
Use of Fund credit and loans	4 766 . .
Liabilities constituting foreign authorities' reserves	4 900 . .
Exceptional financing	4 920 . .
CONVERSION RATES: CURRENCY PER U.S. DOLLAR	0 101 . .

[1]Excludes components that have been classified in the categories of Group E.

Annex II. Standard Presentation

	Data Codes
CURRENT ACCOUNT	4 993 ..
A. GOODS	4 100 ..
Credit	2 100 ..
General merchandise: exports f.o.b.	2 110 ..
Goods for processing: exports f.o.b.	2 150 ..
Repairs on goods	2 160 ..
Goods procured in ports by carriers	2 170 ..
Nonmonetary gold	2 180 ..
Debit	3 100 ..
General merchandise: imports f.o.b.	3 110 ..
Goods for processing: imports f.o.b.	3 150 ..
Repairs on goods	3 160 ..
Goods procured in ports by carriers	3 170 ..
Nonmonetary gold	3 180 ..
B. SERVICES	4 200 ..
Total Credit	2 200 ..
Total Debit	3 200 ..
Transportation services, credit	2 205 ..
Passenger	2 205 BA
Freight	2 205 BB
Other	2 205 BC
Sea transport, passenger	2 207 ..
Sea transport, freight	2 208 ..
Sea transport, other	2 209 ..
Air transport, passenger	2 211 ..
Air transport, freight	2 212 ..
Air transport, other	2 213 ..
Other transport, passenger	2 215 ..
Other transport, freight	2 216 ..
Other transport, other	2 217 ..
Transportation services, debit	3 205 ..
Passenger	3 205 BA
Freight	3 205 BB
Other	3 205 BC
Sea transport, passenger	3 207 ..
Sea transport, freight	3 208 ..
Sea transport, other	3 209 ..
Air transport, passenger	3 211 ..
Air transport, freight	3 212 ..
Air transport, other	3 213 ..
Other transport, passenger	3 215 ..
Other transport, freight	3 216 ..
Other transport, other	3 217 ..
Travel, credit	2 236 ..
Business travel	2 237 ..
Personal travel	2 240 ..
Travel, debit	3 236 ..
Business travel	3 237 ..
Personal travel	3 240 ..

Annex II. Standard Presentation *(continued)*

	Data Codes
Other services, credit	2 200 BA
Communications	2 245 ..
Construction	2 249 ..
Insurance	2 253 ..
Financial	2 260 ..
Computer and information	2 262 ..
Royalties and license fees	2 266 ..
Other business services	2 268 ..
Personal, cultural, and recreational	2 287 ..
Government, n.i.e.	2 291 ..
Other services, debit	3 200 BA
Communications	3 245 ..
Construction	3 249 ..
Insurance	3 253 ..
Financial	3 260 ..
Computer and information	3 262 ..
Royalties and license fees	3 266 ..
Other business services	3 268 ..
Personal, cultural, and recreational	3 287 ..
Government, n.i.e.	3 291 ..
C. INCOME	4 300 ..
Total Credit	2 300 ..
Total Debit	3 300 ..
Compensation of employees, credit	2 310 ..
Compensation of employees, debit	3 310 ..
Investment income, credit	2 320 ..
Direct investment income	2 330 ..
Dividends and distributed branch profits	2 332 ..
Reinvested earnings and undistributed branch profits	2 333 ..
Income on debt (interest)	2 334 ..
Portfolio investment income	2 339 ..
Income on equity	2 340 ..
Income on bonds and notes	2 350 ..
Income on money market instruments and financial derivatives	2 360 ..
Other investment income	2 370 ..
Investment income, debit	3 320 ..
Direct investment income	3 330 ..
Dividends and distributed branch profits	3 332 ..
Reinvested earnings and undistributed branch profits	3 333 ..
Income on debt (interest)	3 334 ..
Portfolio investment income	3 339 ..
Income on equity	3 340 ..
Income on bonds and notes	3 350 ..
Income on money market instruments and financial derivatives	3 360 ..
Other investment income	3 370 ..
D. CURRENT TRANSFERS	4 379 ..
Credit	2 379 ..
General government	2 380 ..
Other sectors	2 390 ..

	Data Codes	
Workers' remittances	2 391	. .
Other current transfers	2 392	. .
Debit	3 379	. .
General government	3 380	. .
Other sectors	3 390	. .
Workers' remittances	3 391	. .
Other current transfers	3 392	. .
CAPITAL AND FINANCIAL ACCOUNT	4 996	. .
CAPITAL ACCOUNT	4 994	. .
Total Credit	2 994	. .
Total Debit	3 994	. .
Capital transfers, credit	2 400	. .
General government	2 401	. .
Debt forgiveness	2 402	. .
Other capital transfers	2 410	. .
Other sectors	2 430	. .
Migrants' transfers	2 431	. .
Debt forgiveness	2 432	. .
Other capital transfers	2 440	. .
Capital transfers, debit	3 400	. .
General government	3 401	. .
Debt forgiveness	3 402	. .
Other capital transfers	3 410	. .
Other sectors	3 430	. .
Migrants' transfers	3 431	. .
Debt forgiveness	3 432	. .
Other capital transfers	3 440	. .
Nonproduced nonfinancial assets, credit	2 480	. .
Nonproduced nonfinancial assets, debit	3 480	. .
FINANCIAL ACCOUNT	4 995	. .
A. DIRECT INVESTMENT	4 500	. .
Direct investment abroad	4 505	. .
Equity capital	4 510	. .
Claims on affiliated enterprises	4 515	. .
Liabilities to affiliated enterprises	4 520	. .
Reinvested earnings	4 525	. .
Other capital	4 530	. .
Claims on affiliated enterprises	4 535	. .
Liabilities to affiliated enterprises	4 540	. .
Direct investment in reporting economy	4 555	. .
Equity capital	4 560	. .
Claims on direct investors	4 565	. .
Liabilities to direct investors	4 570	. .
Reinvested earnings	4 575	. .
Other capital	4 580	. .
Claims on direct investors	4 585	. .
Liabilities to direct investors	4 590	. .

	Data Codes	
B. PORTFOLIO INVESTMENT	4 600	..
Assets	4 602	..
Equity securities	4 610	..
Monetary authorities	4 611	..
General government	4 612	..
Banks	4 613	..
Other sectors	4 614	..
Debt securities	4 619	..
Bonds and notes	4 620	..
Monetary authorities	4 621	..
General government	4 622	..
Banks	4 623	..
Other sectors	4 624	..
Money market instruments	4 630	..
Monetary authorities	4 631	..
General government	4 632	..
Banks	4 633	..
Other sectors	4 634	..
Financial derivatives	4 640	..
Monetary authorities	4 641	..
General government	4 642	..
Banks	4 643	..
Other sectors	4 644	..
Liabilities	4 652	..
Equity securities	4 660	..
Banks	4 663	..
Other sectors	4 664	..
Debt securities	4 669	..
Bonds and notes	4 670	..
Monetary authorities	4 671	..
General government	4 672	..
Banks	4 673	..
Other sectors	4 674	..
Money market instruments	4 680	..
Monetary authorities	4 681	..
General government	4 682	..
Banks	4 683	..
Other sectors	4 684	..
Financial derivatives	4 690	..
Monetary authorities	4 691	..
General government	4 692	..
Banks	4 693	..
Other sectors	4 694	..
C. OTHER INVESTMENT	4 700	..
Assets	4 703	..
Trade credits	4 706	..
General government: long-term	4 708	..
General government: short-term	4 709	..
Other sectors: long-term	4 711	..
Other sectors: short-term	4 712	..
Loans	4 714	..
Monetary authorities: long-term	4 717	..
Monetary authorities: short-term	4 718	..
General government: long-term	4 720	..
General government: short-term	4 721	..

	Data Codes
Banks: long-term	4 723 . .
Banks: short-term	4 724 . .
Other sectors: long-term	4 726 . .
Other sectors: short-term	4 727 . .
Currency and deposits	4 730 . .
Monetary authorities	4 731 . .
General government	4 732 . .
Banks	4 733 . .
Other sectors	4 734 . .
Other assets	4 736 . .
Monetary authorities: long-term	4 738 . .
Monetary authorities: short-term	4 739 . .
General government: long-term	4 741 . .
General governments: short-term	4 742 . .
Banks: long-term	4 744 . .
Banks: short-term	4 745 . .
Other sectors: long-term	4 747 . .
Other sectors: short-term	4 748 . .
Liabilities	4 753 . .
Trade credits	4 756 . .
General government: long-term	4 758 . .
General government: short-term	4 759 . .
Other sectors: long-term	4 761 . .
Other sectors: short-term	4 762 . .
Loans	4 764 . .
Use of Fund credit and loans from the Fund	4 766 . .
Monetary authorities: other long-term	4 767 . .
Monetary authorities: short-term	4 768 . .
General government: long-term	4 770 . .
General government: short-term	4 771 . .
Banks: long-term	4 773 . .
Banks: short-term	4 774 . .
Other sectors: long-term	4 776 . .
Other sectors: short-term	4 777 . .
Currency and deposits	4 780 . .
Monetary authorities	4 781 . .
General government	4 782 . .
Banks	4 783 . .
Other sectors	4 784 . .
Other liabilities	4 786 . .
Monetary authorities: long-term	4 788 . .
Monetary authorities: short-term	4 789 . .
General government: long-term	4 791 . .
General government: short-term	4 792 . .
Banks: long-term	4 794 . .
Banks: short-term	4 795 . .
Other sectors: long-term	4 797 . .
Other sectors: short-term	4 798 . .
D. RESERVE ASSETS	4 800 . .
Monetary gold	4 810 . .
Special drawing rights	4 820 . .
Reserve position in the Fund	4 830 . .
Foreign exchange	4 840 . .
Other claims	4 880 . .
NET ERRORS AND OMISSIONS	4 998 . .

Annex III. IMF/OECD/Eurostat Coding System for Balance of Payments, International Investment Position, and Trade In Services[1]

This coding system incorporates all the standard components and supplementary information lines of the fifth edition of the *Balance of Payments Manual*, as well as the components and memorandum items of the OECD-Eurostat classification for international trade in services.

The code consists of three components or sections as follows:

<position>	one decimal digit (selected from the range of 1 to 8) that describes the position of the subject in the international investment position (IIP)/balance of payments (BOP) accounts;
<BOP topic>	three decimal digits (selected from the range of integers from 100 to 998) that identify all the BOP, trade-in-services, and selected supplementary information components; and
<tag>	a user defined component that may be of any length.

The complete code would take the form <position><topic><tag>. However, the tag component is optional. In contrast, the position and the topic components of the code are always required. Thus, a common implementation of the code will take the form <position><topic>.

The first section of the code describes the position in the IIP and BOP accounts and is defined as follows:

Code	Position in IIP/BOP Accounts
1	stock at the beginning of the period
2	credit flows
3	debit flows
4	net flows
5	price valuation adjustment
6	exchange rate valuation adjustment
7	other adjustments
8	stock at the end of the period
0	other

The first digit of the topic component identifies the section of the balance of payments as follows:

Code	Section of the accounts
1	goods
2	services
3	income and current transfers
4	capital account
5	direct investment
6	portfolio investment
7	other investment
8	reserves
9	aggregates and supplementary information

The second and third digits of the component are generally sequential counts of the components with some gaps to allow for the possibility of additional codes being included at a later time. In addition, with the exception of the direct investment accounts, the second digit of the topic component takes the numbers 0, 1, 2, 3, or 4 for assets and 5, 6, 7, 8, or 9 for liabilities in the financial accounts.

Examples of data codes for "Other Investment" of the financial account are shown below.

Topic	Single Field			Multiple Field		
	Credit	Debit	Net	Credit	Debit	Net
Other investment	2700	3700	4700	2700	3700	4700
Liabilities	2750	3750	4750	2750	3750	4750
Loans	2762	3762	4762	2762	3762	4762
General govt.	2767	3767	4767	2767	3767	4767
Long-term	2768	3768	4768	2768	3768	4768
Short-term	2769	3769	4769	2769	3769	4769
Banks	2770	3770	4770	2770	3770	4770
Long-term	2771	3771	4771	2771	3771	4771
Short-term	2772	3772	4772	2772	3772	4772
Other sectors	2773	3773	4773	2773	3773	4773
Long-term	2774	3774	4774	2774	3774	4774
Short-term	2775	3775	4775	2775	3775	4775

When considering credits and debits for loans, the language that is commonly used is drawings and repayments. The *BPM5* recommends reporting of all drawings and repayments for long-term loans as a supplementary classification. Most other financial account items are presently collected by the Fund on a net basis. Nevertheless, the coding system provides for the identification of all flows on a credit, debit, and net basis.

[1] This is adopted from International Monetary Fund, "Balance of Payments Codes for Standard Components and Additional Items," Washington, D.C., March 3, 1995.

Annex IV. Standard Components of International Investment Position

	Data Codes	
A. ASSETS	8 995 C	.
Direct investment abroad	8 505	..
Equity capital and reinvested earnings	8 506	..
Claims on affiliated enterprises	8 507	..
Liabilities to affiliated enterprises	8 508	..
Other capital	8 530	..
Claims on affiliated enterprises	8 535	..
Liabilities to affiliated enterprises	8 540	..
Portfolio investment	8 602	..
Equity securities	8 610	..
Monetary authorities	8 611	..
General government	8 612	..
Banks	8 613	..
Other sectors	8 614	..
Debt securities	8 619	..
Bonds and notes	8 620	..
Monetary authorities	8 621	..
General government	8 622	..
Banks	8 623	..
Other sectors	8 624	..
Money market instruments	8 630	..
Monetary authorities	8 631	..
General government	8 632	..
Banks	8 633	..
Other sectors	8 634	..
Financial derivatives	8 640	..
Monetary authorities	8 641	..
General government	8 642	..
Banks	8 643	..
Other sectors	8 644	..
Other investment	8 703	..
Trade credits	8 706	..
General government: long-term	8 708	..
General government: short-term	8 709	..
Other sectors: long-term	8 711	..
Other sectors: short-term	8 712	..
Loans	8 714	..
Monetary authorities: long-term	8 717	..
Monetary authorities: short-term	8 718	..
General government: long-term	8 720	..
General government: short-term	8 721	..
Banks: long-term	8 723	..
Banks: short-term	8 724	..
Other sectors: long-term	8 726	..
Other sectors: short-term	8 727	..
Currency and deposits	8 730	..
Monetary authorities	8 731	..
General government	8 732	..
Banks	8 733	..
Other sectors	8 734	..
Other assets	8 736	..
Monetary authorities: long-term	8 738	..
Monetary authorities: short-term	8 739	..
General government: long-term	8 741	..

ANNEX IV. STANDARD COMPONENTS OF INTERNATIONAL INVESTMENT POSITION (continued)

	Data Codes
General government: short-term	8 742 ..
Banks: long-term	8 744 ..
Banks: short-term	8 745 ..
Other sectors: long-term	8 747 ..
Other sectors: short-term	8 748 ..
Reserve assets	8 800 ..
Monetary gold	8 810 ..
Special drawing rights	8 820 ..
Reserve position in the Fund	8 830 ..
Foreign exchange	8 840 ..
Other claims	8 880 ..
B. LIABILITIES	8 995 D .
Direct investment in reporting economy	8 555 ..
Equity capital and reinvested earnings	8 556 ..
Claims on direct investors	8 557 ..
Liabilities to direct investors	8 558 ..
Other capital	8 580 ..
Claims on direct investors	8 585 ..
Liabilities to direct investors	8 590 ..
Portfolio investment	8 652 ..
Equity securities	8 660 ..
Banks	8 663 ..
Other sectors	8 664 ..
Debt securities	8 669 ..
Bonds and notes	8 670 ..
Monetary authorities	8 671 ..
General government	8 672 ..
Banks	8 673 ..
Other sectors	8 674 ..
Money market instruments	8 680 ..
Monetary authorities	8 681 ..
General government	8 682 ..
Banks	8 683 ..
Other sectors	8 684 ..
Financial derivatives	8 690 ..
Monetary authorities	8 691 ..
General government	8 692 ..
Banks	8 693 ..
Other sectors	8 694 ..
Other investment	8 753 ..
Trade credits	8 756 ..
General government: long-term	8 758 ..
General government: short-term	8 759 ..
Other sectors: long-term	8 761 ..
Other sectors: short-term	8 762 ..
Loans	8 764 ..
Use of Fund credit and loans from the Fund	8 766 ..
Monetary authorities: long-term	8 767 ..
Monetary authorities: short-term	8 768 ..
General government: long-term	8 770 ..
General government: short-term	8 771 ..
Banks: long-term	8 773 ..
Banks: short-term	8 774 ..

Annex IV. Standard Components of International Investment Position
(concluded)

	Data Codes	
Other sectors: long-term	8 776	..
Other sectors: short-term	8 777	..
Currency and deposits	8 780	..
Monetary authorities	8 781	..
General government	8 782	..
Banks	8 783	..
Other sectors	8 784	..
Other liabilities	8 786	..
Monetary authorities: long-term	8 788	..
Monetary authorities: short-term	8 789	..
General government: long-term	8 791	..
General government: short-term	8 792	..
Banks: long-term	8 794	..
Banks: short-term	8 795	..
Other sectors: long-term	8 797	..
Other sectors: short-term	8 798	..
NET INTERNATIONAL INVESTMENT POSITION	8 995	..
Conversion rates (end of period)	0 102	..

Annex V. Conceptual Framework of the Balance of Payments and International Investment Position

This annex is reproduced from Chapter II of the BPM5. *Please note that paragraph and page numbers cited in this annex refer to those that appear in the* BPM5.

Definitions

12. Part one of this *Manual* deals with the conceptual framework of balance of payments accounts and the international investment position. Part one covers their relationship to national accounts; to concepts of residence, valuation, and time of recording; and to the unit of account and conversion.

13. The balance of payments is a statistical statement that systematically summarizes, for a specific time period, the economic transactions of an economy with the rest of the world. Transactions, for the most part between residents and nonresidents,[1] consist of those involving goods, services, and income; those involving financial claims on, and liabilities to, the rest of the world; and those (such as gifts) classified as transfers, which involve offsetting entries to balance—in an accounting sense—one-sided transactions. (See paragraph 28.)[2] A transaction itself is defined as an economic flow that reflects the creation, transformation, exchange, transfer, or extinction of economic value and involves changes in ownership of goods and/or financial assets, the provision of services, or the provision of labor and capital.

14. Closely related to the flow-oriented balance of payments framework is the stock-oriented international investment position. Compiled at a specified date such as year end, this investment position is a statistical statement of: (i) the value and composition of the stock of an economy's financial assets or the economy's claims on the rest of the world, and (ii) the value and composition of the stock of an economy's liabilities to the rest of the world. In some instances, it may be of analytic interest to compute the difference between the two sides of the balance sheet. The calculation would provide a measure of the net position, and the measure would be equivalent to that portion of an economy's net worth attributable to, or derived from, its relationship with the rest of the world. A change in stocks during any defined period can be attributable to transactions (flows); to valuation changes reflecting changes in exchange rates, prices, etc.; or to other adjustments (e.g., uncompensated seizures). By contrast, balance of payments accounts reflect only transactions.

Please note that, as stated in this "Introduction," the international investment position is not presented in this volume of the Yearbook.

Principles and Concepts

15. The remainder of this chapter deals with the conceptual framework of international accounts, that is, the set of underlying principles and conventions that ensure the systematized and coherent recording of international transactions and stocks of foreign assets and liabilities. Relevant aspects of these principles, together with practical considerations and limitations, will be thoroughly discussed in subsequent chapters.

Double Entry System

16. The basic convention applied in constructing a balance of payments statement is that every recorded transaction is represented by two entries with equal values. One of these entries is designated a credit with a positive arithmetic sign; the other is designated a debit with a negative sign. In principle, the sum of all credit entries is identical to the sum of all the debit entries, and the net balance of all entries in the statement is zero.

17. In practice, however, the accounts frequently do not balance. Data for balance of payments estimates often are derived independently from different sources; as a result, there may be a summary net credit or net debit (i.e., net errors and omissions in the accounts). A separate entry, equal to that amount with the sign reversed, is then made to balance the accounts. Because inaccurate or missing estimates may be offsetting, the size of the net residual cannot be taken as an indicator of the relative accuracy of the balance of payments statement. Nonetheless, a large, persistent residual that is not reversed should cause concern. Such a residual impedes analysis or interpretation of estimates and diminishes the credibility of both. A large net residual may also have implications for interpretation of the investment position statement. (See the discussion in Chapter XXIII.)

18. Most entries in the balance of payments refer to transactions in which economic values are provided or received in exchange for other economic values; those values consist of real resources (goods, services, and income) and financial items. Therefore, the offsetting credit and debit entries called for by the recording system are often the result of equal amounts having been entered for the two items exchanged. When items are given away rather than exchanged, or when a recording is one-sided for other reasons, special types of entries—referred to as *transfers*—are made as the required offsets. (The various kinds of entries that may be made in the balance of payments are discussed in paragraphs 26 through 31.)

19. Under the conventions of the system, a compiling economy records credit entries (i) for real resources denoting exports and (ii) for financial items reflecting reductions in an economy's foreign assets or increases in an economy's foreign liabilities. Conversely, a compiling economy records debit entries (i) for real resources denoting imports and (ii) for financial items reflecting increases in assets or decreases in liabilities. In other words, for assets—whether real or financial—a positive figure (credit) represents a decrease in holdings, and a negative figure (debit) represents an increase. In contrast, for liabilities, a positive figure shows an increase, and a negative figure shows a decrease. Transfers are shown as credits when the entries to which they provide the offsets are debits and as debits when those entries are credits.

20. The content or coverage of a balance of payments statement depends somewhat on whether transactions are treated on a gross or on a net basis. The recommendations in this *Manual* specify which transactions should be recorded gross or net. The recommendations are appropriately reflected in the list of standard components and in suggested supplementary presentations.

---

[1]The exceptions to the resident/nonresident basis of the balance of payments are the exchange of transferable foreign financial assets between resident sectors and, to a lesser extent, the exchange of transferable foreign financial liabilities between nonresidents. (See paragraph 318.)

[2]The definitions and classifications of international accounts presented in this *Manual* are intended to facilitate reporting of data on international transactions to the Fund. These definitions and classifications do not purport to give effect to, or interpret, various provisions (which pertain to the legal characterization of official action or inaction in relation to such transactions) of the *Articles of Agreement of the International Monetary Fund.*

Concepts of Economic Territory, Residence, and Center of Economic Interest

21. Identical concepts of economic territory, residence, and center of economic interest are used in this *Manual* and in the *SNA*. (These concepts are discussed fully in Chapter IV.) Economic territory may not be identical with boundaries recognized for political purposes. A country's economic territory consists of a geographic territory administered by a government; within this geographic territory, persons, goods, and capital circulate freely. For maritime countries, geographic territory includes any islands subject to the same fiscal and monetary authorities as the mainland.

22. An institutional unit has a center of economic interest and is a resident unit of a country when, from some location (dwelling, place of production, or other premises) within the economic territory of the country, the unit engages and intends to continue engaging (indefinitely or for a finite period) in economic activities and transactions on a significant scale. (One year or more may be used as a guideline but not as an inflexible rule.)

Principles for Valuation and Time of Recording

23. A uniform basis of valuation for the international accounts (both real resources and financial claims and liabilities) is necessary for compiling, on a consistent basis, any aggregate of individual transactions and an asset/liability position consistent with such transactions. This *Manual* generally uses, as the basis of transaction valuations, actual market prices agreed upon by transactors. (This practice is consistent with that of the *SNA*.) Conceptually, all stocks of assets and liabilities are valued at market prices prevailing at the time to which the international investment position relates. A full exposition of valuation principles; recommended practices; limitations; and the valuation of transfers, financial items, and stocks of assets and liabilities appears in Chapter V. (The exposition includes cases in which conditions may not allow for the existence or assumption of market prices.)

24. In the *Manual* and the *SNA*, the principle of accrual accounting governs the *time of recording* for transactions. Therefore, transactions are recorded when economic value is created, transformed, exchanged, transferred, or extinguished. Claims and liabilities arise when there is a change in ownership. The change may be legal or physical (economic). In practice, when a change in ownership is not obvious, the change may be proxied by the time that parties to a transaction record it in their books or accounts. (The recommended timing and conventions for various balance of payments entries, together with exceptions to and departures from the change of ownership principle, are covered in Chapter VI.)

Concept and Types of Transactions

25. Broadly speaking, changes in economic relationships registered by the balance of payments stem primarily from dealings between two parties. These parties are, with one exception (see footnote 1), a resident and a nonresident, and all dealings of this kind are covered in the balance of payments. Recommendations for specific entries are embodied in the list of standard components (see Chapter VIII) and are spelled out in detail from Chapter IX onward.

26. Despite the connotation, the balance of payments is not concerned with *payments*, as that term is generally understood, but with *transactions*. A number of international transactions that are of interest in a balance of payments context may not involve the payment of money, and some are not paid for in any sense. The inclusion of these transactions, in addition to those matched by actual payments, constitutes a principal difference between a balance of payments statement and a record of foreign payments.

Exchanges

27. The most numerous and important transactions found in the balance of payments may be characterized as *exchanges*. A transactor (economic entity) provides an economic value to another transactor and receives in return an equal value. The economic values provided by one economy to another may be categorized broadly as real resources (goods, services, income) and financial items. The parties that engage in the exchange are residents of different economies, except in the case of an exchange of foreign financial items between resident sectors. The provision of a financial item may involve not only a change in the ownership of an existing claim or liability but also the creation of a new claim or liability or the cancellation of existing ones. Moreover, the terms of a contract pertaining to a financial item (e.g., contractual maturity) may be altered by agreement between the parties. Such a case is equivalent to fulfillment of the original contract and replacement by a contract with different terms. All exchanges of these kinds are covered in the balance of payments.

Transfers

28. Transactions involving *transfers* differ from exchanges in that one transactor provides an economic value to another transactor but does not receive a quid pro quo on which, according to the conventions and rules adopted for the system, economic value is placed. This absence of value on one side is represented by an entry referred to as a *transfer*. Such transfers (economic value provided and received without a quid pro quo) are shown in the balance of payments. ***Current transfers*** are included in the **current account** (see Chapter XV) and *capital transfers* appear in the ***capital account***. (See Chapter XVII.)

Migration

29. Because an economy is defined in terms of the economic entities associated with its territory, the scope of an economy is likely to be affected by changes in entities associated with the economy.

30. Migration occurs when the residence of an individual changes from one economy to another because the person moves his or her abode. Certain movable, tangible assets owned by the migrant are, in effect, imported into the new economy. The migrant's immovable assets and certain movable, tangible assets located in the old economy become claims of the new economy on the old economy. The migrant's claims on, or liabilities to, residents of an economy other than the new economy become foreign claims or liabilities of the new economy. The migrant's claims on, or liabilities to, residents of the new economy cease to be claims on, or liabilities to, the rest of the world for any economy. The net sum of all these shifts is equal to the net worth of the migrant, and his or her net worth must also be recorded as an offset if the other shifts are recorded. These entries are made in the balance of payments where the offset is conventionally included with transfers.

Other imputed transactions

31. In some instances, transactions may be imputed and entries may be made in balance of payments accounts when no actual flow occurs. Attribution of reinvested earnings to foreign direct investors is an example. The earnings of a foreign subsidiary or branch include earnings attributable to a direct investor. The earnings, whether distributed or reinvested in the enterprise, are proportionate to the direct investor's equity share in the enterprise. Reinvested earnings are recorded as part of direct investment income. An offsetting entry, with opposite sign, is made in the *financial account*, under direct investment, reinvested earnings, to reflect the direct investor's increased investment in the foreign subsidiary or branch. (Reinvested earnings are discussed in Chapters XIV and XVIII.)

Changes Other Than Transactions

Reclassification of claims and liabilities

32. The classification of financial items in the *Manual* reflects characteristics designed to reveal the motivation of creditor or debtor. Changes in motivation affect the characteristics, and financial items are subject to reclassification in accordance with such changes. A case in point is the distinction drawn between *direct investment* and other types of investment. For example, several independent holders of *portfolio investment* (in the form of corporate equities issued by a single enterprise abroad) may form an associated group to have a lasting, effective voice in the management of the enterprise. Their holdings will then meet the criteria for *direct investment*, and the change in the status of the investment could be recorded as a reclassification. Such a reclassification would be reflected, at the end of the period during which it occurred, in the international investment position but not in the balance of payments. Similarly, claims on nonresidents can come under, or be released from, the control of resident monetary authorities. In such cases, there are reclassifications between *reserve assets* and assets other than reserves.

Valuation changes

33. The values of real resources and financial items are constantly subject to change stemming from either or both of two causes: (i) The price at which transactions in a certain type of item customarily take place may undergo alteration in terms of the currency in which that price is quoted. (ii) The exchange rate for the currency in which the price is quoted may change in relation to the unit of account that is being used. Valuation changes are not included in the balance of payments but are included in the international investment position.

Annex VI. Classification and Standard Components of the Balance of Payments

This annex is reproduced from Chapter VIII of the BPM5. *Please note that paragraph and page numbers cited in this annex refer to those that appear in the* BPM5.

Structure and Classification

139. Part two of this *Manual* deals with the structure and classification of balance of payments accounts and the international investment position. Part two encompasses the standard components of both sets of accounts and contains discussions and elaboration of the ***current account***, the ***capital and financial account***, selected supplementary information, and the international investment position.

140. Balance of payments statistics must be arranged within a coherent structure to facilitate their utilization and adaptation for multiple purposes—policy formulation, analytical studies, projections, bilateral comparisons of particular components or total transactions, regional and global aggregations, etc. (See paragraph 7.)

141. The standard classification and the list of components reflect conceptual and practical considerations, take into account views expressed by national balance of payments experts, and are in general concordance with the *SNA* and with harmonization of the expanded classification of international transactions in services with the Central Product Classification (CPC). (See Appendix III.)

142. The scheme also reflects efforts to link the structure of the ***capital account*** to income accounts and to the international investment position classification. The scheme is designed as a flexible framework to be used by many countries in the long-term development of external statistics. Some countries may not be able to provide data for many items; other countries may be able to provide additional data.

Standard Components

143. The determination of standard components (see list at end of this chapter) is based on a number of considerations. Those that have been given the greatest weight are:

> The item should exhibit distinctive behavior. The economic factor or factors that influence the item should be different from those that influence other items, or the item should respond differently to the same factor or combination. This response to economic influences is what the balance of payments purports to make evident.
>
> The item should be important for a number of countries. Importance may be defined as a function of behavior (unusual variability, for example) or as absolute size.
>
> It should be possible to collect statistics for the item without undue difficulty. However, the desirability of collection should be evaluated according to the two previous criteria.
>
> The item should be needed on a separate basis for other purposes, such as incorporation into, or reconciliation with, the national accounts. The list of standard components should not be unduly long. A large number of countries, including many that are statistically less advanced, are asked to report uniformly on the components.
>
> To the extent practicable, standard components should be in concordance with, and apply to, other IMF statistical systems, the *SNA*, and, for ***services*** in particular, the CPC.

144. The list of standard components carries no implication that recommendations made in this *Manual* are intended to inhibit countries from compiling and publishing additional data of national importance. IMF requests for information will not be limited to standard components when further details are needed to understand the circumstances of particular countries or to analyze new developments. Supplementary information can also be most useful for verifying and reconciling the statistics of partner countries and, for example, analyzing exceptional financing transactions. (See the table entitled *Selected Supplementary Information* at the end of this chapter.) IMF staff will, from time to time, consult with countries to decide on the reporting of additional details.

145. Few countries are likely to have significant information to report for every standard component. Furthermore, several components may be available only in combination, or a minor component may be grouped with one that is more significant. The standard components should nevertheless be reported to the IMF as completely and accurately as possible. National compilers are in better positions than IMF staff to make estimates and adjustments for those components that do not exactly correspond to the basic series of the compiling economy.

Net Errors and Omissions

146. Application of the principles recommended in this *Manual* should result in a consistent body of positive and negative entries with a net (conceptual) total of zero. In practice, however, when all actual entries are totaled, the resulting balance will almost inevitably show a net credit or a net debit. That balance is the result of errors and omissions in compilation of statements. Some of the errors and omissions may be related to recommendations for practical approximation to principles.

147. In balance of payments statements, the standard practice is to show separately an item for net errors and omissions. Labeled by some compilers as a balancing item or statistical discrepancy, that item is intended as an offset to the overstatement or understatement of the recorded components. Thus, if the balance of those components is a credit, the item for net errors and omissions will be shown as a debit of equal value, and vice versa.

148. Some of the errors and omissions that occur in the course of compilation usually offset one another. Therefore, the size of the residual item does not necessarily provide any indication of the overall accuracy of the statement. Nonetheless, interpretation of the statement is hampered by a large net residual.

Major Classifications

149. The standard components, which are listed at the end of this chapter, are comprised of two main groups of accounts:

> The **current account** refers to ***goods and services, income,*** and ***current transfers***.
>
> The **capital and financial account** refers to (i) *capital transfers* and *acquisition/disposal of nonproduced, nonfinancial assets* and (ii) financial assets and liabilities.

This arrangement is based on common historical usage in most countries and on a major change introduced in this *Manual*. The former capital account has been relabeled **capital and financial account**. Reflecting harmonization with the *SNA*, this change introduces that system's distinction between *capital transfers* and ***current transfers*** in balance of payments accounts and concordance of the account with *SNA* capital and financial accounts.

150. **Current account** entries for most items in the list of standard components should show gross debits and credits. Most **capital and financial account** entries should be made on a net basis; that is, each component is shown only as a credit or a debit. (The recommended treatments for specific items and exceptions are discussed in appropriate chapters.) Inflows of real resources, increases in financial assets, and decreases in liabilities should be shown as debits; outflows of real resources, decreases in financial assets, and increases in liabilities should be shown as credits. Transfers, both in sections 1.C and 2.A, should be numerically equal with opposite sign to the entries for which they provide offsets.

Detailed Classifications

151. The following classifications of standard components have been developed in accordance with the criteria set out in paragraph 143. The structure and characteristics of the **current account** and the **capital and financial account** and significant changes from the fourth to the fifth edition of the *Manual* are discussed in chapters IX and XVI, respectively. The standard components of the **current account** are described fully in chapters X through XV, and those of the **capital and financial account** are covered in chapters XVII through XXI.

Current Account (1.)

152. Covered in the **current account** are all transactions (other than those in financial items) that involve economic values and occur between resident and nonresident entities. Also covered are offsets to current economic values provided or acquired without a quid pro quo. Specifically, the major classifications are ***goods and services, income,*** and ***current transfers***.

Goods and services (1.A.)

Goods (1.A.a.)

153. *General merchandise* covers most movable goods that are exported to, or imported from, nonresidents by residents and that, with a few specified exceptions, undergo changes in ownership (actual or imputed).

154. *Goods for processing* cover exports (or imports, in the compiling economy) of goods crossing the frontier for processing abroad and subsequent reimport (or export, in the compiling economy) of the goods, which are valued on a gross basis before and after processing. This item is an exception to the change of ownership principle.

155. *Repairs on goods* cover repair activity on goods provided to or received from nonresidents on ships, aircraft, etc. Although the physical movement of these goods is similar to that described in paragraph 154, the repairs are valued at the prices (fees paid or received) of the repairs and not at the gross values of the goods before and after repairs are made.

156. *Goods procured in ports by carriers* cover all goods (such as fuels, provisions, stores, and supplies) that resident/nonresident carriers—air, shipping, etc.—procure abroad (in the compiling economy). The classification does not cover the provision of auxiliary services (towing, maintenance, etc.), which are covered under *transportation.*

157. *Nonmonetary gold* covers exports and imports of all gold that is not held as a reserve asset (monetary gold) by the authorities. *Nonmonetary gold* is treated the same as any other commodity and is subdivided, when feasible, into gold held as a store of value and other (industrial) gold.

Services (1.A.b.)

158. *Transportation* covers most of the services, performed by residents for nonresidents and vice versa, that were included in shipment and other transportation in the fourth edition of the *Manual.* However, freight insurance is now included with *insurance services* rather than with *transportation. Transportation* includes freight and passenger transportation by all modes of transportation and other distributive and auxiliary services, including rentals of transportation equipment with crew. Certain exceptions are noted in chapters X, XI, and XIII.

159. *Travel* covers goods and services—including those related to health and education—acquired from an economy by nonresident travelers (including excursionists) for business purposes and personal use during their visits (of less than one year) in that economy. *Travel* excludes international passenger services, which are included in *transportation.* Students and medical patients are treated as travelers, regardless of their length of stay. Certain others—military and embassy personnel and nonresident workers—are not regarded as travelers. However, expenditures by nonresident workers are included in *travel,* while those of military and embassy personnel are included in *government services, n.i.e.* These cases are noted in chapters XII and XIII.

160. *Communications services* cover communications transactions between residents and nonresidents. Such services comprise postal, courier, and telecommunications services (transmission of sound, images, and other information by various modes and associated maintenance provided by/for residents by/for nonresidents).

161. *Construction services* cover construction and installation project work that is, on a temporary basis, performed abroad/in the compiling economy or in extraterritorial enclaves by resident/nonresident enterprises and their personnel. Such work does not include that undertaken by a foreign affiliate of a resident enterprise or by an unincorporated site office that, if it meets certain criteria, is equivalent to a foreign affiliate. Such residency aspects are covered in chapters IV and XIII.

162. *Insurance services* cover the provision of insurance to nonresidents by resident insurance enterprises and vice versa. This item comprises services provided for freight insurance (on goods exported and imported), services provided for other types of direct insurance (including life and non-life), and services provided for reinsurance. (For the method of calculating the value of insurance services, see paragraphs 256 and 257.)

163. *Financial services* (other than those related to insurance enterprises and pension funds) cover financial intermediation services and auxiliary services conducted between residents and nonresidents. Included are commissions and fees for letters of credit, lines of credit, financial leasing services, foreign exchange transactions, consumer and business credit services, brokerage services, underwriting services, arrangements for various forms of hedging instruments, etc. Auxiliary services include financial market operational and regulatory services, security custody services, etc.

164. *Computer and information services* cover resident/nonresident transactions related to hardware consultancy, software implementation, information services (data processing, database, news agency), and maintenance and repair of computers and related equipment.

165. *Royalties and license fees* cover receipts (exports) and payments (imports) of residents and nonresidents for: (i) the authorized use of intangible nonproduced, nonfinancial assets and proprietary rights such as trademarks, copyrights, patents, processes, techniques, designs, manufacturing rights, franchises, etc. and (ii) the use, through licensing agreements, of produced originals or prototypes, such as manuscripts, films, etc.

166. *Other business services* provided by residents to nonresidents and vice versa cover merchanting and other trade-related services; operational leasing services; and miscellaneous business, professional, and technical services. (See the table on *Selected Supplementary Information* following this chapter and paragraphs 261 through 264 for details.)

167. *Personal, cultural, and recreational services* cover (i) audiovisual and related services and (ii) other cultural services provided by residents to nonresidents and vice versa. Included under (i) are services associated with the production of motion pictures on films or video tape, radio and television programs, and musical recordings. (Examples of these services are rentals and fees received by actors, producers, etc. for productions and for distribution rights sold to the media.) Included under (ii) are other personal, cultural, and recreational services, such as those associated with libraries, museums, and other cultural and sporting activities.

168. *Government services, n.i.e.* cover all services (such as expenditures of embassies and consulates) associated with government sectors or international and regional organizations and not classified under other items.

Income (1.B.)

169. *Compensation of employees* covers wages, salaries, and other benefits, in cash or in kind, and includes those of border, seasonal, and other nonresident workers (e.g., local staff of embassies).

170. *Investment income* covers receipts and payments of income associated, respectively, with holdings of external financial assets by residents and with liabilities to nonresidents. *Investment income* consists of direct investment income, portfolio investment income, and other investment income. The direct investment component is broken down into income on equity (dividends, branch profits, and reinvested earnings) and income on debt (interest); portfolio investment income is broken down into income on equity (dividends) and income on debt (interest); other investment income covers interest earned on other capital (loans, etc.) and, in principle, imputed income to households from net equity in life insurance reserves and in pension funds.

Current transfers (1.C.)

171. ***Current transfers*** are distinguished from *capital transfers*, which are included in the **capital and financial account** in accordance with the *SNA* treatment of transfers. Transfers are the offsets to changes, which take place between residents and nonresidents, in ownership of real resources or financial items and, whether the changes are voluntary or compulsory, do not involve a quid pro quo in economic value. ***Current transfers*** consist of all transfers that **do not involve**: (i) transfers of ownership of fixed assets; (ii) transfers of funds linked to, or conditioned upon, acquisition or disposal of fixed assets; (iii) forgiveness, without any counterparts being received in return, of liabilities by creditors. All of these are *capital transfers*. ***Current transfers*** include those of general government (e.g., current international cooperation between different governments, payments of current taxes on income and wealth, etc.) and other transfers (e.g., workers' remittances, premiums—less service charges, and claims on non-life insurance). A full discussion of the distinction between ***current transfers*** and *capital transfers* appears in Chapter XV; see also paragraphs 175 and 344.

Capital and Financial Account (2.)

172. The **capital and financial account** has two major components—the ***capital account*** and the ***financial account***—that are in concordance with those same accounts in the *SNA*. Assets represent claims on nonresidents, and liabilities represent indebtedness to nonresidents. The two parties to a transaction in assets or liabilities are usually a resident and a nonresident but, in some instances, both parties may both be residents or nonresidents. (See paragraph 318.)

173. All valuation and other changes in foreign assets and liabilities, which do not reflect transactions (see paragraph 310), are excluded from the **capital and financial account** but are reflected in the international investment position. Supplementary statements identify certain items that are of analytical interest and that affect various accounts. Examples of such items are liabilities constituting foreign authorities' reserves and exceptional financing transactions, which are discussed in Chapter XXII.

174. Classification of the ***financial account*** and the income components of the **current account** are interrelated and must be consistent to facilitate analysis, to form an effective link between the balance of payments and the international investment position, and to be compatible with the *SNA* and other IMF statistical systems.

Capital account (2.A.)

175. The major components of the ***capital account*** are *capital transfers* and *acquisition/disposal of nonproduced, nonfinancial assets*. *Capital transfers* consist of those involving transfers of ownership of fixed assets; transfers of funds linked to, or conditional upon, acquisition or disposal of fixed assets; or cancellation, without any counterparts being received in return, of liabilities by creditors. *Capital transfers* include two components: (i) general government, subdivided into debt forgiveness and other, and (ii) other, subdivided into migrants' transfers, debt forgiveness, and other transfers. (See Chapter XV for discussion of the distinction between *capital transfers* and ***current transfers***. *Acquisition/disposal of nonproduced, nonfinancial assets* largely covers intangibles, such as patented entities, leases or other transferable contracts, goodwill, etc. This item does not cover land in a specific economic territory but may include the purchase or sale of land by a foreign embassy. (See paragraph 312.)

Financial account (2.B.)

176. The classification of standard components in the ***financial account*** is based on these criteria:

All components are classified according to type of investment or by functional breakdown (*direct investment, portfolio investment, other investment, reserve assets*).

For the category of *direct investment*, there are directional distinctions (abroad or in the reporting economy) and, for the equity capital and other capital components within this category, asset or liability distinctions.

For the categories of *portfolio investment* and *other investment*, there are the customary asset/liability distinctions.

Particularly significant for *portfolio investment* and *other investment* is the distinction by type of instrument (equity or debt securities, trade credits, loans, currency and deposits, other assets or liabilities). In this *Manual*, traditional and new money market and other financial instruments and derivatives are included in *portfolio investment*.

For *portfolio investment* and *other investment*, there are distinctions by sector of the domestic creditor for assets or by sector of the domestic debtor for liabilities. These distinctions serve to facilitate links with the income accounts, the international investment position, the *SNA*, and other statistical systems.

The traditional distinction, which is based on original contractual maturity of more than one year or one year or less, between long- and short-term assets and liabilities applies only to *other investment*. In recent years, the significance of this distinction has clearly diminished for many domestic and international transactions. Consequently, the long- and short-term distinction is accorded less importance in the *SNA* and in this *Manual* than in previous editions. However, because the maturity factor remains important for specific purposes—analysis of external debt, for example—it is retained in the *Manual* for *other investment*.

177. *Direct investment*—reflecting the lasting interest of a resident entity in one economy (direct investor) in an entity resident in another economy (direct investment enterprise)—covers all transactions between direct investors and direct investment enterprises. That is, *direct investment* covers the initial transaction between the two and all subsequent transactions between them and among affiliated enterprises, both incorporated and unincorporated. Direct investment transactions (abroad and in the reporting economy) are subclassified into equity capital, reinvested earnings, and other capital (intercompany transactions). For equity capital and other capital, claims on and liabilities to affiliated enterprises and to direct investors are distinguished. Transactions between affiliated banks and between other affiliated financial intermediaries are limited to equity and permanent debt capital. (See paragraph 372.)

178. *Portfolio investment* covers transactions in equity securities and debt securities; the latter are subsectored into bonds and notes, money market instruments, and financial derivatives (such as options) when the derivatives generate financial claims and liabilities. Various new financial instruments are covered under appropriate instrument classifications. (Transactions covered under *direct investment* and *reserve assets* are excluded.)

179. *Other investment* covers short- and long-term trade credits; loans (including use of Fund credit, loans from the Fund, and loans associated with financial leases); currency and deposits (transferable and other—such as savings and term deposits, savings and loan shares, shares in credit unions, etc.); and other accounts receivable and payable. (Transactions covered under *direct investment* are excluded.)

180. *Reserve assets* cover transactions in those assets that are considered, by the monetary authorities of an economy, to be available for use in meeting balance of payments and, in some instances, other needs. Such availability is not closely linked in principle to formal criteria such as ownership or currency of denomination. The items covered are monetary gold, SDRs, reserve position in the Fund, foreign exchange assets (currency, deposits, and securities), and other claims.

181. Coverage and identification of *reserve asset* components are linked to an analytic concept, are in part judgmental, and are not always amenable to application of objective, formal criteria or clear rankings as to conditionality and other considerations. In contrast to the treatment in the fourth edition of the *Manual*, valuation changes in *reserve assets* are excluded, along with counterparts to such changes, in the fifth edition. Also excluded are the allocation/cancellation of SDRs, the monetization/demonetization of gold, and counterpart entries. These changes, which do not constitute transactions, are reflected in the international investment position.

INTRODUCTION[1]

Le volume 47 du *Balance of Payments Yearbook (Yearbook)* (Annuaire de statistiques de balance des paiements), publié par le Fonds monétaire international (FMI), présente les données de balance des paiements communiquées au FMI par ses pays membres. Le FMI est redevable à ceux-ci d'avoir collaboré à cet ouvrage en lui fournissant ces données. Pour certains de ces pays, les données sont parfois complétées par des renseignements que les économistes du FMI ont tirés d'autres sources. Les caractéristiques introduites dans le volume 46 sont conservées dans le présent volume du *Yearbook* et s'accompagnent de nouvelles. En particulier, cet ouvrage offre pour la première fois des données sur la position extérieure globale (PEG), présentées conformément aux recommandations de la cinquième édition du *Manuel de la balance des paiements (Manuel)* du FMI, pour les pays qui établissent cette catégorie de statistiques. En outre, dans une nouvelle partie (la troisième du *Yearbook*), le volume 47 fait montre d'innovation en présentant une analyse détaillée des méthodologies, méthodes de calcul et sources de données utilisées par la plupart des pays qui y sont inclus.

Comme le volume 46, le présent volume du *Yearbook* contient des données de balance des paiements présentées conformément à la classification des composantes types adoptées dans la cinquième édition du *Manuel*[2]. Publiée par le FMI en septembre 1993[3], la cinquième édition apporte un certain nombre de changements à la méthodologie utilisée pour l'établissement des données de balance des paiements. Ces changements sont décrits en détail au chapitre I de la cinquième édition du *Manuel* et sont résumés dans l'encadré figurant à la page F-iii du présent volume. En outre, comme dans le volume précédent, les données présentées ici conformément à la classification des composantes types adoptée dans la cinquième édition s'accompagnent d'une série de codes, établis conjointement par le FMI, l'Organisation de coopération et de développement économiques (OCDE) et l'Office statistique de l'Union européenne (Eurostat). La structure de ces codes est décrite en annexe. Cependant, contrairement à ses prédécesseurs, le présent volume ne présente plus de données trimestrielles de balance des paiements pour les pays qui communiquent des statistiques trimestrielles de ce type au FMI. Ces données trimestrielles continueront à être publiées dans le numéro mensuel de *Statistiques financières internationales*.

La conversion des données par les services du FMI a permis de présenter, selon la classification retenue dans la cinquième édition, les statistiques de la base de données du FMI qui se rapportent à des périodes passées, ainsi que les données communiquées pour des périodes plus récentes par les pays membres qui continuent à suivre les recommandations de la quatrième édition du *Manuel de la balance des paiements*. En 1995, les services du FMI ont mis au point des clés de conversion permettant de mettre sous une forme à peu près conforme à la méthodologie et à la présentation retenues dans la cinquième édition les données de balance des paiements reçues de chaque pays et figurant dans la base de données du FMI. Une fois converties, les données ont été soumises à l'examen des autorités du pays en question, et les observations qui ont été formulées ont été incorporées dans la nouvelle base de données conforme à la cinquième édition. En 1996, avec la collaboration des autorités nationales, les services du FMI ont procédé d'une manière analogue pour présenter conformément à la cinquième édition les données sur la position extérieure globale (PEG) établies selon les recommandations de la quatrième édition. La PEG d'un pays est un relevé du stock de ses avoirs et engagements financiers extérieurs. Pour les pays qui les ont communiquées, ces données de stock sont présentées ici pour la première fois selon la classification des composantes types de la PEG adoptée dans la cinquième édition. Les données converties sur la PEG de certains pays ne sont pas assez détaillées pour être publiées. Dès lors que les autorités des pays membres et les services du FMI continueront d'affiner la méthode de conversion et que des données de stock plus détaillées seront recueillies et transmises au FMI, la base de données sera révisée et une présentation élargie des données de la PEG sera publiée dans les volumes ultérieurs du *Yearbook*.

Le présent volume fournit également pour la première fois une description technique des méthodologies, méthodes de calcul et sources de données utilisées par les pays qui communiquent des statistiques. Ces descriptions se fondent en grande partie sur les renseignements transmis au FMI par les pays. Elles ont pour but de renseigner les utilisateurs sur la couverture et les limitations des données publiées pour les divers pays dans le *Yearbook*, et les statisticiens sur les sources de données et méthodes utilisées par leurs homologues étrangers. Comme il s'agit ici d'une initiative nouvelle, ces descriptions sont appelées à être élargies et améliorées dans les volumes suivants du *Yearbook*, notamment sous la forme d'une uniformisation plus poussée de leur contenu pour tous les pays. Les changements qui seront apportés aux sources et méthodes de calcul seront eux aussi indiqués dans les descriptions ultérieures.

[1]Les versions française et espagnole de la présente introduction font suite aux annexes, lesquelles précèdent immédiatement les pages consacrées aux différents pays.

[2]Le volume 1 du *Yearbook*, paru en 1949, était fondé sur la première édition du *Manuel de la balance des paiements* du FMI, publiée en 1948; les volumes 2 à 12, sur la deuxième édition du *Manuel*, publiée en 1950; les volumes 13 à 23, sur la troisième édition du *Manuel*, publiée en 1961; et les volumes 24 à 29, sur la troisième édition, ainsi que sur le *Manuel de la balance des paiements : supplément à la troisième édition*, paru en 1973. Les volumes 30 à 45 ont été établis sur la base des recommandations de la quatrième édition du *Manuel*, publiée en 1977.

[3]Fonds monétaire international, *Manuel de la balance des paiements*, cinquième édition, Washington, DC, septembre 1993.

Le présent volume du *Yearbook* se compose de trois parties. La première présente les données de la balance des paiements et de la PEG pour les divers pays. La deuxième contient des totaux régionaux et mondiaux pour les principales composantes de la balance des paiements. La troisième partie fournit une description technique des méthodes de certains pays qui ont communiqué les données. La première partie constitue une publication distincte, et les deuxième et troisième parties sont publiées ensemble.

Le reste de la présente introduction s'articule comme suit :

- La section I décrit les caractéristiques fondamentales des tableaux publiés dans la première partie du présent volume du *Yearbook*. (Des détails sur le champ couvert par les données des deuxième et troisième partie sont fournis dans la publication séparée.)
- La section II donne des indications sur l'abonnement aux bandes de données de balance des paiements du FMI.
- Il y a six annexes. L'annexe I contient une présentation analytique des composantes de la balance des paiements (accompagnées des codes correspondants). L'annexe II présente les composantes types définies dans la cinquième édition (et les codes correspondants). L'annexe III explique le système de codage des données. L'annexe IV présente les composantes types de la PEG, telles qu'elles ressortent de la cinquième édition. L'annexe V est consacré au cadre conceptuel de la balance des paiements. L'annexe VI décrit le champ couvert par les principales composantes de la balance des paiements, telles qu'elles sont définies dans la cinquième édition.

I. Première partie du Yearbook : données relatives aux divers pays

La première partie du *Yearbook* présente les pages consacrées aux divers pays suivant un ordre alphabétique. Il convient de noter, toutefois, que, dans la présente publication, le terme «pays» ne désigne pas toujours une entité territoriale constituant un État tel qu'il est défini selon l'usage et le droit internationaux; ce terme recouvre également certaines entités territoriales qui ne sont pas des États souverains mais sur lesquelles des données statistiques sont tenues à jour et fournies, séparément et indépendamment, au niveau international.

Pour la plupart des pays, les données de balance des paiements se présentent sous la forme de deux tableaux. Le tableau 1 est un résumé analytique des données plus détaillées contenues dans le tableau 2. Les composantes de la balance des paiements figurant au tableau 1 sont disposées de manière à mettre en relief les postes de financement (réserves et postes apparentés). (Voir l'annexe I.) Le tableau 2 présente les données correspondant aux composantes types décrites dans la cinquième édition. (Voir l'annexe II.) Dans le cas des pays pour lesquels on dispose de données sur la PEG, celles-ci sont fournies au tableau 3. Les tableaux 1, 2 et 3 présentent, pour chaque pays, des données relatives aux années 1988–95. Les pays ne sont inclus dans les tableaux que si l'on dispose sur eux de données se rapportant au moins à deux années de la période considérée. Sauf indication contraire, les chiffres portent sur l'année civile.

Présentation analytique

Dans la présentation analytique, les composantes de la balance des paiements sont réparties entre cinq grandes catégories (groupes A à E), que le FMI juge utiles à une analyse homogène de l'évolution de la balance des paiements. Cependant, le choix des groupes ne saurait être considéré comme découlant de la recommandation du FMI quant à l'approche analytique à retenir pour chaque pays. Il existe d'autres types de présentation analytique, qui consisteraient à regrouper les composantes types du tableau 2 d'une manière différente, soit pour tenir compte de la situation particulière d'un pays donné, soit pour répondre à des besoins analytiques précis.

Il convient de noter que les données présentées au tableau 1 sur le solde du compte des transactions courantes, du compte de capital et du compte d'opérations financières de certains pays ne concordent pas avec les données correspondantes du tableau 2. Cela tient au fait que, dans le tableau 1, certaines transactions relevant de ces comptes en sont exclus et sont reclassées au poste des «financements exceptionnels» ou des «engagements constituant des avoirs de réserve pour les autorités étrangères» et regroupées sous la rubrique des réserves et postes apparentés. Les «financements exceptionnels» ont trait aux transactions que les autorités effectuent pour répondre aux besoins de financement de la balance des paiements et prennent notamment la forme d'emprunts extérieurs, d'arriérés de paiements et de remises de dette. Les financements exceptionnels ne comprennent pas les réserves et les engagements constituant des avoirs de réserve pour les autorités étrangères, lesquels sont des engagements qui sont considérés comme des avoirs de réserve par le pays créancier.

Présentation type

Comme le montre le tableau 2, la liste des composantes types retenue dans la cinquième édition laisse apparaître une classification plus détaillée des biens et services que celle qui figure dans la quatrième édition. Le compte dénommé «compte de capital et d'opérations financières» comporte deux volets distincts, qui sont le «compte de capital» et le «compte d'opérations financières». Les composantes du «compte d'opérations financières» sont classées selon plusieurs critères : type d'investissement (c'est-à-dire investissements directs, investissements de portefeuille, autres investissements et avoirs de réserve), avoirs et engagments, secteur intérieur (autorités monétaires, administrations publiques, banques et autres secteurs) et échéance (long terme et court terme).

Encadré : Principales différences entre la cinquième et la quatrième édition du *Manuel*

La cinquième édition présente, par rapport à l'édition précédente, d'importants changements, qui ont pour objet de tenir compte de l'évolution du commerce mondial et des finances internationales depuis une dizaine d'années. En outre, les concepts de la cinquième édition ont été dans la mesure du possible harmonisés avec ceux du *Système de comptabilité nationale* de 1993 (*SCN 1993*) et des systèmes de statistiques financières et de statistiques de finances publiques du FMI. Les principales différences entre la méthodologie de la cinquième édition et celle de la quatrième qui influent sensiblement sur la signification et la présentation des données de balance des paiements présentées dans le *Yearbook* sont les suivantes :

1) Le champ couvert par le «compte des transactions courantes» dans la cinquième édition est différent de celui qu'il recouvre dans la quatrième. Dans la cinquième édition, le «compte des transactions courantes» englobe les transactions sur biens, services, revenus avec les non-résidents ainsi que les recettes et paiements au titre des transferts courants; dans la quatrième édition, il recouvre les biens, services et tous les transferts. Dans la cinquième édition, les transferts de capital sont inclus dans un compte élargi et rebaptisé «compte de capital et d'opérations financières». La distinction entre transferts courants et transferts de capital est fondée sur les directives du *SCN 1993*, selon lesquelles a) un transfert en nature est un transfert de capital lorsqu'il y a transfert de propriété d'un actif fixe ou annulation d'un engagement par un créancier qui ne reçoit rien en échange; et b) un transfert en espèces est un transfert de capital lorsqu'il est lié ou subordonné à l'acquisition ou à la cession d'un actif fixe (par exemple un don d'équipement) par l'une des parties ou par les deux parties à la transaction.

2) Dans la cinquième édition, le champ couvert par les biens a été élargi pour inclure a) la valeur (brute) des biens reçus ou expédiés pour être transformés et l'exportation ou importation ultérieure de ces biens après leur transformation; b) la valeur des réparations de biens; et c) la valeur des achats de biens dans les ports par les transporteurs. Dans la quatrième édition, la différence entre la valeur nette des biens importés pour être transformés et celle des biens réexportés par la suite était incluse dans les services de transformation; les réparations de biens et les achats de biens dans les ports par les transporteurs figuraient eux aussi parmi les services.

3) Les revenus, qui étaient une sous-composante des services dans la quatrième édition, sont classés séparément dans la cinquième édition. Les transactions sur certains revenus et services sont elles aussi classées différemment dans la cinquième édition. Selon la quatrième édition, les revenus du travail recouvraient, outre la rémunération des travailleurs, les dépenses des travailleurs non résidents; dans la cinquième édition, la rémunération des travailleurs est classée au poste de la rémunération des salariés sous la rubrique des revenus et leurs dépenses figurent parmi les services de voyage. Dans la quatrième édition, la rémunération du personnel résident des ambassades étrangères et bases militaires, ainsi que des organisations internationales, était incluse dans les services aux administrations publiques. Dans la cinquième édition, cette rémunération est inscrite au crédit du poste de la rémunération des salariés. Par ailleurs, la quatrième édition inclut dans le revenu de la propriété les paiements pour utilisation de brevets, droits d'auteur et autres actifs incorporels non financiers du même type, alors que la cinquième édition en fait des sous-composantes des autres services. En général, dans la cinquième édition, le concept de revenu englobe le revenu des investissements ainsi que la rémunération des salariés sous toutes ses formes, alors que, dans la quatrième édition, il recouvrait le revenu des investissements, la plupart des catégories de revenu du travail (y compris les dépenses des travailleurs à l'étranger) et le revenu de la propriété.

4) Le compte «Capitaux» de la quatrième édition a été modifié dans la cinquième édition et rebaptisé «compte de capital et d'opérations financières»; recouvrant un champ plus vaste que son prédécesseur, ce nouveau compte comporte deux grands volets. Le premier est le compte de capital, dans lequel sont enregistrés a) les recettes ou paiements au titre des transferts de capital et b) les acquisitions et cessions d'actifs non financiers non produits. Le deuxième est le compte d'opérations financières; correspondant à peu près au compte «Capitaux» de la quatrième édition, ce compte retrace toutes les transactions impliquant un transfert de propriété d'actifs et de passifs financiers extérieurs d'une économie à des non-résidents, tel que la création, l'échange et la liquidation de créances sur le reste du monde ou par le reste du monde.

5) Dans la cinquième édition, comme dans la quatrième, les investissements directs sont classés principalement en fonction de leur destination — investissements directs des résidents à l'étranger et investissements directs des non-résidents dans l'économie. Dans la cinquième édition, toutes les transactions entre les entreprises d'investissement direct non financières et leurs maisons mères sont incluses dans les investissements directs. Les transactions entre banques apparentées et entre autres intermédiaires financiers apparentés à classer dans les investissements directs se limitent à celles qui ont un caractère permanent (participations au capital social et capitaux empruntés représentant un intérêt permanent). Les autres transactions entre banques et institutions financières apparentées doivent être classées, selon le cas, parmi les investissements de portefeuille ou les autres investissements. (Dans la quatrième édition, seules les transactions à court terme de ce type étaient exclues des investissements directs.)

6) Dans la cinquième édition, le champ couvert par les investissements de portefeuille a été élargi de façon à tenir compte du développement des nouveaux instruments financiers observé ces dernières années. Le principal changement a trait à l'inclusion dans les investissements de portefeuille des instruments du marché monétaire et des dérivés financiers négociables, lesquels étaient classés parmi les «autres capitaux» dans la quatrième édition.

Il existe encore de nombreuses autres différences dans la présentation des données de balance des paiements entre la cinquième et la quatrième édition. (Pour une description détaillée de la nouvelle méthodologie, voir la cinquième édition du *Manuel*.)

Position extérieure globale

Comme le montre le tableau 3, les données de la PEG sont disposées conformément à la classification des composantes types de la PEG retenue dans la cinquième édition. (Voir l'annexe IV.)

La classification des composantes de la PEG présentée au tableau 3 correspond à celle des composantes du compte d'opérations financières de la balance des paiements figurant au tableau 2, mais il existe pourtant un certain nombre de différences entre les deux tableaux. Comme indiqué précédemment, la PEG est un relevé des avoirs et engagements extérieurs d'un pays à un moment précis. Dans le tableau 3, par conséquent, la présentation de base des composantes de la PEG fait apparaître deux catégories générales, celles des avoirs et des engagements, par opposition à la classification fonctionnelle des investissements retenue au tableau 2 (investissements directs, investissements de portefeuille, autres investissements et avoirs de réserve). En outre, le tableau 3 présente la PEG d'un pays à la fin de la période considérée, alors que le tableau 2 retarce les transactions effectuées pendant cette période. En outre, contrairement au tableau 2, qui indique la valeur des transactions financières pendant une période, le tableau 3 présente de la PEG d'un pays une évaluation qui reflète les transactions financières, réévaluations et autres ajustements opérés durant la période. La PEG nette indiquée au tableau 3 est égale à la différence entre la valeur des avoirs financiers extérieurs et celle des engagements financiers extérieurs.

Voir le chapitre XXIII de la cinquième édition du *Manuel* pour une étude exhaustive du concept de position extérieure globale.

Codage des données

Dans les tableaux 1 et 2, chaque catégorie de données et chaque composante sont accompagnées d'un code. Comme indiqué plus haut, ces codes ont été établis conjointement par le FMI, l'OCDE et Eurostat en vue de faciliter la communication des statistiques au niveau international. Les codes s'appliquent aux composantes types de la balance des paiements et de la position extérieure globale, telles qu'elles sont définies dans la cinquième édition du *Manuel*, ainsi qu'aux composantes de la classification OCDE/Eurostat pour le commerce des services.

Chaque code figurant dans le *Yearbook* est un code alphanumérique à six composantes. Le chiffre placé en première position indique s'il s'agit d'un crédit, d'un débit ou d'un solde; le chiffre «2» désigne un crédit, «3» un crédit et «4» un solde (différence entre crédit et débit). Les trois chiffres suivants correspondent au code attribué à la composante de la balance des paiements. Par exemple, le compte des transactions courantes a pour code 993, le compte de capital, 994, et le compte d'opérations financières, 995.

Les cinquième et sixième chiffres ou lettres du code présenté dans le *Yearbook* servent à signaler l'existence de caractéristiques spéciales pour certaines composantes. Par exemple, dans le tableau 1, la lettre Y, placée en cinquième position, indique que les financements exceptionnels et les engagements constituant des avoirs de réserve pour les autorités étrangères sont exclus de la composante; X signifie que, outre les financements exceptionnels et les engagements constituant des avoirs de réserve pour les autorités étrangères, les données excluent l'utilisation des crédits et prêts du FMI. Les lettres A, B, C et D sont utilisées, dans le tableau 1, pour différencier les divers secteurs intérieurs. Au tableau 2, les lettres A, B et C servent à indiquer qu'il ne s'agit pas de sous-composantes types, comme c'est le cas, par exemple, pour les postes ayant trait aux transports (passagers, fret et autres).

Écritures passées au crédit et au débit

Les données présentées aux tableaux 1 et 2 sur les transactions sont les montants bruts inscrits au crédit ou au débit du compte des transactions courantes et du compte de capital, et les montants nets (correspondant aux variations nettes des engagements et des avoirs) portés au crédit ou au débit du compte d'opérations financières. Les montants inscrits au crédit, qu'ils soient bruts ou nets, sont positifs (mais ne sont pas accompagnés du signe plus) et les montants portés au débit, bruts ou nets, sont négatifs (ils sont affectés du signe moins). En conséquence, la diminution des avoirs et l'augmentation des engagements (crédit) sont indiquées par des chiffres positifs, et l'accroissement des avoirs et la diminution des engagements (débit), par des chiffres négatifs.

Montants nuls ou non disponibles

Lorsqu'il manque des chiffres dans les statistiques communiquées par les pays, il est souvent difficile de savoir si ces données font défaut parce qu'elles ne sont pas disponibles, ou parce qu'il s'agit de montants nuls ou né-gligeables. Dans les tableaux du *Yearbook*, le symbole (...) indique que les données ne sont pas disponibles, ou que les montants sont nuls ou négligeables.

Présentation de chiffres arrondis

La plupart des chiffres des tableaux sont exprimés en millions; il ne faut pas présumer qu'un tableau présentant des chiffres exprimés en unités plus petites fournit nécessairement des données plus exactes. L'unité est choisie pour des raisons de commodité. Étant donné les routines utilisées pour le calcul, il peut exister un écart, dû au fait que les chiffres ont été arrondis, entre le total indiqué et la somme de ses composantes.

Méthodes de conversion

La plupart des données de balance des paiements communiquées au FMI sont exprimées en monnaie nationale ou en dollars E.U bien que quelques pays fournissent certaines données en DTS. Pour faciliter les comparaisons entre pays, tous les états de balance des paiements publiés dans le *Yearbook* sont exprimés en dollars E.U. En outre, dans tous les cas, les données que les pays communiquent sur leurs transactions avec le FMI et sur leurs transactions en DTS sont remplacées par des données tirées des registres du FMI, qui sont exprimées en DTS; celles-ci sont à leur tour converties en dollars E.U.

Pour les pays qui communiquent des données exprimées en unités autres que le dollar E.U., les données sont converties à l'aide des taux de conversion figurant au bas du tableau 1 relatif aux pays en question. Ces taux de conversion sont normalement les taux de change moyens de la monnaie du pays pour la période considérée publiés dans *Statistiques financières internationales (SFI)*. Par exemple, les pages consacrées aux Pays-Bas dans SFI comportent la ligne «rf», qui présente le taux moyen du dollar en florins. Les données de flux exprimées en DTS sont converties en dollars E.U. à l'aide des taux indiqués à la ligne «sb» de la page consacrée aux États-Unis dans SFI. Pour les pays qui transmettent des données trimestrielles exprimées en monnaie nationale, le total annuel en dollars E.U. est égal à la somme des données trimestrielles en dollars E.U.

De plus amples renseignements sur les taux de change utilisés sont fournis dans la section 1 de l'introduction à *SFI*.

II. Abonnement aux bandes

Les statistiques publiées dans le *Yearbook* sont également disponibles sous forme de bandes[1]. Le nombre des pays et des séries chronologiques figurant sur les bandes est légèrement supérieur à celui qui est présenté dans la version imprimée du *Yearbook*, de même que le nombre des périodes auxquelles se rapportent les séries chronologiques. Les abonnés aux bandes reçoivent la première partie de la version imprimée du *Yearbook,* ainsi que douze bandes magnétiques mensuelles, sur lesquelles les données mises à jour et révisées sont enregistrées dès qu'elles sont disponibles. Les demandes de renseignements concernant les bandes doivent être adressées à :

Publication Services
International Monetary Fund
Washington, DC 20431, U.S.A.
Téléphone : (202) 623–7430
Télécopie : (202) 623–7201

[1]Un autre type de support, les disques optiques compacts (CD-ROM), sera disponible à l'avenir.

Annexe I. Présentation analytique

	Codes
A. COMPTE DES TRANSACTIONS COURANTES[1]	4 993 Y .
Biens : exportations, f.à.b.	2 100 . .
Biens : importations, f.à.b.	3 100 . .
Solde au titre des biens	4 100 . .
Services : crédit	2 200 . .
Services : débit	3 200 . .
Solde au titre des biens et services	4 991 . .
Revenus : crédit	2 300 . .
Revenus : débit	3 300 . .
Solde au titre des biens, services et revenus	4 992 . .
Transferts courants : crédit	2 379 Y .
Transferts courants : débit	3 379 . .
B. COMPTE DE CAPITAL[1]	4 994 Y .
Compte de capital : crédit	2 994 Y .
Compte de capital : débit	3 994 . .
Total, groupes A plus B	4 010 . .
C. COMPTE D'OPÉRATIONS FINANCIÈRES[1]	4 995 X .
Investissements directs à l'étranger	4 505 . .
Investissements directs dans l'économie	4 555 Y .
Investissements de portefeuille : avoirs	4 602 . .
Titres de participation	4 610 . .
Titres de créance	4 619 . .
Investissements de portefeuille : engagements	4 652 Y .
Titres de participation	4 660 Y .
Titres d'engagement	4 669 Y .
Autres investissements : avoirs	4 703 . .
Autorités monétaires	4 703 .A
Administrations publiques	4 703 .B
Banques	4 703 .C
Autres secteurs	4 703 .D
Autres investissements : engagements	4 753 X .
Autorités monétaires	4 753 XA
Administrations publiques	4 753 YB
Banques	4 753 YC
Autres secteurs	4 753 YD
Total, groupes A à C inclus	4 020 . .
D. ERREURS ET OMISSIONS NETTES	4 998 . .
Total, groupes A à D inclus	4 030 . .
E. RÉSERVES ET POSTES APPARENTÉS	4 040 . .
Avoirs de réserve	4 800 . .
Utilisation des crédits et prêts du FMI	4 766 . .
Engagements constituant des réserves pour les autorités étrangères	4 900 . .
Financements exceptionnels	4 920 . .
TAUX DE CONVERSION : MONTANT D'UNITÉS MONÉTAIRES POUR UN DOLLAR E.U.	0 101 . .

[1]Non compris les composantes qui font partie des catégories du groupe E.

Annexe II. Composantes types

	Codes
COMPTE DES TRANSACTIONS COURANTES	4 993 . .
A. BIENS	4 100 . .
Crédit	2 100 . .
Marchandises générales : exportations, f.à.b.	2 110 . .
Biens exportés pour transformation, f.à.b.	2 150 . .
Réparations de biens	2 160 . .
Achats de biens dans les ports par les transporteurs	2 170 . .
Or non monétaire	2 180 . .
Débit	3 100 . .
Marchandises générales : importations, f.à.b.	3 110 . .
Biens importés pour transformation, f.à.b.	3 150 . .
Réparations de biens	3 160 . .
Achats de biens dans les ports par les transporteurs	3 170 . .
Or non monétaire	3 180 . .
B. SERVICES	4 200 . .
Total, crédit	2 200 . .
Total, débit	3 200 . .
Services de transport, crédit	2 205 . .
Passagers	2 205 BA
Fret	2 205 BB
Autres	2 205 BC
Transports maritimes, passagers	2 207 . .
Transports maritimes, fret	2 208 . .
Transports maritimes, autres	2 209 . .
Transports aériens, passagers	2 211 . .
Transports aériens, fret	2 212 . .
Transports aériens, autres	2 213 . .
Autres transports, passagers	2 215 . .
Autres transports, fret	2 216 . .
Autres transports, autres	2 217 . .
Services de transport, débit	3 205 . .
Passagers	3 205 BA
Fret	3 205 BB
Autres	3 205 BC
Transports maritimes, passagers	3 207 . .
Transports maritimes, fret	3 208 . .
Transports maritimes, autres	3 209 . .
Transports aériens, passagers	3 211 . .
Transports aériens, fret	3 212 . .
Transports aériens, autres	3 213 . .
Autres transports, passagers	3 215 . .
Autres transports, fret	3 216 . .
Autres transports, autres	3 217 . .
Voyages, crédit	2 236 . .
Voyages à titre professionnel	2 237 . .
Voyages à titre personnel	2 240 . .
Voyages, débit	3 236 . .
Voyages à titre professionnel	3 237 . .
Voyages à titre personnel	3 240 . .

Annexe II. Composantes types *(suite)*

	Codes
Autres services, crédit	2 200 BA
Services de communication	2 245 . .
Services de bâtiment et travaux publics	2 249 . .
Services d'assurance	2 253 . .
Services financiers	2 260 . .
Services d'informatique et d'information	2 262 . .
Redevances et droits de licence	2 266 . .
Autres services aux entreprises	2 268 . .
Services personnels, culturels et relatifs aux loisirs	2 287 . .
Services fournis ou reçus par les administrations publiques, n.c.a.	2 291 . .
Autres services, débit	3 200 BA
Services de communication	3 245 . .
Services de bâtiment et travaux publics	3 249 . .
Services d'assurance	3 253 . .
Services financiers	3 260 . .
Services d'informatique et d'information	3 262 . .
Redevances et droits de licence	3 266 . .
Autres services aux entreprises	3 268 . .
Services personnels, culturels et relatifs aux loisirs	3 287 . .
Services fournis ou reçus par les administrations publiques, n.c.a.	3 291 . .
C. REVENUS	4 300 . .
Total, crédit	2 300 . .
Total, débit	3 300 . .
Rémunération des salariés, crédit	2 310 . .
Rémunération des salariés, débit	3 310 . .
Revenu des investissements, crédit	2 320 . .
Revenu des investissements directs	2 330 . .
Dividendes et bénéfices distribués des succursales	2 332 . .
Bénéfices réinvestis et bénéfices non distribués des succursales	2 333 . .
Revenu des titres de créance (intérêts)	2 334 . .
Revenu des investissements de portefeuille	2 339 . .
Revenu des titres de participation	2 340 . .
Revenu des obligations et autres titres d'emprunt	2 350 . .
Revenu des instruments du marché monétaire et dérivés financiers	2 360 . .
Revenu des autres investissements	2 370 . .
Revenu des investissements, débit	3 320 . .
Revenu des investissements directs	3 330 . .
Dividendes et bénéfices distribués des succursales	3 332 . .
Bénéfices réinvestis et bénéfices non distribués des succursales	3 333 . .
Revenu des titres de créance (intérêts)	3 334 . .
Revenu des investissements de portefeuille	3 339 . .
Revenu des titres de participation	3 340 . .
Revenu des obligations et autres titres d'emprunt	3 350 . .
Revenu des instruments du marché monétaire et dérivés financiers	3 360 . .
Revenu des autres investissements	3 370 . .
D. TRANSFERTS COURANTS	4 379 . .
Crédit	2 379 . .
Administrations publiques	2 380 . .
Autres secteurs	2 390 . .

ANNEXE II. COMPOSANTES TYPES *(suite)*

	Codes	
Envois de fonds des travailleurs	2 391	. .
Autres transferts courants	2 392	. .
Débit	3 379	. .
Administrations publiques	3 380	. .
Autres secteurs	3 390	. .
Envois de fonds des travailleurs	3 391	. .
Autres transferts courants	3 392	. .
COMPTE DE CAPITAL ET D'OPÉRATIONS FINANCIÈRES	4 996	. .
COMPTE DE CAPITAL	4 994	. .
Total, crédit	2 994	. .
Total, débit	3 994	. .
Transferts de capital, crédit	2 400	. .
Administrations publiques	2 401	. .
Remise de dettes	2 402	. .
Autres transferts de capital	2 410	. .
Autres secteurs	2 430	. .
Transferts des migrants	2 431	. .
Remise de dettes	2 432	. .
Autres transferts de capital	2 440	. .
Transferts de capital, débit	3 400	. .
Administrations publiques	3 401	. .
Remise de dettes	3 402	. .
Autres transferts de capital	3 410	. .
Autres secteurs	3 430	. .
Transferts des migrants	3 431	. .
Remise de dettes	3 432	. .
Autres transferts de capital	3 440	. .
Acquisitions et cessions d'actifs non financiers non produits, crédit	2 480	. .
Acquisitions et cessions d'actifs non financiers non produits, débit	3 480	. .
Compte d'opérations financières	4 995	. .
A. INVESTISSEMENTS DIRECTS	4 500	. .
De l'économie à l'étranger	4 505	. .
Capital social	4 510	. .
Créances sur les entreprises apparentées	4 515	. .
Engagements envers les entreprises apparentées	4 520	. .
Bénéfices réinvestis	4 525	. .
Autres transactions	4 530	. .
Créances sur les entreprises apparentées	4 535	. .
Engagements envers les entreprises apparentées	4 540	. .
De l'étranger dans l'économie	4 555	. .
Capital social	4 560	. .
Créances sur les investisseurs directs	4 565	. .
Engagements envers les investisseurs directs	4 570	. .
Bénéfices réinvestis	4 575	. .
Autres transactions	4 580	. .
Créances sur les investisseurs directs	4 585	. .
Engagements envers les investisseurs directs	4 590	. .

Annexe II. Composantes types *(suite)*

	Codes	
B. INVESTISSEMENTS DE PORTEFEUILLE	4 600	. .
Avoirs	4 602	. .
Titres de participation	4 610	. .
Autorités monétaires	4 611	. .
Administrations publiques	4 612	. .
Banques	4 613	. .
Autres secteurs	4 614	. .
Titres de créance	4 619	. .
Obligations et autres titres d'emprunt	4 620	. .
Autorités monétaires	4 621	. .
Administrations publiques	4 622	. .
Banques	4 623	. .
Autres secteurs	4 624	. .
Instruments du marché monétaire	4 630	. .
Autorités monétaires	4 631	. .
Administrations publiques	4 632	. .
Banques	4 633	. .
Autres secteurs	4 634	. .
Produits financiers dérivés	4 640	. .
Autorités monétaires	4 641	. .
Administrations publiques	4 642	. .
Banques	4 643	. .
Autres secteurs	4 644	. .
Engagements	4 652	. .
Titres de participation	4 660	. .
Banques	4 663	. .
Autres secteurs	4 664	. .
Titres d'engagement	4 669	. .
Obligations et autres titres d'emprunt	4 670	. .
Autorités monétaires	4 671	. .
Administrations publiques	4 672	. .
Banques	4 673	. .
Autres secteurs	4 674	. .
Instruments du marché monétaire	4 680	. .
Autorités monétaires	4 681	. .
Administrations publiques	4 682	. .
Banques	4 683	. .
Autres secteurs	4 684	. .
Produits financiers dérivés	4 690	. .
Autorités monétaires	4 691	. .
Administrations publiques	4 692	. .
Banques	4 693	. .
Autres secteurs	4 694	. .
C. AUTRES INVESTISSEMENTS	4 700	. .
Avoirs	4 703	. .
Crédits commerciaux	4 706	. .
Administrations publiques : long terme	4 708	. .
Administrations publiques : court terme	4 709	. .
Autres secteurs : long terme	4 711	. .
Autres secteurs : court terme	4 712	. .

ANNEXE II. COMPOSANTES TYPES *(suite)*

	Codes	
Prêts	4 714	. .
Autorités monétaires : long terme	4 717	. .
Autorités monétaires : court terme	4 718	. .
Administrations publiques : long terme	4 720	. .
Administrations publiques : court terme	4 721	. .
Banques : long terme	4 723	. .
Banques : court terme	4 724	. .
Autres secteurs : long terme	4 726	. .
Autres secteurs : court terme	4 727	. .
Monnaie fiduciaire et dépôts	4 730	. .
Autorités monétaires	4 731	. .
Administrations publiques	4 732	. .
Banques	4 733	. .
Autres secteurs	4 734	. .
Autres avoirs	4 736	. .
Autorités monétaires : long terme	4 738	. .
Autorités monétaires : court terme	4 739	. .
Administrations publiques : long terme	4 741	. .
Administrations publiques : court terme	4 742	. .
Banques : long terme	4 744	. .
Banques : court terme	4 745	. .
Autres secteurs : long terme	4 747	. .
Autres secteurs : court terme	4 748	. .
Engagements	4 753	. .
Crédits commerciaux	4 756	. .
Administrations publiques : long terme	4 758	. .
Administrations publiques : court terme	4 759	. .
Autres secteurs : long terme	4 761	. .
Autres secteurs : court terme	4 762	. .
Prêts	4 764	. .
Utilisation des crédits et prêts du FMI	4 766	. .
Autorités monétaires : autres prêts à long terme	4 767	. .
Autorités monétaires : court terme	4 768	. .
Administrations publiques : long terme	4 770	. .
Administrations publiques : court terme	4 771	. .
Banques : long terme	4 773	. .
Banques : court terme	4 774	. .
Autres secteurs : long terme	4 776	. .
Autres secteurs : court terme	4 777	. .
Monnaie fiduciaire et dépôts	4 780	. .
Autorités monétaires	4 781	. .
Administrations publiques	4 782	. .
Banques	4 783	. .
Autres secteurs	4 784	. .
Autres engagements	4 786	. .
Autorités monétaires : long terme	4 788	. .
Autorités monétaires : court terme	4 789	. .
Administrations publiques : long terme	4 791	. .
Administrations publiques : court terme	4 792	. .
Banques : long terme	4 794	. .
Banques : court terme	4 795	. .
Autres secteurs : long terme	4 797	. .
Autres secteurs : court terme	4 798	. .

ANNEXE II. COMPOSANTES TYPES *(fin)*

	Codes	
D. AVOIRS DE RÉSERVE	4 800	. .
Or monétaire	4 810	. .
Droits de tirage spéciaux	4 820	. .
Position de réserve au FMI	4 830	. .
Avoirs en devises	4 840	. .
Autres créances	4 880	. .
ERREURS ET OMISSIONS NETTES	4 998	. .

Annexe III. Système de codage FMI/OCDE/Eurostat applicable à la balance des paiements, à la position extérieure globale et au commerce international de services[1]

Le système de codage examiné ici s'applique à toutes les composantes types et aux postes complémentaires définis dans la cinquième édition du *Manuel de la balance des paiements*; il s'applique également aux composantes et postes pour mémoire de la classification OCDE-Eurostat des données sur le commerce international de services.

Le code a trois composantes ou sections, qui sont :

<position>	un nombre à un chiffre (compris entre 1 et 8) décrivant la position du poste dans les comptes de la position extérieure globale (PEG) ou de la balance des paiements (BP);
<sujet>	un nombre à trois chiffres (choisi parmi les nombres entiers compris entre 100 et 998) permettant d'identifier toutes les composantes de la balance des paiements et de la classification du commerce international des services et certains postes complémentaires;
<sous-code>	une composante définie par l'utilisateur et de longueur illimitée.

Le code complet comprendrait ces trois éléments dans l'ordre suivant : <position><sujet><sous-code>. Cependant, le sous-code est facultatif, contrairement au code de la position et au code du sujet. En conséquence, le code comportera, sous sa forme couramment utilisée, les composantes suivantes : <position><sujet>.

La première composante du code indique la position du poste dans les comptes de la position extérieure globale (PEG) et de la balance des paiements (BP); elle est définie comme suit :

Code	Position dans les comptes de la PEG et de la BP
1	Stock au début de la période
2	Flux, crédit
3	Flux, débit
4	Flux nets
5	Ajustement de la valeur en fonction des variations du prix
6	Ajustement de la valeur en fonction des variations du taux de change
7	Autres ajustements
8	Stock à la fin de la période
0	Autres

Le premier chiffre de la composante indicative du sujet correspond à la rubrique de la balance des paiements, c'est-à-dire :

Code	Rubrique de la BP
1	Biens
2	Services
3	Revenus et transferts courants
4	Compte de capital
5	Investissements directs
6	Investissements de portefeuille
7	Autres investissements
8	Avoirs de réserve
9	Principaux agrégats et détails complémentaires

Les deuxième et troisième chiffres de la composante sont généralement attribués dans un ordre consécutif et sont séparés par des espaces permettant l'inclusion ultérieure de codes additionnels, le cas échéant. En outre, dans le compte d'opérations financières, à l'exception des comptes des investissements directs, le deuxième chiffre de cette composante est 0, 1, 2, 3 ou 4 pour les avoirs et 5, 6, 7, 8 ou 9 pour les engagements.

Un exemple des codes appliqués aux «Autres investissements» dans le compte d'opérations financières est donné ci-après.

Sujet	Champ unique			Champ multiple		
	Crédit	Débit	Net	Crédit	Débit	Net
Autres investissements	2.700	3.700	4.700	2.700	3.700	4.700
Engagements	2.750	3.750	4.750	2.750	3.750	4.750
Prêts	2.762	3.762	4.762	2.762	3.762	4.762
Administrations publiques	2.767	3.767	4.767	2.767	3.767	4.767
Long terme	2.768	3.768	4.768	2.768	3.768	4.768
Court terme	2.769	3.769	4.769	2.769	3.769	4.769
Banques	2.770	3.770	4.770	2.770	3.770	4.770
Long terme	2.771	3.771	4.771	2.771	3.771	4.771
Court terme	2.772	3.772	4.772	2.772	3.772	4.772
Autres secteurs	2.773	3.773	4.773	2.773	3.773	4.773
Long terme	2.774	3.774	4.774	2.774	3.774	4.774
Court terme	2.775	3.775	4.775	2.775	3.775	4.775

Pour les prêts, les écritures passées au crédit et au débit servent à comptabiliser les transactions communément dénommées tirages et remboursements. La cinquième édition du *Manuel* recommande de classer tous les tirages sur prêts à long terme et tous les remboursements de ces prêts parmi les postes complémentaires. À l'heure actuelle, le FMI recueille des données nettes sur la plupart des autres postes du compte d'opérations financières. Néanmoins, le système de codage permet d'identifier tous les flux, qu'il s'agisse de transactions nettes ou de transactions inscrites au crédit ou au débit.

[1]Tiré de l'ouvrage du FMI intitulé «Balance des paiements : codes utilisés pour les composantes types et les postes complémentaires», Washington, DC, 3 mars 1995.

ANNEXE IV. POSITION EXTÉRIEURE GLOBALE : COMPOSANTES TYPES

	Codes
A. AVOIRS	8 995 C .
Investissements directs à l'étranger	8 505 . .
Capital social et bénéfices réinvestis	8 506 . .
Créances sur les entreprises apparentées	8 507 . .
Engagements envers les entreprises apparentées	8 508 . .
Autres capitaux	8 530 . .
Créances sur les entreprises apparentées	8 535 . .
Engagements envers les entreprises apparentées	8 540 . .
Investissements de portefeuille	8 602 . .
Titres de participation	8 610 . .
Autorités monétaires	8 611 . .
Administrations publiques	8 612 . .
Banques	8 613 . .
Autres secteurs	8 614 . .
Titres de créances	8 619 . .
Obligations et autres titres d'emprunt	8 620 . .
Autorités monétaires	8 621 . .
Administrations publiques	8 622 . .
Banques	8 623 . .
Autres secteurs	8 624 . .
Instruments du marché monétaire	8 630 . .
Autorités monétaires	8 631 . .
Administrations publiques	8 632 . .
Banques	8 633 . .
Autres secteurs	8 634 . .
Produits financiers dérivés	8 640 . .
Autorités monétaires	8 641 . .
Administrations publiques	8 642 . .
Banques	8 643 . .
Autres secteurs	8 644 . .
Autres investissements	8 703 . .
Crédits commerciaux	8 706 . .
Administrations publiques : long terme	8 708 . .
Administrations publiques : court terme	8 709 . .
Autres secteurs : long terme	8 711 . .
Autres secteurs : court terme	8 712 . .
Prêts	8 714 . .
Autorités monétaires : long terme	8 717 . .
Autorités monétaires : court terme	8 718 . .
Administrations publiques : long terme	8 720 . .
Administrations publiques : court terme	8 721 . .
Banques : long terme	8 723 . .
Banques : court terme	8 724 . .
Autres secteurs : long terme	8 726 . .
Autres secteurs : court terme	8 727 . .
Monnaie fiduciaire et dépôts	8 730 . .
Autorités monétaires	8 731 . .
Administrations publiques	8 732 . .
Banques	8 733 . .
Autres secteurs	8 734 . .
Autres avoirs	8 736 . .
Autorités monétaires : long terme	8 738 . .
Autorités monétaires : court terme	8 739 . .
Administrations publiques : long terme	8 741 . .

ANNEXE IV. POSITION EXTÉRIEURE GLOBALE : COMPOSANTES TYPES *(suite)*

	Codes
Administrations publiques : court terme	8 742 ..
Banques : long terme	8 744 ..
Banques : court terme	8 745 ..
Autres secteurs : long terme	8 747 ..
Autres secteurs : court terme	8 748 ..
Avoirs de réserve	8 800 ..
Or monétaire	8 810 ..
Droits de tirage spéciaux	8 820 ..
Position de réserve au FMI	8 830 ..
Devises étrangères	8 840 ..
Autres créances	8 880 ..
B. ENGAGEMENTS	8 995 D .
Investissements directs de l'étranger dans l'économie	8 555 ..
Capital social et bénéfices réinvestis	8 556 ..
Créances sur les investisseurs directs	8 557 ..
Engagements envers les investisseurs directs	8 558 ..
Autres capitaux	8 580 ..
Créances sur les investisseurs directs	8 585 ..
Engagements envers les investisseurs directs	8 590 ..
Investissements de portefeuille	8 652 ..
Titres de participation	8 660 ..
Banques	8 663 ..
Autres secteurs	8 664 ..
Titres d'engagement	8 669 ..
Obligations et autres titres d'emprunt	8 670 ..
Autorités monétaires	8 671 ..
Administrations publiques	8 672 ..
Banques	8 673 ..
Autres secteurs	8 674 ..
Instruments du marché monétaire	8 680 ..
Autorités monétaires	8 681 ..
Administrations publiques	8 682 ..
Banques	8 683 ..
Autres secteurs	8 684 ..
Produits financiers dérivés	8 690 ..
Autorités monétaires	8 691 ..
Administrations publiques	8 692 ..
Banques	8 693 ..
Autres secteurs	8 694 ..
Autres investissements	8 753 ..
Crédits commerciaux	8 756 ..
Administrations publiques : long terme	8 758 ..
Administrations publiques : court terme	8 759 ..
Autres secteurs : long terme	8 761 ..
Autres secteurs : court terme	8 762 ..
Prêts	8 764 ..
Utilisation des crédits et des prêts du FMI	8 766 ..
Autorités monétaires : long terme	8 767 ..
Autorités monétaires : court terme	8 768 ..
Administrations publiques : long terme	8 770 ..
Administrations publiques : court terme	8 771 ..
Banques : long terme	8 773 ..
Banques : court terme	8 774 ..

ANNEXE IV. POSITION EXTÉRIEURE GLOBALE : COMPOSANTES TYPES *(fin)*

	Codes	
Autres secteurs : long terme	8 776	..
Autres secteurs : court terme	8 727	..
Monnaie fiduciaire et dépôts	8 730	..
Autorités monétaires	8 731	..
Administrations publiques	8 732	..
Banques	8 733	..
Autres secteurs	8 734	..
Autres engagements	8 736	..
Autorités monétaires : long terme	8 738	..
Autorités monétaires : court terme	8 739	..
Administrations publiques : long terme	8 741	..
Administrations publiques : court terme	8 742	..
Banques : long terme	8 744	..
Banques : court terme	8 745	..
Autres secteurs : long terme	8 747	..
Autres secteurs : court terme	8 748	..
POSITION EXTÉRIEURE GLOBALE NETTE	8 995	..
Taux de conversion (fin de période)	0 102	..

Annexe V. Cadre conceptuel de la balance des paiements et de la position extérieure globale

La présente annexe reprend le texte du chapitre II de la cinquième édition du Manuel. *Il convient de noter que les numéros de paragraphe et page cités dans cette annexe sont ceux du* Manuel.

Définitions

12. La première partie du présent *Manuel* décrit le cadre conceptuel de la balance des paiements et de la position extérieure globale. Elle traite de leur relation avec la comptabilité nationale, du concept de résidence, des principes d'évaluation et de chronologie, enfin des notions d'unité de compte et de conversion.

13. La balance des paiements est un état statistique où sont systématiquement résumées, pour une période donnée, les transactions économiques d'une économie avec le reste du monde. Les transactions, pour la plupart entre résidents et non-résidents[1], sont celles qui portent sur les biens, services et revenus; celles qui font naître des créances financières sur le reste du monde ou des engagements financiers envers celui-ci; et celles qui, telles les donations, sont considérées comme des transferts, pour lesquels il y a lieu de passer des contre-écritures de manière à solder — au sens comptable du terme — les transactions à sens unique (voir paragraphe 28)[2]. Une transaction se définit comme un flux économique découlant de la création, de la transformation, de l'échange, du transfert ou de l'extinction d'une valeur économique et faisant intervenir le transfert de propriété de biens ou d'actifs financiers, la prestation de services ou la fourniture de travail et de capital.

14. De même que la balance des paiements retrace des flux, la position extérieure globale est un relevé de stocks. C'est un état statistique qui présente, à une date donnée, par exemple en fin d'année, i) la valeur et la composition du stock des actifs financiers d'une économie ou de ses créances sur le reste du monde, ainsi que ii) la valeur et la composition du stock de ses engagements envers le reste du monde. Dans certains cas, il peut être utile, pour les besoins de l'analyse, de calculer la différence entre avoirs et engagements extérieurs de ce bilan pour évaluer la position nette de l'économie, qui équivaut à la partie de la valeur nette de son patrimoine attribuable à ses relations avec le reste du monde ou en résultant. Une variation des stocks pendant une période définie peut être attribuable soit à des transactions (flux), soit à des réévaluations (qui rendent compte des variations des taux de change, des prix, etc.), soit à d'autres ajustements (des confiscations sans dédommagement, par exemple). Au contraire, la balance des paiements n'enregistre que des transactions.

Il y a lieu de noter que, comme l'indique l'«Introduction» au présent ouvrage, la position extérieure globale ne figure pas dans le volume 46 du Yearbook.

[1]Sauf dans le cas d'échanges d'avoirs financiers extérieurs transférables entre secteurs résidents et, dans une moindre mesure, d'engagements financiers extérieurs entre non-résidents (voir paragraphe 318).

[2]Les définitions et classifications des comptes internationaux contenues dans le présent *Manuel* visent à faciliter la communication au FMI des données sur les transactions internationales, et non à donner effet ou à interpréter les diverses dispositions des statuts du Fonds monétaire international qui ont trait aux aspects juridiques de l'action (ou du manque d'action) officielle concernant ces transactions.

Principes et concepts

15. Le reste du présent chapitre est consacré au cadre conceptuel des comptes internationaux — c'est-à-dire l'ensemble de conventions et principes sous-jacents qui assurent l'enregistrement systématisé et cohérent des transactions internationales et des stocks d'avoirs et engagements extérieurs. Les aspects pertinents de ces principes, ainsi que les considérations et contraintes pratiques qui s'y rapportent, seront examinés en détail dans les chapitres suivants.

Système d'enregistrement en partie double

16. La convention de base à respecter pour l'établissement d'un état de balance des paiements est que toute transaction enregistrée doit donner lieu à deux inscriptions de montants égaux. L'un de ces montants est inscrit en crédit et est affecté du signe plus, tandis que l'autre est inscrit en débit et affecté du signe moins. En théorie, donc, la somme des montants inscrits en crédit est censée être identique à celle des montants inscrits en débit et le solde de toutes les inscriptions est égal à zéro.

17. Dans la pratique, toutefois, il arrive fréquemment que les comptes ne s'équilibrent pas. Les données servant à établir les estimations pour la balance des paiements sont souvent obtenues séparément de sources différentes. C'est pourquoi le solde peut être un crédit net ou un débit net, qui correspond au montant net des erreurs et omissions. Une écriture distincte, de montant égal mais de signe contraire, doit alors être passée pour équilibrer les comptes. Comme les estimations erronées ou manquantes peuvent s'annuler, on ne peut juger du degré d'exactitude de l'état de balance des paiements d'après le montant de la différence entre la somme des crédits et celle des débits. Néanmoins, il y a lieu de s'inquiéter lorsqu'il subsiste une différence non négligeable qui n'est pas corrigée, car cela gêne l'analyse ou l'interprétation des estimations et en mine la crédibilité (il peut en aller de même pour l'interprétation de l'état de la position extérieure globale dont il sera question au chapitre XXIII).

18. La plupart des inscriptions à la balance des paiements se rapportent à des transactions dans lesquelles des valeurs économiques sont fournies ou reçues en échange d'autres valeurs économiques; ces valeurs sont soit des ressources réelles (biens, services et revenus), soit des actifs financiers. Les écritures compensatoires en crédit et en débit que requiert le système d'enregistrement résultent donc souvent de l'inscription de montants égaux pour les deux éléments échangés. Dans le cas où il y a don, et non échange, ou quand, pour d'autres raisons, la transaction donne lieu à un enregistrement unique, et non à deux enregistrements, une écriture — dénommée *transfert* — spécifiquement conçue pour assurer la compensation nécessaire doit être passée. (Les diverses sortes d'inscriptions qui peuvent être faites à la balance des paiements sont décrites aux paragraphes 26 à 31.)

19. Par convention de ce système, les inscriptions effectuées en crédit par l'économie qui établit sa balance des paiements reflètent i) des exportations lorsqu'il s'agit de ressources réelles et ii) soit une diminution des avoirs extérieurs de l'économie, soit une augmentation de ses engagements extérieurs, lorsqu'il s'agit d'actifs financiers. Parallèlement, les inscriptions faites en débit par l'économie qui établit les données reflètent i) des importations lorsqu'il s'agit de ressources réelles et ii) soit une augmentation des avoirs, soit une diminution des engagements lorsqu'il s'agit d'actifs financiers. En d'autres termes, pour les avoirs — qu'ils soient réels ou financiers —, un chiffre positif (crédit) dénote une baisse, tandis qu'un chiffre négatif (débit) correspond à une hausse. Par contre, pour les engagements, un chiffre positif indique une augmentation et un chiffre négatif une diminution. Les transferts sont portés au crédit lorsque les inscriptions qu'ils compensent sont faites en débit et ils sont portés au débit lorsque ces inscriptions sont effectuées en crédit.

20. La teneur ou la composition d'un état de balance des paiements varie quelque peu selon que les transactions sont enregistrées sur une base brute ou sur une base nette; les recommandations énoncées dans le présent *Manuel* indiquent quelles transactions sont à enregistrer sur une base brute et lesquelles sont à comptabiliser sur une base nette. Les inscriptions qu'il est recommandé d'effectuer sont énumérées dans la liste des composantes types de la balance des paiements et des renseignements complémentaires qui peuvent être présentés séparément.

Concepts de territoire économique, de résidence et de pôle d'intérêt économique

21. Les concepts de territoire économique, de résidence et de pôle d'intérêt économique utilisés dans le présent *Manuel* sont identiques à ceux qui ont été adoptés dans le *SCN* et seront examinés en détail au chapitre IV. Le territoire économique ne correspond pas forcément à la zone délimitée par les frontières reconnues sur le plan politique. Il recouvre un territoire géographique administré par un gouvernement. À l'intérieur de ce territoire géographique circulent librement des personnes, des biens et des capitaux. Dans le cas de pays maritimes, le territoire géographique comprend toutes les îles régies par les mêmes autorités fiscales et monétaires que le territoire principal.

22. Une unité institutionnelle a son pôle d'intérêt économique dans un pays et est résidente dudit pays lorsqu'il existe, sur le territoire économique de celui-ci, un endroit (domicile, lieu de production ou locaux à autre usage) auquel ou à partir duquel elle exerce et a l'intention de continuer à exercer des activités économiques et effectue ou a l'intention de continuer à effectuer des transactions sur une grande échelle, que ce soit pendant une période de temps indéfinie ou déterminée — en principe d'un an au moins, mais c'est là un critère indicatif et non une règle absolue.

Principes d'évaluation et de chronologie

23. Il est nécessaire d'utiliser une base d'évaluation uniforme pour l'ensemble des transactions internationales (qu'elles portent sur des ressources réelles ou sur des créances et engagements financiers) afin de pouvoir établir de façon systématique et cohérente la somme des transactions individuelles et une position des avoirs et des engagements qui corresponde bien à ces transactions. La base d'évaluation des transactions retenue dans le présent *Manuel* — comme dans le *SCN* — est généralement le prix de marché effectif convenu entre les agents. En théorie, tous les stocks d'avoirs et engagements doivent être évalués aux prix en vigueur sur le marché à la date à laquelle se rapporte la position extérieure globale. Les principes d'évaluation, les pratiques recommandées et leurs limites sont décrits au chapitre V, de même que la méthode d'évaluation des transferts, des actifs financiers et des stocks d'avoirs et engagements. (On y traitera aussi des cas où un prix de marché ne peut ni exister, ni être présumé.)

24. Dans le *Manuel* comme dans le *SCN*, c'est le principe de la comptabilité sur la base des faits générateurs (des droits constatés) qui régit le *moment de l'enregistrement* des transactions. Elles sont donc enregistrées au moment où une valeur économique est créée, transformée, échangée, transférée ou éteinte. Des créances et des engagements se créent lorsqu'il y a transfert de propriété. Le transfert peut être soit juridique, soit matériel (économique). Dans la pratique, lorsque le transfert de propriété n'est pas manifeste, on peut considérer comme une approximation raisonnable de cette date celle à laquelle les parties à une transaction l'enregistrent dans leurs livres ou dans leurs comptes. (Les principes de chronologie et les conventions qu'il est recommandé de respecter pour les diverses inscriptions à la balance des paiements, ainsi que les cas où il est possible de faire exception à la règle du transfert de propriété ou de s'en écarter, sont traités au chapitre VI.)

Le concept et les différents types de transactions

25. En général, les modifications des rapports économiques qu'enregistre la balance des paiements résultent principalement de la relation qui se noue entre deux parties, c'est-à-dire, à une exception près (voir la note 1), entre un résident et un non-résident, et toutes les transactions de cet ordre sont comptabilisées à la balance des paiements. Les inscriptions spécifiques qu'il est recommandé d'effectuer sont celles qui figurent dans la liste des composantes types (voir le chapitre VIII) et elles sont décrites en détail dans les chapitres IX et suivants.

26. En dépit de son appellation, la balance des paiements ne rend pas compte des *paiements*, au sens usuel du terme, mais des *transactions*. Un certain nombre de transactions internationales qui ont leur place à la balance des paiements peuvent ne pas donner lieu à un paiement monétaire et certaines ne comportent même aucun type de paiement. L'enregistrement de ces transactions, en plus de celles qui ont un paiement pour contrepartie, constitue la principale différence entre un état de balance des paiements et un relevé des paiements extérieurs.

Échanges

27. Parmi les transactions qui figurent à la balance des paiements, les plus nombreuses et les plus importantes sont celles qui peuvent être dénommées *échanges*. Un agent économique (entité économique) fournit une valeur économique à un autre et reçoit en échange une valeur égale. Les valeurs économiques fournies par une économie à une autre appartiennent à deux grandes catégories : les ressources réelles (biens, services, revenus), d'une part, et les instruments financiers, d'autre part. Les deux parties à l'échange sont des résidents d'économies différentes, sauf lorsqu'il s'agit d'échanges d'actifs financiers extérieurs entre secteurs résidents. Il se peut que la fourniture d'un instrument financier fasse intervenir non seulement le transfert de propriété d'une créance ou d'un engagement existant, mais aussi la création d'un nouvel avoir ou engagement ou l'annulation d'un avoir ou engagement existant. En outre, les modalités d'un contrat afférent à un instrument financier (par exemple son échéance) peuvent être modifiées par accord entre les parties; on considère dans ce cas que le contrat initial a été exécuté et est remplacé par un autre, assorti de modalités différentes. Tous les échanges de cet ordre doivent être enregistrés à la balance des paiements.

Transferts

28. Les transactions donnant lieu à un *transfert* diffèrent des échanges en ce qu'un agent économique fournit une valeur économique à un autre agent économique sans en recevoir une contrepartie qui, d'après les conventions et règles adoptées aux fins de ce système, a une valeur économique. La valeur qui fait défaut d'un côté de la transaction est représentée par une inscription dénommée *transfert.* Les transferts (valeurs économiques fournies et reçues sans réciprocité) doivent figurer à la balance des paiements. Les ***transferts courants*** figurent au **compte des transactions courantes** (voir le chapitre XV), tandis que les *transferts de capital* sont classés dans le ***compte de capital*** (voir le chapitre XVII).

Migration

29. Comme une économie se définit en fonction des entités économiques qui sont associées à son territoire, il est probable que toute modification touchant ces entités influera sur le champ que recouvre l'économie.

30. Il y a migration lorsqu'un particulier devient résident d'une nouvelle économie parce qu'il y transfère son lieu d'habitation principal. Certains avoirs mobiliers corporels appartenant au migrant sont effectivement importés dans la nouvelle économie; les avoirs immobiliers du migrant et certains de ses avoirs mobiliers corporels qui sont situés sur le territoire de l'ancienne économie deviennent des créances de la nouvelle économie sur l'ancienne; les créances du migrant sur les résidents d'une économie autre que la nouvelle ou ses engagements envers ceux-ci deviennent des créances ou engagements extérieurs de la nouvelle économie; et les créances du migrant sur les résidents de la nouvelle économie ou ses engagements envers ceux-ci cessent d'être des créances d'une économie, quelle qu'elle soit, sur le reste du monde, ou des engagements de cette économie envers celui-ci. La somme nette de tous ces changements est égale à la valeur nette du patrimoine du migrant, qui doit être inscrite en contrepartie si les autres changements sont enregistrés; ces inscriptions doivent être effectuées à la balance des paiements, où, par convention, la contre-écriture est passée sous la rubrique des transferts.

Autres transactions imputées

31. Dans quelques autres cas, des transactions peuvent être imputées et des inscriptions faites à la balance des paiements sans que des flux aient été effectivement engendrés. L'attribution des bénéfices réinvestis aux investisseurs directs étrangers en constitue un exemple. Les bénéfices d'une filiale ou succursale étrangère comprennent les bénéfices attribuables à l'investisseur direct. Ces bénéfices, qu'ils soient distribués ou réinvestis dans l'entreprise, sont proportionnels à sa participation au capital de l'entreprise. Les bénéfices réinvestis sont classés parmi les revenus des investissements directs. Un montant affecté du signe contraire est inscrit en contrepartie au poste investissement direct du *compte d'opérations financières* et représente l'augmentation de la participation des investisseurs directs étrangers au capital de la filiale ou succursale étrangère. (Les bénéfices réinvestis sont traités aux chapitres XIV et XVIII.)

Modifications non dues aux transactions

Reclassement des créances et engagements

32. Dans le *Manuel*, la classification des actifs financiers est établie en fonction de caractéristiques choisies de manière à révéler les intentions du créancier ou du débiteur. Les changements d'intentions influent sur les caractéristiques retenues, et il y a lieu de reclasser les actifs financiers en conséquence. L'un des cas typiques est celui de la distinction qui est faite entre les *investissements directs* et les autres catégories d'opérations financières. Par exemple, plusieurs détenteurs indépendants d'*investissements de portefeuille* (sous forme d'actions émises par une même entreprise à l'étranger) peuvent s'associer de manière à avoir, de façon durable, un pouvoir de décision effectif dans la gestion de l'entreprise. Leurs avoirs répondront alors à la définition de l'*investissement direct*, et la modification de la nature de l'investissement pourrait être assimilée à un reclassement. Ce reclassement se reflétera, à la fin de la période pendant laquelle il aura eu lieu, dans la position extérieure globale, mais non dans la balance des paiements. De même, les créances sur les non-résidents peuvent être soumises, ou cesser d'être assujetties, au contrôle des autorités monétaires résidentes. En pareil cas, il y aura reclassement entre les *actifs de réserve* et les actifs autres que les réserves.

Réévaluations

33. La valeur des ressources réelles et des actifs financiers est constamment sujette à variation. Cette variation peut être due à l'une ou à l'autre des causes suivantes, ou aux deux à la fois : i) le prix auquel les transactions sur une certaine sorte d'avoirs s'effectuent habituellement peut subir des variations qui sont liées à la monnaie dans laquelle le prix est exprimé; ii) le taux de change de la monnaie dans laquelle le prix est exprimé peut varier par rapport à l'unité de compte utilisée. Les réévaluations ne doivent pas être reportées à la balance des paiements, mais doivent figurer dans la position extérieure globale.

Annexe VI. Classification et composantes types de la balance des paiements

La présente annexe reprend le texte du chapitre VIII de la cinquième édition du Manuel. *Il convient de noter que les numéros de paragraphe et de page cités dans cette annexe sont ceux du* Manuel.

Structure et classification

139. La deuxième partie de ce *Manuel* a trait à la structure et à la classification des comptes de la balance des paiements et de la position extérieure globale. À l'examen des composantes types de ces deux séries de comptes succéderont l'analyse et la description détaillée du ***compte des transactions courantes***, du ***compte de capital et d'opérations financières***, des renseignements complémentaires qui peuvent être requis sur certains postes et de la position extérieure globale.

140. Il importe d'ordonner les statistiques de la balance des paiements selon une structure cohérente afin d'en faciliter l'utilisation et l'adaptation à des fins multiples : élaboration de politiques, études analytiques, projections, comparaisons bilatérales de telle ou telle composante ou de l'ensemble des transactions, agrégations régionales ou mondiales, etc. (Voir paragraphe 7.)

141. La classification et la liste des composantes types reposent sur des considérations théoriques et pratiques qui tiennent compte des opinions exprimées par les experts nationaux de la balance des paiements; elles concordent en général avec les définitions que donne le *SCN*. La classification élargie des transactions internationales au titre des services est conforme aux principes de la Classification centrale des produits (CCP). (Voir l'appendice III.)

142. Le système de classification est aussi le résultat d'efforts entrepris pour rattacher la structure du ***compte de capital*** aux comptes de revenu et à la classification de la position extérieure globale. Il a été conçu de manière à offrir un cadre flexible pouvant être utilisé par de nombreux pays pour développer au fil des années leurs statistiques extérieures. Certains pays ne sont peut-être pas en mesure de communiquer des chiffres pour de nombreux postes. D'autres sont peut-être en mesure de fournir des données supplémentaires.

Composantes types

143. Le choix des composantes types (dont la liste figure à la fin du présent chapitre) est fonction d'un certain nombre de considérations; celles qui suivent ont été jugées primordiales.

> Le poste doit manifester un comportement distinct. Il doit être influencé par un facteur économique ou un ensemble de facteurs différents de ceux qui influent sur les autres postes, ou réagir différemment au même facteur ou ensemble de facteurs. C'est cette réaction aux facteurs économiques que la balance des paiements cherche à mettre en évidence.
>
> Le poste doit revêtir de l'importance pour plusieurs pays; cette importance peut être fonction soit de son comportement (par exemple une variabilité exceptionnelle), soit de son ordre de grandeur.
>
> Les données relatives à ce poste ne doivent pas être excessivement difficiles à obtenir. L'utilité qu'il présente doit cependant être évaluée à la lumière des deux considérations qui précèdent.
>
> Le poste doit être utilisable séparément à d'autres fins, par exemple pouvoir être incorporé dans la comptabilité nationale ou servir au rapprochement avec cette dernière. La liste des composantes types ne doit pas être trop longue. En effet, un très grand nombre de pays, dont beaucoup ne disposent pas d'un système statistique très développé, sont censés utiliser les mêmes catégories lorsqu'ils communiquent leurs données.
>
> Dans la mesure du possible, les composantes types doivent être conformes et applicables aux autres systèmes statistiques du FMI et au *SCN* et concorder, pour les *services* en particulier, avec la CCP.

144. La liste type n'implique nullement que les recommandations formulées dans ce *Manuel* empêchent les pays d'établir et de publier d'autres données qu'ils jugent importantes. En fait, lorsque de plus amples détails sont nécessaires pour comprendre les circonstances particulières à tel ou tel pays ou pour analyser les situations nouvelles, les demandes de renseignements que le FMI adresse à ses pays membres ne se limitent pas aux composantes types. Des renseignements complémentaires peuvent être aussi très utiles pour vérifier et rapprocher les statistiques de pays partenaires, et, par exemple, pour analyser les financements exceptionnels. (Voir, à la fin du chapitre, le tableau intitulé *Renseignements complémentaires qui peuvent être requis sur certains postes*.) De temps en temps, les services du FMI tiennent des consultations avec les pays membres afin de déterminer avec eux quelles données complémentaires ils devraient lui communiquer.

145. Rares sont les pays qui ont des renseignements significatifs à communiquer pour chacune des composantes types. Il se peut aussi que certaines des composantes n'existent que regroupées ou qu'une composante mineure soit incluse dans une composante plus importante. Les composantes types doivent néanmoins être communiquées au FMI de manière aussi complète et exacte que possible. Les statisticiens nationaux sont incontestablement mieux placés que les services du FMI pour estimer et ajuster les composantes qui ne correspondent pas exactement aux séries de base de l'économie établissant ses statistiques.

Erreurs et omissions nettes

146. L'application des principes recommandés dans le présent *Manuel* devrait donner un ensemble cohérent d'inscriptions positives et négatives dont la somme est (en principe) égale à zéro. Or, en pratique, si l'on additionne toutes les inscriptions effectuées, on obtient presque inévitablement un crédit net ou un débit net. Ce solde est le résultat d'erreurs et d'omissions dont certaines peuvent être liées aux méthodes d'approximation recommandées pour la mise en pratique des principes.

147. La balance des paiements comprend normalement un poste distinct réservé aux erreurs et omissions nettes, appelé par certains statisticiens «solde» ou «écart statistique». Ce poste vise à compenser la surévaluation ou la sous-évaluation des composantes enregistrées. Ainsi donc, si ces composantes se soldent par un crédit, le poste des erreurs et omissions nettes constituera un débit de valeur égale et vice versa.

148. Certaines erreurs et omissions qui se produisent au cours de l'établissement des données se neutralisent habituellement. C'est pourquoi le montant du solde ne renseigne pas nécessairement sur la précision globale du relevé. Cependant, l'interprétation du relevé devient difficile si ce solde est considérable.

Classification générale

149. Les composantes types, dont la liste est donnée à la fin du présent chapitre, sont réparties en deux principales sections :

> Le compte des transactions courantes, qui se subdivise en : ***biens et services***, ***revenus*** et ***transferts courants***.
>
> Le **compte de capital et d'opérations financières**, qui enregistre i) les *transferts de capital* et les *acquisitions ou cessions d'actifs non financiers non produits*, et ii) les opérations portant sur des avoirs et engagements financiers.

Cette répartition correspond à la pratique suivie par la plupart des pays depuis de longues années et dénote un changement important apporté dans le présent *Manuel*. L'ancien compte des mouvements de capitaux a été rebaptisé **compte de capital et d'opérations financières**. Dicté par un souci d'harmonisation avec le *SCN*, ce changement consiste à adopter pour la balance des paiements la distinction que le *SCN* établit entre les *transferts de capital* et les ***transferts courants*** et à faire concorder le nouveau compte avec le compte de capital et le compte financier du *SCN*.

150. Les inscriptions à la plupart des rubriques du **compte des transactions courantes** doivent faire apparaître les crédits ou débits bruts. La plupart des inscriptions au **compte de capital et d'opérations financières** doivent être effectuées sur une base nette, c'est-à-dire que chaque composante ne doit y figurer que comme un crédit ou un débit (le mode de traitement recommandé pour certains postes spécifiques et les exceptions seront examinés dans les chapitres correspondants). Les entrées de ressources réelles et les augmentations d'avoirs financiers (ou diminutions d'engagements) seront enregistrées au débit; les sorties de ressources réelles et les diminutions d'avoirs financiers (ou augmentations d'engagements) seront enregistrées au crédit. Les transferts, dans les sections 1.C et 2.A, doivent avoir la même valeur numérique, mais affectée du signe opposé, que les inscriptions dont ils sont la contre-écriture.

Classification détaillée

151. La classification des composantes types qui suit a été mise au point conformément aux critères exposés au paragraphe 143. La structure et les caractéristiques du **compte des transactions courantes** et du **compte de capital et d'opérations financières**, sensiblement modifiées par rapport à la quatrième édition du *Manuel*, sont exposées aux chapitres IX et XVI, respectivement. Les composantes types du **compte des transactions courantes** sont décrites en détail aux chapitres X à XV, celles du **compte de capital et d'opérations financières** aux chapitres XVII à XXI.

Transactions courantes (1.)

152. Sont incluses dans le **compte des transactions courantes** toutes les transactions portant sur des valeurs économiques (autres que des actifs financiers) entre entités résidentes et non résidentes. On y inscrit aussi les contreparties des valeurs économiques courantes qui sont fournies ou acquises sans réciprocité. Les grandes subdivisions (postes) sont les ***biens et services***, les ***revenus*** et les ***transferts courants***.

Biens et services (1.A)

Biens (1.A.a.)

153. La rubrique *marchandises générales* recouvre la plupart des biens meubles que les résidents exportent à destination de non-résidents ou qu'ils importent en provenance de non-résidents et qui, à quelques exceptions près, font l'objet d'un transfert de propriété (effectif ou présumé).

154. La rubrique *biens importés ou exportés pour transformation* recouvre les exportations (ou importations dans l'économie établissant sa balance des paiements) de biens franchissant une frontière pour faire l'objet à l'étranger d'une transformation, suivie d'une réimportation (ou exportation) des biens, dont la valeur est établie sur une base brute avant et après la transformation. Cette rubrique fait exception au principe du transfert de propriété.

155. La rubrique *réparations de biens* recouvre les travaux de réparation de biens — bateaux, avions, etc. — fournis à des non-résidents ou reçus de non-résidents. Bien que le mouvement physique de ces biens soit analogue à celui qui est décrit au paragraphe 154, la valeur de la réparation correspond à son prix (c'est-à-dire au montant payé ou reçu pour cette réparation) et non à la valeur brute des biens avant et après la réparation.

156. La rubrique *achats de biens dans les ports par les transporteurs* recouvre tous les biens, tels que carburants, vivres, approvisionnements et fournitures, que les transporteurs résidents ou non résidents — aériens ou maritimes, par exemple — ont achetés à l'étranger (ou dans l'économie établissant sa balance des paiements). Cette rubrique n'enregistre pas les services auxiliaires fournis (remorquage, entretien, etc.), qui sont inclus dans les services de *transports*.

157. La rubrique *or non monétaire* recouvre les exportations et importations de tout or non détenu sous la forme d'avoir de réserve (or monétaire) par les autorités. L'*or non monétaire* est traité comme n'importe quel autre produit et se décompose, lorsque cela est possible, en or détenu à titre de réserve de valeur et or détenu à d'autres fins (industrielles).

Services (1.A.b.)

158. La rubrique *transports* recouvre la plupart des services fournis par les résidents aux non-résidents et vice versa, qui étaient précédemment classés aux rubriques *expéditions* et *autres transports* dans la quatrième édition du *Manuel*. Cependant, l'assurance du fret ne figure pas ici, mais à la rubrique des *services d'assurance*. Sous la rubrique *transports*, on enregistre le transport de marchandises et de passagers, quel qu'en soit le mode, ainsi que les autres services de distribution et services auxiliaires, y compris l'affrètement de véhicules de transport avec leur équipage. Certaines exceptions sont signalées aux chapitres X, XI et XIII.

159. La rubrique *voyages* recouvre les biens et les services acquis dans une économie par les voyageurs non résidents (y compris les excursionnistes), à des fins professionnelles ou personnelles — notamment pour des raisons de santé ou à titre éducatif —, au cours de leur séjour (de moins d'un an) sur le territoire de cette économie. Cette rubrique exclut les services internationaux fournis aux passagers, qui sont inclus dans les *transports*. Les étudiants et les personnes en traitement médical sont considérés comme étant des voyageurs, quelle que soit la durée de leur séjour, contrairement à certaines autres catégories — militaires, personnel des ambassades et travailleurs non résidents. Les dépenses des travailleurs non résidents sont toutefois comprises dans les *voyages*, tandis que celles des militaires et du personnel des ambassades sont incluses dans les *services fournis ou reçus par les administrations publiques, n.c.a.* Ces cas sont signalés aux chapitres XII et XIII.

160. La rubrique *services de communication* recouvre les opérations de communication entre résidents et non-résidents. Ce sont les services postaux (y compris les messageries) et les services de télécommunication (transmission du son, des images et d'autres types d'information par divers moyens et entretien des installations correspondantes, assuré par des résidents pour le compte de non-résidents et vice versa).

161. La rubrique *services de bâtiment et travaux publics (BTP)* recouvre les travaux de construction et d'installation effectués à l'étranger (ou dans l'économie qui établit sa balance des paiements) ou dans les enclaves extraterritoriales, à titre temporaire, par les entreprises résidentes (ou non résidentes) et leur personnel mais qui ne sont effectués ni par une entreprise étrangère apparentée à une entreprise résidente, ni par un bureau sur place non constitué en société qui, dans certaines conditions, équivaut à une entreprise étrangère apparentée. Ces aspects de la résidence sont traités aux chapitres IV et XIII.

162. La rubrique *services d'assurance* recouvre les assurances fournies aux non-résidents par des compagnies d'assurances résidentes et vice versa. On entend par là l'assurance du fret (pour les biens exportés ou importés) et les autres types d'assurance directe (notamment l'assurance-vie et autres formes d'assurances), ainsi que la réassurance. (Pour la méthode de calcul de la valeur des services d'assurance, voir paragraphes 256 et 257.)

163. La rubrique *services financiers* (autres que ceux qui sont offerts par les compagnies d'assurances et les caisses de retraite) recouvre les services d'intermédiation financière et les services auxiliaires entre résidents et non-résidents. Sont inclus les commissions et les frais ayant trait aux services suivants : lettres de crédit, lignes de crédit, crédit-bail, opérations de change, services de crédit aux consommateurs et aux entreprises, opérations de courtage, souscriptions de titres, différentes formes de couverture des opérations à terme, etc. Les services auxiliaires se rapportent à l'administration et à la réglementation des marchés financiers, à la garde de titres, etc.

164. La rubrique *services d'informatique et d'information* recouvre les transactions entre résidents et non-résidents concernant le conseil en matériel, l'installation de logiciels, les services d'information (traitement de données, banques de données, agences de presse) et l'entretien et la réparation des ordinateurs et du matériel connexe.

165. La rubrique *redevances et droits de licence* recouvre les recettes (exportations) et paiements (importations) des résidents et non-résidents se rapportant à i) l'exploitation d'actifs incorporels non financiers non produits et de droits de propriété — marques, droits d'auteur, brevets, procédés, techniques, dessins, licences de fabrication, franchises, etc. — et à ii) l'utilisation, dans le cadre d'accords de licence, de brevets, d'oeuvres originales ou de prototypes, tels que les manuscrits, films, etc.

166. La rubrique *autres services aux entreprises* recouvre les services fournis par des résidents à des non-résidents et vice versa : le négoce international et les autres services liés au commerce, la location-exploitation et divers services aux entreprises, spécialisés et techniques. (Voir, à la fin du chapitre, le tableau des *Renseignements complémentaires qui peuvent être requis sur certains postes*, et les paragraphes 261 à 264 pour de plus amples détails.)

167. La rubrique *services personnels, culturels et relatifs aux loisirs* recouvre i) les services audio-visuels et connexes et ii) les autres services culturels fournis par des résidents à des non-résidents et vice versa. Sont compris dans la catégorie i) les services qui ont trait à la production de films cinématographiques (films ou bandes vidéo), d'émissions de radio ou de télévision et d'enregistrements musicaux, par exemple les droits de location, les redevances perçues par les acteurs, producteurs etc., pour les productions et pour les droits de distribution cédés aux médias. Dans la catégorie ii) figurent les autres services personnels, culturels et relatifs aux loisirs tels que ceux qui ont associés aux bibliothèques, musées et autres activités culturelles ou sportives.

168. La rubrique *services fournis ou reçus par les administrations publiques, n.c.a.* recouvre tous les services (auxquels correspondent par exemple les dépenses des ambassades et consulats) fournis ou reçus par le secteur public ou les organisations internationales ou régionales et non classés ailleurs.

Revenus (1.B.)

169. La rubrique *rémunération des salariés* recouvre les salaires, traitements et autres émoluments versés, en espèces ou en nature, aux travailleurs frontaliers, saisonniers et autres travailleurs non résidents, (par exemple le personnel local des ambassades).

170. La rubrique *revenus des investissements* recouvre les recettes et paiements se rapportant respectivement à la détention d'avoirs financiers extérieurs par les résidents et aux engagements envers les non-résidents. Cela comprend les revenus des investissements directs, les revenus des investissements de portefeuille et les autres revenus d'investissement. La composante investissements directs se subdivise en revenus des participations au capital (dividendes, bénéfices des succursales et bénéfices réinvestis) et en revenus des titres de créance (intérêts); les revenus des investissements de portefeuille se subdivisent en revenus des participations au capital (dividendes) et en revenus des titres de créance (intérêts); les autres revenus d'investissement recouvrent les intérêts provenant d'autres opérations financières (prêts, etc.) et, en principe, les droits nets des ménages sur les réserves techniques d'assurance-vie et les réserves des caisses de retraite.

Transferts courants (1.C.)

171. À l'instar du *SCN*, le *Manuel* distingue les ***transferts courants*** des *transferts de capital* (ces derniers sont enregistrés au **compte de capital et d'opérations financières**). Les transferts sont la contrepartie des transferts de propriété, volontaires ou forcés, de ressources réelles ou d'actifs financiers entre résidents et non-résidents, qui ne reçoivent pas en échange une valeur économique. Les ***transferts courants*** sont tous ceux qui **ne font pas intervenir** i) le transfert de propriété d'un actif fixe, ii) le transfert de fonds lié ou subordonné à l'acquisition ou à la cession d'un actif fixe, ni iii) la remise, sans contrepartie, d'une dette par un créancier (toutes ces opérations sont des *transferts de capital*). Les ***transferts courants*** comprennent ceux des administrations publiques — par exemple la coopération internationale courante (entre des administrations publiques appartenant à différentes économies), les paiements des impôts courants sur le revenu et sur la fortune, etc. — et les autres transferts, tels que les envois de fonds des travailleurs, les primes (moins les commissions de service) et les indemnités au titre des assurances autres que l'assurance-vie, etc. La distinction entre les ***transferts courants*** et les *transferts de capital* fait l'objet d'un examen approfondi au chapitre XV (voir également les paragraphes 175 et 344).

Le compte de capital et d'opérations financières (2.)

172. Le **compte de capital et d'opérations financières** a deux principales composantes — le ***compte de capital*** correspond au compte de capital du *SCN* et le ***compte d'opérations financières*** au compte financier du *SCN*. Les avoirs (ou actifs) sont des créances sur les non-résidents et les engagements (ou passifs) des dettes envers les non-résidents. Les deux parties à une transaction portant sur des avoirs ou des engagements sont en général un résident et un non-résident mais, dans certains cas, il peut s'agir de deux résidents ou de deux non-résidents. (Voir paragraphe 318.)

173. Toutes les réévaluations et toutes les autres variations d'actifs et de passifs extérieurs qui ne sont pas dues à des transactions (voir paragraphe 310) sont exclues du **compte de capital et d'opérations financières** mais apparaissent dans la position extérieure globale. Des relevés complémentaires identifient certains postes qui présentent un intérêt pour l'analyse et qui relèvent de plusieurs comptes. C'est le cas, par exemple, des engagements qui constituent des réserves pour les autorités étrangères et des financements exceptionnels, dont il est question au chapitre XXII.

174. La classification des ***opérations financières*** et celle des composantes des revenus dans les **transactions courantes** sont liées et doivent être cohérentes pour faciliter l'analyse, permettre le rapprochement effectif entre la balance des paiements et la position extérieure globale, et assurer la compatibilité avec le *SCN* et avec les autres systèmes statistiques du FMI.

Compte de capital (2.A.)

175. Les grandes subdivisions du ***compte de capital*** sont les *transferts de capital* et les *acquisitions et cessions d'actifs non financiers non produits*. Les *transferts de capital* sont ceux qui font intervenir le transfert de propriété d'un actif fixe; le transfert de fonds lié ou subordonné à l'acquisition ou à la cession d'un actif fixe; ou la remise, sans contrepartie, d'une dette par un créancier. Ils se subdivisent en deux catégories : i) les transferts des administrations publiques, qui se décomposent en remises de dettes et autres transferts et ii) les autres transferts, qui se subdivisent en transferts des migrants, remises de dettes et autres transferts. (Voir le chapitre XV, qui traite de la distinction entre les *transferts de capital* et les ***transferts courants***). Les *acquisitions et cessions d'actifs non financiers non produits* se rapportent généralement aux avoirs incorporels tels que les brevets, les contrats de location et autres contrats transférables, la marque, etc. Ce poste ne recouvre pas les propriétés non bâties situées sur le territoire d'une économie donnée mais peut inclure l'achat (ou la vente) de terrains par une ambassade étrangère. (Voir paragraphe 312.)

Compte d'opérations financières (2.B.)

176. La classification des composantes types comprises sous ce poste est fondée sur les critères suivants :

> La nature des investissements ou leur ventilation fonctionnelle (*investissements directs*, *investissements de portefeuille*, *autres investissements* et *avoirs de réserve*).
>
> Dans le cas des *investissements directs*, la distinction en fonction du sens des mouvements de capitaux — entre l'étranger et l'économie qui établit sa balance des paiements — étant entendu que, dans chaque sous-catégorie, les avoirs sont distingués des engagements.
>
> Pour ce qui est des *investissements de portefeuille* et des *autres investissements*, la distinction traditionnelle entre avoirs et engagements.
>
> La nature de l'instrument est particulièrement importante pour les *investissements de portefeuille* et les *autres investissements* (titres de participation ou d'engagement, crédits commerciaux, prêts, monnaie et dépôts, autres avoirs ou engagements). Le présent *Manuel* regroupe dans les *investissements de portefeuille* les instruments du marché monétaire, ainsi que les autres instruments financiers et leurs dérivés, tant traditionnels que nouveaux.
>
> Pour ce qui est des *investissements de portefeuille* et des *autres investissements*, on distingue le secteur dont relève le créancier intérieur en ce qui concerne les avoirs et le secteur dont relève le débiteur intérieur en ce qui concerne les engagements. Cette distinction facilite les rapprochements avec les comptes de revenu et la position extérieure globale ainsi qu'avec le *SCN* et les autres systèmes statistiques;
>
> La distinction habituelle entre les avoirs et engagements à long et à court terme, le long terme étant défini par une échéance contractuelle initiale de plus d'un an et le court terme par une échéance ne dépassant pas un an, n'est faite que pour les *autres investissements*. Depuis quelques années, cette distinction a perdu à l'évidence beaucoup de son utilité pour de nombreuses transactions, intérieures ou internationales. C'est pourquoi la différenciation du long et du court terme a moins d'importance dans le présent *Manuel* — et dans le *SCN* — que dans les éditions précédentes. Cependant, parce qu'elle est importante à certains égards, par exemple pour l'analyse de la dette extérieure, elle est retenue dans le présent *Manuel* pour les *autres investissements*.

177. La rubrique *investissements directs* — lesquels témoignent d'un intérêt durable de la part d'une entité résidente d'une économie (l'investisseur direct) pour une entité résidente d'une autre économie (l'entreprise d'investissement direct) — recouvre toutes les transactions entre les investisseurs directs et les entreprises d'investissement direct. Les *investissements directs* recouvrent donc la transaction initiale entre les uns et les autres et toutes les transactions ultérieures entre eux, ainsi que les transactions entre les entreprises apparentées, constituées ou non en sociétés. Les opérations d'investissements directs (à l'étranger et dans l'économie qui établit sa balance des paiements) sont subdivisées en capital social, bénéfices réinvestis et autres transactions entre entreprises apparentées. Dans les catégories capital social et autres transactions entre entreprises apparentées, on fait la distinction entre les créances et engagements à l'égard des entreprises apparentées et les créances et engagements à l'égard des investisseurs directs. Les transactions entre banques apparentées et entre autres intermédiaires financiers apparentés se limitent aux transactions portant sur des titres de participation (capital social) et des dettes/créances permanentes. (Voir paragraphe 372.)

178. La rubrique *investissements de portefeuille* recouvre les transactions portant sur les titres de participation et les titres de créance, ces derniers étant subdivisés en trois catégories : obligations et autres titres d'emprunt, instruments du marché monétaire et produits financiers dérivés (tels que les options), lorsque ces instruments dérivés donnent naissance à des créances et à des engagements financiers. Différents nouveaux instruments financiers sont classés dans la catégorie qui correspond à leurs caractéristiques. (Les transactions classées parmi les *investissements directs* et les *avoirs de réserve* sont exclues des *investissements de portefeuille*.)

179. La rubrique *autres investissements* recouvre les crédits commerciaux et les prêts à court et à long terme (y compris l'utilisation des crédits et des prêts du FMI, ainsi que les prêts/emprunts au titre de la location-vente; la monnaie fiduciaire et les dépôts (transférables et autres, tels que les dépôts d'épargne et les dépôts à terme, les parts des associations d'épargne et de prêt, des associations de crédit mutuel, etc.); et d'autres comptes à payer et à recevoir. (Les transactions classées parmi les *investissements directs* sont exclues de la présente rubrique.)

180. La rubrique *avoirs de réserve* recouvre les transactions portant sur les avoirs dont les autorités monétaires d'une économie considèrent qu'elles disposent pour répondre aux besoins de financement de la balance des paiements et, dans certains cas, à d'autres besoins; en principe, cette disponibilité n'est pas étroitement liée à des critères formels tels que la propriété des avoirs ou la monnaie dans laquelle ils sont libellés. Les rubriques incluses sous ce poste sont l'or monétaire, les DTS, la position de réserve au FMI, les avoirs en devises (monnaie fiduciaire et dépôts, et valeurs mobilières) et les autres créances.

181. Le champ couvert par les composantes des *avoirs de réserve* et leur définition répondent aux besoins de l'analyse, comportent un élément d'appréciation et ne se prêtent pas toujours à l'application de critères objectifs formels ou de systèmes de classement précis fondés sur la conditionnalité ou sur d'autres facteurs. Contrairement à la quatrième édition du *Manuel*, la cinquième édition prescrit d'exclure de ce poste les réévaluations des *avoirs de réserve*, ainsi que leurs contreparties. Sont aussi exclues les allocations ou annulations de DTS, la monétisation ou la démonétisation de l'or et les inscriptions de contrepartie. Ces variations, qui ne sont pas des transactions, apparaissent dans la position extérieure globale.

Introducción

El volumen 47 de *Balance of Payments Statistics Yearbook* (anuario) que publica el Fondo Monetario Internacional (FMI) presenta las estadísticas de balanza de pagos declaradas por los países miembros al FMI. El FMI agradece a los países miembros su cooperación en la declaración de estos datos. En el caso de algunos países, esta información se complementa con detalles que los economistas de la institución obtienen de diferentes fuentes. En este volumen del anuario se mantienen las características introducidas en el volumen 46 y se agregan otras nuevas. Concretamente, a partir del volumen 47 se incluyen, por primera vez, los datos sobre la posición de inversión internacional en el formato de la quinta edición del *Manual de Balanza de Pagos (Manual)* del FMI en el caso de los países que compilan dicha información. Además, en una nueva parte 3 del anuario, se publican por primera vez descripciones detalladas de las metodologías, los procedimientos de compilación y las fuentes de datos que se utilizan en la mayoría de los países incluidos en el presente volumen.

Como en el volumen 46, en este anuario los datos de balanza de pagos se desglosan conforme a los componentes normalizados de la quinta edición del *Manual*[1]. En el *Manual*, publicado por el FMI en septiembre de 1993[2], se introducen varios cambios metodológicos en la compilación de los datos de balanza de pagos, cambios que se describen con detalle en el capítulo I del *Manual* y se resumen en el recuadro de la página S-iii del presente volumen. Además, como en el volumen 46, en este anuario los datos presentados conforme a los componentes normalizados del *Manual* están acompañados de una lista de códigos, preparada conjuntamente por el FMI, la Organización de Cooperación y Desarrollo Económicos (OCDE) y la Oficina Estadística de las Comunidades Europeas (Eurostat). La estructura de estos códigos se explica en un anexo de esta introducción. Sin embargo, en este volumen, a diferencia de los anteriores, no se presentan datos trimestrales de balanza de pagos en el caso de los países que declaran estadísticas trimestrales de balanza de pagos al FMI. Estos datos trimestrales seguirán publicándose en las ediciones mensuales de la publicación del FMI *Estadísticas financieras internacionales (EFI)*.

La conversión de los datos realizada por el personal del FMI ha permitido presentar en el formato de la quinta edición los datos históricos extraídos de la base de datos del FMI, así como los datos más recientes declarados por los países miembros en el formato de la cuarta edición del *Manual de Balanza de Pagos*. En 1995, el personal del FMI elaboró fórmulas para transformar la información de balanza de pagos de cada país incluida en la base de datos del FMI a fin de adaptarla a la metodología y presentación que se establecen en la quinta edición. Seguidamente se enviaron los datos convertidos a las autoridades de los respectivos países para su revisión y se incorporaron los comentarios recibidos a la nueva base de datos. En 1996, el personal del FMI, en colaboración con las autoridades de los países, convirtió en forma similar los datos sobre la posición de inversión internacional declarados en el formato de la cuarta edición a la presentación de la quinta edición. La posición de inversión internacional de un país es un balance general de las tenencias de activos y pasivos financieros frente al exterior. Los datos sobre estas tenencias que declaran los países se desglosan, por primera vez, en este volumen conforme a los componentes normalizados de la posición de inversión internacional que establece la quinta edición del *Manual*. En el caso de algunos países, los datos sobre la posición de inversión internacional convertidos no contienen el detalle suficiente que justifique su publicación. La base de datos se revisará a medida que las autoridades de los países miembros y el personal del FMI sigan efectuando ajustes en el proceso de conversión y se recopilen y declaren al FMI datos más detallados sobre las tenencias, y se publicará una presentación más extensa de los datos sobre la posición de inversión internacional en volúmenes subsiguientes del anuario.

En este volumen también se presentan por primera vez las descripciones técnicas de la metodología, los procedimientos de compilación y las fuentes de datos que utilizan los países que declaran datos. Las descripciones se basan en gran medida en la información que los países suministran al FMI. Se incluyen estas descripciones para que los usuarios comprendan mejor la cobertura de los datos de los distintos países publicados en el anuario, así como sus limitaciones, y para informar a los compiladores sobre las fuentes de datos y los métodos utilizados por los compiladores de otros países. Como se trata de una innovación, se prevé que estas descripciones se amplíen y mejoren en las ediciones futuras del anuario, en particular, en lo que se refiere a una presentación más uniforme de la información sobre los distintos países. Los cambios en las fuentes y los procedimientos de compilación también se reflejarán en las descripciones que se incluyan en las ediciones futuras.

El anuario consta de tres partes. En la parte 1 se presentan datos de balanza de pagos y datos sobre la posición de inversión internacional de cada país. En la parte 2 figuran los totales regionales y mundiales de los componentes principales

[1]El volumen 1 del anuario, publicado en 1949, se basó en la primera edición del *Manual de Balanza de Pagos* del FMI, publicado en 1948; los volúmenes 2–12 se basaron en la segunda edición del manual, publicada en 1950; los volúmenes 13–23 se basaron en la tercera edición, publicada en 1961, y los volúmenes 24–29 se basaron en esa edición así como en el *Manual de Balanza de Pagos: Suplemento a la tercera edición*, que apareció en 1973. Desde el volumen 30 al 45, las presentaciones siguieron las recomendaciones de la cuarta edición del manual, publicada en 1977.

[2]Fondo Monetario Internacional, *Manual de Balanza de Pagos*, quinta edición, Washington, septiembre de 1993.

de la balanza de pagos. En la parte 3 se presentan descripciones técnicas sobre algunos países declarantes. La parte 1 se publica en un tomo separado y las partes 2 y 3 en un mismo tomo.

El resto de esta introducción se ha organizado de la siguiente manera:

- En la sección I se describen las características básicas de los cuadros que se publican en la parte 1 del anuario. (Los detalles sobre cobertura de los datos de las partes 2 y 3 se presentan en el segundo tomo.)
- La sección II contiene información sobre la manera de acceder a la información del FMI sobre balanza de pagos en cintas magnéticas.
- Se han incluido seis anexos. En el anexo I se incluye una presentación analítica sucinta de los componentes de la balanza de pagos (y los códigos correspondientes). En el anexo II se presentan los componentes normalizados (con sus respectivos códigos) de la quinta edición del *Manual*. En el anexo III se explica el sistema de codificación empleado. En el anexo IV se presentan los componentes normalizados de la posición de inversión internacional que figuran en la quinta edición del *Manual*. En el anexo V se describe el marco conceptual de la balanza de pagos y, en el anexo VI, se explica la cobertura de los componentes principales de las cuentas de la balanza de pagos conforme a las directrices establecidas en la quinta edición del *Manual*.

I. Parte 1 del anuario: Datos de cada país

En la parte 1 del anuario se presentan las páginas de países en orden alfabético. Debe hacerse la salvedad de que el término "país", según se emplea en esta publicación, no siempre se refiere a una entidad territorial que constituya un Estado conforme al derecho y la práctica internacionales; el término también abarca ciertas entidades territoriales que no son Estados soberanos, sobre las cuales también se elaboran datos estadísticos y se facilitan a nivel internacional en forma separada e independiente.

Los datos de balanza de pagos de la mayoría de los países se presentan en dos cuadros. El cuadro 1 es un resumen analítico de los datos más detallados que se presentan en el cuadro 2. En el cuadro 1, los componentes de la balanza de pagos están ordenados de tal manera que se destacan las partidas de financiamiento (reservas y partidas conexas). (Véase también el anexo I.) El cuadro 2 presenta los datos correspondientes a los componentes normalizados que se describen en la quinta edición del *Manual*. (Véase también el anexo II.) En el caso de los países sobre los que se dispone de información relativa a la posición de inversión internacional, los datos se presentan en el cuadro 3. En los cuadros 1, 2 y 3, los datos corresponden al período 1988–95 para cada país. Sólo se incluyen los países sobre los que se dispone de datos correspondientes a por lo menos dos años dentro de este período. Los datos se declaran en base a los años calendario, salvo indicación contraria.

Presentación analítica

En la presentación analítica, los componentes de la balanza de pagos se clasifican en cinco categorías principales de datos (grupos A a E) que el FMI considera útiles para analizar de manera uniforme la evolución de la balanza de pagos. No obstante, no debe interpretarse que esta división en grupos refleja una recomendación del FMI sobre el enfoque analítico más apropiado para todos los países. Los componentes normalizados del cuadro 2 podrían agruparse conforme a una presentación analítica diferente en función de las circunstancias especiales de determinado país o de ciertos requisitos analíticos.

Obsérvese que las cifras que aparecen en los cuadros 1 y 2 en lo que respecta a los saldos de la cuenta corriente, la cuenta de capital y la cuenta financiera difieren en el caso de algunos países. Esto se debe a que en el cuadro 1 se excluyen ciertas transacciones que se clasifican en estas cuentas porque han sido reclasificadas como "financiamiento excepcional" o como "pasivos que constituyen reservas de autoridades extranjeras". Estas transacciones forman parte de reservas y partidas conexas. El "financiamiento excepcional" se refiere a las transacciones efectuadas por las autoridades para financiar su balanza de pagos, e incluye la obtención de recursos en préstamo del exterior, los atrasos en los pagos y la condonación de deudas, pero no incluye las reservas ni los pasivos que constituyen reservas de autoridades extranjeras. Estos últimos son pasivos que la economía acreedora considera activos de reserva.

Presentación normalizada

Los componentes normalizados conforme a la quinta edición del *Manual*, que figuran en el cuadro 2, ofrecen una clasificación más detallada de los bienes y servicios que en la cuarta edición. La llamada "cuenta de capital y financiera" agrupa diferentes componentes bajo la "cuenta de capital" y la "cuenta financiera". En esta última se clasifican los componentes según la clase de inversión (es decir, inversión directa, inversión de cartera, otra inversión y activos de reserva), activos/pasivos, sectores internos (autoridades monetarias, gobierno general, bancos y otros sectores) y vencimiento (a largo plazo y a corto plazo).

Posición de inversión internacional

Los datos sobre la posición de inversión internacional, que figuran en el cuadro 3, se agrupan conforme a los componentes normalizados de la posición de inversión internacional que se establecen en la quinta edición del *Manual*. (Véase también el anexo IV.)

Recuadro. Principales diferencias entre la cuarta y la quinta edición del *Manual*

En la quinta edición del *Manual* se han incorporado cambios importantes para tener en cuenta la evolución del comercio y las finanzas internacionales durante la última década. Además, en la medida de lo posible, se han armonizado los conceptos utilizados con la metodología adoptada en el *Sistema de Cuentas Nacionales* de 1993 (*SCN*) y la que emplea el FMI para compilar las estadísticas financieras y de las finanzas públicas. Seguidamente se indican los cambios metodológicos principales que afectan sustancialmente el significado y la presentación de las estadísticas de balanza de pagos en el anuario:

1) La cobertura de la "cuenta corriente" es diferente en la quinta edición del *Manual*. Según la nueva definición, la "cuenta corriente" abarca las transacciones efectuadas con no residentes en bienes, servicios y renta y los pagos recibidos y efectuados por concepto de transferencias corrientes; en la cuarta edición, esta cuenta comprendía los bienes, los servicios y todas las transferencias. En la nueva edición, las transferencias de capital forman parte de la nueva "cuenta de capital y financiera" cuya cobertura es más amplia que la antigua cuenta de capital. La distinción entre transferencias corrientes y de capital se basa en las directrices establecidas en el *SCN* de 1993, el cual caracteriza las transferencias de capital de la siguiente manera: a) una transferencia en especie es una transferencia de capital cuando entraña la transferencia de propiedad de un activo fijo, o la condonación de una obligación por parte de un acreedor sin recibir nada a cambio, y b) una transferencia de efectivo es una transferencia de capital cuando está vinculada o condicionada a la adquisición o enajenación de un activo fijo (por ejemplo, una donación para inversión) por una o ambas partes de la transacción.

2) En la quinta edición se ha ampliado la cobertura de la categoría de bienes, la cual incluye: a) el valor (en cifras brutas) de los bienes recibidos de otro país o enviados al exterior para ser transformados y la subsiguiente exportación/importación una vez efectuada la transformación; b) el valor de las reparaciones de bienes, y c) el valor de los bienes adquiridos en puerto por medios de transporte. En la cuarta edición, el valor neto de los bienes importados para ser transformados y reexportados posteriormente se registraba como servicios de transformación; las reparaciones de bienes y los bienes adquiridos en puerto por medios de transporte también se registraban como servicios.

3) En la quinta edición se clasifican por separado la renta y los servicios; en la cuarta, la renta era un subcomponente de servicios. Además, en la nueva edición se reclasifican ciertas transacciones de renta y de servicios. En la cuarta edición, la renta del trabajo incluía los gastos de los trabajadores no residentes además de sus ingresos; en la quinta, los ingresos de los trabajadores se clasifican bajo remuneración de empleados en la categoría de renta y sus gastos se registran como servicios de viajes. En la cuarta edición, la remuneración del personal residente de embajadas y bases militares situadas en el extranjero y de los funcionarios de organismos internacionales se registraba como parte de los servicios oficiales; en la quinta edición, dicha remuneración se clasifica como partida de crédito en remuneración de empleados. En la cuarta edición, los pagos por el uso de patentes, derechos de autor y otros activos intangibles no financieros de características similares se incluían en el rubro renta de la propiedad; en la quinta edición, se clasifican como subcomponentes de otros servicios. En general, el concepto de renta del nuevo *Manual* abarca la renta de la inversión y todas las demás formas de remuneración de los empleados, en tanto que en la cuarta edición incluía la renta de la inversión, la renta del trabajo en casi todas sus formas (incluidos los gastos de los trabajadores en el extranjero) y la renta de la propiedad.

4) Se amplió la cobertura de la "cuenta de capital" de la cuarta edición y ahora se denomina "cuenta de capital y financiera", que se divide en dos categorías principales. La primera es la cuenta de capital, que cubre todas las transacciones que entrañan: a) pagos recibidos o efectuados por concepto de transferencias de capital y b) la adquisición o enajenación de activos no financieros no producidos. La segunda categoría es la cuenta financiera, muy similar a la cuenta de capital de la cuarta edición, que agrupa todas las transacciones efectuadas con no residentes vinculadas con un traspaso de propiedad de activos y pasivos financieros de una economía sobre el exterior, incluidos la creación, el intercambio y la liquidación de créditos frente al resto del mundo o del resto del mundo frente a la economía.

5) La inversión directa, tanto en la cuarta como en la quinta edición, se clasifica principalmente según su dirección: inversión directa de residentes en el extranjero e inversión directa de no residentes en la economía declarante. En la quinta edición, todas las transacciones entre empresas no financieras de inversión directa y sus empresas matrices se incluyen en inversión directa. Las transacciones entre bancos filiales y entre otros intermediarios financieros filiales se limitan a las relacionadas con el capital accionario o con títulos de deuda que representen una participación permanente. Las demás transacciones entre bancos e instituciones financieras filiales se clasifican como inversión de cartera u otra inversión. (En la cuarta edición, sólo se excluían de la inversión directa las transacciones de estos tipos a corto plazo.)

6) En la quinta edición se amplió la cobertura de la inversión de cartera para reflejar la proliferación de nuevos instrumentos financieros en los últimos años. El principal cambio es que se incluyen ahora en la inversión de cartera los instrumentos de deuda del mercado monetario y los instrumentos financieros derivados negociables; en la cuarta edición se incluían como "otro capital".

Existen muchas otras diferencias en la presentación de los datos de balanza de pagos entre la cuarta y la quinta edición. (Véase la descripción detallada de la nueva metodología en la quinta edición del *Manual*.)

La clasificación de los componentes de la posición de inversión internacional en el cuadro 3 coincide con la de la cuenta financiera de la balanza de pagos que figura en el cuadro 2. Sin embargo, hay varias diferencias entre los dos cuadros. Como se mencionó anteriormente, los datos sobre la posición de inversión internacional reflejan los activos y pasivos financieros de un país frente al exterior en un momento determinado. Por lo tanto, en el cuadro 3 los componentes de la posición de inversión internacional se agrupan en la presentación básica en dos categorías generales, a saber, activos y pasivos, a diferencia de la clasificación funcional de la inversión (es decir, inversión directa, inversión de cartera, otra inversión y activos de reserva) que figura en el cuadro 2. Además, los datos del cuadro 3 reflejan la posición de inversión internacional de un país al final del período de declaración de datos, a diferencia de las transacciones que tuvieron lugar durante el período, que se presentan en el cuadro 2. Asimismo, a diferencia del cuadro 2, en el que se indica el valor de las transacciones a lo largo de un período, la valoración de la posición de inversión internacional de un país, que se presenta en el cuadro 3, refleja el valor de las transacciones financieras, las variaciones por valoración y otras variaciones que tuvieron lugar durante el período. La posición de inversión internacional neta, que figura en el cuadro 3, se calcula como diferencia entre el valor de los activos financieros externos y el de los pasivos financieros externos.

Véase el capítulo XXIII de la quinta edición del *Manual* en el que se presenta un análisis detallado del concepto de posición de inversión internacional.

Códigos de datos

En los cuadros 1 y 2 se indican los códigos de cada categoría y componente. Como se señaló anteriormente, los códigos fueron elaborados conjuntamente por el FMI, la OCDE y Eurostat, a efectos de facilitar la declaración de datos a nivel internacional. Los códigos corresponden a los componentes normalizados de la balanza de pagos y de la posición de inversión internacional según se definen en la quinta edición del *Manual*, así como a los componentes de la clasificación conjunta OCDE/Eurostat para el comercio de servicios.

Cada uno de los códigos que figuran en el anuario está formado por seis dígitos/caracteres. El primer dígito indica si se trata de un crédito, un débito o del valor neto (el número "2" corresponde a un crédito, el "3" a un débito y el "4" al valor neto, es decir, la diferencia entre créditos y débitos). Los siguientes tres dígitos se utilizan para clasificar los componentes de la balanza de pagos. Por ejemplo, para la cuenta corriente se utiliza el código 993, para la cuenta de capital 994 y para la cuenta financiera 995. Los detalles del sistema de codificación figuran en el anexo III.

Los dígitos/caracteres que ocupan los lugares quinto y sexto de los códigos que figuran en el anuario se reservan para indicar características especiales de ciertos componentes específicos. Por ejemplo, en el cuadro 1, la Y del quinto carácter señala que se excluyen de ese componente el financiamiento excepcional y los pasivos que constituyen recursos de las autoridades extranjeras; la X indica que se excluyen estas mismas partidas además del uso del crédito del FMI y préstamos del FMI. Las letras A, B, C y D del cuadro 1 indican los distintos sectores internos. En el cuadro 2, las letras A, B y C se refieren a subcomponentes no normalizados, como los de transportes (pasajeros, fletes y otros).

Créditos y débitos

En los cuadros 1 y 2, los datos sobre transacciones figuran como asientos de crédito bruto o débito bruto en la cuenta corriente y la cuenta de capital, y como asientos de crédito neto o débito neto (para reflejar variaciones netas de los pasivos y de los activos) en la cuenta financiera. Los asientos de crédito, bruto o neto, representan valores positivos (aunque no se indica el signo) y los asientos de débito, bruto o neto, son negativos (y sí se indica el signo). Por lo tanto, toda disminución de los activos y todo aumento de los pasivos (crédito) figuran como valores positivos y todo aumento de los activos y toda disminución de los pasivos (débito) aparecen con signo negativo.

Asientos nulos o carencia de datos

Con frecuencia es difícil discernir en la información declarada por los países si faltan cifras porque no se dispone de datos o porque el valor de esa partida es cero o insignificante. La inclusión de tres puntos (...) en los cuadros del anuario significa cualquiera de las dos posibilidades: bien que no se dispone de datos o bien que el valor es cero o insignificante.

Redondeo de las cifras

La mayor parte de las cifras de los cuadros se expresan en unidades de un millón; no debe suponerse que los cuadros que incluyen unidades más pequeñas representan, necesariamente, cifras más exactas. La unidad se elige con el fin de presentar las cifras de una manera práctica. Debido al redondeo en el cálculo de las cifras, puede haber diferencias entre un total y la suma de sus componentes.

Conversión de monedas

La mayoría de los datos de balanza de pagos declarados al FMI se expresan en unidades de moneda nacional o en dólares de EE.UU., pero algunos países declaran ciertos datos en DEG. Para facilitar la comparación de datos entre los países, todos los estados de balanza de pagos publicados en el anuario se expresan en dólares de EE.UU. Además, los datos sobre transacciones con el FMI y sobre transacciones en DEG declarados por todos los países se remplazan por los datos que figuran en los registros del FMI, expresados en DEG. Esta información se convierte, a su vez, a dólares de EE.UU.

En el caso de los países que no declaran sus estadísticas en dólares de EE.UU., los datos se convierten utilizando el tipo de cambio que figura al pie del cuadro 1 para cada país, que normalmente es el tipo promedio vigente en el país en el período correspondiente y se obtiene de *EFI*. Por ejemplo, en las páginas de *EFI* correspondientes a los Países Bajos figura la línea "rf", en la que se indica el tipo de cambio promedio del florín frente al dólar de EE.UU. La conversión de los datos sobre transacciones de DEG a dólares de EE.UU. se efectúa a los tipos de cambio que se indican en la línea "sb" de las páginas de *EFI* correspondientes a Estados Unidos. En lo que respecta a los países que declaran datos trimestrales en unidades de moneda nacional, los totales anuales en dólares de EE.UU. se obtienen sumando los montos trimestrales en dólares de EE.UU.

En la introducción de *EFI*, sección 1, se presenta mayor información sobre los tipos de cambio empleados.

II. Suscripción a cintas magnéticas

Las estadísticas publicadas en el anuario también se presentan en cintas magnéticas[1]. El número de países y las series cronológicas que cubre la versión para computadora son ligeramente mayores que en la versión impresa del anuario. También es mayor el número de períodos sobre los cuales se incluyen observaciones estadísticas en las series cronológicas. También se incluyen en las cintas los datos trimestrales declarados por los países. Los suscriptores a las cintas magnéticas reciben la parte 1 de la versión impresa del anuario y 12 cintas magnéticas mensuales que incluyen datos actualizados y corregidos a medida que se dispone de los mismos. Para mayor información, sírvase dirigirse a:

Publication Services
International Monetary Fund
Washington, D.C. 20431, EE.UU.
Teléfono: (202) 623-7430
Fax: (202) 623-7201

[1]Se prevé además la presentación en CD-ROM.

ANEXO I. PRESENTACIÓN ANALÍTICA

	Códigos
A. CUENTA CORRIENTE[1]	4 993 Y .
Bienes: exportaciones f.o.b.	2 100 . .
Bienes: importaciones f.o.b.	3 100 . .
Balanza de bienes	4 100 . .
Servicios: crédito	2 200 . .
Servicios: débito	3 200 . .
Balanza de bienes y servicios	4 991 . .
Renta: crédito	2 300 . .
Renta: débito	3 300 . .
Balanza de bienes, servicios y renta	4 992 . .
Transferencias corrientes: crédito	2 379 Y .
Transferencias corrientes: débito	3 379 . .
B. CUENTA DE CAPITAL[1]	4 994 Y .
Cuenta de capital: crédito	2 994 Y .
Cuenta de capital: débito	3 994 . .
Total, grupos A más B	4 010 . .
C. CUENTA FINANCIERA[1]	4 995 X .
Inversión directa en el extranjero	4 505 . .
Inversión directa en la economía declarante	4 555 Y .
Activos de inversión de cartera	4 602 . .
Títulos de participación en el capital	4 610 . .
Títulos de deuda	4 619 . .
Pasivos de inversión de cartera	4 652 Y .
Títulos de participación en el capital	4 660 Y .
Títulos de deuda	4 669 Y .
Activos de otra inversión	4 703 . .
Autoridades monetarias	4 703 .A
Gobierno general	4 703 .B
Bancos	4 703 .C
Otros sectores	4 703 .D
Pasivos de otra inversión	4 753 X .
Autoridades monetarias	4 753 XA
Gobierno general	4 753 YB
Bancos	4 753 YC
Otros sectores	4 753 YD
Total, grupos A a C	4 020 . .
D. ERRORES Y OMISIONES NETOS	4 998 . .
Total, grupos A a D	4 030 . .
E. RESERVAS Y PARTIDAS CONEXAS	4 040 . .
Activos de reserva	4 800 . .
Uso del crédito del FMI y préstamos del FMI	4 766 . .
Pasivos que constituyen reservas de autoridades extranjeras	4 900 . .
Financiamiento excepcional	4 920 . .
TIPOS DE CONVERSIÓN: MONEDA DEL PAÍS POR DÓLAR DE EE.UU.	0 101 . .

[1]Excluidos los componentes que se han clasificado en las categorías del Grupo E.

ANEXO II. PRESENTACIÓN NORMALIZADA

	Códigos	
CUENTA CORRIENTE	4 993	..
A. BIENES	4 100	..
Crédito	2 100	..
Mercancías generales: exportaciones f.o.b.	2 110	..
Bienes para transformación: exportaciones f.o.b.	2 150	..
Reparaciones de bienes	2 160	..
Bienes adquiridos en puerto por medios de transporte	2 170	..
Oro no monetario	2 180	..
Débito	3 100	..
Mercancías generales: importaciones f.o.b.	3 110	..
Bienes para transformación: importaciones f.o.b.	3 150	..
Reparaciones de bienes	3 160	..
Bienes adquiridos en puerto por medios de transporte	3 170	..
Oro no monetario	3 180	..
B. SERVICIOS	4 200	..
Crédito total	2 200	..
Débito total	3 200	..
Servicios de transportes, crédito	2 205	..
Pasajeros	2 205	BA
Fletes	2 205	BB
Otros	2 205	BC
Transporte marítimo, pasajeros	2 207	..
Transporte marítimo, fletes	2 208	..
Transporte marítimo, otros	2 209	..
Transporte aéreo, pasajeros	2 211	..
Transporte aéreo, fletes	2 212	..
Transporte aéreo, otros	2 213	..
Otros transportes, pasajeros	2 215	..
Otros transportes, fletes	2 216	..
Otros transportes, otros	2 217	..
Servicios de transportes, débito	3 205	..
Pasajeros	3 205	BA
Fletes	3 205	BB
Otros	3 205	BC
Transporte marítimo, pasajeros	3 207	..
Transporte marítimo, fletes	3 208	..
Transporte marítimo, otros	3 209	..
Transporte aéreo, pasajeros	3 211	..
Transporte aéreo, fletes	3 212	..
Transporte aéreo, otros	3 213	..
Otros transportes, pasajeros	3 215	..
Otros transportes, fletes	3 216	..
Otros transportes, otros	3 217	..
Viajes, crédito	2 236	..
De negocios	2 237	..
Personales	2 240	..
Viajes, débito	3 236	..
De negocios	3 237	..
Personales	3 240	..
Otros servicios, crédito	2 200	BA
Comunicaciones	2 245	..
Construcción	2 249	..

Anexo II. Presentación Normalizada *(continuación)*

	Códigos	
Seguros	2 253	. .
Financieros	2 260	. .
Informática e información	2 262	. .
Regalías y derechos de licencia	2 266	. .
Otros servicios empresariales	2 268	. .
Personales, culturales y recreativos	2 287	. .
Servicios del gobierno, n.i.o.p.	2 291	. .
Otros servicios, débito	3 200	BA
Comunicaciones	3 245	. .
Construcción	3 249	. .
Seguros	3 253	. .
Financieros	3 260	. .
Informática e información	3 262	. .
Regalías y derechos de licencia	3 266	. .
Otros servicios empresariales	3 268	. .
Personales, culturales y recreativos	3 287	. .
Servicios del gobierno, n.i.o.p.	3 291	. .
C. RENTA	4 300	. .
Crédito total	2 300	. .
Débito total	3 300	. .
Remuneración de empleados, crédito	2 310	. .
Remuneración de empleados, débito	3 310	. .
Renta de la inversión, crédito	2 320	. .
Renta de la inversión directa	2 330	. .
Dividendos y utilidades distribuidas de sucursales	2 332	. .
Utilidades reinvertidas y utilidades no distribuidas de sucursales	2 333	. .
Renta procedente de la deuda (intereses)	2 334	. .
Renta de la inversión de cartera	2 339	. .
Renta procedente de acciones y otras participaciones de capital	2 340	. .
Renta procedente de bonos y pagarés	2 350	. .
Renta procedente de instrumentos del mercado monetario e instrumentos financieros derivados	2 360	. .
Renta de otra inversión	2 370	. .
Renta de la inversión, débito	3 320	. .
Renta de la inversión directa	3 330	. .
Dividendos y utilidades distribuidas de sucursales	3 332	. .
Utilidades reinvertidas y utilidades no distribuidas de sucursales	3 333	. .
Renta procedente de la deuda (intereses)	3 334	. .
Renta de la inversión de cartera	3 339	. .
Renta procedente de acciones y otras participaciones de capital	3 340	. .
Renta procedente de bonos y pagarés	3 350	. .
Renta procedente de instrumentos del mercado monetario e instrumentos financieros derivados	3 360	. .
Renta de otra inversión	3 370	. .
D. Transferencias corrientes	4 379	. .
Crédito	2 379	. .
Gobierno general	2 380	. .
Otros sectores	2 390	. .
Remesas de trabajadores	2 391	. .
Otras transferencias corrientes	2 392	. .
Débito	3 379	. .
Gobierno general	3 380	. .

ANEXO II. PRESENTACIÓN NORMALIZADA *(continuación)*

	Códigos	
Otros sectores	3 390	..
Remesas de trabajadores	3 391	..
Otras transferencias corrientes	3 392	..
CUENTA DE CAPITAL Y FINANCIERA	4 996	..
CUENTA DE CAPITAL	4 994	..
Crédito total	2 994	..
Débito total	3 994	..
Transferencias de capital, crédito	2 400	..
Gobierno general	2 401	..
Condonación de deudas	2 402	..
Otras transferencias de capital	2 410	..
Otros sectores	2 430	..
Transferencias de emigrantes	2 431	..
Condonación de deudas	2 432	..
Otras transferencias de capital	2 440	..
Transferencias de capital, débito	3 400	..
Gobierno general	3 401	..
Condonación de deudas	3 402	..
Otras transferencias de capital	3 410	..
Otros sectores	3 430	..
Transferencias de emigrantes	3 431	..
Condonación de deudas	3 432	..
Otras transferencias de capital	3 440	..
Activos no financieros no producidos, crédito	2 480	..
Activos no financieros no producidos, débito	3 480	..
CUENTA FINANCIERA	4 995	..
A. INVERSIÓN DIRECTA	4 500	..
Inversión directa en el extranjero	4 505	..
Acciones y otras participaciones de capital	4 510	..
Activos frente a empresas filiales	4 515	..
Pasivos frente a empresas filiales	4 520	..
Utilidades reinvertidas	4 525	..
Otro capital	4 530	..
Activos frente a empresas filiales	4 535	..
Pasivos frente a empresas filiales	4 540	..
Inversión directa en la economía declarante	4 555	..
Acciones y otras participaciones de capital	4 560	..
Activos frente a inversionistas directos	4 565	..
Pasivos frente a inversionistas directos	4 570	..
Utilidades reinvertidas	4 575	..
Otro capital	4 580	..
Activos frente a inversionistas directos	4 585	..
Pasivos frente a inversionistas directos	4 590	..
B. INVERSIÓN DE CARTERA	4 600	..
Activos	4 602	..
Títulos de participación en el capital	4 610	..
Autoridades monetarias	4 611	..
Gobierno general	4 612	..
Bancos	4 613	..
Otros sectores	4 614	..

ANEXO II. PRESENTACIÓN NORMALIZADA *(continuación)*

	Códigos	
Títulos de deuda	4 619	..
Bonos y pagarés	4 620	..
Autoridades monetarias	4 621	..
Gobierno general	4 622	..
Bancos	4 623	..
Otros sectores	4 624	..
Instrumentos del mercado monetario	4 630	..
Autoridades monetarias	4 631	..
Gobierno general	4 632	..
Bancos	4 633	..
Otros sectores	4 634	..
Instrumentos financieros derivados	4 640	..
Autoridades monetarias	4 641	..
Gobierno general	4 642	..
Bancos	4 643	..
Otros sectores	4 644	..
Pasivos	4 652	..
Títulos de participación en el capital	4 660	..
Bancos	4 663	..
Otros sectores	4 664	..
Títulos de deuda	4 669	..
Bonos y pagarés	4 670	..
Autoridades monetarias	4 671	..
Gobierno general	4 672	..
Bancos	4 673	..
Otros sectores	4 674	..
Instrumentos del mercado monetario	4 680	..
Autoridades monetarias	4 681	..
Gobierno general	4 682	..
Bancos	4 683	..
Otros sectores	4 684	..
Instrumentos financieros derivados	4 690	..
Autoridades monetarias	4 691	..
Gobierno general	4 692	..
Bancos	4 693	..
Otros sectores	4 694	..
C. OTRA INVERSIÓN	4 700	..
Activos	4 703	..
Créditos comerciales	4 706	..
Gobierno general: a largo plazo	4 708	..
Gobierno general: a corto plazo	4 709	..
Otros sectores: a largo plazo	4 711	..
Otros sectores: a corto plazo	4 712	..
Préstamos	4 714	..
Autoridades monetarias: a largo plazo	4 717	..
Autoridades monetarias: a corto plazo	4 718	..
Gobierno general: a largo plazo	4 720	..
Gobierno general: a corto plazo	4 721	..
Bancos: a largo plazo	4 723	..
Bancos: a corto plazo	4 724	..
Otros sectores: a largo plazo	4 726	..
Otros sectores: a corto plazo	4 727	..
Moneda y depósitos	4 730	..
Autoridades monetarias	4 731	..
Gobierno general	4 732	..

Anexo II. Presentación Normalizada *(conclusión)*

	Códigos	
Bancos	4 733	..
Otros sectores	4 734	..
Otros pasivos	4 736	..
Autoridades monetarias: a largo plazo	4 738	..
Autoridades monetarias: a corto plazo	4 739	..
Gobierno general: a largo plazo	4 741	..
Gobierno general: a corto plazo	4 742	..
Bancos: a largo plazo	4 744	..
Bancos: a corto plazo	4 745	..
Otros sectores: a largo plazo	4 747	..
Otros sectores: a corto plazo	4 748	..
Pasivos	4 753	..
Créditos comerciales	4 756	..
Gobierno general: a largo plazo	4 758	..
Gobierno general: a corto plazo	4 759	..
Otros sectores: a largo plazo	4 761	..
Otros sectores: a corto plazo	4 762	..
Préstamos	4 764	..
Uso del crédito del FMI y préstamos del FMI	4 766	..
Autoridades monetarias: otros a largo plazo	4 767	..
Autoridades monetarias: a corto plazo	4 768	..
Gobierno general: a largo plazo	4 770	..
Gobierno general: a corto plazo	4 771	..
Bancos: a largo plazo	4 773	..
Bancos: a corto plazo	4 774	..
Otros sectores: a largo plazo	4 776	..
Otros sectores: a corto plazo	4 777	..
Moneda y depósitos	4 780	..
Autoridades monetarias	4 781	..
Gobierno general	4 782	..
Bancos	4 783	..
Otros sectores	4 784	..
Otros pasivos	4 786	..
Autoridades monetarias: a largo plazo	4 788	..
Autoridades monetarias: a corto plazo	4 789	..
Gobierno general: a largo plazo	4 791	..
Gobierno general: a corto plazo	4 792	..
Bancos: a largo plazo	4 794	..
Bancos: a corto plazo	4 795	..
Otros sectores: a largo plazo	4 797	..
Otros sectores: a corto plazo	4 798	..
D. ACTIVOS DE RESERVA	4 800	..
Oro monetario	4 810	..
Derechos especiales de giro	4 820	..
Posición de reserva en el FMI	4 830	..
Divisas	4 840	..
Otros activos	4 880	..
ERRORES Y OMISIONES NETOS	4 998	..

ANEXO III. SISTEMA DE CODIFICACIÓN FMI/OCDE/EUROSTAT PARA LA BALANZA DE PAGOS, LA POSICIÓN DE INVERSIÓN INTERNACIONAL Y EL COMERCIO DE SERVICIOS[1]

Este sistema de codificación incorpora todos los componentes normalizados y las líneas de información suplementaria de la quinta edición del *Manual de Balanza de Pagos*, así como los componentes y partidas informativas de la clasificación OCDE/Eurostat para el comercio internacional de servicios.

El código consta de tres partes:

<posición>	Un dígito (del 1 al 8) que describe la posición de la partida en las cuentas de la posición de inversión internacional o de la balanza de pagos.
<tema>	Tres dígitos (del 100 al 998) que identifican todos los componentes de la balanza de pagos, del comercio de servicios y de información suplementaria seleccionada.
<sufijo>	Serie de caracteres definidos por el usuario; puede ser de cualquier longitud.

El código completo deberá tener la siguiente configuración: <posición><tema><sufijo>, aunque el sufijo es optativo. Los dígitos de posición y tema, en cambio, son obligatorios. Por esa razón, en la mayoría de los casos, la configuración del código es <posición><tema>.

El primer dígito del código describe la posición de la partida en las cuentas de la posición de inversión internacional y de la balanza de pagos, a saber:

Código	Posición en las cuentas de la posición de inversión internacional y la balanza de pagos
1	Posición al comienzo del período
2	Flujos de crédito
3	Flujos de débito
4	Flujos netos
5	Ajuste por variaciones de precios
6	Ajuste por variaciones de tipos de cambio
7	Otros ajustes
8	Posición al final del período
0	Otros

El primer dígito del tema identifica la sección de la balanza de pagos, a saber:

Código	Sección de las cuentas
1	Bienes
2	Servicios
3	Renta y transferencias corrientes
4	Cuenta de capital
5	Inversión directa
6	Inversión de cartera
7	Otra inversión
8	Activos de reserva
9	Agregados principales e información suplementaria

El segundo y tercer dígito del tema corresponden al orden consecutivo de los componentes con interrupciones para poder incluir códigos adicionales posteriormente. Además, en la cuenta financiera, salvo las cuentas de inversión directa, el segundo dígito del tema puede ser 0, 1, 2, 3 ó 4 en el caso de los activos y 5, 6, 7, 8 ó 9 en el caso de los pasivos.

A continuación se presentan ejemplos de códigos para "Otra inversión" en la cuenta financiera.

Tema	Campo único			Campo múltiple		
	Crédito	Débito	Neto	Crédito	Débito	Neto
Otra inversión	2700	3700	4700	2700	3700	4700
Pasivos	2750	3750	4750	2750	3750	4750
Préstamos	2762	3762	4762	2762	3762	4762
Gobierno general	2767	3767	4767	2767	3767	4767
A largo plazo	2768	3768	4768	2768	3768	4768
A corto plazo	2769	3769	4769	2769	3769	4769
Bancos	2770	3770	4770	2770	3770	4770
A largo plazo	2771	3771	4771	2771	3771	4771
A corto plazo	2772	3772	4772	2772	3772	4772
Otros sectores	2773	3773	4773	2773	3773	4773
A largo plazo	2774	3774	4774	2774	3774	4774
A corto plazo	2775	3775	4775	2775	3775	4775

Tratándose de créditos y débitos correspondientes a préstamos, los términos que se emplean comúnmente son giros y rembolsos. La quinta edición del *Manual* recomienda declarar todos los giros y rembolsos de los préstamos a largo plazo en una clasificación suplementaria. Actualmente, el FMI recopila la mayoría de las demás partidas de la cuenta financiera en cifras netas. No obstante, el sistema de codificación permite identificar todos los flujos como créditos, débitos o flujos netos.

[1]Adoptado de "Balance of Payments Codes for Standard Components and Additional Items", FMI, Washington, 3 de marzo de 1995.

Anexo IV. Posición de inversión internacional componentes normalizados

	Códigos	
A. ACTIVOS	8 995	C .
Inversión directa en el extranjero	8 505	. .
Acciones y otras participaciones de capital y utilidades reinvertidas	8 506	. .
Activos frente a empresas filiales	8 507	. .
Pasivos frente a empresas filiales	8 508	. .
Otro capital	8 530	. .
Activos frente a empresas filiales	8 535	. .
Pasivos frente a empresas filiales	8 540	. .
Inversión de cartera	8 602	. .
Títulos de participación en el capital	8 610	. .
Autoridades monetarias	8 611	. .
Gobierno general	8 612	. .
Bancos	8 613	. .
Otros sectores	8 614	. .
Títulos de deuda	8 619	. .
Bonos y pagarés	8 620	. .
Autoridades monetarias	8 621	. .
Gobierno general	8 622	. .
Bancos	8 623	. .
Otros sectores	8 624	. .
Instrumentos del mercado monetario	8 630	. .
Autoridades monetarias	8 631	. .
Gobierno general	8 632	. .
Bancos	8 633	. .
Otros sectores	8 634	. .
Instrumentos financieros derivados	8 640	. .
Autoridades monetarias	8 641	. .
Gobierno general	8 642	. .
Bancos	8 643	. .
Otros sectores	8 644	. .
Otra inversión	8 703	. .
Créditos comerciales	8 706	. .
Gobierno general: A largo plazo	8 708	. .
Gobierno general: A corto plazo	8 709	. .
Otros sectores: A largo plazo	8 711	. .
Otros sectores: A corto plazo	8 712	. .
Préstamos	8 714	. .
Autoridades monetarias: A largo plazo	8 717	. .
Autoridades monetarias: A corto plazo	8 718	. .
Gobierno general: A largo plazo	8 720	. .
Gobierno general: A corto plazo	8 721	. .
Bancos: A largo plazo	8 723	. .
Bancos: A corto plazo	8 724	. .
Otros sectores: A largo plazo	8 726	. .
Otros sectores: A corto plazo	8 727	. .
Moneda y depósitos	8 730	. .
Autoridades monetarias	8 731	. .
Gobierno general	8 732	. .
Bancos	8 733	. .
Otros sectores	8 734	. .
Otros activos	8 736	. .
Autoridades monetarias: A largo plazo	8 738	. .
Autoridades monetarias: A corto plazo	8 739	. .
Gobierno general: A largo plazo	8 741	. .
Gobierno general: A corto plazo	8 742	. .

ANEXO IV. POSICIÓN DE INVERSIÓN INTERNACIONAL COMPONENTES NORMALIZADOS *(continuación)*

	Códigos	
Bancos: A largo plazo	8 744	..
Bancos: A corto plazo	8 745	..
Otros sectores: A largo plazo	8 747	..
Otros sectores: A corto plazo	8 748	..
Activos de reserva	8 800	..
Oro monetario	8 810	..
Derechos especiales de giro	8 820	..
Posición de reserva en el FMI	8 830	..
Divisas	8 840	..
Otros activos	8 880	..
B. PASIVOS	8 995	D .
Inversión directa en la economía declarante	8 555	..
Acciones y otras participaciones de capital y utilidades reinvertidas	8 556	..
Activos frente a inversionistas directos	8 557	..
Pasivos frente a inversionistas directos	8 558	..
Otro capital	8 580	..
Activos frente a inversionistas directos	8 585	..
Pasivos frente a inversionistas directos	8 590	..
Inversión de cartera	8 652	..
Títulos de participación en el capital	8 660	..
Bancos	8 663	..
Otros sectores	8 664	..
Títulos de deuda	8 669	..
Bonos y pagarés	8 670	..
Autoridades monetarias	8 671	..
Gobierno general	8 672	..
Bancos	8 673	..
Otros sectores	8 674	..
Instrumentos del mercado monetario	8 680	..
Autoridades monetarias	8 681	..
Gobierno general	8 682	..
Bancos	8 683	..
Otros sectores	8 684	..
Instrumentos financieros derivados	8 690	..
Autoridades monetarias	8 691	..
Gobierno general	8 692	..
Bancos	8 693	..
Otros sectores	8 694	..
Otra inversión	8 753	..
Créditos comerciales	8 756	..
Gobierno general: A largo plazo	8 758	..
Gobierno general: A corto plazo	8 759	..
Otros sectores: A largo plazo	8 761	..
Otros sectores: A corto plazo	8 762	..
Préstamos	8 764	..
Uso del crédito del FMI y préstamos del FMI	8 766	..
Autoridades monetarias: A largo plazo	8 767	..
Autoridades monetarias: A corto plazo	8 768	..
Gobierno general: A largo plazo	8 770	..
Gobierno general: A corto plazo	8 771	..
Bancos: A largo plazo	8 773	..
Bancos: A corto plazo	8 774	..
Otros sectores: A largo plazo	8 776	..
Otros sectores: A corto plazo	8 777	..

ANEXO IV. POSICIÓN DE INVERSIÓN INTERNACIONAL COMPONENTES NORMALIZADOS *(conclusión)*

	Códigos	
Moneda y depósitos	8 780	..
Autoridades monetarias	8 781	..
Gobierno general	8 782	..
Bancos	8 783	..
Otros sectores	8 784	..
Otros pasivos	8 786	..
Autoridades monetarias: A largo plazo	8 788	..
Autoridades monetarias: A corto plazo	8 789	..
Gobierno general: A largo plazo	8 791	..
Gobierno general: A corto plazo	8 792	..
Bancos: A largo plazo	8 794	..
Bancos: A corto plazo	8 795	..
Otros sectores: A largo plazo	8 797	..
Otros sectores: A corto plazo	8 798	..
POSICIÓN DE INVERSIÓN INTERNACIONAL NETA	8 995	..
Tipos de conversión (fin de período)	0 102	..

ANEXO V. MARCO CONCEPTUAL DE LA BALANZA DE PAGOS Y DE LA POSICIÓN DE INVERSIÓN INTERNACIONAL

Este anexo es la reproducción del capítulo II del Manual de Balanza de Pagos, 5a. edición. *Los párrafos y los números de página citados en este anexo corresponden a los del* Manual.

Definiciones

12. La primera parte de este *Manual* abarca el marco conceptual de las cuentas de la balanza de pagos y de la posición de inversión internacional, examinándose su relación con las cuentas nacionales y con los conceptos de residencia, valoración, momento de registro, unidad de cuenta y conversión.

13. La balanza de pagos es un estado estadístico que resume sistemáticamente, para un período específico dado, las transacciones económicas entre una economía y el resto del mundo. Las transacciones, que en su mayoría tienen lugar entre residentes y no residentes[1], comprenden las que se refieren a bienes, servicios y renta, las que entrañan activos y pasivos financieros frente al resto del mundo y las que se clasifican como transferencias (como los regalos), en las que se efectúan asientos compensatorios para equilibrar —desde el punto de vista contable— las transacciones unilaterales (véase el párrafo 28)[2]. Una transacción en sí se define como un flujo económico que refleja la creación, transformación, intercambio, transferencia o extinción de un valor económico y entraña traspasos de propiedad de bienes y/o activos financieros, la prestación de servicios o el suministro de mano de obra y capital.

14. En estrecha relación con el marco de la balanza de pagos, basado en los flujos, se encuentra la posición de inversión internacional, definida por las tenencias de recursos financieros. Esta última, que corresponde a una fecha específica como el fin del año, es un estado estadístico que representa: i) el valor y la composición de las tenencias de activos financieros de una economía, o de los créditos adquiridos por una economía frente al resto del mundo, y ii) el valor y la composición de las tenencias de pasivos de una economía a favor del resto del mundo. En algunos casos, puede ser de interés analítico calcular la diferencia entre los dos lados del balance para tener una medida de la posición neta. Dicha medida sería equivalente a la porción del patrimonio de una economía atribuible a su relación con el resto del mundo, o derivado de ella. Toda variación de las tenencias en cualquier período definido puede atribuirse a transacciones (flujos), a variaciones de valoración debidas a fluctuaciones del tipo de cambio, precios, etc., o a otros ajustes (por ejemplo, confiscaciones sin indemnización). En cambio, las cuentas de la balanza de pagos sólo reflejan transacciones.

Obsérvese que, como se señala en esta introducción, en este volumen del anuario no se presenta la posición de inversión internacional.

[1]En la balanza de pagos, las únicas transacciones que no se efectúan entre residentes y no residentes son el intercambio de activos financieros sobre el exterior transferibles entre sectores residentes y, en menor medida, el intercambio de pasivos financieros sobre el exterior transferibles entre no residentes. (Véase el párrafo 318.)

[2]Cabe destacar que las definiciones y clasificaciones de las cuentas internacionales que se presentan en este *Manual* tienen por objeto facilitar a los países miembros la tarea de declarar al FMI la información sobre transacciones internacionales y no pretenden hacer efectivas ni interpretar las disposiciones del *Convenio Constitutivo del Fondo Monetario Internacional* que se refieren al carácter jurídico de la acción (o falta de acción) oficial en relación con dichas transacciones.

Criterios y conceptos

15. El resto de este capítulo se refiere al marco conceptual de las cuentas internacionales, vale decir, al conjunto de criterios y convenciones básicos que permite el registro sistematizado y coherente de las transacciones internacionales y de las tenencias de activos y pasivos sobre el exterior. En los capítulos subsiguientes se analizarán detenidamente los aspectos sobresalientes de estos criterios, así como sus consideraciones y limitaciones prácticas.

Método de contabilidad por partida doble

16. El criterio básico aplicado a la preparación del estado de balanza de pagos es que toda transacción registrada está representada por dos asientos de igual valor. Uno de ellos se denomina crédito y tiene signo aritmético positivo. El otro se llama débito y tiene signo negativo. En principio, la suma de todos los asientos de crédito es igual a la suma de todos los asientos de débito y el saldo neto de la totalidad de los asientos del estado es igual a cero.

17. En la práctica, sin embargo, las cuentas no suelen estar en equilibrio. A menudo, los datos empleados para estimar la balanza de pagos suelen derivarse en forma independiente de diferentes fuentes; en consecuencia, puede haber un crédito neto o débito neto agregado (es decir, errores y omisiones netos en las cuentas). Para equilibrar las cuentas, se deberá efectuar un asiento separado por un monto equivalente pero de signo contrario. Debe observarse que, como hay estimaciones imprecisas o faltantes de signo contrario que suelen compensarse mutuamente, la magnitud del residuo neto no es indicativa de la exactitud relativa del estado de balanza de pagos. No obstante, la existencia de un residuo significativo y persistente que no se corrige debe ser motivo de preocupación, porque esta situación impide el análisis o la interpretación de las estimaciones y les resta credibilidad. Por otra parte, un residuo neto elevado también puede afectar a la interpretación del estado de la posición de inversión internacional. (Véase la explicación en el capítulo XXIII.)

18. La mayoría de los asientos de la balanza de pagos se refieren a transacciones en las que se entregan o reciben valores económicos a cambio de otros. Dichos valores comprenden recursos reales (bienes, servicios y renta) y financieros. Así, los asientos compensatorios de crédito y débito que exige el método de registro suelen resultar del hecho de que se han anotado montos iguales para los dos recursos que se han intercambiado. Si en vez de ser intercambiados se ceden gratuitamente, o si el registro es unilateral por otras razones, se efectúan asientos especiales —llamados transferencias—para saldarlos. En los párrafos 26 a 31 se describen las distintas clases de asientos que pueden figurar en la balanza de pagos.

19. Conforme a las convenciones del método contable, una economía compiladora registra asientos de crédito i) para los recursos reales que denotan exportaciones y ii) para los recursos financieros que indican reducciones de sus activos sobre el exterior o aumentos de sus pasivos sobre el exterior. A su vez, registra asientos de débito i) para los recursos reales que denotan importaciones y ii) para los recursos financieros que indican aumentos de los activos o disminuciones de los pasivos. En otras palabras, en los activos —reales o financieros— una cifra con signo positivo (crédito) representa una disminución de las tenencias y una cifra con signo negativo (débito) indica un incremento. En cambio, en los pasivos, una cifra con signo positivo significa un aumento, y una cifra con signo negativo, una disminución. Las transferencias aparecen como créditos si compensan asientos de débito, y como débitos si saldan asientos de crédito.

20. El contenido o la cobertura del estado de balanza de pagos depende, en cierto modo, de que las transacciones sean tratadas en base a valores brutos o netos. Las recomendaciones de este *Manual* especifican cuáles deberán registrarse en valores brutos y cuáles en valores netos, como se refleja en la lista de componentes normalizados y en las presentaciones suplementarias sugeridas.

Conceptos de territorio económico, residencia y centro de interés económico

21. Los conceptos de territorio económico, residencia y centro de interés económico que se utilizan en este *Manual* son idénticos a los del *SCN* y se describen detalladamente en el capítulo IV. El territorio económico puede no coincidir con las fronteras políticas reconocidas. El territorio económico de un país comprende el territorio geográfico administrado por un gobierno dentro del cual circulan libremente personas, bienes y capital. En el caso de países marítimos, incluye también las islas que están sujetas a las mismas autoridades fiscales y monetarias que el territorio continental.

22. Una unidad institucional tiene un centro de interés económico y es residente de un país cuando desde algún lugar (vivienda, planta de producción u otro establecimiento), ubicado dentro del territorio económico del país, dicha unidad realiza e intenta seguir realizando (indefinidamente o durante un período finito) actividades económicas y transacciones en gran escala. (Se sugiere emplear un año o más como referencia, aunque no se trata de una regla inflexible.)

Criterios de valoración y momento de registro

23. Para compilar de manera uniforme cualquier agregado de transacciones individuales y registrar la posición de los activos y pasivos que les corresponden, es necesario contar con una base uniforme de valoración de las cuentas internacionales (tanto los recursos reales como los activos y pasivos financieros). En general, en este *Manual* se utiliza como base para la valoración de las transacciones el precio efectivo de mercado acordado por las partes que intervienen en la transacción. (Este criterio coincide con el adoptado en el *SCN*.) Desde el punto de vista conceptual, todas las tenencias de activos y pasivos deberán valorarse de acuerdo a los precios de mercado vigentes en el momento al cual se refiere la posición de inversión internacional. En el capítulo V se presenta una exposición completa de los criterios de valoración, las prácticas recomendadas, las limitaciones y la valoración de transferencias, recursos financieros y tenencias de activos y pasivos. (Se incluyen también casos en que no existe un precio de mercado o no es posible suponerlo.)

24. En el *Manual* y en el *SCN*, el criterio que se aplica con respecto al *momento de registro* de las transacciones es el de contabilidad en valores devengados. Por lo tanto, las transacciones deben registrarse con referencia al momento en que se crea, transforma, intercambia, transfiere o extingue un valor económico. Se crean activos y pasivos cuando tiene lugar un traspaso de propiedad, ya sea de índole legal o física (económica). En la práctica, cuando no sea evidente el traspaso de propiedad, el momento en que éste ocurre puede determinarse de una forma aproximada utilizando la fecha en que las partes de una transacción la registran en sus libros o en sus cuentas. (El capítulo VI trata sobre los momentos de registro y convenciones recomendados para diferentes asientos de la balanza de pagos, e incluye excepciones y desviaciones del criterio de traspaso de propiedad.)

Concepto y clase de transacción

25. En general, las variaciones de las relaciones económicas que se registran en la balanza de pagos provienen básicamente de las transacciones realizadas entre dos partes. Dichas partes son, con una excepción (véase la nota 1), un residente y un no residente, y todas las transacciones de esta clase aparecen en la balanza de pagos. Las recomendaciones sobre los asientos específicos necesarios se hallan incorporadas en la lista de componentes normalizados (véase el capítulo VIII) y se detallan a partir del capítulo IX.

26. A pesar de su nombre, la balanza de pagos no se refiere a *pagos* en su acepción común, sino a *transacciones*. Algunas transacciones internacionales que revisten interés a efectos de la balanza de pagos pueden no entrañar un pago en efectivo y algunas no se pagan en ningún sentido. La inclusión de estas transacciones, además de las que tienen como contrapartida un pago, constituye la diferencia principal entre un estado de balanza de pagos y un registro de pagos externos.

Intercambios

27. Las transacciones más comunes e importantes de la balanza de pagos pueden caracterizarse como *intercambios*. Una parte (entidad económica) suministra un valor económico a otra y recibe a cambio un valor igual. Los valores económicos suministrados por una economía a otra pueden clasificarse en términos generales como recursos reales (bienes, servicios, renta) y recursos financieros. Las partes que intervienen en la transacción son residentes de distintas economías, salvo en el caso de intercambio de recursos financieros externos entre sectores residentes. El suministro de un recurso financiero puede suponer no sólo un traspaso de propiedad de un activo o de un pasivo existente sino también la creación de uno nuevo o la cancelación de uno existente. Es más, las condiciones de un contrato relativo a un recurso financiero (por ejemplo, el plazo de vencimiento contractual) pueden modificarse por acuerdo entre las partes, en cuyo caso se da por cumplido el primer contrato y se considera que éste ha sido remplazado por otro con condiciones distintas. Todos estos intercambios se deberán incluir en la balanza de pagos.

Transferencias

28. Las transacciones que comprenden *transferencias* difieren de los intercambios porque una de las partes entrega un valor económico a la otra sin recibir un quid pro quo que, según las normas y reglas adoptadas en el sistema, tiene valor económico. Esta ausencia de valor por un lado de la transacción está representado por un asiento denominado *transferencia*. Las transferencias de esta clase (valores económicos suministrados y recibidos sin quid pro quo) se registran en la balanza de pagos. Las ***transferencias corrientes*** se incluyen en la **cuenta corriente** (véase el capítulo XV), en tanto que las *transferencias de capital* aparecen en la ***cuenta de capital*** (véase el capítulo XVII).

Migración

29. Como una economía se define en función de las entidades económicas vinculadas a su territorio, su ámbito posiblemente se vea afectado por los cambios que tengan lugar en las entidades vinculadas a ella.

30. Se produce una migración cuando la residencia de una persona se traslada de una economía a otra por haber cambiado su domicilio. Ciertos bienes muebles del emigrante se importan, de hecho, a la nueva economía. Sus bienes inmuebles y ciertos bienes muebles que se encuentran en la economía anterior se transforman en activos de la nueva economía frente a la anterior. Sus activos o pasivos frente a residentes de otra economía distinta de la nueva pasan a ser activos o pasivos sobre el exterior de la nueva economía. Sus activos o pasivos frente a residentes de la nueva economía dejan de ser activos o pasivos de una economía frente al resto del mundo. La suma neta de todas estas variaciones es igual al patrimonio del emigrante, que también debe registrarse como asiento compensatorio, si se registran los demás cambios. Estos asientos se efectúan en la balanza de pagos donde, por norma, se incluyen en las transferencias.

Otras transacciones imputadas

31. En algunos casos, las transacciones pueden ser imputadas y pueden efectuarse asientos en las cuentas de la balanza de pagos cuando no exista un flujo efectivo. Cabe citar como ejemplo la atribución de las utilidades reinvertidas a inversionistas directos extranjeros. Las utilidades de una filial o sucursal extranjera incluyen utilidades atribuibles a un inversionista directo residente. Dichas utilidades, independientemente de que se hayan distribuido o reinvertido en la empresa, son proporcionales a la participación del inversionista directo residente en el capital de la empresa. Las utilidades reinvertidas se registran como parte de la renta de la inversión directa. Se efectúa un asiento compensatorio, con signo contrario, en el rubro inversión directa de la *cuenta financiera* para reflejar el hecho de que aumentó la inversión del inversionista directo extranjero en la filial o sucursal extranjera. (En los capítulos XIV y XVIII se trata el tema de las utilidades reinvertidas.)

Otras variaciones que no entrañan transacciones

Reclasificación de activos y pasivos

32. En este *Manual*, la clasificación de los recursos financieros se basa en características que revelan los motivos del acreedor o del deudor. Si cambian los motivos, varían también dichas características, de modo que los recursos financieros quedan sujetos a reclasificación en función de dichos cambios. Cabe destacar la diferencia que se establece entre la *inversión directa* y otras clases de inversión. Por ejemplo, varios tenedores independientes de *inversiones de cartera* (en forma de acciones y otras participaciones de capital social emitidas por una sola empresa en el extranjero) pueden asociarse para adquirir una participación efectiva duradera en la dirección de la empresa. Sus tenencias reúnen así las condiciones de una *inversión directa* y el cambio de situación de la inversión puede registrarse como reclasificación. Dicha reclasificación se reflejará, al final del período en el que tuvo lugar, en la posición de inversión internacional, pero no en la balanza de pagos. Análogamente, ciertos activos frente a no residentes pueden pasar al control de las autoridades monetarias residentes o quedar fuera de su control, lo cual da lugar a una reclasificación entre *activos de reserva* y activos que no constituyen reservas.

Variaciones de valoración

33. El valor de los recursos reales y financieros está sujeto a constantes cambios, que pueden atribuirse a una de las dos, o a las dos, causas siguientes: i) el precio habitual al que se efectúan transacciones de ciertos tipos de recursos puede variar en relación con la moneda en que se cotiza dicho precio; ii) el tipo de cambio de la moneda en que se cotiza el precio puede variar en relación con la unidad de cuenta utilizada. Las variaciones de valoración no se registran en la balanza de pagos, pero sí en la posición de inversión internacional.

ANEXO VI. CLASIFICACIÓN Y COMPONENTES NORMALIZADOS DE LA BALANZA DE PAGOS

Este anexo es la reproducción del capítulo VIII del Manual de Balanza de Pagos, 5ª edición. *Los párrafos y los números de página citados en este anexo corresponden a los del* Manual.

Estructura y clasificación

139. En la segunda parte de este *Manual* se definen la estructura y la clasificación de las cuentas de la balanza de pagos y de la posición de inversión internacional. Abarca, asimismo, los componentes normalizados de ambos grupos de cuentas; se examina y explica la forma de preparar la **cuenta corriente**, la **cuenta de capital y financiera**, la información suplementaria seleccionada y la posición de inversión internacional.

140. Las estadísticas de balanza de pagos deben organizarse dentro de una estructura coherente para facilitar su utilización y adaptación para diferentes fines, tales como formulación de la política económica, estudios analíticos, proyecciones, comparaciones bilaterales de componentes específicos o transacciones totales, agregados regionales y mundiales, etc. (Véase el párrafo 7.)

141. La clasificación y la lista de componentes normalizados reflejan consideraciones de índole conceptual y práctica, toman en cuenta opiniones expresadas por expertos nacionales en balanza de pagos y, en general, concuerdan con el *SCN* y con la armonización entre la nueva clasificación de las transacciones internacionales de servicios y la Clasificación Central de Productos (CCP). (Véase el apéndice III.)

142. Se ha hecho todo lo posible para vincular la estructura de la ***cuenta de capital*** a las cuentas de renta y a la clasificación de la posición de inversión internacional. El objetivo es que muchos países puedan utilizarla como marco flexible para desarrollar a largo plazo sus estadísticas del sector externo. Si bien puede ocurrir que algunos países no puedan proporcionar datos para muchas partidas, este marco permitirá a otros países declarar datos adicionales.

Componentes normalizados

143. La determinación de los componentes normalizados (véase la lista al final de este capítulo) depende de una serie de factores, considerándose los más importantes los siguientes:

La partida debe exhibir un comportamiento característico, que indique que influyen en ella un factor o una combinación de factores económicos distintos de los que influyen en las demás partidas o que responde de diferente manera ante el mismo factor o combinación de factores. En la balanza de pagos se trata precisamente de poner de manifiesto esta respuesta ante las influencias económicas.

La partida debe ser importante para una serie de países, ya sea en función de su comportamiento (por ejemplo, variabilidad excepcional) o de su valor absoluto.

Deberá ser posible obtener los datos estadísticos de la partida sin demasiada dificultad, aunque cabe tener en cuenta la conveniencia de recopilarlos en razón de las dos primeras consideraciones citadas.

La partida deberá también ser necesaria para otros fines, por ejemplo, para incluirla en las cuentas nacionales o conciliarla con éstas. La lista de componentes normalizados no debe ser demasiada larga, dado el gran número de países, entre ellos muchos con sistemas estadísticos menos adelantados, a los cuales se solicita que presenten esos datos de manera uniforme.

En la medida en que sea posible, los componentes normalizados deberán ser compatibles con otros sistemas estadísticos del FMI, el *SCN* y, en el caso específico de los ***servicios***, con la CCP.

144. La presentación de una lista de componentes normalizados no significa que las recomendaciones formuladas en este *Manual* tengan por objeto disuadir a los países de compilar y publicar otros datos de importancia nacional. Si se requieren mayores datos para comprender las circunstancias que rodean a determinados países o para analizar nuevas situaciones que puedan surgir, la información que solicite el FMI a los países miembros no se limitará a la lista de componentes normalizados. La información suplementaria también puede ser sumamente útil para verificar y conciliar las estadísticas de países que comercian entre sí y, por ejemplo, para analizar transacciones de financiamiento excepcional. (Véase el cuadro *Información suplementaria seleccionada* al final de este capítulo.) El personal del FMI consultará periódicamente con los países para decidir qué otros datos deberán presentar.

145. Es probable que sean pocos los países que cuentan con información significativa sobre todos los componentes normalizados. Tal vez los datos sobre varios de los componentes sólo puedan obtenerse en combinación con otros, o quizás un componente de menor importancia esté agrupado con otro más importante. No obstante, los componentes normalizados deberán declararse al FMI de la manera más completa y exacta que sea posible. En este sentido, los compiladores nacionales se encuentran en mejores condiciones que el personal del FMI para estimar y ajustar los componentes que no correspondan exactamente a los datos básicos de la economía declarante.

Errores y omisiones netos

146. Al aplicar los criterios recomendados en este *Manual*, se obtiene un conjunto coherente de asientos con signo positivo y negativo cuyo total neto es teóricamente igual a cero. En la práctica, sin embargo, una vez sumados todos los asientos, la balanza de pagos casi siempre arroja un crédito neto o un débito neto. Este saldo se debe a errores y omisiones en la compilación de las estadísticas, algunos de los cuales pueden tener relación con recomendaciones para una aproximación práctica a los criterios establecidos.

147. Por regla general, en el estado de balanza de pagos se presenta una partida separada de errores y omisiones netos, que algunos compiladores denominan partida equilibradora o discrepancia estadística, para compensar toda sobrestimación o subestimación de los componentes registrados. Así, si el saldo de estos componentes refleja un crédito, la partida de errores y omisiones netos aparece como un débito de igual valor, y viceversa.

148. Como algunos de los errores y omisiones que se producen al compilar los datos suelen compensarse entre sí, la magnitud de la partida residual no es necesariamente un indicio de la exactitud global del estado. Aun así, cuando el residuo neto es grande, es difícil interpretar un estado.

Clasificaciones principales

149. Los componentes normalizados, cuya lista figura al final de este capítulo, se clasifican en dos grupos principales de cuentas:

La **cuenta corriente**, que comprende ***bienes y servicios, renta*** y ***transferencias corrientes***.

La **cuenta de capital y financiera**, que se refiere a i) *transferencias de capital* y *adquisición/enajenación de activos no financieros no producidos* y ii) activos y pasivos financieros.

Esta presentación general refleja el uso común adoptado en la mayoría de los países en el transcurso de los años y un importante cambio que se introduce en este *Manual*. La cuenta de capital se denomina ahora **cuenta de capital y financiera**. A efectos de mantener la uniformidad con el *SCN*, se hace la distinción entre *transferencias de capital* y ***transferencias corrientes*** en las cuentas de la balanza de pagos, y se procura la concordancia con la cuenta de capital y la cuenta financiera del *SCN*.

150. Los asientos de la mayoría de las partidas de la lista de componentes normalizados de la **cuenta corriente** deberán mostrar créditos y débitos en cifras brutas. La mayoría de los asientos de la **cuenta de capital y financiera** deberán registrarse en cifras netas, es decir, cada componente se indicará únicamente como un crédito o como un débito. (Los tratamientos recomendados para determinadas partidas y las excepciones se describen en los capítulos correspondientes.) Las entradas de recursos reales, los aumentos de activos financieros y las disminuciones de pasivos deberán aparecer como débitos, en tanto que las salidas de recursos reales, las disminuciones de activos financieros y los aumentos de pasivos deberán figurar como créditos. Las transferencias de las secciones 1.C. y 2.A. deben ser numéricamente iguales, pero con signo contrario, a los asientos que saldan.

Clasificaciones detalladas

151. De acuerdo con los criterios establecidos en el párrafo 143, se han determinado las siguientes clasificaciones de los componentes normalizados. En los capítulos IX y XVI, respectivamente, se analizan la estructura y las características de la **cuenta corriente** y de la **cuenta de capital y financiera**, mencionándose los cambios significativos con respecto a la cuarta edición. En los capítulos X al XV se describen detalladamente los componentes normalizados de la **cuenta corriente**, y en los capítulos XVII al XXI, los de la **cuenta de capital y financiera**.

Cuenta corriente (1.)

152. En la **cuenta corriente** se registran todas las transacciones en valores económicos, salvo recursos financieros, que tienen lugar entre entidades residentes y no residentes; asimismo se registran los asientos compensatorios de los valores económicos corrientes que se suministren o adquieran sin un quid pro quo. Concretamente, las clasificaciones principales son ***bienes y servicios, renta*** y ***transferencias corrientes***.

Bienes y servicios (1.A.)
Bienes (1.A.a.)

153. *Mercancías generales* comprende la mayoría de los bienes muebles que los residentes exportan a no residentes, o importan de ellos, dando lugar, salvo algunas excepciones especificadas, a un traspaso de propiedad (efectivo o imputado).

154. *Bienes para transformación* comprende la exportación (o importación, en la economía compiladora) de bienes que cruzan la frontera para ser transformados en el extranjero y la reimportación (o exportación, en la economía compiladora) subsiguiente de dichos bienes, valorados en cifras brutas antes y después de su transformación. Esta partida constituye una excepción al criterio de traspaso de propiedad.

155. *Reparaciones de bienes* comprende las reparaciones de bienes efectuadas para no residentes o recibidas de ellos en embarcaciones, aeronaves, etc. Si bien el movimiento físico de estos bienes es similar al descrito en el párrafo 154, las reparaciones deben valorarse según el precio (derechos pagados o recibidos) de las mismas y no según el valor bruto de los bienes antes y después de las reparaciones.

156. *Bienes adquiridos en puerto por medios de transporte* comprende todos los bienes (como combustibles, víveres, pertrechos y suministros) que las empresas residentes/no residentes de transporte —aéreo, marítimo, etc.— adquieren en el extranjero/en la economía compiladora. Esta clasificación no cubre los servicios auxiliares prestados (remolque, mantenimiento, etc.), que se clasifican en la categoría *transportes*.

157. *Oro no monetario* comprende las exportaciones e importaciones de todo el oro que no esté en poder de las autoridades como activo de reserva (oro monetario). El *oro no monetario* se trata como cualquier otra mercancía y se subdivide, toda vez que sea posible, en oro que se mantiene como reserva de valor y oro para otros usos (industrial).

Servicios (1.A.b.)

158. *Transportes* abarca la mayoría de los servicios prestados por residentes a no residentes, y viceversa, que se incluían en las partidas embarques y otros transportes en la cuarta edición del *Manual*. En esta edición se excluye el seguro de fletes, que ahora forma parte de *servicios de seguros*. *Transportes* incluye el transporte de carga y de pasajeros por todos los medios, así como otros servicios de distribución y auxiliares, incluido el arrendamiento de equipo de transporte tripulado, con ciertas excepciones indicadas en los capítulos X, XI y XIII.

159. *Viajes* comprende bienes y servicios —incluidos los relacionados con salud y educación— adquiridos en una economía por viajeros no residentes (incluidos los excursionistas) para fines de negocios y para uso personal durante su estancia (inferior a un año) en esa economía. En *viajes* no se incluyen los servicios de transporte internacional de pasajeros, que forman parte de *transportes*. Los estudiantes y las personas que están bajo tratamiento médico se tratan como viajeros, independientemente de la duración de su estancia, en tanto que otros individuos —personal militar y de embajadas y trabajadores no residentes— no se consideran viajeros. No obstante, los gastos incurridos por los trabajadores no residentes se incluyen en *viajes*, mientras que los del personal militar y de embajadas se incluyen en *servicios del gobierno, n.i.o.p.* Estos casos se tratan en los capítulos XII y XIII.

160. *Servicios de comunicaciones* abarca las transacciones de comunicaciones entre residentes y no residentes, incluidos los servicios postales, de mensajería y de telecomunicaciones (transmisión de sonido, imagen y otra información por diferentes medios, así como el mantenimiento pertinente proporcionado por residentes a no residentes y viceversa).

161. *Servicios de construcción* incluye las obras de proyectos de construcción e instalación realizadas, con carácter temporal, en el extranjero/en la economía compiladora o en enclaves extraterritoriales por empresas residentes/no residentes y su personal. En este concepto no se incluyen las obras realizadas por una filial extranjera de una empresa residente o una oficina local no constituida en sociedad que sea equivalente siempre y cuando satisfaga ciertos criterios a una filial extranjera. En los capítulos IV y XIII se explica lo relativo a la residencia de esta clase de empresas.

162. *Servicios de seguros* comprende la contratación de seguros de no residentes con aseguradoras residentes y viceversa, incluidos los seguros de fletes (de bienes exportados e importados), los servicios correspondientes a otras clases de seguros directos (de vida y otros) y los servicios correspondientes a reaseguros. (En los párrafos 256 y 257 se describe el método que se emplea para calcular el valor de los servicios de seguros.)

163. *Servicios financieros* (salvo los relacionados con las empresas aseguradoras y las cajas de pensiones) abarca los servicios de intermediación financiera y los servicios auxiliares entre residentes y no residentes. Se incluyen las comisiones y derechos relacionados con cartas de crédito, líneas de crédito, arrendamiento financiero, transacciones en divisas, crédito al consumidor y a las empresas, corretaje, colocación y suscripción de valores, instrumentos de coberturas de riesgo de diferentes clases, etc. En los servicios auxiliares se incluyen los servicios de operación y reglamentación de los mercados financieros, servicios de custodia de valores, etc.

164. *Servicios de informática y de información* abarca las transacciones entre residentes y no residentes relacionadas con el asesoramiento en soporte técnico (*hardware*), aplicación de soporte lógico (*software*), servicios de información (procesamiento de datos, bases de datos, agencias noticiosas), y mantenimiento y reparación de computadores y equipo conexo.

165. *Regalías y derechos de licencia* comprende ingresos (exportación) y pagos (importación) de residentes y no residentes por: i) el uso autorizado de activos intangibles no financieros no producidos y derechos de propiedad como marcas registradas, derechos de autor, patentes, procesos, técnicas, diseños, derechos de fabricación, concesiones, etc., y ii) el uso, mediante convenios de licencia, de originales o prototipos producidos, como manuscritos, películas, etc.

166. *Otros servicios empresariales* prestados por residentes a no residentes y viceversa se refiere a servicios de compraventa y otros servicios relacionados con el comercio, servicios de arrendamiento de explotación y servicios empresariales, profesionales y técnicos varios. (Para información más detallada, véase el cuadro *Información suplementaria seleccionada* al final de este capítulo y los párrafos 261 a 264.)

167. *Servicios personales, culturales y recreativos* abarca i) servicios audiovisuales y conexos y ii) otros servicios culturales prestados por residentes a no residentes y viceversa. En el inciso i) se incluyen servicios relacionados con la producción de películas cinematográficas o videocintas, programas de radio y televisión y grabaciones musicales. (Ejemplos de estos servicios son los alquileres y honorarios percibidos por artistas, productores, etc. por sus producciones y por la venta de derechos de distribución a los medios de comunicación.) En el inciso ii) se incluyen otros servicios personales, culturales y recreativos, como los relacionados con bibliotecas, museos y otras actividades culturales y deportivas.

168. *Servicios del gobierno, n.i.o.p.* incluye todos los servicios (como los gastos incurridos por embajadas y consulados) relacionados con sectores gubernamentales u organismos internacionales y regionales y no clasificados en otras partidas.

Renta (1.B.)

169. *Remuneración de empleados* abarca los salarios, sueldos y otras prestaciones, en efectivo o en especie, incluidos los de los trabajadores fronterizos, de temporada y otros no residentes (por ejemplo, personal local de embajadas).

170. *Renta de la inversión* comprende los ingresos y pagos de la renta derivados, respectivamente, de las tenencias de activos financieros de residentes frente al exterior y de pasivos frente a no residentes, y se divide en renta de la inversión directa, renta de la inversión de cartera y renta de otra inversión. El componente inversión directa se desglosa en renta procedente de acciones y otras participaciones de capital (dividendos, utilidades de sucursales y utilidades reinvertidas) y en renta procedente de la deuda (intereses); la renta de la inversión de cartera se desglosa también en renta procedente de acciones y otras participaciones de capital (dividendos) y renta procedente de la deuda (intereses); en renta de otra inversión se registran los intereses devengados por otra inversión (préstamos, etc.) y, en principio, la renta imputada a las unidades familiares procedente de su participación neta de capital en las reservas de los seguros de vida y en las cajas de pensiones.

Transferencias corrientes (1.C.)

171. Las ***transferencias corrientes*** se distinguen de las *transferencias de capital*, que se incluyen en la **cuenta de capital y financiera** para guardar la uniformidad con el tratamiento de las transferencias que hace el *SCN*. Las transferencias son los asientos compensatorios de los traspasos de propiedad de recursos reales o financieros entre residentes y no residentes, ya sea en forma voluntaria u obligatoria, que no entrañan un quid pro quo en valor económico. Las ***transferencias corrientes*** comprenden todas aquellas en las que **no tiene lugar**: i) un ***traspaso*** de propiedad de activos fijos; ii) un traspaso de fondos vinculados o condicionados a la adquisición o enajenación de activos fijos; iii) una condonación de un pasivo por parte de un acreedor, sin que se reciba a cambio una contrapartida. Todas éstas son *transferencias de capital*. En las ***transferencias corrientes*** se distinguen las del gobierno general (por ejemplo, cooperación internacional corriente entre diferentes gobiernos, pagos de impuestos corrientes sobre la renta y el patrimonio, etc.) y otras transferencias (por ejemplo, remesas de trabajadores, primas —menos cargos por servicio— e indemnizaciones de seguros excepto los de vida). En el capítulo XV se examina en forma detallada la distinción entre ***transferencias corrientes*** y *transferencias de capital*; véanse también los párrafos 175 y 344.

Cuenta de capital y financiera (2.)

172. Esta cuenta tiene dos componentes principales —la ***cuenta de capital*** y la ***cuenta financiera***— coincidiendo así con la clasificación adoptada en el *SCN*. Los activos representan créditos frente a no residentes y los pasivos representan deudas contraídas con no residentes. Las dos partes de una transacción de activos o pasivos son, generalmente, un residente y un no residente pero, en algunos casos, ambas partes pueden ser residentes o bien no residentes. (Véase el párrafo 318.)

173. Todas las variaciones de valoración y de otra índole de los activos y pasivos frente al exterior que no reflejen transacciones (véase el párrafo 310) se excluyen de la **cuenta de capital y financiera** pero figuran en la posición de inversión internacional. Los estados suplementarios identifican ciertas partidas que tienen interés analítico y que afectan a varias cuentas, como los pasivos que constituyen reservas de autoridades extranjeras y las transacciones de financiamiento excepcional, que se describen en el capítulo XXII.

174. La clasificación de la ***cuenta financiera*** y de los componentes de renta de la **cuenta corriente** están interrelacionadas y deben ser coherentes para facilitar el análisis, permitir una vinculación eficaz de la balanza de pagos con la posición de inversión internacional y mantener la compatibilidad con el *SCN* y con otros sistemas estadísticos del FMI.

Cuenta de capital (2.A.)

175. Los componentes principales de la ***cuenta de capital*** son las *transferencias de capital* y la *adquisición/enajenación de activos no financieros no producidos*. Las *transferencias de capital* son aquéllas en las que tiene lugar un traspaso de propiedad de un activo fijo, un traspaso de fondos vinculado o condicionado a la adquisición o enajenación de un activo fijo, o la cancelación de un pasivo por parte de un acreedor sin que se reciba a cambio una contrapartida. Las *transferencias de capital* se dividen en: i) las del gobierno general, que a su vez se subdividen en condonación de deudas y otras y ii) las de otros sectores, haciéndose el desglose en transferencias de emigrantes, condonación de deudas y otras. (Véase el capítulo XV, donde se explica la diferencia entre las *transferencias de capital* y las ***transferencias corrientes***.) La *adquisición/enajenación de activos no financieros no producidos* abarca, en general, los factores intangibles, como las patentes, arrendamientos u otros contratos transferibles, el buen nombre, etc. En esta partida no se incluyen las tierras situadas en un territorio económico específico, pero puede incluirse la compra o venta de tierras por una embajada. (Véase el párrafo 312.)

Cuenta financiera (2.B.)

176. La clasificación de los componentes normalizados de la cuenta financiera se basa en los siguientes criterios:

Todos los componentes se clasifican según la clase de inversión o haciéndose un desglose funcional (*inversión directa, inversión de cartera, otra inversión, activos de reserva*).

Para la categoría *inversión directa*, se hace la distinción según la dirección (en el extranjero o en la economía declarante); para los componentes acciones y otras participaciones de capital y otro capital, dentro de esta categoría, se hace el desglose de activos y pasivos.

En *inversión de cartera* y *otra inversión* se hace la distinción habitual entre activos y pasivos.

Cobra particular importancia en *inversión de cartera* y *otra inversión* la distinción por clases de instrumentos (títulos de participación en el capital, títulos de deuda, créditos comerciales, préstamos, moneda y depósitos, otros activos o pasivos). En este *Manual*, se incluyen en *inversión de cartera* los instrumentos tradicionales y nuevos del mercado monetario y otros instrumentos financieros básicos y derivados.

En *inversión de cartera* y *otra inversión*, se hace la distinción por sectores de acreedores internos en el caso de los activos o por sectores de deudores internos en el caso de los pasivos, a efectos de facilitar la vinculación con las cuentas de renta, la posición de inversión internacional, el *SCN* y otros sistemas estadísticos.

La distinción tradicional entre activos y pasivos a largo y a corto plazo, basada en un plazo contractual original de más de un año o de un año o menos, se efectúa solamente en *otra inversión*. En los últimos años, este desglose ha perdido importancia para muchas transacciones internas e internacionales. En consecuencia, tanto en el *SCN* como en este *Manual*, se da menos importancia a la diferencia entre largo y corto plazo que en ediciones previas. Sin embargo, debido a que el vencimiento sigue siendo importante para fines específicos —el análisis de la deuda externa, por ejemplo—, esta distinción se mantiene en el *Manual* para *otra inversión*.

177. *Inversión directa*, categoría que refleja el interés duradero de una entidad residente de una economía (inversionista directo) en una entidad residente de otra economía (empresa de inversión directa), abarca todas las transacciones entre inversionistas directos y empresas de inversión directa. Es decir, la *inversión directa* abarca la transacción inicial entre las dos partes y todas las transacciones subsiguientes que tienen lugar entre ellas y entre empresas filiales, constituidas o no en sociedad. Las transacciones de inversión directa (en el extranjero y en la economía declarante) se subclasifican en acciones y otras participaciones de capital, utilidades reinvertidas y otro capital (transacciones entre empresas afiliadas). En el caso de las acciones y otras participaciones de capital y de otro capital, se hace la distinción entre activos y pasivos frente a empresas filiales y frente a inversionistas directos. Las transacciones entre bancos filiales y entre otros intermediarios financieros filiales se limitan al capital en acciones y al que está relacionado con la deuda permanente. (Véase el párrafo 372.)

178. *Inversión de cartera* comprende las transacciones en títulos de participación en el capital y títulos de deuda. Los títulos de deuda están subdivididos en bonos y pagarés, instrumentos del mercado monetario e instrumentos financieros derivados (las opciones, por ejemplo) siempre que estos últimos generen activos y pasivos financieros. Se incluyen, asimismo, varios instrumentos financieros nuevos en las clasificaciones de instrumentos. (Se excluyen las transacciones clasificadas como *inversión directa* y *activos de reserva*.)

179. *Otra inversión* incluye créditos comerciales a corto y largo plazo; préstamos (entre ellos, el uso de crédito del FMI, préstamos del FMI y préstamos relacionados con arrendamientos financieros); moneda y depósitos (transferibles y otros, como depósitos de ahorro y a plazo, acciones de asociaciones de ahorro y préstamo, acciones de cooperativas de crédito, etc.); otras cuentas por cobrar y por pagar. (Se excluyen las transacciones clasificadas como *inversión directa*.)

180. *Activos de reserva* comprende las transacciones de aquellos activos que las autoridades monetarias de una economía consideran disponibles para atender necesidades de financiamiento de la balanza de pagos y, en algunos casos, otras necesidades. Tal disponibilidad, en principio, no guarda estrecha relación con criterios formales tales como los de propiedad o moneda de denominación. Esta categoría se divide en oro monetario, DEG, posición de reserva en el FMI, activos en divisas (moneda, depósitos y valores) y otros activos.

181. La cobertura e identificación de los componentes de los *activos de reserva* están relacionadas con un concepto analítico, son en parte resultado de una decisión razonada y no siempre se prestan a la aplicación de criterios objetivos y formales ni a clasificaciones bien delimitadas respecto a la condicionalidad y otras consideraciones. A diferencia de la cuarta edición del *Manual*, en la quinta edición se excluyen las variaciones de valoración de los *activos de reserva* y sus contrapartidas. También se excluyen la asignación y cancelación de DEG, la monetización y desmonetización del oro y los asientos de contrapartida. Estas variaciones, que no constituyen transacciones, figuran en la posición de inversión internacional.

Country Tables

Albania
914

Table 1. ANALYTIC PRESENTATION, 1988–95
(*Millions of U.S. dollars*)

	Code	1988	1989	1990	1991	1992	1993	1994	1995
A. Current Account [1]	4 993 Y.	**–27.1**	**–39.3**	**–118.3**	**–168.0**	**–50.7**	**14.9**	**–157.3**	**–11.5**
Goods: exports f.o.b	2 100 . .	344.6	393.7	322.1	73.0	70.0	111.6	141.3	204.9
Goods: imports f.o.b	3 100 . .	–382.3	–455.8	–455.9	–281.0	–540.5	–601.5	–601.0	–679.7
Balance on Goods	4 100 . .	*–37.7*	*–62.1*	*–133.8*	*–208.0*	*–470.5*	*–489.9*	*–459.7*	*–474.8*
Services: credit	2 200 . .	29.6	40.2	31.5	9.2	20.3	77.6	79.1	98.8
Services: debit	3 200 . .	–26.2	–27.9	–29.1	–33.4	–89.1	–161.9	–132.5	–156.5
Balance on Goods and Services	4 991 . .	*–34.3*	*–49.8*	*–131.4*	*–232.2*	*–539.3*	*–574.2*	*–513.1*	*–532.5*
Income: credit	2 300 . .	.9	.4	. . .	.8	2.6	64.9	55.1	72.0
Income: debit	3 300 . .	–.7	–.5	–1.9	–25.9	–37.7	–31.0	–41.3	–28.4
Balance on Goods, Services, and Income	4 992 . .	*–34.1*	*–49.9*	*–133.3*	*–257.3*	*–574.4*	*–540.3*	*–499.3*	*–488.9*
Current transfers: credit	2 379 Y.	7.0	10.6	15.0	89.3	524.0	556.9	347.5	521.2
Current transfers: debit	3 379 . .	. . .	. . .	. . .	. . .	–.3	–1.7	–5.5	–43.8
B. Capital Account [1]	4 994 Y.	**. . .**	**. . .**	**. . .**	**. . .**	**. . .**	**. . .**	**. . .**	**389.4**
Capital account: credit	2 994 Y.	. . .	. . .	. . .	. . .	. . .	. . .	. . .	389.4
Capital account: debit	3 994 . .	. . .	. . .	. . .	. . .	. . .	. . .	. . .	. . .
Total, Groups A Plus B	4 010 . .	*–27.1*	*–39.3*	*–118.3*	*–168.0*	*–50.7*	*14.9*	*–157.3*	*377.9*
C. Financial Account [1]	4 995 X.	**139.3**	**359.4**	**–117.7**	**–181.2**	**–32.2**	**44.1**	**40.2**	**–411.0**
Direct investment abroad	4 505 . .	. . .	. . .	. . .	. . .	. . .	. . .	. . .	. . .
Direct investment in Albania	4 555 Y.	. . .	. . .	. . .	. . .	20.0	58.0	53.0	70.0
Portfolio investment assets	4 602 . .	. . .	. . .	. . .	. . .	. . .	. . .	. . .	. . .
Equity securities	4 610 . .	. . .	. . .	. . .	. . .	. . .	. . .	. . .	. . .
Debt securities	4 619 . .	. . .	. . .	. . .	. . .	. . .	. . .	. . .	. . .
Portfolio investment liabilities	4 652 Y.	. . .	. . .	. . .	. . .	. . .	. . .	. . .	. . .
Equity securities	4 660 Y.	. . .	. . .	. . .	. . .	. . .	. . .	. . .	. . .
Debt securities	4 669 Y.	. . .	. . .	. . .	. . .	. . .	. . .	. . .	. . .
Other investment assets	4 703 . .	. . .	. . .	. . .	. . .	–73.2	–78.6	–97.3	–97.0
Monetary authorities	4 703 .A	. . .	. . .	. . .	. . .	. . .	. . .	. . .	. . .
General government	4 703 .B	. . .	. . .	. . .	. . .	. . .	. . .	. . .	. . .
Banks	4 703 .C	. . .	. . .	. . .	. . .	–50.0	–25.5	–22.9	–68.4
Other sectors	4 703 .D	. . .	. . .	. . .	. . .	–23.2	–53.1	–74.4	–28.6
Other investment liabilities	4 753 X.	139.3	359.4	–117.7	–181.2	21.0	64.7	84.5	–384.0
Monetary authorities	4 753 XA	141.3	361.4	–144.8	–202.6	. . .	. . .	. . .	–9.1
General government	4 753 YB	–2.0	–2.0	27.1	21.4	22.4	50.5	74.6	–404.5
Banks	4 753 YC	. . .	. . .	. . .	. . .	–1.4	3.4	2.6	–3.3
Other sectors	4 753 YD	. . .	. . .	. . .	. . .	. . .	10.8	7.3	32.9
Total, Groups A Through C	4 020 . .	*112.2*	*320.1*	*–236.0*	*–349.2*	*–82.9*	*59.0*	*–117.1*	*–33.1*
D. Net Errors and Omissions	4 998 . .	**22.0**	**4.8**	**–2.0**	**125.2**	**47.4**	**–10.3**	**123.9**	**53.7**
Total, Groups A Through D	4 030 . .	*134.2*	*324.9*	*–238.0*	*–224.0*	*–35.5*	*48.7*	*6.8*	*20.6*
E. Reserves and Related Items	4 040 . .	**–134.2**	**–324.9**	**238.0**	**224.0**	**35.5**	**–48.7**	**–6.8**	**–20.6**
Reserve assets	4 800 . .	–134.2	–324.9	32.0	28.0	–27.4	–114.9	–55.2	–30.5
Use of Fund credit and loans	4 766 . .	. . .	. . .	. . .	. . .	13.9	16.6	22.3	9.9
Liabilities constituting foreign authorities' reserves	4 900 . .	. . .	. . .	. . .	. . .	. . .	. . .	. . .	. . .
Exceptional financing	4 920 . .	. . .	. . .	206.0	196.0	49.0	49.5	26.1	. . .
Conversion rates: leks per U.S. dollar	0 101 . .	**8.00**	**8.00**	**8.00**	**14.40**	**75.03**	**102.06**	**94.62**	**92.70**

[1] Excludes components that have been classified in the categories of Group E.

Table 2. STANDARD PRESENTATION, 1988–95
(Millions of U.S. dollars)

	Code	1988	1989	1990	1991	1992	1993	1994	1995
CURRENT ACCOUNT	4 993 . .	**–27.1**	**–39.3**	**–118.3**	**–168.0**	**–50.7**	**14.9**	**–157.3**	**–11.5**
A. GOODS	4 100 . .	–37.7	–62.1	–133.8	–208.0	–470.5	–489.9	–459.7	–474.8
Credit	2 100 . .	**344.6**	**393.7**	**322.1**	**73.0**	**70.0**	**111.6**	**141.3**	**204.9**
General merchandise: exports f.o.b.	2 110 . .	344.6	393.7	322.1	73.0	70.0	111.6	141.3	204.9
Goods for processing: exports f.o.b.	2 150 . .	. . .	. . .	. . .	. . .	. . .	. . .	. . .	. . .
Repairs on goods	2 160 . .	. . .	. . .	. . .	. . .	. . .	. . .	. . .	. . .
Goods procured in ports by carriers	2 170 . .	. . .	. . .	. . .	. . .	. . .	. . .	. . .	. . .
Nonmonetary gold	2 180 . .	. . .	. . .	. . .	. . .	. . .	. . .	. . .	. . .
Debit	3 100 . .	**–382.3**	**–455.8**	**–455.9**	**–281.0**	**–540.5**	**–601.5**	**–601.0**	**–679.7**
General merchandise: imports f.o.b.	3 110 . .	–382.3	–455.8	–455.9	–281.0	–540.5	–601.5	–601.0	–679.7
Goods for processing: imports f.o.b.	3 150 . .	. . .	. . .	. . .	. . .	. . .	. . .	. . .	. . .
Repairs on goods	3 160 . .	. . .	. . .	. . .	. . .	. . .	. . .	. . .	. . .
Goods procured in ports by carriers	3 170 . .	. . .	. . .	. . .	. . .	. . .	. . .	. . .	. . .
Nonmonetary gold	3 180 . .	. . .	. . .	. . .	. . .	. . .	. . .	. . .	. . .
B. SERVICES	4 200 . .	3.4	12.3	2.4	–24.2	–68.8	–84.3	–53.4	–57.7
Total credit	2 200 . .	*29.6*	*40.2*	*31.5*	*9.2*	*20.3*	*77.6*	*79.1*	*98.8*
Total debit	3 200 . .	*–26.2*	*–27.9*	*–29.1*	*–33.4*	*–89.1*	*–161.9*	*–132.5*	*–156.5*
Transportation services, credit	2 205 . .	**6.6**	**7.9**	**6.3**	**1.6**	**3.0**	**8.8**	**11.6**	**17.9**
Passenger	2 205 BA	. . .	. . .	. . .	. . .	*1.2*	*1.4*	*2.0*	*5.4*
Freight	2 205 BB	*6.6*	*7.9*	*6.3*	*1.6*	*1.8*	*5.7*	*6.5*	*10.2*
Other	2 205 BC	. . .	. . .	. . .	. . .	. . .	*1.7*	*3.1*	*2.3*
Sea transport, passenger	2 207 . .	. . .	. . .	. . .	. . .	. . .	. . .	. . .	. . .
Sea transport, freight	2 208 . .	. . .	. . .	. . .	. . .	. . .	. . .	. . .	. . .
Sea transport, other	2 209 . .	. . .	. . .	. . .	. . .	. . .	. . .	. . .	. . .
Air transport, passenger	2 211 . .	. . .	. . .	. . .	. . .	. . .	. . .	. . .	. . .
Air transport, freight	2 212 . .	. . .	. . .	. . .	. . .	. . .	. . .	. . .	. . .
Air transport, other	2 213 . .	. . .	. . .	. . .	. . .	. . .	. . .	. . .	. . .
Other transport, passenger	2 215 . .	. . .	. . .	. . .	. . .	. . .	. . .	. . .	. . .
Other transport, freight	2 216 . .	. . .	. . .	. . .	. . .	. . .	. . .	. . .	. . .
Other transport, other	2 217 . .	. . .	. . .	. . .	. . .	. . .	. . .	. . .	. . .
Transportation services, debit	3 205 . .	**–9.1**	**–9.2**	**–7.7**	**–5.0**	**–37.9**	**–50.8**	**–47.4**	**–60.3**
Passenger	3 205 BA	. . .	. . .	. . .	. . .	*–3.8*	*–8.1*	*–7.8*	*–11.6*
Freight	3 205 BB	*–9.1*	*–9.2*	*–7.7*	*–5.0*	*–34.0*	*–39.7*	*–38.9*	*–48.6*
Other	3 205 BC	. . .	. . .	. . .	. . .	*–.1*	*–3.0*	*–.7*	*–.1*
Sea transport, passenger	3 207 . .	. . .	. . .	. . .	. . .	. . .	. . .	. . .	. . .
Sea transport, freight	3 208 . .	. . .	. . .	. . .	. . .	. . .	. . .	. . .	. . .
Sea transport, other	3 209 . .	. . .	. . .	. . .	. . .	. . .	. . .	. . .	. . .
Air transport, passenger	3 211 . .	. . .	. . .	. . .	. . .	. . .	. . .	. . .	. . .
Air transport, freight	3 212 . .	. . .	. . .	. . .	. . .	. . .	. . .	. . .	. . .
Air transport, other	3 213 . .	. . .	. . .	. . .	. . .	. . .	. . .	. . .	. . .
Other transport, passenger	3 215 . .	. . .	. . .	. . .	. . .	. . .	. . .	. . .	. . .
Other transport, freight	3 216 . .	. . .	. . .	. . .	. . .	. . .	. . .	. . .	. . .
Other transport, other	3 217 . .	. . .	. . .	. . .	. . .	. . .	. . .	. . .	. . .
Travel, credit	2 236 . .	**3.0**	**3.3**	**3.5**	**.1**	**12.0**	**56.9**	**58.4**	**65.1**
Business travel	2 237 . .	. . .	. . .	. . .	. . .	. . .	. . .	. . .	. . .
Personal travel	2 240 . .	. . .	. . .	. . .	. . .	. . .	. . .	. . .	. . .
Travel, debit	3 236 . .	**. . .**	**. . .**	**. . .**	**. . .**	**–1.2**	**–7.1**	**–5.6**	**–6.6**
Business travel	3 237 . .	. . .	. . .	. . .	. . .	. . .	. . .	. . .	. . .
Personal travel	3 240 . .	. . .	. . .	. . .	. . .	. . .	. . .	. . .	. . .
Other services, credit	2 200 BA	**20.0**	**29.0**	**21.7**	**7.5**	**5.3**	**11.9**	**9.1**	**15.8**
Communications	2 245 . .	. . .	. . .	. . .	. . .	. . .	. . .	. . .	7.5
Construction	2 249 . .	. . .	. . .	. . .	. . .	. . .	. . .	. . .	. . .
Insurance	2 253 . .	.7	.9	.7	.2	.2	.6	.7	. . .
Financial	2 260 . .	. . .	. . .	. . .	. . .	. . .	. . .	. . .	1.3
Computer and information	2 262 . .	. . .	. . .	. . .	. . .	. . .	. . .	. . .	.8
Royalties and licence fees	2 266 . .	. . .	. . .	. . .	. . .	. . .	. . .	. . .	. . .
Other business services	2 268 . .	19.3	28.1	21.0	7.3	3.7	6.9	7.9	1.3
Personal, cultural, and recreational	2 287 . .	. . .	. . .	. . .	. . .	. . .	. . .	. . .	. . .
Government, n.i.e.	2 291 . .	. . .	. . .	. . .	. . .	1.4	4.4	.5	4.9
Other services, debit	3 200 BA	**–17.1**	**–18.7**	**–21.5**	**–28.4**	**–50.0**	**–104.0**	**–79.5**	**–89.6**
Communications	3 245 . .	. . .	. . .	. . .	. . .	. . .	. . .	. . .	–9.0
Construction	3 249 . .	. . .	. . .	. . .	. . .	. . .	. . .	. . .	. . .
Insurance	3 253 . .	–1.0	–1.0	–.9	–.6	–3.8	–4.4	–4.3	–21.1
Financial	3 260 . .	. . .	. . .	. . .	. . .	. . .	. . .	. . .	–.6
Computer and information	3 262 . .	. . .	. . .	. . .	. . .	. . .	. . .	. . .	. . .
Royalties and licence fees	3 266 . .	. . .	. . .	. . .	. . .	. . .	. . .	. . .	. . .
Other business services	3 268 . .	–16.1	–17.7	–20.6	–27.8	–43.7	–96.1	–70.9	–.6
Personal, cultural, and recreational	3 287 . .	. . .	. . .	. . .	. . .	. . .	. . .	. . .	. . .
Government, n.i.e.	3 291 . .	. . .	. . .	. . .	. . .	–2.5	–3.5	–4.3	–58.3

Table 2 (Continued). STANDARD PRESENTATION, 1988–95
(Millions of U.S. dollars)

	Code	1988	1989	1990	1991	1992	1993	1994	1995
C. INCOME	4 300 . .	.2	–.1	–1.9	–25.1	–35.1	33.9	13.8	43.6
Total credit	2 300 . .	*.9*	*.4*	*. . .*	*.8*	*2.6*	*64.9*	*55.1*	*72.0*
Total debit	3 300 . .	*–.7*	*–.5*	*–1.9*	*–25.9*	*–37.7*	*–31.0*	*–41.3*	*–28.4*
Compensation of employees, credit	2 310 . .	**. . .**	**. . .**	**. . .**	**. . .**	**1.8**	**57.2**	**42.4**	**42.7**
Compensation of employees, debit	3 310 . .	**. . .**	**. . .**	**. . .**	**. . .**	**. . .**	**. . .**	**. . .**	**. . .**
Investment income, credit	2 320 . .	**.9**	**.4**	**. . .**	**.8**	**.8**	**7.7**	**12.7**	**29.3**
Direct investment income	2 330 . .	. . .	. . .	. . .	. . .	. . .	. . .	. . .	.2
Dividends and distributed branch profits	2 332 . .	. . .	. . .	. . .	. . .	. . .	. . .	. . .	. . .
Reinvested earnings and undistributed branch profits	2 333 . .	. . .	. . .	. . .	. . .	. . .	. . .	. . .	. . .
Income on debt (interest)	2 334 . .	. . .	. . .	. . .	. . .	. . .	. . .	. . .	. . .
Portfolio investment income	2 339 . .	. . .	. . .	. . .	. . .	. . .	. . .	. . .	. . .
Income on equity	2 340 . .	. . .	. . .	. . .	. . .	. . .	. . .	. . .	. . .
Income on bonds and notes	2 350 . .	. . .	. . .	. . .	. . .	. . .	. . .	. . .	. . .
Income on money market instruments and financial derivatives	2 360 . .	. . .	. . .	. . .	. . .	. . .	. . .	. . .	. . .
Other investment income	2 370 . .	.9	.4	. . .	.8	.8	7.7	12.7	29.1
Investment income, debit	3 320 . .	**–.7**	**–.5**	**–1.9**	**–25.9**	**–37.7**	**–31.0**	**–41.3**	**–28.4**
Direct investment income	3 330 . .	. . .	. . .	. . .	. . .	. . .	. . .	. . .	–4.0
Dividends and distributed branch profits	3 332 . .	. . .	. . .	. . .	. . .	. . .	. . .	. . .	. . .
Reinvested earnings and undistributed branch profits	3 333 . .	. . .	. . .	. . .	. . .	. . .	. . .	. . .	. . .
Income on debt (interest)	3 334 . .	. . .	. . .	. . .	. . .	. . .	. . .	. . .	. . .
Portfolio investment income	3 339 . .	. . .	. . .	. . .	. . .	. . .	. . .	. . .	. . .
Income on equity	3 340 . .	. . .	. . .	. . .	. . .	. . .	. . .	. . .	. . .
Income on bonds and notes	3 350 . .	. . .	. . .	. . .	. . .	. . .	. . .	. . .	. . .
Income on money market instruments and financial derivatives	3 360 . .	. . .	. . .	. . .	. . .	. . .	. . .	. . .	. . .
Other investment income	3 370 . .	–.7	–.5	–1.9	–25.9	–37.7	–31.0	–41.3	–24.4
D. CURRENT TRANSFERS	4 379 . .	7.0	10.6	15.0	89.3	523.7	555.2	342.0	477.4
Credit	2 379 . .	**7.0**	**10.6**	**15.0**	**89.3**	**524.0**	**556.9**	**347.5**	**521.2**
General government	2 380 . .	. . .	1.5	. . .	81.2	374.0	282.1	82.8	136.6
Other sectors	2 390 . .	7.0	9.1	15.0	8.1	150.0	274.8	264.7	384.6
Workers' remittances	2 391 . .	. . .	. . .	. . .	. . .	150.0	274.8	264.7	384.6
Other current transfers	2 392 . .	7.0	9.1	15.0	8.1	. . .	. . .	. . .	. . .
Debit	3 379 . .	**. . .**	**. . .**	**. . .**	**. . .**	**–.3**	**–1.7**	**–5.5**	**–43.8**
General government	3 380 . .	. . .	. . .	. . .	. . .	. . .	. . .	–1.7	–8.1
Other sectors	3 390 . .	. . .	. . .	. . .	. . .	–.3	–1.7	–3.8	–35.7
Workers' remittances	3 391 . .	. . .	. . .	. . .	. . .	. . .	. . .	. . .	. . .
Other current transfers	3 392 . .	. . .	. . .	. . .	. . .	–.3	–1.7	–3.8	–35.7
CAPITAL AND FINANCIAL ACCOUNT	4 996 . .	**5.1**	**34.5**	**120.3**	**42.8**	**3.3**	**–4.6**	**33.4**	**–42.2**
CAPITAL ACCOUNT	4 994 . .	**. . .**	**. . .**	**. . .**	**. . .**	**. . .**	**. . .**	**. . .**	**389.4**
Total credit	2 994 . .	*. . .*	*. . .*	*. . .*	*. . .*	*. . .*	*. . .*	*. . .*	*389.4*
Total debit	3 994 . .	*. . .*	*. . .*	*. . .*	*. . .*	*. . .*	*. . .*	*. . .*	*. . .*
Capital transfers, credit	2 400 . .	**. . .**	**. . .**	**. . .**	**. . .**	**. . .**	**. . .**	**. . .**	**389.4**
General government	2 401 . .	. . .	. . .	. . .	. . .	. . .	. . .	. . .	389.4
Debt forgiveness	2 402 . .	. . .	. . .	. . .	. . .	. . .	. . .	. . .	383.0
Other capital transfers	2 410 . .	. . .	. . .	. . .	. . .	. . .	. . .	. . .	6.4
Other sectors	2 430 . .	. . .	. . .	. . .	. . .	. . .	. . .	. . .	. . .
Migrants' transfers	2 431 . .	. . .	. . .	. . .	. . .	. . .	. . .	. . .	. . .
Debt forgiveness	2 432 . .	. . .	. . .	. . .	. . .	. . .	. . .	. . .	. . .
Other capital transfers	2 440 . .	. . .	. . .	. . .	. . .	. . .	. . .	. . .	. . .
Capital transfers, debit	3 400 . .	**. . .**	**. . .**	**. . .**	**. . .**	**. . .**	**. . .**	**. . .**	**. . .**
General government	3 401 . .	. . .	. . .	. . .	. . .	. . .	. . .	. . .	. . .
Debt forgiveness	3 402 . .	. . .	. . .	. . .	. . .	. . .	. . .	. . .	. . .
Other capital transfers	3 410 . .	. . .	. . .	. . .	. . .	. . .	. . .	. . .	. . .
Other sectors	3 430 . .	. . .	. . .	. . .	. . .	. . .	. . .	. . .	. . .
Migrants' transfers	3 431 . .	. . .	. . .	. . .	. . .	. . .	. . .	. . .	. . .
Debt forgiveness	3 432 . .	. . .	. . .	. . .	. . .	. . .	. . .	. . .	. . .
Other capital transfers	3 440 . .	. . .	. . .	. . .	. . .	. . .	. . .	. . .	. . .
Nonproduced nonfinancial assets, credit	2 480 . .	**. . .**	**. . .**	**. . .**	**. . .**	**. . .**	**. . .**	**. . .**	**. . .**
Nonproduced nonfinancial assets, debit	3 480 . .	**. . .**	**. . .**	**. . .**	**. . .**	**. . .**	**. . .**	**. . .**	**. . .**

Table 2 (Continued). STANDARD PRESENTATION, 1988–95
(Millions of U.S. dollars)

	Code	1988	1989	1990	1991	1992	1993	1994	1995
FINANCIAL ACCOUNT	4 995	**5.1**	**34.5**	**120.3**	**42.8**	**3.3**	**–4.6**	**33.4**	**–431.6**
A. DIRECT INVESTMENT	4 500	...	...	...	...	20.0	58.0	53.0	70.0
Direct investment abroad	4 505	...	...	...	...	...	...	...	...
Equity capital	4 510	...	...	...	...	...	...	...	...
Claims on affiliated enterprises	4 515	...	...	...	...	...	...	...	...
Liabilities to affiliated enterprises	4 520	...	...	...	...	...	...	...	...
Reinvested earnings	4 525	...	...	...	...	...	...	...	...
Other capital	4 530	...	...	...	...	...	...	...	...
Claims on affiliated enterprises	4 535	...	...	...	...	...	...	...	...
Liabilities to affiliated enterprises	4 540	...	...	...	...	...	...	...	...
Direct investment in Albania	4 555	...	...	...	...	**20.0**	**58.0**	**53.0**	**70.0**
Equity capital	4 560	...	...	...	...	20.0	58.0	53.0	70.0
Claims on direct investors	4 565	...	...	...	...	...	...	...	...
Liabilities to direct investors	4 570	...	...	...	...	...	...	...	70.0
Reinvested earnings	4 575	...	...	...	...	...	...	...	...
Other capital	4 580	...	...	...	...	...	...	...	...
Claims on direct investors	4 585	...	...	...	...	...	...	...	...
Liabilities to direct investors	4 590	...	...	...	...	...	...	...	...
B. PORTFOLIO INVESTMENT	4 600	...	...	...	...	...	...	...	...
Assets	4 602	...	...	...	...	...	...	...	...
Equity securities	4 610	...	...	...	...	...	...	...	...
Monetary authorities	4 611	...	...	...	...	...	...	...	...
General government	4 612	...	...	...	...	...	...	...	...
Banks	4 613	...	...	...	...	...	...	...	...
Other sectors	4 614	...	...	...	...	...	...	...	...
Debt securities	4 619	...	...	...	...	...	...	...	...
Bonds and notes	4 620	...	...	...	...	...	...	...	...
Monetary authorities	4 621	...	...	...	...	...	...	...	...
General government	4 622	...	...	...	...	...	...	...	...
Banks	4 623	...	...	...	...	...	...	...	...
Other sectors	4 624	...	...	...	...	...	...	...	...
Money market instruments	4 630	...	...	...	...	...	...	...	...
Monetary authorities	4 631	...	...	...	...	...	...	...	...
General government	4 632	...	...	...	...	...	...	...	...
Banks	4 633	...	...	...	...	...	...	...	...
Other sectors	4 634	...	...	...	...	...	...	...	...
Financial derivatives	4 640	...	...	...	...	...	...	...	...
Monetary authorities	4 641	...	...	...	...	...	...	...	...
General government	4 642	...	...	...	...	...	...	...	...
Banks	4 643	...	...	...	...	...	...	...	...
Other sectors	4 644	...	...	...	...	...	...	...	...
Liabilities	4 652	...	...	...	...	...	...	...	...
Equity securities	4 660	...	...	...	...	...	...	...	...
Banks	4 663	...	...	...	...	...	...	...	...
Other sectors	4 664	...	...	...	...	...	...	...	...
Debt securities	4 669	...	...	...	...	...	...	...	...
Bonds and notes	4 670	...	...	...	...	...	...	...	...
Monetary authorities	4 671	...	...	...	...	...	...	...	...
General government	4 672	...	...	...	...	...	...	...	...
Banks	4 673	...	...	...	...	...	...	...	...
Other sectors	4 674	...	...	...	...	...	...	...	...
Money market instruments	4 680	...	...	...	...	...	...	...	...
Monetary authorities	4 681	...	...	...	...	...	...	...	...
General government	4 682	...	...	...	...	...	...	...	...
Banks	4 683	...	...	...	...	...	...	...	...
Other sectors	4 684	...	...	...	...	...	...	...	...
Financial derivatives	4 690	...	...	...	...	...	...	...	...
Monetary authorities	4 691	...	...	...	...	...	...	...	...
General government	4 692	...	...	...	...	...	...	...	...
Banks	4 693	...	...	...	...	...	...	...	...
Other sectors	4 694	...	...	...	...	...	...	...	...

Table 2 (Concluded). STANDARD PRESENTATION, 1988–95

(Millions of U.S. dollars)

	Code	1988	1989	1990	1991	1992	1993	1994	1995
C. OTHER INVESTMENT	4 700 . .	139.3	359.4	88.3	14.8	10.7	52.2	35.6	–471.1
Assets	4 703 . .	**. . .**	**. . .**	**. . .**	**. . .**	**–73.2**	**–78.6**	**–97.3**	**–97.0**
Trade credits	4 706 . .	. . .	. . .	. . .	. . .	. . .	. . .	. . .	. . .
General government: long-term	4 708 . .	. . .	. . .	. . .	. . .	. . .	. . .	. . .	. . .
General government: short-term	4 709 . .	. . .	. . .	. . .	. . .	. . .	. . .	. . .	. . .
Other sectors: long-term	4 711 . .	. . .	. . .	. . .	. . .	. . .	. . .	. . .	. . .
Other sectors: short-term	4 712 . .	. . .	. . .	. . .	. . .	. . .	. . .	. . .	. . .
Loans	4 714 . .	. . .	. . .	. . .	. . .	. . .	. . .	. . .	. . .
Monetary authorities: long-term	4 717 . .	. . .	. . .	. . .	. . .	. . .	. . .	. . .	. . .
Monetary authorities: short-term	4 718 . .	. . .	. . .	. . .	. . .	. . .	. . .	. . .	. . .
General government: long-term	4 720 . .	. . .	. . .	. . .	. . .	. . .	. . .	. . .	. . .
General government: short-term	4 721 . .	. . .	. . .	. . .	. . .	. . .	. . .	. . .	. . .
Banks: long-term	4 723 . .	. . .	. . .	. . .	. . .	. . .	. . .	. . .	. . .
Banks: short-term	4 724 . .	. . .	. . .	. . .	. . .	. . .	. . .	. . .	. . .
Other sectors: long-term	4 726 . .	. . .	. . .	. . .	. . .	. . .	. . .	. . .	. . .
Other sectors: short-term	4 727 . .	. . .	. . .	. . .	. . .	. . .	. . .	. . .	. . .
Currency and deposits	4 730 . .	. . .	. . .	. . .	. . .	–73.2	–73.6	–102.3	–96.8
Monetary authorities	4 731 . .	. . .	. . .	. . .	. . .	. . .	. . .	. . .	. . .
General government	4 732 . .	. . .	. . .	. . .	. . .	. . .	. . .	. . .	. . .
Banks	4 733 . .	. . .	. . .	. . .	. . .	–50.0	–25.5	–22.9	–68.2
Other sectors	4 734 . .	. . .	. . .	. . .	. . .	–23.2	–48.1	–79.4	–28.6
Other assets	4 736 . .	. . .	. . .	. . .	. . .	. . .	–5.0	5.0	–.2
Monetary authorities: long-term	4 738 . .	. . .	. . .	. . .	. . .	. . .	. . .	. . .	. . .
Monetary authorities: short-term	4 739 . .	. . .	. . .	. . .	. . .	. . .	. . .	. . .	. . .
General government: long-term	4 741 . .	. . .	. . .	. . .	. . .	. . .	. . .	. . .	. . .
General government: short-term	4 742 . .	. . .	. . .	. . .	. . .	. . .	. . .	. . .	. . .
Banks: long-term	4 744 . .	. . .	. . .	. . .	. . .	. . .	. . .	. . .	. . .
Banks: short-term	4 745 . .	. . .	. . .	. . .	. . .	. . .	. . .	. . .	–.2
Other sectors: long-term	4 747 . .	. . .	. . .	. . .	. . .	. . .	–5.0	5.0	. . .
Other sectors: short-term	4 748 . .	. . .	. . .	. . .	. . .	. . .	. . .	. . .	. . .
Liabilities	4 753 . .	**139.3**	**359.4**	**88.3**	**14.8**	**83.9**	**130.8**	**132.9**	**–374.1**
Trade credits	4 756 . .	. . .	. . .	. . .	. . .	. . .	. . .	. . .	7.8
General government: long-term	4 758 . .	. . .	. . .	. . .	. . .	. . .	. . .	. . .	. . .
General government: short-term	4 759 . .	. . .	. . .	. . .	. . .	. . .	. . .	. . .	. . .
Other sectors: long-term	4 761 . .	. . .	. . .	. . .	. . .	. . .	. . .	. . .	. . .
Other sectors: short-term	4 762 . .	. . .	. . .	. . .	. . .	. . .	. . .	. . .	7.8
Loans	4 764 . .	–2.0	–2.0	27.1	21.4	36.3	77.9	104.2	89.3
Use of Fund credit and loans from the Fund	4 766 . .	. . .	. . .	. . .	. . .	13.9	16.6	22.3	9.9
Monetary authorities: other long term	4 767 . .	. . .	. . .	. . .	. . .	. . .	. . .	. . .	. . .
Monetary authorities: short-term	4 768 . .	. . .	. . .	. . .	. . .	. . .	. . .	. . .	. . .
General government: long-term	4 770 . .	–2.0	–2.0	27.1	21.4	22.4	50.5	74.6	57.5
General government: short-term	4 771 . .	. . .	. . .	. . .	. . .	. . .	. . .	. . .	. . .
Banks: long-term	4 773 . .	. . .	. . .	. . .	. . .	. . .	. . .	. . .	.1
Banks: short-term	4 774 . .	. . .	. . .	. . .	. . .	. . .	. . .	. . .	. . .
Other sectors: long-term	4 776 . .	. . .	. . .	. . .	. . .	. . .	. . .	. . .	21.8
Other sectors: short-term	4 777 . .	. . .	. . .	. . .	. . .	. . .	10.8	7.3	. . .
Currency and deposits	4 780 . .	. . .	. . .	. . .	. . .	. . .	. . .	. . .	–3.4
Monetary authorities	4 781 . .	. . .	. . .	. . .	. . .	. . .	. . .	. . .	. . .
General government	4 782 . .	. . .	. . .	. . .	. . .	. . .	. . .	. . .	. . .
Banks	4 783 . .	. . .	. . .	. . .	. . .	. . .	. . .	. . .	–3.4
Other sectors	4 784 . .	. . .	. . .	. . .	. . .	. . .	. . .	. . .	. . .
Other liabilities	4 786 . .	141.3	361.4	61.2	–6.6	47.6	52.9	28.7	–467.8
Monetary authorities: long-term	4 788 . .	. . .	. . .	. . .	. . .	. . .	. . .	. . .	. . .
Monetary authorities: short-term	4 789 . .	141.3	361.4	–144.8	–202.6	. . .	. . .	. . .	–9.1
General government: long-term	4 791 . .	. . .	. . .	. . .	. . .	. . .	. . .	. . .	. . .
General government: short-term	4 792 . .	. . .	. . .	206.0	196.0	49.0	49.5	26.1	–462.0
Banks: long-term	4 794 . .	. . .	. . .	. . .	. . .	–1.4	3.4	2.6	. . .
Banks: short-term	4 795 . .	. . .	. . .	. . .	. . .	. . .	. . .	. . .	. . .
Other sectors: long-term	4 797 . .	. . .	. . .	. . .	. . .	. . .	. . .	. . .	. . .
Other sectors: short-term	4 798 . .	. . .	. . .	. . .	. . .	. . .	. . .	. . .	3.3
D. RESERVE ASSETS	4 800 . .	–134.2	–324.9	32.0	28.0	–27.4	–114.9	–55.2	–30.5
Monetary gold	4 810 . .	2.4	1.3	4.6	. . .	. . .	. . .	. . .	. . .
Special drawing rights	4 820 . .	. . .	. . .	. . .	. . .	–.1	. . .	–.3	.1
Reserve position in the Fund	4 830 . .	. . .	. . .	. . .	. . .	. . .	. . .	. . .	. . .
Foreign exchange	4 840 . .	–136.6	–326.2	27.4	28.0	–27.3	–114.9	–54.9	–30.6
Other claims	4 880 . .	. . .	. . .	. . .	. . .	. . .	. . .	. . .	. . .
NET ERRORS AND OMISSIONS	4 998 . .	**22.0**	**4.8**	**–2.0**	**125.2**	**47.4**	**–10.3**	**123.9**	**53.7**

Table 1. ANALYTIC PRESENTATION, 1988–95
(*Millions of U.S. dollars*)

	Code			1988	1989	1990	1991	1992	1993	1994	1995
A. Current Account[1]	4	993	Y.	**–2,040**	**–1,081**	**1,420**	**2,367**	**...**	**...**	**...**	**...**
Goods: exports f.o.b	2	100	..	7,620	9,534	12,965	12,330	...	...	...	...
Goods: imports f.o.b	3	100	..	–6,685	–8,390	–8,786	–6,862	...	...	...	...
Balance on Goods	4	100	..	*935*	*1,144*	*4,179*	*5,468*	...	...	...	...
Services: credit	2	200	..	470	496	497	393	...	...	...	...
Services: debit	3	200	..	–1,337	–1,214	–1,321	–1,163	...	...	...	...
Balance on Goods and Services	4	991	..	*68*	*425*	*3,355*	*4,698*	...	...	...	...
Income: credit	2	300	..	71	111	73	70	...	...	...	...
Income: debit	3	300	..	–2,570	–2,157	–2,341	–2,618	...	...	...	...
Balance on Goods, Services, and Income	4	992	..	*–2,430*	*–1,622*	*1,087*	*2,151*	...	...	...	...
Current transfers: credit	2	379	Y.	477	603	400	269	...	...	...	...
Current transfers: debit	3	379	..	–86	–62	–67	–53	...	...	...	...
B. Capital Account[1]	4	994	Y.	**...**	**...**	**...**	**...**	**...**	**...**	**...**	**...**
Capital account: credit	2	994	Y.	...	...	...	...	...	...	...	...
Capital account: debit	3	994	..	...	...	...	...	...	...	...	...
Total, Groups A Plus B	4	010	..	*–2,040*	*–1,081*	*1,420*	*2,367*	...	...	...	...
C. Financial Account[1]	4	995	X.	**744**	**755**	**–1,094**	**–1,020**	**...**	**...**	**...**	**...**
Direct investment abroad	4	505	..	–5	–8	–5	–50	...	...	...	...
Direct investment in Algeria	4	555	Y.	13	12	...	12	...	...	...	...
Portfolio investment assets	4	602	..	2	...	...	...	...	...	...	...
Equity securities	4	610	..	2	...	...	...	...	...	...	...
Debt securities	4	619	..	...	...	...	...	...	...	...	...
Portfolio investment liabilities	4	652	Y.	...	...	...	...	...	...	...	...
Equity securities	4	660	Y.	...	...	...	...	...	...	...	...
Debt securities	4	669	Y.	...	...	...	...	...	...	...	...
Other investment assets	4	703	..	–131	–97	–229	–145	...	...	...	...
Monetary authorities	4	703	.A	...	...	...	...	...	...	...	...
General government	4	703	.B	–45	–14	–4	–37	...	...	...	...
Banks	4	703	.C	–86	–83	–226	–108	...	...	...	...
Other sectors	4	703	.D	...	...	...	...	...	...	...	...
Other investment liabilities	4	753	X.	865	848	–860	–837	...	...	...	...
Monetary authorities	4	753	XA	7	–6	...	–3	...	...	...	...
General government	4	753	YB	240	–51	215	286	...	...	...	...
Banks	4	753	YC	8	138	162	90	...	...	...	...
Other sectors	4	753	YD	609	767	–1,237	–1,210	...	...	...	...
Total, Groups A Through C	4	020	..	*–1,295*	*–326*	*326*	*1,346*	...	...	...	...
D. Net Errors and Omissions	4	998	..	**337**	**–448**	**–336**	**–299**	**...**	**...**	**...**	**...**
Total, Groups A Through D	4	030	..	*–959*	*–774*	*–10*	*1,047*	...	...	...	...
E. Reserves and Related Items	4	040	..	**959**	**774**	**10**	**–1,047**	**...**	**...**	**...**	**...**
Reserve assets	4	800	..	757	121	–138	–1,356	...	...	...	...
Use of Fund credit and loans	4	766	..	...	584	...	308	...	...	...	...
Liabilities constituting foreign authorities' reserves	4	900	..	...	...	...	...	...	...	...	...
Exceptional financing	4	920	..	201	69	148	...	...	...	...	...
Conversion rates: Algerian dinars per U.S. dollar	0	101	..	**5.915**	**7.609**	**8.958**	**18.473**	**21.836**	**23.345**	**35.059**	**47.663**

[1] Excludes components that have been classified in the categories of Group E.

Table 2. STANDARD PRESENTATION, 1988–95

(Millions of U.S. dollars)

	Code	1988	1989	1990	1991	1992	1993	1994	1995
CURRENT ACCOUNT	4 993 . .	**–2,040**	**–1,081**	**1,420**	**2,367**	**...**	**...**	**...**	**...**
A. GOODS	4 100 . .	935	1,144	4,179	5,468	...	...	...	...
Credit	2 100 . .	**7,620**	**9,534**	**12,965**	**12,330**	**...**	**...**	**...**	**...**
General merchandise: exports f.o.b.	2 110 . .	7,620	9,534	12,964	12,330	...	...	...	...
Goods for processing: exports f.o.b.	2 150 . .	...	...	...	...	...	...	...	...
Repairs on goods	2 160 . .	...	...	1	...	...	...	...	...
Goods procured in ports by carriers	2 170 . .	...	...	...	...	...	...	...	...
Nonmonetary gold	2 180 . .	...	...	...	...	...	...	...	...
Debit	3 100 . .	**–6,685**	**–8,390**	**–8,786**	**–6,862**	**...**	**...**	**...**	**...**
General merchandise: imports f.o.b.	3 110 . .	–6,675	–8,372	–8,777	–6,852	...	...	...	...
Goods for processing: imports f.o.b.	3 150 . .	–2	–1	...	...	...	...	...	...
Repairs on goods	3 160 . .	–9	–17	–9	–9	...	...	...	...
Goods procured in ports by carriers	3 170 . .	...	...	...	...	...	...	...	...
Nonmonetary gold	3 180 . .	...	...	...	...	...	...	...	...
B. SERVICES	4 200 . .	–867	–719	–824	–770	...	...	...	...
Total credit	2 200 . .	*470*	*496*	*497*	*393*	...	...	...	...
Total debit	3 200 . .	*–1,337*	*–1,214*	*–1,321*	*–1,163*	...	...	...	...
Transportation services, credit	2 205 . .	**212**	**220**	**199**	**169**	**...**	**...**	**...**	**...**
Passenger	2 205 BA	*63*	*82*	*86*	*86*	...	...	...	...
Freight	2 205 BB	*149*	*138*	*113*	*83*	...	...	...	...
Other	2 205 BC	...	...	...	...	...	...	...	...
Sea transport, passenger	2 207 . .	...	...	...	...	...	...	...	...
Sea transport, freight	2 208 . .	...	...	...	...	...	...	...	...
Sea transport, other	2 209 . .	...	...	...	...	...	...	...	...
Air transport, passenger	2 211 . .	...	...	...	...	...	...	...	...
Air transport, freight	2 212 . .	...	...	...	...	...	...	...	...
Air transport, other	2 213 . .	...	...	...	...	...	...	...	...
Other transport, passenger	2 215 . .	...	...	...	...	...	...	...	...
Other transport, freight	2 216 . .	...	...	...	...	...	...	...	...
Other transport, other	2 217 . .	...	...	...	...	...	...	...	...
Transportation services, debit	3 205 . .	**–618**	**–615**	**–671**	**–566**	**...**	**...**	**...**	**...**
Passenger	3 205 BA	*–94*	*–149*	*–124*	*–89*	...	...	...	...
Freight	3 205 BB	*–524*	*–466*	*–546*	*–477*	...	...	...	...
Other	3 205 BC	...	...	...	...	...	...	...	...
Sea transport, passenger	3 207 . .	...	...	...	...	...	...	...	...
Sea transport, freight	3 208 . .	...	...	...	...	...	...	...	...
Sea transport, other	3 209 . .	...	...	...	...	...	...	...	...
Air transport, passenger	3 211 . .	...	...	...	...	...	...	...	...
Air transport, freight	3 212 . .	...	...	...	...	...	...	...	...
Air transport, other	3 213 . .	...	...	...	...	...	...	...	...
Other transport, passenger	3 215 . .	...	...	...	...	...	...	...	...
Other transport, freight	3 216 . .	...	...	...	...	...	...	...	...
Other transport, other	3 217 . .	...	...	...	...	...	...	...	...
Travel, credit	2 236 . .	**85**	**64**	**64**	**84**	**...**	**...**	**...**	**...**
Business travel	2 237 . .	...	...	...	...	...	...	...	...
Personal travel	2 240 . .	...	...	...	...	...	...	...	...
Travel, debit	3 236 . .	**–294**	**–212**	**–149**	**–140**	**...**	**...**	**...**	**...**
Business travel	3 237 . .	...	...	...	...	...	...	...	...
Personal travel	3 240 . .	...	...	...	...	...	...	...	...
Other services, credit	2 200 BA	**173**	**212**	**233**	**140**	**...**	**...**	**...**	**...**
Communications	2 245 . .	4	5	3	2	...	...	...	...
Construction	2 249 . .	...	...	...	...	...	...	...	...
Insurance	2 253 . .	17	15	13	9	...	...	...	...
Financial	2 260 . .	22	19	16	12	...	...	...	...
Computer and information	2 262 . .	...	...	...	...	...	...	...	...
Royalties and licence fees	2 266 . .	...	...	...	...	...	...	...	...
Other business services	2 268 . .	108	153	184	98	...	...	...	...
Personal, cultural, and recreational	2 287 . .	...	...	...	...	...	...	...	...
Government, n.i.e.	2 291 . .	22	20	18	18	...	...	...	...
Other services, debit	3 200 BA	**–425**	**–388**	**–500**	**–457**	**...**	**...**	**...**	**...**
Communications	3 245 . .	–11	–10	–6	–7	...	...	...	...
Construction	3 249 . .	...	...	...	...	...	...	...	...
Insurance	3 253 . .	–91	–71	–102	–87	...	...	...	...
Financial	3 260 . .	–7	–15	–11	–12	...	...	...	...
Computer and information	3 262 . .	...	...	...	...	...	...	...	...
Royalties and licence fees	3 266 . .	–1	–1	–1	...	...	...	...	...
Other business services	3 268 . .	–206	–172	–211	–184	...	...	...	...
Personal, cultural, and recreational	3 287 . .	–3	–3	–4	–4	...	...	...	...
Government, n.i.e.	3 291 . .	–108	–116	–165	–164	...	...	...	...

Table 2 (Continued). STANDARD PRESENTATION, 1988–95
(Millions of U.S. dollars)

	Code	1988	1989	1990	1991	1992	1993	1994	1995
C. INCOME	4 300	-2,499	-2,047	-2,268	-2,548	...	...	...	...
Total credit	2 300	*71*	*111*	*73*	*70*	...	...	...	...
Total debit	3 300	*-2,570*	*-2,157*	*-2,341*	*-2,618*	...	...	...	...
Compensation of employees, credit	2 310	...	...	...	...	...	...	...	...
Compensation of employees, debit	3 310	...	...	...	...	...	...	...	...
Investment income, credit	2 320	**71**	**111**	**73**	**70**	...	...	...	...
Direct investment income	2 330	3	5	5	15	...	...	...	...
Dividends and distributed branch profits	2 332	3	5	5	15	...	...	...	...
Reinvested earnings and undistributed branch profits	2 333	...	...	...	...	...	...	...	...
Income on debt (interest)	2 334	...	...	...	...	...	...	...	...
Portfolio investment income	2 339	1	6	3	...	...	...	...	...
Income on equity	2 340	1	6	3	...	...	...	...	...
Income on bonds and notes	2 350	...	...	...	...	...	...	...	...
Income on money market instruments and financial derivatives	2 360	...	...	...	...	...	...	...	...
Other investment income	2 370	67	100	66	55	...	...	...	...
Investment income, debit	3 320	**-2,570**	**-2,157**	**-2,341**	**-2,618**	...	...	...	...
Direct investment income	3 330	-487	-153	-151	-332	...	...	...	...
Dividends and distributed branch profits	3 332	-487	-153	-151	-332	...	...	...	...
Reinvested earnings and undistributed branch profits	3 333	...	...	...	...	...	...	...	...
Income on debt (interest)	3 334	...	...	...	...	...	...	...	...
Portfolio investment income	3 339	...	...	-1	...	...	...	...	...
Income on equity	3 340	...	...	-1	...	...	...	...	...
Income on bonds and notes	3 350	...	...	...	...	...	...	...	...
Income on money market instruments and financial derivatives	3 360	...	...	...	...	...	...	...	...
Other investment income	3 370	-2,083	-2,005	-2,189	-2,286	...	...	...	...
D. CURRENT TRANSFERS	4 379	391	541	333	216	...	...	...	...
Credit	2 379	**477**	**603**	**400**	**269**	...	...	...	...
General government	2 380	1	...	...	...	...	...	...	...
Other sectors	2 390	476	603	400	269	...	...	...	...
Workers' remittances	2 391	379	345	352	233	...	...	...	...
Other current transfers	2 392	97	257	47	36	...	...	...	...
Debit	3 379	**-86**	**-62**	**-67**	**-53**	...	...	...	...
General government	3 380	-16	-10	-12	-23	...	...	...	...
Other sectors	3 390	-70	-52	-54	-30	...	...	...	...
Workers' remittances	3 391	-53	-38	-31	-22	...	...	...	...
Other current transfers	3 392	-17	-14	-23	-8	...	...	...	...
CAPITAL AND FINANCIAL ACCOUNT	4 996	**1,703**	**1,529**	**-1,084**	**-2,068**	...	...	...	...
CAPITAL ACCOUNT	4 994	...	...	...	...	...	...	...	...
Total credit	2 994	...	...	...	...	...	...	...	...
Total debit	3 994	...	...	...	...	...	...	...	...
Capital transfers, credit	2 400	...	...	...	...	...	...	...	...
General government	2 401	...	...	...	...	...	...	...	...
Debt forgiveness	2 402	...	...	...	...	...	...	...	...
Other capital transfers	2 410	...	...	...	...	...	...	...	...
Other sectors	2 430	...	...	...	...	...	...	...	...
Migrants' transfers	2 431	...	...	...	...	...	...	...	...
Debt forgiveness	2 432	...	...	...	...	...	...	...	...
Other capital transfers	2 440	...	...	...	...	...	...	...	...
Capital transfers, debit	3 400	...	...	...	...	...	...	...	...
General government	3 401	...	...	...	...	...	...	...	...
Debt forgiveness	3 402	...	...	...	...	...	...	...	...
Other capital transfers	3 410	...	...	...	...	...	...	...	...
Other sectors	3 430	...	...	...	...	...	...	...	...
Migrants' transfers	3 431	...	...	...	...	...	...	...	...
Debt forgiveness	3 432	...	...	...	...	...	...	...	...
Other capital transfers	3 440	...	...	...	...	...	...	...	...
Nonproduced nonfinancial assets, credit	2 480	...	...	...	...	...	...	...	...
Nonproduced nonfinancial assets, debit	3 480	...	...	...	...	...	...	...	...

Table 2 (Continued). STANDARD PRESENTATION, 1988–95
(Millions of U.S. dollars)

	Code	1988	1989	1990	1991	1992	1993	1994	1995
FINANCIAL ACCOUNT	4 995	**1,703**	**1,529**	**–1,084**	**–2,068**	**...**	**...**	**...**	**...**
A. DIRECT INVESTMENT	4 500	8	4	–4	–39	...	...	...	...
Direct investment abroad	4 505	**–5**	**–8**	**–5**	**–50**	**...**	**...**	**...**	**...**
Equity capital	4 510	–5	–8	–5	–50	...	...	...	...
Claims on affiliated enterprises	4 515	...	...	...	...	...	...	...	...
Liabilities to affiliated enterprises	4 520	...	...	...	...	...	...	...	...
Reinvested earnings	4 525	...	...	...	...	...	...	...	...
Other capital	4 530	...	...	...	...	...	...	...	...
Claims on affiliated enterprises	4 535	...	...	...	...	...	...	...	...
Liabilities to affiliated enterprises	4 540	...	...	...	...	...	...	...	...
Direct investment in Algeria	4 555	**13**	**12**	**...**	**12**	**...**	**...**	**...**	**...**
Equity capital	4 560	13	12	...	12	...	...	...	...
Claims on direct investors	4 565	...	...	...	...	...	...	...	...
Liabilities to direct investors	4 570	...	...	...	...	...	...	...	...
Reinvested earnings	4 575	...	...	...	...	...	...	...	...
Other capital	4 580	...	...	...	...	...	...	...	...
Claims on direct investors	4 585	...	...	...	...	...	...	...	...
Liabilities to direct investors	4 590	...	...	...	...	...	...	...	...
B. PORTFOLIO INVESTMENT	4 600	2	...	...	...	...	...	...	...
Assets	4 602	**2**	**...**	**...**	**...**	**...**	**...**	**...**	**...**
Equity securities	4 610	2	...	...	...	...	...	...	...
Monetary authorities	4 611	...	...	...	...	...	...	...	...
General government	4 612	...	...	...	...	...	...	...	...
Banks	4 613	...	...	...	...	...	...	...	...
Other sectors	4 614	...	...	...	...	...	...	...	...
Debt securities	4 619	...	...	...	...	...	...	...	...
Bonds and notes	4 620	...	...	...	...	...	...	...	...
Monetary authorities	4 621	...	...	...	...	...	...	...	...
General government	4 622	...	...	...	...	...	...	...	...
Banks	4 623	...	...	...	...	...	...	...	...
Other sectors	4 624	...	...	...	...	...	...	...	...
Money market instruments	4 630	...	...	...	...	...	...	...	...
Monetary authorities	4 631	...	...	...	...	...	...	...	...
General government	4 632	...	...	...	...	...	...	...	...
Banks	4 633	...	...	...	...	...	...	...	...
Other sectors	4 634	...	...	...	...	...	...	...	...
Financial derivatives	4 640	...	...	...	...	...	...	...	...
Monetary authorities	4 641	...	...	...	...	...	...	...	...
General government	4 642	...	...	...	...	...	...	...	...
Banks	4 643	...	...	...	...	...	...	...	...
Other sectors	4 644	...	...	...	...	...	...	...	...
Liabilities	4 652	**...**	**...**	**...**	**...**	**...**	**...**	**...**	**...**
Equity securities	4 660	...	...	...	...	...	...	...	...
Banks	4 663	...	...	...	...	...	...	...	...
Other sectors	4 664	...	...	...	...	...	...	...	...
Debt securities	4 669	...	...	...	...	...	...	...	...
Bonds and notes	4 670	...	...	...	...	...	...	...	...
Monetary authorities	4 671	...	...	...	...	...	...	...	...
General government	4 672	...	...	...	...	...	...	...	...
Banks	4 673	...	...	...	...	...	...	...	...
Other sectors	4 674	...	...	...	...	...	...	...	...
Money market instruments	4 680	...	...	...	...	...	...	...	...
Monetary authorities	4 681	...	...	...	...	...	...	...	...
General government	4 682	...	...	...	...	...	...	...	...
Banks	4 683	...	...	...	...	...	...	...	...
Other sectors	4 684	...	...	...	...	...	...	...	...
Financial derivatives	4 690	...	...	...	...	...	...	...	...
Monetary authorities	4 691	...	...	...	...	...	...	...	...
General government	4 692	...	...	...	...	...	...	...	...
Banks	4 693	...	...	...	...	...	...	...	...
Other sectors	4 694	...	...	...	...	...	...	...	...

Table 2 (Concluded). STANDARD PRESENTATION, 1988–95
(Millions of U.S. dollars)

	Code	1988	1989	1990	1991	1992	1993	1994	1995
C. OTHER INVESTMENT	4 700 . .	935	1,404	–942	–673	...	...	...	...
Assets	4 703 . .	**–131**	**–97**	**–229**	**–145**	...	...	...	...
Trade credits	4 706 . .	...	...	...	...	...	...	...	...
General government: long-term	4 708 . .	...	...	...	...	...	...	...	...
General government: short-term	4 709 . .	...	...	...	...	...	...	...	...
Other sectors: long-term	4 711 . .	...	...	...	...	...	...	...	...
Other sectors: short-term	4 712 . .	...	...	...	...	...	...	...	...
Loans	4 714 . .	–52	–8	3	–45	...	...	...	...
Monetary authorities: long-term	4 717 . .	...	...	...	...	...	...	...	...
Monetary authorities: short-term	4 718 . .	...	...	...	...	...	...	...	...
General government: long-term	4 720 . .	–52	–8	3	–45	...	...	...	...
General government: short-term	4 721 . .	...	...	...	...	...	...	...	...
Banks: long-term	4 723 . .	...	...	...	...	...	...	...	...
Banks: short-term	4 724 . .	...	...	...	...	...	...	...	...
Other sectors: long-term	4 726 . .	...	...	...	...	...	...	...	...
Other sectors: short-term	4 727 . .	...	...	...	...	...	...	...	...
Currency and deposits	4 730 . .	–72	–83	–226	–100	...	...	...	...
Monetary authorities	4 731 . .	...	...	...	...	...	...	...	...
General government	4 732 . .	14	...	...	8	...	...	...	...
Banks	4 733 . .	–86	–83	–226	–108	...	...	...	...
Other sectors	4 734 . .	...	...	...	...	...	...	...	...
Other assets	4 736 . .	–6	–6	–7	...	...	...	...	...
Monetary authorities: long-term	4 738 . .	...	...	...	...	...	...	...	...
Monetary authorities: short-term	4 739 . .	...	...	...	...	...	...	...	...
General government: long-term	4 741 . .	–6	–6	–7	...	...	...	...	...
General government: short-term	4 742 . .	...	...	...	...	...	...	...	...
Banks: long-term	4 744 . .	...	...	...	...	...	...	...	...
Banks: short-term	4 745 . .	...	...	...	...	...	...	...	...
Other sectors: long-term	4 747 . .	...	...	...	...	...	...	...	...
Other sectors: short-term	4 748 . .	...	...	...	...	...	...	...	...
Liabilities	4 753 . .	**1,066**	**1,501**	**–712**	**–528**	...	...	...	...
Trade credits	4 756 . .	...	...	...	...	...	...	...	...
General government: long-term	4 758 . .	...	...	...	...	...	...	...	...
General government: short-term	4 759 . .	...	...	...	...	...	...	...	...
Other sectors: long-term	4 761 . .	...	...	...	...	...	...	...	...
Other sectors: short-term	4 762 . .	...	...	...	...	...	...	...	...
Loans	4 764 . .	1,017	1,377	–863	–607	...	...	...	...
Use of Fund credit and loans from the Fund	4 766 . .	...	584	...	308	...	...	...	...
Monetary authorities: other long-term	4 767 . .	...	...	...	...	...	...	...	...
Monetary authorities: short-term	4 768 . .	...	...	...	...	...	...	...	...
General government: long-term	4 770 . .	441	17	363	286	...	...	...	...
General government: short-term	4 771 . .	...	...	...	...	...	...	...	...
Banks: long-term	4 773 . .	...	...	...	...	...	...	...	...
Banks: short-term	4 774 . .	...	...	...	...	...	...	...	...
Other sectors: long-term	4 776 . .	576	776	–1,226	–1,202	...	...	...	...
Other sectors: short-term	4 777 . .	...	...	...	...	...	...	...	...
Currency and deposits	4 780 . .	8	138	162	90	...	...	...	...
Monetary authorities	4 781 . .	...	...	...	...	...	...	...	...
General government	4 782 . .	...	...	...	...	...	...	...	...
Banks	4 783 . .	8	138	162	90	...	...	...	...
Other sectors	4 784 . .	...	...	...	...	...	...	...	...
Other liabilities	4 786 . .	41	–14	–11	–11	...	...	...	...
Monetary authorities: long-term	4 788 . .	...	...	...	...	...	...	...	...
Monetary authorities: short-term	4 789 . .	7	–6	...	–3	...	...	...	...
General government: long-term	4 791 . .	...	...	...	...	...	...	...	...
General government: short-term	4 792 . .	...	...	...	...	...	...	...	...
Banks: long-term	4 794 . .	...	...	...	...	...	...	...	...
Banks: short-term	4 795 . .	...	...	...	...	...	...	...	...
Other sectors: long-term	4 797 . .	...	...	...	...	...	...	...	...
Other sectors: short-term	4 798 . .	33	–9	–11	–8	...	...	...	...
D. RESERVE ASSETS	4 800 . .	757	121	–138	–1,356	...	...	...	...
Monetary gold	4 810 . .	...	...	...	...	...	...	...	...
Special drawing rights	4 820 . .	191	–2	1	1	...	...	...	...
Reserve position in the Fund	4 830 . .	146	...	...	...	...	...	...	...
Foreign exchange	4 840 . .	420	139	–108	–1,356	...	...	...	...
Other claims	4 880 . .	...	–16	–31	...	...	...	...	...
NET ERRORS AND OMISSIONS	4 998 . .	**337**	**–448**	**–336**	**–299**	...	...	...	...

Table 1. ANALYTIC PRESENTATION, 1988–95
(Millions of U.S. dollars)

	Code	1988	1989	1990	1991	1992	1993	1994	1995
A. Current Account [1]	4 993 Y.	**–469.0**	**–132.0**	**–235.5**	**–579.6**	**–734.8**	**–768.5**	**. . .**	**. . .**
Goods: exports f.o.b	2 100 . .	2,492.0	3,014.0	3,883.9	3,449.3	3,832.8	2,900.5	. . .	. . .
Goods: imports f.o.b	3 100 . .	–1,372.0	–1,338.0	–1,578.2	–1,347.2	–1,988.0	–1,462.6	. . .	. . .
Balance on Goods	4 100 . .	*1,120.0*	*1,676.0*	*2,305.7*	*2,102.1*	*1,844.8*	*1,437.9*	. . .	. . .
Services: credit	2 200 . .	128.0	150.0	108.5	171.3	142.9	105.8	. . .	. . .
Services: debit	3 200 . .	–1,134.0	–1,175.0	–1,807.3	–1,839.1	–2,042.4	–1,561.9	. . .	. . .
Balance on Goods and Services	4 991 . .	*114.0*	*651.0*	*606.9*	*434.3*	*–54.8*	*–18.2*	. . .	. . .
Income: credit	2 300 . .	. . .	. . .	10.6	15.0	15.7	11.3	. . .	. . .
Income: debit	3 300 . .	–615.0	–779.0	–775.9	–1,057.1	–798.0	–927.4	. . .	. . .
Balance on Goods, Services, and Income	4 992 . .	*–501.0*	*–128.0*	*–158.4*	*–607.8*	*–837.0*	*–934.3*	. . .	. . .
Current transfers: credit	2 379 Y.	42.0	65.0	65.6	111.1	170.9	253.4	. . .	. . .
Current transfers: debit	3 379 . .	–10.0	–69.0	–142.7	–82.9	–68.7	–87.6	. . .	. . .
B. Capital Account [1]	4 994 Y.	**. . .**	**. . .**	**. . .**	**. . .**	**. . .**	**. . .**	**. . .**	**. . .**
Capital account: credit	2 994 Y.	. . .	. . .	. . .	. . .	. . .	. . .	. . .	. . .
Capital account: debit	3 994 . .	. . .	. . .	. . .	. . .	. . .	. . .	. . .	. . .
Total, Groups A Plus B	4 010 . .	*–469.0*	*–132.0*	*–235.5*	*–579.6*	*–734.8*	*–768.5*	. . .	. . .
C. Financial Account [1]	4 995 X.	**–199.0**	**–120.0**	**–954.3**	**–947.2**	**–445.9**	**–274.3**	**. . .**	**. . .**
Direct investment abroad	4 505 . .	. . .	. . .	–.9	. . .	. . .	. . .	. . .	. . .
Direct investment in Angola	4 555 Y.	131.0	200.0	–334.8	664.5	288.0	302.1	. . .	. . .
Portfolio investment assets	4 602 . .	. . .	. . .	. . .	. . .	. . .	. . .	. . .	. . .
Equity securities	4 610 . .	. . .	. . .	. . .	. . .	. . .	. . .	. . .	. . .
Debt securities	4 619 . .	. . .	. . .	. . .	. . .	. . .	. . .	. . .	. . .
Portfolio investment liabilities	4 652 Y.	. . .	. . .	. . .	. . .	. . .	. . .	. . .	. . .
Equity securities	4 660 Y.	. . .	. . .	. . .	. . .	. . .	. . .	. . .	. . .
Debt securities	4 669 Y.	. . .	. . .	. . .	. . .	. . .	. . .	. . .	. . .
Other investment assets	4 703 . .	. . .	. . .	–348.8	–190.2	–255.5	–92.9	. . .	. . .
Monetary authorities	4 703 . A	. . .	. . .	. . .	. . .	. . .	. . .	. . .	. . .
General government	4 703 . B	. . .	. . .	. . .	. . .	–52.6	–156.0	. . .	. . .
Banks	4 703 . C	. . .	. . .	. . .	. . .	. . .	10.0	. . .	. . .
Other sectors	4 703 . D	. . .	. . .	–348.8	–190.2	–202.9	53.1	. . .	. . .
Other investment liabilities	4 753 X.	–330.0	–320.0	–269.8	–1,421.5	–478.4	–483.5	. . .	. . .
Monetary authorities	4 753 XA	. . .	. . .	. . .	14.8	59.8	17.6	. . .	. . .
General government	4 753 YB	–330.0	–320.0	–80.6	–1,031.4	–430.8	–583.6	. . .	. . .
Banks	4 753 YC	. . .	. . .	33.8	–1.3	–9.6	.6	. . .	. . .
Other sectors	4 753 YD	. . .	. . .	–223.0	–403.6	–97.8	81.9	. . .	. . .
Total, Groups A Through C	4 020 . .	*–668.0*	*–252.0*	*–1,189.8*	*–1,526.8*	*–1,180.7*	*–1,042.8*	. . .	. . .
D. Net Errors and Omissions	4 998 . .	**–257.0**	**–678.0**	**–19.1**	**26.9**	**43.0**	**–277.1**	**. . .**	**. . .**
Total, Groups A Through D	4 030 . .	*–925.0*	*–930.0*	*–1,208.9*	*–1,499.9*	*–1,137.7*	*–1,319.9*	. . .	. . .
E. Reserves and Related Items	4 040 . .	**925.0**	**930.0**	**1,208.9**	**1,499.9**	**1,137.7**	**1,319.9**	**. . .**	**. . .**
Reserve assets	4 800 . .	–49.0	6.0	–1.5	–48.3	–227.2	192.9	. . .	. . .
Use of Fund credit and loans	4 766 . .	. . .	. . .	. . .	. . .	. . .	. . .	. . .	. . .
Liabilities constituting foreign authorities' reserves	4 900 . .	. . .	. . .	. . .	. . .	. . .	. . .	. . .	. . .
Exceptional financing	4 920 . .	974.0	924.0	1,210.4	1,548.2	1,364.9	1,127.0	. . .	. . .
Conversion rates: adjusted kwanzas per U.S. dollar	0 101 . .	**30**	**30**	**30**	**55**	**251**	**2,660**	**59,515**	**. . .**

[1] Excludes components that have been classified in the categories of Group E.

Table 2. STANDARD PRESENTATION, 1988–95
(Millions of U.S. dollars)

	Code	1988	1989	1990	1991	1992	1993	1994	1995
CURRENT ACCOUNT	4 993 . .	**–469.0**	**–132.0**	**–235.5**	**–579.6**	**–734.8**	**–768.5**	**. . .**	**. . .**
A. GOODS	4 100 . .	1,120.0	1,676.0	2,305.7	2,102.1	1,844.8	1,437.9	. . .	. . .
Credit	2 100 . .	**2,492.0**	**3,014.0**	**3,883.9**	**3,449.3**	**3,832.8**	**2,900.5**	**. . .**	**. . .**
General merchandise: exports f.o.b.	2 110 . .	2,492.0	3,014.0	3,883.9	3,449.3	3,832.8	2,900.5	. . .	. . .
Goods for processing: exports f.o.b.	2 150 . .	. . .	. . .	. . .	. . .	. . .	. . .	. . .	. . .
Repairs on goods	2 160 . .	. . .	. . .	. . .	. . .	. . .	. . .	. . .	. . .
Goods procured in ports by carriers	2 170 . .	. . .	. . .	. . .	. . .	. . .	. . .	. . .	. . .
Nonmonetary gold	2 180 . .	. . .	. . .	. . .	. . .	. . .	. . .	. . .	. . .
Debit	3 100 . .	**–1,372.0**	**–1,338.0**	**–1,578.2**	**–1,347.2**	**–1,988.0**	**–1,462.6**	**. . .**	**. . .**
General merchandise: imports f.o.b.	3 110 . .	–1,372.0	–1,338.0	–1,578.2	–1,347.2	–1,988.0	–1,462.6	. . .	. . .
Goods for processing: imports f.o.b.	3 150 . .	. . .	. . .	. . .	. . .	. . .	. . .	. . .	. . .
Repairs on goods	3 160 . .	. . .	. . .	. . .	. . .	. . .	. . .	. . .	. . .
Goods procured in ports by carriers	3 170 . .	. . .	. . .	. . .	. . .	. . .	. . .	. . .	. . .
Nonmonetary gold	3 180 . .	. . .	. . .	. . .	. . .	. . .	. . .	. . .	. . .
B. SERVICES	4 200 . .	–1,006.0	–1,025.0	–1,698.8	–1,667.8	–1,899.5	–1,456.1	. . .	. . .
Total credit	2 200 . .	*128.0*	*150.0*	*108.5*	*171.3*	*142.9*	*105.8*	. . .	. . .
Total debit	3 200 . .	*–1,134.0*	*–1,175.0*	*–1,807.3*	*–1,839.1*	*–2,042.4*	*–1,561.9*	. . .	. . .
Transportation services, credit	2 205 . .	**. . .**	**. . .**	**31.5**	**48.5**	**49.0**	**36.2**	**. . .**	**. . .**
Passenger	2 205 BA	. . .	. . .	*13.8*	. . .	. . .	. . .	. . .	. . .
Freight	2 205 BB	. . .	. . .	. . .	*27.3*	*32.9*	*21.1*	. . .	. . .
Other	2 205 BC	. . .	. . .	*17.7*	*21.2*	*16.0*	*15.1*	. . .	. . .
Sea transport, passenger	2 207 . .	. . .	. . .	. . .	. . .	. . .	. . .	. . .	. . .
Sea transport, freight	2 208 . .	. . .	. . .	. . .	. . .	. . .	. . .	. . .	. . .
Sea transport, other	2 209 . .	. . .	. . .	. . .	. . .	. . .	. . .	. . .	. . .
Air transport, passenger	2 211 . .	. . .	. . .	. . .	. . .	. . .	. . .	. . .	. . .
Air transport, freight	2 212 . .	. . .	. . .	. . .	. . .	. . .	. . .	. . .	. . .
Air transport, other	2 213 . .	. . .	. . .	. . .	. . .	. . .	. . .	. . .	. . .
Other transport, passenger	2 215 . .	. . .	. . .	. . .	. . .	. . .	. . .	. . .	. . .
Other transport, freight	2 216 . .	. . .	. . .	. . .	. . .	. . .	. . .	. . .	. . .
Other transport, other	2 217 . .	. . .	. . .	. . .	. . .	. . .	. . .	. . .	. . .
Transportation services, debit	3 205 . .	**–346.6**	**–390.7**	**–493.1**	**–540.1**	**–618.4**	**–439.2**	**. . .**	**. . .**
Passenger	3 205 BA	. . .	. . .	*–144.2*	*–51.5*	*–79.6*	*–46.6*	. . .	. . .
Freight	3 205 BB	*–346.6*	*–390.7*	*–281.2*	*–369.2*	*–411.3*	*–152.1*	. . .	. . .
Other	3 205 BC	. . .	. . .	*–67.7*	*–119.4*	*–127.5*	*–240.5*	. . .	. . .
Sea transport, passenger	3 207 . .	. . .	. . .	. . .	. . .	. . .	. . .	. . .	. . .
Sea transport, freight	3 208 . .	. . .	. . .	. . .	. . .	. . .	. . .	. . .	. . .
Sea transport, other	3 209 . .	. . .	. . .	. . .	. . .	. . .	. . .	. . .	. . .
Air transport, passenger	3 211 . .	. . .	. . .	. . .	. . .	. . .	. . .	. . .	. . .
Air transport, freight	3 212 . .	. . .	. . .	. . .	. . .	. . .	. . .	. . .	. . .
Air transport, other	3 213 . .	. . .	. . .	. . .	. . .	. . .	. . .	. . .	. . .
Other transport, passenger	3 215 . .	. . .	. . .	. . .	. . .	. . .	. . .	. . .	. . .
Other transport, freight	3 216 . .	. . .	. . .	. . .	. . .	. . .	. . .	. . .	. . .
Other transport, other	3 217 . .	. . .	. . .	. . .	. . .	. . .	. . .	. . .	. . .
Travel, credit	2 236 . .	**. . .**	**. . .**	**13.3**	**. . .**	**. . .**	**. . .**	**. . .**	**. . .**
Business travel	2 237 . .	. . .	. . .	. . .	. . .	. . .	. . .	. . .	. . .
Personal travel	2 240 . .	. . .	. . .	. . .	. . .	. . .	. . .	. . .	. . .
Travel, debit	3 236 . .	**–15.0**	**–37.0**	**–38.2**	**–65.2**	**–74.6**	**–65.6**	**. . .**	**. . .**
Business travel	3 237 . .	. . .	. . .	. . .	. . .	. . .	. . .	. . .	. . .
Personal travel	3 240 . .	. . .	. . .	. . .	. . .	. . .	. . .	. . .	. . .
Other services, credit	2 200 BA	**128.0**	**150.0**	**63.7**	**122.8**	**93.9**	**69.6**	**. . .**	**. . .**
Communications	2 245 . .	. . .	. . .	. . .	. . .	. . .	. . .	. . .	. . .
Construction	2 249 . .	. . .	. . .	. . .	. . .	. . .	. . .	. . .	. . .
Insurance	2 253 . .	19.2	22.5	3.0	14.1	11.5	8.8	. . .	. . .
Financial	2 260 . .	. . .	. . .	. . .	. . .	. . .	. . .	. . .	. . .
Computer and information	2 262 . .	. . .	. . .	. . .	. . .	. . .	. . .	. . .	. . .
Royalties and licence fees	2 266 . .	. . .	. . .	. . .	. . .	. . .	14.1	. . .	. . .
Other business services	2 268 . .	108.8	127.5	16.8	54.7	34.7	30.2	. . .	. . .
Personal, cultural, and recreational	2 287 . .	. . .	. . .	. . .	. . .	. . .	. . .	. . .	. . .
Government, n.i.e.	2 291 . .	. . .	. . .	43.9	53.9	47.7	16.6	. . .	. . .
Other services, debit	3 200 BA	**–772.4**	**–747.3**	**–1,276.0**	**–1,233.8**	**–1,349.4**	**–1,057.1**	**. . .**	**. . .**
Communications	3 245 . .	. . .	. . .	. . .	. . .	. . .	. . .	. . .	. . .
Construction	3 249 . .	. . .	. . .	. . .	. . .	. . .	. . .	. . .	. . .
Insurance	3 253 . .	–36.5	–37.2	–34.1	–48.9	–51.4	–33.1	. . .	. . .
Financial	3 260 . .	. . .	. . .	. . .	. . .	. . .	. . .	. . .	. . .
Computer and information	3 262 . .	. . .	. . .	. . .	. . .	. . .	. . .	. . .	. . .
Royalties and licence fees	3 266 . .	. . .	. . .	. . .	. . .	. . .	. . .	. . .	. . .
Other business services	3 268 . .	–713.0	–677.1	–722.6	–1,082.7	–1,109.1	–864.2	. . .	. . .
Personal, cultural, and recreational	3 287 . .	. . .	. . .	. . .	. . .	. . .	. . .	. . .	. . .
Government, n.i.e.	3 291 . .	–23.0	–33.0	–519.4	–102.2	–188.8	–159.9	. . .	. . .

Table 2 (Continued). STANDARD PRESENTATION, 1988–95
(Millions of U.S. dollars)

	Code	1988	1989	1990	1991	1992	1993	1994	1995
C. INCOME	4 300	–615.0	–779.0	–765.3	–1,042.1	–782.3	–916.1	...	...
Total credit	2 300	...	...	*10.6*	*15.0*	*15.7*	*11.3*	...	...
Total debit	3 300	*–615.0*	*–779.0*	*–775.9*	*–1,057.1*	*–798.0*	*–927.4*	...	...
Compensation of employees, credit	2 310	...	...	...	...	...	...	...	...
Compensation of employees, debit	3 310	**–63.0**	**–35.0**	**–10.0**	**–50.2**	**–56.9**	**–50.2**	...	...
Investment income, credit	2 320	...	...	**10.6**	**15.0**	**15.7**	**11.3**	...	...
Direct investment income	2 330	...	...	...	...	...	...	...	...
Dividends and distributed branch profits	2 332	...	...	...	...	...	...	...	...
Reinvested earnings and undistributed branch profits	2 333	...	...	...	...	...	...	...	...
Income on debt (interest)	2 334	...	...	...	...	...	...	...	...
Portfolio investment income	2 339	...	...	...	...	...	...	...	...
Income on equity	2 340	...	...	...	...	...	...	...	...
Income on bonds and notes	2 350	...	...	...	...	...	...	...	...
Income on money market instruments and financial derivatives	2 360	...	...	...	...	...	...	...	...
Other investment income	2 370	...	...	10.6	15.0	15.7	11.3	...	...
Investment income, debit	3 320	**–552.0**	**–744.0**	**–765.9**	**–1,006.9**	**–741.1**	**–877.2**	...	...
Direct investment income	3 330	–185.0	–303.0	–314.1	–313.2	–362.1	–478.6	...	...
Dividends and distributed branch profits	3 332	–185.0	–303.0	–314.1	–286.8	–362.1	–378.6	...	...
Reinvested earnings and undistributed branch profits	3 333	...	...	...	–26.4	...	–100.0	...	...
Income on debt (interest)	3 334	...	...	...	...	...	...	...	...
Portfolio investment income	3 339	...	...	...	...	...	...	...	...
Income on equity	3 340	...	...	...	...	...	...	...	...
Income on bonds and notes	3 350	...	...	...	...	...	...	...	...
Income on money market instruments and financial derivatives	3 360	...	...	...	...	...	...	...	...
Other investment income	3 370	–367.0	–441.0	–451.8	–693.7	–379.0	–398.6	...	...
D. CURRENT TRANSFERS	4 379	32.0	–4.0	–77.1	28.2	102.3	165.8	...	...
Credit	2 379	**42.0**	**65.0**	**65.6**	**111.1**	**170.9**	**253.4**	...	...
General government	2 380	40.0	64.0	65.3	30.7	48.1	31.9	...	...
Other sectors	2 390	2.0	1.0	.3	80.4	122.8	221.5	...	...
Workers' remittances	2 391	...	...	...	...	...	...	...	...
Other current transfers	2 392	2.0	1.0	.3	80.4	122.8	221.5	...	...
Debit	3 379	**–10.0**	**–69.0**	**–142.7**	**–82.9**	**–68.7**	**–87.6**	...	...
General government	3 380	–2.0	...	–2.7	–1.7	–.9	–2.3	...	...
Other sectors	3 390	–8.0	–69.0	–140.0	–81.2	–67.8	–85.3	...	...
Workers' remittances	3 391	–8.0	–69.0	–140.0	–74.3	–64.7	–82.7	...	...
Other current transfers	3 392	...	...	...	–6.9	–3.0	–2.6	...	...
CAPITAL AND FINANCIAL ACCOUNT	4 996	**726.0**	**810.0**	**254.6**	**552.7**	**691.8**	**1,045.6**	...	...
CAPITAL ACCOUNT	4 994	...	...	...	...	...	...	...	...
Total credit	2 994	...	...	...	...	...	...	...	...
Total debit	3 994	...	...	...	...	...	...	...	...
Capital transfers, credit	2 400	...	...	...	...	...	...	...	...
General government	2 401	...	...	...	...	...	...	...	...
Debt forgiveness	2 402	...	...	...	...	...	...	...	...
Other capital transfers	2 410	...	...	...	...	...	...	...	...
Other sectors	2 430	...	...	...	...	...	...	...	...
Migrants' transfers	2 431	...	...	...	...	...	...	...	...
Debt forgiveness	2 432	...	...	...	...	...	...	...	...
Other capital transfers	2 440	...	...	...	...	...	...	...	...
Capital transfers, debit	3 400	...	...	...	...	...	...	...	...
General government	3 401	...	...	...	...	...	...	...	...
Debt forgiveness	3 402	...	...	...	...	...	...	...	...
Other capital transfers	3 410	...	...	...	...	...	...	...	...
Other sectors	3 430	...	...	...	...	...	...	...	...
Migrants' transfers	3 431	...	...	...	...	...	...	...	...
Debt forgiveness	3 432	...	...	...	...	...	...	...	...
Other capital transfers	3 440	...	...	...	...	...	...	...	...
Nonproduced nonfinancial assets, credit	2 480	...	...	...	...	...	...	...	...
Nonproduced nonfinancial assets, debit	3 480	...	...	...	...	...	...	...	...

Table 2 (Continued). STANDARD PRESENTATION, 1988–95
(Millions of U.S. dollars)

	Code	1988	1989	1990	1991	1992	1993	1994	1995
FINANCIAL ACCOUNT	4 995	**726.0**	**810.0**	**254.6**	**552.7**	**691.8**	**1,045.6**	**. . .**	**. . .**
A. DIRECT INVESTMENT	4 500	131.0	200.0	–335.7	664.5	288.0	302.1	. . .	. . .
Direct investment abroad	4 505	**. . .**	**. . .**	**–.9**	**. . .**	**. . .**	**. . .**	**. . .**	**. . .**
Equity capital	4 510	. . .	. . .	–.9	. . .	. . .	. . .	. . .	. . .
Claims on affiliated enterprises	4 515	. . .	. . .	. . .	. . .	. . .	. . .	. . .	. . .
Liabilities to affiliated enterprises	4 520	. . .	. . .	. . .	. . .	. . .	. . .	. . .	. . .
Reinvested earnings	4 525	. . .	. . .	. . .	. . .	. . .	. . .	. . .	. . .
Other capital	4 530	. . .	. . .	. . .	. . .	. . .	. . .	. . .	. . .
Claims on affiliated enterprises	4 535	. . .	. . .	. . .	. . .	. . .	. . .	. . .	. . .
Liabilities to affiliated enterprises	4 540	. . .	. . .	. . .	. . .	. . .	. . .	. . .	. . .
Direct investment in Angola	4 555	**131.0**	**200.0**	**–334.8**	**664.5**	**288.0**	**302.1**	**. . .**	**. . .**
Equity capital	4 560	. . .	. . .	. . .	302.0	. . .	. . .	. . .	. . .
Claims on direct investors	4 565	. . .	. . .	. . .	. . .	. . .	. . .	. . .	. . .
Liabilities to direct investors	4 570	. . .	. . .	. . .	. . .	. . .	. . .	. . .	. . .
Reinvested earnings	4 575	. . .	. . .	. . .	26.4	. . .	100.0	. . .	. . .
Other capital	4 580	131.0	200.0	–334.8	336.1	288.0	202.1	. . .	. . .
Claims on direct investors	4 585	. . .	. . .	. . .	. . .	. . .	. . .	. . .	. . .
Liabilities to direct investors	4 590	. . .	. . .	. . .	. . .	. . .	. . .	. . .	. . .
B. PORTFOLIO INVESTMENT	4 600	. . .	. . .	. . .	. . .	. . .	. . .	. . .	. . .
Assets	4 602	**. . .**	**. . .**	**. . .**	**. . .**	**. . .**	**. . .**	**. . .**	**. . .**
Equity securities	4 610	. . .	. . .	. . .	. . .	. . .	. . .	. . .	. . .
Monetary authorities	4 611	. . .	. . .	. . .	. . .	. . .	. . .	. . .	. . .
General government	4 612	. . .	. . .	. . .	. . .	. . .	. . .	. . .	. . .
Banks	4 613	. . .	. . .	. . .	. . .	. . .	. . .	. . .	. . .
Other sectors	4 614	. . .	. . .	. . .	. . .	. . .	. . .	. . .	. . .
Debt securities	4 619	. . .	. . .	. . .	. . .	. . .	. . .	. . .	. . .
Bonds and notes	4 620	. . .	. . .	. . .	. . .	. . .	. . .	. . .	. . .
Monetary authorities	4 621	. . .	. . .	. . .	. . .	. . .	. . .	. . .	. . .
General government	4 622	. . .	. . .	. . .	. . .	. . .	. . .	. . .	. . .
Banks	4 623	. . .	. . .	. . .	. . .	. . .	. . .	. . .	. . .
Other sectors	4 624	. . .	. . .	. . .	. . .	. . .	. . .	. . .	. . .
Money market instruments	4 630	. . .	. . .	. . .	. . .	. . .	. . .	. . .	. . .
Monetary authorities	4 631	. . .	. . .	. . .	. . .	. . .	. . .	. . .	. . .
General government	4 632	. . .	. . .	. . .	. . .	. . .	. . .	. . .	. . .
Banks	4 633	. . .	. . .	. . .	. . .	. . .	. . .	. . .	. . .
Other sectors	4 634	. . .	. . .	. . .	. . .	. . .	. . .	. . .	. . .
Financial derivatives	4 640	. . .	. . .	. . .	. . .	. . .	. . .	. . .	. . .
Monetary authorities	4 641	. . .	. . .	. . .	. . .	. . .	. . .	. . .	. . .
General government	4 642	. . .	. . .	. . .	. . .	. . .	. . .	. . .	. . .
Banks	4 643	. . .	. . .	. . .	. . .	. . .	. . .	. . .	. . .
Other sectors	4 644	. . .	. . .	. . .	. . .	. . .	. . .	. . .	. . .
Liabilities	4 652	**. . .**	**. . .**	**. . .**	**. . .**	**. . .**	**. . .**	**. . .**	**. . .**
Equity securities	4 660	. . .	. . .	. . .	. . .	. . .	. . .	. . .	. . .
Banks	4 663	. . .	. . .	. . .	. . .	. . .	. . .	. . .	. . .
Other sectors	4 664	. . .	. . .	. . .	. . .	. . .	. . .	. . .	. . .
Debt securities	4 669	. . .	. . .	. . .	. . .	. . .	. . .	. . .	. . .
Bonds and notes	4 670	. . .	. . .	. . .	. . .	. . .	. . .	. . .	. . .
Monetary authorities	4 671	. . .	. . .	. . .	. . .	. . .	. . .	. . .	. . .
General government	4 672	. . .	. . .	. . .	. . .	. . .	. . .	. . .	. . .
Banks	4 673	. . .	. . .	. . .	. . .	. . .	. . .	. . .	. . .
Other sectors	4 674	. . .	. . .	. . .	. . .	. . .	. . .	. . .	. . .
Money market instruments	4 680	. . .	. . .	. . .	. . .	. . .	. . .	. . .	. . .
Monetary authorities	4 681	. . .	. . .	. . .	. . .	. . .	. . .	. . .	. . .
General government	4 682	. . .	. . .	. . .	. . .	. . .	. . .	. . .	. . .
Banks	4 683	. . .	. . .	. . .	. . .	. . .	. . .	. . .	. . .
Other sectors	4 684	. . .	. . .	. . .	. . .	. . .	. . .	. . .	. . .
Financial derivatives	4 690	. . .	. . .	. . .	. . .	. . .	. . .	. . .	. . .
Monetary authorities	4 691	. . .	. . .	. . .	. . .	. . .	. . .	. . .	. . .
General government	4 692	. . .	. . .	. . .	. . .	. . .	. . .	. . .	. . .
Banks	4 693	. . .	. . .	. . .	. . .	. . .	. . .	. . .	. . .
Other sectors	4 694	. . .	. . .	. . .	. . .	. . .	. . .	. . .	. . .

Table 2 (Concluded). STANDARD PRESENTATION, 1988–95
(Millions of U.S. dollars)

	Code	1988	1989	1990	1991	1992	1993	1994	1995
C. OTHER INVESTMENT	4 700 . .	644.0	604.0	591.8	–63.5	631.0	550.6	. . .	. . .
Assets	4 703 . .	**. . .**	**. . .**	**–348.8**	**–190.2**	**–255.5**	**–92.9**	**. . .**	**. . .**
Trade credits	4 706 . .	. . .	. . .	. . .	. . .	. . .	. . .	. . .	. . .
General government: long-term	4 708 . .	. . .	. . .	. . .	. . .	. . .	. . .	. . .	. . .
General government: short-term	4 709 . .	. . .	. . .	. . .	. . .	. . .	. . .	. . .	. . .
Other sectors: long-term	4 711 . .	. . .	. . .	. . .	. . .	. . .	. . .	. . .	. . .
Other sectors: short-term	4 712 . .	. . .	. . .	. . .	. . .	. . .	. . .	. . .	. . .
Loans	4 714 . .	. . .	. . .	–164.6	100.7	–156.2	95.8	. . .	. . .
Monetary authorities: long-term	4 717 . .	. . .	. . .	. . .	. . .	. . .	. . .	. . .	. . .
Monetary authorities: short-term	4 718 . .	. . .	. . .	. . .	. . .	. . .	. . .	. . .	. . .
General government: long-term	4 720 . .	. . .	. . .	. . .	. . .	. . .	. . .	. . .	. . .
General government: short-term	4 721 . .	. . .	. . .	. . .	. . .	. . .	. . .	. . .	. . .
Banks: long-term	4 723 . .	. . .	. . .	. . .	. . .	. . .	. . .	. . .	. . .
Banks: short-term	4 724 . .	. . .	. . .	. . .	. . .	. . .	. . .	. . .	. . .
Other sectors: long-term	4 726 . .	. . .	. . .	. . .	. . .	. . .	. . .	. . .	. . .
Other sectors: short-term	4 727 . .	. . .	. . .	–164.6	100.7	–156.2	95.8	. . .	. . .
Currency and deposits	4 730 . .	. . .	. . .	–184.2	–290.9	–99.3	–188.7	. . .	. . .
Monetary authorities	4 731 . .	. . .	. . .	. . .	. . .	. . .	. . .	. . .	. . .
General government	4 732 . .	. . .	. . .	. . .	. . .	–52.6	–156.0	. . .	. . .
Banks	4 733 . .	. . .	. . .	. . .	. . .	. . .	10.0	. . .	. . .
Other sectors	4 734 . .	. . .	. . .	–184.2	–290.9	–46.7	–42.7	. . .	. . .
Other assets	4 736 . .	. . .	. . .	. . .	. . .	. . .	. . .	. . .	. . .
Monetary authorities: long-term	4 738 . .	. . .	. . .	. . .	. . .	. . .	. . .	. . .	. . .
Monetary authorities: short-term	4 739 . .	. . .	. . .	. . .	. . .	. . .	. . .	. . .	. . .
General government: long-term	4 741 . .	. . .	. . .	. . .	. . .	. . .	. . .	. . .	. . .
General government: short-term	4 742 . .	. . .	. . .	. . .	. . .	. . .	. . .	. . .	. . .
Banks: long-term	4 744 . .	. . .	. . .	. . .	. . .	. . .	. . .	. . .	. . .
Banks: short-term	4 745 . .	. . .	. . .	. . .	. . .	. . .	. . .	. . .	. . .
Other sectors: long-term	4 747 . .	. . .	. . .	. . .	. . .	. . .	. . .	. . .	. . .
Other sectors: short-term	4 748 . .	. . .	. . .	. . .	. . .	. . .	. . .	. . .	. . .
Liabilities	4 753 . .	**644.0**	**604.0**	**940.6**	**126.7**	**886.5**	**643.5**	**. . .**	**. . .**
Trade credits	4 756 . .	. . .	. . .	. . .	. . .	. . .	. . .	. . .	. . .
General government: long-term	4 758 . .	. . .	. . .	. . .	. . .	. . .	. . .	. . .	. . .
General government: short-term	4 759 . .	. . .	. . .	. . .	. . .	. . .	. . .	. . .	. . .
Other sectors: long-term	4 761 . .	. . .	. . .	. . .	. . .	. . .	. . .	. . .	. . .
Other sectors: short-term	4 762 . .	. . .	. . .	. . .	. . .	. . .	. . .	. . .	. . .
Loans	4 764 . .	–323.0	1,499.0	382.3	–1,331.0	–453.0	–486.1	. . .	. . .
Use of Fund credit and loans from the Fund	4 766 . .	. . .	. . .	. . .	. . .	. . .	. . .	. . .	. . .
Monetary authorities: other long-term	4 767 . .	. . .	. . .	. . .	88.2	27.8	–30.2	. . .	. . .
Monetary authorities: short-term	4 768 . .	. . .	. . .	. . .	. . .	. . .	. . .	. . .	. . .
General government: long-term	4 770 . .	–323.0	1,499.0	347.4	–1,029.4	–526.1	–796.8	. . .	. . .
General government: short-term	4 771 . .	. . .	. . .	247.9	13.8	143.2	258.7	. . .	. . .
Banks: long-term	4 773 . .	. . .	. . .	10.0	. . .	–.1	.3	. . .	. . .
Banks: short-term	4 774 . .	. . .	. . .	. . .	. . .	. . .	. . .	. . .	. . .
Other sectors: long-term	4 776 . .	. . .	. . .	39.2	–241.4	–101.8	–1.8	. . .	. . .
Other sectors: short-term	4 777 . .	. . .	. . .	–262.2	–162.2	4.0	83.7	. . .	. . .
Currency and deposits	4 780 . .	. . .	. . .	23.8	–1.3	–9.5	.3	. . .	. . .
Monetary authorities	4 781 . .	. . .	. . .	. . .	. . .	. . .	. . .	. . .	. . .
General government	4 782 . .	. . .	. . .	. . .	. . .	. . .	. . .	. . .	. . .
Banks	4 783 . .	. . .	. . .	23.8	–1.3	–9.5	.3	. . .	. . .
Other sectors	4 784 . .	. . .	. . .	. . .	. . .	. . .	. . .	. . .	. . .
Other liabilities	4 786 . .	967.0	–895.0	534.5	1,459.0	1,349.0	1,129.3	. . .	. . .
Monetary authorities: long-term	4 788 . .	. . .	. . .	. . .	. . .	. . .	. . .	. . .	. . .
Monetary authorities: short-term	4 789 . .	. . .	. . .	. . .	122.6	98.6	57.2	. . .	. . .
General government: long-term	4 791 . .	. . .	. . .	. . .	. . .	. . .	. . .	. . .	. . .
General government: short-term	4 792 . .	967.0	–895.0	522.9	1,249.4	998.9	1,114.2	. . .	. . .
Banks: long-term	4 794 . .	. . .	. . .	. . .	. . .	. . .	. . .	. . .	. . .
Banks: short-term	4 795 . .	. . .	. . .	. . .	. . .	. . .	. . .	. . .	. . .
Other sectors: long-term	4 797 . .	. . .	. . .	. . .	. . .	. . .	. . .	. . .	. . .
Other sectors: short-term	4 798 . .	. . .	. . .	11.6	87.0	251.5	–42.1	. . .	. . .
D. RESERVE ASSETS	4 800 . .	–49.0	6.0	–1.5	–48.3	–227.2	192.9	. . .	. . .
Monetary gold	4 810 . .	. . .	. . .	. . .	. . .	. . .	5.4	. . .	. . .
Special drawing rights	4 820 . .	. . .	. . .	–.1	. . .	. . .	. . .	. . .	. . .
Reserve position in the Fund	4 830 . .	. . .	. . .	. . .	. . .	. . .	. . .	. . .	. . .
Foreign exchange	4 840 . .	–49.0	6.0	–1.4	–48.3	–227.2	187.5	. . .	. . .
Other claims	4 880 . .	. . .	. . .	. . .	. . .	. . .	. . .	. . .	. . .
NET ERRORS AND OMISSIONS	4 998 . .	**–257.0**	**–678.0**	**–19.1**	**26.9**	**43.0**	**–277.1**	**. . .**	**. . .**

Table 1. ANALYTIC PRESENTATION, 1988–95
(Millions of U.S. dollars)

	Code	1988	1989	1990	1991	1992	1993	1994	1995
A. Current Account [1]	4 993 Y .	**. . .**	**. . .**	**–8.51**	**–7.89**	**–16.72**	**–12.77**	**–10.32**	**. . .**
Goods: exports f.o.b	2 100 . .	. . .	. . .	.37	.46	.62	1.14	1.64	. . .
Goods: imports f.o.b	3 100 . .	. . .	. . .	–28.68	–28.21	–33.59	–34.36	–38.28	. . .
Balance on Goods	4 100 . .	. . .	. . .	*–28.31*	*–27.75*	*–32.97*	*–33.22*	*–36.64*	. . .
Services: credit	2 200 . .	. . .	. . .	40.80	42.90	45.01	53.40	61.56	. . .
Services: debit	3 200 . .	. . .	. . .	–14.73	–16.61	–22.20	–25.70	–24.40	. . .
Balance on Goods and Services	4 991 . .	. . .	. . .	*–2.24*	*–1.45*	*–10.15*	*–5.52*	*.52*	. . .
Income: credit	2 300 . .	. . .	. . .	1.86	1.13	1.00	1.11	1.47	. . .
Income: debit	3 300 . .	. . .	. . .	–7.64	–6.66	–8.08	–9.16	–10.77	. . .
Balance on Goods, Services, and Income	4 992 . .	. . .	. . .	*–8.03*	*–6.99*	*–17.23*	*–13.57*	*–8.79*	. . .
Current transfers: credit	2 379 Y .	. . .	. . .	3.15	4.04	6.05	7.28	5.14	. . .
Current transfers: debit	3 379 . .	. . .	. . .	–3.63	–4.95	–5.54	–6.48	–6.67	. . .
B. Capital Account [1]	4 994 Y .	**. . .**	**. . .**	**3.40**	**2.84**	**5.37**	**5.67**	**5.93**	**. . .**
Capital account: credit	2 994 Y .	. . .	. . .	4.29	3.77	6.37	6.97	7.24	. . .
Capital account: debit	3 994 . .	. . .	. . .	–.88	–.93	–1.00	–1.30	–1.31	. . .
Total, Groups A Plus B	4 010 . .	. . .	. . .	*–5.10*	*–5.06*	*–11.35*	*–7.10*	*–4.39*	. . .
C. Financial Account [1]	4 995 X .	**. . .**	**. . .**	**22.23**	**8.96**	**12.02**	**4.31**	**8.41**	**. . .**
Direct investment abroad	4 505 . .	. . .	. . .	. . .	. . .	. . .	. . .	. . .	. . .
Direct investment in Anguilla	4 555 Y .	. . .	. . .	10.82	6.11	15.42	6.45	12.59	. . .
Portfolio investment assets	4 602 . .	. . .	. . .	. . .	. . .	. . .	.05	. . .	. . .
Equity securities	4 610 . .	. . .	. . .	. . .	. . .	. . .	.05	. . .	. . .
Debt securities	4 619 . .	. . .	. . .	. . .	. . .	. . .	. . .	. . .	. . .
Portfolio investment liabilities	4 652 Y .	. . .	. . .	. . .	. . .	. . .	. . .	. . .	. . .
Equity securities	4 660 Y .	. . .	. . .	. . .	. . .	. . .	. . .	. . .	. . .
Debt securities	4 669 Y .	. . .	. . .	. . .	. . .	. . .	. . .	. . .	. . .
Other investment assets	4 703 . .	. . .	. . .	10.19	2.15	3.77	–2.80	–3.33	. . .
Monetary authorities	4 703 . A	. . .	. . .	. . .	. . .	. . .	. . .	. . .	. . .
General government	4 703 . B	. . .	. . .	. . .	. . .	. . .	. . .	. . .	. . .
Banks	4 703 . C	. . .	. . .	10.19	2.15	3.77	–2.80	–3.33	. . .
Other sectors	4 703 . D	. . .	. . .	. . .	. . .	. . .	. . .	. . .	. . .
Other investment liabilities	4 753 X .	. . .	. . .	1.22	.69	–7.17	.61	–.84	. . .
Monetary authorities	4 753 XA	. . .	. . .	. . .	. . .	. . .	. . .	. . .	. . .
General government	4 753 YB	. . .	. . .	1.22	.81	.43	.94	–.37	. . .
Banks	4 753 YC	. . .	. . .	. . .	. . .	. . .	. . .	. . .	. . .
Other sectors	4 753 YD	. . .	. . .	. . .	–.13	–7.60	–.33	–.47	. . .
Total, Groups A Through C	4 020 . .	. . .	. . .	*17.12*	*3.90*	*.67*	*–2.79*	*4.02*	. . .
D. Net Errors and Omissions	4 998 . .	**. . .**	**. . .**	**–14.16**	**–4.07**	**.52**	**3.97**	**–4.19**	**. . .**
Total, Groups A Through D	4 030 . .	. . .	. . .	*2.96*	*–.17*	*1.19*	*1.19*	*–.17*	. . .
E. Reserves and Related Items	4 040 . .	**. . .**	**. . .**	**–2.96**	**.17**	**–1.19**	**–1.19**	**.17**	**. . .**
Reserve assets	4 800 . .	. . .	. . .	–2.96	.17	–1.19	–1.19	.17	. . .
Use of Fund credit and loans	4 766 . .	. . .	. . .	. . .	. . .	. . .	. . .	. . .	. . .
Liabilities constituting foreign authorities' reserves	4 900 . .	. . .	. . .	. . .	. . .	. . .	. . .	. . .	. . .
Exceptional financing	4 920 . .	. . .	. . .	. . .	. . .	. . .	. . .	. . .	. . .
Conversion rates: Eastern Caribbean dollars per U.S. dollar	0 101 . .	**2.7000**	**2.7000**	**2.7000**	**2.7000**	**2.7000**	**2.7000**	**2.7000**	**2.7000**

[1] Excludes components that have been classified in the categories of Group E.

Table 2. STANDARD PRESENTATION, 1988–95
(Millions of U.S. dollars)

	Code		1988	1989	1990	1991	1992	1993	1994	1995
CURRENT ACCOUNT	4 993	. .	**. . .**	**. . .**	**–8.51**	**–7.89**	**–16.72**	**–12.77**	**–10.32**	**. . .**
A. GOODS	4 100	. .	. . .	. . .	–28.31	–27.75	–32.97	–33.22	–36.64	. . .
Credit	2 100	. .	**. . .**	**. . .**	**.37**	**.46**	**.62**	**1.14**	**1.64**	**. . .**
General merchandise: exports f.o.b.	2 110	. .	. . .	. . .	.37	.46	.62	1.14	1.63	. . .
Goods for processing: exports f.o.b.	2 150	. .	. . .	. . .	. . .	. . .	. . .	. . .	. . .	. . .
Repairs on goods	2 160	. .	. . .	. . .	. . .	. . .	. . .	. . .	. . .	. . .
Goods procured in ports by carriers	2 170	. .	. . .	. . .	. . .	. . .	. . .	. . .	. . .	. . .
Nonmonetary gold	2 180	. .	. . .	. . .	. . .	. . .	. . .	. . .	. . .	. . .
Debit	3 100	. .	**. . .**	**. . .**	**–28.68**	**–28.21**	**–33.59**	**–34.36**	**–38.28**	**. . .**
General merchandise: imports f.o.b.	3 110	. .	. . .	. . .	–28.68	–28.11	–33.47	–34.24	–38.13	. . .
Goods for processing: imports f.o.b.	3 150	. .	. . .	. . .	. . .	. . .	. . .	. . .	. . .	. . .
Repairs on goods	3 160	. .	. . .	. . .	. . .	. . .	. . .	. . .	. . .	. . .
Goods procured in ports by carriers	3 170	. .	. . .	. . .	. . .	–.10	–.11	–.11	–.15	. . .
Nonmonetary gold	3 180	. .	. . .	. . .	. . .	. . .	. . .	. . .	. . .	. . .
B. SERVICES	4 200	. .	. . .	. . .	26.07	26.30	22.82	27.70	37.16	. . .
Total credit	2 200	. .	. . .	. . .	*40.80*	*42.90*	*45.01*	*53.40*	*61.56*	. . .
Total debit	3 200	. .	. . .	. . .	*–14.73*	*–16.61*	*–22.20*	*–25.70*	*–24.40*	. . .
Transportation services, credit	2 205	. .	**. . .**	**. . .**	**.25**	**.95**	**.90**	**1.05**	**1.33**	**. . .**
Passenger	2 205	BA	. . .	. . .	. . .	*.37*	*.43*	*.40*	*.55*	. . .
Freight	2 205	BB	. . .	. . .	. . .	*.07*	. . .	. . .	*.01*	. . .
Other	2 205	BC	. . .	. . .	*.25*	*.51*	*.47*	*.64*	*.77*	. . .
Sea transport, passenger	2 207	. .	. . .	. . .	. . .	. . .	. . .	. . .	. . .	. . .
Sea transport, freight	2 208	. .	. . .	. . .	. . .	. . .	. . .	. . .	. . .	. . .
Sea transport, other	2 209	. .	. . .	. . .	. . .	. . .	. . .	. . .	. . .	. . .
Air transport, passenger	2 211	. .	. . .	. . .	. . .	. . .	. . .	. . .	. . .	. . .
Air transport, freight	2 212	. .	. . .	. . .	. . .	. . .	. . .	. . .	. . .	. . .
Air transport, other	2 213	. .	. . .	. . .	. . .	. . .	. . .	. . .	. . .	. . .
Other transport, passenger	2 215	. .	. . .	. . .	. . .	. . .	. . .	. . .	. . .	. . .
Other transport, freight	2 216	. .	. . .	. . .	. . .	. . .	. . .	. . .	. . .	. . .
Other transport, other	2 217	. .	. . .	. . .	. . .	. . .	. . .	. . .	. . .	. . .
Transportation services, debit	3 205	. .	**. . .**	**. . .**	**–5.11**	**–5.74**	**–7.42**	**–8.94**	**–9.51**	**. . .**
Passenger	3 205	BA	. . .	. . .	*–1.85*	*–2.46*	*–3.50*	*–4.94*	*–5.00*	. . .
Freight	3 205	BB	. . .	. . .	*–3.26*	*–3.17*	*–3.81*	*–3.91*	*–4.41*	. . .
Other	3 205	BC	. . .	. . .	. . .	*–.10*	*–.11*	*–.09*	*–.10*	. . .
Sea transport, passenger	3 207	. .	. . .	. . .	. . .	. . .	. . .	. . .	. . .	. . .
Sea transport, freight	3 208	. .	. . .	. . .	. . .	. . .	. . .	. . .	. . .	. . .
Sea transport, other	3 209	. .	. . .	. . .	. . .	. . .	. . .	. . .	. . .	. . .
Air transport, passenger	3 211	. .	. . .	. . .	. . .	. . .	. . .	. . .	. . .	. . .
Air transport, freight	3 212	. .	. . .	. . .	. . .	. . .	. . .	. . .	. . .	. . .
Air transport, other	3 213	. .	. . .	. . .	. . .	. . .	. . .	. . .	. . .	. . .
Other transport, passenger	3 215	. .	. . .	. . .	. . .	. . .	. . .	. . .	. . .	. . .
Other transport, freight	3 216	. .	. . .	. . .	. . .	. . .	. . .	. . .	. . .	. . .
Other transport, other	3 217	. .	. . .	. . .	. . .	. . .	. . .	. . .	. . .	. . .
Travel, credit	2 236	. .	**. . .**	**. . .**	**36.00**	**39.10**	**39.61**	**48.88**	**56.30**	**. . .**
Business travel	2 237	. .	. . .	. . .	. . .	. . .	. . .	. . .	. . .	. . .
Personal travel	2 240	. .	. . .	. . .	. . .	. . .	. . .	. . .	. . .	. . .
Travel, debit	3 236	. .	**. . .**	**. . .**	**–3.70**	**–3.48**	**–3.77**	**–4.77**	**–5.70**	**. . .**
Business travel	3 237	. .	. . .	. . .	. . .	. . .	. . .	. . .	. . .	. . .
Personal travel	3 240	. .	. . .	. . .	. . .	. . .	. . .	. . .	. . .	. . .
Other services, credit	2 200	BA	**. . .**	**. . .**	**4.56**	**2.86**	**4.50**	**3.47**	**3.94**	**. . .**
Communications	2 245	. .	. . .	. . .	. . .	. . .	. . .	. . .	. . .	. . .
Construction	2 249	. .	. . .	. . .	. . .	.23	1.12	. . .	. . .	. . .
Insurance	2 253	. .	. . .	. . .	. . .	.18	.24	.17	.17	. . .
Financial	2 260	. .	. . .	. . .	. . .	. . .	. . .	. . .	. . .	. . .
Computer and information	2 262	. .	. . .	. . .	. . .	. . .	. . .	. . .	. . .	. . .
Royalties and licence fees	2 266	. .	. . .	. . .	. . .	.14	.51	.43	.43	. . .
Other business services	2 268	. .	. . .	. . .	4.56	2.31	2.62	2.87	3.34	. . .
Personal, cultural, and recreational	2 287	. .	. . .	. . .	. . .	. . .	. . .	. . .	. . .	. . .
Government, n.i.e.	2 291	. .	. . .	. . .	. . .	. . .	. . .	. . .	. . .	. . .
Other services, debit	3 200	BA	**. . .**	**. . .**	**–5.92**	**–7.39**	**–11.01**	**–11.98**	**–9.18**	**. . .**
Communications	3 245	. .	. . .	. . .	. . .	. . .	. . .	. . .	. . .	. . .
Construction	3 249	. .	. . .	. . .	. . .	. . .	. . .	. . .	. . .	. . .
Insurance	3 253	. .	. . .	. . .	. . .	–.72	–.86	–.87	–1.09	. . .
Financial	3 260	. .	. . .	. . .	. . .	. . .	. . .	. . .	. . .	. . .
Computer and information	3 262	. .	. . .	. . .	. . .	. . .	. . .	. . .	. . .	. . .
Royalties and licence fees	3 266	. .	. . .	. . .	. . .	. . .	. . .	. . .	–.07	. . .
Other business services	3 268	. .	. . .	. . .	–5.92	–5.93	–7.50	–7.95	–7.45	. . .
Personal, cultural, and recreational	3 287	. .	. . .	. . .	. . .	. . .	. . .	. . .	. . .	. . .
Government, n.i.e.	3 291	. .	. . .	. . .	. . .	–.74	–2.65	–3.16	–.57	. . .

Table 2 (Continued). STANDARD PRESENTATION, 1988–95
(Millions of U.S. dollars)

	Code	1988	1989	1990	1991	1992	1993	1994	1995
C. INCOME	4 300 . .	...	...	–5.79	–5.54	–7.08	–8.06	–9.30	...
Total credit	2 300 . .	...	...	*1.86*	*1.13*	*1.00*	*1.11*	*1.47*	...
Total debit	3 300 . .	...	...	*–7.64*	*–6.66*	*–8.08*	*–9.16*	*–10.77*	...
Compensation of employees, credit	2 310 . .	...	...	...	...	...	...	...	...
Compensation of employees, debit	3 310 . .	...	...	...	...	...	...	...	...
Investment income, credit	2 320 . .	...	...	**1.86**	**1.13**	**1.00**	**1.11**	**1.47**	...
Direct investment income	2 330 . .	...	...	...	...	...	...	...	...
Dividends and distributed branch profits	2 332 . .	...	...	...	...	...	...	...	...
Reinvested earnings and undistributed branch profits	2 333 . .	...	...	...	...	...	...	...	...
Income on debt (interest)	2 334 . .	...	...	...	...	...	...	...	...
Portfolio investment income	2 339 . .	...	...	...	...	...	...	...	...
Income on equity	2 340 . .	...	...	...	...	...	...	...	...
Income on bonds and notes	2 350 . .	...	...	...	...	...	...	...	...
Income on money market instruments and financial derivatives	2 360 . .	...	...	...	...	...	...	...	...
Other investment income	2 370 . .	...	...	1.86	1.13	1.00	1.11	1.47	...
Investment income, debit	3 320 . .	...	...	**–7.64**	**–6.66**	**–8.08**	**–9.16**	**–10.77**	...
Direct investment income	3 330 . .	...	...	–7.03	–5.96	–7.12	–7.84	–9.20	...
Dividends and distributed branch profits	3 332 . .	...	...	–1.85	–3.90	–4.79	–5.12	–4.77	...
Reinvested earnings and undistributed branch profits	3 333 . .	...	...	–5.19	–1.92	–2.10	–1.60	–3.18	...
Income on debt (interest)	3 334 . .	...	...	...	–.14	–.23	–1.12	–1.25	...
Portfolio investment income	3 339 . .	...	...	...	...	...	...	...	...
Income on equity	3 340 . .	...	...	...	...	...	...	...	...
Income on bonds and notes	3 350 . .	...	...	...	...	...	...	...	...
Income on money market instruments and financial derivatives	3 360 . .	...	...	...	...	...	...	...	...
Other investment income	3 370 . .	...	...	–.61	–.70	–.96	–1.32	–1.57	...
D. CURRENT TRANSFERS	4 379 . .	...	...	–.48	–.90	.51	.80	–1.54	...
Credit	2 379 . .	...	...	**3.15**	**4.04**	**6.05**	**7.28**	**5.14**	...
General government	2 380 . .	...	...	...	.91	2.39	2.86	.59	...
Other sectors	2 390 . .	...	...	3.15	3.13	3.66	4.42	4.55	...
Workers' remittances	2 391 . .	...	...	3.15	3.13	3.66	4.41	4.54	...
Other current transfers	2 392 . .	...	...	...	...	...	.01	.01	...
Debit	3 379 . .	...	...	**–3.63**	**–4.95**	**–5.54**	**–6.48**	**–6.67**	...
General government	3 380 . .	...	...	–.10	–.14	–.16	–.12	–.17	...
Other sectors	3 390 . .	...	...	–3.53	–4.81	–5.38	–6.36	–6.50	...
Workers' remittances	3 391 . .	...	...	–3.53	–3.72	–3.99	–5.19	–5.24	...
Other current transfers	3 392 . .	...	...	...	–1.09	–1.39	–1.16	–1.26	...
CAPITAL AND FINANCIAL ACCOUNT	4 996 . .	...	...	**22.67**	**11.96**	**16.20**	**8.80**	**14.51**	...
CAPITAL ACCOUNT	4 994 . .	...	...	**3.40**	**2.84**	**5.37**	**5.67**	**5.93**	...
Total credit	2 994 . .	...	...	*4.29*	*3.77*	*6.37*	*6.97*	*7.24*	...
Total debit	3 994 . .	...	...	*–.88*	*–.93*	*–1.00*	*–1.30*	*–1.31*	...
Capital transfers, credit	2 400 . .	...	...	**4.29**	**3.77**	**6.37**	**6.97**	**7.24**	...
General government	2 401 . .	...	...	1.14	.64	2.71	2.56	2.70	...
Debt forgiveness	2 402 . .	...	...	...	...	...	...	...	...
Other capital transfers	2 410 . .	...	...	1.14	.64	2.71	2.56	2.70	...
Other sectors	2 430 . .	...	...	3.15	3.13	3.66	4.41	4.54	...
Migrants' transfers	2 431 . .	...	...	3.15	3.13	3.66	4.41	4.54	...
Debt forgiveness	2 432 . .	...	...	...	...	...	...	...	...
Other capital transfers	2 440 . .	...	...	...	...	...	...	...	...
Capital transfers, debit	3 400 . .	...	...	**–.88**	**–.93**	**–1.00**	**–1.30**	**–1.31**	...
General government	3 401 . .	...	...	...	...	...	...	...	...
Debt forgiveness	3 402 . .	...	...	...	...	...	...	...	...
Other capital transfers	3 410 . .	...	...	...	...	...	...	...	...
Other sectors	3 430 . .	...	...	–.88	–.93	–1.00	–1.30	–1.31	...
Migrants' transfers	3 431 . .	...	...	–.88	–.93	–1.00	–1.30	–1.31	...
Debt forgiveness	3 432 . .	...	...	...	...	...	...	...	...
Other capital transfers	3 440 . .	...	...	...	...	...	...	...	...
Nonproduced nonfinancial assets, credit	2 480 . .	...	...	...	...	...	...	...	...
Nonproduced nonfinancial assets, debit	3 480 . .	...	...	...	...	...	...	...	...

Table 2 (Continued). STANDARD PRESENTATION, 1988–95
(Millions of U.S. dollars)

	Code	1988	1989	1990	1991	1992	1993	1994	1995
FINANCIAL ACCOUNT	4 995	...	...	**19.26**	**9.12**	**10.83**	**3.13**	**8.58**	...
A. DIRECT INVESTMENT	4 500	...	...	10.82	6.11	15.42	6.45	12.59	...
Direct investment abroad	4 505	...	...	...	...	...	...	...	...
Equity capital	4 510	...	...	...	...	...	...	...	...
Claims on affiliated enterprises	4 515	...	...	...	...	...	...	...	...
Liabilities to affiliated enterprises	4 520	...	...	...	...	...	...	...	...
Reinvested earnings	4 525	...	...	...	...	...	...	...	...
Other capital	4 530	...	...	...	...	...	...	...	...
Claims on affiliated enterprises	4 535	...	...	...	...	...	...	...	...
Liabilities to affiliated enterprises	4 540	...	...	...	...	...	...	...	...
Direct investment in Anguilla	4 555	...	...	**10.82**	**6.11**	**15.42**	**6.45**	**12.59**	...
Equity capital	4 560	...	...	...	.19	...	.84	1.20	...
Claims on direct investors	4 565	...	...	...	...	...	...	...	...
Liabilities to direct investors	4 570	...	...	...	...	...	...	...	...
Reinvested earnings	4 575	...	...	5.19	1.92	2.10	1.60	3.18	...
Other capital	4 580	...	...	5.63	4.01	13.32	4.00	8.21	...
Claims on direct investors	4 585	...	...	...	...	...	...	...	...
Liabilities to direct investors	4 590	...	...	...	...	...	...	...	...
B. PORTFOLIO INVESTMENT	4 600	...	...	...	...	...	.05	...	...
Assets	4 602	...	...	...	...	...	**.05**	...	...
Equity securities	4 610	...	...	...	...	...	.05	...	...
Monetary authorities	4 611	...	...	...	...	...	...	...	...
General government	4 612	...	...	...	...	...	...	...	...
Banks	4 613	...	...	...	...	...	...	...	...
Other sectors	4 614	...	...	...	...	...	...	...	...
Debt securities	4 619	...	...	...	...	...	...	...	...
Bonds and notes	4 620	...	...	...	...	...	...	...	...
Monetary authorities	4 621	...	...	...	...	...	...	...	...
General government	4 622	...	...	...	...	...	...	...	...
Banks	4 623	...	...	...	...	...	...	...	...
Other sectors	4 624	...	...	...	...	...	...	...	...
Money market instruments	4 630	...	...	...	...	...	...	...	...
Monetary authorities	4 631	...	...	...	...	...	...	...	...
General government	4 632	...	...	...	...	...	...	...	...
Banks	4 633	...	...	...	...	...	...	...	...
Other sectors	4 634	...	...	...	...	...	...	...	...
Financial derivatives	4 640	...	...	...	...	...	...	...	...
Monetary authorities	4 641	...	...	...	...	...	...	...	...
General government	4 642	...	...	...	...	...	...	...	...
Banks	4 643	...	...	...	...	...	...	...	...
Other sectors	4 644	...	...	...	...	...	...	...	...
Liabilities	4 652	...	...	...	...	...	...	...	...
Equity securities	4 660	...	...	...	...	...	...	...	...
Banks	4 663	...	...	...	...	...	...	...	...
Other sectors	4 664	...	...	...	...	...	...	...	...
Debt securities	4 669	...	...	...	...	...	...	...	...
Bonds and notes	4 670	...	...	...	...	...	...	...	...
Monetary authorities	4 671	...	...	...	...	...	...	...	...
General government	4 672	...	...	...	...	...	...	...	...
Banks	4 673	...	...	...	...	...	...	...	...
Other sectors	4 674	...	...	...	...	...	...	...	...
Money market instruments	4 680	...	...	...	...	...	...	...	...
Monetary authorities	4 681	...	...	...	...	...	...	...	...
General government	4 682	...	...	...	...	...	...	...	...
Banks	4 683	...	...	...	...	...	...	...	...
Other sectors	4 684	...	...	...	...	...	...	...	...
Financial derivatives	4 690	...	...	...	...	...	...	...	...
Monetary authorities	4 691	...	...	...	...	...	...	...	...
General government	4 692	...	...	...	...	...	...	...	...
Banks	4 693	...	...	...	...	...	...	...	...
Other sectors	4 694	...	...	...	...	...	...	...	...

Table 2 (Concluded). STANDARD PRESENTATION, 1988–95
(Millions of U.S. dollars)

	Code	1988	1989	1990	1991	1992	1993	1994	1995
C. OTHER INVESTMENT	4 700	...	...	11.41	2.84	–3.40	–2.18	–4.17	...
Assets	4 703	...	...	**10.19**	**2.15**	**3.77**	**–2.80**	**–3.33**	...
Trade credits	4 706	...	...	...	...	...	...	...	...
General government: long-term	4 708	...	...	...	...	...	...	...	...
General government: short-term	4 709	...	...	...	...	...	...	...	...
Other sectors: long-term	4 711	...	...	...	...	...	...	...	...
Other sectors: short-term	4 712	...	...	...	...	...	...	...	...
Loans	4 714	...	...	...	...	...	...	...	...
Monetary authorities: long-term	4 717	...	...	...	...	...	...	...	...
Monetary authorities: short-term	4 718	...	...	...	...	...	...	...	...
General government: long-term	4 720	...	...	...	...	...	...	...	...
General government: short-term	4 721	...	...	...	...	...	...	...	...
Banks: long-term	4 723	...	...	...	...	...	...	...	...
Banks: short-term	4 724	...	...	...	...	...	...	...	...
Other sectors: long-term	4 726	...	...	...	...	...	...	...	...
Other sectors: short-term	4 727	...	...	...	...	...	...	...	...
Currency and deposits	4 730	...	...	10.19	2.15	3.77	–2.80	–3.33	...
Monetary authorities	4 731	...	...	...	...	...	...	...	...
General government	4 732	...	...	...	...	...	...	...	...
Banks	4 733	...	...	10.19	2.15	3.77	–2.80	–3.33	...
Other sectors	4 734	...	...	...	...	...	...	...	...
Other assets	4 736	...	...	...	...	...	...	...	...
Monetary authorities: long-term	4 738	...	...	...	...	...	...	...	...
Monetary authorities: short-term	4 739	...	...	...	...	...	...	...	...
General government: long-term	4 741	...	...	...	...	...	...	...	...
General government: short-term	4 742	...	...	...	...	...	...	...	...
Banks: long-term	4 744	...	...	...	...	...	...	...	...
Banks: short-term	4 745	...	...	...	...	...	...	...	...
Other sectors: long-term	4 747	...	...	...	...	...	...	...	...
Other sectors: short-term	4 748	...	...	...	...	...	...	...	...
Liabilities	4 753	...	...	**1.22**	**.69**	**–7.17**	**.61**	**–.84**	...
Trade credits	4 756	...	...	...	...	...	...	...	...
General government: long-term	4 758	...	...	...	...	...	...	...	...
General government: short-term	4 759	...	...	...	...	...	...	...	...
Other sectors: long-term	4 761	...	...	...	...	...	...	...	...
Other sectors: short-term	4 762	...	...	...	...	...	...	...	...
Loans	4 764	...	...	1.22	.69	–7.17	.61	–.84	...
Use of Fund credit and loans from the Fund	4 766	...	...	...	...	...	...	...	...
Monetary authorities: other long term	4 767	...	...	...	...	...	...	...	...
Monetary authorities: short-term	4 768	...	...	...	...	...	...	...	...
General government: long-term	4 770	...	...	1.22	.81	.43	.94	–.37	...
General government: short-term	4 771	...	...	...	...	...	...	...	...
Banks: long-term	4 773	...	...	...	...	...	...	...	...
Banks: short-term	4 774	...	...	...	...	...	...	...	...
Other sectors: long-term	4 776	...	...	...	–.13	–7.60	–.33	–.47	...
Other sectors: short-term	4 777	...	...	...	...	...	...	...	...
Currency and deposits	4 780	...	...	...	...	...	...	...	...
Monetary authorities	4 781	...	...	...	...	...	...	...	...
General government	4 782	...	...	...	...	...	...	...	...
Banks	4 783	...	...	...	...	...	...	...	...
Other sectors	4 784	...	...	...	...	...	...	...	...
Other liabilities	4 786	...	...	...	...	...	...	...	...
Monetary authorities: long-term	4 788	...	...	...	...	...	...	...	...
Monetary authorities: short-term	4 789	...	...	...	...	...	...	...	...
General government: long-term	4 791	...	...	...	...	...	...	...	...
General government: short-term	4 792	...	...	...	...	...	...	...	...
Banks: long-term	4 794	...	...	...	...	...	...	...	...
Banks: short-term	4 795	...	...	...	...	...	...	...	...
Other sectors: long-term	4 797	...	...	...	...	...	...	...	...
Other sectors: short-term	4 798	...	...	...	...	...	...	...	...
D. RESERVE ASSETS	4 800	...	...	–2.96	.17	–1.19	–1.19	.17	...
Monetary gold	4 810	...	...	...	...	...	...	...	...
Special drawing rights	4 820	...	...	...	...	...	...	...	...
Reserve position in the Fund	4 830	...	...	...	...	...	...	...	...
Foreign exchange	4 840	...	...	–2.78	.20	–1.27	–1.07	.19	...
Other claims	4 880	...	...	–.19	–.04	.07	–.11	–.02	...
NET ERRORS AND OMISSIONS	4 998	...	...	**–14.16**	**–4.07**	**.52**	**3.97**	**–4.19**	...

Part 3 of the *Yearbook* contains descriptions of the methodologies, compilation practices, and sources used to compile these data.

Table 1. ANALYTIC PRESENTATION, 1988–95

(Millions of U.S. dollars)

	Code	1988	1989	1990	1991	1992	1993	1994	1995
A. Current Account[1]	4 993 Y.	**–45.04**	**–81.65**	**–30.99**	**–33.37**	**–20.64**	**–.55**	**–17.95**	**. . .**
Goods: exports f.o.b.	2 100 . .	28.19	29.14	33.43	49.50	64.70	62.08	44.45	. . .
Goods: imports f.o.b.	3 100 . .	–204.50	–246.33	–235.44	–258.79	–274.40	–282.58	–298.12	. . .
Balance on Goods	4 100 . .	*–176.31*	*–217.19*	*–202.01*	*–209.29*	*–209.70*	*–220.50*	*–253.67*	. . .
Services: credit	2 200 . .	237.33	261.79	311.87	320.20	342.57	377.20	396.31	. . .
Services: debit	3 200 . .	–79.30	–92.58	–105.12	–113.27	–122.73	–131.64	–134.93	. . .
Balance on Goods and Services	4 991 . .	*–18.27*	*–47.97*	*4.74*	*–2.36*	*10.14*	*25.06*	*7.71*	. . .
Income: credit	2 300 . .	1.43	1.20	2.49	2.66	3.70	3.11	4.26	. . .
Income: debit	3 300 . .	–33.06	–46.69	–47.81	–34.98	–33.36	–26.04	–30.81	. . .
Balance on Goods, Services, and Income	4 992 . .	*–49.90*	*–93.46*	*–40.59*	*–34.67*	*–19.52*	*2.13*	*–18.84*	. . .
Current transfers: credit	2 379 Y.	9.81	17.28	14.89	9.16	8.54	9.07	10.36	. . .
Current transfers: debit	3 379 . .	–4.94	–5.47	–5.29	–7.86	–9.66	–11.75	–9.47	. . .
B. Capital Account[1]	4 994 Y.	**5.49**	**6.74**	**5.21**	**6.43**	**5.74**	**6.81**	**5.91**	**. . .**
Capital account: credit	2 994 Y.	5.49	6.74	5.23	6.43	5.74	6.81	6.53	. . .
Capital account: debit	3 994 . .	. . .	. . .	–.02	. . .	. . .	. . .	–.62	. . .
Total, Groups A Plus B	4 010 . .	*–39.55*	*–74.91*	*–25.78*	*–26.94*	*–14.90*	*6.26*	*–12.04*	. . .
C. Financial Account[1]	4 995 X.	**45.83**	**76.80**	**60.57**	**46.44**	**39.95**	**.49**	**9.59**	**. . .**
Direct investment abroad	4 505 . .	. . .	. . .	. . .	. . .	. . .	. . .	. . .	. . .
Direct investment in Antigua and Barbuda	4 555 Y.	32.95	43.11	60.61	54.71	20.00	15.03	24.81	. . .
Portfolio investment assets	4 602 . .	. . .	. . .	. . .	. . .	. . .	. . .	–1.38	. . .
Equity securities	4 610 . .	. . .	. . .	. . .	. . .	. . .	. . .	–1.38	. . .
Debt securities	4 619 . .	. . .	. . .	. . .	. . .	. . .	. . .	. . .	. . .
Portfolio investment liabilities	4 652 Y.	. . .	. . .	. . .	. . .	. . .	. . .	. . .	. . .
Equity securities	4 660 Y.	. . .	. . .	. . .	. . .	. . .	. . .	. . .	. . .
Debt securities	4 669 Y.	. . .	. . .	. . .	. . .	. . .	. . .	. . .	. . .
Other investment assets	4 703 . .	–3.63	8.69	–2.15	–23.97	8.47	–18.53	–16.67	. . .
Monetary authorities	4 703 . A	. . .	. . .	. . .	. . .	. . .	. . .	. . .	. . .
General government	4 703 . B	. . .	. . .	. . .	. . .	. . .	. . .	. . .	. . .
Banks	4 703 . C	–3.63	8.69	–2.15	–23.97	8.47	–18.53	–16.67	. . .
Other sectors	4 703 . D	. . .	. . .	. . .	. . .	. . .	. . .	. . .	. . .
Other investment liabilities	4 753 X.	16.51	25.01	2.11	15.69	11.47	3.99	2.83	. . .
Monetary authorities	4 753 XA	. . .	. . .	. . .	. . .	. . .	. . .	. . .	. . .
General government	4 753 YB	20.23	28.03	9.27	17.56	6.42	.01	5.67	. . .
Banks	4 753 YC	. . .	. . .	. . .	. . .	. . .	. . .	. . .	. . .
Other sectors	4 753 YD	–3.72	–3.02	–7.15	–1.87	5.05	3.99	–2.84	. . .
Total, Groups A Through C	4 020 . .	*6.28*	*1.89*	*34.80*	*19.50*	*25.05*	*6.75*	*–2.45*	. . .
D. Net Errors and Omissions	4 998 . .	**–3.66**	**–1.85**	**–35.39**	**–14.40**	**–8.65**	**–17.95**	**10.53**	**. . .**
Total, Groups A Through D	4 030 . .	*2.62*	*.04*	*–.59*	*5.10*	*16.40*	*–11.20*	*8.08*	. . .
E. Reserves and Related Items	4 040 . .	**–2.62**	**–.04**	**.59**	**–5.10**	**–16.40**	**11.20**	**–8.08**	**. . .**
Reserve assets	4 800 . .	–2.62	–.04	.59	–5.10	–16.40	11.20	–8.08	. . .
Use of Fund credit and loans	4 766 . .	. . .	. . .	. . .	. . .	. . .	. . .	. . .	. . .
Liabilities constituting foreign authorities' reserves	4 900 . .	. . .	. . .	. . .	. . .	. . .	. . .	. . .	. . .
Exceptional financing	4 920 . .	. . .	. . .	. . .	. . .	. . .	. . .	. . .	. . .
Conversion rates: Eastern Caribbean dollars per U.S. dollar	0 101 . .	**2.7000**	**2.7000**	**2.7000**	**2.7000**	**2.7000**	**2.7000**	**2.7000**	**2.7000**

[1] Excludes components that have been classified in the categories of Group E.

Table 2. STANDARD PRESENTATION, 1988–95
(Millions of U.S. dollars)

	Code	1988	1989	1990	1991	1992	1993	1994	1995
CURRENT ACCOUNT	4 993 . .	**–45.04**	**–81.65**	**–30.99**	**–33.37**	**–20.64**	**–.55**	**–17.95**	. . .
A. GOODS	4 100 . .	–176.31	–217.19	–202.01	–209.29	–209.70	–220.50	–253.67	. . .
Credit	2 100 . .	**28.19**	**29.14**	**33.43**	**49.50**	**64.70**	**62.08**	**44.45**	. . .
General merchandise: exports f.o.b.	2 110 . .	17.00	15.70	18.98	35.43	49.77	47.27	27.42	. . .
Goods for processing: exports f.o.b.	2 150 . .	. . .	. . .	. . .	. . .	. . .	. . .	. . .	. . .
Repairs on goods	2 160 . .	. . .	. . .	. . .	. . .	. . .	. . .	. . .	. . .
Goods procured in ports by carriers	2 170 . .	11.19	13.44	14.44	14.07	14.93	14.81	17.03	. . .
Nonmonetary gold	2 180 . .	. . .	. . .	. . .	. . .	. . .	. . .	. . .	. . .
Debit	3 100 . .	**–204.50**	**–246.33**	**–235.44**	**–258.79**	**–274.40**	**–282.58**	**–298.12**	. . .
General merchandise: imports f.o.b.	3 110 . .	–200.80	–242.03	–230.74	–252.56	–271.43	–278.96	–294.46	. . .
Goods for processing: imports f.o.b.	3 150 . .	. . .	. . .	. . .	. . .	. . .	. . .	. . .	. . .
Repairs on goods	3 160 . .	. . .	. . .	. . .	. . .	. . .	. . .	. . .	. . .
Goods procured in ports by carriers	3 170 . .	–3.70	–4.30	–4.70	–6.23	–2.96	–3.62	–3.66	. . .
Nonmonetary gold	3 180 . .	. . .	. . .	. . .	. . .	. . .	. . .	. . .	. . .
B. SERVICES	4 200 . .	158.03	169.21	206.76	206.93	219.84	245.56	261.38	. . .
Total credit	2 200 . .	*237.33*	*261.79*	*311.87*	*320.20*	*342.57*	*377.20*	*396.31*	. . .
Total debit	3 200 . .	*–79.30*	*–92.58*	*–105.12*	*–113.27*	*–122.73*	*–131.64*	*–134.93*	. . .
Transportation services, credit	2 205 . .	**37.18**	**39.80**	**48.73**	**64.85**	**64.79**	**63.63**	**66.99**	. . .
Passenger	2 205 BA	*30.90*	*33.16*	*41.85*	*55.32*	*53.05*	*51.98*	*52.56*	. . .
Freight	2 205 BB	. . .	. . .	. . .	*1.26*	*2.79*	*2.52*	*2.33*	. . .
Other	2 205 BC	*6.29*	*6.64*	*6.88*	*8.27*	*8.95*	*9.13*	*12.09*	. . .
Sea transport, passenger	2 207 . .	. . .	. . .	. . .	. . .	. . .	. . .	. . .	. . .
Sea transport, freight	2 208 . .	. . .	. . .	. . .	. . .	. . .	. . .	. . .	. . .
Sea transport, other	2 209 . .	. . .	. . .	. . .	. . .	. . .	. . .	. . .	. . .
Air transport, passenger	2 211 . .	. . .	. . .	. . .	. . .	. . .	. . .	. . .	. . .
Air transport, freight	2 212 . .	. . .	. . .	. . .	. . .	. . .	. . .	. . .	. . .
Air transport, other	2 213 . .	. . .	. . .	. . .	. . .	. . .	. . .	. . .	. . .
Other transport, passenger	2 215 . .	. . .	. . .	. . .	. . .	. . .	. . .	. . .	. . .
Other transport, freight	2 216 . .	. . .	. . .	. . .	. . .	. . .	. . .	. . .	. . .
Other transport, other	2 217 . .	. . .	. . .	. . .	. . .	. . .	. . .	. . .	. . .
Transportation services, debit	3 205 . .	**–34.74**	**–41.37**	**–44.47**	**–48.26**	**–48.75**	**–53.48**	**–55.69**	. . .
Passenger	3 205 BA	*–5.91*	*–7.33*	*–9.73*	*–10.94*	*–9.43*	*–11.39*	*–12.29*	. . .
Freight	3 205 BB	*–22.82*	*–27.50*	*–27.80*	*–30.61*	*–33.45*	*–34.44*	*–36.68*	. . .
Other	3 205 BC	*–6.01*	*–6.54*	*–6.94*	*–6.70*	*–5.86*	*–7.65*	*–6.71*	. . .
Sea transport, passenger	3 207 . .	. . .	. . .	. . .	. . .	. . .	. . .	. . .	. . .
Sea transport, freight	3 208 . .	. . .	. . .	. . .	. . .	. . .	. . .	. . .	. . .
Sea transport, other	3 209 . .	. . .	. . .	. . .	. . .	. . .	. . .	. . .	. . .
Air transport, passenger	3 211 . .	. . .	. . .	. . .	. . .	. . .	. . .	. . .	. . .
Air transport, freight	3 212 . .	. . .	. . .	. . .	. . .	. . .	. . .	. . .	. . .
Air transport, other	3 213 . .	. . .	. . .	. . .	. . .	. . .	. . .	. . .	. . .
Other transport, passenger	3 215 . .	. . .	. . .	. . .	. . .	. . .	. . .	. . .	. . .
Other transport, freight	3 216 . .	. . .	. . .	. . .	. . .	. . .	. . .	. . .	. . .
Other transport, other	3 217 . .	. . .	. . .	. . .	. . .	. . .	. . .	. . .	. . .
Travel, credit	2 236 . .	**182.38**	**202.56**	**231.44**	**228.06**	**242.87**	**276.80**	**293.44**	. . .
Business travel	2 237 . .	. . .	. . .	. . .	. . .	. . .	. . .	. . .	. . .
Personal travel	2 240 . .	. . .	. . .	. . .	. . .	. . .	. . .	. . .	. . .
Travel, debit	3 236 . .	**–15.50**	**–16.30**	**–18.00**	**–20.37**	**–22.59**	**–23.42**	**–24.03**	. . .
Business travel	3 237 . .	. . .	. . .	. . .	. . .	. . .	. . .	. . .	. . .
Personal travel	3 240 . .	. . .	. . .	. . .	. . .	. . .	. . .	. . .	. . .
Other services, credit	2 200 BA	**17.77**	**19.43**	**31.70**	**27.29**	**34.91**	**36.78**	**35.88**	. . .
Communications	2 245 . .	. . .	. . .	. . .	. . .	. . .	. . .	. . .	. . .
Construction	2 249 . .	. . .	. . .	. . .	. . .	. . .	. . .	. . .	. . .
Insurance	2 253 . .	1.15	1.28	3.12	4.53	5.07	4.88	6.70	. . .
Financial	2 260 . .	. . .	. . .	. . .	. . .	. . .	. . .	. . .	. . .
Computer and information	2 262 . .	. . .	. . .	. . .	. . .	. . .	. . .	. . .	. . .
Royalties and licence fees	2 266 . .	. . .	. . .	. . .	. . .	. . .	. . .	. . .	. . .
Other business services	2 268 . .	14.19	14.86	25.02	19.36	26.56	28.41	28.61	. . .
Personal, cultural, and recreational	2 287 . .	. . .	. . .	. . .	. . .	. . .	. . .	. . .	. . .
Government, n.i.e.	2 291 . .	2.44	3.29	3.56	3.40	3.27	3.50	.57	. . .
Other services, debit	3 200 BA	**–29.06**	**–34.91**	**–42.64**	**–44.64**	**–51.39**	**–54.74**	**–55.21**	. . .
Communications	3 245 . .	. . .	. . .	. . .	. . .	. . .	. . .	. . .	. . .
Construction	3 249 . .	. . .	. . .	. . .	. . .	. . .	. . .	. . .	. . .
Insurance	3 253 . .	–4.74	–5.86	–8.99	–9.43	–9.53	–14.73	–10.87	. . .
Financial	3 260 . .	. . .	. . .	. . .	. . .	. . .	. . .	. . .	. . .
Computer and information	3 262 . .	. . .	. . .	. . .	. . .	. . .	. . .	. . .	. . .
Royalties and licence fees	3 266 . .	. . .	. . .	. . .	. . .	. . .	. . .	. . .	. . .
Other business services	3 268 . .	–20.67	–24.33	–31.95	–30.76	–37.88	–35.51	–37.42	. . .
Personal, cultural, and recreational	3 287 . .	. . .	. . .	. . .	. . .	. . .	. . .	. . .	. . .
Government, n.i.e.	3 291 . .	–3.66	–4.71	–1.71	–4.44	–3.98	–4.51	–6.93	. . .

Table 2 (Continued). STANDARD PRESENTATION, 1988–95
(Millions of U.S. dollars)

	Code		1988	1989	1990	1991	1992	1993	1994	1995
C. INCOME	4 300	. .	–31.63	–45.48	–45.33	–32.32	–29.66	–22.94	–26.55	. . .
Total credit	2 300	. .	*1.43*	*1.20*	*2.49*	*2.66*	*3.70*	*3.11*	*4.26*	. . .
Total debit	3 300	. .	*–33.06*	*–46.69*	*–47.81*	*–34.98*	*–33.36*	*–26.04*	*–30.81*	. . .
Compensation of employees, credit	2 310	. .	**. . .**	**. . .**	**. . .**	**. . .**	**. . .**	**. . .**	**. . .**	**. . .**
Compensation of employees, debit	3 310	. .	**–1.35**	**–5.25**	**–1.67**	**. . .**	**. . .**	**. . .**	**. . .**	**. . .**
Investment income, credit	2 320	. .	**1.43**	**1.20**	**2.49**	**2.66**	**3.70**	**3.11**	**4.26**	**. . .**
Direct investment income	2 330	. .	. . .	. . .	. . .	. . .	. . .	. . .	. . .	. . .
Dividends and distributed branch profits	2 332	. .	. . .	. . .	. . .	. . .	. . .	. . .	. . .	. . .
Reinvested earnings and undistributed branch profits	2 333	. .	. . .	. . .	. . .	. . .	. . .	. . .	. . .	. . .
Income on debt (interest)	2 334	. .	. . .	. . .	. . .	. . .	. . .	. . .	. . .	. . .
Portfolio investment income	2 339	. .	. . .	. . .	. . .	. . .	. . .	. . .	. . .	. . .
Income on equity	2 340	. .	. . .	. . .	. . .	. . .	. . .	. . .	. . .	. . .
Income on bonds and notes	2 350	. .	. . .	. . .	. . .	. . .	. . .	. . .	. . .	. . .
Income on money market instruments and financial derivatives	2 360	. .	. . .	. . .	. . .	. . .	. . .	. . .	. . .	. . .
Other investment income	2 370	. .	1.43	1.20	2.49	2.66	3.70	3.11	4.26	. . .
Investment income, debit	3 320	. .	**–31.71**	**–41.43**	**–46.15**	**–34.98**	**–33.36**	**–26.04**	**–30.81**	**. . .**
Direct investment income	3 330	. .	–15.76	–17.85	–19.08	–15.23	–15.40	–15.41	–15.84	. . .
Dividends and distributed branch profits	3 332	. .	–13.47	–13.97	–14.07	–10.29	–11.30	–11.43	–10.76	. . .
Reinvested earnings and undistributed branch profits	3 333	. .	–2.29	–3.18	–4.67	–3.36	–3.28	–3.08	–4.68	. . .
Income on debt (interest)	3 334	. .	. . .	–.70	–.34	–1.59	–.82	–.91	–.41	. . .
Portfolio investment income	3 339	. .	. . .	. . .	. . .	. . .	. . .	. . .	. . .	. . .
Income on equity	3 340	. .	. . .	. . .	. . .	. . .	. . .	. . .	. . .	. . .
Income on bonds and notes	3 350	. .	. . .	. . .	. . .	. . .	. . .	. . .	. . .	. . .
Income on money market instruments and financial derivatives	3 360	. .	. . .	. . .	. . .	. . .	. . .	. . .	. . .	. . .
Other investment income	3 370	. .	–15.95	–23.59	–27.07	–19.75	–17.96	–10.63	–14.97	. . .
D. CURRENT TRANSFERS	4 379	. .	4.86	11.81	9.60	1.30	–1.12	–2.67	.90	. . .
Credit	2 379	. .	**9.81**	**17.28**	**14.89**	**9.16**	**8.54**	**9.07**	**10.36**	**. . .**
General government	2 380	. .	.56	1.11	1.11	.05	.40	1.15	1.75	. . .
Other sectors	2 390	. .	9.25	16.17	13.78	9.11	8.14	7.93	8.61	. . .
Workers' remittances	2 391	. .	9.25	9.90	9.40	9.11	8.14	7.93	8.15	. . .
Other current transfers	2 392	. .	. . .	6.27	4.38	. . .	. . .	. . .	.47	. . .
Debit	3 379	. .	**–4.94**	**–5.47**	**–5.29**	**–7.86**	**–9.66**	**–11.75**	**–9.47**	**. . .**
General government	3 380	. .	–.20	–1.25	–.64	–.75	–1.14	–.77	–1.07	. . .
Other sectors	3 390	. .	–4.74	–4.22	–4.64	–7.11	–8.51	–10.98	–8.40	. . .
Workers' remittances	3 391	. .	–2.96	–4.22	–4.64	–5.56	–5.93	–6.07	–5.93	. . .
Other current transfers	3 392	. .	–1.78	. . .	. . .	–1.56	–2.59	–4.91	–2.47	. . .
CAPITAL AND FINANCIAL ACCOUNT	4 996	. .	**48.69**	**83.50**	**66.37**	**47.77**	**29.29**	**18.50**	**7.42**	**. . .**
CAPITAL ACCOUNT	4 994	. .	**5.49**	**6.74**	**5.21**	**6.43**	**5.74**	**6.81**	**5.91**	**. . .**
Total credit	2 994	. .	*5.49*	*6.74*	*5.23*	*6.43*	*5.74*	*6.81*	*6.53*	. . .
Total debit	3 994	. .	. . .	. . .	*–.02*	. . .	. . .	. . .	*–.62*	. . .
Capital transfers, credit	2 400	. .	**5.49**	**6.74**	**5.23**	**6.43**	**5.74**	**6.81**	**6.53**	**. . .**
General government	2 401	. .	2.40	3.44	2.10	3.39	3.02	3.11	3.19	. . .
Debt forgiveness	2 402	. .	. . .	. . .	. . .	. . .	. . .	. . .	. . .	. . .
Other capital transfers	2 410	. .	2.40	3.44	2.10	3.39	3.02	3.11	3.19	. . .
Other sectors	2 430	. .	3.09	3.30	3.13	3.05	2.71	3.70	3.33	. . .
Migrants' transfers	2 431	. .	3.09	3.30	3.13	3.05	2.71	3.70	3.33	. . .
Debt forgiveness	2 432	. .	. . .	. . .	. . .	. . .	. . .	. . .	. . .	. . .
Other capital transfers	2 440	. .	. . .	. . .	. . .	. . .	. . .	. . .	. . .	. . .
Capital transfers, debit	3 400	. .	**. . .**	**. . .**	**–.02**	**. . .**	**. . .**	**. . .**	**. . .**	**. . .**
General government	3 401	. .	. . .	. . .	–.02	. . .	. . .	. . .	. . .	. . .
Debt forgiveness	3 402	. .	. . .	. . .	. . .	. . .	. . .	. . .	. . .	. . .
Other capital transfers	3 410	. .	. . .	. . .	–.02	. . .	. . .	. . .	. . .	. . .
Other sectors	3 430	. .	. . .	. . .	. . .	. . .	. . .	. . .	. . .	. . .
Migrants' transfers	3 431	. .	. . .	. . .	. . .	. . .	. . .	. . .	. . .	. . .
Debt forgiveness	3 432	. .	. . .	. . .	. . .	. . .	. . .	. . .	. . .	. . .
Other capital transfers	3 440	. .	. . .	. . .	. . .	. . .	. . .	. . .	. . .	. . .
Nonproduced nonfinancial assets, credit	2 480	. .	**. . .**	**. . .**	**. . .**	**. . .**	**. . .**	**. . .**	**. . .**	**. . .**
Nonproduced nonfinancial assets, debit	3 480	. .	**. . .**	**. . .**	**. . .**	**. . .**	**. . .**	**. . .**	**–.62**	**. . .**

Table 2 (Continued). STANDARD PRESENTATION, 1988–95
(Millions of U.S. dollars)

	Code		1988	1989	1990	1991	1992	1993	1994	1995
FINANCIAL ACCOUNT	4 995	. .	**43.21**	**76.76**	**61.17**	**41.34**	**23.55**	**11.69**	**1.51**	**...**
A. DIRECT INVESTMENT	4 500	. .	32.95	43.11	60.61	54.71	20.00	15.03	24.81	...
Direct investment abroad	4 505	. .	**...**	**...**	**...**	**...**	**...**	**...**	**...**	**...**
Equity capital	4 510	. .	...	...	...	...	...	...	...	...
Claims on affiliated enterprises	4 515	. .	...	...	...	...	...	...	...	...
Liabilities to affiliated enterprises	4 520	. .	...	...	...	...	...	...	...	...
Reinvested earnings	4 525	. .	...	...	...	...	...	...	...	...
Other capital	4 530	. .	...	...	...	...	...	...	...	...
Claims on affiliated enterprises	4 535	. .	...	...	...	...	...	...	...	...
Liabilities to affiliated enterprises	4 540	. .	...	...	...	...	...	...	...	...
Direct investment in Antigua and Barbuda	4 555	. .	**32.95**	**43.11**	**60.61**	**54.71**	**20.00**	**15.03**	**24.81**	**...**
Equity capital	4 560	. .	27.88	37.56	51.94	39.35	12.20	3.85	6.17	...
Claims on direct investors	4 565	. .	...	...	...	...	...	...	...	...
Liabilities to direct investors	4 570	. .	...	...	...	...	...	...	...	...
Reinvested earnings	4 575	. .	2.29	3.18	4.67	3.36	3.28	3.08	4.68	...
Other capital	4 580	. .	2.78	2.37	4.00	12.01	4.53	8.10	13.97	...
Claims on direct investors	4 585	. .	...	...	...	...	...	...	...	...
Liabilities to direct investors	4 590	. .	...	...	...	...	...	...	...	...
B. PORTFOLIO INVESTMENT	4 600	. .	...	...	...	...	...	...	–1.38	...
Assets	4 602	. .	**...**	**...**	**...**	**...**	**...**	**...**	**–1.38**	**...**
Equity securities	4 610	. .	...	...	...	...	...	...	–1.38	...
Monetary authorities	4 611	. .	...	...	...	...	...	...	...	...
General government	4 612	. .	...	...	...	...	...	...	...	...
Banks	4 613	. .	...	...	...	...	...	...	...	...
Other sectors	4 614	. .	...	...	...	...	...	...	...	...
Debt securities	4 619	. .	...	...	...	...	...	...	...	...
Bonds and notes	4 620	. .	...	...	...	...	...	...	...	...
Monetary authorities	4 621	. .	...	...	...	...	...	...	...	...
General government	4 622	. .	...	...	...	...	...	...	...	...
Banks	4 623	. .	...	...	...	...	...	...	...	...
Other sectors	4 624	. .	...	...	...	...	...	...	...	...
Money market instruments	4 630	. .	...	...	...	...	...	...	...	...
Monetary authorities	4 631	. .	...	...	...	...	...	...	...	...
General government	4 632	. .	...	...	...	...	...	...	...	...
Banks	4 633	. .	...	...	...	...	...	...	...	...
Other sectors	4 634	. .	...	...	...	...	...	...	...	...
Financial derivatives	4 640	. .	...	...	...	...	...	...	...	...
Monetary authorities	4 641	. .	...	...	...	...	...	...	...	...
General government	4 642	. .	...	...	...	...	...	...	...	...
Banks	4 643	. .	...	...	...	...	...	...	...	...
Other sectors	4 644	. .	...	...	...	...	...	...	...	...
Liabilities	4 652	. .	**...**	**...**	**...**	**...**	**...**	**...**	**...**	**...**
Equity securities	4 660	. .	...	...	...	...	...	...	...	...
Banks	4 663	. .	...	...	...	...	...	...	...	...
Other sectors	4 664	. .	...	...	...	...	...	...	...	...
Debt securities	4 669	. .	...	...	...	...	...	...	...	...
Bonds and notes	4 670	. .	...	...	...	...	...	...	...	...
Monetary authorities	4 671	. .	...	...	...	...	...	...	...	...
General government	4 672	. .	...	...	...	...	...	...	...	...
Banks	4 673	. .	...	...	...	...	...	...	...	...
Other sectors	4 674	. .	...	...	...	...	...	...	...	...
Money market instruments	4 680	. .	...	...	...	...	...	...	...	...
Monetary authorities	4 681	. .	...	...	...	...	...	...	...	...
General government	4 682	. .	...	...	...	...	...	...	...	...
Banks	4 683	. .	...	...	...	...	...	...	...	...
Other sectors	4 684	. .	...	...	...	...	...	...	...	...
Financial derivatives	4 690	. .	...	...	...	...	...	...	...	...
Monetary authorities	4 691	. .	...	...	...	...	...	...	...	...
General government	4 692	. .	...	...	...	...	...	...	...	...
Banks	4 693	. .	...	...	...	...	...	...	...	...
Other sectors	4 694	. .	...	...	...	...	...	...	...	...

Table 2 (Concluded). STANDARD PRESENTATION, 1988–95
(Millions of U.S. dollars)

	Code	1988	1989	1990	1991	1992	1993	1994	1995
C. OTHER INVESTMENT	4 700 . .	12.88	33.70	–.03	–8.28	19.94	–14.54	–13.84	. . .
Assets	4 703 . .	**–3.63**	**8.69**	**–2.15**	**–23.97**	**8.47**	**–18.53**	**–16.67**	**. . .**
Trade credits	4 706 . .	. . .	. . .	. . .	. . .	. . .	. . .	. . .	. . .
General government: long-term	4 708 . .	. . .	. . .	. . .	. . .	. . .	. . .	. . .	. . .
General government: short-term	4 709 . .	. . .	. . .	. . .	. . .	. . .	. . .	. . .	. . .
Other sectors: long-term	4 711 . .	. . .	. . .	. . .	. . .	. . .	. . .	. . .	. . .
Other sectors: short-term	4 712 . .	. . .	. . .	. . .	. . .	. . .	. . .	. . .	. . .
Loans	4 714 . .	. . .	. . .	. . .	. . .	. . .	. . .	. . .	. . .
Monetary authorities: long-term	4 717 . .	. . .	. . .	. . .	. . .	. . .	. . .	. . .	. . .
Monetary authorities: short-term	4 718 . .	. . .	. . .	. . .	. . .	. . .	. . .	. . .	. . .
General government: long-term	4 720 . .	. . .	. . .	. . .	. . .	. . .	. . .	. . .	. . .
General government: short-term	4 721 . .	. . .	. . .	. . .	. . .	. . .	. . .	. . .	. . .
Banks: long-term	4 723 . .	. . .	. . .	. . .	. . .	. . .	. . .	. . .	. . .
Banks: short-term	4 724 . .	. . .	. . .	. . .	. . .	. . .	. . .	. . .	. . .
Other sectors: long-term	4 726 . .	. . .	. . .	. . .	. . .	. . .	. . .	. . .	. . .
Other sectors: short-term	4 727 . .	. . .	. . .	. . .	. . .	. . .	. . .	. . .	. . .
Currency and deposits	4 730 . .	–3.63	8.69	–2.15	–23.97	8.47	–18.53	–16.67	. . .
Monetary authorities	4 731 . .	. . .	. . .	. . .	. . .	. . .	. . .	. . .	. . .
General government	4 732 . .	. . .	. . .	. . .	. . .	. . .	. . .	. . .	. . .
Banks	4 733 . .	–3.63	8.69	–2.15	–23.97	8.47	–18.53	–16.67	. . .
Other sectors	4 734 . .	. . .	. . .	. . .	. . .	. . .	. . .	. . .	. . .
Other assets	4 736 . .	. . .	. . .	. . .	. . .	. . .	. . .	. . .	. . .
Monetary authorities: long-term	4 738 . .	. . .	. . .	. . .	. . .	. . .	. . .	. . .	. . .
Monetary authorities: short-term	4 739 . .	. . .	. . .	. . .	. . .	. . .	. . .	. . .	. . .
General government: long-term	4 741 . .	. . .	. . .	. . .	. . .	. . .	. . .	. . .	. . .
General government: short-term	4 742 . .	. . .	. . .	. . .	. . .	. . .	. . .	. . .	. . .
Banks: long-term	4 744 . .	. . .	. . .	. . .	. . .	. . .	. . .	. . .	. . .
Banks: short-term	4 745 . .	. . .	. . .	. . .	. . .	. . .	. . .	. . .	. . .
Other sectors: long-term	4 747 . .	. . .	. . .	. . .	. . .	. . .	. . .	. . .	. . .
Other sectors: short-term	4 748 . .	. . .	. . .	. . .	. . .	. . .	. . .	. . .	. . .
Liabilities	4 753 . .	**16.51**	**25.01**	**2.11**	**15.69**	**11.47**	**3.99**	**2.83**	**. . .**
Trade credits	4 756 . .	. . .	. . .	. . .	. . .	. . .	. . .	. . .	. . .
General government: long-term	4 758 . .	. . .	. . .	. . .	. . .	. . .	. . .	. . .	. . .
General government: short-term	4 759 . .	. . .	. . .	. . .	. . .	. . .	. . .	. . .	. . .
Other sectors: long-term	4 761 . .	. . .	. . .	. . .	. . .	. . .	. . .	. . .	. . .
Other sectors: short-term	4 762 . .	. . .	. . .	. . .	. . .	. . .	. . .	. . .	. . .
Loans	4 764 . .	16.51	25.01	2.11	15.69	11.47	3.99	2.83	. . .
Use of Fund credit and loans from the Fund	4 766 . .	. . .	. . .	. . .	. . .	. . .	. . .	. . .	. . .
Monetary authorities: other long-term	4 767 . .	. . .	. . .	. . .	. . .	. . .	. . .	. . .	. . .
Monetary authorities: short-term	4 768 . .	. . .	. . .	. . .	. . .	. . .	. . .	. . .	. . .
General government: long-term	4 770 . .	20.23	28.03	9.27	17.56	6.42	.01	5.67	. . .
General government: short-term	4 771 . .	. . .	. . .	. . .	. . .	. . .	. . .	. . .	. . .
Banks: long-term	4 773 . .	. . .	. . .	. . .	. . .	. . .	. . .	. . .	. . .
Banks: short-term	4 774 . .	. . .	. . .	. . .	. . .	. . .	. . .	. . .	. . .
Other sectors: long-term	4 776 . .	–3.72	–3.02	–7.15	–1.87	5.05	3.99	–2.84	. . .
Other sectors: short-term	4 777 . .	. . .	. . .	. . .	. . .	. . .	. . .	. . .	. . .
Currency and deposits	4 780 . .	. . .	. . .	. . .	. . .	. . .	. . .	. . .	. . .
Monetary authorities	4 781 . .	. . .	. . .	. . .	. . .	. . .	. . .	. . .	. . .
General government	4 782 . .	. . .	. . .	. . .	. . .	. . .	. . .	. . .	. . .
Banks	4 783 . .	. . .	. . .	. . .	. . .	. . .	. . .	. . .	. . .
Other sectors	4 784 . .	. . .	. . .	. . .	. . .	. . .	. . .	. . .	. . .
Other liabilities	4 786 . .	. . .	. . .	. . .	. . .	. . .	. . .	. . .	. . .
Monetary authorities: long-term	4 788 . .	. . .	. . .	. . .	. . .	. . .	. . .	. . .	. . .
Monetary authorities: short-term	4 789 . .	. . .	. . .	. . .	. . .	. . .	. . .	. . .	. . .
General government: long-term	4 791 . .	. . .	. . .	. . .	. . .	. . .	. . .	. . .	. . .
General government: short-term	4 792 . .	. . .	. . .	. . .	. . .	. . .	. . .	. . .	. . .
Banks: long-term	4 794 . .	. . .	. . .	. . .	. . .	. . .	. . .	. . .	. . .
Banks: short-term	4 795 . .	. . .	. . .	. . .	. . .	. . .	. . .	. . .	. . .
Other sectors: long-term	4 797 . .	. . .	. . .	. . .	. . .	. . .	. . .	. . .	. . .
Other sectors: short-term	4 798 . .	. . .	. . .	. . .	. . .	. . .	. . .	. . .	. . .
D. RESERVE ASSETS	4 800 . .	–2.62	–.04	.59	–5.10	–16.40	11.20	–8.08	. . .
Monetary gold	4 810 . .	. . .	. . .	. . .	. . .	. . .	. . .	. . .	. . .
Special drawing rights	4 820 . .	. . .	. . .	. . .	. . .	. . .	–.01	. . .	. . .
Reserve position in the Fund	4 830 . .	. . .	. . .	. . .	. . .	. . .	. . .	. . .	. . .
Foreign exchange	4 840 . .	–2.62	–.04	.59	–5.10	–16.40	11.21	–8.07	. . .
Other claims	4 880 . .	. . .	. . .	. . .	. . .	. . .	. . .	. . .	. . .
NET ERRORS AND OMISSIONS	4 998 . .	**–3.66**	**–1.85**	**–35.39**	**–14.40**	**–8.65**	**–17.95**	**10.53**	**. . .**

Part 3 of the *Yearbook* contains descriptions of the methodologies, compilation practices, and sources used to compile these data.

Table 1. ANALYTIC PRESENTATION, 1988–95
(Millions of U.S. dollars)

	Code	1988	1989	1990	1991	1992	1993	1994	1995
A. Current Account [1]	4 993 Y.	**–1,572**	**–1,305**	**4,552**	**–647**	**–5,401**	**–7,046**	**–9,363**	**–2,390**
Goods: exports f.o.b.	2 100 . .	9,134	9,573	12,354	11,978	12,235	13,117	15,840	20,964
Goods: imports f.o.b.	3 100 . .	–4,892	–3,864	–3,726	–7,559	–13,685	–15,543	–20,076	–18,727
Balance on Goods	4 100 . .	*4,242*	*5,709*	*8,628*	*4,419*	*–1,450*	*–2,426*	*–4,236*	*2,237*
Services: credit	2 200 . .	2,015	2,193	2,446	2,408	2,494	2,506	2,669	2,889
Services: debit	3 200 . .	–2,702	–2,793	–3,120	–4,007	–4,703	–5,166	–5,525	–5,047
Balance on Goods and Services	4 991 . .	*3,555*	*5,109*	*7,954*	*2,820*	*–3,659*	*–5,086*	*–7,092*	*79*
Income: credit	2 300 . .	211	276	1,854	1,746	1,824	2,159	2,934	4,199
Income: debit	3 300 . .	–5,338	–6,698	–6,254	–6,006	–4,228	–4,531	–5,524	–7,100
Balance on Goods, Services, and Income	4 992 . .	*–1,572*	*–1,313*	*3,554*	*–1,440*	*–6,063*	*–7,458*	*–9,682*	*–2,822*
Current transfers: credit	2 379 Y.	2	18	1,015	821	785	599	541	539
Current transfers: debit	3 379 . .	–2	–10	–17	–28	–123	–187	–222	–107
B. Capital Account [1]	4 994 Y.	**. . .**	**. . .**	**. . .**	**. . .**	**. . .**	**. . .**	**. . .**	**. . .**
Capital account: credit	2 994 Y.	. . .	. . .	. . .	. . .	. . .	. . .	. . .	. . .
Capital account: debit	3 994 . .	. . .	. . .	. . .	. . .	. . .	. . .	. . .	. . .
Total, Groups A Plus B	4 010 . .	*–1,572*	*–1,305*	*4,552*	*–647*	*–5,401*	*–7,046*	*–9,363*	*–2,390*
C. Financial Account [1]	4 995 X.	**431**	**–8,008**	**–5,850**	**160**	**6,967**	**9,956**	**8,681**	**167**
Direct investment abroad	4 505 . .	. . .	. . .	. . .	. . .	7	. . .	–126	–155
Direct investment in Argentina	4 555 Y.	1,147	1,028	1,836	2,439	2,555	3,482	603	1,319
Portfolio investment assets	4 602 . .	. . .	. . .	–241	–8,261	–80	–2,037	–185	64
Equity securities	4 610 . .	. . .	. . .	. . .	. . .	. . .	. . .	. . .	. . .
Debt securities	4 619 . .	. . .	. . .	–241	–8,261	–80	–2,037	–185	64
Portfolio investment liabilities	4 652 Y.	–718	–1,098	–1,105	8,227	795	19,992	3,847	4,637
Equity securities	4 660 Y.	. . .	. . .	. . .	. . .	. . .	. . .	. . .	. . .
Debt securities	4 669 Y.	–718	–1,098	–1,105	8,227	795	19,992	3,847	4,637
Other investment assets	4 703 . .	879	–399	661	426	4,038	399	2,853	–10,458
Monetary authorities	4 703 . A	. . .	366	–669	273	–106	355	27	–489
General government	4 703 . B	. . .	–48	–81	83	–165	–1,144	228	27
Banks	4 703 . C	. . .	. . .	. . .	. . .	–696	–1,728	–301	–683
Other sectors	4 703 . D	879	–717	1,411	70	5,005	2,916	2,899	–9,313
Other investment liabilities	4 753 X.	–877	–7,539	–7,001	–2,671	–348	–11,880	1,689	4,760
Monetary authorities	4 753 XA	488	–1,729	–440	18	3	–41	–32	–20
General government	4 753 YB	5	–438	–420	–3	–637	–12,939	1,027	2,274
Banks	4 753 YC	23	56	100	–31	775	1,151	1,099	3,123
Other sectors	4 753 YD	–1,393	–5,428	–6,241	–2,655	–489	–51	–405	–617
Total, Groups A Through C	4 020 . .	*–1,141*	*–9,313*	*–1,298*	*–487*	*1,566*	*2,910*	*–682*	*–2,223*
D. Net Errors and Omissions	4 998 . .	**–165**	**–249**	**715**	**–341**	**325**	**–254**	**7**	**13**
Total, Groups A Through D	4 030 . .	*–1,306*	*–9,562*	*–583*	*–828*	*1,891*	*2,656*	*–675*	*–2,210*
E. Reserves and Related Items	4 040 . .	**1,306**	**9,562**	**583**	**828**	**–1,891**	**–2,656**	**675**	**2,210**
Reserve assets	4 800 . .	–1,888	1,826	–3,121	–2,040	–3,261	–4,279	–685	81
Use of Fund credit and loans	4 766 . .	30	–478	–257	–590	–73	1,211	455	1,924
Liabilities constituting foreign authorities' reserves	4 900 . .	–62	–75	–34	22	. . .	. . .	. . .	. . .
Exceptional financing	4 920 . .	3,226	8,289	3,996	3,436	1,443	412	904	205
Conversion rates: Argentine pesos per U.S. dollar	0 101 . .	**.00088**	**.04233**	**.48759**	**.95355**	**.99064**	**.99895**	**.99901**	**.99975**

[1] Excludes components that have been classified in the categories of Group E.

Table 2. STANDARD PRESENTATION, 1988–95
(Millions of U.S. dollars)

	Code	1988	1989	1990	1991	1992	1993	1994	1995
CURRENT ACCOUNT	4 993 ..	**–1,572**	**–1,305**	**4,552**	**–647**	**–5,401**	**–7,046**	**–9,363**	**–2,390**
A. GOODS	4 100 ..	4,242	5,709	8,628	4,419	–1,450	–2,426	–4,236	2,237
Credit	2 100 ..	**9,134**	**9,573**	**12,354**	**11,978**	**12,235**	**13,117**	**15,840**	**20,964**
General merchandise: exports f.o.b.	2 110 ..	9,134	9,573	12,354	11,978	12,235	13,117	15,840	20,964
Goods for processing: exports f.o.b.	2 150 ..	...	...	...	...	...	...	...	...
Repairs on goods	2 160 ..	...	...	...	...	...	...	...	...
Goods procured in ports by carriers	2 170 ..	...	...	...	...	...	...	...	...
Nonmonetary gold	2 180 ..	...	...	...	...	...	...	...	...
Debit	3 100 ..	**–4,892**	**–3,864**	**–3,726**	**–7,559**	**–13,685**	**–15,543**	**–20,076**	**–18,727**
General merchandise: imports f.o.b.	3 110 ..	–4,892	–3,864	–3,726	–7,559	–13,685	–15,543	–20,076	–18,727
Goods for processing: imports f.o.b.	3 150 ..	...	...	...	...	...	...	...	...
Repairs on goods	3 160 ..	...	...	...	...	...	...	...	...
Goods procured in ports by carriers	3 170 ..	...	...	...	...	...	...	...	...
Nonmonetary gold	3 180 ..	...	...	...	...	...	...	...	...
B. SERVICES	4 200 ..	–687	–600	–674	–1,599	–2,209	–2,660	–2,856	–2,158
Total credit	2 200 ..	*2,015*	*2,193*	*2,446*	*2,408*	*2,494*	*2,506*	*2,669*	*2,889*
Total debit	3 200 ..	*–2,702*	*–2,793*	*–3,120*	*–4,007*	*–4,703*	*–5,166*	*–5,525*	*–5,047*
Transportation services, credit	2 205 ..	**965**	**1,011**	**1,156**	**1,186**	**1,318**	**1,083**	**1,156**	**1,197**
Passenger	2 205 BA	*269*	*323*	*389*	*400*	*493*	*313*	*317*	*338*
Freight	2 205 BB	*341*	*332*	*303*	*219*	*249*	*218*	*217*	*197*
Other	2 205 BC	*355*	*356*	*464*	*567*	*576*	*552*	*622*	*662*
Sea transport, passenger	2 207 ..	...	...	...	...	...	...	...	...
Sea transport, freight	2 208 ..	...	...	...	...	...	...	...	...
Sea transport, other	2 209 ..	...	...	...	...	...	...	...	...
Air transport, passenger	2 211 ..	...	...	...	...	...	...	...	...
Air transport, freight	2 212 ..	...	...	...	...	...	...	...	...
Air transport, other	2 213 ..	...	...	...	...	...	...	...	...
Other transport, passenger	2 215 ..	...	...	...	...	...	...	...	...
Other transport, freight	2 216 ..	...	...	...	...	...	...	...	...
Other transport, other	2 217 ..	...	...	...	...	...	...	...	...
Transportation services, debit	3 205 ..	**–922**	**–856**	**–937**	**–1,347**	**–1,706**	**–1,829**	**–2,122**	**–2,083**
Passenger	3 205 BA	*–230*	*–219*	*–270*	*–418*	*–557*	*–637*	*–710*	*–693*
Freight	3 205 BB	*–205*	*–144*	*–162*	*–446*	*–764*	*–850*	*–1,070*	*–1,017*
Other	3 205 BC	*–487*	*–493*	*–505*	*–483*	*–385*	*–342*	*–342*	*–373*
Sea transport, passenger	3 207 ..	...	...	...	...	...	...	...	...
Sea transport, freight	3 208 ..	...	...	...	...	...	...	...	...
Sea transport, other	3 209 ..	...	...	...	...	...	...	...	...
Air transport, passenger	3 211 ..	...	...	...	...	...	...	...	...
Air transport, freight	3 212 ..	...	...	...	...	...	...	...	...
Air transport, other	3 213 ..	...	...	...	...	...	...	...	...
Other transport, passenger	3 215 ..	...	...	...	...	...	...	...	...
Other transport, freight	3 216 ..	...	...	...	...	...	...	...	...
Other transport, other	3 217 ..	...	...	...	...	...	...	...	...
Travel, credit	2 236 ..	**634**	**790**	**903**	**782**	**782**	**837**	**936**	**1,057**
Business travel	2 237 ..	...	...	...	...	...	...	...	...
Personal travel	2 240 ..	...	...	...	...	...	...	...	...
Travel, debit	3 236 ..	**–975**	**–1,014**	**–1,171**	**–1,739**	**–2,212**	**–2,445**	**–2,575**	**–2,067**
Business travel	3 237 ..	...	...	...	...	...	...	...	...
Personal travel	3 240 ..	...	...	...	...	...	...	...	...
Other services, credit	2 200 BA	**416**	**392**	**387**	**440**	**394**	**586**	**577**	**635**
Communications	2 245 ..	...	...	...	...	...	...	...	...
Construction	2 249 ..	...	...	...	...	...	...	...	...
Insurance	2 253 ..	1	5	1	3	...	...	...	...
Financial	2 260 ..	...	...	...	...	...	...	...	...
Computer and information	2 262 ..	...	...	...	...	...	...	...	...
Royalties and licence fees	2 266 ..	6	7	4	4	1	7	14	2
Other business services	2 268 ..	288	273	200	199	251	425	398	467
Personal, cultural, and recreational	2 287 ..	...	...	...	...	...	...	...	...
Government, n.i.e.	2 291 ..	121	107	182	234	142	154	165	166
Other services, debit	3 200 BA	**–805**	**–923**	**–1,012**	**–921**	**–785**	**–892**	**–828**	**–897**
Communications	3 245 ..	...	...	...	...	...	...	...	...
Construction	3 249 ..	...	...	...	...	...	...	...	...
Insurance	3 253 ..	...	...	...	...	...	...	...	...
Financial	3 260 ..	...	...	...	...	...	...	...	...
Computer and information	3 262 ..	...	...	...	...	...	...	...	...
Royalties and licence fees	3 266 ..	–288	–403	–409	–420	–193	–184	–192	–206
Other business services	3 268 ..	–270	–261	–359	–263	–316	–466	–375	–416
Personal, cultural, and recreational	3 287 ..	...	...	...	...	...	...	...	...
Government, n.i.e.	3 291 ..	–247	–259	–244	–238	–276	–242	–261	–275

Table 2 (Continued). STANDARD PRESENTATION, 1988–95
(Millions of U.S. dollars)

	Code	1988	1989	1990	1991	1992	1993	1994	1995
C. INCOME	4 300	–5,127	–6,422	–4,400	–4,260	–2,404	–2,372	–2,590	–2,901
Total credit	2 300	*211*	*276*	*1,854*	*1,746*	*1,824*	*2,159*	*2,934*	*4,199*
Total debit	3 300	*–5,338*	*–6,698*	*–6,254*	*–6,006*	*–4,228*	*–4,531*	*–5,524*	*–7,100*
Compensation of employees, credit	2 310	...	...	...	...	...	...	...	...
Compensation of employees, debit	3 310	...	...	...	...	...	...	...	...
Investment income, credit	2 320	**211**	**276**	**1,854**	**1,746**	**1,824**	**2,159**	**2,934**	**4,199**
Direct investment income	2 330	...	11	2	2	...	35	14	32
Dividends and distributed branch profits	2 332	...	11	2	2	...	35	14	32
Reinvested earnings and undistributed branch profits	2 333	...	...	...	...	...	...	...	...
Income on debt (interest)	2 334	...	...	...	...	...	...	...	...
Portfolio investment income	2 339	...	...	...	...	...	...	...	...
Income on equity	2 340	...	...	...	...	...	...	...	...
Income on bonds and notes	2 350	...	...	...	...	...	...	...	...
Income on money market instruments and financial derivatives	2 360	...	...	...	...	...	...	...	...
Other investment income	2 370	211	265	1,852	1,744	1,824	2,124	2,920	4,167
Investment income, debit	3 320	**–5,338**	**–6,698**	**–6,254**	**–6,006**	**–4,228**	**–4,531**	**–5,524**	**–7,100**
Direct investment income	3 330	–660	–675	–637	–807	–845	–1,308	–1,284	–1,656
Dividends and distributed branch profits	3 332	...	–78	–407	–379	–845	–1,308	–1,284	–1,656
Reinvested earnings and undistributed branch profits	3 333	–660	–597	–230	–428	...	...	...	...
Income on debt (interest)	3 334	...	...	...	...	...	...	...	...
Portfolio investment income	3 339	...	...	...	...	...	...	...	...
Income on equity	3 340	...	...	...	...	...	...	...	...
Income on bonds and notes	3 350	...	...	...	...	...	...	...	...
Income on money market instruments and financial derivatives	3 360	...	...	...	...	...	...	...	...
Other investment income	3 370	–4,678	–6,023	–5,617	–5,199	–3,383	–3,223	–4,240	–5,444
D. CURRENT TRANSFERS	4 379	...	8	998	793	662	412	319	432
Credit	2 379	**2**	**18**	**1,015**	**821**	**785**	**599**	**541**	**539**
General government	2 380	...	...	...	...	...	...	...	...
Other sectors	2 390	2	18	1,015	821	785	599	541	539
Workers' remittances	2 391	...	...	...	...	...	...	...	...
Other current transfers	2 392	2	18	1,015	821	785	599	541	539
Debit	3 379	**–2**	**–10**	**–17**	**–28**	**–123**	**–187**	**–222**	**–107**
General government	3 380	...	...	...	...	...	...	...	...
Other sectors	3 390	–2	–10	–17	–28	–123	–187	–222	–107
Workers' remittances	3 391	...	...	...	...	...	...	...	...
Other current transfers	3 392	–2	–10	–17	–28	–123	–187	–222	–107
CAPITAL AND FINANCIAL ACCOUNT	4 996	**1,737**	**1,554**	**–5,267**	**988**	**5,076**	**7,300**	**9,356**	**2,377**
CAPITAL ACCOUNT	4 994	...	...	...	...	...	...	...	...
Total credit	2 994	...	...	...	...	...	...	...	...
Total debit	3 994	...	...	...	...	...	...	...	...
Capital transfers, credit	2 400	...	...	...	...	...	...	...	...
General government	2 401	...	...	...	...	...	...	...	...
Debt forgiveness	2 402	...	...	...	...	...	...	...	...
Other capital transfers	2 410	...	...	...	...	...	...	...	...
Other sectors	2 430	...	...	...	...	...	...	...	...
Migrants' transfers	2 431	...	...	...	...	...	...	...	...
Debt forgiveness	2 432	...	...	...	...	...	...	...	...
Other capital transfers	2 440	...	...	...	...	...	...	...	...
Capital transfers, debit	3 400	...	...	...	...	...	...	...	...
General government	3 401	...	...	...	...	...	...	...	...
Debt forgiveness	3 402	...	...	...	...	...	...	...	...
Other capital transfers	3 410	...	...	...	...	...	...	...	...
Other sectors	3 430	...	...	...	...	...	...	...	...
Migrants' transfers	3 431	...	...	...	...	...	...	...	...
Debt forgiveness	3 432	...	...	...	...	...	...	...	...
Other capital transfers	3 440	...	...	...	...	...	...	...	...
Nonproduced nonfinancial assets, credit	2 480	...	...	...	...	...	...	...	...
Nonproduced nonfinancial assets, debit	3 480	...	...	...	...	...	...	...	...

Table 2 (Continued). STANDARD PRESENTATION, 1988–95
(Millions of U.S. dollars)

	Code	1988	1989	1990	1991	1992	1993	1994	1995
FINANCIAL ACCOUNT	4 995	**1,737**	**1,554**	**–5,267**	**988**	**5,076**	**7,300**	**9,356**	**2,377**
A. DIRECT INVESTMENT	4 500	1,147	1,028	1,836	2,439	2,562	3,482	477	1,164
Direct investment abroad	4 505	**. . .**	**. . .**	**. . .**	**. . .**	**7**	**. . .**	**–126**	**–155**
Equity capital	4 510	. . .	. . .	. . .	. . .	7	. . .	–126	–155
Claims on affiliated enterprises	4 515	. . .	. . .	. . .	. . .	. . .	. . .	. . .	. . .
Liabilities to affiliated enterprises	4 520	. . .	. . .	. . .	. . .	. . .	. . .	. . .	. . .
Reinvested earnings	4 525	. . .	. . .	. . .	. . .	. . .	. . .	. . .	. . .
Other capital	4 530	. . .	. . .	. . .	. . .	. . .	. . .	. . .	. . .
Claims on affiliated enterprises	4 535	. . .	. . .	. . .	. . .	. . .	. . .	. . .	. . .
Liabilities to affiliated enterprises	4 540	. . .	. . .	. . .	. . .	. . .	. . .	. . .	. . .
Direct investment in Argentina	4 555	**1,147**	**1,028**	**1,836**	**2,439**	**2,555**	**3,482**	**603**	**1,319**
Equity capital	4 560	487	431	1,606	2,011	2,555	3,482	603	1,319
Claims on direct investors	4 565	. . .	. . .	. . .	. . .	. . .	. . .	. . .	. . .
Liabilities to direct investors	4 570	. . .	. . .	. . .	. . .	. . .	. . .	. . .	. . .
Reinvested earnings	4 575	660	597	230	428	. . .	. . .	. . .	. . .
Other capital	4 580	. . .	. . .	. . .	. . .	. . .	. . .	. . .	. . .
Claims on direct investors	4 585	. . .	. . .	. . .	. . .	. . .	. . .	. . .	. . .
Liabilities to direct investors	4 590	. . .	. . .	. . .	. . .	. . .	. . .	. . .	. . .
B. PORTFOLIO INVESTMENT	4 600	–656	2,618	–1,309	483	715	26,421	3,662	4,701
Assets	4 602	**. . .**	**. . .**	**–241**	**–8,261**	**–80**	**–2,037**	**–185**	**64**
Equity securities	4 610	. . .	. . .	. . .	. . .	. . .	. . .	. . .	. . .
Monetary authorities	4 611	. . .	. . .	. . .	. . .	. . .	. . .	. . .	. . .
General government	4 612	. . .	. . .	. . .	. . .	. . .	. . .	. . .	. . .
Banks	4 613	. . .	. . .	. . .	. . .	. . .	. . .	. . .	. . .
Other sectors	4 614	. . .	. . .	. . .	. . .	. . .	. . .	. . .	. . .
Debt securities	4 619	. . .	. . .	–241	–8,261	–80	–2,037	–185	64
Bonds and notes	4 620	. . .	. . .	–241	–8,261	–80	–2,037	–185	64
Monetary authorities	4 621	. . .	. . .	. . .	. . .	. . .	. . .	. . .	. . .
General government	4 622	. . .	. . .	. . .	. . .	. . .	. . .	. . .	. . .
Banks	4 623	. . .	. . .	. . .	. . .	. . .	. . .	. . .	. . .
Other sectors	4 624	. . .	. . .	. . .	. . .	. . .	. . .	. . .	. . .
Money market instruments	4 630	. . .	. . .	. . .	. . .	. . .	. . .	. . .	. . .
Monetary authorities	4 631	. . .	. . .	. . .	. . .	. . .	. . .	. . .	. . .
General government	4 632	. . .	. . .	. . .	. . .	. . .	. . .	. . .	. . .
Banks	4 633	. . .	. . .	. . .	. . .	. . .	. . .	. . .	. . .
Other sectors	4 634	. . .	. . .	. . .	. . .	. . .	. . .	. . .	. . .
Financial derivatives	4 640	. . .	. . .	. . .	. . .	. . .	. . .	. . .	. . .
Monetary authorities	4 641	. . .	. . .	. . .	. . .	. . .	. . .	. . .	. . .
General government	4 642	. . .	. . .	. . .	. . .	. . .	. . .	. . .	. . .
Banks	4 643	. . .	. . .	. . .	. . .	. . .	. . .	. . .	. . .
Other sectors	4 644	. . .	. . .	. . .	. . .	. . .	. . .	. . .	. . .
Liabilities	4 652	**–656**	**2,618**	**–1,068**	**8,744**	**795**	**28,458**	**3,847**	**4,637**
Equity securities	4 660	. . .	. . .	. . .	. . .	. . .	. . .	. . .	. . .
Banks	4 663	. . .	. . .	. . .	. . .	. . .	. . .	. . .	. . .
Other sectors	4 664	. . .	. . .	. . .	. . .	. . .	. . .	. . .	. . .
Debt securities	4 669	–656	2,618	–1,068	8,744	795	28,458	3,847	4,637
Bonds and notes	4 670	–656	2,618	–1,068	8,744	795	28,458	3,847	4,637
Monetary authorities	4 671	. . .	. . .	. . .	. . .	. . .	. . .	. . .	. . .
General government	4 672	–656	2,618	–1,071	8,272	–1,125	24,040	1,642	3,512
Banks	4 673	. . .	. . .	. . .	. . .	. . .	. . .	. . .	. . .
Other sectors	4 674	. . .	. . .	3	472	1,920	4,418	2,205	1,125
Money market instruments	4 680	. . .	. . .	. . .	. . .	. . .	. . .	. . .	. . .
Monetary authorities	4 681	. . .	. . .	. . .	. . .	. . .	. . .	. . .	. . .
General government	4 682	. . .	. . .	. . .	. . .	. . .	. . .	. . .	. . .
Banks	4 683	. . .	. . .	. . .	. . .	. . .	. . .	. . .	. . .
Other sectors	4 684	. . .	. . .	. . .	. . .	. . .	. . .	. . .	. . .
Financial derivatives	4 690	. . .	. . .	. . .	. . .	. . .	. . .	. . .	. . .
Monetary authorities	4 691	. . .	. . .	. . .	. . .	. . .	. . .	. . .	. . .
General government	4 692	. . .	. . .	. . .	. . .	. . .	. . .	. . .	. . .
Banks	4 693	. . .	. . .	. . .	. . .	. . .	. . .	. . .	. . .
Other sectors	4 694	. . .	. . .	. . .	. . .	. . .	. . .	. . .	. . .

Table 2 (Concluded). STANDARD PRESENTATION, 1988–95
(Millions of U.S. dollars)

	Code	1988	1989	1990	1991	1992	1993	1994	1995
C. OTHER INVESTMENT	4 700	3,134	–3,918	–2,672	106	5,060	–18,324	5,901	–3,569
Assets	4 703	**879**	**–399**	**661**	**426**	**4,038**	**399**	**2,853**	**–10,458**
Trade credits	4 706	...	...	...	...	...	...	...	...
General government: long-term	4 708	...	...	...	...	...	...	...	...
General government: short-term	4 709	...	...	...	...	...	...	...	...
Other sectors: long-term	4 711	...	...	...	...	...	...	...	...
Other sectors: short-term	4 712	...	...	...	...	...	...	...	...
Loans	4 714	879	–717	1,352	154	...	...	...	...
Monetary authorities: long-term	4 717	...	...	...	...	...	...	...	...
Monetary authorities: short-term	4 718	...	...	...	...	...	...	...	...
General government: long-term	4 720	...	...	–59	84	...	...	...	...
General government: short-term	4 721	...	...	...	...	...	...	...	...
Banks: long-term	4 723	...	...	...	...	...	...	...	...
Banks: short-term	4 724	...	...	...	...	...	...	...	...
Other sectors: long-term	4 726	...	...	...	...	...	...	...	...
Other sectors: short-term	4 727	879	–717	1,411	70	...	...	...	...
Currency and deposits	4 730	...	366	–669	273	4,203	1,543	2,625	–10,485
Monetary authorities	4 731	...	366	–669	273	–106	355	27	–489
General government	4 732	...	...	...	...	...	...	...	...
Banks	4 733	...	...	...	...	–696	–1,728	–301	–683
Other sectors	4 734	...	...	...	...	5,005	2,916	2,899	–9,313
Other assets	4 736	...	–48	–22	–1	–165	–1,144	228	27
Monetary authorities: long-term	4 738	...	...	...	...	...	...	...	...
Monetary authorities: short-term	4 739	...	...	...	...	...	...	...	...
General government: long-term	4 741	...	–48	–22	–1	–165	–1,144	228	27
General government: short-term	4 742	...	...	...	...	...	...	...	...
Banks: long-term	4 744	...	...	...	...	...	...	...	...
Banks: short-term	4 745	...	...	...	...	...	...	...	...
Other sectors: long-term	4 747	...	...	...	...	...	...	...	...
Other sectors: short-term	4 748	...	...	...	...	...	...	...	...
Liabilities	4 753	**2,255**	**–3,519**	**–3,333**	**–320**	**1,022**	**–18,723**	**3,048**	**6,889**
Trade credits	4 756	...	...	...	...	...	...	...	...
General government: long-term	4 758	...	...	...	...	...	...	...	...
General government: short-term	4 759	...	...	...	...	...	...	...	...
Other sectors: long-term	4 761	...	...	...	...	...	...	...	...
Other sectors: short-term	4 762	...	...	...	...	...	...	...	...
Loans	4 764	954	1,544	644	665	–148	–10,660	1,428	3,447
Use of Fund credit and loans from the Fund	4 766	30	–478	–257	–590	–73	1,211	455	1,924
Monetary authorities: other long-term	4 767	542	–55	–111	–32	–1	–4	–3	–3
Monetary authorities: short-term	4 768	...	...	...	...	...	...	...	...
General government: long-term	4 770	325	1,544	533	1,167	415	–11,816	1,381	2,143
General government: short-term	4 771	...	...	...	...	...	...	...	...
Banks: long-term	4 773	23	56	100	–31	...	...	...	...
Banks: short-term	4 774	...	...	...	...	...	...	...	...
Other sectors: long-term	4 776	–1	334	263	116	–489	–51	–405	–617
Other sectors: short-term	4 777	35	143	116	35	...	...	...	...
Currency and deposits	4 780	–62	–75	–34	22	773	1,157	1,066	3,119
Monetary authorities	4 781	–62	–75	–34	22	...	...	...	...
General government	4 782	...	...	...	...	...	...	...	...
Banks	4 783	...	...	...	...	773	1,157	1,066	3,119
Other sectors	4 784	...	...	...	...	...	...	...	...
Other liabilities	4 786	1,363	–4,988	–3,943	–1,007	397	–9,220	554	323
Monetary authorities: long-term	4 788	...	...	37	–4	4	–37	–29	–17
Monetary authorities: short-term	4 789	2,832	1,253	2,685	1,851	392	–9,168	...	...
General government: long-term	4 791	–42	–52	–45	–48	–1	–9	–12	–95
General government: short-term	4 792	...	–284	...	...	...	...	562	431
Banks: long-term	4 794	...	...	...	...	2	–6	33	4
Banks: short-term	4 795	...	...	...	...	...	...	...	...
Other sectors: long-term	4 797	–110	–678	–17	–115	...	...	...	...
Other sectors: short-term	4 798	–1,317	–5,227	–6,603	–2,691	...	...	...	...
D. RESERVE ASSETS	4 800	–1,888	1,826	–3,121	–2,040	–3,261	–4,279	–685	81
Monetary gold	4 810	...	...	54	35	–100	...	...	...
Special drawing rights	4 820	–1	...	–290	102	–190	–75	–82	23
Reserve position in the Fund	4 830	...	...	...	...	...	...	...	...
Foreign exchange	4 840	–1,887	1,826	–2,885	–2,177	–2,971	–4,204	–603	58
Other claims	4 880	...	...	...	...	...	...	...	...
NET ERRORS AND OMISSIONS	4 998	**–165**	**–249**	**715**	**–341**	**325**	**–254**	**7**	**13**

Part 3 of the *Yearbook* contains descriptions of the methodologies, compilation practices, and sources used to compile these data.

Table 1. ANALYTIC PRESENTATION, 1988–95

(Millions of U.S. dollars)

	Code	1988	1989	1990	1991	1992	1993	1994	1995
A. Current Account[1]	4 993 Y.	**...**	**...**	**...**	**...**	**...**	**–66.83**	**–106.22**	**–279.42**
Goods: exports f.o.b	2 100 ..	...	...	...	...	...	156.19	237.85	270.90
Goods: imports f.o.b	3 100 ..	...	...	...	...	...	–254.18	–418.67	–673.90
Balance on Goods	4 100 ..	...	...	...	...	...	*–97.99*	*–180.82*	*–403.00*
Services: credit	2 200 ..	...	...	...	...	...	17.28	13.37	28.60
Services: debit	3 200 ..	...	...	...	...	...	–40.06	–40.50	–52.27
Balance on Goods and Services	4 991 ..	...	...	...	...	...	*–120.77*	*–207.95*	*–426.67*
Income: credit	2 300 ..	...	...	...	...	...	...	...	1.63
Income: debit	3 300 ..	...	...	...	...	...	–1.30	–3.82	–14.61
Balance on Goods, Services, and Income	4 992 ..	...	...	...	...	...	*–122.07*	*–211.77*	*–439.65*
Current transfers: credit	2 379 Y.	...	...	...	...	...	56.29	106.23	161.93
Current transfers: debit	3 379 ..	...	...	...	...	...	–1.05	–.68	–1.70
B. Capital Account[1]	4 994 Y.	**...**	**...**	**...**	**...**	**...**	**5.10**	**5.74**	**8.05**
Capital account: credit	2 994 Y.	...	...	...	...	...	5.10	5.74	8.05
Capital account: debit	3 994 ..	...	...	...	...	...	...	...	...
Total, Groups A Plus B	4 010 ..	...	...	...	...	...	*–61.73*	*–100.48*	*–271.37*
C. Financial Account[1]	4 995 X.	**...**	**...**	**...**	**...**	**...**	**53.03**	**85.46**	**141.40**
Direct investment abroad	4 505 ..	...	...	...	...	...	...	...	...
Direct investment in Armenia	4 555 Y.	...	...	...	...	...	...	8.00	...
Portfolio investment assets	4 602 ..	...	...	...	...	...	...	...	...
Equity securities	4 610 ..	...	...	...	...	...	...	...	...
Debt securities	4 619 ..	...	...	...	...	...	...	...	...
Portfolio investment liabilities	4 652 Y.	...	...	...	...	...	...	...	...
Equity securities	4 660 Y.	...	...	...	...	...	...	...	...
Debt securities	4 669 Y.	...	...	...	...	...	...	...	...
Other investment assets	4 703 ..	...	...	...	...	...	–47.99	35.31	–11.50
Monetary authorities	4 703 .A	...	...	...	...	...	–37.39	.05	–6.99
General government	4 703 .B	...	...	...	...	...	–10.60	–6.50	...
Banks	4 703 .C	...	...	...	...	...	...	...	–4.51
Other sectors	4 703 .D	...	...	...	...	...	...	41.76	...
Other investment liabilities	4 753 X.	...	...	...	...	...	101.02	42.15	152.90
Monetary authorities	4 753 XA	...	...	...	...	...	28.24	–.09	–.04
General government	4 753 YB	...	...	...	...	...	99.05	55.26	151.20
Banks	4 753 YC	...	...	...	...	...	–26.27	–13.02	1.74
Other sectors	4 753 YD	...	...	...	...	...	...	...	...
Total, Groups A Through C	4 020 ..	...	...	...	...	...	*–8.70*	*–15.02*	*–129.97*
D. Net Errors and Omissions	4 998 ..	**...**	**...**	**...**	**...**	**...**	**15.86**	**–12.75**	**70.79**
Total, Groups A Through D	4 030 ..	...	...	...	...	...	*7.16*	*–27.77*	*–59.18*
E. Reserves and Related Items	4 040 ..	**...**	**...**	**...**	**...**	**...**	**–7.16**	**27.77**	**59.18**
Reserve assets	4 800 ..	...	...	...	...	...	–7.16	3.26	12.47
Use of Fund credit and loans	4 766 ..	...	...	...	...	...	...	24.50	46.71
Liabilities constituting foreign authorities' reserves	4 900 ..	...	...	...	...	...	...	...	...
Exceptional financing	4 920 ..	...	...	...	...	...	...	...	...
Conversion rates: dram per U.S. dollar	0 101 ..	**...**	**...**	**...**	**...**	**...**	**8.25**	**287.48**	**405.87**

[1] Excludes components that have been classified in the categories of Group E.

Table 2. STANDARD PRESENTATION, 1988–95
(Millions of U.S. dollars)

	Code	1988	1989	1990	1991	1992	1993	1994	1995
CURRENT ACCOUNT	4 993 . .	**. . .**	**. . .**	**. . .**	**. . .**	**. . .**	**–66.83**	**–106.22**	**–279.42**
A. GOODS	4 100 . .	. . .	. . .	. . .	. . .	. . .	–97.99	–180.82	–403.00
Credit	2 100 . .	**. . .**	**. . .**	**. . .**	**. . .**	**. . .**	**156.19**	**237.85**	**270.90**
General merchandise: exports f.o.b.	2 110 . .	. . .	. . .	. . .	. . .	. . .	156.19	237.85	270.90
Goods for processing: exports f.o.b.	2 150 . .	. . .	. . .	. . .	. . .	. . .	. . .	. . .	. . .
Repairs on goods	2 160 . .	. . .	. . .	. . .	. . .	. . .	. . .	. . .	. . .
Goods procured in ports by carriers	2 170 . .	. . .	. . .	. . .	. . .	. . .	. . .	. . .	. . .
Nonmonetary gold	2 180 . .	. . .	. . .	. . .	. . .	. . .	. . .	. . .	. . .
Debit	3 100 . .	**. . .**	**. . .**	**. . .**	**. . .**	**. . .**	**–254.18**	**–418.67**	**–673.90**
General merchandise: imports f.o.b.	3 110 . .	. . .	. . .	. . .	. . .	. . .	–254.18	–418.67	–673.90
Goods for processing: imports f.o.b.	3 150 . .	. . .	. . .	. . .	. . .	. . .	. . .	. . .	. . .
Repairs on goods	3 160 . .	. . .	. . .	. . .	. . .	. . .	. . .	. . .	. . .
Goods procured in ports by carriers	3 170 . .	. . .	. . .	. . .	. . .	. . .	. . .	. . .	. . .
Nonmonetary gold	3 180 . .	. . .	. . .	. . .	. . .	. . .	. . .	. . .	. . .
B. SERVICES	4 200 . .	. . .	. . .	. . .	. . .	. . .	–22.78	–27.13	–23.67
Total credit	2 200 . .	. . .	. . .	. . .	. . .	. . .	*17.28*	*13.37*	*28.60*
Total debit	3 200 . .	. . .	. . .	. . .	. . .	. . .	*–40.06*	*–40.50*	*–52.27*
Transportation services, credit	2 205 . .	**. . .**	**. . .**	**. . .**	**. . .**	**. . .**	**. . .**	**3.46**	**14.27**
Passenger	2 205 BA	. . .	. . .	. . .	. . .	. . .	. . .	*3.46*	*12.82*
Freight	2 205 BB	. . .	. . .	. . .	. . .	. . .	. . .	. . .	*1.45*
Other	2 205 BC	. . .	. . .	. . .	. . .	. . .	. . .	. . .	. . .
Sea transport, passenger	2 207 . .	. . .	. . .	. . .	. . .	. . .	. . .	. . .	. . .
Sea transport, freight	2 208 . .	. . .	. . .	. . .	. . .	. . .	. . .	. . .	. . .
Sea transport, other	2 209 . .	. . .	. . .	. . .	. . .	. . .	. . .	. . .	. . .
Air transport, passenger	2 211 . .	. . .	. . .	. . .	. . .	. . .	. . .	3.46	12.31
Air transport, freight	2 212 . .	. . .	. . .	. . .	. . .	. . .	. . .	. . .	.95
Air transport, other	2 213 . .	. . .	. . .	. . .	. . .	. . .	. . .	. . .	. . .
Other transport, passenger	2 215 . .	. . .	. . .	. . .	. . .	. . .	. . .	. . .	.51
Other transport, freight	2 216 . .	. . .	. . .	. . .	. . .	. . .	. . .	. . .	.50
Other transport, other	2 217 . .	. . .	. . .	. . .	. . .	. . .	. . .	. . .	. . .
Transportation services, debit	3 205 . .	**. . .**	**. . .**	**. . .**	**. . .**	**. . .**	**–35.73**	**–32.12**	**–43.19**
Passenger	3 205 BA	. . .	. . .	. . .	. . .	. . .	. . .	. . .	*–8.86*
Freight	3 205 BB	. . .	. . .	. . .	. . .	. . .	. . .	. . .	*–34.33*
Other	3 205 BC	. . .	. . .	. . .	. . .	. . .	. . .	. . .	. . .
Sea transport, passenger	3 207 . .	. . .	. . .	. . .	. . .	. . .	. . .	. . .	. . .
Sea transport, freight	3 208 . .	. . .	. . .	. . .	. . .	. . .	. . .	. . .	. . .
Sea transport, other	3 209 . .	. . .	. . .	. . .	. . .	. . .	. . .	. . .	. . .
Air transport, passenger	3 211 . .	. . .	. . .	. . .	. . .	. . .	. . .	. . .	–8.01
Air transport, freight	3 212 . .	. . .	. . .	. . .	. . .	. . .	. . .	. . .	–6.83
Air transport, other	3 213 . .	. . .	. . .	. . .	. . .	. . .	. . .	. . .	. . .
Other transport, passenger	3 215 . .	. . .	. . .	. . .	. . .	. . .	. . .	. . .	–.85
Other transport, freight	3 216 . .	. . .	. . .	. . .	. . .	. . .	. . .	. . .	–27.50
Other transport, other	3 217 . .	. . .	. . .	. . .	. . .	. . .	. . .	. . .	. . .
Travel, credit	2 236 . .	**. . .**	**. . .**	**. . .**	**. . .**	**. . .**	**. . .**	**. . .**	**1.40**
Business travel	2 237 . .	. . .	. . .	. . .	. . .	. . .	. . .	. . .	1.00
Personal travel	2 240 . .	. . .	. . .	. . .	. . .	. . .	. . .	. . .	.40
Travel, debit	3 236 . .	**. . .**	**. . .**	**. . .**	**. . .**	**. . .**	**–.35**	**–.69**	**–3.26**
Business travel	3 237 . .	. . .	. . .	. . .	. . .	. . .	. . .	–.69	–1.71
Personal travel	3 240 . .	. . .	. . .	. . .	. . .	. . .	. . .	. . .	–1.55
Other services, credit	2 200 BA	**. . .**	**. . .**	**. . .**	**. . .**	**. . .**	**17.28**	**9.91**	**12.93**
Communications	2 245 . .	. . .	. . .	. . .	. . .	. . .	16.96	8.47	11.03
Construction	2 249 . .	. . .	. . .	. . .	. . .	. . .	.32	.10	. . .
Insurance	2 253 . .	. . .	. . .	. . .	. . .	. . .	. . .	. . .	. . .
Financial	2 260 . .	. . .	. . .	. . .	. . .	. . .	. . .	. . .	. . .
Computer and information	2 262 . .	. . .	. . .	. . .	. . .	. . .	. . .	. . .	. . .
Royalties and licence fees	2 266 . .	. . .	. . .	. . .	. . .	. . .	. . .	. . .	. . .
Other business services	2 268 . .	. . .	. . .	. . .	. . .	. . .	. . .	. . .	. . .
Personal, cultural, and recreational	2 287 . .	. . .	. . .	. . .	. . .	. . .	. . .	. . .	. . .
Government, n.i.e.	2 291 . .	. . .	. . .	. . .	. . .	. . .	. . .	1.34	1.90
Other services, debit	3 200 BA	**. . .**	**. . .**	**. . .**	**. . .**	**. . .**	**–3.98**	**–7.69**	**–5.82**
Communications	3 245 . .	. . .	. . .	. . .	. . .	. . .	. . .	. . .	–.45
Construction	3 249 . .	. . .	. . .	. . .	. . .	. . .	. . .	–.18	. . .
Insurance	3 253 . .	. . .	. . .	. . .	. . .	. . .	–3.98	–3.58	–5.37
Financial	3 260 . .	. . .	. . .	. . .	. . .	. . .	. . .	. . .	. . .
Computer and information	3 262 . .	. . .	. . .	. . .	. . .	. . .	. . .	. . .	. . .
Royalties and licence fees	3 266 . .	. . .	. . .	. . .	. . .	. . .	. . .	. . .	. . .
Other business services	3 268 . .	. . .	. . .	. . .	. . .	. . .	. . .	–3.93	. . .
Personal, cultural, and recreational	3 287 . .	. . .	. . .	. . .	. . .	. . .	. . .	. . .	. . .
Government, n.i.e.	3 291 . .	. . .	. . .	. . .	. . .	. . .	. . .	. . .	. . .

Table 2 (Continued). STANDARD PRESENTATION, 1988–95

(Millions of U.S. dollars)

	Code	1988	1989	1990	1991	1992	1993	1994	1995
C. INCOME	4 300	...	...	...	...	...	–1.30	–3.82	–12.98
Total credit	2 300	...	...	...	...	...	...	...	*1.63*
Total debit	3 300	...	...	...	...	...	*–1.30*	*–3.82*	*–14.61*
Compensation of employees, credit	2 310	...	...	...	...	...	...	...	...
Compensation of employees, debit	3 310	...	...	...	...	...	...	...	...
Investment income, credit	2 320	...	...	...	...	...	...	...	**1.63**
Direct investment income	2 330	...	...	...	...	...	...	...	...
Dividends and distributed branch profits	2 332	...	...	...	...	...	...	...	...
Reinvested earnings and undistributed branch profits	2 333	...	...	...	...	...	...	...	...
Income on debt (interest)	2 334	...	...	...	...	...	...	...	...
Portfolio investment income	2 339	...	...	...	...	...	...	...	1.00
Income on equity	2 340	...	...	...	...	...	...	...	.50
Income on bonds and notes	2 350	...	...	...	...	...	...	...	.50
Income on money market instruments and financial derivatives	2 360	...	...	...	...	...	...	...	...
Other investment income	2 370	...	...	...	...	...	...	...	.63
Investment income, debit	3 320	...	...	...	...	...	**–1.30**	**–3.82**	**–14.61**
Direct investment income	3 330	...	...	...	...	...	...	...	–12.90
Dividends and distributed branch profits	3 332	...	...	...	...	...	...	...	...
Reinvested earnings and undistributed branch profits	3 333	...	...	...	...	...	...	...	...
Income on debt (interest)	3 334	...	...	...	...	...	...	...	–12.90
Portfolio investment income	3 339	...	...	...	...	...	...	...	...
Income on equity	3 340	...	...	...	...	...	...	...	...
Income on bonds and notes	3 350	...	...	...	...	...	...	...	...
Income on money market instruments and financial derivatives	3 360	...	...	...	...	...	...	...	...
Other investment income	3 370	...	...	...	...	...	–1.30	–3.82	–1.71
D. CURRENT TRANSFERS	4 379	...	...	...	...	...	55.24	105.55	160.23
Credit	2 379	...	...	...	...	...	**56.29**	**106.23**	**161.93**
General government	2 380	...	...	...	...	...	56.08	95.21	143.58
Other sectors	2 390	...	...	...	...	...	.21	11.02	18.35
Workers' remittances	2 391	...	...	...	...	...	...	...	12.35
Other current transfers	2 392	...	...	...	...	...	.21	11.02	6.00
Debit	3 379	...	...	...	...	...	**–1.05**	**–.68**	**–1.70**
General government	3 380	...	...	...	...	...	–1.05	–.68	–1.70
Other sectors	3 390	...	...	...	...	...	...	...	...
Workers' remittances	3 391	...	...	...	...	...	...	...	...
Other current transfers	3 392	...	...	...	...	...	...	...	...
CAPITAL AND FINANCIAL ACCOUNT	4 996	...	...	...	...	...	**50.97**	**118.97**	**208.63**
CAPITAL ACCOUNT	4 994	...	...	...	...	...	**5.10**	**5.74**	**8.05**
Total credit	2 994	...	...	...	...	...	*5.10*	*5.74*	*8.05*
Total debit	3 994	...	...	...	...	...	...	...	...
Capital transfers, credit	2 400	...	...	...	...	...	**5.10**	**5.74**	**8.05**
General government	2 401	...	...	...	...	...	5.10	5.74	8.05
Debt forgiveness	2 402	...	...	...	...	...	...	...	...
Other capital transfers	2 410	...	...	...	...	...	5.10	5.74	8.05
Other sectors	2 430	...	...	...	...	...	...	...	...
Migrants' transfers	2 431	...	...	...	...	...	...	...	...
Debt forgiveness	2 432	...	...	...	...	...	...	...	...
Other capital transfers	2 440	...	...	...	...	...	...	...	...
Capital transfers, debit	3 400	...	...	...	...	...	...	...	...
General government	3 401	...	...	...	...	...	...	...	...
Debt forgiveness	3 402	...	...	...	...	...	...	...	...
Other capital transfers	3 410	...	...	...	...	...	...	...	...
Other sectors	3 430	...	...	...	...	...	...	...	...
Migrants' transfers	3 431	...	...	...	...	...	...	...	...
Debt forgiveness	3 432	...	...	...	...	...	...	...	...
Other capital transfers	3 440	...	...	...	...	...	...	...	...
Nonproduced nonfinancial assets, credit	2 480	...	...	...	...	...	...	...	...
Nonproduced nonfinancial assets, debit	3 480	...	...	...	...	...	...	...	...

Table 2 (Continued). STANDARD PRESENTATION, 1988–95

(Millions of U.S. dollars)

	Code	1988	1989	1990	1991	1992	1993	1994	1995
FINANCIAL ACCOUNT	4 995	...	...	...	...	...	**45.87**	**113.23**	**200.58**
A. DIRECT INVESTMENT	4 500	...	...	...	...	...	...	8.00	...
Direct investment abroad	4 505	...	...	...	...	...	...	...	...
Equity capital	4 510	...	...	...	...	...	...	...	...
Claims on affiliated enterprises	4 515	...	...	...	...	...	...	...	...
Liabilities to affiliated enterprises	4 520	...	...	...	...	...	...	...	...
Reinvested earnings	4 525	...	...	...	...	...	...	...	...
Other capital	4 530	...	...	...	...	...	...	...	...
Claims on affiliated enterprises	4 535	...	...	...	...	...	...	...	...
Liabilities to affiliated enterprises	4 540	...	...	...	...	...	...	...	...
Direct investment in Armenia	4 555	...	...	...	...	...	...	**8.00**	...
Equity capital	4 560	...	...	...	...	...	...	8.00	...
Claims on direct investors	4 565	...	...	...	...	...	...	...	...
Liabilities to direct investors	4 570	...	...	...	...	...	...	8.00	...
Reinvested earnings	4 575	...	...	...	...	...	...	...	...
Other capital	4 580	...	...	...	...	...	...	...	...
Claims on direct investors	4 585	...	...	...	...	...	...	...	...
Liabilities to direct investors	4 590	...	...	...	...	...	...	...	...
B. PORTFOLIO INVESTMENT	4 600	...	...	...	...	...	...	...	...
Assets	4 602	...	...	...	...	...	...	...	...
Equity securities	4 610	...	...	...	...	...	...	...	...
Monetary authorities	4 611	...	...	...	...	...	...	...	...
General government	4 612	...	...	...	...	...	...	...	...
Banks	4 613	...	...	...	...	...	...	...	...
Other sectors	4 614	...	...	...	...	...	...	...	...
Debt securities	4 619	...	...	...	...	...	...	...	...
Bonds and notes	4 620	...	...	...	...	...	...	...	...
Monetary authorities	4 621	...	...	...	...	...	...	...	...
General government	4 622	...	...	...	...	...	...	...	...
Banks	4 623	...	...	...	...	...	...	...	...
Other sectors	4 624	...	...	...	...	...	...	...	...
Money market instruments	4 630	...	...	...	...	...	...	...	...
Monetary authorities	4 631	...	...	...	...	...	...	...	...
General government	4 632	...	...	...	...	...	...	...	...
Banks	4 633	...	...	...	...	...	...	...	...
Other sectors	4 634	...	...	...	...	...	...	...	...
Financial derivatives	4 640	...	...	...	...	...	...	...	...
Monetary authorities	4 641	...	...	...	...	...	...	...	...
General government	4 642	...	...	...	...	...	...	...	...
Banks	4 643	...	...	...	...	...	...	...	...
Other sectors	4 644	...	...	...	...	...	...	...	...
Liabilities	4 652	...	...	...	...	...	...	...	...
Equity securities	4 660	...	...	...	...	...	...	...	...
Banks	4 663	...	...	...	...	...	...	...	...
Other sectors	4 664	...	...	...	...	...	...	...	...
Debt securities	4 669	...	...	...	...	...	...	...	...
Bonds and notes	4 670	...	...	...	...	...	...	...	...
Monetary authorities	4 671	...	...	...	...	...	...	...	...
General government	4 672	...	...	...	...	...	...	...	...
Banks	4 673	...	...	...	...	...	...	...	...
Other sectors	4 674	...	...	...	...	...	...	...	...
Money market instruments	4 680	...	...	...	...	...	...	...	...
Monetary authorities	4 681	...	...	...	...	...	...	...	...
General government	4 682	...	...	...	...	...	...	...	...
Banks	4 683	...	...	...	...	...	...	...	...
Other sectors	4 684	...	...	...	...	...	...	...	...
Financial derivatives	4 690	...	...	...	...	...	...	...	...
Monetary authorities	4 691	...	...	...	...	...	...	...	...
General government	4 692	...	...	...	...	...	...	...	...
Banks	4 693	...	...	...	...	...	...	...	...
Other sectors	4 694	...	...	...	...	...	...	...	...

Table 2 (Concluded). STANDARD PRESENTATION, 1988–95

(Millions of U.S. dollars)

	Code	1988	1989	1990	1991	1992	1993	1994	1995
C. OTHER INVESTMENT	4 700	...	...	...	...	...	53.03	101.96	188.11
Assets	4 703	**...**	**...**	**...**	**...**	**...**	**–47.99**	**35.31**	**–11.50**
Trade credits	4 706	...	...	...	...	...	...	...	...
General government: long-term	4 708	...	...	...	...	...	...	...	...
General government: short-term	4 709	...	...	...	...	...	...	...	...
Other sectors: long-term	4 711	...	...	...	...	...	...	...	...
Other sectors: short-term	4 712	...	...	...	...	...	...	...	...
Loans	4 714	...	...	...	...	...	...	...	–1.22
Monetary authorities: long-term	4 717	...	...	...	...	...	...	...	...
Monetary authorities: short-term	4 718	...	...	...	...	...	...	...	...
General government: long-term	4 720	...	...	...	...	...	...	...	...
General government: short-term	4 721	...	...	...	...	...	...	...	...
Banks: long-term	4 723	...	...	...	...	...	...	...	...
Banks: short-term	4 724	...	...	...	...	...	...	...	–1.22
Other sectors: long-term	4 726	...	...	...	...	...	...	...	...
Other sectors: short-term	4 727	...	...	...	...	...	...	...	...
Currency and deposits	4 730	...	...	...	...	...	–37.39	41.81	.69
Monetary authorities	4 731	...	...	...	...	...	–37.39	.05	1.44
General government	4 732	...	...	...	...	...	...	...	...
Banks	4 733	...	...	...	...	...	...	...	–.75
Other sectors	4 734	...	...	...	...	...	...	41.76	...
Other assets	4 736	...	...	...	...	...	–10.60	–6.50	–10.97
Monetary authorities: long-term	4 738	...	...	...	...	...	...	...	...
Monetary authorities: short-term	4 739	...	...	...	...	...	...	...	–8.43
General government: long-term	4 741	...	...	...	...	...	...	...	...
General government: short-term	4 742	...	...	...	...	...	–10.60	–6.50	...
Banks: long-term	4 744	...	...	...	...	...	...	...	...
Banks: short-term	4 745	...	...	...	...	...	...	...	–2.54
Other sectors: long-term	4 747	...	...	...	...	...	...	...	...
Other sectors: short-term	4 748	...	...	...	...	...	...	...	...
Liabilities	4 753	**...**	**...**	**...**	**...**	**...**	**101.02**	**66.65**	**199.61**
Trade credits	4 756	...	...	...	...	...	...	...	...
General government: long-term	4 758	...	...	...	...	...	...	...	...
General government: short-term	4 759	...	...	...	...	...	...	...	...
Other sectors: long-term	4 761	...	...	...	...	...	...	...	...
Other sectors: short-term	4 762	...	...	...	...	...	...	...	...
Loans	4 764	...	...	...	...	...	99.05	79.76	194.81
Use of Fund credit and loans from the Fund	4 766	...	...	...	...	...	...	24.50	46.71
Monetary authorities: other long term	4 767	...	...	...	...	...	...	...	...
Monetary authorities: short-term	4 768	...	...	...	...	...	...	...	...
General government: long-term	4 770	...	...	...	...	...	99.05	55.26	151.20
General government: short-term	4 771	...	...	...	...	...	...	...	...
Banks: long-term	4 773	...	...	...	...	...	...	...	...
Banks: short-term	4 774	...	...	...	...	...	...	...	–3.10
Other sectors: long-term	4 776	...	...	...	...	...	...	...	...
Other sectors: short-term	4 777	...	...	...	...	...	...	...	...
Currency and deposits	4 780	...	...	...	...	...	28.24	–.09	5.63
Monetary authorities	4 781	...	...	...	...	...	28.24	–.09	–.03
General government	4 782	...	...	...	...	...	...	...	...
Banks	4 783	...	...	...	...	...	...	...	5.66
Other sectors	4 784	...	...	...	...	...	...	...	...
Other liabilities	4 786	...	...	...	...	...	–26.27	–13.02	–.83
Monetary authorities: long-term	4 788	...	...	...	...	...	...	...	–.01
Monetary authorities: short-term	4 789	...	...	...	...	...	...	...	...
General government: long-term	4 791	...	...	...	...	...	...	...	...
General government: short-term	4 792	...	...	...	...	...	...	...	...
Banks: long-term	4 794	...	...	...	...	...	...	...	...
Banks: short-term	4 795	...	...	...	...	...	–26.27	–13.02	–.82
Other sectors: long-term	4 797	...	...	...	...	...	...	...	...
Other sectors: short-term	4 798	...	...	...	...	...	...	...	...
D. RESERVE ASSETS	4 800	...	...	...	...	...	–7.16	3.26	12.47
Monetary gold	4 810	...	...	...	...	...	...	...	–7.93
Special drawing rights	4 820	...	...	...	...	...	...	–.28	–45.59
Reserve position in the Fund	4 830	...	...	...	...	...	.01	...	...
Foreign exchange	4 840	...	...	...	...	...	–7.17	3.54	65.99
Other claims	4 880	...	...	...	...	...	...	...	...
NET ERRORS AND OMISSIONS	4 998	**...**	**...**	**...**	**...**	**...**	**15.86**	**–12.75**	**70.79**

Table 1. ANALYTIC PRESENTATION, 1988–95
(Millions of U.S. dollars)

	Code	1988	1989	1990	1991	1992	1993	1994	1995
A. Current Account [1]	4 993 Y.	**–44.3**	**–46.7**	**–158.2**	**–209.5**	**43.8**	**41.7**	**81.1**	**–.3**
Goods: exports f.o.b.	2 100 . .	87.4	107.5	155.5	878.8	1,069.2	1,154.4	1,296.8	1,347.2
Goods: imports f.o.b.	3 100 . .	–354.6	–397.4	–580.8	–1,402.8	–1,446.7	–1,546.5	–1,607.3	–1,772.5
Balance on Goods	4 100 . .	*–267.3*	*–289.9*	*–425.4*	*–524.1*	*–377.5*	*–392.1*	*–310.6*	*–425.3*
Services: credit	2 200 . .	326.2	351.3	411.0	472.7	571.2	604.1	624.2	645.1
Services: debit	3 200 . .	–85.3	–100.2	–134.9	–147.8	–159.8	–169.1	–228.7	–245.5
Balance on Goods and Services	4 991 . .	*–26.3*	*–38.8*	*–149.3*	*–199.2*	*33.9*	*42.8*	*85.0*	*–25.6*
Income: credit	2 300 . .	10.9	13.4	14.8	17.9	14.5	13.4	9.6	16.4
Income: debit	3 300 . .	–27.9	–24.7	–22.6	–25.7	–21.8	–24.6	–22.3	–24.6
Balance on Goods, Services, and Income	4 992 . .	*–43.4*	*–50.1*	*–157.0*	*–207.0*	*26.5*	*31.6*	*72.3*	*–33.8*
Current transfers: credit	2 379 Y.	14.9	18.0	33.8	38.1	45.9	43.4	47.5	71.5
Current transfers: debit	3 379 . .	–15.8	–14.6	–34.9	–40.6	–28.7	–33.3	–38.7	–37.9
B. Capital Account [1]	4 994 Y.	**. . .**	**. . .**	**. . .**	**–3.0**	**–1.5**	**–1.8**	**–4.1**	**–.5**
Capital account: credit	2 994 Y.	. . .	. . .	. . .	.8	.9	.9	.3	3.1
Capital account: debit	3 994 . .	. . .	. . .	. . .	–3.8	–2.4	–2.8	–4.4	–3.6
Total, Groups A Plus B	4 010 . .	*–44.3*	*–46.7*	*–158.2*	*–212.5*	*42.3*	*39.9*	*76.9*	*–.8*
C. Financial Account [1]	4 995 X.	**56.8**	**47.8**	**172.2**	**228.8**	**–24.1**	**–8.4**	**–75.4**	**41.6**
Direct investment abroad	4 505 . .	. . .	. . .	. . .	. . .	. . .	. . .	. . .	. . .
Direct investment in Aruba	4 555 Y.	. . .	. . .	130.5	184.7	–37.0	–17.9	–73.2	–5.5
Portfolio investment assets	4 602 . .	. . .	. . .	8.7	13.1	11.3	10.8	16.5	–16.6
Equity securities	4 610 . .	. . .	. . .	. . .	. . .	. . .	. . .	. . .	. . .
Debt securities	4 619 . .	. . .	. . .	8.7	13.1	11.3	10.8	16.5	–16.6
Portfolio investment liabilities	4 652 Y.	. . .	. . .	–15.1	–25.4	–18.2	–14.6	–25.8	. . .
Equity securities	4 660 Y.	. . .	. . .	. . .	. . .	. . .	. . .	. . .	. . .
Debt securities	4 669 Y.	. . .	. . .	–15.1	–25.4	–18.2	–14.6	–25.8	. . .
Other investment assets	4 703 . .	–48.9	–19.4	–10.2	–17.1	13.6	–25.8	5.8	12.5
Monetary authorities	4 703 .A	. . .	. . .	. . .	. . .	. . .	. . .	. . .	. . .
General government	4 703 .B	. . .	. . .	. . .	. . .	. . .	. . .	–.8	. . .
Banks	4 703 .C	–48.9	–19.4	–31.3	–33.6	–3.5	–15.7	–3.7	15.6
Other sectors	4 703 .D	. . .	. . .	21.2	16.5	17.2	–10.1	10.4	–3.1
Other investment liabilities	4 753 X.	105.7	67.3	58.3	73.4	6.0	39.2	1.3	51.2
Monetary authorities	4 753 XA	. . .	. . .	. . .	. . .	. . .	. . .	. . .	. . .
General government	4 753 YB	13.8	12.3	1.2	1.9	10.0	.6	.4	.6
Banks	4 753 YC	57.0	–7.4	20.2	19.2	–10.7	18.5	–8.7	10.7
Other sectors	4 753 YD	34.9	62.3	36.9	52.3	6.7	20.1	9.6	39.9
Total, Groups A Through C	4 020 . .	*12.5*	*1.1*	*14.1*	*16.3*	*18.2*	*31.5*	*1.6*	*40.8*
D. Net Errors and Omissions	4 998 . .	**–12.8**	**20.4**	**–2.4**	**6.5**	**4.4**	**2.0**	**–4.7**	**2.0**
Total, Groups A Through D	4 030 . .	*–.4*	*21.5*	*11.7*	*22.8*	*22.6*	*33.4*	*–3.2*	*42.7*
E. Reserves and Related Items	4 040 . .	**.4**	**–21.5**	**–11.7**	**–22.8**	**–22.6**	**–33.4**	**3.2**	**–42.7**
Reserve assets	4 800 . .	.4	–21.5	–11.7	–22.8	–22.6	–33.4	3.2	–42.7
Use of Fund credit and loans	4 766 . .	. . .	. . .	. . .	. . .	. . .	. . .	. . .	. . .
Liabilities constituting foreign authorities' reserves	4 900 . .	. . .	. . .	. . .	. . .	. . .	. . .	. . .	. . .
Exceptional financing	4 920 . .	. . .	. . .	. . .	. . .	. . .	. . .	. . .	. . .
Conversion rates: florins per U.S. dollar	0 101 . .	**1.7900**	**1.7900**	**1.7900**	**1.7900**	**1.7900**	**1.7900**	**1.7900**	**1.7900**

[1] Excludes components that have been classified in the categories of Group E.

Table 2. STANDARD PRESENTATION, 1988–95

(Millions of U.S. dollars)

	Code	1988	1989	1990	1991	1992	1993	1994	1995
CURRENT ACCOUNT	4 993 . .	**–44.3**	**–46.7**	**–158.2**	**–209.5**	**43.8**	**41.7**	**81.1**	**–.3**
A. GOODS	4 100 . .	–267.3	–289.9	–425.4	–524.1	–377.5	–392.1	–310.6	–425.3
Credit	2 100 . .	**87.4**	**107.5**	**155.5**	**878.8**	**1,069.2**	**1,154.4**	**1,296.8**	**1,347.2**
General merchandise: exports f.o.b.	2 110 . .	87.4	107.5	155.5	878.8	1,069.2	1,154.4	1,296.8	1,289.8
Goods for processing: exports f.o.b.	2 150 . .	. . .	. . .	. . .	. . .	. . .	. . .	. . .	. . .
Repairs on goods	2 160 . .	. . .	. . .	. . .	. . .	. . .	. . .	. . .	1.1
Goods procured in ports by carriers	2 170 . .	. . .	. . .	. . .	. . .	. . .	. . .	. . .	56.3
Nonmonetary gold	2 180 . .	. . .	. . .	. . .	. . .	. . .	. . .	. . .	. . .
Debit	3 100 . .	**–354.6**	**–397.4**	**–580.8**	**–1,402.8**	**–1,446.7**	**–1,546.5**	**–1,607.3**	**–1,772.5**
General merchandise: imports f.o.b.	3 110 . .	–354.6	–397.4	–580.8	–1,402.8	–1,446.7	–1,546.5	–1,607.3	–917.9
Goods for processing: imports f.o.b.	3 150 . .	. . .	. . .	. . .	. . .	. . .	. . .	. . .	–838.9
Repairs on goods	3 160 . .	. . .	. . .	. . .	. . .	. . .	. . .	. . .	–6.6
Goods procured in ports by carriers	3 170 . .	. . .	. . .	. . .	. . .	. . .	. . .	. . .	–9.1
Nonmonetary gold	3 180 . .	. . .	. . .	. . .	. . .	. . .	. . .	. . .	. . .
B. SERVICES	4 200 . .	240.9	251.2	276.1	324.9	411.3	435.0	395.6	399.7
Total credit	2 200 . .	*326.2*	*351.3*	*411.0*	*472.7*	*571.2*	*604.1*	*624.2*	*645.1*
Total debit	3 200 . .	*–85.3*	*–100.2*	*–134.9*	*–147.8*	*–159.8*	*–169.1*	*–228.7*	*–245.5*
Transportation services, credit	2 205 . .	**8.7**	**12.3**	**13.3**	**40.2**	**69.2**	**74.1**	**109.4**	**49.0**
Passenger	2 205 BA	. . .	. . .	. . .	*14.1*	*16.5*	*10.7*	*17.8*	*33.4*
Freight	2 205 BB	*8.7*	*12.3*	*13.3*	*2.4*	*5.4*	*8.9*	*11.4*	*15.6*
Other	2 205 BC	. . .	. . .	. . .	*23.7*	*47.3*	*54.5*	*80.2*	. . .
Sea transport, passenger	2 207 . .	. . .	. . .	. . .	. . .	. . .	. . .	. . .	. . .
Sea transport, freight	2 208 . .	. . .	. . .	. . .	. . .	. . .	. . .	. . .	. . .
Sea transport, other	2 209 . .	. . .	. . .	. . .	. . .	. . .	. . .	. . .	. . .
Air transport, passenger	2 211 . .	. . .	. . .	. . .	. . .	. . .	. . .	. . .	. . .
Air transport, freight	2 212 . .	. . .	. . .	. . .	. . .	. . .	. . .	. . .	. . .
Air transport, other	2 213 . .	. . .	. . .	. . .	. . .	. . .	. . .	. . .	. . .
Other transport, passenger	2 215 . .	. . .	. . .	. . .	. . .	. . .	. . .	. . .	. . .
Other transport, freight	2 216 . .	. . .	. . .	. . .	. . .	. . .	. . .	. . .	. . .
Other transport, other	2 217 . .	. . .	. . .	. . .	. . .	. . .	. . .	. . .	. . .
Transportation services, debit	3 205 . .	**–9.3**	**–7.9**	**–12.6**	**–13.2**	**–18.8**	**–18.1**	**–19.2**	**–13.9**
Passenger	3 205 BA	. . .	. . .	. . .	*–3.2*	*–5.6*	*–2.8*	*–4.4*	*–6.4*
Freight	3 205 BB	*–9.3*	*–7.9*	*–12.6*	*–6.3*	*–9.1*	*–11.2*	*–8.5*	*–7.5*
Other	3 205 BC	. . .	. . .	. . .	*–3.6*	*–4.1*	*–4.1*	*–6.3*	. . .
Sea transport, passenger	3 207 . .	. . .	. . .	. . .	. . .	. . .	. . .	. . .	. . .
Sea transport, freight	3 208 . .	. . .	. . .	. . .	. . .	. . .	. . .	. . .	. . .
Sea transport, other	3 209 . .	. . .	. . .	. . .	. . .	. . .	. . .	. . .	. . .
Air transport, passenger	3 211 . .	. . .	. . .	. . .	. . .	. . .	. . .	. . .	. . .
Air transport, freight	3 212 . .	. . .	. . .	. . .	. . .	. . .	. . .	. . .	. . .
Air transport, other	3 213 . .	. . .	. . .	. . .	. . .	. . .	. . .	. . .	. . .
Other transport, passenger	3 215 . .	. . .	. . .	. . .	. . .	. . .	. . .	. . .	. . .
Other transport, freight	3 216 . .	. . .	. . .	. . .	. . .	. . .	. . .	. . .	. . .
Other transport, other	3 217 . .	. . .	. . .	. . .	. . .	. . .	. . .	. . .	. . .
Travel, credit	2 236 . .	**272.8**	**306.4**	**349.5**	**388.4**	**444.9**	**466.7**	**453.2**	**520.6**
Business travel	2 237 . .	. . .	. . .	. . .	. . .	. . .	. . .	. . .	. . .
Personal travel	2 240 . .	. . .	. . .	. . .	. . .	. . .	. . .	. . .	. . .
Travel, debit	3 236 . .	**–23.1**	**–28.4**	**–40.3**	**–47.4**	**–51.2**	**–57.6**	**–65.1**	**–72.7**
Business travel	3 237 . .	. . .	. . .	. . .	. . .	. . .	. . .	. . .	. . .
Personal travel	3 240 . .	. . .	. . .	. . .	. . .	. . .	. . .	. . .	. . .
Other services, credit	2 200 BA	**44.7**	**32.7**	**48.2**	**44.1**	**57.1**	**63.3**	**61.7**	**75.6**
Communications	2 245 . .	. . .	. . .	. . .	. . .	. . .	. . .	. . .	2.3
Construction	2 249 . .	. . .	. . .	. . .	. . .	. . .	. . .	. . .	11.4
Insurance	2 253 . .	1.0	1.4	1.5	.6	1.7	1.4	1.7	2.2
Financial	2 260 . .	. . .	. . .	. . .	14.8	21.3	20.1	22.2	19.7
Computer and information	2 262 . .	. . .	. . .	. . .	. . .	. . .	. . .	. . .	. . .
Royalties and licence fees	2 266 . .	. . .	. . .	. . .	. . .	. . .	. . .	. . .	. . .
Other business services	2 268 . .	30.4	18.3	34.2	19.7	21.6	25.9	18.3	20.8
Personal, cultural, and recreational	2 287 . .	. . .	. . .	. . .	. . .	. . .	. . .	. . .	. . .
Government, n.i.e.	2 291 . .	13.3	13.0	12.6	8.9	12.4	15.9	19.6	19.1
Other services, debit	3 200 BA	**–52.8**	**–63.8**	**–82.0**	**–87.3**	**–89.8**	**–93.4**	**–144.4**	**–158.9**
Communications	3 245 . .	. . .	. . .	. . .	–1.2	–2.7	–1.8	–1.1	–3.2
Construction	3 249 . .	. . .	. . .	. . .	. . .	. . .	. . .	. . .	–47.6
Insurance	3 253 . .	–1.0	–.9	–1.4	–2.8	–7.7	–5.3	–4.5	–3.3
Financial	3 260 . .	. . .	. . .	. . .	–30.8	–32.2	–33.1	–35.7	–53.2
Computer and information	3 262 . .	. . .	. . .	. . .	. . .	. . .	. . .	. . .	. . .
Royalties and licence fees	3 266 . .	. . .	. . .	. . .	. . .	. . .	. . .	. . .	. . .
Other business services	3 268 . .	–31.2	–42.1	–56.4	–27.3	–16.3	–21.1	–72.1	–13.4
Personal, cultural, and recreational	3 287 . .	. . .	. . .	. . .	. . .	. . .	. . .	. . .	. . .
Government, n.i.e.	3 291 . .	–20.6	–20.8	–24.2	–25.3	–31.0	–32.1	–30.9	–38.3

Table 2 (Continued). STANDARD PRESENTATION, 1988–95
(Millions of U.S. dollars)

	Code	1988	1989	1990	1991	1992	1993	1994	1995
C. INCOME	4 300 . .	–17.0	–11.3	–7.8	–7.8	–7.3	–11.2	–12.7	–8.2
Total credit	2 300 . .	*10.9*	*13.4*	*14.8*	*17.9*	*14.5*	*13.4*	*9.6*	*16.4*
Total debit	3 300 . .	*–27.9*	*–24.7*	*–22.6*	*–25.7*	*–21.8*	*–24.6*	*–22.3*	*–24.6*
Compensation of employees, credit	2 310 . .	**. . .**	**. . .**	**. . .**	**. . .**	**. . .**	**. . .**	**. . .**	**. . .**
Compensation of employees, debit	3 310 . .	**. . .**	**. . .**	**. . .**	**. . .**	**. . .**	**. . .**	**. . .**	**. . .**
Investment income, credit	2 320 . .	**10.9**	**13.4**	**14.8**	**17.9**	**14.5**	**13.4**	**9.6**	**16.4**
Direct investment income	2 330 . .	. . .	. . .	. . .	. . .	. . .	.1	. . .	. . .
Dividends and distributed branch profits	2 332 . .	. . .	. . .	. . .	. . .	. . .	.1	. . .	. . .
Reinvested earnings and undistributed branch profits	2 333 . .	. . .	. . .	. . .	. . .	. . .	. . .	. . .	. . .
Income on debt (interest)	2 334 . .	. . .	. . .	. . .	. . .	. . .	. . .	. . .	. . .
Portfolio investment income	2 339 . .	. . .	. . .	. . .	. . .	. . .	. . .	. . .	. . .
Income on equity	2 340 . .	. . .	. . .	. . .	. . .	. . .	. . .	. . .	. . .
Income on bonds and notes	2 350 . .	. . .	. . .	. . .	. . .	. . .	. . .	. . .	. . .
Income on money market instruments and financial derivatives	2 360 . .	. . .	. . .	. . .	. . .	. . .	. . .	. . .	. . .
Other investment income	2 370 . .	10.9	13.4	14.8	17.9	14.5	13.3	9.6	16.4
Investment income, debit	3 320 . .	**–27.9**	**–24.7**	**–22.6**	**–25.7**	**–21.8**	**–24.6**	**–22.3**	**–24.6**
Direct investment income	3 330 . .	. . .	. . .	. . .	–1.9	–2.6	–2.1	–.8	–6.0
Dividends and distributed branch profits	3 332 . .	. . .	. . .	. . .	–1.9	–2.6	–2.1	–.8	–6.0
Reinvested earnings and undistributed branch profits	3 333 . .	. . .	. . .	. . .	. . .	. . .	. . .	. . .	. . .
Income on debt (interest)	3 334 . .	. . .	. . .	. . .	. . .	. . .	. . .	. . .	. . .
Portfolio investment income	3 339 . .	. . .	. . .	. . .	. . .	. . .	. . .	. . .	. . .
Income on equity	3 340 . .	. . .	. . .	. . .	. . .	. . .	. . .	. . .	. . .
Income on bonds and notes	3 350 . .	. . .	. . .	. . .	. . .	. . .	. . .	. . .	. . .
Income on money market instruments and financial derivatives	3 360 . .	. . .	. . .	. . .	. . .	. . .	. . .	. . .	. . .
Other investment income	3 370 . .	–27.9	–24.7	–22.6	–23.8	–19.2	–22.5	–21.5	–18.5
D. CURRENT TRANSFERS	4 379 . .	–.9	3.4	–1.1	–2.5	17.3	10.1	8.8	33.5
Credit	2 379 . .	**14.9**	**18.0**	**33.8**	**38.1**	**45.9**	**43.4**	**47.5**	**71.5**
General government	2 380 . .	. . .	. . .	9.8	11.1	10.1	8.5	11.2	15.1
Other sectors	2 390 . .	14.9	18.0	24.0	27.0	35.8	34.9	36.3	56.3
Workers' remittances	2 391 . .	. . .	. . .	. . .	1.7	1.7	2.4	3.6	1.3
Other current transfers	2 392 . .	14.9	18.0	24.0	25.3	34.1	32.5	32.6	55.0
Debit	3 379 . .	**–15.8**	**–14.6**	**–34.9**	**–40.6**	**–28.7**	**–33.3**	**–38.7**	**–37.9**
General government	3 380 . .	. . .	. . .	–2.0	–2.5	–2.7	–2.7	–2.8	–2.8
Other sectors	3 390 . .	–15.8	–14.6	–33.0	–38.1	–25.9	–30.6	–35.9	–35.1
Workers' remittances	3 391 . .	. . .	. . .	. . .	–16.5	–4.7	–4.3	–3.7	–5.0
Other current transfers	3 392 . .	–15.8	–14.6	–33.0	–21.6	–21.2	–26.3	–32.2	–30.1
CAPITAL AND FINANCIAL ACCOUNT	4 996 . .	**57.2**	**26.3**	**160.6**	**203.0**	**–48.2**	**–43.7**	**–76.3**	**–1.7**
CAPITAL ACCOUNT	4 994 . .	**. . .**	**. . .**	**. . .**	**–3.0**	**–1.5**	**–1.8**	**–4.1**	**–.5**
Total credit	2 994 . .	. . .	. . .	. . .	*.8*	*.9*	*.9*	*.3*	*3.1*
Total debit	3 994 . .	. . .	. . .	. . .	*–3.8*	*–2.4*	*–2.8*	*–4.4*	*–3.6*
Capital transfers, credit	2 400 . .	**. . .**	**. . .**	**. . .**	**.8**	**.9**	**.9**	**.3**	**3.1**
General government	2 401 . .	. . .	. . .	. . .	. . .	. . .	. . .	. . .	. . .
Debt forgiveness	2 402 . .	. . .	. . .	. . .	. . .	. . .	. . .	. . .	. . .
Other capital transfers	2 410 . .	. . .	. . .	. . .	. . .	. . .	. . .	. . .	. . .
Other sectors	2 430 . .	. . .	. . .	. . .	.8	.9	.9	.3	3.1
Migrants' transfers	2 431 . .	. . .	. . .	. . .	.8	.9	.9	.3	3.1
Debt forgiveness	2 432 . .	. . .	. . .	. . .	. . .	. . .	. . .	. . .	. . .
Other capital transfers	2 440 . .	. . .	. . .	. . .	. . .	. . .	. . .	. . .	. . .
Capital transfers, debit	3 400 . .	**. . .**	**. . .**	**. . .**	**–3.8**	**–2.4**	**–2.8**	**–4.4**	**–3.6**
General government	3 401 . .	. . .	. . .	. . .	. . .	. . .	. . .	. . .	. . .
Debt forgiveness	3 402 . .	. . .	. . .	. . .	. . .	. . .	. . .	. . .	. . .
Other capital transfers	3 410 . .	. . .	. . .	. . .	. . .	. . .	. . .	. . .	. . .
Other sectors	3 430 . .	. . .	. . .	. . .	–3.8	–2.4	–2.8	–4.4	–3.6
Migrants' transfers	3 431 . .	. . .	. . .	. . .	–3.8	–2.4	–2.8	–4.4	–3.6
Debt forgiveness	3 432 . .	. . .	. . .	. . .	. . .	. . .	. . .	. . .	. . .
Other capital transfers	3 440 . .	. . .	. . .	. . .	. . .	. . .	. . .	. . .	. . .
Nonproduced nonfinancial assets, credit	2 480 . .	**. . .**	**. . .**	**. . .**	**. . .**	**. . .**	**. . .**	**. . .**	**. . .**
Nonproduced nonfinancial assets, debit	3 480 . .	**. . .**	**. . .**	**. . .**	**. . .**	**. . .**	**. . .**	**. . .**	**. . .**

Table 2 (Continued). STANDARD PRESENTATION, 1988–95
(Millions of U.S. dollars)

	Code	1988	1989	1990	1991	1992	1993	1994	1995
FINANCIAL ACCOUNT	4 995 . .	**57.2**	**26.3**	**160.6**	**205.9**	**−46.7**	**−41.8**	**−72.2**	**−1.2**
A. DIRECT INVESTMENT	4 500 . .	. . .	. . .	130.5	184.7	−37.0	−17.9	−73.2	−5.5
Direct investment abroad	4 505 . .	**. . .**	**. . .**	**. . .**	**. . .**	**. . .**	**. . .**	**. . .**	**. . .**
Equity capital	4 510 . .	. . .	. . .	. . .	. . .	. . .	. . .	. . .	. . .
Claims on affiliated enterprises	4 515 . .	. . .	. . .	. . .	. . .	. . .	. . .	. . .	. . .
Liabilities to affiliated enterprises	4 520 . .	. . .	. . .	. . .	. . .	. . .	. . .	. . .	. . .
Reinvested earnings	4 525 . .	. . .	. . .	. . .	. . .	. . .	. . .	. . .	. . .
Other capital	4 530 . .	. . .	. . .	. . .	. . .	. . .	. . .	. . .	. . .
Claims on affiliated enterprises	4 535 . .	. . .	. . .	. . .	. . .	. . .	. . .	. . .	. . .
Liabilities to affiliated enterprises	4 540 . .	. . .	. . .	. . .	. . .	. . .	. . .	. . .	. . .
Direct investment in Aruba	4 555 . .	**. . .**	**. . .**	**130.5**	**184.7**	**−37.0**	**−17.9**	**−73.2**	**−5.5**
Equity capital	4 560 . .	. . .	. . .	. . .	. . .	. . .	. . .	. . .	. . .
Claims on direct investors	4 565 . .	. . .	. . .	. . .	. . .	. . .	. . .	. . .	. . .
Liabilities to direct investors	4 570 . .	. . .	. . .	. . .	. . .	. . .	. . .	. . .	. . .
Reinvested earnings	4 575 . .	. . .	. . .	. . .	. . .	. . .	. . .	. . .	. . .
Other capital	4 580 . .	. . .	. . .	130.5	184.7	−37.0	−17.9	−73.2	−5.5
Claims on direct investors	4 585 . .	. . .	. . .	. . .	. . .	. . .	. . .	. . .	4.5
Liabilities to direct investors	4 590 . .	. . .	. . .	. . .	. . .	. . .	. . .	. . .	−10.1
B. PORTFOLIO INVESTMENT	4 600 . .	. . .	. . .	−6.4	−12.2	−6.8	−3.9	−9.3	−16.6
Assets	4 602 . .	**. . .**	**. . .**	**8.7**	**13.1**	**11.3**	**10.8**	**16.5**	**−16.6**
Equity securities	4 610 . .	. . .	. . .	. . .	. . .	. . .	. . .	. . .	. . .
Monetary authorities	4 611 . .	. . .	. . .	. . .	. . .	. . .	. . .	. . .	. . .
General government	4 612 . .	. . .	. . .	. . .	. . .	. . .	. . .	. . .	. . .
Banks	4 613 . .	. . .	. . .	. . .	. . .	. . .	. . .	. . .	. . .
Other sectors	4 614 . .	. . .	. . .	. . .	. . .	. . .	. . .	. . .	. . .
Debt securities	4 619 . .	. . .	. . .	8.7	13.1	11.3	10.8	16.5	−16.6
Bonds and notes	4 620 . .	. . .	. . .	8.7	13.1	11.3	10.8	16.5	−16.6
Monetary authorities	4 621 . .	. . .	. . .	. . .	. . .	. . .	. . .	. . .	. . .
General government	4 622 . .	. . .	. . .	. . .	. . .	. . .	. . .	. . .	. . .
Banks	4 623 . .	. . .	. . .	. . .	. . .	. . .	. . .	. . .	. . .
Other sectors	4 624 . .	. . .	. . .	. . .	. . .	. . .	. . .	. . .	−16.6
Money market instruments	4 630 . .	. . .	. . .	. . .	. . .	. . .	. . .	. . .	. . .
Monetary authorities	4 631 . .	. . .	. . .	. . .	. . .	. . .	. . .	. . .	. . .
General government	4 632 . .	. . .	. . .	. . .	. . .	. . .	. . .	. . .	. . .
Banks	4 633 . .	. . .	. . .	. . .	. . .	. . .	. . .	. . .	. . .
Other sectors	4 634 . .	. . .	. . .	. . .	. . .	. . .	. . .	. . .	. . .
Financial derivatives	4 640 . .	. . .	. . .	. . .	. . .	. . .	. . .	. . .	. . .
Monetary authorities	4 641 . .	. . .	. . .	. . .	. . .	. . .	. . .	. . .	. . .
General government	4 642 . .	. . .	. . .	. . .	. . .	. . .	. . .	. . .	. . .
Banks	4 643 . .	. . .	. . .	. . .	. . .	. . .	. . .	. . .	. . .
Other sectors	4 644 . .	. . .	. . .	. . .	. . .	. . .	. . .	. . .	. . .
Liabilities	4 652 . .	**. . .**	**. . .**	**−15.1**	**−25.4**	**−18.2**	**−14.6**	**−25.8**	**. . .**
Equity securities	4 660 . .	. . .	. . .	. . .	. . .	. . .	. . .	. . .	. . .
Banks	4 663 . .	. . .	. . .	. . .	. . .	. . .	. . .	. . .	. . .
Other sectors	4 664 . .	. . .	. . .	. . .	. . .	. . .	. . .	. . .	. . .
Debt securities	4 669 . .	. . .	. . .	−15.1	−25.4	−18.2	−14.6	−25.8	. . .
Bonds and notes	4 670 . .	. . .	. . .	−15.1	−25.4	−18.2	−14.6	−25.8	. . .
Monetary authorities	4 671 . .	. . .	. . .	. . .	. . .	. . .	. . .	. . .	. . .
General government	4 672 . .	. . .	. . .	. . .	. . .	. . .	. . .	. . .	. . .
Banks	4 673 . .	. . .	. . .	. . .	. . .	. . .	. . .	. . .	. . .
Other sectors	4 674 . .	. . .	. . .	−15.1	−25.4	−18.2	−14.6	−25.8	. . .
Money market instruments	4 680 . .	. . .	. . .	. . .	. . .	. . .	. . .	. . .	. . .
Monetary authorities	4 681 . .	. . .	. . .	. . .	. . .	. . .	. . .	. . .	. . .
General government	4 682 . .	. . .	. . .	. . .	. . .	. . .	. . .	. . .	. . .
Banks	4 683 . .	. . .	. . .	. . .	. . .	. . .	. . .	. . .	. . .
Other sectors	4 684 . .	. . .	. . .	. . .	. . .	. . .	. . .	. . .	. . .
Financial derivatives	4 690 . .	. . .	. . .	. . .	. . .	. . .	. . .	. . .	. . .
Monetary authorities	4 691 . .	. . .	. . .	. . .	. . .	. . .	. . .	. . .	. . .
General government	4 692 . .	. . .	. . .	. . .	. . .	. . .	. . .	. . .	. . .
Banks	4 693 . .	. . .	. . .	. . .	. . .	. . .	. . .	. . .	. . .
Other sectors	4 694 . .	. . .	. . .	. . .	. . .	. . .	. . .	. . .	. . .

Table 2 (Concluded). STANDARD PRESENTATION, 1988–95
(Millions of U.S. dollars)

	Code	1988	1989	1990	1991	1992	1993	1994	1995
C. OTHER INVESTMENT	4 700 . .	56.8	47.8	48.2	56.3	19.7	13.4	7.2	63.7
Assets	4 703 . .	**–48.9**	**–19.4**	**–10.2**	**–17.1**	**13.6**	**–25.8**	**5.8**	**12.5**
Trade credits	4 706 . .	. . .	. . .	. . .	. . .	. . .	. . .	. . .	. . .
General government: long-term	4 708 . .	. . .	. . .	. . .	. . .	. . .	. . .	. . .	. . .
General government: short-term	4 709 . .	. . .	. . .	. . .	. . .	. . .	. . .	. . .	. . .
Other sectors: long-term	4 711 . .	. . .	. . .	. . .	. . .	. . .	. . .	. . .	. . .
Other sectors: short-term	4 712 . .	. . .	. . .	. . .	. . .	. . .	. . .	. . .	. . .
Loans	4 714 . .	. . .	. . .	–1.7	–12.3	–2.8	–23.5	–19.7	–10.4
Monetary authorities: long-term	4 717 . .	. . .	. . .	. . .	. . .	. . .	. . .	. . .	. . .
Monetary authorities: short-term	4 718 . .	. . .	. . .	. . .	. . .	. . .	. . .	. . .	. . .
General government: long-term	4 720 . .	. . .	. . .	. . .	. . .	. . .	. . .	. . .	. . .
General government: short-term	4 721 . .	. . .	. . .	. . .	. . .	. . .	. . .	. . .	. . .
Banks: long-term	4 723 . .	. . .	. . .	. . .	. . .	. . .	. . .	. . .	. . .
Banks: short-term	4 724 . .	. . .	. . .	. . .	. . .	. . .	. . .	. . .	. . .
Other sectors: long-term	4 726 . .	. . .	. . .	1.5	1.0	3.1	–.9	1.8	2.8
Other sectors: short-term	4 727 . .	. . .	. . .	–3.2	–13.4	–5.9	–22.6	–21.5	–13.3
Currency and deposits	4 730 . .	–48.9	–19.4	–31.3	–26.5	1.7	–14.0	4.2	23.0
Monetary authorities	4 731 . .	. . .	. . .	. . .	. . .	. . .	. . .	. . .	. . .
General government	4 732 . .	. . .	. . .	. . .	. . .	. . .	. . .	–.8	. . .
Banks	4 733 . .	–48.9	–19.4	–31.3	–33.6	–3.5	–15.7	–3.7	15.6
Other sectors	4 734 . .	. . .	. . .	. . .	7.2	5.3	1.7	8.8	7.4
Other assets	4 736 . .	. . .	. . .	22.9	21.7	14.7	11.7	21.2	. . .
Monetary authorities: long-term	4 738 . .	. . .	. . .	. . .	. . .	. . .	. . .	. . .	. . .
Monetary authorities: short-term	4 739 . .	. . .	. . .	. . .	. . .	. . .	. . .	. . .	. . .
General government: long-term	4 741 . .	. . .	. . .	. . .	. . .	. . .	. . .	. . .	. . .
General government: short-term	4 742 . .	. . .	. . .	. . .	. . .	. . .	. . .	. . .	. . .
Banks: long-term	4 744 . .	. . .	. . .	. . .	. . .	. . .	. . .	. . .	. . .
Banks: short-term	4 745 . .	. . .	. . .	. . .	. . .	. . .	. . .	. . .	. . .
Other sectors: long-term	4 747 . .	. . .	. . .	22.9	21.7	14.7	11.7	21.2	. . .
Other sectors: short-term	4 748 . .	. . .	. . .	. . .	. . .	. . .	. . .	. . .	. . .
Liabilities	4 753 . .	**105.7**	**67.3**	**58.3**	**73.4**	**6.0**	**39.2**	**1.3**	**51.2**
Trade credits	4 756 . .	. . .	. . .	. . .	. . .	. . .	. . .	. . .	. . .
General government: long-term	4 758 . .	. . .	. . .	. . .	. . .	. . .	. . .	. . .	. . .
General government: short-term	4 759 . .	. . .	. . .	. . .	. . .	. . .	. . .	. . .	. . .
Other sectors: long-term	4 761 . .	. . .	. . .	. . .	. . .	. . .	. . .	. . .	. . .
Other sectors: short-term	4 762 . .	. . .	. . .	. . .	. . .	. . .	. . .	. . .	. . .
Loans	4 764 . .	48.7	74.7	40.3	62.2	21.5	27.9	46.3	40.4
Use of Fund credit and loans from the Fund	4 766 . .	. . .	. . .	. . .	. . .	. . .	. . .	. . .	. . .
Monetary authorities: other long-term	4 767 . .	. . .	. . .	. . .	. . .	. . .	. . .	. . .	. . .
Monetary authorities: short-term	4 768 . .	. . .	. . .	. . .	. . .	. . .	. . .	. . .	. . .
General government: long-term	4 770 . .	13.8	12.3	1.2	1.9	10.0	.6	.4	.6
General government: short-term	4 771 . .	. . .	. . .	. . .	. . .	. . .	. . .	. . .	. . .
Banks: long-term	4 773 . .	. . .	. . .	. . .	. . .	. . .	. . .	. . .	. . .
Banks: short-term	4 774 . .	. . .	. . .	. . .	. . .	. . .	. . .	. . .	. . .
Other sectors: long-term	4 776 . .	34.9	62.3	31.8	18.2	–10.6	. . .	34.7	39.9
Other sectors: short-term	4 777 . .	. . .	. . .	7.4	42.1	22.1	27.4	11.1	. . .
Currency and deposits	4 780 . .	57.0	–7.4	20.2	19.2	–10.7	18.5	–8.7	10.7
Monetary authorities	4 781 . .	. . .	. . .	. . .	. . .	. . .	. . .	. . .	. . .
General government	4 782 . .	. . .	. . .	. . .	. . .	. . .	. . .	. . .	. . .
Banks	4 783 . .	57.0	–7.4	20.2	19.2	–10.7	18.5	–8.7	10.7
Other sectors	4 784 . .	. . .	. . .	. . .	. . .	. . .	. . .	. . .	. . .
Other liabilities	4 786 . .	. . .	. . .	–2.2	–8.0	–4.7	–7.3	–36.3	. . .
Monetary authorities: long-term	4 788 . .	. . .	. . .	. . .	. . .	. . .	. . .	. . .	. . .
Monetary authorities: short-term	4 789 . .	. . .	. . .	. . .	. . .	. . .	. . .	. . .	. . .
General government: long-term	4 791 . .	. . .	. . .	. . .	. . .	. . .	. . .	. . .	. . .
General government: short-term	4 792 . .	. . .	. . .	. . .	. . .	. . .	. . .	. . .	. . .
Banks: long-term	4 794 . .	. . .	. . .	. . .	. . .	. . .	. . .	. . .	. . .
Banks: short-term	4 795 . .	. . .	. . .	. . .	. . .	. . .	. . .	. . .	. . .
Other sectors: long-term	4 797 . .	. . .	. . .	–2.1	–2.4	–3.4	–3.3	–28.5	. . .
Other sectors: short-term	4 798 . .	. . .	. . .	–.2	–5.6	–1.4	–4.0	–7.8	. . .
D. RESERVE ASSETS	4 800 . .	.4	–21.5	–11.7	–22.8	–22.6	–33.4	3.2	–42.7
Monetary gold	4 810 . .	. . .	. . .	. . .	. . .	. . .	. . .	. . .	–.7
Special drawing rights	4 820 . .	. . .	. . .	. . .	. . .	. . .	. . .	. . .	. . .
Reserve position in the Fund	4 830 . .	. . .	. . .	. . .	. . .	. . .	. . .	. . .	. . .
Foreign exchange	4 840 . .	.4	–21.5	–11.7	–22.8	–22.6	–33.4	3.2	–42.1
Other claims	4 880 . .	. . .	. . .	. . .	. . .	. . .	. . .	. . .	. . .
NET ERRORS AND OMISSIONS	4 998 . .	**–12.8**	**20.4**	**–2.4**	**6.5**	**4.4**	**2.0**	**–4.7**	**2.0**

Part 3 of the *Yearbook* contains descriptions of the methodologies, compilation practices, and sources used to compile these data.

Table 1. ANALYTIC PRESENTATION, 1988–95
(Millions of U.S. dollars)

	Code	1988	1989	1990	1991	1992	1993	1994	1995
A. Current Account[1]	4 993 Y.	**–11,387**	**–18,772**	**–16,088**	**–11,420**	**–11,542**	**–10,510**	**–17,346**	**–19,184**
Goods: exports f.o.b.	2 100 . .	33,413	37,160	39,642	42,362	42,813	42,637	47,332	53,132
Goods: imports f.o.b.	3 100 . .	–34,090	–40,511	–39,284	–38,833	–41,173	–42,666	–50,611	–57,146
Balance on Goods	4 100 . .	*–677*	*–3,350*	*358*	*3,528*	*1,640*	*–29*	*–3,279*	*–4,014*
Services: credit	2 200 . .	8,670	9,132	10,408	11,111	11,155	11,854	13,869	15,556
Services: debit	3 200 . .	–11,003	–13,390	–14,124	–13,770	–14,124	–13,702	–15,706	–17,611
Balance on Goods and Services	4 991 . .	*–3,010*	*–7,609*	*–3,359*	*869*	*–1,329*	*–1,877*	*–5,117*	*–6,069*
Income: credit	2 300 . .	2,907	3,482	3,162	3,119	3,557	3,825	4,344	5,729
Income: debit	3 300 . .	–11,363	–14,840	–16,335	–15,313	–13,664	–12,248	–16,220	–18,778
Balance on Goods, Services, and Income	4 992 . .	*–11,467*	*–18,967*	*–16,532*	*–11,325*	*–11,437*	*–10,301*	*–16,993*	*–19,117*
Current transfers: credit	2 379 Y.	1,204	1,366	1,749	1,401	1,221	1,103	1,180	1,338
Current transfers: debit	3 379 . .	–1,125	–1,171	–1,305	–1,496	–1,326	–1,313	–1,533	–1,405
B. Capital Account[1]	4 994 Y.	**1,361**	**1,720**	**1,561**	**1,683**	**1,136**	**340**	**387**	**630**
Capital account: credit	2 994 Y.	1,790	2,213	2,077	2,212	1,657	842	976	1,327
Capital account: debit	3 994 . .	–429	–493	–517	–530	–521	–502	–588	–697
Total, Groups A Plus B	4 010 . .	*–10,026*	*–17,051*	*–14,527*	*–9,738*	*–10,406*	*–10,170*	*–16,959*	*–18,554*
C. Financial Account[1]	4 995 X.	**19,365**	**16,670**	**13,223**	**11,028**	**6,468**	**10,048**	**14,894**	**13,075**
Direct investment abroad	4 505 . .	–4,983	–3,372	–185	–3,022	–854	–1,733	–5,686	–4,948
Direct investment in Australia	4 555 Y.	8,145	8,129	6,482	4,037	5,038	3,008	4,708	13,710
Portfolio investment assets	4 602 . .	–1,665	–2,450	1,112	–2,993	–73	–2,366	–572	–2,505
Equity securities	4 610 . .	–1,665	–2,450	1,112	–2,993	–73	–2,366	–572	–2,505
Debt securities	4 619 . .	. . .	. . .	. . .	. . .	. . .	. . .	. . .	. . .
Portfolio investment liabilities	4 652 Y.	7,496	2,819	897	6,664	–2,785	5,859	18,793	–1,571
Equity securities	4 660 Y.	1,106	1,401	1,665	2,416	99	7,460	8,120	2,969
Debt securities	4 669 Y.	6,390	1,418	–768	4,248	–2,884	–1,600	10,673	–4,540
Other investment assets	4 703 . .	404	–2,537	–955	–939	–2,428	–2,698	1,341	–3,573
Monetary authorities	4 703 .A	. . .	. . .	. . .	. . .	. . .	. . .	. . .	. . .
General government	4 703 .B	257	–297	319	348	202	–47	296	–61
Banks	4 703 .C	–215	–131	–833	829	–873	–1,038	–988	–1,111
Other sectors	4 703 .D	361	–2,109	–441	–2,116	–1,757	–1,613	2,033	–2,401
Other investment liabilities	4 753 X.	9,967	14,081	5,872	7,280	7,570	7,979	–3,690	11,963
Monetary authorities	4 753 XA	. . .	. . .	. . .	. . .	. . .	. . .	. . .	. . .
General government	4 753 YB	–1,141	803	–311	1,667	5,065	7,910	47	3,300
Banks	4 753 YC	4,312	9,722	4,556	4,533	1,620	2,661	2,173	7,359
Other sectors	4 753 YD	6,797	3,556	1,627	1,081	885	–2,593	–5,910	1,304
Total, Groups A Through C	4 020 . .	*9,339*	*–381*	*–1,305*	*1,291*	*–3,938*	*–122*	*–2,065*	*–5,479*
D. Net Errors and Omissions	4 998 . .	**–4,088**	**1,009**	**3,032**	**–1,607**	**–799**	**67**	**1,109**	**5,848**
Total, Groups A Through D	4 030 . .	*5,251*	*628*	*1,727*	*–316*	*–4,737*	*–55*	*–955*	*369*
E. Reserves and Related Items	4 040 . .	**–5,251**	**–628**	**–1,727**	**316**	**4,737**	**55**	**955**	**–369**
Reserve assets	4 800 . .	–5,279	–601	–1,740	324	4,726	42	960	–396
Use of Fund credit and loans	4 766 . .	. . .	. . .	. . .	. . .	. . .	. . .	. . .	. . .
Liabilities constituting foreign authorities' reserves	4 900 . .	28	–28	13	–8	11	13	–4	27
Exceptional financing	4 920 . .	. . .	. . .	. . .	. . .	. . .	. . .	. . .	. . .
Conversion rates: Australian dollars per U.S. dollar	0 101 . .	**1.2799**	**1.2646**	**1.2811**	**1.2838**	**1.3616**	**1.4706**	**1.3678**	**1.3490**

[1] Excludes components that have been classified in the categories of Group E.

Table 2. STANDARD PRESENTATION, 1988–95
(Millions of U.S. dollars)

	Code			1988	1989	1990	1991	1992	1993	1994	1995
CURRENT ACCOUNT	4	993	. .	**–11,387**	**–18,772**	**–16,088**	**–11,420**	**–11,542**	**–10,510**	**–17,346**	**–19,184**
A. GOODS	4	100	. .	–677	–3,350	358	3,528	1,640	–29	–3,279	–4,014
Credit	2	100	. .	**33,413**	**37,160**	**39,642**	**42,362**	**42,813**	**42,637**	**47,332**	**53,132**
General merchandise: exports f.o.b.	2	110	. .	30,673	34,312	36,170	38,520	38,859	38,886	43,339	48,672
Goods for processing: exports f.o.b.	2	150	. .	11	23	13	28	12	31	49	61
Repairs on goods	2	160	. .	6	7	9	9	12	10	17	13
Goods procured in ports by carriers	2	170	. .	213	238	288	320	414	384	335	339
Nonmonetary gold	2	180	. .	2,509	2,581	3,161	3,485	3,516	3,326	3,591	4,047
Debit	3	100	. .	**–34,090**	**–40,511**	**–39,284**	**–38,833**	**–41,173**	**–42,666**	**–50,611**	**–57,146**
General merchandise: imports f.o.b.	3	110	. .	–33,670	–40,077	–38,499	–37,704	–39,893	–41,559	–49,508	–56,128
Goods for processing: imports f.o.b.	3	150	. .	–143	–96	–168	–166	–187	–133	–220	–297
Repairs on goods	3	160	. .	–9	–15	–16	–16	–14	–16	–26	–21
Goods procured in ports by carriers	3	170	. .	–175	–181	–273	–277	–268	–278	–295	–159
Nonmonetary gold	3	180	. .	–93	–141	–329	–672	–810	–681	–562	–540
B. SERVICES	4	200	. .	–2,333	–4,259	–3,717	–2,659	–2,969	–1,848	–1,838	–2,055
Total credit	2	200	. .	*8,670*	*9,132*	*10,408*	*11,111*	*11,155*	*11,854*	*13,869*	*15,556*
Total debit	3	200	. .	*–11,003*	*–13,390*	*–14,124*	*–13,770*	*–14,124*	*–13,702*	*–15,706*	*–17,611*
Transportation services, credit	2	205	. .	**3,234**	**3,395**	**3,799**	**3,971**	**4,021**	**4,195**	**4,562**	**4,960**
Passenger	2	205	BA	*1,167*	*1,042*	*1,189*	*1,292*	*1,427*	*1,568*	*1,845*	*2,224*
Freight	2	205	BB	*639*	*721*	*741*	*826*	*850*	*921*	*1,055*	*1,232*
Other	2	205	BC	*1,427*	*1,632*	*1,869*	*1,854*	*1,744*	*1,705*	*1,662*	*1,504*
Sea transport, passenger	2	207	. .	. . .	. . .	. . .	. . .	. . .	. . .	. . .	. . .
Sea transport, freight	2	208	. .	639	721	741	826	850	921	1,055	1,232
Sea transport, other	2	209	. .	832	899	966	837	702	740	729	626
Air transport, passenger	2	211	. .	1,167	1,042	1,189	1,292	1,427	1,568	1,845	2,224
Air transport, freight	2	212	. .	. . .	. . .	. . .	. . .	. . .	. . .	. . .	. . .
Air transport, other	2	213	. .	595	733	903	1,018	1,042	965	933	878
Other transport, passenger	2	215	. .	. . .	. . .	. . .	. . .	. . .	. . .	. . .	. . .
Other transport, freight	2	216	. .	. . .	. . .	. . .	. . .	. . .	. . .	. . .	. . .
Other transport, other	2	217	. .	. . .	. . .	. . .	. . .	. . .	. . .	. . .	. . .
Transportation services, debit	3	205	. .	**–4,391**	**–5,176**	**–5,101**	**–5,023**	**–5,168**	**–4,990**	**–5,720**	**–6,504**
Passenger	3	205	BA	*–1,312*	*–1,658*	*–1,800*	*–1,823*	*–1,851*	*–1,701*	*–1,930*	*–2,165*
Freight	3	205	BB	*–2,317*	*–2,770*	*–2,568*	*–2,422*	*–2,639*	*–2,564*	*–2,968*	*–3,230*
Other	3	205	BC	*–762*	*–747*	*–733*	*–779*	*–677*	*–726*	*–822*	*–1,110*
Sea transport, passenger	3	207	. .	. . .	. . .	. . .	. . .	. . .	. . .	. . .	. . .
Sea transport, freight	3	208	. .	–2,036	–2,446	–2,277	–2,150	–2,389	–2,330	–2,674	–2,880
Sea transport, other	3	209	. .	–762	–747	–733	–779	–677	–726	–822	–1,110
Air transport, passenger	3	211	. .	–1,312	–1,658	–1,800	–1,823	–1,851	–1,701	–1,930	–2,165
Air transport, freight	3	212	. .	–280	–324	–291	–271	–251	–234	–294	–350
Air transport, other	3	213	. .	. . .	. . .	. . .	. . .	. . .	. . .	. . .	. . .
Other transport, passenger	3	215	. .	. . .	. . .	. . .	. . .	. . .	. . .	. . .	. . .
Other transport, freight	3	216	. .	. . .	. . .	. . .	. . .	. . .	. . .	. . .	. . .
Other transport, other	3	217	. .	. . .	. . .	. . .	. . .	. . .	. . .	. . .	. . .
Travel, credit	2	236	. .	**3,635**	**3,611**	**4,245**	**4,631**	**4,591**	**4,946**	**6,098**	**7,341**
Business travel	2	237	. .	. . .	. . .	. . .	. . .	. . .	. . .	. . .	. . .
Personal travel	2	240	. .	3,635	3,611	4,245	4,631	4,591	4,946	6,098	7,341
Travel, debit	3	236	. .	**–2,860**	**–3,820**	**–4,211**	**–3,867**	**–3,891**	**–3,672**	**–4,325**	**–4,979**
Business travel	3	237	. .	. . .	. . .	. . .	. . .	. . .	. . .	. . .	. . .
Personal travel	3	240	. .	–2,860	–3,820	–4,211	–3,867	–3,891	–3,672	–4,325	–4,979
Other services, credit	2	200	BA	**1,802**	**2,126**	**2,363**	**2,508**	**2,543**	**2,713**	**3,208**	**3,255**
Communications	2	245	. .	. . .	. . .	. . .	. . .	. . .	. . .	242	549
Construction	2	249	. .	. . .	. . .	. . .	17	54	42	37	47
Insurance	2	253	. .	74	87	135	139	110	275	387	376
Financial	2	260	. .	118	164	162	239	187	276	321	298
Computer and information	2	262	. .	. . .	. . .	. . .	121	191	147	197	146
Royalties and licence fees	2	266	. .	164	170	162	154	148	186	242	240
Other business services	2	268	. .	1,152	1,352	1,519	1,423	1,380	1,348	1,243	1,034
Personal, cultural, and recreational	2	287	. .	. . .	. . .	. . .	58	126	109	120	150
Government, n.i.e.	2	291	. .	294	352	386	357	346	330	418	415
Other services, debit	3	200	BA	**–3,752**	**–4,395**	**–4,812**	**–4,881**	**–5,065**	**–5,040**	**–5,661**	**–6,128**
Communications	3	245	. .	. . .	. . .	. . .	. . .	. . .	. . .	–342	–732
Construction	3	249	. .	. . .	. . .	. . .	–24	–28	–14	–19	–10
Insurance	3	253	. .	–217	–220	–220	–276	–400	–579	–727	–740
Financial	3	260	. .	–126	–132	–136	–169	–191	–245	–203	–208
Computer and information	3	262	. .	. . .	. . .	. . .	–58	–138	–106	–130	–101
Royalties and licence fees	3	266	. .	–714	–810	–827	–816	–890	–828	–977	–1,015
Other business services	3	268	. .	–2,116	–2,565	–2,845	–2,807	–2,664	–2,571	–2,485	–2,492
Personal, cultural, and recreational	3	287	. .	–245	–312	–325	–340	–347	–314	–385	–411
Government, n.i.e.	3	291	. .	–333	–357	–459	–391	–407	–382	–394	–419

Table 2 (Continued). STANDARD PRESENTATION, 1988–95

(Millions of U.S. dollars)

	Code	1988	1989	1990	1991	1992	1993	1994	1995
C. INCOME	4 300 . .	-8,457	-11,357	-13,173	-12,194	-10,108	-8,424	-11,876	-13,049
Total credit	2 300 . .	*2,907*	*3,482*	*3,162*	*3,119*	*3,557*	*3,825*	*4,344*	*5,729*
Total debit	3 300 . .	*-11,363*	*-14,840*	*-16,335*	*-15,313*	*-13,664*	*-12,248*	*-16,220*	*-18,778*
Compensation of employees, credit	2 310 . .	**127**	**236**	**348**	**337**	**354**	**340**	**387**	**431**
Compensation of employees, debit	3 310 . .	**-177**	**-263**	**-341**	**-300**	**-223**	**-219**	**-235**	**-306**
Investment income, credit	2 320 . .	**2,780**	**3,247**	**2,814**	**2,782**	**3,203**	**3,484**	**3,957**	**5,298**
Direct investment income	2 330 . .	1,715	1,521	757	550	1,146	1,703	2,633	3,418
Dividends and distributed branch profits	2 332 . .	118	117	250	222	212	273	310	368
Reinvested earnings and undistributed branch profits	2 333 . .	1,696	1,404	600	297	940	1,489	2,412	3,074
Income on debt (interest)	2 334 . .	-99	. . .	-93	31	-7	-59	-89	-25
Portfolio investment income	2 339 . .	706	1,203	1,389	1,591	1,513	1,177	659	1,075
Income on equity	2 340 . .	119	259	267	317	335	278	266	350
Income on bonds and notes	2 350 . .	586	945	1,122	1,274	1,178	899	393	724
Income on money market instruments and financial derivatives	2 360 . .	. . .	. . .	. . .	. . .	. . .	. . .	. . .	. . .
Other investment income	2 370 . .	359	522	667	641	544	604	665	806
Investment income, debit	3 320 . .	**-11,186**	**-14,577**	**-15,994**	**-15,013**	**-13,442**	**-12,029**	**-15,986**	**-18,471**
Direct investment income	3 330 . .	-3,665	-4,019	-4,489	-3,836	-4,333	-4,462	-7,599	-8,297
Dividends and distributed branch profits	3 332 . .	-1,171	-1,668	-2,757	-2,372	-2,429	-2,225	-2,508	-3,194
Reinvested earnings and undistributed branch profits	3 333 . .	-1,782	-1,299	-695	-529	-1,124	-1,567	-4,423	-4,367
Income on debt (interest)	3 334 . .	-712	-1,053	-1,037	-935	-780	-669	-668	-736
Portfolio investment income	3 339 . .	-1,648	-2,721	-2,495	-2,211	-1,997	-1,634	-1,923	-2,748
Income on equity	3 340 . .	-583	-1,134	-905	-792	-712	-740	-1,092	-1,595
Income on bonds and notes	3 350 . .	-1,065	-1,588	-1,590	-1,419	-1,285	-894	-831	-1,152
Income on money market instruments and financial derivatives	3 360 . .	. . .	. . .	. . .	. . .	. . .	. . .	. . .	. . .
Other investment income	3 370 . .	-5,873	-7,836	-9,010	-8,967	-7,111	-5,933	-6,464	-7,426
D. CURRENT TRANSFERS	4 379 . .	80	195	444	-95	-105	-210	-353	-67
Credit	2 379 . .	**1,204**	**1,366**	**1,749**	**1,401**	**1,221**	**1,103**	**1,180**	**1,338**
General government	2 380 . .	658	775	910	783	630	551	559	660
Other sectors	2 390 . .	546	591	840	618	591	552	621	678
Workers' remittances	2 391 . .	. . .	. . .	. . .	. . .	. . .	. . .	. . .	. . .
Other current transfers	2 392 . .	546	591	840	618	591	552	621	678
Debit	3 379 . .	**-1,125**	**-1,171**	**-1,305**	**-1,496**	**-1,326**	**-1,313**	**-1,533**	**-1,405**
General government	3 380 . .	-752	-779	-897	-1,079	-929	-939	-1,107	-943
Other sectors	3 390 . .	-373	-392	-408	-417	-397	-373	-427	-462
Workers' remittances	3 391 . .	. . .	. . .	. . .	. . .	. . .	. . .	. . .	. . .
Other current transfers	3 392 . .	-373	-392	-408	-417	-397	-373	-427	-462
CAPITAL AND FINANCIAL ACCOUNT	4 996 . .	**15,475**	**17,762**	**13,056**	**13,027**	**12,341**	**10,443**	**16,237**	**13,336**
CAPITAL ACCOUNT	4 994 . .	**1,361**	**1,720**	**1,561**	**1,683**	**1,136**	**340**	**387**	**630**
Total credit	2 994 . .	*1,790*	*2,213*	*2,077*	*2,212*	*1,657*	*842*	*976*	*1,327*
Total debit	3 994 . .	*-429*	*-493*	*-517*	*-530*	*-521*	*-502*	*-588*	*-697*
Capital transfers, credit	2 400 . .	**1,790**	**2,213**	**2,077**	**2,212**	**1,657**	**842**	**976**	**1,327**
General government	2 401 . .	. . .	. . .	. . .	. . .	. . .	. . .	. . .	. . .
Debt forgiveness	2 402 . .	. . .	. . .	. . .	. . .	. . .	. . .	. . .	. . .
Other capital transfers	2 410 . .	. . .	. . .	. . .	. . .	. . .	. . .	. . .	. . .
Other sectors	2 430 . .	1,790	2,213	2,077	2,212	1,657	842	976	1,327
Migrants' transfers	2 431 . .	1,790	2,213	2,077	2,212	1,657	842	976	1,327
Debt forgiveness	2 432 . .	. . .	. . .	. . .	. . .	. . .	. . .	. . .	. . .
Other capital transfers	2 440 . .	. . .	. . .	. . .	. . .	. . .	. . .	. . .	. . .
Capital transfers, debit	3 400 . .	**-429**	**-493**	**-517**	**-530**	**-521**	**-502**	**-588**	**-697**
General government	3 401 . .	-177	-193	-175	-165	-168	-191	-225	-292
Debt forgiveness	3 402 . .	. . .	. . .	. . .	. . .	. . .	. . .	. . .	. . .
Other capital transfers	3 410 . .	-177	-193	-175	-165	-168	-191	-225	-292
Other sectors	3 430 . .	-252	-300	-342	-365	-353	-311	-363	-405
Migrants' transfers	3 431 . .	-252	-300	-342	-365	-353	-311	-363	-405
Debt forgiveness	3 432 . .	. . .	. . .	. . .	. . .	. . .	. . .	. . .	. . .
Other capital transfers	3 440 . .	. . .	. . .	. . .	. . .	. . .	. . .	. . .	. . .
Nonproduced nonfinancial assets, credit	2 480 . .	. . .	. . .	. . .	. . .	. . .	. . .	. . .	. . .
Nonproduced nonfinancial assets, debit	3 480 . .	. . .	. . .	. . .	. . .	. . .	. . .	. . .	. . .

Table 2 (Continued). STANDARD PRESENTATION, 1988–95
(Millions of U.S. dollars)

	Code	1988	1989	1990	1991	1992	1993	1994	1995
FINANCIAL ACCOUNT	4 995 . .	**14,114**	**16,042**	**11,495**	**11,345**	**11,206**	**10,103**	**15,850**	**12,706**
A. DIRECT INVESTMENT	4 500 . .	3,162	4,757	6,297	1,016	4,185	1,274	–978	8,762
Direct investment abroad	4 505 . .	**–4,983**	**–3,372**	**–185**	**–3,022**	**–854**	**–1,733**	**–5,686**	**–4,948**
Equity capital	4 510 . .	–4,041	–1,762	–1,188	749	–1,107	–1,742	127	–1,528
Claims on affiliated enterprises	4 515 . .	. . .	. . .	. . .	. . .	. . .	. . .	. . .	. . .
Liabilities to affiliated enterprises	4 520 . .	. . .	. . .	. . .	. . .	. . .	. . .	. . .	. . .
Reinvested earnings	4 525 . .	–1,696	–1,404	–600	–297	–940	–1,489	–2,412	–3,074
Other capital	4 530 . .	755	–206	1,603	–3,474	1,193	1,497	–3,401	–346
Claims on affiliated enterprises	4 535 . .	–1,404	–530	–1,354	–659	139	–193	–64	–837
Liabilities to affiliated enterprises	4 540 . .	2,159	324	2,956	–2,815	1,054	1,690	–3,337	491
Direct investment in Australia	4 555 . .	**8,145**	**8,129**	**6,482**	**4,037**	**5,038**	**3,008**	**4,708**	**13,710**
Equity capital	4 560 . .	3,861	3,811	5,312	3,052	2,923	2,781	912	5,485
Claims on direct investors	4 565 . .	. . .	. . .	. . .	. . .	. . .	. . .	. . .	. . .
Liabilities to direct investors	4 570 . .	. . .	. . .	. . .	. . .	. . .	. . .	. . .	. . .
Reinvested earnings	4 575 . .	1,782	1,299	695	529	1,124	1,567	4,423	4,367
Other capital	4 580 . .	2,503	3,019	475	456	992	–1,341	–626	3,858
Claims on direct investors	4 585 . .	–169	67	–483	–988	425	–24	–672	–695
Liabilities to direct investors	4 590 . .	2,672	2,951	959	1,444	567	–1,316	46	4,553
B. PORTFOLIO INVESTMENT	4 600 . .	5,831	370	2,009	3,671	–2,858	3,493	18,221	–4,076
Assets	4 602 . .	**–1,665**	**–2,450**	**1,112**	**–2,993**	**–73**	**–2,366**	**–572**	**–2,505**
Equity securities	4 610 . .	–1,665	–2,450	1,112	–2,993	–73	–2,366	–572	–2,505
Monetary authorities	4 611 . .	. . .	. . .	. . .	. . .	. . .	. . .	. . .	. . .
General government	4 612 . .	. . .	. . .	. . .	. . .	. . .	. . .	. . .	. . .
Banks	4 613 . .	. . .	. . .	. . .	. . .	. . .	. . .	. . .	. . .
Other sectors	4 614 . .	–1,665	–2,450	1,112	–2,993	–73	–2,366	–572	–2,505
Debt securities	4 619 . .	. . .	. . .	. . .	. . .	. . .	. . .	. . .	. . .
Bonds and notes	4 620 . .	. . .	. . .	. . .	. . .	. . .	. . .	. . .	. . .
Monetary authorities	4 621 . .	. . .	. . .	. . .	. . .	. . .	. . .	. . .	. . .
General government	4 622 . .	. . .	. . .	. . .	. . .	. . .	. . .	. . .	. . .
Banks	4 623 . .	. . .	. . .	. . .	. . .	. . .	. . .	. . .	. . .
Other sectors	4 624 . .	. . .	. . .	. . .	. . .	. . .	. . .	. . .	. . .
Money market instruments	4 630 . .	. . .	. . .	. . .	. . .	. . .	. . .	. . .	. . .
Monetary authorities	4 631 . .	. . .	. . .	. . .	. . .	. . .	. . .	. . .	. . .
General government	4 632 . .	. . .	. . .	. . .	. . .	. . .	. . .	. . .	. . .
Banks	4 633 . .	. . .	. . .	. . .	. . .	. . .	. . .	. . .	. . .
Other sectors	4 634 . .	. . .	. . .	. . .	. . .	. . .	. . .	. . .	. . .
Financial derivatives	4 640 . .	. . .	. . .	. . .	. . .	. . .	. . .	. . .	. . .
Monetary authorities	4 641 . .	. . .	. . .	. . .	. . .	. . .	. . .	. . .	. . .
General government	4 642 . .	. . .	. . .	. . .	. . .	. . .	. . .	. . .	. . .
Banks	4 643 . .	. . .	. . .	. . .	. . .	. . .	. . .	. . .	. . .
Other sectors	4 644 . .	. . .	. . .	. . .	. . .	. . .	. . .	. . .	. . .
Liabilities	4 652 . .	**7,496**	**2,819**	**897**	**6,664**	**–2,785**	**5,859**	**18,793**	**–1,571**
Equity securities	4 660 . .	1,106	1,401	1,665	2,416	99	7,460	8,120	2,969
Banks	4 663 . .	. . .	. . .	. . .	. . .	. . .	. . .	. . .	. . .
Other sectors	4 664 . .	1,106	1,401	1,665	2,416	99	7,460	8,120	2,969
Debt securities	4 669 . .	6,390	1,418	–768	4,248	–2,884	–1,600	10,673	–4,540
Bonds and notes	4 670 . .	6,390	1,418	–768	4,248	–2,884	–1,600	10,673	–4,540
Monetary authorities	4 671 . .	. . .	. . .	. . .	. . .	. . .	. . .	. . .	. . .
General government	4 672 . .	5,479	1,866	–439	3,149	–2,693	–917	11,225	–4,266
Banks	4 673 . .	172	496	–732	751	–171	–487	–141	119
Other sectors	4 674 . .	739	–944	404	349	–19	–196	–411	–392
Money market instruments	4 680 . .	. . .	. . .	. . .	. . .	. . .	. . .	. . .	. . .
Monetary authorities	4 681 . .	. . .	. . .	. . .	. . .	. . .	. . .	. . .	. . .
General government	4 682 . .	. . .	. . .	. . .	. . .	. . .	. . .	. . .	. . .
Banks	4 683 . .	. . .	. . .	. . .	. . .	. . .	. . .	. . .	. . .
Other sectors	4 684 . .	. . .	. . .	. . .	. . .	. . .	. . .	. . .	. . .
Financial derivatives	4 690 . .	. . .	. . .	. . .	. . .	. . .	. . .	. . .	. . .
Monetary authorities	4 691 . .	. . .	. . .	. . .	. . .	. . .	. . .	. . .	. . .
General government	4 692 . .	. . .	. . .	. . .	. . .	. . .	. . .	. . .	. . .
Banks	4 693 . .	. . .	. . .	. . .	. . .	. . .	. . .	. . .	. . .
Other sectors	4 694 . .	. . .	. . .	. . .	. . .	. . .	. . .	. . .	. . .

Table 2 (Concluded). STANDARD PRESENTATION, 1988–95
(Millions of U.S. dollars)

	Code	1988	1989	1990	1991	1992	1993	1994	1995
C. OTHER INVESTMENT	4 700	10,399	11,516	4,930	6,334	5,153	5,294	–2,354	8,417
Assets	4 703	**404**	**–2,537**	**–955**	**–939**	**–2,428**	**–2,698**	**1,341**	**–3,573**
Trade credits	4 706	–333	–388	–211	372	504	–205	–73	–700
General government: long-term	4 708	–25	108	–26	–198	225	29	137	–57
General government: short-term	4 709	...	...	...	...	...	...	...	...
Other sectors: long-term	4 711	...	...	...	...	...	...	...	...
Other sectors: short-term	4 712	–308	–496	–185	570	279	–233	–210	–643
Loans	4 714	499	–1,978	123	–2,330	–2,059	–1,470	2,402	–1,762
Monetary authorities: long-term	4 717	...	...	...	...	...	...	...	...
Monetary authorities: short-term	4 718	...	...	...	...	...	...	...	...
General government: long-term	4 720	...	...	...	...	...	...	...	...
General government: short-term	4 721	–171	–365	379	356	–23	–91	159	–4
Banks: long-term	4 723	...	...	...	...	...	...	...	...
Banks: short-term	4 724	...	...	...	...	...	...	...	...
Other sectors: long-term	4 726	669	–1,613	–256	–2,686	–2,036	–1,379	2,243	–1,758
Other sectors: short-term	4 727	...	...	...	...	...	...	...	...
Currency and deposits	4 730	–215	–131	–833	829	–873	–1,038	–988	–1,111
Monetary authorities	4 731	...	...	...	...	...	...	...	...
General government	4 732	...	...	...	...	...	...	...	...
Banks	4 733	–215	–131	–833	829	–873	–1,038	–988	–1,111
Other sectors	4 734	...	...	...	...	...	...	...	...
Other assets	4 736	453	–40	–34	190	...	15	...	...
Monetary authorities: long-term	4 738	...	...	...	...	...	...	...	...
Monetary authorities: short-term	4 739	...	...	...	...	...	...	...	...
General government: long-term	4 741	453	–40	–34	190	...	15	...	...
General government: short-term	4 742	...	...	...	...	...	...	...	...
Banks: long-term	4 744	...	...	...	...	...	...	...	...
Banks: short-term	4 745	...	...	...	...	...	...	...	...
Other sectors: long-term	4 747	...	...	...	...	...	...	...	...
Other sectors: short-term	4 748	...	...	...	...	...	...	...	...
Liabilities	4 753	**9,995**	**14,053**	**5,885**	**7,273**	**7,581**	**7,992**	**–3,694**	**11,990**
Trade credits	4 756	530	59	–409	136	378	378	–163	793
General government: long-term	4 758	...	...	...	...	...	...	...	...
General government: short-term	4 759	...	...	...	...	...	...	...	...
Other sectors: long-term	4 761	...	...	...	...	...	...	...	...
Other sectors: short-term	4 762	530	59	–409	136	378	378	–163	793
Loans	4 764	8,971	12,296	5,710	7,751	6,744	6,765	–4,025	11,343
Use of Fund credit and loans from the Fund	4 766	...	...	...	...	...	...	...	...
Monetary authorities: other long-term	4 767	...	...	...	...	...	...	...	...
Monetary authorities: short-term	4 768	...	...	...	...	...	...	...	...
General government: long-term	4 770	–1,075	928	–204	1,577	5,102	7,864	2	3,409
General government: short-term	4 771	...	...	...	...	...	...	...	...
Banks: long-term	4 773	3,779	7,871	3,879	5,229	1,134	1,872	1,721	7,424
Banks: short-term	4 774	...	...	...	...	...	...	...	...
Other sectors: long-term	4 776	6,267	3,497	2,035	945	507	–2,970	–5,747	510
Other sectors: short-term	4 777	...	...	...	...	...	...	...	...
Currency and deposits	4 780	561	1,823	690	–704	497	803	448	–38
Monetary authorities	4 781	28	–28	13	–8	11	13	–4	27
General government	4 782	...	...	...	...	...	...	...	...
Banks	4 783	533	1,851	677	–696	486	789	452	–65
Other sectors	4 784	...	...	...	...	...	...	...	...
Other liabilities	4 786	–67	–125	–106	90	–38	46	45	–108
Monetary authorities: long-term	4 788	...	...	...	...	...	...	...	...
Monetary authorities: short-term	4 789	...	...	...	...	...	...	...	...
General government: long-term	4 791	...	...	...	...	...	...	...	...
General government: short-term	4 792	–67	–125	–106	90	–38	46	45	–108
Banks: long-term	4 794	...	...	...	...	...	...	...	...
Banks: short-term	4 795	...	...	...	...	...	...	...	...
Other sectors: long-term	4 797	...	...	...	...	...	...	...	...
Other sectors: short-term	4 798	...	...	...	...	...	...	...	...
D. RESERVE ASSETS	4 800	–5,279	–601	–1,740	324	4,726	42	960	–396
Monetary gold	4 810	...	...	...	...	...	13	...	...
Special drawing rights	4 820	16	18	22	22	185	14	14	20
Reserve position in the Fund	4 830	–21	–50	...	...	–242	27	77	14
Foreign exchange	4 840	–5,274	–569	–1,762	303	4,783	–12	869	–430
Other claims	4 880	...	...	...	...	...	...	...	...
NET ERRORS AND OMISSIONS	4 998	**–4,088**	**1,009**	**3,032**	**–1,607**	**–799**	**67**	**1,109**	**5,848**

Part 3 of the *Yearbook* contains descriptions of the methodologies, compilation practices, and sources used to compile these data.

Table 3. INTERNATIONAL INVESTMENT POSITION (End–period stocks), 1988–95
(Millions of U.S. dollars)

	Code		1988	1989	1990	1991	1992	1993	1994	1995
ASSETS	8 995	C.	67,040	74,807	76,012	84,053	78,450	89,532	97,746	111,576
Direct investment abroad	8 505	..	**28,348**	**29,553**	**30,112**	**33,076**	**32,055**	**32,644**	**38,217**	**41,185**
Equity capital and reinvested earnings	8 506	..	29,518	31,114	33,145	32,722	31,947	35,255	38,476	41,622
Claims on affiliated enterprises	8 507	..	...	...	...	...	...	...	...	...
Liabilities to affiliated enterprises	8 508	..	...	...	...	...	...	...	...	...
Other capital	8 530	..	-1,170	-1,561	-3,034	354	108	-2,611	-259	-437
Claims on affiliated enterprises	8 535	..	...	...	...	...	...	...	...	...
Liabilities to affiliated enterprises	8 540	..	...	...	...	...	...	...	...	...
Portfolio investment	8 602	..	**9,523**	**13,664**	**11,344**	**15,695**	**15,157**	**21,571**	**22,970**	**29,668**
Equity securities	8 610	..	9,523	13,664	11,344	15,695	15,157	21,571	22,970	29,668
Monetary authorities	8 611	..	...	...	...	...	...	...	...	...
General government	8 612	..	...	...	...	...	...	...	...	...
Banks	8 613	..	...	...	...	...	...	...	...	...
Other sectors	8 614	..	...	...	...	...	...	...	...	...
Debt securities	8 619	..	...	...	...	...	...	...	...	...
Bonds and notes	8 620	..	...	...	...	...	...	...	...	...
Monetary authorities	8 621	..	...	...	...	...	...	...	...	...
General government	8 622	..	...	...	...	...	...	...	...	...
Banks	8 623	..	...	...	...	...	...	...	...	...
Other sectors	8 624	..	...	...	...	...	...	...	...	...
Money market instruments	8 630	..	...	...	...	...	...	...	...	...
Monetary authorities	8 631	..	...	...	...	...	...	...	...	...
General government	8 632	..	...	...	...	...	...	...	...	...
Banks	8 633	..	...	...	...	...	...	...	...	...
Other sectors	8 634	..	...	...	...	...	...	...	...	...
Financial derivatives	8 640	..	...	...	...	...	...	...	...	...
Monetary authorities	8 641	..	...	...	...	...	...	...	...	...
General government	8 642	..	...	...	...	...	...	...	...	...
Banks	8 643	..	...	...	...	...	...	...	...	...
Other sectors	8 644	..	...	...	...	...	...	...	...	...
Other investment	8 703	..	**12,253**	**14,556**	**15,232**	**15,942**	**17,385**	**21,128**	**22,253**	**25,773**
Trade credits	8 706	..	...	...	...	...	...	...	...	...
General government: long-term	8 708	..	...	...	...	...	...	...	...	...
General government: short-term	8 709	..	...	...	...	...	...	...	...	...
Other sectors: long-term	8 711	..	...	...	...	...	...	...	...	...
Other sectors: short-term	8 712	..	...	...	...	...	...	...	...	...
Loans	8 714	..	7,665	10,219	10,063	11,360	13,236	15,539	19,631	18,313
Monetary authorities: long-term	8 717	..	...	...	...	...	...	...	...	...
Monetary authorities: short-term	8 718	..	...	...	...	...	...	...	...	...
General government: long-term	8 720	..	508	855	504	116	76	182	41	41
General government: short-term	8 721	..	...	...	...	...	...	...	...	...
Banks: long-term	8 723	..	...	...	...	...	...	...	...	...
Banks: short-term	8 724	..	...	...	...	...	...	...	...	...
Other sectors: long-term	8 726	..	3,783	5,265	5,548	8,077	10,897	12,008	15,993	14,247
Other sectors: short-term	8 727	..	3,374	4,099	4,011	3,167	2,263	3,348	3,597	4,024
Currency and deposits	8 730	..	2,459	2,429	3,249	2,492	2,379	3,757	505	5,374
Monetary authorities	8 731	..	...	...	...	...	...	...	...	...
General government	8 732	..	...	...	...	...	...	...	...	...
Banks	8 733	..	2,459	2,429	3,249	2,492	2,379	3,757	505	5,374
Other sectors	8 734	..	...	...	...	...	...	...	...	...
Other assets	8 736	..	2,129	1,909	1,921	2,090	1,770	1,833	2,117	2,086
Monetary authorities: long-term	8 738	..	...	...	...	...	...	...	...	...
Monetary authorities: short-term	8 739	..	...	...	...	...	...	...	...	...
General government: long-term	8 741	..	2,129	1,909	1,921	2,090	1,770	1,833	2,117	2,086
General government: short-term	8 742	..	...	...	...	...	...	...	...	...
Banks: long-term	8 744	..	...	...	...	...	...	...	...	...
Banks: short-term	8 745	..	...	...	...	...	...	...	...	...
Other sectors: long-term	8 747	..	...	...	...	...	...	...	...	...
Other sectors: short-term	8 748	..	...	...	...	...	...	...	...	...
Reserve assets	8 800	..	**16,915**	**17,033**	**19,324**	**19,339**	**13,853**	**14,189**	**14,306**	**14,950**
Monetary gold	8 810	..	3,317	3,253	3,059	2,805	2,645	3,087	3,021	3,053
Special drawing rights	8 820	..	334	307	311	290	96	82	73	55
Reserve position in the Fund	8 830	..	275	322	349	351	577	550	506	502
Foreign exchange	8 840	..	12,989	13,150	15,605	15,893	10,536	10,470	10,706	11,340
Other claims	8 880	..	...	...	...	...	...	...	...	...

Table 3 (Continued). INTERNATIONAL INVESTMENT POSITION (End–period stocks), 1988–95

(Millions of U.S. dollars)

	Code	1988	1989	1990	1991	1992	1993	1994	1995
LIABILITIES	8 995 D.	186,032	203,896	215,662	230,202	218,347	253,055	293,356	318,451
Direct investment in Australia	8 555	**65,023**	**73,471**	**76,055**	**78,037**	**75,157**	**83,671**	**95,056**	**105,485**
Equity capital and reinvested earnings	8 556	49,435	56,225	58,274	60,039	57,058	66,717	76,850	83,783
Claims on direct investors	8 557	...	...	...	...	...	...	...	...
Liabilities to direct investors	8 558	...	...	...	...	...	...	...	...
Other capital	8 580	15,588	17,246	17,780	17,998	18,099	16,955	18,207	21,702
Claims on direct investors	8 585	...	...	...	...	...	...	...	...
Liabilities to direct investors	8 590	...	...	...	...	...	...	...	...
Portfolio investment	8 652	**36,278**	**35,205**	**37,284**	**45,167**	**36,486**	**53,450**	**76,189**	**80,708**
Equity securities	8 660	17,755	17,614	20,034	21,957	18,256	35,916	46,544	53,819
Banks	8 663	...	...	...	...	...	...	...	...
Other sectors	8 664	...	...	...	...	...	...	...	...
Debt securities	8 669	18,523	17,591	17,250	23,210	18,230	17,534	29,646	26,889
Bonds and notes	8 670	18,523	17,591	17,250	23,210	18,230	17,534	29,646	26,889
Monetary authorities	8 671	...	...	...	...	...	...	...	...
General government	8 672	14,959	14,577	14,678	19,531	15,539	15,640	28,015	25,597
Banks	8 673	...	...	...	...	...	...	...	...
Other sectors	8 674	3,564	3,014	2,572	3,679	2,691	1,893	1,631	1,292
Money market instruments	8 680	...	...	...	...	...	...	...	...
Monetary authorities	8 681	...	...	...	...	...	...	...	...
General government	8 682	...	...	...	...	...	...	...	...
Banks	8 683	...	...	...	...	...	...	...	...
Other sectors	8 684	...	...	...	...	...	...	...	...
Financial derivatives	8 690	...	...	...	...	...	...	...	...
Monetary authorities	8 691	...	...	...	...	...	...	...	...
General government	8 692	...	...	...	...	...	...	...	...
Banks	8 692	...	...	...	...	...	...	...	...
Other sectors	8 694	...	...	...	...	...	...	...	...
Other investment	8 753	**84,730**	**95,221**	**102,323**	**106,998**	**106,703**	**115,934**	**122,111**	**132,258**
Trade credits	8 756	...	...	...	...	...	...	...	...
General government: long-term	8 758	...	...	...	...	...	...	...	...
General government: short-term	8 759	...	...	...	...	...	...	...	...
Other sectors: long-term	8 761	...	...	...	...	...	...	...	...
Other sectors: short-term	8 762	...	...	...	...	...	...	...	...
Loans	8 764	81,610	90,452	97,462	102,520	102,362	110,792	115,578	126,324
Use of Fund credit and loans from the Fund	8 766	...	...	...	...	...	...	...	...
Monetary authorities: other long-term	8 767	...	...	...	...	...	...	...	...
Monetary authorities: short-term	8 768	...	...	...	...	...	...	...	...
General government: long-term	8 770	15,279	15,629	16,049	17,380	21,132	28,538	31,421	34,531
General government: short-term	8 771	...	...	...	...	...	...	...	...
Banks: long-term	8 773	...	...	...	...	...	...	...	...
Banks: short-term	8 774	...	...	...	...	...	...	...	...
Other sectors: long-term	8 776	63,153	71,188	78,664	82,461	78,836	78,572	79,878	86,599
Other sectors: short-term	8 777	3,177	3,635	2,749	2,679	2,394	3,681	4,279	5,194
Currency and deposits	8 780	2,868	4,710	4,895	4,432	4,320	5,061	6,401	5,889
Monetary authorities	8 781	...	...	...	...	...	...	...	...
General government	8 782	...	...	...	...	...	...	...	...
Banks	8 783	2,868	4,710	4,895	4,432	4,320	5,061	6,401	5,889
Other sectors	8 784	...	...	...	...	...	...	...	...
Other liabilities	8 786	253	59	–34	46	21	81	132	45
Monetary authorities: long-term	8 788	...	...	...	...	...	...	...	...
Monetary authorities: short-term	8 789	253	59	–34	46	21	81	132	45
General government: long-term	8 791	...	...	...	...	...	...	...	...
General government: short-term	8 792	...	...	...	...	...	...	...	...
Banks: long-term	8 794	...	...	...	...	...	...	...	...
Banks: short-term	8 795	...	...	...	...	...	...	...	...
Other sectors: long-term	8 797	...	...	...	...	...	...	...	...
Other sectors: short-term	8 798	...	...	...	...	...	...	...	...
NET INTERNATIONAL INVESTMENT POSITION	8 995	**–118,992**	**–129,089**	**–139,650**	**–146,149**	**–139,897**	**–163,523**	**–195,610**	**–206,875**
Conversion rates: Australian dollars per U.S. dollar (end of period)	0 102	**1.1689**	**1.2615**	**1.2932**	**1.3161**	**1.4522**	**1.4769**	**1.2873**	**1.3423**

Table 1. ANALYTIC PRESENTATION, 1988–95
(Millions of U.S. dollars)

	Code	1988	1989	1990	1991	1992	1993	1994	1995
A. Current Account [1]	4 993 Y.	**–242**	**248**	**1,166**	**61**	**–79**	**–608**	**–2,209**	**–5,113**
Goods: exports f.o.b	2 100 . .	30,158	31,960	40,414	40,353	43,929	39,845	44,645	72,110
Goods: imports f.o.b	3 100 . .	–34,922	–37,512	–47,383	–48,913	–52,332	–47,112	–53,373	–77,556
Balance on Goods	4 100 . .	*–4,765*	*–5,552*	*–6,969*	*–8,560*	*–8,403*	*–7,267*	*–8,727*	*–5,446*
Services: credit	2 200 . .	17,550	18,377	23,279	25,560	28,352	27,867	29,132	23,506
Services: debit	3 200 . .	–12,077	–11,527	–14,197	–15,333	–18,477	–19,711	–21,189	–21,034
Balance on Goods and Services	4 991 . .	*708*	*1,298*	*2,114*	*1,667*	*1,472*	*889*	*–784*	*–2,975*
Income: credit	2 300 . .	5,324	6,789	9,145	9,544	9,276	9,170	8,825	10,859
Income: debit	3 300 . .	–6,243	–7,723	–10,087	–11,020	–9,844	–9,687	–9,195	–11,495
Balance on Goods, Services, and Income	4 992 . .	*–210*	*364*	*1,172*	*192*	*904*	*372*	*–1,154*	*–3,610*
Current transfers: credit	2 379 Y.	1,258	1,227	1,657	1,699	1,386	1,334	1,443	3,266
Current transfers: debit	3 379 . .	–1,289	–1,343	–1,663	–1,830	–2,369	–2,314	–2,498	–4,769
B. Capital Account [1]	4 994 Y.	**–5**	**–12**	**8**	**55**	**–84**	**–111**	**346**	**10**
Capital account: credit	2 994 Y.	40	50	63	152	168	177	598	317
Capital account: debit	3 994 . .	–44	–62	–55	–97	–252	–288	–252	–307
Total, Groups A Plus B	4 010 . .	*–246*	*236*	*1,174*	*116*	*–164*	*–719*	*–1,862*	*–5,104*
C. Financial Account [1]	4 995 X.	**415**	**1,367**	**–19**	**–12**	**1,961**	**3,415**	**3,099**	**4,649**
Direct investment abroad	4 505 . .	–310	–867	–1,701	–1,293	–1,872	–1,465	–1,203	–1,141
Direct investment in Austria	4 555 Y.	436	587	653	360	947	977	1,311	1,357
Portfolio investment assets	4 602 . .	–1,598	–1,559	–1,608	–2,272	–2,676	–1,912	–4,475	–2,778
Equity securities	4 610 . .	–572	–524	–430	–60	–194	–557	–834	–563
Debt securities	4 619 . .	–1,026	–1,035	–1,178	–2,212	–2,483	–1,355	–3,641	–2,215
Portfolio investment liabilities	4 652 Y.	3,916	4,193	3,239	2,687	9,195	7,912	4,253	12,296
Equity securities	4 660 Y.	389	864	668	186	199	1,184	1,313	1,168
Debt securities	4 669 Y.	3,528	3,329	2,571	2,501	8,996	6,728	2,939	11,128
Other investment assets	4 703 . .	–2,522	–1,606	–1,433	–2,207	–7,086	–5,429	–3,568	–11,396
Monetary authorities	4 703 .A	. . .	. . .	. . .	. . .	. . .	. . .	. . .	. . .
General government	4 703 .B	–106	–24	–244	–331	127	129	–162	–93
Banks	4 703 .C	–1,811	–720	–195	–1,144	–5,787	–5,549	–1,840	–11,765
Other sectors	4 703 .D	–604	–862	–994	–732	–1,426	–8	–1,566	462
Other investment liabilities	4 753 X.	493	618	831	2,714	3,454	3,332	6,781	6,310
Monetary authorities	4 753 XA	–12	4	–3	4	4	–5	6	. . .
General government	4 753 YB	–721	–402	–211	–36	–261	–37	590	1,194
Banks	4 753 YC	749	384	721	2,781	1,708	3,109	4,684	4,610
Other sectors	4 753 YD	478	631	325	–35	2,003	265	1,501	506
Total, Groups A Through C	4 020 . .	*169*	*1,603*	*1,155*	*104*	*1,798*	*2,696*	*1,237*	*–455*
D. Net Errors and Omissions	4 998 . .	**322**	**–613**	**–1,170**	**731**	**795**	**–493**	**–417**	**2,183**
Total, Groups A Through D	4 030 . .	*491*	*990*	*–15*	*835*	*2,593*	*2,202*	*819*	*1,728*
E. Reserves and Related Items	4 040 . .	**–491**	**–990**	**15**	**–835**	**–2,593**	**–2,202**	**–819**	**–1,728**
Reserve assets	4 800 . .	–491	–990	15	–835	–2,593	–2,202	–819	–1,728
Use of Fund credit and loans	4 766 . .	. . .	. . .	. . .	. . .	. . .	. . .	. . .	. . .
Liabilities constituting foreign authorities' reserves	4 900 . .	. . .	. . .	. . .	. . .	. . .	. . .	. . .	. . .
Exceptional financing	4 920 . .	. . .	. . .	. . .	. . .	. . .	. . .	. . .	. . .
Conversion rates: schillings per U.S. dollar	0 101 . .	**12.348**	**13.231**	**11.370**	**11.676**	**10.989**	**11.632**	**11.422**	**10.081**

[1] Excludes components that have been classified in the categories of Group E.

Table 2. STANDARD PRESENTATION, 1988–95
(Millions of U.S. dollars)

	Code	1988	1989	1990	1991	1992	1993	1994	1995
CURRENT ACCOUNT	4 993 . .	**–242**	**248**	**1,166**	**61**	**–79**	**–608**	**–2,209**	**–5,113**
A. GOODS	4 100 . .	–4,765	–5,552	–6,969	–8,560	–8,403	–7,267	–8,727	–5,446
Credit	2 100 . .	**30,158**	**31,960**	**40,414**	**40,353**	**43,929**	**39,845**	**44,645**	**72,110**
General merchandise: exports f.o.b.	2 110 . .	30,108	31,901	40,336	40,285	43,384	39,316	44,180	72,110
Goods for processing: exports f.o.b.	2 150 . .	...	...	...	...	545	528	465	...
Repairs on goods	2 160 . .	49	59	79	68	...	...	...	...
Goods procured in ports by carriers	2 170 . .	...	...	...	...	...	...	...	...
Nonmonetary gold	2 180 . .	...	...	...	...	...	...	...	...
Debit	3 100 . .	**–34,922**	**–37,512**	**–47,383**	**–48,913**	**–52,332**	**–47,112**	**–53,373**	**–77,556**
General merchandise: imports f.o.b.	3 110 . .	–34,889	–37,482	–47,348	–48,882	–52,185	–47,032	–53,286	–77,556
Goods for processing: imports f.o.b.	3 150 . .	...	...	...	...	–147	–80	–87	...
Repairs on goods	3 160 . .	–34	–30	–35	–30	...	...	...	...
Goods procured in ports by carriers	3 170 . .	...	...	...	...	...	...	...	...
Nonmonetary gold	3 180 . .	...	...	...	...	...	...	...	...
B. SERVICES	4 200 . .	5,473	6,850	9,083	10,227	9,875	8,156	7,943	2,471
Total credit	2 200 . .	*17,550*	*18,377*	*23,279*	*25,560*	*28,352*	*27,867*	*29,132*	*23,506*
Total debit	3 200 . .	*–12,077*	*–11,527*	*–14,197*	*–15,333*	*–18,477*	*–19,711*	*–21,189*	*–21,034*
Transportation services, credit	2 205 . .	**1,186**	**1,200**	**1,463**	**1,573**	**2,359**	**2,343**	**2,608**	**2,598**
Passenger	2 205 BA	...	...	...	...	...	...	...	...
Freight	2 205 BB	*1,186*	*1,200*	*1,463*	*1,573*	*2,359*	*2,343*	*2,608*	*2,598*
Other	2 205 BC	...	...	...	...	...	...	...	...
Sea transport, passenger	2 207 . .	...	...	...	...	...	...	...	...
Sea transport, freight	2 208 . .	...	...	...	...	...	...	...	...
Sea transport, other	2 209 . .	...	...	...	...	...	...	...	...
Air transport, passenger	2 211 . .	...	...	...	...	...	...	...	...
Air transport, freight	2 212 . .	...	...	...	...	...	...	...	...
Air transport, other	2 213 . .	...	...	...	...	...	...	...	...
Other transport, passenger	2 215 . .	...	...	...	...	...	...	...	...
Other transport, freight	2 216 . .	...	...	...	...	...	...	...	...
Other transport, other	2 217 . .	...	...	...	...	...	...	...	...
Transportation services, debit	3 205 . .	**–1,060**	**–946**	**–1,184**	**–1,234**	**–1,315**	**–1,180**	**–1,343**	**–1,937**
Passenger	3 205 BA	...	...	...	...	...	...	...	...
Freight	3 205 BB	*–1,060*	*–946*	*–1,184*	*–1,234*	*–1,315*	*–1,180*	*–1,343*	*–1,937*
Other	3 205 BC	...	...	...	...	...	...	...	...
Sea transport, passenger	3 207 . .	...	...	...	...	...	...	...	...
Sea transport, freight	3 208 . .	...	...	...	...	...	...	...	...
Sea transport, other	3 209 . .	...	...	...	...	...	...	...	...
Air transport, passenger	3 211 . .	...	...	...	...	...	...	...	...
Air transport, freight	3 212 . .	...	...	...	...	...	...	...	...
Air transport, other	3 213 . .	...	...	...	...	...	...	...	...
Other transport, passenger	3 215 . .	...	...	...	...	...	...	...	...
Other transport, freight	3 216 . .	...	...	...	...	...	...	...	...
Other transport, other	3 217 . .	...	...	...	...	...	...	...	...
Travel, credit	2 236 . .	**10,076**	**10,707**	**13,417**	**13,854**	**14,608**	**13,537**	**13,102**	**13,085**
Business travel	2 237 . .	...	...	...	...	...	...	...	...
Personal travel	2 240 . .	...	...	...	...	...	...	...	...
Travel, debit	3 236 . .	**–6,276**	**–6,250**	**–7,748**	**–7,362**	**–8,454**	**–8,248**	**–9,470**	**–10,567**
Business travel	3 237 . .	...	...	...	...	...	...	...	...
Personal travel	3 240 . .	...	...	...	...	...	...	...	...
Other services, credit	2 200 BA	**6,287**	**6,470**	**8,399**	**10,134**	**11,385**	**11,986**	**13,422**	**7,823**
Communications	2 245 . .	26	27	33	29	20	20	24	153
Construction	2 249 . .	300	299	501	478	708	586	830	747
Insurance	2 253 . .	466	545	660	723	521	525	541	635
Financial	2 260 . .	...	...	...	139	1,347	1,528	1,467	1,866
Computer and information	2 262 . .	...	...	...	...	...	...	...	...
Royalties and licence fees	2 266 . .	71	76	91	79	122	118	129	132
Other business services	2 268 . .	4,935	5,116	6,525	8,153	8,142	8,681	9,743	3,613
Personal, cultural, and recreational	2 287 . .	29	36	65	69	112	129	162	157
Government, n.i.e.	2 291 . .	461	371	525	464	412	400	525	520
Other services, debit	3 200 BA	**–4,742**	**–4,331**	**–5,264**	**–6,737**	**–8,707**	**–10,282**	**–10,375**	**–8,530**
Communications	3 245 . .	–44	–54	–83	–77	–30	–90	–49	–168
Construction	3 249 . .	–342	–357	–464	–441	–411	–404	–502	–575
Insurance	3 253 . .	–505	–497	–643	–683	–787	–754	–788	–1,035
Financial	3 260 . .	...	...	...	–137	–1,525	–1,522	–1,700	–2,094
Computer and information	3 262 . .	...	...	...	...	...	...	...	...
Royalties and licence fees	3 266 . .	–265	–232	–287	–302	–421	–418	–456	–521
Other business services	3 268 . .	–3,465	–3,060	–3,634	–4,921	–5,278	–6,858	–6,584	–3,795
Personal, cultural, and recreational	3 287 . .	–49	–56	–62	–82	–143	–133	–146	–191
Government, n.i.e.	3 291 . .	–72	–75	–93	–94	–112	–105	–149	–152

Table 2 (Continued). STANDARD PRESENTATION, 1988–95
(Millions of U.S. dollars)

	Code	1988	1989	1990	1991	1992	1993	1994	1995
C. INCOME	4 300 . .	–919	–934	–942	–1,475	–568	–516	–370	–636
Total credit	2 300 . .	*5,324*	*6,789*	*9,145*	*9,544*	*9,276*	*9,170*	*8,825*	*10,859*
Total debit	3 300 . .	*–6,243*	*–7,723*	*–10,087*	*–11,020*	*–9,844*	*–9,687*	*–9,195*	*–11,495*
Compensation of employees, credit	2 310 . .	**. . .**	**. . .**	**. . .**	**82**	**815**	**769**	**845**	**511**
Compensation of employees, debit	3 310 . .	**. . .**	**. . .**	**. . .**	**–21**	**–206**	**–289**	**–292**	**–219**
Investment income, credit	2 320 . .	**5,324**	**6,789**	**9,145**	**9,462**	**8,461**	**8,401**	**7,980**	**10,348**
Direct investment income	2 330 . .	175	235	313	254	51	308	319	185
Dividends and distributed branch profits	2 332 . .	175	235	313	254	51	308	319	185
Reinvested earnings and undistributed branch profits	2 333 . .	. . .	. . .	. . .	. . .	. . .	. . .	. . .	. . .
Income on debt (interest)	2 334 . .	. . .	. . .	. . .	. . .	. . .	. . .	. . .	. . .
Portfolio investment income	2 339 . .	. . .	. . .	. . .	. . .	. . .	. . .	. . .	. . .
Income on equity	2 340 . .	. . .	. . .	. . .	. . .	. . .	. . .	. . .	. . .
Income on bonds and notes	2 350 . .	. . .	. . .	. . .	. . .	. . .	. . .	. . .	. . .
Income on money market instruments and financial derivatives	2 360 . .	. . .	. . .	. . .	. . .	. . .	. . .	. . .	. . .
Other investment income	2 370 . .	5,149	6,554	8,831	9,208	8,409	8,094	7,661	10,163
Investment income, debit	3 320 . .	**–6,243**	**–7,723**	**–10,087**	**–10,999**	**–9,638**	**–9,398**	**–8,903**	**–11,276**
Direct investment income	3 330 . .	–824	–881	–933	–921	–288	–567	–602	–968
Dividends and distributed branch profits	3 332 . .	–824	–881	–933	–921	–288	–567	–602	–968
Reinvested earnings and undistributed branch profits	3 333 . .	. . .	. . .	. . .	. . .	. . .	. . .	. . .	. . .
Income on debt (interest)	3 334 . .	. . .	. . .	. . .	. . .	. . .	. . .	. . .	. . .
Portfolio investment income	3 339 . .	. . .	. . .	. . .	. . .	. . .	. . .	. . .	. . .
Income on equity	3 340 . .	. . .	. . .	. . .	. . .	. . .	. . .	. . .	. . .
Income on bonds and notes	3 350 . .	. . .	. . .	. . .	. . .	. . .	. . .	. . .	. . .
Income on money market instruments and financial derivatives	3 360 . .	. . .	. . .	. . .	. . .	. . .	. . .	. . .	. . .
Other investment income	3 370 . .	–5,419	–6,842	–9,154	–10,078	–9,351	–8,831	–8,301	–10,308
D. CURRENT TRANSFERS	4 379 . .	–31	–116	–6	–131	–983	–980	–1,054	–1,503
Credit	2 379 . .	**1,258**	**1,227**	**1,657**	**1,699**	**1,386**	**1,334**	**1,443**	**3,266**
General government	2 380 . .	. . .	. . .	. . .	. . .	296	252	288	1,644
Other sectors	2 390 . .	1,258	1,227	1,657	1,698	1,090	1,082	1,155	1,621
Workers' remittances	2 391 . .	409	419	572	538	223	228	228	298
Other current transfers	2 392 . .	848	808	1,085	1,160	867	854	927	1,324
Debit	3 379 . .	**–1,289**	**–1,343**	**–1,663**	**–1,830**	**–2,369**	**–2,314**	**–2,498**	**–4,769**
General government	3 380 . .	–74	–71	–108	–107	–787	–840	–914	–2,657
Other sectors	3 390 . .	–1,216	–1,273	–1,555	–1,723	–1,582	–1,475	–1,583	–2,111
Workers' remittances	3 391 . .	–207	–240	–265	–298	–303	–336	–370	–269
Other current transfers	3 392 . .	–1,009	–1,033	–1,290	–1,424	–1,279	–1,139	–1,213	–1,842
CAPITAL AND FINANCIAL ACCOUNT	4 996 . .	**–80**	**365**	**4**	**–792**	**–716**	**1,102**	**2,626**	**2,931**
CAPITAL ACCOUNT	4 994 . .	**–5**	**–12**	**8**	**55**	**–84**	**–111**	**346**	**10**
Total credit	2 994 . .	*40*	*50*	*63*	*152*	*168*	*177*	*598*	*317*
Total debit	3 994 . .	*–44*	*–62*	*–55*	*–97*	*–252*	*–288*	*–252*	*–307*
Capital transfers, credit	2 400 . .	**40**	**50**	**63**	**152**	**168**	**177**	**598**	**317**
General government	2 401 . .	. . .	. . .	. . .	. . .	. . .	. . .	. . .	. . .
Debt forgiveness	2 402 . .	. . .	. . .	. . .	. . .	. . .	. . .	. . .	. . .
Other capital transfers	2 410 . .	. . .	. . .	. . .	. . .	. . .	. . .	. . .	. . .
Other sectors	2 430 . .	40	50	63	152	168	177	598	317
Migrants' transfers	2 431 . .	40	50	63	152	168	177	598	317
Debt forgiveness	2 432 . .	. . .	. . .	. . .	. . .	. . .	. . .	. . .	. . .
Other capital transfers	2 440 . .	. . .	. . .	. . .	. . .	. . .	. . .	. . .	. . .
Capital transfers, debit	3 400 . .	**–44**	**–62**	**–55**	**–97**	**–252**	**–288**	**–252**	**–307**
General government	3 401 . .	. . .	. . .	. . .	. . .	. . .	. . .	. . .	. . .
Debt forgiveness	3 402 . .	. . .	. . .	. . .	. . .	. . .	. . .	. . .	. . .
Other capital transfers	3 410 . .	. . .	. . .	. . .	. . .	. . .	. . .	. . .	. . .
Other sectors	3 430 . .	–44	–62	–55	–97	–252	–288	–252	–307
Migrants' transfers	3 431 . .	–44	–62	–55	–97	–252	–288	–252	–307
Debt forgiveness	3 432 . .	. . .	. . .	. . .	. . .	. . .	. . .	. . .	. . .
Other capital transfers	3 440 . .	. . .	. . .	. . .	. . .	. . .	. . .	. . .	. . .
Nonproduced nonfinancial assets, credit	2 480 . .	**. . .**	**. . .**	**. . .**	**. . .**	**. . .**	**. . .**	**. . .**	**. . .**
Nonproduced nonfinancial assets, debit	3 480 . .	**. . .**	**. . .**	**. . .**	**. . .**	**. . .**	**. . .**	**. . .**	**. . .**

Table 2 (Continued). STANDARD PRESENTATION, 1988–95
(Millions of U.S. dollars)

	Code	1988	1989	1990	1991	1992	1993	1994	1995
FINANCIAL ACCOUNT	4 995	**–76**	**377**	**–4**	**–847**	**–632**	**1,212**	**2,280**	**2,921**
A. DIRECT INVESTMENT	4 500	126	–280	–1,047	–933	–925	–488	109	217
Direct investment abroad	4 505	**–310**	**–867**	**–1,701**	**–1,293**	**–1,872**	**–1,465**	**–1,203**	**–1,141**
Equity capital	4 510	–310	–867	–1,701	–1,293	–1,872	–1,465	–1,203	–1,141
Claims on affiliated enterprises	4 515	...	...	...	...	...	...	...	...
Liabilities to affiliated enterprises	4 520	...	...	...	...	...	...	...	...
Reinvested earnings	4 525	...	...	...	...	...	...	...	...
Other capital	4 530	...	...	...	...	...	...	...	...
Claims on affiliated enterprises	4 535	...	...	...	...	...	...	...	...
Liabilities to affiliated enterprises	4 540	...	...	...	...	...	...	...	...
Direct investment in Austria	4 555	**436**	**587**	**653**	**360**	**947**	**977**	**1,311**	**1,357**
Equity capital	4 560	436	587	653	360	947	977	1,311	1,357
Claims on direct investors	4 565	...	...	...	...	...	...	...	...
Liabilities to direct investors	4 570	...	...	...	...	...	...	...	...
Reinvested earnings	4 575	...	...	...	...	...	...	...	...
Other capital	4 580	...	...	...	...	...	...	...	...
Claims on direct investors	4 585	...	...	...	...	...	...	...	...
Liabilities to direct investors	4 590	...	...	...	...	...	...	...	...
B. PORTFOLIO INVESTMENT	4 600	2,319	2,634	1,631	415	6,519	6,000	–222	9,518
Assets	4 602	**–1,598**	**–1,559**	**–1,608**	**–2,272**	**–2,676**	**–1,912**	**–4,475**	**–2,778**
Equity securities	4 610	–572	–524	–430	–60	–194	–557	–834	–563
Monetary authorities	4 611	...	...	...	...	...	...	...	...
General government	4 612	...	...	...	...	...	...	...	...
Banks	4 613	...	...	...	...	...	...	...	...
Other sectors	4 614	...	...	...	...	...	...	...	...
Debt securities	4 619	–1,026	–1,035	–1,178	–2,212	–2,483	–1,355	–3,641	–2,215
Bonds and notes	4 620	–879	–1,267	–1,264	–1,680	–2,484	–1,216	–3,435	–2,348
Monetary authorities	4 621	...	...	...	...	...	...	...	...
General government	4 622	...	...	...	...	...	...	...	...
Banks	4 623	...	...	...	...	...	...	...	...
Other sectors	4 624	...	...	...	...	...	...	...	...
Money market instruments	4 630	–146	232	86	–532	1	–138	–206	133
Monetary authorities	4 631	...	...	...	...	...	...	...	...
General government	4 632	...	...	...	...	...	...	...	...
Banks	4 633	...	...	...	...	...	...	...	...
Other sectors	4 634	–146	232	86	–532	1	–138	–206	133
Financial derivatives	4 640	...	...	...	...	...	...	...	...
Monetary authorities	4 641	...	...	...	...	...	...	...	...
General government	4 642	...	...	...	...	...	...	...	...
Banks	4 643	...	...	...	...	...	...	...	...
Other sectors	4 644	...	...	...	...	...	...	...	...
Liabilities	4 652	**3,916**	**4,193**	**3,239**	**2,687**	**9,195**	**7,912**	**4,253**	**12,296**
Equity securities	4 660	389	864	668	186	199	1,184	1,313	1,168
Banks	4 663	...	...	...	...	...	...	...	...
Other sectors	4 664	...	...	...	...	...	...	...	...
Debt securities	4 669	3,528	3,329	2,571	2,501	8,996	6,728	2,939	11,128
Bonds and notes	4 670	2,987	2,474	2,395	2,734	5,956	9,102	3,001	11,774
Monetary authorities	4 671	...	...	...	...	...	...	...	...
General government	4 672	...	...	...	...	...	...	...	...
Banks	4 673	...	...	...	...	...	...	...	...
Other sectors	4 674	2,987	2,474	2,395	2,734	...	...	...	...
Money market instruments	4 680	541	855	177	–233	3,039	–2,374	–61	–647
Monetary authorities	4 681	...	...	...	...	...	...	...	...
General government	4 682	...	...	...	...	...	...	...	...
Banks	4 683	...	...	...	...	...	...	...	...
Other sectors	4 684	541	855	177	–233	3,039	–2,374	–61	–647
Financial derivatives	4 690	...	...	...	...	...	...	...	...
Monetary authorities	4 691	...	...	...	...	...	...	...	...
General government	4 692	...	...	...	...	...	...	...	...
Banks	4 693	...	...	...	...	...	...	...	...
Other sectors	4 694	...	...	...	...	...	...	...	...

Table 2 (Concluded). STANDARD PRESENTATION, 1988–95
(Millions of U.S. dollars)

	Code	1988	1989	1990	1991	1992	1993	1994	1995
C. OTHER INVESTMENT	4 700	–2,029	–987	–602	507	–3,632	–2,097	3,212	–5,086
Assets	4 703	**–2,522**	**–1,606**	**–1,433**	**–2,207**	**–7,086**	**–5,429**	**–3,568**	**–11,396**
Trade credits	4 706	–462	–537	141	223	91	183	–391	...
General government: long-term	4 708	...	...	...	...	...	...	...	...
General government: short-term	4 709	...	...	...	...	...	...	...	...
Other sectors: long-term	4 711	...	...	...	...	...	...	...	...
Other sectors: short-term	4 712	–462	–537	141	223	91	183	–391	...
Loans	4 714	–1,137	–955	–1,186	–2,257	–7,587	–5,605	–5,408	–6,153
Monetary authorities: long-term	4 717	...	...	...	...	...	...	...	...
Monetary authorities: short-term	4 718	...	...	...	...	...	...	...	...
General government: long-term	4 720	–58	24	–180	–259	–42	152	–124	184
General government: short-term	4 721	...	...	...	...	...	...	...	...
Banks: long-term	4 723	–1,289	–997	–848	–2,370	–715	–97	–60	–2,446
Banks: short-term	4 724	309	300	885	1,504	–6,079	–4,656	–4,158	–3,924
Other sectors: long-term	4 726	–88	–186	–520	–148	–420	–207	–631	–237
Other sectors: short-term	4 727	–11	–97	–523	–984	–332	–797	–435	270
Currency and deposits	4 730	–63	–263	–385	129	1,092	488	2,484	–2,311
Monetary authorities	4 731	...	...	...	...	...	...	...	...
General government	4 732	...	...	...	...	...	...	...	...
Banks	4 733	–54	–264	–381	158	1,852	–278	2,228	–2,724
Other sectors	4 734	–9	1	–3	–29	–760	766	256	413
Other assets	4 736	–859	148	–3	–303	–682	–494	–253	–2,931
Monetary authorities: long-term	4 738	...	...	...	...	...	...	...	...
Monetary authorities: short-term	4 739	...	...	...	...	...	...	...	...
General government: long-term	4 741	–48	–48	–64	–72	168	–23	–38	–277
General government: short-term	4 742	...	...	...	...	...	...	...	...
Banks: long-term	4 744	–721	218	134	–495	–846	–518	150	–2,670
Banks: short-term	4 745	–56	24	16	59	...	...	...	...
Other sectors: long-term	4 747	–34	–45	–90	–70	–132	–187	–153	–223
Other sectors: short-term	4 748	...	...	1	276	127	234	–212	239
Liabilities	4 753	**493**	**618**	**831**	**2,714**	**3,454**	**3,332**	**6,781**	**6,310**
Trade credits	4 756	308	212	–273	–309	–228	–37	614	...
General government: long-term	4 758	...	...	...	...	...	...	...	...
General government: short-term	4 759	...	...	...	...	...	...	...	...
Other sectors: long-term	4 761	...	...	...	...	...	...	...	...
Other sectors: short-term	4 762	308	212	–273	–309	–228	–37	614	...
Loans	4 764	–7	–11	–1,257	1,613	3,595	1,615	5,815	3,057
Use of Fund credit and loans from the Fund	4 766	...	...	...	...	...	...	...	...
Monetary authorities: other long-term	4 767	...	...	...	...	...	...	...	...
Monetary authorities: short-term	4 768	...	...	...	...	...	...	...	...
General government: long-term	4 770	–720	–402	–211	–35	–103	124	669	1,299
General government: short-term	4 771	...	...	...	...	...	...	...	...
Banks: long-term	4 773	–258	534	–963	–84	–99	–128	–127	66
Banks: short-term	4 774	611	–572	–697	1,347	1,880	1,544	4,797	1,781
Other sectors: long-term	4 776	311	386	245	190	167	302	170	367
Other sectors: short-term	4 777	49	42	369	196	1,750	–227	307	–456
Currency and deposits	4 780	470	645	1,133	473	–444	2,522	–723	1,073
Monetary authorities	4 781	...	...	...	...	...	...	...	...
General government	4 782	...	...	...	...	...	...	...	...
Banks	4 783	470	645	1,133	473	–444	2,522	–723	1,073
Other sectors	4 784	...	...	...	...	...	...	...	...
Other liabilities	4 786	–278	–228	1,228	937	531	–768	1,074	2,180
Monetary authorities: long-term	4 788	...	...	...	...	...	...	...	...
Monetary authorities: short-term	4 789	–12	4	–3	4	4	–5	6	...
General government: long-term	4 791	–1	...	...	–1	–158	–161	–79	–105
General government: short-term	4 792	...	...	...	...	...	...	...	...
Banks: long-term	4 794	–74	–224	1,248	1,045	371	–830	736	1,690
Banks: short-term	4 795	...	...	...	...	...	...	...	...
Other sectors: long-term	4 797	–157	–19	–39	–39	27	1	47	155
Other sectors: short-term	4 798	–34	10	22	–72	287	226	363	441
D. RESERVE ASSETS	4 800	–491	–990	15	–835	–2,593	–2,202	–819	–1,728
Monetary gold	4 810	...	70	41	63	16	210	43	883
Special drawing rights	4 820	10	–31	41	–3	–68	120	–53	116
Reserve position in the Fund	4 830	55	19	45	–48	–159	12	26	–147
Foreign exchange	4 840	–556	–1,051	–116	–849	–2,382	–2,546	–838	–2,560
Other claims	4 880	...	3	4	2	1	1	3	–19
NET ERRORS AND OMISSIONS	4 998	**322**	**–613**	**–1,170**	**731**	**795**	**–493**	**–417**	**2,183**

Part 3 of the *Yearbook* contains descriptions of the methodologies, compilation practices, and sources used to compile these data.

Table 3. INTERNATIONAL INVESTMENT POSITION (End–period stocks), 1988–95
(Millions of U.S. dollars)

	Code			1988	1989	1990	1991	1992	1993	1994	1995
ASSETS	8	995	C.	85,186	94,658	108,096	111,913	117,479	122,090	136,398	160,241
Direct investment abroad	8	505	. .	**1,616**	**3,267**	**4,739**	**6,502**	**6,817**	**8,112**	**9,283**	**11,142**
Equity capital and reinvested earnings	8	506	. .	1,321	1,930	3,681	5,248	5,540	6,415	7,571	9,090
Claims on affiliated enterprises	8	507	. .	...	...	...	...	...	...	...	...
Liabilities to affiliated enterprises	8	508	. .	...	...	...	...	...	...	...	...
Other capital	8	530	. .	294	1,337	1,058	1,254	1,277	1,696	1,712	2,052
Claims on affiliated enterprises	8	535	. .	...	...	...	...	...	...	...	...
Liabilities to affiliated enterprises	8	540	. .	...	...	...	...	...	...	...	...
Portfolio investment	8	602	. .	**8,659**	**10,961**	**13,862**	**14,492**	**16,866**	**17,170**	**22,524**	**27,557**
Equity securities	8	610	. .	1,894	2,607	3,362	3,499	3,435	3,722	4,885	5,868
Monetary authorities	8	611	. .	...	...	...	...	...	...	...	...
General government	8	612	. .	...	...	...	...	...	...	...	...
Banks	8	613	. .	255	398	450	393	326	354	424	456
Other sectors	8	614	. .	1,639	2,209	2,913	3,106	3,109	3,368	4,461	5,412
Debt securities	8	619	. .	6,765	8,354	10,499	10,993	13,431	13,448	17,639	21,689
Bonds and notes	8	620	. .	6,462	8,244	10,480	10,815	13,079	13,193	16,954	20,718
Monetary authorities	8	621	. .	...	...	...	...	...	...	...	...
General government	8	622	. .	56	93	103	150	352	354	352	268
Banks	8	623	. .	2,706	2,869	3,344	3,592	4,184	4,398	5,705	6,483
Other sectors	8	624	. .	3,701	5,281	7,034	7,073	8,543	8,441	10,897	13,967
Money market instruments	8	630	. .	302	110	19	178	352	181	577	803
Monetary authorities	8	631	. .	...	...	...	...	...	...	...	...
General government	8	632	. .	...	...	...	...	...	...	...	...
Banks	8	633	. .	302	110	19	47	88	107	523	406
Other sectors	8	634	. .	...	...	...	131	264	74	54	397
Financial derivatives	8	640	. .	...	...	...	...	...	74	108	169
Monetary authorities	8	641	. .	...	...	...	...	...	...	...	...
General government	8	642	. .	...	...	...	...	...	...	...	...
Banks	8	643	. .	...	...	...	...	...	...	63	119
Other sectors	8	644	. .	...	...	...	...	...	74	45	50
Other investment	8	703	. .	**58,798**	**63,419**	**72,595**	**73,038**	**74,696**	**75,113**	**81,109**	**95,648**
Trade credits	8	706	. .	5,555	6,543	7,090	6,118	6,438	5,773	6,129	6,602
General government: long-term	8	708	. .	...	...	...	...	...	...	...	...
General government: short-term	8	709	. .	...	...	...	...	...	...	...	...
Other sectors: long-term	8	711	. .	...	...	...	...	...	...	...	...
Other sectors: short-term	8	712	. .	...	...	...	...	...	...	...	...
Loans	8	714	. .	21,162	22,996	27,058	29,778	29,267	27,909	25,949	33,347
Monetary authorities: long-term	8	717	. .	...	...	...	...	...	...	...	...
Monetary authorities: short-term	8	718	. .	...	...	...	...	...	...	...	...
General government: long-term	8	720	. .	390	389	618	1,665	1,938	1,878	108	139
General government: short-term	8	721	. .	...	...	...	...	...	...	...	...
Banks: long-term	8	723	. .	20,064	22,074	24,970	27,505	26,466	25,027	25,840	33,208
Banks: short-term	8	724	. .	...	...	...	...	...	...	...	...
Other sectors: long-term	8	726	. .	708	533	1,470	608	863	1,005	...	...
Other sectors: short-term	8	727	. .	...	...	...	...	...	...	...	...
Currency and deposits	8	730	. .	30,959	32,510	36,827	35,083	36,392	38,870	46,048	51,080
Monetary authorities	8	731	. .	...	...	...	...	...	...	...	...
General government	8	732	. .	...	...	...	384	...	82	90	...
Banks	8	733	. .	30,680	32,239	36,115	34,129	36,190	37,462	43,542	49,643
Other sectors	8	734	. .	279	271	712	571	203	1,326	2,416	1,437
Other assets	8	736	. .	1,122	1,371	1,620	2,058	2,598	2,561	2,983	4,619
Monetary authorities: long-term	8	738	. .	...	...	...	...	...	...	...	...
Monetary authorities: short-term	8	739	. .	...	...	...	...	...	...	...	...
General government: long-term	8	741	. .	470	550	590	674	308	156	361	575
General government: short-term	8	742	. .	255	313	356	430	440	412	451	496
Banks: long-term	8	744	. .	135	203	244	187	123	156	198	416
Banks: short-term	8	745	. .	...	...	...	...	...	...	...	169
Other sectors: long-term	8	747	. .	135	195	309	393	493	642	874	1,289
Other sectors: short-term	8	748	. .	127	110	122	374	1,233	1,194	1,100	1,675
Reserve assets	8	800	. .	**16,113**	**17,011**	**16,900**	**17,882**	**19,099**	**21,695**	**23,482**	**25,893**
Monetary gold	8	810	. .	8,675	8,286	7,558	7,503	6,676	7,066	6,967	4,609
Special drawing rights	8	820	. .	268	298	278	282	341	220	283	181
Reserve position in the Fund	8	830	. .	389	361	344	395	536	524	531	682
Foreign exchange	8	840	. .	6,661	7,964	8,617	9,599	11,450	13,802	15,692	20,410
Other claims	8	880	. .	119	102	103	103	97	82	9	10

Table 3 (Continued). INTERNATIONAL INVESTMENT POSITION (End-period stocks), 1988–95
(Millions of U.S. dollars)

	Code	1988	1989	1990	1991	1992	1993	1994	1995
LIABILITIES	8 995 D.	89,733	98,358	114,967	123,342	127,955	133,600	153,772	187,034
Direct investment in Austria	8 555 . .	**7,107**	**8,261**	**10,237**	**11,058**	**11,221**	**11,398**	**13,096**	**15,048**
Equity capital and reinvested earnings	8 556 . .	6,773	7,626	9,609	10,590	10,041	9,709	11,221	12,897
Claims on direct investors	8 557 . .	...	...	...	...	...	...	...	...
Liabilities to direct investors	8 558 . .	...	...	...	...	...	...	...	...
Other capital	8 580 . .	334	635	628	468	1,180	1,688	1,875	2,151
Claims on direct investors	8 585 . .	...	...	...	...	...	...	...	...
Liabilities to direct investors	8 590 . .	...	...	...	...	...	...	...	...
Portfolio investment	8 652 . .	**28,205**	**33,322**	**41,538**	**48,031**	**55,813**	**61,896**	**68,797**	**89,602**
Equity securities	8 660 . .	517	1,244	1,976	2,545	2,633	3,591	5,318	6,989
Banks	8 663 . .	...	...	...	346	352	321	324	367
Other sectors	8 664 . .	517	1,244	1,976	2,199	2,281	3,269	4,993	6,622
Debt securities	8 669 . .	27,688	32,078	39,562	45,486	53,179	58,305	63,479	82,613
Bonds and notes	8 670 . .	25,794	28,845	35,057	40,350	45,068	53,331	58,612	77,716
Monetary authorities	8 671 . .	...	...	...	...	...	...	...	...
General government	8 672 . .	11,277	12,019	14,808	17,410	20,565	26,484	28,580	39,750
Banks	8 673 . .	11,508	13,830	16,119	18,009	19,262	20,003	22,055	27,805
Other sectors	8 674 . .	3,008	2,996	4,130	4,930	5,240	6,843	7,977	10,161
Money market instruments	8 680 . .	1,894	3,233	4,505	5,136	8,112	4,974	4,750	4,768
Monetary authorities	8 681 . .	...	...	...	...	...	...	...	...
General government	8 682 . .	...	...	...	...	...	99	108	59
Banks	8 683 . .	1,894	3,233	4,505	5,136	8,112	4,875	4,615	4,580
Other sectors	8 684 . .	...	...	...	...	...	...	27	129
Financial derivatives	8 690 . .	...	...	...	...	...	...	117	129
Monetary authorities	8 691 . .	...	...	...	...	...	...	...	...
General government	8 692 . .	...	...	...	...	...	...	...	...
Banks	8 692 . .	...	...	...	...	...	...	...	...
Other sectors	8 694 . .	...	...	...	...	...	...	...	...
Other investment	8 753 . .	**54,421**	**56,775**	**63,192**	**64,253**	**60,921**	**60,306**	**71,879**	**82,385**
Trade credits	8 756 . .	3,502	3,961	4,093	3,630	3,673	3,516	4,236	4,421
General government: long-term	8 758 . .	...	...	...	...	...	...	...	...
General government: short-term	8 759 . .	...	...	...	...	...	...	...	...
Other sectors: long-term	8 761 . .	...	...	...	...	...	...	...	...
Other sectors: short-term	8 762 . .	...	...	...	...	...	...	...	...
Loans	8 764 . .	9,280	8,904	9,450	9,150	7,363	5,452	7,805	10,676
Use of Fund credit and loans from the Fund	8 766 . .	...	...	...	...	...	...	...	...
Monetary authorities: other long-term	8 767 . .	...	...	...	...	...	...	...	...
Monetary authorities: short-term	8 768 . .	...	...	...	...	...	...	...	...
General government: long-term	8 770 . .	1,456	1,092	740	870	440	865	1,731	3,033
General government: short-term	8 771 . .	...	...	...	...	...	...	...	...
Banks: long-term	8 773 . .	4,377	4,613	4,964	5,323	4,395	2,405	2,974	4,718
Banks: short-term	8 774 . .	...	...	...	...	...	...	...	...
Other sectors: long-term	8 776 . .	3,446	3,199	3,746	2,956	2,528	2,182	3,100	2,924
Other sectors: short-term	8 777 . .	...	...	...	...	...	...	...	...
Currency and deposits	8 780 . .	40,159	42,082	47,148	48,115	46,495	48,118	56,124	62,272
Monetary authorities	8 781 . .	...	...	...	...	...	...	...	...
General government	8 782 . .	374	...	...	...	440	...	739	446
Banks	8 783 . .	39,777	42,344	46,895	47,348	45,676	47,031	53,961	60,061
Other sectors	8 784 . .	8	–262	253	767	379	1,087	1,424	1,764
Other liabilities	8 786 . .	1,480	1,828	2,501	3,359	3,391	3,220	3,713	5,016
Monetary authorities: long-term	8 788 . .	...	...	...	...	...	...	...	...
Monetary authorities: short-term	8 789 . .	...	...	...	...	...	...	18	20
General government: long-term	8 791 . .	–72	–76	...		...	...	...	...
General government: short-term	8 792 . .	...	–17	–19	543	528	494	541	595
Banks: long-term	8 794 . .	127	102	131	122	97	107	90	416
Banks: short-term	8 795 . .	...	...	...	...	...	...	...	169
Other sectors: long-term	8 797 . .	1,186	1,532	2,061	2,442	2,325	2,174	2,524	2,944
Other sectors: short-term	8 798 . .	239	288	328	253	440	445	541	872
NET INTERNATIONAL INVESTMENT POSITION	8 995 . .	**–4,548**	**–3,700**	**–6,870**	**–11,429**	**–10,476**	**–11,510**	**–17,374**	**–26,794**
Conversion rates: schillings per U.S. dollar (end of period)	0 102 . .	**12.565**	**11.815**	**10.677**	**10.689**	**11.354**	**12.143**	**11.095**	**10.088**

Bahamas, The
313

Table 1. ANALYTIC PRESENTATION, 1988–95
(Millions of U.S. dollars)

	Code	1988	1989	1990	1991	1992	1993	1994	1995
A. Current Account [1]	4 993 Y.	**–66.5**	**–81.6**	**–95.1**	**–107.2**	**–53.5**	**–73.3**	**–224.3**	**–212.2**
Goods: exports f.o.b	2 100 . .	310.8	312.1	375.7	360.2	342.5	286.8	258.5	267.5
Goods: imports f.o.b	3 100 . .	–982.9	–1,136.7	–1,190.2	–1,045.6	–1,069.2	–1,100.5	–1,145.2	–1,168.9
Balance on Goods	4 100 . .	*–672.1*	*–824.6*	*–814.5*	*–685.4*	*–726.7*	*–813.7*	*–886.7*	*–901.4*
Services: credit	2 200 . .	1,275.2	1,438.3	1,463.2	1,315.9	1,352.8	1,429.7	1,482.8	1,507.6
Services: debit	3 200 . .	–491.2	–525.8	–589.3	–546.2	–521.2	–536.6	–631.4	–635.1
Balance on Goods and Services	4 991 . .	*111.9*	*87.9*	*59.4*	*84.3*	*104.9*	*79.4*	*–35.3*	*–28.9*
Income: credit	2 300 . .	15.3	16.1	15.0	15.1	11.6	9.4	5.0	5.3
Income: debit	3 300 . .	–182.2	–189.3	–184.3	–229.1	–187.6	–180.8	–215.0	–217.7
Balance on Goods, Services, and Income	4 992 . .	*–55.0*	*–85.3*	*–109.9*	*–129.7*	*–71.1*	*–92.0*	*–245.3*	*–241.3*
Current transfers: credit	2 379 Y.	17.4	21.6	24.7	30.9	31.1	33.1	33.9	36.3
Current transfers: debit	3 379 . .	–28.9	–17.9	–9.9	–8.4	–13.5	–14.4	–12.9	–7.2
B. Capital Account [1]	4 994 Y.	**–3.0**	**–2.7**	**–4.2**	**–2.9**	**–4.2**	**–4.3**	**–3.0**	**–12.6**
Capital account: credit	2 994 Y.	. . .	. . .	. . .	. . .	. . .	. . .	. . .	. . .
Capital account: debit	3 994 . .	–3.0	–2.7	–4.2	–2.9	–4.2	–4.3	–3.0	–12.6
Total, Groups A Plus B	4 010 . .	*–69.5*	*–84.3*	*–99.3*	*–110.1*	*–57.7*	*–77.6*	*–227.3*	*–224.8*
C. Financial Account [1]	4 995 X.	**73.2**	**94.8**	**57.1**	**176.9**	**12.9**	**9.4**	**77.2**	**104.0**
Direct investment abroad	4 505 . .	. . .	. . .	. . .	. . .	. . .	. . .	. . .	. . .
Direct investment in The Bahamas	4 555 Y.	36.7	25.0	–17.2	. . .	7.4	27.1	26.5	109.1
Portfolio investment assets	4 602 . .	. . .	. . .	. . .	. . .	. . .	. . .	. . .	. . .
Equity securities	4 610 . .	. . .	. . .	. . .	. . .	. . .	. . .	. . .	. . .
Debt securities	4 619 . .	. . .	. . .	. . .	. . .	. . .	. . .	. . .	. . .
Portfolio investment liabilities	4 652 Y.	. . .	. . .	. . .	. . .	. . .	. . .	. . .	. . .
Equity securities	4 660 Y.	. . .	. . .	. . .	. . .	. . .	. . .	. . .	. . .
Debt securities	4 669 Y.	. . .	. . .	. . .	. . .	. . .	. . .	. . .	. . .
Other investment assets	4 703 . .	39.3	44.6	32.9	11.9	–37.9	1.2	11.0	17.2
Monetary authorities	4 703 . A	. . .	. . .	. . .	. . .	. . .	. . .	. . .	. . .
General government	4 703 . B	. . .	. . .	. . .	. . .	. . .	. . .	. . .	. . .
Banks	4 703 . C	39.3	44.6	32.9	11.9	–37.9	1.2	11.0	17.2
Other sectors	4 703 . D	. . .	. . .	. . .	. . .	. . .	. . .	. . .	. . .
Other investment liabilities	4 753 X.	–2.8	25.2	41.4	165.0	43.4	–18.9	39.7	–22.3
Monetary authorities	4 753 XA	. . .	. . .	. . .	. . .	. . .	. . .	. . .	. . .
General government	4 753 YB	–8.1	4.9	12.7	5.9	–3.3	–16.3	–5.9	–9.0
Banks	4 753 YC	. . .	. . .	. . .	. . .	. . .	. . .	. . .	. . .
Other sectors	4 753 YD	5.3	20.3	28.7	159.1	46.7	–2.6	45.6	–13.3
Total, Groups A Through C	4 020 . .	*3.7*	*10.5*	*–42.2*	*66.8*	*–44.8*	*–68.2*	*–150.1*	*–120.8*
D. Net Errors and Omissions	4 998 . .	**–4.4**	**–37.1**	**51.5**	**–53.8**	**16.1**	**87.2**	**159.5**	**117.8**
Total, Groups A Through D	4 030 . .	*–.7*	*–26.6*	*9.3*	*13.0*	*–28.7*	*19.0*	*9.4*	*–3.1*
E. Reserves and Related Items	4 040 . .	**.7**	**26.6**	**–9.3**	**–13.0**	**28.7**	**–19.0**	**–9.4**	**3.1**
Reserve assets	4 800 . .	.7	26.6	–9.3	–13.0	28.7	–19.0	–9.4	3.1
Use of Fund credit and loans	4 766 . .	. . .	. . .	. . .	. . .	. . .	. . .	. . .	. . .
Liabilities constituting foreign authorities' reserves	4 900 . .	. . .	. . .	. . .	. . .	. . .	. . .	. . .	. . .
Exceptional financing	4 920 . .	. . .	. . .	. . .	. . .	. . .	. . .	. . .	. . .
Conversion rates: Bahamian dollar per U.S. dollar	0 101 . .	**1.0000**	**1.0000**	**1.0000**	**1.0000**	**1.0000**	**1.0000**	**1.0000**	**1.0000**

[1] Excludes components that have been classified in the categories of Group E.

Table 2. STANDARD PRESENTATION, 1988–95

(Millions of U.S. dollars)

	Code	1988	1989	1990	1991	1992	1993	1994	1995
CURRENT ACCOUNT	4 993 . .	**–66.5**	**–81.6**	**–95.1**	**–107.2**	**–53.5**	**–73.3**	**–224.3**	**–212.2**
A. GOODS	4 100 . .	–672.1	–824.6	–814.5	–685.4	–726.7	–813.7	–886.7	–901.4
Credit	2 100 . .	**310.8**	**312.1**	**375.7**	**360.2**	**342.5**	**286.8**	**258.5**	**267.5**
General merchandise: exports f.o.b.	2 110 . .	270.5	259.2	307.6	319.8	310.2	256.8	223.9	228.5
Goods for processing: exports f.o.b.	2 150 . .	. . .	. . .	. . .	. . .	. . .	. . .	. . .	. . .
Repairs on goods	2 160 . .	. . .	. . .	. . .	. . .	. . .	. . .	. . .	. . .
Goods procured in ports by carriers	2 170 . .	40.3	52.9	68.1	40.4	32.3	30.0	34.6	39.0
Nonmonetary gold	2 180 . .	. . .	. . .	. . .	. . .	. . .	. . .	. . .	. . .
Debit	3 100 . .	**–982.9**	**–1,136.7**	**–1,190.2**	**–1,045.6**	**–1,069.2**	**–1,100.5**	**–1,145.2**	**–1,168.9**
General merchandise: imports f.o.b.	3 110 . .	–982.9	–1,136.7	–1,190.2	–1,045.6	–1,069.2	–1,100.5	–1,145.2	–1,167.6
Goods for processing: imports f.o.b.	3 150 . .	. . .	. . .	. . .	. . .	. . .	. . .	. . .	. . .
Repairs on goods	3 160 . .	. . .	. . .	. . .	. . .	. . .	. . .	. . .	. . .
Goods procured in ports by carriers	3 170 . .	. . .	. . .	. . .	. . .	. . .	. . .	. . .	–1.3
Nonmonetary gold	3 180 . .	. . .	. . .	. . .	. . .	. . .	. . .	. . .	. . .
B. SERVICES	4 200 . .	784.0	912.5	873.9	769.7	831.6	893.1	851.4	872.5
Total credit	2 200 . .	*1,275.2*	*1,438.3*	*1,463.2*	*1,315.9*	*1,352.8*	*1,429.7*	*1,482.8*	*1,507.6*
Total debit	3 200 . .	*–491.2*	*–525.8*	*–589.3*	*–546.2*	*–521.2*	*–536.6*	*–631.4*	*–635.1*
Transportation services, credit	2 205 . .	**35.8**	**37.2**	**48.1**	**40.1**	**35.1**	**27.1**	**45.6**	**54.8**
Passenger	2 205 BA	*9.4*	*10.4*	*12.2*	*9.3*	*9.2*	*8.7*	*10.4*	*9.6*
Freight	2 205 BB	. . .	. . .	. . .	. . .	. . .	. . .	. . .	. . .
Other	2 205 BC	*26.4*	*26.8*	*35.9*	*30.8*	*25.9*	*18.4*	*35.2*	*45.2*
Sea transport, passenger	2 207 . .	. . .	. . .	. . .	. . .	. . .	. . .	. . .	. . .
Sea transport, freight	2 208 . .	. . .	. . .	. . .	. . .	. . .	. . .	. . .	. . .
Sea transport, other	2 209 . .	. . .	. . .	. . .	. . .	. . .	. . .	. . .	35.6
Air transport, passenger	2 211 . .	. . .	. . .	. . .	. . .	. . .	. . .	. . .	9.6
Air transport, freight	2 212 . .	. . .	. . .	. . .	. . .	. . .	. . .	. . .	. . .
Air transport, other	2 213 . .	. . .	. . .	. . .	. . .	. . .	. . .	. . .	9.6
Other transport, passenger	2 215 . .	. . .	. . .	. . .	. . .	. . .	. . .	. . .	. . .
Other transport, freight	2 216 . .	. . .	. . .	. . .	. . .	. . .	. . .	. . .	. . .
Other transport, other	2 217 . .	. . .	. . .	. . .	. . .	. . .	. . .	. . .	. . .
Transportation services, debit	3 205 . .	**–137.9**	**–138.8**	**–142.3**	**–117.3**	**–111.8**	**–115.0**	**–120.5**	**–129.9**
Passenger	3 205 BA	*–33.5*	*–19.1*	*–20.7*	*–19.6*	*–18.7*	*–15.6*	*–16.7*	*–22.8*
Freight	3 205 BB	*–68.3*	*–77.9*	*–79.1*	*–70.8*	*–74.1*	*–77.6*	*–78.8*	*–80.3*
Other	3 205 BC	*–36.1*	*–41.8*	*–42.5*	*–26.9*	*–19.0*	*–21.8*	*–25.0*	*–26.8*
Sea transport, passenger	3 207 . .	. . .	. . .	. . .	. . .	. . .	. . .	. . .	–1.2
Sea transport, freight	3 208 . .	. . .	. . .	. . .	. . .	. . .	. . .	. . .	–64.2
Sea transport, other	3 209 . .	. . .	. . .	. . .	. . .	. . .	. . .	. . .	–1.6
Air transport, passenger	3 211 . .	. . .	. . .	. . .	. . .	. . .	. . .	. . .	–21.6
Air transport, freight	3 212 . .	. . .	. . .	. . .	. . .	. . .	. . .	. . .	–16.1
Air transport, other	3 213 . .	. . .	. . .	. . .	. . .	. . .	. . .	. . .	–25.2
Other transport, passenger	3 215 . .	. . .	. . .	. . .	. . .	. . .	. . .	. . .	. . .
Other transport, freight	3 216 . .	. . .	. . .	. . .	. . .	. . .	. . .	. . .	. . .
Other transport, other	3 217 . .	. . .	. . .	. . .	. . .	. . .	. . .	. . .	. . .
Travel, credit	2 236 . .	**1,143.9**	**1,302.6**	**1,324.4**	**1,186.1**	**1,237.6**	**1,296.4**	**1,327.3**	**1,340.1**
Business travel	2 237 . .	. . .	. . .	. . .	. . .	. . .	. . .	. . .	. . .
Personal travel	2 240 . .	. . .	. . .	. . .	. . .	. . .	. . .	. . .	. . .
Travel, debit	3 236 . .	**–171.6**	**–183.6**	**–196.2**	**–200.3**	**–186.8**	**–170.9**	**–191.7**	**–211.6**
Business travel	3 237 . .	–48.4	–54.4	–45.0	–37.5	–40.1	–30.0	–31.5	–37.9
Personal travel	3 240 . .	–123.2	–129.2	–151.2	–162.8	–146.7	–140.9	–160.2	–173.7
Other services, credit	2 200 BA	**95.5**	**98.5**	**90.7**	**89.7**	**80.1**	**106.2**	**109.9**	**112.7**
Communications	2 245 . .	. . .	. . .	. . .	. . .	. . .	. . .	. . .	. . .
Construction	2 249 . .	. . .	. . .	. . .	. . .	. . .	. . .	. . .	. . .
Insurance	2 253 . .	. . .	. . .	. . .	. . .	. . .	. . .	. . .	. . .
Financial	2 260 . .	. . .	. . .	. . .	. . .	. . .	. . .	. . .	. . .
Computer and information	2 262 . .	. . .	. . .	. . .	. . .	. . .	. . .	. . .	. . .
Royalties and licence fees	2 266 . .	. . .	. . .	. . .	. . .	. . .	. . .	. . .	. . .
Other business services	2 268 . .	76.9	78.1	68.3	62.8	62.8	86.2	92.9	99.1
Personal, cultural, and recreational	2 287 . .	. . .	. . .	. . .	. . .	. . .	. . .	. . .	. . .
Government, n.i.e.	2 291 . .	18.6	20.4	22.4	26.9	17.3	20.0	17.0	13.6
Other services, debit	3 200 BA	**–181.7**	**–203.4**	**–250.8**	**–228.6**	**–222.6**	**–250.7**	**–319.2**	**–293.6**
Communications	3 245 . .	. . .	. . .	. . .	. . .	. . .	. . .	. . .	–1.2
Construction	3 249 . .	. . .	. . .	. . .	. . .	. . .	. . .	. . .	–4.4
Insurance	3 253 . .	–7.6	–8.6	–8.9	–7.9	–8.1	–8.6	–8.8	–76.3
Financial	3 260 . .	. . .	. . .	. . .	. . .	. . .	. . .	. . .	. . .
Computer and information	3 262 . .	. . .	. . .	. . .	. . .	. . .	. . .	. . .	. . .
Royalties and licence fees	3 266 . .	–3.7	–4.6	–5.2	–5.7	–5.7	–6.5	–7.2	–4.6
Other business services	3 268 . .	–138.8	–159.1	–183.8	–167.0	–168.4	–199.2	–269.5	–170.9
Personal, cultural, and recreational	3 287 . .	. . .	. . .	. . .	. . .	. . .	. . .	. . .	–2.0
Government, n.i.e.	3 291 . .	–31.6	–31.1	–52.9	–48.0	–40.4	–36.4	–33.7	–34.2

Table 2 (Continued). STANDARD PRESENTATION, 1988–95
(Millions of U.S. dollars)

	Code	1988	1989	1990	1991	1992	1993	1994	1995
C. INCOME	4 300 . .	–166.9	–173.2	–169.3	–214.0	–176.0	–171.4	–210.0	–212.4
Total credit	2 300 . .	*15.3*	*16.1*	*15.0*	*15.1*	*11.6*	*9.4*	*5.0*	*5.3*
Total debit	3 300 . .	*–182.2*	*–189.3*	*–184.3*	*–229.1*	*–187.6*	*–180.8*	*–215.0*	*–217.7*
Compensation of employees, credit	2 310 . .	**. . .**	**. . .**	**. . .**	**. . .**	**. . .**	**. . .**	**. . .**	**. . .**
Compensation of employees, debit	3 310 . .	**–17.3**	**–20.8**	**–34.5**	**–47.0**	**–26.9**	**–23.0**	**–24.8**	**–27.9**
Investment income, credit	2 320 . .	**15.3**	**16.1**	**15.0**	**15.1**	**11.6**	**9.4**	**5.0**	**5.3**
Direct investment income	2 330 . .	. . .	. . .	. . .	. . .	. . .	. . .	. . .	. . .
Dividends and distributed branch profits	2 332 . .	. . .	. . .	. . .	. . .	. . .	. . .	. . .	. . .
Reinvested earnings and undistributed branch profits	2 333 . .	. . .	. . .	. . .	. . .	. . .	. . .	. . .	. . .
Income on debt (interest)	2 334 . .	. . .	. . .	. . .	. . .	. . .	. . .	. . .	. . .
Portfolio investment income	2 339 . .	. . .	. . .	. . .	. . .	. . .	. . .	. . .	. . .
Income on equity	2 340 . .	. . .	. . .	. . .	. . .	. . .	. . .	. . .	. . .
Income on bonds and notes	2 350 . .	. . .	. . .	. . .	. . .	. . .	. . .	. . .	. . .
Income on money market instruments and financial derivatives	2 360 . .	. . .	. . .	. . .	. . .	. . .	. . .	. . .	. . .
Other investment income	2 370 . .	15.3	16.1	15.0	15.1	11.6	9.4	5.0	5.3
Investment income, debit	3 320 . .	**–164.9**	**–168.5**	**–149.8**	**–182.1**	**–160.7**	**–157.8**	**–190.2**	**–189.8**
Direct investment income	3 330 . .	. . .	. . .	. . .	. . .	. . .	. . .	. . .	. . .
Dividends and distributed branch profits	3 332 . .	. . .	. . .	. . .	. . .	. . .	. . .	. . .	. . .
Reinvested earnings and undistributed branch profits	3 333 . .	. . .	. . .	. . .	. . .	. . .	. . .	. . .	. . .
Income on debt (interest)	3 334 . .	. . .	. . .	. . .	. . .	. . .	. . .	. . .	. . .
Portfolio investment income	3 339 . .	. . .	. . .	. . .	. . .	. . .	. . .	. . .	. . .
Income on equity	3 340 . .	. . .	. . .	. . .	. . .	. . .	. . .	. . .	. . .
Income on bonds and notes	3 350 . .	. . .	. . .	. . .	. . .	. . .	. . .	. . .	. . .
Income on money market instruments and financial derivatives	3 360 . .	. . .	. . .	. . .	. . .	. . .	. . .	. . .	. . .
Other investment income	3 370 . .	–164.9	–168.5	–149.8	–182.1	–160.7	–157.8	–190.2	–189.8
D. CURRENT TRANSFERS	4 379 . .	–11.5	3.7	14.8	22.5	17.6	18.7	21.0	29.1
Credit	2 379 . .	**17.4**	**21.6**	**24.7**	**30.9**	**31.1**	**33.1**	**33.9**	**36.3**
General government	2 380 . .	16.2	20.4	23.5	29.7	29.9	31.9	32.7	35.1
Other sectors	2 390 . .	1.2	1.2	1.2	1.2	1.2	1.2	1.2	1.2
Workers' remittances	2 391 . .	. . .	. . .	. . .	. . .	. . .	. . .	. . .	. . .
Other current transfers	2 392 . .	1.2	1.2	1.2	1.2	1.2	1.2	1.2	1.2
Debit	3 379 . .	**–28.9**	**–17.9**	**–9.9**	**–8.4**	**–13.5**	**–14.4**	**–12.9**	**–7.2**
General government	3 380 . .	–1.8	–1.5	–2.3	–2.3	–3.7	–5.1	–2.8	–3.3
Other sectors	3 390 . .	–27.1	–16.4	–7.6	–6.1	–9.8	–9.3	–10.1	–3.9
Workers' remittances	3 391 . .	–27.1	–16.4	–7.6	–6.1	–9.8	–9.3	–10.1	–3.9
Other current transfers	3 392 . .	. . .	. . .	. . .	. . .	. . .	. . .	. . .	. . .
CAPITAL AND FINANCIAL ACCOUNT	4 996 . .	**70.9**	**118.7**	**43.6**	**161.0**	**37.4**	**–13.9**	**64.8**	**94.4**
CAPITAL ACCOUNT	4 994 . .	**–3.0**	**–2.7**	**–4.2**	**–2.9**	**–4.2**	**–4.3**	**–3.0**	**–12.6**
Total credit	2 994 . .	*. . .*	*. . .*	*. . .*	*. . .*	*. . .*	*. . .*	*. . .*	*. . .*
Total debit	3 994 . .	*–3.0*	*–2.7*	*–4.2*	*–2.9*	*–4.2*	*–4.3*	*–3.0*	*–12.6*
Capital transfers, credit	2 400 . .	**. . .**	**. . .**	**. . .**	**. . .**	**. . .**	**. . .**	**. . .**	**. . .**
General government	2 401 . .	. . .	. . .	. . .	. . .	. . .	. . .	. . .	. . .
Debt forgiveness	2 402 . .	. . .	. . .	. . .	. . .	. . .	. . .	. . .	. . .
Other capital transfers	2 410 . .	. . .	. . .	. . .	. . .	. . .	. . .	. . .	. . .
Other sectors	2 430 . .	. . .	. . .	. . .	. . .	. . .	. . .	. . .	. . .
Migrants' transfers	2 431 . .	. . .	. . .	. . .	. . .	. . .	. . .	. . .	. . .
Debt forgiveness	2 432 . .	. . .	. . .	. . .	. . .	. . .	. . .	. . .	. . .
Other capital transfers	2 440 . .	. . .	. . .	. . .	. . .	. . .	. . .	. . .	. . .
Capital transfers, debit	3 400 . .	**–3.0**	**–2.7**	**–4.2**	**–2.9**	**–4.2**	**–4.3**	**–3.0**	**–12.6**
General government	3 401 . .	. . .	. . .	. . .	. . .	. . .	. . .	. . .	. . .
Debt forgiveness	3 402 . .	. . .	. . .	. . .	. . .	. . .	. . .	. . .	. . .
Other capital transfers	3 410 . .	. . .	. . .	. . .	. . .	. . .	. . .	. . .	. . .
Other sectors	3 430 . .	–3.0	–2.7	–4.2	–2.9	–4.2	–4.3	–3.0	–12.6
Migrants' transfers	3 431 . .	–3.0	–2.7	–4.2	–2.9	–4.2	–4.3	–3.0	–12.6
Debt forgiveness	3 432 . .	. . .	. . .	. . .	. . .	. . .	. . .	. . .	. . .
Other capital transfers	3 440 . .	. . .	. . .	. . .	. . .	. . .	. . .	. . .	. . .
Nonproduced nonfinancial assets, credit	2 480 . .	**. . .**	**. . .**	**. . .**	**. . .**	**. . .**	**. . .**	**. . .**	**. . .**
Nonproduced nonfinancial assets, debit	3 480 . .	**. . .**	**. . .**	**. . .**	**. . .**	**. . .**	**. . .**	**. . .**	**. . .**

Table 2 (Continued). STANDARD PRESENTATION, 1988–95
(Millions of U.S. dollars)

	Code		1988	1989	1990	1991	1992	1993	1994	1995
FINANCIAL ACCOUNT	4 995	. .	**73.9**	**121.4**	**47.8**	**163.9**	**41.6**	**–9.6**	**67.8**	**107.0**
A. DIRECT INVESTMENT	4 500	. .	36.7	25.0	–17.2	. . .	7.4	27.1	26.5	109.1
Direct investment abroad	4 505	. .	**. . .**	**. . .**	**. . .**	**. . .**	**. . .**	**. . .**	**. . .**	**. . .**
Equity capital	4 510	. .	. . .	. . .	. . .	. . .	. . .	. . .	. . .	. . .
Claims on affiliated enterprises	4 515	. .	. . .	. . .	. . .	. . .	. . .	. . .	. . .	. . .
Liabilities to affiliated enterprises	4 520	. .	. . .	. . .	. . .	. . .	. . .	. . .	. . .	. . .
Reinvested earnings	4 525	. .	. . .	. . .	. . .	. . .	. . .	. . .	. . .	. . .
Other capital	4 530	. .	. . .	. . .	. . .	. . .	. . .	. . .	. . .	. . .
Claims on affiliated enterprises	4 535	. .	. . .	. . .	. . .	. . .	. . .	. . .	. . .	. . .
Liabilities to affiliated enterprises	4 540	. .	. . .	. . .	. . .	. . .	. . .	. . .	. . .	. . .
Direct investment in The Bahamas	4 555	. .	**36.7**	**25.0**	**–17.2**	**. . .**	**7.4**	**27.1**	**26.5**	**109.1**
Equity capital	4 560	. .	45.7	27.4	–4.2	6.7	11.0	28.0	44.7	87.9
Claims on direct investors	4 565	. .	. . .	. . .	. . .	. . .	. . .	. . .	. . .	98.8
Liabilities to direct investors	4 570	. .	. . .	. . .	. . .	. . .	. . .	. . .	. . .	–10.9
Reinvested earnings	4 575	. .	. . .	. . .	. . .	. . .	. . .	. . .	. . .	. . .
Other capital	4 580	. .	–9.0	–2.4	–13.0	–6.7	–3.6	–.9	–18.2	21.2
Claims on direct investors	4 585	. .	. . .	. . .	. . .	. . .	. . .	. . .	. . .	32.7
Liabilities to direct investors	4 590	. .	. . .	. . .	. . .	. . .	. . .	. . .	. . .	–11.5
B. PORTFOLIO INVESTMENT	4 600	. .	. . .	. . .	. . .	. . .	. . .	. . .	. . .	. . .
Assets	4 602	. .	**. . .**	**. . .**	**. . .**	**. . .**	**. . .**	**. . .**	**. . .**	**. . .**
Equity securities	4 610	. .	. . .	. . .	. . .	. . .	. . .	. . .	. . .	. . .
Monetary authorities	4 611	. .	. . .	. . .	. . .	. . .	. . .	. . .	. . .	. . .
General government	4 612	. .	. . .	. . .	. . .	. . .	. . .	. . .	. . .	. . .
Banks	4 613	. .	. . .	. . .	. . .	. . .	. . .	. . .	. . .	. . .
Other sectors	4 614	. .	. . .	. . .	. . .	. . .	. . .	. . .	. . .	. . .
Debt securities	4 619	. .	. . .	. . .	. . .	. . .	. . .	. . .	. . .	. . .
Bonds and notes	4 620	. .	. . .	. . .	. . .	. . .	. . .	. . .	. . .	. . .
Monetary authorities	4 621	. .	. . .	. . .	. . .	. . .	. . .	. . .	. . .	. . .
General government	4 622	. .	. . .	. . .	. . .	. . .	. . .	. . .	. . .	. . .
Banks	4 623	. .	. . .	. . .	. . .	. . .	. . .	. . .	. . .	. . .
Other sectors	4 624	. .	. . .	. . .	. . .	. . .	. . .	. . .	. . .	. . .
Money market instruments	4 630	. .	. . .	. . .	. . .	. . .	. . .	. . .	. . .	. . .
Monetary authorities	4 631	. .	. . .	. . .	. . .	. . .	. . .	. . .	. . .	. . .
General government	4 632	. .	. . .	. . .	. . .	. . .	. . .	. . .	. . .	. . .
Banks	4 633	. .	. . .	. . .	. . .	. . .	. . .	. . .	. . .	. . .
Other sectors	4 634	. .	. . .	. . .	. . .	. . .	. . .	. . .	. . .	. . .
Financial derivatives	4 640	. .	. . .	. . .	. . .	. . .	. . .	. . .	. . .	. . .
Monetary authorities	4 641	. .	. . .	. . .	. . .	. . .	. . .	. . .	. . .	. . .
General government	4 642	. .	. . .	. . .	. . .	. . .	. . .	. . .	. . .	. . .
Banks	4 643	. .	. . .	. . .	. . .	. . .	. . .	. . .	. . .	. . .
Other sectors	4 644	. .	. . .	. . .	. . .	. . .	. . .	. . .	. . .	. . .
Liabilities	4 652	. .	**. . .**	**. . .**	**. . .**	**. . .**	**. . .**	**. . .**	**. . .**	**. . .**
Equity securities	4 660	. .	. . .	. . .	. . .	. . .	. . .	. . .	. . .	. . .
Banks	4 663	. .	. . .	. . .	. . .	. . .	. . .	. . .	. . .	. . .
Other sectors	4 664	. .	. . .	. . .	. . .	. . .	. . .	. . .	. . .	. . .
Debt securities	4 669	. .	. . .	. . .	. . .	. . .	. . .	. . .	. . .	. . .
Bonds and notes	4 670	. .	. . .	. . .	. . .	. . .	. . .	. . .	. . .	. . .
Monetary authorities	4 671	. .	. . .	. . .	. . .	. . .	. . .	. . .	. . .	. . .
General government	4 672	. .	. . .	. . .	. . .	. . .	. . .	. . .	. . .	. . .
Banks	4 673	. .	. . .	. . .	. . .	. . .	. . .	. . .	. . .	. . .
Other sectors	4 674	. .	. . .	. . .	. . .	. . .	. . .	. . .	. . .	. . .
Money market instruments	4 680	. .	. . .	. . .	. . .	. . .	. . .	. . .	. . .	. . .
Monetary authorities	4 681	. .	. . .	. . .	. . .	. . .	. . .	. . .	. . .	. . .
General government	4 682	. .	. . .	. . .	. . .	. . .	. . .	. . .	. . .	. . .
Banks	4 683	. .	. . .	. . .	. . .	. . .	. . .	. . .	. . .	. . .
Other sectors	4 684	. .	. . .	. . .	. . .	. . .	. . .	. . .	. . .	. . .
Financial derivatives	4 690	. .	. . .	. . .	. . .	. . .	. . .	. . .	. . .	. . .
Monetary authorities	4 691	. .	. . .	. . .	. . .	. . .	. . .	. . .	. . .	. . .
General government	4 692	. .	. . .	. . .	. . .	. . .	. . .	. . .	. . .	. . .
Banks	4 693	. .	. . .	. . .	. . .	. . .	. . .	. . .	. . .	. . .
Other sectors	4 694	. .	. . .	. . .	. . .	. . .	. . .	. . .	. . .	. . .

Table 2 (Concluded). STANDARD PRESENTATION, 1988–95
(Millions of U.S. dollars)

	Code		1988	1989	1990	1991	1992	1993	1994	1995
C. OTHER INVESTMENT	4 700	. .	36.5	69.8	74.3	176.9	5.5	–17.7	50.7	–5.1
Assets	4 703	. .	**39.3**	**44.6**	**32.9**	**11.9**	**–37.9**	**1.2**	**11.0**	**17.2**
Trade credits	4 706	. .	. . .	. . .	. . .	. . .	. . .	. . .	. . .	. . .
General government: long-term	4 708	. .	. . .	. . .	. . .	. . .	. . .	. . .	. . .	. . .
General government: short-term	4 709	. .	. . .	. . .	. . .	. . .	. . .	. . .	. . .	. . .
Other sectors: long-term	4 711	. .	. . .	. . .	. . .	. . .	. . .	. . .	. . .	. . .
Other sectors: short-term	4 712	. .	. . .	. . .	. . .	. . .	. . .	. . .	. . .	. . .
Loans	4 714	. .	. . .	. . .	. . .	. . .	. . .	. . .	. . .	. . .
Monetary authorities: long-term	4 717	. .	. . .	. . .	. . .	. . .	. . .	. . .	. . .	. . .
Monetary authorities: short-term	4 718	. .	. . .	. . .	. . .	. . .	. . .	. . .	. . .	. . .
General government: long-term	4 720	. .	. . .	. . .	. . .	. . .	. . .	. . .	. . .	. . .
General government: short-term	4 721	. .	. . .	. . .	. . .	. . .	. . .	. . .	. . .	. . .
Banks: long-term	4 723	. .	. . .	. . .	. . .	. . .	. . .	. . .	. . .	. . .
Banks: short-term	4 724	. .	. . .	. . .	. . .	. . .	. . .	. . .	. . .	. . .
Other sectors: long-term	4 726	. .	. . .	. . .	. . .	. . .	. . .	. . .	. . .	. . .
Other sectors: short-term	4 727	. .	. . .	. . .	. . .	. . .	. . .	. . .	. . .	. . .
Currency and deposits	4 730	. .	39.3	44.6	32.9	11.9	–37.9	1.2	11.0	17.2
Monetary authorities	4 731	. .	. . .	. . .	. . .	. . .	. . .	. . .	. . .	. . .
General government	4 732	. .	. . .	. . .	. . .	. . .	. . .	. . .	. . .	. . .
Banks	4 733	. .	39.3	44.6	32.9	11.9	–37.9	1.2	11.0	17.2
Other sectors	4 734	. .	. . .	. . .	. . .	. . .	. . .	. . .	. . .	. . .
Other assets	4 736	. .	. . .	. . .	. . .	. . .	. . .	. . .	. . .	. . .
Monetary authorities: long-term	4 738	. .	. . .	. . .	. . .	. . .	. . .	. . .	. . .	. . .
Monetary authorities: short-term	4 739	. .	. . .	. . .	. . .	. . .	. . .	. . .	. . .	. . .
General government: long-term	4 741	. .	. . .	. . .	. . .	. . .	. . .	. . .	. . .	. . .
General government: short-term	4 742	. .	. . .	. . .	. . .	. . .	. . .	. . .	. . .	. . .
Banks: long-term	4 744	. .	. . .	. . .	. . .	. . .	. . .	. . .	. . .	. . .
Banks: short-term	4 745	. .	. . .	. . .	. . .	. . .	. . .	. . .	. . .	. . .
Other sectors: long-term	4 747	. .	. . .	. . .	. . .	. . .	. . .	. . .	. . .	. . .
Other sectors: short-term	4 748	. .	. . .	. . .	. . .	. . .	. . .	. . .	. . .	. . .
Liabilities	4 753	. .	**–2.8**	**25.2**	**41.4**	**165.0**	**43.4**	**–18.9**	**39.7**	**–22.3**
Trade credits	4 756	. .	. . .	. . .	. . .	. . .	. . .	. . .	. . .	. . .
General government: long-term	4 758	. .	. . .	. . .	. . .	. . .	. . .	. . .	. . .	. . .
General government: short-term	4 759	. .	. . .	. . .	. . .	. . .	. . .	. . .	. . .	. . .
Other sectors: long-term	4 761	. .	. . .	. . .	. . .	. . .	. . .	. . .	. . .	. . .
Other sectors: short-term	4 762	. .	. . .	. . .	. . .	. . .	. . .	. . .	. . .	. . .
Loans	4 764	. .	–2.8	25.2	41.4	165.0	43.4	–18.9	39.7	–22.3
Use of Fund credit and loans from the Fund	4 766	. .	. . .	. . .	. . .	. . .	. . .	. . .	. . .	. . .
Monetary authorities: other long term	4 767	. .	. . .	. . .	. . .	. . .	. . .	. . .	. . .	. . .
Monetary authorities: short-term	4 768	. .	. . .	. . .	. . .	. . .	. . .	. . .	. . .	. . .
General government: long-term	4 770	. .	–8.1	4.9	12.7	5.9	–3.3	–16.3	–5.9	–9.0
General government: short-term	4 771	. .	. . .	. . .	. . .	. . .	. . .	. . .	. . .	. . .
Banks: long-term	4 773	. .	. . .	. . .	. . .	. . .	. . .	. . .	. . .	. . .
Banks: short-term	4 774	. .	. . .	. . .	. . .	. . .	. . .	. . .	. . .	. . .
Other sectors: long-term	4 776	. .	5.3	20.3	28.7	159.1	46.7	–2.6	45.6	–13.3
Other sectors: short-term	4 777	. .	. . .	. . .	. . .	. . .	. . .	. . .	. . .	. . .
Currency and deposits	4 780	. .	. . .	. . .	. . .	. . .	. . .	. . .	. . .	. . .
Monetary authorities	4 781	. .	. . .	. . .	. . .	. . .	. . .	. . .	. . .	. . .
General government	4 782	. .	. . .	. . .	. . .	. . .	. . .	. . .	. . .	. . .
Banks	4 783	. .	. . .	. . .	. . .	. . .	. . .	. . .	. . .	. . .
Other sectors	4 784	. .	. . .	. . .	. . .	. . .	. . .	. . .	. . .	. . .
Other liabilities	4 786	. .	. . .	. . .	. . .	. . .	. . .	. . .	. . .	. . .
Monetary authorities: long-term	4 788	. .	. . .	. . .	. . .	. . .	. . .	. . .	. . .	. . .
Monetary authorities: short-term	4 789	. .	. . .	. . .	. . .	. . .	. . .	. . .	. . .	. . .
General government: long-term	4 791	. .	. . .	. . .	. . .	. . .	. . .	. . .	. . .	. . .
General government: short-term	4 792	. .	. . .	. . .	. . .	. . .	. . .	. . .	. . .	. . .
Banks: long-term	4 794	. .	. . .	. . .	. . .	. . .	. . .	. . .	. . .	. . .
Banks: short-term	4 795	. .	. . .	. . .	. . .	. . .	. . .	. . .	. . .	. . .
Other sectors: long-term	4 797	. .	. . .	. . .	. . .	. . .	. . .	. . .	. . .	. . .
Other sectors: short-term	4 798	. .	. . .	. . .	. . .	. . .	. . .	. . .	. . .	. . .
D. RESERVE ASSETS	4 800	. .	.7	26.6	–9.3	–13.0	28.7	–19.0	–9.4	3.1
Monetary gold	4 810	. .	. . .	. . .	. . .	. . .	. . .	. . .	. . .	. . .
Special drawing rights	4 820	. .	–.1	.3	–.3	.3	.2	. . .	. . .	. . .
Reserve position in the Fund	4 830	. .	2.3	.5	1.0	1.0	.4	.8	. . .	. . .
Foreign exchange	4 840	. .	–1.5	25.8	–10.0	–14.4	28.1	–19.8	–9.4	3.1
Other claims	4 880	. .	. . .	. . .	. . .	. . .	. . .	. . .	. . .	. . .
NET ERRORS AND OMISSIONS	4 998	. .	**–4.4**	**–37.1**	**51.5**	**–53.8**	**16.1**	**87.2**	**159.5**	**117.8**

Part 3 of the *Yearbook* contains descriptions of the methodologies, compilation practices, and sources used to compile these data.

Table 1. ANALYTIC PRESENTATION, 1988–95
(Millions of U.S. dollars)

	Code	1988	1989	1990	1991	1992	1993	1994	1995
A. Current Account[1]	4 993 Y.	**192.0**	**–193.1**	**244.9**	**–796.0**	**–753.7**	**34.5**	**198.2**	**361.3**
Goods: exports f.o.b	2 100 . .	2,411.4	2,831.1	3,760.6	3,513.0	3,464.4	3,723.4	3,616.8	4,043.6
Goods: imports f.o.b	3 100 . .	–2,334.0	–2,820.2	–3,340.5	–3,703.5	–3,836.7	–3,472.2	–3,373.1	–3,263.2
Balance on Goods	4 100 . .	*77.4*	*10.9*	*420.1*	*–190.4*	*–372.4*	*251.2*	*243.7*	*780.4*
Services: credit	2 200 . .	901.6	809.6	875.5	935.6	1,254.0	1,246.3	1,271.3	1,286.6
Services: debit	3 200 . .	–529.3	–556.4	–651.0	–708.2	–897.0	–825.5	–769.5	–879.7
Balance on Goods and Services	4 991 . .	*449.7*	*264.1*	*644.6*	*37.0*	*–15.4*	*672.0*	*745.5*	*1,187.3*
Income: credit	2 300 . .	263.0	377.7	322.3	282.7	251.1	230.6	129.5	144.9
Income: debit	3 300 . .	–694.1	–738.0	–906.6	–912.2	–818.6	–747.3	–666.5	–748.7
Balance on Goods, Services, and Income	4 992 . .	*18.6*	*–96.3*	*60.3*	*–592.6*	*–582.9*	*155.2*	*208.6*	*583.6*
Current transfers: credit	2 379 Y.	368.1	102.1	456.9	100.0	100.0	201.9	319.4	156.6
Current transfers: debit	3 379 . .	–194.7	–198.9	–272.3	–303.5	–270.7	–322.6	–329.8	–379.0
B. Capital Account[1]	4 994 Y.	**. . .**	**. . .**	**. . .**	**. . .**	**. . .**	**. . .**	**. . .**	**. . .**
Capital account: credit	2 994 Y.	. . .	. . .	. . .	. . .	. . .	. . .	. . .	. . .
Capital account: debit	3 994 . .	. . .	. . .	. . .	. . .	. . .	. . .	. . .	. . .
Total, Groups A Plus B	4 010 . .	*192.0*	*–193.1*	*244.9*	*–796.0*	*–753.7*	*34.5*	*198.2*	*361.3*
C. Financial Account[1]	4 995 X.	**–214.4**	**–264.6**	**407.2**	**469.1**	**967.8**	**153.2**	**–378.5**	**–83.2**
Direct investment abroad	4 505 . .	. . .	. . .	. . .	. . .	. . .	. . .	. . .	. . .
Direct investment in Bahrain	4 555 Y.	222.1	180.9	–3.5	–6.9	–8.5	–5.1	–30.9	–27.1
Portfolio investment assets	4 602 . .	. . .	1.1	–80.6	–35.6	–48.7	–69.4	–69.1	–23.7
Equity securities	4 610 . .	. . .	1.1	–80.6	–35.6	–48.7	–69.4	–69.1	–23.7
Debt securities	4 619 . .	. . .	. . .	. . .	. . .	. . .	. . .	. . .	. . .
Portfolio investment liabilities	4 652 Y.	. . .	. . .	. . .	. . .	. . .	. . .	. . .	. . .
Equity securities	4 660 Y.	. . .	. . .	. . .	. . .	. . .	. . .	. . .	. . .
Debt securities	4 669 Y.	. . .	. . .	. . .	. . .	. . .	. . .	. . .	. . .
Other investment assets	4 703 . .	–437.0	–916.8	601.6	–345.2	165.4	–367.8	–707.3	278.5
Monetary authorities	4 703 . A	. . .	. . .	. . .	. . .	. . .	. . .	. . .	. . .
General government	4 703 . B	–7.4	–79.8	–6.4	–5.9	–6.4	–6.1	–8.8	–6.4
Banks	4 703 . C	–429.5	–837.0	608.0	–339.4	171.8	–361.7	–698.6	284.9
Other sectors	4 703 . D	. . .	. . .	. . .	. . .	. . .	. . .	. . .	. . .
Other investment liabilities	4 753 X.	.5	470.2	–110.4	856.9	859.6	595.5	428.8	–310.9
Monetary authorities	4 753 XA	. . .	17.3	. . .	. . .	. . .	. . .	. . .	. . .
General government	4 753 YB	–10.1	–7.4	–6.1	–10.9	1.1	4.5	3.7	11.2
Banks	4 753 YC	35.9	441.8	–104.8	–2.9	128.5	331.1	454.9	–284.3
Other sectors	4 753 YD	–25.3	18.6	.5	870.7	730.1	259.8	–29.8	–37.8
Total, Groups A Through C	4 020 . .	*–22.3*	*–457.7*	*652.1*	*–326.9*	*214.1*	*187.7*	*–180.3*	*278.0*
D. Net Errors and Omissions	4 998 . .	**114.9**	**269.3**	**–78.4**	**222.0**	**–323.4**	**–278.4**	**44.5**	**–179.9**
Total, Groups A Through D	4 030 . .	*92.5*	*–188.5*	*573.7*	*–104.8*	*–109.3*	*–90.7*	*–135.8*	*98.2*
E. Reserves and Related Items	4 040 . .	**–92.5**	**188.5**	**–573.7**	**104.8**	**109.3**	**90.7**	**135.8**	**–98.2**
Reserve assets	4 800 . .	–92.5	188.5	–573.7	104.8	109.3	90.7	135.8	–98.2
Use of Fund credit and loans	4 766 . .	. . .	. . .	. . .	. . .	. . .	. . .	. . .	. . .
Liabilities constituting foreign authorities' reserves	4 900 . .	. . .	. . .	. . .	. . .	. . .	. . .	. . .	. . .
Exceptional financing	4 920 . .	. . .	. . .	. . .	. . .	. . .	. . .	. . .	. . .
Conversion rates: Bahrain dinar per U.S. dollar	0 101 . .	**.3760**	**.3760**	**.3760**	**.3760**	**.3760**	**.3760**	**.3760**	**.3760**

[1] Excludes components that have been classified in the categories of Group E.

Table 2. STANDARD PRESENTATION, 1988–95
(Millions of U.S. dollars)

	Code	1988	1989	1990	1991	1992	1993	1994	1995
CURRENT ACCOUNT	4 993 . .	**192.0**	**–193.1**	**244.9**	**–796.0**	**–753.7**	**34.5**	**198.2**	**361.3**
A. GOODS	4 100 . .	77.4	10.9	420.1	–190.4	–372.4	251.2	243.7	780.4
Credit	2 100 . .	**2,411.4**	**2,831.1**	**3,760.6**	**3,513.0**	**3,464.4**	**3,723.4**	**3,616.8**	**4,043.6**
General merchandise: exports f.o.b.	2 110 . .	2,411.4	2,831.1	3,760.6	3,513.0	3,464.4	3,723.4	3,616.8	4,043.6
Goods for processing: exports f.o.b.	2 150 . .	. . .	. . .	. . .	. . .	. . .	. . .	. . .	. . .
Repairs on goods	2 160 . .	. . .	. . .	. . .	. . .	. . .	. . .	. . .	. . .
Goods procured in ports by carriers	2 170 . .	. . .	. . .	. . .	. . .	. . .	. . .	. . .	. . .
Nonmonetary gold	2 180 . .	. . .	. . .	. . .	. . .	. . .	. . .	. . .	. . .
Debit	3 100 . .	**–2,334.0**	**–2,820.2**	**–3,340.5**	**–3,703.5**	**–3,836.7**	**–3,472.2**	**–3,373.1**	**–3,263.2**
General merchandise: imports f.o.b.	3 110 . .	–2,334.0	–2,820.2	–3,340.5	–3,703.5	–3,836.7	–3,472.2	–3,373.1	–3,263.2
Goods for processing: imports f.o.b.	3 150 . .	. . .	. . .	. . .	. . .	. . .	. . .	. . .	. . .
Repairs on goods	3 160 . .	. . .	. . .	. . .	. . .	. . .	. . .	. . .	. . .
Goods procured in ports by carriers	3 170 . .	. . .	. . .	. . .	. . .	. . .	. . .	. . .	. . .
Nonmonetary gold	3 180 . .	. . .	. . .	. . .	. . .	. . .	. . .	. . .	. . .
B. SERVICES	4 200 . .	372.3	253.2	224.5	227.4	357.0	420.7	501.9	406.9
Total credit	2 200 . .	*901.6*	*809.6*	*875.5*	*935.6*	*1,254.0*	*1,246.3*	*1,271.3*	*1,286.6*
Total debit	3 200 . .	*–529.3*	*–556.4*	*–651.0*	*–708.2*	*–897.0*	*–825.5*	*–769.5*	*–879.7*
Transportation services, credit	2 205 . .	**212.2**	**216.5**	**231.1**	**260.6**	**467.3**	**479.5**	**492.1**	**504.9**
Passenger	2 205 BA	. . .	. . .	. . .	. . .	. . .	. . .	. . .	. . .
Freight	2 205 BB	. . .	. . .	. . .	. . .	. . .	. . .	. . .	. . .
Other	2 205 BC	*212.2*	*216.5*	*231.1*	*260.6*	*467.3*	*479.5*	*492.1*	*504.9*
Sea transport, passenger	2 207 . .	. . .	. . .	. . .	. . .	. . .	. . .	. . .	. . .
Sea transport, freight	2 208 . .	. . .	. . .	. . .	. . .	. . .	. . .	. . .	. . .
Sea transport, other	2 209 . .	. . .	. . .	. . .	. . .	. . .	. . .	. . .	. . .
Air transport, passenger	2 211 . .	. . .	. . .	. . .	. . .	. . .	. . .	. . .	. . .
Air transport, freight	2 212 . .	. . .	. . .	. . .	. . .	. . .	. . .	. . .	. . .
Air transport, other	2 213 . .	. . .	. . .	. . .	. . .	. . .	. . .	. . .	. . .
Other transport, passenger	2 215 . .	. . .	. . .	. . .	. . .	. . .	. . .	. . .	. . .
Other transport, freight	2 216 . .	. . .	. . .	. . .	. . .	. . .	. . .	. . .	. . .
Other transport, other	2 217 . .	. . .	. . .	. . .	. . .	. . .	. . .	. . .	. . .
Transportation services, debit	3 205 . .	**–352.3**	**–397.7**	**–477.4**	**–520.5**	**–665.3**	**–601.8**	**–521.9**	**–607.3**
Passenger	3 205 BA	. . .	. . .	. . .	. . .	. . .	. . .	. . .	. . .
Freight	3 205 BB	*–233.4*	*–282.0*	*–334.1*	*–370.5*	*–383.7*	*–347.3*	*–337.3*	*–326.3*
Other	3 205 BC	*–118.9*	*–115.7*	*–143.4*	*–150.0*	*–281.6*	*–254.5*	*–184.6*	*–281.0*
Sea transport, passenger	3 207 . .	. . .	. . .	. . .	. . .	. . .	. . .	. . .	. . .
Sea transport, freight	3 208 . .	. . .	. . .	. . .	. . .	. . .	. . .	. . .	. . .
Sea transport, other	3 209 . .	. . .	. . .	. . .	. . .	. . .	. . .	. . .	. . .
Air transport, passenger	3 211 . .	. . .	. . .	. . .	. . .	. . .	. . .	. . .	. . .
Air transport, freight	3 212 . .	. . .	. . .	. . .	. . .	. . .	. . .	. . .	. . .
Air transport, other	3 213 . .	. . .	. . .	. . .	. . .	. . .	. . .	. . .	. . .
Other transport, passenger	3 215 . .	. . .	. . .	. . .	. . .	. . .	. . .	. . .	. . .
Other transport, freight	3 216 . .	. . .	. . .	. . .	. . .	. . .	. . .	. . .	. . .
Other transport, other	3 217 . .	. . .	. . .	. . .	. . .	. . .	. . .	. . .	. . .
Travel, credit	2 236 . .	**113.8**	**116.0**	**135.4**	**162.0**	**176.6**	**222.1**	**302.4**	**287.5**
Business travel	2 237 . .	. . .	. . .	. . .	. . .	. . .	. . .	. . .	. . .
Personal travel	2 240 . .	. . .	. . .	. . .	. . .	. . .	. . .	. . .	. . .
Travel, debit	3 236 . .	**–77.1**	**–76.9**	**–93.6**	**–98.1**	**–140.7**	**–130.1**	**–145.7**	**–163.3**
Business travel	3 237 . .	. . .	. . .	. . .	. . .	. . .	. . .	. . .	. . .
Personal travel	3 240 . .	. . .	. . .	. . .	. . .	. . .	. . .	. . .	. . .
Other services, credit	2 200 BA	**575.5**	**477.1**	**509.0**	**513.0**	**610.1**	**544.7**	**476.9**	**494.1**
Communications	2 245 . .	. . .	. . .	. . .	. . .	. . .	. . .	. . .	. . .
Construction	2 249 . .	. . .	. . .	. . .	. . .	. . .	. . .	. . .	. . .
Insurance	2 253 . .	. . .	. . .	. . .	. . .	. . .	. . .	. . .	. . .
Financial	2 260 . .	. . .	. . .	. . .	. . .	. . .	. . .	. . .	. . .
Computer and information	2 262 . .	. . .	. . .	. . .	. . .	. . .	. . .	. . .	. . .
Royalties and licence fees	2 266 . .	. . .	. . .	. . .	. . .	. . .	. . .	. . .	. . .
Other business services	2 268 . .	569.9	475.0	507.7	510.6	609.8	541.8	473.4	494.1
Personal, cultural, and recreational	2 287 . .	. . .	. . .	. . .	. . .	. . .	. . .	. . .	. . .
Government, n.i.e.	2 291 . .	5.6	2.1	1.3	2.4	.3	2.9	3.5	. . .
Other services, debit	3 200 BA	**–99.9**	**–81.9**	**–80.0**	**–89.6**	**–91.0**	**–93.6**	**–101.8**	**–109.1**
Communications	3 245 . .	. . .	. . .	. . .	. . .	. . .	. . .	. . .	. . .
Construction	3 249 . .	. . .	. . .	. . .	. . .	. . .	. . .	. . .	. . .
Insurance	3 253 . .	–25.9	–31.3	–37.2	–41.2	–43.4	–38.6	–37.5	–36.3
Financial	3 260 . .	. . .	. . .	. . .	. . .	. . .	. . .	. . .	. . .
Computer and information	3 262 . .	. . .	. . .	. . .	. . .	. . .	. . .	. . .	. . .
Royalties and licence fees	3 266 . .	. . .	. . .	. . .	. . .	. . .	. . .	. . .	. . .
Other business services	3 268 . .	–68.1	–50.5	–43.1	–48.1	–46.5	–54.8	–64.4	–72.9
Personal, cultural, and recreational	3 287 . .	. . .	. . .	. . .	. . .	. . .	. . .	. . .	. . .
Government, n.i.e.	3 291 . .	–5.9	. . .	.3	–.3	–1.1	–.3	. . .	. . .

Table 2 (Continued). STANDARD PRESENTATION, 1988–95
(Millions of U.S. dollars)

	Code		1988	1989	1990	1991	1992	1993	1994	1995
C. INCOME	4 300	. .	–431.1	–360.4	–584.3	–629.5	–567.6	–516.8	–537.0	–603.7
Total credit	2 300	. .	*263.0*	*377.7*	*322.3*	*282.7*	*251.1*	*230.6*	*129.5*	*144.9*
Total debit	3 300	. .	*–694.1*	*–738.0*	*–906.6*	*–912.2*	*–818.6*	*–747.3*	*–666.5*	*–748.7*
Compensation of employees, credit	2 310	. .	**. . .**	**. . .**	**. . .**	**. . .**	**. . .**	**. . .**	**. . .**	**. . .**
Compensation of employees, debit	3 310	. .	**–474.5**	**–495.2**	**–626.6**	**–671.0**	**–545.2**	**–464.9**	**–506.4**	**–567.3**
Investment income, credit	2 320	. .	**263.0**	**377.7**	**322.3**	**282.7**	**251.1**	**230.6**	**129.5**	**144.9**
Direct investment income	2 330	. .	. . .	. . .	. . .	. . .	. . .	. . .	. . .	. . .
Dividends and distributed branch profits	2 332	. .	. . .	. . .	. . .	. . .	. . .	. . .	. . .	. . .
Reinvested earnings and undistributed branch profits	2 333	. .	. . .	. . .	. . .	. . .	. . .	. . .	. . .	. . .
Income on debt (interest)	2 334	. .	. . .	. . .	. . .	. . .	. . .	. . .	. . .	. . .
Portfolio investment income	2 339	. .	. . .	. . .	. . .	. . .	. . .	. . .	. . .	. . .
Income on equity	2 340	. .	. . .	. . .	. . .	. . .	. . .	. . .	. . .	. . .
Income on bonds and notes	2 350	. .	. . .	. . .	. . .	. . .	. . .	. . .	. . .	. . .
Income on money market instruments and financial derivatives	2 360	. .	. . .	. . .	. . .	. . .	. . .	. . .	. . .	. . .
Other investment income	2 370	. .	263.0	377.7	322.3	282.7	251.1	230.6	129.5	144.9
Investment income, debit	3 320	. .	**–219.7**	**–242.8**	**–280.1**	**–241.2**	**–273.4**	**–282.4**	**–160.1**	**–181.4**
Direct investment income	3 330	. .	. . .	. . .	. . .	. . .	. . .	. . .	. . .	. . .
Dividends and distributed branch profits	3 332	. .	. . .	. . .	. . .	. . .	. . .	. . .	. . .	. . .
Reinvested earnings and undistributed branch profits	3 333	. .	. . .	. . .	. . .	. . .	. . .	. . .	. . .	. . .
Income on debt (interest)	3 334	. .	. . .	. . .	. . .	. . .	. . .	. . .	. . .	. . .
Portfolio investment income	3 339	. .	. . .	. . .	. . .	. . .	. . .	. . .	. . .	. . .
Income on equity	3 340	. .	. . .	. . .	. . .	. . .	. . .	. . .	. . .	. . .
Income on bonds and notes	3 350	. .	. . .	. . .	. . .	. . .	. . .	. . .	. . .	. . .
Income on money market instruments and financial derivatives	3 360	. .	. . .	. . .	. . .	. . .	. . .	. . .	. . .	. . .
Other investment income	3 370	. .	–219.7	–242.8	–280.1	–241.2	–273.4	–282.4	–160.1	–181.4
D. CURRENT TRANSFERS	4 379	. .	173.4	–96.8	184.6	–203.5	–170.7	–120.7	–10.4	–222.3
Credit	2 379	. .	**368.1**	**102.1**	**456.9**	**100.0**	**100.0**	**201.9**	**319.4**	**156.6**
General government	2 380	. .	368.1	102.1	456.9	100.0	100.0	201.9	319.4	156.6
Other sectors	2 390	. .	. . .	. . .	. . .	. . .	. . .	. . .	. . .	. . .
Workers' remittances	2 391	. .	. . .	. . .	. . .	. . .	. . .	. . .	. . .	. . .
Other current transfers	2 392	. .	. . .	. . .	. . .	. . .	. . .	. . .	. . .	. . .
Debit	3 379	. .	**–194.7**	**–198.9**	**–272.3**	**–303.5**	**–270.7**	**–322.6**	**–329.8**	**–379.0**
General government	3 380	. .	–1.6	. . .	. . .	. . .	. . .	. . .	–.3	. . .
Other sectors	3 390	. .	–193.1	–198.9	–272.3	–303.5	–270.7	–322.6	–329.5	–379.0
Workers' remittances	3 391	. .	–194.1	–198.7	–253.2	–270.5	–218.1	–184.6	–201.1	–236.7
Other current transfers	3 392	. .	1.1	–.3	–19.1	–33.0	–52.7	–138.0	–128.5	–142.3
CAPITAL AND FINANCIAL ACCOUNT	4 996	. .	**–306.9**	**–76.2**	**–166.5**	**574.0**	**1,077.1**	**243.9**	**–242.7**	**–181.4**
CAPITAL ACCOUNT	4 994	. .	. . .	. . .	. . .	. . .	. . .	. . .	. . .	. . .
Total credit	2 994	. .	. . .	. . .	. . .	. . .	. . .	. . .	. . .	. . .
Total debit	3 994	. .	. . .	. . .	. . .	. . .	. . .	. . .	. . .	. . .
Capital transfers, credit	2 400	. .	**. . .**	**. . .**	**. . .**	**. . .**	**. . .**	**. . .**	**. . .**	**. . .**
General government	2 401	. .	. . .	. . .	. . .	. . .	. . .	. . .	. . .	. . .
Debt forgiveness	2 402	. .	. . .	. . .	. . .	. . .	. . .	. . .	. . .	. . .
Other capital transfers	2 410	. .	. . .	. . .	. . .	. . .	. . .	. . .	. . .	. . .
Other sectors	2 430	. .	. . .	. . .	. . .	. . .	. . .	. . .	. . .	. . .
Migrants' transfers	2 431	. .	. . .	. . .	. . .	. . .	. . .	. . .	. . .	. . .
Debt forgiveness	2 432	. .	. . .	. . .	. . .	. . .	. . .	. . .	. . .	. . .
Other capital transfers	2 440	. .	. . .	. . .	. . .	. . .	. . .	. . .	. . .	. . .
Capital transfers, debit	3 400	. .	**. . .**	**. . .**	**. . .**	**. . .**	**. . .**	**. . .**	**. . .**	**. . .**
General government	3 401	. .	. . .	. . .	. . .	. . .	. . .	. . .	. . .	. . .
Debt forgiveness	3 402	. .	. . .	. . .	. . .	. . .	. . .	. . .	. . .	. . .
Other capital transfers	3 410	. .	. . .	. . .	. . .	. . .	. . .	. . .	. . .	. . .
Other sectors	3 430	. .	. . .	. . .	. . .	. . .	. . .	. . .	. . .	. . .
Migrants' transfers	3 431	. .	. . .	. . .	. . .	. . .	. . .	. . .	. . .	. . .
Debt forgiveness	3 432	. .	. . .	. . .	. . .	. . .	. . .	. . .	. . .	. . .
Other capital transfers	3 440	. .	. . .	. . .	. . .	. . .	. . .	. . .	. . .	. . .
Nonproduced nonfinancial assets, credit	2 480	. .	**. . .**	**. . .**	**. . .**	**. . .**	**. . .**	**. . .**	**. . .**	**. . .**
Nonproduced nonfinancial assets, debit	3 480	. .	**. . .**	**. . .**	**. . .**	**. . .**	**. . .**	**. . .**	**. . .**	**. . .**

Table 2 (Continued). STANDARD PRESENTATION, 1988–95
(Millions of U.S. dollars)

	Code	1988	1989	1990	1991	1992	1993	1994	1995
FINANCIAL ACCOUNT	4 995	**–306.9**	**–76.2**	**–166.5**	**574.0**	**1,077.1**	**243.9**	**–242.7**	**–181.4**
A. DIRECT INVESTMENT	4 500	222.1	180.9	–3.5	–6.9	–8.5	–5.1	–30.9	–27.1
Direct investment abroad	4 505	**...**	**...**	**...**	**...**	**...**	**...**	**...**	**...**
Equity capital	4 510	...	...	...	...	...	...	...	...
Claims on affiliated enterprises	4 515	...	...	...	...	...	...	...	...
Liabilities to affiliated enterprises	4 520	...	...	...	...	...	...	...	...
Reinvested earnings	4 525	...	...	...	...	...	...	...	...
Other capital	4 530	...	...	...	...	...	...	...	...
Claims on affiliated enterprises	4 535	...	...	...	...	...	...	...	...
Liabilities to affiliated enterprises	4 540	...	...	...	...	...	...	...	...
Direct investment in Bahrain	4 555	**222.1**	**180.9**	**–3.5**	**–6.9**	**–8.5**	**–5.1**	**–30.9**	**–27.1**
Equity capital	4 560	...	...	...	...	...	...	...	...
Claims on direct investors	4 565	...	...	...	...	...	...	...	...
Liabilities to direct investors	4 570	...	...	...	...	...	...	...	...
Reinvested earnings	4 575	...	...	...	...	...	...	...	...
Other capital	4 580	222.1	180.9	–3.5	–6.9	–8.5	–5.1	–30.9	–27.1
Claims on direct investors	4 585	...	...	...	...	...	...	...	...
Liabilities to direct investors	4 590	...	...	...	...	...	...	...	...
B. PORTFOLIO INVESTMENT	4 600	...	1.1	–80.6	–35.6	–48.7	–69.4	–69.1	–23.7
Assets	4 602	**...**	**1.1**	**–80.6**	**–35.6**	**–48.7**	**–69.4**	**–69.1**	**–23.7**
Equity securities	4 610	...	1.1	–80.6	–35.6	–48.7	–69.4	–69.1	–23.7
Monetary authorities	4 611	...	...	...	...	...	...	...	...
General government	4 612	...	...	...	...	...	...	...	...
Banks	4 613	...	...	...	...	...	...	...	...
Other sectors	4 614	...	...	...	...	...	...	...	...
Debt securities	4 619	...	...	...	...	...	...	...	...
Bonds and notes	4 620	...	...	...	...	...	...	...	...
Monetary authorities	4 621	...	...	...	...	...	...	...	...
General government	4 622	...	...	...	...	...	...	...	...
Banks	4 623	...	...	...	...	...	...	...	...
Other sectors	4 624	...	...	...	...	...	...	...	...
Money market instruments	4 630	...	...	...	...	...	...	...	...
Monetary authorities	4 631	...	...	...	...	...	...	...	...
General government	4 632	...	...	...	...	...	...	...	...
Banks	4 633	...	...	...	...	...	...	...	...
Other sectors	4 634	...	...	...	...	...	...	...	...
Financial derivatives	4 640	...	...	...	...	...	...	...	...
Monetary authorities	4 641	...	...	...	...	...	...	...	...
General government	4 642	...	...	...	...	...	...	...	...
Banks	4 643	...	...	...	...	...	...	...	...
Other sectors	4 644	...	...	...	...	...	...	...	...
Liabilities	4 652	**...**	**...**	**...**	**...**	**...**	**...**	**...**	**...**
Equity securities	4 660	...	...	...	...	...	...	...	...
Banks	4 663	...	...	...	...	...	...	...	...
Other sectors	4 664	...	...	...	...	...	...	...	...
Debt securities	4 669	...	...	...	...	...	...	...	...
Bonds and notes	4 670	...	...	...	...	...	...	...	...
Monetary authorities	4 671	...	...	...	...	...	...	...	...
General government	4 672	...	...	...	...	...	...	...	...
Banks	4 673	...	...	...	...	...	...	...	...
Other sectors	4 674	...	...	...	...	...	...	...	...
Money market instruments	4 680	...	...	...	...	...	...	...	...
Monetary authorities	4 681	...	...	...	...	...	...	...	...
General government	4 682	...	...	...	...	...	...	...	...
Banks	4 683	...	...	...	...	...	...	...	...
Other sectors	4 684	...	...	...	...	...	...	...	...
Financial derivatives	4 690	...	...	...	...	...	...	...	...
Monetary authorities	4 691	...	...	...	...	...	...	...	...
General government	4 692	...	...	...	...	...	...	...	...
Banks	4 693	...	...	...	...	...	...	...	...
Other sectors	4 694	...	...	...	...	...	...	...	...

Table 2 (Concluded). STANDARD PRESENTATION, 1988–95
(Millions of U.S. dollars)

	Code	1988	1989	1990	1991	1992	1993	1994	1995
C. OTHER INVESTMENT	4 700	–436.4	–446.5	491.2	511.7	1,025.0	227.7	–278.5	–32.4
Assets	4 703	**–437.0**	**–916.8**	**601.6**	**–345.2**	**165.4**	**–367.8**	**–707.3**	**278.5**
Trade credits	4 706	...	...	...	...	...	...	...	...
General government: long-term	4 708	...	...	...	...	...	...	...	...
General government: short-term	4 709	...	...	...	...	...	...	...	...
Other sectors: long-term	4 711	...	...	...	...	...	...	...	...
Other sectors: short-term	4 712	...	...	...	...	...	...	...	...
Loans	4 714	...	...	...	...	...	...	...	...
Monetary authorities: long-term	4 717	...	...	...	...	...	...	...	...
Monetary authorities: short-term	4 718	...	...	...	...	...	...	...	...
General government: long-term	4 720	...	...	...	...	...	...	...	...
General government: short-term	4 721	...	...	...	...	...	...	...	...
Banks: long-term	4 723	...	...	...	...	...	...	...	...
Banks: short-term	4 724	...	...	...	...	...	...	...	...
Other sectors: long-term	4 726	...	...	...	...	...	...	...	...
Other sectors: short-term	4 727	...	...	...	...	...	...	...	...
Currency and deposits	4 730	–429.5	–837.0	608.0	–339.4	171.8	–361.7	–698.6	284.9
Monetary authorities	4 731	...	...	...	...	...	...	...	...
General government	4 732	...	...	...	...	...	...	...	...
Banks	4 733	–429.5	–837.0	608.0	–339.4	171.8	–361.7	–698.6	284.9
Other sectors	4 734	...	...	...	...	...	...	...	...
Other assets	4 736	–7.4	–79.8	–6.4	–5.9	–6.4	–6.1	–8.8	–6.4
Monetary authorities: long-term	4 738	...	...	...	...	...	...	...	...
Monetary authorities: short-term	4 739	...	...	...	...	...	...	...	...
General government: long-term	4 741	–7.4	–79.8	–6.4	–5.9	–6.4	–6.1	–8.8	–6.4
General government: short-term	4 742	...	...	...	...	...	...	...	...
Banks: long-term	4 744	...	...	...	...	...	...	...	...
Banks: short-term	4 745	...	...	...	...	...	...	...	...
Other sectors: long-term	4 747	...	...	...	...	...	...	...	...
Other sectors: short-term	4 748	...	...	...	...	...	...	...	...
Liabilities	4 753	**.5**	**470.2**	**–110.4**	**856.9**	**859.6**	**595.5**	**428.8**	**–310.9**
Trade credits	4 756	...	...	...	...	...	...	...	...
General government: long-term	4 758	...	...	...	...	...	...	...	...
General government: short-term	4 759	...	...	...	...	...	...	...	...
Other sectors: long-term	4 761	...	...	...	...	...	...	...	...
Other sectors: short-term	4 762	...	...	...	...	...	...	...	...
Loans	4 764	–9.6	–7.4	–5.6	859.8	731.1	264.4	–26.1	–26.6
Use of Fund credit and loans from the Fund	4 766	...	...	...	...	...	...	...	...
Monetary authorities: other long-term	4 767	...	...	...	...	...	...	...	...
Monetary authorities: short-term	4 768	...	...	...	...	...	...	...	...
General government: long-term	4 770	–10.1	–7.4	–6.1	–10.9	1.1	4.5	3.7	11.2
General government: short-term	4 771	...	...	...	...	...	...	...	...
Banks: long-term	4 773	...	...	...	...	...	...	...	...
Banks: short-term	4 774	...	...	...	...	...	...	...	...
Other sectors: long-term	4 776	.5	...	146.8	473.4	730.1	259.8	–29.8	–37.8
Other sectors: short-term	4 777	...	...	–146.3	397.3	...	...	...	...
Currency and deposits	4 780	35.9	441.8	–104.8	–2.9	128.5	331.1	454.9	–284.3
Monetary authorities	4 781	...	...	...	...	...	...	...	...
General government	4 782	...	...	...	...	...	...	...	...
Banks	4 783	35.9	441.8	–104.8	–2.9	128.5	331.1	454.9	–284.3
Other sectors	4 784	...	...	...	...	...	...	...	...
Other liabilities	4 786	–25.8	35.9	...	...	...	...	...	...
Monetary authorities: long-term	4 788	...	...	...	...	...	...	...	...
Monetary authorities: short-term	4 789	...	17.3	...	...	...	...	...	...
General government: long-term	4 791	...	...	...	...	...	...	...	...
General government: short-term	4 792	...	...	...	...	...	...	...	...
Banks: long-term	4 794	...		...	...	...	...	...	...
Banks: short-term	4 795	...		...	...	...	...	...	...
Other sectors: long-term	4 797	...	...	...	...	...	...	...	...
Other sectors: short-term	4 798	–25.8	18.6	...	...	...	...	...	...
D. RESERVE ASSETS	4 800	–92.5	188.5	–573.7	104.8	109.3	90.7	135.8	–98.2
Monetary gold	4 810	...	...	...	...	...	...	...	...
Special drawing rights	4 820	–.7	–.9	–1.3	–1.3	–1.2	10.9	–.3	–.4
Reserve position in the Fund	4 830	–.6	–2.4	2.1	–2.3	–2.0	–13.5	–1.9	–2.3
Foreign exchange	4 840	–91.2	191.8	–574.5	108.5	112.5	93.4	138.0	–95.5
Other claims	4 880	...	...	...	...	...	...	...	...
NET ERRORS AND OMISSIONS	4 998	**114.9**	**269.3**	**–78.4**	**222.0**	**–323.4**	**–278.4**	**44.5**	**–179.9**

Table 1. ANALYTIC PRESENTATION, 1988–95
(Millions of U.S. dollars)

	Code	1988	1989	1990	1991	1992	1993	1994	1995
A. Current Account [1]	4 993 Y.	**–273.2**	**–1,099.6**	**–397.9**	**64.6**	**180.8**	**359.3**	**199.6**	**–823.9**
Goods: exports f.o.b	2 100 ..	1,291.0	1,304.8	1,672.4	1,688.7	2,097.9	2,544.7	2,934.4	3,733.3
Goods: imports f.o.b	3 100 ..	–2,734.4	–3,300.1	–3,259.4	–3,074.5	–3,353.8	–3,657.3	–4,350.5	–6,057.4
Balance on Goods	4 100 ..	*–1,443.4*	*–1,995.3*	*–1,587.0*	*–1,385.8*	*–1,255.9*	*–1,112.6*	*–1,416.1*	*–2,324.1*
Services: credit	2 200 ..	277.6	334.4	391.6	431.0	483.4	529.4	589.8	698.2
Services: debit	3 200 ..	–613.1	–726.4	–700.5	–695.3	–788.8	–932.2	–1,025.0	–1,531.2
Balance on Goods and Services	4 991 ..	*–1,778.9*	*–2,387.3*	*–1,895.8*	*–1,650.0*	*–1,561.4*	*–1,515.3*	*–1,851.3*	*–3,157.1*
Income: credit	2 300 ..	54.8	88.7	64.2	70.0	100.1	100.1	150.5	270.1
Income: debit	3 300 ..	–180.7	–196.9	–179.8	–166.9	–166.0	–175.8	–188.7	–201.8
Balance on Goods, Services, and Income	4 992 ..	*–1,904.8*	*–2,495.5*	*–2,011.4*	*–1,747.0*	*–1,627.3*	*–1,591.0*	*–1,889.6*	*–3,088.8*
Current transfers: credit	2 379 Y.	1,633.0	1,396.6	1,614.2	1,811.9	1,808.8	1,951.8	2,091.4	2,266.7
Current transfers: debit	3 379 ..	–1.5	–.7	–.7	–.3	–.7	–1.5	–2.2	–1.8
B. Capital Account [1]	4 994 Y.	**...**	**...**	**...**	**...**	**...**	**...**	**...**	**...**
Capital account: credit	2 994 Y.	...	...	...	...	...	...	...	...
Capital account: debit	3 994 ..	...	...	...	...	...	...	...	...
Total, Groups A Plus B	4 010 ..	*–273.2*	*–1,099.6*	*–397.9*	*64.6*	*180.8*	*359.3*	*199.6*	*–823.9*
C. Financial Account [1]	4 995 X.	**398.6**	**833.2**	**697.8**	**467.6**	**538.4**	**268.9**	**748.8**	**178.8**
Direct investment abroad	4 505 ..	...	...	...	...	...	...	...	...
Direct investment in Bangladesh	4 555 Y.	1.8	.2	3.2	1.4	3.7	14.0	11.1	1.9
Portfolio investment assets	4 602 ..	...	...	...	...	...	...	...	...
Equity securities	4 610 ..	...	...	...	...	...	...	...	...
Debt securities	4 619 ..	...	...	...	...	...	...	...	...
Portfolio investment liabilities	4 652 Y.	...	1.7	.3	2.2	8.7	8.4	105.9	–15.2
Equity securities	4 660 Y.	...	1.7	.3	2.2	8.7	8.4	105.9	–15.2
Debt securities	4 669 Y.	...	...	...	...	...	...	...	...
Other investment assets	4 703 ..	–229.1	–152.0	–207.8	–267.1	–196.0	–178.4	–169.3	–292.7
Monetary authorities	4 703 .A	...	...	...	...	...	...	...	...
General government	4 703 .B	–1.6	–.5	–1.6	–.4	...	–.7	–.1	...
Banks	4 703 .C	–227.5	–151.4	–206.1	–266.7	–196.0	–177.7	–169.2	–292.7
Other sectors	4 703 .D	...	...	...	...	...	...	...	...
Other investment liabilities	4 753 X.	625.9	983.2	902.0	731.1	722.0	424.8	801.1	484.9
Monetary authorities	4 753 XA	–7.0	3.5	–.1	1.3	–.9	–.2	15.0	58.3
General government	4 753 YB	618.9	878.1	827.0	533.1	667.6	379.3	718.5	374.2
Banks	4 753 YC	2.8	91.3	40.9	186.8	14.5	...	51.4	14.6
Other sectors	4 753 YD	11.2	10.3	34.2	9.9	40.8	45.8	16.2	37.9
Total, Groups A Through C	4 020 ..	*125.4*	*–266.3*	*299.9*	*532.2*	*719.2*	*628.1*	*948.4*	*–645.1*
D. Net Errors and Omissions	4 998 ..	**6.6**	**–43.1**	**–75.7**	**–98.4**	**–84.0**	**69.4**	**–257.1**	**133.3**
Total, Groups A Through D	4 030 ..	*132.0*	*–309.5*	*224.2*	*433.8*	*635.2*	*697.6*	*691.3*	*–511.7*
E. Reserves and Related Items	4 040 ..	**–132.0**	**309.5**	**–224.2**	**–433.8**	**–635.2**	**–697.6**	**–691.3**	**511.7**
Reserve assets	4 800 ..	–176.1	447.8	–78.9	–544.5	–670.1	–647.0	–636.2	572.8
Use of Fund credit and loans	4 766 ..	43.6	–99.6	–145.3	110.7	34.9	–50.6	–55.1	–61.0
Liabilities constituting foreign authorities' reserves	4 900 ..	...	–38.8	...	...	...	...	...	...
Exceptional financing	4 920 ..	.4	...	...	...	...	...	...	...
Conversion rates: taka per U.S. dollar	0 101 ..	**31.733**	**32.270**	**34.569**	**36.596**	**38.951**	**39.567**	**40.212**	**40.278**

[1] Excludes components that have been classified in the categories of Group E.

Table 2. STANDARD PRESENTATION, 1988–95
(Millions of U.S. dollars)

	Code	1988	1989	1990	1991	1992	1993	1994	1995
CURRENT ACCOUNT	4 993 . .	**–272.8**	**–1,099.6**	**–397.9**	**64.6**	**180.8**	**359.3**	**199.6**	**–823.9**
A. GOODS	4 100 . .	–1,443.4	–1,995.3	–1,587.0	–1,385.8	–1,255.9	–1,112.6	–1,416.1	–2,324.1
Credit	2 100 . .	**1,291.0**	**1,304.8**	**1,672.4**	**1,688.7**	**2,097.9**	**2,544.7**	**2,934.4**	**3,733.3**
General merchandise: exports f.o.b.	2 110 . .	1,291.0	1,304.8	1,672.4	1,688.7	2,097.9	2,544.7	2,934.4	3,733.3
Goods for processing: exports f.o.b.	2 150 . .	. . .	. . .	. . .	. . .	. . .	. . .	. . .	. . .
Repairs on goods	2 160 . .	. . .	. . .	. . .	. . .	. . .	. . .	. . .	. . .
Goods procured in ports by carriers	2 170 . .	. . .	. . .	. . .	. . .	. . .	. . .	. . .	. . .
Nonmonetary gold	2 180 . .	. . .	. . .	. . .	. . .	. . .	. . .	. . .	. . .
Debit	3 100 . .	**–2,734.4**	**–3,300.1**	**–3,259.4**	**–3,074.5**	**–3,353.8**	**–3,657.3**	**–4,350.5**	**–6,057.4**
General merchandise: imports f.o.b.	3 110 . .	–2,734.4	–3,300.1	–3,259.4	–3,074.5	–3,353.8	–3,657.3	–4,350.5	–6,057.4
Goods for processing: imports f.o.b.	3 150 . .	. . .	. . .	. . .	. . .	. . .	. . .	. . .	. . .
Repairs on goods	3 160 . .	. . .	. . .	. . .	. . .	. . .	. . .	. . .	. . .
Goods procured in ports by carriers	3 170 . .	. . .	. . .	. . .	. . .	. . .	. . .	. . .	. . .
Nonmonetary gold	3 180 . .	. . .	. . .	. . .	. . .	. . .	. . .	. . .	. . .
B. SERVICES	4 200 . .	–335.5	–392.0	–308.9	–264.2	–305.4	–402.7	–435.2	–833.0
Total credit	2 200 . .	*277.6*	*334.4*	*391.6*	*431.0*	*483.4*	*529.4*	*589.8*	*698.2*
Total debit	3 200 . .	*–613.1*	*–726.4*	*–700.5*	*–695.3*	*–788.8*	*–932.2*	*–1,025.0*	*–1,531.2*
Transportation services, credit	2 205 . .	**30.0**	**34.1**	**38.3**	**35.7**	**41.0**	**42.5**	**55.1**	**70.2**
Passenger	2 205 BA	. . .	. . .	. . .	. . .	. . .	. . .	. . .	. . .
Freight	2 205 BB	*1.5*	*2.0*	*1.5*	*2.7*	*1.7*	*4.2*	*4.8*	*3.7*
Other	2 205 BC	*28.5*	*32.1*	*36.8*	*33.0*	*39.2*	*38.3*	*50.3*	*66.5*
Sea transport, passenger	2 207 . .	. . .	. . .	. . .	. . .	. . .	. . .	. . .	. . .
Sea transport, freight	2 208 . .	. . .	. . .	. . .	. . .	. . .	. . .	. . .	. . .
Sea transport, other	2 209 . .	. . .	. . .	. . .	. . .	. . .	. . .	. . .	. . .
Air transport, passenger	2 211 . .	. . .	. . .	. . .	. . .	. . .	. . .	. . .	. . .
Air transport, freight	2 212 . .	. . .	. . .	. . .	. . .	. . .	. . .	. . .	. . .
Air transport, other	2 213 . .	. . .	. . .	. . .	. . .	. . .	. . .	. . .	. . .
Other transport, passenger	2 215 . .	. . .	. . .	. . .	. . .	. . .	. . .	. . .	. . .
Other transport, freight	2 216 . .	. . .	. . .	. . .	. . .	. . .	. . .	. . .	. . .
Other transport, other	2 217 . .	. . .	. . .	. . .	. . .	. . .	. . .	. . .	. . .
Transportation services, debit	3 205 . .	**–320.6**	**–384.3**	**–394.0**	**–383.9**	**–450.6**	**–512.2**	**–549.6**	**–775.4**
Passenger	3 205 BA	. . .	. . .	. . .	. . .	. . .	. . .	. . .	. . .
Freight	3 205 BB	*–277.6*	*–323.1*	*–328.4*	*–305.2*	*–344.8*	*–381.7*	*–436.8*	*–603.9*
Other	3 205 BC	*–43.0*	*–61.2*	*–65.6*	*–78.7*	*–105.8*	*–130.6*	*–112.8*	*–171.5*
Sea transport, passenger	3 207 . .	. . .	. . .	. . .	. . .	. . .	. . .	. . .	. . .
Sea transport, freight	3 208 . .	. . .	. . .	. . .	. . .	. . .	. . .	. . .	. . .
Sea transport, other	3 209 . .	. . .	. . .	. . .	. . .	. . .	. . .	. . .	. . .
Air transport, passenger	3 211 . .	. . .	. . .	. . .	. . .	. . .	. . .	. . .	. . .
Air transport, freight	3 212 . .	. . .	. . .	. . .	. . .	. . .	. . .	. . .	. . .
Air transport, other	3 213 . .	. . .	. . .	. . .	. . .	. . .	. . .	. . .	. . .
Other transport, passenger	3 215 . .	. . .	. . .	. . .	. . .	. . .	. . .	. . .	. . .
Other transport, freight	3 216 . .	. . .	. . .	. . .	. . .	. . .	. . .	. . .	. . .
Other transport, other	3 217 . .	. . .	. . .	. . .	. . .	. . .	. . .	. . .	. . .
Travel, credit	2 236 . .	**13.5**	**18.4**	**18.9**	**20.6**	**24.9**	**29.2**	**21.3**	**25.1**
Business travel	2 237 . .	. . .	. . .	. . .	. . .	. . .	. . .	. . .	. . .
Personal travel	2 240 . .	. . .	. . .	. . .	. . .	. . .	. . .	. . .	. . .
Travel, debit	3 236 . .	**–99.1**	**–123.1**	**–78.0**	**–82.9**	**–110.9**	**–153.2**	**–193.6**	**–233.5**
Business travel	3 237 . .	. . .	. . .	. . .	. . .	. . .	. . .	. . .	. . .
Personal travel	3 240 . .	. . .	. . .	. . .	. . .	. . .	. . .	. . .	. . .
Other services, credit	2 200 BA	**234.1**	**281.9**	**334.4**	**374.8**	**417.5**	**457.8**	**513.4**	**602.9**
Communications	2 245 . .	. . .	. . .	. . .	. . .	. . .	. . .	. . .	. . .
Construction	2 249 . .	. . .	. . .	. . .	. . .	. . .	. . .	. . .	. . .
Insurance	2 253 . .	.2	.2	.2	.3	.2	.5	.5	.4
Financial	2 260 . .	. . .	. . .	. . .	. . .	. . .	. . .	. . .	. . .
Computer and information	2 262 . .	. . .	. . .	. . .	. . .	. . .	. . .	. . .	. . .
Royalties and licence fees	2 266 . .	. . .	. . .	. . .	. . .	. . .	. . .	. . .	. . .
Other business services	2 268 . .	188.7	215.2	238.2	287.7	326.7	362.8	341.8	372.8
Personal, cultural, and recreational	2 287 . .	. . .	. . .	. . .	. . .	. . .	. . .	. . .	. . .
Government, n.i.e.	2 291 . .	45.3	66.5	95.9	86.8	90.7	94.5	171.0	229.7
Other services, debit	3 200 BA	**–193.4**	**–218.9**	**–228.5**	**–228.4**	**–227.3**	**–266.7**	**–281.8**	**–522.3**
Communications	3 245 . .	. . .	. . .	. . .	. . .	. . .	. . .	. . .	. . .
Construction	3 249 . .	. . .	. . .	. . .	. . .	. . .	. . .	. . .	. . .
Insurance	3 253 . .	–30.8	–35.9	–36.5	–33.9	–38.3	–42.4	–48.5	–67.1
Financial	3 260 . .	. . .	. . .	. . .	. . .	. . .	. . .	. . .	. . .
Computer and information	3 262 . .	. . .	. . .	. . .	. . .	. . .	. . .	. . .	. . .
Royalties and licence fees	3 266 . .	. . .	. . .	. . .	. . .	. . .	. . .	. . .	. . .
Other business services	3 268 . .	–42.7	–50.7	–46.0	–54.4	–44.5	–73.7	–64.9	–116.1
Personal, cultural, and recreational	3 287 . .	. . .	. . .	. . .	. . .	. . .	. . .	. . .	. . .
Government, n.i.e.	3 291 . .	–119.8	–132.4	–146.0	–140.1	–144.4	–150.6	–168.4	–339.0

Table 2 (Continued). STANDARD PRESENTATION, 1988–95
(Millions of U.S. dollars)

	Code	1988	1989	1990	1991	1992	1993	1994	1995
C. INCOME	4 300	–125.9	–108.2	–115.6	–97.0	–65.9	–75.7	–38.3	68.3
Total credit	2 300	*54.8*	*88.7*	*64.2*	*70.0*	*100.1*	*100.1*	*150.5*	*270.1*
Total debit	3 300	*–180.7*	*–196.9*	*–179.8*	*–166.9*	*–166.0*	*–175.8*	*–188.7*	*–201.8*
Compensation of employees, credit	2 310	...	...	...	...	...	...	...	...
Compensation of employees, debit	3 310	...	...	...	...	...	...	...	...
Investment income, credit	2 320	**54.8**	**88.7**	**64.2**	**70.0**	**100.1**	**100.1**	**150.5**	**270.1**
Direct investment income	2 330	...	...	...	...	...	...	...	...
Dividends and distributed branch profits	2 332	...	...	...	...	...	...	...	...
Reinvested earnings and undistributed branch profits	2 333	...	...	...	...	...	...	...	...
Income on debt (interest)	2 334	...	...	...	...	...	...	...	...
Portfolio investment income	2 339	...	...	...	...	...	...	...	...
Income on equity	2 340	...	...	...	...	...	...	...	...
Income on bonds and notes	2 350	...	...	...	...	...	...	...	...
Income on money market instruments and financial derivatives	2 360	...	...	...	...	...	...	...	...
Other investment income	2 370	54.8	88.7	64.2	70.0	100.1	100.1	150.5	270.1
Investment income, debit	3 320	**–180.7**	**–196.9**	**–179.8**	**–166.9**	**–166.0**	**–175.8**	**–188.7**	**–201.8**
Direct investment income	3 330	...	...	...	...	...	...	...	...
Dividends and distributed branch profits	3 332	...	...	...	...	...	...	...	...
Reinvested earnings and undistributed branch profits	3 333	...	...	...	...	...	...	...	...
Income on debt (interest)	3 334	...	...	...	...	...	...	...	...
Portfolio investment income	3 339	...	...	...	...	...	...	...	...
Income on equity	3 340	...	...	...	...	...	...	...	...
Income on bonds and notes	3 350	...	...	...	...	...	...	...	...
Income on money market instruments and financial derivatives	3 360	...	...	...	...	...	...	...	...
Other investment income	3 370	–180.7	–196.9	–179.8	–166.9	–166.0	–175.8	–188.7	–201.8
D. CURRENT TRANSFERS	4 379	1,631.9	1,396.0	1,613.5	1,811.6	1,808.0	1,950.3	2,089.2	2,264.9
Credit	2 379	**1,633.4**	**1,396.6**	**1,614.2**	**1,811.9**	**1,808.8**	**1,951.8**	**2,091.4**	**2,266.7**
General government	2 380	791.0	571.2	761.9	888.1	760.7	787.4	739.6	810.8
Other sectors	2 390	842.4	825.4	852.3	923.8	1,048.1	1,164.3	1,351.7	1,456.0
Workers' remittances	2 391	763.6	758.0	778.9	769.4	911.8	1,007.4	1,150.9	1,201.7
Other current transfers	2 392	78.7	67.4	73.4	154.5	136.3	157.0	200.8	254.3
Debit	3 379	**–1.5**	**–.7**	**–.7**	**–.3**	**–.7**	**–1.5**	**–2.2**	**–1.8**
General government	3 380	...	...	...	...	...	...	...	...
Other sectors	3 390	–1.5	–.7	–.7	–.3	–.7	–1.5	–2.2	–1.8
Workers' remittances	3 391	...	...	...	...	...	...	...	...
Other current transfers	3 392	–1.5	–.7	–.7	–.3	–.7	–1.5	–2.2	–1.8
CAPITAL AND FINANCIAL ACCOUNT	4 996	**266.2**	**1,142.7**	**473.6**	**33.8**	**–96.8**	**–428.7**	**57.5**	**690.5**
CAPITAL ACCOUNT	4 994	...	...	...	...	...	...	...	...
Total credit	2 994	...	...	...	...	...	...	...	...
Total debit	3 994	...	...	...	...	...	...	...	...
Capital transfers, credit	2 400	...	...	...	...	...	...	...	...
General government	2 401	...	...	...	...	...	...	...	...
Debt forgiveness	2 402	...	...	...	...	...	...	...	...
Other capital transfers	2 410	...	...	...	...	...	...	...	...
Other sectors	2 430	...	...	...	...	...	...	...	...
Migrants' transfers	2 431	...	...	...	...	...	...	...	...
Debt forgiveness	2 432	...	...	...	...	...	...	...	...
Other capital transfers	2 440	...	...	...	...	...	...	...	...
Capital transfers, debit	3 400	...	...	...	...	...	...	...	...
General government	3 401	...	...	...	...	...	...	...	...
Debt forgiveness	3 402	...	...	...	...	...	...	...	...
Other capital transfers	3 410	...	...	...	...	...	...	...	...
Other sectors	3 430	...	...	...	...	...	...	...	...
Migrants' transfers	3 431	...	...	...	...	...	...	...	...
Debt forgiveness	3 432	...	...	...	...	...	...	...	...
Other capital transfers	3 440	...	...	...	...	...	...	...	...
Nonproduced nonfinancial assets, credit	2 480	...	...	...	...	...	...	...	...
Nonproduced nonfinancial assets, debit	3 480	...	...	...	...	...	...	...	...

Table 2 (Continued). STANDARD PRESENTATION, 1988–95

(Millions of U.S. dollars)

	Code		1988	1989	1990	1991	1992	1993	1994	1995
FINANCIAL ACCOUNT	4 995	. .	**266.2**	**1,142.7**	**473.6**	**33.8**	**–96.8**	**–428.7**	**57.5**	**690.5**
A. DIRECT INVESTMENT	4 500	. .	1.8	.2	3.2	1.4	3.7	14.0	11.1	1.9
Direct investment abroad	4 505	. .	**. . .**	**. . .**	**. . .**	**. . .**	**. . .**	**. . .**	**. . .**	**. . .**
Equity capital	4 510	. .	. . .	. . .	. . .	. . .	. . .	. . .	. . .	. . .
Claims on affiliated enterprises	4 515	. .	. . .	. . .	. . .	. . .	. . .	. . .	. . .	. . .
Liabilities to affiliated enterprises	4 520	. .	. . .	. . .	. . .	. . .	. . .	. . .	. . .	. . .
Reinvested earnings	4 525	. .	. . .	. . .	. . .	. . .	. . .	. . .	. . .	. . .
Other capital	4 530	. .	. . .	. . .	. . .	. . .	. . .	. . .	. . .	. . .
Claims on affiliated enterprises	4 535	. .	. . .	. . .	. . .	. . .	. . .	. . .	. . .	. . .
Liabilities to affiliated enterprises	4 540	. .	. . .	. . .	. . .	. . .	. . .	. . .	. . .	. . .
Direct investment in Bangladesh	4 555	. .	**1.8**	**.2**	**3.2**	**1.4**	**3.7**	**14.0**	**11.1**	**1.9**
Equity capital	4 560	. .	1.5	. . .	3.2	1.4	3.7	7.9	5.8	1.8
Claims on direct investors	4 565	. .	. . .	. . .	. . .	. . .	. . .	. . .	. . .	. . .
Liabilities to direct investors	4 570	. .	. . .	. . .	. . .	. . .	. . .	. . .	. . .	. . .
Reinvested earnings	4 575	. .	. . .	. . .	. . .	. . .	. . .	. . .	. . .	. . .
Other capital	4 580	. .	.3	.2	. . .	. . .	. . .	6.2	5.4	.1
Claims on direct investors	4 585	. .	. . .	. . .	. . .	. . .	. . .	. . .	. . .	. . .
Liabilities to direct investors	4 590	. .	. . .	. . .	. . .	. . .	. . .	. . .	. . .	. . .
B. PORTFOLIO INVESTMENT	4 600	. .	. . .	1.7	.3	2.2	8.7	8.4	105.9	–15.2
Assets	4 602	. .	**. . .**	**. . .**	**. . .**	**. . .**	**. . .**	**. . .**	**. . .**	**. . .**
Equity securities	4 610	. .	. . .	. . .	. . .	. . .	. . .	. . .	. . .	. . .
Monetary authorities	4 611	. .	. . .	. . .	. . .	. . .	. . .	. . .	. . .	. . .
General government	4 612	. .	. . .	. . .	. . .	. . .	. . .	. . .	. . .	. . .
Banks	4 613	. .	. . .	. . .	. . .	. . .	. . .	. . .	. . .	. . .
Other sectors	4 614	. .	. . .	. . .	. . .	. . .	. . .	. . .	. . .	. . .
Debt securities	4 619	. .	. . .	. . .	. . .	. . .	. . .	. . .	. . .	. . .
Bonds and notes	4 620	. .	. . .	. . .	. . .	. . .	. . .	. . .	. . .	. . .
Monetary authorities	4 621	. .	. . .	. . .	. . .	. . .	. . .	. . .	. . .	. . .
General government	4 622	. .	. . .	. . .	. . .	. . .	. . .	. . .	. . .	. . .
Banks	4 623	. .	. . .	. . .	. . .	. . .	. . .	. . .	. . .	. . .
Other sectors	4 624	. .	. . .	. . .	. . .	. . .	. . .	. . .	. . .	. . .
Money market instruments	4 630	. .	. . .	. . .	. . .	. . .	. . .	. . .	. . .	. . .
Monetary authorities	4 631	. .	. . .	. . .	. . .	. . .	. . .	. . .	. . .	. . .
General government	4 632	. .	. . .	. . .	. . .	. . .	. . .	. . .	. . .	. . .
Banks	4 633	. .	. . .	. . .	. . .	. . .	. . .	. . .	. . .	. . .
Other sectors	4 634	. .	. . .	. . .	. . .	. . .	. . .	. . .	. . .	. . .
Financial derivatives	4 640	. .	. . .	. . .	. . .	. . .	. . .	. . .	. . .	. . .
Monetary authorities	4 641	. .	. . .	. . .	. . .	. . .	. . .	. . .	. . .	. . .
General government	4 642	. .	. . .	. . .	. . .	. . .	. . .	. . .	. . .	. . .
Banks	4 643	. .	. . .	. . .	. . .	. . .	. . .	. . .	. . .	. . .
Other sectors	4 644	. .	. . .	. . .	. . .	. . .	. . .	. . .	. . .	. . .
Liabilities	4 652	. .	**. . .**	**1.7**	**.3**	**2.2**	**8.7**	**8.4**	**105.9**	**–15.2**
Equity securities	4 660	. .	. . .	1.7	.3	2.2	8.7	8.4	105.9	–15.2
Banks	4 663	. .	. . .	. . .	. . .	. . .	. . .	. . .	. . .	. . .
Other sectors	4 664	. .	. . .	. . .	. . .	. . .	. . .	. . .	. . .	. . .
Debt securities	4 669	. .	. . .	. . .	. . .	. . .	. . .	. . .	. . .	. . .
Bonds and notes	4 670	. .	. . .	. . .	. . .	. . .	. . .	. . .	. . .	. . .
Monetary authorities	4 671	. .	. . .	. . .	. . .	. . .	. . .	. . .	. . .	. . .
General government	4 672	. .	. . .	. . .	. . .	. . .	. . .	. . .	. . .	. . .
Banks	4 673	. .	. . .	. . .	. . .	. . .	. . .	. . .	. . .	. . .
Other sectors	4 674	. .	. . .	. . .	. . .	. . .	. . .	. . .	. . .	. . .
Money market instruments	4 680	. .	. . .	. . .	. . .	. . .	. . .	. . .	. . .	. . .
Monetary authorities	4 681	. .	. . .	. . .	. . .	. . .	. . .	. . .	. . .	. . .
General government	4 682	. .	. . .	. . .	. . .	. . .	. . .	. . .	. . .	. . .
Banks	4 683	. .	. . .	. . .	. . .	. . .	. . .	. . .	. . .	. . .
Other sectors	4 684	. .	. . .	. . .	. . .	. . .	. . .	. . .	. . .	. . .
Financial derivatives	4 690	. .	. . .	. . .	. . .	. . .	. . .	. . .	. . .	. . .
Monetary authorities	4 691	. .	. . .	. . .	. . .	. . .	. . .	. . .	. . .	. . .
General government	4 692	. .	. . .	. . .	. . .	. . .	. . .	. . .	. . .	. . .
Banks	4 693	. .	. . .	. . .	. . .	. . .	. . .	. . .	. . .	. . .
Other sectors	4 694	. .	. . .	. . .	. . .	. . .	. . .	. . .	. . .	. . .

Table 2 (Concluded). STANDARD PRESENTATION, 1988–95
(Millions of U.S. dollars)

	Code	1988	1989	1990	1991	1992	1993	1994	1995
C. OTHER INVESTMENT	4 700	440.4	692.9	549.0	574.7	560.8	195.9	576.7	131.1
Assets	4 703	**–229.1**	**–152.0**	**–207.8**	**–267.1**	**–196.0**	**–178.4**	**–169.3**	**–292.7**
Trade credits	4 706	...	...	...	...	...	...	...	...
General government: long-term	4 708	...	...	...	...	...	...	...	...
General government: short-term	4 709	...	...	...	...	...	...	...	...
Other sectors: long-term	4 711	...	...	...	...	...	...	...	...
Other sectors: short-term	4 712	...	...	...	...	...	...	...	...
Loans	4 714	...	...	...	...	...	...	...	...
Monetary authorities: long-term	4 717	...	...	...	...	...	...	...	...
Monetary authorities: short-term	4 718	...	...	...	...	...	...	...	...
General government: long-term	4 720	...	...	...	...	...	...	...	...
General government: short-term	4 721	...	...	...	...	...	...	...	...
Banks: long-term	4 723	...	...	...	...	...	...	...	...
Banks: short-term	4 724	...	...	...	...	...	...	...	...
Other sectors: long-term	4 726	...	...	...	...	...	...	...	...
Other sectors: short-term	4 727	...	...	...	...	...	...	...	...
Currency and deposits	4 730	–227.5	–151.4	–206.1	–266.7	–196.0	–177.7	–169.2	–292.7
Monetary authorities	4 731	...	...	...	...	...	...	...	...
General government	4 732	...	...	...	...	...	...	...	...
Banks	4 733	–227.5	–151.4	–206.1	–266.7	–196.0	–177.7	–169.2	–292.7
Other sectors	4 734	...	...	...	...	...	...	...	...
Other assets	4 736	–1.6	–.5	–1.6	–.4	...	–.7	–.1	...
Monetary authorities: long-term	4 738	...	...	...	...	...	...	...	...
Monetary authorities: short-term	4 739	...	...	...	...	...	...	...	...
General government: long-term	4 741	–1.6	–.5	–1.6	–.4	...	–.7	–.1	...
General government: short-term	4 742	...	...	...	...	...	...	...	...
Banks: long-term	4 744	...	...	...	...	...	...	...	...
Banks: short-term	4 745	...	...	...	...	...	...	...	...
Other sectors: long-term	4 747	...	...	...	...	...	...	...	...
Other sectors: short-term	4 748	...	...	...	...	...	...	...	...
Liabilities	4 753	**669.5**	**844.9**	**756.7**	**841.8**	**756.9**	**374.3**	**746.0**	**423.9**
Trade credits	4 756	...	...	...	...	...	...	...	...
General government: long-term	4 758	...	...	...	...	...	...	...	...
General government: short-term	4 759	...	...	...	...	...	...	...	...
Other sectors: long-term	4 761	...	...	...	...	...	...	...	...
Other sectors: short-term	4 762	...	...	...	...	...	...	...	...
Loans	4 764	671.7	788.0	702.7	657.5	752.8	373.1	678.2	351.8
Use of Fund credit and loans from the Fund	4 766	43.6	–99.6	–145.3	110.7	34.9	–50.6	–55.1	–61.0
Monetary authorities: other long-term	4 767	...	...	...	...	...	...	...	...
Monetary authorities: short-term	4 768	...	...	...	...	...	...	...	...
General government: long-term	4 770	618.9	878.1	827.0	533.1	667.6	379.3	718.5	374.2
General government: short-term	4 771	...	...	...	...	...	...	...	...
Banks: long-term	4 773	...	...	...	...	...	...	...	...
Banks: short-term	4 774	...	...	...	...	...	...	...	...
Other sectors: long-term	4 776	9.1	9.4	20.9	13.7	50.3	44.4	14.8	38.7
Other sectors: short-term	4 777	...	...	...	...	...	...	...	...
Currency and deposits	4 780	2.8	52.6	40.9	186.8	14.5	...	51.4	14.6
Monetary authorities	4 781	...	–38.8	...	...	...	...	...	...
General government	4 782	...	...	...	...	...	...	...	...
Banks	4 783	2.8	91.3	40.9	186.8	14.5	...	51.4	14.6
Other sectors	4 784	...	...	...	...	...	...	...	...
Other liabilities	4 786	–4.9	4.4	13.2	–2.5	–10.4	1.1	16.4	57.4
Monetary authorities: long-term	4 788	...	...	...	...	...	...	...	...
Monetary authorities: short-term	4 789	–7.0	3.5	–.1	1.3	–.9	–.2	15.0	58.3
General government: long-term	4 791	...	...	...	...	...	...	...	...
General government: short-term	4 792	...	...	...	...	...	...	...	...
Banks: long-term	4 794	...	...	...	...	...	...	...	...
Banks: short-term	4 795	...	...	...	...	...	...	...	...
Other sectors: long-term	4 797	3.3	.8	–.3	1.2	.8	1.4	1.4	–.8
Other sectors: short-term	4 798	–1.2	...	13.6	–5.0	–10.3	...	...	...
D. RESERVE ASSETS	4 800	–176.1	447.8	–78.9	–544.5	–670.1	–647.0	–636.2	572.8
Monetary gold	4 810	...	...	...	...	...	...	...	...
Special drawing rights	4 820	–3.9	50.0	–19.0	–42.3	27.7	19.1	–12.1	–125.4
Reserve position in the Fund	4 830	...	...	29.2	...	...	–.1	...	...
Foreign exchange	4 840	–182.7	421.1	–60.5	–559.8	–654.4	–596.0	–617.2	746.1
Other claims	4 880	10.6	–23.3	–28.5	57.6	–43.4	–70.1	–6.8	–47.9
NET ERRORS AND OMISSIONS	4 998	**6.6**	**–43.1**	**–75.7**	**–98.4**	**–84.0**	**69.4**	**–257.1**	**133.3**

Part 3 of the *Yearbook* contains descriptions of the methodologies, compilation practices, and sources used to compile these data.

Table 1. ANALYTIC PRESENTATION, 1988–95
(Millions of U.S. dollars)

	Code	1988	1989	1990	1991	1992	1993	1994	1995
A. Current Account[1]	4 993 Y.	**42.5**	**23.7**	**–16.4**	**–25.1**	**143.8**	**64.3**	**. . .**	**. . .**
Goods: exports f.o.b	2 100 . .	175.8	185.7	213.1	203.9	190.5	181.5	. . .	. . .
Goods: imports f.o.b	3 100 . .	–518.7	–600.3	–624.1	–617.4	–464.7	–511.3	. . .	. . .
Balance on Goods	4 100 . .	*–342.9*	*–414.7*	*–410.9*	*–413.5*	*–274.2*	*–329.8*	. . .	. . .
Services: credit	2 200 . .	560.2	654.3	579.1	581.3	581.1	646.8	. . .	. . .
Services: debit	3 200 . .	–172.2	–206.9	–194.3	–194.6	–186.5	–244.2	. . .	. . .
Balance on Goods and Services	4 991 . .	*45.1*	*32.7*	*–26.2*	*–26.7*	*120.5*	*72.8*	. . .	. . .
Income: credit	2 300 . .	46.9	47.9	44.2	46.8	50.7	53.8	. . .	. . .
Income: debit	3 300 . .	–66.0	–61.7	–76.9	–78.2	–67.7	–83.1	. . .	. . .
Balance on Goods, Services, and Income	4 992 . .	*26.0*	*18.9*	*–58.9*	*–58.1*	*103.5*	*43.5*	. . .	. . .
Current transfers: credit	2 379 Y.	47.4	51.0	54.4	48.8	54.8	43.1	. . .	. . .
Current transfers: debit	3 379 . .	–31.0	–46.2	–11.9	–15.8	–14.5	–22.3	. . .	. . .
B. Capital Account[1]	4 994 Y.	**. . .**	**. . .**	**. . .**	**. . .**	**. . .**	**. . .**	**. . .**	**. . .**
Capital account: credit	2 994 Y.	. . .	. . .	. . .	. . .	. . .	. . .	. . .	. . .
Capital account: debit	3 994 . .	. . .	. . .	. . .	. . .	. . .	. . .	. . .	. . .
Total, Groups A Plus B	4 010 . .	*42.5*	*23.7*	*–16.4*	*–25.1*	*143.8*	*64.3*	. . .	. . .
C. Financial Account[1]	4 995 X.	**47.5**	**–22.4**	**48.0**	**17.8**	**–94.0**	**1.2**	**. . .**	**. . .**
Direct investment abroad	4 505 . .	–.9	–2.9	–1.4	–1.3	–.8	–2.6	. . .	. . .
Direct investment in Barbados	4 555 Y.	11.5	8.3	11.1	7.3	14.4	9.3	. . .	. . .
Portfolio investment assets	4 602 . .	–.5	–5.1	–6.0	–8.2	–4.1	–9.8	. . .	. . .
Equity securities	4 610 . .	. . .	. . .	. . .	. . .	. . .	. . .	. . .	. . .
Debt securities	4 619 . .	–.5	–5.1	–6.0	–8.2	–4.1	–9.8	. . .	. . .
Portfolio investment liabilities	4 652 Y.	.3	.4	. . .	–.6	. . .	.9	. . .	. . .
Equity securities	4 660 Y.	. . .	. . .	. . .	. . .	. . .	. . .	. . .	. . .
Debt securities	4 669 Y.	.3	.4	. . .	–.6	. . .	.9	. . .	. . .
Other investment assets	4 703 . .	3.1	–23.3	–18.6	–2.2	–4.2	–6.2	. . .	. . .
Monetary authorities	4 703 . A	. . .	. . .	. . .	. . .	. . .	. . .	. . .	. . .
General government	4 703 . B	2.8	–2.5	3.0	–10.2	–3.1	–3.4	. . .	. . .
Banks	4 703 . C	45.5	5.4	–7.9	–11.0	12.2	–.6	. . .	. . .
Other sectors	4 703 . D	–45.3	–26.2	–13.7	18.9	–13.3	–2.1	. . .	. . .
Other investment liabilities	4 753 X.	34.1	.2	62.9	22.9	–99.2	9.6	. . .	. . .
Monetary authorities	4 753 XA	. . .	. . .	. . .	11.9	3.5	. . .	. . .	. . .
General government	4 753 YB	40.5	14.1	8.8	–27.8	–41.7	–25.5	. . .	. . .
Banks	4 753 YC	–35.9	–9.2	18.9	14.3	–6.5	9.0	. . .	. . .
Other sectors	4 753 YD	29.4	–4.6	35.2	24.5	–54.5	26.1	. . .	. . .
Total, Groups A Through C	4 020 . .	*89.9*	*1.3*	*31.7*	*–7.3*	*49.8*	*65.6*	. . .	. . .
D. Net Errors and Omissions	4 998 . .	**–50.4**	**–44.1**	**–70.6**	**–32.6**	**–21.5**	**–44.7**	**. . .**	**. . .**
Total, Groups A Through D	4 030 . .	*39.5*	*–42.8*	*–38.9*	*–39.9*	*28.3*	*20.9*	. . .	. . .
E. Reserves and Related Items	4 040 . .	**–39.5**	**42.8**	**38.9**	**39.9**	**–28.3**	**–20.9**	**. . .**	**. . .**
Reserve assets	4 800 . .	–27.4	48.6	42.0	40.6	–79.8	–20.9	. . .	. . .
Use of Fund credit and loans	4 766 . .	–10.6	–5.8	–3.7	–.7	51.5	. . .	. . .	. . .
Liabilities constituting foreign authorities' reserves	4 900 . .	–1.5	. . .	.6	. . .	. . .	. . .	. . .	. . .
Exceptional financing	4 920 . .	. . .	. . .	. . .	. . .	. . .	. . .	. . .	. . .
Conversion rates: Barbados dollars per U.S. dollar	0 101 . .	**2.0113**	**2.0113**	**2.0113**	**2.0113**	**2.0113**	**2.0113**	**2.0113**	**2.0113**

[1] Excludes components that have been classified in the categories of Group E.

Table 2. STANDARD PRESENTATION, 1988–95

(Millions of U.S. dollars)

	Code	1988	1989	1990	1991	1992	1993	1994	1995
CURRENT ACCOUNT	4 993 . .	**42.5**	**23.7**	**–16.4**	**–25.1**	**143.8**	**64.3**	**. . .**	**. . .**
A. GOODS	4 100 . .	–342.9	–414.7	–410.9	–413.5	–274.2	–329.8	. . .	. . .
Credit	2 100 . .	**175.8**	**185.7**	**213.1**	**203.9**	**190.5**	**181.5**	**. . .**	**. . .**
General merchandise: exports f.o.b.	2 110 . .	144.8	147.0	151.0	143.6	158.0	152.4	. . .	. . .
Goods for processing: exports f.o.b.	2 150 . .	. . .	. . .	. . .	. . .	. . .	. . .	. . .	. . .
Repairs on goods	2 160 . .	. . .	. . .	. . .	. . .	. . .	. . .	. . .	. . .
Goods procured in ports by carriers	2 170 . .	31.0	38.6	62.1	60.3	32.5	29.1	. . .	. . .
Nonmonetary gold	2 180 . .	. . .	. . .	. . .	. . .	. . .	. . .	. . .	. . .
Debit	3 100 . .	**–518.7**	**–600.3**	**–624.1**	**–617.4**	**–464.7**	**–511.3**	**. . .**	**. . .**
General merchandise: imports f.o.b.	3 110 . .	–518.7	–600.3	–624.1	–617.4	–464.7	–511.3	. . .	. . .
Goods for processing: imports f.o.b.	3 150 . .	. . .	. . .	. . .	. . .	. . .	. . .	. . .	. . .
Repairs on goods	3 160 . .	. . .	. . .	. . .	. . .	. . .	. . .	. . .	. . .
Goods procured in ports by carriers	3 170 . .	. . .	. . .	. . .	. . .	. . .	. . .	. . .	. . .
Nonmonetary gold	3 180 . .	. . .	. . .	. . .	. . .	. . .	. . .	. . .	. . .
B. SERVICES	4 200 . .	388.0	447.4	384.8	386.7	394.6	402.6	. . .	. . .
Total credit	2 200 . .	*560.2*	*654.3*	*579.1*	*581.3*	*581.1*	*646.8*	. . .	. . .
Total debit	3 200 . .	*–172.2*	*–206.9*	*–194.3*	*–194.6*	*–186.5*	*–244.2*	. . .	. . .
Transportation services, credit	2 205 . .	**7.0**	**6.1**	**6.6**	**8.7**	**9.2**	**9.5**	**. . .**	**. . .**
Passenger	2 205 BA	. . .	. . .	. . .	*2.0*	*2.6*	*3.0*	. . .	. . .
Freight	2 205 BB	*2.8*	*2.8*	*3.2*	*3.2*	*3.0*	*2.8*	. . .	. . .
Other	2 205 BC	*4.2*	*3.3*	*3.4*	*3.5*	*3.6*	*3.7*	. . .	. . .
Sea transport, passenger	2 207 . .	. . .	. . .	. . .	. . .	. . .	. . .	. . .	. . .
Sea transport, freight	2 208 . .	. . .	. . .	. . .	. . .	. . .	. . .	. . .	. . .
Sea transport, other	2 209 . .	. . .	. . .	. . .	. . .	. . .	. . .	. . .	. . .
Air transport, passenger	2 211 . .	. . .	. . .	. . .	. . .	. . .	. . .	. . .	. . .
Air transport, freight	2 212 . .	. . .	. . .	. . .	. . .	. . .	. . .	. . .	. . .
Air transport, other	2 213 . .	. . .	. . .	. . .	. . .	. . .	. . .	. . .	. . .
Other transport, passenger	2 215 . .	. . .	. . .	. . .	. . .	. . .	. . .	. . .	. . .
Other transport, freight	2 216 . .	. . .	. . .	. . .	. . .	. . .	. . .	. . .	. . .
Other transport, other	2 217 . .	. . .	. . .	. . .	. . .	. . .	. . .	. . .	. . .
Transportation services, debit	3 205 . .	**–83.8**	**–96.6**	**–95.4**	**–95.4**	**–78.3**	**–86.8**	**. . .**	**. . .**
Passenger	3 205 BA	*–25.5*	*–29.1*	*–25.2*	*–25.7*	*–25.8*	*–29.0*	. . .	. . .
Freight	3 205 BB	*–58.2*	*–67.3*	*–70.0*	*–69.4*	*–52.1*	*–57.4*	. . .	. . .
Other	3 205 BC	*–.1*	*–.1*	*–.2*	*–.3*	*–.4*	*–.4*	. . .	. . .
Sea transport, passenger	3 207 . .	. . .	. . .	. . .	. . .	. . .	. . .	. . .	. . .
Sea transport, freight	3 208 . .	. . .	. . .	. . .	. . .	. . .	. . .	. . .	. . .
Sea transport, other	3 209 . .	. . .	. . .	. . .	. . .	. . .	. . .	. . .	. . .
Air transport, passenger	3 211 . .	. . .	. . .	. . .	. . .	. . .	. . .	. . .	. . .
Air transport, freight	3 212 . .	. . .	. . .	. . .	. . .	. . .	. . .	. . .	. . .
Air transport, other	3 213 . .	. . .	. . .	. . .	. . .	. . .	. . .	. . .	. . .
Other transport, passenger	3 215 . .	. . .	. . .	. . .	. . .	. . .	. . .	. . .	. . .
Other transport, freight	3 216 . .	. . .	. . .	. . .	. . .	. . .	. . .	. . .	. . .
Other transport, other	3 217 . .	. . .	. . .	. . .	. . .	. . .	. . .	. . .	. . .
Travel, credit	2 236 . .	**460.4**	**528.7**	**499.9**	**460.9**	**464.5**	**528.3**	**. . .**	**. . .**
Business travel	2 237 . .	. . .	. . .	. . .	. . .	. . .	. . .	. . .	. . .
Personal travel	2 240 . .	460.4	528.7	499.9	460.9	464.5	528.3	. . .	. . .
Travel, debit	3 236 . .	**–37.1**	**–44.9**	**–47.4**	**–43.7**	**–40.7**	**–52.0**	**. . .**	**. . .**
Business travel	3 237 . .	–11.2	–14.9	–15.8	–13.5	–11.7	–17.7	. . .	. . .
Personal travel	3 240 . .	–26.0	–30.0	–31.6	–30.2	–29.0	–34.4	. . .	. . .
Other services, credit	2 200 BA	**92.8**	**119.5**	**72.6**	**111.7**	**107.4**	**109.1**	**. . .**	**. . .**
Communications	2 245 . .	. . .	. . .	. . .	. . .	. . .	. . .	. . .	. . .
Construction	2 249 . .	. . .	. . .	. . .	. . .	. . .	. . .	. . .	. . .
Insurance	2 253 . .	4.9	24.3	3.5	14.3	21.4	15.7	. . .	. . .
Financial	2 260 . .	. . .	. . .	. . .	. . .	. . .	. . .	. . .	. . .
Computer and information	2 262 . .	. . .	. . .	. . .	. . .	. . .	. . .	. . .	. . .
Royalties and licence fees	2 266 . .	.6	.3	.6	.2	.1	.4	. . .	. . .
Other business services	2 268 . .	77.0	82.5	56.2	82.7	68.3	77.1	. . .	. . .
Personal, cultural, and recreational	2 287 . .	. . .	. . .	. . .	. . .	. . .	. . .	. . .	. . .
Government, n.i.e.	2 291 . .	10.2	12.3	12.3	14.5	17.7	16.0	. . .	. . .
Other services, debit	3 200 BA	**–51.3**	**–65.4**	**–51.5**	**–55.5**	**–67.6**	**–105.4**	**. . .**	**. . .**
Communications	3 245 . .	. . .	. . .	. . .	. . .	. . .	. . .	. . .	. . .
Construction	3 249 . .	. . .	. . .	. . .	. . .	. . .	. . .	. . .	. . .
Insurance	3 253 . .	–12.5	–16.5	–11.6	–25.3	–26.2	–42.2	. . .	. . .
Financial	3 260 . .	. . .	. . .	. . .	. . .	. . .	. . .	. . .	. . .
Computer and information	3 262 . .	. . .	. . .	. . .	. . .	. . .	. . .	. . .	. . .
Royalties and licence fees	3 266 . .	–5.5	–6.5	–4.0	–2.7	–7.2	–10.1	. . .	. . .
Other business services	3 268 . .	–20.7	–31.9	–24.9	–19.1	–20.8	–32.3	. . .	. . .
Personal, cultural, and recreational	3 287 . .	. . .	. . .	. . .	. . .	. . .	. . .	. . .	. . .
Government, n.i.e.	3 291 . .	–12.7	–10.5	–11.0	–8.5	–13.3	–20.8	. . .	. . .

Table 2 (Continued). STANDARD PRESENTATION, 1988–95
(Millions of U.S. dollars)

	Code		1988	1989	1990	1991	1992	1993	1994	1995
C. INCOME	4 300	. .	–19.1	–13.8	–32.7	–31.4	–17.0	–29.3	. . .	. . .
Total credit	2 300	. .	*46.9*	*47.9*	*44.2*	*46.8*	*50.7*	*53.8*	. . .	. . .
Total debit	3 300	. .	*–66.0*	*–61.7*	*–76.9*	*–78.2*	*–67.7*	*–83.1*	. . .	. . .
Compensation of employees, credit	2 310	. .	**26.1**	**23.9**	**26.1**	**26.8**	**25.1**	**26.9**	. . .	. . .
Compensation of employees, debit	3 310	. .	**–1.8**	**–3.5**	**–2.3**	**–2.3**	**–2.4**	**–4.1**	. . .	. . .
Investment income, credit	2 320	. .	**20.8**	**24.0**	**18.0**	**20.0**	**25.6**	**26.9**	. . .	. . .
Direct investment income	2 330	. .	6.5	1.8	1.1	1.9	1.9	1.1	. . .	. . .
Dividends and distributed branch profits	2 332	. .	4.1	.7	.3	1.1	1.1	.5	. . .	. . .
Reinvested earnings and undistributed branch profits	2 333	. .	2.4	1.1	.8	.7	.7	.6	. . .	. . .
Income on debt (interest)	2 334	. .	. . .	. . .	. . .	. . .	. . .	. . .	. . .	. . .
Portfolio investment income	2 339	. .	. . .	. . .	. . .	. . .	. . .	. . .	. . .	. . .
Income on equity	2 340	. .	. . .	. . .	. . .	. . .	. . .	. . .	. . .	. . .
Income on bonds and notes	2 350	. .	. . .	. . .	. . .	. . .	. . .	. . .	. . .	. . .
Income on money market instruments and financial derivatives	2 360	. .	. . .	. . .	. . .	. . .	. . .	. . .	. . .	. . .
Other investment income	2 370	. .	14.3	22.2	16.9	18.1	23.7	25.8	. . .	. . .
Investment income, debit	3 320	. .	**–64.2**	**–58.2**	**–74.5**	**–75.9**	**–65.3**	**–79.0**	. . .	. . .
Direct investment income	3 330	. .	–3.9	–7.0	–9.0	–7.7	–9.0	–11.4	. . .	. . .
Dividends and distributed branch profits	3 332	. .	–3.0	–5.9	–6.2	–6.3	–6.5	–9.5	. . .	. . .
Reinvested earnings and undistributed branch profits	3 333	. .	–.8	–1.1	–2.9	–1.4	–2.5	–1.9	. . .	. . .
Income on debt (interest)	3 334	. .	. . .	. . .	. . .	. . .	. . .	. . .	. . .	. . .
Portfolio investment income	3 339	. .	. . .	. . .	. . .	. . .	. . .	. . .	. . .	. . .
Income on equity	3 340	. .	. . .	. . .	. . .	. . .	. . .	. . .	. . .	. . .
Income on bonds and notes	3 350	. .	. . .	. . .	. . .	. . .	. . .	. . .	. . .	. . .
Income on money market instruments and financial derivatives	3 360	. .	. . .	. . .	. . .	. . .	. . .	. . .	. . .	. . .
Other investment income	3 370	. .	–60.3	–51.2	–65.5	–68.2	–56.2	–67.6	. . .	. . .
D. CURRENT TRANSFERS	4 379	. .	16.5	4.8	42.5	33.0	40.3	20.8	. . .	. . .
Credit	2 379	. .	**47.4**	**51.0**	**54.4**	**48.8**	**54.8**	**43.1**	. . .	. . .
General government	2 380	. .	7.7	5.9	5.8	5.0	4.5	2.4	. . .	. . .
Other sectors	2 390	. .	39.7	45.0	48.6	43.8	50.3	40.7	. . .	. . .
Workers' remittances	2 391	. .	. . .	. . .	. . .	. . .	. . .	. . .	. . .	. . .
Other current transfers	2 392	. .	39.7	45.0	48.6	43.8	50.3	40.7	. . .	. . .
Debit	3 379	. .	**–31.0**	**–46.2**	**–11.9**	**–15.8**	**–14.5**	**–22.3**	. . .	. . .
General government	3 380	. .	–25.2	–36.1	–2.3	–6.0	–5.3	–7.6	. . .	. . .
Other sectors	3 390	. .	–5.8	–10.0	–9.6	–9.8	–9.2	–14.7	. . .	. . .
Workers' remittances	3 391	. .	. . .	. . .	. . .	. . .	. . .	. . .	. . .	. . .
Other current transfers	3 392	. .	–5.8	–10.0	–9.6	–9.8	–9.2	–14.7	. . .	. . .
CAPITAL AND FINANCIAL ACCOUNT	4 996	. .	**8.0**	**20.4**	**87.0**	**57.7**	**–122.2**	**–19.7**	. . .	. . .
CAPITAL ACCOUNT	4 994	. .	. . .	. . .	. . .	. . .	. . .	. . .	. . .	. . .
Total credit	2 994	. .	. . .	. . .	. . .	. . .	. . .	. . .	. . .	. . .
Total debit	3 994	. .	. . .	. . .	. . .	. . .	. . .	. . .	. . .	. . .
Capital transfers, credit	2 400	. .	. . .	. . .	. . .	. . .	. . .	. . .	. . .	. . .
General government	2 401	. .	. . .	. . .	. . .	. . .	. . .	. . .	. . .	. . .
Debt forgiveness	2 402	. .	. . .	. . .	. . .	. . .	. . .	. . .	. . .	. . .
Other capital transfers	2 410	. .	. . .	. . .	. . .	. . .	. . .	. . .	. . .	. . .
Other sectors	2 430	. .	. . .	. . .	. . .	. . .	. . .	. . .	. . .	. . .
Migrants' transfers	2 431	. .	. . .	. . .	. . .	. . .	. . .	. . .	. . .	. . .
Debt forgiveness	2 432	. .	. . .	. . .	. . .	. . .	. . .	. . .	. . .	. . .
Other capital transfers	2 440	. .	. . .	. . .	. . .	. . .	. . .	. . .	. . .	. . .
Capital transfers, debit	3 400	. .	. . .	. . .	. . .	. . .	. . .	. . .	. . .	. . .
General government	3 401	. .	. . .	. . .	. . .	. . .	. . .	. . .	. . .	. . .
Debt forgiveness	3 402	. .	. . .	. . .	. . .	. . .	. . .	. . .	. . .	. . .
Other capital transfers	3 410	. .	. . .	. . .	. . .	. . .	. . .	. . .	. . .	. . .
Other sectors	3 430	. .	. . .	. . .	. . .	. . .	. . .	. . .	. . .	. . .
Migrants' transfers	3 431	. .	. . .	. . .	. . .	. . .	. . .	. . .	. . .	. . .
Debt forgiveness	3 432	. .	. . .	. . .	. . .	. . .	. . .	. . .	. . .	. . .
Other capital transfers	3 440	. .	. . .	. . .	. . .	. . .	. . .	. . .	. . .	. . .
Nonproduced nonfinancial assets, credit	2 480	. .	. . .	. . .	. . .	. . .	. . .	. . .	. . .	. . .
Nonproduced nonfinancial assets, debit	3 480	. .	. . .	. . .	. . .	. . .	. . .	. . .	. . .	. . .

Table 2 (Continued). STANDARD PRESENTATION, 1988–95
(Millions of U.S. dollars)

	Code	1988	1989	1990	1991	1992	1993	1994	1995
FINANCIAL ACCOUNT	4 995	**8.0**	**20.4**	**87.0**	**57.7**	**–122.2**	**–19.7**	...	...
A. DIRECT INVESTMENT	4 500	10.5	5.4	9.7	6.0	13.5	6.8	...	...
Direct investment abroad	4 505	**–.9**	**–2.9**	**–1.4**	**–1.3**	**–.8**	**–2.6**	...	...
Equity capital	4 510	–.1	–1.5	...	–.2	–.3	–1.3	...	...
Claims on affiliated enterprises	4 515	...	...	...	...	...	...	...	...
Liabilities to affiliated enterprises	4 520	...	...	...	...	...	...	...	...
Reinvested earnings	4 525	–.7	–1.1	–.8	–.7	–.7	–1.1	...	...
Other capital	4 530	–.1	–.3	–.5	–.3	.2	–.1	...	...
Claims on affiliated enterprises	4 535	...	...	...	...	...	...	...	...
Liabilities to affiliated enterprises	4 540	...	...	...	...	...	...	...	...
Direct investment in Barbados	4 555	**11.5**	**8.3**	**11.1**	**7.3**	**14.4**	**9.3**	...	...
Equity capital	4 560	7.5	5.3	8.0	5.9	7.8	5.4	...	...
Claims on direct investors	4 565	...	...	...	...	...	...	...	...
Liabilities to direct investors	4 570	...	...	...	...	...	...	...	...
Reinvested earnings	4 575	.8	1.1	2.9	1.4	2.5	1.9	...	...
Other capital	4 580	3.1	1.9	.2	...	4.0	2.0	...	...
Claims on direct investors	4 585	...	...	...	...	...	...	...	...
Liabilities to direct investors	4 590	...	...	...	...	...	...	...	...
B. PORTFOLIO INVESTMENT	4 600	–.2	–4.7	–6.0	–8.8	–4.1	–8.9	...	...
Assets	4 602	**–.5**	**–5.1**	**–6.0**	**–8.2**	**–4.1**	**–9.8**	...	...
Equity securities	4 610	...	...	...	...	...	...	...	...
Monetary authorities	4 611	...	...	...	...	...	...	...	...
General government	4 612	...	...	...	...	...	...	...	...
Banks	4 613	...	...	...	...	...	...	...	...
Other sectors	4 614	...	...	...	...	...	...	...	...
Debt securities	4 619	–.5	–5.1	–6.0	–8.2	–4.1	–9.8	...	...
Bonds and notes	4 620	–.5	–5.1	–6.0	–8.2	–4.1	–9.8	...	...
Monetary authorities	4 621	...	...	...	...	...	...	...	...
General government	4 622	...	...	...	...	...	...	...	...
Banks	4 623	...	...	...	...	...	...	...	...
Other sectors	4 624	–.5	–5.1	–6.0	–8.2	–4.1	–9.8	...	...
Money market instruments	4 630	...	...	...	...	...	...	...	...
Monetary authorities	4 631	...	...	...	...	...	...	...	...
General government	4 632	...	...	...	...	...	...	...	...
Banks	4 633	...	...	...	...	...	...	...	...
Other sectors	4 634	...	...	...	...	...	...	...	...
Financial derivatives	4 640	...	...	...	...	...	...	...	...
Monetary authorities	4 641	...	...	...	...	...	...	...	...
General government	4 642	...	...	...	...	...	...	...	...
Banks	4 643	...	...	...	...	...	...	...	...
Other sectors	4 644	...	...	...	...	...	...	...	...
Liabilities	4 652	**.3**	**.4**	...	**–.6**	...	**.9**	...	...
Equity securities	4 660	...	...	...	...	...	...	...	...
Banks	4 663	...	...	...	...	...	...	...	...
Other sectors	4 664	...	...	...	...	...	...	...	...
Debt securities	4 669	.3	.4	...	–.6	...	.9	...	...
Bonds and notes	4 670	.3	.4	...	–.6	...	.9	...	...
Monetary authorities	4 671	...	...	...	...	...	...	...	...
General government	4 672	.3	.4	...	–.6	...	.9	...	...
Banks	4 673	...	...	...	...	...	...	...	...
Other sectors	4 674	...	...	...	...	...	...	...	...
Money market instruments	4 680	...	...	...	...	...	...	...	...
Monetary authorities	4 681	...	...	...	...	...	...	...	...
General government	4 682	...	...	...	...	...	...	...	...
Banks	4 683	...	...	...	...	...	...	...	...
Other sectors	4 684	...	...	...	...	...	...	...	...
Financial derivatives	4 690	...	...	...	...	...	...	...	...
Monetary authorities	4 691	...	...	...	...	...	...	...	...
General government	4 692	...	...	...	...	...	...	...	...
Banks	4 693	...	...	...	...	...	...	...	...
Other sectors	4 694	...	...	...	...	...	...	...	...

Table 2 (Concluded). STANDARD PRESENTATION, 1988–95
(Millions of U.S. dollars)

	Code	1988	1989	1990	1991	1992	1993	1994	1995
C. OTHER INVESTMENT	4 700 . .	25.0	–28.8	41.2	19.9	–51.8	3.4	. . .	. . .
Assets	4 703 . .	**3.1**	**–23.3**	**–18.6**	**–2.2**	**–4.2**	**–6.2**	. . .	. . .
Trade credits	4 706 . .	. . .	. . .	. . .	. . .	. . .	. . .	. . .	. . .
General government: long-term	4 708 . .	. . .	. . .	. . .	. . .	. . .	. . .	. . .	. . .
General government: short-term	4 709 . .	. . .	. . .	. . .	. . .	. . .	. . .	. . .	. . .
Other sectors: long-term	4 711 . .	. . .	. . .	. . .	. . .	. . .	. . .	. . .	. . .
Other sectors: short-term	4 712 . .	. . .	. . .	. . .	. . .	. . .	. . .	. . .	. . .
Loans	4 714 . .	–34.6	–14.7	4.6	24.5	–6.2	18.2	. . .	. . .
Monetary authorities: long-term	4 717 . .	. . .	. . .	. . .	. . .	. . .	. . .	. . .	. . .
Monetary authorities: short-term	4 718 . .	. . .	. . .	. . .	. . .	. . .	. . .	. . .	. . .
General government: long-term	4 720 . .	. . .	. . .	. . .	. . .	. . .	. . .	. . .	. . .
General government: short-term	4 721 . .	–.5	–.5	–.5	–.5	–.6	–.5	. . .	. . .
Banks: long-term	4 723 . .	. . .	. . .	. . .	. . .	. . .	. . .	. . .	. . .
Banks: short-term	4 724 . .	. . .	. . .	. . .	. . .	. . .	. . .	. . .	. . .
Other sectors: long-term	4 726 . .	–.8	–4.8	–.7	–2.0	–1.3	–2.0	. . .	. . .
Other sectors: short-term	4 727 . .	–33.3	–9.4	5.9	27.0	–4.3	20.8	. . .	. . .
Currency and deposits	4 730 . .	35.8	–5.9	–21.9	–15.9	2.7	–20.0	. . .	. . .
Monetary authorities	4 731 . .	. . .	. . .	. . .	. . .	. . .	. . .	. . .	. . .
General government	4 732 . .	.8	–2.1	.6	–1.1	.4	–2.1	. . .	. . .
Banks	4 733 . .	45.5	5.4	–7.9	–11.0	12.2	–.6	. . .	. . .
Other sectors	4 734 . .	–10.5	–9.1	–14.6	–3.7	–9.9	–17.3	. . .	. . .
Other assets	4 736 . .	1.8	–2.7	–1.3	–10.9	–.6	–4.4	. . .	. . .
Monetary authorities: long-term	4 738 . .	. . .	. . .	. . .	. . .	. . .	. . .	. . .	. . .
Monetary authorities: short-term	4 739 . .	. . .	. . .	. . .	. . .	. . .	. . .	. . .	. . .
General government: long-term	4 741 . .	2.5	.1	2.9	–8.6	–2.9	–.8	. . .	. . .
General government: short-term	4 742 . .	. . .	. . .	. . .	. . .	. . .	. . .	. . .	. . .
Banks: long-term	4 744 . .	. . .	. . .	. . .	. . .	. . .	. . .	. . .	. . .
Banks: short-term	4 745 . .	. . .	. . .	. . .	. . .	. . .	. . .	. . .	. . .
Other sectors: long-term	4 747 . .	–.7	–2.8	–4.3	–2.3	2.2	–3.6	. . .	. . .
Other sectors: short-term	4 748 . .	. . .	. . .	. . .	. . .	. . .	. . .	. . .	. . .
Liabilities	4 753 . .	**21.9**	**–5.5**	**59.9**	**22.2**	**–47.7**	**9.6**	. . .	. . .
Trade credits	4 756 . .	. . .	. . .	. . .	. . .	. . .	. . .	. . .	. . .
General government: long-term	4 758 . .	. . .	. . .	. . .	. . .	. . .	. . .	. . .	. . .
General government: short-term	4 759 . .	. . .	. . .	. . .	. . .	. . .	. . .	. . .	. . .
Other sectors: long-term	4 761 . .	. . .	. . .	. . .	. . .	. . .	. . .	. . .	. . .
Other sectors: short-term	4 762 . .	. . .	. . .	. . .	. . .	. . .	. . .	. . .	. . .
Loans	4 764 . .	44.7	–23.8	21.6	–16.0	–77.6	–25.8	. . .	. . .
Use of Fund credit and loans from the Fund	4 766 . .	–10.6	–5.8	–3.7	–.7	51.5	. . .	. . .	. . .
Monetary authorities: other long-term	4 767 . .	. . .	. . .	. . .	. . .	. . .	. . .	. . .	. . .
Monetary authorities: short-term	4 768 . .	. . .	. . .	. . .	. . .	. . .	. . .	. . .	. . .
General government: long-term	4 770 . .	40.5	13.6	8.9	–28.4	–42.2	–26.1	. . .	. . .
General government: short-term	4 771 . .	. . .	. . .	. . .	. . .	. . .	. . .	. . .	. . .
Banks: long-term	4 773 . .	. . .	. . .	. . .	. . .	. . .	. . .	. . .	. . .
Banks: short-term	4 774 . .	. . .	. . .	. . .	. . .	. . .	. . .	. . .	. . .
Other sectors: long-term	4 776 . .	–15.3	–19.7	14.6	31.1	–15.0	–14.6	. . .	. . .
Other sectors: short-term	4 777 . .	30.0	–12.0	1.8	–18.0	–72.0	14.8	. . .	. . .
Currency and deposits	4 780 . .	–37.4	–9.2	19.6	14.3	–6.5	9.0	. . .	. . .
Monetary authorities	4 781 . .	–1.5	. . .	.6	. . .	. . .	. . .	. . .	. . .
General government	4 782 . .	. . .	. . .	. . .	. . .	. . .	. . .	. . .	. . .
Banks	4 783 . .	–35.9	–9.2	18.9	14.3	–6.5	9.0	. . .	. . .
Other sectors	4 784 . .	. . .	. . .	. . .	. . .	. . .	. . .	. . .	. . .
Other liabilities	4 786 . .	14.7	27.5	18.6	23.8	36.4	26.4	. . .	. . .
Monetary authorities: long-term	4 788 . .	. . .	. . .	. . .	. . .	. . .	. . .	. . .	. . .
Monetary authorities: short-term	4 789 . .	. . .	. . .	. . .	11.9	3.5	. . .	. . .	. . .
General government: long-term	4 791 . .	. . .	.4	–.2	.5	.4	.5	. . .	. . .
General government: short-term	4 792 . .	. . .	. . .	. . .	. . .	. . .	. . .	. . .	. . .
Banks: long-term	4 794 . .	. . .	. . .	. . .	. . .	. . .	. . .	. . .	. . .
Banks: short-term	4 795 . .	. . .	. . .	. . .	. . .	. . .	. . .	. . .	. . .
Other sectors: long-term	4 797 . .	1.7	3.2	6.5	9.6	30.3	23.6	. . .	. . .
Other sectors: short-term	4 798 . .	13.0	23.9	12.4	1.7	2.2	2.3	. . .	. . .
D. RESERVE ASSETS	4 800 . .	–27.4	48.6	42.0	40.6	–79.8	–20.9	. . .	. . .
Monetary gold	4 810 . .	. . .	.8	3.1	. . .	. . .	. . .	. . .	. . .
Special drawing rights	4 820 . .	.2	.6	. . .	–.6	.5	.1	. . .	. . .
Reserve position in the Fund	4 830 . .	. . .	. . .	. . .	2.9	. . .	. . .	. . .	. . .
Foreign exchange	4 840 . .	12.3	46.8	4.0	34.3	–80.7	–21.0	. . .	. . .
Other claims	4 880 . .	–40.0	.4	35.0	4.1	.4	. . .	. . .	. . .
NET ERRORS AND OMISSIONS	4 998 . .	**–50.4**	**–44.1**	**–70.6**	**–32.6**	**–21.5**	**–44.7**	. . .	. . .

Part 3 of the *Yearbook* contains descriptions of the methodologies, compilation practices, and sources used to compile these data.

Table 1. ANALYTIC PRESENTATION, 1988–95
(Millions of U.S. dollars)

	Code	1988	1989	1990	1991	1992	1993	1994	1995
A. Current Account [1]	4 993 Y .	**3,592**	**3,600**	**3,627**	**4,746**	**6,650**	**11,237**	**13,021**	**14,960**
Goods: exports f.o.b	2 100 . .	87,436	92,123	110,188	107,990	116,841	106,302	122,879	157,938
Goods: imports f.o.b	3 100 . .	-84,733	-89,845	-108,517	-105,991	-113,141	-100,522	-115,949	-149,124
Balance on Goods	4 100 . .	*2,703*	*2,278*	*1,671*	*1,999*	*3,700*	*5,780*	*6,930*	*8,814*
Services: credit	2 200 . .	21,045	21,840	28,417	30,583	33,658	33,366	53,963	38,655
Services: debit	3 200 . .	-18,898	-21,314	-26,581	-28,789	-30,999	-29,995	-49,768	-35,520
Balance on Goods and Services	4 991 . .	*4,851*	*2,805*	*3,507*	*3,793*	*6,359*	*9,151*	*11,125*	*11,948*
Income: credit	2 300 . .	33,127	48,276	65,544	75,452	88,295	83,011	90,177	108,418
Income: debit	3 300 . .	-32,631	-45,592	-63,228	-72,274	-85,309	-78,138	-85,324	-102,165
Balance on Goods, Services, and Income	4 992 . .	*5,347*	*5,489*	*5,824*	*6,971*	*9,345*	*14,024*	*15,978*	*18,201*
Current transfers: credit	2 379 Y .	2,602	2,329	3,825	4,160	4,368	4,198	4,476	6,073
Current transfers: debit	3 379 . .	-4,357	-4,217	-6,022	-6,385	-7,063	-6,986	-7,434	-9,314
B. Capital Account [1]	4 994 Y .	**...**	**...**	**...**	**...**	**...**	**...**	**...**	**...**
Capital account: credit	2 994 Y .	...	...	...	...	...	...	...	...
Capital account: debit	3 994 . .	...	...	...	...	...	...	...	...
Total, Groups A Plus B	4 010 . .	*3,592*	*3,600*	*3,627*	*4,746*	*6,650*	*11,237*	*13,021*	...
C. Financial Account [1]	4 995 X .	**-3,758**	**-2,664**	**-1,651**	**-3,155**	**-7,806**	**-13,563**	**-10,453**	**...**
Direct investment abroad	4 505 . .	-3,784	-6,486	-6,314	-6,271	-11,407	-4,904	-588	...
Direct investment in Belgium-Luxembourg	4 555 Y .	5,212	7,020	8,047	9,363	11,286	10,750	7,464	...
Portfolio investment assets	4 602 . .	-12,302	-14,324	-9,443	-29,570	-62,887	-58,431	-41,052	...
Equity securities	4 610 . .	-332	-3,839	1,530	-659	-115	-9,465	-10,653	...
Debt securities	4 619 . .	-11,970	-10,485	-10,973	-28,911	-62,773	-48,966	-30,400	...
Portfolio investment liabilities	4 652 Y .	7,729	11,050	7,946	27,490	59,016	50,472	17,201	...
Equity securities	4 660 Y .	6,362	10,082	7,014	20,816	56,272	46,838	22,489	...
Debt securities	4 669 Y .	1,368	968	932	6,674	2,743	3,634	-5,288	...
Other investment assets	4 703 . .	6,361	-55,626	-64,422	-22,023	-49,920	-51,772	11,455	...
Monetary authorities	4 703 . A	...	...	...	...	...	...	...	...
General government	4 703 . B	-99	-242	-184	-440	-536	-802	-290	...
Banks	4 703 . C	8,613	-55,225	-67,666	-25,042	-49,107	-45,916	9,833	...
Other sectors	4 703 . D	-2,153	-159	3,429	3,459	-277	-5,054	1,912	...
Other investment liabilities	4 753 X .	-6,975	55,701	62,536	17,857	46,107	40,321	-4,932	...
Monetary authorities	4 753 XA	2,741	...	...	...	...	...	...	...
General government	4 753 YB	-135	2,167	948	2,417	-2,887	10,758	-5,042	...
Banks	4 753 YC	-11,414	52,731	56,431	7,262	32,419	19,043	64	...
Other sectors	4 753 YD	1,833	804	5,156	8,178	16,575	10,520	47	...
Total, Groups A Through C	4 020 . .	*-166*	*936*	*1,976*	*1,591*	*-1,156*	*-2,326*	*2,568*	...
D. Net Errors and Omissions	4 998 . .	**61**	**-624**	**-1,572**	**-1,007**	**1,726**	**204**	**-2,349**	**...**
Total, Groups A Through D	4 030 . .	*-104*	*312*	*404*	*584*	*569*	*-2,122*	*219*	...
E. Reserves and Related Items	4 040 . .	**104**	**-312**	**-404**	**-584**	**-569**	**2,122**	**-219**	**...**
Reserve assets	4 800 . .	-861	-312	-404	-584	-569	2,122	-219	...
Use of Fund credit and loans	4 766 . .	...	...	...	...	...	...	...	...
Liabilities constituting foreign authorities' reserves	4 900 . .	965	...	...	...	...	...	...	...
Exceptional financing	4 920 . .	...	...	...	...	...	...	...	...
Conversion rates: Belgian francs (or Luxembourg francs) per U.S. dollar	0 101 . .	**36.768**	**39.404**	**33.418**	**34.148**	**32.150**	**34.597**	**33.456**	**29.480**

[1] Excludes components that have been classified in the categories of Group E.

Table 2. STANDARD PRESENTATION, 1988–95
(Millions of U.S. dollars)

	Code	1988	1989	1990	1991	1992	1993	1994	1995
CURRENT ACCOUNT	4 993 . .	**3,592**	**3,600**	**3,627**	**4,746**	**6,650**	**11,237**	**13,021**	**14,960**
A. GOODS	4 100 . .	2,703	2,278	1,671	1,999	3,700	5,780	6,930	8,814
Credit	2 100 . .	**87,436**	**92,123**	**110,188**	**107,990**	**116,841**	**106,302**	**122,879**	**157,938**
General merchandise: exports f.o.b.	2 110 . .	85,496	87,848	105,794	103,836	112,898	102,209	118,842	153,119
Goods for processing: exports f.o.b.	2 150 . .	1,940	2,120	2,530	2,585	2,638	2,730	2,913	3,270
Repairs on goods	2 160 . .	. . .	198	217	247	230	191	200	284
Goods procured in ports by carriers	2 170 . .	. . .	226	300	292	309	238	344	661
Nonmonetary gold	2 180 . .	. . .	1,732	1,348	1,031	766	934	581	604
Debit	3 100 . .	**–84,733**	**–89,845**	**–108,517**	**–105,991**	**–113,141**	**–100,522**	**–115,949**	**–149,124**
General merchandise: imports f.o.b.	3 110 . .	–84,275	–87,328	–105,972	–104,109	–111,456	–98,812	–114,563	–147,142
Goods for processing: imports f.o.b.	3 150 . .	–457	–477	–562	–371	–460	–537	–520	–782
Repairs on goods	3 160 . .	. . .	–99	–108	–120	–122	–137	–155	–314
Goods procured in ports by carriers	3 170 . .	. . .	–371	–382	–248	–228	–243	–244	–455
Nonmonetary gold	3 180 . .	. . .	–1,570	–1,493	–1,142	–876	–793	–467	–430
B. SERVICES	4 200 . .	2,148	526	1,836	1,794	2,659	3,371	4,195	3,134
Total credit	2 200 . .	*21,045*	*21,840*	*28,417*	*30,583*	*33,658*	*33,366*	*53,963*	*38,655*
Total debit	3 200 . .	*–18,898*	*–21,314*	*–26,581*	*–28,789*	*–30,999*	*–29,995*	*–49,768*	*–35,520*
Transportation services, credit	2 205 . .	**5,674**	**5,846**	**7,332**	**7,719**	**7,945**	**7,524**	**9,661**	**9,698**
Passenger	2 205 BA	*759*	*777*	*1,077*	*1,156*	*1,076*	*1,094*	*1,420*	*1,153*
Freight	2 205 BB	*3,483*	*3,987*	*5,051*	*5,317*	*5,653*	*5,228*	*961*	*7,722*
Other	2 205 BC	*1,433*	*1,081*	*1,204*	*1,247*	*1,216*	*1,201*	*7,280*	*823*
Sea transport, passenger	2 207 . .	. . .	. . .	. . .	. . .	. . .	. . .	. . .	5
Sea transport, freight	2 208 . .	. . .	. . .	. . .	. . .	. . .	. . .	. . .	4,079
Sea transport, other	2 209 . .	. . .	. . .	. . .	. . .	. . .	. . .	. . .	601
Air transport, passenger	2 211 . .	. . .	. . .	. . .	. . .	. . .	. . .	. . .	982
Air transport, freight	2 212 . .	. . .	. . .	. . .	. . .	. . .	. . .	. . .	368
Air transport, other	2 213 . .	. . .	. . .	. . .	. . .	. . .	. . .	. . .	57
Other transport, passenger	2 215 . .	. . .	. . .	. . .	. . .	. . .	. . .	1,420	166
Other transport, freight	2 216 . .	. . .	. . .	. . .	. . .	. . .	. . .	961	3,274
Other transport, other	2 217 . .	. . .	. . .	. . .	. . .	. . .	. . .	7,280	165
Transportation services, debit	3 205 . .	**–4,469**	**–4,736**	**–6,041**	**–6,776**	**–6,558**	**–5,869**	**–7,694**	**–7,494**
Passenger	3 205 BA	*–724*	*–546*	*–880*	*–1,002*	*–953*	*–873*	*–1,236*	*–905*
Freight	3 205 BB	*–2,229*	*–2,585*	*–3,541*	*–4,125*	*–4,209*	*–3,841*	*–823*	*–6,046*
Other	3 205 BC	*–1,516*	*–1,605*	*–1,621*	*–1,649*	*–1,396*	*–1,155*	*–5,635*	*–542*
Sea transport, passenger	3 207 . .	. . .	. . .	. . .	. . .	. . .	. . .	. . .	–9
Sea transport, freight	3 208 . .	. . .	. . .	. . .	. . .	. . .	. . .	. . .	–3,345
Sea transport, other	3 209 . .	. . .	. . .	. . .	. . .	. . .	. . .	. . .	–309
Air transport, passenger	3 211 . .	. . .	. . .	. . .	. . .	. . .	. . .	. . .	–757
Air transport, freight	3 212 . .	. . .	. . .	. . .	. . .	. . .	. . .	. . .	–170
Air transport, other	3 213 . .	. . .	. . .	. . .	. . .	. . .	. . .	. . .	–133
Other transport, passenger	3 215 . .	. . .	. . .	. . .	. . .	. . .	. . .	–1,236	–139
Other transport, freight	3 216 . .	. . .	. . .	. . .	. . .	. . .	. . .	–823	–2,531
Other transport, other	3 217 . .	. . .	. . .	. . .	. . .	. . .	. . .	–5,635	–100
Travel, credit	2 236 . .	**3,416**	**3,075**	**3,721**	**3,612**	**4,101**	**4,054**	**5,556**	**5,719**
Business travel	2 237 . .	. . .	. . .	. . .	. . .	. . .	. . .	24	1,128
Personal travel	2 240 . .	. . .	. . .	. . .	. . .	. . .	. . .	5,532	4,591
Travel, debit	3 236 . .	**–4,577**	**–4,320**	**–5,477**	**–5,543**	**–6,714**	**–6,338**	**–8,054**	**–9,215**
Business travel	3 237 . .	. . .	. . .	. . .	. . .	. . .	. . .	. . .	–2,337
Personal travel	3 240 . .	. . .	. . .	. . .	. . .	. . .	. . .	–8,054	–6,878
Other services, credit	2 200 BA	**11,955**	**12,920**	**17,364**	**19,252**	**21,613**	**21,788**	**38,746**	**23,238**
Communications	2 245 . .	. . .	122	224	220	219	118	. . .	606
Construction	2 249 . .	. . .	414	546	628	652	672	735	665
Insurance	2 253 . .	1,397	1,755	3,055	2,950	3,467	3,570	4,061	2,232
Financial	2 260 . .	. . .	1,879	1,792	2,384	2,643	3,686	5,465	4,871
Computer and information	2 262 . .	. . .	. . .	. . .	. . .	. . .	. . .	. . .	649
Royalties and licence fees	2 266 . .	420	705	682	656	867	995	1,070	602
Other business services	2 268 . .	7,554	6,630	9,295	10,368	11,544	10,563	24,391	10,705
Personal, cultural, and recreational	2 287 . .	. . .	. . .	. . .	. . .	. . .	. . .	676	380
Government, n.i.e.	2 291 . .	2,585	1,415	1,772	2,046	2,221	2,184	2,348	2,528
Other services, debit	3 200 BA	**–9,852**	**–12,259**	**–15,063**	**–16,470**	**–17,727**	**–17,788**	**–34,019**	**–18,812**
Communications	3 245 . .	. . .	–600	–372	–282	–350	–107	. . .	–319
Construction	3 249 . .	. . .	–617	–775	–832	–754	–525	–473	–749
Insurance	3 253 . .	–1,320	–1,594	–2,576	–2,656	–3,160	–3,094	–3,403	–1,881
Financial	3 260 . .	. . .	–1,255	–1,248	–1,576	–1,606	–2,149	–4,267	–3,219
Computer and information	3 262 . .	. . .	. . .	. . .	. . .	. . .	. . .	. . .	–516
Royalties and licence fees	3 266 . .	–948	–1,162	–1,328	–1,263	–1,276	–1,394	–1,528	–1,192
Other business services	3 268 . .	–7,153	–6,561	–8,107	–9,147	–9,954	–9,945	–23,103	–9,621
Personal, cultural, and recreational	3 287 . .	. . .	. . .	. . .	. . .	. . .	. . .	–527	–693
Government, n.i.e.	3 291 . .	–431	–471	–657	–713	–628	–574	–719	–624

Table 2 (Continued). STANDARD PRESENTATION, 1988–95
(Millions of U.S. dollars)

	Code		1988	1989	1990	1991	1992	1993	1994	1995
C. INCOME	4 300	. .	496	2,684	2,316	3,178	2,986	4,873	4,853	6,252
Total credit	2 300	. .	*33,127*	*48,276*	*65,544*	*75,452*	*88,295*	*83,011*	*90,177*	*108,418*
Total debit	3 300	. .	*-32,631*	*-45,592*	*-63,228*	*-72,274*	*-85,309*	*-78,138*	*-85,324*	*-102,165*
Compensation of employees, credit	2 310	. .	**802**	**2,220**	**2,821**	**3,127**	**3,541**	**3,442**	**4,097**	**3,866**
Compensation of employees, debit	3 310	. .	**-715**	**-795**	**-1,155**	**-1,274**	**-1,510**	**-1,531**	**-2,589**	**-1,708**
Investment income, credit	2 320	. .	**32,326**	**46,056**	**62,723**	**72,325**	**84,754**	**79,569**	**86,080**	**104,551**
Direct investment income	2 330	. .	...	...	...	...	...	...	...	3,667
Dividends and distributed branch profits	2 332	. .	...	...	...	...	...	...	...	1,977
Reinvested earnings and undistributed branch profits	2 333	. .	...	...	...	...	...	...	...	...
Income on debt (interest)	2 334	. .	...	...	...	...	...	...	...	1,690
Portfolio investment income	2 339	. .	...	...	...	...	...	...	31,667	38,571
Income on equity	2 340	. .	...	...	...	...	...	...	...	2,636
Income on bonds and notes	2 350	. .	...	...	...	...	...	...	31,557	35,360
Income on money market instruments and financial derivatives	2 360	. .	...	...	...	...	...	...	110	575
Other investment income	2 370	. .	32,326	46,056	62,723	72,325	84,754	79,569	54,413	62,313
Investment income, debit	3 320	. .	**-31,916**	**-44,797**	**-62,073**	**-71,000**	**-83,799**	**-76,607**	**-82,734**	**-100,458**
Direct investment income	3 330	. .	...	...	...	...	...	...	...	-5,164
Dividends and distributed branch profits	3 332	. .	...	...	...	...	...	...	...	-3,929
Reinvested earnings and undistributed branch profits	3 333	. .	...	...	...	...	...	...	...	...
Income on debt (interest)	3 334	. .	...	...	...	...	...	...	...	-1,234
Portfolio investment income	3 339	. .	...	...	...	...	...	...	-24,821	-32,076
Income on equity	3 340	. .	...	...	...	...	...	...	...	-4,506
Income on bonds and notes	3 350	. .	...	...	...	...	...	...	-24,642	-26,951
Income on money market instruments and financial derivatives	3 360	. .	...	...	...	...	...	...	-179	-618
Other investment income	3 370	. .	-31,916	-44,797	-62,073	-71,000	-83,799	-76,607	-57,914	-63,218
D. CURRENT TRANSFERS	4 379	. .	-1,755	-1,889	-2,197	-2,225	-2,695	-2,787	-2,958	-3,240
Credit	2 379	. .	**2,602**	**2,329**	**3,825**	**4,160**	**4,368**	**4,198**	**4,476**	**6,073**
General government	2 380	. .	1,209	828	1,820	2,109	2,112	1,732	2,215	2,668
Other sectors	2 390	. .	1,393	1,501	2,005	2,051	2,256	2,466	2,261	3,406
Workers' remittances	2 391	. .	628	516	762	845	934	1,139	754	86
Other current transfers	2 392	. .	765	984	1,243	1,206	1,322	1,327	1,507	3,320
Debit	3 379	. .	**-4,357**	**-4,217**	**-6,022**	**-6,385**	**-7,063**	**-6,986**	**-7,434**	**-9,314**
General government	3 380	. .	-2,819	-2,554	-2,978	-3,508	-3,684	-3,550	-4,698	-5,378
Other sectors	3 390	. .	-1,538	-1,664	-3,043	-2,877	-3,380	-3,435	-2,736	-3,936
Workers' remittances	3 391	. .	-665	-713	-1,155	-1,158	-1,387	-1,498	-1,084	-479
Other current transfers	3 392	. .	-873	-951	-1,889	-1,719	-1,993	-1,937	-1,652	-3,457
CAPITAL AND FINANCIAL ACCOUNT	4 996	. .	**-3,653**	**-2,977**	**-2,055**	**-3,739**	**-8,376**	**-11,441**	**-10,672**	**...**
CAPITAL ACCOUNT	4 994	. .	**...**	**...**	**...**	**...**	**...**	**...**	**...**	**...**
Total credit	2 994	. .	...	...	...	...	...	...	...	...
Total debit	3 994	. .	...	...	...	...	...	...	...	...
Capital transfers, credit	2 400	. .	**...**	**...**	**...**	**...**	**...**	**...**	**...**	**...**
General government	2 401	. .	...	...	...	...	...	...	...	...
Debt forgiveness	2 402	. .	...	...	...	...	...	...	...	...
Other capital transfers	2 410	. .	...	...	...	...	...	...	...	...
Other sectors	2 430	. .	...	...	...	...	...	...	...	...
Migrants' transfers	2 431	. .	...	...	...	...	...	...	...	...
Debt forgiveness	2 432	. .	...	...	...	...	...	...	...	...
Other capital transfers	2 440	. .	...	...	...	...	...	...	...	...
Capital transfers, debit	3 400	. .	**...**	**...**	**...**	**...**	**...**	**...**	**...**	**...**
General government	3 401	. .	...	...	...	...	...	...	...	...
Debt forgiveness	3 402	. .	...	...	...	...	...	...	...	...
Other capital transfers	3 410	. .	...	...	...	...	...	...	...	...
Other sectors	3 430	. .	...	...	...	...	...	...	...	...
Migrants' transfers	3 431	. .	...	...	...	...	...	...	...	...
Debt forgiveness	3 432	. .	...	...	...	...	...	...	...	...
Other capital transfers	3 440	. .	...	...	...	...	...	...	...	...
Nonproduced nonfinancial assets, credit	2 480	. .	**...**	**...**	**...**	**...**	**...**	**...**	**...**	**...**
Nonproduced nonfinancial assets, debit	3 480	. .	**...**	**...**	**...**	**...**	**...**	**...**	**...**	**...**

Table 2 (Continued). STANDARD PRESENTATION, 1988–95
(Millions of U.S. dollars)

	Code	1988	1989	1990	1991	1992	1993	1994	1995
FINANCIAL ACCOUNT	4 995	**–3,653**	**–2,977**	**–2,055**	**–3,739**	**–8,376**	**–11,441**	**–10,672**	...
A. DIRECT INVESTMENT	4 500	1,428	534	1,732	3,092	–121	5,846	6,876	...
Direct investment abroad	4 505	**–3,784**	**–6,486**	**–6,314**	**–6,271**	**–11,407**	**–4,904**	**–588**	...
Equity capital	4 510	–2,054	–3,879	–3,063	–2,370	–1,958	–1,575	–1,534	...
Claims on affiliated enterprises	4 515	...	...	...	...	...	...	...	...
Liabilities to affiliated enterprises	4 520	...	...	...	...	...	...	...	...
Reinvested earnings	4 525	...	...	...	...	...	...	...	...
Other capital	4 530	–1,730	–2,607	–3,251	–3,901	–9,449	–3,329	945	...
Claims on affiliated enterprises	4 535	...	...	...	...	...	...	...	...
Liabilities to affiliated enterprises	4 540	...	...	...	...	...	...	...	...
Direct investment in Belgium-Luxembourg	4 555	**5,212**	**7,020**	**8,047**	**9,363**	**11,286**	**10,750**	**7,464**	...
Equity capital	4 560	3,951	4,458	4,811	6,436	9,680	8,437	6,514	...
Claims on direct investors	4 565	...	...	...	...	...	...	...	...
Liabilities to direct investors	4 570	...	...	...	...	...	...	...	...
Reinvested earnings	4 575	...	...	...	...	...	...	...	...
Other capital	4 580	1,262	2,562	3,236	2,926	1,606	2,313	950	...
Claims on direct investors	4 585	...	...	...	...	...	...	...	...
Liabilities to direct investors	4 590	...	...	...	...	...	...	...	...
B. PORTFOLIO INVESTMENT	4 600	–4,572	–3,274	–1,497	–2,080	–3,872	–7,959	–23,851	...
Assets	4 602	**–12,302**	**–14,324**	**–9,443**	**–29,570**	**–62,887**	**–58,431**	**–41,052**	...
Equity securities	4 610	–332	–3,839	1,530	–659	–115	–9,465	–10,653	...
Monetary authorities	4 611	...	...	...	...	...	...	...	...
General government	4 612	...	...	...	...	...	...	...	...
Banks	4 613	...	...	...	...	...	...	...	...
Other sectors	4 614	...	...	...	...	...	...	–10,653	...
Debt securities	4 619	–11,970	–10,485	–10,973	–28,911	–62,773	–48,966	–30,400	...
Bonds and notes	4 620	–11,970	–10,485	–10,973	–28,911	–62,773	–48,966	–30,400	...
Monetary authorities	4 621	...	...	...	...	...	...	...	...
General government	4 622	...	...	...	...	...	...	...	...
Banks	4 623	...	...	...	...	...	...	...	...
Other sectors	4 624	...	...	...	...	...	...	–30,400	...
Money market instruments	4 630	...	...	...	...	...	...	...	...
Monetary authorities	4 631	...	...	...	...	...	...	...	...
General government	4 632	...	...	...	...	...	...	...	...
Banks	4 633	...	...	...	...	...	...	...	...
Other sectors	4 634	...	...	...	...	...	...	...	...
Financial derivatives	4 640	...	...	...	...	...	...	...	...
Monetary authorities	4 641	...	...	...	...	...	...	...	...
General government	4 642	...	...	...	...	...	...	...	...
Banks	4 643	...	...	...	...	...	...	...	...
Other sectors	4 644	...	...	...	...	...	...	...	...
Liabilities	4 652	**7,729**	**11,050**	**7,946**	**27,490**	**59,016**	**50,472**	**17,201**	...
Equity securities	4 660	6,362	10,082	7,014	20,816	56,272	46,838	22,489	...
Banks	4 663	...	...	...	...	...	...	...	...
Other sectors	4 664	...	...	...	...	...	...	...	...
Debt securities	4 669	1,368	968	932	6,674	2,743	3,634	–5,288	...
Bonds and notes	4 670	1,368	968	932	6,674	2,743	3,634	–6,065	...
Monetary authorities	4 671	...	...	...	...	...	...	...	...
General government	4 672	–63	770	770	6,097	2,447	3,258	–4,883	...
Banks	4 673	...	...	...	...	...	...	...	...
Other sectors	4 674	1,431	198	161	578	296	376	–1,183	...
Money market instruments	4 680	...	...	...	...	...	...	778	...
Monetary authorities	4 681	...	...	...	...	...	...	...	...
General government	4 682	...	...	...	...	...	...	778	...
Banks	4 683	...	...	...	...	...	...	...	...
Other sectors	4 684	...	...	...	...	...	...	...	...
Financial derivatives	4 690	...	...	...	...	...	...	...	...
Monetary authorities	4 691	...	...	...	...	...	...	...	...
General government	4 692	...	...	...	...	...	...	...	...
Banks	4 693	...	...	...	...	...	...	...	...
Other sectors	4 694	...	...	...	...	...	...	...	...

Table 2 (Concluded). STANDARD PRESENTATION, 1988–95
(Millions of U.S. dollars)

	Code	1988	1989	1990	1991	1992	1993	1994	1995
C. OTHER INVESTMENT	4 700 . .	351	76	–1,886	–4,166	–3,813	–11,450	6,523	. . .
Assets	4 703 . .	**6,361**	**–55,626**	**–64,422**	**–22,023**	**–49,920**	**–51,772**	**11,455**	**. . .**
Trade credits	4 706 . .	–1,566	178	1,026	–188	–221	774	. . .	. . .
General government: long-term	4 708 . .	. . .	. . .	. . .	. . .	. . .	. . .	. . .	. . .
General government: short-term	4 709 . .	. . .	. . .	. . .	. . .	. . .	. . .	. . .	. . .
Other sectors: long-term	4 711 . .	. . .	. . .	. . .	. . .	. . .	. . .	. . .	. . .
Other sectors: short-term	4 712 . .	–1,566	178	1,026	–188	–221	774	. . .	. . .
Loans	4 714 . .	–99	–268	–152	–342	–148	–157	4,692	. . .
Monetary authorities: long-term	4 717 . .	. . .	. . .	. . .	. . .	. . .	. . .	. . .	. . .
Monetary authorities: short-term	4 718 . .	. . .	. . .	. . .	. . .	. . .	. . .	. . .	. . .
General government: long-term	4 720 . .	–99	–268	–152	–342	–148	–157	–112	. . .
General government: short-term	4 721 . .	. . .	. . .	. . .	. . .	. . .	. . .	. . .	. . .
Banks: long-term	4 723 . .	. . .	. . .	. . .	. . .	. . .	. . .	. . .	. . .
Banks: short-term	4 724 . .	. . .	. . .	. . .	. . .	. . .	. . .	4,357	. . .
Other sectors: long-term	4 726 . .	. . .	. . .	. . .	. . .	. . .	. . .	. . .	. . .
Other sectors: short-term	4 727 . .	. . .	. . .	. . .	. . .	. . .	. . .	. . .	. . .
Currency and deposits	4 730 . .	8,025	–55,369	–65,293	–21,605	–50,181	–52,047	6,763	. . .
Monetary authorities	4 731 . .	. . .	. . .	. . .	. . .	. . .	. . .	. . .	. . .
General government	4 732 . .	. . .	26	–32	–98	–388	–645	–178	. . .
Banks	4 733 . .	8,613	–55,225	–67,666	–25,042	–49,107	–45,916	5,476	. . .
Other sectors	4 734 . .	–589	–171	2,406	3,535	–685	–5,485	1,465	. . .
Other assets	4 736 . .	2	–166	–3	111	629	–342	. . .	. . .
Monetary authorities: long-term	4 738 . .	. . .	. . .	. . .	. . .	. . .	. . .	. . .	. . .
Monetary authorities: short-term	4 739 . .	. . .	. . .	. . .	. . .	. . .	. . .	. . .	. . .
General government: long-term	4 741 . .	. . .	. . .	. . .	. . .	. . .	. . .	. . .	. . .
General government: short-term	4 742 . .	. . .	. . .	. . .	. . .	. . .	. . .	. . .	. . .
Banks: long-term	4 744 . .	. . .	. . .	. . .	. . .	. . .	. . .	. . .	. . .
Banks: short-term	4 745 . .	. . .	. . .	. . .	. . .	. . .	. . .	. . .	. . .
Other sectors: long-term	4 747 . .	2	–166	–3	111	629	–342	. . .	. . .
Other sectors: short-term	4 748 . .	. . .	. . .	. . .	. . .	. . .	. . .	. . .	. . .
Liabilities	4 753 . .	**–6,010**	**55,701**	**62,536**	**17,857**	**46,107**	**40,321**	**–4,932**	**. . .**
Trade credits	4 756 . .	1,199	. . .	. . .	. . .	. . .	. . .	. . .	. . .
General government: long-term	4 758 . .	. . .	. . .	. . .	. . .	. . .	. . .	. . .	. . .
General government: short-term	4 759 . .	. . .	. . .	. . .	. . .	. . .	. . .	. . .	. . .
Other sectors: long-term	4 761 . .	. . .	. . .	. . .	. . .	. . .	. . .	. . .	. . .
Other sectors: short-term	4 762 . .	1,199	. . .	. . .	. . .	. . .	. . .	. . .	. . .
Loans	4 764 . .	–226	1,600	–126	1,846	–3,048	10,858	–5,328	. . .
Use of Fund credit and loans from the Fund	4 766 . .	. . .	. . .	. . .	. . .	. . .	. . .	. . .	. . .
Monetary authorities: other long-term	4 767 . .	. . .	. . .	. . .	. . .	. . .	. . .	. . .	. . .
Monetary authorities: short-term	4 768 . .	. . .	. . .	. . .	. . .	. . .	. . .	. . .	. . .
General government: long-term	4 770 . .	–135	1,846	998	2,458	–2,969	10,742	. . .	. . .
General government: short-term	4 771 . .	. . .	. . .	. . .	. . .	. . .	. . .	–5,042	. . .
Banks: long-term	4 773 . .	. . .	. . .	. . .	. . .	. . .	. . .	. . .	. . .
Banks: short-term	4 774 . .	. . .	. . .	. . .	. . .	. . .	. . .	. . .	. . .
Other sectors: long-term	4 776 . .	–91	–254	–899	–799	–88	125	–585	. . .
Other sectors: short-term	4 777 . .	. . .	8	–225	186	9	–9	299	. . .
Currency and deposits	4 780 . .	–10,449	52,731	56,431	7,262	32,419	19,043	64	. . .
Monetary authorities	4 781 . .	. . .	. . .	. . .	. . .	. . .	. . .	. . .	. . .
General government	4 782 . .	. . .	. . .	. . .	. . .	. . .	. . .	. . .	. . .
Banks	4 783 . .	–10,449	52,731	56,431	7,262	32,419	19,043	64	. . .
Other sectors	4 784 . .	. . .	. . .	. . .	. . .	. . .	. . .	. . .	. . .
Other liabilities	4 786 . .	3,466	1,371	6,230	8,749	16,735	10,420	332	. . .
Monetary authorities: long-term	4 788 . .	. . .	. . .	. . .	. . .	. . .	. . .	. . .	. . .
Monetary authorities: short-term	4 789 . .	2,741	. . .	. . .	. . .	. . .	. . .	. . .	. . .
General government: long-term	4 791 . .	. . .	. . .	. . .	. . .	. . .	. . .	. . .	. . .
General government: short-term	4 792 . .	. . .	321	–50	–41	82	15	. . .	. . .
Banks: long-term	4 794 . .	. . .	. . .	. . .	. . .	. . .	. . .	. . .	. . .
Banks: short-term	4 795 . .	. . .	. . .	. . .	. . .	. . .	. . .	. . .	. . .
Other sectors: long-term	4 797 . .	–368	951	6,177	8,377	15,880	10,377	. . .	. . .
Other sectors: short-term	4 798 . .	1,093	99	103	413	773	27	332	. . .
D. RESERVE ASSETS	4 800 . .	–861	–312	–404	–584	–569	2,122	–219	. . .
Monetary gold	4 810 . .	. . .	. . .	. . .	. . .	. . .	. . .	. . .	. . .
Special drawing rights	4 820 . .	100	–4	32	–22	418	–1	. . .	. . .
Reserve position in the Fund	4 830 . .	63	3	20	–57	–322	39	6	. . .
Foreign exchange	4 840 . .	–1,018	–311	–457	–505	–665	2,084	–225	. . .
Other claims	4 880 . .	–5	. . .	. . .	. . .	. . .	. . .	. . .	. . .
NET ERRORS AND OMISSIONS	4 998 . .	**61**	**–624**	**–1,572**	**–1,007**	**1,726**	**204**	**–2,349**	**. . .**

Part 3 of the *Yearbook* contains descriptions of the methodologies, compilation practices, and sources used to compile these data.

Table 3. INTERNATIONAL INVESTMENT POSITION (End-period stocks), 1988–95, BELGIUM ONLY
(Millions of U.S. dollars)

	Code	1988	1989	1990	1991	1992	1993	1994	1995
ASSETS	8 995 C.	281,698	331,348	400,613	425,616	438,969	468,153	532,485	...
Direct investment abroad	8 505 . .	**24,903**	**34,676**	**40,636**	**48,385**	**55,636**	**62,642**	**69,541**	...
Equity capital and reinvested earnings	8 506 . .	...	...	...	...	...	...	...	...
Claims on affiliated enterprises	8 507 . .	...	...	...	...	...	...	...	...
Liabilities to affiliated enterprises	8 508 . .	...	...	...	...	...	...	...	...
Other capital	8 530 . .	...	...	...	...	...	...	...	...
Claims on affiliated enterprises	8 535 . .	...	...	...	...	...	...	...	...
Liabilities to affiliated enterprises	8 540 . .	...	...	...	...	...	...	...	...
Portfolio investment	8 602 . .	**70,130**	**86,885**	**106,350**	**116,565**	**124,141**	**145,694**	**161,256**	...
Equity securities	8 610 . .	19,708	27,629	33,858	38,727	42,616	59,319	59,804	...
Monetary authorities	8 611 . .	...	...	...	...	...	...	...	...
General government	8 612 . .	...	...	...	...	753	249	534	...
Banks	8 613 . .	54	56	32	32	30	2,132	565	...
Other sectors	8 614 . .	19,655	27,573	33,826	38,695	41,832	56,937	58,704	...
Debt securities	8 619 . .	50,422	59,256	72,493	77,838	81,525	86,375	101,453	...
Bonds and notes	8 620 . .	47,342	55,117	66,489	71,954	75,015	84,658	100,353	...
Monetary authorities	8 621 . .	...	...	...	...	...	...	...	...
General government	8 622 . .	27	56	65	96	60	83	94	...
Banks	8 623 . .	13,496	14,709	19,882	21,586	26,100	35,309	36,561	...
Other sectors	8 624 . .	33,820	40,352	46,542	50,272	48,855	49,266	63,698	...
Money market instruments	8 630 . .	3,079	4,139	6,003	5,884	6,510	1,717	1,099	...
Monetary authorities	8 631 . .	...	...	...	...	...	...	...	...
General government	8 632 . .	...	...	...	...	...	...	...	...
Banks	8 633 . .	3,079	4,139	6,003	5,884	6,510	1,717	1,099	...
Other sectors	8 634 . .	...	...	...	...	...	...	...	...
Financial derivatives	8 640 . .	...	...	...	...	...	...	...	...
Monetary authorities	8 641 . .	...	...	...	...	...	...	...	...
General government	8 642 . .	...	...	...	...	...	...	...	...
Banks	8 643 . .	...	...	...	...	...	...	...	...
Other sectors	8 644 . .	...	...	...	...	...	...	...	...
Other investment	8 703 . .	**163,610**	**186,997**	**229,775**	**237,544**	**237,342**	**238,244**	**279,199**	...
Trade credits	8 706 . .	3,722	3,691	3,195	3,390	3,466	2,437	2,513	...
General government: long-term	8 708 . .	...	...	...	...	...	...	...	...
General government: short-term	8 709 . .	...	...	...	...	...	...	...	...
Other sectors: long-term	8 711 . .	...	...	...	...	...	...	...	...
Other sectors: short-term	8 712 . .	...	...	...	...	...	...	...	...
Loans	8 714 . .	130,620	145,554	173,098	176,623	170,434	173,442	196,906	...
Monetary authorities: long-term	8 717 . .	...	...	...	...	...	...	...	...
Monetary authorities: short-term	8 718 . .	...	...	...	...	...	...	...	...
General government: long-term	8 720 . .	1,259	1,314	1,775	2,271	2,140	2,049	1,947	...
General government: short-term	8 721 . .	...	...	...	...	...	...	...	...
Banks: long-term	8 723 . .	129,040	143,652	170,548	172,626	166,606	169,704	193,388	...
Banks: short-term	8 724 . .	...	...	...	...	...	...	...	...
Other sectors: long-term	8 726 . .	...	...	...	...	...	...	...	...
Other sectors: short-term	8 727 . .	161	391	516	799	904	914	974	...
Currency and deposits	8 730 . .	20,270	24,664	34,245	35,913	42,435	47,300	55,029	...
Monetary authorities	8 731 . .	...	...	...	...	...	...	...	...
General government	8 732 . .	...	...	...	...	...	...	...	...
Banks	8 733 . .	107	140	161	160	151	138	188	...
Other sectors	8 734 . .	20,163	24,525	34,084	35,753	42,285	47,161	54,841	...
Other assets	8 736 . .	8,997	13,087	19,237	21,618	21,007	15,065	24,751	...
Monetary authorities: long-term	8 738 . .	...	...	...	...	...	...	...	...
Monetary authorities: short-term	8 739 . .	...	...	...	...	...	...	...	...
General government: long-term	8 741 . .	...	...	...	...	...	...	...	...
General government: short-term	8 742 . .	...	...	...	...	...	...	...	...
Banks: long-term	8 744 . .	3,106	4,502	10,780	10,233	10,609	9,083	10,239	...
Banks: short-term	8 745 . .	...	...	...	...	...	...	...	...
Other sectors: long-term	8 747 . .	...	...	...	...	...	...	...	...
Other sectors: short-term	8 748 . .	...	...	...	...	...	...	...	...
Reserve assets	8 800 . .	**23,055**	**22,791**	**23,852**	**23,121**	**21,851**	**21,573**	**22,489**	...
Monetary gold	8 810 . .	...	...	...	...	...	...	...	...
Special drawing rights	8 820 . .	...	...	...	...	...	...	...	...
Reserve position in the Fund	8 830 . .	...	...	...	...	...	...	...	...
Foreign exchange	8 840 . .	...	...	...	...	...	...	...	...
Other claims	8 880 . .	...	...	...	...	...	...	...	...

Table 3 (Continued). INTERNATIONAL INVESTMENT POSITION (End–period stocks), 1988–95, BELGIUM ONLY

(Millions of U.S. dollars)

	Code	1988	1989	1990	1991	1992	1993	1994	1995
LIABILITIES	8 995 D.	278,538	328,384	391,963	408,826	416,667	437,690	495,611	...
Direct investment in Belgium	8 555 ..	**39,309**	**52,824**	**58,388**	**70,163**	**75,678**	**94,295**	**105,881**	...
Equity capital and reinvested earnings	8 556 ..	...	...	...	...	...	...	...	...
Claims on direct investors	8 557 ..	...	...	...	...	...	...	...	...
Liabilities to direct investors	8 558 ..	...	...	...	...	...	...	...	...
Other capital	8 580 ..	...	...	...	...	...	...	...	...
Claims on direct investors	8 585 ..	...	...	...	...	...	...	...	...
Liabilities to direct investors	8 590 ..	...	...	...	...	...	...	...	...
Portfolio investment	8 652 ..	**44,183**	**53,160**	**64,036**	**78,286**	**80,530**	**93,603**	**103,808**	...
Equity securities	8 660 ..	3,749	4,754	5,616	5,980	5,937	8,253	9,737	...
Banks	8 663 ..	...	...	...	...	...	...	...	...
Other sectors	8 664 ..	...	...	...	...	...	...	...	...
Debt securities	8 669 ..	40,434	48,406	58,420	72,306	74,593	85,350	94,071	...
Bonds and notes	8 670 ..	18,316	19,491	25,789	36,073	40,898	53,060	54,841	...
Monetary authorities	8 671 ..	...	...	...	...	...	...	...	...
General government	8 672 ..	15,370	16,555	22,593	31,916	35,202	44,392	44,727	...
Banks	8 673 ..	2,115	2,209	2,711	3,134	4,400	7,089	8,418	...
Other sectors	8 674 ..	830	727	484	1,023	1,296	1,579	1,696	...
Money market instruments	8 680 ..	22,118	28,915	32,631	36,233	33,695	32,290	39,230	...
Monetary authorities	8 681 ..	536	643	226	...	...	...	...	...
General government	8 682 ..	21,583	28,272	32,405	36,233	33,454	30,684	36,843	...
Banks	8 683 ..	...	...	...	...	...	1,135	1,508	...
Other sectors	8 684 ..	...	...	...	...	241	471	879	...
Financial derivatives	8 690 ..	...	...	...	...	...	...	...	...
Monetary authorities	8 691 ..	...	...	...	...	...	...	...	...
General government	8 692 ..	...	...	...	...	...	...	...	...
Banks	8 692 ..	...	...	...	...	...	...	...	...
Other sectors	8 694 ..	...	...	...	...	...	...	...	...
Other investment	8 753 ..	**195,046**	**222,399**	**269,539**	**260,377**	**260,458**	**249,792**	**285,921**	...
Trade credits	8 756 ..	...	...	...	...	...	...	...	...
General government: long-term	8 758 ..	...	...	...	...	...	...	...	...
General government: short-term	8 759 ..	...	...	...	...	...	...	...	...
Other sectors: long-term	8 761 ..	...	...	...	...	...	...	...	...
Other sectors: short-term	8 762 ..	...	...	...	...	...	...	...	...
Loans	8 764 ..	167,412	186,186	217,510	204,637	198,523	190,834	215,092	...
Use of Fund credit and loans from the Fund	8 766 ..	...	...	...	...	...	...	...	...
Monetary authorities: other long-term	8 767 ..	...	...	...	...	...	...	...	...
Monetary authorities: short-term	8 768 ..	...	...	...	...	...	...	...	...
General government: long-term	8 770 ..	54	56	...	160	241	83	534	...
General government: short-term	8 771 ..	...	...	...	...	...	...	...	...
Banks: long-term	8 773 ..	...	...	...	...	...	...	...	...
Banks: short-term	8 774 ..	...	...	...	...	...	...	...	...
Other sectors: long-term	8 776 ..	...	...	...	...	...	...	...	...
Other sectors: short-term	8 777 ..	...	...	...	...	...	...	...	...
Currency and deposits	8 780 ..	24,394	30,872	39,474	41,637	45,871	44,669	52,517	...
Monetary authorities	8 781 ..	616	503	678	768	663	665	848	...
General government	8 782 ..	27	364	355	256	332	222	408	...
Banks	8 783 ..	23,537	29,810	38,215	39,910	43,490	42,454	49,596	...
Other sectors	8 784 ..	214	196	226	704	1,386	1,329	1,665	...
Other liabilities	8 786 ..	3,240	5,341	12,555	14,103	16,064	14,290	18,312	...
Monetary authorities: long-term	8 788 ..	...	...	...	...	...	...	...	...
Monetary authorities: short-term	8 789 ..	...	...	...	...	...	...	...	...
General government: long-term	8 791 ..	...	...	...	...	...	...	...	...
General government: short-term	8 792 ..	...	...	...	...	...	...	...	...
Banks: long-term	8 794 ..	...	...	...	...	...	...	...	...
Banks: short-term	8 795 ..	...	...	...	...	...	...	...	...
Other sectors: long-term	8 797 ..	...	...	...	...	...	...	...	...
Other sectors: short-term	8 798 ..	...	...	...	...	...	...	...	...
NET INTERNATIONAL INVESTMENT POSITION	8 995 ..	**3,160**	**2,964**	**8,650**	**16,789**	**22,303**	**30,462**	**36,875**	...
Conversion rates: Belgian francs per U.S. dollar (end of period)	0 102 ..	**37.345**	**35.760**	**30.983**	**31.270**	**33.180**	**36.110**	**31.838**	**29.415**

Table 1. ANALYTIC PRESENTATION, 1988–95
(Millions of U.S. dollars)

	Code	1988	1989	1990	1991	1992	1993	1994	1995
A. Current Account [1]	4 993 Y.	**–2.6**	**–19.1**	**15.4**	**–25.8**	**–28.6**	**–48.5**	**–40.1**	**–30.4**
Goods: exports f.o.b	2 100 . .	119.4	124.4	129.2	126.1	140.6	132.0	156.5	164.5
Goods: imports f.o.b	3 100 . .	–161.3	–188.5	–188.4	–223.6	–244.5	–250.5	–231.9	–230.6
Balance on Goods	4 100 . .	*–41.9*	*–64.1*	*–59.2*	*–97.5*	*–103.9*	*–118.5*	*–75.4*	*–66.1*
Services: credit	2 200 . .	74.5	85.9	115.4	122.7	142.6	150.5	121.1	120.8
Services: debit	3 200 . .	–53.4	–62.5	–60.0	–68.2	–81.6	–92.5	–88.0	–92.2
Balance on Goods and Services	4 991 . .	*–20.8*	*–40.8*	*–3.9*	*–43.0*	*–42.9*	*–60.5*	*–42.2*	*–37.4*
Income: credit	2 300 . .	8.0	9.7	10.6	8.3	6.7	5.9	2.9	2.8
Income: debit	3 300 . .	–15.7	–19.1	–20.8	–19.1	–22.8	–23.4	–28.2	–28.7
Balance on Goods, Services, and Income	4 992 . .	*–28.5*	*–50.2*	*–14.1*	*–53.8*	*–59.0*	*–78.0*	*–67.5*	*–63.3*
Current transfers: credit	2 379 Y.	29.4	34.5	33.6	32.3	35.4	33.8	34.4	38.3
Current transfers: debit	3 379 . .	–3.6	–3.4	–4.2	–4.3	–5.0	–4.3	–6.9	–5.5
B. Capital Account [1]	4 994 Y.	**. . .**	**. . .**	**. . .**	**. . .**	**. . .**	**. . .**	**. . .**	**. . .**
Capital account: credit	2 994 Y.	. . .	. . .	. . .	. . .	. . .	. . .	. . .	. . .
Capital account: debit	3 994 . .	. . .	. . .	. . .	. . .	. . .	. . .	. . .	. . .
Total, Groups A Plus B	4 010 . .	*–2.6*	*–19.1*	*15.4*	*–25.8*	*–28.6*	*–48.5*	*–40.1*	*–30.4*
C. Financial Account [1]	4 995 X.	**27.3**	**25.5**	**25.1**	**22.2**	**22.4**	**32.8**	**3.6**	**–6.7**
Direct investment abroad	4 505 . .	. . .	. . .	. . .	. . .	. . .	. . .	. . .	. . .
Direct investment in Belize	4 555 Y.	14.0	18.7	17.2	13.6	15.6	9.2	15.4	16.5
Portfolio investment assets	4 602 . .	. . .	. . .	. . .	. . .	. . .	. . .	. . .	. . .
Equity securities	4 610 . .	. . .	. . .	. . .	. . .	. . .	. . .	. . .	. . .
Debt securities	4 619 . .	. . .	. . .	. . .	. . .	. . .	. . .	. . .	. . .
Portfolio investment liabilities	4 652 Y.	. . .	. . .	. . .	. . .	.2	7.0	6.1	3.5
Equity securities	4 660 Y.	. . .	. . .	. . .	. . .	. . .	. . .	. . .	. . .
Debt securities	4 669 Y.	. . .	. . .	. . .	. . .	.2	7.0	6.1	3.5
Other investment assets	4 703 . .	1.8	. . .	. . .	3.0	3.7	–11.6	–17.1	–15.2
Monetary authorities	4 703 .A	. . .	. . .	. . .	. . .	. . .	. . .	. . .	. . .
General government	4 703 .B	.2	. . .	. . .	. . .	. . .	. . .	. . .	. . .
Banks	4 703 .C	1.6	. . .	. . .	3.0	3.7	–11.6	–3.3	–1.7
Other sectors	4 703 .D	. . .	. . .	. . .	. . .	. . .	. . .	–13.8	–13.6
Other investment liabilities	4 753 X.	11.6	6.9	7.9	5.6	3.0	28.2	–.8	–11.5
Monetary authorities	4 753 XA	. . .	. . .	. . .	. . .	. . .	. . .	. . .	. . .
General government	4 753 YB	9.5	11.3	7.9	10.2	6.1	16.3	8.9	–2.6
Banks	4 753 YC	. . .	–9.0	–2.0	2.9	9.1	18.7	–9.3	–12.1
Other sectors	4 753 YD	2.1	4.6	2.1	–7.5	–12.2	–6.8	–.3	3.2
Total, Groups A Through C	4 020 . .	*24.7*	*6.5*	*40.5*	*–3.6*	*–6.2*	*–15.7*	*–36.4*	*–37.1*
D. Net Errors and Omissions	4 998 . .	**–2.9**	**9.1**	**–25.0**	**–12.8**	**6.3**	**1.5**	**32.8**	**41.3**
Total, Groups A Through D	4 030 . .	*21.8*	*15.5*	*15.4*	*–16.4*	*.1*	*–14.2*	*–3.6*	*4.1*
E. Reserves and Related Items	4 040 . .	**–21.8**	**–15.5**	**–15.4**	**16.4**	**–.1**	**14.2**	**3.6**	**–4.1**
Reserve assets	4 800 . .	–18.7	–11.3	–12.5	16.8	–.1	14.2	3.6	–4.1
Use of Fund credit and loans	4 766 . .	–3.0	–4.2	–3.0	–.4	. . .	. . .	. . .	. . .
Liabilities constituting foreign authorities' reserves	4 900 . .	. . .	. . .	. . .	. . .	. . .	. . .	. . .	. . .
Exceptional financing	4 920 . .	. . .	. . .	. . .	. . .	. . .	. . .	. . .	. . .
Conversion rates: Belize dollars per U.S. dollar	0 101 . .	**2.0000**	**2.0000**	**2.0000**	**2.0000**	**2.0000**	**2.0000**	**2.0000**	**2.0000**

[1] Excludes components that have been classified in the categories of Group E.

Table 2. STANDARD PRESENTATION, 1988–95

(Millions of U.S. dollars)

	Code	1988	1989	1990	1991	1992	1993	1994	1995
CURRENT ACCOUNT	4 993 . .	**–2.6**	**–19.1**	**15.4**	**–25.8**	**–28.6**	**–48.5**	**–40.1**	**–30.4**
A. GOODS	4 100 . .	–41.9	–64.1	–59.2	–97.5	–103.9	–118.5	–75.4	–66.1
Credit	2 100 . .	**119.4**	**124.4**	**129.2**	**126.1**	**140.6**	**132.0**	**156.5**	**164.5**
General merchandise: exports f.o.b.	2 110 . .	119.4	124.4	129.2	126.1	140.6	132.0	151.4	162.1
Goods for processing: exports f.o.b.	2 150 . .	...	...	...	...	...	...	...	...
Repairs on goods	2 160 . .	...	...	...	...	...	...	...	...
Goods procured in ports by carriers	2 170 . .	...	...	...	...	...	...	5.0	2.5
Nonmonetary gold	2 180 . .	...	...	...	...	...	...	...	...
Debit	3 100 . .	**–161.3**	**–188.5**	**–188.4**	**–223.6**	**–244.5**	**–250.5**	**–231.9**	**–230.6**
General merchandise: imports f.o.b.	3 110 . .	–161.3	–188.5	–188.4	–223.6	–244.5	–250.5	–231.9	–230.6
Goods for processing: imports f.o.b.	3 150 . .	...	...	...	...	...	...	...	...
Repairs on goods	3 160 . .	...	...	...	...	...	...	...	...
Goods procured in ports by carriers	3 170 . .	...	...	...	...	...	...	...	...
Nonmonetary gold	3 180 . .	...	...	...	...	...	...	...	...
B. SERVICES	4 200 . .	21.1	23.4	55.4	54.5	61.0	58.0	33.2	28.7
Total credit	2 200 . .	*74.5*	*85.9*	*115.4*	*122.7*	*142.6*	*150.5*	*121.1*	*120.8*
Total debit	3 200 . .	*–53.4*	*–62.5*	*–60.0*	*–68.2*	*–81.6*	*–92.5*	*–88.0*	*–92.2*
Transportation services, credit	2 205 . .	**10.2**	**13.5**	**14.6**	**11.4**	**14.1**	**12.5**	**10.3**	**9.1**
Passenger	2 205 BA	...	...	...	...	...	...	...	...
Freight	2 205 BB	...	...	...	...	...	...	...	...
Other	2 205 BC	*10.2*	*13.5*	*14.6*	*11.4*	*14.1*	*12.5*	*10.3*	*9.1*
Sea transport, passenger	2 207 . .	...	...	...	...	...	...	...	...
Sea transport, freight	2 208 . .	...	...	...	...	...	...	...	...
Sea transport, other	2 209 . .	...	...	...	...	...	...	...	...
Air transport, passenger	2 211 . .	...	...	...	...	...	...	...	...
Air transport, freight	2 212 . .	...	...	...	...	...	...	...	...
Air transport, other	2 213 . .	...	...	...	...	...	...	...	...
Other transport, passenger	2 215 . .	...	...	...	...	...	...	...	...
Other transport, freight	2 216 . .	...	...	...	...	...	...	...	...
Other transport, other	2 217 . .	...	...	...	...	...	...	10.3	9.1
Transportation services, debit	3 205 . .	**–24.4**	**–29.3**	**–28.6**	**–33.5**	**–37.1**	**–37.2**	**–37.0**	**–38.1**
Passenger	3 205 BA	*–6.0*	*–7.9*	*–7.5*	*–8.5*	*–9.7*	*–9.2*	*–11.0*	*–12.2*
Freight	3 205 BB	*–18.3*	*–21.3*	*–20.9*	*–24.8*	*–27.2*	*–27.8*	*–26.0*	*–25.9*
Other	3 205 BC	*–.1*	*–.1*	*–.2*	*–.2*	*–.3*	*–.2*	...	...
Sea transport, passenger	3 207 . .	...	...	...	...	...	...	...	...
Sea transport, freight	3 208 . .	...	...	...	...	...	...	...	...
Sea transport, other	3 209 . .	...	...	...	...	...	...	...	...
Air transport, passenger	3 211 . .	...	...	...	...	...	...	...	...
Air transport, freight	3 212 . .	...	...	...	...	...	...	...	...
Air transport, other	3 213 . .	...	...	...	...	...	...	...	...
Other transport, passenger	3 215 . .	...	...	...	...	...	...	...	...
Other transport, freight	3 216 . .	...	...	...	...	...	...	...	...
Other transport, other	3 217 . .	...	...	...	...	...	...	...	...
Travel, credit	2 236 . .	**22.1**	**28.5**	**38.2**	**45.4**	**60.1**	**69.4**	**71.4**	**77.6**
Business travel	2 237 . .	...	...	...	...	...	...	...	...
Personal travel	2 240 . .	...	...	...	...	...	...	71.4	77.6
Travel, debit	3 236 . .	**–6.6**	**–7.6**	**–6.7**	**–7.5**	**–14.3**	**–20.5**	**–18.6**	**–20.8**
Business travel	3 237 . .	...	...	...	...	...	...	–4.1	–2.5
Personal travel	3 240 . .	...	...	...	...	...	...	–14.5	–18.3
Other services, credit	2 200 BA	**42.2**	**43.9**	**62.6**	**65.9**	**68.4**	**68.6**	**39.5**	**34.1**
Communications	2 245 . .	...	...	...	...	...	...	7.4	9.0
Construction	2 249 . .	...	...	...	...	...	...	...	...
Insurance	2 253 . .	...	...	...	...	...	...	1.6	1.3
Financial	2 260 . .	...	...	...	...	...	...	...	...
Computer and information	2 262 . .	...	...	...	...	...	...	...	...
Royalties and licence fees	2 266 . .	2.9	2.9	3.8	.6	...	.1	...	...
Other business services	2 268 . .	15.5	15.8	26.2	32.0	33.7	33.5	18.2	20.8
Personal, cultural, and recreational	2 287 . .	...	...	...	...	...	...	...	...
Government, n.i.e.	2 291 . .	23.9	25.2	32.7	33.3	34.7	35.0	12.3	3.1
Other services, debit	3 200 BA	**–22.4**	**–25.6**	**–24.7**	**–27.2**	**–30.2**	**–34.8**	**–32.3**	**–33.3**
Communications	3 245 . .	...	...	...	...	...	...	–4.1	–4.0
Construction	3 249 . .	...	...	...	...	...	...	...	...
Insurance	3 253 . .	–2.0	–2.4	–2.3	–2.8	–3.0	–3.1	–8.2	–8.3
Financial	3 260 . .	...	...	...	...	...	...	...	...
Computer and information	3 262 . .	...	...	...	...	...	...	...	...
Royalties and licence fees	3 266 . .	–.2	–.2	–.3	–.4	–.3	–.1	–.1	–.1
Other business services	3 268 . .	–8.2	–10.7	–15.9	–14.3	–16.3	–21.5	–18.0	–18.5
Personal, cultural, and recreational	3 287 . .	...	...	...	...	...	...	...	...
Government, n.i.e.	3 291 . .	–12.0	–12.4	–6.3	–9.7	–10.6	–10.1	–2.1	–2.3

Table 2 (Continued). STANDARD PRESENTATION, 1988–95
(Millions of U.S. dollars)

	Code	1988	1989	1990	1991	1992	1993	1994	1995
C. INCOME	4 300 . .	–7.7	–9.4	–10.2	–10.8	–16.1	–17.5	–25.3	–25.9
Total credit	2 300 . .	*8.0*	*9.7*	*10.6*	*8.3*	*6.7*	*5.9*	*2.9*	*2.8*
Total debit	3 300 . .	*–15.7*	*–19.1*	*–20.8*	*–19.1*	*–22.8*	*–23.4*	*–28.2*	*–28.7*
Compensation of employees, credit	2 310 . .	**4.1**	**4.1**	**4.8**	**3.3**	**3.6**	**3.4**	. . .	. . .
Compensation of employees, debit	3 310 . .	**–5.6**	**–5.6**	**–6.5**	**–4.8**	**–4.7**	**–4.7**	**–5.3**	**–5.7**
Investment income, credit	2 320 . .	**4.0**	**5.7**	**5.9**	**5.0**	**3.1**	**2.5**	**2.9**	**2.8**
Direct investment income	2 330 . .	. . .	. . .	. . .	. . .	. . .	. . .	. . .	. . .
Dividends and distributed branch profits	2 332 . .	. . .	. . .	. . .	. . .	. . .	. . .	. . .	. . .
Reinvested earnings and undistributed branch profits	2 333 . .	. . .	. . .	. . .	. . .	. . .	. . .	. . .	. . .
Income on debt (interest)	2 334 . .	. . .	. . .	. . .	. . .	. . .	. . .	. . .	. . .
Portfolio investment income	2 339 . .	. . .	. . .	. . .	. . .	. . .	. . .	. . .	. . .
Income on equity	2 340 . .	. . .	. . .	. . .	. . .	. . .	. . .	. . .	. . .
Income on bonds and notes	2 350 . .	. . .	. . .	. . .	. . .	. . .	. . .	. . .	. . .
Income on money market instruments and financial derivatives	2 360 . .	. . .	. . .	. . .	. . .	. . .	. . .	. . .	. . .
Other investment income	2 370 . .	4.0	5.7	5.9	5.0	3.1	2.5	2.9	2.8
Investment income, debit	3 320 . .	**–10.2**	**–13.6**	**–14.3**	**–14.3**	**–18.1**	**–18.7**	**–22.9**	**–22.9**
Direct investment income	3 330 . .	–4.8	–4.8	–7.5	–8.9	–12.4	–12.4	–13.1	–11.6
Dividends and distributed branch profits	3 332 . .	–3.4	–3.4	–5.9	–6.6	–10.7	–12.4	–10.1	–6.4
Reinvested earnings and undistributed branch profits	3 333 . .	–1.4	–1.4	–1.6	–2.3	–1.7	. . .	–3.0	–5.3
Income on debt (interest)	3 334 . .	. . .	. . .	. . .	. . .	. . .	. . .	. . .	. . .
Portfolio investment income	3 339 . .	. . .	. . .	. . .	. . .	. . .	. . .	. . .	. . .
Income on equity	3 340 . .	. . .	. . .	. . .	. . .	. . .	. . .	. . .	. . .
Income on bonds and notes	3 350 . .	. . .	. . .	. . .	. . .	. . .	. . .	. . .	. . .
Income on money market instruments and financial derivatives	3 360 . .	. . .	. . .	. . .	. . .	. . .	. . .	. . .	. . .
Other investment income	3 370 . .	–5.4	–8.8	–6.9	–5.5	–5.8	–6.4	–9.8	–11.3
D. CURRENT TRANSFERS	4 379 . .	25.9	31.1	29.4	28.0	30.4	29.5	27.5	32.8
Credit	2 379 . .	**29.4**	**34.5**	**33.6**	**32.3**	**35.4**	**33.8**	**34.4**	**38.3**
General government	2 380 . .	11.6	11.4	14.1	14.0	14.3	15.6	15.5	17.8
Other sectors	2 390 . .	17.9	23.1	19.5	18.3	21.1	18.2	18.9	20.5
Workers' remittances	2 391 . .	12.9	17.9	13.7	12.3	16.2	13.1	13.0	13.9
Other current transfers	2 392 . .	5.0	5.2	5.8	6.0	5.0	5.1	5.9	6.6
Debit	3 379 . .	**–3.6**	**–3.4**	**–4.2**	**–4.3**	**–5.0**	**–4.3**	**–6.9**	**–5.5**
General government	3 380 . .	–1.0	–1.0	–1.1	–1.4	–1.5	–1.5	–3.0	–1.8
Other sectors	3 390 . .	–2.6	–2.4	–3.2	–2.9	–3.5	–2.8	–3.9	–3.7
Workers' remittances	3 391 . .	–.5	–.5	–.7	–.9	–1.3	–1.3	–1.3	–1.2
Other current transfers	3 392 . .	–2.2	–1.9	–2.5	–2.0	–2.2	–1.5	–2.6	–2.6
CAPITAL AND FINANCIAL ACCOUNT	4 996 . .	**5.5**	**10.0**	**9.7**	**38.6**	**22.3**	**47.0**	**7.2**	**–10.8**
CAPITAL ACCOUNT	4 994 . .	. . .	. . .	. . .	. . .	. . .	. . .	. . .	. . .
Total credit	2 994 . .	. . .	. . .	. . .	. . .	. . .	. . .	. . .	. . .
Total debit	3 994 . .	. . .	. . .	. . .	. . .	. . .	. . .	. . .	. . .
Capital transfers, credit	2 400 . .	. . .	. . .	. . .	. . .	. . .	. . .	. . .	. . .
General government	2 401 . .	. . .	. . .	. . .	. . .	. . .	. . .	. . .	. . .
Debt forgiveness	2 402 . .	. . .	. . .	. . .	. . .	. . .	. . .	. . .	. . .
Other capital transfers	2 410 . .	. . .	. . .	. . .	. . .	. . .	. . .	. . .	. . .
Other sectors	2 430 . .	. . .	. . .	. . .	. . .	. . .	. . .	. . .	. . .
Migrants' transfers	2 431 . .	. . .	. . .	. . .	. . .	. . .	. . .	. . .	. . .
Debt forgiveness	2 432 . .	. . .	. . .	. . .	. . .	. . .	. . .	. . .	. . .
Other capital transfers	2 440 . .	. . .	. . .	. . .	. . .	. . .	. . .	. . .	. . .
Capital transfers, debit	3 400 . .	. . .	. . .	. . .	. . .	. . .	. . .	. . .	. . .
General government	3 401 . .	. . .	. . .	. . .	. . .	. . .	. . .	. . .	. . .
Debt forgiveness	3 402 . .	. . .	. . .	. . .	. . .	. . .	. . .	. . .	. . .
Other capital transfers	3 410 . .	. . .	. . .	. . .	. . .	. . .	. . .	. . .	. . .
Other sectors	3 430 . .	. . .	. . .	. . .	. . .	. . .	. . .	. . .	. . .
Migrants' transfers	3 431 . .	. . .	. . .	. . .	. . .	. . .	. . .	. . .	. . .
Debt forgiveness	3 432 . .	. . .	. . .	. . .	. . .	. . .	. . .	. . .	. . .
Other capital transfers	3 440 . .	. . .	. . .	. . .	. . .	. . .	. . .	. . .	. . .
Nonproduced nonfinancial assets, credit	2 480 . .	. . .	. . .	. . .	. . .	. . .	. . .	. . .	. . .
Nonproduced nonfinancial assets, debit	3 480 . .	. . .	. . .	. . .	. . .	. . .	. . .	. . .	. . .

Table 2 (Continued). STANDARD PRESENTATION, 1988–95
(Millions of U.S. dollars)

	Code	1988	1989	1990	1991	1992	1993	1994	1995
FINANCIAL ACCOUNT	4 995 . .	**5.5**	**10.0**	**9.7**	**38.6**	**22.3**	**47.0**	**7.2**	**–10.8**
A. DIRECT INVESTMENT	4 500 . .	14.0	18.7	17.2	13.6	15.6	9.2	15.4	16.5
Direct investment abroad	4 505 . .	**. . .**	**. . .**	**. . .**	**. . .**	**. . .**	**. . .**	**. . .**	**. . .**
Equity capital	4 510 . .	. . .	. . .	. . .	. . .	. . .	. . .	. . .	. . .
Claims on affiliated enterprises	4 515 . .	. . .	. . .	. . .	. . .	. . .	. . .	. . .	. . .
Liabilities to affiliated enterprises	4 520 . .	. . .	. . .	. . .	. . .	. . .	. . .	. . .	. . .
Reinvested earnings	4 525 . .	. . .	. . .	. . .	. . .	. . .	. . .	. . .	. . .
Other capital	4 530 . .	. . .	. . .	. . .	. . .	. . .	. . .	. . .	. . .
Claims on affiliated enterprises	4 535 . .	. . .	. . .	. . .	. . .	. . .	. . .	. . .	. . .
Liabilities to affiliated enterprises	4 540 . .	. . .	. . .	. . .	. . .	. . .	. . .	. . .	. . .
Direct investment in Belize	4 555 . .	**14.0**	**18.7**	**17.2**	**13.6**	**15.6**	**9.2**	**15.4**	**16.5**
Equity capital	4 560 . .	12.6	17.3	15.6	11.4	13.9	9.2	5.6	1.3
Claims on direct investors	4 565 . .	. . .	. . .	. . .	. . .	. . .	. . .	. . .	. . .
Liabilities to direct investors	4 570 . .	. . .	. . .	. . .	. . .	. . .	. . .	. . .	. . .
Reinvested earnings	4 575 . .	1.4	1.4	1.6	2.3	1.7	. . .	3.0	5.3
Other capital	4 580 . .	. . .	. . .	. . .	. . .	. . .	. . .	6.8	10.0
Claims on direct investors	4 585 . .	. . .	. . .	. . .	. . .	. . .	. . .	. . .	. . .
Liabilities to direct investors	4 590 . .	. . .	. . .	. . .	. . .	. . .	. . .	. . .	. . .
B. PORTFOLIO INVESTMENT	4 600 . .	. . .	. . .	. . .	. . .	.2	7.0	6.1	3.5
Assets	4 602 . .	**. . .**	**. . .**	**. . .**	**. . .**	**. . .**	**. . .**	**. . .**	**. . .**
Equity securities	4 610 . .	. . .	. . .	. . .	. . .	. . .	. . .	. . .	. . .
Monetary authorities	4 611 . .	. . .	. . .	. . .	. . .	. . .	. . .	. . .	. . .
General government	4 612 . .	. . .	. . .	. . .	. . .	. . .	. . .	. . .	. . .
Banks	4 613 . .	. . .	. . .	. . .	. . .	. . .	. . .	. . .	. . .
Other sectors	4 614 . .	. . .	. . .	. . .	. . .	. . .	. . .	. . .	. . .
Debt securities	4 619 . .	. . .	. . .	. . .	. . .	. . .	. . .	. . .	. . .
Bonds and notes	4 620 . .	. . .	. . .	. . .	. . .	. . .	. . .	. . .	. . .
Monetary authorities	4 621 . .	. . .	. . .	. . .	. . .	. . .	. . .	. . .	. . .
General government	4 622 . .	. . .	. . .	. . .	. . .	. . .	. . .	. . .	. . .
Banks	4 623 . .	. . .	. . .	. . .	. . .	. . .	. . .	. . .	. . .
Other sectors	4 624 . .	. . .	. . .	. . .	. . .	. . .	. . .	. . .	. . .
Money market instruments	4 630 . .	. . .	. . .	. . .	. . .	. . .	. . .	. . .	. . .
Monetary authorities	4 631 . .	. . .	. . .	. . .	. . .	. . .	. . .	. . .	. . .
General government	4 632 . .	. . .	. . .	. . .	. . .	. . .	. . .	. . .	. . .
Banks	4 633 . .	. . .	. . .	. . .	. . .	. . .	. . .	. . .	. . .
Other sectors	4 634 . .	. . .	. . .	. . .	. . .	. . .	. . .	. . .	. . .
Financial derivatives	4 640 . .	. . .	. . .	. . .	. . .	. . .	. . .	. . .	. . .
Monetary authorities	4 641 . .	. . .	. . .	. . .	. . .	. . .	. . .	. . .	. . .
General government	4 642 . .	. . .	. . .	. . .	. . .	. . .	. . .	. . .	. . .
Banks	4 643 . .	. . .	. . .	. . .	. . .	. . .	. . .	. . .	. . .
Other sectors	4 644 . .	. . .	. . .	. . .	. . .	. . .	. . .	. . .	. . .
Liabilities	4 652 . .	**. . .**	**. . .**	**. . .**	**. . .**	**.2**	**7.0**	**6.1**	**3.5**
Equity securities	4 660 . .	. . .	. . .	. . .	. . .	. . .	. . .	. . .	. . .
Banks	4 663 . .	. . .	. . .	. . .	. . .	. . .	. . .	. . .	. . .
Other sectors	4 664 . .	. . .	. . .	. . .	. . .	. . .	. . .	. . .	. . .
Debt securities	4 669 . .	. . .	. . .	. . .	. . .	.2	7.0	6.1	3.5
Bonds and notes	4 670 . .	. . .	. . .	. . .	. . .	.2	7.0	6.1	3.5
Monetary authorities	4 671 . .	. . .	. . .	. . .	. . .	. . .	. . .	. . .	. . .
General government	4 672 . .	. . .	. . .	. . .	. . .	. . .	. . .	. . .	. . .
Banks	4 673 . .	. . .	. . .	. . .	. . .	. . .	. . .	. . .	. . .
Other sectors	4 674 . .	. . .	. . .	. . .	. . .	.2	7.0	6.1	3.5
Money market instruments	4 680 . .	. . .	. . .	. . .	. . .	. . .	. . .	. . .	. . .
Monetary authorities	4 681 . .	. . .	. . .	. . .	. . .	. . .	. . .	. . .	. . .
General government	4 682 . .	. . .	. . .	. . .	. . .	. . .	. . .	. . .	. . .
Banks	4 683 . .	. . .	. . .	. . .	. . .	. . .	. . .	. . .	. . .
Other sectors	4 684 . .	. . .	. . .	. . .	. . .	. . .	. . .	. . .	. . .
Financial derivatives	4 690 . .	. . .	. . .	. . .	. . .	. . .	. . .	. . .	. . .
Monetary authorities	4 691 . .	. . .	. . .	. . .	. . .	. . .	. . .	. . .	. . .
General government	4 692 . .	. . .	. . .	. . .	. . .	. . .	. . .	. . .	. . .
Banks	4 693 . .	. . .	. . .	. . .	. . .	. . .	. . .	. . .	. . .
Other sectors	4 694 . .	. . .	. . .	. . .	. . .	. . .	. . .	. . .	. . .

Table 2 (Concluded). STANDARD PRESENTATION, 1988–95
(Millions of U.S. dollars)

	Code	1988	1989	1990	1991	1992	1993	1994	1995
C. OTHER INVESTMENT	4 700	10.3	2.7	4.9	8.2	6.6	16.6	–17.9	–26.7
Assets	4 703	**1.8**	**. . .**	**. . .**	**3.0**	**3.7**	**–11.6**	**–17.1**	**–15.2**
Trade credits	4 706	. . .	. . .	. . .	. . .	. . .	. . .	. . .	. . .
General government: long-term	4 708	. . .	. . .	. . .	. . .	. . .	. . .	. . .	. . .
General government: short-term	4 709	. . .	. . .	. . .	. . .	. . .	. . .	. . .	. . .
Other sectors: long-term	4 711	. . .	. . .	. . .	. . .	. . .	. . .	. . .	. . .
Other sectors: short-term	4 712	. . .	. . .	. . .	. . .	. . .	. . .	. . .	. . .
Loans	4 714	. . .	. . .	. . .	. . .	. . .	. . .	. . .	. . .
Monetary authorities: long-term	4 717	. . .	. . .	. . .	. . .	. . .	. . .	. . .	. . .
Monetary authorities: short-term	4 718	. . .	. . .	. . .	. . .	. . .	. . .	. . .	. . .
General government: long-term	4 720	. . .	. . .	. . .	. . .	. . .	. . .	. . .	. . .
General government: short-term	4 721	. . .	. . .	. . .	. . .	. . .	. . .	. . .	. . .
Banks: long-term	4 723	. . .	. . .	. . .	. . .	. . .	. . .	. . .	. . .
Banks: short-term	4 724	. . .	. . .	. . .	. . .	. . .	. . .	. . .	. . .
Other sectors: long-term	4 726	. . .	. . .	. . .	. . .	. . .	. . .	. . .	. . .
Other sectors: short-term	4 727	. . .	. . .	. . .	. . .	. . .	. . .	. . .	. . .
Currency and deposits	4 730	1.6	. . .	. . .	3.0	3.7	–11.6	–3.3	–1.7
Monetary authorities	4 731	. . .	. . .	. . .	. . .	. . .	. . .	. . .	. . .
General government	4 732	. . .	. . .	. . .	. . .	. . .	. . .	. . .	. . .
Banks	4 733	1.6	. . .	. . .	3.0	3.7	–11.6	–3.3	–1.7
Other sectors	4 734	. . .	. . .	. . .	. . .	. . .	. . .	. . .	. . .
Other assets	4 736	.2	. . .	. . .	. . .	. . .	. . .	–13.8	–13.6
Monetary authorities: long-term	4 738	. . .	. . .	. . .	. . .	. . .	. . .	. . .	. . .
Monetary authorities: short-term	4 739	. . .	. . .	. . .	. . .	. . .	. . .	. . .	. . .
General government: long-term	4 741	.2	. . .	. . .	. . .	. . .	. . .	. . .	. . .
General government: short-term	4 742	. . .	. . .	. . .	. . .	. . .	. . .	. . .	. . .
Banks: long-term	4 744	. . .	. . .	. . .	. . .	. . .	. . .	. . .	. . .
Banks: short-term	4 745	. . .	. . .	. . .	. . .	. . .	. . .	. . .	. . .
Other sectors: long-term	4 747	. . .	. . .	. . .	. . .	. . .	. . .	–13.8	–13.6
Other sectors: short-term	4 748	. . .	. . .	. . .	. . .	. . .	. . .	. . .	. . .
Liabilities	4 753	**8.5**	**2.7**	**4.9**	**5.2**	**3.0**	**28.2**	**–.8**	**–11.5**
Trade credits	4 756	. . .	. . .	. . .	. . .	. . .	. . .	. . .	. . .
General government: long-term	4 758	. . .	. . .	. . .	. . .	. . .	. . .	. . .	. . .
General government: short-term	4 759	. . .	. . .	. . .	. . .	. . .	. . .	. . .	. . .
Other sectors: long-term	4 761	. . .	. . .	. . .	. . .	. . .	. . .	. . .	. . .
Other sectors: short-term	4 762	. . .	. . .	. . .	. . .	. . .	. . .	. . .	. . .
Loans	4 764	6.4	7.1	11.0	11.5	11.2	18.8	8.5	.6
Use of Fund credit and loans from the Fund	4 766	–3.0	–4.2	–3.0	–.4	. . .	. . .	. . .	. . .
Monetary authorities: other long-term	4 767	. . .	. . .	. . .	. . .	. . .	. . .	. . .	. . .
Monetary authorities: short-term	4 768	. . .	. . .	. . .	. . .	. . .	. . .	. . .	. . .
General government: long-term	4 770	9.5	11.3	8.5	10.3	8.6	16.3	8.9	–2.6
General government: short-term	4 771	. . .	. . .	. . .	. . .	. . .	. . .	. . .	. . .
Banks: long-term	4 773	. . .	. . .	. . .	. . .	. . .	. . .	. . .	. . .
Banks: short-term	4 774	. . .	. . .	. . .	. . .	. . .	. . .	. . .	. . .
Other sectors: long-term	4 776	. . .	. . .	5.5	1.7	2.6	2.5	–.8	1.2
Other sectors: short-term	4 777	. . .	. . .	. . .	. . .	. . .	. . .	.5	2.0
Currency and deposits	4 780	. . .	–9.0	–2.0	2.9	9.1	18.7	–9.3	–12.1
Monetary authorities	4 781	. . .	. . .	. . .	. . .	. . .	. . .	. . .	. . .
General government	4 782	. . .	. . .	. . .	. . .	. . .	. . .	. . .	. . .
Banks	4 783	. . .	–9.0	–2.0	2.9	9.1	18.7	–9.3	–12.1
Other sectors	4 784	. . .	. . .	. . .	. . .	. . .	. . .	. . .	. . .
Other liabilities	4 786	2.1	4.6	–4.1	–9.3	–17.3	–9.3	. . .	. . .
Monetary authorities: long-term	4 788	. . .	. . .	. . .	. . .	. . .	. . .	. . .	. . .
Monetary authorities: short-term	4 789	. . .	. . .	. . .	. . .	. . .	. . .	. . .	. . .
General government: long-term	4 791	. . .	. . .	–.7	. . .	–2.5	. . .	. . .	. . .
General government: short-term	4 792	. . .	. . .	. . .	. . .	. . .	. . .	. . .	. . .
Banks: long-term	4 794	. . .	. . .	. . .	. . .	. . .	. . .	. . .	. . .
Banks: short-term	4 795	. . .	. . .	. . .	. . .	. . .	. . .	. . .	. . .
Other sectors: long-term	4 797	. . .	. . .	–1.2	. . .	. . .	. . .	. . .	. . .
Other sectors: short-term	4 798	2.1	4.6	–2.2	–9.2	–14.8	–9.3	. . .	. . .
D. RESERVE ASSETS	4 800	–18.7	–11.3	–12.5	16.8	–.1	14.2	3.6	–4.1
Monetary gold	4 810	. . .	. . .	. . .	. . .	. . .	. . .	. . .	. . .
Special drawing rights	4 820	.1	. . .	. . .	–.1	–.1	–.2	–.1	–.1
Reserve position in the Fund	4 830	. . .	. . .	. . .	. . .	–1.4	. . .	. . .	. . .
Foreign exchange	4 840	–18.8	–11.4	–12.5	16.9	1.4	14.4	3.7	–4.0
Other claims	4 880	. . .	. . .	. . .	. . .	. . .	. . .	. . .	. . .
NET ERRORS AND OMISSIONS	4 998	**–2.9**	**9.1**	**–25.0**	**–12.8**	**6.3**	**1.5**	**32.8**	**41.3**

Part 3 of the *Yearbook* contains descriptions of the methodologies, compilation practices, and sources used to compile these data.

Table 1. ANALYTIC PRESENTATION, 1988–95
(Millions of U.S. dollars)

	Code	1988	1989	1990	1991	1992	1993	1994	1995
A. Current Account[1]	4 993 Y.	**–52.0**	**81.5**	**18.7**	**–6.7**	**–39.2**	**–14.1**	**36.4**	...
Goods: exports f.o.b	2 100 . .	376.4	214.7	287.2	336.8	371.4	341.1	301.0	...
Goods: imports f.o.b	3 100 . .	–507.6	–316.6	–427.9	–482.4	–560.6	–538.9	–365.8	...
Balance on Goods	4 100 . .	*–131.3*	*–101.9*	*–140.7*	*–145.7*	*–189.2*	*–197.8*	*–64.8*	...
Services: credit	2 200 . .	99.4	87.8	114.6	122.6	142.8	137.4	103.9	...
Services: debit	3 200 . .	–149.4	–111.6	–135.2	–138.6	–158.7	–152.6	–111.1	...
Balance on Goods and Services	4 991 . .	*–181.3*	*–125.7*	*–161.2*	*–161.6*	*–205.1*	*–213.0*	*–72.0*	...
Income: credit	2 300 . .	...	...	...	...	...	...	...	...
Income: debit	3 300 . .	–24.8	–38.2	–38.9	–30.8	–61.6	–39.9	–40.5	...
Balance on Goods, Services, and Income	4 992 . .	*–206.1*	*–163.9*	*–200.2*	*–192.5*	*–266.7*	*–252.9*	*–112.6*	...
Current transfers: credit	2 379 Y.	160.8	252.7	231.4	199.6	244.1	257.8	159.6	...
Current transfers: debit	3 379 . .	–6.7	–7.2	–12.5	–13.8	–16.6	–19.1	–10.6	...
B. Capital Account[1]	4 994 Y.	...	...	...	...	...	...	...	...
Capital account: credit	2 994 Y.	...	...	...	...	...	...	...	...
Capital account: debit	3 994 . .	...	...	...	...	...	...	...	...
Total, Groups A Plus B	4 010 . .	*–52.0*	*81.5*	*18.7*	*–6.7*	*–39.2*	*–14.1*	*36.4*	...
C. Financial Account[1]	4 995 X.	**–25.2**	**2.8**	**54.3**	**47.0**	**–39.9**	**30.4**	**–34.4**	...
Direct investment abroad	4 505 . .	...	...	...	...	...	...	...	...
Direct investment in Benin	4 555 Y.	...	...	...	...	...	...	...	...
Portfolio investment assets	4 602 . .	...	...	...	...	...	...	...	...
Equity securities	4 610 . .	...	...	...	...	...	...	...	...
Debt securities	4 619 . .	...	...	...	...	...	...	...	...
Portfolio investment liabilities	4 652 Y.	...	...	...	...	...	...	...	...
Equity securities	4 660 Y.	...	...	...	...	...	...	...	...
Debt securities	4 669 Y.	...	...	...	...	...	...	...	...
Other investment assets	4 703 . .	–49.4	7.5	–11.0	–26.6	–21.9	–4.9	–70.8	...
Monetary authorities	4 703 . A	...	...	...	...	...	...	...	...
General government	4 703 . B	...	...	...	...	...	...	...	...
Banks	4 703 . C	–49.4	7.5	–11.0	–26.6	–21.9	–4.9	–70.8	...
Other sectors	4 703 . D	...	...	...	...	...	...	...	...
Other investment liabilities	4 753 X.	24.2	–4.7	65.3	73.6	–18.0	35.4	36.4	...
Monetary authorities	4 753 XA	...	...	...	...	...	...	...	...
General government	4 753 YB	22.8	–4.7	64.3	74.1	–45.0	45.6	28.8	...
Banks	4 753 YC	...	–1.3	–.8	–4.0	.5	–3.1	...	...
Other sectors	4 753 YD	1.3	1.3	1.8	3.5	26.4	–7.1	7.6	...
Total, Groups A Through C	4 020 . .	*–77.2*	*84.3*	*73.1*	*40.3*	*–79.1*	*16.3*	*2.0*	...
D. Net Errors and Omissions	4 998 . .	**12.3**	**–150.2**	**–63.1**	**21.6**	**1.6**	**–56.4**	**54.0**	...
Total, Groups A Through D	4 030 . .	*–64.9*	*–65.9*	*10.0*	*61.9*	*–77.5*	*–40.1*	*56.0*	...
E. Reserves and Related Items	4 040 . .	**64.9**	**65.9**	**–10.0**	**–61.9**	**77.5**	**40.1**	**–56.0**	...
Reserve assets	4 800 . .	–.9	.7	–57.6	–116.5	–67.5	–15.3	–117.7	...
Use of Fund credit and loans	4 766 . .	–3.1	5.9	–1.9	12.5	...	21.9	24.9	...
Liabilities constituting foreign authorities' reserves	4 900 . .	...	...	...	...	...	...	...	...
Exceptional financing	4 920 . .	68.8	59.2	49.6	42.2	145.1	33.5	36.7	...
Conversion rates: CFA francs per U.S. dollar	0 101 . .	**297.85**	**319.01**	**272.26**	**282.11**	**264.69**	**283.16**	**555.20**	**499.15**

[1] Excludes components that have been classified in the categories of Group E.

Table 2. STANDARD PRESENTATION, 1988–95
(Millions of U.S. dollars)

	Code	1988	1989	1990	1991	1992	1993	1994	1995
CURRENT ACCOUNT	4 993 . .	**–52.0**	**81.5**	**18.7**	**–6.7**	**–39.2**	**–14.1**	**36.4**	. . .
A. GOODS	4 100 . .	–131.3	–101.9	–140.7	–145.7	–189.2	–197.8	–64.8	. . .
Credit	2 100 . .	**376.4**	**214.7**	**287.2**	**336.8**	**371.4**	**341.1**	**301.0**	. . .
General merchandise: exports f.o.b.	2 110 . .	376.4	214.7	287.2	336.8	371.4	341.1	301.0	. . .
Goods for processing: exports f.o.b.	2 150 . .	. . .	. . .	. . .	. . .	. . .	. . .	. . .	. . .
Repairs on goods	2 160 . .	. . .	. . .	. . .	. . .	. . .	. . .	. . .	. . .
Goods procured in ports by carriers	2 170 . .	. . .	. . .	. . .	. . .	. . .	. . .	. . .	. . .
Nonmonetary gold	2 180 . .	. . .	. . .	. . .	. . .	. . .	. . .	. . .	. . .
Debit	3 100 . .	**–507.6**	**–316.6**	**–427.9**	**–482.4**	**–560.6**	**–538.9**	**–365.8**	. . .
General merchandise: imports f.o.b.	3 110 . .	–507.6	–316.6	–427.9	–482.4	–560.6	–538.9	–365.8	. . .
Goods for processing: imports f.o.b.	3 150 . .	. . .	. . .	. . .	. . .	. . .	. . .	. . .	. . .
Repairs on goods	3 160 . .	. . .	. . .	. . .	. . .	. . .	. . .	. . .	. . .
Goods procured in ports by carriers	3 170 . .	. . .	. . .	. . .	. . .	. . .	. . .	. . .	. . .
Nonmonetary gold	3 180 . .	. . .	. . .	. . .	. . .	. . .	. . .	. . .	. . .
B. SERVICES	4 200 . .	–50.0	–23.8	–20.6	–16.0	–15.9	–15.2	–7.2	. . .
Total credit	2 200 . .	*99.4*	*87.8*	*114.6*	*122.6*	*142.8*	*137.4*	*103.9*	. . .
Total debit	3 200 . .	*–149.4*	*–111.6*	*–135.2*	*–138.6*	*–158.7*	*–152.6*	*–111.1*	. . .
Transportation services, credit	2 205 . .	**57.4**	**48.6**	**65.0**	**71.2**	**84.2**	**79.1**	**59.1**	. . .
Passenger	2 205 BA	. . .	. . .	. . .	. . .	. . .	. . .	. . .	. . .
Freight	2 205 BB	*11.4*	*10.7*	*9.5*	*12.4*	*14.4*	*13.8*	*12.1*	. . .
Other	2 205 BC	*46.0*	*37.9*	*55.5*	*58.8*	*69.9*	*65.3*	*47.0*	. . .
Sea transport, passenger	2 207 . .	. . .	. . .	. . .	. . .	. . .	. . .	. . .	. . .
Sea transport, freight	2 208 . .	. . .	. . .	. . .	. . .	. . .	. . .	. . .	. . .
Sea transport, other	2 209 . .	. . .	. . .	. . .	. . .	. . .	. . .	. . .	. . .
Air transport, passenger	2 211 . .	. . .	. . .	. . .	. . .	. . .	. . .	. . .	. . .
Air transport, freight	2 212 . .	. . .	. . .	. . .	. . .	. . .	. . .	. . .	. . .
Air transport, other	2 213 . .	. . .	. . .	. . .	. . .	. . .	. . .	. . .	. . .
Other transport, passenger	2 215 . .	. . .	. . .	. . .	. . .	. . .	. . .	. . .	. . .
Other transport, freight	2 216 . .	. . .	. . .	. . .	. . .	. . .	. . .	. . .	. . .
Other transport, other	2 217 . .	. . .	. . .	. . .	. . .	. . .	. . .	. . .	. . .
Transportation services, debit	3 205 . .	**–102.8**	**–70.9**	**–86.5**	**–90.7**	**–104.2**	**–101.0**	**–73.1**	. . .
Passenger	3 205 BA	. . .	. . .	. . .	. . .	. . .	. . .	. . .	. . .
Freight	3 205 BB	*–80.7*	*–50.2*	*–68.1*	*–76.6*	*–89.1*	*–85.5*	*–58.2*	. . .
Other	3 205 BC	*–22.2*	*–20.7*	*–18.4*	*–14.2*	*–15.1*	*–15.5*	*–14.9*	. . .
Sea transport, passenger	3 207 . .	. . .	. . .	. . .	. . .	. . .	. . .	. . .	. . .
Sea transport, freight	3 208 . .	. . .	. . .	. . .	. . .	. . .	. . .	. . .	. . .
Sea transport, other	3 209 . .	. . .	. . .	. . .	. . .	. . .	. . .	. . .	. . .
Air transport, passenger	3 211 . .	. . .	. . .	. . .	. . .	. . .	. . .	. . .	. . .
Air transport, freight	3 212 . .	. . .	. . .	. . .	. . .	. . .	. . .	. . .	. . .
Air transport, other	3 213 . .	. . .	. . .	. . .	. . .	. . .	. . .	. . .	. . .
Other transport, passenger	3 215 . .	. . .	. . .	. . .	. . .	. . .	. . .	. . .	. . .
Other transport, freight	3 216 . .	. . .	. . .	. . .	. . .	. . .	. . .	. . .	. . .
Other transport, other	3 217 . .	. . .	. . .	. . .	. . .	. . .	. . .	. . .	. . .
Travel, credit	2 236 . .	**21.8**	**20.4**	**27.5**	**29.4**	**35.1**	**36.4**	**23.4**	. . .
Business travel	2 237 . .	. . .	. . .	. . .	. . .	. . .	. . .	. . .	. . .
Personal travel	2 240 . .	. . .	. . .	. . .	. . .	. . .	. . .	. . .	. . .
Travel, debit	3 236 . .	**–10.7**	**–10.0**	**–11.8**	**–10.3**	**–12.1**	**–11.7**	**–5.9**	. . .
Business travel	3 237 . .	. . .	. . .	. . .	. . .	. . .	. . .	. . .	. . .
Personal travel	3 240 . .	. . .	. . .	. . .	. . .	. . .	. . .	. . .	. . .
Other services, credit	2 200 BA	**20.1**	**18.8**	**22.0**	**22.0**	**23.4**	**21.9**	**21.4**	. . .
Communications	2 245 . .	. . .	. . .	. . .	. . .	. . .	. . .	. . .	. . .
Construction	2 249 . .	. . .	. . .	. . .	. . .	. . .	. . .	. . .	. . .
Insurance	2 253 . .	. . .	. . .	. . .	. . .	. . .	. . .	. . .	. . .
Financial	2 260 . .	. . .	. . .	. . .	. . .	. . .	. . .	. . .	. . .
Computer and information	2 262 . .	. . .	. . .	. . .	. . .	. . .	. . .	. . .	. . .
Royalties and licence fees	2 266 . .	. . .	. . .	. . .	. . .	. . .	. . .	. . .	. . .
Other business services	2 268 . .	3.4	3.1	3.7	3.9	3.8	3.5	3.6	. . .
Personal, cultural, and recreational	2 287 . .	. . .	. . .	. . .	. . .	. . .	. . .	. . .	. . .
Government, n.i.e.	2 291 . .	16.8	15.7	18.4	18.1	19.6	18.4	17.8	. . .
Other services, debit	3 200 BA	**–35.8**	**–30.7**	**–36.9**	**–37.6**	**–42.4**	**–39.9**	**–32.0**	. . .
Communications	3 245 . .	. . .	. . .	. . .	. . .	. . .	. . .	. . .	. . .
Construction	3 249 . .	. . .	. . .	. . .	. . .	. . .	. . .	. . .	. . .
Insurance	3 253 . .	–9.0	–5.6	–7.6	–8.5	–9.9	–9.5	–6.5	. . .
Financial	3 260 . .	. . .	. . .	. . .	. . .	. . .	. . .	. . .	. . .
Computer and information	3 262 . .	. . .	. . .	. . .	. . .	. . .	. . .	. . .	. . .
Royalties and licence fees	3 266 . .	. . .	. . .	. . .	. . .	. . .	. . .	. . .	. . .
Other business services	3 268 . .	–13.4	–12.5	–14.7	–14.9	–17.0	–15.9	–11.2	. . .
Personal, cultural, and recreational	3 287 . .	. . .	. . .	. . .	. . .	. . .	. . .	. . .	. . .
Government, n.i.e.	3 291 . .	–13.4	–12.5	–14.7	–14.2	–15.5	–14.5	–14.4	. . .

Table 2 (Continued). STANDARD PRESENTATION, 1988–95
(Millions of U.S. dollars)

	Code	1988	1989	1990	1991	1992	1993	1994	1995
C. INCOME	4 300 . .	–24.8	–38.2	–38.9	–30.8	–61.6	–39.9	–40.5	. . .
Total credit	2 300 . .	. . .	. . .	. . .	. . .	. . .	. . .	. . .	. . .
Total debit	3 300 . .	*–24.8*	*–38.2*	*–38.9*	*–30.8*	*–61.6*	*–39.9*	*–40.5*	. . .
Compensation of employees, credit	2 310 . .	**. . .**	**. . .**	**. . .**	**. . .**	**. . .**	**. . .**	**. . .**	**. . .**
Compensation of employees, debit	3 310 . .	**. . .**	**. . .**	**. . .**	**. . .**	**. . .**	**. . .**	**. . .**	**. . .**
Investment income, credit	2 320 . .	**. . .**	**. . .**	**. . .**	**. . .**	**. . .**	**. . .**	**. . .**	**. . .**
Direct investment income	2 330 . .	. . .	. . .	. . .	. . .	. . .	. . .	. . .	. . .
Dividends and distributed branch profits	2 332 . .	. . .	. . .	. . .	. . .	. . .	. . .	. . .	. . .
Reinvested earnings and undistributed branch profits	2 333 . .	. . .	. . .	. . .	. . .	. . .	. . .	. . .	. . .
Income on debt (interest)	2 334 . .	. . .	. . .	. . .	. . .	. . .	. . .	. . .	. . .
Portfolio investment income	2 339 . .	. . .	. . .	. . .	. . .	. . .	. . .	. . .	. . .
Income on equity	2 340 . .	. . .	. . .	. . .	. . .	. . .	. . .	. . .	. . .
Income on bonds and notes	2 350 . .	. . .	. . .	. . .	. . .	. . .	. . .	. . .	. . .
Income on money market instruments and financial derivatives	2 360 . .	. . .	. . .	. . .	. . .	. . .	. . .	. . .	. . .
Other investment income	2 370 . .	. . .	. . .	. . .	. . .	. . .	. . .	. . .	. . .
Investment income, debit	3 320 . .	**–24.8**	**–38.2**	**–38.9**	**–30.8**	**–61.6**	**–39.9**	**–40.5**	**. . .**
Direct investment income	3 330 . .	. . .	. . .	. . .	. . .	. . .	. . .	. . .	. . .
Dividends and distributed branch profits	3 332 . .	. . .	. . .	. . .	. . .	. . .	. . .	. . .	. . .
Reinvested earnings and undistributed branch profits	3 333 . .	. . .	. . .	. . .	. . .	. . .	. . .	. . .	. . .
Income on debt (interest)	3 334 . .	. . .	. . .	. . .	. . .	. . .	. . .	. . .	. . .
Portfolio investment income	3 339 . .	. . .	. . .	. . .	. . .	. . .	. . .	. . .	. . .
Income on equity	3 340 . .	. . .	. . .	. . .	. . .	. . .	. . .	. . .	. . .
Income on bonds and notes	3 350 . .	. . .	. . .	. . .	. . .	. . .	. . .	. . .	. . .
Income on money market instruments and financial derivatives	3 360 . .	. . .	. . .	. . .	. . .	. . .	. . .	. . .	. . .
Other investment income	3 370 . .	–24.8	–38.2	–38.9	–30.8	–61.6	–39.9	–40.5	. . .
D. CURRENT TRANSFERS	4 379 . .	154.1	245.4	218.9	185.7	227.4	238.7	149.0	. . .
Credit	2 379 . .	**160.8**	**252.7**	**231.4**	**199.6**	**244.1**	**257.8**	**159.6**	**. . .**
General government	2 380 . .	75.9	168.3	134.1	103.5	135.3	147.3	87.0	. . .
Other sectors	2 390 . .	84.9	84.3	97.3	96.1	108.8	110.5	72.6	. . .
Workers' remittances	2 391 . .	61.4	84.3	97.3	96.1	108.8	110.5	72.6	. . .
Other current transfers	2 392 . .	23.5	. . .	. . .	. . .	. . .	. . .	. . .	. . .
Debit	3 379 . .	**–6.7**	**–7.2**	**–12.5**	**–13.8**	**–16.6**	**–19.1**	**–10.6**	**. . .**
General government	3 380 . .	–3.4	–1.3	–1.5	–1.8	–3.0	–2.8	–2.9	. . .
Other sectors	3 390 . .	–3.4	–6.0	–11.0	–12.1	–13.6	–16.2	–7.7	. . .
Workers' remittances	3 391 . .	–3.4	–6.0	–11.0	–12.1	–13.6	–16.2	–7.7	. . .
Other current transfers	3 392 . .	. . .	. . .	. . .	. . .	. . .	. . .	. . .	. . .
CAPITAL AND FINANCIAL ACCOUNT	4 996 . .	**39.7**	**68.7**	**44.4**	**–14.8**	**37.7**	**70.5**	**–90.4**	**. . .**
CAPITAL ACCOUNT	4 994 . .	**. . .**	**. . .**	**. . .**	**. . .**	**. . .**	**. . .**	**1.1**	**. . .**
Total credit	2 994 . .	. . .	. . .	. . .	. . .	. . .	. . .	*1.1*	. . .
Total debit	3 994 . .	. . .	. . .	. . .	. . .	. . .	. . .	. . .	. . .
Capital transfers, credit	2 400 . .	**. . .**	**. . .**	**. . .**	**. . .**	**. . .**	**. . .**	**1.1**	**. . .**
General government	2 401 . .	. . .	. . .	. . .	. . .	. . .	. . .	1.1	. . .
Debt forgiveness	2 402 . .	. . .	. . .	. . .	. . .	. . .	. . .	1.1	. . .
Other capital transfers	2 410 . .	. . .	. . .	. . .	. . .	. . .	. . .	. . .	. . .
Other sectors	2 430 . .	. . .	. . .	. . .	. . .	. . .	. . .	. . .	. . .
Migrants' transfers	2 431 . .	. . .	. . .	. . .	. . .	. . .	. . .	. . .	. . .
Debt forgiveness	2 432 . .	. . .	. . .	. . .	. . .	. . .	. . .	. . .	. . .
Other capital transfers	2 440 . .	. . .	. . .	. . .	. . .	. . .	. . .	. . .	. . .
Capital transfers, debit	3 400 . .	**. . .**	**. . .**	**. . .**	**. . .**	**. . .**	**. . .**	**. . .**	**. . .**
General government	3 401 . .	. . .	. . .	. . .	. . .	. . .	. . .	. . .	. . .
Debt forgiveness	3 402 . .	. . .	. . .	. . .	. . .	. . .	. . .	. . .	. . .
Other capital transfers	3 410 . .	. . .	. . .	. . .	. . .	. . .	. . .	. . .	. . .
Other sectors	3 430 . .	. . .	. . .	. . .	. . .	. . .	. . .	. . .	. . .
Migrants' transfers	3 431 . .	. . .	. . .	. . .	. . .	. . .	. . .	. . .	. . .
Debt forgiveness	3 432 . .	. . .	. . .	. . .	. . .	. . .	. . .	. . .	. . .
Other capital transfers	3 440 . .	. . .	. . .	. . .	. . .	. . .	. . .	. . .	. . .
Nonproduced nonfinancial assets, credit	2 480 . .	**. . .**	**. . .**	**. . .**	**. . .**	**. . .**	**. . .**	**. . .**	**. . .**
Nonproduced nonfinancial assets, debit	3 480 . .	**. . .**	**. . .**	**. . .**	**. . .**	**. . .**	**. . .**	**. . .**	**. . .**

Table 2 (Continued). STANDARD PRESENTATION, 1988–95
(Millions of U.S. dollars)

	Code		1988	1989	1990	1991	1992	1993	1994	1995
FINANCIAL ACCOUNT	4 995	. .	**39.7**	**68.7**	**44.4**	**–14.8**	**37.7**	**70.5**	**–91.5**	**. . .**
A. DIRECT INVESTMENT	4 500	. .	. . .	. . .	. . .	. . .	. . .	. . .	. . .	. . .
Direct investment abroad	4 505	. .	**. . .**	**. . .**	**. . .**	**. . .**	**. . .**	**. . .**	**. . .**	**. . .**
Equity capital	4 510	. .	. . .	. . .	. . .	. . .	. . .	. . .	. . .	. . .
Claims on affiliated enterprises	4 515	. .	. . .	. . .	. . .	. . .	. . .	. . .	. . .	. . .
Liabilities to affiliated enterprises	4 520	. .	. . .	. . .	. . .	. . .	. . .	. . .	. . .	. . .
Reinvested earnings	4 525	. .	. . .	. . .	. . .	. . .	. . .	. . .	. . .	. . .
Other capital	4 530	. .	. . .	. . .	. . .	. . .	. . .	. . .	. . .	. . .
Claims on affiliated enterprises	4 535	. .	. . .	. . .	. . .	. . .	. . .	. . .	. . .	. . .
Liabilities to affiliated enterprises	4 540	. .	. . .	. . .	. . .	. . .	. . .	. . .	. . .	. . .
Direct investment in Benin	4 555	. .	**. . .**	**. . .**	**. . .**	**. . .**	**. . .**	**. . .**	**. . .**	**. . .**
Equity capital	4 560	. .	. . .	. . .	. . .	. . .	. . .	. . .	. . .	. . .
Claims on direct investors	4 565	. .	. . .	. . .	. . .	. . .	. . .	. . .	. . .	. . .
Liabilities to direct investors	4 570	. .	. . .	. . .	. . .	. . .	. . .	. . .	. . .	. . .
Reinvested earnings	4 575	. .	. . .	. . .	. . .	. . .	. . .	. . .	. . .	. . .
Other capital	4 580	. .	. . .	. . .	. . .	. . .	. . .	. . .	. . .	. . .
Claims on direct investors	4 585	. .	. . .	. . .	. . .	. . .	. . .	. . .	. . .	. . .
Liabilities to direct investors	4 590	. .	. . .	. . .	. . .	. . .	. . .	. . .	. . .	. . .
B. PORTFOLIO INVESTMENT	4 600	. .	. . .	. . .	. . .	. . .	. . .	. . .	. . .	. . .
Assets	4 602	. .	**. . .**	**. . .**	**. . .**	**. . .**	**. . .**	**. . .**	**. . .**	**. . .**
Equity securities	4 610	. .	. . .	. . .	. . .	. . .	. . .	. . .	. . .	. . .
Monetary authorities	4 611	. .	. . .	. . .	. . .	. . .	. . .	. . .	. . .	. . .
General government	4 612	. .	. . .	. . .	. . .	. . .	. . .	. . .	. . .	. . .
Banks	4 613	. .	. . .	. . .	. . .	. . .	. . .	. . .	. . .	. . .
Other sectors	4 614	. .	. . .	. . .	. . .	. . .	. . .	. . .	. . .	. . .
Debt securities	4 619	. .	. . .	. . .	. . .	. . .	. . .	. . .	. . .	. . .
Bonds and notes	4 620	. .	. . .	. . .	. . .	. . .	. . .	. . .	. . .	. . .
Monetary authorities	4 621	. .	. . .	. . .	. . .	. . .	. . .	. . .	. . .	. . .
General government	4 622	. .	. . .	. . .	. . .	. . .	. . .	. . .	. . .	. . .
Banks	4 623	. .	. . .	. . .	. . .	. . .	. . .	. . .	. . .	. . .
Other sectors	4 624	. .	. . .	. . .	. . .	. . .	. . .	. . .	. . .	. . .
Money market instruments	4 630	. .	. . .	. . .	. . .	. . .	. . .	. . .	. . .	. . .
Monetary authorities	4 631	. .	. . .	. . .	. . .	. . .	. . .	. . .	. . .	. . .
General government	4 632	. .	. . .	. . .	. . .	. . .	. . .	. . .	. . .	. . .
Banks	4 633	. .	. . .	. . .	. . .	. . .	. . .	. . .	. . .	. . .
Other sectors	4 634	. .	. . .	. . .	. . .	. . .	. . .	. . .	. . .	. . .
Financial derivatives	4 640	. .	. . .	. . .	. . .	. . .	. . .	. . .	. . .	. . .
Monetary authorities	4 641	. .	. . .	. . .	. . .	. . .	. . .	. . .	. . .	. . .
General government	4 642	. .	. . .	. . .	. . .	. . .	. . .	. . .	. . .	. . .
Banks	4 643	. .	. . .	. . .	. . .	. . .	. . .	. . .	. . .	. . .
Other sectors	4 644	. .	. . .	. . .	. . .	. . .	. . .	. . .	. . .	. . .
Liabilities	4 652	. .	**. . .**	**. . .**	**. . .**	**. . .**	**. . .**	**. . .**	**. . .**	**. . .**
Equity securities	4 660	. .	. . .	. . .	. . .	. . .	. . .	. . .	. . .	. . .
Banks	4 663	. .	. . .	. . .	. . .	. . .	. . .	. . .	. . .	. . .
Other sectors	4 664	. .	. . .	. . .	. . .	. . .	. . .	. . .	. . .	. . .
Debt securities	4 669	. .	. . .	. . .	. . .	. . .	. . .	. . .	. . .	. . .
Bonds and notes	4 670	. .	. . .	. . .	. . .	. . .	. . .	. . .	. . .	. . .
Monetary authorities	4 671	. .	. . .	. . .	. . .	. . .	. . .	. . .	. . .	. . .
General government	4 672	. .	. . .	. . .	. . .	. . .	. . .	. . .	. . .	. . .
Banks	4 673	. .	. . .	. . .	. . .	. . .	. . .	. . .	. . .	. . .
Other sectors	4 674	. .	. . .	. . .	. . .	. . .	. . .	. . .	. . .	. . .
Money market instruments	4 680	. .	. . .	. . .	. . .	. . .	. . .	. . .	. . .	. . .
Monetary authorities	4 681	. .	. . .	. . .	. . .	. . .	. . .	. . .	. . .	. . .
General government	4 682	. .	. . .	. . .	. . .	. . .	. . .	. . .	. . .	. . .
Banks	4 683	. .	. . .	. . .	. . .	. . .	. . .	. . .	. . .	. . .
Other sectors	4 684	. .	. . .	. . .	. . .	. . .	. . .	. . .	. . .	. . .
Financial derivatives	4 690	. .	. . .	. . .	. . .	. . .	. . .	. . .	. . .	. . .
Monetary authorities	4 691	. .	. . .	. . .	. . .	. . .	. . .	. . .	. . .	. . .
General government	4 692	. .	. . .	. . .	. . .	. . .	. . .	. . .	. . .	. . .
Banks	4 693	. .	. . .	. . .	. . .	. . .	. . .	. . .	. . .	. . .
Other sectors	4 694	. .	. . .	. . .	. . .	. . .	. . .	. . .	. . .	. . .

Table 2 (Concluded). STANDARD PRESENTATION, 1988–95
(Millions of U.S. dollars)

	Code	1988	1989	1990	1991	1992	1993	1994	1995
C. OTHER INVESTMENT	4 700	40.6	67.9	102.0	101.7	105.2	85.9	26.2	...
Assets	4 703	**–49.4**	**7.5**	**–11.0**	**–26.6**	**–21.9**	**–4.9**	**–70.8**	**...**
Trade credits	4 706	...	...	...	...	...	...	...	...
General government: long-term	4 708	...	...	...	...	...	...	...	...
General government: short-term	4 709	...	...	...	...	...	...	...	...
Other sectors: long-term	4 711	...	...	...	...	...	...	...	...
Other sectors: short-term	4 712	...	...	...	...	...	...	...	...
Loans	4 714	...	...	...	...	...	...	...	...
Monetary authorities: long-term	4 717	...	...	...	...	...	...	...	...
Monetary authorities: short-term	4 718	...	...	...	...	...	...	...	...
General government: long-term	4 720	...	...	...	...	...	...	...	...
General government: short-term	4 721	...	...	...	...	...	...	...	...
Banks: long-term	4 723	...	...	...	...	...	...	...	...
Banks: short-term	4 724	...	...	...	...	...	...	...	...
Other sectors: long-term	4 726	...	...	...	...	...	...	...	...
Other sectors: short-term	4 727	...	...	...	...	...	...	...	...
Currency and deposits	4 730	–49.4	7.5	–11.0	–26.6	–21.9	–4.9	–70.8	...
Monetary authorities	4 731	...	...	...	...	...	...	...	...
General government	4 732	...	...	...	...	...	...	...	...
Banks	4 733	–49.4	7.5	–11.0	–26.6	–21.9	–4.9	–70.8	...
Other sectors	4 734	...	...	...	...	...	...	...	...
Other assets	4 736	...	...	...	...	...	...	...	...
Monetary authorities: long-term	4 738	...	...	...	...	...	...	...	...
Monetary authorities: short-term	4 739	...	...	...	...	...	...	...	...
General government: long-term	4 741	...	...	...	...	...	...	...	...
General government: short-term	4 742	...	...	...	...	...	...	...	...
Banks: long-term	4 744	...	...	...	...	...	...	...	...
Banks: short-term	4 745	...	...	...	...	...	...	...	...
Other sectors: long-term	4 747	...	...	...	...	...	...	...	...
Other sectors: short-term	4 748	...	...	...	...	...	...	...	...
Liabilities	4 753	**89.9**	**60.4**	**113.0**	**128.3**	**127.1**	**90.8**	**97.0**	**...**
Trade credits	4 756	...	...	...	...	...	...	...	...
General government: long-term	4 758	...	...	...	...	...	...	...	...
General government: short-term	4 759	...	...	...	...	...	...	...	...
Other sectors: long-term	4 761	...	...	...	...	...	...	...	...
Other sectors: short-term	4 762	...	...	...	...	...	...	...	...
Loans	4 764	25.8	314.0	85.9	183.0	126.6	88.3	102.9	...
Use of Fund credit and loans from the Fund	4 766	–3.1	5.9	–1.9	12.5	...	21.9	24.9	...
Monetary authorities: other long-term	4 767	...	...	...	...	...	...	...	...
Monetary authorities: short-term	4 768	...	...	...	...	...	...	...	...
General government: long-term	4 770	27.5	306.9	85.9	167.0	100.1	73.5	70.4	...
General government: short-term	4 771	...	...	...	...	...	...	...	...
Banks: long-term	4 773	...	...	...	...	...	...	...	...
Banks: short-term	4 774	...	...	...	...	...	...	...	...
Other sectors: long-term	4 776	1.3	1.3	1.8	3.5	26.4	–7.1	7.6	...
Other sectors: short-term	4 777	...	...	...	...	...	...	...	...
Currency and deposits	4 780	...	–1.3	–.8	–4.0	.5	–3.1	...	...
Monetary authorities	4 781	...	...	...	...	...	...	...	...
General government	4 782	...	...	...	...	...	...	...	...
Banks	4 783	...	–1.3	–.8	–4.0	.5	–3.1	...	...
Other sectors	4 784	...	...	...	...	...	...	...	...
Other liabilities	4 786	64.1	–252.3	27.9	–50.7	...	5.7	–5.9	...
Monetary authorities: long-term	4 788	...	...	...	...	...	...	...	...
Monetary authorities: short-term	4 789	64.1	–252.3	27.9	–50.7	...	5.7	–5.9	...
General government: long-term	4 791	...	...	...	...	...	...	...	...
General government: short-term	4 792	...	...	...	...	...	...	...	...
Banks: long-term	4 794	...	...	...	...	...	...	...	...
Banks: short-term	4 795	...	...	...	...	...	...	...	...
Other sectors: long-term	4 797	...	...	...	...	...	...	...	...
Other sectors: short-term	4 798	...	...	...	...	...	...	...	...
D. RESERVE ASSETS	4 800	–.9	.7	–57.6	–116.5	–67.5	–15.3	–117.7	...
Monetary gold	4 810	...	...	...	...	...	...	...	...
Special drawing rights	4 820	...	.1	...	–.1	.2	–.1	.1	...
Reserve position in the Fund	4 830	...	...	...	...	–.1	...	...	...
Foreign exchange	4 840	–.8	.7	–57.6	–116.4	–67.7	–15.2	–117.7	...
Other claims	4 880	...	...	...	...	...	...	...	...
NET ERRORS AND OMISSIONS	4 998	**12.3**	**–150.2**	**–63.1**	**21.6**	**1.6**	**–56.4**	**54.0**	**...**

Part 3 of the *Yearbook* contains descriptions of the methodologies, compilation practices, and sources used to compile these data.

Table 1. ANALYTIC PRESENTATION, 1988–95
(Millions of U.S. dollars)

	Code	1988	1989	1990	1991	1992	1993	1994	1995
A. Current Account[1]	4 993 Y.	**–304.4**	**–270.1**	**–198.9**	**–262.6**	**–533.9**	**–505.5**	**–218.4**	...
Goods: exports f.o.b	2 100 ..	542.5	723.5	830.8	760.3	608.4	715.5	985.1	...
Goods: imports f.o.b	3 100 ..	–590.9	–729.5	–775.6	–804.2	–1,040.8	–1,111.7	–1,121.9	...
Balance on Goods	4 100 ..	*–48.4*	*–6.0*	*55.2*	*–43.9*	*–432.4*	*–396.2*	*–136.8*	...
Services: credit	2 200 ..	128.3	143.3	145.9	157.0	164.6	181.4	230.7	...
Services: debit	3 200 ..	–254.8	–298.2	–310.6	–311.2	–311.0	–321.7	–338.2	...
Balance on Goods and Services	4 991 ..	*–174.9*	*–160.9*	*–109.5*	*–198.1*	*–578.8*	*–536.5*	*–244.3*	...
Income: credit	2 300 ..	18.2	23.9	18.8	24.6	17.7	9.2	10.3	...
Income: debit	3 300 ..	–283.0	–283.0	–267.4	–271.6	–215.4	–215.1	–209.6	...
Balance on Goods, Services, and Income	4 992 ..	*–439.7*	*–420.0*	*–358.1*	*–445.1*	*–776.5*	*–742.4*	*–443.6*	...
Current transfers: credit	2 379 Y.	140.0	152.5	161.2	185.8	246.3	241.0	230.4	...
Current transfers: debit	3 379 ..	–4.7	–2.6	–2.0	–3.3	–3.7	–4.1	–5.2	...
B. Capital Account[1]	4 994 Y.	**1.3**	**5.9**	**.8**	**.5**	**.6**	**1.0**	**1.2**	...
Capital account: credit	2 994 Y.	1.3	5.9	.8	.5	.6	1.0	1.2	...
Capital account: debit	3 994 ..	...	...	...	...	...	...	...	...
Total, Groups A Plus B	4 010 ..	*–303.1*	*–264.2*	*–198.1*	*–262.1*	*–533.3*	*–504.5*	*–217.2*	...
C. Financial Account[1]	4 995 X.	**–48.9**	**–124.0**	**76.8**	**87.4**	**316.2**	**206.1**	**242.9**	...
Direct investment abroad	4 505 ..	–1.9	–1.0	–1.1	–2.0	–2.0	2.0	2.2	...
Direct investment in Bolivia	4 555 Y.	–34.3	–45.0	11.0	24.8	35.4	25.0	20.0	...
Portfolio investment assets	4 602 ..	...	...	...	...	...	...	...	...
Equity securities	4 610 ..	...	...	...	...	...	...	...	...
Debt securities	4 619 ..	...	...	...	...	...	...	...	...
Portfolio investment liabilities	4 652 Y.	...	...	...	...	...	...	...	...
Equity securities	4 660 Y.	...	...	...	...	...	...	...	...
Debt securities	4 669 Y.	...	...	...	...	...	...	...	...
Other investment assets	4 703 ..	–85.5	–161.8	–32.1	–16.3	–13.0	...	...	...
Monetary authorities	4 703 .A	...	...	...	...	...	...	...	...
General government	4 703 .B	–2.4	–23.0	–7.4	–9.3	–6.4	...	...	...
Banks	4 703 .C	–2.2	–10.9	3.0	–3.4	–14.3	...	...	...
Other sectors	4 703 .D	–80.9	–127.9	–27.7	–3.6	7.7	...	...	...
Other investment liabilities	4 753 X.	72.8	83.8	99.0	80.9	295.8	179.1	220.7	...
Monetary authorities	4 753 XA	93.8	120.6	73.7	61.5	81.7	66.3	91.4	...
General government	4 753 YB	2.2	–3.3	–60.2	–77.6	–42.6	68.2	75.1	...
Banks	4 753 YC	–44.7	–42.7	30.2	32.9	86.5	–7.6	–6.9	...
Other sectors	4 753 YD	21.5	9.2	55.3	64.1	170.2	52.2	61.1	...
Total, Groups A Through C	4 020 ..	*–352.0*	*–388.2*	*–121.3*	*–174.7*	*–217.1*	*–298.4*	*25.7*	...
D. Net Errors and Omissions	4 998 ..	**70.8**	**–11.5**	**4.8**	**80.5**	**92.0**	**341.9**	**–11.0**	...
Total, Groups A Through D	4 030 ..	*–281.2*	*–399.7*	*–116.5*	*–94.2*	*–125.1*	*43.5*	*14.7*	...
E. Reserves and Related Items	4 040 ..	**281.2**	**399.7**	**116.5**	**94.2**	**125.1**	**–43.5**	**–14.7**	...
Reserve assets	4 800 ..	12.8	57.3	–5.0	–8.4	–41.2	99.7	–23.4	...
Use of Fund credit and loans	4 766 ..	30.6	47.5	–13.2	–13.9	14.7	–28.7	28.7	...
Liabilities constituting foreign authorities' reserves	4 900 ..	–12.4	95.7	–44.9	–52.9	–6.5	–23.8	–8.0	...
Exceptional financing	4 920 ..	250.2	199.2	179.5	169.5	158.1	–90.7	–11.9	...
Conversion rates: bolivianos per U.S. dollar	0 101 ..	**2.3502**	**2.6917**	**3.1727**	**3.5806**	**3.9005**	**4.2651**	**4.6205**	**4.8003**

[1] Excludes components that have been classified in the categories of Group E.

Table 2. STANDARD PRESENTATION, 1988–95
(Millions of U.S. dollars)

	Code	1988	1989	1990	1991	1992	1993	1994	1995
CURRENT ACCOUNT	4 993 . .	**–304.4**	**–270.1**	**–198.9**	**–262.6**	**–533.9**	**–505.5**	**–218.4**	**. . .**
A. GOODS	4 100 . .	–48.4	–6.0	55.2	–43.9	–432.4	–396.2	–136.8	. . .
Credit	2 100 . .	**542.5**	**723.5**	**830.8**	**760.3**	**608.4**	**715.5**	**985.1**	**. . .**
General merchandise: exports f.o.b.	2 110 . .	542.5	723.5	830.8	760.3	608.4	715.5	985.1	. . .
Goods for processing: exports f.o.b.	2 150 . .	. . .	. . .	. . .	. . .	. . .	. . .	. . .	. . .
Repairs on goods	2 160 . .	. . .	. . .	. . .	. . .	. . .	. . .	. . .	. . .
Goods procured in ports by carriers	2 170 . .	. . .	. . .	. . .	. . .	. . .	. . .	. . .	. . .
Nonmonetary gold	2 180 . .	. . .	. . .	. . .	. . .	. . .	. . .	. . .	. . .
Debit	3 100 . .	**–590.9**	**–729.5**	**–775.6**	**–804.2**	**–1,040.8**	**–1,111.7**	**–1,121.9**	**. . .**
General merchandise: imports f.o.b.	3 110 . .	–590.9	–729.5	–775.6	–804.2	–1,040.8	–1,111.7	–1,121.9	. . .
Goods for processing: imports f.o.b.	3 150 . .	. . .	. . .	. . .	. . .	. . .	. . .	. . .	. . .
Repairs on goods	3 160 . .	. . .	. . .	. . .	. . .	. . .	. . .	. . .	. . .
Goods procured in ports by carriers	3 170 . .	. . .	. . .	. . .	. . .	. . .	. . .	. . .	. . .
Nonmonetary gold	3 180 . .	. . .	. . .	. . .	. . .	. . .	. . .	. . .	. . .
B. SERVICES	4 200 . .	–126.5	–154.9	–164.7	–154.2	–146.4	–140.3	–107.5	. . .
Total credit	2 200 . .	*128.3*	*143.3*	*145.9*	*157.0*	*164.6*	*181.4*	*230.7*	. . .
Total debit	3 200 . .	*–254.8*	*–298.2*	*–310.6*	*–311.2*	*–311.0*	*–321.7*	*–338.2*	. . .
Transportation services, credit	2 205 . .	**40.5**	**46.3**	**47.5**	**51.2**	**53.6**	**57.0**	**60.8**	**. . .**
Passenger	2 205 BA	*19.2*	*20.6*	*20.8*	*23.1*	*23.4*	*24.8*	*31.3*	. . .
Freight	2 205 BB	*10.8*	*14.7*	*15.3*	*15.8*	*17.3*	*18.4*	*15.7*	. . .
Other	2 205 BC	*10.5*	*11.0*	*11.4*	*12.3*	*12.9*	*13.8*	*13.8*	. . .
Sea transport, passenger	2 207 . .	. . .	. . .	. . .	. . .	. . .	. . .	. . .	. . .
Sea transport, freight	2 208 . .	. . .	. . .	. . .	. . .	. . .	. . .	. . .	. . .
Sea transport, other	2 209 . .	. . .	. . .	. . .	. . .	. . .	. . .	. . .	. . .
Air transport, passenger	2 211 . .	. . .	. . .	. . .	. . .	. . .	. . .	. . .	. . .
Air transport, freight	2 212 . .	. . .	. . .	. . .	. . .	. . .	. . .	. . .	. . .
Air transport, other	2 213 . .	. . .	. . .	. . .	. . .	. . .	. . .	. . .	. . .
Other transport, passenger	2 215 . .	. . .	. . .	. . .	. . .	. . .	. . .	. . .	. . .
Other transport, freight	2 216 . .	. . .	. . .	. . .	. . .	. . .	. . .	. . .	. . .
Other transport, other	2 217 . .	. . .	. . .	. . .	. . .	. . .	. . .	. . .	. . .
Transportation services, debit	3 205 . .	**–132.2**	**–170.2**	**–179.4**	**–172.0**	**–167.1**	**–174.9**	**–172.2**	**. . .**
Passenger	3 205 BA	*–21.6*	*–22.1*	*–22.5*	*–23.8*	*–25.5*	*–25.0*	*–19.8*	. . .
Freight	3 205 BB	*–97.9*	*–129.3*	*–137.5*	*–128.0*	*–119.7*	*–128.0*	*–120.1*	. . .
Other	3 205 BC	*–12.7*	*–18.8*	*–19.4*	*–20.2*	*–21.9*	*–21.9*	*–32.3*	. . .
Sea transport, passenger	3 207 . .	. . .	. . .	. . .	. . .	. . .	. . .	. . .	. . .
Sea transport, freight	3 208 . .	. . .	. . .	. . .	. . .	. . .	. . .	. . .	. . .
Sea transport, other	3 209 . .	. . .	. . .	. . .	. . .	. . .	. . .	. . .	. . .
Air transport, passenger	3 211 . .	. . .	. . .	. . .	. . .	. . .	. . .	. . .	. . .
Air transport, freight	3 212 . .	. . .	. . .	. . .	. . .	. . .	. . .	. . .	. . .
Air transport, other	3 213 . .	. . .	. . .	. . .	. . .	. . .	. . .	. . .	. . .
Other transport, passenger	3 215 . .	. . .	. . .	. . .	. . .	. . .	. . .	. . .	. . .
Other transport, freight	3 216 . .	. . .	. . .	. . .	. . .	. . .	. . .	. . .	. . .
Other transport, other	3 217 . .	. . .	. . .	. . .	. . .	. . .	. . .	. . .	. . .
Travel, credit	2 236 . .	**53.1**	**57.2**	**57.8**	**62.1**	**65.4**	**69.5**	**72.2**	**. . .**
Business travel	2 237 . .	. . .	. . .	. . .	. . .	. . .	. . .	. . .	. . .
Personal travel	2 240 . .	. . .	. . .	. . .	. . .	. . .	. . .	. . .	. . .
Travel, debit	3 236 . .	**–55.3**	**–58.9**	**–59.9**	**–62.6**	**–67.8**	**–69.4**	**–70.9**	**. . .**
Business travel	3 237 . .	. . .	. . .	. . .	. . .	. . .	. . .	. . .	. . .
Personal travel	3 240 . .	. . .	. . .	. . .	. . .	. . .	. . .	. . .	. . .
Other services, credit	2 200 BA	**34.7**	**39.8**	**40.6**	**43.7**	**45.6**	**54.9**	**97.7**	**. . .**
Communications	2 245 . .	. . .	. . .	. . .	. . .	. . .	. . .	. . .	. . .
Construction	2 249 . .	. . .	. . .	. . .	. . .	. . .	. . .	. . .	. . .
Insurance	2 253 . .	9.2	12.7	13.2	14.2	15.0	18.5	18.1	. . .
Financial	2 260 . .	. . .	. . .	. . .	. . .	. . .	. . .	. . .	. . .
Computer and information	2 262 . .	. . .	. . .	. . .	. . .	. . .	. . .	. . .	. . .
Royalties and licence fees	2 266 . .	. . .	. . .	. . .	. . .	. . .	. . .	. . .	. . .
Other business services	2 268 . .	14.0	14.1	14.1	15.7	16.1	20.4	22.3	. . .
Personal, cultural, and recreational	2 287 . .	. . .	. . .	. . .	. . .	. . .	. . .	. . .	. . .
Government, n.i.e.	2 291 . .	11.5	13.0	13.3	13.8	14.5	16.0	57.3	. . .
Other services, debit	3 200 BA	**–67.3**	**–69.1**	**–71.3**	**–76.6**	**–76.1**	**–77.4**	**–95.1**	**. . .**
Communications	3 245 . .	. . .	. . .	. . .	. . .	. . .	. . .	. . .	. . .
Construction	3 249 . .	. . .	. . .	. . .	. . .	. . .	. . .	. . .	. . .
Insurance	3 253 . .	–24.4	–28.3	–29.1	–29.4	–28.4	–25.9	–18.2	. . .
Financial	3 260 . .	. . .	. . .	. . .	. . .	. . .	. . .	. . .	. . .
Computer and information	3 262 . .	. . .	. . .	. . .	. . .	. . .	. . .	. . .	. . .
Royalties and licence fees	3 266 . .	–3.6	–3.2	–3.2	–3.7	–3.7	–3.9	–4.1	. . .
Other business services	3 268 . .	–19.7	–18.9	–19.0	–22.8	–22.9	–24.5	–26.8	. . .
Personal, cultural, and recreational	3 287 . .	. . .	. . .	. . .	. . .	. . .	. . .	. . .	. . .
Government, n.i.e.	3 291 . .	–19.6	–18.7	–20.0	–20.7	–21.1	–23.1	–46.0	. . .

Table 2 (Continued). STANDARD PRESENTATION, 1988–95
(Millions of U.S. dollars)

	Code		1988	1989	1990	1991	1992	1993	1994	1995
C. INCOME	4 300	. .	–264.8	–259.1	–248.6	–247.0	–197.7	–205.9	–199.3	. . .
Total credit	2 300	. .	*18.2*	*23.9*	*18.8*	*24.6*	*17.7*	*9.2*	*10.3*	. . .
Total debit	3 300	. .	*–283.0*	*–283.0*	*–267.4*	*–271.6*	*–215.4*	*–215.1*	*–209.6*	. . .
Compensation of employees, credit	2 310	. .	**2.4**	**1.8**	**1.8**	**2.3**	**2.4**	**2.3**	**2.1**	**. . .**
Compensation of employees, debit	3 310	. .	**–3.0**	**–6.4**	**–6.4**	**–7.0**	**–7.1**	**–7.3**	**–7.8**	**. . .**
Investment income, credit	2 320	. .	**15.8**	**22.1**	**17.0**	**22.3**	**15.3**	**6.9**	**8.2**	**. . .**
Direct investment income	2 330	. .	. . .	. . .	. . .	. . .	. . .	. . .	. . .	. . .
Dividends and distributed branch profits	2 332	. .	. . .	. . .	. . .	. . .	. . .	. . .	. . .	. . .
Reinvested earnings and undistributed branch profits	2 333	. .	. . .	. . .	. . .	. . .	. . .	. . .	. . .	. . .
Income on debt (interest)	2 334	. .	. . .	. . .	. . .	. . .	. . .	. . .	. . .	. . .
Portfolio investment income	2 339	. .	. . .	. . .	. . .	. . .	. . .	. . .	. . .	. . .
Income on equity	2 340	. .	. . .	. . .	. . .	. . .	. . .	. . .	. . .	. . .
Income on bonds and notes	2 350	. .	. . .	. . .	. . .	. . .	. . .	. . .	. . .	. . .
Income on money market instruments and financial derivatives	2 360	. .	. . .	. . .	. . .	. . .	. . .	. . .	. . .	. . .
Other investment income	2 370	. .	15.8	22.1	17.0	22.3	15.3	6.9	8.2	. . .
Investment income, debit	3 320	. .	**–280.0**	**–276.6**	**–261.0**	**–264.6**	**–208.3**	**–207.8**	**–201.8**	**. . .**
Direct investment income	3 330	. .	–5.2	–15.0	–17.0	–18.0	–20.0	–25.0	–20.0	. . .
Dividends and distributed branch profits	3 332	. .	. . .	–6.4	–3.3	. . .	. . .	. . .	. . .	. . .
Reinvested earnings and undistributed branch profits	3 333	. .	–5.2	–8.6	–13.7	–18.0	–20.0	–25.0	–20.0	. . .
Income on debt (interest)	3 334	. .	. . .	. . .	. . .	. . .	. . .	. . .	. . .	. . .
Portfolio investment income	3 339	. .	. . .	. . .	. . .	. . .	. . .	. . .	. . .	. . .
Income on equity	3 340	. .	. . .	. . .	. . .	. . .	. . .	. . .	. . .	. . .
Income on bonds and notes	3 350	. .	. . .	. . .	. . .	. . .	. . .	. . .	. . .	. . .
Income on money market instruments and financial derivatives	3 360	. .	. . .	. . .	. . .	. . .	. . .	. . .	. . .	. . .
Other investment income	3 370	. .	–274.8	–261.6	–244.0	–246.6	–188.3	–182.8	–181.8	. . .
D. CURRENT TRANSFERS	4 379	. .	135.3	149.9	159.2	182.5	242.6	236.9	225.2	. . .
Credit	2 379	. .	**140.0**	**152.5**	**161.2**	**185.8**	**246.3**	**241.0**	**230.4**	**. . .**
General government	2 380	. .	124.5	136.5	139.1	161.7	222.4	214.1	205.2	. . .
Other sectors	2 390	. .	15.5	16.0	22.1	24.1	23.9	26.9	25.2	. . .
Workers' remittances	2 391	. .	.8	.8	2.0	.6	.8	.9	1.2	. . .
Other current transfers	2 392	. .	14.7	15.2	20.1	23.5	23.1	26.0	24.0	. . .
Debit	3 379	. .	**–4.7**	**–2.6**	**–2.0**	**–3.3**	**–3.7**	**–4.1**	**–5.2**	**. . .**
General government	3 380	. .	–.6	–1.3	–.7	–1.7	–1.9	–1.9	–3.2	. . .
Other sectors	3 390	. .	–4.1	–1.3	–1.3	–1.6	–1.8	–2.2	–2.0	. . .
Workers' remittances	3 391	. .	–4.1	–1.3	–1.3	–1.6	–1.8	–2.2	–2.0	. . .
Other current transfers	3 392	. .	. . .	. . .	. . .	. . .	. . .	. . .	. . .	. . .
CAPITAL AND FINANCIAL ACCOUNT	4 996	. .	**233.6**	**281.6**	**194.1**	**182.1**	**441.9**	**163.6**	**229.4**	**. . .**
CAPITAL ACCOUNT	4 994	. .	**49.0**	**6.4**	**7.4**	**.5**	**.6**	**1.0**	**1.2**	**. . .**
Total credit	2 994	. .	*49.0*	*6.4*	*7.4*	*.5*	*.6*	*1.0*	*1.2*	. . .
Total debit	3 994	. .	. . .	. . .	. . .	. . .	. . .	. . .	. . .	. . .
Capital transfers, credit	2 400	. .	**49.0**	**6.4**	**7.4**	**.5**	**.6**	**1.0**	**1.2**	**. . .**
General government	2 401	. .	47.7	.5	6.6	. . .	. . .	. . .	. . .	. . .
Debt forgiveness	2 402	. .	47.7	.5	6.6	. . .	. . .	. . .	. . .	. . .
Other capital transfers	2 410	. .	. . .	. . .	. . .	. . .	. . .	. . .	. . .	. . .
Other sectors	2 430	. .	1.3	5.9	.8	.5	.6	1.0	1.2	. . .
Migrants' transfers	2 431	. .	1.3	5.9	.8	.5	.6	1.0	1.2	. . .
Debt forgiveness	2 432	. .	. . .	. . .	. . .	. . .	. . .	. . .	. . .	. . .
Other capital transfers	2 440	. .	. . .	. . .	. . .	. . .	. . .	. . .	. . .	. . .
Capital transfers, debit	3 400	. .	**. . .**	**. . .**	**. . .**	**. . .**	**. . .**	**. . .**	**. . .**	**. . .**
General government	3 401	. .	. . .	. . .	. . .	. . .	. . .	. . .	. . .	. . .
Debt forgiveness	3 402	. .	. . .	. . .	. . .	. . .	. . .	. . .	. . .	. . .
Other capital transfers	3 410	. .	. . .	. . .	. . .	. . .	. . .	. . .	. . .	. . .
Other sectors	3 430	. .	. . .	. . .	. . .	. . .	. . .	. . .	. . .	. . .
Migrants' transfers	3 431	. .	. . .	. . .	. . .	. . .	. . .	. . .	. . .	. . .
Debt forgiveness	3 432	. .	. . .	. . .	. . .	. . .	. . .	. . .	. . .	. . .
Other capital transfers	3 440	. .	. . .	. . .	. . .	. . .	. . .	. . .	. . .	. . .
Nonproduced nonfinancial assets, credit	2 480	. .	**. . .**	**. . .**	**. . .**	**. . .**	**. . .**	**. . .**	**. . .**	**. . .**
Nonproduced nonfinancial assets, debit	3 480	. .	**. . .**	**. . .**	**. . .**	**. . .**	**. . .**	**. . .**	**. . .**	**. . .**

Table 2 (Continued). STANDARD PRESENTATION, 1988–95
(Millions of U.S. dollars)

	Code	1988	1989	1990	1991	1992	1993	1994	1995
FINANCIAL ACCOUNT	4 995	**184.6**	**275.2**	**186.7**	**181.6**	**441.3**	**162.6**	**228.2**	...
A. DIRECT INVESTMENT	4 500	–36.2	–46.0	9.9	22.8	33.4	27.0	22.2	...
Direct investment abroad	4 505	**–1.9**	**–1.0**	**–1.1**	**–2.0**	**–2.0**	**2.0**	**2.2**	...
Equity capital	4 510	–1.9	–1.0	–1.1	–2.0	–2.0	2.0	2.2	...
Claims on affiliated enterprises	4 515	...	...	...	...	...	...	...	...
Liabilities to affiliated enterprises	4 520	...	...	...	...	...	...	...	...
Reinvested earnings	4 525	...	...	...	...	...	...	...	...
Other capital	4 530	...	...	...	...	...	...	...	...
Claims on affiliated enterprises	4 535	...	...	...	...	...	...	...	...
Liabilities to affiliated enterprises	4 540	...	...	...	...	...	...	...	...
Direct investment in Bolivia	4 555	**–34.3**	**–45.0**	**11.0**	**24.8**	**35.4**	**25.0**	**20.0**	...
Equity capital	4 560	...	...	...	...	...	...	...	...
Claims on direct investors	4 565	...	...	...	...	...	...	...	...
Liabilities to direct investors	4 570	...	...	...	...	...	...	...	...
Reinvested earnings	4 575	5.2	8.6	13.7	18.0	20.0	25.0	20.0	...
Other capital	4 580	–39.5	–53.6	–2.7	6.8	15.4	...	...	...
Claims on direct investors	4 585	...	...	...	...	...	...	...	...
Liabilities to direct investors	4 590	...	...	...	...	...	...	...	...
B. PORTFOLIO INVESTMENT	4 600	...	...	...	...	...	...	...	...
Assets	4 602	...	...	...	...	...	...	...	...
Equity securities	4 610	...	...	...	...	...	...	...	...
Monetary authorities	4 611	...	...	...	...	...	...	...	...
General government	4 612	...	...	...	...	...	...	...	...
Banks	4 613	...	...	...	...	...	...	...	...
Other sectors	4 614	...	...	...	...	...	...	...	...
Debt securities	4 619	...	...	...	...	...	...	...	...
Bonds and notes	4 620	...	...	...	...	...	...	...	...
Monetary authorities	4 621	...	...	...	...	...	...	...	...
General government	4 622	...	...	...	...	...	...	...	...
Banks	4 623	...	...	...	...	...	...	...	...
Other sectors	4 624	...	...	...	...	...	...	...	...
Money market instruments	4 630	...	...	...	...	...	...	...	...
Monetary authorities	4 631	...	...	...	...	...	...	...	...
General government	4 632	...	...	...	...	...	...	...	...
Banks	4 633	...	...	...	...	...	...	...	...
Other sectors	4 634	...	...	...	...	...	...	...	...
Financial derivatives	4 640	...	...	...	...	...	...	...	...
Monetary authorities	4 641	...	...	...	...	...	...	...	...
General government	4 642	...	...	...	...	...	...	...	...
Banks	4 643	...	...	...	...	...	...	...	...
Other sectors	4 644	...	...	...	...	...	...	...	...
Liabilities	4 652	...	...	...	...	...	...	...	...
Equity securities	4 660	...	...	...	...	...	...	...	...
Banks	4 663	...	...	...	...	...	...	...	...
Other sectors	4 664	...	...	...	...	...	...	...	...
Debt securities	4 669	...	...	...	...	...	...	...	...
Bonds and notes	4 670	...	...	...	...	...	...	...	...
Monetary authorities	4 671	...	...	...	...	...	...	...	...
General government	4 672	...	...	...	...	...	...	...	...
Banks	4 673	...	...	...	...	...	...	...	...
Other sectors	4 674	...	...	...	...	...	...	...	...
Money market instruments	4 680	...	...	...	...	...	...	...	...
Monetary authorities	4 681	...	...	...	...	...	...	...	...
General government	4 682	...	...	...	...	...	...	...	...
Banks	4 683	...	...	...	...	...	...	...	...
Other sectors	4 684	...	...	...	...	...	...	...	...
Financial derivatives	4 690	...	...	...	...	...	...	...	...
Monetary authorities	4 691	...	...	...	...	...	...	...	...
General government	4 692	...	...	...	...	...	...	...	...
Banks	4 693	...	...	...	...	...	...	...	...
Other sectors	4 694	...	...	...	...	...	...	...	...

Table 2 (Concluded). STANDARD PRESENTATION, 1988–95
(Millions of U.S. dollars)

	Code	1988	1989	1990	1991	1992	1993	1994	1995
C. OTHER INVESTMENT	4 700 . .	208.0	263.9	181.7	167.3	449.1	35.9	229.5	. . .
Assets	4 703 . .	**−85.5**	**−161.8**	**−32.1**	**−16.3**	**−13.0**	**. . .**	**. . .**	**. . .**
Trade credits	4 706 . .	. . .	. . .	. . .	. . .	. . .	. . .	. . .	. . .
General government: long-term	4 708 . .	. . .	. . .	. . .	. . .	. . .	. . .	. . .	. . .
General government: short-term	4 709 . .	. . .	. . .	. . .	. . .	. . .	. . .	. . .	. . .
Other sectors: long-term	4 711 . .	. . .	. . .	. . .	. . .	. . .	. . .	. . .	. . .
Other sectors: short-term	4 712 . .	. . .	. . .	. . .	. . .	. . .	. . .	. . .	. . .
Loans	4 714 . .	−38.8	−67.5	−18.9	−3.6	7.7	. . .	. . .	. . .
Monetary authorities: long-term	4 717 . .	. . .	. . .	. . .	. . .	. . .	. . .	. . .	. . .
Monetary authorities: short-term	4 718 . .	. . .	. . .	. . .	. . .	. . .	. . .	. . .	. . .
General government: long-term	4 720 . .	. . .	. . .	. . .	. . .	. . .	. . .	. . .	. . .
General government: short-term	4 721 . .	. . .	. . .	. . .	. . .	. . .	. . .	. . .	. . .
Banks: long-term	4 723 . .	. . .	. . .	. . .	. . .	. . .	. . .	. . .	. . .
Banks: short-term	4 724 . .	. . .	. . .	. . .	. . .	. . .	. . .	. . .	. . .
Other sectors: long-term	4 726 . .	. . .	. . .	. . .	. . .	. . .	. . .	. . .	. . .
Other sectors: short-term	4 727 . .	−38.8	−67.5	−18.9	−3.6	7.7	. . .	. . .	. . .
Currency and deposits	4 730 . .	−44.3	−71.3	−5.8	−3.4	−14.3	. . .	. . .	. . .
Monetary authorities	4 731 . .	. . .	. . .	. . .	. . .	. . .	. . .	. . .	. . .
General government	4 732 . .	. . .	. . .	. . .	. . .	. . .	. . .	. . .	. . .
Banks	4 733 . .	−2.2	−10.9	3.0	−3.4	−14.3	. . .	. . .	. . .
Other sectors	4 734 . .	−42.1	−60.4	−8.8	. . .	. . .	. . .	. . .	. . .
Other assets	4 736 . .	−2.4	−23.0	−7.4	−9.3	−6.4	. . .	. . .	. . .
Monetary authorities: long-term	4 738 . .	. . .	. . .	. . .	. . .	. . .	. . .	. . .	. . .
Monetary authorities: short-term	4 739 . .	. . .	. . .	. . .	. . .	. . .	. . .	. . .	. . .
General government: long-term	4 741 . .	−2.4	−23.0	−7.4	−9.3	−6.4	. . .	. . .	. . .
General government: short-term	4 742 . .	. . .	. . .	. . .	. . .	. . .	. . .	. . .	. . .
Banks: long-term	4 744 . .	. . .	. . .	. . .	. . .	. . .	. . .	. . .	. . .
Banks: short-term	4 745 . .	. . .	. . .	. . .	. . .	. . .	. . .	. . .	. . .
Other sectors: long-term	4 747 . .	. . .	. . .	. . .	. . .	. . .	. . .	. . .	. . .
Other sectors: short-term	4 748 . .	. . .	. . .	. . .	. . .	. . .	. . .	. . .	. . .
Liabilities	4 753 . .	**293.5**	**425.7**	**213.8**	**183.6**	**462.1**	**35.9**	**229.5**	**. . .**
Trade credits	4 756 . .	. . .	. . .	. . .	. . .	. . .	. . .	. . .	. . .
General government: long-term	4 758 . .	. . .	. . .	. . .	. . .	. . .	. . .	. . .	. . .
General government: short-term	4 759 . .	. . .	. . .	. . .	. . .	. . .	. . .	. . .	. . .
Other sectors: long-term	4 761 . .	. . .	. . .	. . .	. . .	. . .	. . .	. . .	. . .
Other sectors: short-term	4 762 . .	. . .	. . .	. . .	. . .	. . .	. . .	. . .	. . .
Loans	4 764 . .	311.2	323.9	304.8	251.3	455.0	170.4	340.2	. . .
Use of Fund credit and loans from the Fund	4 766 . .	30.6	47.5	−13.2	−13.9	14.7	−28.7	28.7	. . .
Monetary authorities: other long-term	4 767 . .	90.3	118.8	70.9	63.7	80.7	63.3	94.9	. . .
Monetary authorities: short-term	4 768 . .	. . .	. . .	17.7	−14.5	−3.2	. . .	. . .	. . .
General government: long-term	4 770 . .	182.8	147.1	159.3	136.5	156.2	91.3	162.4	. . .
General government: short-term	4 771 . .	. . .	. . .	. . .	. . .	. . .	. . .	. . .	. . .
Banks: long-term	4 773 . .	−14.0	1.3	14.8	15.4	36.4	−7.6	−6.9	. . .
Banks: short-term	4 774 . .	. . .	. . .	. . .	. . .	. . .	. . .	. . .	. . .
Other sectors: long-term	4 776 . .	21.5	9.2	55.3	64.1	170.2	52.2	61.1	. . .
Other sectors: short-term	4 777 . .	. . .	. . .	. . .	. . .	. . .	. . .	. . .	. . .
Currency and deposits	4 780 . .	−39.6	53.5	−26.7	−37.6	44.6	−20.8	−11.5	. . .
Monetary authorities	4 781 . .	−8.9	97.5	−42.1	−55.1	−5.5	−20.8	−11.5	. . .
General government	4 782 . .	. . .	. . .	. . .	. . .	. . .	. . .	. . .	. . .
Banks	4 783 . .	−30.7	−44.0	15.4	17.5	50.1	. . .	. . .	. . .
Other sectors	4 784 . .	. . .	. . .	. . .	. . .	. . .	. . .	. . .	. . .
Other liabilities	4 786 . .	21.9	48.3	−64.3	−30.1	−37.5	−113.7	−99.2	. . .
Monetary authorities: long-term	4 788 . .	. . .	. . .	. . .	. . .	. . .	. . .	. . .	. . .
Monetary authorities: short-term	4 789 . .	13.5	9.6	4.4	.2	. . .	. . .	. . .	. . .
General government: long-term	4 791 . .	. . .	. . .	. . .	. . .	. . .	. . .	. . .	. . .
General government: short-term	4 792 . .	. . .	32.4	−67.3	−29.3	−37.4	−113.7	−99.2	. . .
Banks: long-term	4 794 . .	. . .	. . .	. . .	. . .	. . .	. . .	. . .	. . .
Banks: short-term	4 795 . .	−.4	−.5	−1.4	−1.0	−.1	. . .	. . .	. . .
Other sectors: long-term	4 797 . .	. . .	. . .	. . .	. . .	. . .	. . .	. . .	. . .
Other sectors: short-term	4 798 . .	8.8	6.8	. . .	. . .	. . .	. . .	. . .	. . .
D. RESERVE ASSETS	4 800 . .	12.8	57.3	−5.0	−8.4	−41.2	99.7	−23.4	. . .
Monetary gold	4 810 . .	. . .	. . .	. . .	. . .	. . .	. . .	. . .	. . .
Special drawing rights	4 820 . .	.1	. . .	−1.0	1.0	. . .	−14.0	−8.6	. . .
Reserve position in the Fund	4 830 . .	. . .	. . .	. . .	. . .	−12.3	. . .	. . .	. . .
Foreign exchange	4 840 . .	−68.0	2.2	−40.9	21.9	−46.6	90.7	−35.8	. . .
Other claims	4 880 . .	80.7	55.1	36.9	−31.3	17.7	23.0	21.0	. . .
NET ERRORS AND OMISSIONS	4 998 . .	**70.8**	**−11.5**	**4.8**	**80.5**	**92.0**	**341.9**	**−11.0**	**. . .**

Part 3 of the *Yearbook* contains descriptions of the methodologies, compilation practices, and sources used to compile these data.

Table 1. ANALYTIC PRESENTATION, 1988–95
(Millions of U.S. dollars)

	Code	1988	1989	1990	1991	1992	1993	1994	1995
A. Current Account [1]	4 993 Y.	**193.9**	**491.9**	**42.0**	**336.9**	**244.3**	**503.3**	**243.3**	**342.1**
Goods: exports f.o.b	2 100 ..	1,468.9	1,819.7	1,795.4	1,871.1	1,743.9	1,722.2	1,878.4	2,164.4
Goods: imports f.o.b	3 100 ..	-986.9	-1,185.1	-1,610.9	-1,604.0	-1,556.6	-1,455.4	-1,350.0	-1,578.7
Balance on Goods	4 100 ..	*482.0*	*634.6*	*184.4*	*267.2*	*187.3*	*266.8*	*528.4*	*585.7*
Services: credit	2 200 ..	110.3	110.5	209.5	209.9	189.2	191.3	186.1	260.4
Services: debit	3 200 ..	-238.8	-228.0	-375.9	-382.5	-360.1	-325.6	-322.0	-444.2
Balance on Goods and Services	4 991 ..	*353.6*	*517.1*	*18.0*	*94.5*	*16.4*	*132.5*	*392.6*	*401.8*
Income: credit	2 300 ..	220.1	244.8	416.2	483.1	542.1	554.5	230.8	483.2
Income: debit	3 300 ..	-546.8	-483.6	-522.1	-420.2	-429.7	-260.9	-455.0	-515.6
Balance on Goods, Services, and Income	4 992 ..	*26.9*	*278.3*	*-87.9*	*157.4*	*128.8*	*426.1*	*168.4*	*369.4*
Current transfers: credit	2 379 Y.	301.8	266.8	392.0	455.5	391.1	352.3	370.0	342.3
Current transfers: debit	3 379 ..	-134.7	-53.2	-262.1	-276.0	-275.6	-275.1	-295.1	-369.5
B. Capital Account [1]	4 994 Y.	**...**	**6.3**	**3.4**	**3.5**	**6.6**	**8.5**	**6.0**	**2.9**
Capital account: credit	2 994 Y.	...	7.0	4.3	4.6	7.2	9.7	6.5	3.8
Capital account: debit	3 994 ..	...	-.7	-.9	-1.0	-.5	-1.3	-.4	-.9
Total, Groups A Plus B	4 010 ..	*193.9*	*498.2*	*45.4*	*340.4*	*250.9*	*511.8*	*249.3*	*345.0*
C. Financial Account [1]	4 995 X.	**-25.3**	**113.0**	**82.6**	**123.3**	**275.8**	**-40.3**	**41.1**	**-33.9**
Direct investment abroad	4 505 ..	...	...	-7.4	-8.5	-9.9	-9.5	-9.5	-40.9
Direct investment in Botswana	4 555 Y.	39.9	42.2	95.9	-8.2	-1.6	-286.9	-14.3	70.4
Portfolio investment assets	4 602 ..	...	...	...	...	...	...	...	-36.4
Equity securities	4 610 ..	...	...	...	...	...	...	...	-30.8
Debt securities	4 619 ..	...	...	...	...	...	...	...	-5.6
Portfolio investment liabilities	4 652 Y.	...	...	1.3	-1.2	.1	.2	-.1	5.8
Equity securities	4 660 Y.	...	...	...	...	...	...	...	5.5
Debt securities	4 669 Y.	...	...	1.3	-1.2	.1	.2	-.1	.3
Other investment assets	4 703 ..	-68.3	-34.6	-136.9	-53.0	148.9	63.4	15.8	-88.7
Monetary authorities	4 703 .A	...	...	...	...	...	...	...	...
General government	4 703 .B	-41.4	-45.0	-91.8	11.7	139.9	56.1	19.7	-46.1
Banks	4 703 .C	-8.9	10.4	-33.5	-23.4	-7.0	14.3	.4	-8.7
Other sectors	4 703 .D	-18.0	...	-11.7	-41.3	16.1	-6.9	-4.3	-34.0
Other investment liabilities	4 753 X.	3.1	105.4	129.7	194.2	138.2	192.5	49.2	55.9
Monetary authorities	4 753 XA	...	...	...	...	...	...	...	...
General government	4 753 YB	...	28.2	12.3	77.9	54.4	67.0	6.5	-12.3
Banks	4 753 YC	3.1	-4.6	9.5	-3.6	-5.6	23.1	-2.8	-2.5
Other sectors	4 753 YD	...	81.8	108.0	119.9	89.4	102.4	45.5	70.7
Total, Groups A Through C	4 020 ..	*168.6*	*611.2*	*128.0*	*463.8*	*526.7*	*471.5*	*290.4*	*311.1*
D. Net Errors and Omissions	4 998 ..	**213.7**	**-34.7**	**179.2**	**-89.7**	**-121.4**	**-74.5**	**-151.1**	**-104.6**
Total, Groups A Through D	4 030 ..	*382.3*	*576.5*	*307.2*	*374.1*	*405.3*	*397.0*	*139.3*	*206.6*
E. Reserves and Related Items	4 040 ..	**-382.3**	**-576.5**	**-307.2**	**-374.1**	**-405.3**	**-397.0**	**-139.3**	**-206.6**
Reserve assets	4 800 ..	-382.3	-576.5	-307.2	-374.1	-405.3	-397.0	-139.3	-206.6
Use of Fund credit and loans	4 766 ..	...	...	...	...	...	...	...	...
Liabilities constituting foreign authorities' reserves	4 900 ..	...	...	...	...	...	...	...	...
Exceptional financing	4 920 ..	...	...	...	...	...	...	...	...
Conversion rates: pula per U.S. dollar	0 101 ..	**1.8286**	**2.0149**	**1.8605**	**2.0216**	**2.1097**	**2.4231**	**2.6846**	**2.7722**

[1] Excludes components that have been classified in the categories of Group E.

Table 2. STANDARD PRESENTATION, 1988–95
(Millions of U.S. dollars)

	Code	1988	1989	1990	1991	1992	1993	1994	1995
CURRENT ACCOUNT	4 993 . .	**193.9**	**491.9**	**42.0**	**336.9**	**244.3**	**503.3**	**243.3**	**342.1**
A. GOODS	4 100 . .	482.0	634.6	184.4	267.2	187.3	266.8	528.4	585.7
Credit	2 100 . .	**1,468.9**	**1,819.7**	**1,795.4**	**1,871.1**	**1,743.9**	**1,722.2**	**1,878.4**	**2,164.4**
General merchandise: exports f.o.b.	2 110 . .	1,468.9	1,819.7	1,795.4	1,871.1	1,743.9	1,722.2	1,878.4	2,164.4
Goods for processing: exports f.o.b.	2 150 . .	. . .	. . .	. . .	. . .	. . .	. . .	. . .	. . .
Repairs on goods	2 160 . .	. . .	. . .	. . .	. . .	. . .	. . .	. . .	. . .
Goods procured in ports by carriers	2 170 . .	. . .	. . .	. . .	. . .	. . .	. . .	. . .	. . .
Nonmonetary gold	2 180 . .	. . .	. . .	. . .	. . .	. . .	. . .	. . .	. . .
Debit	3 100 . .	**–986.9**	**–1,185.1**	**–1,610.9**	**–1,604.0**	**–1,556.6**	**–1,455.4**	**–1,350.0**	**–1,578.7**
General merchandise: imports f.o.b.	3 110 . .	–986.9	–1,185.1	–1,610.9	–1,604.0	–1,556.6	–1,455.4	–1,350.0	–1,578.7
Goods for processing: imports f.o.b.	3 150 . .	. . .	. . .	. . .	. . .	. . .	. . .	. . .	. . .
Repairs on goods	3 160 . .	. . .	. . .	. . .	. . .	. . .	. . .	. . .	. . .
Goods procured in ports by carriers	3 170 . .	. . .	. . .	. . .	. . .	. . .	. . .	. . .	. . .
Nonmonetary gold	3 180 . .	. . .	. . .	. . .	. . .	. . .	. . .	. . .	. . .
B. SERVICES	4 200 . .	–128.5	–117.5	–166.4	–172.6	–170.9	–134.3	–135.8	–183.9
Total credit	2 200 . .	*110.3*	*110.5*	*209.5*	*209.9*	*189.2*	*191.3*	*186.1*	*260.4*
Total debit	3 200 . .	*–238.8*	*–228.0*	*–375.9*	*–382.5*	*–360.1*	*–325.6*	*–322.0*	*–444.2*
Transportation services, credit	2 205 . .	**24.8**	**23.8**	**37.4**	**37.2**	**42.3**	**36.8**	**35.7**	**38.3**
Passenger	2 205 BA	*7.1*	*4.9*	*11.6*	*11.9*	*11.3*	*9.1*	*9.7*	*14.0*
Freight	2 205 BB	*17.7*	*18.9*	. . .	. . .	. . .	. . .	. . .	. . .
Other	2 205 BC	. . .	. . .	*25.8*	*25.4*	*31.0*	*27.7*	*26.0*	*24.3*
Sea transport, passenger	2 207 . .	. . .	. . .	. . .	. . .	. . .	. . .	. . .	. . .
Sea transport, freight	2 208 . .	. . .	. . .	. . .	. . .	. . .	. . .	. . .	. . .
Sea transport, other	2 209 . .	. . .	. . .	. . .	. . .	. . .	. . .	. . .	. . .
Air transport, passenger	2 211 . .	. . .	. . .	8.5	9.3	8.9	7.9	8.8	13.3
Air transport, freight	2 212 . .	. . .	. . .	. . .	. . .	. . .	. . .	. . .	. . .
Air transport, other	2 213 . .	. . .	. . .	.1	. . .	.7	3.0	2.7	2.1
Other transport, passenger	2 215 . .	. . .	. . .	3.1	2.6	2.4	1.2	.9	.7
Other transport, freight	2 216 . .	. . .	. . .	. . .	. . .	. . .	. . .	. . .	. . .
Other transport, other	2 217 . .	. . .	. . .	25.7	25.3	30.3	24.7	23.3	22.3
Transportation services, debit	3 205 . .	**–96.6**	**–105.0**	**–213.4**	**–232.4**	**–194.8**	**–167.5**	**–164.6**	**–187.4**
Passenger	3 205 BA	*–7.1*	*–36.6*	*–19.6*	*–19.0*	*–16.7*	*–1.7*	*–13.0*	*–8.3*
Freight	3 205 BB	*–78.6*	*–68.4*	*–177.1*	*–164.0*	*–160.0*	*–149.8*	*–139.1*	*–162.7*
Other	3 205 BC	*–10.9*	. . .	*–16.8*	*–49.4*	*–18.2*	*–16.1*	*–12.6*	*–16.5*
Sea transport, passenger	3 207 . .	. . .	. . .	. . .	. . .	. . .	. . .	. . .	. . .
Sea transport, freight	3 208 . .	. . .	. . .	–10.6	–9.8	–9.6	–9.0	–8.3	–8.1
Sea transport, other	3 209 . .	. . .	. . .	–6.9	–5.0	–3.0	–2.6	–1.4	–2.5
Air transport, passenger	3 211 . .	. . .	. . .	–10.3	–19.0	–16.7	–1.7	–6.1	–7.1
Air transport, freight	3 212 . .	. . .	. . .	–62.0	–57.4	–56.0	–52.4	–48.7	–56.9
Air transport, other	3 213 . .	. . .	. . .	–4.5	–3.6	–6.8	–.3	–2.6	–4.5
Other transport, passenger	3 215 . .	. . .	. . .	–9.3	. . .	. . .	. . .	–6.9	–1.1
Other transport, freight	3 216 . .	. . .	. . .	–104.4	–96.8	–94.4	–88.4	–82.1	–97.6
Other transport, other	3 217 . .	. . .	. . .	–5.4	–40.9	–8.3	–13.1	–8.6	–9.6
Travel, credit	2 236 . .	**38.3**	**53.6**	**117.3**	**130.3**	**107.4**	**120.0**	**123.7**	**161.9**
Business travel	2 237 . .	. . .	. . .	4.6	2.8	5.7	4.2	4.5	14.6
Personal travel	2 240 . .	38.3	53.6	112.7	127.6	101.6	115.8	119.3	147.4
Travel, debit	3 236 . .	**–51.8**	**–49.1**	**–55.6**	**–67.3**	**–74.6**	**–78.7**	**–76.2**	**–145.2**
Business travel	3 237 . .	–19.7	–15.0	–12.0	–15.5	–17.2	–17.8	–16.0	–47.9
Personal travel	3 240 . .	–32.1	–34.1	–43.6	–51.8	–57.4	–61.0	–60.2	–97.3
Other services, credit	2 200 BA	**47.2**	**33.1**	**54.8**	**42.3**	**39.5**	**34.5**	**26.7**	**60.1**
Communications	2 245 . .	. . .	. . .	.1	. . .	.2	.2	2.4	2.8
Construction	2 249 . .	. . .	. . .	2.3	3.8	.9	.8	.3	.7
Insurance	2 253 . .	2.0	2.1	6.3	1.0	.7	.6	3.1	8.8
Financial	2 260 . .	. . .	. . .	8.6	7.0	9.8	9.0	5.8	9.8
Computer and information	2 262 . .	. . .	. . .	. . .	. . .	. . .	. . .	. . .	. . .
Royalties and licence fees	2 266 . .	. . .	. . .	. . .	. . .	. . .	. . .	. . .	. . .
Other business services	2 268 . .	9.8	2.4	11.1	6.5	7.2	6.4	3.5	14.1
Personal, cultural, and recreational	2 287 . .	. . .	. . .	. . .	. . .	. . .	. . .	. . .	. . .
Government, n.i.e.	2 291 . .	35.4	28.6	26.5	23.9	20.8	17.5	11.5	24.0
Other services, debit	3 200 BA	**–90.3**	**–73.9**	**–106.9**	**–82.8**	**–90.7**	**–79.4**	**–81.2**	**–111.6**
Communications	3 245 . .	. . .	. . .	–2.7	–3.4	–4.6	–4.4	–.1	–.7
Construction	3 249 . .	. . .	. . .	–18.5	–3.4	–2.4	–2.1	–1.2	–.7
Insurance	3 253 . .	–18.2	–15.4	–14.0	–9.9	–13.0	–11.3	–28.1	–28.1
Financial	3 260 . .	. . .	. . .	–6.4	–5.2	–5.9	–7.5	–10.7	–7.4
Computer and information	3 262 . .	. . .	. . .	. . .	. . .	. . .	. . .	. . .	. . .
Royalties and licence fees	3 266 . .	. . .	. . .	–7.8	–5.8	–10.5	–9.1	–2.1	–5.8
Other business services	3 268 . .	–44.6	–37.1	–52.5	–51.1	–49.4	–41.1	–33.7	–64.5
Personal, cultural, and recreational	3 287 . .	. . .	. . .	–.2	–.1	–.1	–.1	. . .	–.1
Government, n.i.e.	3 291 . .	–27.5	–21.3	–4.7	–3.9	–4.7	–3.8	–5.2	–4.3

Table 2 (Continued). STANDARD PRESENTATION, 1988–95
(Millions of U.S. dollars)

	Code		1988	1989	1990	1991	1992	1993	1994	1995
C. INCOME	4 300	. .	–326.7	–238.8	–105.9	62.9	112.4	293.6	–224.2	–32.4
Total credit	2 300	. .	*220.1*	*244.8*	*416.2*	*483.1*	*542.1*	*554.5*	*230.8*	*483.2*
Total debit	3 300	. .	*–546.8*	*–483.6*	*–522.1*	*–420.2*	*–429.7*	*–260.9*	*–455.0*	*–515.6*
Compensation of employees, credit	2 310	. .	**54.7**	**42.4**	**81.3**	**78.9**	**86.8**	**64.5**	**63.4**	**55.3**
Compensation of employees, debit	3 310	. .	**. . .**	**. . .**	**–58.6**	**–48.9**	**–65.7**	**–50.1**	**–47.4**	**–42.2**
Investment income, credit	2 320	. .	**165.4**	**202.4**	**334.9**	**404.1**	**455.3**	**490.0**	**167.4**	**427.9**
Direct investment income	2 330	. .	8.2	14.6	30.4	32.3	32.2	26.4	25.6	58.3
Dividends and distributed branch profits	2 332	. .	8.2	14.6	20.6	21.3	22.0	16.1	16.1	17.0
Reinvested earnings and undistributed branch profits	2 333	. .	. . .	. . .	7.4	8.5	9.9	9.6	9.1	40.9
Income on debt (interest)	2 334	. .	. . .	. . .	2.5	2.5	.4	.7	.4	.4
Portfolio investment income	2 339	. .	. . .	. . .	297.5	363.4	417.3	458.3	136.1	359.6
Income on equity	2 340	. .	. . .	. . .	297.5	363.4	417.3	458.3	136.1	359.6
Income on bonds and notes	2 350	. .	. . .	. . .	. . .	. . .	. . .	. . .	. . .	. . .
Income on money market instruments and financial derivatives	2 360	. .	. . .	. . .	. . .	. . .	. . .	. . .	. . .	. . .
Other investment income	2 370	. .	157.2	187.8	7.0	8.5	5.8	5.3	5.6	9.9
Investment income, debit	3 320	. .	**–546.8**	**–483.6**	**–463.4**	**–371.3**	**–364.0**	**–210.8**	**–407.6**	**–473.4**
Direct investment income	3 330	. .	–239.4	–323.6	–406.9	–318.8	–287.1	–80.8	–265.3	–415.7
Dividends and distributed branch profits	3 332	. .	–239.4	–309.0	–339.4	–359.9	–338.3	–341.4	–314.5	–346.4
Reinvested earnings and undistributed branch profits	3 333	. .	. . .	–14.6	31.3	148.2	157.3	354.1	69.0	–48.0
Income on debt (interest)	3 334	. .	. . .	. . .	–98.7	–107.1	–106.1	–93.6	–19.8	–21.2
Portfolio investment income	3 339	. .	. . .	. . .	. . .	. . .	. . .	. . .	. . .	. . .
Income on equity	3 340	. .	. . .	. . .	. . .	. . .	. . .	. . .	. . .	. . .
Income on bonds and notes	3 350	. .	. . .	. . .	. . .	. . .	. . .	. . .	. . .	. . .
Income on money market instruments and financial derivatives	3 360	. .	. . .	. . .	. . .	. . .	. . .	. . .	. . .	. . .
Other investment income	3 370	. .	–307.4	–160.0	–56.5	–52.5	–76.9	–130.0	–142.3	–57.8
D. CURRENT TRANSFERS	4 379	. .	167.1	213.6	129.9	179.5	115.5	77.2	74.9	–27.3
Credit	2 379	. .	**301.8**	**266.8**	**392.0**	**455.5**	**391.1**	**352.3**	**370.0**	**342.3**
General government	2 380	. .	284.3	256.0	359.9	395.7	338.2	337.7	358.4	333.3
Other sectors	2 390	. .	17.5	10.8	32.1	59.8	52.9	14.6	11.6	8.9
Workers' remittances	2 391	. .	. . .	. . .	. . .	. . .	. . .	. . .	. . .	. . .
Other current transfers	2 392	. .	17.5	10.8	32.1	59.8	52.9	14.6	11.6	8.9
Debit	3 379	. .	**–134.7**	**–53.2**	**–262.1**	**–276.0**	**–275.6**	**–275.1**	**–295.1**	**–369.5**
General government	3 380	. .	–99.7	–5.5	–198.7	–201.8	–196.6	–187.2	–192.2	–202.9
Other sectors	3 390	. .	–35.0	–47.7	–63.4	–74.2	–79.0	–87.9	–102.9	–166.6
Workers' remittances	3 391	. .	. . .	–35.7	–59.3	–69.0	–73.5	–81.4	–97.9	–156.8
Other current transfers	3 392	. .	–35.0	–12.0	–4.1	–5.2	–5.5	–6.5	–5.0	–9.8
CAPITAL AND FINANCIAL ACCOUNT	4 996	. .	**–407.6**	**–457.2**	**–221.2**	**–247.2**	**–122.9**	**–428.9**	**–92.2**	**–237.5**
CAPITAL ACCOUNT	4 994	. .	**. . .**	**6.3**	**3.4**	**3.5**	**6.6**	**8.5**	**6.0**	**2.9**
Total credit	2 994	. .	. . .	*7.0*	*4.3*	*4.6*	*7.2*	*9.7*	*6.5*	*3.8*
Total debit	3 994	. .	. . .	*–.7*	*–.9*	*–1.0*	*–.5*	*–1.3*	*–.4*	*–.9*
Capital transfers, credit	2 400	. .	**. . .**	**7.0**	**4.3**	**4.6**	**7.2**	**9.7**	**6.5**	**3.8**
General government	2 401	. .	. . .	. . .	. . .	. . .	. . .	. . .	. . .	. . .
Debt forgiveness	2 402	. .	. . .	. . .	. . .	. . .	. . .	. . .	. . .	. . .
Other capital transfers	2 410	. .	. . .	. . .	. . .	. . .	. . .	. . .	. . .	. . .
Other sectors	2 430	. .	. . .	7.0	4.3	4.6	7.2	9.7	6.5	3.8
Migrants' transfers	2 431	. .	. . .	7.0	4.3	4.6	7.2	9.7	6.5	3.8
Debt forgiveness	2 432	. .	. . .	. . .	. . .	. . .	. . .	. . .	. . .	. . .
Other capital transfers	2 440	. .	. . .	. . .	. . .	. . .	. . .	. . .	. . .	. . .
Capital transfers, debit	3 400	. .	**. . .**	**–.7**	**–.9**	**–1.0**	**–.5**	**–1.3**	**–.4**	**–.9**
General government	3 401	. .	. . .	. . .	. . .	. . .	. . .	. . .	. . .	. . .
Debt forgiveness	3 402	. .	. . .	. . .	. . .	. . .	. . .	. . .	. . .	. . .
Other capital transfers	3 410	. .	. . .	. . .	. . .	. . .	. . .	. . .	. . .	. . .
Other sectors	3 430	. .	. . .	–.7	–.9	–1.0	–.5	–1.3	–.4	–.9
Migrants' transfers	3 431	. .	. . .	–.7	–.9	–1.0	–.5	–1.3	–.4	–.9
Debt forgiveness	3 432	. .	. . .	. . .	. . .	. . .	. . .	. . .	. . .	. . .
Other capital transfers	3 440	. .	. . .	. . .	. . .	. . .	. . .	. . .	. . .	. . .
Nonproduced nonfinancial assets, credit	2 480	. .	**. . .**	**. . .**	**. . .**	**. . .**	**. . .**	**. . .**	**. . .**	**. . .**
Nonproduced nonfinancial assets, debit	3 480	. .	**. . .**	**. . .**	**. . .**	**. . .**	**. . .**	**. . .**	**. . .**	**. . .**

Table 2 (Continued). STANDARD PRESENTATION, 1988–95
(Millions of U.S. dollars)

	Code	1988	1989	1990	1991	1992	1993	1994	1995
FINANCIAL ACCOUNT	4 995	**–407.6**	**–463.5**	**–224.6**	**–250.8**	**–129.6**	**–437.3**	**–98.2**	**–240.4**
A. DIRECT INVESTMENT	4 500	39.9	42.2	88.5	–16.7	–11.4	–296.4	–23.8	29.5
Direct investment abroad	4 505	**. . .**	**. . .**	**–7.4**	**–8.5**	**–9.9**	**–9.5**	**–9.5**	**–40.9**
Equity capital	4 510	. . .	. . .	. . .	. . .	. . .	.1	–.4	. . .
Claims on affiliated enterprises	4 515	. . .	. . .	. . .	. . .	. . .	. . .	. . .	. . .
Liabilities to affiliated enterprises	4 520	. . .	. . .	. . .	. . .	. . .	. . .	. . .	. . .
Reinvested earnings	4 525	. . .	. . .	–7.4	–8.5	–9.9	–9.6	–9.1	–40.9
Other capital	4 530	. . .	. . .	. . .	. . .	. . .	. . .	. . .	. . .
Claims on affiliated enterprises	4 535	. . .	. . .	. . .	. . .	. . .	. . .	. . .	. . .
Liabilities to affiliated enterprises	4 540	. . .	. . .	. . .	. . .	. . .	. . .	. . .	. . .
Direct investment in Botswana	4 555	**39.9**	**42.2**	**95.9**	**–8.2**	**–1.6**	**–286.9**	**–14.3**	**70.4**
Equity capital	4 560	. . .	27.5	68.2	6.9	22.1	9.2	12.2	18.4
Claims on direct investors	4 565	. . .	. . .	. . .	. . .	. . .	. . .	. . .	. . .
Liabilities to direct investors	4 570	. . .	. . .	. . .	. . .	. . .	. . .	. . .	. . .
Reinvested earnings	4 575	. . .	14.6	–31.3	–148.2	–157.3	–354.1	–69.0	48.0
Other capital	4 580	39.9	. . .	59.0	133.1	133.7	57.9	42.5	4.0
Claims on direct investors	4 585	. . .	. . .	. . .	. . .	. . .	. . .	. . .	. . .
Liabilities to direct investors	4 590	. . .	. . .	. . .	. . .	. . .	. . .	. . .	. . .
B. PORTFOLIO INVESTMENT	4 600	. . .	. . .	1.3	–1.2	.1	.2	–.1	–30.6
Assets	4 602	**. . .**	**. . .**	**. . .**	**. . .**	**. . .**	**. . .**	**. . .**	**–36.4**
Equity securities	4 610	. . .	. . .	. . .	. . .	. . .	. . .	. . .	–30.8
Monetary authorities	4 611	. . .	. . .	. . .	. . .	. . .	. . .	. . .	. . .
General government	4 612	. . .	. . .	. . .	. . .	. . .	. . .	. . .	. . .
Banks	4 613	. . .	. . .	. . .	. . .	. . .	. . .	. . .	. . .
Other sectors	4 614	. . .	. . .	. . .	. . .	. . .	. . .	. . .	–30.8
Debt securities	4 619	. . .	. . .	. . .	. . .	. . .	. . .	. . .	–5.6
Bonds and notes	4 620	. . .	. . .	. . .	. . .	. . .	. . .	. . .	–5.4
Monetary authorities	4 621	. . .	. . .	. . .	. . .	. . .	. . .	. . .	. . .
General government	4 622	. . .	. . .	. . .	. . .	. . .	. . .	. . .	. . .
Banks	4 623	. . .	. . .	. . .	. . .	. . .	. . .	. . .	. . .
Other sectors	4 624	. . .	. . .	. . .	. . .	. . .	. . .	. . .	–5.4
Money market instruments	4 630	. . .	. . .	. . .	. . .	. . .	. . .	. . .	. . .
Monetary authorities	4 631	. . .	. . .	. . .	. . .	. . .	. . .	. . .	. . .
General government	4 632	. . .	. . .	. . .	. . .	. . .	. . .	. . .	. . .
Banks	4 633	. . .	. . .	. . .	. . .	. . .	. . .	. . .	. . .
Other sectors	4 634	. . .	. . .	. . .	. . .	. . .	. . .	. . .	. . .
Financial derivatives	4 640	. . .	. . .	. . .	. . .	. . .	. . .	. . .	–.2
Monetary authorities	4 641	. . .	. . .	. . .	. . .	. . .	. . .	. . .	. . .
General government	4 642	. . .	. . .	. . .	. . .	. . .	. . .	. . .	. . .
Banks	4 643	. . .	. . .	. . .	. . .	. . .	. . .	. . .	–.2
Other sectors	4 644	. . .	. . .	. . .	. . .	. . .	. . .	. . .	. . .
Liabilities	4 652	**. . .**	**. . .**	**1.3**	**–1.2**	**.1**	**.2**	**–.1**	**5.8**
Equity securities	4 660	. . .	. . .	. . .	. . .	. . .	. . .	. . .	5.5
Banks	4 663	. . .	. . .	. . .	. . .	. . .	. . .	. . .	. . .
Other sectors	4 664	. . .	. . .	. . .	. . .	. . .	. . .	. . .	5.5
Debt securities	4 669	. . .	. . .	1.3	–1.2	.1	.2	–.1	.3
Bonds and notes	4 670	. . .	. . .	. . .	. . .	. . .	. . .	. . .	. . .
Monetary authorities	4 671	. . .	. . .	. . .	. . .	. . .	. . .	. . .	. . .
General government	4 672	. . .	. . .	. . .	. . .	. . .	. . .	. . .	. . .
Banks	4 673	. . .	. . .	. . .	. . .	. . .	. . .	. . .	. . .
Other sectors	4 674	. . .	. . .	. . .	. . .	. . .	. . .	. . .	. . .
Money market instruments	4 680	. . .	. . .	1.3	–1.2	.1	.2	–.1	. . .
Monetary authorities	4 681	. . .	. . .	. . .	. . .	. . .	. . .	. . .	. . .
General government	4 682	. . .	. . .	. . .	. . .	. . .	. . .	. . .	. . .
Banks	4 683	. . .	. . .	. . .	. . .	. . .	. . .	. . .	. . .
Other sectors	4 684	. . .	. . .	1.3	–1.2	.1	.2	–.1	. . .
Financial derivatives	4 690	. . .	. . .	. . .	. . .	. . .	. . .	. . .	.3
Monetary authorities	4 691	. . .	. . .	. . .	. . .	. . .	. . .	. . .	. . .
General government	4 692	. . .	. . .	. . .	. . .	. . .	. . .	. . .	. . .
Banks	4 693	. . .	. . .	. . .	. . .	. . .	. . .	. . .	. . .
Other sectors	4 694	. . .	. . .	. . .	. . .	. . .	. . .	. . .	.3

Table 2 (Concluded). STANDARD PRESENTATION, 1988–95
(Millions of U.S. dollars)

	Code	1988	1989	1990	1991	1992	1993	1994	1995
C. OTHER INVESTMENT	4 700 . .	−65.2	70.8	−7.2	141.2	287.1	255.9	65.0	−32.8
Assets	4 703 . .	**−68.3**	**−34.6**	**−136.9**	**−53.0**	**148.9**	**63.4**	**15.8**	**−88.7**
Trade credits	4 706 . .	. . .	. . .	−6.3	−20.2	6.6	10.4	−11.2	−40.0
General government: long-term	4 708 . .	. . .	. . .	. . .	. . .	. . .	. . .	. . .	. . .
General government: short-term	4 709 . .	. . .	. . .	. . .	. . .	. . .	. . .	. . .	. . .
Other sectors: long-term	4 711 . .	. . .	. . .	−.1	. . .	. . .	. . .	−.1	−.2
Other sectors: short-term	4 712 . .	. . .	. . .	−6.2	−20.3	6.6	10.4	−11.1	−39.8
Loans	4 714 . .	. . .	. . .	−.1	1.5	.1	−1.2	−1.2	−.1
Monetary authorities: long-term	4 717 . .	. . .	. . .	. . .	. . .	. . .	. . .	. . .	. . .
Monetary authorities: short-term	4 718 . .	. . .	. . .	. . .	. . .	. . .	. . .	. . .	. . .
General government: long-term	4 720 . .	. . .	. . .	. . .	. . .	. . .	. . .	. . .	. . .
General government: short-term	4 721 . .	. . .	. . .	. . .	. . .	. . .	. . .	. . .	. . .
Banks: long-term	4 723 . .	. . .	. . .	. . .	. . .	. . .	. . .	. . .	. . .
Banks: short-term	4 724 . .	. . .	. . .	. . .	. . .	. . .	. . .	. . .	. . .
Other sectors: long-term	4 726 . .	. . .	. . .	−.1	1.5	.1	−1.2	−1.2	. . .
Other sectors: short-term	4 727 . .	. . .	. . .	. . .	. . .	. . .	. . .	. . .	. . .
Currency and deposits	4 730 . .	−65.3	10.4	−33.5	−23.4	−7.0	14.3	.4	2.2
Monetary authorities	4 731 . .	. . .	. . .	. . .	. . .	. . .	. . .	. . .	. . .
General government	4 732 . .	−38.4	. . .	. . .	. . .	. . .	. . .	. . .	. . .
Banks	4 733 . .	−8.9	10.4	−33.5	−23.4	−7.0	14.3	.4	−8.7
Other sectors	4 734 . .	−18.0	. . .	. . .	. . .	. . .	. . .	. . .	10.9
Other assets	4 736 . .	−3.0	−45.0	−97.1	−10.8	149.2	40.0	27.8	−50.9
Monetary authorities: long-term	4 738 . .	. . .	. . .	. . .	. . .	. . .	. . .	. . .	. . .
Monetary authorities: short-term	4 739 . .	. . .	. . .	. . .	. . .	. . .	. . .	. . .	. . .
General government: long-term	4 741 . .	. . .	. . .	−91.8	11.7	139.9	56.1	19.7	−46.1
General government: short-term	4 742 . .	−3.0	−45.0	. . .	. . .	. . .	. . .	. . .	. . .
Banks: long-term	4 744 . .	. . .	. . .	. . .	. . .	. . .	. . .	. . .	. . .
Banks: short-term	4 745 . .	. . .	. . .	. . .	. . .	. . .	. . .	. . .	. . .
Other sectors: long-term	4 747 . .	. . .	. . .	−2.1	−2.4	−16.5	1.4	1.2	−2.9
Other sectors: short-term	4 748 . .	. . .	. . .	−3.2	−20.1	25.9	−17.5	6.9	−1.9
Liabilities	4 753 . .	**3.1**	**105.4**	**129.7**	**194.2**	**138.2**	**192.5**	**49.2**	**55.9**
Trade credits	4 756 . .	. . .	72.3	−6.3	19.8	−3.6	16.8	18.8	40.0
General government: long-term	4 758 . .	. . .	. . .	. . .	. . .	. . .	. . .	. . .	. . .
General government: short-term	4 759 . .	. . .	. . .	. . .	. . .	. . .	. . .	. . .	. . .
Other sectors: long-term	4 761 . .	. . .	. . .	−5.9	−.6	.9	−.1	.8	. . .
Other sectors: short-term	4 762 . .	. . .	72.3	−.4	20.4	−4.6	16.8	18.0	40.0
Loans	4 764 . .	. . .	−68.9	114.4	140.4	55.3	92.2	71.2	−34.8
Use of Fund credit and loans from the Fund	4 766 . .	. . .	. . .	. . .	. . .	. . .	. . .	. . .	. . .
Monetary authorities: other long term	4 767 . .	. . .	. . .	. . .	. . .	. . .	. . .	. . .	. . .
Monetary authorities: short-term	4 768 . .	. . .	. . .	. . .	. . .	. . .	. . .	. . .	. . .
General government: long-term	4 770 . .	. . .	28.2	12.3	77.9	54.4	67.0	6.5	−12.3
General government: short-term	4 771 . .	. . .	. . .	. . .	. . .	. . .	. . .	. . .	. . .
Banks: long-term	4 773 . .	. . .	. . .	. . .	. . .	. . .	. . .	. . .	. . .
Banks: short-term	4 774 . .	. . .	. . .	. . .	. . .	. . .	. . .	. . .	. . .
Other sectors: long-term	4 776 . .	. . .	−14.6	102.2	62.5	.9	25.3	64.7	−3.8
Other sectors: short-term	4 777 . .	. . .	−82.5	. . .	. . .	. . .	. . .	. . .	−18.7
Currency and deposits	4 780 . .	3.1	−4.6	9.5	−3.6	−5.6	23.1	−2.8	−2.5
Monetary authorities	4 781 . .	. . .	. . .	. . .	. . .	. . .	. . .	. . .	. . .
General government	4 782 . .	. . .	. . .	. . .	. . .	. . .	. . .	. . .	. . .
Banks	4 783 . .	3.1	−4.6	9.5	−3.6	−5.6	23.1	−2.8	−2.5
Other sectors	4 784 . .	. . .	. . .	. . .	. . .	. . .	. . .	. . .	. . .
Other liabilities	4 786 . .	. . .	106.7	12.1	37.5	92.1	60.4	−38.0	53.2
Monetary authorities: long-term	4 788 . .	. . .	. . .	. . .	. . .	. . .	. . .	. . .	. . .
Monetary authorities: short-term	4 789 . .	. . .	. . .	. . .	. . .	. . .	. . .	. . .	. . .
General government: long-term	4 791 . .	. . .	. . .	. . .	. . .	. . .	. . .	. . .	. . .
General government: short-term	4 792 . .	. . .	. . .	. . .	. . .	. . .	. . .	. . .	. . .
Banks: long-term	4 794 . .	. . .	. . .	. . .	. . .	. . .	. . .	. . .	. . .
Banks: short-term	4 795 . .	. . .	. . .	. . .	. . .	. . .	. . .	. . .	. . .
Other sectors: long-term	4 797 . .	. . .	106.7	10.5	−2.8	79.4	−3.7	−.7	38.1
Other sectors: short-term	4 798 . .	. . .	. . .	1.6	40.3	12.8	64.1	−37.3	15.1
D. RESERVE ASSETS	4 800 . .	−382.3	−576.5	−307.2	−374.1	−405.3	−397.0	−139.3	−206.6
Monetary gold	4 810 . .	. . .	. . .	. . .	. . .	. . .	. . .	. . .	. . .
Special drawing rights	4 820 . .	−1.9	−2.7	−3.8	−3.3	2.2	−2.2	−2.0	−2.5
Reserve position in the Fund	4 830 . .	2.8	−7.0	4.2	3.7	−1.8	−2.5	.4	−4.4
Foreign exchange	4 840 . .	−383.2	−566.7	−527.2	−725.2	−402.3	−791.4	−533.1	−451.3
Other claims	4 880 . .	. . .	. . .	219.6	350.7	−3.4	399.1	395.4	251.7
NET ERRORS AND OMISSIONS	4 998 . .	**213.7**	**−34.7**	**179.2**	**−89.7**	**−121.4**	**−74.5**	**−151.1**	**−104.6**

Part 3 of the *Yearbook* contains descriptions of the methodologies, compilation practices, and sources used to compile these data.

Table 3. INTERNATIONAL INVESTMENT POSITION (End–period stocks), 1988–95
(Millions of U.S. dollars)

	Code		1988	1989	1990	1991	1992	1993	1994	1995
ASSETS	8 995	C.	...	...	...	...	...	...	4,753.8	5,176.9
Direct investment abroad	8 505	. .	**...**	**...**	**...**	**...**	**...**	**...**	**13.5**	**44.5**
Equity capital and reinvested earnings	8 506	. .	...	...	...	...	...	...	10.4	41.6
Claims on affiliated enterprises	8 507	. .	...	...	...	...	...	...	...	...
Liabilities to affiliated enterprises	8 508	. .	...	...	...	...	...	...	...	...
Other capital	8 530	. .	...	...	...	...	...	...	3.1	3.0
Claims on affiliated enterprises	8 535	. .	...	...	...	...	...	...	...	...
Liabilities to affiliated enterprises	8 540	. .	...	...	...	...	...	...	...	...
Portfolio investment	8 602	. .	**...**	**...**	**...**	**...**	**...**	**...**	**26.9**	**61.7**
Equity securities	8 610	. .	...	...	...	...	...	...	16.1	45.8
Monetary authorities	8 611	. .	...	...	...	...	...	...	...	...
General government	8 612	. .	...	...	...	...	...	...	...	...
Banks	8 613	. .	...	...	...	...	...	...	...	...
Other sectors	8 614	. .	...	...	...	...	...	...	16.1	45.8
Debt securities	8 619	. .	...	...	...	...	...	...	10.9	15.9
Bonds and notes	8 620	. .	...	...	...	...	...	...	10.9	15.8
Monetary authorities	8 621	. .	...	...	...	...	...	...	...	...
General government	8 622	. .	...	...	...	...	...	...	...	...
Banks	8 623	. .	...	...	...	...	...	...	...	...
Other sectors	8 624	. .	...	...	...	...	...	...	10.9	15.8
Money market instruments	8 630	. .	...	...	...	...	...	...	...	...
Monetary authorities	8 631	. .	...	...	...	...	...	...	...	...
General government	8 632	. .	...	...	...	...	...	...	...	...
Banks	8 633	. .	...	...	...	...	...	...	...	...
Other sectors	8 634	. .	...	...	...	...	...	...	...	...
Financial derivatives	8 640	. .	...	...	...	...	...	...	...	.2
Monetary authorities	8 641	. .	...	...	...	...	...	...	...	...
General government	8 642	. .	...	...	...	...	...	...	...	...
Banks	8 643	. .	...	...	...	...	...	...	...	...
Other sectors	8 644	. .	...	...	...	...	...	...	...	.2
Other investment	8 703	. .	**...**	**...**	**...**	**...**	**...**	**...**	**311.8**	**374.5**
Trade credits	8 706	. .	...	...	...	...	...	...	38.7	76.5
General government: long-term	8 708	. .	...	...	...	...	...	...	...	...
General government: short-term	8 709	. .	...	...	...	...	...	...	...	...
Other sectors: long-term	8 711	. .	...	...	...	...	...	...	.3	.3
Other sectors: short-term	8 712	. .	...	...	...	...	...	...	38.4	76.2
Loans	8 714	. .	...	...	...	...	...	...	3.1	3.0
Monetary authorities: long-term	8 717	. .	...	...	...	...	...	...	...	...
Monetary authorities: short-term	8 718	. .	...	...	...	...	...	...	...	...
General government: long-term	8 720	. .	...	...	...	...	...	...	...	...
General government: short-term	8 721	. .	...	...	...	...	...	...	...	...
Banks: long-term	8 723	. .	...	...	...	...	...	...	...	...
Banks: short-term	8 724	. .	...	...	...	...	...	...	...	...
Other sectors: long-term	8 726	. .	...	...	...	...	...	...	...	...
Other sectors: short-term	8 727	. .	...	...	...	...	...	...	3.1	3.0
Currency and deposits	8 730	. .	...	...	...	...	...	...	80.7	75.6
Monetary authorities	8 731	. .	...	...	...	...	...	...	...	...
General government	8 732	. .	...	...	...	...	...	...	...	...
Banks	8 733	. .	...	...	...	...	...	...	63.3	69.5
Other sectors	8 734	. .	...	...	...	...	...	...	17.4	6.1
Other assets	8 736	. .	...	...	...	...	...	...	189.4	219.4
Monetary authorities: long-term	8 738	. .	...	...	...	...	...	...	...	...
Monetary authorities: short-term	8 739	. .	...	...	...	...	...	...	...	...
General government: long-term	8 741	. .	...	...	...	...	...	...	...	...
General government: short-term	8 742	. .	...	...	...	...	...	...	...	...
Banks: long-term	8 744	. .	...	...	...	...	...	...	...	...
Banks: short-term	8 745	. .	...	...	...	...	...	...	...	...
Other sectors: long-term	8 747	. .	...	...	...	...	...	...	149.8	187.8
Other sectors: short-term	8 748	. .	...	...	...	...	...	...	39.5	31.6
Reserve assets	8 800	. .	**...**	**...**	**...**	**...**	**...**	**...**	**4,401.5**	**4,696.2**
Monetary gold	8 810	. .	...	...	...	...	...	...	...	...
Special drawing rights	8 820	. .	22.6	24.9	30.9	34.5	30.9	33.0	37.1	40.2
Reserve position in the Fund	8 830	. .	18.4	25.3	23.0	19.2	20.3	22.8	23.9	28.7
Foreign exchange	8 840	. .	...	...	...	...	...	...	4,340.4	4,624.1
Other claims	8 880	. .	...	...	...	...	...	...	...	...

Table 3 (Continued). INTERNATIONAL INVESTMENT POSITION (End–period stocks), 1988–95
(Millions of U.S. dollars)

	Code		1988	1989	1990	1991	1992	1993	1994	1995
LIABILITIES	8 995	D.	...	...	...	...	...	...	1,807.2	1,760.7
Direct investment in Botswana	8 555	..	**...**	**...**	**...**	**...**	**...**	**...**	**321.9**	**373.4**
Equity capital and reinvested earnings	8 556	..	...	...	...	...	...	...	79.3	207.3
Claims on direct investors	8 557	..	...	...	...	...	...	...	...	...
Liabilities to direct investors	8 558	..	...	...	...	...	...	...	...	...
Other capital	8 580	..	...	...	...	...	...	...	242.6	166.1
Claims on direct investors	8 585	..	...	...	...	...	...	...	...	...
Liabilities to direct investors	8 590	..	...	...	...	...	...	...	...	...
Portfolio investment	8 652	..	**...**	**...**	**...**	**...**	**...**	**...**	**10.9**	**16.2**
Equity securities	8 660	..	...	...	...	...	...	...	10.9	15.9
Banks	8 663	..	...	...	...	...	...	...	...	...
Other sectors	8 664	..	...	...	...	...	...	...	10.9	15.9
Debt securities	8 669	..	...	...	...	...	...	...	...	.2
Bonds and notes	8 670	..	...	...	...	...	...	...	...	...
Monetary authorities	8 671	..	...	...	...	...	...	...	...	...
General government	8 672	..	...	...	...	...	...	...	...	...
Banks	8 673	..	...	...	...	...	...	...	...	...
Other sectors	8 674	..	...	...	...	...	...	...	...	...
Money market instruments	8 680	..	...	...	...	...	...	...	...	...
Monetary authorities	8 681	..	...	...	...	...	...	...	...	...
General government	8 682	..	...	...	...	...	...	...	...	...
Banks	8 683	..	...	...	...	...	...	...	...	...
Other sectors	8 684	..	...	...	...	...	...	...	...	...
Financial derivatives	8 690	..	...	...	...	...	...	...	...	.2
Monetary authorities	8 691	..	...	...	...	...	...	...	...	...
General government	8 692	..	...	...	...	...	...	...	...	...
Banks	8 692	..	...	...	...	...	...	...	...	...
Other sectors	8 694	..	...	...	...	...	...	...	...	.2
Other investment	8 753	..	**...**	**...**	**...**	**...**	**...**	**...**	**1,474.4**	**1,371.2**
Trade credits	8 756	..	...	...	...	...	...	...	49.8	87.2
General government: long-term	8 758	..	...	...	...	...	...	...	...	...
General government: short-term	8 759	..	...	...	...	...	...	...	...	...
Other sectors: long-term	8 761	..	...	...	...	...	...	...	.3	.3
Other sectors: short-term	8 762	..	...	...	...	...	...	...	49.5	86.9
Loans	8 764	..	...	...	...	...	...	...	729.0	564.3
Use of Fund credit and loans from the Fund	8 766	..	...	...	...	...	...	...	...	...
Monetary authorities: other long-term	8 767	..	...	...	...	...	...	...	...	...
Monetary authorities: short-term	8 768	..	...	...	...	...	...	...	...	...
General government: long-term	8 770	..	...	...	...	...	...	...	496.9	495.8
General government: short-term	8 771	..	...	...	...	...	...	...	...	...
Banks: long-term	8 773	..	...	...	...	...	...	...	...	...
Banks: short-term	8 774	..	...	...	...	...	...	...	...	...
Other sectors: long-term	8 776	..	...	...	...	...	...	...	194.3	50.3
Other sectors: short-term	8 777	..	...	...	...	...	...	...	37.9	18.1
Currency and deposits	8 780	..	...	...	...	...	...	...	38.9	35.1
Monetary authorities	8 781	..	...	...	...	...	...	...	...	...
General government	8 782	..	...	...	...	...	...	...	...	...
Banks	8 783	..	...	...	...	...	...	...	38.9	35.1
Other sectors	8 784	..	...	...	...	...	...	...	...	...
Other liabilities	8 786	..	...	...	...	...	...	...	656.6	684.6
Monetary authorities: long-term	8 788	..	...	...	...	...	...	...	...	...
Monetary authorities: short-term	8 789	..	...	...	...	...	...	...	...	...
General government: long-term	8 791	..	...	...	...	...	...	...	...	...
General government: short-term	8 792	..	...	...	...	...	...	...	...	...
Banks: long-term	8 794	..	...	...	...	...	...	...	...	...
Banks: short-term	8 795	..	...	...	...	...	...	...	...	...
Other sectors: long-term	8 797	..	...	...	...	...	...	...	634.6	649.5
Other sectors: short-term	8 798	..	...	...	...	...	...	...	22.0	35.2
NET INTERNATIONAL INVESTMENT POSITION	8 995	..	**...**	**...**	**...**	**...**	**...**	**...**	**2,946.6**	**3,416.2**
Conversion rates: pula per U.S. dollar (end of period)	0 102	..	**1.9357**	**1.8723**	**1.8713**	**2.0725**	**2.2568**	**2.5648**	**2.7174**	**2.8217**

Table 1. ANALYTIC PRESENTATION, 1988–95
(Millions of U.S. dollars)

	Code	1988	1989	1990	1991	1992	1993	1994	1995
A. Current Account[1]	4 993 Y.	**4,156**	**1,002**	**–3,823**	**–1,450**	**6,089**	**20**	**–1,153**	**–18,136**
Goods: exports f.o.b.	2 100 . .	33,773	34,375	31,408	31,619	35,793	39,630	44,102	46,506
Goods: imports f.o.b.	3 100 . .	–14,605	–18,263	–20,661	–21,041	–20,554	–25,301	–33,241	–49,663
Balance on Goods	4 100 . .	*19,168*	*16,112*	*10,747*	*10,578*	*15,239*	*14,329*	*10,861*	*–3,157*
Services: credit	2 200 . .	2,279	3,132	3,762	3,319	4,088	3,965	4,908	6,135
Services: debit	3 200 . .	–5,302	–5,917	–7,523	–7,210	–7,430	–9,555	–10,254	–13,630
Balance on Goods and Services	4 991 . .	*16,145*	*13,327*	*6,986*	*6,687*	*11,897*	*8,739*	*5,515*	*–10,652*
Income: credit	2 300 . .	771	1,310	1,157	904	1,118	1,308	2,202	3,457
Income: debit	3 300 . .	–12,851	–13,856	–12,765	–10,555	–9,115	–11,630	–11,293	–14,562
Balance on Goods, Services, and Income	4 992 . .	*4,065*	*781*	*–4,622*	*–2,964*	*3,900*	*–1,583*	*–3,576*	*–21,757*
Current transfers: credit	2 379 Y.	127	238	840	1,556	2,260	1,704	2,577	3,861
Current transfers: debit	3 379 . .	–36	–17	–41	–42	–71	–101	–154	–240
B. Capital Account[1]	4 994 Y.	**3**	**23**	**35**	**42**	**54**	**81**	**173**	**352**
Capital account: credit	2 994 Y.	4	27	36	43	54	86	175	363
Capital account: debit	3 994 . .	–1	–4	–1	–1	. . .	–5	–2	–11
Total, Groups A Plus B	4 010 . .	*4,159*	*1,025*	*–3,788*	*–1,408*	*6,143*	*101*	*–980*	*–17,784*
C. Financial Account[1]	4 995 X.	**–9,210**	**–12,525**	**–5,567**	**–4,129**	**6,516**	**7,604**	**7,965**	**29,310**
Direct investment abroad	4 505 . .	–175	–523	–665	–1,014	–137	–491	–1,037	–1,384
Direct investment in Brazil	4 555 Y.	2,804	1,131	989	1,103	2,061	1,292	3,072	4,859
Portfolio investment assets	4 602 . .	. . .	–30	–67	. . .	. . .	–606	–3,052	–936
Equity securities	4 610 . .	. . .	. . .	. . .	. . .	. . .	–607	. . .	–168
Debt securities	4 619 . .	. . .	–30	–67	. . .	. . .	1	–3,052	–768
Portfolio investment liabilities	4 652 Y.	–498	–391	579	3,808	7,366	12,928	47,784	10,171
Equity securities	4 660 Y.	189	–57	103	578	1,704	6,570	7,280	2,775
Debt securities	4 669 Y.	–687	–334	476	3,230	5,662	6,358	40,504	7,396
Other investment assets	4 703 . .	–1,994	–894	–2,864	–3,140	–99	–2,696	–4,368	–1,783
Monetary authorities	4 703 . A	–17	–5	22	8	. . .	–34	. . .	. . .
General government	4 703 . B	–98	–62	–108	–17	–44	29	. . .	. . .
Banks	4 703 . C	–328	–591	–2,758	–3,357	–37	–2,980	–4,077	–228
Other sectors	4 703 . D	–1,551	–236	–20	226	–18	289	–291	–1,555
Other investment liabilities	4 753 X.	–9,347	–11,818	–3,539	–4,886	–2,675	–2,823	–34,434	18,383
Monetary authorities	4 753 XA	3,230	267	–763	–273	350	–140	–600	–1,648
General government	4 753 YB	–3,729	–6,132	–2,715	–2,876	–1,968	–2,622	–35,609	. . .
Banks	4 753 YC	–1,786	–2,115	–229	386	1,167	–2,269	–1,439	7,071
Other sectors	4 753 YD	–7,062	–3,838	168	–2,123	–2,224	2,208	3,214	12,960
Total, Groups A Through C	4 020 . .	*–5,051*	*–11,500*	*–9,355*	*–5,537*	*12,659*	*7,705*	*6,985*	*11,526*
D. Net Errors and Omissions	4 998 . .	**–827**	**–819**	**–296**	**852**	**–1,393**	**–815**	**–442**	**1,447**
Total, Groups A Through D	4 030 . .	*–5,878*	*–12,319*	*–9,651*	*–4,685*	*11,266*	*6,890*	*6,543*	*12,973*
E. Reserves and Related Items	4 040 . .	**5,878**	**12,319**	**9,651**	**4,685**	**–11,266**	**–6,890**	**–6,543**	**–12,973**
Reserve assets	4 800 . .	–1,250	–893	–474	369	–14,670	–8,709	–7,215	–12,920
Use of Fund credit and loans	4 766 . .	–462	–808	–771	–566	–399	–504	–133	–49
Liabilities constituting foreign authorities' reserves	4 900 . .	73	1,099	126	–739	–627	. . .	55	–4
Exceptional financing	4 920 . .	7,516	12,921	10,771	5,621	4,430	2,323	750	. . .
Conversion rates: real per U.S. dollar	0 101 . .	**. . .**	**. . .**	**.00002**	**.00015**	**.00164**	**.03216**	**.63930**	**.91767**

[1] Excludes components that have been classified in the categories of Group E.

Table 2. STANDARD PRESENTATION, 1988–95

(Millions of U.S. dollars)

	Code	1988	1989	1990	1991	1992	1993	1994	1995
CURRENT ACCOUNT	4 993 . .	**4,156**	**1,002**	**–3,823**	**–1,450**	**6,089**	**20**	**–1,153**	**–18,136**
A. GOODS	4 100 . .	19,168	16,112	10,747	10,578	15,239	14,329	10,861	–3,157
Credit	2 100 . .	**33,773**	**34,375**	**31,408**	**31,619**	**35,793**	**39,630**	**44,102**	**46,506**
General merchandise: exports f.o.b.	2 110 . .	33,773	34,375	31,408	31,619	35,793	38,517	43,558	46,506
Goods for processing: exports f.o.b.	2 150 . .	. . .	. . .	. . .	. . .	. . .	. . .	. . .	. . .
Repairs on goods	2 160 . .	. . .	. . .	. . .	. . .	. . .	6	. . .	. . .
Goods procured in ports by carriers	2 170 . .	. . .	. . .	. . .	. . .	. . .	74	. . .	. . .
Nonmonetary gold	2 180 . .	. . .	. . .	. . .	. . .	. . .	1,033	544	. . .
Debit	3 100 . .	**–14,605**	**–18,263**	**–20,661**	**–21,041**	**–20,554**	**–25,301**	**–33,241**	**–49,663**
General merchandise: imports f.o.b.	3 110 . .	–14,605	–18,263	–20,661	–21,041	–20,554	–25,256	–33,168	–49,663
Goods for processing: imports f.o.b.	3 150 . .	. . .	. . .	. . .	. . .	. . .	. . .	. . .	. . .
Repairs on goods	3 160 . .	. . .	. . .	. . .	. . .	. . .	. . .	. . .	. . .
Goods procured in ports by carriers	3 170 . .	. . .	. . .	. . .	. . .	. . .	. . .	. . .	. . .
Nonmonetary gold	3 180 . .	. . .	. . .	. . .	. . .	. . .	–45	–73	. . .
B. SERVICES	4 200 . .	–3,023	–2,785	–3,761	–3,891	–3,342	–5,590	–5,346	–7,495
Total credit	2 200 . .	*2,279*	*3,132*	*3,762*	*3,319*	*4,088*	*3,965*	*4,908*	*6,135*
Total debit	3 200 . .	*–5,302*	*–5,917*	*–7,523*	*–7,210*	*–7,430*	*–9,555*	*–10,254*	*–13,630*
Transportation services, credit	2 205 . .	**1,318**	**1,349**	**1,348**	**1,457**	**1,924**	**1,638**	**2,200**	**2,600**
Passenger	2 205 BA	*55*	*21*	*32*	*71*	*296*	*149*	*229*	*113*
Freight	2 205 BB	*848*	*898*	*807*	*831*	*957*	*698*	*1,184*	*1,200*
Other	2 205 BC	*415*	*430*	*509*	*555*	*671*	*791*	*787*	*1,287*
Sea transport, passenger	2 207 . .	. . .	. . .	. . .	. . .	. . .	. . .	. . .	. . .
Sea transport, freight	2 208 . .	. . .	. . .	. . .	. . .	. . .	544	. . .	. . .
Sea transport, other	2 209 . .	. . .	. . .	. . .	. . .	. . .	591	. . .	. . .
Air transport, passenger	2 211 . .	. . .	. . .	. . .	. . .	. . .	149	. . .	. . .
Air transport, freight	2 212 . .	. . .	. . .	. . .	. . .	. . .	123	. . .	. . .
Air transport, other	2 213 . .	. . .	. . .	. . .	. . .	. . .	200	. . .	. . .
Other transport, passenger	2 215 . .	. . .	. . .	. . .	. . .	. . .	. . .	. . .	. . .
Other transport, freight	2 216 . .	. . .	. . .	. . .	. . .	. . .	31	. . .	. . .
Other transport, other	2 217 . .	. . .	. . .	. . .	. . .	. . .	. . .	. . .	. . .
Transportation services, debit	3 205 . .	**–2,358**	**–2,801**	**–2,991**	**–3,112**	**–3,284**	**–4,055**	**–4,300**	**–5,800**
Passenger	3 205 BA	*–234*	*–358*	*–346*	*–496*	*–392*	*–490*	*–437*	*–591*
Freight	3 205 BB	*–591*	*–715*	*–810*	*–929*	*–1,051*	*–1,651*	*–1,485*	*–2,200*
Other	3 205 BC	*–1,533*	*–1,728*	*–1,835*	*–1,687*	*–1,841*	*–1,914*	*–2,378*	*–3,009*
Sea transport, passenger	3 207 . .	. . .	. . .	. . .	. . .	. . .	–2	. . .	. . .
Sea transport, freight	3 208 . .	. . .	. . .	. . .	. . .	. . .	–1,589	. . .	. . .
Sea transport, other	3 209 . .	. . .	. . .	. . .	. . .	. . .	–1,204	. . .	. . .
Air transport, passenger	3 211 . .	. . .	. . .	. . .	. . .	. . .	–487	. . .	. . .
Air transport, freight	3 212 . .	. . .	. . .	. . .	. . .	. . .	–31	. . .	. . .
Air transport, other	3 213 . .	. . .	. . .	. . .	. . .	. . .	–708	. . .	. . .
Other transport, passenger	3 215 . .	. . .	. . .	. . .	. . .	. . .	–1	. . .	. . .
Other transport, freight	3 216 . .	. . .	. . .	. . .	. . .	. . .	–31	. . .	. . .
Other transport, other	3 217 . .	. . .	. . .	. . .	. . .	. . .	–2	. . .	. . .
Travel, credit	2 236 . .	**117**	**1,224**	**1,383**	**1,002**	**999**	**1,041**	**944**	**972**
Business travel	2 237 . .	. . .	. . .	. . .	. . .	. . .	20	. . .	20
Personal travel	2 240 . .	. . .	. . .	. . .	. . .	. . .	1,021	. . .	952
Travel, debit	3 236 . .	**–705**	**–750**	**–1,505**	**–1,214**	**–1,318**	**–1,842**	**–2,156**	**–3,391**
Business travel	3 237 . .	. . .	. . .	. . .	. . .	. . .	–132	. . .	–154
Personal travel	3 240 . .	. . .	. . .	. . .	. . .	. . .	–1,710	. . .	–3,237
Other services, credit	2 200 BA	**844**	**559**	**1,031**	**860**	**1,165**	**1,286**	**1,764**	**2,563**
Communications	2 245 . .	. . .	. . .	. . .	. . .	. . .	40	. . .	36
Construction	2 249 . .	. . .	. . .	. . .	. . .	. . .	9	. . .	14
Insurance	2 253 . .	337	60	115	60	115	161	152	186
Financial	2 260 . .	. . .	. . .	. . .	. . .	. . .	251	. . .	827
Computer and information	2 262 . .	. . .	. . .	. . .	. . .	. . .	2	. . .	43
Royalties and licence fees	2 266 . .	6	12	12	13	12	34	19	32
Other business services	2 268 . .	420	425	848	736	952	666	1,502	1,249
Personal, cultural, and recreational	2 287 . .	. . .	. . .	. . .	. . .	. . .	69	. . .	46
Government, n.i.e.	2 291 . .	81	62	56	51	86	54	91	130
Other services, debit	3 200 BA	**–2,239**	**–2,366**	**–3,027**	**–2,884**	**–2,828**	**–3,658**	**–3,798**	**–4,439**
Communications	3 245 . .	. . .	. . .	. . .	. . .	. . .	–16	. . .	–53
Construction	3 249 . .	. . .	. . .	. . .	. . .	. . .	–1	. . .	–4
Insurance	3 253 . .	–200	–172	–184	–192	–173	–206	–262	–308
Financial	3 260 . .	. . .	. . .	. . .	. . .	. . .	–478	. . .	–950
Computer and information	3 262 . .	. . .	. . .	. . .	. . .	. . .	–91	. . .	–251
Royalties and licence fees	3 266 . .	–48	–70	–54	–53	–55	–121	–239	–529
Other business services	3 268 . .	–1,094	–1,299	–1,999	–1,810	–1,779	–2,057	–2,879	–1,619
Personal, cultural, and recreational	3 287 . .	. . .	. . .	. . .	. . .	. . .	–289	. . .	–256
Government, n.i.e.	3 291 . .	–897	–825	–790	–829	–821	–399	–418	–469

Table 2 (Continued). STANDARD PRESENTATION, 1988–95

(Millions of U.S. dollars)

	Code	1988	1989	1990	1991	1992	1993	1994	1995
C. INCOME	4 300	–12,080	–12,546	–11,608	–9,651	–7,997	–10,322	–9,091	–11,105
Total credit	2 300	*771*	*1,310*	*1,157*	*904*	*1,118*	*1,308*	*2,202*	*3,457*
Total debit	3 300	*–12,851*	*–13,856*	*–12,765*	*–10,555*	*–9,115*	*–11,630*	*–11,293*	*–14,562*
Compensation of employees, credit	2 310	**9**	**5**	**10**	**10**	**18**	**38**	**59**	**61**
Compensation of employees, debit	3 310	**–5**	**–4**	**–5**	**–9**	**–13**	**–150**	**–190**	**–218**
Investment income, credit	2 320	**762**	**1,305**	**1,147**	**894**	**1,100**	**1,270**	**2,143**	**3,396**
Direct investment income	2 330	3	1	27	22	75	172	365	770
Dividends and distributed branch profits	2 332	3	1	27	22	75	171	365	770
Reinvested earnings and undistributed branch profits	2 333	. . .	. . .	. . .	. . .	. . .	. . .	. . .	. . .
Income on debt (interest)	2 334	. . .	. . .	. . .	. . .	. . .	1	. . .	. . .
Portfolio investment income	2 339	. . .	. . .	. . .	. . .	. . .	57	35	153
Income on equity	2 340	. . .	. . .	. . .	. . .	. . .	50	35	141
Income on bonds and notes	2 350	. . .	. . .	. . .	. . .	. . .	7	. . .	12
Income on money market instruments and financial derivatives	2 360	. . .	. . .	. . .	. . .	. . .	. . .	. . .	. . .
Other investment income	2 370	759	1,304	1,120	872	1,025	1,041	1,743	2,473
Investment income, debit	3 320	**–12,846**	**–13,852**	**–12,760**	**–10,546**	**–9,102**	**–11,480**	**–11,103**	**–14,344**
Direct investment income	3 330	–2,255	–2,915	–1,892	–1,053	–824	–1,979	–2,315	–2,814
Dividends and distributed branch profits	3 332	–1,541	–2,384	–1,619	–688	–649	–1,583	–2,235	–2,614
Reinvested earnings and undistributed branch profits	3 333	–714	–531	–273	–365	–175	–100	–80	–200
Income on debt (interest)	3 334	. . .	. . .	. . .	. . .	. . .	–296	. . .	. . .
Portfolio investment income	3 339	. . .	. . .	. . .	. . .	. . .	–1,652	–648	–4,896
Income on equity	3 340	. . .	. . .	. . .	. . .	. . .	–468	–648	–887
Income on bonds and notes	3 350	. . .	. . .	. . .	. . .	. . .	–1,184	. . .	–4,009
Income on money market instruments and financial derivatives	3 360	. . .	. . .	. . .	. . .	. . .	. . .	. . .	. . .
Other investment income	3 370	–10,591	–10,937	–10,868	–9,493	–8,278	–7,849	–8,140	–6,634
D. CURRENT TRANSFERS	4 379	91	221	799	1,514	2,189	1,603	2,423	3,621
Credit	2 379	**127**	**238**	**840**	**1,556**	**2,260**	**1,704**	**2,577**	**3,861**
General government	2 380	4	3	3	9	6	20	76	37
Other sectors	2 390	123	235	837	1,547	2,254	1,684	2,501	3,824
Workers' remittances	2 391	19	88	527	1,057	1,719	1,123	1,834	2,891
Other current transfers	2 392	104	147	310	490	535	561	667	933
Debit	3 379	**–36**	**–17**	**–41**	**–42**	**–71**	**–101**	**–154**	**–240**
General government	3 380	–29	–7	–2	–3	–19	–37	–44	–79
Other sectors	3 390	–7	–10	–39	–39	–52	–64	–110	–161
Workers' remittances	3 391	–1	–1	–6	–12	–21	–48	–60	–118
Other current transfers	3 392	–6	–9	–33	–27	–31	–16	–50	–43
CAPITAL AND FINANCIAL ACCOUNT	4 996	**–3,329**	**–183**	**4,119**	**598**	**–4,696**	**795**	**1,595**	**16,689**
CAPITAL ACCOUNT	4 994	**3**	**23**	**35**	**42**	**54**	**81**	**173**	**352**
Total credit	2 994	*4*	*27*	*36*	*43*	*54*	*86*	*175*	*363*
Total debit	3 994	*–1*	*–4*	*–1*	*–1*	. . .	*–5*	*–2*	*–11*
Capital transfers, credit	2 400	**4**	**27**	**36**	**43**	**54**	**86**	**175**	**363**
General government	2 401	. . .	. . .	. . .	. . .	. . .	. . .	. . .	. . .
Debt forgiveness	2 402	. . .	. . .	. . .	. . .	. . .	. . .	. . .	. . .
Other capital transfers	2 410	. . .	. . .	. . .	. . .	. . .	. . .	. . .	. . .
Other sectors	2 430	4	27	36	43	54	86	175	363
Migrants' transfers	2 431	4	27	36	43	54	86	175	363
Debt forgiveness	2 432	. . .	. . .	. . .	. . .	. . .	. . .	. . .	. . .
Other capital transfers	2 440	. . .	. . .	. . .	. . .	. . .	. . .	. . .	. . .
Capital transfers, debit	3 400	**–1**	**–4**	**–1**	**–1**	**. . .**	**–5**	**–2**	**–11**
General government	3 401	. . .	. . .	. . .	. . .	. . .	. . .	. . .	. . .
Debt forgiveness	3 402	. . .	. . .	. . .	. . .	. . .	. . .	. . .	. . .
Other capital transfers	3 410	. . .	. . .	. . .	. . .	. . .	. . .	. . .	. . .
Other sectors	3 430	–1	–4	–1	–1	. . .	–5	–2	–11
Migrants' transfers	3 431	–1	–4	–1	–1	. . .	–5	–2	–11
Debt forgiveness	3 432	. . .	. . .	. . .	. . .	. . .	. . .	. . .	. . .
Other capital transfers	3 440	. . .	. . .	. . .	. . .	. . .	. . .	. . .	. . .
Nonproduced nonfinancial assets, credit	2 480	**. . .**	**. . .**	**. . .**	**. . .**	**. . .**	**. . .**	**. . .**	**. . .**
Nonproduced nonfinancial assets, debit	3 480	**. . .**	**. . .**	**. . .**	**. . .**	**. . .**	**. . .**	**. . .**	**. . .**

Table 2 (Continued). STANDARD PRESENTATION, 1988–95
(Millions of U.S. dollars)

	Code	1988	1989	1990	1991	1992	1993	1994	1995
FINANCIAL ACCOUNT	4 995 . .	**–3,332**	**–206**	**4,084**	**556**	**–4,750**	**714**	**1,422**	**16,337**
A. DIRECT INVESTMENT	4 500 . .	2,629	608	324	89	1,924	801	2,035	3,475
Direct investment abroad	4 505 . .	**–175**	**–523**	**–665**	**–1,014**	**–137**	**–491**	**–1,037**	**–1,384**
Equity capital	4 510 . .	–37	–111	–151	–67	–22	–491	–1,037	–1,384
Claims on affiliated enterprises	4 515 . .	. . .	. . .	. . .	. . .	. . .	–491	–1,037	–1,384
Liabilities to affiliated enterprises	4 520 . .	. . .	. . .	. . .	. . .	. . .	. . .	. . .	. . .
Reinvested earnings	4 525 . .	. . .	. . .	. . .	. . .	. . .	. . .	. . .	. . .
Other capital	4 530 . .	–138	–412	–514	–947	–115	. . .	. . .	. . .
Claims on affiliated enterprises	4 535 . .	. . .	. . .	. . .	. . .	. . .	. . .	. . .	. . .
Liabilities to affiliated enterprises	4 540 . .	. . .	. . .	. . .	. . .	. . .	. . .	. . .	. . .
Direct investment in Brazil	4 555 . .	**2,804**	**1,131**	**989**	**1,103**	**2,061**	**1,292**	**3,072**	**4,859**
Equity capital	4 560 . .	2,255	736	628	607	1,405	614	1,888	3,928
Claims on direct investors	4 565 . .	. . .	. . .	. . .	. . .	. . .	. . .	. . .	. . .
Liabilities to direct investors	4 570 . .	. . .	. . .	. . .	. . .	. . .	614	1,888	3,928
Reinvested earnings	4 575 . .	714	531	273	365	175	100	80	200
Other capital	4 580 . .	–165	–136	88	131	481	578	1,104	731
Claims on direct investors	4 585 . .	. . .	. . .	. . .	. . .	. . .	. . .	. . .	. . .
Liabilities to direct investors	4 590 . .	. . .	. . .	. . .	. . .	. . .	578	1,104	731
B. PORTFOLIO INVESTMENT	4 600 . .	176	–421	512	3,808	14,466	12,322	51,135	9,745
Assets	4 602 . .	**. . .**	**–30**	**–67**	**. . .**	**. . .**	**–606**	**–3,052**	**–936**
Equity securities	4 610 . .	. . .	. . .	. . .	. . .	. . .	–607	. . .	–168
Monetary authorities	4 611 . .	. . .	. . .	. . .	. . .	. . .	. . .	. . .	. . .
General government	4 612 . .	. . .	. . .	. . .	. . .	. . .	. . .	. . .	. . .
Banks	4 613 . .	. . .	. . .	. . .	. . .	. . .	. . .	. . .	. . .
Other sectors	4 614 . .	. . .	. . .	. . .	. . .	. . .	–607	. . .	–168
Debt securities	4 619 . .	. . .	–30	–67	. . .	. . .	1	–3,052	–768
Bonds and notes	4 620 . .	. . .	–30	–67	. . .	. . .	4	–3,052	–768
Monetary authorities	4 621 . .	. . .	. . .	. . .	. . .	. . .	. . .	. . .	. . .
General government	4 622 . .	. . .	. . .	. . .	. . .	. . .	. . .	–3,052	–768
Banks	4 623 . .	. . .	. . .	. . .	. . .	. . .	. . .	. . .	. . .
Other sectors	4 624 . .	. . .	. . .	. . .	. . .	. . .	4	. . .	. . .
Money market instruments	4 630 . .	. . .	. . .	. . .	. . .	. . .	–3	. . .	. . .
Monetary authorities	4 631 . .	. . .	. . .	. . .	. . .	. . .	. . .	. . .	. . .
General government	4 632 . .	. . .	. . .	. . .	. . .	. . .	. . .	. . .	. . .
Banks	4 633 . .	. . .	. . .	. . .	. . .	. . .	. . .	. . .	. . .
Other sectors	4 634 . .	. . .	. . .	. . .	. . .	. . .	–3	. . .	. . .
Financial derivatives	4 640 . .	. . .	. . .	. . .	. . .	. . .	. . .	. . .	. . .
Monetary authorities	4 641 . .	. . .	. . .	. . .	. . .	. . .	. . .	. . .	. . .
General government	4 642 . .	. . .	. . .	. . .	. . .	. . .	. . .	. . .	. . .
Banks	4 643 . .	. . .	. . .	. . .	. . .	. . .	. . .	. . .	. . .
Other sectors	4 644 . .	. . .	. . .	. . .	. . .	. . .	. . .	. . .	. . .
Liabilities	4 652 . .	**176**	**–391**	**579**	**3,808**	**14,466**	**12,928**	**54,187**	**10,681**
Equity securities	4 660 . .	189	–57	103	578	1,704	6,570	7,280	2,775
Banks	4 663 . .	. . .	. . .	. . .	. . .	. . .	. . .	. . .	. . .
Other sectors	4 664 . .	. . .	. . .	. . .	. . .	. . .	6,570	. . .	2,775
Debt securities	4 669 . .	–13	–334	476	3,230	12,762	6,358	46,907	7,906
Bonds and notes	4 670 . .	–13	–334	476	3,230	12,762	6,302	46,907	8,227
Monetary authorities	4 671 . .	. . .	. . .	. . .	. . .	. . .	. . .	. . .	199
General government	4 672 . .	324	–176	–5	–8	7,100	–71	42,612	311
Banks	4 673 . .	. . .	. . .	. . .	. . .	. . .	3,947	. . .	. . .
Other sectors	4 674 . .	–337	–158	481	3,238	5,662	2,426	4,295	7,717
Money market instruments	4 680 . .	. . .	. . .	. . .	. . .	. . .	56	. . .	–321
Monetary authorities	4 681 . .	. . .	. . .	. . .	. . .	. . .	. . .	. . .	. . .
General government	4 682 . .	. . .	. . .	. . .	. . .	. . .	. . .	. . .	. . .
Banks	4 683 . .	. . .	. . .	. . .	. . .	. . .	52	. . .	. . .
Other sectors	4 684 . .	. . .	. . .	. . .	. . .	. . .	4	. . .	–321
Financial derivatives	4 690 . .	. . .	. . .	. . .	. . .	. . .	. . .	. . .	. . .
Monetary authorities	4 691 . .	. . .	. . .	. . .	. . .	. . .	. . .	. . .	. . .
General government	4 692 . .	. . .	. . .	. . .	. . .	. . .	. . .	. . .	. . .
Banks	4 693 . .	. . .	. . .	. . .	. . .	. . .	. . .	. . .	. . .
Other sectors	4 694 . .	. . .	. . .	. . .	. . .	. . .	. . .	. . .	. . .

Table 2 (Concluded). STANDARD PRESENTATION, 1988–95
(Millions of U.S. dollars)

	Code	1988	1989	1990	1991	1992	1993	1994	1995
C. OTHER INVESTMENT	4 700 . .	–4,888	500	3,723	–3,710	–6,470	–3,700	–44,533	16,037
Assets	4 703 . .	**–1,994**	**–894**	**–2,864**	**–3,140**	**–99**	**–2,696**	**–4,368**	**–1,783**
Trade credits	4 706 . .	...	...	...	...	...	...	...	...
General government: long-term	4 708 . .	...	...	...	...	...	...	...	...
General government: short-term	4 709 . .	...	...	...	...	...	...	...	...
Other sectors: long-term	4 711 . .	...	...	...	...	...	...	...	...
Other sectors: short-term	4 712 . .	...	...	...	...	...	...	...	...
Loans	4 714 . .	–139	–154	–255	–102	58	–336	–291	–1,514
Monetary authorities: long-term	4 717 . .	–17	–5	22	8	...	...	...	...
Monetary authorities: short-term	4 718 . .	...	...	...	...	...	...	...	...
General government: long-term	4 720 . .	–9	–19	–13	...	...	29	...	...
General government: short-term	4 721 . .	...	...	...	...	...	...	...	...
Banks: long-term	4 723 . .	...	...	...	...	...	...	...	...
Banks: short-term	4 724 . .	...	...	...	...	...	...	...	...
Other sectors: long-term	4 726 . .	–113	–130	–69	–110	58	–252	–291	–863
Other sectors: short-term	4 727 . .	...	...	–195	...	...	–113	...	–651
Currency and deposits	4 730 . .	–1,808	–712	–2,583	–3,024	–115	–2,285	–4,077	–228
Monetary authorities	4 731 . .	...	...	...	...	...	...	...	...
General government	4 732 . .	–42	–15	–67	...	1	...	...	...
Banks	4 733 . .	–328	–591	–2,758	–3,357	–37	–2,980	–4,077	–228
Other sectors	4 734 . .	–1,438	–106	242	333	–79	695	...	...
Other assets	4 736 . .	–47	–28	–26	–14	–42	–75	...	–41
Monetary authorities: long-term	4 738 . .	...	...	...	...	...	–34	...	...
Monetary authorities: short-term	4 739 . .	...	...	...	...	...	...	...	...
General government: long-term	4 741 . .	–47	–28	–28	–17	–45	...	...	...
General government: short-term	4 742 . .	...	...	...	...	...	...	...	...
Banks: long-term	4 744 . .	...	...	...	...	...	...	...	...
Banks: short-term	4 745 . .	...	...	...	...	...	...	...	...
Other sectors: long-term	4 747 . .	...	...	2	3	3	–41	...	–41
Other sectors: short-term	4 748 . .	...	...	...	...	...	...	...	...
Liabilities	4 753 . .	**–2,894**	**1,394**	**6,587**	**–570**	**–6,371**	**–1,004**	**–40,165**	**17,820**
Trade credits	4 756 . .	...	...	...	...	...	789	5,099	8,659
General government: long-term	4 758 . .	...	...	...	...	...	...	...	...
General government: short-term	4 759 . .	...	...	...	...	...	...	...	...
Other sectors: long-term	4 761 . .	...	...	...	...	...	...	...	...
Other sectors: short-term	4 762 . .	...	...	...	...	...	789	5,099	8,659
Loans	4 764 . .	–2,791	–4,259	–5,457	–6,706	5,961	–815	–40,799	381
Use of Fund credit and loans from the Fund	4 766 . .	–462	–808	–771	–566	–399	–504	–133	–49
Monetary authorities: other long-term	4 767 . .	8,575	7,548	–1,599	–531	–35	–140	...	–1,648
Monetary authorities: short-term	4 768 . .	–115	...	...	...	...	...	–600	...
General government: long-term	4 770 . .	–1,229	–4,759	–1,903	–2,876	9,615	–1,144	–35,609	...
General government: short-term	4 771 . .	...	...	...	...	...	–288	...	...
Banks: long-term	4 773 . .	–2,520	–2,415	–1,354	–616	–463	–275	...	476
Banks: short-term	4 774 . .	...	...	...	...	...	117	...	...
Other sectors: long-term	4 776 . .	–6,993	–3,404	–253	–1,101	–2,977	–2,100	–3,471	–692
Other sectors: short-term	4 777 . .	–47	–421	423	–1,016	220	3,519	–986	2,294
Currency and deposits	4 780 . .	807	1,399	1,251	263	1,003	–2,111	–1,384	6,591
Monetary authorities	4 781 . .	73	1,099	126	–739	–627	...	55	–4
General government	4 782 . .	...	...	...	...	...	...	...	...
Banks	4 783 . .	734	300	1,125	1,002	1,630	–2,111	–1,439	6,595
Other sectors	4 784 . .	...	...	...	...	...	...	...	...
Other liabilities	4 786 . .	–910	4,254	10,793	5,873	–13,335	1,133	–3,081	2,189
Monetary authorities: long-term	4 788 . .	...	...	...	...	...	...	...	...
Monetary authorities: short-term	4 789 . .	–888	4,267	10,795	4,281	–12,270	–365	–5,653	–510
General government: long-term	4 791 . .	...	...	...	...	...	...	...	...
General government: short-term	4 792 . .	...	...	...	...	...	1,498	...	...
Banks: long-term	4 794 . .	...	...	...	...	...	...	...	...
Banks: short-term	4 795 . .	...	...	...	...	...	...	...	...
Other sectors: long-term	4 797 . .	–1	...	...	...	...	...	...	...
Other sectors: short-term	4 798 . .	–21	–13	–2	1,592	–1,065	...	2,572	2,699
D. RESERVE ASSETS	4 800 . .	–1,250	–893	–474	369	–14,670	–8,709	–7,215	–12,920
Monetary gold	4 810 . .	83	–60	–639	966	–74	–233	–297	–331
Special drawing rights	4 820 . .	–1	...	–10	–2	12	–1	2	–1
Reserve position in the Fund	4 830 . .	...	...	...	...	...	...	...	...
Foreign exchange	4 840 . .	–1,332	–826	168	–595	–14,608	–8,475	–6,920	–12,588
Other claims	4 880 . .	...	–7	7	...	...	...	...	...
NET ERRORS AND OMISSIONS	4 998 . .	**–827**	**–819**	**–296**	**852**	**–1,393**	**–815**	**–442**	**1,447**

Part 3 of the *Yearbook* contains descriptions of the methodologies, compilation practices, and sources used to compile these data.

Table 1. ANALYTIC PRESENTATION, 1988–95
(Millions of U.S. dollars)

	Code	1988	1989	1990	1991	1992	1993	1994	1995
A. Current Account[1]	4 993 Y.	**–402**	**–769**	**–1,710**	**–77**	**–360**	**–1,098**	**–32**	**334**
Goods: exports f.o.b.	2 100 ..	9,283	8,268	6,113	3,737	3,956	3,727	3,935	5,110
Goods: imports f.o.b.	3 100 ..	–9,889	–8,960	–7,427	–3,769	–4,169	–4,612	–3,952	–4,683
Balance on Goods	4 100 ..	*–606*	*–692*	*–1,314*	*–32*	*–212*	*–885*	*–17*	*428*
Services: credit	2 200 ..	1,186	1,223	837	400	1,070	1,172	1,257	1,420
Services: debit	3 200 ..	–656	–785	–600	–486	–1,165	–1,229	–1,246	–1,191
Balance on Goods and Services	4 991 ..	*–76*	*–254*	*–1,077*	*–118*	*–308*	*–942*	*–6*	*657*
Income: credit	2 300 ..	82	127	120	56	125	93	85	150
Income: debit	3 300 ..	–511	–719	–878	–84	–221	–285	–277	–605
Balance on Goods, Services, and Income	4 992 ..	*–505*	*–846*	*–1,835*	*–146*	*–403*	*–1,135*	*–199*	*202*
Current transfers: credit	2 379 Y.	183	143	232	123	114	286	357	257
Current transfers: debit	3 379 ..	–80	–66	–107	–54	–71	–249	–190	–125
B. Capital Account[1]	4 994 Y.	**...**	**...**	**...**	**...**	**...**	**...**	**763**	**...**
Capital account: credit	2 994 Y.	...	...	...	...	...	...	763	...
Capital account: debit	3 994 ..	...	...	...	...	...	...	...	...
Total, Groups A Plus B	4 010 ..	*–402*	*–769*	*–1,710*	*–77*	*–360*	*–1,098*	*732*	*334*
C. Financial Account[1]	4 995 X.	**1,545**	**–40**	**–2,814**	**95**	**716**	**755**	**–1,019**	**–148**
Direct investment abroad	4 505 ..	...	...	...	...	...	...	...	8
Direct investment in Bulgaria	4 555 Y.	...	...	4	56	42	55	105	90
Portfolio investment assets	4 602 ..	...	...	...	...	...	...	–222	10
Equity securities	4 610 ..	...	...	...	...	...	...	...	10
Debt securities	4 619 ..	...	...	...	...	...	...	–222	...
Portfolio investment liabilities	4 652 Y.	...	...	...	...	...	...	–10	–51
Equity securities	4 660 Y.	...	...	...	...	...	...	...	...
Debt securities	4 669 Y.	...	...	...	...	...	...	–10	–51
Other investment assets	4 703 ..	–548	–488	384	82	263	338	–209	404
Monetary authorities	4 703 .A	...	...	...	...	...	...	...	...
General government	4 703 .B	...	...	...	...	...	...	90	293
Banks	4 703 .C	–548	–488	384	82	263	338	–299	112
Other sectors	4 703 .D	...	...	...	...	...	...	...	...
Other investment liabilities	4 753 X.	2,093	448	–3,202	–43	412	361	–684	–610
Monetary authorities	4 753 XA	...	...	...	...	...	...	–57	...
General government	4 753 YB	...	...	...	193	...	...	–894	–93
Banks	4 753 YC	2,093	448	–3,202	–236	–106	–46	–40	–113
Other sectors	4 753 YD	...	...	...	...	517	407	307	–404
Total, Groups A Through C	4 020 ..	*1,143*	*–809*	*–4,524*	*18*	*356*	*–343*	*–288*	*185*
D. Net Errors and Omissions	4 998 ..	**–486**	**375**	**70**	**...**	**–85**	**22**	**72**	**178**
Total, Groups A Through D	4 030 ..	*657*	*–434*	*–4,454*	*17*	*271*	*–322*	*–216*	*363*
E. Reserves and Related Items	4 040 ..	**–657**	**434**	**4,454**	**–17**	**–271**	**322**	**216**	**–363**
Reserve assets	4 800 ..	–657	434	878	–417	–639	247	–342	–234
Use of Fund credit and loans	4 766 ..	...	...	...	400	196	43	262	–246
Liabilities constituting foreign authorities' reserves	4 900 ..	...	...	...	...	...	...	...	...
Exceptional financing	4 920 ..	...	...	3,576	...	172	32	295	117
Conversion rates: leva per U.S. dollar	0 101 ..	**.830**	**.840**	**2.190**	**17.788**	**23.341**	**27.594**	**54.134**	**67.171**

[1] Excludes components that have been classified in the categories of Group E.

Table 2. STANDARD PRESENTATION, 1988–95
(Millions of U.S. dollars)

	Code	1988	1989	1990	1991	1992	1993	1994	1995
CURRENT ACCOUNT	4 993 . .	**–402**	**–769**	**–1,710**	**–77**	**–360**	**–1,098**	**–32**	**334**
A. GOODS	4 100 . .	–606	–692	–1,314	–32	–212	–885	–17	428
Credit	2 100 . .	**9,283**	**8,268**	**6,113**	**3,737**	**3,956**	**3,727**	**3,935**	**5,110**
General merchandise: exports f.o.b.	2 110 . .	9,283	8,268	6,113	3,737	3,956	3,727	3,935	5,110
Goods for processing: exports f.o.b.	2 150 . .	...	...	...	...	...	...	...	...
Repairs on goods	2 160 . .	...	...	...	...	...	...	...	...
Goods procured in ports by carriers	2 170 . .	...	...	...	...	...	...	...	...
Nonmonetary gold	2 180 . .	...	...	...	...	...	...	...	...
Debit	3 100 . .	**–9,889**	**–8,960**	**–7,427**	**–3,769**	**–4,169**	**–4,612**	**–3,952**	**–4,683**
General merchandise: imports f.o.b.	3 110 . .	–9,889	–8,960	–7,427	–3,769	–4,169	–4,612	–3,952	–4,683
Goods for processing: imports f.o.b.	3 150 . .	...	...	...	...	...	...	...	...
Repairs on goods	3 160 . .	...	...	...	...	...	...	...	...
Goods procured in ports by carriers	3 170 . .	...	...	...	...	...	...	...	...
Nonmonetary gold	3 180 . .	...	...	...	...	...	...	...	...
B. SERVICES	4 200 . .	530	438	237	–86	–95	–57	11	229
Total credit	2 200 . .	*1,186*	*1,223*	*837*	*400*	*1,070*	*1,172*	*1,257*	*1,420*
Total debit	3 200 . .	*–656*	*–785*	*–600*	*–486*	*–1,165*	*–1,229*	*–1,246*	*–1,191*
Transportation services, credit	2 205 . .	**375**	**338**	**230**	**179**	**457**	**389**	**376**	**482**
Passenger	2 205 BA	...	...	...	...	...	...	*145*	*189*
Freight	2 205 BB	*375*	*338*	*230*	*179*	*457*	*389*	*197*	*256*
Other	2 205 BC	...	...	...	...	...	...	*34*	*37*
Sea transport, passenger	2 207 . .	...	...	...	...	...	...	...	...
Sea transport, freight	2 208 . .	...	...	...	...	...	...	...	...
Sea transport, other	2 209 . .	...	...	...	...	...	...	...	...
Air transport, passenger	2 211 . .	...	...	...	...	...	...	...	...
Air transport, freight	2 212 . .	...	...	...	...	...	...	...	...
Air transport, other	2 213 . .	...	...	...	...	...	...	...	...
Other transport, passenger	2 215 . .	...	...	...	...	...	...	...	...
Other transport, freight	2 216 . .	...	...	...	...	...	...	...	...
Other transport, other	2 217 . .	...	...	...	...	...	...	...	...
Transportation services, debit	3 205 . .	**–349**	**–316**	**–243**	**–192**	**–459**	**–454**	**–466**	**–444**
Passenger	3 205 BA	...	...	...	...	...	...	*–146*	*–117*
Freight	3 205 BB	*–349*	*–316*	*–243*	*–192*	*–459*	*–454*	*–319*	*–327*
Other	3 205 BC	...	...	...	...	...	...	...	...
Sea transport, passenger	3 207 . .	...	...	...	...	...	...	...	...
Sea transport, freight	3 208 . .	...	...	...	...	...	...	...	...
Sea transport, other	3 209 . .	...	...	...	...	...	...	...	...
Air transport, passenger	3 211 . .	...	...	...	...	...	...	...	...
Air transport, freight	3 212 . .	...	...	...	...	...	...	...	...
Air transport, other	3 213 . .	...	...	...	...	...	...	...	...
Other transport, passenger	3 215 . .	...	...	...	...	...	...	...	...
Other transport, freight	3 216 . .	...	...	...	...	...	...	...	...
Other transport, other	3 217 . .	...	...	...	...	...	...	...	...
Travel, credit	2 236 . .	**484**	**495**	**320**	**44**	**215**	**307**	**362**	**473**
Business travel	2 237 . .	...	...	...	...	...	...	...	...
Personal travel	2 240 . .	...	...	...	...	...	...	...	...
Travel, debit	3 236 . .	**–74**	**–113**	**–189**	**–128**	**–313**	**–257**	**–244**	**–195**
Business travel	3 237 . .	...	...	...	...	...	...	...	...
Personal travel	3 240 . .	...	...	...	...	...	...	...	...
Other services, credit	2 200 BA	**327**	**390**	**287**	**177**	**399**	**475**	**520**	**465**
Communications	2 245 . .	...	...	...	...	...	...	...	...
Construction	2 249 . .	...	...	...	...	...	...	...	...
Insurance	2 253 . .	42	38	26	20	51	43	...	...
Financial	2 260 . .	...	...	...	...	...	...	...	...
Computer and information	2 262 . .	...	...	...	...	...	...	...	...
Royalties and licence fees	2 266 . .	...	...	...	...	...	...	...	...
Other business services	2 268 . .	285	352	261	157	348	432	520	465
Personal, cultural, and recreational	2 287 . .	...	...	...	...	...	...	...	...
Government, n.i.e.	2 291 . .	...	...	...	...	...	...	...	...
Other services, debit	3 200 BA	**–233**	**–356**	**–168**	**–166**	**–393**	**–518**	**–537**	**–552**
Communications	3 245 . .	...	...	...	...	...	...	...	...
Construction	3 249 . .	...	...	...	...	...	...	...	...
Insurance	3 253 . .	–39	–35	–27	–21	–51	–50	...	...
Financial	3 260 . .	...	...	...	...	...	...	...	...
Computer and information	3 262 . .	...	...	...	...	...	...	...	...
Royalties and licence fees	3 266 . .	...	...	...	...	...	...	...	...
Other business services	3 268 . .	–194	–321	–141	–145	–342	–467	–537	–552
Personal, cultural, and recreational	3 287 . .	...	...	...	...	...	...	...	...
Government, n.i.e.	3 291 . .	...	...	...	...	...	...	...	...

Table 2 (Continued). STANDARD PRESENTATION, 1988–95
(Millions of U.S. dollars)

	Code	1988	1989	1990	1991	1992	1993	1994	1995
C. INCOME	4 300	–429	–592	–758	–28	–96	–192	–193	–455
Total credit	2 300	*82*	*127*	*120*	*56*	*125*	*93*	*85*	*150*
Total debit	3 300	*–511*	*–719*	*–878*	*–84*	*–221*	*–285*	*–277*	*–605*
Compensation of employees, credit	2 310	...	...	...	...	...	...	...	...
Compensation of employees, debit	3 310	...	...	...	...	...	...	...	...
Investment income, credit	2 320	**82**	**127**	**120**	**56**	**125**	**93**	**85**	**150**
Direct investment income	2 330	...	...	...	...	...	...	...	...
Dividends and distributed branch profits	2 332	...	...	...	...	...	...	...	...
Reinvested earnings and undistributed branch profits	2 333	...	...	...	...	...	...	...	...
Income on debt (interest)	2 334	...	...	...	...	...	...	...	...
Portfolio investment income	2 339	...	...	...	...	...	...	...	...
Income on equity	2 340	...	...	...	...	...	...	...	...
Income on bonds and notes	2 350	...	...	...	...	...	...	...	...
Income on money market instruments and financial derivatives	2 360	...	...	...	...	...	...	...	...
Other investment income	2 370	82	127	120	56	125	93	85	150
Investment income, debit	3 320	**–511**	**–719**	**–878**	**–84**	**–221**	**–285**	**–277**	**–605**
Direct investment income	3 330	...	...	...	...	...	...	...	...
Dividends and distributed branch profits	3 332	...	...	...	...	...	...	...	...
Reinvested earnings and undistributed branch profits	3 333	...	...	...	...	...	...	...	...
Income on debt (interest)	3 334	...	...	...	...	...	...	...	...
Portfolio investment income	3 339	...	...	...	...	...	...	...	...
Income on equity	3 340	...	...	...	...	...	...	...	...
Income on bonds and notes	3 350	...	...	...	...	...	...	...	...
Income on money market instruments and financial derivatives	3 360	...	...	...	...	...	...	...	...
Other investment income	3 370	–511	–719	–878	–84	–221	–285	–277	–605
D. CURRENT TRANSFERS	4 379	103	77	125	69	43	37	167	132
Credit	2 379	**183**	**143**	**232**	**123**	**114**	**286**	**357**	**257**
General government	2 380	...	...	...	19	3	...	10	15
Other sectors	2 390	183	143	232	104	111	286	348	242
Workers' remittances	2 391	...	...	...	...	...	...	...	...
Other current transfers	2 392	183	143	232	104	111	286	348	242
Debit	3 379	**–80**	**–66**	**–107**	**–54**	**–71**	**–249**	**–190**	**–125**
General government	3 380	...	...	...	...	...	...	–7	...
Other sectors	3 390	–80	–66	–107	–54	–71	–249	–183	–125
Workers' remittances	3 391	...	...	...	...	...	...	...	...
Other current transfers	3 392	–80	–66	–107	–54	–71	–249	–183	–125
CAPITAL AND FINANCIAL ACCOUNT	4 996	**888**	**394**	**1,640**	**77**	**445**	**1,076**	**–40**	**–511**
CAPITAL ACCOUNT	4 994	...	...	...	...	...	...	**763**	...
Total credit	2 994	...	...	...	...	...	...	*763*	...
Total debit	3 994	...	...	...	...	...	...	...	...
Capital transfers, credit	2 400	...	...	...	...	...	...	**763**	...
General government	2 401	...	...	...	...	...	...	763	...
Debt forgiveness	2 402	...	...	...	...	...	...	763	...
Other capital transfers	2 410	...	...	...	...	...	...	...	...
Other sectors	2 430	...	...	...	...	...	...	...	...
Migrants' transfers	2 431	...	...	...	...	...	...	...	...
Debt forgiveness	2 432	...	...	...	...	...	...	...	...
Other capital transfers	2 440	...	...	...	...	...	...	...	...
Capital transfers, debit	3 400	...	...	...	...	...	...	...	...
General government	3 401	...	...	...	...	...	...	...	...
Debt forgiveness	3 402	...	...	...	...	...	...	...	...
Other capital transfers	3 410	...	...	...	...	...	...	...	...
Other sectors	3 430	...	...	...	...	...	...	...	...
Migrants' transfers	3 431	...	...	...	...	...	...	...	...
Debt forgiveness	3 432	...	...	...	...	...	...	...	...
Other capital transfers	3 440	...	...	...	...	...	...	...	...
Nonproduced nonfinancial assets, credit	2 480	...	...	...	...	...	...	...	...
Nonproduced nonfinancial assets, debit	3 480	...	...	...	...	...	...	...	...

Table 2 (Continued). STANDARD PRESENTATION, 1988–95
(Millions of U.S. dollars)

	Code	1988	1989	1990	1991	1992	1993	1994	1995
FINANCIAL ACCOUNT	4 995	**888**	**394**	**1,640**	**77**	**445**	**1,076**	**–804**	**–511**
A. DIRECT INVESTMENT	4 500	...	...	4	56	42	55	105	98
Direct investment abroad	4 505	...	...	...	...	...	...	...	**8**
Equity capital	4 510	...	...	...	...	...	...	...	8
Claims on affiliated enterprises	4 515	...	...	...	...	...	...	...	...
Liabilities to affiliated enterprises	4 520	...	...	...	...	...	...	...	...
Reinvested earnings	4 525	...	...	...	...	...	...	...	...
Other capital	4 530	...	...	...	...	...	...	...	...
Claims on affiliated enterprises	4 535	...	...	...	...	...	...	...	...
Liabilities to affiliated enterprises	4 540	...	...	...	...	...	...	...	...
Direct investment in Bulgaria	4 555	...	...	**4**	**56**	**42**	**55**	**105**	**90**
Equity capital	4 560	...	...	4	56	42	55	105	90
Claims on direct investors	4 565	...	...	...	...	...	...	...	...
Liabilities to direct investors	4 570	...	...	...	...	...	...	...	...
Reinvested earnings	4 575	...	...	...	...	...	...	...	...
Other capital	4 580	...	...	...	...	...	...	...	...
Claims on direct investors	4 585	...	...	...	...	...	...	...	...
Liabilities to direct investors	4 590	...	...	...	...	...	...	...	...
B. PORTFOLIO INVESTMENT	4 600	...	...	...	...	...	...	–232	–41
Assets	4 602	...	...	...	...	...	...	**–222**	**10**
Equity securities	4 610	...	...	...	...	...	...	...	10
Monetary authorities	4 611	...	...	...	...	...	...	...	...
General government	4 612	...	...	...	...	...	...	...	...
Banks	4 613	...	...	...	...	...	...	...	10
Other sectors	4 614	...	...	...	...	...	...	...	...
Debt securities	4 619	...	...	...	...	...	...	–222	...
Bonds and notes	4 620	...	...	...	...	...	...	–222	...
Monetary authorities	4 621	...	...	...	...	...	...	...	...
General government	4 622	...	...	...	...	...	...	–222	...
Banks	4 623	...	...	...	...	...	...	...	...
Other sectors	4 624	...	...	...	...	...	...	...	...
Money market instruments	4 630	...	...	...	...	...	...	...	...
Monetary authorities	4 631	...	...	...	...	...	...	...	...
General government	4 632	...	...	...	...	...	...	...	...
Banks	4 633	...	...	...	...	...	...	...	...
Other sectors	4 634	...	...	...	...	...	...	...	...
Financial derivatives	4 640	...	...	...	...	...	...	...	...
Monetary authorities	4 641	...	...	...	...	...	...	...	...
General government	4 642	...	...	...	...	...	...	...	...
Banks	4 643	...	...	...	...	...	...	...	...
Other sectors	4 644	...	...	...	...	...	...	...	...
Liabilities	4 652	...	...	...	...	...	...	**–10**	**–51**
Equity securities	4 660	...	...	...	...	...	...	...	...
Banks	4 663	...	...	...	...	...	...	...	...
Other sectors	4 664	...	...	...	...	...	...	...	...
Debt securities	4 669	...	...	...	...	...	...	–10	–51
Bonds and notes	4 670	...	...	...	...	...	...	–10	–51
Monetary authorities	4 671	...	...	...	...	...	...	...	...
General government	4 672	...	...	...	...	...	...	–10	–51
Banks	4 673	...	...	...	...	...	...	...	...
Other sectors	4 674	...	...	...	...	...	...	...	...
Money market instruments	4 680	...	...	...	...	...	...	...	...
Monetary authorities	4 681	...	...	...	...	...	...	...	...
General government	4 682	...	...	...	...	...	...	...	...
Banks	4 683	...	...	...	...	...	...	...	...
Other sectors	4 684	...	...	...	...	...	...	...	...
Financial derivatives	4 690	...	...	...	...	...	...	...	...
Monetary authorities	4 691	...	...	...	...	...	...	...	...
General government	4 692	...	...	...	...	...	...	...	...
Banks	4 693	...	...	...	...	...	...	...	...
Other sectors	4 694	...	...	...	...	...	...	...	...

Table 2 (Concluded). STANDARD PRESENTATION, 1988–95
(Millions of U.S. dollars)

	Code	1988	1989	1990	1991	1992	1993	1994	1995
C. OTHER INVESTMENT	4 700 . .	1,545	–40	758	439	1,042	774	–336	–335
Assets	4 703 . .	**–548**	**–488**	**384**	**82**	**263**	**338**	**–209**	**404**
Trade credits	4 706 . .	...	...	...	...	...	...	...	...
General government: long-term	4 708 . .	...	...	...	...	...	...	...	...
General government: short-term	4 709 . .	...	...	...	...	...	...	...	...
Other sectors: long-term	4 711 . .	...	...	...	...	...	...	...	...
Other sectors: short-term	4 712 . .	...	...	...	...	...	...	...	...
Loans	4 714 . .	–401	–204	277	295	308	286	263	293
Monetary authorities: long-term	4 717 . .	...	...	...	...	...	...	...	...
Monetary authorities: short-term	4 718 . .	...	...	...	...	...	...	...	...
General government: long-term	4 720 . .	...	...	...	...	...	...	263	293
General government: short-term	4 721 . .	...	...	...	...	...	...	...	...
Banks: long-term	4 723 . .	–401	–204	277	295	308	286	...	...
Banks: short-term	4 724 . .	...	...	...	...	...	...	...	...
Other sectors: long-term	4 726 . .	...	...	...	...	...	...	...	...
Other sectors: short-term	4 727 . .	...	...	...	...	...	...	...	...
Currency and deposits	4 730 . .	–147	–284	107	–213	–45	53	–472	171
Monetary authorities	4 731 . .	...	...	...	...	...	...	...	...
General government	4 732 . .	...	...	...	...	...	...	–173	...
Banks	4 733 . .	–147	–284	107	–213	–45	53	–299	171
Other sectors	4 734 . .	...	...	...	...	...	...	...	...
Other assets	4 736 . .	...	...	...	...	...	...	...	–60
Monetary authorities: long-term	4 738 . .	...	...	...	...	...	...	...	...
Monetary authorities: short-term	4 739 . .	...	...	...	...	...	...	...	...
General government: long-term	4 741 . .	...	...	...	...	...	...	...	...
General government: short-term	4 742 . .	...	...	...	...	...	...	...	...
Banks: long-term	4 744 . .	...	...	...	...	...	...	...	...
Banks: short-term	4 745 . .	...	...	...	...	...	...	...	–60
Other sectors: long-term	4 747 . .	...	...	...	...	...	...	...	...
Other sectors: short-term	4 748 . .	...	...	...	...	...	...	...	...
Liabilities	4 753 . .	**2,093**	**448**	**374**	**357**	**780**	**435**	**–126**	**–739**
Trade credits	4 756 . .	...	...	...	...	...	...	...	...
General government: long-term	4 758 . .	...	...	...	...	...	...	...	...
General government: short-term	4 759 . .	...	...	...	...	...	...	...	...
Other sectors: long-term	4 761 . .	...	...	...	...	...	...	...	...
Other sectors: short-term	4 762 . .	...	...	...	...	...	...	...	...
Loans	4 764 . .	1,955	523	–3,816	545	410	28	–394	–357
Use of Fund credit and loans from the Fund	4 766 . .	...	...	...	400	196	43	262	–246
Monetary authorities: other long-term	4 767 . .	...	...	...	...	...	...	295	64
Monetary authorities: short-term	4 768 . .	...	...	...	...	...	...	...	...
General government: long-term	4 770 . .	...	...	...	193	172	32	–894	–93
General government: short-term	4 771 . .	...	...	...	...	...	...	...	...
Banks: long-term	4 773 . .	1,955	523	–3,816	–48	42	–46	–57	–54
Banks: short-term	4 774 . .	...	...	...	...	...	...	...	–29
Other sectors: long-term	4 776 . .	...	...	...	...	...	...	...	...
Other sectors: short-term	4 777 . .	...	...	...	...	...	...	...	...
Currency and deposits	4 780 . .	138	–75	614	–188	–148	...	17	–30
Monetary authorities	4 781 . .	...	...	...	...	...	...	...	...
General government	4 782 . .	...	...	...	...	...	...	...	...
Banks	4 783 . .	138	–75	614	–188	–148	...	17	–30
Other sectors	4 784 . .	...	...	...	...	...	...	...	...
Other liabilities	4 786 . .	...	...	3,576	...	517	407	250	–352
Monetary authorities: long-term	4 788 . .	...	...	...	...	...	...	...	...
Monetary authorities: short-term	4 789 . .	...	...	...	...	...	...	–57	...
General government: long-term	4 791 . .	...	...	...	...	...	...	...	...
General government: short-term	4 792 . .	...	...	...	...	...	...	...	...
Banks: long-term	4 794 . .	...	...	...	...	...	...	...	...
Banks: short-term	4 795 . .	...	...	3,576	...	...	...	...	52
Other sectors: long-term	4 797 . .	...	...	...	...	...	...	...	...
Other sectors: short-term	4 798 . .	...	...	...	...	517	407	...	...
D. RESERVE ASSETS	4 800 . .	–657	434	878	–417	–639	247	–342	–234
Monetary gold	4 810 . .	...	...	...	...	...	...	...	...
Special drawing rights	4 820 . .	...	...	...	–8	8	–1	–12	–15
Reserve position in the Fund	4 830 . .	...	...	...	...	–54	8	...	...
Foreign exchange	4 840 . .	–657	434	878	–410	–593	239	–330	–219
Other claims	4 880 . .	...	...	...	...	...	...	...	...
NET ERRORS AND OMISSIONS	4 998 . .	**–486**	**375**	**70**	**...**	**–85**	**22**	**72**	**178**

Part 3 of the *Yearbook* contains descriptions of the methodologies, compilation practices, and sources used to compile these data.

Table 1. ANALYTIC PRESENTATION, 1988–95
(Millions of U.S. dollars)

	Code	1988	1989	1990	1991	1992	1993	1994	1995
A. Current Account[1]	4 993 Y.	**–46.5**	**99.3**	**–76.9**	**–90.6**	**–23.0**	**–71.1**	**14.9**	**. . .**
Goods: exports f.o.b	2 100 . .	240.0	184.6	280.5	269.1	237.2	226.1	215.6	. . .
Goods: imports f.o.b	3 100 . .	–477.4	–441.7	–542.5	–490.5	–458.9	–469.1	–344.3	. . .
Balance on Goods	4 100 . .	*–237.3*	*–257.2*	*–261.9*	*–221.4*	*–221.7*	*–243.0*	*–128.7*	. . .
Services: credit	2 200 . .	54.7	51.4	68.7	68.4	64.5	64.6	56.3	. . .
Services: debit	3 200 . .	–243.0	–185.6	–215.7	–253.2	–207.7	–209.0	–138.3	. . .
Balance on Goods and Services	4 991 . .	*–425.6*	*–391.3*	*–409.0*	*–406.2*	*–364.9*	*–387.4*	*–210.7*	. . .
Income: credit	2 300 . .	18.1	17.8	17.6	16.5	21.7	21.5	8.7	. . .
Income: debit	3 300 . .	–26.9	–24.2	–17.7	–16.2	–19.1	–28.6	–38.1	. . .
Balance on Goods, Services, and Income	4 992 . .	*–434.4*	*–397.7*	*–409.2*	*–406.0*	*–362.3*	*–394.5*	*–240.1*	. . .
Current transfers: credit	2 379 Y.	452.0	571.6	430.2	413.1	419.2	389.6	308.0	. . .
Current transfers: debit	3 379 . .	–64.1	–74.6	–97.9	–97.7	–79.9	–66.3	–53.0	. . .
B. Capital Account[1]	4 994 Y.	**. . .**	**. . .**	**. . .**	**. . .**	**. . .**	**. . .**	**. . .**	**. . .**
Capital account: credit	2 994 Y.	. . .	. . .	. . .	. . .	. . .	. . .	. . .	. . .
Capital account: debit	3 994 . .	. . .	. . .	. . .	. . .	. . .	. . .	. . .	. . .
Total, Groups A Plus B	4 010 . .	*–46.5*	*99.3*	*–76.9*	*–90.6*	*–23.0*	*–71.1*	*14.9*	. . .
C. Financial Account[1]	4 995 X.	**63.5**	**–228.6**	**82.4**	**104.8**	**34.7**	**69.1**	**–13.9**	**. . .**
Direct investment abroad	4 505 . .	. . .	. . .	. . .	. . .	. . .	. . .	. . .	. . .
Direct investment in Burkina Faso	4 555 Y.	3.7	5.7	. . .	. . .	. . .	. . .	. . .	. . .
Portfolio investment assets	4 602 . .	. . .	. . .	. . .	. . .	. . .	. . .	. . .	. . .
Equity securities	4 610 . .	. . .	. . .	. . .	. . .	. . .	. . .	. . .	. . .
Debt securities	4 619 . .	. . .	. . .	. . .	. . .	. . .	. . .	. . .	. . .
Portfolio investment liabilities	4 652 Y.	. . .	. . .	. . .	. . .	. . .	. . .	. . .	. . .
Equity securities	4 660 Y.	. . .	. . .	. . .	. . .	. . .	. . .	. . .	. . .
Debt securities	4 669 Y.	. . .	. . .	. . .	. . .	. . .	. . .	. . .	. . .
Other investment assets	4 703 . .	–2.3	–26.7	–6.6	.5	–45.2	24.2	–139.2	. . .
Monetary authorities	4 703 .A	. . .	. . .	. . .	. . .	. . .	. . .	. . .	. . .
General government	4 703 .B	. . .	. . .	. . .	. . .	. . .	. . .	. . .	. . .
Banks	4 703 .C	–.8	–12.8	–3.0	15.9	–21.7	24.2	–135.2	. . .
Other sectors	4 703 .D	–1.5	–13.8	–3.7	–15.4	–23.4	. . .	–4.0	. . .
Other investment liabilities	4 753 X.	62.1	–207.6	89.1	104.3	79.9	44.9	125.3	. . .
Monetary authorities	4 753 XA	. . .	. . .	. . .	. . .	–6.6	. . .	. . .	. . .
General government	4 753 YB	48.4	–226.5	64.3	78.4	100.0	84.4	29.3	. . .
Banks	4 753 YC	1.5	13.0	9.2	–7.0	–12.1	–47.1	41.9	. . .
Other sectors	4 753 YD	12.1	6.0	15.6	32.9	–1.3	7.7	54.0	. . .
Total, Groups A Through C	4 020 . .	*17.0*	*–129.3*	*5.5*	*14.2*	*11.7*	*–2.1*	*1.0*	. . .
D. Net Errors and Omissions	4 998 . .	**1.1**	**–5.9**	**1.6**	**–6.6**	**8.3**	**4.6**	**–8.3**	**. . .**
Total, Groups A Through D	4 030 . .	*18.1*	*–135.2*	*7.1*	*7.7*	*20.0*	*2.5*	*–7.3*	. . .
E. Reserves and Related Items	4 040 . .	**–18.1**	**135.2**	**–7.1**	**–7.7**	**–20.0**	**–2.5**	**7.3**	**. . .**
Reserve assets	4 800 . .	–29.7	50.0	–6.6	–43.6	–15.9	–53.5	–17.4	. . .
Use of Fund credit and loans	4 766 . .	–3.1	–1.9	–.5	8.7	. . .	12.5	25.5	. . .
Liabilities constituting foreign authorities' reserves	4 900 . .	. . .	. . .	. . .	. . .	. . .	. . .	. . .	. . .
Exceptional financing	4 920 . .	14.8	87.1	. . .	27.3	–4.2	38.5	–.7	. . .
Conversion rates: CFA francs per U.S. dollar	0 101 . .	**297.85**	**319.01**	**272.26**	**282.11**	**264.69**	**283.16**	**555.20**	**499.15**

[1] Excludes components that have been classified in the categories of Group E.

Table 2. STANDARD PRESENTATION, 1988–95
(Millions of U.S. dollars)

	Code	1988	1989	1990	1991	1992	1993	1994	1995
CURRENT ACCOUNT	4 993 . .	**–46.5**	**99.3**	**–76.9**	**–90.6**	**–23.0**	**–71.1**	**14.9**	. . .
A. GOODS	4 100 . .	–237.3	–257.2	–261.9	–221.4	–221.7	–243.0	–128.7	. . .
Credit	2 100 . .	**240.0**	**184.6**	**280.5**	**269.1**	**237.2**	**226.1**	**215.6**	. . .
General merchandise: exports f.o.b.	2 110 . .	189.2	148.9	221.6	230.0	205.5	199.3	193.6	. . .
Goods for processing: exports f.o.b.	2 150 . .	. . .	. . .	. . .	. . .	. . .	. . .	. . .	. . .
Repairs on goods	2 160 . .	. . .	. . .	. . .	. . .	. . .	. . .	. . .	. . .
Goods procured in ports by carriers	2 170 . .	. . .	. . .	. . .	. . .	. . .	. . .	. . .	. . .
Nonmonetary gold	2 180 . .	50.9	35.7	58.9	39.1	31.7	26.8	22.0	. . .
Debit	3 100 . .	**–477.4**	**–441.7**	**–542.5**	**–490.5**	**–458.9**	**–469.1**	**–344.3**	. . .
General merchandise: imports f.o.b.	3 110 . .	–476.0	–440.5	–541.2	–489.8	–458.4	–468.6	–344.3	. . .
Goods for processing: imports f.o.b.	3 150 . .	. . .	. . .	. . .	. . .	. . .	. . .	. . .	. . .
Repairs on goods	3 160 . .	. . .	. . .	. . .	. . .	. . .	. . .	. . .	. . .
Goods procured in ports by carriers	3 170 . .	. . .	. . .	. . .	. . .	. . .	. . .	. . .	. . .
Nonmonetary gold	3 180 . .	–1.3	–1.3	–1.3	–.7	–.5	–.5	. . .	. . .
B. SERVICES	4 200 . .	–188.3	–134.2	–147.1	–184.8	–143.2	–144.4	–82.0	. . .
Total credit	2 200 . .	*54.7*	*51.4*	*68.7*	*68.4*	*64.5*	*64.6*	*56.3*	. . .
Total debit	3 200 . .	*–243.0*	*–185.6*	*–215.7*	*–253.2*	*–207.7*	*–209.0*	*–138.3*	. . .
Transportation services, credit	2 205 . .	**9.3**	**12.1**	**12.5**	**9.1**	**7.3**	**7.8**	**6.7**	. . .
Passenger	2 205 BA	*2.9*	*4.9*	*3.2*	*2.0*	. . .	. . .	. . .	. . .
Freight	2 205 BB	. . .	. . .	*.1*	*.1*	*.1*	*.1*	*.1*	. . .
Other	2 205 BC	*6.4*	*7.2*	*9.2*	*7.1*	*7.2*	*7.7*	*6.6*	. . .
Sea transport, passenger	2 207 . .	. . .	. . .	. . .	. . .	. . .	. . .	. . .	. . .
Sea transport, freight	2 208 . .	. . .	. . .	. . .	. . .	. . .	. . .	. . .	. . .
Sea transport, other	2 209 . .	. . .	. . .	. . .	. . .	. . .	. . .	. . .	. . .
Air transport, passenger	2 211 . .	. . .	. . .	. . .	. . .	. . .	. . .	. . .	. . .
Air transport, freight	2 212 . .	. . .	. . .	. . .	. . .	. . .	. . .	. . .	. . .
Air transport, other	2 213 . .	6.4	7.2	9.2	7.1	7.2	7.7	6.6	. . .
Other transport, passenger	2 215 . .	. . .	. . .	. . .	. . .	. . .	. . .	. . .	. . .
Other transport, freight	2 216 . .	. . .	. . .	. . .	. . .	. . .	. . .	. . .	. . .
Other transport, other	2 217 . .	. . .	. . .	. . .	. . .	. . .	. . .	. . .	. . .
Transportation services, debit	3 205 . .	**–133.3**	**–87.8**	**–126.8**	**–147.4**	**–123.6**	**–115.6**	**–64.9**	. . .
Passenger	3 205 BA	*–22.3*	*–5.5*	*–12.8*	*–16.6*	*–39.9*	*–28.2*	*–15.2*	. . .
Freight	3 205 BB	*–92.6*	*–62.2*	*–90.1*	*–107.4*	*–83.7*	*–87.3*	*–49.7*	. . .
Other	3 205 BC	*–18.5*	*–20.1*	*–23.9*	*–23.4*	. . .	. . .	. . .	. . .
Sea transport, passenger	3 207 . .	. . .	. . .	. . .	. . .	. . .	. . .	. . .	. . .
Sea transport, freight	3 208 . .	. . .	. . .	. . .	. . .	. . .	. . .	. . .	. . .
Sea transport, other	3 209 . .	–18.5	–20.1	–23.9	–23.4	. . .	. . .	. . .	. . .
Air transport, passenger	3 211 . .	–22.3	–5.5	–12.8	–16.6	–39.9	–28.2	–15.2	. . .
Air transport, freight	3 212 . .	. . .	. . .	. . .	. . .	. . .	. . .	. . .	. . .
Air transport, other	3 213 . .	. . .	. . .	. . .	. . .	. . .	. . .	. . .	. . .
Other transport, passenger	3 215 . .	. . .	. . .	. . .	. . .	. . .	. . .	. . .	. . .
Other transport, freight	3 216 . .	–92.6	–62.2	–90.1	–107.4	–83.7	–87.3	–49.7	. . .
Other transport, other	3 217 . .	. . .	. . .	. . .	. . .	. . .	. . .	. . .	. . .
Travel, credit	2 236 . .	**10.7**	**10.1**	**11.5**	**16.5**	**24.1**	**23.1**	**18.4**	. . .
Business travel	2 237 . .	. . .	. . .	. . .	. . .	. . .	. . .	. . .	. . .
Personal travel	2 240 . .	. . .	. . .	. . .	. . .	. . .	. . .	. . .	. . .
Travel, debit	3 236 . .	**–24.5**	**–32.0**	**–32.5**	**–22.2**	**–21.2**	**–21.1**	**–22.7**	. . .
Business travel	3 237 . .	. . .	. . .	. . .	. . .	. . .	. . .	. . .	. . .
Personal travel	3 240 . .	. . .	. . .	. . .	. . .	. . .	. . .	. . .	. . .
Other services, credit	2 200 BA	**34.7**	**29.2**	**44.7**	**42.7**	**33.0**	**33.8**	**31.3**	. . .
Communications	2 245 . .	. . .	. . .	. . .	. . .	. . .	. . .	. . .	. . .
Construction	2 249 . .	. . .	. . .	. . .	. . .	. . .	. . .	. . .	. . .
Insurance	2 253 . .	. . .	. . .	. . .	. . .	. . .	. . .	. . .	. . .
Financial	2 260 . .	. . .	. . .	. . .	. . .	. . .	. . .	. . .	. . .
Computer and information	2 262 . .	. . .	. . .	. . .	. . .	. . .	. . .	. . .	. . .
Royalties and licence fees	2 266 . .	. . .	. . .	. . .	. . .	. . .	. . .	. . .	. . .
Other business services	2 268 . .	5.3	5.7	9.7	11.1	10.3	10.3	13.4	. . .
Personal, cultural, and recreational	2 287 . .	. . .	. . .	. . .	. . .	. . .	. . .	. . .	. . .
Government, n.i.e.	2 291 . .	29.4	23.5	35.0	31.6	22.8	23.4	17.9	. . .
Other services, debit	3 200 BA	**–85.2**	**–65.8**	**–56.5**	**–83.6**	**–62.9**	**–72.3**	**–50.7**	. . .
Communications	3 245 . .	. . .	. . .	. . .	. . .	. . .	. . .	. . .	. . .
Construction	3 249 . .	. . .	. . .	. . .	. . .	. . .	. . .	. . .	. . .
Insurance	3 253 . .	–10.3	–6.9	–10.0	–11.9	–9.3	–9.7	–5.5	. . .
Financial	3 260 . .	. . .	. . .	. . .	. . .	. . .	. . .	. . .	. . .
Computer and information	3 262 . .	. . .	. . .	. . .	. . .	. . .	. . .	. . .	. . .
Royalties and licence fees	3 266 . .	. . .	. . .	. . .	. . .	. . .	. . .	. . .	. . .
Other business services	3 268 . .	–57.8	–39.4	–26.6	–37.3	–22.5	–25.5	–22.7	. . .
Personal, cultural, and recreational	3 287 . .	. . .	. . .	. . .	. . .	. . .	. . .	. . .	. . .
Government, n.i.e.	3 291 . .	–17.1	–19.4	–19.9	–34.3	–31.1	–37.1	–22.5	. . .

Table 2 (Continued). STANDARD PRESENTATION, 1988–95
(Millions of U.S. dollars)

	Code		1988	1989	1990	1991	1992	1993	1994	1995
C. INCOME	4 300	. .	–8.8	–6.4	–.2	.2	2.6	–7.1	–29.4	. . .
Total credit	2 300	. .	*18.1*	*17.8*	*17.6*	*16.5*	*21.7*	*21.5*	*8.7*	. . .
Total debit	3 300	. .	*–26.9*	*–24.2*	*–17.7*	*–16.2*	*–19.1*	*–28.6*	*–38.1*	. . .
Compensation of employees, credit	2 310	. .	. . .	. . .	. . .	. . .	. . .	. . .	. . .	. . .
Compensation of employees, debit	3 310	. .	. . .	. . .	. . .	. . .	. . .	. . .	. . .	. . .
Investment income, credit	2 320	. .	**18.1**	**17.8**	**17.6**	**16.5**	**21.7**	**21.5**	**8.7**	. . .
Direct investment income	2 330	. .	. . .	. . .	. . .	. . .	. . .	. . .	. . .	. . .
Dividends and distributed branch profits	2 332	. .	. . .	. . .	. . .	. . .	. . .	. . .	. . .	. . .
Reinvested earnings and undistributed branch profits	2 333	. .		. . .	. . .	. . .	. . .	. . .	. . .	. . .
Income on debt (interest)	2 334	. .	. . .	. . .	. . .	. . .	. . .	. . .	. . .	. . .
Portfolio investment income	2 339	. .	. . .	. . .	. . .	. . .	. . .	. . .	. . .	. . .
Income on equity	2 340	. .	. . .	. . .	. . .	. . .	. . .	. . .	. . .	. . .
Income on bonds and notes	2 350	. .	. . .	. . .	. . .	. . .	. . .	. . .	. . .	. . .
Income on money market instruments and financial derivatives	2 360	. .	. . .	. . .	. . .	. . .	. . .	. . .	. . .	. . .
Other investment income	2 370	. .	18.1	17.8	17.6	16.5	21.7	21.5	8.7	. . .
Investment income, debit	3 320	. .	**–26.9**	**–24.2**	**–17.7**	**–16.2**	**–19.1**	**–28.6**	**–38.1**	. . .
Direct investment income	3 330	. .	–6.3	–6.3	–6.0	–2.0	. . .	. . .	. . .	. . .
Dividends and distributed branch profits	3 332	. .	–6.3	–6.3	–6.0	–2.0	. . .	. . .	. . .	. . .
Reinvested earnings and undistributed branch profits	3 333	. .	. . .	. . .	. . .	. . .	. . .	. . .	. . .	. . .
Income on debt (interest)	3 334	. .	. . .	. . .	. . .	. . .	. . .	. . .	. . .	. . .
Portfolio investment income	3 339	. .	. . .	. . .	. . .	. . .	. . .	. . .	. . .	. . .
Income on equity	3 340	. .	. . .	. . .	. . .	. . .	. . .	. . .	. . .	. . .
Income on bonds and notes	3 350	. .	. . .	. . .	. . .	. . .	. . .	. . .	. . .	. . .
Income on money market instruments and financial derivatives	3 360	. .	. . .	. . .	. . .	. . .	. . .	. . .	. . .	. . .
Other investment income	3 370	. .	–20.6	–17.9	–11.7	–14.2	–19.1	–28.6	–38.1	. . .
D. CURRENT TRANSFERS	4 379	. .	387.8	497.0	332.3	315.4	339.3	323.4	255.0	. . .
Credit	2 379	. .	**452.0**	**571.6**	**430.2**	**413.1**	**419.2**	**389.6**	**308.0**	. . .
General government	2 380	. .	217.1	372.3	240.8	240.4	236.6	222.2	186.5	. . .
Other sectors	2 390	. .	234.9	199.2	189.4	172.7	182.7	167.4	121.6	. . .
Workers' remittances	2 391	. .	187.0	155.3	139.7	113.0	128.8	117.2	80.3	. . .
Other current transfers	2 392	. .	47.8	44.0	49.7	59.8	53.9	50.2	41.2	. . .
Debit	3 379	. .	**–64.1**	**–74.6**	**–97.9**	**–97.7**	**–79.9**	**–66.3**	**–53.0**	. . .
General government	3 380	. .	–4.7	–15.7	–13.6	–23.3	–9.3	–.9	–.9	. . .
Other sectors	3 390	. .	–59.4	–58.8	–84.3	–74.4	–70.6	–65.4	–52.1	. . .
Workers' remittances	3 391	. .	–57.0	–56.1	–80.9	–70.7	–70.1	–61.8	–51.0	. . .
Other current transfers	3 392	. .	–2.4	–2.8	–3.5	–3.8	–.5	–3.6	–1.1	. . .
CAPITAL AND FINANCIAL ACCOUNT	4 996	. .	**45.5**	**–93.3**	**75.4**	**97.1**	**14.7**	**66.6**	**–6.6**	. . .
CAPITAL ACCOUNT	4 994	. .	. . .	**16.6**	. . .	**13.8**	. . .	**1.1**	**3.5**	. . .
Total credit	2 994	. .	. . .	*16.6*	. . .	*13.8*	. . .	*1.1*	*3.5*	. . .
Total debit	3 994	. .	. . .	. . .	. . .	. . .	. . .	. . .	. . .	. . .
Capital transfers, credit	2 400	. .	. . .	**16.6**	. . .	**13.8**	. . .	**1.1**	**3.5**	. . .
General government	2 401	. .	. . .	16.6	. . .	13.8	. . .	1.1	3.5	. . .
Debt forgiveness	2 402	. .	. . .	16.6	. . .	13.8	. . .	1.1	3.5	. . .
Other capital transfers	2 410	. .	. . .	. . .	. . .	. . .	. . .	. . .	. . .	. . .
Other sectors	2 430	. .	. . .	. . .	. . .	. . .	. . .	. . .	. . .	. . .
Migrants' transfers	2 431	. .	. . .	. . .	. . .	. . .	. . .	. . .	. . .	. . .
Debt forgiveness	2 432	. .	. . .	. . .	. . .	. . .	. . .	. . .	. . .	. . .
Other capital transfers	2 440	. .	. . .	. . .	. . .	. . .	. . .	. . .	. . .	. . .
Capital transfers, debit	3 400	. .	. . .	. . .	. . .	. . .	. . .	. . .	. . .	. . .
General government	3 401	. .	. . .	. . .	. . .	. . .	. . .	. . .	. . .	. . .
Debt forgiveness	3 402	. .	. . .	. . .	. . .	. . .	. . .	. . .	. . .	. . .
Other capital transfers	3 410	. .	. . .	. . .	. . .	. . .	. . .	. . .	. . .	. . .
Other sectors	3 430	. .	. . .	. . .	. . .	. . .	. . .	. . .	. . .	. . .
Migrants' transfers	3 431	. .	. . .	. . .	. . .	. . .	. . .	. . .	. . .	. . .
Debt forgiveness	3 432	. .	. . .	. . .	. . .	. . .	. . .	. . .	. . .	. . .
Other capital transfers	3 440	. .	. . .	. . .	. . .	. . .	. . .	. . .	. . .	. . .
Nonproduced nonfinancial assets, credit	2 480	. .	. . .	. . .	. . .	. . .	. . .	. . .	. . .	. . .
Nonproduced nonfinancial assets, debit	3 480	. .	. . .	. . .	. . .	. . .	. . .	. . .	. . .	. . .

Table 2 (Continued). STANDARD PRESENTATION, 1988–95
(Millions of U.S. dollars)

	Code		1988	1989	1990	1991	1992	1993	1994	1995
FINANCIAL ACCOUNT	4 995	. .	**45.5**	**–109.9**	**75.4**	**83.3**	**14.7**	**65.5**	**–10.1**	**. . .**
A. DIRECT INVESTMENT	4 500	. .	3.7	5.7	. . .	. . .	. . .	. . .	. . .	. . .
Direct investment abroad	4 505	. .	**. . .**	**. . .**	**. . .**	**. . .**	**. . .**	**. . .**	**. . .**	**. . .**
Equity capital	4 510	. .	. . .	. . .	. . .	. . .	. . .	. . .	. . .	. . .
Claims on affiliated enterprises	4 515	. .	. . .	. . .	. . .	. . .	. . .	. . .	. . .	. . .
Liabilities to affiliated enterprises	4 520	. .	. . .	. . .	. . .	. . .	. . .	. . .	. . .	. . .
Reinvested earnings	4 525	. .	. . .	. . .	. . .	. . .	. . .	. . .	. . .	. . .
Other capital	4 530	. .	. . .	. . .	. . .	. . .	. . .	. . .	. . .	. . .
Claims on affiliated enterprises	4 535	. .	. . .	. . .	. . .	. . .	. . .	. . .	. . .	. . .
Liabilities to affiliated enterprises	4 540	. .	. . .	. . .	. . .	. . .	. . .	. . .	. . .	. . .
Direct investment in Burkina Faso	4 555	. .	**3.7**	**5.7**	**. . .**	**. . .**	**. . .**	**. . .**	**. . .**	**. . .**
Equity capital	4 560	. .	. . .	. . .	. . .	. . .	. . .	. . .	. . .	. . .
Claims on direct investors	4 565	. .	. . .	. . .	. . .	. . .	. . .	. . .	. . .	. . .
Liabilities to direct investors	4 570	. .	. . .	. . .	. . .	. . .	. . .	. . .	. . .	. . .
Reinvested earnings	4 575	. .	. . .	. . .	. . .	. . .	. . .	. . .	. . .	. . .
Other capital	4 580	. .	3.7	5.7	. . .	. . .	. . .	. . .	. . .	. . .
Claims on direct investors	4 585	. .	. . .	. . .	. . .	. . .	. . .	. . .	. . .	. . .
Liabilities to direct investors	4 590	. .	. . .	. . .	. . .	. . .	. . .	. . .	. . .	. . .
B. PORTFOLIO INVESTMENT	4 600	. .	. . .	. . .	. . .	. . .	. . .	. . .	. . .	. . .
Assets	4 602	. .	**. . .**	**. . .**	**. . .**	**. . .**	**. . .**	**. . .**	**. . .**	**. . .**
Equity securities	4 610	. .	. . .	. . .	. . .	. . .	. . .	. . .	. . .	. . .
Monetary authorities	4 611	. .	. . .	. . .	. . .	. . .	. . .	. . .	. . .	. . .
General government	4 612	. .	. . .	. . .	. . .	. . .	. . .	. . .	. . .	. . .
Banks	4 613	. .	. . .	. . .	. . .	. . .	. . .	. . .	. . .	. . .
Other sectors	4 614	. .	. . .	. . .	. . .	. . .	. . .	. . .	. . .	. . .
Debt securities	4 619	. .	. . .	. . .	. . .	. . .	. . .	. . .	. . .	. . .
Bonds and notes	4 620	. .	. . .	. . .	. . .	. . .	. . .	. . .	. . .	. . .
Monetary authorities	4 621	. .	. . .	. . .	. . .	. . .	. . .	. . .	. . .	. . .
General government	4 622	. .	. . .	. . .	. . .	. . .	. . .	. . .	. . .	. . .
Banks	4 623	. .	. . .	. . .	. . .	. . .	. . .	. . .	. . .	. . .
Other sectors	4 624	. .	. . .	. . .	. . .	. . .	. . .	. . .	. . .	. . .
Money market instruments	4 630	. .	. . .	. . .	. . .	. . .	. . .	. . .	. . .	. . .
Monetary authorities	4 631	. .	. . .	. . .	. . .	. . .	. . .	. . .	. . .	. . .
General government	4 632	. .	. . .	. . .	. . .	. . .	. . .	. . .	. . .	. . .
Banks	4 633	. .	. . .	. . .	. . .	. . .	. . .	. . .	. . .	. . .
Other sectors	4 634	. .	. . .	. . .	. . .	. . .	. . .	. . .	. . .	. . .
Financial derivatives	4 640	. .	. . .	. . .	. . .	. . .	. . .	. . .	. . .	. . .
Monetary authorities	4 641	. .	. . .	. . .	. . .	. . .	. . .	. . .	. . .	. . .
General government	4 642	. .	. . .	. . .	. . .	. . .	. . .	. . .	. . .	. . .
Banks	4 643	. .	. . .	. . .	. . .	. . .	. . .	. . .	. . .	. . .
Other sectors	4 644	. .	. . .	. . .	. . .	. . .	. . .	. . .	. . .	. . .
Liabilities	4 652	. .	**. . .**	**. . .**	**. . .**	**. . .**	**. . .**	**. . .**	**. . .**	**. . .**
Equity securities	4 660	. .	. . .	. . .	. . .	. . .	. . .	. . .	. . .	. . .
Banks	4 663	. .	. . .	. . .	. . .	. . .	. . .	. . .	. . .	. . .
Other sectors	4 664	. .	. . .	. . .	. . .	. . .	. . .	. . .	. . .	. . .
Debt securities	4 669	. .	. . .	. . .	. . .	. . .	. . .	. . .	. . .	. . .
Bonds and notes	4 670	. .	. . .	. . .	. . .	. . .	. . .	. . .	. . .	. . .
Monetary authorities	4 671	. .	. . .	. . .	. . .	. . .	. . .	. . .	. . .	. . .
General government	4 672	. .	. . .	. . .	. . .	. . .	. . .	. . .	. . .	. . .
Banks	4 673	. .	. . .	. . .	. . .	. . .	. . .	. . .	. . .	. . .
Other sectors	4 674	. .	. . .	. . .	. . .	. . .	. . .	. . .	. . .	. . .
Money market instruments	4 680	. .	. . .	. . .	. . .	. . .	. . .	. . .	. . .	. . .
Monetary authorities	4 681	. .	. . .	. . .	. . .	. . .	. . .	. . .	. . .	. . .
General government	4 682	. .	. . .	. . .	. . .	. . .	. . .	. . .	. . .	. . .
Banks	4 683	. .	. . .	. . .	. . .	. . .	. . .	. . .	. . .	. . .
Other sectors	4 684	. .	. . .	. . .	. . .	. . .	. . .	. . .	. . .	. . .
Financial derivatives	4 690	. .	. . .	. . .	. . .	. . .	. . .	. . .	. . .	. . .
Monetary authorities	4 691	. .	. . .	. . .	. . .	. . .	. . .	. . .	. . .	. . .
General government	4 692	. .	. . .	. . .	. . .	. . .	. . .	. . .	. . .	. . .
Banks	4 693	. .	. . .	. . .	. . .	. . .	. . .	. . .	. . .	. . .
Other sectors	4 694	. .	. . .	. . .	. . .	. . .	. . .	. . .	. . .	. . .

Table 2 (Concluded). STANDARD PRESENTATION, 1988–95
(Millions of U.S. dollars)

	Code	1988	1989	1990	1991	1992	1993	1994	1995
C. OTHER INVESTMENT	4 700 . .	71.5	–165.6	81.9	126.9	30.6	119.0	7.4	. . .
Assets	4 703 . .	**–2.3**	**–26.7**	**–6.6**	**.5**	**–45.2**	**24.2**	**–139.2**	**. . .**
Trade credits	4 706 . .	–1.5	–13.8	–3.7	–15.4	–23.4	. . .	–4.0	. . .
General government: long-term	4 708 . .	. . .	. . .	. . .	. . .	. . .	. . .	. . .	. . .
General government: short-term	4 709 . .	. . .	. . .	. . .	. . .	. . .	. . .	. . .	. . .
Other sectors: long-term	4 711 . .	. . .	. . .	. . .	. . .	. . .	. . .	. . .	. . .
Other sectors: short-term	4 712 . .	–1.5	–13.8	–3.7	–15.4	–23.4	. . .	–4.0	. . .
Loans	4 714 . .	. . .	. . .	. . .	. . .	. . .	. . .	. . .	. . .
Monetary authorities: long-term	4 717 . .	. . .	. . .	. . .	. . .	. . .	. . .	. . .	. . .
Monetary authorities: short-term	4 718 . .	. . .	. . .	. . .	. . .	. . .	. . .	. . .	. . .
General government: long-term	4 720 . .	. . .	. . .	. . .	. . .	. . .	. . .	. . .	. . .
General government: short-term	4 721 . .	. . .	. . .	. . .	. . .	. . .	. . .	. . .	. . .
Banks: long-term	4 723 . .	. . .	. . .	. . .	. . .	. . .	. . .	. . .	. . .
Banks: short-term	4 724 . .	. . .	. . .	. . .	. . .	. . .	. . .	. . .	. . .
Other sectors: long-term	4 726 . .	. . .	. . .	. . .	. . .	. . .	. . .	. . .	. . .
Other sectors: short-term	4 727 . .	. . .	. . .	. . .	. . .	. . .	. . .	. . .	. . .
Currency and deposits	4 730 . .	–.8	–12.8	–3.0	15.9	–21.7	24.2	–135.2	. . .
Monetary authorities	4 731 . .	. . .	. . .	. . .	. . .	. . .	. . .	. . .	. . .
General government	4 732 . .	. . .	. . .	. . .	. . .	. . .	. . .	. . .	. . .
Banks	4 733 . .	–.8	–12.8	–3.0	15.9	–21.7	24.2	–135.2	. . .
Other sectors	4 734 . .	. . .	. . .	. . .	. . .	. . .	. . .	. . .	. . .
Other assets	4 736 . .	. . .	. . .	. . .	. . .	. . .	. . .	. . .	. . .
Monetary authorities: long-term	4 738 . .	. . .	. . .	. . .	. . .	. . .	. . .	. . .	. . .
Monetary authorities: short-term	4 739 . .	. . .	. . .	. . .	. . .	. . .	. . .	. . .	. . .
General government: long-term	4 741 . .	. . .	. . .	. . .	. . .	. . .	. . .	. . .	. . .
General government: short-term	4 742 . .	. . .	. . .	. . .	. . .	. . .	. . .	. . .	. . .
Banks: long-term	4 744 . .	. . .	. . .	. . .	. . .	. . .	. . .	. . .	. . .
Banks: short-term	4 745 . .	. . .	. . .	. . .	. . .	. . .	. . .	. . .	. . .
Other sectors: long-term	4 747 . .	. . .	. . .	. . .	. . .	. . .	. . .	. . .	. . .
Other sectors: short-term	4 748 . .	. . .	. . .	. . .	. . .	. . .	. . .	. . .	. . .
Liabilities	4 753 . .	**73.7**	**–138.9**	**88.6**	**126.4**	**75.7**	**94.8**	**146.6**	**. . .**
Trade credits	4 756 . .	. . .	. . .	. . .	. . .	. . .	. . .	. . .	. . .
General government: long-term	4 758 . .	. . .	. . .	. . .	. . .	. . .	. . .	. . .	. . .
General government: short-term	4 759 . .	. . .	. . .	. . .	. . .	. . .	. . .	. . .	. . .
Other sectors: long-term	4 761 . .	. . .	. . .	. . .	. . .	. . .	. . .	. . .	. . .
Other sectors: short-term	4 762 . .	. . .	. . .	. . .	. . .	. . .	. . .	. . .	. . .
Loans	4 764 . .	57.4	–222.4	79.4	133.4	104.5	142.6	116.9	. . .
Use of Fund credit and loans from the Fund	4 766 . .	–3.1	–1.9	–.5	8.7	. . .	12.5	25.5	. . .
Monetary authorities: other long-term	4 767 . .	. . .	. . .	. . .	. . .	. . .	. . .	. . .	. . .
Monetary authorities: short-term	4 768 . .	. . .	. . .	. . .	. . .	–6.6	. . .	. . .	. . .
General government: long-term	4 770 . .	48.4	–226.5	64.3	91.8	112.4	122.4	37.4	. . .
General government: short-term	4 771 . .	. . .	. . .	. . .	. . .	. . .	. . .	. . .	. . .
Banks: long-term	4 773 . .	. . .	. . .	. . .	. . .	. . .	. . .	. . .	. . .
Banks: short-term	4 774 . .	. . .	. . .	. . .	. . .	. . .	. . .	. . .	. . .
Other sectors: long-term	4 776 . .	10.5	5.5	7.9	8.1	–4.4	3.0	25.6	. . .
Other sectors: short-term	4 777 . .	1.7	.5	7.7	24.8	3.1	4.7	28.4	. . .
Currency and deposits	4 780 . .	1.5	13.0	9.2	–7.0	–12.1	–47.1	41.9	. . .
Monetary authorities	4 781 . .	. . .	. . .	. . .	. . .	. . .	. . .	. . .	. . .
General government	4 782 . .	. . .	. . .	. . .	. . .	. . .	. . .	. . .	. . .
Banks	4 783 . .	1.5	13.0	9.2	–7.0	–12.1	–47.1	41.9	. . .
Other sectors	4 784 . .	. . .	. . .	. . .	. . .	. . .	. . .	. . .	. . .
Other liabilities	4 786 . .	14.8	70.5	. . .	. . .	–16.6	–.6	–12.3	. . .
Monetary authorities: long-term	4 788 . .	. . .	. . .	. . .	. . .	. . .	. . .	. . .	. . .
Monetary authorities: short-term	4 789 . .	. . .	. . .	. . .	. . .	. . .	. . .	. . .	. . .
General government: long-term	4 791 . .	. . .	. . .	. . .	. . .	. . .	. . .	. . .	. . .
General government: short-term	4 792 . .	14.8	70.5	. . .	. . .	–16.6	–.6	–12.3	. . .
Banks: long-term	4 794 . .	. . .	. . .	. . .	. . .	. . .	. . .	. . .	. . .
Banks: short-term	4 795 . .	. . .	. . .	. . .	. . .	. . .	. . .	. . .	. . .
Other sectors: long-term	4 797 . .	. . .	. . .	. . .	. . .	. . .	. . .	. . .	. . .
Other sectors: short-term	4 798 . .	. . .	. . .	. . .	. . .	. . .	. . .	. . .	. . .
D. RESERVE ASSETS	4 800 . .	–29.7	50.0	–6.6	–43.6	–15.9	–53.5	–17.4	. . .
Monetary gold	4 810 . .	. . .	. . .	. . .	. . .	. . .	. . .	. . .	. . .
Special drawing rights	4 820 . .	. . .	. . .	. . .	.1	. . .	. . .	. . .	. . .
Reserve position in the Fund	4 830 . .	. . .	. . .	.5	. . .	. . .	. . .	. . .	. . .
Foreign exchange	4 840 . .	–29.7	50.0	–7.0	–43.7	–15.9	–53.5	–17.5	. . .
Other claims	4 880 . .	. . .	. . .	. . .	. . .	. . .	. . .	. . .	. . .
NET ERRORS AND OMISSIONS	4 998 . .	**1.1**	**–5.9**	**1.6**	**–6.6**	**8.3**	**4.6**	**–8.3**	**. . .**

Table 1. ANALYTIC PRESENTATION, 1988–95
(Millions of U.S. dollars)

	Code			1988	1989	1990	1991	1992	1993	1994	1995
A. Current Account [1]	4	993	Y.	**–70.1**	**–11.5**	**–69.4**	**–33.3**	**–59.6**	**–29.2**	**–18.3**	**–6.5**
Goods: exports f.o.b	2	100	. .	124.4	93.2	72.8	93.0	77.0	73.9	80.7	112.5
Goods: imports f.o.b	3	100	. .	–166.1	–151.4	–189.0	–195.9	–181.8	–172.8	–172.6	–175.6
Balance on Goods	4	100	. .	*–41.7*	*–58.2*	*–116.3*	*–103.0*	*–104.8*	*–99.0*	*–91.9*	*–63.1*
Services: credit	2	200	. .	11.9	15.3	16.7	25.7	17.5	14.2	14.6	16.6
Services: debit	3	200	. .	–114.9	–92.6	–129.2	–141.3	–137.3	–115.5	–95.0	–101.8
Balance on Goods and Services	4	991	. .	*–144.7*	*–135.5*	*–228.8*	*–218.6*	*–224.7*	*–200.2*	*–172.3*	*–148.3*
Income: credit	2	300	. .	2.9	8.9	8.2	9.7	14.0	11.2	8.1	10.4
Income: debit	3	300	. .	–25.8	–26.5	–23.0	–20.7	–27.6	–22.2	–19.5	–19.7
Balance on Goods, Services, and Income	4	992	. .	*–167.6*	*–153.1*	*–243.6*	*–229.7*	*–238.2*	*–211.2*	*–183.7*	*–157.6*
Current transfers: credit	2	379	Y.	103.4	142.7	175.5	198.1	180.6	183.8	167.0	153.3
Current transfers: debit	3	379	. .	–5.9	–1.1	–1.3	–1.7	–1.9	–1.8	–1.6	–2.1
B. Capital Account [1]	4	994	Y.	**–.5**	**–.6**	**–.5**	**–.7**	**–.8**	**–1.2**	**–.2**	**–.8**
Capital account: credit	2	994	Y.	. . .	. . .	. . .	. . .	. . .	. . .	. . .	. . .
Capital account: debit	3	994	. .	–.5	–.6	–.5	–.7	–.8	–1.2	–.2	–.8
Total, Groups A Plus B	4	010	. .	*–70.6*	*–12.1*	*–70.0*	*–34.0*	*–60.5*	*–30.4*	*–18.5*	*–7.3*
C. Financial Account [1]	4	995	X.	**84.3**	**64.4**	**78.0**	**70.4**	**98.7**	**52.5**	**31.1**	**26.9**
Direct investment abroad	4	505	. .	. . .	–.1	. . .	. . .	. . .	–.1	–.1	–.6
Direct investment in Burundi	4	555	Y.	1.2	.6	1.3	.9	.6	.5	. . .	2.0
Portfolio investment assets	4	602	. .	. . .	. . .	. . .	. . .	. . .	. . .	. . .	. . .
Equity securities	4	610	. .	. . .	. . .	. . .	. . .	. . .	. . .	. . .	. . .
Debt securities	4	619	. .	. . .	. . .	. . .	. . .	. . .	. . .	. . .	. . .
Portfolio investment liabilities	4	652	Y.	. . .	. . .	. . .	. . .	. . .	. . .	. . .	. . .
Equity securities	4	660	Y.	. . .	. . .	. . .	. . .	. . .	. . .	. . .	. . .
Debt securities	4	669	Y.	. . .	. . .	. . .	. . .	. . .	. . .	. . .	. . .
Other investment assets	4	703	. .	–11.5	–7.6	4.1	–3.5	–1.0	–1.5	–1.6	7.3
Monetary authorities	4	703	. A	. . .	. . .	. . .	. . .	. . .	. . .	. . .	. . .
General government	4	703	. B	–5.8	–1.9	–1.0	–1.1	–.6	–.3	–.8	–.4
Banks	4	703	. C	–.7	.1	–.6	–2.1	–1.3	–4.2	–8.8	–.1
Other sectors	4	703	. D	–5.0	–5.7	5.7	–.4	1.0	3.0	7.9	7.8
Other investment liabilities	4	753	X.	94.6	71.5	72.7	73.1	99.1	53.6	32.9	18.3
Monetary authorities	4	753	XA	. . .	. . .	. . .	. . .	. . .	. . .	. . .	. . .
General government	4	753	YB	83.9	65.4	62.1	57.0	90.8	47.2	25.2	11.1
Banks	4	753	YC	1.3	–.6	1.6	1.4	1.1	.4	4.7	.2
Other sectors	4	753	YD	9.4	6.6	9.0	14.6	7.1	6.0	3.0	7.0
Total, Groups A Through C	4	020	. .	*13.7*	*52.3*	*8.0*	*36.5*	*38.2*	*22.1*	*12.7*	*19.7*
D. Net Errors and Omissions	4	998	. .	**–6.6**	**–14.3**	**–11.3**	**11.7**	**11.7**	**–6.1**	**23.0**	**16.1**
Total, Groups A Through D	4	030	. .	*7.1*	*38.0*	*–3.2*	*48.2*	*49.9*	*16.0*	*35.7*	*35.8*
E. Reserves and Related Items	4	040	. .	**–7.1**	**–38.0**	**3.2**	**–48.2**	**–49.9**	**–16.0**	**–35.7**	**–35.8**
Reserve assets	4	800	. .	–20.5	–46.1	4.0	–54.0	–68.5	–11.9	–29.6	–26.7
Use of Fund credit and loans	4	766	. .	13.3	8.1	–.8	5.8	18.5	–4.1	–6.1	–9.0
Liabilities constituting foreign authorities' reserves	4	900	. .	. . .	. . .	. . .	. . .	. . .	. . .	. . .	. . .
Exceptional financing	4	920	. .	. . .	. . .	. . .	. . .	. . .	. . .	. . .	. . .
Conversion rates: Burundi francs per U.S. dollar	0	101	. .	**140.40**	**158.67**	**171.26**	**181.51**	**208.30**	**242.78**	**252.66**	**249.76**

[1] Excludes components that have been classified in the categories of Group E.

Table 2. STANDARD PRESENTATION, 1988–95
(Millions of U.S. dollars)

	Code	1988	1989	1990	1991	1992	1993	1994	1995
CURRENT ACCOUNT	4 993 . .	**–70.1**	**–11.5**	**–69.4**	**–33.3**	**–59.6**	**–29.2**	**–18.3**	**–6.5**
A. GOODS	4 100 . .	–41.7	–58.2	–116.3	–103.0	–104.8	–99.0	–91.9	–63.1
Credit	2 100 . .	**124.4**	**93.2**	**72.8**	**93.0**	**77.0**	**73.9**	**80.7**	**112.5**
General merchandise: exports f.o.b.	2 110 . .	124.4	93.2	72.8	93.0	77.0	73.9	80.7	112.5
Goods for processing: exports f.o.b.	2 150 . .	. . .	. . .	. . .	. . .	. . .	. . .	. . .	. . .
Repairs on goods	2 160 . .	. . .	. . .	. . .	. . .	. . .	. . .	. . .	. . .
Goods procured in ports by carriers	2 170 . .	. . .	. . .	. . .	. . .	. . .	. . .	. . .	. . .
Nonmonetary gold	2 180 . .	. . .	. . .	. . .	. . .	. . .	. . .	. . .	. . .
Debit	3 100 . .	**–166.1**	**–151.4**	**–189.0**	**–195.9**	**–181.8**	**–172.8**	**–172.6**	**–175.6**
General merchandise: imports f.o.b.	3 110 . .	–166.1	–151.4	–189.0	–195.9	–181.8	–172.8	–172.6	–175.6
Goods for processing: imports f.o.b.	3 150 . .	. . .	. . .	. . .	. . .	. . .	. . .	. . .	. . .
Repairs on goods	3 160 . .	. . .	. . .	. . .	. . .	. . .	. . .	. . .	. . .
Goods procured in ports by carriers	3 170 . .	. . .	. . .	. . .	. . .	. . .	. . .	. . .	. . .
Nonmonetary gold	3 180 . .	. . .	. . .	. . .	. . .	. . .	. . .	. . .	. . .
B. SERVICES	4 200 . .	–103.0	–77.3	–112.5	–115.7	–119.9	–101.2	–80.4	–85.3
Total credit	2 200 . .	*11.9*	*15.3*	*16.7*	*25.7*	*17.5*	*14.2*	*14.6*	*16.6*
Total debit	3 200 . .	*–114.9*	*–92.6*	*–129.2*	*–141.3*	*–137.3*	*–115.5*	*–95.0*	*–101.8*
Transportation services, credit	2 205 . .	**1.3**	**1.8**	**2.5**	**2.9**	**2.3**	**2.0**	**3.1**	**2.0**
Passenger	2 205 BA	*.8*	*1.2*	*1.5*	*1.2*	*.8*	*1.2*	*1.3*	*1.0*
Freight	2 205 BB	*.6*	*.6*	*1.1*	*1.7*	*1.4*	*.8*	*1.8*	*1.0*
Other	2 205 BC	. . .	. . .	. . .	. . .	. . .	. . .	. . .	. . .
Sea transport, passenger	2 207 . .	. . .	. . .	. . .	. . .	. . .	. . .	. . .	. . .
Sea transport, freight	2 208 . .	. . .	. . .	. . .	. . .	. . .	. . .	. . .	. . .
Sea transport, other	2 209 . .	. . .	. . .	. . .	. . .	. . .	. . .	. . .	. . .
Air transport, passenger	2 211 . .	. . .	. . .	. . .	. . .	. . .	. . .	. . .	. . .
Air transport, freight	2 212 . .	. . .	. . .	. . .	. . .	. . .	. . .	. . .	. . .
Air transport, other	2 213 . .	. . .	. . .	. . .	. . .	. . .	. . .	. . .	. . .
Other transport, passenger	2 215 . .	. . .	. . .	. . .	. . .	. . .	. . .	. . .	. . .
Other transport, freight	2 216 . .	. . .	. . .	. . .	. . .	. . .	. . .	. . .	. . .
Other transport, other	2 217 . .	. . .	. . .	. . .	. . .	. . .	. . .	. . .	. . .
Transportation services, debit	3 205 . .	**–29.8**	**–28.9**	**–37.2**	**–42.6**	**–35.9**	**–30.4**	**–35.8**	**–30.6**
Passenger	3 205 BA	. . .	. . .	. . .	. . .	. . .	. . .	. . .	. . .
Freight	3 205 BB	*–29.8*	*–28.9*	*–37.2*	*–42.6*	*–35.9*	*–30.4*	*–35.8*	*–30.6*
Other	3 205 BC	. . .	. . .	. . .	. . .	. . .	. . .	. . .	. . .
Sea transport, passenger	3 207 . .	. . .	. . .	. . .	. . .	. . .	. . .	. . .	. . .
Sea transport, freight	3 208 . .	. . .	. . .	. . .	. . .	. . .	. . .	. . .	. . .
Sea transport, other	3 209 . .	. . .	. . .	. . .	. . .	. . .	. . .	. . .	. . .
Air transport, passenger	3 211 . .	. . .	. . .	. . .	. . .	. . .	. . .	. . .	. . .
Air transport, freight	3 212 . .	. . .	. . .	. . .	. . .	. . .	. . .	. . .	. . .
Air transport, other	3 213 . .	. . .	. . .	. . .	. . .	. . .	. . .	. . .	. . .
Other transport, passenger	3 215 . .	. . .	. . .	. . .	. . .	. . .	. . .	. . .	. . .
Other transport, freight	3 216 . .	. . .	. . .	. . .	. . .	. . .	. . .	. . .	. . .
Other transport, other	3 217 . .	. . .	. . .	. . .	. . .	. . .	. . .	. . .	. . .
Travel, credit	2 236 . .	**. . .**	**2.5**	**3.4**	**4.1**	**3.8**	**3.3**	**1.9**	**1.4**
Business travel	2 237 . .	. . .	. . .	. . .	. . .	. . .	. . .	. . .	. . .
Personal travel	2 240 . .	. . .	. . .	. . .	. . .	. . .	. . .	. . .	. . .
Travel, debit	3 236 . .	**–15.0**	**–14.3**	**–17.2**	**–18.2**	**–20.7**	**–19.6**	**–18.0**	**–25.4**
Business travel	3 237 . .	. . .	. . .	. . .	. . .	. . .	. . .	. . .	. . .
Personal travel	3 240 . .	. . .	. . .	. . .	. . .	. . .	. . .	. . .	. . .
Other services, credit	2 200 BA	**10.6**	**10.9**	**10.8**	**18.7**	**11.4**	**9.0**	**9.6**	**13.2**
Communications	2 245 . .	. . .	. . .	. . .	. . .	. . .	. . .	. . .	. . .
Construction	2 249 . .	. . .	. . .	. . .	. . .	. . .	. . .	. . .	. . .
Insurance	2 253 . .	.1	.1	.1	.2	.1	.1	.2	.2
Financial	2 260 . .	. . .	. . .	. . .	. . .	. . .	. . .	. . .	. . .
Computer and information	2 262 . .	. . .	. . .	. . .	. . .	. . .	. . .	. . .	. . .
Royalties and licence fees	2 266 . .	. . .	. . .	. . .	. . .	. . .	. . .	. . .	. . .
Other business services	2 268 . .	.7	.9	.5	.8	.5	1.0	.9	.9
Personal, cultural, and recreational	2 287 . .	. . .	. . .	. . .	. . .	. . .	. . .	. . .	. . .
Government, n.i.e.	2 291 . .	9.8	9.9	10.1	17.7	10.8	7.9	8.5	12.1
Other services, debit	3 200 BA	**–70.1**	**–49.4**	**–74.8**	**–80.5**	**–80.8**	**–65.5**	**–41.2**	**–45.9**
Communications	3 245 . .	. . .	. . .	. . .	. . .	. . .	. . .	. . .	. . .
Construction	3 249 . .	. . .	. . .	. . .	. . .	. . .	. . .	. . .	. . .
Insurance	3 253 . .	–3.3	–3.2	–3.7	–4.3	–3.6	–3.0	–4.0	–3.9
Financial	3 260 . .	. . .	. . .	. . .	. . .	. . .	. . .	. . .	. . .
Computer and information	3 262 . .	. . .	. . .	. . .	. . .	. . .	. . .	. . .	. . .
Royalties and licence fees	3 266 . .	. . .	. . .	–.1	–.2	–.1	. . .	. . .	–.1
Other business services	3 268 . .	–4.3	–1.2	–1.2	–2.1	–1.4	–1.5	–1.8	–2.2
Personal, cultural, and recreational	3 287 . .	. . .	. . .	. . .	. . .	. . .	. . .	. . .	. . .
Government, n.i.e.	3 291 . .	–62.4	–45.0	–69.8	–74.0	–75.7	–60.9	–35.4	–39.6

Table 2 (Continued). STANDARD PRESENTATION, 1988–95
(Millions of U.S. dollars)

	Code	1988	1989	1990	1991	1992	1993	1994	1995
C. INCOME	4 300	–22.9	–17.6	–14.8	–11.0	–13.6	–11.0	–11.4	–9.3
Total credit	2 300	*2.9*	*8.9*	*8.2*	*9.7*	*14.0*	*11.2*	*8.1*	*10.4*
Total debit	3 300	*–25.8*	*–26.5*	*–23.0*	*–20.7*	*–27.6*	*–22.2*	*–19.5*	*–19.7*
Compensation of employees, credit	2 310	...	...	...	...	...	...	...	...
Compensation of employees, debit	3 310	**–5.4**	**–4.8**	**–5.3**	**–4.4**	**–6.8**	**–6.0**	**–3.9**	**–4.5**
Investment income, credit	2 320	**2.9**	**8.9**	**8.2**	**9.7**	**14.0**	**11.2**	**8.1**	**10.4**
Direct investment income	2 330	...	...	...	...	...	...	...	...
Dividends and distributed branch profits	2 332	...	...	...	...	...	...	...	...
Reinvested earnings and undistributed branch profits	2 333	...	...	...	...	...	...	...	...
Income on debt (interest)	2 334	...	...	...	...	...	...	...	...
Portfolio investment income	2 339	...	...	...	...	...	...	...	...
Income on equity	2 340	...	...	...	...	...	...	...	...
Income on bonds and notes	2 350	...	...	...	...	...	...	...	...
Income on money market instruments and financial derivatives	2 360	...	...	...	...	...	...	...	...
Other investment income	2 370	2.9	8.9	8.2	9.7	14.0	11.2	8.1	10.4
Investment income, debit	3 320	**–20.4**	**–21.7**	**–17.7**	**–16.3**	**–20.7**	**–16.2**	**–15.5**	**–15.2**
Direct investment income	3 330	–2.3	–2.5	–3.3	–2.1	–4.2	–2.9	–3.4	–3.1
Dividends and distributed branch profits	3 332	–2.3	–2.5	–3.3	–2.1	–4.2	–2.9	–3.4	–3.1
Reinvested earnings and undistributed branch profits	3 333	...	...	...	...	...	...	...	...
Income on debt (interest)	3 334	...	...	...	...	...	...	...	...
Portfolio investment income	3 339	...	...	...	...	...	...	...	...
Income on equity	3 340	...	...	...	...	...	...	...	...
Income on bonds and notes	3 350	...	...	...	...	...	...	...	...
Income on money market instruments and financial derivatives	3 360	...	...	...	...	...	...	...	...
Other investment income	3 370	–18.1	–19.3	–14.5	–14.2	–16.5	–13.3	–12.1	–12.1
D. CURRENT TRANSFERS	4 379	97.5	141.6	174.2	196.4	178.6	182.1	165.4	151.1
Credit	2 379	**103.4**	**142.7**	**175.5**	**198.1**	**180.6**	**183.8**	**167.0**	**153.3**
General government	2 380	91.3	132.9	164.6	183.8	166.3	164.7	144.6	137.1
Other sectors	2 390	12.1	9.8	10.9	14.3	14.2	19.2	22.3	16.2
Workers' remittances	2 391	...	...	...	...	...	...	...	...
Other current transfers	2 392	12.1	9.8	10.9	14.3	14.2	19.2	22.3	16.2
Debit	3 379	**–5.9**	**–1.1**	**–1.3**	**–1.7**	**–1.9**	**–1.8**	**–1.6**	**–2.1**
General government	3 380	–4.2	–.6	–1.0	–1.3	–1.4	–1.2	–.8	–1.0
Other sectors	3 390	–1.7	–.6	–.3	–.4	–.5	–.6	–.7	–1.1
Workers' remittances	3 391	...	...	...	...	...	...	...	...
Other current transfers	3 392	–1.7	–.6	–.3	–.4	–.5	–.6	–.7	–1.1
CAPITAL AND FINANCIAL ACCOUNT	4 996	**76.6**	**25.8**	**80.7**	**21.6**	**47.9**	**35.3**	**–4.7**	**–9.6**
CAPITAL ACCOUNT	4 994	**–.5**	**–.6**	**–.5**	**–.7**	**–.8**	**–1.2**	**–.2**	**–.8**
Total credit	2 994	...	...	...	...	...	...	...	...
Total debit	3 994	*–.5*	*–.6*	*–.5*	*–.7*	*–.8*	*–1.2*	*–.2*	*–.8*
Capital transfers, credit	2 400	...	...	...	...	...	...	...	...
General government	2 401	...	...	...	...	...	...	...	...
Debt forgiveness	2 402	...	...	...	...	...	...	...	...
Other capital transfers	2 410	...	...	...	...	...	...	...	...
Other sectors	2 430	...	...	...	...	...	...	...	...
Migrants' transfers	2 431	...	...	...	...	...	...	...	...
Debt forgiveness	2 432	...	...	...	...	...	...	...	...
Other capital transfers	2 440	...	...	...	...	...	...	...	...
Capital transfers, debit	3 400	**–.5**	**–.6**	**–.5**	**–.7**	**–.8**	**–1.2**	**–.2**	**–.8**
General government	3 401	...	...	...	...	...	...	...	...
Debt forgiveness	3 402	...	...	...	...	...	...	...	...
Other capital transfers	3 410	...	...	...	...	...	...	...	...
Other sectors	3 430	–.5	–.6	–.5	–.7	–.8	–1.2	–.2	–.8
Migrants' transfers	3 431	–.5	–.6	–.5	–.7	–.8	–1.2	–.2	–.8
Debt forgiveness	3 432	...	...	...	...	...	...	...	...
Other capital transfers	3 440	...	...	...	...	...	...	...	...
Nonproduced nonfinancial assets, credit	2 480	...	...	...	...	...	...	...	...
Nonproduced nonfinancial assets, debit	3 480	...	...	...	...	...	...	...	...

Table 2 (Continued). STANDARD PRESENTATION, 1988–95
(Millions of U.S. dollars)

	Code	1988	1989	1990	1991	1992	1993	1994	1995
FINANCIAL ACCOUNT	4 995	**77.1**	**26.4**	**81.2**	**22.3**	**48.7**	**36.5**	**–4.5**	**–8.9**
A. DIRECT INVESTMENT	4 500	1.2	.5	1.2	.9	.6	.3	–.1	1.4
Direct investment abroad	4 505	**. . .**	**–.1**	**. . .**	**. . .**	**. . .**	**–.1**	**–.1**	**–.6**
Equity capital	4 510	. . .	–.1	. . .	. . .	. . .	–.1	–.1	–.6
Claims on affiliated enterprises	4 515	. . .	. . .	. . .	. . .	. . .	. . .	. . .	. . .
Liabilities to affiliated enterprises	4 520	. . .	. . .	. . .	. . .	. . .	. . .	. . .	. . .
Reinvested earnings	4 525	. . .	. . .	. . .	. . .	. . .	. . .	. . .	. . .
Other capital	4 530	. . .	. . .	. . .	. . .	. . .	. . .	. . .	. . .
Claims on affiliated enterprises	4 535	. . .	. . .	. . .	. . .	. . .	. . .	. . .	. . .
Liabilities to affiliated enterprises	4 540	. . .	. . .	. . .	. . .	. . .	. . .	. . .	. . .
Direct investment in Burundi	4 555	**1.2**	**.6**	**1.3**	**.9**	**.6**	**.5**	**. . .**	**2.0**
Equity capital	4 560	1.2	.6	1.3	.9	.6	.5	. . .	2.0
Claims on direct investors	4 565	. . .	. . .	. . .	. . .	. . .	. . .	. . .	. . .
Liabilities to direct investors	4 570	. . .	. . .	. . .	. . .	. . .	. . .	. . .	. . .
Reinvested earnings	4 575	. . .	. . .	. . .	. . .	. . .	. . .	. . .	. . .
Other capital	4 580	. . .	. . .	. . .	. . .	. . .	. . .	. . .	. . .
Claims on direct investors	4 585	. . .	. . .	. . .	. . .	. . .	. . .	. . .	. . .
Liabilities to direct investors	4 590	. . .	. . .	. . .	. . .	. . .	. . .	. . .	. . .
B. PORTFOLIO INVESTMENT	4 600	. . .	. . .	. . .	. . .	. . .	. . .	. . .	. . .
Assets	4 602	**. . .**	**. . .**	**. . .**	**. . .**	**. . .**	**. . .**	**. . .**	**. . .**
Equity securities	4 610	. . .	. . .	. . .	. . .	. . .	. . .	. . .	. . .
Monetary authorities	4 611	. . .	. . .	. . .	. . .	. . .	. . .	. . .	. . .
General government	4 612	. . .	. . .	. . .	. . .	. . .	. . .	. . .	. . .
Banks	4 613	. . .	. . .	. . .	. . .	. . .	. . .	. . .	. . .
Other sectors	4 614	. . .	. . .	. . .	. . .	. . .	. . .	. . .	. . .
Debt securities	4 619	. . .	. . .	. . .	. . .	. . .	. . .	. . .	. . .
Bonds and notes	4 620	. . .	. . .	. . .	. . .	. . .	. . .	. . .	. . .
Monetary authorities	4 621	. . .	. . .	. . .	. . .	. . .	. . .	. . .	. . .
General government	4 622	. . .	. . .	. . .	. . .	. . .	. . .	. . .	. . .
Banks	4 623	. . .	. . .	. . .	. . .	. . .	. . .	. . .	. . .
Other sectors	4 624	. . .	. . .	. . .	. . .	. . .	. . .	. . .	. . .
Money market instruments	4 630	. . .	. . .	. . .	. . .	. . .	. . .	. . .	. . .
Monetary authorities	4 631	. . .	. . .	. . .	. . .	. . .	. . .	. . .	. . .
General government	4 632	. . .	. . .	. . .	. . .	. . .	. . .	. . .	. . .
Banks	4 633	. . .	. . .	. . .	. . .	. . .	. . .	. . .	. . .
Other sectors	4 634	. . .	. . .	. . .	. . .	. . .	. . .	. . .	. . .
Financial derivatives	4 640	. . .	. . .	. . .	. . .	. . .	. . .	. . .	. . .
Monetary authorities	4 641	. . .	. . .	. . .	. . .	. . .	. . .	. . .	. . .
General government	4 642	. . .	. . .	. . .	. . .	. . .	. . .	. . .	. . .
Banks	4 643	. . .	. . .	. . .	. . .	. . .	. . .	. . .	. . .
Other sectors	4 644	. . .	. . .	. . .	. . .	. . .	. . .	. . .	. . .
Liabilities	4 652	**. . .**	**. . .**	**. . .**	**. . .**	**. . .**	**. . .**	**. . .**	**. . .**
Equity securities	4 660	. . .	. . .	. . .	. . .	. . .	. . .	. . .	. . .
Banks	4 663	. . .	. . .	. . .	. . .	. . .	. . .	. . .	. . .
Other sectors	4 664	. . .	. . .	. . .	. . .	. . .	. . .	. . .	. . .
Debt securities	4 669	. . .	. . .	. . .	. . .	. . .	. . .	. . .	. . .
Bonds and notes	4 670	. . .	. . .	. . .	. . .	. . .	. . .	. . .	. . .
Monetary authorities	4 671	. . .	. . .	. . .	. . .	. . .	. . .	. . .	. . .
General government	4 672	. . .	. . .	. . .	. . .	. . .	. . .	. . .	. . .
Banks	4 673	. . .	. . .	. . .	. . .	. . .	. . .	. . .	. . .
Other sectors	4 674	. . .	. . .	. . .	. . .	. . .	. . .	. . .	. . .
Money market instruments	4 680	. . .	. . .	. . .	. . .	. . .	. . .	. . .	. . .
Monetary authorities	4 681	. . .	. . .	. . .	. . .	. . .	. . .	. . .	. . .
General government	4 682	. . .	. . .	. . .	. . .	. . .	. . .	. . .	. . .
Banks	4 683	. . .	. . .	. . .	. . .	. . .	. . .	. . .	. . .
Other sectors	4 684	. . .	. . .	. . .	. . .	. . .	. . .	. . .	. . .
Financial derivatives	4 690	. . .	. . .	. . .	. . .	. . .	. . .	. . .	. . .
Monetary authorities	4 691	. . .	. . .	. . .	. . .	. . .	. . .	. . .	. . .
General government	4 692	. . .	. . .	. . .	. . .	. . .	. . .	. . .	. . .
Banks	4 693	. . .	. . .	. . .	. . .	. . .	. . .	. . .	. . .
Other sectors	4 694	. . .	. . .	. . .	. . .	. . .	. . .	. . .	. . .

Table 2 (Concluded). STANDARD PRESENTATION, 1988–95
(Millions of U.S. dollars)

	Code	1988	1989	1990	1991	1992	1993	1994	1995
C. OTHER INVESTMENT	4 700 . .	96.4	72.0	76.0	75.4	116.6	48.0	25.1	16.5
Assets	4 703 . .	**-11.5**	**-7.6**	**4.1**	**-3.5**	**-1.0**	**-1.5**	**-1.6**	**7.3**
Trade credits	4 706 . .	...	...	...	...	...	...	...	...
General government: long-term	4 708 . .	...	...	...	...	...	...	...	...
General government: short-term	4 709 . .	...	...	...	...	...	...	...	...
Other sectors: long-term	4 711 . .	...	...	...	...	...	...	...	...
Other sectors: short-term	4 712 . .	...	...	...	...	...	...	...	...
Loans	4 714 . .	-1.2	2.8	17.3	4.9	10.6	11.2	15.2	12.7
Monetary authorities: long-term	4 717 . .	...	...	...	...	...	...	...	...
Monetary authorities: short-term	4 718 . .	...	...	...	...	...	...	...	...
General government: long-term	4 720 . .	...	...	...	...	...	...	...	...
General government: short-term	4 721 . .	...	...	...	...	...	...	...	...
Banks: long-term	4 723 . .	...	...	...	...	...	...	...	...
Banks: short-term	4 724 . .	...	...	...	...	...	...	...	...
Other sectors: long-term	4 726 . .	...	...	...	...	-.2	-.4	...	...
Other sectors: short-term	4 727 . .	-1.2	2.8	17.3	4.9	10.8	11.5	15.2	12.7
Currency and deposits	4 730 . .	-4.5	-8.4	-12.3	-7.3	-11.0	-12.3	-16.1	-5.1
Monetary authorities	4 731 . .	...	...	...	...	...	...	...	...
General government	4 732 . .	...	...	...	...	...	...	...	...
Banks	4 733 . .	-.7	.1	-.6	-2.1	-1.3	-4.2	-8.8	-.1
Other sectors	4 734 . .	-3.8	-8.5	-11.7	-5.2	-9.7	-8.2	-7.3	-4.9
Other assets	4 736 . .	-5.8	-1.9	-1.0	-1.1	-.6	-.3	-.8	-.4
Monetary authorities: long-term	4 738 . .	...	...	...	...	...	...	...	...
Monetary authorities: short-term	4 739 . .	...	...	...	...	...	...	...	...
General government: long-term	4 741 . .	-5.8	-1.9	-1.0	-1.1	-.6	-.3	-.8	-.4
General government: short-term	4 742 . .	...	...	...	...	...	...	...	...
Banks: long-term	4 744 . .	...	...	...	...	...	...	...	...
Banks: short-term	4 745 . .	...	...	...	...	...	...	...	...
Other sectors: long-term	4 747 . .	...	...	...	...	...	...	...	...
Other sectors: short-term	4 748 . .	...	...	...	...	...	...	...	...
Liabilities	4 753 . .	**107.9**	**79.6**	**71.9**	**78.9**	**117.6**	**49.5**	**26.8**	**9.2**
Trade credits	4 756 . .	...	...	...	...	...	...	...	...
General government: long-term	4 758 . .	...	...	...	...	...	...	...	...
General government: short-term	4 759 . .	...	...	...	...	...	...	...	...
Other sectors: long-term	4 761 . .	...	...	...	...	...	...	...	...
Other sectors: short-term	4 762 . .	...	...	...	...	...	...	...	...
Loans	4 764 . .	97.2	73.6	61.3	62.8	109.2	42.7	19.1	2.1
Use of Fund credit and loans from the Fund	4 766 . .	13.3	8.1	-.8	5.8	18.5	-4.1	-6.1	-9.0
Monetary authorities: other long-term	4 767 . .	...	...	...	...	...	...	...	...
Monetary authorities: short-term	4 768 . .	...	...	...	...	...	...	...	...
General government: long-term	4 770 . .	83.9	65.4	62.1	57.0	90.8	47.2	25.2	11.1
General government: short-term	4 771 . .	...	...	...	...	...	...	...	...
Banks: long-term	4 773 . .	...	...	...	...	...	...	...	...
Banks: short-term	4 774 . .	...	...	...	...	...	...	...	...
Other sectors: long-term	4 776 . .	...	...	...	...	-.2	-.4	...	...
Other sectors: short-term	4 777 . .	...	...	...	...	...	...	...	...
Currency and deposits	4 780 . .	1.3	-.6	1.6	1.4	1.1	.4	4.7	.2
Monetary authorities	4 781 . .	...	...	...	...	...	...	...	...
General government	4 782 . .	...	...	...	...	...	...	...	...
Banks	4 783 . .	1.3	-.6	1.6	1.4	1.1	.4	4.7	.2
Other sectors	4 784 . .	...	...	...	...	...	...	...	...
Other liabilities	4 786 . .	9.4	6.6	9.0	14.7	7.3	6.4	3.0	7.0
Monetary authorities: long-term	4 788 . .	...	...	...	...	...	...	...	...
Monetary authorities: short-term	4 789 . .	...	...	...	...	...	...	...	...
General government: long-term	4 791 . .	...	...	...	...	...	...	...	...
General government: short-term	4 792 . .	...	...	...	...	...	...	...	...
Banks: long-term	4 794 . .	...	...	...	...	...	...	...	...
Banks: short-term	4 795 . .	...	...	...	...	...	...	...	...
Other sectors: long-term	4 797 . .	...	...	...	...	...	...	...	...
Other sectors: short-term	4 798 . .	9.4	6.6	9.0	14.7	7.3	6.4	3.0	7.0
D. RESERVE ASSETS	4 800 . .	-20.5	-46.1	4.0	-54.0	-68.5	-11.9	-29.6	-26.7
Monetary gold	4 810 . .	...	...	...	...	...	...	...	...
Special drawing rights	4 820 . .	-.4	.1	...	-3.6	2.2	.8	.5	.1
Reserve position in the Fund	4 830 . .	...	...	2.2	.4	2.0	...	...	...
Foreign exchange	4 840 . .	-16.6	-47.1	-1.3	-50.8	-72.6	-12.7	-30.1	-26.9
Other claims	4 880 . .	-3.4	.9	3.1	...	...	...	...	...
NET ERRORS AND OMISSIONS	4 998 . .	**-6.6**	**-14.3**	**-11.3**	**11.7**	**11.7**	**-6.1**	**23.0**	**16.1**

Part 3 of the *Yearbook* contains descriptions of the methodologies, compilation practices, and sources used to compile these data.

Table 1. ANALYTIC PRESENTATION, 1988–95
(Millions of U.S. dollars)

	Code	1988	1989	1990	1991	1992	1993	1994	1995
A. Current Account[1]	4 993 Y.	**. . .**	**. . .**	**. . .**	**. . .**	**–93.0**	**–103.9**	**–156.7**	**–185.9**
Goods: exports f.o.b.	2 100 ..	. . .	. . .	. . .	. . .	264.5	283.7	489.9	854.9
Goods: imports f.o.b.	3 100 ..	. . .	. . .	. . .	. . .	–443.4	–471.1	–744.5	–1,186.8
Balance on Goods	4 100 ..	. . .	. . .	. . .	. . .	*–178.9*	*–187.4*	*–254.6*	*–331.9*
Services: credit	2 200 ..	. . .	. . .	. . .	. . .	49.7	63.9	54.5	114.1
Services: debit	3 200 ..	. . .	. . .	. . .	. . .	–63.6	–120.5	–139.6	–187.9
Balance on Goods and Services	4 991 ..	. . .	. . .	. . .	. . .	*–192.8*	*–244.0*	*–339.7*	*–405.7*
Income: credit	2 300 ..	. . .	. . .	. . .	. . .	. . .	.5	2.1	9.7
Income: debit	3 300 ..	. . .	. . .	. . .	. . .	–20.6	–16.6	–49.1	–66.9
Balance on Goods, Services, and Income	4 992 ..	. . .	. . .	. . .	. . .	*–213.4*	*–260.1*	*–386.7*	*–462.9*
Current transfers: credit	2 379 Y.	. . .	. . .	. . .	. . .	120.4	156.4	230.0	277.9
Current transfers: debit	3 379 ..	. . .	. . .	. . .	. . .	. . .	–.2	. . .	–.9
B. Capital Account[1]	4 994 Y.	**. . .**	**. . .**	**. . .**	**. . .**	**126.3**	**123.4**	**73.2**	**78.0**
Capital account: credit	2 994 Y.	. . .	. . .	. . .	. . .	126.3	123.4	73.2	78.0
Capital account: debit	3 994 ..	. . .	. . .	. . .	. . .	. . .	. . .	. . .	. . .
Total, Groups A Plus B	4 010 ..	. . .	. . .	. . .	. . .	*33.3*	*19.5*	*–83.5*	*–107.9*
C. Financial Account[1]	4 995 X.	**. . .**	**. . .**	**. . .**	**. . .**	**13.9**	**2.4**	**54.0**	**122.4**
Direct investment abroad	4 505 ..	. . .	. . .	. . .	. . .	. . .	. . .	. . .	. . .
Direct investment in Cambodia	4 555 Y.	. . .	. . .	. . .	. . .	33.0	54.1	68.9	150.8
Portfolio investment assets	4 602 ..	. . .	. . .	. . .	. . .	. . .	. . .	. . .	. . .
Equity securities	4 610 ..	. . .	. . .	. . .	. . .	. . .	. . .	. . .	. . .
Debt securities	4 619 ..	. . .	. . .	. . .	. . .	. . .	. . .	. . .	. . .
Portfolio investment liabilities	4 652 Y.	. . .	. . .	. . .	. . .	. . .	. . .	. . .	. . .
Equity securities	4 660 Y.	. . .	. . .	. . .	. . .	. . .	. . .	. . .	. . .
Debt securities	4 669 Y.	. . .	. . .	. . .	. . .	. . .	. . .	. . .	. . .
Other investment assets	4 703 ..	. . .	. . .	. . .	. . .	–24.1	–51.1	–46.8	–103.4
Monetary authorities	4 703 .A	. . .	. . .	. . .	. . .	. . .	. . .	. . .	. . .
General government	4 703 .B	. . .	. . .	. . .	. . .	. . .	–.4	. . .	. . .
Banks	4 703 .C	. . .	. . .	. . .	. . .	. . .	–25.6	. . .	–39.8
Other sectors	4 703 .D	. . .	. . .	. . .	. . .	–24.1	–25.1	–46.8	–63.6
Other investment liabilities	4 753 X.	. . .	. . .	. . .	. . .	5.0	–.6	31.9	75.0
Monetary authorities	4 753 XA	. . .	. . .	. . .	. . .	. . .	. . .	. . .	. . .
General government	4 753 YB	. . .	. . .	. . .	. . .	–2.1	5.4	51.4	73.1
Banks	4 753 YC	. . .	. . .	. . .	. . .	7.1	–6.0	–19.5	1.9
Other sectors	4 753 YD	. . .	. . .	. . .	. . .	. . .	. . .	. . .	. . .
Total, Groups A Through C	4 020 ..	. . .	. . .	. . .	. . .	*47.2*	*21.9*	*–29.5*	*14.5*
D. Net Errors and Omissions	4 998 ..	**. . .**	**. . .**	**. . .**	**. . .**	**–34.0**	**–7.3**	**65.7**	**11.7**
Total, Groups A Through D	4 030 ..	. . .	. . .	. . .	. . .	*13.2*	*14.7*	*36.2*	*26.2*
E. Reserves and Related Items	4 040 ..	**. . .**	**. . .**	**. . .**	**. . .**	**–13.2**	**–14.7**	**–36.2**	**–26.2**
Reserve assets	4 800 ..	. . .	. . .	. . .	. . .	–4.5	–23.0	–71.2	–73.2
Use of Fund credit and loans	4 766 ..	. . .	. . .	. . .	. . .	–8.7	. . .	19.8	42.3
Liabilities constituting foreign authorities' reserves	4 900 ..	. . .	. . .	. . .	. . .	. . .	. . .	. . .	. . .
Exceptional financing	4 920 ..	. . .	. . .	. . .	. . .	. . .	8.3	15.2	4.7
Conversion rates: riels per U.S. dollar	0 101 ..	**. . .**	**. . .**	**. . .**	**. . .**	**1,266.6**	**2,689.0**	**2,545.3**	**2,450.8**

[1] Excludes components that have been classified in the categories of Group E.

Table 2. STANDARD PRESENTATION, 1988–95
(Millions of U.S. dollars)

	Code	1988	1989	1990	1991	1992	1993	1994	1995
CURRENT ACCOUNT	4 993 . .	**. . .**	**. . .**	**. . .**	**. . .**	**–93.0**	**–103.9**	**–156.7**	**–185.9**
A. GOODS	4 100 . .	. . .	. . .	. . .	. . .	–178.9	–187.4	–254.6	–331.9
Credit	2 100 . .	**. . .**	**. . .**	**. . .**	**. . .**	**264.5**	**283.7**	**489.9**	**854.9**
General merchandise: exports f.o.b.	2 110 . .	. . .	. . .	. . .	. . .	264.5	280.7	486.5	852.1
Goods for processing: exports f.o.b.	2 150 . .	. . .	. . .	. . .	. . .	. . .	. . .	. . .	. . .
Repairs on goods	2 160 . .	. . .	. . .	. . .	. . .	. . .	. . .	. . .	. . .
Goods procured in ports by carriers	2 170 . .	. . .	. . .	. . .	. . .	. . .	3.0	3.4	2.8
Nonmonetary gold	2 180 . .	. . .	. . .	. . .	. . .	. . .	. . .	. . .	. . .
Debit	3 100 . .	**. . .**	**. . .**	**. . .**	**. . .**	**–443.4**	**–471.1**	**–744.5**	**–1,186.8**
General merchandise: imports f.o.b.	3 110 . .	. . .	. . .	. . .	. . .	–443.4	–470.9	–744.4	–1,186.1
Goods for processing: imports f.o.b.	3 150 . .	. . .	. . .	. . .	. . .	. . .	. . .	. . .	. . .
Repairs on goods	3 160 . .	. . .	. . .	. . .	. . .	. . .	. . .	. . .	. . .
Goods procured in ports by carriers	3 170 . .	. . .	. . .	. . .	. . .	. . .	–.2	–.1	–.7
Nonmonetary gold	3 180 . .	. . .	. . .	. . .	. . .	. . .	. . .	. . .	. . .
B. SERVICES	4 200 . .	. . .	. . .	. . .	. . .	–13.9	–56.6	–85.1	–73.8
Total credit	2 200 . .	. . .	. . .	. . .	. . .	*49.7*	*63.9*	*54.5*	*114.1*
Total debit	3 200 . .	. . .	. . .	. . .	. . .	*–63.6*	*–120.5*	*–139.6*	*–187.9*
Transportation services, credit	2 205 . .	**. . .**	**. . .**	**. . .**	**. . .**	**. . .**	**10.2**	**11.2**	**31.6**
Passenger	2 205 BA	. . .	. . .	. . .	. . .	. . .	*3.0*	*3.7*	*17.7*
Freight	2 205 BB	. . .	. . .	. . .	. . .	. . .	*.4*	*.3*	*.8*
Other	2 205 BC	. . .	. . .	. . .	. . .	. . .	*6.8*	*7.2*	*13.1*
Sea transport, passenger	2 207 . .	. . .	. . .	. . .	. . .	. . .	. . .	. . .	. . .
Sea transport, freight	2 208 . .	. . .	. . .	. . .	. . .	. . .	.3	.3	.5
Sea transport, other	2 209 . .	. . .	. . .	. . .	. . .	. . .	4.6	4.7	11.1
Air transport, passenger	2 211 . .	. . .	. . .	. . .	. . .	. . .	3.0	3.7	17.7
Air transport, freight	2 212 . .	. . .	. . .	. . .	. . .	. . .	.1	. . .	.3
Air transport, other	2 213 . .	. . .	. . .	. . .	. . .	. . .	2.2	2.5	2.0
Other transport, passenger	2 215 . .	. . .	. . .	. . .	. . .	. . .	. . .	. . .	. . .
Other transport, freight	2 216 . .	. . .	. . .	. . .	. . .	. . .	. . .	. . .	. . .
Other transport, other	2 217 . .	. . .	. . .	. . .	. . .	. . .	. . .	. . .	. . .
Transportation services, debit	3 205 . .	**. . .**	**. . .**	**. . .**	**. . .**	**–15.6**	**–52.5**	**–71.7**	**–83.9**
Passenger	3 205 BA	. . .	. . .	. . .	. . .	*–15.6*	*–11.3*	*–13.5*	*–13.9*
Freight	3 205 BB	. . .	. . .	. . .	. . .	. . .	*–41.0*	*–58.2*	*–69.6*
Other	3 205 BC	. . .	. . .	. . .	. . .	. . .	*–.2*	. . .	*–.4*
Sea transport, passenger	3 207 . .	. . .	. . .	. . .	. . .	. . .	. . .	. . .	. . .
Sea transport, freight	3 208 . .	. . .	. . .	. . .	. . .	. . .	–38.7	–56.4	–67.6
Sea transport, other	3 209 . .	. . .	. . .	. . .	. . .	. . .	–.1	. . .	. . .
Air transport, passenger	3 211 . .	. . .	. . .	. . .	. . .	–15.6	–11.3	–13.5	–13.9
Air transport, freight	3 212 . .	. . .	. . .	. . .	. . .	. . .	–2.3	–1.8	–2.0
Air transport, other	3 213 . .	. . .	. . .	. . .	. . .	. . .	–.1	. . .	–.4
Other transport, passenger	3 215 . .	. . .	. . .	. . .	. . .	. . .	. . .	. . .	. . .
Other transport, freight	3 216 . .	. . .	. . .	. . .	. . .	. . .	. . .	. . .	. . .
Other transport, other	3 217 . .	. . .	. . .	. . .	. . .	. . .	. . .	. . .	. . .
Travel, credit	2 236 . .	**. . .**	**. . .**	**. . .**	**. . .**	**49.7**	**48.3**	**33.8**	**53.4**
Business travel	2 237 . .	. . .	. . .	. . .	. . .	. . .	. . .	. . .	. . .
Personal travel	2 240 . .	. . .	. . .	. . .	. . .	. . .	. . .	. . .	. . .
Travel, debit	3 236 . .	**. . .**	**. . .**	**. . .**	**. . .**	**. . .**	**–4.0**	**–7.5**	**–8.3**
Business travel	3 237 . .	. . .	. . .	. . .	. . .	. . .	. . .	. . .	. . .
Personal travel	3 240 . .	. . .	. . .	. . .	. . .	. . .	. . .	. . .	. . .
Other services, credit	2 200 BA	**. . .**	**. . .**	**. . .**	**. . .**	**. . .**	**5.4**	**9.5**	**29.1**
Communications	2 245 . .	. . .	. . .	. . .	. . .	. . .	. . .	. . .	18.3
Construction	2 249 . .	. . .	. . .	. . .	. . .	. . .	. . .	. . .	. . .
Insurance	2 253 . .	. . .	. . .	. . .	. . .	. . .	. . .	. . .	. . .
Financial	2 260 . .	. . .	. . .	. . .	. . .	. . .	. . .	. . .	. . .
Computer and information	2 262 . .	. . .	. . .	. . .	. . .	. . .	. . .	. . .	. . .
Royalties and licence fees	2 266 . .	. . .	. . .	. . .	. . .	. . .	. . .	. . .	. . .
Other business services	2 268 . .	. . .	. . .	. . .	. . .	. . .	. . .	. . .	. . .
Personal, cultural, and recreational	2 287 . .	. . .	. . .	. . .	. . .	. . .	. . .	. . .	. . .
Government, n.i.e.	2 291 . .	. . .	. . .	. . .	. . .	. . .	5.4	9.5	10.8
Other services, debit	3 200 BA	**. . .**	**. . .**	**. . .**	**. . .**	**–48.0**	**–64.0**	**–60.4**	**–95.7**
Communications	3 245 . .	. . .	. . .	. . .	. . .	. . .	–4.9	–3.4	–17.5
Construction	3 249 . .	. . .	. . .	. . .	. . .	–48.0	–53.7	–44.4	–47.4
Insurance	3 253 . .	. . .	. . .	. . .	. . .	. . .	–3.3	–4.4	–7.8
Financial	3 260 . .	. . .	. . .	. . .	. . .	. . .	–.1	–.2	. . .
Computer and information	3 262 . .	. . .	. . .	. . .	. . .	. . .	. . .	. . .	. . .
Royalties and licence fees	3 266 . .	. . .	. . .	. . .	. . .	. . .	. . .	. . .	. . .
Other business services	3 268 . .	. . .	. . .	. . .	. . .	. . .	. . .	. . .	–16.0
Personal, cultural, and recreational	3 287 . .	. . .	. . .	. . .	. . .	. . .	. . .	. . .	. . .
Government, n.i.e.	3 291 . .	. . .	. . .	. . .	. . .	. . .	–2.1	–8.0	–7.0

Table 2 (Continued). STANDARD PRESENTATION, 1988–95
(Millions of U.S. dollars)

	Code		1988	1989	1990	1991	1992	1993	1994	1995
C. INCOME	4 300	. .	...	...	...	...	–20.6	–16.1	–47.0	–57.2
Total credit	2 300	. .	...	...	...	...	...	*.5*	*2.1*	*9.7*
Total debit	3 300	. .	...	...	...	...	*–20.6*	*–16.6*	*–49.1*	*–66.9*
Compensation of employees, credit	2 310	. .	**...**	**...**	**...**	**...**	**...**	**.5**	**1.3**	**1.6**
Compensation of employees, debit	3 310	. .	**...**	**...**	**...**	**...**	**–14.1**	**–14.9**	**–38.4**	**–52.0**
Investment income, credit	2 320	. .	**...**	**...**	**...**	**...**	**...**	**...**	**.8**	**8.1**
Direct investment income	2 330	. .	...	...	...	...	...	...	...	...
Dividends and distributed branch profits	2 332	. .	...	...	...	...	...	...	...	...
Reinvested earnings and undistributed branch profits	2 333	. .	...	...	...	...	...	...	...	...
Income on debt (interest)	2 334	. .	...	...	...	...	...	...	...	...
Portfolio investment income	2 339	. .	...	...	...	...	...	...	...	...
Income on equity	2 340	. .	...	...	...	...	...	...	...	...
Income on bonds and notes	2 350	. .	...	...	...	...	...	...	...	...
Income on money market instruments and financial derivatives	2 360	. .	...	...	...	...	...	...	...	...
Other investment income	2 370	. .	...	...	...	...	...	...	.8	8.1
Investment income, debit	3 320	. .	**...**	**...**	**...**	**...**	**–6.5**	**–1.7**	**–10.7**	**–14.9**
Direct investment income	3 330	. .	...	...	...	...	...	1.5	4.0	3.8
Dividends and distributed branch profits	3 332	. .	...	...	...	...	...	...	...	...
Reinvested earnings and undistributed branch profits	3 333	. .	...	...	...	...	...	1.5	4.0	3.8
Income on debt (interest)	3 334	. .	...	...	...	...	...	...	...	...
Portfolio investment income	3 339	. .	...	...	...	...	...	...	...	...
Income on equity	3 340	. .	...	...	...	...	...	...	...	...
Income on bonds and notes	3 350	. .	...	...	...	...	...	...	...	...
Income on money market instruments and financial derivatives	3 360	. .	...	...	...	...	...	...	...	...
Other investment income	3 370	. .	...	...	...	...	–6.5	–3.2	–14.7	–18.7
D. CURRENT TRANSFERS	4 379	. .	...	...	...	...	120.4	156.2	230.0	277.0
Credit	2 379	. .	**...**	**...**	**...**	**...**	**120.4**	**156.4**	**230.0**	**277.9**
General government	2 380	. .	...	...	...	...	111.4	147.4	210.0	257.9
Other sectors	2 390	. .	...	...	...	...	9.0	9.0	20.0	20.0
Workers' remittances	2 391	. .	...	...	...	...	9.0	9.0	10.0	10.0
Other current transfers	2 392	. .	...	...	...	...	...	...	10.0	10.0
Debit	3 379	. .	**...**	**...**	**...**	**...**	**...**	**–.2**	**...**	**–.9**
General government	3 380	. .	...	...	...	...	...	–.2	...	–.9
Other sectors	3 390	. .	...	...	...	...	...	...	...	...
Workers' remittances	3 391	. .	...	...	...	...	...	...	...	...
Other current transfers	3 392	. .	...	...	...	...	...	...	...	...
CAPITAL AND FINANCIAL ACCOUNT	4 996	. .	**...**	**...**	**...**	**...**	**127.0**	**111.2**	**91.0**	**174.2**
CAPITAL ACCOUNT	4 994	. .	**...**	**...**	**...**	**...**	**126.3**	**178.5**	**73.2**	**91.9**
Total credit	2 994	. .	...	...	...	...	*126.3*	*178.5*	*73.2*	*91.9*
Total debit	3 994	. .	...	...	...	...	...	...	...	...
Capital transfers, credit	2 400	. .	**...**	**...**	**...**	**...**	**126.3**	**178.5**	**73.2**	**91.9**
General government	2 401	. .	...	...	...	...	126.3	178.5	73.2	91.9
Debt forgiveness	2 402	. .	...	...	...	...	...	55.1	...	13.9
Other capital transfers	2 410	. .	...	...	...	...	126.3	123.4	73.2	78.0
Other sectors	2 430	. .	...	...	...	...	...	...	...	...
Migrants' transfers	2 431	. .	...	...	...	...	...	...	...	...
Debt forgiveness	2 432	. .	...	...	...	...	...	...	...	...
Other capital transfers	2 440	. .	...	...	...	...	...	...	...	...
Capital transfers, debit	3 400	. .	**...**	**...**	**...**	**...**	**...**	**...**	**...**	**...**
General government	3 401	. .	...	...	...	...	...	...	...	...
Debt forgiveness	3 402	. .	...	...	...	...	...	...	...	...
Other capital transfers	3 410	. .	...	...	...	...	...	...	...	...
Other sectors	3 430	. .	...	...	...	...	...	...	...	...
Migrants' transfers	3 431	. .	...	...	...	...	...	...	...	...
Debt forgiveness	3 432	. .	...	...	...	...	...	...	...	...
Other capital transfers	3 440	. .	...	...	...	...	...	...	...	...
Nonproduced nonfinancial assets, credit	2 480	. .	**...**	**...**	**...**	**...**	**...**	**...**	**...**	**...**
Nonproduced nonfinancial assets, debit	3 480	. .	**...**	**...**	**...**	**...**	**...**	**...**	**...**	**...**

Table 2 (Continued). STANDARD PRESENTATION, 1988–95

(Millions of U.S. dollars)

	Code	1988	1989	1990	1991	1992	1993	1994	1995
FINANCIAL ACCOUNT	4 995	...	...	...	...	.7	–67.3	17.8	82.3
A. DIRECT INVESTMENT	4 500	...	...	...	...	33.0	54.1	68.9	150.8
Direct investment abroad	4 505	...	...	...	...	...	...	...	...
Equity capital	4 510	...	...	...	...	...	...	...	...
Claims on affiliated enterprises	4 515	...	...	...	...	...	...	...	...
Liabilities to affiliated enterprises	4 520	...	...	...	...	...	...	...	...
Reinvested earnings	4 525	...	...	...	...	...	...	...	...
Other capital	4 530	...	...	...	...	...	...	...	...
Claims on affiliated enterprises	4 535	...	...	...	...	...	...	...	...
Liabilities to affiliated enterprises	4 540	...	...	...	...	...	...	...	...
Direct investment in Cambodia	4 555	...	...	...	...	**33.0**	**54.1**	**68.9**	**150.8**
Equity capital	4 560	...	...	...	...	33.0	55.6	72.9	154.6
Claims on direct investors	4 565	...	...	...	...	...	...	...	...
Liabilities to direct investors	4 570	...	...	...	...	33.0	55.6	72.9	154.6
Reinvested earnings	4 575	...	...	...	...	...	–1.5	–4.0	–3.8
Other capital	4 580	...	...	...	...	...	...	...	...
Claims on direct investors	4 585	...	...	...	...	...	...	...	...
Liabilities to direct investors	4 590	...	...	...	...	...	...	...	...
B. PORTFOLIO INVESTMENT	4 600	...	...	...	...	...	...	...	...
Assets	4 602	...	...	...	...	...	...	...	...
Equity securities	4 610	...	...	...	...	...	...	...	...
Monetary authorities	4 611	...	...	...	...	...	...	...	...
General government	4 612	...	...	...	...	...	...	...	...
Banks	4 613	...	...	...	...	...	...	...	...
Other sectors	4 614	...	...	...	...	...	...	...	...
Debt securities	4 619	...	...	...	...	...	...	...	...
Bonds and notes	4 620	...	...	...	...	...	...	...	...
Monetary authorities	4 621	...	...	...	...	...	...	...	...
General government	4 622	...	...	...	...	...	...	...	...
Banks	4 623	...	...	...	...	...	...	...	...
Other sectors	4 624	...	...	...	...	...	...	...	...
Money market instruments	4 630	...	...	...	...	...	...	...	...
Monetary authorities	4 631	...	...	...	...	...	...	...	...
General government	4 632	...	...	...	...	...	...	...	...
Banks	4 633	...	...	...	...	...	...	...	...
Other sectors	4 634	...	...	...	...	...	...	...	...
Financial derivatives	4 640	...	...	...	...	...	...	...	...
Monetary authorities	4 641	...	...	...	...	...	...	...	...
General government	4 642	...	...	...	...	...	...	...	...
Banks	4 643	...	...	...	...	...	...	...	...
Other sectors	4 644	...	...	...	...	...	...	...	...
Liabilities	4 652	...	...	...	...	...	...	...	...
Equity securities	4 660	...	...	...	...	...	...	...	...
Banks	4 663	...	...	...	...	...	...	...	...
Other sectors	4 664	...	...	...	...	...	...	...	...
Debt securities	4 669	...	...	...	...	...	...	...	...
Bonds and notes	4 670	...	...	...	...	...	...	...	...
Monetary authorities	4 671	...	...	...	...	...	...	...	...
General government	4 672	...	...	...	...	...	...	...	...
Banks	4 673	...	...	...	...	...	...	...	...
Other sectors	4 674	...	...	...	...	...	...	...	...
Money market instruments	4 680	...	...	...	...	...	...	...	...
Monetary authorities	4 681	...	...	...	...	...	...	...	...
General government	4 682	...	...	...	...	...	...	...	...
Banks	4 683	...	...	...	...	...	...	...	...
Other sectors	4 684	...	...	...	...	...	...	...	...
Financial derivatives	4 690	...	...	...	...	...	...	...	...
Monetary authorities	4 691	...	...	...	...	...	...	...	...
General government	4 692	...	...	...	...	...	...	...	...
Banks	4 693	...	...	...	...	...	...	...	...
Other sectors	4 694	...	...	...	...	...	...	...	...

Table 2 (Concluded). STANDARD PRESENTATION, 1988–95
(Millions of U.S. dollars)

	Code	1988	1989	1990	1991	1992	1993	1994	1995
C. OTHER INVESTMENT	4 700	...	...	...	...	–27.8	–98.5	20.1	4.7
Assets	4 703	**...**	**...**	**...**	**...**	**–24.1**	**–51.1**	**–46.8**	**–103.4**
Trade credits	4 706	...	...	...	...	...	–.4	...	...
General government: long-term	4 708	...	...	...	...	...	...	...	...
General government: short-term	4 709	...	...	...	...	...	...	...	...
Other sectors: long-term	4 711	...	...	...	...	...	...	...	...
Other sectors: short-term	4 712	...	...	...	...	...	...	...	...
Loans	4 714	...	...	...	...	...	...	...	...
Monetary authorities: long-term	4 717	...	...	...	...	...	...	...	...
Monetary authorities: short-term	4 718	...	...	...	...	...	...	...	...
General government: long-term	4 720	...	...	...	...	...	...	...	...
General government: short-term	4 721	...	...	...	...	...	...	...	...
Banks: long-term	4 723	...	...	...	...	...	...	...	...
Banks: short-term	4 724	...	...	...	...	...	...	...	...
Other sectors: long-term	4 726	...	...	...	...	...	...	...	...
Other sectors: short-term	4 727	...	...	...	...	...	...	...	...
Currency and deposits	4 730	...	...	...	...	–24.1	–69.4	–38.6	–107.6
Monetary authorities	4 731	...	...	...	...	...	...	...	...
General government	4 732	...	...	...	...	...	...	...	...
Banks	4 733	...	...	...	...	...	–44.3	8.2	–44.0
Other sectors	4 734	...	...	...	...	–24.1	–25.1	–46.8	–63.6
Other assets	4 736	...	...	...	...	...	18.7	–8.2	4.2
Monetary authorities: long-term	4 738	...	...	...	...	...	...	...	...
Monetary authorities: short-term	4 739	...	...	...	...	...	...	...	...
General government: long-term	4 741	...	...	...	...	...	...	...	...
General government: short-term	4 742	...	...	...	...	...	...	...	...
Banks: long-term	4 744	...	...	...	...	...	...	...	...
Banks: short-term	4 745	...	...	...	...	...	...	–8.2	4.2
Other sectors: long-term	4 747	...	...	...	...	...	...	...	...
Other sectors: short-term	4 748	...	...	...	...	...	...	...	...
Liabilities	4 753	**...**	**...**	**...**	**...**	**–3.7**	**–47.4**	**66.9**	**108.1**
Trade credits	4 756	...	...	...	...	...	...	...	...
General government: long-term	4 758	...	...	...	...	...	...	...	...
General government: short-term	4 759	...	...	...	...	...	...	...	...
Other sectors: long-term	4 761	...	...	...	...	...	...	...	...
Other sectors: short-term	4 762	...	...	...	...	...	...	...	...
Loans	4 764	...	...	...	...	–10.8	22.7	50.3	334.2
Use of Fund credit and loans from the Fund	4 766	...	...	...	...	–8.7	...	19.8	42.3
Monetary authorities: other long-term	4 767	...	...	...	...	...	...	...	...
Monetary authorities: short-term	4 768	...	...	...	...	...	...	...	...
General government: long-term	4 770	...	...	...	...	...	5.4	51.4	308.4
General government: short-term	4 771	...	...	...	...	...	...	...	...
Banks: long-term	4 773	...	...	...	...	...	...	...	...
Banks: short-term	4 774	...	...	...	...	...	17.3	...	...
Other sectors: long-term	4 776	...	...	...	...	...	...	...	...
Other sectors: short-term	4 777	...	...	...	...	...	...	...	...
Currency and deposits	4 780	...	...	...	...	7.1	–24.6	1.7	16.8
Monetary authorities	4 781	...	...	...	...	...	...	...	...
General government	4 782	...	...	...	...	...	...	...	...
Banks	4 783	...	...	...	...	7.1	–24.6	1.7	16.8
Other sectors	4 784	...	...	...	...	...	...	...	...
Other liabilities	4 786	...	...	...	...	...	–45.5	14.9	–242.9
Monetary authorities: long-term	4 788	...	...	...	...	...	...	...	...
Monetary authorities: short-term	4 789	...	...	...	...	...	–44.6	...	...
General government: long-term	4 791	...	...	...	...	...	...	...	...
General government: short-term	4 792	...	...	...	...	...	–2.2	15.2	–244.5
Banks: long-term	4 794	...	...	...	...	...	...	...	...
Banks: short-term	4 795	...	...	...	...	...	...	...	...
Other sectors: long-term	4 797	...	...	...	...	...	...	...	...
Other sectors: short-term	4 798	...	...	...	...	...	...	...	...
D. RESERVE ASSETS	4 800	...	...	...	...	–4.5	–23.0	–71.2	–73.2
Monetary gold	4 810	...	...	...	...	...	...	...	...
Special drawing rights	4 820	...	...	...	...	...	–16.1	.8	1.0
Reserve position in the Fund	4 830	...	...	...	...	–1.3	1.3	...	...
Foreign exchange	4 840	...	...	...	...	–3.2	–8.2	–72.0	–74.2
Other claims	4 880	...	...	...	...	...	...	...	...
NET ERRORS AND OMISSIONS	4 998	**...**	**...**	**...**	**...**	**–34.0**	**–7.3**	**65.7**	**11.7**

Part 3 of the *Yearbook* contains descriptions of the methodologies, compilation practices, and sources used to compile these data.

Table 1. ANALYTIC PRESENTATION, 1988–95
(Millions of U.S. dollars)

	Code	1988	1989	1990	1991	1992	1993	1994	1995
A. Current Account [1]	4 993 Y.	**–431.0**	**–298.0**	**–477.8**	**–404.8**	**–338.5**	**–565.4**	**. . .**	**. . .**
Goods: exports f.o.b	2 100 . .	1,841.2	1,853.8	2,125.4	1,957.5	1,934.1	1,507.7	. . .	. . .
Goods: imports f.o.b	3 100 . .	–1,220.8	–1,136.8	–1,347.2	–1,173.1	–983.3	–1,005.3	. . .	. . .
Balance on Goods	4 100 . .	*620.5*	*717.0*	*778.1*	*784.3*	*950.8*	*502.4*	. . .	. . .
Services: credit	2 200 . .	456.2	475.7	382.2	406.0	407.5	390.9	. . .	. . .
Services: debit	3 200 . .	–901.4	–1,032.4	–1,045.1	–1,122.3	–907.3	–741.1	. . .	. . .
Balance on Goods and Services	4 991 . .	*175.3*	*160.3*	*115.2*	*68.0*	*450.9*	*152.2*	. . .	. . .
Income: credit	2 300 . .	16.9	16.8	8.3	18.3	41.8	17.0	. . .	. . .
Income: debit	3 300 . .	–510.9	–430.8	–566.1	–442.7	–823.9	–669.5	. . .	. . .
Balance on Goods, Services, and Income	4 992 . .	*–318.7*	*–253.7*	*–442.6*	*–356.4*	*–331.2*	*–500.3*	. . .	. . .
Current transfers: credit	2 379 Y.	63.8	88.0	82.3	57.0	141.0	65.2	. . .	. . .
Current transfers: debit	3 379 . .	–176.0	–132.3	–117.5	–105.4	–148.3	–130.2	. . .	. . .
B. Capital Account [1]	4 994 Y.	**6.4**	**5.0**	**2.8**	**7.9**	**17.0**	**6.3**	**. . .**	**. . .**
Capital account: credit	2 994 Y.	6.4	5.0	2.9	8.0	17.1	6.4	. . .	. . .
Capital account: debit	3 994 . .	. . .	–.1	–.1	–.1	–.1	–.1	. . .	. . .
Total, Groups A Plus B	4 010 . .	*–424.6*	*–293.0*	*–475.1*	*–396.9*	*–321.5*	*–559.0*	. . .	. . .
C. Financial Account [1]	4 995 X.	**38.7**	**319.4**	**–226.9**	**–362.2**	**–346.4**	**–304.6**	**. . .**	**. . .**
Direct investment abroad	4 505 . .	–28.6	–26.1	–15.1	–21.5	–33.1	–22.1	. . .	. . .
Direct investment in Cameroon	4 555 Y.	92.4	–85.7	–112.8	–14.5	29.2	5.1	. . .	. . .
Portfolio investment assets	4 602 . .	–10.9	–1.0	55.6	–2.2	–46.5	–106.3	. . .	. . .
Equity securities	4 610 . .	3.1	.2	104.1	18.6	53.4	8.0	. . .	. . .
Debt securities	4 619 . .	–14.0	–1.2	–48.4	–20.8	–99.9	–114.4	. . .	. . .
Portfolio investment liabilities	4 652 Y.	. . .	. . .	. . .	. . .	. . .	. . .	. . .	. . .
Equity securities	4 660 Y.	. . .	. . .	. . .	. . .	. . .	. . .	. . .	. . .
Debt securities	4 669 Y.	. . .	. . .	. . .	. . .	. . .	. . .	. . .	. . .
Other investment assets	4 703 . .	–93.9	–8.9	481.5	–112.3	16.8	105.5	. . .	. . .
Monetary authorities	4 703 .A	. . .	. . .	. . .	. . .	. . .	. . .	. . .	. . .
General government	4 703 .B	–.1	. . .	.3	. . .	.1	. . .	. . .	. . .
Banks	4 703 .C	–145.2	–67.4	377.6	–29.7	26.0	42.8	. . .	. . .
Other sectors	4 703 .D	51.4	58.5	103.6	–82.6	–9.2	62.6	. . .	. . .
Other investment liabilities	4 753 X.	79.8	441.1	–636.1	–211.7	–312.9	–286.7	. . .	. . .
Monetary authorities	4 753 XA	. . .	. . .	. . .	. . .	. . .	. . .	. . .	. . .
General government	4 753 YB	226.1	352.0	–84.6	64.1	–175.8	–22.5	. . .	. . .
Banks	4 753 YC	–62.4	301.3	–397.0	–31.2	–41.3	–104.1	. . .	. . .
Other sectors	4 753 YD	–83.9	–212.3	–154.6	–244.6	–95.8	–160.1	. . .	. . .
Total, Groups A Through C	4 020 . .	*–385.9*	*26.4*	*–702.0*	*–759.1*	*–667.9*	*–863.6*	. . .	. . .
D. Net Errors and Omissions	4 998 . .	**221.8**	**–160.7**	**–168.2**	**26.9**	**–640.7**	**–16.2**	**. . .**	**. . .**
Total, Groups A Through D	4 030 . .	*–164.1*	*–134.3*	*–870.2*	*–732.2*	*–1,308.6*	*–879.9*	. . .	. . .
E. Reserves and Related Items	4 040 . .	**164.1**	**134.3**	**870.2**	**732.2**	**1,308.6**	**879.9**	**. . .**	**. . .**
Reserve assets	4 800 . .	–94.6	96.8	64.6	–31.6	20.9	14.9	. . .	. . .
Use of Fund credit and loans	4 766 . .	81.6	14.5	–1.4	–1.2	–54.6	–47.4	. . .	. . .
Liabilities constituting foreign authorities' reserves	4 900 . .	.7	6.2	–.4	1.1	3.5	–5.4	. . .	. . .
Exceptional financing	4 920 . .	176.4	16.7	807.4	763.9	1,338.9	917.8	. . .	. . .
Conversion rates: CFA francs per U.S. dollar	0 101 . .	**297.85**	**319.01**	**272.26**	**282.11**	**264.69**	**283.16**	**555.20**	**499.15**

[1] Excludes components that have been classified in the categories of Group E.

Table 2. STANDARD PRESENTATION, 1988–95
(Millions of U.S. dollars)

	Code	1988	1989	1990	1991	1992	1993	1994	1995
CURRENT ACCOUNT	4 993 . .	**–429.2**	**–289.9**	**–468.4**	**–401.6**	**–307.7**	**–512.3**	**. . .**	**. . .**
A. GOODS	4 100 . .	620.5	717.0	778.1	784.3	950.8	502.4	. . .	. . .
Credit	2 100 . .	**1,841.2**	**1,853.8**	**2,125.4**	**1,957.5**	**1,934.1**	**1,507.7**	**. . .**	**. . .**
General merchandise: exports f.o.b.	2 110 . .	1,841.2	1,853.8	2,125.4	1,957.5	1,934.1	1,507.7	. . .	. . .
Goods for processing: exports f.o.b.	2 150 . .	. . .	. . .	. . .	. . .	. . .	. . .	. . .	. . .
Repairs on goods	2 160 . .	. . .	. . .	. . .	. . .	. . .	. . .	. . .	. . .
Goods procured in ports by carriers	2 170 . .	. . .	. . .	. . .	. . .	. . .	. . .	. . .	. . .
Nonmonetary gold	2 180 . .	. . .	. . .	. . .	. . .	. . .	. . .	. . .	. . .
Debit	3 100 . .	**–1,220.8**	**–1,136.8**	**–1,347.2**	**–1,173.1**	**–983.3**	**–1,005.3**	**. . .**	**. . .**
General merchandise: imports f.o.b.	3 110 . .	–1,220.8	–1,136.8	–1,347.2	–1,173.1	–983.3	–1,005.3	. . .	. . .
Goods for processing: imports f.o.b.	3 150 . .	. . .	. . .	. . .	. . .	. . .	. . .	. . .	. . .
Repairs on goods	3 160 . .	. . .	. . .	. . .	. . .	. . .	. . .	. . .	. . .
Goods procured in ports by carriers	3 170 . .	. . .	. . .	. . .	. . .	. . .	. . .	. . .	. . .
Nonmonetary gold	3 180 . .	. . .	. . .	. . .	. . .	. . .	. . .	. . .	. . .
B. SERVICES	4 200 . .	–445.2	–556.7	–663.0	–716.3	–499.9	–350.2	. . .	. . .
Total credit	2 200 . .	*456.2*	*475.7*	*382.2*	*406.0*	*407.5*	*390.9*	. . .	. . .
Total debit	3 200 . .	*–901.4*	*–1,032.4*	*–1,045.1*	*–1,122.3*	*–907.3*	*–741.1*	. . .	. . .
Transportation services, credit	2 205 . .	**269.7**	**175.8**	**157.1**	**196.9**	**155.2**	**120.5**	**. . .**	**. . .**
Passenger	2 205 BA	*38.9*	*27.4*	*43.3*	*36.3*	*38.5*	*30.2*	. . .	. . .
Freight	2 205 BB	*204.6*	*120.8*	*90.2*	*129.3*	*83.6*	*70.9*	. . .	. . .
Other	2 205 BC	*26.2*	*27.5*	*23.6*	*31.2*	*33.1*	*19.4*	. . .	. . .
Sea transport, passenger	2 207 . .	. . .	. . .	. . .	. . .	. . .	. . .	. . .	. . .
Sea transport, freight	2 208 . .	182.4	97.3	74.4	107.8	68.2	41.0	. . .	. . .
Sea transport, other	2 209 . .	26.2	27.5	23.6	31.2	33.1	19.4	. . .	. . .
Air transport, passenger	2 211 . .	38.9	27.4	43.3	36.3	38.5	30.2	. . .	. . .
Air transport, freight	2 212 . .	22.2	23.5	15.8	21.6	15.4	29.9	. . .	. . .
Air transport, other	2 213 . .	. . .	. . .	. . .	. . .	. . .	. . .	. . .	. . .
Other transport, passenger	2 215 . .	. . .	. . .	. . .	. . .	. . .	. . .	. . .	. . .
Other transport, freight	2 216 . .	. . .	. . .	. . .	. . .	. . .	. . .	. . .	. . .
Other transport, other	2 217 . .	. . .	. . .	. . .	. . .	. . .	. . .	. . .	. . .
Transportation services, debit	3 205 . .	**–285.2**	**–306.7**	**–460.7**	**–357.0**	**–293.9**	**–184.5**	**. . .**	**. . .**
Passenger	3 205 BA	*–46.7*	*–44.1*	*–117.5*	*–54.0*	*–48.9*	*–25.5*	. . .	. . .
Freight	3 205 BB	*–215.4*	*–251.4*	*–329.4*	*–289.0*	*–228.5*	*–140.6*	. . .	. . .
Other	3 205 BC	*–23.2*	*–11.2*	*–13.8*	*–14.0*	*–16.5*	*–18.4*	. . .	. . .
Sea transport, passenger	3 207 . .	. . .	. . .	. . .	. . .	. . .	. . .	. . .	. . .
Sea transport, freight	3 208 . .	–193.9	–241.7	–327.2	–283.7	–225.5	–117.5	. . .	. . .
Sea transport, other	3 209 . .	–23.2	–11.2	–13.8	–14.0	–16.5	–18.4	. . .	. . .
Air transport, passenger	3 211 . .	–46.7	–44.1	–117.5	–54.0	–48.9	–25.5	. . .	. . .
Air transport, freight	3 212 . .	–21.5	–9.7	–2.2	–5.3	–3.0	–23.1	. . .	. . .
Air transport, other	3 213 . .	. . .	. . .	. . .	. . .	. . .	. . .	. . .	. . .
Other transport, passenger	3 215 . .	. . .	. . .	. . .	. . .	. . .	. . .	. . .	. . .
Other transport, freight	3 216 . .	. . .	. . .	. . .	. . .	. . .	. . .	. . .	. . .
Other transport, other	3 217 . .	. . .	. . .	. . .	. . .	. . .	. . .	. . .	. . .
Travel, credit	2 236 . .	**34.4**	**94.2**	**53.3**	**72.9**	**59.4**	**47.3**	**. . .**	**. . .**
Business travel	2 237 . .	14.4	47.1	20.1	35.7	22.6	15.9	. . .	. . .
Personal travel	2 240 . .	20.0	47.1	33.2	37.2	36.8	31.4	. . .	. . .
Travel, debit	3 236 . .	**–282.9**	**–321.3**	**–279.5**	**–414.5**	**–227.5**	**–225.1**	**. . .**	**. . .**
Business travel	3 237 . .	–140.3	–165.7	–140.3	–162.0	–114.2	–109.6	. . .	. . .
Personal travel	3 240 . .	–142.5	–155.5	–139.1	–252.5	–113.3	–115.5	. . .	. . .
Other services, credit	2 200 BA	**152.1**	**205.7**	**171.8**	**136.2**	**192.9**	**223.2**	**. . .**	**. . .**
Communications	2 245 . .	.3	.5	7.3	2.2	2.2	2.4	. . .	. . .
Construction	2 249 . .	46.7	62.2	36.5	31.8	31.1	22.7	. . .	. . .
Insurance	2 253 . .	.2	20.8	33.5	14.7	12.8	32.6	. . .	. . .
Financial	2 260 . .	1.3	16.6	1.2	1.9	2.3	.6	. . .	. . .
Computer and information	2 262 . .	. . .	. . .	. . .	. . .	. . .	. . .	. . .	. . .
Royalties and licence fees	2 266 . .	.2	.7	.6	. . .	13.1	.2	. . .	. . .
Other business services	2 268 . .	72.9	86.0	79.7	76.4	110.4	137.0	. . .	. . .
Personal, cultural, and recreational	2 287 . .	. . .	. . .	. . .	. . .	. . .	. . .	. . .	. . .
Government, n.i.e.	2 291 . .	30.4	19.1	13.0	9.2	21.0	27.8	. . .	. . .
Other services, debit	3 200 BA	**–333.3**	**–404.4**	**–304.9**	**–350.8**	**–385.9**	**–331.4**	**. . .**	**. . .**
Communications	3 245 . .	–1.4	. . .	–1.8	–.2	–.1	. . .	. . .	. . .
Construction	3 249 . .	–216.6	–127.7	–138.9	–133.9	–228.8	–176.7	. . .	. . .
Insurance	3 253 . .	–24.3	–34.0	–59.8	–30.1	–46.0	–40.0	. . .	. . .
Financial	3 260 . .	–10.8	–9.9	–13.7	–11.4	–15.9	–3.7	. . .	. . .
Computer and information	3 262 . .	. . .	. . .	. . .	. . .	. . .	. . .	. . .	. . .
Royalties and licence fees	3 266 . .	–1.3	. . .	–.3	–.4	–.5	–1.7	. . .	. . .
Other business services	3 268 . .	–50.5	–181.2	–63.3	–167.8	–72.2	–91.3	. . .	. . .
Personal, cultural, and recreational	3 287 . .	. . .	. . .	. . .	. . .	. . .	. . .	. . .	. . .
Government, n.i.e.	3 291 . .	–28.4	–51.6	–27.1	–7.1	–22.4	–18.0	. . .	. . .

Table 2 (Continued). STANDARD PRESENTATION, 1988–95
(Millions of U.S. dollars)

	Code	1988	1989	1990	1991	1992	1993	1994	1995
C. INCOME	4 300	–494.0	–414.0	–557.8	–424.3	–782.1	–652.6	...	...
Total credit	2 300	*16.9*	*16.8*	*8.3*	*18.3*	*41.8*	*17.0*	...	...
Total debit	3 300	*–510.9*	*–430.8*	*–566.1*	*–442.7*	*–823.9*	*–669.5*	...	...
Compensation of employees, credit	2 310	**3.3**	**5.6**	**4.0**	**3.7**	**6.2**	**4.7**	**...**	**...**
Compensation of employees, debit	3 310	**–11.3**	**–10.6**	**–14.0**	**–9.4**	**–15.4**	**–6.6**	**...**	**...**
Investment income, credit	2 320	**13.7**	**11.2**	**4.3**	**14.6**	**35.6**	**12.3**	**...**	**...**
Direct investment income	2 330	12.3	9.2	1.9	13.1	32.1	9.1	...	...
Dividends and distributed branch profits	2 332	12.1	8.7	1.7	13.0	32.0	9.1	...	...
Reinvested earnings and undistributed branch profits	2 333	...	.1	.1	.1	...	...	...	...
Income on debt (interest)	2 334	.2	.4	.1	...	.1	.1	...	...
Portfolio investment income	2 339	...	...	...	...	...	...	...	...
Income on equity	2 340	...	...	...	...	...	...	...	...
Income on bonds and notes	2 350	...	...	...	...	...	...	...	...
Income on money market instruments and financial derivatives	2 360	...	...	...	...	...	...	...	...
Other investment income	2 370	1.3	1.9	2.4	1.5	3.5	3.1	...	...
Investment income, debit	3 320	**–499.6**	**–420.3**	**–552.1**	**–433.3**	**–808.6**	**–663.0**	**...**	**...**
Direct investment income	3 330	–234.3	–105.3	–138.5	–87.6	–139.9	–110.6	...	...
Dividends and distributed branch profits	3 332	–157.5	–103.7	–137.4	–80.9	–138.4	–109.5	...	...
Reinvested earnings and undistributed branch profits	3 333	–74.9	...	...	–5.6	...	...	...	...
Income on debt (interest)	3 334	–2.0	–1.7	–1.1	–1.1	–1.5	–1.1	...	...
Portfolio investment income	3 339	...	...	...	...	...	...	...	...
Income on equity	3 340	...	...	...	...	...	...	...	...
Income on bonds and notes	3 350	...	...	...	...	...	...	...	...
Income on money market instruments and financial derivatives	3 360	...	...	...	...	...	...	...	...
Other investment income	3 370	–265.3	–314.9	–413.6	–345.8	–668.7	–552.4	...	...
D. CURRENT TRANSFERS	4 379	–110.5	–36.2	–25.7	–45.3	23.5	–11.9	...	...
Credit	2 379	**65.6**	**96.1**	**91.8**	**60.2**	**171.9**	**118.3**	**...**	**...**
General government	2 380	37.6	40.8	35.8	24.4	121.2	70.3	...	...
Other sectors	2 390	28.0	55.3	56.0	35.7	50.7	48.0	...	...
Workers' remittances	2 391	9.1	26.9	19.0	3.6	18.8	15.6	...	...
Other current transfers	2 392	18.9	28.4	37.0	32.1	31.9	32.3	...	...
Debit	3 379	**–176.0**	**–132.3**	**–117.5**	**–105.4**	**–148.3**	**–130.2**	**...**	**...**
General government	3 380	–13.2	–13.4	–9.6	–3.9	–3.2	–1.6	...	...
Other sectors	3 390	–162.9	–118.9	–107.9	–101.5	–145.1	–128.7	...	...
Workers' remittances	3 391	–149.2	–103.5	–96.9	–86.0	–119.7	–99.9	...	...
Other current transfers	3 392	–13.6	–15.4	–11.1	–15.5	–25.4	–28.7	...	...
CAPITAL AND FINANCIAL ACCOUNT	4 996	**207.4**	**450.6**	**636.6**	**374.8**	**948.4**	**528.5**	**...**	**...**
CAPITAL ACCOUNT	4 994	**6.4**	**5.0**	**2.8**	**7.9**	**17.0**	**6.3**	**...**	**...**
Total credit	2 994	*6.4*	*5.0*	*2.9*	*8.0*	*17.1*	*6.4*	...	...
Total debit	3 994	...	*–.1*	*–.1*	*–.1*	*–.1*	*–.1*	...	...
Capital transfers, credit	2 400	**6.4**	**5.0**	**2.9**	**8.0**	**17.1**	**6.4**	**...**	**...**
General government	2 401	6.4	5.0	2.9	8.0	17.1	6.4	...	...
Debt forgiveness	2 402	...	...	...	...	...	...	...	...
Other capital transfers	2 410	6.4	5.0	2.9	8.0	17.1	6.4	...	...
Other sectors	2 430	...	...	...	...	...	...	...	...
Migrants' transfers	2 431	...	...	...	...	...	...	...	...
Debt forgiveness	2 432	...	...	...	...	...	...	...	...
Other capital transfers	2 440	...	...	...	...	...	...	...	...
Capital transfers, debit	3 400	**...**	**–.1**	**–.1**	**–.1**	**–.1**	**–.1**	**...**	**...**
General government	3 401	...	–.1	–.1	–.1	–.1	–.1	...	...
Debt forgiveness	3 402	...	...	...	...	...	...	...	...
Other capital transfers	3 410	...	–.1	–.1	–.1	–.1	–.1	...	...
Other sectors	3 430	...	...	...	...	...	...	...	...
Migrants' transfers	3 431	...	...	...	...	...	...	...	...
Debt forgiveness	3 432	...	...	...	...	...	...	...	...
Other capital transfers	3 440	...	...	...	...	...	...	...	...
Nonproduced nonfinancial assets, credit	2 480	**...**	**...**	**...**	**...**	**...**	**...**	**...**	**...**
Nonproduced nonfinancial assets, debit	3 480	**...**	**...**	**...**	**...**	**...**	**...**	**...**	**...**

Table 2 (Continued). STANDARD PRESENTATION, 1988–95
(Millions of U.S. dollars)

	Code		1988	1989	1990	1991	1992	1993	1994	1995
FINANCIAL ACCOUNT	4 995	. .	**201.0**	**445.6**	**633.8**	**366.9**	**931.4**	**522.2**	**. . .**	**. . .**
A. DIRECT INVESTMENT	4 500	. .	63.7	–111.8	–127.9	–36.0	–3.9	–17.0	. . .	. . .
Direct investment abroad	4 505	. .	**–28.6**	**–26.1**	**–15.1**	**–21.5**	**–33.1**	**–22.1**	**. . .**	**. . .**
Equity capital	4 510	. .	–28.6	–26.1	–15.1	–21.5	–33.1	–22.1	. . .	. . .
Claims on affiliated enterprises	4 515	. .	. . .	. . .	. . .	. . .	. . .	. . .	. . .	. . .
Liabilities to affiliated enterprises	4 520	. .	. . .	. . .	. . .	. . .	. . .	. . .	. . .	. . .
Reinvested earnings	4 525	. .	. . .	–.1	–.1	–.1	. . .	. . .	. . .	. . .
Other capital	4 530	. .	. . .	.1	.1	.1	. . .	. . .	. . .	. . .
Claims on affiliated enterprises	4 535	. .	. . .	. . .	. . .	. . .	. . .	. . .	. . .	. . .
Liabilities to affiliated enterprises	4 540	. .	. . .	. . .	. . .	. . .	. . .	. . .	. . .	. . .
Direct investment in Cameroon	4 555	. .	**92.4**	**–85.7**	**–112.8**	**–14.5**	**29.2**	**5.1**	**. . .**	**. . .**
Equity capital	4 560	. .	–4.2	–86.0	–112.9	–14.0	29.0	5.0	. . .	. . .
Claims on direct investors	4 565	. .	. . .	. . .	. . .	. . .	. . .	. . .	. . .	. . .
Liabilities to direct investors	4 570	. .	. . .	. . .	. . .	. . .	. . .	. . .	. . .	. . .
Reinvested earnings	4 575	. .	74.9	. . .	. . .	5.6	. . .	. . .	. . .	. . .
Other capital	4 580	. .	21.7	.3	. . .	–6.0	.2	.1	. . .	. . .
Claims on direct investors	4 585	. .	. . .	. . .	. . .	. . .	. . .	. . .	. . .	. . .
Liabilities to direct investors	4 590	. .	. . .	. . .	. . .	. . .	. . .	. . .	. . .	. . .
B. PORTFOLIO INVESTMENT	4 600	. .	–10.9	–1.0	55.6	–2.2	–46.5	–106.3	. . .	. . .
Assets	4 602	. .	**–10.9**	**–1.0**	**55.6**	**–2.2**	**–46.5**	**–106.3**	**. . .**	**. . .**
Equity securities	4 610	. .	3.1	.2	104.1	18.6	53.4	8.0	. . .	. . .
Monetary authorities	4 611	. .	. . .	. . .	. . .	. . .	. . .	. . .	. . .	. . .
General government	4 612	. .	. . .	. . .	. . .	. . .	. . .	. . .	. . .	. . .
Banks	4 613	. .	. . .	. . .	. . .	. . .	. . .	. . .	. . .	. . .
Other sectors	4 614	. .	3.1	.2	104.1	18.6	53.4	8.0	. . .	. . .
Debt securities	4 619	. .	–14.0	–1.2	–48.4	–20.8	–99.9	–114.4	. . .	. . .
Bonds and notes	4 620	. .	–14.0	–1.2	–48.4	–20.8	–99.9	–114.4	. . .	. . .
Monetary authorities	4 621	. .	. . .	. . .	. . .	. . .	. . .	. . .	. . .	. . .
General government	4 622	. .	. . .	. . .	. . .	. . .	. . .	. . .	. . .	. . .
Banks	4 623	. .	. . .	. . .	. . .	. . .	. . .	. . .	. . .	. . .
Other sectors	4 624	. .	–14.0	–1.2	–48.4	–20.8	–99.9	–114.4	. . .	. . .
Money market instruments	4 630	. .	. . .	. . .	. . .	. . .	. . .	. . .	. . .	. . .
Monetary authorities	4 631	. .	. . .	. . .	. . .	. . .	. . .	. . .	. . .	. . .
General government	4 632	. .	. . .	. . .	. . .	. . .	. . .	. . .	. . .	. . .
Banks	4 633	. .	. . .	. . .	. . .	. . .	. . .	. . .	. . .	. . .
Other sectors	4 634	. .	. . .	. . .	. . .	. . .	. . .	. . .	. . .	. . .
Financial derivatives	4 640	. .	. . .	. . .	. . .	. . .	. . .	. . .	. . .	. . .
Monetary authorities	4 641	. .	. . .	. . .	. . .	. . .	. . .	. . .	. . .	. . .
General government	4 642	. .	. . .	. . .	. . .	. . .	. . .	. . .	. . .	. . .
Banks	4 643	. .	. . .	. . .	. . .	. . .	. . .	. . .	. . .	. . .
Other sectors	4 644	. .	. . .	. . .	. . .	. . .	. . .	. . .	. . .	. . .
Liabilities	4 652	. .	**. . .**	**. . .**	**. . .**	**. . .**	**. . .**	**. . .**	**. . .**	**. . .**
Equity securities	4 660	. .	. . .	. . .	. . .	. . .	. . .	. . .	. . .	. . .
Banks	4 663	. .	. . .	. . .	. . .	. . .	. . .	. . .	. . .	. . .
Other sectors	4 664	. .	. . .	. . .	. . .	. . .	. . .	. . .	. . .	. . .
Debt securities	4 669	. .	. . .	. . .	. . .	. . .	. . .	. . .	. . .	. . .
Bonds and notes	4 670	. .	. . .	. . .	. . .	. . .	. . .	. . .	. . .	. . .
Monetary authorities	4 671	. .	. . .	. . .	. . .	. . .	. . .	. . .	. . .	. . .
General government	4 672	. .	. . .	. . .	. . .	. . .	. . .	. . .	. . .	. . .
Banks	4 673	. .	. . .	. . .	. . .	. . .	. . .	. . .	. . .	. . .
Other sectors	4 674	. .	. . .	. . .	. . .	. . .	. . .	. . .	. . .	. . .
Money market instruments	4 680	. .	. . .	. . .	. . .	. . .	. . .	. . .	. . .	. . .
Monetary authorities	4 681	. .	. . .	. . .	. . .	. . .	. . .	. . .	. . .	. . .
General government	4 682	. .	. . .	. . .	. . .	. . .	. . .	. . .	. . .	. . .
Banks	4 683	. .	. . .	. . .	. . .	. . .	. . .	. . .	. . .	. . .
Other sectors	4 684	. .	. . .	. . .	. . .	. . .	. . .	. . .	. . .	. . .
Financial derivatives	4 690	. .	. . .	. . .	. . .	. . .	. . .	. . .	. . .	. . .
Monetary authorities	4 691	. .	. . .	. . .	. . .	. . .	. . .	. . .	. . .	. . .
General government	4 692	. .	. . .	. . .	. . .	. . .	. . .	. . .	. . .	. . .
Banks	4 693	. .	. . .	. . .	. . .	. . .	. . .	. . .	. . .	. . .
Other sectors	4 694	. .	. . .	. . .	. . .	. . .	. . .	. . .	. . .	. . .

Table 2 (Concluded). STANDARD PRESENTATION, 1988–95
(Millions of U.S. dollars)

	Code	1988	1989	1990	1991	1992	1993	1994	1995
C. OTHER INVESTMENT	4 700	242.8	461.6	641.5	436.7	960.9	630.5	...	...
Assets	4 703	**–93.9**	**–8.9**	**481.5**	**–112.3**	**16.8**	**105.5**	**...**	**...**
Trade credits	4 706	236.1	339.1	183.5	213.9	253.1	270.9	...	...
General government: long-term	4 708	...	...	...	...	...	...	...	...
General government: short-term	4 709	...	...	.3	...	...	...	...	...
Other sectors: long-term	4 711	...	...	...	...	...	...	...	...
Other sectors: short-term	4 712	236.1	339.1	183.2	213.9	253.1	270.9	...	...
Loans	4 714	.6	–.9	–4.5	–1.8	2.2	5.1	...	...
Monetary authorities: long-term	4 717	...	...	...	...	...	...	...	...
Monetary authorities: short-term	4 718	...	...	...	...	...	...	...	...
General government: long-term	4 720	–.1	...	...	...	...	...	...	...
General government: short-term	4 721	...	...	...	...	...	...	...	...
Banks: long-term	4 723	...	...	...	...	...	...	...	...
Banks: short-term	4 724	...	...	...	...	...	...	...	...
Other sectors: long-term	4 726	.7	–.9	–4.5	–1.8	2.2	5.1	...	...
Other sectors: short-term	4 727	...	...	...	...	...	...	...	...
Currency and deposits	4 730	–330.7	–347.0	302.6	–324.3	–238.5	–170.5	...	...
Monetary authorities	4 731	...	...	...	...	...	...	...	...
General government	4 732	...	...	...	...	...	...	...	...
Banks	4 733	–145.2	–67.4	377.6	–29.7	26.0	42.8	...	...
Other sectors	4 734	–185.4	–279.7	–75.0	–294.6	–264.5	–213.3	...	...
Other assets	4 736	...	...	...	...	.1	...	...	...
Monetary authorities: long-term	4 738	...	...	...	...	...	...	...	...
Monetary authorities: short-term	4 739	...	...	...	...	...	...	...	...
General government: long-term	4 741	...	...	...	...	.1	...	...	...
General government: short-term	4 742	...	...	...	...	...	...	...	...
Banks: long-term	4 744	...	...	...	...	...	...	...	...
Banks: short-term	4 745	...	...	...	...	...	...	...	...
Other sectors: long-term	4 747	...	...	...	...	...	...	...	...
Other sectors: short-term	4 748	...	...	...	...	...	...	...	...
Liabilities	4 753	**336.7**	**470.5**	**160.0**	**549.0**	**944.0**	**525.1**	**...**	**...**
Trade credits	4 756	–171.5	–366.3	–256.6	–309.1	–243.6	–327.6	...	...
General government: long-term	4 758	...	...	...	...	...	...	...	...
General government: short-term	4 759	...	...	–.1	–5.3	...	...	...	...
Other sectors: long-term	4 761	...	...	...	...	...	...	...	...
Other sectors: short-term	4 762	–171.4	–366.3	–256.6	–303.8	–243.6	–327.6	...	...
Loans	4 764	179.9	268.0	97.9	204.0	31.0	90.9	...	...
Use of Fund credit and loans from the Fund	4 766	81.6	14.5	–1.4	–1.2	–54.6	–47.4	...	...
Monetary authorities: other long-term	4 767	...	...	...	...	...	...	...	...
Monetary authorities: short-term	4 768	–90.0	–80.2	68.1	35.2	147.6	176.4	...	...
General government: long-term	4 770	214.6	352.0	57.4	213.0	–86.9	–29.2	...	...
General government: short-term	4 771	...	...	...	...	...	...	...	...
Banks: long-term	4 773	...	...	...	...	...	...	...	...
Banks: short-term	4 774	...	...	...	...	...	...	...	...
Other sectors: long-term	4 776	–26.4	–18.2	–26.2	–42.9	24.9	–8.8	...	...
Other sectors: short-term	4 777	...	...	...	...	...	...	...	...
Currency and deposits	4 780	–50.2	307.6	–523.0	–30.0	–37.8	–102.8	...	...
Monetary authorities	4 781	.7	6.2	–.4	1.1	3.5	–5.4	...	...
General government	4 782	11.5	...	–125.6	...	...	6.8	...	...
Banks	4 783	–62.4	301.3	–397.0	–31.2	–41.3	–104.1	...	...
Other sectors	4 784	...	...	...	...	...	...	...	...
Other liabilities	4 786	378.4	261.2	841.7	684.1	1,194.5	864.6	...	...
Monetary authorities: long-term	4 788	...	...	...	...	...	...	...	...
Monetary authorities: short-term	4 789	264.6	88.9	713.6	582.0	1,071.6	688.3	...	...
General government: long-term	4 791	...	...	...	...	...	...	...	...
General government: short-term	4 792	...	...	...	...	...	...	...	...
Banks: long-term	4 794	...	...	...	...	...	...	...	...
Banks: short-term	4 795	...	...	...	...	...	...	...	...
Other sectors: long-term	4 797	...	...	...	...	...	...	...	...
Other sectors: short-term	4 798	113.9	172.3	128.1	102.1	122.9	176.3	...	...
D. RESERVE ASSETS	4 800	–94.6	96.8	64.6	–31.6	20.9	14.9	...	...
Monetary gold	4 810	.6	.8	1.9	.8	...	–2.5	...	...
Special drawing rights	4 820	.2	–.3	.1	–4.8	5.1	.3	...	...
Reserve position in the Fund	4 830	...	...	...	...	–.1	–.1	...	...
Foreign exchange	4 840	–95.4	96.3	62.6	–27.6	15.9	17.2	...	...
Other claims	4 880	...	...	...	...	...	...	...	...
NET ERRORS AND OMISSIONS	4 998	**221.8**	**–160.7**	**–168.2**	**26.9**	**–640.7**	**–16.2**	**...**	**...**

Part 3 of the *Yearbook* contains descriptions of the methodologies, compilation practices, and sources used to compile these data.

Table 1. ANALYTIC PRESENTATION, 1988–95
(Millions of U.S. dollars)

	Code	1988	1989	1990	1991	1992	1993	1994	1995
A. Current Account[1]	4 993 Y.	**-18,023**	**-23,790**	**-22,577**	**-24,571**	**-22,592**	**-23,391**	**-17,278**	**-8,693**
Goods: exports f.o.b	2 100 . .	115,431	122,969	128,440	126,153	132,115	143,953	163,813	189,854
Goods: imports f.o.b	3 100 . .	-107,273	-116,984	-120,106	-122,282	-126,415	-136,026	-151,505	-167,513
Balance on Goods	4 100 . .	*8,157*	*5,985*	*8,334*	*3,871*	*5,699*	*7,927*	*12,309*	*22,341*
Services: credit	2 200 . .	14,087	15,448	16,340	17,743	17,729	18,298	19,780	21,770
Services: debit	3 200 . .	-19,798	-23,271	-26,613	-28,567	-28,541	-28,716	-28,908	-30,141
Balance on Goods and Services	4 991 . .	*2,447*	*-1,838*	*-1,938*	*-6,953*	*-5,113*	*-2,491*	*3,181*	*13,971*
Income: credit	2 300 . .	8,372	9,078	9,542	8,938	8,451	7,763	9,987	12,511
Income: debit	3 300 . .	-28,182	-30,230	-29,113	-25,679	-25,038	-27,962	-30,090	-34,804
Balance on Goods, Services, and Income	4 992 . .	*-17,363*	*-22,990*	*-21,510*	*-23,694*	*-21,700*	*-22,690*	*-16,922*	*-8,323*
Current transfers: credit	2 379 Y.	2,066	2,035	2,290	2,292	2,233	2,281	2,258	2,319
Current transfers: debit	3 379 . .	-2,727	-2,835	-3,358	-3,169	-3,125	-2,982	-2,613	-2,689
B. Capital Account[1]	4 994 Y.	**921**	**1,055**	**1,033**	**986**	**1,033**	**1,029**	**1,001**	**650**
Capital account: credit	2 994 Y.	1,100	1,257	1,251	1,260	1,297	1,293	1,265	932
Capital account: debit	3 994 . .	-179	-202	-218	-273	-264	-264	-264	-282
Total, Groups A Plus B	4 010 . .	*-17,102*	*-22,735*	*-21,544*	*-23,585*	*-21,559*	*-22,361*	*-16,277*	*-8,042*
C. Financial Account[1]	4 995 X.	**25,219**	**22,527**	**23,571**	**23,748**	**14,448**	**29,124**	**9,699**	**4,345**
Direct investment abroad	4 505 . .	-3,854	-4,587	-4,725	-5,655	-3,635	-5,825	-7,447	-5,761
Direct investment in Canada	4 555 Y.	6,425	5,029	7,855	2,740	4,517	4,997	7,299	10,786
Portfolio investment assets	4 602 . .	-2,443	-3,393	-2,239	-6,695	-6,933	-10,687	-6,501	-3,938
Equity securities	4 610 . .	-2,373	-2,082	-2,177	-5,689	-6,133	-7,566	-6,878	-3,301
Debt securities	4 619 . .	-71	-1,311	-62	-1,006	-800	-3,121	377	-637
Portfolio investment liabilities	4 652 Y.	18,489	19,220	15,925	27,012	20,679	39,817	12,865	13,365
Equity securities	4 660 Y.	-1,934	3,287	-1,502	-856	830	9,335	4,719	-3,078
Debt securities	4 669 Y.	20,423	15,933	17,427	27,868	19,849	30,482	8,146	16,443
Other investment assets	4 703 . .	4,445	-3,166	-5,371	6,136	679	7,527	-12,743	-9,328
Monetary authorities	4 703 .A	. . .	. . .	. . .	. . .	. . .	. . .	. . .	. . .
General government	4 703 .B	-293	-361	192	-360	-403	-230	-436	-336
Banks	4 703 .C	4,516	-2,785	-4,647	6,084	-1,852	5,903	-12,611	-9,110
Other sectors	4 703 .D	222	-20	-916	411	2,935	1,854	305	118
Other investment liabilities	4 753 X.	2,158	9,425	12,127	209	-859	-6,705	16,225	-780
Monetary authorities	4 753 XA	. . .	. . .	. . .	. . .	. . .	. . .	. . .	. . .
General government	4 753 YB	-820	-742	-360	-105	-238	-111	670	-450
Banks	4 753 YC	-1,457	1,913	6,604	-2,076	-3,202	-6,459	14,511	-4,850
Other sectors	4 753 YD	4,435	8,253	5,883	2,390	2,581	-135	1,044	4,520
Total, Groups A Through C	4 020 . .	*8,116*	*-208*	*2,027*	*163*	*-7,111*	*6,763*	*-6,578*	*-3,697*
D. Net Errors and Omissions	4 998 . .	**-558**	**501**	**-1,402**	**-2,649**	**1,304**	**-7,255**	**1,434**	**3,230**
Total, Groups A Through D	4 030 . .	*7,558*	*293*	*625*	*-2,486*	*-5,807*	*-492*	*-5,144*	*-467*
E. Reserves and Related Items	4 040 . .	**-7,558**	**-293**	**-625**	**2,486**	**5,807**	**492**	**5,144**	**467**
Reserve assets	4 800 . .	-7,558	-293	-625	2,486	5,807	492	1,227	-2,527
Use of Fund credit and loans	4 766 . .	. . .	. . .	. . .	. . .	. . .	. . .	. . .	. . .
Liabilities constituting foreign authorities' reserves	4 900 . .	. . .	. . .	. . .	. . .	. . .	. . .	. . .	. . .
Exceptional financing	4 920 . .	. . .	. . .	. . .	. . .	. . .	. . .	3,917	2,994
Conversion rates: Canadian dollars per U.S. dollar	0 101 . .	**1.2307**	**1.1840**	**1.1668**	**1.1457**	**1.2087**	**1.2901**	**1.3656**	**1.3724**

[1] Excludes components that have been classified in the categories of Group E.

Table 2. STANDARD PRESENTATION, 1988–95
(Millions of U.S. dollars)

	Code	1988	1989	1990	1991	1992	1993	1994	1995
CURRENT ACCOUNT	4 993 . .	**–18,023**	**–23,790**	**–22,577**	**–24,571**	**–22,592**	**–23,391**	**–17,278**	**–8,693**
A. GOODS	4 100 . .	8,157	5,985	8,334	3,871	5,699	7,927	12,309	22,341
Credit	2 100 . .	**115,431**	**122,969**	**128,440**	**126,153**	**132,115**	**143,953**	**163,813**	**189,854**
General merchandise: exports f.o.b.	2 110 . .	113,051	120,684	126,292	124,082	129,567	141,623	161,125	187,707
Goods for processing: exports f.o.b.	2 150 . .	. . .	. . .	. . .	. . .	. . .	. . .	. . .	. . .
Repairs on goods	2 160 . .	. . .	. . .	. . .	. . .	. . .	. . .	. . .	. . .
Goods procured in ports by carriers	2 170 . .	. . .	. . .	. . .	. . .	. . .	. . .	. . .	. . .
Nonmonetary gold	2 180 . .	2,380	2,285	2,149	2,070	2,548	2,330	2,688	2,148
Debit	3 100 . .	**–107,273**	**–116,984**	**–120,106**	**–122,282**	**–126,415**	**–136,026**	**–151,505**	**–167,513**
General merchandise: imports f.o.b.	3 110 . .	–106,419	–116,224	–119,518	–121,636	–125,730	–135,050	–150,876	–166,966
Goods for processing: imports f.o.b.	3 150 . .	. . .	. . .	. . .	. . .	. . .	. . .	. . .	. . .
Repairs on goods	3 160 . .	. . .	. . .	. . .	. . .	. . .	. . .	. . .	. . .
Goods procured in ports by carriers	3 170 . .	. . .	. . .	. . .	. . .	. . .	. . .	. . .	. . .
Nonmonetary gold	3 180 . .	–855	–760	–588	–646	–686	–976	–629	–547
B. SERVICES	4 200 . .	–5,710	–7,823	–10,272	–10,824	–10,812	–10,418	–9,128	–8,370
Total credit	2 200 . .	*14,087*	*15,448*	*16,340*	*17,743*	*17,729*	*18,298*	*19,780*	*21,770*
Total debit	3 200 . .	*–19,798*	*–23,271*	*–26,613*	*–28,567*	*–28,541*	*–28,716*	*–28,908*	*–30,141*
Transportation services, credit	2 205 . .	**1,467**	**1,770**	**1,832**	**2,282**	**2,151**	**2,196**	**3,272**	**3,723**
Passenger	2 205 BA	. . .	. . .	. . .	. . .	. . .	. . .	. . .	. . .
Freight	2 205 BB	*569*	*680*	*644*	*769*	*661*	*752*	*972*	*1,120*
Other	2 205 BC	*897*	*1,090*	*1,188*	*1,513*	*1,490*	*1,444*	*2,300*	*2,602*
Sea transport, passenger	2 207 . .	. . .	. . .	. . .	. . .	. . .	. . .	. . .	. . .
Sea transport, freight	2 208 . .	415	508	471	534	417	555	465	538
Sea transport, other	2 209 . .	330	449	419	770	715	682	479	593
Air transport, passenger	2 211 . .	. . .	. . .	. . .	. . .	. . .	. . .	. . .	. . .
Air transport, freight	2 212 . .	. . .	. . .	. . .	. . .	. . .	. . .	. . .	. . .
Air transport, other	2 213 . .	567	641	769	743	776	762	1,821	2,009
Other transport, passenger	2 215 . .	. . .	. . .	. . .	. . .	. . .	. . .	. . .	. . .
Other transport, freight	2 216 . .	155	172	173	235	244	197	507	582
Other transport, other	2 217 . .	. . .	. . .	. . .	. . .	. . .	. . .	. . .	. . .
Transportation services, debit	3 205 . .	**–2,092**	**–2,453**	**–2,503**	**–2,672**	**–2,825**	**–2,956**	**–5,447**	**–5,997**
Passenger	3 205 BA	. . .	. . .	. . .	. . .	. . .	. . .	. . .	. . .
Freight	3 205 BB	*–1,765*	*–2,048*	*–2,127*	*–2,123*	*–2,232*	*–2,421*	*–5,043*	*–5,541*
Other	3 205 BC	*–327*	*–406*	*–376*	*–549*	*–592*	*–535*	*–405*	*–456*
Sea transport, passenger	3 207 . .	. . .	. . .	. . .	. . .	. . .	. . .	. . .	. . .
Sea transport, freight	3 208 . .	–721	–943	–957	–849	–857	–1,093	–1,280	–1,485
Sea transport, other	3 209 . .	–327	–406	–376	–549	–592	–535	–405	–456
Air transport, passenger	3 211 . .	. . .	. . .	. . .	. . .	. . .	. . .	. . .	. . .
Air transport, freight	3 212 . .	–125	–144	–149	–203	–205	–200	–2,343	–2,579
Air transport, other	3 213 . .	. . .	. . .	. . .	. . .	. . .	. . .	. . .	. . .
Other transport, passenger	3 215 . .	. . .	. . .	. . .	. . .	. . .	. . .	. . .	. . .
Other transport, freight	3 216 . .	–920	–961	–1,022	–1,071	–1,170	–1,129	–1,420	–1,476
Other transport, other	3 217 . .	. . .	. . .	. . .	. . .	. . .	. . .	. . .	. . .
Travel, credit	2 236 . .	**5,946**	**6,490**	**7,099**	**7,279**	**7,148**	**7,265**	**7,108**	**8,046**
Business travel	2 237 . .	. . .	. . .	. . .	. . .	. . .	. . .	. . .	. . .
Personal travel	2 240 . .	. . .	. . .	. . .	. . .	. . .	. . .	. . .	. . .
Travel, debit	3 236 . .	**–8,214**	**–9,992**	**–12,712**	**–13,709**	**–13,764**	**–13,250**	**–10,036**	**–10,213**
Business travel	3 237 . .	. . .	. . .	. . .	. . .	. . .	. . .	. . .	. . .
Personal travel	3 240 . .	. . .	. . .	. . .	. . .	. . .	. . .	. . .	. . .
Other services, credit	2 200 BA	**6,674**	**7,188**	**7,409**	**8,182**	**8,430**	**8,837**	**9,400**	**10,001**
Communications	2 245 . .	. . .	. . .	. . .	. . .	. . .	. . .	. . .	. . .
Construction	2 249 . .	. . .	. . .	. . .	. . .	. . .	. . .	. . .	. . .
Insurance	2 253 . .	. . .	. . .	. . .	. . .	. . .	. . .	. . .	. . .
Financial	2 260 . .	. . .	. . .	. . .	. . .	. . .	. . .	. . .	. . .
Computer and information	2 262 . .	. . .	. . .	. . .	. . .	. . .	. . .	. . .	. . .
Royalties and licence fees	2 266 . .	. . .	. . .	. . .	. . .	. . .	. . .	. . .	. . .
Other business services	2 268 . .	5,782	6,365	6,525	7,316	7,606	8,061	8,691	9,275
Personal, cultural, and recreational	2 287 . .	233	143	152	157	175	187	109	129
Government, n.i.e.	2 291 . .	659	680	732	709	649	589	600	597
Other services, debit	3 200 BA	**–9,492**	**–10,825**	**–11,397**	**–12,186**	**–11,952**	**–12,509**	**–13,424**	**–13,931**
Communications	3 245 . .	. . .	. . .	. . .	. . .	. . .	. . .	. . .	. . .
Construction	3 249 . .	. . .	. . .	. . .	. . .	. . .	. . .	. . .	. . .
Insurance	3 253 . .	. . .	. . .	. . .	. . .	. . .	. . .	. . .	. . .
Financial	3 260 . .	. . .	. . .	. . .	. . .	. . .	. . .	. . .	. . .
Computer and information	3 262 . .	. . .	. . .	. . .	. . .	. . .	. . .	. . .	. . .
Royalties and licence fees	3 266 . .	. . .	. . .	. . .	. . .	. . .	. . .	. . .	. . .
Other business services	3 268 . .	–8,526	–9,601	–9,969	–10,569	–10,489	–11,173	–12,399	–12,904
Personal, cultural, and recreational	3 287 . .	–31	–164	–175	–187	–202	–182	–214	–226
Government, n.i.e.	3 291 . .	–935	–1,061	–1,253	–1,430	–1,261	–1,154	–812	–801

Table 2 (Continued). STANDARD PRESENTATION, 1988–95
(Millions of U.S. dollars)

	Code	1988	1989	1990	1991	1992	1993	1994	1995
C. INCOME	4 300	–19,810	–21,152	–19,571	–16,741	–16,587	–20,199	–20,103	–22,294
Total credit	2 300	*8,372*	*9,078*	*9,542*	*8,938*	*8,451*	*7,763*	*9,987*	*12,511*
Total debit	3 300	*–28,182*	*–30,230*	*–29,113*	*–25,679*	*–25,038*	*–27,962*	*–30,090*	*–34,804*
Compensation of employees, credit	2 310	...	...	...	...	...	...	...	...
Compensation of employees, debit	3 310	...	...	...	...	...	...	...	...
Investment income, credit	2 320	**8,372**	**9,078**	**9,542**	**8,938**	**8,451**	**7,763**	**9,987**	**12,511**
Direct investment income	2 330	3,901	3,840	3,333	3,074	3,564	3,353	5,001	5,828
Dividends and distributed branch profits	2 332	5,144	3,188	2,483	3,262	2,806	3,617	3,175	3,665
Reinvested earnings and undistributed branch profits	2 333	–1,373	348	472	–575	514	–479	1,562	1,854
Income on debt (interest)	2 334	130	304	377	388	245	214	264	310
Portfolio investment income	2 339	1,132	1,359	2,035	2,265	2,231	2,250	2,304	2,339
Income on equity	2 340	822	994	1,387	1,613	1,673	1,757	1,554	1,615
Income on bonds and notes	2 350	310	365	647	652	557	493	750	724
Income on money market instruments and financial derivatives	2 360	...	...	...	...	...	...	...	...
Other investment income	2 370	3,339	3,879	4,175	3,599	2,655	2,160	2,682	4,343
Investment income, debit	3 320	**–28,182**	**–30,230**	**–29,113**	**–25,679**	**–25,038**	**–27,962**	**–30,090**	**–34,804**
Direct investment income	3 330	–10,237	–8,891	–5,420	–1,649	–1,764	–5,365	–6,071	–9,063
Dividends and distributed branch profits	3 332	–6,467	–4,993	–5,109	–3,483	–3,520	–2,889	–3,271	–3,214
Reinvested earnings and undistributed branch profits	3 333	–3,168	–3,341	406	2,928	2,922	–1,132	–1,825	–4,881
Income on debt (interest)	3 334	–601	–557	–717	–1,094	–1,167	–1,344	–975	–968
Portfolio investment income	3 339	–13,702	–15,667	–17,586	–18,785	–19,091	–19,550	–20,293	–21,704
Income on equity	3 340	–952	–698	–757	–668	–535	–650	–707	–736
Income on bonds and notes	3 350	–11,574	–13,040	–14,601	–16,283	–16,879	–17,483	–17,739	–18,568
Income on money market instruments and financial derivatives	3 360	–1,176	–1,928	–2,227	–1,834	–1,677	–1,416	–1,847	–2,401
Other investment income	3 370	–4,244	–5,672	–6,107	–5,245	–4,182	–3,047	–3,727	–4,037
D. CURRENT TRANSFERS	4 379	–661	–800	–1,067	–877	–892	–701	–356	–370
Credit	2 379	**2,066**	**2,035**	**2,290**	**2,292**	**2,233**	**2,281**	**2,258**	**2,319**
General government	2 380	1,365	1,304	1,479	1,320	1,245	1,271	1,238	1,236
Other sectors	2 390	701	732	812	972	988	1,010	1,020	1,083
Workers' remittances	2 391	...	...	...	...	...	...	...	...
Other current transfers	2 392	701	732	812	972	988	1,010	1,020	1,083
Debit	3 379	**–2,727**	**–2,835**	**–3,358**	**–3,169**	**–3,125**	**–2,982**	**–2,613**	**–2,689**
General government	3 380	–1,765	–1,731	–2,273	–1,984	–1,876	–1,748	–1,372	–1,393
Other sectors	3 390	–962	–1,104	–1,085	–1,185	–1,249	–1,234	–1,241	–1,296
Workers' remittances	3 391	...	...	...	...	...	...	...	...
Other current transfers	3 392	–962	–1,104	–1,085	–1,185	–1,249	–1,234	–1,241	–1,296
CAPITAL AND FINANCIAL ACCOUNT	4 996	**18,582**	**23,289**	**23,979**	**27,220**	**21,288**	**30,646**	**15,844**	**5,462**
CAPITAL ACCOUNT	4 994	**921**	**1,055**	**1,033**	**986**	**1,033**	**1,029**	**1,001**	**650**
Total credit	2 994	*1,100*	*1,257*	*1,251*	*1,260*	*1,297*	*1,293*	*1,265*	*932*
Total debit	3 994	*–179*	*–202*	*–218*	*–273*	*–264*	*–264*	*–264*	*–282*
Capital transfers, credit	2 400	**1,100**	**1,257**	**1,251**	**1,260**	**1,297**	**1,293**	**1,265**	**932**
General government	2 401	...	...	...	...	...	...	...	...
Debt forgiveness	2 402	...	...	...	...	...	...	...	...
Other capital transfers	2 410	...	...	...	...	...	...	...	...
Other sectors	2 430	...	...	...	...	...	...	...	...
Migrants' transfers	2 431	...	...	...	...	...	...	...	...
Debt forgiveness	2 432	...	...	...	...	...	...	...	...
Other capital transfers	2 440	...	...	...	...	...	...	...	...
Capital transfers, debit	3 400	**–179**	**–202**	**–218**	**–273**	**–264**	**–264**	**–264**	**–282**
General government	3 401	...	...	...	...	...	...	...	...
Debt forgiveness	3 402	...	...	...	...	...	...	...	...
Other capital transfers	3 410	...	...	...	...	...	...	...	...
Other sectors	3 430	...	...	...	...	...	...	...	...
Migrants' transfers	3 431	...	...	...	...	...	...	...	...
Debt forgiveness	3 432	...	...	...	...	...	...	...	...
Other capital transfers	3 440	...	...	...	...	...	...	...	...
Nonproduced nonfinancial assets, credit	2 480	...	...	...	...	...	...	...	...
Nonproduced nonfinancial assets, debit	3 480	...	...	...	...	...	...	...	...

Table 2 (Continued). STANDARD PRESENTATION, 1988–95
(Millions of U.S. dollars)

	Code		1988	1989	1990	1991	1992	1993	1994	1995
FINANCIAL ACCOUNT	4 995	. .	**17,660**	**22,235**	**22,946**	**26,234**	**20,255**	**29,616**	**14,843**	**4,812**
A. DIRECT INVESTMENT	4 500	. .	2,570	442	3,130	–2,914	882	–827	–148	5,025
Direct investment abroad	4 505	. .	**–3,854**	**–4,587**	**–4,725**	**–5,655**	**–3,635**	**–5,825**	**–7,447**	**–5,761**
Equity capital	4 510	. .	. . .	. . .	. . .	. . .	. . .	. . .	. . .	. . .
Claims on affiliated enterprises	4 515	. .	. . .	. . .	. . .	. . .	. . .	. . .	. . .	. . .
Liabilities to affiliated enterprises	4 520	. .	. . .	. . .	. . .	. . .	. . .	. . .	. . .	. . .
Reinvested earnings	4 525	. .	1,373	–348	–472	575	–514	479	–1,562	–1,854
Other capital	4 530	. .	–5,228	–4,239	–4,253	–6,229	–3,121	–6,303	–5,886	–3,907
Claims on affiliated enterprises	4 535	. .	–5,403	–5,005	–4,387	–6,793	–4,631	–5,123	–6,393	–4,936
Liabilities to affiliated enterprises	4 540	. .	175	766	134	564	1,509	–1,180	508	1,029
Direct investment in Canada	4 555	. .	**6,425**	**5,029**	**7,855**	**2,740**	**4,517**	**4,997**	**7,299**	**10,786**
Equity capital	4 560	. .	. . .	. . .	. . .	. . .	. . .	. . .	. . .	. . .
Claims on direct investors	4 565	. .	. . .	. . .	. . .	. . .	. . .	. . .	. . .	. . .
Liabilities to direct investors	4 570	. .	. . .	. . .	. . .	. . .	. . .	. . .	. . .	. . .
Reinvested earnings	4 575	. .	3,168	3,341	–406	–2,928	–2,922	1,132	1,825	4,881
Other capital	4 580	. .	3,257	1,689	8,260	5,668	7,439	3,865	5,474	5,906
Claims on direct investors	4 585	. .	–363	–171	–158	–57	–464	–593	–969	–1,668
Liabilities to direct investors	4 590	. .	3,620	1,860	8,418	5,725	7,904	4,458	6,444	7,574
B. PORTFOLIO INVESTMENT	4 600	. .	16,045	15,827	13,686	20,317	13,746	29,130	10,281	12,421
Assets	4 602	. .	**–2,443**	**–3,393**	**–2,239**	**–6,695**	**–6,933**	**–10,687**	**–6,501**	**–3,938**
Equity securities	4 610	. .	–2,373	–2,082	–2,177	–5,689	–6,133	–7,566	–6,878	–3,301
Monetary authorities	4 611	. .	. . .	. . .	. . .	. . .	. . .	. . .	. . .	. . .
General government	4 612	. .	. . .	. . .	. . .	. . .	. . .	. . .	. . .	. . .
Banks	4 613	. .	. . .	. . .	. . .	. . .	. . .	. . .	. . .	. . .
Other sectors	4 614	. .	–2,373	–2,082	–2,177	–5,689	–6,133	–7,566	–6,878	–3,301
Debt securities	4 619	. .	–71	–1,311	–62	–1,006	–800	–3,121	377	–637
Bonds and notes	4 620	. .	–71	–1,311	–62	–1,006	–800	–3,121	377	–637
Monetary authorities	4 621	. .	. . .	. . .	. . .	. . .	. . .	. . .	. . .	. . .
General government	4 622	. .	. . .	. . .	. . .	. . .	. . .	. . .	. . .	. . .
Banks	4 623	. .	. . .	. . .	. . .	. . .	. . .	. . .	. . .	. . .
Other sectors	4 624	. .	–71	–1,311	–62	–1,006	–800	–3,121	377	–637
Money market instruments	4 630	. .	. . .	. . .	. . .	. . .	. . .	. . .	. . .	. . .
Monetary authorities	4 631	. .	. . .	. . .	. . .	. . .	. . .	. . .	. . .	. . .
General government	4 632	. .	. . .	. . .	. . .	. . .	. . .	. . .	. . .	. . .
Banks	4 633	. .	. . .	. . .	. . .	. . .	. . .	. . .	. . .	. . .
Other sectors	4 634	. .	. . .	. . .	. . .	. . .	. . .	. . .	. . .	. . .
Financial derivatives	4 640	. .	. . .	. . .	. . .	. . .	. . .	. . .	. . .	. . .
Monetary authorities	4 641	. .	. . .	. . .	. . .	. . .	. . .	. . .	. . .	. . .
General government	4 642	. .	. . .	. . .	. . .	. . .	. . .	. . .	. . .	. . .
Banks	4 643	. .	. . .	. . .	. . .	. . .	. . .	. . .	. . .	. . .
Other sectors	4 644	. .	. . .	. . .	. . .	. . .	. . .	. . .	. . .	. . .
Liabilities	4 652	. .	**18,489**	**19,220**	**15,925**	**27,012**	**20,679**	**39,817**	**16,782**	**16,359**
Equity securities	4 660	. .	–1,934	3,287	–1,502	–856	830	9,335	4,719	–3,078
Banks	4 663	. .	. . .	. . .	. . .	. . .	. . .	. . .	. . .	. . .
Other sectors	4 664	. .	–1,934	3,287	–1,502	–856	830	9,335	4,719	–3,078
Debt securities	4 669	. .	20,423	15,933	17,427	27,868	19,849	30,482	12,063	19,437
Bonds and notes	4 670	. .	12,938	14,946	12,567	23,965	15,781	23,288	11,425	22,021
Monetary authorities	4 671	. .	. . .	. . .	. . .	. . .	. . .	. . .	. . .	. . .
General government	4 672	. .	9,628	8,859	9,303	17,696	12,717	18,774	8,858	15,152
Banks	4 673	. .	698	289	2,417	1,779	3,161	2,787	–367	703
Other sectors	4 674	. .	2,611	5,798	847	4,489	–97	1,728	2,934	6,165
Money market instruments	4 680	. .	7,485	987	4,860	3,903	4,068	7,194	638	–2,584
Monetary authorities	4 681	. .	. . .	. . .	. . .	. . .	. . .	. . .	. . .	. . .
General government	4 682	. .	5,439	676	4,114	2,827	2,790	8,597	1,199	–1,807
Banks	4 683	. .	170	184	871	–649	–586	393	–304	–87
Other sectors	4 684	. .	1,876	127	–125	1,724	1,864	–1,796	–256	–690
Financial derivatives	4 690	. .	. . .	. . .	. . .	. . .	. . .	. . .	. . .	. . .
Monetary authorities	4 691	. .	. . .	. . .	. . .	. . .	. . .	. . .	. . .	. . .
General government	4 692	. .	. . .	. . .	. . .	. . .	. . .	. . .	. . .	. . .
Banks	4 693	. .	. . .	. . .	. . .	. . .	. . .	. . .	. . .	. . .
Other sectors	4 694	. .	. . .	. . .	. . .	. . .	. . .	. . .	. . .	. . .

Table 2 (Concluded). STANDARD PRESENTATION, 1988–95
(Millions of U.S. dollars)

	Code	1988	1989	1990	1991	1992	1993	1994	1995
C. OTHER INVESTMENT	4 700	6,603	6,258	6,756	6,345	–180	821	3,482	–10,107
Assets	4 703	**4,445**	**–3,166**	**–5,371**	**6,136**	**679**	**7,527**	**–12,743**	**–9,328**
Trade credits	4 706	–267	153	233	–157	–171	78	–758	–7
General government: long-term	4 708	...	...	...	...	...	...	...	...
General government: short-term	4 709	...	...	...	...	...	...	...	...
Other sectors: long-term	4 711	...	...	...	...	...	...	...	...
Other sectors: short-term	4 712	...	...	...	...	...	...	...	...
Loans	4 714	–3,598	–1,486	389	–128	–809	–941	109	–3,378
Monetary authorities: long-term	4 717	...	...	...	...	...	...	...	...
Monetary authorities: short-term	4 718	...	...	...	...	...	...	...	...
General government: long-term	4 720	...	...	...	...	...	...	...	...
General government: short-term	4 721	...	...	...	...	...	...	...	...
Banks: long-term	4 723	...	...	...	...	...	...	...	...
Banks: short-term	4 724	...	...	...	...	...	...	...	...
Other sectors: long-term	4 726	...	...	...	...	...	...	...	...
Other sectors: short-term	4 727	...	...	...	...	...	...	...	...
Currency and deposits	4 730	6,658	–2,967	–4,159	5,206	28	8,206	–13,188	–10,196
Monetary authorities	4 731	...	...	...	...	...	...	...	...
General government	4 732	...	...	...	...	...	...	...	...
Banks	4 733	6,914	–2,528	–3,583	5,481	–1,549	7,231	–11,219	–6,738
Other sectors	4 734	–256	–440	–576	–275	1,577	976	–1,969	–3,458
Other assets	4 736	1,652	1,134	–1,835	1,214	1,631	184	1,095	4,253
Monetary authorities: long-term	4 738	...	...	...	...	...	...	...	...
Monetary authorities: short-term	4 739	...	...	...	...	...	...	...	...
General government: long-term	4 741	...	...	...	...	...	...	...	...
General government: short-term	4 742	...	...	...	...	...	...	...	...
Banks: long-term	4 744	...	...	...	...	...	...	...	...
Banks: short-term	4 745	...	...	...	...	...	...	...	...
Other sectors: long-term	4 747	...	...	...	...	...	...	...	...
Other sectors: short-term	4 748	...	...	...	...	...	...	...	...
Liabilities	4 753	**2,158**	**9,425**	**12,127**	**209**	**–859**	**–6,705**	**16,225**	**–780**
Trade credits	4 756	267	134	67	226	317	–233	637	473
General government: long-term	4 758	...	...	...	...	...	...	...	...
General government: short-term	4 759	...	...	...	...	...	...	...	...
Other sectors: long-term	4 761	...	...	...	...	...	...	...	...
Other sectors: short-term	4 762	...	...	...	...	...	...	...	...
Loans	4 764	2,516	7,020	4,524	1,587	1,869	–514	641	4,158
Use of Fund credit and loans from the Fund	4 766	...	...	...	...	...	...	...	...
Monetary authorities: other long-term	4 767	...	...	...	...	...	...	...	...
Monetary authorities: short-term	4 768	...	...	...	...	...	...	...	...
General government: long-term	4 770	...	...	...	...	...	...	...	...
General government: short-term	4 771	...	...	...	...	...	...	...	...
Banks: long-term	4 773	...	...	...	...	...	...	...	...
Banks: short-term	4 774	...	...	...	...	...	...	...	...
Other sectors: long-term	4 776	...	...	...	...	...	...	...	...
Other sectors: short-term	4 777	...	...	...	...	...	...	...	...
Currency and deposits	4 780	–1,549	1,994	6,612	–1,966	–3,255	–6,493	14,662	–4,906
Monetary authorities	4 781	...	...	...	...	...	...	...	...
General government	4 782	...	...	...	...	...	...	...	...
Banks	4 783	–1,457	1,913	6,604	–2,076	–3,202	–6,459	14,511	–4,850
Other sectors	4 784	–92	81	8	110	–53	–34	151	–56
Other liabilities	4 786	924	276	924	361	209	535	285	–504
Monetary authorities: long-term	4 788	...	...	...	...	...	...	...	...
Monetary authorities: short-term	4 789	...	...	...	...	...	...	...	...
General government: long-term	4 791	...	...	...	...	...	...	...	...
General government: short-term	4 792	...	...	...	...	...	...	...	...
Banks: long-term	4 794	...	...	...	...	...	...	...	...
Banks: short-term	4 795	...	...	...	...	...	...	...	...
Other sectors: long-term	4 797	...	...	...	...	...	...	...	...
Other sectors: short-term	4 798	...	...	...	...	...	...	...	...
D. RESERVE ASSETS	4 800	–7,558	–293	–625	2,486	5,807	492	1,227	–2,527
Monetary gold	4 810	593	401	514	638	1,022	1,397	834	182
Special drawing rights	4 820	–1,002	–39	–34	–46	488	–25	–19	1
Reserve position in the Fund	4 830	121	–32	52	–72	–446	63	86	–309
Foreign exchange	4 840	–7,270	–622	–1,158	1,966	4,743	–942	325	–2,402
Other claims	4 880	...	...	...	...	...	...	...	...
NET ERRORS AND OMISSIONS	4 998	**–558**	**501**	**–1,402**	**–2,649**	**1,304**	**–7,255**	**1,434**	**3,230**

Table 3. INTERNATIONAL INVESTMENT POSITION (End-period stocks), 1988–95
(Millions of U.S. dollars)

	Code		1988	1989	1990	1991	1992	1993	1994	1995
ASSETS	8 995	C.	186,184	206,229	226,770	240,435	233,965	242,225	271,494	302,179
Direct investment abroad	8 505	..	**63,860**	**72,787**	**78,826**	**88,060**	**84,533**	**86,752**	**93,666**	**104,268**
Equity capital and reinvested earnings	8 506	..	47,472	54,077	59,812	69,822	68,419	70,696	77,623	86,192
Claims on affiliated enterprises	8 507	..	...	...	...	...	...	...	...	...
Liabilities to affiliated enterprises	8 508	..	...	...	...	...	...	...	...	...
Other capital	8 530	..	16,388	18,710	19,014	18,238	16,114	16,056	16,043	18,076
Claims on affiliated enterprises	8 535	..	...	...	...	...	...	...	...	...
Liabilities to affiliated enterprises	8 540	..	...	...	...	...	...	...	...	...
Portfolio investment	8 602	..	**29,658**	**36,041**	**39,161**	**44,300**	**44,833**	**51,709**	**55,816**	**60,492**
Equity securities	8 610	..	23,231	27,419	30,402	34,547	34,657	38,491	42,759	46,711
Monetary authorities	8 611	..	...	...	...	...	...	...	...	...
General government	8 612	..	...	...	...	...	...	...	...	...
Banks	8 613	..	...	...	...	...	...	...	...	...
Other sectors	8 614	..	...	...	...	...	...	...	...	...
Debt securities	8 619	..	6,427	8,622	8,759	9,753	10,175	13,218	13,057	13,780
Bonds and notes	8 620	..	6,427	8,622	8,759	9,753	10,175	13,218	13,057	13,780
Monetary authorities	8 621	..	...	...	...	...	...	...	...	...
General government	8 622	..	...	...	...	...	...	...	...	...
Banks	8 623	..	...	...	...	...	...	...	...	...
Other sectors	8 624	..	...	...	...	...	...	...	...	...
Money market instruments	8 630	..	...	...	...	...	...	...	...	...
Monetary authorities	8 631	..	...	...	...	...	...	...	...	...
General government	8 632	..	...	...	...	...	...	...	...	...
Banks	8 633	..	...	...	...	...	...	...	...	...
Other sectors	8 634	..	...	...	...	...	...	...	...	...
Financial derivatives	8 640	..	...	...	...	...	...	...	...	...
Monetary authorities	8 641	..	...	...	...	...	...	...	...	...
General government	8 642	..	...	...	...	...	...	...	...	...
Banks	8 643	..	...	...	...	...	...	...	...	...
Other sectors	8 644	..	...	...	...	...	...	...	...	...
Other investment	8 703	..	**76,469**	**80,598**	**90,209**	**91,174**	**92,692**	**91,014**	**109,537**	**122,206**
Trade credits	8 706	..	...	...	...	...	...	...	...	...
General government: long-term	8 708	..	...	...	...	...	...	...	...	...
General government: short-term	8 709	..	...	...	...	...	...	...	...	...
Other sectors: long-term	8 711	..	...	...	...	...	...	...	...	...
Other sectors: short-term	8 712	..	...	...	...	...	...	...	...	...
Loans	8 714	..	15,680	16,993	18,251	18,601	19,256	19,864	20,389	20,866
Monetary authorities: long-term	8 717	..	...	...	...	...	...	...	...	...
Monetary authorities: short-term	8 718	..	...	...	...	...	...	...	...	...
General government: long-term	8 720	..	13,049	13,956	15,095	16,529	17,420	17,129	17,541	17,833
General government: short-term	8 721	..	...	...	...	...	...	...	...	...
Banks: long-term	8 723	..	...	...	...	...	...	...	...	...
Banks: short-term	8 724	..	...	...	...	...	...	...	...	...
Other sectors: long-term	8 726	..	2,632	3,038	3,156	2,072	1,835	2,735	2,848	3,033
Other sectors: short-term	8 727	..	...	...	...	...	...	...	...	...
Currency and deposits	8 730	..	59,477	61,295	65,648	59,615	58,829	53,282	68,266	79,602
Monetary authorities	8 731	..	...	...	...	...	...	...	...	...
General government	8 732	..	...	...	...	...	...	...	...	...
Banks	8 733	..	44,974	46,949	50,270	43,637	44,311	38,350	51,578	60,997
Other sectors	8 734	..	14,502	14,345	15,378	15,978	14,517	14,931	16,687	18,605
Other assets	8 736	..	1,312	2,310	6,310	12,959	14,608	17,868	20,883	21,738
Monetary authorities: long-term	8 738	..	...	...	...	...	...	...	...	...
Monetary authorities: short-term	8 739	..	...	...	...	...	...	...	...	...
General government: long-term	8 741	..	3,282	3,411	3,710	4,069	4,324	4,396	4,505	4,886
General government: short-term	8 742	..	...	...	...	...	...	...	...	...
Banks: long-term	8 744	..	...	...	...	...	...	...	...	...
Banks: short-term	8 745	..	...	...	...	...	...	...	...	...
Other sectors: long-term	8 747	..	–7,084	–6,519	–3,029	1,462	4,280	7,402	9,631	8,795
Other sectors: short-term	8 748	..	5,114	5,418	5,629	7,427	6,004	6,070	6,747	8,057
Reserve assets	8 800	..	**16,197**	**16,803**	**18,575**	**16,900**	**11,907**	**12,750**	**12,475**	**15,214**
Monetary gold	8 810	..	807	741	735	649	478	291	198	177
Special drawing rights	8 820	..	1,369	1,377	1,526	1,582	1,039	1,062	1,148	1,177
Reserve position in the Fund	8 830	..	505	528	517	592	1,011	948	919	1,243
Foreign exchange	8 840	..	13,516	14,157	15,797	14,078	9,380	10,449	10,210	12,616
Other claims	8 880	..	...	...	...	...	...	...	...	...

Table 3 (Continued). INTERNATIONAL INVESTMENT POSITION (End-period stocks), 1988–95
(Millions of U.S. dollars)

	Code	1988	1989	1990	1991	1992	1993	1994	1995
LIABILITIES	8 995 D.	360,376	400,390	439,631	470,031	465,103	486,071	512,039	550,697
Direct investment in Canada	8 555 . .	**95,984**	**106,221**	**113,016**	**117,549**	**109,114**	**107,492**	**108,914**	**123,116**
Equity capital and reinvested earnings	8 556 . .	83,593	92,357	97,302	100,198	89,512	87,665	86,868	103,329
Claims on direct investors	8 557 . .	. . .	. . .	. . .	. . .	. . .	. . .	. . .	. . .
Liabilities to direct investors	8 558 . .	. . .	. . .	. . .	. . .	. . .	. . .	. . .	. . .
Other capital	8 580 . .	12,391	13,864	15,713	17,351	19,602	19,827	22,045	19,787
Claims on direct investors	8 585 . .	. . .	. . .	. . .	. . .	. . .	. . .	. . .	. . .
Liabilities to direct investors	8 590 . .	. . .	. . .	. . .	. . .	. . .	. . .	. . .	. . .
Portfolio investment	8 652 . .	**156,598**	**176,153**	**196,627**	**221,880**	**228,539**	**260,431**	**273,098**	**299,930**
Equity securities	8 660 . .	15,153	17,760	17,752	15,222	14,123	17,853	22,161	23,494
Banks	8 663 . .	. . .	. . .	. . .	. . .	. . .	. . .	. . .	. . .
Other sectors	8 664 . .	. . .	. . .	. . .	. . .	. . .	. . .	. . .	. . .
Debt securities	8 669 . .	141,445	158,393	178,874	206,658	214,416	242,578	250,937	276,436
Bonds and notes	8 670 . .	125,165	140,591	156,120	180,235	186,012	207,909	217,055	241,604
Monetary authorities	8 671 . .	. . .	. . .	. . .	. . .	. . .	. . .	. . .	. . .
General government	8 672 . .	. . .	. . .	. . .	. . .	. . .	. . .	. . .	. . .
Banks	8 673 . .	. . .	. . .	. . .	. . .	. . .	. . .	. . .	. . .
Other sectors	8 674 . .	. . .	. . .	. . .	. . .	. . .	. . .	. . .	. . .
Money market instruments	8 680 . .	16,280	17,802	22,754	26,424	28,404	34,669	33,882	34,832
Monetary authorities	8 681 . .	. . .	. . .	. . .	. . .	. . .	. . .	. . .	. . .
General government	8 682 . .	11,810	12,949	17,049	19,703	20,752	28,474	28,348	28,940
Banks	8 683 . .	. . .	. . .	. . .	. . .	. . .	. . .	. . .	. . .
Other sectors	8 684 . .	4,470	4,853	5,705	6,720	7,652	6,195	5,533	5,892
Financial derivatives	8 690 . .	. . .	. . .	. . .	. . .	. . .	. . .	. . .	. . .
Monetary authorities	8 691 . .	. . .	. . .	. . .	. . .	. . .	. . .	. . .	. . .
General government	8 692 . .	. . .	. . .	. . .	. . .	. . .	. . .	. . .	. . .
Banks	8 692 . .	. . .	. . .	. . .	. . .	. . .	. . .	. . .	. . .
Other sectors	8 694 . .	. . .	. . .	. . .	. . .	. . .	. . .	. . .	. . .
Other investment	8 753 . .	**107,795**	**118,016**	**129,989**	**130,602**	**127,449**	**118,147**	**130,028**	**127,650**
Trade credits	8 756 . .	. . .	. . .	. . .	. . .	. . .	. . .	. . .	. . .
General government: long-term	8 758 . .	. . .	. . .	. . .	. . .	. . .	. . .	. . .	. . .
General government: short-term	8 759 . .	. . .	. . .	. . .	. . .	. . .	. . .	. . .	. . .
Other sectors: long-term	8 761 . .	. . .	. . .	. . .	. . .	. . .	. . .	. . .	. . .
Other sectors: short-term	8 762 . .	. . .	. . .	. . .	. . .	. . .	. . .	. . .	. . .
Loans	8 764 . .	. . .	. . .	. . .	. . .	. . .	. . .	. . .	. . .
Use of Fund credit and loans from the Fund	8 766 . .	. . .	. . .	. . .	. . .	. . .	. . .	. . .	. . .
Monetary authorities: other long-term	8 767 . .	. . .	. . .	. . .	. . .	. . .	. . .	. . .	. . .
Monetary authorities: short-term	8 768 . .	. . .	. . .	. . .	. . .	. . .	. . .	. . .	. . .
General government: long-term	8 770 . .	. . .	. . .	. . .	. . .	. . .	. . .	. . .	. . .
General government: short-term	8 771 . .	. . .	. . .	. . .	. . .	. . .	. . .	. . .	. . .
Banks: long-term	8 773 . .	. . .	. . .	. . .	. . .	. . .	. . .	. . .	. . .
Banks: short-term	8 774 . .	. . .	. . .	. . .	. . .	. . .	. . .	. . .	. . .
Other sectors: long-term	8 776 . .	. . .	. . .	. . .	. . .	. . .	. . .	. . .	. . .
Other sectors: short-term	8 777 . .	. . .	. . .	. . .	. . .	. . .	. . .	. . .	. . .
Currency and deposits	8 780 . .	71,051	73,444	80,881	78,317	75,092	68,050	82,405	77,892
Monetary authorities	8 781 . .	. . .	. . .	. . .	. . .	. . .	. . .	. . .	. . .
General government	8 782 . .	. . .	. . .	. . .	. . .	. . .	. . .	. . .	. . .
Banks	8 783 . .	71,051	73,444	80,881	78,317	75,092	68,050	82,405	77,892
Other sectors	8 784 . .	. . .	. . .	. . .	. . .	. . .	. . .	. . .	. . .
Other liabilities	8 786 . .	36,744	44,572	49,108	52,285	52,357	50,097	47,623	49,758
Monetary authorities: long-term	8 788 . .	. . .	. . .	. . .	. . .	. . .	. . .	. . .	. . .
Monetary authorities: short-term	8 789 . .	. . .	. . .	. . .	. . .	. . .	. . .	. . .	. . .
General government: long-term	8 791 . .	4,851	3,564	3,434	3,486	3,112	3,094	4,064	3,810
General government: short-term	8 792 . .	1,731	1,857	1,831	1,883	1,778	1,763	1,655	1,426
Banks: long-term	8 794 . .	. . .	. . .	. . .	. . .	. . .	. . .	. . .	. . .
Banks: short-term	8 795 . .	. . .	. . .	. . .	. . .	. . .	. . .	. . .	. . .
Other sectors: long-term	8 797 . .	18,384	26,873	29,294	31,680	30,950	29,369	26,782	26,539
Other sectors: short-term	8 798 . .	11,777	12,278	14,549	15,237	16,516	15,872	15,121	17,983
NET INTERNATIONAL INVESTMENT POSITION	8 995 . .	**–174,192**	**–194,162**	**–212,861**	**–229,597**	**–231,137**	**–243,846**	**–240,546**	**–248,518**
Conversion rates: Canadian dollars per U.S. dollar (end of period)	0 102 . .	**1.1927**	**1.1578**	**1.1603**	**1.1556**	**1.2711**	**1.3240**	**1.4028**	**1.3652**

Cape Verde
624

Table 1. ANALYTIC PRESENTATION, 1988–95
(Millions of U.S. dollars)

	Code	1988	1989	1990	1991	1992	1993	1994	1995
A. Current Account[1]	4 993 Y.	**.45**	**-4.58**	**-11.94**	**-7.93**	**-3.55**	**-10.57**	**-29.18**	**-38.77**
Goods: exports f.o.b	2 100 ..	3.28	6.74	5.64	4.14	4.43	3.87	4.86	8.41
Goods: imports f.o.b	3 100 ..	-101.78	-106.86	-119.46	-132.15	-173.29	-151.50	-195.08	-232.25
Balance on Goods	4 100 ..	*-98.50*	*-100.12*	*-113.82*	*-128.00*	*-168.86*	*-147.63*	*-190.22*	*-223.84*
Services: credit	2 200 ..	39.84	50.44	55.20	48.93	53.62	45.15	56.31	74.90
Services: debit	3 200 ..	-19.68	-28.55	-32.78	-19.11	-26.79	-32.49	-35.45	-55.72
Balance on Goods and Services	4 991 ..	*-78.34*	*-78.23*	*-91.40*	*-98.18*	*-142.03*	*-134.98*	*-169.35*	*-204.66*
Income: credit	2 300 ..	5.14	6.84	6.06	5.35	5.51	4.24	3.90	3.45
Income: debit	3 300 ..	-4.54	-3.99	-4.15	-4.13	-4.30	-4.05	-4.47	-6.15
Balance on Goods, Services, and Income	4 992 ..	*-77.74*	*-75.38*	*-89.50*	*-96.97*	*-140.82*	*-134.80*	*-169.92*	*-207.36*
Current transfers: credit	2 379 Y.	80.17	72.88	79.48	94.74	142.98	129.43	145.62	176.84
Current transfers: debit	3 379 ..	-1.98	-2.08	-1.92	-5.70	-5.70	-5.20	-4.88	-8.26
B. Capital Account[1]	4 994 Y.	**...**	**...**	**...**	**...**	**...**	**...**	**...**	**...**
Capital account: credit	2 994 Y.	...	...	...	...	...	...	...	...
Capital account: debit	3 994 ..	...	...	...	...	...	...	...	...
Total, Groups A Plus B	4 010 ..	*.45*	*-4.58*	*-11.94*	*-7.93*	*-3.55*	*-10.57*	*-29.18*	*-38.77*
C. Financial Account[1]	4 995 X.	**-1.74**	**-1.07**	**5.05**	**2.67**	**6.07**	**12.83**	**31.27**	**24.30**
Direct investment abroad	4 505 ..	...	...	...	...	...	...	...	...
Direct investment in Cape Verde	4 555 Y.	.41	-.59	-.06	1.20	-.75	2.98	2.39	9.73
Portfolio investment assets	4 602 ..	...	...	...	...	...	...	...	...
Equity securities	4 610 ..	...	...	...	...	...	...	...	...
Debt securities	4 619 ..	...	...	...	...	...	...	...	...
Portfolio investment liabilities	4 652 Y.	...	...	...	...	...	...	...	...
Equity securities	4 660 Y.	...	...	...	...	...	...	...	...
Debt securities	4 669 Y.	...	...	...	...	...	...	...	...
Other investment assets	4 703 ..	...	...	...	...	...	...	...	...
Monetary authorities	4 703 .A	...	...	...	...	...	...	...	...
General government	4 703 .B	...	...	...	...	...	...	...	...
Banks	4 703 .C	...	...	...	...	...	...	...	...
Other sectors	4 703 .D	...	...	...	...	...	...	...	...
Other investment liabilities	4 753 X.	-2.16	-.48	5.12	1.47	6.82	9.85	28.88	14.56
Monetary authorities	4 753 XA	.11	-.41	-.21	1.27	.68	...	...	...
General government	4 753 YB	1.36	2.93	1.68	2.08	7.98	11.77	15.24	10.02
Banks	4 753 YC	...	...	...	...	...	...	...	...
Other sectors	4 753 YD	-3.63	-3.00	3.65	-1.88	-1.84	-1.93	13.64	4.55
Total, Groups A Through C	4 020 ..	*-1.29*	*-5.65*	*-6.88*	*-5.27*	*2.52*	*2.25*	*2.09*	*-14.48*
D. Net Errors and Omissions	4 998 ..	**-.65**	**-1.22**	**5.15**	**-7.28**	**5.49**	**3.44**	**-8.03**	**.71**
Total, Groups A Through D	4 030 ..	*-1.94*	*-6.86*	*-1.73*	*-12.55*	*8.01*	*5.70*	*-5.94*	*-13.77*
E. Reserves and Related Items	4 040 ..	**1.94**	**6.86**	**1.73**	**12.55**	**-8.01**	**-5.70**	**5.94**	**13.77**
Reserve assets	4 800 ..	-.61	6.60	-2.23	11.87	-13.30	-7.91	2.92	9.52
Use of Fund credit and loans	4 766 ..	...	...	...	...	...	...	...	...
Liabilities constituting foreign authorities' reserves	4 900 ..	...	...	...	...	...	...	...	...
Exceptional financing	4 920 ..	2.55	.27	3.96	.68	5.29	2.21	3.02	4.25
Conversion rates: Cape Verde escudos per U.S. dollar	0 101 ..	**72.068**	**77.978**	**70.031**	**71.408**	**68.018**	**80.427**	**81.891**	**76.853**

[1] Excludes components that have been classified in the categories of Group E.

Table 2. STANDARD PRESENTATION, 1988–95
(Millions of U.S. dollars)

	Code	1988	1989	1990	1991	1992	1993	1994	1995
CURRENT ACCOUNT	4 993 . .	**.45**	**–4.58**	**–11.94**	**–7.93**	**–3.55**	**–10.57**	**–29.18**	**–38.77**
A. GOODS	4 100 . .	–98.50	–100.12	–113.82	–128.00	–168.86	–147.63	–190.22	–223.84
Credit	2 100 . .	**3.28**	**6.74**	**5.64**	**4.14**	**4.43**	**3.87**	**4.86**	**8.41**
General merchandise: exports f.o.b.	2 110 . .	3.28	6.74	5.64	4.14	4.43	3.87	4.86	8.41
Goods for processing: exports f.o.b.	2 150 . .	. . .	. . .	. . .	. . .	. . .	. . .	. . .	. . .
Repairs on goods	2 160 . .	. . .	. . .	. . .	. . .	. . .	. . .	. . .	. . .
Goods procured in ports by carriers	2 170 . .	. . .	. . .	. . .	. . .	. . .	. . .	. . .	. . .
Nonmonetary gold	2 180 . .	. . .	. . .	. . .	. . .	. . .	. . .	. . .	. . .
Debit	3 100 . .	**–101.78**	**–106.86**	**–119.46**	**–132.15**	**–173.29**	**–151.50**	**–195.08**	**–232.25**
General merchandise: imports f.o.b.	3 110 . .	–101.78	–106.86	–119.46	–132.15	–173.29	–151.50	–195.08	–232.25
Goods for processing: imports f.o.b.	3 150 . .	. . .	. . .	. . .	. . .	. . .	. . .	. . .	. . .
Repairs on goods	3 160 . .	. . .	. . .	. . .	. . .	. . .	. . .	. . .	. . .
Goods procured in ports by carriers	3 170 . .	. . .	. . .	. . .	. . .	. . .	. . .	. . .	. . .
Nonmonetary gold	3 180 . .	. . .	. . .	. . .	. . .	. . .	. . .	. . .	. . .
B. SERVICES	4 200 . .	20.16	21.89	22.42	29.82	26.83	12.65	20.86	19.18
Total credit	2 200 . .	*39.84*	*50.44*	*55.20*	*48.93*	*53.62*	*45.15*	*56.31*	*74.90*
Total debit	3 200 . .	*–19.68*	*–28.55*	*–32.78*	*–19.11*	*–26.79*	*–32.49*	*–35.45*	*–55.72*
Transportation services, credit	2 205 . .	**27.76**	**31.14**	**31.28**	**26.61**	**31.37**	**22.46**	**31.58**	**42.18**
Passenger	2 205 BA	*1.21*	*3.28*	*4.09*	*2.38*	*3.23*	*4.94*	*11.42*	*18.73*
Freight	2 205 BB	*.20*	*.08*	*.10*	*.05*	*.09*	*.28*	*.02*	*.01*
Other	2 205 BC	*26.35*	*27.78*	*27.09*	*24.18*	*28.05*	*17.23*	*20.14*	*23.44*
Sea transport, passenger	2 207 . .	. . .	. . .	. . .	. . .	. . .	. . .	. . .	. . .
Sea transport, freight	2 208 . .	. . .	. . .	. . .	. . .	. . .	. . .	. . .	. . .
Sea transport, other	2 209 . .	. . .	. . .	. . .	. . .	. . .	. . .	. . .	. . .
Air transport, passenger	2 211 . .	. . .	. . .	. . .	. . .	. . .	. . .	. . .	. . .
Air transport, freight	2 212 . .	. . .	. . .	. . .	. . .	. . .	. . .	. . .	. . .
Air transport, other	2 213 . .	. . .	. . .	. . .	. . .	. . .	. . .	. . .	. . .
Other transport, passenger	2 215 . .	. . .	. . .	. . .	. . .	. . .	. . .	. . .	. . .
Other transport, freight	2 216 . .	. . .	. . .	. . .	. . .	. . .	. . .	. . .	. . .
Other transport, other	2 217 . .	. . .	. . .	. . .	. . .	. . .	. . .	. . .	. . .
Transportation services, debit	3 205 . .	**–5.73**	**–12.04**	**–13.88**	**–6.36**	**–9.94**	**–7.97**	**–12.19**	**–21.39**
Passenger	3 205 BA	*–1.26*	*–3.71*	*–3.27*	*–2.73*	*–3.98*	*–3.15*	*–2.82*	*–3.56*
Freight	3 205 BB	*–1.30*	*–1.73*	*–2.18*	*–1.46*	*–1.53*	*–2.57*	*–4.23*	*–6.22*
Other	3 205 BC	*–3.17*	*–6.60*	*–8.42*	*–2.17*	*–4.44*	*–2.25*	*–5.14*	*–11.61*
Sea transport, passenger	3 207 . .	. . .	. . .	. . .	. . .	. . .	. . .	. . .	. . .
Sea transport, freight	3 208 . .	. . .	. . .	. . .	. . .	. . .	. . .	. . .	. . .
Sea transport, other	3 209 . .	. . .	. . .	. . .	. . .	. . .	. . .	. . .	. . .
Air transport, passenger	3 211 . .	. . .	. . .	. . .	. . .	. . .	. . .	. . .	. . .
Air transport, freight	3 212 . .	. . .	. . .	. . .	. . .	. . .	. . .	. . .	. . .
Air transport, other	3 213 . .	. . .	. . .	. . .	. . .	. . .	. . .	. . .	. . .
Other transport, passenger	3 215 . .	. . .	. . .	. . .	. . .	. . .	. . .	. . .	. . .
Other transport, freight	3 216 . .	. . .	. . .	. . .	. . .	. . .	. . .	. . .	. . .
Other transport, other	3 217 . .	. . .	. . .	. . .	. . .	. . .	. . .	. . .	. . .
Travel, credit	2 236 . .	**3.28**	**3.45**	**5.92**	**8.08**	**7.10**	**8.63**	**8.76**	**9.68**
Business travel	2 237 . .	. . .	. . .	. . .	. . .	. . .	. . .	. . .	. . .
Personal travel	2 240 . .	. . .	. . .	. . .	. . .	. . .	. . .	. . .	. . .
Travel, debit	3 236 . .	**–3.32**	**–3.28**	**–5.48**	**–3.13**	**–5.92**	**–7.28**	**–9.08**	**–12.29**
Business travel	3 237 . .	. . .	. . .	. . .	. . .	. . .	. . .	. . .	. . .
Personal travel	3 240 . .	. . .	. . .	. . .	. . .	. . .	. . .	. . .	. . .
Other services, credit	2 200 BA	**8.80**	**15.85**	**18.01**	**14.24**	**15.15**	**14.06**	**15.97**	**23.05**
Communications	2 245 . .	. . .	. . .	. . .	. . .	. . .	3.72	7.09	9.84
Construction	2 249 . .	. . .	. . .	. . .	. . .	. . .	1.24	.07	2.30
Insurance	2 253 . .	.02	.01	.01	.01	.01	1.50	.13	.53
Financial	2 260 . .	. . .	. . .	. . .	. . .	. . .	. . .	. . .	. . .
Computer and information	2 262 . .	. . .	. . .	. . .	. . .	. . .	. . .	. . .	. . .
Royalties and licence fees	2 266 . .	. . .	. . .	. . .	.03	.16	.08	.09	.03
Other business services	2 268 . .	3.48	5.22	8.65	6.39	5.95	1.53	.96	.91
Personal, cultural, and recreational	2 287 . .	. . .	. . .	. . .	. . .	. . .	. . .	. . .	. . .
Government, n.i.e.	2 291 . .	5.30	10.62	9.35	7.81	9.03	6.00	7.63	9.43
Other services, debit	3 200 BA	**–10.63**	**–13.22**	**–13.42**	**–9.63**	**–10.93**	**–17.25**	**–14.17**	**–22.04**
Communications	3 245 . .	. . .	. . .	. . .	. . .	. . .	–.43	–1.72	–3.91
Construction	3 249 . .	. . .	. . .	. . .	. . .	. . .	–2.27	–.14	–.23
Insurance	3 253 . .	–.14	–.19	–.24	–.16	–.17	. . .	. . .	–.70
Financial	3 260 . .	. . .	. . .	. . .	. . .	. . .	. . .	. . .	. . .
Computer and information	3 262 . .	. . .	. . .	. . .	. . .	. . .	. . .	. . .	. . .
Royalties and licence fees	3 266 . .	–.12	–.05	–.13	–.04	–.10	–.21	–.06	–.09
Other business services	3 268 . .	–4.56	–7.03	–6.07	–4.09	–5.45	–9.82	–7.49	–11.12
Personal, cultural, and recreational	3 287 . .	. . .	. . .	. . .	. . .	. . .	. . .	. . .	. . .
Government, n.i.e.	3 291 . .	–5.81	–5.95	–6.97	–5.33	–5.20	–4.51	–4.76	–5.98

Table 2 (Continued). STANDARD PRESENTATION, 1988–95
(Millions of U.S. dollars)

	Code		1988	1989	1990	1991	1992	1993	1994	1995
C. INCOME	4 300	..	.60	2.85	1.90	1.21	1.21	.18	–.57	–2.70
Total credit	2 300	..	*5.14*	*6.84*	*6.06*	*5.35*	*5.51*	*4.24*	*3.90*	*3.45*
Total debit	3 300	..	*–4.54*	*–3.99*	*–4.15*	*–4.13*	*–4.30*	*–4.05*	*–4.47*	*–6.15*
Compensation of employees, credit	2 310	..	**2.01**	**3.44**	**2.97**	**2.51**	**2.05**	**2.67**	**2.35**	**1.92**
Compensation of employees, debit	3 310	..	**–1.03**	**–.77**	**–.93**	**–.97**	**–.63**	**–.56**	**–.42**	**–.80**
Investment income, credit	2 320	..	**3.13**	**3.40**	**3.09**	**2.84**	**3.45**	**1.56**	**1.55**	**1.54**
Direct investment income	2 330	..	...	...	...	...	...	...	...	...
Dividends and distributed branch profits	2 332	..	...	...	...	...	...	...	...	...
Reinvested earnings and undistributed branch profits	2 333	..	...	...	...	...	...	...	...	...
Income on debt (interest)	2 334	..	...	...	...	...	...	...	...	...
Portfolio investment income	2 339	..	...	...	...	...	...	...	...	...
Income on equity	2 340	..	...	...	...	...	...	...	...	...
Income on bonds and notes	2 350	..	...	...	...	...	...	...	...	...
Income on money market instruments and financial derivatives	2 360	..	...	...	...	...	...	...	...	...
Other investment income	2 370	..	3.13	3.40	3.09	2.84	3.45	1.56	1.55	1.54
Investment income, debit	3 320	..	**–3.51**	**–3.22**	**–3.22**	**–3.17**	**–3.67**	**–3.49**	**–4.05**	**–5.35**
Direct investment income	3 330	..	...	...	...	...	...	...	...	...
Dividends and distributed branch profits	3 332	..	...	...	...	...	...	...	...	...
Reinvested earnings and undistributed branch profits	3 333	..	...	...	...	...	...	...	...	...
Income on debt (interest)	3 334	..	...	...	...	...	...	...	...	...
Portfolio investment income	3 339	..	...	...	...	...	...	...	...	...
Income on equity	3 340	..	...	...	...	...	...	...	...	...
Income on bonds and notes	3 350	..	...	...	...	...	...	...	...	...
Income on money market instruments and financial derivatives	3 360	..	...	...	...	...	...	...	...	...
Other investment income	3 370	..	–3.51	–3.22	–3.22	–3.17	–3.67	–3.49	–4.05	–5.35
D. CURRENT TRANSFERS	4 379	..	78.19	70.80	77.56	89.04	137.27	124.22	140.74	168.58
Credit	2 379	..	**80.17**	**72.88**	**79.48**	**94.74**	**142.98**	**129.43**	**145.62**	**176.84**
General government	2 380	..	39.44	28.62	26.31	34.87	69.01	55.61	62.52	72.90
Other sectors	2 390	..	40.73	44.26	53.17	59.87	73.97	73.82	83.10	103.94
Workers' remittances	2 391	..	35.65	40.24	46.37	52.98	61.35	63.31	76.74	95.88
Other current transfers	2 392	..	5.08	4.01	6.80	6.89	12.61	10.50	6.36	8.06
Debit	3 379	..	**–1.98**	**–2.08**	**–1.92**	**–5.70**	**–5.70**	**–5.20**	**–4.88**	**–8.26**
General government	3 380	..	–.73	–1.05	–.80	–3.61	–1.60	–2.10	–2.55	–3.89
Other sectors	3 390	..	–1.25	–1.03	–1.12	–2.09	–4.10	–3.10	–2.33	–4.36
Workers' remittances	3 391	..	–.12	–.08	–.17	–.22	–.96	–.70	–.46	–.79
Other current transfers	3 392	..	–1.13	–.95	–.95	–1.86	–3.15	–2.41	–1.87	–3.57
CAPITAL AND FINANCIAL ACCOUNT	4 996	..	**.20**	**5.79**	**6.78**	**15.21**	**–1.94**	**7.13**	**37.21**	**38.06**
CAPITAL ACCOUNT	4 994	..	...	...	...	...	...	...	...	...
Total credit	2 994	..	...	...	...	...	...	...	...	...
Total debit	3 994	..	...	...	...	...	...	...	...	...
Capital transfers, credit	2 400	..	...	...	...	...	...	...	...	...
General government	2 401	..	...	...	...	...	...	...	...	...
Debt forgiveness	2 402	..	...	...	...	...	...	...	...	...
Other capital transfers	2 410	..	...	...	...	...	...	...	...	...
Other sectors	2 430	..	...	...	...	...	...	...	...	...
Migrants' transfers	2 431	..	...	...	...	...	...	...	...	...
Debt forgiveness	2 432	..	...	...	...	...	...	...	...	...
Other capital transfers	2 440	..	...	...	...	...	...	...	...	...
Capital transfers, debit	3 400	..	...	...	...	...	...	...	...	...
General government	3 401	..	...	...	...	...	...	...	...	...
Debt forgiveness	3 402	..	...	...	...	...	...	...	...	...
Other capital transfers	3 410	..	...	...	...	...	...	...	...	...
Other sectors	3 430	..	...	...	...	...	...	...	...	...
Migrants' transfers	3 431	..	...	...	...	...	...	...	...	...
Debt forgiveness	3 432	..	...	...	...	...	...	...	...	...
Other capital transfers	3 440	..	...	...	...	...	...	...	...	...
Nonproduced nonfinancial assets, credit	2 480	..	...	...	...	...	...	...	...	...
Nonproduced nonfinancial assets, debit	3 480	..	...	...	...	...	...	...	...	...

Table 2 (Continued). STANDARD PRESENTATION, 1988–95
(Millions of U.S. dollars)

	Code	1988	1989	1990	1991	1992	1993	1994	1995
FINANCIAL ACCOUNT	4 995 . .	**.20**	**5.79**	**6.78**	**15.21**	**-1.94**	**7.13**	**37.21**	**38.06**
A. DIRECT INVESTMENT	4 500 . .	.41	-.59	-.06	1.20	-.75	2.98	2.39	9.73
Direct investment abroad	4 505 . .	...	...	...	...	...	...	...	...
Equity capital	4 510 . .	...	...	...	...	...	...	...	...
Claims on affiliated enterprises	4 515 . .	...	...	...	...	...	...	...	...
Liabilities to affiliated enterprises	4 520 . .	...	...	...	...	...	...	...	...
Reinvested earnings	4 525 . .	...	...	...	...	...	...	...	...
Other capital	4 530 . .	...	...	...	...	...	...	...	...
Claims on affiliated enterprises	4 535 . .	...	...	...	...	...	...	...	...
Liabilities to affiliated enterprises	4 540 . .	...	...	...	...	...	...	...	...
Direct investment in Cape Verde	4 555 . .	**.41**	**-.59**	**-.06**	**1.20**	**-.75**	**2.98**	**2.39**	**9.73**
Equity capital	4 560 . .	.41	-.59	-.06	1.20	-.75	2.98	2.39	9.73
Claims on direct investors	4 565 . .	...	...	...	...	...	...	...	...
Liabilities to direct investors	4 570 . .	...	...	...	...	...	...	...	...
Reinvested earnings	4 575 . .	...	...	...	...	...	...	...	...
Other capital	4 580 . .	...	...	...	...	...	...	...	...
Claims on direct investors	4 585 . .	...	...	...	...	...	...	...	...
Liabilities to direct investors	4 590 . .	...	...	...	...	...	...	...	...
B. PORTFOLIO INVESTMENT	4 600 . .	...	...	...	...	...	...	...	...
Assets	4 602 . .	...	...	...	...	...	...	...	...
Equity securities	4 610 . .	...	...	...	...	...	...	...	...
Monetary authorities	4 611 . .	...	...	...	...	...	...	...	...
General government	4 612 . .	...	...	...	...	...	...	...	...
Banks	4 613 . .	...	...	...	...	...	...	...	...
Other sectors	4 614 . .	...	...	...	...	...	...	...	...
Debt securities	4 619 . .	...	...	...	...	...	...	...	...
Bonds and notes	4 620 . .	...	...	...	...	...	...	...	...
Monetary authorities	4 621 . .	...	...	...	...	...	...	...	...
General government	4 622 . .	...	...	...	...	...	...	...	...
Banks	4 623 . .	...	...	...	...	...	...	...	...
Other sectors	4 624 . .	...	...	...	...	...	...	...	...
Money market instruments	4 630 . .	...	...	...	...	...	...	...	...
Monetary authorities	4 631 . .	...	...	...	...	...	...	...	...
General government	4 632 . .	...	...	...	...	...	...	...	...
Banks	4 633 . .	...	...	...	...	...	...	...	...
Other sectors	4 634 . .	...	...	...	...	...	...	...	...
Financial derivatives	4 640 . .	...	...	...	...	...	...	...	...
Monetary authorities	4 641 . .	...	...	...	...	...	...	...	...
General government	4 642 . .	...	...	...	...	...	...	...	...
Banks	4 643 . .	...	...	...	...	...	...	...	...
Other sectors	4 644 . .	...	...	...	...	...	...	...	...
Liabilities	4 652 . .	...	...	...	...	...	...	...	...
Equity securities	4 660 . .	...	...	...	...	...	...	...	...
Banks	4 663 . .	...	...	...	...	...	...	...	...
Other sectors	4 664 . .	...	...	...	...	...	...	...	...
Debt securities	4 669 . .	...	...	...	...	...	...	...	...
Bonds and notes	4 670 . .	...	...	...	...	...	...	...	...
Monetary authorities	4 671 . .	...	...	...	...	...	...	...	...
General government	4 672 . .	...	...	...	...	...	...	...	...
Banks	4 673 . .	...	...	...	...	...	...	...	...
Other sectors	4 674 . .	...	...	...	...	...	...	...	...
Money market instruments	4 680 . .	...	...	...	...	...	...	...	...
Monetary authorities	4 681 . .	...	...	...	...	...	...	...	...
General government	4 682 . .	...	...	...	...	...	...	...	...
Banks	4 683 . .	...	...	...	...	...	...	...	...
Other sectors	4 684 . .	...	...	...	...	...	...	...	...
Financial derivatives	4 690 . .	...	...	...	...	...	...	...	...
Monetary authorities	4 691 . .	...	...	...	...	...	...	...	...
General government	4 692 . .	...	...	...	...	...	...	...	...
Banks	4 693 . .	...	...	...	...	...	...	...	...
Other sectors	4 694 . .	...	...	...	...	...	...	...	...

Table 2 (Concluded). STANDARD PRESENTATION, 1988–95

(Millions of U.S. dollars)

	Code	1988	1989	1990	1991	1992	1993	1994	1995
C. OTHER INVESTMENT	4 700	.39	–.21	9.07	2.15	12.11	12.06	31.90	18.81
Assets	4 703	...	...	...	...	...	...	...	...
Trade credits	4 706	...	...	...	...	...	...	...	...
General government: long-term	4 708	...	...	...	...	...	...	...	...
General government: short-term	4 709	...	...	...	...	...	...	...	...
Other sectors: long-term	4 711	...	...	...	...	...	...	...	...
Other sectors: short-term	4 712	...	...	...	...	...	...	...	...
Loans	4 714	...	...	...	...	...	...	...	...
Monetary authorities: long-term	4 717	...	...	...	...	...	...	...	...
Monetary authorities: short-term	4 718	...	...	...	...	...	...	...	...
General government: long-term	4 720	...	...	...	...	...	...	...	...
General government: short-term	4 721	...	...	...	...	...	...	...	...
Banks: long-term	4 723	...	...	...	...	...	...	...	...
Banks: short-term	4 724	...	...	...	...	...	...	...	...
Other sectors: long-term	4 726	...	...	...	...	...	...	...	...
Other sectors: short-term	4 727	...	...	...	...	...	...	...	...
Currency and deposits	4 730	...	...	...	...	...	...	...	...
Monetary authorities	4 731	...	...	...	...	...	...	...	...
General government	4 732	...	...	...	...	...	...	...	...
Banks	4 733	...	...	...	...	...	...	...	...
Other sectors	4 734	...	...	...	...	...	...	...	...
Other assets	4 736	...	...	...	...	...	...	...	...
Monetary authorities: long-term	4 738	...	...	...	...	...	...	...	...
Monetary authorities: short-term	4 739	...	...	...	...	...	...	...	...
General government: long-term	4 741	...	...	...	...	...	...	...	...
General government: short-term	4 742	...	...	...	...	...	...	...	...
Banks: long-term	4 744	...	...	...	...	...	...	...	...
Banks: short-term	4 745	...	...	...	...	...	...	...	...
Other sectors: long-term	4 747	...	...	...	...	...	...	...	...
Other sectors: short-term	4 748	...	...	...	...	...	...	...	...
Liabilities	4 753	**.39**	**–.21**	**9.07**	**2.15**	**12.11**	**12.06**	**31.90**	**18.81**
Trade credits	4 756	...	...	...	...	...	...	...	...
General government: long-term	4 758	...	...	...	...	...	...	...	...
General government: short-term	4 759	...	...	...	...	...	...	...	...
Other sectors: long-term	4 761	...	...	...	...	...	...	...	...
Other sectors: short-term	4 762	...	...	...	...	...	...	...	...
Loans	4 764	–2.26	1.71	5.33	.20	6.14	9.85	28.88	14.56
Use of Fund credit and loans from the Fund	4 766	...	...	...	...	...	...	...	...
Monetary authorities: other long-term	4 767	...	...	...	...	...	...	...	...
Monetary authorities: short-term	4 768	...	...	...	...	...	...	...	...
General government: long-term	4 770	1.36	4.71	1.68	2.08	7.98	11.77	15.24	10.02
General government: short-term	4 771	...	...	...	...	...	...	...	...
Banks: long-term	4 773	...	...	...	...	...	...	...	...
Banks: short-term	4 774	...	...	...	...	...	...	...	...
Other sectors: long-term	4 776	–3.63	–3.00	3.65	–1.88	–1.84	–1.93	13.64	3.29
Other sectors: short-term	4 777	...	...	...	...	...	...	...	1.26
Currency and deposits	4 780	...	...	...	...	...	...	...	...
Monetary authorities	4 781	...	...	...	...	...	...	...	...
General government	4 782	...	...	...	...	...	...	...	...
Banks	4 783	...	...	...	...	...	...	...	...
Other sectors	4 784	...	...	...	...	...	...	...	...
Other liabilities	4 786	2.65	–1.92	3.74	1.95	5.97	2.21	3.02	4.25
Monetary authorities: long-term	4 788	...	...	...	...	...	...	...	...
Monetary authorities: short-term	4 789	2.65	–1.92	3.74	1.95	5.97	...	...	...
General government: long-term	4 791	...	...	...	...	...	...	...	...
General government: short-term	4 792	...	...	...	...	...	2.21	3.02	4.25
Banks: long-term	4 794	...	...	...	...	...	...	...	...
Banks: short-term	4 795	...	...	...	...	...	...	...	...
Other sectors: long-term	4 797	...	...	...	...	...	...	...	...
Other sectors: short-term	4 798	...	...	...	...	...	...	...	...
D. RESERVE ASSETS	4 800	–.61	6.60	–2.23	11.87	–13.30	–7.91	2.92	9.52
Monetary gold	4 810	...	...	...	...	...	...	...	...
Special drawing rights	4 820	.05	–.01	.01	–.01	–.02	.04	–.04	.04
Reserve position in the Fund	4 830	...	...	...	...	...	...	...	...
Foreign exchange	4 840	–.66	6.61	–2.24	11.88	–13.29	–7.95	2.96	9.48
Other claims	4 880	...	...	...	...	...	...	...	...
NET ERRORS AND OMISSIONS	4 998	**–.65**	**–1.22**	**5.15**	**–7.28**	**5.49**	**3.44**	**–8.03**	**.71**

Table 1. ANALYTIC PRESENTATION, 1988–95
(Millions of U.S. dollars)

	Code	1988	1989	1990	1991	1992	1993	1994	1995
A. Current Account[1]	4 993 Y.	**–34.6**	**–33.4**	**–89.1**	**–61.8**	**–83.1**	**–13.0**	**–24.7**	**. . .**
Goods: exports f.o.b	2 100 . .	133.7	148.1	150.5	125.6	115.9	132.5	145.9	. . .
Goods: imports f.o.b	3 100 . .	–179.1	–186.0	–241.6	–178.7	–189.0	–158.1	–130.6	. . .
Balance on Goods	4 100 . .	*–45.4*	*–37.9*	*–91.1*	*–53.0*	*–73.2*	*–25.7*	*15.3*	. . .
Services: credit	2 200 . .	62.3	65.6	69.1	50.5	45.1	49.3	33.1	. . .
Services: debit	3 200 . .	–151.0	–144.4	–168.5	–136.7	–152.7	–131.9	–113.8	. . .
Balance on Goods and Services	4 991 . .	*–134.1*	*–116.8*	*–190.5*	*–139.2*	*–180.7*	*–108.3*	*–65.4*	. . .
Income: credit	2 300 . .	. . .	.7	.8	5.5	6.4	4.5	. . .	. . .
Income: debit	3 300 . .	–21.2	–21.4	–22.4	–19.0	–22.2	–23.2	–22.7	. . .
Balance on Goods, Services, and Income	4 992 . .	*–155.3*	*–137.5*	*–212.1*	*–152.7*	*–196.5*	*–127.1*	*–88.1*	. . .
Current transfers: credit	2 379 Y.	156.7	138.3	164.2	129.7	151.0	152.4	92.6	. . .
Current transfers: debit	3 379 . .	–36.0	–34.2	–41.2	–38.8	–37.6	–38.3	–29.2	. . .
B. Capital Account[1]	4 994 Y.	**. . .**	**. . .**	**. . .**	**. . .**	**. . .**	**. . .**	**. . .**	**. . .**
Capital account: credit	2 994 Y.	. . .	. . .	. . .	. . .	. . .	. . .	. . .	. . .
Capital account: debit	3 994 . .	. . .	. . .	. . .	. . .	. . .	. . .	. . .	. . .
Total, Groups A Plus B	4 010 . .	*–34.6*	*–33.4*	*–89.1*	*–61.8*	*–83.1*	*–13.0*	*–24.7*	. . .
C. Financial Account[1]	4 995 X.	**9.5**	**20.2**	**69.3**	**24.5**	**18.7**	**1.3**	**52.8**	**. . .**
Direct investment abroad	4 505 . .	–4.8	–3.8	–3.8	–3.5	–5.9	–5.3	–7.2	. . .
Direct investment in Central African Republic	4 555 Y.	–3.8	1.3	.7	–4.9	–10.7	–10.0	3.6	. . .
Portfolio investment assets	4 602 . .	. . .	. . .	. . .	. . .	. . .	. . .	. . .	. . .
Equity securities	4 610 . .	. . .	. . .	. . .	. . .	. . .	. . .	. . .	. . .
Debt securities	4 619 . .	. . .	. . .	. . .	. . .	. . .	. . .	. . .	. . .
Portfolio investment liabilities	4 652 Y.	. . .	. . .	. . .	. . .	. . .	. . .	. . .	. . .
Equity securities	4 660 Y.	. . .	. . .	. . .	. . .	. . .	. . .	. . .	. . .
Debt securities	4 669 Y.	. . .	. . .	. . .	. . .	. . .	. . .	. . .	. . .
Other investment assets	4 703 . .	–9.0	–13.3	–16.3	–11.2	–33.2	–18.2	8.1	. . .
Monetary authorities	4 703 .A	. . .	. . .	. . .	. . .	. . .	. . .	. . .	. . .
General government	4 703 .B	–.1	–.1	–.2	. . .	. . .	. . .	. . .	. . .
Banks	4 703 .C	11.8	1.1	–.7	2.8	. . .	2.5	. . .	. . .
Other sectors	4 703 .D	–20.7	–14.3	–15.4	–14.0	–33.2	–20.7	8.1	. . .
Other investment liabilities	4 753 X.	27.1	36.0	88.6	44.1	68.4	34.8	48.3	. . .
Monetary authorities	4 753 XA	–1.1	–.5	–.3	. . .	. . .	. . .	. . .	. . .
General government	4 753 YB	26.9	30.5	83.9	52.3	57.7	23.2	43.9	. . .
Banks	4 753 YC	. . .	.6	.1	–2.5	1.2	3.2	5.9	. . .
Other sectors	4 753 YD	1.3	5.5	4.9	–5.7	9.4	8.4	–1.6	. . .
Total, Groups A Through C	4 020 . .	*–25.1*	*–13.2*	*–19.8*	*–37.2*	*–64.4*	*–11.6*	*28.1*	. . .
D. Net Errors and Omissions	4 998 . .	**11.7**	**1.4**	**1.4**	**–1.9**	**26.2**	**6.3**	**–15.0**	**. . .**
Total, Groups A Through D	4 030 . .	*–13.4*	*–11.9*	*–18.5*	*–39.1*	*–38.2*	*–5.3*	*13.1*	. . .
E. Reserves and Related Items	4 040 . .	**13.4**	**11.9**	**18.5**	**39.1**	**38.2**	**5.3**	**–13.1**	**. . .**
Reserve assets	4 800 . .	–32.4	.8	9.4	13.8	–2.8	–20.1	–56.0	. . .
Use of Fund credit and loans	4 766 . .	1.1	–13.4	–1.6	–3.3	–1.7	–1.6	10.3	. . .
Liabilities constituting foreign authorities' reserves	4 900 . .	.1	–4.8	–2.6	–.5	1.6	–8.4	. . .	. . .
Exceptional financing	4 920 . .	44.6	29.3	13.3	29.2	41.0	35.4	32.6	. . .
Conversion rates: CFA francs per U.S. dollar	0 101 . .	**297.85**	**319.01**	**272.26**	**282.11**	**264.69**	**283.16**	**555.20**	**499.15**

[1] Excludes components that have been classified in the categories of Group E.

Table 2. STANDARD PRESENTATION, 1988–95
(Millions of U.S. dollars)

	Code	1988	1989	1990	1991	1992	1993	1994	1995
CURRENT ACCOUNT	4 993 . .	**–34.6**	**–33.4**	**–89.1**	**–61.8**	**–83.1**	**–13.0**	**–24.7**	**. . .**
A. GOODS	4 100 . .	–45.4	–37.9	–91.1	–53.0	–73.2	–25.7	15.3	. . .
Credit	2 100 . .	**133.7**	**148.1**	**150.5**	**125.6**	**115.9**	**132.5**	**145.9**	**. . .**
General merchandise: exports f.o.b.	2 110 . .	133.7	148.1	150.5	125.6	115.9	132.5	145.9	. . .
Goods for processing: exports f.o.b.	2 150 . .	. . .	. . .	. . .	. . .	. . .	. . .	. . .	. . .
Repairs on goods	2 160 . .	. . .	. . .	. . .	. . .	. . .	. . .	. . .	. . .
Goods procured in ports by carriers	2 170 . .	. . .	. . .	. . .	. . .	. . .	. . .	. . .	. . .
Nonmonetary gold	2 180 . .	. . .	. . .	. . .	. . .	. . .	. . .	. . .	. . .
Debit	3 100 . .	**–179.1**	**–186.0**	**–241.6**	**–178.7**	**–189.0**	**–158.1**	**–130.6**	**. . .**
General merchandise: imports f.o.b.	3 110 . .	–179.1	–186.0	–241.6	–178.7	–189.0	–158.1	–130.6	. . .
Goods for processing: imports f.o.b.	3 150 . .	. . .	. . .	. . .	. . .	. . .	. . .	. . .	. . .
Repairs on goods	3 160 . .	. . .	. . .	. . .	. . .	. . .	. . .	. . .	. . .
Goods procured in ports by carriers	3 170 . .	. . .	. . .	. . .	. . .	. . .	. . .	. . .	. . .
Nonmonetary gold	3 180 . .	. . .	. . .	. . .	. . .	. . .	. . .	. . .	. . .
B. SERVICES	4 200 . .	–88.7	–78.9	–99.5	–86.2	–107.6	–82.6	–80.7	. . .
Total credit	2 200 . .	*62.3*	*65.6*	*69.1*	*50.5*	*45.1*	*49.3*	*33.1*	. . .
Total debit	3 200 . .	*–151.0*	*–144.4*	*–168.5*	*–136.7*	*–152.7*	*–131.9*	*–113.8*	. . .
Transportation services, credit	2 205 . .	**5.9**	**6.0**	**8.8**	**5.5**	**5.7**	**5.8**	**. . .**	**. . .**
Passenger	2 205 BA	. . .	. . .	. . .	. . .	. . .	. . .	. . .	. . .
Freight	2 205 BB	*1.9*	*1.6*	*4.0*	*2.4*	*2.7*	*.5*	. . .	. . .
Other	2 205 BC	*4.0*	*4.4*	*4.9*	*3.2*	*3.0*	*5.3*	. . .	. . .
Sea transport, passenger	2 207 . .	. . .	. . .	. . .	. . .	. . .	. . .	. . .	. . .
Sea transport, freight	2 208 . .	. . .	. . .	. . .	. . .	. . .	. . .	. . .	. . .
Sea transport, other	2 209 . .	. . .	. . .	. . .	. . .	. . .	. . .	. . .	. . .
Air transport, passenger	2 211 . .	. . .	. . .	. . .	. . .	. . .	. . .	. . .	. . .
Air transport, freight	2 212 . .	. . .	. . .	. . .	. . .	. . .	. . .	. . .	. . .
Air transport, other	2 213 . .	. . .	. . .	. . .	. . .	. . .	. . .	. . .	. . .
Other transport, passenger	2 215 . .	. . .	. . .	. . .	. . .	. . .	. . .	. . .	. . .
Other transport, freight	2 216 . .	. . .	. . .	. . .	. . .	. . .	. . .	. . .	. . .
Other transport, other	2 217 . .	. . .	. . .	. . .	. . .	. . .	. . .	. . .	. . .
Transportation services, debit	3 205 . .	**–63.1**	**–64.9**	**–82.8**	**–66.2**	**–69.3**	**–55.4**	**–49.7**	**. . .**
Passenger	3 205 BA	*–10.8*	*–9.1*	*–12.1*	*–12.4*	*–13.3*	*–13.5*	*–14.0*	. . .
Freight	3 205 BB	*–52.3*	*–53.5*	*–68.5*	*–50.4*	*–52.6*	*–41.9*	*–35.7*	. . .
Other	3 205 BC	. . .	*–2.3*	*–2.2*	*–3.4*	*–3.4*	. . .	. . .	. . .
Sea transport, passenger	3 207 . .	. . .	. . .	. . .	. . .	. . .	. . .	. . .	. . .
Sea transport, freight	3 208 . .	. . .	. . .	. . .	. . .	. . .	. . .	. . .	. . .
Sea transport, other	3 209 . .	. . .	. . .	. . .	. . .	. . .	. . .	. . .	. . .
Air transport, passenger	3 211 . .	. . .	. . .	. . .	. . .	. . .	. . .	. . .	. . .
Air transport, freight	3 212 . .	. . .	. . .	. . .	. . .	. . .	. . .	. . .	. . .
Air transport, other	3 213 . .	. . .	. . .	. . .	. . .	. . .	. . .	. . .	. . .
Other transport, passenger	3 215 . .	. . .	. . .	. . .	. . .	. . .	. . .	. . .	. . .
Other transport, freight	3 216 . .	. . .	. . .	. . .	. . .	. . .	. . .	. . .	. . .
Other transport, other	3 217 . .	. . .	. . .	. . .	. . .	. . .	. . .	. . .	. . .
Travel, credit	2 236 . .	**5.0**	**3.2**	**2.8**	**3.4**	**3.0**	**5.8**	**. . .**	**. . .**
Business travel	2 237 . .	. . .	. . .	. . .	. . .	. . .	. . .	. . .	. . .
Personal travel	2 240 . .	. . .	. . .	. . .	. . .	. . .	. . .	. . .	. . .
Travel, debit	3 236 . .	**–44.9**	**–44.6**	**–51.0**	**–43.1**	**–51.3**	**–50.1**	**–43.2**	**. . .**
Business travel	3 237 . .	. . .	. . .	. . .	. . .	. . .	. . .	. . .	. . .
Personal travel	3 240 . .	. . .	. . .	. . .	. . .	. . .	. . .	. . .	. . .
Other services, credit	2 200 BA	**51.4**	**56.4**	**57.5**	**41.5**	**36.4**	**37.7**	**33.1**	**. . .**
Communications	2 245 . .	. . .	. . .	. . .	. . .	. . .	. . .	. . .	. . .
Construction	2 249 . .	. . .	. . .	. . .	. . .	. . .	. . .	. . .	. . .
Insurance	2 253 . .	4.6	2.5	3.3	4.6	4.8	3.3	. . .	. . .
Financial	2 260 . .	. . .	. . .	. . .	. . .	. . .	. . .	. . .	. . .
Computer and information	2 262 . .	. . .	. . .	. . .	. . .	. . .	. . .	. . .	. . .
Royalties and licence fees	2 266 . .	. . .	. . .	. . .	. . .	. . .	. . .	. . .	. . .
Other business services	2 268 . .	2.8	3.3	2.5	2.9	2.3	2.1	. . .	. . .
Personal, cultural, and recreational	2 287 . .	. . .	. . .	. . .	. . .	. . .	. . .	. . .	. . .
Government, n.i.e.	2 291 . .	44.1	50.6	51.7	34.0	29.3	32.2	33.1	. . .
Other services, debit	3 200 BA	**–43.0**	**–35.0**	**–34.7**	**–27.3**	**–32.2**	**–26.4**	**–20.9**	**. . .**
Communications	3 245 . .	. . .	. . .	. . .	. . .	. . .	. . .	. . .	. . .
Construction	3 249 . .	. . .	. . .	. . .	. . .	. . .	. . .	. . .	. . .
Insurance	3 253 . .	–11.0	–10.8	–14.8	–12.1	–12.8	–10.5	–9.0	. . .
Financial	3 260 . .	. . .	. . .	. . .	. . .	. . .	. . .	. . .	. . .
Computer and information	3 262 . .	. . .	. . .	. . .	. . .	. . .	. . .	. . .	. . .
Royalties and licence fees	3 266 . .	. . .	. . .	. . .	. . .	. . .	. . .	. . .	. . .
Other business services	3 268 . .	–20.1	–14.6	–17.9	–13.5	–18.2	–15.1	–11.9	. . .
Personal, cultural, and recreational	3 287 . .	. . .	. . .	. . .	. . .	. . .	. . .	. . .	. . .
Government, n.i.e.	3 291 . .	–11.9	–9.5	–2.1	–1.7	–1.1	–.9	. . .	. . .

Table 2 (Continued). STANDARD PRESENTATION, 1988–95
(Millions of U.S. dollars)

	Code	1988	1989	1990	1991	1992	1993	1994	1995
C. INCOME	4 300 . .	–21.2	–20.8	–21.6	–13.5	–15.7	–18.7	–22.7	. . .
Total credit	2 300 . .	. . .	*.7*	*.8*	*5.5*	*6.4*	*4.5*	. . .	. . .
Total debit	3 300 . .	*–21.2*	*–21.4*	*–22.4*	*–19.0*	*–22.2*	*–23.2*	*–22.7*	. . .
Compensation of employees, credit	2 310 . .	**. . .**	**. . .**	**.1**	**.1**	**. . .**	**.2**	**. . .**	**. . .**
Compensation of employees, debit	3 310 . .	**. . .**	**. . .**	**–.1**	**. . .**	**. . .**	**. . .**	**. . .**	**. . .**
Investment income, credit	2 320 . .	**. . .**	**.6**	**.7**	**5.3**	**6.4**	**4.3**	**. . .**	**. . .**
Direct investment income	2 330 . .	. . .	. . .	. . .	.2	. . .	. . .	. . .	. . .
Dividends and distributed branch profits	2 332 . .	. . .	. . .	. . .	.2	. . .	. . .	. . .	. . .
Reinvested earnings and undistributed branch profits	2 333 . .	. . .	. . .	. . .	. . .	. . .	. . .	. . .	. . .
Income on debt (interest)	2 334 . .	. . .	. . .	. . .	. . .	. . .	. . .	. . .	. . .
Portfolio investment income	2 339 . .	. . .	. . .	. . .	. . .	. . .	. . .	. . .	. . .
Income on equity	2 340 . .	. . .	. . .	. . .	. . .	. . .	. . .	. . .	. . .
Income on bonds and notes	2 350 . .	. . .	. . .	. . .	. . .	. . .	. . .	. . .	. . .
Income on money market instruments and financial derivatives	2 360 . .	. . .	. . .	. . .	. . .	. . .	. . .	. . .	. . .
Other investment income	2 370 . .	. . .	.6	.7	5.2	6.4	4.3	. . .	. . .
Investment income, debit	3 320 . .	**–21.2**	**–21.4**	**–22.3**	**–19.0**	**–22.2**	**–23.2**	**–22.7**	**. . .**
Direct investment income	3 330 . .	. . .	–2.0	–2.1	–1.5	. . .	. . .	. . .	. . .
Dividends and distributed branch profits	3 332 . .	. . .	–1.3	–1.0	–1.5	. . .	. . .	. . .	. . .
Reinvested earnings and undistributed branch profits	3 333 . .	. . .	–.6	–1.1	. . .	. . .	. . .	. . .	. . .
Income on debt (interest)	3 334 . .	. . .	. . .	. . .	. . .	. . .	. . .	. . .	. . .
Portfolio investment income	3 339 . .	. . .	. . .	. . .	. . .	. . .	. . .	. . .	. . .
Income on equity	3 340 . .	. . .	. . .	. . .	. . .	. . .	. . .	. . .	. . .
Income on bonds and notes	3 350 . .	. . .	. . .	. . .	. . .	. . .	. . .	. . .	. . .
Income on money market instruments and financial derivatives	3 360 . .	. . .	. . .	. . .	. . .	. . .	. . .	. . .	. . .
Other investment income	3 370 . .	–21.2	–19.4	–20.2	–17.5	–22.2	–23.2	–22.7	. . .
D. CURRENT TRANSFERS	4 379 . .	120.7	104.1	123.0	90.9	113.4	114.1	63.4	. . .
Credit	2 379 . .	**156.7**	**138.3**	**164.2**	**129.7**	**151.0**	**152.4**	**92.6**	**. . .**
General government	2 380 . .	150.0	119.9	147.3	114.6	142.3	146.0	89.0	. . .
Other sectors	2 390 . .	6.7	18.4	16.9	15.1	8.7	6.4	3.6	. . .
Workers' remittances	2 391 . .	. . .	. . .	. . .	. . .	. . .	. . .	. . .	. . .
Other current transfers	2 392 . .	6.7	18.4	16.9	15.1	8.7	6.4	3.6	. . .
Debit	3 379 . .	**–36.0**	**–34.2**	**–41.2**	**–38.8**	**–37.6**	**–38.3**	**–29.2**	**. . .**
General government	3 380 . .	–1.7	–1.1	–1.4	–1.9	–1.9	–.9	–.9	. . .
Other sectors	3 390 . .	–34.4	–33.1	–39.8	–36.9	–35.7	–37.4	–28.3	. . .
Workers' remittances	3 391 . .	–33.0	–31.2	–35.9	–35.2	–34.6	–36.0	–27.4	. . .
Other current transfers	3 392 . .	–1.3	–1.9	–3.9	–1.7	–1.1	–1.4	–.9	. . .
CAPITAL AND FINANCIAL ACCOUNT	4 996 . .	**22.9**	**32.1**	**87.8**	**63.7**	**56.8**	**6.6**	**39.7**	**. . .**
CAPITAL ACCOUNT	4 994 . .	**. . .**	**. . .**	**. . .**	**. . .**	**. . .**	**. . .**	**. . .**	**. . .**
Total credit	2 994 . .	. . .	. . .	. . .	. . .	. . .	. . .	. . .	. . .
Total debit	3 994 . .	. . .	. . .	. . .	. . .	. . .	. . .	. . .	. . .
Capital transfers, credit	2 400 . .	**. . .**	**. . .**	**. . .**	**. . .**	**. . .**	**. . .**	**. . .**	**. . .**
General government	2 401 . .	. . .	. . .	. . .	. . .	. . .	. . .	. . .	. . .
Debt forgiveness	2 402 . .	. . .	. . .	. . .	. . .	. . .	. . .	. . .	. . .
Other capital transfers	2 410 . .	. . .	. . .	. . .	. . .	. . .	. . .	. . .	. . .
Other sectors	2 430 . .	. . .	. . .	. . .	. . .	. . .	. . .	. . .	. . .
Migrants' transfers	2 431 . .	. . .	. . .	. . .	. . .	. . .	. . .	. . .	. . .
Debt forgiveness	2 432 . .	. . .	. . .	. . .	. . .	. . .	. . .	. . .	. . .
Other capital transfers	2 440 . .	. . .	. . .	. . .	. . .	. . .	. . .	. . .	. . .
Capital transfers, debit	3 400 . .	**. . .**	**. . .**	**. . .**	**. . .**	**. . .**	**. . .**	**. . .**	**. . .**
General government	3 401 . .	. . .	. . .	. . .	. . .	. . .	. . .	. . .	. . .
Debt forgiveness	3 402 . .	. . .	. . .	. . .	. . .	. . .	. . .	. . .	. . .
Other capital transfers	3 410 . .	. . .	. . .	. . .	. . .	. . .	. . .	. . .	. . .
Other sectors	3 430 . .	. . .	. . .	. . .	. . .	. . .	. . .	. . .	. . .
Migrants' transfers	3 431 . .	. . .	. . .	. . .	. . .	. . .	. . .	. . .	. . .
Debt forgiveness	3 432 . .	. . .	. . .	. . .	. . .	. . .	. . .	. . .	. . .
Other capital transfers	3 440 . .	. . .	. . .	. . .	. . .	. . .	. . .	. . .	. . .
Nonproduced nonfinancial assets, credit	2 480 . .	**. . .**	**. . .**	**. . .**	**. . .**	**. . .**	**. . .**	**. . .**	**. . .**
Nonproduced nonfinancial assets, debit	3 480 . .	**. . .**	**. . .**	**. . .**	**. . .**	**. . .**	**. . .**	**. . .**	**. . .**

Table 2 (Continued). STANDARD PRESENTATION, 1988–95

(Millions of U.S. dollars)

	Code	1988	1989	1990	1991	1992	1993	1994	1995
FINANCIAL ACCOUNT	4 995	**22.9**	**32.1**	**87.8**	**63.7**	**56.8**	**6.6**	**39.7**	...
A. DIRECT INVESTMENT	4 500	-8.6	-2.5	-3.1	-8.4	-16.5	-15.3	-3.6	...
Direct investment abroad	4 505	**-4.8**	**-3.8**	**-3.8**	**-3.5**	**-5.9**	**-5.3**	**-7.2**	...
Equity capital	4 510	-4.8	-3.8	-3.8	-3.5	-5.9	-5.3	-7.2	...
Claims on affiliated enterprises	4 515	...	...	...	...	...	...	...	...
Liabilities to affiliated enterprises	4 520	...	...	...	...	...	...	...	...
Reinvested earnings	4 525	...	...	...	...	...	...	...	...
Other capital	4 530	...	...	...	...	...	...	...	...
Claims on affiliated enterprises	4 535	...	...	...	...	...	...	...	...
Liabilities to affiliated enterprises	4 540	...	...	...	...	...	...	...	...
Direct investment in Central African Republic	4 555	**-3.8**	**1.3**	**.7**	**-4.9**	**-10.7**	**-10.0**	**3.6**	...
Equity capital	4 560	...	.2	1.0	.4	...	...	...	...
Claims on direct investors	4 565	...	...	...	...	...	...	...	...
Liabilities to direct investors	4 570	...	...	...	...	...	...	...	...
Reinvested earnings	4 575	...	.6	1.1	...	...	...	...	...
Other capital	4 580	-3.8	.5	-1.4	-5.3	-10.7	-10.0	3.6	...
Claims on direct investors	4 585	...	...	...	...	...	...	...	...
Liabilities to direct investors	4 590	...	...	...	...	...	...	...	...
B. PORTFOLIO INVESTMENT	4 600	...	...	...	...	...	...	...	...
Assets	4 602	...	...	...	...	...	...	...	...
Equity securities	4 610	...	...	...	...	...	...	...	...
Monetary authorities	4 611	...	...	...	...	...	...	...	...
General government	4 612	...	...	...	...	...	...	...	...
Banks	4 613	...	...	...	...	...	...	...	...
Other sectors	4 614	...	...	...	...	...	...	...	...
Debt securities	4 619	...	...	...	...	...	...	...	...
Bonds and notes	4 620	...	...	...	...	...	...	...	...
Monetary authorities	4 621	...	...	...	...	...	...	...	...
General government	4 622	...	...	...	...	...	...	...	...
Banks	4 623	...	...	...	...	...	...	...	...
Other sectors	4 624	...	...	...	...	...	...	...	...
Money market instruments	4 630	...	...	...	...	...	...	...	...
Monetary authorities	4 631	...	...	...	...	...	...	...	...
General government	4 632	...	...	...	...	...	...	...	...
Banks	4 633	...	...	...	...	...	...	...	...
Other sectors	4 634	...	...	...	...	...	...	...	...
Financial derivatives	4 640	...	...	...	...	...	...	...	...
Monetary authorities	4 641	...	...	...	...	...	...	...	...
General government	4 642	...	...	...	...	...	...	...	...
Banks	4 643	...	...	...	...	...	...	...	...
Other sectors	4 644	...	...	...	...	...	...	...	...
Liabilities	4 652	...	...	...	...	...	...	...	...
Equity securities	4 660	...	...	...	...	...	...	...	...
Banks	4 663	...	...	...	...	...	...	...	...
Other sectors	4 664	...	...	...	...	...	...	...	...
Debt securities	4 669	...	...	...	...	...	...	...	...
Bonds and notes	4 670	...	...	...	...	...	...	...	...
Monetary authorities	4 671	...	...	...	...	...	...	...	...
General government	4 672	...	...	...	...	...	...	...	...
Banks	4 673	...	...	...	...	...	...	...	...
Other sectors	4 674	...	...	...	...	...	...	...	...
Money market instruments	4 680	...	...	...	...	...	...	...	...
Monetary authorities	4 681	...	...	...	...	...	...	...	...
General government	4 682	...	...	...	...	...	...	...	...
Banks	4 683	...	...	...	...	...	...	...	...
Other sectors	4 684	...	...	...	...	...	...	...	...
Financial derivatives	4 690	...	...	...	...	...	...	...	...
Monetary authorities	4 691	...	...	...	...	...	...	...	...
General government	4 692	...	...	...	...	...	...	...	...
Banks	4 693	...	...	...	...	...	...	...	...
Other sectors	4 694	...	...	...	...	...	...	...	...

Table 2 (Concluded). STANDARD PRESENTATION, 1988–95

(Millions of U.S. dollars)

	Code	1988	1989	1990	1991	1992	1993	1994	1995
C. OTHER INVESTMENT	4 700 . .	63.8	33.8	81.4	58.2	76.1	42.1	99.3	. . .
Assets	4 703 . .	**–9.0**	**–13.3**	**–16.3**	**–11.2**	**–33.2**	**–18.2**	**8.1**	. . .
Trade credits	4 706 . .	. . .	1.2	1.5	–1.4	. . .	. . .	. . .	. . .
General government: long-term	4 708 . .	. . .	. . .	. . .	. . .	. . .	. . .	. . .	. . .
General government: short-term	4 709 . .	. . .	. . .	. . .	. . .	. . .	. . .	. . .	. . .
Other sectors: long-term	4 711 . .	. . .	. . .	. . .	. . .	. . .	. . .	. . .	. . .
Other sectors: short-term	4 712 . .	. . .	1.2	1.5	–1.4	. . .	. . .	. . .	. . .
Loans	4 714 . .	. . .	. . .	. . .	. . .	. . .	. . .	. . .	. . .
Monetary authorities: long-term	4 717 . .	. . .	. . .	. . .	. . .	. . .	. . .	. . .	. . .
Monetary authorities: short-term	4 718 . .	. . .	. . .	. . .	. . .	. . .	. . .	. . .	. . .
General government: long-term	4 720 . .	. . .	. . .	. . .	. . .	. . .	. . .	. . .	. . .
General government: short-term	4 721 . .	. . .	. . .	. . .	. . .	. . .	. . .	. . .	. . .
Banks: long-term	4 723 . .	. . .	. . .	. . .	. . .	. . .	. . .	. . .	. . .
Banks: short-term	4 724 . .	. . .	. . .	. . .	. . .	. . .	. . .	. . .	. . .
Other sectors: long-term	4 726 . .	. . .	. . .	. . .	. . .	. . .	. . .	. . .	. . .
Other sectors: short-term	4 727 . .	. . .	. . .	. . .	. . .	. . .	. . .	. . .	. . .
Currency and deposits	4 730 . .	–8.9	–14.4	–17.5	–9.8	–33.2	–18.2	8.1	. . .
Monetary authorities	4 731 . .	. . .	. . .	. . .	. . .	. . .	. . .	. . .	. . .
General government	4 732 . .	. . .	. . .	. . .	. . .	. . .	. . .	. . .	. . .
Banks	4 733 . .	11.8	1.1	–.7	2.8	. . .	2.5	. . .	. . .
Other sectors	4 734 . .	–20.7	–15.4	–16.9	–12.6	–33.2	–20.7	8.1	. . .
Other assets	4 736 . .	–.1	–.1	–.2	. . .	. . .	. . .	. . .	. . .
Monetary authorities: long-term	4 738 . .	. . .	. . .	. . .	. . .	. . .	. . .	. . .	. . .
Monetary authorities: short-term	4 739 . .	. . .	. . .	. . .	. . .	. . .	. . .	. . .	. . .
General government: long-term	4 741 . .	–.1	–.1	–.2	. . .	. . .	. . .	. . .	. . .
General government: short-term	4 742 . .	. . .	. . .	. . .	. . .	. . .	. . .	. . .	. . .
Banks: long-term	4 744 . .	. . .	. . .	. . .	. . .	. . .	. . .	. . .	. . .
Banks: short-term	4 745 . .	. . .	. . .	. . .	. . .	. . .	. . .	. . .	. . .
Other sectors: long-term	4 747 . .	. . .	. . .	. . .	. . .	. . .	. . .	. . .	. . .
Other sectors: short-term	4 748 . .	. . .	. . .	. . .	. . .	. . .	. . .	. . .	. . .
Liabilities	4 753 . .	**72.8**	**47.1**	**97.7**	**69.4**	**109.3**	**60.3**	**91.2**	. . .
Trade credits	4 756 . .	–6.6	1.2	1.7	–6.9	3.1	–.4	4.7	. . .
General government: long-term	4 758 . .	. . .	. . .	. . .	. . .	. . .	. . .	. . .	. . .
General government: short-term	4 759 . .	. . .	. . .	. . .	. . .	. . .	. . .	. . .	. . .
Other sectors: long-term	4 761 . .	. . .	. . .	. . .	. . .	. . .	. . .	. . .	. . .
Other sectors: short-term	4 762 . .	–6.6	1.2	1.7	–6.9	3.1	–.4	4.7	. . .
Loans	4 764 . .	84.0	45.2	95.7	49.2	78.0	30.5	47.9	. . .
Use of Fund credit and loans from the Fund	4 766 . .	1.1	–13.4	–1.6	–3.3	–1.7	–1.6	10.3	. . .
Monetary authorities: other long-term	4 767 . .	. . .	. . .	. . .	. . .	. . .	. . .	. . .	. . .
Monetary authorities: short-term	4 768 . .	. . .	. . .	. . .	. . .	. . .	. . .	. . .	. . .
General government: long-term	4 770 . .	75.0	54.8	93.6	52.7	73.4	23.2	43.9	. . .
General government: short-term	4 771 . .	. . .	. . .	. . .	. . .	. . .	. . .	. . .	. . .
Banks: long-term	4 773 . .	. . .	. . .	. . .	. . .	. . .	. . .	. . .	. . .
Banks: short-term	4 774 . .	. . .	. . .	. . .	. . .	. . .	. . .	. . .	. . .
Other sectors: long-term	4 776 . .	7.9	3.9	3.8	–.2	6.3	8.9	–6.3	. . .
Other sectors: short-term	4 777 . .	. . .	. . .	. . .	. . .	. . .	. . .	. . .	. . .
Currency and deposits	4 780 . .	.1	–4.2	–2.5	–3.0	2.8	–5.2	5.9	. . .
Monetary authorities	4 781 . .	.1	–4.8	–2.6	–.5	1.6	–8.4	. . .	. . .
General government	4 782 . .	. . .	. . .	. . .	. . .	. . .	. . .	. . .	. . .
Banks	4 783 . .	. . .	.6	.1	–2.5	1.2	3.2	5.9	. . .
Other sectors	4 784 . .	. . .	. . .	. . .	. . .	. . .	. . .	. . .	. . .
Other liabilities	4 786 . .	–4.6	4.8	2.8	30.2	25.3	35.4	32.6	. . .
Monetary authorities: long-term	4 788 . .	. . .	. . .	. . .	. . .	. . .	. . .	. . .	. . .
Monetary authorities: short-term	4 789 . .	4.4	12.5	7.1	29.2	25.3	35.4	32.6	. . .
General government: long-term	4 791 . .	–9.0	–8.1	–3.7	–.4	. . .	. . .	. . .	. . .
General government: short-term	4 792 . .	. . .	. . .	. . .	. . .	. . .	. . .	. . .	. . .
Banks: long-term	4 794 . .	. . .	. . .	. . .	. . .	. . .	. . .	. . .	. . .
Banks: short-term	4 795 . .	. . .	. . .	. . .	. . .	. . .	. . .	. . .	. . .
Other sectors: long-term	4 797 . .	. . .	. . .	. . .	. . .	. . .	. . .	. . .	. . .
Other sectors: short-term	4 798 . .	. . .	.4	–.6	1.5	. . .	. . .	. . .	. . .
D. RESERVE ASSETS	4 800 . .	–32.4	.8	9.4	13.8	–2.8	–20.1	–56.0	. . .
Monetary gold	4 810 . .	. . .	.3	.7	.3	. . .	–.9	. . .	. . .
Special drawing rights	4 820 . .	–5.7	11.8	–4.3	4.0	.6	. . .	. . .	. . .
Reserve position in the Fund	4 830 . .	. . .	. . .	. . .	. . .	. . .	. . .	. . .	. . .
Foreign exchange	4 840 . .	–26.6	–11.3	13.0	9.5	–3.4	–19.2	–56.0	. . .
Other claims	4 880 . .	. . .	. . .	. . .	. . .	. . .	. . .	. . .	. . .
NET ERRORS AND OMISSIONS	4 998 . .	**11.7**	**1.4**	**1.4**	**–1.9**	**26.2**	**6.3**	**–15.0**	. . .

Table 1. ANALYTIC PRESENTATION, 1988–95
(Millions of U.S. dollars)

	Code	1988	1989	1990	1991	1992	1993	1994	1995
A. Current Account[1]	4 993 Y.	**25.5**	**–55.9**	**–45.6**	**–65.6**	**–85.7**	**–116.6**	**–37.7**	**. . .**
Goods: exports f.o.b.	2 100 . .	145.9	155.4	230.3	193.5	182.3	151.8	135.3	. . .
Goods: imports f.o.b.	3 100 . .	–228.4	–240.3	–259.5	–249.9	–243.0	–215.2	–212.1	. . .
Balance on Goods	4 100 . .	*–82.5*	*–84.9*	*–29.2*	*–56.3*	*–60.7*	*–63.5*	*–76.8*	. . .
Services: credit	2 200 . .	78.7	42.3	40.9	30.9	26.7	47.1	54.8	. . .
Services: debit	3 200 . .	–217.9	–210.0	–228.2	–208.0	–224.1	–235.1	–199.4	. . .
Balance on Goods and Services	4 991 . .	*–221.7*	*–252.6*	*–216.5*	*–233.4*	*–258.1*	*–251.4*	*–221.4*	. . .
Income: credit	2 300 . .	2.1	1.3	3.0	8.9	17.5	4.3	5.0	. . .
Income: debit	3 300 . .	–15.5	–10.8	–23.8	–11.2	–14.9	–15.7	–12.4	. . .
Balance on Goods, Services, and Income	4 992 . .	*–235.0*	*–262.0*	*–237.2*	*–235.7*	*–255.5*	*–262.9*	*–228.7*	. . .
Current transfers: credit	2 379 Y.	301.4	241.4	239.3	215.5	222.3	192.4	209.4	. . .
Current transfers: debit	3 379 . .	–40.8	–35.2	–47.7	–45.3	–52.5	–46.2	–18.4	. . .
B. Capital Account[1]	4 994 Y.	**. . .**	**. . .**	**. . .**	**. . .**	**. . .**	**. . .**	**. . .**	**. . .**
Capital account: credit	2 994 Y.	. . .	. . .	. . .	. . .	. . .	. . .	. . .	. . .
Capital account: debit	3 994 . .	. . .	. . .	. . .	. . .	. . .	. . .	. . .	. . .
Total, Groups A Plus B	4 010 . .	*25.5*	*–55.9*	*–45.6*	*–65.6*	*–85.7*	*–116.6*	*–37.7*	. . .
C. Financial Account[1]	4 995 X.	**24.2**	**74.4**	**56.1**	**59.9**	**40.0**	**74.0**	**76.3**	**. . .**
Direct investment abroad	4 505 . .	–13.8	–12.5	. . .	–10.5	–13.8	–10.9	–.6	. . .
Direct investment in Chad	4 555 Y.	1.3	18.7	. . .	4.2	2.0	15.2	27.1	. . .
Portfolio investment assets	4 602 . .	. . .	. . .	. . .	. . .	. . .	. . .	. . .	. . .
Equity securities	4 610 . .	. . .	. . .	. . .	. . .	. . .	. . .	. . .	. . .
Debt securities	4 619 . .	. . .	. . .	. . .	. . .	. . .	. . .	. . .	. . .
Portfolio investment liabilities	4 652 Y.	. . .	. . .	. . .	. . .	. . .	. . .	. . .	. . .
Equity securities	4 660 Y.	. . .	. . .	. . .	. . .	. . .	. . .	. . .	. . .
Debt securities	4 669 Y.	. . .	. . .	. . .	. . .	. . .	. . .	. . .	. . .
Other investment assets	4 703 . .	10.3	3.5	. . .	24.2	3.9	42.1	.6	. . .
Monetary authorities	4 703 . A	. . .	. . .	. . .	. . .	. . .	. . .	. . .	. . .
General government	4 703 . B	. . .	. . .	. . .	. . .	. . .	. . .	. . .	. . .
Banks	4 703 . C	.8	–3.1	. . .	23.5	–1.8	31.0	–4.8	. . .
Other sectors	4 703 . D	9.5	6.6	. . .	.7	5.7	11.0	5.4	. . .
Other investment liabilities	4 753 X.	26.4	64.7	56.1	42.0	47.9	27.7	49.2	. . .
Monetary authorities	4 753 XA	–.2	–.1	. . .	. . .	. . .	. . .	–.1	. . .
General government	4 753 YB	46.1	79.0	103.4	81.3	71.3	102.1	49.8	. . .
Banks	4 753 YC	1.1	. . .	–36.7	2.2	5.0	. . .	. . .	. . .
Other sectors	4 753 YD	–20.6	–14.2	–10.6	–41.5	–28.3	–74.4	–.6	. . .
Total, Groups A Through C	4 020 . .	*49.7*	*18.5*	*10.5*	*–5.7*	*–45.7*	*–42.6*	*38.5*	. . .
D. Net Errors and Omissions	4 998 . .	**–83.7**	**11.1**	**–33.3**	**–13.0**	**9.2**	**–.1**	**–33.0**	**. . .**
Total, Groups A Through D	4 030 . .	*–34.0*	*29.6*	*–22.9*	*–18.6*	*–36.5*	*–42.7*	*5.5*	. . .
E. Reserves and Related Items	4 040 . .	**34.0**	**–29.6**	**22.9**	**18.6**	**36.5**	**42.7**	**–5.5**	**. . .**
Reserve assets	4 800 . .	14.8	–41.3	3.6	8.2	32.9	39.4	–30.7	. . .
Use of Fund credit and loans	4 766 . .	–2.3	6.9	4.6	. . .	. . .	–1.7	12.7	. . .
Liabilities constituting foreign authorities' reserves	4 900 . .	. . .	. . .	. . .	–.9	–6.3	–5.2	. . .	. . .
Exceptional financing	4 920 . .	21.5	4.8	14.7	11.4	9.9	10.2	12.4	. . .
Conversion rates: CFA francs per U.S. dollar	0 101 . .	**297.85**	**319.01**	**272.26**	**282.11**	**264.69**	**283.16**	**555.20**	**499.15**

[1] Excludes components that have been classified in the categories of Group E.

Table 2. STANDARD PRESENTATION, 1988–95
(Millions of U.S. dollars)

	Code	1988	1989	1990	1991	1992	1993	1994	1995
CURRENT ACCOUNT	4 993 . .	**25.5**	**–51.3**	**–45.6**	**–65.6**	**–85.7**	**–116.6**	**–37.7**	**. . .**
A. GOODS	4 100 . .	–82.5	–84.9	–29.2	–56.3	–60.7	–63.5	–76.8	. . .
Credit	2 100 . .	**145.9**	**155.4**	**230.3**	**193.5**	**182.3**	**151.8**	**135.3**	**. . .**
General merchandise: exports f.o.b.	2 110 . .	145.9	155.4	230.3	193.5	182.3	151.8	135.3	. . .
Goods for processing: exports f.o.b.	2 150 . .	. . .	. . .	. . .	. . .	. . .	. . .	. . .	. . .
Repairs on goods	2 160 . .	. . .	. . .	. . .	. . .	. . .	. . .	. . .	. . .
Goods procured in ports by carriers	2 170 . .	. . .	. . .	. . .	. . .	. . .	. . .	. . .	. . .
Nonmonetary gold	2 180 . .	. . .	. . .	. . .	. . .	. . .	. . .	. . .	. . .
Debit	3 100 . .	**–228.4**	**–240.3**	**–259.5**	**–249.9**	**–243.0**	**–215.2**	**–212.1**	**. . .**
General merchandise: imports f.o.b.	3 110 . .	–228.4	–240.3	–259.5	–249.9	–243.0	–215.2	–212.1	. . .
Goods for processing: imports f.o.b.	3 150 . .	. . .	. . .	. . .	. . .	. . .	. . .	. . .	. . .
Repairs on goods	3 160 . .	. . .	. . .	. . .	. . .	. . .	. . .	. . .	. . .
Goods procured in ports by carriers	3 170 . .	. . .	. . .	. . .	. . .	. . .	. . .	. . .	. . .
Nonmonetary gold	3 180 . .	. . .	. . .	. . .	. . .	. . .	. . .	. . .	. . .
B. SERVICES	4 200 . .	–139.2	–167.7	–187.3	–177.1	–197.4	–188.0	–144.6	. . .
Total credit	2 200 . .	*78.7*	*42.3*	*40.9*	*30.9*	*26.7*	*47.1*	*54.8*	. . .
Total debit	3 200 . .	*–217.9*	*–210.0*	*–228.2*	*–208.0*	*–224.1*	*–235.1*	*–199.4*	. . .
Transportation services, credit	2 205 . .	**2.2**	**2.1**	**4.3**	**4.5**	**1.8**	**2.6**	**1.1**	**. . .**
Passenger	2 205 BA	*.4*	*.9*	*3.9*	*3.7*	*1.6*	*2.4*	*.9*	. . .
Freight	2 205 BB	*.8*	*1.2*	*.5*	*.8*	*.2*	*.2*	*.1*	. . .
Other	2 205 BC	*.9*	. . .	. . .	. . .	. . .	. . .	. . .	. . .
Sea transport, passenger	2 207 . .	. . .	. . .	. . .	. . .	. . .	. . .	. . .	. . .
Sea transport, freight	2 208 . .	. . .	. . .	. . .	. . .	. . .	. . .	. . .	. . .
Sea transport, other	2 209 . .	. . .	. . .	. . .	. . .	. . .	. . .	. . .	. . .
Air transport, passenger	2 211 . .	. . .	. . .	. . .	. . .	. . .	. . .	. . .	. . .
Air transport, freight	2 212 . .	. . .	. . .	. . .	. . .	. . .	. . .	. . .	. . .
Air transport, other	2 213 . .	. . .	. . .	. . .	. . .	. . .	. . .	. . .	. . .
Other transport, passenger	2 215 . .	. . .	. . .	. . .	. . .	. . .	. . .	. . .	. . .
Other transport, freight	2 216 . .	. . .	. . .	. . .	. . .	. . .	. . .	. . .	. . .
Other transport, other	2 217 . .	. . .	. . .	. . .	. . .	. . .	. . .	. . .	. . .
Transportation services, debit	3 205 . .	**–84.3**	**–95.5**	**–100.7**	**–94.4**	**–83.6**	**–78.3**	**–95.9**	**. . .**
Passenger	3 205 BA	*–5.2*	*–8.9*	*–11.5*	*–9.3*	*–5.1*	*–4.6*	*–3.9*	. . .
Freight	3 205 BB	*–75.9*	*–86.6*	*–89.3*	*–85.1*	*–76.6*	*–71.9*	*–91.9*	. . .
Other	3 205 BC	*–3.1*	. . .	. . .	. . .	*–1.9*	*–1.8*	. . .	. . .
Sea transport, passenger	3 207 . .	. . .	. . .	. . .	. . .	. . .	. . .	. . .	. . .
Sea transport, freight	3 208 . .	. . .	. . .	. . .	. . .	. . .	. . .	. . .	. . .
Sea transport, other	3 209 . .	. . .	. . .	. . .	. . .	. . .	. . .	. . .	. . .
Air transport, passenger	3 211 . .	. . .	. . .	. . .	. . .	. . .	. . .	. . .	. . .
Air transport, freight	3 212 . .	. . .	. . .	. . .	. . .	. . .	. . .	. . .	. . .
Air transport, other	3 213 . .	. . .	. . .	. . .	. . .	. . .	. . .	. . .	. . .
Other transport, passenger	3 215 . .	. . .	. . .	. . .	. . .	. . .	. . .	. . .	. . .
Other transport, freight	3 216 . .	. . .	. . .	. . .	. . .	. . .	. . .	. . .	. . .
Other transport, other	3 217 . .	. . .	. . .	. . .	. . .	. . .	. . .	. . .	. . .
Travel, credit	2 236 . .	**7.2**	**7.6**	**8.0**	**6.7**	**7.8**	**7.5**	**11.7**	**. . .**
Business travel	2 237 . .	. . .	. . .	. . .	. . .	. . .	. . .	. . .	. . .
Personal travel	2 240 . .	. . .	. . .	. . .	. . .	. . .	. . .	. . .	. . .
Travel, debit	3 236 . .	**–67.3**	**–53.1**	**–69.7**	**–63.2**	**–79.9**	**–85.6**	**–26.0**	**. . .**
Business travel	3 237 . .	. . .	. . .	. . .	. . .	. . .	. . .	. . .	. . .
Personal travel	3 240 . .	. . .	. . .	. . .	. . .	. . .	. . .	. . .	. . .
Other services, credit	2 200 BA	**69.4**	**32.6**	**28.6**	**19.8**	**17.1**	**37.0**	**42.1**	**. . .**
Communications	2 245 . .	. . .	. . .	. . .	. . .	. . .	. . .	. . .	. . .
Construction	2 249 . .	. . .	. . .	. . .	. . .	. . .	. . .	. . .	. . .
Insurance	2 253 . .	.5	.4	.1	.7	.4	1.1	.4	. . .
Financial	2 260 . .	. . .	. . .	. . .	. . .	. . .	. . .	. . .	. . .
Computer and information	2 262 . .	. . .	. . .	. . .	. . .	. . .	. . .	. . .	. . .
Royalties and licence fees	2 266 . .	. . .	. . .	. . .	. . .	. . .	. . .	. . .	. . .
Other business services	2 268 . .	9.3	18.3	11.1	6.5	3.9	4.4	10.3	. . .
Personal, cultural, and recreational	2 287 . .	. . .	. . .	. . .	. . .	. . .	. . .	. . .	. . .
Government, n.i.e.	2 291 . .	59.6	13.9	17.4	12.5	12.8	31.4	31.4	. . .
Other services, debit	3 200 BA	**–66.3**	**–61.4**	**–57.7**	**–50.4**	**–60.6**	**–71.2**	**–77.6**	**. . .**
Communications	3 245 . .	. . .	. . .	. . .	. . .	. . .	. . .	. . .	. . .
Construction	3 249 . .	. . .	. . .	. . .	. . .	. . .	. . .	. . .	. . .
Insurance	3 253 . .	–11.7	–12.0	–9.9	–14.5	–10.9	–11.5	–2.7	. . .
Financial	3 260 . .	. . .	. . .	. . .	. . .	. . .	. . .	. . .	. . .
Computer and information	3 262 . .	. . .	. . .	. . .	. . .	. . .	. . .	. . .	. . .
Royalties and licence fees	3 266 . .	. . .	. . .	. . .	. . .	. . .	. . .	. . .	. . .
Other business services	3 268 . .	–50.5	–45.5	–42.9	–32.5	–42.6	–50.2	–49.8	. . .
Personal, cultural, and recreational	3 287 . .	. . .	. . .	. . .	. . .	. . .	. . .	. . .	. . .
Government, n.i.e.	3 291 . .	–4.1	–3.8	–4.9	–3.5	–7.1	–9.4	–25.2	. . .

Table 2 (Continued). STANDARD PRESENTATION, 1988–95
(Millions of U.S. dollars)

	Code	1988	1989	1990	1991	1992	1993	1994	1995
C. INCOME	4 300	–13.3	–9.4	–20.8	–2.3	2.6	–11.4	–7.3	...
Total credit	2 300	*2.1*	*1.3*	*3.0*	*8.9*	*17.5*	*4.3*	*5.0*	...
Total debit	3 300	*–15.5*	*–10.8*	*–23.8*	*–11.2*	*–14.9*	*–15.7*	*–12.4*	...
Compensation of employees, credit	2 310	...	...	...	...	...	**.2**	...	...
Compensation of employees, debit	3 310	...	...	...	...	...	...	...	...
Investment income, credit	2 320	**2.1**	**1.3**	**3.0**	**8.9**	**17.5**	**4.1**	**5.0**	...
Direct investment income	2 330	...	...	...	...	...	...	...	...
Dividends and distributed branch profits	2 332	...	...	...	...	...	...	...	...
Reinvested earnings and undistributed branch profits	2 333	...	...	...	...	...	...	...	...
Income on debt (interest)	2 334	...	...	...	...	...	...	...	...
Portfolio investment income	2 339	...	...	...	...	...	...	...	...
Income on equity	2 340	...	...	...	...	...	...	...	...
Income on bonds and notes	2 350	...	...	...	...	...	...	...	...
Income on money market instruments and financial derivatives	2 360	...	...	...	...	...	...	...	...
Other investment income	2 370	2.1	1.3	3.0	8.9	17.5	4.1	5.0	...
Investment income, debit	3 320	**–15.5**	**–10.8**	**–23.8**	**–11.2**	**–14.9**	**–15.6**	**–12.4**	...
Direct investment income	3 330	...	...	...	...	11.2	...	...	...
Dividends and distributed branch profits	3 332	...	...	...	...	...	...	...	...
Reinvested earnings and undistributed branch profits	3 333	...	...	...	...	11.2	...	...	...
Income on debt (interest)	3 334	...	...	...	...	...	...	...	...
Portfolio investment income	3 339	...	...	...	...	...	...	...	...
Income on equity	3 340	...	...	...	...	...	...	...	...
Income on bonds and notes	3 350	...	...	...	...	...	...	...	...
Income on money market instruments and financial derivatives	3 360	...	...	...	...	...	...	...	...
Other investment income	3 370	–15.5	–10.8	–23.8	–11.2	–26.1	–15.6	–12.4	...
D. CURRENT TRANSFERS	4 379	260.5	210.8	191.6	170.2	169.8	146.2	191.0	...
Credit	2 379	**301.4**	**246.0**	**239.3**	**215.5**	**222.3**	**192.4**	**209.4**	...
General government	2 380	270.0	233.1	208.4	186.1	200.1	179.8	201.8	...
Other sectors	2 390	31.3	12.9	30.9	29.4	22.3	12.7	7.6	...
Workers' remittances	2 391	.3	.8	...	...	.2	.2	.7	...
Other current transfers	2 392	31.0	12.2	30.9	29.4	22.1	12.5	6.9	...
Debit	3 379	**–40.8**	**–35.2**	**–47.7**	**–45.3**	**–52.5**	**–46.2**	**–18.4**	...
General government	3 380	–3.8	–1.9	–4.0	–4.4	–1.6	–4.3	–2.5	...
Other sectors	3 390	–37.1	–33.4	–43.7	–41.0	–51.0	–41.9	–16.0	...
Workers' remittances	3 391	–35.2	–31.2	–38.9	–38.8	–46.9	–40.9	–15.4	...
Other current transfers	3 392	–1.9	–2.2	–4.8	–2.2	–4.1	–1.0	–.6	...
CAPITAL AND FINANCIAL ACCOUNT	4 996	**58.2**	**40.2**	**79.0**	**78.5**	**76.4**	**116.7**	**70.7**	...
CAPITAL ACCOUNT	4 994	...	...	...	**5.6**	...	...	...	...
Total credit	2 994	...	...	...	*5.6*	...	...	...	...
Total debit	3 994	...	...	...	...	...	...	...	...
Capital transfers, credit	2 400	...	...	...	**5.6**	...	...	...	...
General government	2 401	...	...	...	5.6	...	...	...	...
Debt forgiveness	2 402	...	...	...	5.6	...	...	...	...
Other capital transfers	2 410	...	...	...	...	...	...	...	...
Other sectors	2 430	...	...	...	...	...	...	...	...
Migrants' transfers	2 431	...	...	...	...	...	...	...	...
Debt forgiveness	2 432	...	...	...	...	...	...	...	...
Other capital transfers	2 440	...	...	...	...	...	...	...	...
Capital transfers, debit	3 400	...	...	...	...	...	...	...	...
General government	3 401	...	...	...	...	...	...	...	...
Debt forgiveness	3 402	...	...	...	...	...	...	...	...
Other capital transfers	3 410	...	...	...	...	...	...	...	...
Other sectors	3 430	...	...	...	...	...	...	...	...
Migrants' transfers	3 431	...	...	...	...	...	...	...	...
Debt forgiveness	3 432	...	...	...	...	...	...	...	...
Other capital transfers	3 440	...	...	...	...	...	...	...	...
Nonproduced nonfinancial assets, credit	2 480	...	...	...	...	...	...	...	...
Nonproduced nonfinancial assets, debit	3 480	...	...	...	...	...	...	...	...

Table 2 (Continued). STANDARD PRESENTATION, 1988–95
(Millions of U.S. dollars)

	Code	1988	1989	1990	1991	1992	1993	1994	1995
FINANCIAL ACCOUNT	4 995	**58.2**	**40.2**	**79.0**	**72.9**	**76.4**	**116.7**	**70.7**	**. . .**
A. DIRECT INVESTMENT	4 500	–12.6	6.2	. . .	–6.3	–11.8	4.2	26.5	. . .
Direct investment abroad	4 505	**–13.8**	**–12.5**	**. . .**	**–10.5**	**–13.8**	**–10.9**	**–.6**	**. . .**
Equity capital	4 510	–13.8	–12.5	. . .	–10.5	–13.8	–10.9	–.6	. . .
Claims on affiliated enterprises	4 515	. . .	. . .	. . .	. . .	. . .	. . .	. . .	. . .
Liabilities to affiliated enterprises	4 520	. . .	. . .	. . .	. . .	. . .	. . .	. . .	. . .
Reinvested earnings	4 525	. . .	. . .	. . .	. . .	. . .	. . .	. . .	. . .
Other capital	4 530	. . .	. . .	. . .	. . .	. . .	. . .	. . .	. . .
Claims on affiliated enterprises	4 535	. . .	. . .	. . .	. . .	. . .	. . .	. . .	. . .
Liabilities to affiliated enterprises	4 540	. . .	. . .	. . .	. . .	. . .	. . .	. . .	. . .
Direct investment in Chad	4 555	**1.3**	**18.7**	**. . .**	**4.2**	**2.0**	**15.2**	**27.1**	**. . .**
Equity capital	4 560	1.3	21.9	. . .	4.2	15.5	15.2	27.1	. . .
Claims on direct investors	4 565	. . .	. . .	. . .	. . .	. . .	. . .	. . .	. . .
Liabilities to direct investors	4 570	. . .	. . .	. . .	. . .	. . .	. . .	. . .	. . .
Reinvested earnings	4 575	. . .	. . .	. . .	. . .	–11.2	. . .	. . .	. . .
Other capital	4 580	. . .	–3.1	. . .	. . .	–2.3	. . .	. . .	. . .
Claims on direct investors	4 585	. . .	. . .	. . .	. . .	. . .	. . .	. . .	. . .
Liabilities to direct investors	4 590	. . .	. . .	. . .	. . .	. . .	. . .	. . .	. . .
B. PORTFOLIO INVESTMENT	4 600	. . .	. . .	. . .	. . .	. . .	. . .	. . .	. . .
Assets	4 602	**. . .**	**. . .**	**. . .**	**. . .**	**. . .**	**. . .**	**. . .**	**. . .**
Equity securities	4 610	. . .	. . .	. . .	. . .	. . .	. . .	. . .	. . .
Monetary authorities	4 611	. . .	. . .	. . .	. . .	. . .	. . .	. . .	. . .
General government	4 612	. . .	. . .	. . .	. . .	. . .	. . .	. . .	. . .
Banks	4 613	. . .	. . .	. . .	. . .	. . .	. . .	. . .	. . .
Other sectors	4 614	. . .	. . .	. . .	. . .	. . .	. . .	. . .	. . .
Debt securities	4 619	. . .	. . .	. . .	. . .	. . .	. . .	. . .	. . .
Bonds and notes	4 620	. . .	. . .	. . .	. . .	. . .	. . .	. . .	. . .
Monetary authorities	4 621	. . .	. . .	. . .	. . .	. . .	. . .	. . .	. . .
General government	4 622	. . .	. . .	. . .	. . .	. . .	. . .	. . .	. . .
Banks	4 623	. . .	. . .	. . .	. . .	. . .	. . .	. . .	. . .
Other sectors	4 624	. . .	. . .	. . .	. . .	. . .	. . .	. . .	. . .
Money market instruments	4 630	. . .	. . .	. . .	. . .	. . .	. . .	. . .	. . .
Monetary authorities	4 631	. . .	. . .	. . .	. . .	. . .	. . .	. . .	. . .
General government	4 632	. . .	. . .	. . .	. . .	. . .	. . .	. . .	. . .
Banks	4 633	. . .	. . .	. . .	. . .	. . .	. . .	. . .	. . .
Other sectors	4 634	. . .	. . .	. . .	. . .	. . .	. . .	. . .	. . .
Financial derivatives	4 640	. . .	. . .	. . .	. . .	. . .	. . .	. . .	. . .
Monetary authorities	4 641	. . .	. . .	. . .	. . .	. . .	. . .	. . .	. . .
General government	4 642	. . .	. . .	. . .	. . .	. . .	. . .	. . .	. . .
Banks	4 643	. . .	. . .	. . .	. . .	. . .	. . .	. . .	. . .
Other sectors	4 644	. . .	. . .	. . .	. . .	. . .	. . .	. . .	. . .
Liabilities	4 652	**. . .**	**. . .**	**. . .**	**. . .**	**. . .**	**. . .**	**. . .**	**. . .**
Equity securities	4 660	. . .	. . .	. . .	. . .	. . .	. . .	. . .	. . .
Banks	4 663	. . .	. . .	. . .	. . .	. . .	. . .	. . .	. . .
Other sectors	4 664	. . .	. . .	. . .	. . .	. . .	. . .	. . .	. . .
Debt securities	4 669	. . .	. . .	. . .	. . .	. . .	. . .	. . .	. . .
Bonds and notes	4 670	. . .	. . .	. . .	. . .	. . .	. . .	. . .	. . .
Monetary authorities	4 671	. . .	. . .	. . .	. . .	. . .	. . .	. . .	. . .
General government	4 672	. . .	. . .	. . .	. . .	. . .	. . .	. . .	. . .
Banks	4 673	. . .	. . .	. . .	. . .	. . .	. . .	. . .	. . .
Other sectors	4 674	. . .	. . .	. . .	. . .	. . .	. . .	. . .	. . .
Money market instruments	4 680	. . .	. . .	. . .	. . .	. . .	. . .	. . .	. . .
Monetary authorities	4 681	. . .	. . .	. . .	. . .	. . .	. . .	. . .	. . .
General government	4 682	. . .	. . .	. . .	. . .	. . .	. . .	. . .	. . .
Banks	4 683	. . .	. . .	. . .	. . .	. . .	. . .	. . .	. . .
Other sectors	4 684	. . .	. . .	. . .	. . .	. . .	. . .	. . .	. . .
Financial derivatives	4 690	. . .	. . .	. . .	. . .	. . .	. . .	. . .	. . .
Monetary authorities	4 691	. . .	. . .	. . .	. . .	. . .	. . .	. . .	. . .
General government	4 692	. . .	. . .	. . .	. . .	. . .	. . .	. . .	. . .
Banks	4 693	. . .	. . .	. . .	. . .	. . .	. . .	. . .	. . .
Other sectors	4 694	. . .	. . .	. . .	. . .	. . .	. . .	. . .	. . .

Table 2 (Concluded). STANDARD PRESENTATION, 1988–95
(Millions of U.S. dollars)

	Code	1988	1989	1990	1991	1992	1993	1994	1995
C. OTHER INVESTMENT	4 700 . .	55.9	75.3	75.3	71.0	55.4	73.1	74.9	. . .
Assets	4 703 . .	**10.3**	**3.5**	**. . .**	**24.2**	**3.9**	**42.1**	**.6**	**. . .**
Trade credits	4 706 . .	5.6	6.6	. . .	.7	5.7	11.0	7.0	. . .
General government: long-term	4 708 . .	. . .	. . .	. . .	. . .	. . .	. . .	. . .	. . .
General government: short-term	4 709 . .	. . .	. . .	. . .	. . .	. . .	. . .	. . .	. . .
Other sectors: long-term	4 711 . .	. . .	. . .	. . .	. . .	. . .	. . .	. . .	. . .
Other sectors: short-term	4 712 . .	5.6	6.6	. . .	.7	5.7	11.0	7.0	. . .
Loans	4 714 . .	. . .	. . .	. . .	. . .	. . .	. . .	. . .	. . .
Monetary authorities: long-term	4 717 . .	. . .	. . .	. . .	. . .	. . .	. . .	. . .	. . .
Monetary authorities: short-term	4 718 . .	. . .	. . .	. . .	. . .	. . .	. . .	. . .	. . .
General government: long-term	4 720 . .	. . .	. . .	. . .	. . .	. . .	. . .	. . .	. . .
General government: short-term	4 721 . .	. . .	. . .	. . .	. . .	. . .	. . .	. . .	. . .
Banks: long-term	4 723 . .	. . .	. . .	. . .	. . .	. . .	. . .	. . .	. . .
Banks: short-term	4 724 . .	. . .	. . .	. . .	. . .	. . .	. . .	. . .	. . .
Other sectors: long-term	4 726 . .	. . .	. . .	. . .	. . .	. . .	. . .	. . .	. . .
Other sectors: short-term	4 727 . .	. . .	. . .	. . .	. . .	. . .	. . .	. . .	. . .
Currency and deposits	4 730 . .	4.7	–3.1	. . .	23.5	–1.8	31.0	–6.4	. . .
Monetary authorities	4 731 . .	. . .	. . .	. . .	. . .	. . .	. . .	. . .	. . .
General government	4 732 . .	. . .	. . .	. . .	. . .	. . .	. . .	. . .	. . .
Banks	4 733 . .	.8	–3.1	. . .	23.5	–1.8	31.0	–4.8	. . .
Other sectors	4 734 . .	3.9	. . .	. . .	. . .	. . .	. . .	–1.6	. . .
Other assets	4 736 . .	. . .	. . .	. . .	. . .	. . .	. . .	. . .	. . .
Monetary authorities: long-term	4 738 . .	. . .	. . .	. . .	. . .	. . .	. . .	. . .	. . .
Monetary authorities: short-term	4 739 . .	. . .	. . .	. . .	. . .	. . .	. . .	. . .	. . .
General government: long-term	4 741 . .	. . .	. . .	. . .	. . .	. . .	. . .	. . .	. . .
General government: short-term	4 742 . .	. . .	. . .	. . .	. . .	. . .	. . .	. . .	. . .
Banks: long-term	4 744 . .	. . .	. . .	. . .	. . .	. . .	. . .	. . .	. . .
Banks: short-term	4 745 . .	. . .	. . .	. . .	. . .	. . .	. . .	. . .	. . .
Other sectors: long-term	4 747 . .	. . .	. . .	. . .	. . .	. . .	. . .	. . .	. . .
Other sectors: short-term	4 748 . .	. . .	. . .	. . .	. . .	. . .	. . .	. . .	. . .
Liabilities	4 753 . .	**45.6**	**71.8**	**75.3**	**46.8**	**51.5**	**31.0**	**74.3**	**. . .**
Trade credits	4 756 . .	. . .	6.3	. . .	–28.6	–5.7	. . .	. . .	. . .
General government: long-term	4 758 . .	. . .	. . .	. . .	. . .	. . .	. . .	. . .	. . .
General government: short-term	4 759 . .	. . .	. . .	. . .	. . .	. . .	. . .	. . .	. . .
Other sectors: long-term	4 761 . .	. . .	. . .	. . .	. . .	. . .	. . .	. . .	. . .
Other sectors: short-term	4 762 . .	. . .	6.3	. . .	–28.6	–5.7	. . .	. . .	. . .
Loans	4 764 . .	79.1	94.3	194.6	93.1	86.3	119.2	67.8	. . .
Use of Fund credit and loans from the Fund	4 766 . .	–2.3	6.9	4.6	. . .	. . .	–1.7	12.7	. . .
Monetary authorities: other long-term	4 767 . .	. . .	. . .	. . .	. . .	. . .	. . .	. . .	. . .
Monetary authorities: short-term	4 768 . .	. . .	. . .	. . .	. . .	. . .	. . .	. . .	. . .
General government: long-term	4 770 . .	64.4	79.0	164.9	81.3	71.3	102.1	49.8	. . .
General government: short-term	4 771 . .	. . .	. . .	. . .	. . .	. . .	. . .	. . .	. . .
Banks: long-term	4 773 . .	. . .	. . .	. . .	. . .	. . .	. . .	. . .	. . .
Banks: short-term	4 774 . .	. . .	. . .	. . .	. . .	. . .	. . .	. . .	. . .
Other sectors: long-term	4 776 . .	17.0	8.3	25.0	11.8	15.0	18.9	5.3	. . .
Other sectors: short-term	4 777 . .	. . .	. . .	. . .	. . .	. . .	. . .	. . .	. . .
Currency and deposits	4 780 . .	1.1	. . .	–36.7	1.2	–1.4	–5.2	–.1	. . .
Monetary authorities	4 781 . .	. . .	. . .	. . .	–.9	–6.3	–5.2	–.1	. . .
General government	4 782 . .	. . .	. . .	. . .	. . .	. . .	. . .	. . .	. . .
Banks	4 783 . .	1.1	. . .	–36.7	2.2	5.0	. . .	. . .	. . .
Other sectors	4 784 . .	. . .	. . .	. . .	. . .	. . .	. . .	. . .	. . .
Other liabilities	4 786 . .	–34.7	–28.8	–82.6	–18.9	–27.8	–83.1	6.6	. . .
Monetary authorities: long-term	4 788 . .	. . .	. . .	. . .	. . .	. . .	. . .	. . .	. . .
Monetary authorities: short-term	4 789 . .	. . .	. . .	. . .	. . .	. . .	. . .	. . .	. . .
General government: long-term	4 791 . .	. . .	. . .	. . .	. . .	. . .	. . .	. . .	. . .
General government: short-term	4 792 . .	3.0	. . .	–46.9	5.7	9.9	10.2	12.4	. . .
Banks: long-term	4 794 . .	. . .	. . .	. . .	. . .	. . .	. . .	. . .	. . .
Banks: short-term	4 795 . .	. . .	. . .	. . .	. . .	. . .	. . .	. . .	. . .
Other sectors: long-term	4 797 . .	. . .	. . .	. . .	. . .	. . .	. . .	. . .	. . .
Other sectors: short-term	4 798 . .	–37.6	–28.8	–35.6	–24.6	–37.7	–93.3	–5.9	. . .
D. RESERVE ASSETS	4 800 . .	14.8	–41.3	3.6	8.2	32.9	39.4	–30.7	. . .
Monetary gold	4 810 . .	.2	.3	. . .	. . .	–.6	1.6	1.2	. . .
Special drawing rights	4 820 . .	.8	5.6	1.7	. . .	.1	. . .	. . .	. . .
Reserve position in the Fund	4 830 . .	. . .	. . .	. . .	. . .	. . .	. . .	. . .	. . .
Foreign exchange	4 840 . .	13.8	–47.2	1.9	8.2	33.4	37.8	–31.9	. . .
Other claims	4 880 . .	. . .	. . .	. . .	. . .	. . .	. . .	. . .	. . .
NET ERRORS AND OMISSIONS	4 998 . .	**–83.7**	**11.1**	**–33.3**	**–13.0**	**9.2**	**–.1**	**–33.0**	**. . .**

Part 3 of the *Yearbook* contains descriptions of the methodologies, compilation practices, and sources used to compile these data.

Table 1. ANALYTIC PRESENTATION, 1988–95
(Millions of U.S. dollars)

	Code	1988	1989	1990	1991	1992	1993	1994	1995
A. Current Account [1]	4 993 Y.	**–234**	**–705**	**–536**	**109**	**–703**	**–2,073**	**–646**	**157**
Goods: exports f.o.b	2 100 . .	7,053	8,080	8,372	8,942	10,008	9,199	11,603	16,038
Goods: imports f.o.b	3 100 . .	–4,844	–6,502	–7,037	–7,354	–9,236	–10,181	–10,879	–14,655
Balance on Goods	4 100 . .	*2,209*	*1,578*	*1,335*	*1,588*	*772*	*–982*	*724*	*1,383*
Services: credit	2 200 . .	1,089	1,495	1,913	2,168	2,431	2,601	2,846	3,153
Services: debit	3 200 . .	–1,781	–2,051	–2,167	–2,177	–2,476	–2,597	–2,827	–3,306
Balance on Goods and Services	4 991 . .	*1,517*	*1,022*	*1,081*	*1,579*	*727*	*–978*	*743*	*1,230*
Income: credit	2 300 . .	185	241	356	472	441	498	498	823
Income: debit	3 300 . .	–2,118	–2,183	–2,173	–2,283	–2,302	–1,963	–2,241	–2,253
Balance on Goods, Services, and Income	4 992 . .	*–416*	*–920*	*–736*	*–232*	*–1,134*	*–2,443*	*–1,000*	*–200*
Current transfers: credit	2 379 Y.	219	241	228	359	450	389	374	376
Current transfers: debit	3 379 . .	–37	–26	–28	–18	–19	–19	–20	–19
B. Capital Account [1]	4 994 Y.	**. . .**	**. . .**	**. . .**	**. . .**	**. . .**	**. . .**	**. . .**	**. . .**
Capital account: credit	2 994 Y.	. . .	. . .	. . .	. . .	. . .	. . .	. . .	. . .
Capital account: debit	3 994 . .	. . .	. . .	. . .	. . .	. . .	. . .	. . .	. . .
Total, Groups A Plus B	4 010 . .	*–234*	*–705*	*–536*	*109*	*–703*	*–2,073*	*–646*	*157*
C. Financial Account [1]	4 995 X.	**–773**	**1,211**	**3,051**	**836**	**2,884**	**2,737**	**4,603**	**1,180**
Direct investment abroad	4 505 . .	–16	–10	–8	–123	–378	–434	–925	–687
Direct investment in Chile	4 555 Y.	968	1,289	590	523	699	809	1,773	1,695
Portfolio investment assets	4 602 . .	. . .	. . .	. . .	. . .	. . .	–90	–351	–14
Equity securities	4 610 . .	. . .	. . .	. . .	. . .	. . .	–90	–351	–14
Debt securities	4 619 . .	. . .	. . .	. . .	. . .	. . .	. . .	. . .	. . .
Portfolio investment liabilities	4 652 Y.	. . .	87	359	186	452	822	1,260	33
Equity securities	4 660 Y.	. . .	87	359	25	332	818	1,260	–264
Debt securities	4 669 Y.	. . .	. . .	. . .	161	120	4	. . .	297
Other investment assets	4 703 . .	370	297	553	1,298	–273	459	–163	–292
Monetary authorities	4 703 . A	. . .	. . .	. . .	. . .	. . .	. . .	. . .	. . .
General government	4 703 . B	–17	–37	37	. . .	47	. . .	. . .	. . .
Banks	4 703 . C	–56	27	–143	–63	–17	3	–22	43
Other sectors	4 703 . D	443	307	659	1,361	–303	456	–141	–335
Other investment liabilities	4 753 X.	–2,095	–452	1,557	–1,048	2,384	1,171	3,009	445
Monetary authorities	4 753 XA	–816	–825	–363	–75	–37	–82	–32	–460
General government	4 753 YB	100	103	247	107	158	–78	–75	–1,357
Banks	4 753 YC	–1,188	–588	–308	–558	1,568	65	417	–254
Other sectors	4 753 YD	–191	858	1,981	–522	695	1,266	2,699	2,516
Total, Groups A Through C	4 020 . .	*–1,007*	*506*	*2,515*	*945*	*2,181*	*664*	*3,957*	*1,337*
D. Net Errors and Omissions	4 998 . .	**–117**	**–119**	**–144**	**302**	**319**	**–79**	**–744**	**–257**
Total, Groups A Through D	4 030 . .	*–1,124*	*387*	*2,371*	*1,247*	*2,500*	*585*	*3,213*	*1,080*
E. Reserves and Related Items	4 040 . .	**1,124**	**–387**	**–2,371**	**–1,247**	**–2,500**	**–585**	**–3,213**	**–1,080**
Reserve assets	4 800 . .	–756	–549	–2,122	–1,049	–2,344	–171	–2,917	–740
Use of Fund credit and loans	4 766 . .	–70	–21	–209	–197	–203	–249	–210	–298
Liabilities constituting foreign authorities' reserves	4 900 . .	93	130	–37	9	47	–156	–64	–22
Exceptional financing	4 920 . .	1,857	53	–3	–11	. . .	–9	–22	–20
Conversion rates: Chilean pesos per U.S. dollar	0 101 . .	**245.05**	**267.16**	**305.06**	**349.37**	**362.59**	**404.35**	**420.08**	**396.78**

[1] Excludes components that have been classified in the categories of Group E.

Table 2. STANDARD PRESENTATION, 1988–95
(Millions of U.S. dollars)

	Code	1988	1989	1990	1991	1992	1993	1994	1995
CURRENT ACCOUNT	4 993 ..	**–234**	**–705**	**–536**	**109**	**–703**	**–2,073**	**–646**	**157**
A. GOODS	4 100 ..	2,209	1,578	1,335	1,588	772	–982	724	1,383
Credit	2 100 ..	**7,053**	**8,080**	**8,372**	**8,942**	**10,008**	**9,199**	**11,603**	**16,038**
General merchandise: exports f.o.b.	2 110 ..	7,053	8,080	8,372	8,942	10,008	9,199	11,603	16,038
Goods for processing: exports f.o.b.	2 150 ..	...	...	...	...	...	...	...	...
Repairs on goods	2 160 ..	...	...	...	...	...	...	...	...
Goods procured in ports by carriers	2 170 ..	...	...	...	...	...	...	...	...
Nonmonetary gold	2 180 ..	...	...	...	...	...	...	...	...
Debit	3 100 ..	**–4,844**	**–6,502**	**–7,037**	**–7,354**	**–9,236**	**–10,181**	**–10,879**	**–14,655**
General merchandise: imports f.o.b.	3 110 ..	–4,844	–6,502	–7,037	–7,354	–9,236	–10,181	–10,879	–14,655
Goods for processing: imports f.o.b.	3 150 ..	...	...	...	...	...	...	...	...
Repairs on goods	3 160 ..	...	...	...	...	...	...	...	...
Goods procured in ports by carriers	3 170 ..	...	...	...	...	...	...	...	...
Nonmonetary gold	3 180 ..	...	...	...	...	...	...	...	...
B. SERVICES	4 200 ..	–692	–556	–254	–9	–45	4	19	–153
Total credit	2 200 ..	*1,089*	*1,495*	*1,913*	*2,168*	*2,431*	*2,601*	*2,846*	*3,153*
Total debit	3 200 ..	*–1,781*	*–2,051*	*–2,167*	*–2,177*	*–2,476*	*–2,597*	*–2,827*	*–3,306*
Transportation services, credit	2 205 ..	**439**	**564**	**801**	**891**	**1,019**	**1,002**	**1,156**	**1,354**
Passenger	2 205 BA	*108*	*125*	*135*	*139*	*150*	*182*	*192*	*205*
Freight	2 205 BB	*239*	*297*	*401*	*396*	*491*	*459*	*545*	*562*
Other	2 205 BC	*92*	*142*	*265*	*356*	*378*	*361*	*419*	*587*
Sea transport, passenger	2 207 ..	...	...	...	...	...	...	...	...
Sea transport, freight	2 208 ..	...	...	...	...	...	...	...	...
Sea transport, other	2 209 ..	...	...	...	...	...	...	...	...
Air transport, passenger	2 211 ..	...	...	...	...	...	...	...	...
Air transport, freight	2 212 ..	...	...	...	...	...	...	...	...
Air transport, other	2 213 ..	...	...	...	...	...	...	...	...
Other transport, passenger	2 215 ..	...	...	...	...	...	...	...	...
Other transport, freight	2 216 ..	...	...	...	...	...	...	...	...
Other transport, other	2 217 ..	...	...	...	...	...	...	...	...
Transportation services, debit	3 205 ..	**–738**	**–937**	**–994**	**–1,076**	**–1,263**	**–1,307**	**–1,379**	**–1,625**
Passenger	3 205 BA	*–168*	*–172*	*–169*	*–174*	*–169*	*–186*	*–193*	*–197*
Freight	3 205 BB	*–226*	*–338*	*–295*	*–341*	*–406*	*–421*	*–430*	*–612*
Other	3 205 BC	*–344*	*–427*	*–530*	*–561*	*–688*	*–700*	*–756*	*–816*
Sea transport, passenger	3 207 ..	...	...	...	...	...	...	...	...
Sea transport, freight	3 208 ..	...	...	...	...	...	...	...	...
Sea transport, other	3 209 ..	...	...	...	...	...	...	...	...
Air transport, passenger	3 211 ..	...	...	...	...	...	...	...	...
Air transport, freight	3 212 ..	...	...	...	...	...	...	...	...
Air transport, other	3 213 ..	...	...	...	...	...	...	...	...
Other transport, passenger	3 215 ..	...	...	...	...	...	...	...	...
Other transport, freight	3 216 ..	...	...	...	...	...	...	...	...
Other transport, other	3 217 ..	...	...	...	...	...	...	...	...
Travel, credit	2 236 ..	**199**	**408**	**531**	**689**	**704**	**834**	**863**	**840**
Business travel	2 237 ..	...	...	...	...	...	...	...	...
Personal travel	2 240 ..	...	...	...	...	...	...	...	...
Travel, debit	3 236 ..	**–442**	**–396**	**–426**	**–446**	**–530**	**–559**	**–639**	**–710**
Business travel	3 237 ..	...	...	...	...	...	...	...	...
Personal travel	3 240 ..	...	...	...	...	...	...	...	...
Other services, credit	2 200 BA	**452**	**523**	**582**	**588**	**708**	**765**	**827**	**959**
Communications	2 245 ..	5	2	17	31	35	53	77	87
Construction	2 249 ..	...	...	...	...	...	...	...	...
Insurance	2 253 ..	69	63	99	58	92	95	105	105
Financial	2 260 ..	...	...	...	...	...	...	...	...
Computer and information	2 262 ..	...	...	...	...	...	...	...	...
Royalties and licence fees	2 266 ..	...	...	...	1	...	2	6	1
Other business services	2 268 ..	326	402	403	432	507	543	563	682
Personal, cultural, and recreational	2 287 ..	...	...	...	...	...	...	...	...
Government, n.i.e.	2 291 ..	52	56	63	66	74	72	76	84
Other services, debit	3 200 BA	**–601**	**–718**	**–747**	**–655**	**–683**	**–731**	**–809**	**–971**
Communications	3 245 ..	–7	–7	–7	–7	–8	–17	–22	–40
Construction	3 249 ..	...	...	...	...	...	...	...	...
Insurance	3 253 ..	–73	–77	–64	–68	–66	–68	–71	–87
Financial	3 260 ..	...	...	...	...	...	...	...	...
Computer and information	3 262 ..	...	...	...	...	...	...	...	...
Royalties and licence fees	3 266 ..	–36	–40	–37	–34	–40	–43	–47	–50
Other business services	3 268 ..	–396	–506	–545	–442	–452	–486	–549	–660
Personal, cultural, and recreational	3 287 ..	...	...	...	...	...	...	...	...
Government, n.i.e.	3 291 ..	–89	–88	–94	–104	–117	–117	–120	–134

Table 2 (Continued). STANDARD PRESENTATION, 1988–95
(Millions of U.S. dollars)

	Code		1988	1989	1990	1991	1992	1993	1994	1995
C. INCOME	4 300	. .	–1,933	–1,942	–1,817	–1,811	–1,861	–1,465	–1,743	–1,430
Total credit	2 300	. .	*185*	*241*	*356*	*472*	*441*	*498*	*498*	*823*
Total debit	3 300	. .	*–2,118*	*–2,183*	*–2,173*	*–2,283*	*–2,302*	*–1,963*	*–2,241*	*–2,253*
Compensation of employees, credit	2 310	. .	**. . .**	**1**	**. . .**	**. . .**	**. . .**	**. . .**	**. . .**	**. . .**
Compensation of employees, debit	3 310	. .	**–14**	**–18**	**–7**	**. . .**	**. . .**	**. . .**	**. . .**	**. . .**
Investment income, credit	2 320	. .	**185**	**240**	**356**	**472**	**441**	**498**	**498**	**823**
Direct investment income	2 330	. .	4	3	2	3	4	6	2	13
Dividends and distributed branch profits	2 332	. .	4	3	2	3	4	6	2	13
Reinvested earnings and undistributed branch profits	2 333	. .	. . .	. . .	. . .	. . .	. . .	. . .	. . .	. . .
Income on debt (interest)	2 334	. .	. . .	. . .	. . .	. . .	. . .	. . .	. . .	. . .
Portfolio investment income	2 339	. .	. . .	. . .	. . .	. . .	. . .	. . .	. . .	. . .
Income on equity	2 340	. .	. . .	. . .	. . .	. . .	. . .	. . .	. . .	. . .
Income on bonds and notes	2 350	. .	. . .	. . .	. . .	. . .	. . .	. . .	. . .	. . .
Income on money market instruments and financial derivatives	2 360	. .	. . .	. . .	. . .	. . .	. . .	. . .	. . .	. . .
Other investment income	2 370	. .	181	237	354	469	437	492	496	810
Investment income, debit	3 320	. .	**–2,104**	**–2,165**	**–2,166**	**–2,283**	**–2,302**	**–1,963**	**–2,241**	**–2,253**
Direct investment income	3 330	. .	–311	–385	–335	–645	–897	–754	–1,058	–903
Dividends and distributed branch profits	3 332	. .	–306	–385	–335	–637	–867	–754	–1,047	–903
Reinvested earnings and undistributed branch profits	3 333	. .	–5	. . .	. . .	–8	–30	. . .	–11	. . .
Income on debt (interest)	3 334	. .	. . .	. . .	. . .	. . .	. . .	. . .	. . .	. . .
Portfolio investment income	3 339	. .	. . .	. . .	. . .	. . .	. . .	. . .	. . .	. . .
Income on equity	3 340	. .	. . .	. . .	. . .	. . .	. . .	. . .	. . .	. . .
Income on bonds and notes	3 350	. .	. . .	. . .	. . .	. . .	. . .	. . .	. . .	. . .
Income on money market instruments and financial derivatives	3 360	. .	. . .	. . .	. . .	. . .	. . .	. . .	. . .	. . .
Other investment income	3 370	. .	–1,793	–1,780	–1,831	–1,638	–1,405	–1,209	–1,183	–1,350
D. CURRENT TRANSFERS	4 379	. .	182	215	200	341	431	370	354	357
Credit	2 379	. .	**219**	**241**	**228**	**359**	**450**	**389**	**374**	**376**
General government	2 380	. .	156	183	174	318	376	328	323	319
Other sectors	2 390	. .	63	58	54	41	74	61	51	57
Workers' remittances	2 391	. .	. . .	. . .	. . .	. . .	. . .	. . .	. . .	. . .
Other current transfers	2 392	. .	63	58	54	41	74	61	51	57
Debit	3 379	. .	**–37**	**–26**	**–28**	**–18**	**–19**	**–19**	**–20**	**–19**
General government	3 380	. .	–20	–9	–9	–12	–13	–13	–14	–14
Other sectors	3 390	. .	–17	–17	–19	–6	–6	–6	–6	–5
Workers' remittances	3 391	. .	. . .	. . .	. . .	. . .	. . .	. . .	. . .	. . .
Other current transfers	3 392	. .	–17	–17	–19	–6	–6	–6	–6	–5
CAPITAL AND FINANCIAL ACCOUNT	4 996	. .	**351**	**824**	**680**	**–411**	**384**	**2,152**	**1,390**	**100**
CAPITAL ACCOUNT	4 994	. .	**. . .**	**. . .**	**. . .**	**. . .**	**. . .**	**. . .**	**. . .**	**. . .**
Total credit	2 994	. .	. . .	. . .	. . .	. . .	. . .	. . .	. . .	. . .
Total debit	3 994	. .	. . .	. . .	. . .	. . .	. . .	. . .	. . .	. . .
Capital transfers, credit	2 400	. .	**. . .**	**. . .**	**. . .**	**. . .**	**. . .**	**. . .**	**. . .**	**. . .**
General government	2 401	. .	. . .	. . .	. . .	. . .	. . .	. . .	. . .	. . .
Debt forgiveness	2 402	. .	. . .	. . .	. . .	. . .	. . .	. . .	. . .	. . .
Other capital transfers	2 410	. .	. . .	. . .	. . .	. . .	. . .	. . .	. . .	. . .
Other sectors	2 430	. .	. . .	. . .	. . .	. . .	. . .	. . .	. . .	. . .
Migrants' transfers	2 431	. .	. . .	. . .	. . .	. . .	. . .	. . .	. . .	. . .
Debt forgiveness	2 432	. .	. . .	. . .	. . .	. . .	. . .	. . .	. . .	. . .
Other capital transfers	2 440	. .	. . .	. . .	. . .	. . .	. . .	. . .	. . .	. . .
Capital transfers, debit	3 400	. .	**. . .**	**. . .**	**. . .**	**. . .**	**. . .**	**. . .**	**. . .**	**. . .**
General government	3 401	. .	. . .	. . .	. . .	. . .	. . .	. . .	. . .	. . .
Debt forgiveness	3 402	. .	. . .	. . .	. . .	. . .	. . .	. . .	. . .	. . .
Other capital transfers	3 410	. .	. . .	. . .	. . .	. . .	. . .	. . .	. . .	. . .
Other sectors	3 430	. .	. . .	. . .	. . .	. . .	. . .	. . .	. . .	. . .
Migrants' transfers	3 431	. .	. . .	. . .	. . .	. . .	. . .	. . .	. . .	. . .
Debt forgiveness	3 432	. .	. . .	. . .	. . .	. . .	. . .	. . .	. . .	. . .
Other capital transfers	3 440	. .	. . .	. . .	. . .	. . .	. . .	. . .	. . .	. . .
Nonproduced nonfinancial assets, credit	2 480	. .	**. . .**	**. . .**	**. . .**	**. . .**	**. . .**	**. . .**	**. . .**	**. . .**
Nonproduced nonfinancial assets, debit	3 480	. .	**. . .**	**. . .**	**. . .**	**. . .**	**. . .**	**. . .**	**. . .**	**. . .**

Table 2 (Continued). STANDARD PRESENTATION, 1988–95
(Millions of U.S. dollars)

	Code	1988	1989	1990	1991	1992	1993	1994	1995
FINANCIAL ACCOUNT	4 995	**351**	**824**	**680**	**–411**	**384**	**2,152**	**1,390**	**100**
A. DIRECT INVESTMENT	4 500	952	1,279	582	400	321	375	848	1,008
Direct investment abroad	4 505	**–16**	**–10**	**–8**	**–123**	**–378**	**–434**	**–925**	**–687**
Equity capital	4 510	–16	–10	–8	–123	–378	–434	–925	–687
Claims on affiliated enterprises	4 515	...	...	...	...	...	...	...	...
Liabilities to affiliated enterprises	4 520	...	...	...	...	...	...	...	...
Reinvested earnings	4 525	...	...	...	...	...	...	...	...
Other capital	4 530	...	...	...	...	...	...	...	...
Claims on affiliated enterprises	4 535	...	...	...	...	...	...	...	...
Liabilities to affiliated enterprises	4 540	...	...	...	...	...	...	...	...
Direct investment in Chile	4 555	**968**	**1,289**	**590**	**523**	**699**	**809**	**1,773**	**1,695**
Equity capital	4 560	963	1,289	590	515	669	809	1,762	1,695
Claims on direct investors	4 565	...	...	...	...	...	...	...	...
Liabilities to direct investors	4 570	...	...	...	...	...	...	...	...
Reinvested earnings	4 575	5	...	...	8	30	...	11	...
Other capital	4 580	...	...	...	...	...	...	...	...
Claims on direct investors	4 585	...	...	...	...	...	...	...	...
Liabilities to direct investors	4 590	...	...	...	...	...	...	...	...
B. PORTFOLIO INVESTMENT	4 600	...	87	359	186	452	732	909	19
Assets	4 602	**...**	**...**	**...**	**...**	**...**	**–90**	**–351**	**–14**
Equity securities	4 610	...	...	...	...	...	–90	–351	–14
Monetary authorities	4 611	...	...	...	...	...	...	...	...
General government	4 612	...	...	...	...	...	...	...	...
Banks	4 613	...	...	...	...	...	...	...	...
Other sectors	4 614	...	...	...	...	...	...	...	...
Debt securities	4 619	...	...	...	...	...	...	...	...
Bonds and notes	4 620	...	...	...	...	...	...	...	...
Monetary authorities	4 621	...	...	...	...	...	...	...	...
General government	4 622	...	...	...	...	...	...	...	...
Banks	4 623	...	...	...	...	...	...	...	...
Other sectors	4 624	...	...	...	...	...	...	...	...
Money market instruments	4 630	...	...	...	...	...	...	...	...
Monetary authorities	4 631	...	...	...	...	...	...	...	...
General government	4 632	...	...	...	...	...	...	...	...
Banks	4 633	...	...	...	...	...	...	...	...
Other sectors	4 634	...	...	...	...	...	...	...	...
Financial derivatives	4 640	...	...	...	...	...	...	...	...
Monetary authorities	4 641	...	...	...	...	...	...	...	...
General government	4 642	...	...	...	...	...	...	...	...
Banks	4 643	...	...	...	...	...	...	...	...
Other sectors	4 644	...	...	...	...	...	...	...	...
Liabilities	4 652	**...**	**87**	**359**	**186**	**452**	**822**	**1,260**	**33**
Equity securities	4 660	...	87	359	25	332	818	1,260	–264
Banks	4 663	...	...	...	...	...	...	...	...
Other sectors	4 664	...	...	...	...	...	...	...	...
Debt securities	4 669	...	...	...	161	120	4	...	297
Bonds and notes	4 670	...	...	...	161	120	4	...	297
Monetary authorities	4 671	...	...	...	...	...	...	...	...
General government	4 672	...	...	...	161	120	–320	...	...
Banks	4 673	...	...	...	...	...	...	...	...
Other sectors	4 674	...	...	...	...	...	324	...	297
Money market instruments	4 680	...	...	...	...	...	...	...	...
Monetary authorities	4 681	...	...	...	...	...	...	...	...
General government	4 682	...	...	...	...	...	...	...	...
Banks	4 683	...	...	...	...	...	...	...	...
Other sectors	4 684	...	...	...	...	...	...	...	...
Financial derivatives	4 690	...	...	...	...	...	...	...	...
Monetary authorities	4 691	...	...	...	...	...	...	...	...
General government	4 692	...	...	...	...	...	...	...	...
Banks	4 693	...	...	...	...	...	...	...	...
Other sectors	4 694	...	...	...	...	...	...	...	...

Table 2 (Concluded). STANDARD PRESENTATION, 1988–95
(Millions of U.S. dollars)

	Code	1988	1989	1990	1991	1992	1993	1994	1995
C. OTHER INVESTMENT	4 700 . .	155	7	1,861	51	1,955	1,216	2,550	–187
Assets	4 703 . .	**370**	**297**	**553**	**1,298**	**–273**	**459**	**–163**	**–292**
Trade credits	4 706 . .	. . .	. . .	. . .	. . .	. . .	. . .	. . .	. . .
General government: long-term	4 708 . .	. . .	. . .	. . .	. . .	. . .	. . .	. . .	. . .
General government: short-term	4 709 . .	. . .	. . .	. . .	. . .	. . .	. . .	. . .	. . .
Other sectors: long-term	4 711 . .	. . .	. . .	. . .	. . .	. . .	. . .	. . .	. . .
Other sectors: short-term	4 712 . .	. . .	. . .	. . .	. . .	. . .	. . .	. . .	. . .
Loans	4 714 . .	–196	47	–147	203	–623	–335	–786	–1,851
Monetary authorities: long-term	4 717 . .	. . .	. . .	. . .	. . .	. . .	. . .	. . .	. . .
Monetary authorities: short-term	4 718 . .	. . .	. . .	. . .	. . .	. . .	. . .	. . .	. . .
General government: long-term	4 720 . .	. . .	. . .	. . .	. . .	. . .	. . .	. . .	. . .
General government: short-term	4 721 . .	. . .	. . .	. . .	. . .	. . .	. . .	. . .	. . .
Banks: long-term	4 723 . .	–1	. . .	. . .	. . .	. . .	. . .	. . .	. . .
Banks: short-term	4 724 . .	. . .	. . .	. . .	. . .	. . .	. . .	. . .	. . .
Other sectors: long-term	4 726 . .	. . .	. . .	. . .	. . .	. . .	. . .	. . .	. . .
Other sectors: short-term	4 727 . .	–195	47	–147	203	–623	–335	–786	–1,851
Currency and deposits	4 730 . .	583	276	660	1,097	299	792	626	1,562
Monetary authorities	4 731 . .	. . .	. . .	. . .	. . .	. . .	. . .	. . .	. . .
General government	4 732 . .	. . .	. . .	. . .	. . .	. . .	. . .	. . .	. . .
Banks	4 733 . .	–55	16	–146	–61	–21	1	–19	46
Other sectors	4 734 . .	638	260	806	1,158	320	791	645	1,516
Other assets	4 736 . .	–17	–26	40	–2	51	2	–3	–3
Monetary authorities: long-term	4 738 . .	. . .	. . .	. . .	. . .	. . .	. . .	. . .	. . .
Monetary authorities: short-term	4 739 . .	. . .	. . .	. . .	. . .	. . .	. . .	. . .	. . .
General government: long-term	4 741 . .	–17	–37	37	. . .	47	. . .	. . .	. . .
General government: short-term	4 742 . .	. . .	. . .	. . .	. . .	. . .	. . .	. . .	. . .
Banks: long-term	4 744 . .	. . .	11	3	–2	4	2	–3	–3
Banks: short-term	4 745 . .	. . .	. . .	. . .	. . .	. . .	. . .	. . .	. . .
Other sectors: long-term	4 747 . .	. . .	. . .	. . .	. . .	. . .	. . .	. . .	. . .
Other sectors: short-term	4 748 . .	. . .	. . .	. . .	. . .	. . .	. . .	. . .	. . .
Liabilities	4 753 . .	**–215**	**–290**	**1,308**	**–1,247**	**2,228**	**757**	**2,713**	**105**
Trade credits	4 756 . .	. . .	. . .	. . .	. . .	. . .	. . .	. . .	. . .
General government: long-term	4 758 . .	. . .	. . .	. . .	. . .	. . .	. . .	. . .	. . .
General government: short-term	4 759 . .	. . .	. . .	. . .	. . .	. . .	. . .	. . .	. . .
Other sectors: long-term	4 761 . .	. . .	. . .	. . .	. . .	. . .	. . .	. . .	. . .
Other sectors: short-term	4 762 . .	. . .	. . .	. . .	. . .	. . .	. . .	. . .	. . .
Loans	4 764 . .	–1,011	–801	1,201	–1,018	621	922	2,476	626
Use of Fund credit and loans from the Fund	4 766 . .	–70	–21	–209	–197	–203	–249	–210	–298
Monetary authorities: other long-term	4 767 . .	–573	–830	–368	–65	–37	–82	–32	–460
Monetary authorities: short-term	4 768 . .	–225	. . .	. . .	. . .	. . .	. . .	. . .	. . .
General government: long-term	4 770 . .	491	119	281	107	158	–78	–75	–1,357
General government: short-term	4 771 . .	. . .	. . .	. . .	. . .	. . .	. . .	. . .	. . .
Banks: long-term	4 773 . .	–958	–927	–439	–353	–6	43	82	219
Banks: short-term	4 774 . .	. . .	. . .	. . .	. . .	. . .	. . .	. . .	. . .
Other sectors: long-term	4 776 . .	5	322	1,170	89	17	669	1,393	1,397
Other sectors: short-term	4 777 . .	319	536	766	–599	692	619	1,318	1,125
Currency and deposits	4 780 . .	398	469	94	–196	1,621	–134	271	–495
Monetary authorities	4 781 . .	93	130	–37	9	47	–156	–64	–22
General government	4 782 . .	. . .	. . .	. . .	. . .	. . .	. . .	. . .	. . .
Banks	4 783 . .	305	339	131	–205	1,574	22	335	–473
Other sectors	4 784 . .	. . .	. . .	. . .	. . .	. . .	. . .	. . .	. . .
Other liabilities	4 786 . .	398	42	13	–33	–14	–31	–34	–26
Monetary authorities: long-term	4 788 . .	. . .	. . .	. . .	. . .	. . .	. . .	. . .	. . .
Monetary authorities: short-term	4 789 . .	. . .	5	5	–10	. . .	–9	–22	–15
General government: long-term	4 791 . .	. . .	. . .	. . .	. . .	. . .	. . .	. . .	. . .
General government: short-term	4 792 . .	196	37	–37	–11	. . .	. . .	. . .	–1
Banks: long-term	4 794 . .	. . .	. . .	. . .	. . .	. . .	. . .	. . .	. . .
Banks: short-term	4 795 . .	139	. . .	. . .	. . .	. . .	. . .	. . .	–4
Other sectors: long-term	4 797 . .	. . .	. . .	45	–12	–14	–22	–12	–6
Other sectors: short-term	4 798 . .	63	. . .	. . .	. . .	. . .	. . .	. . .	. . .
D. RESERVE ASSETS	4 800 . .	–756	–549	–2,122	–1,049	–2,344	–171	–2,917	–740
Monetary gold	4 810 . .	. . .	36	. . .	. . .	. . .	. . .	. . .	. . .
Special drawing rights	4 820 . .	–5	19	24	. . .	. . .	–1	1	–3
Reserve position in the Fund	4 830 . .	. . .	. . .	. . .	. . .	. . .	. . .	. . .	. . .
Foreign exchange	4 840 . .	–751	–604	–2,146	–1,049	–2,344	–170	–2,918	–737
Other claims	4 880 . .	. . .	. . .	. . .	. . .	. . .	. . .	. . .	. . .
NET ERRORS AND OMISSIONS	4 998 . .	**–117**	**–119**	**–144**	**302**	**319**	**–79**	**–744**	**–257**

Part 3 of the *Yearbook* contains descriptions of the methodologies, compilation practices, and sources used to compile these data.

Table 1. ANALYTIC PRESENTATION, 1988–95
(Millions of U.S. dollars)

	Code	1988	1989	1990	1991	1992	1993	1994	1995
A. Current Account [1]	4 993 Y.	**–3,802**	**–4,317**	**11,997**	**13,272**	**6,401**	**–11,609**	**6,908**	**1,618**
Goods: exports f.o.b	2 100 ..	41,054	43,220	51,519	58,919	69,568	75,659	102,561	128,110
Goods: imports f.o.b	3 100 ..	–46,369	–48,840	–42,354	–50,176	–64,385	–86,313	–95,271	–110,060
Balance on Goods	4 100 ..	*–5,315*	*–5,620*	*9,165*	*8,743*	*5,183*	*–10,654*	*7,290*	*18,050*
Services: credit	2 200 ..	4,823	4,550	5,803	6,905	9,189	11,146	16,503	19,130
Services: debit	3 200 ..	–3,603	–3,910	–4,352	–4,121	–9,414	–12,014	–16,201	–25,223
Balance on Goods and Services	4 991 ..	*–4,095*	*–4,980*	*10,616*	*11,527*	*4,958*	*–11,522*	*7,592*	*11,957*
Income: credit	2 300 ..	1,504	1,947	3,069	3,793	5,655	4,437	5,854	5,191
Income: debit	3 300 ..	–1,630	–1,665	–1,962	–2,879	–5,367	–5,696	–6,873	–16,965
Balance on Goods, Services, and Income	4 992 ..	*–4,221*	*–4,698*	*11,723*	*12,441*	*5,246*	*–12,781*	*6,573*	*183*
Current transfers: credit	2 379 Y.	568	477	376	890	1,206	1,290	1,269	1,827
Current transfers: debit	3 379 ..	–149	–96	–102	–59	–51	–118	–934	–392
B. Capital Account [1]	4 994 Y.	**. . .**	**. . .**	**. . .**	**. . .**	**. . .**	**. . .**	**. . .**	**. . .**
Capital account: credit	2 994 Y.	. . .	. . .	. . .	. . .	. . .	. . .	. . .	. . .
Capital account: debit	3 994 ..	. . .	. . .	. . .	. . .	. . .	. . .	. . .	. . .
Total, Groups A Plus B	4 010 ..	*–3,802*	*–4,317*	*11,997*	*13,272*	*6,401*	*–11,609*	*6,908*	*1,618*
C. Financial Account [1]	4 995 X.	**7,133**	**3,723**	**3,255**	**8,032**	**–250**	**23,474**	**32,645**	**38,673**
Direct investment abroad	4 505 ..	–850	–780	–830	–913	–4,000	–4,400	–2,000	–2,000
Direct investment in China	4 555 Y.	3,194	3,393	3,487	4,366	11,156	27,515	33,787	35,849
Portfolio investment assets	4 602 ..	–340	–320	–241	–330	–450	–597	–380	79
Equity securities	4 610 ..	. . .	. . .	. . .	. . .	. . .	. . .	. . .	. . .
Debt securities	4 619 ..	–340	–320	–241	–330	–450	–597	–380	79
Portfolio investment liabilities	4 652 Y.	1,216	140	. . .	565	393	3,646	3,923	710
Equity securities	4 660 Y.	. . .	. . .	. . .	. . .	. . .	. . .	. . .	. . .
Debt securities	4 669 Y.	1,216	140	. . .	565	393	3,646	3,923	710
Other investment assets	4 703 ..	–781	–229	–231	–156	–3,267	–2,114	–1,189	–87
Monetary authorities	4 703 .A	. . .	. . .	. . .	. . .	. . .	. . .	. . .	. . .
General government	4 703 .B	–729	–121	–116	–48	–3,351	–1,741	–1,136	–81
Banks	4 703 .C	. . .	. . .	. . .	. . .	. . .	. . .	. . .	. . .
Other sectors	4 703 .D	–52	–108	–115	–108	84	–373	–53	–6
Other investment liabilities	4 753 X.	4,694	1,519	1,070	4,500	–4,082	–576	–1,496	4,122
Monetary authorities	4 753 XA	198	50	–115	. . .	140	175	1,004	–288
General government	4 753 YB	3,895	4,699	3,129	2,284	–18	1,564	5,178	4,321
Banks	4 753 YC	1,108	–2,661	–2,315	1,655	–786	–415	–5,222	–4,045
Other sectors	4 753 YD	–507	–569	371	561	–3,418	–1,900	–2,456	4,133
Total, Groups A Through C	4 020 ..	*3,331*	*–594*	*15,252*	*21,304*	*6,151*	*11,865*	*39,553*	*40,291*
D. Net Errors and Omissions	4 998 ..	**–957**	**115**	**–3,205**	**–6,767**	**–8,211**	**–10,096**	**–9,100**	**–17,822**
Total, Groups A Through D	4 030 ..	*2,374*	*–479*	*12,047*	*14,537*	*–2,060*	*1,769*	*30,453*	*22,469*
E. Reserves and Related Items	4 040 ..	**–2,374**	**479**	**–12,047**	**–14,537**	**2,060**	**–1,769**	**–30,453**	**–22,469**
Reserve assets	4 800 ..	–2,291	558	–11,555	–14,083	2,060	–1,769	–30,453	–22,469
Use of Fund credit and loans	4 766 ..	–82	–79	–492	–454	. . .	. . .	. . .	. . .
Liabilities constituting foreign authorities' reserves	4 900 ..	. . .	. . .	. . .	. . .	. . .	. . .	. . .	. . .
Exceptional financing	4 920 ..	. . .	. . .	. . .	. . .	. . .	. . .	. . .	. . .
Conversion rates: yuan per U.S. dollar	0 101 ..	**3.7221**	**3.7651**	**4.7832**	**5.3234**	**5.5146**	**5.7620**	**8.6187**	**8.3514**

[1] Excludes components that have been classified in the categories of Group E.

Table 2. STANDARD PRESENTATION, 1988–95

(Millions of U.S. dollars)

	Code	1988	1989	1990	1991	1992	1993	1994	1995
CURRENT ACCOUNT	4 993 . .	**–3,802**	**–4,317**	**11,997**	**13,272**	**6,401**	**–11,609**	**6,908**	**1,618**
A. GOODS	4 100 . .	–5,315	–5,620	9,165	8,743	5,183	–10,654	7,290	18,050
Credit	2 100 . .	**41,054**	**43,220**	**51,519**	**58,919**	**69,568**	**75,659**	**102,561**	**128,110**
General merchandise: exports f.o.b.	2 110 . .	41,054	43,220	51,519	58,919	69,568	75,659	102,561	128,110
Goods for processing: exports f.o.b.	2 150 . .	...	...	...	...	...	...	...	...
Repairs on goods	2 160 . .	...	...	...	...	...	...	...	...
Goods procured in ports by carriers	2 170 . .	...	...	...	...	...	...	...	...
Nonmonetary gold	2 180 . .	...	...	...	...	...	...	...	...
Debit	3 100 . .	**–46,369**	**–48,840**	**–42,354**	**–50,176**	**–64,385**	**–86,313**	**–95,271**	**–110,060**
General merchandise: imports f.o.b.	3 110 . .	–46,369	–48,840	–42,354	–50,176	–64,385	–86,313	–95,271	–110,060
Goods for processing: imports f.o.b.	3 150 . .	...	...	...	...	...	...	...	...
Repairs on goods	3 160 . .	...	...	...	...	...	...	...	...
Goods procured in ports by carriers	3 170 . .	...	...	...	...	...	...	...	...
Nonmonetary gold	3 180 . .	...	...	...	...	...	...	...	...
B. SERVICES	4 200 . .	1,220	640	1,451	2,784	–225	–868	302	–6,093
Total credit	2 200 . .	*4,823*	*4,550*	*5,803*	*6,905*	*9,189*	*11,146*	*16,503*	*19,130*
Total debit	3 200 . .	*–3,603*	*–3,910*	*–4,352*	*–4,121*	*–9,414*	*–12,014*	*–16,201*	*–25,223*
Transportation services, credit	2 205 . .	**2,062**	**1,734**	**2,706**	**2,011**	**2,079**	**1,930**	**3,079**	**3,352**
Passenger	2 205 BA	*450*	*372*	*480*	*494*	*417*	*294*	*254*	...
Freight	2 205 BB	*1,308*	*1,062*	*1,937*	*1,179*	*1,294*	*1,391*	*2,065*	*2,478*
Other	2 205 BC	*304*	*300*	*289*	*338*	*368*	*245*	*760*	*874*
Sea transport, passenger	2 207 . .	...	...	...	...	...	...	...	...
Sea transport, freight	2 208 . .	...	...	...	...	...	...	...	...
Sea transport, other	2 209 . .	...	...	...	...	...	...	...	...
Air transport, passenger	2 211 . .	...	...	...	...	...	...	...	...
Air transport, freight	2 212 . .	...	...	...	...	...	...	...	...
Air transport, other	2 213 . .	...	...	...	...	...	...	...	...
Other transport, passenger	2 215 . .	...	...	...	...	...	...	...	...
Other transport, freight	2 216 . .	...	...	...	...	...	...	...	...
Other transport, other	2 217 . .	...	...	...	...	...	...	...	...
Transportation services, debit	3 205 . .	**–2,276**	**–2,752**	**–3,245**	**–2,508**	**–4,325**	**–5,479**	**–7,621**	**–9,526**
Passenger	3 205 BA	...	...	...	...	...	...	...	...
Freight	3 205 BB	*–1,387*	*–2,382*	*–2,139*	*–2,193*	*–3,876*	*–5,134*	*–6,926*	*–8,727*
Other	3 205 BC	*–889*	*–370*	*–1,106*	*–315*	*–449*	*–345*	*–695*	*–799*
Sea transport, passenger	3 207 . .	...	...	...	...	...	...	...	...
Sea transport, freight	3 208 . .	...	...	...	...	...	...	...	...
Sea transport, other	3 209 . .	...	...	...	...	...	...	...	...
Air transport, passenger	3 211 . .	...	...	...	...	...	...	...	...
Air transport, freight	3 212 . .	...	...	...	...	...	...	...	...
Air transport, other	3 213 . .	...	...	...	...	...	...	...	...
Other transport, passenger	3 215 . .	...	...	...	...	...	...	...	...
Other transport, freight	3 216 . .	...	...	...	...	...	...	...	...
Other transport, other	3 217 . .	...	...	...	...	...	...	...	...
Travel, credit	2 236 . .	**1,797**	**1,488**	**1,738**	**2,346**	**3,530**	**4,683**	**7,323**	**8,730**
Business travel	2 237 . .	...	...	...	...	...	...	...	...
Personal travel	2 240 . .	...	...	...	...	...	...	...	...
Travel, debit	3 236 . .	**–633**	**–429**	**–470**	**–511**	**–2,512**	**–2,797**	**–3,036**	**–3,688**
Business travel	3 237 . .	...	...	...	...	...	...	...	...
Personal travel	3 240 . .	...	...	...	...	...	...	...	...
Other services, credit	2 200 BA	**964**	**1,328**	**1,359**	**2,548**	**3,580**	**4,533**	**6,101**	**7,048**
Communications	2 245 . .	24	118	159	221	349	471	706	756
Construction	2 249 . .	...	...	...	...	...	...	...	...
Insurance	2 253 . .	345	332	227	342	486	452	1,700	1,852
Financial	2 260 . .	...	...	...	...	...	...	...	...
Computer and information	2 262 . .	...	...	...	...	...	...	...	...
Royalties and licence fees	2 266 . .	...	...	...	...	...	...	...	...
Other business services	2 268 . .	458	727	866	1,870	2,604	3,409	3,429	3,740
Personal, cultural, and recreational	2 287 . .	...	...	...	...	...	...	...	...
Government, n.i.e.	2 291 . .	137	151	107	115	141	201	266	700
Other services, debit	3 200 BA	**–694**	**–729**	**–637**	**–1,102**	**–2,577**	**–3,738**	**–5,544**	**–12,009**
Communications	3 245 . .	–11	–16	–13	–15	–72	–85	–146	–217
Construction	3 249 . .	...	...	...	...	...	...	...	...
Insurance	3 253 . .	–213	–187	–94	–214	–274	–362	–1,880	–4,273
Financial	3 260 . .	...	...	...	...	...	...	...	...
Computer and information	3 262 . .	...	...	...	...	...	...	...	...
Royalties and licence fees	3 266 . .	...	...	...	...	...	...	...	...
Other business services	3 268 . .	–193	–189	–291	–689	–2,004	–2,818	–3,000	–6,930
Personal, cultural, and recreational	3 287 . .	...	...	...	...	...	...	...	...
Government, n.i.e.	3 291 . .	–277	–337	–239	–184	–227	–473	–518	–588

Table 2 (Continued). STANDARD PRESENTATION, 1988–95
(Millions of U.S. dollars)

	Code	1988	1989	1990	1991	1992	1993	1994	1995
C. INCOME	4 300	–126	282	1,107	914	288	–1,259	–1,019	–11,774
Total credit	2 300	*1,504*	*1,947*	*3,069*	*3,793*	*5,655*	*4,437*	*5,854*	*5,191*
Total debit	3 300	*–1,630*	*–1,665*	*–1,962*	*–2,879*	*–5,367*	*–5,696*	*–6,873*	*–16,965*
Compensation of employees, credit	2 310	**35**	**53**	**52**	**74**	**60**	**47**	**117**	**...**
Compensation of employees, debit	3 310	**...**	**...**	**...**	**...**	**–20**	**–22**	**–98**	**...**
Investment income, credit	2 320	**1,469**	**1,894**	**3,017**	**3,719**	**5,595**	**4,390**	**5,737**	**5,191**
Direct investment income	2 330	...	6	...	...	...	...	...	1
Dividends and distributed branch profits	2 332	...	6	...	...	...	...	...	1
Reinvested earnings and undistributed branch profits	2 333	...	...	...	...	...	...	...	...
Income on debt (interest)	2 334	...	...	...	...	...	...	...	...
Portfolio investment income	2 339	...	...	...	...	...	...	...	...
Income on equity	2 340	...	...	...	...	...	...	...	...
Income on bonds and notes	2 350	...	...	...	...	...	...	...	...
Income on money market instruments and financial derivatives	2 360	...	...	...	...	...	...	...	...
Other investment income	2 370	1,469	1,888	3,017	3,719	5,595	4,390	5,737	5,190
Investment income, debit	3 320	**–1,630**	**–1,665**	**–1,962**	**–2,879**	**–5,347**	**–5,674**	**–6,775**	**–16,965**
Direct investment income	3 330	–8	–7	–46	–10	–22	–231	–400	–9,953
Dividends and distributed branch profits	3 332	–8	–7	–46	–10	–22	–231	–400	–9,953
Reinvested earnings and undistributed branch profits	3 333	...	...	...	...	...	...	...	...
Income on debt (interest)	3 334	...	...	...	...	...	...	...	...
Portfolio investment income	3 339	...	...	...	...	...	...	...	...
Income on equity	3 340	...	...	...	...	...	...	...	...
Income on bonds and notes	3 350	...	...	...	...	...	...	...	...
Income on money market instruments and financial derivatives	3 360	...	...	...	...	...	...	...	...
Other investment income	3 370	–1,622	–1,658	–1,916	–2,869	–5,325	–5,443	–6,375	–7,012
D. CURRENT TRANSFERS	4 379	419	381	274	831	1,155	1,172	335	1,435
Credit	2 379	**568**	**477**	**376**	**890**	**1,206**	**1,290**	**1,269**	**1,827**
General government	2 380	140	230	143	406	385	389	174	657
Other sectors	2 390	428	247	233	484	821	901	1,095	1,170
Workers' remittances	2 391	129	76	124	207	228	108	395	350
Other current transfers	2 392	299	171	109	277	593	793	700	820
Debit	3 379	**–149**	**–96**	**–102**	**–59**	**–51**	**–118**	**–934**	**–392**
General government	3 380	–137	–87	–91	–19	–34	–100	–675	–32
Other sectors	3 390	–12	–9	–11	–40	–17	–18	–259	–360
Workers' remittances	3 391	–4	–3	–5	–18	–15	–15	–19	...
Other current transfers	3 392	–8	–6	–6	–22	–2	–3	–240	–360
CAPITAL AND FINANCIAL ACCOUNT	4 996	**4,759**	**4,202**	**–8,792**	**–6,505**	**1,810**	**21,705**	**2,192**	**16,204**
CAPITAL ACCOUNT	4 994	**...**	**...**	**...**	**...**	**...**	**...**	**...**	**...**
Total credit	2 994	...	...	...	...	...	...	...	...
Total debit	3 994	...	...	...	...	...	...	...	...
Capital transfers, credit	2 400	**...**	**...**	**...**	**...**	**...**	**...**	**...**	**...**
General government	2 401	...	...	...	...	...	...	...	...
Debt forgiveness	2 402	...	...	...	...	...	...	...	...
Other capital transfers	2 410	...	...	...	...	...	...	...	...
Other sectors	2 430	...	...	...	...	...	...	...	...
Migrants' transfers	2 431	...	...	...	...	...	...	...	...
Debt forgiveness	2 432	...	...	...	...	...	...	...	...
Other capital transfers	2 440	...	...	...	...	...	...	...	...
Capital transfers, debit	3 400	**...**	**...**	**...**	**...**	**...**	**...**	**...**	**...**
General government	3 401	...	...	...	...	...	...	...	...
Debt forgiveness	3 402	...	...	...	...	...	...	...	...
Other capital transfers	3 410	...	...	...	...	...	...	...	...
Other sectors	3 430	...	...	...	...	...	...	...	...
Migrants' transfers	3 431	...	...	...	...	...	...	...	...
Debt forgiveness	3 432	...	...	...	...	...	...	...	...
Other capital transfers	3 440	...	...	...	...	...	...	...	...
Nonproduced nonfinancial assets, credit	2 480	**...**	**...**	**...**	**...**	**...**	**...**	**...**	**...**
Nonproduced nonfinancial assets, debit	3 480	**...**	**...**	**...**	**...**	**...**	**...**	**...**	**...**

Table 2 (Continued). STANDARD PRESENTATION, 1988–95
(Millions of U.S. dollars)

	Code		1988	1989	1990	1991	1992	1993	1994	1995
FINANCIAL ACCOUNT	4 995	. .	**4,759**	**4,202**	**–8,792**	**–6,505**	**1,810**	**21,705**	**2,192**	**16,204**
A. DIRECT INVESTMENT	4 500	. .	2,344	2,613	2,657	3,453	7,156	23,115	31,787	33,849
Direct investment abroad	4 505	. .	**–850**	**–780**	**–830**	**–913**	**–4,000**	**–4,400**	**–2,000**	**–2,000**
Equity capital	4 510	. .	–850	–780	–830	–913	–4,000	–4,400	–2,000	–2,000
Claims on affiliated enterprises	4 515	. .	. . .	. . .	. . .	. . .	. . .	. . .	. . .	. . .
Liabilities to affiliated enterprises	4 520	. .	. . .	. . .	. . .	. . .	. . .	. . .	. . .	. . .
Reinvested earnings	4 525	. .	. . .	. . .	. . .	. . .	. . .	. . .	. . .	. . .
Other capital	4 530	. .	. . .	. . .	. . .	. . .	. . .	. . .	. . .	. . .
Claims on affiliated enterprises	4 535	. .	. . .	. . .	. . .	. . .	. . .	. . .	. . .	. . .
Liabilities to affiliated enterprises	4 540	. .	. . .	. . .	. . .	. . .	. . .	. . .	. . .	. . .
Direct investment in China	4 555	. .	**3,194**	**3,393**	**3,487**	**4,366**	**11,156**	**27,515**	**33,787**	**35,849**
Equity capital	4 560	. .	3,194	3,393	3,487	4,366	11,156	27,515	33,787	35,849
Claims on direct investors	4 565	. .	. . .	. . .	. . .	. . .	. . .	. . .	. . .	. . .
Liabilities to direct investors	4 570	. .	. . .	. . .	. . .	. . .	. . .	. . .	. . .	. . .
Reinvested earnings	4 575	. .	. . .	. . .	. . .	. . .	. . .	. . .	. . .	. . .
Other capital	4 580	. .	. . .	. . .	. . .	. . .	. . .	. . .	. . .	. . .
Claims on direct investors	4 585	. .	. . .	. . .	. . .	. . .	. . .	. . .	. . .	. . .
Liabilities to direct investors	4 590	. .	. . .	. . .	. . .	. . .	. . .	. . .	. . .	. . .
B. PORTFOLIO INVESTMENT	4 600	. .	876	–180	–241	235	–57	3,049	3,543	789
Assets	4 602	. .	**–340**	**–320**	**–241**	**–330**	**–450**	**–597**	**–380**	**79**
Equity securities	4 610	. .	. . .	. . .	. . .	. . .	. . .	. . .	. . .	. . .
Monetary authorities	4 611	. .	. . .	. . .	. . .	. . .	. . .	. . .	. . .	. . .
General government	4 612	. .	. . .	. . .	. . .	. . .	. . .	. . .	. . .	. . .
Banks	4 613	. .	. . .	. . .	. . .	. . .	. . .	. . .	. . .	. . .
Other sectors	4 614	. .	. . .	. . .	. . .	. . .	. . .	. . .	. . .	. . .
Debt securities	4 619	. .	–340	–320	–241	–330	–450	–597	–380	79
Bonds and notes	4 620	. .	–340	–320	–241	–330	–450	–597	–380	79
Monetary authorities	4 621	. .	. . .	. . .	. . .	. . .	. . .	. . .	. . .	. . .
General government	4 622	. .	. . .	. . .	. . .	. . .	. . .	. . .	. . .	. . .
Banks	4 623	. .	. . .	. . .	. . .	. . .	. . .	. . .	. . .	. . .
Other sectors	4 624	. .	. . .	. . .	. . .	. . .	. . .	. . .	. . .	. . .
Money market instruments	4 630	. .	. . .	. . .	. . .	. . .	. . .	. . .	. . .	. . .
Monetary authorities	4 631	. .	. . .	. . .	. . .	. . .	. . .	. . .	. . .	. . .
General government	4 632	. .	. . .	. . .	. . .	. . .	. . .	. . .	. . .	. . .
Banks	4 633	. .	. . .	. . .	. . .	. . .	. . .	. . .	. . .	. . .
Other sectors	4 634	. .	. . .	. . .	. . .	. . .	. . .	. . .	. . .	. . .
Financial derivatives	4 640	. .	. . .	. . .	. . .	. . .	. . .	. . .	. . .	. . .
Monetary authorities	4 641	. .	. . .	. . .	. . .	. . .	. . .	. . .	. . .	. . .
General government	4 642	. .	. . .	. . .	. . .	. . .	. . .	. . .	. . .	. . .
Banks	4 643	. .	. . .	. . .	. . .	. . .	. . .	. . .	. . .	. . .
Other sectors	4 644	. .	. . .	. . .	. . .	. . .	. . .	. . .	. . .	. . .
Liabilities	4 652	. .	**1,216**	**140**	**. . .**	**565**	**393**	**3,646**	**3,923**	**710**
Equity securities	4 660	. .	. . .	. . .	. . .	. . .	. . .	. . .	. . .	. . .
Banks	4 663	. .	. . .	. . .	. . .	. . .	. . .	. . .	. . .	. . .
Other sectors	4 664	. .	. . .	. . .	. . .	. . .	. . .	. . .	. . .	. . .
Debt securities	4 669	. .	1,216	140	. . .	565	393	3,646	3,923	710
Bonds and notes	4 670	. .	1,216	140	. . .	565	393	3,646	3,923	710
Monetary authorities	4 671	. .	. . .	. . .	. . .	. . .	. . .	. . .	. . .	. . .
General government	4 672	. .	. . .	. . .	. . .	. . .	. . .	. . .	. . .	. . .
Banks	4 673	. .	. . .	. . .	. . .	. . .	. . .	. . .	. . .	. . .
Other sectors	4 674	. .	1,216	140	. . .	565	393	3,646	3,923	710
Money market instruments	4 680	. .	. . .	. . .	. . .	. . .	. . .	. . .	. . .	. . .
Monetary authorities	4 681	. .	. . .	. . .	. . .	. . .	. . .	. . .	. . .	. . .
General government	4 682	. .	. . .	. . .	. . .	. . .	. . .	. . .	. . .	. . .
Banks	4 683	. .	. . .	. . .	. . .	. . .	. . .	. . .	. . .	. . .
Other sectors	4 684	. .	. . .	. . .	. . .	. . .	. . .	. . .	. . .	. . .
Financial derivatives	4 690	. .	. . .	. . .	. . .	. . .	. . .	. . .	. . .	. . .
Monetary authorities	4 691	. .	. . .	. . .	. . .	. . .	. . .	. . .	. . .	. . .
General government	4 692	. .	. . .	. . .	. . .	. . .	. . .	. . .	. . .	. . .
Banks	4 693	. .	. . .	. . .	. . .	. . .	. . .	. . .	. . .	. . .
Other sectors	4 694	. .	. . .	. . .	. . .	. . .	. . .	. . .	. . .	. . .

Table 2 (Concluded). STANDARD PRESENTATION, 1988–95

(Millions of U.S. dollars)

	Code	1988	1989	1990	1991	1992	1993	1994	1995
C. OTHER INVESTMENT	4 700	3,831	1,211	347	3,890	–7,349	–2,690	–2,685	4,035
Assets	4 703	**–781**	**–229**	**–231**	**–156**	**–3,267**	**–2,114**	**–1,189**	**–87**
Trade credits	4 706	–52	–108	–115	–108	84	–373	–53	–6
General government: long-term	4 708	...	...	...	...	...	...	...	...
General government: short-term	4 709	...	...	...	...	...	...	...	...
Other sectors: long-term	4 711	–52	–15	–51	22	84	–373	–53	–6
Other sectors: short-term	4 712	...	–93	–64	–130	...	...	...	...
Loans	4 714	–729	–121	–116	–48	–3,351	–1,741	–1,136	–81
Monetary authorities: long-term	4 717	...	...	...	...	...	...	...	...
Monetary authorities: short-term	4 718	...	...	...	...	...	...	...	...
General government: long-term	4 720	–729	–121	–116	–48	–3,351	–1,741	–1,136	–81
General government: short-term	4 721	...	...	...	...	...	...	...	...
Banks: long-term	4 723	...	...	...	...	...	...	...	...
Banks: short-term	4 724	...	...	...	...	...	...	...	...
Other sectors: long-term	4 726	...	...	...	...	...	...	...	...
Other sectors: short-term	4 727	...	...	...	...	...	...	...	...
Currency and deposits	4 730	...	...	...	...	...	...	...	...
Monetary authorities	4 731	...	...	...	...	...	...	...	...
General government	4 732	...	...	...	...	...	...	...	...
Banks	4 733	...	...	...	...	...	...	...	...
Other sectors	4 734	...	...	...	...	...	...	...	...
Other assets	4 736	...	...	...	...	...	...	...	...
Monetary authorities: long-term	4 738	...	...	...	...	...	...	...	...
Monetary authorities: short-term	4 739	...	...	...	...	...	...	...	...
General government: long-term	4 741	...	...	...	...	...	...	...	...
General government: short-term	4 742	...	...	...	...	...	...	...	...
Banks: long-term	4 744	...	...	...	...	...	...	...	...
Banks: short-term	4 745	...	...	...	...	...	...	...	...
Other sectors: long-term	4 747	...	...	...	...	...	...	...	...
Other sectors: short-term	4 748	...	...	...	...	...	...	...	...
Liabilities	4 753	**4,612**	**1,440**	**578**	**4,046**	**–4,082**	**–576**	**–1,496**	**4,122**
Trade credits	4 756	–19	–220	313	48	79	45	447	...
General government: long-term	4 758	...	...	...	...	...	...	...	...
General government: short-term	4 759	...	...	...	...	...	...	...	...
Other sectors: long-term	4 761	–189	10	241	119	79	45	447	...
Other sectors: short-term	4 762	170	–230	72	–71	...	...	...	...
Loans	4 764	4,725	2,855	3,471	3,435	–3,255	3,317	1,169	3,130
Use of Fund credit and loans from the Fund	4 766	–82	–79	–492	–454	...	...	...	...
Monetary authorities: other long-term	4 767	...	...	...	...	...	...	...	...
Monetary authorities: short-term	4 768	...	...	...	...	...	...	...	...
General government: long-term	4 770	3,895	4,699	3,129	2,284	–18	1,564	5,178	4,321
General government: short-term	4 771	...	...	...	...	...	...	...	...
Banks: long-term	4 773	671	–2,079	447	1,097	–3,227	131	–4,808	–2,826
Banks: short-term	4 774	...	...	...	...	...	...	...	–1,219
Other sectors: long-term	4 776	241	314	387	508	–10	1,622	799	1,700
Other sectors: short-term	4 777	...	...	...	...	...	...	...	1,154
Currency and deposits	4 780	437	–582	–2,762	558	2,441	–546	–414	...
Monetary authorities	4 781	...	...	...	...	...	...	...	...
General government	4 782	...	...	...	...	...	...	...	...
Banks	4 783	437	–582	–2,762	558	2,441	–546	–414	...
Other sectors	4 784	...	...	...	...	...	...	...	...
Other liabilities	4 786	–531	–613	–444	5	–3,347	–3,392	–2,698	992
Monetary authorities: long-term	4 788	...	...	...	...	...	...	...	...
Monetary authorities: short-term	4 789	198	50	–115	...	140	175	1,004	–288
General government: long-term	4 791	...	...	...	...	...	...	...	...
General government: short-term	4 792	...	...	...	...	...	...	...	...
Banks: long-term	4 794	...	...	...	...	...	...	...	...
Banks: short-term	4 795	...	...	...	...	...	...	...	...
Other sectors: long-term	4 797	...	...	...	...	...	...	...	789
Other sectors: short-term	4 798	–729	–663	–329	5	–3,487	–3,567	–3,702	490
D. RESERVE ASSETS	4 800	–2,291	558	–11,555	–14,083	2,060	–1,769	–30,453	–22,469
Monetary gold	4 810	...	...	...	...	...	...	...	...
Special drawing rights	4 820	21	31	22	–12	136	–65	–24	–34
Reserve position in the Fund	4 830	...	...	...	...	–345	53	–7	–458
Foreign exchange	4 840	–2,312	527	–11,577	–14,071	2,269	–1,756	–30,421	–21,977
Other claims	4 880	...	...	...	...	...	...	...	...
NET ERRORS AND OMISSIONS	4 998	**–957**	**115**	**–3,205**	**–6,767**	**–8,211**	**–10,096**	**–9,100**	**–17,822**

Part 3 of the *Yearbook* contains descriptions of the methodologies, compilation practices, and sources used to compile these data.

Table 1. ANALYTIC PRESENTATION, 1988–95
(Millions of U.S. dollars)

	Code		1988	1989	1990	1991	1992	1993	1994	1995
A. Current Account[1]	4 993	Y.	**–216**	**–201**	**542**	**2,349**	**901**	**–2,102**	**–3,219**	**–4,116**
Goods: exports f.o.b	2 100	. .	5,343	6,031	7,079	7,507	7,263	7,429	8,754	10,373
Goods: imports f.o.b	3 100	. .	–4,516	–4,557	–5,108	–4,548	–6,029	–9,086	–11,040	–12,921
Balance on Goods	4 100	. .	*827*	*1,474*	*1,971*	*2,959*	*1,234*	*–1,657*	*–2,286*	*–2,548*
Services: credit	2 200	. .	1,408	1,291	1,600	1,593	1,983	2,520	3,193	3,439
Services: debit	3 200	. .	–1,670	–1,565	–1,750	–1,812	–2,028	–2,321	–2,906	–3,349
Balance on Goods and Services	4 991	. .	*565*	*1,200*	*1,821*	*2,740*	*1,189*	*–1,458*	*–1,999*	*–2,457*
Income: credit	2 300	. .	257	287	347	390	449	561	789	981
Income: debit	3 300	. .	–2,002	–2,586	–2,652	–2,480	–2,471	–2,344	–2,871	–3,318
Balance on Goods, Services, and Income	4 992	. .	*–1,180*	*–1,099*	*–484*	*651*	*–833*	*–3,240*	*–4,081*	*–4,794*
Current transfers: credit	2 379	Y.	994	928	1,043	1,743	1,871	1,350	1,055	861
Current transfers: debit	3 379	. .	–30	–30	–17	–45	–137	–212	–193	–182
B. Capital Account[1]	4 994	Y.	**. . .**	**. . .**	**. . .**	**. . .**	**. . .**	**. . .**	**. . .**	**. . .**
Capital account: credit	2 994	Y.	. . .	. . .	. . .	. . .	. . .	. . .	. . .	. . .
Capital account: debit	3 994	. .	. . .	. . .	. . .	. . .	. . .	. . .	. . .	. . .
Total, Groups A Plus B	4 010	. .	*–216*	*–201*	*542*	*2,349*	*901*	*–2,102*	*–3,219*	*–4,116*
C. Financial Account[1]	4 995	X.	**940**	**407**	**26**	**–779**	**299**	**2,686**	**3,086**	**5,002**
Direct investment abroad	4 505	. .	–44	–29	–16	–24	–50	–240	–152	–284
Direct investment in Colombia	4 555	Y.	203	576	500	457	729	959	1,667	2,501
Portfolio investment assets	4 602	. .	. . .	. . .	. . .	. . .	. . .	. . .	. . .	. . .
Equity securities	4 610	. .	. . .	. . .	. . .	. . .	. . .	. . .	. . .	. . .
Debt securities	4 619	. .	. . .	. . .	. . .	. . .	. . .	. . .	. . .	. . .
Portfolio investment liabilities	4 652	Y.	. . .	179	–4	86	126	498	392	–21
Equity securities	4 660	Y.	. . .	. . .	. . .	. . .	. . .	. . .	. . .	. . .
Debt securities	4 669	Y.	. . .	179	–4	86	126	498	392	–21
Other investment assets	4 703	. .	–315	–95	–102	–522	–637	160	–1,511	473
Monetary authorities	4 703	. A	–1	24	. . .	. . .	. . .	–40	. . .	. . .
General government	4 703	. B	. . .	. . .	–82	–100	–346	267	–1,075	494
Banks	4 703	. C	–117	41	17	–272	–110	–74	–274	497
Other sectors	4 703	. D	–197	–160	–37	–150	–182	7	–162	–518
Other investment liabilities	4 753	X.	1,096	–224	–352	–775	131	1,310	2,690	2,333
Monetary authorities	4 753	XA	–3	18	1	–2	–15	–115	–152	102
General government	4 753	YB	371	69	95	–14	–78	–329	–298	–82
Banks	4 753	YC	318	39	10	–362	785	710	577	791
Other sectors	4 753	YD	410	–350	–458	–397	–561	1,043	2,563	1,521
Total, Groups A Through C	4 020	. .	*724*	*206*	*568*	*1,570*	*1,200*	*584*	*–132*	*886*
D. Net Errors and Omissions	4 998	. .	**–530**	**157**	**70**	**191**	**191**	**–135**	**307**	**–523**
Total, Groups A Through D	4 030	. .	*194*	*363*	*638*	*1,761*	*1,390*	*449*	*175*	*362*
E. Reserves and Related Items	4 040	. .	**–194**	**–363**	**–638**	**–1,761**	**–1,390**	**–449**	**–175**	**–362**
Reserve assets	4 800	. .	–193	–434	–610	–1,763	–1,274	–464	–162	–356
Use of Fund credit and loans	4 766	. .	. . .	. . .	. . .	. . .	. . .	. . .	. . .	. . .
Liabilities constituting foreign authorities' reserves	4 900	. .	–1	71	–28	2	–116	15	–13	–6
Exceptional financing	4 920	. .	. . .	. . .	. . .	. . .	. . .	. . .	. . .	. . .
Conversion rates: Colombian pesos per U.S. dollar	0 101	. .	**299.17**	**382.57**	**502.26**	**633.05**	**759.28**	**863.06**	**844.84**	**912.83**

[1] Excludes components that have been classified in the categories of Group E.

Table 2. STANDARD PRESENTATION, 1988–95

(Millions of U.S. dollars)

	Code	1988	1989	1990	1991	1992	1993	1994	1995
CURRENT ACCOUNT	4 993 . .	**–216**	**–201**	**542**	**2,349**	**901**	**–2,102**	**–3,219**	**–4,116**
A. GOODS	4 100 . .	827	1,474	1,971	2,959	1,234	–1,657	–2,286	–2,548
Credit	2 100 . .	**5,343**	**6,031**	**7,079**	**7,507**	**7,263**	**7,429**	**8,754**	**10,373**
General merchandise: exports f.o.b.	2 110 . .	4,930	5,666	6,705	7,098	6,900	7,116	8,449	10,276
Goods for processing: exports f.o.b.	2 150 . .	. . .	. . .	. . .	. . .	. . .	. . .	. . .	. . .
Repairs on goods	2 160 . .	. . .	. . .	. . .	. . .	. . .	. . .	. . .	. . .
Goods procured in ports by carriers	2 170 . .	. . .	. . .	. . .	. . .	. . .	. . .	. . .	. . .
Nonmonetary gold	2 180 . .	413	365	374	409	364	313	305	97
Debit	3 100 . .	**–4,516**	**–4,557**	**–5,108**	**–4,548**	**–6,029**	**–9,086**	**–11,040**	**–12,921**
General merchandise: imports f.o.b.	3 110 . .	–4,516	–4,557	–5,108	–4,548	–6,029	–9,086	–11,040	–12,921
Goods for processing: imports f.o.b.	3 150 . .	. . .	. . .	. . .	. . .	. . .	. . .	. . .	. . .
Repairs on goods	3 160 . .	. . .	. . .	. . .	. . .	. . .	. . .	. . .	. . .
Goods procured in ports by carriers	3 170 . .	. . .	. . .	. . .	. . .	. . .	. . .	. . .	. . .
Nonmonetary gold	3 180 . .	. . .	. . .	. . .	. . .	. . .	. . .	. . .	. . .
B. SERVICES	4 200 . .	–262	–274	–150	–219	–45	199	287	90
Total credit	2 200 . .	*1,408*	*1,291*	*1,600*	*1,593*	*1,983*	*2,520*	*3,193*	*3,439*
Total debit	3 200 . .	*–1,670*	*–1,565*	*–1,750*	*–1,812*	*–2,028*	*–2,321*	*–2,906*	*–3,349*
Transportation services, credit	2 205 . .	**481**	**446**	**484**	**516**	**644**	**973**	**1,176**	**1,429**
Passenger	2 205 BA	*179*	*160*	*168*	*176*	*237*	*364*	*445*	*548*
Freight	2 205 BB	*96*	*101*	*117*	*122*	*120*	*168*	*194*	*218*
Other	2 205 BC	*206*	*185*	*199*	*218*	*287*	*440*	*538*	*663*
Sea transport, passenger	2 207 . .	. . .	. . .	. . .	. . .	. . .	. . .	. . .	. . .
Sea transport, freight	2 208 . .	. . .	. . .	. . .	. . .	. . .	. . .	. . .	. . .
Sea transport, other	2 209 . .	. . .	. . .	. . .	. . .	. . .	. . .	. . .	. . .
Air transport, passenger	2 211 . .	. . .	. . .	. . .	. . .	. . .	. . .	. . .	. . .
Air transport, freight	2 212 . .	. . .	. . .	. . .	. . .	. . .	. . .	. . .	. . .
Air transport, other	2 213 . .	. . .	. . .	. . .	. . .	. . .	. . .	. . .	. . .
Other transport, passenger	2 215 . .	. . .	. . .	. . .	. . .	. . .	. . .	. . .	. . .
Other transport, freight	2 216 . .	. . .	. . .	. . .	. . .	. . .	. . .	. . .	. . .
Other transport, other	2 217 . .	. . .	. . .	. . .	. . .	. . .	. . .	. . .	. . .
Transportation services, debit	3 205 . .	**–568**	**–556**	**–588**	**–569**	**–618**	**–792**	**–891**	**–1,137**
Passenger	3 205 BA	*–104*	*–130*	*–137*	*–143*	*–140*	*–140*	*–167*	*–204*
Freight	3 205 BB	*–254*	*–234*	*–237*	*–214*	*–265*	*–438*	*–470*	*–622*
Other	3 205 BC	*–210*	*–192*	*–214*	*–212*	*–213*	*–213*	*–254*	*–311*
Sea transport, passenger	3 207 . .	. . .	. . .	. . .	. . .	. . .	. . .	. . .	. . .
Sea transport, freight	3 208 . .	. . .	. . .	. . .	. . .	. . .	. . .	. . .	. . .
Sea transport, other	3 209 . .	. . .	. . .	. . .	. . .	. . .	. . .	. . .	. . .
Air transport, passenger	3 211 . .	. . .	. . .	. . .	. . .	. . .	. . .	. . .	. . .
Air transport, freight	3 212 . .	. . .	. . .	. . .	. . .	. . .	. . .	. . .	. . .
Air transport, other	3 213 . .	. . .	. . .	. . .	. . .	. . .	. . .	. . .	. . .
Other transport, passenger	3 215 . .	. . .	. . .	. . .	. . .	. . .	. . .	. . .	. . .
Other transport, freight	3 216 . .	. . .	. . .	. . .	. . .	. . .	. . .	. . .	. . .
Other transport, other	3 217 . .	. . .	. . .	. . .	. . .	. . .	. . .	. . .	. . .
Travel, credit	2 236 . .	**461**	**335**	**406**	**468**	**705**	**755**	**807**	**860**
Business travel	2 237 . .	. . .	. . .	. . .	. . .	. . .	. . .	. . .	. . .
Personal travel	2 240 . .	. . .	. . .	. . .	. . .	. . .	. . .	. . .	. . .
Travel, debit	3 236 . .	**–538**	**–494**	**–454**	**–509**	**–641**	**–694**	**–762**	**–828**
Business travel	3 237 . .	. . .	. . .	. . .	. . .	. . .	. . .	. . .	. . .
Personal travel	3 240 . .	. . .	. . .	. . .	. . .	. . .	. . .	. . .	. . .
Other services, credit	2 200 BA	**466**	**510**	**710**	**609**	**634**	**792**	**1,209**	**1,150**
Communications	2 245 . .	. . .	. . .	. . .	. . .	. . .	. . .	. . .	. . .
Construction	2 249 . .	. . .	. . .	. . .	. . .	. . .	. . .	. . .	. . .
Insurance	2 253 . .	140	181	264	198	222	279	421	403
Financial	2 260 . .	. . .	. . .	. . .	. . .	. . .	. . .	. . .	. . .
Computer and information	2 262 . .	. . .	. . .	. . .	. . .	. . .	. . .	. . .	. . .
Royalties and licence fees	2 266 . .	13	17	21	29	24	30	46	44
Other business services	2 268 . .	279	273	373	329	337	420	645	611
Personal, cultural, and recreational	2 287 . .	. . .	. . .	. . .	. . .	. . .	. . .	. . .	. . .
Government, n.i.e.	2 291 . .	34	39	52	53	51	63	97	92
Other services, debit	3 200 BA	**–564**	**–515**	**–708**	**–734**	**–770**	**–835**	**–1,252**	**–1,383**
Communications	3 245 . .	. . .	. . .	. . .	. . .	. . .	. . .	. . .	. . .
Construction	3 249 . .	. . .	. . .	. . .	. . .	. . .	. . .	. . .	. . .
Insurance	3 253 . .	–227	–219	–230	–232	–251	–286	–426	–473
Financial	3 260 . .	. . .	. . .	. . .	. . .	. . .	. . .	. . .	. . .
Computer and information	3 262 . .	. . .	. . .	. . .	. . .	. . .	. . .	. . .	. . .
Royalties and licence fees	3 266 . .	–10	–12	–13	–19	–17	–19	–29	–32
Other business services	3 268 . .	–257	–222	–391	–413	–424	–448	–667	–738
Personal, cultural, and recreational	3 287 . .	–15	–7	–7	–8	–8	–9	–14	–15
Government, n.i.e.	3 291 . .	–55	–55	–67	–62	–69	–74	–117	–126

Table 2 (Continued). STANDARD PRESENTATION, 1988–95
(Millions of U.S. dollars)

	Code	1988	1989	1990	1991	1992	1993	1994	1995
C. INCOME	4 300	–1,745	–2,299	–2,305	–2,089	–2,022	–1,782	–2,082	–2,337
Total credit	2 300	*257*	*287*	*347*	*390*	*449*	*561*	*789*	*981*
Total debit	3 300	*–2,002*	*–2,586*	*–2,652*	*–2,480*	*–2,471*	*–2,344*	*–2,871*	*–3,318*
Compensation of employees, credit	2 310	**10**	**8**	**7**	**15**	**11**	**13**	**20**	**19**
Compensation of employees, debit	3 310	**–13**	**–16**	**–43**	**–105**	**–79**	**–85**	**–134**	**–144**
Investment income, credit	2 320	**247**	**279**	**340**	**375**	**438**	**548**	**769**	**962**
Direct investment income	2 330	20	20	20	12	8	66	190	64
Dividends and distributed branch profits	2 332	12	12	12	8	5	43	123	42
Reinvested earnings and undistributed branch profits	2 333	8	8	8	4	3	23	66	22
Income on debt (interest)	2 334	...	...	...	...	...	...	...	...
Portfolio investment income	2 339	...	...	...	...	...	...	...	...
Income on equity	2 340	...	...	...	...	...	...	...	...
Income on bonds and notes	2 350	...	...	...	...	...	...	...	...
Income on money market instruments and financial derivatives	2 360	...	...	...	...	...	...	...	...
Other investment income	2 370	227	259	320	363	430	482	579	898
Investment income, debit	3 320	**–1,989**	**–2,570**	**–2,609**	**–2,375**	**–2,391**	**–2,259**	**–2,737**	**–3,174**
Direct investment income	3 330	–592	–983	–964	–884	–1,043	–1,038	–1,179	–1,344
Dividends and distributed branch profits	3 332	–578	–846	–907	–786	–949	–940	–1,029	–1,195
Reinvested earnings and undistributed branch profits	3 333	–14	–137	–57	–98	–94	–98	–150	–149
Income on debt (interest)	3 334	...	...	...	...	...	...	...	...
Portfolio investment income	3 339	...	...	...	...	...	...	...	...
Income on equity	3 340	...	...	...	...	...	...	...	...
Income on bonds and notes	3 350	...	...	...	...	...	...	...	...
Income on money market instruments and financial derivatives	3 360	...	...	...	...	...	...	...	...
Other investment income	3 370	–1,397	–1,587	–1,645	–1,491	–1,348	–1,221	–1,558	–1,830
D. CURRENT TRANSFERS	4 379	964	898	1,026	1,698	1,734	1,138	862	679
Credit	2 379	**994**	**928**	**1,043**	**1,743**	**1,871**	**1,350**	**1,055**	**861**
General government	2 380	...	...	...	...	...	...	...	...
Other sectors	2 390	994	928	1,043	1,743	1,871	1,350	1,055	861
Workers' remittances	2 391	448	459	488	866	630	455	211	172
Other current transfers	2 392	546	469	555	877	1,241	895	844	689
Debit	3 379	**–30**	**–30**	**–17**	**–45**	**–137**	**–212**	**–193**	**–182**
General government	3 380	–11	–14	–15	–14	–14	...	...	...
Other sectors	3 390	–19	–16	–2	–31	–124	–212	–193	–182
Workers' remittances	3 391	–1	–1	–1	...	...	...	...	...
Other current transfers	3 392	–18	–15	–1	–31	–124	–212	–193	–182
CAPITAL AND FINANCIAL ACCOUNT	4 996	**746**	**44**	**–612**	**–2,540**	**–1,091**	**2,237**	**2,911**	**4,639**
CAPITAL ACCOUNT	4 994	...	...	...	...	...	...	...	...
Total credit	2 994	...	...	...	...	...	...	...	...
Total debit	3 994	...	...	...	...	...	...	...	...
Capital transfers, credit	2 400	...	...	...	...	...	...	...	...
General government	2 401	...	...	...	...	...	...	...	...
Debt forgiveness	2 402	...	...	...	...	...	...	...	...
Other capital transfers	2 410	...	...	...	...	...	...	...	...
Other sectors	2 430	...	...	...	...	...	...	...	...
Migrants' transfers	2 431	...	...	...	...	...	...	...	...
Debt forgiveness	2 432	...	...	...	...	...	...	...	...
Other capital transfers	2 440	...	...	...	...	...	...	...	...
Capital transfers, debit	3 400	...	...	...	...	...	...	...	...
General government	3 401	...	...	...	...	...	...	...	...
Debt forgiveness	3 402	...	...	...	...	...	...	...	...
Other capital transfers	3 410	...	...	...	...	...	...	...	...
Other sectors	3 430	...	...	...	...	...	...	...	...
Migrants' transfers	3 431	...	...	...	...	...	...	...	...
Debt forgiveness	3 432	...	...	...	...	...	...	...	...
Other capital transfers	3 440	...	...	...	...	...	...	...	...
Nonproduced nonfinancial assets, credit	2 480	...	...	...	...	...	...	...	...
Nonproduced nonfinancial assets, debit	3 480	...	...	...	...	...	...	...	...

Table 2 (Continued). STANDARD PRESENTATION, 1988–95
(Millions of U.S. dollars)

	Code	1988	1989	1990	1991	1992	1993	1994	1995
FINANCIAL ACCOUNT	4 995 . .	**746**	**44**	**–612**	**–2,540**	**–1,091**	**2,237**	**2,911**	**4,639**
A. DIRECT INVESTMENT	4 500 . .	159	547	484	433	679	719	1,516	2,217
Direct investment abroad	4 505 . .	**–44**	**–29**	**–16**	**–24**	**–50**	**–240**	**–152**	**–284**
Equity capital	4 510 . .	. . .	. . .	. . .	. . .	. . .	. . .	. . .	. . .
Claims on affiliated enterprises	4 515 . .	. . .	. . .	. . .	. . .	. . .	. . .	. . .	. . .
Liabilities to affiliated enterprises	4 520 . .	. . .	. . .	. . .	. . .	. . .	. . .	. . .	. . .
Reinvested earnings	4 525 . .	–8	–8	–8	–4	–3	–23	–66	–22
Other capital	4 530 . .	–36	–21	–8	–20	–47	–217	–85	–262
Claims on affiliated enterprises	4 535 . .	. . .	. . .	. . .	. . .	. . .	. . .	. . .	. . .
Liabilities to affiliated enterprises	4 540 . .	. . .	. . .	. . .	. . .	. . .	. . .	. . .	. . .
Direct investment in Colombia	4 555 . .	**203**	**576**	**500**	**457**	**729**	**959**	**1,667**	**2,501**
Equity capital	4 560 . .	. . .	. . .	. . .	. . .	. . .	. . .	. . .	. . .
Claims on direct investors	4 565 . .	. . .	. . .	. . .	. . .	. . .	. . .	. . .	. . .
Liabilities to direct investors	4 570 . .	. . .	. . .	. . .	. . .	. . .	. . .	. . .	. . .
Reinvested earnings	4 575 . .	14	137	57	98	94	98	150	149
Other capital	4 580 . .	189	439	443	359	634	861	1,517	2,353
Claims on direct investors	4 585 . .	. . .	. . .	. . .	. . .	. . .	. . .	. . .	. . .
Liabilities to direct investors	4 590 . .	. . .	. . .	. . .	. . .	. . .	. . .	. . .	. . .
B. PORTFOLIO INVESTMENT	4 600 . .	. . .	179	–4	86	126	498	392	–21
Assets	4 602 . .	**. . .**	**. . .**	**. . .**	**. . .**	**. . .**	**. . .**	**. . .**	**. . .**
Equity securities	4 610 . .	. . .	. . .	. . .	. . .	. . .	. . .	. . .	. . .
Monetary authorities	4 611 . .	. . .	. . .	. . .	. . .	. . .	. . .	. . .	. . .
General government	4 612 . .	. . .	. . .	. . .	. . .	. . .	. . .	. . .	. . .
Banks	4 613 . .	. . .	. . .	. . .	. . .	. . .	. . .	. . .	. . .
Other sectors	4 614 . .	. . .	. . .	. . .	. . .	. . .	. . .	. . .	. . .
Debt securities	4 619 . .	. . .	. . .	. . .	. . .	. . .	. . .	. . .	. . .
Bonds and notes	4 620 . .	. . .	. . .	. . .	. . .	. . .	. . .	. . .	. . .
Monetary authorities	4 621 . .	. . .	. . .	. . .	. . .	. . .	. . .	. . .	. . .
General government	4 622 . .	. . .	. . .	. . .	. . .	. . .	. . .	. . .	. . .
Banks	4 623 . .	. . .	. . .	. . .	. . .	. . .	. . .	. . .	. . .
Other sectors	4 624 . .	. . .	. . .	. . .	. . .	. . .	. . .	. . .	. . .
Money market instruments	4 630 . .	. . .	. . .	. . .	. . .	. . .	. . .	. . .	. . .
Monetary authorities	4 631 . .	. . .	. . .	. . .	. . .	. . .	. . .	. . .	. . .
General government	4 632 . .	. . .	. . .	. . .	. . .	. . .	. . .	. . .	. . .
Banks	4 633 . .	. . .	. . .	. . .	. . .	. . .	. . .	. . .	. . .
Other sectors	4 634 . .	. . .	. . .	. . .	. . .	. . .	. . .	. . .	. . .
Financial derivatives	4 640 . .	. . .	. . .	. . .	. . .	. . .	. . .	. . .	. . .
Monetary authorities	4 641 . .	. . .	. . .	. . .	. . .	. . .	. . .	. . .	. . .
General government	4 642 . .	. . .	. . .	. . .	. . .	. . .	. . .	. . .	. . .
Banks	4 643 . .	. . .	. . .	. . .	. . .	. . .	. . .	. . .	. . .
Other sectors	4 644 . .	. . .	. . .	. . .	. . .	. . .	. . .	. . .	. . .
Liabilities	4 652 . .	**. . .**	**179**	**–4**	**86**	**126**	**498**	**392**	**–21**
Equity securities	4 660 . .	. . .	. . .	. . .	. . .	. . .	. . .	. . .	. . .
Banks	4 663 . .	. . .	. . .	. . .	. . .	. . .	. . .	. . .	. . .
Other sectors	4 664 . .	. . .	. . .	. . .	. . .	. . .	. . .	. . .	. . .
Debt securities	4 669 . .	. . .	179	–4	86	126	498	392	–21
Bonds and notes	4 670 . .	. . .	179	–4	86	126	498	392	–21
Monetary authorities	4 671 . .	. . .	. . .	. . .	. . .	. . .	. . .	. . .	. . .
General government	4 672 . .	. . .	179	–4	81	60	353	404	401
Banks	4 673 . .	. . .	. . .	. . .	. . .	. . .	. . .	. . .	. . .
Other sectors	4 674 . .	. . .	. . .	. . .	5	66	145	–12	–422
Money market instruments	4 680 . .	. . .	. . .	. . .	. . .	. . .	. . .	. . .	. . .
Monetary authorities	4 681 . .	. . .	. . .	. . .	. . .	. . .	. . .	. . .	. . .
General government	4 682 . .	. . .	. . .	. . .	. . .	. . .	. . .	. . .	. . .
Banks	4 683 . .	. . .	. . .	. . .	. . .	. . .	. . .	. . .	. . .
Other sectors	4 684 . .	. . .	. . .	. . .	. . .	. . .	. . .	. . .	. . .
Financial derivatives	4 690 . .	. . .	. . .	. . .	. . .	. . .	. . .	. . .	. . .
Monetary authorities	4 691 . .	. . .	. . .	. . .	. . .	. . .	. . .	. . .	. . .
General government	4 692 . .	. . .	. . .	. . .	. . .	. . .	. . .	. . .	. . .
Banks	4 693 . .	. . .	. . .	. . .	. . .	. . .	. . .	. . .	. . .
Other sectors	4 694 . .	. . .	. . .	. . .	. . .	. . .	. . .	. . .	. . .

Table 2 (Concluded). STANDARD PRESENTATION, 1988–95
(Millions of U.S. dollars)

	Code	1988	1989	1990	1991	1992	1993	1994	1995
C. OTHER INVESTMENT	4 700 . .	780	–248	–482	–1,296	–622	1,485	1,166	2,799
Assets	4 703 . .	**–315**	**–95**	**–102**	**–522**	**–637**	**160**	**–1,511**	**473**
Trade credits	4 706 . .	–134	–136	–132	–210	–87	–50	–116	–165
General government: long-term	4 708 . .	. . .	. . .	. . .	. . .	. . .	. . .	. . .	. . .
General government: short-term	4 709 . .	. . .	. . .	. . .	. . .	. . .	. . .	. . .	. . .
Other sectors: long-term	4 711 . .	. . .	. . .	. . .	. . .	. . .	. . .	. . .	. . .
Other sectors: short-term	4 712 . .	–134	–136	–132	–210	–87	–50	–116	–165
Loans	4 714 . .	. . .	. . .	. . .	. . .	. . .	. . .	. . .	. . .
Monetary authorities: long-term	4 717 . .	. . .	. . .	. . .	. . .	. . .	. . .	. . .	. . .
Monetary authorities: short-term	4 718 . .	. . .	. . .	. . .	. . .	. . .	. . .	. . .	. . .
General government: long-term	4 720 . .	. . .	. . .	. . .	. . .	. . .	. . .	. . .	. . .
General government: short-term	4 721 . .	. . .	. . .	. . .	. . .	. . .	. . .	. . .	. . .
Banks: long-term	4 723 . .	. . .	. . .	. . .	. . .	. . .	. . .	. . .	. . .
Banks: short-term	4 724 . .	. . .	. . .	. . .	. . .	. . .	. . .	. . .	. . .
Other sectors: long-term	4 726 . .	. . .	. . .	. . .	. . .	. . .	. . .	. . .	. . .
Other sectors: short-term	4 727 . .	. . .	. . .	. . .	. . .	. . .	. . .	. . .	. . .
Currency and deposits	4 730 . .	–181	41	112	–312	–550	222	–1,360	727
Monetary authorities	4 731 . .	–1	24	. . .	. . .	. . .	–40	. . .	. . .
General government	4 732 . .	. . .	. . .	. . .	–100	–346	279	–1,039	582
Banks	4 733 . .	–117	41	17	–272	–110	–74	–274	497
Other sectors	4 734 . .	–63	–24	95	60	–95	57	–47	–353
Other assets	4 736 . .	. . .	. . .	–82	. . .	. . .	–12	–36	–89
Monetary authorities: long-term	4 738 . .	. . .	. . .	. . .	. . .	. . .	. . .	. . .	. . .
Monetary authorities: short-term	4 739 . .	. . .	. . .	. . .	. . .	. . .	. . .	. . .	. . .
General government: long-term	4 741 . .	. . .	. . .	–82	. . .	. . .	–12	–36	–89
General government: short-term	4 742 . .	. . .	. . .	. . .	. . .	. . .	. . .	. . .	. . .
Banks: long-term	4 744 . .	. . .	. . .	. . .	. . .	. . .	. . .	. . .	. . .
Banks: short-term	4 745 . .	. . .	. . .	. . .	. . .	. . .	. . .	. . .	. . .
Other sectors: long-term	4 747 . .	. . .	. . .	. . .	. . .	. . .	. . .	. . .	. . .
Other sectors: short-term	4 748 . .	. . .	. . .	. . .	. . .	. . .	. . .	. . .	. . .
Liabilities	4 753 . .	**1,095**	**–153**	**–380**	**–774**	**15**	**1,325**	**2,677**	**2,326**
Trade credits	4 756 . .	101	–200	–143	–27	–19	247	323	245
General government: long-term	4 758 . .	. . .	. . .	. . .	. . .	. . .	. . .	. . .	. . .
General government: short-term	4 759 . .	. . .	. . .	. . .	. . .	. . .	. . .	. . .	. . .
Other sectors: long-term	4 761 . .	. . .	. . .	. . .	. . .	. . .	. . .	. . .	. . .
Other sectors: short-term	4 762 . .	101	–200	–143	–27	–19	247	323	245
Loans	4 764 . .	675	–73	–202	–369	–635	318	1,743	1,263
Use of Fund credit and loans from the Fund	4 766 . .	. . .	. . .	. . .	. . .	. . .	. . .	. . .	. . .
Monetary authorities: other long-term	4 767 . .	–5	8	18	15	–15	–150	–199	68
Monetary authorities: short-term	4 768 . .	. . .	. . .	. . .	. . .	. . .	. . .	. . .	. . .
General government: long-term	4 770 . .	371	69	95	–14	–78	–329	–298	–82
General government: short-term	4 771 . .	. . .	. . .	. . .	. . .	. . .	. . .	. . .	. . .
Banks: long-term	4 773 . .	. . .	. . .	. . .	. . .	. . .	. . .	. . .	. . .
Banks: short-term	4 774 . .	. . .	. . .	. . .	. . .	. . .	. . .	. . .	. . .
Other sectors: long-term	4 776 . .	309	–150	–315	–370	–541	796	2,240	1,277
Other sectors: short-term	4 777 . .	. . .	. . .	. . .	. . .	. . .	. . .	. . .	. . .
Currency and deposits	4 780 . .	317	110	–18	–360	669	725	565	785
Monetary authorities	4 781 . .	–1	71	–28	2	–116	15	–13	–6
General government	4 782 . .	. . .	. . .	. . .	. . .	. . .	. . .	. . .	. . .
Banks	4 783 . .	318	39	10	–362	785	710	577	791
Other sectors	4 784 . .	. . .	. . .	. . .	. . .	. . .	. . .	. . .	. . .
Other liabilities	4 786 . .	2	10	–17	–17	. . .	35	47	34
Monetary authorities: long-term	4 788 . .	. . .	. . .	. . .	. . .	. . .	. . .	. . .	. . .
Monetary authorities: short-term	4 789 . .	2	10	–17	–17	. . .	35	47	34
General government: long-term	4 791 . .	. . .	. . .	. . .	. . .	. . .	. . .	. . .	. . .
General government: short-term	4 792 . .	. . .	. . .	. . .	. . .	. . .	. . .	. . .	. . .
Banks: long-term	4 794 . .	. . .	. . .	. . .	. . .	. . .	. . .	. . .	. . .
Banks: short-term	4 795 . .	. . .	. . .	. . .	. . .	. . .	. . .	. . .	. . .
Other sectors: long-term	4 797 . .	. . .	. . .	. . .	. . .	. . .	. . .	. . .	. . .
Other sectors: short-term	4 798 . .	. . .	. . .	. . .	. . .	. . .	. . .	. . .	. . .
D. RESERVE ASSETS	4 800 . .	–193	–434	–610	–1,763	–1,274	–464	–162	–356
Monetary gold	4 810 . .	. . .	–1	2	. . .	. . .	. . .	. . .	. . .
Special drawing rights	4 820 . .	. . .	. . .	. . .	. . .	99	–100	–2	–4
Reserve position in the Fund	4 830 . .	. . .	. . .	. . .	. . .	–97	–15	–10	–74
Foreign exchange	4 840 . .	–198	–408	–568	–1,824	–1,387	–50	–137	–263
Other claims	4 880 . .	5	–25	–44	61	110	–300	–13	–15
NET ERRORS AND OMISSIONS	4 998 . .	**–530**	**157**	**70**	**191**	**191**	**–135**	**307**	**–523**

Part 3 of the *Yearbook* contains descriptions of the methodologies, compilation practices, and sources used to compile these data.

Table 3. INTERNATIONAL INVESTMENT POSITION (End–period stocks), 1988–95
(Millions of U.S. dollars)

	Code	1988	1989	1990	1991	1992	1993	1994	1995
ASSETS	8 995 C.	5,157	5,295	5,832	8,041	9,212	...	...	...
Direct investment abroad	8 505 . .	**371**	**392**	**402**	**422**	**472**	...	...	...
Equity capital and reinvested earnings	8 506 . .	371	392	402	422	472	...	...	...
Claims on affiliated enterprises	8 507 . .	...	...	...	...	...	...	...	...
Liabilities to affiliated enterprises	8 508 . .	...	...	...	...	...	...	...	...
Other capital	8 530 . .	...	...	...	...	...	...	...	...
Claims on affiliated enterprises	8 535 . .	...	...	...	...	...	...	...	...
Liabilities to affiliated enterprises	8 540 . .	...	...	...	...	...	...	...	...
Portfolio investment	8 602 . .	...	...	...	...	...	...	...	...
Equity securities	8 610 . .	...	...	...	...	...	...	...	...
Monetary authorities	8 611 . .	...	...	...	...	...	...	...	...
General government	8 612 . .	...	...	...	...	...	...	...	...
Banks	8 613 . .	...	...	...	...	...	...	...	...
Other sectors	8 614 . .	...	...	...	...	...	...	...	...
Debt securities	8 619 . .	...	...	...	...	...	...	...	...
Bonds and notes	8 620 . .	...	...	...	...	...	...	...	...
Monetary authorities	8 621 . .	...	...	...	...	...	...	...	...
General government	8 622 . .	...	...	...	...	...	...	...	...
Banks	8 623 . .	...	...	...	...	...	...	...	...
Other sectors	8 624 . .	...	...	...	...	...	...	...	...
Money market instruments	8 630 . .	...	...	...	...	...	...	...	...
Monetary authorities	8 631 . .	...	...	...	...	...	...	...	...
General government	8 632 . .	...	...	...	...	...	...	...	...
Banks	8 633 . .	...	...	...	...	...	...	...	...
Other sectors	8 634 . .	...	...	...	...	...	...	...	...
Financial derivatives	8 640 . .	...	...	...	...	...	...	...	...
Monetary authorities	8 641 . .	...	...	...	...	...	...	...	...
General government	8 642 . .	...	...	...	...	...	...	...	...
Banks	8 643 . .	...	...	...	...	...	...	...	...
Other sectors	8 644 . .	...	...	...	...	...	...	...	...
Other investment	8 703 . .	**852**	**811**	**699**	**1,012**	**927**	...	...	...
Trade credits	8 706 . .	...	...	...	...	...	...	...	...
General government: long-term	8 708 . .	...	...	...	...	...	...	...	...
General government: short-term	8 709 . .	...	...	...	...	...	...	...	...
Other sectors: long-term	8 711 . .	...	...	...	...	...	...	...	...
Other sectors: short-term	8 712 . .	...	...	...	...	...	...	...	...
Loans	8 714 . .	...	...	...	...	...	...	...	...
Monetary authorities: long-term	8 717 . .	...	...	...	...	...	...	...	...
Monetary authorities: short-term	8 718 . .	...	...	...	...	...	...	...	...
General government: long-term	8 720 . .	...	...	...	...	...	...	...	...
General government: short-term	8 721 . .	...	...	...	...	...	...	...	...
Banks: long-term	8 723 . .	...	...	...	...	...	...	...	...
Banks: short-term	8 724 . .	...	...	...	...	...	...	...	...
Other sectors: long-term	8 726 . .	...	...	...	...	...	...	...	...
Other sectors: short-term	8 727 . .	...	...	...	...	...	...	...	...
Currency and deposits	8 730 . .	239	191	128	628	554	...	...	...
Monetary authorities	8 731 . .	...	...	...	...	...	...	...	...
General government	8 732 . .	24	...	...	100	...	...	...	...
Banks	8 733 . .	215	191	128	528	554	...	...	...
Other sectors	8 734 . .	...	...	...	...	...	...	...	...
Other assets	8 736 . .	613	620	571	384	373	...	...	...
Monetary authorities: long-term	8 738 . .	...	...	...	...	...	...	...	...
Monetary authorities: short-term	8 739 . .	...	...	...	...	...	...	...	...
General government: long-term	8 741 . .	...	...	...	...	...	...	...	...
General government: short-term	8 742 . .	...	...	...	...	...	...	...	...
Banks: long-term	8 744 . .	...	...	...	...	...	...	...	...
Banks: short-term	8 745 . .	...	...	...	...	...	...	...	...
Other sectors: long-term	8 747 . .	...	...	...	...	...	...	...	...
Other sectors: short-term	8 748 . .	613	620	571	384	373	...	...	...
Reserve assets	8 800 . .	**3,934**	**4,092**	**4,731**	**6,607**	**7,813**	...	...	...
Monetary gold	8 810 . .	468	249	248	324	172	...	...	...
Special drawing rights	8 820 . .	154	150	163	163	58	158	170	177
Reserve position in the Fund	8 830 . .	...	...	...	...	95	110	127	201
Foreign exchange	8 840 . .	3,110	3,466	4,049	5,866	7,236	...	...	...
Other claims	8 880 . .	202	227	271	254	252	...	...	...

Table 3 (Continued). INTERNATIONAL INVESTMENT POSITION (End–period stocks), 1988–95
(Millions of U.S. dollars)

	Code	1988	1989	1990	1991	1992	1993	1994	1995
LIABILITIES	8 995 D.	20,839	21,464	23,145	22,890	23,047	...	...	...
Direct investment in Colombia	8 555 . .	**3,827**	**4,404**	**4,904**	**5,362**	**6,152**	...	...	...
Equity capital and reinvested earnings	8 556 . .	3,827	4,404	4,904	5,362	6,152	...	...	...
Claims on direct investors	8 557 . .	...	...	...	...	...	...	...	...
Liabilities to direct investors	8 558 . .	...	...	...	...	...	...	...	...
Other capital	8 580 . .	...	...	...	...	...	...	...	...
Claims on direct investors	8 585 . .	...	...	...	...	...	...	...	...
Liabilities to direct investors	8 590 . .	...	...	...	...	...	...	...	...
Portfolio investment	8 652 . .	**104**	**276**	**275**	**360**	**419**	...	...	...
Equity securities	8 660 . .	...	...	...	...	...	...	...	...
Banks	8 663 . .	...	...	...	...	...	...	...	...
Other sectors	8 664 . .	...	...	...	...	...	...	...	...
Debt securities	8 669 . .	104	276	275	360	419	...	...	...
Bonds and notes	8 670 . .	104	276	275	360	419	...	...	...
Monetary authorities	8 671 . .	...	...	...	...	...	...	...	...
General government	8 672 . .	...	...	...	...	...	...	...	...
Banks	8 673 . .	...	...	...	...	...	...	...	...
Other sectors	8 674 . .	...	...	...	...	...	...	...	...
Money market instruments	8 680 . .	...	...	...	...	...	...	...	...
Monetary authorities	8 681 . .	...	...	...	...	...	...	...	...
General government	8 682 . .	...	...	...	...	...	...	...	...
Banks	8 683 . .	...	...	...	...	...	...	...	...
Other sectors	8 684 . .	...	...	...	...	...	...	...	...
Financial derivatives	8 690 . .	...	...	...	...	...	...	...	...
Monetary authorities	8 691 . .	...	...	...	...	...	...	...	...
General government	8 692 . .	...	...	...	...	...	...	...	...
Banks	8 692 . .	...	...	...	...	...	...	...	...
Other sectors	8 694 . .	...	...	...	...	...	...	...	...
Other investment	8 753 . .	**16,908**	**16,784**	**17,966**	**17,168**	**16,476**	...	...	...
Trade credits	8 756 . .	...	...	...	...	...	...	...	...
General government: long-term	8 758 . .	...	...	...	...	...	...	...	...
General government: short-term	8 759 . .	...	...	...	...	...	...	...	...
Other sectors: long-term	8 761 . .	...	...	...	...	...	...	...	...
Other sectors: short-term	8 762 . .	...	...	...	...	...	...	...	...
Loans	8 764 . .	15,501	15,267	16,468	16,029	14,833	...	...	...
Use of Fund credit and loans from the Fund	8 766 . .	...	...	...	...	...	...	...	...
Monetary authorities: other long-term	8 767 . .	509	528	631	631	635	...	...	...
Monetary authorities: short-term	8 768 . .	...	...	...	...	...	...	...	...
General government: long-term	8 770 . .	4,548	4,855	5,468	5,405	5,589	...	...	...
General government: short-term	8 771 . .	...	...	...	...	...	...	...	...
Banks: long-term	8 773 . .	...	...	...	...	...	...	...	...
Banks: short-term	8 774 . .	...	...	...	...	...	...	...	...
Other sectors: long-term	8 776 . .	9,443	8,974	9,601	9,252	7,887	...	...	...
Other sectors: short-term	8 777 . .	1,001	910	768	741	722	...	...	...
Currency and deposits	8 780 . .	1,130	1,166	1,176	855	1,628	...	...	...
Monetary authorities	8 781 . .	...	...	...	...	...	...	...	...
General government	8 782 . .	...	...	...	...	...	...	...	...
Banks	8 783 . .	1,130	1,166	1,176	855	1,628	...	...	...
Other sectors	8 784 . .	...	...	...	...	...	...	...	...
Other liabilities	8 786 . .	277	351	322	284	15	...	...	...
Monetary authorities: long-term	8 788 . .	...	...	...	...	...	...	...	...
Monetary authorities: short-term	8 789 . .	88	159	130	132	15	...	...	...
General government: long-term	8 791 . .	...	...	...	...	...	...	...	...
General government: short-term	8 792 . .	...	...	...	...	...	...	...	...
Banks: long-term	8 794 . .	...	...	...	...	...	...	...	...
Banks: short-term	8 795 . .	...	...	...	...	...	...	...	...
Other sectors: long-term	8 797 . .	...	...	...	...	...	...	...	...
Other sectors: short-term	8 798 . .	189	192	192	152	...	...	...	...
NET INTERNATIONAL INVESTMENT POSITION	8 995 . .	**–15,682**	**–16,169**	**–17,313**	**–14,848**	**–13,835**	...	...	...
Conversion rates: Colombian pesos per U.S. dollar (end of period)	0 102 . .	**335.86**	**433.92**	**568.73**	**706.86**	**811.77**	**917.33**	**831.27**	**987.65**

Table 1. ANALYTIC PRESENTATION, 1988–95
(Millions of U.S. dollars)

	Code	1988	1989	1990	1991	1992	1993	1994	1995
A. Current Account [1]	4 993 Y.	**–6.52**	**5.41**	**–9.29**	**–8.91**	**. . .**	**. . .**	**. . .**	**. . .**
Goods: exports f.o.b	2 100 . .	21.48	18.05	17.93	24.36	. . .	. . .	. . .	. . .
Goods: imports f.o.b	3 100 . .	–44.29	–35.65	–45.23	–53.60	. . .	. . .	. . .	. . .
Balance on Goods	4 100 . .	*–22.81*	*–17.60*	*–27.29*	*–29.24*	. . .	. . .	. . .	. . .
Services: credit	2 200 . .	16.85	17.54	16.86	24.70	. . .	. . .	. . .	. . .
Services: debit	3 200 . .	–42.29	–39.61	–42.73	–44.38	. . .	. . .	. . .	. . .
Balance on Goods and Services	4 991 . .	*–48.26*	*–39.66*	*–53.17*	*–48.92*	. . .	. . .	. . .	. . .
Income: credit	2 300 . .	1.76	4.30	3.35	2.81	. . .	. . .	. . .	. . .
Income: debit	3 300 . .	–3.94	–2.94	–4.21	–3.74	. . .	. . .	. . .	. . .
Balance on Goods, Services, and Income	4 992 . .	*–50.44*	*–38.31*	*–54.02*	*–49.85*	. . .	. . .	. . .	. . .
Current transfers: credit	2 379 Y.	48.40	49.16	49.41	47.44	. . .	. . .	. . .	. . .
Current transfers: debit	3 379 . .	–4.48	–5.45	–4.67	–6.50	. . .	. . .	. . .	. . .
B. Capital Account [1]	4 994 Y.	**. . .**	**. . .**	**. . .**	**. . .**	**. . .**	**. . .**	**. . .**	**. . .**
Capital account: credit	2 994 Y.	. . .	. . .	. . .	. . .	. . .	. . .	. . .	. . .
Capital account: debit	3 994 . .	. . .	. . .	. . .	. . .	. . .	. . .	. . .	. . .
Total, Groups A Plus B	4 010 . .	*–6.52*	*5.41*	*–9.29*	*–8.91*	. . .	. . .	. . .	. . .
C. Financial Account [1]	4 995 X.	**4.19**	**7.54**	**13.67**	**.58**	**. . .**	**. . .**	**. . .**	**. . .**
Direct investment abroad	4 505 . .	. . .	. . .	–1.10	. . .	. . .	. . .	. . .	. . .
Direct investment in Comoros	4 555 Y.	3.77	3.27	.39	2.51	. . .	. . .	. . .	. . .
Portfolio investment assets	4 602 . .	. . .	. . .	. . .	. . .	. . .	. . .	. . .	. . .
Equity securities	4 610 . .	. . .	. . .	. . .	. . .	. . .	. . .	. . .	. . .
Debt securities	4 619 . .	. . .	. . .	. . .	. . .	. . .	. . .	. . .	. . .
Portfolio investment liabilities	4 652 Y.	. . .	. . .	. . .	. . .	. . .	. . .	. . .	. . .
Equity securities	4 660 Y.	. . .	. . .	. . .	. . .	. . .	. . .	. . .	. . .
Debt securities	4 669 Y.	. . .	. . .	. . .	. . .	. . .	. . .	. . .	. . .
Other investment assets	4 703 . .	–13.70	–6.73	3.05	–17.43	. . .	. . .	. . .	. . .
Monetary authorities	4 703 .A	. . .	. . .	. . .	. . .	. . .	. . .	. . .	. . .
General government	4 703 .B	. . .	. . .	–.74	–13.50	. . .	. . .	. . .	. . .
Banks	4 703 .C	–5.24	.66	.49	–1.83	. . .	. . .	. . .	. . .
Other sectors	4 703 .D	–8.46	–7.39	3.30	–2.11	. . .	. . .	. . .	. . .
Other investment liabilities	4 753 X.	14.13	11.01	11.32	15.51	. . .	. . .	. . .	. . .
Monetary authorities	4 753 XA	8.46	7.20	8.76	4.43	. . .	. . .	. . .	. . .
General government	4 753 YB	1.31	2.79	.66	6.30	. . .	. . .	. . .	. . .
Banks	4 753 YC	.80	. . .	.11	–.40	. . .	. . .	. . .	. . .
Other sectors	4 753 YD	3.57	1.01	1.79	5.18	. . .	. . .	. . .	. . .
Total, Groups A Through C	4 020 . .	*–2.32*	*12.95*	*4.38*	*–8.33*	. . .	. . .	. . .	. . .
D. Net Errors and Omissions	4 998 . .	**–1.39**	**–7.60**	**–9.23**	**1.70**	**. . .**	**. . .**	**. . .**	**. . .**
Total, Groups A Through D	4 030 . .	*–3.72*	*5.35*	*–4.85*	*–6.62*	. . .	. . .	. . .	. . .
E. Reserves and Related Items	4 040 . .	**3.72**	**–5.35**	**4.85**	**6.62**	**. . .**	**. . .**	**. . .**	**. . .**
Reserve assets	4 800 . .	3.72	–5.35	4.85	1.87	. . .	. . .	. . .	. . .
Use of Fund credit and loans	4 766 . .	. . .	. . .	. . .	1.19	. . .	. . .	. . .	. . .
Liabilities constituting foreign authorities' reserves	4 900 . .	. . .	. . .	. . .	. . .	. . .	. . .	. . .	. . .
Exceptional financing	4 920 . .	. . .	. . .	. . .	3.57	. . .	. . .	. . .	. . .
Conversion rates: Comorian francs per U.S. dollar	0 101 . .	**297.85**	**319.01**	**272.27**	**282.11**	**264.69**	**283.16**	**416.40**	**374.36**

[1] Excludes components that have been classified in the categories of Group E.

Table 2. STANDARD PRESENTATION, 1988–95
(Millions of U.S. dollars)

	Code	1988	1989	1990	1991	1992	1993	1994	1995
CURRENT ACCOUNT	4 993 . .	**-6.52**	**5.41**	**-9.29**	**-8.91**	**...**	**...**	**...**	**...**
A. GOODS	4 100 . .	-22.81	-17.60	-27.29	-29.24	...	...	...	...
Credit	2 100 . .	**21.48**	**18.05**	**17.93**	**24.36**	**...**	**...**	**...**	**...**
General merchandise: exports f.o.b.	2 110 . .	21.48	18.05	17.93	24.36	...	...	...	...
Goods for processing: exports f.o.b.	2 150 . .	...	...	...	...	...	...	...	...
Repairs on goods	2 160 . .	...	...	...	...	...	...	...	...
Goods procured in ports by carriers	2 170 . .	...	...	...	...	...	...	...	...
Nonmonetary gold	2 180 . .	...	...	...	...	...	...	...	...
Debit	3 100 . .	**-44.29**	**-35.65**	**-45.23**	**-53.60**	**...**	**...**	**...**	**...**
General merchandise: imports f.o.b.	3 110 . .	-44.29	-35.65	-45.23	-53.60	...	...	...	...
Goods for processing: imports f.o.b.	3 150 . .	...	...	...	...	...	...	...	...
Repairs on goods	3 160 . .	...	...	...	...	...	...	...	...
Goods procured in ports by carriers	3 170 . .	...	...	...	...	...	...	...	...
Nonmonetary gold	3 180 . .	...	...	...	...	...	...	...	...
B. SERVICES	4 200 . .	-25.45	-22.06	-25.87	-19.67	...	...	...	...
Total credit	2 200 . .	*16.85*	*17.54*	*16.86*	*24.70*	...	...	...	...
Total debit	3 200 . .	*-42.29*	*-39.61*	*-42.73*	*-44.38*	...	...	...	...
Transportation services, credit	2 205 . .	**4.14**	**4.10**	**3.95**	**4.47**	**...**	**...**	**...**	**...**
Passenger	2 205 BA	*.99*	*.30*	*1.70*	*1.63*	...	...	...	...
Freight	2 205 BB	...	...	...	...	...	...	...	...
Other	2 205 BC	*3.15*	*3.80*	*2.24*	*2.84*	...	...	...	...
Sea transport, passenger	2 207 . .	...	...	...	...	...	...	...	...
Sea transport, freight	2 208 . .	...	...	...	...	...	...	...	...
Sea transport, other	2 209 . .	...	...	...	...	...	...	...	...
Air transport, passenger	2 211 . .	...	...	...	...	...	...	...	...
Air transport, freight	2 212 . .	...	...	...	...	...	...	...	...
Air transport, other	2 213 . .	...	...	...	...	...	...	...	...
Other transport, passenger	2 215 . .	...	...	...	...	...	...	...	...
Other transport, freight	2 216 . .	...	...	...	...	...	...	...	...
Other transport, other	2 217 . .	...	...	...	...	...	...	...	...
Transportation services, debit	3 205 . .	**-17.37**	**-15.28**	**-18.34**	**-18.42**	**...**	**...**	**...**	**...**
Passenger	3 205 BA	*-5.54*	*-5.80*	*-6.66*	*-5.22*	...	...	...	...
Freight	3 205 BB	*-10.91*	*-8.84*	*-10.71*	*-12.07*	...	...	...	...
Other	3 205 BC	*-.92*	*-.64*	*-.97*	*-1.12*	...	...	...	...
Sea transport, passenger	3 207 . .	...	...	...	...	...	...	...	...
Sea transport, freight	3 208 . .	...	...	...	...	...	...	...	...
Sea transport, other	3 209 . .	...	...	...	...	...	...	...	...
Air transport, passenger	3 211 . .	...	...	...	...	...	...	...	...
Air transport, freight	3 212 . .	...	...	...	...	...	...	...	...
Air transport, other	3 213 . .	...	...	...	...	...	...	...	...
Other transport, passenger	3 215 . .	...	...	...	...	...	...	...	...
Other transport, freight	3 216 . .	...	...	...	...	...	...	...	...
Other transport, other	3 217 . .	...	...	...	...	...	...	...	...
Travel, credit	2 236 . .	**2.50**	**3.26**	**1.78**	**8.62**	**...**	**...**	**...**	**...**
Business travel	2 237 . .	...	...	...	...	...	...	...	...
Personal travel	2 240 . .	...	...	...	...	...	...	...	...
Travel, debit	3 236 . .	**-4.86**	**-4.70**	**-5.93**	**-6.69**	**...**	**...**	**...**	**...**
Business travel	3 237 . .	...	...	...	...	...	...	...	...
Personal travel	3 240 . .	...	...	...	...	...	...	...	...
Other services, credit	2 200 BA	**10.21**	**10.18**	**11.14**	**11.61**	**...**	**...**	**...**	**...**
Communications	2 245 . .	...	...	...	...	...	...	...	...
Construction	2 249 . .	...	...	...	...	...	...	...	...
Insurance	2 253 . .	...	...	...	...	...	...	...	...
Financial	2 260 . .	...	...	...	...	...	...	...	...
Computer and information	2 262 . .	...	...	...	...	...	...	...	...
Royalties and licence fees	2 266 . .	...	...	...	...	...	...	...	...
Other business services	2 268 . .	.44	.39	.47	.39	...	...	...	...
Personal, cultural, and recreational	2 287 . .	...	...	...	...	...	...	...	...
Government, n.i.e.	2 291 . .	9.77	9.79	10.67	11.22	...	...	...	...
Other services, debit	3 200 BA	**-20.07**	**-19.62**	**-18.46**	**-19.26**	**...**	**...**	**...**	**...**
Communications	3 245 . .	...	...	...	...	...	...	...	...
Construction	3 249 . .	...	...	...	...	...	...	...	...
Insurance	3 253 . .	-1.21	-.98	-1.19	-1.34	...	...	...	...
Financial	3 260 . .	...	...	...	...	...	...	...	...
Computer and information	3 262 . .	...	...	...	...	...	...	...	...
Royalties and licence fees	3 266 . .	...	...	...	...	...	...	...	...
Other business services	3 268 . .	-.64	-.40	-.63	-3.29	...	...	...	...
Personal, cultural, and recreational	3 287 . .	...	...	...	...	...	...	...	...
Government, n.i.e.	3 291 . .	-18.21	-18.24	-16.64	-14.63	...	...	...	...

Table 2 (Continued). STANDARD PRESENTATION, 1988–95
(Millions of U.S. dollars)

	Code	1988	1989	1990	1991	1992	1993	1994	1995
C. INCOME	4 300	–2.18	1.36	–.86	–.93	. . .	. . .	. . .	. . .
Total credit	2 300	*1.76*	*4.30*	*3.35*	*2.81*	. . .	. . .	. . .	. . .
Total debit	3 300	*–3.94*	*–2.94*	*–4.21*	*–3.74*	. . .	. . .	. . .	. . .
Compensation of employees, credit	2 310	. . .	. . .	. . .	. . .	. . .	. . .	. . .	. . .
Compensation of employees, debit	3 310	. . .	. . .	. . .	. . .	. . .	. . .	. . .	. . .
Investment income, credit	2 320	**1.76**	**4.30**	**3.35**	**2.81**	. . .	. . .	. . .	. . .
Direct investment income	2 330	. . .	. . .	.18	. . .	. . .	. . .	. . .	. . .
Dividends and distributed branch profits	2 332	. . .	. . .	. . .	. . .	. . .	. . .	. . .	. . .
Reinvested earnings and undistributed branch profits	2 333	. . .	. . .	.18	. . .	. . .	. . .	. . .	. . .
Income on debt (interest)	2 334	. . .	. . .	. . .	. . .	. . .	. . .	. . .	. . .
Portfolio investment income	2 339	. . .	. . .	. . .	. . .	. . .	. . .	. . .	. . .
Income on equity	2 340	. . .	. . .	. . .	. . .	. . .	. . .	. . .	. . .
Income on bonds and notes	2 350	. . .	. . .	. . .	. . .	. . .	. . .	. . .	. . .
Income on money market instruments and financial derivatives	2 360	. . .	. . .	. . .	. . .	. . .	. . .	. . .	. . .
Other investment income	2 370	1.76	4.30	3.17	2.81	. . .	. . .	. . .	. . .
Investment income, debit	3 320	**–3.94**	**–2.94**	**–4.21**	**–3.74**	. . .	. . .	. . .	. . .
Direct investment income	3 330	.01	. . .	–.61	–.76	. . .	. . .	. . .	. . .
Dividends and distributed branch profits	3 332	.11	. . .	–.22	–.30	. . .	. . .	. . .	. . .
Reinvested earnings and undistributed branch profits	3 333	–.10	. . .	–.39	–.46	. . .	. . .	. . .	. . .
Income on debt (interest)	3 334	. . .	. . .	. . .	. . .	. . .	. . .	. . .	. . .
Portfolio investment income	3 339	. . .	. . .	. . .	. . .	. . .	. . .	. . .	. . .
Income on equity	3 340	. . .	. . .	. . .	. . .	. . .	. . .	. . .	. . .
Income on bonds and notes	3 350	. . .	. . .	. . .	. . .	. . .	. . .	. . .	. . .
Income on money market instruments and financial derivatives	3 360	. . .	. . .	. . .	. . .	. . .	. . .	. . .	. . .
Other investment income	3 370	–3.96	–2.94	–3.59	–2.99	. . .	. . .	. . .	. . .
D. CURRENT TRANSFERS	4 379	43.92	43.71	44.74	40.94	. . .	. . .	. . .	. . .
Credit	2 379	**48.40**	**49.16**	**49.41**	**47.44**	. . .	. . .	. . .	. . .
General government	2 380	41.02	41.28	39.47	37.34	. . .	. . .	. . .	. . .
Other sectors	2 390	7.38	7.89	9.94	10.10	. . .	. . .	. . .	. . .
Workers' remittances	2 391	7.38	7.89	9.94	10.10	. . .	. . .	. . .	. . .
Other current transfers	2 392	. . .	. . .	. . .	. . .	. . .	. . .	. . .	. . .
Debit	3 379	**–4.48**	**–5.45**	**–4.67**	**–6.50**	. . .	. . .	. . .	. . .
General government	3 380	–.22	–.22	–.24	–.13	. . .	. . .	. . .	. . .
Other sectors	3 390	–4.26	–5.23	–4.43	–6.37	. . .	. . .	. . .	. . .
Workers' remittances	3 391	–4.26	–5.23	–4.43	–6.37	. . .	. . .	. . .	. . .
Other current transfers	3 392	. . .	. . .	. . .	. . .	. . .	. . .	. . .	. . .
CAPITAL AND FINANCIAL ACCOUNT	4 996	**7.91**	**2.19**	**18.52**	**7.20**	. . .	. . .	. . .	. . .
CAPITAL ACCOUNT	4 994	. . .	. . .	. . .	. . .	. . .	. . .	. . .	. . .
Total credit	2 994	. . .	. . .	. . .	. . .	. . .	. . .	. . .	. . .
Total debit	3 994	. . .	. . .	. . .	. . .	. . .	. . .	. . .	. . .
Capital transfers, credit	2 400	. . .	. . .	. . .	. . .	. . .	. . .	. . .	. . .
General government	2 401	. . .	. . .	. . .	. . .	. . .	. . .	. . .	. . .
Debt forgiveness	2 402	. . .	. . .	. . .	. . .	. . .	. . .	. . .	. . .
Other capital transfers	2 410	. . .	. . .	. . .	. . .	. . .	. . .	. . .	. . .
Other sectors	2 430	. . .	. . .	. . .	. . .	. . .	. . .	. . .	. . .
Migrants' transfers	2 431	. . .	. . .	. . .	. . .	. . .	. . .	. . .	. . .
Debt forgiveness	2 432	. . .	. . .	. . .	. . .	. . .	. . .	. . .	. . .
Other capital transfers	2 440	. . .	. . .	. . .	. . .	. . .	. . .	. . .	. . .
Capital transfers, debit	3 400	. . .	. . .	. . .	. . .	. . .	. . .	. . .	. . .
General government	3 401	. . .	. . .	. . .	. . .	. . .	. . .	. . .	. . .
Debt forgiveness	3 402	. . .	. . .	. . .	. . .	. . .	. . .	. . .	. . .
Other capital transfers	3 410	. . .	. . .	. . .	. . .	. . .	. . .	. . .	. . .
Other sectors	3 430	. . .	. . .	. . .	. . .	. . .	. . .	. . .	. . .
Migrants' transfers	3 431	. . .	. . .	. . .	. . .	. . .	. . .	. . .	. . .
Debt forgiveness	3 432	. . .	. . .	. . .	. . .	. . .	. . .	. . .	. . .
Other capital transfers	3 440	. . .	. . .	. . .	. . .	. . .	. . .	. . .	. . .
Nonproduced nonfinancial assets, credit	2 480	. . .	. . .	. . .	. . .	. . .	. . .	. . .	. . .
Nonproduced nonfinancial assets, debit	3 480	. . .	. . .	. . .	. . .	. . .	. . .	. . .	. . .

Table 2 (Continued). STANDARD PRESENTATION, 1988–95
(Millions of U.S. dollars)

	Code	1988	1989	1990	1991	1992	1993	1994	1995
FINANCIAL ACCOUNT	4 995 . .	**7.91**	**2.19**	**18.52**	**7.20**	...	...	...	...
A. DIRECT INVESTMENT	4 500 . .	3.77	3.27	–.71	2.51	...	...	...	...
Direct investment abroad	4 505 . .	...	...	**–1.10**	...	...	...	...	...
Equity capital	4 510 . .	...	...	–.92	...	...	...	...	...
Claims on affiliated enterprises	4 515 . .	...	...	...	...	...	...	...	...
Liabilities to affiliated enterprises	4 520 . .	...	...	...	...	...	...	...	...
Reinvested earnings	4 525 . .	...	...	–.18	...	...	...	...	...
Other capital	4 530 . .	...	...	...	...	...	...	...	...
Claims on affiliated enterprises	4 535 . .	...	...	...	...	...	...	...	...
Liabilities to affiliated enterprises	4 540 . .	...	...	...	...	...	...	...	...
Direct investment in Comoros	4 555 . .	**3.77**	**3.27**	**.39**	**2.51**	...	...	...	...
Equity capital	4 560 . .	3.67	3.27	...	2.05	...	...	...	...
Claims on direct investors	4 565 . .	...	...	...	...	...	...	...	...
Liabilities to direct investors	4 570 . .	...	...	...	...	...	...	...	...
Reinvested earnings	4 575 . .	.10	...	.39	.46	...	...	...	...
Other capital	4 580 . .	...	...	...	...	...	...	...	...
Claims on direct investors	4 585 . .	...	...	...	...	...	...	...	...
Liabilities to direct investors	4 590 . .	...	...	...	...	...	...	...	...
B. PORTFOLIO INVESTMENT	4 600 . .	...	...	...	...	...	...	...	...
Assets	4 602 . .	...	...	...	...	...	...	...	...
Equity securities	4 610 . .	...	...	...	...	...	...	...	...
Monetary authorities	4 611 . .	...	...	...	...	...	...	...	...
General government	4 612 . .	...	...	...	...	...	...	...	...
Banks	4 613 . .	...	...	...	...	...	...	...	...
Other sectors	4 614 . .	...	...	...	...	...	...	...	...
Debt securities	4 619 . .	...	...	...	...	...	...	...	...
Bonds and notes	4 620 . .	...	...	...	...	...	...	...	...
Monetary authorities	4 621 . .	...	...	...	...	...	...	...	...
General government	4 622 . .	...	...	...	...	...	...	...	...
Banks	4 623 . .	...	...	...	...	...	...	...	...
Other sectors	4 624 . .	...	...	...	...	...	...	...	...
Money market instruments	4 630 . .	...	...	...	...	...	...	...	...
Monetary authorities	4 631 . .	...	...	...	...	...	...	...	...
General government	4 632 . .	...	...	...	...	...	...	...	...
Banks	4 633 . .	...	...	...	...	...	...	...	...
Other sectors	4 634 . .	...	...	...	...	...	...	...	...
Financial derivatives	4 640 . .	...	...	...	...	...	...	...	...
Monetary authorities	4 641 . .	...	...	...	...	...	...	...	...
General government	4 642 . .	...	...	...	...	...	...	...	...
Banks	4 643 . .	...	...	...	...	...	...	...	...
Other sectors	4 644 . .	...	...	...	...	...	...	...	...
Liabilities	4 652 . .	...	...	...	...	...	...	...	...
Equity securities	4 660 . .	...	...	...	...	...	...	...	...
Banks	4 663 . .	...	...	...	...	...	...	...	...
Other sectors	4 664 . .	...	...	...	...	...	...	...	...
Debt securities	4 669 . .	...	...	...	...	...	...	...	...
Bonds and notes	4 670 . .	...	...	...	...	...	...	...	...
Monetary authorities	4 671 . .	...	...	...	...	...	...	...	...
General government	4 672 . .	...	...	...	...	...	...	...	...
Banks	4 673 . .	...	...	...	...	...	...	...	...
Other sectors	4 674 . .	...	...	...	...	...	...	...	...
Money market instruments	4 680 . .	...	...	...	...	...	...	...	...
Monetary authorities	4 681 . .	...	...	...	...	...	...	...	...
General government	4 682 . .	...	...	...	...	...	...	...	...
Banks	4 683 . .	...	...	...	...	...	...	...	...
Other sectors	4 684 . .	...	...	...	...	...	...	...	...
Financial derivatives	4 690 . .	...	...	...	...	...	...	...	...
Monetary authorities	4 691 . .	...	...	...	...	...	...	...	...
General government	4 692 . .	...	...	...	...	...	...	...	...
Banks	4 693 . .	...	...	...	...	...	...	...	...
Other sectors	4 694 . .	...	...	...	...	...	...	...	...

Table 2 (Concluded). STANDARD PRESENTATION, 1988–95

(Millions of U.S. dollars)

	Code	1988	1989	1990	1991	1992	1993	1994	1995
C. OTHER INVESTMENT	4 700	.43	4.27	14.38	2.83	...	...	...	...
Assets	4 703 . .	**–13.70**	**–6.73**	**3.05**	**–17.43**	**...**	**...**	**...**	**...**
Trade credits	4 706 . .	...	...	...	...	...	...	...	...
General government: long-term	4 708 . .	...	...	...	...	...	...	...	...
General government: short-term	4 709 . .	...	...	...	...	...	...	...	...
Other sectors: long-term	4 711 . .	...	...	...	...	...	...	...	...
Other sectors: short-term	4 712 . .	...	...	...	...	...	...	...	...
Loans	4 714 . .	...	...	...	...	...	...	...	...
Monetary authorities: long-term	4 717 . .	...	...	...	...	...	...	...	...
Monetary authorities: short-term	4 718 . .	...	...	...	...	...	...	...	...
General government: long-term	4 720 . .	...	...	...	...	...	...	...	...
General government: short-term	4 721 . .	...	...	...	...	...	...	...	...
Banks: long-term	4 723 . .	...	...	...	...	...	...	...	...
Banks: short-term	4 724 . .	...	...	...	...	...	...	...	...
Other sectors: long-term	4 726 . .	...	...	...	...	...	...	...	...
Other sectors: short-term	4 727 . .	...	...	...	...	...	...	...	...
Currency and deposits	4 730 . .	–13.70	–6.73	3.05	–17.43	...	...	...	...
Monetary authorities	4 731 . .	...	...	...	...	...	...	...	...
General government	4 732 . .	...	...	–.74	–13.50	...	...	...	...
Banks	4 733 . .	–5.24	.66	.49	–1.83	...	...	...	...
Other sectors	4 734 . .	–8.46	–7.39	3.30	–2.11	...	...	...	...
Other assets	4 736 . .	...	...	...	...	...	...	...	...
Monetary authorities: long-term	4 738 . .	...	...	...	...	...	...	...	...
Monetary authorities: short-term	4 739 . .	...	...	...	...	...	...	...	...
General government: long-term	4 741 . .	...	...	...	...	...	...	...	...
General government: short-term	4 742 . .	...	...	...	...	...	...	...	...
Banks: long-term	4 744 . .	...	...	...	...	...	...	...	...
Banks: short-term	4 745 . .	...	...	...	...	...	...	...	...
Other sectors: long-term	4 747 . .	...	...	...	...	...	...	...	...
Other sectors: short-term	4 748 . .	...	...	...	...	...	...	...	...
Liabilities	4 753 . .	**14.13**	**11.01**	**11.32**	**20.26**	**...**	**...**	**...**	**...**
Trade credits	4 756 . .	...	...	...	...	...	...	...	...
General government: long-term	4 758 . .	...	...	...	...	...	...	...	...
General government: short-term	4 759 . .	...	...	...	...	...	...	...	...
Other sectors: long-term	4 761 . .	...	...	...	...	...	...	...	...
Other sectors: short-term	4 762 . .	...	...	...	...	...	...	...	...
Loans	4 764 . .	2.25	3.63	.90	12.47	...	...	...	...
Use of Fund credit and loans from the Fund	4 766 . .	...	...	...	1.19	...	...	...	...
Monetary authorities: other long-term	4 767 . .	...	...	...	...	...	...	...	...
Monetary authorities: short-term	4 768 . .	...	...	...	...	...	...	...	...
General government: long-term	4 770 . .	1.49	2.79	.66	9.87	...	...	...	...
General government: short-term	4 771 . .	...	...	...	...	...	...	...	...
Banks: long-term	4 773 . .	...	...	...	...	...	...	...	...
Banks: short-term	4 774 . .	...	...	...	...	...	...	...	...
Other sectors: long-term	4 776 . .	.76	.83	.24	1.41	...	...	...	...
Other sectors: short-term	4 777 . .	...	...	...	...	...	...	...	...
Currency and deposits	4 780 . .	.80	...	.11	–.40	...	...	...	...
Monetary authorities	4 781 . .	...	...	...	...	...	...	...	...
General government	4 782 . .	...	...	...	...	...	...	...	...
Banks	4 783 . .	.80	...	.11	–.40	...	...	...	...
Other sectors	4 784 . .	...	...	...	...	...	...	...	...
Other liabilities	4 786 . .	11.08	7.38	10.31	8.20	...	...	...	...
Monetary authorities: long-term	4 788 . .	...	...	...	...	...	...	...	...
Monetary authorities: short-term	4 789 . .	8.46	7.20	8.76	4.43	...	...	...	...
General government: long-term	4 791 . .	–.18	...	...	...	...	...	...	...
General government: short-term	4 792 . .	...	...	...	...	...	...	...	...
Banks: long-term	4 794 . .	...	...	...	...	...	...	...	...
Banks: short-term	4 795 . .	...	...	...	...	...	...	...	...
Other sectors: long-term	4 797 . .	...	...	...	...	...	...	...	...
Other sectors: short-term	4 798 . .	2.81	.18	1.55	3.77	...	...	...	...
D. RESERVE ASSETS	4 800 . .	3.72	–5.35	4.85	1.87	...	...	...	...
Monetary gold	4 810 . .	.04	.01	...	.01	...	...	...	...
Special drawing rights	4 820 . .	.04	.06	–.03	.08	...	...	...	...
Reserve position in the Fund	4 830 . .	...	...	...	...	...	...	...	...
Foreign exchange	4 840 . .	3.64	–5.42	4.88	1.78	...	...	...	...
Other claims	4 880 . .	...	...	...	...	...	...	...	...
NET ERRORS AND OMISSIONS	4 998 . .	**–1.39**	**–7.60**	**–9.23**	**1.70**	**...**	**...**	**...**	**...**

Table 1. ANALYTIC PRESENTATION, 1988–95
(Millions of U.S. dollars)

	Code	1988	1989	1990	1991	1992	1993	1994	1995
A. Current Account[1]	4 993 Y.	**–445.5**	**–85.0**	**–251.2**	**–461.5**	**–316.6**	**–552.7**	**–793.4**	**–570.2**
Goods: exports f.o.b	2 100 . .	843.2	1,160.5	1,388.7	1,107.7	1,178.7	1,119.1	958.9	1,172.6
Goods: imports f.o.b	3 100 . .	–522.7	–532.0	–512.7	–494.5	–438.2	–500.1	–612.7	–650.1
Balance on Goods	4 100 . .	*320.5*	*628.5*	*876.0*	*613.2*	*740.5*	*619.1*	*346.2*	*522.5*
Services: credit	2 200 . .	92.3	95.3	99.2	99.3	66.1	56.2	67.0	76.3
Services: debit	3 200 . .	–560.1	–494.0	–769.1	–786.6	–737.5	–845.5	–995.8	–775.1
Balance on Goods and Services	4 991 . .	*–147.4*	*229.8*	*206.0*	*–74.1*	*69.1*	*–170.2*	*–582.7*	*–176.3*
Income: credit	2 300 . .	7.5	2.2	14.7	18.8	12.5	11.3	2.0	3.0
Income: debit	3 300 . .	–313.3	–363.3	–474.9	–401.6	–379.7	–384.9	–291.1	–399.5
Balance on Goods, Services, and Income	4 992 . .	*–453.2*	*–131.3*	*–254.2*	*–456.9*	*–298.1*	*–543.9*	*–871.8*	*–572.8*
Current transfers: credit	2 379 Y.	79.8	119.7	86.3	74.1	54.8	50.5	111.3	40.9
Current transfers: debit	3 379 . .	–72.0	–73.4	–83.4	–78.7	–73.3	–59.3	–33.0	–38.3
B. Capital Account[1]	4 994 Y.	**. . .**	**. . .**	**. . .**	**. . .**	**. . .**	**. . .**	**. . .**	**. . .**
Capital account: credit	2 994 Y.	. . .	. . .	. . .	. . .	. . .	. . .	. . .	. . .
Capital account: debit	3 994 . .	. . .	. . .	. . .	. . .	. . .	. . .	. . .	. . .
Total, Groups A Plus B	4 010 . .	*–445.5*	*–85.0*	*–251.2*	*–461.5*	*–316.6*	*–552.7*	*–793.4*	*–570.2*
C. Financial Account[1]	4 995 X.	**–62.0**	**–325.4**	**–72.0**	**9.6**	**–153.8**	**–111.2**	**605.4**	**–80.3**
Direct investment abroad	4 505 . .	. . .	. . .	. . .	. . .	. . .	. . .	. . .	. . .
Direct investment in Congo	4 555 Y.	9.1	. . .	. . .	. . .	. . .	. . .	. . .	. . .
Portfolio investment assets	4 602 . .	. . .	. . .	. . .	. . .	. . .	. . .	. . .	. . .
Equity securities	4 610 . .	. . .	. . .	. . .	. . .	. . .	. . .	. . .	. . .
Debt securities	4 619 . .	. . .	. . .	. . .	. . .	. . .	. . .	. . .	. . .
Portfolio investment liabilities	4 652 Y.	. . .	. . .	. . .	. . .	. . .	. . .	. . .	. . .
Equity securities	4 660 Y.	. . .	. . .	. . .	. . .	. . .	. . .	. . .	. . .
Debt securities	4 669 Y.	. . .	. . .	. . .	. . .	. . .	. . .	. . .	. . .
Other investment assets	4 703 . .	–59.0	–7.8	–67.9	35.1	–24.9	–22.6	35.5	–10.4
Monetary authorities	4 703 .A	. . .	. . .	. . .	. . .	. . .	. . .	. . .	. . .
General government	4 703 .B	. . .	. . .	. . .	. . .	. . .	. . .	. . .	. . .
Banks	4 703 .C	–13.9	. . .	–56.2	2.5	–18.5	–14.8	33.9	–13.4
Other sectors	4 703 .D	–45.0	–7.8	–11.8	32.6	–6.4	–7.8	1.6	3.0
Other investment liabilities	4 753 X.	–12.1	–317.5	–4.0	–25.5	–128.8	–88.6	569.9	–69.9
Monetary authorities	4 753 XA	. . .	. . .	. . .	. . .	. . .	. . .	. . .	. . .
General government	4 753 YB	–66.5	–233.8	–110.9	–227.6	–257.3	–288.9	88.4	–432.5
Banks	4 753 YC	. . .	. . .	. . .	. . .	. . .	. . .	. . .	. . .
Other sectors	4 753 YD	54.4	–83.7	106.9	202.1	128.5	200.2	481.4	362.6
Total, Groups A Through C	4 020 . .	*–507.4*	*–410.3*	*–323.2*	*–452.0*	*–470.4*	*–663.9*	*–188.0*	*–650.5*
D. Net Errors and Omissions	4 998 . .	**40.6**	**8.5**	**–40.6**	**–6.3**	**40.4**	**244.0**	**33.1**	**75.7**
Total, Groups A Through D	4 030 . .	*–466.8*	*–401.8*	*–363.9*	*–458.2*	*–429.9*	*–420.0*	*–154.9*	*–574.8*
E. Reserves and Related Items	4 040 . .	**466.8**	**401.8**	**363.9**	**458.2**	**429.9**	**420.0**	**154.9**	**574.8**
Reserve assets	4 800 . .	–1.7	. . .	–112.9	32.1	–26.8	–1.7	–55.5	–6.4
Use of Fund credit and loans	4 766 . .	–2.9	–3.4	–1.5	–4.9	. . .	–.7	15.0	–2.3
Liabilities constituting foreign authorities' reserves	4 900 . .	–.4	–1.4	. . .	. . .	. . .	. . .	. . .	. . .
Exceptional financing	4 920 . .	471.8	406.6	478.2	431.0	456.8	422.4	195.4	583.6
Conversion rates: CFA francs per U.S. dollar	0 101 . .	**297.85**	**319.01**	**272.26**	**282.11**	**264.69**	**283.16**	**555.20**	**499.15**

[1] Excludes components that have been classified in the categories of Group E.

Table 2. STANDARD PRESENTATION, 1988–95
(Millions of U.S. dollars)

	Code	1988	1989	1990	1991	1992	1993	1994	1995
CURRENT ACCOUNT	4 993 . .	**–445.5**	**–85.0**	**–251.2**	**–461.5**	**–316.6**	**–552.7**	**–793.4**	**–570.2**
A. GOODS	4 100 . .	320.5	628.5	876.0	613.2	740.5	619.1	346.2	522.5
Credit	2 100 . .	**843.2**	**1,160.5**	**1,388.7**	**1,107.7**	**1,178.7**	**1,119.1**	**958.9**	**1,172.6**
General merchandise: exports f.o.b.	2 110 . .	843.2	1,160.5	1,388.7	1,107.7	1,178.7	1,119.1	958.9	1,172.6
Goods for processing: exports f.o.b.	2 150 . .	...	...	...	...	...	...	...	...
Repairs on goods	2 160 . .	...	...	...	...	...	...	...	...
Goods procured in ports by carriers	2 170 . .	...	...	...	...	...	...	...	...
Nonmonetary gold	2 180 . .	...	...	...	...	...	...	...	...
Debit	3 100 . .	**–522.7**	**–532.0**	**–512.7**	**–494.5**	**–438.2**	**–500.1**	**–612.7**	**–650.1**
General merchandise: imports f.o.b.	3 110 . .	–522.7	–532.0	–512.7	–494.5	–438.2	–500.1	–612.7	–650.1
Goods for processing: imports f.o.b.	3 150 . .	...	...	...	...	...	...	...	...
Repairs on goods	3 160 . .	...	...	...	...	...	...	...	...
Goods procured in ports by carriers	3 170 . .	...	...	...	...	...	...	...	...
Nonmonetary gold	3 180 . .	...	...	...	...	...	...	...	...
B. SERVICES	4 200 . .	–467.8	–398.7	–669.9	–687.3	–671.3	–789.3	–928.8	–698.8
Total credit	2 200 . .	*92.3*	*95.3*	*99.2*	*99.3*	*66.1*	*56.2*	*67.0*	*76.3*
Total debit	3 200 . .	*–560.1*	*–494.0*	*–769.1*	*–786.6*	*–737.5*	*–845.5*	*–995.8*	*–775.1*
Transportation services, credit	2 205 . .	**43.5**	**39.7**	**35.3**	**38.6**	**32.9**	**21.9**	**28.5**	**32.3**
Passenger	2 205 BA	...	...	...	...	...	...	...	...
Freight	2 205 BB	*.2*	*1.1*	...	...	...	...	...	...
Other	2 205 BC	*43.3*	*38.6*	*35.3*	*38.6*	*32.9*	*21.9*	*28.5*	*32.3*
Sea transport, passenger	2 207 . .	...	...	...	...	...	...	...	...
Sea transport, freight	2 208 . .	...	...	...	...	...	...	...	...
Sea transport, other	2 209 . .	...	...	...	...	...	...	...	...
Air transport, passenger	2 211 . .	...	...	...	...	...	...	...	...
Air transport, freight	2 212 . .	...	...	...	...	...	...	...	...
Air transport, other	2 213 . .	...	...	...	...	...	...	...	...
Other transport, passenger	2 215 . .	...	...	...	...	...	...	...	...
Other transport, freight	2 216 . .	...	...	...	...	...	...	...	...
Other transport, other	2 217 . .	...	...	...	...	...	...	...	...
Transportation services, debit	3 205 . .	**–135.7**	**–130.0**	**–137.5**	**–146.7**	**–144.4**	**–156.5**	**–189.7**	**–210.2**
Passenger	3 205 BA	*–24.9*	*–27.3*	*–33.1*	*–47.5*	*–57.0*	*–55.4*	*–63.4*	*–73.3*
Freight	3 205 BB	*–106.5*	*–102.7*	*–104.5*	*–99.2*	*–87.4*	*–101.1*	*–126.3*	*–136.9*
Other	3 205 BC	*–4.3*	...	...	...	...	...	...	...
Sea transport, passenger	3 207 . .	...	...	...	...	...	...	...	...
Sea transport, freight	3 208 . .	...	...	...	...	...	...	...	...
Sea transport, other	3 209 . .	...	...	...	...	...	...	...	...
Air transport, passenger	3 211 . .	...	...	...	...	...	...	...	...
Air transport, freight	3 212 . .	...	...	...	...	...	...	...	...
Air transport, other	3 213 . .	...	...	...	...	...	...	...	...
Other transport, passenger	3 215 . .	...	...	...	...	...	...	...	...
Other transport, freight	3 216 . .	...	...	...	...	...	...	...	...
Other transport, other	3 217 . .	...	...	...	...	...	...	...	...
Travel, credit	2 236 . .	**6.1**	**7.2**	**8.4**	**8.2**	**7.6**	**6.0**	**3.6**	**4.0**
Business travel	2 237 . .	...	...	...	...	...	...	...	...
Personal travel	2 240 . .	...	...	...	...	...	...	...	...
Travel, debit	3 236 . .	**–125.8**	**–85.6**	**–113.5**	**–105.6**	**–94.8**	**–69.9**	**–33.5**	**–39.1**
Business travel	3 237 . .	...	...	...	...	...	...	...	...
Personal travel	3 240 . .	...	...	...	...	...	...	...	...
Other services, credit	2 200 BA	**42.7**	**48.4**	**55.5**	**52.5**	**25.7**	**28.3**	**34.9**	**40.1**
Communications	2 245 . .	...	...	...	...	...	...	...	...
Construction	2 249 . .	...	...	...	...	...	...	...	...
Insurance	2 253 . .	3.7	.1	...	...	...	...	...	...
Financial	2 260 . .	...	...	...	...	...	...	...	...
Computer and information	2 262 . .	...	...	...	...	...	...	...	...
Royalties and licence fees	2 266 . .	...	...	...	...	...	...	...	...
Other business services	2 268 . .	13.0	25.7	21.7	18.1	13.2	12.4	16.6	18.0
Personal, cultural, and recreational	2 287 . .	...	...	...	...	...	...	...	...
Government, n.i.e.	2 291 . .	26.0	22.6	33.8	34.4	12.5	15.9	18.4	22.0
Other services, debit	3 200 BA	**–298.6**	**–278.5**	**–518.1**	**–534.2**	**–498.2**	**–619.0**	**–772.7**	**–525.9**
Communications	3 245 . .	...	...	...	...	...	...	...	...
Construction	3 249 . .	...	...	...	...	...	...	...	...
Insurance	3 253 . .	–24.5	–11.4	–11.6	–11.0	–9.7	–11.2	–14.0	–15.2
Financial	3 260 . .	...	...	...	...	...	...	...	...
Computer and information	3 262 . .	...	...	...	...	...	...	...	...
Royalties and licence fees	3 266 . .	...	...	...	...	...	...	...	...
Other business services	3 268 . .	–232.2	–249.2	–485.6	–516.5	–485.5	–605.0	–745.7	–497.6
Personal, cultural, and recreational	3 287 . .	...	...	...	...	...	...	...	...
Government, n.i.e.	3 291 . .	–41.9	–17.9	–20.9	–6.7	–3.0	–2.8	–13.0	–13.0

Table 2 (Continued). STANDARD PRESENTATION, 1988–95
(Millions of U.S. dollars)

	Code	1988	1989	1990	1991	1992	1993	1994	1995
C. INCOME	4 300 . .	–305.9	–361.1	–460.2	–382.8	–367.2	–373.6	–289.1	–396.5
Total credit	2 300 . .	*7.5*	*2.2*	*14.7*	*18.8*	*12.5*	*11.3*	*2.0*	*3.0*
Total debit	3 300 . .	*–313.3*	*–363.3*	*–474.9*	*–401.6*	*–379.7*	*–384.9*	*–291.1*	*–399.5*
Compensation of employees, credit	2 310 . .	**4.4**	. . .	. . .	. . .	. . .	. . .	. . .	. . .
Compensation of employees, debit	3 310 . .	**–.7**	. . .	. . .	. . .	. . .	. . .	. . .	. . .
Investment income, credit	2 320 . .	**3.0**	**2.2**	**14.7**	**18.8**	**12.5**	**11.3**	**2.0**	**3.0**
Direct investment income	2 330 . .	. . .	. . .	. . .	. . .	. . .	. . .	. . .	. . .
Dividends and distributed branch profits	2 332 . .	. . .	. . .	. . .	. . .	. . .	. . .	. . .	. . .
Reinvested earnings and undistributed branch profits	2 333 . .	. . .	. . .	. . .	. . .	. . .	. . .	. . .	. . .
Income on debt (interest)	2 334 . .	. . .	. . .	. . .	. . .	. . .	. . .	. . .	. . .
Portfolio investment income	2 339 . .	. . .	. . .	. . .	. . .	. . .	. . .	. . .	. . .
Income on equity	2 340 . .	. . .	. . .	. . .	. . .	. . .	. . .	. . .	. . .
Income on bonds and notes	2 350 . .	. . .	. . .	. . .	. . .	. . .	. . .	. . .	. . .
Income on money market instruments and financial derivatives	2 360 . .	. . .	. . .	. . .	. . .	. . .	. . .	. . .	. . .
Other investment income	2 370 . .	3.0	2.2	14.7	18.8	12.5	11.3	2.0	3.0
Investment income, debit	3 320 . .	**–312.7**	**–363.3**	**–474.9**	**–401.6**	**–379.7**	**–384.9**	**–291.1**	**–399.5**
Direct investment income	3 330 . .	–62.5	. . .	. . .	. . .	. . .	. . .	. . .	. . .
Dividends and distributed branch profits	3 332 . .	–62.5	. . .	. . .	. . .	. . .	. . .	. . .	. . .
Reinvested earnings and undistributed branch profits	3 333 . .	. . .	. . .	. . .	. . .	. . .	. . .	. . .	. . .
Income on debt (interest)	3 334 . .	. . .	. . .	. . .	. . .	. . .	. . .	. . .	. . .
Portfolio investment income	3 339 . .	. . .	. . .	. . .	. . .	. . .	. . .	. . .	. . .
Income on equity	3 340 . .	. . .	. . .	. . .	. . .	. . .	. . .	. . .	. . .
Income on bonds and notes	3 350 . .	. . .	. . .	. . .	. . .	. . .	. . .	. . .	. . .
Income on money market instruments and financial derivatives	3 360 . .	. . .	. . .	. . .	. . .	. . .	. . .	. . .	. . .
Other investment income	3 370 . .	–250.2	–363.3	–474.9	–401.6	–379.7	–384.9	–291.1	–399.5
D. CURRENT TRANSFERS	4 379 . .	7.8	46.4	2.9	–4.6	–18.5	–8.8	78.3	2.6
Credit	2 379 . .	**79.8**	**119.7**	**86.3**	**74.1**	**54.8**	**50.5**	**111.3**	**40.9**
General government	2 380 . .	64.2	105.3	74.9	61.0	46.1	45.6	108.2	37.5
Other sectors	2 390 . .	15.6	14.4	11.4	13.1	8.7	4.9	3.1	3.4
Workers' remittances	2 391 . .	. . .	. . .	. . .	. . .	. . .	. . .	. . .	. . .
Other current transfers	2 392 . .	15.6	14.4	11.4	13.1	8.7	4.9	3.1	3.4
Debit	3 379 . .	**–72.0**	**–73.4**	**–83.4**	**–78.7**	**–73.3**	**–59.3**	**–33.0**	**–38.3**
General government	3 380 . .	–3.6	–12.2	–9.2	–5.7	–1.5	–2.5	–1.6	–2.0
Other sectors	3 390 . .	–68.5	–61.1	–74.2	–73.0	–71.8	–56.9	–31.3	–36.3
Workers' remittances	3 391 . .	–54.6	–40.4	–55.5	–52.5	–53.3	–45.2	–23.2	–26.8
Other current transfers	3 392 . .	–13.9	–20.7	–18.7	–20.6	–18.5	–11.7	–8.1	–9.4
CAPITAL AND FINANCIAL ACCOUNT	4 996 . .	**404.9**	**76.4**	**291.9**	**467.8**	**276.2**	**308.7**	**760.3**	**494.5**
CAPITAL ACCOUNT	4 994 . .	. . .	. . .	. . .	. . .	. . .	. . .	. . .	. . .
Total credit	2 994 . .	. . .	. . .	. . .	. . .	. . .	. . .	. . .	. . .
Total debit	3 994 . .	. . .	. . .	. . .	. . .	. . .	. . .	. . .	. . .
Capital transfers, credit	2 400 . .	. . .	. . .	. . .	. . .	. . .	. . .	. . .	. . .
General government	2 401 . .	. . .	. . .	. . .	. . .	. . .	. . .	. . .	. . .
Debt forgiveness	2 402 . .	. . .	. . .	. . .	. . .	. . .	. . .	. . .	. . .
Other capital transfers	2 410 . .	. . .	. . .	. . .	. . .	. . .	. . .	. . .	. . .
Other sectors	2 430 . .	. . .	. . .	. . .	. . .	. . .	. . .	. . .	. . .
Migrants' transfers	2 431 . .	. . .	. . .	. . .	. . .	. . .	. . .	. . .	. . .
Debt forgiveness	2 432 . .	. . .	. . .	. . .	. . .	. . .	. . .	. . .	. . .
Other capital transfers	2 440 . .	. . .	. . .	. . .	. . .	. . .	. . .	. . .	. . .
Capital transfers, debit	3 400 . .	. . .	. . .	. . .	. . .	. . .	. . .	. . .	. . .
General government	3 401 . .	. . .	. . .	. . .	. . .	. . .	. . .	. . .	. . .
Debt forgiveness	3 402 . .	. . .	. . .	. . .	. . .	. . .	. . .	. . .	. . .
Other capital transfers	3 410 . .	. . .	. . .	. . .	. . .	. . .	. . .	. . .	. . .
Other sectors	3 430 . .	. . .	. . .	. . .	. . .	. . .	. . .	. . .	. . .
Migrants' transfers	3 431 . .	. . .	. . .	. . .	. . .	. . .	. . .	. . .	. . .
Debt forgiveness	3 432 . .	. . .	. . .	. . .	. . .	. . .	. . .	. . .	. . .
Other capital transfers	3 440 . .	. . .	. . .	. . .	. . .	. . .	. . .	. . .	. . .
Nonproduced nonfinancial assets, credit	2 480 . .	. . .	. . .	. . .	. . .	. . .	. . .	. . .	. . .
Nonproduced nonfinancial assets, debit	3 480 . .	. . .	. . .	. . .	. . .	. . .	. . .	. . .	. . .

Table 2 (Continued). STANDARD PRESENTATION, 1988–95

(Millions of U.S. dollars)

	Code	1988	1989	1990	1991	1992	1993	1994	1995
FINANCIAL ACCOUNT	4 995 . .	**404.9**	**76.4**	**291.9**	**467.8**	**276.2**	**308.7**	**760.3**	**494.5**
A. DIRECT INVESTMENT	4 500 . .	9.1	...	...	...	...	...	...	...
Direct investment abroad	4 505 . .	...	...	...	...	...	...	...	...
Equity capital	4 510 . .	...	...	...	...	...	...	...	...
Claims on affiliated enterprises	4 515 . .	...	...	...	...	...	...	...	...
Liabilities to affiliated enterprises	4 520 . .	...	...	...	...	...	...	...	...
Reinvested earnings	4 525 . .	...	...	...	...	...	...	...	...
Other capital	4 530 . .	...	...	...	...	...	...	...	...
Claims on affiliated enterprises	4 535 . .	...	...	...	...	...	...	...	...
Liabilities to affiliated enterprises	4 540 . .	...	...	...	...	...	...	...	...
Direct investment in Congo	4 555 . .	**9.1**	...	...	...	...	...	...	...
Equity capital	4 560 . .	...	...	...	...	...	...	...	...
Claims on direct investors	4 565 . .	...	...	...	...	...	...	...	...
Liabilities to direct investors	4 570 . .	...	...	...	...	...	...	...	...
Reinvested earnings	4 575 . .	...	...	...	...	...	...	...	...
Other capital	4 580 . .	9.1	...	...	...	...	...	...	...
Claims on direct investors	4 585 . .	...	...	...	...	...	...	...	...
Liabilities to direct investors	4 590 . .	...	...	...	...	...	...	...	...
B. PORTFOLIO INVESTMENT	4 600 . .	...	...	...	...	...	...	...	...
Assets	4 602 . .	...	...	...	...	...	...	...	...
Equity securities	4 610 . .	...	...	...	...	...	...	...	...
Monetary authorities	4 611 . .	...	...	...	...	...	...	...	...
General government	4 612 . .	...	...	...	...	...	...	...	...
Banks	4 613 . .	...	...	...	...	...	...	...	...
Other sectors	4 614 . .	...	...	...	...	...	...	...	...
Debt securities	4 619 . .	...	...	...	...	...	...	...	...
Bonds and notes	4 620 . .	...	...	...	...	...	...	...	...
Monetary authorities	4 621 . .	...	...	...	...	...	...	...	...
General government	4 622 . .	...	...	...	...	...	...	...	...
Banks	4 623 . .	...	...	...	...	...	...	...	...
Other sectors	4 624 . .	...	...	...	...	...	...	...	...
Money market instruments	4 630 . .	...	...	...	...	...	...	...	...
Monetary authorities	4 631 . .	...	...	...	...	...	...	...	...
General government	4 632 . .	...	...	...	...	...	...	...	...
Banks	4 633 . .	...	...	...	...	...	...	...	...
Other sectors	4 634 . .	...	...	...	...	...	...	...	...
Financial derivatives	4 640 . .	...	...	...	...	...	...	...	...
Monetary authorities	4 641 . .	...	...	...	...	...	...	...	...
General government	4 642 . .	...	...	...	...	...	...	...	...
Banks	4 643 . .	...	...	...	...	...	...	...	...
Other sectors	4 644 . .	...	...	...	...	...	...	...	...
Liabilities	4 652 . .	...	...	...	...	...	...	...	...
Equity securities	4 660 . .	...	...	...	...	...	...	...	...
Banks	4 663 . .	...	...	...	...	...	...	...	...
Other sectors	4 664 . .	...	...	...	...	...	...	...	...
Debt securities	4 669 . .	...	...	...	...	...	...	...	...
Bonds and notes	4 670 . .	...	...	...	...	...	...	...	...
Monetary authorities	4 671 . .	...	...	...	...	...	...	...	...
General government	4 672 . .	...	...	...	...	...	...	...	...
Banks	4 673 . .	...	...	...	...	...	...	...	...
Other sectors	4 674 . .	...	...	...	...	...	...	...	...
Money market instruments	4 680 . .	...	...	...	...	...	...	...	...
Monetary authorities	4 681 . .	...	...	...	...	...	...	...	...
General government	4 682 . .	...	...	...	...	...	...	...	...
Banks	4 683 . .	...	...	...	...	...	...	...	...
Other sectors	4 684 . .	...	...	...	...	...	...	...	...
Financial derivatives	4 690 . .	...	...	...	...	...	...	...	...
Monetary authorities	4 691 . .	...	...	...	...	...	...	...	...
General government	4 692 . .	...	...	...	...	...	...	...	...
Banks	4 693 . .	...	...	...	...	...	...	...	...
Other sectors	4 694 . .	...	...	...	...	...	...	...	...

Table 2 (Concluded). STANDARD PRESENTATION, 1988–95
(Millions of U.S. dollars)

	Code	1988	1989	1990	1991	1992	1993	1994	1995
C. OTHER INVESTMENT	4 700 . .	397.5	76.4	404.8	435.7	303.0	310.4	815.8	501.0
Assets	4 703 . .	**–59.0**	**–7.8**	**–67.9**	**35.1**	**–24.9**	**–22.6**	**35.5**	**–10.4**
Trade credits	4 706 . .	80.1	...	...	...	...	...	...	...
General government: long-term	4 708 . .	...	...	...	...	...	...	...	...
General government: short-term	4 709 . .	...	...	...	...	...	...	...	...
Other sectors: long-term	4 711 . .	...	...	...	...	...	...	...	...
Other sectors: short-term	4 712 . .	80.1	...	...	...	...	...	...	...
Loans	4 714 . .	–13.9	...	–11.8	32.6	–6.4	–7.8	1.6	3.0
Monetary authorities: long-term	4 717 . .	...	...	...	...	...	...	...	...
Monetary authorities: short-term	4 718 . .	...	...	...	...	...	...	...	...
General government: long-term	4 720 . .	...	...	...	...	...	...	...	...
General government: short-term	4 721 . .	...	...	...	...	...	...	...	...
Banks: long-term	4 723 . .	...	...	...	...	...	...	...	...
Banks: short-term	4 724 . .	...	...	...	...	...	...	...	...
Other sectors: long-term	4 726 . .	–13.9	...	–11.8	32.6	–6.4	–7.8	1.6	3.0
Other sectors: short-term	4 727 . .	...	...	...	...	...	...	...	...
Currency and deposits	4 730 . .	–125.2	–7.8	–56.2	2.5	–18.5	–14.8	33.9	–13.4
Monetary authorities	4 731 . .	...	...	...	...	...	...	...	...
General government	4 732 . .	...	...	...	...	...	...	...	...
Banks	4 733 . .	–13.9	...	–56.2	2.5	–18.5	–14.8	33.9	–13.4
Other sectors	4 734 . .	–111.3	–7.8	...	...	...	...	...	...
Other assets	4 736 . .	...	...	...	...	...	...	...	...
Monetary authorities: long-term	4 738 . .	...	...	...	...	...	...	...	...
Monetary authorities: short-term	4 739 . .	...	...	...	...	...	...	...	...
General government: long-term	4 741 . .	...	...	...	...	...	...	...	...
General government: short-term	4 742 . .	...	...	...	...	...	...	...	...
Banks: long-term	4 744 . .	...	...	...	...	...	...	...	...
Banks: short-term	4 745 . .	...	...	...	...	...	...	...	...
Other sectors: long-term	4 747 . .	...	...	...	...	...	...	...	...
Other sectors: short-term	4 748 . .	...	...	...	...	...	...	...	...
Liabilities	4 753 . .	**456.5**	**84.3**	**472.7**	**400.6**	**327.9**	**333.0**	**780.3**	**511.4**
Trade credits	4 756 . .	–47.8	...	...	...	...	...	...	...
General government: long-term	4 758 . .	...	...	...	...	...	...	...	...
General government: short-term	4 759 . .	...	...	...	...	...	...	...	...
Other sectors: long-term	4 761 . .	...	...	...	...	...	...	...	...
Other sectors: short-term	4 762 . .	–47.8	...	...	...	...	...	...	...
Loans	4 764 . .	31.4	–270.3	873.1	–71.9	–244.4	–116.9	1,464.5	–139.3
Use of Fund credit and loans from the Fund	4 766 . .	–2.9	–3.4	–1.5	–4.9	...	–.7	15.0	–2.3
Monetary authorities: other long-term	4 767 . .	...	...	...	...	...	...	...	...
Monetary authorities: short-term	4 768 . .	20.7	13.0	...	...	...	...	...	...
General government: long-term	4 770 . .	70.6	–187.1	880.0	–124.1	–255.0	–287.5	1,208.7	–299.3
General government: short-term	4 771 . .	...	...	...	...	...	...	...	...
Banks: long-term	4 773 . .	...	...	...	...	...	...	...	...
Banks: short-term	4 774 . .	...	...	...	...	...	...	...	...
Other sectors: long-term	4 776 . .	–57.0	–92.8	–5.5	57.1	10.6	171.3	240.8	162.3
Other sectors: short-term	4 777 . .	...	...	...	...	...	...	...	...
Currency and deposits	4 780 . .	–.4	–1.4	...	...	...	...	...	...
Monetary authorities	4 781 . .	–.4	–1.4	...	...	...	...	...	...
General government	4 782 . .	...	...	...	...	...	...	...	...
Banks	4 783 . .	...	...	...	...	...	...	...	...
Other sectors	4 784 . .	...	...	...	...	...	...	...	...
Other liabilities	4 786 . .	473.2	356.0	–400.3	472.5	572.4	449.9	–684.3	650.7
Monetary authorities: long-term	4 788 . .	...	...	...	...	...	...	...	...
Monetary authorities: short-term	4 789 . .	313.9	346.9	–512.7	327.5	454.5	421.0	–924.9	450.4
General government: long-term	4 791 . .	...	...	...	...	...	...	...	...
General government: short-term	4 792 . .	...	...	...	...	...	...	...	...
Banks: long-term	4 794 . .	...	...	...	...	...	...	...	...
Banks: short-term	4 795 . .	...	...	...	...	...	...	...	...
Other sectors: long-term	4 797 . .	...	...	...	...	...	...	...	...
Other sectors: short-term	4 798 . .	159.3	9.1	112.4	145.0	117.9	29.0	240.6	200.3
D. RESERVE ASSETS	4 800 . .	–1.7	...	–112.9	32.1	–26.8	–1.7	–55.5	–6.4
Monetary gold	4 810 . .	...	...	...	...	...	...	...	...
Special drawing rights	4 820 . .	1.4	–.4	.2	1.6	...	...	...	...
Reserve position in the Fund	4 830 . .	...	...	...	...	...	...	...	...
Foreign exchange	4 840 . .	–3.1	.4	–113.1	30.5	–26.8	–1.8	–55.5	–6.4
Other claims	4 880 . .	...	...	...	...	...	...	...	...
NET ERRORS AND OMISSIONS	4 998 . .	**40.6**	**8.5**	**–40.6**	**–6.3**	**40.4**	**244.0**	**33.1**	**75.7**

Part 3 of the *Yearbook* contains descriptions of the methodologies, compilation practices, and sources used to compile these data.

Table 1. ANALYTIC PRESENTATION, 1988–95
(Millions of U.S. dollars)

	Code	1988	1989	1990	1991	1992	1993	1994	1995
A. Current Account [1]	4 993 Y.	**–303.5**	**–479.9**	**–494.0**	**–99.2**	**–380.4**	**–620.2**	**–244.0**	**–143.0**
Goods: exports f.o.b	2 100 . .	1,180.7	1,333.4	1,354.2	1,498.1	1,739.1	1,866.8	2,122.0	2,480.2
Goods: imports f.o.b	3 100 . .	–1,278.6	–1,572.0	–1,796.7	–1,697.6	–2,210.9	–2,627.6	–2,727.8	–2,953.7
Balance on Goods	4 100 . .	*–97.9*	*–238.6*	*–442.5*	*–199.5*	*–471.8*	*–760.8*	*–605.8*	*–473.5*
Services: credit	2 200 . .	430.3	497.9	609.0	691.4	841.3	1,039.3	1,195.0	1,309.9
Services: debit	3 200 . .	–423.7	–496.0	–549.7	–534.8	–710.6	–816.4	–860.1	–947.1
Balance on Goods and Services	4 991 . .	*–91.3*	*–236.7*	*–383.2*	*–42.9*	*–341.1*	*–537.9*	*–270.9*	*–110.7*
Income: credit	2 300 . .	47.8	119.9	130.3	111.4	112.8	111.2	154.6	154.5
Income: debit	3 300 . .	–390.4	–489.5	–363.0	–285.3	–315.4	–336.6	–283.0	–340.3
Balance on Goods, Services, and Income	4 992 . .	*–433.9*	*–606.3*	*–615.9*	*–216.8*	*–543.7*	*–763.3*	*–399.3*	*–296.5*
Current transfers: credit	2 379 Y.	141.9	130.5	126.0	121.1	168.9	149.3	164.5	161.8
Current transfers: debit	3 379 . .	–11.5	–4.1	–4.1	–3.5	–5.6	–6.2	–9.2	–8.3
B. Capital Account [1]	4 994 Y.	**. . .**	**. . .**	**. . .**	**. . .**	**. . .**	**. . .**	**. . .**	**. . .**
Capital account: credit	2 994 Y.	. . .	. . .	. . .	. . .	. . .	. . .	. . .	. . .
Capital account: debit	3 994 . .	. . .	. . .	. . .	. . .	. . .	. . .	. . .	. . .
Total, Groups A Plus B	4 010 . .	*–303.5*	*–479.9*	*–494.0*	*–99.2*	*–380.4*	*–620.2*	*–244.0*	*–143.0*
C. Financial Account [1]	4 995 X.	**–271.9**	**–182.5**	**–83.9**	**155.0**	**199.4**	**91.8**	**–107.9**	**279.3**
Direct investment abroad	4 505 . .	–.9	–6.0	–2.1	–5.6	–4.4	–2.3	–4.7	–5.5
Direct investment in Costa Rica	4 555 Y.	122.3	101.2	162.5	178.4	226.0	246.7	297.6	395.5
Portfolio investment assets	4 602 . .	. . .	. . .	. . .	. . .	. . .	. . .	. . .	. . .
Equity securities	4 610 . .	. . .	. . .	. . .	. . .	. . .	. . .	. . .	. . .
Debt securities	4 619 . .	. . .	. . .	. . .	. . .	. . .	. . .	. . .	. . .
Portfolio investment liabilities	4 652 Y.	–6.0	–13.2	–28.2	–13.0	–16.9	–5.1	–1.2	–24.4
Equity securities	4 660 Y.	. . .	. . .	. . .	. . .	. . .	. . .	. . .	. . .
Debt securities	4 669 Y.	–6.0	–13.2	–28.2	–13.0	–16.9	–5.1	–1.2	–24.4
Other investment assets	4 703 . .	–77.3	–5.9	–124.7	75.6	84.8	54.5	–76.2	–10.0
Monetary authorities	4 703 . A	. . .	. . .	. . .	. . .	. . .	. . .	. . .	. . .
General government	4 703 . B	–.1	–4.9	–4.7	1.2	–8.5	34.9	–4.4	. . .
Banks	4 703 . C	. . .	. . .	. . .	. . .	. . .	. . .	. . .	. . .
Other sectors	4 703 . D	–77.2	–1.0	–120.0	74.4	93.3	19.6	–71.8	–10.0
Other investment liabilities	4 753 X.	–310.0	–258.6	–91.4	–80.4	–90.1	–202.0	–323.4	–76.3
Monetary authorities	4 753 XA	–292.8	–289.1	–134.4	–32.6	–70.0	–227.8	–215.6	–136.1
General government	4 753 YB	–36.1	–17.8	–28.1	–68.3	–47.8	–25.7	–106.2	–32.4
Banks	4 753 YC	–13.5	4.4	–1.0	–8.7	7.1	27.7	–18.8	17.8
Other sectors	4 753 YD	32.4	43.9	72.1	29.2	20.6	23.8	17.2	74.4
Total, Groups A Through C	4 020 . .	*–575.4*	*–662.4*	*–577.9*	*55.8*	*–181.0*	*–528.4*	*–351.9*	*136.3*
D. Net Errors and Omissions	4 998 . .	**224.6**	**208.9**	**43.4**	**99.9**	**201.9**	**299.0**	**249.1**	**94.4**
Total, Groups A Through D	4 030 . .	*–350.8*	*–453.5*	*–534.5*	*155.7*	*20.9*	*–229.4*	*–102.8*	*230.7*
E. Reserves and Related Items	4 040 . .	**350.8**	**453.5**	**534.5**	**–155.7**	**–20.9**	**229.4**	**102.8**	**–230.7**
Reserve assets	4 800 . .	–188.0	–112.3	197.2	–416.1	–176.8	59.6	65.5	–154.1
Use of Fund credit and loans	4 766 . .	–54.1	–33.4	–25.6	67.7	1.7	. . .	–20.3	–44.4
Liabilities constituting foreign authorities' reserves	4 900 . .	8.0	–4.2	–6.9	7.1	–6.6	–29.0	–.5	. . .
Exceptional financing	4 920 . .	585.0	603.3	369.8	185.6	160.8	198.8	58.1	–32.2
Conversion rates: Costa Rican colones per U.S. dollar	0 101 . .	**75.80**	**81.50**	**91.58**	**122.43**	**134.51**	**142.17**	**157.07**	**179.73**

[1] Excludes components that have been classified in the categories of Group E.

Table 2. STANDARD PRESENTATION, 1988–95
(Millions of U.S. dollars)

	Code			1988	1989	1990	1991	1992	1993	1994	1995
CURRENT ACCOUNT	4	993	. .	**–178.5**	**–414.9**	**–424.0**	**–75.2**	**–370.4**	**–620.2**	**–233.6**	**–143.0**
A. GOODS	4	100	. .	–97.9	–238.6	–442.5	–199.5	–471.8	–760.8	–605.8	–473.5
Credit	2	100	. .	**1,180.7**	**1,333.4**	**1,354.2**	**1,498.1**	**1,739.1**	**1,866.8**	**2,122.0**	**2,480.2**
General merchandise: exports f.o.b.	2	110	. .	1,180.7	1,333.4	1,354.2	1,498.1	1,739.1	1,866.8	2,122.0	2,480.2
Goods for processing: exports f.o.b.	2	150	. .	...	...	...	...	...	...	...	...
Repairs on goods	2	160	. .	...	...	...	...	...	...	...	...
Goods procured in ports by carriers	2	170	. .	...	...	...	...	...	...	...	...
Nonmonetary gold	2	180	. .	...	...	...	...	...	...	...	...
Debit	3	100	. .	**–1,278.6**	**–1,572.0**	**–1,796.7**	**–1,697.6**	**–2,210.9**	**–2,627.6**	**–2,727.8**	**–2,953.7**
General merchandise: imports f.o.b.	3	110	. .	–1,278.6	–1,572.0	–1,796.7	–1,697.6	–2,210.9	–2,627.6	–2,727.8	–2,953.7
Goods for processing: imports f.o.b.	3	150	. .	...	...	...	...	...	...	...	...
Repairs on goods	3	160	. .	...	...	...	...	...	...	...	...
Goods procured in ports by carriers	3	170	. .	...	...	...	...	...	...	...	...
Nonmonetary gold	3	180	. .	...	...	...	...	...	...	...	...
B. SERVICES	4	200	. .	6.6	1.9	59.3	156.6	130.7	222.9	334.9	362.8
Total credit	2	200	. .	*430.3*	*497.9*	*609.0*	*691.4*	*841.3*	*1,039.3*	*1,195.0*	*1,309.9*
Total debit	3	200	. .	*–423.7*	*–496.0*	*–549.7*	*–534.8*	*–710.6*	*–816.4*	*–860.1*	*–947.1*
Transportation services, credit	2	205	. .	**72.8**	**80.4**	**95.0**	**105.3**	**133.5**	**147.8**	**172.5**	**179.9**
Passenger	2	205	BA	*37.3*	*41.1*	*45.2*	*45.3*	*64.6*	*74.1*	*81.1*	*81.9*
Freight	2	205	BB	*8.1*	*8.6*	*10.8*	*11.3*	*12.1*	*13.1*	*13.6*	*15.0*
Other	2	205	BC	*27.4*	*30.7*	*39.0*	*48.7*	*56.8*	*60.6*	*77.8*	*83.0*
Sea transport, passenger	2	207	. .	...	...	...	...	...	...	...	...
Sea transport, freight	2	208	. .	...	...	...	...	...	...	...	...
Sea transport, other	2	209	. .	...	...	...	...	...	...	...	...
Air transport, passenger	2	211	. .	...	...	...	...	...	...	...	...
Air transport, freight	2	212	. .	...	...	...	...	...	...	...	...
Air transport, other	2	213	. .	...	...	...	...	...	...	...	...
Other transport, passenger	2	215	. .	...	...	...	...	...	...	...	...
Other transport, freight	2	216	. .	...	...	...	...	...	...	...	...
Other transport, other	2	217	. .	...	...	...	...	...	...	...	...
Transportation services, debit	3	205	. .	**–162.0**	**–192.4**	**–222.5**	**–223.4**	**–276.7**	**–340.3**	**–352.7**	**–380.2**
Passenger	3	205	BA	*–9.8*	*–10.1*	*–10.8*	*–11.1*	*–16.2*	*–11.2*	*–12.5*	*–13.0*
Freight	3	205	BB	*–122.7*	*–152.6*	*–172.8*	*–162.7*	*–211.9*	*–253.0*	*–262.5*	*–287.2*
Other	3	205	BC	*–29.5*	*–29.7*	*–38.9*	*–49.6*	*–48.6*	*–76.1*	*–77.7*	*–80.0*
Sea transport, passenger	3	207	. .	...	...	...	...	...	...	...	...
Sea transport, freight	3	208	. .	...	...	...	...	...	...	...	...
Sea transport, other	3	209	. .	...	...	...	...	...	...	...	...
Air transport, passenger	3	211	. .	...	...	...	...	...	...	...	...
Air transport, freight	3	212	. .	...	...	...	...	...	...	...	...
Air transport, other	3	213	. .	...	...	...	...	...	...	...	...
Other transport, passenger	3	215	. .	...	...	...	...	...	...	...	...
Other transport, freight	3	216	. .	...	...	...	...	...	...	...	...
Other transport, other	3	217	. .	...	...	...	...	...	...	...	...
Travel, credit	2	236	. .	**181.5**	**213.1**	**285.0**	**340.4**	**440.0**	**587.6**	**633.8**	**670.6**
Business travel	2	237	. .	...	...	...	...	...	...	...	...
Personal travel	2	240	. .	...	...	...	...	...	...	...	...
Travel, debit	3	236	. .	**–76.2**	**–119.3**	**–155.5**	**–154.2**	**–227.3**	**–269.7**	**–303.3**	**–327.3**
Business travel	3	237	. .	–.7	–1.0	–3.1	–1.3	–1.4	–.6	–2.1	–2.3
Personal travel	3	240	. .	–75.5	–118.3	–152.4	–152.9	–225.9	–269.1	–301.2	–325.0
Other services, credit	2	200	BA	**176.0**	**204.4**	**229.0**	**245.7**	**267.8**	**303.9**	**388.7**	**459.4**
Communications	2	245	. .	...	...	...	...	...	...	...	...
Construction	2	249	. .	...	...	...	...	...	...	...	...
Insurance	2	253	. .	...	...	...	9.8	...	...	...	...
Financial	2	260	. .	...	...	...	...	...	...	...	...
Computer and information	2	262	. .	...	...	...	...	...	...	...	...
Royalties and licence fees	2	266	. .	...	...	1.2	2.6	2.1	2.5	2.5	3.0
Other business services	2	268	. .	153.6	179.3	201.9	204.2	232.5	267.0	354.0	417.4
Personal, cultural, and recreational	2	287	. .	...	...	...	...	...	...	...	...
Government, n.i.e.	2	291	. .	22.4	25.1	25.9	29.1	33.2	34.4	32.2	39.0
Other services, debit	3	200	BA	**–185.5**	**–184.3**	**–171.7**	**–157.2**	**–206.6**	**–206.4**	**–204.1**	**–239.6**
Communications	3	245	. .	...	...	...	...	...	...	...	...
Construction	3	249	. .	...	...	...	...	...	...	...	...
Insurance	3	253	. .	–31.4	–32.2	–32.5	–12.3	–42.9	–51.5	–54.0	–62.2
Financial	3	260	. .	...	...	...	...	...	...	...	...
Computer and information	3	262	. .	...	...	...	...	...	...	...	...
Royalties and licence fees	3	266	. .	–7.6	–10.0	–9.1	–11.0	–9.2	–5.5	–11.0	–11.6
Other business services	3	268	. .	–138.6	–124.1	–120.4	–122.3	–143.5	–133.7	–124.7	–151.8
Personal, cultural, and recreational	3	287	. .	...	...	...	...	...	...	...	...
Government, n.i.e.	3	291	. .	–7.9	–18.0	–9.7	–11.6	–11.0	–15.7	–14.4	–14.0

Table 2 (Continued). STANDARD PRESENTATION, 1988–95
(Millions of U.S. dollars)

	Code	1988	1989	1990	1991	1992	1993	1994	1995
C. INCOME	4 300	–342.6	–369.6	–232.7	–173.9	–202.6	–225.4	–128.4	–185.8
Total credit	2 300	*47.8*	*119.9*	*130.3*	*111.4*	*112.8*	*111.2*	*154.6*	*154.5*
Total debit	3 300	*–390.4*	*–489.5*	*–363.0*	*–285.3*	*–315.4*	*–336.6*	*–283.0*	*–340.3*
Compensation of employees, credit	2 310	**9.1**	**10.0**	**12.0**	**13.4**	**14.2**	**16.0**	**17.1**	**16.7**
Compensation of employees, debit	3 310	**. . .**	**. . .**	**. . .**	**. . .**	**. . .**	**. . .**	**–7.1**	**–9.0**
Investment income, credit	2 320	**38.7**	**109.9**	**118.3**	**98.0**	**98.6**	**95.2**	**137.5**	**137.8**
Direct investment income	2 330	.9	2.7	3.3	3.0	4.0	5.1	5.7	5.5
Dividends and distributed branch profits	2 332	. . .	. . .	. . .	. . .	. . .	. . .	. . .	. . .
Reinvested earnings and undistributed branch profits	2 333	.9	2.7	3.3	3.0	4.0	5.1	5.7	5.5
Income on debt (interest)	2 334	. . .	. . .	. . .	. . .	. . .	. . .	. . .	. . .
Portfolio investment income	2 339	. . .	. . .	. . .	. . .	. . .	. . .	. . .	. . .
Income on equity	2 340	. . .	. . .	. . .	. . .	. . .	. . .	. . .	. . .
Income on bonds and notes	2 350	. . .	. . .	. . .	. . .	. . .	. . .	. . .	. . .
Income on money market instruments and financial derivatives	2 360	. . .	. . .	. . .	. . .	. . .	. . .	. . .	. . .
Other investment income	2 370	37.8	107.2	115.0	95.0	94.6	90.1	131.8	132.3
Investment income, debit	3 320	**–390.4**	**–489.5**	**–363.0**	**–285.3**	**–315.4**	**–336.6**	**–275.9**	**–331.3**
Direct investment income	3 330	–34.1	–54.9	–59.6	–64.7	–91.8	–101.2	–64.7	–97.0
Dividends and distributed branch profits	3 332	–19.4	–17.3	–17.4	–21.7	–25.8	–11.7	–15.1	–20.0
Reinvested earnings and undistributed branch profits	3 333	–14.7	–37.6	–42.2	–43.0	–66.0	–89.5	–49.6	–77.0
Income on debt (interest)	3 334	. . .	. . .	. . .	. . .	. . .	. . .	. . .	. . .
Portfolio investment income	3 339	. . .	. . .	. . .	. . .	. . .	. . .	. . .	. . .
Income on equity	3 340	. . .	. . .	. . .	. . .	. . .	. . .	. . .	. . .
Income on bonds and notes	3 350	. . .	. . .	. . .	. . .	. . .	. . .	. . .	. . .
Income on money market instruments and financial derivatives	3 360	. . .	. . .	. . .	. . .	. . .	. . .	. . .	. . .
Other investment income	3 370	–356.3	–434.6	–303.4	–220.6	–223.6	–235.4	–211.2	–234.3
D. CURRENT TRANSFERS	4 379	255.4	191.4	191.9	141.6	173.3	143.1	165.7	153.5
Credit	2 379	**266.9**	**195.5**	**196.0**	**145.1**	**178.9**	**149.3**	**174.9**	**161.8**
General government	2 380	217.7	155.1	139.8	93.8	87.7	61.8	50.0	52.0
Other sectors	2 390	49.2	40.4	56.2	51.3	91.2	87.5	124.9	109.8
Workers' remittances	2 391	. . .	. . .	. . .	. . .	. . .	. . .	. . .	. . .
Other current transfers	2 392	49.2	40.4	56.2	51.3	91.2	87.5	124.9	109.8
Debit	3 379	**–11.5**	**–4.1**	**–4.1**	**–3.5**	**–5.6**	**–6.2**	**–9.2**	**–8.3**
General government	3 380	–2.3	–2.9	–3.3	–2.5	–2.7	–3.4	–3.5	–4.0
Other sectors	3 390	–9.2	–1.2	–.8	–1.0	–2.9	–2.8	–5.7	–4.3
Workers' remittances	3 391	. . .	. . .	. . .	. . .	. . .	. . .	. . .	. . .
Other current transfers	3 392	–9.2	–1.2	–.8	–1.0	–2.9	–2.8	–5.7	–4.3
CAPITAL AND FINANCIAL ACCOUNT	4 996	**–46.1**	**206.0**	**380.6**	**–24.7**	**168.5**	**321.2**	**–15.5**	**48.6**
CAPITAL ACCOUNT	4 994	**. . .**	**. . .**	**. . .**	**. . .**	**. . .**	**. . .**	**. . .**	**. . .**
Total credit	2 994	. . .	. . .	. . .	. . .	. . .	. . .	. . .	. . .
Total debit	3 994	. . .	. . .	. . .	. . .	. . .	. . .	. . .	. . .
Capital transfers, credit	2 400	**. . .**	**. . .**	**. . .**	**. . .**	**. . .**	**. . .**	**. . .**	**. . .**
General government	2 401	. . .	. . .	. . .	. . .	. . .	. . .	. . .	. . .
Debt forgiveness	2 402	. . .	. . .	. . .	. . .	. . .	. . .	. . .	. . .
Other capital transfers	2 410	. . .	. . .	. . .	. . .	. . .	. . .	. . .	. . .
Other sectors	2 430	. . .	. . .	. . .	. . .	. . .	. . .	. . .	. . .
Migrants' transfers	2 431	. . .	. . .	. . .	. . .	. . .	. . .	. . .	. . .
Debt forgiveness	2 432	. . .	. . .	. . .	. . .	. . .	. . .	. . .	. . .
Other capital transfers	2 440	. . .	. . .	. . .	. . .	. . .	. . .	. . .	. . .
Capital transfers, debit	3 400	**. . .**	**. . .**	**. . .**	**. . .**	**. . .**	**. . .**	**. . .**	**. . .**
General government	3 401	. . .	. . .	. . .	. . .	. . .	. . .	. . .	. . .
Debt forgiveness	3 402	. . .	. . .	. . .	. . .	. . .	. . .	. . .	. . .
Other capital transfers	3 410	. . .	. . .	. . .	. . .	. . .	. . .	. . .	. . .
Other sectors	3 430	. . .	. . .	. . .	. . .	. . .	. . .	. . .	. . .
Migrants' transfers	3 431	. . .	. . .	. . .	. . .	. . .	. . .	. . .	. . .
Debt forgiveness	3 432	. . .	. . .	. . .	. . .	. . .	. . .	. . .	. . .
Other capital transfers	3 440	. . .	. . .	. . .	. . .	. . .	. . .	. . .	. . .
Nonproduced nonfinancial assets, credit	2 480	**. . .**	**. . .**	**. . .**	**. . .**	**. . .**	**. . .**	**. . .**	**. . .**
Nonproduced nonfinancial assets, debit	3 480	**. . .**	**. . .**	**. . .**	**. . .**	**. . .**	**. . .**	**. . .**	**. . .**

Table 2 (Continued). STANDARD PRESENTATION, 1988–95
(Millions of U.S. dollars)

	Code	1988	1989	1990	1991	1992	1993	1994	1995
FINANCIAL ACCOUNT	4 995	**–46.1**	**206.0**	**380.6**	**–24.7**	**168.5**	**321.2**	**–15.5**	**48.6**
A. DIRECT INVESTMENT	4 500	121.4	95.2	160.4	172.8	221.6	244.4	292.9	390.0
Direct investment abroad	4 505	**–.9**	**–6.0**	**–2.1**	**–5.6**	**–4.4**	**–2.3**	**–4.7**	**–5.5**
Equity capital	4 510	...	–3.3	1.2	–2.5	–.2	2.8	1.0	...
Claims on affiliated enterprises	4 515	...	...	...	...	...	...	...	...
Liabilities to affiliated enterprises	4 520	...	...	...	...	...	...	...	...
Reinvested earnings	4 525	–.9	–2.7	–3.3	–3.0	–4.0	–5.1	–5.7	–5.5
Other capital	4 530	...	...	...	–.1	–.2	...	...	...
Claims on affiliated enterprises	4 535	...	...	...	...	...	...	...	...
Liabilities to affiliated enterprises	4 540	...	...	...	...	...	...	...	...
Direct investment in Costa Rica	4 555	**122.3**	**101.2**	**162.5**	**178.4**	**226.0**	**246.7**	**297.6**	**395.5**
Equity capital	4 560	30.1	11.9	5.6	9.5	60.6	23.7	38.7	...
Claims on direct investors	4 565	...	...	...	...	...	...	...	...
Liabilities to direct investors	4 570	...	...	...	...	...	...	...	...
Reinvested earnings	4 575	14.8	37.5	42.2	43.0	66.0	89.5	49.6	77.0
Other capital	4 580	77.4	51.8	114.7	125.9	99.4	133.5	209.3	318.5
Claims on direct investors	4 585	...	...	...	...	...	...	...	...
Liabilities to direct investors	4 590	...	...	...	...	...	...	...	...
B. PORTFOLIO INVESTMENT	4 600	–6.0	–13.2	–28.2	–13.0	–16.9	–5.1	–1.2	–24.4
Assets	4 602	**...**	**...**	**...**	**...**	**...**	**...**	**...**	**...**
Equity securities	4 610	...	...	...	...	...	...	...	...
Monetary authorities	4 611	...	...	...	...	...	...	...	...
General government	4 612	...	...	...	...	...	...	...	...
Banks	4 613	...	...	...	...	...	...	...	...
Other sectors	4 614	...	...	...	...	...	...	...	...
Debt securities	4 619	...	...	...	...	...	...	...	...
Bonds and notes	4 620	...	...	...	...	...	...	...	...
Monetary authorities	4 621	...	...	...	...	...	...	...	...
General government	4 622	...	...	...	...	...	...	...	...
Banks	4 623	...	...	...	...	...	...	...	...
Other sectors	4 624	...	...	...	...	...	...	...	...
Money market instruments	4 630	...	...	...	...	...	...	...	...
Monetary authorities	4 631	...	...	...	...	...	...	...	...
General government	4 632	...	...	...	...	...	...	...	...
Banks	4 633	...	...	...	...	...	...	...	...
Other sectors	4 634	...	...	...	...	...	...	...	...
Financial derivatives	4 640	...	...	...	...	...	...	...	...
Monetary authorities	4 641	...	...	...	...	...	...	...	...
General government	4 642	...	...	...	...	...	...	...	...
Banks	4 643	...	...	...	...	...	...	...	...
Other sectors	4 644	...	...	...	...	...	...	...	...
Liabilities	4 652	**–6.0**	**–13.2**	**–28.2**	**–13.0**	**–16.9**	**–5.1**	**–1.2**	**–24.4**
Equity securities	4 660	...	...	...	...	...	...	...	...
Banks	4 663	...	...	...	...	...	...	...	...
Other sectors	4 664	...	...	...	...	...	...	...	...
Debt securities	4 669	–6.0	–13.2	–28.2	–13.0	–16.9	–5.1	–1.2	–24.4
Bonds and notes	4 670	–6.0	–13.2	–28.2	–13.0	–16.9	–5.1	–1.2	–24.4
Monetary authorities	4 671	–6.0	–13.2	–28.2	–13.0	–16.9	–5.1	–1.2	–24.4
General government	4 672	...	...	...	...	...	...	...	...
Banks	4 673	...	...	...	...	...	...	...	...
Other sectors	4 674	...	...	...	...	...	...	...	...
Money market instruments	4 680	...	...	...	...	...	...	...	...
Monetary authorities	4 681	...	...	...	...	...	...	...	...
General government	4 682	...	...	...	...	...	...	...	...
Banks	4 683	...	...	...	...	...	...	...	...
Other sectors	4 684	...	...	...	...	...	...	...	...
Financial derivatives	4 690	...	...	...	...	...	...	...	...
Monetary authorities	4 691	...	...	...	...	...	...	...	...
General government	4 692	...	...	...	...	...	...	...	...
Banks	4 693	...	...	...	...	...	...	...	...
Other sectors	4 694	...	...	...	...	...	...	...	...

Table 2 (Concluded). STANDARD PRESENTATION, 1988–95
(Millions of U.S. dollars)

	Code	1988	1989	1990	1991	1992	1993	1994	1995
C. OTHER INVESTMENT	4 700 . .	26.6	236.2	51.2	231.6	140.6	22.3	–372.7	–162.9
Assets	4 703 . .	**–77.3**	**–5.9**	**–124.7**	**75.6**	**84.8**	**54.5**	**–76.2**	**–10.0**
Trade credits	4 706 . .	–23.7	–13.2	–5.5	–26.4	–4.4	–26.5	13.6	–10.0
General government: long-term	4 708 . .	. . .	. . .	. . .	. . .	. . .	. . .	. . .	. . .
General government: short-term	4 709 . .	. . .	. . .	. . .	. . .	. . .	. . .	. . .	. . .
Other sectors: long-term	4 711 . .	. . .	. . .	. . .	. . .	. . .	. . .	. . .	. . .
Other sectors: short-term	4 712 . .	–23.7	–13.2	–5.5	–26.4	–4.4	–26.5	13.6	–10.0
Loans	4 714 . .	. . .	. . .	. . .	. . .	. . .	35.0	. . .	. . .
Monetary authorities: long-term	4 717 . .	. . .	. . .	. . .	. . .	. . .	. . .	. . .	. . .
Monetary authorities: short-term	4 718 . .	. . .	. . .	. . .	. . .	. . .	. . .	. . .	. . .
General government: long-term	4 720 . .	. . .	. . .	. . .	. . .	. . .	. . .	. . .	. . .
General government: short-term	4 721 . .	. . .	. . .	. . .	. . .	. . .	35.0	. . .	. . .
Banks: long-term	4 723 . .	. . .	. . .	. . .	. . .	. . .	. . .	. . .	. . .
Banks: short-term	4 724 . .	. . .	. . .	. . .	. . .	. . .	. . .	. . .	. . .
Other sectors: long-term	4 726 . .	. . .	. . .	. . .	. . .	. . .	. . .	. . .	. . .
Other sectors: short-term	4 727 . .	. . .	. . .	. . .	. . .	. . .	. . .	. . .	. . .
Currency and deposits	4 730 . .	–53.5	12.2	–114.5	100.8	97.7	46.1	–85.4	. . .
Monetary authorities	4 731 . .	. . .	. . .	. . .	. . .	. . .	. . .	. . .	. . .
General government	4 732 . .	. . .	. . .	. . .	. . .	. . .	. . .	. . .	. . .
Banks	4 733 . .	. . .	. . .	. . .	. . .	. . .	. . .	. . .	. . .
Other sectors	4 734 . .	–53.5	12.2	–114.5	100.8	97.7	46.1	–85.4	. . .
Other assets	4 736 . .	–.1	–4.9	–4.7	1.2	–8.5	–.1	–4.4	. . .
Monetary authorities: long-term	4 738 . .	. . .	. . .	. . .	. . .	. . .	. . .	. . .	. . .
Monetary authorities: short-term	4 739 . .	. . .	. . .	. . .	. . .	. . .	. . .	. . .	. . .
General government: long-term	4 741 . .	–.1	–4.9	–4.7	1.2	–8.5	–.1	–4.4	. . .
General government: short-term	4 742 . .	. . .	. . .	. . .	. . .	. . .	. . .	. . .	. . .
Banks: long-term	4 744 . .	. . .	. . .	. . .	. . .	. . .	. . .	. . .	. . .
Banks: short-term	4 745 . .	. . .	. . .	. . .	. . .	. . .	. . .	. . .	. . .
Other sectors: long-term	4 747 . .	. . .	. . .	. . .	. . .	. . .	. . .	. . .	. . .
Other sectors: short-term	4 748 . .	. . .	. . .	. . .	. . .	. . .	. . .	. . .	. . .
Liabilities	4 753 . .	**103.9**	**242.1**	**175.9**	**156.0**	**55.8**	**–32.2**	**–296.5**	**–152.9**
Trade credits	4 756 . .	32.6	35.7	65.8	–19.3	–7.3	45.2	–21.7	35.0
General government: long-term	4 758 . .	. . .	. . .	. . .	. . .	. . .	. . .	. . .	. . .
General government: short-term	4 759 . .	. . .	. . .	. . .	. . .	. . .	. . .	. . .	. . .
Other sectors: long-term	4 761 . .	. . .	. . .	. . .	. . .	. . .	. . .	. . .	. . .
Other sectors: short-term	4 762 . .	32.6	35.7	65.8	–19.3	–7.3	45.2	–21.7	35.0
Loans	4 764 . .	–274.9	–52.9	529.4	282.1	10.1	75.7	–282.4	–154.8
Use of Fund credit and loans from the Fund	4 766 . .	–54.1	–33.4	–25.6	67.7	1.7	. . .	–20.3	–44.4
Monetary authorities: other long-term	4 767 . .	–166.1	–50.1	472.5	281.1	34.4	–3.8	–176.2	–111.1
Monetary authorities: short-term	4 768 . .	–7.5	–2.1	93.6	–88.4	–16.5	55.0	–9.0	–3.0
General government: long-term	4 770 . .	–36.1	22.2	–25.6	–1.9	–22.7	20.5	–106.2	–32.4
General government: short-term	4 771 . .	. . .	. . .	. . .	. . .	. . .	. . .	. . .	. . .
Banks: long-term	4 773 . .	–9.8	–2.7	–2.0	–2.1	–1.1	–1.9	–2.9	–3.3
Banks: short-term	4 774 . .	. . .	. . .	. . .	. . .	. . .	. . .	. . .	. . .
Other sectors: long-term	4 776 . .	–1.3	13.2	16.5	25.7	14.3	5.9	32.2	39.4
Other sectors: short-term	4 777 . .	. . .	. . .	. . .	. . .	. . .	. . .	. . .	. . .
Currency and deposits	4 780 . .	6.9	1.2	3.3	5.8	41.5	2.6	–16.6	21.1
Monetary authorities	4 781 . .	10.6	–5.9	2.3	12.4	33.3	–27.0	–.7	. . .
General government	4 782 . .	. . .	. . .	. . .	. . .	. . .	. . .	. . .	. . .
Banks	4 783 . .	–3.7	7.1	1.0	–6.6	8.2	29.6	–15.9	21.1
Other sectors	4 784 . .	. . .	. . .	. . .	. . .	. . .	. . .	. . .	. . .
Other liabilities	4 786 . .	339.3	258.1	–422.6	–112.6	11.5	–155.7	24.2	–54.2
Monetary authorities: long-term	4 788 . .	. . .	. . .	. . .	. . .	. . .	. . .	. . .	. . .
Monetary authorities: short-term	4 789 . .	253.3	230.5	–491.9	–113.1	–8.9	–17.3	–27.2	–2.9
General government: long-term	4 791 . .	. . .	. . .	–2.5	. . .	. . .	. . .	. . .	. . .
General government: short-term	4 792 . .	72.8	28.7	73.2	–25.1	–5.6	–102.7	46.1	–53.0
Banks: long-term	4 794 . .	. . .	. . .	. . .	. . .	. . .	. . .	. . .	. . .
Banks: short-term	4 795 . .	14.7	–.2	.4	.4	.1	.2	.2	.3
Other sectors: long-term	4 797 . .	. . .	. . .	. . .	. . .	. . .	. . .	. . .	. . .
Other sectors: short-term	4 798 . .	–1.5	–.9	–1.8	25.2	25.9	–35.9	5.1	1.4
D. RESERVE ASSETS	4 800 . .	–188.0	–112.3	197.2	–416.1	–176.8	59.6	65.5	–154.1
Monetary gold	4 810 . .	. . .	. . .	. . .	. . .	. . .	. . .	. . .	. . .
Special drawing rights	4 820 . .	. . .	–.1	–1.5	1.4	. . .	. . .	. . .	.1
Reserve position in the Fund	4 830 . .	. . .	. . .	. . .	. . .	–12.1	. . .	. . .	. . .
Foreign exchange	4 840 . .	–185.5	–67.7	194.8	–411.0	–100.4	10.3	129.9	–176.4
Other claims	4 880 . .	–2.5	–44.5	3.9	–6.5	–64.3	49.2	–64.4	22.2
NET ERRORS AND OMISSIONS	4 998 . .	**224.6**	**208.9**	**43.4**	**99.9**	**201.9**	**299.0**	**249.1**	**94.4**

Table 1. ANALYTIC PRESENTATION, 1988–95
(Millions of U.S. dollars)

	Code	1988	1989	1990	1991	1992	1993	1994	1995
A. Current Account[1]	4 993 Y.	**–1,241.3**	**–967.3**	**–1,214.3**	**–1,074.1**	**–1,012.7**	**–891.7**	**54.8**	**–269.3**
Goods: exports f.o.b	2 100 . .	2,691.3	2,696.8	2,912.6	2,705.0	2,946.8	2,518.7	2,853.7	3,938.9
Goods: imports f.o.b	3 100 . .	–1,769.4	–1,777.1	–1,818.8	–1,781.6	–1,952.1	–1,770.4	–1,637.6	–2,468.4
Balance on Goods	4 100 . .	*921.9*	*919.7*	*1,093.8*	*923.4*	*994.7*	*748.3*	*1,216.1*	*1,470.5*
Services: credit	2 200 . .	555.7	485.9	590.2	614.3	649.2	675.9	487.6	551.3
Services: debit	3 200 . .	–1,342.3	–1,230.4	–1,626.0	–1,393.8	–1,477.2	–1,331.7	–880.4	–1,093.7
Balance on Goods and Services	4 991 . .	*135.3*	*175.2*	*58.0*	*143.9*	*166.8*	*92.5*	*823.3*	*928.2*
Income: credit	2 300 . .	71.8	55.8	58.0	60.3	18.9	97.8	35.7	37.1
Income: debit	3 300 . .	–992.8	–995.9	–1,149.2	–1,171.9	–1,099.8	–887.8	–793.6	–940.4
Balance on Goods, Services, and Income	4 992 . .	*–785.6*	*–764.9*	*–1,033.2*	*–967.7*	*–914.1*	*–697.5*	*65.4*	*24.8*
Current transfers: credit	2 379 Y.	208.8	316.0	370.2	413.7	404.6	270.9	320.1	184.9
Current transfers: debit	3 379 . .	–664.4	–518.5	–551.3	–520.0	–503.2	–465.1	–330.7	–479.0
B. Capital Account[1]	4 994 Y.	**. . .**	**. . .**	**. . .**	**. . .**	**. . .**	**. . .**	**. . .**	**. . .**
Capital account: credit	2 994 Y.	. . .	. . .	. . .	. . .	. . .	. . .	. . .	. . .
Capital account: debit	3 994 . .	. . .	. . .	. . .	. . .	. . .	. . .	. . .	. . .
Total, Groups A Plus B	4 010 . .	*–1,241.3*	*–967.3*	*–1,214.3*	*–1,074.1*	*–1,012.7*	*–891.7*	*54.8*	*–269.3*
C. Financial Account[1]	4 995 X.	**–137.7**	**–304.4**	**–177.8**	**–141.1**	**–417.5**	**–352.4**	**–468.3**	**40.7**
Direct investment abroad	4 505 . .	. . .	. . .	. . .	. . .	. . .	. . .	. . .	. . .
Direct investment in Cote d'Ivoire	4 555 Y.	51.7	18.5	48.1	16.3	–230.8	87.9	17.5	19.4
Portfolio investment assets	4 602 . .	–13.4	1.9	4.4	6.4	. . .	7.4	. . .	. . .
Equity securities	4 610 . .	–13.4	1.9	4.4	6.4	. . .	7.4	. . .	. . .
Debt securities	4 619 . .	. . .	. . .	. . .	. . .	. . .	. . .	. . .	. . .
Portfolio investment liabilities	4 652 Y.	–.7	–.6	. . .	. . .	. . .	. . .	. . .	. . .
Equity securities	4 660 Y.	. . .	. . .	. . .	. . .	. . .	. . .	. . .	. . .
Debt securities	4 669 Y.	–.7	–.6	. . .	. . .	. . .	. . .	. . .	. . .
Other investment assets	4 703 . .	50.4	21.6	–91.8	–25.2	169.6	51.9	–90.6	–38.5
Monetary authorities	4 703 .A	. . .	. . .	. . .	. . .	. . .	. . .	. . .	. . .
General government	4 703 .B	8.4	–25.1	–1.8	–3.2	. . .	. . .	. . .	. . .
Banks	4 703 .C	49.4	36.0	–66.1	2.8	63.8	72.7	–135.6	–92.6
Other sectors	4 703 .D	–7.4	10.7	–23.9	–24.8	105.8	–20.8	45.0	54.1
Other investment liabilities	4 753 X.	–225.6	–345.8	–138.5	–138.6	–356.3	–499.7	–395.2	59.7
Monetary authorities	4 753 XA	. . .	. . .	. . .	. . .	. . .	–40.6	–726.6	. . .
General government	4 753 YB	–353.5	–482.4	–75.7	–141.1	–207.4	–444.6	289.8	33.5
Banks	4 753 YC	65.5	–29.8	–124.5	–18.8	–134.9	7.8	–2.9	70.5
Other sectors	4 753 YD	62.4	166.5	61.7	21.3	–14.0	–22.2	44.5	–44.3
Total, Groups A Through C	4 020 . .	*–1,378.9*	*–1,271.7*	*–1,392.0*	*–1,215.1*	*–1,430.2*	*–1,244.2*	*–413.5*	*–228.6*
D. Net Errors and Omissions	4 998 . .	**–24.4**	**–38.8**	**–109.6**	**–102.2**	**46.6**	**11.1**	**94.2**	**–13.8**
Total, Groups A Through D	4 030 . .	*–1,403.3*	*–1,310.6*	*–1,501.7*	*–1,317.4*	*–1,383.6*	*–1,233.1*	*–319.3*	*–242.4*
E. Reserves and Related Items	4 040 . .	**1,403.3**	**1,310.6**	**1,501.7**	**1,317.4**	**1,383.6**	**1,233.1**	**319.3**	**242.4**
Reserve assets	4 800 . .	–.3	11.3	16.3	–.5	–84.4	4.4	–204.9	–314.3
Use of Fund credit and loans	4 766 . .	–63.0	–123.9	33.4	–58.5	–91.9	–49.0	94.3	94.9
Liabilities constituting foreign authorities' reserves	4 900 . .	–21.5	–.9	55.1	–10.3	–33.2	–3.5	6.7	. . .
Exceptional financing	4 920 . .	1,488.0	1,424.1	1,396.9	1,386.7	1,593.2	1,281.2	423.3	461.8
Conversion rates: CFA francs per U.S. dollar	0 101 . .	**297.85**	**319.01**	**272.26**	**282.11**	**264.69**	**283.16**	**555.20**	**499.15**

[1] Excludes components that have been classified in the categories of Group E.

Côte d'Ivoire
662

Table 2. STANDARD PRESENTATION, 1988–95
(Millions of U.S. dollars)

	Code	1988	1989	1990	1991	1992	1993	1994	1995
CURRENT ACCOUNT	4 993 . .	**–1,238.9**	**–966.4**	**–1,214.2**	**–1,074.1**	**–1,012.7**	**–891.7**	**54.8**	**–269.3**
A. GOODS	4 100 . .	921.9	919.7	1,093.8	923.4	994.7	748.3	1,216.1	1,470.5
Credit	2 100 . .	**2,691.3**	**2,696.8**	**2,912.6**	**2,705.0**	**2,946.8**	**2,518.7**	**2,853.7**	**3,938.9**
General merchandise: exports f.o.b.	2 110 . .	2,691.3	2,696.8	2,912.6	2,705.0	2,946.8	2,518.7	2,853.7	3,938.9
Goods for processing: exports f.o.b.	2 150 . .	...	...	...	...	...	...	...	...
Repairs on goods	2 160 . .	...	...	...	...	...	...	...	...
Goods procured in ports by carriers	2 170 . .	...	...	...	...	...	...	...	...
Nonmonetary gold	2 180 . .	...	...	...	...	...	...	...	...
Debit	3 100 . .	**–1,769.4**	**–1,777.1**	**–1,818.8**	**–1,781.6**	**–1,952.1**	**–1,770.4**	**–1,637.6**	**–2,468.4**
General merchandise: imports f.o.b.	3 110 . .	–1,769.4	–1,777.1	–1,818.8	–1,781.6	–1,952.1	–1,770.4	–1,637.6	–2,468.4
Goods for processing: imports f.o.b.	3 150 . .	...	...	...	...	...	...	...	...
Repairs on goods	3 160 . .	...	...	...	...	...	...	...	...
Goods procured in ports by carriers	3 170 . .	...	...	...	...	...	...	...	...
Nonmonetary gold	3 180 . .	...	...	...	...	...	...	...	...
B. SERVICES	4 200 . .	–786.6	–744.5	–1,035.8	–779.5	–828.0	–655.8	–392.8	–542.3
Total credit	2 200 . .	*555.7*	*485.9*	*590.2*	*614.3*	*649.2*	*675.9*	*487.6*	*551.3*
Total debit	3 200 . .	*–1,342.3*	*–1,230.4*	*–1,626.0*	*–1,393.8*	*–1,477.2*	*–1,331.7*	*–880.4*	*–1,093.7*
Transportation services, credit	2 205 . .	**269.0**	**227.0**	**265.2**	**271.2**	**278.1**	**288.2**	**192.0**	**188.5**
Passenger	2 205 BA	*2.0*	*2.2*	*3.3*	*3.2*	*3.4*	*12.4*	*5.4*	*6.0*
Freight	2 205 BB	*138.4*	*109.7*	*124.1*	*122.6*	*120.5*	*124.0*	*91.7*	*60.3*
Other	2 205 BC	*128.6*	*115.0*	*137.7*	*145.3*	*154.1*	*151.9*	*94.9*	*122.2*
Sea transport, passenger	2 207 . .	...	...	...	...	...	...	...	...
Sea transport, freight	2 208 . .	108.5	79.6	96.2	100.7	120.5	98.9	77.8	36.3
Sea transport, other	2 209 . .	128.6	115.0	137.7	145.3	154.1	131.4	85.2	109.0
Air transport, passenger	2 211 . .	2.0	2.2	3.3	3.2	3.4	8.1	5.4	6.0
Air transport, freight	2 212 . .	...	...	...	...	...	...	...	...
Air transport, other	2 213 . .	...	...	...	...	...	20.5	9.7	13.2
Other transport, passenger	2 215 . .	...	...	...	...	...	4.2	...	...
Other transport, freight	2 216 . .	29.9	30.2	27.9	22.0	...	25.1	13.9	24.0
Other transport, other	2 217 . .	...	...	...	...	...	...	...	...
Transportation services, debit	3 205 . .	**–453.9**	**–395.0**	**–487.8**	**–436.4**	**–477.7**	**–537.5**	**–372.8**	**–477.2**
Passenger	3 205 BA	*–107.1*	*–96.2*	*–135.9*	*–95.0*	*–102.0*	*–135.6*	*–69.9*	*–78.9*
Freight	3 205 BB	*–302.8*	*–262.1*	*–296.0*	*–285.4*	*–294.8*	*–291.0*	*–233.2*	*–351.8*
Other	3 205 BC	*–44.0*	*–36.7*	*–55.8*	*–56.0*	*–80.8*	*–110.9*	*–69.7*	*–46.5*
Sea transport, passenger	3 207 . .	...	...	...	...	...	...	...	...
Sea transport, freight	3 208 . .	–279.2	–239.5	–269.6	–261.6	–294.8	–277.2	–198.1	–326.6
Sea transport, other	3 209 . .	–44.0	–36.7	–55.8	–56.0	–80.8	–97.8	–69.7	–46.5
Air transport, passenger	3 211 . .	–107.1	–96.2	–135.9	–95.0	–102.0	–124.0	–69.9	–78.9
Air transport, freight	3 212 . .	–11.2	–11.8	–11.4	–11.3	...	–13.8	–35.1	–25.2
Air transport, other	3 213 . .	...	...	...	...	...	–13.1	...	...
Other transport, passenger	3 215 . .	...	...	...	...	...	–11.7	...	...
Other transport, freight	3 216 . .	–12.4	–10.7	–15.1	–12.4	...	...	...	...
Other transport, other	3 217 . .	...	...	...	...	...	...	...	...
Travel, credit	2 236 . .	**60.1**	**64.6**	**51.4**	**62.4**	**66.1**	**63.2**	**51.7**	**71.9**
Business travel	2 237 . .	...	...	...	...	...	43.4	...	...
Personal travel	2 240 . .	...	...	...	...	...	19.8	...	...
Travel, debit	3 236 . .	**–235.0**	**–168.3**	**–168.6**	**–162.7**	**–168.1**	**–168.8**	**–117.6**	**–159.1**
Business travel	3 237 . .	–189.4	–127.6	–124.1	–122.6	...	–15.2	...	...
Personal travel	3 240 . .	–45.7	–40.8	–44.4	–40.1	–168.1	–153.6	–117.6	–159.1
Other services, credit	2 200 BA	**226.6**	**194.3**	**273.6**	**280.7**	**305.0**	**324.5**	**243.9**	**290.9**
Communications	2 245 . .	...	...	...	...	...	1.4	...	...
Construction	2 249 . .	...	...	...	...	...	...	...	...
Insurance	2 253 . .	46.3	25.0	35.3	33.7	13.4	19.1	17.5	21.0
Financial	2 260 . .	...	...	...	...	...	2.8	...	...
Computer and information	2 262 . .	...	...	...	...	...	...	...	...
Royalties and licence fees	2 266 . .	–.3	.3	...	...	...	.4	...	...
Other business services	2 268 . .	61.1	58.6	73.1	53.2	121.7	107.7	107.5	130.0
Personal, cultural, and recreational	2 287 . .	...	...	...	...	...	...	...	...
Government, n.i.e.	2 291 . .	119.5	110.3	165.3	193.9	170.0	193.2	118.9	139.8
Other services, debit	3 200 BA	**–653.4**	**–667.0**	**–969.6**	**–794.7**	**–831.4**	**–625.4**	**–389.9**	**–457.4**
Communications	3 245 . .	...	...	...	...	...	–4.2	...	...
Construction	3 249 . .	...	...	...	...	...	...	...	...
Insurance	3 253 . .	–71.9	–58.3	–72.0	–71.2	–32.8	–38.5	–25.2	–28.0
Financial	3 260 . .	...	...	...	...	...	–305.8	...	...
Computer and information	3 262 . .	...	...	...	...	...	...	...	...
Royalties and licence fees	3 266 . .	–1.7	–1.6	...	...	...	–10.6	...	...
Other business services	3 268 . .	–383.1	–490.6	–789.7	–627.4	–670.6	–192.1	–256.1	–303.7
Personal, cultural, and recreational	3 287 . .	...	...	...	...	...	...	...	...
Government, n.i.e.	3 291 . .	–196.7	–116.6	–108.0	–96.1	–128.1	–74.2	–108.6	–125.6

Table 2 (Continued). STANDARD PRESENTATION, 1988–95
(Millions of U.S. dollars)

	Code	1988	1989	1990	1991	1992	1993	1994	1995
C. INCOME	4 300	-920.9	-940.1	-1,091.2	-1,111.6	-1,080.9	-790.0	-757.9	-903.3
Total credit	2 300	*71.8*	*55.8*	*58.0*	*60.3*	*18.9*	*97.8*	*35.7*	*37.1*
Total debit	3 300	*-992.8*	*-995.9*	*-1,149.2*	*-1,171.9*	*-1,099.8*	*-887.8*	*-793.6*	*-940.4*
Compensation of employees, credit	2 310	**42.6**	**35.4**	**44.4**	**41.5**	...	**57.6**	...	...
Compensation of employees, debit	3 310	**-14.4**	**-13.8**	**-13.2**	**-17.4**	...	**-10.2**	...	...
Investment income, credit	2 320	**29.2**	**20.4**	**13.6**	**18.8**	**18.9**	**40.3**	**35.7**	**37.1**
Direct investment income	2 330	...	...	...	...	...	...	...	...
Dividends and distributed branch profits	2 332	...	...	...	...	...	...	...	...
Reinvested earnings and undistributed branch profits	2 333	...	...	...	...	...	...	...	...
Income on debt (interest)	2 334	...	...	...	...	...	...	...	...
Portfolio investment income	2 339	...	...	...	...	...	35.3	35.7	37.1
Income on equity	2 340	...	...	...	...	...	...	...	...
Income on bonds and notes	2 350	...	...	...	...	...	...	...	...
Income on money market instruments and financial derivatives	2 360	...	...	...	...	...	35.3	35.7	37.1
Other investment income	2 370	29.2	20.4	13.6	18.8	18.9	4.9	...	...
Investment income, debit	3 320	**-978.4**	**-982.1**	**-1,136.0**	**-1,154.5**	**-1,099.8**	**-877.6**	**-793.6**	**-940.4**
Direct investment income	3 330	-141.0	-54.5	-74.9	-39.7	-45.7	-52.6	-36.9	-41.1
Dividends and distributed branch profits	3 332	-95.0	-36.7	-43.7	-22.7	-24.2	-35.0	-19.5	-21.6
Reinvested earnings and undistributed branch profits	3 333	-46.0	-17.9	-31.2	-17.0	-21.5	-17.7	-17.5	-19.4
Income on debt (interest)	3 334	...	...	...	...	...	...	...	...
Portfolio investment income	3 339	...	...	...	...	...	-2.5	...	...
Income on equity	3 340	...	...	...	...	...	-1.4	...	...
Income on bonds and notes	3 350	...	...	...	...	...	...	...	...
Income on money market instruments and financial derivatives	3 360	...	...	...	...	...	-1.1	...	...
Other investment income	3 370	-837.3	-927.6	-1,061.1	-1,114.8	-1,054.1	-822.5	-756.7	-899.3
D. CURRENT TRANSFERS	4 379	-453.3	-201.6	-181.0	-106.3	-98.6	-194.2	-10.6	-294.1
Credit	2 379	**211.2**	**316.9**	**370.3**	**413.7**	**404.6**	**270.9**	**320.1**	**184.9**
General government	2 380	199.1	307.2	358.2	378.6	370.6	226.4	288.2	148.5
Other sectors	2 390	12.1	9.7	12.1	35.1	34.0	44.5	31.9	36.5
Workers' remittances	2 391	...	...	...	...	...	...	...	...
Other current transfers	2 392	12.1	9.7	12.1	35.1	34.0	44.5	31.9	36.5
Debit	3 379	**-664.4**	**-518.5**	**-551.3**	**-520.0**	**-503.2**	**-465.1**	**-330.7**	**-479.0**
General government	3 380	-145.7	-115.4	-93.3	-91.5	-46.5	-39.6	-18.2	-30.1
Other sectors	3 390	-518.7	-403.1	-458.0	-428.6	-456.8	-425.6	-312.5	-449.0
Workers' remittances	3 391	-514.4	-398.7	-458.0	-428.6	-456.8	-420.3	-312.5	-449.0
Other current transfers	3 392	-4.4	-4.4	...	...	...	-5.3	...	...
CAPITAL AND FINANCIAL ACCOUNT	4 996	**1,263.3**	**1,005.3**	**1,323.8**	**1,176.3**	**966.2**	**880.6**	**-149.0**	**283.1**
CAPITAL ACCOUNT	4 994	...	...	...	...	...	...	...	...
Total credit	2 994	...	...	...	...	...	...	...	...
Total debit	3 994	...	...	...	...	...	...	...	...
Capital transfers, credit	2 400	...	...	...	...	...	...	...	...
General government	2 401	...	...	...	...	...	...	...	...
Debt forgiveness	2 402	...	...	...	...	...	...	...	...
Other capital transfers	2 410	...	...	...	...	...	...	...	...
Other sectors	2 430	...	...	...	...	...	...	...	...
Migrants' transfers	2 431	...	...	...	...	...	...	...	...
Debt forgiveness	2 432	...	...	...	...	...	...	...	...
Other capital transfers	2 440	...	...	...	...	...	...	...	...
Capital transfers, debit	3 400	...	...	...	...	...	...	...	...
General government	3 401	...	...	...	...	...	...	...	...
Debt forgiveness	3 402	...	...	...	...	...	...	...	...
Other capital transfers	3 410	...	...	...	...	...	...	...	...
Other sectors	3 430	...	...	...	...	...	...	...	...
Migrants' transfers	3 431	...	...	...	...	...	...	...	...
Debt forgiveness	3 432	...	...	...	...	...	...	...	...
Other capital transfers	3 440	...	...	...	...	...	...	...	...
Nonproduced nonfinancial assets, credit	2 480	...	...	...	...	...	...	...	...
Nonproduced nonfinancial assets, debit	3 480	...	...	...	...	...	...	...	...

Table 2 (Continued). STANDARD PRESENTATION, 1988–95

(Millions of U.S. dollars)

	Code	1988	1989	1990	1991	1992	1993	1994	1995
FINANCIAL ACCOUNT	4 995	**1,263.3**	**1,005.3**	**1,323.8**	**1,176.3**	**966.2**	**880.6**	**–149.0**	**283.1**
A. DIRECT INVESTMENT	4 500	51.7	18.5	48.1	16.3	–230.8	87.9	17.5	19.4
Direct investment abroad	4 505	**. . .**	**. . .**	**. . .**	**. . .**	**. . .**	**. . .**	**. . .**	**. . .**
Equity capital	4 510	. . .	. . .	. . .	. . .	. . .	. . .	. . .	. . .
Claims on affiliated enterprises	4 515	. . .	. . .	. . .	. . .	. . .	. . .	. . .	. . .
Liabilities to affiliated enterprises	4 520	. . .	. . .	. . .	. . .	. . .	. . .	. . .	. . .
Reinvested earnings	4 525	. . .	. . .	. . .	. . .	. . .	. . .	. . .	. . .
Other capital	4 530	. . .	. . .	. . .	. . .	. . .	. . .	. . .	. . .
Claims on affiliated enterprises	4 535	. . .	. . .	. . .	. . .	. . .	. . .	. . .	. . .
Liabilities to affiliated enterprises	4 540	. . .	. . .	. . .	. . .	. . .	. . .	. . .	. . .
Direct investment in Cote d'Ivoire	4 555	**51.7**	**18.5**	**48.1**	**16.3**	**–230.8**	**87.9**	**17.5**	**19.4**
Equity capital	4 560	.7	3.4	. . .	. . .	. . .	29.3	. . .	. . .
Claims on direct investors	4 565	. . .	. . .	. . .	. . .	. . .	3.5	. . .	. . .
Liabilities to direct investors	4 570	. . .	. . .	. . .	. . .	. . .	25.8	. . .	. . .
Reinvested earnings	4 575	46.0	17.9	31.2	17.0	21.5	17.7	17.5	19.4
Other capital	4 580	5.0	–2.8	16.9	–.7	–252.4	41.0	. . .	. . .
Claims on direct investors	4 585	. . .	. . .	. . .	. . .	. . .	–14.8	. . .	. . .
Liabilities to direct investors	4 590	. . .	. . .	. . .	. . .	. . .	55.8	. . .	. . .
B. PORTFOLIO INVESTMENT	4 600	–14.1	1.3	4.4	6.4	. . .	7.4	. . .	. . .
Assets	4 602	**–13.4**	**1.9**	**4.4**	**6.4**	**. . .**	**7.4**	**. . .**	**. . .**
Equity securities	4 610	–13.4	1.9	4.4	6.4	. . .	7.4	. . .	. . .
Monetary authorities	4 611	. . .	. . .	. . .	. . .	. . .	. . .	. . .	. . .
General government	4 612	. . .	. . .	. . .	. . .	. . .	7.4	. . .	. . .
Banks	4 613	. . .	. . .	. . .	. . .	. . .	. . .	. . .	. . .
Other sectors	4 614	. . .	. . .	. . .	. . .	. . .	. . .	. . .	. . .
Debt securities	4 619	. . .	. . .	. . .	. . .	. . .	. . .	. . .	. . .
Bonds and notes	4 620	. . .	. . .	. . .	. . .	. . .	. . .	. . .	. . .
Monetary authorities	4 621	. . .	. . .	. . .	. . .	. . .	. . .	. . .	. . .
General government	4 622	. . .	. . .	. . .	. . .	. . .	. . .	. . .	. . .
Banks	4 623	. . .	. . .	. . .	. . .	. . .	. . .	. . .	. . .
Other sectors	4 624	. . .	. . .	. . .	. . .	. . .	. . .	. . .	. . .
Money market instruments	4 630	. . .	. . .	. . .	. . .	. . .	. . .	. . .	. . .
Monetary authorities	4 631	. . .	. . .	. . .	. . .	. . .	. . .	. . .	. . .
General government	4 632	. . .	. . .	. . .	. . .	. . .	. . .	. . .	. . .
Banks	4 633	. . .	. . .	. . .	. . .	. . .	. . .	. . .	. . .
Other sectors	4 634	. . .	. . .	. . .	. . .	. . .	. . .	. . .	. . .
Financial derivatives	4 640	. . .	. . .	. . .	. . .	. . .	. . .	. . .	. . .
Monetary authorities	4 641	. . .	. . .	. . .	. . .	. . .	. . .	. . .	. . .
General government	4 642	. . .	. . .	. . .	. . .	. . .	. . .	. . .	. . .
Banks	4 643	. . .	. . .	. . .	. . .	. . .	. . .	. . .	. . .
Other sectors	4 644	. . .	. . .	. . .	. . .	. . .	. . .	. . .	. . .
Liabilities	4 652	**–.7**	**–.6**	**. . .**	**. . .**	**. . .**	**. . .**	**. . .**	**. . .**
Equity securities	4 660	. . .	. . .	. . .	. . .	. . .	. . .	. . .	. . .
Banks	4 663	. . .	. . .	. . .	. . .	. . .	. . .	. . .	. . .
Other sectors	4 664	. . .	. . .	. . .	. . .	. . .	. . .	. . .	. . .
Debt securities	4 669	–.7	–.6	. . .	. . .	. . .	. . .	. . .	. . .
Bonds and notes	4 670	–.7	–.6	. . .	. . .	. . .	. . .	. . .	. . .
Monetary authorities	4 671	. . .	. . .	. . .	. . .	. . .	. . .	. . .	. . .
General government	4 672	–.7	–.6	. . .	. . .	. . .	. . .	. . .	. . .
Banks	4 673	. . .	. . .	. . .	. . .	. . .	. . .	. . .	. . .
Other sectors	4 674	. . .	. . .	. . .	. . .	. . .	. . .	. . .	. . .
Money market instruments	4 680	. . .	. . .	. . .	. . .	. . .	. . .	. . .	. . .
Monetary authorities	4 681	. . .	. . .	. . .	. . .	. . .	. . .	. . .	. . .
General government	4 682	. . .	. . .	. . .	. . .	. . .	. . .	. . .	. . .
Banks	4 683	. . .	. . .	. . .	. . .	. . .	. . .	. . .	. . .
Other sectors	4 684	. . .	. . .	. . .	. . .	. . .	. . .	. . .	. . .
Financial derivatives	4 690	. . .	. . .	. . .	. . .	. . .	. . .	. . .	. . .
Monetary authorities	4 691	. . .	. . .	. . .	. . .	. . .	. . .	. . .	. . .
General government	4 692	. . .	. . .	. . .	. . .	. . .	. . .	. . .	. . .
Banks	4 693	. . .	. . .	. . .	. . .	. . .	. . .	. . .	. . .
Other sectors	4 694	. . .	. . .	. . .	. . .	. . .	. . .	. . .	. . .

Table 2 (Concluded). STANDARD PRESENTATION, 1988–95
(Millions of U.S. dollars)

	Code		1988	1989	1990	1991	1992	1993	1994	1995
C. OTHER INVESTMENT	4 700	. .	1,225.9	974.2	1,255.0	1,154.1	1,281.4	780.9	38.5	577.9
Assets	4 703	. .	**50.4**	**21.6**	**–91.8**	**–25.2**	**169.6**	**51.9**	**–90.6**	**–38.5**
Trade credits	4 706	. .	1.0	. . .	. . .	. . .	. . .	12.7	. . .	. . .
General government: long-term	4 708	. .	. . .	. . .	. . .	. . .	. . .	. . .	. . .	. . .
General government: short-term	4 709	. .	. . .	. . .	. . .	. . .	. . .	. . .	. . .	. . .
Other sectors: long-term	4 711	. .	1.0	. . .	. . .	. . .	. . .	31.8	. . .	. . .
Other sectors: short-term	4 712	. .	. . .	. . .	. . .	. . .	. . .	–19.1	. . .	. . .
Loans	4 714	. .	2.7	3.4	–8.8	–23.4	105.8	133.8	67.5	54.1
Monetary authorities: long-term	4 717	. .	. . .	. . .	. . .	. . .	. . .	. . .	. . .	. . .
Monetary authorities: short-term	4 718	. .	. . .	. . .	. . .	. . .	. . .	. . .	. . .	. . .
General government: long-term	4 720	. .	. . .	. . .	. . .	. . .	. . .	. . .	. . .	. . .
General government: short-term	4 721	. .	. . .	. . .	. . .	. . .	. . .	. . .	. . .	. . .
Banks: long-term	4 723	. .	. . .	. . .	. . .	. . .	. . .	. . .	. . .	. . .
Banks: short-term	4 724	. .	. . .	. . .	. . .	. . .	. . .	101.4	22.5	. . .
Other sectors: long-term	4 726	. .	. . .	.6	–3.7	–23.7	. . .	49.8	. . .	. . .
Other sectors: short-term	4 727	. .	2.7	2.8	–5.1	.4	105.8	–17.3	45.0	54.1
Currency and deposits	4 730	. .	43.0	16.3	–83.7	.7	63.8	–80.2	–71.7	. . .
Monetary authorities	4 731	. .	. . .	. . .	. . .	. . .	. . .	. . .	. . .	. . .
General government	4 732	. .	9.1	–24.5	–1.1	–2.5	. . .	. . .	. . .	. . .
Banks	4 733	. .	49.4	36.0	–66.1	2.8	63.8	–14.1	–71.7	. . .
Other sectors	4 734	. .	–15.4	4.7	–16.5	.4	. . .	–66.0	. . .	. . .
Other assets	4 736	. .	3.7	1.9	.7	–2.5	. . .	–14.5	–86.5	–92.6
Monetary authorities: long-term	4 738	. .	. . .	. . .	. . .	. . .	. . .	. . .	. . .	. . .
Monetary authorities: short-term	4 739	. .	. . .	. . .	. . .	. . .	. . .	. . .	. . .	. . .
General government: long-term	4 741	. .	–.7	–.6	–.7	–.7	. . .		. . .	. . .
General government: short-term	4 742	. .	. . .	. . .	. . .	. . .	. . .	. . .	. . .	. . .
Banks: long-term	4 744	. .	. . .	. . .	. . .	. . .	. . .	. . .	. . .	. . .
Banks: short-term	4 745	. .	. . .	. . .	. . .	. . .	. . .	–14.5	–86.5	–92.6
Other sectors: long-term	4 747	. .	4.4	2.5	1.5	–1.8	. . .	. . .	. . .	. . .
Other sectors: short-term	4 748	. .	. . .	. . .	. . .	. . .	. . .	. . .	. . .	. . .
Liabilities	4 753	. .	**1,175.6**	**952.6**	**1,346.8**	**1,179.3**	**1,111.8**	**729.0**	**129.1**	**616.4**
Trade credits	4 756	. .	. . .	. . .	. . .	. . .	. . .	–72.4	. . .	. . .
General government: long-term	4 758	. .	. . .	. . .	. . .	. . .	. . .	. . .	. . .	. . .
General government: short-term	4 759	. .	. . .	. . .	. . .	. . .	. . .	. . .	. . .	. . .
Other sectors: long-term	4 761	. .	. . .	. . .	. . .	. . .	. . .	–111.2	. . .	. . .
Other sectors: short-term	4 762	. .	. . .	. . .	. . .	. . .	. . .	38.8	. . .	. . .
Loans	4 764	. .	209.6	187.1	393.3	352.3	51.7	–443.5	1,487.0	545.9
Use of Fund credit and loans from the Fund	4 766	. .	–63.0	–123.9	33.4	–58.5	–91.9	–49.0	94.3	94.9
Monetary authorities: other long-term	4 767	. .	. . .	. . .	. . .	. . .	. . .	. . .	. . .	. . .
Monetary authorities: short-term	4 768	. .	. . .	. . .	. . .	. . .	. . .	. . .	. . .	. . .
General government: long-term	4 770	. .	328.0	109.4	364.0	395.9	157.5	–444.6	1,348.2	495.2
General government: short-term	4 771	. .	. . .	. . .	. . .	. . .	. . .	. . .	. . .	. . .
Banks: long-term	4 773	. .	–87.6	27.0	–31.6	. . .	. . .	. . .	. . .	. . .
Banks: short-term	4 774	. .	. . .	. . .	. . .	. . .	. . .	. . .	. . .	. . .
Other sectors: long-term	4 776	. .	52.7	150.5	–24.2	29.1	20.0	50.5	339.3	494.2
Other sectors: short-term	4 777	. .	–20.5	24.1	51.8	–14.2	–34.0	–.4	–294.8	–538.5
Currency and deposits	4 780	. .	131.6	–57.7	–37.8	–29.1	–168.1	–36.4	–722.8	70.5
Monetary authorities	4 781	. .	–21.5	–.9	55.1	–10.3	–33.2	–44.1	–719.9	. . .
General government	4 782	. .	. . .	. . .	. . .	. . .	. . .	. . .	. . .	. . .
Banks	4 783	. .	153.1	–56.7	–92.9	–18.8	–134.9	7.8	–2.9	70.5
Other sectors	4 784	. .	. . .	. . .	. . .	. . .	. . .	. . .	. . .	. . .
Other liabilities	4 786	. .	834.3	823.2	991.3	856.1	1,228.2	1,281.2	–635.1	. . .
Monetary authorities: long-term	4 788	. .	. . .	. . .	. . .	. . .	. . .	. . .	. . .	. . .
Monetary authorities: short-term	4 789	. .	342.5	120.4	115.7	8.9	327.2	. . .	. . .	. . .
General government: long-term	4 791	. .	. . .	. . .	. . .	. . .	. . .	. . .	. . .	. . .
General government: short-term	4 792	. .	461.6	711.0	841.5	840.8	901.0	1,281.2	–635.1	. . .
Banks: long-term	4 794	. .	. . .	. . .	. . .	. . .	. . .	. . .	. . .	. . .
Banks: short-term	4 795	. .	. . .	. . .	. . .	. . .	. . .	. . .	. . .	. . .
Other sectors: long-term	4 797	. .	–1.0	13.5	30.9	2.8	. . .	. . .		. . .
Other sectors: short-term	4 798	. .	31.2	–21.6	3.3	3.5	. . .	. . .	. . .	. . .
D. RESERVE ASSETS	4 800	. .	–.3	11.3	16.3	–.5	–84.4	4.4	–204.9	–314.3
Monetary gold	4 810	. .	. . .	. . .	. . .	. . .	. . .	. . .	. . .	. . .
Special drawing rights	4 820	. .	.7	–4.7	4.6	–.5	1.7	–.8	1.0	–1.8
Reserve position in the Fund	4 830	. .	. . .	. . .	. . .	. . .	. . .	–.1	. . .	. . .
Foreign exchange	4 840	. .	–2.0	.3	7.7	–7.8	4.2	5.3	–195.6	–312.5
Other claims	4 880	. .	1.0	15.7	4.0	7.8	–90.3	. . .	–10.3	. . .
NET ERRORS AND OMISSIONS	4 998	. .	**–24.4**	**–38.8**	**–109.6**	**–102.2**	**46.6**	**11.1**	**94.2**	**–13.8**

Part 3 of the *Yearbook* contains descriptions of the methodologies, compilation practices, and sources used to compile these data.

Table 1. ANALYTIC PRESENTATION, 1988–95
(Millions of U.S. dollars)

	Code			1988	1989	1990	1991	1992	1993	1994	1995
A. Current Account[1]	4	993	Y.	...	...	...	...	...	**103.99**	**103.44**	**–1,712.16**
Goods: exports f.o.b.	2	100	..	...	...	...	...	...	3,903.82	4,260.37	4,632.66
Goods: imports f.o.b.	3	100	..	...	...	...	...	...	–4,199.73	–4,706.35	–6,758.90
Balance on Goods	4	100	..	...	...	...	...	...	*–295.91*	*–445.98*	*–2,126.24*
Services: credit	2	200	..	...	...	...	...	...	1,806.72	2,292.51	2,569.14
Services: debit	3	200	..	...	...	...	...	...	–1,641.52	–2,077.92	–2,707.52
Balance on Goods and Services	4	991	..	...	...	...	...	...	*–130.71*	*–231.39*	*–2,264.62*
Income: credit	2	300	..	...	...	...	...	...	111.64	101.02	173.41
Income: debit	3	300	..	...	...	...	...	...	–252.91	–225.48	–266.64
Balance on Goods, Services, and Income	4	992	..	...	...	...	...	...	*–271.98*	*–355.85*	*–2,357.85*
Current transfers: credit	2	379	Y.	...	...	...	...	...	554.87	602.08	814.59
Current transfers: debit	3	379	..	...	...	...	...	...	–178.90	–142.79	–168.90
B. Capital Account[1]	4	994	Y.	...	...	...	...	...	...	...	...
Capital account: credit	2	994	Y.	...	...	...	...	...	...	...	...
Capital account: debit	3	994	..	...	...	...	...	...	...	...	...
Total, Groups A Plus B	4	010	..	...	...	...	...	...	*103.99*	*103.44*	*–1,712.16*
C. Financial Account[1]	4	995	X.	...	...	...	...	...	**42.45**	**219.71**	**492.56**
Direct investment abroad	4	505	..	...	...	...	...	...	...	...	...
Direct investment in Croatia	4	555	Y.	...	...	...	...	...	74.33	97.57	80.51
Portfolio investment assets	4	602	..	...	...	...	...	...	...	...	...
Equity securities	4	610	..	...	...	...	...	...	...	...	...
Debt securities	4	619	..	...	...	...	...	...	...	...	...
Portfolio investment liabilities	4	652	Y.	...	...	...	...	...	...	...	...
Equity securities	4	660	Y.	...	...	...	...	...	...	...	...
Debt securities	4	669	Y.	...	...	...	...	...	...	...	...
Other investment assets	4	703	..	...	...	...	...	...	44.18	241.82	49.83
Monetary authorities	4	703	.A	...	...	...	...	...	...	...	...
General government	4	703	.B	...	...	...	...	...	...	...	...
Banks	4	703	.C	...	...	...	...	...	–210.60	–189.50	–467.10
Other sectors	4	703	.D	...	...	...	...	...	254.78	431.32	516.93
Other investment liabilities	4	753	X.	...	...	...	...	...	–76.06	–119.68	362.22
Monetary authorities	4	753	XA	...	...	...	...	...	...	...	...
General government	4	753	YB	...	...	...	...	...	–7.80	–1.80	93.50
Banks	4	753	YC	...	...	...	...	...	–97.39	–34.33	193.11
Other sectors	4	753	YD	...	...	...	...	...	29.13	–83.55	75.61
Total, Groups A Through C	4	020	..	...	...	...	...	...	*146.44*	*323.15*	*–1,219.60*
D. Net Errors and Omissions	4	998	..	...	...	...	...	...	**29.42**	**102.64**	**1,307.19**
Total, Groups A Through D	4	030	..	...	...	...	...	...	*175.86*	*425.79*	*87.59*
E. Reserves and Related Items	4	040	..	...	...	...	...	...	**–175.86**	**–425.79**	**–87.59**
Reserve assets	4	800	..	...	...	...	...	...	–447.00	–791.15	–496.18
Use of Fund credit and loans	4	766	..	...	...	...	...	...	19.83	106.96	97.09
Liabilities constituting foreign authorities' reserves	4	900	..	...	...	...	...	...	...	...	...
Exceptional financing	4	920	..	...	...	...	...	...	251.30	258.40	311.50
Conversion rates: kuna per U.S. dollar	0	101	..	...	...	...	...	...	**3.5774**	**5.9961**	**5.2300**

[1] Excludes components that have been classified in the categories of Group E.

Table 2. STANDARD PRESENTATION, 1988–95
(Millions of U.S. dollars)

	Code	1988	1989	1990	1991	1992	1993	1994	1995
CURRENT ACCOUNT	4 993 . .	...	...	...	...	...	**103.99**	**103.44**	**–1,712.16**
A. GOODS	4 100 . .	...	...	...	...	...	–295.91	–445.98	–2,126.24
Credit	2 100 . .	...	...	...	...	...	**3,903.82**	**4,260.37**	**4,632.66**
General merchandise: exports f.o.b.	2 110 . .	...	...	...	...	...	3,903.82	4,260.37	4,632.66
Goods for processing: exports f.o.b.	2 150 . .	...	...	...	...	...	...	...	...
Repairs on goods	2 160 . .	...	...	...	...	...	...	...	...
Goods procured in ports by carriers	2 170 . .	...	...	...	...	...	...	...	...
Nonmonetary gold	2 180 . .	...	...	...	...	...	...	...	...
Debit	3 100 . .	...	...	...	...	...	**–4,199.73**	**–4,706.35**	**–6,758.90**
General merchandise: imports f.o.b.	3 110 . .	...	...	...	...	...	–4,199.73	–4,706.35	–6,758.90
Goods for processing: imports f.o.b.	3 150 . .	...	...	...	...	...	...	...	...
Repairs on goods	3 160 . .	...	...	...	...	...	...	...	...
Goods procured in ports by carriers	3 170 . .	...	...	...	...	...	...	...	...
Nonmonetary gold	3 180 . .	...	...	...	...	...	...	...	...
B. SERVICES	4 200 . .	...	...	...	...	...	165.20	214.59	–138.38
Total credit	2 200 . .	...	...	...	...	...	*1,806.72*	*2,292.51*	*2,569.14*
Total debit	3 200 . .	...	...	...	...	...	*–1,641.52*	*–2,077.92*	*–2,707.52*
Transportation services, credit	2 205 . .	...	...	...	...	...	**674.79**	**630.91**	**654.54**
Passenger	2 205 BA	...	...	...	...	...	...	...	...
Freight	2 205 BB	...	...	...	...	...	...	...	...
Other	2 205 BC	...	...	...	...	...	...	...	...
Sea transport, passenger	2 207 . .	...	...	...	...	...	...	...	...
Sea transport, freight	2 208 . .	...	...	...	...	...	...	...	...
Sea transport, other	2 209 . .	...	...	...	...	...	...	...	...
Air transport, passenger	2 211 . .	...	...	...	...	...	...	...	...
Air transport, freight	2 212 . .	...	...	...	...	...	...	...	...
Air transport, other	2 213 . .	...	...	...	...	...	...	...	...
Other transport, passenger	2 215 . .	...	...	...	...	...	...	...	...
Other transport, freight	2 216 . .	...	...	...	...	...	...	...	...
Other transport, other	2 217 . .	...	...	...	...	...	...	...	...
Transportation services, debit	3 205 . .	...	...	...	...	...	**–962.86**	**–1,033.48**	**–1,345.62**
Passenger	3 205 BA	...	...	...	...	...	...	...	...
Freight	3 205 BB	...	...	...	...	...	...	...	...
Other	3 205 BC	...	...	...	...	...	...	...	...
Sea transport, passenger	3 207 . .	...	...	...	...	...	...	...	...
Sea transport, freight	3 208 . .	...	...	...	...	...	...	...	...
Sea transport, other	3 209 . .	...	...	...	...	...	...	...	...
Air transport, passenger	3 211 . .	...	...	...	...	...	...	...	...
Air transport, freight	3 212 . .	...	...	...	...	...	...	...	...
Air transport, other	3 213 . .	...	...	...	...	...	...	...	...
Other transport, passenger	3 215 . .	...	...	...	...	...	...	...	...
Other transport, freight	3 216 . .	...	...	...	...	...	...	...	...
Other transport, other	3 217 . .	...	...	...	...	...	...	...	...
Travel, credit	2 236 . .	...	...	...	...	...	**831.58**	**1,426.91**	**1,583.80**
Business travel	2 237 . .	...	...	...	...	...	...	...	...
Personal travel	2 240 . .	...	...	...	...	...	...	...	...
Travel, debit	3 236 . .	...	...	...	...	...	**–298.43**	**–552.25**	**–770.56**
Business travel	3 237 . .	...	...	...	...	...	...	...	...
Personal travel	3 240 . .	...	...	...	...	...	...	...	...
Other services, credit	2 200 BA	...	...	...	...	...	**300.35**	**234.69**	**330.80**
Communications	2 245 . .	...	...	...	...	...	...	...	...
Construction	2 249 . .	...	...	...	...	...	...	...	...
Insurance	2 253 . .	...	...	...	...	...	...	...	...
Financial	2 260 . .	...	...	...	...	...	...	...	...
Computer and information	2 262 . .	...	...	...	...	...	...	...	...
Royalties and licence fees	2 266 . .	...	...	...	...	...	...	...	...
Other business services	2 268 . .	...	...	...	...	...	300.35	234.69	330.80
Personal, cultural, and recreational	2 287 . .	...	...	...	...	...	...	...	...
Government, n.i.e.	2 291 . .	...	...	...	...	...	...	...	...
Other services, debit	3 200 BA	...	...	...	...	...	**–380.23**	**–492.19**	**–591.34**
Communications	3 245 . .	...	...	...	...	...	...	...	...
Construction	3 249 . .	...	...	...	...	...	...	...	...
Insurance	3 253 . .	...	...	...	...	...	...	...	...
Financial	3 260 . .	...	...	...	...	...	...	...	...
Computer and information	3 262 . .	...	...	...	...	...	...	...	...
Royalties and licence fees	3 266 . .	...	...	...	...	...	...	...	...
Other business services	3 268 . .	...	...	...	...	...	–380.23	–492.19	–591.34
Personal, cultural, and recreational	3 287 . .	...	...	...	...	...	...	...	...
Government, n.i.e.	3 291 . .	...	...	...	...	...	...	...	...

Table 2 (Continued). STANDARD PRESENTATION, 1988–95
(Millions of U.S. dollars)

	Code	1988	1989	1990	1991	1992	1993	1994	1995
C. INCOME	4 300	...	...	...	...	...	–141.27	–124.46	–93.23
Total credit	2 300	...	...	...	...	...	*111.64*	*101.02*	*173.41*
Total debit	3 300	...	...	...	...	...	*–252.91*	*–225.48*	*–266.64*
Compensation of employees, credit	2 310	...	...	...	...	...	...	...	...
Compensation of employees, debit	3 310	...	...	...	...	...	...	...	...
Investment income, credit	2 320	...	...	...	...	...	**111.64**	**101.02**	**173.41**
Direct investment income	2 330	...	...	...	...	...	...	...	...
Dividends and distributed branch profits	2 332	...	...	...	...	...	...	...	...
Reinvested earnings and undistributed branch profits	2 333	...	...	...	...	...	...	...	...
Income on debt (interest)	2 334	...	...	...	...	...	...	...	...
Portfolio investment income	2 339	...	...	...	...	...	...	...	...
Income on equity	2 340	...	...	...	...	...	...	...	...
Income on bonds and notes	2 350	...	...	...	...	...	...	...	...
Income on money market instruments and financial derivatives	2 360	...	...	...	...	...	...	...	...
Other investment income	2 370	...	...	...	...	...	111.64	101.02	173.41
Investment income, debit	3 320	...	...	...	...	...	**–252.91**	**–225.48**	**–266.64**
Direct investment income	3 330	...	...	...	...	...	...	...	...
Dividends and distributed branch profits	3 332	...	...	...	...	...	...	...	...
Reinvested earnings and undistributed branch profits	3 333	...	...	...	...	...	...	...	...
Income on debt (interest)	3 334	...	...	...	...	...	...	...	...
Portfolio investment income	3 339	...	...	...	...	...	...	...	...
Income on equity	3 340	...	...	...	...	...	...	...	...
Income on bonds and notes	3 350	...	...	...	...	...	...	...	...
Income on money market instruments and financial derivatives	3 360	...	...	...	...	...	...	...	...
Other investment income	3 370	...	...	...	...	...	–252.91	–225.48	–266.64
D. CURRENT TRANSFERS	4 379	...	...	...	...	...	375.97	459.29	645.69
Credit	2 379	...	...	...	...	...	**554.87**	**602.08**	**814.59**
General government	2 380	...	...	...	...	...	255.72	261.87	309.12
Other sectors	2 390	...	...	...	...	...	299.15	340.21	505.47
Workers' remittances	2 391	...	...	...	...	...	...	...	...
Other current transfers	2 392	...	...	...	...	...	...	...	...
Debit	3 379	...	...	...	...	...	**–178.90**	**–142.79**	**–168.90**
General government	3 380	...	...	...	...	...	–5.96	–26.58	–29.40
Other sectors	3 390	...	...	...	...	...	–172.94	–116.21	–139.50
Workers' remittances	3 391	...	...	...	...	...	...	...	...
Other current transfers	3 392	...	...	...	...	...	...	...	...
CAPITAL AND FINANCIAL ACCOUNT	4 996	...	...	...	...	...	**–133.41**	**–206.08**	**404.97**
CAPITAL ACCOUNT	4 994	...	...	...	...	...	...	...	...
Total credit	2 994	...	...	...	...	...	...	...	...
Total debit	3 994	...	...	...	...	...	...	...	...
Capital transfers, credit	2 400	...	...	...	...	...	...	...	...
General government	2 401	...	...	...	...	...	...	...	...
Debt forgiveness	2 402	...	...	...	...	...	...	...	...
Other capital transfers	2 410	...	...	...	...	...	...	...	...
Other sectors	2 430	...	...	...	...	...	...	...	...
Migrants' transfers	2 431	...	...	...	...	...	...	...	...
Debt forgiveness	2 432	...	...	...	...	...	...	...	...
Other capital transfers	2 440	...	...	...	...	...	...	...	...
Capital transfers, debit	3 400	...	...	...	...	...	...	...	...
General government	3 401	...	...	...	...	...	...	...	...
Debt forgiveness	3 402	...	...	...	...	...	...	...	...
Other capital transfers	3 410	...	...	...	...	...	...	...	...
Other sectors	3 430	...	...	...	...	...	...	...	...
Migrants' transfers	3 431	...	...	...	...	...	...	...	...
Debt forgiveness	3 432	...	...	...	...	...	...	...	...
Other capital transfers	3 440	...	...	...	...	...	...	...	...
Nonproduced nonfinancial assets, credit	2 480	...	...	...	...	...	...	...	...
Nonproduced nonfinancial assets, debit	3 480	...	...	...	...	...	...	...	...

Table 2 (Continued). STANDARD PRESENTATION, 1988–95
(Millions of U.S. dollars)

	Code	1988	1989	1990	1991	1992	1993	1994	1995
FINANCIAL ACCOUNT	4 995 . .	...	...	...	...	...	**–133.41**	**–206.08**	**404.97**
A. DIRECT INVESTMENT	4 500 . .	...	...	...	...	...	74.33	97.57	80.51
Direct investment abroad	4 505 . .	...	...	...	...	...	...	...	...
Equity capital	4 510 . .	...	...	...	...	...	...	...	...
Claims on affiliated enterprises	4 515 . .	...	...	...	...	...	...	...	...
Liabilities to affiliated enterprises	4 520 . .	...	...	...	...	...	...	...	...
Reinvested earnings	4 525 . .	...	...	...	...	...	...	...	...
Other capital	4 530 . .	...	...	...	...	...	...	...	...
Claims on affiliated enterprises	4 535 . .	...	...	...	...	...	...	...	...
Liabilities to affiliated enterprises	4 540 . .	...	...	...	...	...	...	...	...
Direct investment in Croatia	4 555 . .	...	...	...	...	...	**74.33**	**97.57**	**80.51**
Equity capital	4 560 . .	...	...	...	...	...	...	...	...
Claims on direct investors	4 565 . .	...	...	...	...	...	...	...	...
Liabilities to direct investors	4 570 . .	...	...	...	...	...	...	...	...
Reinvested earnings	4 575 . .	...	...	...	...	...	...	...	...
Other capital	4 580 . .	...	...	...	...	...	74.33	97.57	80.51
Claims on direct investors	4 585 . .	...	...	...	...	...	...	...	...
Liabilities to direct investors	4 590 . .	...	...	...	...	...	...	...	...
B. PORTFOLIO INVESTMENT	4 600 . .	...	...	...	...	...	...	...	...
Assets	4 602 . .	...	...	...	...	...	...	...	...
Equity securities	4 610 . .	...	...	...	...	...	...	...	...
Monetary authorities	4 611 . .	...	...	...	...	...	...	...	...
General government	4 612 . .	...	...	...	...	...	...	...	...
Banks	4 613 . .	...	...	...	...	...	...	...	...
Other sectors	4 614 . .	...	...	...	...	...	...	...	...
Debt securities	4 619 . .	...	...	...	...	...	...	...	...
Bonds and notes	4 620 . .	...	...	...	...	...	...	...	...
Monetary authorities	4 621 . .	...	...	...	...	...	...	...	...
General government	4 622 . .	...	...	...	...	...	...	...	...
Banks	4 623 . .	...	...	...	...	...	...	...	...
Other sectors	4 624 . .	...	...	...	...	...	...	...	...
Money market instruments	4 630 . .	...	...	...	...	...	...	...	...
Monetary authorities	4 631 . .	...	...	...	...	...	...	...	...
General government	4 632 . .	...	...	...	...	...	...	...	...
Banks	4 633 . .	...	...	...	...	...	...	...	...
Other sectors	4 634 . .	...	...	...	...	...	...	...	...
Financial derivatives	4 640 . .	...	...	...	...	...	...	...	...
Monetary authorities	4 641 . .	...	...	...	...	...	...	...	...
General government	4 642 . .	...	...	...	...	...	...	...	...
Banks	4 643 . .	...	...	...	...	...	...	...	...
Other sectors	4 644 . .	...	...	...	...	...	...	...	...
Liabilities	4 652 . .	...	...	...	...	...	...	...	...
Equity securities	4 660 . .	...	...	...	...	...	...	...	...
Banks	4 663 . .	...	...	...	...	...	...	...	...
Other sectors	4 664 . .	...	...	...	...	...	...	...	...
Debt securities	4 669 . .	...	...	...	...	...	...	...	...
Bonds and notes	4 670 . .	...	...	...	...	...	...	...	...
Monetary authorities	4 671 . .	...	...	...	...	...	...	...	...
General government	4 672 . .	...	...	...	...	...	...	...	...
Banks	4 673 . .	...	...	...	...	...	...	...	...
Other sectors	4 674 . .	...	...	...	...	...	...	...	...
Money market instruments	4 680 . .	...	...	...	...	...	...	...	...
Monetary authorities	4 681 . .	...	...	...	...	...	...	...	...
General government	4 682 . .	...	...	...	...	...	...	...	...
Banks	4 683 . .	...	...	...	...	...	...	...	...
Other sectors	4 684 . .	...	...	...	...	...	...	...	...
Financial derivatives	4 690 . .	...	...	...	...	...	...	...	...
Monetary authorities	4 691 . .	...	...	...	...	...	...	...	...
General government	4 692 . .	...	...	...	...	...	...	...	...
Banks	4 693 . .	...	...	...	...	...	...	...	...
Other sectors	4 694 . .	...	...	...	...	...	...	...	...

Table 2 (Concluded). STANDARD PRESENTATION, 1988–95
(Millions of U.S. dollars)

	Code	1988	1989	1990	1991	1992	1993	1994	1995
C. OTHER INVESTMENT	4 700	...	...	...	...	...	239.25	487.50	820.64
Assets	4 703	**...**	**...**	**...**	**...**	**...**	**44.18**	**241.82**	**49.83**
Trade credits	4 706	...	...	...	...	...	...	...	...
General government: long-term	4 708	...	...	...	...	...	...	...	...
General government: short-term	4 709	...	...	...	...	...	...	...	...
Other sectors: long-term	4 711	...	...	...	...	...	...	...	...
Other sectors: short-term	4 712	...	...	...	...	...	...	...	...
Loans	4 714	...	...	...	...	...	...	...	...
Monetary authorities: long-term	4 717	...	...	...	...	...	...	...	...
Monetary authorities: short-term	4 718	...	...	...	...	...	...	...	...
General government: long-term	4 720	...	...	...	...	...	...	...	...
General government: short-term	4 721	...	...	...	...	...	...	...	...
Banks: long-term	4 723	...	...	...	...	...	...	...	...
Banks: short-term	4 724	...	...	...	...	...	...	...	...
Other sectors: long-term	4 726	...	...	...	...	...	...	...	...
Other sectors: short-term	4 727	...	...	...	...	...	...	...	...
Currency and deposits	4 730	...	...	...	...	...	44.18	241.82	49.83
Monetary authorities	4 731	...	...	...	...	...	...	...	...
General government	4 732	...	...	...	...	...	...	...	...
Banks	4 733	...	...	...	...	...	–210.60	–189.50	–467.10
Other sectors	4 734	...	...	...	...	...	254.78	431.32	516.93
Other assets	4 736	...	...	...	...	...	...	...	...
Monetary authorities: long-term	4 738	...	...	...	...	...	...	...	...
Monetary authorities: short-term	4 739	...	...	...	...	...	...	...	...
General government: long-term	4 741	...	...	...	...	...	...	...	...
General government: short-term	4 742	...	...	...	...	...	...	...	...
Banks: long-term	4 744	...	...	...	...	...	...	...	...
Banks: short-term	4 745	...	...	...	...	...	...	...	...
Other sectors: long-term	4 747	...	...	...	...	...	...	...	...
Other sectors: short-term	4 748	...	...	...	...	...	...	...	...
Liabilities	4 753	**...**	**...**	**...**	**...**	**...**	**195.07**	**245.68**	**770.81**
Trade credits	4 756	...	...	...	...	...	...	...	...
General government: long-term	4 758	...	...	...	...	...	...	...	...
General government: short-term	4 759	...	...	...	...	...	...	...	...
Other sectors: long-term	4 761	...	...	...	...	...	...	...	...
Other sectors: short-term	4 762	...	...	...	...	...	...	...	...
Loans	4 764	...	...	...	...	...	–74.64	–20.09	432.00
Use of Fund credit and loans from the Fund	4 766	...	...	...	...	...	19.83	106.96	97.09
Monetary authorities: other long term	4 767	...	...	...	...	...	...	...	...
Monetary authorities: short-term	4 768	...	...	...	...	...	...	...	...
General government: long-term	4 770	...	...	...	...	...	–7.80	–1.80	–6.50
General government: short-term	4 771	...	...	...	...	...	...	...	100.00
Banks: long-term	4 773	...	...	...	...	...	–133.20	–56.70	–92.60
Banks: short-term	4 774	...	...	...	...	...	17.40	15.00	270.40
Other sectors: long-term	4 776	...	...	...	...	...	–50.70	–78.30	–35.90
Other sectors: short-term	4 777	...	...	...	...	...	79.83	–5.25	99.51
Currency and deposits	4 780	...	...	...	...	...	...	...	...
Monetary authorities	4 781	...	...	...	...	...	...	...	...
General government	4 782	...	...	...	...	...	...	...	...
Banks	4 783	...	...	...	...	...	...	...	...
Other sectors	4 784	...	...	...	...	...	...	...	...
Other liabilities	4 786	...	...	...	...	...	269.71	265.77	338.81
Monetary authorities: long-term	4 788	...	...	...	...	...	...	...	...
Monetary authorities: short-term	4 789	...	...	...	...	...	...	...	...
General government: long-term	4 791	...	...	...	...	...	...	...	...
General government: short-term	4 792	...	...	...	...	...	...	...	.30
Banks: long-term	4 794	...	...	...	...	...	...	...	...
Banks: short-term	4 795	...	...	...	...	...	221.61	165.77	207.51
Other sectors: long-term	4 797	...	...	...	...	...	...	...	...
Other sectors: short-term	4 798	...	...	...	...	...	48.10	100.00	131.00
D. RESERVE ASSETS	4 800	...	...	...	...	...	–447.00	–791.15	–496.18
Monetary gold	4 810	...	...	...	...	...	...	...	...
Special drawing rights	4 820	...	...	...	...	...	–1.13	–3.40	–141.28
Reserve position in the Fund	4 830	...	...	...	...	...	...	...	...
Foreign exchange	4 840	...	...	...	...	...	–445.87	–787.75	–354.90
Other claims	4 880	...	...	...	...	...	...	...	...
NET ERRORS AND OMISSIONS	4 998	**...**	**...**	**...**	**...**	**...**	**29.42**	**102.64**	**1,307.19**

Table 1. ANALYTIC PRESENTATION, 1988–95
(Millions of U.S. dollars)

	Code	1988	1989	1990	1991	1992	1993	1994	1995
A. Current Account[1]	4 993 Y.	**-107.6**	**-248.7**	**-154.3**	**-420.3**	**-638.2**	**109.8**	**74.4**	**-212.6**
Goods: exports f.o.b	2 100 ..	709.1	795.4	951.6	951.7	985.9	867.7	967.5	1,228.7
Goods: imports f.o.b	3 100 ..	-1,777.4	-2,165.5	-2,504.4	-2,553.5	-3,301.1	-2,374.5	-2,703.0	-3,314.2
Balance on Goods	4 100 ..	*-1,068.3*	*-1,370.1*	*-1,552.8*	*-1,601.8*	*-2,315.2*	*-1,506.8*	*-1,735.5*	*-2,085.5*
Services: credit	2 200 ..	1,411.6	1,618.6	2,003.6	1,857.1	2,521.4	2,335.1	2,646.7	2,960.1
Services: debit	3 200 ..	-501.7	-559.0	-673.9	-729.1	-884.0	-765.0	-862.1	-1,102.7
Balance on Goods and Services	4 991 ..	*-158.4*	*-310.5*	*-223.1*	*-473.7*	*-677.8*	*63.3*	*49.2*	*-228.1*
Income: credit	2 300 ..	87.9	119.1	158.9	175.3	156.8	131.9	121.5	142.3
Income: debit	3 300 ..	-160.7	-172.3	-216.8	-230.8	-234.9	-198.4	-211.1	-244.0
Balance on Goods, Services, and Income	4 992 ..	*-231.2*	*-363.7*	*-281.0*	*-529.3*	*-755.9*	*-3.2*	*-40.4*	*-329.8*
Current transfers: credit	2 379 Y.	126.9	118.5	131.0	114.3	123.2	118.4	125.0	134.8
Current transfers: debit	3 379 ..	-3.2	-3.4	-4.4	-5.4	-5.6	-5.4	-10.2	-17.7
B. Capital Account[1]	4 994 Y.	**...**	**...**	**...**	**...**	**...**	**...**	**...**	**...**
Capital account: credit	2 994 Y.	...	...	...	...	...	...	...	...
Capital account: debit	3 994 ..	...	...	...	...	...	...	...	...
Total, Groups A Plus B	4 010 ..	*-107.6*	*-248.7*	*-154.3*	*-420.3*	*-638.2*	*109.8*	*74.4*	*-212.6*
C. Financial Account[1]	4 995 X.	**166.3**	**451.5**	**436.0**	**278.2**	**323.4**	**-3.8**	**185.7**	**-55.5**
Direct investment abroad	4 505 ..	-.6	-.8	-4.6	-14.6	-14.7	-12.3	-6.1	-6.6
Direct investment in Cyprus	4 555 Y.	62.1	69.7	126.6	81.8	107.4	83.4	75.2	119.1
Portfolio investment assets	4 602 ..	...	...	...	...	-5.1	-18.9	-244.6	-23.7
Equity securities	4 610 ..	...	...	...	...	...	...	...	...
Debt securities	4 619 ..	...	...	...	...	-5.1	-18.9	-244.6	-23.7
Portfolio investment liabilities	4 652 Y.	...	92.6	-38.0	125.7	57.6	-33.4	84.5	-29.4
Equity securities	4 660 Y.	...	...	...	...	...	...	...	...
Debt securities	4 669 Y.	...	92.6	-38.0	125.7	57.6	-33.4	84.5	-29.4
Other investment assets	4 703 ..	-118.5	-231.7	-114.6	-379.0	-321.2	-231.2	56.3	-1,060.7
Monetary authorities	4 703 .A	...	...	...	...	...	...	...	...
General government	4 703 .B	-30.4	-18.6	-29.7	-16.8	57.4	10.1	1.0	-13.9
Banks	4 703 .C	-82.5	-234.7	-83.0	-362.2	-395.5	-246.1	55.3	-1,046.8
Other sectors	4 703 .D	-5.6	21.6	-2.0	...	16.9	4.8	...	...
Other investment liabilities	4 753 X.	223.3	521.6	466.5	464.2	499.4	208.5	220.4	945.8
Monetary authorities	4 753 XA	13.3	6.1	34.9	6.9	9.8	-23.1	.4	29.2
General government	4 753 YB	28.7	110.6	-12.4	60.5	-169.1	-155.0	-228.6	-148.5
Banks	4 753 YC	150.0	221.2	361.5	359.8	463.4	331.3	301.5	921.7
Other sectors	4 753 YD	31.3	183.8	82.5	37.0	195.3	55.3	147.1	143.5
Total, Groups A Through C	4 020 ..	*58.7*	*202.8*	*281.6*	*-142.1*	*-314.8*	*105.9*	*260.1*	*-268.1*
D. Net Errors and Omissions	4 998 ..	**12.0**	**25.3**	**12.2**	**76.5**	**89.9**	**38.8**	**-13.2**	**-94.9**
Total, Groups A Through D	4 030 ..	*70.7*	*228.0*	*293.8*	*-65.6*	*-224.9*	*144.8*	*246.9*	*-363.1*
E. Reserves and Related Items	4 040 ..	**-70.7**	**-228.0**	**-293.8**	**65.6**	**224.9**	**-144.8**	**-246.9**	**363.1**
Reserve assets	4 800 ..	-70.7	-228.0	-293.8	65.6	224.9	-144.8	-246.9	363.1
Use of Fund credit and loans	4 766 ..	...	...	...	...	...	...	...	...
Liabilities constituting foreign authorities' reserves	4 900 ..	...	...	...	...	...	...	...	...
Exceptional financing	4 920 ..	...	...	...	...	...	...	...	...
Conversion rates: Cyprus pound per U.S. dollar	0 101 ..	**.46663**	**.49462**	**.45808**	**.46443**	**.44955**	**.49741**	**.49219**	**.45242**

[1] Excludes components that have been classified in the categories of Group E.

Table 2. STANDARD PRESENTATION, 1988–95
(Millions of U.S. dollars)

	Code	1988	1989	1990	1991	1992	1993	1994	1995
CURRENT ACCOUNT	4 993 . .	**–107.6**	**–248.7**	**–154.3**	**–420.3**	**–638.2**	**109.8**	**74.4**	**–212.6**
A. GOODS	4 100 . .	–1,068.3	–1,370.1	–1,552.8	–1,601.8	–2,315.2	–1,506.8	–1,735.5	–2,085.5
Credit	2 100 . .	**709.1**	**795.4**	**951.6**	**951.7**	**985.9**	**867.7**	**967.5**	**1,228.7**
General merchandise: exports f.o.b.	2 110 . .	645.1	715.7	847.0	869.7	882.0	778.2	879.7	1,127.7
Goods for processing: exports f.o.b.	2 150 . .	. . .	. . .	. . .	. . .	. . .	. . .	. . .	. . .
Repairs on goods	2 160 . .	. . .	. . .	. . .	. . .	. . .	. . .	. . .	. . .
Goods procured in ports by carriers	2 170 . .	64.1	79.7	104.6	82.0	103.9	89.5	87.8	101.0
Nonmonetary gold	2 180 . .	. . .	. . .	. . .	. . .	. . .	. . .	. . .	. . .
Debit	3 100 . .	**–1,777.4**	**–2,165.5**	**–2,504.4**	**–2,553.5**	**–3,301.1**	**–2,374.5**	**–2,703.0**	**–3,314.2**
General merchandise: imports f.o.b.	3 110 . .	–1,777.4	–2,165.5	–2,504.4	–2,553.5	–3,301.1	–2,374.5	–2,703.0	–3,314.2
Goods for processing: imports f.o.b.	3 150 . .	. . .	. . .	. . .	. . .	. . .	. . .	. . .	. . .
Repairs on goods	3 160 . .	. . .	. . .	. . .	. . .	. . .	. . .	. . .	. . .
Goods procured in ports by carriers	3 170 . .	. . .	. . .	. . .	. . .	. . .	. . .	. . .	. . .
Nonmonetary gold	3 180 . .	. . .	. . .	. . .	. . .	. . .	. . .	. . .	. . .
B. SERVICES	4 200 . .	909.9	1,059.6	1,329.7	1,128.1	1,637.4	1,570.1	1,784.7	1,857.3
Total credit	2 200 . .	*1,411.6*	*1,618.6*	*2,003.6*	*1,857.1*	*2,521.4*	*2,335.1*	*2,646.7*	*2,960.1*
Total debit	3 200 . .	*–501.7*	*–559.0*	*–673.9*	*–729.1*	*–884.0*	*–765.0*	*–862.1*	*–1,102.7*
Transportation services, credit	2 205 . .	**204.7**	**215.1**	**260.4**	**268.7**	**316.5**	**301.8**	**343.6**	**384.6**
Passenger	2 205 BA	*143.4*	*151.8*	*185.6*	*194.9*	*227.1*	*211.5*	*246.2*	*260.4*
Freight	2 205 BB	*15.0*	*14.6*	*15.7*	*15.5*	*16.2*	*15.1*	*15.2*	*17.2*
Other	2 205 BC	*46.3*	*48.7*	*59.2*	*58.4*	*73.2*	*75.2*	*82.1*	*107.0*
Sea transport, passenger	2 207 . .	. . .	. . .	. . .	. . .	. . .	. . .	. . .	. . .
Sea transport, freight	2 208 . .	. . .	. . .	. . .	. . .	. . .	. . .	. . .	. . .
Sea transport, other	2 209 . .	. . .	. . .	. . .	. . .	. . .	. . .	. . .	. . .
Air transport, passenger	2 211 . .	. . .	. . .	. . .	. . .	. . .	. . .	. . .	. . .
Air transport, freight	2 212 . .	. . .	. . .	. . .	. . .	. . .	. . .	. . .	. . .
Air transport, other	2 213 . .	. . .	. . .	. . .	. . .	. . .	. . .	. . .	. . .
Other transport, passenger	2 215 . .	. . .	. . .	. . .	. . .	. . .	. . .	. . .	. . .
Other transport, freight	2 216 . .	. . .	. . .	. . .	. . .	. . .	. . .	. . .	. . .
Other transport, other	2 217 . .	. . .	. . .	. . .	. . .	. . .	. . .	. . .	. . .
Transportation services, debit	3 205 . .	**–280.1**	**–325.3**	**–379.6**	**–411.7**	**–508.3**	**–413.3**	**–465.9**	**–583.3**
Passenger	3 205 BA	*–61.5*	*–63.7*	*–76.6*	*–81.8*	*–97.9*	*–97.5*	*–101.6*	*–143.7*
Freight	3 205 BB	*–177.7*	*–216.5*	*–250.4*	*–255.4*	*–330.1*	*–237.4*	*–270.2*	*–331.3*
Other	3 205 BC	*–40.9*	*–45.1*	*–52.6*	*–74.5*	*–80.3*	*–78.4*	*–94.1*	*–108.3*
Sea transport, passenger	3 207 . .	. . .	. . .	. . .	. . .	. . .	. . .	. . .	. . .
Sea transport, freight	3 208 . .	. . .	. . .	. . .	. . .	. . .	. . .	. . .	. . .
Sea transport, other	3 209 . .	. . .	. . .	. . .	. . .	. . .	. . .	. . .	. . .
Air transport, passenger	3 211 . .	. . .	. . .	. . .	. . .	. . .	. . .	. . .	. . .
Air transport, freight	3 212 . .	. . .	. . .	. . .	. . .	. . .	. . .	. . .	. . .
Air transport, other	3 213 . .	. . .	. . .	. . .	. . .	. . .	. . .	. . .	. . .
Other transport, passenger	3 215 . .	. . .	. . .	. . .	. . .	. . .	. . .	. . .	. . .
Other transport, freight	3 216 . .	. . .	. . .	. . .	. . .	. . .	. . .	. . .	. . .
Other transport, other	3 217 . .	. . .	. . .	. . .	. . .	. . .	. . .	. . .	. . .
Travel, credit	2 236 . .	**829.8**	**993.7**	**1,254.1**	**1,029.2**	**1,548.2**	**1,403.9**	**1,650.8**	**1,796.8**
Business travel	2 237 . .	. . .	. . .	. . .	. . .	. . .	. . .	. . .	. . .
Personal travel	2 240 . .	. . .	. . .	. . .	. . .	. . .	. . .	. . .	. . .
Travel, debit	3 236 . .	**–134.4**	**–134.0**	**–177.3**	**–191.2**	**–224.0**	**–217.1**	**–246.2**	**–329.6**
Business travel	3 237 . .	. . .	. . .	. . .	. . .	. . .	. . .	. . .	. . .
Personal travel	3 240 . .	. . .	. . .	. . .	. . .	. . .	. . .	. . .	. . .
Other services, credit	2 200 BA	**377.2**	**409.8**	**489.0**	**559.2**	**656.7**	**629.5**	**652.4**	**778.7**
Communications	2 245 . .	10.9	11.3	10.9	17.2	20.9	15.3	14.6	16.1
Construction	2 249 . .	. . .	. . .	. . .	. . .	. . .	. . .	. . .	. . .
Insurance	2 253 . .	. . .	. . .	. . .	. . .	. . .	. . .	. . .	. . .
Financial	2 260 . .	. . .	. . .	. . .	. . .	. . .	. . .	. . .	. . .
Computer and information	2 262 . .	. . .	. . .	. . .	. . .	. . .	. . .	. . .	. . .
Royalties and licence fees	2 266 . .	. . .	. . .	. . .	. . .	. . .	. . .	. . .	. . .
Other business services	2 268 . .	164.4	177.7	234.7	252.4	331.0	324.1	388.9	486.5
Personal, cultural, and recreational	2 287 . .	. . .	. . .	. . .	. . .	. . .	. . .	. . .	. . .
Government, n.i.e.	2 291 . .	201.9	220.8	243.4	289.6	304.8	290.1	248.9	276.1
Other services, debit	3 200 BA	**–87.2**	**–99.7**	**–117.0**	**–126.2**	**–151.7**	**–134.5**	**–149.9**	**–189.9**
Communications	3 245 . .	–5.8	–7.3	–7.6	–14.4	–19.4	–17.1	–20.7	–27.4
Construction	3 249 . .	. . .	. . .	. . .	. . .	. . .	. . .	. . .	. . .
Insurance	3 253 . .	–27.6	–34.4	–38.9	–38.8	–50.7	–43.4	–48.4	–61.4
Financial	3 260 . .	. . .	. . .	. . .	. . .	. . .	. . .	. . .	. . .
Computer and information	3 262 . .	. . .	. . .	. . .	. . .	. . .	. . .	. . .	. . .
Royalties and licence fees	3 266 . .	–3.0	–3.4	–4.4	–1.5	–7.3	–8.0	–10.0	–11.3
Other business services	3 268 . .	–42.4	–44.9	–55.0	–58.4	–61.6	–53.5	–56.3	–71.4
Personal, cultural, and recreational	3 287 . .	. . .	. . .	. . .	. . .	. . .	. . .	. . .	. . .
Government, n.i.e.	3 291 . .	–8.4	–9.7	–11.1	–13.1	–12.7	–12.5	–14.6	–18.3

Table 2 (Continued). STANDARD PRESENTATION, 1988–95
(Millions of U.S. dollars)

	Code	1988	1989	1990	1991	1992	1993	1994	1995
C. INCOME	4 300 . .	–72.9	–53.2	–57.9	–55.6	–78.1	–66.5	–89.6	–101.7
Total credit	2 300 . .	*87.9*	*119.1*	*158.9*	*175.3*	*156.8*	*131.9*	*121.5*	*142.3*
Total debit	3 300 . .	*–160.7*	*–172.3*	*–216.8*	*–230.8*	*–234.9*	*–198.4*	*–211.1*	*–244.0*
Compensation of employees, credit	2 310 . .	**. . .**	**. . .**	**. . .**	**. . .**	**. . .**	**. . .**	**. . .**	**. . .**
Compensation of employees, debit	3 310 . .	**–10.9**	**–9.7**	**–12.0**	**–18.3**	**–23.8**	**–24.5**	**–33.7**	**–48.0**
Investment income, credit	2 320 . .	**87.9**	**119.1**	**158.9**	**175.3**	**156.8**	**131.9**	**121.5**	**142.3**
Direct investment income	2 330 . .	. . .	. . .	. . .	. . .	. . .	. . .	. . .	. . .
Dividends and distributed branch profits	2 332 . .	. . .	. . .	. . .	. . .	. . .	. . .	. . .	. . .
Reinvested earnings and undistributed branch profits	2 333 . .	. . .	. . .	. . .	. . .	. . .	. . .	. . .	. . .
Income on debt (interest)	2 334 . .	. . .	. . .	. . .	. . .	. . .	. . .	. . .	. . .
Portfolio investment income	2 339 . .	. . .	. . .	. . .	. . .	. . .	. . .	. . .	. . .
Income on equity	2 340 . .	. . .	. . .	. . .	. . .	. . .	. . .	. . .	. . .
Income on bonds and notes	2 350 . .	. . .	. . .	. . .	. . .	. . .	. . .	. . .	. . .
Income on money market instruments and financial derivatives	2 360 . .	. . .	. . .	. . .	. . .	. . .	. . .	. . .	. . .
Other investment income	2 370 . .	87.9	119.1	158.9	175.3	156.8	131.9	121.5	142.3
Investment income, debit	3 320 . .	**–149.8**	**–162.5**	**–204.8**	**–212.5**	**–211.1**	**–173.9**	**–177.4**	**–196.1**
Direct investment income	3 330 . .	–6.9	.2	–4.4	–14.6	–16.5	–12.7	–17.9	–17.7
Dividends and distributed branch profits	3 332 . .	–6.9	.2	–4.4	–14.6	–16.5	–12.7	–17.9	–17.7
Reinvested earnings and undistributed branch profits	3 333 . .	. . .	. . .	. . .	. . .	. . .	. . .	. . .	. . .
Income on debt (interest)	3 334 . .	. . .	. . .	. . .	. . .	. . .	. . .	. . .	. . .
Portfolio investment income	3 339 . .	. . .	. . .	–6.1	–4.7	–11.3	–9.0	–13.2	–15.5
Income on equity	3 340 . .	. . .	. . .	. . .	. . .	. . .	. . .	. . .	. . .
Income on bonds and notes	3 350 . .	. . .	. . .	. . .	. . .	. . .	. . .	. . .	. . .
Income on money market instruments and financial derivatives	3 360 . .	. . .	. . .	–6.1	–4.7	–11.3	–9.0	–13.2	–15.5
Other investment income	3 370 . .	–142.9	–162.7	–194.3	–193.1	–183.3	–152.2	–146.3	–162.9
D. CURRENT TRANSFERS	4 379 . .	123.7	115.0	126.6	109.0	117.7	113.0	114.8	117.1
Credit	2 379 . .	**126.9**	**118.5**	**131.0**	**114.3**	**123.2**	**118.4**	**125.0**	**134.8**
General government	2 380 . .	27.6	23.2	26.2	22.8	14.5	14.9	15.2	19.9
Other sectors	2 390 . .	99.2	95.2	104.8	91.5	108.8	103.5	109.7	114.9
Workers' remittances	2 391 . .	71.4	68.9	78.6	65.7	81.2	79.4	81.3	88.4
Other current transfers	2 392 . .	27.9	26.3	26.2	25.8	27.6	24.1	28.4	26.5
Debit	3 379 . .	**–3.2**	**–3.4**	**–4.4**	**–5.4**	**–5.6**	**–5.4**	**–10.2**	**–17.7**
General government	3 380 . .	. . .	. . .	. . .	. . .	. . .	. . .	. . .	. . .
Other sectors	3 390 . .	–3.2	–3.4	–4.4	–5.4	–5.6	–5.4	–10.2	–17.7
Workers' remittances	3 391 . .	. . .	. . .	. . .	. . .	. . .	. . .	. . .	. . .
Other current transfers	3 392 . .	–3.2	–3.4	–4.4	–5.4	–5.6	–5.4	–10.2	–17.7
CAPITAL AND FINANCIAL ACCOUNT	4 996 . .	**95.6**	**223.4**	**142.2**	**343.8**	**548.3**	**–148.6**	**–61.2**	**307.6**
CAPITAL ACCOUNT	4 994 . .	. . .	. . .	. . .	. . .	. . .	. . .	. . .	. . .
Total credit	2 994 . .	. . .	. . .	. . .	. . .	. . .	. . .	. . .	. . .
Total debit	3 994 . .	. . .	. . .	. . .	. . .	. . .	. . .	. . .	. . .
Capital transfers, credit	2 400 . .	**. . .**	**. . .**	**. . .**	**. . .**	**. . .**	**. . .**	**. . .**	**. . .**
General government	2 401 . .	. . .	. . .	. . .	. . .	. . .	. . .	. . .	. . .
Debt forgiveness	2 402 . .	. . .	. . .	. . .	. . .	. . .	. . .	. . .	. . .
Other capital transfers	2 410 . .	. . .	. . .	. . .	. . .	. . .	. . .	. . .	. . .
Other sectors	2 430 . .	. . .	. . .	. . .	. . .	. . .	. . .	. . .	. . .
Migrants' transfers	2 431 . .	. . .	. . .	. . .	. . .	. . .	. . .	. . .	. . .
Debt forgiveness	2 432 . .	. . .	. . .	. . .	. . .	. . .	. . .	. . .	. . .
Other capital transfers	2 440 . .	. . .	. . .	. . .	. . .	. . .	. . .	. . .	. . .
Capital transfers, debit	3 400 . .	**. . .**	**. . .**	**. . .**	**. . .**	**. . .**	**. . .**	**. . .**	**. . .**
General government	3 401 . .	. . .	. . .	. . .	. . .	. . .	. . .	. . .	. . .
Debt forgiveness	3 402 . .	. . .	. . .	. . .	. . .	. . .	. . .	. . .	. . .
Other capital transfers	3 410 . .	. . .	. . .	. . .	. . .	. . .	. . .	. . .	. . .
Other sectors	3 430 . .	. . .	. . .	. . .	. . .	. . .	. . .	. . .	. . .
Migrants' transfers	3 431 . .	. . .	. . .	. . .	. . .	. . .	. . .	. . .	. . .
Debt forgiveness	3 432 . .	. . .	. . .	. . .	. . .	. . .	. . .	. . .	. . .
Other capital transfers	3 440 . .	. . .	. . .	. . .	. . .	. . .	. . .	. . .	. . .
Nonproduced nonfinancial assets, credit	2 480 . .	**. . .**	**. . .**	**. . .**	**. . .**	**. . .**	**. . .**	**. . .**	**. . .**
Nonproduced nonfinancial assets, debit	3 480 . .	**. . .**	**. . .**	**. . .**	**. . .**	**. . .**	**. . .**	**. . .**	**. . .**

Table 2 (Continued). STANDARD PRESENTATION, 1988–95
(Millions of U.S. dollars)

	Code	1988	1989	1990	1991	1992	1993	1994	1995
FINANCIAL ACCOUNT	4 995	**95.6**	**223.4**	**142.2**	**343.8**	**548.3**	**-148.6**	**-61.2**	**307.6**
A. DIRECT INVESTMENT	4 500	61.5	68.9	122.0	67.2	92.8	71.2	69.1	112.5
Direct investment abroad	4 505	**-.6**	**-.8**	**-4.6**	**-14.6**	**-14.7**	**-12.3**	**-6.1**	**-6.6**
Equity capital	4 510	...	...	...	...	...	...	...	...
Claims on affiliated enterprises	4 515	...	...	...	...	...	...	...	...
Liabilities to affiliated enterprises	4 520	...	...	...	...	...	...	...	...
Reinvested earnings	4 525	...	...	...	...	...	...	...	...
Other capital	4 530	-.6	-.8	-4.6	-14.6	-14.7	-12.3	-6.1	-6.6
Claims on affiliated enterprises	4 535	...	...	...	...	...	...	...	...
Liabilities to affiliated enterprises	4 540	...	...	...	...	...	...	...	...
Direct investment in Cyprus	4 555	**62.1**	**69.7**	**126.6**	**81.8**	**107.4**	**83.4**	**75.2**	**119.1**
Equity capital	4 560	...	...	...	...	...	...	...	...
Claims on direct investors	4 565	...	...	...	...	...	...	...	...
Liabilities to direct investors	4 570	...	...	...	...	...	...	...	...
Reinvested earnings	4 575	...	...	...	...	...	...	...	...
Other capital	4 580	62.1	69.7	126.6	81.8	107.4	83.4	75.2	119.1
Claims on direct investors	4 585	...	...	...	...	...	...	...	...
Liabilities to direct investors	4 590	...	...	...	...	...	...	...	...
B. PORTFOLIO INVESTMENT	4 600	...	92.6	-38.0	125.7	52.5	-52.3	-160.1	-53.0
Assets	4 602	**...**	**...**	**...**	**...**	**-5.1**	**-18.9**	**-244.6**	**-23.7**
Equity securities	4 610	...	...	...	...	...	...	...	...
Monetary authorities	4 611	...	...	...	...	...	...	...	...
General government	4 612	...	...	...	...	...	...	...	...
Banks	4 613	...	...	...	...	...	...	...	...
Other sectors	4 614	...	...	...	...	...	...	...	...
Debt securities	4 619	...	...	...	...	-5.1	-18.9	-244.6	-23.7
Bonds and notes	4 620	...	...	...	...	-5.1	-18.9	-244.6	-23.7
Monetary authorities	4 621	...	...	...	...	...	...	...	...
General government	4 622	...	...	...	...	...	...	...	...
Banks	4 623	...	...	...	...	-5.1	-18.9	-244.6	-23.7
Other sectors	4 624	...	...	...	...	...	...	...	...
Money market instruments	4 630	...	...	...	...	...	...	...	...
Monetary authorities	4 631	...	...	...	...	...	...	...	...
General government	4 632	...	...	...	...	...	...	...	...
Banks	4 633	...	...	...	...	...	...	...	...
Other sectors	4 634	...	...	...	...	...	...	...	...
Financial derivatives	4 640	...	...	...	...	...	...	...	...
Monetary authorities	4 641	...	...	...	...	...	...	...	...
General government	4 642	...	...	...	...	...	...	...	...
Banks	4 643	...	...	...	...	...	...	...	...
Other sectors	4 644	...	...	...	...	...	...	...	...
Liabilities	4 652	**...**	**92.6**	**-38.0**	**125.7**	**57.6**	**-33.4**	**84.5**	**-29.4**
Equity securities	4 660	...	...	...	...	...	...	...	...
Banks	4 663	...	...	...	...	...	...	...	...
Other sectors	4 664	...	...	...	...	...	...	...	...
Debt securities	4 669	...	92.6	-38.0	125.7	57.6	-33.4	84.5	-29.4
Bonds and notes	4 670	...	...	...	...	...	...	...	...
Monetary authorities	4 671	...	...	...	...	...	...	...	...
General government	4 672	...	...	...	...	...	...	...	...
Banks	4 673	...	...	...	...	...	...	...	...
Other sectors	4 674	...	...	...	...	...	...	...	...
Money market instruments	4 680	...	92.6	-38.0	125.7	57.6	-33.4	84.5	-29.4
Monetary authorities	4 681	...	...	...	...	...	...	...	...
General government	4 682	...	92.6	-38.0	125.7	57.6	-33.4	84.5	-29.4
Banks	4 683	...	...	...	...	...	...	...	...
Other sectors	4 684	...	...	...	...	...	...	...	...
Financial derivatives	4 690	...	...	...	...	...	...	...	...
Monetary authorities	4 691	...	...	...	...	...	...	...	...
General government	4 692	...	...	...	...	...	...	...	...
Banks	4 693	...	...	...	...	...	...	...	...
Other sectors	4 694	...	...	...	...	...	...	...	...

Table 2 (Concluded). STANDARD PRESENTATION, 1988–95
(Millions of U.S. dollars)

	Code	1988	1989	1990	1991	1992	1993	1994	1995
C. OTHER INVESTMENT	4 700 . .	104.8	289.9	351.9	85.3	178.2	–22.7	276.7	–114.9
Assets	4 703 . .	**–118.5**	**–231.7**	**–114.6**	**–379.0**	**–321.2**	**–231.2**	**56.3**	**–1,060.7**
Trade credits	4 706 . .	–35.8	2.4	–32.7	–16.4	74.5	15.5	.8	–14.1
General government: long-term	4 708 . .	–30.2	–19.2	–30.8	–16.4	57.6	10.7	.8	–14.1
General government: short-term	4 709 . .	. . .	. . .	. . .	. . .	. . .	. . .	. . .	. . .
Other sectors: long-term	4 711 . .	–5.6	21.6	–2.0	. . .	16.9	4.8	. . .	. . .
Other sectors: short-term	4 712 . .	. . .	. . .	. . .	. . .	. . .	. . .	. . .	. . .
Loans	4 714 . .	. . .	. . .	. . .	. . .	. . .	. . .	. . .	. . .
Monetary authorities: long-term	4 717 . .	. . .	. . .	. . .	. . .	. . .	. . .	. . .	. . .
Monetary authorities: short-term	4 718 . .	. . .	. . .	. . .	. . .	. . .	. . .	. . .	. . .
General government: long-term	4 720 . .	. . .	. . .	. . .	. . .	. . .	. . .	. . .	. . .
General government: short-term	4 721 . .	. . .	. . .	. . .	. . .	. . .	. . .	. . .	. . .
Banks: long-term	4 723 . .	. . .	. . .	. . .	. . .	. . .	. . .	. . .	. . .
Banks: short-term	4 724 . .	. . .	. . .	. . .	. . .	. . .	. . .	. . .	. . .
Other sectors: long-term	4 726 . .	. . .	. . .	. . .	. . .	. . .	. . .	. . .	. . .
Other sectors: short-term	4 727 . .	. . .	. . .	. . .	. . .	. . .	. . .	. . .	. . .
Currency and deposits	4 730 . .	–82.7	–234.1	–81.9	–362.6	–395.7	–246.7	55.5	–1,046.6
Monetary authorities	4 731 . .	. . .	. . .	. . .	. . .	. . .	. . .	. . .	. . .
General government	4 732 . .	–.2	.6	1.1	–.4	–.2	–.6	.2	.2
Banks	4 733 . .	–82.5	–234.7	–83.0	–362.2	–395.5	–246.1	55.3	–1,046.8
Other sectors	4 734 . .	. . .	. . .	. . .	. . .	. . .	. . .	. . .	. . .
Other assets	4 736 . .	. . .	. . .	. . .	. . .	. . .	. . .	. . .	. . .
Monetary authorities: long-term	4 738 . .	. . .	. . .	. . .	. . .	. . .	. . .	. . .	. . .
Monetary authorities: short-term	4 739 . .	. . .	. . .	. . .	. . .	. . .	. . .	. . .	. . .
General government: long-term	4 741 . .	. . .	. . .	. . .	. . .	. . .	. . .	. . .	. . .
General government: short-term	4 742 . .	. . .	. . .	. . .	. . .	. . .	. . .	. . .	. . .
Banks: long-term	4 744 . .	. . .	. . .	. . .	. . .	. . .	. . .	. . .	. . .
Banks: short-term	4 745 . .	. . .	. . .	. . .	. . .	. . .	. . .	. . .	. . .
Other sectors: long-term	4 747 . .	. . .	. . .	. . .	. . .	. . .	. . .	. . .	. . .
Other sectors: short-term	4 748 . .	. . .	. . .	. . .	. . .	. . .	. . .	. . .	. . .
Liabilities	4 753 . .	**223.3**	**521.6**	**466.5**	**464.2**	**499.4**	**208.5**	**220.4**	**945.8**
Trade credits	4 756 . .	17.1	40.4	34.9	36.6	28.9	–28.1	50.8	48.6
General government: long-term	4 758 . .	. . .	. . .	. . .	. . .	. . .	. . .	. . .	. . .
General government: short-term	4 759 . .	. . .	. . .	. . .	. . .	. . .	. . .	. . .	. . .
Other sectors: long-term	4 761 . .	. . .	. . .	. . .	. . .	. . .	. . .	. . .	. . .
Other sectors: short-term	4 762 . .	17.1	40.4	34.9	36.6	28.9	–28.1	50.8	48.6
Loans	4 764 . .	43.5	254.7	35.8	62.9	–1.1	–70.0	–130.6	–51.7
Use of Fund credit and loans from the Fund	4 766 . .	. . .	. . .	. . .	. . .	. . .	. . .	. . .	. . .
Monetary authorities: other long-term	4 767 . .	. . .	. . .	. . .	. . .	. . .	. . .	. . .	. . .
Monetary authorities: short-term	4 768 . .	. . .	. . .	. . .	. . .	. . .	. . .	. . .	. . .
General government: long-term	4 770 . .	29.4	111.4	–11.8	62.4	–167.5	–153.4	–226.9	–146.5
General government: short-term	4 771 . .	. . .	. . .	. . .	. . .	. . .	. . .	. . .	. . .
Banks: long-term	4 773 . .	. . .	. . .	. . .	. . .	. . .	. . .	. . .	. . .
Banks: short-term	4 774 . .	. . .	. . .	. . .	. . .	. . .	. . .	. . .	. . .
Other sectors: long-term	4 776 . .	14.1	143.3	47.6	–14.6	150.8	85.4	103.2	99.2
Other sectors: short-term	4 777 . .	. . .	. . .	. . .	15.1	15.6	–2.0	–6.9	–4.4
Currency and deposits	4 780 . .	163.3	227.6	396.2	366.7	473.1	308.2	301.9	950.9
Monetary authorities	4 781 . .	13.3	6.5	34.7	6.9	9.8	–23.1	.4	29.2
General government	4 782 . .	. . .	. . .	. . .	. . .	. . .	. . .	. . .	. . .
Banks	4 783 . .	150.0	221.2	361.5	359.8	463.4	331.3	301.5	921.7
Other sectors	4 784 . .	. . .	. . .	. . .	. . .	. . .	. . .	. . .	. . .
Other liabilities	4 786 . .	–.6	–1.2	–.4	–1.9	–1.6	–1.6	–1.6	–2.0
Monetary authorities: long-term	4 788 . .	. . .	–.4	.2	. . .	. . .	. . .	. . .	. . .
Monetary authorities: short-term	4 789 . .	. . .	. . .	. . .	. . .	. . .	. . .	. . .	. . .
General government: long-term	4 791 . .	–.6	–.8	–.7	–1.9	–1.6	–1.6	–1.6	–2.0
General government: short-term	4 792 . .	. . .	. . .	. . .	. . .	. . .	. . .	. . .	. . .
Banks: long-term	4 794 . .	. . .	. . .	. . .	. . .	. . .	. . .	. . .	. . .
Banks: short-term	4 795 . .	. . .	. . .	. . .	. . .	. . .	. . .	. . .	. . .
Other sectors: long-term	4 797 . .	. . .	. . .	. . .	. . .	. . .	. . .	. . .	. . .
Other sectors: short-term	4 798 . .	. . .	. . .	. . .	. . .	. . .	. . .	. . .	. . .
D. RESERVE ASSETS	4 800 . .	–70.7	–228.0	–293.8	65.6	224.9	–144.8	–246.9	363.1
Monetary gold	4 810 . .	. . .	. . .	. . .	. . .	. . .	–.2	–.2	–.4
Special drawing rights	4 820 . .	.3	. . .	. . .	. . .	. . .	. . .	–.1	.1
Reserve position in the Fund	4 830 . .	–9.1	–8.1	4.0	–4.0	–10.5	. . .	. . .	. . .
Foreign exchange	4 840 . .	–61.9	–220.0	–297.8	69.5	235.3	–144.6	–246.7	363.4
Other claims	4 880 . .	. . .	. . .	. . .	. . .	. . .	. . .	. . .	. . .
NET ERRORS AND OMISSIONS	4 998 . .	**12.0**	**25.3**	**12.2**	**76.5**	**89.9**	**38.8**	**–13.2**	**–94.9**

Part 3 of the *Yearbook* contains descriptions of the methodologies, compilation practices, and sources used to compile these data.

Table 1. ANALYTIC PRESENTATION, 1988–95
(Millions of U.S. dollars)

	Code		1988	1989	1990	1991	1992	1993	1994	1995
A. Current Account[1]	4 993	Y .	**...**	**...**	**...**	**...**	**...**	**681**	**–81**	**–1,374**
Goods: exports f.o.b	2 100	. .	...	...	...	...	...	13,002	14,037	21,477
Goods: imports f.o.b	3 100	. .	...	...	...	...	...	–13,304	–14,955	–25,162
Balance on Goods	4 100	. .	...	...	...	...	...	*–302*	*–918*	*–3,685*
Services: credit	2 200	. .	...	...	...	...	...	4,721	4,901	6,725
Services: debit	3 200	. .	...	...	...	...	...	–3,709	–4,170	–4,882
Balance on Goods and Services	4 991	. .	...	...	...	...	...	*711*	*–187*	*–1,842*
Income: credit	2 300	. .	...	...	...	...	...	548	791	1,197
Income: debit	3 300	. .	...	...	...	...	...	–664	–812	–1,301
Balance on Goods, Services, and Income	4 992	. .	...	...	...	...	...	*594*	*–208*	*–1,946*
Current transfers: credit	2 379	Y .	...	...	...	...	...	242	298	664
Current transfers: debit	3 379	. .	...	...	...	...	...	–154	–171	–92
B. Capital Account[1]	4 994	Y .	**...**	**...**	**...**	**...**	**...**	**–563**	**...**	**7**
Capital account: credit	2 994	Y .	...	...	...	...	...	208	...	12
Capital account: debit	3 994	. .	...	...	...	...	...	–771	...	–5
Total, Groups A Plus B	4 010	. .	...	...	...	...	...	*118*	*–81*	*–1,367*
C. Financial Account[1]	4 995	X .	**...**	**...**	**...**	**...**	**...**	**3,043**	**4,504**	**8,225**
Direct investment abroad	4 505	. .	...	...	...	...	...	–90	–116	–37
Direct investment in Czech Republic	4 555	Y .	...	...	...	...	...	654	878	2,568
Portfolio investment assets	4 602	. .	...	...	...	...	...	–232	–47	–325
Equity securities	4 610	. .	...	...	...	...	...	–232	–47	–325
Debt securities	4 619	. .	...	...	...	...	...	...	...	...
Portfolio investment liabilities	4 652	Y .	...	...	...	...	...	1,840	893	1,695
Equity securities	4 660	Y .	...	...	...	...	...	1,840	497	1,236
Debt securities	4 669	Y .	...	...	...	...	...	...	396	460
Other investment assets	4 703	. .	...	...	...	...	...	–2,867	–2,536	–2,492
Monetary authorities	4 703	. A	...	...	...	...	...	...	...	...
General government	4 703	. B	...	...	...	...	...	–3,054	–2,461	–2,138
Banks	4 703	. C	...	...	...	...	...	36	–163	–224
Other sectors	4 703	. D	...	...	...	...	...	151	88	–130
Other investment liabilities	4 753	X .	...	...	...	...	...	3,738	5,431	6,816
Monetary authorities	4 753	XA	...	...	...	...	...	106	–47	40
General government	4 753	YB	...	...	...	...	...	3,037	2,919	1,657
Banks	4 753	YC	...	...	...	...	...	4	888	3,310
Other sectors	4 753	YD	...	...	...	...	...	591	1,671	1,809
Total, Groups A Through C	4 020	. .	...	...	...	...	...	*3,161*	*4,423*	*6,858*
D. Net Errors and Omissions	4 998	. .	**...**	**...**	**...**	**...**	**...**	**–98**	**–940**	**596**
Total, Groups A Through D	4 030	. .	...	...	...	...	...	*3,063*	*3,483*	*7,453*
E. Reserves and Related Items	4 040	. .	**...**	**...**	**...**	**...**	**...**	**–3,063**	**–3,483**	**–7,453**
Reserve assets	4 800	. .	...	...	...	...	...	–3,060	–2,366	–7,453
Use of Fund credit and loans	4 766	. .	...	...	...	...	...	–3	–1,117	...
Liabilities constituting foreign authorities' reserves	4 900	. .	...	...	...	...	...	...	...	...
Exceptional financing	4 920	. .	...	...	...	...	...	...	...	...
Conversion rates: Czech koruny per U.S. dollar	0 101	. .	**...**	**...**	**...**	**...**	**...**	**29.153**	**28.785**	**26.541**

[1] Excludes components that have been classified in the categories of Group E.

Table 2. STANDARD PRESENTATION, 1988–95
(Millions of U.S. dollars)

	Code	1988	1989	1990	1991	1992	1993	1994	1995
CURRENT ACCOUNT	4 993 . .	**. . .**	**. . .**	**. . .**	**. . .**	**. . .**	**681**	**–81**	**–1,374**
A. GOODS	4 100 . .	. . .	. . .	. . .	. . .	. . .	–302	–918	–3,685
Credit	2 100 . .	**. . .**	**. . .**	**. . .**	**. . .**	**. . .**	**13,002**	**14,037**	**21,477**
General merchandise: exports f.o.b.	2 110 . .	. . .	. . .	. . .	. . .	. . .	13,002	14,037	21,477
Goods for processing: exports f.o.b.	2 150 . .	. . .	. . .	. . .	. . .	. . .	. . .	. . .	. . .
Repairs on goods	2 160 . .	. . .	. . .	. . .	. . .	. . .	. . .	. . .	. . .
Goods procured in ports by carriers	2 170 . .	. . .	. . .	. . .	. . .	. . .	. . .	. . .	. . .
Nonmonetary gold	2 180 . .	. . .	. . .	. . .	. . .	. . .	. . .	. . .	. . .
Debit	3 100 . .	**. . .**	**. . .**	**. . .**	**. . .**	**. . .**	**–13,304**	**–14,955**	**–25,162**
General merchandise: imports f.o.b.	3 110 . .	. . .	. . .	. . .	. . .	. . .	–13,304	–14,955	–25,162
Goods for processing: imports f.o.b.	3 150 . .	. . .	. . .	. . .	. . .	. . .	. . .	. . .	. . .
Repairs on goods	3 160 . .	. . .	. . .	. . .	. . .	. . .	. . .	. . .	. . .
Goods procured in ports by carriers	3 170 . .	. . .	. . .	. . .	. . .	. . .	. . .	. . .	. . .
Nonmonetary gold	3 180 . .	. . .	. . .	. . .	. . .	. . .	. . .	. . .	. . .
B. SERVICES	4 200 . .	. . .	. . .	. . .	. . .	. . .	1,013	731	1,844
Total credit	2 200 . .	. . .	. . .	. . .	. . .	. . .	*4,721*	*4,901*	*6,725*
Total debit	3 200 . .	. . .	. . .	. . .	. . .	. . .	*–3,709*	*–4,170*	*–4,882*
Transportation services, credit	2 205 . .	**. . .**	**. . .**	**. . .**	**. . .**	**. . .**	**1,241**	**1,244**	**1,463**
Passenger	2 205 BA	. . .	. . .	. . .	. . .	. . .	. . .	. . .	. . .
Freight	2 205 BB	. . .	. . .	. . .	. . .	. . .	. . .	. . .	*8*
Other	2 205 BC	. . .	. . .	. . .	. . .	. . .	. . .	. . .	*1,455*
Sea transport, passenger	2 207 . .	. . .	. . .	. . .	. . .	. . .	. . .	. . .	. . .
Sea transport, freight	2 208 . .	. . .	. . .	. . .	. . .	. . .	. . .	. . .	. . .
Sea transport, other	2 209 . .	. . .	. . .	. . .	. . .	. . .	. . .	. . .	29
Air transport, passenger	2 211 . .	. . .	. . .	. . .	. . .	. . .	. . .	. . .	. . .
Air transport, freight	2 212 . .	. . .	. . .	. . .	. . .	. . .	. . .	. . .	. . .
Air transport, other	2 213 . .	. . .	. . .	. . .	. . .	. . .	. . .	. . .	265
Other transport, passenger	2 215 . .	. . .	. . .	. . .	. . .	. . .	. . .	. . .	. . .
Other transport, freight	2 216 . .	. . .	. . .	. . .	. . .	. . .	. . .	. . .	8
Other transport, other	2 217 . .	. . .	. . .	. . .	. . .	. . .	. . .	. . .	1,161
Transportation services, debit	3 205 . .	**. . .**	**. . .**	**. . .**	**. . .**	**. . .**	**–733**	**–855**	**–800**
Passenger	3 205 BA	. . .	. . .	. . .	. . .	. . .	. . .	. . .	. . .
Freight	3 205 BB	. . .	. . .	. . .	. . .	. . .	. . .	. . .	*–54*
Other	3 205 BC	. . .	. . .	. . .	. . .	. . .	. . .	. . .	*–746*
Sea transport, passenger	3 207 . .	. . .	. . .	. . .	. . .	. . .	. . .	. . .	. . .
Sea transport, freight	3 208 . .	. . .	. . .	. . .	. . .	. . .	. . .	. . .	. . .
Sea transport, other	3 209 . .	. . .	. . .	. . .	. . .	. . .	. . .	. . .	–55
Air transport, passenger	3 211 . .	. . .	. . .	. . .	. . .	. . .	. . .	. . .	. . .
Air transport, freight	3 212 . .	. . .	. . .	. . .	. . .	. . .	. . .	. . .	. . .
Air transport, other	3 213 . .	. . .	. . .	. . .	. . .	. . .	. . .	. . .	–219
Other transport, passenger	3 215 . .	. . .	. . .	. . .	. . .	. . .	. . .	. . .	. . .
Other transport, freight	3 216 . .	. . .	. . .	. . .	. . .	. . .	. . .	. . .	–54
Other transport, other	3 217 . .	. . .	. . .	. . .	. . .	. . .	. . .	. . .	–472
Travel, credit	2 236 . .	**. . .**	**. . .**	**. . .**	**. . .**	**. . .**	**1,558**	**1,971**	**2,880**
Business travel	2 237 . .	. . .	. . .	. . .	. . .	. . .	. . .	. . .	. . .
Personal travel	2 240 . .	. . .	. . .	. . .	. . .	. . .	. . .	. . .	2,880
Travel, debit	3 236 . .	**. . .**	**. . .**	**. . .**	**. . .**	**. . .**	**–526**	**–1,078**	**–1,635**
Business travel	3 237 . .	. . .	. . .	. . .	. . .	. . .	. . .	. . .	. . .
Personal travel	3 240 . .	. . .	. . .	. . .	. . .	. . .	. . .	. . .	–1,635
Other services, credit	2 200 BA	**. . .**	**. . .**	**. . .**	**. . .**	**. . .**	**1,922**	**1,686**	**2,383**
Communications	2 245 . .	. . .	. . .	. . .	. . .	. . .	366	331	292
Construction	2 249 . .	. . .	. . .	. . .	. . .	. . .	24	44	57
Insurance	2 253 . .	. . .	. . .	. . .	. . .	. . .	8	12	17
Financial	2 260 . .	. . .	. . .	. . .	. . .	. . .	440	88	53
Computer and information	2 262 . .	. . .	. . .	. . .	. . .	. . .	. . .	. . .	5
Royalties and licence fees	2 266 . .	. . .	. . .	. . .	. . .	. . .	1	4	13
Other business services	2 268 . .	. . .	. . .	. . .	. . .	. . .	1,040	1,162	1,783
Personal, cultural, and recreational	2 287 . .	. . .	. . .	. . .	. . .	. . .	. . .	. . .	74
Government, n.i.e.	2 291 . .	. . .	. . .	. . .	. . .	. . .	43	47	88
Other services, debit	3 200 BA	**. . .**	**. . .**	**. . .**	**. . .**	**. . .**	**–2,449**	**–2,237**	**–2,446**
Communications	3 245 . .	. . .	. . .	. . .	. . .	. . .	–299	–274	–256
Construction	3 249 . .	. . .	. . .	. . .	. . .	. . .	–108	–124	–141
Insurance	3 253 . .	. . .	. . .	. . .	. . .	. . .	–42	–72	–113
Financial	3 260 . .	. . .	. . .	. . .	. . .	. . .	–476	–114	–141
Computer and information	3 262 . .	. . .	. . .	. . .	. . .	. . .	. . .	. . .	–11
Royalties and licence fees	3 266 . .	. . .	. . .	. . .	. . .	. . .	–20	–26	–53
Other business services	3 268 . .	. . .	. . .	. . .	. . .	. . .	–1,496	–1,626	–1,583
Personal, cultural, and recreational	3 287 . .	. . .	. . .	. . .	. . .	. . .	. . .	. . .	–126
Government, n.i.e.	3 291 . .	. . .	. . .	. . .	. . .	. . .	–8	–1	–22

Table 2 (Continued). STANDARD PRESENTATION, 1988–95
(Millions of U.S. dollars)

	Code	1988	1989	1990	1991	1992	1993	1994	1995
C. INCOME	4 300	...	...	...	...	...	–117	–21	–104
Total credit	2 300	...	...	...	...	...	*548*	*791*	*1,197*
Total debit	3 300	...	...	...	...	...	*–664*	*–812*	*–1,301*
Compensation of employees, credit	2 310	...	...	...	...	...	**138**	**164**	**189**
Compensation of employees, debit	3 310	...	...	...	...	...	**–6**	**–55**	**–100**
Investment income, credit	2 320	...	...	...	...	...	**409**	**627**	**1,008**
Direct investment income	2 330	...	...	...	...	...	3	...	19
Dividends and distributed branch profits	2 332	...	...	...	...	...	3	...	19
Reinvested earnings and undistributed branch profits	2 333	...	...	...	...	...	...	...	...
Income on debt (interest)	2 334	...	...	...	...	...	...	...	...
Portfolio investment income	2 339	...	...	...	...	...	...	...	331
Income on equity	2 340	...	...	...	...	...	...	...	6
Income on bonds and notes	2 350	...	...	...	...	...	...	...	99
Income on money market instruments and financial derivatives	2 360	...	...	...	...	...	...	...	225
Other investment income	2 370	...	...	...	...	...	407	627	658
Investment income, debit	3 320	...	...	...	...	...	**–658**	**–757**	**–1,200**
Direct investment income	3 330	...	...	...	...	...	–4	...	–66
Dividends and distributed branch profits	3 332	...	...	...	...	...	–4	...	–66
Reinvested earnings and undistributed branch profits	3 333	...	...	...	...	...	...	...	...
Income on debt (interest)	3 334	...	...	...	...	...	...	...	...
Portfolio investment income	3 339	...	...	...	...	...	...	...	–248
Income on equity	3 340	...	...	...	...	...	...	...	–20
Income on bonds and notes	3 350	...	...	...	...	...	...	...	–196
Income on money market instruments and financial derivatives	3 360	...	...	...	...	...	...	...	–32
Other investment income	3 370	...	...	...	...	...	–654	–757	–886
D. CURRENT TRANSFERS	4 379	...	...	...	...	...	88	127	572
Credit	2 379	...	...	...	...	...	**242**	**298**	**664**
General government	2 380	...	...	...	...	...	...	...	128
Other sectors	2 390	...	...	...	...	...	...	...	536
Workers' remittances	2 391	...	...	...	...	...	...	...	...
Other current transfers	2 392	...	...	...	...	...	...	...	536
Debit	3 379	...	...	...	...	...	**–154**	**–171**	**–92**
General government	3 380	...	...	...	...	...	...	...	–25
Other sectors	3 390	...	...	...	...	...	...	...	–67
Workers' remittances	3 391	...	...	...	...	...	...	...	...
Other current transfers	3 392	...	...	...	...	...	...	...	–67
CAPITAL AND FINANCIAL ACCOUNT	4 996	...	...	...	...	...	**–583**	**1,021**	**778**
CAPITAL ACCOUNT	4 994	...	...	...	...	...	**–563**	...	**7**
Total credit	2 994	...	...	...	...	...	*208*	...	*12*
Total debit	3 994	...	...	...	...	...	*–771*	...	*–5*
Capital transfers, credit	2 400	...	...	...	...	...	**208**	...	**12**
General government	2 401	...	...	...	...	...	...	...	...
Debt forgiveness	2 402	...	...	...	...	...	...	...	...
Other capital transfers	2 410	...	...	...	...	...	...	...	...
Other sectors	2 430	...	...	...	...	...	208	...	12
Migrants' transfers	2 431	...	...	...	...	...	...	...	1
Debt forgiveness	2 432	...	...	...	...	...	...	...	...
Other capital transfers	2 440	...	...	...	...	...	208	...	10
Capital transfers, debit	3 400	...	...	...	...	...	**–771**	...	**–5**
General government	3 401	...	...	...	...	...	...	...	...
Debt forgiveness	3 402	...	...	...	...	...	...	...	...
Other capital transfers	3 410	...	...	...	...	...	...	...	...
Other sectors	3 430	...	...	...	...	...	–771	...	–5
Migrants' transfers	3 431	...	...	...	...	...	...	...	...
Debt forgiveness	3 432	...	...	...	...	...	...	...	...
Other capital transfers	3 440	...	...	...	...	...	–771	...	–5
Nonproduced nonfinancial assets, credit	2 480	...	...	...	...	...	...	...	...
Nonproduced nonfinancial assets, debit	3 480	...	...	...	...	...	...	...	...

Table 2 (Continued). STANDARD PRESENTATION, 1988–95
(Millions of U.S. dollars)

	Code	1988	1989	1990	1991	1992	1993	1994	1995
FINANCIAL ACCOUNT	4 995 . .	**. . .**	**. . .**	**. . .**	**. . .**	**. . .**	**–20**	**1,021**	**771**
A. DIRECT INVESTMENT	4 500 . .	. . .	. . .	. . .	. . .	. . .	564	762	2,531
Direct investment abroad	4 505 . .	**. . .**	**. . .**	**. . .**	**. . .**	**. . .**	**–90**	**–116**	**–37**
Equity capital	4 510 . .	. . .	. . .	. . .	. . .	. . .	–90	–116	–37
Claims on affiliated enterprises	4 515 . .	. . .	. . .	. . .	. . .	. . .	. . .	. . .	. . .
Liabilities to affiliated enterprises	4 520 . .	. . .	. . .	. . .	. . .	. . .	. . .	. . .	. . .
Reinvested earnings	4 525 . .	. . .	. . .	. . .	. . .	. . .	. . .	. . .	. . .
Other capital	4 530 . .	. . .	. . .	. . .	. . .	. . .	. . .	. . .	. . .
Claims on affiliated enterprises	4 535 . .	. . .	. . .	. . .	. . .	. . .	. . .	. . .	. . .
Liabilities to affiliated enterprises	4 540 . .	. . .	. . .	. . .	. . .	. . .	. . .	. . .	. . .
Direct investment in Czech Republic	4 555 . .	**. . .**	**. . .**	**. . .**	**. . .**	**. . .**	**654**	**878**	**2,568**
Equity capital	4 560 . .	. . .	. . .	. . .	. . .	. . .	654	878	2,568
Claims on direct investors	4 565 . .	. . .	. . .	. . .	. . .	. . .	. . .	. . .	. . .
Liabilities to direct investors	4 570 . .	. . .	. . .	. . .	. . .	. . .	. . .	. . .	. . .
Reinvested earnings	4 575 . .	. . .	. . .	. . .	. . .	. . .	. . .	. . .	. . .
Other capital	4 580 . .	. . .	. . .	. . .	. . .	. . .	. . .	. . .	. . .
Claims on direct investors	4 585 . .	. . .	. . .	. . .	. . .	. . .	. . .	. . .	. . .
Liabilities to direct investors	4 590 . .	. . .	. . .	. . .	. . .	. . .	. . .	. . .	. . .
B. PORTFOLIO INVESTMENT	4 600 . .	. . .	. . .	. . .	. . .	. . .	1,608	847	1,370
Assets	4 602 . .	**. . .**	**. . .**	**. . .**	**. . .**	**. . .**	**–232**	**–47**	**–325**
Equity securities	4 610 . .	. . .	. . .	. . .	. . .	. . .	–232	–47	–325
Monetary authorities	4 611 . .	. . .	. . .	. . .	. . .	. . .	. . .	. . .	. . .
General government	4 612 . .	. . .	. . .	. . .	. . .	. . .	. . .	. . .	. . .
Banks	4 613 . .	. . .	. . .	. . .	. . .	. . .	. . .	. . .	. . .
Other sectors	4 614 . .	. . .	. . .	. . .	. . .	. . .	–232	–47	–325
Debt securities	4 619 . .	. . .	. . .	. . .	. . .	. . .	. . .	. . .	. . .
Bonds and notes	4 620 . .	. . .	. . .	. . .	. . .	. . .	. . .	. . .	. . .
Monetary authorities	4 621 . .	. . .	. . .	. . .	. . .	. . .	. . .	. . .	. . .
General government	4 622 . .	. . .	. . .	. . .	. . .	. . .	. . .	. . .	. . .
Banks	4 623 . .	. . .	. . .	. . .	. . .	. . .	. . .	. . .	. . .
Other sectors	4 624 . .	. . .	. . .	. . .	. . .	. . .	. . .	. . .	. . .
Money market instruments	4 630 . .	. . .	. . .	. . .	. . .	. . .	. . .	. . .	. . .
Monetary authorities	4 631 . .	. . .	. . .	. . .	. . .	. . .	. . .	. . .	. . .
General government	4 632 . .	. . .	. . .	. . .	. . .	. . .	. . .	. . .	. . .
Banks	4 633 . .	. . .	. . .	. . .	. . .	. . .	. . .	. . .	. . .
Other sectors	4 634 . .	. . .	. . .	. . .	. . .	. . .	. . .	. . .	. . .
Financial derivatives	4 640 . .	. . .	. . .	. . .	. . .	. . .	. . .	. . .	. . .
Monetary authorities	4 641 . .	. . .	. . .	. . .	. . .	. . .	. . .	. . .	. . .
General government	4 642 . .	. . .	. . .	. . .	. . .	. . .	. . .	. . .	. . .
Banks	4 643 . .	. . .	. . .	. . .	. . .	. . .	. . .	. . .	. . .
Other sectors	4 644 . .	. . .	. . .	. . .	. . .	. . .	. . .	. . .	. . .
Liabilities	4 652 . .	**. . .**	**. . .**	**. . .**	**. . .**	**. . .**	**1,840**	**893**	**1,695**
Equity securities	4 660 . .	. . .	. . .	. . .	. . .	. . .	1,840	497	1,236
Banks	4 663 . .	. . .	. . .	. . .	. . .	. . .	. . .	425	. . .
Other sectors	4 664 . .	. . .	. . .	. . .	. . .	. . .	1,840	72	1,236
Debt securities	4 669 . .	. . .	. . .	. . .	. . .	. . .	. . .	396	460
Bonds and notes	4 670 . .	. . .	. . .	. . .	. . .	. . .	. . .	60	153
Monetary authorities	4 671 . .	. . .	. . .	. . .	. . .	. . .	. . .	–130	. . .
General government	4 672 . .	. . .	. . .	. . .	. . .	. . .	. . .	. . .	. . .
Banks	4 673 . .	. . .	. . .	. . .	. . .	. . .	. . .	190	153
Other sectors	4 674 . .	. . .	. . .	. . .	. . .	. . .	. . .	. . .	. . .
Money market instruments	4 680 . .	. . .	. . .	. . .	. . .	. . .	. . .	336	307
Monetary authorities	4 681 . .	. . .	. . .	. . .	. . .	. . .	. . .	. . .	. . .
General government	4 682 . .	. . .	. . .	. . .	. . .	. . .	. . .	336	307
Banks	4 683 . .	. . .	. . .	. . .	. . .	. . .	. . .	. . .	. . .
Other sectors	4 684 . .	. . .	. . .	. . .	. . .	. . .	. . .	. . .	. . .
Financial derivatives	4 690 . .	. . .	. . .	. . .	. . .	. . .	. . .	. . .	. . .
Monetary authorities	4 691 . .	. . .	. . .	. . .	. . .	. . .	. . .	. . .	. . .
General government	4 692 . .	. . .	. . .	. . .	. . .	. . .	. . .	. . .	. . .
Banks	4 693 . .	. . .	. . .	. . .	. . .	. . .	. . .	. . .	. . .
Other sectors	4 694 . .	. . .	. . .	. . .	. . .	. . .	. . .	. . .	. . .

Table 2 (Concluded). STANDARD PRESENTATION, 1988–95
(Millions of U.S. dollars)

	Code	1988	1989	1990	1991	1992	1993	1994	1995
C. OTHER INVESTMENT	4 700	...	...	...	...	...	868	1,778	4,324
Assets	4 703	**...**	**...**	**...**	**...**	**...**	**–2,867**	**–2,536**	**–2,492**
Trade credits	4 706	...	...	...	...	...	151	83	–94
General government: long-term	4 708	...	...	...	...	...	...	...	...
General government: short-term	4 709	...	...	...	...	...	...	...	...
Other sectors: long-term	4 711	...	...	...	...	...	220	136	53
Other sectors: short-term	4 712	...	...	...	...	...	–69	–52	–146
Loans	4 714	...	...	...	...	...	...	...	–422
Monetary authorities: long-term	4 717	...	...	...	...	...	...	...	...
Monetary authorities: short-term	4 718	...	...	...	...	...	...	...	...
General government: long-term	4 720	...	...	...	...	...	...	...	...
General government: short-term	4 721	...	...	...	...	...	...	...	...
Banks: long-term	4 723	...	...	...	...	...	...	...	–110
Banks: short-term	4 724	...	...	...	...	...	...	...	–312
Other sectors: long-term	4 726	...	...	...	...	...	...	...	...
Other sectors: short-term	4 727	...	...	...	...	...	...	...	...
Currency and deposits	4 730	...	...	...	...	...	361	–251	153
Monetary authorities	4 731	...	...	...	...	...	...	...	...
General government	4 732	...	...	...	...	...	...	...	...
Banks	4 733	...	...	...	...	...	361	–251	189
Other sectors	4 734	...	...	...	...	...	...	...	–36
Other assets	4 736	...	...	...	...	...	–3,379	–2,368	–2,129
Monetary authorities: long-term	4 738	...	...	...	...	...	...	...	...
Monetary authorities: short-term	4 739	...	...	...	...	...	...	...	...
General government: long-term	4 741	...	...	...	...	...	285	285	126
General government: short-term	4 742	...	...	...	...	...	–3,339	–2,746	–2,264
Banks: long-term	4 744	...	...	...	...	...	–326	88	...
Banks: short-term	4 745	...	...	...	...	...	...	...	9
Other sectors: long-term	4 747	...	...	...	...	...	...	...	...
Other sectors: short-term	4 748	...	...	...	...	...	...	5	...
Liabilities	4 753	**...**	**...**	**...**	**...**	**...**	**3,735**	**4,314**	**6,816**
Trade credits	4 756	...	...	...	...	...	–249	285	231
General government: long-term	4 758	...	...	...	...	...	...	...	...
General government: short-term	4 759	...	...	...	...	...	...	...	...
Other sectors: long-term	4 761	...	...	...	...	...	–187	223	–94
Other sectors: short-term	4 762	...	...	...	...	...	–61	61	325
Loans	4 764	...	...	...	...	...	754	223	2,132
Use of Fund credit and loans from the Fund	4 766	...	...	...	...	...	–3	–1,117	...
Monetary authorities: other long-term	4 767	...	...	...	...	...	45	7	37
Monetary authorities: short-term	4 768	...	...	...	...	...	61	–55	...
General government: long-term	4 770	...	...	...	...	...	–115	–185	–455
General government: short-term	4 771	...	...	...	...	...	...	...	...
Banks: long-term	4 773	...	...	...	...	...	–74	186	774
Banks: short-term	4 774	...	...	...	...	...	...	...	199
Other sectors: long-term	4 776	...	...	...	...	...	680	1,371	1,557
Other sectors: short-term	4 777	...	...	...	...	...	160	16	22
Currency and deposits	4 780	...	...	...	...	...	89	672	2,307
Monetary authorities	4 781	...	...	...	...	...	...	1	3
General government	4 782	...	...	...	...	...	...	...	...
Banks	4 783	...	...	...	...	...	88	671	2,304
Other sectors	4 784	...	...	...	...	...	...	...	...
Other liabilities	4 786	...	...	...	...	...	3,141	3,135	2,145
Monetary authorities: long-term	4 788	...	...	...	...	...	...	...	...
Monetary authorities: short-term	4 789	...	...	...	...	...	...	...	...
General government: long-term	4 791	...	...	...	...	...	...	...	...
General government: short-term	4 792	...	...	...	...	...	3,152	3,105	2,112
Banks: long-term	4 794	...	...	...	...	...	...	...	...
Banks: short-term	4 795	...	...	...	...	...	...	...	33
Other sectors: long-term	4 797	...	...	...	...	...	...	...	...
Other sectors: short-term	4 798	...	...	...	...	...	...	...	...
D. RESERVE ASSETS	4 800	...	...	...	...	...	–3,060	–2,366	–7,453
Monetary gold	4 810	...	...	...	...	...	4	...	3
Special drawing rights	4 820	...	...	...	...	...	–8	9	...
Reserve position in the Fund	4 830	...	...	...	...	...	...	...	...
Foreign exchange	4 840	...	...	...	...	...	–3,056	–2,375	–5,966
Other claims	4 880	...	...	...	...	...	...	...	–1,490
NET ERRORS AND OMISSIONS	4 998	**...**	**...**	**...**	**...**	**...**	**–98**	**–940**	**596**

Part 3 of the *Yearbook* contains descriptions of the methodologies, compilation practices, and sources used to compile these data.

Table 3. INTERNATIONAL INVESTMENT POSITION (End–period stocks), 1988–95
(Millions of U.S. dollars)

	Code	1988	1989	1990	1991	1992	1993	1994	1995
ASSETS	8 995 C.	...	...	...	...	...	17,906	20,424	29,347
Direct investment abroad	8 505 . .	...	...	...	...	...	**181**	**300**	**345**
Equity capital and reinvested earnings	8 506 . .	...	...	...	...	...	181	300	345
Claims on affiliated enterprises	8 507 . .	...	...	...	...	...	...	...	...
Liabilities to affiliated enterprises	8 508 . .	...	...	...	...	...	...	...	...
Other capital	8 530 . .	...	...	...	...	...	...	...	...
Claims on affiliated enterprises	8 535 . .	...	...	...	...	...	...	...	...
Liabilities to affiliated enterprises	8 540 . .	...	...	...	...	...	...	...	...
Portfolio investment	8 602 . .	...	...	...	...	...	**264**	**323**	**659**
Equity securities	8 610 . .	...	...	...	...	...	255	316	653
Monetary authorities	8 611 . .	...	...	...	...	...	...	...	...
General government	8 612 . .	...	...	...	...	...	...	...	...
Banks	8 613 . .	...	...	...	...	...	...	...	...
Other sectors	8 614 . .	...	...	...	...	...	255	316	653
Debt securities	8 619 . .	...	...	...	...	...	10	7	5
Bonds and notes	8 620 . .	...	...	...	...	...	10	7	5
Monetary authorities	8 621 . .	...	...	...	...	...	...	...	...
General government	8 622 . .	...	...	...	...	...	...	...	...
Banks	8 623 . .	...	...	...	...	...	...	...	...
Other sectors	8 624 . .	...	...	...	...	...	10	7	5
Money market instruments	8 630 . .	...	...	...	...	...	...	...	...
Monetary authorities	8 631 . .	...	...	...	...	...	...	...	...
General government	8 632 . .	...	...	...	...	...	...	...	...
Banks	8 633 . .	...	...	...	...	...	...	...	...
Other sectors	8 634 . .	...	...	...	...	...	...	...	...
Financial derivatives	8 640 . .	...	...	...	...	...	...	...	...
Monetary authorities	8 641 . .	...	...	...	...	...	...	...	...
General government	8 642 . .	...	...	...	...	...	...	...	...
Banks	8 643 . .	...	...	...	...	...	...	...	...
Other sectors	8 644 . .	...	...	...	...	...	...	...	...
Other investment	8 703 . .	...	...	...	...	...	**13,589**	**13,557**	**14,320**
Trade credits	8 706 . .	...	...	...	...	...	3,495	3,396	3,833
General government: long-term	8 708 . .	...	...	...	...	...	...	...	...
General government: short-term	8 709 . .	...	...	...	...	...	...	...	...
Other sectors: long-term	8 711 . .	...	...	...	...	...	1,195	995	947
Other sectors: short-term	8 712 . .	...	...	...	...	...	2,299	2,401	2,886
Loans	8 714 . .	...	...	...	...	...	327	419	859
Monetary authorities: long-term	8 717 . .	...	...	...	...	...	...	...	...
Monetary authorities: short-term	8 718 . .	...	...	...	...	...	...	...	...
General government: long-term	8 720 . .	...	...	...	...	...	...	...	...
General government: short-term	8 721 . .	...	...	...	...	...	...	...	...
Banks: long-term	8 723 . .	...	...	...	...	...	38	50	162
Banks: short-term	8 724 . .	...	...	...	...	...	288	369	697
Other sectors: long-term	8 726 . .	...	...	...	...	...	...	...	...
Other sectors: short-term	8 727 . .	...	...	...	...	...	...	...	...
Currency and deposits	8 730 . .	...	...	...	...	...	2,109	2,289	2,673
Monetary authorities	8 731 . .	...	...	...	...	...	...	...	...
General government	8 732 . .	...	...	...	...	...	...	...	...
Banks	8 733 . .	...	...	...	...	...	2,109	2,289	2,673
Other sectors	8 734 . .	...	...	...	...	...	...	...	...
Other assets	8 736 . .	...	...	...	...	...	7,658	7,453	6,955
Monetary authorities: long-term	8 738 . .	...	...	...	...	...	820	876	984
Monetary authorities: short-term	8 739 . .	...	...	...	...	...	...	...	...
General government: long-term	8 741 . .	...	...	...	...	...	6,425	6,231	5,938
General government: short-term	8 742 . .	...	...	...	...	...	...	...	...
Banks: long-term	8 744 . .	...	...	...	...	...	...	...	...
Banks: short-term	8 745 . .	...	...	...	...	...	413	345	33
Other sectors: long-term	8 747 . .	...	...	...	...	...	...	...	...
Other sectors: short-term	8 748 . .	...	...	...	...	...	...	...	...
Reserve assets	8 800 . .	...	...	...	...	...	**3,872**	**6,243**	**14,023**
Monetary gold	8 810 . .	...	...	...	...	...	82	82	84
Special drawing rights	8 820 . .	...	...	...	...	...	8	...	...
Reserve position in the Fund	8 830 . .	...	...	...	...	...	...	...	...
Foreign exchange	8 840 . .	...	...	...	...	...	3,053	5,131	11,339
Other claims	8 880 . .	...	...	...	...	...	728	1,030	2,600

Table 3 (Continued). INTERNATIONAL INVESTMENT POSITION (End–period stocks), 1988–95

(Millions of U.S. dollars)

	Code	1988	1989	1990	1991	1992	1993	1994	1995
LIABILITIES	8 995 D.	...	...	...	...	...	12,854	16,732	25,755
Direct investment in Czech Republic	8 555	**...**	**...**	**...**	**...**	**...**	**2,153**	**3,191**	**5,923**
Equity capital and reinvested earnings	8 556	...	...	...	...	...	2,153	3,191	5,923
Claims on direct investors	8 557	...	...	...	...	...	...	...	...
Liabilities to direct investors	8 558	...	...	...	...	...	...	...	...
Other capital	8 580	...	...	...	...	...	...	...	...
Claims on direct investors	8 585	...	...	...	...	...	...	...	...
Liabilities to direct investors	8 590	...	...	...	...	...	...	...	...
Portfolio investment	8 652	**...**	**...**	**...**	**...**	**...**	**1,956**	**2,910**	**4,696**
Equity securities	8 660	...	...	...	...	...	1,101	1,331	2,642
Banks	8 663	...	...	...	...	...	...	28	190
Other sectors	8 664	...	...	...	...	...	1,101	1,303	2,452
Debt securities	8 669	...	...	...	...	...	855	1,579	2,054
Bonds and notes	8 670	...	...	...	...	...	855	1,239	1,486
Monetary authorities	8 671	...	...	...	...	...	839	754	743
General government	8 672	...	...	...	...	...	...	277	303
Banks	8 673	...	...	...	...	...	...	56	284
Other sectors	8 674	...	...	...	...	...	15	152	156
Money market instruments	8 680	...	...	...	...	...	...	340	568
Monetary authorities	8 681	...	...	...	...	...	...	...	...
General government	8 682	...	...	...	...	...	...	340	568
Banks	8 683	...	...	...	...	...	...	...	...
Other sectors	8 684	...	...	...	...	...	...	...	...
Financial derivatives	8 690	...	...	...	...	...	...	...	...
Monetary authorities	8 691	...	...	...	...	...	...	...	...
General government	8 692	...	...	...	...	...	...	...	...
Banks	8 692	...	...	...	...	...	...	...	...
Other sectors	8 694	...	...	...	...	...	...	...	...
Other investment	8 753	**...**	**...**	**...**	**...**	**...**	**8,744**	**10,631**	**15,136**
Trade credits	8 756	...	...	...	...	...	2,162	2,601	2,757
General government: long-term	8 758	...	...	...	...	...	...	...	...
General government: short-term	8 759	...	...	...	...	...	...	...	...
Other sectors: long-term	8 761	...	...	...	...	...	885	1,182	973
Other sectors: short-term	8 762	...	...	...	...	...	1,277	1,419	1,784
Loans	8 764	...	...	...	...	...	5,018	5,409	7,907
Use of Fund credit and loans from the Fund	8 766	...	...	...	...	...	1,072	...	...
Monetary authorities: other long-term	8 767	...	...	...	...	...	47	60	94
Monetary authorities: short-term	8 768	...	...	...	...	...	58	...	...
General government: long-term	8 770	...	...	...	...	...	1,986	1,925	1,655
General government: short-term	8 771	...	...	...	...	...	...	...	...
Banks: long-term	8 773	...	...	...	...	...	507	690	1,650
Banks: short-term	8 774	...	...	...	...	...	69	75	276
Other sectors: long-term	8 776	...	...	...	...	...	1,126	2,490	4,041
Other sectors: short-term	8 777	...	...	...	...	...	154	168	191
Currency and deposits	8 780	...	...	...	...	...	623	1,512	4,042
Monetary authorities	8 781	...	...	...	...	...	1	1	4
General government	8 782	...	...	...	...	...	...	...	...
Banks	8 783	...	...	...	...	...	623	1,511	4,038
Other sectors	8 784	...	...	...	...	...	...	...	...
Other liabilities	8 786	...	...	...	...	...	941	1,108	429
Monetary authorities: long-term	8 788	...	...	...	...	...	...	...	...
Monetary authorities: short-term	8 789	...	...	...	...	...	94	...	...
General government: long-term	8 791	...	...	...	...	...	762	803	345
General government: short-term	8 792	...	...	...	...	...	...	179	42
Banks: long-term	8 794	...	...	...	...	...	...	...	...
Banks: short-term	8 795	...	...	...	...	...	84	126	43
Other sectors: long-term	8 797	...	...	...	...	...	...	...	...
Other sectors: short-term	8 798	...	...	...	...	...	...	...	...
NET INTERNATIONAL INVESTMENT POSITION	8 995	**...**	**...**	**...**	**...**	**...**	**5,053**	**3,692**	**3,592**
Conversion rates: Czech koruny per U.S. dollar (end of period)	0 102	**...**	**...**	**...**	**...**	**...**	**29.955**	**28.049**	**26.602**

Table 1. ANALYTIC PRESENTATION, 1988–95
(Millions of U.S. dollars)

	Code	1988	1989	1990	1991	1992	1993	1994	1995
A. Current Account [1]	4 993 Y.	**–1,340**	**–1,118**	**1,372**	**1,983**	**4,268**	**4,711**	**2,949**	**1,413**
Goods: exports f.o.b.	2 100 . .	27,537	28,728	36,072	36,783	40,650	37,070	41,777	48,853
Goods: imports f.o.b.	3 100 . .	–25,654	–26,304	–31,197	–32,035	–33,446	–29,073	–34,308	–42,028
Balance on Goods	4 100 . .	*1,883*	*2,425*	*4,875*	*4,748*	*7,204*	*7,998*	*7,469*	*6,825*
Services: credit	2 200 . .	9,623	9,570	12,830	14,264	14,495	12,744	13,848	15,377
Services: debit	3 200 . .	–8,427	–8,638	–10,218	–10,420	–10,896	–10,744	–12,277	–15,111
Balance on Goods and Services	4 991 . .	*3,078*	*3,356*	*7,487*	*8,592*	*10,803*	*9,998*	*9,041*	*7,090*
Income: credit	2 300 . .	3,677	4,718	6,011	8,855	15,569	22,666	22,787	28,542
Income: debit	3 300 . .	–7,876	–9,049	–11,719	–14,599	–21,223	–27,446	–27,674	–33,258
Balance on Goods, Services, and Income	4 992 . .	*–1,121*	*–975*	*1,779*	*2,848*	*5,148*	*5,219*	*4,153*	*2,374*
Current transfers: credit	2 379 Y.	1,799	1,608	2,007	2,083	2,136	2,497	2,261	2,846
Current transfers: debit	3 379 . .	–2,018	–1,750	–2,415	–2,948	–3,016	–3,005	–3,466	–3,807
B. Capital Account [1]	4 994 Y.	**. . .**	**. . .**	**. . .**	**. . .**	**. . .**	**. . .**	**. . .**	**. . .**
Capital account: credit	2 994 Y.	. . .	. . .	. . .	. . .	. . .	. . .	. . .	. . .
Capital account: debit	3 994 . .	. . .	. . .	. . .	. . .	. . .	. . .	. . .	. . .
Total, Groups A Plus B	4 010 . .	*–1,340*	*–1,118*	*1,372*	*1,983*	*4,268*	*4,711*	*2,949*	*1,413*
C. Financial Account [1]	4 995 X.	**3,275**	**–2,357**	**4,409**	**–3,103**	**–4,138**	**–2,079**	**–5,722**	**46**
Direct investment abroad	4 505 . .	–720	–2,066	–1,482	–1,852	–2,236	–1,373	–4,162	–2,969
Direct investment in Denmark	4 555 Y.	503	1,090	1,132	1,553	1,017	1,713	5,006	4,139
Portfolio investment assets	4 602 . .	–585	–1,527	–1,168	–4,378	1,420	2	–1,175	–1,171
Equity securities	4 610 . .	. . .	. . .	. . .	. . .	. . .	. . .	. . .	. . .
Debt securities	4 619 . .	–585	–1,527	–1,168	–4,378	1,420	2	–1,175	–1,171
Portfolio investment liabilities	4 652 Y.	1,815	–1,222	4,068	6,232	8,707	12,659	–10,596	7,673
Equity securities	4 660 Y.	. . .	. . .	. . .	. . .	. . .	. . .	. . .	. . .
Debt securities	4 669 Y.	1,815	–1,222	4,068	6,232	8,707	12,659	–10,596	7,673
Other investment assets	4 703 . .	–7,443	–4,242	–5,442	–3,012	395	–14,812	12,205	–1,330
Monetary authorities	4 703 .A	. . .	. . .	. . .	. . .	. . .	. . .	. . .	. . .
General government	4 703 .B	. . .	. . .	. . .	. . .	. . .	. . .	. . .	. . .
Banks	4 703 .C	–7,443	–4,242	–5,442	–3,012	395	–14,812	12,205	–1,330
Other sectors	4 703 .D	. . .	. . .	. . .	. . .	. . .	. . .	. . .	. . .
Other investment liabilities	4 753 X.	9,704	5,610	7,302	–1,645	–13,442	–268	–7,000	–6,297
Monetary authorities	4 753 XA	. . .	. . .	. . .	. . .	. . .	. . .	. . .	. . .
General government	4 753 YB	–1,480	–679	443	–5,078	1,309	8,648	–4,058	–3,380
Banks	4 753 YC	8,249	5,449	3,867	1,648	–9,437	–6,497	414	15
Other sectors	4 753 YD	2,936	840	2,991	1,785	–5,313	–2,419	–3,356	–2,932
Total, Groups A Through C	4 020 . .	*1,935*	*–3,475*	*5,781*	*–1,119*	*131*	*2,632*	*–2,773*	*1,459*
D. Net Errors and Omissions	4 998 . .	**–619**	**–347**	**–2,407**	**–2,183**	**–357**	**1,220**	**800**	**906**
Total, Groups A Through D	4 030 . .	*1,316*	*–3,821*	*3,374*	*–3,303*	*–226*	*3,851*	*–1,973*	*2,365*
E. Reserves and Related Items	4 040 . .	**–1,316**	**3,821**	**–3,374**	**3,303**	**226**	**–3,851**	**1,973**	**–2,365**
Reserve assets	4 800 . .	–1,436	3,838	–3,385	2,903	–4,075	567	1,851	–2,498
Use of Fund credit and loans	4 766 . .	. . .	. . .	. . .	. . .	. . .	. . .	. . .	. . .
Liabilities constituting foreign authorities' reserves	4 900 . .	120	–16	11	399	4,301	–4,419	122	133
Exceptional financing	4 920 . .	. . .	. . .	. . .	. . .	. . .	. . .	. . .	. . .
Conversion rates: Danish kroner per U.S. dollar	0 101 . .	**6.7315**	**7.3102**	**6.1886**	**6.3965**	**6.0361**	**6.4839**	**6.3606**	**5.6024**

[1] Excludes components that have been classified in the categories of Group E.

Table 2. STANDARD PRESENTATION, 1988–95

(Millions of U.S. dollars)

	Code	1988	1989	1990	1991	1992	1993	1994	1995
CURRENT ACCOUNT	4 993 . .	**–1,340**	**–1,118**	**1,372**	**1,983**	**4,268**	**4,711**	**2,949**	**1,413**
A. GOODS	4 100 . .	1,883	2,425	4,875	4,748	7,204	7,998	7,469	6,825
Credit	2 100 . .	**27,537**	**28,728**	**36,072**	**36,783**	**40,650**	**37,070**	**41,777**	**48,853**
General merchandise: exports f.o.b.	2 110 . .	27,537	28,728	36,072	36,783	40,650	37,070	41,777	48,853
Goods for processing: exports f.o.b.	2 150 . .	...	...	...	...	...	...	...	...
Repairs on goods	2 160 . .	...	...	...	...	...	...	...	...
Goods procured in ports by carriers	2 170 . .	...	...	...	...	...	...	...	...
Nonmonetary gold	2 180 . .	...	...	...	...	...	...	...	...
Debit	3 100 . .	**–25,654**	**–26,304**	**–31,197**	**–32,035**	**–33,446**	**–29,073**	**–34,308**	**–42,028**
General merchandise: imports f.o.b.	3 110 . .	–25,654	–26,304	–31,197	–32,035	–33,446	–29,073	–34,308	–42,028
Goods for processing: imports f.o.b.	3 150 . .	...	...	...	...	...	...	...	...
Repairs on goods	3 160 . .	...	...	...	...	...	...	...	...
Goods procured in ports by carriers	3 170 . .	...	...	...	...	...	...	...	...
Nonmonetary gold	3 180 . .	...	...	...	...	...	...	...	...
B. SERVICES	4 200 . .	1,195	932	2,612	3,844	3,599	2,001	1,572	265
Total credit	2 200 . .	*9,623*	*9,570*	*12,830*	*14,264*	*14,495*	*12,744*	*13,848*	*15,377*
Total debit	3 200 . .	*–8,427*	*–8,638*	*–10,218*	*–10,420*	*–10,896*	*–10,744*	*–12,277*	*–15,111*
Transportation services, credit	2 205 . .	**3,111**	**3,544**	**4,132**	**4,592**	**4,546**	**4,843**	**6,136**	**7,681**
Passenger	2 205 BA	*100*	*114*	*133*	*147*	*146*	*156*	...	...
Freight	2 205 BB	*1,979*	*2,254*	*2,628*	*2,920*	*2,891*	*3,080*	...	...
Other	2 205 BC	*1,033*	*1,176*	*1,371*	*1,524*	*1,509*	*1,607*	...	...
Sea transport, passenger	2 207 . .	...	...	...	...	...	...	...	...
Sea transport, freight	2 208 . .	...	...	...	...	...	...	...	...
Sea transport, other	2 209 . .	...	...	...	...	...	...	...	...
Air transport, passenger	2 211 . .	...	...	...	...	...	...	...	...
Air transport, freight	2 212 . .	...	...	...	...	...	...	...	...
Air transport, other	2 213 . .	...	...	...	...	...	...	...	...
Other transport, passenger	2 215 . .	...	...	...	...	...	...	...	...
Other transport, freight	2 216 . .	...	...	...	...	...	...	...	...
Other transport, other	2 217 . .	...	...	...	...	...	...	...	...
Transportation services, debit	3 205 . .	**–3,174**	**–3,508**	**–3,867**	**–4,361**	**–4,266**	**–4,636**	**–5,763**	**–7,264**
Passenger	3 205 BA	...	...	...	...	...	...	...	...
Freight	3 205 BB	*–1,190*	*–1,315*	*–1,450*	*–1,635*	*–1,600*	*–1,738*	...	...
Other	3 205 BC	*–1,984*	*–2,192*	*–2,417*	*–2,725*	*–2,666*	*–2,897*	...	...
Sea transport, passenger	3 207 . .	...	...	...	...	...	...	...	...
Sea transport, freight	3 208 . .	...	...	...	...	...	...	...	...
Sea transport, other	3 209 . .	...	...	...	...	...	...	...	...
Air transport, passenger	3 211 . .	...	...	...	...	...	...	...	...
Air transport, freight	3 212 . .	...	...	...	...	...	...	...	...
Air transport, other	3 213 . .	...	...	...	...	...	...	...	...
Other transport, passenger	3 215 . .	...	...	...	...	...	...	...	...
Other transport, freight	3 216 . .	...	...	...	...	...	...	...	...
Other transport, other	3 217 . .	...	...	...	...	...	...	...	...
Travel, credit	2 236 . .	**2,404**	**2,303**	**3,338**	**3,441**	**3,835**	**3,041**	**3,302**	**3,691**
Business travel	2 237 . .	...	...	...	...	...	...	...	...
Personal travel	2 240 . .	...	...	...	...	...	...	...	...
Travel, debit	3 236 . .	**–3,129**	**–2,930**	**–3,691**	**–3,369**	**–3,844**	**–3,211**	**–3,597**	**–4,288**
Business travel	3 237 . .	...	...	...	...	...	...	...	...
Personal travel	3 240 . .	...	...	...	...	...	...	...	...
Other services, credit	2 200 BA	**4,107**	**3,723**	**5,360**	**6,231**	**6,113**	**4,861**	**4,410**	**4,005**
Communications	2 245 . .	...	...	...	...	...	...	...	...
Construction	2 249 . .	...	...	...	...	...	...	...	...
Insurance	2 253 . .	220	250	292	324	321	342	...	...
Financial	2 260 . .	...	...	...	...	...	...	...	...
Computer and information	2 262 . .	...	...	...	...	...	...	...	...
Royalties and licence fees	2 266 . .	...	...	...	...	...	...	...	...
Other business services	2 268 . .	3,766	3,346	4,969	5,878	5,744	4,434	4,328	3,869
Personal, cultural, and recreational	2 287 . .	...	...	...	...	...	...	...	...
Government, n.i.e.	2 291 . .	122	127	99	28	48	85	83	136
Other services, debit	3 200 BA	**–2,124**	**–2,200**	**–2,660**	**–2,690**	**–2,786**	**–2,898**	**–2,917**	**–3,559**
Communications	3 245 . .	...	...	...	...	...	...	...	...
Construction	3 249 . .	...	...	...	...	...	...	...	...
Insurance	3 253 . .	–132	–146	–161	–182	–178	–185	...	...
Financial	3 260 . .	...	...	...	...	...	...	...	...
Computer and information	3 262 . .	...	...	...	...	...	...	...	...
Royalties and licence fees	3 266 . .	...	...	...	...	...	...	...	...
Other business services	3 268 . .	–1,822	–1,892	–2,387	–2,459	–2,538	–2,647	–2,847	–3,464
Personal, cultural, and recreational	3 287 . .	...	...	...	...	...	...	...	...
Government, n.i.e.	3 291 . .	–170	–162	–112	–50	–70	–65	–70	–95

Table 2 (Continued). STANDARD PRESENTATION, 1988–95
(Millions of U.S. dollars)

	Code	1988	1989	1990	1991	1992	1993	1994	1995
C. INCOME	4 300	–4,199	–4,331	–5,708	–5,744	–5,655	–4,780	–4,888	–4,716
Total credit	2 300	*3,677*	*4,718*	*6,011*	*8,855*	*15,569*	*22,666*	*22,787*	*28,542*
Total debit	3 300	*–7,876*	*–9,049*	*–11,719*	*–14,599*	*–21,223*	*–27,446*	*–27,674*	*–33,258*
Compensation of employees, credit	2 310	...	...	...	...	...	...	**462**	**550**
Compensation of employees, debit	3 310	...	...	...	...	...	...	**–200**	**–209**
Investment income, credit	2 320	**3,677**	**4,718**	**6,011**	**8,855**	**15,569**	**22,666**	**22,324**	**27,992**
Direct investment income	2 330	...	...	...	...	...	...	...	...
Dividends and distributed branch profits	2 332	...	...	...	...	...	...	...	...
Reinvested earnings and undistributed branch profits	2 333	...	...	...	...	...	...	...	...
Income on debt (interest)	2 334	...	...	...	...	...	...	...	...
Portfolio investment income	2 339	...	...	...	...	...	...	...	...
Income on equity	2 340	...	...	...	...	...	...	...	...
Income on bonds and notes	2 350	...	...	...	...	...	...	...	...
Income on money market instruments and financial derivatives	2 360	...	...	...	...	...	...	...	...
Other investment income	2 370	3,677	4,718	6,011	8,855	15,569	22,666	22,324	27,992
Investment income, debit	3 320	**–7,876**	**–9,049**	**–11,719**	**–14,599**	**–21,223**	**–27,446**	**–27,474**	**–33,049**
Direct investment income	3 330	...	...	...	...	...	...	...	...
Dividends and distributed branch profits	3 332	...	...	...	...	...	...	...	...
Reinvested earnings and undistributed branch profits	3 333	...	...	...	...	...	...	...	...
Income on debt (interest)	3 334	...	...	...	...	...	...	...	...
Portfolio investment income	3 339	...	...	...	...	...	...	...	...
Income on equity	3 340	...	...	...	...	...	...	...	...
Income on bonds and notes	3 350	...	...	...	...	...	...	...	...
Income on money market instruments and financial derivatives	3 360	...	...	...	...	...	...	...	...
Other investment income	3 370	–7,876	–9,049	–11,719	–14,599	–21,223	–27,446	–27,474	–33,049
D. CURRENT TRANSFERS	4 379	–219	–143	–408	–865	–880	–508	–1,204	–961
Credit	2 379	**1,799**	**1,608**	**2,007**	**2,083**	**2,136**	**2,497**	**2,261**	**2,846**
General government	2 380	1,674	1,348	1,749	1,812	1,858	2,219	1,914	2,447
Other sectors	2 390	125	260	258	271	278	278	348	399
Workers' remittances	2 391	...	...	...	...	...	...	...	...
Other current transfers	2 392	125	260	258	271	278	278	348	399
Debit	3 379	**–2,018**	**–1,750**	**–2,415**	**–2,948**	**–3,016**	**–3,005**	**–3,466**	**–3,807**
General government	3 380	–1,805	–1,570	–2,111	–2,527	–2,607	–2,594	–3,025	–3,316
Other sectors	3 390	–213	–180	–304	–421	–409	–411	–441	–491
Workers' remittances	3 391	...	...	...	...	...	...	...	...
Other current transfers	3 392	–213	–180	–304	–421	–409	–411	–441	–491
CAPITAL AND FINANCIAL ACCOUNT	4 996	**1,959**	**1,465**	**1,035**	**200**	**–3,911**	**–5,930**	**–3,749**	**–2,319**
CAPITAL ACCOUNT	4 994	...	...	...	...	...	...	...	...
Total credit	2 994	...	...	...	...	...	...	...	...
Total debit	3 994	...	...	...	...	...	...	...	...
Capital transfers, credit	2 400	...	...	...	...	...	...	...	...
General government	2 401	...	...	...	...	...	...	...	...
Debt forgiveness	2 402	...	...	...	...	...	...	...	...
Other capital transfers	2 410	...	...	...	...	...	...	...	...
Other sectors	2 430	...	...	...	...	...	...	...	...
Migrants' transfers	2 431	...	...	...	...	...	...	...	...
Debt forgiveness	2 432	...	...	...	...	...	...	...	...
Other capital transfers	2 440	...	...	...	...	...	...	...	...
Capital transfers, debit	3 400	...	...	...	...	...	...	...	...
General government	3 401	...	...	...	...	...	...	...	...
Debt forgiveness	3 402	...	...	...	...	...	...	...	...
Other capital transfers	3 410	...	...	...	...	...	...	...	...
Other sectors	3 430	...	...	...	...	...	...	...	...
Migrants' transfers	3 431	...	...	...	...	...	...	...	...
Debt forgiveness	3 432	...	...	...	...	...	...	...	...
Other capital transfers	3 440	...	...	...	...	...	...	...	...
Nonproduced nonfinancial assets, credit	2 480	...	...	...	...	...	...	...	...
Nonproduced nonfinancial assets, debit	3 480	...	...	...	...	...	...	...	...

Table 2 (Continued). STANDARD PRESENTATION, 1988–95
(Millions of U.S. dollars)

	Code	1988	1989	1990	1991	1992	1993	1994	1995
FINANCIAL ACCOUNT	4 995	**1,959**	**1,465**	**1,035**	**200**	**–3,911**	**–5,930**	**–3,749**	**–2,319**
A. DIRECT INVESTMENT	4 500	–217	–976	–350	–299	–1,219	340	844	1,171
Direct investment abroad	4 505	**–720**	**–2,066**	**–1,482**	**–1,852**	**–2,236**	**–1,373**	**–4,162**	**–2,969**
Equity capital	4 510	–720	–2,066	–1,482	–1,852	–2,236	–1,373	–4,162	–2,969
Claims on affiliated enterprises	4 515	...	...	...	...	...	...	...	...
Liabilities to affiliated enterprises	4 520	...	...	...	...	...	...	...	...
Reinvested earnings	4 525	...	...	...	...	...	...	...	...
Other capital	4 530	...	...	...	...	...	...	...	...
Claims on affiliated enterprises	4 535	...	...	...	...	...	...	...	...
Liabilities to affiliated enterprises	4 540	...	...	...	...	...	...	...	...
Direct investment in Denmark	4 555	**503**	**1,090**	**1,132**	**1,553**	**1,017**	**1,713**	**5,006**	**4,139**
Equity capital	4 560	503	1,090	1,132	1,553	1,017	1,713	5,006	4,139
Claims on direct investors	4 565	...	...	...	...	...	...	...	...
Liabilities to direct investors	4 570	...	...	...	...	...	...	...	...
Reinvested earnings	4 575	...	...	...	...	...	...	...	...
Other capital	4 580	...	...	...	...	...	...	...	...
Claims on direct investors	4 585	...	...	...	...	...	...	...	...
Liabilities to direct investors	4 590	...	...	...	...	...	...	...	...
B. PORTFOLIO INVESTMENT	4 600	1,231	–2,749	2,900	1,854	10,127	12,661	–11,771	6,502
Assets	4 602	**–585**	**–1,527**	**–1,168**	**–4,378**	**1,420**	**2**	**–1,175**	**–1,171**
Equity securities	4 610	...	...	...	...	...	...	...	...
Monetary authorities	4 611	...	...	...	...	...	...	...	...
General government	4 612	...	...	...	...	...	...	...	...
Banks	4 613	...	...	...	...	...	...	...	...
Other sectors	4 614	...	...	...	...	...	...	...	...
Debt securities	4 619	–585	–1,527	–1,168	–4,378	1,420	2	–1,175	–1,171
Bonds and notes	4 620	–585	–1,527	–1,168	–4,378	1,420	2	–1,175	–1,171
Monetary authorities	4 621	...	...	...	...	...	...	...	...
General government	4 622	...	...	...	...	...	...	...	...
Banks	4 623	...	...	...	...	...	...	...	...
Other sectors	4 624	...	...	...	...	...	...	...	...
Money market instruments	4 630	...	...	...	...	...	...	...	...
Monetary authorities	4 631	...	...	...	...	...	...	...	...
General government	4 632	...	...	...	...	...	...	...	...
Banks	4 633	...	...	...	...	...	...	...	...
Other sectors	4 634	...	...	...	...	...	...	...	...
Financial derivatives	4 640	...	...	...	...	...	...	...	...
Monetary authorities	4 641	...	...	...	...	...	...	...	...
General government	4 642	...	...	...	...	...	...	...	...
Banks	4 643	...	...	...	...	...	...	...	...
Other sectors	4 644	...	...	...	...	...	...	...	...
Liabilities	4 652	**1,815**	**–1,222**	**4,068**	**6,232**	**8,707**	**12,659**	**–10,596**	**7,673**
Equity securities	4 660	...	...	...	...	...	...	...	...
Banks	4 663	...	...	...	...	...	...	...	...
Other sectors	4 664	...	...	...	...	...	...	...	...
Debt securities	4 669	1,815	–1,222	4,068	6,232	8,707	12,659	–10,596	7,673
Bonds and notes	4 670	1,815	–1,222	4,068	6,232	8,707	12,659	–10,596	7,673
Monetary authorities	4 671	...	...	...	...	...	...	...	...
General government	4 672	1,815	–1,222	4,068	6,232	8,707	12,659	–10,596	7,673
Banks	4 673	...	...	...	...	...	...	...	...
Other sectors	4 674	...	...	...	...	...	...	...	...
Money market instruments	4 680	...	...	...	...	...	...	...	...
Monetary authorities	4 681	...	...	...	...	...	...	...	...
General government	4 682	...	...	...	...	...	...	...	...
Banks	4 683	...	...	...	...	...	...	...	...
Other sectors	4 684	...	...	...	...	...	...	...	...
Financial derivatives	4 690	...	...	...	...	...	...	...	...
Monetary authorities	4 691	...	...	...	...	...	...	...	...
General government	4 692	...	...	...	...	...	...	...	...
Banks	4 693	...	...	...	...	...	...	...	...
Other sectors	4 694	...	...	...	...	...	...	...	...

Table 2 (Concluded). STANDARD PRESENTATION, 1988–95
(Millions of U.S. dollars)

	Code	1988	1989	1990	1991	1992	1993	1994	1995
C. OTHER INVESTMENT	4 700 . .	2,381	1,352	1,870	–4,258	–8,745	–19,499	5,327	–7,494
Assets	4 703 . .	**–7,443**	**–4,242**	**–5,442**	**–3,012**	**395**	**–14,812**	**12,205**	**–1,330**
Trade credits	4 706 . .	. . .	. . .	. . .	. . .	. . .	. . .	. . .	. . .
General government: long-term	4 708 . .	. . .	. . .	. . .	. . .	. . .	. . .	. . .	. . .
General government: short-term	4 709 . .	. . .	. . .	. . .	. . .	. . .	. . .	. . .	. . .
Other sectors: long-term	4 711 . .	. . .	. . .	. . .	. . .	. . .	. . .	. . .	. . .
Other sectors: short-term	4 712 . .	. . .	. . .	. . .	. . .	. . .	. . .	. . .	. . .
Loans	4 714 . .	. . .	. . .	. . .	. . .	. . .	. . .	. . .	. . .
Monetary authorities: long-term	4 717 . .	. . .	. . .	. . .	. . .	. . .	. . .	. . .	. . .
Monetary authorities: short-term	4 718 . .	. . .	. . .	. . .	. . .	. . .	. . .	. . .	. . .
General government: long-term	4 720 . .	. . .	. . .	. . .	. . .	. . .	. . .	. . .	. . .
General government: short-term	4 721 . .	. . .	. . .	. . .	. . .	. . .	. . .	. . .	. . .
Banks: long-term	4 723 . .	. . .	. . .	. . .	. . .	. . .	. . .	. . .	. . .
Banks: short-term	4 724 . .	. . .	. . .	. . .	. . .	. . .	. . .	. . .	. . .
Other sectors: long-term	4 726 . .	. . .	. . .	. . .	. . .	. . .	. . .	. . .	. . .
Other sectors: short-term	4 727 . .	. . .	. . .	. . .	. . .	. . .	. . .	. . .	. . .
Currency and deposits	4 730 . .	–7,443	–4,242	–5,442	–3,012	395	–14,812	12,205	–1,330
Monetary authorities	4 731 . .	. . .	. . .	. . .	. . .	. . .	. . .	. . .	. . .
General government	4 732 . .	. . .	. . .	. . .	. . .	. . .	. . .	. . .	. . .
Banks	4 733 . .	–7,443	–4,242	–5,442	–3,012	395	–14,812	12,205	–1,330
Other sectors	4 734 . .	. . .	. . .	. . .	. . .	. . .	. . .	. . .	. . .
Other assets	4 736 . .	. . .	. . .	. . .	. . .	. . .	. . .	. . .	. . .
Monetary authorities: long-term	4 738 . .	. . .	. . .	. . .	. . .	. . .	. . .	. . .	. . .
Monetary authorities: short-term	4 739 . .	. . .	. . .	. . .	. . .	. . .	. . .	. . .	. . .
General government: long-term	4 741 . .	. . .	. . .	. . .	. . .	. . .	. . .	. . .	. . .
General government: short-term	4 742 . .	. . .	. . .	. . .	. . .	. . .	. . .	. . .	. . .
Banks: long-term	4 744 . .	. . .	. . .	. . .	. . .	. . .	. . .	. . .	. . .
Banks: short-term	4 745 . .	. . .	. . .	. . .	. . .	. . .	. . .	. . .	. . .
Other sectors: long-term	4 747 . .	. . .	. . .	. . .	. . .	. . .	. . .	. . .	. . .
Other sectors: short-term	4 748 . .	. . .	. . .	. . .	. . .	. . .	. . .	. . .	. . .
Liabilities	4 753 . .	**9,825**	**5,594**	**7,312**	**–1,246**	**–9,141**	**–4,687**	**–6,878**	**–6,164**
Trade credits	4 756 . .	. . .	. . .	. . .	. . .	. . .	. . .	. . .	. . .
General government: long-term	4 758 . .	. . .	. . .	. . .	. . .	. . .	. . .	. . .	. . .
General government: short-term	4 759 . .	. . .	. . .	. . .	. . .	. . .	. . .	. . .	. . .
Other sectors: long-term	4 761 . .	. . .	. . .	. . .	. . .	. . .	. . .	. . .	. . .
Other sectors: short-term	4 762 . .	. . .	. . .	. . .	. . .	. . .	. . .	. . .	. . .
Loans	4 764 . .	1,621	322	3,518	–3,181	–3,674	6,593	–7,612	–6,242
Use of Fund credit and loans from the Fund	4 766 . .	. . .	. . .	. . .	. . .	. . .	. . .	. . .	. . .
Monetary authorities: other long-term	4 767 . .	. . .	. . .	. . .	. . .	. . .	. . .	. . .	. . .
Monetary authorities: short-term	4 768 . .	. . .	. . .	. . .	. . .	. . .	. . .	. . .	. . .
General government: long-term	4 770 . .	–1,315	–518	526	–4,966	1,640	9,013	–4,257	–3,310
General government: short-term	4 771 . .	. . .	. . .	. . .	. . .	. . .	. . .	. . .	. . .
Banks: long-term	4 773 . .	. . .	. . .	. . .	. . .	. . .	. . .	. . .	. . .
Banks: short-term	4 774 . .	. . .	. . .	. . .	. . .	. . .	. . .	. . .	. . .
Other sectors: long-term	4 776 . .	2,936	840	2,991	1,785	–5,313	–2,419	–3,356	–2,932
Other sectors: short-term	4 777 . .	. . .	. . .	. . .	. . .	. . .	. . .	. . .	. . .
Currency and deposits	4 780 . .	8,369	5,433	3,878	2,047	–5,136	–10,915	536	148
Monetary authorities	4 781 . .	120	–16	11	399	4,301	–4,419	122	133
General government	4 782 . .	. . .	. . .	. . .	. . .	. . .	. . .	. . .	. . .
Banks	4 783 . .	8,249	5,449	3,867	1,648	–9,437	–6,497	414	15
Other sectors	4 784 . .	. . .	. . .	. . .	. . .	. . .	. . .	. . .	. . .
Other liabilities	4 786 . .	–165	–161	–83	–112	–331	–365	198	–70
Monetary authorities: long-term	4 788 . .	. . .	. . .	. . .	. . .	. . .	. . .	. . .	. . .
Monetary authorities: short-term	4 789 . .	. . .	. . .	. . .	. . .	. . .	. . .	. . .	. . .
General government: long-term	4 791 . .	–165	–161	–83	–112	–331	–365	198	–70
General government: short-term	4 792 . .	. . .	. . .	. . .	. . .	. . .	. . .	. . .	. . .
Banks: long-term	4 794 . .	. . .	. . .	. . .	. . .	. . .	. . .	. . .	. . .
Banks: short-term	4 795 . .	. . .	. . .	. . .	. . .	. . .	. . .	. . .	. . .
Other sectors: long-term	4 797 . .	. . .	. . .	. . .	. . .	. . .	. . .	. . .	. . .
Other sectors: short-term	4 798 . .	. . .	. . .	. . .	. . .	. . .	. . .	. . .	. . .
D. RESERVE ASSETS	4 800 . .	–1,436	3,838	–3,385	2,903	–4,075	567	1,851	–2,498
Monetary gold	4 810 . .	–7	–14	–26	–8	–28	34	9	–30
Special drawing rights	4 820 . .	65	–56	82	–27	142	7	–90	30
Reserve position in the Fund	4 830 . .	–150	–25	47	–40	–135	51	21	–157
Foreign exchange	4 840 . .	–1,344	3,933	–3,488	2,978	–4,054	476	1,911	–2,341
Other claims	4 880 . .	. . .	. . .	. . .	. . .	. . .	. . .	. . .	. . .
NET ERRORS AND OMISSIONS	4 998 . .	**–619**	**–347**	**–2,407**	**–2,183**	**–357**	**1,220**	**800**	**906**

Table 3. INTERNATIONAL INVESTMENT POSITION (End–period stocks), 1988–95

(Millions of U.S. dollars)

	Code	1988	1989	1990	1991	1992	1993	1994	1995
ASSETS	8 995 C.	...	...	...	102,567	100,639	110,957	109,111	126,429
Direct investment abroad	8 505 . .	**...**	**...**	**...**	**15,727**	**15,986**	**15,504**	**19,563**	**24,522**
Equity capital and reinvested earnings	8 506 . .	...	...	...	12,345	12,789	12,403	15,946	20,195
Claims on affiliated enterprises	8 507 . .	...	...	...	12,345	12,789	12,403	15,946	20,195
Liabilities to affiliated enterprises	8 508 . .	...	...	...	...	...	...	...	...
Other capital	8 530 . .	...	...	...	3,382	3,197	3,101	3,617	4,327
Claims on affiliated enterprises	8 535 . .	...	...	...	5,242	5,115	4,873	5,918	7,212
Liabilities to affiliated enterprises	8 540 . .	...	...	...	–1,860	–1,918	–1,772	–2,301	–2,885
Portfolio investment	8 602 . .	**...**	**...**	**...**	**20,462**	**16,945**	**18,752**	**17,426**	**23,440**
Equity securities	8 610 . .	...	...	...	6,764	6,394	8,269	9,042	10,819
Monetary authorities	8 611 . .	...	...	...	...	...	...	...	...
General government	8 612 . .	...	...	...	169	320	591	822	1,262
Banks	8 613 . .	...	...	...	676	480	738	822	902
Other sectors	8 614 . .	...	...	...	5,919	5,595	6,940	7,398	8,655
Debt securities	8 619 . .	...	...	...	13,697	10,551	10,484	8,384	12,622
Bonds and notes	8 620 . .	...	...	...	12,176	9,112	8,859	7,726	10,638
Monetary authorities	8 621 . .	...	...	...	...	...	...	...	...
General government	8 622 . .	...	...	...	169	320	295	493	541
Banks	8 623 . .	...	...	...	3,551	3,517	3,544	2,301	3,787
Other sectors	8 624 . .	...	...	...	8,455	5,275	5,020	4,932	6,311
Money market instruments	8 630 . .	...	...	...	1,522	1,439	1,624	658	1,983
Monetary authorities	8 631 . .	...	...	...	...	...	...	...	...
General government	8 632 . .	...	...	...	...	...	...	...	...
Banks	8 633 . .	...	...	...	1,522	1,439	1,624	658	1,983
Other sectors	8 634 . .	...	...	...	...	...	...	...	...
Financial derivatives	8 640 . .	...	...	...	...	...	...	...	...
Monetary authorities	8 641 . .	...	...	...	...	...	...	...	...
General government	8 642 . .	...	...	...	...	...	...	...	...
Banks	8 643 . .	...	...	...	...	...	...	...	...
Other sectors	8 644 . .	...	...	...	...	...	...	...	...
Other investment	8 703 . .	**...**	**...**	**...**	**58,341**	**56,111**	**65,707**	**62,962**	**66,534**
Trade credits	8 706 . .	...	...	...	7,441	6,554	5,906	6,247	6,491
General government: long-term	8 708 . .	...	...	...	...	...	...	...	...
General government: short-term	8 709 . .	...	...	...	...	...	...	...	...
Other sectors: long-term	8 711 . .	...	...	...	...	...	...	...	...
Other sectors: short-term	8 712 . .	...	...	...	...	...	...	...	...
Loans	8 714 . .	...	...	...	11,330	11,989	16,390	16,439	16,408
Monetary authorities: long-term	8 717 . .	...	...	...	...	...	...	...	...
Monetary authorities: short-term	8 718 . .	...	...	...	...	...	...	...	...
General government: long-term	8 720 . .	...	...	...	...	...	...	...	...
General government: short-term	8 721 . .	...	...	...	...	...	...	...	...
Banks: long-term	8 723 . .	...	...	...	...	...	...	...	...
Banks: short-term	8 724 . .	...	...	...	...	...	...	...	...
Other sectors: long-term	8 726 . .	...	...	...	...	...	...	...	...
Other sectors: short-term	8 727 . .	...	...	...	...	...	...	...	...
Currency and deposits	8 730 . .	...	...	...	37,034	33,411	40,458	36,166	40,209
Monetary authorities	8 731 . .	...	...	...	...	...	...	...	...
General government	8 732 . .	...	...	...	...	...	...	...	...
Banks	8 733 . .	...	...	...	35,005	31,173	38,391	33,700	37,324
Other sectors	8 734 . .	...	...	...	2,029	2,078	2,067	2,466	2,885
Other assets	8 736 . .	...	...	...	2,537	4,156	2,953	4,110	3,426
Monetary authorities: long-term	8 738 . .	...	...	...	...	...	...	...	...
Monetary authorities: short-term	8 739 . .	...	...	...	...	...	...	...	...
General government: long-term	8 741 . .	...	...	...	...	...	...	...	...
General government: short-term	8 742 . .	...	...	...	...	...	...	...	...
Banks: long-term	8 744 . .	...	...	...	...	...	...	...	...
Banks: short-term	8 745 . .	...	...	...	...	...	...	...	...
Other sectors: long-term	8 747 . .	...	...	...	...	...	...	...	...
Other sectors: short-term	8 748 . .	...	...	...	...	...	...	...	...
Reserve assets	8 800 . .	**...**	**...**	**...**	**8,038**	**11,597**	**10,994**	**9,160**	**11,933**
Monetary gold	8 810 . .	...	...	...	507	480	591	658	721
Special drawing rights	8 820 . .	225	280	216	242	92	86	182	159
Reserve position in the Fund	8 830 . .	316	335	313	356	475	425	430	595
Foreign exchange	8 840 . .	...	...	...	6,933	10,551	9,893	7,891	10,458
Other claims	8 880 . .	...	...	...	...	...	...	...	...

Table 3 (Continued). INTERNATIONAL INVESTMENT POSITION (End-period stocks), 1988–95
(Millions of U.S. dollars)

	Code	1988	1989	1990	1991	1992	1993	1994	1995
LIABILITIES	8 995 D.	...	...	...	158,620	151,067	154,153	151,734	173,999
Direct investment in Denmark	8 555 ..	**...**	**...**	**...**	**14,712**	**14,387**	**14,175**	**17,919**	**23,621**
Equity capital and reinvested earnings	8 556 ..	...	...	...	10,992	10,711	10,484	13,316	17,670
Claims on direct investors	8 557 ..	...	...	...	...	...	...	...	...
Liabilities to direct investors	8 558 ..	...	...	...	10,992	10,711	10,484	13,316	17,670
Other capital	8 580 ..	...	...	...	3,720	3,677	3,691	4,603	5,950
Claims on direct investors	8 585 ..	...	...	...	–1,860	–1,918	–2,067	–3,452	–4,868
Liabilities to direct investors	8 590 ..	...	...	...	5,580	5,595	5,759	8,055	10,819
Portfolio investment	8 652 ..	**...**	**...**	**...**	**58,848**	**64,583**	**84,164**	**72,990**	**86,549**
Equity securities	8 660 ..	...	...	...	2,875	2,238	4,282	6,740	8,835
Banks	8 663 ..	...	...	...	1,015	799	2,362	1,480	2,164
Other sectors	8 664 ..	...	...	...	1,860	1,439	1,920	5,261	6,671
Debt securities	8 669 ..	...	...	...	55,974	62,345	79,882	66,250	77,714
Bonds and notes	8 670 ..	...	...	...	52,761	56,590	75,009	65,593	76,632
Monetary authorities	8 671 ..	...	...	...	...	...	...	...	...
General government	8 672 ..	...	...	...	36,527	42,682	60,982	48,989	58,420
Banks	8 673 ..	...	...	...	5,750	3,517	3,101	2,630	2,705
Other sectors	8 674 ..	...	...	...	10,484	10,391	10,927	13,973	15,507
Money market instruments	8 680 ..	...	...	...	3,044	5,595	5,316	493	1,623
Monetary authorities	8 681 ..	...	...	...	...	...	...	...	...
General government	8 682 ..	...	...	...	676	3,197	3,839	164	...
Banks	8 683 ..	...	...	...	2,367	2,398	1,477	329	1,623
Other sectors	8 684 ..	...	...	...	...	...	...	...	...
Financial derivatives	8 690 ..	...	...	...	169	160	–443	164	–541
Monetary authorities	8 691 ..	...	...	...	...	...	...	...	...
General government	8 692 ..	...	...	...	169	160	–443	164	–541
Banks	8 692 ..	...	...	...	169	160	–443	164	–541
Other sectors	8 694 ..	...	...	...	...	...	...	...	...
Other investment	8 753 ..	**...**	**...**	**...**	**85,060**	**72,097**	**55,814**	**60,825**	**63,830**
Trade credits	8 756 ..	...	...	...	3,213	3,037	2,805	3,123	3,426
General government: long-term	8 758 ..	...	...	...	...	...	...	...	...
General government: short-term	8 759 ..	...	...	...	...	...	...	...	...
Other sectors: long-term	8 761 ..	...	...	...	...	...	...	...	...
Other sectors: short-term	8 762 ..	...	...	...	...	...	...	...	...
Loans	8 764 ..	...	...	...	43,967	37,087	33,370	34,358	35,341
Use of Fund credit and loans from the Fund	8 766 ..	...	...	...	...	...	...	...	...
Monetary authorities: other long-term	8 767 ..	...	...	...	...	...	...	...	...
Monetary authorities: short-term	8 768 ..	...	...	...	...	...	...	...	...
General government: long-term	8 770 ..	...	...	...	...	...	...	...	...
General government: short-term	8 771 ..	...	...	...	...	...	...	...	...
Banks: long-term	8 773 ..	...	...	...	...	...	...	...	...
Banks: short-term	8 774 ..	...	...	...	...	...	...	...	...
Other sectors: long-term	8 776 ..	...	...	...	...	...	...	...	...
Other sectors: short-term	8 777 ..	...	...	...	...	...	...	...	...
Currency and deposits	8 780 ..	...	...	...	36,019	31,013	16,980	20,385	20,916
Monetary authorities	8 781 ..	...	...	...	676	4,476	148	329	361
General government	8 782 ..	...	...	...	...	...	...	...	...
Banks	8 783 ..	...	...	...	35,343	26,537	16,833	20,056	20,555
Other sectors	8 784 ..	...	...	...	...	...	...	...	...
Other liabilities	8 786 ..	...	...	...	1,860	959	2,658	2,959	4,147
Monetary authorities: long-term	8 788 ..	...	...	...	...	...	...	...	...
Monetary authorities: short-term	8 789 ..	...	...	...	...	...	...	...	...
General government: long-term	8 791 ..	...	...	...	...	...	...	...	...
General government: short-term	8 792 ..	...	...	...	...	...	...	...	...
Banks: long-term	8 794 ..	...	...	...	...	...	...	...	...
Banks: short-term	8 795 ..	...	...	...	...	...	...	...	...
Other sectors: long-term	8 797 ..	...	...	...	...	...	...	...	...
Other sectors: short-term	8 798 ..	...	...	...	...	...	...	...	...
NET INTERNATIONAL INVESTMENT POSITION	8 995 ..	**...**	**...**	**...**	**–56,053**	**–50,428**	**–43,196**	**–42,623**	**–47,570**
Conversion rates: Danish kroner per U.S. dollar (end of period)	0 102 ..	**6.8740**	**6.6075**	**5.7760**	**5.9135**	**6.2555**	**6.7725**	**6.0830**	**5.5460**

Table 1. ANALYTIC PRESENTATION, 1988–95
(Millions of U.S. dollars)

	Code	1988	1989	1990	1991	1992	1993	1994	1995
A. Current Account [1]	4 993 Y.	...	...	...	...	**–87.5**	**–34.3**	**–46.1**	**–23.0**
Goods: exports f.o.b	2 100 ..	...	...	...	...	53.2	71.2	56.4	33.5
Goods: imports f.o.b	3 100 ..	...	...	...	...	–271.0	–255.1	–237.1	–205.0
Balance on Goods	4 100 ..	...	...	...	...	*–217.8*	*–183.9*	*–180.7*	*–171.5*
Services: credit	2 200 ..	...	...	...	...	145.1	156.9	152.3	151.4
Services: debit	3 200 ..	...	...	...	...	–109.3	–110.8	–89.7	–87.2
Balance on Goods and Services	4 991 ..	...	...	...	...	*–182.0*	*–137.8*	*–118.1*	*–107.3*
Income: credit	2 300 ..	...	...	...	...	29.4	30.3	23.7	25.9
Income: debit	3 300 ..	...	...	...	...	–9.4	–7.2	–7.0	–8.7
Balance on Goods, Services, and Income	4 992 ..	...	...	...	...	*–162.0*	*–114.8*	*–101.4*	*–90.0*
Current transfers: credit	2 379 Y.	...	...	...	...	90.7	96.6	73.7	85.4
Current transfers: debit	3 379 ..	...	...	...	...	–16.3	–16.1	–18.3	–18.4
B. Capital Account [1]	4 994 Y.	...	...	...	...	...	...	...	...
Capital account: credit	2 994 Y.	...	...	...	...	...	...	...	...
Capital account: debit	3 994 ..	...	...	...	...	...	...	...	...
Total, Groups A Plus B	4 010 ..	...	...	...	...	*–87.5*	*–34.3*	*–46.1*	*–23.0*
C. Financial Account [1]	4 995 X.	...	...	...	...	**74.0**	**16.6**	**39.0**	**–2.1**
Direct investment abroad	4 505 ..	...	...	...	...	...	...	...	...
Direct investment in Djibouti	4 555 Y.	...	...	...	...	2.3	1.4	1.4	3.2
Portfolio investment assets	4 602 ..	...	...	...	...	...	...	...	...
Equity securities	4 610 ..	...	...	...	...	...	...	...	...
Debt securities	4 619 ..	...	...	...	...	...	...	...	...
Portfolio investment liabilities	4 652 Y.	...	...	...	...	...	...	...	...
Equity securities	4 660 Y.	...	...	...	...	...	...	...	...
Debt securities	4 669 Y.	...	...	...	...	...	...	...	...
Other investment assets	4 703 ..	...	...	...	...	...	...	...	...
Monetary authorities	4 703 .A	...	...	...	...	...	...	...	...
General government	4 703 .B	...	...	...	...	...	...	...	...
Banks	4 703 .C	...	...	...	...	...	...	...	...
Other sectors	4 703 .D	...	...	...	...	...	...	...	...
Other investment liabilities	4 753 X.	...	...	...	...	71.7	15.2	37.6	–5.4
Monetary authorities	4 753 XA	...	...	...	...	...	...	...	...
General government	4 753 YB	...	...	...	...	8.1	15.9	12.0	–9.4
Banks	4 753 YC	...	...	...	...	37.6	–18.8	11.6	4.0
Other sectors	4 753 YD	...	...	...	...	26.0	18.1	14.1	.1
Total, Groups A Through C	4 020 ..	...	...	...	...	*–13.5*	*–17.6*	*–7.0*	*–25.1*
D. Net Errors and Omissions	4 998 ..	...	...	...	...	**–2.0**	**6.0**	**7.9**	**.7**
Total, Groups A Through D	4 030 ..	...	...	...	...	*–15.5*	*–11.7*	*.8*	*–24.5*
E. Reserves and Related Items	4 040 ..	...	...	...	...	**15.5**	**11.7**	**–.8**	**24.5**
Reserve assets	4 800 ..	...	...	...	...	15.5	11.3	–3.4	7.3
Use of Fund credit and loans	4 766 ..	...	...	...	...	...	...	...	...
Liabilities constituting foreign authorities' reserves	4 900 ..	...	...	...	...	...	...	...	...
Exceptional financing	4 920 ..	...	...	...	...	...	.4	2.6	17.2
Conversion rates: Djibouti francs per U.S. dollar	0 101 ..	**177.72**	**177.72**	**177.72**	**177.72**	**177.72**	**177.72**	**177.72**	**177.72**

[1] Excludes components that have been classified in the categories of Group E.

Table 2. STANDARD PRESENTATION, 1988–95
(Millions of U.S. dollars)

	Code	1988	1989	1990	1991	1992	1993	1994	1995
CURRENT ACCOUNT	4 993 . .	**. . .**	**. . .**	**. . .**	**. . .**	**–87.5**	**–34.3**	**–46.1**	**–23.0**
A. GOODS	4 100 . .	. . .	. . .	. . .	. . .	–217.8	–183.9	–180.7	–171.5
Credit	2 100 . .	**. . .**	**. . .**	**. . .**	**. . .**	**53.2**	**71.2**	**56.4**	**33.5**
General merchandise: exports f.o.b.	2 110 . .	. . .	. . .	. . .	. . .	53.2	71.2	56.4	33.5
Goods for processing: exports f.o.b.	2 150 . .	. . .	. . .	. . .	. . .	. . .	. . .	. . .	. . .
Repairs on goods	2 160 . .	. . .	. . .	. . .	. . .	. . .	. . .	. . .	. . .
Goods procured in ports by carriers	2 170 . .	. . .	. . .	. . .	. . .	. . .	. . .	. . .	. . .
Nonmonetary gold	2 180 . .	. . .	. . .	. . .	. . .	. . .	. . .	. . .	. . .
Debit	3 100 . .	**. . .**	**. . .**	**. . .**	**. . .**	**–271.0**	**–255.1**	**–237.1**	**–205.0**
General merchandise: imports f.o.b.	3 110 . .	. . .	. . .	. . .	. . .	–271.0	–255.1	–237.1	–205.0
Goods for processing: imports f.o.b.	3 150 . .	. . .	. . .	. . .	. . .	. . .	. . .	. . .	. . .
Repairs on goods	3 160 . .	. . .	. . .	. . .	. . .	. . .	. . .	. . .	. . .
Goods procured in ports by carriers	3 170 . .	. . .	. . .	. . .	. . .	. . .	. . .	. . .	. . .
Nonmonetary gold	3 180 . .	. . .	. . .	. . .	. . .	. . .	. . .	. . .	. . .
B. SERVICES	4 200 . .	. . .	. . .	. . .	. . .	35.9	46.1	62.7	64.2
Total credit	2 200 . .	. . .	. . .	. . .	. . .	*145.1*	*156.9*	*152.3*	*151.4*
Total debit	3 200 . .	. . .	. . .	. . .	. . .	*–109.3*	*–110.8*	*–89.7*	*–87.2*
Transportation services, credit	2 205 . .	**. . .**	**. . .**	**. . .**	**. . .**	**21.7**	**21.2**	**23.2**	**16.3**
Passenger	2 205 BA	. . .	. . .	. . .	. . .	*2.8*	*2.8*	*3.1*	*2.3*
Freight	2 205 BB	. . .	. . .	. . .	. . .	*5.5*	*6.3*	*4.2*	*3.5*
Other	2 205 BC	. . .	. . .	. . .	. . .	*13.4*	*12.1*	*15.9*	*10.5*
Sea transport, passenger	2 207 . .	. . .	. . .	. . .	. . .	. . .	. . .	. . .	. . .
Sea transport, freight	2 208 . .	. . .	. . .	. . .	. . .	. . .	. . .	. . .	. . .
Sea transport, other	2 209 . .	. . .	. . .	. . .	. . .	9.4	5.9	6.5	6.2
Air transport, passenger	2 211 . .	. . .	. . .	. . .	. . .	. . .	. . .	. . .	. . .
Air transport, freight	2 212 . .	. . .	. . .	. . .	. . .	. . .	. . .	. . .	. . .
Air transport, other	2 213 . .	. . .	. . .	. . .	. . .	3.9	6.2	9.3	4.3
Other transport, passenger	2 215 . .	. . .	. . .	. . .	. . .	2.8	2.8	3.1	2.3
Other transport, freight	2 216 . .	. . .	. . .	. . .	. . .	5.5	6.3	4.2	3.5
Other transport, other	2 217 . .	. . .	. . .	. . .	. . .	. . .	. . .	. . .	. . .
Transportation services, debit	3 205 . .	**. . .**	**. . .**	**. . .**	**. . .**	**–55.0**	**–55.4**	**–49.9**	**–43.7**
Passenger	3 205 BA	. . .	. . .	. . .	. . .	*–15.9*	*–16.6*	*–14.2*	*–12.5*
Freight	3 205 BB	. . .	. . .	. . .	. . .	*–39.1*	*–38.8*	*–35.7*	*–31.2*
Other	3 205 BC	. . .	. . .	. . .	. . .	. . .	. . .	. . .	. . .
Sea transport, passenger	3 207 . .	. . .	. . .	. . .	. . .	. . .	. . .	. . .	. . .
Sea transport, freight	3 208 . .	. . .	. . .	. . .	. . .	–39.1	–38.8	–35.7	–31.2
Sea transport, other	3 209 . .	. . .	. . .	. . .	. . .	. . .	. . .	. . .	. . .
Air transport, passenger	3 211 . .	. . .	. . .	. . .	. . .	–15.9	–16.6	–14.2	–12.5
Air transport, freight	3 212 . .	. . .	. . .	. . .	. . .	. . .	. . .	. . .	. . .
Air transport, other	3 213 . .	. . .	. . .	. . .	. . .	. . .	. . .	. . .	. . .
Other transport, passenger	3 215 . .	. . .	. . .	. . .	. . .	. . .	. . .	. . .	. . .
Other transport, freight	3 216 . .	. . .	. . .	. . .	. . .	. . .	. . .	. . .	. . .
Other transport, other	3 217 . .	. . .	. . .	. . .	. . .	. . .	. . .	. . .	. . .
Travel, credit	2 236 . .	**. . .**	**. . .**	**. . .**	**. . .**	**5.5**	**11.3**	**3.3**	**4.4**
Business travel	2 237 . .	. . .	. . .	. . .	. . .	. . .	. . .	. . .	. . .
Personal travel	2 240 . .	. . .	. . .	. . .	. . .	. . .	. . .	. . .	. . .
Travel, debit	3 236 . .	**. . .**	**. . .**	**. . .**	**. . .**	**–2.6**	**–5.1**	**–2.6**	**–3.8**
Business travel	3 237 . .	. . .	. . .	. . .	. . .	. . .	. . .	. . .	. . .
Personal travel	3 240 . .	. . .	. . .	. . .	. . .	. . .	. . .	. . .	. . .
Other services, credit	2 200 BA	**. . .**	**. . .**	**. . .**	**. . .**	**117.9**	**124.3**	**125.9**	**130.7**
Communications	2 245 . .	. . .	. . .	. . .	. . .	.2	.2	1.5	1.1
Construction	2 249 . .	. . .	. . .	. . .	. . .	. . .	. . .	. . .	. . .
Insurance	2 253 . .	. . .	. . .	. . .	. . .	. . .	. . .	. . .	. . .
Financial	2 260 . .	. . .	. . .	. . .	. . .	. . .	. . .	. . .	. . .
Computer and information	2 262 . .	. . .	. . .	. . .	. . .	. . .	. . .	. . .	. . .
Royalties and licence fees	2 266 . .	. . .	. . .	. . .	. . .	. . .	. . .	. . .	. . .
Other business services	2 268 . .	. . .	. . .	. . .	. . .	6.5	5.4	5.4	6.1
Personal, cultural, and recreational	2 287 . .	. . .	. . .	. . .	. . .	. . .	. . .	. . .	. . .
Government, n.i.e.	2 291 . .	. . .	. . .	. . .	. . .	111.3	118.7	119.0	123.5
Other services, debit	3 200 BA	**. . .**	**. . .**	**. . .**	**. . .**	**–51.6**	**–50.3**	**–37.1**	**–39.7**
Communications	3 245 . .	. . .	. . .	. . .	. . .	. . .	. . .	. . .	. . .
Construction	3 249 . .	. . .	. . .	. . .	. . .	. . .	. . .	. . .	. . .
Insurance	3 253 . .	. . .	. . .	. . .	. . .	–10.7	–8.6	–7.6	–6.8
Financial	3 260 . .	. . .	. . .	. . .	. . .	. . .	. . .	. . .	. . .
Computer and information	3 262 . .	. . .	. . .	. . .	. . .	. . .	. . .	. . .	. . .
Royalties and licence fees	3 266 . .	. . .	. . .	. . .	. . .	. . .	. . .	. . .	. . .
Other business services	3 268 . .	. . .	. . .	. . .	. . .	–35.8	–36.8	–23.5	–22.3
Personal, cultural, and recreational	3 287 . .	. . .	. . .	. . .	. . .	. . .	. . .	. . .	. . .
Government, n.i.e.	3 291 . .	. . .	. . .	. . .	. . .	–5.1	–4.8	–6.0	–10.6

Table 2 (Continued). STANDARD PRESENTATION, 1988–95
(Millions of U.S. dollars)

	Code		1988	1989	1990	1991	1992	1993	1994	1995
C. INCOME	4 300	..	...	...	...	...	20.0	23.0	16.6	17.2
Total credit	2 300	..	...	...	...	...	*29.4*	*30.3*	*23.7*	*25.9*
Total debit	3 300	..	...	...	...	...	*–9.4*	*–7.2*	*–7.0*	*–8.7*
Compensation of employees, credit	2 310	..	...	...	...	...	**11.6**	**17.5**	**12.0**	**10.9**
Compensation of employees, debit	3 310	..	...	...	...	...	...	...	...	...
Investment income, credit	2 320	..	...	...	...	...	**17.7**	**12.7**	**11.6**	**15.0**
Direct investment income	2 330	..	...	...	...	...	...	...	...	...
Dividends and distributed branch profits	2 332	..	...	...	...	...	...	...	...	...
Reinvested earnings and undistributed branch profits	2 333	..	...	...	...	...	...	...	...	...
Income on debt (interest)	2 334	..	...	...	...	...	...	...	...	...
Portfolio investment income	2 339	..	...	...	...	...	17.7	12.7	11.6	15.0
Income on equity	2 340	..	...	...	...	...	17.7	12.7	11.6	15.0
Income on bonds and notes	2 350	..	...	...	...	...	...	...	...	...
Income on money market instruments and financial derivatives	2 360	..	...	...	...	...	...	...	...	...
Other investment income	2 370	..	...	...	...	...	...	...	...	...
Investment income, debit	3 320	..	...	...	...	...	**–9.4**	**–7.2**	**–7.0**	**–8.7**
Direct investment income	3 330	..	...	...	...	...	–3.3	–2.6	–2.9	–4.6
Dividends and distributed branch profits	3 332	..	...	...	...	...	–1.0	–1.1	–1.4	–1.4
Reinvested earnings and undistributed branch profits	3 333	..	...	...	...	...	–2.3	–1.4	–1.4	–3.2
Income on debt (interest)	3 334	..	...	...	...	...	...	...	...	...
Portfolio investment income	3 339	..	...	...	...	...	...	...	...	...
Income on equity	3 340	..	...	...	...	...	...	...	...	...
Income on bonds and notes	3 350	..	...	...	...	...	...	...	...	...
Income on money market instruments and financial derivatives	3 360	..	...	...	...	...	...	...	...	...
Other investment income	3 370	..	...	...	...	...	–6.0	–4.7	–4.2	–4.0
D. CURRENT TRANSFERS	4 379	..	...	...	...	...	74.5	80.5	55.3	67.0
Credit	2 379	..	...	...	...	...	**90.7**	**96.6**	**73.7**	**85.4**
General government	2 380	..	...	...	...	...	86.8	91.0	67.2	80.7
Other sectors	2 390	..	...	...	...	...	4.0	5.7	6.5	4.7
Workers' remittances	2 391	..	...	...	...	...	1.5	1.5	1.5	1.0
Other current transfers	2 392	..	...	...	...	...	2.5	4.2	5.0	3.7
Debit	3 379	..	...	...	...	...	**–16.3**	**–16.1**	**–18.3**	**–18.4**
General government	3 380	..	...	...	...	...	...	...	–1.0	–.8
Other sectors	3 390	..	...	...	...	...	–16.2	–16.1	–17.3	–17.5
Workers' remittances	3 391	..	...	...	...	...	–16.2	–16.1	–17.3	–17.5
Other current transfers	3 392	..	...	...	...	...	...	...	...	...
CAPITAL AND FINANCIAL ACCOUNT	4 996	..	...	...	...	...	**89.5**	**28.3**	**38.2**	**22.4**
CAPITAL ACCOUNT	4 994	..	...	...	...	...	...	...	...	**18.4**
Total credit	2 994	..	...	...	...	...	...	...	...	*18.4*
Total debit	3 994	..	...	...	...	...	...	...	...	...
Capital transfers, credit	2 400	..	...	...	...	...	...	...	...	**18.4**
General government	2 401	..	...	...	...	...	...	...	...	18.4
Debt forgiveness	2 402	..	...	...	...	...	...	...	...	18.4
Other capital transfers	2 410	..	...	...	...	...	...	...	...	...
Other sectors	2 430	..	...	...	...	...	...	...	...	...
Migrants' transfers	2 431	..	...	...	...	...	...	...	...	...
Debt forgiveness	2 432	..	...	...	...	...	...	...	...	...
Other capital transfers	2 440	..	...	...	...	...	...	...	...	...
Capital transfers, debit	3 400	..	...	...	...	...	...	...	...	...
General government	3 401	..	...	...	...	...	...	...	...	...
Debt forgiveness	3 402	..	...	...	...	...	...	...	...	...
Other capital transfers	3 410	..	...	...	...	...	...	...	...	...
Other sectors	3 430	..	...	...	...	...	...	...	...	...
Migrants' transfers	3 431	..	...	...	...	...	...	...	...	...
Debt forgiveness	3 432	..	...	...	...	...	...	...	...	...
Other capital transfers	3 440	..	...	...	...	...	...	...	...	...
Nonproduced nonfinancial assets, credit	2 480	..	...	...	...	...	...	...	...	...
Nonproduced nonfinancial assets, debit	3 480	..	...	...	...	...	...	...	...	...

Table 2 (Continued). STANDARD PRESENTATION, 1988–95
(Millions of U.S. dollars)

	Code		1988	1989	1990	1991	1992	1993	1994	1995
FINANCIAL ACCOUNT	4 995	. .	**. . .**	**. . .**	**. . .**	**. . .**	**89.5**	**28.3**	**38.2**	**4.0**
A. DIRECT INVESTMENT	4 500	. .	. . .	. . .	. . .	. . .	2.3	1.4	1.4	3.2
Direct investment abroad	4 505	. .	**. . .**	**. . .**	**. . .**	**. . .**	**. . .**	**. . .**	**. . .**	**. . .**
Equity capital	4 510	. .	. . .	. . .	. . .	. . .	. . .	. . .	. . .	. . .
Claims on affiliated enterprises	4 515	. .	. . .	. . .	. . .	. . .	. . .	. . .	. . .	. . .
Liabilities to affiliated enterprises	4 520	. .	. . .	. . .	. . .	. . .	. . .	. . .	. . .	. . .
Reinvested earnings	4 525	. .	. . .	. . .	. . .	. . .	. . .	. . .	. . .	. . .
Other capital	4 530	. .	. . .	. . .	. . .	. . .	. . .	. . .	. . .	. . .
Claims on affiliated enterprises	4 535	. .	. . .	. . .	. . .	. . .	. . .	. . .	. . .	. . .
Liabilities to affiliated enterprises	4 540	. .	. . .	. . .	. . .	. . .	. . .	. . .	. . .	. . .
Direct investment in Djibouti	4 555	. .	**. . .**	**. . .**	**. . .**	**. . .**	**2.3**	**1.4**	**1.4**	**3.2**
Equity capital	4 560	. .	. . .	. . .	. . .	. . .	. . .	. . .	. . .	. . .
Claims on direct investors	4 565	. .	. . .	. . .	. . .	. . .	. . .	. . .	. . .	. . .
Liabilities to direct investors	4 570	. .	. . .	. . .	. . .	. . .	. . .	. . .	. . .	. . .
Reinvested earnings	4 575	. .	. . .	. . .	. . .	. . .	2.3	1.4	1.4	3.2
Other capital	4 580	. .	. . .	. . .	. . .	. . .	. . .	. . .	. . .	. . .
Claims on direct investors	4 585	. .	. . .	. . .	. . .	. . .	. . .	. . .	. . .	. . .
Liabilities to direct investors	4 590	. .	. . .	. . .	. . .	. . .	. . .	. . .	. . .	. . .
B. PORTFOLIO INVESTMENT	4 600	. .	. . .	. . .	. . .	. . .	. . .	. . .	. . .	. . .
Assets	4 602	. .	**. . .**	**. . .**	**. . .**	**. . .**	**. . .**	**. . .**	**. . .**	**. . .**
Equity securities	4 610	. .	. . .	. . .	. . .	. . .	. . .	. . .	. . .	. . .
Monetary authorities	4 611	. .	. . .	. . .	. . .	. . .	. . .	. . .	. . .	. . .
General government	4 612	. .	. . .	. . .	. . .	. . .	. . .	. . .	. . .	. . .
Banks	4 613	. .	. . .	. . .	. . .	. . .	. . .	. . .	. . .	. . .
Other sectors	4 614	. .	. . .	. . .	. . .	. . .	. . .	. . .	. . .	. . .
Debt securities	4 619	. .	. . .	. . .	. . .	. . .	. . .	. . .	. . .	. . .
Bonds and notes	4 620	. .	. . .	. . .	. . .	. . .	. . .	. . .	. . .	. . .
Monetary authorities	4 621	. .	. . .	. . .	. . .	. . .	. . .	. . .	. . .	. . .
General government	4 622	. .	. . .	. . .	. . .	. . .	. . .	. . .	. . .	. . .
Banks	4 623	. .	. . .	. . .	. . .	. . .	. . .	. . .	. . .	. . .
Other sectors	4 624	. .	. . .	. . .	. . .	. . .	. . .	. . .	. . .	. . .
Money market instruments	4 630	. .	. . .	. . .	. . .	. . .	. . .	. . .	. . .	. . .
Monetary authorities	4 631	. .	. . .	. . .	. . .	. . .	. . .	. . .	. . .	. . .
General government	4 632	. .	. . .	. . .	. . .	. . .	. . .	. . .	. . .	. . .
Banks	4 633	. .	. . .	. . .	. . .	. . .	. . .	. . .	. . .	. . .
Other sectors	4 634	. .	. . .	. . .	. . .	. . .	. . .	. . .	. . .	. . .
Financial derivatives	4 640	. .	. . .	. . .	. . .	. . .	. . .	. . .	. . .	. . .
Monetary authorities	4 641	. .	. . .	. . .	. . .	. . .	. . .	. . .	. . .	. . .
General government	4 642	. .	. . .	. . .	. . .	. . .	. . .	. . .	. . .	. . .
Banks	4 643	. .	. . .	. . .	. . .	. . .	. . .	. . .	. . .	. . .
Other sectors	4 644	. .	. . .	. . .	. . .	. . .	. . .	. . .	. . .	. . .
Liabilities	4 652	. .	**. . .**	**. . .**	**. . .**	**. . .**	**. . .**	**. . .**	**. . .**	**. . .**
Equity securities	4 660	. .	. . .	. . .	. . .	. . .	. . .	. . .	. . .	. . .
Banks	4 663	. .	. . .	. . .	. . .	. . .	. . .	. . .	. . .	. . .
Other sectors	4 664	. .	. . .	. . .	. . .	. . .	. . .	. . .	. . .	. . .
Debt securities	4 669	. .	. . .	. . .	. . .	. . .	. . .	. . .	. . .	. . .
Bonds and notes	4 670	. .	. . .	. . .	. . .	. . .	. . .	. . .	. . .	. . .
Monetary authorities	4 671	. .	. . .	. . .	. . .	. . .	. . .	. . .	. . .	. . .
General government	4 672	. .	. . .	. . .	. . .	. . .	. . .	. . .	. . .	. . .
Banks	4 673	. .	. . .	. . .	. . .	. . .	. . .	. . .	. . .	. . .
Other sectors	4 674	. .	. . .	. . .	. . .	. . .	. . .	. . .	. . .	. . .
Money market instruments	4 680	. .	. . .	. . .	. . .	. . .	. . .	. . .	. . .	. . .
Monetary authorities	4 681	. .	. . .	. . .	. . .	. . .	. . .	. . .	. . .	. . .
General government	4 682	. .	. . .	. . .	. . .	. . .	. . .	. . .	. . .	. . .
Banks	4 683	. .	. . .	. . .	. . .	. . .	. . .	. . .	. . .	. . .
Other sectors	4 684	. .	. . .	. . .	. . .	. . .	. . .	. . .	. . .	. . .
Financial derivatives	4 690	. .	. . .	. . .	. . .	. . .	. . .	. . .	. . .	. . .
Monetary authorities	4 691	. .	. . .	. . .	. . .	. . .	. . .	. . .	. . .	. . .
General government	4 692	. .	. . .	. . .	. . .	. . .	. . .	. . .	. . .	. . .
Banks	4 693	. .	. . .	. . .	. . .	. . .	. . .	. . .	. . .	. . .
Other sectors	4 694	. .	. . .	. . .	. . .	. . .	. . .	. . .	. . .	. . .

Table 2 (Concluded). STANDARD PRESENTATION, 1988–95
(Millions of U.S. dollars)

	Code	1988	1989	1990	1991	1992	1993	1994	1995
C. OTHER INVESTMENT	4 700	...	...	...	...	71.7	15.6	40.2	–6.5
Assets	4 703	...	...	...	...	...	...	...	...
Trade credits	4 706	...	...	...	...	...	...	...	...
General government: long-term	4 708	...	...	...	...	...	...	...	...
General government: short-term	4 709	...	...	...	...	...	...	...	...
Other sectors: long-term	4 711	...	...	...	...	...	...	...	...
Other sectors: short-term	4 712	...	...	...	...	...	...	...	...
Loans	4 714	...	...	...	...	...	...	...	...
Monetary authorities: long-term	4 717	...	...	...	...	...	...	...	...
Monetary authorities: short-term	4 718	...	...	...	...	...	...	...	...
General government: long-term	4 720	...	...	...	...	...	...	...	...
General government: short-term	4 721	...	...	...	...	...	...	...	...
Banks: long-term	4 723	...	...	...	...	...	...	...	...
Banks: short-term	4 724	...	...	...	...	...	...	...	...
Other sectors: long-term	4 726	...	...	...	...	...	...	...	...
Other sectors: short-term	4 727	...	...	...	...	...	...	...	...
Currency and deposits	4 730	...	...	...	...	...	...	...	...
Monetary authorities	4 731	...	...	...	...	...	...	...	...
General government	4 732	...	...	...	...	...	...	...	...
Banks	4 733	...	...	...	...	...	...	...	...
Other sectors	4 734	...	...	...	...	...	...	...	...
Other assets	4 736	...	...	...	...	...	...	...	...
Monetary authorities: long-term	4 738	...	...	...	...	...	...	...	...
Monetary authorities: short-term	4 739	...	...	...	...	...	...	...	...
General government: long-term	4 741	...	...	...	...	...	...	...	...
General government: short-term	4 742	...	...	...	...	...	...	...	...
Banks: long-term	4 744	...	...	...	...	...	...	...	...
Banks: short-term	4 745	...	...	...	...	...	...	...	...
Other sectors: long-term	4 747	...	...	...	...	...	...	...	...
Other sectors: short-term	4 748	...	...	...	...	...	...	...	...
Liabilities	4 753	...	...	...	...	**71.7**	**15.6**	**40.2**	**–6.5**
Trade credits	4 756	...	...	...	...	...	...	...	...
General government: long-term	4 758	...	...	...	...	...	...	...	...
General government: short-term	4 759	...	...	...	...	...	...	...	...
Other sectors: long-term	4 761	...	...	...	...	...	...	...	...
Other sectors: short-term	4 762	...	...	...	...	...	...	...	...
Loans	4 764	...	...	...	...	34.1	34.0	26.1	–9.4
Use of Fund credit and loans from the Fund	4 766	...	...	...	...	...	...	...	...
Monetary authorities: other long-term	4 767	...	...	...	...	...	...	...	...
Monetary authorities: short-term	4 768	...	...	...	...	...	...	...	...
General government: long-term	4 770	...	...	...	...	8.1	15.9	12.0	–9.4
General government: short-term	4 771	...	...	...	...	...	...	...	...
Banks: long-term	4 773	...	...	...	...	...	...	...	...
Banks: short-term	4 774	...	...	...	...	...	...	...	...
Other sectors: long-term	4 776	...	...	...	...	26.0	18.1	14.1	.1
Other sectors: short-term	4 777	...	...	...	...	...	...	...	...
Currency and deposits	4 780	...	...	...	...	37.6	–18.8	11.6	4.0
Monetary authorities	4 781	...	...	...	...	...	...	...	...
General government	4 782	...	...	...	...	...	...	...	...
Banks	4 783	...	...	...	...	37.6	–18.8	11.6	4.0
Other sectors	4 784	...	...	...	...	...	...	...	...
Other liabilities	4 786	...	...	...	...	...	.4	2.6	–1.2
Monetary authorities: long-term	4 788	...	...	...	...	...	...	...	...
Monetary authorities: short-term	4 789	...	...	...	...	...	...	...	...
General government: long-term	4 791	...	...	...	...	...	...	...	...
General government: short-term	4 792	...	...	...	...	...	.4	2.6	–1.2
Banks: long-term	4 794	...	...	...	...	...	...	...	...
Banks: short-term	4 795	...	...	...	...	...	...	...	...
Other sectors: long-term	4 797	...	...	...	...	...	...	...	...
Other sectors: short-term	4 798	...	...	...	...	...	...	...	...
D. RESERVE ASSETS	4 800	...	...	...	...	15.5	11.3	–3.4	7.3
Monetary gold	4 810	...	...	...	...	...	...	...	...
Special drawing rights	4 820	...	...	...	...	.1	...	.1	.1
Reserve position in the Fund	4 830	...	...	...	...	–1.2	3.0	...	...
Foreign exchange	4 840	...	...	...	...	16.7	8.3	–3.5	7.2
Other claims	4 880	...	...	...	...	...	...	...	...
NET ERRORS AND OMISSIONS	4 998	...	...	...	...	**–2.0**	**6.0**	**7.9**	**.7**

Part 3 of the *Yearbook* contains descriptions of the methodologies, compilation practices, and sources used to compile these data.

Table 1. ANALYTIC PRESENTATION, 1988–95
(Millions of U.S. dollars)

	Code	1988	1989	1990	1991	1992	1993	1994	1995
A. Current Account [1]	4 993 Y.	**–12.30**	**–45.54**	**–43.53**	**–33.61**	**–25.73**	**–28.16**	**–35.73**	**. . .**
Goods: exports f.o.b	2 100 . .	57.04	46.30	56.07	55.62	55.10	47.29	43.98	. . .
Goods: imports f.o.b	3 100 . .	–77.24	–94.42	–103.95	–96.47	–92.79	–93.87	–95.83	. . .
Balance on Goods	4 100 . .	*–20.21*	*–48.12*	*–47.88*	*–40.86*	*–37.70*	*–46.59*	*–51.85*	. . .
Services: credit	2 200 . .	20.89	24.95	33.38	37.41	44.19	46.93	51.58	. . .
Services: debit	3 200 . .	–21.64	–25.84	–30.00	–29.84	–32.43	–30.59	–32.97	. . .
Balance on Goods and Services	4 991 . .	*–20.96*	*–49.01*	*–44.50*	*–33.29*	*–25.94*	*–30.24*	*–33.24*	. . .
Income: credit	2 300 . .	4.33	3.60	4.03	2.60	2.50	2.97	3.07	. . .
Income: debit	3 300 . .	–5.89	–7.59	–8.92	–10.27	–9.86	–9.58	–13.98	. . .
Balance on Goods, Services, and Income	4 992 . .	*–22.52*	*–53.00*	*–49.39*	*–40.95*	*–33.30*	*–36.85*	*–44.14*	. . .
Current transfers: credit	2 379 Y.	13.16	10.24	10.39	11.20	10.88	12.42	14.82	. . .
Current transfers: debit	3 379 . .	–2.93	–2.78	–4.53	–3.87	–3.31	–3.73	–6.41	. . .
B. Capital Account [1]	4 994 Y.	**11.37**	**13.58**	**13.50**	**13.19**	**9.80**	**9.73**	**8.02**	**. . .**
Capital account: credit	2 994 Y.	12.85	15.58	14.96	14.74	11.28	11.21	8.20	. . .
Capital account: debit	3 994 . .	–1.48	–2.00	–1.45	–1.56	–1.48	–1.48	–.19	. . .
Total, Groups A Plus B	4 010 . .	*–.93*	*–31.96*	*–30.03*	*–20.43*	*–15.93*	*–18.43*	*–27.71*	. . .
C. Financial Account [1]	4 995 X.	**5.11**	**32.03**	**29.32**	**24.59**	**24.29**	**18.06**	**25.83**	**. . .**
Direct investment abroad	4 505 . .	. . .	. . .	. . .	. . .	. . .	. . .	. . .	. . .
Direct investment in Dominica	4 555 Y.	11.93	17.20	12.89	15.22	20.58	13.21	22.13	. . .
Portfolio investment assets	4 602 . .	. . .	. . .	. . .	. . .	. . .	. . .	. . .	. . .
Equity securities	4 610 . .	. . .	. . .	. . .	. . .	. . .	. . .	. . .	. . .
Debt securities	4 619 . .	. . .	. . .	. . .	. . .	. . .	. . .	. . .	. . .
Portfolio investment liabilities	4 652 Y.	. . .	. . .	–.37	. . .	. . .	–.10	. . .	. . .
Equity securities	4 660 Y.	. . .	. . .	–.37	. . .	. . .	–.10	. . .	. . .
Debt securities	4 669 Y.	. . .	. . .	. . .	. . .	. . .	. . .	. . .	. . .
Other investment assets	4 703 . .	–8.48	8.18	10.78	3.06	.90	5.61	5.96	. . .
Monetary authorities	4 703 .A	. . .	. . .	. . .	. . .	. . .	. . .	. . .	. . .
General government	4 703 .B	. . .	. . .	. . .	. . .	. . .	. . .	. . .	. . .
Banks	4 703 .C	–8.48	8.18	10.78	3.06	.90	5.61	5.96	. . .
Other sectors	4 703 .D	. . .	. . .	. . .	. . .	. . .	. . .	. . .	. . .
Other investment liabilities	4 753 X.	1.67	6.66	6.02	6.31	2.81	–.67	–2.26	. . .
Monetary authorities	4 753 XA	. . .	. . .	. . .	. . .	. . .	. . .	. . .	. . .
General government	4 753 YB	1.83	6.95	7.14	8.01	4.04	–.18	–1.79	. . .
Banks	4 753 YC	. . .	. . .	. . .	. . .	. . .	. . .	. . .	. . .
Other sectors	4 753 YD	–.16	–.30	–1.11	–1.70	–1.23	–.49	–.47	. . .
Total, Groups A Through C	4 020 . .	*4.19*	*.07*	*–.70*	*4.16*	*8.36*	*–.37*	*–1.88*	. . .
D. Net Errors and Omissions	4 998 . .	**–5.22**	**.11**	**5.75**	**.07**	**–5.00**	**1.00**	**–1.36**	**. . .**
Total, Groups A Through D	4 030 . .	*–1.03*	*.18*	*5.05*	*4.22*	*3.36*	*.62*	*–3.24*	. . .
E. Reserves and Related Items	4 040 . .	**1.03**	**–.18**	**–5.05**	**–4.22**	**–3.36**	**–.62**	**3.24**	**. . .**
Reserve assets	4 800 . .	3.23	1.83	–3.70	–3.29	–2.60	.11	4.04	. . .
Use of Fund credit and loans	4 766 . .	–2.27	–2.03	–1.35	–.94	–.76	–.73	–.80	. . .
Liabilities constituting foreign authorities' reserves	4 900 . .	. . .	. . .	. . .	. . .	. . .	. . .	. . .	. . .
Exceptional financing	4 920 . .	.07	.03	. . .	. . .	. . .	. . .	. . .	. . .
Conversion rates: Eastern Caribbean dollars per U.S. dollar	0 101 . .	**2.70000**	**2.70000**	**2.70000**	**2.70000**	**2.70000**	**2.70000**	**2.70000**	**2.70000**

[1] Excludes components that have been classified in the categories of Group E.

Table 2. STANDARD PRESENTATION, 1988–95
(Millions of U.S. dollars)

	Code	1988	1989	1990	1991	1992	1993	1994	1995
CURRENT ACCOUNT	4 993 . .	**–12.23**	**–45.51**	**–43.53**	**–33.61**	**–25.73**	**–28.16**	**–35.73**	. . .
A. GOODS	4 100 . .	–20.21	–48.12	–47.88	–40.86	–37.70	–46.59	–51.85	. . .
Credit	2 100 . .	**57.04**	**46.30**	**56.07**	**55.62**	**55.10**	**47.29**	**43.98**	. . .
General merchandise: exports f.o.b.	2 110 . .	57.03	46.30	56.06	55.56	54.56	47.15	43.30	. . .
Goods for processing: exports f.o.b.	2 150 . .	. . .	. . .	. . .	. . .	. . .	. . .	. . .	. . .
Repairs on goods	2 160 . .	. . .	. . .	. . .	. . .	. . .	. . .	. . .	. . .
Goods procured in ports by carriers	2 170 . .	.01	.01	.01	.06	.53	.14	.68	. . .
Nonmonetary gold	2 180 . .	. . .	. . .	. . .	. . .	. . .	. . .	. . .	. . .
Debit	3 100 . .	**–77.24**	**–94.42**	**–103.95**	**–96.47**	**–92.79**	**–93.87**	**–95.83**	. . .
General merchandise: imports f.o.b.	3 110 . .	–77.24	–94.42	–103.95	–96.47	–92.79	–93.80	–95.76	. . .
Goods for processing: imports f.o.b.	3 150 . .	. . .	. . .	. . .	. . .	. . .	. . .	. . .	. . .
Repairs on goods	3 160 . .	. . .	. . .	. . .	. . .	. . .	. . .	. . .	. . .
Goods procured in ports by carriers	3 170 . .	. . .	. . .	. . .	. . .	. . .	–.07	–.07	. . .
Nonmonetary gold	3 180 . .	. . .	. . .	. . .	. . .	. . .	. . .	. . .	. . .
B. SERVICES	4 200 . .	–.75	–.89	3.38	7.57	11.76	16.34	18.61	. . .
Total credit	2 200 . .	*20.89*	*24.95*	*33.38*	*37.41*	*44.19*	*46.93*	*51.58*	. . .
Total debit	3 200 . .	*–21.64*	*–25.84*	*–30.00*	*–29.84*	*–32.43*	*–30.59*	*–32.97*	. . .
Transportation services, credit	2 205 . .	**2.33**	**2.87**	**3.57**	**4.01**	**4.93**	**6.15**	**5.96**	. . .
Passenger	2 205 BA	. . .	. . .	. . .	. . .	. . .	*.07*	*.21*	. . .
Freight	2 205 BB	. . .	. . .	*.47*	*.83*	. . .	*.01*	*.08*	. . .
Other	2 205 BC	*2.33*	*2.87*	*3.10*	*3.18*	*4.93*	*6.06*	*5.67*	. . .
Sea transport, passenger	2 207 . .	. . .	. . .	. . .	. . .	. . .	. . .	. . .	. . .
Sea transport, freight	2 208 . .	. . .	. . .	. . .	. . .	. . .	. . .	. . .	. . .
Sea transport, other	2 209 . .	. . .	. . .	. . .	. . .	. . .	. . .	. . .	. . .
Air transport, passenger	2 211 . .	. . .	. . .	. . .	. . .	. . .	. . .	. . .	. . .
Air transport, freight	2 212 . .	. . .	. . .	. . .	. . .	. . .	. . .	. . .	. . .
Air transport, other	2 213 . .	. . .	. . .	. . .	. . .	. . .	. . .	. . .	. . .
Other transport, passenger	2 215 . .	. . .	. . .	. . .	. . .	. . .	. . .	. . .	. . .
Other transport, freight	2 216 . .	. . .	. . .	. . .	. . .	. . .	. . .	. . .	. . .
Other transport, other	2 217 . .	. . .	. . .	. . .	. . .	. . .	. . .	. . .	. . .
Transportation services, debit	3 205 . .	**–12.11**	**–14.77**	**–15.23**	**–15.25**	**–16.54**	**–16.14**	**–17.71**	. . .
Passenger	3 205 BA	*–3.26*	*–3.92*	*–3.37*	*–4.16*	*–5.95*	*–5.26*	*–6.75*	. . .
Freight	3 205 BB	*–8.85*	*–10.85*	*–11.86*	*–11.09*	*–10.59*	*–10.88*	*–10.95*	. . .
Other	3 205 BC	. . .	. . .	. . .	. . .	. . .	*–.01*	*–.02*	. . .
Sea transport, passenger	3 207 . .	. . .	. . .	. . .	. . .	. . .	. . .	. . .	. . .
Sea transport, freight	3 208 . .	. . .	. . .	. . .	. . .	. . .	. . .	. . .	. . .
Sea transport, other	3 209 . .	. . .	. . .	. . .	. . .	. . .	. . .	. . .	. . .
Air transport, passenger	3 211 . .	. . .	. . .	. . .	. . .	. . .	. . .	. . .	. . .
Air transport, freight	3 212 . .	. . .	. . .	. . .	. . .	. . .	. . .	. . .	. . .
Air transport, other	3 213 . .	. . .	. . .	. . .	. . .	. . .	. . .	. . .	. . .
Other transport, passenger	3 215 . .	. . .	. . .	. . .	. . .	. . .	. . .	. . .	. . .
Other transport, freight	3 216 . .	. . .	. . .	. . .	. . .	. . .	. . .	. . .	. . .
Other transport, other	3 217 . .	. . .	. . .	. . .	. . .	. . .	. . .	. . .	. . .
Travel, credit	2 236 . .	**13.08**	**15.70**	**20.43**	**24.15**	**25.45**	**27.87**	**30.57**	. . .
Business travel	2 237 . .	. . .	. . .	. . .	. . .	. . .	. . .	. . .	. . .
Personal travel	2 240 . .	. . .	. . .	. . .	. . .	. . .	. . .	. . .	. . .
Travel, debit	3 236 . .	**–2.22**	**–3.57**	**–4.41**	**–4.63**	**–5.64**	**–4.96**	**–4.19**	. . .
Business travel	3 237 . .	. . .	. . .	. . .	. . .	. . .	. . .	. . .	. . .
Personal travel	3 240 . .	. . .	. . .	. . .	. . .	. . .	. . .	. . .	. . .
Other services, credit	2 200 BA	**5.48**	**6.38**	**9.37**	**9.26**	**13.80**	**12.91**	**15.05**	. . .
Communications	2 245 . .	. . .	. . .	. . .	. . .	. . .	. . .	. . .	. . .
Construction	2 249 . .	. . .	. . .	. . .	. . .	. . .	. . .	. . .	. . .
Insurance	2 253 . .	1.02	2.07	3.73	1.34	3.62	3.07	2.79	. . .
Financial	2 260 . .	. . .	. . .	. . .	. . .	. . .	. . .	. . .	. . .
Computer and information	2 262 . .	. . .	. . .	. . .	. . .	. . .	. . .	. . .	. . .
Royalties and licence fees	2 266 . .	. . .	. . .	. . .	. . .	. . .	. . .	. . .	. . .
Other business services	2 268 . .	3.79	3.62	5.23	7.17	9.11	8.76	11.88	. . .
Personal, cultural, and recreational	2 287 . .	. . .	. . .	. . .	. . .	. . .	. . .	. . .	. . .
Government, n.i.e.	2 291 . .	.67	.69	.41	.74	1.07	1.08	.39	. . .
Other services, debit	3 200 BA	**–7.31**	**–7.50**	**–10.37**	**–9.97**	**–10.25**	**–9.49**	**–11.07**	. . .
Communications	3 245 . .	. . .	. . .	. . .	. . .	. . .	. . .	. . .	. . .
Construction	3 249 . .	. . .	. . .	. . .	. . .	. . .	. . .	1.36	. . .
Insurance	3 253 . .	–2.32	–3.16	–3.56	–3.32	–3.59	–3.16	–3.49	. . .
Financial	3 260 . .	. . .	. . .	. . .	. . .	. . .	. . .	. . .	. . .
Computer and information	3 262 . .	. . .	. . .	. . .	. . .	. . .	. . .	. . .	. . .
Royalties and licence fees	3 266 . .	–.10	–.10	–.10	–.08	–.10	–.09	.09	. . .
Other business services	3 268 . .	–4.37	–3.57	–6.34	–4.41	–4.38	–3.84	–4.24	. . .
Personal, cultural, and recreational	3 287 . .	. . .	. . .	. . .	. . .	. . .	. . .	. . .	. . .
Government, n.i.e.	3 291 . .	–.52	–.67	–.37	–2.16	–2.18	–2.39	–4.80	. . .

Table 2 (Continued). STANDARD PRESENTATION, 1988–95
(Millions of U.S. dollars)

	Code	1988	1989	1990	1991	1992	1993	1994	1995
C. INCOME	4 300 . .	-1.56	-3.99	-4.89	-7.66	-7.36	-6.61	-10.90	...
Total credit	2 300 . .	*4.33*	*3.60*	*4.03*	*2.60*	*2.50*	*2.97*	*3.07*	...
Total debit	3 300 . .	*-5.89*	*-7.59*	*-8.92*	*-10.27*	*-9.86*	*-9.58*	*-13.98*	...
Compensation of employees, credit	2 310 . .	**.67**	**.78**	**.43**	**.40**	**.24**	**.03**	**.03**	...
Compensation of employees, debit	3 310 . .	**-.33**	**-.45**	**-.16**	**-.20**	**-.12**	**-.02**	**-.37**	...
Investment income, credit	2 320 . .	**3.66**	**2.82**	**3.60**	**2.20**	**2.26**	**2.94**	**3.05**	...
Direct investment income	2 330 . .	...	...	.12	.12	.18	.88	...	...
Dividends and distributed branch profits	2 332 . .	...	...	.12	.12	.18	.88	...	...
Reinvested earnings and undistributed branch profits	2 333 . .	...	...	...	...	...	...	...	...
Income on debt (interest)	2 334 . .	...	...	...	...	...	...	...	...
Portfolio investment income	2 339 . .	...	...	...	...	...	...	...	...
Income on equity	2 340 . .	...	...	...	...	...	...	...	...
Income on bonds and notes	2 350 . .	...	...	...	...	...	...	...	...
Income on money market instruments and financial derivatives	2 360 . .	...	...	...	...	...	...	...	...
Other investment income	2 370 . .	3.66	2.82	3.48	2.09	2.08	2.06	3.05	...
Investment income, debit	3 320 . .	**-5.56**	**-7.14**	**-8.76**	**-10.07**	**-9.74**	**-9.56**	**-13.61**	...
Direct investment income	3 330 . .	-3.04	-4.04	-5.41	-6.43	-6.36	-5.52	-9.62	...
Dividends and distributed branch profits	3 332 . .	-1.00	-2.85	-2.30	-2.76	-3.22	-3.61	-4.52	...
Reinvested earnings and undistributed branch profits	3 333 . .	-2.04	-1.19	-3.11	-3.67	-3.14	-1.87	-5.10	...
Income on debt (interest)	3 334 . .	...	...	...	...	...	-.04	...	...
Portfolio investment income	3 339 . .	...	...	...	...	...	...	...	...
Income on equity	3 340 . .	...	...	...	...	...	...	...	...
Income on bonds and notes	3 350 . .	...	...	...	...	...	...	...	...
Income on money market instruments and financial derivatives	3 360 . .	...	...	...	...	...	...	...	...
Other investment income	3 370 . .	-2.52	-3.10	-3.34	-3.64	-3.38	-4.04	-3.99	...
D. CURRENT TRANSFERS	4 379 . .	10.29	7.49	5.86	7.34	7.57	8.70	8.41	...
Credit	2 379 . .	**13.22**	**10.26**	**10.39**	**11.20**	**10.88**	**12.42**	**14.82**	...
General government	2 380 . .	.37	.37	.38	1.49	1.90	1.37	3.30	...
Other sectors	2 390 . .	12.85	9.89	10.01	9.71	8.98	11.06	11.52	...
Workers' remittances	2 391 . .	12.85	9.26	9.35	8.31	8.22	9.59	10.30	...
Other current transfers	2 392 . .	...	.63	.66	1.40	.76	1.47	1.23	...
Debit	3 379 . .	**-2.93**	**-2.78**	**-4.53**	**-3.87**	**-3.31**	**-3.73**	**-6.41**	...
General government	3 380 . .	-1.63	-1.30	-1.78	-1.93	-1.97	-2.39	-1.97	...
Other sectors	3 390 . .	-1.30	-1.48	-2.75	-1.94	-1.33	-1.34	-4.44	...
Workers' remittances	3 391 . .	...	...	...	...	...	...	.07	...
Other current transfers	3 392 . .	-1.30	-1.48	-2.75	-1.94	-1.33	-1.34	-4.51	...
CAPITAL AND FINANCIAL ACCOUNT	4 996 . .	**17.45**	**45.40**	**37.78**	**33.55**	**30.73**	**27.16**	**37.09**	...
CAPITAL ACCOUNT	4 994 . .	**11.37**	**13.58**	**13.50**	**13.19**	**9.80**	**9.73**	**8.02**	...
Total credit	2 994 . .	*12.85*	*15.58*	*14.96*	*14.74*	*11.28*	*11.21*	*8.20*	...
Total debit	3 994 . .	*-1.48*	*-2.00*	*-1.45*	*-1.56*	*-1.48*	*-1.48*	*-.19*	...
Capital transfers, credit	2 400 . .	**12.85**	**15.58**	**14.96**	**14.74**	**11.28**	**11.21**	**8.20**	...
General government	2 401 . .	10.26	12.25	10.81	10.19	6.35	7.09	5.24	...
Debt forgiveness	2 402 . .	...	...	...	...	...	...	...	...
Other capital transfers	2 410 . .	10.26	12.25	10.81	10.19	6.35	7.09	5.24	...
Other sectors	2 430 . .	2.59	3.33	4.14	4.56	4.93	4.12	2.96	...
Migrants' transfers	2 431 . .	2.59	3.33	4.14	4.56	4.93	4.12	2.96	...
Debt forgiveness	2 432 . .	...	...	...	...	...	...	...	...
Other capital transfers	2 440 . .	...	...	...	...	...	...	...	...
Capital transfers, debit	3 400 . .	**-1.48**	**-2.00**	**-1.45**	**-1.56**	**-1.48**	**-1.48**	**-.19**	...
General government	3 401 . .	...	-.36	...	...	...	...	...	...
Debt forgiveness	3 402 . .	...	...	...	...	...	...	...	...
Other capital transfers	3 410 . .	...	-.36	...	...	...	...	...	...
Other sectors	3 430 . .	-1.48	-1.65	-1.45	-1.56	-1.48	-1.48	-.19	...
Migrants' transfers	3 431 . .	-1.48	-1.65	-1.45	-1.56	-1.48	-1.48	-.19	...
Debt forgiveness	3 432 . .	...	...	...	...	...	...	...	...
Other capital transfers	3 440 . .	...	...	...	...	...	...	...	...
Nonproduced nonfinancial assets, credit	2 480 . .	...	...	...	...	...	...	...	...
Nonproduced nonfinancial assets, debit	3 480 . .	...	...	...	...	...	...	...	...

Table 2 (Continued). STANDARD PRESENTATION, 1988–95
(Millions of U.S. dollars)

	Code	1988	1989	1990	1991	1992	1993	1994	1995
FINANCIAL ACCOUNT	4 995 . .	**6.08**	**31.83**	**24.27**	**20.36**	**20.94**	**17.43**	**29.07**	**. . .**
A. DIRECT INVESTMENT	4 500 . .	11.93	17.20	12.89	15.22	20.58	13.21	22.13	. . .
Direct investment abroad	4 505 . .	**. . .**	**. . .**	**. . .**	**. . .**	**. . .**	**. . .**	**. . .**	**. . .**
Equity capital	4 510 . .	. . .	. . .	. . .	. . .	. . .	. . .	. . .	. . .
Claims on affiliated enterprises	4 515 . .	. . .	. . .	. . .	. . .	. . .	. . .	. . .	. . .
Liabilities to affiliated enterprises	4 520 . .	. . .	. . .	. . .	. . .	. . .	. . .	. . .	. . .
Reinvested earnings	4 525 . .	. . .	. . .	. . .	. . .	. . .	. . .	. . .	. . .
Other capital	4 530 . .	. . .	. . .	. . .	. . .	. . .	. . .	. . .	. . .
Claims on affiliated enterprises	4 535 . .	. . .	. . .	. . .	. . .	. . .	. . .	. . .	. . .
Liabilities to affiliated enterprises	4 540 . .	. . .	. . .	. . .	. . .	. . .	. . .	. . .	. . .
Direct investment in Dominica	4 555 . .	**11.93**	**17.20**	**12.89**	**15.22**	**20.58**	**13.21**	**22.13**	**. . .**
Equity capital	4 560 . .	4.37	6.70	4.26	5.19	4.51	4.80	8.23	. . .
Claims on direct investors	4 565 . .	. . .	. . .	. . .	. . .	. . .	. . .	. . .	. . .
Liabilities to direct investors	4 570 . .	. . .	. . .	. . .	. . .	. . .	. . .	. . .	. . .
Reinvested earnings	4 575 . .	2.04	1.19	3.11	3.67	3.14	1.87	5.10	. . .
Other capital	4 580 . .	5.52	9.30	5.52	6.36	12.93	6.54	8.81	. . .
Claims on direct investors	4 585 . .	. . .	. . .	. . .	. . .	. . .	. . .	. . .	. . .
Liabilities to direct investors	4 590 . .	. . .	. . .	. . .	. . .	. . .	. . .	. . .	. . .
B. PORTFOLIO INVESTMENT	4 600 . .	. . .	. . .	–.37	. . .	. . .	–.10	. . .	. . .
Assets	4 602 . .	**. . .**	**. . .**	**. . .**	**. . .**	**. . .**	**. . .**	**. . .**	**. . .**
Equity securities	4 610 . .	. . .	. . .	. . .	. . .	. . .	. . .	. . .	. . .
Monetary authorities	4 611 . .	. . .	. . .	. . .	. . .	. . .	. . .	. . .	. . .
General government	4 612 . .	. . .	. . .	. . .	. . .	. . .	. . .	. . .	. . .
Banks	4 613 . .	. . .	. . .	. . .	. . .	. . .	. . .	. . .	. . .
Other sectors	4 614 . .	. . .	. . .	. . .	. . .	. . .	. . .	. . .	. . .
Debt securities	4 619 . .	. . .	. . .	. . .	. . .	. . .	. . .	. . .	. . .
Bonds and notes	4 620 . .	. . .	. . .	. . .	. . .	. . .	. . .	. . .	. . .
Monetary authorities	4 621 . .	. . .	. . .	. . .	. . .	. . .	. . .	. . .	. . .
General government	4 622 . .	. . .	. . .	. . .	. . .	. . .	. . .	. . .	. . .
Banks	4 623 . .	. . .	. . .	. . .	. . .	. . .	. . .	. . .	. . .
Other sectors	4 624 . .	. . .	. . .	. . .	. . .	. . .	. . .	. . .	. . .
Money market instruments	4 630 . .	. . .	. . .	. . .	. . .	. . .	. . .	. . .	. . .
Monetary authorities	4 631 . .	. . .	. . .	. . .	. . .	. . .	. . .	. . .	. . .
General government	4 632 . .	. . .	. . .	. . .	. . .	. . .	. . .	. . .	. . .
Banks	4 633 . .	. . .	. . .	. . .	. . .	. . .	. . .	. . .	. . .
Other sectors	4 634 . .	. . .	. . .	. . .	. . .	. . .	. . .	. . .	. . .
Financial derivatives	4 640 . .	. . .	. . .	. . .	. . .	. . .	. . .	. . .	. . .
Monetary authorities	4 641 . .	. . .	. . .	. . .	. . .	. . .	. . .	. . .	. . .
General government	4 642 . .	. . .	. . .	. . .	. . .	. . .	. . .	. . .	. . .
Banks	4 643 . .	. . .	. . .	. . .	. . .	. . .	. . .	. . .	. . .
Other sectors	4 644 . .	. . .	. . .	. . .	. . .	. . .	. . .	. . .	. . .
Liabilities	4 652 . .	**. . .**	**. . .**	**–.37**	**. . .**	**. . .**	**–.10**	**. . .**	**. . .**
Equity securities	4 660 . .	. . .	. . .	–.37	. . .	. . .	–.10	. . .	. . .
Banks	4 663 . .	. . .	. . .	–.37	. . .	. . .	–.10	. . .	. . .
Other sectors	4 664 . .	. . .	. . .	. . .	. . .	. . .	. . .	. . .	. . .
Debt securities	4 669 . .	. . .	. . .	. . .	. . .	. . .	. . .	. . .	. . .
Bonds and notes	4 670 . .	. . .	. . .	. . .	. . .	. . .	. . .	. . .	. . .
Monetary authorities	4 671 . .	. . .	. . .	. . .	. . .	. . .	. . .	. . .	. . .
General government	4 672 . .	. . .	. . .	. . .	. . .	. . .	. . .	. . .	. . .
Banks	4 673 . .	. . .	. . .	. . .	. . .	. . .	. . .	. . .	. . .
Other sectors	4 674 . .	. . .	. . .	. . .	. . .	. . .	. . .	. . .	. . .
Money market instruments	4 680 . .	. . .	. . .	. . .	. . .	. . .	. . .	. . .	. . .
Monetary authorities	4 681 . .	. . .	. . .	. . .	. . .	. . .	. . .	. . .	. . .
General government	4 682 . .	. . .	. . .	. . .	. . .	. . .	. . .	. . .	. . .
Banks	4 683 . .	. . .	. . .	. . .	. . .	. . .	. . .	. . .	. . .
Other sectors	4 684 . .	. . .	. . .	. . .	. . .	. . .	. . .	. . .	. . .
Financial derivatives	4 690 . .	. . .	. . .	. . .	. . .	. . .	. . .	. . .	. . .
Monetary authorities	4 691 . .	. . .	. . .	. . .	. . .	. . .	. . .	. . .	. . .
General government	4 692 . .	. . .	. . .	. . .	. . .	. . .	. . .	. . .	. . .
Banks	4 693 . .	. . .	. . .	. . .	. . .	. . .	. . .	. . .	. . .
Other sectors	4 694 . .	. . .	. . .	. . .	. . .	. . .	. . .	. . .	. . .

Table 2 (Concluded). STANDARD PRESENTATION, 1988–95
(Millions of U.S. dollars)

	Code	1988	1989	1990	1991	1992	1993	1994	1995
C. OTHER INVESTMENT	4 700 . .	–9.08	12.80	15.45	8.43	2.96	4.21	2.90	...
Assets	4 703 . .	**–8.48**	**8.18**	**10.78**	**3.06**	**.90**	**5.61**	**5.96**	**...**
Trade credits	4 706 . .	...	...	...	...	...	...	...	...
General government: long-term	4 708 . .	...	...	...	...	...	...	...	...
General government: short-term	4 709 . .	...	...	...	...	...	...	...	...
Other sectors: long-term	4 711 . .	...	...	...	...	...	...	...	...
Other sectors: short-term	4 712 . .	...	...	...	...	...	...	...	...
Loans	4 714 . .	...	...	...	...	...	...	...	...
Monetary authorities: long-term	4 717 . .	...	...	...	...	...	...	...	...
Monetary authorities: short-term	4 718 . .	...	...	...	...	...	...	...	...
General government: long-term	4 720 . .	...	...	...	...	...	...	...	...
General government: short-term	4 721 . .	...	...	...	...	...	...	...	...
Banks: long-term	4 723 . .	...	...	...	...	...	...	...	...
Banks: short-term	4 724 . .	...	...	...	...	...	...	...	...
Other sectors: long-term	4 726 . .	...	...	...	...	...	...	...	...
Other sectors: short-term	4 727 . .	...	...	...	...	...	...	...	...
Currency and deposits	4 730 . .	–8.48	8.18	10.78	3.06	.90	5.61	5.96	...
Monetary authorities	4 731 . .	...	...	...	...	...	...	...	...
General government	4 732 . .	...	...	...	...	...	...	...	...
Banks	4 733 . .	–8.48	8.18	10.78	3.06	.90	5.61	5.96	...
Other sectors	4 734 . .	...	...	...	...	...	...	...	...
Other assets	4 736 . .	...	...	...	...	...	...	...	...
Monetary authorities: long-term	4 738 . .	...	...	...	...	...	...	...	...
Monetary authorities: short-term	4 739 . .	...	...	...	...	...	...	...	...
General government: long-term	4 741 . .	...	...	...	...	...	...	...	...
General government: short-term	4 742 . .	...	...	...	...	...	...	...	...
Banks: long-term	4 744 . .	...	...	...	...	...	...	...	...
Banks: short-term	4 745 . .	...	...	...	...	...	...	...	...
Other sectors: long-term	4 747 . .	...	...	...	...	...	...	...	...
Other sectors: short-term	4 748 . .	...	...	...	...	...	...	...	...
Liabilities	4 753 . .	**–.60**	**4.62**	**4.68**	**5.38**	**2.06**	**–1.40**	**–3.06**	**...**
Trade credits	4 756 . .	...	...	...	...	...	...	...	...
General government: long-term	4 758 . .	...	...	...	...	...	...	...	...
General government: short-term	4 759 . .	...	...	...	...	...	...	...	...
Other sectors: long-term	4 761 . .	...	...	...	...	...	...	...	...
Other sectors: short-term	4 762 . .	...	...	...	...	...	...	...	...
Loans	4 764 . .	–.60	4.62	4.68	5.38	2.06	–1.40	–3.06	...
Use of Fund credit and loans from the Fund	4 766 . .	–2.27	–2.03	–1.35	–.94	–.76	–.73	–.80	...
Monetary authorities: other long-term	4 767 . .	...	...	...	...	...	...	...	...
Monetary authorities: short-term	4 768 . .	...	...	...	...	...	...	...	...
General government: long-term	4 770 . .	1.83	6.95	7.14	8.01	4.04	–.18	–1.79	...
General government: short-term	4 771 . .	...	...	...	...	...	...	...	...
Banks: long-term	4 773 . .	...	...	...	...	...	...	...	...
Banks: short-term	4 774 . .	...	...	...	...	...	...	...	...
Other sectors: long-term	4 776 . .	–.16	–.30	–1.11	–1.70	–1.23	–.49	–.47	...
Other sectors: short-term	4 777 . .	...	...	...	...	...	...	...	...
Currency and deposits	4 780 . .	...	...	...	...	...	...	...	...
Monetary authorities	4 781 . .	...	...	...	...	...	...	...	...
General government	4 782 . .	...	...	...	...	...	...	...	...
Banks	4 783 . .	...	...	...	...	...	...	...	...
Other sectors	4 784 . .	...	...	...	...	...	...	...	...
Other liabilities	4 786 . .	...	...	...	...	...	...	...	...
Monetary authorities: long-term	4 788 . .	...	...	...	...	...	...	...	...
Monetary authorities: short-term	4 789 . .	...	...	...	...	...	...	...	...
General government: long-term	4 791 . .	...	...	...	...	...	...	...	...
General government: short-term	4 792 . .	...	...	...	...	...	...	...	...
Banks: long-term	4 794 . .	...	...	...	...	...	...	...	...
Banks: short-term	4 795 . .	...	...	...	...	...	...	...	...
Other sectors: long-term	4 797 . .	...	...	...	...	...	...	...	...
Other sectors: short-term	4 798 . .	...	...	...	...	...	...	...	...
D. RESERVE ASSETS	4 800 . .	3.23	1.83	–3.70	–3.29	–2.60	.11	4.04	...
Monetary gold	4 810 . .	...	...	...	...	...	...	...	...
Special drawing rights	4 820 . .	.23	.31	.15	.29	–.09	.09	...	...
Reserve position in the Fund	4 830 . .	...	...	...	...	...	...	...	...
Foreign exchange	4 840 . .	3.37	2.07	–2.93	–3.60	–2.55	.42	4.44	...
Other claims	4 880 . .	–.37	–.56	–.93	.02	.04	–.41	–.41	...
NET ERRORS AND OMISSIONS	4 998 . .	**–5.22**	**.11**	**5.75**	**.07**	**–5.00**	**1.00**	**–1.36**	...

Part 3 of the *Yearbook* contains descriptions of the methodologies, compilation practices, and sources used to compile these data.

Table 1. ANALYTIC PRESENTATION, 1988–95

(Millions of U.S. dollars)

	Code	1988	1989	1990	1991	1992	1993	1994	1995
A. Current Account [1]	4 993 Y.	**–18.9**	**–327.3**	**–279.6**	**–157.3**	**–707.9**	**–447.0**	**–68.3**	**–125.2**
Goods: exports f.o.b	2 100 . .	889.7	924.4	734.5	658.3	562.5	2,738.2	3,296.4	3,051.9
Goods: imports f.o.b	3 100 . .	–1,608.0	–1,963.8	–1,792.8	–1,728.8	–2,174.3	–4,590.3	–5,014.5	–4,843.9
Balance on Goods	4 100 . .	*–718.3*	*–1,039.4*	*–1,058.3*	*–1,070.5*	*–1,611.8*	*–1,852.1*	*–1,718.1*	*–1,792.0*
Services: credit	2 200 . .	1,013.4	1,041.1	1,097.2	1,198.7	1,348.6	1,525.5	1,763.8	1,950.5
Services: debit	3 200 . .	–397.0	–464.7	–440.4	–479.3	–555.1	–517.8	–578.6	–646.6
Balance on Goods and Services	4 991 . .	*–101.9*	*–463.0*	*–401.5*	*–351.1*	*–818.3*	*–844.4*	*–532.9*	*–488.1*
Income: credit	2 300 . .	8.5	107.1	86.3	87.2	54.7	76.4	78.6	103.7
Income: debit	3 300 . .	–279.1	–355.8	–335.0	–279.9	–376.1	–463.7	–478.7	–609.4
Balance on Goods, Services, and Income	4 992 . .	*–372.5*	*–711.7*	*–650.2*	*–543.8*	*–1,139.7*	*–1,231.7*	*–933.0*	*–993.8*
Current transfers: credit	2 379 Y.	353.6	384.4	370.6	386.5	431.8	786.1	864.7	868.8
Current transfers: debit	3 379 . .	...	...	...	...	...	–1.4	...	–.2
B. Capital Account [1]	4 994 Y.	**...**	**...**	**...**	**...**	**...**	**...**	**...**	**...**
Capital account: credit	2 994 Y.	...	...	...	...	...	...	...	...
Capital account: debit	3 994 . .	...	...	...	...	...	...	...	...
Total, Groups A Plus B	4 010 . .	*–18.9*	*–327.3*	*–279.6*	*–157.3*	*–707.9*	*–447.0*	*–68.3*	*–125.2*
C. Financial Account [1]	4 995 X.	**–15.6**	**160.0**	**–17.2**	**–137.7**	**75.7**	**–76.9**	**77.6**	**368.1**
Direct investment abroad	4 505 . .	...	...	...	...	...	...	...	...
Direct investment in Dominican Republic	4 555 Y.	106.1	110.0	132.8	145.0	179.7	91.2	132.4	270.6
Portfolio investment assets	4 602 . .	...	...	...	...	...	...	...	...
Equity securities	4 610 . .	...	...	...	...	...	...	...	...
Debt securities	4 619 . .	...	...	...	...	...	...	...	...
Portfolio investment liabilities	4 652 Y.	...	...	...	...	...	...	...	...
Equity securities	4 660 Y.	...	...	...	...	...	...	...	...
Debt securities	4 669 Y.	...	...	...	...	...	...	...	...
Other investment assets	4 703 . .	–83.0	–98.0	89.3	–196.6	128.8	156.7	–108.0	39.0
Monetary authorities	4 703 .A	...	...	...	...	...	...	...	...
General government	4 703 .B	...	...	...	...	...	...	...	...
Banks	4 703 .C	–83.0	82.0	–.7	–6.6	–1.2	26.7	–18.0	39.0
Other sectors	4 703 .D	...	–180.0	90.0	–190.0	130.0	130.0	–90.0	...
Other investment liabilities	4 753 X.	–38.7	148.0	–239.3	–86.1	–232.8	–324.8	53.2	58.5
Monetary authorities	4 753 XA	–210.6	91.0	–198.9	–75.7	–130.7	–460.5	9.3	74.4
General government	4 753 YB	124.8	–4.2	–64.4	–20.0	–66.2	–66.8	–63.9	–5.1
Banks	4 753 YC	47.1	–3.8	40.8	–4.7	–12.7	–12.6	25.8	9.6
Other sectors	4 753 YD	...	65.0	–16.8	14.3	–23.2	215.1	82.0	–20.4
Total, Groups A Through C	4 020 . .	*–34.5*	*–167.3*	*–296.8*	*–295.0*	*–632.2*	*–523.9*	*9.3*	*242.9*
D. Net Errors and Omissions	4 998 . .	**35.6**	**–73.6**	**–120.7**	**548.3**	**569.0**	**39.1**	**–509.7**	**–116.1**
Total, Groups A Through D	4 030 . .	*1.1*	*–240.9*	*–417.5*	*253.3*	*–63.1*	*–484.8*	*–500.4*	*126.8*
E. Reserves and Related Items	4 040 . .	**–1.1**	**240.9**	**417.5**	**–253.3**	**63.1**	**484.8**	**500.4**	**–126.8**
Reserve assets	4 800 . .	–58.9	90.0	49.0	–357.4	–63.5	–153.5	384.7	–131.2
Use of Fund credit and loans	4 766 . .	–51.2	–88.0	–56.9	15.9	37.3	63.9	–8.1	–34.0
Liabilities constituting foreign authorities' reserves	4 900 . .	...	–22.1	–56.6	3.6	–.9	...	...	...
Exceptional financing	4 920 . .	109.0	261.0	482.0	84.6	90.2	574.4	123.8	38.4
Conversion rates: Dominican pesos per U.S. dollar	0 101 . .	**6.1125**	**6.3400**	**8.5253**	**12.6924**	**12.7742**	**12.6758**	**13.1601**	**13.5974**

[1] Excludes components that have been classified in the categories of Group E.

Table 2. STANDARD PRESENTATION, 1988–95
(Millions of U.S. dollars)

	Code	1988	1989	1990	1991	1992	1993	1994	1995
CURRENT ACCOUNT	4 993 . .	**–18.9**	**–327.3**	**–279.6**	**–157.3**	**–707.9**	**–447.0**	**–68.3**	**–125.2**
A. GOODS	4 100 . .	–718.3	–1,039.4	–1,058.3	–1,070.5	–1,611.8	–1,852.1	–1,718.1	–1,792.0
Credit	2 100 . .	**889.7**	**924.4**	**734.5**	**658.3**	**562.5**	**2,738.2**	**3,296.4**	**3,051.9**
General merchandise: exports f.o.b.	2 110 . .	889.7	924.4	734.5	658.3	562.5	558.3	692.7	782.4
Goods for processing: exports f.o.b.	2 150 . .	. . .	. . .	. . .	. . .	. . .	2,155.3	2,573.4	2,214.6
Repairs on goods	2 160 . .	. . .	. . .	. . .	. . .	. . .	. . .	. . .	. . .
Goods procured in ports by carriers	2 170 . .	. . .	. . .	. . .	. . .	. . .	20.7	13.0	13.6
Nonmonetary gold	2 180 . .	. . .	. . .	. . .	. . .	. . .	3.9	17.3	41.3
Debit	3 100 . .	**–1,608.0**	**–1,963.8**	**–1,792.8**	**–1,728.8**	**–2,174.3**	**–4,590.3**	**–5,014.5**	**–4,843.9**
General merchandise: imports f.o.b.	3 110 . .	–1,608.0	–1,963.8	–1,792.8	–1,728.8	–2,174.3	–2,784.8	–2,816.5	–3,081.3
Goods for processing: imports f.o.b.	3 150 . .	. . .	. . .	. . .	. . .	. . .	–1,805.5	–2,198.0	–1,762.6
Repairs on goods	3 160 . .	. . .	. . .	. . .	. . .	. . .	. . .	. . .	. . .
Goods procured in ports by carriers	3 170 . .	. . .	. . .	. . .	. . .	. . .	. . .	. . .	. . .
Nonmonetary gold	3 180 . .	. . .	. . .	. . .	. . .	. . .	. . .	. . .	. . .
B. SERVICES	4 200 . .	616.4	576.4	656.8	719.4	793.5	1,007.7	1,185.2	1,303.9
Total credit	2 200 . .	*1,013.4*	*1,041.1*	*1,097.2*	*1,198.7*	*1,348.6*	*1,525.5*	*1,763.8*	*1,950.5*
Total debit	3 200 . .	*–397.0*	*–464.7*	*–440.4*	*–479.3*	*–555.1*	*–517.8*	*–578.6*	*–646.6*
Transportation services, credit	2 205 . .	**41.9**	**57.7**	**61.1**	**69.9**	**69.5**	**27.7**	**32.4**	**35.0**
Passenger	2 205 BA	. . .	. . .	. . .	. . .	. . .	. . .	. . .	. . .
Freight	2 205 BB	*10.9*	*24.1*	*18.4*	*16.4*	*14.1*	*.8*	*1.5*	*1.8*
Other	2 205 BC	*31.0*	*33.6*	*42.7*	*53.5*	*55.4*	*26.9*	*30.9*	*33.2*
Sea transport, passenger	2 207 . .	. . .	. . .	. . .	. . .	. . .	. . .	. . .	. . .
Sea transport, freight	2 208 . .	. . .	. . .	. . .	. . .	. . .	. . .	. . .	. . .
Sea transport, other	2 209 . .	. . .	. . .	. . .	. . .	. . .	22.4	26.3	27.9
Air transport, passenger	2 211 . .	. . .	. . .	. . .	. . .	. . .	. . .	. . .	. . .
Air transport, freight	2 212 . .	. . .	. . .	. . .	. . .	. . .	.8	1.5	1.8
Air transport, other	2 213 . .	. . .	. . .	. . .	. . .	. . .	.2	.2	.4
Other transport, passenger	2 215 . .	. . .	. . .	. . .	. . .	. . .	. . .	. . .	. . .
Other transport, freight	2 216 . .	. . .	. . .	. . .	. . .	. . .	. . .	. . .	. . .
Other transport, other	2 217 . .	. . .	. . .	. . .	. . .	. . .	4.3	4.4	4.9
Transportation services, debit	3 205 . .	**–160.1**	**–208.2**	**–174.0**	**–178.2**	**–229.4**	**–298.3**	**–333.0**	**–356.5**
Passenger	3 205 BA	*–15.2*	*–15.0*	*–15.0*	*–20.3*	*–20.8*	*–86.3*	*–87.6*	*–97.5*
Freight	3 205 BB	*–144.9*	*–193.2*	*–159.0*	*–157.9*	*–208.6*	*–212.0*	*–245.4*	*–259.0*
Other	3 205 BC	. . .	. . .	. . .	. . .	. . .	. . .	. . .	. . .
Sea transport, passenger	3 207 . .	. . .	. . .	. . .	. . .	. . .	. . .	. . .	. . .
Sea transport, freight	3 208 . .	. . .	. . .	. . .	. . .	. . .	–173.0	–200.3	–211.3
Sea transport, other	3 209 . .	. . .	. . .	. . .	. . .	. . .	. . .	. . .	. . .
Air transport, passenger	3 211 . .	. . .	. . .	. . .	. . .	. . .	–86.3	–87.6	–97.5
Air transport, freight	3 212 . .	. . .	. . .	. . .	. . .	. . .	–39.0	–45.1	–47.7
Air transport, other	3 213 . .	. . .	. . .	. . .	. . .	. . .	. . .	. . .	. . .
Other transport, passenger	3 215 . .	. . .	. . .	. . .	. . .	. . .	. . .	. . .	. . .
Other transport, freight	3 216 . .	. . .	. . .	. . .	. . .	. . .	. . .	. . .	. . .
Other transport, other	3 217 . .	. . .	. . .	. . .	. . .	. . .	. . .	. . .	. . .
Travel, credit	2 236 . .	**768.3**	**706.7**	**726.1**	**755.6**	**841.0**	**1,234.9**	**1,417.9**	**1,582.1**
Business travel	2 237 . .	. . .	. . .	. . .	. . .	. . .	. . .	. . .	. . .
Personal travel	2 240 . .	. . .	. . .	. . .	. . .	. . .	1,234.9	1,417.9	1,582.1
Travel, debit	3 236 . .	**–127.2**	**–136.0**	**–144.0**	**–153.6**	**–158.8**	**–112.7**	**–135.6**	**–163.3**
Business travel	3 237 . .	. . .	. . .	. . .	. . .	. . .	. . .	. . .	. . .
Personal travel	3 240 . .	. . .	. . .	. . .	. . .	. . .	–112.7	–135.6	–163.3
Other services, credit	2 200 BA	**203.2**	**276.7**	**310.0**	**373.2**	**438.1**	**262.9**	**313.5**	**333.4**
Communications	2 245 . .	. . .	. . .	. . .	. . .	. . .	201.4	237.2	245.9
Construction	2 249 . .	. . .	. . .	. . .	. . .	. . .	. . .	. . .	. . .
Insurance	2 253 . .	1.2	2.7	2.0	1.8	1.6	. . .	. . .	. . .
Financial	2 260 . .	. . .	. . .	. . .	. . .	. . .	. . .	. . .	. . .
Computer and information	2 262 . .	. . .	. . .	. . .	. . .	. . .	. . .	. . .	. . .
Royalties and licence fees	2 266 . .	. . .	. . .	. . .	. . .	. . .	. . .	. . .	. . .
Other business services	2 268 . .	195.0	265.0	297.0	359.9	424.5	15.1	25.1	30.1
Personal, cultural, and recreational	2 287 . .	. . .	. . .	. . .	. . .	. . .	. . .	. . .	. . .
Government, n.i.e.	2 291 . .	7.0	9.0	11.0	11.5	12.0	46.4	51.2	57.4
Other services, debit	3 200 BA	**–109.7**	**–120.5**	**–122.4**	**–147.5**	**–166.9**	**–106.8**	**–110.0**	**–126.8**
Communications	3 245 . .	. . .	. . .	. . .	. . .	. . .	–47.8	–53.4	–75.4
Construction	3 249 . .	. . .	. . .	. . .	. . .	. . .	. . .	. . .	. . .
Insurance	3 253 . .	–16.1	–21.5	–17.7	–17.5	–23.2	–44.7	–37.1	–35.2
Financial	3 260 . .	. . .	. . .	. . .	. . .	. . .	–2.9	–3.5	–1.2
Computer and information	3 262 . .	. . .	. . .	. . .	. . .	. . .	. . .	. . .	. . .
Royalties and licence fees	3 266 . .	. . .	. . .	. . .	. . .	. . .	–2.1	–5.6	–3.6
Other business services	3 268 . .	–88.9	–94.0	–99.4	–125.0	–134.8	–5.4	–6.1	–6.9
Personal, cultural, and recreational	3 287 . .	. . .	. . .	. . .	. . .	. . .	. . .	. . .	. . .
Government, n.i.e.	3 291 . .	–4.7	–5.0	–5.3	–5.0	–8.9	–3.9	–4.3	–4.5

Table 2 (Continued). STANDARD PRESENTATION, 1988–95
(Millions of U.S. dollars)

	Code	1988	1989	1990	1991	1992	1993	1994	1995
C. INCOME	4 300 . .	–270.6	–248.7	–248.7	–192.7	–321.4	–387.3	–400.1	–505.7
Total credit	2 300 . .	*8.5*	*107.1*	*86.3*	*87.2*	*54.7*	*76.4*	*78.6*	*103.7*
Total debit	3 300 . .	*–279.1*	*–355.8*	*–335.0*	*–279.9*	*–376.1*	*–463.7*	*–478.7*	*–609.4*
Compensation of employees, credit	2 310 . .	**. . .**	**. . .**	**. . .**	**. . .**	**. . .**	**1.4**	**1.5**	**1.6**
Compensation of employees, debit	3 310 . .	**. . .**	**. . .**	**. . .**	**. . .**	**. . .**	**–.2**	**–.2**	**–.3**
Investment income, credit	2 320 . .	**8.5**	**107.1**	**86.3**	**87.2**	**54.7**	**75.0**	**77.1**	**102.1**
Direct investment income	2 330 . .	. . .	. . .	. . .	. . .	. . .	. . .	. . .	. . .
Dividends and distributed branch profits	2 332 . .	. . .	. . .	. . .	. . .	. . .	. . .	. . .	. . .
Reinvested earnings and undistributed branch profits	2 333 . .	. . .	. . .	. . .	. . .	. . .	. . .	. . .	. . .
Income on debt (interest)	2 334 . .	. . .	. . .	. . .	. . .	. . .	. . .	. . .	. . .
Portfolio investment income	2 339 . .	. . .	. . .	. . .	. . .	. . .	. . .	. . .	. . .
Income on equity	2 340 . .	. . .	. . .	. . .	. . .	. . .	. . .	. . .	. . .
Income on bonds and notes	2 350 . .	. . .	. . .	. . .	. . .	. . .	. . .	. . .	. . .
Income on money market instruments and financial derivatives	2 360 . .	. . .	. . .	. . .	. . .	. . .	. . .	. . .	. . .
Other investment income	2 370 . .	8.5	107.1	86.3	87.2	54.7	75.0	77.1	102.1
Investment income, debit	3 320 . .	**–279.1**	**–355.8**	**–335.0**	**–279.9**	**–376.1**	**–463.5**	**–478.5**	**–609.1**
Direct investment income	3 330 . .	. . .	–124.3	–90.0	–120.1	–201.9	–187.7	–234.8	–333.5
Dividends and distributed branch profits	3 332 . .	. . .	–124.3	–90.0	–120.1	–201.9	–97.5	–95.4	–98.7
Reinvested earnings and undistributed branch profits	3 333 . .	. . .	. . .	. . .	. . .	. . .	–90.2	–139.4	–234.8
Income on debt (interest)	3 334 . .	. . .	. . .	. . .	. . .	. . .	. . .	. . .	. . .
Portfolio investment income	3 339 . .	. . .	. . .	. . .	. . .	. . .	–1.9	–1.4	–2.9
Income on equity	3 340 . .	. . .	. . .	. . .	. . .	. . .	–1.9	–1.4	–2.9
Income on bonds and notes	3 350 . .	. . .	. . .	. . .	. . .	. . .	. . .	. . .	. . .
Income on money market instruments and financial derivatives	3 360 . .	. . .	. . .	. . .	. . .	. . .	. . .	. . .	. . .
Other investment income	3 370 . .	–279.1	–231.5	–245.0	–159.8	–174.2	–273.9	–242.3	–272.7
D. CURRENT TRANSFERS	4 379 . .	353.6	384.4	370.6	386.5	431.8	784.7	864.7	868.6
Credit	2 379 . .	**353.6**	**384.4**	**370.6**	**386.5**	**431.8**	**786.1**	**864.7**	**868.8**
General government	2 380 . .	64.8	83.9	55.8	57.0	85.2	36.3	71.1	49.1
Other sectors	2 390 . .	288.8	300.5	314.8	329.5	346.6	749.8	793.6	819.7
Workers' remittances	2 391 . .	288.8	300.5	314.8	329.5	346.6	720.6	756.7	794.5
Other current transfers	2 392 . .	. . .	. . .	. . .	. . .	. . .	29.2	36.9	25.2
Debit	3 379 . .	**. . .**	**. . .**	**. . .**	**. . .**	**. . .**	**–1.4**	**. . .**	**–.2**
General government	3 380 . .	. . .	. . .	. . .	. . .	. . .	. . .	. . .	. . .
Other sectors	3 390 . .	. . .	. . .	. . .	. . .	. . .	–1.4	. . .	–.2
Workers' remittances	3 391 . .	. . .	. . .	. . .	. . .	. . .	. . .	. . .	. . .
Other current transfers	3 392 . .	. . .	. . .	. . .	. . .	. . .	–1.4	. . .	–.2
CAPITAL AND FINANCIAL ACCOUNT	4 996 . .	**–16.7**	**400.9**	**400.3**	**–391.0**	**138.9**	**407.9**	**578.0**	**241.3**
CAPITAL ACCOUNT	4 994 . .	**. . .**	**. . .**	**. . .**	**. . .**	**. . .**	**24.0**	**600.6**	**1.2**
Total credit	2 994 . .	. . .	. . .	. . .	. . .	. . .	*24.0*	*600.6*	*1.2*
Total debit	3 994 . .	. . .	. . .	. . .	. . .	. . .	. . .	. . .	. . .
Capital transfers, credit	2 400 . .	**. . .**	**. . .**	**. . .**	**. . .**	**. . .**	**24.0**	**600.6**	**1.2**
General government	2 401 . .	. . .	. . .	. . .	. . .	. . .	24.0	600.6	1.2
Debt forgiveness	2 402 . .	. . .	. . .	. . .	. . .	. . .	24.0	600.6	1.2
Other capital transfers	2 410 . .	. . .	. . .	. . .	. . .	. . .	. . .	. . .	. . .
Other sectors	2 430 . .	. . .	. . .	. . .	. . .	. . .	. . .	. . .	. . .
Migrants' transfers	2 431 . .	. . .	. . .	. . .	. . .	. . .	. . .	. . .	. . .
Debt forgiveness	2 432 . .	. . .	. . .	. . .	. . .	. . .	. . .	. . .	. . .
Other capital transfers	2 440 . .	. . .	. . .	. . .	. . .	. . .	. . .	. . .	. . .
Capital transfers, debit	3 400 . .	**. . .**	**. . .**	**. . .**	**. . .**	**. . .**	**. . .**	**. . .**	**. . .**
General government	3 401 . .	. . .	. . .	. . .	. . .	. . .	. . .	. . .	. . .
Debt forgiveness	3 402 . .	. . .	. . .	. . .	. . .	. . .	. . .	. . .	. . .
Other capital transfers	3 410 . .	. . .	. . .	. . .	. . .	. . .	. . .	. . .	. . .
Other sectors	3 430 . .	. . .	. . .	. . .	. . .	. . .	. . .	. . .	. . .
Migrants' transfers	3 431 . .	. . .	. . .	. . .	. . .	. . .	. . .	. . .	. . .
Debt forgiveness	3 432 . .	. . .	. . .	. . .	. . .	. . .	. . .	. . .	. . .
Other capital transfers	3 440 . .	. . .	. . .	. . .	. . .	. . .	. . .	. . .	. . .
Nonproduced nonfinancial assets, credit	2 480 . .	**. . .**	**. . .**	**. . .**	**. . .**	**. . .**	**. . .**	**. . .**	**. . .**
Nonproduced nonfinancial assets, debit	3 480 . .	**. . .**	**. . .**	**. . .**	**. . .**	**. . .**	**. . .**	**. . .**	**. . .**

Table 2 (Continued). STANDARD PRESENTATION, 1988–95
(Millions of U.S. dollars)

	Code	1988	1989	1990	1991	1992	1993	1994	1995
FINANCIAL ACCOUNT	4 995 . .	**–16.7**	**400.9**	**400.3**	**–391.0**	**138.9**	**383.9**	**–22.6**	**240.1**
A. DIRECT INVESTMENT	4 500 . .	106.1	110.0	132.8	145.0	179.7	91.2	132.4	270.6
Direct investment abroad	4 505 . .	**. . .**	**. . .**	**. . .**	**. . .**	**. . .**	**. . .**	**. . .**	**. . .**
Equity capital	4 510 . .	. . .	. . .	. . .	. . .	. . .	. . .	. . .	. . .
Claims on affiliated enterprises	4 515 . .	. . .	. . .	. . .	. . .	. . .	. . .	. . .	. . .
Liabilities to affiliated enterprises	4 520 . .	. . .	. . .	. . .	. . .	. . .	. . .	. . .	. . .
Reinvested earnings	4 525 . .	. . .	. . .	. . .	. . .	. . .	. . .	. . .	. . .
Other capital	4 530 . .	. . .	. . .	. . .	. . .	. . .	. . .	. . .	. . .
Claims on affiliated enterprises	4 535 . .	. . .	. . .	. . .	. . .	. . .	. . .	. . .	. . .
Liabilities to affiliated enterprises	4 540 . .	. . .	. . .	. . .	. . .	. . .	. . .	. . .	. . .
Direct investment in Dominican Republic	4 555 . .	**106.1**	**110.0**	**132.8**	**145.0**	**179.7**	**91.2**	**132.4**	**270.6**
Equity capital	4 560 . .	106.1	110.0	132.8	145.0	179.7	2.2	11.2	17.4
Claims on direct investors	4 565 . .	. . .	. . .	. . .	. . .	. . .	. . .	. . .	. . .
Liabilities to direct investors	4 570 . .	. . .	. . .	. . .	. . .	. . .	2.2	11.2	17.4
Reinvested earnings	4 575 . .	. . .	. . .	. . .	. . .	. . .	90.2	139.4	234.8
Other capital	4 580 . .	. . .	. . .	. . .	. . .	. . .	–1.2	–18.2	18.4
Claims on direct investors	4 585 . .	. . .	. . .	. . .	. . .	. . .	–1.4	–1.3	–3.1
Liabilities to direct investors	4 590 . .	. . .	. . .	. . .	. . .	. . .	.2	–16.9	21.5
B. PORTFOLIO INVESTMENT	4 600 . .	. . .	. . .	. . .	. . .	. . .	. . .	. . .	. . .
Assets	4 602 . .	**. . .**	**. . .**	**. . .**	**. . .**	**. . .**	**. . .**	**. . .**	**. . .**
Equity securities	4 610 . .	. . .	. . .	. . .	. . .	. . .	. . .	. . .	. . .
Monetary authorities	4 611 . .	. . .	. . .	. . .	. . .	. . .	. . .	. . .	. . .
General government	4 612 . .	. . .	. . .	. . .	. . .	. . .	. . .	. . .	. . .
Banks	4 613 . .	. . .	. . .	. . .	. . .	. . .	. . .	. . .	. . .
Other sectors	4 614 . .	. . .	. . .	. . .	. . .	. . .	. . .	. . .	. . .
Debt securities	4 619 . .	. . .	. . .	. . .	. . .	. . .	. . .	. . .	. . .
Bonds and notes	4 620 . .	. . .	. . .	. . .	. . .	. . .	. . .	. . .	. . .
Monetary authorities	4 621 . .	. . .	. . .	. . .	. . .	. . .	. . .	. . .	. . .
General government	4 622 . .	. . .	. . .	. . .	. . .	. . .	. . .	. . .	. . .
Banks	4 623 . .	. . .	. . .	. . .	. . .	. . .	. . .	. . .	. . .
Other sectors	4 624 . .	. . .	. . .	. . .	. . .	. . .	. . .	. . .	. . .
Money market instruments	4 630 . .	. . .	. . .	. . .	. . .	. . .	. . .	. . .	. . .
Monetary authorities	4 631 . .	. . .	. . .	. . .	. . .	. . .	. . .	. . .	. . .
General government	4 632 . .	. . .	. . .	. . .	. . .	. . .	. . .	. . .	. . .
Banks	4 633 . .	. . .	. . .	. . .	. . .	. . .	. . .	. . .	. . .
Other sectors	4 634 . .	. . .	. . .	. . .	. . .	. . .	. . .	. . .	. . .
Financial derivatives	4 640 . .	. . .	. . .	. . .	. . .	. . .	. . .	. . .	. . .
Monetary authorities	4 641 . .	. . .	. . .	. . .	. . .	. . .	. . .	. . .	. . .
General government	4 642 . .	. . .	. . .	. . .	. . .	. . .	. . .	. . .	. . .
Banks	4 643 . .	. . .	. . .	. . .	. . .	. . .	. . .	. . .	. . .
Other sectors	4 644 . .	. . .	. . .	. . .	. . .	. . .	. . .	. . .	. . .
Liabilities	4 652 . .	**. . .**	**. . .**	**. . .**	**. . .**	**. . .**	**. . .**	**. . .**	**. . .**
Equity securities	4 660 . .	. . .	. . .	. . .	. . .	. . .	. . .	. . .	. . .
Banks	4 663 . .	. . .	. . .	. . .	. . .	. . .	. . .	. . .	. . .
Other sectors	4 664 . .	. . .	. . .	. . .	. . .	. . .	. . .	. . .	. . .
Debt securities	4 669 . .	. . .	. . .	. . .	. . .	. . .	. . .	. . .	. . .
Bonds and notes	4 670 . .	. . .	. . .	. . .	. . .	. . .	. . .	. . .	. . .
Monetary authorities	4 671 . .	. . .	. . .	. . .	. . .	. . .	. . .	. . .	. . .
General government	4 672 . .	. . .	. . .	. . .	. . .	. . .	. . .	. . .	. . .
Banks	4 673 . .	. . .	. . .	. . .	. . .	. . .	. . .	. . .	. . .
Other sectors	4 674 . .	. . .	. . .	. . .	. . .	. . .	. . .	. . .	. . .
Money market instruments	4 680 . .	. . .	. . .	. . .	. . .	. . .	. . .	. . .	. . .
Monetary authorities	4 681 . .	. . .	. . .	. . .	. . .	. . .	. . .	. . .	. . .
General government	4 682 . .	. . .	. . .	. . .	. . .	. . .	. . .	. . .	. . .
Banks	4 683 . .	. . .	. . .	. . .	. . .	. . .	. . .	. . .	. . .
Other sectors	4 684 . .	. . .	. . .	. . .	. . .	. . .	. . .	. . .	. . .
Financial derivatives	4 690 . .	. . .	. . .	. . .	. . .	. . .	. . .	. . .	. . .
Monetary authorities	4 691 . .	. . .	. . .	. . .	. . .	. . .	. . .	. . .	. . .
General government	4 692 . .	. . .	. . .	. . .	. . .	. . .	. . .	. . .	. . .
Banks	4 693 . .	. . .	. . .	. . .	. . .	. . .	. . .	. . .	. . .
Other sectors	4 694 . .	. . .	. . .	. . .	. . .	. . .	. . .	. . .	. . .

Table 2 (Concluded). STANDARD PRESENTATION, 1988–95
(Millions of U.S. dollars)

	Code		1988	1989	1990	1991	1992	1993	1994	1995
C. OTHER INVESTMENT	4 700	. .	–63.9	200.9	218.5	–178.6	22.6	446.2	–539.7	100.7
Assets	4 703	. .	**–83.0**	**–98.0**	**89.3**	**–196.6**	**128.8**	**156.7**	**–108.0**	**39.0**
Trade credits	4 706	. .	. . .	. . .	. . .	. . .	. . .	. . .	. . .	. . .
General government: long-term	4 708	. .	. . .	. . .	. . .	. . .	. . .	. . .	. . .	. . .
General government: short-term	4 709	. .	. . .	. . .	. . .	. . .	. . .	. . .	. . .	. . .
Other sectors: long-term	4 711	. .	. . .	. . .	. . .	. . .	. . .	. . .	. . .	. . .
Other sectors: short-term	4 712	. .	. . .	. . .	. . .	. . .	. . .	. . .	. . .	. . .
Loans	4 714	. .	. . .	. . .	. . .	. . .	. . .	. . .	. . .	. . .
Monetary authorities: long-term	4 717	. .	. . .	. . .	. . .	. . .	. . .	. . .	. . .	. . .
Monetary authorities: short-term	4 718	. .	. . .	. . .	. . .	. . .	. . .	. . .	. . .	. . .
General government: long-term	4 720	. .	. . .	. . .	. . .	. . .	. . .	. . .	. . .	. . .
General government: short-term	4 721	. .	. . .	. . .	. . .	. . .	. . .	. . .	. . .	. . .
Banks: long-term	4 723	. .	. . .	. . .	. . .	. . .	. . .	. . .	. . .	. . .
Banks: short-term	4 724	. .	. . .	. . .	. . .	. . .	. . .	. . .	. . .	. . .
Other sectors: long-term	4 726	. .	. . .	. . .	. . .	. . .	. . .	. . .	. . .	. . .
Other sectors: short-term	4 727	. .	. . .	. . .	. . .	. . .	. . .	. . .	. . .	. . .
Currency and deposits	4 730	. .	–83.0	–98.0	89.3	–196.6	128.8	156.7	–108.0	39.0
Monetary authorities	4 731	. .	. . .	. . .	. . .	. . .	. . .	. . .	. . .	. . .
General government	4 732	. .	. . .	. . .	. . .	. . .	. . .	. . .	. . .	. . .
Banks	4 733	. .	–83.0	82.0	–.7	–6.6	–1.2	26.7	–18.0	39.0
Other sectors	4 734	. .	. . .	–180.0	90.0	–190.0	130.0	130.0	–90.0	. . .
Other assets	4 736	. .	. . .	. . .	. . .	. . .	. . .	. . .	. . .	. . .
Monetary authorities: long-term	4 738	. .	. . .	. . .	. . .	. . .	. . .	. . .	. . .	. . .
Monetary authorities: short-term	4 739	. .	. . .	. . .	. . .	. . .	. . .	. . .	. . .	. . .
General government: long-term	4 741	. .	. . .	. . .	. . .	. . .	. . .	. . .	. . .	. . .
General government: short-term	4 742	. .	. . .	. . .	. . .	. . .	. . .	. . .	. . .	. . .
Banks: long-term	4 744	. .	. . .	. . .	. . .	. . .	. . .	. . .	. . .	. . .
Banks: short-term	4 745	. .	. . .	. . .	. . .	. . .	. . .	. . .	. . .	. . .
Other sectors: long-term	4 747	. .	. . .	. . .	. . .	. . .	. . .	. . .	. . .	. . .
Other sectors: short-term	4 748	. .	. . .	. . .	. . .	. . .	. . .	. . .	. . .	. . .
Liabilities	4 753	. .	**19.1**	**298.9**	**129.2**	**18.0**	**–106.2**	**289.5**	**–431.7**	**61.7**
Trade credits	4 756	. .	. . .	. . .	. . .	. . .	. . .	51.0	–31.4	–17.0
General government: long-term	4 758	. .	. . .	. . .	. . .	. . .	. . .	. . .	. . .	. . .
General government: short-term	4 759	. .	. . .	. . .	. . .	. . .	. . .	. . .	. . .	. . .
Other sectors: long-term	4 761	. .	. . .	. . .	. . .	. . .	. . .	. . .	. . .	. . .
Other sectors: short-term	4 762	. .	. . .	. . .	. . .	. . .	. . .	51.0	–31.4	–17.0
Loans	4 764	. .	85.4	–49.3	–283.1	780.0	7.7	670.2	495.7	25.7
Use of Fund credit and loans from the Fund	4 766	. .	–51.2	–88.0	–56.9	15.9	37.3	63.9	–8.1	–34.0
Monetary authorities: other long-term	4 767	. .	11.8	–22.1	–145.0	–4.1	–25.3	–427.9	269.2	18.6
Monetary authorities: short-term	4 768	. .	. . .	. . .	. . .	. . .	. . .	19.6	27.6	31.9
General government: long-term	4 770	. .	124.8	–7.5	–64.4	753.3	16.6	510.2	10.3	–5.1
General government: short-term	4 771	. .	. . .	3.3	. . .	.6	2.3	–.6	–.2	. . .
Banks: long-term	4 773	. .	. . .	. . .	. . .	. . .	. . .	–1.7	1.0	–.4
Banks: short-term	4 774	. .	. . .	. . .	. . .	. . .	. . .	. . .	4.9	18.1
Other sectors: long-term	4 776	. .	. . .	65.0	–16.8	14.3	–23.2	455.0	218.7	–3.3
Other sectors: short-term	4 777	. .	. . .	. . .	. . .	. . .	. . .	51.7	–27.7	–.1
Currency and deposits	4 780	. .	47.1	–25.9	–15.8	–1.1	–13.6	–49.8	100.8	15.8
Monetary authorities	4 781	. .	. . .	–22.1	–56.6	3.6	–.9	–38.9	79.6	23.9
General government	4 782	. .	. . .	. . .	. . .	. . .	. . .	. . .	. . .	. . .
Banks	4 783	. .	47.1	–3.8	40.8	–4.7	–12.7	–10.9	21.2	–8.1
Other sectors	4 784	. .	. . .	. . .	. . .	. . .	. . .	. . .	. . .	. . .
Other liabilities	4 786	. .	–113.4	374.1	428.1	–760.9	–100.3	–381.9	–996.8	37.2
Monetary authorities: long-term	4 788	. .	. . .	. . .	. . .	. . .	. . .	. . .	. . .	. . .
Monetary authorities: short-term	4 789	. .	–113.4	225.4	222.1	4.7	–98.9	417.8	–785.9	–2.3
General government: long-term	4 791	. .	. . .	. . .	. . .	. . .	. . .	. . .	. . .	. . .
General government: short-term	4 792	. .	. . .	95.0	131.8	–800.7	–28.4	–477.5	–93.9	50.0
Banks: long-term	4 794	. .	. . .	. . .	. . .	. . .	. . .	. . .	. . .	. . .
Banks: short-term	4 795	. .	. . .	.7	.4	.2	–.1	1.1	–2.5	.4
Other sectors: long-term	4 797	. .	. . .	. . .	. . .	. . .	. . .	. . .	. . .	. . .
Other sectors: short-term	4 798	. .	. . .	53.0	73.8	34.9	27.1	–323.3	–114.5	–10.9
D. RESERVE ASSETS	4 800	. .	–58.9	90.0	49.0	–357.4	–63.5	–153.5	384.7	–131.2
Monetary gold	4 810	. .	1.2	.2	.6	.3	.5	–.9	.1	–.2
Special drawing rights	4 820	. .	–.1	. . .	. . .	. . .	. . .	–14.1	11.1	3.0
Reserve position in the Fund	4 830	. .	. . .	. . .	. . .	. . .	. . .	. . .	. . .	. . .
Foreign exchange	4 840	. .	–60.0	89.8	48.4	–357.7	–64.0	–138.5	373.5	–134.0
Other claims	4 880	. .	. . .	. . .	. . .	. . .	. . .	. . .	. . .	. . .
NET ERRORS AND OMISSIONS	4 998	. .	**35.6**	**–73.6**	**–120.7**	**548.3**	**569.0**	**39.1**	**–509.7**	**–116.1**

Part 3 of the *Yearbook* contains descriptions of the methodologies, compilation practices, and sources used to compile these data.

Table 1. ANALYTIC PRESENTATION, 1988–95
(Millions of U.S. dollars)

	Code		1988	1989	1990	1991	1992	1993	1994	1995
A. Current Account [1]	4 993	Y .	**–683**	**–716**	**–366**	**–707**	**–215**	**–682**	**–680**	**–822**
Goods: exports f.o.b	2 100	. .	2,202	2,354	2,714	2,851	3,008	3,062	3,844	4,362
Goods: imports f.o.b	3 100	. .	–1,583	–1,693	–1,711	–2,207	–2,083	–2,474	–3,282	–4,095
Balance on Goods	4 100	. .	*619*	*661*	*1,003*	*644*	*925*	*588*	*562*	*267*
Services: credit	2 200	. .	442	517	539	557	623	654	745	854
Services: debit	3 200	. .	–621	–639	–662	–718	–748	–799	–922	–983
Balance on Goods and Services	4 991	. .	*440*	*539*	*880*	*483*	*800*	*443*	*385*	*138*
Income: credit	2 300	. .	15	19	24	30	29	26	52	82
Income: debit	3 300	. .	–1,235	–1,371	–1,377	–1,330	–1,164	–1,281	–1,262	–1,273
Balance on Goods, Services, and Income	4 992	. .	*–780*	*–813*	*–473*	*–817*	*–335*	*–812*	*–825*	*–1,053*
Current transfers: credit	2 379	Y .	104	106	119	123	134	145	164	250
Current transfers: debit	3 379	. .	–7	–9	–12	–13	–14	–15	–19	–19
B. Capital Account [1]	4 994	Y .	**. . .**	**. . .**	**. . .**	**. . .**	**. . .**	**. . .**	**43**	**. . .**
Capital account: credit	2 994	Y .	. . .	. . .	. . .	. . .	. . .	. . .	43	. . .
Capital account: debit	3 994	. .	. . .	. . .	. . .	. . .	. . .	. . .	. . .	. . .
Total, Groups A Plus B	4 010	. .	*–683*	*–716*	*–366*	*–707*	*–215*	*–682*	*–637*	*–822*
C. Financial Account [1]	4 995	X .	**–588**	**–511**	**–806**	**–481**	**–633**	**156**	**–103**	**1,578**
Direct investment abroad	4 505	. .	. . .	. . .	. . .	. . .	. . .	. . .	. . .	. . .
Direct investment in Ecuador	4 555	Y .	155	160	126	160	178	469	531	470
Portfolio investment assets	4 602	. .	. . .	. . .	. . .	. . .	. . .	. . .	. . .	. . .
Equity securities	4 610	. .	. . .	. . .	. . .	. . .	. . .	. . .	. . .	. . .
Debt securities	4 619	. .	. . .	. . .	. . .	. . .	. . .	. . .	. . .	. . .
Portfolio investment liabilities	4 652	Y .	. . .	. . .	. . .	. . .	. . .	. . .	. . .	. . .
Equity securities	4 660	Y .	. . .	. . .	. . .	. . .	. . .	. . .	. . .	. . .
Debt securities	4 669	Y .	. . .	. . .	. . .	. . .	. . .	. . .	. . .	. . .
Other investment assets	4 703	. .	14	–68	–120	–14	64	–29	–9	–16
Monetary authorities	4 703	. A	. . .	. . .	. . .	. . .	. . .	. . .	. . .	. . .
General government	4 703	. B	1	–15	–114	5	79	–11	–9	–16
Banks	4 703	. C	3	–32	–14	–1	–15	–18	. . .	. . .
Other sectors	4 703	. D	10	–21	8	–18	. . .	. . .	. . .	. . .
Other investment liabilities	4 753	X .	–757	–603	–812	–627	–875	–284	–625	1,124
Monetary authorities	4 753	XA	114	–217	–77	–28	15	102	–114	–16
General government	4 753	YB	–856	–426	–735	–592	–982	–720	–736	404
Banks	4 753	YC	–15	–3	–11	–10	–11	–14	. . .	. . .
Other sectors	4 753	YD	. . .	43	11	3	103	348	225	736
Total, Groups A Through C	4 020	. .	*–1,271*	*–1,227*	*–1,172*	*–1,188*	*–848*	*–526*	*–740*	*756*
D. Net Errors and Omissions	4 998	. .	**28**	**115**	**216**	**163**	**–99**	**–65**	**–22**	**–1,249**
Total, Groups A Through D	4 030	. .	*–1,243*	*–1,112*	*–956*	*–1,025*	*–947*	*–591*	*–762*	*–493*
E. Reserves and Related Items	4 040	. .	**1,243**	**1,112**	**956**	**1,025**	**947**	**591**	**762**	**493**
Reserve assets	4 800	. .	26	–118	–195	–78	–22	–490	–453	233
Use of Fund credit and loans	4 766	. .	–58	–69	–85	–79	–77	–29	122	–29
Liabilities constituting foreign authorities' reserves	4 900	. .	–44	–4	5	15	–19	–33	–4	–26
Exceptional financing	4 920	. .	1,319	1,303	1,231	1,167	1,066	1,143	1,097	315
Conversion rates: sucres per U.S. dollar	0 101	. .	**301.6**	**526.3**	**767.8**	**1,046.2**	**1,534.0**	**1,919.1**	**2,196.7**	**2,564.5**

[1] Excludes components that have been classified in the categories of Group E.

Table 2. STANDARD PRESENTATION, 1988–95

(Millions of U.S. dollars)

	Code	1988	1989	1990	1991	1992	1993	1994	1995
CURRENT ACCOUNT	4 993 . .	**–683**	**–716**	**–366**	**–707**	**–215**	**–682**	**–680**	**–822**
A. GOODS	4 100 . .	619	661	1,003	644	925	588	562	267
Credit	2 100 . .	**2,202**	**2,354**	**2,714**	**2,851**	**3,008**	**3,062**	**3,844**	**4,362**
General merchandise: exports f.o.b.	2 110 . .	2,202	2,354	2,714	2,851	3,008	3,062	3,844	4,362
Goods for processing: exports f.o.b.	2 150 . .	...	...	...	...	...	...	...	...
Repairs on goods	2 160 . .	...	...	...	...	...	...	...	...
Goods procured in ports by carriers	2 170 . .	...	...	...	...	...	...	...	...
Nonmonetary gold	2 180 . .	...	...	...	...	...	...	...	...
Debit	3 100 . .	**–1,583**	**–1,693**	**–1,711**	**–2,207**	**–2,083**	**–2,474**	**–3,282**	**–4,095**
General merchandise: imports f.o.b.	3 110 . .	–1,583	–1,693	–1,711	–2,207	–2,083	–2,474	–3,282	–4,095
Goods for processing: imports f.o.b.	3 150 . .	...	...	...	...	...	...	...	...
Repairs on goods	3 160 . .	...	...	...	...	...	...	...	...
Goods procured in ports by carriers	3 170 . .	...	...	...	...	...	...	...	...
Nonmonetary gold	3 180 . .	...	...	...	...	...	...	...	...
B. SERVICES	4 200 . .	–179	–122	–123	–161	–125	–145	–177	–129
Total credit	2 200 . .	*442*	*517*	*539*	*557*	*623*	*654*	*745*	*854*
Total debit	3 200 . .	*–621*	*–639*	*–662*	*–718*	*–748*	*–799*	*–922*	*–983*
Transportation services, credit	2 205 . .	**200**	**234**	**242**	**241**	**263**	**251**	**296**	**332**
Passenger	2 205 BA	*37*	*48*	*78*	*78*	*78*	*55*	*57*	*60*
Freight	2 205 BB	*112*	*143*	*145*	*143*	*155*	*161*	*197*	*214*
Other	2 205 BC	*51*	*43*	*19*	*20*	*30*	*35*	*42*	*58*
Sea transport, passenger	2 207 . .	...	...	...	...	...	...	...	...
Sea transport, freight	2 208 . .	...	...	...	...	...	...	...	...
Sea transport, other	2 209 . .	...	...	...	...	...	...	...	...
Air transport, passenger	2 211 . .	...	...	...	...	...	...	...	...
Air transport, freight	2 212 . .	...	...	...	...	...	...	...	...
Air transport, other	2 213 . .	...	...	...	...	...	...	...	...
Other transport, passenger	2 215 . .	...	...	...	...	...	...	...	...
Other transport, freight	2 216 . .	...	...	...	...	...	...	...	...
Other transport, other	2 217 . .	...	...	...	...	...	...	...	...
Transportation services, debit	3 205 . .	**–294**	**–300**	**–316**	**–374**	**–387**	**–401**	**–466**	**–469**
Passenger	3 205 BA	*–73*	*–94*	*–69*	*–72*	*–76*	*–66*	*–91*	*–96*
Freight	3 205 BB	*–125*	*–117*	*–131*	*–162*	*–174*	*–181*	*–235*	*–273*
Other	3 205 BC	*–96*	*–89*	*–116*	*–140*	*–137*	*–154*	*–140*	*–100*
Sea transport, passenger	3 207 . .	...	...	...	...	...	...	...	...
Sea transport, freight	3 208 . .	...	...	...	...	...	...	...	...
Sea transport, other	3 209 . .	...	...	...	...	...	...	...	...
Air transport, passenger	3 211 . .	...	...	...	...	...	...	...	...
Air transport, freight	3 212 . .	...	...	...	...	...	...	...	...
Air transport, other	3 213 . .	...	...	...	...	...	...	...	...
Other transport, passenger	3 215 . .	...	...	...	...	...	...	...	...
Other transport, freight	3 216 . .	...	...	...	...	...	...	...	...
Other transport, other	3 217 . .	...	...	...	...	...	...	...	...
Travel, credit	2 236 . .	**173**	**187**	**188**	**189**	**192**	**230**	**252**	**255**
Business travel	2 237 . .	...	...	...	...	...	...	...	...
Personal travel	2 240 . .	...	...	...	...	...	...	...	...
Travel, debit	3 236 . .	**–167**	**–169**	**–175**	**–177**	**–178**	**–190**	**–203**	**–235**
Business travel	3 237 . .	...	...	...	...	...	...	...	...
Personal travel	3 240 . .	...	...	...	...	...	...	...	...
Other services, credit	2 200 BA	**69**	**96**	**109**	**127**	**168**	**173**	**197**	**267**
Communications	2 245 . .	...	...	...	...	...	...	...	...
Construction	2 249 . .	...	...	...	...	...	...	...	...
Insurance	2 253 . .	31	41	47	50	52	45	74	108
Financial	2 260 . .	...	...	...	...	...	...	...	...
Computer and information	2 262 . .	...	...	...	...	...	...	...	...
Royalties and licence fees	2 266 . .	...	...	...	...	...	...	...	...
Other business services	2 268 . .	11	25	32	45	83	95	87	118
Personal, cultural, and recreational	2 287 . .	...	...	...	...	...	...	...	...
Government, n.i.e.	2 291 . .	27	30	30	32	33	33	36	41
Other services, debit	3 200 BA	**–160**	**–170**	**–171**	**–167**	**–183**	**–208**	**–253**	**–279**
Communications	3 245 . .	...	...	...	...	...	...	...	...
Construction	3 249 . .	...	...	...	...	...	...	...	...
Insurance	3 253 . .	–47	–62	–61	–62	–63	–91	–110	–128
Financial	3 260 . .	...	...	...	...	...	...	...	...
Computer and information	3 262 . .	...	...	...	...	...	...	...	...
Royalties and licence fees	3 266 . .	–35	–36	–37	–38	–38	–45	–50	–53
Other business services	3 268 . .	–42	–29	–24	–34	–37	–43	–57	–66
Personal, cultural, and recreational	3 287 . .	...	...	...	...	...	...	...	...
Government, n.i.e.	3 291 . .	–36	–43	–49	–33	–45	–29	–36	–32

Table 2 (Continued). STANDARD PRESENTATION, 1988–95
(Millions of U.S. dollars)

	Code	1988	1989	1990	1991	1992	1993	1994	1995
C. INCOME	4 300 . .	–1,220	–1,352	–1,353	–1,300	–1,135	–1,255	–1,210	–1,191
Total credit	2 300 . .	*15*	*19*	*24*	*30*	*29*	*26*	*52*	*82*
Total debit	3 300 . .	*–1,235*	*–1,371*	*–1,377*	*–1,330*	*–1,164*	*–1,281*	*–1,262*	*–1,273*
Compensation of employees, credit	2 310 . .	**. . .**	**. . .**	**. . .**	**. . .**	**. . .**	**. . .**	**. . .**	**. . .**
Compensation of employees, debit	3 310 . .	**–173**	**–162**	**–144**	**–185**	**–188**	**–330**	**–210**	**–255**
Investment income, credit	2 320 . .	**15**	**19**	**24**	**30**	**29**	**26**	**52**	**82**
Direct investment income	2 330 . .	. . .	. . .	. . .	. . .	. . .	. . .	. . .	. . .
Dividends and distributed branch profits	2 332 . .	. . .	. . .	. . .	. . .	. . .	. . .	. . .	. . .
Reinvested earnings and undistributed branch profits	2 333 . .	. . .	. . .	. . .	. . .	. . .	. . .	. . .	. . .
Income on debt (interest)	2 334 . .	. . .	. . .	. . .	. . .	. . .	. . .	. . .	. . .
Portfolio investment income	2 339 . .	. . .	. . .	. . .	. . .	. . .	. . .	. . .	. . .
Income on equity	2 340 . .	. . .	. . .	. . .	. . .	. . .	. . .	. . .	. . .
Income on bonds and notes	2 350 . .	. . .	. . .	. . .	. . .	. . .	. . .	. . .	. . .
Income on money market instruments and financial derivatives	2 360 . .	. . .	. . .	. . .	. . .	. . .	. . .	. . .	. . .
Other investment income	2 370 . .	15	19	24	30	29	26	52	82
Investment income, debit	3 320 . .	**–1,062**	**–1,209**	**–1,233**	**–1,145**	**–976**	**–951**	**–1,052**	**–1,018**
Direct investment income	3 330 . .	–130	–120	–125	–128	–130	–147	–180	–192
Dividends and distributed branch profits	3 332 . .	–70	–60	–63	–63	–58	–61	–80	–87
Reinvested earnings and undistributed branch profits	3 333 . .	–60	–60	–62	–65	–72	–86	–100	–105
Income on debt (interest)	3 334 . .	. . .	. . .	. . .	. . .	. . .	. . .	. . .	. . .
Portfolio investment income	3 339 . .	. . .	. . .	. . .	. . .	. . .	. . .	. . .	. . .
Income on equity	3 340 . .	. . .	. . .	. . .	. . .	. . .	. . .	. . .	. . .
Income on bonds and notes	3 350 . .	. . .	. . .	. . .	. . .	. . .	. . .	. . .	. . .
Income on money market instruments and financial derivatives	3 360 . .	. . .	. . .	. . .	. . .	. . .	. . .	. . .	. . .
Other investment income	3 370 . .	–932	–1,089	–1,108	–1,017	–846	–804	–872	–826
D. CURRENT TRANSFERS	4 379 . .	97	97	107	110	120	130	145	231
Credit	2 379 . .	**104**	**106**	**119**	**123**	**134**	**145**	**164**	**250**
General government	2 380 . .	104	106	119	123	134	145	164	250
Other sectors	2 390 . .	. . .	. . .	. . .	. . .	. . .	. . .	. . .	. . .
Workers' remittances	2 391 . .	. . .	. . .	. . .	. . .	. . .	. . .	. . .	. . .
Other current transfers	2 392 . .	. . .	. . .	. . .	. . .	. . .	. . .	. . .	. . .
Debit	3 379 . .	**–7**	**–9**	**–12**	**–13**	**–14**	**–15**	**–19**	**–19**
General government	3 380 . .	–7	–9	–12	–13	–14	–15	–19	–19
Other sectors	3 390 . .	. . .	. . .	. . .	. . .	. . .	. . .	. . .	. . .
Workers' remittances	3 391 . .	. . .	. . .	. . .	. . .	. . .	. . .	. . .	. . .
Other current transfers	3 392 . .	. . .	. . .	. . .	. . .	. . .	. . .	. . .	. . .
CAPITAL AND FINANCIAL ACCOUNT	4 996 . .	**655**	**601**	**150**	**544**	**314**	**747**	**702**	**2,071**
CAPITAL ACCOUNT	4 994 . .	**. . .**	**. . .**	**. . .**	**. . .**	**. . .**	**. . .**	**43**	**. . .**
Total credit	2 994 . .	. . .	. . .	. . .	. . .	. . .	. . .	*43*	. . .
Total debit	3 994 . .	. . .	. . .	. . .	. . .	. . .	. . .	. . .	. . .
Capital transfers, credit	2 400 . .	**. . .**	**. . .**	**. . .**	**. . .**	**. . .**	**. . .**	**43**	**. . .**
General government	2 401 . .	. . .	. . .	. . .	. . .	. . .	. . .	43	. . .
Debt forgiveness	2 402 . .	. . .	. . .	. . .	. . .	. . .	. . .	. . .	. . .
Other capital transfers	2 410 . .	. . .	. . .	. . .	. . .	. . .	. . .	43	. . .
Other sectors	2 430 . .	. . .	. . .	. . .	. . .	. . .	. . .	. . .	. . .
Migrants' transfers	2 431 . .	. . .	. . .	. . .	. . .	. . .	. . .	. . .	. . .
Debt forgiveness	2 432 . .	. . .	. . .	. . .	. . .	. . .	. . .	. . .	. . .
Other capital transfers	2 440 . .	. . .	. . .	. . .	. . .	. . .	. . .	. . .	. . .
Capital transfers, debit	3 400 . .	**. . .**	**. . .**	**. . .**	**. . .**	**. . .**	**. . .**	**. . .**	**. . .**
General government	3 401 . .	. . .	. . .	. . .	. . .	. . .	. . .	. . .	. . .
Debt forgiveness	3 402 . .	. . .	. . .	. . .	. . .	. . .	. . .	. . .	. . .
Other capital transfers	3 410 . .	. . .	. . .	. . .	. . .	. . .	. . .	. . .	. . .
Other sectors	3 430 . .	. . .	. . .	. . .	. . .	. . .	. . .	. . .	. . .
Migrants' transfers	3 431 . .	. . .	. . .	. . .	. . .	. . .	. . .	. . .	. . .
Debt forgiveness	3 432 . .	. . .	. . .	. . .	. . .	. . .	. . .	. . .	. . .
Other capital transfers	3 440 . .	. . .	. . .	. . .	. . .	. . .	. . .	. . .	. . .
Nonproduced nonfinancial assets, credit	2 480 . .	**. . .**	**. . .**	**. . .**	**. . .**	**. . .**	**. . .**	**. . .**	**. . .**
Nonproduced nonfinancial assets, debit	3 480 . .	**. . .**	**. . .**	**. . .**	**. . .**	**. . .**	**. . .**	**. . .**	**. . .**

Table 2 (Continued). STANDARD PRESENTATION, 1988–95
(Millions of U.S. dollars)

	Code	1988	1989	1990	1991	1992	1993	1994	1995
FINANCIAL ACCOUNT	4 995 . .	**655**	**601**	**150**	**544**	**314**	**747**	**659**	**2,071**
A. DIRECT INVESTMENT	4 500 . .	155	160	126	160	178	469	531	470
Direct investment abroad	4 505 . .	**...**	**...**	**...**	**...**	**...**	**...**	**...**	**...**
Equity capital	4 510 . .	...	...	...	...	...	...	...	...
Claims on affiliated enterprises	4 515 . .	...	...	...	...	...	...	...	...
Liabilities to affiliated enterprises	4 520 . .	...	...	...	...	...	...	...	...
Reinvested earnings	4 525 . .	...	...	...	...	...	...	...	...
Other capital	4 530 . .	...	...	...	...	...	...	...	...
Claims on affiliated enterprises	4 535 . .	...	...	...	...	...	...	...	...
Liabilities to affiliated enterprises	4 540 . .	...	...	...	...	...	...	...	...
Direct investment in Ecuador	4 555 . .	**155**	**160**	**126**	**160**	**178**	**469**	**531**	**470**
Equity capital	4 560 . .	95	100	64	95	106	383	431	365
Claims on direct investors	4 565 . .	...	...	...	...	...	...	...	...
Liabilities to direct investors	4 570 . .	...	...	...	...	...	...	...	...
Reinvested earnings	4 575 . .	60	60	62	65	72	86	100	105
Other capital	4 580 . .	...	...	...	...	...	...	...	...
Claims on direct investors	4 585 . .	...	...	...	...	...	...	...	...
Liabilities to direct investors	4 590 . .	...	...	...	...	...	...	...	...
B. PORTFOLIO INVESTMENT	4 600 . .	...	...	...	...	...	...	...	...
Assets	4 602 . .	**...**	**...**	**...**	**...**	**...**	**...**	**...**	**...**
Equity securities	4 610 . .	...	...	...	...	...	...	...	...
Monetary authorities	4 611 . .	...	...	...	...	...	...	...	...
General government	4 612 . .	...	...	...	...	...	...	...	...
Banks	4 613 . .	...	...	...	...	...	...	...	...
Other sectors	4 614 . .	...	...	...	...	...	...	...	...
Debt securities	4 619 . .	...	...	...	...	...	...	...	...
Bonds and notes	4 620 . .	...	...	...	...	...	...	...	...
Monetary authorities	4 621 . .	...	...	...	...	...	...	...	...
General government	4 622 . .	...	...	...	...	...	...	...	...
Banks	4 623 . .	...	...	...	...	...	...	...	...
Other sectors	4 624 . .	...	...	...	...	...	...	...	...
Money market instruments	4 630 . .	...	...	...	...	...	...	...	...
Monetary authorities	4 631 . .	...	...	...	...	...	...	...	...
General government	4 632 . .	...	...	...	...	...	...	...	...
Banks	4 633 . .	...	...	...	...	...	...	...	...
Other sectors	4 634 . .	...	...	...	...	...	...	...	...
Financial derivatives	4 640 . .	...	...	...	...	...	...	...	...
Monetary authorities	4 641 . .	...	...	...	...	...	...	...	...
General government	4 642 . .	...	...	...	...	...	...	...	...
Banks	4 643 . .	...	...	...	...	...	...	...	...
Other sectors	4 644 . .	...	...	...	...	...	...	...	...
Liabilities	4 652 . .	**...**	**...**	**...**	**...**	**...**	**...**	**...**	**...**
Equity securities	4 660 . .	...	...	...	...	...	...	...	...
Banks	4 663 . .	...	...	...	...	...	...	...	...
Other sectors	4 664 . .	...	...	...	...	...	...	...	...
Debt securities	4 669 . .	...	...	...	...	...	...	...	...
Bonds and notes	4 670 . .	...	...	...	...	...	...	...	...
Monetary authorities	4 671 . .	...	...	...	...	...	...	...	...
General government	4 672 . .	...	...	...	...	...	...	...	...
Banks	4 673 . .	...	...	...	...	...	...	...	...
Other sectors	4 674 . .	...	...	...	...	...	...	...	...
Money market instruments	4 680 . .	...	...	...	...	...	...	...	...
Monetary authorities	4 681 . .	...	...	...	...	...	...	...	...
General government	4 682 . .	...	...	...	...	...	...	...	...
Banks	4 683 . .	...	...	...	...	...	...	...	...
Other sectors	4 684 . .	...	...	...	...	...	...	...	...
Financial derivatives	4 690 . .	...	...	...	...	...	...	...	...
Monetary authorities	4 691 . .	...	...	...	...	...	...	...	...
General government	4 692 . .	...	...	...	...	...	...	...	...
Banks	4 693 . .	...	...	...	...	...	...	...	...
Other sectors	4 694 . .	...	...	...	...	...	...	...	...

Table 2 (Concluded). STANDARD PRESENTATION, 1988–95
(Millions of U.S. dollars)

	Code	1988	1989	1990	1991	1992	1993	1994	1995
C. OTHER INVESTMENT	4 700	474	559	219	462	159	768	581	1,368
Assets	4 703	**14**	**–68**	**–120**	**–14**	**64**	**–29**	**–9**	**–16**
Trade credits	4 706	...	...	...	...	...	...	...	...
General government: long-term	4 708	...	...	...	...	...	...	...	...
General government: short-term	4 709	...	...	...	...	...	...	...	...
Other sectors: long-term	4 711	...	...	...	...	...	...	...	...
Other sectors: short-term	4 712	...	...	...	...	...	...	...	...
Loans	4 714	...	...	...	...	...	...	...	...
Monetary authorities: long-term	4 717	...	...	...	...	...	...	...	...
Monetary authorities: short-term	4 718	...	...	...	...	...	...	...	...
General government: long-term	4 720	...	...	...	...	...	...	...	...
General government: short-term	4 721	...	...	...	...	...	...	...	...
Banks: long-term	4 723	...	...	...	...	...	...	...	...
Banks: short-term	4 724	...	...	...	...	...	...	...	...
Other sectors: long-term	4 726	...	...	...	...	...	...	...	...
Other sectors: short-term	4 727	...	...	...	...	...	...	...	...
Currency and deposits	4 730	21	–54	–111	–3	74	–16	...	–7
Monetary authorities	4 731	...	...	...	...	...	...	...	...
General government	4 732	5	...	–104	17	89	2	...	–7
Banks	4 733	4	–33	–15	–2	–15	–18	...	...
Other sectors	4 734	12	–21	8	–18	...	...	...	...
Other assets	4 736	–7	–14	–9	–11	–10	–13	–9	–9
Monetary authorities: long-term	4 738	...	...	...	...	...	...	...	...
Monetary authorities: short-term	4 739	...	...	...	...	...	...	...	...
General government: long-term	4 741	–4	–15	–10	–12	–10	–13	–9	–9
General government: short-term	4 742	...	...	...	...	...	...	...	...
Banks: long-term	4 744	–1	1	1	1	...	...	...	...
Banks: short-term	4 745	...	...	...	...	...	...	...	...
Other sectors: long-term	4 747	–2	...	...	...	...	...	...	...
Other sectors: short-term	4 748	...	...	...	...	...	...	...	...
Liabilities	4 753	**460**	**627**	**339**	**476**	**95**	**797**	**590**	**1,384**
Trade credits	4 756	...	...	...	...	...	...	...	...
General government: long-term	4 758	...	...	...	...	...	...	...	...
General government: short-term	4 759	...	...	...	...	...	...	...	...
Other sectors: long-term	4 761	...	...	...	...	...	...	...	...
Other sectors: short-term	4 762	...	...	...	...	...	...	...	...
Loans	4 764	141	4	–659	–689	–637	–263	–290	1,500
Use of Fund credit and loans from the Fund	4 766	–58	–69	–85	–79	–77	–29	122	–29
Monetary authorities: other long-term	4 767	...	...	...	...	...	...	...	...
Monetary authorities: short-term	4 768	114	–217	–77	–28	15	102	–114	–16
General government: long-term	4 770	85	247	–508	–585	–678	–684	–523	809
General government: short-term	4 771	...	...	...	...	...	...	...	...
Banks: long-term	4 773	...	...	...	...	...	...	...	...
Banks: short-term	4 774	...	...	...	...	...	...	...	...
Other sectors: long-term	4 776	...	43	11	3	103	348	225	736
Other sectors: short-term	4 777	...	...	...	...	...	...	...	...
Currency and deposits	4 780	–59	–7	–6	5	–30	–47	–4	–26
Monetary authorities	4 781	–44	–4	5	15	–19	–33	–4	–26
General government	4 782	...	...	...	...	...	...	...	...
Banks	4 783	–15	–3	–11	–10	–11	–14	...	...
Other sectors	4 784	...	...	...	...	...	...	...	...
Other liabilities	4 786	378	630	1,004	1,160	762	1,107	884	–90
Monetary authorities: long-term	4 788	...	...	...	...	...	...	...	...
Monetary authorities: short-term	4 789	–3	4	9	–1	...	...	...	...
General government: long-term	4 791	...	...	...	...	...	...	...	...
General government: short-term	4 792	...	...	...	...	...	...	...	...
Banks: long-term	4 794	...	...	...	...	...	...	...	...
Banks: short-term	4 795	...	...	...	...	...	...	...	...
Other sectors: long-term	4 797	...	...	...	...	...	...	...	...
Other sectors: short-term	4 798	381	626	995	1,161	762	1,107	884	–90
D. RESERVE ASSETS	4 800	26	–118	–195	–78	–22	–490	–453	233
Monetary gold	4 810	...	...	...	...	...	...	...	...
Special drawing rights	4 820	–1	...	–13	–26	40	–4	...	1
Reserve position in the Fund	4 830	...	...	...	...	–24	...	...	...
Foreign exchange	4 840	27	–115	–179	–49	–29	–489	–466	232
Other claims	4 880	...	–3	–3	–3	–10	3	13	...
NET ERRORS AND OMISSIONS	4 998	**28**	**115**	**216**	**163**	**–99**	**–65**	**–22**	**–1,249**

Table 1. ANALYTIC PRESENTATION, 1988–95
(Millions of U.S. dollars)

	Code	1988	1989	1990	1991	1992	1993	1994	1995
A. Current Account [1]	4 993 Y.	**–1,048**	**–1,309**	**185**	**1,903**	**2,812**	**2,299**	**31**	**–254**
Goods: exports f.o.b	2 100 . .	2,770	3,119	3,924	4,164	3,670	3,545	4,044	4,670
Goods: imports f.o.b	3 100 . .	–9,378	–8,841	–10,303	–9,831	–8,901	–9,923	–9,997	–12,267
Balance on Goods	4 100 . .	*–6,608*	*–5,722*	*–6,379*	*–5,667*	*–5,231*	*–6,378*	*–5,953*	*–7,597*
Services: credit	2 200 . .	4,408	4,203	5,971	6,783	7,716	7,895	8,070	8,590
Services: debit	3 200 . .	–3,082	–3,283	–3,788	–3,364	–4,867	–5,367	–5,645	–4,873
Balance on Goods and Services	4 991 . .	*–5,283*	*–4,802*	*–4,196*	*–2,248*	*–2,382*	*–3,850*	*–3,528*	*–3,880*
Income: credit	2 300 . .	575	709	857	860	915	1,110	1,330	1,578
Income: debit	3 300 . .	–776	–1,389	–1,879	–2,143	–2,797	–1,967	–2,114	–1,983
Balance on Goods, Services, and Income	4 992 . .	*–5,484*	*–5,482*	*–5,218*	*–3,531*	*–4,264*	*–4,707*	*–4,312*	*–4,285*
Current transfers: credit	2 379 Y.	4,436	4,183	5,417	5,434	7,076	7,006	4,622	4,284
Current transfers: debit	3 379 . .	. . .	–10	–14	. . .	. . .	. . .	–279	–253
B. Capital Account [1]	4 994 Y.	**. . .**	**. . .**	**. . .**	**. . .**	**. . .**	**. . .**	**. . .**	**. . .**
Capital account: credit	2 994 Y.	. . .	. . .	. . .	. . .	. . .	. . .	. . .	. . .
Capital account: debit	3 994 . .	. . .	. . .	. . .	. . .	. . .	. . .	. . .	. . .
Total, Groups A Plus B	4 010 . .	*–1,048*	*–1,309*	*185*	*1,903*	*2,812*	*2,299*	*31*	*–254*
C. Financial Account [1]	4 995 X.	**1,308**	**361**	**–11,039**	**–4,706**	**–168**	**–762**	**–1,450**	**–1,845**
Direct investment abroad	4 505 . .	–12	–23	–12	–62	–4	. . .	–43	–93
Direct investment in Egypt	4 555 Y.	1,190	1,250	734	253	459	493	1,256	598
Portfolio investment assets	4 602 . .	. . .	. . .	15	21	6	. . .	. . .	. . .
Equity securities	4 610 . .	. . .	. . .	. . .	. . .	. . .	. . .	. . .	. . .
Debt securities	4 619 . .	. . .	. . .	15	21	6	. . .	. . .	. . .
Portfolio investment liabilities	4 652 Y.	. . .	. . .	. . .	. . .	. . .	4	3	20
Equity securities	4 660 Y.	. . .	. . .	. . .	. . .	. . .	. . .	. . .	. . .
Debt securities	4 669 Y.	. . .	. . .	. . .	. . .	. . .	4	3	20
Other investment assets	4 703 . .	546	–1,299	–1,921	–2,298	1,183	319	–905	–396
Monetary authorities	4 703 . A	–7	–25	–16	–46	–13	–21	–25	65
General government	4 703 . B	–17	–26	–2	–18	–104	–4	. . .	. . .
Banks	4 703 . C	571	–1,249	–1,904	–2,234	1,300	523	–634	371
Other sectors	4 703 . D	. . .	. . .	. . .	. . .	. . .	–179	–246	–832
Other investment liabilities	4 753 X.	–416	432	–9,855	–2,620	–1,812	–1,578	–1,761	–1,974
Monetary authorities	4 753 XA	–250	–372	–29	–113	–42	629	–5	–21
General government	4 753 YB	387	688	–10,032	–2,204	–1,175	–1,761	–1,536	–1,783
Banks	4 753 YC	–749	–138	237	–333	–383	–202	–256	–148
Other sectors	4 753 YD	196	254	–31	30	–212	–244	36	–22
Total, Groups A Through C	4 020 . .	*260*	*–948*	*–10,854*	*–2,803*	*2,644*	*1,537*	*–1,419*	*–2,099*
D. Net Errors and Omissions	4 998 . .	**–362**	**414**	**630**	**730**	**716**	**–1,519**	**255**	**272**
Total, Groups A Through D	4 030 . .	*–102*	*–533*	*–10,224*	*–2,073*	*3,360*	*18*	*–1,164*	*–1,827*
E. Reserves and Related Items	4 040 . .	**102**	**533**	**10,224**	**2,073**	**–3,360**	**–18**	**1,164**	**1,827**
Reserve assets	4 800 . .	153	435	–2,508	–2,775	–6,330	–2,809	–1,193	–409
Use of Fund credit and loans	4 766 . .	–59	–24	–48	. . .	81	. . .	–22	–95
Liabilities constituting foreign authorities' reserves	4 900 . .	. . .	. . .	. . .	. . .	. . .	. . .	. . .	. . .
Exceptional financing	4 920 . .	7	122	12,781	4,849	2,889	2,791	2,379	2,331
Conversion rates: Egyptian pounds per U.S. dollar	0 101 . .	**.7000**	**.8667**	**1.5500**	**3.1380**	**3.3217**	**3.3525**	**3.3851**	**3.3922**

[1] Excludes components that have been classified in the categories of Group E.

Table 2. STANDARD PRESENTATION, 1988–95
(Millions of U.S. dollars)

	Code	1988	1989	1990	1991	1992	1993	1994	1995
CURRENT ACCOUNT	4 993 . .	**–1,041**	**–1,309**	**2,327**	**3,369**	**3,270**	**2,538**	**31**	**–254**
A. GOODS	4 100 . .	–6,608	–5,722	–6,379	–5,667	–5,231	–6,378	–5,953	–7,597
Credit	2 100 . .	**2,770**	**3,119**	**3,924**	**4,164**	**3,670**	**3,545**	**4,044**	**4,670**
General merchandise: exports f.o.b.	2 110 . .	2,770	2,907	3,604	3,856	3,400	3,243	3,759	4,256
Goods for processing: exports f.o.b.	2 150 . .	. . .	. . .	. . .	. . .	. . .	. . .	. . .	. . .
Repairs on goods	2 160 . .	. . .	. . .	. . .	. . .	. . .	. . .	. . .	. . .
Goods procured in ports by carriers	2 170 . .	. . .	211	320	308	270	302	285	414
Nonmonetary gold	2 180 . .	. . .	. . .	. . .	. . .	. . .	. . .	. . .	. . .
Debit	3 100 . .	**–9,378**	**–8,841**	**–10,303**	**–9,831**	**–8,901**	**–9,923**	**–9,997**	**–12,267**
General merchandise: imports f.o.b.	3 110 . .	–9,378	–8,841	–10,303	–9,831	–8,901	–9,923	–9,942	–12,102
Goods for processing: imports f.o.b.	3 150 . .	. . .	. . .	. . .	. . .	. . .	. . .	. . .	. . .
Repairs on goods	3 160 . .	. . .	. . .	. . .	. . .	. . .	. . .	. . .	. . .
Goods procured in ports by carriers	3 170 . .	. . .	. . .	. . .	. . .	. . .	. . .	–55	–165
Nonmonetary gold	3 180 . .	. . .	. . .	. . .	. . .	. . .	. . .	. . .	. . .
B. SERVICES	4 200 . .	1,325	920	2,183	3,419	2,849	2,528	2,425	3,717
Total credit	2 200 . .	*4,408*	*4,203*	*5,971*	*6,783*	*7,716*	*7,895*	*8,070*	*8,590*
Total debit	3 200 . .	*–3,082*	*–3,283*	*–3,788*	*–3,364*	*–4,867*	*–5,367*	*–5,645*	*–4,873*
Transportation services, credit	2 205 . .	**2,194**	**2,044**	**2,410**	**2,648**	**2,882**	**2,869**	**3,165**	**3,202**
Passenger	2 205 BA	*375*	*370*	*430*	*300*	*382*	*346*	*213*	*270*
Freight	2 205 BB	. . .	*25*	*26*	*33*	*40*	*11*	*811*	*752*
Other	2 205 BC	*1,819*	*1,649*	*1,955*	*2,315*	*2,460*	*2,512*	*2,141*	*2,180*
Sea transport, passenger	2 207 . .	. . .	. . .	. . .	. . .	. . .	. . .	. . .	3
Sea transport, freight	2 208 . .	. . .	25	26	33	40	11	811	743
Sea transport, other	2 209 . .	. . .	. . .	. . .	. . .	. . .	. . .	. . .	. . .
Air transport, passenger	2 211 . .	375	370	430	300	382	346	213	267
Air transport, freight	2 212 . .	. . .	. . .	. . .	. . .	. . .	. . .	. . .	9
Air transport, other	2 213 . .	. . .	. . .	. . .	. . .	. . .	. . .	. . .	. . .
Other transport, passenger	2 215 . .	. . .	. . .	. . .	. . .	. . .	. . .	. . .	. . .
Other transport, freight	2 216 . .	. . .	. . .	. . .	. . .	. . .	. . .	. . .	. . .
Other transport, other	2 217 . .	1,819	1,649	1,955	2,315	2,460	2,512	2,141	2,180
Transportation services, debit	3 205 . .	**–1,222**	**–1,312**	**–1,465**	**–1,340**	**–1,188**	**–1,301**	**–1,413**	**–1,582**
Passenger	3 205 BA	*–72*	*–52*	*–46*	*–57*	*–31*	*–23*	*–222*	*–93*
Freight	3 205 BB	*–938*	*–1,016*	*–1,204*	*–1,079*	*–967*	*–1,052*	*–1,191*	*–1,477*
Other	3 205 BC	*–212*	*–244*	*–216*	*–204*	*–190*	*–226*	. . .	*–12*
Sea transport, passenger	3 207 . .	. . .	. . .	. . .	. . .	. . .	. . .	–190	–43
Sea transport, freight	3 208 . .	–938	–1,016	–1,204	–1,079	–967	–1,052	–1,191	–1,476
Sea transport, other	3 209 . .	. . .	. . .	. . .	. . .	. . .	. . .	. . .	–3
Air transport, passenger	3 211 . .	–72	–52	–46	–57	–31	–23	–32	–50
Air transport, freight	3 212 . .	. . .	. . .	. . .	. . .	. . .	. . .	. . .	–1
Air transport, other	3 213 . .	. . .	. . .	. . .	. . .	. . .	. . .	. . .	–9
Other transport, passenger	3 215 . .	. . .	. . .	. . .	. . .	. . .	. . .	. . .	. . .
Other transport, freight	3 216 . .	. . .	. . .	. . .	. . .	. . .	. . .	. . .	. . .
Other transport, other	3 217 . .	–212	–244	–216	–204	–190	–226	. . .	. . .
Travel, credit	2 236 . .	**886**	**962**	**1,100**	**1,373**	**2,165**	**1,927**	**2,006**	**2,684**
Business travel	2 237 . .	. . .	. . .	. . .	. . .	. . .	. . .	. . .	. . .
Personal travel	2 240 . .	886	962	1,100	1,373	2,165	1,927	. . .	. . .
Travel, debit	3 236 . .	**–43**	**–87**	**–129**	**–225**	**–918**	**–1,048**	**–1,067**	**–1,278**
Business travel	3 237 . .	. . .	. . .	. . .	. . .	. . .	. . .	–77	–78
Personal travel	3 240 . .	–43	–87	–129	–225	–918	–1,048	–990	–1,200
Other services, credit	2 200 BA	**1,327**	**1,197**	**2,462**	**2,762**	**2,669**	**3,099**	**2,899**	**2,704**
Communications	2 245 . .	. . .	. . .	. . .	. . .	. . .	. . .	105	215
Construction	2 249 . .	. . .	. . .	. . .	. . .	. . .	. . .	. . .	1
Insurance	2 253 . .	59	31	46	42	102	84	34	12
Financial	2 260 . .	. . .	. . .	. . .	. . .	. . .	. . .	84	71
Computer and information	2 262 . .	. . .	. . .	. . .	. . .	. . .	. . .	. . .	1
Royalties and licence fees	2 266 . .	. . .	. . .	. . .	. . .	. . .	. . .	40	47
Other business services	2 268 . .	1,080	336	1,257	2,077	1,905	2,196	2,258	2,027
Personal, cultural, and recreational	2 287 . .	. . .	. . .	. . .	. . .	. . .	. . .	1	2
Government, n.i.e.	2 291 . .	189	831	1,159	643	662	819	377	328
Other services, debit	3 200 BA	**–1,818**	**–1,884**	**–2,195**	**–1,799**	**–2,761**	**–3,018**	**–3,165**	**–2,013**
Communications	3 245 . .	. . .	. . .	. . .	. . .	. . .	. . .	–6	–11
Construction	3 249 . .	. . .	. . .	. . .	. . .	. . .	. . .	. . .	. . .
Insurance	3 253 . .	–151	–124	–155	–122	–124	–138	–130	–167
Financial	3 260 . .	. . .	. . .	. . .	. . .	. . .	. . .	–62	–41
Computer and information	3 262 . .	. . .	. . .	. . .	. . .	. . .	. . .	. . .	–1
Royalties and licence fees	3 266 . .	. . .	. . .	. . .	. . .	. . .	. . .	–508	–97
Other business services	3 268 . .	–1,341	–1,334	–1,579	–1,311	–2,416	–2,677	–2,196	–1,333
Personal, cultural, and recreational	3 287 . .	. . .	. . .	. . .	. . .	. . .	. . .	. . .	–1
Government, n.i.e.	3 291 . .	–325	–427	–462	–366	–221	–203	–263	–362

Table 2 (Continued). STANDARD PRESENTATION, 1988–95
(Millions of U.S. dollars)

	Code	1988	1989	1990	1991	1992	1993	1994	1995
C. INCOME	4 300 . .	–201	–680	–1,022	–1,283	–1,882	–857	–784	–405
Total credit	2 300 . .	*575*	*709*	*857*	*860*	*915*	*1,110*	*1,330*	*1,578*
Total debit	3 300 . .	*–776*	*–1,389*	*–1,879*	*–2,143*	*–2,797*	*–1,967*	*–2,114*	*–1,983*
Compensation of employees, credit	2 310 . .	**. . .**	**. . .**	**. . .**	**. . .**	**. . .**	**. . .**	**. . .**	**. . .**
Compensation of employees, debit	3 310 . .	**. . .**	**–33**	**–27**	**–33**	**–233**	**–140**	**. . .**	**. . .**
Investment income, credit	2 320 . .	**575**	**709**	**857**	**860**	**915**	**1,110**	**1,330**	**1,578**
Direct investment income	2 330 . .	55	189	247	221	318	303	48	79
Dividends and distributed branch profits	2 332 . .	55	189	247	221	318	303	48	79
Reinvested earnings and undistributed branch profits	2 333 . .	. . .	. . .	. . .	. . .	. . .	. . .	. . .	. . .
Income on debt (interest)	2 334 . .	. . .	. . .	. . .	. . .	. . .	. . .	. . .	. . .
Portfolio investment income	2 339 . .	. . .	. . .	. . .	. . .	. . .	. . .	17	1
Income on equity	2 340 . .	. . .	. . .	. . .	. . .	. . .	. . .	. . .	. . .
Income on bonds and notes	2 350 . .	. . .	. . .	. . .	. . .	. . .	. . .	17	1
Income on money market instruments and financial derivatives	2 360 . .	. . .	. . .	. . .	. . .	. . .	. . .	. . .	. . .
Other investment income	2 370 . .	520	520	610	639	597	807	1,265	1,498
Investment income, debit	3 320 . .	**–776**	**–1,355**	**–1,852**	**–2,110**	**–2,564**	**–1,827**	**–2,114**	**–1,983**
Direct investment income	3 330 . .	–24	–25	–14	–7	–14	–13	–329	–228
Dividends and distributed branch profits	3 332 . .	–24	–25	–14	–7	–14	–13	–329	–228
Reinvested earnings and undistributed branch profits	3 333 . .	. . .	. . .	. . .	. . .	. . .	. . .	. . .	. . .
Income on debt (interest)	3 334 . .	. . .	. . .	. . .	. . .	. . .	. . .	. . .	. . .
Portfolio investment income	3 339 . .	. . .	. . .	. . .	. . .	. . .	. . .	. . .	–10
Income on equity	3 340 . .	. . .	. . .	. . .	. . .	. . .	. . .	. . .	. . .
Income on bonds and notes	3 350 . .	. . .	. . .	. . .	. . .	. . .	. . .	. . .	–10
Income on money market instruments and financial derivatives	3 360 . .	. . .	. . .	. . .	. . .	. . .	. . .	. . .	. . .
Other investment income	3 370 . .	–752	–1,330	–1,839	–2,103	–2,550	–1,814	–1,785	–1,745
D. CURRENT TRANSFERS	4 379 . .	4,443	4,173	7,545	6,900	7,534	7,245	4,343	4,031
Credit	2 379 . .	**4,443**	**4,183**	**7,559**	**6,900**	**7,534**	**7,245**	**4,622**	**4,284**
General government	2 380 . .	674	888	3,275	2,846	1,430	1,581	939	1,033
Other sectors	2 390 . .	3,770	3,295	4,284	4,054	6,104	5,664	3,683	3,251
Workers' remittances	2 391 . .	3,770	3,293	4,284	4,054	6,104	5,664	3,672	3,226
Other current transfers	2 392 . .	. . .	2	1	. . .	. . .	. . .	11	25
Debit	3 379 . .	**. . .**	**–10**	**–14**	**. . .**	**. . .**	**. . .**	**–279**	**–253**
General government	3 380 . .	. . .	–7	–14	. . .	. . .	. . .	–22	–30
Other sectors	3 390 . .	. . .	–2	. . .	. . .	. . .	. . .	–257	–223
Workers' remittances	3 391 . .	. . .	. . .	. . .	. . .	. . .	. . .	–255	–223
Other current transfers	3 392 . .	. . .	–2	. . .	. . .	. . .	. . .	–2	. . .
CAPITAL AND FINANCIAL ACCOUNT	4 996 . .	**1,403**	**894**	**–2,957**	**–4,099**	**–3,986**	**–1,019**	**–286**	**–18**
CAPITAL ACCOUNT	4 994 . .	**. . .**	**. . .**	**10,610**	**372**	**. . .**	**437**	**. . .**	**. . .**
Total credit	2 994 . .	. . .	. . .	*10,610*	*372*	. . .	*437*	. . .	. . .
Total debit	3 994 . .	. . .	. . .	. . .	. . .	. . .	. . .	. . .	. . .
Capital transfers, credit	2 400 . .	**. . .**	**. . .**	**10,610**	**372**	**. . .**	**437**	**. . .**	**. . .**
General government	2 401 . .	. . .	. . .	10,610	372	. . .	437	. . .	. . .
Debt forgiveness	2 402 . .	. . .	. . .	10,610	372	. . .	437	. . .	. . .
Other capital transfers	2 410 . .	. . .	. . .	. . .	. . .	. . .	. . .	. . .	. . .
Other sectors	2 430 . .	. . .	. . .	. . .	. . .	. . .	. . .	. . .	. . .
Migrants' transfers	2 431 . .	. . .	. . .	. . .	. . .	. . .	. . .	. . .	. . .
Debt forgiveness	2 432 . .	. . .	. . .	. . .	. . .	. . .	. . .	. . .	. . .
Other capital transfers	2 440 . .	. . .	. . .	. . .	. . .	. . .	. . .	. . .	. . .
Capital transfers, debit	3 400 . .	**. . .**	**. . .**	**. . .**	**. . .**	**. . .**	**. . .**	**. . .**	**. . .**
General government	3 401 . .	. . .	. . .	. . .	. . .	. . .	. . .	. . .	. . .
Debt forgiveness	3 402 . .	. . .	. . .	. . .	. . .	. . .	. . .	. . .	. . .
Other capital transfers	3 410 . .	. . .	. . .	. . .	. . .	. . .	. . .	. . .	. . .
Other sectors	3 430 . .	. . .	. . .	. . .	. . .	. . .	. . .	. . .	. . .
Migrants' transfers	3 431 . .	. . .	. . .	. . .	. . .	. . .	. . .	. . .	. . .
Debt forgiveness	3 432 . .	. . .	. . .	. . .	. . .	. . .	. . .	. . .	. . .
Other capital transfers	3 440 . .	. . .	. . .	. . .	. . .	. . .	. . .	. . .	. . .
Nonproduced nonfinancial assets, credit	2 480 . .	**. . .**	**. . .**	**. . .**	**. . .**	**. . .**	**. . .**	**. . .**	**. . .**
Nonproduced nonfinancial assets, debit	3 480 . .	**. . .**	**. . .**	**. . .**	**. . .**	**. . .**	**. . .**	**. . .**	**. . .**

Table 2 (Continued). STANDARD PRESENTATION, 1988–95
(Millions of U.S. dollars)

	Code		1988	1989	1990	1991	1992	1993	1994	1995
FINANCIAL ACCOUNT	4 995	. .	**1,403**	**894**	**–13,567**	**–4,471**	**–3,986**	**–1,456**	**–286**	**–18**
A. DIRECT INVESTMENT	4 500	. .	1,178	1,228	722	191	455	493	1,213	505
Direct investment abroad	4 505	. .	**–12**	**–23**	**–12**	**–62**	**–4**	**. . .**	**–43**	**–93**
Equity capital	4 510	. .	. . .	. . .	–7	–13	. . .	. . .	. . .	. . .
Claims on affiliated enterprises	4 515	. .	. . .	. . .	. . .	. . .	. . .	. . .	. . .	. . .
Liabilities to affiliated enterprises	4 520	. .	. . .	. . .	. . .	. . .	. . .	. . .	. . .	. . .
Reinvested earnings	4 525	. .	. . .	. . .	. . .	. . .	. . .	. . .	. . .	. . .
Other capital	4 530	. .	–12	–23	–5	–49	–4	. . .	–43	–93
Claims on affiliated enterprises	4 535	. .	. . .	. . .	. . .	. . .	. . .	. . .	–43	–93
Liabilities to affiliated enterprises	4 540	. .	. . .	. . .	. . .	. . .	. . .	. . .	. . .	. . .
Direct investment in Egypt	4 555	. .	**1,190**	**1,250**	**734**	**253**	**459**	**493**	**1,256**	**598**
Equity capital	4 560	. .	. . .	. . .	. . .	. . .	. . .	. . .	. . .	. . .
Claims on direct investors	4 565	. .	. . .	. . .	. . .	. . .	. . .	. . .	. . .	. . .
Liabilities to direct investors	4 570	. .	. . .	. . .	. . .	. . .	. . .	. . .	. . .	. . .
Reinvested earnings	4 575	. .	. . .	. . .	. . .	. . .	. . .	. . .	. . .	. . .
Other capital	4 580	. .	1,190	1,250	734	253	459	493	1,256	598
Claims on direct investors	4 585	. .	. . .	. . .	. . .	. . .	. . .	. . .	. . .	. . .
Liabilities to direct investors	4 590	. .	. . .	. . .	. . .	. . .	. . .	. . .	1,256	598
B. PORTFOLIO INVESTMENT	4 600	. .	. . .	. . .	15	21	6	4	3	20
Assets	4 602	. .	**. . .**	**. . .**	**15**	**21**	**6**	**. . .**	**. . .**	**. . .**
Equity securities	4 610	. .	. . .	. . .	. . .	. . .	. . .	. . .	. . .	. . .
Monetary authorities	4 611	. .	. . .	. . .	. . .	. . .	. . .	. . .	. . .	. . .
General government	4 612	. .	. . .	. . .	. . .	. . .	. . .	. . .	. . .	. . .
Banks	4 613	. .	. . .	. . .	. . .	. . .	. . .	. . .	. . .	. . .
Other sectors	4 614	. .	. . .	. . .	. . .	. . .	. . .	. . .	. . .	. . .
Debt securities	4 619	. .	. . .	. . .	15	21	6	. . .	. . .	. . .
Bonds and notes	4 620	. .	. . .	. . .	15	21	6	. . .	. . .	. . .
Monetary authorities	4 621	. .	. . .	. . .	. . .	. . .	. . .	. . .	. . .	. . .
General government	4 622	. .	. . .	. . .	. . .	. . .	. . .	. . .	. . .	. . .
Banks	4 623	. .	. . .	. . .	. . .	. . .	. . .	. . .	. . .	. . .
Other sectors	4 624	. .	. . .	. . .	. . .	. . .	. . .	. . .	. . .	. . .
Money market instruments	4 630	. .	. . .	. . .	. . .	. . .	. . .	. . .	. . .	. . .
Monetary authorities	4 631	. .	. . .	. . .	. . .	. . .	. . .	. . .	. . .	. . .
General government	4 632	. .	. . .	. . .	. . .	. . .	. . .	. . .	. . .	. . .
Banks	4 633	. .	. . .	. . .	. . .	. . .	. . .	. . .	. . .	. . .
Other sectors	4 634	. .	. . .	. . .	. . .	. . .	. . .	. . .	. . .	. . .
Financial derivatives	4 640	. .	. . .	. . .	. . .	. . .	. . .	. . .	. . .	. . .
Monetary authorities	4 641	. .	. . .	. . .	. . .	. . .	. . .	. . .	. . .	. . .
General government	4 642	. .	. . .	. . .	. . .	. . .	. . .	. . .	. . .	. . .
Banks	4 643	. .	. . .	. . .	. . .	. . .	. . .	. . .	. . .	. . .
Other sectors	4 644	. .	. . .	. . .	. . .	. . .	. . .	. . .	. . .	. . .
Liabilities	4 652	. .	**. . .**	**. . .**	**. . .**	**. . .**	**. . .**	**4**	**3**	**20**
Equity securities	4 660	. .	. . .	. . .	. . .	. . .	. . .	. . .	. . .	. . .
Banks	4 663	. .	. . .	. . .	. . .	. . .	. . .	. . .	. . .	. . .
Other sectors	4 664	. .	. . .	. . .	. . .	. . .	. . .	. . .	. . .	. . .
Debt securities	4 669	. .	. . .	. . .	. . .	. . .	. . .	4	3	20
Bonds and notes	4 670	. .	. . .	. . .	. . .	. . .	. . .	4	3	20
Monetary authorities	4 671	. .	. . .	. . .	. . .	. . .	. . .	4	. . .	. . .
General government	4 672	. .	. . .	. . .	. . .	. . .	. . .	. . .	3	20
Banks	4 673	. .	. . .	. . .	. . .	. . .	. . .	. . .	. . .	. . .
Other sectors	4 674	. .	. . .	. . .	. . .	. . .	. . .	. . .	. . .	. . .
Money market instruments	4 680	. .	. . .	. . .	. . .	. . .	. . .	. . .	. . .	. . .
Monetary authorities	4 681	. .	. . .	. . .	. . .	. . .	. . .	. . .	. . .	. . .
General government	4 682	. .	. . .	. . .	. . .	. . .	. . .	. . .	. . .	. . .
Banks	4 683	. .	. . .	. . .	. . .	. . .	. . .	. . .	. . .	. . .
Other sectors	4 684	. .	. . .	. . .	. . .	. . .	. . .	. . .	. . .	. . .
Financial derivatives	4 690	. .	. . .	. . .	. . .	. . .	. . .	. . .	. . .	. . .
Monetary authorities	4 691	. .	. . .	. . .	. . .	. . .	. . .	. . .	. . .	. . .
General government	4 692	. .	. . .	. . .	. . .	. . .	. . .	. . .	. . .	. . .
Banks	4 693	. .	. . .	. . .	. . .	. . .	. . .	. . .	. . .	. . .
Other sectors	4 694	. .	. . .	. . .	. . .	. . .	. . .	. . .	. . .	. . .

Table 2 (Concluded). STANDARD PRESENTATION, 1988–95
(Millions of U.S. dollars)

	Code	1988	1989	1990	1991	1992	1993	1994	1995
C. OTHER INVESTMENT	4 700 . .	72	–769	–11,796	–1,907	1,883	856	–309	–134
Assets	4 703 . .	**546**	**–1,299**	**–1,921**	**–2,298**	**1,183**	**319**	**–905**	**–396**
Trade credits	4 706 . .	. . .	. . .	. . .	. . .	. . .	. . .	. . .	. . .
General government: long-term	4 708 . .	. . .	. . .	. . .	. . .	. . .	. . .	. . .	. . .
General government: short-term	4 709 . .	. . .	. . .	. . .	. . .	. . .	. . .	. . .	. . .
Other sectors: long-term	4 711 . .	. . .	. . .	. . .	. . .	. . .	. . .	. . .	. . .
Other sectors: short-term	4 712 . .	. . .	. . .	. . .	. . .	. . .	. . .	. . .	. . .
Loans	4 714 . .	. . .	. . .	. . .	. . .	. . .	. . .	. . .	. . .
Monetary authorities: long-term	4 717 . .	. . .	. . .	. . .	. . .	. . .	. . .	. . .	. . .
Monetary authorities: short-term	4 718 . .	. . .	. . .	. . .	. . .	. . .	. . .	. . .	. . .
General government: long-term	4 720 . .	. . .	. . .	. . .	. . .	. . .	. . .	. . .	. . .
General government: short-term	4 721 . .	. . .	. . .	. . .	. . .	. . .	. . .	. . .	. . .
Banks: long-term	4 723 . .	. . .	. . .	. . .	. . .	. . .	. . .	. . .	. . .
Banks: short-term	4 724 . .	. . .	. . .	. . .	. . .	. . .	. . .	. . .	. . .
Other sectors: long-term	4 726 . .	. . .	. . .	. . .	. . .	. . .	. . .	. . .	. . .
Other sectors: short-term	4 727 . .	. . .	. . .	. . .	. . .	. . .	. . .	. . .	. . .
Currency and deposits	4 730 . .	571	–1,249	–1,904	–2,234	1,300	344	–634	371
Monetary authorities	4 731 . .	. . .	. . .	. . .	. . .	. . .	. . .	. . .	. . .
General government	4 732 . .	. . .	. . .	. . .	. . .	. . .	. . .	. . .	. . .
Banks	4 733 . .	571	–1,249	–1,904	–2,234	1,300	523	–634	371
Other sectors	4 734 . .	. . .	. . .	. . .	. . .	. . .	–179	. . .	. . .
Other assets	4 736 . .	–24	–50	–18	–64	–117	–25	–271	–767
Monetary authorities: long-term	4 738 . .	–7	–25	–16	–46	–13	–21	. . .	65
Monetary authorities: short-term	4 739 . .	. . .	. . .	. . .	. . .	. . .	. . .	–25	. . .
General government: long-term	4 741 . .	–17	–26	–2	–18	–104	–4	. . .	. . .
General government: short-term	4 742 . .	. . .	. . .	. . .	. . .	. . .	. . .	. . .	. . .
Banks: long-term	4 744 . .	. . .	. . .	. . .	. . .	. . .	. . .	. . .	. . .
Banks: short-term	4 745 . .	. . .	. . .	. . .	. . .	. . .	. . .	. . .	. . .
Other sectors: long-term	4 747 . .	. . .	. . .	. . .	. . .	. . .	. . .	. . .	. . .
Other sectors: short-term	4 748 . .	. . .	. . .	. . .	. . .	. . .	. . .	–246	–832
Liabilities	4 753 . .	**–475**	**530**	**–9,875**	**391**	**700**	**537**	**596**	**262**
Trade credits	4 756 . .	203	264	–2	101	–157	–240	36	–22
General government: long-term	4 758 . .	. . .	. . .	. . .	. . .	. . .	. . .	. . .	. . .
General government: short-term	4 759 . .	. . .	. . .	. . .	. . .	. . .	. . .	. . .	. . .
Other sectors: long-term	4 761 . .	203	264	–2	101	–157	–240	–163	–265
Other sectors: short-term	4 762 . .	. . .	. . .	. . .	. . .	. . .	. . .	199	243
Loans	4 764 . .	184	433	–7,248	–98	1,185	351	821	453
Use of Fund credit and loans from the Fund	4 766 . .	–59	–24	–48	. . .	81	. . .	–22	–95
Monetary authorities: other long-term	4 767 . .	–250	–250	–29	–113	–42	. . .	. . .	. . .
Monetary authorities: short-term	4 768 . .	. . .	. . .	. . .	. . .	. . .	. . .	. . .	. . .
General government: long-term	4 770 . .	492	715	–7,142	86	1,201	355	843	548
General government: short-term	4 771 . .	. . .	. . .	. . .	. . .	. . .	. . .	. . .	. . .
Banks: long-term	4 773 . .	. . .	. . .	. . .	. . .	. . .	. . .	. . .	. . .
Banks: short-term	4 774 . .	. . .	. . .	. . .	. . .	. . .	. . .	. . .	. . .
Other sectors: long-term	4 776 . .	. . .	–9	–30	–71	–55	–4	. . .	. . .
Other sectors: short-term	4 777 . .	. . .	. . .	. . .	. . .	. . .	. . .	. . .	. . .
Currency and deposits	4 780 . .	–749	–138	237	–333	–383	–202	–256	–148
Monetary authorities	4 781 . .	. . .	. . .	. . .	. . .	. . .	. . .	. . .	. . .
General government	4 782 . .	. . .	. . .	. . .	. . .	. . .	. . .	. . .	. . .
Banks	4 783 . .	–749	–138	237	–333	–383	–202	–256	–148
Other sectors	4 784 . .	. . .	. . .	. . .	. . .	. . .	. . .	. . .	. . .
Other liabilities	4 786 . .	–113	–28	–2,862	721	55	628	–5	–21
Monetary authorities: long-term	4 788 . .	. . .	. . .	. . .	. . .	. . .	. . .	. . .	–2
Monetary authorities: short-term	4 789 . .	. . .	. . .	. . .	. . .	. . .	629	–5	–19
General government: long-term	4 791 . .	–105	–28	–2,862	–53	–43	–50	. . .	. . .
General government: short-term	4 792 . .	. . .	. . .	. . .	774	98	49	. . .	. . .
Banks: long-term	4 794 . .	. . .	. . .	. . .	. . .	. . .	. . .	. . .	. . .
Banks: short-term	4 795 . .	. . .	. . .	. . .	. . .	. . .	. . .	. . .	. . .
Other sectors: long-term	4 797 . .	–8	–1	. . .	. . .	. . .	. . .	. . .	. . .
Other sectors: short-term	4 798 . .	. . .	. . .	. . .	. . .	. . .	. . .	. . .	. . .
D. RESERVE ASSETS	4 800 . .	153	435	–2,508	–2,775	–6,330	–2,809	–1,193	–409
Monetary gold	4 810 . .	. . .	. . .	. . .	. . .	. . .	. . .	. . .	. . .
Special drawing rights	4 820 . .	. . .	. . .	. . .	. . .	–57	–11	–12	–16
Reserve position in the Fund	4 830 . .	. . .	. . .	. . .	. . .	–75	. . .	. . .	. . .
Foreign exchange	4 840 . .	153	436	–2,508	–2,775	–6,198	–2,798	–1,181	–393
Other claims	4 880 . .	. . .	. . .	. . .	. . .	. . .	. . .	. . .	. . .
NET ERRORS AND OMISSIONS	4 998 . .	**–362**	**414**	**630**	**730**	**716**	**–1,519**	**255**	**272**

Part 3 of the *Yearbook* contains descriptions of the methodologies, compilation practices, and sources used to compile these data.

Table 1. ANALYTIC PRESENTATION, 1988–95
(Millions of U.S. dollars)

	Code	1988	1989	1990	1991	1992	1993	1994	1995
A. Current Account[1]	4 993 Y .	**–129.2**	**–369.7**	**–260.8**	**–212.4**	**–195.1**	**–118.2**	**–18.1**	**–70.0**
Goods: exports f.o.b	2 100 . .	610.6	557.5	643.9	586.8	598.1	731.5	1,252.2	1,660.4
Goods: imports f.o.b	3 100 . .	–966.5	–1,220.2	–1,309.5	–1,291.4	–1,560.5	–1,766.4	–2,407.4	–3,183.6
Balance on Goods	4 100 . .	*–355.9*	*–662.7*	*–665.6*	*–704.6*	*–962.3*	*–1,034.9*	*–1,155.3*	*–1,523.2*
Services: credit	2 200 . .	328.0	351.0	329.2	310.9	377.1	406.3	387.2	388.5
Services: debit	3 200 . .	–341.4	–392.1	–314.7	–322.9	–364.7	–382.1	–443.9	–237.5
Balance on Goods and Services	4 991 . .	*–369.3*	*–703.9*	*–651.1*	*–716.6*	*–949.9*	*–1,010.6*	*–1,212.0*	*–1,372.2*
Income: credit	2 300 . .	24.2	26.1	29.5	30.3	31.7	30.8	35.5	54.0
Income: debit	3 300 . .	–129.6	–127.4	–161.1	–151.1	–128.9	–142.4	–130.1	–140.7
Balance on Goods, Services, and Income	4 992 . .	*–474.7*	*–805.2*	*–782.7*	*–837.4*	*–1,047.1*	*–1,122.2*	*–1,306.6*	*–1,458.9*
Current transfers: credit	2 379 Y .	347.6	437.6	524.6	627.5	852.8	1,004.7	1,290.9	1,388.9
Current transfers: debit	3 379 . .	–2.1	–2.1	–2.7	–2.5	–.7	–.7	–2.4	. . .
B. Capital Account[1]	4 994 Y .	**. . .**	**. . .**	**. . .**	**. . .**	**. . .**	**. . .**	**. . .**	**. . .**
Capital account: credit	2 994 Y .	. . .	. . .	. . .	. . .	. . .	. . .	. . .	. . .
Capital account: debit	3 994 . .	. . .	. . .	. . .	. . .	. . .	. . .	. . .	. . .
Total, Groups A Plus B	4 010 . .	*–129.2*	*–369.7*	*–260.8*	*–212.4*	*–195.1*	*–118.2*	*–18.1*	*–70.0*
C. Financial Account[1]	4 995 X .	**52.3**	**118.2**	**–11.4**	**–61.1**	**–4.3**	**86.6**	**83.9**	**432.5**
Direct investment abroad	4 505 . .	. . .	. . .	. . .	. . .	. . .	. . .	. . .	. . .
Direct investment in El Salvador	4 555 Y .	17.0	14.4	1.9	25.2	15.3	16.4	. . .	38.0
Portfolio investment assets	4 602 . .	. . .	. . .	. . .	. . .	. . .	. . .	. . .	. . .
Equity securities	4 610 . .	. . .	. . .	. . .	. . .	. . .	. . .	. . .	. . .
Debt securities	4 619 . .	. . .	. . .	. . .	. . .	. . .	. . .	. . .	. . .
Portfolio investment liabilities	4 652 Y .	. . .	. . .	. . .	. . .	. . .	. . .	. . .	68.5
Equity securities	4 660 Y .	. . .	. . .	. . .	. . .	. . .	. . .	. . .	. . .
Debt securities	4 669 Y .	. . .	. . .	. . .	. . .	. . .	. . .	. . .	68.5
Other investment assets	4 703 . .	10.6	–1.1	–20.9	15.0	. . .	4.1	–7.9	–7.1
Monetary authorities	4 703 . A	. . .	. . .	. . .	. . .	. . .	. . .	. . .	35.0
General government	4 703 . B	–.4	–.3	–.6	–.2	. . .	. . .	. . .	. . .
Banks	4 703 . C	9.5	.8	–17.2	21.3	. . .	4.1	–7.9	–10.2
Other sectors	4 703 . D	1.5	–1.7	–3.1	–6.0	. . .	. . .	. . .	–31.9
Other investment liabilities	4 753 X .	24.7	104.9	7.5	–101.3	–19.6	66.1	91.8	333.0
Monetary authorities	4 753 XA	–42.1	–17.7	–51.1	–139.4	–92.8	–89.2	–147.1	39.5
General government	4 753 YB	67.1	103.2	84.5	14.3	42.2	123.9	158.0	53.5
Banks	4 753 YC	11.4	12.0	–25.3	.7	. . .	14.7	83.2	220.1
Other sectors	4 753 YD	–11.7	7.4	–.7	23.0	31.0	16.7	–2.3	19.9
Total, Groups A Through C	4 020 . .	*–76.9*	*–251.5*	*–272.3*	*–273.5*	*–199.4*	*–31.6*	*65.8*	*362.4*
D. Net Errors and Omissions	4 998 . .	**–107.1**	**140.9**	**299.4**	**125.6**	**65.6**	**90.3**	**47.3**	**–214.1**
Total, Groups A Through D	4 030 . .	*–184.1*	*–110.6*	*27.1*	*–147.9*	*–133.8*	*58.7*	*113.0*	*148.3*
E. Reserves and Related Items	4 040 . .	**184.1**	**110.6**	**–27.1**	**147.9**	**133.8**	**–58.7**	**–113.0**	**–148.3**
Reserve assets	4 800 . .	30.1	–110.0	–164.6	70.0	–91.6	–112.0	–113.0	–148.3
Use of Fund credit and loans	4 766 . .	–10.5	–5.0	–5.2	–.2	. . .	. . .	. . .	. . .
Liabilities constituting foreign authorities' reserves	4 900 . .	. . .	. . .	. . .	. . .	. . .	. . .	. . .	. . .
Exceptional financing	4 920 . .	164.5	225.7	142.7	78.1	225.5	53.3	. . .	. . .
Conversion rates: Salvadoran colones per U.S. dollar	0 101 . .	**5.0000**	**5.0000**	**6.8483**	**8.0167**	**8.3608**	**8.7025**	**8.7288**	**8.7546**

[1] Excludes components that have been classified in the categories of Group E.

Table 2. STANDARD PRESENTATION, 1988–95
(Millions of U.S. dollars)

	Code	1988	1989	1990	1991	1992	1993	1994	1995
CURRENT ACCOUNT	4 993 . .	**25.8**	**–194.4**	**–151.7**	**–167.5**	**–109.0**	**–77.2**	**–18.1**	**–70.0**
A. GOODS	4 100 . .	–355.9	–662.7	–665.6	–704.6	–962.3	–1,034.9	–1,155.3	–1,523.2
Credit	2 100 . .	**610.6**	**557.5**	**643.9**	**586.8**	**598.1**	**731.5**	**1,252.2**	**1,660.4**
General merchandise: exports f.o.b.	2 110 . .	610.6	557.5	643.9	586.8	598.1	731.5	1,252.2	1,004.0
Goods for processing: exports f.o.b.	2 150 . .	. . .	. . .	. . .	. . .	. . .	. . .	. . .	656.3
Repairs on goods	2 160 . .	. . .	. . .	. . .	. . .	. . .	. . .	. . .	. . .
Goods procured in ports by carriers	2 170 . .	. . .	. . .	. . .	. . .	. . .	. . .	. . .	. . .
Nonmonetary gold	2 180 . .	. . .	. . .	. . .	. . .	. . .	. . .	. . .	. . .
Debit	3 100 . .	**–966.5**	**–1,220.2**	**–1,309.5**	**–1,291.4**	**–1,560.5**	**–1,766.4**	**–2,407.4**	**–3,183.6**
General merchandise: imports f.o.b.	3 110 . .	–966.5	–1,220.2	–1,309.5	–1,291.4	–1,560.5	–1,766.4	–2,407.4	–2,638.0
Goods for processing: imports f.o.b.	3 150 . .	. . .	. . .	. . .	. . .	. . .	. . .	. . .	–498.7
Repairs on goods	3 160 . .	. . .	. . .	. . .	. . .	. . .	. . .	. . .	. . .
Goods procured in ports by carriers	3 170 . .	. . .	. . .	. . .	. . .	. . .	. . .	. . .	–46.8
Nonmonetary gold	3 180 . .	. . .	. . .	. . .	. . .	. . .	. . .	. . .	. . .
B. SERVICES	4 200 . .	–13.4	–41.1	14.6	–12.0	12.4	24.2	–56.7	151.0
Total credit	2 200 . .	*328.0*	*351.0*	*329.2*	*310.9*	*377.1*	*406.3*	*387.2*	*388.5*
Total debit	3 200 . .	*–341.4*	*–392.1*	*–314.7*	*–322.9*	*–364.7*	*–382.1*	*–443.9*	*–237.5*
Transportation services, credit	2 205 . .	**98.5**	**96.0**	**78.8**	**73.8**	**79.5**	**80.1**	**94.3**	**96.7**
Passenger	2 205 BA	*57.6*	*66.0*	*54.1*	*50.8*	*54.7*	*55.0*	*64.7*	*66.7*
Freight	2 205 BB	. . .	. . .	. . .	. . .	. . .	. . .	. . .	. . .
Other	2 205 BC	*40.9*	*30.0*	*24.7*	*23.1*	*24.9*	*25.1*	*29.6*	*30.0*
Sea transport, passenger	2 207 . .	. . .	. . .	. . .	. . .	. . .	. . .	. . .	. . .
Sea transport, freight	2 208 . .	. . .	. . .	. . .	. . .	. . .	. . .	. . .	. . .
Sea transport, other	2 209 . .	. . .	. . .	. . .	. . .	. . .	. . .	. . .	. . .
Air transport, passenger	2 211 . .	. . .	. . .	. . .	. . .	. . .	. . .	. . .	. . .
Air transport, freight	2 212 . .	. . .	. . .	. . .	. . .	. . .	. . .	. . .	. . .
Air transport, other	2 213 . .	. . .	. . .	. . .	. . .	. . .	. . .	. . .	. . .
Other transport, passenger	2 215 . .	. . .	. . .	. . .	. . .	. . .	. . .	. . .	. . .
Other transport, freight	2 216 . .	. . .	. . .	. . .	. . .	. . .	. . .	. . .	. . .
Other transport, other	2 217 . .	. . .	. . .	. . .	. . .	. . .	. . .	. . .	. . .
Transportation services, debit	3 205 . .	**–104.3**	**–116.4**	**–135.9**	**–154.9**	**–185.5**	**–193.0**	**–228.6**	**–258.2**
Passenger	3 205 BA	*–3.8*	*–9.2*	*–11.2*	*–11.4*	*–12.4*	*–13.0*	*–15.1*	*–27.3*
Freight	3 205 BB	*–61.5*	*–72.6*	*–82.7*	*–101.0*	*–126.4*	*–131.3*	*–156.4*	*–128.3*
Other	3 205 BC	*–38.9*	*–34.5*	*–42.0*	*–42.5*	*–46.6*	*–48.7*	*–57.1*	*–102.6*
Sea transport, passenger	3 207 . .	. . .	. . .	. . .	. . .	. . .	. . .	. . .	. . .
Sea transport, freight	3 208 . .	. . .	. . .	. . .	. . .	. . .	. . .	. . .	. . .
Sea transport, other	3 209 . .	. . .	. . .	. . .	. . .	. . .	. . .	. . .	. . .
Air transport, passenger	3 211 . .	. . .	. . .	. . .	. . .	. . .	. . .	. . .	. . .
Air transport, freight	3 212 . .	. . .	. . .	. . .	. . .	. . .	. . .	. . .	. . .
Air transport, other	3 213 . .	. . .	. . .	. . .	. . .	. . .	. . .	. . .	. . .
Other transport, passenger	3 215 . .	. . .	. . .	. . .	. . .	. . .	. . .	. . .	. . .
Other transport, freight	3 216 . .	. . .	. . .	. . .	. . .	. . .	. . .	. . .	. . .
Other transport, other	3 217 . .	. . .	. . .	. . .	. . .	. . .	. . .	. . .	. . .
Travel, credit	2 236 . .	**55.5**	**58.1**	**76.0**	**70.9**	**73.4**	**78.5**	**86.4**	**85.4**
Business travel	2 237 . .	. . .	. . .	. . .	. . .	. . .	. . .	. . .	. . .
Personal travel	2 240 . .	. . .	. . .	. . .	. . .	. . .	. . .	. . .	. . .
Travel, debit	3 236 . .	**–75.2**	**–103.8**	**–60.8**	**–56.9**	**–58.0**	**–60.8**	**–70.3**	**72.4**
Business travel	3 237 . .	. . .	. . .	. . .	. . .	. . .	. . .	. . .	. . .
Personal travel	3 240 . .	. . .	. . .	. . .	. . .	. . .	. . .	. . .	. . .
Other services, credit	2 200 BA	**174.0**	**197.0**	**174.4**	**166.2**	**224.1**	**247.7**	**206.6**	**206.3**
Communications	2 245 . .	. . .	. . .	. . .	. . .	. . .	. . .	. . .	70.7
Construction	2 249 . .	. . .	. . .	. . .	. . .	. . .	. . .	. . .	. . .
Insurance	2 253 . .	31.6	31.9	22.6	20.4	21.1	22.5	26.5	26.6
Financial	2 260 . .	. . .	. . .	. . .	. . .	. . .	. . .	. . .	. . .
Computer and information	2 262 . .	. . .	. . .	. . .	. . .	. . .	. . .	. . .	. . .
Royalties and licence fees	2 266 . .	. . .	. . .	. . .	. . .	. . .	.2	. . .	. . .
Other business services	2 268 . .	93.0	134.5	123.6	118.9	163.6	180.6	130.9	62.7
Personal, cultural, and recreational	2 287 . .	. . .	. . .	. . .	. . .	. . .	. . .	. . .	. . .
Government, n.i.e.	2 291 . .	49.3	30.6	28.2	26.9	39.5	44.4	49.1	46.3
Other services, debit	3 200 BA	**–161.9**	**–172.0**	**–117.9**	**–111.1**	**–121.2**	**–128.2**	**–145.0**	**–51.7**
Communications	3 245 . .	. . .	. . .	. . .	. . .	. . .	. . .	. . .	. . .
Construction	3 249 . .	. . .	. . .	. . .	. . .	. . .	. . .	. . .	. . .
Insurance	3 253 . .	–44.0	–53.4	–35.7	–34.9	–40.4	–43.2	–49.3	53.7
Financial	3 260 . .	. . .	. . .	. . .	. . .	. . .	. . .	. . .	. . .
Computer and information	3 262 . .	. . .	. . .	. . .	. . .	. . .	. . .	. . .	. . .
Royalties and licence fees	3 266 . .	–3.4	–1.8	–1.3	–2.2	–5.1	–3.4	–.1	–2.9
Other business services	3 268 . .	–99.6	–87.1	–60.4	–59.0	–59.6	–64.8	–75.4	–80.4
Personal, cultural, and recreational	3 287 . .	–4.0	–2.9	–2.0	. . .	. . .	. . .	. . .	. . .
Government, n.i.e.	3 291 . .	–10.9	–26.8	–18.7	–15.0	–16.0	–16.8	–20.3	–22.2

Table 2 (Continued). STANDARD PRESENTATION, 1988–95
(Millions of U.S. dollars)

	Code	1988	1989	1990	1991	1992	1993	1994	1995
C. INCOME	4 300	–105.5	–101.3	–131.7	–120.8	–97.2	–111.6	–94.6	–86.7
Total credit	2 300	*24.2*	*26.1*	*29.5*	*30.3*	*31.7*	*30.8*	*35.5*	*54.0*
Total debit	3 300	*–129.6*	*–127.4*	*–161.1*	*–151.1*	*–128.9*	*–142.4*	*–130.1*	*–140.7*
Compensation of employees, credit	2 310	**16.4**	**9.7**	**8.8**	**8.3**	**7.1**	**5.4**	**5.0**	**3.2**
Compensation of employees, debit	3 310	**–3.7**	**–4.0**	**–2.8**	**–2.4**	**–.4**	**–.2**	**–.1**	**. . .**
Investment income, credit	2 320	**7.8**	**16.4**	**20.6**	**22.0**	**24.6**	**25.4**	**30.5**	**50.8**
Direct investment income	2 330	. . .	. . .	. . .	. . .	. . .	. . .	. . .	. . .
Dividends and distributed branch profits	2 332	. . .	. . .	. . .	. . .	. . .	. . .	. . .	. . .
Reinvested earnings and undistributed branch profits	2 333	. . .	. . .	. . .	. . .	. . .	. . .	. . .	. . .
Income on debt (interest)	2 334	. . .	. . .	. . .	. . .	. . .	. . .	. . .	. . .
Portfolio investment income	2 339	. . .	. . .	. . .	. . .	. . .	. . .	. . .	. . .
Income on equity	2 340	. . .	. . .	. . .	. . .	. . .	. . .	. . .	. . .
Income on bonds and notes	2 350	. . .	. . .	. . .	. . .	. . .	. . .	. . .	. . .
Income on money market instruments and financial derivatives	2 360	. . .	. . .	. . .	. . .	. . .	. . .	. . .	. . .
Other investment income	2 370	7.8	16.4	20.6	22.0	24.6	25.4	30.5	50.8
Investment income, debit	3 320	**–125.9**	**–123.3**	**–158.3**	**–148.7**	**–128.6**	**–142.1**	**–130.0**	**–140.7**
Direct investment income	3 330	–36.8	–42.9	–31.3	–36.0	–26.2	–25.3	–26.9	–26.8
Dividends and distributed branch profits	3 332	–16.0	–17.3	–12.6	–29.8	–26.2	–25.3	–26.9	. . .
Reinvested earnings and undistributed branch profits	3 333	–20.8	–25.6	–18.7	–6.2	. . .	. . .	. . .	. . .
Income on debt (interest)	3 334	. . .	. . .	. . .	. . .	. . .	. . .	. . .	. . .
Portfolio investment income	3 339	. . .	. . .	. . .	. . .	. . .	. . .	. . .	. . .
Income on equity	3 340	. . .	. . .	. . .	. . .	. . .	. . .	. . .	. . .
Income on bonds and notes	3 350	. . .	. . .	. . .	. . .	. . .	. . .	. . .	. . .
Income on money market instruments and financial derivatives	3 360	. . .	. . .	. . .	. . .	. . .	. . .	. . .	. . .
Other investment income	3 370	–89.2	–80.5	–127.0	–112.7	–102.4	–116.9	–103.1	–113.9
D. CURRENT TRANSFERS	4 379	500.5	610.7	631.0	669.9	938.2	1,045.0	1,288.5	1,388.9
Credit	2 379	**502.6**	**612.9**	**633.7**	**672.4**	**938.9**	**1,045.7**	**1,290.9**	**1,388.9**
General government	2 380	275.0	341.9	249.7	179.9	228.6	222.0	286.6	158.9
Other sectors	2 390	227.6	271.0	384.0	492.5	710.3	823.7	1,004.3	1,230.0
Workers' remittances	2 391	194.4	228.1	357.5	466.9	687.3	789.2	966.7	1,060.8
Other current transfers	2 392	33.3	42.9	26.5	25.5	23.1	34.5	37.6	169.2
Debit	3 379	**–2.1**	**–2.1**	**–2.7**	**–2.5**	**–.7**	**–.7**	**–2.4**	. . .
General government	3 380	–1.9	–1.9	–2.0	–1.8	. . .	. . .	–1.7	. . .
Other sectors	3 390	–.2	–.3	–.7	–.7	–.7	–.7	–.7	. . .
Workers' remittances	3 391	. . .	. . .	. . .	. . .	. . .	. . .	. . .	. . .
Other current transfers	3 392	–.2	–.3	–.7	–.7	–.7	–.7	–.7	. . .
CAPITAL AND FINANCIAL ACCOUNT	4 996	**81.3**	**53.6**	**–147.6**	**41.9**	**43.4**	**–13.1**	**–29.2**	**284.2**
CAPITAL ACCOUNT	4 994	. . .	. . .	. . .	. . .	. . .	. . .	. . .	. . .
Total credit	2 994	. . .	. . .	. . .	. . .	. . .	. . .	. . .	. . .
Total debit	3 994	. . .	. . .	. . .	. . .	. . .	. . .	. . .	. . .
Capital transfers, credit	2 400	. . .	. . .	. . .	. . .	. . .	. . .	. . .	. . .
General government	2 401	. . .	. . .	. . .	. . .	. . .	. . .	. . .	. . .
Debt forgiveness	2 402	. . .	. . .	. . .	. . .	. . .	. . .	. . .	. . .
Other capital transfers	2 410	. . .	. . .	. . .	. . .	. . .	. . .	. . .	. . .
Other sectors	2 430	. . .	. . .	. . .	. . .	. . .	. . .	. . .	. . .
Migrants' transfers	2 431	. . .	. . .	. . .	. . .	. . .	. . .	. . .	. . .
Debt forgiveness	2 432	. . .	. . .	. . .	. . .	. . .	. . .	. . .	. . .
Other capital transfers	2 440	. . .	. . .	. . .	. . .	. . .	. . .	. . .	. . .
Capital transfers, debit	3 400	. . .	. . .	. . .	. . .	. . .	. . .	. . .	. . .
General government	3 401	. . .	. . .	. . .	. . .	. . .	. . .	. . .	. . .
Debt forgiveness	3 402	. . .	. . .	. . .	. . .	. . .	. . .	. . .	. . .
Other capital transfers	3 410	. . .	. . .	. . .	. . .	. . .	. . .	. . .	. . .
Other sectors	3 430	. . .	. . .	. . .	. . .	. . .	. . .	. . .	. . .
Migrants' transfers	3 431	. . .	. . .	. . .	. . .	. . .	. . .	. . .	. . .
Debt forgiveness	3 432	. . .	. . .	. . .	. . .	. . .	. . .	. . .	. . .
Other capital transfers	3 440	. . .	. . .	. . .	. . .	. . .	. . .	. . .	. . .
Nonproduced nonfinancial assets, credit	2 480	. . .	. . .	. . .	. . .	. . .	. . .	. . .	. . .
Nonproduced nonfinancial assets, debit	3 480	. . .	. . .	. . .	. . .	. . .	. . .	. . .	. . .

Table 2 (Continued). STANDARD PRESENTATION, 1988–95
(Millions of U.S. dollars)

	Code	1988	1989	1990	1991	1992	1993	1994	1995
FINANCIAL ACCOUNT	4 995	**81.3**	**53.6**	**–147.6**	**41.9**	**43.4**	**–13.1**	**–29.2**	**284.2**
A. DIRECT INVESTMENT	4 500	17.0	14.4	1.9	25.2	15.3	16.4	...	38.0
Direct investment abroad	4 505	...	...	...	...	...	...	...	...
Equity capital	4 510	...	...	...	...	...	...	...	...
Claims on affiliated enterprises	4 515	...	...	...	...	...	...	...	...
Liabilities to affiliated enterprises	4 520	...	...	...	...	...	...	...	...
Reinvested earnings	4 525	...	...	...	...	...	...	...	...
Other capital	4 530	...	...	...	...	...	...	...	...
Claims on affiliated enterprises	4 535	...	...	...	...	...	...	...	...
Liabilities to affiliated enterprises	4 540	...	...	...	...	...	...	...	...
Direct investment in El Salvador	4 555	**17.0**	**14.4**	**1.9**	**25.2**	**15.3**	**16.4**	...	**38.0**
Equity capital	4 560	3.3	2.0	.9	10.1	15.3	16.4	...	14.8
Claims on direct investors	4 565	...	...	...	...	...	...	...	...
Liabilities to direct investors	4 570	...	...	...	...	...	...	...	...
Reinvested earnings	4 575	20.8	25.6	18.7	6.2	...	...	...	...
Other capital	4 580	–7.2	–13.2	–17.7	8.9	...	...	...	23.2
Claims on direct investors	4 585	...	...	...	...	...	...	...	...
Liabilities to direct investors	4 590	...	...	...	...	...	...	...	...
B. PORTFOLIO INVESTMENT	4 600	...	...	...	...	...	...	...	68.5
Assets	4 602	...	...	...	...	...	...	...	...
Equity securities	4 610	...	...	...	...	...	...	...	...
Monetary authorities	4 611	...	...	...	...	...	...	...	...
General government	4 612	...	...	...	...	...	...	...	...
Banks	4 613	...	...	...	...	...	...	...	...
Other sectors	4 614	...	...	...	...	...	...	...	...
Debt securities	4 619	...	...	...	...	...	...	...	...
Bonds and notes	4 620	...	...	...	...	...	...	...	...
Monetary authorities	4 621	...	...	...	...	...	...	...	...
General government	4 622	...	...	...	...	...	...	...	...
Banks	4 623	...	...	...	...	...	...	...	...
Other sectors	4 624	...	...	...	...	...	...	...	...
Money market instruments	4 630	...	...	...	...	...	...	...	...
Monetary authorities	4 631	...	...	...	...	...	...	...	...
General government	4 632	...	...	...	...	...	...	...	...
Banks	4 633	...	...	...	...	...	...	...	...
Other sectors	4 634	...	...	...	...	...	...	...	...
Financial derivatives	4 640	...	...	...	...	...	...	...	...
Monetary authorities	4 641	...	...	...	...	...	...	...	...
General government	4 642	...	...	...	...	...	...	...	...
Banks	4 643	...	...	...	...	...	...	...	...
Other sectors	4 644	...	...	...	...	...	...	...	...
Liabilities	4 652	...	...	...	...	...	...	...	**68.5**
Equity securities	4 660	...	...	...	...	...	...	...	...
Banks	4 663	...	...	...	...	...	...	...	...
Other sectors	4 664	...	...	...	...	...	...	...	...
Debt securities	4 669	...	...	...	...	...	...	...	68.5
Bonds and notes	4 670	...	...	...	...	...	...	...	68.5
Monetary authorities	4 671	...	...	...	...	...	...	...	...
General government	4 672	...	...	...	...	...	...	...	68.5
Banks	4 673	...	...	...	...	...	...	...	...
Other sectors	4 674	...	...	...	...	...	...	...	...
Money market instruments	4 680	...	...	...	...	...	...	...	...
Monetary authorities	4 681	...	...	...	...	...	...	...	...
General government	4 682	...	...	...	...	...	...	...	...
Banks	4 683	...	...	...	...	...	...	...	...
Other sectors	4 684	...	...	...	...	...	...	...	...
Financial derivatives	4 690	...	...	...	...	...	...	...	...
Monetary authorities	4 691	...	...	...	...	...	...	...	...
General government	4 692	...	...	...	...	...	...	...	...
Banks	4 693	...	...	...	...	...	...	...	...
Other sectors	4 694	...	...	...	...	...	...	...	...

Table 2 (Concluded). STANDARD PRESENTATION, 1988–95
(Millions of U.S. dollars)

	Code	1988	1989	1990	1991	1992	1993	1994	1995
C. OTHER INVESTMENT	4 700	34.3	149.2	15.0	–53.3	119.7	82.5	83.9	325.9
Assets	4 703	**10.6**	**–1.1**	**–20.9**	**15.0**	**. . .**	**4.1**	**–7.9**	**–7.1**
Trade credits	4 706	1.1	–1.4	–3.1	–6.0	. . .	. . .	. . .	–.6
General government: long-term	4 708	. . .	. . .	. . .	. . .	. . .	. . .	. . .	. . .
General government: short-term	4 709	. . .	. . .	. . .	. . .	. . .	. . .	. . .	. . .
Other sectors: long-term	4 711	. . .	. . .	. . .	. . .	. . .	. . .	. . .	. . .
Other sectors: short-term	4 712	1.1	–1.4	–3.1	–6.0	. . .	. . .	. . .	. . .
Loans	4 714	. . .	. . .	. . .	. . .	. . .	. . .	. . .	. . .
Monetary authorities: long-term	4 717	. . .	. . .	. . .	. . .	. . .	. . .	. . .	. . .
Monetary authorities: short-term	4 718	. . .	. . .	. . .	. . .	. . .	. . .	. . .	. . .
General government: long-term	4 720	. . .	. . .	. . .	. . .	. . .	. . .	. . .	. . .
General government: short-term	4 721	. . .	. . .	. . .	. . .	. . .	. . .	. . .	. . .
Banks: long-term	4 723	. . .	. . .	. . .	. . .	. . .	. . .	. . .	. . .
Banks: short-term	4 724	. . .	. . .	. . .	. . .	. . .	. . .	. . .	. . .
Other sectors: long-term	4 726	. . .	. . .	. . .	. . .	. . .	. . .	. . .	. . .
Other sectors: short-term	4 727	. . .	. . .	. . .	. . .	. . .	. . .	. . .	. . .
Currency and deposits	4 730	9.9	.5	–17.2	21.3	. . .	4.1	–7.9	24.8
Monetary authorities	4 731	. . .	. . .	. . .	. . .	. . .	. . .	. . .	35.0
General government	4 732	. . .	. . .	. . .	. . .	. . .	. . .	. . .	. . .
Banks	4 733	9.5	.8	–17.2	21.3	. . .	4.1	–7.9	–10.2
Other sectors	4 734	.4	–.3	. . .	. . .	. . .	. . .	. . .	. . .
Other assets	4 736	–.4	–.3	–.6	–.2	. . .	. . .	. . .	–31.3
Monetary authorities: long-term	4 738	. . .	. . .	. . .	. . .	. . .	. . .	. . .	. . .
Monetary authorities: short-term	4 739	. . .	. . .	. . .	. . .	. . .	. . .	. . .	. . .
General government: long-term	4 741	–.4	–.3	–.6	–.2	. . .	. . .	. . .	. . .
General government: short-term	4 742	. . .	. . .	. . .	. . .	. . .	. . .	. . .	. . .
Banks: long-term	4 744	. . .	. . .	. . .	. . .	. . .	. . .	. . .	. . .
Banks: short-term	4 745	. . .	. . .	. . .	. . .	. . .	. . .	. . .	. . .
Other sectors: long-term	4 747	. . .	. . .	. . .	. . .	. . .	. . .	. . .	–31.3
Other sectors: short-term	4 748	. . .	. . .	. . .	. . .	. . .	. . .	. . .	. . .
Liabilities	4 753	**23.7**	**150.2**	**35.9**	**–68.3**	**119.7**	**78.4**	**91.8**	**333.0**
Trade credits	4 756	–2.2	8.6	4.8	13.1	. . .	. . .	. . .	–5.9
General government: long-term	4 758	. . .	. . .	. . .	. . .	. . .	. . .	. . .	–9.0
General government: short-term	4 759	. . .	. . .	. . .	. . .	. . .	. . .	. . .	. . .
Other sectors: long-term	4 761	. . .	. . .	. . .	. . .	. . .	. . .	. . .	. . .
Other sectors: short-term	4 762	–2.2	8.6	4.8	13.1	. . .	. . .	. . .	3.1
Loans	4 764	9.5	154.5	89.5	–52.4	71.6	95.6	38.7	338.7
Use of Fund credit and loans from the Fund	4 766	–10.5	–5.0	–5.2	–.2	. . .	. . .	. . .	. . .
Monetary authorities: other long-term	4 767	–43.4	62.4	6.3	–79.3	–1.6	–44.9	–117.0	39.6
Monetary authorities: short-term	4 768	9.5	–11.2	5.8	–6.7	. . .	. . .	. . .	–.1
General government: long-term	4 770	67.1	139.9	26.1	99.4	58.5	124.1	158.2	62.5
General government: short-term	4 771	. . .	–36.7	58.4	–85.1	–16.3	–.2	–.2	. . .
Banks: long-term	4 773	–.7	–.2	. . .	. . .	. . .	. . .	. . .	21.1
Banks: short-term	4 774	–1.6	4.5	1.9	2.6	. . .	. . .	. . .	198.8
Other sectors: long-term	4 776	–10.5	.8	–3.9	16.9	31.0	16.7	–2.3	16.8
Other sectors: short-term	4 777	–.4	. . .	. . .	. . .	. . .	. . .	. . .	. . .
Currency and deposits	4 780	13.7	7.7	–27.2	–1.9	. . .	14.7	83.2	7.7
Monetary authorities	4 781	. . .	. . .	. . .	. . .	. . .	. . .	. . .	. . .
General government	4 782	. . .	. . .	. . .	. . .	. . .	. . .	. . .	. . .
Banks	4 783	13.7	7.7	–27.2	–1.9	. . .	14.7	83.2	7.7
Other sectors	4 784	. . .	. . .	. . .	. . .	. . .	. . .	. . .	. . .
Other liabilities	4 786	2.7	–20.5	–31.2	–27.1	48.1	–31.9	–30.1	–7.4
Monetary authorities: long-term	4 788	. . .	. . .	. . .	. . .	. . .	. . .	. . .	. . .
Monetary authorities: short-term	4 789	1.3	–18.5	–29.6	–20.2	48.1	–31.9	–30.1	. . .
General government: long-term	4 791	. . .	. . .	. . .	. . .	. . .	. . .	. . .	. . .
General government: short-term	4 792	. . .	. . .	. . .	. . .	. . .	. . .	. . .	. . .
Banks: long-term	4 794	. . .	. . .	. . .	. . .	. . .	. . .	. . .	. . .
Banks: short-term	4 795	. . .	. . .	. . .	. . .	. . .	. . .	. . .	. . .
Other sectors: long-term	4 797	. . .	. . .	. . .	. . .	. . .	. . .	. . .	. . .
Other sectors: short-term	4 798	1.4	–2.0	–1.6	–7.0	. . .	. . .	. . .	. . .
D. RESERVE ASSETS	4 800	30.1	–110.0	–164.6	70.0	–91.6	–112.0	–113.0	–148.3
Monetary gold	4 810	. . .	. . .	. . .	. . .	. . .	. . .	. . .	. . .
Special drawing rights	4 820	. . .	. . .	. . .	. . .	. . .	. . .	–.1	–38.2
Reserve position in the Fund	4 830	. . .	. . .	. . .	. . .	. . .	. . .	. . .	. . .
Foreign exchange	4 840	30.1	–110.0	–164.6	70.0	–91.6	–112.0	–113.0	–111.0
Other claims	4 880	. . .	. . .	. . .	. . .	. . .	. . .	. . .	.9
NET ERRORS AND OMISSIONS	4 998	**–107.1**	**140.9**	**299.4**	**125.6**	**65.6**	**90.3**	**47.3**	**–214.1**

Part 3 of the *Yearbook* contains descriptions of the methodologies, compilation practices, and sources used to compile these data.

Table 1. ANALYTIC PRESENTATION, 1988–95
(Millions of U.S. dollars)

	Code	1988	1989	1990	1991	1992	1993	1994	1995
A. Current Account [1]	4 993 Y.	**–20.57**	**–21.00**	**–18.99**	**–24.66**	...	...	...	...
Goods: exports f.o.b.	2 100 ..	44.65	32.71	37.82	35.75	...	...	...	...
Goods: imports f.o.b.	3 100 ..	–56.51	–43.61	–53.17	–59.56	...	...	...	...
Balance on Goods	4 100 ..	*–11.86*	*–10.91*	*–15.36*	*–23.81*	...	...	...	...
Services: credit	2 200 ..	5.87	5.84	4.51	6.19	...	...	...	...
Services: debit	3 200 ..	–48.69	–29.77	–35.23	–43.03	...	...	...	...
Balance on Goods and Services	4 991 ..	*–54.68*	*–34.84*	*–46.08*	*–60.65*	...	...	...	...
Income: credit	2 300 ..	...	...	...	...	...	...	...	...
Income: debit	3 300 ..	–7.93	–10.00	–10.78	–9.41	...	...	...	...
Balance on Goods, Services, and Income	4 992 ..	*–62.61*	*–44.84*	*–56.86*	*–70.06*	...	...	...	...
Current transfers: credit	2 379 Y.	46.90	38.10	56.37	63.35	...	...	...	...
Current transfers: debit	3 379 ..	–4.87	–14.25	–18.50	–17.94	...	...	...	...
B. Capital Account [1]	4 994 Y.	...	...	...	...	...	...	...	...
Capital account: credit	2 994 Y.	...	...	...	...	...	...	...	...
Capital account: debit	3 994 ..	...	...	...	...	...	...	...	...
Total, Groups A Plus B	4 010 ..	*–20.57*	*–21.00*	*–18.99*	*–24.66*	...	...	...	...
C. Financial Account [1]	4 995 X.	**4.90**	**10.02**	**11.68**	**32.19**	...	...	...	...
Direct investment abroad	4 505 ..	...	–.14	–.13	–.11	...	...	...	...
Direct investment in Equatorial Guinea	4 555 Y.	...	–.29	9.77	42.26	...	...	...	...
Portfolio investment assets	4 602 ..	...	...	...	...	...	...	...	...
Equity securities	4 610 ..	...	...	...	...	...	...	...	...
Debt securities	4 619 ..	...	...	...	...	...	...	...	...
Portfolio investment liabilities	4 652 Y.	...	...	...	...	...	...	...	...
Equity securities	4 660 Y.	...	...	...	...	...	...	...	...
Debt securities	4 669 Y.	...	...	...	...	...	...	...	...
Other investment assets	4 703 ..	–1.12	–1.08	–2.80	–1.49	...	...	...	...
Monetary authorities	4 703 .A	...	...	...	...	...	...	...	...
General government	4 703 .B	–1.12	–1.90	–1.58	–.73	...	...	...	...
Banks	4 703 .C	...	.82	–1.22	–.63	...	...	...	...
Other sectors	4 703 .D	...	...	...	–.12	...	...	...	...
Other investment liabilities	4 753 X.	6.02	11.53	4.83	–8.48	...	...	...	...
Monetary authorities	4 753 XA	...	...	...	...	...	...	...	...
General government	4 753 YB	10.38	13.40	4.52	–6.57	...	...	...	...
Banks	4 753 YC	2.92	.78	1.45	1.26	...	...	...	...
Other sectors	4 753 YD	–7.28	–2.66	–1.14	–3.17	...	...	...	...
Total, Groups A Through C	4 020 ..	*–15.68*	*–10.97*	*–7.31*	*7.53*	...	...	...	...
D. Net Errors and Omissions	4 998 ..	**–1.70**	**–4.53**	**–2.39**	**–30.72**	...	...	...	...
Total, Groups A Through D	4 030 ..	*–17.37*	*–15.50*	*–9.70*	*–23.19*	...	...	...	...
E. Reserves and Related Items	4 040 ..	**17.37**	**15.50**	**9.70**	**23.19**	...	...	...	...
Reserve assets	4 800 ..	–7.11	4.51	.39	–8.64	...	...	...	...
Use of Fund credit and loans	4 766 ..	3.44	–5.01	–3.53	7.18	...	...	...	...
Liabilities constituting foreign authorities' reserves	4 900 ..	...	...	...	...	...	...	...	...
Exceptional financing	4 920 ..	21.05	16.00	12.84	24.65	...	...	...	...
Conversion rates: CFA francs per U.S. dollar	0 101 ..	**297.85**	**319.01**	**272.26**	**282.11**	**264.69**	**283.16**	**555.20**	**499.15**

[1] Excludes components that have been classified in the categories of Group E.

Table 2. STANDARD PRESENTATION, 1988–95
(Millions of U.S. dollars)

	Code	1988	1989	1990	1991	1992	1993	1994	1995
CURRENT ACCOUNT	4 993 . .	**–16.54**	**–18.55**	**–14.87**	**–22.19**	**. . .**	**. . .**	**. . .**	**. . .**
A. GOODS	4 100 . .	–11.86	–10.91	–15.36	–23.81	. . .	. . .	. . .	. . .
Credit	2 100 . .	**44.65**	**32.71**	**37.82**	**35.75**	**. . .**	**. . .**	**. . .**	**. . .**
General merchandise: exports f.o.b.	2 110 . .	44.65	32.71	37.82	35.75	. . .	. . .	. . .	. . .
Goods for processing: exports f.o.b.	2 150 . .	. . .	. . .	. . .	. . .	. . .	. . .	. . .	. . .
Repairs on goods	2 160 . .	. . .	. . .	. . .	. . .	. . .	. . .	. . .	. . .
Goods procured in ports by carriers	2 170 . .	. . .	. . .	. . .	. . .	. . .	. . .	. . .	. . .
Nonmonetary gold	2 180 . .	. . .	. . .	. . .	. . .	. . .	. . .	. . .	. . .
Debit	3 100 . .	**–56.51**	**–43.61**	**–53.17**	**–59.56**	**. . .**	**. . .**	**. . .**	**. . .**
General merchandise: imports f.o.b.	3 110 . .	–56.51	–43.61	–53.17	–59.56	. . .	. . .	. . .	. . .
Goods for processing: imports f.o.b.	3 150 . .	. . .	. . .	. . .	. . .	. . .	. . .	. . .	. . .
Repairs on goods	3 160 . .	. . .	. . .	. . .	. . .	. . .	. . .	. . .	. . .
Goods procured in ports by carriers	3 170 . .	. . .	. . .	. . .	. . .	. . .	. . .	. . .	. . .
Nonmonetary gold	3 180 . .	. . .	. . .	. . .	. . .	. . .	. . .	. . .	. . .
B. SERVICES	4 200 . .	–42.82	–23.93	–30.72	–36.84	. . .	. . .	. . .	. . .
Total credit	2 200 . .	*5.87*	*5.84*	*4.51*	*6.19*	. . .	. . .	. . .	. . .
Total debit	3 200 . .	*–48.69*	*–29.77*	*–35.23*	*–43.03*	. . .	. . .	. . .	. . .
Transportation services, credit	2 205 . .	**. . .**	**.89**	**1.05**	**1.62**	**. . .**	**. . .**	**. . .**	**. . .**
Passenger	2 205 BA	. . .	. . .	. . .	. . .	. . .	. . .	. . .	. . .
Freight	2 205 BB	. . .	*.14*	*.17*	*.23*	. . .	. . .	. . .	. . .
Other	2 205 BC	. . .	*.75*	*.88*	*1.39*	. . .	. . .	. . .	. . .
Sea transport, passenger	2 207 . .	. . .	. . .	. . .	. . .	. . .	. . .	. . .	. . .
Sea transport, freight	2 208 . .	. . .	. . .	. . .	. . .	. . .	. . .	. . .	. . .
Sea transport, other	2 209 . .	. . .	. . .	. . .	. . .	. . .	. . .	. . .	. . .
Air transport, passenger	2 211 . .	. . .	. . .	. . .	. . .	. . .	. . .	. . .	. . .
Air transport, freight	2 212 . .	. . .	. . .	. . .	. . .	. . .	. . .	. . .	. . .
Air transport, other	2 213 . .	. . .	. . .	. . .	. . .	. . .	. . .	. . .	. . .
Other transport, passenger	2 215 . .	. . .	. . .	. . .	. . .	. . .	. . .	. . .	. . .
Other transport, freight	2 216 . .	. . .	. . .	. . .	. . .	. . .	. . .	. . .	. . .
Other transport, other	2 217 . .	. . .	. . .	. . .	. . .	. . .	. . .	. . .	. . .
Transportation services, debit	3 205 . .	**–6.93**	**–11.86**	**–13.80**	**–14.90**	**. . .**	**. . .**	**. . .**	**. . .**
Passenger	3 205 BA	. . .	. . .	. . .	. . .	. . .	. . .	. . .	. . .
Freight	3 205 BB	*–6.93*	*–6.93*	*–8.45*	*–9.46*	. . .	. . .	. . .	. . .
Other	3 205 BC	. . .	*–4.93*	*–5.36*	*–5.44*	. . .	. . .	. . .	. . .
Sea transport, passenger	3 207 . .	. . .	. . .	. . .	. . .	. . .	. . .	. . .	. . .
Sea transport, freight	3 208 . .	. . .	. . .	. . .	. . .	. . .	. . .	. . .	. . .
Sea transport, other	3 209 . .	. . .	. . .	. . .	. . .	. . .	. . .	. . .	. . .
Air transport, passenger	3 211 . .	. . .	. . .	. . .	. . .	. . .	. . .	. . .	. . .
Air transport, freight	3 212 . .	. . .	. . .	. . .	. . .	. . .	. . .	. . .	. . .
Air transport, other	3 213 . .	. . .	. . .	. . .	. . .	. . .	. . .	. . .	. . .
Other transport, passenger	3 215 . .	. . .	. . .	. . .	. . .	. . .	. . .	. . .	. . .
Other transport, freight	3 216 . .	. . .	. . .	. . .	. . .	. . .	. . .	. . .	. . .
Other transport, other	3 217 . .	. . .	. . .	. . .	. . .	. . .	. . .	. . .	. . .
Travel, credit	2 236 . .	**. . .**	**.84**	**1.11**	**1.80**	**. . .**	**. . .**	**. . .**	**. . .**
Business travel	2 237 . .	. . .	. . .	. . .	. . .	. . .	. . .	. . .	. . .
Personal travel	2 240 . .	. . .	. . .	. . .	. . .	. . .	. . .	. . .	. . .
Travel, debit	3 236 . .	**. . .**	**–7.62**	**–8.07**	**–8.70**	**. . .**	**. . .**	**. . .**	**. . .**
Business travel	3 237 . .	. . .	. . .	. . .	. . .	. . .	. . .	. . .	. . .
Personal travel	3 240 . .	. . .	. . .	. . .	. . .	. . .	. . .	. . .	. . .
Other services, credit	2 200 BA	**5.87**	**4.11**	**2.35**	**2.77**	**. . .**	**. . .**	**. . .**	**. . .**
Communications	2 245 . .	. . .	. . .	. . .	. . .	. . .	. . .	. . .	. . .
Construction	2 249 . .	. . .	. . .	. . .	. . .	. . .	. . .	. . .	. . .
Insurance	2 253 . .	. . .	.02	.02	.03	. . .	. . .	. . .	. . .
Financial	2 260 . .	. . .	. . .	. . .	. . .	. . .	. . .	. . .	. . .
Computer and information	2 262 . .	. . .	. . .	. . .	. . .	. . .	. . .	. . .	. . .
Royalties and licence fees	2 266 . .	. . .	. . .	. . .	. . .	. . .	. . .	. . .	. . .
Other business services	2 268 . .	5.87	4.10	2.33	2.74	. . .	. . .	. . .	. . .
Personal, cultural, and recreational	2 287 . .	. . .	. . .	. . .	. . .	. . .	. . .	. . .	. . .
Government, n.i.e.	2 291 . .	. . .	. . .	. . .	. . .	. . .	. . .	. . .	. . .
Other services, debit	3 200 BA	**–41.75**	**–10.30**	**–13.36**	**–19.43**	**. . .**	**. . .**	**. . .**	**. . .**
Communications	3 245 . .	. . .	. . .	. . .	. . .	. . .	. . .	. . .	. . .
Construction	3 249 . .	. . .	. . .	. . .	. . .	. . .	. . .	. . .	. . .
Insurance	3 253 . .	–.77	–.77	–.94	–1.05	. . .	. . .	. . .	. . .
Financial	3 260 . .	. . .	. . .	. . .	. . .	. . .	. . .	. . .	. . .
Computer and information	3 262 . .	. . .	. . .	. . .	. . .	. . .	. . .	. . .	. . .
Royalties and licence fees	3 266 . .	. . .	. . .	. . .	. . .	. . .	. . .	. . .	. . .
Other business services	3 268 . .	–22.21	–9.53	–12.42	–18.38	. . .	. . .	. . .	. . .
Personal, cultural, and recreational	3 287 . .	. . .	. . .	. . .	. . .	. . .	. . .	. . .	. . .
Government, n.i.e.	3 291 . .	–18.77	. . .	. . .	. . .	. . .	. . .	. . .	. . .

Table 2 (Continued). STANDARD PRESENTATION, 1988–95
(Millions of U.S. dollars)

	Code	1988	1989	1990	1991	1992	1993	1994	1995
C. INCOME	4 300	−7.93	−10.00	−10.78	−9.41	...	...	...	...
Total credit	2 300	...	...	...	...	...	...	...	...
Total debit	3 300	*−7.93*	*−10.00*	*−10.78*	*−9.41*	...	...	...	...
Compensation of employees, credit	2 310	...	...	...	...	...	...	...	...
Compensation of employees, debit	3 310	...	...	...	...	...	...	...	...
Investment income, credit	2 320	...	...	...	...	...	...	...	...
Direct investment income	2 330	...	...	...	...	...	...	...	...
Dividends and distributed branch profits	2 332	...	...	...	...	...	...	...	...
Reinvested earnings and undistributed branch profits	2 333	...	...	...	...	...	...	...	...
Income on debt (interest)	2 334	...	...	...	...	...	...	...	...
Portfolio investment income	2 339	...	...	...	...	...	...	...	...
Income on equity	2 340	...	...	...	...	...	...	...	...
Income on bonds and notes	2 350	...	...	...	...	...	...	...	...
Income on money market instruments and financial derivatives	2 360	...	...	...	...	...	...	...	...
Other investment income	2 370	...	...	...	...	...	...	...	...
Investment income, debit	3 320	**−7.93**	**−10.00**	**−10.78**	**−9.41**	...	...	...	...
Direct investment income	3 330	...	...	...	...	...	...	...	...
Dividends and distributed branch profits	3 332	...	...	...	...	...	...	...	...
Reinvested earnings and undistributed branch profits	3 333	...	...	...	...	...	...	...	...
Income on debt (interest)	3 334	...	...	...	...	...	...	...	...
Portfolio investment income	3 339	...	...	...	...	...	...	...	...
Income on equity	3 340	...	...	...	...	...	...	...	...
Income on bonds and notes	3 350	...	...	...	...	...	...	...	...
Income on money market instruments and financial derivatives	3 360	...	...	...	...	...	...	...	...
Other investment income	3 370	−7.93	−10.00	−10.78	−9.41	...	...	...	...
D. CURRENT TRANSFERS	4 379	46.07	26.29	41.98	47.88	...	...	...	...
Credit	2 379	**50.94**	**40.54**	**60.49**	**65.82**	...	...	...	...
General government	2 380	50.73	40.04	59.86	65.19	...	...	...	...
Other sectors	2 390	.20	.50	.62	.63	...	...	...	...
Workers' remittances	2 391	...	...	...	...	...	...	...	...
Other current transfers	2 392	.20	.50	.62	.63	...	...	...	...
Debit	3 379	**−4.87**	**−14.25**	**−18.50**	**−17.94**	...	...	...	...
General government	3 380	−.89	−.76	−.82	−.76	...	...	...	...
Other sectors	3 390	−3.98	−13.49	−17.68	−17.18	...	...	...	...
Workers' remittances	3 391	...	...	...	...	...	...	...	...
Other current transfers	3 392	−3.98	−13.49	−17.68	−17.18	...	...	...	...
CAPITAL AND FINANCIAL ACCOUNT	4 996	**18.24**	**23.08**	**17.26**	**52.90**	...	...	...	...
CAPITAL ACCOUNT	4 994	...	...	...	...	...	...	...	...
Total credit	2 994	...	...	...	...	...	...	...	...
Total debit	3 994	...	...	...	...	...	...	...	...
Capital transfers, credit	2 400	...	...	...	...	...	...	...	...
General government	2 401	...	...	...	...	...	...	...	...
Debt forgiveness	2 402	...	...	...	...	...	...	...	...
Other capital transfers	2 410	...	...	...	...	...	...	...	...
Other sectors	2 430	...	...	...	...	...	...	...	...
Migrants' transfers	2 431	...	...	...	...	...	...	...	...
Debt forgiveness	2 432	...	...	...	...	...	...	...	...
Other capital transfers	2 440	...	...	...	...	...	...	...	...
Capital transfers, debit	3 400	...	...	...	...	...	...	...	...
General government	3 401	...	...	...	...	...	...	...	...
Debt forgiveness	3 402	...	...	...	...	...	...	...	...
Other capital transfers	3 410	...	...	...	...	...	...	...	...
Other sectors	3 430	...	...	...	...	...	...	...	...
Migrants' transfers	3 431	...	...	...	...	...	...	...	...
Debt forgiveness	3 432	...	...	...	...	...	...	...	...
Other capital transfers	3 440	...	...	...	...	...	...	...	...
Nonproduced nonfinancial assets, credit	2 480	...	...	...	...	...	...	...	...
Nonproduced nonfinancial assets, debit	3 480	...	...	...	...	...	...	...	...

Table 2 (Continued). STANDARD PRESENTATION, 1988–95
(Millions of U.S. dollars)

	Code	1988	1989	1990	1991	1992	1993	1994	1995
FINANCIAL ACCOUNT	4 995 . .	**18.24**	**23.08**	**17.26**	**52.90**	...	...	...	...
A. DIRECT INVESTMENT	4 500 . .	...	–.43	9.65	42.15	...	...	...	...
Direct investment abroad	4 505 . .	...	**–.14**	**–.13**	**–.11**	...	...	...	...
Equity capital	4 510 . .	...	–.14	–.13	–.11	...	...	...	...
Claims on affiliated enterprises	4 515 . .	...	...	...	...	...	...	...	...
Liabilities to affiliated enterprises	4 520 . .	...	...	...	...	...	...	...	...
Reinvested earnings	4 525 . .	...	...	...	...	...	...	...	...
Other capital	4 530 . .	...	...	...	...	...	...	...	...
Claims on affiliated enterprises	4 535 . .	...	...	...	...	...	...	...	...
Liabilities to affiliated enterprises	4 540 . .	...	...	...	...	...	...	...	...
Direct investment in Equatorial Guinea	4 555 . .	...	**–.29**	**9.77**	**42.26**	...	...	...	...
Equity capital	4 560 . .	...	–.29	9.77	42.26	...	...	...	...
Claims on direct investors	4 565 . .	...	...	...	...	...	...	...	...
Liabilities to direct investors	4 570 . .	...	...	...	...	...	...	...	...
Reinvested earnings	4 575 . .	...	...	...	...	...	...	...	...
Other capital	4 580 . .	...	...	...	...	...	...	...	...
Claims on direct investors	4 585 . .	...	...	...	...	...	...	...	...
Liabilities to direct investors	4 590 . .	...	...	...	...	...	...	...	...
B. PORTFOLIO INVESTMENT	4 600 . .	...	...	...	...	...	...	...	...
Assets	4 602 . .	...	...	...	...	...	...	...	...
Equity securities	4 610 . .	...	...	...	...	...	...	...	...
Monetary authorities	4 611 . .	...	...	...	...	...	...	...	...
General government	4 612 . .	...	...	...	...	...	...	...	...
Banks	4 613 . .	...	...	...	...	...	...	...	...
Other sectors	4 614 . .	...	...	...	...	...	...	...	...
Debt securities	4 619 . .	...	...	...	...	...	...	...	...
Bonds and notes	4 620 . .	...	...	...	...	...	...	...	...
Monetary authorities	4 621 . .	...	...	...	...	...	...	...	...
General government	4 622 . .	...	...	...	...	...	...	...	...
Banks	4 623 . .	...	...	...	...	...	...	...	...
Other sectors	4 624 . .	...	...	...	...	...	...	...	...
Money market instruments	4 630 . .	...	...	...	...	...	...	...	...
Monetary authorities	4 631 . .	...	...	...	...	...	...	...	...
General government	4 632 . .	...	...	...	...	...	...	...	...
Banks	4 633 . .	...	...	...	...	...	...	...	...
Other sectors	4 634 . .	...	...	...	...	...	...	...	...
Financial derivatives	4 640 . .	...	...	...	...	...	...	...	...
Monetary authorities	4 641 . .	...	...	...	...	...	...	...	...
General government	4 642 . .	...	...	...	...	...	...	...	...
Banks	4 643 . .	...	...	...	...	...	...	...	...
Other sectors	4 644 . .	...	...	...	...	...	...	...	...
Liabilities	4 652 . .	...	...	...	...	...	...	...	...
Equity securities	4 660 . .	...	...	...	...	...	...	...	...
Banks	4 663 . .	...	...	...	...	...	...	...	...
Other sectors	4 664 . .	...	...	...	...	...	...	...	...
Debt securities	4 669 . .	...	...	...	...	...	...	...	...
Bonds and notes	4 670 . .	...	...	...	...	...	...	...	...
Monetary authorities	4 671 . .	...	...	...	...	...	...	...	...
General government	4 672 . .	...	...	...	...	...	...	...	...
Banks	4 673 . .	...	...	...	...	...	...	...	...
Other sectors	4 674 . .	...	...	...	...	...	...	...	...
Money market instruments	4 680 . .	...	...	...	...	...	...	...	...
Monetary authorities	4 681 . .	...	...	...	...	...	...	...	...
General government	4 682 . .	...	...	...	...	...	...	...	...
Banks	4 683 . .	...	...	...	...	...	...	...	...
Other sectors	4 684 . .	...	...	...	...	...	...	...	...
Financial derivatives	4 690 . .	...	...	...	...	...	...	...	...
Monetary authorities	4 691 . .	...	...	...	...	...	...	...	...
General government	4 692 . .	...	...	...	...	...	...	...	...
Banks	4 693 . .	...	...	...	...	...	...	...	...
Other sectors	4 694 . .	...	...	...	...	...	...	...	...

Table 2 (Concluded). STANDARD PRESENTATION, 1988–95
(Millions of U.S. dollars)

	Code	1988	1989	1990	1991	1992	1993	1994	1995
C. OTHER INVESTMENT	4 700	25.35	19.00	7.23	19.40	...	...	...	...
Assets	4 703	**–1.12**	**–1.08**	**–2.80**	**–1.49**	**...**	**...**	**...**	**...**
Trade credits	4 706	...	...	...	...	...	...	...	...
General government: long-term	4 708	...	...	...	...	...	...	...	...
General government: short-term	4 709	...	...	...	...	...	...	...	...
Other sectors: long-term	4 711	...	...	...	...	...	...	...	...
Other sectors: short-term	4 712	...	...	...	...	...	...	...	...
Loans	4 714	...	...	...	–.12	...	...	...	...
Monetary authorities: long-term	4 717	...	...	...	...	...	...	...	...
Monetary authorities: short-term	4 718	...	...	...	...	...	...	...	...
General government: long-term	4 720	...	...	...	...	...	...	...	...
General government: short-term	4 721	...	...	...	...	...	...	...	...
Banks: long-term	4 723	...	...	...	...	...	...	...	...
Banks: short-term	4 724	...	...	...	...	...	...	...	...
Other sectors: long-term	4 726	...	...	...	–.12	...	...	...	...
Other sectors: short-term	4 727	...	...	...	...	...	...	...	...
Currency and deposits	4 730	...	.82	–1.22	–.63	...	...	...	...
Monetary authorities	4 731	...	...	...	...	...	...	...	...
General government	4 732	...	...	...	...	...	...	...	...
Banks	4 733	...	.82	–1.22	–.63	...	...	...	...
Other sectors	4 734	...	...	...	...	...	...	...	...
Other assets	4 736	–1.12	–1.90	–1.58	–.73	...	...	...	...
Monetary authorities: long-term	4 738	...	...	...	...	...	...	...	...
Monetary authorities: short-term	4 739	...	...	...	...	...	...	...	...
General government: long-term	4 741	–1.12	–1.90	–1.58	–.73	...	...	...	...
General government: short-term	4 742	...	...	...	...	...	...	...	...
Banks: long-term	4 744	...	...	...	...	...	...	...	...
Banks: short-term	4 745	...	...	...	...	...	...	...	...
Other sectors: long-term	4 747	...	...	...	...	...	...	...	...
Other sectors: short-term	4 748	...	...	...	...	...	...	...	...
Liabilities	4 753	**26.47**	**20.08**	**10.03**	**20.88**	**...**	**...**	**...**	**...**
Trade credits	4 756	...	...	...	...	...	...	...	...
General government: long-term	4 758	...	...	...	...	...	...	...	...
General government: short-term	4 759	...	...	...	...	...	...	...	...
Other sectors: long-term	4 761	...	...	...	...	...	...	...	...
Other sectors: short-term	4 762	...	...	...	...	...	...	...	...
Loans	4 764	18.39	13.94	9.90	15.08	...	...	...	...
Use of Fund credit and loans from the Fund	4 766	3.44	–5.01	–3.53	7.18	...	...	...	...
Monetary authorities: other long-term	4 767	...	...	...	...	...	...	...	...
Monetary authorities: short-term	4 768	...	...	...	...	...	...	...	...
General government: long-term	4 770	13.69	18.08	12.50	6.95	...	...	...	...
General government: short-term	4 771	...	...	...	...	...	...	...	...
Banks: long-term	4 773	...	...	...	...	...	...	...	...
Banks: short-term	4 774	...	...	...	...	...	...	...	...
Other sectors: long-term	4 776	1.26	.87	.92	.95	...	...	...	...
Other sectors: short-term	4 777	...	...	...	...	...	...	...	...
Currency and deposits	4 780	2.92	.78	1.45	1.26	...	...	...	...
Monetary authorities	4 781	...	...	...	...	...	...	...	...
General government	4 782	...	...	...	...	...	...	...	...
Banks	4 783	2.92	.78	1.45	1.26	...	...	...	...
Other sectors	4 784	...	...	...	...	...	...	...	...
Other liabilities	4 786	5.16	5.35	–1.33	4.54	...	...	...	...
Monetary authorities: long-term	4 788	...	...	...	...	...	...	...	...
Monetary authorities: short-term	4 789	13.70	8.88	.73	8.66	...	...	...	...
General government: long-term	4 791	...	...	...	...	...	...	...	...
General government: short-term	4 792	...	...	...	...	...	...	...	...
Banks: long-term	4 794	...	...	...	...	...	...	...	...
Banks: short-term	4 795	...	...	...	...	...	...	...	...
Other sectors: long-term	4 797	...	...	...	...	...	...	...	...
Other sectors: short-term	4 798	–8.54	–3.53	–2.06	–4.12	...	...	...	...
D. RESERVE ASSETS	4 800	–7.11	4.51	.39	–8.64	...	...	...	...
Monetary gold	4 810	...	...	...	...	...	...	...	...
Special drawing rights	4 820	.15	–.10	.13	–7.76	...	...	...	...
Reserve position in the Fund	4 830	...	...	...	...	...	...	...	...
Foreign exchange	4 840	–7.27	4.61	.26	–.88	...	...	...	...
Other claims	4 880	...	...	...	...	...	...	...	...
NET ERRORS AND OMISSIONS	4 998	**–1.70**	**–4.53**	**–2.39**	**–30.72**	**...**	**...**	**...**	**...**

Table 1. ANALYTIC PRESENTATION, 1988–95
(Millions of U.S. dollars)

	Code	1988	1989	1990	1991	1992	1993	1994	1995
A. Current Account [1]	4 993 Y.	**. . .**	**. . .**	**. . .**	**. . .**	**36.1**	**23.3**	**–170.8**	**–184.4**
Goods: exports f.o.b	2 100 . .	. . .	. . .	. . .	. . .	460.7	811.7	1,327.4	1,861.4
Goods: imports f.o.b	3 100 . .	. . .	. . .	. . .	. . .	–551.1	–956.6	–1,688.3	–2,553.5
Balance on Goods	4 100 . .	. . .	. . .	. . .	. . .	*–90.4*	*–144.9*	*–361.0*	*–692.2*
Services: credit	2 200 . .	. . .	. . .	. . .	. . .	203.2	334.6	515.3	876.8
Services: debit	3 200 . .	. . .	. . .	. . .	. . .	–160.5	–257.7	–410.8	–497.7
Balance on Goods and Services	4 991 . .	. . .	. . .	. . .	. . .	*–47.7*	*–68.0*	*–256.4*	*–313.1*
Income: credit	2 300 . .	. . .	. . .	. . .	. . .	.5	26.9	37.3	63.2
Income: debit	3 300 . .	. . .	. . .	. . .	. . .	–13.7	–40.8	–66.3	–60.8
Balance on Goods, Services, and Income	4 992 . .	. . .	. . .	. . .	. . .	*–60.9*	*–81.9*	*–285.4*	*–310.7*
Current transfers: credit	2 379 Y.	. . .	. . .	. . .	. . .	97.4	108.4	120.3	134.5
Current transfers: debit	3 379 . .	. . .	. . .	. . .	. . .	–.3	–3.2	–5.7	–8.2
B. Capital Account [1]	4 994 Y.	**. . .**	**. . .**	**. . .**	**. . .**	**27.4**	**. . .**	**–.6**	**–.8**
Capital account: credit	2 994 Y.	. . .	. . .	. . .	. . .	27.4	. . .	.5	1.4
Capital account: debit	3 994 . .	. . .	. . .	. . .	. . .	. . .	. . .	–1.1	–2.2
Total, Groups A Plus B	4 010 . .	. . .	. . .	. . .	. . .	*63.5*	*23.3*	*–171.4*	*–185.2*
C. Financial Account [1]	4 995 X.	**. . .**	**. . .**	**. . .**	**. . .**	**–1.3**	**192.3**	**175.7**	**233.4**
Direct investment abroad	4 505 . .	. . .	. . .	. . .	. . .	–1.9	–7.8	–2.4	–2.5
Direct investment in Estonia	4 555 Y.	. . .	. . .	. . .	. . .	82.3	162.2	214.4	201.5
Portfolio investment assets	4 602 . .	. . .	. . .	. . .	. . .	. . .	–.4	–22.5	–33.2
Equity securities	4 610 . .	. . .	. . .	. . .	. . .	. . .	–.4	–14.5	5.1
Debt securities	4 619 . .	. . .	. . .	. . .	. . .	. . .	. . .	–8.0	–38.2
Portfolio investment liabilities	4 652 Y.	. . .	. . .	. . .	. . .	. . .	.2	8.4	17.2
Equity securities	4 660 Y.	. . .	. . .	. . .	. . .	. . .	.1	8.4	9.9
Debt securities	4 669 Y.	. . .	. . .	. . .	. . .	. . .	.1	. . .	7.3
Other investment assets	4 703 . .	. . .	. . .	. . .	. . .	–122.4	–144.7	–146.7	–98.9
Monetary authorities	4 703 . A	. . .	. . .	. . .	. . .	–72.8	5.0	–3.1	–.2
General government	4 703 . B	. . .	. . .	. . .	. . .	. . .	–17.1	.4	–.4
Banks	4 703 . C	. . .	. . .	. . .	. . .	–48.5	–44.0	–99.6	–41.1
Other sectors	4 703 . D	. . .	. . .	. . .	. . .	–1.1	–88.6	–44.4	–57.2
Other investment liabilities	4 753 X.	. . .	. . .	. . .	. . .	40.7	182.8	124.4	149.4
Monetary authorities	4 753 XA	. . .	. . .	. . .	. . .	21.6	4.5	14.4	–12.7
General government	4 753 YB	. . .	. . .	. . .	. . .	11.1	82.3	28.8	54.9
Banks	4 753 YC	. . .	. . .	. . .	. . .	7.2	7.2	30.3	82.2
Other sectors	4 753 YD	. . .	. . .	. . .	. . .	.7	88.8	50.9	24.9
Total, Groups A Through C	4 020 . .	. . .	. . .	. . .	. . .	*62.3*	*215.6*	*4.3*	*48.2*
D. Net Errors and Omissions	4 998 . .	**. . .**	**. . .**	**. . .**	**. . .**	**–4.3**	**–50.9**	**13.2**	**35.3**
Total, Groups A Through D	4 030 . .	. . .	. . .	. . .	. . .	*57.9*	*164.6*	*17.5*	*83.5*
E. Reserves and Related Items	4 040 . .	**. . .**	**. . .**	**. . .**	**. . .**	**–57.9**	**–164.6**	**–17.5**	**–83.5**
Reserve assets	4 800 . .	. . .	. . .	. . .	. . .	–69.2	–212.4	–17.5	–112.9
Use of Fund credit and loans	4 766 . .	. . .	. . .	. . .	. . .	11.3	47.7	. . .	29.4
Liabilities constituting foreign authorities' reserves	4 900 . .	. . .	. . .	. . .	. . .	. . .	. . .	. . .	. . .
Exceptional financing	4 920 . .	. . .	. . .	. . .	. . .	. . .	. . .	. . .	. . .
Conversion rates: krooni per U.S. dollar	0 101 . .	**. . .**	**. . .**	**. . .**	**. . .**	**12.028**	**13.223**	**12.991**	**11.465**

[1] Excludes components that have been classified in the categories of Group E.

Table 2. STANDARD PRESENTATION, 1988–95
(Millions of U.S. dollars)

	Code	1988	1989	1990	1991	1992	1993	1994	1995
CURRENT ACCOUNT	4 993 . .	...	...	...	...	**36.1**	**23.3**	**–170.8**	**–184.4**
A. GOODS	4 100 . .	...	...	...	...	–90.4	–144.9	–361.0	–692.2
Credit	2 100 . .	...	...	...	...	**460.7**	**811.7**	**1,327.4**	**1,861.4**
General merchandise: exports f.o.b.	2 110 . .	...	...	...	...	460.7	802.7	1,097.5	1,460.8
Goods for processing: exports f.o.b.	2 150 . .	...	...	...	...	...	...	214.4	386.4
Repairs on goods	2 160 . .	...	...	...	...	...	9.1	15.4	14.1
Goods procured in ports by carriers	2 170 . .	...	...	...	...	...	...	...	...
Nonmonetary gold	2 180 . .	...	...	...	...	...	...	.1	.1
Debit	3 100 . .	...	...	...	...	**–551.1**	**–956.6**	**–1,688.3**	**–2,553.5**
General merchandise: imports f.o.b.	3 110 . .	...	...	...	...	–540.6	–927.4	–1,466.5	–2,150.4
Goods for processing: imports f.o.b.	3 150 . .	...	...	...	...	...	...	–187.2	–371.5
Repairs on goods	3 160 . .	...	...	...	...	...	–1.9	–2.6	–6.7
Goods procured in ports by carriers	3 170 . .	...	...	...	...	–10.5	–27.2	–31.5	–23.5
Nonmonetary gold	3 180 . .	...	...	...	...	...	...	–.5	–1.4
B. SERVICES	4 200 . .	...	...	...	...	42.7	76.8	104.6	379.1
Total credit	2 200 . .	...	...	...	...	*203.2*	*334.6*	*515.3*	*876.8*
Total debit	3 200 . .	...	...	...	...	*–160.5*	*–257.7*	*–410.8*	*–497.7*
Transportation services, credit	2 205 . .	...	...	...	...	**149.6**	**223.1**	**337.2**	**373.7**
Passenger	2 205 BA	...	...	...	...	*19.4*	*58.6*	*76.5*	*95.4*
Freight	2 205 BB	...	...	...	...	*109.3*	*107.6*	*174.2*	*173.3*
Other	2 205 BC	...	...	...	...	*20.9*	*57.0*	*86.6*	*105.1*
Sea transport, passenger	2 207 . .	...	...	...	...	16.2	37.8	60.8	71.0
Sea transport, freight	2 208 . .	...	...	...	...	98.6	90.2	128.2	98.1
Sea transport, other	2 209 . .	...	...	...	...	18.9	36.3	54.4	58.9
Air transport, passenger	2 211 . .	...	...	...	...	2.9	19.6	11.1	16.7
Air transport, freight	2 212 . .	...	...	...	...	.1	.6	1.0	1.7
Air transport, other	2 213 . .	...	...	...	...	...	4.0	7.0	10.2
Other transport, passenger	2 215 . .	...	...	...	...	.3	1.2	4.6	7.6
Other transport, freight	2 216 . .	...	...	...	...	10.6	16.7	45.0	73.5
Other transport, other	2 217 . .	...	...	...	...	2.1	16.6	25.1	36.0
Transportation services, debit	3 205 . .	...	...	...	...	**–93.6**	**–124.3**	**–184.5**	**–222.1**
Passenger	3 205 BA	...	...	...	...	*–1.2*	*–13.4*	*–18.5*	*–29.9*
Freight	3 205 BB	...	...	...	...	*–29.1*	*–43.4*	*–100.9*	*–122.1*
Other	3 205 BC	...	...	...	...	*–63.4*	*–67.5*	*–65.2*	*–70.1*
Sea transport, passenger	3 207 . .	...	...	...	...	–1.0	–10.5	–15.5	–19.0
Sea transport, freight	3 208 . .	...	...	...	...	–26.2	–34.3	–77.3	–69.9
Sea transport, other	3 209 . .	...	...	...	...	–57.1	–57.8	–52.1	–50.4
Air transport, passenger	3 211 . .	...	...	...	...	–.2	–2.5	–2.1	–9.6
Air transport, freight	3 212 . .	...	...	...	...	...	–.7	–1.9	–.7
Air transport, other	3 213 . .	...	...	...	...	–.1	–6.2	–5.6	–10.3
Other transport, passenger	3 215 . .	...	...	...	...	...	–.4	–.9	–1.4
Other transport, freight	3 216 . .	...	...	...	...	–2.9	–8.4	–21.7	–51.5
Other transport, other	3 217 . .	...	...	...	...	–6.2	–3.5	–7.4	–9.4
Travel, credit	2 236 . .	...	...	...	...	**27.4**	**49.8**	**91.4**	**356.7**
Business travel	2 237 . .	...	...	...	...	6.9	12.5	22.9	67.5
Personal travel	2 240 . .	...	...	...	...	20.6	37.3	68.5	289.1
Travel, debit	3 236 . .	...	...	...	...	**–18.9**	**–25.3**	**–48.0**	**–90.5**
Business travel	3 237 . .	...	...	...	...	–4.7	–6.3	–12.0	–22.6
Personal travel	3 240 . .	...	...	...	...	–14.2	–19.0	–36.0	–67.9
Other services, credit	2 200 BA	...	...	...	...	**26.1**	**61.6**	**86.7**	**146.4**
Communications	2 245 . .	...	...	...	...	5.7	8.5	11.8	16.7
Construction	2 249 . .	...	...	...	...	5.8	17.8	31.7	63.4
Insurance	2 253 . .	...	...	...	...	.1	.3	.6	1.3
Financial	2 260 . .	...	...	...	...	...	.2	1.0	1.9
Computer and information	2 262 . .	...	...	...	...	...	...	2.7	2.4
Royalties and licence fees	2 266 . .	...	...	...	...	...	...	.9	.9
Other business services	2 268 . .	...	...	...	...	11.7	26.7	30.6	51.1
Personal, cultural, and recreational	2 287 . .	...	...	...	...	...	...	.3	.3
Government, n.i.e.	2 291 . .	...	...	...	...	2.9	8.1	7.2	8.5
Other services, debit	3 200 BA	...	...	...	...	**–48.0**	**–108.1**	**–178.2**	**–185.1**
Communications	3 245 . .	...	...	...	...	–2.0	–8.3	–12.4	–5.5
Construction	3 249 . .	...	...	...	...	–.1	–6.0	–30.5	–28.9
Insurance	3 253 . .	...	...	...	...	–.3	–4.7	–11.7	–14.6
Financial	3 260 . .	...	...	...	...	–.1	–2.9	–2.4	–5.3
Computer and information	3 262 . .	...	...	...	...	...	–4.8	–2.6	–6.4
Royalties and licence fees	3 266 . .	...	...	...	...	...	...	–.8	–1.1
Other business services	3 268 . .	...	...	...	...	–7.7	–8.7	–36.7	–45.0
Personal, cultural, and recreational	3 287 . .	...	...	...	...	...	...	–1.5	–.8
Government, n.i.e.	3 291 . .	...	...	...	...	–37.8	–72.7	–79.6	–77.6

Table 2 (Continued). STANDARD PRESENTATION, 1988–95
(Millions of U.S. dollars)

	Code	1988	1989	1990	1991	1992	1993	1994	1995
C. INCOME	4 300 . .	. . .	. . .	. . .	. . .	–13.2	–13.9	–29.0	2.4
Total credit	2 300 . .	. . .	. . .	. . .	. . .	*.5*	*26.9*	*37.3*	*63.2*
Total debit	3 300 . .	. . .	. . .	. . .	. . .	*–13.7*	*–40.8*	*–66.3*	*–60.8*
Compensation of employees, credit	2 310 . .	**. . .**	**. . .**	**. . .**	**. . .**	**. . .**	**. . .**	**2.8**	**1.3**
Compensation of employees, debit	3 310 . .	**. . .**	**. . .**	**. . .**	**. . .**	**–.1**	**–.1**	**–.5**	**–2.9**
Investment income, credit	2 320 . .	**. . .**	**. . .**	**. . .**	**. . .**	**.5**	**26.9**	**34.5**	**62.0**
Direct investment income	2 330 . .	. . .	. . .	. . .	. . .	.2	.3	.2	.8
Dividends and distributed branch profits	2 332 . .	. . .	. . .	. . .	. . .	.2	.3	. . .	.4
Reinvested earnings and undistributed branch profits	2 333 . .	. . .	. . .	. . .	. . .	. . .	. . .	. . .	. . .
Income on debt (interest)	2 334 . .	. . .	. . .	. . .	. . .	. . .	. . .	.2	.3
Portfolio investment income	2 339 . .	. . .	. . .	. . .	. . .	. . .	10.0	20.4	44.8
Income on equity	2 340 . .	. . .	. . .	. . .	. . .	. . .	. . .	. . .	. . .
Income on bonds and notes	2 350 . .	. . .	. . .	. . .	. . .	. . .	. . .	. . .	. . .
Income on money market instruments and financial derivatives	2 360 . .	. . .	. . .	. . .	. . .	. . .	. . .	. . .	. . .
Other investment income	2 370 . .	. . .	. . .	. . .	. . .	.3	16.5	13.9	16.4
Investment income, debit	3 320 . .	**. . .**	**. . .**	**. . .**	**. . .**	**–13.6**	**–40.7**	**–65.9**	**–57.9**
Direct investment income	3 330 . .	. . .	. . .	. . .	. . .	–9.7	–30.7	–48.3	–26.1
Dividends and distributed branch profits	3 332 . .	. . .	. . .	. . .	. . .	–.4	–1.3	–2.0	–3.1
Reinvested earnings and undistributed branch profits	3 333 . .	. . .	. . .	. . .	. . .	–9.3	–27.6	–42.8	–15.4
Income on debt (interest)	3 334 . .	. . .	. . .	. . .	. . .	. . .	–1.8	–3.5	–7.6
Portfolio investment income	3 339 . .	. . .	. . .	. . .	. . .	. . .	. . .	–4.3	–3.7
Income on equity	3 340 . .	. . .	. . .	. . .	. . .	. . .	. . .	. . .	. . .
Income on bonds and notes	3 350 . .	. . .	. . .	. . .	. . .	. . .	. . .	. . .	. . .
Income on money market instruments and financial derivatives	3 360 . .	. . .	. . .	. . .	. . .	. . .	. . .	. . .	. . .
Other investment income	3 370 . .	. . .	. . .	. . .	. . .	–3.9	–10.0	–13.2	–28.1
D. CURRENT TRANSFERS	4 379 . .	. . .	. . .	. . .	. . .	97.0	105.2	114.7	126.3
Credit	2 379 . .	**. . .**	**. . .**	**. . .**	**. . .**	**97.4**	**108.4**	**120.3**	**134.5**
General government	2 380 . .	. . .	. . .	. . .	. . .	97.4	108.4	110.1	105.3
Other sectors	2 390 . .	. . .	. . .	. . .	. . .	. . .	. . .	10.2	29.2
Workers' remittances	2 391 . .	. . .	. . .	. . .	. . .	. . .	. . .	.1	. . .
Other current transfers	2 392 . .	. . .	. . .	. . .	. . .	. . .	. . .	10.1	29.2
Debit	3 379 . .	**. . .**	**. . .**	**. . .**	**. . .**	**–.3**	**–3.2**	**–5.7**	**–8.2**
General government	3 380 . .	. . .	. . .	. . .	. . .	. . .	–2.8	–1.3	–4.5
Other sectors	3 390 . .	. . .	. . .	. . .	. . .	–.3	–.4	–4.4	–3.7
Workers' remittances	3 391 . .	. . .	. . .	. . .	. . .	–.3	–.1	–.3	–.6
Other current transfers	3 392 . .	. . .	. . .	. . .	. . .	. . .	–.3	–4.1	–3.1
CAPITAL AND FINANCIAL ACCOUNT	4 996 . .	**. . .**	**. . .**	**. . .**	**. . .**	**–31.8**	**27.7**	**157.5**	**149.1**
CAPITAL ACCOUNT	4 994 . .	**. . .**	**. . .**	**. . .**	**. . .**	**27.4**	**. . .**	**–.6**	**–.8**
Total credit	2 994 . .	. . .	. . .	. . .	. . .	*27.4*	. . .	*.5*	*1.4*
Total debit	3 994 . .	. . .	. . .	. . .	. . .	. . .	. . .	*–1.1*	*–2.2*
Capital transfers, credit	2 400 . .	**. . .**	**. . .**	**. . .**	**. . .**	**27.4**	**. . .**	**.5**	**1.4**
General government	2 401 . .	. . .	. . .	. . .	. . .	27.4	. . .	. . .	1.1
Debt forgiveness	2 402 . .	. . .	. . .	. . .	. . .	. . .	. . .	. . .	. . .
Other capital transfers	2 410 . .	. . .	. . .	. . .	. . .	. . .	. . .	. . .	. . .
Other sectors	2 430 . .	. . .	. . .	. . .	. . .	. . .	. . .	.5	.3
Migrants' transfers	2 431 . .	. . .	. . .	. . .	. . .	. . .	. . .	. . .	. . .
Debt forgiveness	2 432 . .	. . .	. . .	. . .	. . .	. . .	. . .	. . .	. . .
Other capital transfers	2 440 . .	. . .	. . .	. . .	. . .	. . .	. . .	. . .	. . .
Capital transfers, debit	3 400 . .	**. . .**	**. . .**	**. . .**	**. . .**	**. . .**	**. . .**	**–1.1**	**–2.2**
General government	3 401 . .	. . .	. . .	. . .	. . .	. . .	. . .	–1.1	–1.9
Debt forgiveness	3 402 . .	. . .	. . .	. . .	. . .	. . .	. . .	. . .	. . .
Other capital transfers	3 410 . .	. . .	. . .	. . .	. . .	. . .	. . .	. . .	. . .
Other sectors	3 430 . .	. . .	. . .	. . .	. . .	. . .	. . .	. . .	–.3
Migrants' transfers	3 431 . .	. . .	. . .	. . .	. . .	. . .	. . .	. . .	. . .
Debt forgiveness	3 432 . .	. . .	. . .	. . .	. . .	. . .	. . .	. . .	. . .
Other capital transfers	3 440 . .	. . .	. . .	. . .	. . .	. . .	. . .	. . .	. . .
Nonproduced nonfinancial assets, credit	2 480 . .	**. . .**	**. . .**	**. . .**	**. . .**	**. . .**	**. . .**	**. . .**	**. . .**
Nonproduced nonfinancial assets, debit	3 480 . .	**. . .**	**. . .**	**. . .**	**. . .**	**. . .**	**. . .**	**. . .**	**. . .**

Table 2 (Continued). STANDARD PRESENTATION, 1988–95
(Millions of U.S. dollars)

	Code	1988	1989	1990	1991	1992	1993	1994	1995
FINANCIAL ACCOUNT	4 995	**...**	**...**	**...**	**...**	**–59.2**	**27.7**	**158.2**	**149.9**
A. DIRECT INVESTMENT	4 500	...	...	...	...	80.4	154.4	212.1	199.0
Direct investment abroad	4 505	**...**	**...**	**...**	**...**	**–1.9**	**–7.8**	**–2.4**	**–2.5**
Equity capital	4 510	...	...	...	...	–1.9	–1.7	–1.8	–.3
Claims on affiliated enterprises	4 515	...	...	...	...	–1.9	–1.7	–1.8	–.3
Liabilities to affiliated enterprises	4 520	...	...	...	...	...	...	...	...
Reinvested earnings	4 525	...	...	...	...	...	...	...	...
Other capital	4 530	...	...	...	...	...	–6.1	–.5	–2.2
Claims on affiliated enterprises	4 535	...	...	...	...	...	–6.1	–.5	–2.3
Liabilities to affiliated enterprises	4 540	...	...	...	...	...	...	...	.1
Direct investment in Estonia	4 555	**...**	**...**	**...**	**...**	**82.3**	**162.2**	**214.4**	**201.5**
Equity capital	4 560	...	...	...	...	65.6	92.9	142.2	101.2
Claims on direct investors	4 565	...	...	...	...	...	...	...	1.2
Liabilities to direct investors	4 570	...	...	...	...	65.6	92.9	142.2	100.0
Reinvested earnings	4 575	...	...	...	...	9.3	27.6	42.8	15.4
Other capital	4 580	...	...	...	...	7.4	41.8	29.5	84.9
Claims on direct investors	4 585	...	...	...	...	...	–6.1	–5.1	–5.2
Liabilities to direct investors	4 590	...	...	...	...	7.4	47.9	34.6	90.1
B. PORTFOLIO INVESTMENT	4 600	...	...	...	...	...	–.2	–14.1	–16.0
Assets	4 602	**...**	**...**	**...**	**...**	**...**	**–.4**	**–22.5**	**–33.2**
Equity securities	4 610	...	...	...	...	...	–.4	–14.5	5.1
Monetary authorities	4 611	...	...	...	...	...	...	...	...
General government	4 612	...	...	...	...	...	...	...	–1.2
Banks	4 613	...	...	...	...	...	...	–2.9	1.5
Other sectors	4 614	...	...	...	...	...	–.4	–11.5	4.7
Debt securities	4 619	...	...	...	...	...	...	–8.0	–38.2
Bonds and notes	4 620	...	...	...	...	...	...	–8.0	–38.2
Monetary authorities	4 621	...	...	...	...	...	...	...	...
General government	4 622	...	...	...	...	...	...	...	...
Banks	4 623	...	...	...	...	...	...	–6.8	–24.3
Other sectors	4 624	...	...	...	...	...	...	–1.2	–13.9
Money market instruments	4 630	...	...	...	...	...	...	...	...
Monetary authorities	4 631	...	...	...	...	...	...	...	...
General government	4 632	...	...	...	...	...	...	...	...
Banks	4 633	...	...	...	...	...	...	...	...
Other sectors	4 634	...	...	...	...	...	...	...	...
Financial derivatives	4 640	...	...	...	...	...	...	...	...
Monetary authorities	4 641	...	...	...	...	...	...	...	...
General government	4 642	...	...	...	...	...	...	...	...
Banks	4 643	...	...	...	...	...	...	...	...
Other sectors	4 644	...	...	...	...	...	...	...	...
Liabilities	4 652	**...**	**...**	**...**	**...**	**...**	**.2**	**8.4**	**17.2**
Equity securities	4 660	...	...	...	...	...	.1	8.4	9.9
Banks	4 663	...	...	...	...	...	...	8.2	9.6
Other sectors	4 664	...	...	...	...	...	.1	.2	.2
Debt securities	4 669	...	...	...	...	...	.1	...	7.3
Bonds and notes	4 670	...	...	...	...	...	.1	...	7.3
Monetary authorities	4 671	...	...	...	...	...	...	...	...
General government	4 672	...	...	...	...	...	...	...	...
Banks	4 673	...	...	...	...	...	...	...	7.0
Other sectors	4 674	...	...	...	...	...	.1	...	.2
Money market instruments	4 680	...	...	...	...	...	...	...	...
Monetary authorities	4 681	...	...	...	...	...	...	...	...
General government	4 682	...	...	...	...	...	...	...	...
Banks	4 683	...	...	...	...	...	...	...	...
Other sectors	4 684	...	...	...	...	...	...	...	...
Financial derivatives	4 690	...	...	...	...	...	...	...	...
Monetary authorities	4 691	...	...	...	...	...	...	...	...
General government	4 692	...	...	...	...	...	...	...	...
Banks	4 693	...	...	...	...	...	...	...	...
Other sectors	4 694	...	...	...	...	...	...	...	...

Table 2 (Concluded). STANDARD PRESENTATION, 1988–95
(Millions of U.S. dollars)

	Code	1988	1989	1990	1991	1992	1993	1994	1995
C. OTHER INVESTMENT	4 700	...	...	...	...	–70.4	85.8	–22.3	79.8
Assets	4 703	**...**	**...**	**...**	**...**	**–122.4**	**–144.7**	**–146.7**	**–98.9**
Trade credits	4 706	...	...	...	...	...	–86.7	–46.0	–5.6
General government: long-term	4 708	...	...	...	...	...	...	...	...
General government: short-term	4 709	...	...	...	...	...	...	...	...
Other sectors: long-term	4 711	...	...	...	...	...	...	...	...
Other sectors: short-term	4 712	...	...	...	...	...	–86.7	–46.0	–5.6
Loans	4 714	...	...	...	...	...	–.6	–2.9	–18.4
Monetary authorities: long-term	4 717	...	...	...	...	...	...	...	...
Monetary authorities: short-term	4 718	...	...	...	...	...	...	...	...
General government: long-term	4 720	...	...	...	...	...	...	...	...
General government: short-term	4 721	...	...	...	...	...	...	...	...
Banks: long-term	4 723	...	...	...	...	...	...	...	...
Banks: short-term	4 724	...	...	...	...	...	...	...	...
Other sectors: long-term	4 726	...	...	...	...	...	–.6	–2.9	–18.4
Other sectors: short-term	4 727	...	...	...	...	...	...	...	...
Currency and deposits	4 730	...	...	...	...	–121.3	–57.3	–97.9	–74.6
Monetary authorities	4 731	...	...	...	...	–72.8	5.0	–3.1	.1
General government	4 732	...	...	...	...	...	–17.1	.4	–.4
Banks	4 733	...	...	...	...	–48.5	–44.0	–99.6	–41.1
Other sectors	4 734	...	...	...	...	...	–1.1	4.3	–33.1
Other assets	4 736	...	...	...	...	–1.1	–.2	.1	–.3
Monetary authorities: long-term	4 738	...	...	...	...	...	...	...	–.3
Monetary authorities: short-term	4 739	...	...	...	...	...	...	...	...
General government: long-term	4 741	...	...	...	...	...	...	...	...
General government: short-term	4 742	...	...	...	...	...	...	...	...
Banks: long-term	4 744	...	...	...	...	...	...	...	...
Banks: short-term	4 745	...	...	...	...	...	...	...	...
Other sectors: long-term	4 747	...	...	...	...	–1.1	–.2	.3	...
Other sectors: short-term	4 748	...	...	...	...	...	...	–.1	...
Liabilities	4 753	**...**	**...**	**...**	**...**	**52.0**	**230.5**	**124.4**	**178.8**
Trade credits	4 756	...	...	...	...	11.1	24.9	77.9	20.5
General government: long-term	4 758	...	...	...	...	10.8	...	...	...
General government: short-term	4 759	...	...	...	...	.2	...	...	...
Other sectors: long-term	4 761	...	...	...	...	...	...	...	...
Other sectors: short-term	4 762	...	...	...	...	...	24.9	77.9	20.5
Loans	4 764	...	...	...	...	13.5	195.6	9.2	101.9
Use of Fund credit and loans from the Fund	4 766	...	...	...	...	11.3	47.7	...	29.4
Monetary authorities: other long-term	4 767	...	...	...	...	1.4	1.5	7.4	–.8
Monetary authorities: short-term	4 768	...	...	...	...	...	...	...	...
General government: long-term	4 770	...	...	...	...	...	82.3	28.8	54.9
General government: short-term	4 771	...	...	...	...	...	...	...	...
Banks: long-term	4 773	...	...	...	...	...	...	...	14.0
Banks: short-term	4 774	...	...	...	...	...	...	...	...
Other sectors: long-term	4 776	...	...	...	...	–.2	19.1	–19.8	2.6
Other sectors: short-term	4 777	...	...	...	...	.9	44.8	–7.1	1.9
Currency and deposits	4 780	...	...	...	...	13.9	20.6	36.4	55.6
Monetary authorities	4 781	...	...	...	...	6.7	13.4	6.1	–12.7
General government	4 782	...	...	...	...	...	...	...	...
Banks	4 783	...	...	...	...	7.2	7.2	30.3	68.3
Other sectors	4 784	...	...	...	...	...	...	...	...
Other liabilities	4 786	...	...	...	...	13.5	–10.5	.9	.7
Monetary authorities: long-term	4 788	...	...	...	...	...	...	.9	.7
Monetary authorities: short-term	4 789	...	...	...	...	13.5	–10.5	...	...
General government: long-term	4 791	...	...	...	...	...	...	...	...
General government: short-term	4 792	...	...	...	...	...	...	...	...
Banks: long-term	4 794	...	...	...	...	...	...	...	...
Banks: short-term	4 795	...	...	...	...	...	...	...	...
Other sectors: long-term	4 797	...	...	...	...	...	...	...	...
Other sectors: short-term	4 798	...	...	...	...	...	...	...	...
D. RESERVE ASSETS	4 800	...	...	...	...	–69.2	–212.4	–17.5	–112.9
Monetary gold	4 810	...	...	...	...	–27.4	22.5	...	...
Special drawing rights	4 820	...	...	...	...	–11.3	–47.4	59.3	2.6
Reserve position in the Fund	4 830	...	...	...	...	...	...	...	...
Foreign exchange	4 840	...	...	...	...	–30.6	–187.5	–76.8	–115.5
Other claims	4 880	...	...	...	...	...	...	...	...
NET ERRORS AND OMISSIONS	4 998	**...**	**...**	**...**	**...**	**–4.3**	**–50.9**	**13.2**	**35.3**

Part 3 of the *Yearbook* contains descriptions of the methodologies, compilation practices, and sources used to compile these data.

Table 1. ANALYTIC PRESENTATION, 1988–95
(Millions of U.S. dollars)

	Code	1988	1989	1990	1991	1992	1993	1994	1995
A. Current Account[1]	4 993 Y.	**–227.5**	**–144.4**	**–293.8**	**103.1**	**–120.0**	**–50.0**	**125.4**	**–28.3**
Goods: exports f.o.b.	2 100 ..	400.0	443.8	292.0	167.6	169.9	198.8	372.0	423.0
Goods: imports f.o.b.	3 100 ..	–956.0	–817.9	–912.1	–470.8	–992.7	–706.0	–925.7	–1,147.9
Balance on Goods	4 100 ..	*–556.0*	*–374.1*	*–620.1*	*–303.2*	*–822.9*	*–507.1*	*–553.7*	*–724.9*
Services: credit	2 200 ..	271.7	289.2	304.6	268.3	267.6	277.2	294.6	344.4
Services: debit	3 200 ..	–330.1	–323.4	–358.8	–284.3	–368.3	–299.0	–310.4	–359.2
Balance on Goods and Services	4 991 ..	*–614.4*	*–408.3*	*–674.3*	*–319.3*	*–923.5*	*–528.9*	*–569.5*	*–739.7*
Income: credit	2 300 ..	17.1	12.7	9.2	14.4	22.3	25.9	42.9	60.7
Income: debit	3 300 ..	–72.8	–85.0	–77.7	–96.7	–104.1	–78.4	–74.6	–85.6
Balance on Goods, Services, and Income	4 992 ..	*–670.0*	*–480.6*	*–742.9*	*–401.5*	*–1,005.3*	*–581.4*	*–601.1*	*–764.5*
Current transfers: credit	2 379 Y.	443.2	337.5	451.3	505.9	887.4	532.6	728.5	737.3
Current transfers: debit	3 379 ..	–.7	–1.3	–2.2	–1.3	–2.0	–1.2	–2.0	–1.1
B. Capital Account[1]	4 994 Y.	**–.3**	**–.1**	**...**	**...**	**...**	**...**	**...**	**...**
Capital account: credit	2 994 Y.	...	...	...	...	...	...	...	...
Capital account: debit	3 994 ..	–.3	–.1	...	...	...	...	...	...
Total, Groups A Plus B	4 010 ..	*–227.9*	*–144.5*	*–293.8*	*103.1*	*–120.0*	*–50.0*	*125.4*	*–28.3*
C. Financial Account[1]	4 995 X.	**299.6**	**222.0**	**230.0**	**–204.1**	**–65.4**	**79.4**	**–243.1**	**113.4**
Direct investment abroad	4 505 ..	...	...	...	...	...	...	...	...
Direct investment in Ethiopia	4 555 Y.	...	...	...	...	...	...	...	...
Portfolio investment assets	4 602 ..	...	...	...	...	...	...	...	...
Equity securities	4 610 ..	...	...	...	...	...	...	...	...
Debt securities	4 619 ..	...	...	...	...	...	...	...	...
Portfolio investment liabilities	4 652 Y.	...	...	...	...	...	...	...	...
Equity securities	4 660 Y.	...	...	...	...	...	...	...	...
Debt securities	4 669 Y.	...	...	...	...	...	...	...	...
Other investment assets	4 703 ..	...	50.0	87.0	–166.7	–87.1	–31.7	–318.5	67.0
Monetary authorities	4 703 .A	...	...	...	...	...	...	...	...
General government	4 703 .B	...	...	...	...	...	...	...	...
Banks	4 703 .C	...	19.2	28.0	–108.9	–26.7	–40.2	–358.5	53.9
Other sectors	4 703 .D	...	30.8	59.0	–57.8	–60.4	8.4	40.0	13.1
Other investment liabilities	4 753 X.	299.6	171.9	143.0	–37.4	21.7	111.2	75.4	46.4
Monetary authorities	4 753 XA	...	8.6	12.0	–41.8	37.3	–50.9	...	7.6
General government	4 753 YB	290.7	266.2	121.7	–41.7	1.0	209.1	107.5	53.6
Banks	4 753 YC	6.8	–3.5	–2.6	8.3	–1.4	8.2	11.5	1.4
Other sectors	4 753 YD	2.1	–99.4	11.9	37.9	–15.2	–55.2	–43.6	–16.2
Total, Groups A Through C	4 020 ..	*71.7*	*77.5*	*–63.7*	*–101.0*	*–185.3*	*29.4*	*–117.6*	*85.1*
D. Net Errors and Omissions	4 998 ..	**–94.0**	**–32.0**	**–134.6**	**–254.9**	**–80.9**	**–15.2**	**–13.1**	**–121.4**
Total, Groups A Through D	4 030 ..	*–22.3*	*45.5*	*–198.3*	*–355.9*	*–266.2*	*14.2*	*–130.7*	*–36.2*
E. Reserves and Related Items	4 040 ..	**22.3**	**–45.5**	**198.3**	**355.9**	**266.2**	**–14.2**	**130.7**	**36.2**
Reserve assets	4 800 ..	39.1	–22.7	34.7	–37.2	–95.9	–296.2	–124.7	–204.8
Use of Fund credit and loans	4 766 ..	–16.8	–22.8	–25.2	–6.5	19.6	29.7	20.8	...
Liabilities constituting foreign authorities' reserves	4 900 ..	...	...	...	...	2.5	18.2	69.2	88.6
Exceptional financing	4 920 ..	...	...	188.8	399.6	340.0	234.0	165.4	152.4
Conversion rates: birr per U.S. dollar	0 101 ..	**2.0700**	**2.0700**	**2.0700**	**2.0700**	**2.8025**	**5.0000**	**5.4650**	**6.1583**

[1] Excludes components that have been classified in the categories of Group E.

Table 2. STANDARD PRESENTATION, 1988–95
(Millions of U.S. dollars)

	Code		1988	1989	1990	1991	1992	1993	1994	1995
CURRENT ACCOUNT	4 993	. .	**–227.5**	**–144.4**	**–293.8**	**103.1**	**–120.0**	**–50.0**	**125.4**	**–28.3**
A. GOODS	4 100	. .	–556.0	–374.1	–620.1	–303.2	–822.9	–507.1	–553.7	–724.9
Credit	2 100	. .	**400.0**	**443.8**	**292.0**	**167.6**	**169.9**	**198.8**	**372.0**	**423.0**
General merchandise: exports f.o.b.	2 110	. .	400.0	443.8	292.0	167.6	169.9	198.8	372.0	423.0
Goods for processing: exports f.o.b.	2 150	. .	. . .	. . .	. . .	. . .	. . .	. . .	. . .	. . .
Repairs on goods	2 160	. .	. . .	. . .	. . .	. . .	. . .	. . .	. . .	. . .
Goods procured in ports by carriers	2 170	. .	. . .	. . .	. . .	. . .	. . .	. . .	. . .	. . .
Nonmonetary gold	2 180	. .	. . .	. . .	. . .	. . .	. . .	. . .	. . .	. . .
Debit	3 100	. .	**–956.0**	**–817.9**	**–912.1**	**–470.8**	**–992.7**	**–706.0**	**–925.7**	**–1,147.9**
General merchandise: imports f.o.b.	3 110	. .	–956.0	–817.9	–912.1	–470.8	–992.7	–706.0	–925.7	–1,147.9
Goods for processing: imports f.o.b.	3 150	. .	. . .	. . .	. . .	. . .	. . .	. . .	. . .	. . .
Repairs on goods	3 160	. .	. . .	. . .	. . .	. . .	. . .	. . .	. . .	. . .
Goods procured in ports by carriers	3 170	. .	. . .	. . .	. . .	. . .	. . .	. . .	. . .	. . .
Nonmonetary gold	3 180	. .	. . .	. . .	. . .	. . .	. . .	. . .	. . .	. . .
B. SERVICES	4 200	. .	–58.4	–34.2	–54.2	–16.1	–100.7	–21.8	–15.8	–14.8
Total credit	2 200	. .	*271.7*	*289.2*	*304.6*	*268.3*	*267.6*	*277.2*	*294.6*	*344.4*
Total debit	3 200	. .	*–330.1*	*–323.4*	*–358.8*	*–284.3*	*–368.3*	*–299.0*	*–310.4*	*–359.2*
Transportation services, credit	2 205	. .	**150.1**	**185.8**	**210.1**	**195.0**	**179.4**	**207.5**	**218.0**	**237.9**
Passenger	2 205	BA	*90.5*	*117.3*	*137.6*	*119.8*	*140.0*	*150.9*	*142.4*	*160.6*
Freight	2 205	BB	. . .	. . .	. . .	. . .	*3.3*	*38.1*	*57.2*	*57.0*
Other	2 205	BC	*59.6*	*68.5*	*72.5*	*75.2*	*36.1*	*18.5*	*18.4*	*20.2*
Sea transport, passenger	2 207	. .	. . .	. . .	. . .	. . .	. . .	. . .	. . .	. . .
Sea transport, freight	2 208	. .	. . .	. . .	. . .	. . .	. . .	18.3	18.3	17.6
Sea transport, other	2 209	. .	. . .	. . .	. . .	. . .	. . .	. . .	. . .	. . .
Air transport, passenger	2 211	. .	. . .	. . .	. . .	. . .	. . .	150.9	142.4	160.6
Air transport, freight	2 212	. .	. . .	. . .	. . .	. . .	. . .	19.8	38.9	39.4
Air transport, other	2 213	. .	. . .	. . .	. . .	. . .	. . .	14.4	13.8	14.8
Other transport, passenger	2 215	. .	. . .	. . .	. . .	. . .	. . .	. . .	. . .	. . .
Other transport, freight	2 216	. .	. . .	. . .	. . .	. . .	. . .	. . .	. . .	. . .
Other transport, other	2 217	. .	. . .	. . .	. . .	. . .	. . .	4.1	4.6	5.5
Transportation services, debit	3 205	. .	**–231.6**	**–236.8**	**–266.0**	**–188.6**	**–266.7**	**–168.7**	**–189.8**	**–219.4**
Passenger	3 205	BA	. . .	. . .	. . .	*–7.8*	*–4.0*	*–4.1*	*–5.3*	*–4.6*
Freight	3 205	BB	*–160.3*	*–138.0*	*–154.1*	*–79.7*	*–150.2*	*–70.5*	*–92.4*	*–114.6*
Other	3 205	BC	*–71.3*	*–98.7*	*–111.9*	*–101.1*	*–112.5*	*–94.1*	*–92.1*	*–100.3*
Sea transport, passenger	3 207	. .	. . .	. . .	. . .	. . .	. . .	. . .	. . .	. . .
Sea transport, freight	3 208	. .	. . .	. . .	. . .	. . .	. . .	. . .	. . .	. . .
Sea transport, other	3 209	. .	. . .	. . .	. . .	. . .	. . .	–16.5	–14.6	–10.9
Air transport, passenger	3 211	. .	. . .	. . .	. . .	. . .	. . .	–4.1	–5.3	–4.6
Air transport, freight	3 212	. .	. . .	. . .	. . .	. . .	. . .	. . .	. . .	. . .
Air transport, other	3 213	. .	. . .	. . .	. . .	. . .	. . .	–75.3	–74.5	–85.7
Other transport, passenger	3 215	. .	. . .	. . .	. . .	. . .	. . .	. . .	. . .	. . .
Other transport, freight	3 216	. .	. . .	. . .	. . .	. . .	. . .	. . .	. . .	. . .
Other transport, other	3 217	. .	. . .	. . .	. . .	. . .	. . .	–2.3	–3.0	–3.7
Travel, credit	2 236	. .	**4.2**	**7.9**	**5.4**	**3.7**	**5.0**	**10.4**	**14.5**	**16.3**
Business travel	2 237	. .	. . .	. . .	. . .	. . .	. . .	. . .	. . .	. . .
Personal travel	2 240	. .	. . .	. . .	. . .	. . .	. . .	. . .	. . .	. . .
Travel, debit	3 236	. .	**–5.5**	**–10.3**	**–11.3**	**–7.1**	**–9.9**	**–10.7**	**–15.2**	**–25.3**
Business travel	3 237	. .	. . .	. . .	. . .	. . .	. . .	. . .	. . .	. . .
Personal travel	3 240	. .	. . .	. . .	. . .	. . .	. . .	. . .	. . .	. . .
Other services, credit	2 200	BA	**117.5**	**95.5**	**89.1**	**69.6**	**83.2**	**59.3**	**62.1**	**90.2**
Communications	2 245	. .	. . .	. . .	. . .	. . .	5.4	17.4	18.5	25.6
Construction	2 249	. .	. . .	. . .	. . .	. . .	.4	2.0	2.1	18.6
Insurance	2 253	. .	. . .	1.4	1.8	2.8	6.1	3.6	2.5	2.1
Financial	2 260	. .	. . .	. . .	. . .	. . .	.4	2.3	2.5	2.6
Computer and information	2 262	. .	. . .	. . .	. . .	. . .	. . .	. . .	. . .	.1
Royalties and licence fees	2 266	. .	. . .	. . .	. . .	. . .	. . .	. . .	. . .	. . .
Other business services	2 268	. .	73.5	57.6	43.2	32.4	27.0	6.3	7.7	6.4
Personal, cultural, and recreational	2 287	. .	. . .	. . .	. . .	. . .	. . .	. . .	. . .	. . .
Government, n.i.e.	2 291	. .	44.0	36.6	44.1	34.4	44.0	27.6	28.8	34.9
Other services, debit	3 200	BA	**–93.0**	**–76.3**	**–81.5**	**–88.6**	**–91.7**	**–119.6**	**–105.4**	**–114.4**
Communications	3 245	. .	. . .	. . .	. . .	. . .	–1.0	–16.4	–6.5	–6.9
Construction	3 249	. .	. . .	. . .	. . .	. . .	–.1	–.8	–3.4	–2.8
Insurance	3 253	. .	–12.4	–10.6	–11.9	–6.1	–14.7	–21.1	–22.9	–24.6
Financial	3 260	. .	. . .	. . .	. . .	. . .	–.1	–.3	–.4	–.9
Computer and information	3 262	. .	. . .	. . .	. . .	. . .	. . .	–.6	–1.0	–.6
Royalties and licence fees	3 266	. .	. . .	. . .	. . .	. . .	. . .	. . .	. . .	. . .
Other business services	3 268	. .	–76.5	–56.2	–58.6	–69.9	–67.9	–69.4	–60.2	–62.9
Personal, cultural, and recreational	3 287	. .	. . .	. . .	. . .	. . .	. . .	. . .	. . .	. . .
Government, n.i.e.	3 291	. .	–4.2	–9.5	–11.0	–12.7	–7.9	–11.0	–11.0	–15.7

Table 2 (Continued). STANDARD PRESENTATION, 1988–95
(Millions of U.S. dollars)

	Code	1988	1989	1990	1991	1992	1993	1994	1995
C. INCOME	4 300	-55.6	-72.4	-68.6	-82.3	-81.8	-52.5	-31.6	-24.8
Total credit	2 300	*17.1*	*12.7*	*9.2*	*14.4*	*22.3*	*25.9*	*42.9*	*60.7*
Total debit	3 300	*-72.8*	*-85.0*	*-77.7*	*-96.7*	*-104.1*	*-78.4*	*-74.6*	*-85.6*
Compensation of employees, credit	2 310	**11.3**	**6.5**	**5.2**	**9.8**	**15.0**	**18.4**	**24.6**	**27.4**
Compensation of employees, debit	3 310	**-.1**	**-.8**	**. . .**	**-.4**	**-.7**	**-.4**	**-.3**	**-.2**
Investment income, credit	2 320	**5.8**	**6.2**	**4.0**	**4.7**	**7.3**	**7.6**	**18.3**	**33.4**
Direct investment income	2 330	. . .	. . .	. . .	. . .	. . .	. . .	. . .	. . .
Dividends and distributed branch profits	2 332	. . .	. . .	. . .	. . .	. . .	. . .	. . .	. . .
Reinvested earnings and undistributed branch profits	2 333	. . .	. . .	. . .	. . .	. . .	. . .	. . .	. . .
Income on debt (interest)	2 334	. . .	. . .	. . .	. . .	. . .	. . .	. . .	. . .
Portfolio investment income	2 339	. . .	. . .	. . .	. . .	. . .	. . .	. . .	. . .
Income on equity	2 340	. . .	. . .	. . .	. . .	. . .	. . .	. . .	. . .
Income on bonds and notes	2 350	. . .	. . .	. . .	. . .	. . .	. . .	. . .	. . .
Income on money market instruments and financial derivatives	2 360	. . .	. . .	. . .	. . .	. . .	. . .	. . .	. . .
Other investment income	2 370	5.8	6.2	4.0	4.7	7.3	7.6	18.3	33.4
Investment income, debit	3 320	**-72.7**	**-84.3**	**-77.7**	**-96.3**	**-103.4**	**-78.0**	**-74.2**	**-85.3**
Direct investment income	3 330	. . .	. . .	. . .	. . .	. . .	. . .	. . .	. . .
Dividends and distributed branch profits	3 332	. . .	. . .	. . .	. . .	. . .	. . .	. . .	. . .
Reinvested earnings and undistributed branch profits	3 333	. . .	. . .	. . .	. . .	. . .	. . .	. . .	. . .
Income on debt (interest)	3 334	. . .	. . .	. . .	. . .	. . .	. . .	. . .	. . .
Portfolio investment income	3 339	. . .	. . .	. . .	. . .	. . .	. . .	. . .	. . .
Income on equity	3 340	. . .	. . .	. . .	. . .	. . .	. . .	. . .	. . .
Income on bonds and notes	3 350	. . .	. . .	. . .	. . .	. . .	. . .	. . .	. . .
Income on money market instruments and financial derivatives	3 360	. . .	. . .	. . .	. . .	. . .	. . .	. . .	. . .
Other investment income	3 370	-72.7	-84.3	-77.7	-96.3	-103.4	-78.0	-74.2	-85.3
D. CURRENT TRANSFERS	4 379	442.5	336.2	449.1	504.6	885.4	531.4	726.6	736.2
Credit	2 379	**443.2**	**337.5**	**451.3**	**505.9**	**887.4**	**532.6**	**728.5**	**737.3**
General government	2 380	261.6	190.5	220.0	282.2	545.3	280.4	422.8	379.9
Other sectors	2 390	181.5	147.1	231.4	223.7	342.2	252.2	305.7	357.4
Workers' remittances	2 391	. . .	. . .	. . .	. . .	. . .	. . .	. . .	. . .
Other current transfers	2 392	181.5	147.1	231.4	223.7	342.2	252.2	305.7	357.4
Debit	3 379	**-.7**	**-1.3**	**-2.2**	**-1.3**	**-2.0**	**-1.2**	**-2.0**	**-1.1**
General government	3 380	. . .	. . .	. . .	. . .	-1.4	-.9	-1.8	-.8
Other sectors	3 390	-.7	-1.3	-2.2	-1.3	-.7	-.4	-.2	-.2
Workers' remittances	3 391	. . .	. . .	. . .	. . .	. . .	. . .	. . .	. . .
Other current transfers	3 392	-.7	-1.3	-2.2	-1.3	-.7	-.4	-.2	-.2
CAPITAL AND FINANCIAL ACCOUNT	4 996	**321.5**	**176.4**	**428.3**	**151.8**	**200.8**	**65.2**	**-112.3**	**149.6**
CAPITAL ACCOUNT	4 994	**-.3**	**-.1**	**. . .**	**70.8**	**. . .**	**. . .**	**. . .**	**. . .**
Total credit	2 994	. . .	. . .	. . .	*70.8*	. . .	. . .	. . .	. . .
Total debit	3 994	*-.3*	*-.1*	. . .	. . .	. . .	. . .	. . .	. . .
Capital transfers, credit	2 400	**. . .**	**. . .**	**. . .**	**70.8**	**. . .**	**. . .**	**. . .**	**. . .**
General government	2 401	. . .	. . .	. . .	70.8	. . .	. . .	. . .	. . .
Debt forgiveness	2 402	. . .	. . .	. . .	70.8	. . .	. . .	. . .	. . .
Other capital transfers	2 410	. . .	. . .	. . .	. . .	. . .	. . .	. . .	. . .
Other sectors	2 430	. . .	. . .	. . .	. . .	. . .	. . .	. . .	. . .
Migrants' transfers	2 431	. . .	. . .	. . .	. . .	. . .	. . .	. . .	. . .
Debt forgiveness	2 432	. . .	. . .	. . .	. . .	. . .	. . .	. . .	. . .
Other capital transfers	2 440	. . .	. . .	. . .	. . .	. . .	. . .	. . .	. . .
Capital transfers, debit	3 400	**-.3**	**-.1**	**. . .**	**. . .**	**. . .**	**. . .**	**. . .**	**. . .**
General government	3 401	. . .	. . .	. . .	. . .	. . .	. . .	. . .	. . .
Debt forgiveness	3 402	. . .	. . .	. . .	. . .	. . .	. . .	. . .	. . .
Other capital transfers	3 410	. . .	. . .	. . .	. . .	. . .	. . .	. . .	. . .
Other sectors	3 430	-.3	-.1	. . .	. . .	. . .	. . .	. . .	. . .
Migrants' transfers	3 431	-.3	-.1	. . .	. . .	. . .	. . .	. . .	. . .
Debt forgiveness	3 432	. . .	. . .	. . .	. . .	. . .	. . .	. . .	. . .
Other capital transfers	3 440	. . .	. . .	. . .	. . .	. . .	. . .	. . .	. . .
Nonproduced nonfinancial assets, credit	2 480	**. . .**	**. . .**	**. . .**	**. . .**	**. . .**	**. . .**	**. . .**	**. . .**
Nonproduced nonfinancial assets, debit	3 480	**. . .**	**. . .**	**. . .**	**. . .**	**. . .**	**. . .**	**. . .**	**. . .**

Table 2 (Continued). STANDARD PRESENTATION, 1988–95
(Millions of U.S. dollars)

	Code	1988	1989	1990	1991	1992	1993	1994	1995
FINANCIAL ACCOUNT	4 995	**321.9**	**176.5**	**428.3**	**81.0**	**200.8**	**65.2**	**–112.3**	**149.6**
A. DIRECT INVESTMENT	4 500	...	...	...	...	...	...	...	...
Direct investment abroad	4 505	...	...	...	...	...	...	...	...
Equity capital	4 510	...	...	...	...	...	...	...	...
Claims on affiliated enterprises	4 515	...	...	...	...	...	...	...	...
Liabilities to affiliated enterprises	4 520	...	...	...	...	...	...	...	...
Reinvested earnings	4 525	...	...	...	...	...	...	...	...
Other capital	4 530	...	...	...	...	...	...	...	...
Claims on affiliated enterprises	4 535	...	...	...	...	...	...	...	...
Liabilities to affiliated enterprises	4 540	...	...	...	...	...	...	...	...
Direct investment in Ethiopia	4 555	...	...	...	...	...	...	...	...
Equity capital	4 560	...	...	...	...	...	...	...	...
Claims on direct investors	4 565	...	...	...	...	...	...	...	...
Liabilities to direct investors	4 570	...	...	...	...	...	...	...	...
Reinvested earnings	4 575	...	...	...	...	...	...	...	...
Other capital	4 580	...	...	...	...	...	...	...	...
Claims on direct investors	4 585	...	...	...	...	...	...	...	...
Liabilities to direct investors	4 590	...	...	...	...	...	...	...	...
B. PORTFOLIO INVESTMENT	4 600	...	...	...	...	...	...	...	...
Assets	4 602	...	...	...	...	...	...	...	...
Equity securities	4 610	...	...	...	...	...	...	...	...
Monetary authorities	4 611	...	...	...	...	...	...	...	...
General government	4 612	...	...	...	...	...	...	...	...
Banks	4 613	...	...	...	...	...	...	...	...
Other sectors	4 614	...	...	...	...	...	...	...	...
Debt securities	4 619	...	...	...	...	...	...	...	...
Bonds and notes	4 620	...	...	...	...	...	...	...	...
Monetary authorities	4 621	...	...	...	...	...	...	...	...
General government	4 622	...	...	...	...	...	...	...	...
Banks	4 623	...	...	...	...	...	...	...	...
Other sectors	4 624	...	...	...	...	...	...	...	...
Money market instruments	4 630	...	...	...	...	...	...	...	...
Monetary authorities	4 631	...	...	...	...	...	...	...	...
General government	4 632	...	...	...	...	...	...	...	...
Banks	4 633	...	...	...	...	...	...	...	...
Other sectors	4 634	...	...	...	...	...	...	...	...
Financial derivatives	4 640	...	...	...	...	...	...	...	...
Monetary authorities	4 641	...	...	...	...	...	...	...	...
General government	4 642	...	...	...	...	...	...	...	...
Banks	4 643	...	...	...	...	...	...	...	...
Other sectors	4 644	...	...	...	...	...	...	...	...
Liabilities	4 652	...	...	...	...	...	...	...	...
Equity securities	4 660	...	...	...	...	...	...	...	...
Banks	4 663	...	...	...	...	...	...	...	...
Other sectors	4 664	...	...	...	...	...	...	...	...
Debt securities	4 669	...	...	...	...	...	...	...	...
Bonds and notes	4 670	...	...	...	...	...	...	...	...
Monetary authorities	4 671	...	...	...	...	...	...	...	...
General government	4 672	...	...	...	...	...	...	...	...
Banks	4 673	...	...	...	...	...	...	...	...
Other sectors	4 674	...	...	...	...	...	...	...	...
Money market instruments	4 680	...	...	...	...	...	...	...	...
Monetary authorities	4 681	...	...	...	...	...	...	...	...
General government	4 682	...	...	...	...	...	...	...	...
Banks	4 683	...	...	...	...	...	...	...	...
Other sectors	4 684	...	...	...	...	...	...	...	...
Financial derivatives	4 690	...	...	...	...	...	...	...	...
Monetary authorities	4 691	...	...	...	...	...	...	...	...
General government	4 692	...	...	...	...	...	...	...	...
Banks	4 693	...	...	...	...	...	...	...	...
Other sectors	4 694	...	...	...	...	...	...	...	...

Table 2 (Concluded). STANDARD PRESENTATION, 1988–95
(Millions of U.S. dollars)

	Code	1988	1989	1990	1991	1992	1993	1994	1995
C. OTHER INVESTMENT	4 700	282.8	199.2	393.6	118.2	296.7	361.4	12.3	354.4
Assets	4 703	**. . .**	**50.0**	**87.0**	**–166.7**	**–87.1**	**–31.7**	**–318.5**	**67.0**
Trade credits	4 706	. . .	15.7	72.9	–30.7	–55.5	–28.7	105.2	–16.3
General government: long-term	4 708	. . .	. . .	. . .	. . .	. . .	. . .	. . .	. . .
General government: short-term	4 709	. . .	. . .	. . .	. . .	. . .	. . .	. . .	. . .
Other sectors: long-term	4 711	. . .	. . .	. . .	. . .	. . .	. . .	. . .	. . .
Other sectors: short-term	4 712	. . .	15.7	72.9	–30.7	–55.5	–28.7	105.2	–16.3
Loans	4 714	. . .	. . .	. . .	. . .	. . .	. . .	. . .	. . .
Monetary authorities: long-term	4 717	. . .	. . .	. . .	. . .	. . .	. . .	. . .	. . .
Monetary authorities: short-term	4 718	. . .	. . .	. . .	. . .	. . .	. . .	. . .	. . .
General government: long-term	4 720	. . .	. . .	. . .	. . .	. . .	. . .	. . .	. . .
General government: short-term	4 721	. . .	. . .	. . .	. . .	. . .	. . .	. . .	. . .
Banks: long-term	4 723	. . .	. . .	. . .	. . .	. . .	. . .	. . .	. . .
Banks: short-term	4 724	. . .	. . .	. . .	. . .	. . .	. . .	. . .	. . .
Other sectors: long-term	4 726	. . .	. . .	. . .	. . .	. . .	. . .	. . .	. . .
Other sectors: short-term	4 727	. . .	. . .	. . .	. . .	. . .	. . .	. . .	. . .
Currency and deposits	4 730	. . .	34.3	14.2	–136.0	–31.6	–3.1	–423.7	83.3
Monetary authorities	4 731	. . .	. . .	. . .	. . .	. . .	. . .	. . .	. . .
General government	4 732	. . .	. . .	. . .	. . .	. . .	. . .	. . .	. . .
Banks	4 733	. . .	19.2	28.0	–108.9	–26.7	–40.2	–358.5	53.9
Other sectors	4 734	. . .	15.1	–13.8	–27.1	–4.9	37.1	–65.2	29.4
Other assets	4 736	. . .	. . .	. . .	. . .	. . .	. . .	. . .	. . .
Monetary authorities: long-term	4 738	. . .	. . .	. . .	. . .	. . .	. . .	. . .	. . .
Monetary authorities: short-term	4 739	. . .	. . .	. . .	. . .	. . .	. . .	. . .	. . .
General government: long-term	4 741	. . .	. . .	. . .	. . .	. . .	. . .	. . .	. . .
General government: short-term	4 742	. . .	. . .	. . .	. . .	. . .	. . .	. . .	. . .
Banks: long-term	4 744	. . .	. . .	. . .	. . .	. . .	. . .	. . .	. . .
Banks: short-term	4 745	. . .	. . .	. . .	. . .	. . .	. . .	. . .	. . .
Other sectors: long-term	4 747	. . .	. . .	. . .	. . .	. . .	. . .	. . .	. . .
Other sectors: short-term	4 748	. . .	. . .	. . .	. . .	. . .	. . .	. . .	. . .
Liabilities	4 753	**282.8**	**149.2**	**306.6**	**284.9**	**383.8**	**393.1**	**330.8**	**287.4**
Trade credits	4 756	. . .	–4.5	1.9	–9.3	9.8	6.6	.9	2.1
General government: long-term	4 758	. . .	. . .	. . .	. . .	. . .	. . .	. . .	. . .
General government: short-term	4 759	. . .	. . .	. . .	. . .	. . .	. . .	. . .	. . .
Other sectors: long-term	4 761	. . .	. . .	. . .	. . .	. . .	. . .	. . .	. . .
Other sectors: short-term	4 762	. . .	–4.5	1.9	–9.3	9.8	6.6	.9	2.1
Loans	4 764	276.0	148.6	106.5	–1.0	–4.4	177.0	83.8	35.4
Use of Fund credit and loans from the Fund	4 766	–16.8	–22.8	–25.2	–6.5	19.6	29.7	20.8	. . .
Monetary authorities: other long term	4 767	. . .	. . .	. . .	. . .	. . .	. . .	. . .	. . .
Monetary authorities: short-term	4 768	. . .	. . .	. . .	. . .	. . .	. . .	. . .	. . .
General government: long-term	4 770	290.7	266.2	121.7	–41.7	1.0	209.1	107.5	53.6
General government: short-term	4 771	. . .	. . .	. . .	. . .	. . .	. . .	. . .	. . .
Banks: long-term	4 773	. . .	. . .	. . .	. . .	. . .	. . .	. . .	. . .
Banks: short-term	4 774	. . .	. . .	. . .	. . .	. . .	. . .	. . .	. . .
Other sectors: long-term	4 776	2.1	–95.5	10.2	47.8	–13.3	–70.1	–72.4	–43.2
Other sectors: short-term	4 777	. . .	.6	–.3	–.6	–11.7	8.3	27.9	25.0
Currency and deposits	4 780	6.8	–3.5	–2.6	8.3	1.1	26.5	80.7	97.6
Monetary authorities	4 781	. . .	. . .	. . .	. . .	. . .	. . .	25.4	7.6
General government	4 782	. . .	. . .	. . .	. . .	. . .	. . .	. . .	. . .
Banks	4 783	6.8	–3.5	–2.6	8.3	1.1	26.5	55.3	90.0
Other sectors	4 784	. . .	. . .	. . .	. . .	. . .	. . .	. . .	. . .
Other liabilities	4 786	. . .	8.6	200.8	287.0	377.3	183.1	165.4	152.4
Monetary authorities: long-term	4 788	. . .	. . .	. . .	. . .	. . .	. . .	. . .	. . .
Monetary authorities: short-term	4 789	. . .	8.6	12.0	–41.8	37.3	–50.9	. . .	. . .
General government: long-term	4 791	. . .	. . .	. . .	. . .	. . .	. . .	. . .	. . .
General government: short-term	4 792	. . .	. . .	182.1	290.9	228.9	181.2	116.8	130.4
Banks: long-term	4 794	. . .	. . .	. . .	. . .	. . .	. . .	. . .	. . .
Banks: short-term	4 795	. . .	. . .	. . .	. . .	. . .	. . .	. . .	. . .
Other sectors: long-term	4 797	. . .	. . .	. . .	. . .	. . .	. . .	. . .	. . .
Other sectors: short-term	4 798	. . .	. . .	6.7	37.9	111.1	52.8	48.6	22.0
D. RESERVE ASSETS	4 800	39.1	–22.7	34.7	–37.2	–95.9	–296.2	–124.7	–204.8
Monetary gold	4 810	. . .	. . .	11.6	–5.7	–16.0	. . .	. . .	. . .
Special drawing rights	4 820	1.6	–.1	–.1	.1	–.2	–.2	–.1	.2
Reserve position in the Fund	4 830	. . .	. . .	. . .	. . .	–9.6	–.1	. . .	. . .
Foreign exchange	4 840	56.8	–2.4	23.2	–31.6	–70.1	–295.8	–124.6	–204.9
Other claims	4 880	–19.3	–20.3	. . .	. . .	. . .	. . .	. . .	. . .
NET ERRORS AND OMISSIONS	4 998	**–94.0**	**–32.0**	**–134.6**	**–254.9**	**–80.9**	**–15.2**	**–13.1**	**–121.4**

Part 3 of the *Yearbook* contains descriptions of the methodologies, compilation practices, and sources used to compile these data.

Table 1. ANALYTIC PRESENTATION, 1988–95
(Millions of U.S. dollars)

	Code	1988	1989	1990	1991	1992	1993	1994	1995
A. Current Account [1]	4 993 Y.	**70.5**	**77.3**	**–9.7**	**52.5**	**59.3**	**13.0**	**–59.4**	**.1**
Goods: exports f.o.b	2 100 . .	372.9	442.0	492.2	446.1	438.5	443.2	484.7	515.5
Goods: imports f.o.b	3 100 . .	–389.2	–488.9	–641.6	–549.3	–539.2	–652.8	–720.7	–761.4
Balance on Goods	4 100 . .	*–16.3*	*–46.9*	*–149.4*	*–103.1*	*–100.7*	*–209.6*	*–236.0*	*–246.0*
Services: credit	2 200 . .	244.7	336.7	377.8	403.2	428.7	491.1	519.9	573.3
Services: debit	3 200 . .	–183.2	–226.4	–257.5	–289.3	–299.3	–298.4	–366.1	–395.7
Balance on Goods and Services	4 991 . .	*45.2*	*63.4*	*–29.1*	*10.7*	*28.7*	*–16.9*	*–82.2*	*–68.4*
Income: credit	2 300 . .	46.2	55.9	63.5	70.9	65.6	65.8	49.2	52.8
Income: debit	3 300 . .	–61.6	–75.0	–62.5	–65.2	–72.1	–78.0	–105.7	–94.6
Balance on Goods, Services, and Income	4 992 . .	*29.9*	*44.3*	*–28.2*	*16.4*	*22.2*	*–29.1*	*–138.7*	*–110.3*
Current transfers: credit	2 379 Y.	53.6	55.4	41.5	64.0	62.9	70.7	114.3	146.1
Current transfers: debit	3 379 . .	–12.9	–22.4	–23.0	–27.9	–25.7	–28.6	–35.0	–35.7
B. Capital Account [1]	4 994 Y.	**–12.1**	**–21.0**	**–24.0**	**–30.6**	**–27.6**	**–26.1**	**–31.1**	**–30.4**
Capital account: credit	2 994 Y.	.1	.1	.6	.1	.1	.2	.1	.2
Capital account: debit	3 994 . .	–12.2	–21.1	–24.6	–30.7	–27.7	–26.3	–31.2	–30.6
Total, Groups A Plus B	4 010 . .	*58.5*	*56.4*	*–33.7*	*21.8*	*31.7*	*–13.1*	*–90.5*	*–30.3*
C. Financial Account [1]	4 995 X.	**46.6**	**–75.6**	**50.9**	**2.0**	**37.5**	**–14.4**	**16.5**	**78.2**
Direct investment abroad	4 505 . .	–1.5	–28.6	–3.8	4.3	–1.5	–6.0	3.7	–9.2
Direct investment in Fiji	4 555 Y.	31.6	8.8	79.8	15.0	50.6	28.5	64.9	67.1
Portfolio investment assets	4 602 . .	. . .	. . .	. . .	. . .	. . .	. . .	. . .	. . .
Equity securities	4 610 . .	. . .	. . .	. . .	. . .	. . .	. . .	. . .	. . .
Debt securities	4 619 . .	. . .	. . .	. . .	. . .	. . .	. . .	. . .	. . .
Portfolio investment liabilities	4 652 Y.	. . .	. . .	. . .	. . .	. . .	. . .	. . .	. . .
Equity securities	4 660 Y.	. . .	. . .	. . .	. . .	. . .	. . .	. . .	. . .
Debt securities	4 669 Y.	. . .	. . .	. . .	. . .	. . .	. . .	. . .	. . .
Other investment assets	4 703 . .	–6.8	–38.7	–11.4	38.7	9.2	–5.3	–10.9	32.9
Monetary authorities	4 703 .A	. . .	. . .	. . .	. . .	. . .	. . .	. . .	. . .
General government	4 703 .B	. . .	. . .	. . .	. . .	. . .	. . .	. . .	. . .
Banks	4 703 .C	–11.2	–22.3	–18.0	27.2	2.6	–13.5	1.2	12.0
Other sectors	4 703 .D	4.4	–16.4	6.6	11.5	6.7	8.2	–12.1	20.9
Other investment liabilities	4 753 X.	23.3	–17.1	–13.6	–55.9	–20.9	–31.6	–41.3	–12.6
Monetary authorities	4 753 XA	. . .	. . .	. . .	. . .	. . .	. . .	. . .	. . .
General government	4 753 YB	9.7	–11.1	–3.1	–18.2	–9.4	–6.9	3.6	–3.7
Banks	4 753 YC	14.3	15.9	21.3	–26.0	3.7	–3.8	–8.1	3.9
Other sectors	4 753 YD	–.7	–21.9	–31.9	–11.7	–15.2	–20.9	–36.8	–12.8
Total, Groups A Through C	4 020 . .	*105.1*	*–19.3*	*17.2*	*23.9*	*69.3*	*–27.5*	*–74.0*	*47.9*
D. Net Errors and Omissions	4 998 . .	**7.1**	**6.0**	**17.8**	**–15.3**	**–16.2**	**–15.0**	**63.4**	**28.6**
Total, Groups A Through D	4 030 . .	*112.2*	*–13.2*	*35.0*	*8.6*	*53.0*	*–42.5*	*–10.7*	*76.5*
E. Reserves and Related Items	4 040 . .	**–112.2**	**13.2**	**–35.0**	**–8.6**	**–53.0**	**42.5**	**10.7**	**–76.5**
Reserve assets	4 800 . .	–109.8	16.3	–34.2	–8.6	–53.0	42.5	10.7	–76.5
Use of Fund credit and loans	4 766 . .	–2.4	–3.1	–.8	. . .	. . .	. . .	. . .	. . .
Liabilities constituting foreign authorities' reserves	4 900 . .	. . .	. . .	. . .	. . .	. . .	. . .	. . .	. . .
Exceptional financing	4 920 . .	. . .	. . .	. . .	. . .	. . .	. . .	. . .	. . .
Conversion rates: Fiji dollars per U.S. dollar	0 101 . .	**1.4303**	**1.4833**	**1.4809**	**1.4756**	**1.5030**	**1.5418**	**1.4641**	**1.4063**

[1] Excludes components that have been classified in the categories of Group E.

Table 2. STANDARD PRESENTATION, 1988–95
(Millions of U.S. dollars)

	Code	1988	1989	1990	1991	1992	1993	1994	1995
CURRENT ACCOUNT	4 993 . .	**70.5**	**77.3**	**–9.7**	**52.5**	**59.3**	**13.0**	**–59.4**	**.1**
A. GOODS	4 100 . .	–16.3	–46.9	–149.4	–103.1	–100.7	–209.6	–236.0	–246.0
Credit	2 100 . .	**372.9**	**442.0**	**492.2**	**446.1**	**438.5**	**443.2**	**484.7**	**515.5**
General merchandise: exports f.o.b.	2 110 . .	355.9	419.9	467.3	427.2	417.2	422.1	470.0	498.1
Goods for processing: exports f.o.b.	2 150 . .	. . .	. . .	. . .	. . .	. . .	. . .	. . .	. . .
Repairs on goods	2 160 . .	. . .	. . .	. . .	. . .	. . .	. . .	. . .	. . .
Goods procured in ports by carriers	2 170 . .	17.0	22.0	24.8	18.9	21.3	21.1	14.8	17.4
Nonmonetary gold	2 180 . .	. . .	. . .	. . .	. . .	. . .	. . .	. . .	. . .
Debit	3 100 . .	**–389.2**	**–488.9**	**–641.6**	**–549.3**	**–539.2**	**–652.8**	**–720.7**	**–761.4**
General merchandise: imports f.o.b.	3 110 . .	–389.2	–488.9	–641.6	–549.3	–539.2	–652.8	–720.7	–761.4
Goods for processing: imports f.o.b.	3 150 . .	. . .	. . .	. . .	. . .	. . .	. . .	. . .	. . .
Repairs on goods	3 160 . .	. . .	. . .	. . .	. . .	. . .	. . .	. . .	. . .
Goods procured in ports by carriers	3 170 . .	. . .	. . .	. . .	. . .	. . .	. . .	. . .	. . .
Nonmonetary gold	3 180 . .	. . .	. . .	. . .	. . .	. . .	. . .	. . .	. . .
B. SERVICES	4 200 . .	61.5	110.3	120.3	113.9	129.3	192.8	153.8	177.6
Total credit	2 200 . .	*244.7*	*336.7*	*377.8*	*403.2*	*428.7*	*491.1*	*519.9*	*573.3*
Total debit	3 200 . .	*–183.2*	*–226.4*	*–257.5*	*–289.3*	*–299.3*	*–298.4*	*–366.1*	*–395.7*
Transportation services, credit	2 205 . .	**46.0**	**78.2**	**101.7**	**120.8**	**121.6**	**145.8**	**135.1**	**153.8**
Passenger	2 205 BA	*31.5*	*54.3*	*71.6*	*84.2*	*85.0*	*86.6*	*73.4*	*78.4*
Freight	2 205 BB	*1.3*	*4.3*	*7.2*	*13.2*	*16.3*	*15.6*	*24.4*	*25.6*
Other	2 205 BC	*13.3*	*19.6*	*22.8*	*23.3*	*20.3*	*43.5*	*37.3*	*49.8*
Sea transport, passenger	2 207 . .	. . .	. . .	. . .	. . .	. . .	. . .	. . .	. . .
Sea transport, freight	2 208 . .	. . .	. . .	. . .	. . .	. . .	. . .	. . .	. . .
Sea transport, other	2 209 . .	. . .	. . .	. . .	. . .	. . .	. . .	. . .	. . .
Air transport, passenger	2 211 . .	. . .	. . .	. . .	. . .	. . .	. . .	. . .	. . .
Air transport, freight	2 212 . .	. . .	. . .	. . .	. . .	. . .	. . .	. . .	. . .
Air transport, other	2 213 . .	. . .	. . .	. . .	. . .	. . .	. . .	. . .	. . .
Other transport, passenger	2 215 . .	. . .	. . .	. . .	. . .	. . .	. . .	. . .	. . .
Other transport, freight	2 216 . .	. . .	. . .	. . .	. . .	. . .	. . .	. . .	. . .
Other transport, other	2 217 . .	. . .	. . .	. . .	. . .	. . .	. . .	. . .	. . .
Transportation services, debit	3 205 . .	**–87.3**	**–112.1**	**–134.1**	**–122.3**	**–126.3**	**–120.4**	**–143.6**	**–156.4**
Passenger	3 205 BA	*–12.0*	*–19.4*	*–20.9*	*–15.0*	*–14.5*	*–14.2*	*–14.3*	*–18.1*
Freight	3 205 BB	*–50.7*	*–63.8*	*–82.7*	*–70.9*	*–70.1*	*–83.2*	*–92.5*	*–98.1*
Other	3 205 BC	*–24.6*	*–28.9*	*–30.5*	*–36.4*	*–41.7*	*–23.1*	*–36.7*	*–40.3*
Sea transport, passenger	3 207 . .	. . .	. . .	. . .	. . .	. . .	. . .	. . .	. . .
Sea transport, freight	3 208 . .	. . .	. . .	. . .	. . .	. . .	. . .	. . .	. . .
Sea transport, other	3 209 . .	. . .	. . .	. . .	. . .	. . .	. . .	. . .	. . .
Air transport, passenger	3 211 . .	. . .	. . .	. . .	. . .	. . .	. . .	. . .	. . .
Air transport, freight	3 212 . .	. . .	. . .	. . .	. . .	. . .	. . .	. . .	. . .
Air transport, other	3 213 . .	. . .	. . .	. . .	. . .	. . .	. . .	. . .	. . .
Other transport, passenger	3 215 . .	. . .	. . .	. . .	. . .	. . .	. . .	. . .	. . .
Other transport, freight	3 216 . .	. . .	. . .	. . .	. . .	. . .	. . .	. . .	. . .
Other transport, other	3 217 . .	. . .	. . .	. . .	. . .	. . .	. . .	. . .	. . .
Travel, credit	2 236 . .	**131.8**	**182.4**	**200.5**	**194.8**	**219.0**	**238.4**	**270.5**	**317.4**
Business travel	2 237 . .	. . .	. . .	. . .	. . .	. . .	. . .	. . .	. . .
Personal travel	2 240 . .	. . .	. . .	. . .	. . .	. . .	. . .	. . .	. . .
Travel, debit	3 236 . .	**–34.6**	**–40.7**	**–40.8**	**–45.3**	**–44.1**	**–46.6**	**–62.4**	**–64.5**
Business travel	3 237 . .	. . .	. . .	. . .	. . .	. . .	. . .	. . .	. . .
Personal travel	3 240 . .	. . .	. . .	. . .	. . .	. . .	. . .	. . .	. . .
Other services, credit	2 200 BA	**66.9**	**76.1**	**75.6**	**87.6**	**88.1**	**106.9**	**114.3**	**102.1**
Communications	2 245 . .	. . .	. . .	. . .	. . .	. . .	. . .	. . .	. . .
Construction	2 249 . .	. . .	. . .	. . .	. . .	. . .	. . .	. . .	. . .
Insurance	2 253 . .	1.7	3.3	4.9	5.1	7.8	16.8	14.9	6.1
Financial	2 260 . .	. . .	. . .	. . .	. . .	. . .	. . .	. . .	. . .
Computer and information	2 262 . .	. . .	. . .	. . .	. . .	. . .	. . .	. . .	. . .
Royalties and licence fees	2 266 . .	. . .	. . .	. . .	. . .	. . .	. . .	. . .	. . .
Other business services	2 268 . .	21.1	34.0	30.4	37.2	40.5	47.3	53.3	56.2
Personal, cultural, and recreational	2 287 . .	. . .	. . .	. . .	. . .	. . .	. . .	. . .	. . .
Government, n.i.e.	2 291 . .	44.0	38.8	40.4	45.3	39.8	42.8	46.1	39.8
Other services, debit	3 200 BA	**–61.3**	**–73.7**	**–82.7**	**–121.6**	**–128.9**	**–131.3**	**–160.2**	**–174.8**
Communications	3 245 . .	. . .	. . .	. . .	. . .	. . .	. . .	. . .	. . .
Construction	3 249 . .	. . .	. . .	. . .	. . .	. . .	. . .	. . .	. . .
Insurance	3 253 . .	–20.5	–21.0	–23.5	–22.4	–26.5	–29.8	–35.2	–32.6
Financial	3 260 . .	. . .	. . .	. . .	. . .	. . .	. . .	. . .	. . .
Computer and information	3 262 . .	. . .	. . .	. . .	. . .	. . .	. . .	. . .	. . .
Royalties and licence fees	3 266 . .	. . .	. . .	. . .	. . .	. . .	. . .	. . .	. . .
Other business services	3 268 . .	–25.1	–32.3	–41.1	–70.5	–76.6	–76.0	–102.9	–117.5
Personal, cultural, and recreational	3 287 . .	. . .	. . .	. . .	. . .	. . .	. . .	. . .	. . .
Government, n.i.e.	3 291 . .	–15.7	–20.4	–18.1	–28.7	–25.8	–25.5	–22.1	–24.7

Table 2 (Continued). STANDARD PRESENTATION, 1988–95
(Millions of U.S. dollars)

	Code	1988	1989	1990	1991	1992	1993	1994	1995
C. INCOME	4 300 . .	–15.4	–19.1	.9	5.7	–6.5	–12.3	–56.6	–41.9
Total credit	2 300 . .	*46.2*	*55.9*	*63.5*	*70.9*	*65.6*	*65.8*	*49.2*	*52.8*
Total debit	3 300 . .	*–61.6*	*–75.0*	*–62.5*	*–65.2*	*–72.1*	*–78.0*	*–105.7*	*–94.6*
Compensation of employees, credit	2 310 . .	**22.6**	**27.5**	**34.1**	**37.5**	**32.1**	**28.4**	**29.6**	**32.7**
Compensation of employees, debit	3 310 . .	. . .	. . .	. . .	. . .	. . .	. . .	. . .	. . .
Investment income, credit	2 320 . .	**23.6**	**28.4**	**29.4**	**33.4**	**33.5**	**37.4**	**19.6**	**20.1**
Direct investment income	2 330 . .	9.3	14.4	12.0	7.9	9.9	11.1	1.1	2.2
Dividends and distributed branch profits	2 332 . .	.8	1.3	.7	.3	1.9	.6	.8	.8
Reinvested earnings and undistributed branch profits	2 333 . .	8.5	13.1	11.2	7.7	8.0	10.5	.3	1.4
Income on debt (interest)	2 334 . .	. . .	. . .	. . .	. . .	. . .	. . .	. . .	. . .
Portfolio investment income	2 339 . .	. . .	. . .	. . .	. . .	. . .	. . .	. . .	. . .
Income on equity	2 340 . .	. . .	. . .	. . .	. . .	. . .	. . .	. . .	. . .
Income on bonds and notes	2 350 . .	. . .	. . .	. . .	. . .	. . .	. . .	. . .	. . .
Income on money market instruments and financial derivatives	2 360 . .	. . .	. . .	. . .	. . .	. . .	. . .	. . .	. . .
Other investment income	2 370 . .	14.3	14.0	17.4	25.5	23.6	26.3	18.5	17.8
Investment income, debit	3 320 . .	**–61.6**	**–75.0**	**–62.5**	**–65.2**	**–72.1**	**–78.0**	**–105.7**	**–94.6**
Direct investment income	3 330 . .	–34.0	–51.5	–39.7	–43.7	–54.2	–62.2	–91.0	–83.7
Dividends and distributed branch profits	3 332 . .	–12.8	–20.9	–21.4	–26.8	–36.9	–45.7	–44.9	–48.9
Reinvested earnings and undistributed branch profits	3 333 . .	–21.3	–30.6	–18.3	–16.9	–17.3	–16.5	–46.0	–34.8
Income on debt (interest)	3 334 . .	. . .	. . .	. . .	. . .	. . .	. . .	. . .	. . .
Portfolio investment income	3 339 . .	. . .	. . .	. . .	. . .	. . .	. . .	. . .	. . .
Income on equity	3 340 . .	. . .	. . .	. . .	. . .	. . .	. . .	. . .	. . .
Income on bonds and notes	3 350 . .	. . .	. . .	. . .	. . .	. . .	. . .	. . .	. . .
Income on money market instruments and financial derivatives	3 360 . .	. . .	. . .	. . .	. . .	. . .	. . .	. . .	. . .
Other investment income	3 370 . .	–27.5	–23.5	–22.8	–21.5	–17.9	–15.8	–14.8	–11.0
D. CURRENT TRANSFERS	4 379 . .	40.7	33.0	18.5	36.1	37.1	42.1	79.4	110.4
Credit	2 379 . .	**53.6**	**55.4**	**41.5**	**64.0**	**62.9**	**70.7**	**114.3**	**146.1**
General government	2 380 . .	32.6	27.1	17.2	31.6	27.9	30.5	76.2	110.1
Other sectors	2 390 . .	21.0	28.3	24.3	32.4	34.9	40.2	38.1	36.0
Workers' remittances	2 391 . .	. . .	. . .	. . .	. . .	. . .	. . .	. . .	. . .
Other current transfers	2 392 . .	21.0	28.3	24.3	32.4	34.9	40.2	38.1	36.0
Debit	3 379 . .	**–12.9**	**–22.4**	**–23.0**	**–27.9**	**–25.7**	**–28.6**	**–35.0**	**–35.7**
General government	3 380 . .	–.4	–.5	–.5	–1.6	–2.1	–3.4	–4.2	–3.6
Other sectors	3 390 . .	–12.4	–21.8	–22.6	–26.4	–23.6	–25.2	–30.7	–32.1
Workers' remittances	3 391 . .	. . .	. . .	. . .	. . .	. . .	. . .	. . .	. . .
Other current transfers	3 392 . .	–12.4	–21.8	–22.6	–26.4	–23.6	–25.2	–30.7	–32.1
CAPITAL AND FINANCIAL ACCOUNT	4 996 . .	**–77.6**	**–83.4**	**–8.1**	**–37.1**	**–43.1**	**2.1**	**–4.0**	**–28.7**
CAPITAL ACCOUNT	4 994 . .	**–12.1**	**–21.0**	**–24.0**	**–30.6**	**–27.6**	**–26.1**	**–31.1**	**–30.4**
Total credit	2 994 . .	*.1*	*.1*	*.6*	*.1*	*.1*	*.2*	*.1*	*.2*
Total debit	3 994 . .	*–12.2*	*–21.1*	*–24.6*	*–30.7*	*–27.7*	*–26.3*	*–31.2*	*–30.6*
Capital transfers, credit	2 400 . .	**.1**	**.1**	**.6**	**.1**	**.1**	**.2**	**.1**	**.2**
General government	2 401 . .	. . .	. . .	. . .	. . .	. . .	. . .	. . .	. . .
Debt forgiveness	2 402 . .	. . .	. . .	. . .	. . .	. . .	. . .	. . .	. . .
Other capital transfers	2 410 . .	. . .	. . .	. . .	. . .	. . .	. . .	. . .	. . .
Other sectors	2 430 . .	.1	.1	.6	.1	.1	.2	.1	.2
Migrants' transfers	2 431 . .	.1	.1	.6	.1	.1	.2	.1	.2
Debt forgiveness	2 432 . .	. . .	. . .	. . .	. . .	. . .	. . .	. . .	. . .
Other capital transfers	2 440 . .	. . .	. . .	. . .	. . .	. . .	. . .	. . .	. . .
Capital transfers, debit	3 400 . .	**–12.2**	**–21.1**	**–24.6**	**–30.7**	**–27.7**	**–26.3**	**–31.2**	**–30.6**
General government	3 401 . .	. . .	. . .	. . .	. . .	. . .	. . .	. . .	. . .
Debt forgiveness	3 402 . .	. . .	. . .	. . .	. . .	. . .	. . .	. . .	. . .
Other capital transfers	3 410 . .	. . .	. . .	. . .	. . .	. . .	. . .	. . .	. . .
Other sectors	3 430 . .	–12.2	–21.1	–24.6	–30.7	–27.7	–26.3	–31.2	–30.6
Migrants' transfers	3 431 . .	–12.2	–21.1	–24.6	–30.7	–27.7	–26.3	–31.2	–30.6
Debt forgiveness	3 432 . .	. . .	. . .	. . .	. . .	. . .	. . .	. . .	. . .
Other capital transfers	3 440 . .	. . .	. . .	. . .	. . .	. . .	. . .	. . .	. . .
Nonproduced nonfinancial assets, credit	2 480 . .	. . .	. . .	. . .	. . .	. . .	. . .	. . .	. . .
Nonproduced nonfinancial assets, debit	3 480 . .	. . .	. . .	. . .	. . .	. . .	. . .	. . .	. . .

Table 2 (Continued). STANDARD PRESENTATION, 1988–95
(Millions of U.S. dollars)

	Code	1988	1989	1990	1991	1992	1993	1994	1995
FINANCIAL ACCOUNT	4 995 . .	**–65.5**	**–62.4**	**15.9**	**–6.5**	**–15.5**	**28.1**	**27.1**	**1.7**
A. DIRECT INVESTMENT	4 500 . .	30.1	–19.8	76.0	19.3	49.2	22.5	68.6	57.9
Direct investment abroad	4 505 . .	**–1.5**	**–28.6**	**–3.8**	**4.3**	**–1.5**	**–6.0**	**3.7**	**–9.2**
Equity capital	4 510 . .	2.7	.9	.8	.4	–.1	. . .	4.0	–7.8
Claims on affiliated enterprises	4 515 . .	. . .	. . .	. . .	. . .	. . .	. . .	. . .	. . .
Liabilities to affiliated enterprises	4 520 . .	. . .	. . .	. . .	. . .	. . .	. . .	. . .	. . .
Reinvested earnings	4 525 . .	–8.5	–13.1	–11.2	–7.7	–8.0	–10.5	–.3	–1.4
Other capital	4 530 . .	4.4	–16.4	6.6	11.5	6.7	4.5	. . .	. . .
Claims on affiliated enterprises	4 535 . .	. . .	. . .	. . .	. . .	. . .	. . .	. . .	. . .
Liabilities to affiliated enterprises	4 540 . .	. . .	. . .	. . .	. . .	. . .	. . .	. . .	. . .
Direct investment in Fiji	4 555 . .	**31.6**	**8.8**	**79.8**	**15.0**	**50.6**	**28.5**	**64.9**	**67.1**
Equity capital	4 560 . .	14.7	7.8	57.3	3.4	26.6	34.4	25.8	23.4
Claims on direct investors	4 565 . .	. . .	. . .	. . .	. . .	. . .	. . .	. . .	. . .
Liabilities to direct investors	4 570 . .	. . .	. . .	. . .	. . .	. . .	. . .	. . .	. . .
Reinvested earnings	4 575 . .	21.3	30.6	18.3	16.9	17.3	16.5	46.0	34.8
Other capital	4 580 . .	–4.3	–29.6	4.2	–5.3	6.7	–22.3	–7.0	8.8
Claims on direct investors	4 585 . .	. . .	. . .	. . .	. . .	. . .	. . .	. . .	. . .
Liabilities to direct investors	4 590 . .	. . .	. . .	. . .	. . .	. . .	. . .	. . .	. . .
B. PORTFOLIO INVESTMENT	4 600 . .	. . .	. . .	. . .	. . .	. . .	. . .	. . .	. . .
Assets	4 602 . .	**. . .**	**. . .**	**. . .**	**. . .**	**. . .**	**. . .**	**. . .**	**. . .**
Equity securities	4 610 . .	. . .	. . .	. . .	. . .	. . .	. . .	. . .	. . .
Monetary authorities	4 611 . .	. . .	. . .	. . .	. . .	. . .	. . .	. . .	. . .
General government	4 612 . .	. . .	. . .	. . .	. . .	. . .	. . .	. . .	. . .
Banks	4 613 . .	. . .	. . .	. . .	. . .	. . .	. . .	. . .	. . .
Other sectors	4 614 . .	. . .	. . .	. . .	. . .	. . .	. . .	. . .	. . .
Debt securities	4 619 . .	. . .	. . .	. . .	. . .	. . .	. . .	. . .	. . .
Bonds and notes	4 620 . .	. . .	. . .	. . .	. . .	. . .	. . .	. . .	. . .
Monetary authorities	4 621 . .	. . .	. . .	. . .	. . .	. . .	. . .	. . .	. . .
General government	4 622 . .	. . .	. . .	. . .	. . .	. . .	. . .	. . .	. . .
Banks	4 623 . .	. . .	. . .	. . .	. . .	. . .	. . .	. . .	. . .
Other sectors	4 624 . .	. . .	. . .	. . .	. . .	. . .	. . .	. . .	. . .
Money market instruments	4 630 . .	. . .	. . .	. . .	. . .	. . .	. . .	. . .	. . .
Monetary authorities	4 631 . .	. . .	. . .	. . .	. . .	. . .	. . .	. . .	. . .
General government	4 632 . .	. . .	. . .	. . .	. . .	. . .	. . .	. . .	. . .
Banks	4 633 . .	. . .	. . .	. . .	. . .	. . .	. . .	. . .	. . .
Other sectors	4 634 . .	. . .	. . .	. . .	. . .	. . .	. . .	. . .	. . .
Financial derivatives	4 640 . .	. . .	. . .	. . .	. . .	. . .	. . .	. . .	. . .
Monetary authorities	4 641 . .	. . .	. . .	. . .	. . .	. . .	. . .	. . .	. . .
General government	4 642 . .	. . .	. . .	. . .	. . .	. . .	. . .	. . .	. . .
Banks	4 643 . .	. . .	. . .	. . .	. . .	. . .	. . .	. . .	. . .
Other sectors	4 644 . .	. . .	. . .	. . .	. . .	. . .	. . .	. . .	. . .
Liabilities	4 652 . .	**. . .**	**. . .**	**. . .**	**. . .**	**. . .**	**. . .**	**. . .**	**. . .**
Equity securities	4 660 . .	. . .	. . .	. . .	. . .	. . .	. . .	. . .	. . .
Banks	4 663 . .	. . .	. . .	. . .	. . .	. . .	. . .	. . .	. . .
Other sectors	4 664 . .	. . .	. . .	. . .	. . .	. . .	. . .	. . .	. . .
Debt securities	4 669 . .	. . .	. . .	. . .	. . .	. . .	. . .	. . .	. . .
Bonds and notes	4 670 . .	. . .	. . .	. . .	. . .	. . .	. . .	. . .	. . .
Monetary authorities	4 671 . .	. . .	. . .	. . .	. . .	. . .	. . .	. . .	. . .
General government	4 672 . .	. . .	. . .	. . .	. . .	. . .	. . .	. . .	. . .
Banks	4 673 . .	. . .	. . .	. . .	. . .	. . .	. . .	. . .	. . .
Other sectors	4 674 . .	. . .	. . .	. . .	. . .	. . .	. . .	. . .	. . .
Money market instruments	4 680 . .	. . .	. . .	. . .	. . .	. . .	. . .	. . .	. . .
Monetary authorities	4 681 . .	. . .	. . .	. . .	. . .	. . .	. . .	. . .	. . .
General government	4 682 . .	. . .	. . .	. . .	. . .	. . .	. . .	. . .	. . .
Banks	4 683 . .	. . .	. . .	. . .	. . .	. . .	. . .	. . .	. . .
Other sectors	4 684 . .	. . .	. . .	. . .	. . .	. . .	. . .	. . .	. . .
Financial derivatives	4 690 . .	. . .	. . .	. . .	. . .	. . .	. . .	. . .	. . .
Monetary authorities	4 691 . .	. . .	. . .	. . .	. . .	. . .	. . .	. . .	. . .
General government	4 692 . .	. . .	. . .	. . .	. . .	. . .	. . .	. . .	. . .
Banks	4 693 . .	. . .	. . .	. . .	. . .	. . .	. . .	. . .	. . .
Other sectors	4 694 . .	. . .	. . .	. . .	. . .	. . .	. . .	. . .	. . .

Table 2 (Concluded). STANDARD PRESENTATION, 1988–95
(Millions of U.S. dollars)

	Code	1988	1989	1990	1991	1992	1993	1994	1995
C. OTHER INVESTMENT	4 700 . .	14.1	–58.9	–25.8	–17.2	–11.6	–36.9	–52.1	20.3
Assets	4 703 . .	**–6.8**	**–38.7**	**–11.4**	**38.7**	**9.2**	**–5.3**	**–10.9**	**32.9**
Trade credits	4 706 . .	. . .	. . .	. . .	. . .	. . .	. . .	. . .	. . .
General government: long-term	4 708 . .	. . .	. . .	. . .	. . .	. . .	. . .	. . .	. . .
General government: short-term	4 709 . .	. . .	. . .	. . .	. . .	. . .	. . .	. . .	. . .
Other sectors: long-term	4 711 . .	. . .	. . .	. . .	. . .	. . .	. . .	. . .	. . .
Other sectors: short-term	4 712 . .	. . .	. . .	. . .	. . .	. . .	. . .	. . .	. . .
Loans	4 714 . .	4.4	–16.4	6.6	11.5	6.7	8.2	–3.4	17.4
Monetary authorities: long-term	4 717 . .	. . .	. . .	. . .	. . .	. . .	. . .	. . .	. . .
Monetary authorities: short-term	4 718 . .	. . .	. . .	. . .	. . .	. . .	. . .	. . .	. . .
General government: long-term	4 720 . .	. . .	. . .	. . .	. . .	. . .	. . .	. . .	. . .
General government: short-term	4 721 . .	. . .	. . .	. . .	. . .	. . .	. . .	. . .	. . .
Banks: long-term	4 723 . .	. . .	. . .	. . .	. . .	. . .	. . .	. . .	. . .
Banks: short-term	4 724 . .	. . .	. . .	. . .	. . .	. . .	. . .	. . .	. . .
Other sectors: long-term	4 726 . .	. . .	. . .	. . .	. . .	. . .	. . .	. . .	. . .
Other sectors: short-term	4 727 . .	4.4	–16.4	6.6	11.5	6.7	8.2	–3.4	17.4
Currency and deposits	4 730 . .	–11.2	–22.3	–18.0	27.2	2.6	–13.5	–7.4	15.6
Monetary authorities	4 731 . .	. . .	. . .	. . .	. . .	. . .	. . .	. . .	. . .
General government	4 732 . .	. . .	. . .	. . .	. . .	. . .	. . .	. . .	. . .
Banks	4 733 . .	–11.2	–22.3	–18.0	27.2	2.6	–13.5	1.2	12.0
Other sectors	4 734 . .	. . .	. . .	. . .	. . .	. . .	. . .	–8.7	3.6
Other assets	4 736 . .	. . .	. . .	. . .	. . .	. . .	. . .	. . .	. . .
Monetary authorities: long-term	4 738 . .	. . .	. . .	. . .	. . .	. . .	. . .	. . .	. . .
Monetary authorities: short-term	4 739 . .	. . .	. . .	. . .	. . .	. . .	. . .	. . .	. . .
General government: long-term	4 741 . .	. . .	. . .	. . .	. . .	. . .	. . .	. . .	. . .
General government: short-term	4 742 . .	. . .	. . .	. . .	. . .	. . .	. . .	. . .	. . .
Banks: long-term	4 744 . .	. . .	. . .	. . .	. . .	. . .	. . .	. . .	. . .
Banks: short-term	4 745 . .	. . .	. . .	. . .	. . .	. . .	. . .	. . .	. . .
Other sectors: long-term	4 747 . .	. . .	. . .	. . .	. . .	. . .	. . .	. . .	. . .
Other sectors: short-term	4 748 . .	. . .	. . .	. . .	. . .	. . .	. . .	. . .	. . .
Liabilities	4 753 . .	**20.9**	**–20.2**	**–14.4**	**–55.9**	**–20.9**	**–31.6**	**–41.3**	**–12.6**
Trade credits	4 756 . .	. . .	. . .	. . .	. . .	. . .	. . .	. . .	. . .
General government: long-term	4 758 . .	. . .	. . .	. . .	. . .	. . .	. . .	. . .	. . .
General government: short-term	4 759 . .	. . .	. . .	. . .	. . .	. . .	. . .	. . .	. . .
Other sectors: long-term	4 761 . .	. . .	. . .	. . .	. . .	. . .	. . .	. . .	. . .
Other sectors: short-term	4 762 . .	. . .	. . .	. . .	. . .	. . .	. . .	. . .	. . .
Loans	4 764 . .	6.6	–36.1	–35.8	–29.9	–24.6	–27.8	–33.2	–16.5
Use of Fund credit and loans from the Fund	4 766 . .	–2.4	–3.1	–.8	. . .	. . .	. . .	. . .	. . .
Monetary authorities: other long-term	4 767 . .	. . .	. . .	. . .	. . .	. . .	. . .	. . .	. . .
Monetary authorities: short-term	4 768 . .	. . .	. . .	. . .	. . .	. . .	. . .	. . .	. . .
General government: long-term	4 770 . .	9.7	–11.1	–3.1	–18.2	–9.4	–6.9	3.6	–3.7
General government: short-term	4 771 . .	. . .	. . .	. . .	. . .	. . .	. . .	. . .	. . .
Banks: long-term	4 773 . .	. . .	. . .	. . .	. . .	. . .	. . .	. . .	. . .
Banks: short-term	4 774 . .	. . .	. . .	. . .	. . .	. . .	. . .	. . .	. . .
Other sectors: long-term	4 776 . .	–.7	–21.9	–31.9	–11.7	–15.2	–20.9	–36.8	–12.8
Other sectors: short-term	4 777 . .	. . .	. . .	. . .	. . .	. . .	. . .	. . .	. . .
Currency and deposits	4 780 . .	14.3	15.9	21.3	–26.0	3.7	–3.8	–8.1	3.9
Monetary authorities	4 781 . .	. . .	. . .	. . .	. . .	. . .	. . .	. . .	. . .
General government	4 782 . .	. . .	. . .	. . .	. . .	. . .	. . .	. . .	. . .
Banks	4 783 . .	14.3	15.9	21.3	–26.0	3.7	–3.8	–8.1	3.9
Other sectors	4 784 . .	. . .	. . .	. . .	. . .	. . .	. . .	. . .	. . .
Other liabilities	4 786 . .	. . .	. . .	. . .	. . .	. . .	. . .	. . .	. . .
Monetary authorities: long-term	4 788 . .	. . .	. . .	. . .	. . .	. . .	. . .	. . .	. . .
Monetary authorities: short-term	4 789 . .	. . .	. . .	. . .	. . .	. . .	. . .	. . .	. . .
General government: long-term	4 791 . .	. . .	. . .	. . .	. . .	. . .	. . .	. . .	. . .
General government: short-term	4 792 . .	. . .	. . .	. . .	. . .	. . .	. . .	. . .	. . .
Banks: long-term	4 794 . .	. . .	. . .	. . .	. . .	. . .	. . .	. . .	. . .
Banks: short-term	4 795 . .	. . .	. . .	. . .	. . .	. . .	. . .	. . .	. . .
Other sectors: long-term	4 797 . .	. . .	. . .	. . .	. . .	. . .	. . .	. . .	. . .
Other sectors: short-term	4 798 . .	. . .	. . .	. . .	. . .	. . .	. . .	. . .	. . .
D. RESERVE ASSETS	4 800 . .	–109.8	16.3	–34.2	–8.6	–53.0	42.5	10.7	–76.5
Monetary gold	4 810 . .	.1	–.1	. . .	.1	. . .	–.1	.1	–.1
Special drawing rights	4 820 . .	–6.9	–1.0	–.8	9.7	4.6	–.4	–1.6	–.4
Reserve position in the Fund	4 830 . .	. . .	. . .	1.1	.5	–5.1	.7	. . .	. . .
Foreign exchange	4 840 . .	–100.5	15.4	–36.4	–19.1	–52.4	42.7	13.0	–76.3
Other claims	4 880 . .	–2.5	2.0	1.9	.3	–.1	–.3	–.8	.3
NET ERRORS AND OMISSIONS	4 998 . .	**7.1**	**6.0**	**17.8**	**–15.3**	**–16.2**	**–15.0**	**63.4**	**28.6**

Table 1. ANALYTIC PRESENTATION, 1988–95
(Millions of U.S. dollars)

	Code	1988	1989	1990	1991	1992	1993	1994	1995
A. Current Account [1]	4 993 Y.	**–2,693**	**–5,797**	**–6,962**	**–6,696**	**–4,945**	**–1,123**	**1,274**	**5,642**
Goods: exports f.o.b	2 100 . .	22,202	23,249	26,531	22,969	23,942	23,478	29,731	40,077
Goods: imports f.o.b	3 100 . .	–21,001	–23,479	–25,829	–20,738	–20,165	–17,217	–22,245	–27,543
Balance on Goods	4 100 . .	*1,200*	*–229*	*701*	*2,231*	*3,777*	*6,261*	*7,486*	*12,534*
Services: credit	2 200 . .	3,948	4,133	4,728	4,377	4,978	4,524	5,795	7,847
Services: debit	3 200 . .	–5,621	–6,275	–7,705	–7,623	–7,440	–6,515	–7,224	–9,834
Balance on Goods and Services	4 991 . .	*–473*	*–2,371*	*–2,276*	*–1,014*	*1,315*	*4,270*	*6,057*	*10,547*
Income: credit	2 300 . .	2,368	2,513	3,505	2,546	1,457	1,098	1,748	2,874
Income: debit	3 300 . .	–4,090	–5,192	–7,239	–7,248	–6,923	–6,063	–6,077	–7,436
Balance on Goods, Services, and Income	4 992 . .	*–2,195*	*–5,050*	*–6,010*	*–5,716*	*–4,152*	*–695*	*1,727*	*5,986*
Current transfers: credit	2 379 Y.	367	222	288	345	427	475	410	1,552
Current transfers: debit	3 379 . .	–865	–969	–1,240	–1,326	–1,221	–903	–863	–1,895
B. Capital Account [1]	4 994 Y.	**. . .**	**. . .**	**. . .**	**–71**	**. . .**	**. . .**	**. . .**	**22**
Capital account: credit	2 994 Y.	. . .	. . .	. . .	. . .	. . .	. . .	. . .	70
Capital account: debit	3 994 . .	. . .	. . .	. . .	–71	. . .	. . .	. . .	–48
Total, Groups A Plus B	4 010 . .	*–2,693*	*–5,797*	*–6,962*	*–6,767*	*–4,945*	*–1,123*	*1,274*	*5,664*
C. Financial Account [1]	4 995 X.	**2,101**	**3,471**	**12,405**	**4,196**	**3,071**	**374**	**4,098**	**–4,045**
Direct investment abroad	4 505 . .	–2,624	–2,968	–2,782	120	757	–1,401	–4,354	–1,512
Direct investment in Finland	4 555 Y.	532	490	812	–233	396	864	1,496	897
Portfolio investment assets	4 602 . .	–481	–61	–469	–334	–622	–604	922	485
Equity securities	4 610 . .	–14	–62	1	87	–10	–151	–52	–123
Debt securities	4 619 . .	–467	1	–470	–421	–612	–452	973	608
Portfolio investment liabilities	4 652 Y.	3,538	3,752	5,696	8,610	8,243	6,836	6,164	–1,233
Equity securities	4 660 Y.	111	304	96	20	89	2,216	2,541	2,027
Debt securities	4 669 Y.	3,427	3,448	5,600	8,590	8,154	4,620	3,623	–3,260
Other investment assets	4 703 . .	–1,722	–1,716	719	–2,964	–3,286	–1,833	–668	–2,612
Monetary authorities	4 703 .A	85	428	151	–1	–416	–29	99	146
General government	4 703 .B	–97	–97	–82	–83	–275	–344	–445	–366
Banks	4 703 .C	–1,135	–1,132	935	–1,899	–896	–987	–511	–1,926
Other sectors	4 703 .D	–575	–915	–284	–981	–1,698	–472	189	–466
Other investment liabilities	4 753 X.	2,858	3,974	8,428	–1,003	–2,418	–3,488	538	–71
Monetary authorities	4 753 XA	–11	59	96	–251	1,244	–298	–107	92
General government	4 753 YB	–436	–344	–104	257	255	983	965	–331
Banks	4 753 YC	3,336	1,936	4,764	–414	–5,034	–4,970	–1,088	869
Other sectors	4 753 YD	–31	2,323	3,672	–595	1,118	796	768	–702
Total, Groups A Through C	4 020 . .	*–592*	*–2,326*	*5,443*	*–2,571*	*–1,874*	*–749*	*5,372*	*1,620*
D. Net Errors and Omissions	4 998 . .	**850**	**1,258**	**–1,511**	**685**	**–276**	**1,041**	**–658**	**–1,991**
Total, Groups A Through D	4 030 . .	*258*	*–1,068*	*3,931*	*–1,886*	*–2,150*	*291*	*4,714*	*–372*
E. Reserves and Related Items	4 040 . .	**–258**	**1,068**	**–3,931**	**1,886**	**2,150**	**–291**	**–4,714**	**372**
Reserve assets	4 800 . .	–258	1,068	–3,931	1,886	2,150	–291	–4,714	372
Use of Fund credit and loans	4 766 . .	. . .	. . .	. . .	. . .	. . .	. . .	. . .	. . .
Liabilities constituting foreign authorities' reserves	4 900 . .	. . .	. . .	. . .	. . .	. . .	. . .	. . .	. . .
Exceptional financing	4 920 . .	. . .	. . .	. . .	. . .	. . .	. . .	. . .	. . .
Conversion rates: markkaa per U.S. dollar	0 101 . .	**4.1828**	**4.2912**	**3.8235**	**4.0440**	**4.4794**	**5.7123**	**5.2235**	**4.3667**

[1] Excludes components that have been classified in the categories of Group E.

Table 2. STANDARD PRESENTATION, 1988–95
(Millions of U.S. dollars)

	Code			1988	1989	1990	1991	1992	1993	1994	1995
CURRENT ACCOUNT	4	993	. .	**–2,693**	**–5,797**	**–6,962**	**–6,696**	**–4,945**	**–1,123**	**1,274**	**5,642**
A. GOODS	4	100	. .	1,200	–229	701	2,231	3,777	6,261	7,486	12,534
Credit	2	100	. .	**22,202**	**23,249**	**26,531**	**22,969**	**23,942**	**23,478**	**29,731**	**40,077**
General merchandise: exports f.o.b.	2	110	. .	21,806	22,860	26,077	22,494	23,558	23,170	29,294	39,582
Goods for processing: exports f.o.b.	2	150	. .	306	282	313	337	285	221	337	358
Repairs on goods	2	160	. .	44	46	79	72	40	38	45	81
Goods procured in ports by carriers	2	170	. .	26	40	39	43	46	39	44	58
Nonmonetary gold	2	180	. .	20	21	24	23	12	12	11	. . .
Debit	3	100	. .	**–21,001**	**–23,479**	**–25,829**	**–20,738**	**–20,165**	**–17,217**	**–22,245**	**–27,543**
General merchandise: imports f.o.b.	3	110	. .	–20,678	–23,092	–25,366	–20,186	–19,612	–16,891	–21,680	–26,948
Goods for processing: imports f.o.b.	3	150	. .	–251	–310	–348	–421	–451	–221	–441	–468
Repairs on goods	3	160	. .	–21	–20	–26	–39	–35	–29	–34	–36
Goods procured in ports by carriers	3	170	. .	–44	–48	–79	–83	–60	–70	–80	–92
Nonmonetary gold	3	180	. .	–7	–9	–9	–9	–7	–7	–10	. . .
B. SERVICES	4	200	. .	–1,673	–2,142	–2,977	–3,246	–2,462	–1,991	–1,429	–1,987
Total credit	2	200	. .	*3,948*	*4,133*	*4,728*	*4,377*	*4,978*	*4,524*	*5,795*	*7,847*
Total debit	3	200	. .	*–5,621*	*–6,275*	*–7,705*	*–7,623*	*–7,440*	*–6,515*	*–7,224*	*–9,834*
Transportation services, credit	2	205	. .	**1,397**	**1,482**	**1,754**	**1,557**	**1,559**	**1,494**	**1,796**	**2,217**
Passenger	2	205	BA	*443*	*490*	*563*	*546*	*575*	*535*	*638*	*806*
Freight	2	205	BB	*598*	*593*	*705*	*500*	*500*	*562*	*681*	*800*
Other	2	205	BC	*356*	*399*	*486*	*511*	*485*	*396*	*478*	*611*
Sea transport, passenger	2	207	. .	195	219	251	262	276	258	300	376
Sea transport, freight	2	208	. .	399	401	489	391	379	442	523	602
Sea transport, other	2	209	. .	312	338	404	419	399	322	417	492
Air transport, passenger	2	211	. .	248	271	312	285	299	277	338	430
Air transport, freight	2	212	. .	61	55	53	50	46	46	57	59
Air transport, other	2	213	. .	44	60	82	77	72	74	59	116
Other transport, passenger	2	215	. .	. . .	. . .	. . .	. . .	. . .	. . .	. . .	. . .
Other transport, freight	2	216	. .	137	138	163	60	75	75	101	139
Other transport, other	2	217	. .	. . .	. . .	. . .	15	13	1	2	4
Transportation services, debit	3	205	. .	**–1,539**	**–1,717**	**–1,942**	**–1,750**	**–1,626**	**–1,502**	**–1,838**	**–2,297**
Passenger	3	205	BA	*–443*	*–492*	*–670*	*–488*	*–412*	*–402*	*–464*	*–575*
Freight	3	205	BB	*–921*	*–1,036*	*–1,027*	*–1,009*	*–973*	*–816*	*–1,049*	*–1,352*
Other	3	205	BC	*–174*	*–189*	*–245*	*–253*	*–241*	*–284*	*–325*	*–370*
Sea transport, passenger	3	207	. .	–196	–221	–298	–234	–199	–196	–223	–269
Sea transport, freight	3	208	. .	–835	–945	–927	–899	–867	–718	–940	–1,205
Sea transport, other	3	209	. .	–98	–111	–136	–149	–153	–192	–221	–228
Air transport, passenger	3	211	. .	–246	–272	–372	–254	–213	–205	–240	–307
Air transport, freight	3	212	. .	–46	–50	–49	–63	–61	–54	–56	–73
Air transport, other	3	213	. .	–77	–79	–108	–105	–88	–87	–95	–119
Other transport, passenger	3	215	. .	. . .	. . .	. . .	. . .	. . .	. . .	. . .	. . .
Other transport, freight	3	216	. .	–40	–41	–50	–47	–45	–45	–52	–73
Other transport, other	3	217	. .	. . .	. . .	. . .	. . .	. . .	–6	–10	–23
Travel, credit	2	236	. .	**984**	**1,015**	**1,179**	**1,191**	**1,328**	**1,201**	**1,365**	**1,683**
Business travel	2	237	. .	541	559	648	655	731	661	751	926
Personal travel	2	240	. .	443	457	530	536	598	540	614	757
Travel, debit	3	236	. .	**–1,841**	**–2,039**	**–2,767**	**–2,683**	**–2,408**	**–1,569**	**–1,619**	**–2,325**
Business travel	3	237	. .	. . .	. . .	. . .	. . .	. . .	. . .	. . .	. . .
Personal travel	3	240	. .	. . .	. . .	. . .	. . .	. . .	. . .	. . .	. . .
Other services, credit	2	200	BA	**1,567**	**1,636**	**1,795**	**1,628**	**2,090**	**1,829**	**2,634**	**3,946**
Communications	2	245	. .	52	56	94	77	145	113	122	153
Construction	2	249	. .	475	172	109	118	170	239	185	338
Insurance	2	253	. .	–138	–141	–214	–295	–370	–257	–118	–131
Financial	2	260	. .	144	117	220	268	425	288	247	275
Computer and information	2	262	. .	226	347	297	307	425	398	608	743
Royalties and licence fees	2	266	. .	40	45	50	54	63	89	75	58
Other business services	2	268	. .	687	939	1,150	1,020	1,136	877	1,440	2,429
Personal, cultural, and recreational	2	287	. .	. . .	. . .	. . .	. . .	. . .	. . .	. . .	. . .
Government, n.i.e.	2	291	. .	82	100	87	80	97	81	75	80
Other services, debit	3	200	BA	**–2,241**	**–2,518**	**–2,997**	**–3,189**	**–3,406**	**–3,443**	**–3,767**	**–5,211**
Communications	3	245	. .	–53	–62	–79	–82	–124	–111	–121	–148
Construction	3	249	. .	–181	–141	–143	–121	–114	–114	–91	–115
Insurance	3	253	. .	–66	–88	27	–34	–47	–68	–81	–166
Financial	3	260	. .	–80	–70	–110	–298	–363	–336	–277	–303
Computer and information	3	262	. .	–323	–421	–562	–520	–650	–450	–497	–757
Royalties and licence fees	3	266	. .	–245	–270	–317	–312	–271	–325	–325	–389
Other business services	3	268	. .	–1,168	–1,321	–1,618	–1,653	–1,686	–1,871	–2,134	–3,167
Personal, cultural, and recreational	3	287	. .	. . .	. . .	. . .	. . .	. . .	. . .	. . .	. . .
Government, n.i.e.	3	291	. .	–126	–145	–195	–170	–153	–168	–242	–166

Table 2 (Continued). STANDARD PRESENTATION, 1988–95
(Millions of U.S. dollars)

	Code	1988	1989	1990	1991	1992	1993	1994	1995
C. INCOME	4 300 . .	–1,722	–2,679	–3,735	–4,701	–5,466	–4,965	–4,330	–4,561
Total credit	2 300 . .	*2,368*	*2,513*	*3,505*	*2,546*	*1,457*	*1,098*	*1,748*	*2,874*
Total debit	3 300 . .	*–4,090*	*–5,192*	*–7,239*	*–7,248*	*–6,923*	*–6,063*	*–6,077*	*–7,436*
Compensation of employees, credit	2 310 . .	**105**	**71**	**63**	**50**	**24**	**21**	**25**	**33**
Compensation of employees, debit	3 310 . .	**–10**	**–6**	**–16**	**–27**	**–11**	**–13**	**–15**	**–19**
Investment income, credit	2 320 . .	**2,263**	**2,442**	**3,442**	**2,497**	**1,432**	**1,077**	**1,722**	**2,841**
Direct investment income	2 330 . .	432	53	–340	–557	–879	–890	374	914
Dividends and distributed branch profits	2 332 . .	63	155	126	415	410	233	495	527
Reinvested earnings and undistributed branch profits	2 333 . .	369	–101	–466	–972	–1,289	–1,123	–52	344
Income on debt (interest)	2 334 . .	. . .	. . .	. . .	. . .	. . .	. . .	–69	43
Portfolio investment income	2 339 . .	. . .	. . .	. . .	. . .	. . .	. . .	460	969
Income on equity	2 340 . .	. . .	. . .	. . .	. . .	. . .	. . .	3	7
Income on bonds and notes	2 350 . .	. . .	. . .	. . .	. . .	. . .	. . .	63	96
Income on money market instruments and financial derivatives	2 360 . .	. . .	. . .	. . .	. . .	. . .	. . .	394	866
Other investment income	2 370 . .	1,831	2,389	3,782	3,054	2,311	1,967	888	958
Investment income, debit	3 320 . .	**–4,081**	**–5,187**	**–7,224**	**–7,221**	**–6,912**	**–6,050**	**–6,062**	**–7,416**
Direct investment income	3 330 . .	–535	–591	–277	–50	–14	–180	–656	–919
Dividends and distributed branch profits	3 332 . .	–232	–408	–454	–278	–184	–157	–252	–330
Reinvested earnings and undistributed branch profits	3 333 . .	–303	–182	176	228	170	–23	–311	–550
Income on debt (interest)	3 334 . .	. . .	. . .	. . .	. . .	. . .	. . .	–93	–39
Portfolio investment income	3 339 . .	28	–45	–84	–90	–110	21	–3,923	–4,902
Income on equity	3 340 . .	28	–45	–84	–90	–110	21	–116	–516
Income on bonds and notes	3 350 . .	. . .	. . .	. . .	. . .	. . .	. . .	–3,699	–4,258
Income on money market instruments and financial derivatives	3 360 . .	. . .	. . .	. . .	. . .	. . .	. . .	–107	–128
Other investment income	3 370 . .	–3,574	–4,551	–6,862	–7,081	–6,789	–5,891	–1,483	–1,595
D. CURRENT TRANSFERS	4 379 . .	–498	–747	–952	–981	–794	–428	–453	–343
Credit	2 379 . .	**367**	**222**	**288**	**345**	**427**	**475**	**410**	**1,552**
General government	2 380 . .	38	30	37	54	57	42	50	1,305
Other sectors	2 390 . .	329	192	252	291	371	433	360	247
Workers' remittances	2 391 . .	. . .	. . .	. . .	. . .	. . .	. . .	. . .	. . .
Other current transfers	2 392 . .	329	192	252	291	371	433	360	247
Debit	3 379 . .	**–865**	**–969**	**–1,240**	**–1,326**	**–1,221**	**–903**	**–863**	**–1,895**
General government	3 380 . .	–463	–540	–670	–751	–588	–393	–408	–1,417
Other sectors	3 390 . .	–402	–430	–570	–575	–632	–511	–456	–478
Workers' remittances	3 391 . .	. . .	. . .	. . .	. . .	. . .	. . .	. . .	. . .
Other current transfers	3 392 . .	–402	–430	–570	–575	–632	–511	–456	–478
CAPITAL AND FINANCIAL ACCOUNT	4 996 . .	**1,843**	**4,539**	**8,474**	**6,012**	**5,221**	**82**	**–615**	**–3,651**
CAPITAL ACCOUNT	4 994 . .	**. . .**	**. . .**	**. . .**	**–71**	**. . .**	**. . .**	**. . .**	**22**
Total credit	2 994 . .	. . .	. . .	. . .	. . .	. . .	. . .	. . .	*70*
Total debit	3 994 . .	. . .	. . .	. . .	*–71*	. . .	. . .	. . .	*–48*
Capital transfers, credit	2 400 . .	**. . .**	**. . .**	**. . .**	**. . .**	**. . .**	**. . .**	**. . .**	**70**
General government	2 401 . .	. . .	. . .	. . .	. . .	. . .	. . .	. . .	70
Debt forgiveness	2 402 . .	. . .	. . .	. . .	. . .	. . .	. . .	. . .	. . .
Other capital transfers	2 410 . .	. . .	. . .	. . .	. . .	. . .	. . .	. . .	70
Other sectors	2 430 . .	. . .	. . .	. . .	. . .	. . .	. . .	. . .	. . .
Migrants' transfers	2 431 . .	. . .	. . .	. . .	. . .	. . .	. . .	. . .	. . .
Debt forgiveness	2 432 . .	. . .	. . .	. . .	. . .	. . .	. . .	. . .	. . .
Other capital transfers	2 440 . .	. . .	. . .	. . .	. . .	. . .	. . .	. . .	. . .
Capital transfers, debit	3 400 . .	**. . .**	**. . .**	**. . .**	**–71**	**. . .**	**. . .**	**. . .**	**–48**
General government	3 401 . .	. . .	. . .	. . .	–71	. . .	. . .	. . .	–48
Debt forgiveness	3 402 . .	. . .	. . .	. . .	–71	. . .	. . .	. . .	–48
Other capital transfers	3 410 . .	. . .	. . .	. . .	. . .	. . .	. . .	. . .	. . .
Other sectors	3 430 . .	. . .	. . .	. . .	. . .	. . .	. . .	. . .	. . .
Migrants' transfers	3 431 . .	. . .	. . .	. . .	. . .	. . .	. . .	. . .	. . .
Debt forgiveness	3 432 . .	. . .	. . .	. . .	. . .	. . .	. . .	. . .	. . .
Other capital transfers	3 440 . .	. . .	. . .	. . .	. . .	. . .	. . .	. . .	. . .
Nonproduced nonfinancial assets, credit	2 480 . .	**. . .**	**. . .**	**. . .**	**. . .**	**. . .**	**. . .**	**. . .**	**. . .**
Nonproduced nonfinancial assets, debit	3 480 . .	**. . .**	**. . .**	**. . .**	**. . .**	**. . .**	**. . .**	**. . .**	**. . .**

Table 2 (Continued). STANDARD PRESENTATION, 1988–95
(Millions of U.S. dollars)

	Code	1988	1989	1990	1991	1992	1993	1994	1995
FINANCIAL ACCOUNT	4 995 . .	**1,843**	**4,539**	**8,474**	**6,082**	**5,221**	**82**	**–615**	**–3,673**
A. DIRECT INVESTMENT	4 500 . .	–2,092	–2,478	–1,970	–113	1,153	–538	–2,858	–614
Direct investment abroad	4 505 . .	**–2,624**	**–2,968**	**–2,782**	**120**	**757**	**–1,401**	**–4,354**	**–1,512**
Equity capital	4 510 . .	–1,365	–2,138	–2,596	–1,838	–1,619	–2,076	–2,268	–1,055
Claims on affiliated enterprises	4 515 . .	. . .	. . .	. . .	. . .	. . .	. . .	. . .	. . .
Liabilities to affiliated enterprises	4 520 . .	. . .	. . .	. . .	. . .	. . .	. . .	. . .	. . .
Reinvested earnings	4 525 . .	–369	101	466	972	1,289	1,123	52	–344
Other capital	4 530 . .	–890	–931	–652	987	1,087	–449	–2,137	–112
Claims on affiliated enterprises	4 535 . .	. . .	. . .	. . .	–228	–217	–877	–804	–549
Liabilities to affiliated enterprises	4 540 . .	. . .	. . .	. . .	1,214	1,305	429	–1,334	436
Direct investment in Finland	4 555 . .	**532**	**490**	**812**	**–233**	**396**	**864**	**1,496**	**897**
Equity capital	4 560 . .	209	104	485	46	430	646	790	524
Claims on direct investors	4 565 . .	. . .	. . .	. . .	. . .	. . .	. . .	. . .	. . .
Liabilities to direct investors	4 570 . .	. . .	. . .	. . .	. . .	. . .	. . .	. . .	. . .
Reinvested earnings	4 575 . .	303	182	–176	–228	–170	23	311	550
Other capital	4 580 . .	20	203	504	–51	137	195	395	–177
Claims on direct investors	4 585 . .	. . .	. . .	. . .	–47	–193	–2	–116	1
Liabilities to direct investors	4 590 . .	. . .	. . .	. . .	–4	331	197	511	–178
B. PORTFOLIO INVESTMENT	4 600 . .	3,057	3,692	5,228	8,276	7,621	6,232	7,086	–748
Assets	4 602 . .	**–481**	**–61**	**–469**	**–334**	**–622**	**–604**	**922**	**485**
Equity securities	4 610 . .	–14	–62	1	87	–10	–151	–52	–123
Monetary authorities	4 611 . .	. . .	. . .	. . .	. . .	. . .	. . .	. . .	. . .
General government	4 612 . .	. . .	. . .	. . .	. . .	. . .	. . .	. . .	. . .
Banks	4 613 . .	–11	–37	–11	–3	2	9	–2	–6
Other sectors	4 614 . .	–3	–25	13	90	–12	–160	–49	–117
Debt securities	4 619 . .	–467	1	–470	–421	–612	–452	973	608
Bonds and notes	4 620 . .	–289	22	–161	6	–66	–129	849	–677
Monetary authorities	4 621 . .	. . .	. . .	. . .	. . .	. . .	. . .	. . .	. . .
General government	4 622 . .	. . .	. . .	. . .	. . .	. . .	. . .	. . .	–10
Banks	4 623 . .	–225	152	–81	–53	90	–127	922	–145
Other sectors	4 624 . .	–65	–131	–80	59	–156	–2	–73	–522
Money market instruments	4 630 . .	–178	–21	–309	–426	–546	–324	73	1,247
Monetary authorities	4 631 . .	. . .	. . .	. . .	. . .	. . .	. . .	. . .	. . .
General government	4 632 . .	. . .	. . .	. . .	. . .	. . .	. . .	. . .	. . .
Banks	4 633 . .	. . .	. . .	. . .	–20	68	–126	85	49
Other sectors	4 634 . .	–178	–21	–309	–406	–614	–198	–12	1,198
Financial derivatives	4 640 . .	. . .	. . .	. . .	. . .	. . .	. . .	51	38
Monetary authorities	4 641 . .	. . .	. . .	. . .	. . .	. . .	. . .	. . .	. . .
General government	4 642 . .	. . .	. . .	. . .	. . .	. . .	. . .	. . .	. . .
Banks	4 643 . .	. . .	. . .	. . .	. . .	. . .	. . .	68	10
Other sectors	4 644 . .	. . .	. . .	. . .	. . .	. . .	. . .	–17	28
Liabilities	4 652 . .	**3,538**	**3,752**	**5,696**	**8,610**	**8,243**	**6,836**	**6,164**	**–1,233**
Equity securities	4 660 . .	111	304	96	20	89	2,216	2,541	2,027
Banks	4 663 . .	. . .	. . .	. . .	–128	. . .	274	15	46
Other sectors	4 664 . .	111	304	96	148	89	1,942	2,526	1,981
Debt securities	4 669 . .	3,427	3,448	5,600	8,590	8,154	4,620	3,623	–3,260
Bonds and notes	4 670 . .	3,354	3,137	5,870	9,583	8,588	5,389	4,092	–4,166
Monetary authorities	4 671 . .	. . .	. . .	. . .	. . .	. . .	. . .	. . .	. . .
General government	4 672 . .	73	–289	1,130	5,268	10,856	7,918	5,070	–166
Banks	4 673 . .	2,862	3,166	4,284	1,841	–2,856	–1,182	–473	–1,980
Other sectors	4 674 . .	419	260	456	2,474	588	–1,347	–504	–2,020
Money market instruments	4 680 . .	73	312	–269	–993	–435	–769	–453	359
Monetary authorities	4 681 . .	. . .	. . .	. . .	. . .	. . .	. . .	–7	1
General government	4 682 . .	. . .	. . .	. . .	195	412	–183	150	389
Banks	4 683 . .	. . .	. . .	. . .	–779	–1,321	–331	–603	–302
Other sectors	4 684 . .	73	312	–269	–410	474	–255	7	272
Financial derivatives	4 690 . .	. . .	. . .	. . .	. . .	. . .	. . .	–16	546
Monetary authorities	4 691 . .	. . .	. . .	. . .	. . .	. . .	. . .	. . .	. . .
General government	4 692 . .	. . .	. . .	. . .	. . .	. . .	. . .	52	228
Banks	4 693 . .	. . .	. . .	. . .	. . .	. . .	. . .	64	58
Other sectors	4 694 . .	. . .	. . .	. . .	. . .	. . .	. . .	–133	261

Table 2 (Concluded). STANDARD PRESENTATION, 1988–95
(Millions of U.S. dollars)

	Code	1988	1989	1990	1991	1992	1993	1994	1995
C. OTHER INVESTMENT	4 700 . .	1,136	2,258	9,147	−3,967	−5,703	−5,321	−130	−2,683
Assets	4 703 . .	**−1,722**	**−1,716**	**719**	**−2,964**	**−3,286**	**−1,833**	**−668**	**−2,612**
Trade credits	4 706 . .	−283	−130	408	222	−795	−339	−278	−634
General government: long-term	4 708 . .	. . .	. . .	. . .	. . .	. . .	. . .	−135	−327
General government: short-term	4 709 . .	. . .	. . .	. . .	−1	. . .	. . .	3	1
Other sectors: long-term	4 711 . .	−153	−20	91	94	−105	−43	87	21
Other sectors: short-term	4 712 . .	−130	−111	317	128	−691	−295	−233	−329
Loans	4 714 . .	−824	−1,198	−739	−611	−718	146	1,438	616
Monetary authorities: long-term	4 717 . .	3	163	169	1	22	77	. . .	. . .
Monetary authorities: short-term	4 718 . .	. . .	. . .	. . .	. . .	. . .	. . .	. . .	. . .
General government: long-term	4 720 . .	−37	−33	−33	59	−18	−91	81	47
General government: short-term	4 721 . .	. . .	. . .	. . .	. . .	. . .	. . .	. . .	. . .
Banks: long-term	4 723 . .	−565	−768	−40	194	−212	458	313	421
Banks: short-term	4 724 . .	. . .	. . .	. . .	−189	−31	−65	452	229
Other sectors: long-term	4 726 . .	−225	−559	−835	−611	−447	−224	519	−33
Other sectors: short-term	4 727 . .	. . .	. . .	. . .	−65	−32	−9	73	−48
Currency and deposits	4 730 . .	9	−27	−242	−342	−933	1,035	−565	289
Monetary authorities	4 731 . .	. . .	. . .	. . .	. . .	. . .	. . .	. . .	. . .
General government	4 732 . .	. . .	. . .	. . .	. . .	−14	−14	−238	168
Banks	4 733 . .	−3	−1	−5	51	−668	823	−23	228
Other sectors	4 734 . .	12	−26	−237	−393	−251	226	−304	−106
Other assets	4 736 . .	−625	−361	1,293	−2,232	−840	−2,675	−1,263	−2,883
Monetary authorities: long-term	4 738 . .	. . .	. . .	. . .	. . .	. . .	. . .	. . .	. . .
Monetary authorities: short-term	4 739 . .	81	265	−19	−2	−438	−106	99	146
General government: long-term	4 741 . .	−71	−64	−77	−140	−198	−318	−156	−255
General government: short-term	4 742 . .	11	. . .	28	−1	−47	79	. . .	. . .
Banks: long-term	4 744 . .	. . .	. . .	. . .	68	43	−200	−27	194
Banks: short-term	4 745 . .	−567	−363	981	−2,023	−28	−2,004	−1,226	−2,998
Other sectors: long-term	4 747 . .	. . .	. . .	. . .	−3	−21	15	20	−7
Other sectors: short-term	4 748 . .	−79	−199	380	−131	−151	−141	27	36
Liabilities	4 753 . .	**2,858**	**3,974**	**8,428**	**−1,003**	**−2,418**	**−3,488**	**538**	**−71**
Trade credits	4 756 . .	−87	346	329	−1,099	831	775	626	−278
General government: long-term	4 758 . .	. . .	. . .	. . .	. . .	. . .	. . .	. . .	. . .
General government: short-term	4 759 . .	. . .	. . .	. . .	. . .	. . .	. . .	. . .	. . .
Other sectors: long-term	4 761 . .	34	−46	51	111	75	255	−30	203
Other sectors: short-term	4 762 . .	−121	392	278	−1,210	757	520	656	−481
Loans	4 764 . .	157	2,537	4,263	1,882	−7	959	249	−1,619
Use of Fund credit and loans from the Fund	4 766 . .	. . .	. . .	. . .	. . .	. . .	. . .	. . .	. . .
Monetary authorities: other long-term	4 767 . .	. . .	. . .	. . .	. . .	. . .	. . .	. . .	. . .
Monetary authorities: short-term	4 768 . .	. . .	. . .	. . .	. . .	. . .	. . .	. . .	. . .
General government: long-term	4 770 . .	−457	−363	−148	218	224	990	997	−295
General government: short-term	4 771 . .	. . .	. . .	. . .	. . .	. . .	. . .	. . .	. . .
Banks: long-term	4 773 . .	566	1,033	1,001	1,347	−510	−33	−907	−902
Banks: short-term	4 774 . .	. . .	. . .	. . .	−188	23	−21	65	189
Other sectors: long-term	4 776 . .	586	1,423	3,631	1,153	143	−443	−680	−489
Other sectors: short-term	4 777 . .	−537	444	−221	−648	114	466	774	−123
Currency and deposits	4 780 . .	6	95	−200	48	368	−936	−41	−179
Monetary authorities	4 781 . .	. . .	. . .	. . .	. . .	. . .	. . .	. . .	. . .
General government	4 782 . .	. . .	. . .	. . .	. . .	. . .	. . .	. . .	. . .
Banks	4 783 . .	. . .	. . .	. . .	52	442	−936	−41	−179
Other sectors	4 784 . .	6	95	−200	−4	−74	. . .	. . .	. . .
Other liabilities	4 786 . .	2,782	996	4,037	−1,834	−3,610	−4,287	−296	2,005
Monetary authorities: long-term	4 788 . .	. . .	. . .	. . .	. . .	. . .	. . .	. . .	. . .
Monetary authorities: short-term	4 789 . .	−11	59	96	−251	1,244	−298	−107	92
General government: long-term	4 791 . .	21	19	45	30	43	−11	−28	−37
General government: short-term	4 792 . .	. . .	. . .	. . .	9	−13	5	−5	1
Banks: long-term	4 794 . .	. . .	. . .	. . .	16	10	−87	−118	546
Banks: short-term	4 795 . .	2,771	903	3,763	−1,641	−4,999	−3,893	−87	1,215
Other sectors: long-term	4 797 . .	. . .	. . .	. . .	. . .	1	. . .	63	59
Other sectors: short-term	4 798 . .	1	15	133	2	103	−2	−15	130
D. RESERVE ASSETS	4 800 . .	−258	1,068	−3,931	1,886	2,150	−291	−4,714	372
Monetary gold	4 810 . .	. . .	−12	. . .	. . .	. . .	. . .	. . .	96
Special drawing rights	4 820 . .	−54	24	39	−9	112	−7	−204	−24
Reserve position in the Fund	4 830 . .	−36	−14	38	−56	−67	29	34	−97
Foreign exchange	4 840 . .	−168	1,070	−4,008	1,952	2,106	−313	−4,544	397
Other claims	4 880 . .	. . .	. . .	. . .	. . .	. . .	. . .	. . .	. . .
NET ERRORS AND OMISSIONS	4 998 . .	**850**	**1,258**	**−1,511**	**685**	**−276**	**1,041**	**−658**	**−1,991**

Part 3 of the *Yearbook* contains descriptions of the methodologies, compilation practices, and sources used to compile these data.

Table 3. INTERNATIONAL INVESTMENT POSITION (End–period stocks), 1988–95
(Millions of U.S. dollars)

	Code	1988	1989	1990	1991	1992	1993	1994	1995
ASSETS	8 995 C.	32,180	35,473	45,048	44,118	39,957	40,838	51,475	57,493
Direct investment abroad	8 505 . .	**5,708**	**7,938**	**11,227**	**10,845**	**8,565**	**9,178**	**12,534**	**14,857**
Equity capital and reinvested earnings	8 506 . .	4,483	5,847	8,608	9,528	9,034	9,131	10,389	12,521
Claims on affiliated enterprises	8 507 . .	...	...	...	...	...	...	...	...
Liabilities to affiliated enterprises	8 508 . .	...	...	...	...	...	...	...	...
Other capital	8 530 . .	1,226	2,092	2,620	1,317	–469	47	2,145	2,336
Claims on affiliated enterprises	8 535 . .	1,322	2,341	3,580	3,568	2,963	3,582	4,734	5,492
Liabilities to affiliated enterprises	8 540 . .	–96	–250	–960	–2,252	–3,432	–3,535	–2,589	–3,156
Portfolio investment	8 602 . .	**2,330**	**2,280**	**2,582**	**2,803**	**3,257**	**4,144**	**3,425**	**3,222**
Equity securities	8 610 . .	30	96	210	103	89	308	393	605
Monetary authorities	8 611 . .	...	...	...	...	...	...	...	...
General government	8 612 . .	...	...	...	...	...	...	...	...
Banks	8 613 . .	25	65	76	57	43	32	37	44
Other sectors	8 614 . .	5	...	...	...	...	277	357	562
Debt securities	8 619 . .	2,300	2,185	2,372	2,700	3,168	3,835	3,032	2,617
Bonds and notes	8 620 . .	1,943	1,797	1,774	1,695	1,658	1,851	1,007	1,948
Monetary authorities	8 621 . .	...	...	...	...	...	...	...	...
General government	8 622 . .	...	...	...	...	...	...	...	10
Banks	8 623 . .	1,614	1,498	1,471	1,459	1,299	1,514	605	801
Other sectors	8 624 . .	329	298	303	236	359	338	402	1,137
Money market instruments	8 630 . .	357	388	598	1,005	1,510	1,907	1,922	628
Monetary authorities	8 631 . .	...	...	...	...	...	...	...	...
General government	8 632 . .	...	...	...	...	...	...	...	...
Banks	8 633 . .	...	...	76	94	...	126	47	...
Other sectors	8 634 . .	357	388	522	911	1,509	1,781	1,875	628
Financial derivatives	8 640 . .	...	...	...	...	...	77	103	42
Monetary authorities	8 641 . .	...	...	...	...	...	...	...	...
General government	8 642 . .	...	...	...	...	...	...	...	...
Banks	8 643 . .	...	...	...	...	...	91	96	29
Other sectors	8 644 . .	...	...	...	...	...	–14	6	13
Other investment	8 703 . .	**17,262**	**19,606**	**20,994**	**22,333**	**22,510**	**21,729**	**24,395**	**28,204**
Trade credits	8 706 . .	5,231	5,499	4,554	3,965	4,078	4,539	5,376	6,406
General government: long-term	8 708 . .	...	...	...	...	...	137	282	618
General government: short-term	8 709 . .	...	...	...	...	...	3	1	...
Other sectors: long-term	8 711 . .	1,383	1,430	614	447	472	364	252	234
Other sectors: short-term	8 712 . .	3,848	4,069	3,940	3,518	3,606	4,035	4,841	5,555
Loans	8 714 . .	3,572	4,942	6,831	6,897	6,721	6,220	5,238	4,812
Monetary authorities: long-term	8 717 . .	471	308	103	104	77	...	...	...
Monetary authorities: short-term	8 718 . .	...	...	...	...	...	...	...	...
General government: long-term	8 720 . .	148	187	236	139	125	207	156	123
General government: short-term	8 721 . .	...	...	...	...	...	...	...	...
Banks: long-term	8 723 . .	2,325	3,201	3,690	3,306	2,878	2,111	1,710	1,271
Banks: short-term	8 724 . .	...	...	370	536	507	986	598	434
Other sectors: long-term	8 726 . .	628	1,247	2,400	2,757	3,069	2,880	2,766	2,901
Other sectors: short-term	8 727 . .	...	...	31	55	66	36	7	82
Currency and deposits	8 730 . .	151	184	1,576	1,850	2,415	1,003	1,741	1,673
Monetary authorities	8 731 . .	...	...	...	...	...	...	...	...
General government	8 732 . .	...	...	...	...	13	26	259	102
Banks	8 733 . .	34	35	940	846	1,305	400	593	530
Other sectors	8 734 . .	118	149	636	1,004	1,096	577	889	1,040
Other assets	8 736 . .	8,308	8,981	8,032	9,621	9,296	9,967	12,039	15,313
Monetary authorities: long-term	8 738 . .	...	...	...	...	...	...	...	...
Monetary authorities: short-term	8 739 . .	805	541	626	555	851	874	969	911
General government: long-term	8 741 . .	596	679	1,125	1,227	1,297	1,468	1,782	2,122
General government: short-term	8 742 . .	67	69	50	48	86	...	...	...
Banks: long-term	8 744 . .	...	...	381	290	208	402	496	300
Banks: short-term	8 745 . .	6,538	7,251	5,616	7,187	6,404	7,034	8,624	11,803
Other sectors: long-term	8 747 . .	...	...	12	14	38	63	46	106
Other sectors: short-term	8 748 . .	302	441	224	300	411	126	122	71
Reserve assets	8 800 . .	**6,880**	**5,648**	**10,245**	**8,137**	**5,626**	**5,788**	**11,122**	**11,210**
Monetary gold	8 810 . .	510	537	600	527	416	377	460	400
Special drawing rights	8 820 . .	269	239	217	226	108	115	325	359
Reserve position in the Fund	8 830 . .	226	235	215	275	331	303	286	386
Foreign exchange	8 840 . .	5,875	4,637	9,213	7,109	4,771	4,993	10,051	9,293
Other claims	8 880 . .	...	...	...	...	...	...	...	772

Table 3 (Continued). INTERNATIONAL INVESTMENT POSITION (End-period stocks), 1988–95
(Millions of U.S. dollars)

	Code		1988	1989	1990	1991	1992	1993	1994	1995
LIABILITIES	8 995	D.	51,754	61,646	84,362	86,073	83,423	85,949	107,052	111,013
Direct investment in Finland	8 555	. .	**3,040**	**3,965**	**5,132**	**4,220**	**3,689**	**4,217**	**6,714**	**8,183**
Equity capital and reinvested earnings	8 556	. .	2,901	3,662	4,286	3,376	2,840	3,162	5,002	6,514
Claims on direct investors	8 557	. .	. . .	. . .	. . .	. . .	. . .	. . .	. . .	. . .
Liabilities to direct investors	8 558	. .	. . .	. . .	. . .	. . .	. . .	. . .	. . .	. . .
Other capital	8 580	. .	139	303	847	844	848	1,054	1,712	1,669
Claims on direct investors	8 585	. .	. . .	. . .	. . .	–46	–201	–184	–614	–655
Liabilities to direct investors	8 590	. .	139	303	847	890	1,049	1,239	2,326	2,325
Portfolio investment	8 652	. .	**17,193**	**21,277**	**34,243**	**40,475**	**44,974**	**52,820**	**68,058**	**69,722**
Equity securities	8 660	. .	1,279	2,007	1,390	1,004	979	5,251	12,767	14,625
Banks	8 663	. .	. . .	. . .	284	118	17	250	270	326
Other sectors	8 664	. .	1,279	2,007	1,106	886	962	5,001	12,497	14,299
Debt securities	8 669	. .	15,914	19,270	32,853	39,471	43,995	47,569	55,291	55,096
Bonds and notes	8 670	. .	15,262	18,272	26,288	34,129	40,298	46,031	54,567	52,465
Monetary authorities	8 671	. .	. . .	. . .	. . .	. . .	. . .	. . .	. . .	. . .
General government	8 672	. .	4,781	4,420	6,793	12,282	21,292	28,645	36,845	38,271
Banks	8 673	. .	7,724	10,865	11,583	10,858	7,984	7,453	7,473	5,786
Other sectors	8 674	. .	2,757	2,986	7,911	10,989	11,022	9,933	10,249	8,409
Money market instruments	8 680	. .	653	998	6,565	5,342	3,697	2,592	2,173	2,317
Monetary authorities	8 681	. .	. . .	. . .	. . .	. . .	. . .	. . .	1	. . .
General government	8 682	. .	. . .	. . .	. . .	301	353	77	218	566
Banks	8 683	. .	. . .	. . .	5,182	4,092	1,998	1,411	683	217
Other sectors	8 684	. .	653	998	1,383	949	1,345	1,104	1,271	1,535
Financial derivatives	8 690	. .	. . .	. . .	. . .	. . .	. . .	–1,055	–1,450	314
Monetary authorities	8 691	. .	. . .	. . .	. . .	. . .	. . .	. . .	. . .	. . .
General government	8 692	. .	. . .	. . .	. . .	. . .	. . .	–614	–184	994
Banks	8 692	. .	. . .	. . .	. . .	. . .	. . .	–614	–184	994
Other sectors	8 694	. .	. . .	. . .	. . .	. . .	. . .	–185	–864	–256
Other investment	8 753	. .	**31,521**	**36,404**	**44,987**	**41,378**	**34,760**	**28,913**	**32,280**	**33,108**
Trade credits	8 756	. .	3,058	3,465	3,829	2,306	2,537	3,147	4,315	4,344
General government: long-term	8 758	. .	. . .	. . .	. . .	. . .	. . .	. . .	. . .	. . .
General government: short-term	8 759	. .	. . .	. . .	. . .	. . .	. . .	. . .	. . .	. . .
Other sectors: long-term	8 761	. .	403	337	342	325	328	569	597	842
Other sectors: short-term	8 762	. .	2,655	3,128	3,487	1,981	2,209	2,578	3,717	3,502
Loans	8 764	. .	7,412	9,906	14,292	16,669	14,934	15,701	17,425	15,888
Use of Fund credit and loans from the Fund	8 766	. .	. . .	. . .	. . .	. . .	. . .	. . .	. . .	. . .
Monetary authorities: other long-term	8 767	. .	. . .	. . .	. . .	. . .	. . .	. . .	. . .	. . .
Monetary authorities: short-term	8 768	. .	. . .	. . .	. . .	. . .	. . .	. . .	. . .	. . .
General government: long-term	8 770	. .	1,572	1,158	1,080	1,244	1,420	2,528	3,762	3,646
General government: short-term	8 771	. .	. . .	. . .	. . .	. . .	. . .	. . .	. . .	. . .
Banks: long-term	8 773	. .	1,418	2,458	2,703	5,033	4,198	4,121	3,626	2,805
Banks: short-term	8 774	. .	. . .	. . .	191	. . .	22	61	178	310
Other sectors: long-term	8 776	. .	3,325	4,696	9,186	9,924	8,971	8,672	8,773	8,211
Other sectors: short-term	8 777	. .	1,098	1,595	1,132	468	324	319	1,086	917
Currency and deposits	8 780	. .	111	214	2,193	2,070	2,265	696	723	589
Monetary authorities	8 781	. .	. . .	. . .	. . .	. . .	. . .	. . .	. . .	. . .
General government	8 782	. .	. . .	. . .	. . .	. . .	. . .	. . .	. . .	. . .
Banks	8 783	. .	. . .	. . .	2,187	2,068	2,263	696	723	589
Other sectors	8 784	. .	111	214	6	2	2	. . .	. . .	. . .
Other liabilities	8 786	. .	20,940	22,819	24,673	20,333	15,024	9,368	9,817	12,287
Monetary authorities: long-term	8 788	. .	. . .	. . .	. . .	. . .	. . .	. . .	. . .	. . .
Monetary authorities: short-term	8 789	. .	610	690	876	558	1,301	908	996	1,176
General government: long-term	8 791	. .	219	245	323	289	261	226	246	230
General government: short-term	8 792	. .	. . .	. . .	10	19	8	13	8	9
Banks: long-term	8 794	. .	. . .	. . .	1,132	901	903	897	817	1,401
Banks: short-term	8 795	. .	20,107	21,865	21,577	17,903	11,962	6,934	7,275	8,720
Other sectors: long-term	8 797	. .	. . .	. . .	. . .	. . .	1	28	97	279
Other sectors: short-term	8 798	. .	3	18	756	664	589	362	378	472
NET INTERNATIONAL INVESTMENT POSITION	8 995	. .	**–19,574**	**–26,173**	**–39,315**	**–41,955**	**–43,466**	**–45,111**	**–55,577**	**–53,520**
Conversion rates: markkaa per U.S. dollar (end of period)	0 102	. .	**4.1690**	**4.0590**	**3.6340**	**4.1330**	**5.2450**	**5.7845**	**4.7432**	**4.3586**

Table 1. ANALYTIC PRESENTATION, 1988–95
(Millions of U.S. dollars)

	Code	1988	1989	1990	1991	1992	1993	1994	1995
A. Current Account [1]	4 993 Y.	**–4,619**	**–4,671**	**–9,944**	**–6,518**	**3,893**	**8,990**	**7,033**	**16,443**
Goods: exports f.o.b.	2 100 . .	161,586	172,186	208,932	209,172	227,442	199,044	224,726	270,400
Goods: imports f.o.b.	3 100 . .	–169,242	–182,491	–222,186	–218,886	–225,071	–191,528	–217,677	–259,225
Balance on Goods	4 100 . .	*–7,656*	*–10,305*	*–13,253*	*–9,714*	*2,371*	*7,516*	*7,049*	*11,175*
Services: credit	2 200 . .	54,523	59,940	76,457	80,100	91,765	86,377	90,390	97,770
Services: debit	3 200 . .	–43,836	–46,342	–61,052	–63,690	–72,647	–69,536	–71,103	–78,530
Balance on Goods and Services	4 991 . .	*3,031*	*3,293*	*2,151*	*6,696*	*21,489*	*24,357*	*26,336*	*30,415*
Income: credit	2 300 . .	34,016	41,287	55,736	69,771	87,596	98,992	110,034	130,033
Income: debit	3 300 . .	–34,969	–41,566	–59,632	–75,503	–96,210	–108,158	–120,972	–137,479
Balance on Goods, Services, and Income	4 992 . .	*2,078*	*3,013*	*–1,745*	*964*	*12,875*	*15,191*	*15,398*	*22,969*
Current transfers: credit	2 379 Y.	13,012	11,524	14,795	18,756	20,726	16,743	15,857	19,351
Current transfers: debit	3 379 . .	–19,709	–19,208	–22,994	–26,238	–29,707	–22,944	–24,222	–25,877
B. Capital Account [1]	4 994 Y.	**–186**	**–211**	**–4,133**	**–27**	**661**	**27**	**–4,641**	**–115**
Capital account: credit	2 994 Y.	217	235	219	252	929	305	271	301
Capital account: debit	3 994 . .	–403	–446	–4,352	–279	–268	–278	–4,912	–415
Total, Groups A Plus B	4 010 . .	*–4,805*	*–4,882*	*–14,077*	*–6,545*	*4,555*	*9,016*	*2,391*	*16,329*
C. Financial Account [1]	4 995 X.	**–1,307**	**10,361**	**24,764**	**–3,066**	**–8,035**	**–16,675**	**–3,934**	**–20,484**
Direct investment abroad	4 505 . .	–14,496	–19,498	–34,823	–23,932	–31,269	–20,605	–22,801	–18,734
Direct investment in France	4 555 Y.	8,490	10,304	13,183	15,153	21,840	20,754	16,628	23,735
Portfolio investment assets	4 602 . .	–4,152	–6,653	–8,409	–15,716	–18,463	–31,499	–24,659	–22,901
Equity securities	4 610 . .	–1,164	–1,455	501	–2,979	–1,550	–2,522	–1,952	606
Debt securities	4 619 . .	–2,988	–5,198	–8,910	–12,737	–16,912	–28,977	–22,706	–23,507
Portfolio investment liabilities	4 652 Y.	11,945	32,045	43,219	29,535	52,500	34,516	–30,109	9,700
Equity securities	4 660 Y.	1,746	6,999	5,898	7,663	5,407	13,579	4,807	7,070
Debt securities	4 669 Y.	10,199	25,046	37,322	21,873	47,093	20,937	–34,916	2,630
Other investment assets	4 703 . .	–28,178	–62,794	–61,543	151	–61,086	–13,380	26,316	–25,604
Monetary authorities	4 703 . A	. . .	. . .	. . .	. . .	. . .	. . .	. . .	. . .
General government	4 703 . B	–5,157	–4,468	–1,574	–5,125	–4,961	–3,911	1,683	–1,349
Banks	4 703 . C	–23,525	–52,303	–52,831	8,739	–65,086	–46,688	22,630	–46,719
Other sectors	4 703 . D	504	–6,023	–7,138	–3,463	8,961	37,219	2,002	22,464
Other investment liabilities	4 753 X.	25,084	56,956	73,136	–8,257	28,444	–6,460	30,689	13,320
Monetary authorities	4 753 XA	–4,104	3,541	–325	644	22,022	–1,070	–9,910	2,713
General government	4 753 YB	–231	–17	–556	–135	112	231	328	465
Banks	4 753 YC	27,355	57,505	80,259	–5,074	10,394	–5,688	32,499	15,217
Other sectors	4 753 YD	2,063	–4,072	–6,242	–3,692	–4,084	66	7,772	–5,076
Total, Groups A Through C	4 020 . .	*–6,112*	*5,479*	*10,687*	*–9,611*	*–3,481*	*–7,658*	*–1,543*	*–4,155*
D. Net Errors and Omissions	4 998 . .	**953**	**–6,336**	**262**	**4,416**	**1,905**	**2,652**	**3,991**	**4,868**
Total, Groups A Through D	4 030 . .	*–5,159*	*–857*	*10,949*	*–5,194*	*–1,576*	*–5,006*	*2,448*	*712*
E. Reserves and Related Items	4 040 . .	**5,159**	**857**	**–10,949**	**5,194**	**1,576**	**5,006**	**–2,448**	**–712**
Reserve assets	4 800 . .	5,159	857	–10,949	5,194	1,576	5,006	–2,448	–712
Use of Fund credit and loans	4 766 . .	. . .	. . .	. . .	. . .	. . .	. . .	. . .	. . .
Liabilities constituting foreign authorities' reserves	4 900 . .	. . .	. . .	. . .	. . .	. . .	. . .	. . .	. . .
Exceptional financing	4 920 . .	. . .	. . .	. . .	. . .	. . .	. . .	. . .	. . .
Conversion rates: French francs per U.S. dollar	0 101 . .	**5.9569**	**6.3801**	**5.4453**	**5.6421**	**5.2938**	**5.6632**	**5.5520**	**4.9915**

[1] Excludes components that have been classified in the categories of Group E.

Table 2. STANDARD PRESENTATION, 1988–95

(Millions of U.S. dollars)

	Code		1988	1989	1990	1991	1992	1993	1994	1995
CURRENT ACCOUNT	4 993	. .	**–4,619**	**–4,671**	**–9,944**	**–6,518**	**3,893**	**8,990**	**7,033**	**16,443**
A. GOODS	4 100	. .	–7,656	–10,305	–13,253	–9,714	2,371	7,516	7,049	11,175
Credit	2 100	. .	**161,586**	**172,186**	**208,932**	**209,172**	**227,442**	**199,044**	**224,726**	**270,400**
General merchandise: exports f.o.b.	2 110	. .	159,749	170,307	206,154	206,625	224,833	196,396	222,165	267,562
Goods for processing: exports f.o.b.	2 150	. .	. . .	. . .	. . .	. . .	. . .	. . .	. . .	. . .
Repairs on goods	2 160	. .	1,397	1,233	1,887	1,751	1,670	1,710	2,024	2,209
Goods procured in ports by carriers	2 170	. .	. . .	190	376	295	452	524	536	629
Nonmonetary gold	2 180	. .	439	455	515	501	487	415	. . .	. . .
Debit	3 100	. .	**–169,242**	**–182,491**	**–222,186**	**–218,886**	**–225,071**	**–191,528**	**–217,677**	**–259,225**
General merchandise: imports f.o.b.	3 110	. .	–168,275	–180,825	–219,350	–216,752	–222,972	–189,584	–216,649	–258,063
Goods for processing: imports f.o.b.	3 150	. .	. . .	. . .	. . .	. . .	. . .	. . .	. . .	. . .
Repairs on goods	3 160	. .	–511	–805	–1,397	–1,169	–1,081	–969	–731	–891
Goods procured in ports by carriers	3 170	. .	. . .	–277	–451	–418	–421	–458	–297	–271
Nonmonetary gold	3 180	. .	–455	–585	–988	–547	–597	–517	. . .	. . .
B. SERVICES	4 200	. .	10,687	13,598	15,405	16,410	19,118	16,841	19,287	19,240
Total credit	2 200	. .	*54,523*	*59,940*	*76,457*	*80,100*	*91,765*	*86,377*	*90,390*	*97,770*
Total debit	3 200	. .	*–43,836*	*–46,342*	*–61,052*	*–63,690*	*–72,647*	*–69,536*	*–71,103*	*–78,530*
Transportation services, credit	2 205	. .	**12,623**	**13,736**	**16,257**	**17,136**	**18,215**	**17,509**	**17,235**	**20,464**
Passenger	2 205	BA	*2,049*	*3,032*	*3,585*	*3,680*	*3,939*	*3,480*	*3,269*	*3,708*
Freight	2 205	BB	*3,123*	*3,144*	*3,447*	*3,800*	*3,883*	*3,796*	*4,190*	*4,856*
Other	2 205	BC	*7,451*	*7,561*	*9,225*	*9,656*	*10,392*	*10,233*	*9,777*	*11,899*
Sea transport, passenger	2 207	. .	140	123	165	183	219	202	195	192
Sea transport, freight	2 208	. .	1,618	1,509	1,678	1,716	1,607	1,558	1,842	2,177
Sea transport, other	2 209	. .	1,258	1,136	1,349	1,513	1,627	1,596	1,225	1,341
Air transport, passenger	2 211	. .	1,556	2,519	2,961	3,079	3,226	2,940	2,749	3,075
Air transport, freight	2 212	. .	437	630	793	874	836	729	783	889
Air transport, other	2 213	. .	1,586	2,557	2,799	2,882	3,152	3,467	3,698	4,526
Other transport, passenger	2 215	. .	353	390	460	418	494	338	325	441
Other transport, freight	2 216	. .	1,068	1,004	976	1,210	1,440	1,510	1,565	1,789
Other transport, other	2 217	. .	4,607	3,867	5,076	5,260	5,613	5,170	4,854	6,033
Transportation services, debit	3 205	. .	**–11,585**	**–13,931**	**–17,523**	**–18,186**	**–19,843**	**–18,814**	**–18,035**	**–21,252**
Passenger	3 205	BA	*–2,770*	*–2,923*	*–3,668*	*–3,594*	*–4,101*	*–3,727*	*–3,746*	*–4,341*
Freight	3 205	BB	*–2,695*	*–2,957*	*–3,326*	*–3,873*	*–3,997*	*–3,841*	*–4,024*	*–4,724*
Other	3 205	BC	*–6,121*	*–8,051*	*–10,530*	*–10,719*	*–11,745*	*–11,247*	*–10,264*	*–12,187*
Sea transport, passenger	3 207	. .	–37	–33	–37	–48	–72	–55	–58	–38
Sea transport, freight	3 208	. .	–1,929	–2,211	–2,477	–3,002	–3,078	–2,991	–3,084	–3,506
Sea transport, other	3 209	. .	–1,423	–1,291	–1,520	–1,645	–1,626	–1,568	–1,295	–1,259
Air transport, passenger	3 211	. .	–2,526	–2,681	–3,409	–3,306	–3,759	–3,482	–3,532	–4,092
Air transport, freight	3 212	. .	–444	–425	–469	–459	–450	–436	–630	–800
Air transport, other	3 213	. .	–497	–2,074	–2,544	–2,671	–3,146	–3,402	–3,371	–3,822
Other transport, passenger	3 215	. .	–207	–209	–221	–240	–270	–189	–156	–211
Other transport, freight	3 216	. .	–323	–320	–380	–412	–469	–414	–309	–418
Other transport, other	3 217	. .	–4,201	–4,686	–6,466	–6,403	–6,973	–6,277	–5,599	–7,106
Travel, credit	2 236	. .	**13,717**	**16,200**	**20,270**	**21,185**	**25,406**	**23,511**	**24,796**	**27,587**
Business travel	2 237	. .	. . .	. . .	. . .	. . .	. . .	. . .	. . .	. . .
Personal travel	2 240	. .	. . .	. . .	. . .	. . .	. . .	. . .	. . .	. . .
Travel, debit	3 236	. .	**–9,651**	**–10,010**	**–12,331**	**–12,245**	**–14,053**	**–12,803**	**–13,853**	**–16,359**
Business travel	3 237	. .	. . .	. . .	. . .	. . .	. . .	. . .	. . .	. . .
Personal travel	3 240	. .	. . .	. . .	. . .	. . .	. . .	. . .	. . .	. . .
Other services, credit	2 200	BA	**28,184**	**30,004**	**39,929**	**41,779**	**48,144**	**45,356**	**48,359**	**49,720**
Communications	2 245	. .	165	159	207	216	360	401	365	472
Construction	2 249	. .	1,359	1,355	1,771	2,122	2,754	2,438	2,236	3,013
Insurance	2 253	. .	3,087	2,895	4,109	4,806	5,810	6,583	7,247	7,504
Financial	2 260	. .	1,947	3,780	7,014	6,090	14,210	7,564	10,805	9,867
Computer and information	2 262	. .	29	19	76	91	151	164	250	360
Royalties and licence fees	2 266	. .	1,082	998	1,295	1,388	1,579	1,456	1,531	1,850
Other business services	2 268	. .	18,872	19,243	23,549	25,176	21,000	24,800	23,820	24,219
Personal, cultural, and recreational	2 287	. .	175	220	399	387	627	438	504	666
Government, n.i.e.	2 291	. .	1,468	1,334	1,508	1,503	1,655	1,514	1,600	1,768
Other services, debit	3 200	BA	**–22,599**	**–22,401**	**–31,198**	**–33,259**	**–38,750**	**–37,918**	**–39,215**	**–40,920**
Communications	3 245	. .	–211	–162	–213	–295	–367	–419	–406	–406
Construction	3 249	. .	–644	–642	–599	–751	–988	–955	–728	–893
Insurance	3 253	. .	–2,915	–3,126	–4,170	–4,936	–6,112	–6,925	–6,782	–7,021
Financial	3 260	. .	–2,342	–3,801	–7,267	–6,751	–14,667	–8,239	–10,171	–9,356
Computer and information	3 262	. .	–279	–229	–411	–416	–483	–474	–469	–518
Royalties and licence fees	3 266	. .	–1,721	–1,417	–1,629	–1,748	–2,073	–1,798	–1,909	–2,320
Other business services	3 268	. .	–12,628	–11,305	–14,843	–16,103	–11,537	–16,793	–16,337	–17,942
Personal, cultural, and recreational	3 287	. .	–425	–396	–576	–709	–897	–678	–916	–870
Government, n.i.e.	3 291	. .	–1,434	–1,324	–1,492	–1,550	–1,626	–1,638	–1,498	–1,594

Table 2 (Continued). STANDARD PRESENTATION, 1988–95
(Millions of U.S. dollars)

	Code	1988	1989	1990	1991	1992	1993	1994	1995
C. INCOME	4 300 . .	-953	-279	-3,896	-5,732	-8,615	-9,166	-10,938	-7,446
Total credit	2 300 . .	*34,016*	*41,287*	*55,736*	*69,771*	*87,596*	*98,992*	*110,034*	*130,033*
Total debit	3 300 . .	*-34,969*	*-41,566*	*-59,632*	*-75,503*	*-96,210*	*-108,158*	*-120,972*	*-137,479*
Compensation of employees, credit	2 310 . .	**2,795**	**2,472**	**3,032**	**3,461**	**3,660**	**3,539**	**3,695**	**4,460**
Compensation of employees, debit	3 310 . .	**-3,826**	**-3,220**	**-3,986**	**-4,137**	**-4,871**	**-4,524**	**-4,769**	**-5,362**
Investment income, credit	2 320 . .	**31,221**	**38,814**	**52,704**	**66,309**	**83,935**	**95,453**	**106,338**	**125,573**
Direct investment income	2 330 . .	339	883	2,267	2,554	3,842	4,335	4,832	5,286
Dividends and distributed branch profits	2 332 . .	339	883	2,267	2,554	3,842	4,335	4,832	5,286
Reinvested earnings and undistributed branch profits	2 333 . .	...	...	...	...	...	...	...	...
Income on debt (interest)	2 334 . .	...	...	...	...	...	...	...	...
Portfolio investment income	2 339 . .	7,295	7,117	8,224	9,677	12,386	48,365	77,129	90,731
Income on equity	2 340 . .	2,467	2,378	2,015	1,746	1,978	2,199	1,967	1,874
Income on bonds and notes	2 350 . .	4,828	4,740	6,209	7,930	10,408	35,750	37,711	42,653
Income on money market instruments and financial derivatives	2 360 . .	...	...	...	...	...	10,415	37,451	46,205
Other investment income	2 370 . .	23,587	30,814	42,213	54,079	67,707	42,753	24,377	29,555
Investment income, debit	3 320 . .	**-31,143**	**-38,346**	**-55,646**	**-71,366**	**-91,339**	**-103,634**	**-116,203**	**-132,116**
Direct investment income	3 330 . .	-445	-1,150	-2,698	-1,818	-1,998	-2,512	-3,638	-3,621
Dividends and distributed branch profits	3 332 . .	-445	-1,150	-2,698	-1,818	-1,998	-2,512	-3,638	-3,621
Reinvested earnings and undistributed branch profits	3 333 . .	...	...	...	...	...	...	...	...
Income on debt (interest)	3 334 . .	...	...	...	...	...	...	...	...
Portfolio investment income	3 339 . .	-9,225	-8,339	-12,258	-17,404	-23,171	-61,348	-91,935	-104,324
Income on equity	3 340 . .	-2,476	-1,689	-1,843	-1,353	-1,660	-1,834	-2,472	-3,313
Income on bonds and notes	3 350 . .	-6,749	-6,650	-10,415	-16,051	-21,511	-49,190	-51,097	-55,369
Income on money market instruments and financial derivatives	3 360 . .	...	...	...	...	...	-10,324	-38,367	-45,642
Other investment income	3 370 . .	-21,473	-28,857	-40,690	-52,144	-66,170	-39,774	-20,629	-24,171
D. CURRENT TRANSFERS	4 379 . .	-6,697	-7,684	-8,199	-7,482	-8,981	-6,201	-8,365	-6,526
Credit	2 379 . .	**13,012**	**11,524**	**14,795**	**18,756**	**20,726**	**16,743**	**15,857**	**19,351**
General government	2 380 . .	9,410	7,034	8,655	12,301	12,904	12,759	11,922	14,154
Other sectors	2 390 . .	3,602	4,490	6,140	6,455	7,822	3,984	3,935	5,198
Workers' remittances	2 391 . .	445	541	807	968	1,300	1,231	1,413	1,782
Other current transfers	2 392 . .	3,157	3,949	5,333	5,487	6,521	2,753	2,522	3,416
Debit	3 379 . .	**-19,709**	**-19,208**	**-22,994**	**-26,238**	**-29,707**	**-22,944**	**-24,222**	**-25,877**
General government	3 380 . .	-13,646	-12,729	-14,057	-17,174	-18,559	-18,163	-19,373	-20,320
Other sectors	3 390 . .	-6,063	-6,480	-8,937	-9,064	-11,148	-4,781	-4,849	-5,557
Workers' remittances	3 391 . .	-2,399	-2,228	-2,787	-2,754	-3,108	-2,761	-2,704	-3,146
Other current transfers	3 392 . .	-3,664	-4,251	-6,150	-6,309	-8,041	-2,020	-2,146	-2,412
CAPITAL AND FINANCIAL ACCOUNT	4 996 . .	**3,666**	**11,007**	**9,682**	**2,102**	**-5,798**	**-11,642**	**-11,023**	**-21,311**
CAPITAL ACCOUNT	4 994 . .	**-186**	**-211**	**-4,133**	**-27**	**661**	**27**	**-4,641**	**-115**
Total credit	2 994 . .	*217*	*235*	*219*	*252*	*929*	*305*	*271*	*301*
Total debit	3 994 . .	*-403*	*-446*	*-4,352*	*-279*	*-268*	*-278*	*-4,912*	*-415*
Capital transfers, credit	2 400 . .	**179**	**210**	**195**	**190**	**879**	**262**	**206**	**207**
General government	2 401 . .	...	...	...	...	...	...	...	...
Debt forgiveness	2 402 . .	...	...	...	...	...	...	...	...
Other capital transfers	2 410 . .	...	...	...	...	...	...	...	...
Other sectors	2 430 . .	179	210	195	190	879	262	206	207
Migrants' transfers	2 431 . .	179	210	195	190	252	262	205	206
Debt forgiveness	2 432 . .	...	...	...	...	627	...	1	1
Other capital transfers	2 440 . .	...	...	...	...	...	...	...	...
Capital transfers, debit	3 400 . .	**-163**	**-290**	**-4,317**	**-218**	**-203**	**-195**	**-4,823**	**-234**
General government	3 401 . .	...	-170	-4,059	-88	-29	-46	-4,249	-90
Debt forgiveness	3 402 . .	...	-170	-4,059	-88	-29	-46	-4,249	-90
Other capital transfers	3 410 . .	...	...	...	...	...	...	...	...
Other sectors	3 430 . .	-163	-121	-258	-130	-174	-149	-574	-143
Migrants' transfers	3 431 . .	-163	-121	-176	-130	-174	-149	-132	-140
Debt forgiveness	3 432 . .	...	...	-82	...	...	...	-442	-3
Other capital transfers	3 440 . .	...	...	...	...	...	...	...	...
Nonproduced nonfinancial assets, credit	2 480 . .	**39**	**25**	**24**	**62**	**50**	**43**	**64**	**94**
Nonproduced nonfinancial assets, debit	3 480 . .	**-241**	**-156**	**-35**	**-61**	**-64**	**-84**	**-89**	**-182**

Table 2 (Continued). STANDARD PRESENTATION, 1988–95
(Millions of U.S. dollars)

	Code	1988	1989	1990	1991	1992	1993	1994	1995
FINANCIAL ACCOUNT	4 995 . .	**3,852**	**11,218**	**13,815**	**2,129**	**–6,459**	**–11,668**	**–6,382**	**–21,196**
A. DIRECT INVESTMENT	4 500 . .	–6,006	–9,194	–21,640	–8,779	–9,430	150	–6,172	5,001
Direct investment abroad	4 505 . .	**–14,496**	**–19,498**	**–34,823**	**–23,932**	**–31,269**	**–20,605**	**–22,801**	**–18,734**
Equity capital	4 510 . .	–10,290	–15,878	–23,998	–18,433	–16,816	–10,153	–9,985	–7,899
Claims on affiliated enterprises	4 515 . .	–10,290	–15,878	–23,998	–18,433	–16,816	–10,153	–9,985	–7,899
Liabilities to affiliated enterprises	4 520 . .	. . .	. . .	. . .	. . .	. . .	. . .	. . .	. . .
Reinvested earnings	4 525 . .	. . .	. . .	. . .	. . .	. . .	. . .	. . .	. . .
Other capital	4 530 . .	–4,206	–3,620	–10,825	–5,499	–14,453	–10,451	–12,816	–10,835
Claims on affiliated enterprises	4 535 . .	–4,206	–3,620	–10,825	–5,499	–14,453	–10,451	–12,816	–10,835
Liabilities to affiliated enterprises	4 540 . .	. . .	. . .	. . .	. . .	. . .	. . .	. . .	. . .
Direct investment in France	4 555 . .	**8,490**	**10,304**	**13,183**	**15,153**	**21,840**	**20,754**	**16,628**	**23,735**
Equity capital	4 560 . .	6,688	8,511	7,073	10,027	14,151	11,478	9,355	11,856
Claims on direct investors	4 565 . .	. . .	. . .	. . .	. . .	. . .	. . .	. . .	. . .
Liabilities to direct investors	4 570 . .	6,688	8,511	7,073	10,027	14,151	11,478	9,355	11,856
Reinvested earnings	4 575 . .	. . .	. . .	. . .	. . .	. . .	. . .	. . .	. . .
Other capital	4 580 . .	1,802	1,793	6,111	5,125	7,689	9,276	7,274	11,879
Claims on direct investors	4 585 . .	. . .	. . .	. . .	. . .	. . .	. . .	. . .	. . .
Liabilities to direct investors	4 590 . .	1,802	1,793	6,111	5,125	7,689	9,276	7,274	11,879
B. PORTFOLIO INVESTMENT	4 600 . .	7,793	25,392	34,811	13,819	34,037	3,016	–54,767	–13,201
Assets	4 602 . .	**–4,152**	**–6,653**	**–8,409**	**–15,716**	**–18,463**	**–31,499**	**–24,659**	**–22,901**
Equity securities	4 610 . .	–1,164	–1,455	501	–2,979	–1,550	–2,522	–1,952	606
Monetary authorities	4 611 . .	. . .	. . .	. . .	. . .	. . .	. . .	. . .	. . .
General government	4 612 . .	. . .	. . .	. . .	. . .	. . .	. . .	. . .	. . .
Banks	4 613 . .	. . .	. . .	. . .	. . .	. . .	. . .	. . .	. . .
Other sectors	4 614 . .	. . .	. . .	. . .	. . .	. . .	. . .	. . .	. . .
Debt securities	4 619 . .	–2,988	–5,198	–8,910	–12,737	–16,912	–28,977	–22,706	–23,507
Bonds and notes	4 620 . .	–2,988	–5,198	–8,910	–12,348	–17,957	–28,640	–22,389	–24,507
Monetary authorities	4 621 . .	. . .	. . .	. . .	. . .	. . .	. . .	. . .	. . .
General government	4 622 . .	. . .	. . .	. . .	. . .	. . .	. . .	. . .	. . .
Banks	4 623 . .	. . .	. . .	. . .	. . .	. . .	. . .	. . .	. . .
Other sectors	4 624 . .	. . .	. . .	. . .	. . .	. . .	. . .	. . .	. . .
Money market instruments	4 630 . .	. . .	. . .	. . .	. . .	. . .	. . .	. . .	. . .
Monetary authorities	4 631 . .	. . .	. . .	. . .	. . .	. . .	. . .	. . .	. . .
General government	4 632 . .	. . .	. . .	. . .	. . .	. . .	. . .	. . .	. . .
Banks	4 633 . .	. . .	. . .	. . .	. . .	. . .	. . .	. . .	. . .
Other sectors	4 634 . .	. . .	. . .	. . .	. . .	. . .	. . .	. . .	. . .
Financial derivatives	4 640 . .	. . .	. . .	. . .	–389	1,045	–338	–317	1,001
Monetary authorities	4 641 . .	. . .	. . .	. . .	. . .	. . .	. . .	. . .	. . .
General government	4 642 . .	. . .	. . .	. . .	. . .	. . .	. . .	. . .	. . .
Banks	4 643 . .	. . .	. . .	. . .	. . .	. . .	. . .	. . .	. . .
Other sectors	4 644 . .	. . .	. . .	. . .	–389	1,045	–338	–317	1,001
Liabilities	4 652 . .	**11,945**	**32,045**	**43,219**	**29,535**	**52,500**	**34,516**	**–30,109**	**9,700**
Equity securities	4 660 . .	1,746	6,999	5,898	7,663	5,407	13,579	4,807	7,070
Banks	4 663 . .	. . .	. . .	. . .	. . .	. . .	. . .	. . .	. . .
Other sectors	4 664 . .	. . .	. . .	. . .	. . .	. . .	. . .	. . .	. . .
Debt securities	4 669 . .	10,199	25,046	37,322	21,873	47,093	20,937	–34,916	2,630
Bonds and notes	4 670 . .	10,199	25,046	37,322	21,873	47,093	20,937	–34,916	2,630
Monetary authorities	4 671 . .	. . .	. . .	. . .	. . .	. . .	. . .	. . .	. . .
General government	4 672 . .	–204	13,375	14,445	2,090	24,001	10,241	–18,932	–6,119
Banks	4 673 . .	. . .	. . .	. . .	. . .	. . .	. . .	. . .	. . .
Other sectors	4 674 . .	10,404	11,670	22,876	19,783	23,092	10,696	–15,984	8,749
Money market instruments	4 680 . .	. . .	. . .	. . .	. . .	. . .	. . .	. . .	. . .
Monetary authorities	4 681 . .	. . .	. . .	. . .	. . .	. . .	. . .	. . .	. . .
General government	4 682 . .	. . .	. . .	. . .	. . .	. . .	. . .	. . .	. . .
Banks	4 683 . .	. . .	. . .	. . .	. . .	. . .	. . .	. . .	. . .
Other sectors	4 684 . .	. . .	. . .	. . .	. . .	. . .	. . .	. . .	. . .
Financial derivatives	4 690 . .	. . .	. . .	. . .	. . .	. . .	. . .	. . .	. . .
Monetary authorities	4 691 . .	. . .	. . .	. . .	. . .	. . .	. . .	. . .	. . .
General government	4 692 . .	. . .	. . .	. . .	. . .	. . .	. . .	. . .	. . .
Banks	4 693 . .	. . .	. . .	. . .	. . .	. . .	. . .	. . .	. . .
Other sectors	4 694 . .	. . .	. . .	. . .	. . .	. . .	. . .	. . .	. . .

Table 2 (Concluded). STANDARD PRESENTATION, 1988–95
(Millions of U.S. dollars)

	Code	1988	1989	1990	1991	1992	1993	1994	1995
C. OTHER INVESTMENT	4 700 . .	–3,094	–5,837	11,593	–8,106	–32,643	–19,840	57,005	–12,284
Assets	4 703 . .	**–28,178**	**–62,794**	**–61,543**	**151**	**–61,086**	**–13,380**	**26,316**	**–25,604**
Trade credits	4 706 . .	2,315	–634	1,100	4,235	4,908	7,405	–1,522	1,509
General government: long-term	4 708 . .	...	...	...	...	...	...	...	...
General government: short-term	4 709 . .	...	...	...	...	...	...	...	...
Other sectors: long-term	4 711 . .	...	...	...	...	...	...	...	...
Other sectors: short-term	4 712 . .	...	...	...	...	...	...	...	...
Loans	4 714 . .	–5,766	–5,082	–4,629	–4,012	–9,013	–2,426	7,632	–2,961
Monetary authorities: long-term	4 717 . .	...	...	...	...	...	...	...	...
Monetary authorities: short-term	4 718 . .	...	...	...	...	...	...	...	...
General government: long-term	4 720 . .	–4,157	–4,063	–1,438	–4,200	–3,677	–2,775	1,890	–1,153
General government: short-term	4 721 . .	...	...	...	...	...	...	...	...
Banks: long-term	4 723 . .	–1,241	–194	–2,640	697	–4,253	983	6,153	–1,368
Banks: short-term	4 724 . .	...	...	...	...	...	...	...	...
Other sectors: long-term	4 726 . .	–41	–48	–692	–461	–791	–94	–29	–107
Other sectors: short-term	4 727 . .	–326	–777	140	–49	–292	–540	–383	–333
Currency and deposits	4 730 . .	–24,305	–56,607	–57,499	648	–56,334	–17,672	20,859	–23,461
Monetary authorities	4 731 . .	...	...	...	...	...	...	...	...
General government	4 732 . .	–578	65	378	–206	–636	–450	446	495
Banks	4 733 . .	–22,284	–52,109	–50,191	8,041	–60,833	–47,671	16,477	–45,351
Other sectors	4 734 . .	–1,444	–4,564	–7,686	–7,188	5,136	30,448	3,936	21,395
Other assets	4 736 . .	–422	–470	–515	–720	–647	–687	–653	–691
Monetary authorities: long-term	4 738 . .	...	...	...	...	...	...	...	...
Monetary authorities: short-term	4 739 . .	...	...	...	...	...	...	...	...
General government: long-term	4 741 . .	–422	–470	–515	–720	–647	–687	–653	–691
General government: short-term	4 742 . .	...	...	...	...	...	...	...	...
Banks: long-term	4 744 . .	...	...	...	...	...	...	...	...
Banks: short-term	4 745 . .	...	...	...	...	...	...	...	...
Other sectors: long-term	4 747 . .	...	...	...	...	...	...	...	...
Other sectors: short-term	4 748 . .	...	...	...	...	...	...	...	...
Liabilities	4 753 . .	**25,084**	**56,956**	**73,136**	**–8,257**	**28,444**	**–6,460**	**30,689**	**13,320**
Trade credits	4 756 . .	899	–3,804	–6,901	–4,808	–5,426	–1,714	3,246	–5,494
General government: long-term	4 758 . .	...	...	...	...	...	...	...	...
General government: short-term	4 759 . .	...	...	...	...	...	...	...	...
Other sectors: long-term	4 761 . .	...	...	...	...	...	...	...	...
Other sectors: short-term	4 762 . .	899	–3,804	–6,901	–4,808	–5,426	–1,714	3,246	–5,494
Loans	4 764 . .	–740	–893	4,889	2,175	692	–542	90	5,929
Use of Fund credit and loans from the Fund	4 766 . .	...	...	...	...	...	...	...	...
Monetary authorities: other long-term	4 767 . .	–4,186	...	...	...	...	4,082	–3,914	...
Monetary authorities: short-term	4 768 . .	...	...	...	...	...	...	...	...
General government: long-term	4 770 . .	–231	–17	–556	–135	112	231	328	465
General government: short-term	4 771 . .	...	...	...	...	...	...	...	...
Banks: long-term	4 773 . .	2,710	–395	5,078	1,281	–3,420	–5,249	1,850	5,689
Banks: short-term	4 774 . .	...	...	...	...	...	...	...	...
Other sectors: long-term	4 776 . .	1,075	–447	–196	195	2,268	365	913	–987
Other sectors: short-term	4 777 . .	–108	–34	562	835	1,733	28	913	762
Currency and deposits	4 780 . .	24,842	60,014	74,887	–6,658	22,722	–9,348	36,444	10,931
Monetary authorities	4 781 . .	...	1,901	–587	–390	11,567	–10,297	3,096	759
General government	4 782 . .	...	...	...	...	...	...	...	...
Banks	4 783 . .	24,646	57,899	75,181	–6,355	13,814	–439	30,649	9,529
Other sectors	4 784 . .	197	213	293	87	–2,659	1,387	2,699	643
Other liabilities	4 786 . .	83	1,640	262	1,034	10,455	5,144	–9,091	1,954
Monetary authorities: long-term	4 788 . .	...	...	...	...	...	...	...	...
Monetary authorities: short-term	4 789 . .	83	1,640	262	1,034	10,455	5,144	–9,091	1,954
General government: long-term	4 791 . .	...	...	...	...	...	...	...	...
General government: short-term	4 792 . .	...	...	...	...	...	...	...	...
Banks: long-term	4 794 . .	...	...	...	...	...	...	...	...
Banks: short-term	4 795 . .	...	...	...	...	...	...	...	...
Other sectors: long-term	4 797 . .	...	...	...	...	...	...	...	...
Other sectors: short-term	4 798 . .	...	...	...	...	...	...	...	...
D. RESERVE ASSETS	4 800 . .	5,159	857	–10,949	5,194	1,576	5,006	–2,448	–712
Monetary gold	4 810 . .	...	...	...	...	...	...	...	...
Special drawing rights	4 820 . .	33	32	145	–36	1,125	–171	–11	–589
Reserve position in the Fund	4 830 . .	202	162	94	–226	–887	173	78	–343
Foreign exchange	4 840 . .	4,924	663	–11,188	5,456	1,338	5,004	–2,515	220
Other claims	4 880 . .	...	...	...	...	...	...	...	...
NET ERRORS AND OMISSIONS	4 998 . .	**953**	**–6,336**	**262**	**4,416**	**1,905**	**2,652**	**3,991**	**4,868**

Part 3 of the *Yearbook* contains descriptions of the methodologies, compilation practices, and sources used to compile these data.

Table 3. INTERNATIONAL INVESTMENT POSITION (End–period stocks), 1988–95

(Millions of U.S. dollars)

	Code	1988	1989	1990	1991	1992	1993	1994	1995
ASSETS	8 995 C.	...	587,465	736,314	754,913	812,075	905,943	967,612	1,104,636
Direct investment abroad	8 505 . .	**51,461**	**75,415**	**110,119**	**129,903**	**140,579**	**141,430**	**163,075**	**197,959**
Equity capital and reinvested earnings	8 506 . .	44,925	66,690	98,440	116,448	122,256	123,806	138,982	115,102
Claims on affiliated enterprises	8 507 . .	...	...	...	...	...	...	...	...
Liabilities to affiliated enterprises	8 508 . .	...	...	...	...	...	...	...	...
Other capital	8 530 . .	6,536	8,725	11,679	13,456	18,324	17,624	24,093	82,857
Claims on affiliated enterprises	8 535 . .	...	...	...	...	...	...	...	...
Liabilities to affiliated enterprises	8 540 . .	...	...	...	...	...	...	...	...
Portfolio investment	8 602 . .	**...**	**73,652**	**81,049**	**91,506**	**96,105**	**130,184**	**155,051**	**200,551**
Equity securities	8 610 . .	...	45,232	40,203	44,421	42,513	51,836	54,433	65,551
Monetary authorities	8 611 . .	...	...	...	...	...	...	...	...
General government	8 612 . .	...	...	...	...	...	...	...	...
Banks	8 613 . .	...	...	...	...	...	...	...	...
Other sectors	8 614 . .	...	...	...	...	...	...	...	...
Debt securities	8 619 . .	...	28,421	40,846	47,085	53,591	78,348	100,617	135,000
Bonds and notes	8 620 . .	...	28,421	40,846	47,085	53,591	70,461	91,246	117,735
Monetary authorities	8 621 . .	...	...	...	...	...	...	...	...
General government	8 622 . .	...	...	...	...	...	...	...	...
Banks	8 623 . .	...	...	...	...	...	...	...	...
Other sectors	8 624 . .	...	...	...	...	...	...	...	...
Money market instruments	8 630 . .	...	...	...	...	...	7,887	9,371	17,265
Monetary authorities	8 631 . .	...	...	...	...	...	...	...	...
General government	8 632 . .	...	...	...	...	...	...	...	...
Banks	8 633 . .	...	...	...	...	...	...	...	...
Other sectors	8 634 . .	...	...	...	...	...	...	...	...
Financial derivatives	8 640 . .	...	...	...	...	...	...	...	...
Monetary authorities	8 641 . .	...	...	...	...	...	...	...	...
General government	8 642 . .	...	...	...	...	...	...	...	...
Banks	8 643 . .	...	...	...	...	...	...	...	...
Other sectors	8 644 . .	...	...	...	...	...	...	...	...
Other investment	8 703 . .	**289,399**	**379,599**	**476,450**	**470,243**	**521,772**	**581,817**	**591,545**	**647,490**
Trade credits	8 706 . .	...	...	...	...	...	35,162	38,028	41,510
General government: long-term	8 708 . .	...	...	...	...	...	...	...	...
General government: short-term	8 709 . .	...	...	...	...	...	...	...	...
Other sectors: long-term	8 711 . .	...	...	...	...	...	...	...	...
Other sectors: short-term	8 712 . .	...	...	...	...	...	...	...	...
Loans	8 714 . .	103,614	114,045	127,709	131,004	131,287	126,921	128,620	138,531
Monetary authorities: long-term	8 717 . .	...	...	...	...	...	...	...	...
Monetary authorities: short-term	8 718 . .	...	...	...	...	...	...	...	...
General government: long-term	8 720 . .	26,465	32,379	37,890	42,069	43,107	42,829	45,455	50,776
General government: short-term	8 721 . .	...	...	...	...	...	...	...	...
Banks: long-term	8 723 . .	74,882	79,575	87,577	87,236	86,763	84,091	83,165	87,755
Banks: short-term	8 724 . .	...	...	...	...	...	...	...	...
Other sectors: long-term	8 726 . .	2,268	2,091	2,242	1,699	1,417	...	...	...
Other sectors: short-term	8 727 . .	...	...	...	...	...	...	...	...
Currency and deposits	8 730 . .	185,785	237,082	303,975	298,236	348,118	384,274	386,532	443,143
Monetary authorities	8 731 . .	...	...	...	...	...	...	...	...
General government	8 732 . .	2,799	2,802	2,589	2,718	3,361	3,783	2,282	1,980
Banks	8 733 . .	182,986	234,280	301,386	295,517	344,756	380,492	384,250	441,163
Other sectors	8 734 . .	...	...	...	...	...	...	...	...
Other assets	8 736 . .	...	28,473	44,765	41,004	42,368	35,459	38,365	24,306
Monetary authorities: long-term	8 738 . .	...	...	...	...	...	...	...	...
Monetary authorities: short-term	8 739 . .	...	...	...	...	...	...	...	...
General government: long-term	8 741 . .	...	...	...	...	...	...	...	...
General government: short-term	8 742 . .	...	...	...	...	...	...	...	...
Banks: long-term	8 744 . .	...	...	...	...	...	...	...	...
Banks: short-term	8 745 . .	...	...	...	...	...	...	...	...
Other sectors: long-term	8 747 . .	...	...	...	...	...	...	...	...
Other sectors: short-term	8 748 . .	...	28,473	44,765	41,004	42,368	27,860	30,172	14,776
Reserve assets	8 800 . .	**59,764**	**58,799**	**68,696**	**63,260**	**53,619**	**52,513**	**57,941**	**58,636**
Monetary gold	8 810 . .	34,009	33,993	31,523	31,736	26,354	30,206	31,270	31,731
Special drawing rights	8 820 . .	1,390	1,329	1,283	1,326	163	331	362	955
Reserve position in the Fund	8 830 . .	1,615	1,414	1,428	1,666	2,482	2,310	2,375	2,756
Foreign exchange	8 840 . .	22,573	21,873	34,287	28,320	24,422	19,666	23,934	23,194
Other claims	8 880 . .	177	190	175	212	198	...	...	...

Table 3 (Continued). INTERNATIONAL INVESTMENT POSITION (End–period stocks), 1988–95
(Millions of U.S. dollars)

	Code	1988	1989	1990	1991	1992	1993	1994	1995
LIABILITIES	8 995 D.	...	561,515	757,994	813,846	848,020	955,812	1,036,433	1,178,429
Direct investment in France	8 555 ..	**...**	**60,523**	**84,929**	**97,452**	**100,209**	**103,197**	**123,887**	**159,306**
Equity capital and reinvested earnings	8 556 ..	...	56,308	78,846	88,514	90,693	96,599	116,667	...
Claims on direct investors	8 557 ..	...	...	...	...	...	...	...	...
Liabilities to direct investors	8 558 ..	...	...	...	...	...	...	...	...
Other capital	8 580 ..	...	4,216	6,083	8,938	9,516	6,598	7,220	...
Claims on direct investors	8 585 ..	...	...	...	...	...	...	...	...
Liabilities to direct investors	8 590 ..	...	...	...	...	...	...	...	...
Portfolio investment	8 652 ..	**...**	**153,438**	**215,266**	**260,849**	**287,424**	**366,127**	**348,541**	**399,816**
Equity securities	8 660 ..	...	50,294	54,826	71,178	71,388	103,604	102,282	116,837
Banks	8 663 ..	...	...	...	...	...	...	...	...
Other sectors	8 664 ..	...	...	...	...	...	...	...	...
Debt securities	8 669 ..	27,485	103,144	160,441	189,672	216,036	262,522	246,259	282,980
Bonds and notes	8 670 ..	27,485	103,144	160,441	189,672	216,036	217,522	208,848	231,571
Monetary authorities	8 671 ..	...	...	...	...	...	...	...	...
General government	8 672 ..	...	...	...	...	...	...	...	...
Banks	8 673 ..	...	...	...	...	...	...	...	...
Other sectors	8 674 ..	...	...	...	...	...	...	...	...
Money market instruments	8 680 ..	...	...	...	...	...	45,000	37,411	51,408
Monetary authorities	8 681 ..	...	...	...	...	...	...	...	...
General government	8 682 ..	...	...	...	...	...	...	...	...
Banks	8 683 ..	...	...	...	...	...	...	...	...
Other sectors	8 684 ..	...	...	...	...	...	...	...	...
Financial derivatives	8 690 ..	...	...	...	...	...	...	...	...
Monetary authorities	8 691 ..	...	...	...	...	...	...	...	...
General government	8 692 ..	...	...	...	...	...	...	...	...
Banks	8 692 ..	...	...	...	...	...	...	...	...
Other sectors	8 694 ..	...	...	...	...	...	...	...	...
Other investment	8 753 ..	**280,132**	**347,554**	**457,799**	**455,544**	**460,387**	**486,488**	**564,005**	**619,306**
Trade credits	8 756 ..	...	...	...	...	...	58,248	79,405	89,939
General government: long-term	8 758 ..	...	...	...	...	...	...	...	...
General government: short-term	8 759 ..	...	...	...	...	...	...	...	...
Other sectors: long-term	8 761 ..	...	...	...	...	...	...	...	...
Other sectors: short-term	8 762 ..	...	...	...	...	...	...	...	...
Loans	8 764 ..	53,994	51,702	59,579	63,263	58,965	52,021	60,363	71,061
Use of Fund credit and loans from the Fund	8 766 ..	...	...	...	...	...	...	...	...
Monetary authorities: other long-term	8 767 ..	...	...	...	...	...	...	...	...
Monetary authorities: short-term	8 768 ..	...	...	...	...	...	...	...	...
General government: long-term	8 770 ..	957	933	487	373	381	305	973	1,531
General government: short-term	8 771 ..	...	...	...	...	...	...	...	...
Banks: long-term	8 773 ..	33,331	31,090	37,391	40,322	38,135	31,565	35,784	43,367
Banks: short-term	8 774 ..	...	...	...	...	...	...	...	...
Other sectors: long-term	8 776 ..	...	...	...	...	...	...	...	...
Other sectors: short-term	8 777 ..	...	...	...	...	...	...	...	...
Currency and deposits	8 780 ..	219,409	287,533	389,789	384,069	375,162	357,849	414,042	446,367
Monetary authorities	8 781 ..	...	...	...	...	...	...	...	...
General government	8 782 ..	...	...	...	...	...	...	...	...
Banks	8 783 ..	219,409	287,533	389,789	384,069	375,162	357,849	414,042	446,367
Other sectors	8 784 ..	...	...	...	...	...	...	...	...
Other liabilities	8 786 ..	6,729	8,319	8,430	8,212	26,260	18,370	10,195	11,939
Monetary authorities: long-term	8 788 ..	...	...	...	...	...	...	...	...
Monetary authorities: short-term	8 789 ..	6,729	8,319	8,430	8,212	26,260	18,370	10,195	11,939
General government: long-term	8 791 ..	...	...	...	...	...	...	...	...
General government: short-term	8 792 ..	...	...	...	...	...	...	...	...
Banks: long-term	8 794 ..	...	...	...	...	...	...	...	...
Banks: short-term	8 795 ..	...	...	...	...	...	...	...	...
Other sectors: long-term	8 797 ..	...	...	...	...	...	...	...	...
Other sectors: short-term	8 798 ..	...	...	...	...	...	...	...	...
NET INTERNATIONAL INVESTMENT POSITION	8 995 ..	**...**	**25,950**	**–21,680**	**–58,933**	**–35,945**	**–49,869**	**–68,821**	**–73,793**
Conversion rates: French francs per U.S. dollar (end of period)	0 102 ..	**6.0590**	**5.7880**	**5.1290**	**5.1800**	**5.5065**	**5.8955**	**5.3460**	**4.9000**

Gabon
646

Table 1. ANALYTIC PRESENTATION, 1988–95
(Millions of U.S. dollars)

	Code	1988	1989	1990	1991	1992	1993	1994	1995
A. Current Account[1]	4 993 Y.	**–615.5**	**–192.2**	**167.7**	**74.8**	**–168.1**	**–49.1**	**319.7**	**...**
Goods: exports f.o.b	2 100 . .	1,195.6	1,626.0	2,488.8	2,227.9	2,259.2	2,326.2	2,349.4	...
Goods: imports f.o.b	3 100 . .	–791.2	–751.7	–805.1	–861.0	–886.3	–845.1	–756.5	...
Balance on Goods	4 100 . .	*404.3*	*874.3*	*1,683.7*	*1,366.9*	*1,372.9*	*1,481.1*	*1,592.9*	...
Services: credit	2 200 . .	213.0	289.0	241.6	324.0	347.6	311.1	219.6	...
Services: debit	3 200 . .	–811.0	–900.8	–1,006.6	–881.6	–924.8	–1,022.7	–812.1	...
Balance on Goods and Services	4 991 . .	*–193.7*	*262.5*	*918.7*	*809.3*	*795.6*	*769.5*	*1,000.4*	...
Income: credit	2 300 . .	15.1	19.0	20.1	28.0	47.2	32.1	11.9	...
Income: debit	3 300 . .	–292.7	–347.8	–636.7	–642.7	–868.9	–658.3	–569.0	...
Balance on Goods, Services, and Income	4 992 . .	*–471.2*	*–66.2*	*302.0*	*194.6*	*–26.1*	*143.4*	*443.3*	...
Current transfers: credit	2 379 Y.	53.8	42.3	58.9	44.0	51.4	48.0	59.3	...
Current transfers: debit	3 379 . .	–198.1	–168.3	–193.3	–163.8	–193.4	–240.5	–182.8	...
B. Capital Account[1]	4 994 Y.	**...**	**...**	**...**	**...**	**...**	**...**	**...**	**...**
Capital account: credit	2 994 Y.	...	...	...	...	...	...	...	...
Capital account: debit	3 994 . .	...	...	...	...	...	...	...	...
Total, Groups A Plus B	4 010 . .	*–615.5*	*–192.2*	*167.7*	*74.8*	*–168.1*	*–49.1*	*319.7*	...
C. Financial Account[1]	4 995 X.	**716.6**	**61.1**	**–366.5**	**–303.8**	**–220.6**	**–382.8**	**–480.4**	**...**
Direct investment abroad	4 505 . .	–9.7	–8.0	–28.8	–14.9	–25.7	–2.5	–.7	...
Direct investment in Gabon	4 555 Y.	132.5	–30.5	73.5	–54.6	126.9	–113.7	–102.8	...
Portfolio investment assets	4 602 . .	...	...	...	...	...	...	...	...
Equity securities	4 610 . .	...	...	...	...	...	...	...	...
Debt securities	4 619 . .	...	...	...	...	...	...	...	...
Portfolio investment liabilities	4 652 Y.	...	...	...	...	...	...	...	...
Equity securities	4 660 Y.	...	...	...	...	...	...	...	...
Debt securities	4 669 Y.	...	...	...	...	...	...	...	...
Other investment assets	4 703 . .	42.1	–278.3	–285.1	–14.2	–27.2	–7.8	–258.8	...
Monetary authorities	4 703 . A	...	...	...	...	...	...	...	...
General government	4 703 . B	...	...	...	...	...	...	...	...
Banks	4 703 . C	–6.1	–36.4	10.0	.7	6.8	4.6	–40.9	...
Other sectors	4 703 . D	48.2	–241.9	–295.0	–14.9	–34.0	–12.4	–217.9	...
Other investment liabilities	4 753 X.	551.7	378.0	–126.1	–220.1	–294.7	–258.9	–118.0	...
Monetary authorities	4 753 XA	...	...	...	...	...	...	...	...
General government	4 753 YB	288.1	223.0	–187.7	–149.2	–236.1	–174.1	–133.1	...
Banks	4 753 YC	–32.6	16.6	29.0	11.3	–2.6	1.8	7.7	...
Other sectors	4 753 YD	296.3	138.4	32.6	–82.2	–55.9	–86.5	7.4	...
Total, Groups A Through C	4 020 . .	*101.1*	*–131.1*	*–198.8*	*–229.0*	*–388.8*	*–431.9*	*–160.7*	...
D. Net Errors and Omissions	4 998 . .	**–101.9**	**35.0**	**–38.0**	**8.6**	**–55.1**	**–13.6**	**6.7**	**...**
Total, Groups A Through D	4 030 . .	*–.8*	*–96.1*	*–236.8*	*–220.4*	*–443.8*	*–445.5*	*–153.9*	...
E. Reserves and Related Items	4 040 . .	**.8**	**96.1**	**236.8**	**220.4**	**443.8**	**445.5**	**153.9**	**...**
Reserve assets	4 800 . .	–55.7	29.8	–219.3	–54.0	246.3	67.5	–167.4	...
Use of Fund credit and loans	4 766 . .	74.6	5.0	–5.9	–19.4	–36.3	–35.9	40.9	...
Liabilities constituting foreign authorities' reserves	4 900 . .	...	...	–31.8	–2.9	1.9	–6.4	–26.3	...
Exceptional financing	4 920 . .	–18.1	61.3	493.8	296.7	232.0	420.3	306.7	...
Conversion rates: CFA francs per U.S. dollar	0 101 . .	**297.85**	**319.01**	**272.26**	**282.11**	**264.69**	**283.16**	**555.20**	**499.15**

[1] Excludes components that have been classified in the categories of Group E.

Table 2. STANDARD PRESENTATION, 1988–95
(Millions of U.S. dollars)

	Code	1988	1989	1990	1991	1992	1993	1994	1995
CURRENT ACCOUNT	4 993 . .	**–615.5**	**–192.2**	**167.7**	**74.8**	**–168.1**	**–49.1**	**319.7**	...
A. GOODS	4 100 . .	404.3	874.3	1,683.7	1,366.9	1,372.9	1,481.1	1,592.9	...
Credit	2 100 . .	**1,195.6**	**1,626.0**	**2,488.8**	**2,227.9**	**2,259.2**	**2,326.2**	**2,349.4**	...
General merchandise: exports f.o.b.	2 110 . .	1,195.6	1,626.0	2,488.8	2,227.9	2,259.2	2,326.2	2,349.4	...
Goods for processing: exports f.o.b.	2 150 . .	...	...	...	...	...	...	...	...
Repairs on goods	2 160 . .	...	...	...	...	...	...	...	...
Goods procured in ports by carriers	2 170 . .	...	...	...	...	...	...	...	...
Nonmonetary gold	2 180 . .	...	...	...	...	...	...	...	...
Debit	3 100 . .	**–791.2**	**–751.7**	**–805.1**	**–861.0**	**–886.3**	**–845.1**	**–756.5**	...
General merchandise: imports f.o.b.	3 110 . .	–791.2	–751.7	–805.1	–861.0	–886.3	–845.1	–756.5	...
Goods for processing: imports f.o.b.	3 150 . .	...	...	...	...	...	...	...	...
Repairs on goods	3 160 . .	...	...	...	...	...	...	...	...
Goods procured in ports by carriers	3 170 . .	...	...	...	...	...	...	...	...
Nonmonetary gold	3 180 . .	...	...	...	...	...	...	...	...
B. SERVICES	4 200 . .	–598.0	–611.8	–765.0	–557.6	–577.3	–711.6	–592.6	...
Total credit	2 200 . .	*213.0*	*289.0*	*241.6*	*324.0*	*347.6*	*311.1*	*219.6*	...
Total debit	3 200 . .	*–811.0*	*–900.8*	*–1,006.6*	*–881.6*	*–924.8*	*–1,022.7*	*–812.1*	...
Transportation services, credit	2 205 . .	**59.0**	**77.7**	**71.5**	**97.1**	**95.6**	**79.5**	**70.2**	...
Passenger	2 205 BA	*44.4*	*42.9*	*29.6*	*97.1*	*95.6*	*79.5*	*70.2*	...
Freight	2 205 BB	*4.9*	*5.6*	*5.0*	...	...	...	...	...
Other	2 205 BC	*9.6*	*29.2*	*36.9*	...	...	...	...	...
Sea transport, passenger	2 207 . .	...	...	...	...	...	...	...	...
Sea transport, freight	2 208 . .	...	...	...	...	...	...	...	...
Sea transport, other	2 209 . .	...	...	...	...	...	...	...	...
Air transport, passenger	2 211 . .	...	...	...	...	...	...	...	...
Air transport, freight	2 212 . .	...	...	...	...	...	...	...	...
Air transport, other	2 213 . .	...	...	...	...	...	...	...	...
Other transport, passenger	2 215 . .	...	...	...	...	...	...	...	...
Other transport, freight	2 216 . .	...	...	...	...	...	...	...	...
Other transport, other	2 217 . .	...	...	...	...	...	...	...	...
Transportation services, debit	3 205 . .	**–189.3**	**–198.0**	**–228.6**	**–244.1**	**–250.1**	**–241.0**	**–217.7**	...
Passenger	3 205 BA	*–35.8*	*–36.0*	*–41.8*	*–98.9*	*–97.5*	*–73.8*	*–67.9*	...
Freight	3 205 BB	*–146.0*	*–138.7*	*–137.2*	*–145.2*	*–152.7*	*–167.2*	*–149.8*	...
Other	3 205 BC	*–7.5*	*–23.3*	*–49.5*	...	...	...	...	...
Sea transport, passenger	3 207 . .	...	...	...	...	...	...	...	...
Sea transport, freight	3 208 . .	...	...	...	...	...	...	...	...
Sea transport, other	3 209 . .	...	...	...	...	...	...	...	...
Air transport, passenger	3 211 . .	...	...	...	...	...	...	...	...
Air transport, freight	3 212 . .	...	...	...	...	...	...	...	...
Air transport, other	3 213 . .	...	...	...	...	...	...	...	...
Other transport, passenger	3 215 . .	...	...	...	...	...	...	...	...
Other transport, freight	3 216 . .	...	...	...	...	...	...	...	...
Other transport, other	3 217 . .	...	...	...	...	...	...	...	...
Travel, credit	2 236 . .	**7.2**	**3.9**	**3.1**	**4.3**	**5.3**	**3.9**	**5.2**	...
Business travel	2 237 . .	...	...	...	...	...	...	...	...
Personal travel	2 240 . .	...	...	...	...	...	...	...	...
Travel, debit	3 236 . .	**–133.8**	**–123.9**	**–136.6**	**–111.7**	**–142.8**	**–154.0**	**–142.8**	...
Business travel	3 237 . .	...	...	...	...	...	...	...	...
Personal travel	3 240 . .	...	...	...	...	...	...	...	...
Other services, credit	2 200 BA	**146.8**	**207.3**	**167.0**	**222.6**	**246.7**	**227.8**	**144.1**	...
Communications	2 245 . .	...	...	...	...	...	...	...	...
Construction	2 249 . .	...	...	...	...	...	...	...	...
Insurance	2 253 . .	8.7	10.0	12.3	10.3	11.3	5.7	11.9	...
Financial	2 260 . .	...	...	...	...	...	...	...	...
Computer and information	2 262 . .	...	...	...	...	...	...	...	...
Royalties and licence fees	2 266 . .	...	...	...	...	...	...	...	...
Other business services	2 268 . .	107.1	174.4	127.2	179.4	199.9	196.7	112.2	...
Personal, cultural, and recreational	2 287 . .	...	...	...	...	...	...	...	...
Government, n.i.e.	2 291 . .	31.0	22.9	27.5	33.0	35.5	25.4	20.0	...
Other services, debit	3 200 BA	**–487.8**	**–578.8**	**–641.4**	**–525.9**	**–531.9**	**–627.8**	**–451.6**	...
Communications	3 245 . .	...	...	...	...	...	...	...	...
Construction	3 249 . .	...	...	...	...	...	...	...	...
Insurance	3 253 . .	–47.8	–43.6	–51.8	–51.9	–52.9	–50.4	–46.7	...
Financial	3 260 . .	...	...	...	...	...	...	...	...
Computer and information	3 262 . .	...	...	...	...	...	...	...	...
Royalties and licence fees	3 266 . .	...	...	...	...	...	...	...	...
Other business services	3 268 . .	–402.1	–501.4	–566.8	–429.3	–421.2	–558.7	–387.6	...
Personal, cultural, and recreational	3 287 . .	...	...	...	...	...	...	...	...
Government, n.i.e.	3 291 . .	–37.9	–33.8	–22.8	–44.7	–57.8	–18.7	–17.3	...

Table 2 (Continued). STANDARD PRESENTATION, 1988–95
(Millions of U.S. dollars)

	Code	1988	1989	1990	1991	1992	1993	1994	1995
C. INCOME	4 300 . .	−277.6	−328.8	−616.6	−614.7	−821.7	−626.1	−557.1	. . .
Total credit	2 300 . .	*15.1*	*19.0*	*20.1*	*28.0*	*47.2*	*32.1*	*11.9*	. . .
Total debit	3 300 . .	*−292.7*	*−347.8*	*−636.7*	*−642.7*	*−868.9*	*−658.3*	*−569.0*	. . .
Compensation of employees, credit	2 310 . .	. . .	. . .	. . .	. . .	. . .	. . .	. . .	. . .
Compensation of employees, debit	3 310 . .	**−1.6**	**−3.3**	**−3.3**	**−2.8**	**−3.4**	**−3.9**	**−2.2**	. . .
Investment income, credit	2 320 . .	**15.1**	**19.0**	**20.1**	**28.0**	**47.2**	**32.1**	**11.9**	. . .
Direct investment income	2 330 . .	7.1	14.5	13.2	3.9	12.1	1.4	1.8	. . .
Dividends and distributed branch profits	2 332 . .	7.1	14.5	13.2	3.9	12.1	1.4	1.8	. . .
Reinvested earnings and undistributed branch profits	2 333 . .	. . .	. . .	. . .	. . .	. . .	. . .	. . .	. . .
Income on debt (interest)	2 334 . .	. . .	. . .	. . .	. . .	. . .	. . .	. . .	. . .
Portfolio investment income	2 339 . .	. . .	. . .	. . .	. . .	. . .	. . .	. . .	. . .
Income on equity	2 340 . .	. . .	. . .	. . .	. . .	. . .	. . .	. . .	. . .
Income on bonds and notes	2 350 . .	. . .	. . .	. . .	. . .	. . .	. . .	. . .	. . .
Income on money market instruments and financial derivatives	2 360 . .	. . .	. . .	. . .	. . .	. . .	. . .	. . .	. . .
Other investment income	2 370 . .	8.0	4.5	6.9	24.1	35.1	30.7	10.1	. . .
Investment income, debit	3 320 . .	**−291.1**	**−344.5**	**−633.4**	**−639.8**	**−865.5**	**−654.4**	**−566.8**	. . .
Direct investment income	3 330 . .	−31.8	51.7	−116.4	−141.4	−156.4	−163.2	−150.8	. . .
Dividends and distributed branch profits	3 332 . .	−5.9	−6.0	−60.8	−69.1	−80.8	−40.3	−46.8	. . .
Reinvested earnings and undistributed branch profits	3 333 . .	−25.9	57.7	−55.6	−72.3	−75.6	−122.9	−103.9	. . .
Income on debt (interest)	3 334 . .	. . .	. . .	. . .	. . .	. . .	. . .	. . .	. . .
Portfolio investment income	3 339 . .	. . .	. . .	. . .	. . .	. . .	. . .	. . .	. . .
Income on equity	3 340 . .	. . .	. . .	. . .	. . .	. . .	. . .	. . .	. . .
Income on bonds and notes	3 350 . .	. . .	. . .	. . .	. . .	. . .	. . .	. . .	. . .
Income on money market instruments and financial derivatives	3 360 . .	. . .	. . .	. . .	. . .	. . .	. . .	. . .	. . .
Other investment income	3 370 . .	−259.3	−396.2	−517.0	−498.4	−709.1	−491.2	−416.1	. . .
D. CURRENT TRANSFERS	4 379 . .	−144.3	−126.0	−134.3	−119.8	−142.1	−192.5	−123.6	. . .
Credit	2 379 . .	**53.8**	**42.3**	**58.9**	**44.0**	**51.4**	**48.0**	**59.3**	. . .
General government	2 380 . .	49.3	39.7	55.2	41.1	48.4	46.3	55.7	. . .
Other sectors	2 390 . .	4.5	2.7	3.8	2.8	3.0	1.8	3.6	. . .
Workers' remittances	2 391 . .	.1	.2	. . .	. . .	. . .	. . .	. . .	. . .
Other current transfers	2 392 . .	4.4	2.5	3.8	2.8	3.0	1.8	3.6	. . .
Debit	3 379 . .	**−198.1**	**−168.3**	**−193.3**	**−163.8**	**−193.4**	**−240.5**	**−182.8**	. . .
General government	3 380 . .	−26.9	−20.7	−18.9	−18.1	−19.3	−30.0	−18.0	. . .
Other sectors	3 390 . .	−171.2	−147.6	−174.4	−145.7	−174.2	−210.5	−164.8	. . .
Workers' remittances	3 391 . .	−151.8	−125.3	−144.0	−114.5	−142.4	−192.5	−152.2	. . .
Other current transfers	3 392 . .	−19.3	−22.3	−30.4	−31.2	−31.7	−18.0	−12.6	. . .
CAPITAL AND FINANCIAL ACCOUNT	4 996 . .	**717.4**	**157.2**	**−129.7**	**−83.4**	**223.2**	**62.7**	**−326.4**	. . .
CAPITAL ACCOUNT	4 994 . .	. . .	. . .	. . .	. . .	. . .	. . .	. . .	. . .
Total credit	2 994 . .	. . .	. . .	. . .	. . .	. . .	. . .	. . .	. . .
Total debit	3 994 . .	. . .	. . .	. . .	. . .	. . .	. . .	. . .	. . .
Capital transfers, credit	2 400 . .	. . .	. . .	. . .	. . .	. . .	. . .	. . .	. . .
General government	2 401 . .	. . .	. . .	. . .	. . .	. . .	. . .	. . .	. . .
Debt forgiveness	2 402 . .	. . .	. . .	. . .	. . .	. . .	. . .	. . .	. . .
Other capital transfers	2 410 . .	. . .	. . .	. . .	. . .	. . .	. . .	. . .	. . .
Other sectors	2 430 . .	. . .	. . .	. . .	. . .	. . .	. . .	. . .	. . .
Migrants' transfers	2 431 . .	. . .	. . .	. . .	. . .	. . .	. . .	. . .	. . .
Debt forgiveness	2 432 . .	. . .	. . .	. . .	. . .	. . .	. . .	. . .	. . .
Other capital transfers	2 440 . .	. . .	. . .	. . .	. . .	. . .	. . .	. . .	. . .
Capital transfers, debit	3 400 . .	. . .	. . .	. . .	. . .	. . .	. . .	. . .	. . .
General government	3 401 . .	. . .	. . .	. . .	. . .	. . .	. . .	. . .	. . .
Debt forgiveness	3 402 . .	. . .	. . .	. . .	. . .	. . .	. . .	. . .	. . .
Other capital transfers	3 410 . .	. . .	. . .	. . .	. . .	. . .	. . .	. . .	. . .
Other sectors	3 430 . .	. . .	. . .	. . .	. . .	. . .	. . .	. . .	. . .
Migrants' transfers	3 431 . .	. . .	. . .	. . .	. . .	. . .	. . .	. . .	. . .
Debt forgiveness	3 432 . .	. . .	. . .	. . .	. . .	. . .	. . .	. . .	. . .
Other capital transfers	3 440 . .	. . .	. . .	. . .	. . .	. . .	. . .	. . .	. . .
Nonproduced nonfinancial assets, credit	2 480 . .	. . .	. . .	. . .	. . .	. . .	. . .	. . .	. . .
Nonproduced nonfinancial assets, debit	3 480 . .	. . .	. . .	. . .	. . .	. . .	. . .	. . .	. . .

Table 2 (Continued). STANDARD PRESENTATION, 1988–95
(Millions of U.S. dollars)

	Code	1988	1989	1990	1991	1992	1993	1994	1995
FINANCIAL ACCOUNT	4 995	**717.4**	**157.2**	**–129.7**	**–83.4**	**223.2**	**62.7**	**–326.4**	. . .
A. DIRECT INVESTMENT	4 500	122.8	–38.6	44.7	–69.5	101.2	–116.2	–103.6	. . .
Direct investment abroad	4 505	**–9.7**	**–8.0**	**–28.8**	**–14.9**	**–25.7**	**–2.5**	**–.7**	. . .
Equity capital	4 510	–9.7	–8.0	–28.8	–14.9	–25.7	–2.5	–.7	. . .
Claims on affiliated enterprises	4 515	. . .	. . .	. . .	. . .	. . .	. . .	. . .	. . .
Liabilities to affiliated enterprises	4 520	. . .	. . .	. . .	. . .	. . .	. . .	. . .	. . .
Reinvested earnings	4 525	. . .	. . .	. . .	. . .	. . .	. . .	. . .	. . .
Other capital	4 530	. . .	. . .	. . .	. . .	. . .	. . .	. . .	. . .
Claims on affiliated enterprises	4 535	. . .	. . .	. . .	. . .	. . .	. . .	. . .	. . .
Liabilities to affiliated enterprises	4 540	. . .	. . .	. . .	. . .	. . .	. . .	. . .	. . .
Direct investment in Gabon	4 555	**132.5**	**–30.5**	**73.5**	**–54.6**	**126.9**	**–113.7**	**–102.8**	. . .
Equity capital	4 560	22.2	36.4	215.9	110.2	242.9	. . .	. . .	. . .
Claims on direct investors	4 565	. . .	. . .	. . .	. . .	. . .	. . .	. . .	. . .
Liabilities to direct investors	4 570	. . .	. . .	. . .	. . .	. . .	. . .	. . .	. . .
Reinvested earnings	4 575	25.9	–57.7	55.6	72.3	75.6	122.9	103.9	. . .
Other capital	4 580	84.5	–9.2	–198.0	–237.1	–191.5	–236.6	–206.8	. . .
Claims on direct investors	4 585	. . .	. . .	. . .	. . .	. . .	. . .	. . .	. . .
Liabilities to direct investors	4 590	. . .	. . .	. . .	. . .	. . .	. . .	. . .	. . .
B. PORTFOLIO INVESTMENT	4 600	. . .	. . .	. . .	. . .	. . .	. . .	. . .	. . .
Assets	4 602	. . .	. . .	. . .	. . .	. . .	. . .	. . .	. . .
Equity securities	4 610	. . .	. . .	. . .	. . .	. . .	. . .	. . .	. . .
Monetary authorities	4 611	. . .	. . .	. . .	. . .	. . .	. . .	. . .	. . .
General government	4 612	. . .	. . .	. . .	. . .	. . .	. . .	. . .	. . .
Banks	4 613	. . .	. . .	. . .	. . .	. . .	. . .	. . .	. . .
Other sectors	4 614	. . .	. . .	. . .	. . .	. . .	. . .	. . .	. . .
Debt securities	4 619	. . .	. . .	. . .	. . .	. . .	. . .	. . .	. . .
Bonds and notes	4 620	. . .	. . .	. . .	. . .	. . .	. . .	. . .	. . .
Monetary authorities	4 621	. . .	. . .	. . .	. . .	. . .	. . .	. . .	. . .
General government	4 622	. . .	. . .	. . .	. . .	. . .	. . .	. . .	. . .
Banks	4 623	. . .	. . .	. . .	. . .	. . .	. . .	. . .	. . .
Other sectors	4 624	. . .	. . .	. . .	. . .	. . .	. . .	. . .	. . .
Money market instruments	4 630	. . .	. . .	. . .	. . .	. . .	. . .	. . .	. . .
Monetary authorities	4 631	. . .	. . .	. . .	. . .	. . .	. . .	. . .	. . .
General government	4 632	. . .	. . .	. . .	. . .	. . .	. . .	. . .	. . .
Banks	4 633	. . .	. . .	. . .	. . .	. . .	. . .	. . .	. . .
Other sectors	4 634	. . .	. . .	. . .	. . .	. . .	. . .	. . .	. . .
Financial derivatives	4 640	. . .	. . .	. . .	. . .	. . .	. . .	. . .	. . .
Monetary authorities	4 641	. . .	. . .	. . .	. . .	. . .	. . .	. . .	. . .
General government	4 642	. . .	. . .	. . .	. . .	. . .	. . .	. . .	. . .
Banks	4 643	. . .	. . .	. . .	. . .	. . .	. . .	. . .	. . .
Other sectors	4 644	. . .	. . .	. . .	. . .	. . .	. . .	. . .	. . .
Liabilities	4 652	. . .	. . .	. . .	. . .	. . .	. . .	. . .	. . .
Equity securities	4 660	. . .	. . .	. . .	. . .	. . .	. . .	. . .	. . .
Banks	4 663	. . .	. . .	. . .	. . .	. . .	. . .	. . .	. . .
Other sectors	4 664	. . .	. . .	. . .	. . .	. . .	. . .	. . .	. . .
Debt securities	4 669	. . .	. . .	. . .	. . .	. . .	. . .	. . .	. . .
Bonds and notes	4 670	. . .	. . .	. . .	. . .	. . .	. . .	. . .	. . .
Monetary authorities	4 671	. . .	. . .	. . .	. . .	. . .	. . .	. . .	. . .
General government	4 672	. . .	. . .	. . .	. . .	. . .	. . .	. . .	. . .
Banks	4 673	. . .	. . .	. . .	. . .	. . .	. . .	. . .	. . .
Other sectors	4 674	. . .	. . .	. . .	. . .	. . .	. . .	. . .	. . .
Money market instruments	4 680	. . .	. . .	. . .	. . .	. . .	. . .	. . .	. . .
Monetary authorities	4 681	. . .	. . .	. . .	. . .	. . .	. . .	. . .	. . .
General government	4 682	. . .	. . .	. . .	. . .	. . .	. . .	. . .	. . .
Banks	4 683	. . .	. . .	. . .	. . .	. . .	. . .	. . .	. . .
Other sectors	4 684	. . .	. . .	. . .	. . .	. . .	. . .	. . .	. . .
Financial derivatives	4 690	. . .	. . .	. . .	. . .	. . .	. . .	. . .	. . .
Monetary authorities	4 691	. . .	. . .	. . .	. . .	. . .	. . .	. . .	. . .
General government	4 692	. . .	. . .	. . .	. . .	. . .	. . .	. . .	. . .
Banks	4 693	. . .	. . .	. . .	. . .	. . .	. . .	. . .	. . .
Other sectors	4 694	. . .	. . .	. . .	. . .	. . .	. . .	. . .	. . .

Table 2 (Concluded). STANDARD PRESENTATION, 1988–95
(Millions of U.S. dollars)

	Code	1988	1989	1990	1991	1992	1993	1994	1995
C. OTHER INVESTMENT	4 700 . .	650.3	166.0	44.9	40.1	–124.4	111.4	–55.5	. . .
Assets	4 703 . .	**42.1**	**–278.3**	**–285.1**	**–14.2**	**–27.2**	**–7.8**	**–258.8**	**. . .**
Trade credits	4 706 . .	. . .	–125.1	–281.6	–11.3	–30.2	–8.8	–239.0	. . .
General government: long-term	4 708 . .	. . .	. . .	. . .	. . .	. . .	. . .	. . .	. . .
General government: short-term	4 709 . .	. . .	. . .	. . .	. . .	. . .	. . .	. . .	. . .
Other sectors: long-term	4 711 . .	. . .	. . .	. . .	. . .	. . .	. . .	. . .	. . .
Other sectors: short-term	4 712 . .	. . .	–125.1	–281.6	–11.3	–30.2	–8.8	–239.0	. . .
Loans	4 714 . .	6.2	–43.8	–13.4	–3.5	–3.8	–3.5	21.1	. . .
Monetary authorities: long-term	4 717 . .	. . .	. . .	. . .	. . .	. . .	. . .	. . .	. . .
Monetary authorities: short-term	4 718 . .	. . .	. . .	. . .	. . .	. . .	. . .	. . .	. . .
General government: long-term	4 720 . .	. . .	. . .	. . .	. . .	. . .	. . .	. . .	. . .
General government: short-term	4 721 . .	. . .	. . .	. . .	. . .	. . .	. . .	. . .	. . .
Banks: long-term	4 723 . .	. . .	. . .	. . .	. . .	. . .	. . .	. . .	. . .
Banks: short-term	4 724 . .	. . .	. . .	. . .	. . .	. . .	. . .	. . .	. . .
Other sectors: long-term	4 726 . .	6.2	–43.8	–13.4	–3.5	–3.8	–3.5	21.1	. . .
Other sectors: short-term	4 727 . .	. . .	. . .	. . .	. . .	. . .	. . .	. . .	. . .
Currency and deposits	4 730 . .	35.9	–109.5	10.0	.7	6.8	4.6	–41.1	. . .
Monetary authorities	4 731 . .	. . .	. . .	. . .	. . .	. . .	. . .	. . .	. . .
General government	4 732 . .	. . .	. . .	. . .	. . .	. . .	. . .	. . .	. . .
Banks	4 733 . .	–6.1	–36.4	10.0	.7	6.8	4.6	–41.1	. . .
Other sectors	4 734 . .	42.0	–73.1	. . .	. . .	. . .	. . .	. . .	. . .
Other assets	4 736 . .	. . .	. . .	. . .	. . .	. . .	. . .	.2	. . .
Monetary authorities: long-term	4 738 . .	. . .	. . .	. . .	. . .	. . .	. . .	. . .	. . .
Monetary authorities: short-term	4 739 . .	. . .	. . .	. . .	. . .	. . .	. . .	. . .	. . .
General government: long-term	4 741 . .	. . .	. . .	. . .	. . .	. . .	. . .	. . .	. . .
General government: short-term	4 742 . .	. . .	. . .	. . .	. . .	. . .	. . .	. . .	. . .
Banks: long-term	4 744 . .	. . .	. . .	. . .	. . .	. . .	. . .	.2	. . .
Banks: short-term	4 745 . .	. . .	. . .	. . .	. . .	. . .	. . .	. . .	. . .
Other sectors: long-term	4 747 . .	. . .	. . .	. . .	. . .	. . .	. . .	. . .	. . .
Other sectors: short-term	4 748 . .	. . .	. . .	. . .	. . .	. . .	. . .	. . .	. . .
Liabilities	4 753 . .	**608.2**	**444.3**	**330.0**	**54.3**	**–97.2**	**119.2**	**203.3**	**. . .**
Trade credits	4 756 . .	20.4	4.1	136.3	1.4	23.4	56.9	65.4	. . .
General government: long-term	4 758 . .	. . .	. . .	. . .	. . .	. . .	. . .	. . .	. . .
General government: short-term	4 759 . .	. . .	. . .	. . .	. . .	. . .	. . .	. . .	. . .
Other sectors: long-term	4 761 . .	. . .	. . .	. . .	. . .	. . .	. . .	. . .	. . .
Other sectors: short-term	4 762 . .	20.4	4.1	136.3	1.4	23.4	56.9	65.4	. . .
Loans	4 764 . .	580.2	301.1	–300.5	–252.3	–351.8	–284.1	1,429.4	. . .
Use of Fund credit and loans from the Fund	4 766 . .	74.6	5.0	–5.9	–19.4	–36.3	–35.9	40.9	. . .
Monetary authorities: other long-term	4 767 . .	. . .	. . .	. . .	. . .	. . .	. . .	. . .	. . .
Monetary authorities: short-term	4 768 . .	–18.1	–44.7	–3.2	. . .	. . .	. . .	. . .	. . .
General government: long-term	4 770 . .	288.1	223.0	–187.7	–149.2	–236.1	–174.1	–133.1	. . .
General government: short-term	4 771 . .	. . .	. . .	. . .	. . .	. . .	. . .	1,572.6	. . .
Banks: long-term	4 773 . .	. . .	. . .	. . .	. . .	. . .	. . .	. . .	. . .
Banks: short-term	4 774 . .	. . .	. . .	. . .	. . .	. . .	. . .	. . .	. . .
Other sectors: long-term	4 776 . .	235.7	117.7	–103.7	–83.7	–79.3	–74.2	–51.0	. . .
Other sectors: short-term	4 777 . .	. . .	. . .	. . .	. . .	. . .	. . .	. . .	. . .
Currency and deposits	4 780 . .	–32.6	16.6	–2.8	8.5	–.8	–4.6	–18.6	. . .
Monetary authorities	4 781 . .	. . .	. . .	–31.8	–2.9	1.9	–6.4	–26.3	. . .
General government	4 782 . .	. . .	. . .	. . .	. . .	. . .	. . .	. . .	. . .
Banks	4 783 . .	–32.6	16.6	29.0	11.3	–2.6	1.8	7.7	. . .
Other sectors	4 784 . .	. . .	. . .	. . .	. . .	. . .	. . .	. . .	. . .
Other liabilities	4 786 . .	40.2	122.6	496.9	296.7	232.0	351.0	–1,272.9	. . .
Monetary authorities: long-term	4 788 . .	. . .	. . .	. . .	. . .	. . .	. . .	. . .	. . .
Monetary authorities: short-term	4 789 . .	. . .	106.0	496.9	296.7	232.0	420.3	–1,265.8	. . .
General government: long-term	4 791 . .	. . .	. . .	. . .	. . .	. . .	. . .	. . .	. . .
General government: short-term	4 792 . .	. . .	. . .	. . .	. . .	. . .	. . .	. . .	. . .
Banks: long-term	4 794 . .	. . .	. . .	. . .	. . .	. . .	. . .	. . .	. . .
Banks: short-term	4 795 . .	. . .	. . .	. . .	. . .	. . .	. . .	. . .	. . .
Other sectors: long-term	4 797 . .	. . .	. . .	. . .	. . .	. . .	. . .	. . .	. . .
Other sectors: short-term	4 798 . .	40.2	16.6	. . .	. . .	. . .	–69.2	–7.0	. . .
D. RESERVE ASSETS	4 800 . .	–55.7	29.8	–219.3	–54.0	246.3	67.5	–167.4	. . .
Monetary gold	4 810 . .	. . .	. . .	. . .	. . .	–1.9	–1.1	.5	. . .
Special drawing rights	4 820 . .	2.2	8.2	.5	–5.9	6.0	. . .	–.2	. . .
Reserve position in the Fund	4 830 . .	. . .	. . .	. . .	. . .	. . .	. . .	. . .	. . .
Foreign exchange	4 840 . .	–57.8	24.7	–220.5	–47.6	242.2	68.5	–167.7	. . .
Other claims	4 880 . .	. . .	–3.1	.7	–.5	. . .	. . .	. . .	. . .
NET ERRORS AND OMISSIONS	4 998 . .	**–101.9**	**35.0**	**–38.0**	**8.6**	**–55.1**	**–13.6**	**6.7**	**. . .**

Table 1. ANALYTIC PRESENTATION, FISCAL YEARS 1988–95 ENDING JUNE 30
(Millions of U.S. dollars)

	Code	1988	1989	1990	1991	1992	1993	1994	1995
A. Current Account [1]	4 993 Y.	**26.50**	**15.02**	**21.63**	**13.15**	**37.16**	**–5.32**	**8.17**	**–8.19**
Goods: exports f.o.b	2 100 ..	83.06	100.20	110.62	142.87	146.95	157.03	124.97	122.96
Goods: imports f.o.b	3 100 ..	–105.92	–125.35	–140.51	–185.00	–177.76	–214.46	–181.62	–162.53
Balance on Goods	4 100 ..	*–22.86*	*–25.16*	*–29.88*	*–42.13*	*–30.81*	*–57.43*	*–56.65*	*–39.57*
Services: credit	2 200 ..	62.21	65.73	57.48	80.53	80.86	79.57	90.47	53.71
Services: debit	3 200 ..	–48.17	–50.60	–51.83	–72.23	–66.93	–74.56	–67.04	–69.25
Balance on Goods and Services	4 991 ..	*–8.83*	*–10.03*	*–24.23*	*–33.83*	*–16.89*	*–52.42*	*–33.22*	*–55.11*
Income: credit	2 300 ..	1.44	2.01	1.59	3.78	4.85	5.82	4.87	4.37
Income: debit	3 300 ..	–13.24	–15.81	–13.04	–11.30	–7.31	–5.11	–5.14	–9.58
Balance on Goods, Services, and Income	4 992 ..	*–20.62*	*–23.84*	*–35.67*	*–41.35*	*–19.35*	*–51.71*	*–33.50*	*–60.32*
Current transfers: credit	2 379 Y.	54.45	46.36	59.98	58.58	60.51	49.99	45.85	55.81
Current transfers: debit	3 379 ..	–7.33	–7.51	–2.67	–4.08	–4.00	–3.60	–4.18	–3.68
B. Capital Account [1]	4 994 Y.	**...**	**...**	**...**	**...**	**...**	**...**	**...**	**...**
Capital account: credit	2 994 Y.	...	...	...	...	...	...	...	...
Capital account: debit	3 994 ..	...	...	...	...	...	...	...	...
Total, Groups A Plus B	4 010 ..	*26.50*	*15.02*	*21.63*	*13.15*	*37.16*	*–5.32*	*8.17*	*–8.19*
C. Financial Account [1]	4 995 X.	**9.63**	**9.48**	**–6.09**	**20.76**	**18.71**	**39.39**	**33.13**	**24.77**
Direct investment abroad	4 505 ..	...	...	...	...	...	...	...	...
Direct investment in The Gambia	4 555 Y.	1.17	14.79	...	10.20	6.16	11.07	9.81	7.78
Portfolio investment assets	4 602 ..	...	...	...	...	...	...	...	...
Equity securities	4 610 ..	...	...	...	...	...	...	...	...
Debt securities	4 619 ..	...	...	...	...	...	...	...	...
Portfolio investment liabilities	4 652 Y.	...	...	...	...	...	...	...	...
Equity securities	4 660 Y.	...	...	...	...	...	...	...	...
Debt securities	4 669 Y.	...	...	...	...	...	...	...	...
Other investment assets	4 703 ..	1.63	–2.42	–1.04	–.60	–1.52	1.40	3.79	–3.66
Monetary authorities	4 703 .A	...	...	...	...	...	...	...	...
General government	4 703 .B	...	...	...	...	...	...	...	...
Banks	4 703 .C	1.63	–2.42	–1.04	–.60	–1.52	1.40	3.79	–3.66
Other sectors	4 703 .D	...	...	...	...	...	...	...	...
Other investment liabilities	4 753 X.	6.83	–2.89	–5.05	11.17	14.07	26.92	19.54	20.65
Monetary authorities	4 753 XA	...	...	...	...	...	...	...	...
General government	4 753 YB	6.39	–4.14	–4.85	11.64	13.82	23.12	17.79	22.60
Banks	4 753 YC	1.02	1.39	.81	–.32	.47	3.80	1.75	–1.95
Other sectors	4 753 YD	–.57	–.15	–1.01	–.15	–.22	...	...	...
Total, Groups A Through C	4 020 ..	*36.13*	*24.49*	*15.54*	*33.91*	*55.87*	*34.07*	*41.31*	*16.58*
D. Net Errors and Omissions	4 998 ..	**–11.29**	**–20.84**	**–11.71**	**–16.66**	**–36.65**	**–22.72**	**–35.12**	**–15.63**
Total, Groups A Through D	4 030 ..	*24.83*	*3.65*	*3.83*	*17.26*	*19.22*	*11.35*	*6.19*	*.95*
E. Reserves and Related Items	4 040 ..	**–24.83**	**–3.65**	**–3.83**	**–17.26**	**–19.22**	**–11.35**	**–6.19**	**–.95**
Reserve assets	4 800 ..	–30.07	3.91	–2.86	–25.64	–35.34	–8.92	–3.30	4.23
Use of Fund credit and loans	4 766 ..	2.39	3.52	4.13	–1.76	.28	–2.42	–2.89	–5.17
Liabilities constituting foreign authorities' reserves	4 900 ..	...	...	...	...	...	...	...	...
Exceptional financing	4 920 ..	2.85	–11.08	–5.10	10.14	15.84	...	...	...
Conversion rates: dalasis per U.S. dollar	0 101 ..	**6.7493**	**7.0338**	**8.1313**	**7.9407**	**9.1360**	**8.8475**	**9.4936**	**9.4790**

[1] Excludes components that have been classified in the categories of Group E.

Table 2. STANDARD PRESENTATION, FISCAL YEARS 1988–95 ENDING JUNE 30
(Millions of U.S. dollars)

	Code	1988	1989	1990	1991	1992	1993	1994	1995
CURRENT ACCOUNT	4 993 . .	**32.06**	**16.72**	**23.42**	**13.15**	**37.16**	**–5.32**	**8.17**	**–8.19**
A. GOODS	4 100 . .	–22.86	–25.16	–29.88	–42.13	–30.81	–57.43	–56.65	–39.57
Credit	2 100 . .	**83.06**	**100.20**	**110.62**	**142.87**	**146.95**	**157.03**	**124.97**	**122.96**
General merchandise: exports f.o.b.	2 110 . .	83.06	100.20	110.62	142.87	146.95	157.03	124.97	122.96
Goods for processing: exports f.o.b.	2 150 . .	. . .	. . .	. . .	. . .	. . .	. . .	. . .	. . .
Repairs on goods	2 160 . .	. . .	. . .	. . .	. . .	. . .	. . .	. . .	. . .
Goods procured in ports by carriers	2 170 . .	. . .	. . .	. . .	. . .	. . .	. . .	. . .	. . .
Nonmonetary gold	2 180 . .	. . .	. . .	. . .	. . .	. . .	. . .	. . .	. . .
Debit	3 100 . .	**–105.92**	**–125.35**	**–140.51**	**–185.00**	**–177.76**	**–214.46**	**–181.62**	**–162.53**
General merchandise: imports f.o.b.	3 110 . .	–105.92	–125.35	–140.51	–185.00	–177.76	–214.46	–181.62	–162.53
Goods for processing: imports f.o.b.	3 150 . .	. . .	. . .	. . .	. . .	. . .	. . .	. . .	. . .
Repairs on goods	3 160 . .	. . .	. . .	. . .	. . .	. . .	. . .	. . .	. . .
Goods procured in ports by carriers	3 170 . .	. . .	. . .	. . .	. . .	. . .	. . .	. . .	. . .
Nonmonetary gold	3 180 . .	. . .	. . .	. . .	. . .	. . .	. . .	. . .	. . .
B. SERVICES	4 200 . .	14.03	15.12	5.65	8.31	13.93	5.00	23.43	–15.54
Total credit	2 200 . .	*62.21*	*65.73*	*57.48*	*80.53*	*80.86*	*79.57*	*90.47*	*53.71*
Total debit	3 200 . .	*–48.17*	*–50.60*	*–51.83*	*–72.23*	*–66.93*	*–74.56*	*–67.04*	*–69.25*
Transportation services, credit	2 205 . .	**4.61**	**4.96**	**4.66**	**8.23**	**9.45**	**9.07**	**7.87**	**8.31**
Passenger	2 205 BA	. . .	. . .	. . .	. . .	. . .	. . .	. . .	. . .
Freight	2 205 BB	*.96*	*.78*	*.33*	*.37*	*.34*	*.81*	*.88*	*.96*
Other	2 205 BC	*3.64*	*4.18*	*4.33*	*7.86*	*9.11*	*8.26*	*6.99*	*7.36*
Sea transport, passenger	2 207 . .	. . .	. . .	. . .	. . .	. . .	. . .	. . .	. . .
Sea transport, freight	2 208 . .	. . .	. . .	. . .	. . .	. . .	. . .	. . .	. . .
Sea transport, other	2 209 . .	. . .	. . .	. . .	. . .	. . .	. . .	. . .	7.36
Air transport, passenger	2 211 . .	. . .	. . .	. . .	. . .	. . .	. . .	. . .	. . .
Air transport, freight	2 212 . .	. . .	. . .	. . .	. . .	. . .	. . .	. . .	. . .
Air transport, other	2 213 . .	. . .	. . .	. . .	. . .	. . .	. . .	. . .	. . .
Other transport, passenger	2 215 . .	. . .	. . .	. . .	. . .	. . .	. . .	. . .	. . .
Other transport, freight	2 216 . .	. . .	. . .	. . .	. . .	. . .	. . .	. . .	. . .
Other transport, other	2 217 . .	. . .	. . .	. . .	. . .	. . .	. . .	. . .	. . .
Transportation services, debit	3 205 . .	**–21.65**	**–24.58**	**–22.62**	**–35.25**	**–33.74**	**–35.99**	**–30.71**	**–27.93**
Passenger	3 205 BA	*–1.69*	*–.93*	*–1.96*	*–2.01*	*–1.81*	*–1.92*	*–1.79*	*–1.85*
Freight	3 205 BB	*–19.03*	*–22.52*	*–20.66*	*–33.23*	*–31.93*	*–32.28*	*–27.33*	*–24.40*
Other	3 205 BC	*–.93*	*–1.14*	. . .	. . .	. . .	*–1.79*	*–1.58*	*–1.68*
Sea transport, passenger	3 207 . .	. . .	. . .	. . .	. . .	. . .	. . .	. . .	. . .
Sea transport, freight	3 208 . .	. . .	. . .	. . .	. . .	. . .	. . .	. . .	. . .
Sea transport, other	3 209 . .	. . .	. . .	. . .	. . .	. . .	. . .	. . .	–1.68
Air transport, passenger	3 211 . .	. . .	. . .	. . .	. . .	. . .	. . .	. . .	. . .
Air transport, freight	3 212 . .	. . .	. . .	. . .	. . .	. . .	. . .	. . .	. . .
Air transport, other	3 213 . .	. . .	. . .	. . .	. . .	. . .	. . .	. . .	. . .
Other transport, passenger	3 215 . .	. . .	. . .	. . .	. . .	. . .	. . .	. . .	. . .
Other transport, freight	3 216 . .	. . .	. . .	. . .	. . .	. . .	. . .	. . .	. . .
Other transport, other	3 217 . .	. . .	. . .	. . .	. . .	. . .	. . .	. . .	. . .
Travel, credit	2 236 . .	**43.10**	**42.56**	**46.46**	**55.45**	**56.24**	**53.95**	**66.29**	**28.14**
Business travel	2 237 . .	. . .	. . .	. . .	. . .	. . .	. . .	. . .	. . .
Personal travel	2 240 . .	. . .	. . .	. . .	. . .	. . .	. . .	. . .	. . .
Travel, debit	3 236 . .	**–4.89**	**–4.65**	**–8.02**	**–14.69**	**–12.70**	**–13.85**	**–13.55**	**–14.25**
Business travel	3 237 . .	. . .	. . .	. . .	. . .	. . .	. . .	. . .	. . .
Personal travel	3 240 . .	. . .	. . .	. . .	. . .	. . .	. . .	. . .	. . .
Other services, credit	2 200 BA	**14.50**	**18.20**	**6.36**	**16.86**	**15.16**	**16.54**	**16.31**	**17.26**
Communications	2 245 . .	. . .	. . .	. . .	. . .	. . .	. . .	. . .	. . .
Construction	2 249 . .	. . .	. . .	. . .	. . .	. . .	. . .	. . .	. . .
Insurance	2 253 . .	.11	.09	.04	.04	.04	.09	.10	.11
Financial	2 260 . .	. . .	. . .	. . .	. . .	. . .	. . .	. . .	. . .
Computer and information	2 262 . .	. . .	. . .	. . .	. . .	. . .	. . .	. . .	. . .
Royalties and licence fees	2 266 . .	. . .	. . .	. . .	. . .	. . .	. . .	. . .	. . .
Other business services	2 268 . .	1.93	1.92	1.72	1.83	1.64	1.75	1.69	1.79
Personal, cultural, and recreational	2 287 . .	. . .	. . .	. . .	. . .	. . .	. . .	. . .	. . .
Government, n.i.e.	2 291 . .	12.46	16.19	4.60	14.99	13.48	14.70	14.52	15.36
Other services, debit	3 200 BA	**–21.63**	**–21.37**	**–21.19**	**–22.29**	**–20.49**	**–24.73**	**–22.78**	**–27.07**
Communications	3 245 . .	. . .	. . .	. . .	. . .	. . .	. . .	. . .	. . .
Construction	3 249 . .	. . .	. . .	. . .	. . .	. . .	. . .	. . .	. . .
Insurance	3 253 . .	–1.90	–2.25	–3.14	–3.32	–3.19	–3.50	–2.97	–2.71
Financial	3 260 . .	. . .	. . .	. . .	. . .	. . .	. . .	. . .	. . .
Computer and information	3 262 . .	. . .	. . .	. . .	. . .	. . .	. . .	. . .	. . .
Royalties and licence fees	3 266 . .	. . .	. . .	. . .	. . .	. . .	. . .	. . .	. . .
Other business services	3 268 . .	–3.10	–2.87	–.96	–1.29	–1.58	–1.72	–1.70	–1.97
Personal, cultural, and recreational	3 287 . .	. . .	. . .	. . .	. . .	. . .	. . .	. . .	. . .
Government, n.i.e.	3 291 . .	–16.63	–16.25	–17.09	–17.68	–15.72	–19.50	–18.12	–22.39

Table 2 (Continued). STANDARD PRESENTATION, FISCAL YEARS 1988–95 ENDING JUNE 30
(Millions of U.S. dollars)

	Code		1988	1989	1990	1991	1992	1993	1994	1995
C. INCOME	4 300	. .	−11.80	−13.80	−11.44	−7.52	−2.46	.71	−.27	−5.21
Total credit	2 300	. .	*1.44*	*2.01*	*1.59*	*3.78*	*4.85*	*5.82*	*4.87*	*4.37*
Total debit	3 300	. .	*−13.24*	*−15.81*	*−13.04*	*−11.30*	*−7.31*	*−5.11*	*−5.14*	*−9.58*
Compensation of employees, credit	2 310	. .	**. . .**	**. . .**	**. . .**	**. . .**	**. . .**	**. . .**	**. . .**	**. . .**
Compensation of employees, debit	3 310	. .	**. . .**	**. . .**	**. . .**	**. . .**	**. . .**	**. . .**	**. . .**	**. . .**
Investment income, credit	2 320	. .	**1.44**	**2.01**	**1.59**	**3.78**	**4.85**	**5.82**	**4.87**	**4.37**
Direct investment income	2 330	. .	. . .	. . .	. . .	. . .	. . .	. . .	. . .	. . .
Dividends and distributed branch profits	2 332	. .	. . .	. . .	. . .	. . .	. . .	. . .	. . .	. . .
Reinvested earnings and undistributed branch profits	2 333	. .	. . .	. . .	. . .	. . .	. . .	. . .	. . .	. . .
Income on debt (interest)	2 334	. .	. . .	. . .	. . .	. . .	. . .	. . .	. . .	. . .
Portfolio investment income	2 339	. .	. . .	. . .	. . .	. . .	. . .	. . .	. . .	. . .
Income on equity	2 340	. .	. . .	. . .	. . .	. . .	. . .	. . .	. . .	. . .
Income on bonds and notes	2 350	. .	. . .	. . .	. . .	. . .	. . .	. . .	. . .	. . .
Income on money market instruments and financial derivatives	2 360	. .	. . .	. . .	. . .	. . .	. . .	. . .	. . .	. . .
Other investment income	2 370	. .	1.44	2.01	1.59	3.78	4.85	5.82	4.87	4.37
Investment income, debit	3 320	. .	**−13.24**	**−15.81**	**−13.04**	**−11.30**	**−7.31**	**−5.11**	**−5.14**	**−9.58**
Direct investment income	3 330	. .	.56	. . .	. . .	. . .	. . .	. . .	. . .	. . .
Dividends and distributed branch profits	3 332	. .	−.24	. . .	. . .	. . .	. . .	. . .	. . .	. . .
Reinvested earnings and undistributed branch profits	3 333	. .	.80	. . .	. . .	. . .	. . .	. . .	. . .	. . .
Income on debt (interest)	3 334	. .	. . .	. . .	. . .	. . .	. . .	. . .	. . .	. . .
Portfolio investment income	3 339	. .	. . .	. . .	. . .	. . .	. . .	. . .	. . .	. . .
Income on equity	3 340	. .	. . .	. . .	. . .	. . .	. . .	. . .	. . .	. . .
Income on bonds and notes	3 350	. .	. . .	. . .	. . .	. . .	. . .	. . .	. . .	. . .
Income on money market instruments and financial derivatives	3 360	. .	. . .	. . .	. . .	. . .	. . .	. . .	. . .	. . .
Other investment income	3 370	. .	−13.80	−15.81	−13.04	−11.30	−7.31	−5.11	−5.14	−9.58
D. CURRENT TRANSFERS	4 379	. .	52.69	40.56	59.10	54.50	56.51	46.39	41.67	52.12
Credit	2 379	. .	**60.01**	**48.07**	**61.77**	**58.58**	**60.51**	**49.99**	**45.85**	**55.81**
General government	2 380	. .	42.44	36.23	44.97	40.94	44.88	33.89	30.00	30.53
Other sectors	2 390	. .	17.57	11.84	16.80	17.64	15.64	16.10	15.85	25.28
Workers' remittances	2 391	. .	. . .	. . .	. . .	. . .	. . .	. . .	. . .	. . .
Other current transfers	2 392	. .	17.57	11.84	16.80	17.64	15.64	16.10	15.85	25.28
Debit	3 379	. .	**−7.33**	**−7.51**	**−2.67**	**−4.08**	**−4.00**	**−3.60**	**−4.18**	**−3.68**
General government	3 380	. .	−2.53	−2.35	. . .	−1.56	−1.65	−1.11	−1.81	−1.26
Other sectors	3 390	. .	−4.79	−5.16	−2.67	−2.52	−2.35	−2.49	−2.37	−2.43
Workers' remittances	3 391	. .	. . .	. . .	. . .	. . .	. . .	. . .	. . .	. . .
Other current transfers	3 392	. .	−4.79	−5.16	−2.67	−2.52	−2.35	−2.49	−2.37	−2.43
CAPITAL AND FINANCIAL ACCOUNT	4 996	. .	**−20.77**	**4.12**	**−11.71**	**3.50**	**−.51**	**28.04**	**26.94**	**23.83**
CAPITAL ACCOUNT	4 994	. .	**2.00**	**. . .**	**. . .**	**3.61**	**2.88**	**. . .**	**. . .**	**. . .**
Total credit	2 994	. .	*2.00*	. . .	. . .	*3.61*	*2.88*	. . .	. . .	. . .
Total debit	3 994	. .	. . .	. . .	. . .	. . .	. . .	. . .	. . .	. . .
Capital transfers, credit	2 400	. .	**2.00**	**. . .**	**. . .**	**3.61**	**2.88**	**. . .**	**. . .**	**. . .**
General government	2 401	. .	2.00	. . .	. . .	3.61	2.88	. . .	. . .	. . .
Debt forgiveness	2 402	. .	2.00	. . .	. . .	3.61	2.88	. . .	. . .	. . .
Other capital transfers	2 410	. .	. . .	. . .	. . .	. . .	. . .	. . .	. . .	. . .
Other sectors	2 430	. .	. . .	. . .	. . .	. . .	. . .	. . .	. . .	. . .
Migrants' transfers	2 431	. .	. . .	. . .	. . .	. . .	. . .	. . .	. . .	. . .
Debt forgiveness	2 432	. .	. . .	. . .	. . .	. . .	. . .	. . .	. . .	. . .
Other capital transfers	2 440	. .	. . .	. . .	. . .	. . .	. . .	. . .	. . .	. . .
Capital transfers, debit	3 400	. .	**. . .**	**. . .**	**. . .**	**. . .**	**. . .**	**. . .**	**. . .**	**. . .**
General government	3 401	. .	. . .	. . .	. . .	. . .	. . .	. . .	. . .	. . .
Debt forgiveness	3 402	. .	. . .	. . .	. . .	. . .	. . .	. . .	. . .	. . .
Other capital transfers	3 410	. .	. . .	. . .	. . .	. . .	. . .	. . .	. . .	. . .
Other sectors	3 430	. .	. . .	. . .	. . .	. . .	. . .	. . .	. . .	. . .
Migrants' transfers	3 431	. .	. . .	. . .	. . .	. . .	. . .	. . .	. . .	. . .
Debt forgiveness	3 432	. .	. . .	. . .	. . .	. . .	. . .	. . .	. . .	. . .
Other capital transfers	3 440	. .	. . .	. . .	. . .	. . .	. . .	. . .	. . .	. . .
Nonproduced nonfinancial assets, credit	2 480	. .	**. . .**	**. . .**	**. . .**	**. . .**	**. . .**	**. . .**	**. . .**	**. . .**
Nonproduced nonfinancial assets, debit	3 480	. .	**. . .**	**. . .**	**. . .**	**. . .**	**. . .**	**. . .**	**. . .**	**. . .**

Table 2 (Continued). STANDARD PRESENTATION, FISCAL YEARS 1988–95 ENDING JUNE 30
(Millions of U.S. dollars)

	Code	1988	1989	1990	1991	1992	1993	1994	1995
FINANCIAL ACCOUNT	4 995 . .	**–22.77**	**4.12**	**–11.71**	**–.11**	**–3.39**	**28.04**	**26.94**	**23.83**
A. DIRECT INVESTMENT	4 500 . .	1.17	14.79	...	10.20	6.16	11.07	9.81	7.78
Direct investment abroad	4 505 . .	...	...	...	...	...	...	...	...
Equity capital	4 510 . .	...	...	...	...	...	...	...	...
Claims on affiliated enterprises	4 515 . .	...	...	...	...	...	...	...	...
Liabilities to affiliated enterprises	4 520 . .	...	...	...	...	...	...	...	...
Reinvested earnings	4 525 . .	...	...	...	...	...	...	...	...
Other capital	4 530 . .	...	...	...	...	...	...	...	...
Claims on affiliated enterprises	4 535 . .	...	...	...	...	...	...	...	...
Liabilities to affiliated enterprises	4 540 . .	...	...	...	...	...	...	...	...
Direct investment in The Gambia	4 555 . .	**1.17**	**14.79**	...	**10.20**	**6.16**	**11.07**	**9.81**	**7.78**
Equity capital	4 560 . .	1.97	14.79	...	10.20	6.16	11.07	9.81	7.78
Claims on direct investors	4 565 . .	...	...	...	...	...	...	...	...
Liabilities to direct investors	4 570 . .	...	...	...	...	...	...	...	...
Reinvested earnings	4 575 . .	–.80	...	...	...	...	...	...	...
Other capital	4 580 . .	...	...	...	...	...	...	...	...
Claims on direct investors	4 585 . .	...	...	...	...	...	...	...	...
Liabilities to direct investors	4 590 . .	...	...	...	...	...	...	...	...
B. PORTFOLIO INVESTMENT	4 600 . .	...	...	...	...	...	...	...	...
Assets	4 602 . .	...	...	...	...	...	...	...	...
Equity securities	4 610 . .	...	...	...	...	...	...	...	...
Monetary authorities	4 611 . .	...	...	...	...	...	...	...	...
General government	4 612 . .	...	...	...	...	...	...	...	...
Banks	4 613 . .	...	...	...	...	...	...	...	...
Other sectors	4 614 . .	...	...	...	...	...	...	...	...
Debt securities	4 619 . .	...	...	...	...	...	...	...	...
Bonds and notes	4 620 . .	...	...	...	...	...	...	...	...
Monetary authorities	4 621 . .	...	...	...	...	...	...	...	...
General government	4 622 . .	...	...	...	...	...	...	...	...
Banks	4 623 . .	...	...	...	...	...	...	...	...
Other sectors	4 624 . .	...	...	...	...	...	...	...	...
Money market instruments	4 630 . .	...	...	...	...	...	...	...	...
Monetary authorities	4 631 . .	...	...	...	...	...	...	...	...
General government	4 632 . .	...	...	...	...	...	...	...	...
Banks	4 633 . .	...	...	...	...	...	...	...	...
Other sectors	4 634 . .	...	...	...	...	...	...	...	...
Financial derivatives	4 640 . .	...	...	...	...	...	...	...	...
Monetary authorities	4 641 . .	...	...	...	...	...	...	...	...
General government	4 642 . .	...	...	...	...	...	...	...	...
Banks	4 643 . .	...	...	...	...	...	...	...	...
Other sectors	4 644 . .	...	...	...	...	...	...	...	...
Liabilities	4 652 . .	...	...	...	...	...	...	...	...
Equity securities	4 660 . .	...	...	...	...	...	...	...	...
Banks	4 663 . .	...	...	...	...	...	...	...	...
Other sectors	4 664 . .	...	...	...	...	...	...	...	...
Debt securities	4 669 . .	...	...	...	...	...	...	...	...
Bonds and notes	4 670 . .	...	...	...	...	...	...	...	...
Monetary authorities	4 671 . .	...	...	...	...	...	...	...	...
General government	4 672 . .	...	...	...	...	...	...	...	...
Banks	4 673 . .	...	...	...	...	...	...	...	...
Other sectors	4 674 . .	...	...	...	...	...	...	...	...
Money market instruments	4 680 . .	...	...	...	...	...	...	...	...
Monetary authorities	4 681 . .	...	...	...	...	...	...	...	...
General government	4 682 . .	...	...	...	...	...	...	...	...
Banks	4 683 . .	...	...	...	...	...	...	...	...
Other sectors	4 684 . .	...	...	...	...	...	...	...	...
Financial derivatives	4 690 . .	...	...	...	...	...	...	...	...
Monetary authorities	4 691 . .	...	...	...	...	...	...	...	...
General government	4 692 . .	...	...	...	...	...	...	...	...
Banks	4 693 . .	...	...	...	...	...	...	...	...
Other sectors	4 694 . .	...	...	...	...	...	...	...	...

Table 2 (Concluded). STANDARD PRESENTATION, FISCAL YEARS 1988–95 ENDING JUNE 30
(Millions of U.S. dollars)

	Code	1988	1989	1990	1991	1992	1993	1994	1995
C. OTHER INVESTMENT	4 700	6.12	–14.58	–8.85	15.33	25.79	25.90	20.43	11.82
Assets	4 703	**1.63**	**–2.42**	**–1.04**	**–.60**	**–1.52**	**1.40**	**3.79**	**–3.66**
Trade credits	4 706	. . .	. . .	. . .	. . .	. . .	. . .	. . .	. . .
General government: long-term	4 708	. . .	. . .	. . .	. . .	. . .	. . .	. . .	. . .
General government: short-term	4 709	. . .	. . .	. . .	. . .	. . .	. . .	. . .	. . .
Other sectors: long-term	4 711	. . .	. . .	. . .	. . .	. . .	. . .	. . .	. . .
Other sectors: short-term	4 712	. . .	. . .	. . .	. . .	. . .	. . .	. . .	. . .
Loans	4 714	. . .	. . .	. . .	. . .	. . .	. . .	. . .	. . .
Monetary authorities: long-term	4 717	. . .	. . .	. . .	. . .	. . .	. . .	. . .	. . .
Monetary authorities: short-term	4 718	. . .	. . .	. . .	. . .	. . .	. . .	. . .	. . .
General government: long-term	4 720	. . .	. . .	. . .	. . .	. . .	. . .	. . .	. . .
General government: short-term	4 721	. . .	. . .	. . .	. . .	. . .	. . .	. . .	. . .
Banks: long-term	4 723	. . .	. . .	. . .	. . .	. . .	. . .	. . .	. . .
Banks: short-term	4 724	. . .	. . .	. . .	. . .	. . .	. . .	. . .	. . .
Other sectors: long-term	4 726	. . .	. . .	. . .	. . .	. . .	. . .	. . .	. . .
Other sectors: short-term	4 727	. . .	. . .	. . .	. . .	. . .	. . .	. . .	. . .
Currency and deposits	4 730	1.63	–2.42	–1.04	–.60	–1.52	1.40	3.79	–3.66
Monetary authorities	4 731	. . .	. . .	. . .	. . .	. . .	. . .	. . .	. . .
General government	4 732	. . .	. . .	. . .	. . .	. . .	. . .	. . .	. . .
Banks	4 733	1.63	–2.42	–1.04	–.60	–1.52	1.40	3.79	–3.66
Other sectors	4 734	. . .	. . .	. . .	. . .	. . .	. . .	. . .	. . .
Other assets	4 736	. . .	. . .	. . .	. . .	. . .	. . .	. . .	. . .
Monetary authorities: long-term	4 738	. . .	. . .	. . .	. . .	. . .	. . .	. . .	. . .
Monetary authorities: short-term	4 739	. . .	. . .	. . .	. . .	. . .	. . .	. . .	. . .
General government: long-term	4 741	. . .	. . .	. . .	. . .	. . .	. . .	. . .	. . .
General government: short-term	4 742	. . .	. . .	. . .	. . .	. . .	. . .	. . .	. . .
Banks: long-term	4 744	. . .	. . .	. . .	. . .	. . .	. . .	. . .	. . .
Banks: short-term	4 745	. . .	. . .	. . .	. . .	. . .	. . .	. . .	. . .
Other sectors: long-term	4 747	. . .	. . .	. . .	. . .	. . .	. . .	. . .	. . .
Other sectors: short-term	4 748	. . .	. . .	. . .	. . .	. . .	. . .	. . .	. . .
Liabilities	4 753	**4.50**	**–12.16**	**–7.82**	**15.94**	**27.31**	**24.50**	**16.64**	**15.47**
Trade credits	4 756	. . .	. . .	. . .	. . .	. . .	. . .	. . .	. . .
General government: long-term	4 758	. . .	. . .	. . .	. . .	. . .	. . .	. . .	. . .
General government: short-term	4 759	. . .	. . .	. . .	. . .	. . .	. . .	. . .	. . .
Other sectors: long-term	4 761	. . .	. . .	. . .	. . .	. . .	. . .	. . .	. . .
Other sectors: short-term	4 762	. . .	. . .	. . .	. . .	. . .	. . .	. . .	. . .
Loans	4 764	12.70	1.62	10.78	16.58	26.85	20.70	14.90	17.43
Use of Fund credit and loans from the Fund	4 766	2.39	3.52	4.13	–1.76	.28	–2.42	–2.89	–5.17
Monetary authorities: other long-term	4 767	. . .	. . .	. . .	. . .	. . .	. . .	. . .	. . .
Monetary authorities: short-term	4 768	. . .	. . .	. . .	. . .	. . .	. . .	. . .	. . .
General government: long-term	4 770	10.89	–1.75	7.66	18.49	26.78	23.12	17.79	22.60
General government: short-term	4 771	. . .	. . .	. . .	. . .	. . .	. . .	. . .	. . .
Banks: long-term	4 773	. . .	. . .	. . .	. . .	. . .	. . .	. . .	. . .
Banks: short-term	4 774	. . .	. . .	. . .	. . .	. . .	. . .	. . .	. . .
Other sectors: long-term	4 776	–.57	–.15	–1.01	–.15	–.22	. . .	. . .	. . .
Other sectors: short-term	4 777	. . .	. . .	. . .	. . .	. . .	. . .	. . .	. . .
Currency and deposits	4 780	1.02	1.39	.81	–.32	.47	3.80	1.75	–1.95
Monetary authorities	4 781	. . .	. . .	. . .	. . .	. . .	. . .	. . .	. . .
General government	4 782	. . .	. . .	. . .	. . .	. . .	. . .	. . .	. . .
Banks	4 783	1.02	1.39	.81	–.32	.47	3.80	1.75	–1.95
Other sectors	4 784	. . .	. . .	. . .	. . .	. . .	. . .	. . .	. . .
Other liabilities	4 786	–9.22	–15.17	–19.40	–.32	. . .	. . .	. . .	. . .
Monetary authorities: long-term	4 788	. . .	. . .	. . .	. . .	. . .	. . .	. . .	. . .
Monetary authorities: short-term	4 789	–9.22	–15.17	–19.40	–.32	. . .	. . .	. . .	. . .
General government: long-term	4 791	. . .	. . .	. . .	. . .	. . .	. . .	. . .	. . .
General government: short-term	4 792	. . .	. . .	. . .	. . .	. . .	. . .	. . .	. . .
Banks: long-term	4 794	. . .	. . .	. . .	. . .	. . .	. . .	. . .	. . .
Banks: short-term	4 795	. . .	. . .	. . .	. . .	. . .	. . .	. . .	. . .
Other sectors: long-term	4 797	. . .	. . .	. . .	. . .	. . .	. . .	. . .	. . .
Other sectors: short-term	4 798	. . .	. . .	. . .	. . .	. . .	. . .	. . .	. . .
D. RESERVE ASSETS	4 800	–30.07	3.91	–2.86	–25.64	–35.34	–8.92	–3.30	4.23
Monetary gold	4 810	. . .	. . .	. . .	. . .	. . .	. . .	. . .	. . .
Special drawing rights	4 820	–2.11	2.29	–1.01	–.07	–.05	.98	.18	.25
Reserve position in the Fund	4 830	. . .	. . .	. . .	.03	. . .	–2.01	–.01	. . .
Foreign exchange	4 840	–27.96	1.61	–1.85	–25.60	–35.30	–7.88	–3.47	3.97
Other claims	4 880	. . .	. . .	. . .	. . .	. . .	. . .	. . .	. . .
NET ERRORS AND OMISSIONS	4 998	**–11.29**	**–20.84**	**–11.71**	**–16.66**	**–36.65**	**–22.72**	**–35.12**	**–15.63**

Part 3 of the *Yearbook* contains descriptions of the methodologies, compilation practices, and sources used to compile these data.

Table 1. ANALYTIC PRESENTATION, 1988–95
(Billions of U.S. dollars)

	Code	1988	1989	1990	1991	1992	1993	1994	1995
A. Current Account [1]	4 993 Y.	**50.23**	**56.73**	**48.11**	**-17.88**	**-19.39**	**-13.40**	**-20.31**	**-20.98**
Goods: exports f.o.b.	2 100 ..	321.99	340.01	410.92	403.37	430.23	382.49	430.27	523.22
Goods: imports f.o.b.	3 100 ..	-245.35	-264.73	-341.88	-383.45	-401.51	-340.73	-378.59	-457.10
Balance on Goods	4 100 ..	*76.64*	*75.28*	*69.04*	*19.92*	*28.72*	*41.75*	*51.68*	*66.12*
Services: credit	2 200 ..	49.00	51.83	66.57	68.56	73.55	68.43	70.80	86.02
Services: debit	3 200 ..	-61.96	-64.34	-83.78	-89.66	-104.15	-101.50	-110.77	-132.52
Balance on Goods and Services	4 991 ..	*63.68*	*62.77*	*51.84*	*-1.18*	*-1.87*	*8.68*	*11.70*	*19.62*
Income: credit	2 300 ..	36.20	45.62	65.85	74.37	80.68	78.28	78.31	97.26
Income: debit	3 300 ..	-29.75	-31.88	-45.78	-53.41	-63.50	-65.05	-71.51	-96.89
Balance on Goods, Services, and Income	4 992 ..	*70.13*	*76.51*	*71.91*	*19.78*	*15.31*	*21.91*	*18.50*	*19.99*
Current transfers: credit	2 379 Y.	11.68	10.48	13.07	13.42	14.90	13.39	13.90	16.75
Current transfers: debit	3 379 ..	-31.58	-30.25	-36.87	-51.08	-49.60	-48.70	-52.71	-57.72
B. Capital Account [1]	4 994 Y.	**-.01**	**.08**	**-1.33**	**-.65**	**.60**	**.49**	**.15**	**-.65**
Capital account: credit	2 994 Y.	.27	.39	.41	.77	1.12	1.38	1.56	1.68
Capital account: debit	3 994 ..	-.28	-.32	-1.73	-1.41	-.52	-.89	-1.42	-2.33
Total, Groups A Plus B	4 010 ..	*50.22*	*56.81*	*46.78*	*-18.53*	*-18.79*	*-12.92*	*-20.16*	*-21.63*
C. Financial Account [1]	4 995 X.	**-67.56**	**-59.08**	**-54.78**	**5.22**	**51.80**	**15.71**	**25.76**	**33.24**
Direct investment abroad	4 505 ..	-12.07	-15.26	-24.20	-23.72	-19.67	-15.28	-16.69	-34.89
Direct investment in Germany	4 555 Y.	1.02	7.15	2.53	4.11	2.64	1.82	.81	8.94
Portfolio investment assets	4 602 ..	-40.82	-26.63	-15.17	-17.96	-48.06	-32.73	-55.28	-30.26
Equity securities	4 610 ..	-10.18	-4.97	1.06	-8.64	-40.45	-16.88	-21.13	.94
Debt securities	4 619 ..	-30.64	-21.66	-16.23	-9.31	-7.61	-15.85	-34.15	-31.20
Portfolio investment liabilities	4 652 Y.	4.17	24.40	13.44	42.25	80.00	152.14	22.10	56.99
Equity securities	4 660 Y.	3.02	12.08	-1.90	1.64	-2.80	7.54	3.72	-1.81
Debt securities	4 669 Y.	1.16	12.32	15.34	40.61	82.80	144.60	18.37	58.80
Other investment assets	4 703 ..	-34.92	-90.85	-74.67	-24.28	-7.29	-131.42	-.85	-64.49
Monetary authorities	4 703 .A	...	...	...	...	-.02	-.01	.17	.28
General government	4 703 .B	-2.58	-4.58	-7.93	-5.17	-6.36	-7.07	2.39	-7.48
Banks	4 703 .C	-15.16	-47.13	-38.20	-2.19	3.63	-88.21	14.99	-54.44
Other sectors	4 703 .D	-17.18	-39.15	-28.54	-16.92	-4.54	-36.13	-18.40	-2.84
Other investment liabilities	4 753 X.	15.06	42.12	43.28	24.82	44.18	41.18	75.67	96.94
Monetary authorities	4 753 XA	3.62	12.91	.40	-5.81	-9.53	-1.57	-2.04	-2.65
General government	4 753 YB	-5.80	-2.80	.24	-.55	-1.19	3.73	1.95	3.74
Banks	4 753 YC	11.24	22.58	26.22	10.51	48.01	35.33	69.17	83.67
Other sectors	4 753 YD	6.01	9.43	16.42	20.67	6.88	3.69	6.59	12.18
Total, Groups A Through C	4 020 ..	*-17.34*	*-2.27*	*-8.00*	*-13.31*	*33.01*	*2.80*	*5.60*	*11.61*
D. Net Errors and Omissions	4 998 ..	**1.74**	**5.12**	**15.26**	**7.12**	**4.16**	**-17.00**	**-7.64**	**-4.38**
Total, Groups A Through D	4 030 ..	*-15.60*	*2.86*	*7.25*	*-6.18*	*37.18*	*-14.20*	*-2.04*	*7.22*
E. Reserves and Related Items	4 040 ..	**15.60**	**-2.86**	**-7.25**	**6.18**	**-37.18**	**14.20**	**2.04**	**-7.22**
Reserve assets	4 800 ..	15.60	-2.86	-7.25	6.18	-37.18	14.20	2.04	-7.22
Use of Fund credit and loans	4 766 ..	...	...	...	...	...	...	...	...
Liabilities constituting foreign authorities' reserves	4 900 ..	...	...	...	...	...	...	...	...
Exceptional financing	4 920 ..	...	...	...	...	...	...	...	...
Conversion rates: deutsche mark per U.S. dollar	0 101 ..	**1.7562**	**1.8800**	**1.6157**	**1.6595**	**1.5617**	**1.6533**	**1.6228**	**1.4331**

[1] Excludes components that have been classified in the categories of Group E.

Table 2. STANDARD PRESENTATION, 1988–95

(Billions of U.S. dollars)

	Code			1988	1989	1990	1991	1992	1993	1994	1995
CURRENT ACCOUNT	4	993	. .	**50.23**	**56.73**	**48.11**	**–17.88**	**–19.39**	**–13.40**	**–20.31**	**–20.98**
A. GOODS	4	100	. .	76.64	75.28	69.04	19.92	28.72	41.75	51.68	66.12
Credit	2	100	. .	**321.99**	**340.01**	**410.92**	**403.37**	**430.23**	**382.49**	**430.27**	**523.22**
General merchandise: exports f.o.b.	2	110	. .	. . .	. . .	389.31	378.88	405.62	361.72	405.75	494.81
Goods for processing: exports f.o.b.	2	150	. .	. . .	. . .	16.92	19.03	19.45	16.27	19.10	22.86
Repairs on goods	2	160	. .	. . .	. . .	4.19	4.65	4.51	3.96	4.63	4.72
Goods procured in ports by carriers	2	170	. .	. . .	. . .	. . .	. . .	. . .	. . .	. . .	. . .
Nonmonetary gold	2	180	. .	. . .	. . .	.50	.82	.66	.55	.79	.83
Debit	3	100	. .	**–245.35**	**–264.73**	**–341.88**	**–383.45**	**–401.51**	**–340.73**	**–378.59**	**–457.10**
General merchandise: imports f.o.b.	3	110	. .	. . .	. . .	–319.30	–357.44	–374.54	–317.38	–351.26	–424.12
Goods for processing: imports f.o.b.	3	150	. .	. . .	. . .	–18.41	–21.59	–22.41	–18.55	–22.21	–27.36
Repairs on goods	3	160	. .	. . .	. . .	–2.72	–3.20	–3.15	–3.28	–3.78	–4.19
Goods procured in ports by carriers	3	170	. .	. . .	. . .	. . .	. . .	. . .	. . .	. . .	. . .
Nonmonetary gold	3	180	. .	. . .	. . .	–1.45	–1.22	–1.40	–1.52	–1.34	–1.44
B. SERVICES	4	200	. .	–12.97	–12.50	–17.21	–21.10	–30.60	–33.07	–39.97	–46.50
Total credit	2	200	. .	*49.00*	*51.83*	*66.57*	*68.56*	*73.55*	*68.43*	*70.80*	*86.02*
Total debit	3	200	. .	*–61.96*	*–64.34*	*–83.78*	*–89.66*	*–104.15*	*–101.50*	*–110.77*	*–132.52*
Transportation services, credit	2	205	. .	**11.29**	**11.82**	**14.98**	**15.64**	**17.17**	**16.24**	**17.09**	**19.35**
Passenger	2	205	BA	*3.65*	*3.93*	*5.17*	*5.30*	*5.83*	*5.24*	*5.39*	*6.17*
Freight	2	205	BB	*5.16*	*5.36*	*6.44*	*6.82*	*7.51*	*7.42*	*8.01*	*9.12*
Other	2	205	BC	*2.48*	*2.53*	*3.37*	*3.53*	*3.83*	*3.58*	*3.69*	*4.05*
Sea transport, passenger	2	207	. .	.04	.04	.06	.06	.05	.03	.02	.03
Sea transport, freight	2	208	. .	2.75	2.84	3.31	3.26	3.77	4.01	4.49	5.08
Sea transport, other	2	209	. .	.91	.93	1.35	1.12	1.11	1.09	.97	1.02
Air transport, passenger	2	211	. .	3.04	3.37	4.48	4.53	4.93	4.54	4.82	5.77
Air transport, freight	2	212	. .	1.03	1.06	1.23	1.37	1.38	1.28	1.23	1.35
Air transport, other	2	213	. .	1.18	1.18	1.50	1.90	2.21	2.06	2.27	2.53
Other transport, passenger	2	215	. .	.56	.52	.63	.70	.85	.67	.55	.38
Other transport, freight	2	216	. .	1.38	1.46	1.89	2.18	2.37	2.13	2.30	2.68
Other transport, other	2	217	. .	.39	.41	.52	.52	.51	.43	.46	.50
Transportation services, debit	3	205	. .	**–13.36**	**–13.78**	**–17.99**	**–19.84**	**–21.94**	**–20.46**	**–22.11**	**–26.12**
Passenger	3	205	BA	*–4.11*	*–4.02*	*–5.32*	*–5.67*	*–6.33*	*–5.68*	*–5.83*	*–6.62*
Freight	3	205	BB	*–5.75*	*–5.89*	*–7.33*	*–8.93*	*–9.59*	*–8.91*	*–9.96*	*–12.03*
Other	3	205	BC	*–3.51*	*–3.87*	*–5.34*	*–5.24*	*–6.02*	*–5.88*	*–6.31*	*–7.47*
Sea transport, passenger	3	207	. .	–.47	–.48	–.59	–.64	–.43	–.49	–.56	–.41
Sea transport, freight	3	208	. .	–3.19	–3.17	–3.54	–4.32	–4.30	–3.83	–4.33	–5.02
Sea transport, other	3	209	. .	–1.56	–1.71	–2.15	–2.10	–2.38	–2.33	–2.75	–3.40
Air transport, passenger	3	211	. .	–3.12	–3.12	–4.18	–4.47	–5.14	–4.58	–4.78	–5.90
Air transport, freight	3	212	. .	–.14	–.29	–.33	–.36	–.28	–.26	–.26	–.34
Air transport, other	3	213	. .	–.94	–1.01	–1.75	–1.81	–2.23	–2.16	–2.08	–2.36
Other transport, passenger	3	215	. .	–.52	–.43	–.55	–.56	–.76	–.62	–.50	–.31
Other transport, freight	3	216	. .	–2.42	–2.44	–3.45	–4.26	–5.01	–4.82	–5.37	–6.68
Other transport, other	3	217	. .	–1.00	–1.15	–1.43	–1.33	–1.40	–1.39	–1.49	–1.71
Travel, credit	2	236	. .	**9.72**	**10.15**	**13.60**	**14.15**	**15.11**	**14.02**	**14.00**	**16.25**
Business travel	2	237	. .	. . .	. . .	. . .	. . .	. . .	. . .	. . .	. . .
Personal travel	2	240	. .	. . .	. . .	. . .	. . .	. . .	. . .	. . .	. . .
Travel, debit	3	236	. .	**–25.81**	**–25.95**	**–33.14**	**–34.71**	**–40.71**	**–40.02**	**–44.53**	**–50.75**
Business travel	3	237	. .	. . .	. . .	. . .	. . .	. . .	. . .	. . .	. . .
Personal travel	3	240	. .	. . .	. . .	. . .	. . .	. . .	. . .	. . .	. . .
Other services, credit	2	200	BA	**28.00**	**29.86**	**38.00**	**38.77**	**41.27**	**38.17**	**39.71**	**50.43**
Communications	2	245	. .	1.19	1.06	1.41	1.17	2.18	.54	.68	2.04
Construction	2	249	. .	2.77	2.75	3.29	3.89	4.39	4.15	3.76	5.01
Insurance	2	253	. .	2.84	3.01	3.74	4.28	5.47	5.44	7.24	8.67
Financial	2	260	. .	.75	.72	.75	.92	1.37	1.85	1.44	2.42
Computer and information	2	262	. .	.23	.25	.26	.36	.48	.70	.88	1.36
Royalties and licence fees	2	266	. .	1.27	1.34	1.99	1.89	2.07	2.04	2.18	2.78
Other business services	2	268	. .	8.88	10.48	14.40	14.60	15.01	15.26	16.23	21.44
Personal, cultural, and recreational	2	287	. .	.06	.08	.12	.10	.09	.14	.15	.16
Government, n.i.e.	2	291	. .	10.02	10.18	12.04	11.55	10.20	8.06	7.15	6.56
Other services, debit	3	200	BA	**–22.80**	**–24.60**	**–32.65**	**–35.12**	**–41.50**	**–41.01**	**–44.13**	**–55.65**
Communications	3	245	. .	–1.42	–1.22	–1.69	–1.63	–2.70	–1.32	–1.48	–2.95
Construction	3	249	. .	–2.18	–2.21	–2.98	–3.35	–3.92	–4.25	–4.54	–5.87
Insurance	3	253	. .	–3.04	–3.37	–4.49	–5.20	–6.24	–5.95	–7.34	–8.84
Financial	3	260	. .	–.12	–.20	–.30	–.30	–.35	–.41	–.44	–.55
Computer and information	3	262	. .	–.23	–.29	–.35	–.45	–.57	–.83	–.87	–1.41
Royalties and licence fees	3	266	. .	–2.74	–3.03	–3.80	–4.24	–4.50	–4.43	–4.50	–5.44
Other business services	3	268	. .	–11.20	–12.36	–16.38	–17.17	–20.20	–20.29	–21.34	–26.71
Personal, cultural, and recreational	3	287	. .	–.43	–.45	–.88	–1.07	–1.18	–1.48	–1.77	–1.97
Government, n.i.e.	3	291	. .	–1.43	–1.48	–1.79	–1.70	–1.83	–2.05	–1.85	–1.89

Table 2 (Continued). STANDARD PRESENTATION, 1988–95
(Billions of U.S. dollars)

	Code	1988	1989	1990	1991	1992	1993	1994	1995
C. INCOME	4 300 . .	6.45	13.74	20.07	20.96	17.18	13.23	6.79	.37
Total credit	2 300 . .	*36.20*	*45.62*	*65.85*	*74.37*	*80.68*	*78.28*	*78.31*	*97.26*
Total debit	3 300 . .	*-29.75*	*-31.88*	*-45.78*	*-53.41*	*-63.50*	*-65.05*	*-71.51*	*-96.89*
Compensation of employees, credit	2 310 . .	**4.02**	**3.95**	**5.10**	**5.03**	**5.15**	**4.62**	**4.34**	**4.46**
Compensation of employees, debit	3 310 . .	**-2.12**	**-2.05**	**-3.17**	**-3.74**	**-4.80**	**-5.14**	**-5.35**	**-6.01**
Investment income, credit	2 320 . .	**32.18**	**41.67**	**60.74**	**69.34**	**75.53**	**73.66**	**73.97**	**92.81**
Direct investment income	2 330 . .	2.81	4.70	5.77	5.67	4.62	3.59	5.17	7.55
Dividends and distributed branch profits	2 332 . .	1.50	1.65	2.41	1.74	3.48	4.32	4.89	5.68
Reinvested earnings and undistributed branch profits	2 333 . .	1.02	2.66	3.10	3.63	.97	-.91	. . .	1.40
Income on debt (interest)	2 334 . .	.29	.39	.27	.29	.18	.18	.28	.47
Portfolio investment income	2 339 . .	7.33	10.40	14.60	15.86	18.10	18.90	20.92	23.48
Income on equity	2 340 . .	.91	1.41	2.11	2.37	3.97	6.90	7.08	7.35
Income on bonds and notes	2 350 . .	. . .	. . .	. . .	. . .	. . .	. . .	. . .	. . .
Income on money market instruments and financial derivatives	2 360 . .	. . .	. . .	. . .	. . .	. . .	. . .	. . .	. . .
Other investment income	2 370 . .	22.05	26.57	40.37	47.82	52.81	51.16	47.87	61.78
Investment income, debit	3 320 . .	**-27.63**	**-29.84**	**-42.61**	**-49.67**	**-58.70**	**-59.90**	**-66.17**	**-90.89**
Direct investment income	3 330 . .	-5.59	-5.54	-6.28	-6.53	-7.26	-2.79	-1.71	-8.19
Dividends and distributed branch profits	3 332 . .	-5.28	-3.03	-7.03	-4.19	-6.33	-3.24	-6.31	-7.23
Reinvested earnings and undistributed branch profits	3 333 . .	-.06	-1.92	1.43	-1.51	. . .	1.81	6.17	.70
Income on debt (interest)	3 334 . .	-.25	-.59	-.67	-.83	-.93	-1.36	-1.57	-1.66
Portfolio investment income	3 339 . .	-7.94	-7.17	-9.91	-11.83	-15.87	-22.70	-29.56	-34.02
Income on equity	3 340 . .	-1.57	-1.64	-2.56	-2.31	-2.66	-3.43	-4.05	-5.04
Income on bonds and notes	3 350 . .	. . .	. . .	. . .	. . .	. . .	. . .	. . .	. . .
Income on money market instruments and financial derivatives	3 360 . .	. . .	. . .	. . .	. . .	. . .	. . .	. . .	. . .
Other investment income	3 370 . .	-14.10	-17.13	-26.42	-31.30	-35.56	-34.41	-34.90	-48.68
D. CURRENT TRANSFERS	4 379 . .	-19.90	-19.77	-23.80	-37.67	-34.70	-35.32	-38.81	-40.97
Credit	2 379 . .	**11.68**	**10.48**	**13.07**	**13.42**	**14.90**	**13.39**	**13.90**	**16.75**
General government	2 380 . .	9.97	8.01	10.06	10.55	12.03	10.45	10.66	12.88
Other sectors	2 390 . .	1.71	2.47	3.02	2.87	2.87	2.93	3.24	3.88
Workers' remittances	2 391 . .	. . .	. . .	. . .	. . .	. . .	. . .	. . .	. . .
Other current transfers	2 392 . .	1.71	2.47	3.02	2.87	2.87	2.93	3.24	3.88
Debit	3 379 . .	**-31.58**	**-30.25**	**-36.87**	**-51.08**	**-49.60**	**-48.70**	**-52.71**	**-57.72**
General government	3 380 . .	-22.75	-21.20	-25.95	-40.50	-37.16	-36.26	-39.39	-42.46
Other sectors	3 390 . .	-8.82	-9.05	-10.92	-10.58	-12.44	-12.45	-13.32	-15.26
Workers' remittances	3 391 . .	-4.25	-3.99	-4.38	-3.86	-4.38	-4.13	-4.63	-5.31
Other current transfers	3 392 . .	-4.58	-5.06	-6.54	-6.72	-8.05	-8.31	-8.68	-9.96
CAPITAL AND FINANCIAL ACCOUNT	4 996 . .	**-51.97**	**-61.86**	**-63.36**	**10.76**	**15.22**	**30.40**	**27.94**	**25.36**
CAPITAL ACCOUNT	4 994 . .	**-.01**	**.08**	**-1.33**	**-.65**	**.60**	**.49**	**.15**	**-.65**
Total credit	2 994 . .	*.27*	*.39*	*.41*	*.77*	*1.12*	*1.38*	*1.56*	*1.68*
Total debit	3 994 . .	*-.28*	*-.32*	*-1.73*	*-1.41*	*-.52*	*-.89*	*-1.42*	*-2.33*
Capital transfers, credit	2 400 . .	**.27**	**.39**	**.41**	**.77**	**1.12**	**1.38**	**1.56**	**1.68**
General government	2 401 . .	. . .	. . .	. . .	. . .	. . .	. . .	. . .	. . .
Debt forgiveness	2 402 . .	. . .	. . .	. . .	. . .	. . .	. . .	. . .	. . .
Other capital transfers	2 410 . .	. . .	. . .	. . .	. . .	. . .	. . .	. . .	. . .
Other sectors	2 430 . .	.27	.39	.41	.77	1.12	1.38	1.56	1.68
Migrants' transfers	2 431 . .	.02	.02	.02	.01	.01	.01	.02	.02
Debt forgiveness	2 432 . .	. . .	. . .	. . .	. . .	. . .	. . .	. . .	. . .
Other capital transfers	2 440 . .	.26	.37	.39	.75	1.11	1.37	1.55	1.66
Capital transfers, debit	3 400 . .	**-.28**	**-.32**	**-1.73**	**-1.41**	**-.52**	**-.89**	**-1.42**	**-2.33**
General government	3 401 . .	. . .	-.09	-1.42	-1.12	-.16	-.55	-.39	-1.86
Debt forgiveness	3 402 . .	. . .	-.09	-1.42	-1.12	-.16	-.15	-.19	-1.65
Other capital transfers	3 410 . .	. . .	. . .	. . .	. . .	. . .	-.40	-.19	-.21
Other sectors	3 430 . .	-.28	-.22	-.31	-.30	-.37	-.34	-1.03	-.47
Migrants' transfers	3 431 . .	-.28	-.22	-.31	-.30	-.37	-.34	-.41	-.46
Debt forgiveness	3 432 . .	. . .	. . .	. . .	. . .	. . .	. . .	-.62	-.01
Other capital transfers	3 440 . .	. . .	. . .	. . .	. . .	. . .	. . .	. . .	. . .
Nonproduced nonfinancial assets, credit	2 480 . .	. . .	. . .	. . .	. . .	. . .	. . .	. . .	. . .
Nonproduced nonfinancial assets, debit	3 480 . .	. . .	. . .	. . .	. . .	. . .	. . .	. . .	. . .

Table 2 (Continued). STANDARD PRESENTATION, 1988–95
(Billions of U.S. dollars)

	Code		1988	1989	1990	1991	1992	1993	1994	1995
FINANCIAL ACCOUNT	4 995	. .	**–51.96**	**–61.94**	**–62.04**	**11.41**	**14.63**	**29.91**	**27.80**	**26.01**
A. DIRECT INVESTMENT	4 500	. .	–11.05	–8.11	–21.66	–19.61	–17.02	–13.46	–15.87	–25.96
Direct investment abroad	4 505	. .	**–12.07**	**–15.26**	**–24.20**	**–23.72**	**–19.67**	**–15.28**	**–16.69**	**–34.89**
Equity capital	4 510	. .	–9.59	–11.29	–19.55	–18.81	–16.89	–13.92	–14.55	–28.90
Claims on affiliated enterprises	4 515	. .	. . .	. . .	. . .	. . .	. . .	. . .	. . .	. . .
Liabilities to affiliated enterprises	4 520	. .	. . .	. . .	. . .	. . .	. . .	. . .	. . .	. . .
Reinvested earnings	4 525	. .	–1.02	–2.66	–3.10	–3.63	–.97	.91	. . .	–1.40
Other capital	4 530	. .	–1.45	–1.31	–1.54	–1.28	–1.81	–2.26	–2.14	–4.60
Claims on affiliated enterprises	4 535	. .	. . .	. . .	. . .	. . .	. . .	. . .	. . .	. . .
Liabilities to affiliated enterprises	4 540	. .	. . .	. . .	. . .	. . .	. . .	. . .	. . .	. . .
Direct investment in Germany	4 555	. .	**1.02**	**7.15**	**2.53**	**4.11**	**2.64**	**1.82**	**.81**	**8.94**
Equity capital	4 560	. .	–1.56	2.88	3.20	.55	.41	3.55	3.32	6.42
Claims on direct investors	4 565	. .	. . .	. . .	. . .	. . .	. . .	. . .	. . .	. . .
Liabilities to direct investors	4 570	. .	. . .	. . .	. . .	. . .	. . .	. . .	. . .	. . .
Reinvested earnings	4 575	. .	.06	1.92	–1.43	1.51	. . .	–1.81	–6.17	–.70
Other capital	4 580	. .	2.52	2.36	.76	2.05	2.23	.08	3.66	3.22
Claims on direct investors	4 585	. .	. . .	. . .	. . .	. . .	. . .	. . .	. . .	. . .
Liabilities to direct investors	4 590	. .	. . .	. . .	. . .	. . .	. . .	. . .	. . .	. . .
B. PORTFOLIO INVESTMENT	4 600	. .	–36.65	–2.23	–1.74	24.29	31.94	119.41	–33.18	26.74
Assets	4 602	. .	**–40.82**	**–26.63**	**–15.17**	**–17.96**	**–48.06**	**–32.73**	**–55.28**	**–30.26**
Equity securities	4 610	. .	–10.18	–4.97	1.06	–8.64	–40.45	–16.88	–21.13	.94
Monetary authorities	4 611	. .	. . .	. . .	. . .	. . .	. . .	. . .	. . .	. . .
General government	4 612	. .	. . .	. . .	. . .	. . .	. . .	. . .	. . .	. . .
Banks	4 613	. .	. . .	. . .	. . .	. . .	. . .	. . .	. . .	. . .
Other sectors	4 614	. .	. . .	. . .	. . .	. . .	. . .	. . .	. . .	. . .
Debt securities	4 619	. .	–30.64	–21.66	–16.23	–9.31	–7.61	–15.85	–34.15	–31.20
Bonds and notes	4 620	. .	–30.43	–21.20	–14.91	–7.64	–4.15	–7.74	–16.99	–17.02
Monetary authorities	4 621	. .	. . .	. . .	. . .	. . .	. . .	. . .	. . .	. . .
General government	4 622	. .	. . .	. . .	. . .	. . .	. . .	. . .	. . .	. . .
Banks	4 623	. .	. . .	. . .	. . .	. . .	. . .	. . .	. . .	. . .
Other sectors	4 624	. .	. . .	. . .	. . .	. . .	. . .	. . .	. . .	. . .
Money market instruments	4 630	. .	.09	–.06	–.14	–.97	–.12	–.79	–6.61	–8.67
Monetary authorities	4 631	. .	. . .	. . .	. . .	. . .	. . .	. . .	. . .	. . .
General government	4 632	. .	. . .	. . .	. . .	. . .	. . .	. . .	. . .	. . .
Banks	4 633	. .	. . .	. . .	. . .	. . .	. . .	. . .	. . .	. . .
Other sectors	4 634	. .	. . .	. . .	. . .	. . .	. . .	. . .	. . .	. . .
Financial derivatives	4 640	. .	–.30	–.40	–1.18	–.71	–3.35	–7.33	–10.55	–5.51
Monetary authorities	4 641	. .	. . .	. . .	. . .	. . .	. . .	. . .	. . .	. . .
General government	4 642	. .	. . .	. . .	. . .	. . .	. . .	. . .	. . .	. . .
Banks	4 643	. .	. . .	. . .	. . .	. . .	. . .	. . .	. . .	. . .
Other sectors	4 644	. .	. . .	. . .	. . .	. . .	. . .	. . .	. . .	. . .
Liabilities	4 652	. .	**4.17**	**24.40**	**13.44**	**42.25**	**80.00**	**152.14**	**22.10**	**56.99**
Equity securities	4 660	. .	3.02	12.08	–1.90	1.64	–2.80	7.54	3.72	–1.81
Banks	4 663	. .	. . .	. . .	. . .	. . .	. . .	. . .	. . .	. . .
Other sectors	4 664	. .	. . .	. . .	. . .	. . .	. . .	. . .	. . .	. . .
Debt securities	4 669	. .	1.16	12.32	15.34	40.61	82.80	144.60	18.37	58.80
Bonds and notes	4 670	. .	1.17	11.71	13.74	35.21	79.00	137.17	7.16	55.34
Monetary authorities	4 671	. .	.04	–.03	–.04	–.14	–.70	9.51	–7.75	–2.72
General government	4 672	. .	8.53	11.57	10.67	26.42	50.86	93.26	3.32	33.72
Banks	4 673	. .	. . .	. . .	. . .	. . .	. . .	. . .	. . .	. . .
Other sectors	4 674	. .	–7.40	.17	3.11	8.92	28.85	34.41	11.60	24.34
Money market instruments	4 680	. .	. . .	. . .	.45	4.34	.73	.76	–.04	–1.32
Monetary authorities	4 681	. .	. . .	. . .	. . .	. . .	. . .	. . .	. . .	. . .
General government	4 682	. .	. . .	. . .	.45	. . .	–1.39	–.25	–.33	.06
Banks	4 683	. .	. . .	. . .	. . .	. . .	–.04	.33	.47	–.06
Other sectors	4 684	. .	. . .	. . .	. . .	. . .	2.16	.68	–.17	–1.32
Financial derivatives	4 690	. .	–.01	.60	1.15	1.06	3.07	6.67	11.25	4.78
Monetary authorities	4 691	. .	. . .	. . .	. . .	. . .	. . .	. . .	. . .	. . .
General government	4 692	. .	. . .	. . .	. . .	. . .	. . .	. . .	. . .	. . .
Banks	4 693	. .	. . .	. . .	. . .	. . .	. . .	. . .	. . .	. . .
Other sectors	4 694	. .	. . .	. . .	. . .	. . .	. . .	. . .	. . .	. . .

Table 2 (Concluded). STANDARD PRESENTATION, 1988–95
(Billions of U.S. dollars)

	Code		1988	1989	1990	1991	1992	1993	1994	1995
C. OTHER INVESTMENT	4 700	. .	–19.86	–48.73	–31.39	.55	36.89	–90.24	74.82	32.46
Assets	4 703	. .	**–34.92**	**–90.85**	**–74.67**	**–24.28**	**–7.29**	**–131.42**	**–.85**	**–64.49**
Trade credits	4 706	. .	–9.40	–7.98	–4.80	–5.71	17.36	1.77	–7.99	–5.46
General government: long-term	4 708	. .	. . .	. . .	. . .	. . .	. . .	. . .	. . .	. . .
General government: short-term	4 709	. .	. . .	. . .	. . .	. . .	. . .	. . .	. . .	. . .
Other sectors: long-term	4 711	. .	. . .	. . .	. . .	. . .	. . .	. . .	. . .	. . .
Other sectors: short-term	4 712	. .	. . .	. . .	. . .	. . .	. . .	. . .	. . .	. . .
Loans	4 714	. .	–24.54	–81.72	–68.57	–16.70	–22.99	–131.65	8.73	–56.68
Monetary authorities: long-term	4 717	. .	. . .	. . .	. . .	. . .	. . .	. . .	. . .	. . .
Monetary authorities: short-term	4 718	. .	. . .	. . .	. . .	. . .	. . .	. . .	. . .	. . .
General government: long-term	4 720	. .	–2.61	–2.29	–3.37	–1.43	–2.63	–3.96	–3.15	–2.35
General government: short-term	4 721	. .	.02	–2.28	–4.56	–3.74	–3.72	–3.12	5.54	–5.13
Banks: long-term	4 723	. .	1.13	–2.81	–22.71	–13.37	–6.11	–15.84	–13.37	–14.49
Banks: short-term	4 724	. .	–16.28	–44.32	–15.49	11.18	9.74	–72.37	28.36	–39.95
Other sectors: long-term	4 726	. .	–.04	–2.51	–.33	–.93	–.40	–.35	.23	–2.02
Other sectors: short-term	4 727	. .	–6.77	–27.51	–22.11	–8.41	–19.85	–36.01	–9.05	6.99
Currency and deposits	4 730	. .	. . .	. . .	. . .	. . .	. . .	. . .	. . .	. . .
Monetary authorities	4 731	. .	. . .	. . .	. . .	. . .	. . .	. . .	. . .	. . .
General government	4 732	. .	. . .	. . .	. . .	. . .	. . .	. . .	. . .	. . .
Banks	4 733	. .	. . .	. . .	. . .	. . .	. . .	. . .	. . .	. . .
Other sectors	4 734	. .	. . .	. . .	. . .	. . .	. . .	. . .	. . .	. . .
Other assets	4 736	. .	–.98	–1.15	–1.30	–1.87	–1.66	–1.54	–1.60	–2.34
Monetary authorities: long-term	4 738	. .	. . .	. . .	. . .	. . .	. . .	. . .	. . .	. . .
Monetary authorities: short-term	4 739	. .	. . .	. . .	. . .	. . .	. . .	. . .	. . .	. . .
General government: long-term	4 741	. .	. . .	. . .	. . .	. . .	. . .	. . .	. . .	. . .
General government: short-term	4 742	. .	. . .	. . .	. . .	. . .	. . .	. . .	. . .	. . .
Banks: long-term	4 744	. .	. . .	. . .	. . .	. . .	. . .	. . .	. . .	. . .
Banks: short-term	4 745	. .	. . .	. . .	. . .	. . .	. . .	. . .	. . .	. . .
Other sectors: long-term	4 747	. .	. . .	. . .	. . .	. . .	. . .	. . .	. . .	. . .
Other sectors: short-term	4 748	. .	–.98	–1.15	–1.30	–1.87	–1.66	–1.54	–1.60	–2.34
Liabilities	4 753	. .	**15.06**	**42.12**	**43.28**	**24.82**	**44.18**	**41.18**	**75.67**	**96.94**
Trade credits	4 756	. .	4.45	2.55	4.27	2.70	–.84	–1.18	7.38	4.40
General government: long-term	4 758	. .	. . .	. . .	. . .	. . .	. . .	. . .	. . .	. . .
General government: short-term	4 759	. .	. . .	. . .	. . .	. . .	. . .	. . .	. . .	. . .
Other sectors: long-term	4 761	. .	. . .	. . .	. . .	. . .	. . .	. . .	. . .	. . .
Other sectors: short-term	4 762	. .	. . .	. . .	. . .	. . .	. . .	. . .	. . .	. . .
Loans	4 764	. .	7.02	26.70	38.88	27.98	54.67	43.95	69.78	95.88
Use of Fund credit and loans from the Fund	4 766	. .	. . .	. . .	. . .	. . .	. . .	. . .	. . .	. . .
Monetary authorities: other long-term	4 767	. .	. . .	. . .	. . .	. . .	. . .	. . .	. . .	. . .
Monetary authorities: short-term	4 768	. .	. . .	. . .	. . .	. . .	. . .	. . .	. . .	. . .
General government: long-term	4 770	. .	–6.19	–2.66	–.83	–.28	–1.75	2.09	–1.11	1.65
General government: short-term	4 771	. .	.40	–.14	1.07	–.28	.56	1.65	3.06	2.09
Banks: long-term	4 773	. .	5.55	9.66	10.63	–3.17	14.92	23.04	23.13	42.21
Banks: short-term	4 774	. .	5.68	12.92	15.58	13.68	33.10	12.29	46.04	41.46
Other sectors: long-term	4 776	. .	1.49	.63	2.77	3.54	4.65	5.00	–1.61	.11
Other sectors: short-term	4 777	. .	.10	6.29	9.65	14.49	3.19	–.11	.27	8.35
Currency and deposits	4 780	. .	. . .	. . .	. . .	. . .	. . .	. . .	. . .	. . .
Monetary authorities	4 781	. .	. . .	. . .	. . .	. . .	. . .	. . .	. . .	. . .
General government	4 782	. .	. . .	. . .	. . .	. . .	. . .	. . .	. . .	. . .
Banks	4 783	. .	. . .	. . .	. . .	. . .	. . .	. . .	. . .	. . .
Other sectors	4 784	. .	. . .	. . .	. . .	. . .	. . .	. . .	. . .	. . .
Other liabilities	4 786	. .	3.59	12.86	.14	–5.86	–9.66	–1.59	–1.49	–3.34
Monetary authorities: long-term	4 788	. .	. . .	. . .	. . .	. . .	. . .	. . .	. . .	. . .
Monetary authorities: short-term	4 789	. .	. . .	. . .	. . .	. . .	. . .	. . .	. . .	. . .
General government: long-term	4 791	. .	. . .	. . .	. . .	. . .	. . .	. . .	. . .	. . .
General government: short-term	4 792	. .	. . .	. . .	. . .	. . .	. . .	. . .	. . .	. . .
Banks: long-term	4 794	. .	. . .	. . .	. . .	. . .	. . .	. . .	. . .	. . .
Banks: short-term	4 795	. .	. . .	. . .	. . .	. . .	. . .	. . .	. . .	. . .
Other sectors: long-term	4 797	. .	. . .	. . .	. . .	. . .	. . .	. . .	. . .	. . .
Other sectors: short-term	4 798	. .	. . .	. . .	. . .	. . .	. . .	. . .	. . .	. . .
D. RESERVE ASSETS	4 800	. .	15.60	–2.86	–7.25	6.18	–37.18	14.20	2.04	–7.22
Monetary gold	4 810	. .	. . .	. . .	. . .	. . .	. . .	. . .	. . .	. . .
Special drawing rights	4 820	. .	.01	.01	.07	–.03	1.01	–.12	–.09	–.86
Reserve position in the Fund	4 830	. .	.35	.22	.22	–.48	–.82	.29	.16	–1.13
Foreign exchange	4 840	. .	15.23	–3.09	–7.54	6.70	–37.37	14.03	1.96	–5.23
Other claims	4 880	. .	. . .	. . .	. . .	. . .	. . .	. . .	. . .	. . .
NET ERRORS AND OMISSIONS	4 998	. .	**1.74**	**5.12**	**15.26**	**7.12**	**4.16**	**–17.00**	**–7.64**	**–4.38**

Part 3 of the *Yearbook* contains descriptions of the methodologies, compilation practices, and sources used to compile these data.

Table 3. INTERNATIONAL INVESTMENT POSITION (End–period stocks), 1988–95

(Billions of U.S. dollars)

	Code	1988	1989	1990	1991	1992	1993	1994	1995
ASSETS	8 995 C.	689.50	863.59	1,099.97	1,145.81	1,174.69	1,275.97	1,449.19	1,671.91
Direct investment abroad	8 505 . .	**80.20**	**94.99**	**125.95**	**144.08**	**149.61**	**157.65**	**189.77**	**231.41**
Equity capital and reinvested earnings	8 506 . .	...	...	...	...	...	...	...	...
Claims on affiliated enterprises	8 507 . .	...	...	...	...	...	...	...	...
Liabilities to affiliated enterprises	8 508 . .	...	...	...	...	...	...	...	...
Other capital	8 530 . .	...	...	...	...	...	...	...	...
Claims on affiliated enterprises	8 535 . .	...	...	...	...	...	...	...	...
Liabilities to affiliated enterprises	8 540 . .	...	...	...	...	...	...	...	...
Portfolio investment	8 602 . .	**135.51**	**171.29**	**197.75**	**216.38**	**246.48**	**266.83**	**331.75**	**386.13**
Equity securities	8 610 . .	32.96	43.95	42.70	55.07	90.53	108.66	137.58	156.92
Monetary authorities	8 611 . .	...	...	...	...	...	...	...	...
General government	8 612 . .	...	...	...	...	...	...	...	...
Banks	8 613 . .	...	...	...	...	...	...	...	...
Other sectors	8 614 . .	32.96	43.95	42.70	55.07	90.53	108.66	137.58	156.92
Debt securities	8 619 . .	102.54	127.33	155.05	161.31	155.95	158.17	194.17	229.21
Bonds and notes	8 620 . .	101.06	125.80	153.23	159.79	153.33	154.87	183.99	209.96
Monetary authorities	8 621 . .	...	...	...	...	...	...	...	...
General government	8 622 . .	...	...	...	...	...	...	...	...
Banks	8 623 . .	12.57	16.54	25.36	31.25	40.92	50.48	57.81	72.25
Other sectors	8 624 . .	88.49	109.27	127.86	128.54	112.41	104.39	126.17	137.70
Money market instruments	8 630 . .	1.48	1.53	1.82	1.52	2.63	3.30	10.18	19.25
Monetary authorities	8 631 . .	...	...	...	...	...	...	...	...
General government	8 632 . .	...	...	...	...	...	...	...	...
Banks	8 633 . .	.69	.56	.96	.90	.25	.09	.43	1.24
Other sectors	8 634 . .	.79	.97	.86	.62	2.38	3.21	9.76	18.01
Financial derivatives	8 640 . .	...	...	...	...	...	...	...	...
Monetary authorities	8 641 . .	...	...	...	...	...	...	...	...
General government	8 642 . .	...	...	...	...	...	...	...	...
Banks	8 643 . .	...	...	...	...	...	...	...	...
Other sectors	8 644 . .	...	...	...	...	...	...	...	...
Other investment	8 703 . .	**420.61**	**539.87**	**706.64**	**722.83**	**691.02**	**781.91**	**854.32**	**969.75**
Trade credits	8 706 . .	87.09	100.03	123.49	124.19	101.39	92.54	111.02	120.00
General government: long-term	8 708 . .	...	...	...	...	...	...	...	...
General government: short-term	8 709 . .	...	...	...	...	...	...	...	...
Other sectors: long-term	8 711 . .	...	...	...	...	...	...	...	...
Other sectors: short-term	8 712 . .	87.09	100.03	123.49	124.19	101.39	92.54	111.02	120.00
Loans	8 714 . .	242.11	306.87	405.98	408.39	383.87	452.54	473.32	560.34
Monetary authorities: long-term	8 717 . .	1.37	1.43	1.62	1.71	1.62	1.52	1.52	1.36
Monetary authorities: short-term	8 718 . .	...	...	...	...	...	...	...	...
General government: long-term	8 720 . .	35.15	37.91	44.73	45.69	45.77	46.70	55.49	62.32
General government: short-term	8 721 . .	...	...	...	...	...	...	...	...
Banks: long-term	8 723 . .	69.39	76.50	115.57	144.10	141.70	146.23	172.37	195.22
Banks: short-term	8 724 . .	122.33	173.71	224.03	195.93	174.96	238.79	223.04	275.05
Other sectors: long-term	8 726 . .	13.87	17.33	20.02	20.95	19.83	19.30	20.90	26.40
Other sectors: short-term	8 727 . .	...	...	...	...	...	...	...	...
Currency and deposits	8 730 . .	73.09	110.37	150.71	161.83	177.25	208.40	237.22	252.35
Monetary authorities	8 731 . .	...	...	...	...	...	...	...	...
General government	8 732 . .	2.43	4.97	9.96	13.97	16.96	18.97	15.53	21.90
Banks	8 733 . .	...	...	...	...	...	...	...	...
Other sectors	8 734 . .	70.66	105.40	140.75	147.86	160.30	189.43	221.69	230.45
Other assets	8 736 . .	18.32	22.60	26.46	28.44	28.50	28.43	32.76	37.06
Monetary authorities: long-term	8 738 . .	...	...	...	...	...	...	...	...
Monetary authorities: short-term	8 739 . .	...	...	...	...	...	...	...	...
General government: long-term	8 741 . .	6.60	7.28	8.73	9.96	10.33	10.80	12.52	14.11
General government: short-term	8 742 . .	...	...	...	...	...	...	...	...
Banks: long-term	8 744 . .	1.34	1.84	1.90	1.88	1.88	1.86	2.09	2.31
Banks: short-term	8 745 . .	...	...	...	...	...	...	...	...
Other sectors: long-term	8 747 . .	10.04	13.10	15.36	16.10	15.80	15.30	17.66	20.17
Other sectors: short-term	8 748 . .	.34	.38	.48	.50	.49	.46	.49	.47
Reserve assets	8 800 . .	**53.19**	**57.44**	**69.63**	**62.50**	**87.58**	**69.59**	**73.35**	**84.62**
Monetary gold	8 810 . .	7.69	8.06	9.16	9.03	8.48	7.93	8.84	9.55
Special drawing rights	8 820 . .	1.86	1.80	1.88	1.92	.84	.96	1.11	2.00
Reserve position in the Fund	8 830 . .	3.35	3.04	3.06	3.57	4.24	3.95	4.03	5.21
Foreign exchange	8 840 . .	49.52	53.27	62.84	55.77	79.00	63.57	67.56	74.57
Other claims	8 880 . .	–9.22	–8.73	–7.31	–7.78	–4.98	–6.83	–8.19	–6.70

Table 3 (Continued). INTERNATIONAL INVESTMENT POSITION (End–period stocks), 1988–95
(Billions of U.S. dollars)

	Code	1988	1989	1990	1991	1992	1993	1994	1995
LIABILITIES	8 995 D.	480.66	595.02	751.07	817.57	881.01	1,033.19	1,233.14	1,484.48
Direct investment in Germany	8 555 . .	**39.81**	**44.10**	**65.73**	**69.03**	**66.64**	**64.46**	**78.77**	**90.87**
Equity capital and reinvested earnings	8 556 . .	. . .	. . .	. . .	. . .	. . .	. . .	. . .	. . .
Claims on direct investors	8 557 . .	. . .	. . .	. . .	. . .	. . .	. . .	. . .	. . .
Liabilities to direct investors	8 558 . .	. . .	. . .	. . .	. . .	. . .	. . .	. . .	. . .
Other capital	8 580 . .	. . .	. . .	. . .	. . .	. . .	. . .	. . .	. . .
Claims on direct investors	8 585 . .	. . .	. . .	. . .	. . .	. . .	. . .	. . .	. . .
Liabilities to direct investors	8 590 . .	. . .	. . .	. . .	. . .	. . .	. . .	. . .	. . .
Portfolio investment	8 652 . .	**176.16**	**225.39**	**251.78**	**292.20**	**336.68**	**477.30**	**529.55**	**638.09**
Equity securities	8 660 . .	48.32	81.04	74.94	77.56	64.06	88.55	92.99	104.16
Banks	8 663 . .	. . .	. . .	. . .	. . .	. . .	. . .	. . .	. . .
Other sectors	8 664 . .	48.32	81.04	74.94	77.56	64.06	88.55	92.99	104.16
Debt securities	8 669 . .	127.84	144.36	176.84	214.64	272.62	388.75	436.56	533.92
Bonds and notes	8 670 . .	127.84	144.36	176.28	212.26	271.68	388.11	436.21	533.48
Monetary authorities	8 671 . .	. . .	. . .	. . .	. . .	. . .	9.48	2.98	. . .
General government	8 672 . .	104.70	120.91	146.13	172.53	207.25	284.69	319.73	388.60
Banks	8 673 . .	14.28	15.01	20.09	29.50	53.81	83.99	103.79	134.67
Other sectors	8 674 . .	8.85	8.43	10.06	10.23	10.61	9.94	9.71	10.21
Money market instruments	8 680 . .	. . .	. . .	.56	2.39	.94	.64	.35	.44
Monetary authorities	8 681 . .	. . .	. . .	. . .	. . .	. . .	. . .	. . .	. . .
General government	8 682 . .	. . .	. . .	.56	2.39	.94	.64	.35	.44
Banks	8 683 . .	. . .	. . .	. . .	. . .	. . .	. . .	. . .	. . .
Other sectors	8 684 . .	. . .	. . .	. . .	. . .	. . .	. . .	. . .	. . .
Financial derivatives	8 690 . .	. . .	. . .	. . .	. . .	. . .	. . .	. . .	. . .
Monetary authorities	8 691 . .	. . .	. . .	. . .	. . .	. . .	. . .	. . .	. . .
General government	8 692 . .	. . .	. . .	. . .	. . .	. . .	. . .	. . .	. . .
Banks	8 692 . .	. . .	. . .	. . .	. . .	. . .	. . .	. . .	. . .
Other sectors	8 694 . .	. . .	. . .	. . .	. . .	. . .	. . .	. . .	. . .
Other investment	8 753 . .	**264.69**	**325.52**	**433.56**	**456.34**	**477.68**	**491.43**	**624.83**	**755.52**
Trade credits	8 756 . .	46.65	52.29	64.53	66.51	61.81	56.69	71.03	77.92
General government: long-term	8 758 . .	. . .	. . .	. . .	. . .	. . .	. . .	. . .	. . .
General government: short-term	8 759 . .	. . .	. . .	. . .	. . .	. . .	. . .	. . .	. . .
Other sectors: long-term	8 761 . .	. . .	. . .	. . .	. . .	. . .	. . .	. . .	. . .
Other sectors: short-term	8 762 . .	46.65	52.29	64.53	66.51	61.81	56.69	71.03	77.92
Loans	8 764 . .	126.60	150.94	213.80	229.02	241.35	257.05	316.26	385.63
Use of Fund credit and loans from the Fund	8 766 . .	. . .	. . .	. . .	. . .	. . .	. . .	. . .	. . .
Monetary authorities: other long-term	8 767 . .	. . .	. . .	. . .	. . .	. . .	. . .	. . .	. . .
Monetary authorities: short-term	8 768 . .	. . .	. . .	. . .	. . .	. . .	. . .	. . .	. . .
General government: long-term	8 770 . .	. . .	. . .	. . .	. . .	. . .	. . .	. . .	. . .
General government: short-term	8 771 . .	.69	1.02	1.06	.81	1.20	2.13	5.49	6.43
Banks: long-term	8 773 . .	60.92	73.34	110.35	106.13	114.00	129.72	163.97	213.91
Banks: short-term	8 774 . .	. . .	. . .	. . .	. . .	. . .	. . .	. . .	. . .
Other sectors: long-term	8 776 . .	29.84	33.06	42.05	46.42	52.26	55.38	68.31	74.60
Other sectors: short-term	8 777 . .	35.16	43.53	60.34	75.67	73.89	69.82	78.49	90.70
Currency and deposits	8 780 . .	68.26	83.86	109.98	122.39	148.02	154.18	213.08	266.28
Monetary authorities	8 781 . .	. . .	. . .	. . .	. . .	. . .	. . .	. . .	. . .
General government	8 782 . .	. . .	. . .	. . .	. . .	. . .	. . .	. . .	. . .
Banks	8 783 . .	68.26	83.86	109.98	122.39	148.02	154.18	213.08	266.28
Other sectors	8 784 . .	. . .	. . .	. . .	. . .	. . .	. . .	. . .	. . .
Other liabilities	8 786 . .	23.17	38.43	45.24	38.42	26.50	23.51	24.45	25.70
Monetary authorities: long-term	8 788 . .	. . .	. . .	. . .	. . .	. . .	. . .	. . .	. . .
Monetary authorities: short-term	8 789 . .	21.89	36.97	43.68	36.79	25.00	22.01	22.13	23.78
General government: long-term	8 791 . .	.07	.06	.06	.08	.16	.18	.22	.22
General government: short-term	8 792 . .	. . .	. . .	. . .	. . .	. . .	. . .	. . .	. . .
Banks: long-term	8 794 . .	.38	.39	.48	.49	.51	.47	.50	.55
Banks: short-term	8 795 . .	. . .	. . .	. . .	. . .	. . .	. . .	. . .	. . .
Other sectors: long-term	8 797 . .	.83	1.01	1.03	1.06	.84	.85	1.60	1.15
Other sectors: short-term	8 798 . .	. . .	. . .	. . .	. . .	. . .	. . .	. . .	. . .
NET INTERNATIONAL INVESTMENT POSITION	8 995 . .	**208.85**	**268.58**	**348.90**	**328.23**	**293.68**	**242.78**	**216.05**	**187.43**
Conversion rates: deutsche mark per U.S. dollar (end of period)	0 102 . .	**1.7803**	**1.6978**	**1.4940**	**1.5160**	**1.6140**	**1.7263**	**1.5488**	**1.4335**

Table 1. ANALYTIC PRESENTATION, 1988–95
(Millions of U.S. dollars)

	Code	1988	1989	1990	1991	1992	1993	1994	1995
A. Current Account [1]	4 993 Y.	**–65.1**	**–97.8**	**–223.6**	**–250.8**	**–375.3**	**–557.9**	**–263.8**	**. . .**
Goods: exports f.o.b	2 100 . .	881.0	807.2	890.6	997.6	986.4	1,063.7	1,226.8	. . .
Goods: imports f.o.b	3 100 . .	–993.4	–1,002.2	–1,205.0	–1,318.7	–1,456.7	–1,728.0	–1,579.9	. . .
Balance on Goods	4 100 . .	*–112.4*	*–195.0*	*–314.4*	*–321.1*	*–470.3*	*–664.3*	*–353.1*	. . .
Services: credit	2 200 . .	71.4	75.5	79.3	95.1	110.3	136.6	139.4	. . .
Services: debit	3 200 . .	–255.1	–270.9	–285.1	–319.3	–372.2	–428.2	–400.7	. . .
Balance on Goods and Services	4 991 . .	*–296.1*	*–390.4*	*–520.2*	*–545.3*	*–732.2*	*–955.9*	*–614.4*	. . .
Income: credit	2 300 . .	6.3	6.4	13.8	15.2	18.6	19.7	19.9	. . .
Income: debit	3 300 . .	–144.5	–136.9	–133.4	–143.5	–132.9	–140.1	–142.1	. . .
Balance on Goods, Services, and Income	4 992 . .	*–434.3*	*–520.9*	*–639.8*	*–673.6*	*–846.5*	*–1,076.3*	*–736.6*	. . .
Current transfers: credit	2 379 Y.	377.8	432.2	426.3	434.1	484.8	532.0	487.3	. . .
Current transfers: debit	3 379 . .	–8.6	–9.1	–10.1	–11.3	–13.6	–13.6	–14.5	. . .
B. Capital Account [1]	4 994 Y.	**–.7**	**–.8**	**–.5**	**–.9**	**–1.0**	**–1.0**	**–1.0**	**. . .**
Capital account: credit	2 994 Y.	. . .	. . .	. . .	. . .	. . .	. . .	. . .	. . .
Capital account: debit	3 994 . .	–.7	–.8	–.5	–.9	–1.0	–1.0	–1.0	. . .
Total, Groups A Plus B	4 010 . .	*–65.8*	*–98.6*	*–224.1*	*–251.7*	*–376.3*	*–558.9*	*–264.8*	. . .
C. Financial Account [1]	4 995 X.	**209.0**	**178.6**	**259.2**	**338.1**	**321.6**	**648.1**	**511.2**	**. . .**
Direct investment abroad	4 505 . .	. . .	. . .	. . .	. . .	. . .	. . .	. . .	. . .
Direct investment in Ghana	4 555 Y.	5.0	15.0	14.8	20.0	22.5	125.0	233.0	. . .
Portfolio investment assets	4 602 . .	. . .	. . .	. . .	. . .	. . .	. . .	. . .	. . .
Equity securities	4 610 . .	. . .	. . .	. . .	. . .	. . .	. . .	. . .	. . .
Debt securities	4 619 . .	. . .	. . .	. . .	. . .	. . .	. . .	. . .	. . .
Portfolio investment liabilities	4 652 Y.	. . .	. . .	. . .	. . .	. . .	. . .	. . .	. . .
Equity securities	4 660 Y.	. . .	. . .	. . .	. . .	. . .	. . .	. . .	. . .
Debt securities	4 669 Y.	. . .	. . .	. . .	. . .	. . .	. . .	. . .	. . .
Other investment assets	4 703 . .	–.4	–49.8	–76.5	–1.3	–3.5	11.3	–90.1	. . .
Monetary authorities	4 703 .A	. . .	. . .	. . .	. . .	. . .	. . .	. . .	. . .
General government	4 703 .B	.4	4.2	–11.8	–19.6	1.6	12.5	3.2	. . .
Banks	4 703 .C	–.8	–54.0	–64.7	18.3	–5.1	–1.2	–93.3	. . .
Other sectors	4 703 .D	. . .	. . .	. . .	. . .	. . .	. . .	. . .	. . .
Other investment liabilities	4 753 X.	204.4	213.4	320.9	319.4	302.6	511.8	368.3	. . .
Monetary authorities	4 753 XA	–1.9	10.5	–2.3	–4.1	–.3	. . .	. . .	. . .
General government	4 753 YB	179.9	171.2	281.4	354.4	386.5	370.2	295.3	. . .
Banks	4 753 YC	7.4	19.0	–4.0	–6.1	–16.2	44.8	64.8	. . .
Other sectors	4 753 YD	19.0	12.7	45.8	–24.8	–67.4	96.8	8.2	. . .
Total, Groups A Through C	4 020 . .	*143.2*	*80.0*	*35.1*	*86.4*	*–54.7*	*89.2*	*246.4*	. . .
D. Net Errors and Omissions	4 998 . .	**71.2**	**57.7**	**21.3**	**165.2**	**–177.8**	**53.4**	**–153.0**	**. . .**
Total, Groups A Through D	4 030 . .	*214.4*	*137.7*	*56.4*	*251.6*	*–232.5*	*142.6*	*93.4*	. . .
E. Reserves and Related Items	4 040 . .	**–214.4**	**–137.7**	**–56.4**	**–251.6**	**232.5**	**–142.6**	**–93.4**	**. . .**
Reserve assets	4 800 . .	–65.1	–22.3	–53.8	–249.5	234.9	–78.1	–85.7	. . .
Use of Fund credit and loans	4 766 . .	–76.2	–21.0	31.4	–2.1	–2.4	–64.5	–7.7	. . .
Liabilities constituting foreign authorities' reserves	4 900 . .	. . .	. . .	. . .	. . .	. . .	. . .	. . .	. . .
Exceptional financing	4 920 . .	–73.2	–94.4	–34.0	. . .	. . .	. . .	. . .	. . .
Conversion rates: cedis per U.S. dollar	0 101 . .	**202.35**	**270.00**	**326.33**	**367.83**	**437.09**	**649.06**	**956.71**	**1,200.43**

[1] Excludes components that have been classified in the categories of Group E.

Table 2. STANDARD PRESENTATION, 1988–95
(Millions of U.S. dollars)

	Code	1988	1989	1990	1991	1992	1993	1994	1995
CURRENT ACCOUNT	4 993 . .	**–65.1**	**–97.8**	**–223.6**	**–250.8**	**–375.3**	**–557.9**	**–263.8**	**. . .**
A. GOODS	4 100 . .	–112.4	–195.0	–314.4	–321.1	–470.3	–664.3	–353.1	. . .
Credit	2 100 . .	**881.0**	**807.2**	**890.6**	**997.6**	**986.4**	**1,063.7**	**1,226.8**	**. . .**
General merchandise: exports f.o.b.	2 110 . .	712.5	647.3	689.0	693.6	643.0	629.7	678.2	. . .
Goods for processing: exports f.o.b.	2 150 . .	. . .	. . .	. . .	. . .	. . .	. . .	. . .	. . .
Repairs on goods	2 160 . .	. . .	. . .	. . .	. . .	. . .	. . .	. . .	. . .
Goods procured in ports by carriers	2 170 . .	. . .	. . .	. . .	. . .	. . .	. . .	. . .	. . .
Nonmonetary gold	2 180 . .	168.5	159.9	201.6	304.0	343.4	434.0	548.6	. . .
Debit	3 100 . .	**–993.4**	**–1,002.2**	**–1,205.0**	**–1,318.7**	**–1,456.7**	**–1,728.0**	**–1,579.9**	**. . .**
General merchandise: imports f.o.b.	3 110 . .	–993.4	–1,002.2	–1,205.0	–1,318.7	–1,456.7	–1,728.0	–1,579.9	. . .
Goods for processing: imports f.o.b.	3 150 . .	. . .	. . .	. . .	. . .	. . .	. . .	. . .	. . .
Repairs on goods	3 160 . .	. . .	. . .	. . .	. . .	. . .	. . .	. . .	. . .
Goods procured in ports by carriers	3 170 . .	. . .	. . .	. . .	. . .	. . .	. . .	. . .	. . .
Nonmonetary gold	3 180 . .	. . .	. . .	. . .	. . .	. . .	. . .	. . .	. . .
B. SERVICES	4 200 . .	–183.7	–195.4	–205.8	–224.2	–261.9	–291.6	–261.3	. . .
Total credit	2 200 . .	*71.4*	*75.5*	*79.3*	*95.1*	*110.3*	*136.6*	*139.4*	. . .
Total debit	3 200 . .	*–255.1*	*–270.9*	*–285.1*	*–319.3*	*–372.2*	*–428.2*	*–400.7*	. . .
Transportation services, credit	2 205 . .	**34.1**	**36.2**	**38.8**	**49.4**	**58.0**	**78.7**	**80.2**	**. . .**
Passenger	2 205 BA	*12.3*	*11.8*	*10.2*	*14.1*	*13.7*	*20.1*	*18.4*	. . .
Freight	2 205 BB	*15.6*	*17.1*	*18.8*	*22.8*	*27.4*	*32.8*	*33.4*	. . .
Other	2 205 BC	*6.2*	*7.3*	*9.8*	*12.5*	*16.9*	*25.8*	*28.4*	. . .
Sea transport, passenger	2 207 . .	. . .	. . .	. . .	. . .	. . .	. . .	. . .	. . .
Sea transport, freight	2 208 . .	. . .	. . .	. . .	. . .	. . .	. . .	. . .	. . .
Sea transport, other	2 209 . .	. . .	. . .	. . .	. . .	. . .	. . .	. . .	. . .
Air transport, passenger	2 211 . .	. . .	. . .	. . .	. . .	. . .	. . .	. . .	. . .
Air transport, freight	2 212 . .	. . .	. . .	. . .	. . .	. . .	. . .	. . .	. . .
Air transport, other	2 213 . .	. . .	. . .	. . .	. . .	. . .	. . .	. . .	. . .
Other transport, passenger	2 215 . .	. . .	. . .	. . .	. . .	. . .	. . .	. . .	. . .
Other transport, freight	2 216 . .	. . .	. . .	. . .	. . .	. . .	. . .	. . .	. . .
Other transport, other	2 217 . .	. . .	. . .	. . .	. . .	. . .	. . .	. . .	. . .
Transportation services, debit	3 205 . .	**–130.8**	**–133.4**	**–139.2**	**–155.9**	**–178.4**	**–212.6**	**–199.3**	**. . .**
Passenger	3 205 BA	*–27.2*	*–26.8*	*–27.0*	*–29.9*	*–38.9*	*–45.5*	*–50.5*	. . .
Freight	3 205 BB	*–87.5*	*–89.2*	*–94.1*	*–106.4*	*–119.0*	*–144.3*	*–129.6*	. . .
Other	3 205 BC	*–16.1*	*–17.4*	*–18.1*	*–19.6*	*–20.5*	*–22.8*	*–19.2*	. . .
Sea transport, passenger	3 207 . .	. . .	. . .	. . .	. . .	. . .	. . .	. . .	. . .
Sea transport, freight	3 208 . .	. . .	. . .	. . .	. . .	. . .	. . .	. . .	. . .
Sea transport, other	3 209 . .	. . .	. . .	. . .	. . .	. . .	. . .	. . .	. . .
Air transport, passenger	3 211 . .	. . .	. . .	. . .	. . .	. . .	. . .	. . .	. . .
Air transport, freight	3 212 . .	. . .	. . .	. . .	. . .	. . .	. . .	. . .	. . .
Air transport, other	3 213 . .	. . .	. . .	. . .	. . .	. . .	. . .	. . .	. . .
Other transport, passenger	3 215 . .	. . .	. . .	. . .	. . .	. . .	. . .	. . .	. . .
Other transport, freight	3 216 . .	. . .	. . .	. . .	. . .	. . .	. . .	. . .	. . .
Other transport, other	3 217 . .	. . .	. . .	. . .	. . .	. . .	. . .	. . .	. . .
Travel, credit	2 236 . .	**2.6**	**3.4**	**4.4**	**5.9**	**7.1**	**10.6**	**10.8**	**. . .**
Business travel	2 237 . .	. . .	. . .	. . .	. . .	. . .	. . .	. . .	. . .
Personal travel	2 240 . .	. . .	. . .	. . .	. . .	. . .	. . .	. . .	. . .
Travel, debit	3 236 . .	**–12.1**	**–12.7**	**–13.3**	**–14.3**	**–17.2**	**–19.7**	**–20.1**	**. . .**
Business travel	3 237 . .	. . .	. . .	. . .	. . .	. . .	. . .	. . .	. . .
Personal travel	3 240 . .	. . .	. . .	. . .	. . .	. . .	. . .	. . .	. . .
Other services, credit	2 200 BA	**34.7**	**35.9**	**36.1**	**39.8**	**45.2**	**47.3**	**48.4**	**. . .**
Communications	2 245 . .	. . .	. . .	. . .	. . .	. . .	. . .	. . .	. . .
Construction	2 249 . .	. . .	. . .	. . .	. . .	. . .	. . .	. . .	. . .
Insurance	2 253 . .	1.7	1.9	2.1	2.5	3.0	3.6	3.7	. . .
Financial	2 260 . .	. . .	. . .	. . .	. . .	. . .	. . .	. . .	. . .
Computer and information	2 262 . .	. . .	. . .	. . .	. . .	. . .	. . .	. . .	. . .
Royalties and licence fees	2 266 . .	. . .	. . .	. . .	. . .	. . .	. . .	. . .	. . .
Other business services	2 268 . .	26.8	27.2	26.5	29.1	32.4	32.4	33.2	. . .
Personal, cultural, and recreational	2 287 . .	. . .	. . .	. . .	. . .	. . .	. . .	. . .	. . .
Government, n.i.e.	2 291 . .	6.2	6.8	7.5	8.2	9.8	11.3	11.5	. . .
Other services, debit	3 200 BA	**–112.2**	**–124.8**	**–132.7**	**–149.1**	**–176.6**	**–195.9**	**–181.3**	**. . .**
Communications	3 245 . .	. . .	. . .	. . .	. . .	. . .	. . .	. . .	. . .
Construction	3 249 . .	. . .	. . .	. . .	. . .	. . .	. . .	. . .	. . .
Insurance	3 253 . .	–19.4	–20.4	–25.2	–25.6	–28.1	–30.9	–27.2	. . .
Financial	3 260 . .	. . .	. . .	. . .	. . .	. . .	. . .	. . .	. . .
Computer and information	3 262 . .	. . .	. . .	. . .	. . .	. . .	. . .	. . .	. . .
Royalties and licence fees	3 266 . .	–.1	–.2	–.2	–.5	–.9	–.9	–.7	. . .
Other business services	3 268 . .	–29.1	–31.9	–32.4	–38.1	–50.8	–50.8	–51.6	. . .
Personal, cultural, and recreational	3 287 . .	. . .	. . .	. . .	. . .	. . .	. . .	. . .	. . .
Government, n.i.e.	3 291 . .	–63.6	–72.3	–74.9	–84.9	–96.8	–113.3	–101.8	. . .

Table 2 (Continued). STANDARD PRESENTATION, 1988–95
(Millions of U.S. dollars)

	Code	1988	1989	1990	1991	1992	1993	1994	1995
C. INCOME	4 300	−138.2	−130.5	−119.6	−128.3	−114.3	−120.4	−122.2	...
Total credit	2 300	*6.3*	*6.4*	*13.8*	*15.2*	*18.6*	*19.7*	*19.9*	...
Total debit	3 300	*−144.5*	*−136.9*	*−133.4*	*−143.5*	*−132.9*	*−140.1*	*−142.1*	...
Compensation of employees, credit	2 310	**5.3**	**5.4**	**7.0**	**7.7**	**8.1**	**8.1**	**8.1**	...
Compensation of employees, debit	3 310	**−12.7**	**−14.2**	**−15.2**	**−16.6**	**−16.2**	**−16.2**	**−19.4**	...
Investment income, credit	2 320	**1.0**	**1.0**	**6.8**	**7.5**	**10.5**	**11.6**	**11.8**	...
Direct investment income	2 330	...	...	...	...	...	...	...	...
Dividends and distributed branch profits	2 332	...	...	...	...	...	...	...	...
Reinvested earnings and undistributed branch profits	2 333	...	...	...	...	...	...	...	...
Income on debt (interest)	2 334	...	...	...	...	...	...	...	...
Portfolio investment income	2 339	...	...	...	...	...	...	...	...
Income on equity	2 340	...	...	...	...	...	...	...	...
Income on bonds and notes	2 350	...	...	...	...	...	...	...	...
Income on money market instruments and financial derivatives	2 360	...	...	...	...	...	...	...	...
Other investment income	2 370	1.0	1.0	6.8	7.5	10.5	11.6	11.8	...
Investment income, debit	3 320	**−131.8**	**−122.7**	**−118.2**	**−126.9**	**−116.7**	**−123.9**	**−122.7**	...
Direct investment income	3 330	−5.5	−6.6	−7.0	−7.7	−9.2	−9.2	−10.6	...
Dividends and distributed branch profits	3 332	−5.5	−6.6	−7.0	−7.7	−9.2	−9.2	−10.6	...
Reinvested earnings and undistributed branch profits	3 333	...	...	...	...	...	...	...	...
Income on debt (interest)	3 334	...	...	...	...	...	...	...	...
Portfolio investment income	3 339	...	...	...	...	...	...	...	...
Income on equity	3 340	...	...	...	...	...	...	...	...
Income on bonds and notes	3 350	...	...	...	...	...	...	...	...
Income on money market instruments and financial derivatives	3 360	...	...	...	...	...	...	...	...
Other investment income	3 370	−126.3	−116.1	−111.2	−119.2	−107.5	−114.7	−112.1	...
D. CURRENT TRANSFERS	4 379	369.2	423.1	416.2	422.8	471.2	518.4	472.8	...
Credit	2 379	**377.8**	**432.2**	**426.3**	**434.1**	**484.8**	**532.0**	**487.3**	...
General government	2 380	201.8	226.2	220.3	210.0	224.4	265.3	210.8	...
Other sectors	2 390	176.0	206.0	206.0	224.1	260.4	266.7	276.5	...
Workers' remittances	2 391	6.0	6.0	6.0	6.2	7.3	10.1	15.7	...
Other current transfers	2 392	170.0	200.0	200.0	217.9	253.1	256.6	260.8	...
Debit	3 379	**−8.6**	**−9.1**	**−10.1**	**−11.3**	**−13.6**	**−13.6**	**−14.5**	...
General government	3 380	−5.7	−6.0	−6.5	−7.6	−9.1	−9.1	−10.0	...
Other sectors	3 390	−2.9	−3.1	−3.6	−3.7	−4.5	−4.5	−4.5	...
Workers' remittances	3 391	−2.5	−2.7	−3.4	−3.5	−3.9	−3.9	−3.9	...
Other current transfers	3 392	−.4	−.4	−.2	−.2	−.6	−.6	−.6	...
CAPITAL AND FINANCIAL ACCOUNT	4 996	**−6.1**	**40.1**	**202.3**	**85.6**	**553.1**	**504.5**	**416.8**	...
CAPITAL ACCOUNT	4 994	**−.7**	**−.8**	**−.5**	**−.9**	**−1.0**	**−1.0**	**−1.0**	...
Total credit	2 994	...	...	...	...	...	...	...	...
Total debit	3 994	*−.7*	*−.8*	*−.5*	*−.9*	*−1.0*	*−1.0*	*−1.0*	...
Capital transfers, credit	2 400	...	...	...	...	...	...	...	...
General government	2 401	...	...	...	...	...	...	...	...
Debt forgiveness	2 402	...	...	...	...	...	...	...	...
Other capital transfers	2 410	...	...	...	...	...	...	...	...
Other sectors	2 430	...	...	...	...	...	...	...	...
Migrants' transfers	2 431	...	...	...	...	...	...	...	...
Debt forgiveness	2 432	...	...	...	...	...	...	...	...
Other capital transfers	2 440	...	...	...	...	...	...	...	...
Capital transfers, debit	3 400	**−.7**	**−.8**	**−.5**	**−.9**	**−1.0**	**−1.0**	**−1.0**	...
General government	3 401	...	...	...	...	...	...	...	...
Debt forgiveness	3 402	...	...	...	...	...	...	...	...
Other capital transfers	3 410	...	...	...	...	...	...	...	...
Other sectors	3 430	−.7	−.8	−.5	−.9	−1.0	−1.0	−1.0	...
Migrants' transfers	3 431	−.7	−.8	−.5	−.9	−1.0	−1.0	−1.0	...
Debt forgiveness	3 432	...	...	...	...	...	...	...	...
Other capital transfers	3 440	...	...	...	...	...	...	...	...
Nonproduced nonfinancial assets, credit	2 480	...	...	...	...	...	...	...	...
Nonproduced nonfinancial assets, debit	3 480	...	...	...	...	...	...	...	...

Table 2 (Continued). STANDARD PRESENTATION, 1988–95

(Millions of U.S. dollars)

	Code	1988	1989	1990	1991	1992	1993	1994	1995
FINANCIAL ACCOUNT	4 995	**-5.4**	**40.9**	**202.8**	**86.5**	**554.1**	**505.5**	**417.8**	**...**
A. DIRECT INVESTMENT	4 500	5.0	15.0	14.8	20.0	22.5	125.0	233.0	...
Direct investment abroad	4 505	**...**	**...**	**...**	**...**	**...**	**...**	**...**	**...**
Equity capital	4 510	...	...	...	...	...	...	...	...
Claims on affiliated enterprises	4 515	...	...	...	...	...	...	...	...
Liabilities to affiliated enterprises	4 520	...	...	...	...	...	...	...	...
Reinvested earnings	4 525	...	...	...	...	...	...	...	...
Other capital	4 530	...	...	...	...	...	...	...	...
Claims on affiliated enterprises	4 535	...	...	...	...	...	...	...	...
Liabilities to affiliated enterprises	4 540	...	...	...	...	...	...	...	...
Direct investment in Ghana	4 555	**5.0**	**15.0**	**14.8**	**20.0**	**22.5**	**125.0**	**233.0**	**...**
Equity capital	4 560	5.0	15.0	14.8	20.0	22.5	125.0	233.0	...
Claims on direct investors	4 565	...	...	...	...	...	...	...	...
Liabilities to direct investors	4 570	...	...	...	...	...	...	...	...
Reinvested earnings	4 575	...	...	...	...	...	...	...	...
Other capital	4 580	...	...	...	...	...	...	...	...
Claims on direct investors	4 585	...	...	...	...	...	...	...	...
Liabilities to direct investors	4 590	...	...	...	...	...	...	...	...
B. PORTFOLIO INVESTMENT	4 600	...	...	...	...	...	...	...	...
Assets	4 602	**...**	**...**	**...**	**...**	**...**	**...**	**...**	**...**
Equity securities	4 610	...	...	...	...	...	...	...	...
Monetary authorities	4 611	...	...	...	...	...	...	...	...
General government	4 612	...	...	...	...	...	...	...	...
Banks	4 613	...	...	...	...	...	...	...	...
Other sectors	4 614	...	...	...	...	...	...	...	...
Debt securities	4 619	...	...	...	...	...	...	...	...
Bonds and notes	4 620	...	...	...	...	...	...	...	...
Monetary authorities	4 621	...	...	...	...	...	...	...	...
General government	4 622	...	...	...	...	...	...	...	...
Banks	4 623	...	...	...	...	...	...	...	...
Other sectors	4 624	...	...	...	...	...	...	...	...
Money market instruments	4 630	...	...	...	...	...	...	...	...
Monetary authorities	4 631	...	...	...	...	...	...	...	...
General government	4 632	...	...	...	...	...	...	...	...
Banks	4 633	...	...	...	...	...	...	...	...
Other sectors	4 634	...	...	...	...	...	...	...	...
Financial derivatives	4 640	...	...	...	...	...	...	...	...
Monetary authorities	4 641	...	...	...	...	...	...	...	...
General government	4 642	...	...	...	...	...	...	...	...
Banks	4 643	...	...	...	...	...	...	...	...
Other sectors	4 644	...	...	...	...	...	...	...	...
Liabilities	4 652	**...**	**...**	**...**	**...**	**...**	**...**	**...**	**...**
Equity securities	4 660	...	...	...	...	...	...	...	...
Banks	4 663	...	...	...	...	...	...	...	...
Other sectors	4 664	...	...	...	...	...	...	...	...
Debt securities	4 669	...	...	...	...	...	...	...	...
Bonds and notes	4 670	...	...	...	...	...	...	...	...
Monetary authorities	4 671	...	...	...	...	...	...	...	...
General government	4 672	...	...	...	...	...	...	...	...
Banks	4 673	...	...	...	...	...	...	...	...
Other sectors	4 674	...	...	...	...	...	...	...	...
Money market instruments	4 680	...	...	...	...	...	...	...	...
Monetary authorities	4 681	...	...	...	...	...	...	...	...
General government	4 682	...	...	...	...	...	...	...	...
Banks	4 683	...	...	...	...	...	...	...	...
Other sectors	4 684	...	...	...	...	...	...	...	...
Financial derivatives	4 690	...	...	...	...	...	...	...	...
Monetary authorities	4 691	...	...	...	...	...	...	...	...
General government	4 692	...	...	...	...	...	...	...	...
Banks	4 693	...	...	...	...	...	...	...	...
Other sectors	4 694	...	...	...	...	...	...	...	...

Table 2 (Concluded). STANDARD PRESENTATION, 1988–95
(Millions of U.S. dollars)

	Code	1988	1989	1990	1991	1992	1993	1994	1995
C. OTHER INVESTMENT	4 700 . .	54.7	48.2	241.8	316.0	296.7	458.6	270.5	. . .
Assets	4 703 . .	**–.4**	**–49.8**	**–76.5**	**–1.3**	**–3.5**	**11.3**	**–90.1**	**. . .**
Trade credits	4 706 . .	. . .	. . .	. . .	. . .	. . .	. . .	. . .	. . .
General government: long-term	4 708 . .	. . .	. . .	. . .	. . .	. . .	. . .	. . .	. . .
General government: short-term	4 709 . .	. . .	. . .	. . .	. . .	. . .	. . .	. . .	. . .
Other sectors: long-term	4 711 . .	. . .	. . .	. . .	. . .	. . .	. . .	. . .	. . .
Other sectors: short-term	4 712 . .	. . .	. . .	. . .	. . .	. . .	. . .	. . .	. . .
Loans	4 714 . .	. . .	. . .	. . .	. . .	. . .	. . .	. . .	. . .
Monetary authorities: long-term	4 717 . .	. . .	. . .	. . .	. . .	. . .	. . .	. . .	. . .
Monetary authorities: short-term	4 718 . .	. . .	. . .	. . .	. . .	. . .	. . .	. . .	. . .
General government: long-term	4 720 . .	. . .	. . .	. . .	. . .	. . .	. . .	. . .	. . .
General government: short-term	4 721 . .	. . .	. . .	. . .	. . .	. . .	. . .	. . .	. . .
Banks: long-term	4 723 . .	. . .	. . .	. . .	. . .	. . .	. . .	. . .	. . .
Banks: short-term	4 724 . .	. . .	. . .	. . .	. . .	. . .	. . .	. . .	. . .
Other sectors: long-term	4 726 . .	. . .	. . .	. . .	. . .	. . .	. . .	. . .	. . .
Other sectors: short-term	4 727 . .	. . .	. . .	. . .	. . .	. . .	. . .	. . .	. . .
Currency and deposits	4 730 . .	–.8	–54.0	–64.7	18.3	–5.1	–1.2	–93.3	. . .
Monetary authorities	4 731 . .	. . .	. . .	. . .	. . .	. . .	. . .	. . .	. . .
General government	4 732 . .	. . .	. . .	. . .	. . .	. . .	. . .	. . .	. . .
Banks	4 733 . .	–.8	–54.0	–64.7	18.3	–5.1	–1.2	–93.3	. . .
Other sectors	4 734 . .	. . .	. . .	. . .	. . .	. . .	. . .	. . .	. . .
Other assets	4 736 . .	.4	4.2	–11.8	–19.6	1.6	12.5	3.2	. . .
Monetary authorities: long-term	4 738 . .	. . .	. . .	. . .	. . .	. . .	. . .	. . .	. . .
Monetary authorities: short-term	4 739 . .	. . .	. . .	. . .	. . .	. . .	. . .	. . .	. . .
General government: long-term	4 741 . .	. . .	. . .	. . .	. . .	. . .	. . .	. . .	. . .
General government: short-term	4 742 . .	.4	4.2	–11.8	–19.6	1.6	12.5	3.2	. . .
Banks: long-term	4 744 . .	. . .	. . .	. . .	. . .	. . .	. . .	. . .	. . .
Banks: short-term	4 745 . .	. . .	. . .	. . .	. . .	. . .	. . .	. . .	. . .
Other sectors: long-term	4 747 . .	. . .	. . .	. . .	. . .	. . .	. . .	. . .	. . .
Other sectors: short-term	4 748 . .	. . .	. . .	. . .	. . .	. . .	. . .	. . .	. . .
Liabilities	4 753 . .	**55.1**	**98.0**	**318.3**	**317.3**	**300.2**	**447.3**	**360.6**	**. . .**
Trade credits	4 756 . .	–75.1	–107.5	–58.0	–4.3	57.3	–9.3	38.3	. . .
General government: long-term	4 758 . .	–85.8	–115.1	–41.0	–18.6	74.9	–92.6	–16.8	. . .
General government: short-term	4 759 . .	. . .	. . .	. . .	. . .	. . .	. . .	. . .	. . .
Other sectors: long-term	4 761 . .	. . .	. . .	. . .	. . .	. . .	. . .	. . .	. . .
Other sectors: short-term	4 762 . .	10.7	7.6	–17.0	14.3	–17.6	83.3	55.1	. . .
Loans	4 764 . .	159.4	223.7	399.9	331.8	259.4	411.8	257.5	. . .
Use of Fund credit and loans from the Fund	4 766 . .	–76.2	–21.0	31.4	–2.1	–2.4	–64.5	–7.7	. . .
Monetary authorities: other long-term	4 767 . .	. . .	. . .	. . .	. . .	. . .	. . .	. . .	. . .
Monetary authorities: short-term	4 768 . .	. . .	. . .	. . .	. . .	. . .	. . .	. . .	. . .
General government: long-term	4 770 . .	265.7	286.3	322.4	373.0	311.6	462.8	312.1	. . .
General government: short-term	4 771 . .	–38.4	–46.7	–16.7	. . .	. . .	. . .	. . .	. . .
Banks: long-term	4 773 . .	. . .	. . .	. . .	. . .	. . .	. . .	. . .	. . .
Banks: short-term	4 774 . .	. . .	. . .	. . .	. . .	. . .	. . .	. . .	. . .
Other sectors: long-term	4 776 . .	–1.0	–6.0	38.0	–.9	–16.1	–18.7	–27.5	. . .
Other sectors: short-term	4 777 . .	9.3	11.1	24.8	–38.2	–33.7	32.2	–19.4	. . .
Currency and deposits	4 780 . .	7.4	19.0	–4.0	–6.1	–16.2	44.8	64.8	. . .
Monetary authorities	4 781 . .	. . .	. . .	. . .	. . .	. . .	. . .	. . .	. . .
General government	4 782 . .	. . .	. . .	. . .	. . .	. . .	. . .	. . .	. . .
Banks	4 783 . .	7.4	19.0	–4.0	–6.1	–16.2	44.8	64.8	. . .
Other sectors	4 784 . .	. . .	. . .	. . .	. . .	. . .	. . .	. . .	. . .
Other liabilities	4 786 . .	–36.7	–37.2	–19.6	–4.1	–.3	. . .	. . .	. . .
Monetary authorities: long-term	4 788 . .	. . .	. . .	. . .	. . .	. . .	. . .	. . .	. . .
Monetary authorities: short-term	4 789 . .	–1.9	10.5	–2.3	–4.1	–.3	. . .	. . .	. . .
General government: long-term	4 791 . .	. . .	. . .	. . .	. . .	. . .	. . .	. . .	. . .
General government: short-term	4 792 . .	. . .	. . .	. . .	. . .	. . .	. . .	. . .	. . .
Banks: long-term	4 794 . .	. . .	. . .	. . .	. . .	. . .	. . .	. . .	. . .
Banks: short-term	4 795 . .	. . .	. . .	. . .	. . .	. . .	. . .	. . .	. . .
Other sectors: long-term	4 797 . .	. . .	. . .	. . .	. . .	. . .	. . .	. . .	. . .
Other sectors: short-term	4 798 . .	–34.8	–47.7	–17.3	. . .	. . .	. . .	. . .	. . .
D. RESERVE ASSETS	4 800 . .	–65.1	–22.3	–53.8	–249.5	234.9	–78.1	–85.7	. . .
Monetary gold	4 810 . .	–46.0	. . .	. . .	. . .	. . .	. . .	. . .	. . .
Special drawing rights	4 820 . .	–1.4	.5	–10.1	–38.6	47.9	2.0	–4.5	. . .
Reserve position in the Fund	4 830 . .	. . .	. . .	. . .	. . .	. . .	–24.1	. . .	. . .
Foreign exchange	4 840 . .	–17.7	–22.8	–43.7	–210.9	187.0	–56.0	–81.2	. . .
Other claims	4 880 . .	. . .	. . .	. . .	. . .	. . .	. . .	. . .	. . .
NET ERRORS AND OMISSIONS	4 998 . .	**71.2**	**57.7**	**21.3**	**165.2**	**–177.8**	**53.4**	**–153.0**	**. . .**

Table 1. ANALYTIC PRESENTATION, 1988–95
(Millions of U.S. dollars)

	Code	1988	1989	1990	1991	1992	1993	1994	1995
A. Current Account[1]	4 993 Y.	**–958**	**–2,561**	**–3,537**	**–1,574**	**–2,140**	**–747**	**–146**	**–2,864**
Goods: exports f.o.b	2 100 ..	6,015	6,074	6,458	6,911	6,076	5,112	5,338	5,918
Goods: imports f.o.b	3 100 ..	–12,042	–13,401	–16,564	–16,933	–17,637	–15,611	–16,611	–20,343
Balance on Goods	4 100 ..	*–6,027*	*–7,327*	*–10,106*	*–10,022*	*–11,561*	*–10,499*	*–11,273*	*–14,425*
Services: credit	2 200 ..	5,094	4,828	6,560	7,222	8,697	8,214	9,213	9,605
Services: debit	3 200 ..	–2,164	–2,415	–3,000	–3,193	–3,701	–3,521	–3,774	–4,368
Balance on Goods and Services	4 991 ..	*–3,097*	*–4,914*	*–6,546*	*–5,993*	*–6,565*	*–5,806*	*–5,834*	*–9,188*
Income: credit	2 300 ..	269	283	315	421	555	927	1,099	1,312
Income: debit	3 300 ..	–1,779	–1,913	–2,024	–2,185	–2,605	–2,367	–2,347	–2,996
Balance on Goods, Services, and Income	4 992 ..	*–4,607*	*–6,544*	*–8,255*	*–7,757*	*–8,615*	*–7,246*	*–7,082*	*–10,872*
Current transfers: credit	2 379 Y.	3,663	3,996	4,730	6,199	6,489	6,516	6,964	8,039
Current transfers: debit	3 379 ..	–14	–13	–12	–16	–14	–17	–28	–31
B. Capital Account[1]	4 994 Y.	**...**	**...**	**...**	**...**	**...**	**...**	**...**	**...**
Capital account: credit	2 994 Y.	...	...	...	...	...	...	...	...
Capital account: debit	3 994 ..	...	...	...	...	...	...	...	...
Total, Groups A Plus B	4 010 ..	*–958*	*–2,561*	*–3,537*	*–1,574*	*–2,140*	*–747*	*–146*	*–2,864*
C. Financial Account[1]	4 995 X.	**1,854**	**2,751**	**4,002**	**3,961**	**2,619**	**4,817**	**6,903**	**3,162**
Direct investment abroad	4 505 ..	...	...	...	...	...	...	...	...
Direct investment in Greece	4 555 Y.	907	752	1,005	1,135	1,144	977	981	1,053
Portfolio investment assets	4 602 ..	...	...	...	...	...	...	...	...
Equity securities	4 610 ..	...	...	...	...	...	...	...	...
Debt securities	4 619 ..	...	...	...	...	...	...	...	...
Portfolio investment liabilities	4 652 Y.	...	...	...	...	...	...	...	...
Equity securities	4 660 Y.	...	...	...	...	...	...	...	...
Debt securities	4 669 Y.	...	...	...	...	...	...	...	...
Other investment assets	4 703 ..	...	...	...	...	...	...	...	...
Monetary authorities	4 703 .A	...	...	...	...	...	...	...	...
General government	4 703 .B	...	...	...	...	...	...	...	...
Banks	4 703 .C	...	...	...	...	...	...	...	...
Other sectors	4 703 .D	...	...	...	...	...	...	...	...
Other investment liabilities	4 753 X.	947	1,999	2,997	2,826	1,475	3,840	5,922	2,109
Monetary authorities	4 753 XA	288	736	367	710	1,460	2,584	–1,791	–2,385
General government	4 753 YB	–145	255	936	688	–1,773	884	4,703	3,441
Banks	4 753 YC	143	503	581	175	–2	78	89	–2,110
Other sectors	4 753 YD	661	505	1,113	1,253	1,790	294	2,921	3,163
Total, Groups A Through C	4 020 ..	*896*	*190*	*465*	*2,387*	*479*	*4,070*	*6,757*	*298*
D. Net Errors and Omissions	4 998 ..	**41**	**–538**	**–185**	**–183**	**–853**	**–631**	**–448**	**–321**
Total, Groups A Through D	4 030 ..	*937*	*–348*	*280*	*2,204*	*–374*	*3,439*	*6,309*	*–23*
E. Reserves and Related Items	4 040 ..	**–937**	**348**	**–280**	**–2,204**	**374**	**–3,439**	**–6,309**	**23**
Reserve assets	4 800 ..	–1,148	341	–40	–1,660	188	–3,019	–6,309	23
Use of Fund credit and loans	4 766 ..	...	...	...	...	...	...	...	...
Liabilities constituting foreign authorities' reserves	4 900 ..	...	...	...	...	...	...	...	...
Exceptional financing	4 920 ..	211	7	–240	–544	186	–420	...	...
Conversion rates: drachmas per U.S. dollar	0 101 ..	**141.86**	**162.42**	**158.51**	**182.27**	**190.62**	**229.25**	**242.60**	**231.66**

[1] Excludes components that have been classified in the categories of Group E.

Table 2. STANDARD PRESENTATION, 1988–95
(Millions of U.S. dollars)

	Code	1988	1989	1990	1991	1992	1993	1994	1995
CURRENT ACCOUNT	4 993 . .	**–958**	**–2,561**	**–3,537**	**–1,574**	**–2,140**	**–747**	**–146**	**–2,864**
A. GOODS	4 100 . .	–6,027	–7,327	–10,106	–10,022	–11,561	–10,499	–11,273	–14,425
Credit	2 100 . .	**6,015**	**6,074**	**6,458**	**6,911**	**6,076**	**5,112**	**5,338**	**5,918**
General merchandise: exports f.o.b.	2 110 . .	5,933	5,994	6,365	6,797	6,009	5,035	5,219	5,783
Goods for processing: exports f.o.b.	2 150 . .	...	...	...	...	...	...	...	...
Repairs on goods	2 160 . .	...	...	...	...	...	...	...	...
Goods procured in ports by carriers	2 170 . .	82	80	93	114	67	77	119	135
Nonmonetary gold	2 180 . .	...	...	...	...	...	...	...	...
Debit	3 100 . .	**–12,042**	**–13,401**	**–16,564**	**–16,933**	**–17,637**	**–15,611**	**–16,611**	**–20,343**
General merchandise: imports f.o.b.	3 110 . .	–12,005	–13,377	–16,543	–16,909	–17,612	–15,592	–16,588	–20,292
Goods for processing: imports f.o.b.	3 150 . .	...	...	...	...	...	...	...	...
Repairs on goods	3 160 . .	...	...	...	...	...	...	...	...
Goods procured in ports by carriers	3 170 . .	–37	–24	–21	–24	–25	–19	–23	–51
Nonmonetary gold	3 180 . .	...	...	...	...	...	...	...	...
B. SERVICES	4 200 . .	2,930	2,413	3,560	4,029	4,996	4,693	5,439	5,237
Total credit	2 200 . .	*5,094*	*4,828*	*6,560*	*7,222*	*8,697*	*8,214*	*9,213*	*9,605*
Total debit	3 200 . .	*–2,164*	*–2,415*	*–3,000*	*–3,193*	*–3,701*	*–3,521*	*–3,774*	*–4,368*
Transportation services, credit	2 205 . .	**303**	**200**	**321**	**262**	**469**	**554**	**466**	**376**
Passenger	2 205 BA	*29*	*16*	*30*	*45*	*92*	*67*	*48*	*47*
Freight	2 205 BB	*137*	*143*	*193*	*154*	*128*	*118*	*100*	*48*
Other	2 205 BC	*137*	*41*	*98*	*63*	*249*	*369*	*318*	*281*
Sea transport, passenger	2 207 . .	...	...	...	...	...	...	...	...
Sea transport, freight	2 208 . .	...	...	...	...	...	...	...	...
Sea transport, other	2 209 . .	...	...	...	...	...	...	...	...
Air transport, passenger	2 211 . .	...	...	...	...	...	...	...	...
Air transport, freight	2 212 . .	...	...	...	...	...	...	...	...
Air transport, other	2 213 . .	...	...	...	...	...	...	...	...
Other transport, passenger	2 215 . .	...	...	...	...	...	...	...	...
Other transport, freight	2 216 . .	...	...	...	...	...	...	...	...
Other transport, other	2 217 . .	...	...	...	...	...	...	...	...
Transportation services, debit	3 205 . .	**–691**	**–772**	**–938**	**–1,041**	**–1,115**	**–910**	**–966**	**–1,197**
Passenger	3 205 BA	*–113*	*–114*	*–147*	*–158*	*–164*	*–99*	*–130*	*–172*
Freight	3 205 BB	*–489*	*–545*	*–674*	*–688*	*–718*	*–635*	*–675*	*–826*
Other	3 205 BC	*–89*	*–113*	*–117*	*–195*	*–233*	*–176*	*–161*	*–199*
Sea transport, passenger	3 207 . .	...	...	...	...	...	...	...	...
Sea transport, freight	3 208 . .	...	...	...	...	...	...	...	...
Sea transport, other	3 209 . .	...	...	...	...	...	...	...	...
Air transport, passenger	3 211 . .	...	...	...	...	...	...	...	...
Air transport, freight	3 212 . .	...	...	...	...	...	...	...	...
Air transport, other	3 213 . .	...	...	...	...	...	...	...	...
Other transport, passenger	3 215 . .	...	...	...	...	...	...	...	...
Other transport, freight	3 216 . .	...	...	...	...	...	...	...	...
Other transport, other	3 217 . .	...	...	...	...	...	...	...	...
Travel, credit	2 236 . .	**2,396**	**1,976**	**2,587**	**2,567**	**3,272**	**3,335**	**3,905**	**4,135**
Business travel	2 237 . .	...	...	...	...	...	...	...	...
Personal travel	2 240 . .	...	...	...	...	...	...	...	...
Travel, debit	3 236 . .	**–733**	**–816**	**–1,089**	**–1,015**	**–1,188**	**–1,004**	**–1,125**	**–1,323**
Business travel	3 237 . .	...	...	...	...	...	...	...	...
Personal travel	3 240 . .	...	...	...	...	...	...	...	...
Other services, credit	2 200 BA	**2,395**	**2,652**	**3,652**	**4,393**	**4,956**	**4,325**	**4,842**	**5,094**
Communications	2 245 . .	...	...	...	...	...	...	...	...
Construction	2 249 . .	...	...	...	...	...	...	...	...
Insurance	2 253 . .	8	7	8	11	10	13	17	24
Financial	2 260 . .	...	...	...	...	...	...	...	...
Computer and information	2 262 . .	...	...	...	...	...	...	...	...
Royalties and licence fees	2 266 . .	...	...	...	...	...	...	...	...
Other business services	2 268 . .	2,357	2,583	3,598	4,302	4,890	4,251	4,754	4,993
Personal, cultural, and recreational	2 287 . .	...	...	...	...	...	...	...	...
Government, n.i.e.	2 291 . .	30	62	46	80	56	61	71	77
Other services, debit	3 200 BA	**–740**	**–827**	**–973**	**–1,137**	**–1,398**	**–1,607**	**–1,683**	**–1,848**
Communications	3 245 . .	...	...	...	...	...	...	...	...
Construction	3 249 . .	...	...	...	...	...	...	...	...
Insurance	3 253 . .	–106	–115	–150	–140	–152	–151	–151	–182
Financial	3 260 . .	...	...	...	...	...	...	...	...
Computer and information	3 262 . .	...	...	...	...	...	...	...	...
Royalties and licence fees	3 266 . .	–13	–15	–15	–13	–19	–27	–46	–58
Other business services	3 268 . .	–432	–484	–564	–741	–962	–1,095	–1,132	–1,243
Personal, cultural, and recreational	3 287 . .	...	...	...	...	...	...	...	...
Government, n.i.e.	3 291 . .	–189	–213	–244	–243	–265	–334	–354	–365

Table 2 (Continued). STANDARD PRESENTATION, 1988–95
(Millions of U.S. dollars)

	Code	1988	1989	1990	1991	1992	1993	1994	1995
C. INCOME	4 300 . .	–1,510	–1,630	–1,709	–1,764	–2,050	–1,440	–1,248	–1,684
Total credit	2 300 . .	*269*	*283*	*315*	*421*	*555*	*927*	*1,099*	*1,312*
Total debit	3 300 . .	*–1,779*	*–1,913*	*–2,024*	*–2,185*	*–2,605*	*–2,367*	*–2,347*	*–2,996*
Compensation of employees, credit	2 310 . .	**62**	**37**	**42**	**58**	**165**	**295**	**310**	**304**
Compensation of employees, debit	3 310 . .	**–95**	**–118**	**–122**	**–118**	**–173**	**–250**	**–222**	**–300**
Investment income, credit	2 320 . .	**207**	**246**	**273**	**363**	**390**	**632**	**789**	**1,008**
Direct investment income	2 330 . .	4	3	19	16	32	65	45	22
Dividends and distributed branch profits	2 332 . .	4	3	19	16	32	65	45	22
Reinvested earnings and undistributed branch profits	2 333 . .	. . .	. . .	. . .	. . .	. . .	. . .	. . .	. . .
Income on debt (interest)	2 334 . .	. . .	. . .	. . .	. . .	. . .	. . .	. . .	. . .
Portfolio investment income	2 339 . .	. . .	. . .	. . .	. . .	. . .	. . .	. . .	. . .
Income on equity	2 340 . .	. . .	. . .	. . .	. . .	. . .	. . .	. . .	. . .
Income on bonds and notes	2 350 . .	. . .	. . .	. . .	. . .	. . .	. . .	. . .	. . .
Income on money market instruments and financial derivatives	2 360 . .	. . .	. . .	. . .	. . .	. . .	. . .	. . .	. . .
Other investment income	2 370 . .	203	243	254	347	358	567	744	986
Investment income, debit	3 320 . .	**–1,684**	**–1,795**	**–1,902**	**–2,067**	**–2,432**	**–2,117**	**–2,125**	**–2,696**
Direct investment income	3 330 . .	–56	–68	–78	–131	–170	–133	–141	–206
Dividends and distributed branch profits	3 332 . .	–56	–68	–78	–78	–108	–102	–116	–193
Reinvested earnings and undistributed branch profits	3 333 . .	. . .	. . .	. . .	–53	–62	–31	–25	–13
Income on debt (interest)	3 334 . .	. . .	. . .	. . .	. . .	. . .	. . .	. . .	. . .
Portfolio investment income	3 339 . .	. . .	. . .	. . .	. . .	. . .	. . .	. . .	. . .
Income on equity	3 340 . .	. . .	. . .	. . .	. . .	. . .	. . .	. . .	. . .
Income on bonds and notes	3 350 . .	. . .	. . .	. . .	. . .	. . .	. . .	. . .	. . .
Income on money market instruments and financial derivatives	3 360 . .	. . .	. . .	. . .	. . .	. . .	. . .	. . .	. . .
Other investment income	3 370 . .	–1,628	–1,727	–1,824	–1,936	–2,262	–1,984	–1,984	–2,490
D. CURRENT TRANSFERS	4 379 . .	3,649	3,983	4,718	6,183	6,475	6,499	6,936	8,008
Credit	2 379 . .	**3,663**	**3,996**	**4,730**	**6,199**	**6,489**	**6,516**	**6,964**	**8,039**
General government	2 380 . .	1,936	2,602	2,901	4,034	4,058	4,085	4,307	4,968
Other sectors	2 390 . .	1,727	1,394	1,829	2,165	2,431	2,431	2,657	3,071
Workers' remittances	2 391 . .	1,675	1,350	1,775	2,115	2,366	2,360	2,576	2,982
Other current transfers	2 392 . .	52	44	54	50	65	71	81	89
Debit	3 379 . .	**–14**	**–13**	**–12**	**–16**	**–14**	**–17**	**–28**	**–31**
General government	3 380 . .	. . .	. . .	. . .	. . .	. . .	. . .	. . .	. . .
Other sectors	3 390 . .	–14	–13	–12	–16	–14	–17	–28	–31
Workers' remittances	3 391 . .	. . .	. . .	. . .	. . .	. . .	. . .	. . .	. . .
Other current transfers	3 392 . .	–14	–13	–12	–16	–14	–17	–28	–31
CAPITAL AND FINANCIAL ACCOUNT	4 996 . .	**917**	**3,099**	**3,722**	**1,757**	**2,993**	**1,378**	**594**	**3,185**
CAPITAL ACCOUNT	4 994 . .	**. . .**	**. . .**	**. . .**	**. . .**	**. . .**	**. . .**	**. . .**	**. . .**
Total credit	2 994 . .	. . .	. . .	. . .	. . .	. . .	. . .	. . .	. . .
Total debit	3 994 . .	. . .	. . .	. . .	. . .	. . .	. . .	. . .	. . .
Capital transfers, credit	2 400 . .	**. . .**	**. . .**	**. . .**	**. . .**	**. . .**	**. . .**	**. . .**	**. . .**
General government	2 401 . .	. . .	. . .	. . .	. . .	. . .	. . .	. . .	. . .
Debt forgiveness	2 402 . .	. . .	. . .	. . .	. . .	. . .	. . .	. . .	. . .
Other capital transfers	2 410 . .	. . .	. . .	. . .	. . .	. . .	. . .	. . .	. . .
Other sectors	2 430 . .	. . .	. . .	. . .	. . .	. . .	. . .	. . .	. . .
Migrants' transfers	2 431 . .	. . .	. . .	. . .	. . .	. . .	. . .	. . .	. . .
Debt forgiveness	2 432 . .	. . .	. . .	. . .	. . .	. . .	. . .	. . .	. . .
Other capital transfers	2 440 . .	. . .	. . .	. . .	. . .	. . .	. . .	. . .	. . .
Capital transfers, debit	3 400 . .	**. . .**	**. . .**	**. . .**	**. . .**	**. . .**	**. . .**	**. . .**	**. . .**
General government	3 401 . .	. . .	. . .	. . .	. . .	. . .	. . .	. . .	. . .
Debt forgiveness	3 402 . .	. . .	. . .	. . .	. . .	. . .	. . .	. . .	. . .
Other capital transfers	3 410 . .	. . .	. . .	. . .	. . .	. . .	. . .	. . .	. . .
Other sectors	3 430 . .	. . .	. . .	. . .	. . .	. . .	. . .	. . .	. . .
Migrants' transfers	3 431 . .	. . .	. . .	. . .	. . .	. . .	. . .	. . .	. . .
Debt forgiveness	3 432 . .	. . .	. . .	. . .	. . .	. . .	. . .	. . .	. . .
Other capital transfers	3 440 . .	. . .	. . .	. . .	. . .	. . .	. . .	. . .	. . .
Nonproduced nonfinancial assets, credit	2 480 . .	**. . .**	**. . .**	**. . .**	**. . .**	**. . .**	**. . .**	**. . .**	**. . .**
Nonproduced nonfinancial assets, debit	3 480 . .	**. . .**	**. . .**	**. . .**	**. . .**	**. . .**	**. . .**	**. . .**	**. . .**

Table 2 (Continued). STANDARD PRESENTATION, 1988–95
(Millions of U.S. dollars)

	Code	1988	1989	1990	1991	1992	1993	1994	1995
FINANCIAL ACCOUNT	4 995 . .	**917**	**3,099**	**3,722**	**1,757**	**2,993**	**1,378**	**594**	**3,185**
A. DIRECT INVESTMENT	4 500 . .	907	752	1,005	1,135	1,144	977	981	1,053
Direct investment abroad	4 505 . .	**. . .**	**. . .**	**. . .**	**. . .**	**. . .**	**. . .**	**. . .**	**. . .**
Equity capital	4 510 . .	. . .	. . .	. . .	. . .	. . .	. . .	. . .	. . .
Claims on affiliated enterprises	4 515 . .	. . .	. . .	. . .	. . .	. . .	. . .	. . .	. . .
Liabilities to affiliated enterprises	4 520 . .	. . .	. . .	. . .	. . .	. . .	. . .	. . .	. . .
Reinvested earnings	4 525 . .	. . .	. . .	. . .	. . .	. . .	. . .	. . .	. . .
Other capital	4 530 . .	. . .	. . .	. . .	. . .	. . .	. . .	. . .	. . .
Claims on affiliated enterprises	4 535 . .	. . .	. . .	. . .	. . .	. . .	. . .	. . .	. . .
Liabilities to affiliated enterprises	4 540 . .	. . .	. . .	. . .	. . .	. . .	. . .	. . .	. . .
Direct investment in Greece	4 555 . .	**907**	**752**	**1,005**	**1,135**	**1,144**	**977**	**981**	**1,053**
Equity capital	4 560 . .	896	740	991	1,082	1,082	946	956	1,040
Claims on direct investors	4 565 . .	. . .	. . .	. . .	. . .	. . .	. . .	. . .	. . .
Liabilities to direct investors	4 570 . .	. . .	. . .	. . .	. . .	. . .	. . .	. . .	. . .
Reinvested earnings	4 575 . .	. . .	. . .	. . .	53	62	31	25	13
Other capital	4 580 . .	11	12	14	. . .	. . .	. . .	. . .	. . .
Claims on direct investors	4 585 . .	. . .	. . .	. . .	. . .	. . .	. . .	. . .	. . .
Liabilities to direct investors	4 590 . .	. . .	. . .	. . .	. . .	. . .	. . .	. . .	. . .
B. PORTFOLIO INVESTMENT	4 600 . .	. . .	. . .	. . .	. . .	. . .	. . .	. . .	. . .
Assets	4 602 . .	**. . .**	**. . .**	**. . .**	**. . .**	**. . .**	**. . .**	**. . .**	**. . .**
Equity securities	4 610 . .	. . .	. . .	. . .	. . .	. . .	. . .	. . .	. . .
Monetary authorities	4 611 . .	. . .	. . .	. . .	. . .	. . .	. . .	. . .	. . .
General government	4 612 . .	. . .	. . .	. . .	. . .	. . .	. . .	. . .	. . .
Banks	4 613 . .	. . .	. . .	. . .	. . .	. . .	. . .	. . .	. . .
Other sectors	4 614 . .	. . .	. . .	. . .	. . .	. . .	. . .	. . .	. . .
Debt securities	4 619 . .	. . .	. . .	. . .	. . .	. . .	. . .	. . .	. . .
Bonds and notes	4 620 . .	. . .	. . .	. . .	. . .	. . .	. . .	. . .	. . .
Monetary authorities	4 621 . .	. . .	. . .	. . .	. . .	. . .	. . .	. . .	. . .
General government	4 622 . .	. . .	. . .	. . .	. . .	. . .	. . .	. . .	. . .
Banks	4 623 . .	. . .	. . .	. . .	. . .	. . .	. . .	. . .	. . .
Other sectors	4 624 . .	. . .	. . .	. . .	. . .	. . .	. . .	. . .	. . .
Money market instruments	4 630 . .	. . .	. . .	. . .	. . .	. . .	. . .	. . .	. . .
Monetary authorities	4 631 . .	. . .	. . .	. . .	. . .	. . .	. . .	. . .	. . .
General government	4 632 . .	. . .	. . .	. . .	. . .	. . .	. . .	. . .	. . .
Banks	4 633 . .	. . .	. . .	. . .	. . .	. . .	. . .	. . .	. . .
Other sectors	4 634 . .	. . .	. . .	. . .	. . .	. . .	. . .	. . .	. . .
Financial derivatives	4 640 . .	. . .	. . .	. . .	. . .	. . .	. . .	. . .	. . .
Monetary authorities	4 641 . .	. . .	. . .	. . .	. . .	. . .	. . .	. . .	. . .
General government	4 642 . .	. . .	. . .	. . .	. . .	. . .	. . .	. . .	. . .
Banks	4 643 . .	. . .	. . .	. . .	. . .	. . .	. . .	. . .	. . .
Other sectors	4 644 . .	. . .	. . .	. . .	. . .	. . .	. . .	. . .	. . .
Liabilities	4 652 . .	**. . .**	**. . .**	**. . .**	**. . .**	**. . .**	**. . .**	**. . .**	**. . .**
Equity securities	4 660 . .	. . .	. . .	. . .	. . .	. . .	. . .	. . .	. . .
Banks	4 663 . .	. . .	. . .	. . .	. . .	. . .	. . .	. . .	. . .
Other sectors	4 664 . .	. . .	. . .	. . .	. . .	. . .	. . .	. . .	. . .
Debt securities	4 669 . .	. . .	. . .	. . .	. . .	. . .	. . .	. . .	. . .
Bonds and notes	4 670 . .	. . .	. . .	. . .	. . .	. . .	. . .	. . .	. . .
Monetary authorities	4 671 . .	. . .	. . .	. . .	. . .	. . .	. . .	. . .	. . .
General government	4 672 . .	. . .	. . .	. . .	. . .	. . .	. . .	. . .	. . .
Banks	4 673 . .	. . .	. . .	. . .	. . .	. . .	. . .	. . .	. . .
Other sectors	4 674 . .	. . .	. . .	. . .	. . .	. . .	. . .	. . .	. . .
Money market instruments	4 680 . .	. . .	. . .	. . .	. . .	. . .	. . .	. . .	. . .
Monetary authorities	4 681 . .	. . .	. . .	. . .	. . .	. . .	. . .	. . .	. . .
General government	4 682 . .	. . .	. . .	. . .	. . .	. . .	. . .	. . .	. . .
Banks	4 683 . .	. . .	. . .	. . .	. . .	. . .	. . .	. . .	. . .
Other sectors	4 684 . .	. . .	. . .	. . .	. . .	. . .	. . .	. . .	. . .
Financial derivatives	4 690 . .	. . .	. . .	. . .	. . .	. . .	. . .	. . .	. . .
Monetary authorities	4 691 . .	. . .	. . .	. . .	. . .	. . .	. . .	. . .	. . .
General government	4 692 . .	. . .	. . .	. . .	. . .	. . .	. . .	. . .	. . .
Banks	4 693 . .	. . .	. . .	. . .	. . .	. . .	. . .	. . .	. . .
Other sectors	4 694 . .	. . .	. . .	. . .	. . .	. . .	. . .	. . .	. . .

Table 2 (Concluded). STANDARD PRESENTATION, 1988–95
(Millions of U.S. dollars)

	Code	1988	1989	1990	1991	1992	1993	1994	1995
C. OTHER INVESTMENT	4 700 . .	1,158	2,006	2,757	2,282	1,661	3,420	5,922	2,109
Assets	4 703 . .	...	...	...	...	...	...	...	...
Trade credits	4 706 . .	...	...	...	...	...	...	...	...
General government: long-term	4 708 . .	...	...	...	...	...	...	...	...
General government: short-term	4 709 . .	...	...	...	...	...	...	...	...
Other sectors: long-term	4 711 . .	...	...	...	...	...	...	...	...
Other sectors: short-term	4 712 . .	...	...	...	...	...	...	...	...
Loans	4 714 . .	...	...	...	...	...	...	...	...
Monetary authorities: long-term	4 717 . .	...	...	...	...	...	...	...	...
Monetary authorities: short-term	4 718 . .	...	...	...	...	...	...	...	...
General government: long-term	4 720 . .	...	...	...	...	...	...	...	...
General government: short-term	4 721 . .	...	...	...	...	...	...	...	...
Banks: long-term	4 723 . .	...	...	...	...	...	...	...	...
Banks: short-term	4 724 . .	...	...	...	...	...	...	...	...
Other sectors: long-term	4 726 . .	...	...	...	...	...	...	...	...
Other sectors: short-term	4 727 . .	...	...	...	...	...	...	...	...
Currency and deposits	4 730 . .	...	...	...	...	...	...	...	...
Monetary authorities	4 731 . .	...	...	...	...	...	...	...	...
General government	4 732 . .	...	...	...	...	...	...	...	...
Banks	4 733 . .	...	...	...	...	...	...	...	...
Other sectors	4 734 . .	...	...	...	...	...	...	...	...
Other assets	4 736 . .	...	...	...	...	...	...	...	...
Monetary authorities: long-term	4 738 . .	...	...	...	...	...	...	...	...
Monetary authorities: short-term	4 739 . .	...	...	...	...	...	...	...	...
General government: long-term	4 741 . .	...	...	...	...	...	...	...	...
General government: short-term	4 742 . .	...	...	...	...	...	...	...	...
Banks: long-term	4 744 . .	...	...	...	...	...	...	...	...
Banks: short-term	4 745 . .	...	...	...	...	...	...	...	...
Other sectors: long-term	4 747 . .	...	...	...	...	...	...	...	...
Other sectors: short-term	4 748 . .	...	...	...	...	...	...	...	...
Liabilities	4 753 . .	**1,158**	**2,006**	**2,757**	**2,282**	**1,661**	**3,420**	**5,922**	**2,109**
Trade credits	4 756 . .	192	124	441	327	428	–428	269	527
General government: long-term	4 758 . .	...	...	...	...	...	...	...	...
General government: short-term	4 759 . .	...	...	...	...	...	...	...	...
Other sectors: long-term	4 761 . .	–24	–48	–34	–18	–2	–15	...	...
Other sectors: short-term	4 762 . .	216	172	475	345	430	–413	269	527
Loans	4 764 . .	735	1,511	1,879	1,968	1,526	4,392	5,216	4,539
Use of Fund credit and loans from the Fund	4 766 . .	...	...	...	...	...	...	...	...
Monetary authorities: other long-term	4 767 . .	255	744	359	718	1,463	2,588	–1,791	–2,385
Monetary authorities: short-term	4 768 . .	211	7	–240	–544	186	–420	...	...
General government: long-term	4 770 . .	–145	255	936	688	–1,773	884	4,703	3,441
General government: short-term	4 771 . .	...	...	...	...	...	...	...	...
Banks: long-term	4 773 . .	...	...	...	...	...	...	...	...
Banks: short-term	4 774 . .	...	...	...	...	...	...	...	...
Other sectors: long-term	4 776 . .	372	409	898	1,210	1,625	1,503	2,398	3,483
Other sectors: short-term	4 777 . .	42	96	–74	–104	25	–163	–94	...
Currency and deposits	4 780 . .	125	550	618	141	–24	46	60	–2,115
Monetary authorities	4 781 . .	...	...	...	...	...	...	...	...
General government	4 782 . .	...	...	...	...	...	...	...	...
Banks	4 783 . .	125	550	618	141	–24	46	60	–2,115
Other sectors	4 784 . .	...	...	...	...	...	...	...	...
Other liabilities	4 786 . .	106	–179	–181	–154	–269	–590	377	–842
Monetary authorities: long-term	4 788 . .	...	...	...	...	...	...	...	...
Monetary authorities: short-term	4 789 . .	33	–8	8	–8	–3	–4	...	...
General government: long-term	4 791 . .	...	...	...	...	...	...	...	...
General government: short-term	4 792 . .	...	...	...	...	...	...	...	...
Banks: long-term	4 794 . .	18	–47	–37	34	22	32	29	5
Banks: short-term	4 795 . .	...	...	...	...	...	...	...	...
Other sectors: long-term	4 797 . .	55	–124	–152	–180	–288	–618	348	–847
Other sectors: short-term	4 798 . .	...	...	...	...	...	...	...	...
D. RESERVE ASSETS	4 800 . .	–1,148	341	–40	–1,660	188	–3,019	–6,309	23
Monetary gold	4 810 . .	–94	–13	–6	–15	–68	–83	51	–13
Special drawing rights	4 820 . .	...	...	...	...	...	...	...	...
Reserve position in the Fund	4 830 . .	–1	–23	20	...	–58	4	...	...
Foreign exchange	4 840 . .	–1,053	377	–54	–1,645	314	–2,940	–6,360	36
Other claims	4 880 . .	...	...	...	...	...	...	...	...
NET ERRORS AND OMISSIONS	4 998 . .	**41**	**–538**	**–185**	**–183**	**–853**	**–631**	**–448**	**–321**

Table 1. ANALYTIC PRESENTATION, 1988–95
(Millions of U.S. dollars)

	Code	1988	1989	1990	1991	1992	1993	1994	1995
A. Current Account [1]	4 993 Y.	**–27.77**	**–36.32**	**–46.24**	**–46.58**	**–33.14**	**–43.54**	**–32.86**	...
Goods: exports f.o.b	2 100 . .	33.19	31.11	29.29	26.71	23.33	22.53	25.75	...
Goods: imports f.o.b	3 100 . .	–92.19	–99.04	–106.26	–113.58	–103.18	–118.13	–125.09	...
Balance on Goods	4 100 . .	*–59.00*	*–67.93*	*–76.98*	*–86.87*	*–79.85*	*–95.59*	*–99.34*	...
Services: credit	2 200 . .	53.00	54.22	63.81	71.81	76.00	87.73	101.93	...
Services: debit	3 200 . .	–27.70	–29.59	–32.54	–35.54	–35.10	–41.01	–42.87	...
Balance on Goods and Services	4 991 . .	*–33.70*	*–43.30*	*–45.71*	*–50.59*	*–38.95*	*–48.87*	*–40.28*	...
Income: credit	2 300 . .	2.73	2.43	2.51	2.48	2.55	2.80	3.61	...
Income: debit	3 300 . .	–9.00	–11.96	–14.38	–9.77	–8.74	–11.16	–12.43	...
Balance on Goods, Services, and Income	4 992 . .	*–39.98*	*–52.83*	*–57.58*	*–57.88*	*–45.14*	*–57.23*	*–49.10*	...
Current transfers: credit	2 379 Y.	13.04	17.39	12.46	13.25	14.26	16.10	19.75	...
Current transfers: debit	3 379 . .	–.83	–.88	–1.11	–1.96	–2.25	–2.41	–3.51	...
B. Capital Account [1]	4 994 Y.	**12.93**	**9.87**	**22.10**	**17.51**	**13.43**	**16.89**	**21.67**	...
Capital account: credit	2 994 Y.	20.85	10.69	23.36	18.51	14.80	18.27	23.04	...
Capital account: debit	3 994 . .	–7.93	–.81	–1.26	–1.01	–1.38	–1.38	–1.38	...
Total, Groups A Plus B	4 010 . .	*–14.84*	*–26.45*	*–24.13*	*–29.08*	*–19.71*	*–26.65*	*–11.19*	...
C. Financial Account [1]	4 995 X.	**11.43**	**33.16**	**18.54**	**23.39**	**18.29**	**18.96**	**6.28**	...
Direct investment abroad	4 505 . .	...	...	...	...	...	...	...	...
Direct investment in Grenada	4 555 Y.	14.98	10.48	12.87	15.27	22.58	20.20	19.31	...
Portfolio investment assets	4 602 . .	...	...	...	...	...	...	...	...
Equity securities	4 610 . .	...	...	...	...	...	...	...	...
Debt securities	4 619 . .	...	...	...	...	...	...	...	...
Portfolio investment liabilities	4 652 Y.	.15	...	.02	.05	–.16	.20	–.38	...
Equity securities	4 660 Y.	.15	...	.02	.05	–.16	.20	–.38	...
Debt securities	4 669 Y.	...	...	...	...	...	...	...	...
Other investment assets	4 703 . .	–8.35	17.52	–11.48	2.02	–2.30	–.19	–12.31	...
Monetary authorities	4 703 .A	...	...	...	...	...	...	...	...
General government	4 703 .B	...	...	...	...	...	...	...	...
Banks	4 703 .C	–8.35	17.52	–11.48	2.02	–2.30	–.19	–12.31	...
Other sectors	4 703 .D	...	...	...	...	...	...	...	...
Other investment liabilities	4 753 X.	4.65	5.16	17.13	6.04	–1.83	–1.26	–.34	...
Monetary authorities	4 753 XA	...	...	...	...	...	...	...	...
General government	4 753 YB	6.19	6.56	16.19	8.59	.75	1.29	3.41	...
Banks	4 753 YC	...	...	...	...	...	...	...	...
Other sectors	4 753 YD	–1.54	–1.40	.94	–2.54	–2.57	–2.56	–3.75	...
Total, Groups A Through C	4 020 . .	*–3.41*	*6.71*	*–5.59*	*–5.69*	*–1.42*	*–7.70*	*–4.91*	...
D. Net Errors and Omissions	4 998 . .	**–1.72**	**–7.55**	**8.12**	**8.15**	**9.52**	**8.14**	**9.45**	...
Total, Groups A Through D	4 030 . .	*–5.14*	*–.84*	*2.53*	*2.46*	*8.10*	*.44*	*4.54*	...
E. Reserves and Related Items	4 040 . .	**5.14**	**.84**	**–2.53**	**–2.46**	**–8.10**	**–.44**	**–4.54**	...
Reserve assets	4 800 . .	5.89	1.56	–2.07	–2.44	–8.10	–.44	–4.54	...
Use of Fund credit and loans	4 766 . .	–.75	–.72	–.46	–.01	...	...	...	...
Liabilities constituting foreign authorities' reserves	4 900 . .	...	...	...	...	...	...	...	...
Exceptional financing	4 920 . .	...	...	...	...	...	...	...	...
Conversion rates: Eastern Caribbean dollars per U.S. dollar	0 101 . .	**2.7000**	**2.7000**	**2.7000**	**2.7000**	**2.7000**	**2.7000**	**2.7000**	**2.7000**

[1] Excludes components that have been classified in the categories of Group E.

Table 2. STANDARD PRESENTATION, 1988–95
(Millions of U.S. dollars)

	Code	1988	1989	1990	1991	1992	1993	1994	1995
CURRENT ACCOUNT	4 993 . .	**-27.77**	**-36.32**	**-46.24**	**-46.58**	**-33.14**	**-43.54**	**-32.86**	**. . .**
A. GOODS	4 100 . .	-59.00	-67.93	-76.98	-86.87	-79.85	-95.59	-99.34	. . .
Credit	2 100 . .	**33.19**	**31.11**	**29.29**	**26.71**	**23.33**	**22.53**	**25.75**	**. . .**
General merchandise: exports f.o.b.	2 110 . .	32.78	30.33	27.87	24.92	21.54	21.51	23.84	. . .
Goods for processing: exports f.o.b.	2 150 . .	. . .	. . .	. . .	. . .	. . .	. . .	. . .	. . .
Repairs on goods	2 160 . .	. . .	. . .	. . .	. . .	. . .	. . .	. . .	. . .
Goods procured in ports by carriers	2 170 . .	.41	.78	1.42	1.79	1.79	1.02	1.90	. . .
Nonmonetary gold	2 180 . .	. . .	. . .	. . .	. . .	. . .	. . .	. . .	. . .
Debit	3 100 . .	**-92.19**	**-99.04**	**-106.26**	**-113.58**	**-103.18**	**-118.13**	**-125.09**	**. . .**
General merchandise: imports f.o.b.	3 110 . .	-92.19	-99.04	-106.26	-113.58	-103.18	-118.13	-125.09	. . .
Goods for processing: imports f.o.b.	3 150 . .	. . .	. . .	. . .	. . .	. . .	. . .	. . .	. . .
Repairs on goods	3 160 . .	. . .	. . .	. . .	. . .	. . .	. . .	. . .	. . .
Goods procured in ports by carriers	3 170 . .	. . .	. . .	. . .	. . .	. . .	. . .	. . .	. . .
Nonmonetary gold	3 180 . .	. . .	. . .	. . .	. . .	. . .	. . .	. . .	. . .
B. SERVICES	4 200 . .	25.30	24.63	31.27	36.28	40.90	46.72	59.06	. . .
Total credit	2 200 . .	*53.00*	*54.22*	*63.81*	*71.81*	*76.00*	*87.73*	*101.93*	. . .
Total debit	3 200 . .	*-27.70*	*-29.59*	*-32.54*	*-35.54*	*-35.10*	*-41.01*	*-42.87*	. . .
Transportation services, credit	2 205 . .	**2.78**	**2.19**	**1.95**	**3.90**	**3.77**	**3.64**	**4.64**	**. . .**
Passenger	2 205 BA	. . .	. . .	. . .	. . .	. . .	. . .	. . .	. . .
Freight	2 205 BB	. . .	. . .	. . .	*.41*	. . .	. . .	. . .	. . .
Other	2 205 BC	*2.78*	*2.19*	*1.94*	*3.49*	*3.77*	*3.64*	*4.64*	. . .
Sea transport, passenger	2 207 . .	. . .	. . .	. . .	. . .	. . .	. . .	. . .	. . .
Sea transport, freight	2 208 . .	. . .	. . .	. . .	. . .	. . .	. . .	. . .	. . .
Sea transport, other	2 209 . .	. . .	. . .	. . .	. . .	. . .	. . .	. . .	. . .
Air transport, passenger	2 211 . .	. . .	. . .	. . .	. . .	. . .	. . .	. . .	. . .
Air transport, freight	2 212 . .	. . .	. . .	. . .	. . .	. . .	. . .	. . .	. . .
Air transport, other	2 213 . .	. . .	. . .	. . .	. . .	. . .	. . .	. . .	. . .
Other transport, passenger	2 215 . .	. . .	. . .	. . .	. . .	. . .	. . .	. . .	. . .
Other transport, freight	2 216 . .	. . .	. . .	. . .	. . .	. . .	. . .	. . .	. . .
Other transport, other	2 217 . .	. . .	. . .	. . .	. . .	. . .	. . .	. . .	. . .
Transportation services, debit	3 205 . .	**-15.08**	**-15.98**	**-17.43**	**-18.54**	**-17.58**	**-19.03**	**-22.72**	**. . .**
Passenger	3 205 BA	*-5.63*	*-5.93*	*-6.25*	*-6.65*	*-6.90*	*-6.48*	*-8.99*	. . .
Freight	3 205 BB	*-9.45*	*-10.06*	*-11.18*	*-11.89*	*-10.68*	*-12.55*	*-13.73*	. . .
Other	3 205 BC	. . .	. . .	. . .	. . .	. . .	. . .	. . .	. . .
Sea transport, passenger	3 207 . .	. . .	. . .	. . .	. . .	. . .	. . .	. . .	. . .
Sea transport, freight	3 208 . .	. . .	. . .	. . .	. . .	. . .	. . .	. . .	. . .
Sea transport, other	3 209 . .	. . .	. . .	. . .	. . .	. . .	. . .	. . .	. . .
Air transport, passenger	3 211 . .	. . .	. . .	. . .	. . .	. . .	. . .	. . .	. . .
Air transport, freight	3 212 . .	. . .	. . .	. . .	. . .	. . .	. . .	. . .	. . .
Air transport, other	3 213 . .	. . .	. . .	. . .	. . .	. . .	. . .	. . .	. . .
Other transport, passenger	3 215 . .	. . .	. . .	. . .	. . .	. . .	. . .	. . .	. . .
Other transport, freight	3 216 . .	. . .	. . .	. . .	. . .	. . .	. . .	. . .	. . .
Other transport, other	3 217 . .	. . .	. . .	. . .	. . .	. . .	. . .	. . .	. . .
Travel, credit	2 236 . .	**37.41**	**40.74**	**49.57**	**54.47**	**55.84**	**63.70**	**77.61**	**. . .**
Business travel	2 237 . .	. . .	. . .	. . .	. . .	. . .	. . .	. . .	. . .
Personal travel	2 240 . .	. . .	. . .	. . .	. . .	. . .	. . .	. . .	. . .
Travel, debit	3 236 . .	**-4.00**	**-4.48**	**-4.70**	**-4.92**	**-3.72**	**-4.09**	**-4.24**	**. . .**
Business travel	3 237 . .	. . .	. . .	. . .	. . .	. . .	. . .	. . .	. . .
Personal travel	3 240 . .	. . .	. . .	. . .	. . .	. . .	. . .	. . .	. . .
Other services, credit	2 200 BA	**12.81**	**11.30**	**12.29**	**13.44**	**16.39**	**20.38**	**19.68**	**. . .**
Communications	2 245 . .	. . .	. . .	. . .	. . .	. . .	. . .	. . .	. . .
Construction	2 249 . .	. . .	. . .	. . .	. . .	. . .	. . .	. . .	. . .
Insurance	2 253 . .	.63	.48	.70	.97	1.13	1.31	1.59	. . .
Financial	2 260 . .	. . .	. . .	. . .	. . .	. . .	. . .	. . .	. . .
Computer and information	2 262 . .	. . .	. . .	. . .	. . .	. . .	. . .	. . .	. . .
Royalties and licence fees	2 266 . .	. . .	. . .	. . .	. . .	. . .	. . .	. . .	. . .
Other business services	2 268 . .	8.52	9.30	10.80	11.64	14.34	17.90	16.64	. . .
Personal, cultural, and recreational	2 287 . .	. . .	. . .	. . .	. . .	. . .	. . .	. . .	. . .
Government, n.i.e.	2 291 . .	3.67	1.52	.79	.83	.91	1.16	1.45	. . .
Other services, debit	3 200 BA	**-8.62**	**-9.13**	**-10.40**	**-12.07**	**-13.80**	**-17.89**	**-15.91**	**. . .**
Communications	3 245 . .	. . .	. . .	. . .	. . .	. . .	. . .	. . .	. . .
Construction	3 249 . .	. . .	. . .	. . .	. . .	. . .	. . .	. . .	. . .
Insurance	3 253 . .	-2.36	-2.50	-2.38	-3.14	-3.38	-4.43	-4.56	. . .
Financial	3 260 . .	. . .	. . .	. . .	. . .	. . .	. . .	. . .	. . .
Computer and information	3 262 . .	. . .	. . .	. . .	. . .	. . .	. . .	. . .	. . .
Royalties and licence fees	3 266 . .	-.33	-.37	-.37	-.37	-.44	-.35	-.27	. . .
Other business services	3 268 . .	-3.85	-4.74	-5.53	-5.84	-7.53	-7.75	-8.77	. . .
Personal, cultural, and recreational	3 287 . .	. . .	. . .	. . .	. . .	. . .	. . .	. . .	. . .
Government, n.i.e.	3 291 . .	-2.07	-1.52	-2.12	-2.72	-2.44	-5.36	-2.32	. . .

Table 2 (Continued). STANDARD PRESENTATION, 1988–95
(Millions of U.S. dollars)

	Code		1988	1989	1990	1991	1992	1993	1994	1995
C. INCOME	4 300	. .	–6.27	–9.53	–11.87	–7.29	–6.19	–8.36	–8.81	. . .
Total credit	2 300	. .	*2.73*	*2.43*	*2.51*	*2.48*	*2.55*	*2.80*	*3.61*	. . .
Total debit	3 300	. .	*–9.00*	*–11.96*	*–14.38*	*–9.77*	*–8.74*	*–11.16*	*–12.43*	. . .
Compensation of employees, credit	2 310	. .	**.26**	**.15**	**.09**	**.08**	**.08**	**.08**	**.08**	. . .
Compensation of employees, debit	3 310	. .	**–.11**	**–.11**	**–.03**	**–.02**	**–.02**	**–.02**	**–.02**	. . .
Investment income, credit	2 320	. .	**2.47**	**2.28**	**2.42**	**2.40**	**2.48**	**2.72**	**3.54**	. . .
Direct investment income	2 330	. .	. . .	. . .	.11	.09	. . .	.17	.05	. . .
Dividends and distributed branch profits	2 332	. .	. . .	. . .	. . .	. . .	. . .	. . .	. . .	. . .
Reinvested earnings and undistributed branch profits	2 333	. .	. . .	. . .	. . .	. . .	. . .	. . .	. . .	. . .
Income on debt (interest)	2 334	. .	. . .	. . .	.11	.09	. . .	.17	.05	. . .
Portfolio investment income	2 339	. .	. . .	. . .	. . .	. . .	. . .	. . .	. . .	. . .
Income on equity	2 340	. .	. . .	. . .	. . .	. . .	. . .	. . .	. . .	. . .
Income on bonds and notes	2 350	. .	. . .	. . .	. . .	. . .	. . .	. . .	. . .	. . .
Income on money market instruments and financial derivatives	2 360	. .	. . .	. . .	. . .	. . .	. . .	. . .	. . .	. . .
Other investment income	2 370	. .	2.47	2.28	2.31	2.31	2.48	2.55	3.49	. . .
Investment income, debit	3 320	. .	**–8.89**	**–11.85**	**–14.36**	**–9.75**	**–8.73**	**–11.14**	**–12.41**	. . .
Direct investment income	3 330	. .	–4.19	–5.89	–8.43	–5.80	–6.13	–7.22	–7.60	. . .
Dividends and distributed branch profits	3 332	. .	–3.44	–4.59	–5.34	–3.44	–2.81	–5.22	–4.59	. . .
Reinvested earnings and undistributed branch profits	3 333	. .	–.74	–.81	–2.01	–1.43	–1.87	–1.12	–1.75	. . .
Income on debt (interest)	3 334	. .	. . .	–.48	–1.07	–.93	–1.44	–.88	–1.26	. . .
Portfolio investment income	3 339	. .	. . .	. . .	. . .	. . .	. . .	. . .	. . .	. . .
Income on equity	3 340	. .	. . .	. . .	. . .	. . .	. . .	. . .	. . .	. . .
Income on bonds and notes	3 350	. .	. . .	. . .	. . .	. . .	. . .	. . .	. . .	. . .
Income on money market instruments and financial derivatives	3 360	. .	. . .	. . .	. . .	. . .	. . .	. . .	. . .	. . .
Other investment income	3 370	. .	–4.70	–5.96	–5.92	–3.95	–2.60	–3.91	–4.81	. . .
D. CURRENT TRANSFERS	4 379	. .	12.21	16.51	11.34	11.30	12.00	13.69	16.24	. . .
Credit	2 379	. .	**13.04**	**17.39**	**12.46**	**13.25**	**14.26**	**16.10**	**19.75**	. . .
General government	2 380	. .	1.41	9.04	2.22	1.94	3.16	5.63	5.41	. . .
Other sectors	2 390	. .	11.63	8.35	10.24	11.31	11.10	10.47	14.34	. . .
Workers' remittances	2 391	. .	11.63	8.35	9.87	10.90	10.72	10.11	13.52	. . .
Other current transfers	2 392	. .	. . .	. . .	.37	.42	.38	.36	.82	. . .
Debit	3 379	. .	**–.83**	**–.88**	**–1.11**	**–1.96**	**–2.25**	**–2.41**	**–3.51**	. . .
General government	3 380	. .	–.83	–.88	–1.11	–1.96	–2.25	–2.41	–1.88	. . .
Other sectors	3 390	. .	. . .	. . .	. . .	. . .	. . .	. . .	–1.63	. . .
Workers' remittances	3 391	. .	. . .	. . .	. . .	. . .	. . .	. . .	. . .	. . .
Other current transfers	3 392	. .	. . .	. . .	. . .	. . .	. . .	. . .	–1.63	. . .
CAPITAL AND FINANCIAL ACCOUNT	4 996	. .	**29.49**	**43.87**	**38.11**	**38.43**	**23.62**	**35.40**	**23.41**	. . .
CAPITAL ACCOUNT	4 994	. .	**12.93**	**9.87**	**22.10**	**17.51**	**13.43**	**16.89**	**21.67**	. . .
Total credit	2 994	. .	*20.85*	*10.69*	*23.36*	*18.51*	*14.80*	*18.27*	*23.04*	. . .
Total debit	3 994	. .	*–7.93*	*–.81*	*–1.26*	*–1.01*	*–1.38*	*–1.38*	*–1.38*	. . .
Capital transfers, credit	2 400	. .	**20.85**	**10.69**	**23.36**	**18.51**	**14.80**	**18.27**	**23.04**	. . .
General government	2 401	. .	9.22	2.33	15.34	10.31	6.29	10.10	10.48	. . .
Debt forgiveness	2 402	. .	. . .	. . .	. . .	. . .	. . .	. . .	. . .	. . .
Other capital transfers	2 410	. .	9.22	2.33	15.34	10.31	6.29	10.10	10.48	. . .
Other sectors	2 430	. .	11.63	8.35	8.02	8.20	8.52	8.17	12.56	. . .
Migrants' transfers	2 431	. .	11.63	8.35	8.02	8.20	8.52	8.17	12.56	. . .
Debt forgiveness	2 432	. .	. . .	. . .	. . .	. . .	. . .	. . .	. . .	. . .
Other capital transfers	2 440	. .	. . .	. . .	. . .	. . .	. . .	. . .	. . .	. . .
Capital transfers, debit	3 400	. .	**–7.93**	**–.81**	**–1.26**	**–1.01**	**–1.38**	**–1.38**	**–1.38**	. . .
General government	3 401	. .	. . .	. . .	. . .	. . .	. . .	. . .	. . .	. . .
Debt forgiveness	3 402	. .	. . .	. . .	. . .	. . .	. . .	. . .	. . .	. . .
Other capital transfers	3 410	. .	. . .	. . .	. . .	. . .	. . .	. . .	. . .	. . .
Other sectors	3 430	. .	–7.93	–.81	–1.26	–1.01	–1.38	–1.38	–1.38	. . .
Migrants' transfers	3 431	. .	–7.41	. . .	–1.26	–1.01	–1.38	–1.38	–1.38	. . .
Debt forgiveness	3 432	. .	. . .	. . .	. . .	. . .	. . .	. . .	. . .	. . .
Other capital transfers	3 440	. .	–.52	–.81	. . .	. . .	. . .	. . .	. . .	. . .
Nonproduced nonfinancial assets, credit	2 480	. .	. . .	. . .	. . .	. . .	. . .	. . .	. . .	. . .
Nonproduced nonfinancial assets, debit	3 480	. .	. . .	. . .	. . .	. . .	. . .	. . .	. . .	. . .

Table 2 (Continued). STANDARD PRESENTATION, 1988–95

(Millions of U.S. dollars)

	Code	1988	1989	1990	1991	1992	1993	1994	1995
FINANCIAL ACCOUNT	4 995 . .	**16.57**	**34.00**	**16.01**	**20.93**	**10.19**	**18.51**	**1.74**	. . .
A. DIRECT INVESTMENT	4 500 . .	14.98	10.48	12.87	15.27	22.58	20.20	19.31	. . .
Direct investment abroad	4 505 . .	. . .	. . .	. . .	. . .	. . .	. . .	. . .	. . .
Equity capital	4 510 . .	. . .	. . .	. . .	. . .	. . .	. . .	. . .	. . .
Claims on affiliated enterprises	4 515 . .	. . .	. . .	. . .	. . .	. . .	. . .	. . .	. . .
Liabilities to affiliated enterprises	4 520 . .	. . .	. . .	. . .	. . .	. . .	. . .	. . .	. . .
Reinvested earnings	4 525 . .	. . .	. . .	. . .	. . .	. . .	. . .	. . .	. . .
Other capital	4 530 . .	. . .	. . .	. . .	. . .	. . .	. . .	. . .	. . .
Claims on affiliated enterprises	4 535 . .	. . .	. . .	. . .	. . .	. . .	. . .	. . .	. . .
Liabilities to affiliated enterprises	4 540 . .	. . .	. . .	. . .	. . .	. . .	. . .	. . .	. . .
Direct investment in Grenada	4 555 . .	**14.98**	**10.48**	**12.87**	**15.27**	**22.58**	**20.20**	**19.31**	. . .
Equity capital	4 560 . .	11.69	9.67	8.89	11.93	6.27	11.58	7.31	. . .
Claims on direct investors	4 565 . .	. . .	. . .	. . .	. . .	. . .	. . .	. . .	. . .
Liabilities to direct investors	4 570 . .	. . .	. . .	. . .	. . .	. . .	. . .	. . .	. . .
Reinvested earnings	4 575 . .	.74	.81	2.01	1.43	1.87	1.12	1.75	. . .
Other capital	4 580 . .	2.56	. . .	1.97	1.91	14.44	7.50	10.25	. . .
Claims on direct investors	4 585 . .	. . .	. . .	. . .	. . .	. . .	. . .	. . .	. . .
Liabilities to direct investors	4 590 . .	. . .	. . .	. . .	. . .	. . .	. . .	. . .	. . .
B. PORTFOLIO INVESTMENT	4 600 . .	.15	. . .	.02	.05	–.16	.20	–.38	. . .
Assets	4 602 . .	. . .	. . .	. . .	. . .	. . .	. . .	. . .	. . .
Equity securities	4 610 . .	. . .	. . .	. . .	. . .	. . .	. . .	. . .	. . .
Monetary authorities	4 611 . .	. . .	. . .	. . .	. . .	. . .	. . .	. . .	. . .
General government	4 612 . .	. . .	. . .	. . .	. . .	. . .	. . .	. . .	. . .
Banks	4 613 . .	. . .	. . .	. . .	. . .	. . .	. . .	. . .	. . .
Other sectors	4 614 . .	. . .	. . .	. . .	. . .	. . .	. . .	. . .	. . .
Debt securities	4 619 . .	. . .	. . .	. . .	. . .	. . .	. . .	. . .	. . .
Bonds and notes	4 620 . .	. . .	. . .	. . .	. . .	. . .	. . .	. . .	. . .
Monetary authorities	4 621 . .	. . .	. . .	. . .	. . .	. . .	. . .	. . .	. . .
General government	4 622 . .	. . .	. . .	. . .	. . .	. . .	. . .	. . .	. . .
Banks	4 623 . .	. . .	. . .	. . .	. . .	. . .	. . .	. . .	. . .
Other sectors	4 624 . .	. . .	. . .	. . .	. . .	. . .	. . .	. . .	. . .
Money market instruments	4 630 . .	. . .	. . .	. . .	. . .	. . .	. . .	. . .	. . .
Monetary authorities	4 631 . .	. . .	. . .	. . .	. . .	. . .	. . .	. . .	. . .
General government	4 632 . .	. . .	. . .	. . .	. . .	. . .	. . .	. . .	. . .
Banks	4 633 . .	. . .	. . .	. . .	. . .	. . .	. . .	. . .	. . .
Other sectors	4 634 . .	. . .	. . .	. . .	. . .	. . .	. . .	. . .	. . .
Financial derivatives	4 640 . .	. . .	. . .	. . .	. . .	. . .	. . .	. . .	. . .
Monetary authorities	4 641 . .	. . .	. . .	. . .	. . .	. . .	. . .	. . .	. . .
General government	4 642 . .	. . .	. . .	. . .	. . .	. . .	. . .	. . .	. . .
Banks	4 643 . .	. . .	. . .	. . .	. . .	. . .	. . .	. . .	. . .
Other sectors	4 644 . .	. . .	. . .	. . .	. . .	. . .	. . .	. . .	. . .
Liabilities	4 652 . .	**.15**	. . .	**.02**	**.05**	**–.16**	**.20**	**–.38**	. . .
Equity securities	4 660 . .	.15	. . .	.02	.05	–.16	.20	–.38	. . .
Banks	4 663 . .	. . .	. . .	. . .	. . .	. . .	. . .	. . .	. . .
Other sectors	4 664 . .	. . .	. . .	. . .	. . .	. . .	. . .	. . .	. . .
Debt securities	4 669 . .	. . .	. . .	. . .	. . .	. . .	. . .	. . .	. . .
Bonds and notes	4 670 . .	. . .	. . .	. . .	. . .	. . .	. . .	. . .	. . .
Monetary authorities	4 671 . .	. . .	. . .	. . .	. . .	. . .	. . .	. . .	. . .
General government	4 672 . .	. . .	. . .	. . .	. . .	. . .	. . .	. . .	. . .
Banks	4 673 . .	. . .	. . .	. . .	. . .	. . .	. . .	. . .	. . .
Other sectors	4 674 . .	. . .	. . .	. . .	. . .	. . .	. . .	. . .	. . .
Money market instruments	4 680 . .	. . .	. . .	. . .	. . .	. . .	. . .	. . .	. . .
Monetary authorities	4 681 . .	. . .	. . .	. . .	. . .	. . .	. . .	. . .	. . .
General government	4 682 . .	. . .	. . .	. . .	. . .	. . .	. . .	. . .	. . .
Banks	4 683 . .	. . .	. . .	. . .	. . .	. . .	. . .	. . .	. . .
Other sectors	4 684 . .	. . .	. . .	. . .	. . .	. . .	. . .	. . .	. . .
Financial derivatives	4 690 . .	. . .	. . .	. . .	. . .	. . .	. . .	. . .	. . .
Monetary authorities	4 691 . .	. . .	. . .	. . .	. . .	. . .	. . .	. . .	. . .
General government	4 692 . .	. . .	. . .	. . .	. . .	. . .	. . .	. . .	. . .
Banks	4 693 . .	. . .	. . .	. . .	. . .	. . .	. . .	. . .	. . .
Other sectors	4 694 . .	. . .	. . .	. . .	. . .	. . .	. . .	. . .	. . .

Table 2 (Concluded). STANDARD PRESENTATION, 1988–95
(Millions of U.S. dollars)

	Code	1988	1989	1990	1991	1992	1993	1994	1995
C. OTHER INVESTMENT	4 700 . .	–4.45	21.96	5.19	8.05	–4.13	–1.45	–12.65	. . .
Assets	4 703 . .	**–8.35**	**17.52**	**–11.48**	**2.02**	**–2.30**	**–.19**	**–12.31**	**. . .**
Trade credits	4 706 . .	. . .	. . .	. . .	. . .	. . .	. . .	. . .	. . .
General government: long-term	4 708 . .	. . .	. . .	. . .	. . .	. . .	. . .	. . .	. . .
General government: short-term	4 709 . .	. . .	. . .	. . .	. . .	. . .	. . .	. . .	. . .
Other sectors: long-term	4 711 . .	. . .	. . .	. . .	. . .	. . .	. . .	. . .	. . .
Other sectors: short-term	4 712 . .	. . .	. . .	. . .	. . .	. . .	. . .	. . .	. . .
Loans	4 714 . .	. . .	. . .	. . .	. . .	. . .	. . .	. . .	. . .
Monetary authorities: long-term	4 717 . .	. . .	. . .	. . .	. . .	. . .	. . .	. . .	. . .
Monetary authorities: short-term	4 718 . .	. . .	. . .	. . .	. . .	. . .	. . .	. . .	. . .
General government: long-term	4 720 . .	. . .	. . .	. . .	. . .	. . .	. . .	. . .	. . .
General government: short-term	4 721 . .	. . .	. . .	. . .	. . .	. . .	. . .	. . .	. . .
Banks: long-term	4 723 . .	. . .	. . .	. . .	. . .	. . .	. . .	. . .	. . .
Banks: short-term	4 724 . .	. . .	. . .	. . .	. . .	. . .	. . .	. . .	. . .
Other sectors: long-term	4 726 . .	. . .	. . .	. . .	. . .	. . .	. . .	. . .	. . .
Other sectors: short-term	4 727 . .	. . .	. . .	. . .	. . .	. . .	. . .	. . .	. . .
Currency and deposits	4 730 . .	–8.35	17.52	–11.48	2.02	–2.30	–.19	–12.31	. . .
Monetary authorities	4 731 . .	. . .	. . .	. . .	. . .	. . .	. . .	. . .	. . .
General government	4 732 . .	. . .	. . .	. . .	. . .	. . .	. . .	. . .	. . .
Banks	4 733 . .	–8.35	17.52	–11.48	2.02	–2.30	–.19	–12.31	. . .
Other sectors	4 734 . .	. . .	. . .	. . .	. . .	. . .	. . .	. . .	. . .
Other assets	4 736 . .	. . .	. . .	. . .	. . .	. . .	. . .	. . .	. . .
Monetary authorities: long-term	4 738 . .	. . .	. . .	. . .	. . .	. . .	. . .	. . .	. . .
Monetary authorities: short-term	4 739 . .	. . .	. . .	. . .	. . .	. . .	. . .	. . .	. . .
General government: long-term	4 741 . .	. . .	. . .	. . .	. . .	. . .	. . .	. . .	. . .
General government: short-term	4 742 . .	. . .	. . .	. . .	. . .	. . .	. . .	. . .	. . .
Banks: long-term	4 744 . .	. . .	. . .	. . .	. . .	. . .	. . .	. . .	. . .
Banks: short-term	4 745 . .	. . .	. . .	. . .	. . .	. . .	. . .	. . .	. . .
Other sectors: long-term	4 747 . .	. . .	. . .	. . .	. . .	. . .	. . .	. . .	. . .
Other sectors: short-term	4 748 . .	. . .	. . .	. . .	. . .	. . .	. . .	. . .	. . .
Liabilities	4 753 . .	**3.90**	**4.44**	**16.67**	**6.03**	**–1.83**	**–1.26**	**–.34**	**. . .**
Trade credits	4 756 . .	. . .	. . .	. . .	. . .	. . .	. . .	. . .	. . .
General government: long-term	4 758 . .	. . .	. . .	. . .	. . .	. . .	. . .	. . .	. . .
General government: short-term	4 759 . .	. . .	. . .	. . .	. . .	. . .	. . .	. . .	. . .
Other sectors: long-term	4 761 . .	. . .	. . .	. . .	. . .	. . .	. . .	. . .	. . .
Other sectors: short-term	4 762 . .	. . .	. . .	. . .	. . .	. . .	. . .	. . .	. . .
Loans	4 764 . .	3.90	4.44	16.67	6.03	–1.83	–1.26	–.34	. . .
Use of Fund credit and loans from the Fund	4 766 . .	–.75	–.72	–.46	–.01	. . .	. . .	. . .	. . .
Monetary authorities: other long-term	4 767 . .	. . .	. . .	. . .	. . .	. . .	. . .	. . .	. . .
Monetary authorities: short-term	4 768 . .	. . .	. . .	. . .	. . .	. . .	. . .	. . .	. . .
General government: long-term	4 770 . .	6.19	6.56	16.19	8.59	.75	1.29	3.41	. . .
General government: short-term	4 771 . .	. . .	. . .	. . .	. . .	. . .	. . .	. . .	. . .
Banks: long-term	4 773 . .	. . .	. . .	. . .	. . .	. . .	. . .	. . .	. . .
Banks: short-term	4 774 . .	. . .	. . .	. . .	. . .	. . .	. . .	. . .	. . .
Other sectors: long-term	4 776 . .	–1.54	–1.40	.94	–2.54	–2.57	–2.56	–3.75	. . .
Other sectors: short-term	4 777 . .	. . .	. . .	. . .	. . .	. . .	. . .	. . .	. . .
Currency and deposits	4 780 . .	. . .	. . .	. . .	. . .	. . .	. . .	. . .	. . .
Monetary authorities	4 781 . .	. . .	. . .	. . .	. . .	. . .	. . .	. . .	. . .
General government	4 782 . .	. . .	. . .	. . .	. . .	. . .	. . .	. . .	. . .
Banks	4 783 . .	. . .	. . .	. . .	. . .	. . .	. . .	. . .	. . .
Other sectors	4 784 . .	. . .	. . .	. . .	. . .	. . .	. . .	. . .	. . .
Other liabilities	4 786 . .	. . .	. . .	. . .	. . .	. . .	. . .	. . .	. . .
Monetary authorities: long-term	4 788 . .	. . .	. . .	. . .	. . .	. . .	. . .	. . .	. . .
Monetary authorities: short-term	4 789 . .	. . .	. . .	. . .	. . .	. . .	. . .	. . .	. . .
General government: long-term	4 791 . .	. . .	. . .	. . .	. . .	. . .	. . .	. . .	. . .
General government: short-term	4 792 . .	. . .	. . .	. . .	. . .	. . .	. . .	. . .	. . .
Banks: long-term	4 794 . .	. . .	. . .	. . .	. . .	. . .	. . .	. . .	. . .
Banks: short-term	4 795 . .	. . .	. . .	. . .	. . .	. . .	. . .	. . .	. . .
Other sectors: long-term	4 797 . .	. . .	. . .	. . .	. . .	. . .	. . .	. . .	. . .
Other sectors: short-term	4 798 . .	. . .	. . .	. . .	. . .	. . .	. . .	. . .	. . .
D. RESERVE ASSETS	4 800 . .	5.89	1.56	–2.07	–2.44	–8.10	–.44	–4.54	. . .
Monetary gold	4 810 . .	. . .	. . .	. . .	. . .	. . .	. . .	. . .	. . .
Special drawing rights	4 820 . .	. . .	. . .	. . .	. . .	. . .	. . .	–.03	. . .
Reserve position in the Fund	4 830 . .	. . .	. . .	. . .	. . .	. . .	. . .	. . .	. . .
Foreign exchange	4 840 . .	5.89	1.56	–2.07	–2.44	–8.10	–.44	–4.10	. . .
Other claims	4 880 . .	. . .	. . .	. . .	. . .	. . .	. . .	–.41	. . .
NET ERRORS AND OMISSIONS	4 998 . .	**–1.72**	**–7.55**	**8.12**	**8.15**	**9.52**	**8.14**	**9.45**	**. . .**

Part 3 of the *Yearbook* contains descriptions of the methodologies, compilation practices, and sources used to compile these data.

Table 1. ANALYTIC PRESENTATION, 1988–95
(Millions of U.S. dollars)

	Code	1988	1989	1990	1991	1992	1993	1994	1995
A. Current Account[1]	4 993 Y .	**–414.0**	**–367.1**	**–232.9**	**–183.7**	**–705.9**	**–701.7**	**–625.3**	**–572.2**
Goods: exports f.o.b	2 100 . .	1,073.3	1,126.1	1,211.4	1,230.0	1,283.7	1,363.2	1,550.1	2,155.5
Goods: imports f.o.b	3 100 . .	–1,413.2	–1,484.4	–1,428.0	–1,673.0	–2,327.8	–2,384.0	–2,546.6	–3,032.6
Balance on Goods	4 100 . .	*–339.9*	*–358.3*	*–216.6*	*–443.0*	*–1,044.1*	*–1,020.8*	*–996.5*	*–877.1*
Services: credit	2 200 . .	195.8	297.7	356.1	458.8	614.0	660.4	697.5	665.8
Services: debit	3 200 . .	–317.9	–376.9	–383.7	–356.4	–525.3	–586.1	–644.9	–695.0
Balance on Goods and Services	4 991 . .	*–462.0*	*–437.5*	*–244.2*	*–340.6*	*–955.4*	*–946.5*	*–943.9*	*–906.3*
Income: credit	2 300 . .	31.6	31.0	20.9	63.9	69.1	61.1	63.6	46.6
Income: debit	3 300 . .	–207.9	–210.4	–216.6	–166.7	–210.1	–179.5	–193.6	–205.7
Balance on Goods, Services, and Income	4 992 . .	*–638.3*	*–616.9*	*–439.9*	*–443.4*	*–1,096.4*	*–1,064.9*	*–1,073.9*	*–1,065.4*
Current transfers: credit	2 379 Y .	227.7	255.1	217.6	276.7	406.2	371.4	456.4	510.4
Current transfers: debit	3 379 . .	–3.4	–5.3	–10.6	–17.0	–15.7	–8.2	–7.8	–17.2
B. Capital Account[1]	4 994 Y .	**. . .**	**. . .**	**. . .**	**. . .**	**. . .**	**. . .**	**. . .**	**59.3**
Capital account: credit	2 994 Y .	. . .	. . .	. . .	. . .	. . .	. . .	. . .	59.3
Capital account: debit	3 994 . .	. . .	. . .	. . .	. . .	. . .	. . .	. . .	. . .
Total, Groups A Plus B	4 010 . .	*–414.0*	*–367.1*	*–232.9*	*–183.7*	*–705.9*	*–701.7*	*–625.3*	*–512.9*
C. Financial Account[1]	4 995 X .	**80.5**	**225.3**	**–46.2**	**732.8**	**610.5**	**789.2**	**655.2**	**496.8**
Direct investment abroad	4 505 . .	. . .	. . .	. . .	. . .	. . .	. . .	. . .	. . .
Direct investment in Guatemala	4 555 Y .	329.7	76.2	47.6	90.7	94.1	142.5	65.2	75.2
Portfolio investment assets	4 602 . .	. . .	. . .	–1.8	–.2	1.8	112.4	–9.8	–22.2
Equity securities	4 610 . .	. . .	. . .	. . .	. . .	. . .	. . .	. . .	. . .
Debt securities	4 619 . .	. . .	. . .	–1.8	–.2	1.8	112.4	–9.8	–22.2
Portfolio investment liabilities	4 652 Y .	–372.2	–63.9	–19.5	71.3	9.6	–27.0	7.1	5.9
Equity securities	4 660 Y .	. . .	. . .	. . .	. . .	. . .	. . .	. . .	. . .
Debt securities	4 669 Y .	–372.2	–63.9	–19.5	71.3	9.6	–27.0	7.1	5.9
Other investment assets	4 703 . .	29.4	98.7	–78.0	68.1	57.2	–3.0	116.8	125.1
Monetary authorities	4 703 . A	. . .	. . .	. . .	. . .	. . .	. . .	. . .	. . .
General government	4 703 . B	29.4	98.7	–90.7	. . .	. . .	–45.9	–49.2	. . .
Banks	4 703 . C	. . .	. . .	. . .	. . .	. . .	. . .	. . .	. . .
Other sectors	4 703 . D	. . .	. . .	12.7	68.1	57.2	42.9	166.0	125.1
Other investment liabilities	4 753 X .	93.6	114.3	5.5	502.9	447.8	564.3	475.9	312.8
Monetary authorities	4 753 XA	–85.3	–96.9	–102.5	–65.1	.6	–71.1	–63.9	–78.3
General government	4 753 YB	31.6	60.6	3.6	–25.8	–16.3	–51.3	132.7	11.8
Banks	4 753 YC	16.9	–14.3	–17.0	–3.9	14.4	. . .	. . .	7.3
Other sectors	4 753 YD	130.4	164.9	121.4	597.7	449.1	686.7	407.1	372.0
Total, Groups A Through C	4 020 . .	*–333.5*	*–141.8*	*–279.1*	*549.1*	*–95.4*	*87.5*	*29.9*	*–16.1*
D. Net Errors and Omissions	4 998 . .	**–2.4**	**54.7**	**36.2**	**83.3**	**81.8**	**85.2**	**–23.6**	**–135.9**
Total, Groups A Through D	4 030 . .	*–336.0*	*–87.1*	*–242.9*	*632.4*	*–13.6*	*172.7*	*6.3*	*–152.0*
E. Reserves and Related Items	4 040 . .	**336.0**	**87.1**	**242.9**	**–632.4**	**13.6**	**–172.7**	**–6.3**	**152.0**
Reserve assets	4 800 . .	110.6	–59.0	41.8	–551.3	51.6	–120.5	–47.3	157.3
Use of Fund credit and loans	4 766 . .	30.8	–12.7	–11.9	–2.8	–31.7	–31.3	. . .	. . .
Liabilities constituting foreign authorities' reserves	4 900 . .	–2.5	3.0	. . .	–1.0	. . .	27.0	. . .	. . .
Exceptional financing	4 920 . .	197.0	155.8	213.0	–77.3	–6.4	–47.9	41.0	–5.3
Conversion rates: quetzales per U.S. dollar	0 101 . .	**2.6196**	**2.8161**	**4.4858**	**5.0289**	**5.1706**	**5.6354**	**5.7512**	**5.8103**

[1] Excludes components that have been classified in the categories of Group E.

Table 2. STANDARD PRESENTATION, 1988–95
(Millions of U.S. dollars)

	Code	1988	1989	1990	1991	1992	1993	1994	1995
CURRENT ACCOUNT	4 993 . .	**–414.0**	**–367.1**	**–212.9**	**–183.7**	**–705.9**	**–701.7**	**–625.3**	**–572.0**
A. GOODS	4 100 . .	–339.9	–358.3	–216.6	–443.0	–1,044.1	–1,020.8	–996.5	–877.1
Credit	2 100 . .	**1,073.3**	**1,126.1**	**1,211.4**	**1,230.0**	**1,283.7**	**1,363.2**	**1,550.1**	**2,155.5**
General merchandise: exports f.o.b.	2 110 . .	1,073.3	1,126.1	1,211.4	1,230.0	1,283.7	1,363.2	1,550.1	1,989.0
Goods for processing: exports f.o.b.	2 150 . .	. . .	. . .	. . .	. . .	. . .	. . .	. . .	166.5
Repairs on goods	2 160 . .	. . .	. . .	. . .	. . .	. . .	. . .	. . .	. . .
Goods procured in ports by carriers	2 170 . .	. . .	. . .	. . .	. . .	. . .	. . .	. . .	. . .
Nonmonetary gold	2 180 . .	. . .	. . .	. . .	. . .	. . .	. . .	. . .	. . .
Debit	3 100 . .	**–1,413.2**	**–1,484.4**	**–1,428.0**	**–1,673.0**	**–2,327.8**	**–2,384.0**	**–2,546.6**	**–3,032.6**
General merchandise: imports f.o.b.	3 110 . .	–1,413.2	–1,484.4	–1,428.0	–1,673.0	–2,327.8	–2,384.0	–2,546.6	–3,032.6
Goods for processing: imports f.o.b.	3 150 . .	. . .	. . .	. . .	. . .	. . .	. . .	. . .	. . .
Repairs on goods	3 160 . .	. . .	. . .	. . .	. . .	. . .	. . .	. . .	. . .
Goods procured in ports by carriers	3 170 . .	. . .	. . .	. . .	. . .	. . .	. . .	. . .	. . .
Nonmonetary gold	3 180 . .	. . .	. . .	. . .	. . .	. . .	. . .	. . .	. . .
B. SERVICES	4 200 . .	–122.1	–79.2	–27.6	102.4	88.7	74.3	52.6	–29.2
Total credit	2 200 . .	*195.8*	*297.7*	*356.1*	*458.8*	*614.0*	*660.4*	*697.5*	*665.8*
Total debit	3 200 . .	*–317.9*	*–376.9*	*–383.7*	*–356.4*	*–525.3*	*–586.1*	*–644.9*	*–695.0*
Transportation services, credit	2 205 . .	**16.6**	**26.0**	**23.1**	**24.2**	**41.2**	**34.4**	**39.8**	**53.6**
Passenger	2 205 BA	. . .	. . .	. . .	. . .	. . .	. . .	. . .	*3.3*
Freight	2 205 BB	*.4*	*2.1*	*6.8*	*6.8*	*2.2*	*4.4*	*6.6*	*13.8*
Other	2 205 BC	*16.2*	*23.9*	*16.3*	*17.4*	*39.0*	*30.0*	*33.2*	*36.5*
Sea transport, passenger	2 207 . .	. . .	. . .	. . .	. . .	. . .	. . .	. . .	. . .
Sea transport, freight	2 208 . .	. . .	. . .	. . .	. . .	. . .	. . .	. . .	8.6
Sea transport, other	2 209 . .	. . .	. . .	. . .	. . .	. . .	. . .	. . .	8.4
Air transport, passenger	2 211 . .	. . .	. . .	. . .	. . .	. . .	. . .	. . .	2.7
Air transport, freight	2 212 . .	. . .	. . .	. . .	. . .	. . .	. . .	. . .	.8
Air transport, other	2 213 . .	. . .	. . .	. . .	. . .	. . .	. . .	. . .	21.4
Other transport, passenger	2 215 . .	. . .	. . .	. . .	. . .	. . .	. . .	. . .	.6
Other transport, freight	2 216 . .	. . .	. . .	. . .	. . .	. . .	. . .	. . .	4.4
Other transport, other	2 217 . .	. . .	. . .	. . .	. . .	. . .	. . .	. . .	6.7
Transportation services, debit	3 205 . .	**–152.4**	**–165.6**	**–148.8**	**–183.9**	**–224.9**	**–231.6**	**–255.9**	**–278.6**
Passenger	3 205 BA	*–7.7*	*–6.3*	*–7.2*	*–7.7*	*–20.1*	*–17.4*	*–18.3*	*–25.7*
Freight	3 205 BB	*–136.3*	*–148.3*	*–135.7*	*–168.8*	*–192.9*	*–203.9*	*–222.2*	*–251.7*
Other	3 205 BC	*–8.4*	*–11.0*	*–5.9*	*–7.4*	*–11.9*	*–10.3*	*–15.4*	*–1.2*
Sea transport, passenger	3 207 . .	. . .	. . .	. . .	. . .	. . .	. . .	. . .	. . .
Sea transport, freight	3 208 . .	. . .	. . .	. . .	. . .	. . .	. . .	. . .	–159.1
Sea transport, other	3 209 . .	. . .	. . .	. . .	. . .	. . .	. . .	. . .	. . .
Air transport, passenger	3 211 . .	. . .	. . .	. . .	. . .	. . .	. . .	. . .	–20.9
Air transport, freight	3 212 . .	. . .	. . .	. . .	. . .	. . .	. . .	. . .	–12.0
Air transport, other	3 213 . .	. . .	. . .	. . .	. . .	. . .	. . .	. . .	. . .
Other transport, passenger	3 215 . .	. . .	. . .	. . .	. . .	. . .	. . .	. . .	–4.8
Other transport, freight	3 216 . .	. . .	. . .	. . .	. . .	. . .	. . .	. . .	–80.6
Other transport, other	3 217 . .	. . .	. . .	. . .	. . .	. . .	. . .	. . .	–1.2
Travel, credit	2 236 . .	**62.1**	**108.9**	**117.9**	**145.2**	**186.0**	**204.5**	**205.0**	**212.5**
Business travel	2 237 . .	8.8	20.6	22.0	24.4	35.6	39.0	53.6	1.8
Personal travel	2 240 . .	53.3	88.3	95.9	120.8	150.4	165.5	151.4	210.7
Travel, debit	3 236 . .	**–95.2**	**–123.5**	**–99.6**	**–100.2**	**–102.9**	**–117.1**	**–150.7**	**–141.2**
Business travel	3 237 . .	–12.3	–23.5	–28.8	–25.9	–23.5	–23.5	–33.3	–1.9
Personal travel	3 240 . .	–82.9	–100.0	–70.8	–74.3	–79.4	–93.6	–117.4	–139.3
Other services, credit	2 200 BA	**117.1**	**162.8**	**215.1**	**289.4**	**386.8**	**421.5**	**452.7**	**399.7**
Communications	2 245 . .	. . .	. . .	. . .	. . .	. . .	. . .	. . .	66.1
Construction	2 249 . .	. . .	. . .	. . .	. . .	. . .	. . .	. . .	. . .
Insurance	2 253 . .	2.0	6.8	6.1	5.5	11.9	4.6	5.3	8.2
Financial	2 260 . .	. . .	. . .	. . .	. . .	. . .	. . .	. . .	17.0
Computer and information	2 262 . .	. . .	. . .	. . .	. . .	. . .	. . .	. . .	1.7
Royalties and licence fees	2 266 . .	. . .	. . .	. . .	1.6	. . .	. . .	. . .	. . .
Other business services	2 268 . .	53.7	77.5	166.2	245.5	340.6	381.8	408.4	268.5
Personal, cultural, and recreational	2 287 . .	. . .	. . .	. . .	. . .	. . .	. . .	. . .	. . .
Government, n.i.e.	2 291 . .	61.4	78.5	42.8	36.8	34.3	35.1	39.0	38.2
Other services, debit	3 200 BA	**–70.3**	**–87.8**	**–135.3**	**–72.3**	**–197.5**	**–237.4**	**–238.3**	**–275.2**
Communications	3 245 . .	. . .	. . .	. . .	. . .	. . .	. . .	. . .	–6.5
Construction	3 249 . .	. . .	. . .	. . .	. . .	. . .	. . .	. . .	–23.6
Insurance	3 253 . .	–14.3	–18.3	–12.5	–14.5	–19.1	–27.2	–31.2	–31.7
Financial	3 260 . .	. . .	. . .	. . .	. . .	. . .	. . .	. . .	–26.5
Computer and information	3 262 . .	. . .	. . .	. . .	. . .	. . .	. . .	. . .	–2.1
Royalties and licence fees	3 266 . .	. . .	. . .	. . .	–.1	. . .	. . .	. . .	. . .
Other business services	3 268 . .	–37.1	–48.5	–102.3	–29.3	–153.4	–172.2	–163.9	–162.3
Personal, cultural, and recreational	3 287 . .	. . .	. . .	. . .	. . .	. . .	. . .	. . .	. . .
Government, n.i.e.	3 291 . .	–18.9	–21.0	–20.5	–28.4	–25.0	–38.0	–43.2	–22.5

Table 2 (Continued). STANDARD PRESENTATION, 1988–95
(Millions of U.S. dollars)

	Code	1988	1989	1990	1991	1992	1993	1994	1995
C. INCOME	4 300 . .	–176.3	–179.4	–195.7	–102.8	–141.0	–118.4	–130.0	–159.1
Total credit	2 300 . .	*31.6*	*31.0*	*20.9*	*63.9*	*69.1*	*61.1*	*63.6*	*46.6*
Total debit	3 300 . .	*–207.9*	*–210.4*	*–216.6*	*–166.7*	*–210.1*	*–179.5*	*–193.6*	*–205.7*
Compensation of employees, credit	2 310 . .	**3.0**	**16.4**	**12.1**	**39.9**	**43.9**	**35.5**	**21.9**	**. . .**
Compensation of employees, debit	3 310 . .	**–2.3**	**–4.4**	**–3.4**	**–2.8**	**–6.4**	**–2.2**	**–3.2**	**. . .**
Investment income, credit	2 320 . .	**28.6**	**14.6**	**8.8**	**24.0**	**25.2**	**25.6**	**41.7**	**46.6**
Direct investment income	2 330 . .	1.5	.2	.9	.6	. . .	.1	6.8	11.9
Dividends and distributed branch profits	2 332 . .	1.5	.2	.9	.6	. . .	.1	6.8	7.0
Reinvested earnings and undistributed branch profits	2 333 . .	. . .	. . .	. . .	. . .	. . .	. . .	. . .	. . .
Income on debt (interest)	2 334 . .	. . .	. . .	. . .	. . .	. . .	. . .	. . .	4.9
Portfolio investment income	2 339 . .	. . .	. . .	. . .	. . .	. . .	. . .	. . .	. . .
Income on equity	2 340 . .	. . .	. . .	. . .	. . .	. . .	. . .	. . .	. . .
Income on bonds and notes	2 350 . .	. . .	. . .	. . .	. . .	. . .	. . .	. . .	. . .
Income on money market instruments and financial derivatives	2 360 . .	. . .	. . .	. . .	. . .	. . .	. . .	. . .	. . .
Other investment income	2 370 . .	27.1	14.4	7.9	23.4	25.2	25.5	34.9	34.7
Investment income, debit	3 320 . .	**–205.6**	**–206.0**	**–213.2**	**–163.9**	**–203.7**	**–177.3**	**–190.4**	**–205.7**
Direct investment income	3 330 . .	–29.4	–44.4	–37.0	–43.9	–36.0	–52.3	–58.6	–95.3
Dividends and distributed branch profits	3 332 . .	–14.2	–24.4	–17.3	–21.4	–21.9	–25.3	–25.3	–35.2
Reinvested earnings and undistributed branch profits	3 333 . .	–15.2	–20.0	–19.7	–22.5	–14.1	–27.0	–33.3	–37.1
Income on debt (interest)	3 334 . .	. . .	. . .	. . .	. . .	. . .	. . .	. . .	–23.0
Portfolio investment income	3 339 . .	. . .	. . .	. . .	. . .	. . .	. . .	. . .	. . .
Income on equity	3 340 . .	. . .	. . .	. . .	. . .	. . .	. . .	. . .	. . .
Income on bonds and notes	3 350 . .	. . .	. . .	. . .	. . .	. . .	. . .	. . .	. . .
Income on money market instruments and financial derivatives	3 360 . .	. . .	. . .	. . .	. . .	. . .	. . .	. . .	. . .
Other investment income	3 370 . .	–176.2	–161.6	–176.2	–120.0	–167.7	–125.0	–131.8	–110.4
D. CURRENT TRANSFERS	4 379 . .	224.3	249.8	227.0	259.7	390.5	363.2	448.6	493.4
Credit	2 379 . .	**227.7**	**255.1**	**237.6**	**276.7**	**406.2**	**371.4**	**456.4**	**510.6**
General government	2 380 . .	82.8	71.3	21.7	2.4	52.7	2.6	12.4	2.4
Other sectors	2 390 . .	144.9	183.8	215.9	274.3	353.5	368.8	444.0	508.2
Workers' remittances	2 391 . .	42.7	68.6	106.6	139.0	186.7	205.3	262.6	357.5
Other current transfers	2 392 . .	102.2	115.2	109.3	135.3	166.8	163.5	181.4	150.7
Debit	3 379 . .	**–3.4**	**–5.3**	**–10.6**	**–17.0**	**–15.7**	**–8.2**	**–7.8**	**–17.2**
General government	3 380 . .	–.2	–.3	. . .	–.4	–1.0	–1.4	. . .	–.2
Other sectors	3 390 . .	–3.2	–5.0	–10.6	–16.6	–14.7	–6.8	–7.8	–17.0
Workers' remittances	3 391 . .	–3.2	–4.9	–10.1	–16.4	–13.3	–6.4	–7.4	–7.8
Other current transfers	3 392 . .	. . .	–.1	–.5	–.2	–1.4	–.4	–.4	–9.2
CAPITAL AND FINANCIAL ACCOUNT	4 996 . .	**416.4**	**312.4**	**176.7**	**100.4**	**624.1**	**616.5**	**648.9**	**707.9**
CAPITAL ACCOUNT	4 994 . .	**. . .**	**. . .**	**. . .**	**. . .**	**. . .**	**. . .**	**. . .**	**59.3**
Total credit	2 994 . .	. . .	. . .	. . .	. . .	. . .	. . .	. . .	*59.3*
Total debit	3 994 . .	. . .	. . .	. . .	. . .	. . .	. . .	. . .	. . .
Capital transfers, credit	2 400 . .	**. . .**	**. . .**	**. . .**	**. . .**	**. . .**	**. . .**	**. . .**	**59.3**
General government	2 401 . .	. . .	. . .	. . .	. . .	. . .	. . .	. . .	59.3
Debt forgiveness	2 402 . .	. . .	. . .	. . .	. . .	. . .	. . .	. . .	. . .
Other capital transfers	2 410 . .	. . .	. . .	. . .	. . .	. . .	. . .	. . .	59.3
Other sectors	2 430 . .	. . .	. . .	. . .	. . .	. . .	. . .	. . .	. . .
Migrants' transfers	2 431 . .	. . .	. . .	. . .	. . .	. . .	. . .	. . .	. . .
Debt forgiveness	2 432 . .	. . .	. . .	. . .	. . .	. . .	. . .	. . .	. . .
Other capital transfers	2 440 . .	. . .	. . .	. . .	. . .	. . .	. . .	. . .	. . .
Capital transfers, debit	3 400 . .	**. . .**	**. . .**	**. . .**	**. . .**	**. . .**	**. . .**	**. . .**	**. . .**
General government	3 401 . .	. . .	. . .	. . .	. . .	. . .	. . .	. . .	. . .
Debt forgiveness	3 402 . .	. . .	. . .	. . .	. . .	. . .	. . .	. . .	. . .
Other capital transfers	3 410 . .	. . .	. . .	. . .	. . .	. . .	. . .	. . .	. . .
Other sectors	3 430 . .	. . .	. . .	. . .	. . .	. . .	. . .	. . .	. . .
Migrants' transfers	3 431 . .	. . .	. . .	. . .	. . .	. . .	. . .	. . .	. . .
Debt forgiveness	3 432 . .	. . .	. . .	. . .	. . .	. . .	. . .	. . .	. . .
Other capital transfers	3 440 . .	. . .	. . .	. . .	. . .	. . .	. . .	. . .	. . .
Nonproduced nonfinancial assets, credit	2 480 . .	**. . .**	**. . .**	**. . .**	**. . .**	**. . .**	**. . .**	**. . .**	**. . .**
Nonproduced nonfinancial assets, debit	3 480 . .	**. . .**	**. . .**	**. . .**	**. . .**	**. . .**	**. . .**	**. . .**	**. . .**

Table 2 (Continued). STANDARD PRESENTATION, 1988–95
(Millions of U.S. dollars)

	Code	1988	1989	1990	1991	1992	1993	1994	1995
FINANCIAL ACCOUNT	4 995	**416.4**	**312.4**	**176.7**	**100.4**	**624.1**	**616.5**	**648.9**	**648.6**
A. DIRECT INVESTMENT	4 500	329.7	76.2	47.6	90.7	94.1	142.5	65.2	75.2
Direct investment abroad	4 505	**...**	**...**	**...**	**...**	**...**	**...**	**...**	**...**
Equity capital	4 510	...	...	...	...	...	...	...	...
Claims on affiliated enterprises	4 515	...	...	...	...	...	...	...	...
Liabilities to affiliated enterprises	4 520	...	...	...	...	...	...	...	...
Reinvested earnings	4 525	...	...	...	...	...	...	...	...
Other capital	4 530	...	...	...	...	...	...	...	...
Claims on affiliated enterprises	4 535	...	...	...	...	...	...	...	...
Liabilities to affiliated enterprises	4 540	...	...	...	...	...	...	...	...
Direct investment in Guatemala	4 555	**329.7**	**76.2**	**47.6**	**90.7**	**94.1**	**142.5**	**65.2**	**75.2**
Equity capital	4 560	152.8	14.5	6.0	68.2	79.7	111.1	27.2	32.5
Claims on direct investors	4 565	...	...	...	...	...	...	...	488.4
Liabilities to direct investors	4 570	...	...	...	...	...	...	...	–455.9
Reinvested earnings	4 575	15.0	20.0	19.6	22.5	14.1	27.0	33.3	37.1
Other capital	4 580	161.9	41.7	22.0	...	.3	4.4	4.7	5.6
Claims on direct investors	4 585	...	...	...	...	...	...	...	5.6
Liabilities to direct investors	4 590	...	...	...	...	...	...	...	...
B. PORTFOLIO INVESTMENT	4 600	–220.6	–24.8	–16.6	74.9	11.7	85.4	–4.0	–16.3
Assets	4 602	**...**	**...**	**–1.8**	**–.2**	**1.8**	**112.4**	**–9.8**	**–22.2**
Equity securities	4 610	...	...	...	...	...	...	...	...
Monetary authorities	4 611	...	...	...	...	...	...	...	...
General government	4 612	...	...	...	...	...	...	...	...
Banks	4 613	...	...	...	...	...	...	...	...
Other sectors	4 614	...	...	...	...	...	...	...	...
Debt securities	4 619	...	...	–1.8	–.2	1.8	112.4	–9.8	–22.2
Bonds and notes	4 620	...	...	–1.8	–.2	1.8	112.4	–9.8	–22.2
Monetary authorities	4 621	...	...	...	...	...	...	...	...
General government	4 622	...	...	...	...	...	...	...	...
Banks	4 623	...	...	...	...	...	...	...	...
Other sectors	4 624	...	...	...	...	...	...	...	–22.2
Money market instruments	4 630	...	...	...	...	...	...	...	...
Monetary authorities	4 631	...	...	...	...	...	...	...	...
General government	4 632	...	...	...	...	...	...	...	...
Banks	4 633	...	...	...	...	...	...	...	...
Other sectors	4 634	...	...	...	...	...	...	...	...
Financial derivatives	4 640	...	...	...	...	...	...	...	...
Monetary authorities	4 641	...	...	...	...	...	...	...	...
General government	4 642	...	...	...	...	...	...	...	...
Banks	4 643	...	...	...	...	...	...	...	...
Other sectors	4 644	...	...	...	...	...	...	...	...
Liabilities	4 652	**–220.6**	**–24.8**	**–14.8**	**75.1**	**9.9**	**–27.0**	**5.8**	**5.9**
Equity securities	4 660	...	...	...	...	...	...	...	...
Banks	4 663	...	...	...	...	...	...	...	...
Other sectors	4 664	...	...	...	...	...	...	...	...
Debt securities	4 669	–220.6	–24.8	–14.8	75.1	9.9	–27.0	5.8	5.9
Bonds and notes	4 670	–220.6	–24.8	–14.8	75.1	9.9	–27.0	5.8	5.9
Monetary authorities	4 671	–220.6	–24.8	–14.8	–17.4	–16.9	–27.0	–26.7	...
General government	4 672	...	...	...	...	...	...	32.5	5.9
Banks	4 673	...	...	...	...	...	...	...	...
Other sectors	4 674	...	...	...	92.5	26.8	...	...	...
Money market instruments	4 680	...	...	...	...	...	...	...	...
Monetary authorities	4 681	...	...	...	...	...	...	...	...
General government	4 682	...	...	...	...	...	...	...	...
Banks	4 683	...	...	...	...	...	...	...	...
Other sectors	4 684	...	...	...	...	...	...	...	...
Financial derivatives	4 690	...	...	...	...	...	...	...	...
Monetary authorities	4 691	...	...	...	...	...	...	...	...
General government	4 692	...	...	...	...	...	...	...	...
Banks	4 693	...	...	...	...	...	...	...	...
Other sectors	4 694	...	...	...	...	...	...	...	...

Table 2 (Concluded). STANDARD PRESENTATION, 1988–95
(Millions of U.S. dollars)

	Code	1988	1989	1990	1991	1992	1993	1994	1995
C. OTHER INVESTMENT	4 700	196.7	320.0	103.9	486.1	466.6	509.1	635.0	432.4
Assets	4 703	**29.4**	**98.7**	**–78.0**	**68.1**	**57.2**	**–3.0**	**116.8**	**125.1**
Trade credits	4 706	. . .	. . .	. . .	. . .	. . .	. . .	. . .	. . .
General government: long-term	4 708	. . .	. . .	. . .	. . .	. . .	. . .	. . .	. . .
General government: short-term	4 709	. . .	. . .	. . .	. . .	. . .	. . .	. . .	. . .
Other sectors: long-term	4 711	. . .	. . .	. . .	. . .	. . .	. . .	. . .	. . .
Other sectors: short-term	4 712	. . .	. . .	. . .	. . .	. . .	. . .	. . .	. . .
Loans	4 714	29.4	98.7	–90.7	. . .	. . .	–45.9	–49.2	. . .
Monetary authorities: long-term	4 717	. . .	. . .	. . .	. . .	. . .	. . .	. . .	. . .
Monetary authorities: short-term	4 718	. . .	. . .	. . .	. . .	. . .	. . .	. . .	. . .
General government: long-term	4 720	. . .	. . .	. . .	. . .	. . .	. . .	. . .	. . .
General government: short-term	4 721	29.4	98.7	–90.7	. . .	. . .	–45.9	–49.2	. . .
Banks: long-term	4 723	. . .	. . .	. . .	. . .	. . .	. . .	. . .	. . .
Banks: short-term	4 724	. . .	. . .	. . .	. . .	. . .	. . .	. . .	. . .
Other sectors: long-term	4 726	. . .	. . .	. . .	. . .	. . .	. . .	. . .	. . .
Other sectors: short-term	4 727	. . .	. . .	. . .	. . .	. . .	. . .	. . .	. . .
Currency and deposits	4 730	. . .	. . .	. . .	–1.0	. . .	. . .	. . .	. . .
Monetary authorities	4 731	. . .	. . .	. . .	. . .	. . .	. . .	. . .	. . .
General government	4 732	. . .	. . .	. . .	. . .	. . .	. . .	. . .	. . .
Banks	4 733	. . .	. . .	. . .	. . .	. . .	. . .	. . .	. . .
Other sectors	4 734	. . .	. . .	. . .	–1.0	. . .	. . .	. . .	. . .
Other assets	4 736	. . .	. . .	12.7	69.1	57.2	42.9	166.0	125.1
Monetary authorities: long-term	4 738	. . .	. . .	. . .	. . .	. . .	. . .	. . .	. . .
Monetary authorities: short-term	4 739	. . .	. . .	. . .	. . .	. . .	. . .	. . .	. . .
General government: long-term	4 741	. . .	. . .	. . .	. . .	. . .	. . .	. . .	. . .
General government: short-term	4 742	. . .	. . .	. . .	. . .	. . .	. . .	. . .	. . .
Banks: long-term	4 744	. . .	. . .	. . .	. . .	. . .	. . .	. . .	. . .
Banks: short-term	4 745	. . .	. . .	. . .	. . .	. . .	. . .	. . .	. . .
Other sectors: long-term	4 747	. . .	. . .	12.7	69.1	57.2	42.9	166.0	125.1
Other sectors: short-term	4 748	. . .	. . .	. . .	. . .	. . .	. . .	. . .	. . .
Liabilities	4 753	**167.3**	**221.3**	**181.9**	**418.0**	**409.4**	**512.1**	**518.2**	**307.3**
Trade credits	4 756	122.1	139.8	23.3	524.0	333.8	330.8	267.8	479.7
General government: long-term	4 758	. . .	. . .	. . .	. . .	. . .	. . .	. . .	. . .
General government: short-term	4 759	. . .	. . .	. . .	. . .	. . .	. . .	. . .	. . .
Other sectors: long-term	4 761	. . .	. . .	. . .	. . .	. . .	. . .	. . .	. . .
Other sectors: short-term	4 762	122.1	139.8	23.3	524.0	333.8	330.8	267.8	479.7
Loans	4 764	43.4	68.5	–130.4	–1.1	59.9	59.1	251.3	16.3
Use of Fund credit and loans from the Fund	4 766	30.8	–12.7	–11.9	–2.8	–31.7	–31.3	. . .	. . .
Monetary authorities: other long-term	4 767	–35.4	–6.9	–19.7	–39.1	92.4	–26.3	–54.9	–77.7
Monetary authorities: short-term	4 768	. . .	. . .	–113.3	–6.3	–49.3	. . .	. . .	. . .
General government: long-term	4 770	38.7	63.9	10.5	–25.8	–16.3	–51.3	132.7	11.8
General government: short-term	4 771	. . .	. . .	. . .	. . .	. . .	. . .	. . .	. . .
Banks: long-term	4 773	. . .	. . .	. . .	. . .	. . .	. . .	. . .	. . .
Banks: short-term	4 774	. . .	. . .	. . .	. . .	. . .	. . .	. . .	. . .
Other sectors: long-term	4 776	2.7	20.6	5.7	53.9	36.3	120.6	135.7	63.0
Other sectors: short-term	4 777	6.6	3.6	–1.7	19.0	28.5	47.4	37.8	19.2
Currency and deposits	4 780	14.4	–11.3	–17.0	–4.9	14.4	27.0	. . .	–.4
Monetary authorities	4 781	–2.5	3.0	. . .	–1.0	. . .	27.0	. . .	. . .
General government	4 782	. . .	. . .	. . .	. . .	. . .	. . .	. . .	. . .
Banks	4 783	16.9	–14.3	–17.0	–3.9	14.4	. . .	. . .	. . .
Other sectors	4 784	. . .	. . .	. . .	. . .	. . .	. . .	. . .	–.4
Other liabilities	4 786	–12.6	24.3	306.0	–100.0	1.3	95.2	–.9	–188.3
Monetary authorities: long-term	4 788	. . .	. . .	. . .	. . .	. . .	. . .	. . .	. . .
Monetary authorities: short-term	4 789	–4.5	26.7	218.8	–100.8	–49.2	–92.7	33.3	–.6
General government: long-term	4 791	–7.1	–3.3	–6.9	. . .	. . .	. . .	. . .	. . .
General government: short-term	4 792	. . .	. . .	. . .	. . .	. . .	. . .	. . .	–5.5
Banks: long-term	4 794	. . .	. . .	. . .	. . .	. . .	. . .	. . .	. . .
Banks: short-term	4 795	. . .	. . .	. . .	. . .	. . .	. . .	. . .	7.3
Other sectors: long-term	4 797	. . .	. . .	. . .	. . .	2.2	. . .	. . .	. . .
Other sectors: short-term	4 798	–1.0	.9	94.1	.8	48.3	187.9	–34.2	–189.5
D. RESERVE ASSETS	4 800	110.6	–59.0	41.8	–551.3	51.6	–120.5	–47.3	157.3
Monetary gold	4 810	. . .	. . .	. . .	. . .	3.7	–3.7	. . .	. . .
Special drawing rights	4 820	1.5	–.6	.7	. . .	–15.8	–.1	.1	1.2
Reserve position in the Fund	4 830	. . .	. . .	. . .	. . .	. . .	. . .	. . .	. . .
Foreign exchange	4 840	85.0	–93.9	23.3	–525.3	57.7	–102.5	5.6	156.1
Other claims	4 880	24.1	35.5	17.7	–26.0	6.0	–14.2	–53.0	. . .
NET ERRORS AND OMISSIONS	4 998	**–2.4**	**54.7**	**36.2**	**83.3**	**81.8**	**85.2**	**–23.6**	**–135.9**

Part 3 of the *Yearbook* contains descriptions of the methodologies, compilation practices, and sources used to compile these data.

Table 1. ANALYTIC PRESENTATION, 1988–95
(Millions of U.S. dollars)

	Code	1988	1989	1990	1991	1992	1993	1994	1995
A. Current Account[1]	4 993 Y.	**–221.5**	**–179.7**	**–203.0**	**–288.8**	**–262.7**	**–56.8**	**–248.0**	**–196.7**
Goods: exports f.o.b	2 100 . .	511.9	595.6	671.2	687.1	517.2	561.1	515.7	582.8
Goods: imports f.o.b	3 100 . .	–510.6	–531.6	–585.8	–694.9	–608.4	–582.7	–685.4	–621.7
Balance on Goods	4 100 . .	*1.3*	*64.0*	*85.5*	*–7.8*	*–91.2*	*–21.6*	*–169.7*	*–39.0*
Services: credit	2 200 . .	52.6	103.7	157.5	144.7	159.7	186.8	152.9	118.7
Services: debit	3 200 . .	–230.8	–259.8	–367.3	–347.8	–322.6	–334.8	–366.0	–370.8
Balance on Goods and Services	4 991 . .	*–177.0*	*–92.1*	*–124.3*	*–210.9*	*–254.0*	*–169.6*	*–382.9*	*–291.1*
Income: credit	2 300 . .	11.2	8.6	12.6	15.5	7.9	9.3	6.5	12.9
Income: debit	3 300 . .	–142.4	–178.5	–161.5	–181.4	–148.9	–92.6	–79.8	–97.5
Balance on Goods, Services, and Income	4 992 . .	*–308.1*	*–261.9*	*–273.2*	*–376.8*	*–395.0*	*–252.9*	*–456.1*	*–375.7*
Current transfers: credit	2 379 Y.	121.3	143.6	118.8	136.2	193.5	260.3	280.6	258.3
Current transfers: debit	3 379 . .	–34.7	–61.3	–48.6	–48.2	–61.2	–64.2	–72.5	–79.3
B. Capital Account[1]	4 994 Y.	**. . .**	**198.7**	**. . .**	**. . .**	**8.0**	**12.4**	**. . .**	**35.2**
Capital account: credit	2 994 Y.	. . .	198.7	. . .	. . .	8.0	12.4	. . .	35.2
Capital account: debit	3 994 . .	. . .	. . .	. . .	. . .	. . .	. . .	. . .	. . .
Total, Groups A Plus B	4 010 . .	*–221.5*	*19.0*	*–203.0*	*–288.8*	*–254.7*	*–44.4*	*–248.0*	*–161.6*
C. Financial Account[1]	4 995 X.	**34.8**	**–158.9**	**53.8**	**10.4**	**67.4**	**62.6**	**84.2**	**120.9**
Direct investment abroad	4 505 . .	. . .	. . .	. . .	. . .	. . .	. . .	. . .	. . .
Direct investment in Guinea	4 555 Y.	15.7	12.3	17.9	38.8	19.7	2.7	.2	.8
Portfolio investment assets	4 602 . .	. . .	. . .	. . .	. . .	. . .	. . .	. . .	. . .
Equity securities	4 610 . .	. . .	. . .	. . .	. . .	. . .	. . .	. . .	. . .
Debt securities	4 619 . .	. . .	. . .	. . .	. . .	. . .	. . .	. . .	. . .
Portfolio investment liabilities	4 652 Y.	. . .	. . .	. . .	. . .	. . .	. . .	. . .	. . .
Equity securities	4 660 Y.	. . .	. . .	. . .	. . .	. . .	. . .	. . .	. . .
Debt securities	4 669 Y.	. . .	. . .	. . .	. . .	. . .	. . .	. . .	. . .
Other investment assets	4 703 . .	–5.2	–39.1	–52.7	–47.0	–27.5	–20.1	–14.5	–73.7
Monetary authorities	4 703 .A	. . .	. . .	. . .	. . .	. . .	. . .	–6.5	9.0
General government	4 703 .B	3.1	–.9	–10.6	–1.1	–4.1	2.2	. . .	. . .
Banks	4 703 .C	6.6	–7.6	–12.5	–11.4	–5.0	. . .	–2.2	–4.6
Other sectors	4 703 .D	–15.0	–30.6	–29.6	–34.5	–18.4	–22.3	–5.8	–78.2
Other investment liabilities	4 753 X.	24.4	–132.1	88.7	18.6	75.3	80.0	98.5	193.9
Monetary authorities	4 753 XA	. . .	. . .	. . .	. . .	. . .	. . .	.1	–.5
General government	4 753 YB	–28.8	–153.8	54.3	–34.1	15.4	54.6	79.6	118.2
Banks	4 753 YC	23.7	–2.6	9.4	2.4	–6.5	.1	8.3	26.0
Other sectors	4 753 YD	29.5	24.2	25.0	50.3	66.4	25.3	10.5	50.2
Total, Groups A Through C	4 020 . .	*–186.7*	*–139.9*	*–149.2*	*–278.4*	*–187.3*	*18.3*	*–163.8*	*–40.7*
D. Net Errors and Omissions	4 998 . .	**57.3**	**–50.5**	**50.4**	**117.5**	**33.4**	**–124.5**	**57.6**	**–39.3**
Total, Groups A Through D	4 030 . .	*–129.4*	*–190.5*	*–98.8*	*–160.9*	*–153.9*	*–106.2*	*–106.2*	*–80.0*
E. Reserves and Related Items	4 040 . .	**129.4**	**190.5**	**98.8**	**160.9**	**153.9**	**106.2**	**106.2**	**80.0**
Reserve assets	4 800 . .	–37.6	–10.8	–3.3	21.7	–10.1	–46.6	24.8	–32.0
Use of Fund credit and loans	4 766 . .	5.0	17.0	–12.3	–13.3	7.9	10.5	–3.2	17.8
Liabilities constituting foreign authorities' reserves	4 900 . .	. . .	. . .	. . .	8.4	–5.7	–.1	. . .	. . .
Exceptional financing	4 920 . .	162.0	184.3	114.4	144.1	161.8	142.4	84.7	94.2
Conversion rates: Guinean francs per U.S. dollar	0 101 . .	**474.40**	**591.65**	**660.17**	**753.86**	**902.00**	**955.49**	**976.64**	**991.41**

[1] Excludes components that have been classified in the categories of Group E.

Table 2. STANDARD PRESENTATION, 1988–95
(Millions of U.S. dollars)

	Code			1988	1989	1990	1991	1992	1993	1994	1995
CURRENT ACCOUNT	4	993	. .	**–221.5**	**–179.7**	**–203.0**	**–288.8**	**–262.7**	**–56.8**	**–248.0**	**–196.7**
A. GOODS	4	100	. .	1.3	64.0	85.5	–7.8	–91.2	–21.6	–169.7	–39.0
Credit	2	100	. .	**511.9**	**595.6**	**671.2**	**687.1**	**517.2**	**561.1**	**515.7**	**582.8**
General merchandise: exports f.o.b.	2	110	. .	511.9	595.6	671.2	687.1	517.2	561.1	452.5	521.2
Goods for processing: exports f.o.b.	2	150	. .	. . .	. . .	. . .	. . .	. . .	. . .	. . .	. . .
Repairs on goods	2	160	. .	. . .	. . .	. . .	. . .	. . .	. . .	. . .	. . .
Goods procured in ports by carriers	2	170	. .	. . .	. . .	. . .	. . .	. . .	. . .	.3	.9
Nonmonetary gold	2	180	. .	. . .	. . .	. . .	. . .	. . .	. . .	62.9	60.7
Debit	3	100	. .	**–510.6**	**–531.6**	**–585.8**	**–694.9**	**–608.4**	**–582.7**	**–685.4**	**–621.7**
General merchandise: imports f.o.b.	3	110	. .	–510.6	–531.6	–585.8	–694.9	–608.4	–582.7	–685.4	–621.5
Goods for processing: imports f.o.b.	3	150	. .	. . .	. . .	. . .	. . .	. . .	. . .	. . .	. . .
Repairs on goods	3	160	. .	. . .	. . .	. . .	. . .	. . .	. . .	. . .	. . .
Goods procured in ports by carriers	3	170	. .	. . .	. . .	. . .	. . .	. . .	. . .	. . .	–.3
Nonmonetary gold	3	180	. .	. . .	. . .	. . .	. . .	. . .	. . .	. . .	. . .
B. SERVICES	4	200	. .	–178.2	–156.1	–209.8	–203.1	–162.8	–148.0	–213.2	–252.1
Total credit	2	200	. .	*52.6*	*103.7*	*157.5*	*144.7*	*159.7*	*186.8*	*152.9*	*118.7*
Total debit	3	200	. .	*–230.8*	*–259.8*	*–367.3*	*–347.8*	*–322.6*	*–334.8*	*–366.0*	*–370.8*
Transportation services, credit	2	205	. .	**6.9**	**4.2**	**12.9**	**6.9**	**7.0**	**4.3**	**11.5**	**12.7**
Passenger	2	205	BA	*5.0*	. . .	*5.0*	*2.8*	*2.9*	*3.3*	*.4*	. . .
Freight	2	205	BB	. . .	*.3*	*1.1*	. . .	*.2*	. . .	. . .	. . .
Other	2	205	BC	*1.8*	*3.8*	*6.8*	*4.1*	*3.9*	*1.0*	*11.2*	*12.7*
Sea transport, passenger	2	207	. .	. . .	. . .	. . .	. . .	. . .	. . .	. . .	. . .
Sea transport, freight	2	208	. .	. . .	. . .	. . .	. . .	. . .	. . .	. . .	. . .
Sea transport, other	2	209	. .	. . .	. . .	. . .	. . .	. . .	. . .	3.4	12.1
Air transport, passenger	2	211	. .	. . .	. . .	. . .	. . .	. . .	. . .	. . .	. . .
Air transport, freight	2	212	. .	. . .	. . .	. . .	. . .	. . .	. . .	. . .	. . .
Air transport, other	2	213	. .	. . .	. . .	. . .	. . .	. . .	. . .	7.8	.7
Other transport, passenger	2	215	. .	. . .	. . .	. . .	. . .	. . .	. . .	.4	. . .
Other transport, freight	2	216	. .	. . .	. . .	. . .	. . .	. . .	. . .	. . .	. . .
Other transport, other	2	217	. .	. . .	. . .	. . .	. . .	. . .	. . .	. . .	. . .
Transportation services, debit	3	205	. .	**–93.2**	**–107.8**	**–139.4**	**–112.5**	**–91.5**	**–107.3**	**–131.5**	**–144.1**
Passenger	3	205	BA	*–13.1*	*–25.5*	*–19.4*	*–16.7*	*–12.3*	*–20.9*	*–6.8*	*–7.9*
Freight	3	205	BB	*–79.4*	*–82.2*	*–120.1*	*–95.6*	*–79.1*	*–83.5*	*–124.7*	*–129.9*
Other	3	205	BC	*–.7*	*–.1*	. . .	*–.2*	. . .	*–2.8*	*–.1*	*–6.3*
Sea transport, passenger	3	207	. .	. . .	. . .	. . .	. . .	. . .	. . .	. . .	. . .
Sea transport, freight	3	208	. .	. . .	. . .	. . .	. . .	. . .	. . .	–124.7	–119.7
Sea transport, other	3	209	. .	. . .	. . .	. . .	. . .	. . .	. . .	–.1	–4.4
Air transport, passenger	3	211	. .	. . .	. . .	. . .	. . .	. . .	. . .	–6.5	–7.9
Air transport, freight	3	212	. .	. . .	. . .	. . .	. . .	. . .	. . .	. . .	–10.2
Air transport, other	3	213	. .	. . .	. . .	. . .	. . .	. . .	. . .	. . .	–1.9
Other transport, passenger	3	215	. .	. . .	. . .	. . .	. . .	. . .	. . .	–.3	. . .
Other transport, freight	3	216	. .	. . .	. . .	. . .	. . .	. . .	. . .	. . .	. . .
Other transport, other	3	217	. .	. . .	. . .	. . .	. . .	. . .	. . .	. . .	. . .
Travel, credit	2	236	. .	**. . .**	**23.9**	**29.7**	**12.9**	**11.0**	**6.0**	**.5**	**.9**
Business travel	2	237	. .	. . .	. . .	. . .	. . .	. . .	. . .	.5	.3
Personal travel	2	240	. .	. . .	. . .	. . .	. . .	. . .	. . .	. . .	.6
Travel, debit	3	236	. .	**–28.6**	**–22.9**	**–29.5**	**–27.0**	**–17.4**	**–28.0**	**–23.5**	**–21.2**
Business travel	3	237	. .	. . .	. . .	. . .	. . .	. . .	. . .	–7.7	–8.8
Personal travel	3	240	. .	. . .	. . .	. . .	. . .	. . .	. . .	–15.8	–12.4
Other services, credit	2	200	BA	**45.7**	**75.6**	**114.8**	**124.9**	**141.7**	**176.5**	**140.8**	**105.1**
Communications	2	245	. .	. . .	. . .	. . .	. . .	. . .	. . .	. . .	. . .
Construction	2	249	. .	. . .	. . .	. . .	. . .	. . .	. . .	. . .	. . .
Insurance	2	253	. .	. . .	. . .	.1	. . .	. . .	. . .	.9	.2
Financial	2	260	. .	. . .	. . .	. . .	. . .	. . .	. . .	. . .	. . .
Computer and information	2	262	. .	. . .	. . .	. . .	. . .	. . .	. . .	. . .	. . .
Royalties and licence fees	2	266	. .	. . .	. . .	. . .	. . .	. . .	. . .	. . .	. . .
Other business services	2	268	. .	22.8	36.2	48.5	67.6	65.5	35.5	1.0	4.3
Personal, cultural, and recreational	2	287	. .	. . .	. . .	. . .	. . .	. . .	. . .	. . .	. . .
Government, n.i.e.	2	291	. .	22.9	39.4	66.1	57.3	76.2	141.0	138.9	100.5
Other services, debit	3	200	BA	**–108.9**	**–129.1**	**–198.3**	**–208.3**	**–213.8**	**–199.4**	**–211.0**	**–205.5**
Communications	3	245	. .	. . .	. . .	. . .	. . .	. . .	. . .	–1.0	–.6
Construction	3	249	. .	. . .	. . .	. . .	. . .	. . .	. . .	. . .	. . .
Insurance	3	253	. .	–8.8	–9.1	–13.3	–10.6	–8.8	–9.3	–26.2	–18.1
Financial	3	260	. .	. . .	. . .	. . .	. . .	. . .	. . .	. . .	. . .
Computer and information	3	262	. .	. . .	. . .	. . .	. . .	. . .	. . .	. . .	. . .
Royalties and licence fees	3	266	. .	. . .	. . .	. . .	. . .	. . .	. . .	. . .	. . .
Other business services	3	268	. .	–46.8	–43.1	–60.3	–102.0	–81.3	–104.5	–46.7	–59.1
Personal, cultural, and recreational	3	287	. .	. . .	. . .	. . .	. . .	. . .	. . .	–4.1	–.3
Government, n.i.e.	3	291	. .	–53.3	–76.9	–124.7	–95.7	–123.7	–85.6	–133.0	–127.4

Table 2 (Continued). STANDARD PRESENTATION, 1988–95
(Millions of U.S. dollars)

	Code	1988	1989	1990	1991	1992	1993	1994	1995
C. INCOME	4 300 . .	–131.2	–169.9	–148.9	–165.9	–141.0	–83.3	–73.2	–84.6
Total credit	2 300 . .	*11.2*	*8.6*	*12.6*	*15.5*	*7.9*	*9.3*	*6.5*	*12.9*
Total debit	3 300 . .	*–142.4*	*–178.5*	*–161.5*	*–181.4*	*–148.9*	*–92.6*	*–79.8*	*–97.5*
Compensation of employees, credit	2 310 . .	**. . .**	**. . .**	**. . .**	**. . .**	**. . .**	**. . .**	**. . .**	**.2**
Compensation of employees, debit	3 310 . .	**. . .**	**. . .**	**. . .**	**. . .**	**. . .**	**. . .**	**–.3**	**. . .**
Investment income, credit	2 320 . .	**11.2**	**8.6**	**12.6**	**15.5**	**7.9**	**9.3**	**6.5**	**12.6**
Direct investment income	2 330 . .	. . .	. . .	. . .	. . .	. . .	. . .	. . .	. . .
Dividends and distributed branch profits	2 332 . .	. . .	. . .	. . .	. . .	. . .	. . .	. . .	. . .
Reinvested earnings and undistributed branch profits	2 333 . .	. . .	. . .	. . .	. . .	. . .	. . .	. . .	. . .
Income on debt (interest)	2 334 . .	. . .	. . .	. . .	. . .	. . .	. . .	. . .	. . .
Portfolio investment income	2 339 . .	. . .	. . .	. . .	. . .	. . .	. . .	. . .	. . .
Income on equity	2 340 . .	. . .	. . .	. . .	. . .	. . .	. . .	. . .	. . .
Income on bonds and notes	2 350 . .	. . .	. . .	. . .	. . .	. . .	. . .	. . .	. . .
Income on money market instruments and financial derivatives	2 360 . .	. . .	. . .	. . .	. . .	. . .	. . .	. . .	. . .
Other investment income	2 370 . .	11.2	8.6	12.6	15.5	7.9	9.3	6.5	12.6
Investment income, debit	3 320 . .	**–142.4**	**–178.5**	**–161.5**	**–181.4**	**–148.9**	**–92.6**	**–79.5**	**–97.5**
Direct investment income	3 330 . .	–44.1	–71.1	–60.7	–91.4	–59.7	–26.2	–15.9	–23.3
Dividends and distributed branch profits	3 332 . .	–35.0	–63.0	–44.0	–54.2	–40.4	–26.2	–15.7	–23.2
Reinvested earnings and undistributed branch profits	3 333 . .	–9.0	–8.1	–16.6	–37.2	–19.3	. . .	–.2	–.1
Income on debt (interest)	3 334 . .	. . .	. . .	. . .	. . .	. . .	. . .	. . .	. . .
Portfolio investment income	3 339 . .	. . .	. . .	. . .	. . .	. . .	. . .	. . .	. . .
Income on equity	3 340 . .	. . .	. . .	. . .	. . .	. . .	. . .	. . .	. . .
Income on bonds and notes	3 350 . .	. . .	. . .	. . .	. . .	. . .	. . .	. . .	. . .
Income on money market instruments and financial derivatives	3 360 . .	. . .	. . .	. . .	. . .	. . .	. . .	. . .	. . .
Other investment income	3 370 . .	–98.3	–107.4	–100.8	–90.0	–89.2	–66.4	–63.6	–74.3
D. CURRENT TRANSFERS	4 379 . .	86.6	82.2	70.3	88.0	132.3	196.1	208.1	179.0
Credit	2 379 . .	**121.3**	**143.6**	**118.8**	**136.2**	**193.5**	**260.3**	**280.6**	**258.3**
General government	2 380 . .	81.7	81.6	97.4	117.0	134.0	125.0	208.1	148.4
Other sectors	2 390 . .	39.6	61.9	21.4	19.2	59.5	135.3	72.6	109.9
Workers' remittances	2 391 . .	26.7	. . .	. . .	. . .	. . .	. . .	.5	.5
Other current transfers	2 392 . .	12.9	61.9	21.4	19.2	59.5	135.3	72.1	109.4
Debit	3 379 . .	**–34.7**	**–61.3**	**–48.6**	**–48.2**	**–61.2**	**–64.2**	**–72.5**	**–79.3**
General government	3 380 . .	–1.1	–2.5	–2.4	–2.8	–3.0	–1.2	–.9	–1.3
Other sectors	3 390 . .	–33.6	–58.9	–46.2	–45.4	–58.2	–63.1	–71.6	–78.0
Workers' remittances	3 391 . .	–19.7	–18.3	–20.4	–20.9	–21.6	–19.9	–21.9	–10.4
Other current transfers	3 392 . .	–13.8	–40.5	–25.8	–24.5	–36.7	–43.1	–49.7	–67.6
CAPITAL AND FINANCIAL ACCOUNT	4 996 . .	**164.2**	**230.2**	**152.6**	**171.3**	**229.3**	**181.3**	**190.4**	**236.0**
CAPITAL ACCOUNT	4 994 . .	**. . .**	**235.4**	**6.6**	**. . .**	**59.4**	**14.3**	**.7**	**80.0**
Total credit	2 994 . .	. . .	*235.4*	*6.6*	. . .	*59.4*	*14.3*	*.7*	*80.0*
Total debit	3 994 . .	. . .	. . .	. . .	. . .	. . .	. . .	. . .	. . .
Capital transfers, credit	2 400 . .	**. . .**	**235.4**	**6.6**	**. . .**	**59.4**	**14.3**	**.7**	**80.0**
General government	2 401 . .	. . .	235.4	6.6	. . .	59.4	14.3	.7	80.0
Debt forgiveness	2 402 . .	. . .	235.4	6.6	. . .	59.4	14.3	.7	80.0
Other capital transfers	2 410 . .	. . .	. . .	. . .	. . .	. . .	. . .	. . .	. . .
Other sectors	2 430 . .	. . .	. . .	. . .	. . .	. . .	. . .	. . .	. . .
Migrants' transfers	2 431 . .	. . .	. . .	. . .	. . .	. . .	. . .	. . .	. . .
Debt forgiveness	2 432 . .	. . .	. . .	. . .	. . .	. . .	. . .	. . .	. . .
Other capital transfers	2 440 . .	. . .	. . .	. . .	. . .	. . .	. . .	. . .	. . .
Capital transfers, debit	3 400 . .	**. . .**	**. . .**	**. . .**	**. . .**	**. . .**	**. . .**	**. . .**	**. . .**
General government	3 401 . .	. . .	. . .	. . .	. . .	. . .	. . .	. . .	. . .
Debt forgiveness	3 402 . .	. . .	. . .	. . .	. . .	. . .	. . .	. . .	. . .
Other capital transfers	3 410 . .	. . .	. . .	. . .	. . .	. . .	. . .	. . .	. . .
Other sectors	3 430 . .	. . .	. . .	. . .	. . .	. . .	. . .	. . .	. . .
Migrants' transfers	3 431 . .	. . .	. . .	. . .	. . .	. . .	. . .	. . .	. . .
Debt forgiveness	3 432 . .	. . .	. . .	. . .	. . .	. . .	. . .	. . .	. . .
Other capital transfers	3 440 . .	. . .	. . .	. . .	. . .	. . .	. . .	. . .	. . .
Nonproduced nonfinancial assets, credit	2 480 . .	**. . .**	**. . .**	**. . .**	**. . .**	**. . .**	**. . .**	**. . .**	**. . .**
Nonproduced nonfinancial assets, debit	3 480 . .	**. . .**	**. . .**	**. . .**	**. . .**	**. . .**	**. . .**	**. . .**	**. . .**

Table 2 (Continued). STANDARD PRESENTATION, 1988–95

(Millions of U.S. dollars)

	Code	1988	1989	1990	1991	1992	1993	1994	1995
FINANCIAL ACCOUNT	4 995 . .	**164.2**	**–5.2**	**146.0**	**171.3**	**169.9**	**167.0**	**189.7**	**156.1**
A. DIRECT INVESTMENT	4 500 . .	15.7	12.3	17.9	38.8	19.7	2.7	.2	.8
Direct investment abroad	4 505 . .	...	...	...	...	...	...	...	...
Equity capital	4 510 . .	...	...	...	...	...	...	...	...
Claims on affiliated enterprises	4 515 . .	...	...	...	...	...	...	...	...
Liabilities to affiliated enterprises	4 520 . .	...	...	...	...	...	...	...	...
Reinvested earnings	4 525 . .	...	...	...	...	...	...	...	...
Other capital	4 530 . .	...	...	...	...	...	...	...	...
Claims on affiliated enterprises	4 535 . .	...	...	...	...	...	...	...	...
Liabilities to affiliated enterprises	4 540 . .	...	...	...	...	...	...	...	...
Direct investment in Guinea	4 555 . .	**15.7**	**12.3**	**17.9**	**38.8**	**19.7**	**2.7**	**.2**	**.8**
Equity capital	4 560 . .	6.7	1.5	.6	1.6	...	2.7	...	.7
Claims on direct investors	4 565 . .	...	...	...	...	...	...	...	...
Liabilities to direct investors	4 570 . .	...	...	...	...	...	...	...	.7
Reinvested earnings	4 575 . .	9.0	8.1	16.6	37.2	19.3	...	.2	.1
Other capital	4 580 . .	...	2.7	.6	...	.4	...	...	...
Claims on direct investors	4 585 . .	...	...	...	...	...	...	...	...
Liabilities to direct investors	4 590 . .	...	...	...	...	...	...	...	...
B. PORTFOLIO INVESTMENT	4 600 . .	...	...	...	...	...	...	...	...
Assets	4 602 . .	...	...	...	...	...	...	...	...
Equity securities	4 610 . .	...	...	...	...	...	...	...	...
Monetary authorities	4 611 . .	...	...	...	...	...	...	...	...
General government	4 612 . .	...	...	...	...	...	...	...	...
Banks	4 613 . .	...	...	...	...	...	...	...	...
Other sectors	4 614 . .	...	...	...	...	...	...	...	...
Debt securities	4 619 . .	...	...	...	...	...	...	...	...
Bonds and notes	4 620 . .	...	...	...	...	...	...	...	...
Monetary authorities	4 621 . .	...	...	...	...	...	...	...	...
General government	4 622 . .	...	...	...	...	...	...	...	...
Banks	4 623 . .	...	...	...	...	...	...	...	...
Other sectors	4 624 . .	...	...	...	...	...	...	...	...
Money market instruments	4 630 . .	...	...	...	...	...	...	...	...
Monetary authorities	4 631 . .	...	...	...	...	...	...	...	...
General government	4 632 . .	...	...	...	...	...	...	...	...
Banks	4 633 . .	...	...	...	...	...	...	...	...
Other sectors	4 634 . .	...	...	...	...	...	...	...	...
Financial derivatives	4 640 . .	...	...	...	...	...	...	...	...
Monetary authorities	4 641 . .	...	...	...	...	...	...	...	...
General government	4 642 . .	...	...	...	...	...	...	...	...
Banks	4 643 . .	...	...	...	...	...	...	...	...
Other sectors	4 644 . .	...	...	...	...	...	...	...	...
Liabilities	4 652 . .	...	...	...	...	...	...	...	...
Equity securities	4 660 . .	...	...	...	...	...	...	...	...
Banks	4 663 . .	...	...	...	...	...	...	...	...
Other sectors	4 664 . .	...	...	...	...	...	...	...	...
Debt securities	4 669 . .	...	...	...	...	...	...	...	...
Bonds and notes	4 670 . .	...	...	...	...	...	...	...	...
Monetary authorities	4 671 . .	...	...	...	...	...	...	...	...
General government	4 672 . .	...	...	...	...	...	...	...	...
Banks	4 673 . .	...	...	...	...	...	...	...	...
Other sectors	4 674 . .	...	...	...	...	...	...	...	...
Money market instruments	4 680 . .	...	...	...	...	...	...	...	...
Monetary authorities	4 681 . .	...	...	...	...	...	...	...	...
General government	4 682 . .	...	...	...	...	...	...	...	...
Banks	4 683 . .	...	...	...	...	...	...	...	...
Other sectors	4 684 . .	...	...	...	...	...	...	...	...
Financial derivatives	4 690 . .	...	...	...	...	...	...	...	...
Monetary authorities	4 691 . .	...	...	...	...	...	...	...	...
General government	4 692 . .	...	...	...	...	...	...	...	...
Banks	4 693 . .	...	...	...	...	...	...	...	...
Other sectors	4 694 . .	...	...	...	...	...	...	...	...

Table 2 (Concluded). STANDARD PRESENTATION, 1988–95
(Millions of U.S. dollars)

	Code	1988	1989	1990	1991	1992	1993	1994	1995
C. OTHER INVESTMENT	4 700	186.1	–6.7	131.5	110.8	160.3	210.9	164.7	187.3
Assets	4 703	**–5.2**	**–39.1**	**–52.7**	**–47.0**	**–27.5**	**–20.1**	**–14.5**	**–73.7**
Trade credits	4 706	...	...	...	...	...	...	–.2	11.1
General government: long-term	4 708	...	...	...	...	...	...	...	...
General government: short-term	4 709	...	...	...	...	...	...	...	...
Other sectors: long-term	4 711	...	...	...	...	...	...	...	...
Other sectors: short-term	4 712	...	...	...	...	...	...	–.2	11.1
Loans	4 714	.8	–41.7	–34.9	–30.4	–18.4	–.8	...	...
Monetary authorities: long-term	4 717	...	...	...	...	...	...	...	...
Monetary authorities: short-term	4 718	...	...	...	...	...	...	...	...
General government: long-term	4 720	...	...	...	...	...	...	...	...
General government: short-term	4 721	...	...	–.1	.1	...	.1	...	...
Banks: long-term	4 723	...	...	...	...	...	...	...	...
Banks: short-term	4 724	...	...	...	...	...	...	...	...
Other sectors: long-term	4 726	...	...	...	...	...	...	...	...
Other sectors: short-term	4 727	.8	–41.6	–34.8	–30.4	–18.4	–.9	...	...
Currency and deposits	4 730	–2.7	1.7	–17.8	–16.6	–9.2	–18.7	–6.0	–29.7
Monetary authorities	4 731	...	...	...	...	...	...	...	...
General government	4 732	3.1	–.9	–10.5	–1.2	–4.1	2.1	...	...
Banks	4 733	6.6	–7.6	–12.5	–11.4	–5.0	...	–.4	–4.6
Other sectors	4 734	–12.4	10.2	5.2	–4.0	–.1	–20.8	–5.6	–25.1
Other assets	4 736	–3.3	.9	...	...	...	–.6	–8.3	–55.1
Monetary authorities: long-term	4 738	...	...	...	...	...	...	...	...
Monetary authorities: short-term	4 739	...	...	...	...	...	...	–6.5	9.0
General government: long-term	4 741	...	...	...	...	...	...	...	...
General government: short-term	4 742	...	...	...	...	...	...	...	...
Banks: long-term	4 744	...	...	...	...	...	...	...	...
Banks: short-term	4 745	...	...	...	...	...	...	–1.8	...
Other sectors: long-term	4 747	–3.3	.9	...	...	...	–.6	...	...
Other sectors: short-term	4 748	...	...	...	...	...	...	...	–64.1
Liabilities	4 753	**191.3**	**32.4**	**184.2**	**157.8**	**187.8**	**230.9**	**179.3**	**261.0**
Trade credits	4 756	...	...	...	...	...	...	–3.5	–1.7
General government: long-term	4 758	...	...	...	...	...	...	...	...
General government: short-term	4 759	...	...	...	...	...	...	...	...
Other sectors: long-term	4 761	...	...	...	...	...	...	–3.5	...
Other sectors: short-term	4 762	...	...	...	...	...	...	...	–1.7
Loans	4 764	59.5	290.4	121.4	149.3	310.1	281.7	118.6	340.3
Use of Fund credit and loans from the Fund	4 766	5.0	17.0	–12.3	–13.3	7.9	10.5	–3.2	17.8
Monetary authorities: other long-term	4 767	40.0	75.8	14.0	36.0	39.0	63.8	12.1	...
Monetary authorities: short-term	4 768	...	...	...	...	...	...	...	...
General government: long-term	4 770	–15.9	172.0	73.2	85.0	188.5	205.8	94.8	272.6
General government: short-term	4 771	6.7	2.3	10.0	–8.5	9.8	–23.5	...	...
Banks: long-term	4 773	...	–.1	12.5	–.1	–.1	–.1	1.0	–1.9
Banks: short-term	4 774	...	...	...	...	...	...	...	...
Other sectors: long-term	4 776	31.0	17.5	5.9	11.6	24.2	17.4	–2.5	35.3
Other sectors: short-term	4 777	–7.4	6.0	18.1	38.7	40.8	7.9	16.5	16.6
Currency and deposits	4 780	23.7	–2.5	–3.1	11.0	–12.1	.1	7.4	27.9
Monetary authorities	4 781	...	...	...	8.4	–5.7	–.1	.1	...
General government	4 782	...	...	...	...	...	...	...	...
Banks	4 783	23.7	–2.5	–3.1	2.6	–6.4	.2	7.3	27.9
Other sectors	4 784	...	...	...	...	...	...	...	...
Other liabilities	4 786	108.2	–255.6	66.0	–2.5	–110.2	–50.9	56.8	–105.4
Monetary authorities: long-term	4 788	...	...	...	...	...	...	...	...
Monetary authorities: short-term	4 789	...	...	...	...	...	...	...	–.4
General government: long-term	4 791	...	–198.7	...	...	–8.0	–5.0	...	...
General government: short-term	4 792	102.4	–57.7	65.0	–2.5	–103.6	–45.9	56.8	–105.0
Banks: long-term	4 794	...	...	...	...	...	...	...	...
Banks: short-term	4 795	...	...	...	...	...	...	...	...
Other sectors: long-term	4 797	...	...	...	...	...	...	...	...
Other sectors: short-term	4 798	5.8	.8	1.0	...	1.4	...	...	...
D. RESERVE ASSETS	4 800	–37.6	–10.8	–3.3	21.7	–10.1	–46.6	24.8	–32.0
Monetary gold	4 810	...	...	...	...	...	...	–11.5	–28.6
Special drawing rights	4 820	–2.2	2.8	...	–1.0	–9.6	2.5	–.8	9.9
Reserve position in the Fund	4 830	...	...	...	...	...	–.1	...	...
Foreign exchange	4 840	–35.4	–13.6	–3.3	22.7	–.5	–49.0	37.1	–13.3
Other claims	4 880	...	...	...	...	...	...	...	...
NET ERRORS AND OMISSIONS	4 998	**57.3**	**–50.5**	**50.4**	**117.5**	**33.4**	**–124.5**	**57.6**	**–39.3**

Part 3 of the *Yearbook* contains descriptions of the methodologies, compilation practices, and sources used to compile these data.

Table 1. ANALYTIC PRESENTATION, 1988–95
(Millions of U.S. dollars)

	Code	1988	1989	1990	1991	1992	1993	1994	1995
A. Current Account [1]	4 993 Y.	**–68.40**	**–92.80**	**–60.40**	**–79.04**	**–104.18**	**–65.48**	**–50.63**	**–41.45**
Goods: exports f.o.b	2 100 . .	15.90	14.20	19.26	20.44	6.47	15.96	33.21	23.90
Goods: imports f.o.b	3 100 . .	–58.90	–68.90	–68.07	–67.47	–83.51	–53.82	–53.80	–59.34
Balance on Goods	4 100 . .	*–43.00*	*–54.70*	*–48.81*	*–47.03*	*–77.04*	*–37.86*	*–20.59*	*–35.44*
Services: credit	2 200 . .	. . .	. . .	. . .	. . .	. . .	. . .	. . .	. . .
Services: debit	3 200 . .	–17.10	–20.95	–13.17	–14.35	–16.00	–11.38	–24.50	–21.09
Balance on Goods and Services	4 991 . .	*–60.10*	*–75.65*	*–61.98*	*–61.38*	*–93.04*	*–49.24*	*–45.09*	*–56.53*
Income: credit	2 300 . .	. . .	. . .	. . .	. . .	. . .	. . .	. . .	. . .
Income: debit	3 300 . .	–19.90	–28.05	–22.28	–32.91	–27.78	–28.98	–26.27	–15.02
Balance on Goods, Services, and Income	4 992 . .	*–80.00*	*–103.70*	*–84.26*	*–94.29*	*–120.82*	*–78.22*	*–71.36*	*–71.55*
Current transfers: credit	2 379 Y.	11.60	10.90	23.86	19.39	17.28	14.39	21.79	31.42
Current transfers: debit	3 379 . .	. . .	. . .	. . .	–4.14	–.64	–1.65	–1.06	–1.32
B. Capital Account [1]	4 994 Y.	**26.90**	**41.60**	**28.96**	**32.72**	**28.49**	**36.58**	**44.42**	**49.20**
Capital account: credit	2 994 Y.	26.90	41.60	28.96	32.72	28.49	36.58	44.42	49.20
Capital account: debit	3 994 . .	. . .	. . .	. . .	. . .	. . .	. . .	. . .	. . .
Total, Groups A Plus B	4 010 . .	*–41.50*	*–51.20*	*–31.44*	*–46.32*	*–75.69*	*–28.90*	*–6.21*	*7.75*
C. Financial Account [1]	4 995 X.	**–3.44**	**–7.00**	**1.22**	**–8.75**	**2.13**	**–13.55**	**–26.98**	**–25.60**
Direct investment abroad	4 505 . .	. . .	. . .	. . .	. . .	. . .	. . .	. . .	. . .
Direct investment in Guinea-Bissau	4 555 Y.	. . .	. . .	. . .	. . .	. . .	. . .	. . .	. . .
Portfolio investment assets	4 602 . .	. . .	. . .	. . .	. . .	. . .	. . .	. . .	. . .
Equity securities	4 610 . .	. . .	. . .	. . .	. . .	. . .	. . .	. . .	. . .
Debt securities	4 619 . .	. . .	. . .	. . .	. . .	. . .	. . .	. . .	. . .
Portfolio investment liabilities	4 652 Y.	. . .	. . .	. . .	. . .	. . .	. . .	. . .	. . .
Equity securities	4 660 Y.	. . .	. . .	. . .	. . .	. . .	. . .	. . .	. . .
Debt securities	4 669 Y.	. . .	. . .	. . .	. . .	. . .	. . .	. . .	. . .
Other investment assets	4 703 . .	. . .	. . .	. . .	. . .	. . .	. . .	. . .	. . .
Monetary authorities	4 703 . A	. . .	. . .	. . .	. . .	. . .	. . .	. . .	. . .
General government	4 703 . B	. . .	. . .	. . .	. . .	. . .	. . .	. . .	. . .
Banks	4 703 . C	. . .	. . .	. . .	. . .	. . .	. . .	. . .	. . .
Other sectors	4 703 . D	. . .	. . .	. . .	. . .	. . .	. . .	. . .	. . .
Other investment liabilities	4 753 X.	–3.44	–7.00	1.22	–8.75	2.13	–13.55	–26.98	–25.60
Monetary authorities	4 753 XA	. . .	. . .	. . .	. . .	. . .	. . .	. . .	. . .
General government	4 753 YB	–3.44	–7.00	1.22	–8.75	2.13	–13.55	–26.98	–25.60
Banks	4 753 YC	. . .	. . .	. . .	. . .	. . .	. . .	. . .	. . .
Other sectors	4 753 YD	. . .	. . .	. . .	. . .	. . .	. . .	. . .	. . .
Total, Groups A Through C	4 020 . .	*–44.94*	*–58.20*	*–30.22*	*–55.07*	*–73.56*	*–42.45*	*–33.19*	*–17.85*
D. Net Errors and Omissions	4 998 . .	**3.50**	**–11.60**	**–1.47**	**–16.27**	**22.01**	**–15.98**	**–21.36**	**–25.53**
Total, Groups A Through D	4 030 . .	*–41.44*	*–69.81*	*–31.69*	*–71.34*	*–51.55*	*–58.43*	*–54.55*	*–43.38*
E. Reserves and Related Items	4 040 . .	**41.44**	**69.81**	**31.69**	**71.34**	**51.55**	**58.43**	**54.55**	**43.38**
Reserve assets	4 800 . .	–11.83	6.70	–5.20	8.89	–5.10	9.02	6.24	–3.64
Use of Fund credit and loans	4 766 . .	–1.26	1.97	. . .	. . .	. . .	–.42	–.43	1.19
Liabilities constituting foreign authorities' reserves	4 900 . .	. . .	. . .	. . .	. . .	. . .	. . .	. . .	. . .
Exceptional financing	4 920 . .	54.53	61.13	36.89	62.45	56.65	49.83	48.75	45.83
Conversion rates: Guinea-Bissau pesos per U.S. dollar	0 101 . .	**1,110**	**1,810**	**2,185**	**3,659**	**6,934**	**10,082**	**12,892**	**18,073**

[1] Excludes components that have been classified in the categories of Group E.

Table 2. STANDARD PRESENTATION, 1988–95
(Millions of U.S. dollars)

	Code	1988	1989	1990	1991	1992	1993	1994	1995
CURRENT ACCOUNT	4 993 . .	**–55.80**	**–80.20**	**–45.20**	**–75.40**	**–96.98**	**–61.98**	**–48.94**	**–25.98**
A. GOODS	4 100 . .	–43.00	–54.70	–48.81	–47.03	–77.04	–37.86	–20.59	–35.44
Credit	2 100 . .	**15.90**	**14.20**	**19.26**	**20.44**	**6.47**	**15.96**	**33.21**	**23.90**
General merchandise: exports f.o.b.	2 110 . .	15.90	14.20	19.26	20.44	6.47	15.96	33.21	23.90
Goods for processing: exports f.o.b.	2 150 . .	...	...	...	...	...	...	...	...
Repairs on goods	2 160 . .	...	...	...	...	...	...	...	...
Goods procured in ports by carriers	2 170 . .	...	...	...	...	...	...	...	...
Nonmonetary gold	2 180 . .	...	...	...	...	...	...	...	...
Debit	3 100 . .	**–58.90**	**–68.90**	**–68.07**	**–67.47**	**–83.51**	**–53.82**	**–53.80**	**–59.34**
General merchandise: imports f.o.b.	3 110 . .	–58.90	–68.90	–68.07	–67.47	–83.51	–53.82	–53.80	–59.34
Goods for processing: imports f.o.b.	3 150 . .	...	...	...	...	...	...	...	...
Repairs on goods	3 160 . .	...	...	...	...	...	...	...	...
Goods procured in ports by carriers	3 170 . .	...	...	...	...	...	...	...	...
Nonmonetary gold	3 180 . .	...	...	...	...	...	...	...	...
B. SERVICES	4 200 . .	–17.10	–20.95	–13.17	–14.35	–16.00	–11.38	–24.50	–21.09
Total credit	2 200 . .	...	...	...	...	...	...	...	...
Total debit	3 200 . .	*–17.10*	*–20.95*	*–13.17*	*–14.35*	*–16.00*	*–11.38*	*–24.50*	*–21.09*
Transportation services, credit	2 205 . .	...	...	...	...	...	...	...	...
Passenger	2 205 BA	...	...	...	...	...	...	...	...
Freight	2 205 BB	...	...	...	...	...	...	...	...
Other	2 205 BC	...	...	...	...	...	...	...	...
Sea transport, passenger	2 207 . .	...	...	...	...	...	...	...	...
Sea transport, freight	2 208 . .	...	...	...	...	...	...	...	...
Sea transport, other	2 209 . .	...	...	...	...	...	...	...	...
Air transport, passenger	2 211 . .	...	...	...	...	...	...	...	...
Air transport, freight	2 212 . .	...	...	...	...	...	...	...	...
Air transport, other	2 213 . .	...	...	...	...	...	...	...	...
Other transport, passenger	2 215 . .	...	...	...	...	...	...	...	...
Other transport, freight	2 216 . .	...	...	...	...	...	...	...	...
Other transport, other	2 217 . .	...	...	...	...	...	...	...	...
Transportation services, debit	3 205 . .	**–6.62**	**–7.75**	**–8.75**	**–8.16**	**–10.74**	**–6.92**	**–10.28**	**–11.10**
Passenger	3 205 BA	...	...	...	...	...	...	...	...
Freight	3 205 BB	*–6.62*	*–7.75*	*–8.75*	*–8.16*	*–10.74*	*–6.92*	*–10.28*	*–11.10*
Other	3 205 BC	...	...	...	...	...	...	...	...
Sea transport, passenger	3 207 . .	...	...	...	...	...	...	...	...
Sea transport, freight	3 208 . .	...	...	...	...	...	...	...	...
Sea transport, other	3 209 . .	...	...	...	...	...	...	...	...
Air transport, passenger	3 211 . .	...	...	...	...	...	...	...	...
Air transport, freight	3 212 . .	...	...	...	...	...	...	...	...
Air transport, other	3 213 . .	...	...	...	...	...	...	...	...
Other transport, passenger	3 215 . .	...	...	...	...	...	...	...	...
Other transport, freight	3 216 . .	...	...	...	...	...	...	...	...
Other transport, other	3 217 . .	...	...	...	...	...	...	...	...
Travel, credit	2 236 . .	...	...	...	...	...	...	...	...
Business travel	2 237 . .	...	...	...	...	...	...	...	...
Personal travel	2 240 . .	...	...	...	...	...	...	...	...
Travel, debit	3 236 . .	...	...	...	...	...	...	...	...
Business travel	3 237 . .	...	...	...	...	...	...	...	...
Personal travel	3 240 . .	...	...	...	...	...	...	...	...
Other services, credit	2 200 BA	...	...	...	...	...	...	...	...
Communications	2 245 . .	...	...	...	...	...	...	...	...
Construction	2 249 . .	...	...	...	...	...	...	...	...
Insurance	2 253 . .	...	...	...	...	...	...	...	...
Financial	2 260 . .	...	...	...	...	...	...	...	...
Computer and information	2 262 . .	...	...	...	...	...	...	...	...
Royalties and licence fees	2 266 . .	...	...	...	...	...	...	...	...
Other business services	2 268 . .	...	...	...	...	...	...	...	...
Personal, cultural, and recreational	2 287 . .	...	...	...	...	...	...	...	...
Government, n.i.e.	2 291 . .	...	...	...	...	...	...	...	...
Other services, debit	3 200 BA	**–10.48**	**–13.20**	**–4.42**	**–6.19**	**–5.26**	**–4.46**	**–14.22**	**–9.99**
Communications	3 245 . .	...	...	...	...	...	...	...	...
Construction	3 249 . .	...	...	...	...	...	...	...	...
Insurance	3 253 . .	–.74	–.86	–.97	–.91	–1.19	–.77	–1.14	–1.23
Financial	3 260 . .	...	...	...	...	...	...	...	...
Computer and information	3 262 . .	...	...	...	...	...	...	...	...
Royalties and licence fees	3 266 . .	...	...	...	...	...	...	...	...
Other business services	3 268 . .	–9.74	–12.34	–3.45	–5.28	–4.07	–3.69	–13.08	–8.76
Personal, cultural, and recreational	3 287 . .	...	...	...	...	...	...	...	...
Government, n.i.e.	3 291 . .	...	...	...	...	...	...	...	...

Table 2 (Continued). STANDARD PRESENTATION, 1988–95
(Millions of U.S. dollars)

	Code	1988	1989	1990	1991	1992	1993	1994	1995
C. INCOME	4 300 . .	–19.90	–28.05	–22.28	–32.91	–27.78	–28.98	–26.27	–15.02
Total credit	2 300 . .	...	...	...	...	...	...	...	...
Total debit	3 300 . .	*–19.90*	*–28.05*	*–22.28*	*–32.91*	*–27.78*	*–28.98*	*–26.27*	*–15.02*
Compensation of employees, credit	2 310 . .	...	...	...	...	...	...	...	...
Compensation of employees, debit	3 310 . .	**–9.90**	**–15.75**	**–11.64**	**–15.87**	**–14.32**	**–13.17**	**–12.18**	**–13.92**
Investment income, credit	2 320 . .	...	...	...	...	...	...	...	...
Direct investment income	2 330 . .	...	...	...	...	...	...	...	...
Dividends and distributed branch profits	2 332 . .	...	...	...	...	...	...	...	...
Reinvested earnings and undistributed branch profits	2 333 . .	...	...	...	...	...	...	...	...
Income on debt (interest)	2 334 . .	...	...	...	...	...	...	...	...
Portfolio investment income	2 339 . .	...	...	...	...	...	...	...	...
Income on equity	2 340 . .	...	...	...	...	...	...	...	...
Income on bonds and notes	2 350 . .	...	...	...	...	...	...	...	...
Income on money market instruments and financial derivatives	2 360 . .	...	...	...	...	...	...	...	...
Other investment income	2 370 . .	...	...	...	...	...	...	...	...
Investment income, debit	3 320 . .	**–10.00**	**–12.30**	**–10.64**	**–17.04**	**–13.46**	**–15.81**	**–14.09**	**–1.10**
Direct investment income	3 330 . .	...	...	...	...	...	...	...	...
Dividends and distributed branch profits	3 332 . .	...	...	...	...	...	...	...	...
Reinvested earnings and undistributed branch profits	3 333 . .	...	...	...	...	...	...	...	...
Income on debt (interest)	3 334 . .	...	...	...	...	...	...	...	...
Portfolio investment income	3 339 . .	...	...	...	...	...	...	...	...
Income on equity	3 340 . .	...	...	...	...	...	...	...	...
Income on bonds and notes	3 350 . .	...	...	...	...	...	...	...	...
Income on money market instruments and financial derivatives	3 360 . .	...	...	...	...	...	...	...	...
Other investment income	3 370 . .	–10.00	–12.30	–10.64	–17.04	–13.46	–15.81	–14.09	–1.10
D. CURRENT TRANSFERS	4 379 . .	24.20	23.50	39.06	18.89	23.84	16.24	22.42	45.57
Credit	2 379 . .	**24.20**	**23.50**	**39.06**	**23.03**	**24.48**	**17.89**	**23.48**	**46.89**
General government	2 380 . .	22.70	22.30	38.06	23.03	24.48	17.89	23.48	46.89
Other sectors	2 390 . .	1.50	1.20	1.00	...	...	...	...	...
Workers' remittances	2 391 . .	1.50	1.20	1.00	...	...	...	...	...
Other current transfers	2 392 . .	...	...	...	...	...	...	...	...
Debit	3 379 . .	...	...	...	**–4.14**	**–.64**	**–1.65**	**–1.06**	**–1.32**
General government	3 380 . .	...	...	...	...	...	...	...	...
Other sectors	3 390 . .	...	...	...	–4.14	–.64	–1.65	–1.06	–1.32
Workers' remittances	3 391 . .	...	...	...	–4.14	–.64	–1.65	–1.06	–1.32
Other current transfers	3 392 . .	...	...	...	...	...	...	...	...
CAPITAL AND FINANCIAL ACCOUNT	4 996 . .	**52.30**	**91.80**	**46.67**	**91.67**	**74.97**	**77.96**	**70.30**	**51.51**
CAPITAL ACCOUNT	4 994 . .	**26.90**	**41.60**	**28.96**	**32.72**	**28.49**	**36.58**	**44.42**	**49.20**
Total credit	2 994 . .	*26.90*	*41.60*	*28.96*	*32.72*	*28.49*	*36.58*	*44.42*	*49.20*
Total debit	3 994 . .	...	...	...	...	...	...	...	...
Capital transfers, credit	2 400 . .	**26.90**	**41.60**	**28.96**	**32.72**	**28.49**	**36.58**	**44.42**	**49.20**
General government	2 401 . .	26.90	41.60	28.96	32.72	28.49	36.58	44.42	49.20
Debt forgiveness	2 402 . .	...	...	...	...	...	...	...	...
Other capital transfers	2 410 . .	...	...	...	...	...	...	...	...
Other sectors	2 430 . .	...	...	...	...	...	...	...	...
Migrants' transfers	2 431 . .	...	...	...	...	...	...	...	...
Debt forgiveness	2 432 . .	...	...	...	...	...	...	...	...
Other capital transfers	2 440 . .	...	...	...	...	...	...	...	...
Capital transfers, debit	3 400 . .	...	...	...	...	...	...	...	...
General government	3 401 . .	...	...	...	...	...	...	...	...
Debt forgiveness	3 402 . .	...	...	...	...	...	...	...	...
Other capital transfers	3 410 . .	...	...	...	...	...	...	...	...
Other sectors	3 430 . .	...	...	...	...	...	...	...	...
Migrants' transfers	3 431 . .	...	...	...	...	...	...	...	...
Debt forgiveness	3 432 . .	...	...	...	...	...	...	...	...
Other capital transfers	3 440 . .	...	...	...	...	...	...	...	...
Nonproduced nonfinancial assets, credit	2 480 . .	...	...	...	...	...	...	...	...
Nonproduced nonfinancial assets, debit	3 480 . .	...	...	...	...	...	...	...	...

Table 2 (Continued). STANDARD PRESENTATION, 1988–95
(Millions of U.S. dollars)

	Code		1988	1989	1990	1991	1992	1993	1994	1995
FINANCIAL ACCOUNT	4 995	. .	**25.40**	**50.20**	**17.71**	**58.95**	**46.48**	**41.38**	**25.88**	**2.31**
A. DIRECT INVESTMENT	4 500	. .	. . .	. . .	. . .	. . .	. . .	. . .	. . .	. . .
Direct investment abroad	4 505	. .	. . .	. . .	. . .	. . .	. . .	. . .	. . .	. . .
Equity capital	4 510	. .	. . .	. . .	. . .	. . .	. . .	. . .	. . .	. . .
Claims on affiliated enterprises	4 515	. .	. . .	. . .	. . .	. . .	. . .	. . .	. . .	. . .
Liabilities to affiliated enterprises	4 520	. .	. . .	. . .	. . .	. . .	. . .	. . .	. . .	. . .
Reinvested earnings	4 525	. .	. . .	. . .	. . .	. . .	. . .	. . .	. . .	. . .
Other capital	4 530	. .	. . .	. . .	. . .	. . .	. . .	. . .	. . .	. . .
Claims on affiliated enterprises	4 535	. .	. . .	. . .	. . .	. . .	. . .	. . .	. . .	. . .
Liabilities to affiliated enterprises	4 540	. .	. . .	. . .	. . .	. . .	. . .	. . .	. . .	. . .
Direct investment in Guinea-Bissau	4 555	. .	. . .	. . .	. . .	. . .	. . .	. . .	. . .	. . .
Equity capital	4 560	. .	. . .	. . .	. . .	. . .	. . .	. . .	. . .	. . .
Claims on direct investors	4 565	. .	. . .	. . .	. . .	. . .	. . .	. . .	. . .	. . .
Liabilities to direct investors	4 570	. .	. . .	. . .	. . .	. . .	. . .	. . .	. . .	. . .
Reinvested earnings	4 575	. .	. . .	. . .	. . .	. . .	. . .	. . .	. . .	. . .
Other capital	4 580	. .	. . .	. . .	. . .	. . .	. . .	. . .	. . .	. . .
Claims on direct investors	4 585	. .	. . .	. . .	. . .	. . .	. . .	. . .	. . .	. . .
Liabilities to direct investors	4 590	. .	. . .	. . .	. . .	. . .	. . .	. . .	. . .	. . .
B. PORTFOLIO INVESTMENT	4 600	. .	. . .	. . .	. . .	. . .	. . .	. . .	. . .	. . .
Assets	4 602	. .	. . .	. . .	. . .	. . .	. . .	. . .	. . .	. . .
Equity securities	4 610	. .	. . .	. . .	. . .	. . .	. . .	. . .	. . .	. . .
Monetary authorities	4 611	. .	. . .	. . .	. . .	. . .	. . .	. . .	. . .	. . .
General government	4 612	. .	. . .	. . .	. . .	. . .	. . .	. . .	. . .	. . .
Banks	4 613	. .	. . .	. . .	. . .	. . .	. . .	. . .	. . .	. . .
Other sectors	4 614	. .	. . .	. . .	. . .	. . .	. . .	. . .	. . .	. . .
Debt securities	4 619	. .	. . .	. . .	. . .	. . .	. . .	. . .	. . .	. . .
Bonds and notes	4 620	. .	. . .	. . .	. . .	. . .	. . .	. . .	. . .	. . .
Monetary authorities	4 621	. .	. . .	. . .	. . .	. . .	. . .	. . .	. . .	. . .
General government	4 622	. .	. . .	. . .	. . .	. . .	. . .	. . .	. . .	. . .
Banks	4 623	. .	. . .	. . .	. . .	. . .	. . .	. . .	. . .	. . .
Other sectors	4 624	. .	. . .	. . .	. . .	. . .	. . .	. . .	. . .	. . .
Money market instruments	4 630	. .	. . .	. . .	. . .	. . .	. . .	. . .	. . .	. . .
Monetary authorities	4 631	. .	. . .	. . .	. . .	. . .	. . .	. . .	. . .	. . .
General government	4 632	. .	. . .	. . .	. . .	. . .	. . .	. . .	. . .	. . .
Banks	4 633	. .	. . .	. . .	. . .	. . .	. . .	. . .	. . .	. . .
Other sectors	4 634	. .	. . .	. . .	. . .	. . .	. . .	. . .	. . .	. . .
Financial derivatives	4 640	. .	. . .	. . .	. . .	. . .	. . .	. . .	. . .	. . .
Monetary authorities	4 641	. .	. . .	. . .	. . .	. . .	. . .	. . .	. . .	. . .
General government	4 642	. .	. . .	. . .	. . .	. . .	. . .	. . .	. . .	. . .
Banks	4 643	. .	. . .	. . .	. . .	. . .	. . .	. . .	. . .	. . .
Other sectors	4 644	. .	. . .	. . .	. . .	. . .	. . .	. . .	. . .	. . .
Liabilities	4 652	. .	. . .	. . .	. . .	. . .	. . .	. . .	. . .	. . .
Equity securities	4 660	. .	. . .	. . .	. . .	. . .	. . .	. . .	. . .	. . .
Banks	4 663	. .	. . .	. . .	. . .	. . .	. . .	. . .	. . .	. . .
Other sectors	4 664	. .	. . .	. . .	. . .	. . .	. . .	. . .	. . .	. . .
Debt securities	4 669	. .	. . .	. . .	. . .	. . .	. . .	. . .	. . .	. . .
Bonds and notes	4 670	. .	. . .	. . .	. . .	. . .	. . .	. . .	. . .	. . .
Monetary authorities	4 671	. .	. . .	. . .	. . .	. . .	. . .	. . .	. . .	. . .
General government	4 672	. .	. . .	. . .	. . .	. . .	. . .	. . .	. . .	. . .
Banks	4 673	. .	. . .	. . .	. . .	. . .	. . .	. . .	. . .	. . .
Other sectors	4 674	. .	. . .	. . .	. . .	. . .	. . .	. . .	. . .	. . .
Money market instruments	4 680	. .	. . .	. . .	. . .	. . .	. . .	. . .	. . .	. . .
Monetary authorities	4 681	. .	. . .	. . .	. . .	. . .	. . .	. . .	. . .	. . .
General government	4 682	. .	. . .	. . .	. . .	. . .	. . .	. . .	. . .	. . .
Banks	4 683	. .	. . .	. . .	. . .	. . .	. . .	. . .	. . .	. . .
Other sectors	4 684	. .	. . .	. . .	. . .	. . .	. . .	. . .	. . .	. . .
Financial derivatives	4 690	. .	. . .	. . .	. . .	. . .	. . .	. . .	. . .	. . .
Monetary authorities	4 691	. .	. . .	. . .	. . .	. . .	. . .	. . .	. . .	. . .
General government	4 692	. .	. . .	. . .	. . .	. . .	. . .	. . .	. . .	. . .
Banks	4 693	. .	. . .	. . .	. . .	. . .	. . .	. . .	. . .	. . .
Other sectors	4 694	. .	. . .	. . .	. . .	. . .	. . .	. . .	. . .	. . .

Table 2 (Concluded). STANDARD PRESENTATION, 1988–95
(Millions of U.S. dollars)

	Code		1988	1989	1990	1991	1992	1993	1994	1995
C. OTHER INVESTMENT	4 700	..	37.23	43.50	22.91	50.06	51.58	32.36	19.65	5.95
Assets	4 703	..	**...**	**...**	**...**	**...**	**...**	**...**	**...**	**...**
Trade credits	4 706	..	...	...	...	...	...	...	...	...
General government: long-term	4 708	..	...	...	...	...	...	...	...	...
General government: short-term	4 709	..	...	...	...	...	...	...	...	...
Other sectors: long-term	4 711	..	...	...	...	...	...	...	...	...
Other sectors: short-term	4 712	..	...	...	...	...	...	...	...	...
Loans	4 714	..	...	...	...	...	...	...	...	...
Monetary authorities: long-term	4 717	..	...	...	...	...	...	...	...	...
Monetary authorities: short-term	4 718	..	...	...	...	...	...	...	...	...
General government: long-term	4 720	..	...	...	...	...	...	...	...	...
General government: short-term	4 721	..	...	...	...	...	...	...	...	...
Banks: long-term	4 723	..	...	...	...	...	...	...	...	...
Banks: short-term	4 724	..	...	...	...	...	...	...	...	...
Other sectors: long-term	4 726	..	...	...	...	...	...	...	...	...
Other sectors: short-term	4 727	..	...	...	...	...	...	...	...	...
Currency and deposits	4 730	..	...	...	...	...	...	...	...	...
Monetary authorities	4 731	..	...	...	...	...	...	...	...	...
General government	4 732	..	...	...	...	...	...	...	...	...
Banks	4 733	..	...	...	...	...	...	...	...	...
Other sectors	4 734	..	...	...	...	...	...	...	...	...
Other assets	4 736	..	...	...	...	...	...	...	...	...
Monetary authorities: long-term	4 738	..	...	...	...	...	...	...	...	...
Monetary authorities: short-term	4 739	..	...	...	...	...	...	...	...	...
General government: long-term	4 741	..	...	...	...	...	...	...	...	...
General government: short-term	4 742	..	...	...	...	...	...	...	...	...
Banks: long-term	4 744	..	...	...	...	...	...	...	...	...
Banks: short-term	4 745	..	...	...	...	...	...	...	...	...
Other sectors: long-term	4 747	..	...	...	...	...	...	...	...	...
Other sectors: short-term	4 748	..	...	...	...	...	...	...	...	...
Liabilities	4 753	..	**37.23**	**43.50**	**22.91**	**50.06**	**51.58**	**32.36**	**19.65**	**5.95**
Trade credits	4 756	..	...	...	...	...	...	...	...	...
General government: long-term	4 758	..	...	...	...	...	...	...	...	...
General government: short-term	4 759	..	...	...	...	...	...	...	...	...
Other sectors: long-term	4 761	..	...	...	...	...	...	...	...	...
Other sectors: short-term	4 762	..	...	...	...	...	...	...	...	...
Loans	4 764	..	34.14	26.27	39.56	17.98	12.63	2.11	–24.15	152.79
Use of Fund credit and loans from the Fund	4 766	..	–1.26	1.97	...	...	...	–.42	–.43	1.19
Monetary authorities: other long-term	4 767	..	...	...	...	...	...	...	...	...
Monetary authorities: short-term	4 768	..	...	...	...	...	...	...	...	...
General government: long-term	4 770	..	35.40	24.30	39.56	17.98	12.63	2.53	–23.72	151.60
General government: short-term	4 771	..	...	...	...	...	...	...	...	...
Banks: long-term	4 773	..	...	...	...	...	...	...	...	...
Banks: short-term	4 774	..	...	...	...	...	...	...	...	...
Other sectors: long-term	4 776	..	...	...	...	...	...	...	...	...
Other sectors: short-term	4 777	..	...	...	...	...	...	...	...	...
Currency and deposits	4 780	..	...	...	...	...	...	...	...	...
Monetary authorities	4 781	..	...	...	...	...	...	...	...	...
General government	4 782	..	...	...	...	...	...	...	...	...
Banks	4 783	..	...	...	...	...	...	...	...	...
Other sectors	4 784	..	...	...	...	...	...	...	...	...
Other liabilities	4 786	..	3.09	17.23	–16.65	32.08	38.95	30.25	43.80	–146.84
Monetary authorities: long-term	4 788	..	...	...	...	...	...	...	...	...
Monetary authorities: short-term	4 789	..	4.03	17.83	–16.65	32.08	38.95	30.25	43.80	–146.84
General government: long-term	4 791	..	–.94	–.60	...	...	...	...	...	...
General government: short-term	4 792	..	...	...	...	...	...	...	...	...
Banks: long-term	4 794	..	...	...	...	...	...	...	...	...
Banks: short-term	4 795	..	...	...	...	...	...	...	...	...
Other sectors: long-term	4 797	..	...	...	...	...	...	...	...	...
Other sectors: short-term	4 798	..	...	...	...	...	...	...	...	...
D. RESERVE ASSETS	4 800	..	–11.83	6.70	–5.20	8.89	–5.10	9.02	6.24	–3.64
Monetary gold	4 810	..	...	...	...	...	...	...	...	...
Special drawing rights	4 820	..	.07	...	...	...	...	–.01	.01	–.01
Reserve position in the Fund	4 830	..	...	...	...	...	...	...	...	...
Foreign exchange	4 840	..	–11.90	6.70	–5.20	8.89	–5.10	9.03	6.23	–3.63
Other claims	4 880	..	...	...	...	...	...	...	...	...
NET ERRORS AND OMISSIONS	4 998	..	**3.50**	**–11.60**	**–1.47**	**–16.27**	**22.01**	**–15.98**	**–21.36**	**–25.53**

Part 3 of the *Yearbook* contains descriptions of the methodologies, compilation practices, and sources used to compile these data.

Table 1. ANALYTIC PRESENTATION, 1988–95
(Millions of U.S. dollars)

	Code	1988	1989	1990	1991	1992	1993	1994	1995
A. Current Account[1]	4 993 Y.	...	...	...	...	**–138.5**	**–140.2**	**–124.9**	**–134.8**
Goods: exports f.o.b	2 100 ..	...	...	...	...	381.7	415.5	463.4	495.7
Goods: imports f.o.b	3 100 ..	...	...	...	...	–442.7	–483.8	–504.0	–536.5
Balance on Goods	4 100 ..	...	...	...	...	*–61.0*	*–68.3*	*–40.6*	*–40.8*
Services: credit	2 200 ..	...	...	...	...	105.9	115.3	120.7	133.5
Services: debit	3 200 ..	...	...	...	...	–139.8	–148.1	–160.9	–171.8
Balance on Goods and Services	4 991 ..	...	...	...	...	*–95.0*	*–101.1*	*–80.8*	*–79.2*
Income: credit	2 300 ..	...	...	...	...	4.9	5.1	8.7	12.2
Income: debit	3 300 ..	...	...	...	...	–101.5	–106.8	–114.8	–129.9
Balance on Goods, Services, and Income	4 992 ..	...	...	...	...	*–191.6*	*–202.9*	*–186.9*	*–196.8*
Current transfers: credit	2 379 Y.	...	...	...	...	62.9	70.0	68.1	67.4
Current transfers: debit	3 379 ..	...	...	...	...	–9.9	–7.4	–6.2	–5.3
B. Capital Account[1]	4 994 Y.	...	...	...	...	**81.7**	**65.7**	**16.4**	**10.2**
Capital account: credit	2 994 Y.	...	...	...	...	83.5	67.9	19.1	13.2
Capital account: debit	3 994 ..	...	...	...	...	–1.8	–2.2	–2.7	–3.0
Total, Groups A Plus B	4 010 ..	...	...	...	...	*–56.9*	*–74.5*	*–108.5*	*–124.6*
C. Financial Account[1]	4 995 X.	...	...	...	...	**86.9**	**111.6**	**155.4**	**122.4**
Direct investment abroad	4 505 ..	...	...	...	...	...	...	...	...
Direct investment in Guyana	4 555 Y.	...	...	...	...	146.6	69.5	106.7	74.4
Portfolio investment assets	4 602 ..	...	...	...	...	...	...	...	...
Equity securities	4 610 ..	...	...	...	...	...	...	...	...
Debt securities	4 619 ..	...	...	...	...	...	...	...	...
Portfolio investment liabilities	4 652 Y.	...	...	...	...	2.8	3.6	15.8	3.2
Equity securities	4 660 Y.	...	...	...	...	...	...	...	...
Debt securities	4 669 Y.	...	...	...	...	2.8	3.6	15.8	3.2
Other investment assets	4 703 ..	...	...	...	...	–19.9	8.8	–5.8	–8.9
Monetary authorities	4 703 .A	...	...	...	...	...	...	...	...
General government	4 703 .B	...	...	...	...	–3.4	1.4	1.3	–2.2
Banks	4 703 .C	...	...	...	...	–6.4	3.2	4.2	–2.8
Other sectors	4 703 .D	...	...	...	...	–10.2	4.2	–11.2	–3.9
Other investment liabilities	4 753 X.	...	...	...	...	–42.5	29.6	38.7	53.6
Monetary authorities	4 753 XA	...	...	...	...	–4.7	–13.9	1.3	18.6
General government	4 753 YB	...	...	...	...	–49.7	50.2	27.5	46.0
Banks	4 753 YC	...	...	...	...	–5.5	–4.9	–2.9	–.4
Other sectors	4 753 YD	...	...	...	...	17.4	–1.8	12.9	–10.5
Total, Groups A Through C	4 020 ..	...	...	...	...	*30.1*	*37.1*	*46.9*	*–2.2*
D. Net Errors and Omissions	4 998 ..	...	...	...	...	**12.2**	**11.0**	**–16.3**	**11.2**
Total, Groups A Through D	4 030 ..	...	...	...	...	*42.3*	*48.1*	*30.6*	*8.9*
E. Reserves and Related Items	4 040 ..	...	...	...	...	**–42.3**	**–48.1**	**–30.6**	**–8.9**
Reserve assets	4 800 ..	...	...	...	...	–67.1	–57.1	–21.8	.8
Use of Fund credit and loans	4 766 ..	...	...	...	...	24.8	9.1	–8.8	–9.7
Liabilities constituting foreign authorities' reserves	4 900 ..	...	...	...	...	...	...	...	...
Exceptional financing	4 920 ..	...	...	...	...	...	...	...	...
Conversion Rates: Guyana dollars per U.S. dollar	0 101 ..	**10.000**	**27.159**	**39.533**	**111.811**	**125.003**	**126.730**	**138.290**	**141.989**

[1] Excludes components that have been classified in the categories of Group E.

Table 2. STANDARD PRESENTATION, 1988–95
(Millions of U.S. dollars)

	Code	1988	1989	1990	1991	1992	1993	1994	1995
CURRENT ACCOUNT	4 993 . .	**. . .**	**. . .**	**. . .**	**. . .**	**–138.5**	**–140.2**	**–124.9**	**–134.8**
A. GOODS	4 100 . .	. . .	. . .	. . .	. . .	–61.0	–68.3	–40.6	–40.8
Credit	2 100 . .	**. . .**	**. . .**	**. . .**	**. . .**	**381.7**	**415.5**	**463.4**	**495.7**
General merchandise: exports f.o.b.	2 110 . .	. . .	. . .	. . .	. . .	381.7	415.5	463.4	495.7
Goods for processing: exports f.o.b.	2 150 . .	. . .	. . .	. . .	. . .	. . .	. . .	. . .	. . .
Repairs on goods	2 160 . .	. . .	. . .	. . .	. . .	. . .	. . .	. . .	. . .
Goods procured in ports by carriers	2 170 . .	. . .	. . .	. . .	. . .	. . .	. . .	. . .	. . .
Nonmonetary gold	2 180 . .	. . .	. . .	. . .	. . .	. . .	. . .	. . .	. . .
Debit	3 100 . .	**. . .**	**. . .**	**. . .**	**. . .**	**–442.7**	**–483.8**	**–504.0**	**–536.5**
General merchandise: imports f.o.b.	3 110 . .	. . .	. . .	. . .	. . .	–442.7	–483.8	–504.0	–536.5
Goods for processing: imports f.o.b.	3 150 . .	. . .	. . .	. . .	. . .	. . .	. . .	. . .	. . .
Repairs on goods	3 160 . .	. . .	. . .	. . .	. . .	. . .	. . .	. . .	. . .
Goods procured in ports by carriers	3 170 . .	. . .	. . .	. . .	. . .	. . .	. . .	. . .	. . .
Nonmonetary gold	3 180 . .	. . .	. . .	. . .	. . .	. . .	. . .	. . .	. . .
B. SERVICES	4 200 . .	. . .	. . .	. . .	. . .	–34.0	–32.8	–40.2	–38.4
Total credit	2 200 . .	. . .	. . .	. . .	. . .	*105.9*	*115.3*	*120.7*	*133.5*
Total debit	3 200 . .	. . .	. . .	. . .	. . .	*–139.8*	*–148.1*	*–160.9*	*–171.8*
Transportation services, credit	2 205 . .	**. . .**	**. . .**	**. . .**	**. . .**	**28.3**	**29.4**	**26.7**	**33.1**
Passenger	2 205 BA	. . .	. . .	. . .	. . .	. . .	. . .	. . .	. . .
Freight	2 205 BB	. . .	. . .	. . .	. . .	. . .	. . .	. . .	. . .
Other	2 205 BC	. . .	. . .	. . .	. . .	. . .	. . .	. . .	. . .
Sea transport, passenger	2 207 . .	. . .	. . .	. . .	. . .	. . .	. . .	. . .	. . .
Sea transport, freight	2 208 . .	. . .	. . .	. . .	. . .	. . .	. . .	. . .	. . .
Sea transport, other	2 209 . .	. . .	. . .	. . .	. . .	. . .	. . .	. . .	. . .
Air transport, passenger	2 211 . .	. . .	. . .	. . .	. . .	. . .	. . .	. . .	. . .
Air transport, freight	2 212 . .	. . .	. . .	. . .	. . .	. . .	. . .	. . .	. . .
Air transport, other	2 213 . .	. . .	. . .	. . .	. . .	. . .	. . .	. . .	. . .
Other transport, passenger	2 215 . .	. . .	. . .	. . .	. . .	. . .	. . .	. . .	. . .
Other transport, freight	2 216 . .	. . .	. . .	. . .	. . .	. . .	. . .	. . .	. . .
Other transport, other	2 217 . .	. . .	. . .	. . .	. . .	. . .	. . .	. . .	. . .
Transportation services, debit	3 205 . .	**. . .**	**. . .**	**. . .**	**. . .**	**–67.7**	**–66.7**	**–63.1**	**–68.7**
Passenger	3 205 BA	. . .	. . .	. . .	. . .	. . .	. . .	. . .	. . .
Freight	3 205 BB	. . .	. . .	. . .	. . .	. . .	. . .	. . .	. . .
Other	3 205 BC	. . .	. . .	. . .	. . .	. . .	. . .	. . .	. . .
Sea transport, passenger	3 207 . .	. . .	. . .	. . .	. . .	. . .	. . .	. . .	. . .
Sea transport, freight	3 208 . .	. . .	. . .	. . .	. . .	. . .	. . .	. . .	. . .
Sea transport, other	3 209 . .	. . .	. . .	. . .	. . .	. . .	. . .	. . .	. . .
Air transport, passenger	3 211 . .	. . .	. . .	. . .	. . .	. . .	. . .	. . .	. . .
Air transport, freight	3 212 . .	. . .	. . .	. . .	. . .	. . .	. . .	. . .	. . .
Air transport, other	3 213 . .	. . .	. . .	. . .	. . .	. . .	. . .	. . .	. . .
Other transport, passenger	3 215 . .	. . .	. . .	. . .	. . .	. . .	. . .	. . .	. . .
Other transport, freight	3 216 . .	. . .	. . .	. . .	. . .	. . .	. . .	. . .	. . .
Other transport, other	3 217 . .	. . .	. . .	. . .	. . .	. . .	. . .	. . .	. . .
Travel, credit	2 236 . .	**. . .**	**. . .**	**. . .**	**. . .**	**32.8**	**35.5**	**34.0**	**32.6**
Business travel	2 237 . .	. . .	. . .	. . .	. . .	. . .	. . .	. . .	. . .
Personal travel	2 240 . .	. . .	. . .	. . .	. . .	. . .	. . .	. . .	. . .
Travel, debit	3 236 . .	**. . .**	**. . .**	**. . .**	**. . .**	**–14.1**	**–17.5**	**–23.0**	**–21.1**
Business travel	3 237 . .	. . .	. . .	. . .	. . .	. . .	. . .	. . .	. . .
Personal travel	3 240 . .	. . .	. . .	. . .	. . .	. . .	. . .	. . .	. . .
Other services, credit	2 200 BA	**. . .**	**. . .**	**. . .**	**. . .**	**44.8**	**50.5**	**60.0**	**67.8**
Communications	2 245 . .	. . .	. . .	. . .	. . .	38.2	45.2	53.2	60.5
Construction	2 249 . .	. . .	. . .	. . .	. . .	. . .	. . .	. . .	. . .
Insurance	2 253 . .	. . .	. . .	. . .	. . .	. . .	. . .	. . .	. . .
Financial	2 260 . .	. . .	. . .	. . .	. . .	. . .	. . .	. . .	. . .
Computer and information	2 262 . .	. . .	. . .	. . .	. . .	. . .	. . .	. . .	. . .
Royalties and licence fees	2 266 . .	. . .	. . .	. . .	. . .	. . .	. . .	. . .	. . .
Other business services	2 268 . .	. . .	. . .	. . .	. . .	3.2	1.9	3.2	3.4
Personal, cultural, and recreational	2 287 . .	. . .	. . .	. . .	. . .	. . .	. . .	. . .	. . .
Government, n.i.e.	2 291 . .	. . .	. . .	. . .	. . .	3.5	3.5	3.6	3.9
Other services, debit	3 200 BA	**. . .**	**. . .**	**. . .**	**. . .**	**–58.1**	**–63.9**	**–74.8**	**–82.0**
Communications	3 245 . .	. . .	. . .	. . .	. . .	–12.2	–19.0	–36.1	–50.5
Construction	3 249 . .	. . .	. . .	. . .	. . .	–21.8	–15.8	–9.0	–5.7
Insurance	3 253 . .	. . .	. . .	. . .	. . .	–4.4	–4.8	–5.0	–5.4
Financial	3 260 . .	. . .	. . .	. . .	. . .	. . .	. . .	. . .	. . .
Computer and information	3 262 . .	. . .	. . .	. . .	. . .	. . .	. . .	. . .	. . .
Royalties and licence fees	3 266 . .	. . .	. . .	. . .	. . .	. . .	. . .	. . .	. . .
Other business services	3 268 . .	. . .	. . .	. . .	. . .	–10.9	–17.3	–20.4	–16.1
Personal, cultural, and recreational	3 287 . .	. . .	. . .	. . .	. . .	. . .	. . .	. . .	. . .
Government, n.i.e.	3 291 . .	. . .	. . .	. . .	. . .	–8.7	–6.9	–4.3	–4.3

Table 2 (Continued). STANDARD PRESENTATION, 1988–95
(Millions of U.S. dollars)

	Code	1988	1989	1990	1991	1992	1993	1994	1995
C. INCOME	4 300	...	...	...	...	–96.6	–101.8	–106.1	–117.7
Total credit	2 300	...	...	...	...	*4.9*	*5.1*	*8.7*	*12.2*
Total debit	3 300	...	...	...	...	*–101.5*	*–106.8*	*–114.8*	*–129.9*
Compensation of employees, credit	2 310	...	...	...	...	...	...	...	...
Compensation of employees, debit	3 310	...	...	...	...	**–2.7**	**–9.1**	**–8.6**	**–9.0**
Investment income, credit	2 320	...	...	...	...	**4.9**	**5.1**	**8.7**	**12.2**
Direct investment income	2 330	...	...	...	...	...	...	...	...
Dividends and distributed branch profits	2 332	...	...	...	...	...	...	...	...
Reinvested earnings and undistributed branch profits	2 333	...	...	...	...	...	...	...	...
Income on debt (interest)	2 334	...	...	...	...	...	...	...	...
Portfolio investment income	2 339	...	...	...	...	...	...	...	...
Income on equity	2 340	...	...	...	...	...	...	...	...
Income on bonds and notes	2 350	...	...	...	...	...	...	...	...
Income on money market instruments and financial derivatives	2 360	...	...	...	...	...	...	...	...
Other investment income	2 370	...	...	...	...	4.9	5.1	8.7	12.2
Investment income, debit	3 320	...	...	...	...	**–98.8**	**–97.8**	**–106.3**	**–120.9**
Direct investment income	3 330	...	...	...	...	...	...	...	...
Dividends and distributed branch profits	3 332	...	...	...	...	...	...	...	...
Reinvested earnings and undistributed branch profits	3 333	...	...	...	...	...	...	...	...
Income on debt (interest)	3 334	...	...	...	...	...	...	...	...
Portfolio investment income	3 339	...	...	...	...	–74.9	–61.6	–66.9	–70.3
Income on equity	3 340	...	...	...	...	...	...	...	...
Income on bonds and notes	3 350	...	...	...	...	–74.9	–61.6	–66.9	–70.3
Income on money market instruments and financial derivatives	3 360	...	...	...	...	...	...	...	...
Other investment income	3 370	...	...	...	...	–24.0	–36.2	–39.4	–50.6
D. CURRENT TRANSFERS	4 379	...	...	...	...	53.0	62.6	61.9	62.1
Credit	2 379	...	...	...	...	**62.9**	**70.0**	**68.1**	**67.4**
General government	2 380	...	...	...	...	20.6	19.6	15.0	6.1
Other sectors	2 390	...	...	...	...	42.3	50.4	53.1	61.3
Workers' remittances	2 391	...	...	...	...	...	...	...	...
Other current transfers	2 392	...	...	...	...	...	...	...	...
Debit	3 379	...	...	...	...	**–9.9**	**–7.4**	**–6.2**	**–5.3**
General government	3 380	...	...	...	...	–8.2	–5.3	–4.2	–3.2
Other sectors	3 390	...	...	...	...	–1.7	–2.1	–2.0	–2.1
Workers' remittances	3 391	...	...	...	...	...	...	...	...
Other current transfers	3 392	...	...	...	...	...	...	...	...
CAPITAL AND FINANCIAL ACCOUNT	4 996	...	...	...	...	**126.3**	**129.2**	**141.2**	**123.6**
CAPITAL ACCOUNT	4 994	...	...	...	...	**81.7**	**65.7**	**16.4**	**10.2**
Total credit	2 994	...	...	...	...	*83.5*	*67.9*	*19.1*	*13.2*
Total debit	3 994	...	...	...	...	*–1.8*	*–2.2*	*–2.7*	*–3.0*
Capital transfers, credit	2 400	...	...	...	...	**83.5**	**67.9**	**19.1**	**13.2**
General government	2 401	...	...	...	...	81.6	66.7	17.7	11.5
Debt forgiveness	2 402	...	...	...	...	80.1	61.3	8.1	.7
Other capital transfers	2 410	...	...	...	...	1.5	5.4	9.7	10.8
Other sectors	2 430	...	...	...	...	1.9	1.2	1.3	1.7
Migrants' transfers	2 431	...	...	...	...	1.0	1.2	1.3	1.7
Debt forgiveness	2 432	...	...	...	...	...	...	...	...
Other capital transfers	2 440	...	...	...	...	.9	...	...	...
Capital transfers, debit	3 400	...	...	...	...	**–1.8**	**–2.2**	**–2.7**	**–3.0**
General government	3 401	...	...	...	...	...	...	...	...
Debt forgiveness	3 402	...	...	...	...	...	...	...	...
Other capital transfers	3 410	...	...	...	...	...	...	...	...
Other sectors	3 430	...	...	...	...	–1.8	–2.2	–2.7	–3.0
Migrants' transfers	3 431	...	...	...	...	–1.8	–2.2	–2.7	–3.0
Debt forgiveness	3 432	...	...	...	...	...	...	...	...
Other capital transfers	3 440	...	...	...	...	...	...	...	...
Nonproduced nonfinancial assets, credit	2 480	...	...	...	...	...	...	...	...
Nonproduced nonfinancial assets, debit	3 480	...	...	...	...	...	...	...	...

Table 2 (Continued). STANDARD PRESENTATION, 1988–95
(Millions of U.S. dollars)

	Code	1988	1989	1990	1991	1992	1993	1994	1995
FINANCIAL ACCOUNT	4 995	...	...	...	...	**44.6**	**63.5**	**124.8**	**113.4**
A. DIRECT INVESTMENT	4 500	...	...	...	...	146.6	69.5	106.7	74.4
Direct investment abroad	4 505	...	...	...	...	...	...	...	...
Equity capital	4 510	...	...	...	...	...	...	...	...
Claims on affiliated enterprises	4 515	...	...	...	...	...	...	...	...
Liabilities to affiliated enterprises	4 520	...	...	...	...	...	...	...	...
Reinvested earnings	4 525	...	...	...	...	...	...	...	...
Other capital	4 530	...	...	...	...	...	...	...	...
Claims on affiliated enterprises	4 535	...	...	...	...	...	...	...	...
Liabilities to affiliated enterprises	4 540	...	...	...	...	...	...	...	...
Direct investment in Guyana	4 555	...	...	...	...	**146.6**	**69.5**	**106.7**	**74.4**
Equity capital	4 560	...	...	...	...	...	...	...	...
Claims on direct investors	4 565	...	...	...	...	...	...	...	...
Liabilities to direct investors	4 570	...	...	...	...	...	...	...	...
Reinvested earnings	4 575	...	...	...	...	...	...	...	...
Other capital	4 580	...	...	...	...	146.6	69.5	106.7	74.4
Claims on direct investors	4 585	...	...	...	...	...	...	...	...
Liabilities to direct investors	4 590	...	...	...	...	...	...	...	...
B. PORTFOLIO INVESTMENT	4 600	...	...	...	...	2.8	3.6	15.8	3.2
Assets	4 602	...	...	...	...	...	...	...	...
Equity securities	4 610	...	...	...	...	...	...	...	...
Monetary authorities	4 611	...	...	...	...	...	...	...	...
General government	4 612	...	...	...	...	...	...	...	...
Banks	4 613	...	...	...	...	...	...	...	...
Other sectors	4 614	...	...	...	...	...	...	...	...
Debt securities	4 619	...	...	...	...	...	...	...	...
Bonds and notes	4 620	...	...	...	...	...	...	...	...
Monetary authorities	4 621	...	...	...	...	...	...	...	...
General government	4 622	...	...	...	...	...	...	...	...
Banks	4 623	...	...	...	...	...	...	...	...
Other sectors	4 624	...	...	...	...	...	...	...	...
Money market instruments	4 630	...	...	...	...	...	...	...	...
Monetary authorities	4 631	...	...	...	...	...	...	...	...
General government	4 632	...	...	...	...	...	...	...	...
Banks	4 633	...	...	...	...	...	...	...	...
Other sectors	4 634	...	...	...	...	...	...	...	...
Financial derivatives	4 640	...	...	...	...	...	...	...	...
Monetary authorities	4 641	...	...	...	...	...	...	...	...
General government	4 642	...	...	...	...	...	...	...	...
Banks	4 643	...	...	...	...	...	...	...	...
Other sectors	4 644	...	...	...	...	...	...	...	...
Liabilities	4 652	...	...	...	...	**2.8**	**3.6**	**15.8**	**3.2**
Equity securities	4 660	...	...	...	...	...	...	...	...
Banks	4 663	...	...	...	...	...	...	...	...
Other sectors	4 664	...	...	...	...	...	...	...	...
Debt securities	4 669	...	...	...	...	2.8	3.6	15.8	3.2
Bonds and notes	4 670	...	...	...	...	2.8	3.6	15.8	3.2
Monetary authorities	4 671	...	...	...	...	...	...	...	...
General government	4 672	...	...	...	...	...	...	...	...
Banks	4 673	...	...	...	...	...	...	...	...
Other sectors	4 674	...	...	...	...	...	...	...	...
Money market instruments	4 680	...	...	...	...	...	...	...	...
Monetary authorities	4 681	...	...	...	...	...	...	...	...
General government	4 682	...	...	...	...	...	...	...	...
Banks	4 683	...	...	...	...	...	...	...	...
Other sectors	4 684	...	...	...	...	...	...	...	...
Financial derivatives	4 690	...	...	...	...	...	...	...	...
Monetary authorities	4 691	...	...	...	...	...	...	...	...
General government	4 692	...	...	...	...	...	...	...	...
Banks	4 693	...	...	...	...	...	...	...	...
Other sectors	4 694	...	...	...	...	...	...	...	...

Table 2 (Concluded). STANDARD PRESENTATION, 1988–95
(Millions of U.S. dollars)

	Code	1988	1989	1990	1991	1992	1993	1994	1995
C. OTHER INVESTMENT	4 700 . .	...	...	...	...	–37.7	47.5	24.1	35.1
Assets	4 703 . .	**...**	**...**	**...**	**...**	**–19.9**	**8.8**	**–5.8**	**–8.9**
Trade credits	4 706 . .	...	...	...	...	...	...	...	...
General government: long-term	4 708 . .	...	...	...	...	...	...	...	...
General government: short-term	4 709 . .	...	...	...	...	...	...	...	...
Other sectors: long-term	4 711 . .	...	...	...	...	...	...	...	...
Other sectors: short-term	4 712 . .	...	...	...	...	...	...	...	...
Loans	4 714 . .	...	...	...	...	...	...	...	...
Monetary authorities: long-term	4 717 . .	...	...	...	...	...	...	...	...
Monetary authorities: short-term	4 718 . .	...	...	...	...	...	...	...	...
General government: long-term	4 720 . .	...	...	...	...	...	...	...	...
General government: short-term	4 721 . .	...	...	...	...	...	...	...	...
Banks: long-term	4 723 . .	...	...	...	...	...	...	...	...
Banks: short-term	4 724 . .	...	...	...	...	...	...	...	...
Other sectors: long-term	4 726 . .	...	...	...	...	...	...	...	...
Other sectors: short-term	4 727 . .	...	...	...	...	...	...	...	...
Currency and deposits	4 730 . .	...	...	...	...	...	...	...	...
Monetary authorities	4 731 . .	...	...	...	...	...	...	...	...
General government	4 732 . .	...	...	...	...	...	...	...	...
Banks	4 733 . .	...	...	...	...	...	...	...	...
Other sectors	4 734 . .	...	...	...	...	...	...	...	...
Other assets	4 736 . .	...	...	...	...	–19.9	8.8	–5.8	–8.9
Monetary authorities: long-term	4 738 . .	...	...	...	...	...	...	...	...
Monetary authorities: short-term	4 739 . .	...	...	...	...	...	...	...	...
General government: long-term	4 741 . .	...	...	...	...	...	...	...	...
General government: short-term	4 742 . .	...	...	...	...	–3.4	1.4	1.3	–2.2
Banks: long-term	4 744 . .	...	...	...	...	...	...	...	...
Banks: short-term	4 745 . .	...	...	...	...	–6.4	3.2	4.2	–2.8
Other sectors: long-term	4 747 . .	...	...	...	...	...	...	...	...
Other sectors: short-term	4 748 . .	...	...	...	...	–10.2	4.2	–11.2	–3.9
Liabilities	4 753 . .	**...**	**...**	**...**	**...**	**–17.7**	**38.7**	**29.9**	**43.9**
Trade credits	4 756 . .	...	...	...	...	...	...	...	...
General government: long-term	4 758 . .	...	...	...	...	...	...	...	...
General government: short-term	4 759 . .	...	...	...	...	...	...	...	...
Other sectors: long-term	4 761 . .	...	...	...	...	...	...	...	...
Other sectors: short-term	4 762 . .	...	...	...	...	...	...	...	...
Loans	4 764 . .	...	...	...	...	–25.6	24.8	4.4	–25.2
Use of Fund credit and loans from the Fund	4 766 . .	...	...	...	...	24.8	9.1	–8.8	–9.7
Monetary authorities: other long term	4 767 . .	...	...	...	...	7.3	–6.4	1.2	.4
Monetary authorities: short-term	4 768 . .	...	...	...	...	...	...	...	...
General government: long-term	4 770 . .	...	...	...	...	–73.6	27.3	–1.0	–5.4
General government: short-term	4 771 . .	...	...	...	...	...	...	...	...
Banks: long-term	4 773 . .	...	...	...	...	...	...	1.0	.6
Banks: short-term	4 774 . .	...	...	...	...	...	...	...	...
Other sectors: long-term	4 776 . .	...	...	...	...	15.9	–5.2	12.0	–11.1
Other sectors: short-term	4 777 . .	...	...	...	...	...	...	...	...
Currency and deposits	4 780 . .	...	...	...	...	...	...	...	...
Monetary authorities	4 781 . .	...	...	...	...	...	...	...	...
General government	4 782 . .	...	...	...	...	...	...	...	...
Banks	4 783 . .	...	...	...	...	...	...	...	...
Other sectors	4 784 . .	...	...	...	...	...	...	...	...
Other liabilities	4 786 . .	...	...	...	...	7.9	13.8	25.5	69.1
Monetary authorities: long-term	4 788 . .	...	...	...	...	–2.1	–1.8	5.5	17.6
Monetary authorities: short-term	4 789 . .	...	...	...	...	–9.9	–5.7	–5.4	.6
General government: long-term	4 791 . .	...	...	...	...	...	...	...	...
General government: short-term	4 792 . .	...	...	...	...	23.9	22.9	28.5	51.3
Banks: long-term	4 794 . .	...	...	...	...	...	...	...	...
Banks: short-term	4 795 . .	...	...	...	...	–5.5	–4.9	–3.9	–1.0
Other sectors: long-term	4 797 . .	...	...	...	...	...	...	...	...
Other sectors: short-term	4 798 . .	...	...	...	...	1.5	3.3	.8	.6
D. RESERVE ASSETS	4 800 . .	...	...	...	...	–67.1	–57.1	–21.8	.8
Monetary gold	4 810 . .	...	...	...	...	...	–.2	–1.5	.4
Special drawing rights	4 820 . .	...	...	...	...	1.1	.3	–.1	–.2
Reserve position in the Fund	4 830 . .	...	...	...	...	...	...	...	...
Foreign exchange	4 840 . .	...	...	...	...	–68.2	–57.3	–20.2	.6
Other claims	4 880 . .	...	...	...	...	...	...	...	...
NET ERRORS AND OMISSIONS	4 998 . .	**...**	**...**	**...**	**...**	**12.2**	**11.0**	**–16.3**	**11.2**

Table 3. INTERNATIONAL INVESTMENT POSITION (End–period stocks), 1988–95
(Millions of U.S. dollars)

	Code	1988	1989	1990	1991	1992	1993	1994	1995
ASSETS	8 995 C.	...	...	...	...	281.1	310.1	345.9	348.0
Direct investment abroad	8 505 ..	...	...	...	...	...	...	...	...
Equity capital and reinvested earnings	8 506 ..	...	...	...	...	...	...	...	...
Claims on affiliated enterprises	8 507 ..	...	...	...	...	...	...	...	...
Liabilities to affiliated enterprises	8 508 ..	...	...	...	...	...	...	...	...
Other capital	8 530 ..	...	...	...	...	...	...	...	...
Claims on affiliated enterprises	8 535 ..	...	...	...	...	...	...	...	...
Liabilities to affiliated enterprises	8 540 ..	...	...	...	...	...	...	...	...
Portfolio investment	8 602 ..	...	...	...	...	**7.2**	**.7**	**7.2**	**2.3**
Equity securities	8 610 ..	...	...	...	...	...	...	...	...
Monetary authorities	8 611 ..	...	...	...	...	...	...	...	...
General government	8 612 ..	...	...	...	...	...	...	...	...
Banks	8 613 ..	...	...	...	...	...	...	...	...
Other sectors	8 614 ..	...	...	...	...	...	...	...	...
Debt securities	8 619 ..	...	...	...	...	7.2	.7	7.2	2.3
Bonds and notes	8 620 ..	...	...	...	...	7.2	.7	7.2	2.3
Monetary authorities	8 621 ..	...	...	...	...	...	...	...	...
General government	8 622 ..	...	...	...	...	.4	.6	.8	.5
Banks	8 623 ..	...	...	...	...	...	...	...	...
Other sectors	8 624 ..	...	...	...	...	6.8	.1	6.4	1.8
Money market instruments	8 630 ..	...	...	...	...	...	...	...	...
Monetary authorities	8 631 ..	...	...	...	...	...	...	...	...
General government	8 632 ..	...	...	...	...	...	...	...	...
Banks	8 633 ..	...	...	...	...	...	...	...	...
Other sectors	8 634 ..	...	...	...	...	...	...	...	...
Financial derivatives	8 640 ..	...	...	...	...	...	...	...	...
Monetary authorities	8 641 ..	...	...	...	...	...	...	...	...
General government	8 642 ..	...	...	...	...	...	...	...	...
Banks	8 643 ..	...	...	...	...	...	...	...	...
Other sectors	8 644 ..	...	...	...	...	...	...	...	...
Other investment	8 703 ..	...	...	...	...	**82.1**	**60.5**	**68.0**	**76.0**
Trade credits	8 706 ..	...	...	...	...	...	...	...	...
General government: long-term	8 708 ..	...	...	...	...	...	...	...	...
General government: short-term	8 709 ..	...	...	...	...	...	...	...	...
Other sectors: long-term	8 711 ..	...	...	...	...	...	...	...	...
Other sectors: short-term	8 712 ..	...	...	...	...	...	...	...	...
Loans	8 714 ..	...	...	...	...	...	...	...	...
Monetary authorities: long-term	8 717 ..	...	...	...	...	...	...	...	...
Monetary authorities: short-term	8 718 ..	...	...	...	...	...	...	...	...
General government: long-term	8 720 ..	...	...	...	...	...	...	...	...
General government: short-term	8 721 ..	...	...	...	...	...	...	...	...
Banks: long-term	8 723 ..	...	...	...	...	...	...	...	...
Banks: short-term	8 724 ..	...	...	...	...	...	...	...	...
Other sectors: long-term	8 726 ..	...	...	...	...	...	...	...	...
Other sectors: short-term	8 727 ..	...	...	...	...	...	...	...	...
Currency and deposits	8 730 ..	...	...	...	...	58.9	36.8	32.5	38.2
Monetary authorities	8 731 ..	...	...	...	...	...	...	...	...
General government	8 732 ..	...	...	...	...	10.0	8.6	7.3	9.5
Banks	8 733 ..	...	...	...	...	27.6	20.7	17.3	20.0
Other sectors	8 734 ..	...	...	...	...	21.4	7.5	8.0	8.8
Other assets	8 736 ..	...	...	...	...	23.2	23.8	35.5	37.8
Monetary authorities: long-term	8 738 ..	...	...	...	...	...	...	...	...
Monetary authorities: short-term	8 739 ..	...	...	...	...	...	...	...	...
General government: long-term	8 741 ..	...	...	...	...	...	...	...	...
General government: short-term	8 742 ..	...	...	...	...	...	...	...	...
Banks: long-term	8 744 ..	...	...	...	...	...	...	...	...
Banks: short-term	8 745 ..	...	...	...	...	...	...	...	...
Other sectors: long-term	8 747 ..	...	...	...	...	...	...	...	...
Other sectors: short-term	8 748 ..	...	...	...	...	...	...	...	...
Reserve assets	8 800 ..	...	...	...	...	**191.7**	**248.9**	**270.7**	**269.7**
Monetary gold	8 810 ..	...	...	...	...	...	.2	1.7	1.3
Special drawing rights	8 820 ..	...	...	2.1	1.4	.3	...	.1	.1
Reserve position in the Fund	8 830 ..	...	...	...	...	...	...	...	...
Foreign exchange	8 840 ..	...	...	...	...	191.4	248.7	268.9	268.3
Other claims	8 880 ..	...	...	...	...	...	...	...	...

Table 3 (Continued). INTERNATIONAL INVESTMENT POSITION (End–period stocks), 1988–95
(Millions of U.S. dollars)

	Code	1988	1989	1990	1991	1992	1993	1994	1995
LIABILITIES	8 995 D.	...	...	...	...	2,357.2	2,279.0	2,315.2	2,391.2
Direct investment in Guyana	8 555 ..	...	...	...	...	**146.6**	**69.5**	**106.5**	**74.4**
Equity capital and reinvested earnings	8 556 ..	...	...	...	...	...	...	...	...
Claims on direct investors	8 557 ..	...	...	...	...	...	...	...	...
Liabilities to direct investors	8 558 ..	...	...	...	...	...	...	...	...
Other capital	8 580 ..	...	...	...	...	...	...	...	...
Claims on direct investors	8 585 ..	...	...	...	...	...	...	...	...
Liabilities to direct investors	8 590 ..	...	...	...	...	...	...	...	...
Portfolio investment	8 652 ..	...	...	...	...	**10.0**	**4.4**	**10.2**	**5.5**
Equity securities	8 660 ..	...	...	...	...	...	...	...	...
Banks	8 663 ..	...	...	...	...	...	...	...	...
Other sectors	8 664 ..	...	...	...	...	...	...	...	...
Debt securities	8 669 ..	...	...	...	...	...	...	...	...
Bonds and notes	8 670 ..	...	...	...	...	...	...	...	...
Monetary authorities	8 671 ..	...	...	...	...	...	...	...	...
General government	8 672 ..	...	...	...	...	...	...	...	...
Banks	8 673 ..	...	...	...	...	...	...	...	...
Other sectors	8 674 ..	...	...	...	...	...	...	...	...
Money market instruments	8 680 ..	...	...	...	...	...	...	...	...
Monetary authorities	8 681 ..	...	...	...	...	...	...	...	...
General government	8 682 ..	...	...	...	...	...	...	...	...
Banks	8 683 ..	...	...	...	...	...	...	...	...
Other sectors	8 684 ..	...	...	...	...	...	...	...	...
Financial derivatives	8 690 ..	...	...	...	...	...	...	...	...
Monetary authorities	8 691 ..	...	...	...	...	...	...	...	...
General government	8 692 ..	...	...	...	...	...	...	...	...
Banks	8 692 ..	...	...	...	...	...	...	...	...
Other sectors	8 694 ..	...	...	...	...	...	...	...	...
Other investment	8 753 ..	...	...	...	...	**2,200.6**	**2,205.1**	**2,198.5**	**2,311.3**
Trade credits	8 756 ..	...	...	...	...	...	...	...	...
General government: long-term	8 758 ..	...	...	...	...	...	...	...	...
General government: short-term	8 759 ..	...	...	...	...	...	...	...	...
Other sectors: long-term	8 761 ..	...	...	...	...	...	...	...	...
Other sectors: short-term	8 762 ..	...	...	...	...	...	...	...	...
Loans	8 764 ..	...	...	...	...	2,160.6	2,157.8	2,149.3	2,262.0
Use of Fund credit and loans from the Fund	8 766 ..	110.0	106.3	112.9	149.4	168.0	176.7	178.5	171.8
Monetary authorities: other long-term	8 767 ..	...	...	...	...	297.0	280.5	219.6	276.0
Monetary authorities: short-term	8 768 ..	...	...	...	...	600.6	611.4	615.5	627.3
General government: long-term	8 770 ..	...	...	...	...	1,095.0	1,089.2	1,135.7	1,186.9
General government: short-term	8 771 ..	...	...	...	...	...	...	...	...
Banks: long-term	8 773 ..	...	...	...	...	...	...	...	...
Banks: short-term	8 774 ..	...	...	...	...	...	...	...	...
Other sectors: long-term	8 776 ..	...	...	...	...	...	...	...	...
Other sectors: short-term	8 777 ..	...	...	...	...	...	...	...	...
Currency and deposits	8 780 ..	...	...	...	...	5.8	2.1	2.8	2.8
Monetary authorities	8 781 ..	...	...	...	...	...	...	...	...
General government	8 782 ..	...	...	...	...	...	...	...	...
Banks	8 783 ..	...	...	...	...	5.8	2.1	2.8	2.8
Other sectors	8 784 ..	...	...	...	...	...	...	...	...
Other liabilities	8 786 ..	...	...	...	...	34.2	45.2	46.4	46.5
Monetary authorities: long-term	8 788 ..	...	...	...	...	...	...	...	...
Monetary authorities: short-term	8 789 ..	...	...	...	...	...	...	...	...
General government: long-term	8 791 ..	...	...	...	...	...	...	...	...
General government: short-term	8 792 ..	...	...	...	...	...	...	...	...
Banks: long-term	8 794 ..	...	...	...	...	...	...	...	...
Banks: short-term	8 795 ..	...	...	...	...	...	...	...	...
Other sectors: long-term	8 797 ..	...	...	...	...	...	...	...	...
Other sectors: short-term	8 798 ..	...	...	...	...	...	...	...	...
NET INTERNATIONAL INVESTMENT POSITION	8 995 ..	...	...	...	...	**–2,076.1**	**–1,968.9**	**–1,969.4**	**–2,043.2**
Conversion rates: Guyana dollars per U.S. dollar (end of period)	0 102 ..	**10.00**	**33.00**	**45.00**	**122.00**	**126.00**	**130.75**	**142.50**	**140.50**

Table 1. ANALYTIC PRESENTATION, FISCAL YEARS 1988–95 ENDING SEPTEMBER 30
(Millions of U.S. dollars)

	Code	1988	1989	1990	1991	1992	1993	1994	1995
A. Current Account[1]	4 993 Y.	**–40.4**	**–62.7**	**–21.9**	**–56.1**	**7.9**	**–16.6**	**4.0**	**–66.6**
Goods: exports f.o.b.	2 100 . .	180.4	148.3	265.8	202.0	75.6	81.6	57.4	105.3
Goods: imports f.o.b.	3 100 . .	–283.9	–259.3	–442.6	–448.6	–214.1	–266.6	–141.2	–520.0
Balance on Goods	4 100 . .	*–103.5*	*–111.0*	*–176.8*	*–246.6*	*–138.5*	*–185.0*	*–83.8*	*–414.7*
Services: credit	2 200 . .	94.5	88.5	52.2	57.6	38.5	35.8	6.7	100.1
Services: debit	3 200 . .	–197.1	–188.8	–72.0	–83.3	–35.2	–30.2	–63.9	–233.5
Balance on Goods and Services	4 991 . .	*–206.1*	*–211.4*	*–196.6*	*–272.3*	*–135.2*	*–179.4*	*–141.0*	*–548.1*
Income: credit	2 300 . .	6.2	4.6	6.9	2.0	1.0	2.0	. . .	3.2
Income: debit	3 300 . .	–33.4	–30.2	–25.1	–20.0	–12.9	–12.6	–11.2	–26.9
Balance on Goods, Services, and Income	4 992 . .	*–233.2*	*–236.9*	*–214.8*	*–290.3*	*–147.1*	*–190.0*	*–152.2*	*–571.7*
Current transfers: credit	2 379 Y.	253.6	237.7	192.9	234.2	155.0	173.4	156.2	505.1
Current transfers: debit	3 379 . .	–60.7	–63.5	. . .	. . .	. . .	. . .	. . .	. . .
B. Capital Account[1]	4 994 Y.	**. . .**	**. . .**	**. . .**	**. . .**	**. . .**	**. . .**	**. . .**	**. . .**
Capital account: credit	2 994 Y.	. . .	. . .	. . .	. . .	. . .	. . .	. . .	. . .
Capital account: debit	3 994 . .	. . .	. . .	. . .	. . .	. . .	. . .	. . .	. . .
Total, Groups A Plus B	4 010 . .	*–40.4*	*–62.7*	*–21.9*	*–56.1*	*7.9*	*–16.6*	*4.0*	*–66.6*
C. Financial Account[1]	4 995 X.	**26.3**	**60.1**	**33.0**	**25.9**	**–20.6**	**–43.7**	**–15.8**	**82.6**
Direct investment abroad	4 505 . .	. . .	. . .	8.0	13.6	. . .	. . .	. . .	. . .
Direct investment in Haiti	4 555 Y.	10.1	9.4	. . .	. . .	. . .	. . .	. . .	. . .
Portfolio investment assets	4 602 . .	. . .	. . .	. . .	. . .	. . .	. . .	. . .	. . .
Equity securities	4 610 . .	. . .	. . .	. . .	. . .	. . .	. . .	. . .	. . .
Debt securities	4 619 . .	. . .	. . .	. . .	. . .	. . .	. . .	. . .	. . .
Portfolio investment liabilities	4 652 Y.	. . .	. . .	. . .	. . .	. . .	. . .	. . .	. . .
Equity securities	4 660 Y.	. . .	. . .	. . .	. . .	. . .	. . .	. . .	. . .
Debt securities	4 669 Y.	. . .	. . .	. . .	. . .	. . .	. . .	. . .	. . .
Other investment assets	4 703 . .	–3.1	21.5	–23.1	–16.2	–12.6	–30.6	–5.5	–10.9
Monetary authorities	4 703 . A	. . .	. . .	. . .	. . .	. . .	. . .	. . .	. . .
General government	4 703 . B	. . .	. . .	. . .	. . .	. . .	. . .	. . .	. . .
Banks	4 703 . C	–3.1	21.5	–23.1	–16.2	–12.6	–30.6	–5.5	–10.9
Other sectors	4 703 . D	. . .	. . .	. . .	. . .	. . .	. . .	. . .	. . .
Other investment liabilities	4 753 X.	19.3	29.3	48.1	28.5	–8.0	–13.1	–10.3	93.4
Monetary authorities	4 753 XA	–2.1	–.4	–.6	. . .	2.9	2.2	2.1	. . .
General government	4 753 YB	–4.5	2.3	48.7	28.5	–10.9	–15.3	–12.4	93.4
Banks	4 753 YC	8.1	9.1	. . .	. . .	. . .	. . .	. . .	. . .
Other sectors	4 753 YD	17.9	18.3	. . .	. . .	. . .	. . .	. . .	. . .
Total, Groups A Through C	4 020 . .	*–14.0*	*–2.5*	*11.1*	*–30.2*	*–12.7*	*–60.3*	*–11.8*	*15.9*
D. Net Errors and Omissions	4 998 . .	**14.3**	**–10.7**	**–46.3**	**42.9**	**6.4**	**37.3**	**–37.9**	**205.0**
Total, Groups A Through D	4 030 . .	*.3*	*–13.2*	*–35.2*	*12.7*	*–6.3*	*–23.0*	*–49.7*	*221.0*
E. Reserves and Related Items	4 040 . .	**–.3**	**13.2**	**35.2**	**–12.7**	**6.3**	**23.0**	**49.7**	**–221.0**
Reserve assets	4 800 . .	1.2	3.9	39.0	–20.0	–11.3	–19.1	12.8	–187.5
Use of Fund credit and loans	4 766 . .	–26.6	–5.6	–7.0	–4.5	. . .	. . .	. . .	–5.6
Liabilities constituting foreign authorities' reserves	4 900 . .	. . .	. . .	. . .	. . .	. . .	. . .	. . .	. . .
Exceptional financing	4 920 . .	25.1	14.9	3.2	11.8	17.6	42.1	36.9	–27.8
Conversion rates: gourdes per U.S. dollar	0 101 . .	**5.000**	**5.000**	**5.000**	**5.204**	**9.169**	**12.332**	**14.744**	**14.477**

[1] Excludes components that have been classified in the categories of Group E.

Table 2. STANDARD PRESENTATION, FISCAL YEARS 1988–95 ENDING SEPTEMBER 30
(Millions of U.S. dollars)

	Code	1988	1989	1990	1991	1992	1993	1994	1995
CURRENT ACCOUNT	4 993 . .	**–40.4**	**–62.7**	**–21.9**	**–56.1**	**7.9**	**–16.6**	**4.0**	**–66.6**
A. GOODS	4 100 . .	–103.5	–111.0	–176.8	–246.6	–138.5	–185.0	–83.8	–414.7
Credit	2 100 . .	**180.4**	**148.3**	**265.8**	**202.0**	**75.6**	**81.6**	**57.4**	**105.3**
General merchandise: exports f.o.b.	2 110 . .	180.4	148.3	265.8	202.0	75.6	81.6	57.4	105.3
Goods for processing: exports f.o.b.	2 150 . .	. . .	. . .	. . .	. . .	. . .	. . .	. . .	. . .
Repairs on goods	2 160 . .	. . .	. . .	. . .	. . .	. . .	. . .	. . .	. . .
Goods procured in ports by carriers	2 170 . .	. . .	. . .	. . .	. . .	. . .	. . .	. . .	. . .
Nonmonetary gold	2 180 . .	. . .	. . .	. . .	. . .	. . .	. . .	. . .	. . .
Debit	3 100 . .	**–283.9**	**–259.3**	**–442.6**	**–448.6**	**–214.1**	**–266.6**	**–141.2**	**–520.0**
General merchandise: imports f.o.b.	3 110 . .	–283.9	–259.3	–442.6	–448.6	–214.1	–266.6	–141.2	–520.0
Goods for processing: imports f.o.b.	3 150 . .	. . .	. . .	. . .	. . .	. . .	. . .	. . .	. . .
Repairs on goods	3 160 . .	. . .	. . .	. . .	. . .	. . .	. . .	. . .	. . .
Goods procured in ports by carriers	3 170 . .	. . .	. . .	. . .	. . .	. . .	. . .	. . .	. . .
Nonmonetary gold	3 180 . .	. . .	. . .	. . .	. . .	. . .	. . .	. . .	. . .
B. SERVICES	4 200 . .	–102.6	–100.4	–19.8	–25.7	3.3	5.6	–57.2	–133.4
Total credit	2 200 . .	*94.5*	*88.5*	*52.2*	*57.6*	*38.5*	*35.8*	*6.7*	*100.1*
Total debit	3 200 . .	*–197.1*	*–188.8*	*–72.0*	*–83.3*	*–35.2*	*–30.2*	*–63.9*	*–233.5*
Transportation services, credit	2 205 . .	**6.6**	**6.6**	**8.5**	**7.6**	**2.9**	**3.0**	**2.1**	**5.0**
Passenger	2 205 BA	. . .	. . .	*3.6*	*4.0*	*1.5*	*1.6*	*1.1*	. . .
Freight	2 205 BB	*3.2*	*3.0*	*4.9*	*3.6*	*1.4*	*1.4*	*1.0*	. . .
Other	2 205 BC	*3.5*	*3.6*	. . .	. . .	. . .	. . .	. . .	. . .
Sea transport, passenger	2 207 . .	. . .	. . .	. . .	. . .	. . .	. . .	. . .	. . .
Sea transport, freight	2 208 . .	. . .	. . .	. . .	. . .	. . .	. . .	. . .	. . .
Sea transport, other	2 209 . .	. . .	. . .	. . .	. . .	. . .	. . .	. . .	. . .
Air transport, passenger	2 211 . .	. . .	. . .	. . .	. . .	. . .	. . .	. . .	. . .
Air transport, freight	2 212 . .	. . .	. . .	. . .	. . .	. . .	. . .	. . .	. . .
Air transport, other	2 213 . .	. . .	. . .	. . .	. . .	. . .	. . .	. . .	. . .
Other transport, passenger	2 215 . .	. . .	. . .	. . .	. . .	. . .	. . .	. . .	. . .
Other transport, freight	2 216 . .	. . .	. . .	. . .	. . .	. . .	. . .	. . .	. . .
Other transport, other	2 217 . .	. . .	. . .	. . .	. . .	. . .	. . .	. . .	. . .
Transportation services, debit	3 205 . .	**–87.5**	**–84.2**	**–34.0**	**–38.4**	**–24.4**	**–19.8**	**–47.0**	**–132.0**
Passenger	3 205 BA	*–40.1*	*–38.1*	*–34.0*	*–38.4*	*–24.4*	*–19.8*	*–17.7*	. . .
Freight	3 205 BB	*–47.4*	*–46.2*	. . .	. . .	. . .	. . .	*–29.3*	. . .
Other	3 205 BC	. . .	. . .	. . .	. . .	. . .	. . .	. . .	. . .
Sea transport, passenger	3 207 . .	. . .	. . .	. . .	. . .	. . .	. . .	. . .	. . .
Sea transport, freight	3 208 . .	. . .	. . .	. . .	. . .	. . .	. . .	. . .	. . .
Sea transport, other	3 209 . .	. . .	. . .	. . .	. . .	. . .	. . .	. . .	. . .
Air transport, passenger	3 211 . .	. . .	. . .	. . .	. . .	. . .	. . .	. . .	. . .
Air transport, freight	3 212 . .	. . .	. . .	. . .	. . .	. . .	. . .	. . .	. . .
Air transport, other	3 213 . .	. . .	. . .	. . .	. . .	. . .	. . .	. . .	. . .
Other transport, passenger	3 215 . .	. . .	. . .	. . .	. . .	. . .	. . .	. . .	. . .
Other transport, freight	3 216 . .	. . .	. . .	. . .	. . .	. . .	. . .	. . .	. . .
Other transport, other	3 217 . .	. . .	. . .	. . .	. . .	. . .	. . .	. . .	. . .
Travel, credit	2 236 . .	**74.0**	**70.0**	**33.7**	**40.1**	**29.5**	**23.1**	**4.5**	**82.2**
Business travel	2 237 . .	. . .	. . .	. . .	. . .	. . .	. . .	. . .	. . .
Personal travel	2 240 . .	. . .	. . .	. . .	. . .	. . .	. . .	. . .	. . .
Travel, debit	3 236 . .	**–34.4**	**–32.8**	**–37.0**	**–34.9**	**–10.8**	**–10.4**	**–13.7**	**–34.7**
Business travel	3 237 . .	. . .	. . .	. . .	. . .	. . .	. . .	. . .	. . .
Personal travel	3 240 . .	. . .	. . .	. . .	. . .	. . .	. . .	. . .	. . .
Other services, credit	2 200 BA	**13.8**	**11.8**	**10.0**	**9.9**	**6.2**	**9.7**	**.1**	**13.0**
Communications	2 245 . .	. . .	. . .	. . .	. . .	. . .	. . .	. . .	. . .
Construction	2 249 . .	. . .	. . .	. . .	. . .	. . .	. . .	. . .	. . .
Insurance	2 253 . .	1.4	1.1	.5	.4	.2	.2	.1	.6
Financial	2 260 . .	. . .	. . .	. . .	. . .	. . .	. . .	. . .	. . .
Computer and information	2 262 . .	. . .	. . .	. . .	. . .	. . .	. . .	. . .	. . .
Royalties and licence fees	2 266 . .	. . .	. . .	. . .	. . .	. . .	. . .	. . .	. . .
Other business services	2 268 . .	2.1	1.5	. . .	. . .	. . .	. . .	. . .	2.4
Personal, cultural, and recreational	2 287 . .	. . .	. . .	. . .	. . .	. . .	. . .	. . .	. . .
Government, n.i.e.	2 291 . .	10.3	9.2	9.5	9.5	6.0	9.5	. . .	10.0
Other services, debit	3 200 BA	**–75.2**	**–71.9**	**–1.0**	**–10.0**	**. . .**	**. . .**	**–3.2**	**–66.8**
Communications	3 245 . .	. . .	. . .	. . .	. . .	. . .	. . .	. . .	. . .
Construction	3 249 . .	. . .	. . .	. . .	. . .	. . .	. . .	. . .	. . .
Insurance	3 253 . .	–9.8	–9.6	. . .	. . .	. . .	. . .	–3.2	–4.0
Financial	3 260 . .	. . .	. . .	. . .	. . .	. . .	. . .	. . .	. . .
Computer and information	3 262 . .	. . .	. . .	. . .	. . .	. . .	. . .	. . .	. . .
Royalties and licence fees	3 266 . .	. . .	. . .	. . .	. . .	. . .	. . .	. . .	. . .
Other business services	3 268 . .	–18.2	–16.6	. . .	. . .	. . .	. . .	. . .	–14.0
Personal, cultural, and recreational	3 287 . .	. . .	. . .	. . .	. . .	. . .	. . .	. . .	. . .
Government, n.i.e.	3 291 . .	–47.2	–45.7	–1.0	–10.0	. . .	. . .	. . .	–48.8

Table 2 (Continued). STANDARD PRESENTATION, FISCAL YEARS 1988–95 ENDING SEPTEMBER 30
(Millions of U.S. dollars)

	Code	1988	1989	1990	1991	1992	1993	1994	1995
C. INCOME	4 300 . .	−27.1	−25.6	−18.2	−18.0	−11.9	−10.6	−11.2	−23.7
Total credit	2 300 . .	*6.2*	*4.6*	*6.9*	*2.0*	*1.0*	*2.0*	*. . .*	*3.2*
Total debit	3 300 . .	*−33.4*	*−30.2*	*−25.1*	*−20.0*	*−12.9*	*−12.6*	*−11.2*	*−26.9*
Compensation of employees, credit	2 310 . .	**. . .**	**. . .**	**. . .**	**. . .**	**. . .**	**. . .**	**. . .**	**. . .**
Compensation of employees, debit	3 310 . .	**. . .**	**. . .**	**. . .**	**. . .**	**. . .**	**. . .**	**. . .**	**. . .**
Investment income, credit	2 320 . .	**6.2**	**4.6**	**6.9**	**2.0**	**1.0**	**2.0**	**. . .**	**3.2**
Direct investment income	2 330 . .	6.2	4.6	6.9	2.0	1.0	2.0	. . .	3.2
Dividends and distributed branch profits	2 332 . .	6.2	4.6	6.9	2.0	1.0	2.0	. . .	. . .
Reinvested earnings and undistributed branch profits	2 333 . .	. . .	. . .	. . .	. . .	. . .	. . .	. . .	. . .
Income on debt (interest)	2 334 . .	. . .	. . .	. . .	. . .	. . .	. . .	. . .	. . .
Portfolio investment income	2 339 . .	. . .	. . .	. . .	. . .	. . .	. . .	. . .	. . .
Income on equity	2 340 . .	. . .	. . .	. . .	. . .	. . .	. . .	. . .	. . .
Income on bonds and notes	2 350 . .	. . .	. . .	. . .	. . .	. . .	. . .	. . .	. . .
Income on money market instruments and financial derivatives	2 360 . .	. . .	. . .	. . .	. . .	. . .	. . .	. . .	. . .
Other investment income	2 370 . .	. . .	. . .	. . .	. . .	. . .	. . .	. . .	. . .
Investment income, debit	3 320 . .	**−33.4**	**−30.2**	**−25.1**	**−20.0**	**−12.9**	**−12.6**	**−11.2**	**−26.9**
Direct investment income	3 330 . .	−10.7	−7.6	. . .	. . .	. . .	. . .	. . .	. . .
Dividends and distributed branch profits	3 332 . .	−10.7	−7.6	. . .	. . .	. . .	. . .	. . .	. . .
Reinvested earnings and undistributed branch profits	3 333 . .	. . .	. . .	. . .	. . .	. . .	. . .	. . .	. . .
Income on debt (interest)	3 334 . .	. . .	. . .	. . .	. . .	. . .	. . .	. . .	. . .
Portfolio investment income	3 339 . .	. . .	. . .	. . .	. . .	. . .	. . .	. . .	. . .
Income on equity	3 340 . .	. . .	. . .	. . .	. . .	. . .	. . .	. . .	. . .
Income on bonds and notes	3 350 . .	. . .	. . .	. . .	. . .	. . .	. . .	. . .	. . .
Income on money market instruments and financial derivatives	3 360 . .	. . .	. . .	. . .	. . .	. . .	. . .	. . .	. . .
Other investment income	3 370 . .	−22.7	−22.6	−25.1	−20.0	−12.9	−12.6	−11.2	−26.9
D. CURRENT TRANSFERS	4 379 . .	192.9	174.3	192.9	234.2	155.0	173.4	156.2	505.1
Credit	2 379 . .	**253.6**	**237.7**	**192.9**	**234.2**	**155.0**	**173.4**	**156.2**	**505.1**
General government	2 380 . .	129.5	114.9	131.9	164.7	85.0	100.0	113.3	396.6
Other sectors	2 390 . .	124.1	122.8	61.0	69.5	70.0	73.4	42.9	108.5
Workers' remittances	2 391 . .	124.1	122.8	. . .	. . .	. . .	. . .	. . .	. . .
Other current transfers	2 392 . .	. . .	. . .	61.0	69.5	70.0	73.4	42.9	108.5
Debit	3 379 . .	**−60.7**	**−63.5**	**. . .**	**. . .**	**. . .**	**. . .**	**. . .**	**. . .**
General government	3 380 . .	. . .	. . .	. . .	. . .	. . .	. . .	. . .	. . .
Other sectors	3 390 . .	−60.7	−63.5	. . .	. . .	. . .	. . .	. . .	. . .
Workers' remittances	3 391 . .	−60.7	−63.5	. . .	. . .	. . .	. . .	. . .	. . .
Other current transfers	3 392 . .	. . .	. . .	. . .	. . .	. . .	. . .	. . .	. . .
CAPITAL AND FINANCIAL ACCOUNT	4 996 . .	**26.0**	**73.4**	**68.2**	**13.2**	**−14.3**	**−20.7**	**33.9**	**−138.4**
CAPITAL ACCOUNT	4 994 . .	**. . .**	**. . .**	**. . .**	**. . .**	**. . .**	**. . .**	**. . .**	**. . .**
Total credit	2 994 . .	. . .	. . .	. . .	. . .	. . .	. . .	. . .	. . .
Total debit	3 994 . .	. . .	. . .	. . .	. . .	. . .	. . .	. . .	. . .
Capital transfers, credit	2 400 . .	**. . .**	**. . .**	**. . .**	**. . .**	**. . .**	**. . .**	**. . .**	**. . .**
General government	2 401 . .	. . .	. . .	. . .	. . .	. . .	. . .	. . .	. . .
Debt forgiveness	2 402 . .	. . .	. . .	. . .	. . .	. . .	. . .	. . .	. . .
Other capital transfers	2 410 . .	. . .	. . .	. . .	. . .	. . .	. . .	. . .	. . .
Other sectors	2 430 . .	. . .	. . .	. . .	. . .	. . .	. . .	. . .	. . .
Migrants' transfers	2 431 . .	. . .	. . .	. . .	. . .	. . .	. . .	. . .	. . .
Debt forgiveness	2 432 . .	. . .	. . .	. . .	. . .	. . .	. . .	. . .	. . .
Other capital transfers	2 440 . .	. . .	. . .	. . .	. . .	. . .	. . .	. . .	. . .
Capital transfers, debit	3 400 . .	**. . .**	**. . .**	**. . .**	**. . .**	**. . .**	**. . .**	**. . .**	**. . .**
General government	3 401 . .	. . .	. . .	. . .	. . .	. . .	. . .	. . .	. . .
Debt forgiveness	3 402 . .	. . .	. . .	. . .	. . .	. . .	. . .	. . .	. . .
Other capital transfers	3 410 . .	. . .	. . .	. . .	. . .	. . .	. . .	. . .	. . .
Other sectors	3 430 . .	. . .	. . .	. . .	. . .	. . .	. . .	. . .	. . .
Migrants' transfers	3 431 . .	. . .	. . .	. . .	. . .	. . .	. . .	. . .	. . .
Debt forgiveness	3 432 . .	. . .	. . .	. . .	. . .	. . .	. . .	. . .	. . .
Other capital transfers	3 440 . .	. . .	. . .	. . .	. . .	. . .	. . .	. . .	. . .
Nonproduced nonfinancial assets, credit	2 480 . .	**. . .**	**. . .**	**. . .**	**. . .**	**. . .**	**. . .**	**. . .**	**. . .**
Nonproduced nonfinancial assets, debit	3 480 . .	**. . .**	**. . .**	**. . .**	**. . .**	**. . .**	**. . .**	**. . .**	**. . .**

Table 2 (Continued). STANDARD PRESENTATION, FISCAL YEARS 1988–95 ENDING SEPTEMBER 30
(Millions of U.S. dollars)

	Code	1988	1989	1990	1991	1992	1993	1994	1995
FINANCIAL ACCOUNT	4 995 . .	**26.0**	**73.4**	**68.2**	**13.2**	**–14.3**	**–20.7**	**33.9**	**–138.4**
A. DIRECT INVESTMENT	4 500 . .	10.1	9.4	8.0	13.6	. . .	. . .	. . .	. . .
Direct investment abroad	4 505 . .	**. . .**	**. . .**	**8.0**	**13.6**	**. . .**	**. . .**	**. . .**	**. . .**
Equity capital	4 510 . .	. . .	. . .	. . .	. . .	. . .	. . .	. . .	. . .
Claims on affiliated enterprises	4 515 . .	. . .	. . .	. . .	. . .	. . .	. . .	. . .	. . .
Liabilities to affiliated enterprises	4 520 . .	. . .	. . .	. . .	. . .	. . .	. . .	. . .	. . .
Reinvested earnings	4 525 . .	. . .	. . .	. . .	. . .	. . .	. . .	. . .	. . .
Other capital	4 530 . .	. . .	. . .	8.0	13.6	. . .	. . .	. . .	. . .
Claims on affiliated enterprises	4 535 . .	. . .	. . .	. . .	. . .	. . .	. . .	. . .	. . .
Liabilities to affiliated enterprises	4 540 . .	. . .	. . .	. . .	. . .	. . .	. . .	. . .	. . .
Direct investment in Haiti	4 555 . .	**10.1**	**9.4**	**. . .**	**. . .**	**. . .**	**. . .**	**. . .**	**. . .**
Equity capital	4 560 . .	10.1	9.4	. . .	. . .	. . .	. . .	. . .	. . .
Claims on direct investors	4 565 . .	. . .	. . .	. . .	. . .	. . .	. . .	. . .	. . .
Liabilities to direct investors	4 570 . .	. . .	. . .	. . .	. . .	. . .	. . .	. . .	. . .
Reinvested earnings	4 575 . .	. . .	. . .	. . .	. . .	. . .	. . .	. . .	. . .
Other capital	4 580 . .	. . .	. . .	. . .	. . .	. . .	. . .	. . .	. . .
Claims on direct investors	4 585 . .	. . .	. . .	. . .	. . .	. . .	. . .	. . .	. . .
Liabilities to direct investors	4 590 . .	. . .	. . .	. . .	. . .	. . .	. . .	. . .	. . .
B. PORTFOLIO INVESTMENT	4 600 . .	. . .	. . .	. . .	. . .	. . .	. . .	. . .	. . .
Assets	4 602 . .	**. . .**	**. . .**	**. . .**	**. . .**	**. . .**	**. . .**	**. . .**	**. . .**
Equity securities	4 610 . .	. . .	. . .	. . .	. . .	. . .	. . .	. . .	. . .
Monetary authorities	4 611 . .	. . .	. . .	. . .	. . .	. . .	. . .	. . .	. . .
General government	4 612 . .	. . .	. . .	. . .	. . .	. . .	. . .	. . .	. . .
Banks	4 613 . .	. . .	. . .	. . .	. . .	. . .	. . .	. . .	. . .
Other sectors	4 614 . .	. . .	. . .	. . .	. . .	. . .	. . .	. . .	. . .
Debt securities	4 619 . .	. . .	. . .	. . .	. . .	. . .	. . .	. . .	. . .
Bonds and notes	4 620 . .	. . .	. . .	. . .	. . .	. . .	. . .	. . .	. . .
Monetary authorities	4 621 . .	. . .	. . .	. . .	. . .	. . .	. . .	. . .	. . .
General government	4 622 . .	. . .	. . .	. . .	. . .	. . .	. . .	. . .	. . .
Banks	4 623 . .	. . .	. . .	. . .	. . .	. . .	. . .	. . .	. . .
Other sectors	4 624 . .	. . .	. . .	. . .	. . .	. . .	. . .	. . .	. . .
Money market instruments	4 630 . .	. . .	. . .	. . .	. . .	. . .	. . .	. . .	. . .
Monetary authorities	4 631 . .	. . .	. . .	. . .	. . .	. . .	. . .	. . .	. . .
General government	4 632 . .	. . .	. . .	. . .	. . .	. . .	. . .	. . .	. . .
Banks	4 633 . .	. . .	. . .	. . .	. . .	. . .	. . .	. . .	. . .
Other sectors	4 634 . .	. . .	. . .	. . .	. . .	. . .	. . .	. . .	. . .
Financial derivatives	4 640 . .	. . .	. . .	. . .	. . .	. . .	. . .	. . .	. . .
Monetary authorities	4 641 . .	. . .	. . .	. . .	. . .	. . .	. . .	. . .	. . .
General government	4 642 . .	. . .	. . .	. . .	. . .	. . .	. . .	. . .	. . .
Banks	4 643 . .	. . .	. . .	. . .	. . .	. . .	. . .	. . .	. . .
Other sectors	4 644 . .	. . .	. . .	. . .	. . .	. . .	. . .	. . .	. . .
Liabilities	4 652 . .	**. . .**	**. . .**	**. . .**	**. . .**	**. . .**	**. . .**	**. . .**	**. . .**
Equity securities	4 660 . .	. . .	. . .	. . .	. . .	. . .	. . .	. . .	. . .
Banks	4 663 . .	. . .	. . .	. . .	. . .	. . .	. . .	. . .	. . .
Other sectors	4 664 . .	. . .	. . .	. . .	. . .	. . .	. . .	. . .	. . .
Debt securities	4 669 . .	. . .	. . .	. . .	. . .	. . .	. . .	. . .	. . .
Bonds and notes	4 670 . .	. . .	. . .	. . .	. . .	. . .	. . .	. . .	. . .
Monetary authorities	4 671 . .	. . .	. . .	. . .	. . .	. . .	. . .	. . .	. . .
General government	4 672 . .	. . .	. . .	. . .	. . .	. . .	. . .	. . .	. . .
Banks	4 673 . .	. . .	. . .	. . .	. . .	. . .	. . .	. . .	. . .
Other sectors	4 674 . .	. . .	. . .	. . .	. . .	. . .	. . .	. . .	. . .
Money market instruments	4 680 . .	. . .	. . .	. . .	. . .	. . .	. . .	. . .	. . .
Monetary authorities	4 681 . .	. . .	. . .	. . .	. . .	. . .	. . .	. . .	. . .
General government	4 682 . .	. . .	. . .	. . .	. . .	. . .	. . .	. . .	. . .
Banks	4 683 . .	. . .	. . .	. . .	. . .	. . .	. . .	. . .	. . .
Other sectors	4 684 . .	. . .	. . .	. . .	. . .	. . .	. . .	. . .	. . .
Financial derivatives	4 690 . .	. . .	. . .	. . .	. . .	. . .	. . .	. . .	. . .
Monetary authorities	4 691 . .	. . .	. . .	. . .	. . .	. . .	. . .	. . .	. . .
General government	4 692 . .	. . .	. . .	. . .	. . .	. . .	. . .	. . .	. . .
Banks	4 693 . .	. . .	. . .	. . .	. . .	. . .	. . .	. . .	. . .
Other sectors	4 694 . .	. . .	. . .	. . .	. . .	. . .	. . .	. . .	. . .

Table 2 (Concluded). STANDARD PRESENTATION, FISCAL YEARS 1988–95 ENDING SEPTEMBER 30
(Millions of U.S. dollars)

	Code	1988	1989	1990	1991	1992	1993	1994	1995
C. OTHER INVESTMENT	4 700	14.7	60.1	21.2	19.6	–3.0	–1.6	21.1	49.1
Assets	4 703	**–3.1**	**21.5**	**–23.1**	**–16.2**	**–12.6**	**–30.6**	**–5.5**	**–10.9**
Trade credits	4 706	...	...	...	...	...	...	...	...
General government: long-term	4 708	...	...	...	...	...	...	...	...
General government: short-term	4 709	...	...	...	...	...	...	...	...
Other sectors: long-term	4 711	...	...	...	...	...	...	...	...
Other sectors: short-term	4 712	...	...	...	...	...	...	...	...
Loans	4 714	...	...	...	...	...	...	...	...
Monetary authorities: long-term	4 717	...	...	...	...	...	...	...	...
Monetary authorities: short-term	4 718	...	...	...	...	...	...	...	...
General government: long-term	4 720	...	...	...	...	...	...	...	...
General government: short-term	4 721	...	...	...	...	...	...	...	...
Banks: long-term	4 723	...	...	...	...	...	...	...	...
Banks: short-term	4 724	...	...	...	...	...	...	...	...
Other sectors: long-term	4 726	...	...	...	...	...	...	...	...
Other sectors: short-term	4 727	...	...	...	...	...	...	...	...
Currency and deposits	4 730	–3.1	21.5	–23.1	–16.2	–12.6	–30.6	–5.5	–10.9
Monetary authorities	4 731	...	...	...	...	...	...	...	...
General government	4 732	...	...	...	...	...	...	...	...
Banks	4 733	–3.1	21.5	–23.1	–16.2	–12.6	–30.6	–5.5	–10.9
Other sectors	4 734	...	...	...	...	...	...	...	...
Other assets	4 736	...	...	...	...	...	...	...	...
Monetary authorities: long-term	4 738	...	...	...	...	...	...	...	...
Monetary authorities: short-term	4 739	...	...	...	...	...	...	...	...
General government: long-term	4 741	...	...	...	...	...	...	...	...
General government: short-term	4 742	...	...	...	...	...	...	...	...
Banks: long-term	4 744	...	...	...	...	...	...	...	...
Banks: short-term	4 745	...	...	...	...	...	...	...	...
Other sectors: long-term	4 747	...	...	...	...	...	...	...	...
Other sectors: short-term	4 748	...	...	...	...	...	...	...	...
Liabilities	4 753	**17.8**	**38.6**	**44.3**	**35.8**	**9.6**	**29.0**	**26.6**	**59.9**
Trade credits	4 756	...	...	...	...	...	...	...	...
General government: long-term	4 758	...	...	...	...	...	...	...	...
General government: short-term	4 759	...	...	...	...	...	...	...	...
Other sectors: long-term	4 761	...	...	...	...	...	...	...	...
Other sectors: short-term	4 762	...	...	...	...	...	...	...	...
Loans	4 764	1.5	10.4	41.7	24.0	–10.9	–15.3	–12.4	87.8
Use of Fund credit and loans from the Fund	4 766	–26.6	–5.6	–7.0	–4.5	...	...	...	–5.6
Monetary authorities: other long-term	4 767	...	...	...	...	...	...	...	...
Monetary authorities: short-term	4 768	...	...	...	...	...	...	...	...
General government: long-term	4 770	20.9	10.4	48.7	28.5	–10.9	–15.3	–12.4	93.4
General government: short-term	4 771	...	...	...	...	...	...	...	...
Banks: long-term	4 773	...	...	...	...	...	...	...	...
Banks: short-term	4 774	...	...	...	...	...	...	...	...
Other sectors: long-term	4 776	7.2	5.6	...	...	...	...	...	...
Other sectors: short-term	4 777	...	...	...	...	...	...	...	...
Currency and deposits	4 780	8.1	9.1	...	...	...	...	...	...
Monetary authorities	4 781	...	...	...	...	...	...	...	...
General government	4 782	...	...	...	...	...	...	...	...
Banks	4 783	8.1	9.1	...	...	...	...	...	...
Other sectors	4 784	...	...	...	...	...	...	...	...
Other liabilities	4 786	8.2	19.1	2.6	11.8	20.5	44.3	39.0	–27.8
Monetary authorities: long-term	4 788	...	...	...	...	...	...	...	...
Monetary authorities: short-term	4 789	22.9	14.5	1.6	3.1	2.9	2.2	2.1	–34.4
General government: long-term	4 791	–25.5	–8.1	...	...	...	...	...	91.0
General government: short-term	4 792	...	...	1.0	8.7	17.6	42.1	36.9	–84.4
Banks: long-term	4 794	...	...	...	...	...	...	...	...
Banks: short-term	4 795	...	...	...	...	...	...	...	...
Other sectors: long-term	4 797	10.7	12.7	...	...	...	...	...	...
Other sectors: short-term	4 798	...	...	...	...	...	...	...	...
D. RESERVE ASSETS	4 800	1.2	3.9	39.0	–20.0	–11.3	–19.1	12.8	–187.5
Monetary gold	4 810	–.4	–.5	...	...	...	...	...	...
Special drawing rights	4 820	.9	–1.6	1.6	...	...	...	...	–.6
Reserve position in the Fund	4 830	...	...	...	...	...	...	...	...
Foreign exchange	4 840	.7	6.0	37.4	–20.0	–11.3	–19.1	12.8	–186.9
Other claims	4 880	...	...	...	...	...	...	...	...
NET ERRORS AND OMISSIONS	4 998	**14.3**	**–10.7**	**–46.3**	**42.9**	**6.4**	**37.3**	**–37.9**	**205.0**

Part 3 of the *Yearbook* contains descriptions of the methodologies, compilation practices, and sources used to compile these data.

Table 1. ANALYTIC PRESENTATION, 1988–95
(Millions of U.S. dollars)

	Code	1988	1989	1990	1991	1992	1993	1994	1995
A. Current Account [1]	4 993 Y.	**–181.0**	**–206.3**	**–227.9**	**–258.4**	**–351.0**	**–308.7**	**–343.3**	**–200.9**
Goods: exports f.o.b	2 100 . .	889.5	911.2	895.2	840.6	839.3	999.6	1,101.5	1,377.2
Goods: imports f.o.b	3 100 . .	–923.4	–955.7	–907.0	–912.5	–990.2	–1,203.1	–1,351.1	–1,518.6
Balance on Goods	4 100 . .	*–34.0*	*–44.5*	*–11.8*	*–71.9*	*–150.9*	*–203.5*	*–249.6*	*–141.4*
Services: credit	2 200 . .	136.4	149.7	137.3	175.0	202.0	223.9	242.4	257.6
Services: debit	3 200 . .	–217.5	–230.5	–219.8	–226.7	–243.2	–294.7	–311.0	–333.7
Balance on Goods and Services	4 991 . .	*–115.1*	*–125.3*	*–94.3*	*–123.6*	*–192.1*	*–274.3*	*–318.2*	*–217.5*
Income: credit	2 300 . .	22.0	24.3	20.7	39.8	61.4	16.6	24.0	32.3
Income: debit	3 300 . .	–253.3	–261.9	–257.5	–285.9	–343.4	–215.3	–238.1	–258.2
Balance on Goods, Services, and Income	4 992 . .	*–346.4*	*–362.9*	*–331.1*	*–369.7*	*–474.1*	*–473.0*	*–532.3*	*–443.4*
Current transfers: credit	2 379 Y.	168.4	159.6	106.2	114.3	126.1	165.5	190.2	243.7
Current transfers: debit	3 379 . .	–3.0	–3.0	–3.0	–3.0	–3.0	–1.2	–1.2	–1.2
B. Capital Account [1]	4 994 Y.	**20.0**	**26.0**	**41.5**	**45.0**	**52.8**	**54.0**	**31.9**	**17.4**
Capital account: credit	2 994 Y.	30.0	35.0	50.0	52.0	60.0	54.0	31.9	17.4
Capital account: debit	3 994 . .	–10.0	–9.0	–8.5	–7.0	–7.2	. . .	. . .	. . .
Total, Groups A Plus B	4 010 . .	*–161.0*	*–180.3*	*–186.4*	*–213.4*	*–298.2*	*–254.7*	*–311.4*	*–183.5*
C. Financial Account [1]	4 995 X.	**55.8**	**–65.2**	**–4.8**	**–97.0**	**22.5**	**22.9**	**157.5**	**114.6**
Direct investment abroad	4 505 . .	. . .	. . .	. . .	. . .	. . .	. . .	. . .	. . .
Direct investment in Honduras	4 555 Y.	48.3	51.0	43.5	52.1	47.6	26.7	34.8	50.0
Portfolio investment assets	4 602 . .	–.2	.1	.1	.1	.1	. . .	. . .	. . .
Equity securities	4 610 . .	–.2	.1	.1	.1	.1	. . .	. . .	. . .
Debt securities	4 619 . .	. . .	. . .	. . .	. . .	. . .	. . .	. . .	. . .
Portfolio investment liabilities	4 652 Y.	. . .	. . .	. . .	. . .	. . .	. . .	. . .	. . .
Equity securities	4 660 Y.	. . .	. . .	. . .	. . .	. . .	. . .	. . .	. . .
Debt securities	4 669 Y.	. . .	. . .	. . .	. . .	. . .	. . .	. . .	. . .
Other investment assets	4 703 . .	–12.5	–6.2	–39.5	–17.4	–63.4	–139.6	8.9	–12.8
Monetary authorities	4 703 . A	. . .	. . .	. . .	. . .	. . .	3.9	3.3	11.7
General government	4 703 . B	–7.2	–.7	12.9	1.6	–26.3	–132.0	14.4	14.4
Banks	4 703 . C	–5.3	–5.5	–52.4	–19.0	–37.1	–11.5	–8.8	–38.9
Other sectors	4 703 . D	. . .	. . .	. . .	. . .	. . .	. . .	. . .	. . .
Other investment liabilities	4 753 X.	20.2	–110.1	–8.9	–131.8	38.2	135.8	113.8	77.4
Monetary authorities	4 753 XA	1.4	–29.0	–19.3	–124.1	–84.3	–73.5	–60.7	–73.1
General government	4 753 YB	68.5	–1.6	128.7	184.1	104.7	224.8	96.2	101.7
Banks	4 753 YC	–6.1	–15.5	–24.6	–15.6	–7.3	1.7	–2.2	6.3
Other sectors	4 753 YD	–43.6	–64.1	–93.7	–176.2	25.1	–17.2	80.5	42.5
Total, Groups A Through C	4 020 . .	*–105.1*	*–245.5*	*–191.2*	*–310.4*	*–275.7*	*–231.8*	*–153.9*	*–68.9*
D. Net Errors and Omissions	4 998 . .	**–93.1**	**–138.9**	**–107.4**	**152.0**	**29.2**	**–101.5**	**83.6**	**27.6**
Total, Groups A Through D	4 030 . .	*–198.3*	*–384.3*	*–298.6*	*–158.4*	*–246.5*	*–333.3*	*–70.3*	*–41.3*
E. Reserves and Related Items	4 040 . .	**198.3**	**384.3**	**298.6**	**158.4**	**246.5**	**333.3**	**70.3**	**41.3**
Reserve assets	4 800 . .	21.6	29.0	–20.1	–66.9	–92.0	99.6	–74.1	–90.3
Use of Fund credit and loans	4 766 . .	–36.0	–.4	–4.2	1.1	80.7	6.4	–16.1	–13.7
Liabilities constituting foreign authorities' reserves	4 900 . .	–10.4	16.6	–11.9	–1.3	–.5	–.1	. . .	. . .
Exceptional financing	4 920 . .	223.1	339.2	334.8	225.5	258.3	227.4	160.4	145.3
Conversion rates: lempiras per U.S. dollar	0 101 . .	**2.0000**	**2.0000**	**4.1120**	**5.3167**	**5.4979**	**6.4716**	**8.4088**	**9.4710**

[1] Excludes components that have been classified in the categories of Group E.

Table 2. STANDARD PRESENTATION, 1988–95
(Millions of U.S. dollars)

	Code	1988	1989	1990	1991	1992	1993	1994	1995
CURRENT ACCOUNT	4 993 . .	**–130.8**	**–196.3**	**–92.9**	**–217.4**	**–310.8**	**–254.7**	**–311.4**	**–183.5**
A. GOODS	4 100 . .	–34.0	–44.5	–11.8	–71.9	–150.9	–203.5	–249.6	–141.4
Credit	2 100 . .	**889.5**	**911.2**	**895.2**	**840.6**	**839.3**	**999.6**	**1,101.5**	**1,377.2**
General merchandise: exports f.o.b.	2 110 . .	881.1	903.2	886.9	834.7	833.1	872.8	939.5	1,189.7
Goods for processing: exports f.o.b.	2 150 . .	. . .	. . .	. . .	. . .	. . .	126.8	162.0	187.5
Repairs on goods	2 160 . .	. . .	. . .	. . .	. . .	. . .	. . .	. . .	. . .
Goods procured in ports by carriers	2 170 . .	8.4	8.0	8.3	5.9	6.2	. . .	. . .	. . .
Nonmonetary gold	2 180 . .	. . .	. . .	. . .	. . .	. . .	. . .	. . .	. . .
Debit	3 100 . .	**–923.4**	**–955.7**	**–907.0**	**–912.5**	**–990.2**	**–1,203.1**	**–1,351.1**	**–1,518.6**
General merchandise: imports f.o.b.	3 110 . .	–923.4	–955.7	–907.0	–912.5	–990.2	–1,203.1	–1,351.1	–1,518.6
Goods for processing: imports f.o.b.	3 150 . .	. . .	. . .	. . .	. . .	. . .	. . .	. . .	. . .
Repairs on goods	3 160 . .	. . .	. . .	. . .	. . .	. . .	. . .	. . .	. . .
Goods procured in ports by carriers	3 170 . .	. . .	. . .	. . .	. . .	. . .	. . .	. . .	. . .
Nonmonetary gold	3 180 . .	. . .	. . .	. . .	. . .	. . .	. . .	. . .	. . .
B. SERVICES	4 200 . .	–81.1	–80.8	–82.5	–51.7	–41.2	–70.8	–68.6	–76.1
Total credit	2 200 . .	*136.4*	*149.7*	*137.3*	*175.0*	*202.0*	*223.9*	*242.4*	*257.6*
Total debit	3 200 . .	*–217.5*	*–230.5*	*–219.8*	*–226.7*	*–243.2*	*–294.7*	*–311.0*	*–333.7*
Transportation services, credit	2 205 . .	**39.5**	**42.5**	**42.4**	**47.4**	**49.8**	**60.8**	**59.3**	**56.4**
Passenger	2 205 BA	*15.0*	*16.0*	*15.0*	*15.4*	*14.6*	*15.3*	*11.0*	*5.0*
Freight	2 205 BB	*9.8*	*10.7*	*10.4*	*10.0*	*9.9*	*10.0*	*12.0*	*13.3*
Other	2 205 BC	*14.7*	*15.8*	*17.0*	*22.0*	*25.3*	*35.5*	*36.3*	*38.1*
Sea transport, passenger	2 207 . .	. . .	. . .	. . .	. . .	. . .	. . .	. . .	. . .
Sea transport, freight	2 208 . .	. . .	. . .	. . .	. . .	. . .	. . .	. . .	. . .
Sea transport, other	2 209 . .	. . .	. . .	. . .	. . .	. . .	. . .	. . .	. . .
Air transport, passenger	2 211 . .	. . .	. . .	. . .	. . .	. . .	. . .	. . .	. . .
Air transport, freight	2 212 . .	. . .	. . .	. . .	. . .	. . .	. . .	. . .	. . .
Air transport, other	2 213 . .	. . .	. . .	. . .	. . .	. . .	. . .	. . .	. . .
Other transport, passenger	2 215 . .	. . .	. . .	. . .	. . .	. . .	. . .	. . .	. . .
Other transport, freight	2 216 . .	. . .	. . .	. . .	. . .	. . .	. . .	. . .	. . .
Other transport, other	2 217 . .	. . .	. . .	. . .	. . .	. . .	. . .	. . .	. . .
Transportation services, debit	3 205 . .	**–96.6**	**–101.2**	**–96.7**	**–99.1**	**–105.4**	**–156.0**	**–177.3**	**–196.7**
Passenger	3 205 BA	*–6.0*	*–8.0*	*–7.0*	*–8.0*	*–8.0*	*–29.4*	*–39.0*	*–42.0*
Freight	3 205 BB	*–80.8*	*–83.2*	*–79.5*	*–81.2*	*–87.4*	*–116.4*	*–130.3*	*–146.7*
Other	3 205 BC	*–9.8*	*–10.0*	*–10.2*	*–9.9*	*–10.0*	*–10.2*	*–8.0*	*–8.0*
Sea transport, passenger	3 207 . .	. . .	. . .	. . .	. . .	. . .	. . .	. . .	. . .
Sea transport, freight	3 208 . .	. . .	. . .	. . .	. . .	. . .	. . .	. . .	. . .
Sea transport, other	3 209 . .	. . .	. . .	. . .	. . .	. . .	. . .	. . .	. . .
Air transport, passenger	3 211 . .	. . .	. . .	. . .	. . .	. . .	. . .	. . .	. . .
Air transport, freight	3 212 . .	. . .	. . .	. . .	. . .	. . .	. . .	. . .	. . .
Air transport, other	3 213 . .	. . .	. . .	. . .	. . .	. . .	. . .	. . .	. . .
Other transport, passenger	3 215 . .	. . .	. . .	. . .	. . .	. . .	. . .	. . .	. . .
Other transport, freight	3 216 . .	. . .	. . .	. . .	. . .	. . .	. . .	. . .	. . .
Other transport, other	3 217 . .	. . .	. . .	. . .	. . .	. . .	. . .	. . .	. . .
Travel, credit	2 236 . .	**27.5**	**28.0**	**29.0**	**30.6**	**31.8**	**60.0**	**72.0**	**80.0**
Business travel	2 237 . .	. . .	. . .	. . .	. . .	. . .	. . .	. . .	. . .
Personal travel	2 240 . .	. . .	. . .	. . .	. . .	. . .	. . .	. . .	. . .
Travel, debit	3 236 . .	**–37.0**	**–38.0**	**–37.5**	**–36.8**	**–38.2**	**–55.0**	**–57.0**	**–57.0**
Business travel	3 237 . .	. . .	. . .	. . .	. . .	. . .	. . .	. . .	. . .
Personal travel	3 240 . .	. . .	. . .	. . .	. . .	. . .	. . .	. . .	. . .
Other services, credit	2 200 BA	**69.4**	**79.2**	**65.9**	**97.0**	**120.4**	**103.1**	**111.1**	**121.2**
Communications	2 245 . .	. . .	. . .	. . .	. . .	. . .	51.1	60.5	67.5
Construction	2 249 . .	. . .	. . .	. . .	. . .	. . .	. . .	. . .	. . .
Insurance	2 253 . .	17.3	20.7	15.6	18.0	20.0	6.3	3.9	4.5
Financial	2 260 . .	. . .	. . .	. . .	. . .	. . .	. . .	. . .	. . .
Computer and information	2 262 . .	. . .	. . .	. . .	. . .	. . .	. . .	. . .	. . .
Royalties and licence fees	2 266 . .	. . .	. . .	. . .	. . .	. . .	. . .	. . .	. . .
Other business services	2 268 . .	35.9	42.0	33.8	63.0	84.2	12.7	11.7	12.2
Personal, cultural, and recreational	2 287 . .	. . .	. . .	. . .	. . .	. . .	. . .	. . .	. . .
Government, n.i.e.	2 291 . .	16.2	16.5	16.5	16.0	16.2	33.0	35.0	37.0
Other services, debit	3 200 BA	**–83.9**	**–91.3**	**–85.6**	**–90.8**	**–99.6**	**–83.7**	**–76.7**	**–80.0**
Communications	3 245 . .	. . .	. . .	. . .	. . .	. . .	–14.4	–14.9	–16.0
Construction	3 249 . .	. . .	. . .	. . .	. . .	. . .	. . .	. . .	. . .
Insurance	3 253 . .	–31.2	–35.2	–31.9	–32.1	–35.4	–11.9	–7.5	–8.0
Financial	3 260 . .	. . .	. . .	. . .	. . .	. . .	. . .	. . .	. . .
Computer and information	3 262 . .	. . .	. . .	. . .	. . .	. . .	. . .	. . .	. . .
Royalties and licence fees	3 266 . .	–2.2	–2.5	–3.0	–4.0	–4.5	–4.9	–5.4	–8.9
Other business services	3 268 . .	–44.0	–46.6	–43.9	–47.9	–52.7	–45.4	–41.7	–39.1
Personal, cultural, and recreational	3 287 . .	. . .	. . .	. . .	. . .	. . .	. . .	. . .	. . .
Government, n.i.e.	3 291 . .	–6.5	–7.0	–6.8	–6.8	–7.0	–7.1	–7.2	–8.0

Table 2 (Continued). STANDARD PRESENTATION, 1988–95
(Millions of U.S. dollars)

	Code	1988	1989	1990	1991	1992	1993	1994	1995
C. INCOME	4 300	–231.3	–237.6	–236.8	–246.1	–282.0	–198.7	–214.1	–225.9
Total credit	2 300	*22.0*	*24.3*	*20.7*	*39.8*	*61.4*	*16.6*	*24.0*	*32.3*
Total debit	3 300	*–253.3*	*–261.9*	*–257.5*	*–285.9*	*–343.4*	*–215.3*	*–238.1*	*–258.2*
Compensation of employees, credit	2 310	**11.8**	**13.6**	**12.9**	**30.6**	**52.0**	**3.8**	**4.0**	**4.0**
Compensation of employees, debit	3 310	...	...	...	...	...	...	...	...
Investment income, credit	2 320	**10.2**	**10.7**	**7.8**	**9.2**	**9.4**	**12.8**	**20.0**	**28.3**
Direct investment income	2 330	...	...	...	...	...	...	...	...
Dividends and distributed branch profits	2 332	...	...	...	...	...	...	...	...
Reinvested earnings and undistributed branch profits	2 333	...	...	...	...	...	...	...	...
Income on debt (interest)	2 334	...	...	...	...	...	...	...	...
Portfolio investment income	2 339	...	...	...	...	...	...	...	...
Income on equity	2 340	...	...	...	...	...	...	...	...
Income on bonds and notes	2 350	...	...	...	...	...	...	...	...
Income on money market instruments and financial derivatives	2 360	...	...	...	...	...	...	...	...
Other investment income	2 370	10.2	10.7	7.8	9.2	9.4	12.8	20.0	28.3
Investment income, debit	3 320	**–253.3**	**–261.9**	**–257.5**	**–285.9**	**–343.4**	**–215.3**	**–238.1**	**–258.2**
Direct investment income	3 330	–72.5	–74.7	–72.0	–72.0	–73.9	–27.0	–30.0	–40.0
Dividends and distributed branch profits	3 332	–37.8	–36.0	–37.2	–37.1	–26.4	–16.2	–18.0	–30.0
Reinvested earnings and undistributed branch profits	3 333	–34.7	–38.7	–34.8	–34.9	–47.5	–10.8	–12.0	–10.0
Income on debt (interest)	3 334	...	...	...	...	...	...	...	...
Portfolio investment income	3 339	...	...	...	...	...	...	...	...
Income on equity	3 340	...	...	...	...	...	...	...	...
Income on bonds and notes	3 350	...	...	...	...	...	...	...	...
Income on money market instruments and financial derivatives	3 360	...	...	...	...	...	...	...	...
Other investment income	3 370	–180.8	–187.2	–185.5	–213.9	–269.5	–188.3	–208.1	–218.2
D. CURRENT TRANSFERS	4 379	215.6	166.6	238.2	152.3	163.3	218.3	220.9	259.9
Credit	2 379	**218.6**	**169.6**	**241.2**	**155.3**	**166.3**	**219.5**	**222.1**	**261.1**
General government	2 380	210.6	161.4	233.9	147.3	158.0	151.0	128.6	133.1
Other sectors	2 390	8.0	8.2	7.3	8.0	8.3	68.5	93.5	128.0
Workers' remittances	2 391	...	...	...	...	...	60.0	85.0	120.0
Other current transfers	2 392	8.0	8.2	7.3	8.0	8.3	8.5	8.5	8.0
Debit	3 379	**–3.0**	**–3.0**	**–3.0**	**–3.0**	**–3.0**	**–1.2**	**–1.2**	**–1.2**
General government	3 380	–3.0	–3.0	–3.0	–3.0	–3.0	–.7	–.7	–.7
Other sectors	3 390	...	...	...	...	...	–.5	–.5	–.5
Workers' remittances	3 391	...	...	...	...	...	...	...	...
Other current transfers	3 392	...	...	...	...	...	–.5	–.5	–.5
CAPITAL AND FINANCIAL ACCOUNT	4 996	**223.9**	**335.1**	**200.3**	**65.4**	**281.6**	**356.2**	**227.8**	**155.9**
CAPITAL ACCOUNT	4 994	**20.0**	**26.0**	**41.5**	**45.0**	**52.8**	**54.0**	**31.9**	**17.4**
Total credit	2 994	*30.0*	*35.0*	*50.0*	*52.0*	*60.0*	*54.0*	*31.9*	*17.4*
Total debit	3 994	*–10.0*	*–9.0*	*–8.5*	*–7.0*	*–7.2*	...	...	...
Capital transfers, credit	2 400	**30.0**	**35.0**	**50.0**	**52.0**	**60.0**	**54.0**	**31.9**	**17.4**
General government	2 401	...	...	...	...	...	...	...	...
Debt forgiveness	2 402	...	...	...	...	...	...	...	...
Other capital transfers	2 410	...	...	...	...	...	...	...	...
Other sectors	2 430	30.0	35.0	50.0	52.0	60.0	54.0	31.9	17.4
Migrants' transfers	2 431	30.0	35.0	50.0	52.0	60.0	...	...	...
Debt forgiveness	2 432	...	...	...	...	...	54.0	31.9	17.4
Other capital transfers	2 440	...	...	...	...	...	...	...	...
Capital transfers, debit	3 400	**–10.0**	**–9.0**	**–8.5**	**–7.0**	**–7.2**	...	...	...
General government	3 401	...	...	...	...	...	...	...	...
Debt forgiveness	3 402	...	...	...	...	...	...	...	...
Other capital transfers	3 410	...	...	...	...	...	...	...	...
Other sectors	3 430	–10.0	–9.0	–8.5	–7.0	–7.2	...	...	...
Migrants' transfers	3 431	–10.0	–9.0	–8.5	–7.0	–7.2	...	...	...
Debt forgiveness	3 432	...	...	...	...	...	...	...	...
Other capital transfers	3 440	...	...	...	...	...	...	...	...
Nonproduced nonfinancial assets, credit	2 480	...	...	...	...	...	...	...	...
Nonproduced nonfinancial assets, debit	3 480	...	...	...	...	...	...	...	...

Table 2 (Continued). STANDARD PRESENTATION, 1988–95
(Millions of U.S. dollars)

	Code	1988	1989	1990	1991	1992	1993	1994	1995
FINANCIAL ACCOUNT	4 995	**203.9**	**309.1**	**158.8**	**20.4**	**228.8**	**302.2**	**195.9**	**138.5**
A. DIRECT INVESTMENT	4 500	48.3	51.0	43.5	52.1	47.6	26.7	34.8	50.0
Direct investment abroad	4 505	**...**	**...**	**...**	**...**	**...**	**...**	**...**	**...**
Equity capital	4 510	...	...	...	...	...	...	...	...
Claims on affiliated enterprises	4 515	...	...	...	...	...	...	...	...
Liabilities to affiliated enterprises	4 520	...	...	...	...	...	...	...	...
Reinvested earnings	4 525	...	...	...	...	...	...	...	...
Other capital	4 530	...	...	...	...	...	...	...	...
Claims on affiliated enterprises	4 535	...	...	...	...	...	...	...	...
Liabilities to affiliated enterprises	4 540	...	...	...	...	...	...	...	...
Direct investment in Honduras	4 555	**48.3**	**51.0**	**43.5**	**52.1**	**47.6**	**26.7**	**34.8**	**50.0**
Equity capital	4 560	6.6	4.1	...	...	...	12.8	11.9	13.2
Claims on direct investors	4 565	...	...	...	...	...	...	...	...
Liabilities to direct investors	4 570	...	...	...	...	...	...	...	...
Reinvested earnings	4 575	34.7	38.7	34.8	34.9	47.5	10.8	12.0	10.0
Other capital	4 580	7.0	8.2	8.7	17.2	.1	3.1	10.9	26.8
Claims on direct investors	4 585	...	...	...	...	...	...	...	...
Liabilities to direct investors	4 590	...	...	...	...	...	...	...	...
B. PORTFOLIO INVESTMENT	4 600	–.2	.1	.1	.1	.1	...	...	...
Assets	4 602	**–.2**	**.1**	**.1**	**.1**	**.1**	**...**	**...**	**...**
Equity securities	4 610	–.2	.1	.1	.1	.1	...	...	...
Monetary authorities	4 611	...	...	...	...	...	...	...	...
General government	4 612	...	...	...	...	...	...	...	...
Banks	4 613	...	...	...	...	...	...	...	...
Other sectors	4 614	...	...	...	...	...	...	...	...
Debt securities	4 619	...	...	...	...	...	...	...	...
Bonds and notes	4 620	...	...	...	...	...	...	...	...
Monetary authorities	4 621	...	...	...	...	...	...	...	...
General government	4 622	...	...	...	...	...	...	...	...
Banks	4 623	...	...	...	...	...	...	...	...
Other sectors	4 624	...	...	...	...	...	...	...	...
Money market instruments	4 630	...	...	...	...	...	...	...	...
Monetary authorities	4 631	...	...	...	...	...	...	...	...
General government	4 632	...	...	...	...	...	...	...	...
Banks	4 633	...	...	...	...	...	...	...	...
Other sectors	4 634	...	...	...	...	...	...	...	...
Financial derivatives	4 640	...	...	...	...	...	...	...	...
Monetary authorities	4 641	...	...	...	...	...	...	...	...
General government	4 642	...	...	...	...	...	...	...	...
Banks	4 643	...	...	...	...	...	...	...	...
Other sectors	4 644	...	...	...	...	...	...	...	...
Liabilities	4 652	**...**	**...**	**...**	**...**	**...**	**...**	**...**	**...**
Equity securities	4 660	...	...	...	...	...	...	...	...
Banks	4 663	...	...	...	...	...	...	...	...
Other sectors	4 664	...	...	...	...	...	...	...	...
Debt securities	4 669	...	...	...	...	...	...	...	...
Bonds and notes	4 670	...	...	...	...	...	...	...	...
Monetary authorities	4 671	...	...	...	...	...	...	...	...
General government	4 672	...	...	...	...	...	...	...	...
Banks	4 673	...	...	...	...	...	...	...	...
Other sectors	4 674	...	...	...	...	...	...	...	...
Money market instruments	4 680	...	...	...	...	...	...	...	...
Monetary authorities	4 681	...	...	...	...	...	...	...	...
General government	4 682	...	...	...	...	...	...	...	...
Banks	4 683	...	...	...	...	...	...	...	...
Other sectors	4 684	...	...	...	...	...	...	...	...
Financial derivatives	4 690	...	...	...	...	...	...	...	...
Monetary authorities	4 691	...	...	...	...	...	...	...	...
General government	4 692	...	...	...	...	...	...	...	...
Banks	4 693	...	...	...	...	...	...	...	...
Other sectors	4 694	...	...	...	...	...	...	...	...

Table 2 (Concluded). STANDARD PRESENTATION, 1988–95
(Millions of U.S. dollars)

	Code	1988	1989	1990	1991	1992	1993	1994	1995
C. OTHER INVESTMENT	4 700 . .	134.2	229.1	135.3	35.1	273.1	175.9	235.1	178.8
Assets	4 703 . .	**–12.5**	**–6.2**	**–39.5**	**–17.4**	**–63.4**	**–139.6**	**8.9**	**–12.8**
Trade credits	4 706 . .	. . .	. . .	. . .	. . .	. . .	. . .	. . .	. . .
General government: long-term	4 708 . .	. . .	. . .	. . .	. . .	. . .	. . .	. . .	. . .
General government: short-term	4 709 . .	. . .	. . .	. . .	. . .	. . .	. . .	. . .	. . .
Other sectors: long-term	4 711 . .	. . .	. . .	. . .	. . .	. . .	. . .	. . .	. . .
Other sectors: short-term	4 712 . .	. . .	. . .	. . .	. . .	. . .	. . .	. . .	. . .
Loans	4 714 . .	. . .	. . .	. . .	. . .	. . .	. . .	. . .	. . .
Monetary authorities: long-term	4 717 . .	. . .	. . .	. . .	. . .	. . .	. . .	. . .	. . .
Monetary authorities: short-term	4 718 . .	. . .	. . .	. . .	. . .	. . .	. . .	. . .	. . .
General government: long-term	4 720 . .	. . .	. . .	. . .	. . .	. . .	. . .	. . .	. . .
General government: short-term	4 721 . .	. . .	. . .	. . .	. . .	. . .	. . .	. . .	. . .
Banks: long-term	4 723 . .	. . .	. . .	. . .	. . .	. . .	. . .	. . .	. . .
Banks: short-term	4 724 . .	. . .	. . .	. . .	. . .	. . .	. . .	. . .	. . .
Other sectors: long-term	4 726 . .	. . .	. . .	. . .	. . .	. . .	. . .	. . .	. . .
Other sectors: short-term	4 727 . .	. . .	. . .	. . .	. . .	. . .	. . .	. . .	. . .
Currency and deposits	4 730 . .	–5.3	–5.5	–52.4	–19.0	–37.1	–143.7	6.6	6.8
Monetary authorities	4 731 . .	. . .	. . .	. . .	. . .	. . .	. . .	. . .	. . .
General government	4 732 . .	. . .	. . .	. . .	. . .	. . .	–132.2	15.4	45.7
Banks	4 733 . .	–5.3	–5.5	–52.4	–19.0	–37.1	–11.5	–8.8	–38.9
Other sectors	4 734 . .	. . .	. . .	. . .	. . .	. . .	. . .	. . .	. . .
Other assets	4 736 . .	–7.2	–.7	12.9	1.6	–26.3	4.1	2.3	–19.6
Monetary authorities: long-term	4 738 . .	. . .	. . .	. . .	. . .	. . .	3.9	3.3	11.7
Monetary authorities: short-term	4 739 . .	. . .	. . .	. . .	. . .	. . .	. . .	. . .	. . .
General government: long-term	4 741 . .	–7.2	–.7	12.9	1.6	–26.3	.2	–1.0	–31.3
General government: short-term	4 742 . .	. . .	. . .	. . .	. . .	. . .	. . .	. . .	. . .
Banks: long-term	4 744 . .	. . .	. . .	. . .	. . .	. . .	. . .	. . .	. . .
Banks: short-term	4 745 . .	. . .	. . .	. . .	. . .	. . .	. . .	. . .	. . .
Other sectors: long-term	4 747 . .	. . .	. . .	. . .	. . .	. . .	. . .	. . .	. . .
Other sectors: short-term	4 748 . .	. . .	. . .	. . .	. . .	. . .	. . .	. . .	. . .
Liabilities	4 753 . .	**146.7**	**235.2**	**174.8**	**52.5**	**336.5**	**315.5**	**226.2**	**191.6**
Trade credits	4 756 . .	–5.0	–13.5	–14.5	3.2	–64.3	–1.3	83.5	40.1
General government: long-term	4 758 . .	. . .	. . .	. . .	. . .	. . .	. . .	. . .	. . .
General government: short-term	4 759 . .	. . .	. . .	. . .	. . .	. . .	. . .	. . .	. . .
Other sectors: long-term	4 761 . .	. . .	. . .	. . .	. . .	. . .	. . .	. . .	. . .
Other sectors: short-term	4 762 . .	–5.0	–13.5	–14.5	3.2	–64.3	–1.3	83.5	40.1
Loans	4 764 . .	40.2	–13.4	55.1	–89.0	223.6	306.0	95.3	194.8
Use of Fund credit and loans from the Fund	4 766 . .	–36.0	–.4	–4.2	1.1	80.7	6.4	–16.1	–13.7
Monetary authorities: other long-term	4 767 . .	17.6	20.6	6.7	–90.5	–37.9	–38.6	–22.7	7.6
Monetary authorities: short-term	4 768 . .	. . .	. . .	. . .	. . .	. . .	5.6	–68.7	2.8
General government: long-term	4 770 . .	85.5	37.1	145.9	196.6	126.8	424.8	206.9	130.4
General government: short-term	4 771 . .	12.6	–18.4	–9.6	–12.5	–22.1	–76.7	–16.5	39.0
Banks: long-term	4 773 . .	–.9	–1.7	–4.5	–4.3	–13.3	.4	15.4	26.3
Banks: short-term	4 774 . .	. . .	. . .	. . .	. . .	. . .	. . .	. . .	. . .
Other sectors: long-term	4 776 . .	–49.1	–48.3	–61.1	–200.2	71.8	3.7	.1	5.0
Other sectors: short-term	4 777 . .	10.5	–2.4	–18.1	20.8	17.6	–19.6	–3.1	–2.6
Currency and deposits	4 780 . .	–15.6	2.8	–32.0	–12.6	5.5	1.7	–1.2	–.8
Monetary authorities	4 781 . .	–10.4	16.6	–11.9	–1.3	–.5	–.1	. . .	. . .
General government	4 782 . .	. . .	. . .	. . .	. . .	. . .	. . .	. . .	. . .
Banks	4 783 . .	–5.2	–13.8	–20.1	–11.3	6.0	1.8	–1.2	–.8
Other sectors	4 784 . .	. . .	. . .	. . .	. . .	. . .	. . .	. . .	. . .
Other liabilities	4 786 . .	127.1	259.3	166.2	150.9	171.7	9.1	48.6	–42.5
Monetary authorities: long-term	4 788 . .	. . .	. . .	. . .	. . .	. . .	. . .	. . .	. . .
Monetary authorities: short-term	4 789 . .	156.6	273.8	168.7	77.7	162.3	7.1	65.0	–23.3
General government: long-term	4 791 . .	–29.6	–20.3	–7.6	. . .	. . .	. . .	. . .	. . .
General government: short-term	4 792 . .	. . .	. . .	. . .	. . .	. . .	. . .	. . .	. . .
Banks: long-term	4 794 . .	. . .	. . .	. . .	. . .	. . .	. . .	. . .	. . .
Banks: short-term	4 795 . .	. . .	. . .	.1	.1	. . .	–.4	–16.4	–19.2
Other sectors: long-term	4 797 . .	. . .	. . .	. . .	. . .	. . .	. . .	. . .	. . .
Other sectors: short-term	4 798 . .	. . .	5.8	5.0	73.1	9.4	2.4	. . .	. . .
D. RESERVE ASSETS	4 800 . .	21.6	29.0	–20.1	–66.9	–92.0	99.6	–74.1	–90.3
Monetary gold	4 810 . .	. . .	. . .	. . .	–2.5	. . .	. . .	. . .	. . .
Special drawing rights	4 820 . .	. . .	. . .	. . .	. . .	–.2	. . .	–.1	. . .
Reserve position in the Fund	4 830 . .	. . .	. . .	. . .	. . .	. . .	. . .	. . .	. . .
Foreign exchange	4 840 . .	22.9	29.0	–19.5	–64.4	–91.8	99.6	–74.0	–90.3
Other claims	4 880 . .	–1.3	. . .	–.6	. . .	. . .	. . .	. . .	. . .
NET ERRORS AND OMISSIONS	4 998 . .	**–93.1**	**–138.9**	**–107.4**	**152.0**	**29.2**	**–101.5**	**83.6**	**27.6**

Part 3 of the *Yearbook* contains descriptions of the methodologies, compilation practices, and sources used to compile these data.

Table 1. ANALYTIC PRESENTATION, 1988–95
(Millions of U.S. dollars)

	Code			1988	1989	1990	1991	1992	1993	1994	1995
A. Current Account [1]	4	993	Y.	**–572**	**–588**	**379**	**403**	**352**	**–4,262**	**–4,054**	**–2,535**
Goods: exports f.o.b	2	100	. .	9,989	10,493	9,151	9,688	10,097	8,119	7,648	12,864
Goods: imports f.o.b	3	100	. .	–9,406	–9,450	–8,617	–9,330	–10,108	–12,140	–11,364	–15,297
Balance on Goods	4	100	. .	*583*	*1,043*	*534*	*358*	*–11*	*–4,021*	*–3,716*	*–2,433*
Services: credit	2	200	. .	1,047	1,291	2,884	2,526	3,405	2,836	3,117	4,271
Services: debit	3	200	. .	–1,227	–1,658	–2,400	–1,991	–2,641	–2,620	–2,958	–3,629
Balance on Goods and Services	4	991	. .	*403*	*676*	*1,019*	*892*	*753*	*–3,805*	*–3,557*	*–1,791*
Income: credit	2	300	. .	240	231	280	322	424	465	676	798
Income: debit	3	300	. .	–1,332	–1,625	–1,707	–1,678	–1,684	–1,655	–2,082	–2,602
Balance on Goods, Services, and Income	4	992	. .	*–689*	*–718*	*–408*	*–464*	*–506*	*–4,995*	*–4,963*	*–3,595*
Current transfers: credit	2	379	Y.	117	130	1,595	2,604	2,866	2,694	2,871	3,575
Current transfers: debit	3	379	. .	. . .	. . .	–808	–1,737	–2,008	–1,961	–1,961	–2,515
B. Capital Account [1]	4	994	Y.	**. . .**	**. . .**	**. . .**	**. . .**	**. . .**	**. . .**	**. . .**	**59**
Capital account: credit	2	994	Y.	. . .	. . .	. . .	. . .	. . .	. . .	. . .	80
Capital account: debit	3	994	. .	. . .	. . .	. . .	. . .	. . .	. . .	. . .	–20
Total, Groups A Plus B	4	010	. .	*–572*	*–588*	*379*	*403*	*352*	*–4,262*	*–4,054*	*–2,476*
C. Financial Account [1]	4	995	X.	**680**	**901**	**–801**	**1,474**	**416**	**6,083**	**3,370**	**6,577**
Direct investment abroad	4	505	. .	. . .	. . .	. . .	. . .	. . .	–11	–49	–43
Direct investment in Hungary	4	555	Y.	. . .	. . .	. . .	1,462	1,479	2,350	1,144	4,519
Portfolio investment assets	4	602	. .	. . .	. . .	. . .	. . .	. . .	–8	6	–1
Equity securities	4	610	. .	. . .	. . .	. . .	. . .	. . .	. . .	–10	. . .
Debt securities	4	619	. .	. . .	. . .	. . .	. . .	. . .	–8	16	–1
Portfolio investment liabilities	4	652	Y.	. . .	. . .	. . .	. . .	. . .	3,927	2,458	2,213
Equity securities	4	660	Y.	. . .	. . .	. . .	. . .	. . .	46	224	. . .
Debt securities	4	669	Y.	. . .	. . .	. . .	. . .	. . .	3,881	2,234	2,213
Other investment assets	4	703	. .	–83	–322	–524	–13	–421	881	362	88
Monetary authorities	4	703	.A	. . .	. . .	. . .	. . .	. . .	. . .	. . .	–15
General government	4	703	.B	–95	–95	–524	–136	–899	811	156	27
Banks	4	703	.C	–116	–227	. . .	116	616	–127	191	125
Other sectors	4	703	.D	128	. . .	. . .	6	–138	198	15	–48
Other investment liabilities	4	753	X.	763	1,223	–278	25	–642	–1,055	–551	–199
Monetary authorities	4	753	XA	173	–358	–570	–431	174	54	17	–904
General government	4	753	YB	517	1,375	292	815	–787	–1,541	–1,761	–438
Banks	4	753	YC	73	206	. . .	–359	–29	–69	365	321
Other sectors	4	753	YD	. . .	. . .	. . .	. . .	. . .	501	828	823
Total, Groups A Through C	4	020	. .	*108*	*313*	*–423*	*1,877*	*768*	*1,821*	*–684*	*4,101*
D. Net Errors and Omissions	4	998	. .	**50**	**–141**	**10**	**–82**	**2**	**724**	**209**	**1,298**
Total, Groups A Through D	4	030	. .	*158*	*172*	*–413*	*1,795*	*770*	*2,545*	*–475*	*5,399*
E. Reserves and Related Items	4	040	. .	**–158**	**–172**	**413**	**–1,795**	**–770**	**–2,545**	**475**	**–5,399**
Reserve assets	4	800	. .	–25	–14	558	–2,700	–763	–2,574	640	–4,614
Use of Fund credit and loans	4	766	. .	–132	–158	–145	905	–7	30	–165	–785
Liabilities constituting foreign authorities' reserves	4	900	. .	. . .	. . .	. . .	. . .	. . .	. . .	. . .	. . .
Exceptional financing	4	920	. .	. . .	. . .	. . .	. . .	. . .	. . .	. . .	. . .
Conversion rates: forint per U.S. dollar	0	101	. .	**50.41**	**59.07**	**63.21**	**74.74**	**78.99**	**91.93**	**105.16**	**125.68**

[1] Excludes components that have been classified in the categories of Group E.

Table 2. STANDARD PRESENTATION, 1988–95
(Millions of U.S. dollars)

	Code	1988	1989	1990	1991	1992	1993	1994	1995
CURRENT ACCOUNT	4 993 . .	**–572**	**–588**	**379**	**403**	**352**	**–4,262**	**–4,054**	**–2,535**
A. GOODS	4 100 . .	583	1,043	534	358	–11	–4,021	–3,716	–2,433
Credit	2 100 . .	**9,989**	**10,493**	**9,151**	**9,688**	**10,097**	**8,119**	**7,648**	**12,864**
General merchandise: exports f.o.b.	2 110 . .	9,989	10,493	9,151	9,688	10,097	8,119	7,648	12,864
Goods for processing: exports f.o.b.	2 150 . .	...	...	...	...	...	...	...	...
Repairs on goods	2 160 . .	...	...	...	...	...	...	...	...
Goods procured in ports by carriers	2 170 . .	...	...	...	...	...	...	...	...
Nonmonetary gold	2 180 . .	...	...	...	...	...	...	...	...
Debit	3 100 . .	**–9,406**	**–9,450**	**–8,617**	**–9,330**	**–10,108**	**–12,140**	**–11,364**	**–15,297**
General merchandise: imports f.o.b.	3 110 . .	–9,406	–9,450	–8,617	–9,330	–10,108	–12,140	–11,364	–15,297
Goods for processing: imports f.o.b.	3 150 . .	...	...	...	...	...	...	...	...
Repairs on goods	3 160 . .	...	...	...	...	...	...	...	...
Goods procured in ports by carriers	3 170 . .	...	...	...	...	...	...	...	...
Nonmonetary gold	3 180 . .	...	...	...	...	...	...	...	...
B. SERVICES	4 200 . .	–180	–367	484	534	765	216	159	642
Total credit	2 200 . .	*1,047*	*1,291*	*2,884*	*2,526*	*3,405*	*2,836*	*3,117*	*4,271*
Total debit	3 200 . .	*–1,227*	*–1,658*	*–2,400*	*–1,991*	*–2,641*	*–2,620*	*–2,958*	*–3,629*
Transportation services, credit	2 205 . .	**59**	**62**	**42**	**49**	**17**	**66**	**51**	**446**
Passenger	2 205 BA	...	...	...	...	...	...	...	*10*
Freight	2 205 BB	*59*	*62*	*42*	*49*	*17*	*66*	*51*	*394*
Other	2 205 BC	...	...	...	...	...	...	...	*42*
Sea transport, passenger	2 207 . .	...	...	...	...	...	...	...	...
Sea transport, freight	2 208 . .	...	...	...	...	...	...	...	29
Sea transport, other	2 209 . .	...	...	...	...	...	...	...	...
Air transport, passenger	2 211 . .	...	...	...	...	...	...	...	...
Air transport, freight	2 212 . .	...	...	...	...	...	...	...	71
Air transport, other	2 213 . .	...	...	...	...	...	...	...	...
Other transport, passenger	2 215 . .	...	...	...	...	...	...	...	...
Other transport, freight	2 216 . .	...	...	...	...	...	...	...	294
Other transport, other	2 217 . .	...	...	...	...	...	...	...	42
Transportation services, debit	3 205 . .	**–397**	**–411**	**–200**	**–128**	**–121**	**–161**	**–210**	**–370**
Passenger	3 205 BA	...	...	...	...	...	...	...	*–3*
Freight	3 205 BB	*–397*	*–411*	*–200*	*–128*	*–121*	*–161*	*–210*	*–139*
Other	3 205 BC	...	...	...	...	...	...	...	*–228*
Sea transport, passenger	3 207 . .	...	...	...	...	...	...	...	...
Sea transport, freight	3 208 . .	...	...	...	...	...	...	...	–9
Sea transport, other	3 209 . .	...	...	...	...	...	...	...	...
Air transport, passenger	3 211 . .	...	...	...	...	...	...	...	...
Air transport, freight	3 212 . .	...	...	...	...	...	...	...	–4
Air transport, other	3 213 . .	...	...	...	...	...	...	...	...
Other transport, passenger	3 215 . .	...	...	...	...	...	...	...	...
Other transport, freight	3 216 . .	...	...	...	...	...	...	...	–126
Other transport, other	3 217 . .	...	...	...	...	...	...	...	–228
Travel, credit	2 236 . .	**865**	**984**	**985**	**1,036**	**1,250**	**1,188**	**1,435**	**1,724**
Business travel	2 237 . .	...	...	...	...	...	...	...	...
Personal travel	2 240 . .	...	...	...	...	...	...	...	1,724
Travel, debit	3 236 . .	**–711**	**–1,144**	**–585**	**–497**	**–664**	**–746**	**–935**	**–1,071**
Business travel	3 237 . .	...	...	...	...	...	...	...	–164
Personal travel	3 240 . .	...	...	...	...	...	...	...	–907
Other services, credit	2 200 BA	**124**	**245**	**1,857**	**1,441**	**2,139**	**1,582**	**1,631**	**2,101**
Communications	2 245 . .	...	...	...	...	...	...	...	38
Construction	2 249 . .	...	...	...	...	...	...	...	21
Insurance	2 253 . .	7	7	5	5	2	7	6	62
Financial	2 260 . .	...	...	...	...	...	...	...	100
Computer and information	2 262 . .	...	...	...	...	...	...	...	...
Royalties and licence fees	2 266 . .	...	...	49	18	38	33	31	32
Other business services	2 268 . .	96	210	1,596	1,246	1,906	1,474	1,523	1,789
Personal, cultural, and recreational	2 287 . .	...	...	...	...	...	...	...	...
Government, n.i.e.	2 291 . .	21	28	208	172	193	67	71	60
Other services, debit	3 200 BA	**–119**	**–103**	**–1,615**	**–1,365**	**–1,856**	**–1,713**	**–1,813**	**–2,188**
Communications	3 245 . .	...	...	...	...	...	...	...	–22
Construction	3 249 . .	...	...	...	...	...	...	...	–36
Insurance	3 253 . .	–44	–46	–22	–14	–13	–18	–23	–31
Financial	3 260 . .	...	...	...	...	...	...	...	–152
Computer and information	3 262 . .	...	...	...	...	...	...	...	...
Royalties and licence fees	3 266 . .	...	...	–36	–39	–30	–39	–75	–70
Other business services	3 268 . .	...	...	–1,421	–1,202	–1,698	–1,571	–1,632	–1,803
Personal, cultural, and recreational	3 287 . .	...	...	...	...	...	...	...	...
Government, n.i.e.	3 291 . .	–75	–57	–136	–110	–114	–85	–83	–73

Table 2 (Continued). STANDARD PRESENTATION, 1988–95
(Millions of U.S. dollars)

	Code	1988	1989	1990	1991	1992	1993	1994	1995
C. INCOME	4 300	–1,092	–1,394	–1,427	–1,356	–1,260	–1,190	–1,406	–1,804
Total credit	2 300	*240*	*231*	*280*	*322*	*424*	*465*	*676*	*798*
Total debit	3 300	*–1,332*	*–1,625*	*–1,707*	*–1,678*	*–1,684*	*–1,655*	*–2,082*	*–2,602*
Compensation of employees, credit	2 310	**...**	**...**	**...**	**...**	**...**	**...**	**...**	**21**
Compensation of employees, debit	3 310	**...**	**...**	**...**	**...**	**...**	**...**	**...**	**–34**
Investment income, credit	2 320	**240**	**231**	**280**	**322**	**424**	**465**	**676**	**778**
Direct investment income	2 330	...	...	27	11	6	10	15	12
Dividends and distributed branch profits	2 332	...	...	27	11	6	10	15	12
Reinvested earnings and undistributed branch profits	2 333	...	...	...	...	...	...	...	...
Income on debt (interest)	2 334	...	...	...	...	...	...	...	...
Portfolio investment income	2 339	...	...	...	...	...	...	...	349
Income on equity	2 340	...	...	...	...	...	...	...	...
Income on bonds and notes	2 350	...	...	...	...	...	...	...	9
Income on money market instruments and financial derivatives	2 360	...	...	...	...	...	...	...	340
Other investment income	2 370	240	231	253	310	418	455	660	417
Investment income, debit	3 320	**–1,332**	**–1,625**	**–1,707**	**–1,678**	**–1,684**	**–1,655**	**–2,082**	**–2,568**
Direct investment income	3 330	...	...	–37	–43	–51	–66	–132	–206
Dividends and distributed branch profits	3 332	...	...	–37	–43	–51	–66	–132	–206
Reinvested earnings and undistributed branch profits	3 333	...	...	...	...	...	...	...	...
Income on debt (interest)	3 334	...	...	...	...	...	...	...	...
Portfolio investment income	3 339	...	...	...	...	...	...	...	–1,136
Income on equity	3 340	...	...	...	...	...	...	...	...
Income on bonds and notes	3 350	...	...	...	...	...	...	...	–1,135
Income on money market instruments and financial derivatives	3 360	...	...	...	...	...	...	...	–1
Other investment income	3 370	–1,332	–1,625	–1,670	–1,634	–1,633	–1,589	–1,950	–1,226
D. CURRENT TRANSFERS	4 379	117	130	787	867	858	733	910	1,060
Credit	2 379	**117**	**130**	**1,595**	**2,604**	**2,866**	**2,694**	**2,871**	**3,575**
General government	2 380	...	...	3	62	52	67	82	62
Other sectors	2 390	117	130	1,592	2,542	2,815	2,627	2,789	3,513
Workers' remittances	2 391	...	...	...	...	...	...	...	6
Other current transfers	2 392	117	130	1,592	2,542	2,815	2,627	2,789	3,507
Debit	3 379	**...**	**...**	**–808**	**–1,737**	**–2,008**	**–1,961**	**–1,961**	**–2,515**
General government	3 380	...	...	–10	–29	–36	–45	–68	–49
Other sectors	3 390	...	...	–798	–1,708	–1,972	–1,916	–1,893	–2,466
Workers' remittances	3 391	...	...	...	...	...	...	...	–20
Other current transfers	3 392	...	...	–798	–1,708	–1,972	–1,916	–1,893	–2,446
CAPITAL AND FINANCIAL ACCOUNT	4 996	**522**	**729**	**–388**	**–321**	**–354**	**3,538**	**3,845**	**1,237**
CAPITAL ACCOUNT	4 994	**...**	**...**	**...**	**...**	**...**	**...**	**...**	**59**
Total credit	2 994	...	...	...	...	...	...	...	*80*
Total debit	3 994	...	...	...	...	...	...	...	*–20*
Capital transfers, credit	2 400	**...**	**...**	**...**	**...**	**...**	**...**	**...**	**80**
General government	2 401	...	...	...	...	...	...	...	24
Debt forgiveness	2 402	...	...	...	...	...	...	...	...
Other capital transfers	2 410	...	...	...	...	...	...	...	24
Other sectors	2 430	...	...	...	...	...	...	...	56
Migrants' transfers	2 431	...	...	...	...	...	...	...	5
Debt forgiveness	2 432	...	...	...	...	...	...	...	...
Other capital transfers	2 440	...	...	...	...	...	...	...	50
Capital transfers, debit	3 400	**...**	**...**	**...**	**...**	**...**	**...**	**...**	**–20**
General government	3 401	...	...	...	...	...	...	...	–15
Debt forgiveness	3 402	...	...	...	...	...	...	...	...
Other capital transfers	3 410	...	...	...	...	...	...	...	–15
Other sectors	3 430	...	...	...	...	...	...	...	–5
Migrants' transfers	3 431	...	...	...	...	...	...	...	...
Debt forgiveness	3 432	...	...	...	...	...	...	...	...
Other capital transfers	3 440	...	...	...	...	...	...	...	–5
Nonproduced nonfinancial assets, credit	2 480	**...**	**...**	**...**	**...**	**...**	**...**	**...**	**...**
Nonproduced nonfinancial assets, debit	3 480	**...**	**...**	**...**	**...**	**...**	**...**	**...**	**...**

Table 2 (Continued). STANDARD PRESENTATION, 1988–95
(Millions of U.S. dollars)

	Code	1988	1989	1990	1991	1992	1993	1994	1995
FINANCIAL ACCOUNT	4 995 . .	**522**	**729**	**–388**	**–321**	**–354**	**3,538**	**3,845**	**1,178**
A. DIRECT INVESTMENT	4 500 . .	...	...	...	1,462	1,479	2,339	1,095	4,476
Direct investment abroad	4 505 . .	**...**	**...**	**...**	**...**	**...**	**–11**	**–49**	**–43**
Equity capital	4 510 . .	...	...	...	...	...	–11	–49	–43
Claims on affiliated enterprises	4 515 . .	...	...	...	...	...	...	...	...
Liabilities to affiliated enterprises	4 520 . .	...	...	...	...	...	...	...	...
Reinvested earnings	4 525 . .	...	...	...	...	...	...	...	...
Other capital	4 530 . .	...	...	...	...	...	...	...	...
Claims on affiliated enterprises	4 535 . .	...	...	...	...	...	...	...	...
Liabilities to affiliated enterprises	4 540 . .	...	...	...	...	...	...	...	...
Direct investment in Hungary	4 555 . .	**...**	**...**	**...**	**1,462**	**1,479**	**2,350**	**1,144**	**4,519**
Equity capital	4 560 . .	...	...	...	1,462	1,479	2,350	1,144	4,519
Claims on direct investors	4 565 . .	...	...	...	...	...	...	...	...
Liabilities to direct investors	4 570 . .	...	...	...	...	...	...	...	...
Reinvested earnings	4 575 . .	...	...	...	...	...	...	...	...
Other capital	4 580 . .	...	...	...	...	...	...	...	...
Claims on direct investors	4 585 . .	...	...	...	...	...	...	...	...
Liabilities to direct investors	4 590 . .	...	...	...	...	...	...	...	...
B. PORTFOLIO INVESTMENT	4 600 . .	...	...	...	...	...	3,918	2,464	2,212
Assets	4 602 . .	**...**	**...**	**...**	**...**	**...**	**–8**	**6**	**–1**
Equity securities	4 610 . .	...	...	...	...	...	...	–10	...
Monetary authorities	4 611 . .	...	...	...	...	...	...	...	...
General government	4 612 . .	...	...	...	...	...	...	...	...
Banks	4 613 . .	...	...	...	...	...	...	...	...
Other sectors	4 614 . .	...	...	...	...	...	...	...	...
Debt securities	4 619 . .	...	...	...	...	...	–8	16	–1
Bonds and notes	4 620 . .	...	...	...	...	...	–8	16	...
Monetary authorities	4 621 . .	...	...	...	...	...	...	...	...
General government	4 622 . .	...	...	...	...	...	...	...	...
Banks	4 623 . .	...	...	...	...	...	...	...	...
Other sectors	4 624 . .	...	...	...	...	...	...	...	...
Money market instruments	4 630 . .	...	...	...	...	...	...	...	...
Monetary authorities	4 631 . .	...	...	...	...	...	...	...	...
General government	4 632 . .	...	...	...	...	...	...	...	...
Banks	4 633 . .	...	...	...	...	...	...	...	...
Other sectors	4 634 . .	...	...	...	...	...	...	...	...
Financial derivatives	4 640 . .	...	...	...	...	...	...	...	...
Monetary authorities	4 641 . .	...	...	...	...	...	...	...	...
General government	4 642 . .	...	...	...	...	...	...	...	...
Banks	4 643 . .	...	...	...	...	...	...	...	...
Other sectors	4 644 . .	...	...	...	...	...	...	...	...
Liabilities	4 652 . .	**...**	**...**	**...**	**...**	**...**	**3,927**	**2,458**	**2,213**
Equity securities	4 660 . .	...	...	...	...	...	46	224	...
Banks	4 663 . .	...	...	...	...	...	...	...	...
Other sectors	4 664 . .	...	...	...	...	...	...	...	...
Debt securities	4 669 . .	...	...	...	...	...	3,881	2,234	2,213
Bonds and notes	4 670 . .	...	...	...	...	...	3,881	2,234	2,021
Monetary authorities	4 671 . .	...	...	...	...	...	...	...	2,056
General government	4 672 . .	...	...	...	...	...	3,815	2,136	28
Banks	4 673 . .	...	...	...	...	...	...	...	...
Other sectors	4 674 . .	...	...	...	...	...	66	98	–62
Money market instruments	4 680 . .	...	...	...	...	...	...	...	192
Monetary authorities	4 681 . .	...	...	...	...	...	...	...	...
General government	4 682 . .	...	...	...	...	...	...	...	88
Banks	4 683 . .	...	...	...	...	...	...	...	...
Other sectors	4 684 . .	...	...	...	...	...	...	...	103
Financial derivatives	4 690 . .	...	...	...	...	...	...	...	...
Monetary authorities	4 691 . .	...	...	...	...	...	...	...	...
General government	4 692 . .	...	...	...	...	...	...	...	...
Banks	4 693 . .	...	...	...	...	...	...	...	...
Other sectors	4 694 . .	...	...	...	...	...	...	...	...

Table 2 (Concluded). STANDARD PRESENTATION, 1988–95
(Millions of U.S. dollars)

	Code	1988	1989	1990	1991	1992	1993	1994	1995
C. OTHER INVESTMENT	4 700 . .	548	743	–946	917	–1,070	–144	–355	–896
Assets	4 703 . .	**–83**	**–322**	**–524**	**–13**	**–421**	**881**	**362**	**88**
Trade credits	4 706 . .	. . .	. . .	. . .	. . .	. . .	. . .	. . .	56
General government: long-term	4 708 . .	. . .	. . .	. . .	. . .	. . .	. . .	. . .	9
General government: short-term	4 709 . .	. . .	. . .	. . .	. . .	. . .	. . .	. . .	. . .
Other sectors: long-term	4 711 . .	. . .	. . .	. . .	. . .	. . .	. . .	. . .	2
Other sectors: short-term	4 712 . .	. . .	. . .	. . .	. . .	. . .	. . .	. . .	45
Loans	4 714 . .	. . .	. . .	–282	–136	–899	1,004	152	98
Monetary authorities: long-term	4 717 . .	. . .	. . .	. . .	. . .	. . .	. . .	. . .	–17
Monetary authorities: short-term	4 718 . .	. . .	. . .	. . .	. . .	. . .	. . .	. . .	. . .
General government: long-term	4 720 . .	. . .	. . .	–52	–56	–909	790	105	18
General government: short-term	4 721 . .	. . .	. . .	–230	–80	10	1	32	. . .
Banks: long-term	4 723 . .	. . .	. . .	. . .	. . .	. . .	–23	. . .	86
Banks: short-term	4 724 . .	. . .	. . .	. . .	. . .	. . .	. . .	. . .	11
Other sectors: long-term	4 726 . .	. . .	. . .	. . .	. . .	. . .	66	12	. . .
Other sectors: short-term	4 727 . .	. . .	. . .	. . .	. . .	. . .	169	3	. . .
Currency and deposits	4 730 . .	12	–227	–242	123	478	–317	192	–66
Monetary authorities	4 731 . .	. . .	. . .	. . .	. . .	. . .	. . .	. . .	1
General government	4 732 . .	. . .	. . .	–242	. . .	. . .	2	. . .	. . .
Banks	4 733 . .	–116	–227	. . .	116	616	–282	192	28
Other sectors	4 734 . .	128	. . .	. . .	6	–138	–37	. . .	–95
Other assets	4 736 . .	–95	–95	. . .	. . .	. . .	195	18	. . .
Monetary authorities: long-term	4 738 . .	. . .	. . .	. . .	. . .	. . .	. . .	. . .	. . .
Monetary authorities: short-term	4 739 . .	. . .	. . .	. . .	. . .	. . .	. . .	. . .	. . .
General government: long-term	4 741 . .	–95	–95	. . .	. . .	. . .	18	19	. . .
General government: short-term	4 742 . .	. . .	. . .	. . .	. . .	. . .	. . .	. . .	. . .
Banks: long-term	4 744 . .	. . .	. . .	. . .	. . .	. . .	177	–1	. . .
Banks: short-term	4 745 . .	. . .	. . .	. . .	. . .	. . .	. . .	. . .	. . .
Other sectors: long-term	4 747 . .	. . .	. . .	. . .	. . .	. . .	. . .	. . .	. . .
Other sectors: short-term	4 748 . .	. . .	. . .	. . .	. . .	. . .	. . .	. . .	. . .
Liabilities	4 753 . .	**631**	**1,065**	**–423**	**930**	**–650**	**–1,026**	**–716**	**–985**
Trade credits	4 756 . .	. . .	. . .	. . .	. . .	. . .	. . .	. . .	–51
General government: long-term	4 758 . .	. . .	. . .	. . .	. . .	. . .	. . .	. . .	53
General government: short-term	4 759 . .	. . .	. . .	. . .	. . .	. . .	. . .	. . .	. . .
Other sectors: long-term	4 761 . .	. . .	. . .	. . .	. . .	. . .	. . .	. . .	–225
Other sectors: short-term	4 762 . .	. . .	. . .	. . .	. . .	. . .	. . .	. . .	122
Loans	4 764 . .	385	1,217	147	1,720	–795	766	204	–526
Use of Fund credit and loans from the Fund	4 766 . .	–132	–158	–145	905	–7	30	–165	–785
Monetary authorities: other long-term	4 767 . .	. . .	. . .	. . .	. . .	. . .	. . .	. . .	–625
Monetary authorities: short-term	4 768 . .	. . .	. . .	. . .	. . .	. . .	. . .	. . .	3
General government: long-term	4 770 . .	517	1,375	292	815	–787	172	–201	–491
General government: short-term	4 771 . .	. . .	. . .	. . .	. . .	. . .	. . .	. . .	. . .
Banks: long-term	4 773 . .	. . .	. . .	. . .	. . .	. . .	–4	–11	271
Banks: short-term	4 774 . .	. . .	. . .	. . .	. . .	. . .	. . .	. . .	175
Other sectors: long-term	4 776 . .	. . .	. . .	. . .	. . .	. . .	670	561	801
Other sectors: short-term	4 777 . .	. . .	. . .	. . .	. . .	. . .	–102	20	125
Currency and deposits	4 780 . .	73	206	. . .	–359	–29	–46	211	–408
Monetary authorities	4 781 . .	. . .	. . .	. . .	. . .	. . .	. . .	. . .	–282
General government	4 782 . .	. . .	. . .	. . .	. . .	. . .	. . .	. . .	. . .
Banks	4 783 . .	73	206	. . .	–359	–29	–46	211	–126
Other sectors	4 784 . .	. . .	. . .	. . .	. . .	. . .	. . .	. . .	. . .
Other liabilities	4 786 . .	173	–358	–570	–431	174	–1,746	–1,131	. . .
Monetary authorities: long-term	4 788 . .	. . .	. . .	. . .	. . .	. . .	. . .	. . .	. . .
Monetary authorities: short-term	4 789 . .	173	–358	–570	–431	174	54	17	. . .
General government: long-term	4 791 . .	. . .	. . .	. . .	. . .	. . .	–1,713	–1,560	. . .
General government: short-term	4 792 . .	. . .	. . .	. . .	. . .	. . .	. . .	. . .	. . .
Banks: long-term	4 794 . .	. . .	. . .	. . .	. . .	. . .	–20	165	. . .
Banks: short-term	4 795 . .	. . .	. . .	. . .	. . .	. . .	. . .	. . .	. . .
Other sectors: long-term	4 797 . .	. . .	. . .	. . .	. . .	. . .	. . .	. . .	. . .
Other sectors: short-term	4 798 . .	. . .	. . .	. . .	. . .	. . .	–67	247	. . .
D. RESERVE ASSETS	4 800 . .	–25	–14	558	–2,700	–763	–2,574	640	–4,614
Monetary gold	4 810 . .	. . .	. . .	383	14	50	–5	1	. . .
Special drawing rights	4 820 . .	. . .	. . .	–1	. . .	–2	–1	2	. . .
Reserve position in the Fund	4 830 . .	. . .	. . .	. . .	. . .	–78	. . .	. . .	. . .
Foreign exchange	4 840 . .	–25	–15	176	–2,714	–733	–2,569	637	–4,614
Other claims	4 880 . .	. . .	. . .	. . .	. . .	. . .	. . .	. . .	. . .
NET ERRORS AND OMISSIONS	4 998 . .	**50**	**–141**	**10**	**–82**	**2**	**724**	**209**	**1,298**

Part 3 of the *Yearbook* contains descriptions of the methodologies, compilation practices, and sources used to compile these data.

Table 1. ANALYTIC PRESENTATION, 1988–95
(Millions of U.S. dollars)

	Code	1988	1989	1990	1991	1992	1993	1994	1995
A. Current Account [1]	4 993 Y.	**–231.2**	**–102.0**	**–135.0**	**–318.0**	**–214.0**	**–5.0**	**111.0**	**51.0**
Goods: exports f.o.b	2 100 . .	1,425.4	1,401.5	1,588.0	1,552.0	1,529.0	1,398.0	1,561.0	1,804.0
Goods: imports f.o.b	3 100 . .	–1,439.4	–1,267.3	–1,509.0	–1,599.0	–1,527.0	–1,217.0	–1,288.0	–1,598.0
Balance on Goods	4 100 . .	*–14.0*	*134.2*	*79.0*	*–47.0*	*2.0*	*181.0*	*273.0*	*206.0*
Services: credit	2 200 . .	531.6	516.9	549.0	558.0	575.0	590.0	603.0	670.0
Services: debit	3 200 . .	–535.6	–494.8	–549.0	–605.0	–591.0	–594.0	–577.0	–641.0
Balance on Goods and Services	4 991 . .	*–18.0*	*156.3*	*79.0*	*–94.0*	*–14.0*	*177.0*	*299.0*	*235.0*
Income: credit	2 300 . .	26.2	32.5	78.0	82.0	94.0	83.0	79.0	91.0
Income: debit	3 300 . .	–228.5	–269.7	–290.0	–297.0	–291.0	–262.0	–259.0	–270.0
Balance on Goods, Services, and Income	4 992 . .	*–220.3*	*–80.9*	*–133.0*	*–309.0*	*–211.0*	*–2.0*	*119.0*	*56.0*
Current transfers: credit	2 379 Y.	9.0	10.5	26.0	13.0	19.0	18.0	12.0	15.0
Current transfers: debit	3 379 . .	–19.9	–31.6	–28.0	–22.0	–22.0	–21.0	–20.0	–20.0
B. Capital Account [1]	4 994 Y.	**9.7**	**18.1**	**3.0**	**4.0**	**–1.0**	**2.0**	**–4.0**	**–1.0**
Capital account: credit	2 994 Y.	18.4	25.9	17.0	15.0	11.0	12.0	6.0	13.0
Capital account: debit	3 994 . .	–8.7	–7.8	–14.0	–11.0	–12.0	–10.0	–10.0	–14.0
Total, Groups A Plus B	4 010 . .	*–221.5*	*–83.9*	*–132.0*	*–314.0*	*–215.0*	*–3.0*	*107.0*	*50.0*
C. Financial Account [1]	4 995 X.	**226.8**	**125.0**	**237.0**	**299.0**	**287.0**	**–25.0**	**–266.0**	**36.0**
Direct investment abroad	4 505 . .	–1.1	–8.2	–6.0	–5.0	–6.0	–3.0	–3.0	–6.0
Direct investment in Iceland	4 555 Y.	–14.8	–27.4	3.0	33.0	14.0	8.0	–1.0	4.0
Portfolio investment assets	4 602 . .	. . .	.5	. . .	–4.0	–4.0	–30.0	–109.0	–43.0
Equity securities	4 610 . .	. . .	. . .	. . .	–3.0	–4.0	–4.0	–23.0	–38.0
Debt securities	4 619 . .	. . .	.5	. . .	–1.0	. . .	–26.0	–86.0	–5.0
Portfolio investment liabilities	4 652 Y.	. . .	.1	. . .	26.0	–11.0	–10.0	4.0	–9.0
Equity securities	4 660 Y.	. . .	. . .	. . .	. . .	. . .	. . .	. . .	. . .
Debt securities	4 669 Y.	. . .	.1	. . .	26.0	–11.0	–10.0	4.0	–9.0
Other investment assets	4 703 . .	–65.3	11.8	–37.0	–1.0	52.0	–22.0	–66.0	25.0
Monetary authorities	4 703 . A	. . .	. . .	. . .	. . .	7.0	. . .	–49.0	–17.0
General government	4 703 . B	. . .	. . .	. . .	. . .	. . .	. . .	. . .	. . .
Banks	4 703 . C	–6.9	3.0	–26.0	–3.0	13.0	–28.0	–5.0	64.0
Other sectors	4 703 . D	–58.4	8.8	–11.0	2.0	32.0	6.0	–12.0	–22.0
Other investment liabilities	4 753 X.	308.0	148.2	277.0	250.0	242.0	32.0	–91.0	65.0
Monetary authorities	4 753 XA	20.2	–24.7	–1.0	2.0	–6.0	22.0	93.0	37.0
General government	4 753 YB	144.3	191.7	46.0	104.0	181.0	78.0	157.0	226.0
Banks	4 753 YC	74.2	62.8	–21.0	10.0	–9.0	–69.0	–166.0	–84.0
Other sectors	4 753 YD	69.3	–81.6	253.0	134.0	76.0	1.0	–175.0	–114.0
Total, Groups A Through C	4 020 . .	*5.3*	*41.1*	*105.0*	*–15.0*	*72.0*	*–28.0*	*–159.0*	*86.0*
D. Net Errors and Omissions	4 998 . .	**–4.1**	**13.5**	**–31.1**	**24.0**	**6.4**	**–31.9**	**8.8**	**–82.0**
Total, Groups A Through D	4 030 . .	*1.2*	*54.6*	*73.9*	*9.0*	*78.4*	*–59.9*	*–150.2*	*4.0*
E. Reserves and Related Items	4 040 . .	**–1.2**	**–54.6**	**–73.9**	**–9.0**	**–78.4**	**59.9**	**150.2**	**–4.0**
Reserve assets	4 800 . .	–1.2	–54.6	–73.9	–9.0	–78.4	59.9	150.2	–4.0
Use of Fund credit and loans	4 766 . .	. . .	. . .	. . .	. . .	. . .	. . .	. . .	. . .
Liabilities constituting foreign authorities' reserves	4 900 . .	. . .	. . .	. . .	. . .	. . .	. . .	. . .	. . .
Exceptional financing	4 920 . .	. . .	. . .	. . .	. . .	. . .	. . .	. . .	. . .
Conversion rates: krónur per U.S. dollar	0 101 . .	**43.014**	**57.042**	**58.284**	**58.996**	**57.546**	**67.603**	**69.944**	**64.692**

[1] Excludes components that have been classified in the categories of Group E.

Table 2. STANDARD PRESENTATION, 1988–95
(Millions of U.S. dollars)

	Code			1988	1989	1990	1991	1992	1993	1994	1995
CURRENT ACCOUNT	4	993	. .	**–231.2**	**–102.0**	**–135.0**	**–318.0**	**–214.0**	**–5.0**	**111.0**	**51.0**
A. GOODS	4	100	. .	–14.0	134.2	79.0	–47.0	2.0	181.0	273.0	206.0
Credit	2	100	. .	**1,425.4**	**1,401.5**	**1,588.0**	**1,552.0**	**1,529.0**	**1,398.0**	**1,561.0**	**1,804.0**
General merchandise: exports f.o.b.	2	110	. .	1,425.4	1,401.5	1,588.0	1,552.0	1,529.0	1,398.0	1,561.0	1,804.0
Goods for processing: exports f.o.b.	2	150	. .	. . .	. . .	. . .	. . .	. . .	. . .	. . .	. . .
Repairs on goods	2	160	. .	. . .	. . .	. . .	. . .	. . .	. . .	. . .	. . .
Goods procured in ports by carriers	2	170	. .	. . .	. . .	. . .	. . .	. . .	. . .	. . .	. . .
Nonmonetary gold	2	180	. .	. . .	. . .	. . .	. . .	. . .	. . .	. . .	. . .
Debit	3	100	. .	**–1,439.4**	**–1,267.3**	**–1,509.0**	**–1,599.0**	**–1,527.0**	**–1,217.0**	**–1,288.0**	**–1,598.0**
General merchandise: imports f.o.b.	3	110	. .	–1,439.4	–1,267.3	–1,509.0	–1,599.0	–1,527.0	–1,217.0	–1,288.0	–1,598.0
Goods for processing: imports f.o.b.	3	150	. .	. . .	. . .	. . .	. . .	. . .	. . .	. . .	. . .
Repairs on goods	3	160	. .	. . .	. . .	. . .	. . .	. . .	. . .	. . .	. . .
Goods procured in ports by carriers	3	170	. .	. . .	. . .	. . .	. . .	. . .	. . .	. . .	. . .
Nonmonetary gold	3	180	. .	. . .	. . .	. . .	. . .	. . .	. . .	. . .	. . .
B. SERVICES	4	200	. .	–4.0	22.1	. . .	–47.0	–16.0	–4.0	26.0	29.0
Total credit	2	200	. .	*531.6*	*516.9*	*549.0*	*558.0*	*575.0*	*590.0*	*603.0*	*670.0*
Total debit	3	200	. .	*–535.6*	*–494.8*	*–549.0*	*–605.0*	*–591.0*	*–594.0*	*–577.0*	*–641.0*
Transportation services, credit	2	205	. .	**208.6**	**193.9**	**226.0**	**224.0**	**209.0**	**236.0**	**250.0**	**268.0**
Passenger	2	205	BA	*118.7*	*83.4*	*82.0*	*91.0*	*93.0*	*88.0*	*99.0*	*123.0*
Freight	2	205	BB	*63.9*	*71.4*	*78.0*	*77.0*	*75.0*	*79.0*	*91.0*	*82.0*
Other	2	205	BC	*26.0*	*39.1*	*66.0*	*56.0*	*41.0*	*69.0*	*60.0*	*63.0*
Sea transport, passenger	2	207	. .	. . .	. . .	. . .	. . .	. . .	. . .	. . .	. . .
Sea transport, freight	2	208	. .	. . .	. . .	73.0	73.0	71.0	75.0	86.0	77.0
Sea transport, other	2	209	. .	11.4	15.8	31.0	19.0	9.0	22.0	17.0	23.0
Air transport, passenger	2	211	. .	. . .	. . .	82.0	91.0	93.0	88.0	99.0	123.0
Air transport, freight	2	212	. .	. . .	. . .	5.0	4.0	4.0	4.0	5.0	5.0
Air transport, other	2	213	. .	14.6	23.3	35.0	37.0	32.0	47.0	43.0	40.0
Other transport, passenger	2	215	. .	. . .	. . .	. . .	. . .	. . .	. . .	. . .	. . .
Other transport, freight	2	216	. .	. . .	. . .	. . .	. . .	. . .	. . .	. . .	. . .
Other transport, other	2	217	. .	. . .	. . .	. . .	. . .	. . .	. . .	. . .	. . .
Transportation services, debit	3	205	. .	**–203.7**	**–179.9**	**–161.0**	**–181.0**	**–165.0**	**–160.0**	**–167.0**	**–206.0**
Passenger	3	205	BA	. . .	. . .	. . .	. . .	. . .	. . .	. . .	. . .
Freight	3	205	BB	*–7.8*	*–7.5*	. . .	*–15.0*	*–17.0*	*–13.0*	*–15.0*	*–17.0*
Other	3	205	BC	*–195.9*	*–172.4*	*–161.0*	*–166.0*	*–148.0*	*–147.0*	*–152.0*	*–189.0*
Sea transport, passenger	3	207	. .	. . .	. . .	. . .	. . .	. . .	. . .	. . .	. . .
Sea transport, freight	3	208	. .	. . .	. . .	. . .	–15.0	–17.0	–13.0	–15.0	–17.0
Sea transport, other	3	209	. .	. . .	. . .	–85.0	–83.0	–69.0	–70.0	–73.0	–87.0
Air transport, passenger	3	211	. .	. . .	. . .	. . .	. . .	. . .	. . .	. . .	. . .
Air transport, freight	3	212	. .	. . .	. . .	. . .	. . .	. . .	. . .	. . .	. . .
Air transport, other	3	213	. .	. . .	. . .	–76.0	–83.0	–79.0	–77.0	–79.0	–102.0
Other transport, passenger	3	215	. .	. . .	. . .	. . .	. . .	. . .	. . .	. . .	. . .
Other transport, freight	3	216	. .	. . .	. . .	. . .	. . .	. . .	. . .	. . .	. . .
Other transport, other	3	217	. .	. . .	. . .	. . .	. . .	. . .	. . .	. . .	. . .
Travel, credit	2	236	. .	**106.1**	**107.3**	**139.0**	**132.0**	**129.0**	**130.0**	**133.0**	**166.0**
Business travel	2	237	. .	. . .	. . .	. . .	. . .	. . .	. . .	. . .	. . .
Personal travel	2	240	. .	. . .	. . .	139.0	132.0	129.0	130.0	133.0	166.0
Travel, debit	3	236	. .	**–224.5**	**–203.5**	**–286.0**	**–299.0**	**–294.0**	**–270.0**	**–247.0**	**–282.0**
Business travel	3	237	. .	. . .	. . .	. . .	. . .	. . .	. . .	. . .	. . .
Personal travel	3	240	. .	–224.5	–203.5	–286.0	–299.0	–294.0	–270.0	–247.0	–282.0
Other services, credit	2	200	BA	**216.9**	**215.7**	**184.0**	**202.0**	**237.0**	**224.0**	**220.0**	**236.0**
Communications	2	245	. .	. . .	. . .	15.0	16.0	16.0	18.0	20.0	23.0
Construction	2	249	. .	. . .	. . .	. . .	2.0	7.0	8.0	2.0	5.0
Insurance	2	253	. .	3.8	4.0	6.0	7.0	12.0	11.0	5.0	4.0
Financial	2	260	. .	. . .	. . .	. . .	. . .	. . .	. . .	. . .	. . .
Computer and information	2	262	. .	. . .	. . .	. . .	. . .	. . .	. . .	. . .	. . .
Royalties and licence fees	2	266	. .	. . .	. . .	. . .	. . .	. . .	. . .	. . .	. . .
Other business services	2	268	. .	77.3	66.9	41.0	59.0	70.0	87.0	105.0	99.0
Personal, cultural, and recreational	2	287	. .	. . .	. . .	. . .	. . .	. . .	. . .	. . .	2.0
Government, n.i.e.	2	291	. .	135.8	144.8	122.0	118.0	132.0	100.0	88.0	103.0
Other services, debit	3	200	BA	**–107.4**	**–111.4**	**–102.0**	**–125.0**	**–132.0**	**–164.0**	**–163.0**	**–153.0**
Communications	3	245	. .	. . .	. . .	–11.0	–12.0	–13.0	–15.0	–17.0	–19.0
Construction	3	249	. .	. . .	. . .	–4.0	–6.0	–8.0	–19.0	–21.0	–16.0
Insurance	3	253	. .	–37.7	–28.7	–15.0	–22.0	–17.0	–18.0	–25.0	–21.0
Financial	3	260	. .	. . .	. . .	. . .	. . .	. . .	–5.0	–5.0	. . .
Computer and information	3	262	. .	. . .	. . .	. . .	. . .	. . .	. . .	. . .	. . .
Royalties and licence fees	3	266	. .	. . .	. . .	. . .	. . .	. . .	. . .	. . .	. . .
Other business services	3	268	. .	–46.3	–59.8	–63.0	–75.0	–85.0	–101.0	–85.0	–81.0
Personal, cultural, and recreational	3	287	. .	. . .	. . .	. . .	. . .	. . .	. . .	. . .	–5.0
Government, n.i.e.	3	291	. .	–23.4	–22.9	–9.0	–10.0	–9.0	–6.0	–10.0	–11.0

Table 2 (Continued). STANDARD PRESENTATION, 1988–95
(Millions of U.S. dollars)

	Code		1988	1989	1990	1991	1992	1993	1994	1995
C. INCOME	4 300	. .	−202.3	−237.2	−212.0	−215.0	−197.0	−179.0	−180.0	−179.0
Total credit	2 300	. .	*26.2*	*32.5*	*78.0*	*82.0*	*94.0*	*83.0*	*79.0*	*91.0*
Total debit	3 300	. .	*−228.5*	*−269.7*	*−290.0*	*−297.0*	*−291.0*	*−262.0*	*−259.0*	*−270.0*
Compensation of employees, credit	2 310	. .	**4.0**	**4.3**	**47.0**	**51.0**	**53.0**	**47.0**	**42.0**	**51.0**
Compensation of employees, debit	3 310	. .	**−7.8**	**−9.0**	**−12.0**	**−15.0**	**−12.0**	**−11.0**	**−8.0**	**−6.0**
Investment income, credit	2 320	. .	**22.2**	**28.2**	**31.0**	**31.0**	**41.0**	**36.0**	**37.0**	**40.0**
Direct investment income	2 330	. .	. . .	. . .	. . .	. . .	. . .	5.0	. . .	. . .
Dividends and distributed branch profits	2 332	. .	. . .	. . .	. . .	. . .	. . .	5.0	. . .	. . .
Reinvested earnings and undistributed branch profits	2 333	. .	. . .	. . .	. . .	. . .	. . .	. . .	. . .	. . .
Income on debt (interest)	2 334	. .	. . .	. . .	. . .	. . .	. . .	. . .	. . .	. . .
Portfolio investment income	2 339	. .	. . .	. . .	. . .	. . .	. . .	. . .	6.0	11.0
Income on equity	2 340	. .	. . .	. . .	. . .	. . .	. . .	. . .	. . .	. . .
Income on bonds and notes	2 350	. .	. . .	. . .	. . .	. . .	. . .	. . .	6.0	11.0
Income on money market instruments and financial derivatives	2 360	. .	. . .	. . .	. . .	. . .	. . .	. . .	. . .	. . .
Other investment income	2 370	. .	22.2	28.2	31.0	31.0	41.0	31.0	31.0	29.0
Investment income, debit	3 320	. .	**−220.7**	**−260.7**	**−278.0**	**−282.0**	**−279.0**	**−251.0**	**−251.0**	**−264.0**
Direct investment income	3 330	. .	−8.8	−6.0	. . .	−9.0	−13.0	−11.0	−9.0	−4.0
Dividends and distributed branch profits	3 332	. .	−8.8	−6.0	. . .	−5.0	−7.0	−7.0	−5.0	. . .
Reinvested earnings and undistributed branch profits	3 333	. .	. . .	. . .	. . .	. . .	. . .	. . .	. . .	. . .
Income on debt (interest)	3 334	. .	. . .	. . .	. . .	−4.0	−6.0	−4.0	−4.0	−4.0
Portfolio investment income	3 339	. .	. . .	. . .	. . .	. . .	−1.0	−1.0	−2.0	. . .
Income on equity	3 340	. .	. . .	. . .	. . .	. . .	. . .	. . .	. . .	. . .
Income on bonds and notes	3 350	. .	. . .	. . .	. . .	. . .	−1.0	−1.0	−2.0	. . .
Income on money market instruments and financial derivatives	3 360	. .	. . .	. . .	. . .	. . .	. . .	. . .	. . .	. . .
Other investment income	3 370	. .	−211.9	−254.7	−278.0	−273.0	−265.0	−239.0	−240.0	−260.0
D. CURRENT TRANSFERS	4 379	. .	−10.9	−21.1	−2.0	−9.0	−3.0	−3.0	−8.0	−5.0
Credit	2 379	. .	**9.0**	**10.5**	**26.0**	**13.0**	**19.0**	**18.0**	**12.0**	**15.0**
General government	2 380	. .	. . .	. . .	. . .	. . .	. . .	. . .	. . .	. . .
Other sectors	2 390	. .	9.0	10.5	26.0	13.0	19.0	18.0	12.0	15.0
Workers' remittances	2 391	. .	. . .	. . .	. . .	. . .	. . .	. . .	. . .	. . .
Other current transfers	2 392	. .	9.0	10.5	26.0	13.0	19.0	18.0	12.0	15.0
Debit	3 379	. .	**−19.9**	**−31.6**	**−28.0**	**−22.0**	**−22.0**	**−21.0**	**−20.0**	**−20.0**
General government	3 380	. .	−1.9	−3.9	−6.0	−8.0	−7.0	−8.0	−7.0	−10.0
Other sectors	3 390	. .	−18.0	−27.7	−22.0	−14.0	−15.0	−13.0	−13.0	−10.0
Workers' remittances	3 391	. .	. . .	. . .	. . .	. . .	. . .	. . .	. . .	. . .
Other current transfers	3 392	. .	−18.0	−27.7	−22.0	−14.0	−15.0	−13.0	−13.0	−10.0
CAPITAL AND FINANCIAL ACCOUNT	4 996	. .	**235.3**	**88.5**	**166.1**	**294.0**	**207.6**	**36.9**	**−119.8**	**31.0**
CAPITAL ACCOUNT	4 994	. .	**9.7**	**18.1**	**3.0**	**4.0**	**−1.0**	**2.0**	**−4.0**	**−1.0**
Total credit	2 994	. .	*18.4*	*25.9*	*17.0*	*15.0*	*11.0*	*12.0*	*6.0*	*13.0*
Total debit	3 994	. .	*−8.7*	*−7.8*	*−14.0*	*−11.0*	*−12.0*	*−10.0*	*−10.0*	*−14.0*
Capital transfers, credit	2 400	. .	**18.4**	**25.9**	**17.0**	**15.0**	**11.0**	**12.0**	**6.0**	**13.0**
General government	2 401	. .	. . .	. . .	. . .	. . .	. . .	. . .	. . .	. . .
Debt forgiveness	2 402	. .	. . .	. . .	. . .	. . .	. . .	. . .	. . .	. . .
Other capital transfers	2 410	. .	. . .	. . .	. . .	. . .	. . .	. . .	. . .	. . .
Other sectors	2 430	. .	18.4	25.9	17.0	15.0	11.0	12.0	6.0	13.0
Migrants' transfers	2 431	. .	18.4	25.9	17.0	15.0	11.0	12.0	6.0	13.0
Debt forgiveness	2 432	. .	. . .	. . .	. . .	. . .	. . .	. . .	. . .	. . .
Other capital transfers	2 440	. .	. . .	. . .	. . .	. . .	. . .	. . .	. . .	. . .
Capital transfers, debit	3 400	. .	**−8.7**	**−7.8**	**−14.0**	**−11.0**	**−12.0**	**−10.0**	**−10.0**	**−14.0**
General government	3 401	. .	. . .	. . .	. . .	. . .	. . .	. . .	. . .	. . .
Debt forgiveness	3 402	. .	. . .	. . .	. . .	. . .	. . .	. . .	. . .	. . .
Other capital transfers	3 410	. .	. . .	. . .	. . .	. . .	. . .	. . .	. . .	. . .
Other sectors	3 430	. .	−8.7	−7.8	−14.0	−11.0	−12.0	−10.0	−10.0	−14.0
Migrants' transfers	3 431	. .	−8.7	−7.8	−14.0	−11.0	−12.0	−10.0	−10.0	−14.0
Debt forgiveness	3 432	. .	. . .	. . .	. . .	. . .	. . .	. . .	. . .	. . .
Other capital transfers	3 440	. .	. . .	. . .	. . .	. . .	. . .	. . .	. . .	. . .
Nonproduced nonfinancial assets, credit	2 480	. .	**. . .**	**. . .**	**. . .**	**. . .**	**. . .**	**. . .**	**. . .**	**. . .**
Nonproduced nonfinancial assets, debit	3 480	. .	**. . .**	**. . .**	**. . .**	**. . .**	**. . .**	**. . .**	**. . .**	**. . .**

Table 2 (Continued). STANDARD PRESENTATION, 1988–95
(Millions of U.S. dollars)

	Code	1988	1989	1990	1991	1992	1993	1994	1995
FINANCIAL ACCOUNT	4 995 . .	**225.6**	**70.4**	**163.1**	**290.0**	**208.6**	**34.9**	**–115.8**	**32.0**
A. DIRECT INVESTMENT	4 500 . .	–15.9	–35.6	–3.0	28.0	8.0	5.0	–4.0	–2.0
Direct investment abroad	4 505 . .	**–1.1**	**–8.2**	**–6.0**	**–5.0**	**–6.0**	**–3.0**	**–3.0**	**–6.0**
Equity capital	4 510 . .	–.5	–6.4	–6.0	–5.0	–6.0	–3.0	–3.0	–6.0
Claims on affiliated enterprises	4 515 . .	. . .	. . .	. . .	. . .	. . .	. . .	. . .	. . .
Liabilities to affiliated enterprises	4 520 . .	. . .	. . .	. . .	. . .	. . .	. . .	. . .	. . .
Reinvested earnings	4 525 . .	. . .	. . .	. . .	. . .	. . .	. . .	. . .	. . .
Other capital	4 530 . .	–.6	–1.8	. . .	. . .	. . .	. . .	. . .	. . .
Claims on affiliated enterprises	4 535 . .	. . .	. . .	. . .	. . .	. . .	. . .	. . .	. . .
Liabilities to affiliated enterprises	4 540 . .	. . .	. . .	. . .	. . .	. . .	. . .	. . .	. . .
Direct investment in Iceland	4 555 . .	**–14.8**	**–27.4**	**3.0**	**33.0**	**14.0**	**8.0**	**–1.0**	**4.0**
Equity capital	4 560 . .	3.8	4.6	3.0	33.0	14.0	8.0	–1.0	4.0
Claims on direct investors	4 565 . .	. . .	. . .	. . .	. . .	. . .	. . .	. . .	. . .
Liabilities to direct investors	4 570 . .	. . .	. . .	. . .	. . .	. . .	. . .	. . .	. . .
Reinvested earnings	4 575 . .	. . .	. . .	. . .	. . .	. . .	. . .	. . .	. . .
Other capital	4 580 . .	–18.6	–32.0	. . .	. . .	. . .	. . .	. . .	. . .
Claims on direct investors	4 585 . .	. . .	. . .	. . .	. . .	. . .	. . .	. . .	. . .
Liabilities to direct investors	4 590 . .	. . .	. . .	. . .	. . .	. . .	. . .	. . .	. . .
B. PORTFOLIO INVESTMENT	4 600 . .	. . .	.6	. . .	22.0	–15.0	–40.0	–105.0	–52.0
Assets	4 602 . .	**. . .**	**.5**	**. . .**	**–4.0**	**–4.0**	**–30.0**	**–109.0**	**–43.0**
Equity securities	4 610 . .	. . .	. . .	. . .	–3.0	–4.0	–4.0	–23.0	–38.0
Monetary authorities	4 611 . .	. . .	. . .	. . .	. . .	. . .	. . .	. . .	. . .
General government	4 612 . .	. . .	. . .	. . .	. . .	. . .	. . .	. . .	. . .
Banks	4 613 . .	. . .	. . .	. . .	. . .	. . .	. . .	. . .	. . .
Other sectors	4 614 . .	. . .	. . .	. . .	. . .	. . .	. . .	. . .	. . .
Debt securities	4 619 . .	. . .	.5	. . .	–1.0	. . .	–26.0	–86.0	–5.0
Bonds and notes	4 620 . .	. . .	.5	. . .	–1.0	. . .	–26.0	–86.0	–5.0
Monetary authorities	4 621 . .	. . .	. . .	. . .	. . .	. . .	. . .	. . .	. . .
General government	4 622 . .	. . .	. . .	. . .	. . .	. . .	. . .	. . .	. . .
Banks	4 623 . .	. . .	. . .	. . .	. . .	. . .	. . .	. . .	. . .
Other sectors	4 624 . .	. . .	. . .	. . .	–1.0	. . .	–26.0	–86.0	–5.0
Money market instruments	4 630 . .	. . .	. . .	. . .	. . .	. . .	. . .	. . .	. . .
Monetary authorities	4 631 . .	. . .	. . .	. . .	. . .	. . .	. . .	. . .	. . .
General government	4 632 . .	. . .	. . .	. . .	. . .	. . .	. . .	. . .	. . .
Banks	4 633 . .	. . .	. . .	. . .	. . .	. . .	. . .	. . .	. . .
Other sectors	4 634 . .	. . .	. . .	. . .	. . .	. . .	. . .	. . .	. . .
Financial derivatives	4 640 . .	. . .	. . .	. . .	. . .	. . .	. . .	. . .	. . .
Monetary authorities	4 641 . .	. . .	. . .	. . .	. . .	. . .	. . .	. . .	. . .
General government	4 642 . .	. . .	. . .	. . .	. . .	. . .	. . .	. . .	. . .
Banks	4 643 . .	. . .	. . .	. . .	. . .	. . .	. . .	. . .	. . .
Other sectors	4 644 . .	. . .	. . .	. . .	. . .	. . .	. . .	. . .	. . .
Liabilities	4 652 . .	**. . .**	**.1**	**. . .**	**26.0**	**–11.0**	**–10.0**	**4.0**	**–9.0**
Equity securities	4 660 . .	. . .	. . .	. . .	. . .	. . .	. . .	. . .	. . .
Banks	4 663 . .	. . .	. . .	. . .	. . .	. . .	. . .	. . .	. . .
Other sectors	4 664 . .	. . .	. . .	. . .	. . .	. . .	. . .	. . .	. . .
Debt securities	4 669 . .	. . .	.1	. . .	26.0	–11.0	–10.0	4.0	–9.0
Bonds and notes	4 670 . .	. . .	.1	. . .	26.0	–11.0	–10.0	4.0	–9.0
Monetary authorities	4 671 . .	. . .	. . .	. . .	. . .	. . .	. . .	. . .	. . .
General government	4 672 . .	. . .	. . .	. . .	26.0	–11.0	–10.0	4.0	–9.0
Banks	4 673 . .	. . .	. . .	. . .	. . .	. . .	. . .	. . .	. . .
Other sectors	4 674 . .	. . .	.1	. . .	. . .	. . .	. . .	. . .	. . .
Money market instruments	4 680 . .	. . .	. . .	. . .	. . .	. . .	. . .	. . .	. . .
Monetary authorities	4 681 . .	. . .	. . .	. . .	. . .	. . .	. . .	. . .	. . .
General government	4 682 . .	. . .	. . .	. . .	. . .	. . .	. . .	. . .	. . .
Banks	4 683 . .	. . .	. . .	. . .	. . .	. . .	. . .	. . .	. . .
Other sectors	4 684 . .	. . .	. . .	. . .	. . .	. . .	. . .	. . .	. . .
Financial derivatives	4 690 . .	. . .	. . .	. . .	. . .	. . .	. . .	. . .	. . .
Monetary authorities	4 691 . .	. . .	. . .	. . .	. . .	. . .	. . .	. . .	. . .
General government	4 692 . .	. . .	. . .	. . .	. . .	. . .	. . .	. . .	. . .
Banks	4 693 . .	. . .	. . .	. . .	. . .	. . .	. . .	. . .	. . .
Other sectors	4 694 . .	. . .	. . .	. . .	. . .	. . .	. . .	. . .	. . .

Table 2 (Concluded). STANDARD PRESENTATION, 1988–95
(Millions of U.S. dollars)

	Code	1988	1989	1990	1991	1992	1993	1994	1995
C. OTHER INVESTMENT	4 700	242.7	160.0	240.0	249.0	294.0	10.0	−157.0	90.0
Assets	4 703	**−65.3**	**11.8**	**−37.0**	**−1.0**	**52.0**	**−22.0**	**−66.0**	**25.0**
Trade credits	4 706	−22.2	19.4	−9.0	26.0	8.0	4.0	4.0	−7.0
General government: long-term	4 708	...	...	...	...	...	...	...	...
General government: short-term	4 709	...	...	...	...	...	...	...	...
Other sectors: long-term	4 711	...	...	...	...	...	...	...	...
Other sectors: short-term	4 712	−22.2	19.4	...	...	...	...	...	...
Loans	4 714	...	...	...	...	...	...	...	...
Monetary authorities: long-term	4 717	...	...	...	...	...	...	...	...
Monetary authorities: short-term	4 718	...	...	...	...	...	...	...	...
General government: long-term	4 720	...	...	...	...	...	...	...	...
General government: short-term	4 721	...	...	...	...	...	...	...	...
Banks: long-term	4 723	...	...	...	...	...	...	...	...
Banks: short-term	4 724	...	...	...	...	...	...	...	...
Other sectors: long-term	4 726	...	...	...	...	...	...	...	...
Other sectors: short-term	4 727	...	...	...	...	...	...	...	...
Currency and deposits	4 730	−43.1	−7.6	−24.0	−28.0	36.0	−28.0	−18.0	51.0
Monetary authorities	4 731	...	...	...	...	...	...	...	...
General government	4 732	...	...	...	...	...	...	...	...
Banks	4 733	−6.9	3.0	−26.0	−3.0	13.0	−28.0	−5.0	64.0
Other sectors	4 734	−36.2	−10.6	2.0	−25.0	23.0	...	−13.0	−13.0
Other assets	4 736	...	...	−4.0	1.0	8.0	2.0	−52.0	−19.0
Monetary authorities: long-term	4 738	...	...	...	...	...	...	...	...
Monetary authorities: short-term	4 739	...	...	...	...	...	...	...	...
General government: long-term	4 741	...	...	...	...	...	...	...	...
General government: short-term	4 742	...	...	...	...	...	...	...	...
Banks: long-term	4 744	...	...	...	...	...	...	...	...
Banks: short-term	4 745	...	...	...	...	...	...	...	...
Other sectors: long-term	4 747	...	...	...	...	...	...	...	...
Other sectors: short-term	4 748	...	...	...	...	...	...	...	...
Liabilities	4 753	**308.0**	**148.2**	**277.0**	**250.0**	**242.0**	**32.0**	**−91.0**	**65.0**
Trade credits	4 756	−19.1	2.7	19.0	−8.0	−15.0	−23.0	2.0	2.0
General government: long-term	4 758	...	...	...	...	...	...	...	...
General government: short-term	4 759	...	...	...	...	...	...	...	...
Other sectors: long-term	4 761	...	...	...	...	...	...	...	...
Other sectors: short-term	4 762	−19.1	2.7	...	...	...	...	...	...
Loans	4 764	303.9	158.0	259.0	257.0	243.0	58.0	−134.0	38.0
Use of Fund credit and loans from the Fund	4 766	...	...	...	...	...	...	...	...
Monetary authorities: other long-term	4 767	...	...	−1.0	−1.0	−1.0	−1.0	...	...
Monetary authorities: short-term	4 768	...	...	...	3.0	−5.0	23.0	50.0	19.0
General government: long-term	4 770	142.9	191.0	46.0	104.0	181.0	78.0	157.0	226.0
General government: short-term	4 771	1.4	.7	...	...	...	...	...	...
Banks: long-term	4 773	84.7	73.9	−15.0	−5.0	−21.0	−20.0	−77.0	−128.0
Banks: short-term	4 774	...	...	−6.0	15.0	12.0	−49.0	−89.0	44.0
Other sectors: long-term	4 776	−3.9	30.8	250.0	142.0	71.0	47.0	−167.0	−120.0
Other sectors: short-term	4 777	78.8	−138.4	−15.0	−1.0	6.0	−20.0	−8.0	−3.0
Currency and deposits	4 780	−10.5	−11.1	...	...	...	...	−11.0	2.0
Monetary authorities	4 781	...	...	...	...	...	...	−11.0	2.0
General government	4 782	...	...	...	...	...	...	...	...
Banks	4 783	−10.5	−11.1	...	...	...	...	...	...
Other sectors	4 784	...	...	...	...	...	...	...	...
Other liabilities	4 786	33.7	−1.4	−1.0	1.0	14.0	−3.0	52.0	23.0
Monetary authorities: long-term	4 788	...	...	...	...	...	...	...	...
Monetary authorities: short-term	4 789	20.2	−24.7	...	...	...	...	...	...
General government: long-term	4 791	...	...	...	...	...	...	...	...
General government: short-term	4 792	...	...	...	...	...	...	...	...
Banks: long-term	4 794	...	...	...	...	...	...	...	...
Banks: short-term	4 795	...	...	...	...	...	...	...	...
Other sectors: long-term	4 797	...	...	...	...	...	...	...	...
Other sectors: short-term	4 798	13.5	23.3	...	...	...	...	...	...
D. RESERVE ASSETS	4 800	−1.2	−54.6	−73.9	−9.0	−78.4	59.9	150.2	−4.0
Monetary gold	4 810	...	...	...	...	...	...	...	...
Special drawing rights	4 820	1.2	1.2	−.3	.3	...	...	−.1	.1
Reserve position in the Fund	4 830	...	...	...	...	−8.9	...	...	...
Foreign exchange	4 840	−2.4	−55.8	−73.6	−9.3	−69.5	59.9	150.3	−4.1
Other claims	4 880	...	...	...	...	...	...	...	...
NET ERRORS AND OMISSIONS	4 998	**−4.1**	**13.5**	**−31.1**	**24.0**	**6.4**	**−31.9**	**8.8**	**−82.0**

Part 3 of the *Yearbook* contains descriptions of the methodologies, compilation practices, and sources used to compile these data.

Table 1. ANALYTIC PRESENTATION, 1988–95
(Millions of U.S. dollars)

	Code	1988	1989	1990	1991	1992	1993	1994	1995
A. Current Account [1]	4 993 Y.	**–6,986**	**–6,735**	**–6,836**	**–4,028**	**–4,105**	**. . .**	**. . .**	**. . .**
Goods: exports f.o.b	2 100 . .	13,510	16,144	18,286	18,095	20,019	. . .	. . .	. . .
Goods: imports f.o.b	3 100 . .	–20,091	–22,254	–23,437	–21,087	–22,150	. . .	. . .	. . .
Balance on Goods	4 100 . .	*–6,581*	*–6,110*	*–5,151*	*–2,992*	*–2,130*	. . .	. . .	. . .
Services: credit	2 200 . .	3,791	4,140	4,625	4,925	4,926	. . .	. . .	. . .
Services: debit	3 200 . .	–5,164	–5,783	–5,889	–5,681	–6,323	. . .	. . .	. . .
Balance on Goods and Services	4 991 . .	*–7,954*	*–7,754*	*–6,415*	*–3,748*	*–3,527*	. . .	. . .	. . .
Income: credit	2 300 . .	427	446	436	232	377	. . .	. . .	. . .
Income: debit	3 300 . .	–2,211	–2,498	–3,693	–4,235	–4,289	. . .	. . .	. . .
Balance on Goods, Services, and Income	4 992 . .	*–9,738*	*–9,806*	*–9,672*	*–7,751*	*–7,439*	. . .	. . .	. . .
Current transfers: credit	2 379 Y.	2,768	3,093	2,853	3,736	3,353	. . .	. . .	. . .
Current transfers: debit	3 379 . .	–16	–23	–17	–13	–18	. . .	. . .	. . .
B. Capital Account [1]	4 994 Y.	**. . .**	**. . .**	**. . .**	**. . .**	**. . .**	**. . .**	**. . .**	**. . .**
Capital account: credit	2 994 Y.	. . .	. . .	. . .	. . .	. . .	. . .	. . .	. . .
Capital account: debit	3 994 . .	. . .	. . .	. . .	. . .	. . .	. . .	. . .	. . .
Total, Groups A Plus B	4 010 . .	*–6,986*	*–6,735*	*–6,836*	*–4,028*	*–4,105*	. . .	. . .	. . .
C. Financial Account [1]	4 995 X.	**7,175**	**7,212**	**5,528**	**3,485**	**4,131**	**. . .**	**. . .**	**. . .**
Direct investment abroad	4 505 . .	. . .	. . .	. . .	. . .	. . .	. . .	. . .	. . .
Direct investment in India	4 555 Y.	. . .	. . .	. . .	. . .	. . .	. . .	. . .	. . .
Portfolio investment assets	4 602 . .	. . .	. . .	. . .	. . .	. . .	. . .	. . .	. . .
Equity securities	4 610 . .	. . .	. . .	. . .	. . .	. . .	. . .	. . .	. . .
Debt securities	4 619 . .	. . .	. . .	. . .	. . .	. . .	. . .	. . .	. . .
Portfolio investment liabilities	4 652 Y.	. . .	. . .	. . .	. . .	. . .	. . .	. . .	. . .
Equity securities	4 660 Y.	. . .	. . .	. . .	. . .	. . .	. . .	. . .	. . .
Debt securities	4 669 Y.	. . .	. . .	. . .	. . .	. . .	. . .	. . .	. . .
Other investment assets	4 703 . .	276	114	–611	–781	2,147	. . .	. . .	. . .
Monetary authorities	4 703 .A	. . .	. . .	. . .	. . .	. . .	. . .	. . .	. . .
General government	4 703 .B	43	–186	–868	218	431	. . .	. . .	. . .
Banks	4 703 .C	240	310	333	–1,003	1,732	. . .	. . .	. . .
Other sectors	4 703 .D	–6	–10	–76	3	–16	. . .	. . .	. . .
Other investment liabilities	4 753 X.	6,899	7,099	6,139	4,267	1,984	. . .	. . .	. . .
Monetary authorities	4 753 XA	1,296	1,344	1,867	–758	–2,131	. . .	. . .	. . .
General government	4 753 YB	3,877	3,605	2,999	2,281	125	. . .	. . .	. . .
Banks	4 753 YC	–297	–281	–450	–218	–459	. . .	. . .	. . .
Other sectors	4 753 YD	2,023	2,431	1,723	2,962	4,450	. . .	. . .	. . .
Total, Groups A Through C	4 020 . .	*190*	*477*	*–1,308*	*–543*	*26*	. . .	. . .	. . .
D. Net Errors and Omissions	4 998 . .	**–205**	**–240**	**–633**	**343**	**1,102**	**. . .**	**. . .**	**. . .**
Total, Groups A Through D	4 030 . .	*–16*	*237*	*–1,941*	*–200*	*1,128*	. . .	. . .	. . .
E. Reserves and Related Items	4 040 . .	**16**	**–237**	**1,941**	**200**	**–1,128**	**. . .**	**. . .**	**. . .**
Reserve assets	4 800 . .	1,184	836	2,798	–2,075	–2,309	. . .	. . .	. . .
Use of Fund credit and loans	4 766 . .	–1,197	–1,086	–858	2,275	1,181	. . .	. . .	. . .
Liabilities constituting foreign authorities' reserves	4 900 . .	. . .	. . .	. . .	. . .	. . .	. . .	. . .	. . .
Exceptional financing	4 920 . .	29	13	1	. . .	. . .	. . .	. . .	. . .
Conversion rates: Indian rupees per U.S. dollar	0 101 . .	**13.917**	**16.226**	**17.504**	**22.742**	**25.918**	**30.493**	**31.374**	**32.427**

[1] Excludes components that have been classified in the categories of Group E.

Table 2. STANDARD PRESENTATION, 1988–95
(Millions of U.S. dollars)

	Code	1988	1989	1990	1991	1992	1993	1994	1995
CURRENT ACCOUNT	4 993 . .	**–6,956**	**–6,723**	**–6,835**	**–4,028**	**–4,105**	...	...	...
A. GOODS	4 100 . .	–6,581	–6,110	–5,151	–2,992	–2,130	...	...	...
Credit	2 100 . .	**13,510**	**16,144**	**18,286**	**18,095**	**20,019**	...	...	...
General merchandise: exports f.o.b.	2 110 . .	13,510	16,144	18,286	18,095	20,019	...	...	...
Goods for processing: exports f.o.b.	2 150 . .	...	...	...	...	...	...	...	...
Repairs on goods	2 160 . .	...	...	...	...	...	...	...	...
Goods procured in ports by carriers	2 170 . .	...	...	...	...	...	...	...	...
Nonmonetary gold	2 180 . .	...	...	...	...	...	...	...	...
Debit	3 100 . .	**–20,091**	**–22,254**	**–23,437**	**–21,087**	**–22,150**	...	...	...
General merchandise: imports f.o.b.	3 110 . .	–20,091	–22,254	–23,437	–21,087	–22,150	...	...	...
Goods for processing: imports f.o.b.	3 150 . .	...	...	...	...	...	...	...	...
Repairs on goods	3 160 . .	...	...	...	...	...	...	...	...
Goods procured in ports by carriers	3 170 . .	...	...	...	...	...	...	...	...
Nonmonetary gold	3 180 . .	...	...	...	...	...	...	...	...
B. SERVICES	4 200 . .	–1,373	–1,644	–1,264	–756	–1,397	...	...	...
Total credit	2 200 . .	*3,791*	*4,140*	*4,625*	*4,925*	*4,926*	...	...	...
Total debit	3 200 . .	*–5,164*	*–5,783*	*–5,889*	*–5,681*	*–6,323*	...	...	...
Transportation services, credit	2 205 . .	**864**	**850**	**959**	**975**	**1,035**	...	...	...
Passenger	2 205 BA	...	...	...	...	...	...	...	...
Freight	2 205 BB	*535*	*636*	*714*	*695*	*768*	...	...	...
Other	2 205 BC	*329*	*214*	*246*	*280*	*267*	...	...	...
Sea transport, passenger	2 207 . .	...	...	...	...	...	...	...	...
Sea transport, freight	2 208 . .	...	...	...	...	...	...	...	...
Sea transport, other	2 209 . .	...	...	...	...	...	...	...	...
Air transport, passenger	2 211 . .	...	...	...	...	...	...	...	...
Air transport, freight	2 212 . .	...	...	...	...	...	...	...	...
Air transport, other	2 213 . .	...	...	...	...	...	...	...	...
Other transport, passenger	2 215 . .	...	...	...	...	...	...	...	...
Other transport, freight	2 216 . .	...	...	...	...	...	...	...	...
Other transport, other	2 217 . .	...	...	...	...	...	...	...	...
Transportation services, debit	3 205 . .	**–2,915**	**–3,294**	**–3,301**	**–3,094**	**–3,761**	...	...	...
Passenger	3 205 BA	...	...	...	...	...	...	...	...
Freight	3 205 BB	*–2,050*	*–2,225*	*–2,344*	*–2,109*	*–2,213*	...	...	...
Other	3 205 BC	*–865*	*–1,068*	*–958*	*–985*	*–1,548*	...	...	...
Sea transport, passenger	3 207 . .	...	...	...	...	...	...	...	...
Sea transport, freight	3 208 . .	...	...	...	...	...	...	...	...
Sea transport, other	3 209 . .	...	...	...	...	...	...	...	...
Air transport, passenger	3 211 . .	...	...	...	...	...	...	...	...
Air transport, freight	3 212 . .	...	...	...	...	...	...	...	...
Air transport, other	3 213 . .	...	...	...	...	...	...	...	...
Other transport, passenger	3 215 . .	...	...	...	...	...	...	...	...
Other transport, freight	3 216 . .	...	...	...	...	...	...	...	...
Other transport, other	3 217 . .	...	...	...	...	...	...	...	...
Travel, credit	2 236 . .	**1,407**	**1,449**	**1,558**	**1,842**	**2,295**	...	...	...
Business travel	2 237 . .	...	...	...	...	...	...	...	...
Personal travel	2 240 . .	...	...	...	...	...	...	...	...
Travel, debit	3 236 . .	**–397**	**–416**	**–393**	**–434**	**–470**	...	...	...
Business travel	3 237 . .	...	...	...	...	...	...	...	...
Personal travel	3 240 . .	...	...	...	...	...	...	...	...
Other services, credit	2 200 BA	**1,520**	**1,841**	**2,107**	**2,108**	**1,595**	...	...	...
Communications	2 245 . .	...	...	...	...	...	...	...	...
Construction	2 249 . .	...	...	...	...	...	...	...	...
Insurance	2 253 . .	71	110	123	107	150	...	...	...
Financial	2 260 . .	...	...	...	...	...	...	...	...
Computer and information	2 262 . .	...	...	...	...	...	...	...	...
Royalties and licence fees	2 266 . .	1	1	1	1	1	...	...	...
Other business services	2 268 . .	1,375	1,683	1,967	1,981	1,412	...	...	...
Personal, cultural, and recreational	2 287 . .	...	...	...	...	...	...	...	...
Government, n.i.e.	2 291 . .	72	48	15	19	32	...	...	...
Other services, debit	3 200 BA	**–1,852**	**–2,074**	**–2,195**	**–2,153**	**–2,092**	...	...	...
Communications	3 245 . .	...	...	...	...	...	...	...	...
Construction	3 249 . .	...	...	...	...	...	...	...	...
Insurance	3 253 . .	–223	–247	–260	–234	–244	...	...	...
Financial	3 260 . .	...	...	...	...	...	...	...	...
Computer and information	3 262 . .	...	...	...	...	...	...	...	...
Royalties and licence fees	3 266 . .	–108	–127	–72	–50	–69	...	...	...
Other business services	3 268 . .	–1,367	–1,564	–1,715	–1,722	–1,668	...	...	...
Personal, cultural, and recreational	3 287 . .	...	...	...	...	...	...	...	...
Government, n.i.e.	3 291 . .	–154	–135	–147	–148	–112	...	...	...

Table 2 (Continued). STANDARD PRESENTATION, 1988–95
(Millions of U.S. dollars)

	Code	1988	1989	1990	1991	1992	1993	1994	1995
C. INCOME	4 300 . .	–1,784	–2,052	–3,257	–4,003	–3,912	...	...	...
Total credit	2 300 . .	*427*	*446*	*436*	*232*	*377*	...	...	...
Total debit	3 300 . .	*–2,211*	*–2,498*	*–3,693*	*–4,235*	*–4,289*	...	...	...
Compensation of employees, credit	2 310 . .	**7**	**30**	**32**	**14**	**6**	...	...	...
Compensation of employees, debit	3 310 . .	**–93**	**–99**	**–106**	**–52**	**–68**	...	...	...
Investment income, credit	2 320 . .	**420**	**416**	**405**	**217**	**371**	...	...	...
Direct investment income	2 330 . .	...	...	...	...	...	...	...	...
Dividends and distributed branch profits	2 332 . .	...	...	...	...	...	...	...	...
Reinvested earnings and undistributed branch profits	2 333 . .	...	...	...	...	...	...	...	...
Income on debt (interest)	2 334 . .	...	...	...	...	...	...	...	...
Portfolio investment income	2 339 . .	...	...	...	...	...	...	...	...
Income on equity	2 340 . .	...	...	...	...	...	...	...	...
Income on bonds and notes	2 350 . .	...	...	...	...	...	...	...	...
Income on money market instruments and financial derivatives	2 360 . .	...	...	...	...	...	...	...	...
Other investment income	2 370 . .	420	416	405	217	371	...	...	...
Investment income, debit	3 320 . .	**–2,118**	**–2,399**	**–3,588**	**–4,183**	**–4,221**	...	...	...
Direct investment income	3 330 . .	...	...	...	...	...	...	...	...
Dividends and distributed branch profits	3 332 . .	...	...	...	...	...	...	...	...
Reinvested earnings and undistributed branch profits	3 333 . .	...	...	...	...	...	...	...	...
Income on debt (interest)	3 334 . .	...	...	...	...	...	...	...	...
Portfolio investment income	3 339 . .	...	...	...	...	...	...	...	...
Income on equity	3 340 . .	...	...	...	...	...	...	...	...
Income on bonds and notes	3 350 . .	...	...	...	...	...	...	...	...
Income on money market instruments and financial derivatives	3 360 . .	...	...	...	...	...	...	...	...
Other investment income	3 370 . .	–2,118	–2,399	–3,588	–4,183	–4,221	...	...	...
D. CURRENT TRANSFERS	4 379 . .	2,781	3,083	2,837	3,723	3,335	...	...	...
Credit	2 379 . .	**2,797**	**3,106**	**2,854**	**3,736**	**3,353**	...	...	...
General government	2 380 . .	489	522	502	461	461	...	...	...
Other sectors	2 390 . .	2,309	2,584	2,352	3,275	2,891	...	...	...
Workers' remittances	2 391 . .	2,309	2,584	2,352	3,275	2,891	...	...	...
Other current transfers	2 392 . .	...	...	...	...	...	...	...	...
Debit	3 379 . .	**–16**	**–23**	**–17**	**–13**	**–18**	...	...	...
General government	3 380 . .	–2	–6	–2	–1	–1	...	...	...
Other sectors	3 390 . .	–14	–17	–15	–12	–17	...	...	...
Workers' remittances	3 391 . .	...	...	...	...	...	...	...	...
Other current transfers	3 392 . .	–14	–17	–15	–12	–17	...	...	...
CAPITAL AND FINANCIAL ACCOUNT	4 996 . .	**7,162**	**6,962**	**7,468**	**3,685**	**3,003**	...	...	...
CAPITAL ACCOUNT	4 994 . .	...	...	...	...	...	...	...	...
Total credit	2 994 . .	...	...	...	...	...	...	...	...
Total debit	3 994 . .	...	...	...	...	...	...	...	...
Capital transfers, credit	2 400 . .	...	...	...	...	...	...	...	...
General government	2 401 . .	...	...	...	...	...	...	...	...
Debt forgiveness	2 402 . .	...	...	...	...	...	...	...	...
Other capital transfers	2 410 . .	...	...	...	...	...	...	...	...
Other sectors	2 430 . .	...	...	...	...	...	...	...	...
Migrants' transfers	2 431 . .	...	...	...	...	...	...	...	...
Debt forgiveness	2 432 . .	...	...	...	...	...	...	...	...
Other capital transfers	2 440 . .	...	...	...	...	...	...	...	...
Capital transfers, debit	3 400 . .	...	...	...	...	...	...	...	...
General government	3 401 . .	...	...	...	...	...	...	...	...
Debt forgiveness	3 402 . .	...	...	...	...	...	...	...	...
Other capital transfers	3 410 . .	...	...	...	...	...	...	...	...
Other sectors	3 430 . .	...	...	...	...	...	...	...	...
Migrants' transfers	3 431 . .	...	...	...	...	...	...	...	...
Debt forgiveness	3 432 . .	...	...	...	...	...	...	...	...
Other capital transfers	3 440 . .	...	...	...	...	...	...	...	...
Nonproduced nonfinancial assets, credit	2 480 . .	...	...	...	...	...	...	...	...
Nonproduced nonfinancial assets, debit	3 480 . .	...	...	...	...	...	...	...	...

Table 2 (Continued). STANDARD PRESENTATION, 1988–95
(Millions of U.S. dollars)

	Code		1988	1989	1990	1991	1992	1993	1994	1995
FINANCIAL ACCOUNT	4 995	. .	**7,162**	**6,962**	**7,468**	**3,685**	**3,003**	**. . .**	**. . .**	**. . .**
A. DIRECT INVESTMENT	4 500	. .	. . .	. . .	. . .	. . .	. . .	. . .	. . .	. . .
Direct investment abroad	4 505	. .	**. . .**	**. . .**	**. . .**	**. . .**	**. . .**	**. . .**	**. . .**	**. . .**
Equity capital	4 510	. .	. . .	. . .	. . .	. . .	. . .	. . .	. . .	. . .
Claims on affiliated enterprises	4 515	. .	. . .	. . .	. . .	. . .	. . .	. . .	. . .	. . .
Liabilities to affiliated enterprises	4 520	. .	. . .	. . .	. . .	. . .	. . .	. . .	. . .	. . .
Reinvested earnings	4 525	. .	. . .	. . .	. . .	. . .	. . .	. . .	. . .	. . .
Other capital	4 530	. .	. . .	. . .	. . .	. . .	. . .	. . .	. . .	. . .
Claims on affiliated enterprises	4 535	. .	. . .	. . .	. . .	. . .	. . .	. . .	. . .	. . .
Liabilities to affiliated enterprises	4 540	. .	. . .	. . .	. . .	. . .	. . .	. . .	. . .	. . .
Direct investment in India	4 555	. .	**. . .**	**. . .**	**. . .**	**. . .**	**. . .**	**. . .**	**. . .**	**. . .**
Equity capital	4 560	. .	. . .	. . .	. . .	. . .	. . .	. . .	. . .	. . .
Claims on direct investors	4 565	. .	. . .	. . .	. . .	. . .	. . .	. . .	. . .	. . .
Liabilities to direct investors	4 570	. .	. . .	. . .	. . .	. . .	. . .	. . .	. . .	. . .
Reinvested earnings	4 575	. .	. . .	. . .	. . .	. . .	. . .	. . .	. . .	. . .
Other capital	4 580	. .	. . .	. . .	. . .	. . .	. . .	. . .	. . .	. . .
Claims on direct investors	4 585	. .	. . .	. . .	. . .	. . .	. . .	. . .	. . .	. . .
Liabilities to direct investors	4 590	. .	. . .	. . .	. . .	. . .	. . .	. . .	. . .	. . .
B. PORTFOLIO INVESTMENT	4 600	. .	. . .	. . .	. . .	. . .	. . .	. . .	. . .	. . .
Assets	4 602	. .	**. . .**	**. . .**	**. . .**	**. . .**	**. . .**	**. . .**	**. . .**	**. . .**
Equity securities	4 610	. .	. . .	. . .	. . .	. . .	. . .	. . .	. . .	. . .
Monetary authorities	4 611	. .	. . .	. . .	. . .	. . .	. . .	. . .	. . .	. . .
General government	4 612	. .	. . .	. . .	. . .	. . .	. . .	. . .	. . .	. . .
Banks	4 613	. .	. . .	. . .	. . .	. . .	. . .	. . .	. . .	. . .
Other sectors	4 614	. .	. . .	. . .	. . .	. . .	. . .	. . .	. . .	. . .
Debt securities	4 619	. .	. . .	. . .	. . .	. . .	. . .	. . .	. . .	. . .
Bonds and notes	4 620	. .	. . .	. . .	. . .	. . .	. . .	. . .	. . .	. . .
Monetary authorities	4 621	. .	. . .	. . .	. . .	. . .	. . .	. . .	. . .	. . .
General government	4 622	. .	. . .	. . .	. . .	. . .	. . .	. . .	. . .	. . .
Banks	4 623	. .	. . .	. . .	. . .	. . .	. . .	. . .	. . .	. . .
Other sectors	4 624	. .	. . .	. . .	. . .	. . .	. . .	. . .	. . .	. . .
Money market instruments	4 630	. .	. . .	. . .	. . .	. . .	. . .	. . .	. . .	. . .
Monetary authorities	4 631	. .	. . .	. . .	. . .	. . .	. . .	. . .	. . .	. . .
General government	4 632	. .	. . .	. . .	. . .	. . .	. . .	. . .	. . .	. . .
Banks	4 633	. .	. . .	. . .	. . .	. . .	. . .	. . .	. . .	. . .
Other sectors	4 634	. .	. . .	. . .	. . .	. . .	. . .	. . .	. . .	. . .
Financial derivatives	4 640	. .	. . .	. . .	. . .	. . .	. . .	. . .	. . .	. . .
Monetary authorities	4 641	. .	. . .	. . .	. . .	. . .	. . .	. . .	. . .	. . .
General government	4 642	. .	. . .	. . .	. . .	. . .	. . .	. . .	. . .	. . .
Banks	4 643	. .	. . .	. . .	. . .	. . .	. . .	. . .	. . .	. . .
Other sectors	4 644	. .	. . .	. . .	. . .	. . .	. . .	. . .	. . .	. . .
Liabilities	4 652	. .	**. . .**	**. . .**	**. . .**	**. . .**	**. . .**	**. . .**	**. . .**	**. . .**
Equity securities	4 660	. .	. . .	. . .	. . .	. . .	. . .	. . .	. . .	. . .
Banks	4 663	. .	. . .	. . .	. . .	. . .	. . .	. . .	. . .	. . .
Other sectors	4 664	. .	. . .	. . .	. . .	. . .	. . .	. . .	. . .	. . .
Debt securities	4 669	. .	. . .	. . .	. . .	. . .	. . .	. . .	. . .	. . .
Bonds and notes	4 670	. .	. . .	. . .	. . .	. . .	. . .	. . .	. . .	. . .
Monetary authorities	4 671	. .	. . .	. . .	. . .	. . .	. . .	. . .	. . .	. . .
General government	4 672	. .	. . .	. . .	. . .	. . .	. . .	. . .	. . .	. . .
Banks	4 673	. .	. . .	. . .	. . .	. . .	. . .	. . .	. . .	. . .
Other sectors	4 674	. .	. . .	. . .	. . .	. . .	. . .	. . .	. . .	. . .
Money market instruments	4 680	. .	. . .	. . .	. . .	. . .	. . .	. . .	. . .	. . .
Monetary authorities	4 681	. .	. . .	. . .	. . .	. . .	. . .	. . .	. . .	. . .
General government	4 682	. .	. . .	. . .	. . .	. . .	. . .	. . .	. . .	. . .
Banks	4 683	. .	. . .	. . .	. . .	. . .	. . .	. . .	. . .	. . .
Other sectors	4 684	. .	. . .	. . .	. . .	. . .	. . .	. . .	. . .	. . .
Financial derivatives	4 690	. .	. . .	. . .	. . .	. . .	. . .	. . .	. . .	. . .
Monetary authorities	4 691	. .	. . .	. . .	. . .	. . .	. . .	. . .	. . .	. . .
General government	4 692	. .	. . .	. . .	. . .	. . .	. . .	. . .	. . .	. . .
Banks	4 693	. .	. . .	. . .	. . .	. . .	. . .	. . .	. . .	. . .
Other sectors	4 694	. .	. . .	. . .	. . .	. . .	. . .	. . .	. . .	. . .

Table 2 (Concluded). STANDARD PRESENTATION, 1988–95
(Millions of U.S. dollars)

	Code	1988	1989	1990	1991	1992	1993	1994	1995
C. OTHER INVESTMENT	4 700	5,978	6,126	4,670	5,760	5,312	...	...	...
Assets	4 703	**276**	**114**	**–611**	**–781**	**2,147**	...	...	...
Trade credits	4 706	...	...	...	...	...	...	...	...
General government: long-term	4 708	...	...	...	...	...	...	...	...
General government: short-term	4 709	...	...	...	...	...	...	...	...
Other sectors: long-term	4 711	...	...	...	...	...	...	...	...
Other sectors: short-term	4 712	...	...	...	...	...	...	...	...
Loans	4 714	60	–165	–845	27	412	...	...	...
Monetary authorities: long-term	4 717	...	...	...	...	...	...	...	...
Monetary authorities: short-term	4 718	...	...	...	...	...	...	...	...
General government: long-term	4 720	–12	2	4	–1	–1	...	...	...
General government: short-term	4 721	72	–166	–850	28	412	...	...	...
Banks: long-term	4 723	...	...	...	...	...	...	...	...
Banks: short-term	4 724	...	...	...	...	...	...	...	...
Other sectors: long-term	4 726	...	...	...	...	...	...	...	...
Other sectors: short-term	4 727	...	...	...	...	...	...	...	...
Currency and deposits	4 730	241	310	333	–1,002	1,732	...	...	...
Monetary authorities	4 731	...	...	...	...	...	...	...	...
General government	4 732	...	...	...	...	...	...	...	...
Banks	4 733	240	310	333	–1,003	1,732	...	...	...
Other sectors	4 734	...	...	...	...	...	...	...	...
Other assets	4 736	–25	–31	–98	194	3	...	...	...
Monetary authorities: long-term	4 738	...	...	...	...	...	...	...	...
Monetary authorities: short-term	4 739	...	...	...	...	...	...	...	...
General government: long-term	4 741	–18	–22	–22	191	20	...	...	...
General government: short-term	4 742	...	...	...	...	...	...	...	...
Banks: long-term	4 744	...	...	...	...	...	...	...	...
Banks: short-term	4 745	...	...	...	...	...	...	...	...
Other sectors: long-term	4 747	–7	–10	–76	3	–17	...	...	...
Other sectors: short-term	4 748	...	...	...	...	...	...	...	...
Liabilities	4 753	**5,702**	**6,013**	**5,281**	**6,541**	**3,165**	...	...	...
Trade credits	4 756	...	...	...	...	...	...	...	...
General government: long-term	4 758	...	...	...	...	...	...	...	...
General government: short-term	4 759	...	...	...	...	...	...	...	...
Other sectors: long-term	4 761	...	...	...	...	...	...	...	...
Other sectors: short-term	4 762	...	...	...	...	...	...	...	...
Loans	4 764	2,865	3,166	2,501	5,177	4,508	...	...	...
Use of Fund credit and loans from the Fund	4 766	–1,197	–1,086	–858	2,275	1,181	...	...	...
Monetary authorities: other long-term	4 767	...	...	...	...	...	...	...	...
Monetary authorities: short-term	4 768	...	...	...	...	...	...	...	...
General government: long-term	4 770	3,879	3,605	2,999	2,281	125	...	...	...
General government: short-term	4 771	...	...	...	...	...	...	...	...
Banks: long-term	4 773	...	...	...	...	...	...	...	...
Banks: short-term	4 774	...	...	...	...	...	...	...	...
Other sectors: long-term	4 776	183	647	360	621	3,202	...	...	...
Other sectors: short-term	4 777	...	...	...	...	...	...	...	...
Currency and deposits	4 780	–297	–281	–450	–218	–459	...	...	...
Monetary authorities	4 781	...	...	...	...	...	...	...	...
General government	4 782	...	...	...	...	...	...	...	...
Banks	4 783	–297	–281	–450	–218	–459	...	...	...
Other sectors	4 784	...	...	...	...	...	...	...	...
Other liabilities	4 786	3,134	3,127	3,230	1,582	–884	...	...	...
Monetary authorities: long-term	4 788	...	...	...	...	...	...	...	...
Monetary authorities: short-term	4 789	1,296	1,344	1,867	–758	–2,131	...	...	...
General government: long-term	4 791	–2	...	...	...	–1	...	...	...
General government: short-term	4 792	...	...	...	...	...	...	...	...
Banks: long-term	4 794	...	...	...	...	...	...	...	...
Banks: short-term	4 795	...	...	...	...	...	...	...	...
Other sectors: long-term	4 797	1,824	1,802	1,352	1,428	2,150	...	...	...
Other sectors: short-term	4 798	16	–19	11	912	–902	...	...	...
D. RESERVE ASSETS	4 800	1,184	836	2,798	–2,075	–2,309	...	...	...
Monetary gold	4 810	...	...	...	...	...	...	...	...
Special drawing rights	4 820	56	–21	–182	270	45	...	...	...
Reserve position in the Fund	4 830	...	...	670	...	–295	...	...	...
Foreign exchange	4 840	1,249	806	2,111	–2,501	–2,022	...	...	...
Other claims	4 880	–121	52	198	156	–37	...	...	...
NET ERRORS AND OMISSIONS	4 998	**–205**	**–240**	**–633**	**343**	**1,102**	...	...	...

Part 3 of the *Yearbook* contains descriptions of the methodologies, compilation practices, and sources used to compile these data.

Table 1. ANALYTIC PRESENTATION, 1988–95
(Millions of U.S. dollars)

	Code	1988	1989	1990	1991	1992	1993	1994	1995
A. Current Account [1]	4 993 Y.	**–1,397**	**–1,108**	**–2,988**	**–4,260**	**–2,780**	**–2,106**	**–2,792**	**–7,023**
Goods: exports f.o.b	2 100 . .	19,509	22,974	26,807	29,635	33,796	36,607	40,223	45,479
Goods: imports f.o.b	3 100 . .	–13,831	–16,310	–21,455	–24,834	–26,774	–28,376	–32,322	–39,769
Balance on Goods	4 100 . .	*5,678*	*6,664*	*5,352*	*4,801*	*7,022*	*8,231*	*7,901*	*5,710*
Services: credit	2 200 . .	1,369	1,875	2,488	2,822	3,391	3,959	4,797	5,681
Services: debit	3 200 . .	–4,606	–5,439	–6,056	–6,564	–8,100	–9,846	–11,416	–13,475
Balance on Goods and Services	4 991 . .	*2,441*	*3,100*	*1,784*	*1,059*	*2,313*	*2,344*	*1,282*	*–2,084*
Income: credit	2 300 . .	492	562	409	917	818	1,028	1,048	1,345
Income: debit	3 300 . .	–4,584	–5,109	–5,599	–6,498	–6,482	–6,015	–5,741	–7,123
Balance on Goods, Services, and Income	4 992 . .	*–1,651*	*–1,447*	*–3,406*	*–4,522*	*–3,351*	*–2,643*	*–3,411*	*–7,862*
Current transfers: credit	2 379 Y.	254	339	418	262	571	537	619	839
Current transfers: debit	3 379 . .	. . .	. . .	. . .	. . .	. . .	. . .	. . .	. . .
B. Capital Account [1]	4 994 Y.	**. . .**	**. . .**	**. . .**	**. . .**	**. . .**	**. . .**	**. . .**	**. . .**
Capital account: credit	2 994 Y.	. . .	. . .	. . .	. . .	. . .	. . .	. . .	. . .
Capital account: debit	3 994 . .	. . .	. . .	. . .	. . .	. . .	. . .	. . .	. . .
Total, Groups A Plus B	4 010 . .	*–1,397*	*–1,108*	*–2,988*	*–4,260*	*–2,780*	*–2,106*	*–2,792*	*–7,023*
C. Financial Account [1]	4 995 X.	**2,217**	**2,918**	**4,495**	**5,697**	**6,129**	**5,632**	**3,839**	**10,386**
Direct investment abroad	4 505 . .	. . .	. . .	. . .	. . .	. . .	–356	–609	–603
Direct investment in Indonesia	4 555 Y.	576	682	1,093	1,482	1,777	2,004	2,109	4,348
Portfolio investment assets	4 602 . .	. . .	. . .	. . .	. . .	. . .	. . .	. . .	. . .
Equity securities	4 610 . .	. . .	. . .	. . .	. . .	. . .	. . .	. . .	. . .
Debt securities	4 619 . .	. . .	. . .	. . .	. . .	. . .	. . .	. . .	. . .
Portfolio investment liabilities	4 652 Y.	–98	–173	–93	–12	–88	1,805	3,877	4,100
Equity securities	4 660 Y.	. . .	. . .	. . .	. . .	. . .	1,805	1,900	1,493
Debt securities	4 669 Y.	–98	–173	–93	–12	–88	. . .	1,977	2,607
Other investment assets	4 703 . .	. . .	. . .	. . .	. . .	. . .	. . .	. . .	. . .
Monetary authorities	4 703 .A	. . .	. . .	. . .	. . .	. . .	. . .	. . .	. . .
General government	4 703 .B	. . .	. . .	. . .	. . .	. . .	. . .	. . .	. . .
Banks	4 703 .C	. . .	. . .	. . .	. . .	. . .	. . .	. . .	. . .
Other sectors	4 703 .D	. . .	. . .	. . .	. . .	. . .	. . .	. . .	. . .
Other investment liabilities	4 753 X.	1,739	2,409	3,495	4,227	4,440	2,179	–1,538	2,541
Monetary authorities	4 753 XA	. . .	. . .	. . .	. . .	. . .	. . .	. . .	. . .
General government	4 753 YB	1,908	2,777	474	1,299	858	552	137	131
Banks	4 753 YC	. . .	. . .	. . .	. . .	. . .	1,357	527	1,953
Other sectors	4 753 YD	–169	–368	3,021	2,928	3,582	270	–2,202	457
Total, Groups A Through C	4 020 . .	*820*	*1,810*	*1,507*	*1,437*	*3,349*	*3,526*	*1,047*	*3,363*
D. Net Errors and Omissions	4 998 . .	**–933**	**–1,315**	**744**	**91**	**–1,279**	**–2,932**	**–263**	**–1,790**
Total, Groups A Through D	4 030 . .	*–113*	*495*	*2,251*	*1,528*	*2,070*	*594*	*784*	*1,573*
E. Reserves and Related Items	4 040 . .	**113**	**–495**	**–2,251**	**–1,528**	**–2,070**	**–594**	**–784**	**–1,573**
Reserve assets	4 800 . .	167	–495	–2,088	–1,210	–1,909	–594	–784	–1,573
Use of Fund credit and loans	4 766 . .	–54	. . .	–163	–319	–161	. . .	. . .	. . .
Liabilities constituting foreign authorities' reserves	4 900 . .	. . .	. . .	. . .	. . .	. . .	. . .	. . .	. . .
Exceptional financing	4 920 . .	. . .	. . .	. . .	. . .	. . .	. . .	. . .	. . .
Conversion rates: rupiah per U.S. dollar	0 101 . .	**1,686**	**1,770**	**1,843**	**1,950**	**2,030**	**2,087**	**2,161**	**2,249**

[1] Excludes components that have been classified in the categories of Group E.

Table 2. STANDARD PRESENTATION, 1988–95
(Millions of U.S. dollars)

	Code	1988	1989	1990	1991	1992	1993	1994	1995
CURRENT ACCOUNT	4 993 . .	**–1,397**	**–1,108**	**–2,988**	**–4,260**	**–2,780**	**–2,106**	**–2,792**	**–7,023**
A. GOODS	4 100 . .	5,678	6,664	5,352	4,801	7,022	8,231	7,901	5,710
Credit	2 100 . .	**19,509**	**22,974**	**26,807**	**29,635**	**33,796**	**36,607**	**40,223**	**45,479**
General merchandise: exports f.o.b.	2 110 . .	19,509	22,974	26,807	29,635	33,796	36,607	40,223	45,479
Goods for processing: exports f.o.b.	2 150 . .	. . .	. . .	. . .	. . .	. . .	. . .	. . .	. . .
Repairs on goods	2 160 . .	. . .	. . .	. . .	. . .	. . .	. . .	. . .	. . .
Goods procured in ports by carriers	2 170 . .	. . .	. . .	. . .	. . .	. . .	. . .	. . .	. . .
Nonmonetary gold	2 180 . .	. . .	. . .	. . .	. . .	. . .	. . .	. . .	. . .
Debit	3 100 . .	**–13,831**	**–16,310**	**–21,455**	**–24,834**	**–26,774**	**–28,376**	**–32,322**	**–39,769**
General merchandise: imports f.o.b.	3 110 . .	–13,831	–16,310	–21,455	–24,834	–26,774	–28,376	–32,322	–39,769
Goods for processing: imports f.o.b.	3 150 . .	. . .	. . .	. . .	. . .	. . .	. . .	. . .	. . .
Repairs on goods	3 160 . .	. . .	. . .	. . .	. . .	. . .	. . .	. . .	. . .
Goods procured in ports by carriers	3 170 . .	. . .	. . .	. . .	. . .	. . .	. . .	. . .	. . .
Nonmonetary gold	3 180 . .	. . .	. . .	. . .	. . .	. . .	. . .	. . .	. . .
B. SERVICES	4 200 . .	–3,237	–3,564	–3,568	–3,742	–4,709	–5,887	–6,619	–7,794
Total credit	2 200 . .	*1,369*	*1,875*	*2,488*	*2,822*	*3,391*	*3,959*	*4,797*	*5,681*
Total debit	3 200 . .	*–4,606*	*–5,439*	*–6,056*	*–6,564*	*–8,100*	*–9,846*	*–11,416*	*–13,475*
Transportation services, credit	2 205 . .	**44**	**54**	**70**	**81**	**89**	**44**	**. . .**	**. . .**
Passenger	2 205 BA	. . .	. . .	. . .	. . .	. . .	. . .	. . .	. . .
Freight	2 205 BB	. . .	. . .	. . .	. . .	. . .	. . .	. . .	. . .
Other	2 205 BC	*44*	*54*	*70*	*81*	*89*	*44*	. . .	. . .
Sea transport, passenger	2 207 . .	. . .	. . .	. . .	. . .	. . .	. . .	. . .	. . .
Sea transport, freight	2 208 . .	. . .	. . .	. . .	. . .	. . .	. . .	. . .	. . .
Sea transport, other	2 209 . .	. . .	. . .	. . .	. . .	. . .	. . .	. . .	. . .
Air transport, passenger	2 211 . .	. . .	. . .	. . .	. . .	. . .	. . .	. . .	. . .
Air transport, freight	2 212 . .	. . .	. . .	. . .	. . .	. . .	. . .	. . .	. . .
Air transport, other	2 213 . .	. . .	. . .	. . .	. . .	. . .	. . .	. . .	. . .
Other transport, passenger	2 215 . .	. . .	. . .	. . .	. . .	. . .	. . .	. . .	. . .
Other transport, freight	2 216 . .	. . .	. . .	. . .	. . .	. . .	. . .	. . .	. . .
Other transport, other	2 217 . .	. . .	. . .	. . .	. . .	. . .	. . .	. . .	. . .
Transportation services, debit	3 205 . .	**–1,666**	**–2,081**	**–2,795**	**–3,187**	**–3,574**	**–3,667**	**–3,913**	**–4,747**
Passenger	3 205 BA	. . .	. . .	. . .	. . .	. . .	. . .	. . .	. . .
Freight	3 205 BB	*–1,352*	*–1,595*	*–2,109*	*–2,449*	*–2,642*	*–2,800*	*–3,196*	*–3,939*
Other	3 205 BC	*–314*	*–486*	*–686*	*–738*	*–932*	*–867*	*–717*	*–808*
Sea transport, passenger	3 207 . .	. . .	. . .	. . .	. . .	. . .	. . .	. . .	. . .
Sea transport, freight	3 208 . .	. . .	. . .	. . .	. . .	. . .	. . .	. . .	. . .
Sea transport, other	3 209 . .	. . .	. . .	. . .	. . .	. . .	. . .	. . .	. . .
Air transport, passenger	3 211 . .	. . .	. . .	. . .	. . .	. . .	. . .	. . .	. . .
Air transport, freight	3 212 . .	. . .	. . .	. . .	. . .	. . .	. . .	. . .	. . .
Air transport, other	3 213 . .	. . .	. . .	. . .	. . .	. . .	. . .	. . .	. . .
Other transport, passenger	3 215 . .	. . .	. . .	. . .	. . .	. . .	. . .	. . .	. . .
Other transport, freight	3 216 . .	. . .	. . .	. . .	. . .	. . .	. . .	. . .	. . .
Other transport, other	3 217 . .	. . .	. . .	. . .	. . .	. . .	. . .	. . .	. . .
Travel, credit	2 236 . .	**1,283**	**1,628**	**2,153**	**2,515**	**3,051**	**3,651**	**4,575**	**5,449**
Business travel	2 237 . .	. . .	. . .	. . .	. . .	. . .	. . .	1,190	1,417
Personal travel	2 240 . .	. . .	. . .	. . .	. . .	. . .	. . .	3,385	4,032
Travel, debit	3 236 . .	**–592**	**–722**	**–836**	**–969**	**–1,166**	**–1,539**	**–1,900**	**–2,172**
Business travel	3 237 . .	. . .	. . .	. . .	. . .	. . .	. . .	. . .	. . .
Personal travel	3 240 . .	. . .	. . .	. . .	. . .	. . .	. . .	–1,900	–2,172
Other services, credit	2 200 BA	**42**	**193**	**265**	**226**	**251**	**264**	**222**	**232**
Communications	2 245 . .	. . .	. . .	. . .	. . .	. . .	49	105	105
Construction	2 249 . .	. . .	. . .	. . .	. . .	. . .	. . .	. . .	. . .
Insurance	2 253 . .	. . .	. . .	. . .	. . .	. . .	. . .	. . .	. . .
Financial	2 260 . .	. . .	. . .	. . .	. . .	. . .	. . .	. . .	. . .
Computer and information	2 262 . .	. . .	. . .	. . .	. . .	. . .	. . .	. . .	. . .
Royalties and licence fees	2 266 . .	. . .	. . .	. . .	. . .	. . .	. . .	. . .	. . .
Other business services	2 268 . .	42	193	265	226	251	134	. . .	. . .
Personal, cultural, and recreational	2 287 . .	. . .	. . .	. . .	. . .	. . .	. . .	. . .	. . .
Government, n.i.e.	2 291 . .	. . .	. . .	. . .	. . .	. . .	81	117	127
Other services, debit	3 200 BA	**–2,348**	**–2,636**	**–2,425**	**–2,408**	**–3,360**	**–4,640**	**–5,603**	**–6,556**
Communications	3 245 . .	. . .	. . .	. . .	. . .	. . .	–27	–57	–49
Construction	3 249 . .	. . .	. . .	. . .	. . .	. . .	. . .	. . .	. . .
Insurance	3 253 . .	–150	–177	–234	–272	–294	–311	–355	–437
Financial	3 260 . .	. . .	. . .	. . .	. . .	. . .	. . .	. . .	. . .
Computer and information	3 262 . .	. . .	. . .	. . .	. . .	. . .	. . .	. . .	. . .
Royalties and licence fees	3 266 . .	. . .	. . .	. . .	. . .	. . .	. . .	. . .	. . .
Other business services	3 268 . .	–2,061	–2,311	–2,033	–1,948	–2,850	–4,051	–4,911	–5,760
Personal, cultural, and recreational	3 287 . .	. . .	. . .	. . .	. . .	. . .	. . .	. . .	. . .
Government, n.i.e.	3 291 . .	–137	–148	–158	–188	–216	–251	–280	–310

Table 2 (Continued). STANDARD PRESENTATION, 1988–95
(Millions of U.S. dollars)

	Code		1988	1989	1990	1991	1992	1993	1994	1995
C. INCOME	4 300	. .	-4,092	-4,547	-5,190	-5,581	-5,664	-4,987	-4,693	-5,778
Total credit	2 300	. .	*492*	*562*	*409*	*917*	*818*	*1,028*	*1,048*	*1,345*
Total debit	3 300	. .	*-4,584*	*-5,109*	*-5,599*	*-6,498*	*-6,482*	*-6,015*	*-5,741*	*-7,123*
Compensation of employees, credit	2 310	. .	...	...	...	...	...	...	...	...
Compensation of employees, debit	3 310	. .	...	...	...	...	...	...	...	...
Investment income, credit	2 320	. .	**492**	**562**	**409**	**917**	**818**	**1,028**	**1,048**	**1,345**
Direct investment income	2 330	. .	...	...	...	...	...	...	...	...
Dividends and distributed branch profits	2 332	. .	...	...	...	...	...	...	...	...
Reinvested earnings and undistributed branch profits	2 333	. .	...	...	...	...	...	...	...	...
Income on debt (interest)	2 334	. .	...	...	...	...	...	...	...	...
Portfolio investment income	2 339	. .	...	...	...	...	...	...	...	...
Income on equity	2 340	. .	...	...	...	...	...	...	...	...
Income on bonds and notes	2 350	. .	...	...	...	...	...	...	...	...
Income on money market instruments and financial derivatives	2 360	. .	...	...	...	...	...	...	...	...
Other investment income	2 370	. .	492	562	409	917	818	1,028	1,048	1,345
Investment income, debit	3 320	. .	**-4,584**	**-5,109**	**-5,599**	**-6,498**	**-6,482**	**-6,015**	**-5,741**	**-7,123**
Direct investment income	3 330	. .	-1,318	-1,794	-2,192	-2,318	-2,623	-1,583	-597	-719
Dividends and distributed branch profits	3 332	. .	-1,318	-1,794	-2,192	-2,318	-2,623	-1,583	-597	-719
Reinvested earnings and undistributed branch profits	3 333	. .	...	...	...	...	...	...	...	...
Income on debt (interest)	3 334	. .	...	...	...	...	...	...	...	...
Portfolio investment income	3 339	. .	...	...	...	...	...	...	...	...
Income on equity	3 340	. .	...	...	...	...	...	...	...	...
Income on bonds and notes	3 350	. .	...	...	...	...	...	...	...	...
Income on money market instruments and financial derivatives	3 360	. .	...	...	...	...	...	...	...	...
Other investment income	3 370	. .	-3,266	-3,315	-3,407	-4,180	-3,859	-4,432	-5,144	-6,404
D. CURRENT TRANSFERS	4 379	. .	254	339	418	262	571	537	619	839
Credit	2 379	. .	**254**	**339**	**418**	**262**	**571**	**537**	**619**	**839**
General government	2 380	. .	155	172	252	132	342	191	170	210
Other sectors	2 390	. .	99	167	166	130	229	346	449	629
Workers' remittances	2 391	. .	99	167	166	130	229	346	449	629
Other current transfers	2 392	. .	...	...	...	...	...	...	...	...
Debit	3 379	. .	...	...	...	...	...	...	...	...
General government	3 380	. .	...	...	...	...	...	...	...	...
Other sectors	3 390	. .	...	...	...	...	...	...	...	...
Workers' remittances	3 391	. .	...	...	...	...	...	...	...	...
Other current transfers	3 392	. .	...	...	...	...	...	...	...	...
CAPITAL AND FINANCIAL ACCOUNT	4 996	. .	**2,330**	**2,423**	**2,244**	**4,169**	**4,059**	**5,038**	**3,055**	**8,813**
CAPITAL ACCOUNT	4 994	. .	...	...	...	...	...	...	...	...
Total credit	2 994	. .	...	...	...	...	...	...	...	...
Total debit	3 994	. .	...	...	...	...	...	...	...	...
Capital transfers, credit	2 400	. .	...	...	...	...	...	...	...	...
General government	2 401	. .	...	...	...	...	...	...	...	...
Debt forgiveness	2 402	. .	...	...	...	...	...	...	...	...
Other capital transfers	2 410	. .	...	...	...	...	...	...	...	...
Other sectors	2 430	. .	...	...	...	...	...	...	...	...
Migrants' transfers	2 431	. .	...	...	...	...	...	...	...	...
Debt forgiveness	2 432	. .	...	...	...	...	...	...	...	...
Other capital transfers	2 440	. .	...	...	...	...	...	...	...	...
Capital transfers, debit	3 400	. .	...	...	...	...	...	...	...	...
General government	3 401	. .	...	...	...	...	...	...	...	...
Debt forgiveness	3 402	. .	...	...	...	...	...	...	...	...
Other capital transfers	3 410	. .	...	...	...	...	...	...	...	...
Other sectors	3 430	. .	...	...	...	...	...	...	...	...
Migrants' transfers	3 431	. .	...	...	...	...	...	...	...	...
Debt forgiveness	3 432	. .	...	...	...	...	...	...	...	...
Other capital transfers	3 440	. .	...	...	...	...	...	...	...	...
Nonproduced nonfinancial assets, credit	2 480	. .	...	...	...	...	...	...	...	...
Nonproduced nonfinancial assets, debit	3 480	. .	...	...	...	...	...	...	...	...

Table 2 (Continued). STANDARD PRESENTATION, 1988–95
(Millions of U.S. dollars)

	Code	1988	1989	1990	1991	1992	1993	1994	1995
FINANCIAL ACCOUNT	4 995	**2,330**	**2,423**	**2,244**	**4,169**	**4,059**	**5,038**	**3,055**	**8,813**
A. DIRECT INVESTMENT	4 500	576	682	1,093	1,482	1,777	1,648	1,500	3,745
Direct investment abroad	4 505	**...**	**...**	**...**	**...**	**...**	**–356**	**–609**	**–603**
Equity capital	4 510	...	...	...	...	...	–356	...	...
Claims on affiliated enterprises	4 515	...	...	...	...	...	...	...	...
Liabilities to affiliated enterprises	4 520	...	...	...	...	...	...	...	...
Reinvested earnings	4 525	...	...	...	...	...	...	...	...
Other capital	4 530	...	...	...	...	...	...	...	...
Claims on affiliated enterprises	4 535	...	...	...	...	...	...	...	...
Liabilities to affiliated enterprises	4 540	...	...	...	...	...	...	...	...
Direct investment in Indonesia	4 555	**576**	**682**	**1,093**	**1,482**	**1,777**	**2,004**	**2,109**	**4,348**
Equity capital	4 560	247	308	433	589	747	887	1,024	1,793
Claims on direct investors	4 565	...	...	...	...	...	...	...	...
Liabilities to direct investors	4 570	...	...	...	...	...	...	...	...
Reinvested earnings	4 575	...	...	...	...	...	...	...	...
Other capital	4 580	329	374	660	893	1,030	1,117	1,085	2,555
Claims on direct investors	4 585	...	...	...	...	...	...	...	...
Liabilities to direct investors	4 590	...	...	...	...	...	...	...	...
B. PORTFOLIO INVESTMENT	4 600	–98	–173	–93	–12	–88	1,805	3,877	4,100
Assets	4 602	**...**	**...**	**...**	**...**	**...**	**...**	**...**	**...**
Equity securities	4 610	...	...	...	...	...	...	...	...
Monetary authorities	4 611	...	...	...	...	...	...	...	...
General government	4 612	...	...	...	...	...	...	...	...
Banks	4 613	...	...	...	...	...	...	...	...
Other sectors	4 614	...	...	...	...	...	...	...	...
Debt securities	4 619	...	...	...	...	...	...	...	...
Bonds and notes	4 620	...	...	...	...	...	...	...	...
Monetary authorities	4 621	...	...	...	...	...	...	...	...
General government	4 622	...	...	...	...	...	...	...	...
Banks	4 623	...	...	...	...	...	...	...	...
Other sectors	4 624	...	...	...	...	...	...	...	...
Money market instruments	4 630	...	...	...	...	...	...	...	...
Monetary authorities	4 631	...	...	...	...	...	...	...	...
General government	4 632	...	...	...	...	...	...	...	...
Banks	4 633	...	...	...	...	...	...	...	...
Other sectors	4 634	...	...	...	...	...	...	...	...
Financial derivatives	4 640	...	...	...	...	...	...	...	...
Monetary authorities	4 641	...	...	...	...	...	...	...	...
General government	4 642	...	...	...	...	...	...	...	...
Banks	4 643	...	...	...	...	...	...	...	...
Other sectors	4 644	...	...	...	...	...	...	...	...
Liabilities	4 652	**–98**	**–173**	**–93**	**–12**	**–88**	**1,805**	**3,877**	**4,100**
Equity securities	4 660	...	...	...	...	...	1,805	1,900	1,493
Banks	4 663	...	...	...	...	...	...	...	...
Other sectors	4 664	...	...	...	...	...	1,805	1,900	1,493
Debt securities	4 669	–98	–173	–93	–12	–88	...	1,977	2,607
Bonds and notes	4 670	–98	–173	–93	–12	–88	...	1,977	2,607
Monetary authorities	4 671	...	...	...	...	...	...	...	...
General government	4 672	–98	–173	–93	–12	–88	...	...	...
Banks	4 673	...	...	...	...	...	...	...	...
Other sectors	4 674	...	...	...	...	...	...	1,977	2,607
Money market instruments	4 680	...	...	...	...	...	...	...	...
Monetary authorities	4 681	...	...	...	...	...	...	...	...
General government	4 682	...	...	...	...	...	...	...	...
Banks	4 683	...	...	...	...	...	...	...	...
Other sectors	4 684	...	...	...	...	...	...	...	...
Financial derivatives	4 690	...	...	...	...	...	...	...	...
Monetary authorities	4 691	...	...	...	...	...	...	...	...
General government	4 692	...	...	...	...	...	...	...	...
Banks	4 693	...	...	...	...	...	...	...	...
Other sectors	4 694	...	...	...	...	...	...	...	...

Table 2 (Concluded). STANDARD PRESENTATION, 1988–95
(Millions of U.S. dollars)

	Code		1988	1989	1990	1991	1992	1993	1994	1995
C. OTHER INVESTMENT	4 700	. .	1,685	2,409	3,332	3,908	4,279	2,179	−1,538	2,541
Assets	4 703	. .	...	...	...	...	...	...	...	...
Trade credits	4 706	. .	...	...	...	...	...	...	...	...
General government: long-term	4 708	. .	...	...	...	...	...	...	...	...
General government: short-term	4 709	. .	...	...	...	...	...	...	...	...
Other sectors: long-term	4 711	. .	...	...	...	...	...	...	...	...
Other sectors: short-term	4 712	. .	...	...	...	...	...	...	...	...
Loans	4 714	. .	...	...	...	...	...	...	...	...
Monetary authorities: long-term	4 717	. .	...	...	...	...	...	...	...	...
Monetary authorities: short-term	4 718	. .	...	...	...	...	...	...	...	...
General government: long-term	4 720	. .	...	...	...	...	...	...	...	...
General government: short-term	4 721	. .	...	...	...	...	...	...	...	...
Banks: long-term	4 723	. .	...	...	...	...	...	...	...	...
Banks: short-term	4 724	. .	...	...	...	...	...	...	...	...
Other sectors: long-term	4 726	. .	...	...	...	...	...	...	...	...
Other sectors: short-term	4 727	. .	...	...	...	...	...	...	...	...
Currency and deposits	4 730	. .	...	...	...	...	...	...	...	...
Monetary authorities	4 731	. .	...	...	...	...	...	...	...	...
General government	4 732	. .	...	...	...	...	...	...	...	...
Banks	4 733	. .	...	...	...	...	...	...	...	...
Other sectors	4 734	. .	...	...	...	...	...	...	...	...
Other assets	4 736	. .	...	...	...	...	...	...	...	...
Monetary authorities: long-term	4 738	. .	...	...	...	...	...	...	...	...
Monetary authorities: short-term	4 739	. .	...	...	...	...	...	...	...	...
General government: long-term	4 741	. .	...	...	...	...	...	...	...	...
General government: short-term	4 742	. .	...	...	...	...	...	...	...	...
Banks: long-term	4 744	. .	...	...	...	...	...	...	...	...
Banks: short-term	4 745	. .	...	...	...	...	...	...	...	...
Other sectors: long-term	4 747	. .	...	...	...	...	...	...	...	...
Other sectors: short-term	4 748	. .	...	...	...	...	...	...	...	...
Liabilities	4 753	. .	**1,685**	**2,409**	**3,332**	**3,908**	**4,279**	**2,179**	**−1,538**	**2,541**
Trade credits	4 756	. .	...	...	...	...	...	83	280	117
General government: long-term	4 758	. .	...	...	...	...	...	...	...	...
General government: short-term	4 759	. .	...	...	...	...	...	...	...	...
Other sectors: long-term	4 761	. .	...	...	...	...	...	...	...	...
Other sectors: short-term	4 762	. .	...	...	...	...	...	83	280	117
Loans	4 764	. .	1,277	2,507	3,561	3,694	4,142	2,096	−1,818	2,424
Use of Fund credit and loans from the Fund	4 766	. .	−54	...	−163	−319	−161	...	...	...
Monetary authorities: other long-term	4 767	. .	...	...	...	...	...	...	...	...
Monetary authorities: short-term	4 768	. .	...	...	...	...	...	...	...	...
General government: long-term	4 770	. .	1,908	2,777	474	1,299	858	552	137	131
General government: short-term	4 771	. .	...	...	...	...	...	...	...	...
Banks: long-term	4 773	. .	...	...	...	...	...	1,357	527	1,953
Banks: short-term	4 774	. .	...	...	...	...	...	...	...	...
Other sectors: long-term	4 776	. .	−577	−270	3,250	2,714	3,445	187	192	1,056
Other sectors: short-term	4 777	. .	...	...	...	...	...	...	−2,674	−716
Currency and deposits	4 780	. .	...	...	...	...	...	...	...	...
Monetary authorities	4 781	. .	...	...	...	...	...	...	...	...
General government	4 782	. .	...	...	...	...	...	...	...	...
Banks	4 783	. .	...	...	...	...	...	...	...	...
Other sectors	4 784	. .	...	...	...	...	...	...	...	...
Other liabilities	4 786	. .	408	−98	−229	214	137	...	...	...
Monetary authorities: long-term	4 788	. .	...	...	...	...	...	...	...	...
Monetary authorities: short-term	4 789	. .	...	...	...	...	...	...	...	...
General government: long-term	4 791	. .	...	...	...	...	...	...	...	...
General government: short-term	4 792	. .	...	...	...	...	...	...	...	...
Banks: long-term	4 794	. .	...	...	...	...	...	...	...	...
Banks: short-term	4 795	. .	...	...	...	...	...	...	...	...
Other sectors: long-term	4 797	. .	...	...	...	...	...	...	...	...
Other sectors: short-term	4 798	. .	408	−98	−229	214	137	...	...	...
D. RESERVE ASSETS	4 800	. .	167	−495	−2,088	−1,210	−1,909	−594	−784	−1,573
Monetary gold	4 810	. .	...	−46	22	73	21	−272	−89	−2
Special drawing rights	4 820	. .	3	1	−1	...	3	...	...	−1
Reserve position in the Fund	4 830	. .	...	...	...	...	−169	−7	−21	−86
Foreign exchange	4 840	. .	164	−450	−2,109	−1,283	−1,764	−315	−674	−1,484
Other claims	4 880	. .	...	...	...	...	...	...	...	...
NET ERRORS AND OMISSIONS	4 998	. .	**−933**	**−1,315**	**744**	**91**	**−1,279**	**−2,932**	**−263**	**−1,790**

Part 3 of the *Yearbook* contains descriptions of the methodologies, compilation practices, and sources used to compile these data.

Table 1. ANALYTIC PRESENTATION, 1988–95 YEARS BEGINNING MARCH 21
(Millions of U.S. dollars)

	Code	1988	1989	1990	1991	1992	1993	1994	1995
A. Current Account [1]	4 993 Y.	**–1,869**	**–191**	**327**	**–9,448**	**–6,504**	**–4,215**	**4,777**	**. . .**
Goods: exports f.o.b	2 100 . .	10,709	13,081	19,305	18,661	19,868	18,080	19,434	. . .
Goods: imports f.o.b	3 100 . .	–10,608	–13,448	–18,330	–25,190	–23,274	–19,287	–12,617	. . .
Balance on Goods	4 100 . .	*101*	*–367*	*975*	*–6,529*	*–3,406*	*–1,207*	*6,817*	. . .
Services: credit	2 200 . .	244	446	436	668	559	1,084	438	. . .
Services: debit	3 200 . .	–2,355	–3,018	–3,962	–5,715	–5,783	–5,600	–3,405	. . .
Balance on Goods and Services	4 991 . .	*–2,010*	*–2,939*	*–2,551*	*–11,576*	*–8,630*	*–5,723*	*3,850*	. . .
Income: credit	2 300 . .	223	352	456	213	287	151	142	. . .
Income: debit	3 300 . .	–82	–104	–78	–85	–157	–143	–413	. . .
Balance on Goods, Services, and Income	4 992 . .	*–1,869*	*–2,691*	*–2,173*	*–11,448*	*–8,500*	*–5,715*	*3,579*	. . .
Current transfers: credit	2 379 Y.	. . .	2,500	2,500	2,000	1,996	1,500	1,200	. . .
Current transfers: debit	3 379 . .	. . .	. . .	. . .	. . .	. . .	. . .	–2	. . .
B. Capital Account [1]	4 994 Y.	**. . .**	**. . .**	**. . .**	**. . .**	**. . .**	**. . .**	**. . .**	**. . .**
Capital account: credit	2 994 Y.	. . .	. . .	. . .	. . .	. . .	. . .	. . .	. . .
Capital account: debit	3 994 . .	. . .	. . .	. . .	. . .	. . .	. . .	. . .	. . .
Total, Groups A Plus B	4 010 . .	*–1,869*	*–191*	*327*	*–9,448*	*–6,504*	*–4,215*	*4,777*	. . .
C. Financial Account [1]	4 995 X.	**320**	**3,261**	**295**	**6,033**	**4,703**	**5,563**	**–2,227**	**. . .**
Direct investment abroad	4 505 . .	. . .	. . .	. . .	. . .	. . .	. . .	. . .	. . .
Direct investment in Iran	4 555 Y.	. . .	. . .	. . .	. . .	. . .	. . .	. . .	. . .
Portfolio investment assets	4 602 . .	. . .	. . .	. . .	. . .	. . .	. . .	. . .	. . .
Equity securities	4 610 . .	. . .	. . .	. . .	. . .	. . .	. . .	. . .	. . .
Debt securities	4 619 . .	. . .	. . .	. . .	. . .	. . .	. . .	. . .	. . .
Portfolio investment liabilities	4 652 Y.	. . .	. . .	. . .	. . .	. . .	. . .	. . .	. . .
Equity securities	4 660 Y.	. . .	. . .	. . .	. . .	. . .	. . .	. . .	. . .
Debt securities	4 669 Y.	. . .	. . .	. . .	. . .	. . .	. . .	. . .	. . .
Other investment assets	4 703 . .	10	539	–1,510	1,082	1,000	1,250	–456	. . .
Monetary authorities	4 703 .A	. . .	. . .	. . .	. . .	. . .	. . .	. . .	. . .
General government	4 703 .B	140	1,099	142	910	342	44	–42	. . .
Banks	4 703 .C	–130	–560	–1,652	172	658	1,206	–414	. . .
Other sectors	4 703 .D	. . .	. . .	. . .	. . .	. . .	. . .	. . .	. . .
Other investment liabilities	4 753 X.	310	2,722	1,805	4,951	3,703	4,313	–1,771	. . .
Monetary authorities	4 753 XA	117	501	387	–372	63	68	–504	. . .
General government	4 753 YB	–144	–71	–41	440	4,556	–1,358	9,202	. . .
Banks	4 753 YC	–29	344	1,101	489	. . .	. . .	. . .	. . .
Other sectors	4 753 YD	366	1,948	358	4,394	–916	5,603	–10,469	. . .
Total, Groups A Through C	4 020 . .	*–1,549*	*3,070*	*622*	*–3,415*	*–1,801*	*1,348*	*2,550*	. . .
D. Net Errors and Omissions	4 998 . .	**539**	**–770**	**–947**	**1,322**	**1,637**	**–1,119**	**–1,318**	**. . .**
Total, Groups A Through D	4 030 . .	*–1,010*	*2,300*	*–325*	*–2,093*	*–164*	*229*	*1,232*	. . .
E. Reserves and Related Items	4 040 . .	**1,010**	**–2,300**	**325**	**2,093**	**164**	**–229**	**–1,232**	**. . .**
Reserve assets	4 800 . .	1,010	–2,300	325	2,093	164	–229	–1,232	. . .
Use of Fund credit and loans	4 766 . .	. . .	. . .	. . .	. . .	. . .	. . .	. . .	. . .
Liabilities constituting foreign authorities' reserves	4 900 . .	. . .	. . .	. . .	. . .	. . .	. . .	. . .	. . .
Exceptional financing	4 920 . .	. . .	. . .	. . .	. . .	. . .	. . .	. . .	. . .
Conversion rates: Iranian rials per U.S. dollar	0 101 . .	**69.35**	**72.03**	**66.86**	**67.82**	**96.41**	**1,657.40**	**1,748.32**	**1,748.23**

[1] Excludes components that have been classified in the categories of Group E.

Table 2. STANDARD PRESENTATION, 1988–95 YEARS BEGINNING MARCH 21

(Millions of U.S. dollars)

	Code	1988	1989	1990	1991	1992	1993	1994	1995
CURRENT ACCOUNT	4 993 . .	**–1,869**	**–191**	**327**	**–9,448**	**–6,504**	**–4,215**	**4,777**	. . .
A. GOODS	4 100 . .	101	–367	975	–6,529	–3,406	–1,207	6,817	. . .
Credit	2 100 . .	**10,709**	**13,081**	**19,305**	**18,661**	**19,868**	**18,080**	**19,434**	. . .
General merchandise: exports f.o.b.	2 110 . .	10,709	13,081	19,305	18,661	19,868	18,080	19,434	. . .
Goods for processing: exports f.o.b.	2 150 . .	. . .	. . .	. . .	. . .	. . .	. . .	. . .	. . .
Repairs on goods	2 160 . .	. . .	. . .	. . .	. . .	. . .	. . .	. . .	. . .
Goods procured in ports by carriers	2 170 . .	. . .	. . .	. . .	. . .	. . .	. . .	. . .	. . .
Nonmonetary gold	2 180 . .	. . .	. . .	. . .	. . .	. . .	. . .	. . .	. . .
Debit	3 100 . .	**–10,608**	**–13,448**	**–18,330**	**–25,190**	**–23,274**	**–19,287**	**–12,617**	. . .
General merchandise: imports f.o.b.	3 110 . .	–10,608	–13,448	–18,330	–25,190	–23,274	–19,287	–12,617	. . .
Goods for processing: imports f.o.b.	3 150 . .	. . .	. . .	. . .	. . .	. . .	. . .	. . .	. . .
Repairs on goods	3 160 . .	. . .	. . .	. . .	. . .	. . .	. . .	. . .	. . .
Goods procured in ports by carriers	3 170 . .	. . .	. . .	. . .	. . .	. . .	. . .	. . .	. . .
Nonmonetary gold	3 180 . .	. . .	. . .	. . .	. . .	. . .	. . .	. . .	. . .
B. SERVICES	4 200 . .	–2,111	–2,572	–3,526	–5,047	–5,224	–4,516	–2,967	. . .
Total credit	2 200 . .	*244*	*446*	*436*	*668*	*559*	*1,084*	*438*	. . .
Total debit	3 200 . .	*–2,355*	*–3,018*	*–3,962*	*–5,715*	*–5,783*	*–5,600*	*–3,405*	. . .
Transportation services, credit	2 205 . .	**55**	**68**	**36**	**61**	**40**	**19**	**91**	. . .
Passenger	2 205 BA	*55*	*68*	*36*	*61*	*40*	*19*	*91*	. . .
Freight	2 205 BB	. . .	. . .	. . .	. . .	. . .	. . .	. . .	. . .
Other	2 205 BC	. . .	. . .	. . .	. . .	. . .	. . .	. . .	. . .
Sea transport, passenger	2 207 . .	. . .	. . .	. . .	. . .	. . .	. . .	. . .	. . .
Sea transport, freight	2 208 . .	. . .	. . .	. . .	. . .	. . .	. . .	. . .	. . .
Sea transport, other	2 209 . .	. . .	. . .	. . .	. . .	. . .	. . .	. . .	. . .
Air transport, passenger	2 211 . .	. . .	. . .	. . .	. . .	. . .	. . .	. . .	. . .
Air transport, freight	2 212 . .	. . .	. . .	. . .	. . .	. . .	. . .	. . .	. . .
Air transport, other	2 213 . .	. . .	. . .	. . .	. . .	. . .	. . .	. . .	. . .
Other transport, passenger	2 215 . .	. . .	. . .	. . .	. . .	. . .	. . .	. . .	. . .
Other transport, freight	2 216 . .	. . .	. . .	. . .	. . .	. . .	. . .	. . .	. . .
Other transport, other	2 217 . .	. . .	. . .	. . .	. . .	. . .	. . .	. . .	. . .
Transportation services, debit	3 205 . .	**–1,015**	**–1,167**	**–1,751**	**–2,445**	**–2,247**	**–1,828**	**–990**	. . .
Passenger	3 205 BA	*–103*	*–43*	*–64*	*–127*	*–49*	*–9*	*–12*	. . .
Freight	3 205 BB	*–912*	*–1,124*	*–1,687*	*–2,318*	*–2,198*	*–1,819*	*–978*	. . .
Other	3 205 BC	. . .	. . .	. . .	. . .	. . .	. . .	. . .	. . .
Sea transport, passenger	3 207 . .	. . .	. . .	. . .	. . .	. . .	. . .	. . .	. . .
Sea transport, freight	3 208 . .	. . .	. . .	. . .	. . .	. . .	. . .	. . .	. . .
Sea transport, other	3 209 . .	. . .	. . .	. . .	. . .	. . .	. . .	. . .	. . .
Air transport, passenger	3 211 . .	. . .	. . .	. . .	. . .	. . .	. . .	. . .	. . .
Air transport, freight	3 212 . .	. . .	. . .	. . .	. . .	. . .	. . .	. . .	. . .
Air transport, other	3 213 . .	. . .	. . .	. . .	. . .	. . .	. . .	. . .	. . .
Other transport, passenger	3 215 . .	. . .	. . .	. . .	. . .	. . .	. . .	. . .	. . .
Other transport, freight	3 216 . .	. . .	. . .	. . .	. . .	. . .	. . .	. . .	. . .
Other transport, other	3 217 . .	. . .	. . .	. . .	. . .	. . .	. . .	. . .	. . .
Travel, credit	2 236 . .	**11**	**15**	**28**	**57**	**31**	**71**	**11**	. . .
Business travel	2 237 . .	. . .	. . .	. . .	. . .	. . .	. . .	. . .	. . .
Personal travel	2 240 . .	11	15	28	57	31	71	11	. . .
Travel, debit	3 236 . .	**–69**	**–129**	**–340**	**–734**	**–1,109**	**–862**	**–149**	. . .
Business travel	3 237 . .	. . .	. . .	. . .	. . .	. . .	. . .	. . .	. . .
Personal travel	3 240 . .	–69	–129	–340	–734	–1,109	–862	–149	. . .
Other services, credit	2 200 BA	**178**	**363**	**372**	**550**	**488**	**994**	**336**	. . .
Communications	2 245 . .	. . .	. . .	. . .	. . .	. . .	. . .	. . .	. . .
Construction	2 249 . .	. . .	. . .	. . .	. . .	. . .	. . .	. . .	. . .
Insurance	2 253 . .	. . .	. . .	. . .	. . .	. . .	. . .	. . .	. . .
Financial	2 260 . .	72	132	22	161	53	56	49	. . .
Computer and information	2 262 . .	. . .	. . .	. . .	. . .	. . .	. . .	. . .	. . .
Royalties and licence fees	2 266 . .	. . .	. . .	. . .	. . .	. . .	. . .	. . .	. . .
Other business services	2 268 . .	71	106	257	205	333	902	259	. . .
Personal, cultural, and recreational	2 287 . .	. . .	. . .	. . .	. . .	. . .	. . .	. . .	. . .
Government, n.i.e.	2 291 . .	35	125	93	184	102	36	28	. . .
Other services, debit	3 200 BA	**–1,271**	**–1,722**	**–1,871**	**–2,536**	**–2,427**	**–2,910**	**–2,266**	. . .
Communications	3 245 . .	. . .	. . .	. . .	. . .	. . .	. . .	. . .	. . .
Construction	3 249 . .	. . .	. . .	. . .	. . .	. . .	. . .	. . .	. . .
Insurance	3 253 . .	–176	–222	–305	–419	–388	–321	–179	. . .
Financial	3 260 . .	–32	–41	–94	–71	–202	–92	–73	. . .
Computer and information	3 262 . .	. . .	. . .	. . .	. . .	. . .	. . .	. . .	. . .
Royalties and licence fees	3 266 . .	. . .	. . .	. . .	. . .	. . .	. . .	. . .	. . .
Other business services	3 268 . .	–928	–859	–1,213	–1,734	–1,595	–2,381	–1,850	. . .
Personal, cultural, and recreational	3 287 . .	. . .	. . .	. . .	. . .	. . .	. . .	. . .	. . .
Government, n.i.e.	3 291 . .	–135	–600	–259	–312	–242	–116	–164	. . .

Table 2 (Continued). STANDARD PRESENTATION, 1988–95 YEARS BEGINNING MARCH 21
(Millions of U.S. dollars)

	Code	1988	1989	1990	1991	1992	1993	1994	1995
C. INCOME	4 300	141	248	378	128	130	8	–271	...
Total credit	2 300	*223*	*352*	*456*	*213*	*287*	*151*	*142*	...
Total debit	3 300	*–82*	*–104*	*–78*	*–85*	*–157*	*–143*	*–413*	...
Compensation of employees, credit	2 310	...	...	...	...	...	...	...	...
Compensation of employees, debit	3 310	...	...	...	...	...	...	...	...
Investment income, credit	2 320	**223**	**352**	**456**	**213**	**287**	**151**	**142**	...
Direct investment income	2 330	...	...	...	...	...	...	...	...
Dividends and distributed branch profits	2 332	...	...	...	...	...	...	...	...
Reinvested earnings and undistributed branch profits	2 333	...	...	...	...	...	...	...	...
Income on debt (interest)	2 334	...	...	...	...	...	...	...	...
Portfolio investment income	2 339	...	...	...	...	...	...	...	...
Income on equity	2 340	...	...	...	...	...	...	...	...
Income on bonds and notes	2 350	...	...	...	...	...	...	...	...
Income on money market instruments and financial derivatives	2 360	...	...	...	...	...	...	...	...
Other investment income	2 370	223	352	456	213	287	151	142	...
Investment income, debit	3 320	**–82**	**–104**	**–78**	**–85**	**–157**	**–143**	**–413**	...
Direct investment income	3 330	...	...	...	...	...	...	...	...
Dividends and distributed branch profits	3 332	...	...	...	...	...	...	...	...
Reinvested earnings and undistributed branch profits	3 333	...	...	...	...	...	...	...	...
Income on debt (interest)	3 334	...	...	...	...	...	...	...	...
Portfolio investment income	3 339	...	...	...	...	...	...	...	...
Income on equity	3 340	...	...	...	...	...	...	...	...
Income on bonds and notes	3 350	...	...	...	...	...	...	...	...
Income on money market instruments and financial derivatives	3 360	...	...	...	...	...	...	...	...
Other investment income	3 370	–82	–104	–78	–85	–157	–143	–413	...
D. CURRENT TRANSFERS	4 379	...	2,500	2,500	2,000	1,996	1,500	1,198	...
Credit	2 379	...	**2,500**	**2,500**	**2,000**	**1,996**	**1,500**	**1,200**	...
General government	2 380	...	...	...	...	...	...	...	...
Other sectors	2 390	...	2,500	2,500	2,000	1,996	1,500	1,200	...
Workers' remittances	2 391	...	...	...	...	...	...	...	...
Other current transfers	2 392	...	2,500	2,500	2,000	1,996	1,500	1,200	...
Debit	3 379	...	...	...	...	...	...	**–2**	...
General government	3 380	...	...	...	...	...	...	–2	...
Other sectors	3 390	...	...	...	...	...	...	...	...
Workers' remittances	3 391	...	...	...	...	...	...	...	...
Other current transfers	3 392	...	...	...	...	...	...	...	...
CAPITAL AND FINANCIAL ACCOUNT	4 996	**1,330**	**961**	**620**	**8,126**	**4,867**	**5,334**	**–3,459**	...
CAPITAL ACCOUNT	4 994	...	...	...	...	...	...	...	...
Total credit	2 994	...	...	...	...	...	...	...	...
Total debit	3 994	...	...	...	...	...	...	...	...
Capital transfers, credit	2 400	...	...	...	...	...	...	...	...
General government	2 401	...	...	...	...	...	...	...	...
Debt forgiveness	2 402	...	...	...	...	...	...	...	...
Other capital transfers	2 410	...	...	...	...	...	...	...	...
Other sectors	2 430	...	...	...	...	...	...	...	...
Migrants' transfers	2 431	...	...	...	...	...	...	...	...
Debt forgiveness	2 432	...	...	...	...	...	...	...	...
Other capital transfers	2 440	...	...	...	...	...	...	...	...
Capital transfers, debit	3 400	...	...	...	...	...	...	...	...
General government	3 401	...	...	...	...	...	...	...	...
Debt forgiveness	3 402	...	...	...	...	...	...	...	...
Other capital transfers	3 410	...	...	...	...	...	...	...	...
Other sectors	3 430	...	...	...	...	...	...	...	...
Migrants' transfers	3 431	...	...	...	...	...	...	...	...
Debt forgiveness	3 432	...	...	...	...	...	...	...	...
Other capital transfers	3 440	...	...	...	...	...	...	...	...
Nonproduced nonfinancial assets, credit	2 480	...	...	...	...	...	...	...	...
Nonproduced nonfinancial assets, debit	3 480	...	...	...	...	...	...	...	...

Table 2 (Continued). STANDARD PRESENTATION, 1988–95 YEARS BEGINNING MARCH 21
(Millions of U.S. dollars)

	Code		1988	1989	1990	1991	1992	1993	1994	1995
FINANCIAL ACCOUNT	4 995	. .	**1,330**	**961**	**620**	**8,126**	**4,867**	**5,334**	**–3,459**	**. . .**
A. DIRECT INVESTMENT	4 500	. .	. . .	. . .	. . .	. . .	. . .	. . .	. . .	. . .
Direct investment abroad	4 505	. .	**. . .**	**. . .**	**. . .**	**. . .**	**. . .**	**. . .**	**. . .**	**. . .**
Equity capital	4 510	. .	. . .	. . .	. . .	. . .	. . .	. . .	. . .	. . .
Claims on affiliated enterprises	4 515	. .	. . .	. . .	. . .	. . .	. . .	. . .	. . .	. . .
Liabilities to affiliated enterprises	4 520	. .	. . .	. . .	. . .	. . .	. . .	. . .	. . .	. . .
Reinvested earnings	4 525	. .	. . .	. . .	. . .	. . .	. . .	. . .	. . .	. . .
Other capital	4 530	. .	. . .	. . .	. . .	. . .	. . .	. . .	. . .	. . .
Claims on affiliated enterprises	4 535	. .	. . .	. . .	. . .	. . .	. . .	. . .	. . .	. . .
Liabilities to affiliated enterprises	4 540	. .	. . .	. . .	. . .	. . .	. . .	. . .	. . .	. . .
Direct investment in Iran	4 555	. .	**. . .**	**. . .**	**. . .**	**. . .**	**. . .**	**. . .**	**. . .**	**. . .**
Equity capital	4 560	. .	. . .	. . .	. . .	. . .	. . .	. . .	. . .	. . .
Claims on direct investors	4 565	. .	. . .	. . .	. . .	. . .	. . .	. . .	. . .	. . .
Liabilities to direct investors	4 570	. .	. . .	. . .	. . .	. . .	. . .	. . .	. . .	. . .
Reinvested earnings	4 575	. .	. . .	. . .	. . .	. . .	. . .	. . .	. . .	. . .
Other capital	4 580	. .	. . .	. . .	. . .	. . .	. . .	. . .	. . .	. . .
Claims on direct investors	4 585	. .	. . .	. . .	. . .	. . .	. . .	. . .	. . .	. . .
Liabilities to direct investors	4 590	. .	. . .	. . .	. . .	. . .	. . .	. . .	. . .	. . .
B. PORTFOLIO INVESTMENT	4 600	. .	. . .	. . .	. . .	. . .	. . .	. . .	. . .	. . .
Assets	4 602	. .	**. . .**	**. . .**	**. . .**	**. . .**	**. . .**	**. . .**	**. . .**	**. . .**
Equity securities	4 610	. .	. . .	. . .	. . .	. . .	. . .	. . .	. . .	. . .
Monetary authorities	4 611	. .	. . .	. . .	. . .	. . .	. . .	. . .	. . .	. . .
General government	4 612	. .	. . .	. . .	. . .	. . .	. . .	. . .	. . .	. . .
Banks	4 613	. .	. . .	. . .	. . .	. . .	. . .	. . .	. . .	. . .
Other sectors	4 614	. .	. . .	. . .	. . .	. . .	. . .	. . .	. . .	. . .
Debt securities	4 619	. .	. . .	. . .	. . .	. . .	. . .	. . .	. . .	. . .
Bonds and notes	4 620	. .	. . .	. . .	. . .	. . .	. . .	. . .	. . .	. . .
Monetary authorities	4 621	. .	. . .	. . .	. . .	. . .	. . .	. . .	. . .	. . .
General government	4 622	. .	. . .	. . .	. . .	. . .	. . .	. . .	. . .	. . .
Banks	4 623	. .	. . .	. . .	. . .	. . .	. . .	. . .	. . .	. . .
Other sectors	4 624	. .	. . .	. . .	. . .	. . .	. . .	. . .	. . .	. . .
Money market instruments	4 630	. .	. . .	. . .	. . .	. . .	. . .	. . .	. . .	. . .
Monetary authorities	4 631	. .	. . .	. . .	. . .	. . .	. . .	. . .	. . .	. . .
General government	4 632	. .	. . .	. . .	. . .	. . .	. . .	. . .	. . .	. . .
Banks	4 633	. .	. . .	. . .	. . .	. . .	. . .	. . .	. . .	. . .
Other sectors	4 634	. .	. . .	. . .	. . .	. . .	. . .	. . .	. . .	. . .
Financial derivatives	4 640	. .	. . .	. . .	. . .	. . .	. . .	. . .	. . .	. . .
Monetary authorities	4 641	. .	. . .	. . .	. . .	. . .	. . .	. . .	. . .	. . .
General government	4 642	. .	. . .	. . .	. . .	. . .	. . .	. . .	. . .	. . .
Banks	4 643	. .	. . .	. . .	. . .	. . .	. . .	. . .	. . .	. . .
Other sectors	4 644	. .	. . .	. . .	. . .	. . .	. . .	. . .	. . .	. . .
Liabilities	4 652	. .	**. . .**	**. . .**	**. . .**	**. . .**	**. . .**	**. . .**	**. . .**	**. . .**
Equity securities	4 660	. .	. . .	. . .	. . .	. . .	. . .	. . .	. . .	. . .
Banks	4 663	. .	. . .	. . .	. . .	. . .	. . .	. . .	. . .	. . .
Other sectors	4 664	. .	. . .	. . .	. . .	. . .	. . .	. . .	. . .	. . .
Debt securities	4 669	. .	. . .	. . .	. . .	. . .	. . .	. . .	. . .	. . .
Bonds and notes	4 670	. .	. . .	. . .	. . .	. . .	. . .	. . .	. . .	. . .
Monetary authorities	4 671	. .	. . .	. . .	. . .	. . .	. . .	. . .	. . .	. . .
General government	4 672	. .	. . .	. . .	. . .	. . .	. . .	. . .	. . .	. . .
Banks	4 673	. .	. . .	. . .	. . .	. . .	. . .	. . .	. . .	. . .
Other sectors	4 674	. .	. . .	. . .	. . .	. . .	. . .	. . .	. . .	. . .
Money market instruments	4 680	. .	. . .	. . .	. . .	. . .	. . .	. . .	. . .	. . .
Monetary authorities	4 681	. .	. . .	. . .	. . .	. . .	. . .	. . .	. . .	. . .
General government	4 682	. .	. . .	. . .	. . .	. . .	. . .	. . .	. . .	. . .
Banks	4 683	. .	. . .	. . .	. . .	. . .	. . .	. . .	. . .	. . .
Other sectors	4 684	. .	. . .	. . .	. . .	. . .	. . .	. . .	. . .	. . .
Financial derivatives	4 690	. .	. . .	. . .	. . .	. . .	. . .	. . .	. . .	. . .
Monetary authorities	4 691	. .	. . .	. . .	. . .	. . .	. . .	. . .	. . .	. . .
General government	4 692	. .	. . .	. . .	. . .	. . .	. . .	. . .	. . .	. . .
Banks	4 693	. .	. . .	. . .	. . .	. . .	. . .	. . .	. . .	. . .
Other sectors	4 694	. .	. . .	. . .	. . .	. . .	. . .	. . .	. . .	. . .

Table 2 (Concluded). STANDARD PRESENTATION, 1988–95 YEARS BEGINNING MARCH 21

(Millions of U.S. dollars)

	Code	1988	1989	1990	1991	1992	1993	1994	1995
C. OTHER INVESTMENT	4 700 . .	320	3,261	295	6,033	4,703	5,563	–2,227	. . .
Assets	4 703 . .	**10**	**539**	**–1,510**	**1,082**	**1,000**	**1,250**	**–456**	**. . .**
Trade credits	4 706 . .	. . .	. . .	. . .	. . .	. . .	. . .	. . .	. . .
General government: long-term	4 708 . .	. . .	. . .	. . .	. . .	. . .	. . .	. . .	. . .
General government: short-term	4 709 . .	. . .	. . .	. . .	. . .	. . .	. . .	. . .	. . .
Other sectors: long-term	4 711 . .	. . .	. . .	. . .	. . .	. . .	. . .	. . .	. . .
Other sectors: short-term	4 712 . .	. . .	. . .	. . .	. . .	. . .	. . .	. . .	. . .
Loans	4 714 . .	140	1,099	142	910	342	44	–42	. . .
Monetary authorities: long-term	4 717 . .	. . .	. . .	. . .	. . .	. . .	. . .	. . .	. . .
Monetary authorities: short-term	4 718 . .	. . .	. . .	. . .	. . .	. . .	. . .	. . .	. . .
General government: long-term	4 720 . .	140	1,099	142	910	342	44	–42	. . .
General government: short-term	4 721 . .	. . .	. . .	. . .	. . .	. . .	. . .	. . .	. . .
Banks: long-term	4 723 . .	. . .	. . .	. . .	. . .	. . .	. . .	. . .	. . .
Banks: short-term	4 724 . .	. . .	. . .	. . .	. . .	. . .	. . .	. . .	. . .
Other sectors: long-term	4 726 . .	. . .	. . .	. . .	. . .	. . .	. . .	. . .	. . .
Other sectors: short-term	4 727 . .	. . .	. . .	. . .	. . .	. . .	. . .	. . .	. . .
Currency and deposits	4 730 . .	–130	–560	–1,652	172	658	1,206	–414	. . .
Monetary authorities	4 731 . .	. . .	. . .	. . .	. . .	. . .	. . .	. . .	. . .
General government	4 732 . .	. . .	. . .	. . .	. . .	. . .	. . .	. . .	. . .
Banks	4 733 . .	–130	–560	–1,652	172	658	1,206	–414	. . .
Other sectors	4 734 . .	. . .	. . .	. . .	. . .	. . .	. . .	. . .	. . .
Other assets	4 736 . .	. . .	. . .	. . .	. . .	. . .	. . .	. . .	. . .
Monetary authorities: long-term	4 738 . .	. . .	. . .	. . .	. . .	. . .	. . .	. . .	. . .
Monetary authorities: short-term	4 739 . .	. . .	. . .	. . .	. . .	. . .	. . .	. . .	. . .
General government: long-term	4 741 . .	. . .	. . .	. . .	. . .	. . .	. . .	. . .	. . .
General government: short-term	4 742 . .	. . .	. . .	. . .	. . .	. . .	. . .	. . .	. . .
Banks: long-term	4 744 . .	. . .	. . .	. . .	. . .	. . .	. . .	. . .	. . .
Banks: short-term	4 745 . .	. . .	. . .	. . .	. . .	. . .	. . .	. . .	. . .
Other sectors: long-term	4 747 . .	. . .	. . .	. . .	. . .	. . .	. . .	. . .	. . .
Other sectors: short-term	4 748 . .	. . .	. . .	. . .	. . .	. . .	. . .	. . .	. . .
Liabilities	4 753 . .	**310**	**2,722**	**1,805**	**4,951**	**3,703**	**4,313**	**–1,771**	**. . .**
Trade credits	4 756 . .	399	1,940	410	4,869	3,684	4,276	–1,236	. . .
General government: long-term	4 758 . .	–20	–10	52	476	4,600	–1,328	9,233	. . .
General government: short-term	4 759 . .	. . .	. . .	. . .	. . .	. . .	. . .	. . .	. . .
Other sectors: long-term	4 761 . .	. . .	. . .	. . .	. . .	. . .	. . .	. . .	. . .
Other sectors: short-term	4 762 . .	419	1,950	358	4,393	–916	5,604	–10,469	. . .
Loans	4 764 . .	–177	–63	–93	–35	–44	–31	–31	. . .
Use of Fund credit and loans from the Fund	4 766 . .	. . .	. . .	. . .	. . .	. . .	. . .	. . .	. . .
Monetary authorities: other long-term	4 767 . .	. . .	. . .	. . .	. . .	. . .	. . .	. . .	. . .
Monetary authorities: short-term	4 768 . .	. . .	. . .	. . .	. . .	. . .	. . .	. . .	. . .
General government: long-term	4 770 . .	–124	–61	–93	–36	–44	–30	–31	. . .
General government: short-term	4 771 . .	. . .	. . .	. . .	. . .	. . .	. . .	. . .	. . .
Banks: long-term	4 773 . .	. . .	. . .	. . .	. . .	. . .	. . .	. . .	. . .
Banks: short-term	4 774 . .	. . .	. . .	. . .	. . .	. . .	. . .	. . .	. . .
Other sectors: long-term	4 776 . .	–53	–2	. . .	1	. . .	–1	. . .	. . .
Other sectors: short-term	4 777 . .	. . .	. . .	. . .	. . .	. . .	. . .	. . .	. . .
Currency and deposits	4 780 . .	–29	344	1,101	489	. . .	. . .	. . .	. . .
Monetary authorities	4 781 . .	. . .	. . .	. . .	. . .	. . .	. . .	. . .	. . .
General government	4 782 . .	. . .	. . .	. . .	. . .	. . .	. . .	. . .	. . .
Banks	4 783 . .	–29	344	1,101	489	. . .	. . .	. . .	. . .
Other sectors	4 784 . .	. . .	. . .	. . .	. . .	. . .	. . .	. . .	. . .
Other liabilities	4 786 . .	117	501	387	–372	63	68	–504	. . .
Monetary authorities: long-term	4 788 . .	. . .	. . .	. . .	. . .	. . .	. . .	. . .	. . .
Monetary authorities: short-term	4 789 . .	117	501	387	–372	63	68	–504	. . .
General government: long-term	4 791 . .	. . .	. . .	. . .	. . .	. . .	. . .	. . .	. . .
General government: short-term	4 792 . .	. . .	. . .	. . .	. . .	. . .	. . .	. . .	. . .
Banks: long-term	4 794 . .	. . .	. . .	. . .	. . .	. . .	. . .	. . .	. . .
Banks: short-term	4 795 . .	. . .	. . .	. . .	. . .	. . .	. . .	. . .	. . .
Other sectors: long-term	4 797 . .	. . .	. . .	. . .	. . .	. . .	. . .	. . .	. . .
Other sectors: short-term	4 798 . .	. . .	. . .	. . .	. . .	. . .	. . .	. . .	. . .
D. RESERVE ASSETS	4 800 . .	1,010	–2,300	325	2,093	164	–229	–1,232	. . .
Monetary gold	4 810 . .	454	–279	–133	629	6	6	–28	. . .
Special drawing rights	4 820 . .	175	–111	–8	133	145	9	11	. . .
Reserve position in the Fund	4 830 . .	95	. . .	. . .	. . .	–1	. . .	. . .	. . .
Foreign exchange	4 840 . .	–30	–1,841	478	1,332	174	–228	–1,177	. . .
Other claims	4 880 . .	315	–69	–12	–1	–160	–16	–38	. . .
NET ERRORS AND OMISSIONS	4 998 . .	**539**	**–770**	**–947**	**1,322**	**1,637**	**–1,119**	**–1,318**	**. . .**

Part 3 of the *Yearbook* contains descriptions of the methodologies, compilation practices, and sources used to compile these data.

Table 1. ANALYTIC PRESENTATION, 1988–95
(Millions of U.S. dollars)

	Code	1988	1989	1990	1991	1992	1993	1994	1995
A. Current Account [1]	4 993 Y .	**–25**	**–581**	**–361**	**284**	**607**	**1,765**	**1,510**	**1,379**
Goods: exports f.o.b	2 100 . .	18,389	20,356	23,341	23,659	28,107	28,728	33,642	43,319
Goods: imports f.o.b	3 100 . .	–14,567	–16,352	–19,397	–19,366	–21,062	–20,553	–24,275	–30,194
Balance on Goods	4 100 . .	*3,822*	*4,003*	*3,944*	*4,294*	*7,045*	*8,175*	*9,366*	*13,125*
Services: credit	2 200 . .	2,414	2,533	3,445	3,667	4,054	3,769	4,110	4,802
Services: debit	3 200 . .	–3,837	–4,342	–5,178	–5,662	–7,084	–6,760	–8,310	–10,516
Balance on Goods and Services	4 991 . .	*2,399*	*2,194*	*2,211*	*2,298*	*4,015*	*5,185*	*5,167*	*7,411*
Income: credit	2 300 . .	1,411	1,795	3,280	3,259	3,282	2,780	3,513	5,006
Income: debit	3 300 . .	–5,282	–6,075	–8,235	–7,858	–8,827	–8,116	–8,919	–12,820
Balance on Goods, Services, and Income	4 992 . .	*–1,473*	*–2,086*	*–2,745*	*–2,301*	*–1,530*	*–151*	*–240*	*–403*
Current transfers: credit	2 379 Y .	1,908	1,976	3,089	3,395	3,033	2,858	2,850	3,014
Current transfers: debit	3 379 . .	–460	–471	–705	–809	–896	–941	–1,100	–1,231
B. Capital Account [1]	4 994 Y .	**95**	**103**	**387**	**601**	**787**	**775**	**387**	**817**
Capital account: credit	2 994 Y .	247	231	486	698	889	863	477	914
Capital account: debit	3 994 . .	–152	–127	–99	–97	–102	–89	–90	–96
Total, Groups A Plus B	4 010 . .	*70*	*–478*	*26*	*886*	*1,394*	*2,540*	*1,897*	*2,196*
C. Financial Account [1]	4 995 X .	**200**	**–1,574**	**–1,877**	**–2,296**	**–5,341**	**346**	**–3,752**	**–673**
Direct investment abroad	4 505 . .	. . .	. . .	–365	–195	–215	–220	–438	–820
Direct investment in Ireland	4 555 Y .	92	85	760	1,062	1,438	1,113	934	2,317
Portfolio investment assets	4 602 . .	–485	–1,120	–465	–1,717	–439	–272	–1,019	–1,056
Equity securities	4 610 . .	. . .	. . .	. . .	. . .	. . .	. . .	. . .	. . .
Debt securities	4 619 . .	–485	–1,120	–465	–1,717	–439	–272	–1,019	–1,056
Portfolio investment liabilities	4 652 Y .	1,475	1,770	266	648	–2,750	2,723	–379	771
Equity securities	4 660 Y .	. . .	. . .	. . .	. . .	. . .	. . .	. . .	. . .
Debt securities	4 669 Y .	1,475	1,770	266	648	–2,750	2,723	–379	771
Other investment assets	4 703 . .	–1,941	–4,483	–5,284	–1,860	–8,489	–10,642	–4,368	–18,078
Monetary authorities	4 703 . A	. . .	. . .	. . .	. . .	. . .	. . .	. . .	. . .
General government	4 703 . B	. . .	. . .	. . .	. . .	. . .	. . .	–76	76
Banks	4 703 . C	–1,214	–2,942	–2,310	–662	–6,414	–9,486	–2,803	–14,204
Other sectors	4 703 . D	–727	–1,541	–2,973	–1,197	–2,075	–1,157	–1,489	–3,950
Other investment liabilities	4 753 X .	1,060	2,175	3,211	–234	5,114	7,644	1,519	16,192
Monetary authorities	4 753 XA	. . .	. . .	. . .	. . .	. . .	. . .	. . .	. . .
General government	4 753 YB	–615	–413	–195	–239	1,142	–580	–1,585	–808
Banks	4 753 YC	1,675	2,588	3,406	5	3,972	8,224	3,103	17,000
Other sectors	4 753 YD	. . .	. . .	. . .	. . .	. . .	. . .	. . .	. . .
Total, Groups A Through C	4 020 . .	*270*	*–2,051*	*–1,851*	*–1,410*	*–3,947*	*2,886*	*–1,854*	*1,523*
D. Net Errors and Omissions	4 998 . .	**322**	**1,115**	**2,476**	**1,873**	**405**	**1,029**	**1,679**	**816**
Total, Groups A Through D	4 030 . .	*592*	*–937*	*626*	*463*	*–3,541*	*3,915*	*–176*	*2,339*
E. Reserves and Related Items	4 040 . .	**–592**	**937**	**–626**	**–463**	**3,541**	**–3,915**	**176**	**–2,339**
Reserve assets	4 800 . .	–592	937	–626	–463	2,166	–2,660	176	–2,339
Use of Fund credit and loans	4 766 . .	. . .	. . .	. . .	. . .	. . .	. . .	. . .	. . .
Liabilities constituting foreign authorities' reserves	4 900 . .	. . .	. . .	. . .	. . .	1,376	–1,255	. . .	. . .
Exceptional financing	4 920 . .	. . .	. . .	. . .	. . .	. . .	. . .	. . .	. . .
Conversion rates: Irish pound per U.S. dollar	0 101 . .	**.65647**	**.70554**	**.60459**	**.62130**	**.58772**	**.67725**	**.66863**	**.62373**

[1] Excludes components that have been classified in the categories of Group E.

Table 2. STANDARD PRESENTATION, 1988–95
(Millions of U.S. dollars)

	Code	1988	1989	1990	1991	1992	1993	1994	1995
CURRENT ACCOUNT	4 993 . .	**–25**	**–581**	**–361**	**284**	**607**	**1,765**	**1,510**	**1,379**
A. GOODS	4 100 . .	3,822	4,003	3,944	4,294	7,045	8,175	9,366	13,125
Credit	2 100 . .	**18,389**	**20,356**	**23,341**	**23,659**	**28,107**	**28,728**	**33,642**	**43,319**
General merchandise: exports f.o.b.	2 110 . .	18,386	20,353	23,339	23,658	28,102	28,728	33,642	43,319
Goods for processing: exports f.o.b.	2 150 . .	. . .	. . .	. . .	. . .	. . .	. . .	. . .	. . .
Repairs on goods	2 160 . .	. . .	. . .	. . .	. . .	. . .	. . .	. . .	. . .
Goods procured in ports by carriers	2 170 . .	. . .	. . .	. . .	. . .	. . .	. . .	. . .	. . .
Nonmonetary gold	2 180 . .	2	2	2	2	5	. . .	. . .	. . .
Debit	3 100 . .	**–14,567**	**–16,352**	**–19,397**	**–19,366**	**–21,062**	**–20,553**	**–24,275**	**–30,194**
General merchandise: imports f.o.b.	3 110 . .	–14,557	–16,343	–19,386	–19,356	–21,052	–20,544	–24,263	–30,180
Goods for processing: imports f.o.b.	3 150 . .	. . .	. . .	. . .	. . .	. . .	. . .	. . .	. . .
Repairs on goods	3 160 . .	. . .	. . .	. . .	. . .	. . .	. . .	. . .	. . .
Goods procured in ports by carriers	3 170 . .	. . .	. . .	. . .	. . .	. . .	. . .	. . .	. . .
Nonmonetary gold	3 180 . .	–10	–10	–11	–10	–10	–9	–12	–14
B. SERVICES	4 200 . .	–1,423	–1,809	–1,733	–1,995	–3,030	–2,990	–4,200	–5,714
Total credit	2 200 . .	*2,414*	*2,533*	*3,445*	*3,667*	*4,054*	*3,769*	*4,110*	*4,802*
Total debit	3 200 . .	*–3,837*	*–4,342*	*–5,178*	*–5,662*	*–7,084*	*–6,760*	*–8,310*	*–10,516*
Transportation services, credit	2 205 . .	**801**	**811**	**1,020**	**1,017**	**1,089**	**936**	**975**	**1,071**
Passenger	2 205 BA	*283*	*327*	*438*	*441*	*486*	*406*	*444*	*487*
Freight	2 205 BB	*30*	*23*	*35*	*32*	*31*	*24*	*26*	*32*
Other	2 205 BC	*488*	*461*	*548*	*544*	*573*	*506*	*506*	*552*
Sea transport, passenger	2 207 . .	. . .	. . .	. . .	. . .	. . .	. . .	. . .	. . .
Sea transport, freight	2 208 . .	. . .	. . .	. . .	. . .	. . .	. . .	. . .	. . .
Sea transport, other	2 209 . .	. . .	. . .	. . .	. . .	. . .	. . .	. . .	. . .
Air transport, passenger	2 211 . .	. . .	. . .	. . .	. . .	. . .	. . .	. . .	. . .
Air transport, freight	2 212 . .	. . .	. . .	. . .	. . .	. . .	. . .	. . .	. . .
Air transport, other	2 213 . .	. . .	. . .	. . .	. . .	. . .	. . .	. . .	. . .
Other transport, passenger	2 215 . .	. . .	. . .	. . .	. . .	. . .	. . .	. . .	. . .
Other transport, freight	2 216 . .	. . .	. . .	. . .	. . .	. . .	. . .	. . .	. . .
Other transport, other	2 217 . .	. . .	. . .	. . .	. . .	. . .	. . .	. . .	. . .
Transportation services, debit	3 205 . .	**–977**	**–1,057**	**–1,251**	**–1,262**	**–1,358**	**–1,293**	**–1,461**	**–1,760**
Passenger	3 205 BA	. . .	. . .	. . .	. . .	. . .	. . .	. . .	. . .
Freight	3 205 BB	*–578*	*–666*	*–781*	*–786*	*–853*	*–854*	*–1,021*	*–1,284*
Other	3 205 BC	*–399*	*–391*	*–470*	*–476*	*–505*	*–440*	*–440*	*–476*
Sea transport, passenger	3 207 . .	. . .	. . .	. . .	. . .	. . .	. . .	. . .	. . .
Sea transport, freight	3 208 . .	. . .	. . .	. . .	. . .	. . .	. . .	. . .	. . .
Sea transport, other	3 209 . .	. . .	. . .	. . .	. . .	. . .	. . .	. . .	. . .
Air transport, passenger	3 211 . .	. . .	. . .	. . .	. . .	. . .	. . .	. . .	. . .
Air transport, freight	3 212 . .	. . .	. . .	. . .	. . .	. . .	. . .	. . .	. . .
Air transport, other	3 213 . .	. . .	. . .	. . .	. . .	. . .	. . .	. . .	. . .
Other transport, passenger	3 215 . .	. . .	. . .	. . .	. . .	. . .	. . .	. . .	. . .
Other transport, freight	3 216 . .	. . .	. . .	. . .	. . .	. . .	. . .	. . .	. . .
Other transport, other	3 217 . .	. . .	. . .	. . .	. . .	. . .	. . .	. . .	. . .
Travel, credit	2 236 . .	**984**	**1,058**	**1,459**	**1,485**	**1,641**	**1,593**	**1,811**	**2,211**
Business travel	2 237 . .	. . .	. . .	. . .	. . .	. . .	. . .	. . .	. . .
Personal travel	2 240 . .	. . .	. . .	. . .	. . .	. . .	. . .	. . .	. . .
Travel, debit	3 236 . .	**–947**	**–982**	**–1,163**	**–1,111**	**–1,375**	**–1,220**	**–1,615**	**–2,034**
Business travel	3 237 . .	. . .	. . .	. . .	. . .	. . .	. . .	. . .	. . .
Personal travel	3 240 . .	. . .	. . .	. . .	. . .	. . .	. . .	. . .	. . .
Other services, credit	2 200 BA	**629**	**664**	**965**	**1,165**	**1,324**	**1,241**	**1,323**	**1,520**
Communications	2 245 . .	. . .	. . .	. . .	. . .	. . .	. . .	. . .	. . .
Construction	2 249 . .	. . .	. . .	. . .	. . .	. . .	. . .	. . .	. . .
Insurance	2 253 . .	. . .	. . .	. . .	. . .	. . .	. . .	. . .	. . .
Financial	2 260 . .	. . .	. . .	. . .	. . .	. . .	. . .	. . .	. . .
Computer and information	2 262 . .	. . .	. . .	. . .	. . .	. . .	. . .	. . .	. . .
Royalties and licence fees	2 266 . .	. . .	. . .	38	44	39	67	91	114
Other business services	2 268 . .	510	537	768	947	1,081	978	1,059	1,204
Personal, cultural, and recreational	2 287 . .	. . .	. . .	. . .	. . .	. . .	. . .	. . .	. . .
Government, n.i.e.	2 291 . .	119	128	159	174	204	195	174	202
Other services, debit	3 200 BA	**–1,912**	**–2,303**	**–2,765**	**–3,288**	**–4,352**	**–4,247**	**–5,234**	**–6,722**
Communications	3 245 . .	. . .	. . .	. . .	. . .	. . .	. . .	. . .	. . .
Construction	3 249 . .	. . .	. . .	. . .	. . .	. . .	. . .	. . .	. . .
Insurance	3 253 . .	–75	–84	–98	–98	–107	–105	–123	–154
Financial	3 260 . .	. . .	. . .	. . .	. . .	. . .	. . .	. . .	. . .
Computer and information	3 262 . .	. . .	. . .	. . .	. . .	. . .	. . .	. . .	. . .
Royalties and licence fees	3 266 . .	–346	–422	–591	–811	–1,154	–1,390	–1,917	–2,554
Other business services	3 268 . .	–1,465	–1,767	–2,043	–2,346	–3,056	–2,716	–3,145	–3,963
Personal, cultural, and recreational	3 287 . .	. . .	. . .	. . .	. . .	. . .	. . .	. . .	. . .
Government, n.i.e.	3 291 . .	–27	–30	–33	–32	–34	–36	–48	–51

Table 2 (Continued). STANDARD PRESENTATION, 1988–95
(Millions of U.S. dollars)

	Code	1988	1989	1990	1991	1992	1993	1994	1995
C. INCOME	4 300 . .	–3,871	–4,280	–4,955	–4,600	–5,545	–5,336	–5,406	–7,814
Total credit	2 300 . .	*1,411*	*1,795*	*3,280*	*3,259*	*3,282*	*2,780*	*3,513*	*5,006*
Total debit	3 300 . .	*–5,282*	*–6,075*	*–8,235*	*–7,858*	*–8,827*	*–8,116*	*–8,919*	*–12,820*
Compensation of employees, credit	2 310 . .	**. . .**	**. . .**	**286**	**278**	**322**	**297**	**324**	**347**
Compensation of employees, debit	3 310 . .	**. . .**	**. . .**	**–66**	**–71**	**–75**	**–71**	**–72**	**–77**
Investment income, credit	2 320 . .	**1,411**	**1,795**	**2,994**	**2,981**	**2,960**	**2,483**	**3,189**	**4,659**
Direct investment income	2 330 . .	. . .	. . .	395	301	268	223	444	891
Dividends and distributed branch profits	2 332 . .	. . .	. . .	30	106	53	3	6	71
Reinvested earnings and undistributed branch profits	2 333 . .	. . .	. . .	365	195	215	220	438	820
Income on debt (interest)	2 334 . .	. . .	. . .	. . .	. . .	. . .	. . .	. . .	. . .
Portfolio investment income	2 339 . .	. . .	. . .	. . .	. . .	. . .	. . .	. . .	. . .
Income on equity	2 340 . .	. . .	. . .	. . .	. . .	. . .	. . .	. . .	. . .
Income on bonds and notes	2 350 . .	. . .	. . .	. . .	. . .	. . .	. . .	. . .	. . .
Income on money market instruments and financial derivatives	2 360 . .	. . .	. . .	. . .	. . .	. . .	. . .	. . .	. . .
Other investment income	2 370 . .	1,411	1,795	2,599	2,680	2,692	2,260	2,746	3,768
Investment income, debit	3 320 . .	**–5,282**	**–6,075**	**–8,169**	**–7,787**	**–8,752**	**–8,045**	**–8,847**	**–12,743**
Direct investment income	3 330 . .	–2,847	–3,217	–4,350	–4,077	–5,174	–4,989	–5,645	–8,719
Dividends and distributed branch profits	3 332 . .	–2,847	–3,217	–3,690	–3,111	–3,838	–3,965	–4,801	–6,498
Reinvested earnings and undistributed branch profits	3 333 . .	. . .	. . .	–660	–966	–1,336	–1,024	–844	–2,221
Income on debt (interest)	3 334 . .	. . .	. . .	. . .	. . .	. . .	. . .	. . .	. . .
Portfolio investment income	3 339 . .	. . .	. . .	. . .	. . .	. . .	. . .	. . .	. . .
Income on equity	3 340 . .	. . .	. . .	. . .	. . .	. . .	. . .	. . .	. . .
Income on bonds and notes	3 350 . .	. . .	. . .	. . .	. . .	. . .	. . .	. . .	. . .
Income on money market instruments and financial derivatives	3 360 . .	. . .	. . .	. . .	. . .	. . .	. . .	. . .	. . .
Other investment income	3 370 . .	–2,435	–2,858	–3,818	–3,711	–3,578	–3,057	–3,203	–4,024
D. CURRENT TRANSFERS	4 379 . .	1,448	1,505	2,384	2,586	2,137	1,917	1,750	1,782
Credit	2 379 . .	**1,908**	**1,976**	**3,089**	**3,395**	**3,033**	**2,858**	**2,850**	**3,014**
General government	2 380 . .	49	49	378	761	722	712	587	591
Other sectors	2 390 . .	1,859	1,927	2,711	2,634	2,311	2,146	2,263	2,423
Workers' remittances	2 391 . .	. . .	. . .	. . .	. . .	. . .	. . .	. . .	. . .
Other current transfers	2 392 . .	1,859	1,927	2,711	2,634	2,311	2,146	2,263	2,423
Debit	3 379 . .	**–460**	**–471**	**–705**	**–809**	**–896**	**–941**	**–1,100**	**–1,231**
General government	3 380 . .	–414	–432	–106	–174	–194	–240	–311	–328
Other sectors	3 390 . .	–46	–39	–599	–635	–702	–701	–789	–903
Workers' remittances	3 391 . .	. . .	. . .	. . .	. . .	. . .	. . .	. . .	. . .
Other current transfers	3 392 . .	–46	–39	–599	–635	–702	–701	–789	–903
CAPITAL AND FINANCIAL ACCOUNT	4 996 . .	**–298**	**–534**	**–2,116**	**–2,157**	**–1,012**	**–2,795**	**–3,189**	**–2,195**
CAPITAL ACCOUNT	4 994 . .	**95**	**103**	**387**	**601**	**787**	**775**	**387**	**817**
Total credit	2 994 . .	*247*	*231*	*486*	*698*	*889*	*863*	*477*	*914*
Total debit	3 994 . .	*–152*	*–127*	*–99*	*–97*	*–102*	*–89*	*–90*	*–96*
Capital transfers, credit	2 400 . .	**247**	**231**	**486**	**698**	**889**	**863**	**477**	**914**
General government	2 401 . .	247	231	473	692	883	852	471	907
Debt forgiveness	2 402 . .	. . .	. . .	. . .	. . .	. . .	. . .	. . .	. . .
Other capital transfers	2 410 . .	. . .	. . .	473	692	883	852	471	907
Other sectors	2 430 . .	. . .	. . .	13	6	7	12	6	6
Migrants' transfers	2 431 . .	. . .	. . .	. . .	. . .	. . .	. . .	. . .	. . .
Debt forgiveness	2 432 . .	. . .	. . .	. . .	. . .	. . .	. . .	. . .	. . .
Other capital transfers	2 440 . .	. . .	. . .	13	6	7	12	6	6
Capital transfers, debit	3 400 . .	**–152**	**–127**	**–99**	**–97**	**–102**	**–89**	**–90**	**–96**
General government	3 401 . .	. . .	. . .	. . .	. . .	. . .	. . .	. . .	. . .
Debt forgiveness	3 402 . .	. . .	. . .	. . .	. . .	. . .	. . .	. . .	. . .
Other capital transfers	3 410 . .	. . .	. . .	. . .	. . .	. . .	. . .	. . .	. . .
Other sectors	3 430 . .	–152	–127	–99	–97	–102	–89	–90	–96
Migrants' transfers	3 431 . .	–152	–127	–99	–97	–102	–89	–90	–96
Debt forgiveness	3 432 . .	. . .	. . .	. . .	. . .	. . .	. . .	. . .	. . .
Other capital transfers	3 440 . .	. . .	. . .	. . .	. . .	. . .	. . .	. . .	. . .
Nonproduced nonfinancial assets, credit	2 480 . .	**. . .**	**. . .**	**. . .**	**. . .**	**. . .**	**. . .**	**. . .**	**. . .**
Nonproduced nonfinancial assets, debit	3 480 . .	**. . .**	**. . .**	**. . .**	**. . .**	**. . .**	**. . .**	**. . .**	**. . .**

Table 2 (Continued). STANDARD PRESENTATION, 1988–95
(Millions of U.S. dollars)

	Code	1988	1989	1990	1991	1992	1993	1994	1995
FINANCIAL ACCOUNT	4 995	**–392**	**–637**	**–2,503**	**–2,759**	**–1,799**	**–3,569**	**–3,576**	**–3,012**
A. DIRECT INVESTMENT	4 500	92	85	395	867	1,223	893	496	1,497
Direct investment abroad	4 505	**. . .**	**. . .**	**–365**	**–195**	**–215**	**–220**	**–438**	**–820**
Equity capital	4 510	. . .	. . .	. . .	. . .	. . .	. . .	. . .	. . .
Claims on affiliated enterprises	4 515	. . .	. . .	. . .	. . .	. . .	. . .	. . .	. . .
Liabilities to affiliated enterprises	4 520	. . .	. . .	. . .	. . .	. . .	. . .	. . .	. . .
Reinvested earnings	4 525	. . .	. . .	–365	–195	–215	–220	–438	–820
Other capital	4 530	. . .	. . .	. . .	. . .	. . .	. . .	. . .	. . .
Claims on affiliated enterprises	4 535	. . .	. . .	. . .	. . .	. . .	. . .	. . .	. . .
Liabilities to affiliated enterprises	4 540	. . .	. . .	. . .	. . .	. . .	. . .	. . .	. . .
Direct investment in Ireland	4 555	**92**	**85**	**760**	**1,062**	**1,438**	**1,113**	**934**	**2,317**
Equity capital	4 560	. . .	. . .	. . .	. . .	. . .	. . .	. . .	. . .
Claims on direct investors	4 565	. . .	. . .	. . .	. . .	. . .	. . .	. . .	. . .
Liabilities to direct investors	4 570	. . .	. . .	. . .	. . .	. . .	. . .	. . .	. . .
Reinvested earnings	4 575	. . .	. . .	660	966	1,336	1,024	844	2,221
Other capital	4 580	92	85	99	97	102	89	90	96
Claims on direct investors	4 585	. . .	. . .	. . .	. . .	. . .	. . .	. . .	. . .
Liabilities to direct investors	4 590	. . .	. . .	. . .	. . .	. . .	. . .	. . .	. . .
B. PORTFOLIO INVESTMENT	4 600	990	650	–200	–1,069	–3,189	2,451	–1,399	–285
Assets	4 602	**–485**	**–1,120**	**–465**	**–1,717**	**–439**	**–272**	**–1,019**	**–1,056**
Equity securities	4 610	. . .	. . .	. . .	. . .	. . .	. . .	. . .	. . .
Monetary authorities	4 611	. . .	. . .	. . .	. . .	. . .	. . .	. . .	. . .
General government	4 612	. . .	. . .	. . .	. . .	. . .	. . .	. . .	. . .
Banks	4 613	. . .	. . .	. . .	. . .	. . .	. . .	. . .	. . .
Other sectors	4 614	. . .	. . .	. . .	. . .	. . .	. . .	. . .	. . .
Debt securities	4 619	–485	–1,120	–465	–1,717	–439	–272	–1,019	–1,056
Bonds and notes	4 620	–485	–1,120	–465	–1,717	–439	–272	–1,019	–1,056
Monetary authorities	4 621	. . .	. . .	. . .	. . .	. . .	. . .	. . .	. . .
General government	4 622	. . .	. . .	. . .	. . .	. . .	. . .	. . .	. . .
Banks	4 623	. . .	. . .	. . .	. . .	. . .	. . .	. . .	. . .
Other sectors	4 624	. . .	. . .	–465	–1,717	–439	–272	–1,019	–1,056
Money market instruments	4 630	. . .	. . .	. . .	. . .	. . .	. . .	. . .	. . .
Monetary authorities	4 631	. . .	. . .	. . .	. . .	. . .	. . .	. . .	. . .
General government	4 632	. . .	. . .	. . .	. . .	. . .	. . .	. . .	. . .
Banks	4 633	. . .	. . .	. . .	. . .	. . .	. . .	. . .	. . .
Other sectors	4 634	. . .	. . .	. . .	. . .	. . .	. . .	. . .	. . .
Financial derivatives	4 640	. . .	. . .	. . .	. . .	. . .	. . .	. . .	. . .
Monetary authorities	4 641	. . .	. . .	. . .	. . .	. . .	. . .	. . .	. . .
General government	4 642	. . .	. . .	. . .	. . .	. . .	. . .	. . .	. . .
Banks	4 643	. . .	. . .	. . .	. . .	. . .	. . .	. . .	. . .
Other sectors	4 644	. . .	. . .	. . .	. . .	. . .	. . .	. . .	. . .
Liabilities	4 652	**1,475**	**1,770**	**266**	**648**	**–2,750**	**2,723**	**–379**	**771**
Equity securities	4 660	. . .	. . .	. . .	. . .	. . .	. . .	. . .	. . .
Banks	4 663	. . .	. . .	. . .	. . .	. . .	. . .	. . .	. . .
Other sectors	4 664	. . .	. . .	. . .	. . .	. . .	. . .	. . .	. . .
Debt securities	4 669	1,475	1,770	266	648	–2,750	2,723	–379	771
Bonds and notes	4 670	1,475	1,770	266	648	–2,750	2,723	–379	771
Monetary authorities	4 671	. . .	. . .	. . .	. . .	. . .	. . .	. . .	. . .
General government	4 672	1,475	1,770	266	648	–2,750	2,723	–379	771
Banks	4 673	. . .	. . .	. . .	. . .	. . .	. . .	. . .	. . .
Other sectors	4 674	. . .	. . .	. . .	. . .	. . .	. . .	. . .	. . .
Money market instruments	4 680	. . .	. . .	. . .	. . .	. . .	. . .	. . .	. . .
Monetary authorities	4 681	. . .	. . .	. . .	. . .	. . .	. . .	. . .	. . .
General government	4 682	. . .	. . .	. . .	. . .	. . .	. . .	. . .	. . .
Banks	4 683	. . .	. . .	. . .	. . .	. . .	. . .	. . .	. . .
Other sectors	4 684	. . .	. . .	. . .	. . .	. . .	. . .	. . .	. . .
Financial derivatives	4 690	. . .	. . .	. . .	. . .	. . .	. . .	. . .	. . .
Monetary authorities	4 691	. . .	. . .	. . .	. . .	. . .	. . .	. . .	. . .
General government	4 692	. . .	. . .	. . .	. . .	. . .	. . .	. . .	. . .
Banks	4 693	. . .	. . .	. . .	. . .	. . .	. . .	. . .	. . .
Other sectors	4 694	. . .	. . .	. . .	. . .	. . .	. . .	. . .	. . .

Table 2 (Concluded). STANDARD PRESENTATION, 1988–95
(Millions of U.S. dollars)

	Code	1988	1989	1990	1991	1992	1993	1994	1995
C. OTHER INVESTMENT	4 700 . .	–881	–2,308	–2,072	–2,094	–2,000	–4,253	–2,849	–1,886
Assets	4 703 . .	**–1,941**	**–4,483**	**–5,284**	**–1,860**	**–8,489**	**–10,642**	**–4,368**	**–18,078**
Trade credits	4 706 . .	...	...	...	...	...	...	...	...
General government: long-term	4 708 . .	...	...	...	...	...	...	...	...
General government: short-term	4 709 . .	...	...	...	...	...	...	...	...
Other sectors: long-term	4 711 . .	...	...	...	...	...	...	...	...
Other sectors: short-term	4 712 . .	...	...	...	...	...	...	...	...
Loans	4 714 . .	...	...	...	...	...	...	...	...
Monetary authorities: long-term	4 717 . .	...	...	...	...	...	...	...	...
Monetary authorities: short-term	4 718 . .	...	...	...	...	...	...	...	...
General government: long-term	4 720 . .	...	...	...	...	...	...	...	...
General government: short-term	4 721 . .	...	...	...	...	...	...	...	...
Banks: long-term	4 723 . .	...	...	...	...	...	...	...	...
Banks: short-term	4 724 . .	...	...	...	...	...	...	...	...
Other sectors: long-term	4 726 . .	...	...	...	...	...	...	...	...
Other sectors: short-term	4 727 . .	...	...	...	...	...	...	...	...
Currency and deposits	4 730 . .	–1,214	–2,942	–2,310	–662	–6,414	–9,486	–2,879	–14,129
Monetary authorities	4 731 . .	...	...	...	...	...	...	...	...
General government	4 732 . .	...	...	...	...	...	...	–76	76
Banks	4 733 . .	–1,214	–2,942	–2,310	–662	–6,414	–9,486	–2,803	–14,204
Other sectors	4 734 . .	...	...	...	...	...	...	...	...
Other assets	4 736 . .	–727	–1,541	–2,973	–1,197	–2,075	–1,157	–1,489	–3,950
Monetary authorities: long-term	4 738 . .	...	...	...	...	...	...	...	...
Monetary authorities: short-term	4 739 . .	...	...	...	...	...	...	...	...
General government: long-term	4 741 . .	...	...	...	...	...	...	...	...
General government: short-term	4 742 . .	...	...	...	...	...	...	...	...
Banks: long-term	4 744 . .	...	...	...	...	...	...	...	...
Banks: short-term	4 745 . .	...	...	...	...	...	...	...	...
Other sectors: long-term	4 747 . .	–727	–1,541	–2,973	–1,197	–2,075	–1,157	–1,489	–3,950
Other sectors: short-term	4 748 . .	...	...	...	...	...	...	...	...
Liabilities	4 753 . .	**1,060**	**2,175**	**3,211**	**–234**	**6,489**	**6,389**	**1,519**	**16,192**
Trade credits	4 756 . .	...	...	...	...	...	...	...	...
General government: long-term	4 758 . .	...	...	...	...	...	...	...	...
General government: short-term	4 759 . .	...	...	...	...	...	...	...	...
Other sectors: long-term	4 761 . .	...	...	...	...	...	...	...	...
Other sectors: short-term	4 762 . .	...	...	...	...	...	...	...	...
Loans	4 764 . .	–615	–410	–195	–233	1,149	–580	–1,579	–795
Use of Fund credit and loans from the Fund	4 766 . .	...	...	...	...	...	...	...	...
Monetary authorities: other long-term	4 767 . .	...	...	...	...	...	...	...	...
Monetary authorities: short-term	4 768 . .	...	...	...	...	...	...	...	...
General government: long-term	4 770 . .	–615	–410	–195	–233	1,149	–580	–1,579	–795
General government: short-term	4 771 . .	...	...	...	...	...	...	...	...
Banks: long-term	4 773 . .	...	...	...	...	...	...	...	...
Banks: short-term	4 774 . .	...	...	...	...	...	...	...	...
Other sectors: long-term	4 776 . .	...	...	...	...	...	...	...	...
Other sectors: short-term	4 777 . .	...	...	...	...	...	...	...	...
Currency and deposits	4 780 . .	1,675	2,588	3,406	5	5,347	6,969	3,103	17,000
Monetary authorities	4 781 . .	...	...	...	...	1,376	–1,255	...	...
General government	4 782 . .	...	...	...	...	...	...	...	...
Banks	4 783 . .	1,675	2,588	3,406	5	3,972	8,224	3,103	17,000
Other sectors	4 784 . .	...	...	...	...	...	...	...	...
Other liabilities	4 786 . .	...	–4	...	–6	–7	...	–6	–13
Monetary authorities: long-term	4 788 . .	...	...	...	...	...	...	...	...
Monetary authorities: short-term	4 789 . .	...	...	...	...	...	...	...	...
General government: long-term	4 791 . .	...	...	...	...	...	...	...	...
General government: short-term	4 792 . .	...	–4	...	–6	–7	...	–6	–13
Banks: long-term	4 794 . .	...	...	...	...	...	...	...	...
Banks: short-term	4 795 . .	...	...	...	...	...	...	...	...
Other sectors: long-term	4 797 . .	...	...	...	...	...	...	...	...
Other sectors: short-term	4 798 . .	...	...	...	...	...	...	...	...
D. RESERVE ASSETS	4 800 . .	–592	937	–626	–463	2,166	–2,660	176	–2,339
Monetary gold	4 810 . .	12	8	13	5	16	–72	19	2
Special drawing rights	4 820 . .	–11	–14	–18	–16	111	–9	–7	–9
Reserve position in the Fund	4 830 . .	–4	11	28	–27	–66	23	5	–69
Foreign exchange	4 840 . .	–589	932	–649	–425	2,105	–2,602	159	–2,262
Other claims	4 880 . .	...	...	...	...	...	...	...	...
NET ERRORS AND OMISSIONS	4 998 . .	**322**	**1,115**	**2,476**	**1,873**	**405**	**1,029**	**1,679**	**816**

Part 3 of the *Yearbook* contains descriptions of the methodologies, compilation practices, and sources used to compile these data.

Table 1. ANALYTIC PRESENTATION, 1988–95
(Millions of U.S. dollars)

	Code	1988	1989	1990	1991	1992	1993	1994	1995
A. Current Account [1]	4 993 Y.	**–361**	**573**	**–89**	**–1,046**	**–752**	**–2,069**	**–3,589**	**–5,491**
Goods: exports f.o.b	2 100 ..	10,334	11,123	12,214	12,092	13,382	14,888	16,783	18,994
Goods: imports f.o.b	3 100 ..	–13,231	–13,045	–15,305	–17,101	–18,389	–20,518	–22,745	–26,742
Balance on Goods	4 100 ..	*–2,897*	*–1,922*	*–3,091*	*–5,010*	*–5,007*	*–5,630*	*–5,963*	*–7,748*
Services: credit	2 200 ..	4,115	4,334	4,559	4,665	5,896	6,156	6,649	7,741
Services: debit	3 200 ..	–4,456	–4,928	–5,683	–5,913	–6,596	–7,179	–8,284	–9,257
Balance on Goods and Services	4 991 ..	*–3,238*	*–2,515*	*–4,215*	*–6,258*	*–5,707*	*–6,653*	*–7,598*	*–9,264*
Income: credit	2 300 ..	1,132	1,410	1,628	1,711	1,642	1,263	1,194	1,925
Income: debit	3 300 ..	–2,690	–2,689	–2,763	–2,583	–2,586	–2,488	–2,924	–3,751
Balance on Goods, Services, and Income	4 992 ..	*–4,796*	*–3,795*	*–5,350*	*–7,130*	*–6,651*	*–7,878*	*–9,328*	*–11,090*
Current transfers: credit	2 379 Y.	4,619	4,508	5,451	6,320	6,192	6,095	5,968	6,093
Current transfers: debit	3 379 ..	–185	–140	–189	–236	–294	–286	–229	–493
B. Capital Account [1]	4 994 Y.	**433**	**677**	**624**	**688**	**924**	**950**	**1,254**	**1,404**
Capital account: credit	2 994 Y.	433	677	624	688	924	950	1,254	1,404
Capital account: debit	3 994 ..	...	...	...	...	...	...	...	...
Total, Groups A Plus B	4 010 ..	*71*	*1,250*	*535*	*–359*	*172*	*–1,119*	*–2,334*	*–4,087*
C. Financial Account [1]	4 995 X.	**–503**	**–890**	**455**	**195**	**–826**	**2,414**	**1,617**	**3,085**
Direct investment abroad	4 505 ..	–62	–38	–165	–424	–651	–763	–735	–831
Direct investment in Israel	4 555 Y.	235	125	101	351	539	580	442	1,637
Portfolio investment assets	4 602 ..	–39	–102	–345	–262	–1,268	–730	–267	234
Equity securities	4 610 ..	5	–3	14	–345	–926	79	303	113
Debt securities	4 619 ..	–44	–99	–358	83	–341	–809	–570	122
Portfolio investment liabilities	4 652 Y.	4,211	1,124	134	811	553	2,599	2,796	1,277
Equity securities	4 660 Y.	...	...	...	...	...	...	...	...
Debt securities	4 669 Y.	4,211	1,124	134	811	553	2,599	2,796	1,277
Other investment assets	4 703 ..	–118	–1,229	–801	–543	–1,276	898	–1,699	–878
Monetary authorities	4 703 .A	...	...	...	...	...	...	...	...
General government	4 703 .B	497	–323	–190	–180	78	261	–28	–1,197
Banks	4 703 .C	–413	–538	–244	–604	–1,657	1,140	–1,702	–316
Other sectors	4 703 .D	–202	–369	–367	242	303	–502	31	635
Other investment liabilities	4 753 X.	–4,730	–771	1,531	262	1,276	–170	1,080	1,646
Monetary authorities	4 753 XA	23	30	–26	–4	–14	–2	42	19
General government	4 753 YB	–4,810	–1,080	–162	–156	118	–408	–499	–212
Banks	4 753 YC	–59	–31	376	151	937	281	968	1,232
Other sectors	4 753 YD	115	310	1,342	271	235	–40	570	607
Total, Groups A Through C	4 020 ..	*–432*	*360*	*990*	*–164*	*–654*	*1,296*	*–717*	*–1,002*
D. Net Errors and Omissions	4 998 ..	**–739**	**1,038**	**–475**	**–10**	**–803**	**185**	**786**	**2,252**
Total, Groups A Through D	4 030 ..	*–1,170*	*1,398*	*515*	*–173*	*–1,457*	*1,481*	*69*	*1,250*
E. Reserves and Related Items	4 040 ..	**1,170**	**–1,398**	**–515**	**173**	**1,457**	**–1,481**	**–69**	**–1,250**
Reserve assets	4 800 ..	1,170	–1,398	–515	173	1,212	–1,481	–69	–1,149
Use of Fund credit and loans	4 766 ..	...	...	...	...	245	...	...	–101
Liabilities constituting foreign authorities' reserves	4 900 ..	...	...	...	...	...	...	...	...
Exceptional financing	4 920 ..	...	...	...	...	...	...	...	...
Conversion rates: new sheqalim per U.S. dollar	0 101 ..	**1.5989**	**1.9164**	**2.0162**	**2.2791**	**2.4591**	**2.8301**	**3.0111**	**3.0113**

[1] Excludes components that have been classified in the categories of Group E.

Table 2. STANDARD PRESENTATION, 1988–95
(Millions of U.S. dollars)

	Code	1988	1989	1990	1991	1992	1993	1994	1995
CURRENT ACCOUNT	4 993 . .	**–361**	**573**	**–89**	**–1,046**	**–752**	**–2,069**	**–3,589**	**–5,491**
A. GOODS	4 100 . .	–2,897	–1,922	–3,091	–5,010	–5,007	–5,630	–5,963	–7,748
Credit	2 100 . .	**10,334**	**11,123**	**12,214**	**12,092**	**13,382**	**14,888**	**16,783**	**18,994**
General merchandise: exports f.o.b.	2 110 . .	10,286	11,067	12,139	12,029	13,314	14,804	16,691	18,893
Goods for processing: exports f.o.b.	2 150 . .	. . .	. . .	. . .	. . .	. . .	. . .	. . .	. . .
Repairs on goods	2 160 . .	. . .	. . .	. . .	. . .	. . .	. . .	. . .	. . .
Goods procured in ports by carriers	2 170 . .	48	56	75	63	68	84	91	101
Nonmonetary gold	2 180 . .	. . .	. . .	. . .	. . .	. . .	. . .	. . .	. . .
Debit	3 100 . .	**–13,231**	**–13,045**	**–15,305**	**–17,101**	**–18,389**	**–20,518**	**–22,745**	**–26,742**
General merchandise: imports f.o.b.	3 110 . .	–13,099	–12,900	–15,120	–16,931	–18,237	–20,380	–22,613	–26,577
Goods for processing: imports f.o.b.	3 150 . .	. . .	. . .	. . .	. . .	. . .	. . .	. . .	. . .
Repairs on goods	3 160 . .	. . .	. . .	. . .	. . .	. . .	. . .	. . .	. . .
Goods procured in ports by carriers	3 170 . .	–132	–145	–185	–170	–152	–139	–132	–165
Nonmonetary gold	3 180 . .	. . .	. . .	. . .	. . .	. . .	. . .	. . .	. . .
B. SERVICES	4 200 . .	–341	–593	–1,124	–1,248	–700	–1,023	–1,635	–1,516
Total credit	2 200 . .	*4,115*	*4,334*	*4,559*	*4,665*	*5,896*	*6,156*	*6,649*	*7,741*
Total debit	3 200 . .	*–4,456*	*–4,928*	*–5,683*	*–5,913*	*–6,596*	*–7,179*	*–8,284*	*–9,257*
Transportation services, credit	2 205 . .	**1,214**	**1,285**	**1,420**	**1,483**	**1,614**	**1,680**	**1,701**	**2,015**
Passenger	2 205 BA	*303*	*321*	*361*	*369*	*455*	*467*	*412*	*519*
Freight	2 205 BB	*743*	*762*	*834*	*869*	*952*	*996*	*1,045*	*1,157*
Other	2 205 BC	*169*	*201*	*225*	*246*	*207*	*218*	*244*	*339*
Sea transport, passenger	2 207 . .	. . .	. . .	. . .	. . .	. . .	. . .	. . .	. . .
Sea transport, freight	2 208 . .	. . .	. . .	. . .	. . .	. . .	. . .	. . .	. . .
Sea transport, other	2 209 . .	. . .	. . .	. . .	. . .	. . .	. . .	. . .	. . .
Air transport, passenger	2 211 . .	. . .	. . .	. . .	. . .	. . .	. . .	. . .	. . .
Air transport, freight	2 212 . .	. . .	. . .	. . .	. . .	. . .	. . .	. . .	. . .
Air transport, other	2 213 . .	. . .	. . .	. . .	. . .	. . .	. . .	. . .	. . .
Other transport, passenger	2 215 . .	. . .	. . .	. . .	. . .	. . .	. . .	. . .	. . .
Other transport, freight	2 216 . .	. . .	. . .	. . .	. . .	. . .	. . .	. . .	. . .
Other transport, other	2 217 . .	. . .	. . .	. . .	. . .	. . .	. . .	. . .	. . .
Transportation services, debit	3 205 . .	**–1,540**	**–1,648**	**–1,852**	**–2,034**	**–2,264**	**–2,509**	**–2,759**	**–3,135**
Passenger	3 205 BA	*–202*	*–210*	*–252*	*–259*	*–316*	*–409*	*–434*	*–440*
Freight	3 205 BB	*–458*	*–453*	*–535*	*–621*	*–680*	*–761*	*–890*	*–1,088*
Other	3 205 BC	*–880*	*–985*	*–1,065*	*–1,154*	*–1,269*	*–1,339*	*–1,435*	*–1,608*
Sea transport, passenger	3 207 . .	. . .	. . .	. . .	. . .	. . .	. . .	. . .	. . .
Sea transport, freight	3 208 . .	. . .	. . .	. . .	. . .	. . .	. . .	. . .	. . .
Sea transport, other	3 209 . .	. . .	. . .	. . .	. . .	. . .	. . .	. . .	. . .
Air transport, passenger	3 211 . .	. . .	. . .	. . .	. . .	. . .	. . .	. . .	. . .
Air transport, freight	3 212 . .	. . .	. . .	. . .	. . .	. . .	. . .	. . .	. . .
Air transport, other	3 213 . .	. . .	. . .	. . .	. . .	. . .	. . .	. . .	. . .
Other transport, passenger	3 215 . .	. . .	. . .	. . .	. . .	. . .	. . .	. . .	. . .
Other transport, freight	3 216 . .	. . .	. . .	. . .	. . .	. . .	. . .	. . .	. . .
Other transport, other	3 217 . .	. . .	. . .	. . .	. . .	. . .	. . .	. . .	. . .
Travel, credit	2 236 . .	**1,519**	**1,641**	**1,594**	**1,495**	**2,150**	**2,352**	**2,498**	**2,878**
Business travel	2 237 . .	172	173	197	191	255	159	99	94
Personal travel	2 240 . .	1,347	1,468	1,396	1,304	1,895	2,193	2,399	2,784
Travel, debit	3 236 . .	**–1,727**	**–1,919**	**–2,216**	**–2,261**	**–2,588**	**–2,638**	**–2,996**	**–3,549**
Business travel	3 237 . .	–644	–659	–774	–711	–914	–586	–400	–401
Personal travel	3 240 . .	–1,083	–1,261	–1,442	–1,551	–1,674	–2,052	–2,596	–3,148
Other services, credit	2 200 BA	**1,382**	**1,408**	**1,545**	**1,687**	**2,132**	**2,124**	**2,450**	**2,847**
Communications	2 245 . .	189	218	256	302	309	359	393	435
Construction	2 249 . .	. . .	. . .	. . .	. . .	. . .	. . .	. . .	. . .
Insurance	2 253 . .	9	–24	–11	–4	–14	11	10	14
Financial	2 260 . .	. . .	. . .	. . .	. . .	. . .	. . .	. . .	. . .
Computer and information	2 262 . .	. . .	. . .	. . .	. . .	. . .	. . .	. . .	. . .
Royalties and licence fees	2 266 . .	62	55	63	70	96	92	108	124
Other business services	2 268 . .	1,088	1,117	1,190	1,270	1,687	1,615	1,889	2,210
Personal, cultural, and recreational	2 287 . .	. . .	. . .	. . .	. . .	. . .	. . .	. . .	. . .
Government, n.i.e.	2 291 . .	35	42	47	48	53	47	50	64
Other services, debit	3 200 BA	**–1,190**	**–1,360**	**–1,614**	**–1,618**	**–1,744**	**–2,032**	**–2,530**	**–2,572**
Communications	3 245 . .	–120	–142	–159	–180	–220	–221	–273	–315
Construction	3 249 . .	. . .	. . .	. . .	. . .	. . .	. . .	. . .	. . .
Insurance	3 253 . .	–108	–128	–214	–139	–43	–208	–212	–235
Financial	3 260 . .	. . .	. . .	. . .	. . .	. . .	. . .	. . .	. . .
Computer and information	3 262 . .	. . .	. . .	. . .	. . .	. . .	. . .	. . .	. . .
Royalties and licence fees	3 266 . .	–56	–64	–73	–86	–103	–111	–143	–152
Other business services	3 268 . .	–805	–912	–1,048	–1,075	–1,214	–1,300	–1,697	–1,650
Personal, cultural, and recreational	3 287 . .	. . .	. . .	. . .	. . .	. . .	. . .	. . .	. . .
Government, n.i.e.	3 291 . .	–101	–114	–120	–138	–164	–192	–204	–221

Table 2 (Continued). STANDARD PRESENTATION, 1988–95
(Millions of U.S. dollars)

	Code	1988	1989	1990	1991	1992	1993	1994	1995
C. INCOME	4 300 . .	–1,558	–1,280	–1,135	–872	–944	–1,225	–1,730	–1,827
Total credit	2 300 . .	*1,132*	*1,410*	*1,628*	*1,711*	*1,642*	*1,263*	*1,194*	*1,925*
Total debit	3 300 . .	*–2,690*	*–2,689*	*–2,763*	*–2,583*	*–2,586*	*–2,488*	*–2,924*	*–3,751*
Compensation of employees, credit	2 310 . .	**85**	**79**	**76**	**96**	**119**	**144**	**115**	**221**
Compensation of employees, debit	3 310 . .	**–34**	**. . .**	**. . .**	**. . .**	**–20**	**–132**	**–269**	**–556**
Investment income, credit	2 320 . .	**1,047**	**1,331**	**1,552**	**1,615**	**1,523**	**1,119**	**1,079**	**1,704**
Direct investment income	2 330 . .	93	97	73	–1	15	–43	65	50
Dividends and distributed branch profits	2 332 . .	51	61	56	45	51	31	36	40
Reinvested earnings and undistributed branch profits	2 333 . .	43	36	17	–46	–36	–74	28	10
Income on debt (interest)	2 334 . .	. . .	. . .	. . .	. . .	. . .	. . .	. . .	. . .
Portfolio investment income	2 339 . .	17	26	29	41	62	53	35	68
Income on equity	2 340 . .	17	26	29	41	62	53	35	68
Income on bonds and notes	2 350 . .	. . .	. . .	. . .	. . .	. . .	. . .	. . .	. . .
Income on money market instruments and financial derivatives	2 360 . .	. . .	. . .	. . .	. . .	. . .	. . .	. . .	. . .
Other investment income	2 370 . .	937	1,207	1,450	1,575	1,446	1,109	980	1,587
Investment income, debit	3 320 . .	**–2,657**	**–2,689**	**–2,763**	**–2,583**	**–2,566**	**–2,356**	**–2,656**	**–3,195**
Direct investment income	3 330 . .	–147	–176	–186	–165	–244	–220	–292	–297
Dividends and distributed branch profits	3 332 . .	–124	–154	–164	–146	–215	–194	–255	–260
Reinvested earnings and undistributed branch profits	3 333 . .	–22	–22	–22	–19	–28	–26	–37	–37
Income on debt (interest)	3 334 . .	. . .	. . .	. . .	. . .	. . .	. . .	. . .	. . .
Portfolio investment income	3 339 . .	–378	–876	–942	–945	–980	–972	–1,145	–1,315
Income on equity	3 340 . .	. . .	. . .	. . .	. . .	. . .	. . .	. . .	. . .
Income on bonds and notes	3 350 . .	–378	–876	–942	–945	–980	–972	–1,145	–1,315
Income on money market instruments and financial derivatives	3 360 . .	. . .	. . .	. . .	. . .	. . .	. . .	. . .	. . .
Other investment income	3 370 . .	–2,132	–1,638	–1,635	–1,473	–1,342	–1,164	–1,219	–1,583
D. CURRENT TRANSFERS	4 379 . .	4,434	4,368	5,262	6,083	5,899	5,809	5,739	5,600
Credit	2 379 . .	**4,619**	**4,508**	**5,451**	**6,320**	**6,192**	**6,095**	**5,968**	**6,093**
General government	2 380 . .	3,277	3,159	3,856	4,490	4,107	3,835	3,410	2,695
Other sectors	2 390 . .	1,342	1,349	1,595	1,829	2,085	2,261	2,558	3,397
Workers' remittances	2 391 . .	. . .	. . .	. . .	. . .	. . .	. . .	. . .	. . .
Other current transfers	2 392 . .	1,342	1,349	1,595	1,829	2,085	2,261	2,558	3,397
Debit	3 379 . .	**–185**	**–140**	**–189**	**–236**	**–294**	**–286**	**–229**	**–493**
General government	3 380 . .	–95	–66	–90	–109	–139	–106	–29	–260
Other sectors	3 390 . .	–89	–74	–100	–127	–155	–180	–200	–233
Workers' remittances	3 391 . .	. . .	. . .	. . .	. . .	. . .	. . .	. . .	. . .
Other current transfers	3 392 . .	–89	–74	–100	–127	–155	–180	–200	–233
CAPITAL AND FINANCIAL ACCOUNT	4 996 . .	**1,100**	**–1,611**	**564**	**1,056**	**1,555**	**1,884**	**2,802**	**3,239**
CAPITAL ACCOUNT	4 994 . .	**433**	**677**	**624**	**688**	**924**	**950**	**1,254**	**1,404**
Total credit	2 994 . .	*433*	*677*	*624*	*688*	*924*	*950*	*1,254*	*1,404*
Total debit	3 994 . .	. . .	. . .	. . .	. . .	. . .	. . .	. . .	. . .
Capital transfers, credit	2 400 . .	**433**	**677**	**624**	**688**	**924**	**950**	**1,254**	**1,404**
General government	2 401 . .	. . .	. . .	. . .	. . .	. . .	. . .	. . .	. . .
Debt forgiveness	2 402 . .	. . .	. . .	. . .	. . .	. . .	. . .	. . .	. . .
Other capital transfers	2 410 . .	. . .	. . .	. . .	. . .	. . .	. . .	. . .	. . .
Other sectors	2 430 . .	433	677	624	688	924	950	1,254	1,404
Migrants' transfers	2 431 . .	433	677	624	688	924	950	1,254	1,404
Debt forgiveness	2 432 . .	. . .	. . .	. . .	. . .	. . .	. . .	. . .	. . .
Other capital transfers	2 440 . .	. . .	. . .	. . .	. . .	. . .	. . .	. . .	. . .
Capital transfers, debit	3 400 . .	**. . .**	**. . .**	**. . .**	**. . .**	**. . .**	**. . .**	**. . .**	**. . .**
General government	3 401 . .	. . .	. . .	. . .	. . .	. . .	. . .	. . .	. . .
Debt forgiveness	3 402 . .	. . .	. . .	. . .	. . .	. . .	. . .	. . .	. . .
Other capital transfers	3 410 . .	. . .	. . .	. . .	. . .	. . .	. . .	. . .	. . .
Other sectors	3 430 . .	. . .	. . .	. . .	. . .	. . .	. . .	. . .	. . .
Migrants' transfers	3 431 . .	. . .	. . .	. . .	. . .	. . .	. . .	. . .	. . .
Debt forgiveness	3 432 . .	. . .	. . .	. . .	. . .	. . .	. . .	. . .	. . .
Other capital transfers	3 440 . .	. . .	. . .	. . .	. . .	. . .	. . .	. . .	. . .
Nonproduced nonfinancial assets, credit	2 480 . .	**. . .**	**. . .**	**. . .**	**. . .**	**. . .**	**. . .**	**. . .**	**. . .**
Nonproduced nonfinancial assets, debit	3 480 . .	**. . .**	**. . .**	**. . .**	**. . .**	**. . .**	**. . .**	**. . .**	**. . .**

Table 2 (Continued). STANDARD PRESENTATION, 1988–95
(Millions of U.S. dollars)

	Code		1988	1989	1990	1991	1992	1993	1994	1995
FINANCIAL ACCOUNT	4 995	. .	**667**	**–2,288**	**–60**	**368**	**631**	**934**	**1,548**	**1,835**
A. DIRECT INVESTMENT	4 500	. .	173	87	–65	–73	–112	–183	–293	806
Direct investment abroad	4 505	. .	**–62**	**–38**	**–165**	**–424**	**–651**	**–763**	**–735**	**–831**
Equity capital	4 510	. .	...	...	...	...	...	...	...	...
Claims on affiliated enterprises	4 515	. .	...	...	...	...	...	...	...	...
Liabilities to affiliated enterprises	4 520	. .	...	...	...	...	...	...	...	...
Reinvested earnings	4 525	. .	–43	–36	–17	46	36	74	–28	–10
Other capital	4 530	. .	–19	–2	–148	–470	–686	–837	–707	–821
Claims on affiliated enterprises	4 535	. .	...	...	...	...	...	...	...	...
Liabilities to affiliated enterprises	4 540	. .	...	...	...	...	...	...	...	...
Direct investment in Israel	4 555	. .	**235**	**125**	**101**	**351**	**539**	**580**	**442**	**1,637**
Equity capital	4 560	. .	...	...	...	...	...	...	...	...
Claims on direct investors	4 565	. .	...	...	...	...	...	...	...	...
Liabilities to direct investors	4 570	. .	...	...	...	...	...	...	...	...
Reinvested earnings	4 575	. .	22	22	22	19	28	26	37	37
Other capital	4 580	. .	213	104	79	332	510	554	406	1,600
Claims on direct investors	4 585	. .	...	...	...	...	...	...	...	...
Liabilities to direct investors	4 590	. .	...	...	...	...	...	...	...	...
B. PORTFOLIO INVESTMENT	4 600	. .	4,172	1,023	–210	548	–714	1,869	2,529	1,511
Assets	4 602	. .	**–39**	**–102**	**–345**	**–262**	**–1,268**	**–730**	**–267**	**234**
Equity securities	4 610	. .	5	–3	14	–345	–926	79	303	113
Monetary authorities	4 611	. .	...	...	...	...	...	...	...	...
General government	4 612	. .	...	...	...	...	...	...	...	...
Banks	4 613	. .	...	...	...	...	...	...	...	...
Other sectors	4 614	. .	...	...	...	...	...	...	...	...
Debt securities	4 619	. .	–44	–99	–358	83	–341	–809	–570	122
Bonds and notes	4 620	. .	–44	–99	–358	83	–341	–809	–570	122
Monetary authorities	4 621	. .	...	...	...	...	...	...	...	...
General government	4 622	. .	...	...	...	...	...	...	...	...
Banks	4 623	. .	...	...	...	...	...	...	...	...
Other sectors	4 624	. .	...	...	...	...	...	...	...	...
Money market instruments	4 630	. .	...	...	...	...	...	...	...	...
Monetary authorities	4 631	. .	...	...	...	...	...	...	...	...
General government	4 632	. .	...	...	...	...	...	...	...	...
Banks	4 633	. .	...	...	...	...	...	...	...	...
Other sectors	4 634	. .	...	...	...	...	...	...	...	...
Financial derivatives	4 640	. .	...	...	...	...	...	...	...	...
Monetary authorities	4 641	. .	...	...	...	...	...	...	...	...
General government	4 642	. .	...	...	...	...	...	...	...	...
Banks	4 643	. .	...	...	...	...	...	...	...	...
Other sectors	4 644	. .	...	...	...	...	...	...	...	...
Liabilities	4 652	. .	**4,211**	**1,124**	**134**	**811**	**553**	**2,599**	**2,796**	**1,277**
Equity securities	4 660	. .	...	...	...	...	...	...	...	...
Banks	4 663	. .	...	...	...	...	...	...	...	...
Other sectors	4 664	. .	...	...	...	...	...	...	...	...
Debt securities	4 669	. .	4,211	1,124	134	811	553	2,599	2,796	1,277
Bonds and notes	4 670	. .	4,211	1,124	134	811	553	2,599	2,796	1,277
Monetary authorities	4 671	. .	...	...	...	...	...	...	...	...
General government	4 672	. .	4,981	1,144	154	796	588	2,423	2,612	884
Banks	4 673	. .	...	...	...	...	...	...	...	...
Other sectors	4 674	. .	–771	–20	–20	15	–35	176	183	393
Money market instruments	4 680	. .	...	...	...	...	...	...	...	...
Monetary authorities	4 681	. .	...	...	...	...	...	...	...	...
General government	4 682	. .	...	...	...	...	...	...	...	...
Banks	4 683	. .	...	...	...	...	...	...	...	...
Other sectors	4 684	. .	...	...	...	...	...	...	...	...
Financial derivatives	4 690	. .	...	...	...	...	...	...	...	...
Monetary authorities	4 691	. .	...	...	...	...	...	...	...	...
General government	4 692	. .	...	...	...	...	...	...	...	...
Banks	4 693	. .	...	...	...	...	...	...	...	...
Other sectors	4 694	. .	...	...	...	...	...	...	...	...

Table 2 (Concluded). STANDARD PRESENTATION, 1988–95
(Millions of U.S. dollars)

	Code	1988	1989	1990	1991	1992	1993	1994	1995
C. OTHER INVESTMENT	4 700	–4,848	–2,000	730	–281	245	728	–619	667
Assets	4 703	**–118**	**–1,229**	**–801**	**–543**	**–1,276**	**898**	**–1,699**	**–878**
Trade credits	4 706	...	...	...	...	...	...	...	...
General government: long-term	4 708	...	...	...	...	...	...	...	...
General government: short-term	4 709	...	...	...	...	...	...	...	...
Other sectors: long-term	4 711	...	...	...	...	...	...	...	...
Other sectors: short-term	4 712	...	...	...	...	...	...	...	...
Loans	4 714	–71	–489	–377	129	382	–695	–389	210
Monetary authorities: long-term	4 717	...	...	...	...	...	...	...	...
Monetary authorities: short-term	4 718	...	...	...	...	...	...	...	...
General government: long-term	4 720	...	...	...	...	...	...	...	...
General government: short-term	4 721	101	–100	...	...	...	...	...	...
Banks: long-term	4 723	...	...	...	...	...	...	...	...
Banks: short-term	4 724	...	...	...	...	...	...	...	...
Other sectors: long-term	4 726	...	...	...	...	...	...	...	...
Other sectors: short-term	4 727	–172	–389	–377	129	382	–695	–389	210
Currency and deposits	4 730	–46	–740	–424	–672	–1,658	1,593	–1,310	–1,088
Monetary authorities	4 731	...	...	...	...	...	...	...	...
General government	4 732	397	–222	–190	–180	78	261	–28	–1,197
Banks	4 733	–413	–538	–244	–604	–1,657	1,140	–1,702	–316
Other sectors	4 734	–30	20	10	113	–79	192	420	425
Other assets	4 736	...	...	...	...	...	...	...	...
Monetary authorities: long-term	4 738	...	...	...	...	...	...	...	...
Monetary authorities: short-term	4 739	...	...	...	...	...	...	...	...
General government: long-term	4 741	...	...	...	...	...	...	...	...
General government: short-term	4 742	...	...	...	...	...	...	...	...
Banks: long-term	4 744	...	...	...	...	...	...	...	...
Banks: short-term	4 745	...	...	...	...	...	...	...	...
Other sectors: long-term	4 747	...	...	...	...	...	...	...	...
Other sectors: short-term	4 748	...	...	...	...	...	...	...	...
Liabilities	4 753	**–4,730**	**–771**	**1,531**	**262**	**1,521**	**–170**	**1,080**	**1,545**
Trade credits	4 756	–51	–107	–92	–47	...	...	...	–5
General government: long-term	4 758	...	...	...	...	...	...	...	...
General government: short-term	4 759	...	...	...	...	...	...	...	...
Other sectors: long-term	4 761	–51	–107	–92	–47	...	...	...	–5
Other sectors: short-term	4 762	...	...	...	...	...	...	...	...
Loans	4 764	–4,786	–981	735	–193	756	–403	–69	59
Use of Fund credit and loans from the Fund	4 766	...	...	...	...	245	...	...	–101
Monetary authorities: other long-term	4 767	...	...	...	...	...	...	...	...
Monetary authorities: short-term	4 768	...	...	...	...	...	...	...	...
General government: long-term	4 770	–4,810	–1,080	–162	–156	118	–408	–499	–212
General government: short-term	4 771	...	...	...	...	...	...	...	...
Banks: long-term	4 773	...	...	...	...	...	...	...	...
Banks: short-term	4 774	...	...	...	...	...	...	...	...
Other sectors: long-term	4 776	–20	122	383	–55	–98	48	552	252
Other sectors: short-term	4 777	43	–23	514	18	491	–42	–122	121
Currency and deposits	4 780	–59	–31	376	151	937	281	968	1,232
Monetary authorities	4 781	...	...	...	...	...	...	...	...
General government	4 782	...	...	...	...	...	...	...	...
Banks	4 783	–59	–31	376	151	937	281	968	1,232
Other sectors	4 784	...	...	...	...	...	...	...	...
Other liabilities	4 786	165	348	511	351	–172	–48	181	259
Monetary authorities: long-term	4 788	...	...	...	...	...	...	...	...
Monetary authorities: short-term	4 789	23	30	–26	–4	–14	–2	42	19
General government: long-term	4 791	...	...	...	...	...	...	...	...
General government: short-term	4 792	...	...	...	...	...	...	...	...
Banks: long-term	4 794	...	...	...	...	...	...	...	...
Banks: short-term	4 795	...	...	...	...	...	...	...	...
Other sectors: long-term	4 797	...	...	...	...	...	...	...	...
Other sectors: short-term	4 798	142	318	537	355	–158	–45	139	239
D. RESERVE ASSETS	4 800	1,170	–1,398	–515	173	1,212	–1,481	–69	–1,149
Monetary gold	4 810	...	...	9	19	21	...	...	...
Special drawing rights	4 820	...	...	...	...	...	...	...	...
Reserve position in the Fund	4 830	...	...	...	...	...	...	...	...
Foreign exchange	4 840	1,798	–1,258	–762	111	1,169	–1,345	–196	–1,161
Other claims	4 880	–628	–140	238	43	23	–135	127	12
NET ERRORS AND OMISSIONS	4 998	**–739**	**1,038**	**–475**	**–10**	**–803**	**185**	**786**	**2,252**

Part 3 of the *Yearbook* contains descriptions of the methodologies, compilation practices, and sources used to compile these data.

Table 1. ANALYTIC PRESENTATION, 1988–95
(Millions of U.S. dollars)

	Code	1988	1989	1990	1991	1992	1993	1994	1995
A. Current Account[1]	4 993 Y.	**–7,181**	**–12,812**	**–17,587**	**–24,650**	**–29,461**	**9,404**	**14,125**	**25,706**
Goods: exports f.o.b.	2 100 . .	127,860	140,556	170,304	169,465	178,155	169,153	191,422	231,336
Goods: imports f.o.b.	3 100 . .	–128,784	–142,219	–168,931	–169,911	–175,070	–136,328	–155,819	–187,254
Balance on Goods	4 100 . .	*–924*	*–1,664*	*1,373*	*–445*	*3,085*	*32,825*	*35,602*	*44,082*
Services: credit	2 200 . .	30,187	31,790	48,750	47,583	58,816	54,009	55,998	65,043
Services: debit	3 200 . .	–29,060	–32,121	–49,833	–47,374	–62,118	–53,097	–53,800	–63,332
Balance on Goods and Services	4 991 . .	*203*	*–1,995*	*290*	*–237*	*–217*	*33,737*	*37,800*	*45,793*
Income: credit	2 300 . .	11,025	14,585	18,997	21,930	28,730	31,789	28,489	33,907
Income: debit	3 300 . .	–16,536	–21,906	–33,709	–39,477	–50,480	–48,940	–45,056	–49,368
Balance on Goods, Services, and Income	4 992 . .	*–5,308*	*–9,315*	*–14,422*	*–17,783*	*–21,967*	*16,586*	*21,233*	*30,332*
Current transfers: credit	2 379 Y.	10,394	11,214	12,560	13,741	14,261	12,962	12,259	14,276
Current transfers: debit	3 379 . .	–12,267	–14,710	–15,725	–20,608	–21,755	–20,144	–19,367	–18,902
B. Capital Account[1]	4 994 Y.	**580**	**912**	**759**	**588**	**820**	**1,650**	**1,028**	**1,666**
Capital account: credit	2 994 Y.	1,514	1,608	1,822	1,717	2,265	2,799	2,216	2,796
Capital account: debit	3 994 . .	–934	–696	–1,063	–1,129	–1,445	–1,149	–1,187	–1,130
Total, Groups A Plus B	4 010 . .	*–6,600*	*–11,900*	*–16,828*	*–24,062*	*–28,642*	*11,054*	*15,153*	*27,372*
C. Financial Account[1]	4 995 X.	**16,710**	**24,738**	**42,638**	**24,213**	**11,555**	**5,260**	**–14,209**	**–3,258**
Direct investment abroad	4 505 . .	–4,703	–2,160	–7,394	–6,928	–6,502	–9,271	–5,639	–6,926
Direct investment in Italy	4 555 Y.	6,801	2,166	6,411	2,401	3,950	4,383	2,163	4,879
Portfolio investment assets	4 602 . .	–5,497	–9,068	–19,285	–22,715	–26,559	–8,416	–19,207	–2,704
Equity securities	4 610 . .	924	–4,742	–6,135	428	3,699	386	–3,361	1,014
Debt securities	4 619 . .	–6,421	–4,326	–13,150	–23,143	–30,258	–8,802	–15,846	–3,718
Portfolio investment liabilities	4 652 Y.	5,809	12,245	19,259	19,169	26,257	65,738	25,408	38,652
Equity securities	4 660 Y.	. . .	4,242	3,950	70	–433	4,133	–1,395	5,358
Debt securities	4 669 Y.	5,809	8,004	15,309	19,100	26,690	61,606	26,803	33,294
Other investment assets	4 703 . .	–10,938	–21,492	–13,894	–17,693	–16,921	–21,660	–15,933	–32,780
Monetary authorities	4 703 .A	. . .	. . .	. . .	. . .	. . .	. . .	. . .	. . .
General government	4 703 .B	–2,556	–1,365	–1,341	–1,772	–1,817	–1,539	–2,025	–2,147
Banks	4 703 .C	–7,281	–16,818	–4,384	–7,230	–4,152	–10,764	4,575	–21,872
Other sectors	4 703 .D	–1,101	–3,310	–8,169	–8,691	–10,953	–9,358	–18,483	–8,761
Other investment liabilities	4 753 X.	25,239	43,047	57,542	49,979	31,329	–25,514	–1,001	–4,378
Monetary authorities	4 753 XA	68	161	7	43	7,198	–4,602	–95	1,062
General government	4 753 YB	3,870	2,318	5,814	87	1,423	765	–1,812	4,893
Banks	4 753 YC	15,350	27,906	23,589	37,702	15,033	–21,239	3,624	–14,744
Other sectors	4 753 YD	5,950	12,662	28,132	12,147	7,675	–439	–2,719	4,410
Total, Groups A Through C	4 020 . .	*10,110*	*12,838*	*25,810*	*151*	*–17,086*	*16,314*	*945*	*24,115*
D. Net Errors and Omissions	4 998 . .	**–1,693**	**–1,480**	**–14,187**	**–6,869**	**–6,906**	**–19,449**	**631**	**–21,311**
Total, Groups A Through D	4 030 . .	*8,417*	*11,358*	*11,623*	*–6,718*	*–23,992*	*–3,135*	*1,575*	*2,804*
E. Reserves and Related Items	4 040 . .	**–8,417**	**–11,358**	**–11,623**	**6,718**	**23,992**	**3,135**	**–1,575**	**–2,804**
Reserve assets	4 800 . .	–8,417	–11,358	–11,623	6,718	23,992	3,135	–1,575	–2,804
Use of Fund credit and loans	4 766 . .	. . .	. . .	. . .	. . .	. . .	. . .	. . .	. . .
Liabilities constituting foreign authorities' reserves	4 900 . .	. . .	. . .	. . .	. . .	. . .	. . .	. . .	. . .
Exceptional financing	4 920 . .	. . .	. . .	. . .	. . .	. . .	. . .	. . .	. . .
Conversion rates: lire per U.S. dollar	0 101 . .	**1,301.6**	**1,372.1**	**1,198.1**	**1,240.6**	**1,232.4**	**1,573.7**	**1,612.4**	**1,628.9**

[1] Excludes components that have been classified in the categories of Group E.

Table 2. STANDARD PRESENTATION, 1988–95
(Millions of U.S. dollars)

	Code	1988	1989	1990	1991	1992	1993	1994	1995
CURRENT ACCOUNT	4 993 . .	**-7,181**	**-12,812**	**-17,587**	**-24,650**	**-29,461**	**9,404**	**14,125**	**25,706**
A. GOODS	4 100 . .	-924	-1,664	1,373	-445	3,085	32,825	35,602	44,082
Credit	2 100 . .	**127,860**	**140,556**	**170,304**	**169,465**	**178,155**	**169,153**	**191,422**	**231,336**
General merchandise: exports f.o.b.	2 110 . .	127,404	140,051	169,662	168,766	177,585	168,364	190,601	230,406
Goods for processing: exports f.o.b.	2 150 . .	. . .	. . .	. . .	. . .	. . .	. . .	. . .	. . .
Repairs on goods	2 160 . .	. . .	. . .	. . .	. . .	. . .	. . .	. . .	. . .
Goods procured in ports by carriers	2 170 . .	430	471	611	667	519	644	742	870
Nonmonetary gold	2 180 . .	26	34	31	32	51	146	79	59
Debit	3 100 . .	**-128,784**	**-142,219**	**-168,931**	**-169,911**	**-175,070**	**-136,328**	**-155,819**	**-187,254**
General merchandise: imports f.o.b.	3 110 . .	-125,672	-138,698	-164,989	-165,397	-170,465	-132,037	-151,215	-182,568
Goods for processing: imports f.o.b.	3 150 . .	. . .	. . .	. . .	. . .	. . .	. . .	. . .	. . .
Repairs on goods	3 160 . .	. . .	. . .	. . .	. . .	. . .	. . .	. . .	. . .
Goods procured in ports by carriers	3 170 . .	. . .	. . .	. . .	-352	-438	-438	-455	-477
Nonmonetary gold	3 180 . .	-3,111	-3,522	-3,942	-4,162	-4,167	-3,854	-4,150	-4,208
B. SERVICES	4 200 . .	1,127	-331	-1,083	209	-3,302	912	2,197	1,711
Total credit	2 200 . .	*30,187*	*31,790*	*48,750*	*47,583*	*58,816*	*54,009*	*55,998*	*65,043*
Total debit	3 200 . .	*-29,060*	*-32,121*	*-49,833*	*-47,374*	*-62,118*	*-53,097*	*-53,800*	*-63,332*
Transportation services, credit	2 205 . .	**7,635**	**8,472**	**9,663**	**11,051**	**11,147**	**11,846**	**12,808**	**14,912**
Passenger	2 205 BA	*1,326*	*1,413*	*1,682*	*1,712*	*2,025*	*2,057*	*2,288*	*2,658*
Freight	2 205 BB	*6,017*	*6,694*	*7,587*	*8,825*	*8,567*	*9,063*	*9,907*	*11,554*
Other	2 205 BC	*292*	*366*	*394*	*514*	*556*	*725*	*613*	*700*
Sea transport, passenger	2 207 . .	249	278	341	375	389	516	577	652
Sea transport, freight	2 208 . .	5,628	6,338	7,144	7,507	7,150	7,773	8,526	9,860
Sea transport, other	2 209 . .	227	249	283	289	314	446	336	377
Air transport, passenger	2 211 . .	1,077	1,134	1,341	1,266	1,545	1,461	1,641	1,927
Air transport, freight	2 212 . .	207	151	213	258	262	314	322	322
Air transport, other	2 213 . .	60	66	82	80	68	95	137	146
Other transport, passenger	2 215 . .	. . .	. . .	. . .	71	91	80	70	79
Other transport, freight	2 216 . .	182	204	230	1,060	1,155	977	1,060	1,371
Other transport, other	2 217 . .	4	51	29	144	174	184	140	178
Transportation services, debit	3 205 . .	**-10,515**	**-11,683**	**-14,479**	**-14,877**	**-17,098**	**-16,072**	**-18,560**	**-23,267**
Passenger	3 205 BA	*-1,040*	*-1,191*	*-1,762*	*-2,114*	*-2,516*	*-2,208*	*-2,638*	*-3,413*
Freight	3 205 BB	*-7,571*	*-8,364*	*-10,135*	*-10,206*	*-10,754*	*-9,668*	*-10,775*	*-13,496*
Other	3 205 BC	*-1,903*	*-2,128*	*-2,582*	*-2,557*	*-3,829*	*-4,196*	*-5,148*	*-6,358*
Sea transport, passenger	3 207 . .	-98	-112	-170	-192	-216	-193	-199	-242
Sea transport, freight	3 208 . .	-6,326	-6,988	-8,471	-8,352	-8,580	-7,570	-8,718	-10,922
Sea transport, other	3 209 . .	-1,496	-1,705	-2,071	-2,043	-3,182	-3,575	-4,385	-5,377
Air transport, passenger	3 211 . .	-942	-1,079	-1,592	-1,853	-2,227	-1,941	-2,372	-3,094
Air transport, freight	3 212 . .	-357	-394	-476	-472	-540	-429	-459	-656
Air transport, other	3 213 . .	-407	-393	-491	-463	-564	-520	-647	-846
Other transport, passenger	3 215 . .	. . .	. . .	. . .	-69	-72	-74	-67	-77
Other transport, freight	3 216 . .	-888	-981	-1,189	-1,383	-1,634	-1,669	-1,597	-1,919
Other transport, other	3 217 . .	. . .	-30	-20	-50	-83	-101	-115	-134
Travel, credit	2 236 . .	**12,235**	**11,912**	**16,324**	**18,315**	**23,045**	**22,019**	**23,906**	**27,449**
Business travel	2 237 . .	. . .	. . .	. . .	. . .	. . .	. . .	. . .	. . .
Personal travel	2 240 . .	12,235	11,912	16,324	18,315	23,045	22,019	23,906	27,449
Travel, debit	3 236 . .	**-6,016**	**-6,809**	**-10,081**	**-11,747**	**-18,370**	**-14,273**	**-12,423**	**-12,712**
Business travel	3 237 . .	. . .	. . .	. . .	. . .	. . .	. . .	. . .	. . .
Personal travel	3 240 . .	-6,016	-6,809	-10,081	-11,747	-18,370	-14,273	-12,423	-12,712
Other services, credit	2 200 BA	**10,317**	**11,406**	**22,763**	**18,217**	**24,623**	**20,144**	**19,283**	**22,681**
Communications	2 245 . .	192	195	247	271	217	273	310	292
Construction	2 249 . .	6	8	500	1,254	2,508	2,343	2,568	3,166
Insurance	2 253 . .	317	271	223	198	1,065	1,229	1,511	1,394
Financial	2 260 . .	1,721	2,278	2,455	2,536	3,064	3,048	2,353	2,635
Computer and information	2 262 . .	. . .	. . .	133	90	270	141	139	160
Royalties and licence fees	2 266 . .	113	110	1,040	248	241	234	323	462
Other business services	2 268 . .	6,823	7,567	16,256	12,314	16,031	12,080	11,194	13,897
Personal, cultural, and recreational	2 287 . .	100	112	820	310	345	257	375	368
Government, n.i.e.	2 291 . .	1,046	866	1,088	996	883	540	511	307
Other services, debit	3 200 BA	**-12,530**	**-13,629**	**-25,272**	**-20,750**	**-26,650**	**-22,753**	**-22,817**	**-27,352**
Communications	3 245 . .	-179	-213	-228	-332	-488	-467	-631	-627
Construction	3 249 . .	-18	-53	-284	-630	-1,082	-1,100	-1,102	-1,511
Insurance	3 253 . .	-720	-662	-1,039	-961	-1,319	-1,181	-1,402	-862
Financial	3 260 . .	-2,672	-2,849	-3,795	-3,615	-4,587	-3,830	-3,634	-4,438
Computer and information	3 262 . .	. . .	. . .	-273	-244	-293	-384	-401	-455
Royalties and licence fees	3 266 . .	-780	-616	-1,959	-1,472	-1,442	-1,215	-1,179	-1,166
Other business services	3 268 . .	-7,011	-8,454	-16,210	-12,389	-16,317	-13,549	-13,478	-16,744
Personal, cultural, and recreational	3 287 . .	-498	-562	-1,292	-964	-950	-817	-828	-1,113
Government, n.i.e.	3 291 . .	-650	-220	-193	-143	-172	-209	-163	-436

Table 2 (Continued). STANDARD PRESENTATION, 1988–95
(Millions of U.S. dollars)

	Code	1988	1989	1990	1991	1992	1993	1994	1995
C. INCOME	4 300 . .	–5,511	–7,321	–14,712	–17,547	–21,750	–17,151	–16,567	–15,461
Total credit	2 300 . .	*11,025*	*14,585*	*18,997*	*21,930*	*28,730*	*31,789*	*28,489*	*33,907*
Total debit	3 300 . .	*–16,536*	*–21,906*	*–33,709*	*–39,477*	*–50,480*	*–48,940*	*–45,056*	*–49,368*
Compensation of employees, credit	2 310 . .	**3,114**	**3,584**	**3,764**	**2,712**	**2,205**	**1,967**	**1,791**	**1,688**
Compensation of employees, debit	3 310 . .	**–1,529**	**–2,641**	**–3,640**	**–2,484**	**–2,127**	**–2,021**	**–1,672**	**–982**
Investment income, credit	2 320 . .	**7,911**	**11,002**	**15,233**	**19,218**	**26,525**	**29,822**	**26,699**	**32,219**
Direct investment income	2 330 . .	174	188	264	552	459	326	1,124	1,494
Dividends and distributed branch profits	2 332 . .	174	188	264	552	459	326	1,124	1,494
Reinvested earnings and undistributed branch profits	2 333 . .	. . .	. . .	. . .	. . .	. . .	. . .	. . .	. . .
Income on debt (interest)	2 334 . .	. . .	. . .	. . .	. . .	. . .	. . .	. . .	. . .
Portfolio investment income	2 339 . .	548	954	1,653	2,951	5,464	8,222	6,376	7,396
Income on equity	2 340 . .	. . .	. . .	. . .	. . .	. . .	. . .	. . .	. . .
Income on bonds and notes	2 350 . .	. . .	. . .	. . .	. . .	. . .	. . .	. . .	. . .
Income on money market instruments and financial derivatives	2 360 . .	. . .	. . .	. . .	. . .	. . .	. . .	. . .	. . .
Other investment income	2 370 . .	7,189	9,860	13,315	15,715	20,602	21,274	19,198	23,330
Investment income, debit	3 320 . .	**–15,007**	**–19,266**	**–30,069**	**–36,993**	**–48,353**	**–46,919**	**–43,384**	**–48,386**
Direct investment income	3 330 . .	–1,615	–1,571	–613	–490	–493	–440	–412	–738
Dividends and distributed branch profits	3 332 . .	–1,615	–1,571	–613	–490	–493	–440	–412	–738
Reinvested earnings and undistributed branch profits	3 333 . .	. . .	. . .	. . .	. . .	. . .	. . .	. . .	. . .
Income on debt (interest)	3 334 . .	. . .	. . .	. . .	. . .	. . .	. . .	. . .	. . .
Portfolio investment income	3 339 . .	–633	–1,412	–3,017	–6,048	–9,346	–11,653	–13,841	–15,415
Income on equity	3 340 . .	. . .	. . .	. . .	. . .	. . .	. . .	. . .	. . .
Income on bonds and notes	3 350 . .	. . .	. . .	. . .	. . .	. . .	. . .	. . .	. . .
Income on money market instruments and financial derivatives	3 360 . .	. . .	. . .	. . .	. . .	. . .	. . .	. . .	. . .
Other investment income	3 370 . .	–12,760	–16,283	–26,438	–30,455	–38,515	–34,826	–29,131	–32,233
D. CURRENT TRANSFERS	4 379 . .	–1,873	–3,496	–3,165	–6,867	–7,494	–7,182	–7,108	–4,626
Credit	2 379 . .	**10,394**	**11,214**	**12,560**	**13,741**	**14,261**	**12,962**	**12,259**	**14,276**
General government	2 380 . .	6,505	7,050	7,462	8,950	8,724	7,992	5,781	6,307
Other sectors	2 390 . .	3,890	4,163	5,098	4,791	5,537	4,970	6,478	7,969
Workers' remittances	2 391 . .	1,480	1,460	1,263	903	693	588	461	346
Other current transfers	2 392 . .	2,410	2,703	3,835	3,888	4,845	4,382	6,017	7,623
Debit	3 379 . .	**–12,267**	**–14,710**	**–15,725**	**–20,608**	**–21,755**	**–20,144**	**–19,367**	**–18,902**
General government	3 380 . .	–10,151	–11,661	–11,830	–15,653	–15,938	–15,802	–12,956	–11,711
Other sectors	3 390 . .	–2,116	–3,049	–3,895	–4,955	–5,817	–4,342	–6,411	–7,191
Workers' remittances	3 391 . .	. . .	. . .	–27	–89	–162	–155	–209	–248
Other current transfers	3 392 . .	–2,116	–3,049	–3,869	–4,866	–5,655	–4,187	–6,202	–6,944
CAPITAL AND FINANCIAL ACCOUNT	4 996 . .	**8,874**	**14,292**	**31,774**	**31,519**	**36,367**	**10,045**	**–14,756**	**–4,395**
CAPITAL ACCOUNT	4 994 . .	**580**	**912**	**759**	**588**	**820**	**1,650**	**1,028**	**1,666**
Total credit	2 994 . .	*1,514*	*1,608*	*1,822*	*1,717*	*2,265*	*2,799*	*2,216*	*2,796*
Total debit	3 994 . .	*–934*	*–696*	*–1,063*	*–1,129*	*–1,445*	*–1,149*	*–1,187*	*–1,130*
Capital transfers, credit	2 400 . .	**1,171**	**1,336**	**1,373**	**1,463**	**2,045**	**2,576**	**1,903**	**2,379**
General government	2 401 . .	935	1,300	1,325	1,379	1,999	2,515	1,846	2,295
Debt forgiveness	2 402 . .	. . .	. . .	. . .	. . .	. . .	. . .	. . .	. . .
Other capital transfers	2 410 . .	935	1,300	1,325	1,379	1,999	2,515	1,846	2,295
Other sectors	2 430 . .	236	36	48	84	46	60	57	84
Migrants' transfers	2 431 . .	236	36	48	84	46	60	57	84
Debt forgiveness	2 432 . .	. . .	. . .	. . .	. . .	. . .	. . .	. . .	. . .
Other capital transfers	2 440 . .	. . .	. . .	. . .	. . .	. . .	. . .	. . .	. . .
Capital transfers, debit	3 400 . .	**–690**	**–469**	**–534**	**–685**	**–938**	**–790**	**–640**	**–686**
General government	3 401 . .	–294	–408	–436	–473	–705	–552	–526	–551
Debt forgiveness	3 402 . .	. . .	. . .	. . .	. . .	. . .	. . .	. . .	. . .
Other capital transfers	3 410 . .	–294	–408	–436	–473	–705	–552	–526	–551
Other sectors	3 430 . .	–396	–60	–98	–212	–234	–238	–115	–135
Migrants' transfers	3 431 . .	–396	–60	–98	–212	–234	–238	–115	–135
Debt forgiveness	3 432 . .	. . .	. . .	. . .	. . .	. . .	. . .	. . .	. . .
Other capital transfers	3 440 . .	. . .	. . .	. . .	. . .	. . .	. . .	. . .	. . .
Nonproduced nonfinancial assets, credit	2 480 . .	**344**	**272**	**449**	**255**	**220**	**223**	**312**	**417**
Nonproduced nonfinancial assets, debit	3 480 . .	**–244**	**–227**	**–530**	**–444**	**–507**	**–359**	**–547**	**–444**

Table 2 (Continued). STANDARD PRESENTATION, 1988–95
(Millions of U.S. dollars)

	Code	1988	1989	1990	1991	1992	1993	1994	1995
FINANCIAL ACCOUNT	4 995 . .	**8,293**	**13,380**	**31,015**	**30,931**	**35,547**	**8,395**	**-15,784**	**-6,061**
A. DIRECT INVESTMENT	4 500 . .	2,098	6	-983	-4,528	-2,551	-4,888	-3,476	-2,048
Direct investment abroad	4 505 . .	**-4,703**	**-2,160**	**-7,394**	**-6,928**	**-6,502**	**-9,271**	**-5,639**	**-6,926**
Equity capital	4 510 . .	-4,703	-2,160	-7,394	-6,928	-6,502	-9,271	-5,639	-6,926
Claims on affiliated enterprises	4 515 . .	...	...	...	...	...	...	...	...
Liabilities to affiliated enterprises	4 520 . .	...	...	...	...	...	...	...	...
Reinvested earnings	4 525 . .	...	...	...	...	...	...	...	...
Other capital	4 530 . .	...	...	...	...	...	...	...	...
Claims on affiliated enterprises	4 535 . .	...	...	...	...	...	...	...	...
Liabilities to affiliated enterprises	4 540 . .	...	...	...	...	...	...	...	...
Direct investment in Italy	4 555 . .	**6,801**	**2,166**	**6,411**	**2,401**	**3,950**	**4,383**	**2,163**	**4,879**
Equity capital	4 560 . .	6,801	2,166	6,411	2,401	3,950	4,383	2,163	4,879
Claims on direct investors	4 565 . .	...	...	...	...	...	...	...	...
Liabilities to direct investors	4 570 . .	...	...	...	...	...	...	...	...
Reinvested earnings	4 575 . .	...	...	...	...	...	...	...	...
Other capital	4 580 . .	...	...	...	...	...	...	...	...
Claims on direct investors	4 585 . .	...	...	...	...	...	...	...	...
Liabilities to direct investors	4 590 . .	...	...	...	...	...	...	...	...
B. PORTFOLIO INVESTMENT	4 600 . .	312	3,177	-26	-3,546	-301	57,322	6,201	35,948
Assets	4 602 . .	**-5,497**	**-9,068**	**-19,285**	**-22,715**	**-26,559**	**-8,416**	**-19,207**	**-2,704**
Equity securities	4 610 . .	924	-4,742	-6,135	428	3,699	386	-3,361	1,014
Monetary authorities	4 611 . .	...	...	...	...	...	...	...	...
General government	4 612 . .	...	...	...	...	...	...	...	...
Banks	4 613 . .	...	...	...	...	...	...	...	...
Other sectors	4 614 . .	924	-4,742	-6,135	428	3,699	386	-3,361	1,014
Debt securities	4 619 . .	-6,421	-4,326	-13,150	-23,143	-30,258	-8,802	-15,846	-3,718
Bonds and notes	4 620 . .	-6,422	-4,319	-13,190	-23,125	-30,110	-8,793	-15,932	-2,866
Monetary authorities	4 621 . .	...	...	...	...	...	...	...	...
General government	4 622 . .	...	...	...	...	...	...	...	...
Banks	4 623 . .	...	...	...	...	-5,387	-20,314	6,751	1,418
Other sectors	4 624 . .	-6,422	-4,319	-13,190	-23,125	-24,722	11,520	-22,684	-4,283
Money market instruments	4 630 . .	...	...	...	...	...	...	...	...
Monetary authorities	4 631 . .	...	...	...	...	...	...	...	...
General government	4 632 . .	...	...	...	...	...	...	...	...
Banks	4 633 . .	...	...	...	...	...	...	...	...
Other sectors	4 634 . .	...	...	...	...	...	...	...	...
Financial derivatives	4 640 . .	1	-7	39	-18	-148	-8	87	-852
Monetary authorities	4 641 . .	...	...	...	...	...	...	...	...
General government	4 642 . .	...	...	...	...	...	...	...	...
Banks	4 643 . .	...	...	...	...	...	...	...	...
Other sectors	4 644 . .	1	-7	39	-18	-148	-8	87	-852
Liabilities	4 652 . .	**5,809**	**12,245**	**19,259**	**19,169**	**26,257**	**65,738**	**25,408**	**38,652**
Equity securities	4 660 . .	...	4,242	3,950	70	-433	4,133	-1,395	5,358
Banks	4 663 . .	...	...	...	...	...	...	...	...
Other sectors	4 664 . .	...	4,242	3,950	70	-433	4,133	-1,395	5,358
Debt securities	4 669 . .	5,809	8,004	15,309	19,100	26,690	61,606	26,803	33,294
Bonds and notes	4 670 . .	5,088	7,108	14,468	18,914	26,784	60,987	25,549	29,130
Monetary authorities	4 671 . .	...	...	...	...	...	...	...	...
General government	4 672 . .	3,351	6,084	12,502	15,699	13,581	55,008	23,770	27,984
Banks	4 673 . .	...	...	...	...	4,260	625	-122	501
Other sectors	4 674 . .	1,737	1,024	1,965	3,215	8,943	5,355	1,901	645
Money market instruments	4 680 . .	717	912	798	203	14	840	625	3,085
Monetary authorities	4 681 . .	...	...	...	...	...	...	...	...
General government	4 682 . .	717	912	798	203	14	840	625	3,085
Banks	4 683 . .	...	...	...	...	...	...	...	...
Other sectors	4 684 . .	...	...	...	...	...	...	...	...
Financial derivatives	4 690 . .	4	-17	43	-18	-108	-221	628	1,079
Monetary authorities	4 691 . .	...	...	...	...	...	...	...	...
General government	4 692 . .	...	...	...	...	...	...	...	...
Banks	4 693 . .	...	...	...	...	...	...	...	...
Other sectors	4 694 . .	4	-17	43	-18	-108	-221	628	1,079

Table 2 (Concluded). STANDARD PRESENTATION, 1988–95
(Millions of U.S. dollars)

	Code	1988	1989	1990	1991	1992	1993	1994	1995
C. OTHER INVESTMENT	4 700 . .	14,300	21,555	43,648	32,287	14,408	–47,175	–16,934	–37,158
Assets	4 703 . .	**–10,938**	**–21,492**	**–13,894**	**–17,693**	**–16,921**	**–21,660**	**–15,933**	**–32,780**
Trade credits	4 706 . .	–974	–3,389	–4,844	–1,508	–3,131	–2,368	–6,350	–4,812
General government: long-term	4 708 . .	. . .	. . .	. . .	. . .	. . .	. . .	. . .	. . .
General government: short-term	4 709 . .	. . .	. . .	. . .	. . .	. . .	. . .	. . .	. . .
Other sectors: long-term	4 711 . .	–678	–1,099	–1,872	–1,458	–2,797	–892	–1,557	–1,927
Other sectors: short-term	4 712 . .	–296	–2,290	–2,972	–51	–333	–1,476	–4,793	–2,885
Loans	4 714 . .	–1,785	–1,255	–3,980	–6,169	–16,484	–7,499	–12,942	–13,588
Monetary authorities: long-term	4 717 . .	. . .	. . .	. . .	. . .	. . .	. . .	. . .	. . .
Monetary authorities: short-term	4 718 . .	. . .	. . .	. . .	. . .	. . .	. . .	. . .	. . .
General government: long-term	4 720 . .	–1,675	–1,365	–1,151	–1,478	–1,529	–1,233	–1,703	–1,888
General government: short-term	4 721 . .	. . .	. . .	. . .	. . .	. . .	. . .	. . .	. . .
Banks: long-term	4 723 . .	. . .	. . .	. . .	. . .	. . .	. . .	. . .	. . .
Banks: short-term	4 724 . .	. . .	. . .	. . .	. . .	–11,440	–4,303	–4,547	–10,897
Other sectors: long-term	4 726 . .	–110	109	–2,829	–4,691	–3,514	–1,963	–6,692	–802
Other sectors: short-term	4 727 . .	. . .	. . .	. . .	. . .	. . .	. . .	. . .	. . .
Currency and deposits	4 730 . .	–7,299	–16,848	–4,714	–9,722	2,980	–11,488	3,680	–14,121
Monetary authorities	4 731 . .	. . .	. . .	. . .	. . .	. . .	. . .	. . .	. . .
General government	4 732 . .	. . .	. . .	. . .	. . .	. . .	. . .	. . .	. . .
Banks	4 733 . .	–7,281	–16,818	–4,384	–7,230	7,288	–6,461	9,122	–10,974
Other sectors	4 734 . .	–17	–30	–330	–2,491	–4,308	–5,027	–5,441	–3,147
Other assets	4 736 . .	–880	. . .	–356	–294	–287	–306	–322	–259
Monetary authorities: long-term	4 738 . .	. . .	. . .	. . .	. . .	. . .	. . .	. . .	. . .
Monetary authorities: short-term	4 739 . .	. . .	. . .	. . .	. . .	. . .	. . .	. . .	. . .
General government: long-term	4 741 . .	–880	. . .	–191	–294	–287	–306	–322	–259
General government: short-term	4 742 . .	. . .	. . .	. . .	. . .	. . .	. . .	. . .	. . .
Banks: long-term	4 744 . .	. . .	. . .	. . .	. . .	. . .	. . .	. . .	. . .
Banks: short-term	4 745 . .	. . .	. . .	. . .	. . .	. . .	. . .	. . .	. . .
Other sectors: long-term	4 747 . .	. . .	. . .	–166	. . .	. . .	. . .	. . .	. . .
Other sectors: short-term	4 748 . .	. . .	. . .	. . .	. . .	. . .	. . .	. . .	. . .
Liabilities	4 753 . .	**25,239**	**43,047**	**57,542**	**49,979**	**31,329**	**–25,514**	**–1,001**	**–4,378**
Trade credits	4 756 . .	1,232	589	4,337	–462	969	–262	4,348	3,500
General government: long-term	4 758 . .	. . .	. . .	. . .	. . .	. . .	. . .	. . .	. . .
General government: short-term	4 759 . .	. . .	. . .	. . .	. . .	. . .	. . .	. . .	. . .
Other sectors: long-term	4 761 . .	57	35	39	15	252	–99	73	460
Other sectors: short-term	4 762 . .	1,175	553	4,298	–477	716	–163	4,274	3,040
Loans	4 764 . .	8,589	14,391	29,468	12,696	9,498	993	–4,249	8,630
Use of Fund credit and loans from the Fund	4 766 . .	. . .	. . .	. . .	. . .	. . .	. . .	. . .	. . .
Monetary authorities: other long term	4 767 . .	. . .	. . .	. . .	. . .	. . .	. . .	. . .	. . .
Monetary authorities: short-term	4 768 . .	. . .	. . .	. . .	. . .	. . .	. . .	. . .	. . .
General government: long-term	4 770 . .	3,870	2,318	5,814	87	1,423	765	–1,812	4,893
General government: short-term	4 771 . .	. . .	. . .	. . .	. . .	. . .	. . .	. . .	. . .
Banks: long-term	4 773 . .	. . .	. . .	. . .	. . .	. . .	. . .	. . .	. . .
Banks: short-term	4 774 . .	. . .	. . .	. . .	. . .	1,369	405	4,629	2,827
Other sectors: long-term	4 776 . .	4,718	12,073	23,654	12,609	6,706	–177	–7,066	910
Other sectors: short-term	4 777 . .	. . .	. . .	. . .	. . .	. . .	. . .	. . .	. . .
Currency and deposits	4 780 . .	15,350	27,906	23,589	37,702	13,664	–21,643	–1,005	–17,571
Monetary authorities	4 781 . .	. . .	. . .	. . .	. . .	. . .	. . .	. . .	. . .
General government	4 782 . .	. . .	. . .	. . .	. . .	. . .	. . .	. . .	. . .
Banks	4 783 . .	15,350	27,906	23,589	37,702	13,664	–21,643	–1,005	–17,571
Other sectors	4 784 . .	. . .	. . .	. . .	. . .	. . .	. . .	. . .	. . .
Other liabilities	4 786 . .	68	161	148	43	7,198	–4,602	–95	1,062
Monetary authorities: long-term	4 788 . .	. . .	. . .	. . .	. . .	. . .	. . .	. . .	. . .
Monetary authorities: short-term	4 789 . .	68	161	7	43	7,198	–4,602	–95	1,062
General government: long-term	4 791 . .	. . .	. . .	. . .	. . .	. . .	. . .	. . .	. . .
General government: short-term	4 792 . .	. . .	. . .	. . .	. . .	. . .	. . .	. . .	. . .
Banks: long-term	4 794 . .	. . .	. . .	. . .	. . .	. . .	. . .	. . .	. . .
Banks: short-term	4 795 . .	. . .	. . .	. . .	. . .	. . .	. . .	. . .	. . .
Other sectors: long-term	4 797 . .	. . .	. . .	141	. . .	. . .	. . .	. . .	. . .
Other sectors: short-term	4 798 . .	. . .	. . .	. . .	. . .	. . .	. . .	. . .	. . .
D. RESERVE ASSETS	4 800 . .	–8,417	–11,358	–11,623	6,718	23,992	3,135	–1,575	–2,804
Monetary gold	4 810 . .	. . .	. . .	. . .	. . .	. . .	. . .	. . .	. . .
Special drawing rights	4 820 . .	–50	–70	48	105	662	–4	126	130
Reserve position in the Fund	4 830 . .	106	–202	–156	–521	–273	276	262	109
Foreign exchange	4 840 . .	–8,473	–11,086	–11,515	7,134	23,603	2,863	–1,963	–3,042
Other claims	4 880 . .	. . .	. . .	. . .	. . .	. . .	. . .	. . .	. . .
NET ERRORS AND OMISSIONS	4 998 . .	**–1,693**	**–1,480**	**–14,187**	**–6,869**	**–6,906**	**–19,449**	**631**	**–21,311**

Part 3 of the *Yearbook* contains descriptions of the methodologies, compilation practices, and sources used to compile these data.

Table 3. INTERNATIONAL INVESTMENT POSITION (End–period stocks), 1988–95

(Millions of U.S. dollars)

	Code	1988	1989	1990	1991	1992	1993	1994	1995
ASSETS	8 995 C.	238,415	296,776	380,738	424,366	410,960	450,985	516,340	598,585
Direct investment abroad	8 505 . .	**37,432**	**43,462**	**57,261**	**67,233**	**71,004**	**81,892**	**91,097**	**109,176**
Equity capital and reinvested earnings	8 506 . .	37,432	43,462	57,261	67,233	71,004	81,892	91,097	109,176
Claims on affiliated enterprises	8 507 . .	...	...	...	...	...	...	...	...
Liabilities to affiliated enterprises	8 508 . .	...	...	...	...	...	...	...	...
Other capital	8 530 . .	...	...	...	...	...	...	...	...
Claims on affiliated enterprises	8 535 . .	...	...	...	...	...	...	...	...
Liabilities to affiliated enterprises	8 540 . .	...	...	...	...	...	...	...	...
Portfolio investment	8 602 . .	**24,411**	**38,054**	**62,844**	**94,847**	**111,123**	**130,667**	**150,413**	**171,840**
Equity securities	8 610 . .	8,327	14,070	22,040	21,342	16,454	15,783	20,143	19,386
Monetary authorities	8 611 . .	...	...	...	...	...	...	...	...
General government	8 612 . .	...	...	...	...	...	...	...	...
Banks	8 613 . .	...	...	...	...	...	...	...	...
Other sectors	8 614 . .	8,327	14,070	22,040	21,342	16,454	15,783	20,143	19,386
Debt securities	8 619 . .	16,084	23,983	40,803	73,505	94,670	114,884	130,270	152,455
Bonds and notes	8 620 . .	16,084	23,983	40,803	73,505	94,670	114,884	130,270	152,455
Monetary authorities	8 621 . .	...	...	...	...	...	...	...	...
General government	8 622 . .	...	...	...	...	...	...	...	...
Banks	8 623 . .	...	...	...	2,230	5,472	20,862	10,270	9,178
Other sectors	8 624 . .	16,084	23,983	40,803	71,276	89,197	94,022	120,000	143,276
Money market instruments	8 630 . .	...	...	...	...	...	...	...	...
Monetary authorities	8 631 . .	...	...	...	...	...	...	...	...
General government	8 632 . .	...	...	...	...	...	...	...	...
Banks	8 633 . .	...	...	...	...	...	...	...	...
Other sectors	8 634 . .	...	...	...	...	...	...	...	...
Financial derivatives	8 640 . .	...	...	...	...	...	...	...	...
Monetary authorities	8 641 . .	...	...	...	...	...	...	...	...
General government	8 642 . .	...	...	...	...	...	...	...	...
Banks	8 643 . .	...	...	...	...	...	...	...	...
Other sectors	8 644 . .	...	...	...	...	...	...	...	...
Other investment	8 703 . .	**112,179**	**140,633**	**167,787**	**178,957**	**176,796**	**187,622**	**217,216**	**257,247**
Trade credits	8 706 . .	32,413	36,382	45,576	46,377	38,969	35,757	43,637	50,688
General government: long-term	8 708 . .	...	...	...	...	...	...	...	...
General government: short-term	8 709 . .	...	...	...	...	...	...	...	...
Other sectors: long-term	8 711 . .	14,202	15,306	19,197	20,412	17,979	16,329	18,618	21,244
Other sectors: short-term	8 712 . .	18,211	21,076	26,379	25,965	20,990	19,428	25,019	29,444
Loans	8 714 . .	6,695	11,030	16,521	20,264	32,410	34,569	50,287	65,513
Monetary authorities: long-term	8 717 . .	...	...	...	...	...	...	...	...
Monetary authorities: short-term	8 718 . .	...	...	...	...	...	...	...	...
General government: long-term	8 720 . .	5,042	7,742	9,875	11,112	10,689	10,971	13,340	16,073
General government: short-term	8 721 . .	...	...	...	...	...	...	...	...
Banks: long-term	8 723 . .	...	...	...	...	...	...	...	...
Banks: short-term	8 724 . .	...	...	...	...	10,102	12,693	18,905	30,314
Other sectors: long-term	8 726 . .	1,653	3,288	6,646	9,152	11,618	10,906	18,042	19,126
Other sectors: short-term	8 727 . .	...	...	...	...	...	...	...	...
Currency and deposits	8 730 . .	70,082	90,150	102,767	109,126	102,652	114,626	120,173	137,576
Monetary authorities	8 731 . .	...	...	...	...	...	...	...	...
General government	8 732 . .	...	...	...	...	...	...	...	...
Banks	8 733 . .	70,064	90,098	102,381	106,122	95,943	103,414	102,821	116,631
Other sectors	8 734 . .	18	51	386	3,003	6,708	11,211	17,352	20,946
Other assets	8 736 . .	2,989	3,072	2,924	3,190	2,766	2,670	3,120	3,469
Monetary authorities: long-term	8 738 . .	...	...	...	...	...	...	...	...
Monetary authorities: short-term	8 739 . .	...	...	...	...	...	...	...	...
General government: long-term	8 741 . .	2,989	3,072	2,924	3,190	2,766	2,670	3,120	3,469
General government: short-term	8 742 . .	...	...	...	...	...	...	...	...
Banks: long-term	8 744 . .	...	...	...	...	...	...	...	...
Banks: short-term	8 745 . .	...	...	...	...	...	...	...	...
Other sectors: long-term	8 747 . .	...	...	...	...	...	...	...	...
Other sectors: short-term	8 748 . .	...	...	...	...	...	...	...	...
Reserve assets	8 800 . .	**64,394**	**74,627**	**92,845**	**83,329**	**52,037**	**50,803**	**57,615**	**60,321**
Monetary gold	8 810 . .	28,521	26,496	27,057	25,444	20,358	21,661	25,365	25,403
Special drawing rights	8 820 . .	949	998	1,037	930	238	241	125	...
Reserve position in the Fund	8 830 . .	1,266	1,444	1,714	2,255	2,439	2,164	2,033	1,963
Foreign exchange	8 840 . .	33,658	45,690	63,037	54,700	29,001	26,737	30,091	32,955
Other claims	8 880 . .	...	...	...	...	...	...	...	...

Table 3 (Continued). INTERNATIONAL INVESTMENT POSITION (End-period stocks), 1988–95
(Millions of U.S. dollars)

	Code	1988	1989	1990	1991	1992	1993	1994	1995
LIABILITIES	8 995 D.	257,711	342,678	465,424	530,368	521,563	535,352	587,612	650,391
Direct investment in Italy	8 555 ..	**38,529**	**50,937**	**59,997**	**61,576**	**50,730**	**54,538**	**60,955**	**65,980**
Equity capital and reinvested earnings	8 556 ..	38,529	50,937	59,997	61,576	50,730	54,538	60,955	65,980
Claims on direct investors	8 557 ..	...	...	...	...	...	...	...	...
Liabilities to direct investors	8 558 ..	...	...	...	...	...	...	...	...
Other capital	8 580 ..	...	...	...	...	...	...	...	...
Claims on direct investors	8 585 ..	...	...	...	...	...	...	...	...
Liabilities to direct investors	8 590 ..	...	...	...	...	...	...	...	...
Portfolio investment	8 652 ..	**15,900**	**32,097**	**53,320**	**91,396**	**101,229**	**160,403**	**188,594**	**237,861**
Equity securities	8 660 ..	451	5,129	10,243	10,363	8,719	11,662	11,366	16,952
Banks	8 663 ..	...	...	...	...	...	...	...	...
Other sectors	8 664 ..	451	5,129	10,243	10,363	8,719	11,662	11,366	16,952
Debt securities	8 669 ..	15,449	26,969	43,077	81,032	92,510	148,741	177,228	220,909
Bonds and notes	8 670 ..	15,098	25,619	40,757	78,527	90,544	146,226	173,923	214,375
Monetary authorities	8 671 ..	...	...	...	...	...	...	...	...
General government	8 672 ..	11,601	18,455	34,522	63,859	66,337	119,588	140,055	177,541
Banks	8 673 ..	...	...	...	219	1,345	1,005	918	1,444
Other sectors	8 674 ..	3,496	7,164	6,235	14,448	22,862	25,631	32,949	35,389
Money market instruments	8 680 ..	352	1,350	2,320	2,505	1,965	2,515	3,305	6,534
Monetary authorities	8 681 ..	...	...	...	...	...	...	...	...
General government	8 682 ..	352	1,350	2,320	2,505	1,965	2,515	3,305	6,534
Banks	8 683 ..	...	...	...	...	...	...	...	...
Other sectors	8 684 ..	...	...	...	...	...	...	...	...
Financial derivatives	8 690 ..	...	...	...	...	...	...	...	...
Monetary authorities	8 691 ..	...	...	...	...	...	...	...	...
General government	8 692 ..	...	...	...	...	...	...	...	...
Banks	8 692 ..	...	...	...	...	...	...	...	...
Other sectors	8 694 ..	...	...	...	...	...	...	...	...
Other investment	8 753 ..	**203,282**	**259,644**	**352,107**	**377,396**	**369,604**	**320,411**	**338,063**	**346,550**
Trade credits	8 756 ..	22,264	23,322	30,553	29,579	23,957	20,358	25,596	30,237
General government: long-term	8 758 ..	...	...	...	...	...	...	...	...
General government: short-term	8 759 ..	...	...	...	...	...	...	...	...
Other sectors: long-term	8 761 ..	3,700	3,702	4,206	4,147	3,121	2,589	2,783	3,425
Other sectors: short-term	8 762 ..	18,564	19,621	26,347	25,432	20,836	17,769	22,813	26,812
Loans	8 764 ..	51,606	74,065	118,303	107,901	98,698	86,977	88,402	94,428
Use of Fund credit and loans from the Fund	8 766 ..	...	...	...	...	...	...	...	...
Monetary authorities: other long-term	8 767 ..	...	...	...	...	...	...	...	...
Monetary authorities: short-term	8 768 ..	...	...	...	...	...	...	...	...
General government: long-term	8 770 ..	30,705	37,702	47,179	25,542	21,579	21,506	21,551	26,328
General government: short-term	8 771 ..	...	...	...	...	...	...	...	...
Banks: long-term	8 773 ..	...	...	...	...	...	...	...	...
Banks: short-term	8 774 ..	...	...	...	...	1,136	1,026	5,540	8,528
Other sectors: long-term	8 776 ..	20,901	36,364	71,124	82,359	75,983	64,445	61,312	59,573
Other sectors: short-term	8 777 ..	...	...	...	...	...	...	...	...
Currency and deposits	8 780 ..	129,264	161,942	202,898	239,554	241,633	212,497	223,580	220,331
Monetary authorities	8 781 ..	...	...	...	...	...	...	...	...
General government	8 782 ..	...	...	...	...	...	...	...	...
Banks	8 783 ..	129,264	161,942	202,898	239,554	241,633	212,497	223,580	220,331
Other sectors	8 784 ..	...	...	...	...	...	...	...	...
Other liabilities	8 786 ..	147	315	354	363	5,316	578	485	1,554
Monetary authorities: long-term	8 788 ..	...	...	...	...	...	...	...	...
Monetary authorities: short-term	8 789 ..	147	315	354	363	5,316	578	485	1,554
General government: long-term	8 791 ..	...	...	...	...	...	...	...	...
General government: short-term	8 792 ..	...	...	...	...	...	...	...	...
Banks: long-term	8 794 ..	...	...	...	...	...	...	...	...
Banks: short-term	8 795 ..	...	...	...	...	...	...	...	...
Other sectors: long-term	8 797 ..	...	...	...	...	...	...	...	...
Other sectors: short-term	8 798 ..	...	...	...	...	...	...	...	...
NET INTERNATIONAL INVESTMENT POSITION	8 995 ..	**–19,295**	**–45,902**	**–84,686**	**–106,003**	**–110,603**	**–84,367**	**–71,271**	**–51,806**
Conversion rates: lire per U.S. dollar (end of period)	0 102 ..	**1,305.8**	**1,270.5**	**1,130.2**	**1,151.1**	**1,470.9**	**1,704.0**	**1,629.7**	**1,584.7**

Table 1. ANALYTIC PRESENTATION, 1988–95
(Millions of U.S. dollars)

	Code	1988	1989	1990	1991	1992	1993	1994	1995
A. Current Account [1]	4 993 Y.	**46.6**	**–282.6**	**–312.1**	**–240.1**	**28.5**	**–184.0**	**16.9**	**–245.2**
Goods: exports f.o.b	2 100 ..	898.4	1,028.9	1,190.6	1,196.7	1,116.5	1,105.4	1,551.0	1,792.7
Goods: imports f.o.b	3 100 ..	–1,255.3	–1,618.7	–1,692.7	–1,588.3	–1,541.1	–1,920.5	–2,064.8	–2,605.9
Balance on Goods	4 100 ..	*–356.9*	*–589.8*	*–502.1*	*–391.6*	*–424.6*	*–815.1*	*–513.8*	*–813.2*
Services: credit	2 200 ..	785.3	876.1	1,026.5	992.1	1,104.0	1,260.7	1,272.4	1,387.8
Services: debit	3 200 ..	–567.6	–720.8	–697.4	–670.3	–714.4	–823.5	–905.2	–1,034.3
Balance on Goods and Services	4 991 ..	*–139.2*	*–434.5*	*–173.0*	*–69.8*	*–35.0*	*–377.9*	*–146.6*	*–459.7*
Income: credit	2 300 ..	88.0	104.0	107.6	59.7	75.0	117.0	104.6	146.6
Income: debit	3 300 ..	–423.2	–454.1	–537.6	–498.5	–368.9	–312.9	–398.7	–466.7
Balance on Goods, Services, and Income	4 992 ..	*–474.4*	*–784.6*	*–603.0*	*–508.6*	*–328.9*	*–573.8*	*–440.7*	*–779.8*
Current transfers: credit	2 379 Y.	587.8	523.8	314.9	294.8	387.2	415.9	498.4	597.2
Current transfers: debit	3 379 ..	–66.8	–21.8	–24.0	–26.3	–29.8	–26.1	–40.8	–62.6
B. Capital Account [1]	4 994 Y.	**–15.4**	**–15.0**	**–15.9**	**–15.7**	**–17.6**	**–12.9**	**14.7**	**37.1**
Capital account: credit	2 994 Y.	...	...	...	...	...	...	1.5	3.4
Capital account: debit	3 994 ..	–15.4	–15.0	–15.9	–15.7	–17.6	–12.9	13.2	33.7
Total, Groups A Plus B	4 010 ..	*31.2*	*–297.6*	*–328.0*	*–255.8*	*10.9*	*–196.9*	*31.6*	*–208.1*
C. Financial Account [1]	4 995 X.	**88.0**	**98.2**	**404.5**	**271.4**	**354.5**	**296.4**	**324.7**	**201.4**
Direct investment abroad	4 505 ..	...	...	...	...	...	...	...	...
Direct investment in Jamaica	4 555 Y.	–12.0	57.1	137.9	133.2	142.4	77.9	116.8	166.7
Portfolio investment assets	4 602 ..	...	...	...	...	...	...	...	...
Equity securities	4 610 ..	...	...	...	...	...	...	...	...
Debt securities	4 619 ..	...	...	...	...	...	...	...	...
Portfolio investment liabilities	4 652 Y.	...	...	...	...	...	...	...	...
Equity securities	4 660 Y.	...	...	...	...	...	...	...	...
Debt securities	4 669 Y.	...	...	...	...	...	...	...	...
Other investment assets	4 703 ..	1.3	12.0	–2.5	105.7	10.2	1.1	127.1	...
Monetary authorities	4 703 .A	...	...	...	...	...	...	...	...
General government	4 703 .B	–22.9	–6.1	–7.4	–8.0	–1.0	–1.4	–2.6	...
Banks	4 703 .C	24.2	18.1	4.9	113.7	11.2	2.5	129.7	...
Other sectors	4 703 .D	...	...	...	...	...	...	...	...
Other investment liabilities	4 753 X.	98.7	29.1	269.1	32.5	201.9	217.4	80.8	34.7
Monetary authorities	4 753 XA	–2.9	–18.9	–23.2	–38.8	6.4	3.4	–40.1	–41.3
General government	4 753 YB	61.3	216.8	94.7	94.9	–10.0	37.8	–137.2	–97.2
Banks	4 753 YC	–28.8	–19.9	–21.7	–151.3	–46.4	–6.0	–145.5	–144.4
Other sectors	4 753 YD	69.1	–148.9	219.3	127.7	251.9	182.2	403.6	317.6
Total, Groups A Through C	4 020 ..	*119.2*	*–199.4*	*76.5*	*15.6*	*365.4*	*99.5*	*356.3*	*–6.7*
D. Net Errors and Omissions	4 998 ..	**–46.0**	**10.0**	**29.3**	**–20.4**	**–59.9**	**49.7**	**12.9**	**36.1**
Total, Groups A Through D	4 030 ..	*73.2*	*–189.4*	*105.8*	*–4.8*	*305.5*	*149.2*	*369.2*	*29.4*
E. Reserves and Related Items	4 040 ..	**–73.2**	**189.4**	**–105.8**	**4.8**	**–305.5**	**–149.2**	**–369.2**	**–29.4**
Reserve assets	4 800 ..	25.2	39.9	–65.3	52.9	–192.2	–92.9	–331.0	55.3
Use of Fund credit and loans	4 766 ..	–160.2	–86.0	–53.2	32.6	–19.4	–21.3	–38.2	–84.6
Liabilities constituting foreign authorities' reserves	4 900 ..	4.8	17.6	23.7	–16.5	–57.2	–39.3	...	...
Exceptional financing	4 920 ..	57.0	217.9	–11.1	–64.2	–36.7	4.4	...	...
Conversion rates: Jamaica dollars per U.S. dollar	0 101 ..	**5.489**	**5.745**	**7.184**	**12.116**	**22.960**	**24.949**	**33.086**	**35.142**

[1] Excludes components that have been classified in the categories of Group E.

Table 2. STANDARD PRESENTATION, 1988–95
(Millions of U.S. dollars)

	Code	1988	1989	1990	1991	1992	1993	1994	1995
CURRENT ACCOUNT	4 993 . .	**47.5**	**–282.4**	**–312.1**	**–240.1**	**28.5**	**–184.0**	**16.9**	**–245.2**
A. GOODS	4 100 . .	–356.9	–589.8	–502.1	–391.6	–424.6	–815.1	–513.8	–813.2
Credit	2 100 . .	**898.4**	**1,028.9**	**1,190.6**	**1,196.7**	**1,116.5**	**1,105.4**	**1,551.0**	**1,792.7**
General merchandise: exports f.o.b.	2 110 . .	883.0	1,000.4	1,157.5	1,150.7	1,053.6	1,075.4	1,522.0	1,764.4
Goods for processing: exports f.o.b.	2 150 . .	. . .	. . .	. . .	. . .	. . .	. . .	. . .	. . .
Repairs on goods	2 160 . .	. . .	. . .	. . .	. . .	. . .	. . .	. . .	. . .
Goods procured in ports by carriers	2 170 . .	15.4	28.5	33.1	46.0	62.9	30.0	29.0	28.3
Nonmonetary gold	2 180 . .	. . .	. . .	. . .	. . .	. . .	. . .	. . .	. . .
Debit	3 100 . .	**–1,255.3**	**–1,618.7**	**–1,692.7**	**–1,588.3**	**–1,541.1**	**–1,920.5**	**–2,064.8**	**–2,605.9**
General merchandise: imports f.o.b.	3 110 . .	–1,240.3	–1,606.4	–1,679.6	–1,575.0	–1,529.2	–1,882.8	–2,038.2	–2,544.9
Goods for processing: imports f.o.b.	3 150 . .	. . .	. . .	. . .	. . .	. . .	. . .	. . .	. . .
Repairs on goods	3 160 . .	. . .	. . .	. . .	. . .	. . .	. . .	. . .	. . .
Goods procured in ports by carriers	3 170 . .	–15.0	–12.3	–13.1	–13.3	–11.9	–37.7	–26.6	–61.0
Nonmonetary gold	3 180 . .	. . .	. . .	. . .	. . .	. . .	. . .	. . .	. . .
B. SERVICES	4 200 . .	217.7	155.3	329.1	321.8	389.6	437.2	367.2	353.5
Total credit	2 200 . .	*785.3*	*876.1*	*1,026.5*	*992.1*	*1,104.0*	*1,260.7*	*1,272.4*	*1,387.8*
Total debit	3 200 . .	*–567.6*	*–720.8*	*–697.4*	*–670.3*	*–714.4*	*–823.5*	*–905.2*	*–1,034.3*
Transportation services, credit	2 205 . .	**152.1**	**168.5**	**175.9**	**124.2**	**131.5**	**142.6**	**215.8**	**250.9**
Passenger	2 205 BA	*107.9*	*115.7*	*117.6*	*88.9*	*96.4*	*99.4*	*127.0*	*130.0*
Freight	2 205 BB	*10.1*	*12.2*	*14.0*	*9.0*	*5.4*	*5.3*	*13.4*	*3.6*
Other	2 205 BC	*34.1*	*40.6*	*44.3*	*26.3*	*29.7*	*37.9*	*75.4*	*117.3*
Sea transport, passenger	2 207 . .	. . .	. . .	. . .	. . .	. . .	. . .	. . .	. . .
Sea transport, freight	2 208 . .	. . .	. . .	. . .	. . .	. . .	. . .	. . .	. . .
Sea transport, other	2 209 . .	. . .	. . .	. . .	. . .	. . .	. . .	. . .	. . .
Air transport, passenger	2 211 . .	. . .	. . .	. . .	. . .	. . .	. . .	. . .	. . .
Air transport, freight	2 212 . .	. . .	. . .	. . .	. . .	. . .	. . .	. . .	. . .
Air transport, other	2 213 . .	. . .	. . .	. . .	. . .	. . .	. . .	. . .	. . .
Other transport, passenger	2 215 . .	. . .	. . .	. . .	. . .	. . .	. . .	. . .	. . .
Other transport, freight	2 216 . .	. . .	. . .	. . .	. . .	. . .	. . .	. . .	. . .
Other transport, other	2 217 . .	. . .	. . .	. . .	. . .	. . .	. . .	. . .	. . .
Transportation services, debit	3 205 . .	**–244.8**	**–339.7**	**–319.2**	**–290.6**	**–310.4**	**–366.9**	**–404.5**	**–492.6**
Passenger	3 205 BA	*–12.5*	*–14.1*	*–11.9*	*–12.0*	*–12.6*	*–10.5*	*–24.2*	*–24.5*
Freight	3 205 BB	*–183.3*	*–239.3*	*–234.9*	*–226.1*	*–220.1*	*–278.1*	*–307.8*	*–393.1*
Other	3 205 BC	*–49.0*	*–86.3*	*–72.4*	*–52.5*	*–77.7*	*–78.3*	*–72.5*	*–75.0*
Sea transport, passenger	3 207 . .	. . .	. . .	. . .	. . .	. . .	. . .	. . .	. . .
Sea transport, freight	3 208 . .	. . .	. . .	. . .	. . .	. . .	. . .	. . .	. . .
Sea transport, other	3 209 . .	. . .	. . .	. . .	. . .	. . .	. . .	. . .	. . .
Air transport, passenger	3 211 . .	. . .	. . .	. . .	. . .	. . .	. . .	. . .	. . .
Air transport, freight	3 212 . .	. . .	. . .	. . .	. . .	. . .	. . .	. . .	. . .
Air transport, other	3 213 . .	. . .	. . .	. . .	. . .	. . .	. . .	. . .	. . .
Other transport, passenger	3 215 . .	. . .	. . .	. . .	. . .	. . .	. . .	. . .	. . .
Other transport, freight	3 216 . .	. . .	. . .	. . .	. . .	. . .	. . .	. . .	. . .
Other transport, other	3 217 . .	. . .	. . .	. . .	. . .	. . .	. . .	. . .	. . .
Travel, credit	2 236 . .	**544.1**	**604.3**	**751.3**	**774.0**	**863.6**	**945.0**	**923.3**	**1,022.1**
Business travel	2 237 . .	. . .	. . .	. . .	. . .	. . .	. . .	. . .	. . .
Personal travel	2 240 . .	. . .	. . .	. . .	. . .	. . .	. . .	. . .	. . .
Travel, debit	3 236 . .	**–112.3**	**–113.9**	**–113.6**	**–70.5**	**–87.1**	**–82.4**	**–80.9**	**–147.6**
Business travel	3 237 . .	. . .	. . .	. . .	. . .	. . .	. . .	. . .	. . .
Personal travel	3 240 . .	. . .	. . .	. . .	. . .	. . .	. . .	. . .	. . .
Other services, credit	2 200 BA	**89.1**	**103.3**	**99.4**	**93.9**	**108.9**	**173.1**	**133.3**	**114.8**
Communications	2 245 . .	. . .	. . .	. . .	. . .	. . .	. . .	. . .	. . .
Construction	2 249 . .	. . .	. . .	. . .	. . .	. . .	. . .	. . .	. . .
Insurance	2 253 . .	10.9	10.1	13.6	11.0	9.1	9.8	21.6	11.3
Financial	2 260 . .	. . .	. . .	. . .	. . .	. . .	. . .	4.3	.9
Computer and information	2 262 . .	. . .	. . .	. . .	. . .	. . .	. . .	30.0	31.3
Royalties and licence fees	2 266 . .	15.3	2.7	3.3	2.0	3.3	9.2	5.1	3.9
Other business services	2 268 . .	23.7	43.3	31.5	38.9	52.7	104.5	27.1	14.9
Personal, cultural, and recreational	2 287 . .	. . .	. . .	. . .	. . .	. . .	. . .	.2	. . .
Government, n.i.e.	2 291 . .	39.2	47.2	51.0	42.0	43.8	49.6	45.0	52.5
Other services, debit	3 200 BA	**–210.5**	**–267.2**	**–264.6**	**–309.2**	**–316.9**	**–374.2**	**–419.8**	**–394.1**
Communications	3 245 . .	. . .	. . .	. . .	. . .	. . .	. . .	. . .	. . .
Construction	3 249 . .	. . .	. . .	. . .	. . .	. . .	. . .	. . .	. . .
Insurance	3 253 . .	–39.3	–43.1	–44.5	–44.3	–43.8	–58.6	–79.4	–95.6
Financial	3 260 . .	. . .	. . .	. . .	. . .	. . .	. . .	–1.1	–1.9
Computer and information	3 262 . .	. . .	. . .	. . .	. . .	. . .	. . .	. . .	–.6
Royalties and licence fees	3 266 . .	–7.9	–11.5	–7.1	–9.4	–2.7	–3.2	–10.5	–19.4
Other business services	3 268 . .	–138.9	–179.1	–181.1	–222.7	–229.8	–272.7	–288.8	–253.8
Personal, cultural, and recreational	3 287 . .	. . .	–2.5	–1.3	–1.3	–.5	–1.6	–2.2	–2.2
Government, n.i.e.	3 291 . .	–24.4	–31.0	–30.6	–31.5	–40.1	–38.1	–37.8	–20.6

Table 2 (Continued). STANDARD PRESENTATION, 1988–95
(Millions of U.S. dollars)

	Code	1988	1989	1990	1991	1992	1993	1994	1995
C. INCOME	4 300 . .	–335.2	–350.1	–430.0	–438.8	–293.9	–195.9	–294.1	–320.1
Total credit	2 300 . .	*88.0*	*104.0*	*107.6*	*59.7*	*75.0*	*117.0*	*104.6*	*146.6*
Total debit	3 300 . .	*–423.2*	*–454.1*	*–537.6*	*–498.5*	*–368.9*	*–312.9*	*–398.7*	*–466.7*
Compensation of employees, credit	2 310 . .	**77.9**	**92.3**	**92.5**	**45.7**	**57.9**	**52.0**	**49.2**	**56.8**
Compensation of employees, debit	3 310 . .	**–5.7**	**–7.0**	**–5.4**	**–5.6**	**–3.6**	**–7.7**	**–7.8**	**–10.3**
Investment income, credit	2 320 . .	**10.1**	**11.7**	**15.1**	**14.0**	**17.1**	**65.0**	**55.4**	**89.8**
Direct investment income	2 330 . .	1.0	1.2	1.0	1.0	1.0	42.7	8.6	14.9
Dividends and distributed branch profits	2 332 . .	1.0	1.2	1.0	1.0	1.0	42.7	8.6	14.9
Reinvested earnings and undistributed branch profits	2 333 . .	...	...	...	...	...	...	...	...
Income on debt (interest)	2 334 . .	...	...	...	...	...	...	...	...
Portfolio investment income	2 339 . .	...	...	...	...	...	...	...	...
Income on equity	2 340 . .	...	...	...	...	...	...	...	...
Income on bonds and notes	2 350 . .	...	...	...	...	...	...	...	...
Income on money market instruments and financial derivatives	2 360 . .	...	...	...	...	...	...	...	...
Other investment income	2 370 . .	9.1	10.5	14.1	13.0	16.1	22.3	46.8	74.9
Investment income, debit	3 320 . .	**–417.5**	**–447.1**	**–532.2**	**–492.9**	**–365.3**	**–305.2**	**–390.9**	**–456.4**
Direct investment income	3 330 . .	–109.5	–108.5	–189.1	–159.4	–56.8	–5.0	–124.0	–179.5
Dividends and distributed branch profits	3 332 . .	–100.5	–97.6	–178.2	–147.6	–46.8	–1.5	–117.9	–162.1
Reinvested earnings and undistributed branch profits	3 333 . .	–9.0	–10.9	–10.9	–11.8	–10.0	–3.5	–6.1	–17.4
Income on debt (interest)	3 334 . .	...	...	...	...	...	...	...	...
Portfolio investment income	3 339 . .	...	...	...	...	...	...	...	...
Income on equity	3 340 . .	...	...	...	...	...	...	...	...
Income on bonds and notes	3 350 . .	...	...	...	...	...	...	...	...
Income on money market instruments and financial derivatives	3 360 . .	...	...	...	...	...	...	...	...
Other investment income	3 370 . .	–308.0	–338.6	–343.1	–333.5	–308.5	–300.2	–266.9	–276.9
D. CURRENT TRANSFERS	4 379 . .	521.9	502.2	290.9	268.5	357.4	389.8	457.6	534.6
Credit	2 379 . .	**588.7**	**524.0**	**314.9**	**294.8**	**387.2**	**415.9**	**498.4**	**597.2**
General government	2 380 . .	127.7	196.4	127.1	111.5	102.0	84.9	14.9	21.8
Other sectors	2 390 . .	461.0	327.6	187.8	183.3	285.2	331.0	483.5	575.4
Workers' remittances	2 391 . .	76.0	116.2	136.2	135.6	157.7	187.2	332.2	443.2
Other current transfers	2 392 . .	385.0	211.4	51.6	47.7	127.5	143.8	151.3	132.2
Debit	3 379 . .	**–66.8**	**–21.8**	**–24.0**	**–26.3**	**–29.8**	**–26.1**	**–40.8**	**–62.6**
General government	3 380 . .	–57.7	–8.7	–11.1	–12.0	–10.4	–14.4	–5.0	–4.8
Other sectors	3 390 . .	–9.1	–13.1	–12.9	–14.3	–19.4	–11.7	–35.8	–57.8
Workers' remittances	3 391 . .	–2.1	–2.1	–5.4	–5.6	–7.9	–6.0	–12.3	–29.5
Other current transfers	3 392 . .	–7.0	–11.0	–7.5	–8.7	–11.5	–5.7	–23.5	–28.3
CAPITAL AND FINANCIAL ACCOUNT	4 996 . .	**–1.4**	**272.4**	**282.8**	**260.5**	**31.4**	**134.3**	**–29.8**	**209.1**
CAPITAL ACCOUNT	4 994 . .	**–15.4**	**–15.0**	**–15.9**	**–15.7**	**–17.6**	**–12.9**	**14.7**	**37.1**
Total credit	2 994 . .	...	...	...	...	...	...	*1.5*	*3.4*
Total debit	3 994 . .	*–15.4*	*–15.0*	*–15.9*	*–15.7*	*–17.6*	*–12.9*	*13.2*	*33.7*
Capital transfers, credit	2 400 . .	...	...	...	...	...	...	**1.5**	**3.4**
General government	2 401 . .	...	...	...	...	...	...	...	...
Debt forgiveness	2 402 . .	...	...	...	...	...	...	...	...
Other capital transfers	2 410 . .	...	...	...	...	...	...	...	...
Other sectors	2 430 . .	...	...	...	...	...	...	1.5	3.4
Migrants' transfers	2 431 . .	...	...	...	...	...	...	1.5	3.4
Debt forgiveness	2 432 . .	...	...	...	...	...	...	...	...
Other capital transfers	2 440 . .	...	...	...	...	...	...	...	...
Capital transfers, debit	3 400 . .	**–15.4**	**–15.0**	**–15.9**	**–15.7**	**–17.6**	**–12.9**	**13.2**	**33.7**
General government	3 401 . .	...	...	...	...	...	...	18.2	40.7
Debt forgiveness	3 402 . .	...	...	...	...	...	...	...	...
Other capital transfers	3 410 . .	...	...	...	...	...	...	18.2	40.7
Other sectors	3 430 . .	–15.4	–15.0	–15.9	–15.7	–17.6	–12.9	–5.0	–7.0
Migrants' transfers	3 431 . .	–15.4	–15.0	–15.9	–15.7	–17.6	–12.9	–5.0	–7.0
Debt forgiveness	3 432 . .	...	...	...	...	...	...	...	...
Other capital transfers	3 440 . .	...	...	...	...	...	...	...	...
Nonproduced nonfinancial assets, credit	2 480 . .	...	...	...	...	...	...	...	...
Nonproduced nonfinancial assets, debit	3 480 . .	...	...	...	...	...	...	...	...

Table 2 (Continued). STANDARD PRESENTATION, 1988–95
(Millions of U.S. dollars)

	Code	1988	1989	1990	1991	1992	1993	1994	1995
FINANCIAL ACCOUNT	4 995 . .	**14.0**	**287.4**	**298.7**	**276.2**	**49.0**	**147.2**	**–44.5**	**172.0**
A. DIRECT INVESTMENT	4 500 . .	–12.0	57.1	137.9	133.2	142.4	77.9	116.8	166.7
Direct investment abroad	4 505 . .	**. . .**	**. . .**	**. . .**	**. . .**	**. . .**	**. . .**	**. . .**	**. . .**
Equity capital	4 510 . .	. . .	. . .	. . .	. . .	. . .	. . .	. . .	. . .
Claims on affiliated enterprises	4 515 . .	. . .	. . .	. . .	. . .	. . .	. . .	. . .	. . .
Liabilities to affiliated enterprises	4 520 . .	. . .	. . .	. . .	. . .	. . .	. . .	. . .	. . .
Reinvested earnings	4 525 . .	. . .	. . .	. . .	. . .	. . .	. . .	. . .	. . .
Other capital	4 530 . .	. . .	. . .	. . .	. . .	. . .	. . .	. . .	. . .
Claims on affiliated enterprises	4 535 . .	. . .	. . .	. . .	. . .	. . .	. . .	. . .	. . .
Liabilities to affiliated enterprises	4 540 . .	. . .	. . .	. . .	. . .	. . .	. . .	. . .	. . .
Direct investment in Jamaica	4 555 . .	**–12.0**	**57.1**	**137.9**	**133.2**	**142.4**	**77.9**	**116.8**	**166.7**
Equity capital	4 560 . .	. . .	52.1	62.6	15.1	9.8	5.6	17.3	. . .
Claims on direct investors	4 565 . .	. . .	. . .	. . .	. . .	. . .	. . .	. . .	. . .
Liabilities to direct investors	4 570 . .	. . .	. . .	. . .	. . .	. . .	. . .	17.3	. . .
Reinvested earnings	4 575 . .	9.0	10.9	10.9	11.8	10.0	3.5	6.1	17.4
Other capital	4 580 . .	–21.0	–5.9	64.4	106.3	122.6	68.8	93.4	149.3
Claims on direct investors	4 585 . .	. . .	. . .	. . .	. . .	. . .	. . .	. . .	. . .
Liabilities to direct investors	4 590 . .	. . .	. . .	. . .	. . .	. . .	. . .	93.4	149.3
B. PORTFOLIO INVESTMENT	4 600 . .	. . .	. . .	. . .	. . .	. . .	. . .	. . .	. . .
Assets	4 602 . .	**. . .**	**. . .**	**. . .**	**. . .**	**. . .**	**. . .**	**. . .**	**. . .**
Equity securities	4 610 . .	. . .	. . .	. . .	. . .	. . .	. . .	. . .	. . .
Monetary authorities	4 611 . .	. . .	. . .	. . .	. . .	. . .	. . .	. . .	. . .
General government	4 612 . .	. . .	. . .	. . .	. . .	. . .	. . .	. . .	. . .
Banks	4 613 . .	. . .	. . .	. . .	. . .	. . .	. . .	. . .	. . .
Other sectors	4 614 . .	. . .	. . .	. . .	. . .	. . .	. . .	. . .	. . .
Debt securities	4 619 . .	. . .	. . .	. . .	. . .	. . .	. . .	. . .	. . .
Bonds and notes	4 620 . .	. . .	. . .	. . .	. . .	. . .	. . .	. . .	. . .
Monetary authorities	4 621 . .	. . .	. . .	. . .	. . .	. . .	. . .	. . .	. . .
General government	4 622 . .	. . .	. . .	. . .	. . .	. . .	. . .	. . .	. . .
Banks	4 623 . .	. . .	. . .	. . .	. . .	. . .	. . .	. . .	. . .
Other sectors	4 624 . .	. . .	. . .	. . .	. . .	. . .	. . .	. . .	. . .
Money market instruments	4 630 . .	. . .	. . .	. . .	. . .	. . .	. . .	. . .	. . .
Monetary authorities	4 631 . .	. . .	. . .	. . .	. . .	. . .	. . .	. . .	. . .
General government	4 632 . .	. . .	. . .	. . .	. . .	. . .	. . .	. . .	. . .
Banks	4 633 . .	. . .	. . .	. . .	. . .	. . .	. . .	. . .	. . .
Other sectors	4 634 . .	. . .	. . .	. . .	. . .	. . .	. . .	. . .	. . .
Financial derivatives	4 640 . .	. . .	. . .	. . .	. . .	. . .	. . .	. . .	. . .
Monetary authorities	4 641 . .	. . .	. . .	. . .	. . .	. . .	. . .	. . .	. . .
General government	4 642 . .	. . .	. . .	. . .	. . .	. . .	. . .	. . .	. . .
Banks	4 643 . .	. . .	. . .	. . .	. . .	. . .	. . .	. . .	. . .
Other sectors	4 644 . .	. . .	. . .	. . .	. . .	. . .	. . .	. . .	. . .
Liabilities	4 652 . .	**. . .**	**. . .**	**. . .**	**. . .**	**. . .**	**. . .**	**. . .**	**. . .**
Equity securities	4 660 . .	. . .	. . .	. . .	. . .	. . .	. . .	. . .	. . .
Banks	4 663 . .	. . .	. . .	. . .	. . .	. . .	. . .	. . .	. . .
Other sectors	4 664 . .	. . .	. . .	. . .	. . .	. . .	. . .	. . .	. . .
Debt securities	4 669 . .	. . .	. . .	. . .	. . .	. . .	. . .	. . .	. . .
Bonds and notes	4 670 . .	. . .	. . .	. . .	. . .	. . .	. . .	. . .	. . .
Monetary authorities	4 671 . .	. . .	. . .	. . .	. . .	. . .	. . .	. . .	. . .
General government	4 672 . .	. . .	. . .	. . .	. . .	. . .	. . .	. . .	. . .
Banks	4 673 . .	. . .	. . .	. . .	. . .	. . .	. . .	. . .	. . .
Other sectors	4 674 . .	. . .	. . .	. . .	. . .	. . .	. . .	. . .	. . .
Money market instruments	4 680 . .	. . .	. . .	. . .	. . .	. . .	. . .	. . .	. . .
Monetary authorities	4 681 . .	. . .	. . .	. . .	. . .	. . .	. . .	. . .	. . .
General government	4 682 . .	. . .	. . .	. . .	. . .	. . .	. . .	. . .	. . .
Banks	4 683 . .	. . .	. . .	. . .	. . .	. . .	. . .	. . .	. . .
Other sectors	4 684 . .	. . .	. . .	. . .	. . .	. . .	. . .	. . .	. . .
Financial derivatives	4 690 . .	. . .	. . .	. . .	. . .	. . .	. . .	. . .	. . .
Monetary authorities	4 691 . .	. . .	. . .	. . .	. . .	. . .	. . .	. . .	. . .
General government	4 692 . .	. . .	. . .	. . .	. . .	. . .	. . .	. . .	. . .
Banks	4 693 . .	. . .	. . .	. . .	. . .	. . .	. . .	. . .	. . .
Other sectors	4 694 . .	. . .	. . .	. . .	. . .	. . .	. . .	. . .	. . .

Table 2 (Concluded). STANDARD PRESENTATION, 1988–95
(Millions of U.S. dollars)

	Code	1988	1989	1990	1991	1992	1993	1994	1995
C. OTHER INVESTMENT	4 700	.7	190.4	226.0	90.1	98.8	162.3	169.7	–49.9
Assets	4 703	**1.3**	**12.0**	**–2.5**	**105.7**	**10.2**	**1.1**	**127.1**	**. . .**
Trade credits	4 706	. . .	. . .	. . .	. . .	. . .	. . .	. . .	. . .
General government: long-term	4 708	. . .	. . .	. . .	. . .	. . .	. . .	. . .	. . .
General government: short-term	4 709	. . .	. . .	. . .	. . .	. . .	. . .	. . .	. . .
Other sectors: long-term	4 711	. . .	. . .	. . .	. . .	. . .	. . .	. . .	. . .
Other sectors: short-term	4 712	. . .	. . .	. . .	. . .	. . .	. . .	. . .	. . .
Loans	4 714	. . .	. . .	. . .	. . .	. . .	. . .	. . .	. . .
Monetary authorities: long-term	4 717	. . .	. . .	. . .	. . .	. . .	. . .	. . .	. . .
Monetary authorities: short-term	4 718	. . .	. . .	. . .	. . .	. . .	. . .	. . .	. . .
General government: long-term	4 720	. . .	. . .	. . .	. . .	. . .	. . .	. . .	. . .
General government: short-term	4 721	. . .	. . .	. . .	. . .	. . .	. . .	. . .	. . .
Banks: long-term	4 723	. . .	. . .	. . .	. . .	. . .	. . .	. . .	. . .
Banks: short-term	4 724	. . .	. . .	. . .	. . .	. . .	. . .	. . .	. . .
Other sectors: long-term	4 726	. . .	. . .	. . .	. . .	. . .	. . .	. . .	. . .
Other sectors: short-term	4 727	. . .	. . .	. . .	. . .	. . .	. . .	. . .	. . .
Currency and deposits	4 730	24.2	18.1	4.9	113.7	11.2	2.5	129.7	. . .
Monetary authorities	4 731	. . .	. . .	. . .	. . .	. . .	. . .	. . .	. . .
General government	4 732	. . .	. . .	. . .	. . .	. . .	. . .	. . .	. . .
Banks	4 733	24.2	18.1	4.9	113.7	11.2	2.5	129.7	. . .
Other sectors	4 734	. . .	. . .	. . .	. . .	. . .	. . .	. . .	. . .
Other assets	4 736	–22.9	–6.1	–7.4	–8.0	–1.0	–1.4	–2.6	. . .
Monetary authorities: long-term	4 738	. . .	. . .	. . .	. . .	. . .	. . .	. . .	. . .
Monetary authorities: short-term	4 739	. . .	. . .	. . .	. . .	. . .	. . .	. . .	. . .
General government: long-term	4 741	–22.9	–6.1	–7.4	–8.0	–1.0	–1.4	–2.6	. . .
General government: short-term	4 742	. . .	. . .	. . .	. . .	. . .	. . .	. . .	. . .
Banks: long-term	4 744	. . .	. . .	. . .	. . .	. . .	. . .	. . .	. . .
Banks: short-term	4 745	. . .	. . .	. . .	. . .	. . .	. . .	. . .	. . .
Other sectors: long-term	4 747	. . .	. . .	. . .	. . .	. . .	. . .	. . .	. . .
Other sectors: short-term	4 748	. . .	. . .	. . .	. . .	. . .	. . .	. . .	. . .
Liabilities	4 753	**–.6**	**178.4**	**228.5**	**–15.6**	**88.6**	**161.2**	**42.6**	**–49.9**
Trade credits	4 756	. . .	. . .	. . .	. . .	. . .	. . .	. . .	. . .
General government: long-term	4 758	. . .	. . .	. . .	. . .	. . .	. . .	. . .	. . .
General government: short-term	4 759	. . .	. . .	. . .	. . .	. . .	. . .	. . .	. . .
Other sectors: long-term	4 761	. . .	. . .	. . .	. . .	. . .	. . .	. . .	. . .
Other sectors: short-term	4 762	. . .	. . .	. . .	. . .	. . .	. . .	. . .	. . .
Loans	4 764	18.3	–17.6	261.7	265.9	226.6	214.9	239.5	137.7
Use of Fund credit and loans from the Fund	4 766	–160.2	–86.0	–53.2	32.6	–19.4	–21.3	–38.2	–84.6
Monetary authorities: other long-term	4 767	–8.0	–12.8	–.3	6.4	4.1	4.4	1.9	1.9
Monetary authorities: short-term	4 768	. . .	. . .	. . .	. . .	. . .	. . .	–.4	. . .
General government: long-term	4 770	117.4	230.1	95.9	99.2	–10.0	49.6	–127.4	–97.2
General government: short-term	4 771	. . .	. . .	. . .	. . .	. . .	. . .	. . .	. . .
Banks: long-term	4 773	. . .	. . .	. . .	. . .	. . .	. . .	. . .	. . .
Banks: short-term	4 774	. . .	. . .	. . .	. . .	. . .	. . .	. . .	. . .
Other sectors: long-term	4 776	–6.0	–5.5	60.7	30.0	9.0	.7	17.3	56.8
Other sectors: short-term	4 777	75.1	–143.4	158.6	97.7	242.9	181.5	386.3	260.8
Currency and deposits	4 780	–24.0	–2.3	2.0	–167.8	–103.6	–45.3	–176.7	–187.6
Monetary authorities	4 781	4.8	17.6	23.7	–16.5	–57.2	–39.3	–31.2	–43.2
General government	4 782	. . .	. . .	. . .	. . .	. . .	. . .	. . .	. . .
Banks	4 783	–28.8	–19.9	–21.7	–151.3	–46.4	–6.0	–145.5	–144.4
Other sectors	4 784	. . .	. . .	. . .	. . .	. . .	. . .	. . .	. . .
Other liabilities	4 786	5.1	198.3	–35.2	–113.7	–34.4	–8.4	–20.2	. . .
Monetary authorities: long-term	4 788	. . .	. . .	. . .	. . .	. . .	. . .	. . .	. . .
Monetary authorities: short-term	4 789	61.2	7.3	–20.0	–25.7	3.8	3.4	–10.4	. . .
General government: long-term	4 791	–56.1	–13.3	–1.2	–4.3	. . .	. . .	. . .	. . .
General government: short-term	4 792	. . .	204.3	–14.0	–83.7	–38.2	–11.8	–9.8	. . .
Banks: long-term	4 794	. . .	. . .	. . .	. . .	. . .	. . .	. . .	. . .
Banks: short-term	4 795	. . .	. . .	. . .	. . .	. . .	. . .	. . .	. . .
Other sectors: long-term	4 797	. . .	. . .	. . .	. . .	. . .	. . .	. . .	. . .
Other sectors: short-term	4 798	. . .	. . .	. . .	. . .	. . .	. . .	. . .	. . .
D. RESERVE ASSETS	4 800	25.2	39.9	–65.3	52.9	–192.2	–92.9	–331.0	55.3
Monetary gold	4 810	. . .	. . .	. . .	. . .	. . .	. . .	. . .	. . .
Special drawing rights	4 820	1.3	. . .	–.4	.4	–12.3	–.2	12.7	–.4
Reserve position in the Fund	4 830	. . .	. . .	. . .	. . .	. . .	. . .	. . .	. . .
Foreign exchange	4 840	21.7	40.1	–65.1	52.1	–179.6	–93.1	–343.7	55.9
Other claims	4 880	2.2	–.2	.2	.4	–.3	.4	. . .	–.2
NET ERRORS AND OMISSIONS	4 998	**–46.0**	**10.0**	**29.3**	**–20.4**	**–59.9**	**49.7**	**12.9**	**36.1**

Part 3 of the *Yearbook* contains descriptions of the methodologies, compilation practices, and sources used to compile these data.

Table 1. ANALYTIC PRESENTATION, 1988–95
(Billions of U.S. dollars)

	Code	1988	1989	1990	1991	1992	1993	1994	1995
A. Current Account[1]	4 993 Y.	**79.61**	**56.99**	**35.87**	**68.37**	**112.33**	**131.98**	**130.56**	**111.25**
Goods: exports f.o.b.	2 100 . .	259.77	269.55	280.35	308.10	332.50	352.90	385.99	429.32
Goods: imports f.o.b.	3 100 . .	–164.77	–192.66	–216.77	–212.03	–207.80	–213.32	–241.55	–297.24
Balance on Goods	4 100 . .	*95.00*	*76.89*	*63.58*	*96.07*	*124.70*	*139.58*	*144.44*	*132.07*
Services: credit	2 200 . .	36.67	41.72	43.34	44.83	49.05	53.25	58.31	65.21
Services: debit	3 200 . .	–68.55	–80.33	–88.03	–86.61	–93.01	–96.34	–106.38	–122.70
Balance on Goods and Services	4 991 . .	*63.12*	*38.28*	*18.89*	*54.29*	*80.74*	*96.50*	*96.37*	*74.59*
Income: credit	2 300 . .	75.11	102.19	122.64	140.89	142.69	148.23	155.37	192.61
Income: debit	3 300 . .	–54.50	–79.20	–100.14	–114.98	–107.26	–107.63	–115.06	–148.20
Balance on Goods, Services, and Income	4 992 . .	*83.73*	*61.27*	*41.39*	*80.19*	*116.17*	*137.10*	*136.67*	*118.99*
Current transfers: credit	2 379 Y.	1.09	1.01	1.00	1.42	1.67	1.58	1.83	1.98
Current transfers: debit	3 379 . .	–5.21	–5.29	–6.52	–13.24	–5.51	–6.70	–7.95	–9.73
B. Capital Account[1]	4 994 Y.	**. . .**	**. . .**	**. . .**	**–1.20**	**–1.29**	**–1.46**	**–1.86**	**–2.26**
Capital account: credit	2 994 Y.	. . .	. . .	. . .	. . .	. . .	. . .	. . .	.01
Capital account: debit	3 994 . .	. . .	. . .	. . .	–1.20	–1.29	–1.46	–1.86	–2.27
Total, Groups A Plus B	4 010 . .	*79.61*	*56.99*	*35.87*	*67.17*	*111.04*	*130.52*	*128.70*	*108.98*
C. Financial Account[1]	4 995 X.	**–66.22**	**–47.93**	**–21.54**	**–67.54**	**–99.93**	**–102.59**	**–85.53**	**–64.40**
Direct investment abroad	4 505 . .	–34.21	–44.16	–48.05	–31.49	–17.36	–13.83	–18.10	–22.66
Direct investment in Japan	4 555 Y.	–.52	–1.06	1.76	1.30	2.76	.13	.92	.06
Portfolio investment assets	4 602 . .	–87.12	–113.24	–40.20	–81.72	–34.93	–64.03	–91.13	–88.07
Equity securities	4 610 . .	–2.98	–17.89	–6.26	–3.63	3.01	–15.33	–14.06	.16
Debt securities	4 619 . .	–84.14	–95.35	–33.94	–78.08	–37.94	–48.71	–77.07	–88.23
Portfolio investment liabilities	4 652 Y.	21.01	84.48	35.39	125.87	7.50	–6.68	64.46	51.96
Equity securities	4 660 Y.	6.81	6.99	–13.26	46.71	8.73	19.99	49.01	50.70
Debt securities	4 669 Y.	14.20	77.49	48.65	79.15	–1.23	–26.67	15.46	1.26
Other investment assets	4 703 . .	–189.99	–171.54	–89.14	26.94	47.60	13.04	–35.88	–105.71
Monetary authorities	4 703 .A	. . .	. . .	. . .	. . .	. . .	. . .	. . .	. . .
General government	4 703 .B	–6.32	–8.04	–10.12	. . .	. . .	. . .	. . .	. . .
Banks	4 703 .C	–153.34	–140.20	–64.16	. . .	. . .	. . .	. . .	. . .
Other sectors	4 703 .D	–30.33	–23.30	–14.86	. . .	. . .	. . .	. . .	. . .
Other investment liabilities	4 753 X.	224.61	197.59	118.70	–108.45	–105.51	–31.22	–5.80	100.04
Monetary authorities	4 753 XA	1.49	11.51	14.46	. . .	. . .	. . .	. . .	. . .
General government	4 753 YB	–.58	–.43	–.36	. . .	. . .	. . .	. . .	. . .
Banks	4 753 YC	191.73	143.88	44.46	–80.66	–36.48	–29.44	–1.38	4.42
Other sectors	4 753 YD	31.97	42.63	60.14	–27.79	–69.02	–1.79	–4.41	95.62
Total, Groups A Through C	4 020 . .	*13.39*	*9.06*	*14.33*	*–.37*	*11.11*	*27.93*	*43.17*	*44.58*
D. Net Errors and Omissions	4 998 . .	**3.13**	**–21.82**	**–20.92**	**–7.88**	**–10.44**	**–.28**	**–17.80**	**14.06**
Total, Groups A Through D	4 030 . .	*16.52*	*–12.76*	*–6.59*	*–8.26*	*.67*	*27.65*	*25.36*	*58.64*
E. Reserves and Related Items	4 040 . .	**–16.52**	**12.76**	**6.59**	**8.26**	**–.67**	**–27.65**	**–25.36**	**–58.64**
Reserve assets	4 800 . .	–16.52	12.76	6.59	8.26	–.67	–27.65	–25.36	–58.64
Use of Fund credit and loans	4 766 . .	. . .	. . .	. . .	. . .	. . .	. . .	. . .	. . .
Liabilities constituting foreign authorities' reserves	4 900 . .	. . .	. . .	. . .	. . .	. . .	. . .	. . .	. . .
Exceptional financing	4 920 . .	. . .	. . .	. . .	. . .	. . .	. . .	. . .	. . .
Conversion rates: yen per U.S. dollar	0 101 . .	**128.15**	**137.96**	**144.79**	**134.71**	**126.65**	**111.20**	**102.21**	**94.06**

[1] Excludes components that have been classified in the categories of Group E.

Table 2. STANDARD PRESENTATION, 1988–95
(Billions of U.S. dollars)

	Code	1988	1989	1990	1991	1992	1993	1994	1995
CURRENT ACCOUNT	4 993 . .	**79.61**	**56.99**	**35.87**	**68.37**	**112.33**	**131.98**	**130.56**	**111.25**
A. GOODS	4 100 . .	95.00	76.89	63.58	96.07	124.70	139.58	144.44	132.07
Credit	2 100 . .	**259.77**	**269.55**	**280.35**	**308.10**	**332.50**	**352.90**	**385.99**	**429.32**
General merchandise: exports f.o.b.	2 110 . .	259.77	269.55	280.35	. . .	. . .	. . .	. . .	. . .
Goods for processing: exports f.o.b.	2 150 . .	. . .	. . .	. . .	. . .	. . .	. . .	. . .	. . .
Repairs on goods	2 160 . .	. . .	. . .	. . .	. . .	. . .	. . .	. . .	. . .
Goods procured in ports by carriers	2 170 . .	. . .	. . .	. . .	. . .	. . .	. . .	. . .	. . .
Nonmonetary gold	2 180 . .	. . .	. . .	. . .	. . .	. . .	. . .	. . .	. . .
Debit	3 100 . .	**-164.77**	**-192.66**	**-216.77**	**-212.03**	**-207.80**	**-213.32**	**-241.55**	**-297.24**
General merchandise: imports f.o.b.	3 110 . .	-162.19	-184.60	-206.24	. . .	. . .	. . .	. . .	. . .
Goods for processing: imports f.o.b.	3 150 . .	. . .	. . .	. . .	. . .	. . .	. . .	. . .	. . .
Repairs on goods	3 160 . .	. . .	. . .	. . .	. . .	. . .	. . .	. . .	. . .
Goods procured in ports by carriers	3 170 . .	. . .	. . .	. . .	. . .	. . .	. . .	. . .	. . .
Nonmonetary gold	3 180 . .	-2.58	-8.06	-10.53	. . .	. . .	. . .	. . .	. . .
B. SERVICES	4 200 . .	-31.88	-38.61	-44.69	-41.78	-43.96	-43.08	-48.08	-57.49
Total credit	2 200 . .	*36.67*	*41.72*	*43.34*	*44.83*	*49.05*	*53.25*	*58.31*	*65.21*
Total debit	3 200 . .	*-68.55*	*-80.33*	*-88.03*	*-86.61*	*-93.01*	*-96.34*	*-106.38*	*-122.70*
Transportation services, credit	2 205 . .	**15.09**	**17.71**	**17.75**	**17.56**	**18.46**	**18.93**	**20.32**	**22.37**
Passenger	2 205 BA	*1.14*	*1.48*	*1.29*	*1.26*	*1.32*	*1.40*	*1.52*	*1.61*
Freight	2 205 BB	*8.24*	*9.00*	*9.09*	*9.87*	*9.94*	*9.71*	*10.26*	*11.43*
Other	2 205 BC	*5.71*	*7.23*	*7.37*	*6.43*	*7.20*	*7.83*	*8.53*	*9.34*
Sea transport, passenger	2 207 . .	. . .	. . .	. . .	. . .	. . .	.01	. . .	. . .
Sea transport, freight	2 208 . .	. . .	. . .	. . .	8.43	8.58	8.29	8.53	9.44
Sea transport, other	2 209 . .	. . .	. . .	. . .	3.62	3.99	4.30	4.78	5.27
Air transport, passenger	2 211 . .	. . .	. . .	. . .	1.26	1.32	1.38	1.52	1.61
Air transport, freight	2 212 . .	. . .	. . .	. . .	1.44	1.36	1.42	1.73	1.99
Air transport, other	2 213 . .	. . .	. . .	. . .	2.81	3.21	3.52	3.76	4.07
Other transport, passenger	2 215 . .	. . .	. . .	. . .	. . .	. . .	. . .	. . .	. . .
Other transport, freight	2 216 . .	. . .	. . .	. . .	. . .	. . .	. . .	. . .	. . .
Other transport, other	2 217 . .	. . .	. . .	. . .	. . .	. . .	. . .	. . .	. . .
Transportation services, debit	3 205 . .	**-22.09**	**-24.96**	**-26.65**	**-26.43**	**-27.15**	**-28.90**	**-31.70**	**-35.97**
Passenger	3 205 BA	*-4.83*	*-6.55*	*-7.26*	*-7.47*	*-8.56*	*-8.90*	*-9.54*	*-10.20*
Freight	3 205 BB	*-7.31*	*-7.01*	*-7.21*	*-7.75*	*-7.30*	*-8.36*	*-9.50*	*-11.93*
Other	3 205 BC	*-9.95*	*-11.40*	*-12.18*	*-11.21*	*-11.29*	*-11.64*	*-12.66*	*-13.84*
Sea transport, passenger	3 207 . .	. . .	. . .	. . .	. . .	. . .	. . .	. . .	. . .
Sea transport, freight	3 208 . .	. . .	. . .	. . .	-6.90	-6.50	-7.35	-8.21	-10.27
Sea transport, other	3 209 . .	. . .	. . .	. . .	-10.03	-10.17	-10.69	-11.79	-12.85
Air transport, passenger	3 211 . .	. . .	. . .	. . .	-7.47	-8.56	-8.90	-9.54	-10.20
Air transport, freight	3 212 . .	. . .	. . .	. . .	-.85	-.80	-1.00	-1.29	-1.66
Air transport, other	3 213 . .	. . .	. . .	. . .	-1.18	-1.12	-.96	-.87	-.99
Other transport, passenger	3 215 . .	. . .	. . .	. . .	. . .	. . .	. . .	. . .	. . .
Other transport, freight	3 216 . .	. . .	. . .	. . .	. . .	. . .	. . .	. . .	. . .
Other transport, other	3 217 . .	. . .	. . .	. . .	. . .	. . .	. . .	. . .	. . .
Travel, credit	2 236 . .	**2.89**	**3.15**	**3.59**	**3.43**	**3.59**	**3.56**	**3.48**	**3.22**
Business travel	2 237 . .	. . .	. . .	. . .	. . .	. . .	. . .	. . .	. . .
Personal travel	2 240 . .	. . .	. . .	. . .	. . .	. . .	. . .	. . .	. . .
Travel, debit	3 236 . .	**-18.67**	**-22.50**	**-24.93**	**-23.95**	**-26.84**	**-26.86**	**-30.72**	**-36.74**
Business travel	3 237 . .	. . .	. . .	. . .	. . .	. . .	. . .	. . .	. . .
Personal travel	3 240 . .	. . .	. . .	. . .	. . .	. . .	. . .	. . .	. . .
Other services, credit	2 200 BA	**18.69**	**20.86**	**22.00**	**23.84**	**27.00**	**30.77**	**34.51**	**39.62**
Communications	2 245 . .	. . .	. . .	. . .	.24	.19	.22	.47	.47
Construction	2 249 . .	. . .	. . .	. . .	3.32	4.86	4.86	4.96	6.57
Insurance	2 253 . .	.25	.19	.05	-.25	-.17	.09	.36	.30
Financial	2 260 . .	. . .	. . .	. . .	.09	.15	.23	.19	.30
Computer and information	2 262 . .	. . .	. . .	. . .	. . .	. . .	. . .	. . .	. . .
Royalties and licence fees	2 266 . .	1.64	2.02	2.49	2.86	3.05	3.88	5.19	6.01
Other business services	2 268 . .	14.02	16.01	17.25	16.07	17.37	19.80	21.70	24.52
Personal, cultural, and recreational	2 287 . .	. . .	. . .	. . .	.14	.10	.09	.11	.13
Government, n.i.e.	2 291 . .	2.78	2.64	2.21	1.37	1.45	1.61	1.52	1.31
Other services, debit	3 200 BA	**-27.79**	**-32.87**	**-36.45**	**-36.24**	**-39.03**	**-40.58**	**-43.96**	**-49.99**
Communications	3 245 . .	. . .	. . .	. . .	-.59	-.79	-.74	-.79	-.83
Construction	3 249 . .	. . .	. . .	. . .	-2.04	-2.24	-2.12	-2.34	-3.20
Insurance	3 253 . .	-1.34	-1.33	-1.35	.32	-.91	-1.91	-2.57	-2.48
Financial	3 260 . .	. . .	. . .	. . .	-1.49	-1.11	-1.15	-.56	-.46
Computer and information	3 262 . .	. . .	. . .	. . .	. . .	. . .	. . .	. . .	. . .
Royalties and licence fees	3 266 . .	-5.02	-5.32	-6.04	-6.05	-7.19	-7.18	-8.30	-9.36
Other business services	3 268 . .	-20.90	-25.65	-28.45	-25.32	-25.63	-26.15	-28.02	-32.02
Personal, cultural, and recreational	3 287 . .	. . .	. . .	. . .	-.38	-.45	-.52	-.48	-.56
Government, n.i.e.	3 291 . .	-.53	-.57	-.61	-.68	-.71	-.81	-.91	-1.09

Table 2 (Continued). STANDARD PRESENTATION, 1988–95
(Billions of U.S. dollars)

	Code	1988	1989	1990	1991	1992	1993	1994	1995
C. INCOME	4 300 . .	20.61	22.99	22.50	25.91	35.43	40.60	40.31	44.41
Total credit	2 300 . .	*75.11*	*102.19*	*122.64*	*140.89*	*142.69*	*148.23*	*155.37*	*192.61*
Total debit	3 300 . .	*–54.50*	*–79.20*	*–100.14*	*–114.98*	*–107.26*	*–107.63*	*–115.06*	*–148.20*
Compensation of employees, credit	2 310 . .	**.29**	**.37**	**.46**	**.51**	**.58**	**.78**	**.87**	**1.15**
Compensation of employees, debit	3 310 . .	**–.69**	**–.81**	**–1.17**	**–1.30**	**–1.37**	**–1.58**	**–1.58**	**–1.83**
Investment income, credit	2 320 . .	**74.82**	**101.82**	**122.18**	**140.38**	**142.11**	**147.45**	**154.50**	**191.45**
Direct investment income	2 330 . .	3.74	4.59	4.81	6.37	7.79	8.31	9.75	9.44
Dividends and distributed branch profits	2 332 . .	3.74	4.59	4.81	. . .	. . .	. . .	. . .	. . .
Reinvested earnings and undistributed branch profits	2 333 . .	. . .	. . .	. . .	. . .	. . .	. . .	. . .	. . .
Income on debt (interest)	2 334 . .	. . .	. . .	. . .	. . .	. . .	. . .	. . .	. . .
Portfolio investment income	2 339 . .	. . .	. . .	. . .	47.09	48.22	51.23	48.68	56.81
Income on equity	2 340 . .	. . .	. . .	. . .	. . .	. . .	. . .	. . .	. . .
Income on bonds and notes	2 350 . .	. . .	. . .	. . .	. . .	. . .	. . .	. . .	. . .
Income on money market instruments and financial derivatives	2 360 . .	. . .	. . .	. . .	. . .	. . .	. . .	. . .	. . .
Other investment income	2 370 . .	71.08	97.23	117.37	86.92	86.10	87.92	96.06	125.21
Investment income, debit	3 320 . .	**–53.81**	**–78.39**	**–98.97**	**–113.68**	**–105.89**	**–106.05**	**–113.48**	**–146.37**
Direct investment income	3 330 . .	–2.00	–2.29	–2.26	–2.07	–1.87	–1.85	–1.94	–2.59
Dividends and distributed branch profits	3 332 . .	–2.00	–2.29	–2.26	. . .	. . .	. . .	. . .	. . .
Reinvested earnings and undistributed branch profits	3 333 . .	. . .	. . .	. . .	. . .	. . .	. . .	. . .	. . .
Income on debt (interest)	3 334 . .	. . .	. . .	. . .	. . .	. . .	. . .	. . .	. . .
Portfolio investment income	3 339 . .	. . .	. . .	. . .	–14.67	–17.03	–19.09	–18.27	–19.94
Income on equity	3 340 . .	. . .	. . .	. . .	. . .	. . .	. . .	. . .	. . .
Income on bonds and notes	3 350 . .	. . .	. . .	. . .	. . .	. . .	. . .	. . .	. . .
Income on money market instruments and financial derivatives	3 360 . .	. . .	. . .	. . .	. . .	. . .	. . .	. . .	. . .
Other investment income	3 370 . .	–51.81	–76.10	–96.71	–96.94	–87.00	–85.11	–93.27	–123.85
D. CURRENT TRANSFERS	4 379 . .	–4.12	–4.28	–5.52	–11.83	–3.84	–5.12	–6.12	–7.75
Credit	2 379 . .	**1.09**	**1.01**	**1.00**	**1.42**	**1.67**	**1.58**	**1.83**	**1.98**
General government	2 380 . .	.07	.10	.08	.14	.28	.24	.28	.33
Other sectors	2 390 . .	1.02	.91	.92	1.28	1.39	1.34	1.55	1.65
Workers' remittances	2 391 . .	. . .	. . .	. . .	. . .	. . .	. . .	. . .	. . .
Other current transfers	2 392 . .	1.02	.91	.92	. . .	. . .	. . .	. . .	. . .
Debit	3 379 . .	**–5.21**	**–5.29**	**–6.52**	**–13.24**	**–5.51**	**–6.70**	**–7.95**	**–9.73**
General government	3 380 . .	–2.15	–2.91	–4.13	–10.77	–2.35	–2.65	–3.12	–3.64
Other sectors	3 390 . .	–3.06	–2.38	–2.39	–2.47	–3.15	–4.05	–4.83	–6.10
Workers' remittances	3 391 . .	. . .	. . .	. . .	. . .	. . .	. . .	. . .	. . .
Other current transfers	3 392 . .	–3.06	–2.38	–2.39	. . .	. . .	. . .	. . .	. . .
CAPITAL AND FINANCIAL ACCOUNT	4 996 . .	**–82.74**	**–35.17**	**–14.95**	**–60.48**	**–101.89**	**–131.71**	**–112.75**	**–125.31**
CAPITAL ACCOUNT	4 994 . .	**. . .**	**. . .**	**. . .**	**–1.20**	**–1.29**	**–1.46**	**–1.86**	**–2.26**
Total credit	2 994 . .	. . .	. . .	. . .	. . .	. . .	. . .	. . .	*.01*
Total debit	3 994 . .	. . .	. . .	. . .	*–1.20*	*–1.29*	*–1.46*	*–1.86*	*–2.27*
Capital transfers, credit	2 400 . .	**. . .**	**. . .**	**. . .**	**. . .**	**. . .**	**. . .**	**. . .**	**.01**
General government	2 401 . .	. . .	. . .	. . .	. . .	. . .	. . .	. . .	.01
Debt forgiveness	2 402 . .	. . .	. . .	. . .	. . .	. . .	. . .	. . .	. . .
Other capital transfers	2 410 . .	. . .	. . .	. . .	. . .	. . .	. . .	. . .	. . .
Other sectors	2 430 . .	. . .	. . .	. . .	. . .	. . .	. . .	. . .	. . .
Migrants' transfers	2 431 . .	. . .	. . .	. . .	. . .	. . .	. . .	. . .	. . .
Debt forgiveness	2 432 . .	. . .	. . .	. . .	. . .	. . .	. . .	. . .	. . .
Other capital transfers	2 440 . .	. . .	. . .	. . .	. . .	. . .	. . .	. . .	. . .
Capital transfers, debit	3 400 . .	**. . .**	**. . .**	**. . .**	**–1.20**	**–1.29**	**–1.46**	**–1.86**	**–2.27**
General government	3 401 . .	. . .	. . .	. . .	–1.20	–1.29	–1.46	–1.86	–2.27
Debt forgiveness	3 402 . .	. . .	. . .	. . .	. . .	. . .	. . .	. . .	. . .
Other capital transfers	3 410 . .	. . .	. . .	. . .	. . .	. . .	. . .	. . .	. . .
Other sectors	3 430 . .	. . .	. . .	. . .	. . .	. . .	. . .	. . .	. . .
Migrants' transfers	3 431 . .	. . .	. . .	. . .	. . .	. . .	. . .	. . .	. . .
Debt forgiveness	3 432 . .	. . .	. . .	. . .	. . .	. . .	. . .	. . .	. . .
Other capital transfers	3 440 . .	. . .	. . .	. . .	. . .	. . .	. . .	. . .	. . .
Nonproduced nonfinancial assets, credit	2 480 . .	**. . .**	**. . .**	**. . .**	**. . .**	**. . .**	**. . .**	**. . .**	**. . .**
Nonproduced nonfinancial assets, debit	3 480 . .	**. . .**	**. . .**	**. . .**	**. . .**	**. . .**	**. . .**	**. . .**	**. . .**

Table 2 (Continued). STANDARD PRESENTATION, 1988–95
(Billions of U.S. dollars)

	Code	1988	1989	1990	1991	1992	1993	1994	1995
FINANCIAL ACCOUNT	4 995 . .	**–82.74**	**–35.17**	**–14.95**	**–59.29**	**–100.60**	**–130.25**	**–110.90**	**–123.04**
A. DIRECT INVESTMENT	4 500 . .	–34.73	–45.22	–46.29	–30.19	–14.60	–13.70	–17.19	–22.61
Direct investment abroad	4 505 . .	**–34.21**	**–44.16**	**–48.05**	**–31.49**	**–17.36**	**–13.83**	**–18.10**	**–22.66**
Equity capital	4 510 . .	–21.66	–26.30	–33.97	–27.11	–17.67	–15.08	–16.54	–23.32
Claims on affiliated enterprises	4 515 . .	. . .	. . .	. . .	. . .	. . .	. . .	. . .	. . .
Liabilities to affiliated enterprises	4 520 . .	. . .	. . .	. . .	. . .	. . .	. . .	. . .	. . .
Reinvested earnings	4 525 . .	. . .	. . .	. . .	. . .	. . .	. . .	. . .	. . .
Other capital	4 530 . .	–12.55	–17.86	–14.08	–4.38	.31	1.25	–1.56	.66
Claims on affiliated enterprises	4 535 . .	. . .	. . .	. . .	. . .	. . .	. . .	. . .	. . .
Liabilities to affiliated enterprises	4 540 . .	. . .	. . .	. . .	. . .	. . .	. . .	. . .	. . .
Direct investment in Japan	4 555 . .	**–.52**	**–1.06**	**1.76**	**1.30**	**2.76**	**.13**	**.92**	**.06**
Equity capital	4 560 . .	–.32	–1.43	1.02	.97	2.22	–.02	.69	.31
Claims on direct investors	4 565 . .	. . .	. . .	. . .	. . .	. . .	. . .	. . .	. . .
Liabilities to direct investors	4 570 . .	. . .	. . .	. . .	. . .	. . .	. . .	. . .	. . .
Reinvested earnings	4 575 . .	. . .	. . .	. . .	. . .	. . .	. . .	. . .	. . .
Other capital	4 580 . .	–.20	.37	.74	.33	.54	.14	.22	–.25
Claims on direct investors	4 585 . .	. . .	. . .	. . .	. . .	. . .	. . .	. . .	. . .
Liabilities to direct investors	4 590 . .	. . .	. . .	. . .	. . .	. . .	. . .	. . .	. . .
B. PORTFOLIO INVESTMENT	4 600 . .	–66.11	–28.76	–4.81	44.15	–27.43	–70.71	–26.67	–36.12
Assets	4 602 . .	**–87.12**	**–113.24**	**–40.20**	**–81.72**	**–34.93**	**–64.03**	**–91.13**	**–88.07**
Equity securities	4 610 . .	–2.98	–17.89	–6.26	–3.63	3.01	–15.33	–14.06	.16
Monetary authorities	4 611 . .	. . .	. . .	. . .	. . .	. . .	. . .	. . .	. . .
General government	4 612 . .	. . .	. . .	. . .	. . .	. . .	. . .	. . .	. . .
Banks	4 613 . .	. . .	. . .	. . .	. . .	. . .	. . .	. . .	. . .
Other sectors	4 614 . .	. . .	. . .	. . .	. . .	. . .	. . .	. . .	. . .
Debt securities	4 619 . .	–84.14	–95.35	–33.94	–78.08	–37.94	–48.71	–77.07	–88.23
Bonds and notes	4 620 . .	–84.14	–95.35	–33.94	–70.94	–36.75	–36.53	–69.68	–93.15
Monetary authorities	4 621 . .	. . .	. . .	. . .	. . .	. . .	. . .	. . .	. . .
General government	4 622 . .	. . .	. . .	. . .	. . .	. . .	. . .	. . .	. . .
Banks	4 623 . .	. . .	. . .	. . .	. . .	. . .	. . .	. . .	. . .
Other sectors	4 624 . .	. . .	. . .	. . .	. . .	. . .	. . .	. . .	. . .
Money market instruments	4 630 . .	. . .	. . .	. . .	–7.12	–.58	–11.68	–7.82	6.10
Monetary authorities	4 631 . .	. . .	. . .	. . .	. . .	. . .	. . .	. . .	. . .
General government	4 632 . .	. . .	. . .	. . .	. . .	. . .	. . .	. . .	. . .
Banks	4 633 . .	. . .	. . .	. . .	. . .	. . .	. . .	. . .	. . .
Other sectors	4 634 . .	. . .	. . .	. . .	. . .	. . .	. . .	. . .	. . .
Financial derivatives	4 640 . .	. . .	. . .	. . .	–.02	–.61	–.49	.43	–1.18
Monetary authorities	4 641 . .	. . .	. . .	. . .	. . .	. . .	. . .	. . .	. . .
General government	4 642 . .	. . .	. . .	. . .	. . .	. . .	. . .	. . .	. . .
Banks	4 643 . .	. . .	. . .	. . .	. . .	. . .	. . .	. . .	. . .
Other sectors	4 644 . .	. . .	. . .	. . .	. . .	. . .	. . .	. . .	. . .
Liabilities	4 652 . .	**21.01**	**84.48**	**35.39**	**125.87**	**7.50**	**–6.68**	**64.46**	**51.96**
Equity securities	4 660 . .	6.81	6.99	–13.26	46.71	8.73	19.99	49.01	50.70
Banks	4 663 . .	. . .	. . .	. . .	. . .	. . .	. . .	. . .	. . .
Other sectors	4 664 . .	. . .	. . .	. . .	. . .	. . .	. . .	. . .	. . .
Debt securities	4 669 . .	14.20	77.49	48.65	79.15	–1.23	–26.67	15.46	1.26
Bonds and notes	4 670 . .	14.20	77.49	48.65	68.35	–.56	–31.07	–14.34	–10.08
Monetary authorities	4 671 . .	. . .	. . .	. . .	. . .	. . .	. . .	. . .	. . .
General government	4 672 . .	–22.35	.22	17.57	. . .	. . .	. . .	. . .	. . .
Banks	4 673 . .	. . .	. . .	. . .	. . .	. . .	. . .	. . .	. . .
Other sectors	4 674 . .	36.55	77.27	31.08	68.35	–.56	–31.07	–14.34	–10.08
Money market instruments	4 680 . .	. . .	. . .	. . .	12.10	1.28	4.91	30.00	20.42
Monetary authorities	4 681 . .	. . .	. . .	. . .	. . .	. . .	. . .	. . .	. . .
General government	4 682 . .	. . .	. . .	. . .	. . .	. . .	. . .	. . .	. . .
Banks	4 683 . .	. . .	. . .	. . .	. . .	. . .	. . .	. . .	. . .
Other sectors	4 684 . .	. . .	. . .	. . .	12.10	1.28	4.91	30.00	20.42
Financial derivatives	4 690 . .	. . .	. . .	. . .	–1.30	–1.95	–.52	–.20	–9.09
Monetary authorities	4 691 . .	. . .	. . .	. . .	. . .	. . .	. . .	. . .	. . .
General government	4 692 . .	. . .	. . .	. . .	. . .	. . .	. . .	. . .	. . .
Banks	4 693 . .	. . .	. . .	. . .	. . .	. . .	. . .	. . .	. . .
Other sectors	4 694 . .	. . .	. . .	. . .	–1.30	–1.95	–.52	–.20	–9.09

Table 2 (Concluded). STANDARD PRESENTATION, 1988–95

(Billions of U.S. dollars)

	Code	1988	1989	1990	1991	1992	1993	1994	1995
C. OTHER INVESTMENT	4 700 . .	34.62	26.05	29.56	–81.50	–57.91	–18.18	–41.68	–5.67
Assets	4 703 . .	**–189.99**	**–171.54**	**–89.14**	**26.94**	**47.60**	**13.04**	**–35.88**	**–105.71**
Trade credits	4 706 . .	–8.39	–5.85	–.11	2.49	4.03	5.14	2.49	2.01
General government: long-term	4 708 . .	. . .	. . .	. . .	. . .	. . .	. . .	. . .	. . .
General government: short-term	4 709 . .	. . .	. . .	. . .	. . .	. . .	. . .	. . .	. . .
Other sectors: long-term	4 711 . .	–7.02	–4.12	.58	. . .	. . .	. . .	. . .	. . .
Other sectors: short-term	4 712 . .	–1.37	–1.73	–.69	. . .	. . .	. . .	. . .	. . .
Loans	4 714 . .	–15.65	–23.05	–23.11	15.95	57.44	27.96	–11.72	–166.17
Monetary authorities: long-term	4 717 . .	. . .	. . .	. . .	. . .	. . .	. . .	. . .	. . .
Monetary authorities: short-term	4 718 . .	. . .	. . .	. . .	. . .	. . .	. . .	. . .	. . .
General government: long-term	4 720 . .	–3.99	–6.04	–8.21	. . .	. . .	. . .	. . .	. . .
General government: short-term	4 721 . .	. . .	. . .	. . .	. . .	. . .	. . .	. . .	. . .
Banks: long-term	4 723 . .	–5.68	–6.61	–7.60	. . .	. . .	. . .	. . .	. . .
Banks: short-term	4 724 . .	. . .	. . .	. . .	. . .	. . .	. . .	. . .	. . .
Other sectors: long-term	4 726 . .	–5.47	–9.74	–6.27	. . .	. . .	. . .	. . .	. . .
Other sectors: short-term	4 727 . .	–.51	–.66	–1.03	. . .	. . .	. . .	. . .	. . .
Currency and deposits	4 730 . .	–159.37	–134.31	–54.34	5.44	–14.11	–15.78	–25.19	38.29
Monetary authorities	4 731 . .	. . .	. . .	. . .	. . .	. . .	. . .	. . .	. . .
General government	4 732 . .	.01	.04	–.07	. . .	. . .	. . .	. . .	. . .
Banks	4 733 . .	–147.47	–133.88	–56.01	. . .	. . .	. . .	. . .	. . .
Other sectors	4 734 . .	–11.91	–.47	1.74	. . .	. . .	. . .	. . .	. . .
Other assets	4 736 . .	–6.58	–8.33	–11.58	3.06	.24	–4.28	–1.46	20.17
Monetary authorities: long-term	4 738 . .	. . .	. . .	. . .	. . .	. . .	. . .	. . .	. . .
Monetary authorities: short-term	4 739 . .	. . .	. . .	. . .	. . .	. . .	. . .	. . .	. . .
General government: long-term	4 741 . .	–2.34	–2.04	–1.84	. . .	. . .	. . .	. . .	. . .
General government: short-term	4 742 . .	. . .	. . .	. . .	. . .	. . .	. . .	. . .	. . .
Banks: long-term	4 744 . .	–.19	.29	–.55	. . .	. . .	. . .	. . .	. . .
Banks: short-term	4 745 . .	. . .	. . .	. . .	. . .	. . .	. . .	. . .	. . .
Other sectors: long-term	4 747 . .	–4.05	–6.58	–9.19	. . .	. . .	. . .	. . .	. . .
Other sectors: short-term	4 748 . .	. . .	. . .	. . .	. . .	. . .	. . .	. . .	. . .
Liabilities	4 753 . .	**224.61**	**197.59**	**118.70**	**–108.45**	**–105.51**	**–31.22**	**–5.80**	**100.04**
Trade credits	4 756 . .	.52	–.76	1.63	–.56	.32	–.91	–1.59	–.24
General government: long-term	4 758 . .	. . .	. . .	. . .	. . .	. . .	. . .	. . .	. . .
General government: short-term	4 759 . .	. . .	. . .	. . .	. . .	. . .	. . .	. . .	. . .
Other sectors: long-term	4 761 . .	–.01	.03	. . .	. . .	. . .	. . .	. . .	. . .
Other sectors: short-term	4 762 . .	.53	–.79	1.63	–.56	.32	–.91	–1.59	–.24
Loans	4 764 . .	30.68	40.71	60.04	–19.96	–72.54	–6.85	–.10	105.75
Use of Fund credit and loans from the Fund	4 766 . .	. . .	. . .	. . .	. . .	. . .	. . .	. . .	. . .
Monetary authorities: other long term	4 767 . .	. . .	. . .	. . .	. . .	. . .	. . .	. . .	. . .
Monetary authorities: short-term	4 768 . .	. . .	. . .	. . .	. . .	. . .	. . .	. . .	. . .
General government: long-term	4 770 . .	–.05	–.02	–.01	. . .	. . .	. . .	. . .	. . .
General government: short-term	4 771 . .	. . .	. . .	. . .	. . .	. . .	. . .	. . .	. . .
Banks: long-term	4 773 . .	. . .	. . .	. . .	. . .	. . .	. . .	. . .	. . .
Banks: short-term	4 774 . .	. . .	. . .	. . .	. . .	. . .	. . .	. . .	. . .
Other sectors: long-term	4 776 . .	–.05	17.84	39.13	. . .	. . .	. . .	. . .	. . .
Other sectors: short-term	4 777 . .	30.78	22.89	20.92	–19.96	–72.54	–6.85	–.10	105.75
Currency and deposits	4 780 . .	191.93	142.46	42.35	–80.66	–36.48	–29.44	–1.38	4.42
Monetary authorities	4 781 . .	. . .	. . .	. . .	. . .	. . .	. . .	. . .	. . .
General government	4 782 . .	. . .	. . .	. . .	. . .	. . .	. . .	. . .	. . .
Banks	4 783 . .	191.93	142.46	42.35	–80.66	–36.48	–29.44	–1.38	4.42
Other sectors	4 784 . .	. . .	. . .	. . .	. . .	. . .	. . .	. . .	. . .
Other liabilities	4 786 . .	1.48	15.18	14.68	–7.27	3.20	5.98	–2.72	–9.88
Monetary authorities: long-term	4 788 . .	. . .	. . .	. . .	. . .	. . .	. . .	. . .	. . .
Monetary authorities: short-term	4 789 . .	1.49	11.51	14.46	. . .	. . .	. . .	. . .	. . .
General government: long-term	4 791 . .	–.53	–.41	–.35	. . .	. . .	. . .	. . .	. . .
General government: short-term	4 792 . .	. . .	. . .	. . .	. . .	. . .	. . .	. . .	. . .
Banks: long-term	4 794 . .	–.20	1.42	2.11	. . .	. . .	. . .	. . .	. . .
Banks: short-term	4 795 . .	. . .	. . .	. . .	. . .	. . .	. . .	. . .	. . .
Other sectors: long-term	4 797 . .	–.03	–.03	–.10	. . .	. . .	. . .	. . .	. . .
Other sectors: short-term	4 798 . .	.75	2.69	–1.44	–7.27	3.20	5.98	–2.72	–9.88
D. RESERVE ASSETS	4 800 . .	–16.52	12.76	6.59	8.26	–.67	–27.65	–25.36	–58.64
Monetary gold	4 810 . .	. . .	. . .	. . .	. . .	. . .	. . .	. . .	. . .
Special drawing rights	4 820 . .	–.61	.42	–.38	.47	1.40	–.46	–.44	–.54
Reserve position in the Fund	4 830 . .	–.57	–.31	–2.04	–1.68	–1.22	.38	.14	.69
Foreign exchange	4 840 . .	–15.34	12.66	9.01	9.46	–.85	–27.57	–25.07	–58.79
Other claims	4 880 . .	. . .	. . .	. . .	. . .	. . .	. . .	. . .	. . .
NET ERRORS AND OMISSIONS	4 998 . .	**3.13**	**–21.82**	**–20.92**	**–7.88**	**–10.44**	**–.28**	**–17.80**	**14.06**

Part 3 of the *Yearbook* contains descriptions of the methodologies, compilation practices, and sources used to compile these data.

Table 3. INTERNATIONAL INVESTMENT POSITION (End–period stocks), 1988–95
(Billions of U.S. dollars)

	Code	1988	1989	1990	1991	1992	1993	1994	1995
ASSETS	8 995 C.	1,469.34	1,771.01	1,857.88	2,006.51	2,035.24	2,180.88	2,424.24	2,724.79
Direct investment abroad	8 505 . .	**110.78**	**154.37**	**201.44**	**231.79**	**248.06**	**259.80**	**275.57**	**296.22**
Equity capital and reinvested earnings	8 506 . .	68.66	94.74	128.03	154.53	171.54	184.41	199.43	221.23
Claims on affiliated enterprises	8 507 . .	...	...	...	...	...	...	...	...
Liabilities to affiliated enterprises	8 508 . .	...	...	...	...	...	...	...	...
Other capital	8 530 . .	42.12	59.63	73.41	77.26	76.52	75.39	76.14	74.99
Claims on affiliated enterprises	8 535 . .	...	...	...	...	...	...	...	...
Liabilities to affiliated enterprises	8 540 . .	...	...	...	...	...	...	...	...
Portfolio investment	8 602 . .	**449.31**	**561.85**	**595.84**	**679.18**	**715.45**	**771.11**	**858.69**	**942.90**
Equity securities	8 610 . .	...	...	...	...	...	...	...	...
Monetary authorities	8 611 . .	...	...	...	...	...	...	...	...
General government	8 612 . .	...	...	...	...	...	...	...	...
Banks	8 613 . .	...	...	...	...	...	...	...	...
Other sectors	8 614 . .	...	...	...	...	...	...	...	...
Debt securities	8 619 . .	449.31	561.85	595.84	679.18	715.45	771.11	858.69	942.90
Bonds and notes	8 620 . .	449.31	561.85	595.84	679.18	715.45	771.11	858.69	942.90
Monetary authorities	8 621 . .	...	...	...	...	...	...	...	...
General government	8 622 . .	...	...	...	...	...	...	...	...
Banks	8 623 . .	...	...	...	...	...	...	...	...
Other sectors	8 624 . .	...	...	...	...	...	...	...	...
Money market instruments	8 630 . .	...	...	...	...	...	...	...	...
Monetary authorities	8 631 . .	...	...	...	...	...	...	...	...
General government	8 632 . .	...	...	...	...	...	...	...	...
Banks	8 633 . .	...	...	...	...	...	...	...	...
Other sectors	8 634 . .	...	...	...	...	...	...	...	...
Financial derivatives	8 640 . .	...	...	...	...	...	...	...	...
Monetary authorities	8 641 . .	...	...	...	...	...	...	...	...
General government	8 642 . .	...	...	...	...	...	...	...	...
Banks	8 643 . .	...	...	...	...	...	...	...	...
Other sectors	8 644 . .	...	...	...	...	...	...	...	...
Other investment	8 703 . .	**811.39**	**969.72**	**980.89**	**1,022.27**	**998.94**	**1,050.29**	**1,162.87**	**1,301.03**
Trade credits	8 706 . .	...	...	...	...	...	...	...	...
General government: long-term	8 708 . .	...	...	...	...	...	...	...	...
General government: short-term	8 709 . .	...	...	...	...	...	...	...	...
Other sectors: long-term	8 711 . .	...	...	...	...	...	...	...	...
Other sectors: short-term	8 712 . .	...	...	...	...	...	...	...	...
Loans	8 714 . .	239.40	263.53	252.10	281.94	294.66	320.26	348.33	366.42
Monetary authorities: long-term	8 717 . .	...	...	...	...	...	...	...	...
Monetary authorities: short-term	8 718 . .	...	...	...	...	...	...	...	...
General government: long-term	8 720 . .	57.46	62.22	62.35	78.75	89.67	105.03	122.50	136.05
General government: short-term	8 721 . .	...	...	...	...	...	...	...	...
Banks: long-term	8 723 . .	77.39	83.96	75.82	83.10	84.15	85.42	74.19	71.07
Banks: short-term	8 724 . .	...	...	...	...	...	...	...	...
Other sectors: long-term	8 726 . .	95.07	105.99	101.40	105.44	103.83	108.78	126.19	130.41
Other sectors: short-term	8 727 . .	9.48	11.36	12.53	14.65	17.01	21.03	25.45	28.89
Currency and deposits	8 730 . .	502.26	627.85	644.52	640.83	599.89	607.80	670.51	782.16
Monetary authorities	8 731 . .	...	...	...	...	...	...	...	...
General government	8 732 . .	...	...	...	...	...	...	...	...
Banks	8 733 . .	502.26	627.85	644.52	640.83	599.89	607.80	670.51	782.16
Other sectors	8 734 . .	...	...	...	...	...	...	...	...
Other assets	8 736 . .	69.73	78.34	84.27	99.50	104.39	122.23	144.03	152.45
Monetary authorities: long-term	8 738 . .	...	...	...	...	...	...	...	...
Monetary authorities: short-term	8 739 . .	...	...	...	...	...	...	...	...
General government: long-term	8 741 . .	24.95	27.20	28.09	31.98	33.73	37.19	42.51	47.25
General government: short-term	8 742 . .	...	...	...	...	...	...	...	...
Banks: long-term	8 744 . .	5.44	4.89	5.06	5.74	6.28	8.25	7.42	7.33
Banks: short-term	8 745 . .	...	...	...	...	...	...	...	...
Other sectors: long-term	8 747 . .	12.28	18.75	26.10	31.86	34.38	37.36	41.50	46.87
Other sectors: short-term	8 748 . .	27.06	27.50	25.02	29.92	30.00	39.43	52.60	50.99
Reserve assets	8 800 . .	**97.86**	**85.07**	**79.71**	**73.27**	**72.79**	**99.68**	**127.10**	**184.65**
Monetary gold	8 810 . .	1.14	1.11	1.21	1.21	1.17	1.16	1.24	1.26
Special drawing rights	8 820 . .	2.94	2.45	3.04	2.58	1.09	1.54	2.08	2.71
Reserve position in the Fund	8 830 . .	3.28	3.52	5.97	7.72	8.64	8.26	8.63	8.10
Foreign exchange	8 840 . .	90.51	77.99	69.49	61.76	61.89	88.72	115.15	172.58
Other claims	8 880 . .	...	...	...	...	...	...	...	...

Table 3 (Continued). INTERNATIONAL INVESTMENT POSITION (End–period stocks), 1988–95
(Billions of U.S. dollars)

	Code	1988	1989	1990	1991	1992	1993	1994	1995
LIABILITIES	8 995 D.	1,176.41	1,476.62	1,528.52	1,622.17	1,520.39	1,568.84	1,733.92	1,887.54
Direct investment in Japan	8 555 ..	**10.42**	**9.16**	**9.85**	**12.29**	**15.51**	**16.89**	**19.17**	**19.85**
Equity capital and reinvested earnings	8 556 ..	7.07	5.47	5.74	7.34	9.76	9.83	11.40	11.97
Claims on direct investors	8 557 ..	...	...	...	...	...	...	...	...
Liabilities to direct investors	8 558 ..	...	...	...	...	...	...	...	...
Other capital	8 580 ..	3.35	3.69	4.11	4.95	5.75	7.06	7.77	7.88
Claims on direct investors	8 585 ..	...	...	...	...	...	...	...	...
Liabilities to direct investors	8 590 ..	...	...	...	...	...	...	...	...
Portfolio investment	8 652 ..	**317.73**	**431.88**	**395.97**	**527.69**	**513.10**	**545.32**	**630.67**	**723.86**
Equity securities	8 660 ..	113.52	162.08	90.38	141.78	124.59	171.17	250.88	329.57
Banks	8 663 ..	...	...	...	...	...	...	...	...
Other sectors	8 664 ..	...	...	...	...	...	...	...	...
Debt securities	8 669 ..	204.21	269.80	305.59	385.91	388.51	374.15	379.79	394.29
Bonds and notes	8 670 ..	204.21	269.80	305.59	385.91	388.51	374.15	379.79	394.29
Monetary authorities	8 671 ..	...	...	...	...	...	...	...	...
General government	8 672 ..	...	...	...	...	...	...	...	...
Banks	8 673 ..	...	...	...	...	...	...	...	...
Other sectors	8 674 ..	...	...	...	...	...	...	...	...
Money market instruments	8 680 ..	...	...	...	...	...	...	...	...
Monetary authorities	8 681 ..	...	...	...	...	...	...	...	...
General government	8 682 ..	...	...	...	...	...	...	...	...
Banks	8 683 ..	...	...	...	...	...	...	...	...
Other sectors	8 684 ..	...	...	...	...	...	...	...	...
Financial derivatives	8 690 ..	...	...	...	...	...	...	...	...
Monetary authorities	8 691 ..	...	...	...	...	...	...	...	...
General government	8 692 ..	...	...	...	...	...	...	...	...
Banks	8 692 ..	...	...	...	...	...	...	...	...
Other sectors	8 694 ..	...	...	...	...	...	...	...	...
Other investment	8 753 ..	**848.26**	**1,035.58**	**1,122.70**	**1,082.19**	**991.78**	**1,006.63**	**1,084.08**	**1,143.83**
Trade credits	8 756 ..	...	...	...	...	...	...	...	...
General government: long-term	8 758 ..	...	...	...	...	...	...	...	...
General government: short-term	8 759 ..	...	...	...	...	...	...	...	...
Other sectors: long-term	8 761 ..	...	...	...	...	...	...	...	...
Other sectors: short-term	8 762 ..	...	...	...	...	...	...	...	...
Loans	8 764 ..	65.46	108.45	180.20	215.31	237.27	263.00	284.76	285.44
Use of Fund credit and loans from the Fund	8 766 ..	...	...	...	...	...	...	...	...
Monetary authorities: other long-term	8 767 ..	...	...	...	...	...	...	...	...
Monetary authorities: short-term	8 768 ..	...	...	...	...	...	...	...	...
General government: long-term	8 770 ..	.03	.01	...	...	...	...	...	...
General government: short-term	8 771 ..	...	...	...	...	...	...	...	...
Banks: long-term	8 773 ..	...	...	...	...	...	...	...	...
Banks: short-term	8 774 ..	...	...	...	...	...	...	...	...
Other sectors: long-term	8 776 ..	1.08	18.91	58.02	99.71	119.70	135.76	139.35	142.72
Other sectors: short-term	8 777 ..	64.35	89.53	122.18	115.60	117.57	127.24	145.41	142.72
Currency and deposits	8 780 ..	765.17	894.68	898.89	803.52	684.68	659.65	678.96	709.58
Monetary authorities	8 781 ..	...	...	...	...	...	...	...	...
General government	8 782 ..	...	...	...	...	...	...	...	...
Banks	8 783 ..	765.17	894.68	898.89	803.52	684.68	659.65	678.96	709.58
Other sectors	8 784 ..	...	...	...	...	...	...	...	...
Other liabilities	8 786 ..	17.63	32.45	43.61	63.36	69.83	83.98	120.36	148.81
Monetary authorities: long-term	8 788 ..	...	...	...	...	...	...	...	...
Monetary authorities: short-term	8 789 ..	13.81	25.03	35.74	50.11	54.72	65.52	99.85	123.45
General government: long-term	8 791 ..	...	...	...	...	...	...	...	...
General government: short-term	8 792 ..	...	...	...	...	...	...	...	...
Banks: long-term	8 794 ..	1.76	3.20	5.52	9.30	12.03	13.93	15.98	18.69
Banks: short-term	8 795 ..	...	...	...	...	...	...	...	...
Other sectors: long-term	8 797 ..	.28	.24	.15	.13	.16	.20	.37	.39
Other sectors: short-term	8 798 ..	1.78	3.98	2.20	3.82	2.92	4.33	4.16	6.28
NET INTERNATIONAL INVESTMENT POSITION	8 995 ..	**292.93**	**294.39**	**329.36**	**384.34**	**514.85**	**612.04**	**690.32**	**837.25**
Conversion rates: yen per U.S. dollar (end of period)	0 102 ..	**125.85**	**143.45**	**134.40**	**125.20**	**124.75**	**111.85**	**99.74**	**102.83**

Table 1. ANALYTIC PRESENTATION, 1988–95
(Millions of U.S. dollars)

	Code	1988	1989	1990	1991	1992	1993	1994	1995
A. Current Account[1]	4 993 Y.	**–293.7**	**384.9**	**–227.1**	**–393.5**	**–835.2**	**–629.1**	**–398.0**	...
Goods: exports f.o.b	2 100 ..	1,007.4	1,109.4	1,063.8	1,129.5	1,218.9	1,246.3	1,424.5	...
Goods: imports f.o.b	3 100 ..	–2,418.7	–1,882.5	–2,300.7	–2,302.2	–2,998.7	–3,145.2	–3,003.8	...
Balance on Goods	4 100 ..	*–1,411.3*	*–773.1*	*–1,236.9*	*–1,172.7*	*–1,779.7*	*–1,898.8*	*–1,579.4*	...
Services: credit	2 200 ..	1,420.6	1,239.2	1,447.2	1,351.2	1,449.2	1,573.7	1,562.0	...
Services: debit	3 200 ..	–1,340.5	–1,063.3	–1,267.9	–1,122.5	–1,324.7	–1,347.2	–1,392.7	...
Balance on Goods and Services	4 991 ..	*–1,331.1*	*–597.1*	*–1,057.6*	*–944.0*	*–1,655.2*	*–1,672.3*	*–1,410.1*	...
Income: credit	2 300 ..	40.6	39.0	67.3	114.3	112.4	99.0	72.7	...
Income: debit	3 300 ..	–354.8	–235.6	–281.8	–447.7	–460.0	–409.4	–387.5	...
Balance on Goods, Services, and Income	4 992 ..	*–1,645.2*	*–793.7*	*–1,272.1*	*–1,277.4*	*–2,002.8*	*–1,982.8*	*–1,724.9*	...
Current transfers: credit	2 379 Y.	1,532.0	1,284.5	1,123.1	949.5	1,263.6	1,441.1	1,447.4	...
Current transfers: debit	3 379 ..	–180.5	–105.8	–78.2	–65.7	–96.1	–87.4	–120.5	...
B. Capital Account[1]	4 994 Y.	...	...	...	...	...	...	...	...
Capital account: credit	2 994 Y.	...	...	...	...	...	...	...	...
Capital account: debit	3 994 ..	...	...	...	...	...	...	...	...
Total, Groups A Plus B	4 010 ..	*–293.7*	*384.9*	*–227.1*	*–393.5*	*–835.2*	*–629.1*	*–398.0*	...
C. Financial Account[1]	4 995 X.	**374.2**	**79.5**	**572.7**	**2,097.3**	**615.1**	**–530.0**	**188.9**	...
Direct investment abroad	4 505 ..	.1	–16.7	31.5	–13.7	3.4	53.0	23.1	...
Direct investment in Jordan	4 555 Y.	23.7	–1.3	37.6	–11.9	40.7	–33.5	2.9	...
Portfolio investment assets	4 602 ..	...	...	...	...	...	...	...	...
Equity securities	4 610 ..	...	...	...	...	...	...	...	...
Debt securities	4 619 ..	...	...	...	...	...	...	...	...
Portfolio investment liabilities	4 652 Y.	...	...	...	...	...	...	...	...
Equity securities	4 660 Y.	...	...	...	...	...	...	...	...
Debt securities	4 669 Y.	...	...	...	...	...	...	...	...
Other investment assets	4 703 ..	...	...	222.2	561.5	609.2	384.8	62.5	...
Monetary authorities	4 703 .A	...	...	110.1	–241.7	–113.6	–94.9	–163.5	...
General government	4 703 .B	...	...	...	...	...	–.3	...	...
Banks	4 703 .C	...	...	...	...	...	...	...	...
Other sectors	4 703 .D	...	...	112.1	803.2	722.8	480.0	225.9	...
Other investment liabilities	4 753 X.	350.4	97.6	281.4	1,561.4	–38.3	–934.3	100.4	...
Monetary authorities	4 753 XA	–133.2	5.2	.2	...	.6	.7	–8.7	...
General government	4 753 YB	13.4	202.6	353.2	296.5	–532.1	–675.8	–235.4	...
Banks	4 753 YC	457.2	–75.9	–66.7	1,267.9	495.1	–257.5	344.5	...
Other sectors	4 753 YD	13.0	–34.3	–5.3	–3.1	–1.9	–1.7	...	...
Total, Groups A Through C	4 020 ..	*80.5*	*464.5*	*345.6*	*1,703.8*	*–220.2*	*–1,159.1*	*–209.1*	...
D. Net Errors and Omissions	4 998 ..	**123.4**	**.3**	**75.4**	**321.4**	**83.1**	**298.0**	**–55.8**	...
Total, Groups A Through D	4 030 ..	*203.9*	*464.7*	*421.0*	*2,025.2*	*–137.1*	*–861.1*	*–264.9*	...
E. Reserves and Related Items	4 040 ..	**–203.9**	**–464.7**	**–421.0**	**–2,025.2**	**137.1**	**861.1**	**264.9**	...
Reserve assets	4 800 ..	–175.2	–512.0	–411.5	–2,025.2	–432.0	402.9	–216.8	...
Use of Fund credit and loans	4 766 ..	–28.7	47.2	–9.5	...	21.1	–31.0	57.6	...
Liabilities constituting foreign authorities' reserves	4 900 ..	...	...	...	...	...	...	...	...
Exceptional financing	4 920 ..	...	...	...	...	548.0	489.1	424.1	...
Conversion rates: Jordan dinar per U.S. dollar	0 101 ..	**.37429**	**.57458**	**.66371**	**.68087**	**.67982**	**.69285**	**.69876**	**.70038**

[1] Excludes components that have been classified in the categories of Group E.

Table 2. STANDARD PRESENTATION, 1988–95
(Millions of U.S. dollars)

	Code		1988	1989	1990	1991	1992	1993	1994	1995
CURRENT ACCOUNT	4 993	. .	**–293.7**	**384.9**	**–227.1**	**–393.5**	**–835.2**	**–629.1**	**–398.0**	. . .
A. GOODS	4 100	. .	–1,411.3	–773.1	–1,236.9	–1,172.7	–1,779.7	–1,898.8	–1,579.4	. . .
Credit	2 100	. .	**1,007.4**	**1,109.4**	**1,063.8**	**1,129.5**	**1,218.9**	**1,246.3**	**1,424.5**	. . .
General merchandise: exports f.o.b.	2 110	. .	1,007.4	1,109.4	1,063.8	1,129.5	1,218.9	1,246.3	1,424.5	. . .
Goods for processing: exports f.o.b.	2 150	. .	. . .	. . .	. . .	. . .	. . .	. . .	. . .	. . .
Repairs on goods	2 160	. .	. . .	. . .	. . .	. . .	. . .	. . .	. . .	. . .
Goods procured in ports by carriers	2 170	. .	. . .	. . .	. . .	. . .	. . .	. . .	. . .	. . .
Nonmonetary gold	2 180	. .	. . .	. . .	. . .	. . .	. . .	. . .	. . .	. . .
Debit	3 100	. .	**–2,418.7**	**–1,882.5**	**–2,300.7**	**–2,302.2**	**–2,998.7**	**–3,145.2**	**–3,003.8**	. . .
General merchandise: imports f.o.b.	3 110	. .	–2,418.7	–1,882.5	–2,300.7	–2,302.2	–2,998.7	–3,145.2	–3,003.8	. . .
Goods for processing: imports f.o.b.	3 150	. .	. . .	. . .	. . .	. . .	. . .	. . .	. . .	. . .
Repairs on goods	3 160	. .	. . .	. . .	. . .	. . .	. . .	. . .	. . .	. . .
Goods procured in ports by carriers	3 170	. .	. . .	. . .	. . .	. . .	. . .	. . .	. . .	. . .
Nonmonetary gold	3 180	. .	. . .	. . .	. . .	. . .	. . .	. . .	. . .	. . .
B. SERVICES	4 200	. .	80.2	176.0	179.3	228.7	124.5	226.5	169.3	. . .
Total credit	2 200	. .	*1,420.6*	*1,239.2*	*1,447.2*	*1,351.2*	*1,449.2*	*1,573.7*	*1,562.0*	. . .
Total debit	3 200	. .	*–1,340.5*	*–1,063.3*	*–1,267.9*	*–1,122.5*	*–1,324.7*	*–1,347.2*	*–1,392.7*	. . .
Transportation services, credit	2 205	. .	**409.9**	**293.1**	**371.2**	**250.7**	**333.8**	**367.6**	**352.8**	. . .
Passenger	2 205	BA	*292.7*	*204.8*	*276.6*	*187.2*	*247.1*	*274.4*	*262.7*	. . .
Freight	2 205	BB	*19.3*	*20.0*	*2.4*	*1.3*	*4.3*	*1.9*	*2.4*	. . .
Other	2 205	BC	*98.0*	*68.3*	*92.2*	*62.2*	*82.5*	*91.3*	*87.6*	. . .
Sea transport, passenger	2 207	. .	. . .	. . .	. . .	. . .	. . .	. . .	. . .	. . .
Sea transport, freight	2 208	. .	. . .	. . .	. . .	. . .	. . .	. . .	. . .	. . .
Sea transport, other	2 209	. .	. . .	. . .	. . .	. . .	. . .	. . .	. . .	. . .
Air transport, passenger	2 211	. .	. . .	. . .	. . .	. . .	. . .	. . .	. . .	. . .
Air transport, freight	2 212	. .	. . .	. . .	. . .	. . .	. . .	. . .	. . .	. . .
Air transport, other	2 213	. .	. . .	. . .	. . .	. . .	. . .	. . .	. . .	. . .
Other transport, passenger	2 215	. .	. . .	. . .	. . .	. . .	. . .	. . .	. . .	. . .
Other transport, freight	2 216	. .	. . .	. . .	. . .	. . .	. . .	. . .	. . .	. . .
Other transport, other	2 217	. .	. . .	. . .	. . .	. . .	. . .	. . .	. . .	. . .
Transportation services, debit	3 205	. .	**–593.1**	**–430.0**	**–581.5**	**–402.1**	**–598.8**	**–617.1**	**–607.4**	. . .
Passenger	3 205	BA	*–261.2*	*–179.7*	*–261.8*	*–127.0*	*–221.7*	*–224.3*	*–227.9*	. . .
Freight	3 205	BB	*–244.6*	*–190.3*	*–232.6*	*–232.8*	*–303.2*	*–318.1*	*–303.6*	. . .
Other	3 205	BC	*–87.3*	*–60.0*	*–87.1*	*–42.4*	*–73.9*	*–74.8*	*–75.9*	. . .
Sea transport, passenger	3 207	. .	. . .	. . .	. . .	. . .	. . .	. . .	. . .	. . .
Sea transport, freight	3 208	. .	. . .	. . .	. . .	. . .	. . .	. . .	. . .	. . .
Sea transport, other	3 209	. .	. . .	. . .	. . .	. . .	. . .	. . .	. . .	. . .
Air transport, passenger	3 211	. .	. . .	. . .	. . .	. . .	. . .	. . .	. . .	. . .
Air transport, freight	3 212	. .	. . .	. . .	. . .	. . .	. . .	. . .	. . .	. . .
Air transport, other	3 213	. .	. . .	. . .	. . .	. . .	. . .	. . .	. . .	. . .
Other transport, passenger	3 215	. .	. . .	. . .	. . .	. . .	. . .	. . .	. . .	. . .
Other transport, freight	3 216	. .	. . .	. . .	. . .	. . .	. . .	. . .	. . .	. . .
Other transport, other	3 217	. .	. . .	. . .	. . .	. . .	. . .	. . .	. . .	. . .
Travel, credit	2 236	. .	**625.5**	**545.8**	**511.2**	**316.6**	**463.1**	**562.9**	**582.0**	. . .
Business travel	2 237	. .	. . .	. . .	. . .	. . .	. . .	. . .	. . .	. . .
Personal travel	2 240	. .	. . .	. . .	. . .	. . .	. . .	. . .	. . .	. . .
Travel, debit	3 236	. .	**–480.4**	**–418.6**	**–336.3**	**–281.3**	**–350.5**	**–345.1**	**–394.1**	. . .
Business travel	3 237	. .	. . .	. . .	. . .	. . .	. . .	. . .	. . .	. . .
Personal travel	3 240	. .	–480.4	–418.6	–336.3	–281.3	–350.5	–345.1	–394.1	. . .
Other services, credit	2 200	BA	**385.2**	**400.3**	**564.7**	**783.9**	**652.3**	**643.2**	**627.2**	. . .
Communications	2 245	. .	. . .	. . .	. . .	. . .	. . .	. . .	. . .	. . .
Construction	2 249	. .	. . .	. . .	. . .	. . .	. . .	. . .	. . .	. . .
Insurance	2 253	. .	. . .	. . .	. . .	. . .	. . .	. . .	. . .	. . .
Financial	2 260	. .	. . .	. . .	. . .	. . .	. . .	. . .	. . .	. . .
Computer and information	2 262	. .	. . .	. . .	. . .	. . .	. . .	. . .	. . .	. . .
Royalties and licence fees	2 266	. .	. . .	. . .	. . .	. . .	. . .	. . .	. . .	. . .
Other business services	2 268	. .	372.9	382.3	547.6	765.2	637.9	629.2	608.5	. . .
Personal, cultural, and recreational	2 287	. .	. . .	. . .	. . .	. . .	. . .	. . .	. . .	. . .
Government, n.i.e.	2 291	. .	12.3	18.0	17.2	18.7	14.4	14.0	18.8	. . .
Other services, debit	3 200	BA	**–267.0**	**–214.8**	**–350.0**	**–439.1**	**–375.3**	**–384.9**	**–391.2**	. . .
Communications	3 245	. .	. . .	. . .	. . .	. . .	. . .	. . .	. . .	. . .
Construction	3 249	. .	. . .	. . .	. . .	. . .	. . .	. . .	. . .	. . .
Insurance	3 253	. .	–64.2	–48.5	–58.3	–57.3	–73.1	–76.7	–73.3	. . .
Financial	3 260	. .	. . .	. . .	. . .	. . .	. . .	. . .	. . .	. . .
Computer and information	3 262	. .	. . .	. . .	. . .	. . .	. . .	. . .	. . .	. . .
Royalties and licence fees	3 266	. .	. . .	. . .	. . .	. . .	. . .	. . .	. . .	. . .
Other business services	3 268	. .	–62.7	–61.7	–141.8	–222.4	–145.5	–109.8	–121.8	. . .
Personal, cultural, and recreational	3 287	. .	. . .	. . .	. . .	. . .	. . .	. . .	. . .	. . .
Government, n.i.e.	3 291	. .	–140.1	–104.6	–149.9	–159.4	–156.7	–198.4	–196.1	. . .

Table 2 (Continued). STANDARD PRESENTATION, 1988–95

(Millions of U.S. dollars)

	Code	1988	1989	1990	1991	1992	1993	1994	1995
C. INCOME	4 300	–314.1	–196.6	–214.5	–333.4	–347.6	–310.5	–314.7	. . .
Total credit	2 300	*40.6*	*39.0*	*67.3*	*114.3*	*112.4*	*99.0*	*72.7*	. . .
Total debit	3 300	*–354.8*	*–235.6*	*–281.8*	*–447.7*	*–460.0*	*–409.4*	*–387.5*	. . .
Compensation of employees, credit	2 310	. . .	. . .	. . .	. . .	. . .	. . .	. . .	. . .
Compensation of employees, debit	3 310	. . .	. . .	. . .	. . .	. . .	. . .	. . .	. . .
Investment income, credit	2 320	**40.6**	**39.0**	**67.3**	**114.3**	**112.4**	**99.0**	**72.7**	. . .
Direct investment income	2 330	. . .	. . .	. . .	. . .	. . .	. . .	. . .	. . .
Dividends and distributed branch profits	2 332	. . .	. . .	. . .	. . .	. . .	. . .	. . .	. . .
Reinvested earnings and undistributed branch profits	2 333	. . .	. . .	. . .	. . .	. . .	. . .	. . .	. . .
Income on debt (interest)	2 334	. . .	. . .	. . .	. . .	. . .	. . .	. . .	. . .
Portfolio investment income	2 339	. . .	. . .	. . .	. . .	. . .	. . .	. . .	. . .
Income on equity	2 340	. . .	. . .	. . .	. . .	. . .	. . .	. . .	. . .
Income on bonds and notes	2 350	. . .	. . .	. . .	. . .	. . .	. . .	. . .	. . .
Income on money market instruments and financial derivatives	2 360	. . .	. . .	. . .	. . .	. . .	. . .	. . .	. . .
Other investment income	2 370	40.6	39.0	67.3	114.3	112.4	99.0	72.7	. . .
Investment income, debit	3 320	**–354.8**	**–235.6**	**–281.8**	**–447.7**	**–460.0**	**–409.4**	**–387.5**	. . .
Direct investment income	3 330	. . .	. . .	. . .	. . .	. . .	. . .	. . .	. . .
Dividends and distributed branch profits	3 332	. . .	. . .	. . .	. . .	. . .	. . .	. . .	. . .
Reinvested earnings and undistributed branch profits	3 333	. . .	. . .	. . .	. . .	. . .	. . .	. . .	. . .
Income on debt (interest)	3 334	. . .	. . .	. . .	. . .	. . .	. . .	. . .	. . .
Portfolio investment income	3 339	. . .	. . .	. . .	. . .	. . .	. . .	. . .	. . .
Income on equity	3 340	. . .	. . .	. . .	. . .	. . .	. . .	. . .	. . .
Income on bonds and notes	3 350	. . .	. . .	. . .	. . .	. . .	. . .	. . .	. . .
Income on money market instruments and financial derivatives	3 360	. . .	. . .	. . .	. . .	. . .	. . .	. . .	. . .
Other investment income	3 370	–354.8	–235.6	–281.8	–447.7	–460.0	–409.4	–387.5	. . .
D. CURRENT TRANSFERS	4 379	1,351.5	1,178.7	1,044.9	883.8	1,167.5	1,353.7	1,326.9	. . .
Credit	2 379	**1,532.0**	**1,284.5**	**1,123.1**	**949.5**	**1,263.6**	**1,441.1**	**1,447.4**	. . .
General government	2 380	551.7	613.2	587.6	475.7	386.3	356.6	324.1	. . .
Other sectors	2 390	980.3	671.3	535.6	473.8	877.4	1,084.6	1,123.2	. . .
Workers' remittances	2 391	895.0	627.1	499.3	447.9	843.7	1,040.1	1,093.9	. . .
Other current transfers	2 392	85.3	44.2	36.3	25.8	33.7	44.4	29.3	. . .
Debit	3 379	**–180.5**	**–105.8**	**–78.2**	**–65.7**	**–96.1**	**–87.4**	**–120.5**	. . .
General government	3 380	. . .	. . .	. . .	. . .	. . .	. . .	. . .	. . .
Other sectors	3 390	–180.5	–105.8	–78.2	–65.7	–96.1	–87.4	–120.5	. . .
Workers' remittances	3 391	–154.7	–91.1	–70.5	–61.1	–86.1	–78.1	–93.0	. . .
Other current transfers	3 392	–25.8	–14.8	–7.7	–4.6	–10.0	–9.4	–27.5	. . .
CAPITAL AND FINANCIAL ACCOUNT	4 996	**170.3**	**–385.2**	**151.7**	**72.1**	**752.2**	**331.1**	**453.8**	. . .
CAPITAL ACCOUNT	4 994	. . .	. . .	. . .	. . .	. . .	. . .	. . .	. . .
Total credit	2 994	. . .	. . .	. . .	. . .	. . .	. . .	. . .	. . .
Total debit	3 994	. . .	. . .	. . .	. . .	. . .	. . .	. . .	. . .
Capital transfers, credit	2 400	. . .	. . .	. . .	. . .	. . .	. . .	. . .	. . .
General government	2 401	. . .	. . .	. . .	. . .	. . .	. . .	. . .	. . .
Debt forgiveness	2 402	. . .	. . .	. . .	. . .	. . .	. . .	. . .	. . .
Other capital transfers	2 410	. . .	. . .	. . .	. . .	. . .	. . .	. . .	. . .
Other sectors	2 430	. . .	. . .	. . .	. . .	. . .	. . .	. . .	. . .
Migrants' transfers	2 431	. . .	. . .	. . .	. . .	. . .	. . .	. . .	. . .
Debt forgiveness	2 432	. . .	. . .	. . .	. . .	. . .	. . .	. . .	. . .
Other capital transfers	2 440	. . .	. . .	. . .	. . .	. . .	. . .	. . .	. . .
Capital transfers, debit	3 400	. . .	. . .	. . .	. . .	. . .	. . .	. . .	. . .
General government	3 401	. . .	. . .	. . .	. . .	. . .	. . .	. . .	. . .
Debt forgiveness	3 402	. . .	. . .	. . .	. . .	. . .	. . .	. . .	. . .
Other capital transfers	3 410	. . .	. . .	. . .	. . .	. . .	. . .	. . .	. . .
Other sectors	3 430	. . .	. . .	. . .	. . .	. . .	. . .	. . .	. . .
Migrants' transfers	3 431	. . .	. . .	. . .	. . .	. . .	. . .	. . .	. . .
Debt forgiveness	3 432	. . .	. . .	. . .	. . .	. . .	. . .	. . .	. . .
Other capital transfers	3 440	. . .	. . .	. . .	. . .	. . .	. . .	. . .	. . .
Nonproduced nonfinancial assets, credit	2 480	. . .	. . .	. . .	. . .	. . .	. . .	. . .	. . .
Nonproduced nonfinancial assets, debit	3 480	. . .	. . .	. . .	. . .	. . .	. . .	. . .	. . .

Table 2 (Continued). STANDARD PRESENTATION, 1988–95

(Millions of U.S. dollars)

	Code	1988	1989	1990	1991	1992	1993	1994	1995
FINANCIAL ACCOUNT	4 995	**170.3**	**–385.2**	**151.7**	**72.1**	**752.2**	**331.1**	**453.8**	...
A. DIRECT INVESTMENT	4 500	23.8	–18.1	69.1	–25.6	44.1	19.5	26.0	...
Direct investment abroad	4 505	**.1**	**–16.7**	**31.5**	**–13.7**	**3.4**	**53.0**	**23.1**	...
Equity capital	4 510	...	...	...	...	...	...	...	...
Claims on affiliated enterprises	4 515	...	...	...	...	...	...	...	...
Liabilities to affiliated enterprises	4 520	...	...	...	...	...	...	...	...
Reinvested earnings	4 525	...	...	...	...	...	...	...	...
Other capital	4 530	.1	–16.7	31.5	–13.7	3.4	53.0	23.1	...
Claims on affiliated enterprises	4 535	...	...	...	...	...	...	...	...
Liabilities to affiliated enterprises	4 540	...	...	...	...	...	...	...	...
Direct investment in Jordan	4 555	**23.7**	**–1.3**	**37.6**	**–11.9**	**40.7**	**–33.5**	**2.9**	...
Equity capital	4 560	...	...	...	...	...	...	...	...
Claims on direct investors	4 565	...	...	...	...	...	...	...	...
Liabilities to direct investors	4 570	...	...	...	...	...	...	...	...
Reinvested earnings	4 575	...	...	...	...	...	...	...	...
Other capital	4 580	23.7	–1.3	37.6	–11.9	40.7	–33.5	2.9	...
Claims on direct investors	4 585	...	...	...	...	...	...	...	...
Liabilities to direct investors	4 590	...	...	...	...	...	...	...	...
B. PORTFOLIO INVESTMENT	4 600	...	...	...	...	...	...	...	...
Assets	4 602	...	...	...	...	...	...	...	...
Equity securities	4 610	...	...	...	...	...	...	...	...
Monetary authorities	4 611	...	...	...	...	...	...	...	...
General government	4 612	...	...	...	...	...	...	...	...
Banks	4 613	...	...	...	...	...	...	...	...
Other sectors	4 614	...	...	...	...	...	...	...	...
Debt securities	4 619	...	...	...	...	...	...	...	...
Bonds and notes	4 620	...	...	...	...	...	...	...	...
Monetary authorities	4 621	...	...	...	...	...	...	...	...
General government	4 622	...	...	...	...	...	...	...	...
Banks	4 623	...	...	...	...	...	...	...	...
Other sectors	4 624	...	...	...	...	...	...	...	...
Money market instruments	4 630	...	...	...	...	...	...	...	...
Monetary authorities	4 631	...	...	...	...	...	...	...	...
General government	4 632	...	...	...	...	...	...	...	...
Banks	4 633	...	...	...	...	...	...	...	...
Other sectors	4 634	...	...	...	...	...	...	...	...
Financial derivatives	4 640	...	...	...	...	...	...	...	...
Monetary authorities	4 641	...	...	...	...	...	...	...	...
General government	4 642	...	...	...	...	...	...	...	...
Banks	4 643	...	...	...	...	...	...	...	...
Other sectors	4 644	...	...	...	...	...	...	...	...
Liabilities	4 652	...	...	...	...	...	...	...	...
Equity securities	4 660	...	...	...	...	...	...	...	...
Banks	4 663	...	...	...	...	...	...	...	...
Other sectors	4 664	...	...	...	...	...	...	...	...
Debt securities	4 669	...	...	...	...	...	...	...	...
Bonds and notes	4 670	...	...	...	...	...	...	...	...
Monetary authorities	4 671	...	...	...	...	...	...	...	...
General government	4 672	...	...	...	...	...	...	...	...
Banks	4 673	...	...	...	...	...	...	...	...
Other sectors	4 674	...	...	...	...	...	...	...	...
Money market instruments	4 680	...	...	...	...	...	...	...	...
Monetary authorities	4 681	...	...	...	...	...	...	...	...
General government	4 682	...	...	...	...	...	...	...	...
Banks	4 683	...	...	...	...	...	...	...	...
Other sectors	4 684	...	...	...	...	...	...	...	...
Financial derivatives	4 690	...	...	...	...	...	...	...	...
Monetary authorities	4 691	...	...	...	...	...	...	...	...
General government	4 692	...	...	...	...	...	...	...	...
Banks	4 693	...	...	...	...	...	...	...	...
Other sectors	4 694	...	...	...	...	...	...	...	...

Table 2 (Concluded). STANDARD PRESENTATION, 1988–95
(Millions of U.S. dollars)

	Code	1988	1989	1990	1991	1992	1993	1994	1995
C. OTHER INVESTMENT	4 700	321.6	144.8	494.1	2,122.9	1,140.0	–91.3	644.6	...
Assets	4 703	**...**	**...**	**222.2**	**561.5**	**609.2**	**384.8**	**62.5**	**...**
Trade credits	4 706	...	...	...	...	...	...	...	...
General government: long-term	4 708	...	...	...	...	...	...	...	...
General government: short-term	4 709	...	...	...	...	...	...	...	...
Other sectors: long-term	4 711	...	...	...	...	...	...	...	...
Other sectors: short-term	4 712	...	...	...	...	...	...	...	...
Loans	4 714	...	...	110.1	–241.7	–113.6	–94.9	–163.5	...
Monetary authorities: long-term	4 717	...	...	...	...	...	...	...	...
Monetary authorities: short-term	4 718	...	...	110.1	–241.7	–113.6	–94.9	–163.5	...
General government: long-term	4 720	...	...	...	...	...	...	...	...
General government: short-term	4 721	...	...	...	...	...	...	...	...
Banks: long-term	4 723	...	...	...	...	...	...	...	...
Banks: short-term	4 724	...	...	...	...	...	...	...	...
Other sectors: long-term	4 726	...	...	...	...	...	...	...	...
Other sectors: short-term	4 727	...	...	...	...	...	...	...	...
Currency and deposits	4 730	...	...	112.1	803.2	722.8	480.0	225.9	...
Monetary authorities	4 731	...	...	...	...	...	...	...	...
General government	4 732	...	...	...	...	...	...	...	...
Banks	4 733	...	...	...	...	...	...	...	...
Other sectors	4 734	...	...	112.1	803.2	722.8	480.0	225.9	...
Other assets	4 736	...	...	...	...	...	–.3	...	...
Monetary authorities: long-term	4 738	...	...	...	...	...	...	...	...
Monetary authorities: short-term	4 739	...	...	...	...	...	...	...	...
General government: long-term	4 741	...	...	...	...	...	–.3	...	...
General government: short-term	4 742	...	...	...	...	...	...	...	...
Banks: long-term	4 744	...	...	...	...	...	...	...	...
Banks: short-term	4 745	...	...	...	...	...	...	...	...
Other sectors: long-term	4 747	...	...	...	...	...	...	...	...
Other sectors: short-term	4 748	...	...	...	...	...	...	...	...
Liabilities	4 753	**321.6**	**144.8**	**271.9**	**1,561.4**	**530.8**	**–476.1**	**582.1**	**...**
Trade credits	4 756	...	...	...	...	...	...	...	...
General government: long-term	4 758	...	...	...	...	...	...	...	...
General government: short-term	4 759	...	...	...	...	...	...	...	...
Other sectors: long-term	4 761	...	...	...	...	...	...	...	...
Other sectors: short-term	4 762	...	...	...	...	...	...	...	...
Loans	4 764	–15.4	249.9	343.7	296.5	37.0	–217.6	246.3	...
Use of Fund credit and loans from the Fund	4 766	–28.7	47.2	–9.5	...	21.1	–31.0	57.6	...
Monetary authorities: other long-term	4 767	...	...	...	...	...	...	...	...
Monetary authorities: short-term	4 768	...	...	...	...	...	...	...	...
General government: long-term	4 770	13.4	202.6	353.2	296.5	15.9	–186.6	188.7	...
General government: short-term	4 771	...	...	...	...	...	...	...	...
Banks: long-term	4 773	...	...	...	...	...	...	...	...
Banks: short-term	4 774	...	...	...	...	...	...	...	...
Other sectors: long-term	4 776	...	...	...	...	...	...	...	...
Other sectors: short-term	4 777	...	...	...	...	...	...	...	...
Currency and deposits	4 780	457.2	–75.9	–66.7	1,267.9	495.1	–257.5	344.5	...
Monetary authorities	4 781	...	...	...	...	...	...	...	...
General government	4 782	...	...	...	...	...	...	...	...
Banks	4 783	457.2	–75.9	–66.7	1,267.9	495.1	–257.5	344.5	...
Other sectors	4 784	...	...	...	...	...	...	...	...
Other liabilities	4 786	–120.2	–29.1	–5.1	–3.1	–1.3	–1.0	–8.7	...
Monetary authorities: long-term	4 788	...	...	...	...	...	...	...	...
Monetary authorities: short-term	4 789	–133.2	5.2	.2	...	.6	.7	–8.7	...
General government: long-term	4 791	...	...	...	...	...	...	...	...
General government: short-term	4 792	...	...	...	...	...	...	...	...
Banks: long-term	4 794	...	...	...	...	...	...	...	...
Banks: short-term	4 795	...	...	...	...	...	...	...	...
Other sectors: long-term	4 797	...	...	...	...	...	...	...	...
Other sectors: short-term	4 798	13.0	–34.3	–5.3	–3.1	–1.9	–1.7	...	...
D. RESERVE ASSETS	4 800	–175.2	–512.0	–411.5	–2,025.2	–432.0	402.9	–216.8	...
Monetary gold	4 810	...	...	...	...	...	...	...	...
Special drawing rights	4 820	11.1	–10.9	10.3	...	.4	–4.9	5.8	...
Reserve position in the Fund	4 830	...	...	...	...	–16.6	16.5	...	...
Foreign exchange	4 840	134.5	–430.6	–171.1	–603.0	53.5	149.7	–47.9	...
Other claims	4 880	–320.7	–70.5	–250.7	–1,422.2	–469.4	241.7	–174.7	...
NET ERRORS AND OMISSIONS	4 998	**123.4**	**.3**	**75.4**	**321.4**	**83.1**	**298.0**	**–55.8**	**...**

Part 3 of the *Yearbook* contains descriptions of the methodologies, compilation practices, and sources used to compile these data.

Table 1. ANALYTIC PRESENTATION, 1988–95
(Millions of U.S. dollars)

	Code		1988	1989	1990	1991	1992	1993	1994	1995
A. Current Account [1]	4 993	Y.	**–472.1**	**–590.6**	**–527.1**	**–213.3**	**–180.2**	**71.2**	**97.9**	**–400.4**
Goods: exports f.o.b.	2 100	. .	1,072.7	1,001.5	1,090.2	1,185.3	1,108.5	1,262.6	1,537.0	1,914.3
Goods: imports f.o.b.	3 100	. .	–1,802.2	–1,963.4	–2,005.3	–1,697.3	–1,608.7	–1,509.6	–1,775.3	–2,652.4
Balance on Goods	4 100	. .	*–729.5*	*–961.9*	*–915.2*	*–511.9*	*–500.2*	*–247.0*	*–238.4*	*–738.1*
Services: credit	2 200	. .	798.9	921.4	1,138.3	1,014.4	1,042.2	1,063.5	1,117.3	1,034.5
Services: debit	3 200	. .	–530.0	–603.1	–699.7	–632.7	–563.7	–569.4	–686.8	–871.3
Balance on Goods and Services	4 991	. .	*–460.5*	*–643.7*	*–476.5*	*–130.2*	*–21.7*	*247.0*	*192.2*	*–574.9*
Income: credit	2 300	. .	20.1	11.8	4.8	5.9	1.7	3.3	20.9	25.6
Income: debit	3 300	. .	–365.5	–330.1	–423.2	–434.7	–359.6	–392.2	–385.7	–350.5
Balance on Goods, Services, and Income	4 992	. .	*–805.9*	*–962.0*	*–894.9*	*–559.0*	*–379.6*	*–141.8*	*–172.6*	*–899.8*
Current transfers: credit	2 379	Y.	372.9	420.6	422.9	396.7	392.9	276.0	333.7	544.8
Current transfers: debit	3 379	. .	–39.1	–49.1	–55.1	–51.1	–193.5	–63.0	–63.2	–45.5
B. Capital Account [1]	4 994	Y.	**11.5**	**11.0**	**6.8**	**3.2**	**83.1**	**28.1**	**–.4**	**–.4**
Capital account: credit	2 994	Y.	11.8	11.2	7.6	3.6	83.5	28.5	. . .	. . .
Capital account: debit	3 994	. .	–.3	–.2	–.8	–.4	–.4	–.4	–.4	–.4
Total, Groups A Plus B	4 010	. .	*–460.6*	*–579.6*	*–520.3*	*–210.1*	*–97.1*	*99.2*	*97.5*	*–400.9*
C. Financial Account [1]	4 995	X.	**382.3**	**633.9**	**360.9**	**96.6**	**–270.1**	**55.1**	**–41.7**	**247.5**
Direct investment abroad	4 505	. .	–2.2	–1.4	. . .	. . .	. . .	. . .	. . .	. . .
Direct investment in Kenya	4 555	Y.	.4	62.2	57.1	18.8	6.4	1.6	3.7	32.5
Portfolio investment assets	4 602	. .	. . .	. . .	. . .	. . .	. . .	. . .	. . .	6.0
Equity securities	4 610	. .	. . .	. . .	. . .	. . .	. . .	. . .	. . .	6.0
Debt securities	4 619	. .	. . .	. . .	. . .	. . .	. . .	. . .	. . .	. . .
Portfolio investment liabilities	4 652	Y.	. . .	. . .	. . .	. . .	. . .	. . .	. . .	. . .
Equity securities	4 660	Y.	. . .	. . .	. . .	. . .	. . .	. . .	. . .	. . .
Debt securities	4 669	Y.	. . .	. . .	. . .	. . .	. . .	. . .	. . .	. . .
Other investment assets	4 703	. .	–14.4	–56.5	72.7	–77.5	–125.0	–31.4	171.1	261.6
Monetary authorities	4 703	. A	. . .	. . .	. . .	. . .	. . .	. . .	. . .	. . .
General government	4 703	. B	. . .	. . .	. . .	. . .	–4.3	. . .	. . .	. . .
Banks	4 703	. C	–11.2	–26.4	–7.8	–11.7	–117.5	–310.7	–61.2	–15.5
Other sectors	4 703	. D	–3.2	–30.1	80.5	–65.8	–3.2	279.3	232.3	277.1
Other investment liabilities	4 753	X.	398.4	629.6	231.1	155.3	–151.5	85.0	–216.5	–52.5
Monetary authorities	4 753	XA	. . .	. . .	. . .	. . .	. . .	. . .	. . .	. . .
General government	4 753	YB	289.0	378.8	91.8	83.8	–64.8	152.7	–113.3	–5.7
Banks	4 753	YC	5.1	5.8	–3.5	–11.2	13.8	25.4	32.1	15.2
Other sectors	4 753	YD	104.4	245.0	142.8	82.7	–100.5	–93.0	–135.3	–61.9
Total, Groups A Through C	4 020	. .	*–78.4*	*54.3*	*–159.4*	*–113.5*	*–367.2*	*154.4*	*55.8*	*–153.4*
D. Net Errors and Omissions	4 998	. .	**34.7**	**67.7**	**66.9**	**69.6**	**110.3**	**257.5**	**5.8**	**11.4**
Total, Groups A Through D	4 030	. .	*–43.6*	*121.9*	*–92.5*	*–43.9*	*–256.9*	*411.8*	*61.6*	*–142.0*
E. Reserves and Related Items	4 040	. .	**43.6**	**–121.9**	**92.5**	**43.9**	**256.9**	**–411.8**	**–61.6**	**142.0**
Reserve assets	4 800	. .	–30.8	–92.9	58.8	36.9	–27.4	–477.3	–95.3	174.5
Use of Fund credit and loans	4 766	. .	73.6	–29.2	33.7	7.0	–82.9	–30.6	19.3	–39.1
Liabilities constituting foreign authorities' reserves	4 900	. .	. . .	. . .	. . .	. . .	. . .	. . .	. . .	. . .
Exceptional financing	4 920	. .	.8	.2	. . .	. . .	367.1	96.2	14.4	6.5
Conversion rates: Kenya shillings per U.S. dollar	0 101	. .	**17.747**	**20.572**	**22.915**	**27.508**	**32.217**	**58.001**	**56.051**	**51.430**

[1] Excludes components that have been classified in the categories of Group E.

Table 2. STANDARD PRESENTATION, 1988–95
(Millions of U.S. dollars)

	Code		1988	1989	1990	1991	1992	1993	1994	1995
CURRENT ACCOUNT	4 993	. .	**–471.3**	**–590.4**	**–527.1**	**–213.3**	**–180.2**	**71.2**	**97.9**	**–400.4**
A. GOODS	4 100	. .	–729.5	–961.9	–915.2	–511.9	–500.2	–247.0	–238.4	–738.1
Credit	2 100	. .	**1,072.7**	**1,001.5**	**1,090.2**	**1,185.3**	**1,108.5**	**1,262.6**	**1,537.0**	**1,914.3**
General merchandise: exports f.o.b.	2 110	. .	1,017.5	926.1	1,010.5	1,053.8	1,004.0	1,185.6	1,481.1	1,875.4
Goods for processing: exports f.o.b.	2 150	. .	...	...	...	...	...	...	...	...
Repairs on goods	2 160	. .	...	1.0	...	...	9.1	9.1	9.8	21.7
Goods procured in ports by carriers	2 170	. .	55.3	74.4	79.7	131.5	95.4	67.9	46.0	17.2
Nonmonetary gold	2 180	. .	...	...	...	...	...	...	...	...
Debit	3 100	. .	**–1,802.2**	**–1,963.4**	**–2,005.3**	**–1,697.3**	**–1,608.7**	**–1,509.6**	**–1,775.3**	**–2,652.4**
General merchandise: imports f.o.b.	3 110	. .	–1,802.2	–1,963.4	–2,005.3	–1,697.3	–1,594.0	–1,492.8	–1,761.3	–2,639.4
Goods for processing: imports f.o.b.	3 150	. .	...	...	...	...	...	...	...	...
Repairs on goods	3 160	. .	...	...	...	...	–14.7	–16.8	–14.0	–13.0
Goods procured in ports by carriers	3 170	. .	...	...	...	...	...	...	...	...
Nonmonetary gold	3 180	. .	...	...	...	...	...	...	...	...
B. SERVICES	4 200	. .	268.9	318.2	438.6	381.7	478.5	494.1	430.6	163.2
Total credit	2 200	. .	*798.9*	*921.4*	*1,138.3*	*1,014.4*	*1,042.2*	*1,063.5*	*1,117.3*	*1,034.5*
Total debit	3 200	. .	*–530.0*	*–603.1*	*–699.7*	*–632.7*	*–563.7*	*–569.4*	*–686.8*	*–871.3*
Transportation services, credit	2 205	. .	**177.7**	**181.9**	**247.9**	**233.8**	**239.6**	**257.6**	**242.2**	**311.5**
Passenger	2 205	BA	*99.9*	*92.7*	*112.8*	*107.5*	*112.0*	*124.3*	*113.5*	*123.2*
Freight	2 205	BB	*41.3*	*45.8*	*45.8*	*43.7*	*49.4*	*58.6*	*49.0*	*103.5*
Other	2 205	BC	*36.5*	*43.4*	*89.3*	*82.6*	*78.2*	*74.7*	*79.8*	*84.8*
Sea transport, passenger	2 207	. .	...	...	...	...	...	...	...	...
Sea transport, freight	2 208	. .	...	...	...	...	...	...	...	...
Sea transport, other	2 209	. .	...	...	...	...	...	...	...	...
Air transport, passenger	2 211	. .	...	...	...	...	...	...	...	...
Air transport, freight	2 212	. .	...	...	...	...	...	...	...	...
Air transport, other	2 213	. .	...	...	...	...	...	...	...	...
Other transport, passenger	2 215	. .	...	...	...	...	...	...	...	...
Other transport, freight	2 216	. .	...	...	...	...	...	...	...	...
Other transport, other	2 217	. .	...	...	...	...	...	...	...	...
Transportation services, debit	3 205	. .	**–313.3**	**–361.8**	**–395.6**	**–362.9**	**–319.5**	**–315.2**	**–353.6**	**–482.5**
Passenger	3 205	BA	*–16.2*	*–23.8*	*–26.1*	*–45.8*	*–31.7*	*–32.7*	*–34.0*	*–37.7*
Freight	3 205	BB	*–259.6*	*–288.2*	*–289.0*	*–244.6*	*–229.8*	*–215.1*	*–253.8*	*–380.3*
Other	3 205	BC	*–37.5*	*–49.8*	*–80.5*	*–72.5*	*–58.0*	*–67.4*	*–65.8*	*–64.5*
Sea transport, passenger	3 207	. .	...	...	...	...	...	...	...	...
Sea transport, freight	3 208	. .	...	...	...	...	...	...	...	...
Sea transport, other	3 209	. .	...	...	...	...	...	...	...	...
Air transport, passenger	3 211	. .	...	...	...	...	...	...	...	...
Air transport, freight	3 212	. .	...	...	...	...	...	...	...	...
Air transport, other	3 213	. .	...	...	...	...	...	...	...	...
Other transport, passenger	3 215	. .	...	...	...	...	...	...	...	...
Other transport, freight	3 216	. .	...	...	...	...	...	...	...	...
Other transport, other	3 217	. .	...	...	...	...	...	...	...	...
Travel, credit	2 236	. .	**393.6**	**420.0**	**465.5**	**431.7**	**442.4**	**421.5**	**501.3**	**486.0**
Business travel	2 237	. .	...	...	...	...	...	...	...	...
Personal travel	2 240	. .	...	...	...	...	...	...	...	...
Travel, debit	3 236	. .	**–23.0**	**–26.8**	**–38.3**	**–24.0**	**–28.6**	**–47.9**	**–113.8**	**–144.8**
Business travel	3 237	. .	...	...	...	...	...	...	...	...
Personal travel	3 240	. .	...	...	...	...	...	...	...	...
Other services, credit	2 200	BA	**227.6**	**319.5**	**424.9**	**348.9**	**360.2**	**384.4**	**373.8**	**237.0**
Communications	2 245	. .	...	...	...	...	52.3	65.8	54.6	57.2
Construction	2 249	. .	...	...	...	...	...	...	...	...
Insurance	2 253	. .	4.6	5.1	5.1	4.9	5.5	6.5	5.4	11.5
Financial	2 260	. .	...	...	...	...	...	...	...	...
Computer and information	2 262	. .	...	...	...	...	...	...	...	...
Royalties and licence fees	2 266	. .	...	12.1	9.4	11.1	7.0	6.5	6.9	5.5
Other business services	2 268	. .	16.8	4.8	45.7	57.9	1.6	2.9	4.3	1.2
Personal, cultural, and recreational	2 287	. .	...	...	...	...	...	...	...	...
Government, n.i.e.	2 291	. .	206.2	297.5	364.7	275.0	293.8	302.7	302.6	161.6
Other services, debit	3 200	BA	**–193.7**	**–214.5**	**–265.8**	**–245.8**	**–215.6**	**–206.4**	**–219.4**	**–243.9**
Communications	3 245	. .	–5.2	–2.5	–40.9	–35.6	–30.4	–29.9	–21.4	–33.5
Construction	3 249	. .	...	...	...	...	...	...	...	...
Insurance	3 253	. .	–46.9	–51.8	–53.2	–42.5	–44.3	–36.3	–46.5	–48.0
Financial	3 260	. .	...	...	...	...	...	...	...	...
Computer and information	3 262	. .	...	...	...	...	...	...	...	...
Royalties and licence fees	3 266	. .	...	–4.2	–6.0	–3.8	–3.4	–3.5	–3.5	...
Other business services	3 268	. .	–54.1	–36.3	–46.5	–73.0	–60.1	–66.5	–61.9	–46.1
Personal, cultural, and recreational	3 287	. .	–.5	–16.3	–17.2	...	...	...	...	...
Government, n.i.e.	3 291	. .	–86.9	–103.4	–102.0	–90.8	–77.5	–70.1	–86.1	–116.3

Table 2 (Continued). STANDARD PRESENTATION, 1988–95
(Millions of U.S. dollars)

	Code	1988	1989	1990	1991	1992	1993	1994	1995
C. INCOME	4 300	–345.4	–318.4	–418.3	–428.7	–357.9	–388.9	–364.8	–324.9
Total credit	2 300	*20.1*	*11.8*	*4.8*	*5.9*	*1.7*	*3.3*	*20.9*	*25.6*
Total debit	3 300	*–365.5*	*–330.1*	*–423.2*	*–434.7*	*–359.6*	*–392.2*	*–385.7*	*–350.5*
Compensation of employees, credit	2 310	**.2**	**...**	**.2**	**.2**	**...**	**...**	**...**	**...**
Compensation of employees, debit	3 310	**–4.5**	**...**	**–4.1**	**–3.4**	**–3.6**	**...**	**...**	**...**
Investment income, credit	2 320	**19.9**	**11.8**	**4.6**	**5.7**	**1.7**	**3.3**	**20.9**	**25.6**
Direct investment income	2 330	...	...	...	...	...	...	...	...
Dividends and distributed branch profits	2 332	...	...	...	...	...	...	...	...
Reinvested earnings and undistributed branch profits	2 333	...	...	...	...	...	...	...	...
Income on debt (interest)	2 334	...	...	...	...	...	...	...	...
Portfolio investment income	2 339	...	...	...	...	...	...	...	...
Income on equity	2 340	...	...	...	...	...	...	...	...
Income on bonds and notes	2 350	...	...	...	...	...	...	...	...
Income on money market instruments and financial derivatives	2 360	...	...	...	...	...	...	...	...
Other investment income	2 370	19.9	11.8	4.6	5.7	1.7	3.3	20.9	25.6
Investment income, debit	3 320	**–361.0**	**–330.1**	**–419.0**	**–431.3**	**–356.0**	**–392.2**	**–385.7**	**–350.5**
Direct investment income	3 330	–90.0	–99.5	–132.1	–59.0	–125.6	–170.4	–86.9	–90.7
Dividends and distributed branch profits	3 332	–69.1	–75.7	–87.0	–43.0	–124.0	–168.8	–83.2	–86.4
Reinvested earnings and undistributed branch profits	3 333	–20.8	–23.8	–45.1	–16.0	–1.6	–1.6	–3.7	–4.3
Income on debt (interest)	3 334	...	...	...	...	...	...	...	...
Portfolio investment income	3 339	...	...	...	...	...	...	...	...
Income on equity	3 340	...	...	...	...	...	...	...	...
Income on bonds and notes	3 350	...	...	...	...	...	...	...	...
Income on money market instruments and financial derivatives	3 360	...	...	...	...	...	...	...	...
Other investment income	3 370	–271.0	–230.6	–286.9	–372.3	–230.4	–221.9	–298.8	–259.8
D. CURRENT TRANSFERS	4 379	334.6	371.6	367.8	345.7	199.4	213.0	270.5	499.3
Credit	2 379	**373.7**	**420.7**	**422.9**	**396.7**	**392.9**	**276.0**	**333.7**	**544.8**
General government	2 380	258.1	286.2	212.1	209.1	218.8	96.6	125.4	92.9
Other sectors	2 390	115.6	134.5	210.8	187.6	174.1	179.4	208.3	451.9
Workers' remittances	2 391	...	...	...	...	...	...	...	...
Other current transfers	2 392	115.6	134.5	210.8	187.6	174.1	179.4	208.3	451.9
Debit	3 379	**–39.1**	**–49.1**	**–55.1**	**–51.1**	**–193.5**	**–63.0**	**–63.2**	**–45.5**
General government	3 380	–1.1	–5.1	–5.3	–4.6	–4.5	–2.6	–2.5	–2.3
Other sectors	3 390	–38.0	–44.0	–49.8	–46.4	–188.9	–60.4	–60.6	–43.2
Workers' remittances	3 391	–2.8	–2.7	–2.2	...	–3.4	–3.5	–3.5	–3.6
Other current transfers	3 392	–35.2	–41.3	–47.6	–46.4	–185.6	–56.9	–57.2	–39.6
CAPITAL AND FINANCIAL ACCOUNT	4 996	**436.6**	**522.8**	**460.2**	**143.7**	**69.8**	**–328.6**	**–103.8**	**389.1**
CAPITAL ACCOUNT	4 994	**11.5**	**11.0**	**6.8**	**3.2**	**83.1**	**28.1**	**–.4**	**–.4**
Total credit	2 994	*11.8*	*11.2*	*7.6*	*3.6*	*83.5*	*28.5*	*...*	*...*
Total debit	3 994	*–.3*	*–.2*	*–.8*	*–.4*	*–.4*	*–.4*	*–.4*	*–.4*
Capital transfers, credit	2 400	**11.8**	**11.2**	**7.6**	**3.6**	**83.5**	**28.5**	**...**	**...**
General government	2 401	...	...	...	...	...	...	...	...
Debt forgiveness	2 402	...	...	...	...	...	...	...	...
Other capital transfers	2 410	...	...	...	...	...	...	...	...
Other sectors	2 430	11.8	11.2	7.6	3.6	83.5	28.5	...	...
Migrants' transfers	2 431	11.8	11.2	7.6	3.6	83.5	28.5	...	...
Debt forgiveness	2 432	...	...	...	...	...	...	...	...
Other capital transfers	2 440	...	...	...	...	...	...	...	...
Capital transfers, debit	3 400	**–.3**	**–.2**	**–.8**	**–.4**	**–.4**	**–.4**	**–.4**	**–.4**
General government	3 401	...	...	...	...	...	...	...	...
Debt forgiveness	3 402	...	...	...	...	...	...	...	...
Other capital transfers	3 410	...	...	...	...	...	...	...	...
Other sectors	3 430	–.3	–.2	–.8	–.4	–.4	–.4	–.4	–.4
Migrants' transfers	3 431	–.3	–.2	–.8	–.4	–.4	–.4	–.4	–.4
Debt forgiveness	3 432	...	...	...	...	...	...	...	...
Other capital transfers	3 440	...	...	...	...	...	...	...	...
Nonproduced nonfinancial assets, credit	2 480	...	...	...	...	...	...	...	...
Nonproduced nonfinancial assets, debit	3 480	...	...	...	...	...	...	...	...

Table 2 (Continued). STANDARD PRESENTATION, 1988–95
(Millions of U.S. dollars)

	Code	1988	1989	1990	1991	1992	1993	1994	1995
FINANCIAL ACCOUNT	4 995 . .	**425.1**	**511.8**	**453.4**	**140.5**	**–13.2**	**–356.7**	**–103.4**	**389.5**
A. DIRECT INVESTMENT	4 500 . .	–1.8	60.8	57.1	18.8	6.4	1.6	3.7	32.5
Direct investment abroad	4 505 . .	**–2.2**	**–1.4**	**. . .**	**. . .**	**. . .**	**. . .**	**. . .**	**. . .**
Equity capital	4 510 . .	. . .	–.8	. . .	. . .	. . .	. . .	. . .	. . .
Claims on affiliated enterprises	4 515 . .	. . .	. . .	. . .	. . .	. . .	. . .	. . .	. . .
Liabilities to affiliated enterprises	4 520 . .	. . .	. . .	. . .	. . .	. . .	. . .	. . .	. . .
Reinvested earnings	4 525 . .	. . .	. . .	. . .	. . .	. . .	. . .	. . .	. . .
Other capital	4 530 . .	–2.2	–.6	. . .	. . .	. . .	. . .	. . .	. . .
Claims on affiliated enterprises	4 535 . .	. . .	. . .	. . .	. . .	. . .	. . .	. . .	. . .
Liabilities to affiliated enterprises	4 540 . .	. . .	. . .	. . .	. . .	. . .	. . .	. . .	. . .
Direct investment in Kenya	4 555 . .	**.4**	**62.2**	**57.1**	**18.8**	**6.4**	**1.6**	**3.7**	**32.5**
Equity capital	4 560 . .	.8	8.6	12.0	2.8	4.8	. . .	. . .	28.2
Claims on direct investors	4 565 . .	. . .	. . .	. . .	. . .	4.8	. . .	. . .	28.2
Liabilities to direct investors	4 570 . .	. . .	. . .	. . .	. . .	. . .	. . .	. . .	. . .
Reinvested earnings	4 575 . .	20.8	23.8	45.1	16.0	1.6	1.6	3.7	4.3
Other capital	4 580 . .	–21.2	29.8	. . .	. . .	. . .	. . .	. . .	. . .
Claims on direct investors	4 585 . .	. . .	. . .	. . .	. . .	. . .	. . .	. . .	. . .
Liabilities to direct investors	4 590 . .	. . .	. . .	. . .	. . .	. . .	. . .	. . .	. . .
B. PORTFOLIO INVESTMENT	4 600 . .	. . .	. . .	. . .	. . .	. . .	. . .	. . .	6.0
Assets	4 602 . .	**. . .**	**. . .**	**. . .**	**. . .**	**. . .**	**. . .**	**. . .**	**6.0**
Equity securities	4 610 . .	. . .	. . .	. . .	. . .	. . .	. . .	. . .	6.0
Monetary authorities	4 611 . .	. . .	. . .	. . .	. . .	. . .	. . .	. . .	. . .
General government	4 612 . .	. . .	. . .	. . .	. . .	. . .	. . .	. . .	. . .
Banks	4 613 . .	. . .	. . .	. . .	. . .	. . .	. . .	. . .	. . .
Other sectors	4 614 . .	. . .	. . .	. . .	. . .	. . .	. . .	. . .	6.0
Debt securities	4 619 . .	. . .	. . .	. . .	. . .	. . .	. . .	. . .	. . .
Bonds and notes	4 620 . .	. . .	. . .	. . .	. . .	. . .	. . .	. . .	. . .
Monetary authorities	4 621 . .	. . .	. . .	. . .	. . .	. . .	. . .	. . .	. . .
General government	4 622 . .	. . .	. . .	. . .	. . .	. . .	. . .	. . .	. . .
Banks	4 623 . .	. . .	. . .	. . .	. . .	. . .	. . .	. . .	. . .
Other sectors	4 624 . .	. . .	. . .	. . .	. . .	. . .	. . .	. . .	. . .
Money market instruments	4 630 . .	. . .	. . .	. . .	. . .	. . .	. . .	. . .	. . .
Monetary authorities	4 631 . .	. . .	. . .	. . .	. . .	. . .	. . .	. . .	. . .
General government	4 632 . .	. . .	. . .	. . .	. . .	. . .	. . .	. . .	. . .
Banks	4 633 . .	. . .	. . .	. . .	. . .	. . .	. . .	. . .	. . .
Other sectors	4 634 . .	. . .	. . .	. . .	. . .	. . .	. . .	. . .	. . .
Financial derivatives	4 640 . .	. . .	. . .	. . .	. . .	. . .	. . .	. . .	. . .
Monetary authorities	4 641 . .	. . .	. . .	. . .	. . .	. . .	. . .	. . .	. . .
General government	4 642 . .	. . .	. . .	. . .	. . .	. . .	. . .	. . .	. . .
Banks	4 643 . .	. . .	. . .	. . .	. . .	. . .	. . .	. . .	. . .
Other sectors	4 644 . .	. . .	. . .	. . .	. . .	. . .	. . .	. . .	. . .
Liabilities	4 652 . .	**. . .**	**. . .**	**. . .**	**. . .**	**. . .**	**. . .**	**. . .**	**. . .**
Equity securities	4 660 . .	. . .	. . .	. . .	. . .	. . .	. . .	. . .	. . .
Banks	4 663 . .	. . .	. . .	. . .	. . .	. . .	. . .	. . .	. . .
Other sectors	4 664 . .	. . .	. . .	. . .	. . .	. . .	. . .	. . .	. . .
Debt securities	4 669 . .	. . .	. . .	. . .	. . .	. . .	. . .	. . .	. . .
Bonds and notes	4 670 . .	. . .	. . .	. . .	. . .	. . .	. . .	. . .	. . .
Monetary authorities	4 671 . .	. . .	. . .	. . .	. . .	. . .	. . .	. . .	. . .
General government	4 672 . .	. . .	. . .	. . .	. . .	. . .	. . .	. . .	. . .
Banks	4 673 . .	. . .	. . .	. . .	. . .	. . .	. . .	. . .	. . .
Other sectors	4 674 . .	. . .	. . .	. . .	. . .	. . .	. . .	. . .	. . .
Money market instruments	4 680 . .	. . .	. . .	. . .	. . .	. . .	. . .	. . .	. . .
Monetary authorities	4 681 . .	. . .	. . .	. . .	. . .	. . .	. . .	. . .	. . .
General government	4 682 . .	. . .	. . .	. . .	. . .	. . .	. . .	. . .	. . .
Banks	4 683 . .	. . .	. . .	. . .	. . .	. . .	. . .	. . .	. . .
Other sectors	4 684 . .	. . .	. . .	. . .	. . .	. . .	. . .	. . .	. . .
Financial derivatives	4 690 . .	. . .	. . .	. . .	. . .	. . .	. . .	. . .	. . .
Monetary authorities	4 691 . .	. . .	. . .	. . .	. . .	. . .	. . .	. . .	. . .
General government	4 692 . .	. . .	. . .	. . .	. . .	. . .	. . .	. . .	. . .
Banks	4 693 . .	. . .	. . .	. . .	. . .	. . .	. . .	. . .	. . .
Other sectors	4 694 . .	. . .	. . .	. . .	. . .	. . .	. . .	. . .	. . .

Table 2 (Concluded). STANDARD PRESENTATION, 1988–95
(Millions of U.S. dollars)

	Code		1988	1989	1990	1991	1992	1993	1994	1995
C. OTHER INVESTMENT	4 700	. .	457.7	543.9	337.5	84.8	7.8	119.1	−11.8	176.5
Assets	4 703	. .	**−14.4**	**−56.5**	**72.7**	**−77.5**	**−125.0**	**−31.4**	**171.1**	**261.6**
Trade credits	4 706	. .	. . .	. . .	. . .	. . .	. . .	. . .	. . .	. . .
General government: long-term	4 708	. .	. . .	. . .	. . .	. . .	. . .	. . .	. . .	. . .
General government: short-term	4 709	. .	. . .	. . .	. . .	. . .	. . .	. . .	. . .	. . .
Other sectors: long-term	4 711	. .	. . .	. . .	. . .	. . .	. . .	. . .	. . .	. . .
Other sectors: short-term	4 712	. .	. . .	. . .	. . .	. . .	. . .	. . .	. . .	. . .
Loans	4 714	. .	. . .	. . .	86.5	−28.0	. . .	. . .	. . .	. . .
Monetary authorities: long-term	4 717	. .	. . .	. . .	. . .	. . .	. . .	. . .	. . .	. . .
Monetary authorities: short-term	4 718	. .	. . .	. . .	. . .	. . .	. . .	. . .	. . .	. . .
General government: long-term	4 720	. .	. . .	. . .	. . .	. . .	. . .	. . .	. . .	. . .
General government: short-term	4 721	. .	. . .	. . .	. . .	. . .	. . .	. . .	. . .	. . .
Banks: long-term	4 723	. .	. . .	. . .	. . .	. . .	. . .	. . .	. . .	. . .
Banks: short-term	4 724	. .	. . .	. . .	. . .	. . .	. . .	. . .	. . .	. . .
Other sectors: long-term	4 726	. .	. . .	. . .	. . .	. . .	. . .	. . .	. . .	. . .
Other sectors: short-term	4 727	. .	. . .	. . .	86.5	−28.0	. . .	. . .	. . .	. . .
Currency and deposits	4 730	. .	−14.4	−56.5	−11.0	−45.2	−121.8	−31.4	171.1	274.2
Monetary authorities	4 731	. .	. . .	. . .	. . .	. . .	. . .	. . .	. . .	. . .
General government	4 732	. .	. . .	. . .	. . .	. . .	−4.3	. . .	. . .	. . .
Banks	4 733	. .	−11.2	−26.4	−7.8	−11.7	−117.5	−310.7	−61.2	−15.5
Other sectors	4 734	. .	−3.2	−30.1	−3.2	−33.5	. . .	279.3	232.3	289.7
Other assets	4 736	. .	. . .	. . .	−2.8	−4.4	−3.2	. . .	−.1	−12.6
Monetary authorities: long-term	4 738	. .	. . .	. . .	. . .	. . .	. . .	. . .	. . .	. . .
Monetary authorities: short-term	4 739	. .	. . .	. . .	. . .	. . .	. . .	. . .	. . .	. . .
General government: long-term	4 741	. .	. . .	. . .	. . .	. . .	. . .	. . .	. . .	. . .
General government: short-term	4 742	. .	. . .	. . .	. . .	. . .	. . .	. . .	. . .	. . .
Banks: long-term	4 744	. .	. . .	. . .	. . .	. . .	. . .	. . .	. . .	. . .
Banks: short-term	4 745	. .	. . .	. . .	. . .	. . .	. . .	. . .	. . .	. . .
Other sectors: long-term	4 747	. .	. . .	. . .	−2.8	−4.4	−3.2	. . .	−.1	−12.6
Other sectors: short-term	4 748	. .	. . .	. . .	. . .	. . .	. . .	. . .	. . .	. . .
Liabilities	4 753	. .	**472.0**	**600.4**	**264.8**	**162.3**	**132.8**	**150.5**	**−182.8**	**−85.0**
Trade credits	4 756	. .	. . .	. . .	. . .	. . .	. . .	. . .	. . .	. . .
General government: long-term	4 758	. .	. . .	. . .	. . .	. . .	. . .	. . .	. . .	. . .
General government: short-term	4 759	. .	. . .	. . .	. . .	. . .	. . .	. . .	. . .	. . .
Other sectors: long-term	4 761	. .	. . .	. . .	. . .	. . .	. . .	. . .	. . .	. . .
Other sectors: short-term	4 762	. .	. . .	. . .	. . .	. . .	. . .	. . .	. . .	. . .
Loans	4 764	. .	461.1	522.8	217.3	129.3	−248.2	12.8	−242.7	−135.8
Use of Fund credit and loans from the Fund	4 766	. .	73.6	−29.2	33.7	7.0	−82.9	−30.6	19.3	−39.1
Monetary authorities: other long-term	4 767	. .	. . .	. . .	. . .	. . .	. . .	. . .	. . .	. . .
Monetary authorities: short-term	4 768	. .	. . .	. . .	. . .	. . .	. . .	. . .	. . .	. . .
General government: long-term	4 770	. .	289.0	378.8	91.8	83.8	−64.8	152.7	−113.3	−5.7
General government: short-term	4 771	. .	. . .	. . .	. . .	. . .	. . .	. . .	. . .	. . .
Banks: long-term	4 773	. .	. . .	. . .	. . .	. . .	. . .	. . .	. . .	. . .
Banks: short-term	4 774	. .	. . .	. . .	. . .	. . .	. . .	. . .	. . .	. . .
Other sectors: long-term	4 776	. .	44.4	162.3	77.2	38.5	−100.5	−109.2	−148.7	−91.0
Other sectors: short-term	4 777	. .	54.0	10.9	14.7	. . .	. . .	. . .	. . .	. . .
Currency and deposits	4 780	. .	5.1	5.8	−3.5	−11.2	13.8	25.4	32.1	15.2
Monetary authorities	4 781	. .	. . .	. . .	. . .	. . .	. . .	. . .	. . .	. . .
General government	4 782	. .	. . .	. . .	. . .	. . .	. . .	. . .	. . .	. . .
Banks	4 783	. .	5.1	5.8	−3.5	−11.2	13.8	25.4	32.1	15.2
Other sectors	4 784	. .	. . .	. . .	. . .	. . .	. . .	. . .	. . .	. . .
Other liabilities	4 786	. .	5.9	71.8	51.0	44.2	367.1	112.3	27.8	35.6
Monetary authorities: long-term	4 788	. .	. . .	. . .	. . .	. . .	. . .	. . .	. . .	. . .
Monetary authorities: short-term	4 789	. .	. . .	. . .	. . .	. . .	367.1	96.2	14.4	6.5
General government: long-term	4 791	. .	. . .	. . .	. . .	. . .	. . .	. . .	. . .	. . .
General government: short-term	4 792	. .	. . .	. . .	. . .	. . .	. . .	. . .	. . .	. . .
Banks: long-term	4 794	. .	. . .	. . .	. . .	. . .	. . .	. . .	. . .	. . .
Banks: short-term	4 795	. .	. . .	. . .	. . .	. . .	. . .	. . .	. . .	. . .
Other sectors: long-term	4 797	. .	. . .	. . .	. . .	. . .	. . .	. . .	. . .	. . .
Other sectors: short-term	4 798	. .	5.9	71.8	51.0	44.2	. . .	16.1	13.4	29.0
D. RESERVE ASSETS	4 800	. .	−30.8	−92.9	58.8	36.9	−27.4	−477.3	−95.3	174.5
Monetary gold	4 810	. .	. . .	. . .	. . .	. . .	. . .	. . .	. . .	. . .
Special drawing rights	4 820	. .	15.7	−10.5	8.1	2.8	.6	−.3	.5	.3
Reserve position in the Fund	4 830	. .	. . .	. . .	. . .	. . .	. . .	. . .	−.1	. . .
Foreign exchange	4 840	. .	−45.9	−82.4	32.7	54.5	168.1	−473.5	−97.8	180.3
Other claims	4 880	. .	−.6	. . .	18.1	−20.4	−196.1	−3.5	2.1	−6.1
NET ERRORS AND OMISSIONS	4 998	. .	**34.7**	**67.7**	**66.9**	**69.6**	**110.3**	**257.5**	**5.8**	**11.4**

Table 1. ANALYTIC PRESENTATION, 1988–95
(Millions of U.S. dollars)

	Code		1988	1989	1990	1991	1992	1993	1994	1995
A. Current Account [1]	4 993	Y.	**–1.836**	**–1.537**	**–9.187**	**4.287**	**–9.094**	**–4.105**	**1.383**	**. . .**
Goods: exports f.o.b	2 100	. .	5.593	5.507	3.342	3.632	5.518	4.282	6.149	. . .
Goods: imports f.o.b	3 100	. .	–22.943	–23.575	–27.655	–26.318	–37.489	–29.345	–27.275	. . .
Balance on Goods	4 100	. .	*–17.350*	*–18.068*	*–24.313*	*–22.687*	*–31.972*	*–25.063*	*–21.126*	. . .
Services: credit	2 200	. .	5.743	6.412	7.746	12.646	13.870	14.538	17.559	. . .
Services: debit	3 200	. .	–14.095	–15.629	–18.678	–17.527	–19.169	–19.179	–17.229	. . .
Balance on Goods and Services	4 991	. .	*–25.702*	*–27.285*	*–35.244*	*–27.568*	*–37.271*	*–29.704*	*–20.796*	. . .
Income: credit	2 300	. .	15.743	16.888	19.247	20.555	19.294	16.398	17.053	. . .
Income: debit	3 300	. .	–.729	–1.030	–2.472	–1.543	–1.224	–1.682	–2.220	. . .
Balance on Goods, Services, and Income	4 992	. .	*–10.688*	*–11.427*	*–18.469*	*–8.556*	*–19.200*	*–14.987*	*–5.963*	. . .
Current transfers: credit	2 379	Y.	10.842	12.118	11.145	15.106	12.443	12.911	8.954	. . .
Current transfers: debit	3 379	. .	–1.990	–2.228	–1.863	–2.263	–2.337	–2.028	–1.608	. . .
B. Capital Account [1]	4 994	Y.	**6.688**	**6.559**	**12.469**	**6.127**	**16.404**	**5.713**	**2.543**	**. . .**
Capital account: credit	2 994	Y.	6.688	6.559	12.469	6.127	16.404	5.713	2.543	. . .
Capital account: debit	3 994	. .	. . .	. . .	. . .	. . .	. . .	. . .	. . .	. . .
Total, Groups A Plus B	4 010	. .	*4.852*	*5.021*	*3.282*	*10.413*	*7.310*	*1.608*	*3.925*	. . .
C. Financial Account [1]	4 995	X.	**–3.592**	**–5.416**	**–5.033**	**–11.809**	**–14.939**	**–7.460**	**–4.786**	**. . .**
Direct investment abroad	4 505	. .	. . .	. . .	. . .	. . .	. . .	. . .	–.028	. . .
Direct investment in Kiribati	4 555	Y.	.257	.180	.300	.428	.407	–.770	.431	. . .
Portfolio investment assets	4 602	. .	–4.586	–6.401	–8.359	–13.062	–17.710	–6.691	–6.604	. . .
Equity securities	4 610	. .	. . .	. . .	. . .	. . .	. . .	. . .	. . .	. . .
Debt securities	4 619	. .	–4.586	–6.401	–8.359	–13.062	–17.710	–6.691	–6.604	. . .
Portfolio investment liabilities	4 652	Y.	. . .	. . .	. . .	. . .	. . .	. . .	. . .	. . .
Equity securities	4 660	Y.	. . .	. . .	. . .	. . .	. . .	. . .	. . .	. . .
Debt securities	4 669	Y.	. . .	. . .	. . .	. . .	. . .	. . .	. . .	. . .
Other investment assets	4 703	. .	. . .	. . .	. . .	. . .	. . .	. . .	. . .	. . .
Monetary authorities	4 703	. A	. . .	. . .	. . .	. . .	. . .	. . .	. . .	. . .
General government	4 703	. B	. . .	. . .	. . .	. . .	. . .	. . .	. . .	. . .
Banks	4 703	. C	. . .	. . .	. . .	. . .	. . .	. . .	. . .	. . .
Other sectors	4 703	. D	. . .	. . .	. . .	. . .	. . .	. . .	. . .	. . .
Other investment liabilities	4 753	X.	.738	.805	3.026	.825	2.365	. . .	1.414	. . .
Monetary authorities	4 753	XA	. . .	. . .	. . .	. . .	. . .	. . .	. . .	. . .
General government	4 753	YB	.738	.805	3.026	.825	2.365	. . .	1.414	. . .
Banks	4 753	YC	. . .	. . .	. . .	. . .	. . .	. . .	. . .	. . .
Other sectors	4 753	YD	. . .	. . .	. . .	. . .	. . .	. . .	. . .	. . .
Total, Groups A Through C	4 020	. .	*1.260*	*–.395*	*–1.751*	*–1.396*	*–7.628*	*–5.853*	*–.861*	. . .
D. Net Errors and Omissions	4 998	. .	**–4.220**	**–4.725**	**–4.996**	**–9.637**	**–8.984**	**.766**	**–5.113**	**. . .**
Total, Groups A Through D	4 030	. .	*–2.960*	*–5.119*	*–6.747*	*–11.033*	*–16.612*	*–5.087*	*–5.974*	. . .
E. Reserves and Related Items	4 040	. .	**2.960**	**5.119**	**6.747**	**11.033**	**16.612**	**5.087**	**5.974**	**. . .**
Reserve assets	4 800	. .	2.960	5.119	6.747	11.033	16.612	5.087	5.974	. . .
Use of Fund credit and loans	4 766	. .	. . .	. . .	. . .	. . .	. . .	. . .	. . .	. . .
Liabilities constituting foreign authorities' reserves	4 900	. .	. . .	. . .	. . .	. . .	. . .	. . .	. . .	. . .
Exceptional financing	4 920	. .	. . .	. . .	. . .	. . .	. . .	. . .	. . .	. . .
Conversion rates: Australian dollars per U.S. dollar	0 101	. .	**1.2799**	**1.2646**	**1.2811**	**1.2838**	**1.3616**	**1.4706**	**1.3678**	**1.3490**

[1] Excludes components that have been classified in the categories of Group E.

Table 2. STANDARD PRESENTATION, 1988–95
(Millions of U.S. dollars)

	Code	1988	1989	1990	1991	1992	1993	1994	1995
CURRENT ACCOUNT	4 993 . .	**–1.836**	**–1.537**	**–9.187**	**4.287**	**–9.094**	**–4.105**	**1.383**	. . .
A. GOODS	4 100 . .	–17.350	–18.068	–24.313	–22.687	–31.972	–25.063	–21.126	. . .
Credit	2 100 . .	**5.593**	**5.507**	**3.342**	**3.632**	**5.518**	**4.282**	**6.149**	. . .
General merchandise: exports f.o.b.	2 110 . .	5.211	5.089	2.873	2.880	4.783	3.447	5.198	. . .
Goods for processing: exports f.o.b.	2 150 . .	. . .	. . .	. . .	. . .	. . .	. . .	. . .	. . .
Repairs on goods	2 160 . .	. . .	. . .	. . .	. . .	. . .	. . .	. . .	. . .
Goods procured in ports by carriers	2 170 . .	.382	.418	.468	.752	.734	.835	.950	. . .
Nonmonetary gold	2 180 . .	. . .	. . .	. . .	. . .	. . .	. . .	. . .	. . .
Debit	3 100 . .	**–22.943**	**–23.575**	**–27.655**	**–26.318**	**–37.489**	**–29.345**	**–27.275**	. . .
General merchandise: imports f.o.b.	3 110 . .	–22.021	–22.613	–26.889	–25.882	–37.109	–28.814	–26.405	. . .
Goods for processing: imports f.o.b.	3 150 . .	. . .	. . .	. . .	. . .	. . .	. . .	. . .	. . .
Repairs on goods	3 160 . .	–.877	–.911	–.720	–.387	–.322	–.476	–.804	. . .
Goods procured in ports by carriers	3 170 . .	–.045	–.051	–.045	–.049	–.057	–.054	–.066	. . .
Nonmonetary gold	3 180 . .	. . .	. . .	. . .	. . .	. . .	. . .	. . .	. . .
B. SERVICES	4 200 . .	–8.352	–9.216	–10.932	–4.881	–5.299	–4.641	.330	. . .
Total credit	2 200 . .	*5.743*	*6.412*	*7.746*	*12.646*	*13.870*	*14.538*	*17.559*	. . .
Total debit	3 200 . .	*–14.095*	*–15.629*	*–18.678*	*–17.527*	*–19.169*	*–19.179*	*–17.229*	. . .
Transportation services, credit	2 205 . .	**2.399**	**2.401**	**2.965**	**1.666**	**2.368**	**2.939**	**2.053**	. . .
Passenger	2 205 BA	*.754*	*.718*	*.989*	. . .	*.537*	*1.076*	*.152*	. . .
Freight	2 205 BB	*.388*	*.496*	*.793*	*.853*	*.947*	*.979*	*.804*	. . .
Other	2 205 BC	*1.257*	*1.187*	*1.183*	*.813*	*.884*	*.884*	*1.097*	. . .
Sea transport, passenger	2 207 . .	. . .	. . .	. . .	. . .	. . .	. . .	. . .	. . .
Sea transport, freight	2 208 . .	.105	.100	.244	.230	.286	.299	.366	. . .
Sea transport, other	2 209 . .	1.257	1.187	1.183	.813	.884	.884	1.097	. . .
Air transport, passenger	2 211 . .	.754	.718	.989	. . .	.537	1.076	.152	. . .
Air transport, freight	2 212 . .	.283	.395	.550	.623	.661	.680	.439	. . .
Air transport, other	2 213 . .	. . .	. . .	. . .	. . .	. . .	. . .	. . .	. . .
Other transport, passenger	2 215 . .	. . .	. . .	. . .	. . .	. . .	. . .	. . .	. . .
Other transport, freight	2 216 . .	. . .	. . .	. . .	. . .	. . .	. . .	. . .	. . .
Other transport, other	2 217 . .	. . .	. . .	. . .	. . .	. . .	. . .	. . .	. . .
Transportation services, debit	3 205 . .	**–8.782**	**–9.680**	**–12.149**	**–9.741**	**–12.154**	**–11.194**	**–10.534**	. . .
Passenger	3 205 BA	*–2.639*	*–2.588*	*–3.907*	*–2.827*	*–3.494*	*–3.975*	*–3.760*	. . .
Freight	3 205 BB	*–5.361*	*–5.307*	*–5.869*	*–5.538*	*–8.028*	*–6.587*	*–5.999*	. . .
Other	3 205 BC	*–.782*	*–1.785*	*–2.372*	*–1.376*	*–.632*	*–.632*	*–.775*	. . .
Sea transport, passenger	3 207 . .	. . .	. . .	. . .	. . .	. . .	. . .	. . .	. . .
Sea transport, freight	3 208 . .	–5.361	–5.307	–5.869	–5.538	–8.028	–6.587	–5.999	. . .
Sea transport, other	3 209 . .	–.595	–.607	–.561	–.342	–.478	–.476	–.585	. . .
Air transport, passenger	3 211 . .	–2.639	–2.588	–3.907	–2.827	–3.494	–3.975	–3.760	. . .
Air transport, freight	3 212 . .	. . .	. . .	. . .	. . .	. . .	. . .	. . .	. . .
Air transport, other	3 213 . .	–.187	–1.177	–1.811	–1.034	–.154	–.156	–.190	. . .
Other transport, passenger	3 215 . .	. . .	. . .	. . .	. . .	. . .	. . .	. . .	. . .
Other transport, freight	3 216 . .	. . .	. . .	. . .	. . .	. . .	. . .	. . .	. . .
Other transport, other	3 217 . .	. . .	. . .	. . .	. . .	. . .	. . .	. . .	. . .
Travel, credit	2 236 . .	**.920**	**.876**	**1.009**	**.891**	**1.109**	**1.270**	**1.305**	. . .
Business travel	2 237 . .	. . .	. . .	. . .	. . .	. . .	. . .	. . .	. . .
Personal travel	2 240 . .	. . .	. . .	. . .	. . .	. . .	. . .	. . .	. . .
Travel, debit	3 236 . .	**–1.781**	**–1.733**	**–2.597**	**–2.409**	**–2.601**	**–2.691**	**–3.075**	. . .
Business travel	3 237 . .	. . .	. . .	. . .	. . .	. . .	. . .	. . .	. . .
Personal travel	3 240 . .	. . .	. . .	. . .	. . .	. . .	. . .	. . .	. . .
Other services, credit	2 200 BA	**2.424**	**3.135**	**3.773**	**10.089**	**10.393**	**10.329**	**14.201**	. . .
Communications	2 245 . .	.216	.262	.304	.418	.433	.406	.439	. . .
Construction	2 249 . .	. . .	. . .	. . .	. . .	. . .	. . .	. . .	. . .
Insurance	2 253 . .	. . .	. . .	. . .	. . .	. . .	. . .	. . .	. . .
Financial	2 260 . .	.123	.124	.123	.135	.142	.216	.219	. . .
Computer and information	2 262 . .	. . .	. . .	. . .	. . .	. . .	. . .	. . .	. . .
Royalties and licence fees	2 266 . .	1.729	2.328	3.102	9.283	9.552	9.607	13.433	. . .
Other business services	2 268 . .	. . .	. . .	. . .	. . .	. . .	. . .	. . .	. . .
Personal, cultural, and recreational	2 287 . .	. . .	. . .	. . .	. . .	. . .	. . .	. . .	. . .
Government, n.i.e.	2 291 . .	.355	.421	.244	.254	.266	.101	.110	. . .
Other services, debit	3 200 BA	**–3.532**	**–4.216**	**–3.932**	**–5.378**	**–4.414**	**–5.294**	**–3.620**	. . .
Communications	3 245 . .	–.398	–.550	–.471	–.322	–.634	–.475	–.585	. . .
Construction	3 249 . .	. . .	. . .	. . .	. . .	. . .	. . .	. . .	. . .
Insurance	3 253 . .	–.391	–.293	–.447	–.486	–.328	–.390	–.461	. . .
Financial	3 260 . .	–.398	–.210	–.672	–.675	–.514	–1.029	–1.112	. . .
Computer and information	3 262 . .	. . .	. . .	. . .	. . .	. . .	. . .	. . .	. . .
Royalties and licence fees	3 266 . .	. . .	. . .	. . .	. . .	. . .	. . .	. . .	. . .
Other business services	3 268 . .	. . .	. . .	. . .	. . .	. . .	. . .	. . .	. . .
Personal, cultural, and recreational	3 287 . .	. . .	. . .	. . .	. . .	. . .	. . .	. . .	. . .
Government, n.i.e.	3 291 . .	–2.344	–3.163	–2.342	–3.895	–2.938	–3.400	–1.462	. . .

Table 2 (Continued). STANDARD PRESENTATION, 1988–95
(Millions of U.S. dollars)

	Code	1988	1989	1990	1991	1992	1993	1994	1995
C. INCOME	4 300 . .	15.014	15.857	16.775	19.011	18.071	14.716	14.833	. . .
Total credit	2 300 . .	*15.743*	*16.888*	*19.247*	*20.555*	*19.294*	*16.398*	*17.053*	. . .
Total debit	3 300 . .	*–.729*	*–1.030*	*–2.472*	*–1.543*	*–1.224*	*–1.682*	*–2.220*	. . .
Compensation of employees, credit	2 310 . .	**2.266**	**2.451**	**2.576**	**3.661**	**3.452**	**3.468**	**4.021**	. . .
Compensation of employees, debit	3 310 . .	. . .	. . .	. . .	. . .	. . .	. . .	. . .	. . .
Investment income, credit	2 320 . .	**13.477**	**14.436**	**16.671**	**16.893**	**15.843**	**12.930**	**13.032**	. . .
Direct investment income	2 330 . .	. . .	. . .	. . .	. . .	. . .	. . .	.028	. . .
Dividends and distributed branch profits	2 332 . .	. . .	. . .	. . .	. . .	. . .	. . .	. . .	. . .
Reinvested earnings and undistributed branch profits	2 333 . .	. . .	. . .	. . .	. . .	. . .	. . .	.028	. . .
Income on debt (interest)	2 334 . .	. . .	. . .	. . .	. . .	. . .	. . .	. . .	. . .
Portfolio investment income	2 339 . .	13.477	14.436	16.671	16.893	15.843	12.930	13.004	. . .
Income on equity	2 340 . .	.353	1.031	1.485	1.941	2.519	2.141	2.121	. . .
Income on bonds and notes	2 350 . .	. . .	. . .	. . .	. . .	. . .	. . .	. . .	. . .
Income on money market instruments and financial derivatives	2 360 . .	. . .	. . .	. . .	. . .	. . .	. . .	. . .	. . .
Other investment income	2 370 . .	. . .	. . .	. . .	. . .	. . .	. . .	. . .	. . .
Investment income, debit	3 320 . .	**–.729**	**–1.030**	**–2.472**	**–1.543**	**–1.224**	**–1.682**	**–2.220**	. . .
Direct investment income	3 330 . .	–.729	–1.030	–2.472	–1.543	–1.224	–1.682	–2.220	. . .
Dividends and distributed branch profits	3 332 . .	–.466	–.848	–2.168	–1.072	–.734	–1.284	–1.701	. . .
Reinvested earnings and undistributed branch profits	3 333 . .	–.257	–.180	–.300	–.468	–.441	–.305	–.475	. . .
Income on debt (interest)	3 334 . .	–.005	–.002	–.005	–.003	–.048	–.093	–.043	. . .
Portfolio investment income	3 339 . .	. . .	. . .	. . .	. . .	. . .	. . .	. . .	. . .
Income on equity	3 340 . .	. . .	. . .	. . .	. . .	. . .	. . .	. . .	. . .
Income on bonds and notes	3 350 . .	. . .	. . .	. . .	. . .	. . .	. . .	. . .	. . .
Income on money market instruments and financial derivatives	3 360 . .	. . .	. . .	. . .	. . .	. . .	. . .	. . .	. . .
Other investment income	3 370 . .	. . .	. . .	. . .	. . .	. . .	. . .	. . .	. . .
D. CURRENT TRANSFERS	4 379 . .	8.852	9.890	9.282	12.843	10.106	10.882	7.346	. . .
Credit	2 379 . .	**10.842**	**12.118**	**11.145**	**15.106**	**12.443**	**12.911**	**8.954**	. . .
General government	2 380 . .	8.715	9.783	8.053	11.777	9.628	10.141	5.783	. . .
Other sectors	2 390 . .	2.127	2.336	3.093	3.329	2.815	2.770	3.171	. . .
Workers' remittances	2 391 . .	1.790	1.739	2.567	2.397	2.572	2.634	2.878	. . .
Other current transfers	2 392 . .	.337	.597	.525	.932	.243	.136	.292	. . .
Debit	3 379 . .	**–1.990**	**–2.228**	**–1.863**	**–2.263**	**–2.337**	**–2.028**	**–1.608**	. . .
General government	3 380 . .	–.506	–.805	–.536	–.705	–.721	–.804	–.877	. . .
Other sectors	3 390 . .	–1.484	–1.423	–1.327	–1.558	–1.616	–1.224	–.731	. . .
Workers' remittances	3 391 . .	–1.484	–1.423	–1.327	–1.558	–1.616	–1.224	–.731	. . .
Other current transfers	3 392 . .	. . .	. . .	. . .	. . .	. . .	. . .	. . .	. . .
CAPITAL AND FINANCIAL ACCOUNT	4 996 . .	**6.056**	**6.262**	**14.183**	**5.350**	**18.078**	**3.340**	**3.731**	. . .
CAPITAL ACCOUNT	4 994 . .	**6.688**	**6.559**	**12.469**	**6.127**	**16.404**	**5.713**	**2.543**	. . .
Total credit	2 994 . .	*6.688*	*6.559*	*12.469*	*6.127*	*16.404*	*5.713*	*2.543*	. . .
Total debit	3 994 . .	. . .	. . .	. . .	. . .	. . .	. . .	. . .	. . .
Capital transfers, credit	2 400 . .	**6.688**	**6.559**	**12.469**	**6.127**	**16.404**	**5.713**	**2.543**	. . .
General government	2 401 . .	6.688	6.559	12.469	6.127	16.404	5.713	2.543	. . .
Debt forgiveness	2 402 . .	. . .	. . .	. . .	. . .	. . .	. . .	. . .	. . .
Other capital transfers	2 410 . .	6.688	6.559	12.469	6.127	16.404	5.713	2.543	. . .
Other sectors	2 430 . .	. . .	. . .	. . .	. . .	. . .	. . .	. . .	. . .
Migrants' transfers	2 431 . .	. . .	. . .	. . .	. . .	. . .	. . .	. . .	. . .
Debt forgiveness	2 432 . .	. . .	. . .	. . .	. . .	. . .	. . .	. . .	. . .
Other capital transfers	2 440 . .	. . .	. . .	. . .	. . .	. . .	. . .	. . .	. . .
Capital transfers, debit	3 400 . .	. . .	. . .	. . .	. . .	. . .	. . .	. . .	. . .
General government	3 401 . .	. . .	. . .	. . .	. . .	. . .	. . .	. . .	. . .
Debt forgiveness	3 402 . .	. . .	. . .	. . .	. . .	. . .	. . .	. . .	. . .
Other capital transfers	3 410 . .	. . .	. . .	. . .	. . .	. . .	. . .	. . .	. . .
Other sectors	3 430 . .	. . .	. . .	. . .	. . .	. . .	. . .	. . .	. . .
Migrants' transfers	3 431 . .	. . .	. . .	. . .	. . .	. . .	. . .	. . .	. . .
Debt forgiveness	3 432 . .	. . .	. . .	. . .	. . .	. . .	. . .	. . .	. . .
Other capital transfers	3 440 . .	. . .	. . .	. . .	. . .	. . .	. . .	. . .	. . .
Nonproduced nonfinancial assets, credit	2 480 . .	. . .	. . .	. . .	. . .	. . .	. . .	. . .	. . .
Nonproduced nonfinancial assets, debit	3 480 . .	. . .	. . .	. . .	. . .	. . .	. . .	. . .	. . .

Table 2 (Continued). STANDARD PRESENTATION, 1988–95
(Millions of U.S. dollars)

	Code		1988	1989	1990	1991	1992	1993	1994	1995
FINANCIAL ACCOUNT	4 995	. .	**–.632**	**–.297**	**1.714**	**–.776**	**1.674**	**–2.373**	**1.188**	. . .
A. DIRECT INVESTMENT	4 500	. .	.257	.180	.300	.428	.407	–.770	.404	. . .
Direct investment abroad	4 505	. .	. . .	. . .	. . .	. . .	. . .	. . .	**–.028**	. . .
Equity capital	4 510	. .	. . .	. . .	. . .	. . .	. . .	. . .	. . .	. . .
Claims on affiliated enterprises	4 515	. .	. . .	. . .	. . .	. . .	. . .	. . .	. . .	. . .
Liabilities to affiliated enterprises	4 520	. .	. . .	. . .	. . .	. . .	. . .	. . .	. . .	. . .
Reinvested earnings	4 525	. .	. . .	. . .	. . .	. . .	. . .	. . .	. . .	. . .
Other capital	4 530	. .	. . .	. . .	. . .	. . .	. . .	. . .	–.028	. . .
Claims on affiliated enterprises	4 535	. .	. . .	. . .	. . .	. . .	. . .	. . .	. . .	. . .
Liabilities to affiliated enterprises	4 540	. .	. . .	. . .	. . .	. . .	. . .	. . .	. . .	. . .
Direct investment in Kiribati	4 555	. .	**.257**	**.180**	**.300**	**.428**	**.407**	**–.770**	**.431**	. . .
Equity capital	4 560	. .	. . .	. . .	. . .	–.041	–.035	–1.074	–.044	. . .
Claims on direct investors	4 565	. .	. . .	. . .	. . .	. . .	. . .	. . .	. . .	. . .
Liabilities to direct investors	4 570	. .	. . .	. . .	. . .	–.041	–.035	–1.074	–.044	. . .
Reinvested earnings	4 575	. .	.257	.180	.300	.468	.441	.305	.475	. . .
Other capital	4 580	. .	. . .	. . .	. . .	. . .	. . .	. . .	. . .	. . .
Claims on direct investors	4 585	. .	. . .	. . .	. . .	. . .	. . .	. . .	. . .	. . .
Liabilities to direct investors	4 590	. .	. . .	. . .	. . .	. . .	. . .	. . .	. . .	. . .
B. PORTFOLIO INVESTMENT	4 600	. .	–4.586	–6.401	–8.359	–13.062	–17.710	–6.691	–6.604	. . .
Assets	4 602	. .	**–4.586**	**–6.401**	**–8.359**	**–13.062**	**–17.710**	**–6.691**	**–6.604**	. . .
Equity securities	4 610	. .	. . .	. . .	. . .	. . .	. . .	. . .	. . .	. . .
Monetary authorities	4 611	. .	. . .	. . .	. . .	. . .	. . .	. . .	. . .	. . .
General government	4 612	. .	. . .	. . .	. . .	. . .	. . .	. . .	. . .	. . .
Banks	4 613	. .	. . .	. . .	. . .	. . .	. . .	. . .	. . .	. . .
Other sectors	4 614	. .	. . .	. . .	. . .	. . .	. . .	. . .	. . .	. . .
Debt securities	4 619	. .	–4.586	–6.401	–8.359	–13.062	–17.710	–6.691	–6.604	. . .
Bonds and notes	4 620	. .	–4.586	–6.401	–8.359	–13.062	–17.710	–6.691	–6.604	. . .
Monetary authorities	4 621	. .	. . .	. . .	. . .	. . .	. . .	. . .	. . .	. . .
General government	4 622	. .	–4.586	–6.401	–8.359	–13.062	–17.710	–6.691	–6.604	. . .
Banks	4 623	. .	. . .	. . .	. . .	. . .	. . .	. . .	. . .	. . .
Other sectors	4 624	. .	. . .	. . .	. . .	. . .	. . .	. . .	. . .	. . .
Money market instruments	4 630	. .	. . .	. . .	. . .	. . .	. . .	. . .	. . .	. . .
Monetary authorities	4 631	. .	. . .	. . .	. . .	. . .	. . .	. . .	. . .	. . .
General government	4 632	. .	. . .	. . .	. . .	. . .	. . .	. . .	. . .	. . .
Banks	4 633	. .	. . .	. . .	. . .	. . .	. . .	. . .	. . .	. . .
Other sectors	4 634	. .	. . .	. . .	. . .	. . .	. . .	. . .	. . .	. . .
Financial derivatives	4 640	. .	. . .	. . .	. . .	. . .	. . .	. . .	. . .	. . .
Monetary authorities	4 641	. .	. . .	. . .	. . .	. . .	. . .	. . .	. . .	. . .
General government	4 642	. .	. . .	. . .	. . .	. . .	. . .	. . .	. . .	. . .
Banks	4 643	. .	. . .	. . .	. . .	. . .	. . .	. . .	. . .	. . .
Other sectors	4 644	. .	. . .	. . .	. . .	. . .	. . .	. . .	. . .	. . .
Liabilities	4 652	. .	. . .	. . .	. . .	. . .	. . .	. . .	. . .	. . .
Equity securities	4 660	. .	. . .	. . .	. . .	. . .	. . .	. . .	. . .	. . .
Banks	4 663	. .	. . .	. . .	. . .	. . .	. . .	. . .	. . .	. . .
Other sectors	4 664	. .	. . .	. . .	. . .	. . .	. . .	. . .	. . .	. . .
Debt securities	4 669	. .	. . .	. . .	. . .	. . .	. . .	. . .	. . .	. . .
Bonds and notes	4 670	. .	. . .	. . .	. . .	. . .	. . .	. . .	. . .	. . .
Monetary authorities	4 671	. .	. . .	. . .	. . .	. . .	. . .	. . .	. . .	. . .
General government	4 672	. .	. . .	. . .	. . .	. . .	. . .	. . .	. . .	. . .
Banks	4 673	. .	. . .	. . .	. . .	. . .	. . .	. . .	. . .	. . .
Other sectors	4 674	. .	. . .	. . .	. . .	. . .	. . .	. . .	. . .	. . .
Money market instruments	4 680	. .	. . .	. . .	. . .	. . .	. . .	. . .	. . .	. . .
Monetary authorities	4 681	. .	. . .	. . .	. . .	. . .	. . .	. . .	. . .	. . .
General government	4 682	. .	. . .	. . .	. . .	. . .	. . .	. . .	. . .	. . .
Banks	4 683	. .	. . .	. . .	. . .	. . .	. . .	. . .	. . .	. . .
Other sectors	4 684	. .	. . .	. . .	. . .	. . .	. . .	. . .	. . .	. . .
Financial derivatives	4 690	. .	. . .	. . .	. . .	. . .	. . .	. . .	. . .	. . .
Monetary authorities	4 691	. .	. . .	. . .	. . .	. . .	. . .	. . .	. . .	. . .
General government	4 692	. .	. . .	. . .	. . .	. . .	. . .	. . .	. . .	. . .
Banks	4 693	. .	. . .	. . .	. . .	. . .	. . .	. . .	. . .	. . .
Other sectors	4 694	. .	. . .	. . .	. . .	. . .	. . .	. . .	. . .	. . .

Table 2 (Concluded). STANDARD PRESENTATION, 1988–95
(Millions of U.S. dollars)

	Code	1988	1989	1990	1991	1992	1993	1994	1995
C. OTHER INVESTMENT	4 700	.738	.805	3.026	.825	2.365	...	1.414	...
Assets	4 703	...	...	...	...	...	...	...	...
Trade credits	4 706	...	...	...	...	...	...	...	...
General government: long-term	4 708	...	...	...	...	...	...	...	...
General government: short-term	4 709	...	...	...	...	...	...	...	...
Other sectors: long-term	4 711	...	...	...	...	...	...	...	...
Other sectors: short-term	4 712	...	...	...	...	...	...	...	...
Loans	4 714	...	...	...	...	...	...	...	...
Monetary authorities: long-term	4 717	...	...	...	...	...	...	...	...
Monetary authorities: short-term	4 718	...	...	...	...	...	...	...	...
General government: long-term	4 720	...	...	...	...	...	...	...	...
General government: short-term	4 721	...	...	...	...	...	...	...	...
Banks: long-term	4 723	...	...	...	...	...	...	...	...
Banks: short-term	4 724	...	...	...	...	...	...	...	...
Other sectors: long-term	4 726	...	...	...	...	...	...	...	...
Other sectors: short-term	4 727	...	...	...	...	...	...	...	...
Currency and deposits	4 730	...	...	...	...	...	...	...	...
Monetary authorities	4 731	...	...	...	...	...	...	...	...
General government	4 732	...	...	...	...	...	...	...	...
Banks	4 733	...	...	...	...	...	...	...	...
Other sectors	4 734	...	...	...	...	...	...	...	...
Other assets	4 736	...	...	...	...	...	...	...	...
Monetary authorities: long-term	4 738	...	...	...	...	...	...	...	...
Monetary authorities: short-term	4 739	...	...	...	...	...	...	...	...
General government: long-term	4 741	...	...	...	...	...	...	...	...
General government: short-term	4 742	...	...	...	...	...	...	...	...
Banks: long-term	4 744	...	...	...	...	...	...	...	...
Banks: short-term	4 745	...	...	...	...	...	...	...	...
Other sectors: long-term	4 747	...	...	...	...	...	...	...	...
Other sectors: short-term	4 748	...	...	...	...	...	...	...	...
Liabilities	4 753	**.738**	**.805**	**3.026**	**.825**	**2.365**	...	**1.414**	...
Trade credits	4 756	...	...	...	...	...	...	...	...
General government: long-term	4 758	...	...	...	...	...	...	...	...
General government: short-term	4 759	...	...	...	...	...	...	...	...
Other sectors: long-term	4 761	...	...	...	...	...	...	...	...
Other sectors: short-term	4 762	...	...	...	...	...	...	...	...
Loans	4 764	.738	.805	3.026	.825	2.365	...	1.414	...
Use of Fund credit and loans from the Fund	4 766	...	...	...	...	...	...	...	...
Monetary authorities: other long-term	4 767	...	...	...	...	...	...	...	...
Monetary authorities: short-term	4 768	...	...	...	...	...	...	...	...
General government: long-term	4 770	.738	.805	3.026	.825	2.365	...	1.414	...
General government: short-term	4 771	...	...	...	...	...	...	...	...
Banks: long-term	4 773	...	...	...	...	...	...	...	...
Banks: short-term	4 774	...	...	...	...	...	...	...	...
Other sectors: long-term	4 776	...	...	...	...	...	...	...	...
Other sectors: short-term	4 777	...	...	...	...	...	...	...	...
Currency and deposits	4 780	...	...	...	...	...	...	...	...
Monetary authorities	4 781	...	...	...	...	...	...	...	...
General government	4 782	...	...	...	...	...	...	...	...
Banks	4 783	...	...	...	...	...	...	...	...
Other sectors	4 784	...	...	...	...	...	...	...	...
Other liabilities	4 786	...	...	...	...	...	...	...	...
Monetary authorities: long-term	4 788	...	...	...	...	...	...	...	...
Monetary authorities: short-term	4 789	...	...	...	...	...	...	...	...
General government: long-term	4 791	...	...	...	...	...	...	...	...
General government: short-term	4 792	...	...	...	...	...	...	...	...
Banks: long-term	4 794	...	...	...	...	...	...	...	...
Banks: short-term	4 795	...	...	...	...	...	...	...	...
Other sectors: long-term	4 797	...	...	...	...	...	...	...	...
Other sectors: short-term	4 798	...	...	...	...	...	...	...	...
D. RESERVE ASSETS	4 800	2.960	5.119	6.747	11.033	16.612	5.087	5.974	...
Monetary gold	4 810	...	...	...	...	...	...	...	...
Special drawing rights	4 820	...	...	–.013	...	...	.004	...	...
Reserve position in the Fund	4 830	...	...	...	...	...	...	...	...
Foreign exchange	4 840	2.960	5.119	6.760	11.033	16.612	5.083	5.973	...
Other claims	4 880	...	...	...	...	...	...	...	...
NET ERRORS AND OMISSIONS	4 998	**–4.220**	**–4.725**	**–4.996**	**–9.637**	**–8.984**	**.766**	**–5.113**	...

Table 1. ANALYTIC PRESENTATION, 1988–95
(Millions of U.S. dollars)

	Code	1988	1989	1990	1991	1992	1993	1994	1995
A. Current Account [1]	4 993 Y.	**14,538**	**5,387**	**–1,745**	**–8,291**	**–3,939**	**1,016**	**–3,855**	**–8,251**
Goods: exports f.o.b.	2 100 . .	59,648	61,408	63,123	69,581	75,169	80,950	93,676	123,203
Goods: imports f.o.b.	3 100 . .	–48,203	–56,811	–65,127	–76,561	–77,315	–79,090	–96,822	–127,949
Balance on Goods	4 100 . .	*11,445*	*4,597*	*–2,004*	*–6,980*	*–2,146*	*1,860*	*–3,146*	*–4,746*
Services: credit	2 200 . .	9,707	10,347	11,208	12,221	12,750	15,545	19,814	26,243
Services: debit	3 200 . .	–6,888	–9,452	–11,268	–13,422	–14,823	–16,714	–20,529	–27,885
Balance on Goods and Services	4 991 . .	*14,264*	*5,492*	*–2,064*	*–8,181*	*–4,219*	*691*	*–3,861*	*–6,388*
Income: credit	2 300 . .	1,029	1,680	2,079	2,068	1,782	1,564	1,671	2,380
Income: debit	3 300 . .	–3,048	–2,945	–2,956	–3,021	–2,777	–2,810	–3,225	–4,656
Balance on Goods, Services, and Income	4 992 . .	*12,245*	*4,227*	*–2,941*	*–9,134*	*–5,214*	*–555*	*–5,415*	*–8,664*
Current transfers: credit	2 379 Y.	2,538	2,103	2,439	2,794	3,358	3,644	3,937	4,315
Current transfers: debit	3 379 . .	–245	–943	–1,243	–1,951	–2,083	–2,073	–2,377	–3,902
B. Capital Account [1]	4 994 Y.	**–353**	**–318**	**–331**	**–328**	**–407**	**–475**	**–437**	**–487**
Capital account: credit	2 994 Y.	6	9	7	7	5	2	8	15
Capital account: debit	3 994 . .	–359	–327	–338	–335	–412	–477	–445	–502
Total, Groups A Plus B	4 010 . .	*14,185*	*5,069*	*–2,076*	*–8,619*	*–4,346*	*541*	*–4,292*	*–8,738*
C. Financial Account [1]	4 995 X.	**–4,279**	**–2,640**	**2,866**	**6,714**	**6,969**	**3,188**	**10,610**	**17,221**
Direct investment abroad	4 505 . .	–643	–613	–1,056	–1,500	–1,208	–1,361	–2,524	–3,529
Direct investment in Korea	4 555 Y.	1,014	1,118	788	1,180	727	588	809	1,776
Portfolio investment assets	4 602 . .	–37	–66	240	492	845	232	–230	–311
Equity securities	4 610 . .	–18	–46	–70	–30	–15	–238	–376	–318
Debt securities	4 619 . .	–19	–20	310	522	860	470	146	7
Portfolio investment liabilities	4 652 Y.	–606	–2	82	2,442	4,857	10,298	7,097	11,136
Equity securities	4 660 Y.	29	30	380	. . .	2,478	6,586	3,648	4,836
Debt securities	4 669 Y.	–635	–32	–298	2,442	2,379	3,712	3,449	6,300
Other investment assets	4 703 . .	–1,958	–1,382	–2,330	–6,378	–2,515	–4,224	–7,627	–13,084
Monetary authorities	4 703 .A	–29	–16	–44	–23	–23	–27	–27	–24
General government	4 703 .B	. . .	–133	14	–962	–163	–509	–336	–328
Banks	4 703 .C	–2,007	–253	–2,282	–5,821	–3,137	–4,135	–6,250	–10,712
Other sectors	4 703 .D	78	–980	–18	428	808	447	–1,014	–2,020
Other investment liabilities	4 753 X.	–2,049	–1,695	5,142	10,478	4,263	–2,345	13,085	21,233
Monetary authorities	4 753 XA	19	9	22	2	7	15	–1	–10
General government	4 753 YB	–2,769	–1,944	–901	–52	–638	–2,726	–157	10
Banks	4 753 YC	–799	634	1,980	8,315	1,706	751	7,832	12,249
Other sectors	4 753 YD	1,500	–394	4,041	2,213	3,188	–385	5,411	8,984
Total, Groups A Through C	4 020 . .	*9,906*	*2,429*	*790*	*–1,905*	*2,623*	*3,729*	*6,318*	*8,483*
D. Net Errors and Omissions	4 998 . .	**–590**	**691**	**–1,998**	**757**	**1,101**	**–720**	**–1,704**	**–1,443**
Total, Groups A Through D	4 030 . .	*9,316*	*3,120*	*–1,208*	*–1,148*	*3,724*	*3,009*	*4,614*	*7,040*
E. Reserves and Related Items	4 040 . .	**–9,316**	**–3,120**	**1,208**	**1,148**	**–3,724**	**–3,009**	**–4,614**	**–7,040**
Reserve assets	4 800 . .	–8,826	–3,120	1,208	1,148	–3,724	–3,009	–4,614	–7,040
Use of Fund credit and loans	4 766 . .	–490	. . .	. . .	. . .	. . .	. . .	. . .	. . .
Liabilities constituting foreign authorities' reserves	4 900 . .	. . .	. . .	. . .	. . .	. . .	. . .	. . .	. . .
Exceptional financing	4 920 . .	. . .	. . .	. . .	. . .	. . .	. . .	. . .	. . .
Conversion rates: won per U.S. dollar	0 101 . .	**731.47**	**671.46**	**707.76**	**733.35**	**780.65**	**802.67**	**803.45**	**771.27**

[1] Excludes components that have been classified in the categories of Group E.

Table 2. STANDARD PRESENTATION, 1988–95
(Millions of U.S. dollars)

	Code			1988	1989	1990	1991	1992	1993	1994	1995
CURRENT ACCOUNT	4	993	..	**14,538**	**5,387**	**–1,745**	**–8,291**	**–3,939**	**1,016**	**–3,855**	**–8,251**
A. GOODS	4	100	..	11,445	4,597	–2,004	–6,980	–2,146	1,860	–3,146	–4,746
Credit	2	100	..	**59,648**	**61,408**	**63,123**	**69,581**	**75,169**	**80,950**	**93,676**	**123,203**
General merchandise: exports f.o.b.	2	110	..	59,648	61,408	63,123	69,581	75,169	80,950	93,676	123,203
Goods for processing: exports f.o.b.	2	150	..	...	...	...	...	...	...	...	...
Repairs on goods	2	160	..	...	...	...	...	...	...	...	...
Goods procured in ports by carriers	2	170	..	...	...	...	...	...	...	...	...
Nonmonetary gold	2	180	..	...	...	...	...	...	...	...	...
Debit	3	100	..	**–48,203**	**–56,811**	**–65,127**	**–76,561**	**–77,315**	**–79,090**	**–96,822**	**–127,949**
General merchandise: imports f.o.b.	3	110	..	–48,203	–56,811	–65,127	–76,561	–77,315	–79,090	–96,822	–127,949
Goods for processing: imports f.o.b.	3	150	..	...	...	...	...	...	...	...	...
Repairs on goods	3	160	..	...	...	...	...	...	...	...	...
Goods procured in ports by carriers	3	170	..	...	...	...	...	...	...	...	...
Nonmonetary gold	3	180	..	...	...	...	...	...	...	...	...
B. SERVICES	4	200	..	2,819	895	–60	–1,201	–2,073	–1,169	–715	–1,642
Total credit	2	200	..	*9,707*	*10,347*	*11,208*	*12,221*	*12,750*	*15,545*	*19,814*	*26,243*
Total debit	3	200	..	*–6,888*	*–9,452*	*–11,268*	*–13,422*	*–14,823*	*–16,714*	*–20,529*	*–27,885*
Transportation services, credit	2	205	..	**2,951**	**3,430**	**3,702**	**4,440**	**5,029**	**6,134**	**8,106**	**10,578**
Passenger	2	205	BA	*707*	*818*	*849*	*933*	*992*	*1,179*	*1,317*	*1,520*
Freight	2	205	BB	*2,017*	*2,274*	*2,379*	*2,943*	*3,267*	*3,993*	*5,334*	*7,014*
Other	2	205	BC	*227*	*338*	*474*	*564*	*770*	*962*	*1,455*	*2,044*
Sea transport, passenger	2	207	..	...	...	...	...	...	...	...	...
Sea transport, freight	2	208	..	...	...	...	...	...	...	...	...
Sea transport, other	2	209	..	...	...	...	...	...	...	...	...
Air transport, passenger	2	211	..	...	...	...	...	...	...	...	...
Air transport, freight	2	212	..	...	...	...	...	...	...	...	...
Air transport, other	2	213	..	...	...	...	...	...	...	...	...
Other transport, passenger	2	215	..	...	...	...	...	...	...	...	...
Other transport, freight	2	216	..	...	...	...	...	...	...	...	...
Other transport, other	2	217	..	...	...	...	...	...	...	...	...
Transportation services, debit	3	205	..	**–3,094**	**–3,718**	**–4,499**	**–5,465**	**–6,041**	**–6,777**	**–7,866**	**–10,653**
Passenger	3	205	BA	*–182*	*–231*	*–352*	*–490*	*–473*	*–389*	*–452*	*–606*
Freight	3	205	BB	*–1,219*	*–1,497*	*–1,813*	*–2,335*	*–2,199*	*–2,381*	*–2,892*	*–4,645*
Other	3	205	BC	*–1,693*	*–1,990*	*–2,334*	*–2,640*	*–3,369*	*–4,007*	*–4,522*	*–5,402*
Sea transport, passenger	3	207	..	...	...	...	...	...	...	...	...
Sea transport, freight	3	208	..	...	...	...	...	...	...	...	...
Sea transport, other	3	209	..	...	...	...	...	...	...	...	...
Air transport, passenger	3	211	..	...	...	...	...	...	...	...	...
Air transport, freight	3	212	..	...	...	...	...	...	...	...	...
Air transport, other	3	213	..	...	...	...	...	...	...	...	...
Other transport, passenger	3	215	..	...	...	...	...	...	...	...	...
Other transport, freight	3	216	..	...	...	...	...	...	...	...	...
Other transport, other	3	217	..	...	...	...	...	...	...	...	...
Travel, credit	2	236	..	**3,116**	**3,311**	**3,161**	**2,856**	**2,690**	**2,964**	**3,340**	**5,150**
Business travel	2	237	..	...	...	...	...	...	...	...	...
Personal travel	2	240	..	...	...	...	...	...	...	...	...
Travel, debit	3	236	..	**–1,205**	**–2,356**	**–2,768**	**–3,214**	**–3,213**	**–3,533**	**–4,513**	**–6,341**
Business travel	3	237	..	...	...	...	...	...	...	...	...
Personal travel	3	240	..	...	...	...	...	...	...	...	...
Other services, credit	2	200	BA	**3,640**	**3,606**	**4,345**	**4,925**	**5,031**	**6,447**	**8,368**	**10,515**
Communications	2	245	..	457	213	284	217	209	189	178	186
Construction	2	249	..	360	239	353	306	196	406	757	576
Insurance	2	253	..	275	316	404	470	379	468	445	538
Financial	2	260	..	1	...	1	2	23	63	92	105
Computer and information	2	262	..	3	4	3	5	5	7	7	5
Royalties and licence fees	2	266	..	42	23	37	61	105	129	155	299
Other business services	2	268	..	1,537	1,760	2,302	3,090	3,464	4,299	5,736	7,665
Personal, cultural, and recreational	2	287	..	...	...	...	...	...	...	...	...
Government, n.i.e.	2	291	..	965	1,051	961	774	650	886	998	1,141
Other services, debit	3	200	BA	**–2,589**	**–3,378**	**–4,001**	**–4,743**	**–5,569**	**–6,404**	**–8,150**	**–10,891**
Communications	3	245	..	–17	–28	–50	–66	–92	–136	–213	–212
Construction	3	249	..	...	...	...	...	...	...	...	...
Insurance	3	253	..	–286	–278	–325	–440	–492	–549	–578	–824
Financial	3	260	..	–10	–5	–7	–5	–13	–18	–17	–31
Computer and information	3	262	..	–36	–43	–50	–58	–63	–64	–73	–94
Royalties and licence fees	3	266	..	–82	–112	–136	–158	–163	–141	–172	–2,385
Other business services	3	268	..	–1,953	–2,634	–3,194	–3,706	–4,354	–5,098	–6,680	–6,835
Personal, cultural, and recreational	3	287	..	–17	–14	–19	–35	–49	–44	–57	–98
Government, n.i.e.	3	291	..	–188	–264	–220	–275	–343	–354	–360	–412

Table 2 (Continued). STANDARD PRESENTATION, 1988–95
(Millions of U.S. dollars)

	Code	1988	1989	1990	1991	1992	1993	1994	1995
C. INCOME	4 300	–2,019	–1,265	–877	–953	–995	–1,246	–1,554	–2,276
Total credit	2 300	*1,029*	*1,680*	*2,079*	*2,068*	*1,782*	*1,564*	*1,671*	*2,380*
Total debit	3 300	*–3,048*	*–2,945*	*–2,956*	*–3,021*	*–2,777*	*–2,810*	*–3,225*	*–4,656*
Compensation of employees, credit	2 310	...	...	...	...	...	...	...	...
Compensation of employees, debit	3 310	...	...	...	...	...	...	...	...
Investment income, credit	2 320	**1,029**	**1,680**	**2,079**	**2,068**	**1,782**	**1,564**	**1,671**	**2,380**
Direct investment income	2 330	129	130	121	148	227	138	182	238
Dividends and distributed branch profits	2 332	129	130	100	148	227	138	182	238
Reinvested earnings and undistributed branch profits	2 333	...	...	21	...	...	...	...	...
Income on debt (interest)	2 334	...	...	...	...	...	...	...	...
Portfolio investment income	2 339	...	...	...	704	632	640	758	999
Income on equity	2 340	...	...	...	...	...	...	...	...
Income on bonds and notes	2 350	...	...	...	704	632	640	758	999
Income on money market instruments and financial derivatives	2 360	...	...	...	...	...	...	...	...
Other investment income	2 370	900	1,550	1,958	1,216	923	786	731	1,143
Investment income, debit	3 320	**–3,048**	**–2,945**	**–2,956**	**–3,021**	**–2,777**	**–2,810**	**–3,225**	**–4,656**
Direct investment income	3 330	–179	–222	–266	–296	–247	–253	–353	–480
Dividends and distributed branch profits	3 332	–179	–208	–250	–279	–232	–239	–326	–471
Reinvested earnings and undistributed branch profits	3 333	...	–14	–16	–17	–15	–14	–27	–9
Income on debt (interest)	3 334	...	...	...	...	...	...	...	...
Portfolio investment income	3 339	–21	–23	–35	–289	–337	–507	–670	–900
Income on equity	3 340	...	...	...	...	...	...	...	...
Income on bonds and notes	3 350	...	...	...	–263	–310	–497	–659	–838
Income on money market instruments and financial derivatives	3 360	–21	–23	–35	–26	–27	–10	–11	–62
Other investment income	3 370	–2,848	–2,700	–2,655	–2,436	–2,193	–2,050	–2,202	–3,276
D. CURRENT TRANSFERS	4 379	2,293	1,160	1,196	843	1,275	1,571	1,560	413
Credit	2 379	**2,538**	**2,103**	**2,439**	**2,794**	**3,358**	**3,644**	**3,937**	**4,315**
General government	2 380	44	48	76	51	69	101	90	90
Other sectors	2 390	2,494	2,055	2,363	2,743	3,289	3,543	3,847	4,225
Workers' remittances	2 391	517	615	616	722	705	696	615	618
Other current transfers	2 392	1,977	1,440	1,747	2,021	2,584	2,847	3,232	3,607
Debit	3 379	**–245**	**–943**	**–1,243**	**–1,951**	**–2,083**	**–2,073**	**–2,377**	**–3,902**
General government	3 380	...	...	–67	–224	–94	–243	–318	–348
Other sectors	3 390	–245	–943	–1,176	–1,727	–1,989	–1,830	–2,059	–3,554
Workers' remittances	3 391	–25	–21	–26	–54	–69	–91	–96	–132
Other current transfers	3 392	–220	–922	–1,150	–1,673	–1,920	–1,739	–1,963	–3,422
CAPITAL AND FINANCIAL ACCOUNT	4 996	**–13,948**	**–6,078**	**3,743**	**7,534**	**2,838**	**–296**	**5,559**	**9,694**
CAPITAL ACCOUNT	4 994	**–353**	**–318**	**–331**	**–328**	**–407**	**–475**	**–437**	**–487**
Total credit	2 994	*6*	*9*	*7*	*7*	*5*	*2*	*8*	*15*
Total debit	3 994	*–359*	*–327*	*–338*	*–335*	*–412*	*–477*	*–445*	*–502*
Capital transfers, credit	2 400	**6**	**9**	**7**	**7**	**5**	**2**	**8**	**15**
General government	2 401	...	...	...	...	...	...	...	...
Debt forgiveness	2 402	...	...	...	...	...	...	...	...
Other capital transfers	2 410	...	...	...	...	...	...	...	...
Other sectors	2 430	6	9	7	7	5	2	8	15
Migrants' transfers	2 431	6	9	7	7	5	2	8	15
Debt forgiveness	2 432	...	...	...	...	...	...	...	...
Other capital transfers	2 440	...	...	...	...	...	...	...	...
Capital transfers, debit	3 400	**–359**	**–327**	**–338**	**–335**	**–412**	**–477**	**–445**	**–502**
General government	3 401	...	...	...	...	...	...	...	...
Debt forgiveness	3 402	...	...	...	...	...	...	...	...
Other capital transfers	3 410	...	...	...	...	...	...	...	...
Other sectors	3 430	–359	–327	–338	–335	–412	–477	–445	–502
Migrants' transfers	3 431	–359	–327	–338	–335	–412	–477	–445	–502
Debt forgiveness	3 432	...	...	...	...	...	...	...	...
Other capital transfers	3 440	...	...	...	...	...	...	...	...
Nonproduced nonfinancial assets, credit	2 480	...	...	...	...	...	...	...	...
Nonproduced nonfinancial assets, debit	3 480	...	...	...	...	...	...	...	...

Table 2 (Continued). STANDARD PRESENTATION, 1988–95
(Millions of U.S. dollars)

	Code	1988	1989	1990	1991	1992	1993	1994	1995
FINANCIAL ACCOUNT	4 995	**–13,595**	**–5,760**	**4,074**	**7,862**	**3,245**	**179**	**5,996**	**10,181**
A. DIRECT INVESTMENT	4 500	371	505	–268	–320	–481	–773	–1,715	–1,753
Direct investment abroad	4 505	**–643**	**–613**	**–1,056**	**–1,500**	**–1,208**	**–1,361**	**–2,524**	**–3,529**
Equity capital	4 510	–197	–356	–934	–1,427	–1,168	–1,349	–2,466	–3,446
Claims on affiliated enterprises	4 515	...	...	...	...	...	...	...	...
Liabilities to affiliated enterprises	4 520	...	...	...	...	...	...	...	...
Reinvested earnings	4 525	...	...	–21	...	...	...	...	...
Other capital	4 530	–446	–257	–101	–73	–40	–12	–58	–83
Claims on affiliated enterprises	4 535	...	...	...	...	...	...	...	...
Liabilities to affiliated enterprises	4 540	...	...	...	...	...	...	...	...
Direct investment in Korea	4 555	**1,014**	**1,118**	**788**	**1,180**	**727**	**588**	**809**	**1,776**
Equity capital	4 560	1,014	1,104	772	1,163	712	574	782	1,767
Claims on direct investors	4 565	...	...	...	...	...	...	...	...
Liabilities to direct investors	4 570	...	...	...	...	...	...	...	...
Reinvested earnings	4 575	...	14	16	17	15	14	27	9
Other capital	4 580	...	...	...	...	...	...	...	...
Claims on direct investors	4 585	...	...	...	...	...	...	...	...
Liabilities to direct investors	4 590	...	...	...	...	...	...	...	...
B. PORTFOLIO INVESTMENT	4 600	–643	–68	322	2,934	5,702	10,530	6,867	10,825
Assets	4 602	**–37**	**–66**	**240**	**492**	**845**	**232**	**–230**	**–311**
Equity securities	4 610	–18	–46	–70	–30	–15	–238	–376	–318
Monetary authorities	4 611	...	...	...	...	...	...	...	...
General government	4 612	...	...	...	...	...	...	...	...
Banks	4 613	...	...	...	...	...	...	...	...
Other sectors	4 614	...	...	...	...	...	...	...	...
Debt securities	4 619	–19	–20	310	522	860	470	146	7
Bonds and notes	4 620	–19	–20	–56	3	87	22	–306	–616
Monetary authorities	4 621	...	...	...	...	...	...	...	...
General government	4 622	...	...	...	...	...	...	...	...
Banks	4 623	...	...	...	...	...	...	...	...
Other sectors	4 624	...	...	...	...	...	...	...	...
Money market instruments	4 630	...	...	...	...	...	...	...	...
Monetary authorities	4 631	...	...	...	...	...	...	...	...
General government	4 632	...	...	...	...	...	...	...	...
Banks	4 633	...	...	...	...	...	...	...	...
Other sectors	4 634	...	...	...	...	...	...	...	...
Financial derivatives	4 640	...	...	366	519	773	448	452	623
Monetary authorities	4 641	...	...	...	...	...	...	...	...
General government	4 642	...	...	...	...	...	...	...	...
Banks	4 643	...	...	...	...	...	...	...	...
Other sectors	4 644	...	...	...	...	...	...	...	...
Liabilities	4 652	**–606**	**–2**	**82**	**2,442**	**4,857**	**10,298**	**7,097**	**11,136**
Equity securities	4 660	29	30	380	...	2,478	6,586	3,648	4,836
Banks	4 663	...	...	...	...	...	...	...	...
Other sectors	4 664	...	...	...	...	...	...	...	...
Debt securities	4 669	–635	–32	–298	2,442	2,379	3,712	3,449	6,300
Bonds and notes	4 670	–617	–31	143	3,000	3,301	4,253	4,014	7,046
Monetary authorities	4 671	...	...	...	...	...	...	...	...
General government	4 672	–516	–14	299	1,853	2,623	3,496	2,971	2,896
Banks	4 673	–192	–37	–594	47	56	–159	234	2,123
Other sectors	4 674	91	20	438	1,100	622	916	809	2,027
Money market instruments	4 680	–18	–1	3	10	–1	–6	...	–2
Monetary authorities	4 681	...	...	...	...	...	...	...	...
General government	4 682	...	...	...	...	...	...	...	...
Banks	4 683	...	...	...	...	...	...	...	...
Other sectors	4 684	–18	–1	3	10	–1	–6	...	–2
Financial derivatives	4 690	...	...	–444	–568	–921	–535	–565	–744
Monetary authorities	4 691	...	...	...	...	...	...	...	...
General government	4 692	...	...	...	...	...	...	...	...
Banks	4 693	...	...	...	...	...	...	...	...
Other sectors	4 694	...	...	...	...	...	...	...	...

Table 2 (Concluded). STANDARD PRESENTATION, 1988–95

(Millions of U.S. dollars)

	Code	1988	1989	1990	1991	1992	1993	1994	1995
C. OTHER INVESTMENT	4 700 . .	–4,497	–3,077	2,812	4,100	1,748	–6,569	5,458	8,149
Assets	4 703 . .	**–1,958**	**–1,382**	**–2,330**	**–6,378**	**–2,515**	**–4,224**	**–7,627**	**–13,084**
Trade credits	4 706 . .	271	–726	302	503	1,744	732	–130	–1,011
General government: long-term	4 708 . .	. . .	. . .	. . .	. . .	. . .	. . .	. . .	. . .
General government: short-term	4 709 . .	. . .	. . .	. . .	. . .	. . .	. . .	. . .	. . .
Other sectors: long-term	4 711 . .	267	–709	332	595	1,757	804	–51	–843
Other sectors: short-term	4 712 . .	4	–17	–30	–92	–13	–72	–79	–168
Loans	4 714 . .	4	–77	–42	–627	–91	42	–92	–281
Monetary authorities: long-term	4 717 . .	. . .	. . .	. . .	. . .	. . .	. . .	. . .	. . .
Monetary authorities: short-term	4 718 . .	. . .	. . .	. . .	. . .	. . .	. . .	. . .	. . .
General government: long-term	4 720 . .	. . .	–53	–44	–625	34	46	–78	–216
General government: short-term	4 721 . .	. . .	. . .	. . .	. . .	. . .	. . .	. . .	. . .
Banks: long-term	4 723 . .	. . .	–18	. . .	. . .	–127	–18	–14	–65
Banks: short-term	4 724 . .	. . .	. . .	. . .	. . .	. . .	. . .	. . .	. . .
Other sectors: long-term	4 726 . .	4	–6	2	–2	2	14	. . .	. . .
Other sectors: short-term	4 727 . .	. . .	. . .	. . .	. . .	. . .	. . .	. . .	. . .
Currency and deposits	4 730 . .	–4	–98	59	–410	–1,135	–656	–1,013	–1,085
Monetary authorities	4 731 . .	. . .	. . .	. . .	. . .	. . .	. . .	. . .	. . .
General government	4 732 . .	. . .	–80	58	–337	–197	–555	–258	–112
Banks	4 733 . .	. . .	. . .	. . .	. . .	. . .	. . .	. . .	. . .
Other sectors	4 734 . .	–4	–18	1	–73	–938	–101	–755	–973
Other assets	4 736 . .	–2,229	–481	–2,649	–5,844	–3,033	–4,342	–6,392	–10,707
Monetary authorities: long-term	4 738 . .	–29	–16	–44	–23	–23	–27	–27	–24
Monetary authorities: short-term	4 739 . .	. . .	. . .	. . .	. . .	. . .	. . .	. . .	. . .
General government: long-term	4 741 . .	. . .	. . .	. . .	. . .	. . .	. . .	. . .	. . .
General government: short-term	4 742 . .	. . .	. . .	. . .	. . .	. . .	. . .	. . .	. . .
Banks: long-term	4 744 . .	–106	–996	–1,377	–4,900	–918	–809	–1,681	–4,480
Banks: short-term	4 745 . .	–1,901	761	–905	–921	–2,092	–3,308	–4,555	–6,167
Other sectors: long-term	4 747 . .	. . .	. . .	. . .	. . .	. . .	. . .	. . .	. . .
Other sectors: short-term	4 748 . .	–193	–230	–323	. . .	. . .	–198	–129	–36
Liabilities	4 753 . .	**–2,539**	**–1,695**	**5,142**	**10,478**	**4,263**	**–2,345**	**13,085**	**21,233**
Trade credits	4 756 . .	1,352	470	3,441	1,255	2,127	–1,693	2,857	4,142
General government: long-term	4 758 . .	. . .	. . .	. . .	. . .	. . .	. . .	. . .	. . .
General government: short-term	4 759 . .	. . .	. . .	. . .	. . .	. . .	. . .	. . .	. . .
Other sectors: long-term	4 761 . .	27	518	549	724	218	–459	–331	–190
Other sectors: short-term	4 762 . .	1,325	–48	2,892	531	1,909	–1,234	3,188	4,332
Loans	4 764 . .	–3,870	–3,139	472	4,671	982	–1,484	8,938	13,107
Use of Fund credit and loans from the Fund	4 766 . .	–490	. . .	. . .	. . .	. . .	. . .	. . .	. . .
Monetary authorities: other long-term	4 767 . .	. . .	. . .	. . .	. . .	. . .	. . .	. . .	. . .
Monetary authorities: short-term	4 768 . .	. . .	. . .	. . .	. . .	. . .	. . .	. . .	. . .
General government: long-term	4 770 . .	–2,745	–2,020	–1,042	–26	–863	–2,849	–578	–1,115
General government: short-term	4 771 . .	–24	76	141	–26	225	123	421	1,125
Banks: long-term	4 773 . .	–513	–552	31	1,021	217	61	–318	–46
Banks: short-term	4 774 . .	–246	221	742	2,744	342	–127	6,859	8,301
Other sectors: long-term	4 776 . .	–113	–1,250	–29	941	1,027	1,367	1,567	2,881
Other sectors: short-term	4 777 . .	261	386	629	17	34	–59	987	1,961
Currency and deposits	4 780 . .	–132	–150	1	–55	–2	31	15	60
Monetary authorities	4 781 . .	. . .	. . .	. . .	. . .	. . .	. . .	. . .	. . .
General government	4 782 . .	. . .	. . .	. . .	. . .	. . .	. . .	. . .	. . .
Banks	4 783 . .	–132	–150	1	–55	–2	31	15	60
Other sectors	4 784 . .	. . .	. . .	. . .	. . .	. . .	. . .	. . .	. . .
Other liabilities	4 786 . .	111	1,124	1,228	4,607	1,156	801	1,275	3,924
Monetary authorities: long-term	4 788 . .	19	9	22	2	7	15	–1	–10
Monetary authorities: short-term	4 789 . .	. . .	. . .	. . .	. . .	. . .	. . .	. . .	. . .
General government: long-term	4 791 . .	. . .	. . .	. . .	. . .	. . .	. . .	. . .	. . .
General government: short-term	4 792 . .	. . .	. . .	. . .	. . .	. . .	. . .	. . .	. . .
Banks: long-term	4 794 . .	16	738	777	5,662	884	446	1,077	3,925
Banks: short-term	4 795 . .	76	377	429	–1,057	265	340	199	9
Other sectors: long-term	4 797 . .	. . .	. . .	. . .	. . .	. . .	. . .	. . .	. . .
Other sectors: short-term	4 798 . .	. . .	. . .	. . .	. . .	. . .	. . .	. . .	. . .
D. RESERVE ASSETS	4 800 . .	–8,826	–3,120	1,208	1,148	–3,724	–3,009	–4,614	–7,040
Monetary gold	4 810 . .	. . .	. . .	. . .	. . .	. . .	. . .	. . .	–1
Special drawing rights	4 820 . .	10	4	–12	–15	–14	–16	–14	–20
Reserve position in the Fund	4 830 . .	. . .	–223	–62	–44	–88	–28	–35	–116
Foreign exchange	4 840 . .	–8,836	–2,901	1,282	1,207	–3,622	–2,965	–4,564	–6,902
Other claims	4 880 . .	. . .	. . .	. . .	. . .	. . .	. . .	. . .	. . .
NET ERRORS AND OMISSIONS	4 998 . .	**–590**	**691**	**–1,998**	**757**	**1,101**	**–720**	**–1,704**	**–1,443**

Part 3 of the *Yearbook* contains descriptions of the methodologies, compilation practices, and sources used to compile these data.

Table 3. INTERNATIONAL INVESTMENT POSITION (End–period stocks), 1988–95
(Millions of U.S. dollars)

	Code	1988	1989	1990	1991	1992	1993	1994	1995
ASSETS	8 995 C.	24,093	26,915	28,639	30,369	38,068	46,762	60,612	...
Direct investment abroad	8 505 . .	**970**	**1,275**	**2,095**	**3,452**	**4,499**	**5,555**	**7,630**	...
Equity capital and reinvested earnings	8 506 . .	970	1,275	2,095	3,452	4,499	5,555	7,630	...
Claims on affiliated enterprises	8 507 . .	...	...	...	...	...	...	...	...
Liabilities to affiliated enterprises	8 508 . .	...	...	...	...	...	...	...	...
Other capital	8 530 . .	...	...	...	...	...	...	...	...
Claims on affiliated enterprises	8 535 . .	...	...	...	...	...	...	...	...
Liabilities to affiliated enterprises	8 540 . .	...	...	...	...	...	...	...	...
Portfolio investment	8 602 . .	**22**	**80**	**168**	**206**	**225**	**522**	**992**	...
Equity securities	8 610 . .	...	...	...	...	...	...	...	...
Monetary authorities	8 611 . .	...	...	...	...	...	...	...	...
General government	8 612 . .	...	...	...	...	...	...	...	...
Banks	8 613 . .	...	...	...	...	...	...	...	...
Other sectors	8 614 . .	...	...	...	...	...	...	...	...
Debt securities	8 619 . .	22	80	168	206	225	522	992	...
Bonds and notes	8 620 . .	22	80	168	206	225	522	992	...
Monetary authorities	8 621 . .	...	...	...	...	...	...	...	...
General government	8 622 . .	...	...	...	...	...	...	...	...
Banks	8 623 . .	...	...	...	...	...	...	...	...
Other sectors	8 624 . .	...	...	...	...	...	...	...	...
Money market instruments	8 630 . .	...	...	...	...	...	...	...	...
Monetary authorities	8 631 . .	...	...	...	...	...	...	...	...
General government	8 632 . .	...	...	...	...	...	...	...	...
Banks	8 633 . .	...	...	...	...	...	...	...	...
Other sectors	8 634 . .	...	...	...	...	...	...	...	...
Financial derivatives	8 640 . .	...	...	...	...	...	...	...	...
Monetary authorities	8 641 . .	...	...	...	...	...	...	...	...
General government	8 642 . .	...	...	...	...	...	...	...	...
Banks	8 643 . .	...	...	...	...	...	...	...	...
Other sectors	8 644 . .	...	...	...	...	...	...	...	...
Other investment	8 703 . .	**10,723**	**10,315**	**11,552**	**12,979**	**16,192**	**20,423**	**26,317**	...
Trade credits	8 706 . .	...	...	...	...	...	...	...	...
General government: long-term	8 708 . .	...	...	...	...	...	...	...	...
General government: short-term	8 709 . .	...	...	...	...	...	...	...	...
Other sectors: long-term	8 711 . .	...	...	...	...	...	...	...	...
Other sectors: short-term	8 712 . .	...	...	...	...	...	...	...	...
Loans	8 714 . .	540	540	540	558	540	540	540	...
Monetary authorities: long-term	8 717 . .	...	...	...	...	...	...	...	...
Monetary authorities: short-term	8 718 . .	...	...	...	...	...	...	...	...
General government: long-term	8 720 . .	...	...	...	18	...	...	...	...
General government: short-term	8 721 . .	...	...	...	...	...	...	...	...
Banks: long-term	8 723 . .	...	...	...	...	...	...	...	...
Banks: short-term	8 724 . .	...	...	...	...	...	...	...	...
Other sectors: long-term	8 726 . .	540	540	540	540	540	540	540	...
Other sectors: short-term	8 727 . .	...	...	...	...	...	...	...	...
Currency and deposits	8 730 . .	8,924	8,163	9,068	9,989	12,081	15,389	19,944	...
Monetary authorities	8 731 . .	...	...	...	...	...	...	...	...
General government	8 732 . .	...	...	...	...	...	...	...	...
Banks	8 733 . .	8,924	8,163	9,068	9,989	12,081	15,389	19,944	...
Other sectors	8 734 . .	...	...	...	...	...	...	...	...
Other assets	8 736 . .	1,259	1,612	1,944	2,432	3,571	4,494	5,833	...
Monetary authorities: long-term	8 738 . .	...	...	...	...	...	...	...	...
Monetary authorities: short-term	8 739 . .	...	...	...	...	...	...	...	...
General government: long-term	8 741 . .	...	...	...	...	...	...	...	...
General government: short-term	8 742 . .	...	...	...	...	...	...	...	...
Banks: long-term	8 744 . .	...	...	...	...	...	...	...	...
Banks: short-term	8 745 . .	...	...	...	...	...	...	...	...
Other sectors: long-term	8 747 . .	...	...	...	...	...	...	...	...
Other sectors: short-term	8 748 . .	1,259	1,612	1,944	2,432	3,571	4,494	5,833	...
Reserve assets	8 800 . .	**12,378**	**15,245**	**14,824**	**13,732**	**17,152**	**20,262**	**25,673**	...
Monetary gold	8 810 . .	31	31	31	31	31	31	31	...
Special drawing rights	8 820 . .	6	2	14	30	42	58	76	98
Reserve position in the Fund	8 830 . .	1	234	319	365	439	466	531	652
Foreign exchange	8 840 . .	12,340	14,978	14,459	13,306	16,640	19,707	25,035	...
Other claims	8 880 . .	...	...	...	...	...	...	...	...

Table 3 (Continued). INTERNATIONAL INVESTMENT POSITION (End-period stocks), 1988–95
(Millions of U.S. dollars)

	Code	1988	1989	1990	1991	1992	1993	1994	1995
LIABILITIES	8 995 D.	15,710	17,463	20,564	33,264	41,508	53,706	69,830	...
Direct investment in Korea	8 555 . .	**3,358**	**4,116**	**4,831**	**5,947**	**6,482**	**6,984**	**7,715**	...
Equity capital and reinvested earnings	8 556 . .	3,358	4,116	4,831	5,947	6,482	6,984	7,715	...
Claims on direct investors	8 557 . .	...	...	...	...	...	...	...	...
Liabilities to direct investors	8 558 . .	...	...	...	...	...	...	...	...
Other capital	8 580 . .	...	...	...	...	...	...	...	...
Claims on direct investors	8 585 . .	...	...	...	...	...	...	...	...
Liabilities to direct investors	8 590 . .	...	...	...	...	...	...	...	...
Portfolio investment	8 652 . .	**1,573**	**1,602**	**2,501**	**5,655**	**11,416**	**22,438**	**29,714**	...
Equity securities	8 660 . .	292	322	702	702	3,030	9,316	11,796	...
Banks	8 663 . .	...	...	...	...	...	...	...	...
Other sectors	8 664 . .	...	...	...	...	...	...	...	...
Debt securities	8 669 . .	1,281	1,280	1,799	4,953	8,386	13,122	17,918	...
Bonds and notes	8 670 . .	1,281	1,280	1,799	4,953	8,386	13,122	17,918	...
Monetary authorities	8 671 . .	...	...	...	...	...	...	...	...
General government	8 672 . .	...	...	...	...	...	...	...	...
Banks	8 673 . .	...	...	...	...	...	...	...	...
Other sectors	8 674 . .	...	...	...	...	...	...	...	...
Money market instruments	8 680 . .	...	...	...	...	...	...	...	...
Monetary authorities	8 681 . .	...	...	...	...	...	...	...	...
General government	8 682 . .	...	...	...	...	...	...	...	...
Banks	8 683 . .	...	...	...	...	...	...	...	...
Other sectors	8 684 . .	...	...	...	...	...	...	...	...
Financial derivatives	8 690 . .	...	...	...	...	...	...	...	...
Monetary authorities	8 691 . .	...	...	...	...	...	...	...	...
General government	8 692 . .	...	...	...	...	...	...	...	...
Banks	8 692 . .	...	...	...	...	...	...	...	...
Other sectors	8 694 . .	...	...	...	...	...	...	...	...
Other investment	8 753 . .	**10,779**	**11,745**	**13,232**	**21,662**	**23,610**	**24,284**	**32,401**	...
Trade credits	8 756 . .	...	...	...	...	...	...	...	...
General government: long-term	8 758 . .	...	...	...	...	...	...	...	...
General government: short-term	8 759 . .	...	...	...	...	...	...	...	...
Other sectors: long-term	8 761 . .	...	...	...	...	...	...	...	...
Other sectors: short-term	8 762 . .	...	...	...	...	...	...	...	...
Loans	8 764 . .	...	...	...	...	...	...	...	...
Use of Fund credit and loans from the Fund	8 766 . .	...	...	...	...	...	...	...	...
Monetary authorities: other long-term	8 767 . .	...	...	...	...	...	...	...	...
Monetary authorities: short-term	8 768 . .	...	...	...	...	...	...	...	...
General government: long-term	8 770 . .	...	...	...	...	...	...	...	...
General government: short-term	8 771 . .	...	...	...	...	...	...	...	...
Banks: long-term	8 773 . .	...	...	...	...	...	...	...	...
Banks: short-term	8 774 . .	...	...	...	...	...	...	...	...
Other sectors: long-term	8 776 . .	...	...	...	...	...	...	...	...
Other sectors: short-term	8 777 . .	...	...	...	...	...	...	...	...
Currency and deposits	8 780 . .	9,323	9,780	10,958	12,592	13,199	13,438	20,512	...
Monetary authorities	8 781 . .	...	...	...	...	...	...	...	...
General government	8 782 . .	...	...	...	...	...	...	...	...
Banks	8 783 . .	9,323	9,780	10,958	12,592	13,199	13,438	20,512	...
Other sectors	8 784 . .	...	...	...	...	...	...	...	...
Other liabilities	8 786 . .	1,456	1,965	2,274	9,070	10,411	10,846	11,889	...
Monetary authorities: long-term	8 788 . .	...	...	...	...	...	...	...	...
Monetary authorities: short-term	8 789 . .	162	162	184	186	193	208	207	...
General government: long-term	8 791 . .	...	...	...	...	...	...	...	...
General government: short-term	8 792 . .	...	...	...	...	...	...	...	...
Banks: long-term	8 794 . .	1,294	1,803	2,090	8,884	10,218	10,638	11,682	...
Banks: short-term	8 795 . .	...	...	...	...	...	...	...	...
Other sectors: long-term	8 797 . .	...	...	...	...	...	...	...	...
Other sectors: short-term	8 798 . .	...	...	...	...	...	...	...	...
NET INTERNATIONAL INVESTMENT POSITION	8 995 . .	**8,383**	**9,452**	**8,075**	**–2,895**	**–3,440**	**–6,944**	**–9,218**	...
Conversion rates: won per U.S. dollar (end of period)	0 102 . .	**684.10**	**679.60**	**716.40**	**760.80**	**788.40**	**808.10**	**788.70**	**774.70**

Table 1. ANALYTIC PRESENTATION, 1988–95
(Millions of U.S. dollars)

	Code	1988	1989	1990	1991	1992	1993	1994	1995
A. Current Account[1]	4 993 Y.	**4,602**	**9,136**	**3,886**	**-26,478**	**-450**	**1,938**	**2,489**	**4,198**
Goods: exports f.o.b	2 100 ..	7,709	11,396	6,989	1,080	6,548	10,141	11,129	12,632
Goods: imports f.o.b	3 100 ..	-5,999	-6,410	-3,810	-5,073	-7,237	-6,954	-6,670	-7,154
Balance on Goods	4 100 ..	*1,709*	*4,987*	*3,179*	*-3,993*	*-689*	*3,187*	*4,460*	*5,478*
Services: credit	2 200 ..	1,158	1,345	1,279	992	1,494	1,302	1,512	1,491
Services: debit	3 200 ..	-4,204	-4,119	-3,359	-5,090	-4,590	-4,628	-4,564	-4,936
Balance on Goods and Services	4 991 ..	*-1,337*	*2,213*	*1,099*	*-8,091*	*-3,786*	*-139*	*1,408*	*2,034*
Income: credit	2 300 ..	7,863	9,211	8,584	6,093	5,907	4,486	3,675	5,153
Income: debit	3 300 ..	-606	-793	-846	-682	-662	-898	-889	-1,143
Balance on Goods, Services, and Income	4 992 ..	*5,921*	*10,630*	*8,837*	*-2,681*	*1,460*	*3,449*	*4,194*	*6,045*
Current transfers: credit	2 379 Y.	...	...	...	...	17	109	94	57
Current transfers: debit	3 379 ..	-1,319	-1,494	-4,951	-23,798	-1,927	-1,620	-1,799	-1,903
B. Capital Account[1]	4 994 Y.	**...**	**...**	**...**	**...**	**...**	**...**	**...**	**...**
Capital account: credit	2 994 Y.	...	...	...	...	...	...	...	...
Capital account: debit	3 994 ..	...	...	...	...	...	...	...	...
Total, Groups A Plus B	4 010 ..	*4,602*	*9,136*	*3,886*	*-26,478*	*-450*	*1,938*	*2,489*	*4,198*
C. Financial Account[1]	4 995 X.	**-7,340**	**-8,323**	**413**	**38,766**	**11,067**	**-1,090**	**1,839**	**-6,912**
Direct investment abroad	4 505 ..	-477	-994	-239	186	-1,211	-848	-1,031	-717
Direct investment in Kuwait	4 555 Y.	...	...	...	...	...	...	...	...
Portfolio investment assets	4 602 ..	-720	-623	-919	-813	-3	-89	-451	-34
Equity securities	4 610 ..	...	...	...	...	...	...	...	...
Debt securities	4 619 ..	-720	-623	-919	-813	-3	-89	-451	-34
Portfolio investment liabilities	4 652 Y.	280	24	537	211	276	252	475	452
Equity securities	4 660 Y.	...	...	...	...	...	...	...	...
Debt securities	4 669 Y.	280	24	537	211	276	252	475	452
Other investment assets	4 703 ..	-6,042	-7,295	829	43,061	11,261	-248	2,452	-5,947
Monetary authorities	4 703 .A	-5,121	-5,647	-281	38,745	10,490	454	3,571	-4,007
General government	4 703 .B	-434	-701	783	...	-634	-93	-505	-1,471
Banks	4 703 .C	-699	-1,236	55	3,785	1,385	-404	-401	-680
Other sectors	4 703 .D	211	289	270	531	20	-205	-212	211
Other investment liabilities	4 753 X.	-380	565	205	-3,880	743	-156	394	-667
Monetary authorities	4 753 XA	...	...	...	...	...	...	...	...
General government	4 753 YB	...	...	...	...	...	...	...	...
Banks	4 753 YC	201	742	205	-4,176	720	-172	600	-194
Other sectors	4 753 YD	-581	-177	...	295	24	17	-205	-472
Total, Groups A Through C	4 020 ..	*-2,738*	*814*	*4,299*	*12,288*	*10,617*	*848*	*4,328*	*-2,714*
D. Net Errors and Omissions	4 998 ..	**810**	**462**	**-5,196**	**-11,012**	**-8,765**	**-2,333**	**-4,275**	**2,627**
Total, Groups A Through D	4 030 ..	*-1,928*	*1,275*	*-897*	*1,276*	*1,851*	*-1,485*	*53*	*-87*
E. Reserves and Related Items	4 040 ..	**1,928**	**-1,275**	**897**	**-1,276**	**-1,851**	**1,485**	**-53**	**87**
Reserve assets	4 800 ..	1,928	-1,275	897	-1,276	-1,851	1,485	-53	87
Use of Fund credit and loans	4 766 ..	...	...	...	...	...	...	...	...
Liabilities constituting foreign authorities' reserves	4 900 ..	...	...	...	...	...	...	...	...
Exceptional financing	4 920 ..	...	...	...	...	...	...	...	...
Conversion rates: Kuwaiti dinar per U.S. dollar	0 101 ..	**.27903**	**.29378**	**.28846**	**.28427**	**.29322**	**.30184**	**.29687**	**.29845**

[1] Excludes components that have been classified in the categories of Group E.

Table 2. STANDARD PRESENTATION, 1988–95
(Millions of U.S. dollars)

	Code	1988	1989	1990	1991	1992	1993	1994	1995
CURRENT ACCOUNT	4 993 . .	**4,602**	**9,136**	**3,886**	**–26,478**	**–450**	**1,938**	**2,489**	**4,198**
A. GOODS	4 100 . .	1,709	4,987	3,179	–3,993	–689	3,187	4,460	5,478
Credit	2 100 . .	**7,709**	**11,396**	**6,989**	**1,080**	**6,548**	**10,141**	**11,129**	**12,632**
General merchandise: exports f.o.b.	2 110 . .	7,673	11,366	6,940	1,076	6,514	10,141	11,129	12,632
Goods for processing: exports f.o.b.	2 150 . .	. . .	. . .	. . .	. . .	. . .	. . .	. . .	. . .
Repairs on goods	2 160 . .	. . .	. . .	. . .	. . .	. . .	. . .	. . .	. . .
Goods procured in ports by carriers	2 170 . .	. . .	. . .	. . .	. . .	. . .	. . .	. . .	. . .
Nonmonetary gold	2 180 . .	36	31	49	4	34	. . .	. . .	. . .
Debit	3 100 . .	**–5,999**	**–6,410**	**–3,810**	**–5,073**	**–7,237**	**–6,954**	**–6,670**	**–7,154**
General merchandise: imports f.o.b.	3 110 . .	–5,827	–6,290	–3,775	–5,066	–7,117	–6,898	–6,579	–7,154
Goods for processing: imports f.o.b.	3 150 . .	. . .	. . .	. . .	. . .	. . .	. . .	. . .	. . .
Repairs on goods	3 160 . .	. . .	. . .	. . .	. . .	. . .	. . .	. . .	. . .
Goods procured in ports by carriers	3 170 . .	. . .	. . .	. . .	. . .	. . .	. . .	. . .	. . .
Nonmonetary gold	3 180 . .	–172	–119	–35	–7	–119	–56	–91	. . .
B. SERVICES	4 200 . .	–3,046	–2,774	–2,080	–4,098	–3,097	–3,326	–3,052	–3,444
Total credit	2 200 . .	*1,158*	*1,345*	*1,279*	*992*	*1,494*	*1,302*	*1,512*	*1,491*
Total debit	3 200 . .	*–4,204*	*–4,119*	*–3,359*	*–5,090*	*–4,590*	*–4,628*	*–4,564*	*–4,936*
Transportation services, credit	2 205 . .	**835**	**980**	**922**	**503**	**996**	**1,004**	**1,186**	**1,143**
Passenger	2 205 BA	*183*	*214*	*340*	*186*	*273*	*149*	*340*	*265*
Freight	2 205 BB	*434*	*487*	*347*	*162*	*491*	*669*	*637*	*623*
Other	2 205 BC	*219*	*279*	*236*	*155*	*232*	*186*	*209*	*255*
Sea transport, passenger	2 207 . .	. . .	. . .	. . .	. . .	. . .	. . .	. . .	. . .
Sea transport, freight	2 208 . .	. . .	. . .	. . .	. . .	. . .	. . .	. . .	. . .
Sea transport, other	2 209 . .	. . .	. . .	. . .	. . .	. . .	. . .	. . .	. . .
Air transport, passenger	2 211 . .	. . .	. . .	. . .	. . .	. . .	. . .	. . .	. . .
Air transport, freight	2 212 . .	. . .	. . .	. . .	. . .	. . .	. . .	. . .	. . .
Air transport, other	2 213 . .	. . .	. . .	. . .	. . .	. . .	. . .	. . .	. . .
Other transport, passenger	2 215 . .	. . .	. . .	. . .	. . .	. . .	. . .	. . .	. . .
Other transport, freight	2 216 . .	. . .	. . .	. . .	. . .	. . .	. . .	. . .	. . .
Other transport, other	2 217 . .	. . .	. . .	. . .	. . .	. . .	. . .	. . .	. . .
Transportation services, debit	3 205 . .	**–1,190**	**–1,174**	**–894**	**–960**	**–1,374**	**–1,488**	**–1,445**	**–1,605**
Passenger	3 205 BA	*–147*	*–133*	*–173*	*–141*	*–205*	*–209*	*–222*	*–265*
Freight	3 205 BB	*–817*	*–837*	*–527*	*–633*	*–965*	*–934*	*–889*	*–1,035*
Other	3 205 BC	*–226*	*–204*	*–194*	*–186*	*–205*	*–345*	*–333*	*–305*
Sea transport, passenger	3 207 . .	. . .	. . .	. . .	. . .	. . .	. . .	. . .	. . .
Sea transport, freight	3 208 . .	. . .	. . .	. . .	. . .	. . .	. . .	. . .	. . .
Sea transport, other	3 209 . .	. . .	. . .	. . .	. . .	. . .	. . .	. . .	. . .
Air transport, passenger	3 211 . .	. . .	. . .	. . .	. . .	. . .	. . .	. . .	. . .
Air transport, freight	3 212 . .	. . .	. . .	. . .	. . .	. . .	. . .	. . .	. . .
Air transport, other	3 213 . .	. . .	. . .	. . .	. . .	. . .	. . .	. . .	. . .
Other transport, passenger	3 215 . .	. . .	. . .	. . .	. . .	. . .	. . .	. . .	. . .
Other transport, freight	3 216 . .	. . .	. . .	. . .	. . .	. . .	. . .	. . .	. . .
Other transport, other	3 217 . .	. . .	. . .	. . .	. . .	. . .	. . .	. . .	. . .
Travel, credit	2 236 . .	**108**	**143**	**132**	**253**	**273**	**83**	**101**	**107**
Business travel	2 237 . .	. . .	. . .	. . .	. . .	. . .	. . .	. . .	. . .
Personal travel	2 240 . .	. . .	. . .	. . .	. . .	. . .	. . .	. . .	. . .
Travel, debit	3 236 . .	**–2,358**	**–2,250**	**–1,837**	**–2,012**	**–1,797**	**–1,819**	**–2,146**	**–2,322**
Business travel	3 237 . .	. . .	. . .	. . .	. . .	. . .	. . .	. . .	. . .
Personal travel	3 240 . .	. . .	. . .	. . .	. . .	. . .	. . .	. . .	. . .
Other services, credit	2 200 BA	**215**	**221**	**225**	**236**	**225**	**215**	**226**	**241**
Communications	2 245 . .	. . .	. . .	. . .	. . .	. . .	. . .	. . .	. . .
Construction	2 249 . .	. . .	. . .	. . .	. . .	. . .	. . .	. . .	. . .
Insurance	2 253 . .	. . .	. . .	. . .	. . .	. . .	. . .	. . .	. . .
Financial	2 260 . .	. . .	. . .	. . .	. . .	. . .	. . .	. . .	. . .
Computer and information	2 262 . .	. . .	. . .	. . .	. . .	. . .	. . .	. . .	. . .
Royalties and licence fees	2 266 . .	. . .	. . .	. . .	. . .	. . .	. . .	. . .	. . .
Other business services	2 268 . .	. . .	. . .	. . .	. . .	. . .	. . .	. . .	13
Personal, cultural, and recreational	2 287 . .	. . .	. . .	. . .	. . .	. . .	. . .	. . .	. . .
Government, n.i.e.	2 291 . .	215	221	225	236	225	215	226	228
Other services, debit	3 200 BA	**–656**	**–694**	**–627**	**–2,118**	**–1,419**	**–1,322**	**–973**	**–1,009**
Communications	3 245 . .	. . .	. . .	. . .	. . .	. . .	. . .	. . .	. . .
Construction	3 249 . .	. . .	. . .	. . .	. . .	. . .	. . .	. . .	. . .
Insurance	3 253 . .	–50	–51	–35	–39	–58	–56	–54	–64
Financial	3 260 . .	. . .	. . .	. . .	. . .	. . .	. . .	. . .	. . .
Computer and information	3 262 . .	. . .	. . .	. . .	. . .	. . .	. . .	. . .	. . .
Royalties and licence fees	3 266 . .	. . .	. . .	. . .	. . .	. . .	. . .	. . .	. . .
Other business services	3 268 . .	–50	–54	–38	–63	–44	–50	–30	–30
Personal, cultural, and recreational	3 287 . .	. . .	. . .	. . .	. . .	. . .	. . .	. . .	. . .
Government, n.i.e.	3 291 . .	–555	–589	–555	–2,016	–1,316	–1,216	–889	–915

Table 2 (Continued). STANDARD PRESENTATION, 1988–95
(Millions of U.S. dollars)

	Code		1988	1989	1990	1991	1992	1993	1994	1995
C. INCOME	4 300	..	7,257	8,418	7,738	5,410	5,245	3,588	2,786	4,011
Total credit	2 300	..	*7,863*	*9,211*	*8,584*	*6,093*	*5,907*	*4,486*	*3,675*	*5,153*
Total debit	3 300	..	*–606*	*–793*	*–846*	*–682*	*–662*	*–898*	*–889*	*–1,143*
Compensation of employees, credit	2 310	..	...	...	...	...	...	...	...	...
Compensation of employees, debit	3 310	..	...	...	...	...	...	...	...	...
Investment income, credit	2 320	..	**7,863**	**9,211**	**8,584**	**6,093**	**5,907**	**4,486**	**3,675**	**5,153**
Direct investment income	2 330	..	...	...	...	...	...	...	...	...
Dividends and distributed branch profits	2 332	..	...	...	...	...	...	...	...	...
Reinvested earnings and undistributed branch profits	2 333	..	...	...	...	...	...	...	...	...
Income on debt (interest)	2 334	..	...	...	...	...	...	...	...	...
Portfolio investment income	2 339	..	...	...	...	...	...	...	...	...
Income on equity	2 340	..	...	...	...	...	...	...	...	...
Income on bonds and notes	2 350	..	...	...	...	...	...	...	...	...
Income on money market instruments and financial derivatives	2 360	..	...	...	...	...	...	...	...	...
Other investment income	2 370	..	7,863	9,211	8,584	6,093	5,907	4,486	3,675	5,153
Investment income, debit	3 320	..	**–606**	**–793**	**–846**	**–682**	**–662**	**–898**	**–889**	**–1,143**
Direct investment income	3 330	..	...	...	...	...	...	...	...	...
Dividends and distributed branch profits	3 332	..	...	...	...	...	...	...	...	...
Reinvested earnings and undistributed branch profits	3 333	..	...	...	...	...	...	...	...	...
Income on debt (interest)	3 334	..	...	...	...	...	...	...	...	...
Portfolio investment income	3 339	..	...	...	...	...	...	...	...	...
Income on equity	3 340	..	...	...	...	...	...	...	...	...
Income on bonds and notes	3 350	..	...	...	...	...	...	...	...	...
Income on money market instruments and financial derivatives	3 360	..	...	...	...	...	...	...	...	...
Other investment income	3 370	..	–606	–793	–846	–682	–662	–898	–889	–1,143
D. CURRENT TRANSFERS	4 379	..	–1,319	–1,494	–4,951	–23,798	–1,910	–1,511	–1,704	–1,846
Credit	2 379	..	...	...	...	...	**17**	**109**	**94**	**57**
General government	2 380	..	...	...	...	...	17	109	94	57
Other sectors	2 390	..	...	...	...	...	...	...	...	...
Workers' remittances	2 391	..	...	...	...	...	...	...	...	...
Other current transfers	2 392	..	...	...	...	...	...	...	...	...
Debit	3 379	..	**–1,319**	**–1,494**	**–4,951**	**–23,798**	**–1,927**	**–1,620**	**–1,799**	**–1,903**
General government	3 380	..	–140	–211	–4,181	–23,372	–1,098	–391	–468	–556
Other sectors	3 390	..	–1,179	–1,283	–770	–426	–829	–1,229	–1,331	–1,347
Workers' remittances	3 391	..	–1,179	–1,283	–770	–426	–829	–1,229	–1,331	–1,347
Other current transfers	3 392	..	...	...	...	...	...	...	...	...
CAPITAL AND FINANCIAL ACCOUNT	4 996	..	**–5,412**	**–9,598**	**1,310**	**37,490**	**9,215**	**395**	**1,786**	**–6,826**
CAPITAL ACCOUNT	4 994	..	...	...	...	...	...	...	...	...
Total credit	2 994	..	...	...	...	...	...	...	...	...
Total debit	3 994	..	...	...	...	...	...	...	...	...
Capital transfers, credit	2 400	..	...	...	...	...	...	...	...	...
General government	2 401	..	...	...	...	...	...	...	...	...
Debt forgiveness	2 402	..	...	...	...	...	...	...	...	...
Other capital transfers	2 410	..	...	...	...	...	...	...	...	...
Other sectors	2 430	..	...	...	...	...	...	...	...	...
Migrants' transfers	2 431	..	...	...	...	...	...	...	...	...
Debt forgiveness	2 432	..	...	...	...	...	...	...	...	...
Other capital transfers	2 440	..	...	...	...	...	...	...	...	...
Capital transfers, debit	3 400	..	...	...	...	...	...	...	...	...
General government	3 401	..	...	...	...	...	...	...	...	...
Debt forgiveness	3 402	..	...	...	...	...	...	...	...	...
Other capital transfers	3 410	..	...	...	...	...	...	...	...	...
Other sectors	3 430	..	...	...	...	...	...	...	...	...
Migrants' transfers	3 431	..	...	...	...	...	...	...	...	...
Debt forgiveness	3 432	..	...	...	...	...	...	...	...	...
Other capital transfers	3 440	..	...	...	...	...	...	...	...	...
Nonproduced nonfinancial assets, credit	2 480	..	...	...	...	...	...	...	...	...
Nonproduced nonfinancial assets, debit	3 480	..	...	...	...	...	...	...	...	...

Table 2 (Continued). STANDARD PRESENTATION, 1988–95
(Millions of U.S. dollars)

	Code		1988	1989	1990	1991	1992	1993	1994	1995
FINANCIAL ACCOUNT	4 995	. .	**–5,412**	**–9,598**	**1,310**	**37,490**	**9,215**	**395**	**1,786**	**–6,826**
A. DIRECT INVESTMENT	4 500	. .	–477	–994	–239	186	–1,211	–848	–1,031	–717
Direct investment abroad	4 505	. .	**–477**	**–994**	**–239**	**186**	**–1,211**	**–848**	**–1,031**	**–717**
Equity capital	4 510	. .	–477	–994	–239	186	–1,211	–848	–1,031	–717
Claims on affiliated enterprises	4 515	. .	...	...	...	...	...	...	...	...
Liabilities to affiliated enterprises	4 520	. .	...	...	...	...	...	...	...	...
Reinvested earnings	4 525	. .	...	...	...	...	...	...	...	...
Other capital	4 530	. .	...	...	...	...	...	...	...	...
Claims on affiliated enterprises	4 535	. .	...	...	...	...	...	...	...	...
Liabilities to affiliated enterprises	4 540	. .	...	...	...	...	...	...	...	...
Direct investment in Kuwait	4 555	. .	**...**	**...**	**...**	**...**	**...**	**...**	**...**	**...**
Equity capital	4 560	. .	...	...	...	...	...	...	...	...
Claims on direct investors	4 565	. .	...	...	...	...	...	...	...	...
Liabilities to direct investors	4 570	. .	...	...	...	...	...	...	...	...
Reinvested earnings	4 575	. .	...	...	...	...	...	...	...	...
Other capital	4 580	. .	...	...	...	...	...	...	...	...
Claims on direct investors	4 585	. .	...	...	...	...	...	...	...	...
Liabilities to direct investors	4 590	. .	...	...	...	...	...	...	...	...
B. PORTFOLIO INVESTMENT	4 600	. .	–441	–599	–381	–602	273	162	24	419
Assets	4 602	. .	**–720**	**–623**	**–919**	**–813**	**–3**	**–89**	**–451**	**–34**
Equity securities	4 610	. .	...	...	...	...	...	...	...	...
Monetary authorities	4 611	. .	...	...	...	...	...	...	...	...
General government	4 612	. .	...	...	...	...	...	...	...	...
Banks	4 613	. .	...	...	...	...	...	...	...	...
Other sectors	4 614	. .	...	...	...	...	...	...	...	...
Debt securities	4 619	. .	–720	–623	–919	–813	–3	–89	–451	–34
Bonds and notes	4 620	. .	–720	–623	–919	–813	–3	–89	–451	–34
Monetary authorities	4 621	. .	...	...	...	...	...	...	...	...
General government	4 622	. .	...	...	...	...	...	...	...	...
Banks	4 623	. .	...	...	...	...	...	...	...	...
Other sectors	4 624	. .	...	...	...	...	...	...	...	...
Money market instruments	4 630	. .	...	...	...	...	...	...	...	...
Monetary authorities	4 631	. .	...	...	...	...	...	...	...	...
General government	4 632	. .	...	...	...	...	...	...	...	...
Banks	4 633	. .	...	...	...	...	...	...	...	...
Other sectors	4 634	. .	...	...	...	...	...	...	...	...
Financial derivatives	4 640	. .	...	...	...	...	...	...	...	...
Monetary authorities	4 641	. .	...	...	...	...	...	...	...	...
General government	4 642	. .	...	...	...	...	...	...	...	...
Banks	4 643	. .	...	...	...	...	...	...	...	...
Other sectors	4 644	. .	...	...	...	...	...	...	...	...
Liabilities	4 652	. .	**280**	**24**	**537**	**211**	**276**	**252**	**475**	**452**
Equity securities	4 660	. .	...	...	...	...	...	...	...	...
Banks	4 663	. .	...	...	...	...	...	...	...	...
Other sectors	4 664	. .	...	...	...	...	...	...	...	...
Debt securities	4 669	. .	280	24	537	211	276	252	475	452
Bonds and notes	4 670	. .	280	24	537	211	276	252	475	452
Monetary authorities	4 671	. .	...	...	...	...	...	...	...	...
General government	4 672	. .	280	24	537	211	276	252	475	452
Banks	4 673	. .	...	...	...	...	...	...	...	...
Other sectors	4 674	. .	...	...	...	...	...	...	...	...
Money market instruments	4 680	. .	...	...	...	...	...	...	...	...
Monetary authorities	4 681	. .	...	...	...	...	...	...	...	...
General government	4 682	. .	...	...	...	...	...	...	...	...
Banks	4 683	. .	...	...	...	...	...	...	...	...
Other sectors	4 684	. .	...	...	...	...	...	...	...	...
Financial derivatives	4 690	. .	...	...	...	...	...	...	...	...
Monetary authorities	4 691	. .	...	...	...	...	...	...	...	...
General government	4 692	. .	...	...	...	...	...	...	...	...
Banks	4 693	. .	...	...	...	...	...	...	...	...
Other sectors	4 694	. .	...	...	...	...	...	...	...	...

Table 2 (Concluded). STANDARD PRESENTATION, 1988–95
(Millions of U.S. dollars)

	Code	1988	1989	1990	1991	1992	1993	1994	1995
C. OTHER INVESTMENT	4 700 . .	–6,422	–6,730	1,033	39,181	12,005	–404	2,846	–6,614
Assets	4 703 . .	**–6,042**	**–7,295**	**829**	**43,061**	**11,261**	**–248**	**2,452**	**–5,947**
Trade credits	4 706 . .	. . .	. . .	. . .	. . .	. . .	. . .	. . .	. . .
General government: long-term	4 708 . .	. . .	. . .	. . .	. . .	. . .	. . .	. . .	. . .
General government: short-term	4 709 . .	. . .	. . .	. . .	. . .	. . .	. . .	. . .	. . .
Other sectors: long-term	4 711 . .	. . .	. . .	. . .	. . .	. . .	. . .	. . .	. . .
Other sectors: short-term	4 712 . .	. . .	. . .	. . .	. . .	. . .	. . .	. . .	. . .
Loans	4 714 . .	–448	–266	–839	109	–17	–613	–664	–218
Monetary authorities: long-term	4 717 . .	. . .	. . .	. . .	. . .	. . .	. . .	. . .	. . .
Monetary authorities: short-term	4 718 . .	. . .	. . .	. . .	. . .	. . .	. . .	. . .	. . .
General government: long-term	4 720 . .	–394	–248	–170	109	–14	–99	–307	–211
General government: short-term	4 721 . .	. . .	. . .	. . .	. . .	. . .	. . .	. . .	. . .
Banks: long-term	4 723 . .	. . .	. . .	. . .	. . .	. . .	. . .	. . .	. . .
Banks: short-term	4 724 . .	. . .	. . .	. . .	. . .	. . .	. . .	. . .	. . .
Other sectors: long-term	4 726 . .	–54	–17	–669	. . .	–3	–514	–357	–7
Other sectors: short-term	4 727 . .	. . .	. . .	. . .	. . .	. . .	. . .	. . .	. . .
Currency and deposits	4 730 . .	–5,594	–7,029	1,668	42,952	11,278	364	3,116	–5,730
Monetary authorities	4 731 . .	–5,121	–5,647	–281	38,745	10,490	454	3,571	–4,007
General government	4 732 . .	–39	–453	953	–109	–621	7	–199	–1,260
Banks	4 733 . .	–699	–1,236	55	3,785	1,385	–404	–401	–680
Other sectors	4 734 . .	265	306	939	531	24	308	145	218
Other assets	4 736 . .	. . .	. . .	. . .	. . .	. . .	. . .	. . .	. . .
Monetary authorities: long-term	4 738 . .	. . .	. . .	. . .	. . .	. . .	. . .	. . .	. . .
Monetary authorities: short-term	4 739 . .	. . .	. . .	. . .	. . .	. . .	. . .	. . .	. . .
General government: long-term	4 741 . .	. . .	. . .	. . .	. . .	. . .	. . .	. . .	. . .
General government: short-term	4 742 . .	. . .	. . .	. . .	. . .	. . .	. . .	. . .	. . .
Banks: long-term	4 744 . .	. . .	. . .	. . .	. . .	. . .	. . .	. . .	. . .
Banks: short-term	4 745 . .	. . .	. . .	. . .	. . .	. . .	. . .	. . .	. . .
Other sectors: long-term	4 747 . .	. . .	. . .	. . .	. . .	. . .	. . .	. . .	. . .
Other sectors: short-term	4 748 . .	. . .	. . .	. . .	. . .	. . .	. . .	. . .	. . .
Liabilities	4 753 . .	**–380**	**565**	**205**	**–3,880**	**743**	**–156**	**394**	**–667**
Trade credits	4 756 . .	. . .	. . .	. . .	. . .	. . .	. . .	. . .	. . .
General government: long-term	4 758 . .	. . .	. . .	. . .	. . .	. . .	. . .	. . .	. . .
General government: short-term	4 759 . .	. . .	. . .	. . .	. . .	. . .	. . .	. . .	. . .
Other sectors: long-term	4 761 . .	. . .	. . .	. . .	. . .	. . .	. . .	. . .	. . .
Other sectors: short-term	4 762 . .	. . .	. . .	. . .	. . .	. . .	. . .	. . .	. . .
Loans	4 764 . .	548	82	. . .	792	249	176	27	67
Use of Fund credit and loans from the Fund	4 766 . .	. . .	. . .	. . .	. . .	. . .	. . .	. . .	. . .
Monetary authorities: other long-term	4 767 . .	. . .	. . .	. . .	. . .	. . .	. . .	. . .	. . .
Monetary authorities: short-term	4 768 . .	. . .	. . .	. . .	. . .	. . .	. . .	. . .	. . .
General government: long-term	4 770 . .	. . .	. . .	. . .	. . .	. . .	. . .	. . .	. . .
General government: short-term	4 771 . .	. . .	. . .	. . .	. . .	. . .	. . .	. . .	. . .
Banks: long-term	4 773 . .	. . .	. . .	. . .	. . .	. . .	. . .	. . .	. . .
Banks: short-term	4 774 . .	. . .	. . .	. . .	. . .	. . .	. . .	. . .	. . .
Other sectors: long-term	4 776 . .	548	82	. . .	792	249	176	27	67
Other sectors: short-term	4 777 . .	. . .	. . .	. . .	. . .	. . .	. . .	. . .	. . .
Currency and deposits	4 780 . .	201	742	205	–4,176	720	–172	600	–194
Monetary authorities	4 781 . .	. . .	. . .	. . .	. . .	. . .	. . .	. . .	. . .
General government	4 782 . .	. . .	. . .	. . .	. . .	. . .	. . .	. . .	. . .
Banks	4 783 . .	201	742	205	–4,176	720	–172	600	–194
Other sectors	4 784 . .	. . .	. . .	. . .	. . .	. . .	. . .	. . .	. . .
Other liabilities	4 786 . .	–1,129	–259	. . .	–496	–225	–159	–232	–539
Monetary authorities: long-term	4 788 . .	. . .	. . .	. . .	. . .	. . .	. . .	. . .	. . .
Monetary authorities: short-term	4 789 . .	. . .	. . .	. . .	. . .	. . .	. . .	. . .	. . .
General government: long-term	4 791 . .	. . .	. . .	. . .	. . .	. . .	. . .	. . .	. . .
General government: short-term	4 792 . .	. . .	. . .	. . .	. . .	. . .	. . .	. . .	. . .
Banks: long-term	4 794 . .	. . .	. . .	. . .	. . .	. . .	. . .	. . .	. . .
Banks: short-term	4 795 . .	. . .	. . .	. . .	. . .	. . .	. . .	. . .	. . .
Other sectors: long-term	4 797 . .	. . .	. . .	. . .	. . .	. . .	. . .	. . .	. . .
Other sectors: short-term	4 798 . .	–1,129	–259	. . .	–496	–225	–159	–232	–539
D. RESERVE ASSETS	4 800 . .	1,928	–1,275	897	–1,276	–1,851	1,485	–53	87
Monetary gold	4 810 . .	. . .	. . .	. . .	. . .	. . .	. . .	. . .	. . .
Special drawing rights	4 820 . .	–24	91	–22	–20	–3	112	–9	–9
Reserve position in the Fund	4 830 . .	175	114	46	17	21	–97	36	6
Foreign exchange	4 840 . .	1,778	–1,481	874	–1,273	–1,869	1,471	–81	90
Other claims	4 880 . .	. . .	. . .	. . .	. . .	. . .	. . .	. . .	. . .
NET ERRORS AND OMISSIONS	4 998 . .	**810**	**462**	**–5,196**	**–11,012**	**–8,765**	**–2,333**	**–4,275**	**2,627**

Part 3 of the *Yearbook* contains descriptions of the methodologies, compilation practices, and sources used to compile these data.

Table 1. ANALYTIC PRESENTATION, 1988–95
(Millions of U.S. dollars)

	Code	1988	1989	1990	1991	1992	1993	1994	1995
A. Current Account[1]	4 993 Y.	**–103.2**	**–136.5**	**–110.8**	**–115.1**	**–111.3**	**–165.9**	**–243.1**	**–223.6**
Goods: exports f.o.b	2 100 ..	57.8	63.3	78.7	96.6	132.6	240.5	300.4	347.8
Goods: imports f.o.b	3 100 ..	–149.4	–193.8	–185.5	–197.9	–232.8	–397.4	–519.1	–540.2
Balance on Goods	4 100 ..	*–91.6*	*–130.5*	*–106.8*	*–101.3*	*–100.2*	*–156.9*	*–218.7*	*–192.4*
Services: credit	2 200 ..	17.8	22.5	23.7	37.8	61.4	86.7	87.1	97.4
Services: debit	3 200 ..	–26.7	–25.8	–26.4	–47.6	–71.3	–96.7	–108.9	–125.4
Balance on Goods and Services	4 991 ..	*–100.5*	*–133.8*	*–109.5*	*–111.1*	*–110.1*	*–166.9*	*–240.5*	*–220.4*
Income: credit	2 300 ..	.4	.8	2.2	3.3	5.6	8.6	6.8	7.4
Income: debit	3 300 ..	–2.5	–3.1	–3.2	–4.4	–4.6	–5.6	–6.2	–7.2
Balance on Goods, Services, and Income	4 992 ..	*–102.6*	*–136.1*	*–110.5*	*–112.2*	*–109.1*	*–163.9*	*–239.9*	*–220.2*
Current transfers: credit	2 379 Y.	...	...	...	...	...	...	...	...
Current transfers: debit	3 379 ..	–.6	–.4	–.3	–2.9	–2.2	–2.0	–3.2	–3.4
B. Capital Account[1]	4 994 Y.	**6.7**	**8.3**	**10.9**	**10.4**	**8.6**	**9.5**	**9.5**	**13.4**
Capital account: credit	2 994 Y.	6.7	8.3	10.9	10.4	8.6	9.5	9.5	13.4
Capital account: debit	3 994 ..	...	...	...	...	...	...	...	...
Total, Groups A Plus B	4 010 ..	*–96.5*	*–128.2*	*–99.9*	*–104.7*	*–102.7*	*–156.4*	*–233.6*	*–210.2*
C. Financial Account[1]	4 995 X.	**–25.2**	**–4.4**	**14.2**	**39.5**	**–3.0**	**28.0**	**8.7**	**55.1**
Direct investment abroad	4 505 ..	...	...	...	...	...	...	...	...
Direct investment in Lao PDR	4 555 Y.	2.0	4.0	6.0	6.9	7.8	47.6	42.4	77.2
Portfolio investment assets	4 602 ..	...	...	...	...	...	...	...	...
Equity securities	4 610 ..	...	...	...	...	...	...	...	...
Debt securities	4 619 ..	...	...	...	...	...	...	...	...
Portfolio investment liabilities	4 652 Y.	...	...	...	1.1	1.2	30.3	1.0	13.4
Equity securities	4 660 Y.	...	...	...	1.1	1.2	30.3	1.0	13.4
Debt securities	4 669 Y.	...	...	...	...	...	...	...	...
Other investment assets	4 703 ..	–28.7	–29.4	–4.5	34.2	–16.1	–43.2	–9.4	–5.7
Monetary authorities	4 703 .A	...	...	...	...	...	...	...	...
General government	4 703 .B	...	...	...	...	...	...	...	...
Banks	4 703 .C	–28.7	–29.4	–4.5	34.2	–16.1	–43.2	–9.4	–5.7
Other sectors	4 703 .D	...	...	...	...	...	...	...	...
Other investment liabilities	4 753 X.	1.5	21.0	12.7	–2.7	4.1	–6.7	–25.3	–29.8
Monetary authorities	4 753 XA	...	...	...	...	...	...	...	...
General government	4 753 YB	–9.2	–10.6	–7.3	–12.0	–9.0	–8.3	–8.3	–14.0
Banks	4 753 YC	1.5	–1.2	–.9	–.7	–1.2	–7.4	–17.0	–15.8
Other sectors	4 753 YD	9.2	32.8	20.9	10.0	14.3	9.0	...	...
Total, Groups A Through C	4 020 ..	*–121.7*	*–132.6*	*–85.7*	*–65.2*	*–105.7*	*–128.4*	*–224.9*	*–155.1*
D. Net Errors and Omissions	4 998 ..	**17.4**	**–31.2**	**–40.2**	**–60.3**	**–16.3**	**–29.4**	**44.2**	**–74.6**
Total, Groups A Through D	4 030 ..	*–104.3*	*–163.8*	*–125.9*	*–125.5*	*–122.0*	*–157.8*	*–180.7*	*–229.7*
E. Reserves and Related Items	4 040 ..	**104.3**	**163.8**	**125.9**	**125.5**	**122.0**	**157.8**	**180.7**	**229.7**
Reserve assets	4 800 ..	–.7	–1.0	–.7	–27.0	–12.8	–23.8	–5.6	–13.2
Use of Fund credit and loans	4 766 ..	–3.4	5.4	–.5	11.8	8.1	8.3	8.1	15.6
Liabilities constituting foreign authorities' reserves	4 900 ..	...	...	...	...	...	...	...	...
Exceptional financing	4 920 ..	108.4	159.4	127.1	140.7	126.7	173.3	178.2	227.3
Conversion rates: kip per U.S. dollar	0 101 ..	**400.37**	**591.50**	**707.75**	**702.08**	**716.08**	**716.25**	**717.67**	**804.69**

[1] Excludes components that have been classified in the categories of Group E.

Table 2. STANDARD PRESENTATION, 1988–95

(Millions of U.S. dollars)

	Code	1988	1989	1990	1991	1992	1993	1994	1995
CURRENT ACCOUNT	4 993 . .	**–77.7**	**–81.3**	**–54.9**	**–29.6**	**–48.4**	**–62.4**	**–118.5**	**–114.3**
A. GOODS	4 100 . .	–91.6	–130.5	–106.8	–101.3	–100.2	–156.9	–218.7	–192.4
Credit	2 100 . .	**57.8**	**63.3**	**78.7**	**96.6**	**132.6**	**240.5**	**300.4**	**347.8**
General merchandise: exports f.o.b.	2 110 . .	57.8	63.3	78.7	96.6	132.6	117.2	147.5	207.2
Goods for processing: exports f.o.b.	2 150 . .	. . .	. . .	. . .	. . .	. . .	19.6	24.8	24.1
Repairs on goods	2 160 . .	. . .	. . .	. . .	. . .	. . .	85.0	104.4	94.4
Goods procured in ports by carriers	2 170 . .	. . .	. . .	. . .	. . .	. . .	14.5	4.9	.4
Nonmonetary gold	2 180 . .	. . .	. . .	. . .	. . .	. . .	4.2	18.8	21.7
Debit	3 100 . .	**–149.4**	**–193.8**	**–185.5**	**–197.9**	**–232.8**	**–397.4**	**–519.1**	**–540.2**
General merchandise: imports f.o.b.	3 110 . .	–149.4	–193.8	–185.5	–197.9	–190.4	–311.4	–388.8	–435.2
Goods for processing: imports f.o.b.	3 150 . .	. . .	. . .	. . .	. . .	. . .	–2.2	–2.2	–2.7
Repairs on goods	3 160 . .	. . .	. . .	. . .	. . .	–42.4	–58.1	–79.0	–73.2
Goods procured in ports by carriers	3 170 . .	. . .	. . .	. . .	. . .	. . .	–13.8	–6.0	–2.0
Nonmonetary gold	3 180 . .	. . .	. . .	. . .	. . .	. . .	–11.9	–43.1	–27.1
B. SERVICES	4 200 . .	–8.9	–3.3	–2.7	–9.8	–9.9	–10.0	–21.8	–28.0
Total credit	2 200 . .	*17.8*	*22.5*	*23.7*	*37.8*	*61.4*	*86.7*	*87.1*	*97.4*
Total debit	3 200 . .	*–26.7*	*–25.8*	*–26.4*	*–47.6*	*–71.3*	*–96.7*	*–108.9*	*–125.4*
Transportation services, credit	2 205 . .	**6.2**	**8.5**	**8.0**	**10.6**	**14.1**	**19.2**	**11.4**	**15.2**
Passenger	2 205 BA	. . .	. . .	. . .	. . .	. . .	*3.1*	*1.9*	*1.2*
Freight	2 205 BB	*.5*	*.9*	*.9*	*2.3*	*3.7*	*4.8*	*1.1*	*3.7*
Other	2 205 BC	*5.7*	*7.6*	*7.1*	*8.3*	*10.4*	*11.3*	*8.4*	*10.3*
Sea transport, passenger	2 207 . .	. . .	. . .	. . .	. . .	. . .	. . .	. . .	. . .
Sea transport, freight	2 208 . .	. . .	. . .	. . .	. . .	. . .	2.0	.1	2.8
Sea transport, other	2 209 . .	. . .	. . .	. . .	. . .	. . .	. . .	. . .	. . .
Air transport, passenger	2 211 . .	. . .	. . .	. . .	. . .	. . .	3.1	1.9	1.2
Air transport, freight	2 212 . .	. . .	. . .	. . .	. . .	. . .	. . .	. . .	. . .
Air transport, other	2 213 . .	5.7	7.6	7.1	8.3	10.4	11.3	8.4	10.3
Other transport, passenger	2 215 . .	. . .	. . .	. . .	. . .	. . .	. . .	. . .	. . .
Other transport, freight	2 216 . .	.5	.9	.9	2.3	3.7	2.8	1.0	.9
Other transport, other	2 217 . .	. . .	. . .	. . .	. . .	. . .	. . .	. . .	. . .
Transportation services, debit	3 205 . .	**–13.6**	**–19.1**	**–18.4**	**–22.2**	**–31.4**	**–33.5**	**–45.5**	**–40.8**
Passenger	3 205 BA	*–.6*	*–2.2*	*–2.3*	*–2.9*	*–3.0*	*–3.6*	*–6.9*	*–3.3*
Freight	3 205 BB	*–13.0*	*–16.9*	*–16.1*	*–19.3*	*–28.4*	*–29.9*	*–38.6*	*–37.2*
Other	3 205 BC	. . .	. . .	. . .	. . .	. . .	. . .	. . .	*–.3*
Sea transport, passenger	3 207 . .	. . .	. . .	. . .	. . .	. . .	. . .	. . .	. . .
Sea transport, freight	3 208 . .	–13.0	–16.9	–16.1	–17.2	–26.3	–27.0	–35.3	–36.8
Sea transport, other	3 209 . .	. . .	. . .	. . .	. . .	. . .	. . .	. . .	. . .
Air transport, passenger	3 211 . .	–.6	–2.2	–2.3	–2.9	–3.0	–3.6	–6.9	–3.3
Air transport, freight	3 212 . .	. . .	. . .	. . .	. . .	. . .	. . .	. . .	. . .
Air transport, other	3 213 . .	. . .	. . .	. . .	. . .	. . .	. . .	. . .	–.3
Other transport, passenger	3 215 . .	. . .	. . .	. . .	. . .	. . .	. . .	. . .	. . .
Other transport, freight	3 216 . .	. . .	. . .	. . .	–2.1	–2.1	–2.9	–3.3	–.4
Other transport, other	3 217 . .	. . .	. . .	. . .	. . .	. . .	. . .	. . .	. . .
Travel, credit	2 236 . .	**.6**	**1.7**	**2.6**	**7.5**	**18.1**	**34.0**	**42.7**	**51.4**
Business travel	2 237 . .	. . .	. . .	. . .	. . .	. . .	. . .	. . .	. . .
Personal travel	2 240 . .	.6	1.7	2.6	7.5	18.1	34.0	42.7	51.4
Travel, debit	3 236 . .	**. . .**	**. . .**	**. . .**	**–6.2**	**–9.7**	**–11.0**	**–18.0**	**–29.6**
Business travel	3 237 . .	. . .	. . .	. . .	. . .	. . .	. . .	. . .	. . .
Personal travel	3 240 . .	. . .	. . .	. . .	–6.2	–9.7	–11.0	–18.0	–29.6
Other services, credit	2 200 BA	**11.0**	**12.3**	**13.1**	**19.7**	**29.2**	**33.5**	**33.0**	**30.8**
Communications	2 245 . .	. . .	. . .	. . .	1.0	3.6	2.6	1.0	.4
Construction	2 249 . .	. . .	. . .	. . .	. . .	. . .	. . .	. . .	. . .
Insurance	2 253 . .	.1	.1	.1	.3	.4	.3	.4	.4
Financial	2 260 . .	. . .	. . .	. . .	. . .	. . .	. . .	. . .	. . .
Computer and information	2 262 . .	. . .	. . .	. . .	. . .	. . .	. . .	. . .	. . .
Royalties and licence fees	2 266 . .	. . .	. . .	. . .	. . .	. . .	. . .	. . .	. . .
Other business services	2 268 . .	. . .	. . .	. . .	. . .	. . .	.2	.4	.8
Personal, cultural, and recreational	2 287 . .	. . .	. . .	. . .	. . .	. . .	. . .	. . .	. . .
Government, n.i.e.	2 291 . .	10.9	12.2	13.0	18.4	25.2	30.4	31.2	29.2
Other services, debit	3 200 BA	**–13.1**	**–6.7**	**–8.0**	**–19.2**	**–30.2**	**–52.2**	**–45.4**	**–55.0**
Communications	3 245 . .	. . .	. . .	. . .	–.9	–.9	–1.1	–.8	–.4
Construction	3 249 . .	. . .	. . .	. . .	. . .	. . .	–20.7	–20.5	–30.8
Insurance	3 253 . .	–1.3	–1.7	–1.6	–1.9	–2.8	–4.6	–.9	–.9
Financial	3 260 . .	. . .	. . .	. . .	. . .	. . .	. . .	. . .	. . .
Computer and information	3 262 . .	. . .	. . .	. . .	. . .	. . .	. . .	. . .	. . .
Royalties and licence fees	3 266 . .	. . .	. . .	. . .	. . .	. . .	. . .	. . .	. . .
Other business services	3 268 . .	–10.9	–4.3	–5.2	–15.3	–23.8	–23.0	–20.5	–19.9
Personal, cultural, and recreational	3 287 . .	. . .	. . .	. . .	. . .	. . .	. . .	. . .	. . .
Government, n.i.e.	3 291 . .	–.9	–.7	–1.2	–1.1	–2.7	–2.8	–2.7	–3.0

Table 2 (Continued). STANDARD PRESENTATION, 1988–95
(Millions of U.S. dollars)

	Code	1988	1989	1990	1991	1992	1993	1994	1995
C. INCOME	4 300 . .	−2.1	−2.3	−1.0	−1.1	1.0	3.0	.6	.2
Total credit	2 300 . .	*.4*	*.8*	*2.2*	*3.3*	*5.6*	*8.6*	*6.8*	*7.4*
Total debit	3 300 . .	*−2.5*	*−3.1*	*−3.2*	*−4.4*	*−4.6*	*−5.6*	*−6.2*	*−7.2*
Compensation of employees, credit	2 310 . .	. . .	. . .	. . .	. . .	**2.2**	**2.6**	**.5**	**.4**
Compensation of employees, debit	3 310 . .	. . .	. . .	. . .	. . .	**−.2**	**−.2**	**−.5**	**−.4**
Investment income, credit	2 320 . .	**.4**	**.8**	**2.2**	**3.3**	**3.4**	**6.0**	**6.3**	**7.0**
Direct investment income	2 330 . .	. . .	. . .	. . .	. . .	. . .	. . .	. . .	. . .
Dividends and distributed branch profits	2 332 . .	. . .	. . .	. . .	. . .	. . .	. . .	. . .	. . .
Reinvested earnings and undistributed branch profits	2 333 . .	. . .	. . .	. . .	. . .	. . .	. . .	. . .	. . .
Income on debt (interest)	2 334 . .	. . .	. . .	. . .	. . .	. . .	. . .	. . .	. . .
Portfolio investment income	2 339 . .	. . .	. . .	. . .	. . .	. . .	. . .	. . .	. . .
Income on equity	2 340 . .	. . .	. . .	. . .	. . .	. . .	. . .	. . .	. . .
Income on bonds and notes	2 350 . .	. . .	. . .	. . .	. . .	. . .	. . .	. . .	. . .
Income on money market instruments and financial derivatives	2 360 . .	. . .	. . .	. . .	. . .	. . .	. . .	. . .	. . .
Other investment income	2 370 . .	.4	.8	2.2	3.3	3.4	6.0	6.3	7.0
Investment income, debit	3 320 . .	**−2.5**	**−3.1**	**−3.2**	**−4.4**	**−4.4**	**−5.4**	**−5.7**	**−6.8**
Direct investment income	3 330 . .	. . .	. . .	. . .	. . .	. . .	. . .	. . .	. . .
Dividends and distributed branch profits	3 332 . .	. . .	. . .	. . .	. . .	. . .	. . .	. . .	. . .
Reinvested earnings and undistributed branch profits	3 333 . .	. . .	. . .	. . .	. . .	. . .	. . .	. . .	. . .
Income on debt (interest)	3 334 . .	. . .	. . .	. . .	. . .	. . .	. . .	. . .	. . .
Portfolio investment income	3 339 . .	. . .	. . .	. . .	. . .	. . .	. . .	. . .	. . .
Income on equity	3 340 . .	. . .	. . .	. . .	. . .	. . .	. . .	. . .	. . .
Income on bonds and notes	3 350 . .	. . .	. . .	. . .	. . .	. . .	. . .	. . .	. . .
Income on money market instruments and financial derivatives	3 360 . .	. . .	. . .	. . .	. . .	. . .	. . .	. . .	. . .
Other investment income	3 370 . .	−2.5	−3.1	−3.2	−4.4	−4.4	−5.4	−5.7	−6.8
D. CURRENT TRANSFERS	4 379 . .	24.9	54.8	55.6	82.6	60.7	101.5	121.4	105.9
Credit	2 379 . .	**25.5**	**55.2**	**55.9**	**85.5**	**62.9**	**103.5**	**124.6**	**109.3**
General government	2 380 . .	25.5	55.2	55.9	85.5	62.9	103.5	124.6	109.3
Other sectors	2 390 . .	. . .	. . .	. . .	. . .	. . .	. . .	. . .	. . .
Workers' remittances	2 391 . .	. . .	. . .	. . .	. . .	. . .	. . .	. . .	. . .
Other current transfers	2 392 . .	. . .	. . .	. . .	. . .	. . .	. . .	. . .	. . .
Debit	3 379 . .	**−.6**	**−.4**	**−.3**	**−2.9**	**−2.2**	**−2.0**	**−3.2**	**−3.4**
General government	3 380 . .	−.6	−.4	−.3	−2.9	−2.2	−2.0	−3.2	−3.4
Other sectors	3 390 . .	. . .	. . .	. . .	. . .	. . .	. . .	. . .	. . .
Workers' remittances	3 391 . .	. . .	. . .	. . .	. . .	. . .	. . .	. . .	. . .
Other current transfers	3 392 . .	. . .	. . .	. . .	. . .	. . .	. . .	. . .	. . .
CAPITAL AND FINANCIAL ACCOUNT	4 996 . .	**60.3**	**112.5**	**95.1**	**89.9**	**64.7**	**91.8**	**74.3**	**188.9**
CAPITAL ACCOUNT	4 994 . .	**6.7**	**8.3**	**10.9**	**10.4**	**8.6**	**9.5**	**9.5**	**13.4**
Total credit	2 994 . .	*6.7*	*8.3*	*10.9*	*10.4*	*8.6*	*9.5*	*9.5*	*13.4*
Total debit	3 994 . .	. . .	. . .	. . .	. . .	. . .	. . .	. . .	. . .
Capital transfers, credit	2 400 . .	**6.7**	**8.3**	**10.9**	**10.4**	**8.6**	**9.5**	**9.5**	**13.4**
General government	2 401 . .	. . .	. . .	. . .	. . .	. . .	. . .	. . .	. . .
Debt forgiveness	2 402 . .	. . .	. . .	. . .	. . .	. . .	. . .	. . .	. . .
Other capital transfers	2 410 . .	. . .	. . .	. . .	. . .	. . .	. . .	. . .	. . .
Other sectors	2 430 . .	6.7	8.3	10.9	10.4	8.6	9.5	9.5	13.4
Migrants' transfers	2 431 . .	6.7	8.3	10.9	10.4	8.6	9.5	9.5	13.4
Debt forgiveness	2 432 . .	. . .	. . .	. . .	. . .	. . .	. . .	. . .	. . .
Other capital transfers	2 440 . .	. . .	. . .	. . .	. . .	. . .	. . .	. . .	. . .
Capital transfers, debit	3 400 . .	. . .	. . .	. . .	. . .	. . .	. . .	. . .	. . .
General government	3 401 . .	. . .	. . .	. . .	. . .	. . .	. . .	. . .	. . .
Debt forgiveness	3 402 . .	. . .	. . .	. . .	. . .	. . .	. . .	. . .	. . .
Other capital transfers	3 410 . .	. . .	. . .	. . .	. . .	. . .	. . .	. . .	. . .
Other sectors	3 430 . .	. . .	. . .	. . .	. . .	. . .	. . .	. . .	. . .
Migrants' transfers	3 431 . .	. . .	. . .	. . .	. . .	. . .	. . .	. . .	. . .
Debt forgiveness	3 432 . .	. . .	. . .	. . .	. . .	. . .	. . .	. . .	. . .
Other capital transfers	3 440 . .	. . .	. . .	. . .	. . .	. . .	. . .	. . .	. . .
Nonproduced nonfinancial assets, credit	2 480 . .	. . .	. . .	. . .	. . .	. . .	. . .	. . .	. . .
Nonproduced nonfinancial assets, debit	3 480 . .	. . .	. . .	. . .	. . .	. . .	. . .	. . .	. . .

Table 2 (Continued). STANDARD PRESENTATION, 1988–95

(Millions of U.S. dollars)

	Code	1988	1989	1990	1991	1992	1993	1994	1995
FINANCIAL ACCOUNT	4 995 . .	**53.6**	**104.2**	**84.2**	**79.5**	**56.1**	**82.3**	**64.8**	**175.5**
A. DIRECT INVESTMENT	4 500 . .	2.0	4.0	6.0	6.9	7.8	47.6	42.4	77.2
Direct investment abroad	4 505 . .	**. . .**	**. . .**	**. . .**	**. . .**	**. . .**	**. . .**	**. . .**	**. . .**
Equity capital	4 510 . .	. . .	. . .	. . .	. . .	. . .	. . .	. . .	. . .
Claims on affiliated enterprises	4 515 . .	. . .	. . .	. . .	. . .	. . .	. . .	. . .	. . .
Liabilities to affiliated enterprises	4 520 . .	. . .	. . .	. . .	. . .	. . .	. . .	. . .	. . .
Reinvested earnings	4 525 . .	. . .	. . .	. . .	. . .	. . .	. . .	. . .	. . .
Other capital	4 530 . .	. . .	. . .	. . .	. . .	. . .	. . .	. . .	. . .
Claims on affiliated enterprises	4 535 . .	. . .	. . .	. . .	. . .	. . .	. . .	. . .	. . .
Liabilities to affiliated enterprises	4 540 . .	. . .	. . .	. . .	. . .	. . .	. . .	. . .	. . .
Direct investment in Lao PDR	4 555 . .	**2.0**	**4.0**	**6.0**	**6.9**	**7.8**	**47.6**	**42.4**	**77.2**
Equity capital	4 560 . .	. . .	. . .	. . .	. . .	. . .	. . .	. . .	. . .
Claims on direct investors	4 565 . .	. . .	. . .	. . .	. . .	. . .	. . .	. . .	. . .
Liabilities to direct investors	4 570 . .	. . .	. . .	. . .	. . .	. . .	. . .	. . .	. . .
Reinvested earnings	4 575 . .	. . .	. . .	. . .	. . .	. . .	. . .	. . .	. . .
Other capital	4 580 . .	2.0	4.0	6.0	6.9	7.8	47.6	42.4	77.2
Claims on direct investors	4 585 . .	2.0	4.0	6.0	6.9	7.8	47.6	42.4	77.2
Liabilities to direct investors	4 590 . .	. . .	. . .	. . .	. . .	. . .	. . .	. . .	. . .
B. PORTFOLIO INVESTMENT	4 600 . .	. . .	. . .	. . .	1.1	1.2	30.3	1.0	13.4
Assets	4 602 . .	**. . .**	**. . .**	**. . .**	**. . .**	**. . .**	**. . .**	**. . .**	**. . .**
Equity securities	4 610 . .	. . .	. . .	. . .	. . .	. . .	. . .	. . .	. . .
Monetary authorities	4 611 . .	. . .	. . .	. . .	. . .	. . .	. . .	. . .	. . .
General government	4 612 . .	. . .	. . .	. . .	. . .	. . .	. . .	. . .	. . .
Banks	4 613 . .	. . .	. . .	. . .	. . .	. . .	. . .	. . .	. . .
Other sectors	4 614 . .	. . .	. . .	. . .	. . .	. . .	. . .	. . .	. . .
Debt securities	4 619 . .	. . .	. . .	. . .	. . .	. . .	. . .	. . .	. . .
Bonds and notes	4 620 . .	. . .	. . .	. . .	. . .	. . .	. . .	. . .	. . .
Monetary authorities	4 621 . .	. . .	. . .	. . .	. . .	. . .	. . .	. . .	. . .
General government	4 622 . .	. . .	. . .	. . .	. . .	. . .	. . .	. . .	. . .
Banks	4 623 . .	. . .	. . .	. . .	. . .	. . .	. . .	. . .	. . .
Other sectors	4 624 . .	. . .	. . .	. . .	. . .	. . .	. . .	. . .	. . .
Money market instruments	4 630 . .	. . .	. . .	. . .	. . .	. . .	. . .	. . .	. . .
Monetary authorities	4 631 . .	. . .	. . .	. . .	. . .	. . .	. . .	. . .	. . .
General government	4 632 . .	. . .	. . .	. . .	. . .	. . .	. . .	. . .	. . .
Banks	4 633 . .	. . .	. . .	. . .	. . .	. . .	. . .	. . .	. . .
Other sectors	4 634 . .	. . .	. . .	. . .	. . .	. . .	. . .	. . .	. . .
Financial derivatives	4 640 . .	. . .	. . .	. . .	. . .	. . .	. . .	. . .	. . .
Monetary authorities	4 641 . .	. . .	. . .	. . .	. . .	. . .	. . .	. . .	. . .
General government	4 642 . .	. . .	. . .	. . .	. . .	. . .	. . .	. . .	. . .
Banks	4 643 . .	. . .	. . .	. . .	. . .	. . .	. . .	. . .	. . .
Other sectors	4 644 . .	. . .	. . .	. . .	. . .	. . .	. . .	. . .	. . .
Liabilities	4 652 . .	**. . .**	**. . .**	**. . .**	**1.1**	**1.2**	**30.3**	**1.0**	**13.4**
Equity securities	4 660 . .	. . .	. . .	. . .	1.1	1.2	30.3	1.0	13.4
Banks	4 663 . .	. . .	. . .	. . .	. . .	. . .	17.0	. . .	6.7
Other sectors	4 664 . .	. . .	. . .	. . .	1.1	1.2	13.3	1.0	6.7
Debt securities	4 669 . .	. . .	. . .	. . .	. . .	. . .	. . .	. . .	. . .
Bonds and notes	4 670 . .	. . .	. . .	. . .	. . .	. . .	. . .	. . .	. . .
Monetary authorities	4 671 . .	. . .	. . .	. . .	. . .	. . .	. . .	. . .	. . .
General government	4 672 . .	. . .	. . .	. . .	. . .	. . .	. . .	. . .	. . .
Banks	4 673 . .	. . .	. . .	. . .	. . .	. . .	. . .	. . .	. . .
Other sectors	4 674 . .	. . .	. . .	. . .	. . .	. . .	. . .	. . .	. . .
Money market instruments	4 680 . .	. . .	. . .	. . .	. . .	. . .	. . .	. . .	. . .
Monetary authorities	4 681 . .	. . .	. . .	. . .	. . .	. . .	. . .	. . .	. . .
General government	4 682 . .	. . .	. . .	. . .	. . .	. . .	. . .	. . .	. . .
Banks	4 683 . .	. . .	. . .	. . .	. . .	. . .	. . .	. . .	. . .
Other sectors	4 684 . .	. . .	. . .	. . .	. . .	. . .	. . .	. . .	. . .
Financial derivatives	4 690 . .	. . .	. . .	. . .	. . .	. . .	. . .	. . .	. . .
Monetary authorities	4 691 . .	. . .	. . .	. . .	. . .	. . .	. . .	. . .	. . .
General government	4 692 . .	. . .	. . .	. . .	. . .	. . .	. . .	. . .	. . .
Banks	4 693 . .	. . .	. . .	. . .	. . .	. . .	. . .	. . .	. . .
Other sectors	4 694 . .	. . .	. . .	. . .	. . .	. . .	. . .	. . .	. . .

Table 2 (Concluded). STANDARD PRESENTATION, 1988–95
(Millions of U.S. dollars)

	Code	1988	1989	1990	1991	1992	1993	1994	1995
C. OTHER INVESTMENT	4 700 . .	52.3	101.2	78.9	98.5	59.9	28.2	27.0	98.1
Assets	4 703 . .	**–28.7**	**–29.4**	**–4.5**	**34.2**	**–16.1**	**–43.2**	**–9.4**	**–5.7**
Trade credits	4 706 . .	...	...	...	...	...	...	...	...
General government: long-term	4 708 . .	...	...	...	...	...	...	...	...
General government: short-term	4 709 . .	...	...	...	...	...	...	...	...
Other sectors: long-term	4 711 . .	...	...	...	...	...	...	...	...
Other sectors: short-term	4 712 . .	...	...	...	...	...	...	...	...
Loans	4 714 . .	...	...	...	...	...	...	...	...
Monetary authorities: long-term	4 717 . .	...	...	...	...	...	...	...	...
Monetary authorities: short-term	4 718 . .	...	...	...	...	...	...	...	...
General government: long-term	4 720 . .	...	...	...	...	...	...	...	...
General government: short-term	4 721 . .	...	...	...	...	...	...	...	...
Banks: long-term	4 723 . .	...	...	...	...	...	...	...	...
Banks: short-term	4 724 . .	...	...	...	...	...	...	...	...
Other sectors: long-term	4 726 . .	...	...	...	...	...	...	...	...
Other sectors: short-term	4 727 . .	...	...	...	...	...	...	...	...
Currency and deposits	4 730 . .	–28.7	–29.4	–4.5	34.2	–16.1	–43.2	–9.4	–5.7
Monetary authorities	4 731 . .	...	...	...	...	...	...	...	...
General government	4 732 . .	...	...	...	...	...	...	...	...
Banks	4 733 . .	–28.7	–29.4	–4.5	34.2	–16.1	–43.2	–9.4	–5.7
Other sectors	4 734 . .	...	...	...	...	...	...	...	...
Other assets	4 736 . .	...	...	...	...	...	...	...	...
Monetary authorities: long-term	4 738 . .	...	...	...	...	...	...	...	...
Monetary authorities: short-term	4 739 . .	...	...	...	...	...	...	...	...
General government: long-term	4 741 . .	...	...	...	...	...	...	...	...
General government: short-term	4 742 . .	...	...	...	...	...	...	...	...
Banks: long-term	4 744 . .	...	...	...	...	...	...	...	...
Banks: short-term	4 745 . .	...	...	...	...	...	...	...	...
Other sectors: long-term	4 747 . .	...	...	...	...	...	...	...	...
Other sectors: short-term	4 748 . .	...	...	...	...	...	...	...	...
Liabilities	4 753 . .	**81.0**	**130.6**	**83.4**	**64.3**	**76.0**	**71.4**	**36.4**	**103.8**
Trade credits	4 756 . .	...	...	...	...	...	...	...	...
General government: long-term	4 758 . .	...	...	...	...	...	...	...	...
General government: short-term	4 759 . .	...	...	...	...	...	...	...	...
Other sectors: long-term	4 761 . .	...	...	...	...	...	...	...	...
Other sectors: short-term	4 762 . .	...	...	...	...	...	...	...	...
Loans	4 764 . .	28.1	86.7	65.5	56.9	84.5	86.8	63.8	124.8
Use of Fund credit and loans from the Fund	4 766 . .	–3.4	5.4	–.5	11.8	8.1	8.3	8.1	15.6
Monetary authorities: other long term	4 767 . .	...	...	...	...	...	...	...	...
Monetary authorities: short-term	4 768 . .	...	...	...	...	...	...	...	...
General government: long-term	4 770 . .	22.3	48.5	45.1	35.1	62.1	69.5	55.7	109.2
General government: short-term	4 771 . .	...	...	...	...	...	...	...	...
Banks: long-term	4 773 . .	...	...	...	...	...	...	...	...
Banks: short-term	4 774 . .	...	...	...	...	...	...	...	...
Other sectors: long-term	4 776 . .	...	...	...	...	...	...	...	...
Other sectors: short-term	4 777 . .	9.2	32.8	20.9	10.0	14.3	9.0	...	...
Currency and deposits	4 780 . .	1.5	–1.2	–.9	–.7	–1.2	–7.4	–17.0	–15.8
Monetary authorities	4 781 . .	...	...	...	...	...	...	...	...
General government	4 782 . .	...	...	...	...	...	...	...	...
Banks	4 783 . .	1.5	–1.2	–.9	–.7	–1.2	–7.4	–17.0	–15.8
Other sectors	4 784 . .	...	...	...	...	...	...	...	...
Other liabilities	4 786 . .	51.4	45.1	18.8	8.1	–7.3	–8.0	–10.4	–5.2
Monetary authorities: long-term	4 788 . .	...	...	...	...	...	...	...	...
Monetary authorities: short-term	4 789 . .	51.4	45.1	18.8	8.1	–7.3	–8.0	–10.4	–5.2
General government: long-term	4 791 . .	...	...	...	...	...	...	...	...
General government: short-term	4 792 . .	...	...	...	...	...	...	...	...
Banks: long-term	4 794 . .	...	...	...	...	...	...	...	...
Banks: short-term	4 795 . .	...	...	...	...	...	...	...	...
Other sectors: long-term	4 797 . .	...	...	...	...	...	...	...	...
Other sectors: short-term	4 798 . .	...	...	...	...	...	...	...	...
D. RESERVE ASSETS	4 800 . .	–.7	–1.0	–.7	–27.0	–12.8	–23.8	–5.6	–13.2
Monetary gold	4 810 . .	...	...	...	...	...	...	...	...
Special drawing rights	4 820 . .	...	...	...	–.4	–.3	–1.9	–7.7	–3.0
Reserve position in the Fund	4 830 . .	...	...	...	...	...	...	...	...
Foreign exchange	4 840 . .	–.7	–1.0	–.7	–26.6	–12.5	–21.9	2.1	–10.2
Other claims	4 880 . .	...	...	...	...	...	...	...	...
NET ERRORS AND OMISSIONS	4 998 . .	**17.4**	**–31.2**	**–40.2**	**–60.3**	**–16.3**	**–29.4**	**44.2**	**–74.6**

Latvia
941

Table 1. ANALYTIC PRESENTATION, 1988–95
(Millions of U.S. dollars)

	Code	1988	1989	1990	1991	1992	1993	1994	1995
A. Current Account [1]	4 993 Y.	...	...	...	...	**191**	**417**	**201**	**–27**
Goods: exports f.o.b	2 100 . .	...	...	...	...	800	1,054	1,022	1,368
Goods: imports f.o.b	3 100 . .	...	...	...	...	–840	–1,051	–1,322	–1,947
Balance on Goods	4 100 . .	...	...	...	...	*–40*	*3*	*–301*	*–580*
Services: credit	2 200 . .	...	...	...	...	291	533	657	712
Services: debit	3 200 . .	...	...	...	...	–156	–205	–297	–246
Balance on Goods and Services	4 991 . .	...	...	...	...	*94*	*332*	*60*	*–113*
Income: credit	2 300 . .	...	...	...	...	3	17	51	71
Income: debit	3 300 . .	...	...	...	...	–1	–10	–42	–53
Balance on Goods, Services, and Income	4 992 . .	...	...	...	...	*95*	*339*	*68*	*–95*
Current transfers: credit	2 379 Y.	...	...	...	...	97	81	136	72
Current transfers: debit	3 379 . .	...	...	...	...	–1	–3	–3	–5
B. Capital Account [1]	4 994 Y.	...	...	...	...	...	...	...	...
Capital account: credit	2 994 Y.	...	...	...	...	...	...	...	...
Capital account: debit	3 994 . .	...	...	...	...	...	...	...	...
Total, Groups A Plus B	4 010 . .	...	...	...	...	*191*	*417*	*201*	*–27*
C. Financial Account [1]	4 995 X.	...	...	...	...	**–110**	**67**	**363**	**692**
Direct investment abroad	4 505 . .	...	...	...	...	–2	5	65	65
Direct investment in Latvia	4 555 Y.	...	...	...	...	29	45	214	180
Portfolio investment assets	4 602 . .	...	...	...	...	...	...	–22	–37
Equity securities	4 610 . .	...	...	...	...	...	...	–12	–7
Debt securities	4 619 . .	...	...	...	...	...	...	–10	–30
Portfolio investment liabilities	4 652 Y.	...	...	...	...	...	...	...	...
Equity securities	4 660 Y.	...	...	...	...	...	...	...	...
Debt securities	4 669 Y.	...	...	...	...	...	...	...	...
Other investment assets	4 703 . .	...	...	...	...	–371	–129	–386	–31
Monetary authorities	4 703 .A	...	...	...	...	–24	39	5	1
General government	4 703 .B	...	...	...	...	3	...	...	...
Banks	4 703 .C	...	...	...	...	–59	–119	–400	99
Other sectors	4 703 .D	...	...	...	...	–291	–50	8	–130
Other investment liabilities	4 753 X.	...	...	...	...	234	146	493	514
Monetary authorities	4 753 XA	...	...	...	...	10	–4	–5	...
General government	4 753 YB	...	...	...	...	22	99	54	53
Banks	4 753 YC	...	...	...	...	5	76	272	147
Other sectors	4 753 YD	...	...	...	...	198	–25	172	315
Total, Groups A Through C	4 020 . .	...	...	...	...	*81*	*484*	*565*	*664*
D. Net Errors and Omissions	4 998 . .	...	...	...	...	**–44**	**–186**	**–508**	**–698**
Total, Groups A Through D	4 030 . .	...	...	...	...	*37*	*298*	*57*	*–33*
E. Reserves and Related Items	4 040 . .	...	...	...	...	**–37**	**–298**	**–57**	**33**
Reserve assets	4 800 . .	...	...	...	...	–73	–371	–103	36
Use of Fund credit and loans	4 766 . .	...	...	...	...	36	74	47	–3
Liabilities constituting foreign authorities' reserves	4 900 . .	...	...	...	...	...	...	...	...
Exceptional financing	4 920 . .	...	...	...	...	...	...	...	...
Conversion rates: lats per U.S. dollar	0 101 . .	...	...	...	...	**.7365**	**.6753**	**.5598**	**.5276**

[1] Excludes components that have been classified in the categories of Group E.

Table 2. STANDARD PRESENTATION, 1988–95
(Millions of U.S. dollars)

	Code			1988	1989	1990	1991	1992	1993	1994	1995
CURRENT ACCOUNT	4	993	. .	...	...	...	...	**191**	**417**	**201**	**–27**
A. GOODS	4	100	. .	...	...	...	...	–40	3	–301	–580
Credit	2	100	. .	...	...	...	...	**800**	**1,054**	**1,022**	**1,368**
General merchandise: exports f.o.b.	2	110	. .	...	...	...	...	783	1,041	1,022	1,368
Goods for processing: exports f.o.b.	2	150	. .	...	...	...	...	...	...	...	...
Repairs on goods	2	160	. .	...	...	...	...	...	...	...	...
Goods procured in ports by carriers	2	170	. .	...	...	...	...	...	...	...	...
Nonmonetary gold	2	180	. .	...	...	...	...	16	13	...	...
Debit	3	100	. .	...	...	...	...	**–840**	**–1,051**	**–1,322**	**–1,947**
General merchandise: imports f.o.b.	3	110	. .	...	...	...	...	–797	–1,004	–1,282	–1,897
Goods for processing: imports f.o.b.	3	150	. .	...	...	...	...	...	...	...	...
Repairs on goods	3	160	. .	...	...	...	...	...	...	...	...
Goods procured in ports by carriers	3	170	. .	...	...	...	...	–43	–47	–40	–51
Nonmonetary gold	3	180	. .	...	...	...	...	...	...	...	...
B. SERVICES	4	200	. .	...	...	...	...	134	329	360	466
Total credit	2	200	. .	...	...	...	...	*291*	*533*	*657*	*712*
Total debit	3	200	. .	...	...	...	...	*–156*	*–205*	*–297*	*–246*
Transportation services, credit	2	205	. .	...	...	...	...	**275**	**425**	**600**	**652**
Passenger	2	205	BA	...	...	...	...	*1*	*3*	*8*	*9*
Freight	2	205	BB	...	...	...	...	*233*	*329*	*320*	*417*
Other	2	205	BC	...	...	...	...	*42*	*93*	*273*	*225*
Sea transport, passenger	2	207	. .	...	...	...	...	...	...	...	...
Sea transport, freight	2	208	. .	...	...	...	...	220	210	211	168
Sea transport, other	2	209	. .	...	...	...	...	32	73	106	149
Air transport, passenger	2	211	. .	...	...	...	...	...	2	5	4
Air transport, freight	2	212	. .	...	...	...	...	...	...	...	...
Air transport, other	2	213	. .	...	...	...	...	2	5	4	6
Other transport, passenger	2	215	. .	...	...	...	...	1	2	3	6
Other transport, freight	2	216	. .	...	...	...	...	13	119	109	248
Other transport, other	2	217	. .	...	...	...	...	8	16	163	70
Transportation services, debit	3	205	. .	...	...	...	...	**–99**	**–130**	**–136**	**–153**
Passenger	3	205	BA	...	...	...	...	*–1*	*–29*	*–34*	*–38*
Freight	3	205	BB	...	...	...	...	*–16*	*–16*	*–34*	*–48*
Other	3	205	BC	...	...	...	...	*–81*	*–85*	*–68*	*–67*
Sea transport, passenger	3	207	. .	...	...	...	...	...	...	...	...
Sea transport, freight	3	208	. .	...	...	...	...	...	...	...	...
Sea transport, other	3	209	. .	...	...	...	...	–78	–76	–58	–53
Air transport, passenger	3	211	. .	...	...	...	...	–1	–29	–34	–38
Air transport, freight	3	212	. .	...	...	...	...	...	...	...	...
Air transport, other	3	213	. .	...	...	...	...	...	–3	–3	–5
Other transport, passenger	3	215	. .	...	...	...	...	...	...	...	...
Other transport, freight	3	216	. .	...	...	...	...	–16	–16	–34	–48
Other transport, other	3	217	. .	...	...	...	...	–3	–6	–7	–9
Travel, credit	2	236	. .	...	...	...	...	**7**	**15**	**18**	**20**
Business travel	2	237	. .	...	...	...	...	...	...	...	...
Personal travel	2	240	. .	...	...	...	...	7	15	18	20
Travel, debit	3	236	. .	...	...	...	...	**–13**	**–29**	**–31**	**–24**
Business travel	3	237	. .	...	...	...	...	–1	–1	–2	–4
Personal travel	3	240	. .	...	...	...	...	–13	–28	–29	–21
Other services, credit	2	200	BA	...	...	...	...	**8**	**93**	**39**	**41**
Communications	2	245	. .	...	...	...	...	...	3	5	5
Construction	2	249	. .	...	...	...	...	4	5	12	8
Insurance	2	253	. .	...	...	...	...	...	...	...	...
Financial	2	260	. .	...	...	...	...	...	...	6	17
Computer and information	2	262	. .	...	...	...	...	...	1	...	...
Royalties and licence fees	2	266	. .	...	...	...	...	...	...	...	...
Other business services	2	268	. .	...	...	...	...	3	79	10	8
Personal, cultural, and recreational	2	287	. .	...	...	...	...	...	...	...	...
Government, n.i.e.	2	291	. .	...	...	...	...	1	5	6	2
Other services, debit	3	200	BA	...	...	...	...	**–44**	**–46**	**–130**	**–68**
Communications	3	245	. .	...	...	...	...	...	–1	–5	–4
Construction	3	249	. .	...	...	...	...	–2	–2	–1	–13
Insurance	3	253	. .	...	...	...	...	–6	–11	–14	–10
Financial	3	260	. .	...	...	...	...	...	–1	–13	–6
Computer and information	3	262	. .	...	...	...	...	...	–1	...	...
Royalties and licence fees	3	266	. .	...	...	...	...	...	...	...	...
Other business services	3	268	. .	...	...	...	...	–1	–4	–11	–15
Personal, cultural, and recreational	3	287	. .	...	...	...	...	...	...	...	...
Government, n.i.e.	3	291	. .	...	...	...	...	–36	–26	–86	–21

Table 2 (Continued). STANDARD PRESENTATION, 1988–95
(Millions of U.S. dollars)

	Code	1988	1989	1990	1991	1992	1993	1994	1995
C. INCOME	4 300 . .	. . .	. . .	. . .	. . .	2	7	9	19
Total credit	2 300 . .	. . .	. . .	. . .	. . .	*3*	*17*	*51*	*71*
Total debit	3 300 . .	. . .	. . .	. . .	. . .	*–1*	*–10*	*–42*	*–53*
Compensation of employees, credit	2 310 . .	. . .	. . .	. . .	. . .	. . .	. . .	. . .	. . .
Compensation of employees, debit	3 310 . .	. . .	. . .	. . .	. . .	. . .	. . .	**–2**	**–1**
Investment income, credit	2 320 . .	. . .	. . .	. . .	. . .	**3**	**17**	**51**	**71**
Direct investment income	2 330 . .	. . .	. . .	. . .	. . .	. . .	5	. . .	. . .
Dividends and distributed branch profits	2 332 . .	. . .	. . .	. . .	. . .	. . .	5	. . .	. . .
Reinvested earnings and undistributed branch profits	2 333 . .	. . .	. . .	. . .	. . .	. . .	. . .	. . .	. . .
Income on debt (interest)	2 334 . .	. . .	. . .	. . .	. . .	. . .	. . .	. . .	. . .
Portfolio investment income	2 339 . .	. . .	. . .	. . .	. . .	. . .	2	9	38
Income on equity	2 340 . .	. . .	. . .	. . .	. . .	. . .	. . .	. . .	38
Income on bonds and notes	2 350 . .	. . .	. . .	. . .	. . .	. . .	1	8	. . .
Income on money market instruments and financial derivatives	2 360 . .	. . .	. . .	. . .	. . .	. . .	. . .	. . .	. . .
Other investment income	2 370 . .	. . .	. . .	. . .	. . .	2	11	42	33
Investment income, debit	3 320 . .	. . .	. . .	. . .	. . .	**–1**	**–10**	**–40**	**–51**
Direct investment income	3 330 . .	. . .	. . .	. . .	. . .	. . .	. . .	. . .	. . .
Dividends and distributed branch profits	3 332 . .	. . .	. . .	. . .	. . .	. . .	. . .	. . .	. . .
Reinvested earnings and undistributed branch profits	3 333 . .	. . .	. . .	. . .	. . .	. . .	. . .	. . .	. . .
Income on debt (interest)	3 334 . .	. . .	. . .	. . .	. . .	. . .	. . .	. . .	. . .
Portfolio investment income	3 339 . .	. . .	. . .	. . .	. . .	. . .	. . .	. . .	. . .
Income on equity	3 340 . .	. . .	. . .	. . .	. . .	. . .	. . .	. . .	. . .
Income on bonds and notes	3 350 . .	. . .	. . .	. . .	. . .	. . .	. . .	. . .	. . .
Income on money market instruments and financial derivatives	3 360 . .	. . .	. . .	. . .	. . .	. . .	. . .	. . .	. . .
Other investment income	3 370 . .	. . .	. . .	. . .	. . .	–1	–10	–40	–51
D. CURRENT TRANSFERS	4 379 . .	. . .	. . .	. . .	. . .	96	78	133	68
Credit	2 379 . .	. . .	. . .	. . .	. . .	**97**	**81**	**136**	**72**
General government	2 380 . .	. . .	. . .	. . .	. . .	91	50	110	36
Other sectors	2 390 . .	. . .	. . .	. . .	. . .	6	31	26	36
Workers' remittances	2 391 . .	. . .	. . .	. . .	. . .	. . .	. . .	. . .	. . .
Other current transfers	2 392 . .	. . .	. . .	. . .	. . .	6	31	26	36
Debit	3 379 . .	. . .	. . .	. . .	. . .	**–1**	**–3**	**–3**	**–5**
General government	3 380 . .	. . .	. . .	. . .	. . .	–1	–3	–3	–5
Other sectors	3 390 . .	. . .	. . .	. . .	. . .	. . .	. . .	. . .	. . .
Workers' remittances	3 391 . .	. . .	. . .	. . .	. . .	. . .	. . .	. . .	. . .
Other current transfers	3 392 . .	. . .	. . .	. . .	. . .	. . .	. . .	. . .	. . .
CAPITAL AND FINANCIAL ACCOUNT	4 996 . .	. . .	. . .	. . .	. . .	**–148**	**–231**	**307**	**725**
CAPITAL ACCOUNT	4 994 . .	. . .	. . .	. . .	. . .	. . .	. . .	. . .	. . .
Total credit	2 994 . .	. . .	. . .	. . .	. . .	. . .	. . .	. . .	. . .
Total debit	3 994 . .	. . .	. . .	. . .	. . .	. . .	. . .	. . .	. . .
Capital transfers, credit	2 400 . .	. . .	. . .	. . .	. . .	. . .	. . .	. . .	. . .
General government	2 401 . .	. . .	. . .	. . .	. . .	. . .	. . .	. . .	. . .
Debt forgiveness	2 402 . .	. . .	. . .	. . .	. . .	. . .	. . .	. . .	. . .
Other capital transfers	2 410 . .	. . .	. . .	. . .	. . .	. . .	. . .	. . .	. . .
Other sectors	2 430 . .	. . .	. . .	. . .	. . .	. . .	. . .	. . .	. . .
Migrants' transfers	2 431 . .	. . .	. . .	. . .	. . .	. . .	. . .	. . .	. . .
Debt forgiveness	2 432 . .	. . .	. . .	. . .	. . .	. . .	. . .	. . .	. . .
Other capital transfers	2 440 . .	. . .	. . .	. . .	. . .	. . .	. . .	. . .	. . .
Capital transfers, debit	3 400 . .	. . .	. . .	. . .	. . .	. . .	. . .	. . .	. . .
General government	3 401 . .	. . .	. . .	. . .	. . .	. . .	. . .	. . .	. . .
Debt forgiveness	3 402 . .	. . .	. . .	. . .	. . .	. . .	. . .	. . .	. . .
Other capital transfers	3 410 . .	. . .	. . .	. . .	. . .	. . .	. . .	. . .	. . .
Other sectors	3 430 . .	. . .	. . .	. . .	. . .	. . .	. . .	. . .	. . .
Migrants' transfers	3 431 . .	. . .	. . .	. . .	. . .	. . .	. . .	. . .	. . .
Debt forgiveness	3 432 . .	. . .	. . .	. . .	. . .	. . .	. . .	. . .	. . .
Other capital transfers	3 440 . .	. . .	. . .	. . .	. . .	. . .	. . .	. . .	. . .
Nonproduced nonfinancial assets, credit	2 480 . .	. . .	. . .	. . .	. . .	. . .	. . .	. . .	. . .
Nonproduced nonfinancial assets, debit	3 480 . .	. . .	. . .	. . .	. . .	. . .	. . .	. . .	. . .

Table 2 (Continued). STANDARD PRESENTATION, 1988–95
(Millions of U.S. dollars)

	Code	1988	1989	1990	1991	1992	1993	1994	1995
FINANCIAL ACCOUNT	4 995 . .	...	...	...	...	**–148**	**–231**	**307**	**725**
A. DIRECT INVESTMENT	4 500 . .	...	...	...	...	27	50	279	245
Direct investment abroad	4 505 . .	...	...	...	...	**–2**	**5**	**65**	**65**
Equity capital	4 510 . .	...	...	...	...	–1	–5	26	2
Claims on affiliated enterprises	4 515 . .	...	...	...	...	–1	–5	1	2
Liabilities to affiliated enterprises	4 520 . .	...	...	...	...	...	...	25	...
Reinvested earnings	4 525 . .	...	...	...	...	...	...	...	...
Other capital	4 530 . .	...	...	...	...	–1	9	38	63
Claims on affiliated enterprises	4 535 . .	...	...	...	...	–1	...	–9	1
Liabilities to affiliated enterprises	4 540 . .	...	...	...	...	...	9	47	62
Direct investment in Latvia	4 555 . .	...	...	...	...	**29**	**45**	**214**	**180**
Equity capital	4 560 . .	...	...	...	...	29	45	214	180
Claims on direct investors	4 565 . .	...	...	...	...	–1	–2	4	–3
Liabilities to direct investors	4 570 . .	...	...	...	...	30	47	210	182
Reinvested earnings	4 575 . .	...	...	...	...	...	...	...	...
Other capital	4 580 . .	...	...	...	...	...	...	...	...
Claims on direct investors	4 585 . .	...	...	...	...	...	...	...	...
Liabilities to direct investors	4 590 . .	...	...	...	...	...	...	...	...
B. PORTFOLIO INVESTMENT	4 600 . .	...	...	...	...	...	...	–22	–37
Assets	4 602 . .	...	...	...	...	...	...	**–22**	**–37**
Equity securities	4 610 . .	...	...	...	...	...	...	–12	–7
Monetary authorities	4 611 . .	...	...	...	...	...	...	...	...
General government	4 612 . .	...	...	...	...	...	...	...	...
Banks	4 613 . .	...	...	...	...	...	...	–12	–5
Other sectors	4 614 . .	...	...	...	...	...	...	...	–1
Debt securities	4 619 . .	...	...	...	...	...	...	–10	–30
Bonds and notes	4 620 . .	...	...	...	...	...	...	–10	–30
Monetary authorities	4 621 . .	...	...	...	...	...	...	...	...
General government	4 622 . .	...	...	...	...	...	...	...	...
Banks	4 623 . .	...	...	...	...	...	...	–9	–30
Other sectors	4 624 . .	...	...	...	...	...	...	–1	...
Money market instruments	4 630 . .	...	...	...	...	...	...	...	...
Monetary authorities	4 631 . .	...	...	...	...	...	...	...	...
General government	4 632 . .	...	...	...	...	...	...	...	...
Banks	4 633 . .	...	...	...	...	...	...	...	...
Other sectors	4 634 . .	...	...	...	...	...	...	...	...
Financial derivatives	4 640 . .	...	...	...	...	...	...	...	...
Monetary authorities	4 641 . .	...	...	...	...	...	...	...	...
General government	4 642 . .	...	...	...	...	...	...	...	...
Banks	4 643 . .	...	...	...	...	...	...	...	...
Other sectors	4 644 . .	...	...	...	...	...	...	...	...
Liabilities	4 652 . .	...	...	...	...	...	...	...	...
Equity securities	4 660 . .	...	...	...	...	...	...	...	...
Banks	4 663 . .	...	...	...	...	...	...	...	...
Other sectors	4 664 . .	...	...	...	...	...	...	...	...
Debt securities	4 669 . .	...	...	...	...	...	...	...	...
Bonds and notes	4 670 . .	...	...	...	...	...	...	...	...
Monetary authorities	4 671 . .	...	...	...	...	...	...	...	...
General government	4 672 . .	...	...	...	...	...	...	...	...
Banks	4 673 . .	...	...	...	...	...	...	...	...
Other sectors	4 674 . .	...	...	...	...	...	...	...	...
Money market instruments	4 680 . .	...	...	...	...	...	...	...	...
Monetary authorities	4 681 . .	...	...	...	...	...	...	...	...
General government	4 682 . .	...	...	...	...	...	...	...	...
Banks	4 683 . .	...	...	...	...	...	...	...	...
Other sectors	4 684 . .	...	...	...	...	...	...	...	...
Financial derivatives	4 690 . .	...	...	...	...	...	...	...	...
Monetary authorities	4 691 . .	...	...	...	...	...	...	...	...
General government	4 692 . .	...	...	...	...	...	...	...	...
Banks	4 693 . .	...	...	...	...	...	...	...	...
Other sectors	4 694 . .	...	...	...	...	...	...	...	...

Table 2 (Concluded). STANDARD PRESENTATION, 1988–95
(Millions of U.S. dollars)

	Code	1988	1989	1990	1991	1992	1993	1994	1995
C. OTHER INVESTMENT	4 700 . .	...	...	...	...	–101	91	153	481
Assets	4 703 . .	**...**	**...**	**...**	**...**	**–371**	**–129**	**–386**	**–31**
Trade credits	4 706 . .	...	...	...	...	–177	–34	39	–23
General government: long-term	4 708 . .	...	...	...	...	...	...	...	...
General government: short-term	4 709 . .	...	...	...	...	...	...	...	...
Other sectors: long-term	4 711 . .	...	...	...	...	...	...	...	...
Other sectors: short-term	4 712 . .	...	...	...	...	–177	–34	39	–23
Loans	4 714 . .	...	...	...	...	–11	–21	–180	161
Monetary authorities: long-term	4 717 . .	...	...	...	...	...	...	...	...
Monetary authorities: short-term	4 718 . .	...	...	...	...	...	...	...	...
General government: long-term	4 720 . .	...	...	...	...	...	...	...	...
General government: short-term	4 721 . .	...	...	...	...	...	...	...	...
Banks: long-term	4 723 . .	...	...	...	...	...	...	...	22
Banks: short-term	4 724 . .	...	...	...	...	...	–33	–180	143
Other sectors: long-term	4 726 . .	...	...	...	...	...	...	...	...
Other sectors: short-term	4 727 . .	...	...	...	...	...	...	–1	–4
Currency and deposits	4 730 . .	...	...	...	...	–81	–70	–197	–65
Monetary authorities	4 731 . .	...	...	...	...	–13	27	4	1
General government	4 732 . .	...	...	...	...	3	...	...	...
Banks	4 733 . .	...	...	...	...	–59	–86	–217	–59
Other sectors	4 734 . .	...	...	...	...	–12	–11	16	–7
Other assets	4 736 . .	...	...	...	...	–102	–4	–49	–104
Monetary authorities: long-term	4 738 . .	...	...	...	...	...	...	...	...
Monetary authorities: short-term	4 739 . .	...	...	...	...	...	...	...	...
General government: long-term	4 741 . .	...	...	...	...	...	...	...	...
General government: short-term	4 742 . .	...	...	...	...	...	...	...	...
Banks: long-term	4 744 . .	...	...	...	...	...	...	...	...
Banks: short-term	4 745 . .	...	...	...	...	...	...	–3	–8
Other sectors: long-term	4 747 . .	...	...	...	...	...	...	...	...
Other sectors: short-term	4 748 . .	...	...	...	...	–102	–4	–45	–96
Liabilities	4 753 . .	**...**	**...**	**...**	**...**	**270**	**220**	**540**	**512**
Trade credits	4 756 . .	...	...	...	...	79	–22	51	139
General government: long-term	4 758 . .	...	...	...	...	...	...	...	...
General government: short-term	4 759 . .	...	...	...	...	...	...	...	...
Other sectors: long-term	4 761 . .	...	...	...	...	...	...	...	...
Other sectors: short-term	4 762 . .	...	...	...	...	79	–22	51	139
Loans	4 764 . .	...	...	...	...	62	195	221	62
Use of Fund credit and loans from the Fund	4 766 . .	...	...	...	...	36	74	47	–3
Monetary authorities: other long term	4 767 . .	...	...	...	...	...	...	...	...
Monetary authorities: short-term	4 768 . .	...	...	...	...	...	...	...	...
General government: long-term	4 770 . .	...	...	...	...	22	99	54	53
General government: short-term	4 771 . .	...	...	...	...	...	...	...	...
Banks: long-term	4 773 . .	...	...	...	...	...	...	...	...
Banks: short-term	4 774 . .	...	...	...	...	...	...	75	–60
Other sectors: long-term	4 776 . .	...	...	...	...	...	...	...	...
Other sectors: short-term	4 777 . .	...	...	...	...	5	23	45	72
Currency and deposits	4 780 . .	...	...	...	...	15	72	178	114
Monetary authorities	4 781 . .	...	...	...	...	10	–4	–5	...
General government	4 782 . .	...	...	...	...	...	...	...	...
Banks	4 783 . .	...	...	...	...	5	76	183	115
Other sectors	4 784 . .	...	...	...	...	...	...	...	...
Other liabilities	4 786 . .	...	...	...	...	114	–25	90	196
Monetary authorities: long-term	4 788 . .	...	...	...	...	...	...	...	...
Monetary authorities: short-term	4 789 . .	...	...	...	...	...	...	...	...
General government: long-term	4 791 . .	...	...	...	...	...	...	...	...
General government: short-term	4 792 . .	...	...	...	...	...	...	...	...
Banks: long-term	4 794 . .	...	...	...	...	...	...	...	...
Banks: short-term	4 795 . .	...	...	...	...	...	...	13	92
Other sectors: long-term	4 797 . .	...	...	...	...	114	–25	76	104
Other sectors: short-term	4 798 . .	...	...	...	...	...	...	...	...
D. RESERVE ASSETS	4 800 . .	...	...	...	...	–73	–371	–103	36
Monetary gold	4 810 . .	...	...	...	...	...	...	...	...
Special drawing rights	4 820 . .	...	...	...	...	–28	–72	103	–2
Reserve position in the Fund	4 830 . .	...	...	...	...	...	...	...	...
Foreign exchange	4 840 . .	...	...	...	...	–46	–295	–208	39
Other claims	4 880 . .	...	...	...	...	...	–3	2	–1
NET ERRORS AND OMISSIONS	4 998 . .	**...**	**...**	**...**	**...**	**–44**	**–186**	**–508**	**–698**

Part 3 of the *Yearbook* contains descriptions of the methodologies, compilation practices, and sources used to compile these data.

Table 1. ANALYTIC PRESENTATION, 1988–95
(Millions of U.S. dollars)

	Code	1988	1989	1990	1991	1992	1993	1994	1995
A. Current Account [1]	4 993 Y.	**–24.6**	**10.4**	**65.0**	**83.1**	**37.6**	**29.3**	**108.1**	**...**
Goods: exports f.o.b.	2 100 ..	63.7	66.4	59.5	67.2	109.2	134.0	143.5	...
Goods: imports f.o.b.	3 100 ..	–559.4	–592.6	–672.6	–803.5	–932.6	–868.1	–810.2	...
Balance on Goods	4 100 ..	*–495.7*	*–526.2*	*–613.2*	*–736.4*	*–823.4*	*–734.1*	*–666.7*	...
Services: credit	2 200 ..	32.1	32.9	40.6	40.9	41.3	37.0	37.8	...
Services: debit	3 200 ..	–69.1	–70.9	–81.4	–83.9	–82.8	–70.5	–64.2	...
Balance on Goods and Services	4 991 ..	*–532.7*	*–564.2*	*–654.0*	*–779.5*	*–864.9*	*–767.6*	*–693.2*	...
Income: credit	2 300 ..	384.9	380.0	455.0	476.8	496.3	444.5	369.6	...
Income: debit	3 300 ..	–14.9	–20.3	–21.8	–20.4	–32.6	–22.8	–39.4	...
Balance on Goods, Services, and Income	4 992 ..	*–162.8*	*–204.5*	*–220.9*	*–323.1*	*–401.1*	*–345.9*	*–363.0*	...
Current transfers: credit	2 379 Y.	197.0	281.7	362.3	492.8	542.1	376.5	472.1	...
Current transfers: debit	3 379 ..	–58.8	–66.8	–76.4	–86.6	–103.3	–1.3	–.9	...
B. Capital Account [1]	4 994 Y.	**...**	**...**	**...**	**...**	**...**	**...**	**...**	**...**
Capital account: credit	2 994 Y.	...	...	...	...	...	...	...	...
Capital account: debit	3 994 ..	...	...	...	...	...	...	...	...
Total, Groups A Plus B	4 010 ..	*–24.6*	*10.4*	*65.0*	*83.1*	*37.6*	*29.3*	*108.1*	...
C. Financial Account [1]	4 995 X.	**–8.0**	**–20.2**	**–45.0**	**–60.8**	**–67.0**	**55.2**	**33.0**	**...**
Direct investment abroad	4 505 ..	–.1	...	...	...	...	...	...	...
Direct investment in Lesotho	4 555 Y.	21.0	13.4	17.1	7.5	2.7	15.0	18.7	...
Portfolio investment assets	4 602 ..	...	...	...	...	...	...	...	...
Equity securities	4 610 ..	...	...	...	...	...	...	...	...
Debt securities	4 619 ..	...	...	...	...	...	...	...	...
Portfolio investment liabilities	4 652 Y.	...	...	...	...	...	...	...	...
Equity securities	4 660 Y.	...	...	...	...	...	...	...	...
Debt securities	4 669 Y.	...	...	...	...	...	...	...	...
Other investment assets	4 703 ..	–80.0	–64.8	–109.7	–103.6	–106.4	8.9	–13.4	...
Monetary authorities	4 703 .A	...	...	...	...	...	...	...	...
General government	4 703 .B	–64.6	–61.4	–71.5	–105.1	–73.2	...	...	...
Banks	4 703 .C	–15.4	–3.5	–38.2	1.5	–33.3	8.9	–13.4	...
Other sectors	4 703 .D	...	...	...	...	...	...	...	...
Other investment liabilities	4 753 X.	51.0	31.3	47.6	35.4	36.8	31.3	27.6	...
Monetary authorities	4 753 XA	.1	...	6.0	1.4	–.1	...	.3	...
General government	4 753 YB	41.3	33.0	43.4	36.0	37.1	27.7	26.0	...
Banks	4 753 YC	12.8	–1.2	–2.6	–1.3	.5	1.5	1.9	...
Other sectors	4 753 YD	–3.2	–.5	.8	–.7	–.7	2.1	–.5	...
Total, Groups A Through C	4 020 ..	*–32.6*	*–9.8*	*20.0*	*22.3*	*–29.4*	*84.5*	*141.1*	...
D. Net Errors and Omissions	4 998 ..	**26.5**	**1.9**	**–2.8**	**20.1**	**79.2**	**17.8**	**–20.3**	**...**
Total, Groups A Through D	4 030 ..	*–6.1*	*–7.9*	*17.2*	*42.4*	*49.9*	*102.3*	*120.9*	...
E. Reserves and Related Items	4 040 ..	**6.1**	**7.9**	**–17.2**	**–42.4**	**–49.9**	**–102.3**	**–120.9**	**...**
Reserve assets	4 800 ..	3.3	3.0	–21.0	–45.4	–57.3	–111.7	–124.6	...
Use of Fund credit and loans	4 766 ..	2.8	4.9	3.8	3.0	7.5	9.5	3.8	...
Liabilities constituting foreign authorities' reserves	4 900 ..	...	...	...	...	...	...	...	...
Exceptional financing	4 920 ..	...	...	...	...	...	...	...	...
Conversion rates: maloti per U.S. dollar	0 101 ..	**2.2735**	**2.6227**	**2.5873**	**2.7613**	**2.8520**	**3.2677**	**3.5508**	**3.6271**

[1] Excludes components that have been classified in the categories of Group E.

Table 2. STANDARD PRESENTATION, 1988–95
(Millions of U.S. dollars)

	Code	1988	1989	1990	1991	1992	1993	1994	1995
CURRENT ACCOUNT	4 993 . .	**–24.6**	**10.4**	**65.0**	**83.1**	**37.6**	**29.3**	**108.1**	**. . .**
A. GOODS	4 100 . .	–495.7	–526.2	–613.2	–736.4	–823.4	–734.1	–666.7	. . .
Credit	2 100 . .	**63.7**	**66.4**	**59.5**	**67.2**	**109.2**	**134.0**	**143.5**	**. . .**
General merchandise: exports f.o.b.	2 110 . .	63.7	66.4	59.5	67.2	109.2	134.0	143.5	. . .
Goods for processing: exports f.o.b.	2 150 . .	. . .	. . .	. . .	. . .	. . .	. . .	. . .	. . .
Repairs on goods	2 160 . .	. . .	. . .	. . .	. . .	. . .	. . .	. . .	. . .
Goods procured in ports by carriers	2 170 . .	. . .	. . .	. . .	. . .	. . .	. . .	. . .	. . .
Nonmonetary gold	2 180 . .	. . .	. . .	. . .	. . .	. . .	. . .	. . .	. . .
Debit	3 100 . .	**–559.4**	**–592.6**	**–672.6**	**–803.5**	**–932.6**	**–868.1**	**–810.2**	**. . .**
General merchandise: imports f.o.b.	3 110 . .	–559.4	–592.6	–672.6	–803.5	–932.6	–868.1	–810.2	. . .
Goods for processing: imports f.o.b.	3 150 . .	. . .	. . .	. . .	. . .	. . .	. . .	. . .	. . .
Repairs on goods	3 160 . .	. . .	. . .	. . .	. . .	. . .	. . .	. . .	. . .
Goods procured in ports by carriers	3 170 . .	. . .	. . .	. . .	. . .	. . .	. . .	. . .	. . .
Nonmonetary gold	3 180 . .	. . .	. . .	. . .	. . .	. . .	. . .	. . .	. . .
B. SERVICES	4 200 . .	–37.0	–38.0	–40.8	–43.1	–41.5	–33.5	–26.4	. . .
Total credit	2 200 . .	*32.1*	*32.9*	*40.6*	*40.9*	*41.3*	*37.0*	*37.8*	. . .
Total debit	3 200 . .	*–69.1*	*–70.9*	*–81.4*	*–83.9*	*–82.8*	*–70.5*	*–64.2*	. . .
Transportation services, credit	2 205 . .	**3.8**	**3.8**	**4.8**	**2.8**	**2.6**	**2.4**	**3.1**	**. . .**
Passenger	2 205 BA	*3.3*	*3.7*	*4.2*	*2.6*	*2.5*	*2.1*	*2.9*	. . .
Freight	2 205 BB	. . .	. . .	. . .	. . .	. . .	. . .	. . .	. . .
Other	2 205 BC	*.5*	*.1*	*.6*	*.2*	*.1*	*.3*	*.2*	. . .
Sea transport, passenger	2 207 . .	. . .	. . .	. . .	. . .	. . .	. . .	. . .	. . .
Sea transport, freight	2 208 . .	. . .	. . .	. . .	. . .	. . .	. . .	. . .	. . .
Sea transport, other	2 209 . .	. . .	. . .	. . .	. . .	. . .	. . .	. . .	. . .
Air transport, passenger	2 211 . .	. . .	. . .	. . .	. . .	. . .	. . .	. . .	. . .
Air transport, freight	2 212 . .	. . .	. . .	. . .	. . .	. . .	. . .	. . .	. . .
Air transport, other	2 213 . .	. . .	. . .	. . .	. . .	. . .	. . .	. . .	. . .
Other transport, passenger	2 215 . .	. . .	. . .	. . .	. . .	. . .	. . .	. . .	. . .
Other transport, freight	2 216 . .	. . .	. . .	. . .	. . .	. . .	. . .	. . .	. . .
Other transport, other	2 217 . .	. . .	. . .	. . .	. . .	. . .	. . .	. . .	. . .
Transportation services, debit	3 205 . .	**–28.8**	**–29.8**	**–32.7**	**–36.8**	**–40.5**	**–37.1**	**–32.6**	**. . .**
Passenger	3 205 BA	*–7.3*	*–7.4*	*–7.6*	*–7.0*	*–6.3*	*–5.5*	*–3.5*	. . .
Freight	3 205 BB	*–20.1*	*–21.4*	*–24.3*	*–28.9*	*–33.5*	*–31.2*	*–29.1*	. . .
Other	3 205 BC	*–1.3*	*–1.0*	*–.8*	*–1.0*	*–.7*	*–.4*	. . .	. . .
Sea transport, passenger	3 207 . .	. . .	. . .	. . .	. . .	. . .	. . .	. . .	. . .
Sea transport, freight	3 208 . .	. . .	. . .	. . .	. . .	. . .	. . .	. . .	. . .
Sea transport, other	3 209 . .	. . .	. . .	. . .	. . .	. . .	. . .	. . .	. . .
Air transport, passenger	3 211 . .	. . .	. . .	. . .	. . .	. . .	. . .	. . .	. . .
Air transport, freight	3 212 . .	. . .	. . .	. . .	. . .	. . .	. . .	. . .	. . .
Air transport, other	3 213 . .	. . .	. . .	. . .	. . .	. . .	. . .	. . .	. . .
Other transport, passenger	3 215 . .	. . .	. . .	. . .	. . .	. . .	. . .	. . .	. . .
Other transport, freight	3 216 . .	. . .	. . .	. . .	. . .	. . .	. . .	. . .	. . .
Other transport, other	3 217 . .	. . .	. . .	. . .	. . .	. . .	. . .	. . .	. . .
Travel, credit	2 236 . .	**12.1**	**12.9**	**17.4**	**18.0**	**18.8**	**17.2**	**17.4**	**. . .**
Business travel	2 237 . .	. . .	. . .	. . .	. . .	. . .	. . .	. . .	. . .
Personal travel	2 240 . .	. . .	. . .	. . .	. . .	. . .	. . .	. . .	. . .
Travel, debit	3 236 . .	**–11.2**	**–9.7**	**–11.9**	**–10.9**	**–11.3**	**–6.5**	**–6.8**	**. . .**
Business travel	3 237 . .	–.7	–.6	–.5	–.6	–.3	. . .	. . .	. . .
Personal travel	3 240 . .	–10.6	–9.2	–11.4	–10.3	–11.0	. . .	. . .	. . .
Other services, credit	2 200 BA	**16.2**	**16.2**	**18.4**	**20.1**	**19.8**	**17.4**	**17.3**	**. . .**
Communications	2 245 . .	. . .	. . .	. . .	. . .	. . .	. . .	. . .	. . .
Construction	2 249 . .	. . .	. . .	. . .	. . .	. . .	. . .	. . .	. . .
Insurance	2 253 . .	. . .	. . .	. . .	. . .	. . .	. . .	. . .	. . .
Financial	2 260 . .	. . .	. . .	. . .	. . .	. . .	. . .	. . .	. . .
Computer and information	2 262 . .	. . .	. . .	. . .	. . .	. . .	. . .	. . .	. . .
Royalties and licence fees	2 266 . .	. . .	. . .	. . .	. . .	. . .	. . .	. . .	. . .
Other business services	2 268 . .	10.5	10.5	11.8	12.9	11.6	9.3	9.1	. . .
Personal, cultural, and recreational	2 287 . .	. . .	. . .	. . .	. . .	. . .	. . .	. . .	. . .
Government, n.i.e.	2 291 . .	5.7	5.7	6.6	7.2	8.2	8.1	8.2	. . .
Other services, debit	3 200 BA	**–29.1**	**–31.3**	**–36.8**	**–36.3**	**–31.0**	**–26.9**	**–24.8**	**. . .**
Communications	3 245 . .	. . .	. . .	. . .	. . .	. . .	. . .	. . .	. . .
Construction	3 249 . .	. . .	. . .	. . .	. . .	. . .	. . .	. . .	. . .
Insurance	3 253 . .	–2.2	–2.4	–2.7	–3.2	–3.7	–3.5	–3.2	. . .
Financial	3 260 . .	. . .	. . .	. . .	. . .	. . .	. . .	. . .	. . .
Computer and information	3 262 . .	. . .	. . .	. . .	. . .	. . .	. . .	. . .	. . .
Royalties and licence fees	3 266 . .	–.7	–1.4	–1.0	–.4	–1.1	. . .	. . .	. . .
Other business services	3 268 . .	–.5	–.3	.2	–.1	–.5	–1.7	. . .	. . .
Personal, cultural, and recreational	3 287 . .	. . .	. . .	. . .	. . .	. . .	. . .	. . .	. . .
Government, n.i.e.	3 291 . .	–25.7	–27.2	–33.3	–32.5	–25.7	–21.7	–21.6	. . .

Table 2 (Continued). STANDARD PRESENTATION, 1988–95
(Millions of U.S. dollars)

	Code	1988	1989	1990	1991	1992	1993	1994	1995
C. INCOME	4 300 . .	370.0	359.7	433.1	456.3	463.7	421.7	330.2	. . .
Total credit	2 300 . .	*384.9*	*380.0*	*455.0*	*476.8*	*496.3*	*444.5*	*369.6*	. . .
Total debit	3 300 . .	*–14.9*	*–20.3*	*–21.8*	*–20.4*	*–32.6*	*–22.8*	*–39.4*	. . .
Compensation of employees, credit	2 310 . .	**371.5**	**365.0**	**427.9**	**437.1**	**455.4**	**400.8**	**319.7**	. . .
Compensation of employees, debit	3 310 . .	. . .	. . .	. . .	. . .	. . .	. . .	. . .	. . .
Investment income, credit	2 320 . .	**13.4**	**15.1**	**27.1**	**39.7**	**40.8**	**43.7**	**49.9**	. . .
Direct investment income	2 330 . .	. . .	. . .	. . .	. . .	. . .	. . .	. . .	. . .
Dividends and distributed branch profits	2 332 . .	. . .	. . .	. . .	. . .	. . .	. . .	. . .	. . .
Reinvested earnings and undistributed branch profits	2 333 . .	. . .	. . .	. . .	. . .	. . .	. . .	. . .	. . .
Income on debt (interest)	2 334 . .	. . .	. . .	. . .	. . .	. . .	. . .	. . .	. . .
Portfolio investment income	2 339 . .	. . .	. . .	. . .	. . .	. . .	. . .	. . .	. . .
Income on equity	2 340 . .	. . .	. . .	. . .	. . .	. . .	. . .	. . .	. . .
Income on bonds and notes	2 350 . .	. . .	. . .	. . .	. . .	. . .	. . .	. . .	. . .
Income on money market instruments and financial derivatives	2 360 . .	. . .	. . .	. . .	. . .	. . .	. . .	. . .	. . .
Other investment income	2 370 . .	13.4	15.1	27.1	39.7	40.8	43.7	49.9	. . .
Investment income, debit	3 320 . .	**–14.9**	**–20.3**	**–21.8**	**–20.4**	**–32.6**	**–22.8**	**–39.4**	. . .
Direct investment income	3 330 . .	–8.5	–12.6	–12.7	–11.3	–23.2	–16.5	–26.9	. . .
Dividends and distributed branch profits	3 332 . .	–8.5	–12.6	–12.7	–11.3	–23.2	–16.5	–26.9	. . .
Reinvested earnings and undistributed branch profits	3 333 . .	. . .	. . .	. . .	. . .	. . .	. . .	. . .	. . .
Income on debt (interest)	3 334 . .	. . .	. . .	. . .	. . .	. . .	. . .	. . .	. . .
Portfolio investment income	3 339 . .	. . .	. . .	. . .	. . .	. . .	. . .	. . .	. . .
Income on equity	3 340 . .	. . .	. . .	. . .	. . .	. . .	. . .	. . .	. . .
Income on bonds and notes	3 350 . .	. . .	. . .	. . .	. . .	. . .	. . .	. . .	. . .
Income on money market instruments and financial derivatives	3 360 . .	. . .	. . .	. . .	. . .	. . .	. . .	. . .	. . .
Other investment income	3 370 . .	–6.4	–7.7	–9.2	–9.2	–9.3	–6.3	–12.5	. . .
D. CURRENT TRANSFERS	4 379 . .	138.1	214.9	285.9	406.2	438.8	375.2	471.2	. . .
Credit	2 379 . .	**197.0**	**281.7**	**362.3**	**492.8**	**542.1**	**376.5**	**472.1**	. . .
General government	2 380 . .	179.6	272.1	343.2	478.8	525.6	363.4	459.4	. . .
Other sectors	2 390 . .	17.4	9.6	19.1	14.0	16.5	13.1	12.7	. . .
Workers' remittances	2 391 . .	. . .	. . .	. . .	. . .	. . .	. . .	. . .	. . .
Other current transfers	2 392 . .	17.4	9.6	19.1	14.0	16.5	13.1	12.7	. . .
Debit	3 379 . .	**–58.8**	**–66.8**	**–76.4**	**–86.6**	**–103.3**	**–1.3**	**–.9**	. . .
General government	3 380 . .	–58.7	–66.5	–76.2	–86.5	–103.2	–1.2	–.9	. . .
Other sectors	3 390 . .	–.1	–.3	–.2	–.1	–.1	–.1	–.1	. . .
Workers' remittances	3 391 . .	. . .	. . .	. . .	. . .	. . .	. . .	. . .	. . .
Other current transfers	3 392 . .	–.1	–.3	–.2	–.1	–.1	–.1	–.1	. . .
CAPITAL AND FINANCIAL ACCOUNT	4 996 . .	**–1.9**	**–12.3**	**–62.2**	**–103.2**	**–116.8**	**–47.1**	**–87.9**	. . .
CAPITAL ACCOUNT	4 994 . .	. . .	. . .	. . .	. . .	. . .	. . .	. . .	. . .
Total credit	2 994 . .	. . .	. . .	. . .	. . .	. . .	. . .	. . .	. . .
Total debit	3 994 . .	. . .	. . .	. . .	. . .	. . .	. . .	. . .	. . .
Capital transfers, credit	2 400 . .	. . .	. . .	. . .	. . .	. . .	. . .	. . .	. . .
General government	2 401 . .	. . .	. . .	. . .	. . .	. . .	. . .	. . .	. . .
Debt forgiveness	2 402 . .	. . .	. . .	. . .	. . .	. . .	. . .	. . .	. . .
Other capital transfers	2 410 . .	. . .	. . .	. . .	. . .	. . .	. . .	. . .	. . .
Other sectors	2 430 . .	. . .	. . .	. . .	. . .	. . .	. . .	. . .	. . .
Migrants' transfers	2 431 . .	. . .	. . .	. . .	. . .	. . .	. . .	. . .	. . .
Debt forgiveness	2 432 . .	. . .	. . .	. . .	. . .	. . .	. . .	. . .	. . .
Other capital transfers	2 440 . .	. . .	. . .	. . .	. . .	. . .	. . .	. . .	. . .
Capital transfers, debit	3 400 . .	. . .	. . .	. . .	. . .	. . .	. . .	. . .	. . .
General government	3 401 . .	. . .	. . .	. . .	. . .	. . .	. . .	. . .	. . .
Debt forgiveness	3 402 . .	. . .	. . .	. . .	. . .	. . .	. . .	. . .	. . .
Other capital transfers	3 410 . .	. . .	. . .	. . .	. . .	. . .	. . .	. . .	. . .
Other sectors	3 430 . .	. . .	. . .	. . .	. . .	. . .	. . .	. . .	. . .
Migrants' transfers	3 431 . .	. . .	. . .	. . .	. . .	. . .	. . .	. . .	. . .
Debt forgiveness	3 432 . .	. . .	. . .	. . .	. . .	. . .	. . .	. . .	. . .
Other capital transfers	3 440 . .	. . .	. . .	. . .	. . .	. . .	. . .	. . .	. . .
Nonproduced nonfinancial assets, credit	2 480 . .	. . .	. . .	. . .	. . .	. . .	. . .	. . .	. . .
Nonproduced nonfinancial assets, debit	3 480 . .	. . .	. . .	. . .	. . .	. . .	. . .	. . .	. . .

Table 2 (Continued). STANDARD PRESENTATION, 1988–95

(Millions of U.S. dollars)

	Code	1988	1989	1990	1991	1992	1993	1994	1995
FINANCIAL ACCOUNT	4 995 . .	**–1.9**	**–12.3**	**–62.2**	**–103.2**	**–116.8**	**–47.1**	**–87.9**	**. . .**
A. DIRECT INVESTMENT	4 500 . .	21.0	13.4	17.1	7.5	2.7	15.0	18.7	. . .
Direct investment abroad	4 505 . .	**–.1**	**. . .**	**. . .**	**. . .**	**. . .**	**. . .**	**. . .**	**. . .**
Equity capital	4 510 . .	. . .	. . .	. . .	. . .	. . .	. . .	. . .	. . .
Claims on affiliated enterprises	4 515 . .	. . .	. . .	. . .	. . .	. . .	. . .	. . .	. . .
Liabilities to affiliated enterprises	4 520 . .	. . .	. . .	. . .	. . .	. . .	. . .	. . .	. . .
Reinvested earnings	4 525 . .	. . .	. . .	. . .	. . .	. . .	. . .	. . .	. . .
Other capital	4 530 . .	–.1	. . .	. . .	. . .	. . .	. . .	. . .	. . .
Claims on affiliated enterprises	4 535 . .	. . .	. . .	. . .	. . .	. . .	. . .	. . .	. . .
Liabilities to affiliated enterprises	4 540 . .	. . .	. . .	. . .	. . .	. . .	. . .	. . .	. . .
Direct investment in Lesotho	4 555 . .	**21.0**	**13.4**	**17.1**	**7.5**	**2.7**	**15.0**	**18.7**	**. . .**
Equity capital	4 560 . .	21.0	13.4	17.1	7.5	2.7	15.0	18.7	. . .
Claims on direct investors	4 565 . .	. . .	. . .	. . .	. . .	. . .	. . .	. . .	. . .
Liabilities to direct investors	4 570 . .	. . .	. . .	. . .	. . .	. . .	. . .	. . .	. . .
Reinvested earnings	4 575 . .	. . .	. . .	. . .	. . .	. . .	. . .	. . .	. . .
Other capital	4 580 . .	. . .	. . .	. . .	. . .	. . .	. . .	. . .	. . .
Claims on direct investors	4 585 . .	. . .	. . .	. . .	. . .	. . .	. . .	. . .	. . .
Liabilities to direct investors	4 590 . .	. . .	. . .	. . .	. . .	. . .	. . .	. . .	. . .
B. PORTFOLIO INVESTMENT	4 600 . .	. . .	. . .	. . .	. . .	. . .	. . .	. . .	. . .
Assets	4 602 . .	**. . .**	**. . .**	**. . .**	**. . .**	**. . .**	**. . .**	**. . .**	**. . .**
Equity securities	4 610 . .	. . .	. . .	. . .	. . .	. . .	. . .	. . .	. . .
Monetary authorities	4 611 . .	. . .	. . .	. . .	. . .	. . .	. . .	. . .	. . .
General government	4 612 . .	. . .	. . .	. . .	. . .	. . .	. . .	. . .	. . .
Banks	4 613 . .	. . .	. . .	. . .	. . .	. . .	. . .	. . .	. . .
Other sectors	4 614 . .	. . .	. . .	. . .	. . .	. . .	. . .	. . .	. . .
Debt securities	4 619 . .	. . .	. . .	. . .	. . .	. . .	. . .	. . .	. . .
Bonds and notes	4 620 . .	. . .	. . .	. . .	. . .	. . .	. . .	. . .	. . .
Monetary authorities	4 621 . .	. . .	. . .	. . .	. . .	. . .	. . .	. . .	. . .
General government	4 622 . .	. . .	. . .	. . .	. . .	. . .	. . .	. . .	. . .
Banks	4 623 . .	. . .	. . .	. . .	. . .	. . .	. . .	. . .	. . .
Other sectors	4 624 . .	. . .	. . .	. . .	. . .	. . .	. . .	. . .	. . .
Money market instruments	4 630 . .	. . .	. . .	. . .	. . .	. . .	. . .	. . .	. . .
Monetary authorities	4 631 . .	. . .	. . .	. . .	. . .	. . .	. . .	. . .	. . .
General government	4 632 . .	. . .	. . .	. . .	. . .	. . .	. . .	. . .	. . .
Banks	4 633 . .	. . .	. . .	. . .	. . .	. . .	. . .	. . .	. . .
Other sectors	4 634 . .	. . .	. . .	. . .	. . .	. . .	. . .	. . .	. . .
Financial derivatives	4 640 . .	. . .	. . .	. . .	. . .	. . .	. . .	. . .	. . .
Monetary authorities	4 641 . .	. . .	. . .	. . .	. . .	. . .	. . .	. . .	. . .
General government	4 642 . .	. . .	. . .	. . .	. . .	. . .	. . .	. . .	. . .
Banks	4 643 . .	. . .	. . .	. . .	. . .	. . .	. . .	. . .	. . .
Other sectors	4 644 . .	. . .	. . .	. . .	. . .	. . .	. . .	. . .	. . .
Liabilities	4 652 . .	**. . .**	**. . .**	**. . .**	**. . .**	**. . .**	**. . .**	**. . .**	**. . .**
Equity securities	4 660 . .	. . .	. . .	. . .	. . .	. . .	. . .	. . .	. . .
Banks	4 663 . .	. . .	. . .	. . .	. . .	. . .	. . .	. . .	. . .
Other sectors	4 664 . .	. . .	. . .	. . .	. . .	. . .	. . .	. . .	. . .
Debt securities	4 669 . .	. . .	. . .	. . .	. . .	. . .	. . .	. . .	. . .
Bonds and notes	4 670 . .	. . .	. . .	. . .	. . .	. . .	. . .	. . .	. . .
Monetary authorities	4 671 . .	. . .	. . .	. . .	. . .	. . .	. . .	. . .	. . .
General government	4 672 . .	. . .	. . .	. . .	. . .	. . .	. . .	. . .	. . .
Banks	4 673 . .	. . .	. . .	. . .	. . .	. . .	. . .	. . .	. . .
Other sectors	4 674 . .	. . .	. . .	. . .	. . .	. . .	. . .	. . .	. . .
Money market instruments	4 680 . .	. . .	. . .	. . .	. . .	. . .	. . .	. . .	. . .
Monetary authorities	4 681 . .	. . .	. . .	. . .	. . .	. . .	. . .	. . .	. . .
General government	4 682 . .	. . .	. . .	. . .	. . .	. . .	. . .	. . .	. . .
Banks	4 683 . .	. . .	. . .	. . .	. . .	. . .	. . .	. . .	. . .
Other sectors	4 684 . .	. . .	. . .	. . .	. . .	. . .	. . .	. . .	. . .
Financial derivatives	4 690 . .	. . .	. . .	. . .	. . .	. . .	. . .	. . .	. . .
Monetary authorities	4 691 . .	. . .	. . .	. . .	. . .	. . .	. . .	. . .	. . .
General government	4 692 . .	. . .	. . .	. . .	. . .	. . .	. . .	. . .	. . .
Banks	4 693 . .	. . .	. . .	. . .	. . .	. . .	. . .	. . .	. . .
Other sectors	4 694 . .	. . .	. . .	. . .	. . .	. . .	. . .	. . .	. . .

Table 2 (Concluded). STANDARD PRESENTATION, 1988–95
(Millions of U.S. dollars)

	Code	1988	1989	1990	1991	1992	1993	1994	1995
C. OTHER INVESTMENT	4 700 . .	–26.2	–28.6	–58.3	–65.2	–62.2	49.7	18.0	. . .
Assets	4 703 . .	**–80.0**	**–64.8**	**–109.7**	**–103.6**	**–106.4**	**8.9**	**–13.4**	. . .
Trade credits	4 706 . .	. . .	. . .	. . .	. . .	. . .	. . .	. . .	. . .
General government: long-term	4 708 . .	. . .	. . .	. . .	. . .	. . .	. . .	. . .	. . .
General government: short-term	4 709 . .	. . .	. . .	. . .	. . .	. . .	. . .	. . .	. . .
Other sectors: long-term	4 711 . .	. . .	. . .	. . .	. . .	. . .	. . .	. . .	. . .
Other sectors: short-term	4 712 . .	. . .	. . .	. . .	. . .	. . .	. . .	. . .	. . .
Loans	4 714 . .	. . .	. . .	. . .	. . .	. . .	. . .	. . .	. . .
Monetary authorities: long-term	4 717 . .	. . .	. . .	. . .	. . .	. . .	. . .	. . .	. . .
Monetary authorities: short-term	4 718 . .	. . .	. . .	. . .	. . .	. . .	. . .	. . .	. . .
General government: long-term	4 720 . .	. . .	. . .	. . .	. . .	. . .	. . .	. . .	. . .
General government: short-term	4 721 . .	. . .	. . .	. . .	. . .	. . .	. . .	. . .	. . .
Banks: long-term	4 723 . .	. . .	. . .	. . .	. . .	. . .	. . .	. . .	. . .
Banks: short-term	4 724 . .	. . .	. . .	. . .	. . .	. . .	. . .	. . .	. . .
Other sectors: long-term	4 726 . .	. . .	. . .	. . .	. . .	. . .	. . .	. . .	. . .
Other sectors: short-term	4 727 . .	. . .	. . .	. . .	. . .	. . .	. . .	. . .	. . .
Currency and deposits	4 730 . .	–80.0	–64.8	–109.7	–103.6	–106.4	8.9	–13.4	. . .
Monetary authorities	4 731 . .	. . .	. . .	. . .	. . .	. . .	. . .	. . .	. . .
General government	4 732 . .	–64.6	–61.4	–71.5	–105.1	–73.2	. . .	. . .	. . .
Banks	4 733 . .	–15.4	–3.5	–38.2	1.5	–33.3	8.9	–13.4	. . .
Other sectors	4 734 . .	. . .	. . .	. . .	. . .	. . .	. . .	. . .	. . .
Other assets	4 736 . .	. . .	. . .	. . .	. . .	. . .	. . .	. . .	. . .
Monetary authorities: long-term	4 738 . .	. . .	. . .	. . .	. . .	. . .	. . .	. . .	. . .
Monetary authorities: short-term	4 739 . .	. . .	. . .	. . .	. . .	. . .	. . .	. . .	. . .
General government: long-term	4 741 . .	. . .	. . .	. . .	. . .	. . .	. . .	. . .	. . .
General government: short-term	4 742 . .	. . .	. . .	. . .	. . .	. . .	. . .	. . .	. . .
Banks: long-term	4 744 . .	. . .	. . .	. . .	. . .	. . .	. . .	. . .	. . .
Banks: short-term	4 745 . .	. . .	. . .	. . .	. . .	. . .	. . .	. . .	. . .
Other sectors: long-term	4 747 . .	. . .	. . .	. . .	. . .	. . .	. . .	. . .	. . .
Other sectors: short-term	4 748 . .	. . .	. . .	. . .	. . .	. . .	. . .	. . .	. . .
Liabilities	4 753 . .	**53.8**	**36.2**	**51.4**	**38.4**	**44.2**	**40.8**	**31.4**	. . .
Trade credits	4 756 . .	. . .	. . .	. . .	. . .	. . .	. . .	. . .	. . .
General government: long-term	4 758 . .	. . .	. . .	. . .	. . .	. . .	. . .	. . .	. . .
General government: short-term	4 759 . .	. . .	. . .	. . .	. . .	. . .	. . .	. . .	. . .
Other sectors: long-term	4 761 . .	. . .	. . .	. . .	. . .	. . .	. . .	. . .	. . .
Other sectors: short-term	4 762 . .	. . .	. . .	. . .	. . .	. . .	. . .	. . .	. . .
Loans	4 764 . .	40.9	37.4	48.1	38.4	43.9	39.3	29.3	. . .
Use of Fund credit and loans from the Fund	4 766 . .	2.8	4.9	3.8	3.0	7.5	9.5	3.8	. . .
Monetary authorities: other long-term	4 767 . .	. . .	. . .	. . .	. . .	. . .	. . .	. . .	. . .
Monetary authorities: short-term	4 768 . .	. . .	. . .	. . .	. . .	. . .	. . .	. . .	. . .
General government: long-term	4 770 . .	41.3	33.0	43.4	36.0	37.1	27.7	26.0	. . .
General government: short-term	4 771 . .	. . .	. . .	. . .	. . .	. . .	. . .	. . .	. . .
Banks: long-term	4 773 . .	. . .	. . .	. . .	. . .	. . .	. . .	. . .	. . .
Banks: short-term	4 774 . .	. . .	. . .	. . .	. . .	. . .	. . .	. . .	. . .
Other sectors: long-term	4 776 . .	–3.2	–.5	.8	–.7	–.7	2.1	–.5	. . .
Other sectors: short-term	4 777 . .	. . .	. . .	. . .	. . .	. . .	. . .	. . .	. . .
Currency and deposits	4 780 . .	12.8	–1.2	–2.6	–1.3	.5	1.5	1.9	. . .
Monetary authorities	4 781 . .	. . .	. . .	. . .	. . .	. . .	. . .	. . .	. . .
General government	4 782 . .	. . .	. . .	. . .	. . .	. . .	. . .	. . .	. . .
Banks	4 783 . .	12.8	–1.2	–2.6	–1.3	.5	1.5	1.9	. . .
Other sectors	4 784 . .	. . .	. . .	. . .	. . .	. . .	. . .	. . .	. . .
Other liabilities	4 786 . .	.1	. . .	6.0	1.4	–.1	. . .	.3	. . .
Monetary authorities: long-term	4 788 . .	. . .	. . .	. . .	. . .	. . .	. . .	. . .	. . .
Monetary authorities: short-term	4 789 . .	.1	. . .	6.0	1.4	–.1	. . .	.3	. . .
General government: long-term	4 791 . .	. . .	. . .	. . .	. . .	. . .	. . .	. . .	. . .
General government: short-term	4 792 . .	. . .	. . .	. . .	. . .	. . .	. . .	. . .	. . .
Banks: long-term	4 794 . .	. . .	. . .	. . .	. . .	. . .	. . .	. . .	. . .
Banks: short-term	4 795 . .	. . .	. . .	. . .	. . .	. . .	. . .	. . .	. . .
Other sectors: long-term	4 797 . .	. . .	. . .	. . .	. . .	. . .	. . .	. . .	. . .
Other sectors: short-term	4 798 . .	. . .	. . .	. . .	. . .	. . .	. . .	. . .	. . .
D. RESERVE ASSETS	4 800 . .	3.3	3.0	–21.0	–45.4	–57.3	–111.7	–124.6	. . .
Monetary gold	4 810 . .	. . .	. . .	. . .	. . .	. . .	. . .	. . .	. . .
Special drawing rights	4 820 . .	–.5	.3	.4	.4	–.4	.1	.1	. . .
Reserve position in the Fund	4 830 . .	. . .	. . .	. . .	. . .	–3.1	. . .	. . .	. . .
Foreign exchange	4 840 . .	3.8	2.7	–21.4	–45.8	–53.9	–111.8	–124.8	. . .
Other claims	4 880 . .	. . .	. . .	. . .	. . .	. . .	. . .	. . .	. . .
NET ERRORS AND OMISSIONS	4 998 . .	**26.5**	**1.9**	**–2.8**	**20.1**	**79.2**	**17.8**	**–20.3**	. . .

Table 1. ANALYTIC PRESENTATION, 1988–95
(Millions of U.S. dollars)

	Code	1988	1989	1990	1991	1992	1993	1994	1995
A. Current Account[1]	4 993 Y .	**-1,826**	**-1,026**	**2,201**	...	...	...	...	...
Goods: exports f.o.b	2 100 . .	5,653	7,274	11,352	...	...	...	...	...
Goods: imports f.o.b	3 100 . .	-5,762	-6,509	-7,575	...	...	...	...	...
Balance on Goods	4 100 . .	*-109*	*765*	*3,777*	...	...	...	...	...
Services: credit	2 200 . .	128	117	117	...	...	...	...	...
Services: debit	3 200 . .	-1,637	-1,481	-1,385	...	...	...	...	...
Balance on Goods and Services	4 991 . .	*-1,617*	*-598*	*2,508*	...	...	...	...	...
Income: credit	2 300 . .	762	447	666	...	...	...	...	...
Income: debit	3 300 . .	-437	-388	-493	...	...	...	...	...
Balance on Goods, Services, and Income	4 992 . .	*-1,292*	*-539*	*2,682*	...	...	...	...	...
Current transfers: credit	2 379 Y .	7	6	7	...	...	...	...	...
Current transfers: debit	3 379 . .	-541	-493	-488	...	...	...	...	...
B. Capital Account[1]	4 994 Y .	...	...	...	...	...	...	...	...
Capital account: credit	2 994 Y .	...	...	...	...	...	...	...	...
Capital account: debit	3 994 . .	...	...	...	...	...	...	...	...
Total, Groups A Plus B	4 010 . .	*-1,826*	*-1,026*	*2,201*	...	...	...	...	...
C. Financial Account[1]	4 995 X .	**163**	**1,188**	**-1,006**	...	...	...	...	...
Direct investment abroad	4 505 . .	-56	-35	-105	...	...	...	...	...
Direct investment in Libya	4 555 Y .	98	125	159	...	...	...	...	...
Portfolio investment assets	4 602 . .	-222	-52	-115	...	...	...	...	...
Equity securities	4 610 . .	-222	-52	-115	...	...	...	...	...
Debt securities	4 619 . .	...	...	...	...	...	...	...	...
Portfolio investment liabilities	4 652 Y .	...	...	...	...	...	...	...	...
Equity securities	4 660 Y .	...	...	...	...	...	...	...	...
Debt securities	4 669 Y .	...	...	...	...	...	...	...	...
Other investment assets	4 703 . .	-670	320	-715	...	...	...	...	...
Monetary authorities	4 703 . A	...	...	...	...	...	...	...	...
General government	4 703 . B	-150	-109	-230	...	...	...	...	...
Banks	4 703 . C	-26	186	-90	...	...	...	...	...
Other sectors	4 703 . D	-494	242	-395	...	...	...	...	...
Other investment liabilities	4 753 X .	1,013	830	-230	...	...	...	...	...
Monetary authorities	4 753 XA	196	598	-130	...	...	...	...	...
General government	4 753 YB	...	...	...	...	...	...	...	...
Banks	4 753 YC	486	214	21	...	...	...	...	...
Other sectors	4 753 YD	331	18	-121	...	...	...	...	...
Total, Groups A Through C	4 020 . .	*-1,663*	*162*	*1,195*	...	...	...	...	...
D. Net Errors and Omissions	4 998 . .	**271**	**130**	**-37**	...	...	...	...	...
Total, Groups A Through D	4 030 . .	*-1,392*	*292*	*1,158*	...	...	...	...	...
E. Reserves and Related Items	4 040 . .	**1,392**	**-292**	**-1,158**	...	...	...	...	...
Reserve assets	4 800 . .	1,392	-292	-1,158	...	...	...	...	...
Use of Fund credit and loans	4 766 . .	...	...	...	...	...	...	...	...
Liabilities constituting foreign authorities' reserves	4 900 . .	...	...	...	...	...	...	...	...
Exceptional financing	4 920 . .	...	...	...	...	...	...	...	...
Conversion rates: Libyan dinar per U.S. dollar	0 101 . .	**.28576**	**.29960**	**.28317**	**.28072**	**.28471**	**.30516**	**.32086**	**.34620**

[1] Excludes components that have been classified in the categories of Group E.

Table 2. STANDARD PRESENTATION, 1988–95
(Millions of U.S. dollars)

	Code	1988	1989	1990	1991	1992	1993	1994	1995
CURRENT ACCOUNT	4 993 . .	**–1,826**	**–1,026**	**2,201**	...	...	...	...	...
A. GOODS	4 100 . .	–109	765	3,777	...	...	...	...	...
Credit	2 100 . .	**5,653**	**7,274**	**11,352**	...	...	...	...	...
General merchandise: exports f.o.b.	2 110 . .	5,653	7,274	11,352	...	...	...	...	...
Goods for processing: exports f.o.b.	2 150 . .	...	...	...	...	...	...	...	...
Repairs on goods	2 160 . .	...	...	...	...	...	...	...	...
Goods procured in ports by carriers	2 170 . .	...	...	...	...	...	...	...	...
Nonmonetary gold	2 180 . .	...	...	...	...	...	...	...	...
Debit	3 100 . .	**–5,762**	**–6,509**	**–7,575**	...	...	...	...	...
General merchandise: imports f.o.b.	3 110 . .	–5,762	–6,509	–7,575	...	...	...	...	...
Goods for processing: imports f.o.b.	3 150 . .	...	...	...	...	...	...	...	...
Repairs on goods	3 160 . .	...	...	...	...	...	...	...	...
Goods procured in ports by carriers	3 170 . .	...	...	...	...	...	...	...	...
Nonmonetary gold	3 180 . .	...	...	...	...	...	...	...	...
B. SERVICES	4 200 . .	–1,508	–1,364	–1,268	...	...	...	...	...
Total credit	2 200 . .	*128*	*117*	*117*	...	...	...	...	...
Total debit	3 200 . .	*–1,637*	*–1,481*	*–1,385*	...	...	...	...	...
Transportation services, credit	2 205 . .	**71**	**66**	**70**	...	...	...	...	...
Passenger	2 205 BA	*9*	*8*	*8*	...	...	...	...	...
Freight	2 205 BB	...	...	...	...	...	...	...	...
Other	2 205 BC	*62*	*58*	*61*	...	...	...	...	...
Sea transport, passenger	2 207 . .	...	...	...	...	...	...	...	...
Sea transport, freight	2 208 . .	...	...	...	...	...	...	...	...
Sea transport, other	2 209 . .	...	...	...	...	...	...	...	...
Air transport, passenger	2 211 . .	...	...	...	...	...	...	...	...
Air transport, freight	2 212 . .	...	...	...	...	...	...	...	...
Air transport, other	2 213 . .	...	...	...	...	...	...	...	...
Other transport, passenger	2 215 . .	...	...	...	...	...	...	...	...
Other transport, freight	2 216 . .	...	...	...	...	...	...	...	...
Other transport, other	2 217 . .	...	...	...	...	...	...	...	...
Transportation services, debit	3 205 . .	**–380**	**–363**	**–388**	...	...	...	...	...
Passenger	3 205 BA	*–56*	*–49*	*–19*	...	...	...	...	...
Freight	3 205 BB	*–290*	*–288*	*–340*	...	...	...	...	...
Other	3 205 BC	*–34*	*–26*	*–29*	...	...	...	...	...
Sea transport, passenger	3 207 . .	...	...	...	...	...	...	...	...
Sea transport, freight	3 208 . .	...	...	...	...	...	...	...	...
Sea transport, other	3 209 . .	...	...	...	...	...	...	...	...
Air transport, passenger	3 211 . .	...	...	...	...	...	...	...	...
Air transport, freight	3 212 . .	...	...	...	...	...	...	...	...
Air transport, other	3 213 . .	...	...	...	...	...	...	...	...
Other transport, passenger	3 215 . .	...	...	...	...	...	...	...	...
Other transport, freight	3 216 . .	...	...	...	...	...	...	...	...
Other transport, other	3 217 . .	...	...	...	...	...	...	...	...
Travel, credit	2 236 . .	**7**	**5**	**6**	...	...	...	...	...
Business travel	2 237 . .	...	...	...	...	...	...	...	...
Personal travel	2 240 . .	...	...	...	...	...	...	...	...
Travel, debit	3 236 . .	**–552**	**–512**	**–424**	...	...	...	...	...
Business travel	3 237 . .	...	...	...	...	...	...	...	...
Personal travel	3 240 . .	...	...	...	...	...	...	...	...
Other services, credit	2 200 BA	**50**	**47**	**41**	...	...	...	...	...
Communications	2 245 . .	...	...	...	...	...	...	...	...
Construction	2 249 . .	...	...	...	...	...	...	...	...
Insurance	2 253 . .	...	...	...	...	...	...	...	...
Financial	2 260 . .	...	...	...	...	...	...	...	...
Computer and information	2 262 . .	...	...	...	...	...	...	...	...
Royalties and licence fees	2 266 . .	...	...	...	...	...	...	...	...
Other business services	2 268 . .	9	9	7	...	...	...	...	...
Personal, cultural, and recreational	2 287 . .	...	...	...	...	...	...	...	...
Government, n.i.e.	2 291 . .	41	38	34	...	...	...	...	...
Other services, debit	3 200 BA	**–705**	**–605**	**–574**	...	...	...	...	...
Communications	3 245 . .	...	...	...	...	...	...	...	...
Construction	3 249 . .	...	...	...	...	...	...	...	...
Insurance	3 253 . .	–32	–32	–38	...	...	...	...	...
Financial	3 260 . .	...	...	...	...	...	...	...	...
Computer and information	3 262 . .	...	...	...	...	...	...	...	...
Royalties and licence fees	3 266 . .	...	...	...	...	...	...	...	...
Other business services	3 268 . .	–62	–83	–77	...	...	...	...	...
Personal, cultural, and recreational	3 287 . .	...	...	...	...	...	...	...	...
Government, n.i.e.	3 291 . .	–611	–490	–459	...	...	...	...	...

Table 2 (Continued). STANDARD PRESENTATION, 1988–95
(Millions of U.S. dollars)

	Code		1988	1989	1990	1991	1992	1993	1994	1995
C. INCOME	4 300	. .	325	60	174	. . .	. . .	. . .	. . .	. . .
Total credit	2 300	. .	*762*	*447*	*666*	. . .	. . .	. . .	. . .	. . .
Total debit	3 300	. .	*–437*	*–388*	*–493*	. . .	. . .	. . .	. . .	. . .
Compensation of employees, credit	2 310	. .	**. . .**	**. . .**	**. . .**	**. . .**	**. . .**	**. . .**	**. . .**	**. . .**
Compensation of employees, debit	3 310	. .	**. . .**	**. . .**	**. . .**	**. . .**	**. . .**	**. . .**	**. . .**	**. . .**
Investment income, credit	2 320	. .	**762**	**447**	**666**	**. . .**	**. . .**	**. . .**	**. . .**	**. . .**
Direct investment income	2 330	. .	18	18	18	. . .	. . .	. . .	. . .	. . .
Dividends and distributed branch profits	2 332	. .	18	18	18	. . .	. . .	. . .	. . .	. . .
Reinvested earnings and undistributed branch profits	2 333	. .	. . .	. . .	. . .	. . .	. . .	. . .	. . .	. . .
Income on debt (interest)	2 334	. .	. . .	. . .	. . .	. . .	. . .	. . .	. . .	. . .
Portfolio investment income	2 339	. .	. . .	. . .	. . .	. . .	. . .	. . .	. . .	. . .
Income on equity	2 340	. .	. . .	. . .	. . .	. . .	. . .	. . .	. . .	. . .
Income on bonds and notes	2 350	. .	. . .	. . .	. . .	. . .	. . .	. . .	. . .	. . .
Income on money market instruments and financial derivatives	2 360	. .	. . .	. . .	. . .	. . .	. . .	. . .	. . .	. . .
Other investment income	2 370	. .	744	429	649	. . .	. . .	. . .	. . .	. . .
Investment income, debit	3 320	. .	**–437**	**–388**	**–493**	**. . .**	**. . .**	**. . .**	**. . .**	**. . .**
Direct investment income	3 330	. .	–350	–322	–436	. . .	. . .	. . .	. . .	. . .
Dividends and distributed branch profits	3 332	. .	–350	–322	–436	. . .	. . .	. . .	. . .	. . .
Reinvested earnings and undistributed branch profits	3 333	. .	. . .	. . .	. . .	. . .	. . .	. . .	. . .	. . .
Income on debt (interest)	3 334	. .	. . .	. . .	. . .	. . .	. . .	. . .	. . .	. . .
Portfolio investment income	3 339	. .	. . .	. . .	. . .	. . .	. . .	. . .	. . .	. . .
Income on equity	3 340	. .	. . .	. . .	. . .	. . .	. . .	. . .	. . .	. . .
Income on bonds and notes	3 350	. .	. . .	. . .	. . .	. . .	. . .	. . .	. . .	. . .
Income on money market instruments and financial derivatives	3 360	. .	. . .	. . .	. . .	. . .	. . .	. . .	. . .	. . .
Other investment income	3 370	. .	–87	–65	–57	. . .	. . .	. . .	. . .	. . .
D. CURRENT TRANSFERS	4 379	. .	–534	–488	–481	. . .	. . .	. . .	. . .	. . .
Credit	2 379	. .	**7**	**6**	**7**	**. . .**	**. . .**	**. . .**	**. . .**	**. . .**
General government	2 380	. .	7	6	7	. . .	. . .	. . .	. . .	. . .
Other sectors	2 390	. .	. . .	. . .	. . .	. . .	. . .	. . .	. . .	. . .
Workers' remittances	2 391	. .	. . .	. . .	. . .	. . .	. . .	. . .	. . .	. . .
Other current transfers	2 392	. .	. . .	. . .	. . .	. . .	. . .	. . .	. . .	. . .
Debit	3 379	. .	**–541**	**–493**	**–488**	**. . .**	**. . .**	**. . .**	**. . .**	**. . .**
General government	3 380	. .	–44	–22	–42	. . .	. . .	. . .	. . .	. . .
Other sectors	3 390	. .	–497	–472	–446	. . .	. . .	. . .	. . .	. . .
Workers' remittances	3 391	. .	–497	–472	–446	. . .	. . .	. . .	. . .	. . .
Other current transfers	3 392	. .	. . .	. . .	. . .	. . .	. . .	. . .	. . .	. . .
CAPITAL AND FINANCIAL ACCOUNT	4 996	. .	**1,556**	**896**	**–2,164**	**. . .**	**. . .**	**. . .**	**. . .**	**. . .**
CAPITAL ACCOUNT	4 994	. .	**. . .**	**. . .**	**. . .**	**. . .**	**. . .**	**. . .**	**. . .**	**. . .**
Total credit	2 994	. .	. . .	. . .	. . .	. . .	. . .	. . .	. . .	. . .
Total debit	3 994	. .	. . .	. . .	. . .	. . .	. . .	. . .	. . .	. . .
Capital transfers, credit	2 400	. .	**. . .**	**. . .**	**. . .**	**. . .**	**. . .**	**. . .**	**. . .**	**. . .**
General government	2 401	. .	. . .	. . .	. . .	. . .	. . .	. . .	. . .	. . .
Debt forgiveness	2 402	. .	. . .	. . .	. . .	. . .	. . .	. . .	. . .	. . .
Other capital transfers	2 410	. .	. . .	. . .	. . .	. . .	. . .	. . .	. . .	. . .
Other sectors	2 430	. .	. . .	. . .	. . .	. . .	. . .	. . .	. . .	. . .
Migrants' transfers	2 431	. .	. . .	. . .	. . .	. . .	. . .	. . .	. . .	. . .
Debt forgiveness	2 432	. .	. . .	. . .	. . .	. . .	. . .	. . .	. . .	. . .
Other capital transfers	2 440	. .	. . .	. . .	. . .	. . .	. . .	. . .	. . .	. . .
Capital transfers, debit	3 400	. .	**. . .**	**. . .**	**. . .**	**. . .**	**. . .**	**. . .**	**. . .**	**. . .**
General government	3 401	. .	. . .	. . .	. . .	. . .	. . .	. . .	. . .	. . .
Debt forgiveness	3 402	. .	. . .	. . .	. . .	. . .	. . .	. . .	. . .	. . .
Other capital transfers	3 410	. .	. . .	. . .	. . .	. . .	. . .	. . .	. . .	. . .
Other sectors	3 430	. .	. . .	. . .	. . .	. . .	. . .	. . .	. . .	. . .
Migrants' transfers	3 431	. .	. . .	. . .	. . .	. . .	. . .	. . .	. . .	. . .
Debt forgiveness	3 432	. .	. . .	. . .	. . .	. . .	. . .	. . .	. . .	. . .
Other capital transfers	3 440	. .	. . .	. . .	. . .	. . .	. . .	. . .	. . .	. . .
Nonproduced nonfinancial assets, credit	2 480	. .	**. . .**	**. . .**	**. . .**	**. . .**	**. . .**	**. . .**	**. . .**	**. . .**
Nonproduced nonfinancial assets, debit	3 480	. .	**. . .**	**. . .**	**. . .**	**. . .**	**. . .**	**. . .**	**. . .**	**. . .**

Table 2 (Continued). STANDARD PRESENTATION, 1988–95
(Millions of U.S. dollars)

	Code		1988	1989	1990	1991	1992	1993	1994	1995
FINANCIAL ACCOUNT	4 995	. .	**1,556**	**896**	**–2,164**	...	...	...	...	...
A. DIRECT INVESTMENT	4 500	. .	42	90	54	...	...	...	...	...
Direct investment abroad	4 505	. .	**–56**	**–35**	**–105**	...	...	...	...	...
Equity capital	4 510	. .	–56	–35	–105	...	...	...	...	...
Claims on affiliated enterprises	4 515	. .	...	...	...	...	...	...	...	...
Liabilities to affiliated enterprises	4 520	. .	...	...	...	...	...	...	...	...
Reinvested earnings	4 525	. .	...	...	...	...	...	...	...	...
Other capital	4 530	. .	...	...	...	...	...	...	...	...
Claims on affiliated enterprises	4 535	. .	...	...	...	...	...	...	...	...
Liabilities to affiliated enterprises	4 540	. .	...	...	...	...	...	...	...	...
Direct investment in Libya	4 555	. .	**98**	**125**	**159**	...	...	...	...	...
Equity capital	4 560	. .	...	...	...	...	...	...	...	...
Claims on direct investors	4 565	. .	...	...	...	...	...	...	...	...
Liabilities to direct investors	4 570	. .	...	...	...	...	...	...	...	...
Reinvested earnings	4 575	. .	...	...	...	...	...	...	...	...
Other capital	4 580	. .	98	125	159	...	...	...	...	...
Claims on direct investors	4 585	. .	...	...	...	...	...	...	...	...
Liabilities to direct investors	4 590	. .	...	...	...	...	...	...	...	...
B. PORTFOLIO INVESTMENT	4 600	. .	–222	–52	–115	...	...	...	...	...
Assets	4 602	. .	**–222**	**–52**	**–115**	...	...	...	...	...
Equity securities	4 610	. .	–222	–52	–115	...	...	...	...	...
Monetary authorities	4 611	. .	...	...	...	...	...	...	...	...
General government	4 612	. .	...	...	...	...	...	...	...	...
Banks	4 613	. .	...	...	...	...	...	...	...	...
Other sectors	4 614	. .	...	...	...	...	...	...	...	...
Debt securities	4 619	. .	...	...	...	...	...	...	...	...
Bonds and notes	4 620	. .	...	...	...	...	...	...	...	...
Monetary authorities	4 621	. .	...	...	...	...	...	...	...	...
General government	4 622	. .	...	...	...	...	...	...	...	...
Banks	4 623	. .	...	...	...	...	...	...	...	...
Other sectors	4 624	. .	...	...	...	...	...	...	...	...
Money market instruments	4 630	. .	...	...	...	...	...	...	...	...
Monetary authorities	4 631	. .	...	...	...	...	...	...	...	...
General government	4 632	. .	...	...	...	...	...	...	...	...
Banks	4 633	. .	...	...	...	...	...	...	...	...
Other sectors	4 634	. .	...	...	...	...	...	...	...	...
Financial derivatives	4 640	. .	...	...	...	...	...	...	...	...
Monetary authorities	4 641	. .	...	...	...	...	...	...	...	...
General government	4 642	. .	...	...	...	...	...	...	...	...
Banks	4 643	. .	...	...	...	...	...	...	...	...
Other sectors	4 644	. .	...	...	...	...	...	...	...	...
Liabilities	4 652	. .	...	...	...	...	...	...	...	...
Equity securities	4 660	. .	...	...	...	...	...	...	...	...
Banks	4 663	. .	...	...	...	...	...	...	...	...
Other sectors	4 664	. .	...	...	...	...	...	...	...	...
Debt securities	4 669	. .	...	...	...	...	...	...	...	...
Bonds and notes	4 670	. .	...	...	...	...	...	...	...	...
Monetary authorities	4 671	. .	...	...	...	...	...	...	...	...
General government	4 672	. .	...	...	...	...	...	...	...	...
Banks	4 673	. .	...	...	...	...	...	...	...	...
Other sectors	4 674	. .	...	...	...	...	...	...	...	...
Money market instruments	4 680	. .	...	...	...	...	...	...	...	...
Monetary authorities	4 681	. .	...	...	...	...	...	...	...	...
General government	4 682	. .	...	...	...	...	...	...	...	...
Banks	4 683	. .	...	...	...	...	...	...	...	...
Other sectors	4 684	. .	...	...	...	...	...	...	...	...
Financial derivatives	4 690	. .	...	...	...	...	...	...	...	...
Monetary authorities	4 691	. .	...	...	...	...	...	...	...	...
General government	4 692	. .	...	...	...	...	...	...	...	...
Banks	4 693	. .	...	...	...	...	...	...	...	...
Other sectors	4 694	. .	...	...	...	...	...	...	...	...

Table 2 (Concluded). STANDARD PRESENTATION, 1988–95
(Millions of U.S. dollars)

	Code	1988	1989	1990	1991	1992	1993	1994	1995
C. OTHER INVESTMENT	4 700 . .	343	1,150	–945	...	...	...	...	...
Assets	4 703 . .	**–670**	**320**	**–715**	...	...	...	...	...
Trade credits	4 706 . .	...	...	...	...	...	...	...	...
General government: long-term	4 708 . .	...	...	...	...	...	...	...	...
General government: short-term	4 709 . .	...	...	...	...	...	...	...	...
Other sectors: long-term	4 711 . .	...	...	...	...	...	...	...	...
Other sectors: short-term	4 712 . .	...	...	...	...	...	...	...	...
Loans	4 714 . .	–891	–322	–45	...	...	...	...	...
Monetary authorities: long-term	4 717 . .	...	...	...	...	...	...	...	...
Monetary authorities: short-term	4 718 . .	...	...	...	...	...	...	...	...
General government: long-term	4 720 . .	–265	–121	–310	...	...	...	...	...
General government: short-term	4 721 . .	...	...	...	...	...	...	...	...
Banks: long-term	4 723 . .	...	...	...	...	...	...	...	...
Banks: short-term	4 724 . .	...	...	...	...	...	...	...	...
Other sectors: long-term	4 726 . .	–590	–163	216	...	...	...	...	...
Other sectors: short-term	4 727 . .	–36	–38	49	...	...	...	...	...
Currency and deposits	4 730 . .	460	406	–669	...	...	...	...	...
Monetary authorities	4 731 . .	...	...	...	...	...	...	...	...
General government	4 732 . .	114	12	81	...	...	...	...	...
Banks	4 733 . .	212	–53	–95	...	...	...	...	...
Other sectors	4 734 . .	133	446	–655	...	...	...	...	...
Other assets	4 736 . .	–239	237	–1	...	...	...	...	...
Monetary authorities: long-term	4 738 . .	...	...	...	...	...	...	...	...
Monetary authorities: short-term	4 739 . .	...	...	...	...	...	...	...	...
General government: long-term	4 741 . .	...	...	...	...	...	...	...	...
General government: short-term	4 742 . .	...	...	...	...	...	...	...	...
Banks: long-term	4 744 . .	–238	239	4	...	...	...	...	...
Banks: short-term	4 745 . .	...	...	...	...	...	...	...	...
Other sectors: long-term	4 747 . .	–1	–2	–5	...	...	...	...	...
Other sectors: short-term	4 748 . .	...	...	...	...	...	...	...	...
Liabilities	4 753 . .	**1,013**	**830**	**–230**	...	...	...	...	...
Trade credits	4 756 . .	...	...	...	...	...	...	...	...
General government: long-term	4 758 . .	...	...	...	...	...	...	...	...
General government: short-term	4 759 . .	...	...	...	...	...	...	...	...
Other sectors: long-term	4 761 . .	...	...	...	...	...	...	...	...
Other sectors: short-term	4 762 . .	...	...	...	...	...	...	...	...
Loans	4 764 . .	520	158	–83	...	...	...	...	...
Use of Fund credit and loans from the Fund	4 766 . .	...	...	...	...	...	...	...	...
Monetary authorities: other long-term	4 767 . .	...	...	...	...	...	...	...	...
Monetary authorities: short-term	4 768 . .	...	...	...	...	...	...	...	...
General government: long-term	4 770 . .	...	...	...	...	...	...	...	...
General government: short-term	4 771 . .	...	...	...	...	...	...	...	...
Banks: long-term	4 773 . .	496	161	–48	...	...	...	...	...
Banks: short-term	4 774 . .	...	...	...	...	...	...	...	...
Other sectors: long-term	4 776 . .	...	...	–4	...	...	...	...	...
Other sectors: short-term	4 777 . .	24	–3	–32	...	...	...	...	...
Currency and deposits	4 780 . .	1	2	45	...	...	...	...	...
Monetary authorities	4 781 . .	...	...	...	...	...	...	...	...
General government	4 782 . .	...	...	...	...	...	...	...	...
Banks	4 783 . .	1	2	45	...	...	...	...	...
Other sectors	4 784 . .	...	...	...	...	...	...	...	...
Other liabilities	4 786 . .	493	671	–192	...	...	...	...	...
Monetary authorities: long-term	4 788 . .	...	...	...	...	...	...	...	...
Monetary authorities: short-term	4 789 . .	196	598	–130	...	...	...	...	...
General government: long-term	4 791 . .	...	...	...	...	...	...	...	...
General government: short-term	4 792 . .	...	...	...	...	...	...	...	...
Banks: long-term	4 794 . .	–10	51	23	...	...	...	...	...
Banks: short-term	4 795 . .	...	...	...	...	...	...	...	...
Other sectors: long-term	4 797 . .	357	–114	–322	...	...	...	...	...
Other sectors: short-term	4 798 . .	–50	136	237	...	...	...	...	...
D. RESERVE ASSETS	4 800 . .	1,392	–292	–1,158	...	...	...	...	...
Monetary gold	4 810 . .	...	...	...	...	...	...	...	...
Special drawing rights	4 820 . .	–28	–39	–52	...	...	...	...	...
Reserve position in the Fund	4 830 . .	...	...	...	...	...	...	...	...
Foreign exchange	4 840 . .	1,421	–253	–1,106	...	...	...	...	...
Other claims	4 880 . .	...	...	...	...	...	...	...	...
NET ERRORS AND OMISSIONS	4 998 . .	**271**	**130**	**–37**	...	...	...	...	...

Table 1. ANALYTIC PRESENTATION, 1988–95
(Millions of U.S. dollars)

	Code	1988	1989	1990	1991	1992	1993	1994	1995
A. Current Account[1]	4 993 Y.	...	...	...	...	...	**–85.7**	**–94.0**	**–614.4**
Goods: exports f.o.b	2 100 ..	...	...	...	...	...	2,025.8	2,029.2	2,706.1
Goods: imports f.o.b	3 100 ..	...	...	...	...	...	–2,180.5	–2,234.1	–3,404.0
Balance on Goods	4 100 ..	...	...	...	...	...	*–154.7*	*–204.9*	*–697.9*
Services: credit	2 200 ..	...	...	...	...	...	197.8	321.9	485.2
Services: debit	3 200 ..	...	...	...	...	...	–252.9	–376.5	–498.1
Balance on Goods and Services	4 991 ..	...	...	...	...	...	*–209.8*	*–259.4*	*–710.8*
Income: credit	2 300 ..	...	...	...	...	...	12.5	21.4	50.9
Income: debit	3 300 ..	...	...	...	...	...	–4.3	–12.8	–63.7
Balance on Goods, Services, and Income	4 992 ..	...	...	...	...	...	*–201.5*	*–250.8*	*–723.7*
Current transfers: credit	2 379 Y.	...	...	...	...	...	115.9	161.6	112.3
Current transfers: debit	3 379 ..	...	...	...	...	...	...	–4.8	–3.0
B. Capital Account[1]	4 994 Y.	...	...	...	...	...	...	**12.9**	**–39.0**
Capital account: credit	2 994 Y.	...	...	...	...	...	...	12.9	3.3
Capital account: debit	3 994 ..	...	...	...	...	...	...	...	–42.3
Total, Groups A Plus B	4 010 ..	...	...	...	...	...	*–85.7*	*–81.1*	*–653.4*
C. Financial Account[1]	4 995 X.	...	...	...	...	...	**301.5**	**103.3**	**236.7**
Direct investment abroad	4 505 ..	...	...	...	...	...	...	...	–1.0
Direct investment in Lithuania	4 555 Y.	...	...	...	...	...	30.2	31.3	72.6
Portfolio investment assets	4 602 ..	...	...	...	...	...	–.9	–.2	–10.5
Equity securities	4 610 ..	...	...	...	...	...	–.9	–.2	–3.0
Debt securities	4 619 ..	...	...	...	...	...	...	...	–7.5
Portfolio investment liabilities	4 652 Y.	...	...	...	...	...	.6	4.6	26.6
Equity securities	4 660 Y.	...	...	...	...	...	.6	4.6	6.2
Debt securities	4 669 Y.	...	...	...	...	...	...	...	20.4
Other investment assets	4 703 ..	...	...	...	...	...	95.3	–26.4	–36.1
Monetary authorities	4 703 .A	...	...	...	...	...	...	...	67.0
General government	4 703 .B	...	...	...	...	...	...	...	...
Banks	4 703 .C	...	...	...	...	...	108.9	–17.3	–18.0
Other sectors	4 703 .D	...	...	...	...	...	–13.6	–9.2	–85.0
Other investment liabilities	4 753 X.	...	...	...	...	...	176.5	94.1	185.0
Monetary authorities	4 753 XA	...	...	...	...	...	...	–.9	–25.1
General government	4 753 YB	...	...	...	...	...	255.7	–30.0	–2.5
Banks	4 753 YC	...	...	...	...	...	–62.9	75.8	10.8
Other sectors	4 753 YD	...	...	...	...	...	–16.3	49.1	201.8
Total, Groups A Through C	4 020 ..	...	...	...	...	...	*215.9*	*22.2*	*–416.7*
D. Net Errors and Omissions	4 998 ..	...	...	...	...	...	**–7.4**	**–46.9**	**287.2**
Total, Groups A Through D	4 030 ..	...	...	...	...	...	*208.5*	*–24.7*	*–129.5*
E. Reserves and Related Items	4 040 ..	...	...	...	...	...	**–208.5**	**24.7**	**129.5**
Reserve assets	4 800 ..	...	...	...	...	...	–308.0	–179.7	–231.3
Use of Fund credit and loans	4 766 ..	...	...	...	...	...	99.5	66.9	63.0
Liabilities constituting foreign authorities' reserves	4 900 ..	...	...	...	...	...	...	...	...
Exceptional financing	4 920 ..	...	...	...	...	...	...	137.6	297.8
Conversion rates: litai per U.S. dollar	0 101 ..	...	...	...	...	**1.7728**	**4.3441**	**3.9778**	**4.0000**

[1] Excludes components that have been classified in the categories of Group E.

Table 2. STANDARD PRESENTATION, 1988–95

(Millions of U.S. dollars)

	Code	1988	1989	1990	1991	1992	1993	1994	1995
CURRENT ACCOUNT	4 993 . .	...	...	...	...	...	**–85.7**	**–94.0**	**–614.4**
A. GOODS	4 100 . .	...	...	...	...	...	–154.7	–204.9	–697.9
Credit	2 100 . .	...	...	...	...	...	**2,025.8**	**2,029.2**	**2,706.1**
General merchandise: exports f.o.b.	2 110 . .	...	...	...	...	...	2,025.8	2,029.2	2,705.0
Goods for processing: exports f.o.b.	2 150 . .	...	...	...	...	...	...	...	...
Repairs on goods	2 160 . .	...	...	...	...	...	...	...	...
Goods procured in ports by carriers	2 170 . .	...	...	...	...	...	...	...	1.1
Nonmonetary gold	2 180 . .	...	...	...	...	...	...	...	...
Debit	3 100 . .	...	...	...	...	...	**–2,180.5**	**–2,234.1**	**–3,404.0**
General merchandise: imports f.o.b.	3 110 . .	...	...	...	...	...	–2,180.5	–2,234.1	–3,389.8
Goods for processing: imports f.o.b.	3 150 . .	...	...	...	...	...	...	...	...
Repairs on goods	3 160 . .	...	...	...	...	...	...	...	...
Goods procured in ports by carriers	3 170 . .	...	...	...	...	...	...	...	–14.2
Nonmonetary gold	3 180 . .	...	...	...	...	...	...	...	...
B. SERVICES	4 200 . .	...	...	...	...	...	–55.1	–54.5	–12.9
Total credit	2 200 . .	...	...	...	...	...	*197.8*	*321.9*	*485.2*
Total debit	3 200 . .	...	...	...	...	...	*–252.9*	*–376.5*	*–498.1*
Transportation services, credit	2 205 . .	...	...	...	...	...	**165.4**	**207.6**	**287.5**
Passenger	2 205 BA	...	...	...	...	...	...	*13.8*	*25.4*
Freight	2 205 BB	...	...	...	...	...	...	*161.4*	*187.3*
Other	2 205 BC	...	...	...	...	...	...	*32.4*	*74.9*
Sea transport, passenger	2 207 . .	...	...	...	...	...	...	1.6	3.8
Sea transport, freight	2 208 . .	...	...	...	...	...	...	95.6	88.9
Sea transport, other	2 209 . .	...	...	...	...	...	...	...	10.5
Air transport, passenger	2 211 . .	...	...	...	...	...	...	9.3	16.3
Air transport, freight	2 212 . .	...	...	...	...	...	...	.2	.8
Air transport, other	2 213 . .	...	...	...	...	...	...	2.3	4.4
Other transport, passenger	2 215 . .	...	...	...	...	...	...	3.0	5.2
Other transport, freight	2 216 . .	...	...	...	...	...	...	65.6	97.6
Other transport, other	2 217 . .	...	...	...	...	...	...	30.1	60.0
Transportation services, debit	3 205 . .	...	...	...	...	...	**–160.7**	**–197.0**	**–292.2**
Passenger	3 205 BA	...	...	...	...	...	...	*–.9*	*–.5*
Freight	3 205 BB	...	...	...	...	...	...	*–152.6*	*–247.1*
Other	3 205 BC	...	...	...	...	...	...	*–43.5*	*–44.5*
Sea transport, passenger	3 207 . .	...	...	...	...	...	...	...	...
Sea transport, freight	3 208 . .	...	...	...	...	...	...	...	...
Sea transport, other	3 209 . .	...	...	...	...	...	...	–19.8	–19.8
Air transport, passenger	3 211 . .	...	...	...	...	...	...	...	...
Air transport, freight	3 212 . .	...	...	...	...	...	...	...	...
Air transport, other	3 213 . .	...	...	...	...	...	...	–20.7	–18.9
Other transport, passenger	3 215 . .	...	...	...	...	...	...	–.9	–.5
Other transport, freight	3 216 . .	...	...	...	...	...	...	–152.6	–247.1
Other transport, other	3 217 . .	...	...	...	...	...	...	–3.0	–5.8
Travel, credit	2 236 . .	...	...	...	...	...	**21.6**	**68.6**	**77.0**
Business travel	2 237 . .	...	...	...	...	...	...	...	...
Personal travel	2 240 . .	...	...	...	...	...	...	...	77.0
Travel, debit	3 236 . .	...	...	...	...	...	**–12.1**	**–50.3**	**–106.3**
Business travel	3 237 . .	...	...	...	...	...	...	...	...
Personal travel	3 240 . .	...	...	...	...	...	...	...	–106.3
Other services, credit	2 200 BA	...	...	...	...	...	**10.8**	**45.7**	**120.7**
Communications	2 245 . .	...	...	...	...	...	2.4	9.7	23.9
Construction	2 249 . .	...	...	...	...	...	6.3	31.2	64.9
Insurance	2 253 . .	...	...	...	...	...	...	1.2	2.8
Financial	2 260 . .	...	...	...	...	...	...	.1	1.7
Computer and information	2 262 . .	...	...	...	...	...	...	...	.3
Royalties and licence fees	2 266 . .	...	...	...	...	...	...	...	...
Other business services	2 268 . .	...	...	...	...	...	2.1	3.5	24.1
Personal, cultural, and recreational	2 287 . .	...	...	...	...	...	...	...	...
Government, n.i.e.	2 291 . .	...	...	...	...	...	...	...	3.0
Other services, debit	3 200 BA	...	...	...	...	...	**–80.0**	**–129.2**	**–99.6**
Communications	3 245 . .	...	...	...	...	...	–1.3	–7.6	–20.8
Construction	3 249 . .	...	...	...	...	...	–.1	–1.7	–10.3
Insurance	3 253 . .	...	...	...	...	...	...	...	–2.5
Financial	3 260 . .	...	...	...	...	...	...	–.2	–2.4
Computer and information	3 262 . .	...	...	...	...	...	...	–.4	–.7
Royalties and licence fees	3 266 . .	...	...	...	...	...	...	–.2	–1.4
Other business services	3 268 . .	...	...	...	...	...	–2.9	–8.3	–20.4
Personal, cultural, and recreational	3 287 . .	...	...	...	...	...	...	...	...
Government, n.i.e.	3 291 . .	...	...	...	...	...	–75.8	–110.7	–41.1

Table 2 (Continued). STANDARD PRESENTATION, 1988–95
(Millions of U.S. dollars)

	Code	1988	1989	1990	1991	1992	1993	1994	1995
C. INCOME	4 300 . .	...	...	...	...	...	8.3	8.6	–12.9
Total credit	2 300 . .	...	...	...	...	...	*12.5*	*21.4*	*50.9*
Total debit	3 300 . .	...	...	...	...	...	*–4.3*	*–12.8*	*–63.7*
Compensation of employees, credit	2 310 . .	...	...	...	...	...	...	...	...
Compensation of employees, debit	3 310 . .	...	...	...	...	...	**–.1**	**–.3**	**–.4**
Investment income, credit	2 320 . .	...	...	...	...	...	**12.5**	**21.4**	**50.9**
Direct investment income	2 330 . .	...	...	...	...	...	...	...	...
Dividends and distributed branch profits	2 332 . .	...	...	...	...	...	...	...	...
Reinvested earnings and undistributed branch profits	2 333 . .	...	...	...	...	...	...	...	...
Income on debt (interest)	2 334 . .	...	...	...	...	...	...	...	...
Portfolio investment income	2 339 . .	...	...	...	...	...	.1	...	28.1
Income on equity	2 340 . .	...	...	...	...	...	...	...	.2
Income on bonds and notes	2 350 . .	...	...	...	...	...	...	...	27.9
Income on money market instruments and financial derivatives	2 360 . .	...	...	...	...	...	...	...	...
Other investment income	2 370 . .	...	...	...	...	...	12.4	21.4	22.8
Investment income, debit	3 320 . .	...	...	...	...	...	**–4.2**	**–12.5**	**–63.3**
Direct investment income	3 330 . .	...	...	...	...	...	–.1	–.5	–8.1
Dividends and distributed branch profits	3 332 . .	...	...	...	...	...	–.1	–.5	–1.0
Reinvested earnings and undistributed branch profits	3 333 . .	...	...	...	...	...	...	...	–7.1
Income on debt (interest)	3 334 . .	...	...	...	...	...	...	...	...
Portfolio investment income	3 339 . .	...	...	...	...	...	–3.5	...	–12.3
Income on equity	3 340 . .	...	...	...	...	...	...	...	...
Income on bonds and notes	3 350 . .	...	...	...	...	...	...	...	–12.3
Income on money market instruments and financial derivatives	3 360 . .	...	...	...	...	...	...	...	...
Other investment income	3 370 . .	...	...	...	...	...	–.6	–12.0	–42.9
D. CURRENT TRANSFERS	4 379 . .	...	...	...	...	...	115.9	156.8	109.3
Credit	2 379 . .	...	...	...	...	...	**115.9**	**161.6**	**112.3**
General government	2 380 . .	...	...	...	...	...	94.9	122.7	63.7
Other sectors	2 390 . .	...	...	...	...	...	21.0	38.9	48.6
Workers' remittances	2 391 . .	...	...	...	...	...	...	.7	1.1
Other current transfers	2 392 . .	...	...	...	...	...	20.9	38.2	47.5
Debit	3 379 . .	...	...	...	...	...	...	**–4.8**	**–3.0**
General government	3 380 . .	...	...	...	...	...	...	–4.5	–2.3
Other sectors	3 390 . .	...	...	...	...	...	...	–.3	–.6
Workers' remittances	3 391 . .	...	...	...	...	...	...	–.3	–.6
Other current transfers	3 392 . .	...	...	...	...	...	...	...	–.1
CAPITAL AND FINANCIAL ACCOUNT	4 996 . .	...	...	...	...	...	**93.1**	**140.9**	**327.1**
CAPITAL ACCOUNT	4 994 . .	...	...	...	...	...	...	**12.9**	**–39.0**
Total credit	2 994 . .	...	...	...	...	...	...	*12.9*	*3.3*
Total debit	3 994 . .	...	...	...	...	...	...	...	*–42.3*
Capital transfers, credit	2 400 . .	...	...	...	...	...	...	**12.9**	**3.3**
General government	2 401 . .	...	...	...	...	...	...	12.9	1.4
Debt forgiveness	2 402 . .	...	...	...	...	...	...	...	...
Other capital transfers	2 410 . .	...	...	...	...	...	...	12.9	1.4
Other sectors	2 430 . .	...	...	...	...	...	...	...	1.9
Migrants' transfers	2 431 . .	...	...	...	...	...	...	...	...
Debt forgiveness	2 432 . .	...	...	...	...	...	...	...	...
Other capital transfers	2 440 . .	...	...	...	...	...	...	...	1.9
Capital transfers, debit	3 400 . .	...	...	...	...	...	...	...	**–42.3**
General government	3 401 . .	...	...	...	...	...	...	...	–42.0
Debt forgiveness	3 402 . .	...	...	...	...	...	...	...	...
Other capital transfers	3 410 . .	...	...	...	...	...	...	...	...
Other sectors	3 430 . .	...	...	...	...	...	...	...	–.3
Migrants' transfers	3 431 . .	...	...	...	...	...	...	...	...
Debt forgiveness	3 432 . .	...	...	...	...	...	...	...	–.3
Other capital transfers	3 440 . .	...	...	...	...	...	...	...	...
Nonproduced nonfinancial assets, credit	2 480 . .	...	...	...	...	...	...	...	...
Nonproduced nonfinancial assets, debit	3 480 . .	...	...	...	...	...	...	...	...

Table 2 (Continued). STANDARD PRESENTATION, 1988–95
(Millions of U.S. dollars)

	Code	1988	1989	1990	1991	1992	1993	1994	1995
FINANCIAL ACCOUNT	4 995	**. . .**	**. . .**	**. . .**	**. . .**	**. . .**	**93.1**	**128.1**	**366.1**
A. DIRECT INVESTMENT	4 500	. . .	. . .	. . .	. . .	. . .	30.2	31.3	71.6
Direct investment abroad	4 505	**. . .**	**. . .**	**. . .**	**. . .**	**. . .**	**. . .**	**. . .**	**–1.0**
Equity capital	4 510	. . .	. . .	. . .	. . .	. . .	. . .	. . .	–1.0
Claims on affiliated enterprises	4 515	. . .	. . .	. . .	. . .	. . .	. . .	. . .	–1.0
Liabilities to affiliated enterprises	4 520	. . .	. . .	. . .	. . .	. . .	. . .	. . .	. . .
Reinvested earnings	4 525	. . .	. . .	. . .	. . .	. . .	. . .	. . .	. . .
Other capital	4 530	. . .	. . .	. . .	. . .	. . .	. . .	. . .	. . .
Claims on affiliated enterprises	4 535	. . .	. . .	. . .	. . .	. . .	. . .	. . .	. . .
Liabilities to affiliated enterprises	4 540	. . .	. . .	. . .	. . .	. . .	. . .	. . .	. . .
Direct investment in Lithuania	4 555	**. . .**	**. . .**	**. . .**	**. . .**	**. . .**	**30.2**	**31.3**	**72.6**
Equity capital	4 560	. . .	. . .	. . .	. . .	. . .	30.2	31.3	65.4
Claims on direct investors	4 565	. . .	. . .	. . .	. . .	. . .	. . .	. . .	. . .
Liabilities to direct investors	4 570	. . .	. . .	. . .	. . .	. . .	. . .	31.3	65.4
Reinvested earnings	4 575	. . .	. . .	. . .	. . .	. . .	. . .	. . .	7.1
Other capital	4 580	. . .	. . .	. . .	. . .	. . .	. . .	. . .	.1
Claims on direct investors	4 585	. . .	. . .	. . .	. . .	. . .	. . .	. . .	. . .
Liabilities to direct investors	4 590	. . .	. . .	. . .	. . .	. . .	. . .	. . .	.1
B. PORTFOLIO INVESTMENT	4 600	. . .	. . .	. . .	. . .	. . .	–.4	4.4	16.2
Assets	4 602	**. . .**	**. . .**	**. . .**	**. . .**	**. . .**	**–.9**	**–.2**	**–10.5**
Equity securities	4 610	. . .	. . .	. . .	. . .	. . .	–.9	–.2	–3.0
Monetary authorities	4 611	. . .	. . .	. . .	. . .	. . .	. . .	. . .	–1.9
General government	4 612	. . .	. . .	. . .	. . .	. . .	. . .	. . .	. . .
Banks	4 613	. . .	. . .	. . .	. . .	. . .	–.9	. . .	–.8
Other sectors	4 614	. . .	. . .	. . .	. . .	. . .	. . .	–.1	–.3
Debt securities	4 619	. . .	. . .	. . .	. . .	. . .	. . .	. . .	–7.5
Bonds and notes	4 620	. . .	. . .	. . .	. . .	. . .	. . .	. . .	–7.5
Monetary authorities	4 621	. . .	. . .	. . .	. . .	. . .	. . .	. . .	. . .
General government	4 622	. . .	. . .	. . .	. . .	. . .	. . .	. . .	. . .
Banks	4 623	. . .	. . .	. . .	. . .	. . .	. . .	. . .	–7.3
Other sectors	4 624	. . .	. . .	. . .	. . .	. . .	. . .	. . .	–.2
Money market instruments	4 630	. . .	. . .	. . .	. . .	. . .	. . .	. . .	. . .
Monetary authorities	4 631	. . .	. . .	. . .	. . .	. . .	. . .	. . .	. . .
General government	4 632	. . .	. . .	. . .	. . .	. . .	. . .	. . .	. . .
Banks	4 633	. . .	. . .	. . .	. . .	. . .	. . .	. . .	. . .
Other sectors	4 634	. . .	. . .	. . .	. . .	. . .	. . .	. . .	. . .
Financial derivatives	4 640	. . .	. . .	. . .	. . .	. . .	. . .	. . .	. . .
Monetary authorities	4 641	. . .	. . .	. . .	. . .	. . .	. . .	. . .	. . .
General government	4 642	. . .	. . .	. . .	. . .	. . .	. . .	. . .	. . .
Banks	4 643	. . .	. . .	. . .	. . .	. . .	. . .	. . .	. . .
Other sectors	4 644	. . .	. . .	. . .	. . .	. . .	. . .	. . .	. . .
Liabilities	4 652	**. . .**	**. . .**	**. . .**	**. . .**	**. . .**	**.6**	**4.6**	**26.6**
Equity securities	4 660	. . .	. . .	. . .	. . .	. . .	.6	4.6	6.2
Banks	4 663	. . .	. . .	. . .	. . .	. . .	.6	4.6	5.9
Other sectors	4 664	. . .	. . .	. . .	. . .	. . .	. . .	. . .	.3
Debt securities	4 669	. . .	. . .	. . .	. . .	. . .	. . .	. . .	20.4
Bonds and notes	4 670	. . .	. . .	. . .	. . .	. . .	. . .	. . .	20.4
Monetary authorities	4 671	. . .	. . .	. . .	. . .	. . .	. . .	. . .	. . .
General government	4 672	. . .	. . .	. . .	. . .	. . .	. . .	. . .	20.4
Banks	4 673	. . .	. . .	. . .	. . .	. . .	. . .	. . .	. . .
Other sectors	4 674	. . .	. . .	. . .	. . .	. . .	. . .	. . .	. . .
Money market instruments	4 680	. . .	. . .	. . .	. . .	. . .	. . .	. . .	. . .
Monetary authorities	4 681	. . .	. . .	. . .	. . .	. . .	. . .	. . .	. . .
General government	4 682	. . .	. . .	. . .	. . .	. . .	. . .	. . .	. . .
Banks	4 683	. . .	. . .	. . .	. . .	. . .	. . .	. . .	. . .
Other sectors	4 684	. . .	. . .	. . .	. . .	. . .	. . .	. . .	. . .
Financial derivatives	4 690	. . .	. . .	. . .	. . .	. . .	. . .	. . .	. . .
Monetary authorities	4 691	. . .	. . .	. . .	. . .	. . .	. . .	. . .	. . .
General government	4 692	. . .	. . .	. . .	. . .	. . .	. . .	. . .	. . .
Banks	4 693	. . .	. . .	. . .	. . .	. . .	. . .	. . .	. . .
Other sectors	4 694	. . .	. . .	. . .	. . .	. . .	. . .	. . .	. . .

Table 2 (Concluded). STANDARD PRESENTATION, 1988–95
(Millions of U.S. dollars)

	Code	1988	1989	1990	1991	1992	1993	1994	1995
C. OTHER INVESTMENT	4 700 . .	...	...	...	...	...	371.3	272.1	509.7
Assets	4 703 . .	**...**	**...**	**...**	**...**	**...**	**95.3**	**–26.4**	**–36.1**
Trade credits	4 706 . .	...	...	...	...	...	...	...	–64.3
General government: long-term	4 708 . .	...	...	...	...	...	...	...	...
General government: short-term	4 709 . .	...	...	...	...	...	...	...	...
Other sectors: long-term	4 711 . .	...	...	...	...	...	...	...	...
Other sectors: short-term	4 712 . .	...	...	...	...	...	...	...	–64.3
Loans	4 714 . .	...	...	...	...	...	–.7	–11.6	–13.1
Monetary authorities: long-term	4 717 . .	...	...	...	...	...	...	...	...
Monetary authorities: short-term	4 718 . .	...	...	...	...	...	...	...	...
General government: long-term	4 720 . .	...	...	...	...	...	...	...	...
General government: short-term	4 721 . .	...	...	...	...	...	...	...	...
Banks: long-term	4 723 . .	...	...	...	...	...	...	...	–4.9
Banks: short-term	4 724 . .	...	...	...	...	...	–.7	–11.6	–8.3
Other sectors: long-term	4 726 . .	...	...	...	...	...	...	...	.1
Other sectors: short-term	4 727 . .	...	...	...	...	...	...	...	–.1
Currency and deposits	4 730 . .	...	...	...	...	...	109.0	–7.2	43.3
Monetary authorities	4 731 . .	...	...	...	...	...	...	...	67.0
General government	4 732 . .	...	...	...	...	...	...	...	...
Banks	4 733 . .	...	...	...	...	...	109.5	–5.7	–2.8
Other sectors	4 734 . .	...	...	...	...	...	–.6	–1.6	–20.8
Other assets	4 736 . .	...	...	...	...	...	–13.1	–7.6	–2.0
Monetary authorities: long-term	4 738 . .	...	...	...	...	...	...	...	...
Monetary authorities: short-term	4 739 . .	...	...	...	...	...	...	...	...
General government: long-term	4 741 . .	...	...	...	...	...	...	...	...
General government: short-term	4 742 . .	...	...	...	...	...	...	...	...
Banks: long-term	4 744 . .	...	...	...	...	...	...	...	...
Banks: short-term	4 745 . .	...	...	...	...	...	...	...	–2.0
Other sectors: long-term	4 747 . .	...	...	...	...	...	...	...	...
Other sectors: short-term	4 748 . .	...	...	...	...	...	–13.1	–7.6	...
Liabilities	4 753 . .	**...**	**...**	**...**	**...**	**...**	**276.0**	**298.5**	**545.7**
Trade credits	4 756 . .	...	...	...	...	...	...	...	195.1
General government: long-term	4 758 . .	...	...	...	...	...	...	...	...
General government: short-term	4 759 . .	...	...	...	...	...	...	...	...
Other sectors: long-term	4 761 . .	...	...	...	...	...	...	...	...
Other sectors: short-term	4 762 . .	...	...	...	...	...	...	...	195.1
Loans	4 764 . .	...	...	...	...	...	355.3	206.8	370.6
Use of Fund credit and loans from the Fund	4 766 . .	...	...	...	...	...	99.5	66.9	63.0
Monetary authorities: other long term	4 767 . .	...	...	...	...	...	...	...	...
Monetary authorities: short-term	4 768 . .	...	...	...	...	...	...	...	...
General government: long-term	4 770 . .	...	...	...	...	...	255.7	85.5	178.5
General government: short-term	4 771 . .	...	...	...	...	...	...	...	...
Banks: long-term	4 773 . .	...	...	...	...	...	...	12.1	6.3
Banks: short-term	4 774 . .	...	...	...	...	...	...	7.2	–.7
Other sectors: long-term	4 776 . .	...	...	...	...	...	...	35.1	100.8
Other sectors: short-term	4 777 . .	...	...	...	...	...	...	...	22.7
Currency and deposits	4 780 . .	...	...	...	...	...	–62.9	55.6	–21.0
Monetary authorities	4 781 . .	...	...	...	...	...	...	–.9	–25.1
General government	4 782 . .	...	...	...	...	...	...	...	...
Banks	4 783 . .	...	...	...	...	...	–62.9	56.4	4.1
Other sectors	4 784 . .	...	...	...	...	...	...	...	...
Other liabilities	4 786 . .	...	...	...	...	...	–16.3	36.1	1.1
Monetary authorities: long-term	4 788 . .	...	...	...	...	...	...	...	...
Monetary authorities: short-term	4 789 . .	...	...	...	...	...	...	...	...
General government: long-term	4 791 . .	...	...	...	...	...	...	...	...
General government: short-term	4 792 . .	...	...	...	...	...	...	...	...
Banks: long-term	4 794 . .	...	...	...	...	...	...	...	...
Banks: short-term	4 795 . .	...	...	...	...	...	...	...	1.1
Other sectors: long-term	4 797 . .	...	...	...	...	...	–16.3	...	...
Other sectors: short-term	4 798 . .	...	...	...	...	...	...	36.1	...
D. RESERVE ASSETS	4 800 . .	...	...	...	...	...	–308.0	–179.7	–231.3
Monetary gold	4 810 . .	...	...	...	...	...	...	...	–.1
Special drawing rights	4 820 . .	...	...	...	...	...	–75.7	62.5	–2.7
Reserve position in the Fund	4 830 . .	...	...	...	...	...	...	...	...
Foreign exchange	4 840 . .	...	...	...	...	...	–232.4	–242.2	–228.6
Other claims	4 880 . .	...	...	...	...	...	...	...	...
NET ERRORS AND OMISSIONS	4 998 . .	**...**	**...**	**...**	**...**	**...**	**–7.4**	**–46.9**	**287.2**

Table 3. INTERNATIONAL INVESTMENT POSITION (End–period stocks), 1988–95
(Millions of U.S. dollars)

	Code		1988	1989	1990	1991	1992	1993	1994	1995
ASSETS	8 995	C.	...	...	...	...	...	...	997.6	1,274.6
Direct investment abroad	8 505	. .	...	...	...	...	...	...	**.2**	**1.2**
Equity capital and reinvested earnings	8 506	. .	...	...	...	...	...	...	.2	1.2
Claims on affiliated enterprises	8 507	. .	...	...	...	...	...	...	.2	1.2
Liabilities to affiliated enterprises	8 508	. .	...	...	...	...	...	...	...	...
Other capital	8 530	. .	...	...	...	...	...	...	...	...
Claims on affiliated enterprises	8 535	. .	...	...	...	...	...	...	...	...
Liabilities to affiliated enterprises	8 540	. .	...	...	...	...	...	...	...	...
Portfolio investment	8 602	. .	...	...	...	...	...	...	**.6**	**11.1**
Equity securities	8 610	. .	...	...	...	...	...	...	.2	3.1
Monetary authorities	8 611	. .	...	...	...	...	...	...	...	1.9
General government	8 612	. .	...	...	...	...	...	...	...	...
Banks	8 613	. .	...	...	...	...	...	...	...	.8
Other sectors	8 614	. .	...	...	...	...	...	...	.2	.4
Debt securities	8 619	. .	...	...	...	...	...	...	.5	7.9
Bonds and notes	8 620	. .	...	...	...	...	...	...	.5	7.9
Monetary authorities	8 621	. .	...	...	...	...	...	...	...	...
General government	8 622	. .	...	...	...	...	...	...	...	...
Banks	8 623	. .	...	...	...	...	...	...	...	7.3
Other sectors	8 624	. .	...	...	...	...	...	...	.4	.6
Money market instruments	8 630	. .	...	...	...	...	...	...	...	...
Monetary authorities	8 631	. .	...	...	...	...	...	...	...	...
General government	8 632	. .	...	...	...	...	...	...	...	...
Banks	8 633	. .	...	...	...	...	...	...	...	...
Other sectors	8 634	. .	...	...	...	...	...	...	...	...
Financial derivatives	8 640	. .	...	...	...	...	...	...	...	...
Monetary authorities	8 641	. .	...	...	...	...	...	...	...	...
General government	8 642	. .	...	...	...	...	...	...	...	...
Banks	8 643	. .	...	...	...	...	...	...	...	...
Other sectors	8 644	. .	...	...	...	...	...	...	...	...
Other investment	8 703	. .	...	...	...	...	...	...	**409.4**	**443.4**
Trade credits	8 706	. .	...	...	...	...	...	...	173.6	237.9
General government: long-term	8 708	. .	...	...	...	...	...	...	...	...
General government: short-term	8 709	. .	...	...	...	...	...	...	...	...
Other sectors: long-term	8 711	. .	...	...	...	...	...	...	...	...
Other sectors: short-term	8 712	. .	...	...	...	...	...	...	173.6	237.9
Loans	8 714	. .	...	...	...	...	...	...	16.5	27.5
Monetary authorities: long-term	8 717	. .	...	...	...	...	...	...	...	...
Monetary authorities: short-term	8 718	. .	...	...	...	...	...	...	...	...
General government: long-term	8 720	. .	...	...	...	...	...	...	...	...
General government: short-term	8 721	. .	...	...	...	...	...	...	...	...
Banks: long-term	8 723	. .	...	...	...	...	...	...	...	...
Banks: short-term	8 724	. .	...	...	...	...	...	...	...	...
Other sectors: long-term	8 726	. .	...	...	...	...	...	...	1.2	1.1
Other sectors: short-term	8 727	. .	...	...	...	...	...	...	.2	.3
Currency and deposits	8 730	. .	...	...	...	...	...	...	219.2	175.9
Monetary authorities	8 731	. .	...	...	...	...	...	...	67.2	.2
General government	8 732	. .	...	...	...	...	...	...	...	...
Banks	8 733	. .	...	...	...	...	...	...	88.2	91.0
Other sectors	8 734	. .	...	...	...	...	...	...	63.9	84.7
Other assets	8 736	. .	...	...	...	...	...	...	...	2.0
Monetary authorities: long-term	8 738	. .	...	...	...	...	...	...	...	...
Monetary authorities: short-term	8 739	. .	...	...	...	...	...	...	...	...
General government: long-term	8 741	. .	...	...	...	...	...	...	...	...
General government: short-term	8 742	. .	...	...	...	...	...	...	...	...
Banks: long-term	8 744	. .	...	...	...	...	...	...	...	...
Banks: short-term	8 745	. .	...	...	...	...	...	...	...	2.0
Other sectors: long-term	8 747	. .	...	...	...	...	...	...	...	...
Other sectors: short-term	8 748	. .	...	...	...	...	...	...	...	...
Reserve assets	8 800	. .	...	...	...	...	...	...	**587.4**	**819.0**
Monetary gold	8 810	. .	...	...	...	...	...	...	61.9	62.0
Special drawing rights	8 820	. .	...	...	...	...	1.3	75.1	15.1	18.2
Reserve position in the Fund	8 830	. .	...	...	...	...	...	...	...	...
Foreign exchange	8 840	. .	...	...	...	...	...	...	510.3	738.9
Other claims	8 880	. .	...	...	...	...	...	...	...	...

Table 3 (Continued). INTERNATIONAL INVESTMENT POSITION (End–period stocks), 1988–95
(Millions of U.S. dollars)

	Code	1988	1989	1990	1991	1992	1993	1994	1995
LIABILITIES	8 995 D.	...	...	...	...	...	...	1,114.3	1,795.8
Direct investment in Lithuania	8 555 . .	...	...	...	...	...	...	**262.2**	**353.9**
Equity capital and reinvested earnings	8 556 . .	...	...	...	...	...	...	262.2	353.9
Claims on direct investors	8 557 . .	...	...	...	...	...	...	...	...
Liabilities to direct investors	8 558 . .	...	...	...	...	...	...	262.2	353.9
Other capital	8 580 . .	...	...	...	...	...	...	...	...
Claims on direct investors	8 585 . .	...	...	...	...	...	...	...	...
Liabilities to direct investors	8 590 . .	...	...	...	...	...	...	...	...
Portfolio investment	8 652 . .	...	...	...	...	...	...	**12.9**	**40.5**
Equity securities	8 660 . .	...	...	...	...	...	...	5.8	12.4
Banks	8 663 . .	...	...	...	...	...	...	5.4	11.6
Other sectors	8 664 . .	...	...	...	...	...	...	.4	.7
Debt securities	8 669 . .	...	...	...	...	...	...	7.2	28.1
Bonds and notes	8 670 . .	...	...	...	...	...	...	7.2	28.1
Monetary authorities	8 671 . .	...	...	...	...	...	...	...	...
General government	8 672 . .	...	...	...	...	...	...	7.2	28.1
Banks	8 673 . .	...	...	...	...	...	...	...	...
Other sectors	8 674 . .	...	...	...	...	...	...	...	...
Money market instruments	8 680 . .	...	...	...	...	...	...	...	...
Monetary authorities	8 681 . .	...	...	...	...	...	...	...	...
General government	8 682 . .	...	...	...	...	...	...	...	...
Banks	8 683 . .	...	...	...	...	...	...	...	...
Other sectors	8 684 . .	...	...	...	...	...	...	...	...
Financial derivatives	8 690 . .	...	...	...	...	...	...	...	...
Monetary authorities	8 691 . .	...	...	...	...	...	...	...	...
General government	8 692 . .	...	...	...	...	...	...	...	...
Banks	8 692 . .	...	...	...	...	...	...	...	...
Other sectors	8 694 . .	...	...	...	...	...	...	...	...
Other investment	8 753 . .	...	...	...	...	...	...	**839.1**	**1,401.4**
Trade credits	8 756 . .	...	...	...	...	...	...	188.2	383.3
General government: long-term	8 758 . .	...	...	...	...	...	...	...	...
General government: short-term	8 759 . .	...	...	...	...	...	...	...	...
Other sectors: long-term	8 761 . .	...	...	...	...	...	...	...	...
Other sectors: short-term	8 762 . .	...	...	...	...	...	...	188.2	383.3
Loans	8 764 . .	...	...	...	...	...	...	560.5	947.7
Use of Fund credit and loans from the Fund	8 766 . .	...	...	...	...	23.7	120.8	196.4	261.5
Monetary authorities: other long-term	8 767 . .	...	...	...	...	...	...	...	...
Monetary authorities: short-term	8 768 . .	...	...	...	...	...	...	...	...
General government: long-term	8 770 . .	...	...	...	...	...	...	235.2	424.0
General government: short-term	8 771 . .	...	...	...	...	...	...	...	...
Banks: long-term	8 773 . .	...	...	...	...	...	...	...	...
Banks: short-term	8 774 . .	...	...	...	...	...	...	...	...
Other sectors: long-term	8 776 . .	...	...	...	...	...	...	94.3	195.5
Other sectors: short-term	8 777 . .	...	...	...	...	...	...	15.3	37.9
Currency and deposits	8 780 . .	...	...	...	...	...	...	90.3	69.4
Monetary authorities	8 781 . .	...	...	...	...	...	...	25.2	.1
General government	8 782 . .	...	...	...	...	...	...	...	...
Banks	8 783 . .	...	...	...	...	...	...	65.2	69.3
Other sectors	8 784 . .	...	...	...	...	...	...	...	...
Other liabilities	8 786 . .	...	...	...	...	...	...	...	1.1
Monetary authorities: long-term	8 788 . .	...	...	...	...	...	...	...	...
Monetary authorities: short-term	8 789 . .	...	...	...	...	...	...	...	...
General government: long-term	8 791 . .	...	...	...	...	...	...	...	...
General government: short-term	8 792 . .	...	...	...	...	...	...	...	...
Banks: long-term	8 794 . .	...	...	...	...	...	...	...	...
Banks: short-term	8 795 . .	...	...	...	...	...	...	...	1.1
Other sectors: long-term	8 797 . .	...	...	...	...	...	...	...	...
Other sectors: short-term	8 798 . .	...	...	...	...	...	...	...	...
NET INTERNATIONAL INVESTMENT POSITION	8 995 . .	...	...	...	...	...	...	**–116.7**	**–521.2**
Conversion rates: litai per U.S. dollar (end of period)	0 102 . .	...	...	...	...	**3.7900**	**3.9000**	**4.0000**	**4.0000**

Table 1. ANALYTIC PRESENTATION, 1988–95

(Millions of U.S. dollars)

	Code	1988	1989	1990	1991	1992	1993	1994	1995
A. Current Account [1]	4 993 Y.	**–150**	**–84**	**–265**	**–230**	**–198**	**–258**	**–277**	**–276**
Goods: exports f.o.b	2 100 ..	284	321	318	335	327	335	450	507
Goods: imports f.o.b	3 100 ..	–319	–320	–566	–446	–471	–514	–546	–628
Balance on Goods	4 100 ..	*–34*	*1*	*–249*	*–111*	*–144*	*–180*	*–96*	*–122*
Services: credit	2 200 ..	118	132	153	148	174	187	206	242
Services: debit	3 200 ..	–250	–229	–242	–233	–260	–302	–328	–359
Balance on Goods and Services	4 991 ..	*–166*	*–96*	*–338*	*–196*	*–230*	*–295*	*–218*	*–238*
Income: credit	2 300 ..	13	18	15	4	6	3	2	7
Income: debit	3 300 ..	–193	–208	–176	–166	–153	–154	–158	–174
Balance on Goods, Services, and Income	4 992 ..	*–345*	*–285*	*–499*	*–357*	*–377*	*–446*	*–374*	*–405*
Current transfers: credit	2 379 Y.	225	230	270	142	197	202	114	141
Current transfers: debit	3 379 ..	–30	–29	–36	–15	–17	–14	–17	–12
B. Capital Account [1]	4 994 Y.	**1**	**2**	**3**	**49**	**50**	**78**	**62**	**45**
Capital account: credit	2 994 Y.	1	2	3	49	50	78	62	45
Capital account: debit	3 994 ..	...	...	...	...	...	...	...	...
Total, Groups A Plus B	4 010 ..	*–149*	*–82*	*–262*	*–181*	*–148*	*–180*	*–215*	*–231*
C. Financial Account [1]	4 995 X.	**–22**	**–49**	**–18**	**–59**	**–100**	**–158**	**–122**	**–198**
Direct investment abroad	4 505 ..	...	...	...	...	...	...	...	...
Direct investment in Madagascar	4 555 Y.	...	13	22	14	21	15	6	10
Portfolio investment assets	4 602 ..	...	...	...	...	...	...	...	...
Equity securities	4 610 ..	...	...	...	...	...	...	...	...
Debt securities	4 619 ..	...	...	...	...	...	...	...	...
Portfolio investment liabilities	4 652 Y.	...	...	...	...	...	...	...	...
Equity securities	4 660 Y.	...	...	...	...	...	...	...	...
Debt securities	4 669 Y.	...	...	...	...	...	...	...	...
Other investment assets	4 703 ..	9	–18	–7	–27	–3	–47	19	–62
Monetary authorities	4 703 .A	...	...	...	–25	9	–19	38	–45
General government	4 703 .B	...	...	...	...	...	...	...	...
Banks	4 703 .C	9	–18	–7	–3	–13	–28	–18	–12
Other sectors	4 703 .D	...	...	...	...	...	...	–1	–5
Other investment liabilities	4 753 X.	–31	–44	–33	–45	–117	–126	–147	–145
Monetary authorities	4 753 XA	...	...	...	–204	–238	–254	–235	–230
General government	4 753 YB	–1	–29	–59	180	124	123	79	91
Banks	4 753 YC	–29	–15	26	–21	–3	5	6	–8
Other sectors	4 753 YD	...	...	...	...	...	...	3	3
Total, Groups A Through C	4 020 ..	*–171*	*–131*	*–280*	*–240*	*–247*	*–338*	*–338*	*–428*
D. Net Errors and Omissions	4 998 ..	**53**	**–42**	**2**	**–52**	**–31**	**4**	**61**	**98**
Total, Groups A Through D	4 030 ..	*–118*	*–174*	*–278*	*–292*	*–278*	*–334*	*–277*	*–330*
E. Reserves and Related Items	4 040 ..	**118**	**174**	**278**	**292**	**278**	**334**	**277**	**330**
Reserve assets	4 800 ..	–42	–26	167	28	–8	23	–14	–2
Use of Fund credit and loans	4 766 ..	–35	–20	–34	–16	–16	–14	–12	–14
Liabilities constituting foreign authorities' reserves	4 900 ..	1	13	...	...	...	...	...	...
Exceptional financing	4 920 ..	195	207	145	280	303	326	303	347
Conversion rates: Malagasy francs per U.S. dollar	0 101 ..	**1,407.1**	**1,603.4**	**1,494.1**	**1,835.4**	**1,864.0**	**1,913.8**	**3,067.3**	**4,265.6**

[1] Excludes components that have been classified in the categories of Group E.

Table 2. STANDARD PRESENTATION, 1988–95
(Millions of U.S. dollars)

	Code	1988	1989	1990	1991	1992	1993	1994	1995
CURRENT ACCOUNT	4 993 . .	**–150**	**–84**	**–265**	**–230**	**–198**	**–258**	**–277**	**–276**
A. GOODS	4 100 . .	–34	1	–249	–111	–144	–180	–96	–122
Credit	2 100 . .	**284**	**321**	**318**	**335**	**327**	**335**	**450**	**507**
General merchandise: exports f.o.b.	2 110 . .	284	321	318	334	324	332	447	502
Goods for processing: exports f.o.b.	2 150 . .	. . .	. . .	. . .	. . .	. . .	. . .	. . .	. . .
Repairs on goods	2 160 . .	. . .	. . .	. . .	. . .	. . .	. . .	. . .	2
Goods procured in ports by carriers	2 170 . .	. . .	. . .	. . .	1	2	2	2	3
Nonmonetary gold	2 180 . .	. . .	. . .	. . .	. . .	. . .	. . .	. . .	. . .
Debit	3 100 . .	**–319**	**–320**	**–566**	**–446**	**–471**	**–514**	**–546**	**–628**
General merchandise: imports f.o.b.	3 110 . .	–319	–320	–566	–430	–445	–465	–491	–528
Goods for processing: imports f.o.b.	3 150 . .	. . .	. . .	. . .	–10	–21	–45	–54	–100
Repairs on goods	3 160 . .	. . .	. . .	. . .	–6	–5	–5	. . .	. . .
Goods procured in ports by carriers	3 170 . .	. . .	. . .	. . .	. . .	. . .	. . .	. . .	. . .
Nonmonetary gold	3 180 . .	. . .	. . .	. . .	. . .	. . .	. . .	. . .	. . .
B. SERVICES	4 200 . .	–132	–97	–89	–85	–86	–115	–123	–116
Total credit	2 200 . .	*118*	*132*	*153*	*148*	*174*	*187*	*206*	*242*
Total debit	3 200 . .	*–250*	*–229*	*–242*	*–233*	*–260*	*–302*	*–328*	*–359*
Transportation services, credit	2 205 . .	**59**	**52**	**41**	**46**	**47**	**47**	**58**	**65**
Passenger	2 205 BA	*30*	*29*	*38*	*32*	*34*	*33*	*39*	*48*
Freight	2 205 BB	*4*	*3*	*3*	*2*	*1*	*3*	*4*	*5*
Other	2 205 BC	*26*	*20*	. . .	*12*	*12*	*11*	*15*	*13*
Sea transport, passenger	2 207 . .	. . .	. . .	. . .	. . .	. . .	. . .	. . .	. . .
Sea transport, freight	2 208 . .	. . .	. . .	. . .	2	1	3	4	5
Sea transport, other	2 209 . .	. . .	. . .	. . .	6	5	7	12	9
Air transport, passenger	2 211 . .	. . .	. . .	. . .	32	34	33	39	48
Air transport, freight	2 212 . .	. . .	. . .	. . .	. . .	. . .	. . .	. . .	. . .
Air transport, other	2 213 . .	. . .	. . .	. . .	6	8	3	3	3
Other transport, passenger	2 215 . .	. . .	. . .	. . .	. . .	. . .	. . .	. . .	. . .
Other transport, freight	2 216 . .	. . .	. . .	. . .	. . .	. . .	. . .	. . .	. . .
Other transport, other	2 217 . .	. . .	. . .	. . .	. . .	. . .	. . .	. . .	. . .
Transportation services, debit	3 205 . .	**–117**	**–73**	**–75**	**–101**	**–123**	**–123**	**–134**	**–154**
Passenger	3 205 BA	*–15*	*–15*	*–20*	*–17*	*–22*	*–18*	*–17*	*–20*
Freight	3 205 BB	*–53*	*–34*	*–55*	*–50*	*–69*	*–81*	*–88*	*–102*
Other	3 205 BC	*–49*	*–24*	. . .	*–34*	*–32*	*–24*	*–29*	*–32*
Sea transport, passenger	3 207 . .	. . .	. . .	. . .	. . .	. . .	. . .	. . .	. . .
Sea transport, freight	3 208 . .	. . .	. . .	. . .	–50	–69	–81	–88	–102
Sea transport, other	3 209 . .	. . .	. . .	. . .	–15	–19	–7	–9	–10
Air transport, passenger	3 211 . .	. . .	. . .	. . .	–17	–22	–18	–17	–20
Air transport, freight	3 212 . .	. . .	. . .	. . .	. . .	. . .	. . .	. . .	. . .
Air transport, other	3 213 . .	. . .	. . .	. . .	–19	–13	–17	–20	–22
Other transport, passenger	3 215 . .	. . .	. . .	. . .	. . .	. . .	. . .	. . .	. . .
Other transport, freight	3 216 . .	. . .	. . .	. . .	. . .	. . .	. . .	. . .	. . .
Other transport, other	3 217 . .	. . .	. . .	. . .	. . .	. . .	. . .	. . .	. . .
Travel, credit	2 236 . .	**20**	**28**	**40**	**27**	**39**	**40**	**46**	**58**
Business travel	2 237 . .	. . .	. . .	. . .	. . .	. . .	. . .	. . .	. . .
Personal travel	2 240 . .	. . .	. . .	. . .	27	39	40	46	58
Travel, debit	3 236 . .	**–30**	**–38**	**–40**	**–32**	**–37**	**–34**	**–47**	**–59**
Business travel	3 237 . .	. . .	. . .	. . .	–1	–2	–2	–1	–3
Personal travel	3 240 . .	. . .	. . .	. . .	–31	–35	–32	–46	–56
Other services, credit	2 200 BA	**39**	**52**	**71**	**75**	**88**	**100**	**101**	**120**
Communications	2 245 . .	. . .	. . .	. . .	5	5	9	6	4
Construction	2 249 . .	. . .	. . .	. . .	. . .	. . .	. . .	. . .	. . .
Insurance	2 253 . .	. . .	. . .	. . .	4	5	6	3	4
Financial	2 260 . .	. . .	. . .	. . .	1	2	4	1	1
Computer and information	2 262 . .	. . .	. . .	. . .	. . .	. . .	. . .	. . .	. . .
Royalties and licence fees	2 266 . .	. . .	. . .	. . .	2	1	1	1	1
Other business services	2 268 . .	19	32	47	40	44	45	67	86
Personal, cultural, and recreational	2 287 . .	. . .	. . .	. . .	. . .	. . .	. . .	. . .	. . .
Government, n.i.e.	2 291 . .	19	20	24	23	32	34	22	24
Other services, debit	3 200 BA	**–103**	**–118**	**–127**	**–100**	**–100**	**–145**	**–147**	**–146**
Communications	3 245 . .	. . .	. . .	. . .	–1	–2	–1	–1	–5
Construction	3 249 . .	. . .	. . .	. . .	. . .	. . .	. . .	. . .	. . .
Insurance	3 253 . .	–6	–4	–6	–3	–3	–2	–4	–7
Financial	3 260 . .	. . .	. . .	. . .	–4	–3	–6	–2	–3
Computer and information	3 262 . .	. . .	. . .	. . .	. . .	. . .	. . .	. . .	. . .
Royalties and licence fees	3 266 . .	. . .	. . .	. . .	–4	–4	–6	–9	–9
Other business services	3 268 . .	–15	–37	–51	–34	–25	–32	–52	–40
Personal, cultural, and recreational	3 287 . .	. . .	. . .	. . .	. . .	. . .	. . .	. . .	. . .
Government, n.i.e.	3 291 . .	–82	–78	–70	–55	–63	–98	–79	–81

Table 2 (Continued). STANDARD PRESENTATION, 1988–95
(Millions of U.S. dollars)

	Code	1988	1989	1990	1991	1992	1993	1994	1995
C. INCOME	4 300 . .	–179	–189	–161	–161	–147	–151	–155	–167
Total credit	2 300 . .	*13*	*18*	*15*	*4*	*6*	*3*	*2*	*7*
Total debit	3 300 . .	*–193*	*–208*	*–176*	*–166*	*–153*	*–154*	*–158*	*–174*
Compensation of employees, credit	2 310 . .	**. . .**	**. . .**	**. . .**	**. . .**	**. . .**	**. . .**	**. . .**	**. . .**
Compensation of employees, debit	3 310 . .	**. . .**	**–1**	**–1**	**–2**	**–2**	**. . .**	**. . .**	**. . .**
Investment income, credit	2 320 . .	**13**	**18**	**15**	**4**	**5**	**3**	**2**	**7**
Direct investment income	2 330 . .	. . .	. . .	. . .	. . .	. . .	. . .	. . .	. . .
Dividends and distributed branch profits	2 332 . .	. . .	. . .	. . .	. . .	. . .	. . .	. . .	. . .
Reinvested earnings and undistributed branch profits	2 333 . .	. . .	. . .	. . .	. . .	. . .	. . .	. . .	. . .
Income on debt (interest)	2 334 . .	. . .	. . .	. . .	. . .	. . .	. . .	. . .	. . .
Portfolio investment income	2 339 . .	. . .	. . .	. . .	. . .	. . .	. . .	. . .	. . .
Income on equity	2 340 . .	. . .	. . .	. . .	. . .	. . .	. . .	. . .	. . .
Income on bonds and notes	2 350 . .	. . .	. . .	. . .	. . .	. . .	. . .	. . .	. . .
Income on money market instruments and financial derivatives	2 360 . .	. . .	. . .	. . .	. . .	. . .	. . .	. . .	. . .
Other investment income	2 370 . .	13	18	15	4	5	3	2	7
Investment income, debit	3 320 . .	**–192**	**–207**	**–174**	**–164**	**–151**	**–154**	**–158**	**–174**
Direct investment income	3 330 . .	–1	–1	–1	–2	–1	–4	–1	–3
Dividends and distributed branch profits	3 332 . .	–1	–1	–1	–2	–1	–4	–1	–3
Reinvested earnings and undistributed branch profits	3 333 . .	. . .	. . .	. . .	. . .	. . .	. . .	. . .	. . .
Income on debt (interest)	3 334 . .	. . .	. . .	. . .	. . .	. . .	. . .	. . .	. . .
Portfolio investment income	3 339 . .	. . .	. . .	. . .	. . .	. . .	. . .	. . .	. . .
Income on equity	3 340 . .	. . .	. . .	. . .	. . .	. . .	. . .	. . .	. . .
Income on bonds and notes	3 350 . .	. . .	. . .	. . .	. . .	. . .	. . .	. . .	. . .
Income on money market instruments and financial derivatives	3 360 . .	. . .	. . .	. . .	. . .	. . .	. . .	. . .	. . .
Other investment income	3 370 . .	–192	–206	–174	–162	–149	–150	–156	–170
D. CURRENT TRANSFERS	4 379 . .	195	201	234	127	180	187	97	129
Credit	2 379 . .	**225**	**230**	**270**	**142**	**197**	**202**	**114**	**141**
General government	2 380 . .	129	114	154	74	88	89	64	63
Other sectors	2 390 . .	97	117	117	67	108	113	49	78
Workers' remittances	2 391 . .	3	8	4	9	12	12	11	9
Other current transfers	2 392 . .	94	109	112	59	96	102	38	69
Debit	3 379 . .	**–30**	**–29**	**–36**	**–15**	**–17**	**–14**	**–17**	**–12**
General government	3 380 . .	–8	–2	–7	–7	–10	–8	–9	–2
Other sectors	3 390 . .	–22	–28	–29	–8	–7	–6	–8	–11
Workers' remittances	3 391 . .	–13	–13	–16	–8	–7	–6	–8	–11
Other current transfers	3 392 . .	–8	–15	–13	. . .	. . .	. . .	. . .	. . .
CAPITAL AND FINANCIAL ACCOUNT	4 996 . .	**97**	**126**	**263**	**282**	**229**	**254**	**216**	**178**
CAPITAL ACCOUNT	4 994 . .	**1**	**2**	**3**	**54**	**54**	**83**	**62**	**45**
Total credit	2 994 . .	*1*	*2*	*3*	*54*	*54*	*83*	*62*	*45*
Total debit	3 994 . .	. . .	. . .	. . .	. . .	. . .	. . .	. . .	. . .
Capital transfers, credit	2 400 . .	**1**	**2**	**3**	**54**	**54**	**83**	**62**	**45**
General government	2 401 . .	. . .	. . .	. . .	50	51	81	60	40
Debt forgiveness	2 402 . .	. . .	. . .	. . .	5	4	5	. . .	. . .
Other capital transfers	2 410 . .	. . .	. . .	. . .	45	47	76	60	40
Other sectors	2 430 . .	1	2	3	4	3	2	2	5
Migrants' transfers	2 431 . .	1	2	3	4	3	2	2	5
Debt forgiveness	2 432 . .	. . .	. . .	. . .	. . .	. . .	. . .	. . .	. . .
Other capital transfers	2 440 . .	. . .	. . .	. . .	. . .	. . .	. . .	. . .	. . .
Capital transfers, debit	3 400 . .	**. . .**	**. . .**	**. . .**	**. . .**	**. . .**	**. . .**	**. . .**	**. . .**
General government	3 401 . .	. . .	. . .	. . .	. . .	. . .	. . .	. . .	. . .
Debt forgiveness	3 402 . .	. . .	. . .	. . .	. . .	. . .	. . .	. . .	. . .
Other capital transfers	3 410 . .	. . .	. . .	. . .	. . .	. . .	. . .	. . .	. . .
Other sectors	3 430 . .	. . .	. . .	. . .	. . .	. . .	. . .	. . .	. . .
Migrants' transfers	3 431 . .	. . .	. . .	. . .	. . .	. . .	. . .	. . .	. . .
Debt forgiveness	3 432 . .	. . .	. . .	. . .	. . .	. . .	. . .	. . .	. . .
Other capital transfers	3 440 . .	. . .	. . .	. . .	. . .	. . .	. . .	. . .	. . .
Nonproduced nonfinancial assets, credit	2 480 . .	**. . .**	**. . .**	**. . .**	**. . .**	**. . .**	**. . .**	**. . .**	**. . .**
Nonproduced nonfinancial assets, debit	3 480 . .	**. . .**	**. . .**	**. . .**	**. . .**	**. . .**	**. . .**	**. . .**	**. . .**

Table 2 (Continued). STANDARD PRESENTATION, 1988–95
(Millions of U.S. dollars)

	Code	1988	1989	1990	1991	1992	1993	1994	1995
FINANCIAL ACCOUNT	4 995 . .	**96**	**124**	**260**	**228**	**175**	**171**	**154**	**133**
A. DIRECT INVESTMENT	4 500 . .	...	13	22	14	21	15	6	10
Direct investment abroad	4 505 . .	...	...	...	...	...	...	...	...
Equity capital	4 510 . .	...	...	...	...	...	...	...	...
Claims on affiliated enterprises	4 515 . .	...	...	...	...	...	...	...	...
Liabilities to affiliated enterprises	4 520 . .	...	...	...	...	...	...	...	...
Reinvested earnings	4 525 . .	...	...	...	...	...	...	...	...
Other capital	4 530 . .	...	...	...	...	...	...	...	...
Claims on affiliated enterprises	4 535 . .	...	...	...	...	...	...	...	...
Liabilities to affiliated enterprises	4 540 . .	...	...	...	...	...	...	...	...
Direct investment in Madagascar	4 555 . .	...	**13**	**22**	**14**	**21**	**15**	**6**	**10**
Equity capital	4 560 . .	...	13	22	14	21	15	6	10
Claims on direct investors	4 565 . .	...	...	...	14	21	15	6	10
Liabilities to direct investors	4 570 . .	...	...	...	...	...	...	...	...
Reinvested earnings	4 575 . .	...	...	...	...	...	...	...	...
Other capital	4 580 . .	...	...	...	...	...	...	...	...
Claims on direct investors	4 585 . .	...	...	...	...	...	...	...	...
Liabilities to direct investors	4 590 . .	...	...	...	...	...	...	...	...
B. PORTFOLIO INVESTMENT	4 600 . .	...	...	...	...	...	...	...	...
Assets	4 602 . .	...	...	...	...	...	...	...	...
Equity securities	4 610 . .	...	...	...	...	...	...	...	...
Monetary authorities	4 611 . .	...	...	...	...	...	...	...	...
General government	4 612 . .	...	...	...	...	...	...	...	...
Banks	4 613 . .	...	...	...	...	...	...	...	...
Other sectors	4 614 . .	...	...	...	...	...	...	...	...
Debt securities	4 619 . .	...	...	...	...	...	...	...	...
Bonds and notes	4 620 . .	...	...	...	...	...	...	...	...
Monetary authorities	4 621 . .	...	...	...	...	...	...	...	...
General government	4 622 . .	...	...	...	...	...	...	...	...
Banks	4 623 . .	...	...	...	...	...	...	...	...
Other sectors	4 624 . .	...	...	...	...	...	...	...	...
Money market instruments	4 630 . .	...	...	...	...	...	...	...	...
Monetary authorities	4 631 . .	...	...	...	...	...	...	...	...
General government	4 632 . .	...	...	...	...	...	...	...	...
Banks	4 633 . .	...	...	...	...	...	...	...	...
Other sectors	4 634 . .	...	...	...	...	...	...	...	...
Financial derivatives	4 640 . .	...	...	...	...	...	...	...	...
Monetary authorities	4 641 . .	...	...	...	...	...	...	...	...
General government	4 642 . .	...	...	...	...	...	...	...	...
Banks	4 643 . .	...	...	...	...	...	...	...	...
Other sectors	4 644 . .	...	...	...	...	...	...	...	...
Liabilities	4 652 . .	...	...	...	...	...	...	...	...
Equity securities	4 660 . .	...	...	...	...	...	...	...	...
Banks	4 663 . .	...	...	...	...	...	...	...	...
Other sectors	4 664 . .	...	...	...	...	...	...	...	...
Debt securities	4 669 . .	...	...	...	...	...	...	...	...
Bonds and notes	4 670 . .	...	...	...	...	...	...	...	...
Monetary authorities	4 671 . .	...	...	...	...	...	...	...	...
General government	4 672 . .	...	...	...	...	...	...	...	...
Banks	4 673 . .	...	...	...	...	...	...	...	...
Other sectors	4 674 . .	...	...	...	...	...	...	...	...
Money market instruments	4 680 . .	...	...	...	...	...	...	...	...
Monetary authorities	4 681 . .	...	...	...	...	...	...	...	...
General government	4 682 . .	...	...	...	...	...	...	...	...
Banks	4 683 . .	...	...	...	...	...	...	...	...
Other sectors	4 684 . .	...	...	...	...	...	...	...	...
Financial derivatives	4 690 . .	...	...	...	...	...	...	...	...
Monetary authorities	4 691 . .	...	...	...	...	...	...	...	...
General government	4 692 . .	...	...	...	...	...	...	...	...
Banks	4 693 . .	...	...	...	...	...	...	...	...
Other sectors	4 694 . .	...	...	...	...	...	...	...	...

Table 2 (Concluded). STANDARD PRESENTATION, 1988–95
(Millions of U.S. dollars)

	Code	1988	1989	1990	1991	1992	1993	1994	1995
C. OTHER INVESTMENT	4 700 . .	138	138	71	185	162	133	163	125
Assets	4 703 . .	**9**	**–18**	**–7**	**–27**	**–3**	**–47**	**19**	**–62**
Trade credits	4 706 . .	...	...	...	...	...	...	...	...
General government: long-term	4 708 . .	...	...	...	...	...	...	...	...
General government: short-term	4 709 . .	...	...	...	...	...	...	...	...
Other sectors: long-term	4 711 . .	...	...	...	...	...	...	...	...
Other sectors: short-term	4 712 . .	...	...	...	...	...	...	...	...
Loans	4 714 . .	...	...	...	...	...	...	...	...
Monetary authorities: long-term	4 717 . .	...	...	...	...	...	...	...	...
Monetary authorities: short-term	4 718 . .	...	...	...	...	...	...	...	...
General government: long-term	4 720 . .	...	...	...	...	...	...	...	...
General government: short-term	4 721 . .	...	...	...	...	...	...	...	...
Banks: long-term	4 723 . .	...	...	...	...	...	...	...	...
Banks: short-term	4 724 . .	...	...	...	...	...	...	...	...
Other sectors: long-term	4 726 . .	...	...	...	...	...	...	...	...
Other sectors: short-term	4 727 . .	...	...	...	...	...	...	...	...
Currency and deposits	4 730 . .	9	–18	–7	–3	–13	–28	–26	–6
Monetary authorities	4 731 . .	...	...	...	...	...	...	...	...
General government	4 732 . .	...	...	...	...	...	...	...	...
Banks	4 733 . .	9	–18	–7	–3	–13	–28	–26	–6
Other sectors	4 734 . .	...	...	...	...	...	...	...	...
Other assets	4 736 . .	...	...	...	–25	9	–19	46	–57
Monetary authorities: long-term	4 738 . .	...	...	...	...	...	...	...	...
Monetary authorities: short-term	4 739 . .	...	...	...	–25	9	–19	38	–45
General government: long-term	4 741 . .	...	...	...	...	...	...	...	...
General government: short-term	4 742 . .	...	...	...	...	...	...	...	...
Banks: long-term	4 744 . .	...	...	...	...	...	...	9	–6
Banks: short-term	4 745 . .	...	...	...	...	...	...	...	...
Other sectors: long-term	4 747 . .	...	...	...	...	...	...	...	...
Other sectors: short-term	4 748 . .	...	...	...	...	...	...	–1	–5
Liabilities	4 753 . .	**129**	**156**	**78**	**213**	**165**	**180**	**144**	**187**
Trade credits	4 756 . .	...	...	...	...	...	...	...	...
General government: long-term	4 758 . .	...	...	...	...	...	...	...	...
General government: short-term	4 759 . .	...	...	...	...	...	...	...	...
Other sectors: long-term	4 761 . .	...	...	...	...	...	...	...	...
Other sectors: short-term	4 762 . .	...	...	...	...	...	...	...	...
Loans	4 764 . .	175	186	85	4	–128	–140	–166	–155
Use of Fund credit and loans from the Fund	4 766 . .	–35	–20	–34	–16	–16	–14	–12	–14
Monetary authorities: other long-term	4 767 . .	...	...	...	–201	–236	–248	–233	–232
Monetary authorities: short-term	4 768 . .	...	...	...	...	...	...	...	...
General government: long-term	4 770 . .	209	209	119	221	124	123	79	91
General government: short-term	4 771 . .	1	–4	...	...	...	...	...	...
Banks: long-term	4 773 . .	...	...	...	...	...	...	...	...
Banks: short-term	4 774 . .	...	...	...	...	...	...	...	...
Other sectors: long-term	4 776 . .	...	...	...	...	...	...	...	...
Other sectors: short-term	4 777 . .	...	...	...	...	...	...	...	...
Currency and deposits	4 780 . .	–29	–2	27	–25	–5	–1	4	–7
Monetary authorities	4 781 . .	1	13	...	–4	–2	–6	–2	1
General government	4 782 . .	...	...	...	...	...	...	...	...
Banks	4 783 . .	–29	–15	26	–21	–3	5	6	–8
Other sectors	4 784 . .	...	...	...	...	...	...	...	...
Other liabilities	4 786 . .	–17	–27	–33	234	299	320	306	349
Monetary authorities: long-term	4 788 . .	...	...	...	...	...	...	...	...
Monetary authorities: short-term	4 789 . .	–17	–27	–33	...	...	...	...	...
General government: long-term	4 791 . .	...	...	...	...	...	...	...	...
General government: short-term	4 792 . .	...	...	...	234	299	320	303	347
Banks: long-term	4 794 . .	...	...	...	...	...	...	...	...
Banks: short-term	4 795 . .	...	...	...	...	...	...	...	...
Other sectors: long-term	4 797 . .	...	...	...	...	...	...	...	...
Other sectors: short-term	4 798 . .	...	...	...	...	...	...	3	3
D. RESERVE ASSETS	4 800 . .	–42	–26	167	28	–8	23	–14	–2
Monetary gold	4 810 . .	...	...	...	...	...	...	...	...
Special drawing rights	4 820 . .	...	...	...	...	...	...	...	...
Reserve position in the Fund	4 830 . .	...	...	...	...	...	...	...	...
Foreign exchange	4 840 . .	–42	–26	167	28	–8	23	–14	–2
Other claims	4 880 . .	...	...	...	...	...	...	...	...
NET ERRORS AND OMISSIONS	4 998 . .	**53**	**–42**	**2**	**–52**	**–31**	**4**	**61**	**98**

Table 1. ANALYTIC PRESENTATION, 1988–95
(Millions of U.S. dollars)

	Code	1988	1989	1990	1991	1992	1993	1994	1995
A. Current Account[1]	4 993 Y.	**–87.0**	**–51.2**	**–86.2**	**–227.7**	**–284.9**	**–165.6**	**–449.6**	**. . .**
Goods: exports f.o.b	2 100 . .	293.5	268.8	406.4	475.5	399.9	317.5	362.6	. . .
Goods: imports f.o.b	3 100 . .	–253.0	–204.8	–280.3	–415.8	–415.0	–340.2	–639.0	. . .
Balance on Goods	4 100 . .	*40.4*	*64.0*	*126.1*	*59.7*	*–15.0*	*–22.8*	*–276.4*	. . .
Services: credit	2 200 . .	38.5	30.5	36.6	38.5	28.5	30.0	22.2	. . .
Services: debit	3 200 . .	–197.9	–231.3	–268.4	–356.5	–338.8	–260.1	–233.7	. . .
Balance on Goods and Services	4 991 . .	*–119.0*	*–136.8*	*–105.6*	*–258.3*	*–325.4*	*–252.9*	*–488.0*	. . .
Income: credit	2 300 . .	9.6	10.5	9.3	7.4	6.3	2.2	1.9	. . .
Income: debit	3 300 . .	–108.3	–99.2	–88.9	–92.9	–83.4	–70.9	–87.8	. . .
Balance on Goods, Services, and Income	4 992 . .	*–217.7*	*–225.4*	*–185.2*	*–343.8*	*–402.5*	*–321.6*	*–573.9*	. . .
Current transfers: credit	2 379 Y.	169.2	208.0	134.1	159.0	155.2	167.9	139.7	. . .
Current transfers: debit	3 379 . .	–38.6	–33.9	–35.1	–42.9	–37.7	–11.9	–15.4	. . .
B. Capital Account[1]	4 994 Y.	**. . .**	**. . .**	**. . .**	**. . .**	**. . .**	**. . .**	**. . .**	**. . .**
Capital account: credit	2 994 Y.	. . .	. . .	. . .	. . .	. . .	. . .	. . .	. . .
Capital account: debit	3 994 . .	. . .	. . .	. . .	. . .	. . .	. . .	. . .	. . .
Total, Groups A Plus B	4 010 . .	*–87.0*	*–51.2*	*–86.2*	*–227.7*	*–284.9*	*–165.6*	*–449.6*	. . .
C. Financial Account[1]	4 995 X.	**68.9**	**92.0**	**128.6**	**104.3**	**93.6**	**188.9**	**122.0**	**. . .**
Direct investment abroad	4 505 . .	. . .	. . .	. . .	. . .	. . .	. . .	. . .	. . .
Direct investment in Malawi	4 555 Y.	. . .	. . .	. . .	. . .	. . .	. . .	. . .	. . .
Portfolio investment assets	4 602 . .	. . .	. . .	. . .	. . .	. . .	. . .	. . .	. . .
Equity securities	4 610 . .	. . .	. . .	. . .	. . .	. . .	. . .	. . .	. . .
Debt securities	4 619 . .	. . .	. . .	. . .	. . .	. . .	. . .	. . .	. . .
Portfolio investment liabilities	4 652 Y.	.8	2.6	.8	. . .	. . .	. . .	. . .	. . .
Equity securities	4 660 Y.	.8	2.6	.8	. . .	. . .	. . .	. . .	. . .
Debt securities	4 669 Y.	. . .	. . .	. . .	. . .	. . .	. . .	. . .	. . .
Other investment assets	4 703 . .	6.7	42.8	33.9	–5.8	11.9	–11.8	. . .	. . .
Monetary authorities	4 703 .A	. . .	. . .	. . .	. . .	. . .	. . .	. . .	. . .
General government	4 703 .B	. . .	. . .	. . .	. . .	. . .	. . .	. . .	. . .
Banks	4 703 .C	6.7	42.8	33.9	–5.8	11.9	–11.8	. . .	. . .
Other sectors	4 703 .D	. . .	. . .	. . .	. . .	. . .	. . .	. . .	. . .
Other investment liabilities	4 753 X.	61.4	46.7	93.9	110.0	81.7	200.6	122.0	. . .
Monetary authorities	4 753 XA	. . .	. . .	. . .	. . .	. . .	. . .	. . .	. . .
General government	4 753 YB	44.8	38.7	68.9	62.7	41.4	150.9	98.5	. . .
Banks	4 753 YC	. . .	. . .	. . .	. . .	. . .	. . .	. . .	. . .
Other sectors	4 753 YD	16.6	8.0	25.0	47.3	40.3	49.7	23.5	. . .
Total, Groups A Through C	4 020 . .	*–18.1*	*40.8*	*42.4*	*–123.4*	*–191.3*	*23.3*	*–327.6*	. . .
D. Net Errors and Omissions	4 998 . .	**78.3**	**–92.5**	**–13.7**	**139.2**	**144.8**	**.7**	**292.6**	**. . .**
Total, Groups A Through D	4 030 . .	*60.2*	*–51.7*	*28.7*	*15.7*	*–46.5*	*24.0*	*–35.1*	. . .
E. Reserves and Related Items	4 040 . .	**–60.2**	**51.7**	**–28.7**	**–15.7**	**46.5**	**–24.0**	**35.1**	**. . .**
Reserve assets	4 800 . .	–102.1	36.7	–34.3	–15.8	65.7	–18.1	14.3	. . .
Use of Fund credit and loans	4 766 . .	–5.4	–2.6	5.6	.1	–19.2	–5.9	20.8	. . .
Liabilities constituting foreign authorities' reserves	4 900 . .	. . .	. . .	. . .	. . .	. . .	. . .	. . .	. . .
Exceptional financing	4 920 . .	47.4	17.7	. . .	. . .	. . .	. . .	. . .	. . .
Conversion rates: Malawi kwacha per U.S. dollar	0 101 . .	**2.561**	**2.760**	**2.729**	**2.803**	**3.603**	**4.403**	**8.736**	**15.284**

[1] Excludes components that have been classified in the categories of Group E.

Table 2. STANDARD PRESENTATION, 1988–95
(Millions of U.S. dollars)

	Code	1988	1989	1990	1991	1992	1993	1994	1995
CURRENT ACCOUNT	4 993 . .	**–86.9**	**–51.2**	**–86.2**	**–227.7**	**–284.9**	**–165.6**	**–449.6**	. . .
A. GOODS	4 100 . .	40.4	64.0	126.1	59.7	–15.0	–22.8	–276.4	. . .
Credit	2 100 . .	**293.5**	**268.8**	**406.4**	**475.5**	**399.9**	**317.5**	**362.6**	. . .
General merchandise: exports f.o.b.	2 110 . .	293.5	268.8	406.4	475.5	399.9	317.5	362.6	. . .
Goods for processing: exports f.o.b.	2 150 . .	. . .	. . .	. . .	. . .	. . .	. . .	. . .	. . .
Repairs on goods	2 160 . .	. . .	. . .	. . .	. . .	. . .	. . .	. . .	. . .
Goods procured in ports by carriers	2 170 . .	. . .	. . .	. . .	. . .	. . .	. . .	. . .	. . .
Nonmonetary gold	2 180 . .	. . .	. . .	. . .	. . .	. . .	. . .	. . .	. . .
Debit	3 100 . .	**–253.0**	**–204.8**	**–280.3**	**–415.8**	**–415.0**	**–340.2**	**–639.0**	. . .
General merchandise: imports f.o.b.	3 110 . .	–253.0	–204.8	–280.3	–415.8	–415.0	–340.2	–639.0	. . .
Goods for processing: imports f.o.b.	3 150 . .	. . .	. . .	. . .	. . .	. . .	. . .	. . .	. . .
Repairs on goods	3 160 . .	. . .	. . .	. . .	. . .	. . .	. . .	. . .	. . .
Goods procured in ports by carriers	3 170 . .	. . .	. . .	. . .	. . .	. . .	. . .	. . .	. . .
Nonmonetary gold	3 180 . .	. . .	. . .	. . .	. . .	. . .	. . .	. . .	. . .
B. SERVICES	4 200 . .	–159.4	–200.8	–231.8	–317.9	–310.3	–230.1	–211.5	. . .
Total credit	2 200 . .	*38.5*	*30.5*	*36.6*	*38.5*	*28.5*	*30.0*	*22.2*	. . .
Total debit	3 200 . .	*–197.9*	*–231.3*	*–268.4*	*–356.5*	*–338.8*	*–260.1*	*–233.7*	. . .
Transportation services, credit	2 205 . .	**16.9**	**13.9**	**16.9**	**15.4**	**16.2**	**16.4**	**13.0**	. . .
Passenger	2 205 BA	*11.2*	*9.6*	*10.8*	*8.1*	*3.9*	*4.4*	*6.5*	. . .
Freight	2 205 BB	*.4*	*.3*	*.4*	*.5*	*.9*	*.7*	*.6*	. . .
Other	2 205 BC	*5.4*	*3.9*	*5.7*	*6.8*	*11.4*	*11.2*	*5.9*	. . .
Sea transport, passenger	2 207 . .	. . .	. . .	. . .	. . .	. . .	. . .	. . .	. . .
Sea transport, freight	2 208 . .	. . .	. . .	. . .	. . .	. . .	. . .	. . .	. . .
Sea transport, other	2 209 . .	. . .	. . .	. . .	. . .	. . .	. . .	. . .	. . .
Air transport, passenger	2 211 . .	. . .	. . .	. . .	. . .	. . .	. . .	. . .	. . .
Air transport, freight	2 212 . .	. . .	. . .	. . .	. . .	. . .	. . .	. . .	. . .
Air transport, other	2 213 . .	. . .	. . .	. . .	. . .	. . .	. . .	. . .	. . .
Other transport, passenger	2 215 . .	. . .	. . .	. . .	. . .	. . .	. . .	. . .	. . .
Other transport, freight	2 216 . .	. . .	. . .	. . .	. . .	. . .	. . .	. . .	. . .
Other transport, other	2 217 . .	. . .	. . .	. . .	. . .	. . .	. . .	. . .	. . .
Transportation services, debit	3 205 . .	**–164.7**	**–194.4**	**–219.5**	**–276.5**	**–275.4**	**–220.3**	**–193.9**	. . .
Passenger	3 205 BA	*–9.8*	*–7.8*	*–7.8*	*–12.1*	*–13.5*	*–20.9*	*–13.2*	. . .
Freight	3 205 BB	*–151.8*	*–182.5*	*–209.0*	*–260.1*	*–259.0*	*–196.6*	*–178.1*	. . .
Other	3 205 BC	*–3.1*	*–4.2*	*–2.7*	*–4.3*	*–3.0*	*–2.8*	*–2.6*	. . .
Sea transport, passenger	3 207 . .	. . .	. . .	. . .	. . .	. . .	. . .	. . .	. . .
Sea transport, freight	3 208 . .	. . .	. . .	. . .	. . .	. . .	. . .	. . .	. . .
Sea transport, other	3 209 . .	. . .	. . .	. . .	. . .	. . .	. . .	. . .	. . .
Air transport, passenger	3 211 . .	. . .	. . .	. . .	. . .	. . .	. . .	. . .	. . .
Air transport, freight	3 212 . .	. . .	. . .	. . .	. . .	. . .	. . .	. . .	. . .
Air transport, other	3 213 . .	. . .	. . .	. . .	. . .	. . .	. . .	. . .	. . .
Other transport, passenger	3 215 . .	. . .	. . .	. . .	. . .	. . .	. . .	. . .	. . .
Other transport, freight	3 216 . .	. . .	. . .	. . .	. . .	. . .	. . .	. . .	. . .
Other transport, other	3 217 . .	. . .	. . .	. . .	. . .	. . .	. . .	. . .	. . .
Travel, credit	2 236 . .	**10.7**	**12.7**	**15.6**	**11.8**	**8.3**	**6.8**	**4.6**	. . .
Business travel	2 237 . .	. . .	. . .	. . .	. . .	. . .	. . .	. . .	. . .
Personal travel	2 240 . .	. . .	. . .	. . .	. . .	. . .	. . .	. . .	. . .
Travel, debit	3 236 . .	**–8.7**	**–9.5**	**–15.8**	**–27.4**	**–23.8**	**–11.4**	**–15.3**	. . .
Business travel	3 237 . .	. . .	. . .	. . .	. . .	. . .	. . .	. . .	. . .
Personal travel	3 240 . .	. . .	. . .	. . .	. . .	. . .	. . .	. . .	. . .
Other services, credit	2 200 BA	**10.8**	**3.9**	**4.1**	**11.3**	**4.0**	**6.7**	**4.6**	. . .
Communications	2 245 . .	. . .	. . .	. . .	. . .	. . .	. . .	. . .	. . .
Construction	2 249 . .	. . .	. . .	. . .	. . .	. . .	. . .	. . .	. . .
Insurance	2 253 . .	. . .	. . .	. . .	.1	.1	.1	.1	. . .
Financial	2 260 . .	. . .	. . .	. . .	. . .	. . .	. . .	. . .	. . .
Computer and information	2 262 . .	. . .	. . .	. . .	. . .	. . .	. . .	. . .	. . .
Royalties and licence fees	2 266 . .	. . .	. . .	. . .	. . .	. . .	. . .	. . .	. . .
Other business services	2 268 . .	10.8	3.9	4.1	11.2	3.9	6.7	4.6	. . .
Personal, cultural, and recreational	2 287 . .	. . .	. . .	. . .	. . .	. . .	. . .	. . .	. . .
Government, n.i.e.	2 291 . .	. . .	. . .	. . .	. . .	. . .	. . .	. . .	. . .
Other services, debit	3 200 BA	**–24.4**	**–27.3**	**–33.1**	**–52.6**	**–39.7**	**–28.4**	**–24.6**	. . .
Communications	3 245 . .	. . .	. . .	. . .	. . .	. . .	. . .	. . .	. . .
Construction	3 249 . .	. . .	. . .	. . .	. . .	. . .	. . .	. . .	. . .
Insurance	3 253 . .	–16.9	–20.3	–23.2	–28.9	–28.8	–21.8	–19.8	. . .
Financial	3 260 . .	. . .	. . .	. . .	. . .	. . .	. . .	. . .	. . .
Computer and information	3 262 . .	. . .	. . .	. . .	. . .	. . .	. . .	. . .	. . .
Royalties and licence fees	3 266 . .	. . .	. . .	. . .	. . .	. . .	. . .	. . .	. . .
Other business services	3 268 . .	–7.6	–7.1	–9.9	–23.7	–10.9	–6.5	–4.8	. . .
Personal, cultural, and recreational	3 287 . .	. . .	. . .	. . .	. . .	. . .	. . .	. . .	. . .
Government, n.i.e.	3 291 . .	. . .	. . .	. . .	. . .	. . .	. . .	. . .	. . .

Table 2 (Continued). STANDARD PRESENTATION, 1988–95
(Millions of U.S. dollars)

	Code	1988	1989	1990	1991	1992	1993	1994	1995
C. INCOME	4 300	–98.7	–88.6	–79.6	–85.5	–77.1	–68.7	–85.9	...
Total credit	2 300	*9.6*	*10.5*	*9.3*	*7.4*	*6.3*	*2.2*	*1.9*	...
Total debit	3 300	*–108.3*	*–99.2*	*–88.9*	*–92.9*	*–83.4*	*–70.9*	*–87.8*	...
Compensation of employees, credit	2 310	...	...	...	...	...	...	...	...
Compensation of employees, debit	3 310	**–.2**	**–.4**	...	...	**–.1**	**–.1**	**–.1**	...
Investment income, credit	2 320	**9.6**	**10.5**	**9.3**	**7.4**	**6.3**	**2.2**	**1.9**	...
Direct investment income	2 330	...	...	...	...	...	...	...	...
Dividends and distributed branch profits	2 332	...	...	...	...	...	...	...	...
Reinvested earnings and undistributed branch profits	2 333	...	...	...	...	...	...	...	...
Income on debt (interest)	2 334	...	...	...	...	...	...	...	...
Portfolio investment income	2 339	...	...	...	...	...	...	...	...
Income on equity	2 340	...	...	...	...	...	...	...	...
Income on bonds and notes	2 350	...	...	...	...	...	...	...	...
Income on money market instruments and financial derivatives	2 360	...	...	...	...	...	...	...	...
Other investment income	2 370	9.6	10.5	9.3	7.4	6.3	2.2	1.9	...
Investment income, debit	3 320	**–108.1**	**–98.8**	**–88.9**	**–92.9**	**–83.3**	**–70.7**	**–87.7**	...
Direct investment income	3 330	–7.7	–6.9	–5.3	–9.3	–8.6	–3.1	–7.3	...
Dividends and distributed branch profits	3 332	–7.7	–6.9	–5.3	–9.3	–8.6	–3.1	–7.3	...
Reinvested earnings and undistributed branch profits	3 333	...	...	...	...	...	...	...	...
Income on debt (interest)	3 334	...	...	...	...	...	...	...	...
Portfolio investment income	3 339	...	...	...	...	...	...	...	...
Income on equity	3 340	...	...	...	...	...	...	...	...
Income on bonds and notes	3 350	...	...	...	...	...	...	...	...
Income on money market instruments and financial derivatives	3 360	...	...	...	...	...	...	...	...
Other investment income	3 370	–100.4	–91.9	–83.6	–83.6	–74.7	–67.6	–80.5	...
D. CURRENT TRANSFERS	4 379	130.8	174.2	99.1	116.1	117.6	156.0	124.3	...
Credit	2 379	**169.4**	**208.0**	**134.1**	**159.0**	**155.2**	**167.9**	**139.7**	...
General government	2 380	83.1	76.9	75.5	62.6	53.3	86.1	103.1	...
Other sectors	2 390	86.2	131.1	58.7	96.4	102.0	81.7	36.6	...
Workers' remittances	2 391	...	...	...	...	...	...	...	...
Other current transfers	2 392	86.2	131.1	58.7	96.4	102.0	81.7	36.6	...
Debit	3 379	**–38.6**	**–33.9**	**–35.1**	**–42.9**	**–37.7**	**–11.9**	**–15.4**	...
General government	3 380	–2.6	2.4	3.0	3.2	3.2	4.0	3.1	...
Other sectors	3 390	–36.0	–36.3	–38.1	–46.2	–40.9	–15.9	–18.5	...
Workers' remittances	3 391	...	...	...	...	...	...	...	...
Other current transfers	3 392	–36.0	–36.3	–38.1	–46.2	–40.9	–15.9	–18.5	...
CAPITAL AND FINANCIAL ACCOUNT	4 996	**8.6**	**143.7**	**99.9**	**88.5**	**140.1**	**164.9**	**157.0**	...
CAPITAL ACCOUNT	4 994	...	...	...	...	...	...	...	...
Total credit	2 994	...	...	...	...	...	...	...	...
Total debit	3 994	...	...	...	...	...	...	...	...
Capital transfers, credit	2 400	...	...	...	...	...	...	...	...
General government	2 401	...	...	...	...	...	...	...	...
Debt forgiveness	2 402	...	...	...	...	...	...	...	...
Other capital transfers	2 410	...	...	...	...	...	...	...	...
Other sectors	2 430	...	...	...	...	...	...	...	...
Migrants' transfers	2 431	...	...	...	...	...	...	...	...
Debt forgiveness	2 432	...	...	...	...	...	...	...	...
Other capital transfers	2 440	...	...	...	...	...	...	...	...
Capital transfers, debit	3 400	...	...	...	...	...	...	...	...
General government	3 401	...	...	...	...	...	...	...	...
Debt forgiveness	3 402	...	...	...	...	...	...	...	...
Other capital transfers	3 410	...	...	...	...	...	...	...	...
Other sectors	3 430	...	...	...	...	...	...	...	...
Migrants' transfers	3 431	...	...	...	...	...	...	...	...
Debt forgiveness	3 432	...	...	...	...	...	...	...	...
Other capital transfers	3 440	...	...	...	...	...	...	...	...
Nonproduced nonfinancial assets, credit	2 480	...	...	...	...	...	...	...	...
Nonproduced nonfinancial assets, debit	3 480	...	...	...	...	...	...	...	...

Table 2 (Continued). STANDARD PRESENTATION, 1988–95
(Millions of U.S. dollars)

	Code	1988	1989	1990	1991	1992	1993	1994	1995
FINANCIAL ACCOUNT	4 995 . .	**8.6**	**143.7**	**99.9**	**88.5**	**140.1**	**164.9**	**157.0**	...
A. DIRECT INVESTMENT	4 500 . .	...	...	...	...	...	...	...	...
Direct investment abroad	4 505 . .	...	...	...	...	...	...	...	...
Equity capital	4 510 . .	...	...	...	...	...	...	...	...
Claims on affiliated enterprises	4 515 . .	...	...	...	...	...	...	...	...
Liabilities to affiliated enterprises	4 520 . .	...	...	...	...	...	...	...	...
Reinvested earnings	4 525 . .	...	...	...	...	...	...	...	...
Other capital	4 530 . .	...	...	...	...	...	...	...	...
Claims on affiliated enterprises	4 535 . .	...	...	...	...	...	...	...	...
Liabilities to affiliated enterprises	4 540 . .	...	...	...	...	...	...	...	...
Direct investment in Malawi	4 555 . .	...	...	...	...	...	...	...	...
Equity capital	4 560 . .	...	...	...	...	...	...	...	...
Claims on direct investors	4 565 . .	...	...	...	...	...	...	...	...
Liabilities to direct investors	4 570 . .	...	...	...	...	...	...	...	...
Reinvested earnings	4 575 . .	...	...	...	...	...	...	...	...
Other capital	4 580 . .	...	...	...	...	...	...	...	...
Claims on direct investors	4 585 . .	...	...	...	...	...	...	...	...
Liabilities to direct investors	4 590 . .	...	...	...	...	...	...	...	...
B. PORTFOLIO INVESTMENT	4 600 . .	.8	2.6	.8	...	...	...	...	...
Assets	4 602 . .	...	...	...	...	...	...	...	...
Equity securities	4 610 . .	...	...	...	...	...	...	...	...
Monetary authorities	4 611 . .	...	...	...	...	...	...	...	...
General government	4 612 . .	...	...	...	...	...	...	...	...
Banks	4 613 . .	...	...	...	...	...	...	...	...
Other sectors	4 614 . .	...	...	...	...	...	...	...	...
Debt securities	4 619 . .	...	...	...	...	...	...	...	...
Bonds and notes	4 620 . .	...	...	...	...	...	...	...	...
Monetary authorities	4 621 . .	...	...	...	...	...	...	...	...
General government	4 622 . .	...	...	...	...	...	...	...	...
Banks	4 623 . .	...	...	...	...	...	...	...	...
Other sectors	4 624 . .	...	...	...	...	...	...	...	...
Money market instruments	4 630 . .	...	...	...	...	...	...	...	...
Monetary authorities	4 631 . .	...	...	...	...	...	...	...	...
General government	4 632 . .	...	...	...	...	...	...	...	...
Banks	4 633 . .	...	...	...	...	...	...	...	...
Other sectors	4 634 . .	...	...	...	...	...	...	...	...
Financial derivatives	4 640 . .	...	...	...	...	...	...	...	...
Monetary authorities	4 641 . .	...	...	...	...	...	...	...	...
General government	4 642 . .	...	...	...	...	...	...	...	...
Banks	4 643 . .	...	...	...	...	...	...	...	...
Other sectors	4 644 . .	...	...	...	...	...	...	...	...
Liabilities	4 652 . .	**.8**	**2.6**	**.8**	...	...	...	...	...
Equity securities	4 660 . .	.8	2.6	.8	...	...	...	...	...
Banks	4 663 . .	...	...	...	...	...	...	...	...
Other sectors	4 664 . .	...	...	...	...	...	...	...	...
Debt securities	4 669 . .	...	...	...	...	...	...	...	...
Bonds and notes	4 670 . .	...	...	...	...	...	...	...	...
Monetary authorities	4 671 . .	...	...	...	...	...	...	...	...
General government	4 672 . .	...	...	...	...	...	...	...	...
Banks	4 673 . .	...	...	...	...	...	...	...	...
Other sectors	4 674 . .	...	...	...	...	...	...	...	...
Money market instruments	4 680 . .	...	...	...	...	...	...	...	...
Monetary authorities	4 681 . .	...	...	...	...	...	...	...	...
General government	4 682 . .	...	...	...	...	...	...	...	...
Banks	4 683 . .	...	...	...	...	...	...	...	...
Other sectors	4 684 . .	...	...	...	...	...	...	...	...
Financial derivatives	4 690 . .	...	...	...	...	...	...	...	...
Monetary authorities	4 691 . .	...	...	...	...	...	...	...	...
General government	4 692 . .	...	...	...	...	...	...	...	...
Banks	4 693 . .	...	...	...	...	...	...	...	...
Other sectors	4 694 . .	...	...	...	...	...	...	...	...

Table 2 (Concluded). STANDARD PRESENTATION, 1988–95
(Millions of U.S. dollars)

	Code	1988	1989	1990	1991	1992	1993	1994	1995
C. OTHER INVESTMENT	4 700 . .	109.9	104.5	133.4	104.4	74.4	183.0	142.8	. . .
Assets	4 703 . .	**6.7**	**42.8**	**33.9**	**–5.8**	**11.9**	**–11.8**	. . .	. . .
Trade credits	4 706 . .	. . .	. . .	. . .	. . .	. . .	. . .	. . .	. . .
General government: long-term	4 708 . .	. . .	. . .	. . .	. . .	. . .	. . .	. . .	. . .
General government: short-term	4 709 . .	. . .	. . .	. . .	. . .	. . .	. . .	. . .	. . .
Other sectors: long-term	4 711 . .	. . .	. . .	. . .	. . .	. . .	. . .	. . .	. . .
Other sectors: short-term	4 712 . .	. . .	. . .	. . .	. . .	. . .	. . .	. . .	. . .
Loans	4 714 . .	. . .	. . .	. . .	. . .	. . .	. . .	. . .	. . .
Monetary authorities: long-term	4 717 . .	. . .	. . .	. . .	. . .	. . .	. . .	. . .	. . .
Monetary authorities: short-term	4 718 . .	. . .	. . .	. . .	. . .	. . .	. . .	. . .	. . .
General government: long-term	4 720 . .	. . .	. . .	. . .	. . .	. . .	. . .	. . .	. . .
General government: short-term	4 721 . .	. . .	. . .	. . .	. . .	. . .	. . .	. . .	. . .
Banks: long-term	4 723 . .	. . .	. . .	. . .	. . .	. . .	. . .	. . .	. . .
Banks: short-term	4 724 . .	. . .	. . .	. . .	. . .	. . .	. . .	. . .	. . .
Other sectors: long-term	4 726 . .	. . .	. . .	. . .	. . .	. . .	. . .	. . .	. . .
Other sectors: short-term	4 727 . .	. . .	. . .	. . .	. . .	. . .	. . .	. . .	. . .
Currency and deposits	4 730 . .	6.7	42.8	33.9	–5.8	11.9	–11.8	. . .	. . .
Monetary authorities	4 731 . .	. . .	. . .	. . .	. . .	. . .	. . .	. . .	. . .
General government	4 732 . .	. . .	. . .	. . .	. . .	. . .	. . .	. . .	. . .
Banks	4 733 . .	6.7	42.8	33.9	–5.8	11.9	–11.8	. . .	. . .
Other sectors	4 734 . .	. . .	. . .	. . .	. . .	. . .	. . .	. . .	. . .
Other assets	4 736 . .	. . .	. . .	. . .	. . .	. . .	. . .	. . .	. . .
Monetary authorities: long-term	4 738 . .	. . .	. . .	. . .	. . .	. . .	. . .	. . .	. . .
Monetary authorities: short-term	4 739 . .	. . .	. . .	. . .	. . .	. . .	. . .	. . .	. . .
General government: long-term	4 741 . .	. . .	. . .	. . .	. . .	. . .	. . .	. . .	. . .
General government: short-term	4 742 . .	. . .	. . .	. . .	. . .	. . .	. . .	. . .	. . .
Banks: long-term	4 744 . .	. . .	. . .	. . .	. . .	. . .	. . .	. . .	. . .
Banks: short-term	4 745 . .	. . .	. . .	. . .	. . .	. . .	. . .	. . .	. . .
Other sectors: long-term	4 747 . .	. . .	. . .	. . .	. . .	. . .	. . .	. . .	. . .
Other sectors: short-term	4 748 . .	. . .	. . .	. . .	. . .	. . .	. . .	. . .	. . .
Liabilities	4 753 . .	**103.2**	**61.7**	**99.5**	**110.1**	**62.5**	**194.7**	**142.8**	. . .
Trade credits	4 756 . .	. . .	. . .	. . .	. . .	. . .	. . .	. . .	. . .
General government: long-term	4 758 . .	. . .	. . .	. . .	. . .	. . .	. . .	. . .	. . .
General government: short-term	4 759 . .	. . .	. . .	. . .	. . .	. . .	. . .	. . .	. . .
Other sectors: long-term	4 761 . .	. . .	. . .	. . .	. . .	. . .	. . .	. . .	. . .
Other sectors: short-term	4 762 . .	. . .	. . .	. . .	. . .	. . .	. . .	. . .	. . .
Loans	4 764 . .	103.2	61.7	99.5	110.1	62.5	194.7	142.8	. . .
Use of Fund credit and loans from the Fund	4 766 . .	–5.4	–2.6	5.6	.1	–19.2	–5.9	20.8	. . .
Monetary authorities: other long-term	4 767 . .	. . .	. . .	. . .	. . .	. . .	. . .	. . .	. . .
Monetary authorities: short-term	4 768 . .	. . .	. . .	. . .	. . .	. . .	. . .	. . .	. . .
General government: long-term	4 770 . .	92.1	56.4	68.9	62.7	41.4	150.9	98.5	. . .
General government: short-term	4 771 . .	. . .	. . .	. . .	. . .	. . .	. . .	. . .	. . .
Banks: long-term	4 773 . .	. . .	. . .	. . .	. . .	. . .	. . .	. . .	. . .
Banks: short-term	4 774 . .	. . .	. . .	. . .	. . .	. . .	. . .	. . .	. . .
Other sectors: long-term	4 776 . .	16.6	8.0	25.0	47.3	40.3	49.7	23.5	. . .
Other sectors: short-term	4 777 . .	. . .	. . .	. . .	. . .	. . .	. . .	. . .	. . .
Currency and deposits	4 780 . .	. . .	. . .	. . .	. . .	. . .	. . .	. . .	. . .
Monetary authorities	4 781 . .	. . .	. . .	. . .	. . .	. . .	. . .	. . .	. . .
General government	4 782 . .	. . .	. . .	. . .	. . .	. . .	. . .	. . .	. . .
Banks	4 783 . .	. . .	. . .	. . .	. . .	. . .	. . .	. . .	. . .
Other sectors	4 784 . .	. . .	. . .	. . .	. . .	. . .	. . .	. . .	. . .
Other liabilities	4 786 . .	. . .	. . .	. . .	. . .	. . .	. . .	. . .	. . .
Monetary authorities: long-term	4 788 . .	. . .	. . .	. . .	. . .	. . .	. . .	. . .	. . .
Monetary authorities: short-term	4 789 . .	. . .	. . .	. . .	. . .	. . .	. . .	. . .	. . .
General government: long-term	4 791 . .	. . .	. . .	. . .	. . .	. . .	. . .	. . .	. . .
General government: short-term	4 792 . .	. . .	. . .	. . .	. . .	. . .	. . .	. . .	. . .
Banks: long-term	4 794 . .	. . .	. . .	. . .	. . .	. . .	. . .	. . .	. . .
Banks: short-term	4 795 . .	. . .	. . .	. . .	. . .	. . .	. . .	. . .	. . .
Other sectors: long-term	4 797 . .	. . .	. . .	. . .	. . .	. . .	. . .	. . .	. . .
Other sectors: short-term	4 798 . .	. . .	. . .	. . .	. . .	. . .	. . .	. . .	. . .
D. RESERVE ASSETS	4 800 . .	–102.1	36.7	–34.3	–15.8	65.7	–18.1	14.3	. . .
Monetary gold	4 810 . .	. . .	. . .	–.1	. . .	–.3	. . .	. . .	. . .
Special drawing rights	4 820 . .	–3.2	2.8	–2.6	2.9	.2	–.1	–6.0	. . .
Reserve position in the Fund	4 830 . .	. . .	. . .	. . .	. . .	. . .	. . .	. . .	. . .
Foreign exchange	4 840 . .	–98.9	33.9	–31.6	–18.8	65.8	–17.9	20.2	. . .
Other claims	4 880 . .	. . .	. . .	. . .	. . .	. . .	. . .	. . .	. . .
NET ERRORS AND OMISSIONS	4 998 . .	**78.3**	**–92.5**	**–13.7**	**139.2**	**144.8**	**.7**	**292.6**	. . .

Table 1. ANALYTIC PRESENTATION, 1988–95
(Millions of U.S. dollars)

	Code	1988	1989	1990	1991	1992	1993	1994	1995
A. Current Account [1]	4 993 Y.	**1,867**	**315**	**–870**	**–4,183**	**–2,167**	**–2,809**	**–4,147**	**. . .**
Goods: exports f.o.b	2 100 . .	20,980	24,776	28,806	33,712	39,823	46,226	56,906	. . .
Goods: imports f.o.b	3 100 . .	–15,553	–20,498	–26,280	–33,321	–36,673	–43,201	–55,325	. . .
Balance on Goods	4 100 . .	*5,427*	*4,277*	*2,525*	*391*	*3,150*	*3,026*	*1,581*	. . .
Services: credit	2 200 . .	2,379	2,870	3,859	4,374	4,989	5,218	6,546	. . .
Services: debit	3 200 . .	–4,205	–4,792	–5,485	–6,564	–7,336	–8,054	–8,883	. . .
Balance on Goods and Services	4 991 . .	*3,600*	*2,356*	*900*	*–1,799*	*804*	*190*	*–756*	. . .
Income: credit	2 300 . .	1,090	1,172	1,849	1,425	1,609	2,006	2,343	. . .
Income: debit	3 300 . .	–3,032	–3,351	–3,721	–3,898	–4,752	–5,214	–5,897	. . .
Balance on Goods, Services, and Income	4 992 . .	*1,659*	*177*	*–972*	*–4,271*	*–2,339*	*–3,019*	*–4,311*	. . .
Current transfers: credit	2 379 Y.	288	212	249	215	296	345	290	. . .
Current transfers: debit	3 379 . .	–80	–74	–147	–126	–124	–135	–127	. . .
B. Capital Account [1]	4 994 Y.	**–58**	**–57**	**–48**	**–51**	**–40**	**–61**	**–43**	**. . .**
Capital account: credit	2 994 Y.	. . .	. . .	. . .	. . .	. . .	. . .	. . .	. . .
Capital account: debit	3 994 . .	–58	–57	–48	–51	–40	–61	–43	. . .
Total, Groups A Plus B	4 010 . .	*1,810*	*258*	*–918*	*–4,234*	*–2,207*	*–2,869*	*–4,191*	. . .
C. Financial Account [1]	4 995 X.	**–1,973**	**1,330**	**1,786**	**5,623**	**8,743**	**10,798**	**1,511**	**. . .**
Direct investment abroad	4 505 . .	. . .	. . .	. . .	. . .	. . .	. . .	. . .	. . .
Direct investment in Malaysia	4 555 Y.	719	1,668	2,332	3,998	5,183	5,006	4,348	. . .
Portfolio investment assets	4 602 . .	. . .	. . .	. . .	. . .	. . .	. . .	. . .	. . .
Equity securities	4 610 . .	. . .	. . .	. . .	. . .	. . .	. . .	. . .	. . .
Debt securities	4 619 . .	. . .	. . .	. . .	. . .	. . .	. . .	. . .	. . .
Portfolio investment liabilities	4 652 Y.	–448	–107	–255	170	–1,122	–709	–1,649	. . .
Equity securities	4 660 Y.	. . .	. . .	. . .	. . .	. . .	. . .	. . .	. . .
Debt securities	4 669 Y.	–448	–107	–255	170	–1,122	–709	–1,649	. . .
Other investment assets	4 703 . .	–1,083	32	–205	957	1,502	–934	682	. . .
Monetary authorities	4 703 .A	. . .	. . .	. . .	. . .	. . .	. . .	. . .	. . .
General government	4 703 .B	–4	72	4	–13	–42	–64	–52	. . .
Banks	4 703 .C	–920	–196	135	414	481	–2,057	–1,173	. . .
Other sectors	4 703 .D	–159	157	–344	556	1,063	1,187	1,907	. . .
Other investment liabilities	4 753 X.	–1,162	–262	–87	497	3,181	7,434	–1,870	. . .
Monetary authorities	4 753 XA	. . .	. . .	. . .	. . .	. . .	. . .	. . .	. . .
General government	4 753 YB	–734	–276	–36	–132	–122	–509	–163	. . .
Banks	4 753 YC	330	616	712	898	3,150	6,282	–3,754	. . .
Other sectors	4 753 YD	–758	–602	–763	–269	153	1,662	2,047	. . .
Total, Groups A Through C	4 020 . .	*–163*	*1,588*	*868*	*1,389*	*6,537*	*7,929*	*–2,680*	. . .
D. Net Errors and Omissions	4 998 . .	**–267**	**–358**	**1,085**	**–151**	**79**	**3,414**	**–476**	**. . .**
Total, Groups A Through D	4 030 . .	*–430*	*1,230*	*1,953*	*1,238*	*6,615*	*11,343*	*–3,157*	. . .
E. Reserves and Related Items	4 040 . .	**430**	**–1,230**	**–1,953**	**–1,238**	**–6,615**	**–11,343**	**3,157**	**. . .**
Reserve assets	4 800 . .	458	–1,235	–1,951	–1,236	–6,618	–11,350	3,160	. . .
Use of Fund credit and loans	4 766 . .	. . .	. . .	. . .	. . .	. . .	. . .	. . .	. . .
Liabilities constituting foreign authorities' reserves	4 900 . .	–28	5	–1	–1	3	7	–3	. . .
Exceptional financing	4 920 . .	. . .	. . .	. . .	. . .	. . .	. . .	. . .	. . .
Conversion rates: ringgit per U.S. dollar	0 101 . .	**2.6188**	**2.7088**	**2.7049**	**2.7501**	**2.5474**	**2.5741**	**2.6243**	**2.5044**

[1] Excludes components that have been classified in the categories of Group E.

Table 2. STANDARD PRESENTATION, 1988–95
(Millions of U.S. dollars)

	Code		1988	1989	1990	1991	1992	1993	1994	1995
CURRENT ACCOUNT	4 993	. .	**1,867**	**315**	**–870**	**–4,183**	**–2,167**	**–2,809**	**–4,147**	...
A. GOODS	4 100	. .	5,427	4,277	2,525	391	3,150	3,026	1,581	...
Credit	2 100	. .	**20,980**	**24,776**	**28,806**	**33,712**	**39,823**	**46,226**	**56,906**	...
General merchandise: exports f.o.b.	2 110	. .	20,852	24,633	28,636	33,534	39,613	45,990	56,590	...
Goods for processing: exports f.o.b.	2 150	. .	...	...	...	...	...	...	...	...
Repairs on goods	2 160	. .	...	...	...	...	...	...	...	...
Goods procured in ports by carriers	2 170	. .	128	143	169	178	210	236	317	...
Nonmonetary gold	2 180	. .	...	...	...	...	...	...	...	...
Debit	3 100	. .	**–15,553**	**–20,498**	**–26,280**	**–33,321**	**–36,673**	**–43,201**	**–55,325**	...
General merchandise: imports f.o.b.	3 110	. .	–15,008	–19,369	–24,612	–31,639	–35,535	–41,821	–53,341	...
Goods for processing: imports f.o.b.	3 150	. .	...	...	...	...	...	...	...	...
Repairs on goods	3 160	. .	...	...	...	...	...	...	...	...
Goods procured in ports by carriers	3 170	. .	–247	–248	–266	–314	–439	–408	–473	...
Nonmonetary gold	3 180	. .	–298	–882	–1,402	–1,368	–699	–972	–1,511	...
B. SERVICES	4 200	. .	–1,826	–1,921	–1,626	–2,190	–2,347	–2,836	–2,337	...
Total credit	2 200	. .	*2,379*	*2,870*	*3,859*	*4,374*	*4,989*	*5,218*	*6,546*	...
Total debit	3 200	. .	*–4,205*	*–4,792*	*–5,485*	*–6,564*	*–7,336*	*–8,054*	*–8,883*	...
Transportation services, credit	2 205	. .	**1,104**	**1,127**	**1,198**	**1,389**	**1,593**	**1,613**	**1,876**	...
Passenger	2 205	BA	*357*	*413*	*447*	*591*	*678*	*682*	*835*	...
Freight	2 205	BB	*615*	*577*	*560*	*610*	*727*	*744*	*777*	...
Other	2 205	BC	*132*	*137*	*191*	*188*	*189*	*187*	*265*	...
Sea transport, passenger	2 207	. .	...	...	...	...	...	...	...	...
Sea transport, freight	2 208	. .	...	...	...	...	...	...	...	...
Sea transport, other	2 209	. .	...	...	...	...	...	...	...	...
Air transport, passenger	2 211	. .	...	...	...	...	...	...	...	...
Air transport, freight	2 212	. .	...	...	...	...	...	...	...	...
Air transport, other	2 213	. .	...	...	...	...	...	...	...	...
Other transport, passenger	2 215	. .	...	...	...	...	...	...	...	...
Other transport, freight	2 216	. .	...	...	...	...	...	...	...	...
Other transport, other	2 217	. .	...	...	...	...	...	...	...	...
Transportation services, debit	3 205	. .	**–1,795**	**–2,144**	**–2,531**	**–3,023**	**–3,181**	**–3,433**	**–4,352**	...
Passenger	3 205	BA	*–206*	*–224*	*–243*	*–292*	*–318*	*–350*	*–365*	...
Freight	3 205	BB	*–1,409*	*–1,697*	*–1,982*	*–2,376*	*–2,404*	*–2,648*	*–3,590*	...
Other	3 205	BC	*–180*	*–223*	*–306*	*–355*	*–459*	*–435*	*–397*	...
Sea transport, passenger	3 207	. .	...	...	...	...	...	...	...	...
Sea transport, freight	3 208	. .	...	...	...	...	...	...	...	...
Sea transport, other	3 209	. .	...	...	...	...	...	...	...	...
Air transport, passenger	3 211	. .	...	...	...	...	...	...	...	...
Air transport, freight	3 212	. .	...	...	...	...	...	...	...	...
Air transport, other	3 213	. .	...	...	...	...	...	...	...	...
Other transport, passenger	3 215	. .	...	...	...	...	...	...	...	...
Other transport, freight	3 216	. .	...	...	...	...	...	...	...	...
Other transport, other	3 217	. .	...	...	...	...	...	...	...	...
Travel, credit	2 236	. .	**770**	**1,036**	**1,684**	**1,783**	**2,028**	**2,190**	**3,376**	...
Business travel	2 237	. .	...	...	...	...	...	...	...	...
Personal travel	2 240	. .	...	...	...	...	...	...	...	...
Travel, debit	3 236	. .	**–1,306**	**–1,365**	**–1,450**	**–1,584**	**–1,770**	**–1,838**	**–1,737**	...
Business travel	3 237	. .	...	...	...	...	...	...	...	...
Personal travel	3 240	. .	...	...	...	...	...	...	...	...
Other services, credit	2 200	BA	**505**	**707**	**977**	**1,202**	**1,368**	**1,414**	**1,294**	...
Communications	2 245	. .	...	...	...	...	...	...	...	...
Construction	2 249	. .	...	...	...	...	...	...	...	...
Insurance	2 253	. .	2	3	3	3	4	5	6	...
Financial	2 260	. .	...	...	...	...	...	...	...	...
Computer and information	2 262	. .	...	...	...	...	...	...	...	...
Royalties and licence fees	2 266	. .	...	...	...	...	...	...	...	...
Other business services	2 268	. .	406	612	885	1,109	1,256	1,292	1,168	...
Personal, cultural, and recreational	2 287	. .	...	...	...	...	...	...	...	...
Government, n.i.e.	2 291	. .	97	92	89	89	109	117	120	...
Other services, debit	3 200	BA	**–1,105**	**–1,282**	**–1,503**	**–1,957**	**–2,385**	**–2,782**	**–2,794**	...
Communications	3 245	. .	...	...	...	...	...	...	...	...
Construction	3 249	. .	...	...	...	...	...	...	...	...
Insurance	3 253	. .	...	...	...	...	...	...	...	...
Financial	3 260	. .	...	...	...	...	...	...	...	...
Computer and information	3 262	. .	...	...	...	...	...	...	...	...
Royalties and licence fees	3 266	. .	...	...	...	...	...	...	...	...
Other business services	3 268	. .	–925	–1,094	–1,412	–1,848	–2,297	–2,637	–2,660	...
Personal, cultural, and recreational	3 287	. .	...	...	...	...	...	...	...	...
Government, n.i.e.	3 291	. .	–180	–188	–91	–109	–88	–145	–134	...

Table 2 (Continued). STANDARD PRESENTATION, 1988–95
(Millions of U.S. dollars)

	Code	1988	1989	1990	1991	1992	1993	1994	1995
C. INCOME	4 300 . .	–1,941	–2,179	–1,872	–2,472	–3,143	–3,208	–3,555	. . .
Total credit	2 300 . .	*1,090*	*1,172*	*1,849*	*1,425*	*1,609*	*2,006*	*2,343*	. . .
Total debit	3 300 . .	*–3,032*	*–3,351*	*–3,721*	*–3,898*	*–4,752*	*–5,214*	*–5,897*	. . .
Compensation of employees, credit	2 310 . .	**100**	**139**	**185**	**130**	**153**	**175**	**110**	**. . .**
Compensation of employees, debit	3 310 . .	**–124**	**–127**	**–182**	**–154**	**–187**	**–207**	**–88**	**. . .**
Investment income, credit	2 320 . .	**991**	**1,033**	**1,664**	**1,295**	**1,456**	**1,831**	**2,233**	**. . .**
Direct investment income	2 330 . .	42	78	63	54	79	127	61	. . .
Dividends and distributed branch profits	2 332 . .	37	61	41	47	74	91	32	. . .
Reinvested earnings and undistributed branch profits	2 333 . .	. . .	. . .	. . .	. . .	. . .	. . .	. . .	. . .
Income on debt (interest)	2 334 . .	5	17	22	7	5	36	28	. . .
Portfolio investment income	2 339 . .	60	75	94	100	182	354	450	. . .
Income on equity	2 340 . .	60	75	94	100	182	354	450	. . .
Income on bonds and notes	2 350 . .	. . .	. . .	. . .	. . .	. . .	. . .	. . .	. . .
Income on money market instruments and financial derivatives	2 360 . .	. . .	. . .	. . .	. . .	. . .	. . .	. . .	. . .
Other investment income	2 370 . .	889	879	1,508	1,142	1,195	1,350	1,722	. . .
Investment income, debit	3 320 . .	**–2,907**	**–3,224**	**–3,539**	**–3,744**	**–4,565**	**–5,007**	**–5,809**	**. . .**
Direct investment income	3 330 . .	–1,329	–1,630	–1,926	–2,275	–2,939	–3,222	–3,846	. . .
Dividends and distributed branch profits	3 332 . .	–1,265	–1,553	–1,856	–2,213	–2,863	–3,132	–3,781	. . .
Reinvested earnings and undistributed branch profits	3 333 . .	. . .	. . .	. . .	. . .	. . .	. . .	. . .	. . .
Income on debt (interest)	3 334 . .	–64	–76	–70	–62	–77	–89	–65	. . .
Portfolio investment income	3 339 . .	–187	–292	–350	–340	–433	–512	–621	. . .
Income on equity	3 340 . .	–187	–292	–350	–340	–433	–512	–621	. . .
Income on bonds and notes	3 350 . .	. . .	. . .	. . .	. . .	. . .	. . .	. . .	. . .
Income on money market instruments and financial derivatives	3 360 . .	. . .	. . .	. . .	. . .	. . .	. . .	. . .	. . .
Other investment income	3 370 . .	–1,391	–1,302	–1,263	–1,128	–1,193	–1,273	–1,342	. . .
D. CURRENT TRANSFERS	4 379 . .	208	138	102	88	172	210	163	. . .
Credit	2 379 . .	**288**	**212**	**249**	**215**	**296**	**345**	**290**	**. . .**
General government	2 380 . .	108	111	109	36	91	101	99	. . .
Other sectors	2 390 . .	181	100	140	179	205	244	190	. . .
Workers' remittances	2 391 . .	. . .	. . .	. . .	. . .	. . .	. . .	. . .	. . .
Other current transfers	2 392 . .	181	100	140	179	205	244	190	. . .
Debit	3 379 . .	**–80**	**–74**	**–147**	**–126**	**–124**	**–135**	**–127**	**. . .**
General government	3 380 . .	–27	–14	–58	–28	–24	–21	–28	. . .
Other sectors	3 390 . .	–53	–60	–89	–99	–100	–114	–98	. . .
Workers' remittances	3 391 . .	. . .	. . .	. . .	. . .	. . .	. . .	. . .	. . .
Other current transfers	3 392 . .	–53	–60	–89	–99	–100	–114	–98	. . .
CAPITAL AND FINANCIAL ACCOUNT	4 996 . .	**–1,600**	**44**	**–215**	**4,334**	**2,088**	**–606**	**4,624**	**. . .**
CAPITAL ACCOUNT	4 994 . .	**–58**	**–57**	**–48**	**–51**	**–40**	**–61**	**–43**	**. . .**
Total credit	2 994 . .	. . .	. . .	. . .	. . .	. . .	. . .	. . .	. . .
Total debit	3 994 . .	*–58*	*–57*	*–48*	*–51*	*–40*	*–61*	*–43*	. . .
Capital transfers, credit	2 400 . .	**. . .**	**. . .**	**. . .**	**. . .**	**. . .**	**. . .**	**. . .**	**. . .**
General government	2 401 . .	. . .	. . .	. . .	. . .	. . .	. . .	. . .	. . .
Debt forgiveness	2 402 . .	. . .	. . .	. . .	. . .	. . .	. . .	. . .	. . .
Other capital transfers	2 410 . .	. . .	. . .	. . .	. . .	. . .	. . .	. . .	. . .
Other sectors	2 430 . .	. . .	. . .	. . .	. . .	. . .	. . .	. . .	. . .
Migrants' transfers	2 431 . .	. . .	. . .	. . .	. . .	. . .	. . .	. . .	. . .
Debt forgiveness	2 432 . .	. . .	. . .	. . .	. . .	. . .	. . .	. . .	. . .
Other capital transfers	2 440 . .	. . .	. . .	. . .	. . .	. . .	. . .	. . .	. . .
Capital transfers, debit	3 400 . .	**–58**	**–57**	**–48**	**–51**	**–40**	**–61**	**–43**	**. . .**
General government	3 401 . .	. . .	. . .	. . .	. . .	. . .	. . .	. . .	. . .
Debt forgiveness	3 402 . .	. . .	. . .	. . .	. . .	. . .	. . .	. . .	. . .
Other capital transfers	3 410 . .	. . .	. . .	. . .	. . .	. . .	. . .	. . .	. . .
Other sectors	3 430 . .	–58	–57	–48	–51	–40	–61	–43	. . .
Migrants' transfers	3 431 . .	–58	–57	–48	–51	–40	–61	–43	. . .
Debt forgiveness	3 432 . .	. . .	. . .	. . .	. . .	. . .	. . .	. . .	. . .
Other capital transfers	3 440 . .	. . .	. . .	. . .	. . .	. . .	. . .	. . .	. . .
Nonproduced nonfinancial assets, credit	2 480 . .	**. . .**	**. . .**	**. . .**	**. . .**	**. . .**	**. . .**	**. . .**	**. . .**
Nonproduced nonfinancial assets, debit	3 480 . .	**. . .**	**. . .**	**. . .**	**. . .**	**. . .**	**. . .**	**. . .**	**. . .**

Table 2 (Continued). STANDARD PRESENTATION, 1988–95
(Millions of U.S. dollars)

	Code	1988	1989	1990	1991	1992	1993	1994	1995
FINANCIAL ACCOUNT	4 995	**–1,543**	**100**	**–167**	**4,385**	**2,128**	**–545**	**4,667**	**. . .**
A. DIRECT INVESTMENT	4 500	719	1,668	2,332	3,998	5,183	5,006	4,348	. . .
Direct investment abroad	4 505	**. . .**	**. . .**	**. . .**	**. . .**	**. . .**	**. . .**	**. . .**	**. . .**
Equity capital	4 510	. . .	. . .	. . .	. . .	. . .	. . .	. . .	. . .
Claims on affiliated enterprises	4 515	. . .	. . .	. . .	. . .	. . .	. . .	. . .	. . .
Liabilities to affiliated enterprises	4 520	. . .	. . .	. . .	. . .	. . .	. . .	. . .	. . .
Reinvested earnings	4 525	. . .	. . .	. . .	. . .	. . .	. . .	. . .	. . .
Other capital	4 530	. . .	. . .	. . .	. . .	. . .	. . .	. . .	. . .
Claims on affiliated enterprises	4 535	. . .	. . .	. . .	. . .	. . .	. . .	. . .	. . .
Liabilities to affiliated enterprises	4 540	. . .	. . .	. . .	. . .	. . .	. . .	. . .	. . .
Direct investment in Malaysia	4 555	**719**	**1,668**	**2,332**	**3,998**	**5,183**	**5,006**	**4,348**	**. . .**
Equity capital	4 560	. . .	. . .	. . .	. . .	. . .	. . .	. . .	. . .
Claims on direct investors	4 565	. . .	. . .	. . .	. . .	. . .	. . .	. . .	. . .
Liabilities to direct investors	4 570	. . .	. . .	. . .	. . .	. . .	. . .	. . .	. . .
Reinvested earnings	4 575	. . .	. . .	. . .	. . .	. . .	. . .	. . .	. . .
Other capital	4 580	719	1,668	2,332	3,998	5,183	5,006	4,348	. . .
Claims on direct investors	4 585	. . .	. . .	. . .	. . .	. . .	. . .	. . .	. . .
Liabilities to direct investors	4 590	. . .	. . .	. . .	. . .	. . .	. . .	. . .	. . .
B. PORTFOLIO INVESTMENT	4 600	–448	–107	–255	170	–1,122	–709	–1,649	. . .
Assets	4 602	**. . .**	**. . .**	**. . .**	**. . .**	**. . .**	**. . .**	**. . .**	**. . .**
Equity securities	4 610	. . .	. . .	. . .	. . .	. . .	. . .	. . .	. . .
Monetary authorities	4 611	. . .	. . .	. . .	. . .	. . .	. . .	. . .	. . .
General government	4 612	. . .	. . .	. . .	. . .	. . .	. . .	. . .	. . .
Banks	4 613	. . .	. . .	. . .	. . .	. . .	. . .	. . .	. . .
Other sectors	4 614	. . .	. . .	. . .	. . .	. . .	. . .	. . .	. . .
Debt securities	4 619	. . .	. . .	. . .	. . .	. . .	. . .	. . .	. . .
Bonds and notes	4 620	. . .	. . .	. . .	. . .	. . .	. . .	. . .	. . .
Monetary authorities	4 621	. . .	. . .	. . .	. . .	. . .	. . .	. . .	. . .
General government	4 622	. . .	. . .	. . .	. . .	. . .	. . .	. . .	. . .
Banks	4 623	. . .	. . .	. . .	. . .	. . .	. . .	. . .	. . .
Other sectors	4 624	. . .	. . .	. . .	. . .	. . .	. . .	. . .	. . .
Money market instruments	4 630	. . .	. . .	. . .	. . .	. . .	. . .	. . .	. . .
Monetary authorities	4 631	. . .	. . .	. . .	. . .	. . .	. . .	. . .	. . .
General government	4 632	. . .	. . .	. . .	. . .	. . .	. . .	. . .	. . .
Banks	4 633	. . .	. . .	. . .	. . .	. . .	. . .	. . .	. . .
Other sectors	4 634	. . .	. . .	. . .	. . .	. . .	. . .	. . .	. . .
Financial derivatives	4 640	. . .	. . .	. . .	. . .	. . .	. . .	. . .	. . .
Monetary authorities	4 641	. . .	. . .	. . .	. . .	. . .	. . .	. . .	. . .
General government	4 642	. . .	. . .	. . .	. . .	. . .	. . .	. . .	. . .
Banks	4 643	. . .	. . .	. . .	. . .	. . .	. . .	. . .	. . .
Other sectors	4 644	. . .	. . .	. . .	. . .	. . .	. . .	. . .	. . .
Liabilities	4 652	**–448**	**–107**	**–255**	**170**	**–1,122**	**–709**	**–1,649**	**. . .**
Equity securities	4 660	. . .	. . .	. . .	. . .	. . .	. . .	. . .	. . .
Banks	4 663	. . .	. . .	. . .	. . .	. . .	. . .	. . .	. . .
Other sectors	4 664	. . .	. . .	. . .	. . .	. . .	. . .	. . .	. . .
Debt securities	4 669	–448	–107	–255	170	–1,122	–709	–1,649	. . .
Bonds and notes	4 670	–448	–107	–255	170	–1,122	–709	–1,649	. . .
Monetary authorities	4 671	. . .	. . .	. . .	. . .	. . .	. . .	. . .	. . .
General government	4 672	–448	–107	–255	170	–1,122	–709	–1,649	. . .
Banks	4 673	. . .	. . .	. . .	. . .	. . .	. . .	. . .	. . .
Other sectors	4 674	. . .	. . .	. . .	. . .	. . .	. . .	. . .	. . .
Money market instruments	4 680	. . .	. . .	. . .	. . .	. . .	. . .	. . .	. . .
Monetary authorities	4 681	. . .	. . .	. . .	. . .	. . .	. . .	. . .	. . .
General government	4 682	. . .	. . .	. . .	. . .	. . .	. . .	. . .	. . .
Banks	4 683	. . .	. . .	. . .	. . .	. . .	. . .	. . .	. . .
Other sectors	4 684	. . .	. . .	. . .	. . .	. . .	. . .	. . .	. . .
Financial derivatives	4 690	. . .	. . .	. . .	. . .	. . .	. . .	. . .	. . .
Monetary authorities	4 691	. . .	. . .	. . .	. . .	. . .	. . .	. . .	. . .
General government	4 692	. . .	. . .	. . .	. . .	. . .	. . .	. . .	. . .
Banks	4 693	. . .	. . .	. . .	. . .	. . .	. . .	. . .	. . .
Other sectors	4 694	. . .	. . .	. . .	. . .	. . .	. . .	. . .	. . .

Table 2 (Concluded). STANDARD PRESENTATION, 1988–95
(Millions of U.S. dollars)

	Code	1988	1989	1990	1991	1992	1993	1994	1995
C. OTHER INVESTMENT	4 700	–2,272	–226	–294	1,453	4,685	6,508	–1,191	...
Assets	4 703	**–1,083**	**32**	**–205**	**957**	**1,502**	**–934**	**682**	...
Trade credits	4 706	...	...	...	...	...	...	...	...
General government: long-term	4 708	...	...	...	...	...	...	...	...
General government: short-term	4 709	...	...	...	...	...	...	...	...
Other sectors: long-term	4 711	...	...	...	...	...	...	...	...
Other sectors: short-term	4 712	...	...	...	...	...	...	...	...
Loans	4 714	...	...	...	...	...	...	...	...
Monetary authorities: long-term	4 717	...	...	...	...	...	...	...	...
Monetary authorities: short-term	4 718	...	...	...	...	...	...	...	...
General government: long-term	4 720	...	...	...	...	...	...	...	...
General government: short-term	4 721	...	...	...	...	...	...	...	...
Banks: long-term	4 723	...	...	...	...	...	...	...	...
Banks: short-term	4 724	...	...	...	...	...	...	...	...
Other sectors: long-term	4 726	...	...	...	...	...	...	...	...
Other sectors: short-term	4 727	...	...	...	...	...	...	...	...
Currency and deposits	4 730	–1,079	–40	–209	971	1,544	–870	734	...
Monetary authorities	4 731	...	...	...	...	...	...	...	...
General government	4 732	...	...	...	...	...	...	...	...
Banks	4 733	–920	–196	135	414	481	–2,057	–1,173	...
Other sectors	4 734	–159	157	–344	556	1,063	1,187	1,907	...
Other assets	4 736	–4	72	4	–13	–42	–64	–52	...
Monetary authorities: long-term	4 738	...	...	...	...	...	...	...	...
Monetary authorities: short-term	4 739	...	...	...	...	...	...	...	...
General government: long-term	4 741	–4	72	4	–13	–42	–64	–52	...
General government: short-term	4 742	...	...	...	...	...	...	...	...
Banks: long-term	4 744	...	...	...	...	...	...	...	...
Banks: short-term	4 745	...	...	...	...	...	...	...	...
Other sectors: long-term	4 747	...	...	...	...	...	...	...	...
Other sectors: short-term	4 748	...	...	...	...	...	...	...	...
Liabilities	4 753	**–1,189**	**–258**	**–89**	**496**	**3,183**	**7,441**	**–1,873**	...
Trade credits	4 756	...	...	...	...	...	...	...	...
General government: long-term	4 758	...	...	...	...	...	...	...	...
General government: short-term	4 759	...	...	...	...	...	...	...	...
Other sectors: long-term	4 761	...	...	...	...	...	...	...	...
Other sectors: short-term	4 762	...	...	...	...	...	...	...	...
Loans	4 764	–1,492	–878	–799	–401	31	1,153	1,884	...
Use of Fund credit and loans from the Fund	4 766	...	...	...	...	...	...	...	...
Monetary authorities: other long-term	4 767	...	...	...	...	...	...	...	...
Monetary authorities: short-term	4 768	...	...	...	...	...	...	...	...
General government: long-term	4 770	–734	–276	–36	–132	–122	–509	–163	...
General government: short-term	4 771	...	...	...	...	...	...	...	...
Banks: long-term	4 773	...	...	...	...	...	...	...	...
Banks: short-term	4 774	...	...	...	...	...	...	...	...
Other sectors: long-term	4 776	–758	–602	–763	–269	153	1,662	2,047	...
Other sectors: short-term	4 777	...	...	...	...	...	...	...	...
Currency and deposits	4 780	302	621	711	896	3,153	6,288	–3,757	...
Monetary authorities	4 781	–28	5	–1	–1	3	7	–3	...
General government	4 782	...	...	...	...	...	...	...	...
Banks	4 783	330	616	712	898	3,150	6,282	–3,754	...
Other sectors	4 784	...	...	...	...	...	...	...	...
Other liabilities	4 786	...	...	...	...	...	...	...	...
Monetary authorities: long-term	4 788	...	...	...	...	...	...	...	...
Monetary authorities: short-term	4 789	...	...	...	...	...	...	...	...
General government: long-term	4 791	...	...	...	...	...	...	...	...
General government: short-term	4 792	...	...	...	...	...	...	...	...
Banks: long-term	4 794	...	...	...	...	...	...	...	...
Banks: short-term	4 795	...	...	...	...	...	...	...	...
Other sectors: long-term	4 797	...	...	...	...	...	...	...	...
Other sectors: short-term	4 798	...	...	...	...	...	...	...	...
D. RESERVE ASSETS	4 800	458	–1,235	–1,951	–1,236	–6,618	–11,350	3,160	...
Monetary gold	4 810	...	...	...	...	...	...	...	...
Special drawing rights	4 820	–6	–9	–13	–12	87	–8	–7	...
Reserve position in the Fund	4 830	–25	4	7	–23	–84	15	–63	...
Foreign exchange	4 840	495	–1,236	–1,947	–1,204	–6,626	–11,357	3,231	...
Other claims	4 880	–5	7	1	3	5	...	...	...
NET ERRORS AND OMISSIONS	4 998	**–267**	**–358**	**1,085**	**–151**	**79**	**3,414**	**–476**	...

Part 3 of the *Yearbook* contains descriptions of the methodologies, compilation practices, and sources used to compile these data.

Table 3. INTERNATIONAL INVESTMENT POSITION (End–period stocks), 1988–95
(Millions of U.S. dollars)

	Code	1988	1989	1990	1991	1992	1993	1994	1995
ASSETS	8 995 C.	11,032	14,967	14,000	14,817	21,600	...	...	...
Direct investment abroad	8 505 ..	**1,146**	**967**	**753**	**763**	**1,058**	...	...	...
Equity capital and reinvested earnings	8 506 ..	1,146	967	753	763	1,058	...	...	...
Claims on affiliated enterprises	8 507 ..	...	...	...	...	...	...	...	...
Liabilities to affiliated enterprises	8 508 ..	...	...	...	...	...	...	...	...
Other capital	8 530 ..	...	...	...	...	...	...	...	...
Claims on affiliated enterprises	8 535 ..	...	...	...	...	...	...	...	...
Liabilities to affiliated enterprises	8 540 ..	...	...	...	...	...	...	...	...
Portfolio investment	8 602 ..	**356**	**999**	**393**	**429**	**429**	...	...	...
Equity securities	8 610 ..	356	371	393	429	429	...	...	...
Monetary authorities	8 611 ..	...	...	...	...	...	...	...	...
General government	8 612 ..	...	...	...	...	...	...	...	...
Banks	8 613 ..	...	...	...	...	...	...	...	...
Other sectors	8 614 ..	...	...	...	...	...	...	...	...
Debt securities	8 619 ..	...	628	...	...	...	...	...	...
Bonds and notes	8 620 ..	...	628	...	...	...	...	...	...
Monetary authorities	8 621 ..	...	...	...	...	...	...	...	...
General government	8 622 ..	...	...	...	...	...	...	...	...
Banks	8 623 ..	...	...	...	...	...	...	...	...
Other sectors	8 624 ..	...	...	...	...	...	...	...	...
Money market instruments	8 630 ..	...	...	...	...	...	...	...	...
Monetary authorities	8 631 ..	...	...	...	...	...	...	...	...
General government	8 632 ..	...	...	...	...	...	...	...	...
Banks	8 633 ..	...	...	...	...	...	...	...	...
Other sectors	8 634 ..	...	...	...	...	...	...	...	...
Financial derivatives	8 640 ..	...	...	...	...	...	...	...	...
Monetary authorities	8 641 ..	...	...	...	...	...	...	...	...
General government	8 642 ..	...	...	...	...	...	...	...	...
Banks	8 643 ..	...	...	...	...	...	...	...	...
Other sectors	8 644 ..	...	...	...	...	...	...	...	...
Other investment	8 703 ..	**2,732**	**4,945**	**2,807**	**2,407**	**1,999**	**3,892**	**4,164**	...
Trade credits	8 706 ..	...	...	...	...	...	...	...	...
General government: long-term	8 708 ..	...	...	...	...	...	...	...	...
General government: short-term	8 709 ..	...	...	...	...	...	...	...	...
Other sectors: long-term	8 711 ..	...	...	...	...	...	...	...	...
Other sectors: short-term	8 712 ..	...	...	...	...	...	...	...	...
Loans	8 714 ..	...	6	...	41	...	...	...	...
Monetary authorities: long-term	8 717 ..	...	...	...	...	...	...	...	...
Monetary authorities: short-term	8 718 ..	...	...	...	...	...	...	...	...
General government: long-term	8 720 ..	...	...	...	...	...	...	...	...
General government: short-term	8 721 ..	...	...	...	...	...	...	...	...
Banks: long-term	8 723 ..	...	6	...	27	...	...	...	...
Banks: short-term	8 724 ..	...	...	...	...	...	...	...	...
Other sectors: long-term	8 726 ..	...	...	...	14	...	...	...	...
Other sectors: short-term	8 727 ..	...	...	...	...	...	...	...	...
Currency and deposits	8 730 ..	2,732	2,940	2,807	2,366	1,999	3,892	4,164	...
Monetary authorities	8 731 ..	...	...	...	...	...	...	...	...
General government	8 732 ..	...	...	...	...	...	...	...	...
Banks	8 733 ..	2,732	2,940	2,807	2,366	1,999	3,892	4,164	...
Other sectors	8 734 ..	...	...	...	...	...	...	...	...
Other assets	8 736 ..	...	1,998	...	...	...	...	...	...
Monetary authorities: long-term	8 738 ..	...	...	...	...	...	...	...	...
Monetary authorities: short-term	8 739 ..	...	...	...	...	...	...	...	...
General government: long-term	8 741 ..	...	...	...	...	...	...	...	...
General government: short-term	8 742 ..	...	...	...	...	...	...	...	...
Banks: long-term	8 744 ..	...	...	...	...	...	...	...	...
Banks: short-term	8 745 ..	...	...	...	...	...	...	...	...
Other sectors: long-term	8 747 ..	...	...	...	...	...	...	...	...
Other sectors: short-term	8 748 ..	...	1,998	...	...	...	...	...	...
Reserve assets	8 800 ..	**6,798**	**8,056**	**10,047**	**11,218**	**18,115**	**28,343**	**26,673**	...
Monetary gold	8 810 ..	...	...	...	...	...	...	...	...
Special drawing rights	8 820 ..	161	167	194	207	113	121	135	151
Reserve position in the Fund	8 830 ..	231	223	233	257	330	315	400	678
Foreign exchange	8 840 ..	6,361	7,627	9,582	10,718	17,640	27,877	26,106	...
Other claims	8 880 ..	45	38	37	35	31	31	32	...

Table 3 (Continued). INTERNATIONAL INVESTMENT POSITION (End–period stocks), 1988–95

(Millions of U.S. dollars)

	Code	1988	1989	1990	1991	1992	1993	1994	1995
LIABILITIES	8 995 D.	20,494	25,674	25,008	32,059	35,247	...	...	...
Direct investment in Malaysia	8 555 . .	**7,054**	**8,096**	**10,318**	**12,440**	**16,860**	...	...	...
Equity capital and reinvested earnings	8 556 . .	4,757	5,523	6,702	8,138	11,081	...	...	...
Claims on direct investors	8 557 . .	...	...	...	...	...	...	...	...
Liabilities to direct investors	8 558 . .	...	...	...	...	...	...	...	...
Other capital	8 580 . .	2,297	2,574	3,616	4,302	5,779	...	...	...
Claims on direct investors	8 585 . .	...	...	...	...	...	...	...	...
Liabilities to direct investors	8 590 . .	...	...	...	...	...	...	...	...
Portfolio investment	8 652 . .	**8,335**	**8,151**	**8,504**	**8,808**	**8,136**	...	...	...
Equity securities	8 660 . .	1,976	2,094	2,514	2,680	3,223	...	...	...
Banks	8 663 . .	...	...	...	...	...	...	...	...
Other sectors	8 664 . .	...	...	...	...	...	...	...	...
Debt securities	8 669 . .	6,358	6,057	5,990	6,128	4,913	4,292	3,709	...
Bonds and notes	8 670 . .	6,358	6,057	5,990	6,128	4,913	4,292	3,709	...
Monetary authorities	8 671 . .	...	...	...	...	...	...	...	...
General government	8 672 . .	...	...	...	...	...	...	...	...
Banks	8 673 . .	...	...	...	...	...	...	...	...
Other sectors	8 674 . .	...	...	...	...	...	...	...	...
Money market instruments	8 680 . .	...	...	...	...	...	...	...	...
Monetary authorities	8 681 . .	...	...	...	...	...	...	...	...
General government	8 682 . .	...	...	...	...	...	...	...	...
Banks	8 683 . .	...	...	...	...	...	...	...	...
Other sectors	8 684 . .	...	...	...	...	...	...	...	...
Financial derivatives	8 690 . .	...	...	...	...	...	...	...	...
Monetary authorities	8 691 . .	...	...	...	...	...	...	...	...
General government	8 692 . .	...	...	...	...	...	...	...	...
Banks	8 692 . .	...	...	...	...	...	...	...	...
Other sectors	8 694 . .	...	...	...	...	...	...	...	...
Other investment	8 753 . .	**5,105**	**9,427**	**6,185**	**10,810**	**10,252**	**14,530**	**9,676**	...
Trade credits	8 756 . .	...	...	...	...	...	...	...	...
General government: long-term	8 758 . .	...	...	...	...	...	...	...	...
General government: short-term	8 759 . .	...	...	...	...	...	...	...	...
Other sectors: long-term	8 761 . .	...	...	...	...	...	...	...	...
Other sectors: short-term	8 762 . .	...	...	...	...	...	...	...	...
Loans	8 764 . .	3,188	5,938	3,163	6,489	3,097	2,875	3,033	...
Use of Fund credit and loans from the Fund	8 766 . .	...	...	...	...	...	...	...	...
Monetary authorities: other long-term	8 767 . .	...	...	...	...	...	...	...	...
Monetary authorities: short-term	8 768 . .	...	...	...	...	...	...	...	...
General government: long-term	8 770 . .	3,188	2,888	3,163	3,203	3,097	2,875	3,033	...
General government: short-term	8 771 . .	...	...	...	...	...	...	...	...
Banks: long-term	8 773 . .	...	421	...	466	...	...	...	...
Banks: short-term	8 774 . .	...	...	...	...	...	...	...	...
Other sectors: long-term	8 776 . .	...	2,629	...	2,819	...	...	...	...
Other sectors: short-term	8 777 . .	...	...	...	...	...	...	...	...
Currency and deposits	8 780 . .	1,917	2,389	3,023	4,322	7,155	11,656	6,643	...
Monetary authorities	8 781 . .	...	...	...	...	...	...	...	...
General government	8 782 . .	...	...	...	...	...	...	...	...
Banks	8 783 . .	1,917	2,389	3,023	4,322	7,155	11,656	6,643	...
Other sectors	8 784 . .	...	...	...	...	...	...	...	...
Other liabilities	8 786 . .	...	1,099	...	...	...	...	...	...
Monetary authorities: long-term	8 788 . .	...	...	...	...	...	...	...	...
Monetary authorities: short-term	8 789 . .	...	...	...	...	...	...	...	...
General government: long-term	8 791 . .	...	...	...	...	...	...	...	...
General government: short-term	8 792 . .	...	...	...	...	...	...	...	...
Banks: long-term	8 794 . .	...	...	...	...	...	...	...	...
Banks: short-term	8 795 . .	...	...	...	...	...	...	...	...
Other sectors: long-term	8 797 . .	...	...	...	...	...	...	...	...
Other sectors: short-term	8 798 . .	...	1,099	...	...	...	...	...	...
NET INTERNATIONAL INVESTMENT POSITION	8 995 . .	**-9,462**	**-10,708**	**-11,008**	**-17,242**	**-13,647**	...	...	...
Conversion rates: ringgit per U.S. dollar (end of period)	0 102 . .	**2.7153**	**2.7033**	**2.7015**	**2.7240**	**2.6120**	**2.7015**	**2.5600**	**2.5420**

Table 1. ANALYTIC PRESENTATION, 1988–95
(Millions of U.S. dollars)

	Code	1988	1989	1990	1991	1992	1993	1994	1995
A. Current Account [1]	4 993 Y.	**8.9**	**10.6**	**8.6**	**–9.0**	**–19.7**	**–47.6**	**. . .**	**. . .**
Goods: exports f.o.b.	2 100 . .	44.6	51.3	58.1	59.2	51.1	38.5	. . .	. . .
Goods: imports f.o.b.	3 100 . .	–87.3	–111.3	–121.2	–141.8	–167.9	–177.8	. . .	. . .
Balance on Goods	4 100 . .	*–42.7*	*–60.0*	*–63.1*	*–82.6*	*–116.8*	*–139.3*	. . .	. . .
Services: credit	2 200 . .	83.3	98.8	119.7	125.1	168.2	178.2	. . .	. . .
Services: debit	3 200 . .	–28.5	–28.9	–38.0	–42.1	–49.4	–55.8	. . .	. . .
Balance on Goods and Services	4 991 . .	*12.1*	*9.9*	*18.6*	*.4*	*2.0*	*–16.9*	. . .	. . .
Income: credit	2 300 . .	2.0	3.8	4.7	3.8	2.9	3.0	. . .	. . .
Income: debit	3 300 . .	–11.7	–16.3	–18.5	–18.7	–20.0	–22.0	. . .	. . .
Balance on Goods, Services, and Income	4 992 . .	*2.4*	*–2.6*	*4.8*	*–14.5*	*–15.1*	*–35.9*	. . .	. . .
Current transfers: credit	2 379 Y.	11.5	18.3	11.2	22.1	14.3	8.3	. . .	. . .
Current transfers: debit	3 379 . .	–5.0	–5.1	–7.4	–16.6	–18.9	–20.0	. . .	. . .
B. Capital Account [1]	4 994 Y.	**. . .**	**. . .**	**. . .**	**. . .**	**. . .**	**. . .**	**. . .**	**. . .**
Capital account: credit	2 994 Y.	. . .	. . .	. . .	. . .	. . .	. . .	. . .	. . .
Capital account: debit	3 994 . .	. . .	. . .	. . .	. . .	. . .	. . .	. . .	. . .
Total, Groups A Plus B	4 010 . .	*8.9*	*10.6*	*8.6*	*–9.0*	*–19.7*	*–47.6*	. . .	. . .
C. Financial Account [1]	4 995 X.	**–1.5**	**11.8**	**8.1**	**5.4**	**25.5**	**24.9**	**. . .**	**. . .**
Direct investment abroad	4 505 . .	. . .	. . .	. . .	. . .	. . .	. . .	. . .	. . .
Direct investment in Maldives	4 555 Y.	1.2	4.4	5.6	6.5	6.6	6.9	. . .	. . .
Portfolio investment assets	4 602 . .	. . .	. . .	. . .	. . .	. . .	. . .	. . .	. . .
Equity securities	4 610 . .	. . .	. . .	. . .	. . .	. . .	. . .	. . .	. . .
Debt securities	4 619 . .	. . .	. . .	. . .	. . .	. . .	. . .	. . .	. . .
Portfolio investment liabilities	4 652 Y.	. . .	. . .	. . .	. . .	. . .	. . .	. . .	. . .
Equity securities	4 660 Y.	. . .	. . .	. . .	. . .	. . .	. . .	. . .	. . .
Debt securities	4 669 Y.	. . .	. . .	. . .	. . .	. . .	. . .	. . .	. . .
Other investment assets	4 703 . .	1.6	–2.9	–2.2	–2.2	–1.8	4.3	. . .	. . .
Monetary authorities	4 703 .A	. . .	. . .	. . .	. . .	. . .	. . .	. . .	. . .
General government	4 703 .B	. . .	. . .	. . .	. . .	. . .	. . .	. . .	. . .
Banks	4 703 .C	1.6	–2.9	–2.2	–2.2	–1.8	4.3	. . .	. . .
Other sectors	4 703 .D	. . .	. . .	. . .	. . .	. . .	. . .	. . .	. . .
Other investment liabilities	4 753 X.	–4.3	10.3	4.7	1.1	20.7	13.7	. . .	. . .
Monetary authorities	4 753 XA	.1	. . .	. . .	. . .	. . .	15.2	. . .	. . .
General government	4 753 YB	–2.2	1.0	5.1	11.2	16.4	2.2	. . .	. . .
Banks	4 753 YC	–2.2	9.3	–.4	–10.1	4.3	–3.7	. . .	. . .
Other sectors	4 753 YD	. . .	. . .	. . .	. . .	. . .	. . .	. . .	. . .
Total, Groups A Through C	4 020 . .	*7.4*	*22.4*	*16.7*	*–3.6*	*5.8*	*–22.7*	. . .	. . .
D. Net Errors and Omissions	4 998 . .	**6.2**	**–20.1**	**–17.8**	**2.6**	**–1.0**	**22.6**	**. . .**	**. . .**
Total, Groups A Through D	4 030 . .	*13.6*	*2.3*	*–1.1*	*–1.0*	*4.8*	*–.1*	. . .	. . .
E. Reserves and Related Items	4 040 . .	**–13.6**	**–2.3**	**1.1**	**1.0**	**–4.8**	**.1**	**. . .**	**. . .**
Reserve assets	4 800 . .	–13.6	–2.3	.3	1.0	–4.8	.1	. . .	. . .
Use of Fund credit and loans	4 766 . .	. . .	. . .	. . .	. . .	. . .	. . .	. . .	. . .
Liabilities constituting foreign authorities' reserves	4 900 . .	. . .	. . .	. . .	. . .	. . .	. . .	. . .	. . .
Exceptional financing	4 920 . .	. . .	. . .	.8	. . .	. . .	. . .	. . .	. . .
Conversion rates: rufiyaa per U.S. dollar	0 101 . .	**8.785**	**9.041**	**9.552**	**10.253**	**10.569**	**10.957**	**11.586**	**11.770**

[1] Excludes components that have been classified in the categories of Group E.

Table 2. STANDARD PRESENTATION, 1988–95
(Millions of U.S. dollars)

	Code	1988	1989	1990	1991	1992	1993	1994	1995
CURRENT ACCOUNT	4 993 . .	**8.9**	**10.6**	**8.6**	**–9.0**	**–19.7**	**–47.6**	**. . .**	**. . .**
A. GOODS	4 100 . .	–42.7	–60.0	–63.1	–82.6	–116.8	–139.3	. . .	. . .
Credit	2 100 . .	**44.6**	**51.3**	**58.1**	**59.2**	**51.1**	**38.5**	**. . .**	**. . .**
General merchandise: exports f.o.b.	2 110 . .	44.6	51.3	58.1	59.2	51.1	38.5	. . .	. . .
Goods for processing: exports f.o.b.	2 150 . .	. . .	. . .	. . .	. . .	. . .	. . .	. . .	. . .
Repairs on goods	2 160 . .	. . .	. . .	. . .	. . .	. . .	. . .	. . .	. . .
Goods procured in ports by carriers	2 170 . .	. . .	. . .	. . .	. . .	. . .	. . .	. . .	. . .
Nonmonetary gold	2 180 . .	. . .	. . .	. . .	. . .	. . .	. . .	. . .	. . .
Debit	3 100 . .	**–87.3**	**–111.3**	**–121.2**	**–141.8**	**–167.9**	**–177.8**	**. . .**	**. . .**
General merchandise: imports f.o.b.	3 110 . .	–87.3	–111.3	–121.2	–141.8	–167.9	–177.8	. . .	. . .
Goods for processing: imports f.o.b.	3 150 . .	. . .	. . .	. . .	. . .	. . .	. . .	. . .	. . .
Repairs on goods	3 160 . .	. . .	. . .	. . .	. . .	. . .	. . .	. . .	. . .
Goods procured in ports by carriers	3 170 . .	. . .	. . .	. . .	. . .	. . .	. . .	. . .	. . .
Nonmonetary gold	3 180 . .	. . .	. . .	. . .	. . .	. . .	. . .	. . .	. . .
B. SERVICES	4 200 . .	54.8	69.9	81.7	83.0	118.8	122.4	. . .	. . .
Total credit	2 200 . .	*83.3*	*98.8*	*119.7*	*125.1*	*168.2*	*178.2*	. . .	. . .
Total debit	3 200 . .	*–28.5*	*–28.9*	*–38.0*	*–42.1*	*–49.4*	*–55.8*	. . .	. . .
Transportation services, credit	2 205 . .	**20.9**	**23.4**	**28.5**	**27.0**	**23.9**	**24.4**	**. . .**	**. . .**
Passenger	2 205 BA	. . .	. . .	. . .	. . .	. . .	. . .	. . .	. . .
Freight	2 205 BB	*7.7*	*7.3*	*5.7*	*5.9*	*3.6*	*4.1*	. . .	. . .
Other	2 205 BC	*13.2*	*16.1*	*22.8*	*21.1*	*20.3*	*20.3*	. . .	. . .
Sea transport, passenger	2 207 . .	. . .	. . .	. . .	. . .	. . .	. . .	. . .	. . .
Sea transport, freight	2 208 . .	. . .	. . .	. . .	. . .	. . .	. . .	. . .	. . .
Sea transport, other	2 209 . .	. . .	. . .	. . .	. . .	. . .	. . .	. . .	. . .
Air transport, passenger	2 211 . .	. . .	. . .	. . .	. . .	. . .	. . .	. . .	. . .
Air transport, freight	2 212 . .	. . .	. . .	. . .	. . .	. . .	. . .	. . .	. . .
Air transport, other	2 213 . .	. . .	. . .	. . .	. . .	. . .	. . .	. . .	. . .
Other transport, passenger	2 215 . .	. . .	. . .	. . .	. . .	. . .	. . .	. . .	. . .
Other transport, freight	2 216 . .	. . .	. . .	. . .	. . .	. . .	. . .	. . .	. . .
Other transport, other	2 217 . .	. . .	. . .	. . .	. . .	. . .	. . .	. . .	. . .
Transportation services, debit	3 205 . .	**–16.8**	**–15.7**	**–19.7**	**–19.3**	**–23.7**	**–21.9**	**. . .**	**. . .**
Passenger	3 205 BA	*–3.6*	*–5.5*	*–6.3*	*–7.5*	*–8.2*	*–7.9*	. . .	. . .
Freight	3 205 BB	*–7.9*	*–8.1*	*–9.3*	*–11.0*	*–13.6*	*–13.8*	. . .	. . .
Other	3 205 BC	*–5.3*	*–2.1*	*–4.1*	*–.8*	*–1.9*	*–.2*	. . .	. . .
Sea transport, passenger	3 207 . .	. . .	. . .	. . .	. . .	. . .	. . .	. . .	. . .
Sea transport, freight	3 208 . .	. . .	. . .	. . .	. . .	. . .	. . .	. . .	. . .
Sea transport, other	3 209 . .	. . .	. . .	. . .	. . .	. . .	. . .	. . .	. . .
Air transport, passenger	3 211 . .	. . .	. . .	. . .	. . .	. . .	. . .	. . .	. . .
Air transport, freight	3 212 . .	. . .	. . .	. . .	. . .	. . .	. . .	. . .	. . .
Air transport, other	3 213 . .	. . .	. . .	. . .	. . .	. . .	. . .	. . .	. . .
Other transport, passenger	3 215 . .	. . .	. . .	. . .	. . .	. . .	. . .	. . .	. . .
Other transport, freight	3 216 . .	. . .	. . .	. . .	. . .	. . .	. . .	. . .	. . .
Other transport, other	3 217 . .	. . .	. . .	. . .	. . .	. . .	. . .	. . .	. . .
Travel, credit	2 236 . .	**55.0**	**73.4**	**88.7**	**95.3**	**138.0**	**146.4**	**. . .**	**. . .**
Business travel	2 237 . .	. . .	. . .	. . .	. . .	. . .	. . .	. . .	. . .
Personal travel	2 240 . .	. . .	. . .	. . .	. . .	. . .	. . .	. . .	. . .
Travel, debit	3 236 . .	**–7.6**	**–10.0**	**–15.0**	**–19.1**	**–21.5**	**–29.4**	**. . .**	**. . .**
Business travel	3 237 . .	. . .	. . .	. . .	. . .	. . .	. . .	. . .	. . .
Personal travel	3 240 . .	. . .	. . .	. . .	. . .	. . .	. . .	. . .	. . .
Other services, credit	2 200 BA	**7.4**	**2.0**	**2.5**	**2.9**	**6.3**	**7.4**	**. . .**	**. . .**
Communications	2 245 . .	. . .	. . .	. . .	. . .	. . .	. . .	. . .	. . .
Construction	2 249 . .	. . .	. . .	. . .	. . .	. . .	. . .	. . .	. . .
Insurance	2 253 . .	.9	.8	.6	.7	.4	.5	. . .	. . .
Financial	2 260 . .	. . .	. . .	. . .	. . .	. . .	. . .	. . .	. . .
Computer and information	2 262 . .	. . .	. . .	. . .	. . .	. . .	. . .	. . .	. . .
Royalties and licence fees	2 266 . .	. . .	. . .	. . .	. . .	. . .	. . .	. . .	. . .
Other business services	2 268 . .	3.4	1.0	1.6	1.2	4.3	4.3	. . .	. . .
Personal, cultural, and recreational	2 287 . .	. . .	. . .	. . .	. . .	. . .	. . .	. . .	. . .
Government, n.i.e.	2 291 . .	3.1	.2	.3	1.0	1.6	2.6	. . .	. . .
Other services, debit	3 200 BA	**–4.1**	**–3.2**	**–3.3**	**–3.7**	**–4.2**	**–4.5**	**. . .**	**. . .**
Communications	3 245 . .	. . .	. . .	. . .	. . .	. . .	. . .	. . .	. . .
Construction	3 249 . .	. . .	. . .	. . .	. . .	. . .	. . .	. . .	. . .
Insurance	3 253 . .	–.9	–.9	–1.0	–1.2	–1.5	–1.5	. . .	. . .
Financial	3 260 . .	. . .	. . .	. . .	. . .	. . .	. . .	. . .	. . .
Computer and information	3 262 . .	. . .	. . .	. . .	. . .	. . .	. . .	. . .	. . .
Royalties and licence fees	3 266 . .	. . .	. . .	. . .	. . .	. . .	. . .	. . .	. . .
Other business services	3 268 . .	–2.0	–1.5	–1.4	–1.7	–1.9	–1.9	. . .	. . .
Personal, cultural, and recreational	3 287 . .	. . .	. . .	. . .	. . .	. . .	. . .	. . .	. . .
Government, n.i.e.	3 291 . .	–1.2	–.8	–.9	–.8	–.8	–1.1	. . .	. . .

Table 2 (Continued). STANDARD PRESENTATION, 1988–95
(Millions of U.S. dollars)

	Code	1988	1989	1990	1991	1992	1993	1994	1995
C. INCOME	4 300 . .	-9.7	-12.5	-13.8	-14.9	-17.1	-19.0	...	...
Total credit	2 300 . .	*2.0*	*3.8*	*4.7*	*3.8*	*2.9*	*3.0*	...	...
Total debit	3 300 . .	*-11.7*	*-16.3*	*-18.5*	*-18.7*	*-20.0*	*-22.0*	...	...
Compensation of employees, credit	2 310 . .	**1.2**	**1.4**	**1.7**	**1.8**	**1.6**	**1.3**	...	...
Compensation of employees, debit	3 310 . .	**-.9**	**-.9**	**-.8**	**-.6**	**-.4**	**-.3**	...	...
Investment income, credit	2 320 . .	**.8**	**2.4**	**3.0**	**2.0**	**1.3**	**1.7**	...	...
Direct investment income	2 330 . .	...	...	...	...	...	...	...	...
Dividends and distributed branch profits	2 332 . .	...	...	...	...	...	...	...	...
Reinvested earnings and undistributed branch profits	2 333 . .	...	...	...	...	...	...	...	...
Income on debt (interest)	2 334 . .	...	...	...	...	...	...	...	...
Portfolio investment income	2 339 . .	...	...	...	...	...	...	...	...
Income on equity	2 340 . .	...	...	...	...	...	...	...	...
Income on bonds and notes	2 350 . .	...	...	...	...	...	...	...	...
Income on money market instruments and financial derivatives	2 360 . .	...	...	...	...	...	...	...	...
Other investment income	2 370 . .	.8	2.4	3.0	2.0	1.3	1.7	...	...
Investment income, debit	3 320 . .	**-10.8**	**-15.4**	**-17.7**	**-18.1**	**-19.6**	**-21.7**	...	...
Direct investment income	3 330 . .	-7.8	-12.1	-13.9	-15.6	-16.8	-17.6	...	...
Dividends and distributed branch profits	3 332 . .	-6.6	-7.7	-8.3	-9.1	-10.2	-10.7	...	...
Reinvested earnings and undistributed branch profits	3 333 . .	-1.2	-4.4	-5.6	-6.5	-6.6	-6.9	...	...
Income on debt (interest)	3 334 . .	...	...	...	...	...	...	...	...
Portfolio investment income	3 339 . .	...	...	...	...	...	...	...	...
Income on equity	3 340 . .	...	...	...	...	...	...	...	...
Income on bonds and notes	3 350 . .	...	...	...	...	...	...	...	...
Income on money market instruments and financial derivatives	3 360 . .	...	...	...	...	...	...	...	...
Other investment income	3 370 . .	-3.0	-3.3	-3.8	-2.5	-2.8	-4.1	...	...
D. CURRENT TRANSFERS	4 379 . .	6.5	13.2	3.8	5.5	-4.6	-11.7	...	...
Credit	2 379 . .	**11.5**	**18.3**	**11.2**	**22.1**	**14.3**	**8.3**	...	...
General government	2 380 . .	11.5	18.3	11.2	22.1	14.3	8.3	...	...
Other sectors	2 390 . .	...	...	...	...	...	...	...	...
Workers' remittances	2 391 . .	...	...	...	...	...	...	...	...
Other current transfers	2 392 . .	...	...	...	...	...	...	...	...
Debit	3 379 . .	**-5.0**	**-5.1**	**-7.4**	**-16.6**	**-18.9**	**-20.0**	...	...
General government	3 380 . .	...	...	...	...	...	...	...	...
Other sectors	3 390 . .	-5.0	-5.1	-7.4	-16.6	-18.9	-20.0	...	...
Workers' remittances	3 391 . .	-5.0	-5.1	-7.4	-16.6	-18.9	-20.0	...	...
Other current transfers	3 392 . .	...	...	...	...	...	...	...	...
CAPITAL AND FINANCIAL ACCOUNT	4 996 . .	**-15.1**	**9.5**	**9.2**	**6.4**	**20.7**	**25.0**	...	...
CAPITAL ACCOUNT	4 994 . .	...	...	...	...	...	...	...	...
Total credit	2 994 . .	...	...	...	...	...	...	...	...
Total debit	3 994 . .	...	...	...	...	...	...	...	...
Capital transfers, credit	2 400 . .	...	...	...	...	...	...	...	...
General government	2 401 . .	...	...	...	...	...	...	...	...
Debt forgiveness	2 402 . .	...	...	...	...	...	...	...	...
Other capital transfers	2 410 . .	...	...	...	...	...	...	...	...
Other sectors	2 430 . .	...	...	...	...	...	...	...	...
Migrants' transfers	2 431 . .	...	...	...	...	...	...	...	...
Debt forgiveness	2 432 . .	...	...	...	...	...	...	...	...
Other capital transfers	2 440 . .	...	...	...	...	...	...	...	...
Capital transfers, debit	3 400 . .	...	...	...	...	...	...	...	...
General government	3 401 . .	...	...	...	...	...	...	...	...
Debt forgiveness	3 402 . .	...	...	...	...	...	...	...	...
Other capital transfers	3 410 . .	...	...	...	...	...	...	...	...
Other sectors	3 430 . .	...	...	...	...	...	...	...	...
Migrants' transfers	3 431 . .	...	...	...	...	...	...	...	...
Debt forgiveness	3 432 . .	...	...	...	...	...	...	...	...
Other capital transfers	3 440 . .	...	...	...	...	...	...	...	...
Nonproduced nonfinancial assets, credit	2 480 . .	...	...	...	...	...	...	...	...
Nonproduced nonfinancial assets, debit	3 480 . .	...	...	...	...	...	...	...	...

Table 2 (Continued). STANDARD PRESENTATION, 1988–95
(Millions of U.S. dollars)

	Code		1988	1989	1990	1991	1992	1993	1994	1995
FINANCIAL ACCOUNT	4 995	. .	**–15.1**	**9.5**	**9.2**	**6.4**	**20.7**	**25.0**	**. . .**	**. . .**
A. DIRECT INVESTMENT	4 500	. .	1.2	4.4	5.6	6.5	6.6	6.9	. . .	. . .
Direct investment abroad	4 505	. .	**. . .**	**. . .**	**. . .**	**. . .**	**. . .**	**. . .**	**. . .**	**. . .**
Equity capital	4 510	. .	. . .	. . .	. . .	. . .	. . .	. . .	. . .	. . .
Claims on affiliated enterprises	4 515	. .	. . .	. . .	. . .	. . .	. . .	. . .	. . .	. . .
Liabilities to affiliated enterprises	4 520	. .	. . .	. . .	. . .	. . .	. . .	. . .	. . .	. . .
Reinvested earnings	4 525	. .	. . .	. . .	. . .	. . .	. . .	. . .	. . .	. . .
Other capital	4 530	. .	. . .	. . .	. . .	. . .	. . .	. . .	. . .	. . .
Claims on affiliated enterprises	4 535	. .	. . .	. . .	. . .	. . .	. . .	. . .	. . .	. . .
Liabilities to affiliated enterprises	4 540	. .	. . .	. . .	. . .	. . .	. . .	. . .	. . .	. . .
Direct investment in Maldives	4 555	. .	**1.2**	**4.4**	**5.6**	**6.5**	**6.6**	**6.9**	**. . .**	**. . .**
Equity capital	4 560	. .	. . .	. . .	. . .	. . .	. . .	. . .	. . .	. . .
Claims on direct investors	4 565	. .	. . .	. . .	. . .	. . .	. . .	. . .	. . .	. . .
Liabilities to direct investors	4 570	. .	. . .	. . .	. . .	. . .	. . .	. . .	. . .	. . .
Reinvested earnings	4 575	. .	1.2	4.4	5.6	6.5	6.6	6.9	. . .	. . .
Other capital	4 580	. .	. . .	. . .	. . .	. . .	. . .	. . .	. . .	. . .
Claims on direct investors	4 585	. .	. . .	. . .	. . .	. . .	. . .	. . .	. . .	. . .
Liabilities to direct investors	4 590	. .	. . .	. . .	. . .	. . .	. . .	. . .	. . .	. . .
B. PORTFOLIO INVESTMENT	4 600	. .	. . .	. . .	. . .	. . .	. . .	. . .	. . .	. . .
Assets	4 602	. .	**. . .**	**. . .**	**. . .**	**. . .**	**. . .**	**. . .**	**. . .**	**. . .**
Equity securities	4 610	. .	. . .	. . .	. . .	. . .	. . .	. . .	. . .	. . .
Monetary authorities	4 611	. .	. . .	. . .	. . .	. . .	. . .	. . .	. . .	. . .
General government	4 612	. .	. . .	. . .	. . .	. . .	. . .	. . .	. . .	. . .
Banks	4 613	. .	. . .	. . .	. . .	. . .	. . .	. . .	. . .	. . .
Other sectors	4 614	. .	. . .	. . .	. . .	. . .	. . .	. . .	. . .	. . .
Debt securities	4 619	. .	. . .	. . .	. . .	. . .	. . .	. . .	. . .	. . .
Bonds and notes	4 620	. .	. . .	. . .	. . .	. . .	. . .	. . .	. . .	. . .
Monetary authorities	4 621	. .	. . .	. . .	. . .	. . .	. . .	. . .	. . .	. . .
General government	4 622	. .	. . .	. . .	. . .	. . .	. . .	. . .	. . .	. . .
Banks	4 623	. .	. . .	. . .	. . .	. . .	. . .	. . .	. . .	. . .
Other sectors	4 624	. .	. . .	. . .	. . .	. . .	. . .	. . .	. . .	. . .
Money market instruments	4 630	. .	. . .	. . .	. . .	. . .	. . .	. . .	. . .	. . .
Monetary authorities	4 631	. .	. . .	. . .	. . .	. . .	. . .	. . .	. . .	. . .
General government	4 632	. .	. . .	. . .	. . .	. . .	. . .	. . .	. . .	. . .
Banks	4 633	. .	. . .	. . .	. . .	. . .	. . .	. . .	. . .	. . .
Other sectors	4 634	. .	. . .	. . .	. . .	. . .	. . .	. . .	. . .	. . .
Financial derivatives	4 640	. .	. . .	. . .	. . .	. . .	. . .	. . .	. . .	. . .
Monetary authorities	4 641	. .	. . .	. . .	. . .	. . .	. . .	. . .	. . .	. . .
General government	4 642	. .	. . .	. . .	. . .	. . .	. . .	. . .	. . .	. . .
Banks	4 643	. .	. . .	. . .	. . .	. . .	. . .	. . .	. . .	. . .
Other sectors	4 644	. .	. . .	. . .	. . .	. . .	. . .	. . .	. . .	. . .
Liabilities	4 652	. .	**. . .**	**. . .**	**. . .**	**. . .**	**. . .**	**. . .**	**. . .**	**. . .**
Equity securities	4 660	. .	. . .	. . .	. . .	. . .	. . .	. . .	. . .	. . .
Banks	4 663	. .	. . .	. . .	. . .	. . .	. . .	. . .	. . .	. . .
Other sectors	4 664	. .	. . .	. . .	. . .	. . .	. . .	. . .	. . .	. . .
Debt securities	4 669	. .	. . .	. . .	. . .	. . .	. . .	. . .	. . .	. . .
Bonds and notes	4 670	. .	. . .	. . .	. . .	. . .	. . .	. . .	. . .	. . .
Monetary authorities	4 671	. .	. . .	. . .	. . .	. . .	. . .	. . .	. . .	. . .
General government	4 672	. .	. . .	. . .	. . .	. . .	. . .	. . .	. . .	. . .
Banks	4 673	. .	. . .	. . .	. . .	. . .	. . .	. . .	. . .	. . .
Other sectors	4 674	. .	. . .	. . .	. . .	. . .	. . .	. . .	. . .	. . .
Money market instruments	4 680	. .	. . .	. . .	. . .	. . .	. . .	. . .	. . .	. . .
Monetary authorities	4 681	. .	. . .	. . .	. . .	. . .	. . .	. . .	. . .	. . .
General government	4 682	. .	. . .	. . .	. . .	. . .	. . .	. . .	. . .	. . .
Banks	4 683	. .	. . .	. . .	. . .	. . .	. . .	. . .	. . .	. . .
Other sectors	4 684	. .	. . .	. . .	. . .	. . .	. . .	. . .	. . .	. . .
Financial derivatives	4 690	. .	. . .	. . .	. . .	. . .	. . .	. . .	. . .	. . .
Monetary authorities	4 691	. .	. . .	. . .	. . .	. . .	. . .	. . .	. . .	. . .
General government	4 692	. .	. . .	. . .	. . .	. . .	. . .	. . .	. . .	. . .
Banks	4 693	. .	. . .	. . .	. . .	. . .	. . .	. . .	. . .	. . .
Other sectors	4 694	. .	. . .	. . .	. . .	. . .	. . .	. . .	. . .	. . .

Table 2 (Concluded). STANDARD PRESENTATION, 1988–95
(Millions of U.S. dollars)

	Code	1988	1989	1990	1991	1992	1993	1994	1995
C. OTHER INVESTMENT	4 700	−2.7	7.4	3.3	−1.1	18.9	18.0	...	...
Assets	4 703	**1.6**	**−2.9**	**−2.2**	**−2.2**	**−1.8**	**4.3**	...	...
Trade credits	4 706	...	...	...	...	...	...	...	...
General government: long-term	4 708	...	...	...	...	...	...	...	...
General government: short-term	4 709	...	...	...	...	...	...	...	...
Other sectors: long-term	4 711	...	...	...	...	...	...	...	...
Other sectors: short-term	4 712	...	...	...	...	...	...	...	...
Loans	4 714	...	...	...	...	...	...	...	...
Monetary authorities: long-term	4 717	...	...	...	...	...	...	...	...
Monetary authorities: short-term	4 718	...	...	...	...	...	...	...	...
General government: long-term	4 720	...	...	...	...	...	...	...	...
General government: short-term	4 721	...	...	...	...	...	...	...	...
Banks: long-term	4 723	...	...	...	...	...	...	...	...
Banks: short-term	4 724	...	...	...	...	...	...	...	...
Other sectors: long-term	4 726	...	...	...	...	...	...	...	...
Other sectors: short-term	4 727	...	...	...	...	...	...	...	...
Currency and deposits	4 730	1.6	−2.9	−2.2	−2.2	−1.8	4.3	...	...
Monetary authorities	4 731	...	...	...	...	...	...	...	...
General government	4 732	...	...	...	...	...	...	...	...
Banks	4 733	1.6	−2.9	−2.2	−2.2	−1.8	4.3	...	...
Other sectors	4 734	...	...	...	...	...	...	...	...
Other assets	4 736	...	...	...	...	...	...	...	...
Monetary authorities: long-term	4 738	...	...	...	...	...	...	...	...
Monetary authorities: short-term	4 739	...	...	...	...	...	...	...	...
General government: long-term	4 741	...	...	...	...	...	...	...	...
General government: short-term	4 742	...	...	...	...	...	...	...	...
Banks: long-term	4 744	...	...	...	...	...	...	...	...
Banks: short-term	4 745	...	...	...	...	...	...	...	...
Other sectors: long-term	4 747	...	...	...	...	...	...	...	...
Other sectors: short-term	4 748	...	...	...	...	...	...	...	...
Liabilities	4 753	**−4.3**	**10.3**	**5.5**	**1.1**	**20.7**	**13.7**	...	...
Trade credits	4 756	...	...	...	...	...	...	...	...
General government: long-term	4 758	...	...	...	...	...	...	...	...
General government: short-term	4 759	...	...	...	...	...	...	...	...
Other sectors: long-term	4 761	...	...	...	...	...	...	...	...
Other sectors: short-term	4 762	...	...	...	...	...	...	...	...
Loans	4 764	−2.2	1.0	5.9	11.2	16.4	2.2	...	...
Use of Fund credit and loans from the Fund	4 766	...	...	...	...	...	...	...	...
Monetary authorities: other long-term	4 767	...	...	...	...	...	...	...	...
Monetary authorities: short-term	4 768	...	...	...	...	...	...	...	...
General government: long-term	4 770	−2.2	1.0	5.9	11.2	16.4	2.2	...	...
General government: short-term	4 771	...	...	...	...	...	...	...	...
Banks: long-term	4 773	...	...	...	...	...	...	...	...
Banks: short-term	4 774	...	...	...	...	...	...	...	...
Other sectors: long-term	4 776	...	...	...	...	...	...	...	...
Other sectors: short-term	4 777	...	...	...	...	...	...	...	...
Currency and deposits	4 780	−2.2	9.3	−.4	−10.1	4.3	−3.7	...	...
Monetary authorities	4 781	...	...	...	...	...	...	...	...
General government	4 782	...	...	...	...	...	...	...	...
Banks	4 783	−2.2	9.3	−.4	−10.1	4.3	−3.7	...	...
Other sectors	4 784	...	...	...	...	...	...	...	...
Other liabilities	4 786	.1	...	...	...	...	15.2	...	...
Monetary authorities: long-term	4 788	...	...	...	...	...	...	...	...
Monetary authorities: short-term	4 789	.1	...	...	...	...	15.2	...	...
General government: long-term	4 791	...	...	...	...	...	...	...	...
General government: short-term	4 792	...	...	...	...	...	...	...	...
Banks: long-term	4 794	...	...	...	...	...	...	...	...
Banks: short-term	4 795	...	...	...	...	...	...	...	...
Other sectors: long-term	4 797	...	...	...	...	...	...	...	...
Other sectors: short-term	4 798	...	...	...	...	...	...	...	...
D. RESERVE ASSETS	4 800	−13.6	−2.3	.3	1.0	−4.8	.1	...	...
Monetary gold	4 810	...	...	...	...	...	...	...	...
Special drawing rights	4 820	...	...	...	...	...	...	...	...
Reserve position in the Fund	4 830	...	...	...	...	−1.2	...	...	...
Foreign exchange	4 840	−13.6	−2.3	.3	1.0	−3.6	.1	...	...
Other claims	4 880	...	...	...	...	...	...	...	...
NET ERRORS AND OMISSIONS	4 998	**6.2**	**−20.1**	**−17.8**	**2.6**	**−1.0**	**22.6**	...	...

Part 3 of the *Yearbook* contains descriptions of the methodologies, compilation practices, and sources used to compile these data.

Table 1. ANALYTIC PRESENTATION, 1988–95
(Millions of U.S. dollars)

	Code	1988	1989	1990	1991	1992	1993	1994	1995
A. Current Account[1]	4 993 Y.	**–233.7**	**–190.6**	**–250.1**	**–175.9**	**–253.1**	**–213.4**	**–164.4**	**. . .**
Goods: exports f.o.b	2 100 . .	251.5	269.3	337.9	355.9	335.9	341.1	319.7	. . .
Goods: imports f.o.b	3 100 . .	–359.1	–338.8	–432.4	–446.9	–484.5	–446.5	–421.6	. . .
Balance on Goods	4 100 . .	*–107.6*	*–69.5*	*–94.5*	*–91.0*	*–148.6*	*–105.3*	*–101.9*	. . .
Services: credit	2 200 . .	83.6	69.0	80.1	69.8	75.0	75.4	66.8	. . .
Services: debit	3 200 . .	–344.6	–317.0	–395.1	–374.9	–406.5	–388.6	–324.0	. . .
Balance on Goods and Services	4 991 . .	*–368.6*	*–317.5*	*–409.5*	*–396.1*	*–480.2*	*–418.6*	*–359.1*	. . .
Income: credit	2 300 . .	4.4	6.6	19.5	11.7	12.8	25.1	5.4	. . .
Income: debit	3 300 . .	–27.5	–36.7	–61.0	–36.9	–43.1	–38.1	–41.2	. . .
Balance on Goods, Services, and Income	4 992 . .	*–391.8*	*–347.6*	*–451.0*	*–421.2*	*–510.4*	*–431.7*	*–395.0*	. . .
Current transfers: credit	2 379 Y.	235.7	232.1	291.5	333.0	344.9	300.2	275.8	. . .
Current transfers: debit	3 379 . .	–77.6	–75.0	–90.6	–87.7	–87.6	–81.9	–45.2	. . .
B. Capital Account[1]	4 994 Y.	**142.0**	**107.8**	**105.8**	**137.5**	**143.6**	**111.9**	**111.7**	**. . .**
Capital account: credit	2 994 Y.	142.0	107.8	105.8	137.5	143.6	111.9	111.7	. . .
Capital account: debit	3 994 . .	. . .	. . .	. . .	. . .	. . .	. . .	. . .	. . .
Total, Groups A Plus B	4 010 . .	*–91.7*	*–82.8*	*–144.3*	*–38.4*	*–109.6*	*–101.5*	*–52.8*	. . .
C. Financial Account[1]	4 995 X.	**138.8**	**96.9**	**77.6**	**52.8**	**3.0**	**–25.8**	**–5.9**	**. . .**
Direct investment abroad	4 505 . .	. . .	. . .	. . .	. . .	. . .	. . .	. . .	. . .
Direct investment in Mali	4 555 Y.	.7	15.0	–6.6	3.5	–7.6	–20.1	45.0	. . .
Portfolio investment assets	4 602 . .	. . .	. . .	. . .	. . .	. . .	. . .	. . .	. . .
Equity securities	4 610 . .	. . .	. . .	. . .	. . .	. . .	. . .	. . .	. . .
Debt securities	4 619 . .	. . .	. . .	. . .	. . .	. . .	. . .	. . .	. . .
Portfolio investment liabilities	4 652 Y.	. . .	. . .	. . .	. . .	. . .	. . .	. . .	. . .
Equity securities	4 660 Y.	. . .	. . .	. . .	. . .	. . .	. . .	. . .	. . .
Debt securities	4 669 Y.	. . .	. . .	. . .	. . .	. . .	. . .	. . .	. . .
Other investment assets	4 703 . .	4.6	–39.4	–.1	9.6	17.5	11.9	–100.3	. . .
Monetary authorities	4 703 .A	. . .	. . .	. . .	. . .	. . .	. . .	. . .	. . .
General government	4 703 .B	. . .	. . .	. . .	. . .	. . .	. . .	. . .	. . .
Banks	4 703 .C	4.6	–39.4	–.1	9.6	17.5	11.9	–100.3	. . .
Other sectors	4 703 .D	. . .	. . .	. . .	. . .	. . .	. . .	. . .	. . .
Other investment liabilities	4 753 X.	133.5	121.3	84.4	39.6	–7.0	–17.6	49.4	. . .
Monetary authorities	4 753 XA	. . .	. . .	. . .	. . .	. . .	. . .	. . .	. . .
General government	4 753 YB	126.5	121.3	82.6	65.2	12.8	–18.0	44.7	. . .
Banks	4 753 YC	6.9	–.1	1.7	–25.6	–19.8	.4	4.7	. . .
Other sectors	4 753 YD	. . .	. . .	. . .	. . .	. . .	. . .	. . .	. . .
Total, Groups A Through C	4 020 . .	*47.1*	*14.1*	*–66.7*	*14.4*	*–106.5*	*–127.3*	*–58.6*	. . .
D. Net Errors and Omissions	4 998 . .	**–1.5**	**–1.5**	**1.1**	**14.6**	**–31.0**	**30.1**	**–5.1**	**. . .**
Total, Groups A Through D	4 030 . .	*45.7*	*12.6*	*–65.6*	*29.0*	*–137.6*	*–97.2*	*–63.7*	. . .
E. Reserves and Related Items	4 040 . .	**–45.7**	**–12.6**	**65.6**	**–29.0**	**137.6**	**97.2**	**63.7**	**. . .**
Reserve assets	4 800 . .	–61.9	–71.9	–54.8	–119.8	–7.6	–45.8	–30.7	. . .
Use of Fund credit and loans	4 766 . .	–7.6	–16.6	8.3	–9.2	8.4	5.6	32.7	. . .
Liabilities constituting foreign authorities' reserves	4 900 . .	. . .	. . .	. . .	. . .	. . .	. . .	. . .	. . .
Exceptional financing	4 920 . .	23.9	75.9	112.0	100.0	136.8	137.4	61.8	. . .
Conversion rates: CFA francs per U.S. dollar	0 101 . .	**297.85**	**319.01**	**272.26**	**282.11**	**264.69**	**283.16**	**555.20**	**499.15**

[1] Excludes components that have been classified in the categories of Group E.

Table 2. STANDARD PRESENTATION, 1988–95
(*Millions of U.S. dollars*)

	Code		1988	1989	1990	1991	1992	1993	1994	1995
CURRENT ACCOUNT	4 993	. .	**–232.0**	**–185.6**	**–250.1**	**–175.9**	**–253.1**	**–213.4**	**–164.4**	. . .
A. GOODS	4 100	. .	–107.6	–69.5	–94.5	–91.0	–148.6	–105.3	–101.9	. . .
Credit	2 100	. .	**251.5**	**269.3**	**337.9**	**355.9**	**335.9**	**341.1**	**319.7**	. . .
General merchandise: exports f.o.b.	2 110	. .	251.5	269.3	337.9	355.9	335.9	341.1	319.7	. . .
Goods for processing: exports f.o.b.	2 150	. .	. . .	. . .	. . .	. . .	. . .	. . .	. . .	. . .
Repairs on goods	2 160	. .	. . .	. . .	. . .	. . .	. . .	. . .	. . .	. . .
Goods procured in ports by carriers	2 170	. .	. . .	. . .	. . .	. . .	. . .	. . .	. . .	. . .
Nonmonetary gold	2 180	. .	. . .	. . .	. . .	. . .	. . .	. . .	. . .	. . .
Debit	3 100	. .	**–359.1**	**–338.8**	**–432.4**	**–446.9**	**–484.5**	**–446.5**	**–421.6**	. . .
General merchandise: imports f.o.b.	3 110	. .	–359.1	–338.8	–432.4	–446.9	–484.5	–446.5	–421.6	. . .
Goods for processing: imports f.o.b.	3 150	. .	. . .	. . .	. . .	. . .	. . .	. . .	. . .	. . .
Repairs on goods	3 160	. .	. . .	. . .	. . .	. . .	. . .	. . .	. . .	. . .
Goods procured in ports by carriers	3 170	. .	. . .	. . .	. . .	. . .	. . .	. . .	. . .	. . .
Nonmonetary gold	3 180	. .	. . .	. . .	. . .	. . .	. . .	. . .	. . .	. . .
B. SERVICES	4 200	. .	–261.0	–248.0	–315.0	–305.1	–331.6	–313.3	–257.2	. . .
Total credit	2 200	. .	*83.6*	*69.0*	*80.1*	*69.8*	*75.0*	*75.4*	*66.8*	. . .
Total debit	3 200	. .	*–344.6*	*–317.0*	*–395.1*	*–374.9*	*–406.5*	*–388.6*	*–324.0*	. . .
Transportation services, credit	2 205	. .	**19.5**	**3.1**	**4.0**	**30.5**	**32.5**	**31.1**	**25.5**	. . .
Passenger	2 205	BA	*11.1*	. . .	. . .	*24.8*	*27.2*	*25.4*	*20.0*	. . .
Freight	2 205	BB	*8.5*	*3.1*	*4.0*	*5.7*	*5.3*	*5.7*	*5.5*	. . .
Other	2 205	BC	. . .	. . .	. . .	. . .	. . .	. . .	. . .	. . .
Sea transport, passenger	2 207	. .	. . .	. . .	. . .	. . .	. . .	. . .	. . .	. . .
Sea transport, freight	2 208	. .	. . .	. . .	. . .	. . .	. . .	. . .	. . .	. . .
Sea transport, other	2 209	. .	. . .	. . .	. . .	. . .	. . .	. . .	. . .	. . .
Air transport, passenger	2 211	. .	. . .	. . .	. . .	. . .	. . .	. . .	. . .	. . .
Air transport, freight	2 212	. .	. . .	. . .	. . .	. . .	. . .	. . .	. . .	. . .
Air transport, other	2 213	. .	. . .	. . .	. . .	. . .	. . .	. . .	. . .	. . .
Other transport, passenger	2 215	. .	11.1	. . .	. . .	24.8	27.2	25.4	20.0	. . .
Other transport, freight	2 216	. .	8.5	3.1	4.0	5.7	5.3	5.7	5.5	. . .
Other transport, other	2 217	. .	. . .	. . .	. . .	. . .	. . .	. . .	. . .	. . .
Transportation services, debit	3 205	. .	**–169.4**	**–160.8**	**–193.6**	**–199.0**	**–215.1**	**–207.0**	**–165.5**	. . .
Passenger	3 205	BA	. . .	. . .	. . .	. . .	. . .	. . .	. . .	. . .
Freight	3 205	BB	*–138.5*	*–130.7*	*–166.8*	*–172.8*	*–185.6*	*–178.8*	*–162.6*	. . .
Other	3 205	BC	*–30.9*	*–30.1*	*–26.8*	*–26.2*	*–29.5*	*–28.3*	*–2.9*	. . .
Sea transport, passenger	3 207	. .	. . .	. . .	. . .	. . .	. . .	. . .	. . .	. . .
Sea transport, freight	3 208	. .	–55.4	–52.3	–66.7	–69.3	–74.6	–71.5	–65.0	. . .
Sea transport, other	3 209	. .	–30.9	–30.1	–26.8	–26.2	–29.5	–28.3	–2.9	. . .
Air transport, passenger	3 211	. .	. . .	. . .	. . .	. . .	. . .	. . .	. . .	. . .
Air transport, freight	3 212	. .	. . .	. . .	. . .	. . .	. . .	. . .	. . .	. . .
Air transport, other	3 213	. .	. . .	. . .	. . .	. . .	. . .	. . .	. . .	. . .
Other transport, passenger	3 215	. .	. . .	. . .	. . .	. . .	. . .	. . .	. . .	. . .
Other transport, freight	3 216	. .	–83.1	–78.4	–100.1	–103.5	–111.0	–107.3	–97.6	. . .
Other transport, other	3 217	. .	. . .	. . .	. . .	. . .	. . .	. . .	. . .	. . .
Travel, credit	2 236	. .	**37.6**	**38.6**	**47.4**	**10.6**	**11.3**	**13.1**	**18.0**	. . .
Business travel	2 237	. .	. . .	. . .	. . .	. . .	. . .	. . .	. . .	. . .
Personal travel	2 240	. .	. . .	. . .	. . .	. . .	. . .	. . .	. . .	. . .
Travel, debit	3 236	. .	**–57.7**	**–55.8**	**–62.4**	**–60.3**	**–64.6**	**–60.0**	**–54.0**	. . .
Business travel	3 237	. .	. . .	. . .	. . .	. . .	. . .	. . .	. . .	. . .
Personal travel	3 240	. .	. . .	. . .	. . .	. . .	. . .	. . .	. . .	. . .
Other services, credit	2 200	BA	**26.5**	**27.3**	**28.7**	**28.7**	**31.1**	**31.2**	**23.3**	. . .
Communications	2 245	. .	. . .	. . .	. . .	. . .	. . .	. . .	. . .	. . .
Construction	2 249	. .	. . .	. . .	. . .	. . .	. . .	. . .	. . .	. . .
Insurance	2 253	. .	.9	.3	.4	1.1	.5	.5	.6	. . .
Financial	2 260	. .	. . .	. . .	. . .	. . .	. . .	. . .	. . .	. . .
Computer and information	2 262	. .	. . .	. . .	. . .	. . .	. . .	. . .	. . .	. . .
Royalties and licence fees	2 266	. .	. . .	. . .	. . .	. . .	. . .	. . .	. . .	. . .
Other business services	2 268	. .	8.1	10.3	8.1	7.4	7.9	8.1	7.7	. . .
Personal, cultural, and recreational	2 287	. .	. . .	. . .	. . .	. . .	. . .	. . .	. . .	. . .
Government, n.i.e.	2 291	. .	17.5	16.6	20.2	20.2	22.7	22.6	14.9	. . .
Other services, debit	3 200	BA	**–117.5**	**–100.4**	**–139.0**	**–115.6**	**–126.8**	**–121.6**	**–104.5**	. . .
Communications	3 245	. .	. . .	. . .	. . .	. . .	. . .	. . .	. . .	. . .
Construction	3 249	. .	. . .	. . .	. . .	. . .	. . .	. . .	. . .	. . .
Insurance	3 253	. .	–15.4	–14.5	–18.5	–19.2	–20.6	–19.9	–18.1	. . .
Financial	3 260	. .	. . .	. . .	. . .	. . .	. . .	. . .	. . .	. . .
Computer and information	3 262	. .	. . .	. . .	. . .	. . .	. . .	. . .	. . .	. . .
Royalties and licence fees	3 266	. .	. . .	. . .	. . .	. . .	. . .	. . .	. . .	. . .
Other business services	3 268	. .	–76.9	–63.3	–92.9	–69.5	–76.7	–74.2	–64.8	. . .
Personal, cultural, and recreational	3 287	. .	. . .	. . .	. . .	. . .	. . .	. . .	. . .	. . .
Government, n.i.e.	3 291	. .	–25.2	–22.6	–27.5	–26.9	–29.5	–27.5	–21.6	. . .

Table 2 (Continued). STANDARD PRESENTATION, 1988–95
(Millions of U.S. dollars)

	Code	1988	1989	1990	1991	1992	1993	1994	1995
C. INCOME	4 300 . .	–23.2	–30.1	–41.5	–25.2	–30.2	–13.1	–35.8	. . .
Total credit	2 300 . .	*4.4*	*6.6*	*19.5*	*11.7*	*12.8*	*25.1*	*5.4*	. . .
Total debit	3 300 . .	*–27.5*	*–36.7*	*–61.0*	*–36.9*	*–43.1*	*–38.1*	*–41.2*	. . .
Compensation of employees, credit	2 310 . .	**. . .**	**. . .**	**. . .**	**. . .**	**. . .**	**. . .**	**. . .**	**. . .**
Compensation of employees, debit	3 310 . .	**. . .**	**. . .**	**. . .**	**. . .**	**. . .**	**. . .**	**. . .**	**. . .**
Investment income, credit	2 320 . .	**4.4**	**6.6**	**19.5**	**11.7**	**12.8**	**25.1**	**5.4**	**. . .**
Direct investment income	2 330 . .	. . .	. . .	. . .	. . .	. . .	. . .	. . .	. . .
Dividends and distributed branch profits	2 332 . .	. . .	. . .	. . .	. . .	. . .	. . .	. . .	. . .
Reinvested earnings and undistributed branch profits	2 333 . .	. . .	. . .	. . .	. . .	. . .	. . .	. . .	. . .
Income on debt (interest)	2 334 . .	. . .	. . .	. . .	. . .	. . .	. . .	. . .	. . .
Portfolio investment income	2 339 . .	. . .	. . .	. . .	. . .	. . .	. . .	. . .	. . .
Income on equity	2 340 . .	. . .	. . .	. . .	. . .	. . .	. . .	. . .	. . .
Income on bonds and notes	2 350 . .	. . .	. . .	. . .	. . .	. . .	. . .	. . .	. . .
Income on money market instruments and financial derivatives	2 360 . .	. . .	. . .	. . .	. . .	. . .	. . .	. . .	. . .
Other investment income	2 370 . .	4.4	6.6	19.5	11.7	12.8	25.1	5.4	. . .
Investment income, debit	3 320 . .	**–27.5**	**–36.7**	**–61.0**	**–36.9**	**–43.1**	**–38.1**	**–41.2**	**. . .**
Direct investment income	3 330 . .	. . .	–8.2	–23.9	–.7	–1.9	–4.2	–1.8	. . .
Dividends and distributed branch profits	3 332 . .	. . .	–3.4	–14.7	–.7	–1.9	–4.2	–1.8	. . .
Reinvested earnings and undistributed branch profits	3 333 . .	. . .	–4.7	–9.2	. . .	. . .	. . .	. . .	. . .
Income on debt (interest)	3 334 . .	. . .	. . .	. . .	. . .	. . .	. . .	. . .	. . .
Portfolio investment income	3 339 . .	. . .	. . .	. . .	. . .	. . .	. . .	. . .	. . .
Income on equity	3 340 . .	. . .	. . .	. . .	. . .	. . .	. . .	. . .	. . .
Income on bonds and notes	3 350 . .	. . .	. . .	. . .	. . .	. . .	. . .	. . .	. . .
Income on money market instruments and financial derivatives	3 360 . .	. . .	. . .	. . .	. . .	. . .	. . .	. . .	. . .
Other investment income	3 370 . .	–27.5	–28.5	–37.1	–36.2	–41.2	–33.9	–39.4	. . .
D. CURRENT TRANSFERS	4 379 . .	159.8	162.1	200.9	245.3	257.3	218.2	230.5	. . .
Credit	2 379 . .	**237.4**	**237.1**	**291.5**	**333.0**	**344.9**	**300.2**	**275.8**	**. . .**
General government	2 380 . .	107.8	104.7	128.2	164.5	171.1	121.1	150.2	. . .
Other sectors	2 390 . .	129.6	132.4	163.3	168.5	173.8	179.0	125.5	. . .
Workers' remittances	2 391 . .	94.3	99.3	124.9	127.6	141.7	134.2	94.0	. . .
Other current transfers	2 392 . .	35.3	33.1	38.4	40.9	32.1	44.9	31.5	. . .
Debit	3 379 . .	**–77.6**	**–75.0**	**–90.6**	**–87.7**	**–87.6**	**–81.9**	**–45.2**	**. . .**
General government	3 380 . .	–6.7	–6.6	–7.7	–7.8	–8.3	–7.8	–4.5	. . .
Other sectors	3 390 . .	–70.8	–68.5	–82.9	–79.9	–79.3	–74.2	–40.7	. . .
Workers' remittances	3 391 . .	–45.3	–44.3	–53.8	–51.9	–51.0	–47.7	–25.2	. . .
Other current transfers	3 392 . .	–25.5	–24.1	–29.1	–28.0	–28.3	–26.5	–15.5	. . .
CAPITAL AND FINANCIAL ACCOUNT	4 996 . .	**233.5**	**187.1**	**249.0**	**161.3**	**284.1**	**183.3**	**169.5**	**. . .**
CAPITAL ACCOUNT	4 994 . .	**144.0**	**111.0**	**116.8**	**149.2**	**155.3**	**123.6**	**115.8**	**. . .**
Total credit	2 994 . .	*144.0*	*111.0*	*116.8*	*149.2*	*155.3*	*123.6*	*115.8*	. . .
Total debit	3 994 . .	. . .	. . .	. . .	. . .	. . .	. . .	. . .	. . .
Capital transfers, credit	2 400 . .	**144.0**	**111.0**	**116.8**	**149.2**	**155.3**	**123.6**	**115.8**	**. . .**
General government	2 401 . .	144.0	111.0	116.8	149.2	155.3	123.6	115.8	. . .
Debt forgiveness	2 402 . .	2.0	3.1	11.0	11.7	11.7	11.7	4.1	. . .
Other capital transfers	2 410 . .	142.0	107.8	105.8	137.5	143.6	111.9	111.7	. . .
Other sectors	2 430 . .	. . .	. . .	. . .	. . .	. . .	. . .	. . .	. . .
Migrants' transfers	2 431 . .	. . .	. . .	. . .	. . .	. . .	. . .	. . .	. . .
Debt forgiveness	2 432 . .	. . .	. . .	. . .	. . .	. . .	. . .	. . .	. . .
Other capital transfers	2 440 . .	. . .	. . .	. . .	. . .	. . .	. . .	. . .	. . .
Capital transfers, debit	3 400 . .	**. . .**	**. . .**	**. . .**	**. . .**	**. . .**	**. . .**	**. . .**	**. . .**
General government	3 401 . .	. . .	. . .	. . .	. . .	. . .	. . .	. . .	. . .
Debt forgiveness	3 402 . .	. . .	. . .	. . .	. . .	. . .	. . .	. . .	. . .
Other capital transfers	3 410 . .	. . .	. . .	. . .	. . .	. . .	. . .	. . .	. . .
Other sectors	3 430 . .	. . .	. . .	. . .	. . .	. . .	. . .	. . .	. . .
Migrants' transfers	3 431 . .	. . .	. . .	. . .	. . .	. . .	. . .	. . .	. . .
Debt forgiveness	3 432 . .	. . .	. . .	. . .	. . .	. . .	. . .	. . .	. . .
Other capital transfers	3 440 . .	. . .	. . .	. . .	. . .	. . .	. . .	. . .	. . .
Nonproduced nonfinancial assets, credit	2 480 . .	**. . .**	**. . .**	**. . .**	**. . .**	**. . .**	**. . .**	**. . .**	**. . .**
Nonproduced nonfinancial assets, debit	3 480 . .	**. . .**	**. . .**	**. . .**	**. . .**	**. . .**	**. . .**	**. . .**	**. . .**

Table 2 (Continued). STANDARD PRESENTATION, 1988–95
(Millions of U.S. dollars)

	Code		1988	1989	1990	1991	1992	1993	1994	1995
FINANCIAL ACCOUNT	4 995	. .	**89.4**	**76.1**	**132.2**	**12.1**	**128.9**	**59.7**	**53.7**	...
A. DIRECT INVESTMENT	4 500	. .	.7	15.0	–6.6	3.5	–7.6	–20.1	45.0	...
Direct investment abroad	4 505	. .	...	...	...	...	...	...	...	...
Equity capital	4 510	. .	...	...	...	...	...	...	...	...
Claims on affiliated enterprises	4 515	. .	...	...	...	...	...	...	...	...
Liabilities to affiliated enterprises	4 520	. .	...	...	...	...	...	...	...	...
Reinvested earnings	4 525	. .	...	...	...	...	...	...	...	...
Other capital	4 530	. .	...	...	...	...	...	...	...	...
Claims on affiliated enterprises	4 535	. .	...	...	...	...	...	...	...	...
Liabilities to affiliated enterprises	4 540	. .	...	...	...	...	...	...	...	...
Direct investment in Mali	4 555	. .	**.7**	**15.0**	**–6.6**	**3.5**	**–7.6**	**–20.1**	**45.0**	...
Equity capital	4 560	. .	...	...	...	...	...	...	...	...
Claims on direct investors	4 565	. .	...	...	...	...	...	...	...	...
Liabilities to direct investors	4 570	. .	...	...	...	...	...	...	...	...
Reinvested earnings	4 575	. .	...	4.7	9.2	...	...	...	...	...
Other capital	4 580	. .	.7	10.3	–15.8	3.5	–7.6	–20.1	45.0	...
Claims on direct investors	4 585	. .	...	...	...	...	...	...	...	...
Liabilities to direct investors	4 590	. .	...	...	...	...	...	...	...	...
B. PORTFOLIO INVESTMENT	4 600	. .	...	...	...	...	...	...	...	...
Assets	4 602	. .	...	...	...	...	...	...	...	...
Equity securities	4 610	. .	...	...	...	...	...	...	...	...
Monetary authorities	4 611	. .	...	...	...	...	...	...	...	...
General government	4 612	. .	...	...	...	...	...	...	...	...
Banks	4 613	. .	...	...	...	...	...	...	...	...
Other sectors	4 614	. .	...	...	...	...	...	...	...	...
Debt securities	4 619	. .	...	...	...	...	...	...	...	...
Bonds and notes	4 620	. .	...	...	...	...	...	...	...	...
Monetary authorities	4 621	. .	...	...	...	...	...	...	...	...
General government	4 622	. .	...	...	...	...	...	...	...	...
Banks	4 623	. .	...	...	...	...	...	...	...	...
Other sectors	4 624	. .	...	...	...	...	...	...	...	...
Money market instruments	4 630	. .	...	...	...	...	...	...	...	...
Monetary authorities	4 631	. .	...	...	...	...	...	...	...	...
General government	4 632	. .	...	...	...	...	...	...	...	...
Banks	4 633	. .	...	...	...	...	...	...	...	...
Other sectors	4 634	. .	...	...	...	...	...	...	...	...
Financial derivatives	4 640	. .	...	...	...	...	...	...	...	...
Monetary authorities	4 641	. .	...	...	...	...	...	...	...	...
General government	4 642	. .	...	...	...	...	...	...	...	...
Banks	4 643	. .	...	...	...	...	...	...	...	...
Other sectors	4 644	. .	...	...	...	...	...	...	...	...
Liabilities	4 652	. .	...	...	...	...	...	...	...	...
Equity securities	4 660	. .	...	...	...	...	...	...	...	...
Banks	4 663	. .	...	...	...	...	...	...	...	...
Other sectors	4 664	. .	...	...	...	...	...	...	...	...
Debt securities	4 669	. .	...	...	...	...	...	...	...	...
Bonds and notes	4 670	. .	...	...	...	...	...	...	...	...
Monetary authorities	4 671	. .	...	...	...	...	...	...	...	...
General government	4 672	. .	...	...	...	...	...	...	...	...
Banks	4 673	. .	...	...	...	...	...	...	...	...
Other sectors	4 674	. .	...	...	...	...	...	...	...	...
Money market instruments	4 680	. .	...	...	...	...	...	...	...	...
Monetary authorities	4 681	. .	...	...	...	...	...	...	...	...
General government	4 682	. .	...	...	...	...	...	...	...	...
Banks	4 683	. .	...	...	...	...	...	...	...	...
Other sectors	4 684	. .	...	...	...	...	...	...	...	...
Financial derivatives	4 690	. .	...	...	...	...	...	...	...	...
Monetary authorities	4 691	. .	...	...	...	...	...	...	...	...
General government	4 692	. .	...	...	...	...	...	...	...	...
Banks	4 693	. .	...	...	...	...	...	...	...	...
Other sectors	4 694	. .	...	...	...	...	...	...	...	...

Table 2 (Concluded). STANDARD PRESENTATION, 1988–95

(Millions of U.S. dollars)

	Code	1988	1989	1990	1991	1992	1993	1994	1995
C. OTHER INVESTMENT	4 700	150.7	133.0	193.6	128.4	144.0	125.7	39.4	...
Assets	4 703	**4.6**	**–39.4**	**–.1**	**9.6**	**17.5**	**11.9**	**–100.3**	**...**
Trade credits	4 706	...	...	...	...	...	...	...	...
General government: long-term	4 708	...	...	...	...	...	...	...	...
General government: short-term	4 709	...	...	...	...	...	...	...	...
Other sectors: long-term	4 711	...	...	...	...	...	...	...	...
Other sectors: short-term	4 712	...	...	...	...	...	...	...	...
Loans	4 714	...	...	...	...	...	...	...	...
Monetary authorities: long-term	4 717	...	...	...	...	...	...	...	...
Monetary authorities: short-term	4 718	...	...	...	...	...	...	...	...
General government: long-term	4 720	...	...	...	...	...	...	...	...
General government: short-term	4 721	...	...	...	...	...	...	...	...
Banks: long-term	4 723	...	...	...	...	...	...	...	...
Banks: short-term	4 724	...	...	...	...	...	...	...	...
Other sectors: long-term	4 726	...	...	...	...	...	...	...	...
Other sectors: short-term	4 727	...	...	...	...	...	...	...	...
Currency and deposits	4 730	4.6	–39.4	–.1	9.6	17.5	11.9	–100.3	...
Monetary authorities	4 731	...	...	...	...	...	...	...	...
General government	4 732	...	...	...	...	...	...	...	...
Banks	4 733	4.6	–39.4	–.1	9.6	17.5	11.9	–100.3	...
Other sectors	4 734	...	...	...	...	...	...	...	...
Other assets	4 736	...	...	...	...	...	...	...	...
Monetary authorities: long-term	4 738	...	...	...	...	...	...	...	...
Monetary authorities: short-term	4 739	...	...	...	...	...	...	...	...
General government: long-term	4 741	...	...	...	...	...	...	...	...
General government: short-term	4 742	...	...	...	...	...	...	...	...
Banks: long-term	4 744	...	...	...	...	...	...	...	...
Banks: short-term	4 745	...	...	...	...	...	...	...	...
Other sectors: long-term	4 747	...	...	...	...	...	...	...	...
Other sectors: short-term	4 748	...	...	...	...	...	...	...	...
Liabilities	4 753	**146.0**	**172.4**	**193.7**	**118.7**	**126.5**	**113.8**	**139.7**	**...**
Trade credits	4 756	...	...	...	...	...	...	...	...
General government: long-term	4 758	...	...	...	...	...	...	...	...
General government: short-term	4 759	...	...	...	...	...	...	...	...
Other sectors: long-term	4 761	...	...	...	...	...	...	...	...
Other sectors: short-term	4 762	...	...	...	...	...	...	...	...
Loans	4 764	204.6	222.6	192.0	140.4	132.3	95.7	170.6	...
Use of Fund credit and loans from the Fund	4 766	–7.6	–16.6	8.3	–9.2	8.4	5.6	32.7	...
Monetary authorities: other long-term	4 767	...	...	...	...	...	...	...	...
Monetary authorities: short-term	4 768	...	...	...	...	...	...	...	...
General government: long-term	4 770	212.2	239.2	183.6	149.6	123.9	90.1	138.0	...
General government: short-term	4 771	...	...	...	...	...	...	...	...
Banks: long-term	4 773	...	...	...	...	...	...	...	...
Banks: short-term	4 774	...	...	...	...	...	...	...	...
Other sectors: long-term	4 776	...	...	...	...	...	...	...	...
Other sectors: short-term	4 777	...	...	...	...	...	...	...	...
Currency and deposits	4 780	6.9	–.1	1.7	–25.6	–19.8	.4	4.7	...
Monetary authorities	4 781	...	...	...	...	...	...	...	...
General government	4 782	...	...	...	...	...	...	...	...
Banks	4 783	6.9	–.1	1.7	–25.6	–19.8	.4	4.7	...
Other sectors	4 784	...	...	...	...	...	...	...	...
Other liabilities	4 786	–65.5	–50.2	...	3.9	14.0	17.7	–35.7	...
Monetary authorities: long-term	4 788	...	...	...	...	...	...	...	...
Monetary authorities: short-term	4 789	...	...	...	...	...	...	...	...
General government: long-term	4 791	–1.0	...	...	...	...	...	...	...
General government: short-term	4 792	–64.4	–50.2	...	3.9	14.0	17.7	–35.7	...
Banks: long-term	4 794	...	...	...	...	...	...	...	...
Banks: short-term	4 795	...	...	...	...	...	...	...	...
Other sectors: long-term	4 797	...	...	...	...	...	...	...	...
Other sectors: short-term	4 798	...	...	...	...	...	...	...	...
D. RESERVE ASSETS	4 800	–61.9	–71.9	–54.8	–119.8	–7.6	–45.8	–30.7	...
Monetary gold	4 810	...	...	...	...	...	...	...	...
Special drawing rights	4 820	...	...	–.2	.1	.3	...	–.1	...
Reserve position in the Fund	4 830	...	...	...	...	...	–.1	...	...
Foreign exchange	4 840	–20.8	–77.3	–66.6	–119.8	–7.9	–45.8	–30.7	...
Other claims	4 880	–41.1	5.4	12.0	...	...	...	...	...
NET ERRORS AND OMISSIONS	4 998	**–1.5**	**–1.5**	**1.1**	**14.6**	**–31.0**	**30.1**	**–5.1**	**...**

Table 1. ANALYTIC PRESENTATION, 1988–95
(Millions of U.S. dollars)

	Code	1988	1989	1990	1991	1992	1993	1994	1995
A. Current Account[1]	4 993 Y.	**61.1**	**–9.5**	**–41.1**	**5.9**	**34.5**	**–65.2**	**–136.2**	**–405.6**
Goods: exports f.o.b	2 100 . .	780.1	891.3	1,198.1	1,330.7	1,609.8	1,408.1	1,618.5	1,939.0
Goods: imports f.o.b	3 100 . .	–1,222.3	–1,327.7	–1,769.2	–1,913.1	–2,122.9	–1,976.4	–2,221.0	–2,686.5
Balance on Goods	4 100 . .	*–442.2*	*–436.5*	*–571.1*	*–582.4*	*–513.0*	*–568.3*	*–602.5*	*–747.6*
Services: credit	2 200 . .	653.2	644.5	730.9	787.5	846.0	868.7	928.8	967.2
Services: debit	3 200 . .	–412.3	–433.3	–478.5	–489.1	–546.6	–541.4	–624.0	–719.3
Balance on Goods and Services	4 991 . .	*–201.3*	*–225.3*	*–318.7*	*–284.0*	*–213.6*	*–241.0*	*–297.8*	*–499.6*
Income: credit	2 300 . .	156.6	190.5	269.0	268.3	271.2	241.8	218.0	285.1
Income: debit	3 300 . .	–53.5	–73.2	–78.9	–93.9	–116.9	–126.8	–150.6	–241.1
Balance on Goods, Services, and Income	4 992 . .	*–98.2*	*–107.9*	*–128.6*	*–109.7*	*–59.3*	*–126.1*	*–230.4*	*–455.6*
Current transfers: credit	2 379 Y.	170.5	114.5	110.6	120.6	98.6	64.9	101.2	63.8
Current transfers: debit	3 379 . .	–11.2	–16.1	–23.1	–5.1	–4.8	–4.1	–7.1	–13.9
B. Capital Account[1]	4 994 Y.	**7.0**	**6.0**	**. . .**	**. . .**	**. . .**	**13.1**	**32.1**	**30.2**
Capital account: credit	2 994 Y.	7.0	6.0	. . .	. . .	. . .	13.1	32.1	30.2
Capital account: debit	3 994 . .	. . .	. . .	. . .	. . .	. . .	. . .	. . .	. . .
Total, Groups A Plus B	4 010 . .	*68.0*	*–3.4*	*–41.1*	*5.9*	*34.5*	*–52.1*	*–104.1*	*–375.4*
C. Financial Account[1]	4 995 X.	**17.2**	**–46.8**	**–43.1**	**13.3**	**27.0**	**188.7**	**448.7**	**14.8**
Direct investment abroad	4 505 . .	. . .	. . .	. . .	. . .	. . .	–.9	1.0	–8.7
Direct investment in Malta	4 555 Y.	40.8	51.7	45.8	77.0	39.5	56.4	119.6	98.0
Portfolio investment assets	4 602 . .	–38.4	–57.7	–1.9	–245.2	–214.1	–266.6	304.4	–614.3
Equity securities	4 610 . .	–5.4	. . .	.7	4.0	4.7	13.2	247.2	26.0
Debt securities	4 619 . .	–32.9	–57.7	–2.6	–249.3	–218.8	–279.8	57.2	–640.3
Portfolio investment liabilities	4 652 Y.	. . .	. . .	. . .	. . .	. . .	. . .	. . .	. . .
Equity securities	4 660 Y.	. . .	. . .	. . .	. . .	. . .	. . .	. . .	. . .
Debt securities	4 669 Y.	. . .	. . .	. . .	. . .	. . .	. . .	. . .	. . .
Other investment assets	4 703 . .	–105.5	–100.1	–242.6	67.5	–96.1	131.1	103.4	–283.3
Monetary authorities	4 703 . A	. . .	. . .	. . .	. . .	. . .	. . .	. . .	. . .
General government	4 703 . B	. . .	. . .	. . .	. . .	. . .	. . .	–.5	–.5
Banks	4 703 . C	–111.5	–98.1	–218.4	77.8	–99.7	146.4	79.6	–322.2
Other sectors	4 703 . D	6.0	–2.0	–24.1	–10.3	3.6	–15.3	24.4	39.4
Other investment liabilities	4 753 X.	120.3	59.4	155.6	114.0	297.7	268.7	–79.7	823.1
Monetary authorities	4 753 XA	. . .	. . .	. . .	. . .	. . .	. . .	. . .	. . .
General government	4 753 YB	–4.5	4.0	38.6	26.6	102.8	35.3	6.0	–38.3
Banks	4 753 YC	94.6	39.3	53.2	25.8	48.5	111.2	–274.6	748.2
Other sectors	4 753 YD	30.2	16.1	63.7	61.6	146.4	122.2	188.8	113.1
Total, Groups A Through C	4 020 . .	*85.2*	*–50.2*	*–84.2*	*19.1*	*61.5*	*136.6*	*344.6*	*–360.5*
D. Net Errors and Omissions	4 998 . .	**–50.4**	**64.4**	**–12.1**	**–97.9**	**–16.9**	**–1.8**	**38.1**	**326.0**
Total, Groups A Through D	4 030 . .	*34.8*	*14.2*	*–96.3*	*–78.8*	*44.6*	*134.8*	*382.8*	*–34.5*
E. Reserves and Related Items	4 040 . .	**–34.8**	**–14.2**	**96.3**	**78.8**	**–44.6**	**–134.8**	**–382.8**	**34.5**
Reserve assets	4 800 . .	–34.8	–14.2	96.3	78.8	–44.6	–134.8	–382.8	34.5
Use of Fund credit and loans	4 766 . .	. . .	. . .	. . .	. . .	. . .	. . .	. . .	. . .
Liabilities constituting foreign authorities' reserves	4 900 . .	. . .	. . .	. . .	. . .	. . .	. . .	. . .	. . .
Exceptional financing	4 920 . .	. . .	. . .	. . .	. . .	. . .	. . .	. . .	. . .
Conversion rates: Maltese lira per U.S. dollar	0 101 . .	**.33086**	**.34849**	**.31779**	**.32324**	**.31892**	**.38229**	**.37792**	**.35306**

[1] Excludes components that have been classified in the categories of Group E.

Table 2. STANDARD PRESENTATION, 1988–95
(Millions of U.S. dollars)

	Code	1988	1989	1990	1991	1992	1993	1994	1995
CURRENT ACCOUNT	4 993 . .	**61.1**	**–9.5**	**–41.1**	**5.9**	**34.5**	**–65.2**	**–136.2**	**–405.6**
A. GOODS	4 100 . .	–442.2	–436.5	–571.1	–582.4	–513.0	–568.3	–602.5	–747.6
Credit	2 100 . .	**780.1**	**891.3**	**1,198.1**	**1,330.7**	**1,609.8**	**1,408.1**	**1,618.5**	**1,939.0**
General merchandise: exports f.o.b.	2 110 . .	758.3	866.3	1,154.2	1,283.6	1,557.3	1,355.4	1,569.9	1,887.8
Goods for processing: exports f.o.b.	2 150 . .	. . .	. . .	. . .	. . .	. . .	. . .	. . .	. . .
Repairs on goods	2 160 . .	. . .	. . .	6.3	6.2	6.3	7.2	4.8	4.5
Goods procured in ports by carriers	2 170 . .	21.8	25.0	37.6	41.0	46.3	45.4	43.7	46.6
Nonmonetary gold	2 180 . .	. . .	. . .	. . .	. . .	. . .	. . .	. . .	. . .
Debit	3 100 . .	**–1,222.3**	**–1,327.7**	**–1,769.2**	**–1,913.1**	**–2,122.9**	**–1,976.4**	**–2,221.0**	**–2,686.5**
General merchandise: imports f.o.b.	3 110 . .	–1,200.2	–1,317.7	–1,725.9	–1,878.3	–2,082.1	–1,942.2	–2,175.1	–2,634.8
Goods for processing: imports f.o.b.	3 150 . .	. . .	. . .	. . .	. . .	. . .	. . .	. . .	. . .
Repairs on goods	3 160 . .	. . .	. . .	–5.5	–6.4	–9.9	–10.5	–9.5	–14.1
Goods procured in ports by carriers	3 170 . .	. . .	. . .	–10.6	–9.5	–8.8	–12.2	–13.0	–14.7
Nonmonetary gold	3 180 . .	–22.1	–10.0	–27.2	–18.9	–22.0	–11.5	–23.5	–22.9
B. SERVICES	4 200 . .	240.9	211.2	252.4	298.3	299.4	327.3	304.8	247.9
Total credit	2 200 . .	*653.2*	*644.5*	*730.9*	*787.5*	*846.0*	*868.7*	*928.8*	*967.2*
Total debit	3 200 . .	*–412.3*	*–433.3*	*–478.5*	*–489.1*	*–546.6*	*–541.4*	*–624.0*	*–719.3*
Transportation services, credit	2 205 . .	**172.5**	**162.7**	**168.0**	**172.0**	**214.6**	**199.4**	**221.7**	**238.3**
Passenger	2 205 BA	*58.0*	*56.5*	*117.4*	*120.7*	*141.8*	*130.8*	*148.2*	*155.7*
Freight	2 205 BB	*22.6*	*20.7*	*20.8*	*14.6*	*13.4*	*12.6*	*12.4*	*9.9*
Other	2 205 BC	*91.9*	*85.5*	*29.8*	*36.7*	*59.4*	*56.0*	*61.2*	*72.7*
Sea transport, passenger	2 207 . .	. . .	. . .	. . .	. . .	. . .	. . .	. . .	. . .
Sea transport, freight	2 208 . .	. . .	. . .	. . .	. . .	. . .	. . .	. . .	. . .
Sea transport, other	2 209 . .	. . .	. . .	. . .	. . .	. . .	. . .	. . .	. . .
Air transport, passenger	2 211 . .	. . .	. . .	. . .	. . .	. . .	. . .	. . .	. . .
Air transport, freight	2 212 . .	. . .	. . .	. . .	. . .	. . .	. . .	. . .	. . .
Air transport, other	2 213 . .	. . .	. . .	. . .	. . .	. . .	. . .	. . .	. . .
Other transport, passenger	2 215 . .	. . .	. . .	. . .	. . .	. . .	. . .	. . .	. . .
Other transport, freight	2 216 . .	. . .	. . .	. . .	. . .	. . .	. . .	. . .	. . .
Other transport, other	2 217 . .	. . .	. . .	. . .	. . .	. . .	. . .	. . .	. . .
Transportation services, debit	3 205 . .	**–186.8**	**–205.5**	**–235.7**	**–233.5**	**–262.3**	**–272.1**	**–309.5**	**–360.4**
Passenger	3 205 BA	*–14.5*	*–10.6*	*–10.9*	*–6.2*	*–8.9*	*–23.6*	*–23.3*	*–24.9*
Freight	3 205 BB	*–121.5*	*–133.1*	*–175.7*	*–185.1*	*–204.4*	*–188.0*	*–208.0*	*–251.7*
Other	3 205 BC	*–50.8*	*–61.7*	*–49.0*	*–42.2*	*–49.0*	*–60.4*	*–78.3*	*–83.7*
Sea transport, passenger	3 207 . .	. . .	. . .	. . .	. . .	. . .	. . .	. . .	. . .
Sea transport, freight	3 208 . .	. . .	. . .	. . .	. . .	. . .	. . .	. . .	. . .
Sea transport, other	3 209 . .	. . .	. . .	. . .	. . .	. . .	. . .	. . .	. . .
Air transport, passenger	3 211 . .	. . .	. . .	. . .	. . .	. . .	. . .	. . .	. . .
Air transport, freight	3 212 . .	. . .	. . .	. . .	. . .	. . .	. . .	. . .	. . .
Air transport, other	3 213 . .	. . .	. . .	. . .	. . .	. . .	. . .	. . .	. . .
Other transport, passenger	3 215 . .	. . .	. . .	. . .	. . .	. . .	. . .	. . .	. . .
Other transport, freight	3 216 . .	. . .	. . .	. . .	. . .	. . .	. . .	. . .	. . .
Other transport, other	3 217 . .	. . .	. . .	. . .	. . .	. . .	. . .	. . .	. . .
Travel, credit	2 236 . .	**427.4**	**412.6**	**495.3**	**542.3**	**566.0**	**607.5**	**640.0**	**659.4**
Business travel	2 237 . .	. . .	. . .	. . .	. . .	. . .	. . .	. . .	. . .
Personal travel	2 240 . .	. . .	. . .	. . .	. . .	. . .	. . .	. . .	. . .
Travel, debit	3 236 . .	**–120.3**	**–107.0**	**–136.9**	**–132.3**	**–137.8**	**–154.2**	**–177.3**	**–213.6**
Business travel	3 237 . .	. . .	. . .	. . .	. . .	. . .	. . .	. . .	. . .
Personal travel	3 240 . .	. . .	. . .	. . .	. . .	. . .	. . .	. . .	. . .
Other services, credit	2 200 BA	**53.3**	**69.2**	**67.6**	**73.1**	**65.5**	**61.9**	**67.0**	**69.5**
Communications	2 245 . .	. . .	. . .	9.4	10.0	18.3	12.0	16.3	14.5
Construction	2 249 . .	. . .	. . .	. . .	. . .	. . .	. . .	. . .	. . .
Insurance	2 253 . .	21.9	25.8	27.3	30.4	24.9	29.7	31.0	32.8
Financial	2 260 . .	. . .	. . .	. . .	. . .	. . .	. . .	. . .	. . .
Computer and information	2 262 . .	. . .	. . .	. . .	. . .	. . .	. . .	. . .	. . .
Royalties and licence fees	2 266 . .	.3	.3	.2	.1	.1	.1	.1	.2
Other business services	2 268 . .	17.8	26.1	. . .	. . .	. . .	. . .	. . .	. . .
Personal, cultural, and recreational	2 287 . .	. . .	. . .	. . .	. . .	. . .	. . .	. . .	. . .
Government, n.i.e.	2 291 . .	13.3	16.9	30.8	32.6	22.2	20.1	19.6	22.0
Other services, debit	3 200 BA	**–105.2**	**–120.8**	**–106.0**	**–123.4**	**–146.5**	**–115.1**	**–137.2**	**–145.3**
Communications	3 245 . .	. . .	. . .	–8.2	–10.2	–11.7	–12.9	–21.3	–15.9
Construction	3 249 . .	. . .	. . .	. . .	. . .	. . .	. . .	. . .	. . .
Insurance	3 253 . .	–62.9	–70.3	–79.9	–84.9	–105.1	–81.4	–87.0	–99.3
Financial	3 260 . .	. . .	. . .	. . .	. . .	. . .	. . .	. . .	. . .
Computer and information	3 262 . .	. . .	. . .	. . .	. . .	. . .	. . .	. . .	. . .
Royalties and licence fees	3 266 . .	–2.1	–2.0	–2.5	–2.6	–2.8	–2.7	–5.5	–6.6
Other business services	3 268 . .	–30.2	–31.9	. . .	. . .	. . .	. . .	. . .	. . .
Personal, cultural, and recreational	3 287 . .	. . .	. . .	–.5	–.2	–2.4	–1.8	–4.8	–5.1
Government, n.i.e.	3 291 . .	–10.0	–16.6	–14.8	–25.5	–24.6	–16.3	–18.6	–18.4

Table 2 (Continued). STANDARD PRESENTATION, 1988–95
(Millions of U.S. dollars)

	Code	1988	1989	1990	1991	1992	1993	1994	1995
C. INCOME	4 300 . .	103.1	117.4	190.1	174.4	154.3	115.0	67.4	44.1
Total credit	2 300 . .	*156.6*	*190.5*	*269.0*	*268.3*	*271.2*	*241.8*	*218.0*	*285.1*
Total debit	3 300 . .	*–53.5*	*–73.2*	*–78.9*	*–93.9*	*–116.9*	*–126.8*	*–150.6*	*–241.1*
Compensation of employees, credit	2 310 . .	**17.8**	**23.5**	**21.1**	**26.6**	**27.5**	**24.2**	**18.2**	**11.4**
Compensation of employees, debit	3 310 . .	**–.3**	**–8.9**	**–4.1**	**–5.8**	**–3.9**	**–1.6**	**–.5**	**–1.6**
Investment income, credit	2 320 . .	**138.7**	**167.0**	**247.9**	**241.7**	**243.7**	**217.6**	**199.8**	**273.7**
Direct investment income	2 330 . .	. . .	. . .	247.9	241.7	243.7	217.6	199.8	273.7
Dividends and distributed branch profits	2 332 . .	. . .	. . .	. . .	. . .	. . .	.4	.1	13.0
Reinvested earnings and undistributed branch profits	2 333 . .	. . .	. . .	. . .	. . .	. . .	. . .	–1.4	. . .
Income on debt (interest)	2 334 . .	. . .	. . .	247.9	241.7	243.7	217.2	201.1	260.6
Portfolio investment income	2 339 . .	. . .	. . .	. . .	. . .	. . .	. . .	. . .	. . .
Income on equity	2 340 . .	. . .	. . .	. . .	. . .	. . .	. . .	. . .	. . .
Income on bonds and notes	2 350 . .	. . .	. . .	. . .	. . .	. . .	. . .	. . .	. . .
Income on money market instruments and financial derivatives	2 360 . .	. . .	. . .	. . .	. . .	. . .	. . .	. . .	. . .
Other investment income	2 370 . .	138.7	167.0	. . .	. . .	. . .	. . .	. . .	. . .
Investment income, debit	3 320 . .	**–53.2**	**–64.3**	**–74.8**	**–88.1**	**–112.9**	**–125.2**	**–150.1**	**–239.5**
Direct investment income	3 330 . .	–32.6	–39.3	–73.7	–86.2	–111.9	–124.9	–149.4	–239.1
Dividends and distributed branch profits	3 332 . .	–17.2	–14.3	–7.8	–7.7	–12.8	–16.8	–26.4	–34.8
Reinvested earnings and undistributed branch profits	3 333 . .	–15.4	–25.0	–24.5	–24.8	–32.4	–36.9	–57.5	–91.9
Income on debt (interest)	3 334 . .	. . .	. . .	–41.4	–53.8	–66.6	–71.2	–65.5	–112.4
Portfolio investment income	3 339 . .	. . .	. . .	. . .	. . .	. . .	. . .	. . .	. . .
Income on equity	3 340 . .	. . .	. . .	. . .	. . .	. . .	. . .	. . .	. . .
Income on bonds and notes	3 350 . .	. . .	. . .	. . .	. . .	. . .	. . .	. . .	. . .
Income on money market instruments and financial derivatives	3 360 . .	. . .	. . .	. . .	. . .	. . .	. . .	. . .	. . .
Other investment income	3 370 . .	–20.6	–25.0	–1.1	–1.9	–1.1	–.4	–.7	–.4
D. CURRENT TRANSFERS	4 379 . .	159.3	98.4	87.5	115.5	93.8	60.9	94.1	49.9
Credit	2 379 . .	**170.5**	**114.5**	**110.6**	**120.6**	**98.6**	**64.9**	**101.2**	**63.8**
General government	2 380 . .	43.5	24.4	25.2	51.4	53.0	22.9	34.9	13.3
Other sectors	2 390 . .	126.9	90.1	85.4	69.3	45.6	42.1	66.3	50.5
Workers' remittances	2 391 . .	26.9	40.5	37.2	15.5	3.0	1.3	5.3	6.6
Other current transfers	2 392 . .	100.0	49.6	48.2	53.8	42.6	40.8	61.0	43.9
Debit	3 379 . .	**–11.2**	**–16.1**	**–23.1**	**–5.1**	**–4.8**	**–4.1**	**–7.1**	**–13.9**
General government	3 380 . .	–1.8	–1.1	–2.2	–2.0	–2.0	–2.2	–2.7	–2.9
Other sectors	3 390 . .	–9.4	–14.9	–21.0	–3.1	–2.8	–1.9	–4.4	–11.0
Workers' remittances	3 391 . .	–9.1	–14.6	–20.7	–2.5	–1.2	–.2	–2.4	–5.0
Other current transfers	3 392 . .	–.3	–.3	–.2	–.5	–1.6	–1.7	–2.0	–6.0
CAPITAL AND FINANCIAL ACCOUNT	4 996 . .	**–10.7**	**–55.0**	**53.3**	**92.1**	**–17.6**	**67.0**	**98.1**	**79.6**
CAPITAL ACCOUNT	4 994 . .	**7.0**	**6.0**	**. . .**	**. . .**	**. . .**	**13.1**	**32.1**	**30.2**
Total credit	2 994 . .	*7.0*	*6.0*	. . .	. . .	. . .	*13.1*	*32.1*	*30.2*
Total debit	3 994 . .	. . .	. . .	. . .	. . .	. . .	. . .	. . .	. . .
Capital transfers, credit	2 400 . .	**7.0**	**6.0**	**. . .**	**. . .**	**. . .**	**. . .**	**. . .**	**. . .**
General government	2 401 . .	. . .	. . .	. . .	. . .	. . .	. . .	. . .	. . .
Debt forgiveness	2 402 . .	. . .	. . .	. . .	. . .	. . .	. . .	. . .	. . .
Other capital transfers	2 410 . .	. . .	. . .	. . .	. . .	. . .	. . .	. . .	. . .
Other sectors	2 430 . .	7.0	6.0	. . .	. . .	. . .	. . .	. . .	. . .
Migrants' transfers	2 431 . .	7.0	6.0	. . .	. . .	. . .	. . .	. . .	. . .
Debt forgiveness	2 432 . .	. . .	. . .	. . .	. . .	. . .	. . .	. . .	. . .
Other capital transfers	2 440 . .	. . .	. . .	. . .	. . .	. . .	. . .	. . .	. . .
Capital transfers, debit	3 400 . .	**. . .**	**. . .**	**. . .**	**. . .**	**. . .**	**. . .**	**. . .**	**. . .**
General government	3 401 . .	. . .	. . .	. . .	. . .	. . .	. . .	. . .	. . .
Debt forgiveness	3 402 . .	. . .	. . .	. . .	. . .	. . .	. . .	. . .	. . .
Other capital transfers	3 410 . .	. . .	. . .	. . .	. . .	. . .	. . .	. . .	. . .
Other sectors	3 430 . .	. . .	. . .	. . .	. . .	. . .	. . .	. . .	. . .
Migrants' transfers	3 431 . .	. . .	. . .	. . .	. . .	. . .	. . .	. . .	. . .
Debt forgiveness	3 432 . .	. . .	. . .	. . .	. . .	. . .	. . .	. . .	. . .
Other capital transfers	3 440 . .	. . .	. . .	. . .	. . .	. . .	. . .	. . .	. . .
Nonproduced nonfinancial assets, credit	2 480 . .	**. . .**	**. . .**	**. . .**	**. . .**	**. . .**	**13.1**	**32.1**	**30.2**
Nonproduced nonfinancial assets, debit	3 480 . .	**. . .**	**. . .**	**. . .**	**. . .**	**. . .**	**. . .**	**. . .**	**. . .**

Table 2 (Continued). STANDARD PRESENTATION, 1988–95
(Millions of U.S. dollars)

	Code		1988	1989	1990	1991	1992	1993	1994	1995
FINANCIAL ACCOUNT	4 995	. .	**–17.6**	**–61.0**	**53.3**	**92.1**	**–17.6**	**53.9**	**66.0**	**49.3**
A. DIRECT INVESTMENT	4 500	. .	40.8	51.7	45.8	77.0	39.5	55.5	120.6	89.3
Direct investment abroad	4 505	. .	**. . .**	**. . .**	**. . .**	**. . .**	**. . .**	**–.9**	**1.0**	**–8.7**
Equity capital	4 510	. .	. . .	. . .	. . .	. . .	. . .	–.9	–4.6	–7.4
Claims on affiliated enterprises	4 515	. .	. . .	. . .	. . .	. . .	. . .	–.9	–4.6	–7.4
Liabilities to affiliated enterprises	4 520	. .	. . .	. . .	. . .	. . .	. . .	. . .	. . .	. . .
Reinvested earnings	4 525	. .	. . .	. . .	. . .	. . .	. . .	. . .	1.4	. . .
Other capital	4 530	. .	. . .	. . .	. . .	. . .	. . .	. . .	4.1	–1.3
Claims on affiliated enterprises	4 535	. .	. . .	. . .	. . .	. . .	. . .	. . .	4.1	–1.3
Liabilities to affiliated enterprises	4 540	. .	. . .	. . .	. . .	. . .	. . .	. . .	. . .	. . .
Direct investment in Malta	4 555	. .	**40.8**	**51.7**	**45.8**	**77.0**	**39.5**	**56.4**	**119.6**	**98.0**
Equity capital	4 560	. .	–.3	6.9	3.3	21.1	17.6	17.4	61.1	27.5
Claims on direct investors	4 565	. .	. . .	. . .	. . .	. . .	. . .	. . .	. . .	. . .
Liabilities to direct investors	4 570	. .	. . .	. . .	3.3	21.1	17.6	17.4	61.1	27.5
Reinvested earnings	4 575	. .	15.4	25.0	24.5	24.8	32.4	36.9	57.5	91.9
Other capital	4 580	. .	25.7	19.8	18.0	31.1	–10.5	2.1	1.0	–21.4
Claims on direct investors	4 585	. .	. . .	. . .	15.8	–13.1	–45.2	. . .	. . .	–52.3
Liabilities to direct investors	4 590	. .	. . .	. . .	2.2	44.1	34.6	2.1	1.0	30.9
B. PORTFOLIO INVESTMENT	4 600	. .	–38.4	–57.7	–1.9	–245.2	–214.1	–266.6	304.4	–614.3
Assets	4 602	. .	**–38.4**	**–57.7**	**–1.9**	**–245.2**	**–214.1**	**–266.6**	**304.4**	**–614.3**
Equity securities	4 610	. .	–5.4	. . .	.7	4.0	4.7	13.2	247.2	26.0
Monetary authorities	4 611	. .	. . .	. . .	. . .	. . .	. . .	. . .	. . .	. . .
General government	4 612	. .	. . .	. . .	. . .	. . .	. . .	. . .	. . .	. . .
Banks	4 613	. .	. . .	. . .	. . .	. . .	. . .	. . .	. . .	. . .
Other sectors	4 614	. .	. . .	. . .	.7	4.0	4.7	13.2	247.2	26.0
Debt securities	4 619	. .	–32.9	–57.7	–2.6	–249.3	–218.8	–279.8	57.2	–640.3
Bonds and notes	4 620	. .	–32.9	–57.7	–2.6	–249.3	–218.8	–279.8	57.2	–640.3
Monetary authorities	4 621	. .	. . .	. . .	. . .	. . .	. . .	. . .	. . .	. . .
General government	4 622	. .	. . .	. . .	. . .	. . .	. . .	. . .	. . .	. . .
Banks	4 623	. .	. . .	. . .	–2.6	–249.3	–218.8	–279.8	57.2	–640.3
Other sectors	4 624	. .	. . .	. . .	. . .	. . .	. . .	. . .	. . .	. . .
Money market instruments	4 630	. .	. . .	. . .	. . .	. . .	. . .	. . .	. . .	. . .
Monetary authorities	4 631	. .	. . .	. . .	. . .	. . .	. . .	. . .	. . .	. . .
General government	4 632	. .	. . .	. . .	. . .	. . .	. . .	. . .	. . .	. . .
Banks	4 633	. .	. . .	. . .	. . .	. . .	. . .	. . .	. . .	. . .
Other sectors	4 634	. .	. . .	. . .	. . .	. . .	. . .	. . .	. . .	. . .
Financial derivatives	4 640	. .	. . .	. . .	. . .	. . .	. . .	. . .	. . .	. . .
Monetary authorities	4 641	. .	. . .	. . .	. . .	. . .	. . .	. . .	. . .	. . .
General government	4 642	. .	. . .	. . .	. . .	. . .	. . .	. . .	. . .	. . .
Banks	4 643	. .	. . .	. . .	. . .	. . .	. . .	. . .	. . .	. . .
Other sectors	4 644	. .	. . .	. . .	. . .	. . .	. . .	. . .	. . .	. . .
Liabilities	4 652	. .	**. . .**	**. . .**	**. . .**	**. . .**	**. . .**	**. . .**	**. . .**	**. . .**
Equity securities	4 660	. .	. . .	. . .	. . .	. . .	. . .	. . .	. . .	. . .
Banks	4 663	. .	. . .	. . .	. . .	. . .	. . .	. . .	. . .	. . .
Other sectors	4 664	. .	. . .	. . .	. . .	. . .	. . .	. . .	. . .	. . .
Debt securities	4 669	. .	. . .	. . .	. . .	. . .	. . .	. . .	. . .	. . .
Bonds and notes	4 670	. .	. . .	. . .	. . .	. . .	. . .	. . .	. . .	. . .
Monetary authorities	4 671	. .	. . .	. . .	. . .	. . .	. . .	. . .	. . .	. . .
General government	4 672	. .	. . .	. . .	. . .	. . .	. . .	. . .	. . .	. . .
Banks	4 673	. .	. . .	. . .	. . .	. . .	. . .	. . .	. . .	. . .
Other sectors	4 674	. .	. . .	. . .	. . .	. . .	. . .	. . .	. . .	. . .
Money market instruments	4 680	. .	. . .	. . .	. . .	. . .	. . .	. . .	. . .	. . .
Monetary authorities	4 681	. .	. . .	. . .	. . .	. . .	. . .	. . .	. . .	. . .
General government	4 682	. .	. . .	. . .	. . .	. . .	. . .	. . .	. . .	. . .
Banks	4 683	. .	. . .	. . .	. . .	. . .	. . .	. . .	. . .	. . .
Other sectors	4 684	. .	. . .	. . .	. . .	. . .	. . .	. . .	. . .	. . .
Financial derivatives	4 690	. .	. . .	. . .	. . .	. . .	. . .	. . .	. . .	. . .
Monetary authorities	4 691	. .	. . .	. . .	. . .	. . .	. . .	. . .	. . .	. . .
General government	4 692	. .	. . .	. . .	. . .	. . .	. . .	. . .	. . .	. . .
Banks	4 693	. .	. . .	. . .	. . .	. . .	. . .	. . .	. . .	. . .
Other sectors	4 694	. .	. . .	. . .	. . .	. . .	. . .	. . .	. . .	. . .

Table 2 (Concluded). STANDARD PRESENTATION, 1988–95
(Millions of U.S. dollars)

	Code	1988	1989	1990	1991	1992	1993	1994	1995
C. OTHER INVESTMENT	4 700 . .	14.8	–40.7	–87.0	181.5	201.6	399.8	23.7	539.8
Assets	4 703 . .	**–105.5**	**–100.1**	**–242.6**	**67.5**	**–96.1**	**131.1**	**103.4**	**–283.3**
Trade credits	4 706 . .	...	...	–14.9	–7.6	4.2	11.4	–46.4	–3.4
General government: long-term	4 708 . .	...	...	...	...	...	...	...	...
General government: short-term	4 709 . .	...	...	...	...	...	...	...	...
Other sectors: long-term	4 711 . .	...	...	...	...	...	...	...	...
Other sectors: short-term	4 712 . .	...	...	–14.9	–7.6	4.2	11.4	–46.4	–3.4
Loans	4 714 . .	–73.7	–17.8	–50.1	–51.1	–24.5	30.9	134.4	–251.5
Monetary authorities: long-term	4 717 . .	...	...	...	...	...	...	...	...
Monetary authorities: short-term	4 718 . .	...	...	...	...	...	...	...	...
General government: long-term	4 720 . .	...	...	...	...	...	...	...	...
General government: short-term	4 721 . .	...	...	...	...	...	...	...	...
Banks: long-term	4 723 . .	–73.7	–17.8	–50.1	–51.1	–24.5	30.9	134.4	–251.5
Banks: short-term	4 724 . .	...	...	...	...	...	...	...	...
Other sectors: long-term	4 726 . .	...	...	...	...	...	...	...	...
Other sectors: short-term	4 727 . .	...	...	...	...	...	...	...	...
Currency and deposits	4 730 . .	–31.7	–82.4	–168.3	128.9	–75.2	109.4	–30.1	–73.3
Monetary authorities	4 731 . .	...	...	...	...	...	...	...	...
General government	4 732 . .	...	...	...	...	...	...	...	...
Banks	4 733 . .	–37.8	–80.3	–168.3	128.9	–75.2	115.4	–54.9	–70.7
Other sectors	4 734 . .	6.0	–2.0	...	...	...	–6.1	24.8	–2.5
Other assets	4 736 . .	...	...	–9.2	–2.8	–.6	–20.6	45.5	44.9
Monetary authorities: long-term	4 738 . .	...	...	...	...	...	...	...	...
Monetary authorities: short-term	4 739 . .	...	...	...	...	...	...	...	...
General government: long-term	4 741 . .	...	...	...	...	...	...	–.5	–.5
General government: short-term	4 742 . .	...	...	...	...	...	...	...	...
Banks: long-term	4 744 . .	...	...	...	...	...	...	...	...
Banks: short-term	4 745 . .	...	...	...	...	...	...	...	...
Other sectors: long-term	4 747 . .	...	...	...	...	...	...	...	...
Other sectors: short-term	4 748 . .	...	...	–9.2	–2.8	–.6	–20.6	46.0	45.3
Liabilities	4 753 . .	**120.3**	**59.4**	**155.6**	**114.0**	**297.7**	**268.7**	**–79.7**	**823.1**
Trade credits	4 756 . .	...	...	–3.6	7.0	–4.9	40.7	24.1	–2.8
General government: long-term	4 758 . .	...	...	...	...	...	...	...	...
General government: short-term	4 759 . .	...	...	...	...	...	...	...	...
Other sectors: long-term	4 761 . .	...	...	...	...	...	...	...	...
Other sectors: short-term	4 762 . .	...	...	–3.6	7.0	–4.9	40.7	24.1	–2.8
Loans	4 764 . .	–3.6	–22.7	38.6	26.6	102.8	39.0	13.2	–38.0
Use of Fund credit and loans from the Fund	4 766 . .	...	...	...	...	...	...	...	...
Monetary authorities: other long-term	4 767 . .	...	...	...	...	...	...	...	...
Monetary authorities: short-term	4 768 . .	...	...	...	...	...	...	...	...
General government: long-term	4 770 . .	–4.5	4.0	38.6	26.6	102.8	35.3	6.0	–38.3
General government: short-term	4 771 . .	...	...	...	...	...	...	...	...
Banks: long-term	4 773 . .	...	...	...	...	...	...	...	...
Banks: short-term	4 774 . .	...	...	...	...	...	...	...	...
Other sectors: long-term	4 776 . .	...	...	...	...	...	...	...	...
Other sectors: short-term	4 777 . .	.9	–26.7	...	...	...	3.7	7.2	.3
Currency and deposits	4 780 . .	94.6	39.3	120.6	80.4	199.7	181.5	–127.1	854.8
Monetary authorities	4 781 . .	...	...	...	...	...	...	...	...
General government	4 782 . .	...	...	...	...	...	...	...	...
Banks	4 783 . .	94.6	39.3	53.2	25.8	48.5	111.2	–274.6	748.2
Other sectors	4 784 . .	...	...	67.3	54.6	151.2	70.2	147.5	106.6
Other liabilities	4 786 . .	29.3	42.8	...	...	...	7.6	10.1	9.1
Monetary authorities: long-term	4 788 . .	...	...	...	...	...	...	...	...
Monetary authorities: short-term	4 789 . .	...	...	...	...	...	...	...	...
General government: long-term	4 791 . .	...	...	...	...	...	...	...	...
General government: short-term	4 792 . .	...	...	...	...	...	...	...	...
Banks: long-term	4 794 . .	...	...	...	...	...	...	...	...
Banks: short-term	4 795 . .	...	...	...	...	...	...	...	...
Other sectors: long-term	4 797 . .	...	...	...	...	...	...	...	...
Other sectors: short-term	4 798 . .	29.3	42.8	...	...	...	7.6	10.1	9.1
D. RESERVE ASSETS	4 800 . .	–34.8	–14.2	96.3	78.8	–44.6	–134.8	–382.8	34.5
Monetary gold	4 810 . .	...	...	25.2	19.0	–2.6	.6	6.4	9.4
Special drawing rights	4 820 . .	–4.7	–4.4	–7.6	–7.0	43.0	–3.0	–.5	–3.1
Reserve position in the Fund	4 830 . .	5.3	4.8	5.4	–1.9	–6.3	.1	–.3	–2.9
Foreign exchange	4 840 . .	–35.4	–14.6	77.1	61.1	–78.1	–135.8	–235.7	30.3
Other claims	4 880 . .	...	...	–3.8	7.5	–.7	3.3	–152.7	.8
NET ERRORS AND OMISSIONS	4 998 . .	**–50.4**	**64.4**	**–12.1**	**–97.9**	**–16.9**	**–1.8**	**38.1**	**326.0**

Part 3 of the *Yearbook* contains descriptions of the methodologies, compilation practices, and sources used to compile these data.

Mauritania
682

Table 1. ANALYTIC PRESENTATION, 1988–95

(Millions of U.S. dollars)

	Code	1988	1989	1990	1991	1992	1993	1994	1995
A. Current Account[1]	4 993 Y .	**-96.0**	**-18.6**	**-9.6**	**-29.9**	**-118.3**	**-174.0**	**-69.9**	**. . .**
Goods: exports f.o.b	2 100 . .	437.6	447.9	443.9	435.8	406.8	403.0	399.7	. . .
Goods: imports f.o.b	3 100 . .	-348.9	-349.3	-382.9	-399.1	-461.3	-400.4	-352.3	. . .
Balance on Goods	4 100 . .	*88.8*	*98.6*	*61.0*	*36.7*	*-54.5*	*2.6*	*47.4*	. . .
Services: credit	2 200 . .	35.3	33.6	26.8	31.2	20.2	21.4	26.0	. . .
Services: debit	3 200 . .	-217.0	-196.0	-136.8	-151.0	-179.1	-184.9	-181.1	. . .
Balance on Goods and Services	4 991 . .	*-93.0*	*-63.9*	*-49.1*	*-83.1*	*-213.4*	*-160.9*	*-107.7*	. . .
Income: credit	2 300 . .	4.1	5.6	3.8	2.0	1.1	.8	1.1	. . .
Income: debit	3 300 . .	-89.7	-55.6	-50.2	-34.9	-29.9	-97.6	-47.7	. . .
Balance on Goods, Services, and Income	4 992 . .	*-178.6*	*-113.9*	*-95.5*	*-115.9*	*-242.2*	*-257.8*	*-154.3*	. . .
Current transfers: credit	2 379 Y .	123.3	130.0	120.2	118.9	157.4	110.3	113.3	. . .
Current transfers: debit	3 379 . .	-40.8	-34.7	-34.3	-32.8	-33.4	-26.5	-28.9	. . .
B. Capital Account[1]	4 994 Y .	**. . .**	**. . .**	**. . .**	**. . .**	**. . .**	**. . .**	**. . .**	**. . .**
Capital account: credit	2 994 Y .	. . .	. . .	. . .	. . .	. . .	. . .	. . .	. . .
Capital account: debit	3 994 . .	. . .	. . .	. . .	. . .	. . .	. . .	. . .	. . .
Total, Groups A Plus B	4 010 . .	*-96.0*	*-18.6*	*-9.6*	*-29.9*	*-118.3*	*-174.0*	*-69.9*	. . .
C. Financial Account[1]	4 995 X .	**39.4**	**16.9**	**-.5**	**26.7**	**77.9**	**-134.7**	**-11.2**	**. . .**
Direct investment abroad	4 505 . .	-.9	. . .	. . .	. . .	. . .	. . .	. . .	. . .
Direct investment in Mauritania	4 555 Y .	1.9	3.5	6.7	2.3	7.5	16.1	2.1	. . .
Portfolio investment assets	4 602 . .	. . .	. . .	. . .	. . .	. . .	. . .	. . .	. . .
Equity securities	4 610 . .	. . .	. . .	. . .	. . .	. . .	. . .	. . .	. . .
Debt securities	4 619 . .	. . .	. . .	. . .	. . .	. . .	. . .	. . .	. . .
Portfolio investment liabilities	4 652 Y .	. . .	. . .	. . .	. . .	. . .	. . .	. . .	. . .
Equity securities	4 660 Y .	. . .	. . .	. . .	. . .	. . .	. . .	. . .	. . .
Debt securities	4 669 Y .	. . .	. . .	. . .	. . .	. . .	. . .	. . .	. . .
Other investment assets	4 703 . .	2.2	-9.9	205.8	194.0	168.7	170.5	169.3	. . .
Monetary authorities	4 703 . A	. . .	. . .	. . .	. . .	. . .	. . .	. . .	. . .
General government	4 703 . B	-.1	. . .	. . .	. . .	. . .	-.8	-2.2	. . .
Banks	4 703 . C	11.4	-6.5	. . .	. . .	. . .	. . .	. . .	. . .
Other sectors	4 703 . D	-9.0	-3.4	205.8	194.0	168.7	171.3	171.5	. . .
Other investment liabilities	4 753 X .	36.2	23.3	-213.0	-169.6	-98.3	-321.3	-182.6	. . .
Monetary authorities	4 753 XA	. . .	. . .	-1.6	2.4	. . .	. . .	. . .	. . .
General government	4 753 YB	-8.9	29.0	-36.2	34.7	35.6	-137.6	-7.0	. . .
Banks	4 753 YC	5.0	5.8	-.6	-1.5	-.8	-18.8	. . .	. . .
Other sectors	4 753 YD	40.1	-11.5	-174.5	-205.1	-133.1	-164.9	-175.5	. . .
Total, Groups A Through C	4 020 . .	*-56.6*	*-1.8*	*-10.1*	*-3.2*	*-40.3*	*-308.8*	*-81.0*	. . .
D. Net Errors and Omissions	4 998 . .	**-16.0**	**-3.6**	**-62.3**	**19.5**	**57.4**	**26.7**	**-23.5**	**. . .**
Total, Groups A Through D	4 030 . .	*-72.6*	*-5.3*	*-72.5*	*16.3*	*17.0*	*-282.0*	*-104.5*	. . .
E. Reserves and Related Items	4 040 . .	**72.6**	**5.3**	**72.5**	**-16.3**	**-17.0**	**282.0**	**104.5**	**. . .**
Reserve assets	4 800 . .	10.6	-16.8	40.6	-3.1	-20.4	69.0	46.9	. . .
Use of Fund credit and loans	4 766 . .	-1.9	-.7	-4.5	-13.2	3.4	5.6	17.9	. . .
Liabilities constituting foreign authorities' reserves	4 900 . .	9.4	-.6	. . .	. . .	. . .	-.1	-.2	. . .
Exceptional financing	4 920 . .	54.5	23.3	36.4	. . .	. . .	207.5	40.0	. . .
Conversion rates: ouguiyas per U.S. dollar	0 101 . .	**75.26**	**83.05**	**80.61**	**81.95**	**87.03**	**120.81**	**123.58**	**129.77**

[1] Excludes components that have been classified in the categories of Group E.

Table 2. STANDARD PRESENTATION, 1988–95
(Millions of U.S. dollars)

	Code	1988	1989	1990	1991	1992	1993	1994	1995
CURRENT ACCOUNT	4 993 . .	**–95.9**	**–18.6**	**–9.6**	**–29.9**	**–118.3**	**–174.0**	**–69.9**	. . .
A. GOODS	4 100 . .	88.8	98.6	61.0	36.7	–54.5	2.6	47.4	. . .
Credit	2 100 . .	**437.6**	**447.9**	**443.9**	**435.8**	**406.8**	**403.0**	**399.7**	. . .
General merchandise: exports f.o.b.	2 110 . .	437.6	447.9	443.9	435.8	406.8	403.0	399.7	. . .
Goods for processing: exports f.o.b.	2 150 . .	. . .	. . .	. . .	. . .	. . .	. . .	. . .	. . .
Repairs on goods	2 160 . .	. . .	. . .	. . .	. . .	. . .	. . .	. . .	. . .
Goods procured in ports by carriers	2 170 . .	. . .	. . .	. . .	. . .	. . .	. . .	. . .	. . .
Nonmonetary gold	2 180 . .	. . .	. . .	. . .	. . .	. . .	. . .	. . .	. . .
Debit	3 100 . .	**–348.9**	**–349.3**	**–382.9**	**–399.1**	**–461.3**	**–400.4**	**–352.3**	. . .
General merchandise: imports f.o.b.	3 110 . .	–348.9	–349.3	–382.9	–399.1	–461.3	–400.4	–352.3	. . .
Goods for processing: imports f.o.b.	3 150 . .	. . .	. . .	. . .	. . .	. . .	. . .	. . .	. . .
Repairs on goods	3 160 . .	. . .	. . .	. . .	. . .	. . .	. . .	. . .	. . .
Goods procured in ports by carriers	3 170 . .	. . .	. . .	. . .	. . .	. . .	. . .	. . .	. . .
Nonmonetary gold	3 180 . .	. . .	. . .	. . .	. . .	. . .	. . .	. . .	. . .
B. SERVICES	4 200 . .	–181.8	–162.4	–110.1	–119.7	–158.9	–163.6	–155.1	. . .
Total credit	2 200 . .	*35.3*	*33.6*	*26.8*	*31.2*	*20.2*	*21.4*	*26.0*	. . .
Total debit	3 200 . .	*–217.0*	*–196.0*	*–136.8*	*–151.0*	*–179.1*	*–184.9*	*–181.1*	. . .
Transportation services, credit	2 205 . .	**6.9**	**6.0**	**4.9**	**6.5**	**2.2**	**2.6**	**1.7**	. . .
Passenger	2 205 BA	. . .	. . .	. . .	. . .	. . .	. . .	*.6*	. . .
Freight	2 205 BB	. . .	. . .	. . .	. . .	. . .	. . .	. . .	. . .
Other	2 205 BC	*6.9*	*6.0*	*4.9*	*6.5*	*2.2*	*2.6*	*1.1*	. . .
Sea transport, passenger	2 207 . .	. . .	. . .	. . .	. . .	. . .	. . .	. . .	. . .
Sea transport, freight	2 208 . .	. . .	. . .	. . .	. . .	. . .	. . .	. . .	. . .
Sea transport, other	2 209 . .	. . .	. . .	. . .	. . .	. . .	. . .	. . .	. . .
Air transport, passenger	2 211 . .	. . .	. . .	. . .	. . .	. . .	. . .	. . .	. . .
Air transport, freight	2 212 . .	. . .	. . .	. . .	. . .	. . .	. . .	. . .	. . .
Air transport, other	2 213 . .	. . .	. . .	. . .	. . .	. . .	. . .	. . .	. . .
Other transport, passenger	2 215 . .	. . .	. . .	. . .	. . .	. . .	. . .	. . .	. . .
Other transport, freight	2 216 . .	. . .	. . .	. . .	. . .	. . .	. . .	. . .	. . .
Other transport, other	2 217 . .	. . .	. . .	. . .	. . .	. . .	. . .	. . .	. . .
Transportation services, debit	3 205 . .	**–116.0**	**–97.2**	**–96.7**	**–103.4**	**–114.2**	**–92.0**	**–93.8**	. . .
Passenger	3 205 BA	*–10.1*	*–9.0*	*–11.5*	*–11.6*	*–10.3*	*–6.3*	*–5.9*	. . .
Freight	3 205 BB	*–36.0*	*–28.3*	*–34.9*	*–31.4*	*–39.5*	*–36.4*	*–31.5*	. . .
Other	3 205 BC	*–69.9*	*–59.9*	*–50.2*	*–60.4*	*–64.4*	*–49.3*	*–56.4*	. . .
Sea transport, passenger	3 207 . .	. . .	. . .	. . .	. . .	. . .	. . .	. . .	. . .
Sea transport, freight	3 208 . .	. . .	. . .	. . .	. . .	. . .	. . .	. . .	. . .
Sea transport, other	3 209 . .	. . .	. . .	. . .	. . .	. . .	. . .	. . .	. . .
Air transport, passenger	3 211 . .	. . .	. . .	. . .	. . .	. . .	. . .	. . .	. . .
Air transport, freight	3 212 . .	. . .	. . .	. . .	. . .	. . .	. . .	. . .	. . .
Air transport, other	3 213 . .	. . .	. . .	. . .	. . .	. . .	. . .	. . .	. . .
Other transport, passenger	3 215 . .	. . .	. . .	. . .	. . .	. . .	. . .	. . .	. . .
Other transport, freight	3 216 . .	. . .	. . .	. . .	. . .	. . .	. . .	. . .	. . .
Other transport, other	3 217 . .	. . .	. . .	. . .	. . .	. . .	. . .	. . .	. . .
Travel, credit	2 236 . .	**12.0**	**12.7**	**9.1**	**12.1**	**8.2**	**8.4**	**10.8**	. . .
Business travel	2 237 . .	. . .	. . .	. . .	. . .	. . .	. . .	. . .	. . .
Personal travel	2 240 . .	. . .	. . .	. . .	. . .	. . .	. . .	. . .	. . .
Travel, debit	3 236 . .	**–23.4**	**–30.7**	**–23.0**	**–26.2**	**–31.5**	**–19.7**	**–17.9**	. . .
Business travel	3 237 . .	. . .	. . .	. . .	. . .	. . .	. . .	. . .	. . .
Personal travel	3 240 . .	. . .	. . .	. . .	. . .	. . .	. . .	. . .	. . .
Other services, credit	2 200 BA	**16.4**	**14.9**	**12.7**	**12.7**	**9.8**	**10.4**	**13.5**	. . .
Communications	2 245 . .	. . .	. . .	. . .	. . .	. . .	. . .	. . .	. . .
Construction	2 249 . .	. . .	. . .	. . .	. . .	. . .	. . .	. . .	. . .
Insurance	2 253 . .	. . .	. . .	. . .	. . .	. . .	. . .	. . .	. . .
Financial	2 260 . .	. . .	. . .	. . .	. . .	. . .	. . .	. . .	. . .
Computer and information	2 262 . .	. . .	. . .	. . .	. . .	. . .	. . .	. . .	. . .
Royalties and licence fees	2 266 . .	. . .	. . .	. . .	. . .	. . .	. . .	. . .	. . .
Other business services	2 268 . .	4.1	3.5	. . .	. . .	. . .	4.4	4.1	. . .
Personal, cultural, and recreational	2 287 . .	. . .	. . .	. . .	. . .	. . .	. . .	. . .	. . .
Government, n.i.e.	2 291 . .	12.3	11.3	12.7	12.7	9.8	6.1	9.4	. . .
Other services, debit	3 200 BA	**–77.6**	**–68.1**	**–17.1**	**–21.4**	**–33.4**	**–73.2**	**–69.4**	. . .
Communications	3 245 . .	. . .	. . .	. . .	. . .	. . .	. . .	. . .	. . .
Construction	3 249 . .	. . .	. . .	. . .	. . .	. . .	. . .	. . .	. . .
Insurance	3 253 . .	–4.0	–3.1	–3.9	–3.5	–4.4	–4.0	–3.5	. . .
Financial	3 260 . .	. . .	. . .	. . .	. . .	. . .	. . .	. . .	. . .
Computer and information	3 262 . .	. . .	. . .	. . .	. . .	. . .	. . .	. . .	. . .
Royalties and licence fees	3 266 . .	. . .	. . .	. . .	. . .	. . .	. . .	. . .	. . .
Other business services	3 268 . .	–62.3	–56.8	–2.1	–2.9	–10.1	–50.8	–46.7	. . .
Personal, cultural, and recreational	3 287 . .	. . .	. . .	. . .	. . .	. . .	. . .	. . .	. . .
Government, n.i.e.	3 291 . .	–11.3	–8.1	–11.1	–14.9	–18.9	–18.4	–19.2	. . .

Table 2 (Continued). STANDARD PRESENTATION, 1988–95
(Millions of U.S. dollars)

	Code	1988	1989	1990	1991	1992	1993	1994	1995
C. INCOME	4 300 . .	–85.5	–50.0	–46.4	–32.9	–28.8	–96.8	–46.6	. . .
Total credit	2 300 . .	*4.1*	*5.6*	*3.8*	*2.0*	*1.1*	*.8*	*1.1*	. . .
Total debit	3 300 . .	*–89.7*	*–55.6*	*–50.2*	*–34.9*	*–29.9*	*–97.6*	*–47.7*	. . .
Compensation of employees, credit	2 310 . .	. . .	. . .	. . .	. . .	. . .	. . .	. . .	. . .
Compensation of employees, debit	3 310 . .	. . .	. . .	. . .	. . .	. . .	. . .	. . .	. . .
Investment income, credit	2 320 . .	**4.1**	**5.6**	**3.8**	**2.0**	**1.1**	**.8**	**1.1**	. . .
Direct investment income	2 330 . .	. . .	. . .	. . .	. . .	. . .	. . .	. . .	. . .
Dividends and distributed branch profits	2 332 . .	. . .	. . .	. . .	. . .	. . .	. . .	. . .	. . .
Reinvested earnings and undistributed branch profits	2 333 . .	. . .	. . .	. . .	. . .	. . .	. . .	. . .	. . .
Income on debt (interest)	2 334 . .	. . .	. . .	. . .	. . .	. . .	. . .	. . .	. . .
Portfolio investment income	2 339 . .	. . .	. . .	. . .	. . .	. . .	. . .	. . .	. . .
Income on equity	2 340 . .	. . .	. . .	. . .	. . .	. . .	. . .	. . .	. . .
Income on bonds and notes	2 350 . .	. . .	. . .	. . .	. . .	. . .	. . .	. . .	. . .
Income on money market instruments and financial derivatives	2 360 . .	. . .	. . .	. . .	. . .	. . .	. . .	. . .	. . .
Other investment income	2 370 . .	4.1	5.6	3.8	2.0	1.1	.8	1.1	. . .
Investment income, debit	3 320 . .	**–89.7**	**–55.6**	**–50.2**	**–34.9**	**–29.9**	**–97.6**	**–47.7**	. . .
Direct investment income	3 330 . .	–34.1	–12.8	–.7	–.7	–2.0	–1.8	–2.3	. . .
Dividends and distributed branch profits	3 332 . .	–34.1	–12.8	–.7	–.7	–2.0	–1.8	–2.3	. . .
Reinvested earnings and undistributed branch profits	3 333 . .	. . .	. . .	. . .	. . .	. . .	. . .	. . .	. . .
Income on debt (interest)	3 334 . .	. . .	. . .	. . .	. . .	. . .	. . .	. . .	. . .
Portfolio investment income	3 339 . .	. . .	. . .	. . .	. . .	. . .	. . .	. . .	. . .
Income on equity	3 340 . .	. . .	. . .	. . .	. . .	. . .	. . .	. . .	. . .
Income on bonds and notes	3 350 . .	. . .	. . .	. . .	. . .	. . .	. . .	. . .	. . .
Income on money market instruments and financial derivatives	3 360 . .	. . .	. . .	. . .	. . .	. . .	. . .	. . .	. . .
Other investment income	3 370 . .	–55.6	–42.8	–49.5	–34.1	–27.9	–95.8	–45.3	. . .
D. CURRENT TRANSFERS	4 379 . .	82.7	95.3	85.9	86.1	124.0	83.8	84.4	. . .
Credit	2 379 . .	**123.5**	**130.0**	**120.2**	**118.9**	**157.4**	**110.3**	**113.3**	. . .
General government	2 380 . .	107.8	119.0	100.7	101.2	98.0	102.4	101.8	. . .
Other sectors	2 390 . .	15.6	11.1	19.4	17.7	59.3	7.8	11.6	. . .
Workers' remittances	2 391 . .	9.3	4.8	13.7	11.7	50.1	2.3	4.9	. . .
Other current transfers	2 392 . .	6.3	6.3	5.7	6.0	9.2	5.6	6.7	. . .
Debit	3 379 . .	**–40.8**	**–34.7**	**–34.3**	**–32.8**	**–33.4**	**–26.5**	**–28.9**	. . .
General government	3 380 . .	–6.0	–1.8	–2.4	–1.7	–1.8	–2.8	–2.2	. . .
Other sectors	3 390 . .	–34.8	–33.0	–31.9	–31.1	–31.6	–23.7	–26.7	. . .
Workers' remittances	3 391 . .	–34.0	–32.5	–31.2	–29.4	–30.4	–22.8	–24.9	. . .
Other current transfers	3 392 . .	–.7	–.5	–.7	–1.7	–1.2	–.9	–1.8	. . .
CAPITAL AND FINANCIAL ACCOUNT	4 996 . .	**111.9**	**22.1**	**72.0**	**10.4**	**60.9**	**147.3**	**93.3**	. . .
CAPITAL ACCOUNT	4 994 . .	. . .	. . .	. . .	. . .	. . .	. . .	. . .	. . .
Total credit	2 994 . .	. . .	. . .	. . .	. . .	. . .	. . .	. . .	. . .
Total debit	3 994 . .	. . .	. . .	. . .	. . .	. . .	. . .	. . .	. . .
Capital transfers, credit	2 400 . .	. . .	. . .	. . .	. . .	. . .	. . .	. . .	. . .
General government	2 401 . .	. . .	. . .	. . .	. . .	. . .	. . .	. . .	. . .
Debt forgiveness	2 402 . .	. . .	. . .	. . .	. . .	. . .	. . .	. . .	. . .
Other capital transfers	2 410 . .	. . .	. . .	. . .	. . .	. . .	. . .	. . .	. . .
Other sectors	2 430 . .	. . .	. . .	. . .	. . .	. . .	. . .	. . .	. . .
Migrants' transfers	2 431 . .	. . .	. . .	. . .	. . .	. . .	. . .	. . .	. . .
Debt forgiveness	2 432 . .	. . .	. . .	. . .	. . .	. . .	. . .	. . .	. . .
Other capital transfers	2 440 . .	. . .	. . .	. . .	. . .	. . .	. . .	. . .	. . .
Capital transfers, debit	3 400 . .	. . .	. . .	. . .	. . .	. . .	. . .	. . .	. . .
General government	3 401 . .	. . .	. . .	. . .	. . .	. . .	. . .	. . .	. . .
Debt forgiveness	3 402 . .	. . .	. . .	. . .	. . .	. . .	. . .	. . .	. . .
Other capital transfers	3 410 . .	. . .	. . .	. . .	. . .	. . .	. . .	. . .	. . .
Other sectors	3 430 . .	. . .	. . .	. . .	. . .	. . .	. . .	. . .	. . .
Migrants' transfers	3 431 . .	. . .	. . .	. . .	. . .	. . .	. . .	. . .	. . .
Debt forgiveness	3 432 . .	. . .	. . .	. . .	. . .	. . .	. . .	. . .	. . .
Other capital transfers	3 440 . .	. . .	. . .	. . .	. . .	. . .	. . .	. . .	. . .
Nonproduced nonfinancial assets, credit	2 480 . .	. . .	. . .	. . .	. . .	. . .	. . .	. . .	. . .
Nonproduced nonfinancial assets, debit	3 480 . .	. . .	. . .	. . .	. . .	. . .	. . .	. . .	. . .

Table 2 (Continued). STANDARD PRESENTATION, 1988–95
(Millions of U.S. dollars)

	Code		1988	1989	1990	1991	1992	1993	1994	1995
FINANCIAL ACCOUNT	4 995	. .	**111.9**	**22.1**	**72.0**	**10.4**	**60.9**	**147.3**	**93.3**	**. . .**
A. DIRECT INVESTMENT	4 500	. .	1.0	3.5	6.7	2.3	7.5	16.1	2.1	. . .
Direct investment abroad	4 505	. .	**–.9**	**. . .**	**. . .**	**. . .**	**. . .**	**. . .**	**. . .**	**. . .**
Equity capital	4 510	. .	–.9	. . .	. . .	. . .	. . .	. . .	. . .	. . .
Claims on affiliated enterprises	4 515	. .	. . .	. . .	. . .	. . .	. . .	. . .	. . .	. . .
Liabilities to affiliated enterprises	4 520	. .	. . .	. . .	. . .	. . .	. . .	. . .	. . .	. . .
Reinvested earnings	4 525	. .	. . .	. . .	. . .	. . .	. . .	. . .	. . .	. . .
Other capital	4 530	. .	. . .	. . .	. . .	. . .	. . .	. . .	. . .	. . .
Claims on affiliated enterprises	4 535	. .	. . .	. . .	. . .	. . .	. . .	. . .	. . .	. . .
Liabilities to affiliated enterprises	4 540	. .	. . .	. . .	. . .	. . .	. . .	. . .	. . .	. . .
Direct investment in Mauritania	4 555	. .	**1.9**	**3.5**	**6.7**	**2.3**	**7.5**	**16.1**	**2.1**	**. . .**
Equity capital	4 560	. .	1.9	3.5	6.7	2.3	7.5	16.1	2.1	. . .
Claims on direct investors	4 565	. .	. . .	. . .	. . .	. . .	. . .	. . .	. . .	. . .
Liabilities to direct investors	4 570	. .	. . .	. . .	. . .	. . .	. . .	. . .	. . .	. . .
Reinvested earnings	4 575	. .	. . .	. . .	. . .	. . .	. . .	. . .	. . .	. . .
Other capital	4 580	. .	. . .	. . .	. . .	. . .	. . .	. . .	. . .	. . .
Claims on direct investors	4 585	. .	. . .	. . .	. . .	. . .	. . .	. . .	. . .	. . .
Liabilities to direct investors	4 590	. .	. . .	. . .	. . .	. . .	. . .	. . .	. . .	. . .
B. PORTFOLIO INVESTMENT	4 600	. .	. . .	. . .	. . .	. . .	. . .	–.1	–.2	. . .
Assets	4 602	. .	**. . .**	**. . .**	**. . .**	**. . .**	**. . .**	**. . .**	**. . .**	**. . .**
Equity securities	4 610	. .	. . .	. . .	. . .	. . .	. . .	. . .	. . .	. . .
Monetary authorities	4 611	. .	. . .	. . .	. . .	. . .	. . .	. . .	. . .	. . .
General government	4 612	. .	. . .	. . .	. . .	. . .	. . .	. . .	. . .	. . .
Banks	4 613	. .	. . .	. . .	. . .	. . .	. . .	. . .	. . .	. . .
Other sectors	4 614	. .	. . .	. . .	. . .	. . .	. . .	. . .	. . .	. . .
Debt securities	4 619	. .	. . .	. . .	. . .	. . .	. . .	. . .	. . .	. . .
Bonds and notes	4 620	. .	. . .	. . .	. . .	. . .	. . .	. . .	. . .	. . .
Monetary authorities	4 621	. .	. . .	. . .	. . .	. . .	. . .	. . .	. . .	. . .
General government	4 622	. .	. . .	. . .	. . .	. . .	. . .	. . .	. . .	. . .
Banks	4 623	. .	. . .	. . .	. . .	. . .	. . .	. . .	. . .	. . .
Other sectors	4 624	. .	. . .	. . .	. . .	. . .	. . .	. . .	. . .	. . .
Money market instruments	4 630	. .	. . .	. . .	. . .	. . .	. . .	. . .	. . .	. . .
Monetary authorities	4 631	. .	. . .	. . .	. . .	. . .	. . .	. . .	. . .	. . .
General government	4 632	. .	. . .	. . .	. . .	. . .	. . .	. . .	. . .	. . .
Banks	4 633	. .	. . .	. . .	. . .	. . .	. . .	. . .	. . .	. . .
Other sectors	4 634	. .	. . .	. . .	. . .	. . .	. . .	. . .	. . .	. . .
Financial derivatives	4 640	. .	. . .	. . .	. . .	. . .	. . .	. . .	. . .	. . .
Monetary authorities	4 641	. .	. . .	. . .	. . .	. . .	. . .	. . .	. . .	. . .
General government	4 642	. .	. . .	. . .	. . .	. . .	. . .	. . .	. . .	. . .
Banks	4 643	. .	. . .	. . .	. . .	. . .	. . .	. . .	. . .	. . .
Other sectors	4 644	. .	. . .	. . .	. . .	. . .	. . .	. . .	. . .	. . .
Liabilities	4 652	. .	**. . .**	**. . .**	**. . .**	**. . .**	**. . .**	**–.1**	**–.2**	**. . .**
Equity securities	4 660	. .	. . .	. . .	. . .	. . .	. . .	. . .	. . .	. . .
Banks	4 663	. .	. . .	. . .	. . .	. . .	. . .	. . .	. . .	. . .
Other sectors	4 664	. .	. . .	. . .	. . .	. . .	. . .	. . .	. . .	. . .
Debt securities	4 669	. .	. . .	. . .	. . .	. . .	. . .	–.1	–.2	. . .
Bonds and notes	4 670	. .	. . .	. . .	. . .	. . .	. . .	–.1	–.2	. . .
Monetary authorities	4 671	. .	. . .	. . .	. . .	. . .	. . .	. . .	. . .	. . .
General government	4 672	. .	. . .	. . .	. . .	. . .	. . .	–.1	–.2	. . .
Banks	4 673	. .	. . .	. . .	. . .	. . .	. . .	. . .	. . .	. . .
Other sectors	4 674	. .	. . .	. . .	. . .	. . .	. . .	. . .	. . .	. . .
Money market instruments	4 680	. .	. . .	. . .	. . .	. . .	. . .	. . .	. . .	. . .
Monetary authorities	4 681	. .	. . .	. . .	. . .	. . .	. . .	. . .	. . .	. . .
General government	4 682	. .	. . .	. . .	. . .	. . .	. . .	. . .	. . .	. . .
Banks	4 683	. .	. . .	. . .	. . .	. . .	. . .	. . .	. . .	. . .
Other sectors	4 684	. .	. . .	. . .	. . .	. . .	. . .	. . .	. . .	. . .
Financial derivatives	4 690	. .	. . .	. . .	. . .	. . .	. . .	. . .	. . .	. . .
Monetary authorities	4 691	. .	. . .	. . .	. . .	. . .	. . .	. . .	. . .	. . .
General government	4 692	. .	. . .	. . .	. . .	. . .	. . .	. . .	. . .	. . .
Banks	4 693	. .	. . .	. . .	. . .	. . .	. . .	. . .	. . .	. . .
Other sectors	4 694	. .	. . .	. . .	. . .	. . .	. . .	. . .	. . .	. . .

Table 2 (Concluded). STANDARD PRESENTATION, 1988–95

(Millions of U.S. dollars)

	Code	1988	1989	1990	1991	1992	1993	1994	1995
C. OTHER INVESTMENT	4 700 . .	100.3	35.4	24.6	11.2	73.8	62.3	44.6	. . .
Assets	4 703 . .	**2.2**	**–9.9**	**205.8**	**194.0**	**168.7**	**170.5**	**169.3**	**. . .**
Trade credits	4 706 . .	. . .	. . .	. . .	. . .	. . .	. . .	. . .	. . .
General government: long-term	4 708 . .	. . .	. . .	. . .	. . .	. . .	. . .	. . .	. . .
General government: short-term	4 709 . .	. . .	. . .	. . .	. . .	. . .	. . .	. . .	. . .
Other sectors: long-term	4 711 . .	. . .	. . .	. . .	. . .	. . .	. . .	. . .	. . .
Other sectors: short-term	4 712 . .	. . .	. . .	. . .	. . .	. . .	. . .	. . .	. . .
Loans	4 714 . .	. . .	. . .	. . .	. . .	. . .	. . .	. . .	. . .
Monetary authorities: long-term	4 717 . .	. . .	. . .	. . .	. . .	. . .	. . .	. . .	. . .
Monetary authorities: short-term	4 718 . .	. . .	. . .	. . .	. . .	. . .	. . .	. . .	. . .
General government: long-term	4 720 . .	. . .	. . .	. . .	. . .	. . .	. . .	. . .	. . .
General government: short-term	4 721 . .	. . .	. . .	. . .	. . .	. . .	. . .	. . .	. . .
Banks: long-term	4 723 . .	. . .	. . .	. . .	. . .	. . .	. . .	. . .	. . .
Banks: short-term	4 724 . .	. . .	. . .	. . .	. . .	. . .	. . .	. . .	. . .
Other sectors: long-term	4 726 . .	. . .	. . .	. . .	. . .	. . .	. . .	. . .	. . .
Other sectors: short-term	4 727 . .	. . .	. . .	. . .	. . .	. . .	. . .	. . .	. . .
Currency and deposits	4 730 . .	2.3	–9.9	205.8	194.0	168.7	171.3	171.5	. . .
Monetary authorities	4 731 . .	. . .	. . .	. . .	. . .	. . .	. . .	. . .	. . .
General government	4 732 . .	. . .	. . .	. . .	. . .	. . .	. . .	. . .	. . .
Banks	4 733 . .	11.4	–6.5	. . .	. . .	. . .	. . .	. . .	. . .
Other sectors	4 734 . .	–9.0	–3.4	205.8	194.0	168.7	171.3	171.5	. . .
Other assets	4 736 . .	–.1	. . .	. . .	. . .	. . .	–.8	–2.2	. . .
Monetary authorities: long-term	4 738 . .	. . .	. . .	. . .	. . .	. . .	. . .	. . .	. . .
Monetary authorities: short-term	4 739 . .	. . .	. . .	. . .	. . .	. . .	. . .	. . .	. . .
General government: long-term	4 741 . .	–.1	. . .	. . .	. . .	. . .	–.8	–2.2	. . .
General government: short-term	4 742 . .	. . .	. . .	. . .	. . .	. . .	. . .	. . .	. . .
Banks: long-term	4 744 . .	. . .	. . .	. . .	. . .	. . .	. . .	. . .	. . .
Banks: short-term	4 745 . .	. . .	. . .	. . .	. . .	. . .	. . .	. . .	. . .
Other sectors: long-term	4 747 . .	. . .	. . .	. . .	. . .	. . .	. . .	. . .	. . .
Other sectors: short-term	4 748 . .	. . .	. . .	. . .	. . .	. . .	. . .	. . .	. . .
Liabilities	4 753 . .	**98.1**	**45.3**	**–181.2**	**–182.8**	**–94.9**	**–108.2**	**–124.7**	**. . .**
Trade credits	4 756 . .	. . .	. . .	. . .	. . .	. . .	. . .	. . .	. . .
General government: long-term	4 758 . .	. . .	. . .	. . .	. . .	. . .	. . .	. . .	. . .
General government: short-term	4 759 . .	. . .	. . .	. . .	. . .	. . .	. . .	. . .	. . .
Other sectors: long-term	4 761 . .	. . .	. . .	. . .	. . .	. . .	. . .	. . .	. . .
Other sectors: short-term	4 762 . .	. . .	. . .	. . .	. . .	. . .	. . .	. . .	. . .
Loans	4 764 . .	70.3	33.2	46.3	37.3	77.9	103.7	60.8	. . .
Use of Fund credit and loans from the Fund	4 766 . .	–1.9	–.7	–4.5	–13.2	3.4	5.6	17.9	. . .
Monetary authorities: other long-term	4 767 . .	. . .	. . .	. . .	. . .	. . .	. . .	. . .	. . .
Monetary authorities: short-term	4 768 . .	. . .	. . .	. . .	. . .	. . .	. . .	. . .	. . .
General government: long-term	4 770 . .	32.3	32.2	–5.8	34.7	35.6	51.9	25.2	. . .
General government: short-term	4 771 . .	. . .	. . .	. . .	. . .	. . .	. . .	. . .	. . .
Banks: long-term	4 773 . .	–1.7	–5.3	–1.0	–.4	–.8	–.8	. . .	. . .
Banks: short-term	4 774 . .	. . .	. . .	. . .	. . .	. . .	. . .	. . .	. . .
Other sectors: long-term	4 776 . .	39.3	12.2	36.3	–1.3	39.7	46.9	17.7	. . .
Other sectors: short-term	4 777 . .	2.3	–5.2	21.4	17.5	. . .	. . .	. . .	. . .
Currency and deposits	4 780 . .	16.2	10.6	.4	–1.1	. . .	–18.1	. . .	. . .
Monetary authorities	4 781 . .	9.4	–.6	. . .	. . .	. . .	. . .	. . .	. . .
General government	4 782 . .	. . .	. . .	. . .	. . .	. . .	. . .	. . .	. . .
Banks	4 783 . .	6.7	11.1	.4	–1.1	. . .	–18.1	. . .	. . .
Other sectors	4 784 . .	. . .	. . .	. . .	. . .	. . .	. . .	. . .	. . .
Other liabilities	4 786 . .	11.7	1.5	–227.9	–219.0	–172.8	–193.9	–185.5	. . .
Monetary authorities: long-term	4 788 . .	. . .	. . .	. . .	. . .	. . .	. . .	. . .	. . .
Monetary authorities: short-term	4 789 . .	. . .	. . .	–1.6	2.4	. . .	. . .	. . .	. . .
General government: long-term	4 791 . .	. . .	. . .	. . .	. . .	. . .	. . .	. . .	. . .
General government: short-term	4 792 . .	. . .	. . .	. . .	. . .	. . .	. . .	. . .	. . .
Banks: long-term	4 794 . .	. . .	. . .	. . .	. . .	. . .	. . .	. . .	. . .
Banks: short-term	4 795 . .	. . .	. . .	. . .	. . .	. . .	. . .	. . .	. . .
Other sectors: long-term	4 797 . .	. . .	. . .	. . .	. . .	. . .	. . .	. . .	. . .
Other sectors: short-term	4 798 . .	11.7	1.5	–226.3	–221.3	–172.8	–193.9	–185.5	. . .
D. RESERVE ASSETS	4 800 . .	10.6	–16.8	40.6	–3.1	–20.4	69.0	46.9	. . .
Monetary gold	4 810 . .	. . .	. . .	.5	. . .	. . .	. . .	. . .	. . .
Special drawing rights	4 820 . .	16.3	–.1	–.6	.7	. . .	–.1	.1	. . .
Reserve position in the Fund	4 830 . .	. . .	. . .	. . .	. . .	. . .	. . .	. . .	. . .
Foreign exchange	4 840 . .	–5.8	–16.7	40.9	–4.9	–20.5	69.0	46.8	. . .
Other claims	4 880 . .	. . .	. . .	–.1	1.1	. . .	. . .	. . .	. . .
NET ERRORS AND OMISSIONS	4 998 . .	**–16.0**	**–3.6**	**–62.3**	**19.5**	**57.4**	**26.7**	**–23.5**	**. . .**

Table 1. ANALYTIC PRESENTATION, 1988–95
(Millions of U.S. dollars)

	Code	1988	1989	1990	1991	1992	1993	1994	1995
A. Current Account[1]	4 993 Y .	**–56.4**	**–103.5**	**–119.3**	**–18.2**	**–.1**	**–92.0**	**–232.1**	**–21.9**
Goods: exports f.o.b	2 100 . .	1,030.2	1,025.3	1,238.1	1,253.4	1,334.7	1,334.4	1,376.9	1,571.7
Goods: imports f.o.b	3 100 . .	–1,177.8	–1,217.7	–1,494.8	–1,438.5	–1,493.9	–1,576.0	–1,773.9	–1,812.2
Balance on Goods	4 100 . .	*–147.6*	*–192.4*	*–256.7*	*–185.1*	*–159.2*	*–241.6*	*–397.0*	*–240.5*
Services: credit	2 200 . .	348.8	372.7	483.9	528.3	577.5	566.2	632.7	777.7
Services: debit	3 200 . .	–307.1	–340.3	–421.0	–448.4	–522.8	–521.7	–546.4	–641.3
Balance on Goods and Services	4 991 . .	*–105.9*	*–160.0*	*–193.8*	*–105.2*	*–104.5*	*–197.1*	*–310.6*	*–104.2*
Income: credit	2 300 . .	26.6	51.1	55.9	82.5	91.0	70.0	31.7	52.2
Income: debit	3 300 . .	–70.7	–70.9	–78.7	–78.5	–80.1	–66.5	–56.4	–71.3
Balance on Goods, Services, and Income	4 992 . .	*–150.0*	*–179.8*	*–216.6*	*–101.1*	*–93.6*	*–193.6*	*–335.3*	*–123.3*
Current transfers: credit	2 379 Y .	103.3	84.9	108.5	98.6	109.9	115.9	129.6	146.8
Current transfers: debit	3 379 . .	–9.7	–8.7	–11.2	–15.7	–16.4	–14.4	–26.3	–45.4
B. Capital Account[1]	4 994 Y .	**–1.1**	**–.9**	**–.6**	**–1.6**	**–1.4**	**–1.5**	**–1.3**	**–1.1**
Capital account: credit	2 994 Y .	. . .	. . .	. . .	. . .	. . .	. . .	. . .	. . .
Capital account: debit	3 994 . .	–1.1	–.9	–.6	–1.6	–1.4	–1.5	–1.3	–1.1
Total, Groups A Plus B	4 010 . .	*–57.5*	*–104.4*	*–119.9*	*–19.8*	*–1.5*	*–93.5*	*–233.4*	*–22.9*
C. Financial Account[1]	4 995 X .	**121.2**	**50.2**	**138.6**	**41.8**	**–14.8**	**19.3**	**41.4**	**25.1**
Direct investment abroad	4 505 . .	–.1	–.6	–.6	–10.9	–43.3	–33.2	–1.1	–3.6
Direct investment in Mauritius	4 555 Y .	23.7	35.8	41.0	19.0	14.7	14.7	20.0	18.7
Portfolio investment assets	4 602 . .	. . .	. . .	–2.2	–.4	. . .	–2.2	–.3	. . .
Equity securities	4 610 . .	. . .	. . .	. . .	. . .	. . .	. . .	. . .	. . .
Debt securities	4 619 . .	. . .	. . .	–2.2	–.4	. . .	–2.2	–.3	. . .
Portfolio investment liabilities	4 652 Y .	. . .	. . .	. . .	. . .	. . .	. . .	2.1	175.9
Equity securities	4 660 Y .	. . .	. . .	. . .	. . .	. . .	. . .	2.1	22.0
Debt securities	4 669 Y .	. . .	. . .	. . .	. . .	. . .	. . .	. . .	154.0
Other investment assets	4 703 . .	–33.7	–49.4	–7.1	–36.2	14.3	–26.7	–64.6	–136.4
Monetary authorities	4 703 . A	. . .	. . .	. . .	. . .	. . .	. . .	. . .	. . .
General government	4 703 . B	. . .	–2.2	. . .	. . .	. . .	. . .	. . .	. . .
Banks	4 703 . C	–19.1	–19.3	–14.9	–16.8	33.0	–49.0	–11.5	–85.2
Other sectors	4 703 . D	–14.6	–27.9	7.7	–19.4	–18.7	22.3	–53.1	–51.2
Other investment liabilities	4 753 X .	131.3	64.4	107.4	70.4	–.5	66.6	85.2	–29.5
Monetary authorities	4 753 XA	. . .	. . .	. . .	. . .	. . .	. . .	. . .	. . .
General government	4 753 YB	–15.4	1.6	–5.3	–22.0	–34.7	1.4	–14.1	–18.8
Banks	4 753 YC	3.6	1.4	3.3	–2.4	–5.8	26.6	9.2	27.7
Other sectors	4 753 YD	143.0	61.4	109.5	94.7	40.0	38.6	90.1	–38.5
Total, Groups A Through C	4 020 . .	*63.6*	*–54.2*	*18.7*	*22.0*	*–16.3*	*–74.2*	*–192.0*	*2.1*
D. Net Errors and Omissions	4 998 . .	**121.2**	**199.8**	**213.2**	**168.8**	**59.6**	**81.2**	**148.5**	**106.7**
Total, Groups A Through D	4 030 . .	*184.8*	*145.6*	*231.9*	*190.8*	*43.3*	*7.0*	*–43.5*	*108.8*
E. Reserves and Related Items	4 040 . .	**–184.8**	**–145.6**	**–231.9**	**–190.8**	**–43.3**	**–7.0**	**43.5**	**–108.8**
Reserve assets	4 800 . .	–144.0	–108.5	–188.3	–168.9	–43.3	–7.0	43.5	–108.8
Use of Fund credit and loans	4 766 . .	–41.0	–37.1	–43.6	–21.9	. . .	. . .	. . .	. . .
Liabilities constituting foreign authorities' reserves	4 900 . .	. . .	. . .	. . .	. . .	. . .	. . .	. . .	. . .
Exceptional financing	4 920 . .	.2	. . .	. . .	. . .	. . .	. . .	. . .	. . .
Conversion rates: Mauritian rupees per U.S. dollar	0 101 . .	**13.438**	**15.250**	**14.863**	**15.652**	**15.563**	**17.648**	**17.960**	**17.386**

[1] Excludes components that have been classified in the categories of Group E.

Table 2. STANDARD PRESENTATION, 1988–95
(Millions of U.S. dollars)

	Code	1988	1989	1990	1991	1992	1993	1994	1995
CURRENT ACCOUNT	4 993 . .	**–56.2**	**–103.5**	**–119.3**	**–18.2**	**–.1**	**–92.0**	**–232.1**	**–21.9**
A. GOODS	4 100 . .	–147.6	–192.4	–256.7	–185.1	–159.2	–241.6	–397.0	–240.5
Credit	2 100 . .	**1,030.2**	**1,025.3**	**1,238.1**	**1,253.4**	**1,334.7**	**1,334.4**	**1,376.9**	**1,571.7**
General merchandise: exports f.o.b.	2 110 . .	1,001.3	994.4	1,205.2	1,215.1	1,302.6	1,304.4	1,343.5	1,538.9
Goods for processing: exports f.o.b.	2 150 . .	. . .	. . .	. . .	. . .	. . .	. . .	. . .	. . .
Repairs on goods	2 160 . .	. . .	. . .	. . .	. . .	. . .	. . .	. . .	. . .
Goods procured in ports by carriers	2 170 . .	28.9	30.8	32.8	38.3	32.1	30.0	33.4	32.8
Nonmonetary gold	2 180 . .	. . .	. . .	. . .	. . .	. . .	. . .	. . .	. . .
Debit	3 100 . .	**–1,177.8**	**–1,217.7**	**–1,494.8**	**–1,438.5**	**–1,493.9**	**–1,576.0**	**–1,773.9**	**–1,812.2**
General merchandise: imports f.o.b.	3 110 . .	–1,163.0	–1,205.6	–1,474.8	–1,419.1	–1,473.4	–1,558.6	–1,759.5	–1,797.2
Goods for processing: imports f.o.b.	3 150 . .	. . .	. . .	. . .	. . .	. . .	. . .	. . .	. . .
Repairs on goods	3 160 . .	. . .	. . .	. . .	. . .	. . .	. . .	. . .	. . .
Goods procured in ports by carriers	3 170 . .	–14.8	–12.1	–20.0	–19.4	–20.5	–17.4	–14.4	–15.1
Nonmonetary gold	3 180 . .	. . .	. . .	. . .	. . .	. . .	. . .	. . .	. . .
B. SERVICES	4 200 . .	41.7	32.4	62.9	79.9	54.7	44.5	86.4	136.4
Total credit	2 200 . .	*348.8*	*372.7*	*483.9*	*528.3*	*577.5*	*566.2*	*632.7*	*777.7*
Total debit	3 200 . .	*–307.1*	*–340.3*	*–421.0*	*–448.4*	*–522.8*	*–521.7*	*–546.4*	*–641.3*
Transportation services, credit	2 205 . .	**106.1**	**113.6**	**157.4**	**173.6**	**187.3**	**155.7**	**170.7**	**199.7**
Passenger	2 205 BA	*89.7*	*97.8*	*141.1*	*156.2*	*171.6*	*144.3*	*157.3*	*185.5*
Freight	2 205 BB	*3.3*	*3.7*	*4.2*	*6.6*	*1.4*	*.7*	*.8*	*.9*
Other	2 205 BC	*13.1*	*12.1*	*12.1*	*10.8*	*14.2*	*10.8*	*12.5*	*13.3*
Sea transport, passenger	2 207 . .	. . .	. . .	. . .	. . .	. . .	. . .	. . .	. . .
Sea transport, freight	2 208 . .	. . .	. . .	. . .	. . .	. . .	. . .	. . .	. . .
Sea transport, other	2 209 . .	. . .	. . .	. . .	. . .	. . .	. . .	. . .	. . .
Air transport, passenger	2 211 . .	. . .	. . .	. . .	. . .	. . .	. . .	. . .	. . .
Air transport, freight	2 212 . .	. . .	. . .	. . .	. . .	. . .	. . .	. . .	. . .
Air transport, other	2 213 . .	. . .	. . .	. . .	. . .	. . .	. . .	. . .	. . .
Other transport, passenger	2 215 . .	. . .	. . .	. . .	. . .	. . .	. . .	. . .	. . .
Other transport, freight	2 216 . .	. . .	. . .	. . .	. . .	. . .	. . .	. . .	. . .
Other transport, other	2 217 . .	. . .	. . .	. . .	. . .	. . .	. . .	. . .	. . .
Transportation services, debit	3 205 . .	**–165.3**	**–173.7**	**–209.9**	**–208.8**	**–233.9**	**–236.9**	**–233.5**	**–251.7**
Passenger	3 205 BA	*–17.4*	*–15.6*	*–17.4*	*–18.4*	*–22.0*	*–23.1*	*–23.7*	*–25.0*
Freight	3 205 BB	*–104.7*	*–106.5*	*–126.4*	*–122.4*	*–126.7*	*–135.7*	*–135.6*	*–149.3*
Other	3 205 BC	*–43.2*	*–51.7*	*–66.1*	*–68.0*	*–85.1*	*–78.1*	*–74.2*	*–77.4*
Sea transport, passenger	3 207 . .	. . .	. . .	. . .	. . .	. . .	. . .	. . .	. . .
Sea transport, freight	3 208 . .	. . .	. . .	. . .	. . .	. . .	. . .	. . .	. . .
Sea transport, other	3 209 . .	. . .	. . .	. . .	. . .	. . .	. . .	. . .	. . .
Air transport, passenger	3 211 . .	. . .	. . .	. . .	. . .	. . .	. . .	. . .	. . .
Air transport, freight	3 212 . .	. . .	. . .	. . .	. . .	. . .	. . .	. . .	. . .
Air transport, other	3 213 . .	. . .	. . .	. . .	. . .	. . .	. . .	. . .	. . .
Other transport, passenger	3 215 . .	. . .	. . .	. . .	. . .	. . .	. . .	. . .	. . .
Other transport, freight	3 216 . .	. . .	. . .	. . .	. . .	. . .	. . .	. . .	. . .
Other transport, other	3 217 . .	. . .	. . .	. . .	. . .	. . .	. . .	. . .	. . .
Travel, credit	2 236 . .	**177.2**	**183.3**	**244.2**	**251.7**	**299.1**	**303.8**	**357.2**	**429.8**
Business travel	2 237 . .	. . .	. . .	. . .	. . .	. . .	. . .	. . .	. . .
Personal travel	2 240 . .	. . .	. . .	. . .	. . .	. . .	. . .	. . .	. . .
Travel, debit	3 236 . .	**–63.8**	**–79.3**	**–93.5**	**–110.0**	**–142.0**	**–127.5**	**–142.9**	**–159.0**
Business travel	3 237 . .	. . .	. . .	. . .	. . .	. . .	. . .	. . .	. . .
Personal travel	3 240 . .	. . .	. . .	. . .	. . .	. . .	. . .	. . .	. . .
Other services, credit	2 200 BA	**65.6**	**75.8**	**82.2**	**103.0**	**91.1**	**106.7**	**104.9**	**148.2**
Communications	2 245 . .	. . .	. . .	. . .	. . .	. . .	. . .	. . .	. . .
Construction	2 249 . .	. . .	. . .	. . .	. . .	. . .	. . .	. . .	. . .
Insurance	2 253 . .	.4	.4	.5	.7	.2	.1	.1	.1
Financial	2 260 . .	. . .	. . .	. . .	. . .	. . .	. . .	. . .	. . .
Computer and information	2 262 . .	. . .	. . .	. . .	. . .	. . .	. . .	. . .	. . .
Royalties and licence fees	2 266 . .	. . .	. . .	. . .	. . .	. . .	. . .	. . .	. . .
Other business services	2 268 . .	59.6	70.3	75.7	96.4	86.7	101.7	101.1	143.1
Personal, cultural, and recreational	2 287 . .	. . .	. . .	. . .	. . .	. . .	. . .	. . .	. . .
Government, n.i.e.	2 291 . .	5.6	5.0	6.1	5.9	4.2	4.9	3.7	5.0
Other services, debit	3 200 BA	**–78.0**	**–87.3**	**–117.6**	**–129.6**	**–146.9**	**–157.3**	**–170.0**	**–230.6**
Communications	3 245 . .	. . .	. . .	. . .	. . .	. . .	. . .	. . .	. . .
Construction	3 249 . .	. . .	. . .	. . .	. . .	. . .	. . .	. . .	. . .
Insurance	3 253 . .	–17.9	–20.6	–22.2	–22.6	–23.9	–29.1	–22.7	–28.9
Financial	3 260 . .	. . .	. . .	. . .	. . .	. . .	. . .	. . .	. . .
Computer and information	3 262 . .	. . .	. . .	. . .	. . .	. . .	. . .	. . .	. . .
Royalties and licence fees	3 266 . .	. . .	. . .	. . .	. . .	. . .	. . .	. . .	. . .
Other business services	3 268 . .	–51.1	–59.3	–81.0	–94.1	–107.6	–109.0	–126.8	–190.9
Personal, cultural, and recreational	3 287 . .	. . .	. . .	. . .	. . .	. . .	. . .	. . .	. . .
Government, n.i.e.	3 291 . .	–9.0	–7.5	–14.3	–12.9	–15.4	–19.2	–20.4	–10.8

Table 2 (Continued). STANDARD PRESENTATION, 1988–95
(Millions of U.S. dollars)

	Code		1988	1989	1990	1991	1992	1993	1994	1995
C. INCOME	4 300	. .	–44.1	–19.8	–22.8	4.1	11.0	3.5	–24.7	–19.1
Total credit	2 300	. .	*26.6*	*51.1*	*55.9*	*82.5*	*91.0*	*70.0*	*31.7*	*52.2*
Total debit	3 300	. .	*–70.7*	*–70.9*	*–78.7*	*–78.5*	*–80.1*	*–66.5*	*–56.4*	*–71.3*
Compensation of employees, credit	2 310	. .	**. . .**	**. . .**	**. . .**	**. . .**	**. . .**	**. . .**	**. . .**	**. . .**
Compensation of employees, debit	3 310	. .	**. . .**	**. . .**	**. . .**	**. . .**	**. . .**	**. . .**	**. . .**	**. . .**
Investment income, credit	2 320	. .	**26.6**	**51.1**	**55.9**	**82.5**	**91.0**	**70.0**	**31.7**	**52.2**
Direct investment income	2 330	. .	1.6	3.4	2.0	3.5	5.2	2.0	1.1	1.6
Dividends and distributed branch profits	2 332	. .	1.6	3.3	2.0	3.5	5.2	2.0	1.1	1.6
Reinvested earnings and undistributed branch profits	2 333	. .	. . .	.1	. . .	. . .	. . .	. . .	. . .	. . .
Income on debt (interest)	2 334	. .	. . .	. . .	. . .	. . .	. . .	. . .	. . .	. . .
Portfolio investment income	2 339	. .	. . .	. . .	. . .	. . .	. . .	. . .	. . .	. . .
Income on equity	2 340	. .	. . .	. . .	. . .	. . .	. . .	. . .	. . .	. . .
Income on bonds and notes	2 350	. .	. . .	. . .	. . .	. . .	. . .	. . .	. . .	. . .
Income on money market instruments and financial derivatives	2 360	. .	. . .	. . .	. . .	. . .	. . .	. . .	. . .	. . .
Other investment income	2 370	. .	24.9	47.7	53.9	79.0	85.8	67.9	30.6	50.7
Investment income, debit	3 320	. .	**–70.7**	**–70.9**	**–78.7**	**–78.5**	**–80.1**	**–66.5**	**–56.4**	**–71.3**
Direct investment income	3 330	. .	–16.0	–16.9	–22.5	–22.2	–22.0	–20.1	–11.6	–15.5
Dividends and distributed branch profits	3 332	. .	–14.7	–16.5	–17.8	–20.6	–21.1	–20.0	–11.6	–15.5
Reinvested earnings and undistributed branch profits	3 333	. .	–1.3	–.4	–4.6	–1.6	–.9	–.1	. . .	. . .
Income on debt (interest)	3 334	. .	. . .	. . .	. . .	. . .	. . .	. . .	. . .	. . .
Portfolio investment income	3 339	. .	. . .	. . .	. . .	. . .	. . .	. . .	. . .	. . .
Income on equity	3 340	. .	. . .	. . .	. . .	. . .	. . .	. . .	. . .	. . .
Income on bonds and notes	3 350	. .	. . .	. . .	. . .	. . .	. . .	. . .	. . .	. . .
Income on money market instruments and financial derivatives	3 360	. .	. . .	. . .	. . .	. . .	. . .	. . .	. . .	. . .
Other investment income	3 370	. .	–54.7	–54.0	–56.2	–56.2	–58.1	–46.4	–44.8	–55.8
D. CURRENT TRANSFERS	4 379	. .	93.8	76.3	97.4	82.9	93.4	101.5	103.2	101.4
Credit	2 379	. .	**103.5**	**84.9**	**108.5**	**98.6**	**109.9**	**115.9**	**129.6**	**146.8**
General government	2 380	. .	22.9	9.5	16.7	3.8	7.7	11.4	12.0	9.6
Other sectors	2 390	. .	80.6	75.4	91.8	94.9	102.2	104.5	117.5	137.2
Workers' remittances	2 391	. .	. . .	. . .	. . .	. . .	. . .	. . .	. . .	. . .
Other current transfers	2 392	. .	80.6	75.4	91.8	94.9	102.2	104.5	117.5	137.2
Debit	3 379	. .	**–9.7**	**–8.7**	**–11.2**	**–15.7**	**–16.4**	**–14.4**	**–26.3**	**–45.4**
General government	3 380	. .	–1.8	–2.2	–2.2	–1.9	–2.3	–3.1	–3.3	–3.3
Other sectors	3 390	. .	–7.9	–6.4	–8.9	–13.8	–14.1	–11.3	–23.0	–42.1
Workers' remittances	3 391	. .	. . .	. . .	. . .	. . .	. . .	. . .	. . .	. . .
Other current transfers	3 392	. .	–7.9	–6.4	–8.9	–13.8	–14.1	–11.3	–23.0	–42.1
CAPITAL AND FINANCIAL ACCOUNT	4 996	. .	**–65.0**	**–96.3**	**–94.0**	**–150.6**	**–59.5**	**10.8**	**83.5**	**–84.8**
CAPITAL ACCOUNT	4 994	. .	**–1.1**	**–.9**	**–.6**	**–1.6**	**–1.4**	**–1.5**	**–1.3**	**–1.1**
Total credit	2 994	. .	. . .	. . .	. . .	. . .	. . .	. . .	. . .	. . .
Total debit	3 994	. .	*–1.1*	*–.9*	*–.6*	*–1.6*	*–1.4*	*–1.5*	*–1.3*	*–1.1*
Capital transfers, credit	2 400	. .	**. . .**	**. . .**	**. . .**	**. . .**	**. . .**	**. . .**	**. . .**	**. . .**
General government	2 401	. .	. . .	. . .	. . .	. . .	. . .	. . .	. . .	. . .
Debt forgiveness	2 402	. .	. . .	. . .	. . .	. . .	. . .	. . .	. . .	. . .
Other capital transfers	2 410	. .	. . .	. . .	. . .	. . .	. . .	. . .	. . .	. . .
Other sectors	2 430	. .	. . .	. . .	. . .	. . .	. . .	. . .	. . .	. . .
Migrants' transfers	2 431	. .	. . .	. . .	. . .	. . .	. . .	. . .	. . .	. . .
Debt forgiveness	2 432	. .	. . .	. . .	. . .	. . .	. . .	. . .	. . .	. . .
Other capital transfers	2 440	. .	. . .	. . .	. . .	. . .	. . .	. . .	. . .	. . .
Capital transfers, debit	3 400	. .	**–1.1**	**–.9**	**–.6**	**–1.6**	**–1.4**	**–1.5**	**–1.3**	**–1.1**
General government	3 401	. .	. . .	. . .	. . .	. . .	. . .	. . .	. . .	. . .
Debt forgiveness	3 402	. .	. . .	. . .	. . .	. . .	. . .	. . .	. . .	. . .
Other capital transfers	3 410	. .	. . .	. . .	. . .	. . .	. . .	. . .	. . .	. . .
Other sectors	3 430	. .	–1.1	–.9	–.6	–1.6	–1.4	–1.5	–1.3	–1.1
Migrants' transfers	3 431	. .	–1.1	–.9	–.6	–1.6	–1.4	–1.5	–1.3	–1.1
Debt forgiveness	3 432	. .	. . .	. . .	. . .	. . .	. . .	. . .	. . .	. . .
Other capital transfers	3 440	. .	. . .	. . .	. . .	. . .	. . .	. . .	. . .	. . .
Nonproduced nonfinancial assets, credit	2 480	. .	**. . .**	**. . .**	**. . .**	**. . .**	**. . .**	**. . .**	**. . .**	**. . .**
Nonproduced nonfinancial assets, debit	3 480	. .	**. . .**	**. . .**	**. . .**	**. . .**	**. . .**	**. . .**	**. . .**	**. . .**

Table 2 (Continued). STANDARD PRESENTATION, 1988–95

(Millions of U.S. dollars)

	Code	1988	1989	1990	1991	1992	1993	1994	1995
FINANCIAL ACCOUNT	4 995 . .	**–63.9**	**–95.4**	**–93.4**	**–149.0**	**–58.1**	**12.3**	**84.9**	**–83.7**
A. DIRECT INVESTMENT	4 500 . .	23.6	35.2	40.4	8.1	–28.6	–18.5	18.9	15.1
Direct investment abroad	4 505 . .	**–.1**	**–.6**	**–.6**	**–10.9**	**–43.3**	**–33.2**	**–1.1**	**–3.6**
Equity capital	4 510 . .	. . .	. . .	. . .	. . .	. . .	. . .	. . .	. . .
Claims on affiliated enterprises	4 515 . .	. . .	. . .	. . .	. . .	. . .	. . .	. . .	. . .
Liabilities to affiliated enterprises	4 520 . .	. . .	. . .	. . .	. . .	. . .	. . .	. . .	. . .
Reinvested earnings	4 525 . .	. . .	–.1	. . .	. . .	. . .	. . .	. . .	. . .
Other capital	4 530 . .	–.1	–.5	–.6	–10.9	–43.3	–33.2	–1.1	–3.6
Claims on affiliated enterprises	4 535 . .	. . .	. . .	. . .	. . .	. . .	. . .	. . .	. . .
Liabilities to affiliated enterprises	4 540 . .	. . .	. . .	. . .	. . .	. . .	. . .	. . .	. . .
Direct investment in Mauritius	4 555 . .	**23.7**	**35.8**	**41.0**	**19.0**	**14.7**	**14.7**	**20.0**	**18.7**
Equity capital	4 560 . .	. . .	. . .	. . .	. . .	. . .	. . .	. . .	. . .
Claims on direct investors	4 565 . .	. . .	. . .	. . .	. . .	. . .	. . .	. . .	. . .
Liabilities to direct investors	4 570 . .	. . .	. . .	. . .	. . .	. . .	. . .	. . .	. . .
Reinvested earnings	4 575 . .	1.3	.4	4.6	1.6	.9	.1	. . .	. . .
Other capital	4 580 . .	22.4	35.4	36.4	17.4	13.8	14.7	20.0	18.7
Claims on direct investors	4 585 . .	. . .	. . .	. . .	. . .	. . .	. . .	. . .	. . .
Liabilities to direct investors	4 590 . .	. . .	. . .	. . .	. . .	. . .	. . .	. . .	. . .
B. PORTFOLIO INVESTMENT	4 600 . .	. . .	. . .	–2.2	–.4	. . .	–2.2	1.8	175.9
Assets	4 602 . .	**. . .**	**. . .**	**–2.2**	**–.4**	**. . .**	**–2.2**	**–.3**	**. . .**
Equity securities	4 610 . .	. . .	. . .	. . .	. . .	. . .	. . .	. . .	. . .
Monetary authorities	4 611 . .	. . .	. . .	. . .	. . .	. . .	. . .	. . .	. . .
General government	4 612 . .	. . .	. . .	. . .	. . .	. . .	. . .	. . .	. . .
Banks	4 613 . .	. . .	. . .	. . .	. . .	. . .	. . .	. . .	. . .
Other sectors	4 614 . .	. . .	. . .	. . .	. . .	. . .	. . .	. . .	. . .
Debt securities	4 619 . .	. . .	. . .	–2.2	–.4	. . .	–2.2	–.3	. . .
Bonds and notes	4 620 . .	. . .	. . .	–2.2	–.4	. . .	–2.2	–.3	. . .
Monetary authorities	4 621 . .	. . .	. . .	. . .	. . .	. . .	. . .	. . .	. . .
General government	4 622 . .	. . .	. . .	. . .	. . .	. . .	. . .	. . .	. . .
Banks	4 623 . .	. . .	. . .	. . .	. . .	. . .	. . .	. . .	. . .
Other sectors	4 624 . .	. . .	. . .	. . .	. . .	. . .	. . .	. . .	. . .
Money market instruments	4 630 . .	. . .	. . .	. . .	. . .	. . .	. . .	. . .	. . .
Monetary authorities	4 631 . .	. . .	. . .	. . .	. . .	. . .	. . .	. . .	. . .
General government	4 632 . .	. . .	. . .	. . .	. . .	. . .	. . .	. . .	. . .
Banks	4 633 . .	. . .	. . .	. . .	. . .	. . .	. . .	. . .	. . .
Other sectors	4 634 . .	. . .	. . .	. . .	. . .	. . .	. . .	. . .	. . .
Financial derivatives	4 640 . .	. . .	. . .	. . .	. . .	. . .	. . .	. . .	. . .
Monetary authorities	4 641 . .	. . .	. . .	. . .	. . .	. . .	. . .	. . .	. . .
General government	4 642 . .	. . .	. . .	. . .	. . .	. . .	. . .	. . .	. . .
Banks	4 643 . .	. . .	. . .	. . .	. . .	. . .	. . .	. . .	. . .
Other sectors	4 644 . .	. . .	. . .	. . .	. . .	. . .	. . .	. . .	. . .
Liabilities	4 652 . .	**. . .**	**. . .**	**. . .**	**. . .**	**. . .**	**. . .**	**2.1**	**175.9**
Equity securities	4 660 . .	. . .	. . .	. . .	. . .	. . .	. . .	2.1	22.0
Banks	4 663 . .	. . .	. . .	. . .	. . .	. . .	. . .	. . .	. . .
Other sectors	4 664 . .	. . .	. . .	. . .	. . .	. . .	. . .	. . .	22.0
Debt securities	4 669 . .	. . .	. . .	. . .	. . .	. . .	. . .	. . .	154.0
Bonds and notes	4 670 . .	. . .	. . .	. . .	. . .	. . .	. . .	. . .	154.0
Monetary authorities	4 671 . .	. . .	. . .	. . .	. . .	. . .	. . .	. . .	. . .
General government	4 672 . .	. . .	. . .	. . .	. . .	. . .	. . .	. . .	. . .
Banks	4 673 . .	. . .	. . .	. . .	. . .	. . .	. . .	. . .	. . .
Other sectors	4 674 . .	. . .	. . .	. . .	. . .	. . .	. . .	. . .	. . .
Money market instruments	4 680 . .	. . .	. . .	. . .	. . .	. . .	. . .	. . .	. . .
Monetary authorities	4 681 . .	. . .	. . .	. . .	. . .	. . .	. . .	. . .	. . .
General government	4 682 . .	. . .	. . .	. . .	. . .	. . .	. . .	. . .	. . .
Banks	4 683 . .	. . .	. . .	. . .	. . .	. . .	. . .	. . .	. . .
Other sectors	4 684 . .	. . .	. . .	. . .	. . .	. . .	. . .	. . .	. . .
Financial derivatives	4 690 . .	. . .	. . .	. . .	. . .	. . .	. . .	. . .	. . .
Monetary authorities	4 691 . .	. . .	. . .	. . .	. . .	. . .	. . .	. . .	. . .
General government	4 692 . .	. . .	. . .	. . .	. . .	. . .	. . .	. . .	. . .
Banks	4 693 . .	. . .	. . .	. . .	. . .	. . .	. . .	. . .	. . .
Other sectors	4 694 . .	. . .	. . .	. . .	. . .	. . .	. . .	. . .	. . .

Table 2 (Concluded). STANDARD PRESENTATION, 1988–95
(Millions of U.S. dollars)

	Code	1988	1989	1990	1991	1992	1993	1994	1995
C. OTHER INVESTMENT	4 700 . .	56.5	–22.1	56.7	12.3	13.8	39.9	20.6	–165.9
Assets	4 703 . .	**–33.7**	**–49.4**	**–7.1**	**–36.2**	**14.3**	**–26.7**	**–64.6**	**–136.4**
Trade credits	4 706 . .	. . .	. . .	. . .	. . .	. . .	. . .	. . .	. . .
General government: long-term	4 708 . .	. . .	. . .	. . .	. . .	. . .	. . .	. . .	. . .
General government: short-term	4 709 . .	. . .	. . .	. . .	. . .	. . .	. . .	. . .	. . .
Other sectors: long-term	4 711 . .	. . .	. . .	. . .	. . .	. . .	. . .	. . .	. . .
Other sectors: short-term	4 712 . .	. . .	. . .	. . .	. . .	. . .	. . .	. . .	. . .
Loans	4 714 . .	–3.5	–19.8	12.1	–3.0	–16.6	18.1	.2	–23.0
Monetary authorities: long-term	4 717 . .	. . .	. . .	. . .	. . .	. . .	. . .	. . .	. . .
Monetary authorities: short-term	4 718 . .	. . .	. . .	. . .	. . .	. . .	. . .	. . .	. . .
General government: long-term	4 720 . .	. . .	. . .	. . .	. . .	. . .	. . .	. . .	. . .
General government: short-term	4 721 . .	. . .	–2.2	. . .	. . .	. . .	. . .	. . .	. . .
Banks: long-term	4 723 . .	. . .	. . .	. . .	. . .	. . .	. . .	. . .	. . .
Banks: short-term	4 724 . .	. . .	. . .	. . .	. . .	. . .	. . .	. . .	. . .
Other sectors: long-term	4 726 . .	. . .	. . .	. . .	. . .	. . .	. . .	. . .	. . .
Other sectors: short-term	4 727 . .	–3.5	–17.6	12.1	–3.0	–16.6	18.1	.2	–23.0
Currency and deposits	4 730 . .	–30.2	–29.6	–19.2	–33.2	30.9	–44.8	–49.2	–98.1
Monetary authorities	4 731 . .	. . .	. . .	. . .	. . .	. . .	. . .	. . .	. . .
General government	4 732 . .	. . .	. . .	. . .	. . .	. . .	. . .	. . .	. . .
Banks	4 733 . .	–19.1	–19.3	–14.9	–16.8	33.0	–49.0	–11.5	–85.2
Other sectors	4 734 . .	–11.1	–10.4	–4.4	–16.4	–2.1	4.1	–37.7	–12.8
Other assets	4 736 . .	. . .	. . .	. . .	. . .	. . .	. . .	–15.5	–15.4
Monetary authorities: long-term	4 738 . .	. . .	. . .	. . .	. . .	. . .	. . .	. . .	. . .
Monetary authorities: short-term	4 739 . .	. . .	. . .	. . .	. . .	. . .	. . .	. . .	. . .
General government: long-term	4 741 . .	. . .	. . .	. . .	. . .	. . .	. . .	. . .	. . .
General government: short-term	4 742 . .	. . .	. . .	. . .	. . .	. . .	. . .	. . .	. . .
Banks: long-term	4 744 . .	. . .	. . .	. . .	. . .	. . .	. . .	. . .	. . .
Banks: short-term	4 745 . .	. . .	. . .	. . .	. . .	. . .	. . .	. . .	. . .
Other sectors: long-term	4 747 . .	. . .	. . .	. . .	. . .	. . .	. . .	–15.5	–15.4
Other sectors: short-term	4 748 . .	. . .	. . .	. . .	. . .	. . .	. . .	. . .	. . .
Liabilities	4 753 . .	**90.2**	**27.3**	**63.8**	**48.5**	**–.5**	**66.6**	**85.2**	**–29.5**
Trade credits	4 756 . .	. . .	. . .	. . .	. . .	. . .	. . .	. . .	. . .
General government: long-term	4 758 . .	. . .	. . .	. . .	. . .	. . .	. . .	. . .	. . .
General government: short-term	4 759 . .	. . .	. . .	. . .	. . .	. . .	. . .	. . .	. . .
Other sectors: long-term	4 761 . .	. . .	. . .	. . .	. . .	. . .	. . .	. . .	. . .
Other sectors: short-term	4 762 . .	. . .	. . .	. . .	. . .	. . .	. . .	. . .	. . .
Loans	4 764 . .	85.8	26.4	62.3	48.7	5.1	40.9	76.3	–57.2
Use of Fund credit and loans from the Fund	4 766 . .	–41.0	–37.1	–43.6	–21.9	. . .	. . .	. . .	. . .
Monetary authorities: other long-term	4 767 . .	. . .	. . .	. . .	. . .	. . .	. . .	. . .	. . .
Monetary authorities: short-term	4 768 . .	. . .	. . .	. . .	. . .	. . .	. . .	. . .	. . .
General government: long-term	4 770 . .	–15.4	1.6	–5.3	–22.0	–34.7	1.4	–14.1	–18.8
General government: short-term	4 771 . .	. . .	. . .	. . .	. . .	. . .	. . .	. . .	. . .
Banks: long-term	4 773 . .	. . .	. . .	. . .	. . .	. . .	. . .	. . .	. . .
Banks: short-term	4 774 . .	. . .	. . .	. . .	. . .	. . .	. . .	. . .	. . .
Other sectors: long-term	4 776 . .	134.2	70.7	111.2	92.6	39.8	39.4	90.4	–38.5
Other sectors: short-term	4 777 . .	8.0	–8.8	. . .	. . .	. . .	. . .	. . .	. . .
Currency and deposits	4 780 . .	3.6	1.4	3.3	–2.4	–5.8	26.6	9.2	27.7
Monetary authorities	4 781 . .	. . .	. . .	. . .	. . .	. . .	. . .	. . .	. . .
General government	4 782 . .	. . .	. . .	. . .	. . .	. . .	. . .	. . .	. . .
Banks	4 783 . .	3.6	1.4	3.3	–2.4	–5.8	26.6	9.2	27.7
Other sectors	4 784 . .	. . .	. . .	. . .	. . .	. . .	. . .	. . .	. . .
Other liabilities	4 786 . .	.8	–.5	–1.7	2.2	.2	–.8	–.3	. . .
Monetary authorities: long-term	4 788 . .	. . .	. . .	. . .	. . .	. . .	. . .	. . .	. . .
Monetary authorities: short-term	4 789 . .	. . .	. . .	. . .	. . .	. . .	. . .	. . .	. . .
General government: long-term	4 791 . .	. . .	. . .	. . .	. . .	. . .	. . .	. . .	. . .
General government: short-term	4 792 . .	. . .	. . .	. . .	. . .	. . .	. . .	. . .	. . .
Banks: long-term	4 794 . .	. . .	. . .	. . .	. . .	. . .	. . .	. . .	. . .
Banks: short-term	4 795 . .	. . .	. . .	. . .	. . .	. . .	. . .	. . .	. . .
Other sectors: long-term	4 797 . .	. . .	. . .	. . .	. . .	. . .	. . .	. . .	. . .
Other sectors: short-term	4 798 . .	.8	–.5	–1.7	2.2	.2	–.8	–.3	. . .
D. RESERVE ASSETS	4 800 . .	–144.0	–108.5	–188.3	–168.9	–43.3	–7.0	43.5	–108.8
Monetary gold	4 810 . .	. . .	. . .	. . .	. . .	. . .	. . .	. . .	. . .
Special drawing rights	4 820 . .	.5	–1.6	–7.5	–10.4	.5	–4.7	–.4	–.5
Reserve position in the Fund	4 830 . .	. . .	. . .	. . .	–1.6	–6.9	–1.6	. . .	. . .
Foreign exchange	4 840 . .	–145.2	–107.1	–180.8	–156.8	–36.9	–.8	44.0	–108.3
Other claims	4 880 . .	.7	.2	. . .	–.1	–.1	.1	–.1	. . .
NET ERRORS AND OMISSIONS	4 998 . .	**121.2**	**199.8**	**213.2**	**168.8**	**59.6**	**81.2**	**148.5**	**106.7**

Table 1. ANALYTIC PRESENTATION, 1988–95
(Millions of U.S. dollars)

	Code		1988	1989	1990	1991	1992	1993	1994	1995
A. Current Account [1]	4 993	Y .	**–2,374**	**–5,825**	**–7,451**	**–14,888**	**–24,442**	**–23,400**	**–29,418**	**–654**
Goods: exports f.o.b	2 100	. .	30,692	35,171	40,711	42,687	46,196	51,885	60,879	79,543
Goods: imports f.o.b	3 100	. .	–28,081	–34,766	–41,592	–49,966	–62,130	–65,366	–79,346	–72,454
Balance on Goods	4 100	. .	*2,611*	*405*	*–881*	*–7,279*	*–15,934*	*–13,481*	*–18,467*	*7,089*
Services: credit	2 200	. .	6,084	7,208	8,094	8,869	9,275	9,517	10,323	10,281
Services: debit	3 200	. .	–6,281	–7,880	–10,323	–10,959	–11,959	–12,046	–12,925	–9,407
Balance on Goods and Services	4 991	. .	*2,414*	*–267*	*–3,110*	*–9,369*	*–18,618*	*–16,010*	*–21,069*	*7,963*
Income: credit	2 300	. .	3,049	3,160	3,273	3,523	2,789	2,694	3,348	3,705
Income: debit	3 300	. .	–10,092	–11,261	–11,589	–11,788	–11,998	–13,724	–15,709	–16,284
Balance on Goods, Services, and Income	4 992	. .	*–4,629*	*–8,368*	*–11,426*	*–17,634*	*–27,827*	*–27,040*	*–33,430*	*–4,616*
Current transfers: credit	2 379	Y .	2,270	2,559	3,990	2,765	3,404	3,656	4,042	3,993
Current transfers: debit	3 379	. .	–15	–16	–15	–19	–19	–16	–30	–31
B. Capital Account [1]	4 994	Y .	**. . .**	**. . .**	**. . .**	**. . .**	**. . .**	**. . .**	**. . .**	**. . .**
Capital account: credit	2 994	Y .	. . .	. . .	. . .	. . .	. . .	. . .	. . .	. . .
Capital account: debit	3 994	. .	. . .	. . .	. . .	. . .	. . .	. . .	. . .	. . .
Total, Groups A Plus B	4 010	. .	*–2,374*	*–5,825*	*–7,451*	*–14,888*	*–24,442*	*–23,400*	*–29,418*	*–654*
C. Financial Account [1]	4 995	X .	**–4,495**	**1,110**	**8,441**	**25,139**	**27,039**	**33,760**	**15,787**	**–11,781**
Direct investment abroad	4 505	. .	. . .	. . .	. . .	. . .	. . .	. . .	. . .	. . .
Direct investment in Mexico	4 555	Y .	2,011	2,785	2,549	4,742	4,393	4,389	10,972	6,963
Portfolio investment assets	4 602	. .	–880	–56	–7,354	–603	1,165	–564	–615	–663
Equity securities	4 610	. .	. . .	. . .	. . .	. . .	. . .	. . .	. . .	. . .
Debt securities	4 619	. .	–880	–56	–7,354	–603	1,165	–564	–615	–663
Portfolio investment liabilities	4 652	Y .	1,001	354	3,369	12,741	18,041	28,919	8,185	–10,140
Equity securities	4 660	Y .	. . .	494	1,995	6,331	4,783	10,716	4,085	519
Debt securities	4 669	Y .	1,001	–140	1,374	6,410	13,258	18,203	4,100	–10,659
Other investment assets	4 703	. .	–874	–1,114	–1,345	–395	4,387	–3,038	–5,057	–5,296
Monetary authorities	4 703	. A	. . .	. . .	. . .	. . .	. . .	. . .	. . .	. . .
General government	4 703	. B	. . .	. . .	. . .	. . .	. . .	. . .	. . .	–1,000
Banks	4 703	. C	–338	–719	–749	–1,097	22	–1,683	–1,179	–2,080
Other sectors	4 703	. D	–536	–395	–596	702	4,365	–1,355	–3,878	–2,216
Other investment liabilities	4 753	X .	–5,753	–859	11,222	8,654	–947	4,054	2,302	–2,645
Monetary authorities	4 753	XA	. . .	. . .	. . .	. . .	. . .	. . .	. . .	–787
General government	4 753	YB	–4,112	–104	1,657	–1,454	–5,867	–1,136	–985	210
Banks	4 753	YC	320	680	9,061	7,845	1,626	3,622	2,802	–5,295
Other sectors	4 753	YD	–1,961	–1,435	504	2,263	3,294	1,568	485	3,227
Total, Groups A Through C	4 020	. .	*–6,869*	*–4,715*	*990*	*10,251*	*2,597*	*10,360*	*–13,631*	*–12,435*
D. Net Errors and Omissions	4 998	. .	**–3,193**	**4,504**	**1,228**	**–2,278**	**–852**	**–3,128**	**–4,035**	**–2,871**
Total, Groups A Through D	4 030	. .	*–10,062*	*–211*	*2,218*	*7,973*	*1,745*	*7,232*	*–17,667*	*–15,306*
E. Reserves and Related Items	4 040	. .	**10,062**	**211**	**–2,218**	**–7,973**	**–1,745**	**–7,232**	**17,667**	**15,306**
Reserve assets	4 800	. .	6,721	–542	–3,261	–8,154	–1,173	–6,057	18,865	–10,654
Use of Fund credit and loans	4 766	. .	–84	364	958	161	–572	–1,175	–1,199	11,950
Liabilities constituting foreign authorities' reserves	4 900	. .	. . .	. . .	. . .	. . .	. . .	. . .	. . .	. . .
Exceptional financing	4 920	. .	3,424	389	85	20	. . .	. . .	. . .	14,010
Conversion rates: new Mexican pesos per U.S. dollar	0 101	. .	**2.2731**	**2.4615**	**2.8126**	**3.0184**	**3.0949**	**3.1156**	**3.3751**	**6.4194**

[1] Excludes components that have been classified in the categories of Group E.

Table 2. STANDARD PRESENTATION, 1988–95
(Millions of U.S. dollars)

	Code	1988	1989	1990	1991	1992	1993	1994	1995
CURRENT ACCOUNT	4 993 . .	**–2,374**	**–5,825**	**–7,451**	**–14,888**	**–24,442**	**–23,400**	**–29,418**	**–654**
A. GOODS	4 100 . .	2,611	405	–881	–7,279	–15,934	–13,481	–18,467	7,089
Credit	2 100 . .	**30,692**	**35,171**	**40,711**	**42,687**	**46,196**	**51,885**	**60,879**	**79,543**
General merchandise: exports f.o.b.	2 110 . .	20,547	22,842	26,838	26,855	27,516	30,031	34,611	48,440
Goods for processing: exports f.o.b.	2 150 . .	10,145	12,329	13,873	15,832	18,680	21,854	26,268	31,103
Repairs on goods	2 160 . .	. . .	. . .	. . .	. . .	. . .	. . .	. . .	. . .
Goods procured in ports by carriers	2 170 . .	. . .	. . .	. . .	. . .	. . .	. . .	. . .	. . .
Nonmonetary gold	2 180 . .	. . .	. . .	. . .	. . .	. . .	. . .	. . .	. . .
Debit	3 100 . .	**–28,081**	**–34,766**	**–41,592**	**–49,966**	**–62,130**	**–65,366**	**–79,346**	**–72,454**
General merchandise: imports f.o.b.	3 110 . .	–20,273	–25,438	–31,271	–38,184	–48,193	–48,924	–58,880	–46,276
Goods for processing: imports f.o.b.	3 150 . .	–7,808	–9,328	–10,321	–11,782	–13,937	–16,442	–20,466	–26,178
Repairs on goods	3 160 . .	. . .	. . .	. . .	. . .	. . .	. . .	. . .	. . .
Goods procured in ports by carriers	3 170 . .	. . .	. . .	. . .	. . .	. . .	. . .	. . .	. . .
Nonmonetary gold	3 180 . .	. . .	. . .	. . .	. . .	. . .	. . .	. . .	. . .
B. SERVICES	4 200 . .	–197	–672	–2,229	–2,090	–2,684	–2,529	–2,602	874
Total credit	2 200 . .	*6,084*	*7,208*	*8,094*	*8,869*	*9,275*	*9,517*	*10,323*	*10,281*
Total debit	3 200 . .	*–6,281*	*–7,880*	*–10,323*	*–10,959*	*–11,959*	*–12,046*	*–12,925*	*–9,407*
Transportation services, credit	2 205 . .	**690**	**691**	**892**	**901**	**980**	**938**	**1,065**	**1,174**
Passenger	2 205 BA	*386*	*356*	*441*	*446*	*498*	*454*	*618*	*675*
Freight	2 205 BB	. . .	. . .	. . .	. . .	. . .	. . .	. . .	. . .
Other	2 205 BC	*304*	*335*	*451*	*455*	*482*	*484*	*447*	*499*
Sea transport, passenger	2 207 . .	. . .	. . .	. . .	. . .	. . .	. . .	. . .	. . .
Sea transport, freight	2 208 . .	. . .	. . .	. . .	. . .	. . .	. . .	. . .	. . .
Sea transport, other	2 209 . .	. . .	. . .	. . .	. . .	. . .	. . .	. . .	. . .
Air transport, passenger	2 211 . .	. . .	. . .	. . .	. . .	. . .	. . .	. . .	. . .
Air transport, freight	2 212 . .	. . .	. . .	. . .	. . .	. . .	. . .	. . .	. . .
Air transport, other	2 213 . .	. . .	. . .	. . .	. . .	. . .	. . .	. . .	. . .
Other transport, passenger	2 215 . .	. . .	. . .	. . .	. . .	. . .	. . .	. . .	. . .
Other transport, freight	2 216 . .	. . .	. . .	. . .	. . .	. . .	. . .	. . .	. . .
Other transport, other	2 217 . .	. . .	. . .	. . .	. . .	. . .	. . .	. . .	. . .
Transportation services, debit	3 205 . .	**–1,482**	**–1,957**	**–2,511**	**–2,853**	**–3,225**	**–3,326**	**–4,547**	**–3,254**
Passenger	3 205 BA	*–299*	*–388*	*–476*	*–515*	*–525*	*–490*	*–541*	*–379*
Freight	3 205 BB	*–740*	*–1,043*	*–1,378*	*–1,582*	*–1,875*	*–1,963*	*–2,639*	*–1,975*
Other	3 205 BC	*–443*	*–526*	*–657*	*–756*	*–825*	*–873*	*–1,367*	*–900*
Sea transport, passenger	3 207 . .	. . .	. . .	. . .	. . .	. . .	. . .	. . .	. . .
Sea transport, freight	3 208 . .	. . .	. . .	. . .	. . .	. . .	. . .	. . .	. . .
Sea transport, other	3 209 . .	. . .	. . .	. . .	. . .	. . .	. . .	. . .	. . .
Air transport, passenger	3 211 . .	. . .	. . .	. . .	. . .	. . .	. . .	. . .	. . .
Air transport, freight	3 212 . .	. . .	. . .	. . .	. . .	. . .	. . .	. . .	. . .
Air transport, other	3 213 . .	. . .	. . .	. . .	. . .	. . .	. . .	. . .	. . .
Other transport, passenger	3 215 . .	. . .	. . .	. . .	. . .	. . .	. . .	. . .	. . .
Other transport, freight	3 216 . .	. . .	. . .	. . .	. . .	. . .	. . .	. . .	. . .
Other transport, other	3 217 . .	. . .	. . .	. . .	. . .	. . .	. . .	. . .	. . .
Travel, credit	2 236 . .	**4,049**	**4,821**	**5,527**	**5,959**	**6,084**	**6,167**	**6,363**	**6,164**
Business travel	2 237 . .	. . .	. . .	. . .	. . .	. . .	. . .	. . .	. . .
Personal travel	2 240 . .	. . .	. . .	. . .	. . .	. . .	. . .	. . .	. . .
Travel, debit	3 236 . .	**–3,202**	**–4,247**	**–5,520**	**–5,812**	**–6,107**	**–5,562**	**–5,338**	**–3,153**
Business travel	3 237 . .	. . .	. . .	. . .	. . .	. . .	. . .	. . .	. . .
Personal travel	3 240 . .	. . .	. . .	. . .	. . .	. . .	. . .	. . .	. . .
Other services, credit	2 200 BA	**1,345**	**1,696**	**1,675**	**2,009**	**2,211**	**2,412**	**2,895**	**2,943**
Communications	2 245 . .	. . .	. . .	. . .	. . .	. . .	. . .	. . .	. . .
Construction	2 249 . .	. . .	. . .	. . .	. . .	. . .	. . .	. . .	. . .
Insurance	2 253 . .	379	412	335	510	528	572	664	708
Financial	2 260 . .	. . .	. . .	. . .	. . .	. . .	. . .	. . .	. . .
Computer and information	2 262 . .	. . .	. . .	. . .	. . .	. . .	. . .	. . .	. . .
Royalties and licence fees	2 266 . .	14	21	73	78	85	96	20	114
Other business services	2 268 . .	277	451	395	428	473	523	575	626
Personal, cultural, and recreational	2 287 . .	. . .	. . .	. . .	. . .	. . .	. . .	. . .	. . .
Government, n.i.e.	2 291 . .	675	812	872	993	1,125	1,221	1,636	1,495
Other services, debit	3 200 BA	**–1,597**	**–1,676**	**–2,292**	**–2,294**	**–2,627**	**–3,158**	**–3,040**	**–3,000**
Communications	3 245 . .	. . .	. . .	. . .	. . .	. . .	. . .	. . .	. . .
Construction	3 249 . .	. . .	. . .	. . .	. . .	. . .	. . .	. . .	. . .
Insurance	3 253 . .	–501	–553	–621	–653	–703	–1,186	–996	–1,020
Financial	3 260 . .	. . .	. . .	. . .	. . .	. . .	. . .	. . .	. . .
Computer and information	3 262 . .	. . .	. . .	. . .	. . .	. . .	. . .	. . .	. . .
Royalties and licence fees	3 266 . .	–217	–221	–380	–419	–472	–494	–669	–484
Other business services	3 268 . .	–678	–676	–1,031	–939	–1,135	–1,203	–1,220	–1,375
Personal, cultural, and recreational	3 287 . .	. . .	. . .	. . .	. . .	. . .	. . .	. . .	. . .
Government, n.i.e.	3 291 . .	–201	–226	–260	–283	–317	–275	–155	–121

Table 2 (Continued). STANDARD PRESENTATION, 1988–95
(Millions of U.S. dollars)

	Code	1988	1989	1990	1991	1992	1993	1994	1995
C. INCOME	4 300 . .	-7,043	-8,101	-8,316	-8,265	-9,209	-11,030	-12,361	-12,579
Total credit	2 300 . .	*3,049*	*3,160*	*3,273*	*3,523*	*2,789*	*2,694*	*3,348*	*3,705*
Total debit	3 300 . .	*-10,092*	*-11,261*	*-11,589*	*-11,788*	*-11,998*	*-13,724*	*-15,709*	*-16,284*
Compensation of employees, credit	2 310 . .	**542**	**580**	**606**	**616**	**630**	**647**	**647**	**695**
Compensation of employees, debit	3 310 . .	**. . .**	**. . .**	**. . .**	**. . .**	**. . .**	**. . .**	**. . .**	**. . .**
Investment income, credit	2 320 . .	**2,507**	**2,580**	**2,667**	**2,907**	**2,159**	**2,047**	**2,701**	**3,010**
Direct investment income	2 330 . .	. . .	. . .	. . .	. . .	. . .	. . .	. . .	. . .
Dividends and distributed branch profits	2 332 . .	. . .	. . .	. . .	. . .	. . .	. . .	. . .	. . .
Reinvested earnings and undistributed branch profits	2 333 . .	. . .	. . .	. . .	. . .	. . .	. . .	. . .	. . .
Income on debt (interest)	2 334 . .	. . .	. . .	. . .	. . .	. . .	. . .	. . .	. . .
Portfolio investment income	2 339 . .	. . .	. . .	. . .	. . .	. . .	. . .	. . .	. . .
Income on equity	2 340 . .	. . .	. . .	. . .	. . .	. . .	. . .	. . .	. . .
Income on bonds and notes	2 350 . .	. . .	. . .	. . .	. . .	. . .	. . .	. . .	. . .
Income on money market instruments and financial derivatives	2 360 . .	. . .	. . .	. . .	. . .	. . .	. . .	. . .	. . .
Other investment income	2 370 . .	2,507	2,580	2,667	2,907	2,159	2,047	2,701	3,010
Investment income, debit	3 320 . .	**-10,092**	**-11,261**	**-11,589**	**-11,788**	**-11,998**	**-13,724**	**-15,709**	**-16,284**
Direct investment income	3 330 . .	-1,407	-1,949	-2,304	-2,492	-2,312	-2,512	-3,627	-2,664
Dividends and distributed branch profits	3 332 . .	-716	-875	-1,237	-1,084	-1,292	-1,113	-1,260	-1,199
Reinvested earnings and undistributed branch profits	3 333 . .	-691	-1,074	-1,067	-1,408	-1,020	-1,399	-2,367	-1,465
Income on debt (interest)	3 334 . .	. . .	. . .	. . .	. . .	. . .	. . .	. . .	. . .
Portfolio investment income	3 339 . .	. . .	. . .	. . .	. . .	. . .	. . .	. . .	. . .
Income on equity	3 340 . .	. . .	. . .	. . .	. . .	. . .	. . .	. . .	. . .
Income on bonds and notes	3 350 . .	. . .	. . .	. . .	. . .	. . .	. . .	. . .	. . .
Income on money market instruments and financial derivatives	3 360 . .	. . .	. . .	. . .	. . .	. . .	. . .	. . .	. . .
Other investment income	3 370 . .	-8,685	-9,312	-9,285	-9,296	-9,686	-11,212	-12,082	-13,620
D. CURRENT TRANSFERS	4 379 . .	2,255	2,543	3,975	2,746	3,385	3,640	4,012	3,962
Credit	2 379 . .	**2,270**	**2,559**	**3,990**	**2,765**	**3,404**	**3,656**	**4,042**	**3,993**
General government	2 380 . .	185	168	1,311	126	132	112	103	95
Other sectors	2 390 . .	2,085	2,391	2,679	2,639	3,272	3,544	3,939	3,898
Workers' remittances	2 391 . .	1,897	2,213	2,492	2,414	3,070	3,332	3,694	3,672
Other current transfers	2 392 . .	188	178	187	225	202	212	245	226
Debit	3 379 . .	**-15**	**-16**	**-15**	**-19**	**-19**	**-16**	**-30**	**-31**
General government	3 380 . .	-15	-16	-15	-19	-19	-16	-30	-31
Other sectors	3 390 . .	. . .	. . .	. . .	. . .	. . .	. . .	. . .	. . .
Workers' remittances	3 391 . .	. . .	. . .	. . .	. . .	. . .	. . .	. . .	. . .
Other current transfers	3 392 . .	. . .	. . .	. . .	. . .	. . .	. . .	. . .	. . .
CAPITAL AND FINANCIAL ACCOUNT	4 996 . .	**5,567**	**1,321**	**6,223**	**17,166**	**25,294**	**26,528**	**33,454**	**3,525**
CAPITAL ACCOUNT	4 994 . .	**. . .**	**. . .**	**. . .**	**. . .**	**. . .**	**. . .**	**. . .**	**. . .**
Total credit	2 994 . .	. . .	. . .	. . .	. . .	. . .	. . .	. . .	. . .
Total debit	3 994 . .	. . .	. . .	. . .	. . .	. . .	. . .	. . .	. . .
Capital transfers, credit	2 400 . .	**. . .**	**. . .**	**. . .**	**. . .**	**. . .**	**. . .**	**. . .**	**. . .**
General government	2 401 . .	. . .	. . .	. . .	. . .	. . .	. . .	. . .	. . .
Debt forgiveness	2 402 . .	. . .	. . .	. . .	. . .	. . .	. . .	. . .	. . .
Other capital transfers	2 410 . .	. . .	. . .	. . .	. . .	. . .	. . .	. . .	. . .
Other sectors	2 430 . .	. . .	. . .	. . .	. . .	. . .	. . .	. . .	. . .
Migrants' transfers	2 431 . .	. . .	. . .	. . .	. . .	. . .	. . .	. . .	. . .
Debt forgiveness	2 432 . .	. . .	. . .	. . .	. . .	. . .	. . .	. . .	. . .
Other capital transfers	2 440 . .	. . .	. . .	. . .	. . .	. . .	. . .	. . .	. . .
Capital transfers, debit	3 400 . .	**. . .**	**. . .**	**. . .**	**. . .**	**. . .**	**. . .**	**. . .**	**. . .**
General government	3 401 . .	. . .	. . .	. . .	. . .	. . .	. . .	. . .	. . .
Debt forgiveness	3 402 . .	. . .	. . .	. . .	. . .	. . .	. . .	. . .	. . .
Other capital transfers	3 410 . .	. . .	. . .	. . .	. . .	. . .	. . .	. . .	. . .
Other sectors	3 430 . .	. . .	. . .	. . .	. . .	. . .	. . .	. . .	. . .
Migrants' transfers	3 431 . .	. . .	. . .	. . .	. . .	. . .	. . .	. . .	. . .
Debt forgiveness	3 432 . .	. . .	. . .	. . .	. . .	. . .	. . .	. . .	. . .
Other capital transfers	3 440 . .	. . .	. . .	. . .	. . .	. . .	. . .	. . .	. . .
Nonproduced nonfinancial assets, credit	2 480 . .	**. . .**	**. . .**	**. . .**	**. . .**	**. . .**	**. . .**	**. . .**	**. . .**
Nonproduced nonfinancial assets, debit	3 480 . .	**. . .**	**. . .**	**. . .**	**. . .**	**. . .**	**. . .**	**. . .**	**. . .**

Table 2 (Continued). STANDARD PRESENTATION, 1988–95
(Millions of U.S. dollars)

	Code	1988	1989	1990	1991	1992	1993	1994	1995
FINANCIAL ACCOUNT	4 995 . .	**5,567**	**1,321**	**6,223**	**17,166**	**25,294**	**26,528**	**33,454**	**3,525**
A. DIRECT INVESTMENT	4 500 . .	2,879	3,174	2,634	4,762	4,393	4,389	10,972	6,963
Direct investment abroad	4 505 . .	...	...	...	...	...	...	...	...
Equity capital	4 510 . .	...	...	...	...	...	...	...	...
Claims on affiliated enterprises	4 515 . .	...	...	...	...	...	...	...	...
Liabilities to affiliated enterprises	4 520 . .	...	...	...	...	...	...	...	...
Reinvested earnings	4 525 . .	...	...	...	...	...	...	...	...
Other capital	4 530 . .	...	...	...	...	...	...	...	...
Claims on affiliated enterprises	4 535 . .	...	...	...	...	...	...	...	...
Liabilities to affiliated enterprises	4 540 . .	...	...	...	...	...	...	...	...
Direct investment in Mexico	4 555 . .	**2,879**	**3,174**	**2,634**	**4,762**	**4,393**	**4,389**	**10,972**	**6,963**
Equity capital	4 560 . .	2,205	1,659	1,118	3,423	3,012	3,041	5,672	4,397
Claims on direct investors	4 565 . .	...	...	...	...	...	...	...	...
Liabilities to direct investors	4 570 . .	2,205	1,659	1,118	3,423	3,012	3,041	5,672	4,397
Reinvested earnings	4 575 . .	691	1,074	1,067	1,408	1,020	1,399	2,367	1,465
Other capital	4 580 . .	–17	441	449	–69	361	–51	2,933	1,101
Claims on direct investors	4 585 . .	...	...	...	...	...	...	...	...
Liabilities to direct investors	4 590 . .	...	...	...	...	...	...	...	...
B. PORTFOLIO INVESTMENT	4 600 . .	2,677	298	–3,985	12,138	19,206	28,355	7,570	–10,803
Assets	4 602 . .	**–880**	**–56**	**–7,354**	**–603**	**1,165**	**–564**	**–615**	**–663**
Equity securities	4 610 . .	...	...	...	...	...	...	...	...
Monetary authorities	4 611 . .	...	...	...	...	...	...	...	...
General government	4 612 . .	...	...	...	...	...	...	...	...
Banks	4 613 . .	...	...	...	...	...	...	...	...
Other sectors	4 614 . .	...	...	...	...	...	...	...	...
Debt securities	4 619 . .	–880	–56	–7,354	–603	1,165	–564	–615	–663
Bonds and notes	4 620 . .	–880	–56	–7,354	–603	1,165	–564	–615	–663
Monetary authorities	4 621 . .	...	...	...	...	...	...	...	...
General government	4 622 . .	...	...	...	...	...	...	...	...
Banks	4 623 . .	...	...	...	...	...	...	...	...
Other sectors	4 624 . .	...	...	...	...	...	...	...	...
Money market instruments	4 630 . .	...	...	...	...	...	...	...	...
Monetary authorities	4 631 . .	...	...	...	...	...	...	...	...
General government	4 632 . .	...	...	...	...	...	...	...	...
Banks	4 633 . .	...	...	...	...	...	...	...	...
Other sectors	4 634 . .	...	...	...	...	...	...	...	...
Financial derivatives	4 640 . .	...	...	...	...	...	...	...	...
Monetary authorities	4 641 . .	...	...	...	...	...	...	...	...
General government	4 642 . .	...	...	...	...	...	...	...	...
Banks	4 643 . .	...	...	...	...	...	...	...	...
Other sectors	4 644 . .	...	...	...	...	...	...	...	...
Liabilities	4 652 . .	**3,557**	**354**	**3,369**	**12,741**	**18,041**	**28,919**	**8,185**	**–10,140**
Equity securities	4 660 . .	...	494	1,995	6,331	4,783	10,716	4,085	519
Banks	4 663 . .	...	...	...	...	...	...	...	...
Other sectors	4 664 . .	...	...	...	...	...	...	...	...
Debt securities	4 669 . .	3,557	–140	1,374	6,410	13,258	18,203	4,100	–10,659
Bonds and notes	4 670 . .	3,557	–140	1,374	6,410	13,258	18,203	4,100	–10,659
Monetary authorities	4 671 . .	...	...	...	...	...	...	...	...
General government	4 672 . .	3,946	–148	276	5,070	9,699	11,885	2,039	–11,222
Banks	4 673 . .	...	...	...	...	...	...	...	...
Other sectors	4 674 . .	–389	8	1,098	1,340	3,559	6,318	2,061	563
Money market instruments	4 680 . .	...	...	...	...	...	...	...	...
Monetary authorities	4 681 . .	...	...	...	...	...	...	...	...
General government	4 682 . .	...	...	...	...	...	...	...	...
Banks	4 683 . .	...	...	...	...	...	...	...	...
Other sectors	4 684 . .	...	...	...	...	...	...	...	...
Financial derivatives	4 690 . .	...	...	...	...	...	...	...	...
Monetary authorities	4 691 . .	...	...	...	...	...	...	...	...
General government	4 692 . .	...	...	...	...	...	...	...	...
Banks	4 693 . .	...	...	...	...	...	...	...	...
Other sectors	4 694 . .	...	...	...	...	...	...	...	...

Table 2 (Concluded). STANDARD PRESENTATION, 1988–95

(Millions of U.S. dollars)

	Code	1988	1989	1990	1991	1992	1993	1994	1995
C. OTHER INVESTMENT	4 700	–6,711	–1,609	10,835	8,420	2,868	–159	–3,954	18,019
Assets	4 703	**–874**	**–1,114**	**–1,345**	**–395**	**4,387**	**–3,038**	**–5,057**	**–5,296**
Trade credits	4 706	...	...	...	...	...	...	...	...
General government: long-term	4 708	...	...	...	...	...	...	...	...
General government: short-term	4 709	...	...	...	...	...	...	...	...
Other sectors: long-term	4 711	...	...	...	...	...	...	...	...
Other sectors: short-term	4 712	...	...	...	...	...	...	...	...
Loans	4 714	–14	–225	–73	59	–4	–11	–1	–27
Monetary authorities: long-term	4 717	...	...	...	...	...	...	...	...
Monetary authorities: short-term	4 718	...	...	...	...	...	...	...	...
General government: long-term	4 720	...	...	...	...	...	...	...	...
General government: short-term	4 721	...	...	...	...	...	...	...	...
Banks: long-term	4 723	–14	–225	–73	59	–4	–11	–1	–27
Banks: short-term	4 724	...	...	...	...	...	...	...	...
Other sectors: long-term	4 726	...	...	...	...	...	...	...	...
Other sectors: short-term	4 727	...	...	...	...	...	...	...	...
Currency and deposits	4 730	–860	–889	–1,272	–454	4,391	–3,027	–5,056	–5,269
Monetary authorities	4 731	...	...	...	...	...	...	...	...
General government	4 732	...	...	...	...	...	...	...	–1,000
Banks	4 733	–324	–494	–676	–1,156	26	–1,672	–1,178	–2,053
Other sectors	4 734	–536	–395	–596	702	4,365	–1,355	–3,878	–2,216
Other assets	4 736	...	...	...	...	...	...	...	...
Monetary authorities: long-term	4 738	...	...	...	...	...	...	...	...
Monetary authorities: short-term	4 739	...	...	...	...	...	...	...	...
General government: long-term	4 741	...	...	...	...	...	...	...	...
General government: short-term	4 742	...	...	...	...	...	...	...	...
Banks: long-term	4 744	...	...	...	...	...	...	...	...
Banks: short-term	4 745	...	...	...	...	...	...	...	...
Other sectors: long-term	4 747	...	...	...	...	...	...	...	...
Other sectors: short-term	4 748	...	...	...	...	...	...	...	...
Liabilities	4 753	**–5,837**	**–495**	**12,180**	**8,815**	**–1,519**	**2,879**	**1,103**	**23,315**
Trade credits	4 756	...	...	...	...	...	...	...	...
General government: long-term	4 758	...	...	...	...	...	...	...	...
General government: short-term	4 759	...	...	...	...	...	...	...	...
Other sectors: long-term	4 761	...	...	...	...	...	...	...	...
Other sectors: short-term	4 762	...	...	...	...	...	...	...	...
Loans	4 764	–6,254	–492	8,230	5,721	–2,759	–467	–1,760	26,444
Use of Fund credit and loans from the Fund	4 766	–84	364	958	161	–572	–1,175	–1,199	11,950
Monetary authorities: other long-term	4 767	...	...	...	...	...	...	...	1,450
Monetary authorities: short-term	4 768	...	...	...	...	...	...	...	...
General government: long-term	4 770	–4,117	–101	1,685	–1,467	–5,438	–1,165	–985	10,040
General government: short-term	4 771	5	–3	–28	13	–429	29	...	670
Banks: long-term	4 773	–97	683	5,111	4,751	386	276	–61	–893
Banks: short-term	4 774	...	...	...	...	...	...	...	...
Other sectors: long-term	4 776	–3,220	–1,394	307	1,573	1,648	201	1,018	1,955
Other sectors: short-term	4 777	1,259	–41	197	690	1,646	1,367	–533	1,272
Currency and deposits	4 780	417	–3	3,950	3,094	1,240	3,346	2,863	–3,129
Monetary authorities	4 781	...	...	...	...	...	...	...	...
General government	4 782	...	...	...	...	...	...	...	...
Banks	4 783	417	–3	3,950	3,094	1,240	3,346	2,863	–3,129
Other sectors	4 784	...	...	...	...	...	...	...	...
Other liabilities	4 786	...	...	...	...	...	...	...	...
Monetary authorities: long-term	4 788	...	...	...	...	...	...	...	...
Monetary authorities: short-term	4 789	...	...	...	...	...	...	...	...
General government: long-term	4 791	...	...	...	...	...	...	...	...
General government: short-term	4 792	...	...	...	...	...	...	...	...
Banks: long-term	4 794	...	...	...	...	...	...	...	...
Banks: short-term	4 795	...	...	...	...	...	...	...	...
Other sectors: long-term	4 797	...	...	...	...	...	...	...	...
Other sectors: short-term	4 798	...	...	...	...	...	...	...	...
D. RESERVE ASSETS	4 800	6,721	–542	–3,261	–8,154	–1,173	–6,057	18,865	–10,654
Monetary gold	4 810	–18	611	268	–282	98	39	26	–35
Special drawing rights	4 820	280	–1	3	–172	29	329	55	–1,475
Reserve position in the Fund	4 830	...	...	...	...	...	...	...	...
Foreign exchange	4 840	6,459	–1,152	–3,532	–7,700	–1,300	–6,425	18,784	–9,144
Other claims	4 880	...	...	...	...	...	...	...	...
NET ERRORS AND OMISSIONS	4 998	**–3,193**	**4,504**	**1,228**	**–2,278**	**–852**	**–3,128**	**–4,035**	**–2,871**

Part 3 of the *Yearbook* contains descriptions of the methodologies, compilation practices, and sources used to compile these data.

Table 1. ANALYTIC PRESENTATION, 1988–95
(Millions of U.S. dollars)

	Code	1988	1989	1990	1991	1992	1993	1994	1995
A. Current Account[1]	4 993 Y.	...	...	...	...	...	...	**–82.0**	**–94.7**
Goods: exports f.o.b	2 100 ..	...	...	...	...	...	...	618.5	740.6
Goods: imports f.o.b	3 100 ..	...	...	...	...	...	...	–672.4	–773.1
Balance on Goods	4 100 ..	...	...	...	...	...	...	*–53.9*	*–32.4*
Services: credit	2 200 ..	...	...	...	...	...	...	32.8	103.2
Services: debit	3 200 ..	...	...	...	...	...	...	–79.0	–184.6
Balance on Goods and Services	4 991 ..	...	...	...	...	...	...	*–100.0*	*–113.7*
Income: credit	2 300 ..	...	...	...	...	...	...	10.8	20.9
Income: debit	3 300 ..	...	...	...	...	...	...	–26.1	–41.4
Balance on Goods, Services, and Income	4 992 ..	...	...	...	...	...	...	*–115.4*	*–134.2*
Current transfers: credit	2 379 Y.	...	...	...	...	...	...	36.9	49.6
Current transfers: debit	3 379 ..	...	...	...	...	...	...	–3.6	–10.0
B. Capital Account[1]	4 994 Y.	...	...	...	...	...	...	**–1.0**	**–.4**
Capital account: credit	2 994 Y.	...	...	...	...	...	...	...	...
Capital account: debit	3 994 ..	...	...	...	...	...	...	–1.0	–.4
Total, Groups A Plus B	4 010 ..	...	...	...	...	...	...	*–83.0*	*–95.1*
C. Financial Account[1]	4 995 X.	...	...	...	...	...	...	**211.9**	**78.1**
Direct investment abroad	4 505 ..	...	...	...	...	...	...	...	–.5
Direct investment in Moldova	4 555 Y.	...	...	...	...	...	...	11.6	64.2
Portfolio investment assets	4 602 ..	...	...	...	...	...	...	–.4	...
Equity securities	4 610 ..	...	...	...	...	...	...	–.4	...
Debt securities	4 619 ..	...	...	...	...	...	...	...	...
Portfolio investment liabilities	4 652 Y.	...	...	...	...	...	...	.7	–.3
Equity securities	4 660 Y.	...	...	...	...	...	...	.7	–.4
Debt securities	4 669 Y.	...	...	...	...	...	...	...	...
Other investment assets	4 703 ..	...	...	...	...	...	...	–81.7	–120.9
Monetary authorities	4 703 .A	...	...	...	...	...	...	–1.3	2.9
General government	4 703 .B	...	...	...	...	...	...	–4.1	6.0
Banks	4 703 .C	...	...	...	...	...	...	–10.1	–13.1
Other sectors	4 703 .D	...	...	...	...	...	...	–66.2	–116.8
Other investment liabilities	4 753 X.	...	...	...	...	...	...	281.7	135.7
Monetary authorities	4 753 XA	...	...	...	...	...	...	3.1	2.2
General government	4 753 YB	...	...	...	...	...	...	147.4	56.9
Banks	4 753 YC	...	...	...	...	...	...	–.8	12.0
Other sectors	4 753 YD	...	...	...	...	...	...	131.9	64.6
Total, Groups A Through C	4 020 ..	...	...	...	...	...	...	*128.9*	*–17.0*
D. Net Errors and Omissions	4 998 ..	...	...	...	...	...	...	**–115.3**	**9.3**
Total, Groups A Through D	4 030 ..	...	...	...	...	...	...	*13.6*	*–7.7*
E. Reserves and Related Items	4 040 ..	...	...	...	...	...	...	**–13.6**	**7.7**
Reserve assets	4 800 ..	...	...	...	...	...	...	–103.1	–76.7
Use of Fund credit and loans	4 766 ..	...	...	...	...	...	...	71.5	64.8
Liabilities constituting foreign authorities' reserves	4 900 ..	...	...	...	...	...	...	...	...
Exceptional financing	4 920 ..	...	...	...	...	...	...	18.0	19.6
Conversion rates: lei per U.S. dollar	0 101 ..	...	...	...	...	...	...	...	**4.4958**

[1] Excludes components that have been classified in the categories of Group E.

Table 2. STANDARD PRESENTATION, 1988–95

(Millions of U.S. dollars)

	Code	1988	1989	1990	1991	1992	1993	1994	1995
CURRENT ACCOUNT	4 993 ..	...	...	...	...	...	...	**–82.0**	**–94.7**
A. GOODS	4 100 ..	...	...	...	...	...	...	–53.9	–32.4
Credit	2 100 ..	...	...	...	...	...	...	**618.5**	**740.6**
General merchandise: exports f.o.b.	2 110 ..	...	...	...	...	...	...	618.5	740.6
Goods for processing: exports f.o.b.	2 150 ..	...	...	...	...	...	...	...	...
Repairs on goods	2 160 ..	...	...	...	...	...	...	...	...
Goods procured in ports by carriers	2 170 ..	...	...	...	...	...	...	...	...
Nonmonetary gold	2 180 ..	...	...	...	...	...	...	...	...
Debit	3 100 ..	...	...	...	...	...	...	**–672.4**	**–773.1**
General merchandise: imports f.o.b.	3 110 ..	...	...	...	...	...	...	–672.4	–773.1
Goods for processing: imports f.o.b.	3 150 ..	...	...	...	...	...	...	...	...
Repairs on goods	3 160 ..	...	...	...	...	...	...	...	...
Goods procured in ports by carriers	3 170 ..	...	...	...	...	...	...	...	...
Nonmonetary gold	3 180 ..	...	...	...	...	...	...	...	...
B. SERVICES	4 200 ..	...	...	...	...	...	...	–46.1	–81.3
Total credit	2 200 ..	...	...	...	...	...	...	*32.8*	*103.2*
Total debit	3 200 ..	...	...	...	...	...	...	*–79.0*	*–184.6*
Transportation services, credit	2 205 ..	...	...	...	...	...	...	**10.2**	**1.1**
Passenger	2 205 BA	...	...	...	...	...	...	...	...
Freight	2 205 BB	...	...	...	...	...	...	...	...
Other	2 205 BC	...	...	...	...	...	...	...	...
Sea transport, passenger	2 207 ..	...	...	...	...	...	...	...	...
Sea transport, freight	2 208 ..	...	...	...	...	...	...	...	...
Sea transport, other	2 209 ..	...	...	...	...	...	...	...	...
Air transport, passenger	2 211 ..	...	...	...	...	...	...	...	...
Air transport, freight	2 212 ..	...	...	...	...	...	...	...	...
Air transport, other	2 213 ..	...	...	...	...	...	...	...	...
Other transport, passenger	2 215 ..	...	...	...	...	...	...	...	...
Other transport, freight	2 216 ..	...	...	...	...	...	...	...	...
Other transport, other	2 217 ..	...	...	...	...	...	...	...	...
Transportation services, debit	3 205 ..	...	...	...	...	...	...	**–51.0**	**–95.7**
Passenger	3 205 BA	...	...	...	...	...	...	...	...
Freight	3 205 BB	...	...	...	...	...	...	...	...
Other	3 205 BC	...	...	...	...	...	...	...	...
Sea transport, passenger	3 207 ..	...	...	...	...	...	...	...	...
Sea transport, freight	3 208 ..	...	...	...	...	...	...	...	...
Sea transport, other	3 209 ..	...	...	...	...	...	...	...	...
Air transport, passenger	3 211 ..	...	...	...	...	...	...	...	...
Air transport, freight	3 212 ..	...	...	...	...	...	...	...	...
Air transport, other	3 213 ..	...	...	...	...	...	...	...	...
Other transport, passenger	3 215 ..	...	...	...	...	...	...	...	...
Other transport, freight	3 216 ..	...	...	...	...	...	...	...	...
Other transport, other	3 217 ..	...	...	...	...	...	...	...	...
Travel, credit	2 236 ..	...	...	...	...	...	...	**7.5**	**56.9**
Business travel	2 237 ..	...	...	...	...	...	...	...	...
Personal travel	2 240 ..	...	...	...	...	...	...	...	...
Travel, debit	3 236 ..	...	...	...	...	...	...	**–10.3**	**–56.4**
Business travel	3 237 ..	...	...	...	...	...	...	...	...
Personal travel	3 240 ..	...	...	...	...	...	...	...	...
Other services, credit	2 200 BA	...	...	...	...	...	...	**15.1**	**45.3**
Communications	2 245 ..	...	...	...	...	...	...	.9	3.7
Construction	2 249 ..	...	...	...	...	...	...	1.0	.3
Insurance	2 253 ..	...	...	...	...	...	...	.1	.6
Financial	2 260 ..	...	...	...	...	...	...	1.0	16.0
Computer and information	2 262 ..	...	...	...	...	...	...	1.3	.2
Royalties and licence fees	2 266 ..	...	...	...	...	...	...	...	...
Other business services	2 268 ..	...	...	...	...	...	...	10.8	23.1
Personal, cultural, and recreational	2 287 ..	...	...	...	...	...	...	...	...
Government, n.i.e.	2 291 ..	...	...	...	...	...	...	...	1.3
Other services, debit	3 200 BA	...	...	...	...	...	...	**–17.7**	**–32.5**
Communications	3 245 ..	...	...	...	...	...	...	–.8	–1.7
Construction	3 249 ..	...	...	...	...	...	...	–.1	–.8
Insurance	3 253 ..	...	...	...	...	...	...	–.3	–.9
Financial	3 260 ..	...	...	...	...	...	...	–3.0	–17.0
Computer and information	3 262 ..	...	...	...	...	...	...	–.3	–.4
Royalties and licence fees	3 266 ..	...	...	...	...	...	...	...	...
Other business services	3 268 ..	...	...	...	...	...	...	–8.7	–8.3
Personal, cultural, and recreational	3 287 ..	...	...	...	...	...	...	...	...
Government, n.i.e.	3 291 ..	...	...	...	...	...	...	–4.5	–3.5

Table 2 (Continued). STANDARD PRESENTATION, 1988–95
(Millions of U.S. dollars)

	Code		1988	1989	1990	1991	1992	1993	1994	1995
C. INCOME	4 300	. .	...	...	...	...	...	...	–15.3	–20.5
Total credit	2 300	. .	...	...	...	...	...	...	*10.8*	*20.9*
Total debit	3 300	. .	...	...	...	...	...	...	*–26.1*	*–41.4*
Compensation of employees, credit	2 310	. .	...	...	...	...	...	...	...	...
Compensation of employees, debit	3 310	. .	...	...	...	...	...	...	**–9.5**	**–9.5**
Investment income, credit	2 320	. .	...	...	...	...	...	...	**10.8**	**20.9**
Direct investment income	2 330	. .	...	...	...	...	...	...	...	...
Dividends and distributed branch profits	2 332	. .	...	...	...	...	...	...	...	...
Reinvested earnings and undistributed branch profits	2 333	. .	...	...	...	...	...	...	...	...
Income on debt (interest)	2 334	. .	...	...	...	...	...	...	...	...
Portfolio investment income	2 339	. .	...	...	...	...	...	...	.9	...
Income on equity	2 340	. .	...	...	...	...	...	...	...	...
Income on bonds and notes	2 350	. .	...	...	...	...	...	...	...	...
Income on money market instruments and financial derivatives	2 360	. .	...	...	...	...	...	...	...	...
Other investment income	2 370	. .	...	...	...	...	...	...	9.9	20.9
Investment income, debit	3 320	. .	...	...	...	...	...	...	**–16.6**	**–31.8**
Direct investment income	3 330	. .	...	...	...	...	...	...	...	–.1
Dividends and distributed branch profits	3 332	. .	...	...	...	...	...	...	...	...
Reinvested earnings and undistributed branch profits	3 333	. .	...	...	...	...	...	...	...	...
Income on debt (interest)	3 334	. .	...	...	...	...	...	...	...	...
Portfolio investment income	3 339	. .	...	...	...	...	...	...	...	...
Income on equity	3 340	. .	...	...	...	...	...	...	...	...
Income on bonds and notes	3 350	. .	...	...	...	...	...	...	...	...
Income on money market instruments and financial derivatives	3 360	. .	...	...	...	...	...	...	...	...
Other investment income	3 370	. .	...	...	...	...	...	...	–16.6	–31.8
D. CURRENT TRANSFERS	4 379	. .	...	...	...	...	...	...	33.3	39.5
Credit	2 379	. .	...	...	...	...	...	...	**36.9**	**49.6**
General government	2 380	. .	...	...	...	...	...	...	...	...
Other sectors	2 390	. .	...	...	...	...	...	...	...	...
Workers' remittances	2 391	. .	...	...	...	...	...	...	...	...
Other current transfers	2 392	. .	...	...	...	...	...	...	...	...
Debit	3 379	. .	...	...	...	...	...	...	**–3.6**	**–10.0**
General government	3 380	. .	...	...	...	...	...	...	...	...
Other sectors	3 390	. .	...	...	...	...	...	...	...	...
Workers' remittances	3 391	. .	...	...	...	...	...	...	...	...
Other current transfers	3 392	. .	...	...	...	...	...	...	...	...
CAPITAL AND FINANCIAL ACCOUNT	4 996	. .	...	...	...	...	...	...	**197.3**	**85.5**
CAPITAL ACCOUNT	4 994	. .	...	...	...	...	...	...	**–1.0**	**–.4**
Total credit	2 994	. .	...	...	...	...	...	...	...	...
Total debit	3 994	. .	...	...	...	...	...	...	*–1.0*	*–.4*
Capital transfers, credit	2 400	. .	...	...	...	...	...	...	...	...
General government	2 401	. .	...	...	...	...	...	...	...	...
Debt forgiveness	2 402	. .	...	...	...	...	...	...	...	...
Other capital transfers	2 410	. .	...	...	...	...	...	...	...	...
Other sectors	2 430	. .	...	...	...	...	...	...	...	...
Migrants' transfers	2 431	. .	...	...	...	...	...	...	...	...
Debt forgiveness	2 432	. .	...	...	...	...	...	...	...	...
Other capital transfers	2 440	. .	...	...	...	...	...	...	...	...
Capital transfers, debit	3 400	. .	...	...	...	...	...	...	**–1.0**	**–.4**
General government	3 401	. .	...	...	...	...	...	...	...	...
Debt forgiveness	3 402	. .	...	...	...	...	...	...	...	...
Other capital transfers	3 410	. .	...	...	...	...	...	...	...	...
Other sectors	3 430	. .	...	...	...	...	...	...	...	...
Migrants' transfers	3 431	. .	...	...	...	...	...	...	...	...
Debt forgiveness	3 432	. .	...	...	...	...	...	...	...	...
Other capital transfers	3 440	. .	...	...	...	...	...	...	...	...
Nonproduced nonfinancial assets, credit	2 480	. .	...	...	...	...	...	...	...	...
Nonproduced nonfinancial assets, debit	3 480	. .	...	...	...	...	...	...	...	...

Table 2 (Continued). STANDARD PRESENTATION, 1988–95

(Millions of U.S. dollars)

	Code	1988	1989	1990	1991	1992	1993	1994	1995
FINANCIAL ACCOUNT	4 995	...	...	...	...	...	...	**198.3**	**85.8**
A. DIRECT INVESTMENT	4 500	...	...	...	...	...	...	11.6	63.7
Direct investment abroad	4 505	...	...	...	...	...	...	...	**–.5**
Equity capital	4 510	...	...	...	...	...	...	...	...
Claims on affiliated enterprises	4 515	...	...	...	...	...	...	...	...
Liabilities to affiliated enterprises	4 520	...	...	...	...	...	...	...	...
Reinvested earnings	4 525	...	...	...	...	...	...	...	...
Other capital	4 530	...	...	...	...	...	...	...	–.5
Claims on affiliated enterprises	4 535	...	...	...	...	...	...	...	–.5
Liabilities to affiliated enterprises	4 540	...	...	...	...	...	...	...	...
Direct investment in Moldova	4 555	...	...	...	...	...	...	**11.6**	**64.2**
Equity capital	4 560	...	...	...	...	...	...	...	63.5
Claims on direct investors	4 565	...	...	...	...	...	...	...	...
Liabilities to direct investors	4 570	...	...	...	...	...	...	...	63.5
Reinvested earnings	4 575	...	...	...	...	...	...	...	...
Other capital	4 580	...	...	...	...	...	...	...	.7
Claims on direct investors	4 585	...	...	...	...	...	...	...	...
Liabilities to direct investors	4 590	...	...	...	...	...	...	...	.7
B. PORTFOLIO INVESTMENT	4 600	...	...	...	...	...	...	.3	–.3
Assets	4 602	...	...	...	...	...	...	**–.4**	...
Equity securities	4 610	...	...	...	...	...	...	–.4	...
Monetary authorities	4 611	...	...	...	...	...	...	...	...
General government	4 612	...	...	...	...	...	...	–.4	...
Banks	4 613	...	...	...	...	...	...	...	...
Other sectors	4 614	...	...	...	...	...	...	...	...
Debt securities	4 619	...	...	...	...	...	...	...	...
Bonds and notes	4 620	...	...	...	...	...	...	...	...
Monetary authorities	4 621	...	...	...	...	...	...	...	...
General government	4 622	...	...	...	...	...	...	...	...
Banks	4 623	...	...	...	...	...	...	...	...
Other sectors	4 624	...	...	...	...	...	...	...	...
Money market instruments	4 630	...	...	...	...	...	...	...	...
Monetary authorities	4 631	...	...	...	...	...	...	...	...
General government	4 632	...	...	...	...	...	...	...	...
Banks	4 633	...	...	...	...	...	...	...	...
Other sectors	4 634	...	...	...	...	...	...	...	...
Financial derivatives	4 640	...	...	...	...	...	...	...	...
Monetary authorities	4 641	...	...	...	...	...	...	...	...
General government	4 642	...	...	...	...	...	...	...	...
Banks	4 643	...	...	...	...	...	...	...	...
Other sectors	4 644	...	...	...	...	...	...	...	...
Liabilities	4 652	...	...	...	...	...	...	**.7**	**–.3**
Equity securities	4 660	...	...	...	...	...	...	.7	–.4
Banks	4 663	...	...	...	...	...	...	...	...
Other sectors	4 664	...	...	...	...	...	...	.7	–.4
Debt securities	4 669	...	...	...	...	...	...	...	...
Bonds and notes	4 670	...	...	...	...	...	...	...	...
Monetary authorities	4 671	...	...	...	...	...	...	...	...
General government	4 672	...	...	...	...	...	...	...	...
Banks	4 673	...	...	...	...	...	...	...	...
Other sectors	4 674	...	...	...	...	...	...	...	...
Money market instruments	4 680	...	...	...	...	...	...	...	...
Monetary authorities	4 681	...	...	...	...	...	...	...	...
General government	4 682	...	...	...	...	...	...	...	...
Banks	4 683	...	...	...	...	...	...	...	...
Other sectors	4 684	...	...	...	...	...	...	...	...
Financial derivatives	4 690	...	...	...	...	...	...	...	...
Monetary authorities	4 691	...	...	...	...	...	...	...	...
General government	4 692	...	...	...	...	...	...	...	...
Banks	4 693	...	...	...	...	...	...	...	...
Other sectors	4 694	...	...	...	...	...	...	...	...

Table 2 (Concluded). STANDARD PRESENTATION, 1988–95
(Millions of U.S. dollars)

	Code	1988	1989	1990	1991	1992	1993	1994	1995
C. OTHER INVESTMENT	4 700 . .	...	...	...	...	...	...	289.5	99.2
Assets	4 703 . .	**...**	**...**	**...**	**...**	**...**	**...**	**–81.7**	**–120.9**
Trade credits	4 706 . .	...	...	...	...	...	...	–65.8	–137.0
General government: long-term	4 708 . .	...	...	...	...	...	...	...	...
General government: short-term	4 709 . .	...	...	...	...	...	...	–.3	–1.6
Other sectors: long-term	4 711 . .	...	...	...	...	...	...	...	...
Other sectors: short-term	4 712 . .	...	...	...	...	...	...	–65.6	–135.4
Loans	4 714 . .	...	...	...	...	...	...	9.2	9.6
Monetary authorities: long-term	4 717 . .	...	...	...	...	...	...	...	...
Monetary authorities: short-term	4 718 . .	...	...	...	...	...	...	...	...
General government: long-term	4 720 . .	...	...	...	...	...	...	9.5	9.5
General government: short-term	4 721 . .	...	...	...	...	...	...	...	...
Banks: long-term	4 723 . .	...	...	...	...	...	...	...	.1
Banks: short-term	4 724 . .	...	...	...	...	...	...	–.2	.1
Other sectors: long-term	4 726 . .	...	...	...	...	...	...	...	...
Other sectors: short-term	4 727 . .	...	...	...	...	...	...	...	...
Currency and deposits	4 730 . .	...	...	...	...	...	...	–11.3	8.9
Monetary authorities	4 731 . .	...	...	...	...	...	...	–1.3	2.9
General government	4 732 . .	...	...	...	...	...	...	...	...
Banks	4 733 . .	...	...	...	...	...	...	–9.9	–13.2
Other sectors	4 734 . .	...	...	...	...	...	...	–.1	19.3
Other assets	4 736 . .	...	...	...	...	...	...	–13.8	–2.5
Monetary authorities: long-term	4 738 . .	...	...	...	...	...	...	...	...
Monetary authorities: short-term	4 739 . .	...	...	...	...	...	...	...	...
General government: long-term	4 741 . .	...	...	...	...	...	...	...	...
General government: short-term	4 742 . .	...	...	...	...	...	...	...	–1.9
Banks: long-term	4 744 . .	...	...	...	...	...	...	...	...
Banks: short-term	4 745 . .	...	...	...	...	...	...	...	...
Other sectors: long-term	4 747 . .	...	...	...	...	...	...	...	...
Other sectors: short-term	4 748 . .	...	...	...	...	...	...	...	–.6
Liabilities	4 753 . .	**...**	**...**	**...**	**...**	**...**	**...**	**371.2**	**220.1**
Trade credits	4 756 . .	...	...	...	...	...	...	123.2	47.0
General government: long-term	4 758 . .	...	...	...	...	...	...	...	...
General government: short-term	4 759 . .	...	...	...	...	...	...	–3.6	.5
Other sectors: long-term	4 761 . .	...	...	...	...	...	...	...	...
Other sectors: short-term	4 762 . .	...	...	...	...	...	...	126.8	46.5
Loans	4 764 . .	...	...	...	...	...	...	223.2	130.8
Use of Fund credit and loans from the Fund	4 766 . .	...	...	...	...	...	...	71.5	64.8
Monetary authorities: other long term	4 767 . .	...	...	...	...	...	...	...	...
Monetary authorities: short-term	4 768 . .	...	...	...	...	...	...	...	...
General government: long-term	4 770 . .	...	...	...	...	...	...	151.5	55.0
General government: short-term	4 771 . .	...	...	...	...	...	...	...	...
Banks: long-term	4 773 . .	...	...	...	...	...	...	...	6.3
Banks: short-term	4 774 . .	...	...	...	...	...	...	.2	.1
Other sectors: long-term	4 776 . .	...	...	...	...	...	...	...	4.4
Other sectors: short-term	4 777 . .	...	...	...	...	...	...	.1	.2
Currency and deposits	4 780 . .	...	...	...	...	...	...	2.2	7.6
Monetary authorities	4 781 . .	...	...	...	...	...	...	3.1	2.2
General government	4 782 . .	...	...	...	...	...	...	...	...
Banks	4 783 . .	...	...	...	...	...	...	–1.0	5.4
Other sectors	4 784 . .	...	...	...	...	...	...	...	...
Other liabilities	4 786 . .	...	...	...	...	...	...	22.6	34.7
Monetary authorities: long-term	4 788 . .	...	...	...	...	...	...	...	...
Monetary authorities: short-term	4 789 . .	...	...	...	...	...	...	...	...
General government: long-term	4 791 . .	...	...	...	...	...	...	...	...
General government: short-term	4 792 . .	...	...	...	...	...	...	17.5	21.0
Banks: long-term	4 794 . .	...	...	...	...	...	...	...	...
Banks: short-term	4 795 . .	...	...	...	...	...	...	...	.2
Other sectors: long-term	4 797 . .	...	...	...	...	...	...	...	...
Other sectors: short-term	4 798 . .	...	...	...	...	...	...	5.1	13.5
D. RESERVE ASSETS	4 800 . .	...	...	...	...	...	...	–103.1	–76.7
Monetary gold	4 810 . .	...	...	...	...	...	...	...	...
Special drawing rights	4 820 . .	...	...	...	...	...	...	14.6	8.8
Reserve position in the Fund	4 830 . .	...	...	...	...	...	...	...	...
Foreign exchange	4 840 . .	...	...	...	...	...	...	–117.7	–85.5
Other claims	4 880 . .	...	...	...	...	...	...	...	...
NET ERRORS AND OMISSIONS	4 998 . .	**...**	**...**	**...**	**...**	**...**	**...**	**–115.3**	**9.3**

Mongolia
948

Table 1. ANALYTIC PRESENTATION, 1988–95

(Millions of U.S. dollars)

	Code	1988	1989	1990	1991	1992	1993	1994	1995
A. Current Account[1]	4 993 Y .	**–1,033.3**	**–1,228.7**	**–639.5**	**–104.2**	**–55.7**	**31.1**	**46.4**	**38.9**
Goods: exports f.o.b	2 100 . .	829.1	795.8	444.8	346.5	355.8	365.8	367.0	451.0
Goods: imports f.o.b	3 100 . .	–1,701.9	–1,758.9	–941.7	–447.6	–384.9	–344.5	–333.3	–425.7
Balance on Goods	4 100 . .	*–872.8*	*–963.1*	*–496.9*	*–101.1*	*–29.1*	*21.3*	*33.7*	*25.3*
Services: credit	2 200 . .	94.3	36.4	48.1	26.5	34.8	26.0	45.4	57.3
Services: debit	3 200 . .	–220.3	–257.0	–154.5	–66.3	–69.7	–66.9	–91.2	–95.4
Balance on Goods and Services	4 991 . .	*–998.8*	*–1,183.7*	*–603.3*	*–140.9*	*–64.0*	*–19.6*	*–12.1*	*–12.8*
Income: credit	2 300 . .	.2	7.5	5.1	. . .	.2	.8	3.2	3.0
Income: debit	3 300 . .	–34.4	–56.4	–48.7	–4.9	–27.1	–21.0	–22.5	–28.4
Balance on Goods, Services, and Income	4 992 . .	*–1,033.0*	*–1,232.6*	*–646.9*	*–145.8*	*–90.9*	*–39.8*	*–31.4*	*–38.2*
Current transfers: credit	2 379 Y .	. . .	3.9	7.4	41.6	38.7	66.7	77.8	77.1
Current transfers: debit	3 379 . .	–.3	. . .	. . .	. . .	–3.5	4.2	. . .	. . .
B. Capital Account[1]	4 994 Y .	**. . .**	**. . .**	**. . .**	**. . .**	**. . .**	**. . .**	**. . .**	**. . .**
Capital account: credit	2 994 Y .	. . .	. . .	. . .	. . .	. . .	. . .	. . .	. . .
Capital account: debit	3 994 . .	. . .	. . .	. . .	. . .	. . .	. . .	. . .	. . .
Total, Groups A Plus B	4 010 . .	*–1,033.3*	*–1,228.7*	*–639.5*	*–104.2*	*–55.7*	*31.1*	*46.4*	*38.9*
C. Financial Account[1]	4 995 X .	**1,019.4**	**1,313.0**	**541.0**	**10.8**	**–44.0**	**–11.8**	**–39.0**	**–16.9**
Direct investment abroad	4 505 . .	. . .	. . .	. . .	. . .	. . .	. . .	. . .	. . .
Direct investment in Mongolia	4 555 Y .	. . .	. . .	. . .	. . .	2.0	7.7	6.9	9.8
Portfolio investment assets	4 602 . .	. . .	. . .	. . .	. . .	. . .	. . .	. . .	. . .
Equity securities	4 610 . .	. . .	. . .	. . .	. . .	. . .	. . .	. . .	. . .
Debt securities	4 619 . .	. . .	. . .	. . .	. . .	. . .	. . .	. . .	. . .
Portfolio investment liabilities	4 652 Y .	. . .	. . .	. . .	. . .	. . .	. . .	. . .	. . .
Equity securities	4 660 Y .	. . .	. . .	. . .	. . .	. . .	. . .	. . .	. . .
Debt securities	4 669 Y .	. . .	. . .	. . .	. . .	. . .	. . .	. . .	. . .
Other investment assets	4 703 . .	. . .	. . .	–2.0	. . .	–64.0	–35.4	–51.0	–49.2
Monetary authorities	4 703 . A	. . .	. . .	. . .	. . .	. . .	. . .	. . .	. . .
General government	4 703 . B	. . .	. . .	–2.0	. . .	. . .	. . .	. . .	. . .
Banks	4 703 . C	. . .	. . .	. . .	. . .	–11.6	–24.9	–15.3	–15.3
Other sectors	4 703 . D	. . .	. . .	. . .	. . .	–52.4	–10.5	–35.7	–33.9
Other investment liabilities	4 753 X .	1,019.4	1,313.0	543.0	10.8	18.0	15.9	5.1	22.5
Monetary authorities	4 753 XA	–89.1	84.6	26.3	–32.8	–69.8	–11.2	. . .	. . .
General government	4 753 YB	1,108.5	1,228.4	516.7	36.2	45.6	32.5	7.9	22.5
Banks	4 753 YC	. . .	. . .	. . .	. . .	. . .	3.6	. . .	. . .
Other sectors	4 753 YD	. . .	. . .	. . .	7.4	42.2	–9.0	–2.8	. . .
Total, Groups A Through C	4 020 . .	*–13.9*	*84.3*	*–98.5*	*–93.4*	*–99.7*	*19.3*	*7.4*	*22.0*
D. Net Errors and Omissions	4 998 . .	**14.6**	**45.4**	**–3.1**	**–36.4**	**17.4**	**–4.8**	**–1.0**	**10.1**
Total, Groups A Through D	4 030 . .	*.7*	*129.7*	*–101.6*	*–129.8*	*–82.3*	*14.5*	*6.4*	*32.1*
E. Reserves and Related Items	4 040 . .	**–.7**	**–129.7**	**101.6**	**129.8**	**82.3**	**–14.5**	**–6.4**	**–32.1**
Reserve assets	4 800 . .	–.7	–129.7	101.6	51.2	72.3	–23.5	–27.4	–22.6
Use of Fund credit and loans	4 766 . .	. . .	. . .	. . .	15.3	3.5	13.1	21.1	–9.5
Liabilities constituting foreign authorities' reserves	4 900 . .	. . .	. . .	. . .	. . .	. . .	. . .	. . .	. . .
Exceptional financing	4 920 . .	. . .	. . .	. . .	63.3	6.5	–4.1	. . .	. . .
Conversion rates: tugriks per U.S. dollar	0 101 . .	**. . .**	**. . .**	**. . .**	**9.52**	**42.56**	**300.87**	**412.72**	**448.61**

[1] Excludes components that have been classified in the categories of Group E.

Table 2. STANDARD PRESENTATION, 1988–95
(Millions of U.S. dollars)

	Code	1988	1989	1990	1991	1992	1993	1994	1995
CURRENT ACCOUNT	4 993 . .	**–1,033.3**	**–1,228.7**	**–639.5**	**–104.2**	**–55.7**	**31.1**	**46.4**	**38.9**
A. GOODS	4 100 . .	–872.8	–963.1	–496.9	–101.1	–29.1	21.3	33.7	25.3
Credit	2 100 . .	**829.1**	**795.8**	**444.8**	**346.5**	**355.8**	**365.8**	**367.0**	**451.0**
General merchandise: exports f.o.b.	2 110 . .	829.1	795.8	444.8	346.5	355.8	365.8	367.0	451.0
Goods for processing: exports f.o.b.	2 150 . .	...	...	...	...	...	...	...	...
Repairs on goods	2 160 . .	...	...	...	...	...	...	...	...
Goods procured in ports by carriers	2 170 . .	...	...	...	...	...	...	...	...
Nonmonetary gold	2 180 . .	...	...	...	...	...	...	...	...
Debit	3 100 . .	**–1,701.9**	**–1,758.9**	**–941.7**	**–447.6**	**–384.9**	**–344.5**	**–333.3**	**–425.7**
General merchandise: imports f.o.b.	3 110 . .	–1,701.9	–1,758.9	–941.7	–447.6	–384.9	–344.5	–333.3	–425.7
Goods for processing: imports f.o.b.	3 150 . .	...	...	...	...	...	...	...	...
Repairs on goods	3 160 . .	...	...	...	...	...	...	...	...
Goods procured in ports by carriers	3 170 . .	...	...	...	...	...	...	...	...
Nonmonetary gold	3 180 . .	...	...	...	...	...	...	...	...
B. SERVICES	4 200 . .	–126.0	–220.6	–106.4	–39.8	–34.9	–40.9	–45.8	–38.1
Total credit	2 200 . .	*94.3*	*36.4*	*48.1*	*26.5*	*34.8*	*26.0*	*45.4*	*57.3*
Total debit	3 200 . .	*–220.3*	*–257.0*	*–154.5*	*–66.3*	*–69.7*	*–66.9*	*–91.2*	*–95.4*
Transportation services, credit	2 205 . .	**26.0**	**19.3**	**20.1**	**...**	**17.8**	**14.0**	**20.7**	**15.0**
Passenger	2 205 BA	...	...	...	...	*8.1*	*7.3*	*8.1*	*12.0*
Freight	2 205 BB	*26.0*	*19.3*	*20.1*	...	*4.6*	*4.9*	*5.5*	...
Other	2 205 BC	...	...	...	...	*5.1*	*1.8*	*7.1*	*3.0*
Sea transport, passenger	2 207 . .	...	...	...	...	...	...	...	...
Sea transport, freight	2 208 . .	...	...	...	...	...	...	...	...
Sea transport, other	2 209 . .	...	...	...	...	...	...	...	...
Air transport, passenger	2 211 . .	...	...	...	...	7.4	6.2	6.4	8.0
Air transport, freight	2 212 . .	...	...	...	...	...	...	...	...
Air transport, other	2 213 . .	...	...	...	...	...	...	...	...
Other transport, passenger	2 215 . .	...	...	...	...	.7	1.1	1.7	4.0
Other transport, freight	2 216 . .	...	...	...	...	...	...	5.5	...
Other transport, other	2 217 . .	...	...	...	...	...	...	7.1	3.0
Transportation services, debit	3 205 . .	**–155.6**	**–157.0**	**–86.8**	**–35.0**	**–46.5**	**–51.3**	**–60.7**	**–60.8**
Passenger	3 205 BA	...	...	...	...	*–7.5*	*–11.0*	*–4.9*	*–1.5*
Freight	3 205 BB	*–155.6*	*–157.0*	*–86.8*	*–35.0*	*–31.3*	*–27.0*	*–37.1*	*–47.3*
Other	3 205 BC	...	...	...	...	*–7.7*	*–13.3*	*–18.7*	*–12.0*
Sea transport, passenger	3 207 . .	...	...	...	...	...	...	...	...
Sea transport, freight	3 208 . .	...	...	...	...	...	...	...	...
Sea transport, other	3 209 . .	...	...	...	...	...	...	...	...
Air transport, passenger	3 211 . .	...	...	...	...	–3.0	–7.8	...	...
Air transport, freight	3 212 . .	...	...	...	...	...	...	...	...
Air transport, other	3 213 . .	...	...	...	...	...	...	...	...
Other transport, passenger	3 215 . .	...	...	...	...	–4.5	–3.2	–4.9	–1.5
Other transport, freight	3 216 . .	...	...	...	...	...	...	–37.1	–47.3
Other transport, other	3 217 . .	...	...	...	...	...	...	–18.7	–12.0
Travel, credit	2 236 . .	**4.8**	**4.4**	**5.0**	**...**	**3.2**	**3.5**	**6.6**	**20.6**
Business travel	2 237 . .	...	...	...	...	...	...	...	...
Personal travel	2 240 . .	...	...	...	...	...	...	...	...
Travel, debit	3 236 . .	**–.4**	**–.4**	**–1.2**	**...**	**–3.5**	**–2.5**	**–3.4**	**–19.5**
Business travel	3 237 . .	...	...	...	...	...	...	...	...
Personal travel	3 240 . .	...	...	...	...	...	...	...	...
Other services, credit	2 200 BA	**63.5**	**12.7**	**23.0**	**26.5**	**13.8**	**8.5**	**18.1**	**21.7**
Communications	2 245 . .	...	...	...	...	2.3	2.2	3.8	5.0
Construction	2 249 . .	...	...	...	...	...	...	...	...
Insurance	2 253 . .	2.9	2.1	2.2	...	.5	.6	...	...
Financial	2 260 . .	...	...	...	...	.4	1.6	3.1	2.5
Computer and information	2 262 . .	...	...	...	...	...	...	...	...
Royalties and licence fees	2 266 . .	...	...	...	...	...	...	...	...
Other business services	2 268 . .	60.6	10.6	20.8	26.5	4.3	2.7	.3	4.2
Personal, cultural, and recreational	2 287 . .	...	...	...	...	...	...	...	...
Government, n.i.e.	2 291 . .	...	...	...	...	6.3	1.4	10.9	10.0
Other services, debit	3 200 BA	**–64.3**	**–99.6**	**–66.5**	**–31.3**	**–19.7**	**–13.1**	**–27.1**	**–15.1**
Communications	3 245 . .	...	...	...	...	–.8	–.9	–4.1	–4.0
Construction	3 249 . .	...	...	...	...	...	...	...	...
Insurance	3 253 . .	–17.3	–17.4	–9.7	–3.9	–3.5	–3.0	...	...
Financial	3 260 . .	...	...	...	...	–.1	–.3	...	...
Computer and information	3 262 . .	...	...	...	...	...	...	...	...
Royalties and licence fees	3 266 . .	...	...	...	...	...	...	...	...
Other business services	3 268 . .	–47.0	–82.2	–56.8	–27.4	–7.9	–7.4	–20.0	–3.1
Personal, cultural, and recreational	3 287 . .	...	...	...	...	...	...	...	...
Government, n.i.e.	3 291 . .	...	...	...	...	–7.4	–1.5	–3.0	–8.0

Table 2 (Continued). STANDARD PRESENTATION, 1988–95
(Millions of U.S. dollars)

	Code	1988	1989	1990	1991	1992	1993	1994	1995
C. INCOME	4 300	–34.2	–48.9	–43.6	–4.9	–26.9	–20.2	–19.3	–25.4
Total credit	2 300	*.2*	*7.5*	*5.1*	. . .	*.2*	*.8*	*3.2*	*3.0*
Total debit	3 300	*–34.4*	*–56.4*	*–48.7*	*–4.9*	*–27.1*	*–21.0*	*–22.5*	*–28.4*
Compensation of employees, credit	2 310	. . .	. . .	. . .	. . .	. . .	. . .	. . .	. . .
Compensation of employees, debit	3 310	. . .	. . .	. . .	. . .	. . .	. . .	. . .	. . .
Investment income, credit	2 320	**.2**	**7.5**	**5.1**	. . .	**.2**	**.8**	**3.2**	**3.0**
Direct investment income	2 330	. . .	. . .	. . .	. . .	. . .	. . .	. . .	. . .
Dividends and distributed branch profits	2 332	. . .	. . .	. . .	. . .	. . .	. . .	. . .	. . .
Reinvested earnings and undistributed branch profits	2 333	. . .	. . .	. . .	. . .	. . .	. . .	. . .	. . .
Income on debt (interest)	2 334	. . .	. . .	. . .	. . .	. . .	. . .	. . .	. . .
Portfolio investment income	2 339	. . .	. . .	. . .	. . .	. . .	. . .	. . .	. . .
Income on equity	2 340	. . .	. . .	. . .	. . .	. . .	. . .	. . .	. . .
Income on bonds and notes	2 350	. . .	. . .	. . .	. . .	. . .	. . .	. . .	. . .
Income on money market instruments and financial derivatives	2 360	. . .	. . .	. . .	. . .	. . .	. . .	. . .	. . .
Other investment income	2 370	.2	7.5	5.1	. . .	.2	.8	3.2	3.0
Investment income, debit	3 320	**–34.4**	**–56.4**	**–48.7**	**–4.9**	**–27.1**	**–21.0**	**–22.5**	**–28.4**
Direct investment income	3 330	. . .	. . .	. . .	. . .	–12.5	–11.8	–8.2	–17.8
Dividends and distributed branch profits	3 332	. . .	. . .	. . .	. . .	. . .	. . .	. . .	. . .
Reinvested earnings and undistributed branch profits	3 333	. . .	. . .	. . .	. . .	. . .	. . .	. . .	. . .
Income on debt (interest)	3 334	. . .	. . .	. . .	. . .	. . .	. . .	. . .	. . .
Portfolio investment income	3 339	. . .	. . .	. . .	. . .	. . .	. . .	. . .	. . .
Income on equity	3 340	. . .	. . .	. . .	. . .	. . .	. . .	. . .	. . .
Income on bonds and notes	3 350	. . .	. . .	. . .	. . .	. . .	. . .	. . .	. . .
Income on money market instruments and financial derivatives	3 360	. . .	. . .	. . .	. . .	. . .	. . .	. . .	. . .
Other investment income	3 370	–34.4	–56.4	–48.7	–4.9	–14.6	–9.2	–14.3	–10.6
D. CURRENT TRANSFERS	4 379	–.3	3.9	7.4	41.6	35.2	70.9	77.8	77.1
Credit	2 379	. . .	**3.9**	**7.4**	**41.6**	**38.7**	**66.7**	**77.8**	**77.1**
General government	2 380	. . .	3.9	7.4	41.6	38.7	66.7	77.7	77.1
Other sectors	2 390	. . .	. . .	. . .	. . .	. . .	. . .	.1	. . .
Workers' remittances	2 391	. . .	. . .	. . .	. . .	. . .	. . .	. . .	. . .
Other current transfers	2 392	. . .	. . .	. . .	. . .	. . .	. . .	.1	. . .
Debit	3 379	**–.3**	. . .	. . .	. . .	**–3.5**	**4.2**	. . .	. . .
General government	3 380	. . .	. . .	. . .	. . .	–.8	4.3	. . .	. . .
Other sectors	3 390	–.3	. . .	. . .	. . .	–2.7	–.1	. . .	. . .
Workers' remittances	3 391	. . .	. . .	. . .	. . .	. . .	. . .	. . .	. . .
Other current transfers	3 392	–.3	. . .	. . .	. . .	–2.7	–.1	. . .	. . .
CAPITAL AND FINANCIAL ACCOUNT	4 996	**1,018.7**	**1,183.3**	**642.6**	**140.6**	**38.3**	**–26.3**	**–45.4**	**–49.0**
CAPITAL ACCOUNT	4 994	. . .	. . .	. . .	. . .	. . .	. . .	. . .	. . .
Total credit	2 994	. . .	. . .	. . .	. . .	. . .	. . .	. . .	. . .
Total debit	3 994	. . .	. . .	. . .	. . .	. . .	. . .	. . .	. . .
Capital transfers, credit	2 400	. . .	. . .	. . .	. . .	. . .	. . .	. . .	. . .
General government	2 401	. . .	. . .	. . .	. . .	. . .	. . .	. . .	. . .
Debt forgiveness	2 402	. . .	. . .	. . .	. . .	. . .	. . .	. . .	. . .
Other capital transfers	2 410	. . .	. . .	. . .	. . .	. . .	. . .	. . .	. . .
Other sectors	2 430	. . .	. . .	. . .	. . .	. . .	. . .	. . .	. . .
Migrants' transfers	2 431	. . .	. . .	. . .	. . .	. . .	. . .	. . .	. . .
Debt forgiveness	2 432	. . .	. . .	. . .	. . .	. . .	. . .	. . .	. . .
Other capital transfers	2 440	. . .	. . .	. . .	. . .	. . .	. . .	. . .	. . .
Capital transfers, debit	3 400	. . .	. . .	. . .	. . .	. . .	. . .	. . .	. . .
General government	3 401	. . .	. . .	. . .	. . .	. . .	. . .	. . .	. . .
Debt forgiveness	3 402	. . .	. . .	. . .	. . .	. . .	. . .	. . .	. . .
Other capital transfers	3 410	. . .	. . .	. . .	. . .	. . .	. . .	. . .	. . .
Other sectors	3 430	. . .	. . .	. . .	. . .	. . .	. . .	. . .	. . .
Migrants' transfers	3 431	. . .	. . .	. . .	. . .	. . .	. . .	. . .	. . .
Debt forgiveness	3 432	. . .	. . .	. . .	. . .	. . .	. . .	. . .	. . .
Other capital transfers	3 440	. . .	. . .	. . .	. . .	. . .	. . .	. . .	. . .
Nonproduced nonfinancial assets, credit	2 480	. . .	. . .	. . .	. . .	. . .	. . .	. . .	. . .
Nonproduced nonfinancial assets, debit	3 480	. . .	. . .	. . .	. . .	. . .	. . .	. . .	. . .

Table 2 (Continued). STANDARD PRESENTATION, 1988–95
(Millions of U.S. dollars)

	Code	1988	1989	1990	1991	1992	1993	1994	1995
FINANCIAL ACCOUNT	4 995 . .	**1,018.7**	**1,183.3**	**642.6**	**140.6**	**38.3**	**–26.3**	**–45.4**	**–49.0**
A. DIRECT INVESTMENT	4 500 . .	. . .	. . .	. . .	. . .	2.0	7.7	6.9	9.8
Direct investment abroad	4 505 . .	**. . .**	**. . .**	**. . .**	**. . .**	**. . .**	**. . .**	**. . .**	**. . .**
Equity capital	4 510 . .	. . .	. . .	. . .	. . .	. . .	. . .	. . .	. . .
Claims on affiliated enterprises	4 515 . .	. . .	. . .	. . .	. . .	. . .	. . .	. . .	. . .
Liabilities to affiliated enterprises	4 520 . .	. . .	. . .	. . .	. . .	. . .	. . .	. . .	. . .
Reinvested earnings	4 525 . .	. . .	. . .	. . .	. . .	. . .	. . .	. . .	. . .
Other capital	4 530 . .	. . .	. . .	. . .	. . .	. . .	. . .	. . .	. . .
Claims on affiliated enterprises	4 535 . .	. . .	. . .	. . .	. . .	. . .	. . .	. . .	. . .
Liabilities to affiliated enterprises	4 540 . .	. . .	. . .	. . .	. . .	. . .	. . .	. . .	. . .
Direct investment in Mongolia	4 555 . .	**. . .**	**. . .**	**. . .**	**. . .**	**2.0**	**7.7**	**6.9**	**9.8**
Equity capital	4 560 . .	. . .	. . .	. . .	. . .	2.0	7.7	6.9	9.8
Claims on direct investors	4 565 . .	. . .	. . .	. . .	. . .	. . .	. . .	. . .	. . .
Liabilities to direct investors	4 570 . .	. . .	. . .	. . .	. . .	. . .	. . .	. . .	. . .
Reinvested earnings	4 575 . .	. . .	. . .	. . .	. . .	. . .	. . .	. . .	. . .
Other capital	4 580 . .	. . .	. . .	. . .	. . .	. . .	. . .	. . .	. . .
Claims on direct investors	4 585 . .	. . .	. . .	. . .	. . .	. . .	. . .	. . .	. . .
Liabilities to direct investors	4 590 . .	. . .	. . .	. . .	. . .	. . .	. . .	. . .	. . .
B. PORTFOLIO INVESTMENT	4 600 . .	. . .	. . .	. . .	. . .	. . .	. . .	. . .	. . .
Assets	4 602 . .	**. . .**	**. . .**	**. . .**	**. . .**	**. . .**	**. . .**	**. . .**	**. . .**
Equity securities	4 610 . .	. . .	. . .	. . .	. . .	. . .	. . .	. . .	. . .
Monetary authorities	4 611 . .	. . .	. . .	. . .	. . .	. . .	. . .	. . .	. . .
General government	4 612 . .	. . .	. . .	. . .	. . .	. . .	. . .	. . .	. . .
Banks	4 613 . .	. . .	. . .	. . .	. . .	. . .	. . .	. . .	. . .
Other sectors	4 614 . .	. . .	. . .	. . .	. . .	. . .	. . .	. . .	. . .
Debt securities	4 619 . .	. . .	. . .	. . .	. . .	. . .	. . .	. . .	. . .
Bonds and notes	4 620 . .	. . .	. . .	. . .	. . .	. . .	. . .	. . .	. . .
Monetary authorities	4 621 . .	. . .	. . .	. . .	. . .	. . .	. . .	. . .	. . .
General government	4 622 . .	. . .	. . .	. . .	. . .	. . .	. . .	. . .	. . .
Banks	4 623 . .	. . .	. . .	. . .	. . .	. . .	. . .	. . .	. . .
Other sectors	4 624 . .	. . .	. . .	. . .	. . .	. . .	. . .	. . .	. . .
Money market instruments	4 630 . .	. . .	. . .	. . .	. . .	. . .	. . .	. . .	. . .
Monetary authorities	4 631 . .	. . .	. . .	. . .	. . .	. . .	. . .	. . .	. . .
General government	4 632 . .	. . .	. . .	. . .	. . .	. . .	. . .	. . .	. . .
Banks	4 633 . .	. . .	. . .	. . .	. . .	. . .	. . .	. . .	. . .
Other sectors	4 634 . .	. . .	. . .	. . .	. . .	. . .	. . .	. . .	. . .
Financial derivatives	4 640 . .	. . .	. . .	. . .	. . .	. . .	. . .	. . .	. . .
Monetary authorities	4 641 . .	. . .	. . .	. . .	. . .	. . .	. . .	. . .	. . .
General government	4 642 . .	. . .	. . .	. . .	. . .	. . .	. . .	. . .	. . .
Banks	4 643 . .	. . .	. . .	. . .	. . .	. . .	. . .	. . .	. . .
Other sectors	4 644 . .	. . .	. . .	. . .	. . .	. . .	. . .	. . .	. . .
Liabilities	4 652 . .	**. . .**	**. . .**	**. . .**	**. . .**	**. . .**	**. . .**	**. . .**	**. . .**
Equity securities	4 660 . .	. . .	. . .	. . .	. . .	. . .	. . .	. . .	. . .
Banks	4 663 . .	. . .	. . .	. . .	. . .	. . .	. . .	. . .	. . .
Other sectors	4 664 . .	. . .	. . .	. . .	. . .	. . .	. . .	. . .	. . .
Debt securities	4 669 . .	. . .	. . .	. . .	. . .	. . .	. . .	. . .	. . .
Bonds and notes	4 670 . .	. . .	. . .	. . .	. . .	. . .	. . .	. . .	. . .
Monetary authorities	4 671 . .	. . .	. . .	. . .	. . .	. . .	. . .	. . .	. . .
General government	4 672 . .	. . .	. . .	. . .	. . .	. . .	. . .	. . .	. . .
Banks	4 673 . .	. . .	. . .	. . .	. . .	. . .	. . .	. . .	. . .
Other sectors	4 674 . .	. . .	. . .	. . .	. . .	. . .	. . .	. . .	. . .
Money market instruments	4 680 . .	. . .	. . .	. . .	. . .	. . .	. . .	. . .	. . .
Monetary authorities	4 681 . .	. . .	. . .	. . .	. . .	. . .	. . .	. . .	. . .
General government	4 682 . .	. . .	. . .	. . .	. . .	. . .	. . .	. . .	. . .
Banks	4 683 . .	. . .	. . .	. . .	. . .	. . .	. . .	. . .	. . .
Other sectors	4 684 . .	. . .	. . .	. . .	. . .	. . .	. . .	. . .	. . .
Financial derivatives	4 690 . .	. . .	. . .	. . .	. . .	. . .	. . .	. . .	. . .
Monetary authorities	4 691 . .	. . .	. . .	. . .	. . .	. . .	. . .	. . .	. . .
General government	4 692 . .	. . .	. . .	. . .	. . .	. . .	. . .	. . .	. . .
Banks	4 693 . .	. . .	. . .	. . .	. . .	. . .	. . .	. . .	. . .
Other sectors	4 694 . .	. . .	. . .	. . .	. . .	. . .	. . .	. . .	. . .

Table 2 (Concluded). STANDARD PRESENTATION, 1988–95

(Millions of U.S. dollars)

	Code	1988	1989	1990	1991	1992	1993	1994	1995
C. OTHER INVESTMENT	4 700	1,019.4	1,313.0	541.0	89.4	–36.0	–10.5	–24.8	–36.2
Assets	4 703	**. . .**	**. . .**	**–2.0**	**. . .**	**–64.0**	**–35.4**	**–51.0**	**–49.2**
Trade credits	4 706	. . .	. . .	. . .	. . .	–52.4	–10.5	–35.7	–33.9
General government: long-term	4 708	. . .	. . .	. . .	. . .	. . .	. . .	. . .	. . .
General government: short-term	4 709	. . .	. . .	. . .	. . .	. . .	. . .	. . .	. . .
Other sectors: long-term	4 711	. . .	. . .	. . .	. . .	. . .	. . .	. . .	. . .
Other sectors: short-term	4 712	. . .	. . .	. . .	. . .	–52.4	–10.5	–35.7	–33.9
Loans	4 714	. . .	. . .	. . .	. . .	. . .	. . .	. . .	. . .
Monetary authorities: long-term	4 717	. . .	. . .	. . .	. . .	. . .	. . .	. . .	. . .
Monetary authorities: short-term	4 718	. . .	. . .	. . .	. . .	. . .	. . .	. . .	. . .
General government: long-term	4 720	. . .	. . .	. . .	. . .	. . .	. . .	. . .	. . .
General government: short-term	4 721	. . .	. . .	. . .	. . .	. . .	. . .	. . .	. . .
Banks: long-term	4 723	. . .	. . .	. . .	. . .	. . .	. . .	. . .	. . .
Banks: short-term	4 724	. . .	. . .	. . .	. . .	. . .	. . .	. . .	. . .
Other sectors: long-term	4 726	. . .	. . .	. . .	. . .	. . .	. . .	. . .	. . .
Other sectors: short-term	4 727	. . .	. . .	. . .	. . .	. . .	. . .	. . .	. . .
Currency and deposits	4 730	. . .	. . .	–2.0	. . .	–11.6	–24.9	–15.3	–15.3
Monetary authorities	4 731	. . .	. . .	. . .	. . .	. . .	. . .	. . .	. . .
General government	4 732	. . .	. . .	–2.0	. . .	. . .	. . .	. . .	. . .
Banks	4 733	. . .	. . .	. . .	. . .	–11.6	–24.9	–15.3	–15.3
Other sectors	4 734	. . .	. . .	. . .	. . .	. . .	. . .	. . .	. . .
Other assets	4 736	. . .	. . .	. . .	. . .	. . .	. . .	. . .	. . .
Monetary authorities: long-term	4 738	. . .	. . .	. . .	. . .	. . .	. . .	. . .	. . .
Monetary authorities: short-term	4 739	. . .	. . .	. . .	. . .	. . .	. . .	. . .	. . .
General government: long-term	4 741	. . .	. . .	. . .	. . .	. . .	. . .	. . .	. . .
General government: short-term	4 742	. . .	. . .	. . .	. . .	. . .	. . .	. . .	. . .
Banks: long-term	4 744	. . .	. . .	. . .	. . .	. . .	. . .	. . .	. . .
Banks: short-term	4 745	. . .	. . .	. . .	. . .	. . .	. . .	. . .	. . .
Other sectors: long-term	4 747	. . .	. . .	. . .	. . .	. . .	. . .	. . .	. . .
Other sectors: short-term	4 748	. . .	. . .	. . .	. . .	. . .	. . .	. . .	. . .
Liabilities	4 753	**1,019.4**	**1,313.0**	**543.0**	**89.4**	**28.0**	**24.9**	**26.2**	**13.0**
Trade credits	4 756	. . .	. . .	. . .	–23.4	3.7	–11.1	–2.8	. . .
General government: long-term	4 758	. . .	. . .	. . .	. . .	. . .	. . .	. . .	. . .
General government: short-term	4 759	. . .	. . .	. . .	. . .	. . .	. . .	. . .	. . .
Other sectors: long-term	4 761	. . .	. . .	. . .	. . .	. . .	. . .	. . .	. . .
Other sectors: short-term	4 762	. . .	. . .	. . .	–23.4	3.7	–11.1	–2.8	. . .
Loans	4 764	1,108.5	1,228.4	516.7	82.3	107.8	52.5	29.0	13.0
Use of Fund credit and loans from the Fund	4 766	. . .	. . .	. . .	15.3	3.5	13.1	21.1	–9.5
Monetary authorities: other long-term	4 767	. . .	. . .	. . .	. . .	. . .	. . .	. . .	. . .
Monetary authorities: short-term	4 768	. . .	. . .	. . .	. . .	. . .	. . .	. . .	. . .
General government: long-term	4 770	1,108.5	1,228.4	516.7	36.2	63.6	39.4	7.9	22.5
General government: short-term	4 771	. . .	. . .	. . .	. . .	. . .	. . .	. . .	. . .
Banks: long-term	4 773	. . .	. . .	. . .	. . .	. . .	. . .	. . .	. . .
Banks: short-term	4 774	. . .	. . .	. . .	. . .	. . .	. . .	. . .	. . .
Other sectors: long-term	4 776	. . .	. . .	. . .	30.8	40.7	. . .	. . .	. . .
Other sectors: short-term	4 777	. . .	. . .	. . .	. . .	. . .	. . .	. . .	. . .
Currency and deposits	4 780	. . .	. . .	. . .	. . .	. . .	3.6	. . .	. . .
Monetary authorities	4 781	. . .	. . .	. . .	. . .	. . .	. . .	. . .	. . .
General government	4 782	. . .	. . .	. . .	. . .	. . .	. . .	. . .	. . .
Banks	4 783	. . .	. . .	. . .	. . .	. . .	3.6	. . .	. . .
Other sectors	4 784	. . .	. . .	. . .	. . .	. . .	. . .	. . .	. . .
Other liabilities	4 786	–89.1	84.6	26.3	30.5	–83.5	–20.1	. . .	. . .
Monetary authorities: long-term	4 788	. . .	. . .	. . .	. . .	. . .	. . .	. . .	. . .
Monetary authorities: short-term	4 789	–89.1	84.6	26.3	–32.8	–69.8	–11.2	. . .	. . .
General government: long-term	4 791	. . .	. . .	. . .	. . .	. . .	. . .	. . .	. . .
General government: short-term	4 792	. . .	. . .	. . .	63.3	–11.5	–11.0	. . .	. . .
Banks: long-term	4 794	. . .	. . .	. . .	. . .	. . .	. . .	. . .	. . .
Banks: short-term	4 795	. . .	. . .	. . .	. . .	. . .	. . .	. . .	. . .
Other sectors: long-term	4 797	. . .	. . .	. . .	. . .	. . .	. . .	. . .	. . .
Other sectors: short-term	4 798	. . .	. . .	. . .	. . .	–2.2	2.1	. . .	. . .
D. RESERVE ASSETS	4 800	–.7	–129.7	101.6	51.2	72.3	–23.5	–27.4	–22.6
Monetary gold	4 810	1.2	.1	–35.9	2.9	27.0	19.5	–5.7	–23.5
Special drawing rights	4 820	. . .	. . .	. . .	. . .	. . .	. . .	–2.8	.4
Reserve position in the Fund	4 830	. . .	. . .	. . .	. . .	. . .	. . .	. . .	. . .
Foreign exchange	4 840	–1.9	–129.8	137.5	48.3	45.3	–43.0	–18.9	.5
Other claims	4 880	. . .	. . .	. . .	. . .	. . .	. . .	. . .	. . .
NET ERRORS AND OMISSIONS	4 998	**14.6**	**45.4**	**–3.1**	**–36.4**	**17.4**	**–4.8**	**–1.0**	**10.1**

Table 1. ANALYTIC PRESENTATION, 1988–95
(Millions of U.S. dollars)

	Code	1988	1989	1990	1991	1992	1993	1994	1995
A. Current Account [1]	4 993 Y.	**−16.00**	**5.39**	**−22.91**	**−21.34**	**−12.83**	**−10.11**	**−19.36**	...
Goods: exports f.o.b	2 100 . .	2.30	1.26	1.48	1.03	1.58	2.27	2.92	...
Goods: imports f.o.b	3 100 . .	−23.37	−32.59	−42.37	−34.13	−29.83	−24.23	−30.04	...
Balance on Goods	4 100 . .	*−21.07*	*−31.33*	*−40.89*	*−33.10*	*−28.25*	*−21.96*	*−27.12*	...
Services: credit	2 200 . .	14.70	15.34	17.64	18.63	19.97	23.34	27.15	...
Services: debit	3 200 . .	−8.59	−9.96	−12.27	−11.40	−12.28	−11.29	−14.72	...
Balance on Goods and Services	4 991 . .	*−14.97*	*−25.95*	*−35.52*	*−25.87*	*−20.56*	*−9.91*	*−14.69*	...
Income: credit	2 300 . .	.78	1.68	1.75	.72	.53	.42	.44	...
Income: debit	3 300 . .	−1.06	−2.45	−2.95	−2.36	−1.58	−3.89	−4.94	...
Balance on Goods, Services, and Income	4 992 . .	*−15.24*	*−26.72*	*−36.73*	*−27.51*	*−21.61*	*−13.38*	*−19.20*	...
Current transfers: credit	2 379 Y.	...	35.40	18.36	11.67	12.14	9.71	3.27	...
Current transfers: debit	3 379 . .	−.76	−3.29	−4.55	−5.50	−3.36	−6.44	−3.44	...
B. Capital Account [1]	4 994 Y.	**4.56**	**6.97**	**4.54**	**5.23**	**2.07**	**5.41**	**10.10**	...
Capital account: credit	2 994 Y.	4.56	6.97	4.54	5.23	2.07	5.41	10.10	...
Capital account: debit	3 994 . .	...	...	...	...	...	...	...	...
Total, Groups A Plus B	4 010 . .	*−11.44*	*12.36*	*−18.37*	*−16.11*	*−10.76*	*−4.70*	*−9.26*	...
C. Financial Account [1]	4 995 X.	**4.80**	**−9.17**	**23.61**	**5.10**	**4.73**	**5.47**	**−4.27**	...
Direct investment abroad	4 505 . .	...	...	...	...	...	...	...	...
Direct investment in Montserrat	4 555 Y.	9.51	4.91	9.58	8.03	4.61	4.86	1.24	...
Portfolio investment assets	4 602 . .	...	...	...	...	...	...	−.03	...
Equity securities	4 610 . .	...	...	...	...	...	...	−.03	...
Debt securities	4 619 . .	...	...	...	...	...	...	...	...
Portfolio investment liabilities	4 652 Y.	...	...	...	...	...	...	...	...
Equity securities	4 660 Y.	...	...	...	...	...	...	...	...
Debt securities	4 669 Y.	...	...	...	...	...	...	...	...
Other investment assets	4 703 . .	−3.97	−13.42	15.21	−3.15	.43	−2.67	−4.73	...
Monetary authorities	4 703 . A	...	...	...	...	...	...	...	...
General government	4 703 . B	...	...	...	...	...	...	...	...
Banks	4 703 . C	−3.97	−13.42	15.21	−3.15	.43	−2.67	−4.73	...
Other sectors	4 703 . D	...	...	...	...	...	...	...	...
Other investment liabilities	4 753 X.	−.74	−.66	−1.17	.21	−.31	3.29	−.75	...
Monetary authorities	4 753 XA	...	...	...	...	...	...	...	...
General government	4 753 YB	.09	−.07	−.74	.68	−.09	5.14	.08	...
Banks	4 753 YC	...	...	...	...	...	...	...	...
Other sectors	4 753 YD	−.83	−.60	−.43	−.47	−.22	−1.86	−.83	...
Total, Groups A Through C	4 020 . .	*−6.64*	*3.18*	*5.24*	*−11.01*	*−6.02*	*.77*	*−13.53*	...
D. Net Errors and Omissions	4 998 . .	**6.93**	**−2.86**	**−2.69**	**7.41**	**6.11**	**−1.16**	**15.12**	...
Total, Groups A Through D	4 030 . .	*.30*	*.32*	*2.56*	*−3.60*	*.09*	*−.39*	*1.60*	...
E. Reserves and Related Items	4 040 . .	**−.30**	**−.32**	**−2.56**	**3.60**	**−.09**	**.39**	**−1.60**	...
Reserve assets	4 800 . .	−.30	−.32	−2.56	3.60	−.09	.39	−1.60	...
Use of Fund credit and loans	4 766 . .	...	...	...	...	...	...	...	...
Liabilities constituting foreign authorities' reserves	4 900 . .	...	...	...	...	...	...	...	...
Exceptional financing	4 920 . .	...	...	...	...	...	...	...	...
Conversion rates: Eastern Carribean dollars per U.S. dollar	0 101 . .	**2.7000**	**2.7000**	**2.7000**	**2.7000**	**2.7000**	**2.7000**	**2.7000**	**2.7000**

[1] Excludes components that have been classified in the categories of Group E.

Table 2. STANDARD PRESENTATION, 1988–95

(Millions of U.S. dollars)

	Code	1988	1989	1990	1991	1992	1993	1994	1995
CURRENT ACCOUNT	4 993 . .	**–16.00**	**5.39**	**–22.91**	**–21.34**	**–12.83**	**–10.11**	**–19.36**	. . .
A. GOODS	4 100 . .	–21.07	–31.33	–40.89	–33.10	–28.25	–21.96	–27.12	. . .
Credit	2 100 . .	**2.30**	**1.26**	**1.48**	**1.03**	**1.58**	**2.27**	**2.92**	. . .
General merchandise: exports f.o.b.	2 110 . .	2.30	1.26	1.48	1.03	1.58	2.27	2.91	. . .
Goods for processing: exports f.o.b.	2 150 . .	. . .	. . .	. . .	. . .	. . .	. . .	. . .	. . .
Repairs on goods	2 160 . .	. . .	. . .	. . .	. . .	. . .	. . .	. . .	. . .
Goods procured in ports by carriers	2 170 . .	. . .	. . .	. . .	. . .	. . .	. . .	.01	. . .
Nonmonetary gold	2 180 . .	. . .	. . .	. . .	. . .	. . .	. . .	. . .	. . .
Debit	3 100 . .	**–23.37**	**–32.59**	**–42.37**	**–34.13**	**–29.83**	**–24.23**	**–30.04**	. . .
General merchandise: imports f.o.b.	3 110 . .	–23.37	–32.59	–42.37	–34.13	–29.83	–24.23	–29.93	. . .
Goods for processing: imports f.o.b.	3 150 . .	. . .	. . .	. . .	. . .	. . .	. . .	. . .	. . .
Repairs on goods	3 160 . .	. . .	. . .	. . .	. . .	. . .	. . .	. . .	. . .
Goods procured in ports by carriers	3 170 . .	. . .	. . .	. . .	. . .	. . .	. . .	–.11	. . .
Nonmonetary gold	3 180 . .	. . .	. . .	. . .	. . .	. . .	. . .	. . .	. . .
B. SERVICES	4 200 . .	6.11	5.39	5.37	7.23	7.69	12.05	12.43	. . .
Total credit	2 200 . .	*14.70*	*15.34*	*17.64*	*18.63*	*19.97*	*23.34*	*27.15*	. . .
Total debit	3 200 . .	*–8.59*	*–9.96*	*–12.27*	*–11.40*	*–12.28*	*–11.29*	*–14.72*	. . .
Transportation services, credit	2 205 . .	**1.16**	**1.65**	**2.31**	**1.76**	**1.68**	**1.56**	**2.33**	. . .
Passenger	2 205 BA	. . .	. . .	. . .	. . .	. . .	. . .	. . .	. . .
Freight	2 205 BB	. . .	. . .	. . .	. . .	. . .	. . .	*.18*	. . .
Other	2 205 BC	*1.16*	*1.65*	*2.31*	*1.76*	*1.68*	*1.56*	*2.14*	. . .
Sea transport, passenger	2 207 . .	. . .	. . .	. . .	. . .	. . .	. . .	. . .	. . .
Sea transport, freight	2 208 . .	. . .	. . .	. . .	. . .	. . .	. . .	. . .	. . .
Sea transport, other	2 209 . .	. . .	. . .	. . .	. . .	. . .	. . .	. . .	. . .
Air transport, passenger	2 211 . .	. . .	. . .	. . .	. . .	. . .	. . .	. . .	. . .
Air transport, freight	2 212 . .	. . .	. . .	. . .	. . .	. . .	. . .	. . .	. . .
Air transport, other	2 213 . .	. . .	. . .	. . .	. . .	. . .	. . .	. . .	. . .
Other transport, passenger	2 215 . .	. . .	. . .	. . .	. . .	. . .	. . .	. . .	. . .
Other transport, freight	2 216 . .	. . .	. . .	. . .	. . .	. . .	. . .	. . .	. . .
Other transport, other	2 217 . .	. . .	. . .	. . .	. . .	. . .	. . .	. . .	. . .
Transportation services, debit	3 205 . .	**–4.71**	**–5.70**	**–7.48**	**–6.93**	**–6.59**	**–5.61**	**–6.52**	. . .
Passenger	3 205 BA	*–2.06*	*–2.00*	*–2.67*	*–2.97*	*–2.88*	*–2.74*	*–2.99*	. . .
Freight	3 205 BB	*–2.66*	*–3.70*	*–4.81*	*–3.88*	*–3.39*	*–2.75*	*–3.41*	. . .
Other	3 205 BC	. . .	. . .	. . .	*–.08*	*–.32*	*–.11*	*–.12*	. . .
Sea transport, passenger	3 207 . .	. . .	. . .	. . .	. . .	. . .	. . .	. . .	. . .
Sea transport, freight	3 208 . .	. . .	. . .	. . .	. . .	. . .	. . .	. . .	. . .
Sea transport, other	3 209 . .	. . .	. . .	. . .	. . .	. . .	. . .	. . .	. . .
Air transport, passenger	3 211 . .	. . .	. . .	. . .	. . .	. . .	. . .	. . .	. . .
Air transport, freight	3 212 . .	. . .	. . .	. . .	. . .	. . .	. . .	. . .	. . .
Air transport, other	3 213 . .	. . .	. . .	. . .	. . .	. . .	. . .	. . .	. . .
Other transport, passenger	3 215 . .	. . .	. . .	. . .	. . .	. . .	. . .	. . .	. . .
Other transport, freight	3 216 . .	. . .	. . .	. . .	. . .	. . .	. . .	. . .	. . .
Other transport, other	3 217 . .	. . .	. . .	. . .	. . .	. . .	. . .	. . .	. . .
Travel, credit	2 236 . .	**10.96**	**10.40**	**11.19**	**11.91**	**13.70**	**18.08**	**20.07**	. . .
Business travel	2 237 . .	. . .	. . .	. . .	. . .	. . .	. . .	. . .	. . .
Personal travel	2 240 . .	. . .	. . .	. . .	. . .	. . .	. . .	. . .	. . .
Travel, debit	3 236 . .	**–1.85**	**–2.04**	**–1.77**	**–1.84**	**–1.45**	**–2.59**	**–3.22**	. . .
Business travel	3 237 . .	. . .	. . .	. . .	. . .	. . .	. . .	. . .	. . .
Personal travel	3 240 . .	. . .	. . .	. . .	. . .	. . .	. . .	. . .	. . .
Other services, credit	2 200 BA	**2.57**	**3.29**	**4.14**	**4.95**	**4.59**	**3.70**	**4.76**	. . .
Communications	2 245 . .	. . .	. . .	. . .	. . .	. . .	. . .	. . .	. . .
Construction	2 249 . .	. . .	. . .	. . .	. . .	. . .	. . .	. . .	. . .
Insurance	2 253 . .	. . .	.55	.57	1.01	1.08	.59	.60	. . .
Financial	2 260 . .	. . .	. . .	. . .	. . .	. . .	. . .	. . .	. . .
Computer and information	2 262 . .	. . .	. . .	. . .	. . .	. . .	. . .	. . .	. . .
Royalties and licence fees	2 266 . .	. . .	. . .	. . .	. . .	. . .	. . .	. . .	. . .
Other business services	2 268 . .	2.57	2.74	3.58	3.94	3.50	3.11	4.16	. . .
Personal, cultural, and recreational	2 287 . .	. . .	. . .	. . .	. . .	. . .	. . .	. . .	. . .
Government, n.i.e.	2 291 . .	. . .	. . .	. . .	. . .	. . .	. . .	. . .	. . .
Other services, debit	3 200 BA	**–2.03**	**–2.21**	**–3.01**	**–2.63**	**–4.24**	**–3.09**	**–4.98**	. . .
Communications	3 245 . .	. . .	. . .	. . .	. . .	. . .	. . .	. . .	. . .
Construction	3 249 . .	. . .	. . .	. . .	. . .	. . .	. . .	–.16	. . .
Insurance	3 253 . .	–.53	–.84	–1.08	–.91	–.80	–.71	–.86	. . .
Financial	3 260 . .	. . .	. . .	. . .	. . .	. . .	. . .	. . .	. . .
Computer and information	3 262 . .	. . .	. . .	. . .	. . .	. . .	. . .	. . .	. . .
Royalties and licence fees	3 266 . .	. . .	. . .	. . .	. . .	. . .	. . .	. . .	. . .
Other business services	3 268 . .	–1.50	–1.37	–1.72	–1.49	–1.80	–1.85	–2.20	. . .
Personal, cultural, and recreational	3 287 . .	. . .	. . .	. . .	. . .	. . .	. . .	. . .	. . .
Government, n.i.e.	3 291 . .	. . .	. . .	–.21	–.23	–1.64	–.53	–1.76	. . .

Table 2 (Continued). STANDARD PRESENTATION, 1988–95
(Millions of U.S. dollars)

	Code		1988	1989	1990	1991	1992	1993	1994	1995
C. INCOME	4 300	. .	–.28	–.77	–1.20	–1.64	–1.05	–3.47	–4.50	. . .
Total credit	2 300	. .	*.78*	*1.68*	*1.75*	*.72*	*.53*	*.42*	*.44*	. . .
Total debit	3 300	. .	*–1.06*	*–2.45*	*–2.95*	*–2.36*	*–1.58*	*–3.89*	*–4.94*	. . .
Compensation of employees, credit	2 310	. .	. . .	. . .	. . .	. . .	**.01**	. . .	**.07**	. . .
Compensation of employees, debit	3 310	. .	. . .	**–.74**	**–.74**	. . .	. . .	. . .	. . .	. . .
Investment income, credit	2 320	. .	**.78**	**1.67**	**1.74**	**.72**	**.51**	**.42**	**.36**	. . .
Direct investment income	2 330	. .	. . .	. . .	. . .	. . .	. . .	. . .	. . .	. . .
Dividends and distributed branch profits	2 332	. .	. . .	. . .	. . .	. . .	. . .	. . .	. . .	. . .
Reinvested earnings and undistributed branch profits	2 333	. .	. . .	. . .	. . .	. . .	. . .	. . .	. . .	. . .
Income on debt (interest)	2 334	. .	. . .	. . .	. . .	. . .	. . .	. . .	. . .	. . .
Portfolio investment income	2 339	. .	. . .	. . .	. . .	. . .	. . .	. . .	. . .	. . .
Income on equity	2 340	. .	. . .	. . .	. . .	. . .	. . .	. . .	. . .	. . .
Income on bonds and notes	2 350	. .	. . .	. . .	. . .	. . .	. . .	. . .	. . .	. . .
Income on money market instruments and financial derivatives	2 360	. .	. . .	. . .	. . .	. . .	. . .	. . .	. . .	. . .
Other investment income	2 370	. .	.78	1.67	1.74	.72	.51	.42	.36	. . .
Investment income, debit	3 320	. .	**–1.06**	**–1.71**	**–2.21**	**–2.36**	**–1.58**	**–3.89**	**–4.94**	. . .
Direct investment income	3 330	. .	–.72	–1.30	–1.65	–1.90	–1.25	–3.40	–3.86	. . .
Dividends and distributed branch profits	3 332	. .	–.25	–.45	–1.24	–1.70	–.86	–1.32	–2.02	. . .
Reinvested earnings and undistributed branch profits	3 333	. .	–.47	–.86	–.41	–.19	–.14	–1.84	–1.48	. . .
Income on debt (interest)	3 334	. .	. . .	. . .	. . .	–.01	–.26	–.24	–.36	. . .
Portfolio investment income	3 339	. .	. . .	. . .	. . .	. . .	. . .	. . .	. . .	. . .
Income on equity	3 340	. .	. . .	. . .	. . .	. . .	. . .	. . .	. . .	. . .
Income on bonds and notes	3 350	. .	. . .	. . .	. . .	. . .	. . .	. . .	. . .	. . .
Income on money market instruments and financial derivatives	3 360	. .	. . .	. . .	. . .	. . .	. . .	. . .	. . .	. . .
Other investment income	3 370	. .	–.34	–.41	–.56	–.46	–.33	–.49	–1.08	. . .
D. CURRENT TRANSFERS	4 379	. .	–.76	32.11	13.81	6.17	8.78	3.27	–.17	. . .
Credit	2 379	. .	. . .	**35.40**	**18.36**	**11.67**	**12.14**	**9.71**	**3.27**	. . .
General government	2 380	. .	. . .	.21	.21	.29	1.67	.60	1.55	. . .
Other sectors	2 390	. .	. . .	35.19	18.15	11.38	10.47	9.11	1.72	. . .
Workers' remittances	2 391	. .	. . .	35.19	18.15	11.38	10.47	9.11	1.55	. . .
Other current transfers	2 392	. .	. . .	. . .	. . .	. . .	. . .	. . .	.17	. . .
Debit	3 379	. .	**–.76**	**–3.29**	**–4.55**	**–5.50**	**–3.36**	**–6.44**	**–3.44**	. . .
General government	3 380	. .	–.38	–.49	–.50	–.40	–.25	–.38	–.62	. . .
Other sectors	3 390	. .	–.38	–2.79	–4.05	–5.10	–3.11	–6.07	–2.81	. . .
Workers' remittances	3 391	. .	–.38	–1.48	–2.59	–3.47	–1.46	–3.79	–.62	. . .
Other current transfers	3 392	. .	. . .	–1.31	–1.46	–1.62	–1.65	–2.28	–2.19	. . .
CAPITAL AND FINANCIAL ACCOUNT	4 996	. .	**9.07**	**–2.53**	**25.60**	**13.93**	**6.72**	**11.27**	**4.24**	. . .
CAPITAL ACCOUNT	4 994	. .	**4.56**	**6.97**	**4.54**	**5.23**	**2.07**	**5.41**	**10.10**	. . .
Total credit	2 994	. .	*4.56*	*6.97*	*4.54*	*5.23*	*2.07*	*5.41*	*10.10*	. . .
Total debit	3 994	. .	. . .	. . .	. . .	. . .	. . .	. . .	. . .	. . .
Capital transfers, credit	2 400	. .	**4.56**	**6.97**	**4.54**	**5.23**	**2.07**	**5.41**	**10.10**	. . .
General government	2 401	. .	4.56	6.97	4.54	5.23	2.07	5.41	10.10	. . .
Debt forgiveness	2 402	. .	. . .	. . .	. . .	. . .	. . .	. . .	. . .	. . .
Other capital transfers	2 410	. .	. . .	. . .	. . .	. . .	. . .	. . .	. . .	. . .
Other sectors	2 430	. .	. . .	. . .	. . .	. . .	. . .	. . .	. . .	. . .
Migrants' transfers	2 431	. .	. . .	. . .	. . .	. . .	. . .	. . .	. . .	. . .
Debt forgiveness	2 432	. .	. . .	. . .	. . .	. . .	. . .	. . .	. . .	. . .
Other capital transfers	2 440	. .	. . .	. . .	. . .	. . .	. . .	. . .	. . .	. . .
Capital transfers, debit	3 400	. .	. . .	. . .	. . .	. . .	. . .	. . .	. . .	. . .
General government	3 401	. .	. . .	. . .	. . .	. . .	. . .	. . .	. . .	. . .
Debt forgiveness	3 402	. .	. . .	. . .	. . .	. . .	. . .	. . .	. . .	. . .
Other capital transfers	3 410	. .	. . .	. . .	. . .	. . .	. . .	. . .	. . .	. . .
Other sectors	3 430	. .	. . .	. . .	. . .	. . .	. . .	. . .	. . .	. . .
Migrants' transfers	3 431	. .	. . .	. . .	. . .	. . .	. . .	. . .	. . .	. . .
Debt forgiveness	3 432	. .	. . .	. . .	. . .	. . .	. . .	. . .	. . .	. . .
Other capital transfers	3 440	. .	. . .	. . .	. . .	. . .	. . .	. . .	. . .	. . .
Nonproduced nonfinancial assets, credit	2 480	. .	. . .	. . .	. . .	. . .	. . .	. . .	. . .	. . .
Nonproduced nonfinancial assets, debit	3 480	. .	. . .	. . .	. . .	. . .	. . .	. . .	. . .	. . .

Table 2 (Continued). STANDARD PRESENTATION, 1988–95
(Millions of U.S. dollars)

	Code		1988	1989	1990	1991	1992	1993	1994	1995
FINANCIAL ACCOUNT	4 995	. .	**4.50**	**–9.50**	**21.06**	**8.70**	**4.65**	**5.86**	**–5.86**	. . .
A. DIRECT INVESTMENT	4 500	. .	9.51	4.91	9.58	8.03	4.61	4.86	1.24	. . .
Direct investment abroad	4 505	. .	. . .	. . .	. . .	. . .	. . .	. . .	. . .	. . .
Equity capital	4 510	. .	. . .	. . .	. . .	. . .	. . .	. . .	. . .	. . .
Claims on affiliated enterprises	4 515	. .	. . .	. . .	. . .	. . .	. . .	. . .	. . .	. . .
Liabilities to affiliated enterprises	4 520	. .	. . .	. . .	. . .	. . .	. . .	. . .	. . .	. . .
Reinvested earnings	4 525	. .	. . .	. . .	. . .	. . .	. . .	. . .	. . .	. . .
Other capital	4 530	. .	. . .	. . .	. . .	. . .	. . .	. . .	. . .	. . .
Claims on affiliated enterprises	4 535	. .	. . .	. . .	. . .	. . .	. . .	. . .	. . .	. . .
Liabilities to affiliated enterprises	4 540	. .	. . .	. . .	. . .	. . .	. . .	. . .	. . .	. . .
Direct investment in Montserrat	4 555	. .	**9.51**	**4.91**	**9.58**	**8.03**	**4.61**	**4.86**	**1.24**	. . .
Equity capital	4 560	. .	. . .	. . .	. . .	3.00	. . .	.57	.02	. . .
Claims on direct investors	4 565	. .	. . .	. . .	. . .	. . .	. . .	. . .	. . .	. . .
Liabilities to direct investors	4 570	. .	. . .	. . .	. . .	. . .	. . .	. . .	. . .	. . .
Reinvested earnings	4 575	. .	.47	.86	.41	.19	.14	1.84	1.48	. . .
Other capital	4 580	. .	9.04	4.05	9.17	4.84	4.48	2.44	–.26	. . .
Claims on direct investors	4 585	. .	. . .	. . .	. . .	. . .	. . .	. . .	. . .	. . .
Liabilities to direct investors	4 590	. .	. . .	. . .	. . .	. . .	. . .	. . .	. . .	. . .
B. PORTFOLIO INVESTMENT	4 600	. .	. . .	. . .	. . .	. . .	. . .	. . .	–.03	. . .
Assets	4 602	. .	. . .	. . .	. . .	. . .	. . .	. . .	**–.03**	. . .
Equity securities	4 610	. .	. . .	. . .	. . .	. . .	. . .	. . .	–.03	. . .
Monetary authorities	4 611	. .	. . .	. . .	. . .	. . .	. . .	. . .	. . .	. . .
General government	4 612	. .	. . .	. . .	. . .	. . .	. . .	. . .	. . .	. . .
Banks	4 613	. .	. . .	. . .	. . .	. . .	. . .	. . .	. . .	. . .
Other sectors	4 614	. .	. . .	. . .	. . .	. . .	. . .	. . .	. . .	. . .
Debt securities	4 619	. .	. . .	. . .	. . .	. . .	. . .	. . .	. . .	. . .
Bonds and notes	4 620	. .	. . .	. . .	. . .	. . .	. . .	. . .	. . .	. . .
Monetary authorities	4 621	. .	. . .	. . .	. . .	. . .	. . .	. . .	. . .	. . .
General government	4 622	. .	. . .	. . .	. . .	. . .	. . .	. . .	. . .	. . .
Banks	4 623	. .	. . .	. . .	. . .	. . .	. . .	. . .	. . .	. . .
Other sectors	4 624	. .	. . .	. . .	. . .	. . .	. . .	. . .	. . .	. . .
Money market instruments	4 630	. .	. . .	. . .	. . .	. . .	. . .	. . .	. . .	. . .
Monetary authorities	4 631	. .	. . .	. . .	. . .	. . .	. . .	. . .	. . .	. . .
General government	4 632	. .	. . .	. . .	. . .	. . .	. . .	. . .	. . .	. . .
Banks	4 633	. .	. . .	. . .	. . .	. . .	. . .	. . .	. . .	. . .
Other sectors	4 634	. .	. . .	. . .	. . .	. . .	. . .	. . .	. . .	. . .
Financial derivatives	4 640	. .	. . .	. . .	. . .	. . .	. . .	. . .	. . .	. . .
Monetary authorities	4 641	. .	. . .	. . .	. . .	. . .	. . .	. . .	. . .	. . .
General government	4 642	. .	. . .	. . .	. . .	. . .	. . .	. . .	. . .	. . .
Banks	4 643	. .	. . .	. . .	. . .	. . .	. . .	. . .	. . .	. . .
Other sectors	4 644	. .	. . .	. . .	. . .	. . .	. . .	. . .	. . .	. . .
Liabilities	4 652	. .	. . .	. . .	. . .	. . .	. . .	. . .	. . .	. . .
Equity securities	4 660	. .	. . .	. . .	. . .	. . .	. . .	. . .	. . .	. . .
Banks	4 663	. .	. . .	. . .	. . .	. . .	. . .	. . .	. . .	. . .
Other sectors	4 664	. .	. . .	. . .	. . .	. . .	. . .	. . .	. . .	. . .
Debt securities	4 669	. .	. . .	. . .	. . .	. . .	. . .	. . .	. . .	. . .
Bonds and notes	4 670	. .	. . .	. . .	. . .	. . .	. . .	. . .	. . .	. . .
Monetary authorities	4 671	. .	. . .	. . .	. . .	. . .	. . .	. . .	. . .	. . .
General government	4 672	. .	. . .	. . .	. . .	. . .	. . .	. . .	. . .	. . .
Banks	4 673	. .	. . .	. . .	. . .	. . .	. . .	. . .	. . .	. . .
Other sectors	4 674	. .	. . .	. . .	. . .	. . .	. . .	. . .	. . .	. . .
Money market instruments	4 680	. .	. . .	. . .	. . .	. . .	. . .	. . .	. . .	. . .
Monetary authorities	4 681	. .	. . .	. . .	. . .	. . .	. . .	. . .	. . .	. . .
General government	4 682	. .	. . .	. . .	. . .	. . .	. . .	. . .	. . .	. . .
Banks	4 683	. .	. . .	. . .	. . .	. . .	. . .	. . .	. . .	. . .
Other sectors	4 684	. .	. . .	. . .	. . .	. . .	. . .	. . .	. . .	. . .
Financial derivatives	4 690	. .	. . .	. . .	. . .	. . .	. . .	. . .	. . .	. . .
Monetary authorities	4 691	. .	. . .	. . .	. . .	. . .	. . .	. . .	. . .	. . .
General government	4 692	. .	. . .	. . .	. . .	. . .	. . .	. . .	. . .	. . .
Banks	4 693	. .	. . .	. . .	. . .	. . .	. . .	. . .	. . .	. . .
Other sectors	4 694	. .	. . .	. . .	. . .	. . .	. . .	. . .	. . .	. . .

Table 2 (Concluded). STANDARD PRESENTATION, 1988–95
(Millions of U.S. dollars)

	Code	1988	1989	1990	1991	1992	1993	1994	1995
C. OTHER INVESTMENT	4 700 . .	–4.71	–14.08	14.03	–2.93	.12	.61	–5.48	. . .
Assets	4 703 . .	**–3.97**	**–13.42**	**15.21**	**–3.15**	**.43**	**–2.67**	**–4.73**	. . .
Trade credits	4 706 . .	. . .	. . .	. . .	. . .	. . .	. . .	. . .	. . .
General government: long-term	4 708 . .	. . .	. . .	. . .	. . .	. . .	. . .	. . .	. . .
General government: short-term	4 709 . .	. . .	. . .	. . .	. . .	. . .	. . .	. . .	. . .
Other sectors: long-term	4 711 . .	. . .	. . .	. . .	. . .	. . .	. . .	. . .	. . .
Other sectors: short-term	4 712 . .	. . .	. . .	. . .	. . .	. . .	. . .	. . .	. . .
Loans	4 714 . .	. . .	. . .	. . .	. . .	. . .	. . .	. . .	. . .
Monetary authorities: long-term	4 717 . .	. . .	. . .	. . .	. . .	. . .	. . .	. . .	. . .
Monetary authorities: short-term	4 718 . .	. . .	. . .	. . .	. . .	. . .	. . .	. . .	. . .
General government: long-term	4 720 . .	. . .	. . .	. . .	. . .	. . .	. . .	. . .	. . .
General government: short-term	4 721 . .	. . .	. . .	. . .	. . .	. . .	. . .	. . .	. . .
Banks: long-term	4 723 . .	. . .	. . .	. . .	. . .	. . .	. . .	. . .	. . .
Banks: short-term	4 724 . .	. . .	. . .	. . .	. . .	. . .	. . .	. . .	. . .
Other sectors: long-term	4 726 . .	. . .	. . .	. . .	. . .	. . .	. . .	. . .	. . .
Other sectors: short-term	4 727 . .	. . .	. . .	. . .	. . .	. . .	. . .	. . .	. . .
Currency and deposits	4 730 . .	–3.97	–13.42	15.21	–3.15	.43	–2.67	–4.73	. . .
Monetary authorities	4 731 . .	. . .	. . .	. . .	. . .	. . .	. . .	. . .	. . .
General government	4 732 . .	. . .	. . .	. . .	. . .	. . .	. . .	. . .	. . .
Banks	4 733 . .	–3.97	–13.42	15.21	–3.15	.43	–2.67	–4.73	. . .
Other sectors	4 734 . .	. . .	. . .	. . .	. . .	. . .	. . .	. . .	. . .
Other assets	4 736 . .	. . .	. . .	. . .	. . .	. . .	. . .	. . .	. . .
Monetary authorities: long-term	4 738 . .	. . .	. . .	. . .	. . .	. . .	. . .	. . .	. . .
Monetary authorities: short-term	4 739 . .	. . .	. . .	. . .	. . .	. . .	. . .	. . .	. . .
General government: long-term	4 741 . .	. . .	. . .	. . .	. . .	. . .	. . .	. . .	. . .
General government: short-term	4 742 . .	. . .	. . .	. . .	. . .	. . .	. . .	. . .	. . .
Banks: long-term	4 744 . .	. . .	. . .	. . .	. . .	. . .	. . .	. . .	. . .
Banks: short-term	4 745 . .	. . .	. . .	. . .	. . .	. . .	. . .	. . .	. . .
Other sectors: long-term	4 747 . .	. . .	. . .	. . .	. . .	. . .	. . .	. . .	. . .
Other sectors: short-term	4 748 . .	. . .	. . .	. . .	. . .	. . .	. . .	. . .	. . .
Liabilities	4 753 . .	**–.74**	**–.66**	**–1.17**	**.21**	**–.31**	**3.29**	**–.75**	. . .
Trade credits	4 756 . .	. . .	. . .	. . .	. . .	. . .	. . .	. . .	. . .
General government: long-term	4 758 . .	. . .	. . .	. . .	. . .	. . .	. . .	. . .	. . .
General government: short-term	4 759 . .	. . .	. . .	. . .	. . .	. . .	. . .	. . .	. . .
Other sectors: long-term	4 761 . .	. . .	. . .	. . .	. . .	. . .	. . .	. . .	. . .
Other sectors: short-term	4 762 . .	. . .	. . .	. . .	. . .	. . .	. . .	. . .	. . .
Loans	4 764 . .	–.74	–.66	–1.17	.21	–.31	3.29	–.75	. . .
Use of Fund credit and loans from the Fund	4 766 . .	. . .	. . .	. . .	. . .	. . .	. . .	. . .	. . .
Monetary authorities: other long term	4 767 . .	. . .	. . .	. . .	. . .	. . .	. . .	. . .	. . .
Monetary authorities: short-term	4 768 . .	. . .	. . .	. . .	. . .	. . .	. . .	. . .	. . .
General government: long-term	4 770 . .	.09	–.07	–.74	.68	–.09	5.14	.08	. . .
General government: short-term	4 771 . .	. . .	. . .	. . .	. . .	. . .	. . .	. . .	. . .
Banks: long-term	4 773 . .	. . .	. . .	. . .	. . .	. . .	. . .	. . .	. . .
Banks: short-term	4 774 . .	. . .	. . .	. . .	. . .	. . .	. . .	. . .	. . .
Other sectors: long-term	4 776 . .	–.83	–.60	–.43	–.47	–.22	–1.86	–.83	. . .
Other sectors: short-term	4 777 . .	. . .	. . .	. . .	. . .	. . .	. . .	. . .	. . .
Currency and deposits	4 780 . .	. . .	. . .	. . .	. . .	. . .	. . .	. . .	. . .
Monetary authorities	4 781 . .	. . .	. . .	. . .	. . .	. . .	. . .	. . .	. . .
General government	4 782 . .	. . .	. . .	. . .	. . .	. . .	. . .	. . .	. . .
Banks	4 783 . .	. . .	. . .	. . .	. . .	. . .	. . .	. . .	. . .
Other sectors	4 784 . .	. . .	. . .	. . .	. . .	. . .	. . .	. . .	. . .
Other liabilities	4 786 . .	. . .	. . .	. . .	. . .	. . .	. . .	. . .	. . .
Monetary authorities: long-term	4 788 . .	. . .	. . .	. . .	. . .	. . .	. . .	. . .	. . .
Monetary authorities: short-term	4 789 . .	. . .	. . .	. . .	. . .	. . .	. . .	. . .	. . .
General government: long-term	4 791 . .	. . .	. . .	. . .	. . .	. . .	. . .	. . .	. . .
General government: short-term	4 792 . .	. . .	. . .	. . .	. . .	. . .	. . .	. . .	. . .
Banks: long-term	4 794 . .	. . .	. . .	. . .	. . .	. . .	. . .	. . .	. . .
Banks: short-term	4 795 . .	. . .	. . .	. . .	. . .	. . .	. . .	. . .	. . .
Other sectors: long-term	4 797 . .	. . .	. . .	. . .	. . .	. . .	. . .	. . .	. . .
Other sectors: short-term	4 798 . .	. . .	. . .	. . .	. . .	. . .	. . .	. . .	. . .
D. RESERVE ASSETS	4 800 . .	–.30	–.32	–2.56	3.60	–.09	.39	–1.60	. . .
Monetary gold	4 810 . .	. . .	. . .	. . .	. . .	. . .	. . .	. . .	. . .
Special drawing rights	4 820 . .	. . .	. . .	. . .	. . .	. . .	. . .	. . .	. . .
Reserve position in the Fund	4 830 . .	. . .	. . .	. . .	. . .	. . .	. . .	. . .	. . .
Foreign exchange	4 840 . .	–.30	–.26	–2.56	3.60	–.09	.39	–1.49	. . .
Other claims	4 880 . .	. . .	–.06	. . .	. . .	. . .	. . .	–.10	. . .
NET ERRORS AND OMISSIONS	4 998 . .	**6.93**	**–2.86**	**–2.69**	**7.41**	**6.11**	**–1.16**	**15.12**	. . .

Part 3 of the *Yearbook* contains descriptions of the methodologies, compilation practices, and sources used to compile these data.

Table 1. ANALYTIC PRESENTATION, 1988–95
(Millions of U.S. dollars)

	Code	1988	1989	1990	1991	1992	1993	1994	1995
A. Current Account[1]	4 993 Y.	**473**	**–787**	**–196**	**–413**	**–433**	**–521**	**–723**	**–1,521**
Goods: exports f.o.b	2 100 . .	3,624	3,331	4,229	5,094	5,010	4,936	5,541	6,871
Goods: imports f.o.b	3 100 . .	–4,384	–5,027	–6,338	–6,858	–7,473	–7,001	–7,648	–9,268
Balance on Goods	4 100 . .	*–760*	*–1,697*	*–2,108*	*–1,764*	*–2,463*	*–2,065*	*–2,107*	*–2,397*
Services: credit	2 200 . .	1,764	1,650	2,009	1,618	2,125	2,050	2,014	1,996
Services: debit	3 200 . .	–1,106	–1,204	–1,445	–1,427	–1,571	–1,593	–1,730	–2,063
Balance on Goods and Services	4 991 . .	*–102*	*–1,251*	*–1,544*	*–1,573*	*–1,909*	*–1,608*	*–1,822*	*–2,464*
Income: credit	2 300 . .	18	32	83	199	292	224	224	251
Income: debit	3 300 . .	–1,055	–1,191	–1,071	–1,315	–1,349	–1,431	–1,394	–1,569
Balance on Goods, Services, and Income	4 992 . .	*–1,139*	*–2,411*	*–2,532*	*–2,688*	*–2,966*	*–2,816*	*–2,992*	*–3,782*
Current transfers: credit	2 379 Y.	1,663	1,669	2,383	2,356	2,614	2,361	2,355	2,339
Current transfers: debit	3 379 . .	–51	–46	–47	–81	–81	–66	–86	–78
B. Capital Account[1]	4 994 Y.	**–6**	**–3**	**–5**	**–5**	**–6**	**–3**	**–3**	**–6**
Capital account: credit	2 994 Y.	1	. . .	. . .	. . .	. . .	. . .	. . .	. . .
Capital account: debit	3 994 . .	–7	–3	–5	–5	–6	–3	–4	–6
Total, Groups A Plus B	4 010 . .	*467*	*–790*	*–200*	*–418*	*–439*	*–524*	*–726*	*–1,527*
C. Financial Account[1]	4 995 X.	**–226**	**822**	**1,889**	**1,379**	**1,242**	**973**	**1,253**	**148**
Direct investment abroad	4 505 . .	. . .	. . .	. . .	–23	–32	–23	–24	–12
Direct investment in Morocco	4 555 Y.	85	167	165	317	422	491	551	290
Portfolio investment assets	4 602 . .	. . .	. . .	. . .	. . .	. . .	. . .	. . .	. . .
Equity securities	4 610 . .	. . .	. . .	. . .	. . .	. . .	. . .	. . .	. . .
Debt securities	4 619 . .	. . .	. . .	. . .	. . .	. . .	. . .	. . .	. . .
Portfolio investment liabilities	4 652 Y.	. . .	. . .	. . .	2	1	24	238	20
Equity securities	4 660 Y.	. . .	. . .	. . .	. . .	. . .	24	238	20
Debt securities	4 669 Y.	. . .	. . .	. . .	2	1	1	. . .	. . .
Other investment assets	4 703 . .	–376	–94	–267	. . .	. . .	. . .	344	216
Monetary authorities	4 703 .A	. . .	. . .	. . .	. . .	. . .	. . .	. . .	. . .
General government	4 703 .B	–10	–18	–11	. . .	. . .	. . .	. . .	. . .
Banks	4 703 .C	–78	–65	–202	. . .	. . .	. . .	. . .	. . .
Other sectors	4 703 .D	–287	–11	–54	. . .	. . .	. . .	344	216
Other investment liabilities	4 753 X.	65	749	1,991	1,082	851	480	144	–366
Monetary authorities	4 753 XA	. . .	. . .	. . .	1	–7	. . .	24	16
General government	4 753 YB	339	336	1,002	648	157	59	–421	–323
Banks	4 753 YC	35	25	101	. . .	. . .	. . .	–48	–136
Other sectors	4 753 YD	–308	388	887	433	702	422	588	77
Total, Groups A Through C	4 020 . .	*241*	*32*	*1,688*	*961*	*803*	*448*	*527*	*–1,378*
D. Net Errors and Omissions	4 998 . .	**22**	**–11**	**9**	**3**	**–10**	**–5**	**–39**	**615**
Total, Groups A Through D	4 030 . .	*264*	*21*	*1,697*	*963*	*794*	*443*	*488*	*–763*
E. Reserves and Related Items	4 040 . .	**–264**	**–21**	**–1,697**	**–963**	**–794**	**–443**	**–488**	**763**
Reserve assets	4 800 . .	–158	63	–1,537	–785	–675	–280	–362	861
Use of Fund credit and loans	4 766 . .	–105	–83	–161	–171	–116	–156	–152	–101
Liabilities constituting foreign authorities' reserves	4 900 . .	. . .	. . .	. . .	–7	–3	–7	–5	–13
Exceptional financing	4 920 . .	. . .	. . .	. . .	. . .	. . .	. . .	31	16
Conversion rates: Moroccan dirhams per U.S. dollar	0 101 . .	**8.2092**	**8.4882**	**8.2423**	**8.7066**	**8.5379**	**9.2987**	**9.2027**	**8.5402**

[1] Excludes components that have been classified in the categories of Group E.

Table 2. STANDARD PRESENTATION, 1988–95
(Millions of U.S. dollars)

	Code	1988	1989	1990	1991	1992	1993	1994	1995
CURRENT ACCOUNT	4 993 . .	**473**	**–787**	**–196**	**–413**	**–433**	**–521**	**–723**	**–1,521**
A. GOODS	4 100 . .	–760	–1,697	–2,108	–1,764	–2,463	–2,065	–2,107	–2,397
Credit	2 100 . .	**3,624**	**3,331**	**4,229**	**5,094**	**5,010**	**4,936**	**5,541**	**6,871**
General merchandise: exports f.o.b.	2 110 . .	3,608	3,312	4,210	4,278	3,956	3,682	3,957	4,687
Goods for processing: exports f.o.b.	2 150 . .	. . .	. . .	. . .	812	1,032	1,240	1,567	2,158
Repairs on goods	2 160 . .	. . .	. . .	. . .	. . .	. . .	. . .	. . .	. . .
Goods procured in ports by carriers	2 170 . .	16	18	19	5	21	14	17	26
Nonmonetary gold	2 180 . .	. . .	. . .	. . .	. . .	. . .	. . .	. . .	. . .
Debit	3 100 . .	**–4,384**	**–5,027**	**–6,338**	**–6,858**	**–7,473**	**–7,001**	**–7,648**	**–9,268**
General merchandise: imports f.o.b.	3 110 . .	–4,360	–4,991	–6,282	–6,253	–6,692	–6,062	–6,531	–7,773
Goods for processing: imports f.o.b.	3 150 . .	. . .	. . .	. . .	–594	–757	–919	–1,097	–1,478
Repairs on goods	3 160 . .	. . .	. . .	. . .	. . .	. . .	. . .	. . .	. . .
Goods procured in ports by carriers	3 170 . .	–24	–36	–56	–10	–23	–20	–19	–17
Nonmonetary gold	3 180 . .	. . .	. . .	. . .	. . .	. . .	. . .	. . .	. . .
B. SERVICES	4 200 . .	657	446	564	191	554	457	285	–67
Total credit	2 200 . .	*1,764*	*1,650*	*2,009*	*1,618*	*2,125*	*2,050*	*2,014*	*1,996*
Total debit	3 200 . .	*–1,106*	*–1,204*	*–1,445*	*–1,427*	*–1,571*	*–1,593*	*–1,730*	*–2,063*
Transportation services, credit	2 205 . .	**225**	**155**	**179**	**270**	**315**	**357**	**342**	**422**
Passenger	2 205 BA	*40*	*31*	*38*	*78*	*105*	*117*	*142*	*173*
Freight	2 205 BB	*183*	*122*	*139*	*192*	*209*	*239*	*200*	*248*
Other	2 205 BC	*2*	*2*	*3*	. . .	. . .	. . .	. . .	. . .
Sea transport, passenger	2 207 . .	. . .	. . .	. . .	. . .	. . .	. . .	. . .	. . .
Sea transport, freight	2 208 . .	. . .	. . .	. . .	192	209	228	194	235
Sea transport, other	2 209 . .	. . .	. . .	. . .	. . .	. . .	. . .	. . .	. . .
Air transport, passenger	2 211 . .	. . .	. . .	. . .	74	99	116	141	173
Air transport, freight	2 212 . .	. . .	. . .	. . .	. . .	. . .	3	. . .	. . .
Air transport, other	2 213 . .	. . .	. . .	. . .	. . .	. . .	. . .	. . .	. . .
Other transport, passenger	2 215 . .	. . .	. . .	. . .	4	7	1	1	. . .
Other transport, freight	2 216 . .	. . .	. . .	. . .	. . .	. . .	8	6	13
Other transport, other	2 217 . .	. . .	. . .	. . .	. . .	. . .	. . .	. . .	. . .
Transportation services, debit	3 205 . .	**–359**	**–437**	**–548**	**–604**	**–657**	**–576**	**–625**	**–746**
Passenger	3 205 BA	*–31*	*–29*	*–31*	*–47*	*–59*	*–37*	*–43*	*–54*
Freight	3 205 BB	*–313*	*–396*	*–503*	*–558*	*–598*	*–540*	*–581*	*–692*
Other	3 205 BC	*–16*	*–11*	*–13*	. . .	. . .	. . .	. . .	. . .
Sea transport, passenger	3 207 . .	. . .	. . .	. . .	. . .	. . .	–7	–7	–1
Sea transport, freight	3 208 . .	. . .	. . .	. . .	–558	–598	–435	–523	–669
Sea transport, other	3 209 . .	. . .	. . .	. . .	. . .	. . .	. . .	. . .	. . .
Air transport, passenger	3 211 . .	. . .	. . .	. . .	–33	–42	–29	–37	–51
Air transport, freight	3 212 . .	. . .	. . .	. . .	. . .	. . .	–62	–19	–9
Air transport, other	3 213 . .	. . .	. . .	. . .	. . .	. . .	. . .	. . .	. . .
Other transport, passenger	3 215 . .	. . .	. . .	. . .	–14	–17	–1	. . .	–3
Other transport, freight	3 216 . .	. . .	. . .	. . .	. . .	. . .	–42	–40	–14
Other transport, other	3 217 . .	. . .	. . .	. . .	. . .	. . .	. . .	. . .	. . .
Travel, credit	2 236 . .	**1,102**	**1,015**	**1,280**	**1,013**	**1,371**	**1,234**	**1,231**	**1,163**
Business travel	2 237 . .	. . .	. . .	. . .	. . .	. . .	. . .	. . .	. . .
Personal travel	2 240 . .	. . .	. . .	. . .	. . .	. . .	. . .	. . .	. . .
Travel, debit	3 236 . .	**–164**	**–153**	**–187**	**–193**	**–244**	**–244**	**–302**	**–302**
Business travel	3 237 . .	. . .	. . .	. . .	–33	–30	–29	–33	–37
Personal travel	3 240 . .	. . .	. . .	. . .	–160	–214	–215	–269	–265
Other services, credit	2 200 BA	**437**	**480**	**550**	**334**	**439**	**459**	**441**	**411**
Communications	2 245 . .	. . .	. . .	. . .	30	35	37	47	54
Construction	2 249 . .	. . .	. . .	. . .	. . .	. . .	. . .	. . .	. . .
Insurance	2 253 . .	20	14	15	40	55	36	39	27
Financial	2 260 . .	. . .	. . .	. . .	. . .	. . .	. . .	. . .	. . .
Computer and information	2 262 . .	. . .	. . .	. . .	. . .	. . .	. . .	. . .	. . .
Royalties and licence fees	2 266 . .	1	9	4	4	1	6	2	3
Other business services	2 268 . .	277	340	392	134	190	188	215	190
Personal, cultural, and recreational	2 287 . .	. . .	. . .	. . .	. . .	. . .	. . .	. . .	. . .
Government, n.i.e.	2 291 . .	139	117	138	126	157	193	138	137
Other services, debit	3 200 BA	**–583**	**–614**	**–711**	**–629**	**–669**	**–773**	**–803**	**–1,014**
Communications	3 245 . .	. . .	. . .	. . .	–8	–8	–17	–22	–14
Construction	3 249 . .	. . .	. . .	. . .	. . .	. . .	. . .	. . .	. . .
Insurance	3 253 . .	–35	–44	–56	–93	–106	–75	–84	–124
Financial	3 260 . .	. . .	. . .	. . .	. . .	. . .	. . .	. . .	. . .
Computer and information	3 262 . .	. . .	. . .	. . .	. . .	. . .	. . .	. . .	. . .
Royalties and licence fees	3 266 . .	–44	–49	–60	–60	–67	–78	–100	–125
Other business services	3 268 . .	–101	–83	–90	–55	–66	–60	–75	–211
Personal, cultural, and recreational	3 287 . .	. . .	. . .	. . .	. . .	. . .	. . .	. . .	. . .
Government, n.i.e.	3 291 . .	–404	–438	–505	–412	–423	–545	–522	–540

Table 2 (Continued). STANDARD PRESENTATION, 1988–95
(Millions of U.S. dollars)

	Code	1988	1989	1990	1991	1992	1993	1994	1995
C. INCOME	4 300 . .	–1,037	–1,159	–988	–1,115	–1,057	–1,208	–1,170	–1,318
Total credit	2 300 . .	*18*	*32*	*83*	*199*	*292*	*224*	*224*	*251*
Total debit	3 300 . .	*–1,055*	*–1,191*	*–1,071*	*–1,315*	*–1,349*	*–1,431*	*–1,394*	*–1,569*
Compensation of employees, credit	2 310 . .	**. . .**	**. . .**	**. . .**	**. . .**	**. . .**	**. . .**	**. . .**	**. . .**
Compensation of employees, debit	3 310 . .	**. . .**	**. . .**	**. . .**	**. . .**	**. . .**	**. . .**	**. . .**	**. . .**
Investment income, credit	2 320 . .	**18**	**32**	**83**	**199**	**292**	**224**	**224**	**251**
Direct investment income	2 330 . .	. . .	. . .	. . .	3	2	7	14	11
Dividends and distributed branch profits	2 332 . .	. . .	. . .	. . .	2	1	. . .	2	1
Reinvested earnings and undistributed branch profits	2 333 . .	. . .	. . .	. . .	. . .	. . .	. . .	. . .	3
Income on debt (interest)	2 334 . .	. . .	. . .	. . .	1	1	6	13	7
Portfolio investment income	2 339 . .	. . .	. . .	. . .	. . .	. . .	. . .	. . .	. . .
Income on equity	2 340 . .	. . .	. . .	. . .	. . .	. . .	. . .	. . .	. . .
Income on bonds and notes	2 350 . .	. . .	. . .	. . .	. . .	. . .	. . .	. . .	. . .
Income on money market instruments and financial derivatives	2 360 . .	. . .	. . .	. . .	. . .	. . .	. . .	. . .	. . .
Other investment income	2 370 . .	18	32	83	196	290	217	210	240
Investment income, debit	3 320 . .	**–1,055**	**–1,191**	**–1,071**	**–1,315**	**–1,349**	**–1,431**	**–1,394**	**–1,569**
Direct investment income	3 330 . .	–61	–56	–69	–95	–171	–62	–94	–100
Dividends and distributed branch profits	3 332 . .	–54	–43	–58	–51	–58	–44	–67	–85
Reinvested earnings and undistributed branch profits	3 333 . .	–7	–13	–11	–40	–106	–16	–25	–5
Income on debt (interest)	3 334 . .	. . .	. . .	. . .	–4	–8	–1	–2	–11
Portfolio investment income	3 339 . .	. . .	. . .	. . .	. . .	. . .	–41	–11	–14
Income on equity	3 340 . .	. . .	. . .	. . .	. . .	. . .	. . .	. . .	. . .
Income on bonds and notes	3 350 . .	. . .	. . .	. . .	. . .	. . .	–41	–11	–14
Income on money market instruments and financial derivatives	3 360 . .	. . .	. . .	. . .	. . .	. . .	. . .	. . .	. . .
Other investment income	3 370 . .	–994	–1,135	–1,001	–1,220	–1,177	–1,329	–1,290	–1,454
D. CURRENT TRANSFERS	4 379 . .	1,612	1,623	2,336	2,275	2,533	2,295	2,270	2,261
Credit	2 379 . .	**1,663**	**1,669**	**2,383**	**2,356**	**2,614**	**2,361**	**2,355**	**2,339**
General government	2 380 . .	216	189	216	175	255	192	232	110
Other sectors	2 390 . .	1,446	1,480	2,167	2,181	2,359	2,169	2,123	2,228
Workers' remittances	2 391 . .	1,303	1,336	2,006	1,990	2,170	1,959	1,827	1,904
Other current transfers	2 392 . .	143	144	161	191	189	210	296	324
Debit	3 379 . .	**–51**	**–46**	**–47**	**–81**	**–81**	**–66**	**–86**	**–78**
General government	3 380 . .	–33	–29	–30	–57	–46	–38	–59	–41
Other sectors	3 390 . .	–18	–17	–17	–24	–34	–28	–27	–37
Workers' remittances	3 391 . .	–14	–11	–11	–17	–23	–14	–13	–15
Other current transfers	3 392 . .	–4	–5	–5	–6	–12	–14	–14	–22
CAPITAL AND FINANCIAL ACCOUNT	4 996 . .	**–495**	**799**	**186**	**411**	**442**	**526**	**762**	**906**
CAPITAL ACCOUNT	4 994 . .	**–6**	**–3**	**–5**	**–5**	**–6**	**–3**	**–3**	**–6**
Total credit	2 994 . .	*1*	. . .	. . .	. . .	. . .	. . .	. . .	. . .
Total debit	3 994 . .	*–7*	*–3*	*–5*	*–5*	*–6*	*–3*	*–4*	*–6*
Capital transfers, credit	2 400 . .	**1**	**. . .**	**. . .**	**. . .**	**. . .**	**. . .**	**. . .**	**. . .**
General government	2 401 . .	. . .	. . .	. . .	. . .	. . .	. . .	. . .	. . .
Debt forgiveness	2 402 . .	. . .	. . .	. . .	. . .	. . .	. . .	. . .	. . .
Other capital transfers	2 410 . .	. . .	. . .	. . .	. . .	. . .	. . .	. . .	. . .
Other sectors	2 430 . .	1	. . .	. . .	. . .	. . .	. . .	. . .	. . .
Migrants' transfers	2 431 . .	1	. . .	. . .	. . .	. . .	. . .	. . .	. . .
Debt forgiveness	2 432 . .	. . .	. . .	. . .	. . .	. . .	. . .	. . .	. . .
Other capital transfers	2 440 . .	. . .	. . .	. . .	. . .	. . .	. . .	. . .	. . .
Capital transfers, debit	3 400 . .	**–7**	**–3**	**–5**	**–5**	**–6**	**–3**	**–4**	**–6**
General government	3 401 . .	. . .	. . .	. . .	. . .	. . .	. . .	. . .	. . .
Debt forgiveness	3 402 . .	. . .	. . .	. . .	. . .	. . .	. . .	. . .	. . .
Other capital transfers	3 410 . .	. . .	. . .	. . .	. . .	. . .	. . .	. . .	. . .
Other sectors	3 430 . .	–7	–3	–5	–5	–6	–3	–4	–6
Migrants' transfers	3 431 . .	–7	–3	–5	–5	–6	–3	–4	–6
Debt forgiveness	3 432 . .	. . .	. . .	. . .	. . .	. . .	. . .	. . .	. . .
Other capital transfers	3 440 . .	. . .	. . .	. . .	. . .	. . .	. . .	. . .	. . .
Nonproduced nonfinancial assets, credit	2 480 . .	**. . .**	**. . .**	**. . .**	**. . .**	**. . .**	**. . .**	**. . .**	**. . .**
Nonproduced nonfinancial assets, debit	3 480 . .	**. . .**	**. . .**	**. . .**	**. . .**	**. . .**	**. . .**	**. . .**	**. . .**

Table 2 (Continued). STANDARD PRESENTATION, 1988–95
(Millions of U.S. dollars)

	Code	1988	1989	1990	1991	1992	1993	1994	1995
FINANCIAL ACCOUNT	4 995	**–490**	**802**	**191**	**415**	**449**	**530**	**765**	**912**
A. DIRECT INVESTMENT	4 500	85	167	165	295	390	468	527	278
Direct investment abroad	4 505	**...**	**...**	**...**	**–23**	**–32**	**–23**	**–24**	**–12**
Equity capital	4 510	...	...	...	–23	–32	–23	–24	–9
Claims on affiliated enterprises	4 515	...	...	...	–23	–32	–23	–24	–9
Liabilities to affiliated enterprises	4 520	...	...	...	...	...	...	...	...
Reinvested earnings	4 525	...	...	...	...	...	...	...	–3
Other capital	4 530	...	...	...	...	...	...	...	...
Claims on affiliated enterprises	4 535	...	...	...	...	...	...	...	...
Liabilities to affiliated enterprises	4 540	...	...	...	...	...	...	...	...
Direct investment in Morocco	4 555	**85**	**167**	**165**	**317**	**422**	**491**	**551**	**290**
Equity capital	4 560	...	...	...	272	271	431	192	200
Claims on direct investors	4 565	...	...	...	...	...	...	...	...
Liabilities to direct investors	4 570	...	...	...	272	271	431	192	200
Reinvested earnings	4 575	7	13	11	40	106	16	25	5
Other capital	4 580	78	154	154	6	46	44	334	85
Claims on direct investors	4 585	...	...	...	...	...	...	...	...
Liabilities to direct investors	4 590	...	...	...	...	...	...	...	...
B. PORTFOLIO INVESTMENT	4 600	...	...	...	2	1	24	238	20
Assets	4 602	**...**	**...**	**...**	**...**	**...**	**...**	**...**	**...**
Equity securities	4 610	...	...	...	...	...	...	...	...
Monetary authorities	4 611	...	...	...	...	...	...	...	...
General government	4 612	...	...	...	...	...	...	...	...
Banks	4 613	...	...	...	...	...	...	...	...
Other sectors	4 614	...	...	...	...	...	...	...	...
Debt securities	4 619	...	...	...	...	...	...	...	...
Bonds and notes	4 620	...	...	...	...	...	...	...	...
Monetary authorities	4 621	...	...	...	...	...	...	...	...
General government	4 622	...	...	...	...	...	...	...	...
Banks	4 623	...	...	...	...	...	...	...	...
Other sectors	4 624	...	...	...	...	...	...	...	...
Money market instruments	4 630	...	...	...	...	...	...	...	...
Monetary authorities	4 631	...	...	...	...	...	...	...	...
General government	4 632	...	...	...	...	...	...	...	...
Banks	4 633	...	...	...	...	...	...	...	...
Other sectors	4 634	...	...	...	...	...	...	...	...
Financial derivatives	4 640	...	...	...	...	...	...	...	...
Monetary authorities	4 641	...	...	...	...	...	...	...	...
General government	4 642	...	...	...	...	...	...	...	...
Banks	4 643	...	...	...	...	...	...	...	...
Other sectors	4 644	...	...	...	...	...	...	...	...
Liabilities	4 652	**...**	**...**	**...**	**2**	**1**	**24**	**238**	**20**
Equity securities	4 660	...	...	...	...	...	24	238	20
Banks	4 663	...	...	...	...	...	...	...	...
Other sectors	4 664	...	...	...	...	...	24	238	20
Debt securities	4 669	...	...	...	2	1	1	...	...
Bonds and notes	4 670	...	...	...	2	1	1	...	...
Monetary authorities	4 671	...	...	...	...	...	...	...	...
General government	4 672	...	...	...	2	1	1	...	...
Banks	4 673	...	...	...	...	...	...	...	...
Other sectors	4 674	...	...	...	...	...	...	...	...
Money market instruments	4 680	...	...	...	...	...	...	...	...
Monetary authorities	4 681	...	...	...	...	...	...	...	...
General government	4 682	...	...	...	...	...	...	...	...
Banks	4 683	...	...	...	...	...	...	...	...
Other sectors	4 684	...	...	...	...	...	...	...	...
Financial derivatives	4 690	...	...	...	...	...	...	...	...
Monetary authorities	4 691	...	...	...	...	...	...	...	...
General government	4 692	...	...	...	...	...	...	...	...
Banks	4 693	...	...	...	...	...	...	...	...
Other sectors	4 694	...	...	...	...	...	...	...	...

Table 2 (Concluded). STANDARD PRESENTATION, 1988–95
(Millions of U.S. dollars)

	Code	1988	1989	1990	1991	1992	1993	1994	1995
C. OTHER INVESTMENT	4 700 . .	–416	572	1,563	903	732	317	362	–248
Assets	4 703 . .	**–376**	**–94**	**–267**	**. . .**	**. . .**	**. . .**	**344**	**216**
Trade credits	4 706 . .	. . .	. . .	. . .	. . .	. . .	. . .	. . .	. . .
General government: long-term	4 708 . .	. . .	. . .	. . .	. . .	. . .	. . .	. . .	. . .
General government: short-term	4 709 . .	. . .	. . .	. . .	. . .	. . .	. . .	. . .	. . .
Other sectors: long-term	4 711 . .	. . .	. . .	. . .	. . .	. . .	. . .	. . .	. . .
Other sectors: short-term	4 712 . .	. . .	. . .	. . .	. . .	. . .	. . .	. . .	. . .
Loans	4 714 . .	–215	–10	–41	. . .	. . .	. . .	. . .	. . .
Monetary authorities: long-term	4 717 . .	. . .	. . .	. . .	. . .	. . .	. . .	. . .	. . .
Monetary authorities: short-term	4 718 . .	. . .	. . .	. . .	. . .	. . .	. . .	. . .	. . .
General government: long-term	4 720 . .	. . .	. . .	. . .	. . .	. . .	. . .	. . .	. . .
General government: short-term	4 721 . .	. . .	. . .	. . .	. . .	. . .	. . .	. . .	. . .
Banks: long-term	4 723 . .	. . .	. . .	. . .	. . .	. . .	. . .	. . .	. . .
Banks: short-term	4 724 . .	. . .	. . .	. . .	. . .	. . .	. . .	. . .	. . .
Other sectors: long-term	4 726 . .	. . .	. . .	. . .	. . .	. . .	. . .	. . .	. . .
Other sectors: short-term	4 727 . .	–215	–10	–41	. . .	. . .	. . .	. . .	. . .
Currency and deposits	4 730 . .	–141	–65	–202	. . .	. . .	. . .	344	216
Monetary authorities	4 731 . .	. . .	. . .	. . .	. . .	. . .	. . .	. . .	. . .
General government	4 732 . .	. . .	. . .	. . .	. . .	. . .	. . .	. . .	. . .
Banks	4 733 . .	–78	–65	–202	. . .	. . .	. . .	. . .	. . .
Other sectors	4 734 . .	–63	. . .	. . .	. . .	. . .	. . .	344	216
Other assets	4 736 . .	–19	–19	–24	. . .	. . .	. . .	. . .	. . .
Monetary authorities: long-term	4 738 . .	. . .	. . .	. . .	. . .	. . .	. . .	. . .	. . .
Monetary authorities: short-term	4 739 . .	. . .	. . .	. . .	. . .	. . .	. . .	. . .	. . .
General government: long-term	4 741 . .	–10	–18	–11	. . .	. . .	. . .	. . .	. . .
General government: short-term	4 742 . .	. . .	. . .	. . .	. . .	. . .	. . .	. . .	. . .
Banks: long-term	4 744 . .	. . .	. . .	. . .	. . .	. . .	. . .	. . .	. . .
Banks: short-term	4 745 . .	. . .	. . .	. . .	. . .	. . .	. . .	. . .	. . .
Other sectors: long-term	4 747 . .	–9	–2	–13	. . .	. . .	. . .	. . .	. . .
Other sectors: short-term	4 748 . .	. . .	. . .	. . .	. . .	. . .	. . .	. . .	. . .
Liabilities	4 753 . .	**–40**	**665**	**1,830**	**903**	**732**	**317**	**18**	**–463**
Trade credits	4 756 . .	124	164	476	120	824	260	62	–466
General government: long-term	4 758 . .	22	–26	68	–258	39	–350	–538	–518
General government: short-term	4 759 . .	. . .	. . .	. . .	. . .	. . .	. . .	. . .	. . .
Other sectors: long-term	4 761 . .	102	190	408	367	400	452	351	93
Other sectors: short-term	4 762 . .	. . .	. . .	. . .	11	385	158	249	–41
Loans	4 764 . .	–164	476	1,249	790	–82	64	–63	–1
Use of Fund credit and loans from the Fund	4 766 . .	–105	–83	–161	–171	–116	–156	–152	–101
Monetary authorities: other long-term	4 767 . .	. . .	. . .	. . .	. . .	. . .	. . .	. . .	. . .
Monetary authorities: short-term	4 768 . .	. . .	. . .	. . .	. . .	. . .	. . .	. . .	. . .
General government: long-term	4 770 . .	352	362	931	906	118	409	118	196
General government: short-term	4 771 . .	. . .	. . .	. . .	. . .	. . .	. . .	. . .	. . .
Banks: long-term	4 773 . .	. . .	. . .	. . .	. . .	. . .	. . .	–17	–120
Banks: short-term	4 774 . .	. . .	. . .	. . .	. . .	. . .	. . .	. . .	. . .
Other sectors: long-term	4 776 . .	–43	–63	165	55	–84	–188	–12	25
Other sectors: short-term	4 777 . .	–367	260	314	. . .	. . .	. . .	. . .	. . .
Currency and deposits	4 780 . .	35	25	101	. . .	. . .	. . .	. . .	. . .
Monetary authorities	4 781 . .	. . .	. . .	. . .	. . .	. . .	. . .	. . .	. . .
General government	4 782 . .	. . .	. . .	. . .	. . .	. . .	. . .	. . .	. . .
Banks	4 783 . .	35	25	101	. . .	. . .	. . .	. . .	. . .
Other sectors	4 784 . .	. . .	. . .	. . .	. . .	. . .	. . .	. . .	. . .
Other liabilities	4 786 . .	–35	–1	4	–7	–11	–7	19	4
Monetary authorities: long-term	4 788 . .	. . .	. . .	. . .	–7	–11	–7	19	4
Monetary authorities: short-term	4 789 . .	. . .	. . .	. . .	. . .	. . .	. . .	. . .	. . .
General government: long-term	4 791 . .	. . .	. . .	. . .	. . .	. . .	. . .	. . .	. . .
General government: short-term	4 792 . .	–35	–1	4	. . .	. . .	. . .	. . .	. . .
Banks: long-term	4 794 . .	. . .	. . .	. . .	. . .	. . .	. . .	. . .	. . .
Banks: short-term	4 795 . .	. . .	. . .	. . .	. . .	. . .	. . .	. . .	. . .
Other sectors: long-term	4 797 . .	. . .	. . .	. . .	. . .	. . .	. . .	. . .	. . .
Other sectors: short-term	4 798 . .	. . .	. . .	. . .	. . .	. . .	. . .	. . .	. . .
D. RESERVE ASSETS	4 800 . .	–158	63	–1,537	–785	–675	–280	–362	861
Monetary gold	4 810 . .	. . .	. . .	. . .	. . .	. . .	. . .	. . .	. . .
Special drawing rights	4 820 . .	2	. . .	–1	–139	66	43	10	1
Reserve position in the Fund	4 830 . .	. . .	. . .	. . .	. . .	–42	. . .	. . .	. . .
Foreign exchange	4 840 . .	–160	62	–1,534	–780	–826	–298	–611	1,135
Other claims	4 880 . .	. . .	1	–2	134	128	–26	239	–275
NET ERRORS AND OMISSIONS	4 998 . .	**22**	**–11**	**9**	**3**	**–10**	**–5**	**–39**	**615**

Part 3 of the *Yearbook* contains descriptions of the methodologies, compilation practices, and sources used to compile these data.

Table 1. ANALYTIC PRESENTATION, 1988–95
(Millions of U.S. dollars)

	Code			1988	1989	1990	1991	1992	1993	1994	1995
A. Current Account[1]	4	993	Y .	**–358.5**	**–460.2**	**–415.3**	**–344.3**	**–381.3**	**. . .**	**. . .**	**. . .**
Goods: exports f.o.b	2	100	. .	103.0	104.8	126.4	162.3	139.3	. . .	. . .	. . .
Goods: imports f.o.b	3	100	. .	–662.0	–726.9	–789.7	–808.8	–798.5	. . .	. . .	. . .
Balance on Goods	4	100	. .	*–559.0*	*–622.1*	*–663.3*	*–646.5*	*–659.2*	. . .	. . .	. . .
Services: credit	2	200	. .	85.0	95.4	103.0	147.2	164.6	. . .	. . .	. . .
Services: debit	3	200	. .	–190.9	–195.5	–206.0	–236.8	–246.4	. . .	. . .	. . .
Balance on Goods and Services	4	991	. .	*–664.9*	*–722.2*	*–766.3*	*–736.1*	*–741.0*	. . .	. . .	. . .
Income: credit	2	300	. .	71.6	71.3	70.4	55.6	58.0	. . .	. . .	. . .
Income: debit	3	300	. .	–142.0	–196.8	–167.8	–165.5	–197.7	. . .	. . .	. . .
Balance on Goods, Services, and Income	4	992	. .	*–735.3*	*–847.7*	*–863.7*	*–846.0*	*–880.7*	. . .	. . .	. . .
Current transfers: credit	2	379	Y .	376.8	387.5	448.4	501.7	499.4	. . .	. . .	. . .
Current transfers: debit	3	379	. .	. . .	. . .	. . .	. . .	. . .	. . .	. . .	. . .
B. Capital Account[1]	4	994	Y .	**. . .**	**. . .**	**. . .**	**. . .**	**. . .**	**. . .**	**. . .**	**. . .**
Capital account: credit	2	994	Y .	. . .	. . .	. . .	. . .	. . .	. . .	. . .	. . .
Capital account: debit	3	994	. .	. . .	. . .	. . .	. . .	. . .	. . .	. . .	. . .
Total, Groups A Plus B	4	010	. .	*–358.5*	*–460.2*	*–415.3*	*–344.3*	*–381.3*	. . .	. . .	. . .
C. Financial Account[1]	4	995	X .	**–126.2**	**–55.0**	**–83.5**	**–187.5**	**–122.9**	**. . .**	**. . .**	**. . .**
Direct investment abroad	4	505	. .	. . .	. . .	. . .	. . .	. . .	. . .	. . .	. . .
Direct investment in Mozambique	4	555	Y .	4.5	3.4	9.2	22.5	25.3	. . .	. . .	. . .
Portfolio investment assets	4	602	. .	. . .	. . .	. . .	. . .	. . .	. . .	. . .	. . .
Equity securities	4	610	. .	. . .	. . .	. . .	. . .	. . .	. . .	. . .	. . .
Debt securities	4	619	. .	. . .	. . .	. . .	. . .	. . .	. . .	. . .	. . .
Portfolio investment liabilities	4	652	Y .	. . .	. . .	. . .	. . .	. . .	. . .	. . .	. . .
Equity securities	4	660	Y .	. . .	. . .	. . .	. . .	. . .	. . .	. . .	. . .
Debt securities	4	669	Y .	. . .	. . .	. . .	. . .	. . .	. . .	. . .	. . .
Other investment assets	4	703	. .	. . .	. . .	. . .	. . .	. . .	. . .	. . .	. . .
Monetary authorities	4	703	. A	. . .	. . .	. . .	. . .	. . .	. . .	. . .	. . .
General government	4	703	. B	. . .	. . .	. . .	. . .	. . .	. . .	. . .	. . .
Banks	4	703	. C	. . .	. . .	. . .	. . .	. . .	. . .	. . .	. . .
Other sectors	4	703	. D	. . .	. . .	. . .	. . .	. . .	. . .	. . .	. . .
Other investment liabilities	4	753	X .	–130.7	–58.4	–92.7	–210.0	–148.2	. . .	. . .	. . .
Monetary authorities	4	753	XA	. . .	. . .	. . .	. . .	. . .	. . .	. . .	. . .
General government	4	753	YB	–130.7	–58.4	–92.7	–210.0	–148.2	. . .	. . .	. . .
Banks	4	753	YC	. . .	. . .	. . .	. . .	. . .	. . .	. . .	. . .
Other sectors	4	753	YD	. . .	. . .	. . .	. . .	. . .	. . .	. . .	. . .
Total, Groups A Through C	4	020	. .	*–484.7*	*–515.2*	*–498.8*	*–531.8*	*–504.2*	. . .	. . .	. . .
D. Net Errors and Omissions	4	998	. .	**84.7**	**56.7**	**66.3**	**–3.9**	**32.5**	**. . .**	**. . .**	**. . .**
Total, Groups A Through D	4	030	. .	*–400.0*	*–458.5*	*–432.5*	*–535.7*	*–471.7*	. . .	. . .	. . .
E. Reserves and Related Items	4	040	. .	**400.0**	**458.5**	**432.5**	**535.7**	**471.7**	**. . .**	**. . .**	**. . .**
Reserve assets	4	800	. .	–25.2	2.9	–5.9	–12.7	–37.2	. . .	. . .	. . .
Use of Fund credit and loans	4	766	. .	25.3	15.9	12.0	41.2	62.5	. . .	. . .	. . .
Liabilities constituting foreign authorities' reserves	4	900	. .	. . .	. . .	. . .	. . .	. . .	. . .	. . .	. . .
Exceptional financing	4	920	. .	399.9	439.7	426.4	507.2	446.4	. . .	. . .	. . .
Conversion rates: meticais per U.S. dollar	0	101	. .	**524.6**	**744.9**	**929.1**	**1,434.5**	**2,516.5**	**3,874.2**	**6,038.6**	**9,024.3**

[1] Excludes components that have been classified in the categories of Group E.

Table 2. STANDARD PRESENTATION, 1988–95
(Millions of U.S. dollars)

	Code	1988	1989	1990	1991	1992	1993	1994	1995
CURRENT ACCOUNT	4 993 . .	**–358.5**	**–460.2**	**–415.3**	**–344.3**	**–381.3**	**. . .**	**. . .**	**. . .**
A. GOODS	4 100 . .	–559.0	–622.1	–663.3	–646.5	–659.2	. . .	. . .	. . .
Credit	2 100 . .	**103.0**	**104.8**	**126.4**	**162.3**	**139.3**	**. . .**	**. . .**	**. . .**
General merchandise: exports f.o.b.	2 110 . .	103.0	104.8	126.4	162.3	139.3	. . .	. . .	. . .
Goods for processing: exports f.o.b.	2 150 . .	. . .	. . .	. . .	. . .	. . .	. . .	. . .	. . .
Repairs on goods	2 160 . .	. . .	. . .	. . .	. . .	. . .	. . .	. . .	. . .
Goods procured in ports by carriers	2 170 . .	. . .	. . .	. . .	. . .	. . .	. . .	. . .	. . .
Nonmonetary gold	2 180 . .	. . .	. . .	. . .	. . .	. . .	. . .	. . .	. . .
Debit	3 100 . .	**–662.0**	**–726.9**	**–789.7**	**–808.8**	**–798.5**	**. . .**	**. . .**	**. . .**
General merchandise: imports f.o.b.	3 110 . .	–662.0	–726.9	–789.7	–808.8	–798.5	. . .	. . .	. . .
Goods for processing: imports f.o.b.	3 150 . .	. . .	. . .	. . .	. . .	. . .	. . .	. . .	. . .
Repairs on goods	3 160 . .	. . .	. . .	. . .	. . .	. . .	. . .	. . .	. . .
Goods procured in ports by carriers	3 170 . .	. . .	. . .	. . .	. . .	. . .	. . .	. . .	. . .
Nonmonetary gold	3 180 . .	. . .	. . .	. . .	. . .	. . .	. . .	. . .	. . .
B. SERVICES	4 200 . .	–105.9	–100.1	–103.0	–89.6	–81.8	. . .	. . .	. . .
Total credit	2 200 . .	*85.0*	*95.4*	*103.0*	*147.2*	*164.6*	. . .	. . .	. . .
Total debit	3 200 . .	*–190.9*	*–195.5*	*–206.0*	*–236.8*	*–246.4*	. . .	. . .	. . .
Transportation services, credit	2 205 . .	**41.5**	**52.9**	**63.1**	**60.2**	**69.5**	**. . .**	**. . .**	**. . .**
Passenger	2 205 BA	. . .	. . .	. . .	. . .	. . .	. . .	. . .	. . .
Freight	2 205 BB	*41.5*	*52.9*	*63.1*	*60.2*	*69.5*	. . .	. . .	. . .
Other	2 205 BC	. . .	. . .	. . .	. . .	. . .	. . .	. . .	. . .
Sea transport, passenger	2 207 . .	. . .	. . .	. . .	. . .	. . .	. . .	. . .	. . .
Sea transport, freight	2 208 . .	. . .	. . .	. . .	. . .	. . .	. . .	. . .	. . .
Sea transport, other	2 209 . .	. . .	. . .	. . .	. . .	. . .	. . .	. . .	. . .
Air transport, passenger	2 211 . .	. . .	. . .	. . .	. . .	. . .	. . .	. . .	. . .
Air transport, freight	2 212 . .	. . .	. . .	. . .	. . .	. . .	. . .	. . .	. . .
Air transport, other	2 213 . .	. . .	. . .	. . .	. . .	. . .	. . .	. . .	. . .
Other transport, passenger	2 215 . .	. . .	. . .	. . .	. . .	. . .	. . .	. . .	. . .
Other transport, freight	2 216 . .	. . .	. . .	. . .	. . .	. . .	. . .	. . .	. . .
Other transport, other	2 217 . .	. . .	. . .	. . .	. . .	. . .	. . .	. . .	. . .
Transportation services, debit	3 205 . .	**–107.5**	**–110.2**	**–118.8**	**–131.1**	**–128.3**	**. . .**	**. . .**	**. . .**
Passenger	3 205 BA	. . .	. . .	. . .	. . .	. . .	. . .	. . .	. . .
Freight	3 205 BB	*–66.2*	*–72.7*	*–79.0*	*–80.9*	*–79.8*	. . .	. . .	. . .
Other	3 205 BC	*–41.3*	*–37.5*	*–39.8*	*–50.2*	*–48.5*	. . .	. . .	. . .
Sea transport, passenger	3 207 . .	. . .	. . .	. . .	. . .	. . .	. . .	. . .	. . .
Sea transport, freight	3 208 . .	. . .	. . .	. . .	. . .	. . .	. . .	. . .	. . .
Sea transport, other	3 209 . .	. . .	. . .	. . .	. . .	. . .	. . .	. . .	. . .
Air transport, passenger	3 211 . .	. . .	. . .	. . .	. . .	. . .	. . .	. . .	. . .
Air transport, freight	3 212 . .	. . .	. . .	. . .	. . .	. . .	. . .	. . .	. . .
Air transport, other	3 213 . .	. . .	. . .	. . .	. . .	. . .	. . .	. . .	. . .
Other transport, passenger	3 215 . .	. . .	. . .	. . .	. . .	. . .	. . .	. . .	. . .
Other transport, freight	3 216 . .	. . .	. . .	. . .	. . .	. . .	. . .	. . .	. . .
Other transport, other	3 217 . .	. . .	. . .	. . .	. . .	. . .	. . .	. . .	. . .
Travel, credit	2 236 . .	**. . .**	**. . .**	**. . .**	**. . .**	**. . .**	**. . .**	**. . .**	**. . .**
Business travel	2 237 . .	. . .	. . .	. . .	. . .	. . .	. . .	. . .	. . .
Personal travel	2 240 . .	. . .	. . .	. . .	. . .	. . .	. . .	. . .	. . .
Travel, debit	3 236 . .	**. . .**	**. . .**	**. . .**	**. . .**	**. . .**	**. . .**	**. . .**	**. . .**
Business travel	3 237 . .	. . .	. . .	. . .	. . .	. . .	. . .	. . .	. . .
Personal travel	3 240 . .	. . .	. . .	. . .	. . .	. . .	. . .	. . .	. . .
Other services, credit	2 200 BA	**43.5**	**42.5**	**39.9**	**87.0**	**95.1**	**. . .**	**. . .**	**. . .**
Communications	2 245 . .	. . .	. . .	. . .	. . .	. . .	. . .	. . .	. . .
Construction	2 249 . .	. . .	. . .	. . .	. . .	. . .	. . .	. . .	. . .
Insurance	2 253 . .	. . .	. . .	. . .	. . .	. . .	. . .	. . .	. . .
Financial	2 260 . .	. . .	. . .	. . .	. . .	. . .	. . .	. . .	. . .
Computer and information	2 262 . .	. . .	. . .	. . .	. . .	. . .	. . .	. . .	. . .
Royalties and licence fees	2 266 . .	. . .	. . .	. . .	. . .	. . .	. . .	. . .	. . .
Other business services	2 268 . .	43.5	42.5	39.9	87.0	95.1	. . .	. . .	. . .
Personal, cultural, and recreational	2 287 . .	. . .	. . .	. . .	. . .	. . .	. . .	. . .	. . .
Government, n.i.e.	2 291 . .	. . .	. . .	. . .	. . .	. . .	. . .	. . .	. . .
Other services, debit	3 200 BA	**–83.4**	**–85.3**	**–87.2**	**–105.7**	**–118.1**	**. . .**	**. . .**	**. . .**
Communications	3 245 . .	. . .	. . .	. . .	. . .	. . .	. . .	. . .	. . .
Construction	3 249 . .	. . .	. . .	. . .	. . .	. . .	. . .	. . .	. . .
Insurance	3 253 . .	–7.4	–8.1	–8.8	–9.0	–8.9	. . .	. . .	. . .
Financial	3 260 . .	. . .	. . .	. . .	. . .	. . .	. . .	. . .	. . .
Computer and information	3 262 . .	. . .	. . .	. . .	. . .	. . .	. . .	. . .	. . .
Royalties and licence fees	3 266 . .	. . .	. . .	. . .	. . .	. . .	. . .	. . .	. . .
Other business services	3 268 . .	–76.0	–77.2	–78.4	–96.7	–109.2	. . .	. . .	. . .
Personal, cultural, and recreational	3 287 . .	. . .	. . .	. . .	. . .	. . .	. . .	. . .	. . .
Government, n.i.e.	3 291 . .	. . .	. . .	. . .	. . .	. . .	. . .	. . .	. . .

Table 2 (Continued). STANDARD PRESENTATION, 1988–95
(Millions of U.S. dollars)

	Code	1988	1989	1990	1991	1992	1993	1994	1995
C. INCOME	4 300 . .	–70.4	–125.5	–97.4	–109.9	–139.7	...	...	...
Total credit	2 300 . .	*71.6*	*71.3*	*70.4*	*55.6*	*58.0*	...	...	...
Total debit	3 300 . .	*–142.0*	*–196.8*	*–167.8*	*–165.5*	*–197.7*	...	...	...
Compensation of employees, credit	2 310 . .	**71.6**	**71.3**	**70.4**	**55.6**	**58.0**	...	...	...
Compensation of employees, debit	3 310 . .	**–25.3**	**–27.5**	**–25.4**	**–29.6**	**–26.6**	...	...	...
Investment income, credit	2 320 . .	...	...	...	...	...	...	...	...
Direct investment income	2 330 . .	...	...	...	...	...	...	...	...
Dividends and distributed branch profits	2 332 . .	...	...	...	...	...	...	...	...
Reinvested earnings and undistributed branch profits	2 333 . .	...	...	...	...	...	...	...	...
Income on debt (interest)	2 334 . .	...	...	...	...	...	...	...	...
Portfolio investment income	2 339 . .	...	...	...	...	...	...	...	...
Income on equity	2 340 . .	...	...	...	...	...	...	...	...
Income on bonds and notes	2 350 . .	...	...	...	...	...	...	...	...
Income on money market instruments and financial derivatives	2 360 . .	...	...	...	...	...	...	...	...
Other investment income	2 370 . .	...	...	...	...	...	...	...	...
Investment income, debit	3 320 . .	**–116.7**	**–169.3**	**–142.4**	**–135.9**	**–171.1**	...	...	...
Direct investment income	3 330 . .	...	...	...	...	...	...	...	...
Dividends and distributed branch profits	3 332 . .	...	...	...	...	...	...	...	...
Reinvested earnings and undistributed branch profits	3 333 . .	...	...	...	...	...	...	...	...
Income on debt (interest)	3 334 . .	...	...	...	...	...	...	...	...
Portfolio investment income	3 339 . .	...	...	...	...	...	...	...	...
Income on equity	3 340 . .	...	...	...	...	...	...	...	...
Income on bonds and notes	3 350 . .	...	...	...	...	...	...	...	...
Income on money market instruments and financial derivatives	3 360 . .	...	...	...	...	...	...	...	...
Other investment income	3 370 . .	–116.7	–169.3	–142.4	–135.9	–171.1	...	...	...
D. CURRENT TRANSFERS	4 379 . .	376.8	387.5	448.4	501.7	499.4	...	...	...
Credit	2 379 . .	**376.8**	**387.5**	**448.4**	**501.7**	**499.4**	...	...	...
General government	2 380 . .	376.8	387.5	448.4	501.7	499.4	...	...	...
Other sectors	2 390 . .	...	...	...	...	...	...	...	...
Workers' remittances	2 391 . .	...	...	...	...	...	...	...	...
Other current transfers	2 392 . .	...	...	...	...	...	...	...	...
Debit	3 379 . .	...	...	...	...	...	...	...	...
General government	3 380 . .	...	...	...	...	...	...	...	...
Other sectors	3 390 . .	...	...	...	...	...	...	...	...
Workers' remittances	3 391 . .	...	...	...	...	...	...	...	...
Other current transfers	3 392 . .	...	...	...	...	...	...	...	...
CAPITAL AND FINANCIAL ACCOUNT	4 996 . .	**273.8**	**403.5**	**349.0**	**348.2**	**348.8**	...	...	...
CAPITAL ACCOUNT	4 994 . .	**1.6**	**21.1**	**22.3**	**36.6**	...	...	...	...
Total credit	2 994 . .	*1.6*	*21.1*	*22.3*	*36.6*	...	...	...	...
Total debit	3 994 . .	...	...	...	...	...	...	...	...
Capital transfers, credit	2 400 . .	**1.6**	**21.1**	**22.3**	**36.6**	...	...	...	...
General government	2 401 . .	1.6	21.1	22.3	36.6	...	...	...	...
Debt forgiveness	2 402 . .	1.6	21.1	22.3	36.6	...	...	...	...
Other capital transfers	2 410 . .	...	...	...	...	...	...	...	...
Other sectors	2 430 . .	...	...	...	...	...	...	...	...
Migrants' transfers	2 431 . .	...	...	...	...	...	...	...	...
Debt forgiveness	2 432 . .	...	...	...	...	...	...	...	...
Other capital transfers	2 440 . .	...	...	...	...	...	...	...	...
Capital transfers, debit	3 400 . .	...	...	...	...	...	...	...	...
General government	3 401 . .	...	...	...	...	...	...	...	...
Debt forgiveness	3 402 . .	...	...	...	...	...	...	...	...
Other capital transfers	3 410 . .	...	...	...	...	...	...	...	...
Other sectors	3 430 . .	...	...	...	...	...	...	...	...
Migrants' transfers	3 431 . .	...	...	...	...	...	...	...	...
Debt forgiveness	3 432 . .	...	...	...	...	...	...	...	...
Other capital transfers	3 440 . .	...	...	...	...	...	...	...	...
Nonproduced nonfinancial assets, credit	2 480 . .	...	...	...	...	...	...	...	...
Nonproduced nonfinancial assets, debit	3 480 . .	...	...	...	...	...	...	...	...

Table 2 (Continued). STANDARD PRESENTATION, 1988–95

(Millions of U.S. dollars)

	Code		1988	1989	1990	1991	1992	1993	1994	1995
FINANCIAL ACCOUNT	4 995	. .	**272.2**	**382.4**	**326.7**	**311.6**	**348.8**	**. . .**	**. . .**	**. . .**
A. DIRECT INVESTMENT	4 500	. .	4.5	3.4	9.2	22.5	25.3	. . .	. . .	. . .
Direct investment abroad	4 505	. .	**. . .**	**. . .**	**. . .**	**. . .**	**. . .**	**. . .**	**. . .**	**. . .**
Equity capital	4 510	. .	. . .	. . .	. . .	. . .	. . .	. . .	. . .	. . .
Claims on affiliated enterprises	4 515	. .	. . .	. . .	. . .	. . .	. . .	. . .	. . .	. . .
Liabilities to affiliated enterprises	4 520	. .	. . .	. . .	. . .	. . .	. . .	. . .	. . .	. . .
Reinvested earnings	4 525	. .	. . .	. . .	. . .	. . .	. . .	. . .	. . .	. . .
Other capital	4 530	. .	. . .	. . .	. . .	. . .	. . .	. . .	. . .	. . .
Claims on affiliated enterprises	4 535	. .	. . .	. . .	. . .	. . .	. . .	. . .	. . .	. . .
Liabilities to affiliated enterprises	4 540	. .	. . .	. . .	. . .	. . .	. . .	. . .	. . .	. . .
Direct investment in Mozambique	4 555	. .	**4.5**	**3.4**	**9.2**	**22.5**	**25.3**	**. . .**	**. . .**	**. . .**
Equity capital	4 560	. .	4.5	3.4	9.2	22.5	25.3	. . .	. . .	. . .
Claims on direct investors	4 565	. .	. . .	. . .	. . .	. . .	. . .	. . .	. . .	. . .
Liabilities to direct investors	4 570	. .	. . .	. . .	. . .	. . .	. . .	. . .	. . .	. . .
Reinvested earnings	4 575	. .	. . .	. . .	. . .	. . .	. . .	. . .	. . .	. . .
Other capital	4 580	. .	. . .	. . .	. . .	. . .	. . .	. . .	. . .	. . .
Claims on direct investors	4 585	. .	. . .	. . .	. . .	. . .	. . .	. . .	. . .	. . .
Liabilities to direct investors	4 590	. .	. . .	. . .	. . .	. . .	. . .	. . .	. . .	. . .
B. PORTFOLIO INVESTMENT	4 600	. .	. . .	. . .	. . .	. . .	. . .	. . .	. . .	. . .
Assets	4 602	. .	**. . .**	**. . .**	**. . .**	**. . .**	**. . .**	**. . .**	**. . .**	**. . .**
Equity securities	4 610	. .	. . .	. . .	. . .	. . .	. . .	. . .	. . .	. . .
Monetary authorities	4 611	. .	. . .	. . .	. . .	. . .	. . .	. . .	. . .	. . .
General government	4 612	. .	. . .	. . .	. . .	. . .	. . .	. . .	. . .	. . .
Banks	4 613	. .	. . .	. . .	. . .	. . .	. . .	. . .	. . .	. . .
Other sectors	4 614	. .	. . .	. . .	. . .	. . .	. . .	. . .	. . .	. . .
Debt securities	4 619	. .	. . .	. . .	. . .	. . .	. . .	. . .	. . .	. . .
Bonds and notes	4 620	. .	. . .	. . .	. . .	. . .	. . .	. . .	. . .	. . .
Monetary authorities	4 621	. .	. . .	. . .	. . .	. . .	. . .	. . .	. . .	. . .
General government	4 622	. .	. . .	. . .	. . .	. . .	. . .	. . .	. . .	. . .
Banks	4 623	. .	. . .	. . .	. . .	. . .	. . .	. . .	. . .	. . .
Other sectors	4 624	. .	. . .	. . .	. . .	. . .	. . .	. . .	. . .	. . .
Money market instruments	4 630	. .	. . .	. . .	. . .	. . .	. . .	. . .	. . .	. . .
Monetary authorities	4 631	. .	. . .	. . .	. . .	. . .	. . .	. . .	. . .	. . .
General government	4 632	. .	. . .	. . .	. . .	. . .	. . .	. . .	. . .	. . .
Banks	4 633	. .	. . .	. . .	. . .	. . .	. . .	. . .	. . .	. . .
Other sectors	4 634	. .	. . .	. . .	. . .	. . .	. . .	. . .	. . .	. . .
Financial derivatives	4 640	. .	. . .	. . .	. . .	. . .	. . .	. . .	. . .	. . .
Monetary authorities	4 641	. .	. . .	. . .	. . .	. . .	. . .	. . .	. . .	. . .
General government	4 642	. .	. . .	. . .	. . .	. . .	. . .	. . .	. . .	. . .
Banks	4 643	. .	. . .	. . .	. . .	. . .	. . .	. . .	. . .	. . .
Other sectors	4 644	. .	. . .	. . .	. . .	. . .	. . .	. . .	. . .	. . .
Liabilities	4 652	. .	**. . .**	**. . .**	**. . .**	**. . .**	**. . .**	**. . .**	**. . .**	**. . .**
Equity securities	4 660	. .	. . .	. . .	. . .	. . .	. . .	. . .	. . .	. . .
Banks	4 663	. .	. . .	. . .	. . .	. . .	. . .	. . .	. . .	. . .
Other sectors	4 664	. .	. . .	. . .	. . .	. . .	. . .	. . .	. . .	. . .
Debt securities	4 669	. .	. . .	. . .	. . .	. . .	. . .	. . .	. . .	. . .
Bonds and notes	4 670	. .	. . .	. . .	. . .	. . .	. . .	. . .	. . .	. . .
Monetary authorities	4 671	. .	. . .	. . .	. . .	. . .	. . .	. . .	. . .	. . .
General government	4 672	. .	. . .	. . .	. . .	. . .	. . .	. . .	. . .	. . .
Banks	4 673	. .	. . .	. . .	. . .	. . .	. . .	. . .	. . .	. . .
Other sectors	4 674	. .	. . .	. . .	. . .	. . .	. . .	. . .	. . .	. . .
Money market instruments	4 680	. .	. . .	. . .	. . .	. . .	. . .	. . .	. . .	. . .
Monetary authorities	4 681	. .	. . .	. . .	. . .	. . .	. . .	. . .	. . .	. . .
General government	4 682	. .	. . .	. . .	. . .	. . .	. . .	. . .	. . .	. . .
Banks	4 683	. .	. . .	. . .	. . .	. . .	. . .	. . .	. . .	. . .
Other sectors	4 684	. .	. . .	. . .	. . .	. . .	. . .	. . .	. . .	. . .
Financial derivatives	4 690	. .	. . .	. . .	. . .	. . .	. . .	. . .	. . .	. . .
Monetary authorities	4 691	. .	. . .	. . .	. . .	. . .	. . .	. . .	. . .	. . .
General government	4 692	. .	. . .	. . .	. . .	. . .	. . .	. . .	. . .	. . .
Banks	4 693	. .	. . .	. . .	. . .	. . .	. . .	. . .	. . .	. . .
Other sectors	4 694	. .	. . .	. . .	. . .	. . .	. . .	. . .	. . .	. . .

Table 2 (Concluded). STANDARD PRESENTATION, 1988–95
(Millions of U.S. dollars)

	Code		1988	1989	1990	1991	1992	1993	1994	1995
C. OTHER INVESTMENT	4 700	. .	292.9	376.1	323.4	301.8	360.7	. . .	. . .	. . .
Assets	4 703	. .	**. . .**	**. . .**	**. . .**	**. . .**	**. . .**	**. . .**	**. . .**	**. . .**
Trade credits	4 706	. .	. . .	. . .	. . .	. . .	. . .	. . .	. . .	. . .
General government: long-term	4 708	. .	. . .	. . .	. . .	. . .	. . .	. . .	. . .	. . .
General government: short-term	4 709	. .	. . .	. . .	. . .	. . .	. . .	. . .	. . .	. . .
Other sectors: long-term	4 711	. .	. . .	. . .	. . .	. . .	. . .	. . .	. . .	. . .
Other sectors: short-term	4 712	. .	. . .	. . .	. . .	. . .	. . .	. . .	. . .	. . .
Loans	4 714	. .	. . .	. . .	. . .	. . .	. . .	. . .	. . .	. . .
Monetary authorities: long-term	4 717	. .	. . .	. . .	. . .	. . .	. . .	. . .	. . .	. . .
Monetary authorities: short-term	4 718	. .	. . .	. . .	. . .	. . .	. . .	. . .	. . .	. . .
General government: long-term	4 720	. .	. . .	. . .	. . .	. . .	. . .	. . .	. . .	. . .
General government: short-term	4 721	. .	. . .	. . .	. . .	. . .	. . .	. . .	. . .	. . .
Banks: long-term	4 723	. .	. . .	. . .	. . .	. . .	. . .	. . .	. . .	. . .
Banks: short-term	4 724	. .	. . .	. . .	. . .	. . .	. . .	. . .	. . .	. . .
Other sectors: long-term	4 726	. .	. . .	. . .	. . .	. . .	. . .	. . .	. . .	. . .
Other sectors: short-term	4 727	. .	. . .	. . .	. . .	. . .	. . .	. . .	. . .	. . .
Currency and deposits	4 730	. .	. . .	. . .	. . .	. . .	. . .	. . .	. . .	. . .
Monetary authorities	4 731	. .	. . .	. . .	. . .	. . .	. . .	. . .	. . .	. . .
General government	4 732	. .	. . .	. . .	. . .	. . .	. . .	. . .	. . .	. . .
Banks	4 733	. .	. . .	. . .	. . .	. . .	. . .	. . .	. . .	. . .
Other sectors	4 734	. .	. . .	. . .	. . .	. . .	. . .	. . .	. . .	. . .
Other assets	4 736	. .	. . .	. . .	. . .	. . .	. . .	. . .	. . .	. . .
Monetary authorities: long-term	4 738	. .	. . .	. . .	. . .	. . .	. . .	. . .	. . .	. . .
Monetary authorities: short-term	4 739	. .	. . .	. . .	. . .	. . .	. . .	. . .	. . .	. . .
General government: long-term	4 741	. .	. . .	. . .	. . .	. . .	. . .	. . .	. . .	. . .
General government: short-term	4 742	. .	. . .	. . .	. . .	. . .	. . .	. . .	. . .	. . .
Banks: long-term	4 744	. .	. . .	. . .	. . .	. . .	. . .	. . .	. . .	. . .
Banks: short-term	4 745	. .	. . .	. . .	. . .	. . .	. . .	. . .	. . .	. . .
Other sectors: long-term	4 747	. .	. . .	. . .	. . .	. . .	. . .	. . .	. . .	. . .
Other sectors: short-term	4 748	. .	. . .	. . .	. . .	. . .	. . .	. . .	. . .	. . .
Liabilities	4 753	. .	**292.9**	**376.1**	**323.4**	**301.8**	**360.7**	**. . .**	**. . .**	**. . .**
Trade credits	4 756	. .	. . .	. . .	. . .	. . .	. . .	. . .	. . .	. . .
General government: long-term	4 758	. .	. . .	. . .	. . .	. . .	. . .	. . .	. . .	. . .
General government: short-term	4 759	. .	. . .	. . .	. . .	. . .	. . .	. . .	. . .	. . .
Other sectors: long-term	4 761	. .	. . .	. . .	. . .	. . .	. . .	. . .	. . .	. . .
Other sectors: short-term	4 762	. .	. . .	. . .	. . .	. . .	. . .	. . .	. . .	. . .
Loans	4 764	. .	292.9	–21.4	272.6	216.1	582.9	. . .	. . .	. . .
Use of Fund credit and loans from the Fund	4 766	. .	25.3	15.9	12.0	41.2	62.5	. . .	. . .	. . .
Monetary authorities: other long-term	4 767	. .	. . .	. . .	. . .	. . .	. . .	. . .	. . .	. . .
Monetary authorities: short-term	4 768	. .	. . .	. . .	. . .	. . .	. . .	. . .	. . .	. . .
General government: long-term	4 770	. .	267.6	–37.3	260.6	174.9	520.4	. . .	. . .	. . .
General government: short-term	4 771	. .	. . .	. . .	. . .	. . .	. . .	. . .	. . .	. . .
Banks: long-term	4 773	. .	. . .	. . .	. . .	. . .	. . .	. . .	. . .	. . .
Banks: short-term	4 774	. .	. . .	. . .	. . .	. . .	. . .	. . .	. . .	. . .
Other sectors: long-term	4 776	. .	. . .	. . .	. . .	. . .	. . .	. . .	. . .	. . .
Other sectors: short-term	4 777	. .	. . .	. . .	. . .	. . .	. . .	. . .	. . .	. . .
Currency and deposits	4 780	. .	. . .	. . .	. . .	. . .	. . .	. . .	. . .	. . .
Monetary authorities	4 781	. .	. . .	. . .	. . .	. . .	. . .	. . .	. . .	. . .
General government	4 782	. .	. . .	. . .	. . .	. . .	. . .	. . .	. . .	. . .
Banks	4 783	. .	. . .	. . .	. . .	. . .	. . .	. . .	. . .	. . .
Other sectors	4 784	. .	. . .	. . .	. . .	. . .	. . .	. . .	. . .	. . .
Other liabilities	4 786	. .	. . .	397.5	50.8	85.7	–222.2	. . .	. . .	. . .
Monetary authorities: long-term	4 788	. .	. . .	. . .	. . .	. . .	. . .	. . .	. . .	. . .
Monetary authorities: short-term	4 789	. .	. . .	397.5	50.8	85.7	–222.2	. . .	. . .	. . .
General government: long-term	4 791	. .	. . .	. . .	. . .	. . .	. . .	. . .	. . .	. . .
General government: short-term	4 792	. .	. . .	. . .	. . .	. . .	. . .	. . .	. . .	. . .
Banks: long-term	4 794	. .	. . .	. . .	. . .	. . .	. . .	. . .	. . .	. . .
Banks: short-term	4 795	. .	. . .	. . .	. . .	. . .	. . .	. . .	. . .	. . .
Other sectors: long-term	4 797	. .	. . .	. . .	. . .	. . .	. . .	. . .	. . .	. . .
Other sectors: short-term	4 798	. .	. . .	. . .	. . .	. . .	. . .	. . .	. . .	. . .
D. RESERVE ASSETS	4 800	. .	–25.2	2.9	–5.9	–12.7	–37.2	. . .	. . .	. . .
Monetary gold	4 810	. .	. . .	. . .	. . .	. . .	. . .	. . .	. . .	. . .
Special drawing rights	4 820	. .	. . .	. . .	. . .	. . .	. . .	. . .	. . .	. . .
Reserve position in the Fund	4 830	. .	. . .	. . .	. . .	. . .	. . .	. . .	. . .	. . .
Foreign exchange	4 840	. .	–25.2	2.9	–5.9	–12.7	–37.2	. . .	. . .	. . .
Other claims	4 880	. .	. . .	. . .	. . .	. . .	. . .	. . .	. . .	. . .
NET ERRORS AND OMISSIONS	4 998	. .	**84.7**	**56.7**	**66.3**	**–3.9**	**32.5**	**. . .**	**. . .**	**. . .**

Table 1. ANALYTIC PRESENTATION, 1988–95
(Millions of U.S. dollars)

	Code	1988	1989	1990	1991	1992	1993	1994	1995
A. Current Account[1]	4 993 Y.	**–175.9**	**–68.0**	**–431.3**	**–267.4**	**–114.4**	**. . .**	**. . .**	**. . .**
Goods: exports f.o.b	2 100 . .	165.7	222.8	222.6	248.2	531.3	. . .	. . .	. . .
Goods: imports f.o.b	3 100 . .	–370.2	–304.3	–524.3	–301.5	–636.2	. . .	. . .	. . .
Balance on Goods	4 100 . .	*–204.5*	*–81.5*	*–301.7*	*–53.3*	*–104.9*	. . .	. . .	. . .
Services: credit	2 200 . .	46.9	56.6	93.5	56.0	112.4	. . .	. . .	. . .
Services: debit	3 200 . .	–34.5	–44.3	–72.3	–54.3	–42.4	. . .	. . .	. . .
Balance on Goods and Services	4 991 . .	*–192.0*	*–69.2*	*–280.6*	*–51.6*	*–34.9*	. . .	. . .	. . .
Income: credit	2 300 . .	2.7	2.7	2.4	1.0	3.4	. . .	. . .	. . .
Income: debit	3 300 . .	–79.1	–57.1	–192.1	–272.2	–151.4	. . .	. . .	. . .
Balance on Goods, Services, and Income	4 992 . .	*–268.4*	*–123.6*	*–470.3*	*–322.8*	*–182.9*	. . .	. . .	. . .
Current transfers: credit	2 379 Y.	93.1	55.6	39.0	55.5	70.3	. . .	. . .	. . .
Current transfers: debit	3 379 . .	–.5	. . .	. . .	–.1	–1.8	. . .	. . .	. . .
B. Capital Account[1]	4 994 Y.	**. . .**	**84.0**	**232.9**	**. . .**	**. . .**	**. . .**	**. . .**	**. . .**
Capital account: credit	2 994 Y.	. . .	84.0	232.9	. . .	. . .	. . .	. . .	. . .
Capital account: debit	3 994 . .	. . .	. . .	. . .	. . .	. . .	. . .	. . .	. . .
Total, Groups A Plus B	4 010 . .	*–175.9*	*16.0*	*–198.4*	*–267.4*	*–114.4*	. . .	. . .	. . .
C. Financial Account[1]	4 995 X.	**139.7**	**82.0**	**185.8**	**275.0**	**191.0**	**. . .**	**. . .**	**. . .**
Direct investment abroad	4 505 . .	. . .	. . .	. . .	. . .	. . .	. . .	. . .	. . .
Direct investment in Myanmar	4 555 Y.	. . .	7.8	161.1	238.1	171.6	. . .	. . .	. . .
Portfolio investment assets	4 602 . .	. . .	. . .	. . .	. . .	. . .	. . .	. . .	. . .
Equity securities	4 610 . .	. . .	. . .	. . .	. . .	. . .	. . .	. . .	. . .
Debt securities	4 619 . .	. . .	. . .	. . .	. . .	. . .	. . .	. . .	. . .
Portfolio investment liabilities	4 652 Y.	. . .	. . .	. . .	. . .	. . .	. . .	. . .	. . .
Equity securities	4 660 Y.	. . .	. . .	. . .	. . .	. . .	. . .	. . .	. . .
Debt securities	4 669 Y.	. . .	. . .	. . .	. . .	. . .	. . .	. . .	. . .
Other investment assets	4 703 . .	. . .	. . .	. . .	. . .	. . .	. . .	. . .	. . .
Monetary authorities	4 703 .A	. . .	. . .	. . .	. . .	. . .	. . .	. . .	. . .
General government	4 703 .B	. . .	. . .	. . .	. . .	. . .	. . .	. . .	. . .
Banks	4 703 .C	. . .	. . .	. . .	. . .	. . .	. . .	. . .	. . .
Other sectors	4 703 .D	. . .	. . .	. . .	. . .	. . .	. . .	. . .	. . .
Other investment liabilities	4 753 X.	139.7	74.2	24.6	37.0	19.4	. . .	. . .	. . .
Monetary authorities	4 753 XA	–3.3	–.6	–1.8	–2.8	–.7	. . .	. . .	. . .
General government	4 753 YB	143.0	74.8	26.4	39.8	20.2	. . .	. . .	. . .
Banks	4 753 YC	. . .	. . .	. . .	. . .	. . .	. . .	. . .	. . .
Other sectors	4 753 YD	. . .	. . .	. . .	. . .	. . .	. . .	. . .	. . .
Total, Groups A Through C	4 020 . .	*–36.2*	*98.0*	*–12.7*	*7.6*	*76.6*	. . .	. . .	. . .
D. Net Errors and Omissions	4 998 . .	**116.7**	**52.6**	**21.4**	**–53.9**	**17.7**	**. . .**	**. . .**	**. . .**
Total, Groups A Through D	4 030 . .	*80.5*	*150.6*	*8.7*	*–46.3*	*94.3*	. . .	. . .	. . .
E. Reserves and Related Items	4 040 . .	**–80.5**	**–150.6**	**–8.7**	**46.3**	**–94.3**	**. . .**	**. . .**	**. . .**
Reserve assets	4 800 . .	–52.4	–142.9	–6.3	46.6	–94.3	. . .	. . .	. . .
Use of Fund credit and loans	4 766 . .	–28.1	–7.7	–2.4	–.3	. . .	. . .	. . .	. . .
Liabilities constituting foreign authorities' reserves	4 900 . .	. . .	. . .	. . .	. . .	. . .	. . .	. . .	. . .
Exceptional financing	4 920 . .	. . .	. . .	. . .	. . .	. . .	. . .	. . .	. . .
Conversion rates: kyats per U.S. dollar	0 101 . .	**6.3945**	**6.7049**	**6.3386**	**6.2837**	**6.1045**	**6.1570**	**5.9749**	**5.6670**

[1] Excludes components that have been classified in the categories of Group E.

Table 2. STANDARD PRESENTATION, 1988–95
(Millions of U.S. dollars)

	Code	1988	1989	1990	1991	1992	1993	1994	1995
CURRENT ACCOUNT	4 993 . .	**–175.9**	**–68.0**	**–431.3**	**–267.4**	**–114.4**	. . .	. . .	. . .
A. GOODS	4 100 . .	–204.5	–81.5	–301.7	–53.3	–104.9	. . .	. . .	. . .
Credit	2 100 . .	**165.7**	**222.8**	**222.6**	**248.2**	**531.3**	. . .	. . .	. . .
General merchandise: exports f.o.b.	2 110 . .	165.7	222.8	222.6	248.2	531.3	. . .	. . .	. . .
Goods for processing: exports f.o.b.	2 150 . .	. . .	. . .	. . .	. . .	. . .	. . .	. . .	. . .
Repairs on goods	2 160 . .	. . .	. . .	. . .	. . .	. . .	. . .	. . .	. . .
Goods procured in ports by carriers	2 170 . .	. . .	. . .	. . .	. . .	. . .	. . .	. . .	. . .
Nonmonetary gold	2 180 . .	. . .	. . .	. . .	. . .	. . .	. . .	. . .	. . .
Debit	3 100 . .	**–370.2**	**–304.3**	**–524.3**	**–301.5**	**–636.2**	. . .	. . .	. . .
General merchandise: imports f.o.b.	3 110 . .	–370.2	–304.3	–524.3	–301.5	–636.2	. . .	. . .	. . .
Goods for processing: imports f.o.b.	3 150 . .	. . .	. . .	. . .	. . .	. . .	. . .	. . .	. . .
Repairs on goods	3 160 . .	. . .	. . .	. . .	. . .	. . .	. . .	. . .	. . .
Goods procured in ports by carriers	3 170 . .	. . .	. . .	. . .	. . .	. . .	. . .	. . .	. . .
Nonmonetary gold	3 180 . .	. . .	. . .	. . .	. . .	. . .	. . .	. . .	. . .
B. SERVICES	4 200 . .	12.5	12.3	21.1	1.7	70.0	. . .	. . .	. . .
Total credit	2 200 . .	*46.9*	*56.6*	*93.5*	*56.0*	*112.4*	. . .	. . .	. . .
Total debit	3 200 . .	*–34.5*	*–44.3*	*–72.3*	*–54.3*	*–42.4*	. . .	. . .	. . .
Transportation services, credit	2 205 . .	**5.4**	**4.5**	**9.6**	**4.4**	**3.2**	. . .	. . .	. . .
Passenger	2 205 BA	*1.4*	*.4*	*1.2*	*3.3*	*2.3*	. . .	. . .	. . .
Freight	2 205 BB	*2.0*	*2.1*	*3.6*	*1.1*	*.9*	. . .	. . .	. . .
Other	2 205 BC	*2.1*	*2.0*	*4.8*	. . .	. . .	. . .	. . .	. . .
Sea transport, passenger	2 207 . .	. . .	. . .	. . .	. . .	. . .	. . .	. . .	. . .
Sea transport, freight	2 208 . .	. . .	. . .	. . .	. . .	. . .	. . .	. . .	. . .
Sea transport, other	2 209 . .	. . .	. . .	. . .	. . .	. . .	. . .	. . .	. . .
Air transport, passenger	2 211 . .	. . .	. . .	. . .	. . .	. . .	. . .	. . .	. . .
Air transport, freight	2 212 . .	. . .	. . .	. . .	. . .	. . .	. . .	. . .	. . .
Air transport, other	2 213 . .	. . .	. . .	. . .	. . .	. . .	. . .	. . .	. . .
Other transport, passenger	2 215 . .	. . .	. . .	. . .	. . .	. . .	. . .	. . .	. . .
Other transport, freight	2 216 . .	. . .	. . .	. . .	. . .	. . .	. . .	. . .	. . .
Other transport, other	2 217 . .	. . .	. . .	. . .	. . .	. . .	. . .	. . .	. . .
Transportation services, debit	3 205 . .	**–8.3**	**–14.9**	**–25.6**	**–1.2**	**–10.8**	. . .	. . .	. . .
Passenger	3 205 BA	*–.2*	. . .	*–.1*	. . .	. . .	. . .	. . .	. . .
Freight	3 205 BB	*–8.1*	*–14.9*	*–25.6*	*–1.2*	*–10.8*	. . .	. . .	. . .
Other	3 205 BC	. . .	. . .	. . .	. . .	. . .	. . .	. . .	. . .
Sea transport, passenger	3 207 . .	. . .	. . .	. . .	. . .	. . .	. . .	. . .	. . .
Sea transport, freight	3 208 . .	. . .	. . .	. . .	. . .	. . .	. . .	. . .	. . .
Sea transport, other	3 209 . .	. . .	. . .	. . .	. . .	. . .	. . .	. . .	. . .
Air transport, passenger	3 211 . .	. . .	. . .	. . .	. . .	. . .	. . .	. . .	. . .
Air transport, freight	3 212 . .	. . .	. . .	. . .	. . .	. . .	. . .	. . .	. . .
Air transport, other	3 213 . .	. . .	. . .	. . .	. . .	. . .	. . .	. . .	. . .
Other transport, passenger	3 215 . .	. . .	. . .	. . .	. . .	. . .	. . .	. . .	. . .
Other transport, freight	3 216 . .	. . .	. . .	. . .	. . .	. . .	. . .	. . .	. . .
Other transport, other	3 217 . .	. . .	. . .	. . .	. . .	. . .	. . .	. . .	. . .
Travel, credit	2 236 . .	**12.2**	**9.6**	**19.5**	**11.1**	**90.7**	. . .	. . .	. . .
Business travel	2 237 . .	2.0	4.3	7.2	8.4	4.2	. . .	. . .	. . .
Personal travel	2 240 . .	10.2	5.2	12.3	2.8	86.5	. . .	. . .	. . .
Travel, debit	3 236 . .	**–5.4**	**–7.9**	**–16.3**	**–24.0**	**–16.2**	. . .	. . .	. . .
Business travel	3 237 . .	. . .	. . .	. . .	. . .	–16.0	. . .	. . .	. . .
Personal travel	3 240 . .	. . .	. . .	. . .	. . .	–.2	. . .	. . .	. . .
Other services, credit	2 200 BA	**29.3**	**42.5**	**64.3**	**40.5**	**18.5**	. . .	. . .	. . .
Communications	2 245 . .	. . .	. . .	. . .	. . .	. . .	. . .	. . .	. . .
Construction	2 249 . .	. . .	. . .	. . .	. . .	. . .	. . .	. . .	. . .
Insurance	2 253 . .	. . .	. . .	.5	. . .	. . .	. . .	. . .	. . .
Financial	2 260 . .	. . .	. . .	. . .	. . .	. . .	. . .	. . .	. . .
Computer and information	2 262 . .	. . .	. . .	. . .	. . .	. . .	. . .	. . .	. . .
Royalties and licence fees	2 266 . .	.5	.2	.2	. . .	. . .	. . .	. . .	. . .
Other business services	2 268 . .	28.9	42.3	63.7	40.5	7.7	. . .	. . .	. . .
Personal, cultural, and recreational	2 287 . .	. . .	. . .	. . .	. . .	. . .	. . .	. . .	. . .
Government, n.i.e.	2 291 . .	. . .	. . .	. . .	. . .	10.7	. . .	. . .	. . .
Other services, debit	3 200 BA	**–20.7**	**–21.4**	**–30.4**	**–29.2**	**–15.4**	. . .	. . .	. . .
Communications	3 245 . .	. . .	. . .	. . .	. . .	. . .	. . .	. . .	. . .
Construction	3 249 . .	. . .	. . .	. . .	. . .	. . .	. . .	. . .	. . .
Insurance	3 253 . .	–2.3	–2.1	–1.8	–2.8	–4.7	. . .	. . .	. . .
Financial	3 260 . .	. . .	. . .	. . .	. . .	. . .	. . .	. . .	. . .
Computer and information	3 262 . .	. . .	. . .	. . .	. . .	. . .	. . .	. . .	. . .
Royalties and licence fees	3 266 . .	–.3	. . .	–.2	. . .	. . .	. . .	. . .	. . .
Other business services	3 268 . .	–18.1	–19.3	–28.4	–26.4	–1.6	. . .	. . .	. . .
Personal, cultural, and recreational	3 287 . .	. . .	. . .	. . .	. . .	. . .	. . .	. . .	. . .
Government, n.i.e.	3 291 . .	. . .	. . .	. . .	. . .	–9.1	. . .	. . .	. . .

Table 2 (Continued). STANDARD PRESENTATION, 1988–95

(Millions of U.S. dollars)

	Code		1988	1989	1990	1991	1992	1993	1994	1995
C. INCOME	4 300	. .	−76.4	−54.4	−189.7	−271.2	−147.9	. . .	. . .	. . .
Total credit	2 300	. .	*2.7*	*2.7*	*2.4*	*1.0*	*3.4*	. . .	. . .	. . .
Total debit	3 300	. .	*−79.1*	*−57.1*	*−192.1*	*−272.2*	*−151.4*	. . .	. . .	. . .
Compensation of employees, credit	2 310	. .	**. . .**	**. . .**	**. . .**	**. . .**	**. . .**	**. . .**	**. . .**	**. . .**
Compensation of employees, debit	3 310	. .	**. . .**	**. . .**	**. . .**	**. . .**	**. . .**	**. . .**	**. . .**	**. . .**
Investment income, credit	2 320	. .	**2.7**	**2.7**	**2.4**	**1.0**	**3.4**	**. . .**	**. . .**	**. . .**
Direct investment income	2 330	. .	. . .	. . .	. . .	. . .	. . .	. . .	. . .	. . .
Dividends and distributed branch profits	2 332	. .	. . .	. . .	. . .	. . .	. . .	. . .	. . .	. . .
Reinvested earnings and undistributed branch profits	2 333	. .	. . .		. . .	. . .	. . .	. . .	. . .	. . .
Income on debt (interest)	2 334	. .	. . .	. . .	. . .	. . .	. . .	. . .	. . .	. . .
Portfolio investment income	2 339	. .	. . .	. . .	. . .	. . .	. . .	. . .	. . .	. . .
Income on equity	2 340	. .	. . .	. . .	. . .	. . .	. . .	. . .	. . .	. . .
Income on bonds and notes	2 350	. .	. . .	. . .	. . .	. . .	. . .	. . .	. . .	. . .
Income on money market instruments and financial derivatives	2 360	. .	. . .	. . .	. . .	. . .	. . .	. . .	. . .	. . .
Other investment income	2 370	. .	2.7	2.7	2.4	1.0	. . .	. . .	. . .	. . .
Investment income, debit	3 320	. .	**−79.1**	**−57.1**	**−192.1**	**−272.2**	**−151.4**	**. . .**	**. . .**	**. . .**
Direct investment income	3 330	. .	. . .	−7.1	−145.8	−227.0	−151.4	. . .	. . .	. . .
Dividends and distributed branch profits	3 332	. .	. . .	−7.1	−145.8	−227.0	−151.4	. . .	. . .	. . .
Reinvested earnings and undistributed branch profits	3 333	. .	. . .	. . .	. . .	. . .	. . .	. . .	. . .	. . .
Income on debt (interest)	3 334	. .	. . .	. . .	. . .	. . .	. . .	. . .	. . .	. . .
Portfolio investment income	3 339	. .	. . .	. . .	. . .	. . .	. . .	. . .	. . .	. . .
Income on equity	3 340	. .	. . .	. . .	. . .	. . .	. . .	. . .	. . .	. . .
Income on bonds and notes	3 350	. .	. . .	. . .	. . .	. . .	. . .	. . .	. . .	. . .
Income on money market instruments and financial derivatives	3 360	. .	. . .	. . .	. . .	. . .	. . .	. . .	. . .	. . .
Other investment income	3 370	. .	−79.1	−50.1	−46.3	−45.2	. . .	. . .	. . .	. . .
D. CURRENT TRANSFERS	4 379	. .	92.5	55.6	39.0	55.4	68.5	. . .	. . .	. . .
Credit	2 379	. .	**93.1**	**55.6**	**39.0**	**55.5**	**70.3**	**. . .**	**. . .**	**. . .**
General government	2 380	. .	83.9	41.4	28.8	53.3	69.7	. . .	. . .	. . .
Other sectors	2 390	. .	9.1	14.3	10.2	2.2	.5	. . .	. . .	. . .
Workers' remittances	2 391	. .	6.8	9.2	5.9	1.5	.3	. . .	. . .	. . .
Other current transfers	2 392	. .	2.4	5.1	4.3	.7	.3	. . .	. . .	. . .
Debit	3 379	. .	**−.5**	**. . .**	**. . .**	**−.1**	**−1.8**	**. . .**	**. . .**	**. . .**
General government	3 380	. .	. . .	. . .	. . .	. . .	. . .	. . .	. . .	. . .
Other sectors	3 390	. .	−.5	. . .	. . .	−.1	−1.8	. . .	. . .	. . .
Workers' remittances	3 391	. .	−.4	. . .	. . .	. . .	. . .	. . .	. . .	. . .
Other current transfers	3 392	. .	−.1	. . .	. . .	−.1	−1.8	. . .	. . .	. . .
CAPITAL AND FINANCIAL ACCOUNT	4 996	. .	**59.2**	**15.4**	**409.9**	**321.3**	**96.7**	**. . .**	**. . .**	**. . .**
CAPITAL ACCOUNT	4 994	. .	**. . .**	**84.0**	**232.9**	**. . .**	**. . .**	**. . .**	**. . .**	**. . .**
Total credit	2 994	. .	. . .	*84.0*	*232.9*	. . .	. . .	. . .	. . .	. . .
Total debit	3 994	. .	. . .	. . .	. . .	. . .	. . .	. . .	. . .	. . .
Capital transfers, credit	2 400	. .	**. . .**	**. . .**	**. . .**	**. . .**	**. . .**	**. . .**	**. . .**	**. . .**
General government	2 401	. .	. . .	. . .	. . .	. . .	. . .	. . .	. . .	. . .
Debt forgiveness	2 402	. .	. . .	. . .	. . .	. . .	. . .	. . .	. . .	. . .
Other capital transfers	2 410	. .	. . .	. . .	. . .	. . .	. . .	. . .	. . .	. . .
Other sectors	2 430	. .	. . .	. . .	. . .	. . .	. . .	. . .	. . .	. . .
Migrants' transfers	2 431	. .	. . .	. . .	. . .	. . .	. . .	. . .	. . .	. . .
Debt forgiveness	2 432	. .	. . .	. . .	. . .	. . .	. . .	. . .	. . .	. . .
Other capital transfers	2 440	. .	. . .	. . .	. . .	. . .	. . .	. . .	. . .	. . .
Capital transfers, debit	3 400	. .	**. . .**	**. . .**	**. . .**	**. . .**	**. . .**	**. . .**	**. . .**	**. . .**
General government	3 401	. .	. . .	. . .	. . .	. . .	. . .	. . .	. . .	. . .
Debt forgiveness	3 402	. .	. . .	. . .	. . .	. . .	. . .	. . .	. . .	. . .
Other capital transfers	3 410	. .	. . .	. . .	. . .	. . .	. . .	. . .	. . .	. . .
Other sectors	3 430	. .	. . .	. . .	. . .	. . .	. . .	. . .	. . .	. . .
Migrants' transfers	3 431	. .	. . .	. . .	. . .	. . .	. . .	. . .	. . .	. . .
Debt forgiveness	3 432	. .	. . .	. . .	. . .	. . .	. . .	. . .	. . .	. . .
Other capital transfers	3 440	. .	. . .	. . .	. . .	. . .	. . .	. . .	. . .	. . .
Nonproduced nonfinancial assets, credit	2 480	. .	**. . .**	**84.0**	**232.9**	**. . .**	**. . .**	**. . .**	**. . .**	**. . .**
Nonproduced nonfinancial assets, debit	3 480	. .	**. . .**	**. . .**	**. . .**	**. . .**	**. . .**	**. . .**	**. . .**	**. . .**

Table 2 (Continued). STANDARD PRESENTATION, 1988–95
(Millions of U.S. dollars)

	Code	1988	1989	1990	1991	1992	1993	1994	1995
FINANCIAL ACCOUNT	4 995 . .	**59.2**	**–68.7**	**177.1**	**321.3**	**96.7**	...	...	...
A. DIRECT INVESTMENT	4 500 . .	...	7.8	161.1	238.1	171.6	...	...	...
Direct investment abroad	4 505 . .	...	...	...	...	...	...	...	...
Equity capital	4 510 . .	...	...	...	...	...	...	...	...
Claims on affiliated enterprises	4 515 . .	...	...	...	...	...	...	...	...
Liabilities to affiliated enterprises	4 520 . .	...	...	...	...	...	...	...	...
Reinvested earnings	4 525 . .	...	...	...	...	...	...	...	...
Other capital	4 530 . .	...	...	...	...	...	...	...	...
Claims on affiliated enterprises	4 535 . .	...	...	...	...	...	...	...	...
Liabilities to affiliated enterprises	4 540 . .	...	...	...	...	...	...	...	...
Direct investment in Myanmar	4 555 . .	...	**7.8**	**161.1**	**238.1**	**171.6**	...	...	...
Equity capital	4 560 . .	...	7.8	161.1	238.1	171.6	...	...	...
Claims on direct investors	4 565 . .	...	...	...	...	...	...	...	...
Liabilities to direct investors	4 570 . .	...	...	...	...	...	...	...	...
Reinvested earnings	4 575 . .	...	...	...	...	...	...	...	...
Other capital	4 580 . .	...	...	...	...	...	...	...	...
Claims on direct investors	4 585 . .	...	...	...	...	...	...	...	...
Liabilities to direct investors	4 590 . .	...	...	...	...	...	...	...	...
B. PORTFOLIO INVESTMENT	4 600 . .	...	...	...	...	...	...	...	...
Assets	4 602 . .	...	...	...	...	...	...	...	...
Equity securities	4 610 . .	...	...	...	...	...	...	...	...
Monetary authorities	4 611 . .	...	...	...	...	...	...	...	...
General government	4 612 . .	...	...	...	...	...	...	...	...
Banks	4 613 . .	...	...	...	...	...	...	...	...
Other sectors	4 614 . .	...	...	...	...	...	...	...	...
Debt securities	4 619 . .	...	...	...	...	...	...	...	...
Bonds and notes	4 620 . .	...	...	...	...	...	...	...	...
Monetary authorities	4 621 . .	...	...	...	...	...	...	...	...
General government	4 622 . .	...	...	...	...	...	...	...	...
Banks	4 623 . .	...	...	...	...	...	...	...	...
Other sectors	4 624 . .	...	...	...	...	...	...	...	...
Money market instruments	4 630 . .	...	...	...	...	...	...	...	...
Monetary authorities	4 631 . .	...	...	...	...	...	...	...	...
General government	4 632 . .	...	...	...	...	...	...	...	...
Banks	4 633 . .	...	...	...	...	...	...	...	...
Other sectors	4 634 . .	...	...	...	...	...	...	...	...
Financial derivatives	4 640 . .	...	...	...	...	...	...	...	...
Monetary authorities	4 641 . .	...	...	...	...	...	...	...	...
General government	4 642 . .	...	...	...	...	...	...	...	...
Banks	4 643 . .	...	...	...	...	...	...	...	...
Other sectors	4 644 . .	...	...	...	...	...	...	...	...
Liabilities	4 652 . .	...	...	...	...	...	...	...	...
Equity securities	4 660 . .	...	...	...	...	...	...	...	...
Banks	4 663 . .	...	...	...	...	...	...	...	...
Other sectors	4 664 . .	...	...	...	...	...	...	...	...
Debt securities	4 669 . .	...	...	...	...	...	...	...	...
Bonds and notes	4 670 . .	...	...	...	...	...	...	...	...
Monetary authorities	4 671 . .	...	...	...	...	...	...	...	...
General government	4 672 . .	...	...	...	...	...	...	...	...
Banks	4 673 . .	...	...	...	...	...	...	...	...
Other sectors	4 674 . .	...	...	...	...	...	...	...	...
Money market instruments	4 680 . .	...	...	...	...	...	...	...	...
Monetary authorities	4 681 . .	...	...	...	...	...	...	...	...
General government	4 682 . .	...	...	...	...	...	...	...	...
Banks	4 683 . .	...	...	...	...	...	...	...	...
Other sectors	4 684 . .	...	...	...	...	...	...	...	...
Financial derivatives	4 690 . .	...	...	...	...	...	...	...	...
Monetary authorities	4 691 . .	...	...	...	...	...	...	...	...
General government	4 692 . .	...	...	...	...	...	...	...	...
Banks	4 693 . .	...	...	...	...	...	...	...	...
Other sectors	4 694 . .	...	...	...	...	...	...	...	...

Table 2 (Concluded). STANDARD PRESENTATION, 1988–95
(Millions of U.S. dollars)

	Code	1988	1989	1990	1991	1992	1993	1994	1995
C. OTHER INVESTMENT	4 700 . .	111.6	66.5	22.2	36.7	19.4	...	...	...
Assets	4 703 . .	...	...	...	...	...	...	...	...
Trade credits	4 706 . .	...	...	...	...	...	...	...	...
General government: long-term	4 708 . .	...	...	...	...	...	...	...	...
General government: short-term	4 709 . .	...	...	...	...	...	...	...	...
Other sectors: long-term	4 711 . .	...	...	...	...	...	...	...	...
Other sectors: short-term	4 712 . .	...	...	...	...	...	...	...	...
Loans	4 714 . .	...	...	...	...	...	...	...	...
Monetary authorities: long-term	4 717 . .	...	...	...	...	...	...	...	...
Monetary authorities: short-term	4 718 . .	...	...	...	...	...	...	...	...
General government: long-term	4 720 . .	...	...	...	...	...	...	...	...
General government: short-term	4 721 . .	...	...	...	...	...	...	...	...
Banks: long-term	4 723 . .	...	...	...	...	...	...	...	...
Banks: short-term	4 724 . .	...	...	...	...	...	...	...	...
Other sectors: long-term	4 726 . .	...	...	...	...	...	...	...	...
Other sectors: short-term	4 727 . .	...	...	...	...	...	...	...	...
Currency and deposits	4 730 . .	...	...	...	...	...	...	...	...
Monetary authorities	4 731 . .	...	...	...	...	...	...	...	...
General government	4 732 . .	...	...	...	...	...	...	...	...
Banks	4 733 . .	...	...	...	...	...	...	...	...
Other sectors	4 734 . .	...	...	...	...	...	...	...	...
Other assets	4 736 . .	...	...	...	...	...	...	...	...
Monetary authorities: long-term	4 738 . .	...	...	...	...	...	...	...	...
Monetary authorities: short-term	4 739 . .	...	...	...	...	...	...	...	...
General government: long-term	4 741 . .	...	...	...	...	...	...	...	...
General government: short-term	4 742 . .	...	...	...	...	...	...	...	...
Banks: long-term	4 744 . .	...	...	...	...	...	...	...	...
Banks: short-term	4 745 . .	...	...	...	...	...	...	...	...
Other sectors: long-term	4 747 . .	...	...	...	...	...	...	...	...
Other sectors: short-term	4 748 . .	...	...	...	...	...	...	...	...
Liabilities	4 753 . .	**111.6**	**66.5**	**22.2**	**36.7**	**19.4**	...	...	...
Trade credits	4 756 . .	–37.3	–57.2	–59.3	–15.0	–9.5	...	...	...
General government: long-term	4 758 . .	–37.3	–57.2	–59.3	–15.0	–9.5	...	...	...
General government: short-term	4 759 . .	...	...	...	...	...	...	...	...
Other sectors: long-term	4 761 . .	...	...	...	...	...	...	...	...
Other sectors: short-term	4 762 . .	...	...	...	...	...	...	...	...
Loans	4 764 . .	152.1	124.2	83.3	54.5	29.7	...	...	...
Use of Fund credit and loans from the Fund	4 766 . .	–28.1	–7.7	–2.4	–.3	...	...	...	...
Monetary authorities: other long-term	4 767 . .	...	...	...	...	...	...	...	...
Monetary authorities: short-term	4 768 . .	...	...	...	...	...	...	...	...
General government: long-term	4 770 . .	188.4	132.2	89.3	54.0	57.0	...	...	...
General government: short-term	4 771 . .	–8.2	–.3	–3.6	.8	–27.3	...	...	...
Banks: long-term	4 773 . .	...	...	...	...	...	...	...	...
Banks: short-term	4 774 . .	...	...	...	...	...	...	...	...
Other sectors: long-term	4 776 . .	...	...	...	...	...	...	...	...
Other sectors: short-term	4 777 . .	...	...	...	...	...	...	...	...
Currency and deposits	4 780 . .	...	...	...	...	...	...	...	...
Monetary authorities	4 781 . .	...	...	...	...	...	...	...	...
General government	4 782 . .	...	...	...	...	...	...	...	...
Banks	4 783 . .	...	...	...	...	...	...	...	...
Other sectors	4 784 . .	...	...	...	...	...	...	...	...
Other liabilities	4 786 . .	–3.3	–.6	–1.8	–2.8	–.7	...	...	...
Monetary authorities: long-term	4 788 . .	...	...	...	...	...	...	...	...
Monetary authorities: short-term	4 789 . .	–3.3	–.6	–1.8	–2.8	–.7	...	...	...
General government: long-term	4 791 . .	...	...	...	...	...	...	...	...
General government: short-term	4 792 . .	...	...	...	...	...	...	...	...
Banks: long-term	4 794 . .	...	...	...	...	...	...	...	...
Banks: short-term	4 795 . .	...	...	...	...	...	...	...	...
Other sectors: long-term	4 797 . .	...	...	...	...	...	...	...	...
Other sectors: short-term	4 798 . .	...	...	...	...	...	...	...	...
D. RESERVE ASSETS	4 800 . .	–52.4	–142.9	–6.3	46.6	–94.3	...	...	...
Monetary gold	4 810 . .	...	...	...	...	...	...	...	...
Special drawing rights	4 820 . .	...	–.5	–.1	.6	.1	...	...	...
Reserve position in the Fund	4 830 . .	...	...	...	...	...	...	...	...
Foreign exchange	4 840 . .	–52.3	–142.5	–6.2	46.0	–94.5	...	...	...
Other claims	4 880 . .	...	...	...	...	...	...	...	...
NET ERRORS AND OMISSIONS	4 998 . .	**116.7**	**52.6**	**21.4**	**–53.9**	**17.7**	...	...	...

Part 3 of the *Yearbook* contains descriptions of the methodologies, compilation practices, and sources used to compile these data.

Table 1. ANALYTIC PRESENTATION, 1988–95
(Millions of U.S. dollars)

	Code	1988	1989	1990	1991	1992	1993	1994	1995
A. Current Account [1]	4 993 Y.	**. . .**	**. . .**	**23.2**	**129.0**	**84.6**	**120.9**	**169.2**	**50.0**
Goods: exports f.o.b.	2 100 . .	. . .	. . .	1,085.8	1,213.9	1,326.9	1,279.4	1,336.7	1,369.1
Goods: imports f.o.b.	3 100 . .	. . .	. . .	-1,117.8	-1,119.8	-1,262.5	-1,212.2	-1,279.0	-1,467.1
Balance on Goods	4 100 . .	. . .	. . .	*-32.0*	*94.1*	*64.4*	*67.3*	*57.8*	*-98.1*
Services: credit	2 200 . .	. . .	. . .	136.0	148.2	172.3	235.7	254.8	297.4
Services: debit	3 200 . .	. . .	. . .	-364.2	-480.6	-529.0	-497.6	-455.4	-466.8
Balance on Goods and Services	4 991 . .	. . .	. . .	*-260.2*	*-238.4*	*-292.4*	*-194.6*	*-142.9*	*-267.5*
Income: credit	2 300 . .	. . .	. . .	183.6	243.4	202.3	223.9	235.8	232.9
Income: debit	3 300 . .	. . .	. . .	-150.3	-150.0	-163.8	-147.1	-129.0	-148.5
Balance on Goods, Services, and Income	4 992 . .	. . .	. . .	*-226.9*	*-145.0*	*-253.9*	*-117.9*	*-36.0*	*-183.1*
Current transfers: credit	2 379 Y.	. . .	. . .	375.8	398.1	476.7	371.1	346.6	390.0
Current transfers: debit	3 379 . .	. . .	. . .	-125.8	-124.1	-138.3	-132.3	-141.3	-156.9
B. Capital Account [1]	4 994 Y.	**. . .**	**. . .**	**42.6**	**29.2**	**32.4**	**27.3**	**43.3**	**43.6**
Capital account: credit	2 994 Y.	. . .	. . .	46.5	32.8	32.4	27.3	43.3	43.6
Capital account: debit	3 994 . .	. . .	. . .	-3.9	-3.6	. . .	. . .	. . .	. . .
Total, Groups A Plus B	4 010 . .	. . .	. . .	*65.8*	*158.2*	*116.9*	*148.2*	*212.5*	*93.6*
C. Financial Account [1]	4 995 X.	**. . .**	**. . .**	**-202.7**	**-187.4**	**-104.8**	**-60.2**	**-169.5**	**-79.0**
Direct investment abroad	4 505 . .	. . .	. . .	-1.4	-6.4	1.6	-10.6	-3.5	-6.1
Direct investment in Namibia	4 555 Y.	. . .	. . .	29.6	120.4	104.2	38.6	51.5	47.1
Portfolio investment assets	4 602 . .	. . .	. . .	-4.6	-10.7	.9	15.5	-19.4	-2.6
Equity securities	4 610 . .	. . .	. . .	-8.9	-12.4	-6.9	-4.9	-5.0	-8.3
Debt securities	4 619 . .	. . .	. . .	4.4	1.7	7.8	20.4	-14.5	5.7
Portfolio investment liabilities	4 652 Y.	. . .	. . .	15.5	-15.0	24.5	60.1	55.8	107.6
Equity securities	4 660 Y.	. . .	. . .	. . .	-4.1	6.0	1.1	28.5	43.6
Debt securities	4 669 Y.	. . .	. . .	15.5	-10.9	18.5	59.1	27.3	64.0
Other investment assets	4 703 . .	. . .	. . .	-328.4	-269.3	-219.5	-193.5	-301.8	-280.4
Monetary authorities	4 703 . A	. . .	. . .	. . .	. . .	. . .	. . .	. . .	. . .
General government	4 703 . B	. . .	. . .	-105.6	94.7	-6.0	-9.4	9.5	-1.4
Banks	4 703 . C	. . .	. . .	-7.6	-86.8	88.8	44.5	-1.2	14.9
Other sectors	4 703 . D	. . .	. . .	-215.2	-277.2	-302.3	-228.6	-310.2	-293.9
Other investment liabilities	4 753 X.	. . .	. . .	86.6	-6.5	-16.4	29.7	48.1	55.4
Monetary authorities	4 753 XA	. . .	. . .	. . .	. . .	4.0	18.0	28.3	17.6
General government	4 753 YB	. . .	. . .	38.4	39.8	3.5	18.5	5.9	15.7
Banks	4 753 YC	. . .	. . .	30.1	-66.0	-9.9	19.9	63.8	24.8
Other sectors	4 753 YD	. . .	. . .	18.1	19.7	-14.0	-26.7	-50.0	-2.8
Total, Groups A Through C	4 020 . .	. . .	. . .	*-136.9*	*-29.2*	*12.2*	*88.0*	*42.9*	*14.6*
D. Net Errors and Omissions	4 998 . .	**. . .**	**. . .**	**173.7**	**16.8**	**-18.7**	**3.3**	**32.0**	**14.5**
Total, Groups A Through D	4 030 . .	. . .	. . .	*36.8*	*-12.4*	*-6.6*	*91.3*	*75.0*	*29.1*
E. Reserves and Related Items	4 040 . .	**. . .**	**. . .**	**-36.8**	**12.4**	**6.6**	**-91.3**	**-75.0**	**-29.1**
Reserve assets	4 800 . .	. . .	. . .	-36.8	12.4	6.6	-91.3	-75.0	-29.1
Use of Fund credit and loans	4 766 . .	. . .	. . .	. . .	. . .	. . .	. . .	. . .	. . .
Liabilities constituting foreign authorities' reserves	4 900 . .	. . .	. . .	. . .	. . .	. . .	. . .	. . .	. . .
Exceptional financing	4 920 . .	. . .	. . .	. . .	. . .	. . .	. . .	. . .	. . .
Conversion rates: Namibia dollars per U.S. dollar	0 101 . .	**2.2735**	**2.6227**	**2.5873**	**2.7613**	**2.8520**	**3.2677**	**3.5508**	**3.6271**

[1] Excludes components that have been classified in the categories of Group E.

Table 2. STANDARD PRESENTATION, 1988–95
(Millions of U.S. dollars)

	Code		1988	1989	1990	1991	1992	1993	1994	1995
CURRENT ACCOUNT	4 993	. .	**. . .**	**. . .**	**23.2**	**129.0**	**84.6**	**120.9**	**169.2**	**50.0**
A. GOODS	4 100	. .	. . .	. . .	–32.0	94.1	64.4	67.3	57.8	–98.1
Credit	2 100	. .	**. . .**	**. . .**	**1,085.8**	**1,213.9**	**1,326.9**	**1,279.4**	**1,336.7**	**1,369.1**
General merchandise: exports f.o.b.	2 110	. .	. . .	. . .	1,085.8	1,213.9	1,326.9	1,279.4	1,336.7	1,369.1
Goods for processing: exports f.o.b.	2 150	. .	. . .	. . .	. . .	. . .	. . .	. . .	. . .	. . .
Repairs on goods	2 160	. .	. . .	. . .	. . .	. . .	. . .	. . .	. . .	. . .
Goods procured in ports by carriers	2 170	. .	. . .	. . .	. . .	. . .	. . .	. . .	. . .	. . .
Nonmonetary gold	2 180	. .	. . .	. . .	. . .	. . .	. . .	. . .	. . .	. . .
Debit	3 100	. .	**. . .**	**. . .**	**–1,117.8**	**–1,119.8**	**–1,262.5**	**–1,212.2**	**–1,279.0**	**–1,467.1**
General merchandise: imports f.o.b.	3 110	. .	. . .	. . .	–1,117.8	–1,119.8	–1,262.5	–1,212.2	–1,279.0	–1,467.1
Goods for processing: imports f.o.b.	3 150	. .	. . .	. . .	. . .	. . .	. . .	. . .	. . .	. . .
Repairs on goods	3 160	. .	. . .	. . .	. . .	. . .	. . .	. . .	. . .	. . .
Goods procured in ports by carriers	3 170	. .	. . .	. . .	. . .	. . .	. . .	. . .	. . .	. . .
Nonmonetary gold	3 180	. .	. . .	. . .	. . .	. . .	. . .	. . .	. . .	. . .
B. SERVICES	4 200	. .	. . .	. . .	–228.2	–332.5	–356.8	–261.9	–200.7	–169.5
Total credit	2 200	. .	. . .	. . .	*136.0*	*148.2*	*172.3*	*235.7*	*254.8*	*297.4*
Total debit	3 200	. .	. . .	. . .	*–364.2*	*–480.6*	*–529.0*	*–497.6*	*–455.4*	*–466.8*
Transportation services, credit	2 205	. .	**. . .**	**. . .**	**. . .**	**. . .**	**. . .**	**. . .**	**. . .**	**. . .**
Passenger	2 205	BA	. . .	. . .	. . .	. . .	. . .	. . .	. . .	. . .
Freight	2 205	BB	. . .	. . .	. . .	. . .	. . .	. . .	. . .	. . .
Other	2 205	BC	. . .	. . .	. . .	. . .	. . .	. . .	. . .	. . .
Sea transport, passenger	2 207	. .	. . .	. . .	. . .	. . .	. . .	. . .	. . .	. . .
Sea transport, freight	2 208	. .	. . .	. . .	. . .	. . .	. . .	. . .	. . .	. . .
Sea transport, other	2 209	. .	. . .	. . .	. . .	. . .	. . .	. . .	. . .	. . .
Air transport, passenger	2 211	. .	. . .	. . .	. . .	. . .	. . .	. . .	. . .	. . .
Air transport, freight	2 212	. .	. . .	. . .	. . .	. . .	. . .	. . .	. . .	. . .
Air transport, other	2 213	. .	. . .	. . .	. . .	. . .	. . .	. . .	. . .	. . .
Other transport, passenger	2 215	. .	. . .	. . .	. . .	. . .	. . .	. . .	. . .	. . .
Other transport, freight	2 216	. .	. . .	. . .	. . .	. . .	. . .	. . .	. . .	. . .
Other transport, other	2 217	. .	. . .	. . .	. . .	. . .	. . .	. . .	. . .	. . .
Transportation services, debit	3 205	. .	**. . .**	**. . .**	**–94.8**	**–96.0**	**–115.3**	**–108.7**	**–116.9**	**–121.6**
Passenger	3 205	BA	. . .	. . .	. . .	. . .	. . .	. . .	. . .	. . .
Freight	3 205	BB	. . .	. . .	*–94.8*	*–96.0*	*–115.3*	*–108.7*	*–116.9*	*–121.6*
Other	3 205	BC	. . .	. . .	. . .	. . .	. . .	. . .	. . .	. . .
Sea transport, passenger	3 207	. .	. . .	. . .	. . .	. . .	. . .	. . .	. . .	. . .
Sea transport, freight	3 208	. .	. . .	. . .	. . .	. . .	. . .	. . .	. . .	. . .
Sea transport, other	3 209	. .	. . .	. . .	. . .	. . .	. . .	. . .	. . .	. . .
Air transport, passenger	3 211	. .	. . .	. . .	. . .	. . .	. . .	. . .	. . .	. . .
Air transport, freight	3 212	. .	. . .	. . .	. . .	. . .	. . .	. . .	. . .	. . .
Air transport, other	3 213	. .	. . .	. . .	. . .	. . .	. . .	. . .	. . .	. . .
Other transport, passenger	3 215	. .	. . .	. . .	. . .	. . .	. . .	. . .	. . .	. . .
Other transport, freight	3 216	. .	. . .	. . .	. . .	. . .	. . .	. . .	. . .	. . .
Other transport, other	3 217	. .	. . .	. . .	. . .	. . .	. . .	. . .	. . .	. . .
Travel, credit	2 236	. .	**. . .**	**. . .**	**89.7**	**103.7**	**132.0**	**200.2**	**220.8**	**262.6**
Business travel	2 237	. .	. . .	. . .	. . .	. . .	. . .	. . .	. . .	. . .
Personal travel	2 240	. .	. . .	. . .	. . .	. . .	. . .	. . .	. . .	. . .
Travel, debit	3 236	. .	**. . .**	**. . .**	**–63.0**	**–69.0**	**–72.5**	**–71.4**	**–73.6**	**–81.6**
Business travel	3 237	. .	. . .	. . .	. . .	. . .	. . .	. . .	. . .	. . .
Personal travel	3 240	. .	. . .	. . .	. . .	. . .	. . .	. . .	. . .	. . .
Other services, credit	2 200	BA	**. . .**	**. . .**	**46.3**	**44.4**	**40.3**	**35.5**	**34.0**	**34.8**
Communications	2 245	. .	. . .	. . .	5.4	5.2	7.6	8.2	8.6	9.0
Construction	2 249	. .	. . .	. . .	1.6	.4	1.1	.9	1.1	1.4
Insurance	2 253	. .	. . .	. . .	6.1	8.6	5.4	4.9	5.4	5.2
Financial	2 260	. .	. . .	. . .	.1	.2	.2	.2	.3	.3
Computer and information	2 262	. .	. . .	. . .	.1	. . .	. . .	. . .	.2	.1
Royalties and licence fees	2 266	. .	. . .	. . .	1.3	.3	.4	.3	.3	.3
Other business services	2 268	. .	. . .	. . .	5.4	8.1	5.9	4.3	3.7	4.1
Personal, cultural, and recreational	2 287	. .	. . .	. . .	. . .	. . .	. . .	. . .	. . .	. . .
Government, n.i.e.	2 291	. .	. . .	. . .	26.2	21.7	19.7	16.6	14.3	14.3
Other services, debit	3 200	BA	**. . .**	**. . .**	**–206.4**	**–315.6**	**–341.2**	**–317.5**	**–264.9**	**–263.7**
Communications	3 245	. .	. . .	. . .	–.2	–.2	–.1	–.2	–.1	–.1
Construction	3 249	. .	. . .	. . .	–9.5	–10.3	–9.1	–8.3	–8.4	–15.2
Insurance	3 253	. .	. . .	. . .	–22.8	–26.2	–30.4	–26.3	–29.0	–35.6
Financial	3 260	. .	. . .	. . .	–.7	–1.3	–3.6	–4.4	–.6	–2.8
Computer and information	3 262	. .	. . .	. . .	–6.5	–9.2	–9.5	–14.8	–11.3	–10.6
Royalties and licence fees	3 266	. .	. . .	. . .	–2.5	–4.3	–3.5	–2.4	–3.9	–2.8
Other business services	3 268	. .	. . .	. . .	–151.5	–249.2	–268.4	–247.2	–198.5	–183.3
Personal, cultural, and recreational	3 287	. .	. . .	. . .	. . .	. . .	. . .	. . .	. . .	. . .
Government, n.i.e.	3 291	. .	. . .	. . .	–12.8	–14.9	–16.6	–14.0	–13.0	–13.4

Table 2 (Continued). STANDARD PRESENTATION, 1988–95
(Millions of U.S. dollars)

	Code		1988	1989	1990	1991	1992	1993	1994	1995
C. INCOME	4 300	. .	. . .	. . .	33.2	93.4	38.5	76.7	106.8	84.4
Total credit	2 300	. .	. . .	. . .	*183.6*	*243.4*	*202.3*	*223.9*	*235.8*	*232.9*
Total debit	3 300	. .	. . .	. . .	*–150.3*	*–150.0*	*–163.8*	*–147.1*	*–129.0*	*–148.5*
Compensation of employees, credit	2 310	. .	. . .	. . .	**4.9**	**5.8**	**6.9**	**6.5**	**6.3**	**6.6**
Compensation of employees, debit	3 310	. .	. . .	. . .	**–22.6**	**–18.3**	**–12.7**	**–9.4**	**–6.1**	**–10.1**
Investment income, credit	2 320	. .	. . .	. . .	**178.6**	**237.6**	**195.4**	**217.4**	**229.5**	**226.3**
Direct investment income	2 330	. .	. . .	. . .	3.5	8.0	9.2	14.3	18.4	13.0
Dividends and distributed branch profits	2 332	. .	. . .	. . .	3.6	5.8	7.3	13.3	13.5	11.0
Reinvested earnings and undistributed branch profits	2 333	. .	. . .	. . .	–.2	2.2	1.9	1.0	4.8	1.9
Income on debt (interest)	2 334	. .	. . .	. . .	.2	. . .	. . .	. . .	.1	.1
Portfolio investment income	2 339	. .	. . .	. . .	19.1	13.1	15.0	12.6	10.2	11.1
Income on equity	2 340	. .	. . .	. . .	1.5	1.8	1.8	2.9	3.7	3.0
Income on bonds and notes	2 350	. .	. . .	. . .	17.6	11.3	13.3	9.6	6.5	8.1
Income on money market instruments and financial derivatives	2 360	. .	. . .	. . .	. . .	. . .	. . .	. . .	. . .	. . .
Other investment income	2 370	. .	. . .	. . .	156.1	216.5	171.2	190.5	200.9	202.2
Investment income, debit	3 320	. .	. . .	. . .	**–127.7**	**–131.7**	**–151.1**	**–137.8**	**–122.9**	**–138.4**
Direct investment income	3 330	. .	. . .	. . .	–66.7	–75.5	–126.3	–113.9	–94.4	–100.9
Dividends and distributed branch profits	3 332	. .	. . .	. . .	–107.6	–51.1	–69.4	–86.9	–58.8	–61.5
Reinvested earnings and undistributed branch profits	3 333	. .	. . .	. . .	43.5	–22.7	–56.3	–25.2	–34.5	–38.6
Income on debt (interest)	3 334	. .	. . .	. . .	–2.6	–1.6	–.6	–1.7	–1.1	–.8
Portfolio investment income	3 339	. .	. . .	. . .	–23.6	–34.0	–8.2	–8.8	–15.0	–20.4
Income on equity	3 340	. .	. . .	. . .	–6.1	. . .	. . .	. . .	. . .	. . .
Income on bonds and notes	3 350	. .	. . .	. . .	–17.5	–33.9	–8.1	–8.0	–14.7	–19.5
Income on money market instruments and financial derivatives	3 360	. .	. . .	. . .	. . .	–.1	. . .	–.8	–.3	–.8
Other investment income	3 370	. .	. . .	. . .	–37.4	–22.2	–16.6	–15.1	–13.5	–17.1
D. CURRENT TRANSFERS	4 379	. .	. . .	. . .	250.1	274.0	338.4	238.8	205.2	233.1
Credit	2 379	. .	. . .	. . .	**375.8**	**398.1**	**476.7**	**371.1**	**346.6**	**390.0**
General government	2 380	. .	. . .	. . .	337.4	360.8	416.8	338.0	321.8	366.3
Other sectors	2 390	. .	. . .	. . .	38.5	37.3	60.0	33.1	24.8	23.7
Workers' remittances	2 391	. .	. . .	. . .	6.2	6.9	8.1	7.7	8.4	8.8
Other current transfers	2 392	. .	. . .	. . .	32.3	30.4	51.9	25.4	16.3	14.9
Debit	3 379	. .	. . .	. . .	**–125.8**	**–124.1**	**–138.3**	**–132.3**	**–141.3**	**–156.9**
General government	3 380	. .	. . .	. . .	–112.6	–112.9	–127.8	–123.4	–132.6	–148.6
Other sectors	3 390	. .	. . .	. . .	–13.1	–11.2	–10.5	–8.9	–8.7	–8.3
Workers' remittances	3 391	. .	. . .	. . .	–8.5	–8.3	–7.7	–6.4	–5.6	–5.2
Other current transfers	3 392	. .	. . .	. . .	–4.6	–2.9	–2.8	–2.4	–3.1	–3.0
CAPITAL AND FINANCIAL ACCOUNT	4 996	. .	. . .	. . .	**–196.9**	**–145.7**	**–65.8**	**–124.2**	**–201.3**	**–64.4**
CAPITAL ACCOUNT	4 994	. .	. . .	. . .	**42.6**	**29.2**	**32.4**	**27.3**	**43.3**	**43.6**
Total credit	2 994	. .	. . .	. . .	*46.5*	*32.8*	*32.4*	*27.3*	*43.3*	*43.6*
Total debit	3 994	. .	. . .	. . .	*–3.9*	*–3.6*	. . .	. . .	. . .	. . .
Capital transfers, credit	2 400	. .	. . .	. . .	**46.5**	**32.8**	**32.4**	**27.3**	**43.3**	**43.6**
General government	2 401	. .	. . .	. . .	43.9	31.6	29.3	26.0	41.4	42.0
Debt forgiveness	2 402	. .	. . .	. . .	. . .	. . .	. . .	. . .	. . .	. . .
Other capital transfers	2 410	. .	. . .	. . .	43.9	31.6	29.3	26.0	41.4	42.0
Other sectors	2 430	. .	. . .	. . .	2.6	1.3	3.1	1.3	1.9	1.5
Migrants' transfers	2 431	. .	. . .	. . .	1.9	.7	.4	. . .	. . .	. . .
Debt forgiveness	2 432	. .	. . .	. . .	. . .	. . .	. . .	. . .	. . .	. . .
Other capital transfers	2 440	. .	. . .	. . .	.7	.5	2.7	1.3	1.9	1.5
Capital transfers, debit	3 400	. .	. . .	. . .	**–3.9**	**–3.6**	. . .	. . .	. . .	. . .
General government	3 401	. .	. . .	. . .	. . .	. . .	. . .	. . .	. . .	. . .
Debt forgiveness	3 402	. .	. . .	. . .	. . .	. . .	. . .	. . .	. . .	. . .
Other capital transfers	3 410	. .	. . .	. . .	. . .	. . .	. . .	. . .	. . .	. . .
Other sectors	3 430	. .	. . .	. . .	–3.9	–3.6	. . .	. . .	. . .	. . .
Migrants' transfers	3 431	. .	. . .	. . .	–3.9	–3.6	. . .	. . .	. . .	. . .
Debt forgiveness	3 432	. .	. . .	. . .	. . .	. . .	. . .	. . .	. . .	. . .
Other capital transfers	3 440	. .	. . .	. . .	. . .	. . .	. . .	. . .	. . .	. . .
Nonproduced nonfinancial assets, credit	2 480	. .	. . .	. . .	. . .	. . .	. . .	. . .	. . .	. . .
Nonproduced nonfinancial assets, debit	3 480	. .	. . .	. . .	. . .	. . .	. . .	. . .	. . .	. . .

Table 2 (Continued). STANDARD PRESENTATION, 1988–95
(Millions of U.S. dollars)

	Code		1988	1989	1990	1991	1992	1993	1994	1995
FINANCIAL ACCOUNT	4 995	. .	**. . .**	**. . .**	**–239.5**	**–174.9**	**–98.2**	**–151.5**	**–244.5**	**–108.0**
A. DIRECT INVESTMENT	4 500	. .	. . .	. . .	28.2	114.0	105.7	28.0	47.9	41.1
Direct investment abroad	4 505	. .	**. . .**	**. . .**	**–1.4**	**–6.4**	**1.6**	**–10.6**	**–3.5**	**–6.1**
Equity capital	4 510	. .	. . .	. . .	–.1	–.3	3.4	–1.2	.7	–1.4
Claims on affiliated enterprises	4 515	. .	. . .	. . .	. . .	. . .	. . .	. . .	. . .	. . .
Liabilities to affiliated enterprises	4 520	. .	. . .	. . .	. . .	. . .	. . .	. . .	. . .	. . .
Reinvested earnings	4 525	. .	. . .	. . .	.2	–2.2	–1.9	–1.0	–4.8	–1.9
Other capital	4 530	. .	. . .	. . .	–1.5	–4.0	. . .	–8.5	.6	–2.8
Claims on affiliated enterprises	4 535	. .	. . .	. . .	–1.5	–4.0	. . .	–8.5	.6	–2.8
Liabilities to affiliated enterprises	4 540	. .	. . .	. . .	. . .	. . .	. . .	. . .	. . .	. . .
Direct investment in Namibia	4 555	. .	**. . .**	**. . .**	**29.6**	**120.4**	**104.2**	**38.6**	**51.5**	**47.1**
Equity capital	4 560	. .	. . .	. . .	36.3	28.4	8.7	3.9	20.3	26.7
Claims on direct investors	4 565	. .	. . .	. . .	. . .	. . .	. . .	. . .	. . .	. . .
Liabilities to direct investors	4 570	. .	. . .	. . .	. . .	. . .	. . .	. . .	. . .	. . .
Reinvested earnings	4 575	. .	. . .	. . .	–43.5	22.7	56.3	25.2	34.5	38.6
Other capital	4 580	. .	. . .	. . .	36.8	69.3	39.2	9.6	–3.4	–18.2
Claims on direct investors	4 585	. .	. . .	. . .	. . .	. . .	. . .	. . .	. . .	. . .
Liabilities to direct investors	4 590	. .	. . .	. . .	. . .	. . .	. . .	. . .	. . .	. . .
B. PORTFOLIO INVESTMENT	4 600	. .	. . .	. . .	10.9	–25.7	25.4	75.6	36.3	105.0
Assets	4 602	. .	**. . .**	**. . .**	**–4.6**	**–10.7**	**.9**	**15.5**	**–19.4**	**–2.6**
Equity securities	4 610	. .	. . .	. . .	–8.9	–12.4	–6.9	–4.9	–5.0	–8.3
Monetary authorities	4 611	. .	. . .	. . .	. . .	. . .	. . .	. . .	. . .	. . .
General government	4 612	. .	. . .	. . .	–2.1	–2.4	–.1	2.9	–2.9	.1
Banks	4 613	. .	. . .	. . .	. . .	. . .	. . .	. . .	. . .	. . .
Other sectors	4 614	. .	. . .	. . .	–6.8	–10.0	–6.8	–7.7	–2.0	–8.4
Debt securities	4 619	. .	. . .	. . .	4.4	1.7	7.8	20.4	–14.5	5.7
Bonds and notes	4 620	. .	. . .	. . .	4.4	1.7	7.8	20.4	–14.5	5.7
Monetary authorities	4 621	. .	. . .	. . .	. . .	. . .	. . .	. . .	. . .	. . .
General government	4 622	. .	. . .	. . .	.2	.2	.2	.2	.2	.2
Banks	4 623	. .	. . .	. . .	.7	13.0	–12.3	12.0	1.4	. . .
Other sectors	4 624	. .	. . .	. . .	3.5	–11.5	20.0	8.2	–16.1	5.5
Money market instruments	4 630	. .	. . .	. . .	. . .	. . .	. . .	. . .	. . .	. . .
Monetary authorities	4 631	. .	. . .	. . .	. . .	. . .	. . .	. . .	. . .	. . .
General government	4 632	. .	. . .	. . .	. . .	. . .	. . .	. . .	. . .	. . .
Banks	4 633	. .	. . .	. . .	. . .	. . .	. . .	. . .	. . .	. . .
Other sectors	4 634	. .	. . .	. . .	. . .	. . .	. . .	. . .	. . .	. . .
Financial derivatives	4 640	. .	. . .	. . .	. . .	. . .	. . .	. . .	. . .	. . .
Monetary authorities	4 641	. .	. . .	. . .	. . .	. . .	. . .	. . .	. . .	. . .
General government	4 642	. .	. . .	. . .	. . .	. . .	. . .	. . .	. . .	. . .
Banks	4 643	. .	. . .	. . .	. . .	. . .	. . .	. . .	. . .	. . .
Other sectors	4 644	. .	. . .	. . .	. . .	. . .	. . .	. . .	. . .	. . .
Liabilities	4 652	. .	**. . .**	**. . .**	**15.5**	**–15.0**	**24.5**	**60.1**	**55.8**	**107.6**
Equity securities	4 660	. .	. . .	. . .	. . .	–4.1	6.0	1.1	28.5	43.6
Banks	4 663	. .	. . .	. . .	. . .	. . .	–.4	. . .	. . .	. . .
Other sectors	4 664	. .	. . .	. . .	. . .	–4.1	6.5	1.1	28.5	43.6
Debt securities	4 669	. .	. . .	. . .	15.5	–10.9	18.5	59.1	27.3	64.0
Bonds and notes	4 670	. .	. . .	. . .	15.5	–11.8	9.8	63.1	30.1	52.7
Monetary authorities	4 671	. .	. . .	. . .	. . .	. . .	. . .	. . .	. . .	. . .
General government	4 672	. .	. . .	. . .	15.5	–11.8	9.8	63.1	30.1	52.7
Banks	4 673	. .	. . .	. . .	. . .	. . .	. . .	. . .	. . .	. . .
Other sectors	4 674	. .	. . .	. . .	. . .	. . .	. . .	. . .	. . .	. . .
Money market instruments	4 680	. .	. . .	. . .	. . .	.9	8.7	–4.0	–2.9	11.4
Monetary authorities	4 681	. .	. . .	. . .	. . .	. . .	. . .	. . .	. . .	. . .
General government	4 682	. .	. . .	. . .	. . .	.9	8.7	–4.0	–2.9	11.4
Banks	4 683	. .	. . .	. . .	. . .	. . .	. . .	. . .	. . .	. . .
Other sectors	4 684	. .	. . .	. . .	. . .	. . .	. . .	. . .	. . .	. . .
Financial derivatives	4 690	. .	. . .	. . .	. . .	. . .	. . .	. . .	. . .	. . .
Monetary authorities	4 691	. .	. . .	. . .	. . .	. . .	. . .	. . .	. . .	. . .
General government	4 692	. .	. . .	. . .	. . .	. . .	. . .	. . .	. . .	. . .
Banks	4 693	. .	. . .	. . .	. . .	. . .	. . .	. . .	. . .	. . .
Other sectors	4 694	. .	. . .	. . .	. . .	. . .	. . .	. . .	. . .	. . .

Table 2 (Concluded). STANDARD PRESENTATION, 1988–95
(Millions of U.S. dollars)

	Code		1988	1989	1990	1991	1992	1993	1994	1995
C. OTHER INVESTMENT	4 700	. .	...	...	–241.8	–275.7	–235.9	–163.8	–253.7	–225.1
Assets	4 703	. .	**...**	**...**	**–328.4**	**–269.3**	**–219.5**	**–193.5**	**–301.8**	**–280.4**
Trade credits	4 706	. .	...	...	...	...	...	...	...	...
General government: long-term	4 708	. .	...	...	...	...	...	...	...	...
General government: short-term	4 709	. .	...	...	...	...	...	...	...	...
Other sectors: long-term	4 711	. .	...	...	...	...	...	...	...	...
Other sectors: short-term	4 712	. .	...	...	...	...	...	...	...	...
Loans	4 714	. .	...	...	...	...	...	...	...	...
Monetary authorities: long-term	4 717	. .	...	...	...	...	...	...	...	...
Monetary authorities: short-term	4 718	. .	...	...	...	...	...	...	...	...
General government: long-term	4 720	. .	...	...	...	...	...	...	...	...
General government: short-term	4 721	. .	...	...	...	...	...	...	...	...
Banks: long-term	4 723	. .	...	...	...	...	...	...	...	...
Banks: short-term	4 724	. .	...	...	...	...	...	...	...	...
Other sectors: long-term	4 726	. .	...	...	...	...	...	...	...	...
Other sectors: short-term	4 727	. .	...	...	...	...	...	...	...	...
Currency and deposits	4 730	. .	...	...	–26.3	–72.8	69.6	37.2	–14.6	7.2
Monetary authorities	4 731	. .	...	...	...	...	...	...	...	...
General government	4 732	. .	...	...	...	...	...	...	...	...
Banks	4 733	. .	...	...	–7.6	–86.8	88.8	44.5	–1.2	14.9
Other sectors	4 734	. .	...	...	–18.7	14.0	–19.1	–7.3	–13.3	–7.7
Other assets	4 736	. .	...	...	–302.2	–196.4	–289.1	–230.7	–287.3	–287.6
Monetary authorities: long-term	4 738	. .	...	...	...	...	...	...	...	...
Monetary authorities: short-term	4 739	. .	...	...	...	...	...	...	...	...
General government: long-term	4 741	. .	...	...	...	...	...	...	...	...
General government: short-term	4 742	. .	...	...	–105.6	94.7	–6.0	–9.4	9.5	–1.4
Banks: long-term	4 744	. .	...	...	...	...	...	...	...	...
Banks: short-term	4 745	. .	...	...	...	...	...	...	...	...
Other sectors: long-term	4 747	. .	...	...	–196.6	–291.1	–283.1	–221.3	–296.8	–286.2
Other sectors: short-term	4 748	. .	...	...	...	...	...	...	...	...
Liabilities	4 753	. .	**...**	**...**	**86.6**	**–6.5**	**–16.4**	**29.7**	**48.1**	**55.4**
Trade credits	4 756	. .	...	...	...	...	...	...	...	...
General government: long-term	4 758	. .	...	...	...	...	...	...	...	...
General government: short-term	4 759	. .	...	...	...	...	...	...	...	...
Other sectors: long-term	4 761	. .	...	...	...	...	...	...	...	...
Other sectors: short-term	4 762	. .	...	...	...	...	...	...	...	...
Loans	4 764	. .	...	...	38.4	39.8	3.5	18.5	5.9	15.7
Use of Fund credit and loans from the Fund	4 766	. .	...	...	...	...	...	...	...	...
Monetary authorities: other long-term	4 767	. .	...	...	...	...	...	...	...	...
Monetary authorities: short-term	4 768	. .	...	...	...	...	...	...	...	...
General government: long-term	4 770	. .	...	...	38.4	39.8	3.5	18.5	5.9	15.7
General government: short-term	4 771	. .	...	...	...	...	...	...	...	...
Banks: long-term	4 773	. .	...	...	...	...	...	...	...	...
Banks: short-term	4 774	. .	...	...	...	...	...	...	...	...
Other sectors: long-term	4 776	. .	...	...	...	...	...	...	...	...
Other sectors: short-term	4 777	. .	...	...	...	...	...	...	...	...
Currency and deposits	4 780	. .	...	...	30.0	–58.3	–4.8	20.4	62.6	30.1
Monetary authorities	4 781	. .	...	...	...	...	...	...	...	...
General government	4 782	. .	...	...	...	...	...	...	...	...
Banks	4 783	. .	...	...	30.0	–58.3	–4.8	20.4	62.6	30.1
Other sectors	4 784	. .	...	...	...	...	...	...	...	...
Other liabilities	4 786	. .	...	...	18.2	12.0	–15.1	–9.2	–20.5	9.6
Monetary authorities: long-term	4 788	. .	...	...	...	...	4.0	18.0	28.3	17.6
Monetary authorities: short-term	4 789	. .	...	...	...	...	...	...	...	...
General government: long-term	4 791	. .	...	...	...	...	...	...	...	...
General government: short-term	4 792	. .	...	...	...	...	...	...	...	...
Banks: long-term	4 794	. .	...	...	–5.8	–6.7	–3.8	–2.9	–4.1	–2.8
Banks: short-term	4 795	. .	...	...	5.9	–1.1	–1.3	2.4	5.3	–2.5
Other sectors: long-term	4 797	. .	...	...	5.0	15.1	–9.0	–48.2	–54.5	2.8
Other sectors: short-term	4 798	. .	...	...	13.1	4.6	–5.0	21.5	4.5	–5.5
D. RESERVE ASSETS	4 800	. .	...	...	–36.8	12.4	6.6	–91.3	–75.0	–29.1
Monetary gold	4 810	. .	...	...	...	...	...	...	...	...
Special drawing rights	4 820	. .	...	...	...	...	...	...	...	...
Reserve position in the Fund	4 830	. .	...	...	...	...	...	...	...	...
Foreign exchange	4 840	. .	...	...	–36.8	12.5	6.6	–91.3	–75.0	–29.1
Other claims	4 880	. .	...	...	...	...	...	...	...	...
NET ERRORS AND OMISSIONS	4 998	. .	**...**	**...**	**173.7**	**16.8**	**–18.7**	**3.3**	**32.0**	**14.5**

Part 3 of the *Yearbook* contains descriptions of the methodologies, compilation practices, and sources used to compile these data.

Table 3. INTERNATIONAL INVESTMENT POSITION (End–period stocks), 1988–95
(Millions of U.S. dollars)

	Code	1988	1989	1990	1991	1992	1993	1994	1995
ASSETS	8 995 C.	...	1,772.9	2,102.6	2,343.8	2,261.1	2,571.0	2,960.3	3,397.9
Direct investment abroad	8 505 . .	**...**	**64.3**	**79.6**	**98.1**	**81.6**	**82.4**	**92.6**	**100.1**
Equity capital and reinvested earnings	8 506 . .	...	56.8	60.1	76.2	62.2	58.3	66.6	73.5
Claims on affiliated enterprises	8 507 . .	...	...	...	...	...	...	...	...
Liabilities to affiliated enterprises	8 508 . .	...	...	...	...	...	...	...	...
Other capital	8 530 . .	...	7.5	19.5	21.9	19.3	24.1	26.0	26.6
Claims on affiliated enterprises	8 535 . .	...	...	...	...	...	...	...	...
Liabilities to affiliated enterprises	8 540 . .	...	...	...	...	...	...	...	...
Portfolio investment	8 602 . .	**...**	**160.9**	**161.2**	**167.3**	**145.1**	**118.0**	**126.1**	**132.1**
Equity securities	8 610 . .	...	23.7	29.7	45.2	43.6	45.6	52.8	60.9
Monetary authorities	8 611 . .	...	...	...	...	...	...	...	...
General government	8 612 . .	...	...	1.6	4.0	3.6	.6	.6	.5
Banks	8 613 . .	...	...	...	...	...	...	...	...
Other sectors	8 614 . .	...	...	28.1	41.2	40.0	45.0	52.2	60.3
Debt securities	8 619 . .	...	137.2	131.5	122.1	101.5	72.4	73.4	71.3
Bonds and notes	8 620 . .	...	137.2	131.5	122.1	101.5	72.4	73.4	71.3
Monetary authorities	8 621 . .	...	...	...	...	...	...	...	...
General government	8 622 . .	...	8.3	7.8	7.3	6.2	5.6	5.1	4.9
Banks	8 623 . .	...	20.5	19.5	5.1	16.0	2.9	1.4	4.1
Other sectors	8 624 . .	...	108.4	104.2	109.7	79.3	63.9	66.9	62.2
Money market instruments	8 630 . .	...	...	...	...	...	...	...	...
Monetary authorities	8 631 . .	...	...	...	...	...	...	...	...
General government	8 632 . .	...	...	...	...	...	...	...	...
Banks	8 633 . .	...	...	...	...	...	...	...	...
Other sectors	8 634 . .	...	...	...	...	...	...	...	...
Financial derivatives	8 640 . .	...	...	...	...	...	...	...	...
Monetary authorities	8 641 . .	...	...	...	...	...	...	...	...
General government	8 642 . .	...	...	...	...	...	...	...	...
Banks	8 643 . .	...	...	...	...	...	...	...	...
Other sectors	8 644 . .	...	...	...	...	...	...	...	...
Other investment	8 703 . .	**...**	**1,504.3**	**1,786.5**	**2,020.4**	**1,988.2**	**2,241.1**	**2,542.1**	**2,943.7**
Trade credits	8 706 . .	...	...	...	...	...	...	...	...
General government: long-term	8 708 . .	...	...	...	...	...	...	...	...
General government: short-term	8 709 . .	...	...	...	...	...	...	...	...
Other sectors: long-term	8 711 . .	...	...	...	...	...	...	...	...
Other sectors: short-term	8 712 . .	...	...	...	...	...	...	...	...
Loans	8 714 . .	...	...	...	...	...	...	...	...
Monetary authorities: long-term	8 717 . .	...	...	...	...	...	...	...	...
Monetary authorities: short-term	8 718 . .	...	...	...	...	...	...	...	...
General government: long-term	8 720 . .	...	...	...	...	...	...	...	...
General government: short-term	8 721 . .	...	...	...	...	...	...	...	...
Banks: long-term	8 723 . .	...	...	...	...	...	...	...	...
Banks: short-term	8 724 . .	...	...	...	...	...	...	...	...
Other sectors: long-term	8 726 . .	...	...	...	...	...	...	...	...
Other sectors: short-term	8 727 . .	...	...	...	...	...	...	...	...
Currency and deposits	8 730 . .	...	137.6	136.2	216.2	114.6	62.1	61.2	105.3
Monetary authorities	8 731 . .	...	...	...	...	...	...	...	...
General government	8 732 . .	...	...	...	...	...	...	...	...
Banks	8 733 . .	...	129.7	128.4	208.2	106.8	54.5	53.3	97.1
Other sectors	8 734 . .	...	7.9	7.8	8.0	7.9	7.7	7.9	8.2
Other assets	8 736 . .	...	1,366.7	1,650.3	1,804.2	1,873.6	2,179.0	2,480.9	2,838.4
Monetary authorities: long-term	8 738 . .	...	...	...	...	...	...	...	...
Monetary authorities: short-term	8 739 . .	...	...	...	...	...	...	...	...
General government: long-term	8 741 . .	...	...	1.2	4.4	5.6	6.2	7.3	8.5
General government: short-term	8 742 . .	...	...	105.4	...	3.9	11.5	30.2	38.9
Banks: long-term	8 744 . .	...	...	...	...	...	...	...	...
Banks: short-term	8 745 . .	...	...	...	...	...	...	...	...
Other sectors: long-term	8 747 . .	...	1,272.9	1,408.8	1,689.7	1,753.4	2,052.4	2,325.7	2,665.1
Other sectors: short-term	8 748 . .	...	93.8	135.0	110.1	110.7	108.9	117.7	125.8
Reserve assets	8 800 . .	**...**	**43.4**	**75.3**	**58.0**	**46.2**	**129.5**	**199.5**	**222.1**
Monetary gold	8 810 . .	...	...	...	...	...	...	...	...
Special drawing rights	8 820 . .	...	...	...	...	...	...	...	...
Reserve position in the Fund	8 830 . .	...	...	...	...	...	...	...	...
Foreign exchange	8 840 . .	...	43.4	75.3	58.0	46.2	129.5	199.5	222.1
Other claims	8 880 . .	...	...	...	...	...	...	...	...

Table 3 (Continued). INTERNATIONAL INVESTMENT POSITION (End–period stocks), 1988–95
(Millions of U.S. dollars)

	Code	1988	1989	1990	1991	1992	1993	1994	1995
LIABILITIES	8 995 D.	...	2,667.6	2,845.7	2,824.2	2,811.0	2,363.2	2,511.1	2,659.1
Direct investment in Namibia	8 555 . .	**...**	**1,957.8**	**2,046.8**	**2,114.8**	**2,141.8**	**1,662.1**	**1,703.7**	**1,813.8**
Equity capital and reinvested earnings	8 556 . .	...	1,845.4	1,895.0	1,904.8	1,943.3	1,473.4	1,563.1	1,702.5
Claims on direct investors	8 557 . .	...	...	...	...	...	...	...	...
Liabilities to direct investors	8 558 . .	...	...	...	...	...	...	...	...
Other capital	8 580 . .	...	112.4	151.8	210.0	198.5	188.7	140.5	111.3
Claims on direct investors	8 585 . .	...	...	...	...	...	...	...	...
Liabilities to direct investors	8 590 . .	...	...	...	...	...	...	...	...
Portfolio investment	8 652 . .	**...**	**213.3**	**220.5**	**182.6**	**183.8**	**223.4**	**250.6**	**277.5**
Equity securities	8 660 . .	...	33.1	26.5	12.4	22.6	21.8	30.8	31.3
Banks	8 663 . .	...	...	...	...	...	...	...	...
Other sectors	8 664 . .	...	...	...	...	...	...	...	...
Debt securities	8 669 . .	...	180.2	194.0	170.2	161.2	201.6	219.8	246.2
Bonds and notes	8 670 . .	...	180.2	194.0	169.2	152.3	197.5	218.7	246.2
Monetary authorities	8 671 . .	...	...	...	...	...	...	...	...
General government	8 672 . .	...	180.2	194.0	169.2	152.3	197.5	218.7	246.2
Banks	8 673 . .	...	...	...	...	...	...	...	...
Other sectors	8 674 . .	...	...	...	...	...	...	...	...
Money market instruments	8 680 . .	...	...	...	1.1	8.8	4.1	1.1	...
Monetary authorities	8 681 . .	...	...	...	...	...	...	...	...
General government	8 682 . .	...	...	...	1.1	8.8	4.1	1.1	...
Banks	8 683 . .	...	...	...	...	...	...	...	...
Other sectors	8 684 . .	...	...	...	...	...	...	...	...
Financial derivatives	8 690 . .	...	...	...	...	...	...	...	...
Monetary authorities	8 691 . .	...	...	...	...	...	...	...	...
General government	8 692 . .	...	...	...	...	...	...	...	...
Banks	8 692 . .	...	...	...	...	...	...	...	...
Other sectors	8 694 . .	...	...	...	...	...	...	...	...
Other investment	8 753 . .	**...**	**496.4**	**578.3**	**526.8**	**485.4**	**477.7**	**556.8**	**567.8**
Trade credits	8 756 . .	...	...	...	...	...	...	...	...
General government: long-term	8 758 . .	...	...	...	...	...	...	...	...
General government: short-term	8 759 . .	...	...	...	...	...	...	...	...
Other sectors: long-term	8 761 . .	...	...	...	...	...	...	...	...
Other sectors: short-term	8 762 . .	...	...	...	...	...	...	...	...
Loans	8 764 . .	...	85.2	124.9	159.7	8.5	25.3	27.4	32.1
Use of Fund credit and loans from the Fund	8 766 . .	...	...	...	...	...	...	...	...
Monetary authorities: other long-term	8 767 . .	...	...	...	...	...	...	...	...
Monetary authorities: short-term	8 768 . .	...	...	...	...	...	...	...	...
General government: long-term	8 770 . .	...	85.2	124.9	159.7	8.5	25.3	27.4	32.1
General government: short-term	8 771 . .	...	...	...	...	...	...	...	...
Banks: long-term	8 773 . .	...	...	...	...	...	...	...	...
Banks: short-term	8 774 . .	...	...	...	...	...	...	...	...
Other sectors: long-term	8 776 . .	...	...	...	...	...	...	...	...
Other sectors: short-term	8 777 . .	...	...	...	...	...	...	...	...
Currency and deposits	8 780 . .	...	87.9	...	...	...	...	...	...
Monetary authorities	8 781 . .	...	...	...	...	...	...	...	...
General government	8 782 . .	...	...	...	...	...	...	...	...
Banks	8 783 . .	...	87.9	...	...	...	...	...	...
Other sectors	8 784 . .	...	...	...	...	...	...	...	...
Other liabilities	8 786 . .	...	323.3	453.5	367.1	476.9	452.4	529.4	535.7
Monetary authorities: long-term	8 788 . .	...	...	...	...	164.4	177.5	197.3	195.5
Monetary authorities: short-term	8 789 . .	...	...	...	...	...	...	...	...
General government: long-term	8 791 . .	...	...	...	...	...	...	...	...
General government: short-term	8 792 . .	...	...	...	...	...	...	...	...
Banks: long-term	8 794 . .	...	49.7	43.3	33.9	26.9	21.2	17.8	14.3
Banks: short-term	8 795 . .	...	...	122.9	55.4	43.9	61.5	121.6	128.6
Other sectors: long-term	8 797 . .	...	111.2	115.1	123.6	105.1	50.9	54.5	61.1
Other sectors: short-term	8 798 . .	...	162.5	172.1	154.2	136.6	141.3	138.3	136.3
NET INTERNATIONAL INVESTMENT POSITION	8 995 . .	**...**	**–894.7**	**–743.0**	**–480.5**	**–550.0**	**207.8**	**449.3**	**738.9**
Conversion rates: Namibia dollars per U.S. dollar (end of period)	0 102 . .	**2.3777**	**2.5360**	**2.5625**	**2.7430**	**3.0530**	**3.3975**	**3.5435**	**3.6475**

Table 1. ANALYTIC PRESENTATION, 1988–95
(Millions of U.S. dollars)

	Code	1988	1989	1990	1991	1992	1993	1994	1995
A. Current Account[1]	4 993 Y.	**-271.5**	**-243.3**	**-289.2**	**-304.4**	**-181.3**	**-222.5**	**-351.9**	**-356.4**
Goods: exports f.o.b	2 100 . .	193.8	161.2	217.9	274.5	376.3	397.0	368.7	349.9
Goods: imports f.o.b	3 100 . .	-664.9	-568.1	-666.6	-756.9	-752.1	-858.6	-1,158.9	-1,310.8
Balance on Goods	4 100 . .	*-471.1*	*-407.0*	*-448.7*	*-482.4*	*-375.8*	*-461.6*	*-790.3*	*-961.0*
Services: credit	2 200 . .	223.8	203.1	204.4	239.8	273.8	333.2	579.2	679.0
Services: debit	3 200 . .	-150.8	-147.7	-167.3	-183.9	-225.0	-251.8	-296.6	-313.3
Balance on Goods and Services	4 991 . .	*-398.1*	*-351.6*	*-411.7*	*-426.4*	*-327.0*	*-380.2*	*-507.6*	*-595.2*
Income: credit	2 300 . .	16.2	21.2	25.1	27.0	33.5	28.9	34.6	43.6
Income: debit	3 300 . .	-14.4	-10.5	-11.2	-16.2	-16.8	-23.7	-30.8	-34.9
Balance on Goods, Services, and Income	4 992 . .	*-396.3*	*-340.9*	*-397.8*	*-415.6*	*-310.3*	*-375.0*	*-503.9*	*-586.5*
Current transfers: credit	2 379 Y.	130.5	109.2	115.7	121.3	133.6	155.5	160.7	239.2
Current transfers: debit	3 379 . .	-5.6	-11.6	-7.1	-10.1	-4.6	-3.0	-8.7	-9.1
B. Capital Account[1]	4 994 Y.	**. . .**	**. . .**	**. . .**	**. . .**	**. . .**	**. . .**	**. . .**	**. . .**
Capital account: credit	2 994 Y.	. . .	. . .	. . .	. . .	. . .	. . .	. . .	. . .
Capital account: debit	3 994 . .	. . .	. . .	. . .	. . .	. . .	. . .	. . .	. . .
Total, Groups A Plus B	4 010 . .	*-271.5*	*-243.3*	*-289.2*	*-304.4*	*-181.3*	*-222.5*	*-351.9*	*-356.4*
C. Financial Account[1]	4 995 X.	**252.7**	**196.1**	**304.5**	**457.1**	**335.9**	**283.5**	**407.3**	**368.5**
Direct investment abroad	4 505 . .	. . .	. . .	. . .	. . .	. . .	. . .	. . .	. . .
Direct investment in Nepal	4 555 Y.	. . .	. . .	. . .	. . .	. . .	. . .	. . .	. . .
Portfolio investment assets	4 602 . .	. . .	. . .	. . .	. . .	. . .	. . .	. . .	. . .
Equity securities	4 610 . .	. . .	. . .	. . .	. . .	. . .	. . .	. . .	. . .
Debt securities	4 619 . .	. . .	. . .	. . .	. . .	. . .	. . .	. . .	. . .
Portfolio investment liabilities	4 652 Y.	. . .	. . .	. . .	. . .	. . .	. . .	. . .	. . .
Equity securities	4 660 Y.	. . .	. . .	. . .	. . .	. . .	. . .	. . .	. . .
Debt securities	4 669 Y.	. . .	. . .	. . .	. . .	. . .	. . .	. . .	. . .
Other investment assets	4 703 . .	38.5	-19.0	116.2	220.0	182.3	149.6	159.2	264.4
Monetary authorities	4 703 . A	. . .	. . .	. . .	. . .	. . .	. . .	. . .	. . .
General government	4 703 . B	. . .	. . .	. . .	. . .	. . .	. . .	. . .	. . .
Banks	4 703 . C	. . .	. . .	. . .	. . .	. . .	. . .	. . .	. . .
Other sectors	4 703 . D	38.5	-19.0	116.2	220.0	182.3	149.6	159.2	264.4
Other investment liabilities	4 753 X.	214.2	215.1	188.3	237.1	153.7	133.9	248.0	104.1
Monetary authorities	4 753 XA	-10.5	2.5	2.3	.3	1.5	-4.0	4.3	.1
General government	4 753 YB	196.8	210.3	175.7	214.6	130.1	125.7	237.5	106.8
Banks	4 753 YC	10.8	.6	6.8	12.5	22.1	11.7	5.4	-4.5
Other sectors	4 753 YD	17.0	1.7	3.6	9.8	. . .	.4	.8	1.7
Total, Groups A Through C	4 020 . .	*-18.8*	*-47.2*	*15.3*	*152.7*	*154.6*	*61.0*	*55.4*	*12.1*
D. Net Errors and Omissions	4 998 . .	**12.5**	**5.2**	**4.9**	**10.7**	**.8**	**4.6**	**7.1**	**2.8**
Total, Groups A Through D	4 030 . .	*-6.3*	*-42.1*	*20.2*	*163.4*	*155.4*	*65.6*	*62.5*	*15.0*
E. Reserves and Related Items	4 040 . .	**6.3**	**42.1**	**-20.2**	**-163.4**	**-155.4**	**-65.6**	**-62.5**	**-15.0**
Reserve assets	4 800 . .	-5.7	41.2	-8.1	-157.9	-162.3	-71.4	-65.0	-7.0
Use of Fund credit and loans	4 766 . .	12.0	.9	-12.2	-5.4	6.9	5.8	2.5	-8.0
Liabilities constituting foreign authorities' reserves	4 900 . .	. . .	. . .	. . .	. . .	. . .	. . .	. . .	. . .
Exceptional financing	4 920 . .	. . .	. . .	. . .	. . .	. . .	. . .	. . .	. . .
Conversion rates: Nepalese rupees per U.S. dollar	0 101 . .	**23.289**	**27.189**	**29.369**	**37.255**	**42.718**	**48.607**	**49.398**	**51.890**

[1] Excludes components that have been classified in the categories of Group E.

Table 2. STANDARD PRESENTATION, 1988–95
(Millions of U.S. dollars)

	Code	1988	1989	1990	1991	1992	1993	1994	1995
CURRENT ACCOUNT	4 993 . .	**–271.5**	**–243.3**	**–289.2**	**–304.4**	**–181.3**	**–222.5**	**–351.9**	**–356.4**
A. GOODS	4 100 . .	–471.1	–407.0	–448.7	–482.4	–375.8	–461.6	–790.3	–961.0
Credit	2 100 . .	**193.8**	**161.2**	**217.9**	**274.5**	**376.3**	**397.0**	**368.7**	**349.9**
General merchandise: exports f.o.b.	2 110 . .	193.8	161.2	217.9	274.5	376.3	397.0	368.7	349.9
Goods for processing: exports f.o.b.	2 150 . .	...	...	...	...	...	...	...	...
Repairs on goods	2 160 . .	...	...	...	...	...	...	...	...
Goods procured in ports by carriers	2 170 . .	...	...	...	...	...	...	...	...
Nonmonetary gold	2 180 . .	...	...	...	...	...	...	...	...
Debit	3 100 . .	**–664.9**	**–568.1**	**–666.6**	**–756.9**	**–752.1**	**–858.6**	**–1,158.9**	**–1,310.8**
General merchandise: imports f.o.b.	3 110 . .	–664.9	–568.1	–666.6	–756.9	–752.1	–858.6	–1,158.9	–1,310.8
Goods for processing: imports f.o.b.	3 150 . .	...	...	...	...	...	...	...	...
Repairs on goods	3 160 . .	...	...	...	...	...	...	...	...
Goods procured in ports by carriers	3 170 . .	...	...	...	...	...	...	...	...
Nonmonetary gold	3 180 . .	...	...	...	...	...	...	...	...
B. SERVICES	4 200 . .	73.0	55.4	37.0	55.9	48.8	81.4	282.6	365.8
Total credit	2 200 . .	*223.8*	*203.1*	*204.4*	*239.8*	*273.8*	*333.2*	*579.2*	*679.0*
Total debit	3 200 . .	*–150.8*	*–147.7*	*–167.3*	*–183.9*	*–225.0*	*–251.8*	*–296.6*	*–313.3*
Transportation services, credit	2 205 . .	**5.9**	**2.4**	**6.0**	**21.5**	**39.3**	**44.9**	**46.1**	**55.3**
Passenger	2 205 BA	*5.9*	*2.4*	*6.0*	*21.5*	*39.3*	*44.9*	*46.1*	*55.3*
Freight	2 205 BB	...	...	...	...	...	...	...	...
Other	2 205 BC	...	...	...	...	...	...	...	...
Sea transport, passenger	2 207 . .	...	...	...	...	...	...	...	...
Sea transport, freight	2 208 . .	...	...	...	...	...	...	...	...
Sea transport, other	2 209 . .	...	...	...	...	...	...	...	...
Air transport, passenger	2 211 . .	...	...	...	...	...	...	...	...
Air transport, freight	2 212 . .	...	...	...	...	...	...	...	...
Air transport, other	2 213 . .	...	...	...	...	...	...	...	...
Other transport, passenger	2 215 . .	...	...	...	...	...	...	...	...
Other transport, freight	2 216 . .	...	...	...	...	...	...	...	...
Other transport, other	2 217 . .	...	...	...	...	...	...	...	...
Transportation services, debit	3 205 . .	**–48.9**	**–39.2**	**–64.8**	**–83.4**	**–86.0**	**–78.3**	**–95.9**	**–110.7**
Passenger	3 205 BA	*–12.2*	*–4.2*	*–18.7*	*–30.7*	*–30.9*	*–15.3*	*–22.9*	*–31.1*
Freight	3 205 BB	*–36.8*	*–35.0*	*–46.2*	*–52.7*	*–55.1*	*–63.0*	*–73.0*	*–79.6*
Other	3 205 BC	...	...	...	...	...	...	...	...
Sea transport, passenger	3 207 . .	...	...	...	...	...	...	...	...
Sea transport, freight	3 208 . .	...	...	...	...	...	...	...	...
Sea transport, other	3 209 . .	...	...	...	...	...	...	...	...
Air transport, passenger	3 211 . .	...	...	...	...	...	...	...	...
Air transport, freight	3 212 . .	...	...	...	...	...	...	...	...
Air transport, other	3 213 . .	...	...	...	...	...	...	...	...
Other transport, passenger	3 215 . .	...	...	...	...	...	...	...	...
Other transport, freight	3 216 . .	...	...	...	...	...	...	...	...
Other transport, other	3 217 . .	...	...	...	...	...	...	...	...
Travel, credit	2 236 . .	**94.4**	**106.9**	**109.1**	**126.4**	**109.6**	**157.0**	**172.1**	**177.4**
Business travel	2 237 . .	...	...	...	...	...	...	...	...
Personal travel	2 240 . .	...	...	...	...	...	...	...	...
Travel, debit	3 236 . .	**–43.6**	**–47.8**	**–45.3**	**–38.1**	**–51.9**	**–92.9**	**–112.4**	**–136.3**
Business travel	3 237 . .	...	...	...	...	...	...	...	...
Personal travel	3 240 . .	...	...	...	...	...	...	...	...
Other services, credit	2 200 BA	**123.5**	**93.9**	**89.3**	**92.0**	**124.9**	**131.3**	**361.0**	**446.4**
Communications	2 245 . .	...	...	...	...	...	...	...	...
Construction	2 249 . .	...	...	...	...	...	...	...	...
Insurance	2 253 . .	...	...	...	...	...	...	...	...
Financial	2 260 . .	...	...	...	...	...	...	...	...
Computer and information	2 262 . .	...	...	...	...	...	...	...	...
Royalties and licence fees	2 266 . .	...	...	...	...	...	...	...	...
Other business services	2 268 . .	61.0	51.4	51.3	53.4	61.0	81.8	308.5	359.2
Personal, cultural, and recreational	2 287 . .	...	...	...	...	...	...	...	...
Government, n.i.e.	2 291 . .	62.5	42.5	38.0	38.6	63.9	49.5	52.5	87.1
Other services, debit	3 200 BA	**–58.3**	**–60.8**	**–57.2**	**–62.5**	**–87.1**	**–80.6**	**–88.3**	**–66.2**
Communications	3 245 . .	...	...	...	...	...	...	...	...
Construction	3 249 . .	...	...	...	...	...	...	...	...
Insurance	3 253 . .	–4.1	–3.9	–5.1	–5.9	–6.1	–7.0	–8.1	–9.2
Financial	3 260 . .	...	...	...	...	...	...	...	...
Computer and information	3 262 . .	...	...	...	...	...	...	...	...
Royalties and licence fees	3 266 . .	...	...	...	...	...	...	...	...
Other business services	3 268 . .	–47.5	–50.2	–43.7	–51.5	–76.0	–68.0	–73.1	–48.5
Personal, cultural, and recreational	3 287 . .	...	...	...	...	...	...	...	...
Government, n.i.e.	3 291 . .	–6.7	–6.7	–8.4	–5.2	–5.0	–5.6	–7.1	–8.5

Table 2 (Continued). STANDARD PRESENTATION, 1988–95
(Millions of U.S. dollars)

	Code	1988	1989	1990	1991	1992	1993	1994	1995
C. INCOME	4 300	1.8	10.7	13.9	10.8	16.7	5.2	3.8	8.7
Total credit	2 300	*16.2*	*21.2*	*25.1*	*27.0*	*33.5*	*28.9*	*34.6*	*43.6*
Total debit	3 300	*–14.4*	*–10.5*	*–11.2*	*–16.2*	*–16.8*	*–23.7*	*–30.8*	*–34.9*
Compensation of employees, credit	2 310	...	...	...	...	...	...	...	...
Compensation of employees, debit	3 310	...	...	...	...	...	...	...	...
Investment income, credit	2 320	**16.2**	**21.2**	**25.1**	**27.0**	**33.5**	**28.9**	**34.6**	**43.6**
Direct investment income	2 330	...	...	...	...	...	...	...	...
Dividends and distributed branch profits	2 332	...	...	...	...	...	...	...	...
Reinvested earnings and undistributed branch profits	2 333	...	...	...	...	...	...	...	...
Income on debt (interest)	2 334	...	...	...	...	...	...	...	...
Portfolio investment income	2 339	...	...	...	...	...	...	...	...
Income on equity	2 340	...	...	...	...	...	...	...	...
Income on bonds and notes	2 350	...	...	...	...	...	...	...	...
Income on money market instruments and financial derivatives	2 360	...	...	...	...	...	...	...	...
Other investment income	2 370	16.2	21.2	25.1	27.0	33.5	28.9	34.6	43.6
Investment income, debit	3 320	**–14.4**	**–10.5**	**–11.2**	**–16.2**	**–16.8**	**–23.7**	**–30.8**	**–34.9**
Direct investment income	3 330	...	...	...	...	...	...	...	...
Dividends and distributed branch profits	3 332	...	...	...	...	...	...	...	...
Reinvested earnings and undistributed branch profits	3 333	...	...	...	...	...	...	...	...
Income on debt (interest)	3 334	...	...	...	...	...	...	...	...
Portfolio investment income	3 339	...	...	...	...	...	...	...	...
Income on equity	3 340	...	...	...	...	...	...	...	...
Income on bonds and notes	3 350	...	...	...	...	...	...	...	...
Income on money market instruments and financial derivatives	3 360	...	...	...	...	...	...	...	...
Other investment income	3 370	–14.4	–10.5	–11.2	–16.2	–16.8	–23.7	–30.8	–34.9
D. CURRENT TRANSFERS	4 379	124.9	97.6	108.6	111.2	129.0	152.5	152.0	230.1
Credit	2 379	**130.5**	**109.2**	**115.7**	**121.3**	**133.6**	**155.5**	**160.7**	**239.2**
General government	2 380	64.9	49.0	48.2	57.6	83.3	78.2	80.9	145.8
Other sectors	2 390	65.6	60.2	67.5	63.8	50.3	77.3	79.8	93.4
Workers' remittances	2 391	...	...	...	...	...	...	...	...
Other current transfers	2 392	65.6	60.2	67.5	63.8	50.3	77.3	79.8	93.4
Debit	3 379	**–5.6**	**–11.6**	**–7.1**	**–10.1**	**–4.6**	**–3.0**	**–8.7**	**–9.1**
General government	3 380	–.1	...	...	...	...	...	...	...
Other sectors	3 390	–5.5	–11.6	–7.1	–10.1	–4.5	–3.0	–8.7	–9.1
Workers' remittances	3 391	...	...	...	...	...	...	...	...
Other current transfers	3 392	–5.5	–11.6	–7.1	–10.1	–4.5	–3.0	–8.7	–9.1
CAPITAL AND FINANCIAL ACCOUNT	4 996	**259.0**	**238.1**	**284.3**	**293.7**	**180.5**	**217.9**	**344.7**	**353.5**
CAPITAL ACCOUNT	4 994	...	...	...	...	...	...	...	...
Total credit	2 994	...	...	...	...	...	...	...	...
Total debit	3 994	...	...	...	...	...	...	...	...
Capital transfers, credit	2 400	...	...	...	...	...	...	...	...
General government	2 401	...	...	...	...	...	...	...	...
Debt forgiveness	2 402	...	...	...	...	...	...	...	...
Other capital transfers	2 410	...	...	...	...	...	...	...	...
Other sectors	2 430	...	...	...	...	...	...	...	...
Migrants' transfers	2 431	...	...	...	...	...	...	...	...
Debt forgiveness	2 432	...	...	...	...	...	...	...	...
Other capital transfers	2 440	...	...	...	...	...	...	...	...
Capital transfers, debit	3 400	...	...	...	...	...	...	...	...
General government	3 401	...	...	...	...	...	...	...	...
Debt forgiveness	3 402	...	...	...	...	...	...	...	...
Other capital transfers	3 410	...	...	...	...	...	...	...	...
Other sectors	3 430	...	...	...	...	...	...	...	...
Migrants' transfers	3 431	...	...	...	...	...	...	...	...
Debt forgiveness	3 432	...	...	...	...	...	...	...	...
Other capital transfers	3 440	...	...	...	...	...	...	...	...
Nonproduced nonfinancial assets, credit	2 480	...	...	...	...	...	...	...	...
Nonproduced nonfinancial assets, debit	3 480	...	...	...	...	...	...	...	...

Table 2 (Continued). STANDARD PRESENTATION, 1988–95
(Millions of U.S. dollars)

	Code		1988	1989	1990	1991	1992	1993	1994	1995
FINANCIAL ACCOUNT	4 995	. .	**259.0**	**238.1**	**284.3**	**293.7**	**180.5**	**217.9**	**344.7**	**353.5**
A. DIRECT INVESTMENT	4 500	. .	. . .	. . .	. . .	. . .	. . .	. . .	. . .	. . .
Direct investment abroad	4 505	. .	. . .	. . .	. . .	. . .	. . .	. . .	. . .	. . .
Equity capital	4 510	. .	. . .	. . .	. . .	. . .	. . .	. . .	. . .	. . .
Claims on affiliated enterprises	4 515	. .	. . .	. . .	. . .	. . .	. . .	. . .	. . .	. . .
Liabilities to affiliated enterprises	4 520	. .	. . .	. . .	. . .	. . .	. . .	. . .	. . .	. . .
Reinvested earnings	4 525	. .	. . .	. . .	. . .	. . .	. . .	. . .	. . .	. . .
Other capital	4 530	. .	. . .	. . .	. . .	. . .	. . .	. . .	. . .	. . .
Claims on affiliated enterprises	4 535	. .	. . .	. . .	. . .	. . .	. . .	. . .	. . .	. . .
Liabilities to affiliated enterprises	4 540	. .	. . .	. . .	. . .	. . .	. . .	. . .	. . .	. . .
Direct investment in Nepal	4 555	. .	. . .	. . .	. . .	. . .	. . .	. . .	. . .	. . .
Equity capital	4 560	. .	. . .	. . .	. . .	. . .	. . .	. . .	. . .	. . .
Claims on direct investors	4 565	. .	. . .	. . .	. . .	. . .	. . .	. . .	. . .	. . .
Liabilities to direct investors	4 570	. .	. . .	. . .	. . .	. . .	. . .	. . .	. . .	. . .
Reinvested earnings	4 575	. .	. . .	. . .	. . .	. . .	. . .	. . .	. . .	. . .
Other capital	4 580	. .	. . .	. . .	. . .	. . .	. . .	. . .	. . .	. . .
Claims on direct investors	4 585	. .	. . .	. . .	. . .	. . .	. . .	. . .	. . .	. . .
Liabilities to direct investors	4 590	. .	. . .	. . .	. . .	. . .	. . .	. . .	. . .	. . .
B. PORTFOLIO INVESTMENT	4 600	. .	. . .	. . .	. . .	. . .	. . .	. . .	. . .	. . .
Assets	4 602	. .	. . .	. . .	. . .	. . .	. . .	. . .	. . .	. . .
Equity securities	4 610	. .	. . .	. . .	. . .	. . .	. . .	. . .	. . .	. . .
Monetary authorities	4 611	. .	. . .	. . .	. . .	. . .	. . .	. . .	. . .	. . .
General government	4 612	. .	. . .	. . .	. . .	. . .	. . .	. . .	. . .	. . .
Banks	4 613	. .	. . .	. . .	. . .	. . .	. . .	. . .	. . .	. . .
Other sectors	4 614	. .	. . .	. . .	. . .	. . .	. . .	. . .	. . .	. . .
Debt securities	4 619	. .	. . .	. . .	. . .	. . .	. . .	. . .	. . .	. . .
Bonds and notes	4 620	. .	. . .	. . .	. . .	. . .	. . .	. . .	. . .	. . .
Monetary authorities	4 621	. .	. . .	. . .	. . .	. . .	. . .	. . .	. . .	. . .
General government	4 622	. .	. . .	. . .	. . .	. . .	. . .	. . .	. . .	. . .
Banks	4 623	. .	. . .	. . .	. . .	. . .	. . .	. . .	. . .	. . .
Other sectors	4 624	. .	. . .	. . .	. . .	. . .	. . .	. . .	. . .	. . .
Money market instruments	4 630	. .	. . .	. . .	. . .	. . .	. . .	. . .	. . .	. . .
Monetary authorities	4 631	. .	. . .	. . .	. . .	. . .	. . .	. . .	. . .	. . .
General government	4 632	. .	. . .	. . .	. . .	. . .	. . .	. . .	. . .	. . .
Banks	4 633	. .	. . .	. . .	. . .	. . .	. . .	. . .	. . .	. . .
Other sectors	4 634	. .	. . .	. . .	. . .	. . .	. . .	. . .	. . .	. . .
Financial derivatives	4 640	. .	. . .	. . .	. . .	. . .	. . .	. . .	. . .	. . .
Monetary authorities	4 641	. .	. . .	. . .	. . .	. . .	. . .	. . .	. . .	. . .
General government	4 642	. .	. . .	. . .	. . .	. . .	. . .	. . .	. . .	. . .
Banks	4 643	. .	. . .	. . .	. . .	. . .	. . .	. . .	. . .	. . .
Other sectors	4 644	. .	. . .	. . .	. . .	. . .	. . .	. . .	. . .	. . .
Liabilities	4 652	. .	. . .	. . .	. . .	. . .	. . .	. . .	. . .	. . .
Equity securities	4 660	. .	. . .	. . .	. . .	. . .	. . .	. . .	. . .	. . .
Banks	4 663	. .	. . .	. . .	. . .	. . .	. . .	. . .	. . .	. . .
Other sectors	4 664	. .	. . .	. . .	. . .	. . .	. . .	. . .	. . .	. . .
Debt securities	4 669	. .	. . .	. . .	. . .	. . .	. . .	. . .	. . .	. . .
Bonds and notes	4 670	. .	. . .	. . .	. . .	. . .	. . .	. . .	. . .	. . .
Monetary authorities	4 671	. .	. . .	. . .	. . .	. . .	. . .	. . .	. . .	. . .
General government	4 672	. .	. . .	. . .	. . .	. . .	. . .	. . .	. . .	. . .
Banks	4 673	. .	. . .	. . .	. . .	. . .	. . .	. . .	. . .	. . .
Other sectors	4 674	. .	. . .	. . .	. . .	. . .	. . .	. . .	. . .	. . .
Money market instruments	4 680	. .	. . .	. . .	. . .	. . .	. . .	. . .	. . .	. . .
Monetary authorities	4 681	. .	. . .	. . .	. . .	. . .	. . .	. . .	. . .	. . .
General government	4 682	. .	. . .	. . .	. . .	. . .	. . .	. . .	. . .	. . .
Banks	4 683	. .	. . .	. . .	. . .	. . .	. . .	. . .	. . .	. . .
Other sectors	4 684	. .	. . .	. . .	. . .	. . .	. . .	. . .	. . .	. . .
Financial derivatives	4 690	. .	. . .	. . .	. . .	. . .	. . .	. . .	. . .	. . .
Monetary authorities	4 691	. .	. . .	. . .	. . .	. . .	. . .	. . .	. . .	. . .
General government	4 692	. .	. . .	. . .	. . .	. . .	. . .	. . .	. . .	. . .
Banks	4 693	. .	. . .	. . .	. . .	. . .	. . .	. . .	. . .	. . .
Other sectors	4 694	. .	. . .	. . .	. . .	. . .	. . .	. . .	. . .	. . .

Table 2 (Concluded). STANDARD PRESENTATION, 1988–95
(Millions of U.S. dollars)

	Code	1988	1989	1990	1991	1992	1993	1994	1995
C. OTHER INVESTMENT	4 700	264.7	196.9	292.4	451.7	342.9	289.3	409.7	360.5
Assets	4 703	**38.5**	**–19.0**	**116.2**	**220.0**	**182.3**	**149.6**	**159.2**	**264.4**
Trade credits	4 706	...	...	...	...	...	...	...	...
General government: long-term	4 708	...	...	...	...	...	...	...	...
General government: short-term	4 709	...	...	...	...	...	...	...	...
Other sectors: long-term	4 711	...	...	...	...	...	...	...	...
Other sectors: short-term	4 712	...	...	...	...	...	...	...	...
Loans	4 714	38.5	–19.0	116.2	220.0	182.3	149.6	159.2	264.4
Monetary authorities: long-term	4 717	...	...	...	...	...	...	...	...
Monetary authorities: short-term	4 718	...	...	...	...	...	...	...	...
General government: long-term	4 720	...	...	...	...	...	...	...	...
General government: short-term	4 721	...	...	...	...	...	...	...	...
Banks: long-term	4 723	...	...	...	...	...	...	...	...
Banks: short-term	4 724	...	...	...	...	...	...	...	...
Other sectors: long-term	4 726	...	...	...	...	...	...	...	...
Other sectors: short-term	4 727	38.5	–19.0	116.2	220.0	182.3	149.6	159.2	264.4
Currency and deposits	4 730	...	...	...	...	...	...	...	...
Monetary authorities	4 731	...	...	...	...	...	...	...	...
General government	4 732	...	...	...	...	...	...	...	...
Banks	4 733	...	...	...	...	...	...	...	...
Other sectors	4 734	...	...	...	...	...	...	...	...
Other assets	4 736	...	...	...	...	...	...	...	...
Monetary authorities: long-term	4 738	...	...	...	...	...	...	...	...
Monetary authorities: short-term	4 739	...	...	...	...	...	...	...	...
General government: long-term	4 741	...	...	...	...	...	...	...	...
General government: short-term	4 742	...	...	...	...	...	...	...	...
Banks: long-term	4 744	...	...	...	...	...	...	...	...
Banks: short-term	4 745	...	...	...	...	...	...	...	...
Other sectors: long-term	4 747	...	...	...	...	...	...	...	...
Other sectors: short-term	4 748	...	...	...	...	...	...	...	...
Liabilities	4 753	**226.2**	**215.9**	**176.1**	**231.7**	**160.6**	**139.7**	**250.5**	**96.1**
Trade credits	4 756	...	...	...	...	...	...	...	...
General government: long-term	4 758	...	...	...	...	...	...	...	...
General government: short-term	4 759	...	...	...	...	...	...	...	...
Other sectors: long-term	4 761	...	...	...	...	...	...	...	...
Other sectors: short-term	4 762	...	...	...	...	...	...	...	...
Loans	4 764	225.0	212.5	166.5	218.2	137.1	131.6	240.0	98.9
Use of Fund credit and loans from the Fund	4 766	12.0	.9	–12.2	–5.4	6.9	5.8	2.5	–8.0
Monetary authorities: other long-term	4 767	...	...	...	...	...	...	...	...
Monetary authorities: short-term	4 768	...	...	...	...	...	...	...	...
General government: long-term	4 770	196.8	210.3	175.7	214.6	130.1	125.7	237.5	106.8
General government: short-term	4 771	...	...	...	...	...	...	...	...
Banks: long-term	4 773	...	...	...	...	...	...	...	...
Banks: short-term	4 774	...	...	...	...	...	...	...	...
Other sectors: long-term	4 776	16.1	1.3	3.1	9.1	...	...	...	...
Other sectors: short-term	4 777	...	...	...	...	...	...	...	...
Currency and deposits	4 780	10.8	.6	6.8	12.5	22.1	11.7	5.4	–4.5
Monetary authorities	4 781	...	...	...	...	...	...	...	...
General government	4 782	...	...	...	...	...	...	...	...
Banks	4 783	10.8	.6	6.8	12.5	22.1	11.7	5.4	–4.5
Other sectors	4 784	...	...	...	...	...	...	...	...
Other liabilities	4 786	–9.6	2.9	2.8	1.0	1.5	–3.5	5.1	1.7
Monetary authorities: long-term	4 788	...	...	...	...	...	...	...	...
Monetary authorities: short-term	4 789	–10.5	2.5	2.3	.3	1.5	–4.0	4.3	.1
General government: long-term	4 791	...	...	...	...	...	...	...	...
General government: short-term	4 792	...	...	...	...	...	...	...	...
Banks: long-term	4 794	...	...	...	...	...	...	...	...
Banks: short-term	4 795	...	...	...	...	...	...	...	...
Other sectors: long-term	4 797	...	...	...	...	...	...	...	...
Other sectors: short-term	4 798	.9	.4	.5	.7	...	.4	.8	1.7
D. RESERVE ASSETS	4 800	–5.7	41.2	–8.1	–157.9	–162.3	–71.4	–65.0	–7.0
Monetary gold	4 810	–.9	–.8	–.5	–2.3	–.1	–.8	–.1	–.8
Special drawing rights	4 820	...	–.1	.1	.1	–.1	.1	–.1	.1
Reserve position in the Fund	4 830	...	...	...	...	...	...	...	...
Foreign exchange	4 840	–4.8	42.1	–7.6	–155.7	–162.2	–70.7	–64.8	–6.3
Other claims	4 880	...	...	...	...	...	...	...	...
NET ERRORS AND OMISSIONS	4 998	**12.5**	**5.2**	**4.9**	**10.7**	**.8**	**4.6**	**7.1**	**2.8**

Table 1. ANALYTIC PRESENTATION, 1988–95
(Millions of U.S. dollars)

	Code			1988	1989	1990	1991	1992	1993	1994	1995
A. Current Account [1]	4	993	Y.	**7,132**	**10,013**	**9,207**	**7,729**	**7,332**	**12,249**	**15,008**	**16,191**
Goods: exports f.o.b	2	100	. .	103,389	108,155	130,002	130,759	137,330	127,123	140,230	173,302
Goods: imports f.o.b	3	100	. .	-93,317	-98,330	-117,944	-118,780	-125,024	-111,589	-124,392	-154,022
Balance on Goods	4	100	. .	*10,072*	*9,825*	*12,058*	*11,979*	*12,306*	*15,535*	*15,839*	*19,281*
Services: credit	2	200	. .	22,318	25,091	30,924	33,647	39,323	39,253	43,377	48,377
Services: debit	3	200	. .	-24,505	-25,775	-30,189	-34,341	-39,059	-38,578	-41,891	-46,317
Balance on Goods and Services	4	991	. .	*7,885*	*9,141*	*12,793*	*11,285*	*12,570*	*16,209*	*17,325*	*21,341*
Income: credit	2	300	. .	18,365	23,592	26,258	27,801	27,550	28,130	29,065	29,311
Income: debit	3	300	. .	-17,247	-20,781	-26,902	-27,226	-28,431	-27,603	-26,104	-28,122
Balance on Goods, Services, and Income	4	992	. .	*9,003*	*11,952*	*12,149*	*11,860*	*11,688*	*16,737*	*20,286*	*22,530*
Current transfers: credit	2	379	Y.	5,592	5,142	4,478	4,603	4,642	4,359	4,197	4,810
Current transfers: debit	3	379	. .	-7,464	-7,081	-7,421	-8,733	-8,997	-8,847	-9,474	-11,150
B. Capital Account [1]	4	994	Y.	**-198**	**-314**	**-301**	**-282**	**-631**	**-714**	**-981**	**-1,209**
Capital account: credit	2	994	Y.	293	299	314	343	369	577	560	729
Capital account: debit	3	994	. .	-490	-613	-615	-625	-1,000	-1,291	-1,540	-1,938
Total, Groups A Plus B	4	010	. .	*6,934*	*9,699*	*8,906*	*7,447*	*6,701*	*11,535*	*14,027*	*14,982*
C. Financial Account [1]	4	995	X.	**-668**	**-7,884**	**-4,635**	**-5,828**	**-7,421**	**-9,794**	**-8,547**	**-7,477**
Direct investment abroad	4	505	. .	-7,117	-14,893	-15,388	-13,565	-14,257	-11,708	-16,738	-12,060
Direct investment in the Netherlands	4	555	Y.	4,781	8,563	12,349	6,316	7,790	7,661	5,616	10,228
Portfolio investment assets	4	602	. .	-6,971	-724	-3,588	-4,792	-13,430	-10,438	-8,601	-15,285
Equity securities	4	610	. .	-1,642	-2,321	-2,521	-3,789	-2,703	-4,236	-6,625	-8,446
Debt securities	4	619	. .	-5,329	1,596	-1,067	-1,002	-10,727	-6,202	-1,977	-6,839
Portfolio investment liabilities	4	652	Y.	10,340	8,307	-1,378	4,218	3,825	12,346	617	4,638
Equity securities	4	660	Y.	832	2,211	-2,736	-1,214	-1,512	3,495	113	-972
Debt securities	4	669	Y.	9,508	6,096	1,358	5,432	5,337	8,852	503	5,610
Other investment assets	4	703	. .	-14,054	-27,911	-24,250	-5,773	-7,426	-11,306	7,598	-19,125
Monetary authorities	4	703	. A	. . .	-1	. . .	-1	. . .	. . .	. . .	. . .
General government	4	703	. B	-983	-658	-368	265	-324	-189	-44	10
Banks	4	703	. C	-11,337	-27,160	-22,212	-4,637	-4,200	-7,884	9,440	-16,859
Other sectors	4	703	. D	-1,734	-93	-1,670	-1,400	-2,903	-3,233	-1,799	-2,276
Other investment liabilities	4	753	X.	12,352	18,775	27,620	7,767	16,078	3,651	2,963	24,128
Monetary authorities	4	753	XA	-59	57	-9	430	-309	99	91	-135
General government	4	753	YB	239	209	-20	-185	-183	166	1,151	24
Banks	4	753	YC	10,962	12,984	20,914	3,940	17,023	3,122	-513	20,634
Other sectors	4	753	YD	1,210	5,525	6,736	3,583	-453	264	2,234	3,605
Total, Groups A Through C	4	020	. .	*6,266*	*1,815*	*4,271*	*1,619*	*-719*	*1,741*	*5,480*	*7,505*
D. Net Errors and Omissions	4	998	. .	**-4,698**	**-1,308**	**-4,003**	**-1,113**	**6,837**	**4,900**	**-4,980**	**-9,417**
Total, Groups A Through D	4	030	. .	*1,568*	*507*	*268*	*506*	*6,118*	*6,641*	*500*	*-1,912*
E. Reserves and Related Items	4	040	. .	**-1,568**	**-507**	**-268**	**-506**	**-6,118**	**-6,641**	**-500**	**1,912**
Reserve assets	4	800	. .	-1,568	-507	-268	-506	-6,118	-6,641	-500	1,912
Use of Fund credit and loans	4	766	. .	. . .	. . .	. . .	. . .	. . .	. . .	. . .	. . .
Liabilities constituting foreign authorities' reserves	4	900	. .	. . .	. . .	. . .	. . .	. . .	. . .	. . .	. . .
Exceptional financing	4	920	. .	. . .	. . .	. . .	. . .	. . .	. . .	. . .	. . .
Conversion rates: Netherlands guilders per U.S. dollar	0	101	. .	**1.9766**	**2.1207**	**1.8209**	**1.8697**	**1.7585**	**1.8573**	**1.8200**	**1.6057**

[1] Excludes components that have been classified in the categories of Group E.

Table 2. STANDARD PRESENTATION, 1988–95
(Millions of U.S. dollars)

	Code	1988	1989	1990	1991	1992	1993	1994	1995
CURRENT ACCOUNT	4 993 . .	**7,132**	**10,013**	**9,207**	**7,729**	**7,332**	**12,249**	**15,008**	**16,191**
A. GOODS	4 100 . .	10,072	9,825	12,058	11,979	12,306	15,535	15,839	19,281
Credit	2 100 . .	**103,389**	**108,155**	**130,002**	**130,759**	**137,330**	**127,123**	**140,230**	**173,302**
General merchandise: exports f.o.b.	2 110 . .	96,715	100,851	121,529	122,017	128,408	119,713	132,512	164,696
Goods for processing: exports f.o.b.	2 150 . .	4,846	5,684	6,851	7,570	7,830	6,283	6,346	6,636
Repairs on goods	2 160 . .	372	244	265	219	228	169	180	448
Goods procured in ports by carriers	2 170 . .	1,099	1,310	1,334	925	839	888	1,087	1,371
Nonmonetary gold	2 180 . .	357	66	24	28	25	71	104	152
Debit	3 100 . .	**–93,317**	**–98,330**	**–117,944**	**–118,780**	**–125,024**	**–111,589**	**–124,392**	**–154,022**
General merchandise: imports f.o.b.	3 110 . .	–88,922	–93,122	–111,685	–111,814	–117,761	–105,675	–118,169	–146,189
Goods for processing: imports f.o.b.	3 150 . .	–4,352	–5,168	–6,203	–6,895	–7,165	–5,820	–5,992	–6,364
Repairs on goods	3 160 . .	. . .	. . .	. . .	. . .	. . .	. . .	. . .	–221
Goods procured in ports by carriers	3 170 . .	. . .	. . .	. . .	. . .	. . .	. . .	. . .	–1,024
Nonmonetary gold	3 180 . .	–44	–40	–56	–71	–98	–93	–231	–224
B. SERVICES	4 200 . .	–2,188	–684	735	–694	264	675	1,486	2,061
Total credit	2 200 . .	*22,318*	*25,091*	*30,924*	*33,647*	*39,323*	*39,253*	*43,377*	*48,377*
Total debit	3 200 . .	*–24,505*	*–25,775*	*–30,189*	*–34,341*	*–39,059*	*–38,578*	*–41,891*	*–46,317*
Transportation services, credit	2 205 . .	**10,493**	**11,071**	**13,418**	**14,201**	**16,726**	**16,031**	**17,217**	**19,582**
Passenger	2 205 BA	*1,516*	*1,523*	*1,789*	*2,075*	*3,298*	*3,361*	*3,566*	*4,723*
Freight	2 205 BB	*6,344*	*6,785*	*8,172*	*8,620*	*9,576*	*8,996*	*9,635*	*10,698*
Other	2 205 BC	*2,633*	*2,763*	*3,457*	*3,506*	*3,852*	*3,674*	*4,016*	*4,161*
Sea transport, passenger	2 207 . .	14	16	17	14	15	13	15	16
Sea transport, freight	2 208 . .	3,508	3,763	4,220	4,192	4,424	4,106	4,485	4,845
Sea transport, other	2 209 . .	. . .	. . .	. . .	. . .	. . .	. . .	. . .	. . .
Air transport, passenger	2 211 . .	1,430	1,452	1,739	1,962	3,188	3,228	3,482	4,657
Air transport, freight	2 212 . .	357	362	434	490	796	807	871	1,165
Air transport, other	2 213 . .	. . .	. . .	. . .	. . .	. . .	. . .	. . .	. . .
Other transport, passenger	2 215 . .	73	55	33	98	95	121	69	50
Other transport, freight	2 216 . .	2,479	2,659	3,517	3,938	4,356	4,084	4,279	4,688
Other transport, other	2 217 . .	2,633	2,763	3,457	3,506	3,852	3,674	4,016	4,161
Transportation services, debit	3 205 . .	**–9,500**	**–9,840**	**–11,411**	**–11,874**	**–13,111**	**–13,029**	**–13,814**	**–14,236**
Passenger	3 205 BA	*–1,099*	*–1,154*	*–1,284*	*–1,451*	*–1,627*	*–1,588*	*–1,578*	*–2,286*
Freight	3 205 BB	*–7,360*	*–7,455*	*–8,449*	*–8,759*	*–9,137*	*–9,217*	*–9,748*	*–10,521*
Other	3 205 BC	*–1,040*	*–1,232*	*–1,678*	*–1,664*	*–2,347*	*–2,224*	*–2,487*	*–1,429*
Sea transport, passenger	3 207 . .	–45	–50	–54	–48	–59	–61	–82	–97
Sea transport, freight	3 208 . .	–6,035	–6,054	–6,736	–6,847	–7,104	–7,123	–7,530	–8,007
Sea transport, other	3 209 . .	. . .	. . .	. . .	. . .	. . .	. . .	. . .	. . .
Air transport, passenger	3 211 . .	–926	–996	–1,150	–1,230	–1,389	–1,307	–1,363	–2,081
Air transport, freight	3 212 . .	–103	–111	–128	–137	–154	–145	–151	–231
Air transport, other	3 213 . .	. . .	. . .	. . .	. . .	. . .	. . .	. . .	. . .
Other transport, passenger	3 215 . .	–128	–109	–80	–173	–179	–220	–133	–108
Other transport, freight	3 216 . .	–1,222	–1,289	–1,585	–1,775	–1,879	–1,949	–2,067	–2,283
Other transport, other	3 217 . .	–1,040	–1,232	–1,678	–1,664	–2,347	–2,224	–2,487	–1,429
Travel, credit	2 236 . .	**3,258**	**3,449**	**4,155**	**4,825**	**6,000**	**5,391**	**5,434**	**6,579**
Business travel	2 237 . .	. . .	. . .	. . .	. . .	. . .	. . .	. . .	. . .
Personal travel	2 240 . .	. . .	. . .	. . .	. . .	. . .	. . .	. . .	. . .
Travel, debit	3 236 . .	**–6,701**	**–6,461**	**–7,376**	**–8,149**	**–9,665**	**–8,917**	**–9,396**	**–11,670**
Business travel	3 237 . .	. . .	. . .	. . .	. . .	. . .	. . .	. . .	. . .
Personal travel	3 240 . .	. . .	. . .	. . .	. . .	. . .	. . .	. . .	. . .
Other services, credit	2 200 BA	**8,567**	**10,571**	**13,350**	**14,621**	**16,596**	**17,831**	**20,726**	**22,217**
Communications	2 245 . .	300	356	422	405	441	435	618	618
Construction	2 249 . .	1,073	1,701	1,711	2,058	1,682	2,099	3,435	3,272
Insurance	2 253 . .	. . .	. . .	. . .	. . .	. . .	. . .	. . .	157
Financial	2 260 . .	198	207	220	223	242	342	303	354
Computer and information	2 262 . .	. . .	. . .	. . .	. . .	. . .	. . .	. . .	618
Royalties and licence fees	2 266 . .	863	954	1,086	1,496	1,613	1,917	2,208	2,350
Other business services	2 268 . .	5,258	6,666	9,087	9,480	11,782	12,169	13,126	13,109
Personal, cultural, and recreational	2 287 . .	. . .	. . .	. . .	. . .	. . .	. . .	. . .	467
Government, n.i.e.	2 291 . .	874	687	824	958	837	868	1,037	1,272
Other services, debit	3 200 BA	**–8,305**	**–9,474**	**–11,401**	**–14,318**	**–16,283**	**–16,632**	**–18,681**	**–20,410**
Communications	3 245 . .	–309	–299	–327	–365	–395	–378	–417	–675
Construction	3 249 . .	–682	–841	–965	–1,301	–1,215	–1,124	–1,893	–1,618
Insurance	3 253 . .	–342	–339	55	–259	–417	–211	–525	–939
Financial	3 260 . .	–191	–201	–223	–227	–249	–263	–272	–415
Computer and information	3 262 . .	. . .	. . .	. . .	. . .	. . .	. . .	. . .	–534
Royalties and licence fees	3 266 . .	–1,412	–1,818	–1,751	–2,267	–2,308	–2,668	–2,668	–3,050
Other business services	3 268 . .	–4,868	–5,448	–7,477	–9,286	–11,047	–11,224	–11,919	–11,531
Personal, cultural, and recreational	3 287 . .	. . .	. . .	. . .	. . .	. . .	. . .	. . .	–498
Government, n.i.e.	3 291 . .	–500	–528	–713	–613	–652	–763	–988	–1,151

Table 2 (Continued). STANDARD PRESENTATION, 1988–95
(Millions of U.S. dollars)

	Code	1988	1989	1990	1991	1992	1993	1994	1995
C. INCOME	4 300 . .	1,119	2,811	–644	575	–882	527	2,961	1,189
Total credit	2 300 . .	*18,365*	*23,592*	*26,258*	*27,801*	*27,550*	*28,130*	*29,065*	*29,311*
Total debit	3 300 . .	*–17,247*	*–20,781*	*–26,902*	*–27,226*	*–28,431*	*–27,603*	*–26,104*	*–28,122*
Compensation of employees, credit	2 310 . .	**604**	**526**	**465**	**440**	**497**	**480**	**511**	**665**
Compensation of employees, debit	3 310 . .	**–606**	**–594**	**–620**	**–627**	**–943**	**–823**	**–758**	**–1,083**
Investment income, credit	2 320 . .	**17,761**	**23,066**	**25,793**	**27,361**	**27,053**	**27,650**	**28,554**	**28,646**
Direct investment income	2 330 . .	5,870	8,285	6,365	7,051	7,349	7,947	10,366	8,353
Dividends and distributed branch profits	2 332 . .	2,356	3,788	3,216	4,187	5,578	6,318	6,485	6,661
Reinvested earnings and undistributed branch profits	2 333 . .	2,747	3,439	1,689	1,266	87	282	2,396	. . .
Income on debt (interest)	2 334 . .	767	1,058	1,460	1,598	1,685	1,346	1,485	1,692
Portfolio investment income	2 339 . .	2,731	2,563	2,982	3,311	4,295	3,672	4,630	6,711
Income on equity	2 340 . .	444	422	523	641	906	953	1,006	1,502
Income on bonds and notes	2 350 . .	2,287	2,222	2,487	2,405	3,277	3,073	4,291	6,320
Income on money market instruments and financial derivatives	2 360 . .	. . .	–82	–27	265	112	–354	–667	–1,110
Other investment income	2 370 . .	9,160	12,219	16,445	16,999	15,409	16,032	13,558	13,582
Investment income, debit	3 320 . .	**–16,641**	**–20,187**	**–26,282**	**–26,599**	**–27,488**	**–26,780**	**–25,346**	**–27,039**
Direct investment income	3 330 . .	–4,877	–5,441	–7,098	–6,247	–6,610	–5,434	–6,437	–5,774
Dividends and distributed branch profits	3 332 . .	–3,340	–2,784	–2,763	–3,095	–4,375	–3,375	–3,935	–3,916
Reinvested earnings and undistributed branch profits	3 333 . .	–929	–1,814	–2,994	–1,523	–576	–340	–978	. . .
Income on debt (interest)	3 334 . .	–608	–843	–1,341	–1,629	–1,658	–1,718	–1,524	–1,859
Portfolio investment income	3 339 . .	–4,062	–4,033	–4,956	–5,508	–6,671	–6,728	–7,448	–9,864
Income on equity	3 340 . .	–1,709	–1,546	–1,976	–2,127	–2,309	–2,107	–1,944	–3,246
Income on bonds and notes	3 350 . .	–2,353	–2,487	–2,980	–3,381	–4,362	–4,620	–5,503	–6,617
Income on money market instruments and financial derivatives	3 360 . .	–1	. . .	. . .	. . .	. . .	–1	–1	. . .
Other investment income	3 370 . .	–7,702	–10,713	–14,229	–14,844	–14,208	–14,618	–11,462	–11,401
D. CURRENT TRANSFERS	4 379 . .	–1,871	–1,939	–2,943	–4,130	–4,355	–4,488	–5,278	–6,339
Credit	2 379 . .	**5,592**	**5,142**	**4,478**	**4,603**	**4,642**	**4,359**	**4,197**	**4,810**
General government	2 380 . .	4,931	4,396	3,655	3,698	3,678	3,389	3,056	3,558
Other sectors	2 390 . .	662	746	823	905	963	970	1,141	1,253
Workers' remittances	2 391 . .	. . .	. . .	. . .	. . .	. . .	. . .	. . .	. . .
Other current transfers	2 392 . .	662	746	823	905	963	970	1,141	1,253
Debit	3 379 . .	**–7,464**	**–7,081**	**–7,421**	**–8,733**	**–8,997**	**–8,847**	**–9,474**	**–11,150**
General government	3 380 . .	–6,123	–5,738	–5,814	–7,015	–7,057	–6,983	–7,292	–8,760
Other sectors	3 390 . .	–1,341	–1,343	–1,607	–1,718	–1,940	–1,864	–2,182	–2,390
Workers' remittances	3 391 . .	–273	–253	–301	–321	–363	–357	–403	–423
Other current transfers	3 392 . .	–1,068	–1,090	–1,305	–1,397	–1,577	–1,507	–1,779	–1,967
CAPITAL AND FINANCIAL ACCOUNT	4 996 . .	**–2,434**	**–8,705**	**–5,204**	**–6,616**	**–14,170**	**–17,149**	**–10,028**	**–6,774**
CAPITAL ACCOUNT	4 994 . .	**–198**	**–314**	**–301**	**–282**	**–631**	**–714**	**–981**	**–1,209**
Total credit	2 994 . .	*293*	*299*	*314*	*343*	*369*	*577*	*560*	*729*
Total debit	3 994 . .	*–490*	*–613*	*–615*	*–625*	*–1,000*	*–1,291*	*–1,540*	*–1,938*
Capital transfers, credit	2 400 . .	**293**	**299**	**314**	**343**	**369**	**577**	**560**	**729**
General government	2 401 . .	17	22	23	5	1	12	5	13
Debt forgiveness	2 402 . .	. . .	. . .	. . .	. . .	. . .	. . .	. . .	. . .
Other capital transfers	2 410 . .	. . .	. . .	. . .	. . .	. . .	. . .	. . .	. . .
Other sectors	2 430 . .	276	277	291	337	368	565	555	716
Migrants' transfers	2 431 . .	210	243	243	233	295	422	470	658
Debt forgiveness	2 432 . .	. . .	. . .	. . .	. . .	. . .	. . .	. . .	. . .
Other capital transfers	2 440 . .	66	34	48	105	72	143	84	59
Capital transfers, debit	3 400 . .	**–490**	**–613**	**–615**	**–625**	**–1,000**	**–1,291**	**–1,540**	**–1,938**
General government	3 401 . .	–107	–120	–73	–9	–103	–114	–140	–160
Debt forgiveness	3 402 . .	. . .	. . .	. . .	. . .	. . .	. . .	. . .	. . .
Other capital transfers	3 410 . .	. . .	. . .	. . .	. . .	. . .	. . .	. . .	. . .
Other sectors	3 430 . .	–383	–494	–541	–616	–896	–1,177	–1,400	–1,778
Migrants' transfers	3 431 . .	–285	–347	–471	–468	–803	–1,095	–1,329	–1,281
Debt forgiveness	3 432 . .	. . .	. . .	. . .	. . .	. . .	. . .	. . .	. . .
Other capital transfers	3 440 . .	–99	–147	–70	–148	–94	–83	–71	–497
Nonproduced nonfinancial assets, credit	2 480 . .	. . .	. . .	. . .	. . .	. . .	. . .	. . .	. . .
Nonproduced nonfinancial assets, debit	3 480 . .	. . .	. . .	. . .	. . .	. . .	. . .	. . .	. . .

Table 2 (Continued). STANDARD PRESENTATION, 1988–95
(Millions of U.S. dollars)

	Code	1988	1989	1990	1991	1992	1993	1994	1995
FINANCIAL ACCOUNT	4 995 . .	**–2,236**	**–8,391**	**–4,903**	**–6,334**	**–13,539**	**–16,435**	**–9,047**	**–5,565**
A. DIRECT INVESTMENT	4 500 . .	–2,336	–6,330	–3,039	–7,249	–6,467	–4,048	–11,122	–1,832
Direct investment abroad	4 505 . .	**–7,117**	**–14,893**	**–15,388**	**–13,565**	**–14,257**	**–11,708**	**–16,738**	**–12,060**
Equity capital	4 510 . .	–3,742	–6,876	–7,776	–7,321	–9,300	–6,034	–8,319	–9,585
Claims on affiliated enterprises	4 515 . .	...	...	...	...	...	...	...	...
Liabilities to affiliated enterprises	4 520 . .	...	...	...	...	...	...	...	...
Reinvested earnings	4 525 . .	–2,747	–3,439	–1,689	–1,266	–87	–282	–2,396	...
Other capital	4 530 . .	–628	–4,578	–5,923	–4,978	–4,870	–5,392	–6,023	–2,475
Claims on affiliated enterprises	4 535 . .	...	...	...	...	...	...	...	...
Liabilities to affiliated enterprises	4 540 . .	...	...	...	...	...	...	...	...
Direct investment in the Netherlands	4 555 . .	**4,781**	**8,563**	**12,349**	**6,316**	**7,790**	**7,661**	**5,616**	**10,228**
Equity capital	4 560 . .	887	2,273	4,801	1,225	2,702	4,241	2,226	3,928
Claims on direct investors	4 565 . .	...	...	...	...	...	...	...	...
Liabilities to direct investors	4 570 . .	...	...	...	...	...	...	...	...
Reinvested earnings	4 575 . .	929	1,814	2,994	1,523	576	340	978	...
Other capital	4 580 . .	2,965	4,476	4,554	3,568	4,511	3,080	2,412	6,299
Claims on direct investors	4 585 . .	...	...	...	...	...	...	...	...
Liabilities to direct investors	4 590 . .	...	...	...	...	...	...	...	...
B. PORTFOLIO INVESTMENT	4 600 . .	3,369	7,582	–4,966	–574	–9,605	1,908	–7,985	–10,647
Assets	4 602 . .	**–6,971**	**–724**	**–3,588**	**–4,792**	**–13,430**	**–10,438**	**–8,601**	**–15,285**
Equity securities	4 610 . .	–1,642	–2,321	–2,521	–3,789	–2,703	–4,236	–6,625	–8,446
Monetary authorities	4 611 . .	...	...	...	...	...	...	...	...
General government	4 612 . .	...	...	...	...	...	...	...	...
Banks	4 613 . .	...	...	...	...	...	...	...	...
Other sectors	4 614 . .	...	...	...	...	...	...	...	...
Debt securities	4 619 . .	–5,329	1,596	–1,067	–1,002	–10,727	–6,202	–1,977	–6,839
Bonds and notes	4 620 . .	–5,279	1,728	–1,046	–1,178	–10,334	–7,078	–4,787	–8,100
Monetary authorities	4 621 . .	...	...	...	...	...	...	...	...
General government	4 622 . .	...	...	...	...	...	...	...	...
Banks	4 623 . .	...	...	...	...	...	...	...	...
Other sectors	4 624 . .	...	...	...	...	...	...	...	...
Money market instruments	4 630 . .	–27	–64	20	160	–361	611	2,519	1,879
Monetary authorities	4 631 . .	...	...	...	...	...	...	...	...
General government	4 632 . .	...	...	...	...	...	...	...	...
Banks	4 633 . .	...	...	...	...	...	...	...	...
Other sectors	4 634 . .	...	...	...	...	...	...	...	...
Financial derivatives	4 640 . .	–24	–68	–41	15	–32	265	291	–618
Monetary authorities	4 641 . .	...	...	...	...	...	...	...	...
General government	4 642 . .	...	...	...	...	...	...	...	...
Banks	4 643 . .	...	...	...	...	...	...	...	...
Other sectors	4 644 . .	...	...	...	...	...	...	...	...
Liabilities	4 652 . .	**10,340**	**8,307**	**–1,378**	**4,218**	**3,825**	**12,346**	**617**	**4,638**
Equity securities	4 660 . .	832	2,211	–2,736	–1,214	–1,512	3,495	113	–972
Banks	4 663 . .	...	...	...	...	...	...	...	...
Other sectors	4 664 . .	...	...	...	...	...	...	...	...
Debt securities	4 669 . .	9,508	6,096	1,358	5,432	5,337	8,852	503	5,610
Bonds and notes	4 670 . .	9,462	5,635	1,128	5,326	5,391	9,489	–646	5,362
Monetary authorities	4 671 . .	...	...	...	...	...	...	...	...
General government	4 672 . .	6,108	4,149	899	4,259	1,975	4,537	–12,097	–4,727
Banks	4 673 . .	...	...	...	...	...	...	...	...
Other sectors	4 674 . .	3,354	1,486	229	1,067	3,417	4,953	11,451	10,089
Money market instruments	4 680 . .	46	460	230	105	–54	–638	1,149	248
Monetary authorities	4 681 . .	...	...	...	...	...	...	...	...
General government	4 682 . .	–6	–12	–1	–1	–41	–56	231	713
Banks	4 683 . .	–35	–9	–235	52	–31	623	1,085	–96
Other sectors	4 684 . .	87	482	467	54	18	–1,205	–167	–370
Financial derivatives	4 690 . .	...	...	...	...	...	...	...	...
Monetary authorities	4 691 . .	...	...	...	...	...	...	...	...
General government	4 692 . .	...	...	...	...	...	...	...	...
Banks	4 693 . .	...	...	...	...	...	...	...	...
Other sectors	4 694 . .	...	...	...	...	...	...	...	...

Table 2 (Concluded). STANDARD PRESENTATION, 1988–95
(Millions of U.S. dollars)

	Code	1988	1989	1990	1991	1992	1993	1994	1995
C. OTHER INVESTMENT	4 700 . .	–1,702	–9,136	3,370	1,995	8,651	–7,654	10,560	5,003
Assets	4 703 . .	**–14,054**	**–27,911**	**–24,250**	**–5,773**	**–7,426**	**–11,306**	**7,598**	**–19,125**
Trade credits	4 706 . .	–40	–36	2	246	149	–95	148	–82
General government: long-term	4 708 . .	–80	–210	33	163	143	28	–38	–117
General government: short-term	4 709 . .	. . .	. . .	. . .	. . .	. . .	. . .	. . .	. . .
Other sectors: long-term	4 711 . .	41	174	–31	83	6	–123	186	36
Other sectors: short-term	4 712 . .	. . .	. . .	. . .	. . .	. . .	. . .	. . .	. . .
Loans	4 714 . .	–3,671	–2,809	–3,513	–1,058	–3,423	–1,131	4,562	–4,148
Monetary authorities: long-term	4 717 . .	. . .	. . .	. . .	. . .	. . .	. . .	. . .	. . .
Monetary authorities: short-term	4 718 . .	. . .	. . .	. . .	. . .	. . .	. . .	. . .	. . .
General government: long-term	4 720 . .	–512	–309	–144	125	126	124	340	419
General government: short-term	4 721 . .	. . .	. . .	. . .	. . .	. . .	. . .	. . .	. . .
Banks: long-term	4 723 . .	–3,356	–2,389	–2,710	–722	–3,145	–1,036	4,000	–4,681
Banks: short-term	4 724 . .	. . .	. . .	. . .	. . .	. . .	. . .	. . .	. . .
Other sectors: long-term	4 726 . .	266	–50	–599	–453	–359	–186	228	232
Other sectors: short-term	4 727 . .	–69	–61	–60	–8	–45	–33	–6	–118
Currency and deposits	4 730 . .	–8,654	–24,837	–20,350	–4,639	–3,208	–9,548	4,153	–13,856
Monetary authorities	4 731 . .	. . .	–1	. . .	–1	. . .	. . .	. . .	. . .
General government	4 732 . .	. . .	. . .	. . .	. . .	. . .	. . .	. . .	. . .
Banks	4 733 . .	–7,981	–24,771	–19,502	–3,915	–1,055	–6,848	5,440	–12,178
Other sectors	4 734 . .	–673	–65	–848	–723	–2,154	–2,700	–1,287	–1,678
Other assets	4 736 . .	–1,690	–230	–390	–321	–945	–531	–1,266	–1,038
Monetary authorities: long-term	4 738 . .	. . .	. . .	. . .	. . .	. . .	. . .	. . .	. . .
Monetary authorities: short-term	4 739 . .	. . .	. . .	. . .	. . .	. . .	. . .	. . .	. . .
General government: long-term	4 741 . .	–391	–140	–257	–22	–593	–341	–346	–292
General government: short-term	4 742 . .	. . .	. . .	. . .	. . .	. . .	. . .	. . .	. . .
Banks: long-term	4 744 . .	. . .	. . .	. . .	. . .	. . .	. . .	. . .	. . .
Banks: short-term	4 745 . .	. . .	. . .	. . .	. . .	. . .	. . .	. . .	. . .
Other sectors: long-term	4 747 . .	65	52	14	40	4	7	–21	73
Other sectors: short-term	4 748 . .	–1,364	–143	–147	–338	–356	–197	–899	–819
Liabilities	4 753 . .	**12,352**	**18,775**	**27,620**	**7,767**	**16,078**	**3,651**	**2,963**	**24,128**
Trade credits	4 756 . .	–793	132	–22	96	11	130	–172	8
General government: long-term	4 758 . .	. . .	. . .	. . .	. . .	. . .	. . .	. . .	. . .
General government: short-term	4 759 . .	. . .	. . .	. . .	. . .	. . .	. . .	. . .	. . .
Other sectors: long-term	4 761 . .	–793	132	–22	96	11	130	–172	8
Other sectors: short-term	4 762 . .	. . .	. . .	. . .	. . .	. . .	. . .	. . .	. . .
Loans	4 764 . .	5,289	7,554	7,991	3,746	1,074	1,782	–170	770
Use of Fund credit and loans from the Fund	4 766 . .	. . .	. . .	. . .	. . .	. . .	. . .	. . .	. . .
Monetary authorities: other long-term	4 767 . .	. . .	. . .	. . .	. . .	. . .	. . .	. . .	. . .
Monetary authorities: short-term	4 768 . .	. . .	. . .	. . .	. . .	. . .	. . .	. . .	. . .
General government: long-term	4 770 . .	–18	–42	–16	–5	–1	. . .	. . .	. . .
General government: short-term	4 771 . .	. . .	. . .	. . .	. . .	. . .	. . .	271	38
Banks: long-term	4 773 . .	4,177	3,273	2,041	374	1,704	1,481	–653	–397
Banks: short-term	4 774 . .	. . .	. . .	. . .	. . .	. . .	. . .	. . .	. . .
Other sectors: long-term	4 776 . .	889	3,338	3,640	3,220	–127	103	535	1,237
Other sectors: short-term	4 777 . .	241	985	2,327	157	–503	198	–322	–109
Currency and deposits	4 780 . .	6,898	10,120	19,035	3,867	14,229	1,766	969	21,088
Monetary authorities	4 781 . .	–59	57	–9	430	–309	99	91	–135
General government	4 782 . .	67	295	–19	36	–459	37	777	–5
Banks	4 783 . .	6,788	9,704	18,867	3,558	15,317	1,626	139	21,031
Other sectors	4 784 . .	102	64	196	–156	–320	5	–39	197
Other liabilities	4 786 . .	958	970	617	59	764	–27	2,336	2,262
Monetary authorities: long-term	4 788 . .	. . .	. . .	. . .	. . .	. . .	. . .	. . .	. . .
Monetary authorities: short-term	4 789 . .	. . .	. . .	. . .	. . .	. . .	. . .	. . .	. . .
General government: long-term	4 791 . .	. . .	. . .	. . .	. . .	. . .	. . .	. . .	. . .
General government: short-term	4 792 . .	191	–44	15	–216	277	130	103	–9
Banks: long-term	4 794 . .	. . .	. . .	. . .	. . .	. . .	. . .	. . .	. . .
Banks: short-term	4 795 . .	–3	7	6	9	2	15	1	. . .
Other sectors: long-term	4 797 . .	927	1,098	668	404	197	–361	1,431	2,471
Other sectors: short-term	4 798 . .	–156	–91	–73	–138	289	189	801	–200
D. RESERVE ASSETS	4 800 . .	–1,568	–507	–268	–506	–6,118	–6,641	–500	1,912
Monetary gold	4 810 . .	. . .	. . .	. . .	. . .	. . .	3,358	61	. . .
Special drawing rights	4 820 . .	78	–14	113	–35	177	–30	–25	–255
Reserve position in the Fund	4 830 . .	123	33	21	–58	–384	54	–8	–557
Foreign exchange	4 840 . .	–1,768	–526	–402	–412	–5,911	–10,022	–528	2,723
Other claims	4 880 . .	. . .	. . .	. . .	. . .	. . .	. . .	. . .	. . .
NET ERRORS AND OMISSIONS	4 998 . .	**–4,698**	**–1,308**	**–4,003**	**–1,113**	**6,837**	**4,900**	**–4,980**	**–9,417**

Part 3 of the *Yearbook* contains descriptions of the methodologies, compilation practices, and sources used to compile these data.

Table 3. INTERNATIONAL INVESTMENT POSITION (End–period stocks), 1988–95

(Millions of U.S. dollars)

	Code	1988	1989	1990	1991	1992	1993	1994	1995
ASSETS	8 995 C.	301,802	352,011	417,958	451,939	456,151	494,484	544,588	...
Direct investment abroad	8 505 ..	**76,580**	**92,242**	**113,476**	**124,889**	**129,396**	**132,438**	**157,194**	**...**
Equity capital and reinvested earnings	8 506 ..	61,668	72,562	85,271	90,399	92,710	91,840	107,269	...
Claims on affiliated enterprises	8 507 ..	...	...	...	...	...	...	...	...
Liabilities to affiliated enterprises	8 508 ..	...	...	...	...	...	...	...	...
Other capital	8 530 ..	14,912	19,680	28,205	34,490	36,686	40,598	49,925	...
Claims on affiliated enterprises	8 535 ..	...	...	...	...	...	...	...	...
Liabilities to affiliated enterprises	8 540 ..	...	...	...	...	...	...	...	...
Portfolio investment	8 602 ..	**54,275**	**61,169**	**64,205**	**78,038**	**84,501**	**106,470**	**121,425**	**157,780**
Equity securities	8 610 ..	25,856	34,038	33,254	42,095	44,209	59,663	68,642	91,935
Monetary authorities	8 611 ..	50	52	118	117	165	206	288	374
General government	8 612 ..	...	...	...	...	...	...	...	...
Banks	8 613 ..	350	313	237	351	331	464	461	686
Other sectors	8 614 ..	25,456	33,673	32,899	41,628	43,713	58,993	67,892	90,875
Debt securities	8 619 ..	28,419	27,131	30,951	35,943	40,292	46,807	52,784	65,845
Bonds and notes	8 620 ..	25,706	24,223	27,692	32,916	37,043	44,361	51,236	65,009
Monetary authorities	8 621 ..	...	...	...	...	...	206	231	249
General government	8 622 ..	...	...	...	...	...	...	...	...
Banks	8 623 ..	11,303	11,746	14,675	16,195	16,978	16,178	20,518	24,807
Other sectors	8 624 ..	14,404	12,477	13,018	16,721	20,065	27,977	30,488	39,953
Money market instruments	8 630 ..	2,712	2,908	3,259	3,027	3,248	2,446	1,547	836
Monetary authorities	8 631 ..	...	...	...	...	...	...	...	...
General government	8 632 ..	...	...	...	...	...	...	...	...
Banks	8 633 ..	...	...	...	...	...	...	...	...
Other sectors	8 634 ..	...	...	...	...	...	...	...	...
Financial derivatives	8 640 ..	...	...	...	...	...	...	...	...
Monetary authorities	8 641 ..	...	...	...	...	...	...	...	...
General government	8 642 ..	...	...	...	...	...	...	...	...
Banks	8 643 ..	...	...	...	...	...	...	...	...
Other sectors	8 644 ..	...	...	...	...	...	...	...	...
Other investment	8 703 ..	**136,461**	**164,096**	**205,222**	**215,304**	**205,326**	**210,847**	**218,065**	**...**
Trade credits	8 706 ..	578	543	598	519	567	692	541	...
General government: long-term	8 708 ..	...	...	...	...	...	...	...	...
General government: short-term	8 709 ..	...	...	...	...	...	...	...	...
Other sectors: long-term	8 711 ..	578	543	598	519	567	692	541	...
Other sectors: short-term	8 712 ..	...	...	...	...	...	...	...	...
Loans	8 714 ..	31,670	33,685	41,480	44,379	47,494	43,229	41,802	...
Monetary authorities: long-term	8 717 ..	...	...	...	...	...	...	...	...
Monetary authorities: short-term	8 718 ..	...	...	...	...	...	...	...	...
General government: long-term	8 720 ..	6,726	7,644	9,278	9,234	8,597	7,995	8,994	8,434
General government: short-term	8 721 ..	...	...	...	...	...	...	...	...
Banks: long-term	8 723 ..	17,454	18,612	22,753	25,271	29,223	25,819	22,864	26,774
Banks: short-term	8 724 ..	...	...	...	...	...	...	...	...
Other sectors: long-term	8 726 ..	7,328	7,211	9,150	9,578	9,350	9,073	9,591	...
Other sectors: short-term	8 727 ..	163	217	299	296	325	341	353	...
Currency and deposits	8 730 ..	86,703	109,803	140,664	144,816	132,742	142,704	148,156	167,714
Monetary authorities	8 731 ..	...	...	...	...	...	...	...	...
General government	8 732 ..	1,614	724	148	...	54	61	...	...
Banks	8 733 ..	81,476	105,266	135,309	138,904	124,957	132,954	136,166	153,052
Other sectors	8 734 ..	3,613	3,813	5,208	5,911	7,731	9,688	11,990	14,662
Other assets	8 736 ..	17,510	20,065	22,480	25,590	24,523	24,222	27,567	30,603
Monetary authorities: long-term	8 738 ..	...	...	...	...	...	...	...	...
Monetary authorities: short-term	8 739 ..	...	...	...	...	...	...	...	...
General government: long-term	8 741 ..	7,214	9,168	9,998	12,879	12,154	12,436	13,447	14,519
General government: short-term	8 742 ..	...	...	...	...	...	...	...	...
Banks: long-term	8 744 ..	...	...	...	...	...	...	...	...
Banks: short-term	8 745 ..	...	...	...	...	...	...	...	...
Other sectors: long-term	8 747 ..	–55	–73	–76	–68	–17	20	31	24
Other sectors: short-term	8 748 ..	10,351	10,970	12,558	12,778	12,386	11,766	14,089	16,059
Reserve assets	8 800 ..	**34,487**	**34,504**	**35,054**	**33,708**	**36,928**	**44,729**	**47,904**	**47,182**
Monetary gold	8 810 ..	18,023	17,620	17,181	15,526	14,628	13,150	13,306	13,452
Special drawing rights	8 820 ..	776	776	718	758	554	583	645	916
Reserve position in the Fund	8 830 ..	757	706	738	800	1,147	1,092	1,171	1,738
Foreign exchange	8 840 ..	14,932	15,402	16,418	16,625	20,599	29,904	32,782	31,075
Other claims	8 880 ..	...	...	...	...	...	...	...	...

Table 3 (Continued). INTERNATIONAL INVESTMENT POSITION (End–period stocks), 1988–95

(Millions of U.S. dollars)

	Code		1988	1989	1990	1991	1992	1993	1994	1995
LIABILITIES	8 995	D.	241,619	292,453	354,382	386,520	400,965	434,093	479,278	...
Direct investment in the Netherlands	8 555	. .	**45,937**	**56,660**	**75,763**	**81,277**	**82,941**	**85,241**	**102,803**	...
Equity capital and reinvested earnings	8 556	. .	32,037	37,299	49,195	50,623	50,036	50,951	62,430	...
Claims on direct investors	8 557	. .	...	...	...	...	...	...	...	...
Liabilities to direct investors	8 558	. .	...	...	...	...	...	...	...	...
Other capital	8 580	. .	13,900	19,361	26,569	30,654	32,906	34,291	40,373	...
Claims on direct investors	8 585	. .	...	...	...	...	...	...	...	...
Liabilities to direct investors	8 590	. .	...	...	...	...	...	...	...	...
Portfolio investment	8 652	. .	**77,163**	**99,783**	**102,484**	**120,912**	**132,134**	**164,631**	**178,315**	**227,348**
Equity securities	8 660	. .	42,661	57,478	55,976	66,476	65,818	92,380	107,141	132,012
Banks	8 663	. .	...	...	...	...	...	...	...	...
Other sectors	8 664	. .	...	...	...	...	...	...	...	...
Debt securities	8 669	. .	34,502	42,305	46,508	54,436	66,317	72,252	71,174	95,336
Bonds and notes	8 670	. .	33,658	40,929	44,675	52,502	64,550	71,204	68,699	92,371
Monetary authorities	8 671	. .	...	...	...	...	...	...	...	...
General government	8 672	. .	25,006	30,488	33,609	40,517	49,005	53,789	46,049	62,391
Banks	8 673	. .	...	...	...	...	...	...	...	...
Other sectors	8 674	. .	8,652	10,441	11,065	11,986	15,545	17,415	22,650	29,980
Money market instruments	8 680	. .	844	1,376	1,833	1,934	1,767	1,047	2,475	2,965
Monetary authorities	8 681	. .	...	...	...	...	...	...	...	...
General government	8 682	. .	...	...	...	...	...	...	...	...
Banks	8 683	. .	...	...	...	...	...	...	...	...
Other sectors	8 684	. .	...	...	...	...	...	...	...	...
Financial derivatives	8 690	. .	...	...	...	...	...	...	...	...
Monetary authorities	8 691	. .	...	...	...	...	...	...	...	...
General government	8 692	. .	...	...	...	...	...	...	...	...
Banks	8 692	. .	...	...	...	...	...	...	...	...
Other sectors	8 694	. .	...	...	...	...	...	...	...	...
Other investment	8 753	. .	**118,519**	**136,009**	**176,135**	**184,331**	**185,889**	**184,220**	**198,161**	...
Trade credits	8 756	. .	362	498	534	623	614	720	587	...
General government: long-term	8 758	. .	...	...	...	...	...	...	...	...
General government: short-term	8 759	. .	...	...	...	...	...	...	...	...
Other sectors: long-term	8 761	. .	362	498	534	623	614	720	587	...
Other sectors: short-term	8 762	. .	...	...	...	...	...	...	...	...
Loans	8 764	. .	14,040	20,755	30,217	34,900	35,745	34,038	36,075	...
Use of Fund credit and loans from the Fund	8 766	. .	...	...	...	...	...	...	...	...
Monetary authorities: other long-term	8 767	. .	...	...	...	...	...	...	...	...
Monetary authorities: short-term	8 768	. .	...	...	...	...	...	...	...	...
General government: long-term	8 770	. .	111	73	67	60	23	21	24	...
General government: short-term	8 771	. .	13	14	15	15	...	...	...	...
Banks: long-term	8 773	. .	4,536	6,296	8,068	9,173	12,266	10,875	10,225	...
Banks: short-term	8 774	. .	...	...	...	...	...	...	...	...
Other sectors: long-term	8 776	. .	6,910	10,489	15,765	19,179	17,976	17,681	20,100	...
Other sectors: short-term	8 777	. .	2,470	3,883	6,301	6,472	5,480	5,460	5,727	...
Currency and deposits	8 780	. .	97,928	106,691	136,765	137,411	139,151	138,573	149,200	175,527
Monetary authorities	8 781	. .	...	...	...	...	...	...	...	...
General government	8 782	. .	...	...	...	...	...	...	803	889
Banks	8 783	. .	97,359	106,034	135,821	136,649	138,765	138,150	147,811	174,150
Other sectors	8 784	. .	569	657	944	762	386	423	587	487
Other liabilities	8 786	. .	6,190	8,066	8,620	11,397	10,379	10,889	12,298	12,783
Monetary authorities: long-term	8 788	. .	...	...	...	...	...	...	...	...
Monetary authorities: short-term	8 789	. .	26	87	85	245	38	152	263	141
General government: long-term	8 791	. .	5,347	7,066	7,421	9,956	9,086	9,318	9,759	10,279
General government: short-term	8 792	. .	335	339	414	459	190	165	...	302
Banks: long-term	8 794	. .	...	...	...	...	...	...	...	...
Banks: short-term	8 795	. .	...	...	...	...	...	...	...	...
Other sectors: long-term	8 797	. .	1,342	1,570	1,893	2,000	2,036	2,008	2,274	2,283
Other sectors: short-term	8 798	. .	–860	–997	–1,194	–1,262	–971	–754	2	–223
NET INTERNATIONAL INVESTMENT POSITION	8 995	. .	**60,183**	**59,559**	**63,576**	**65,419**	**55,186**	**60,391**	**65,310**	...
Conversion rates: Netherlands guilders per U.S. dollar (end of period)	0 102	. .	**1.9995**	**1.9155**	**1.6900**	**1.7104**	**1.8141**	**1.9409**	**1.7351**	**1.6044**

Table 1. ANALYTIC PRESENTATION, 1988–95
(Millions of U.S. dollars)

	Code	1988	1989	1990	1991	1992	1993	1994	1995
A. Current Account [1]	4 993 Y.	**75.2**	**38.1**	**–44.0**	**–6.2**	**9.9**	**1.2**	**–97.9**	**86.5**
Goods: exports f.o.b	2 100 ..	225.8	313.4	302.7	301.8	332.3	306.0	351.1	354.2
Goods: imports f.o.b	3 100 ..	–879.4	–1,017.8	–1,112.3	–1,118.9	–1,168.4	–1,143.8	–1,271.6	–1,318.7
Balance on Goods	4 100 ..	*–653.6*	*–704.4*	*–809.7*	*–817.2*	*–836.1*	*–837.8*	*–920.5*	*–964.4*
Services: credit	2 200 ..	892.6	960.8	1,161.4	1,227.9	1,339.6	1,346.0	1,414.2	1,686.8
Services: debit	3 200 ..	–378.2	–407.5	–518.2	–544.2	–606.9	–596.0	–670.5	–724.9
Balance on Goods and Services	4 991 ..	*–139.1*	*–151.1*	*–166.5*	*–133.5*	*–103.5*	*–87.8*	*–176.8*	*–2.6*
Income: credit	2 300 ..	80.9	108.9	126.1	126.8	158.1	122.7	133.7	122.7
Income: debit	3 300 ..	–41.3	–73.0	–109.6	–109.6	–146.6	–140.3	–99.4	–130.9
Balance on Goods, Services, and Income	4 992 ..	*–99.5*	*–115.2*	*–149.9*	*–116.3*	*–92.0*	*–105.4*	*–142.5*	*–10.8*
Current transfers: credit	2 379 Y.	268.7	260.9	213.1	228.7	217.4	250.3	217.9	245.9
Current transfers: debit	3 379 ..	–94.1	–107.6	–107.3	–118.6	–115.5	–143.7	–173.3	–148.5
B. Capital Account [1]	4 994 Y.	**–2.9**	**–3.2**	**–1.7**	**–.7**	**–.6**	**–.8**	**–.7**	**–.8**
Capital account: credit	2 994 Y.	.4	.1	.5	.9	1.7	.8	1.0	1.4
Capital account: debit	3 994 ..	–3.3	–3.3	–2.2	–1.7	–2.3	–1.7	–1.7	–2.2
Total, Groups A Plus B	4 010 ..	*72.2*	*34.9*	*–45.7*	*–6.9*	*9.4*	*.4*	*–98.5*	*85.7*
C. Financial Account [1]	4 995 X.	**–58.3**	**–93.7**	**9.4**	**–41.5**	**41.7**	**32.2**	**–2.3**	**31.1**
Direct investment abroad	4 505 ..	–2.8	–4.8	–2.4	–1.1	–1.5	2.2	–1.0	–.7
Direct investment in the Netherlands Antilles	4 555 Y.	6.7	17.4	8.1	33.4	40.1	11.0	21.5	9.8
Portfolio investment assets	4 602 ..	–55.1	–76.9	–50.3	–29.2	–21.6	–13.9	–69.1	–24.7
Equity securities	4 610 ..	...	...	...	...	...	...	...	...
Debt securities	4 619 ..	–55.1	–76.9	–50.3	–29.2	–21.6	–13.9	–69.1	–24.7
Portfolio investment liabilities	4 652 Y.	–2.1	1.1	1.2	–1.5	2.8	1.5	10.9	1.7
Equity securities	4 660 Y.	...	...	...	...	...	...	...	...
Debt securities	4 669 Y.	–2.1	1.1	1.2	–1.5	2.8	1.5	10.9	1.7
Other investment assets	4 703 ..	–194.2	–335.5	–249.4	–165.8	–68.7	–38.4	15.3	83.6
Monetary authorities	4 703 .A	...	...	...	...	...	...	...	...
General government	4 703 .B	.7	–13.0	24.1	–40.5	...	...	...	...
Banks	4 703 .C	–182.1	–297.9	–290.8	–120.1	–61.0	–46.9	–55.8	–10.1
Other sectors	4 703 .D	–12.8	–24.6	17.4	–5.3	–7.7	8.5	71.1	93.7
Other investment liabilities	4 753 X.	189.1	305.0	302.1	122.7	90.6	69.8	20.1	–38.7
Monetary authorities	4 753 XA	...	...	...	...	...	...	...	...
General government	4 753 YB	6.3	14.3	–3.3	–7.9	.4	–9.5	–38.3	–17.6
Banks	4 753 YC	177.6	303.9	290.1	114.6	60.6	59.7	59.7	4.4
Other sectors	4 753 YD	5.2	–13.2	15.3	16.0	29.7	19.6	–1.3	–25.4
Total, Groups A Through C	4 020 ..	*13.9*	*–58.8*	*–36.3*	*–48.4*	*51.1*	*32.6*	*–100.8*	*116.8*
D. Net Errors and Omissions	4 998 ..	**19.5**	**14.6**	**6.5**	**6.2**	**8.2**	**11.5**	**24.9**	**22.5**
Total, Groups A Through D	4 030 ..	*33.4*	*–44.2*	*–29.8*	*–42.2*	*59.2*	*44.0*	*–75.9*	*139.3*
E. Reserves and Related Items	4 040 ..	**–33.4**	**44.2**	**29.8**	**42.2**	**–59.2**	**–44.0**	**75.9**	**–139.3**
Reserve assets	4 800 ..	–33.4	44.2	29.8	42.2	–59.2	–44.0	75.9	–139.3
Use of Fund credit and loans	4 766 ..	...	...	...	...	...	...	...	...
Liabilities constituting foreign authorities' reserves	4 900 ..	...	...	...	...	...	...	...	...
Exceptional financing	4 920 ..	...	...	...	...	...	...	...	...
Conversion rates: Netherlands Antillean guilders per U.S. dollar	0 101 ..	**1.8000**	**1.7933**	**1.7900**	**1.7900**	**1.7900**	**1.7900**	**1.7900**	**1.7900**

[1] Excludes components that have been classified in the categories of Group E.

Table 2. STANDARD PRESENTATION, 1988–95
(Millions of U.S. dollars)

	Code	1988	1989	1990	1991	1992	1993	1994	1995
CURRENT ACCOUNT	4 993 . .	**75.2**	**38.1**	**–44.0**	**–6.2**	**9.9**	**1.2**	**–97.9**	**86.5**
A. GOODS	4 100 . .	–653.6	–704.4	–809.7	–817.2	–836.1	–837.8	–920.5	–964.4
Credit	2 100 . .	**225.8**	**313.4**	**302.7**	**301.8**	**332.3**	**306.0**	**351.1**	**354.2**
General merchandise: exports f.o.b.	2 110 . .	172.8	253.8	208.3	210.9	242.6	222.9	245.2	222.2
Goods for processing: exports f.o.b.	2 150 . .	. . .	. . .	. . .	. . .	. . .	. . .	. . .	. . .
Repairs on goods	2 160 . .	. . .	. . .	. . .	. . .	. . .	. . .	. . .	. . .
Goods procured in ports by carriers	2 170 . .	53.0	59.7	94.4	90.9	89.7	83.1	105.9	132.0
Nonmonetary gold	2 180 . .	. . .	. . .	. . .	. . .	. . .	. . .	. . .	. . .
Debit	3 100 . .	**–879.4**	**–1,017.8**	**–1,112.3**	**–1,118.9**	**–1,168.4**	**–1,143.8**	**–1,271.6**	**–1,318.7**
General merchandise: imports f.o.b.	3 110 . .	–879.4	–1,017.8	–1,112.3	–1,118.9	–1,168.4	–1,143.8	–1,271.6	–1,318.7
Goods for processing: imports f.o.b.	3 150 . .	. . .	. . .	. . .	. . .	. . .	. . .	. . .	. . .
Repairs on goods	3 160 . .	. . .	. . .	. . .	. . .	. . .	. . .	. . .	. . .
Goods procured in ports by carriers	3 170 . .	. . .	. . .	. . .	. . .	. . .	. . .	. . .	. . .
Nonmonetary gold	3 180 . .	. . .	. . .	. . .	. . .	. . .	. . .	. . .	. . .
B. SERVICES	4 200 . .	514.4	553.3	643.2	683.7	732.7	750.0	743.7	961.8
Total credit	2 200 . .	*892.6*	*960.8*	*1,161.4*	*1,227.9*	*1,339.6*	*1,346.0*	*1,414.2*	*1,686.8*
Total debit	3 200 . .	*–378.2*	*–407.5*	*–518.2*	*–544.2*	*–606.9*	*–596.0*	*–670.5*	*–724.9*
Transportation services, credit	2 205 . .	**132.7**	**164.3**	**186.9**	**200.6**	**220.4**	**204.4**	**219.7**	**239.8**
Passenger	2 205 BA	*39.2*	*40.4*	*55.6*	*58.2*	*59.4*	*58.7*	*65.9*	*59.8*
Freight	2 205 BB	. . .	. . .	. . .	. . .	. . .	. . .	. . .	. . .
Other	2 205 BC	*93.5*	*124.0*	*131.3*	*142.5*	*161.1*	*145.6*	*153.8*	*180.0*
Sea transport, passenger	2 207 . .	. . .	. . .	. . .	. . .	. . .	. . .	. . .	. . .
Sea transport, freight	2 208 . .	. . .	. . .	. . .	. . .	. . .	. . .	. . .	. . .
Sea transport, other	2 209 . .	. . .	. . .	. . .	. . .	. . .	. . .	. . .	. . .
Air transport, passenger	2 211 . .	. . .	. . .	. . .	. . .	. . .	. . .	. . .	. . .
Air transport, freight	2 212 . .	. . .	. . .	. . .	. . .	. . .	. . .	. . .	. . .
Air transport, other	2 213 . .	. . .	. . .	. . .	. . .	. . .	. . .	. . .	. . .
Other transport, passenger	2 215 . .	. . .	. . .	. . .	. . .	. . .	. . .	. . .	. . .
Other transport, freight	2 216 . .	. . .	. . .	. . .	. . .	. . .	. . .	. . .	. . .
Other transport, other	2 217 . .	. . .	. . .	. . .	. . .	. . .	. . .	. . .	. . .
Transportation services, debit	3 205 . .	**–163.7**	**–163.9**	**–184.1**	**–177.2**	**–182.5**	**–176.2**	**–203.2**	**–211.0**
Passenger	3 205 BA	*–8.7*	*–19.4*	*–17.3*	*–10.9*	*–11.5*	*–5.9*	*–8.0*	*–8.0*
Freight	3 205 BB	*–94.9*	*–105.6*	*–116.8*	*–120.5*	*–127.0*	*–124.3*	*–135.6*	*–143.5*
Other	3 205 BC	*–60.2*	*–38.8*	*–49.9*	*–45.8*	*–44.0*	*–46.0*	*–59.7*	*–59.5*
Sea transport, passenger	3 207 . .	. . .	. . .	. . .	. . .	. . .	. . .	. . .	. . .
Sea transport, freight	3 208 . .	. . .	. . .	. . .	. . .	. . .	. . .	. . .	. . .
Sea transport, other	3 209 . .	. . .	. . .	. . .	. . .	. . .	. . .	. . .	. . .
Air transport, passenger	3 211 . .	. . .	. . .	. . .	. . .	. . .	. . .	. . .	. . .
Air transport, freight	3 212 . .	. . .	. . .	. . .	. . .	. . .	. . .	. . .	. . .
Air transport, other	3 213 . .	. . .	. . .	. . .	. . .	. . .	. . .	. . .	. . .
Other transport, passenger	3 215 . .	. . .	. . .	. . .	. . .	. . .	. . .	. . .	. . .
Other transport, freight	3 216 . .	. . .	. . .	. . .	. . .	. . .	. . .	. . .	. . .
Other transport, other	3 217 . .	. . .	. . .	. . .	. . .	. . .	. . .	. . .	. . .
Travel, credit	2 236 . .	**319.8**	**371.0**	**449.2**	**470.9**	**521.2**	**604.6**	**637.8**	**561.1**
Business travel	2 237 . .	. . .	. . .	. . .	. . .	521.2	604.6	637.8	. . .
Personal travel	2 240 . .	. . .	. . .	. . .	. . .	. . .	. . .	. . .	. . .
Travel, debit	3 236 . .	**–82.4**	**–88.9**	**–127.4**	**–131.8**	**–157.3**	**–189.9**	**–206.0**	**–223.5**
Business travel	3 237 . .	. . .	. . .	. . .	. . .	–157.3	–189.9	–206.0	. . .
Personal travel	3 240 . .	. . .	. . .	. . .	. . .	. . .	. . .	. . .	. . .
Other services, credit	2 200 BA	**440.2**	**425.5**	**525.4**	**556.4**	**597.9**	**537.0**	**556.7**	**885.9**
Communications	2 245 . .	. . .	. . .	. . .	. . .	. . .	. . .	. . .	. . .
Construction	2 249 . .	. . .	. . .	. . .	. . .	. . .	. . .	. . .	. . .
Insurance	2 253 . .	. . .	. . .	. . .	. . .	. . .	. . .	. . .	. . .
Financial	2 260 . .	. . .	. . .	. . .	. . .	. . .	. . .	. . .	. . .
Computer and information	2 262 . .	. . .	. . .	. . .	. . .	. . .	. . .	. . .	. . .
Royalties and licence fees	2 266 . .	.2	.7	.2	.3	.2	1.1	.1	.1
Other business services	2 268 . .	416.0	395.9	493.6	518.8	560.3	512.6	524.2	854.6
Personal, cultural, and recreational	2 287 . .	. . .	. . .	. . .	. . .	. . .	. . .	. . .	. . .
Government, n.i.e.	2 291 . .	24.0	28.8	31.6	37.3	37.4	23.3	32.5	31.2
Other services, debit	3 200 BA	**–132.1**	**–154.7**	**–206.8**	**–235.2**	**–267.2**	**–229.9**	**–261.3**	**–290.4**
Communications	3 245 . .	. . .	. . .	. . .	. . .	. . .	. . .	. . .	. . .
Construction	3 249 . .	. . .	. . .	. . .	. . .	. . .	. . .	. . .	. . .
Insurance	3 253 . .	–10.5	–11.7	–13.0	–13.4	–14.1	–13.8	–15.1	–15.9
Financial	3 260 . .	. . .	. . .	. . .	. . .	. . .	. . .	. . .	. . .
Computer and information	3 262 . .	. . .	. . .	. . .	. . .	. . .	. . .	. . .	. . .
Royalties and licence fees	3 266 . .	–1.2	–1.9	–1.1	–1.8	–2.0	–1.1	–.8	–.6
Other business services	3 268 . .	–116.7	–135.4	–185.0	–210.5	–247.3	–207.3	–239.5	–267.7
Personal, cultural, and recreational	3 287 . .	. . .	. . .	. . .	. . .	. . .	. . .	. . .	. . .
Government, n.i.e.	3 291 . .	–3.7	–5.7	–7.8	–9.4	–3.9	–7.7	–5.9	–6.1

Table 2 (Continued). STANDARD PRESENTATION, 1988–95
(Millions of U.S. dollars)

	Code	1988	1989	1990	1991	1992	1993	1994	1995
C. INCOME	4 300 . .	39.6	35.9	16.6	17.2	11.5	–17.6	34.2	–8.2
Total credit	2 300 . .	*80.9*	*108.9*	*126.1*	*126.8*	*158.1*	*122.7*	*133.7*	*122.7*
Total debit	3 300 . .	*–41.3*	*–73.0*	*–109.6*	*–109.6*	*–146.6*	*–140.3*	*–99.4*	*–130.9*
Compensation of employees, credit	2 310 . .	**3.3**	**3.6**	**4.0**	**4.7**	**6.0**	**6.5**	**8.3**	**6.5**
Compensation of employees, debit	3 310 . .	**–9.7**	**–10.4**	**–8.4**	**–10.1**	**–15.5**	**–19.7**	**–16.8**	**–14.4**
Investment income, credit	2 320 . .	**77.6**	**105.3**	**122.1**	**122.1**	**152.1**	**116.1**	**125.4**	**116.2**
Direct investment income	2 330 . .	.6	5.6	14.7	33.5	45.0	28.4	14.5	7.9
Dividends and distributed branch profits	2 332 . .	.6	5.6	13.2	32.5	44.0	28.0	13.7	7.5
Reinvested earnings and undistributed branch profits	2 333 . .	...	...	1.6	1.1	1.0	.4	.8	.4
Income on debt (interest)	2 334 . .	...	...	...	...	...	...	...	...
Portfolio investment income	2 339 . .	...	...	...	...	...	...	...	...
Income on equity	2 340 . .	...	...	...	...	...	...	...	...
Income on bonds and notes	2 350 . .	...	...	...	...	...	...	...	...
Income on money market instruments and financial derivatives	2 360 . .	...	...	...	...	...	...	...	...
Other investment income	2 370 . .	77.0	99.6	107.4	88.5	107.0	87.7	110.8	108.3
Investment income, debit	3 320 . .	**–31.6**	**–62.7**	**–101.1**	**–99.5**	**–131.1**	**–120.6**	**–82.7**	**–116.5**
Direct investment income	3 330 . .	–7.3	–48.2	–73.2	–49.4	–103.5	–88.8	–41.8	–67.5
Dividends and distributed branch profits	3 332 . .	–15.8	–44.3	–65.7	–47.3	–85.6	–78.0	–20.7	–50.4
Reinvested earnings and undistributed branch profits	3 333 . .	8.4	–3.8	–7.5	–2.2	–17.9	–10.8	–21.1	–17.1
Income on debt (interest)	3 334 . .	...	...	...	...	...	...	...	...
Portfolio investment income	3 339 . .	...	...	...	...	...	...	...	...
Income on equity	3 340 . .	...	...	...	...	...	...	...	...
Income on bonds and notes	3 350 . .	...	...	...	...	...	...	...	...
Income on money market instruments and financial derivatives	3 360 . .	...	...	...	...	...	...	...	...
Other investment income	3 370 . .	–24.2	–14.5	–27.9	–50.1	–27.6	–31.8	–40.9	–49.0
D. CURRENT TRANSFERS	4 379 . .	174.7	153.3	105.9	110.1	102.0	106.6	44.6	97.3
Credit	2 379 . .	**268.7**	**260.9**	**213.1**	**228.7**	**217.4**	**250.3**	**217.9**	**245.9**
General government	2 380 . .	233.6	197.3	152.7	170.3	147.7	167.3	127.2	159.4
Other sectors	2 390 . .	35.1	63.6	60.4	58.3	69.8	83.0	90.7	86.5
Workers' remittances	2 391 . .	...	...	...	...	...	...	...	...
Other current transfers	2 392 . .	35.1	63.6	60.4	58.3	69.8	83.0	90.7	86.5
Debit	3 379 . .	**–94.1**	**–107.6**	**–107.3**	**–118.6**	**–115.5**	**–143.7**	**–173.3**	**–148.5**
General government	3 380 . .	...	...	...	...	...	...	...	...
Other sectors	3 390 . .	–94.1	–107.6	–107.3	–118.6	–115.5	–143.7	–173.3	–148.5
Workers' remittances	3 391 . .	...	...	...	...	...	...	...	...
Other current transfers	3 392 . .	–94.1	–107.6	–107.3	–118.6	–115.5	–143.7	–173.3	–148.5
CAPITAL AND FINANCIAL ACCOUNT	4 996 . .	**–94.7**	**–52.7**	**37.5**	**...**	**–18.1**	**–12.7**	**73.0**	**–109.0**
CAPITAL ACCOUNT	4 994 . .	**–2.9**	**–3.2**	**–1.7**	**–.7**	**–.6**	**–.8**	**–.7**	**–.8**
Total credit	2 994 . .	*.4*	*.1*	*.5*	*.9*	*1.7*	*.8*	*1.0*	*1.4*
Total debit	3 994 . .	*–3.3*	*–3.3*	*–2.2*	*–1.7*	*–2.3*	*–1.7*	*–1.7*	*–2.2*
Capital transfers, credit	2 400 . .	**.4**	**.1**	**.5**	**.9**	**1.7**	**.8**	**1.0**	**1.4**
General government	2 401 . .	...	...	...	...	...	...	...	...
Debt forgiveness	2 402 . .	...	...	...	...	...	...	...	...
Other capital transfers	2 410 . .	...	...	...	...	...	...	...	...
Other sectors	2 430 . .	.4	.1	.5	.9	1.7	.8	1.0	1.4
Migrants' transfers	2 431 . .	.4	.1	.5	.9	1.7	.8	1.0	1.4
Debt forgiveness	2 432 . .	...	...	...	...	...	...	...	...
Other capital transfers	2 440 . .	...	...	...	...	...	...	...	...
Capital transfers, debit	3 400 . .	**–3.3**	**–3.3**	**–2.2**	**–1.7**	**–2.3**	**–1.7**	**–1.7**	**–2.2**
General government	3 401 . .	...	...	...	...	...	...	...	...
Debt forgiveness	3 402 . .	...	...	...	...	...	...	...	...
Other capital transfers	3 410 . .	...	...	...	...	...	...	...	...
Other sectors	3 430 . .	–3.3	–3.3	–2.2	–1.7	–2.3	–1.7	–1.7	–2.2
Migrants' transfers	3 431 . .	–3.3	–3.3	–2.2	–1.7	–2.3	–1.7	–1.7	–2.2
Debt forgiveness	3 432 . .	...	...	...	...	...	...	...	...
Other capital transfers	3 440 . .	...	...	...	...	...	...	...	...
Nonproduced nonfinancial assets, credit	2 480 . .	**...**	**...**	**...**	**...**	**...**	**...**	**...**	**...**
Nonproduced nonfinancial assets, debit	3 480 . .	**...**	**...**	**...**	**...**	**...**	**...**	**...**	**...**

Table 2 (Continued). STANDARD PRESENTATION, 1988–95
(Millions of U.S. dollars)

	Code	1988	1989	1990	1991	1992	1993	1994	1995
FINANCIAL ACCOUNT	4 995 . .	**–91.7**	**–49.5**	**39.2**	**.7**	**–17.5**	**–11.8**	**73.6**	**–108.2**
A. DIRECT INVESTMENT	4 500 . .	3.8	12.6	5.7	32.3	38.5	13.2	20.5	9.1
Direct investment abroad	4 505 . .	**–2.8**	**–4.8**	**–2.4**	**–1.1**	**–1.5**	**2.2**	**–1.0**	**–.7**
Equity capital	4 510 . .	–.4	–.2	–.8	–.1	–.5	2.6	–.2	.5
Claims on affiliated enterprises	4 515 . .	. . .	. . .	. . .	. . .	. . .	. . .	. . .	. . .
Liabilities to affiliated enterprises	4 520 . .	. . .	. . .	. . .	. . .	. . .	. . .	. . .	. . .
Reinvested earnings	4 525 . .	. . .	. . .	–1.6	–1.1	–1.0	–.4	–.8	–.4
Other capital	4 530 . .	–2.4	–4.6	. . .	. . .	. . .	. . .	. . .	–.7
Claims on affiliated enterprises	4 535 . .	. . .	. . .	. . .	. . .	. . .	. . .	. . .	. . .
Liabilities to affiliated enterprises	4 540 . .	. . .	. . .	. . .	. . .	. . .	. . .	. . .	. . .
Direct investment in the Netherlands Antilles	4 555 . .	**6.7**	**17.4**	**8.1**	**33.4**	**40.1**	**11.0**	**21.5**	**9.8**
Equity capital	4 560 . .	.2	3.3	8.6	25.4	11.3	9.3	7.8	–.9
Claims on direct investors	4 565 . .	. . .	. . .	. . .	. . .	. . .	. . .	. . .	. . .
Liabilities to direct investors	4 570 . .	. . .	. . .	. . .	. . .	. . .	. . .	. . .	. . .
Reinvested earnings	4 575 . .	–8.4	3.8	7.5	2.2	17.9	10.8	21.1	17.1
Other capital	4 580 . .	14.9	10.2	–8.0	5.9	10.8	–9.1	–7.4	–6.4
Claims on direct investors	4 585 . .	. . .	. . .	. . .	. . .	. . .	. . .	. . .	. . .
Liabilities to direct investors	4 590 . .	. . .	. . .	. . .	. . .	. . .	. . .	. . .	. . .
B. PORTFOLIO INVESTMENT	4 600 . .	–57.1	–75.8	–49.1	–30.7	–18.8	–12.5	–58.2	–23.0
Assets	4 602 . .	**–55.1**	**–76.9**	**–50.3**	**–29.2**	**–21.6**	**–13.9**	**–69.1**	**–24.7**
Equity securities	4 610 . .	. . .	. . .	. . .	. . .	. . .	. . .	. . .	. . .
Monetary authorities	4 611 . .	. . .	. . .	. . .	. . .	. . .	. . .	. . .	. . .
General government	4 612 . .	. . .	. . .	. . .	. . .	. . .	. . .	. . .	. . .
Banks	4 613 . .	. . .	. . .	. . .	. . .	. . .	. . .	. . .	. . .
Other sectors	4 614 . .	. . .	. . .	. . .	. . .	. . .	. . .	. . .	. . .
Debt securities	4 619 . .	–55.1	–76.9	–50.3	–29.2	–21.6	–13.9	–69.1	–24.7
Bonds and notes	4 620 . .	–55.1	–76.9	–50.3	–29.2	–21.6	–13.9	–69.1	–24.7
Monetary authorities	4 621 . .	. . .	. . .	. . .	. . .	. . .	. . .	. . .	. . .
General government	4 622 . .	. . .	. . .	. . .	. . .	. . .	. . .	. . .	. . .
Banks	4 623 . .	. . .	. . .	. . .	. . .	. . .	. . .	. . .	. . .
Other sectors	4 624 . .	. . .	. . .	. . .	. . .	. . .	. . .	. . .	. . .
Money market instruments	4 630 . .	. . .	. . .	. . .	. . .	. . .	. . .	. . .	. . .
Monetary authorities	4 631 . .	. . .	. . .	. . .	. . .	. . .	. . .	. . .	. . .
General government	4 632 . .	. . .	. . .	. . .	. . .	. . .	. . .	. . .	. . .
Banks	4 633 . .	. . .	. . .	. . .	. . .	. . .	. . .	. . .	. . .
Other sectors	4 634 . .	. . .	. . .	. . .	. . .	. . .	. . .	. . .	. . .
Financial derivatives	4 640 . .	. . .	. . .	. . .	. . .	. . .	. . .	. . .	. . .
Monetary authorities	4 641 . .	. . .	. . .	. . .	. . .	. . .	. . .	. . .	. . .
General government	4 642 . .	. . .	. . .	. . .	. . .	. . .	. . .	. . .	. . .
Banks	4 643 . .	. . .	. . .	. . .	. . .	. . .	. . .	. . .	. . .
Other sectors	4 644 . .	. . .	. . .	. . .	. . .	. . .	. . .	. . .	. . .
Liabilities	4 652 . .	**–2.1**	**1.1**	**1.2**	**–1.5**	**2.8**	**1.5**	**10.9**	**1.7**
Equity securities	4 660 . .	. . .	. . .	. . .	. . .	. . .	. . .	. . .	. . .
Banks	4 663 . .	. . .	. . .	. . .	. . .	. . .	. . .	. . .	. . .
Other sectors	4 664 . .	. . .	. . .	. . .	. . .	. . .	. . .	. . .	. . .
Debt securities	4 669 . .	–2.1	1.1	1.2	–1.5	2.8	1.5	10.9	1.7
Bonds and notes	4 670 . .	–2.1	1.1	1.2	–1.5	2.8	1.5	10.9	1.7
Monetary authorities	4 671 . .	. . .	. . .	. . .	. . .	. . .	. . .	. . .	. . .
General government	4 672 . .	. . .	. . .	. . .	. . .	. . .	. . .	. . .	. . .
Banks	4 673 . .	. . .	. . .	. . .	. . .	. . .	. . .	. . .	. . .
Other sectors	4 674 . .	–2.1	1.1	1.2	–1.5	2.8	1.5	10.9	1.7
Money market instruments	4 680 . .	. . .	. . .	. . .	. . .	. . .	. . .	. . .	. . .
Monetary authorities	4 681 . .	. . .	. . .	. . .	. . .	. . .	. . .	. . .	. . .
General government	4 682 . .	. . .	. . .	. . .	. . .	. . .	. . .	. . .	. . .
Banks	4 683 . .	. . .	. . .	. . .	. . .	. . .	. . .	. . .	. . .
Other sectors	4 684 . .	. . .	. . .	. . .	. . .	. . .	. . .	. . .	. . .
Financial derivatives	4 690 . .	. . .	. . .	. . .	. . .	. . .	. . .	. . .	. . .
Monetary authorities	4 691 . .	. . .	. . .	. . .	. . .	. . .	. . .	. . .	. . .
General government	4 692 . .	. . .	. . .	. . .	. . .	. . .	. . .	. . .	. . .
Banks	4 693 . .	. . .	. . .	. . .	. . .	. . .	. . .	. . .	. . .
Other sectors	4 694 . .	. . .	. . .	. . .	. . .	. . .	. . .	. . .	. . .

Table 2 (Concluded). STANDARD PRESENTATION, 1988–95
(Millions of U.S. dollars)

	Code	1988	1989	1990	1991	1992	1993	1994	1995
C. OTHER INVESTMENT	4 700 . .	–5.1	–30.4	52.7	–43.1	22.0	31.5	35.4	45.0
Assets	4 703 . .	**–194.2**	**–335.5**	**–249.4**	**–165.8**	**–68.7**	**–38.4**	**15.3**	**83.6**
Trade credits	4 706 . .	...	...	...	...	...	...	...	...
General government: long-term	4 708 . .	...	...	...	...	...	...	...	...
General government: short-term	4 709 . .	...	...	...	...	...	...	...	...
Other sectors: long-term	4 711 . .	...	...	...	...	...	...	...	...
Other sectors: short-term	4 712 . .	...	...	...	...	...	...	...	...
Loans	4 714 . .	3.9	–.3	4.7	.5	–3.0	7.8	1.3	–.8
Monetary authorities: long-term	4 717 . .	...	...	...	...	...	...	...	...
Monetary authorities: short-term	4 718 . .	...	...	...	...	...	...	...	...
General government: long-term	4 720 . .	...	...	...	...	...	...	...	...
General government: short-term	4 721 . .	...	...	...	...	...	...	...	...
Banks: long-term	4 723 . .	...	...	...	...	...	...	...	...
Banks: short-term	4 724 . .	...	...	...	...	...	...	...	...
Other sectors: long-term	4 726 . .	3.9	–.3	4.7	.5	–3.0	7.8	1.3	–.8
Other sectors: short-term	4 727 . .	...	...	...	...	...	...	...	...
Currency and deposits	4 730 . .	–198.1	–334.2	–253.1	–163.2	–63.7	–45.5	14.0	84.5
Monetary authorities	4 731 . .	...	...	...	...	...	...	...	...
General government	4 732 . .	.7	–13.0	24.1	–40.5	...	...	...	...
Banks	4 733 . .	–182.1	–297.9	–290.8	–120.1	–61.0	–46.9	–55.8	–10.1
Other sectors	4 734 . .	–16.7	–23.3	13.7	–2.7	–2.7	1.3	69.8	94.6
Other assets	4 736 . .	...	–1.0	–1.0	–3.1	–2.0	–.7	...	...
Monetary authorities: long-term	4 738 . .	...	...	...	...	...	...	...	...
Monetary authorities: short-term	4 739 . .	...	...	...	...	...	...	...	...
General government: long-term	4 741 . .	...	...	...	...	...	...	...	...
General government: short-term	4 742 . .	...	...	...	...	...	...	...	...
Banks: long-term	4 744 . .	...	...	...	...	...	...	...	...
Banks: short-term	4 745 . .	...	...	...	...	...	...	...	...
Other sectors: long-term	4 747 . .	...	–1.0	–1.0	–3.1	–2.0	–.7	...	...
Other sectors: short-term	4 748 . .	...	...	...	...	...	...	...	...
Liabilities	4 753 . .	**189.1**	**305.0**	**302.1**	**122.7**	**90.6**	**69.8**	**20.1**	**–38.7**
Trade credits	4 756 . .	...	...	...	...	...	...	...	...
General government: long-term	4 758 . .	...	...	...	...	...	...	...	...
General government: short-term	4 759 . .	...	...	...	...	...	...	...	...
Other sectors: long-term	4 761 . .	...	...	...	...	...	...	...	...
Other sectors: short-term	4 762 . .	...	...	...	...	...	...	...	...
Loans	4 764 . .	7.0	6.1	5.8	2.6	27.7	19.7	–38.1	–48.8
Use of Fund credit and loans from the Fund	4 766 . .	...	...	...	...	...	...	...	...
Monetary authorities: other long-term	4 767 . .	...	...	...	...	...	...	...	...
Monetary authorities: short-term	4 768 . .	...	...	...	...	...	...	...	...
General government: long-term	4 770 . .	6.3	14.3	–3.3	–7.9	.4	–9.5	–38.3	–17.6
General government: short-term	4 771 . .	...	...	...	...	...	...	...	...
Banks: long-term	4 773 . .	–4.5	6.0	–.7	–5.4	–.4	12.8	3.9	–5.8
Banks: short-term	4 774 . .	...	...	...	...	...	...	...	...
Other sectors: long-term	4 776 . .	5.2	–14.2	9.8	16.0	27.7	16.3	–3.7	–25.4
Other sectors: short-term	4 777 . .	...	...	...	...	...	...	...	...
Currency and deposits	4 780 . .	182.1	297.9	290.8	120.1	60.9	46.9	55.8	10.2
Monetary authorities	4 781 . .	...	...	...	...	...	...	...	...
General government	4 782 . .	...	...	...	...	...	...	...	...
Banks	4 783 . .	182.1	297.9	290.8	120.1	60.9	46.9	55.8	10.2
Other sectors	4 784 . .	...	...	...	...	...	...	...	...
Other liabilities	4 786 . .	...	1.0	5.5	.1	2.0	3.3	2.5	...
Monetary authorities: long-term	4 788 . .	...	...	...	...	...	...	...	...
Monetary authorities: short-term	4 789 . .	...	...	...	...	...	...	...	...
General government: long-term	4 791 . .	...	...	...	...	...	...	...	...
General government: short-term	4 792 . .	...	...	...	...	...	...	...	...
Banks: long-term	4 794 . .	...	...	...	...	...	...	...	...
Banks: short-term	4 795 . .	...	...	...	...	...	...	...	...
Other sectors: long-term	4 797 . .	...	1.0	5.5	.1	2.0	3.3	2.5	...
Other sectors: short-term	4 798 . .	...	...	...	...	...	...	...	...
D. RESERVE ASSETS	4 800 . .	–33.4	44.2	29.8	42.2	–59.2	–44.0	75.9	–139.3
Monetary gold	4 810 . .	...	.1	...	.1	...	...	...	–78.8
Special drawing rights	4 820 . .	...	...	...	...	...	...	...	...
Reserve position in the Fund	4 830 . .	...	...	...	...	...	...	...	...
Foreign exchange	4 840 . .	–43.7	51.6	–4.7	38.7	–43.1	–14.5	55.2	–53.5
Other claims	4 880 . .	10.3	–7.5	34.5	3.5	–16.1	–29.6	20.7	–6.9
NET ERRORS AND OMISSIONS	4 998 . .	**19.5**	**14.6**	**6.5**	**6.2**	**8.2**	**11.5**	**24.9**	**22.5**

Table 1. ANALYTIC PRESENTATION, 1988–95
(Millions of U.S. dollars)

	Code	1988	1989	1990	1991	1992	1993	1994	1995
A. Current Account[1]	4 993 Y.	**–1,863**	**–1,525**	**–1,453**	**–1,159**	**–1,370**	**–1,070**	**–2,371**	**–3,778**
Goods: exports f.o.b	2 100 . .	8,831	8,846	9,190	9,555	9,735	10,468	11,984	13,485
Goods: imports f.o.b	3 100 . .	–6,658	–7,873	–8,375	–7,485	–8,108	–8,749	–10,648	–12,584
Balance on Goods	4 100 . .	*2,173*	*973*	*815*	*2,070*	*1,627*	*1,719*	*1,336*	*901*
Services: credit	2 200 . .	2,549	2,395	2,494	2,579	2,634	2,854	3,668	4,297
Services: debit	3 200 . .	–3,153	–3,167	–3,324	–3,414	–3,582	–3,505	–3,992	–4,600
Balance on Goods and Services	4 991 . .	*1,569*	*201*	*–15*	*1,235*	*679*	*1,068*	*1,011*	*598*
Income: credit	2 300 . .	451	661	719	33	–115	274	481	790
Income: debit	3 300 . .	–4,033	–2,545	–2,295	–2,566	–2,062	–2,544	–3,964	–5,244
Balance on Goods, Services, and Income	4 992 . .	*–2,014*	*–1,684*	*–1,591*	*–1,298*	*–1,498*	*–1,202*	*–2,472*	*–3,856*
Current transfers: credit	2 379 Y.	309	314	317	321	310	310	334	339
Current transfers: debit	3 379 . .	–159	–156	–179	–182	–182	–178	–233	–261
B. Capital Account[1]	4 994 Y.	**–49**	**47**	**213**	**252**	**292**	**542**	**806**	**1,239**
Capital account: credit	2 994 Y.	228	331	507	586	602	833	1,155	1,667
Capital account: debit	3 994 . .	–277	–284	–294	–334	–311	–291	–349	–427
Total, Groups A Plus B	4 010 . .	*–1,913*	*–1,478*	*–1,240*	*–907*	*–1,078*	*–528*	*–1,565*	*–2,539*
C. Financial Account[1]	4 995 X.	**–1,790**	**–739**	**875**	**–709**	**702**	**–520**	**1,133**	**527**
Direct investment abroad	4 505 . .	–373	–1,896	–1,594	–690	792	–1,300	–1,571	–924
Direct investment in New Zealand	4 555 Y.	1,717	1,627	1,735	1,290	2,086	2,469	2,524	2,509
Portfolio investment assets	4 602 . .	. . .	–40	–111	–68	–14	–286	75	63
Equity securities	4 610 . .	. . .	–50	–97	–53	–11	–185	–4	22
Debt securities	4 619 . .	. . .	10	–14	–15	–2	–101	79	41
Portfolio investment liabilities	4 652 Y.	. . .	70	282	–83	382	2,435	1,457	234
Equity securities	4 660 Y.	. . .	12	146	129	52	116	21	–6
Debt securities	4 669 Y.	. . .	58	136	–212	331	2,319	1,436	241
Other investment assets	4 703 . .	628	–254	–81	–207	113	–618	261	174
Monetary authorities	4 703 .A	. . .	. . .	. . .	. . .	. . .	. . .	. . .	. . .
General government	4 703 .B	. . .	–24	–45	–47	–47	–62	–81	–23
Banks	4 703 .C	628	–411	–42	31	7	86	–41	–26
Other sectors	4 703 .D	. . .	181	6	–191	154	–642	383	223
Other investment liabilities	4 753 X.	–3,762	–247	644	–952	–2,658	–3,219	–1,614	–1,528
Monetary authorities	4 753 XA	. . .	. . .	. . .	. . .	. . .	. . .	. . .	. . .
General government	4 753 YB	–2,673	–1,231	–832	–1,239	–2,352	–2,774	–2,631	–1,933
Banks	4 753 YC	95	–397	–58	–23	19	–85	75	38
Other sectors	4 753 YD	–1,183	1,382	1,534	310	–326	–360	942	366
Total, Groups A Through C	4 020 . .	*–3,703*	*–2,217*	*–365*	*–1,615*	*–376*	*–1,048*	*–433*	*–2,011*
D. Net Errors and Omissions	4 998 . .	**782**	**1,000**	**544**	**104**	**–1,101**	**–725**	**–788**	**2,345**
Total, Groups A Through D	4 030 . .	*–2,921*	*–1,217*	*179*	*–1,511*	*–1,477*	*–1,773*	*–1,220*	*334*
E. Reserves and Related Items	4 040 . .	**2,921**	**1,217**	**–179**	**1,511**	**1,477**	**1,773**	**1,220**	**–334**
Reserve assets	4 800 . .	735	–248	–1,014	1,319	–131	74	–422	–384
Use of Fund credit and loans	4 766 . .	. . .	. . .	. . .	. . .	. . .	. . .	. . .	. . .
Liabilities constituting foreign authorities' reserves	4 900 . .	. . .	. . .	. . .	. . .	. . .	. . .	. . .	. . .
Exceptional financing	4 920 . .	2,186	1,466	835	192	1,608	1,699	1,642	50
Conversion rates: New Zealand dollars per U.S. dollar	0 101 . .	**1.5264**	**1.6721**	**1.6762**	**1.7335**	**1.8618**	**1.8505**	**1.6865**	**1.5239**

[1] Excludes components that have been classified in the categories of Group E.

Table 2. STANDARD PRESENTATION, 1988–95
(Millions of U.S. dollars)

	Code	1988	1989	1990	1991	1992	1993	1994	1995
CURRENT ACCOUNT	4 993 . .	**–1,863**	**–1,525**	**–1,453**	**–1,159**	**–1,370**	**–1,070**	**–2,371**	**–3,778**
A. GOODS	4 100 . .	2,173	973	815	2,070	1,627	1,719	1,336	901
Credit	2 100 . .	**8,831**	**8,846**	**9,190**	**9,555**	**9,735**	**10,468**	**11,984**	**13,485**
General merchandise: exports f.o.b.	2 110 . .	8,831	8,846	9,190	9,555	9,735	10,468	11,984	13,485
Goods for processing: exports f.o.b.	2 150 . .	. . .	. . .	. . .	. . .	. . .	. . .	. . .	. . .
Repairs on goods	2 160 . .	. . .	. . .	. . .	. . .	. . .	. . .	. . .	. . .
Goods procured in ports by carriers	2 170 . .	. . .	. . .	. . .	. . .	. . .	. . .	. . .	. . .
Nonmonetary gold	2 180 . .	. . .	. . .	. . .	. . .	. . .	. . .	. . .	. . .
Debit	3 100 . .	**–6,658**	**–7,873**	**–8,375**	**–7,485**	**–8,108**	**–8,749**	**–10,648**	**–12,584**
General merchandise: imports f.o.b.	3 110 . .	–6,658	–7,873	–8,375	–7,485	–8,108	–8,749	–10,648	–12,584
Goods for processing: imports f.o.b.	3 150 . .	. . .	. . .	. . .	. . .	. . .	. . .	. . .	. . .
Repairs on goods	3 160 . .	. . .	. . .	. . .	. . .	. . .	. . .	. . .	. . .
Goods procured in ports by carriers	3 170 . .	. . .	. . .	. . .	. . .	. . .	. . .	. . .	. . .
Nonmonetary gold	3 180 . .	. . .	. . .	. . .	. . .	. . .	. . .	. . .	. . .
B. SERVICES	4 200 . .	–604	–772	–830	–834	–948	–651	–324	–303
Total credit	2 200 . .	*2,549*	*2,395*	*2,494*	*2,579*	*2,634*	*2,854*	*3,668*	*4,297*
Total debit	3 200 . .	*–3,153*	*–3,167*	*–3,324*	*–3,414*	*–3,582*	*–3,505*	*–3,992*	*–4,600*
Transportation services, credit	2 205 . .	**1,034**	**944**	**1,049**	**1,086**	**1,109**	**1,149**	**1,465**	**1,529**
Passenger	2 205 BA	*294*	*416*	*469*	*488*	*554*	*573*	*785*	*804*
Freight	2 205 BB	*431*	*144*	*143*	*157*	*134*	*150*	*164*	*168*
Other	2 205 BC	*310*	*384*	*437*	*440*	*420*	*426*	*517*	*557*
Sea transport, passenger	2 207 . .	. . .	. . .	. . .	. . .	. . .	. . .	. . .	. . .
Sea transport, freight	2 208 . .	. . .	. . .	. . .	. . .	. . .	. . .	. . .	. . .
Sea transport, other	2 209 . .	. . .	. . .	. . .	. . .	. . .	. . .	. . .	. . .
Air transport, passenger	2 211 . .	. . .	. . .	. . .	. . .	. . .	. . .	. . .	. . .
Air transport, freight	2 212 . .	. . .	. . .	. . .	. . .	. . .	. . .	. . .	. . .
Air transport, other	2 213 . .	. . .	. . .	. . .	. . .	. . .	. . .	. . .	. . .
Other transport, passenger	2 215 . .	. . .	. . .	. . .	. . .	. . .	. . .	. . .	. . .
Other transport, freight	2 216 . .	. . .	. . .	. . .	. . .	. . .	. . .	. . .	. . .
Other transport, other	2 217 . .	. . .	. . .	. . .	. . .	. . .	. . .	. . .	. . .
Transportation services, debit	3 205 . .	**–1,117**	**–1,253**	**–1,319**	**–1,311**	**–1,287**	**–1,310**	**–1,526**	**–1,824**
Passenger	3 205 BA	*–312*	*–381*	*–371*	*–365*	*–332*	*–309*	*–352*	*–422*
Freight	3 205 BB	*–626*	*–618*	*–663*	*–591*	*–597*	*–634*	*–733*	*–868*
Other	3 205 BC	*–180*	*–255*	*–285*	*–355*	*–357*	*–366*	*–442*	*–534*
Sea transport, passenger	3 207 . .	. . .	. . .	. . .	. . .	. . .	. . .	. . .	. . .
Sea transport, freight	3 208 . .	. . .	. . .	. . .	. . .	. . .	. . .	. . .	. . .
Sea transport, other	3 209 . .	. . .	. . .	. . .	. . .	. . .	. . .	. . .	. . .
Air transport, passenger	3 211 . .	. . .	. . .	. . .	. . .	. . .	. . .	. . .	. . .
Air transport, freight	3 212 . .	. . .	. . .	. . .	. . .	. . .	. . .	. . .	. . .
Air transport, other	3 213 . .	. . .	. . .	. . .	. . .	. . .	. . .	. . .	. . .
Other transport, passenger	3 215 . .	. . .	. . .	. . .	. . .	. . .	. . .	. . .	. . .
Other transport, freight	3 216 . .	. . .	. . .	. . .	. . .	. . .	. . .	. . .	. . .
Other transport, other	3 217 . .	. . .	. . .	. . .	. . .	. . .	. . .	. . .	. . .
Travel, credit	2 236 . .	**1,014**	**1,005**	**1,030**	**1,070**	**1,097**	**1,245**	**1,669**	**2,163**
Business travel	2 237 . .	. . .	. . .	. . .	. . .	. . .	. . .	. . .	. . .
Personal travel	2 240 . .	. . .	. . .	. . .	. . .	. . .	. . .	. . .	. . .
Travel, debit	3 236 . .	**–988**	**–944**	**–958**	**–987**	**–977**	**–1,002**	**–1,148**	**–1,283**
Business travel	3 237 . .	. . .	. . .	. . .	. . .	. . .	. . .	. . .	. . .
Personal travel	3 240 . .	. . .	. . .	. . .	. . .	. . .	. . .	. . .	. . .
Other services, credit	2 200 BA	**502**	**446**	**415**	**423**	**428**	**460**	**534**	**605**
Communications	2 245 . .	. . .	. . .	. . .	. . .	. . .	. . .	. . .	. . .
Construction	2 249 . .	. . .	. . .	. . .	. . .	. . .	. . .	. . .	. . .
Insurance	2 253 . .	7	8	–6	–12	–25	–17	–14	–11
Financial	2 260 . .	. . .	. . .	. . .	. . .	. . .	. . .	. . .	. . .
Computer and information	2 262 . .	. . .	. . .	. . .	. . .	. . .	. . .	. . .	. . .
Royalties and licence fees	2 266 . .	. . .	. . .	. . .	. . .	. . .	. . .	. . .	. . .
Other business services	2 268 . .	425	386	342	365	399	427	496	568
Personal, cultural, and recreational	2 287 . .	. . .	. . .	. . .	. . .	. . .	. . .	. . .	. . .
Government, n.i.e.	2 291 . .	70	52	79	70	54	50	52	49
Other services, debit	3 200 BA	**–1,048**	**–969**	**–1,047**	**–1,115**	**–1,318**	**–1,194**	**–1,318**	**–1,493**
Communications	3 245 . .	. . .	. . .	. . .	. . .	. . .	. . .	. . .	. . .
Construction	3 249 . .	. . .	. . .	. . .	. . .	. . .	. . .	. . .	. . .
Insurance	3 253 . .	–71	–66	–81	–117	–120	–162	–202	–230
Financial	3 260 . .	. . .	. . .	. . .	. . .	. . .	. . .	. . .	. . .
Computer and information	3 262 . .	. . .	. . .	. . .	. . .	. . .	. . .	. . .	. . .
Royalties and licence fees	3 266 . .	. . .	. . .	. . .	. . .	. . .	. . .	. . .	. . .
Other business services	3 268 . .	–839	–815	–894	–935	–1,130	–982	–1,053	–1,187
Personal, cultural, and recreational	3 287 . .	. . .	. . .	. . .	. . .	. . .	. . .	. . .	. . .
Government, n.i.e.	3 291 . .	–138	–88	–73	–63	–68	–50	–63	–76

Table 2 (Continued). STANDARD PRESENTATION, 1988–95
(Millions of U.S. dollars)

	Code		1988	1989	1990	1991	1992	1993	1994	1995
C. INCOME	4 300	. .	–3,582	–1,884	–1,576	–2,533	–2,177	–2,270	–3,483	–4,454
Total credit	2 300	. .	*451*	*661*	*719*	*33*	*–115*	*274*	*481*	*790*
Total debit	3 300	. .	*–4,033*	*–2,545*	*–2,295*	*–2,566*	*–2,062*	*–2,544*	*–3,964*	*–5,244*
Compensation of employees, credit	2 310	. .	...	...	...	...	...	...	...	...
Compensation of employees, debit	3 310	. .	...	...	...	...	...	...	...	...
Investment income, credit	2 320	. .	**451**	**661**	**719**	**33**	**–115**	**274**	**481**	**790**
Direct investment income	2 330	. .	101	346	305	–341	–373	39	275	446
Dividends and distributed branch profits	2 332	. .	...	...	...	...	...	...	...	...
Reinvested earnings and undistributed branch profits	2 333	. .	375	596	555	116	–150	154	408	683
Income on debt (interest)	2 334	. .	–274	–250	–250	–456	–222	–115	–132	–237
Portfolio investment income	2 339	. .	...	...	...	...	...	...	...	...
Income on equity	2 340	. .	...	...	...	...	...	...	...	...
Income on bonds and notes	2 350	. .	...	...	...	...	...	...	...	...
Income on money market instruments and financial derivatives	2 360	. .	...	...	...	...	...	...	...	...
Other investment income	2 370	. .	350	314	414	374	258	235	205	344
Investment income, debit	3 320	. .	**–4,033**	**–2,545**	**–2,295**	**–2,566**	**–2,062**	**–2,544**	**–3,964**	**–5,244**
Direct investment income	3 330	. .	–1,757	–462	–129	–554	–689	–1,348	–2,395	–3,370
Dividends and distributed branch profits	3 332	. .	–348	–318	–318	–405	–214	–728	–1,180	–1,155
Reinvested earnings and undistributed branch profits	3 333	. .	–1,410	–144	189	–148	–475	–620	–1,215	–2,215
Income on debt (interest)	3 334	. .	...	...	...	...	...	...	...	...
Portfolio investment income	3 339	. .	...	...	...	...	...	...	...	...
Income on equity	3 340	. .	...	...	...	...	...	...	...	...
Income on bonds and notes	3 350	. .	...	...	...	...	...	...	...	...
Income on money market instruments and financial derivatives	3 360	. .	...	...	...	...	...	...	...	...
Other investment income	3 370	. .	–2,276	–2,082	–2,166	–2,013	–1,373	–1,196	–1,569	–1,874
D. CURRENT TRANSFERS	4 379	. .	150	158	138	139	129	132	101	78
Credit	2 379	. .	**309**	**314**	**317**	**321**	**310**	**310**	**334**	**339**
General government	2 380	. .	45	61	63	63	54	57	67	64
Other sectors	2 390	. .	264	254	254	258	257	253	267	275
Workers' remittances	2 391	. .	264	254	254	258	257	253	267	275
Other current transfers	2 392	. .	...	...	...	...	...	...	...	...
Debit	3 379	. .	**–159**	**–156**	**–179**	**–182**	**–182**	**–178**	**–233**	**–261**
General government	3 380	. .	–89	–87	–107	–108	–109	–103	–145	–160
Other sectors	3 390	. .	–70	–69	–72	–74	–72	–75	–88	–101
Workers' remittances	3 391	. .	–70	–69	–72	–74	–72	–75	–88	–101
Other current transfers	3 392	. .	...	...	...	...	...	...	...	...
CAPITAL AND FINANCIAL ACCOUNT	4 996	. .	**1,081**	**525**	**910**	**1,055**	**2,471**	**1,795**	**3,159**	**1,433**
CAPITAL ACCOUNT	4 994	. .	**–49**	**47**	**213**	**252**	**292**	**542**	**806**	**1,239**
Total credit	2 994	. .	*228*	*331*	*507*	*586*	*602*	*833*	*1,155*	*1,667*
Total debit	3 994	. .	*–277*	*–284*	*–294*	*–334*	*–311*	*–291*	*–349*	*–427*
Capital transfers, credit	2 400	. .	**228**	**331**	**507**	**586**	**602**	**833**	**1,155**	**1,667**
General government	2 401	. .	...	...	...	...	...	...	...	...
Debt forgiveness	2 402	. .	...	...	...	...	...	...	...	...
Other capital transfers	2 410	. .	...	...	...	...	...	...	...	...
Other sectors	2 430	. .	228	331	507	586	602	833	1,155	1,667
Migrants' transfers	2 431	. .	228	331	507	586	602	833	1,155	1,667
Debt forgiveness	2 432	. .	...	...	...	...	...	...	...	...
Other capital transfers	2 440	. .	...	...	...	...	...	...	...	...
Capital transfers, debit	3 400	. .	**–277**	**–284**	**–294**	**–334**	**–311**	**–291**	**–349**	**–427**
General government	3 401	. .	...	...	...	...	...	...	...	...
Debt forgiveness	3 402	. .	...	...	...	...	...	...	...	...
Other capital transfers	3 410	. .	...	...	...	...	...	...	...	...
Other sectors	3 430	. .	–277	–284	–294	–334	–311	–291	–349	–427
Migrants' transfers	3 431	. .	–277	–284	–294	–334	–311	–291	–349	–427
Debt forgiveness	3 432	. .	...	...	...	...	...	...	...	...
Other capital transfers	3 440	. .	...	...	...	...	...	...	...	...
Nonproduced nonfinancial assets, credit	2 480	. .	...	...	...	...	...	...	...	...
Nonproduced nonfinancial assets, debit	3 480	. .	...	...	...	...	...	...	...	...

Table 2 (Continued). STANDARD PRESENTATION, 1988–95
(Millions of U.S. dollars)

	Code	1988	1989	1990	1991	1992	1993	1994	1995
FINANCIAL ACCOUNT	4 995	**1,131**	**478**	**697**	**802**	**2,179**	**1,253**	**2,353**	**193**
A. DIRECT INVESTMENT	4 500	1,344	–269	141	600	2,878	1,169	953	1,584
Direct investment abroad	4 505	**–373**	**–1,896**	**–1,594**	**–690**	**792**	**–1,300**	**–1,571**	**–924**
Equity capital	4 510	–55	–691	–1,688	–837	–641	–1,322	–336	23
Claims on affiliated enterprises	4 515	...	...	...	...	...	...	...	...
Liabilities to affiliated enterprises	4 520	...	...	...	...	...	...	...	...
Reinvested earnings	4 525	–375	–596	–555	–116	150	–154	–408	–683
Other capital	4 530	57	–608	649	263	1,283	176	–828	–265
Claims on affiliated enterprises	4 535	...	...	...	...	...	...	...	...
Liabilities to affiliated enterprises	4 540	...	...	...	...	...	...	...	...
Direct investment in New Zealand	4 555	**1,717**	**1,627**	**1,735**	**1,290**	**2,086**	**2,469**	**2,524**	**2,509**
Equity capital	4 560	247	1,396	330	730	1,028	1,030	1,121	303
Claims on direct investors	4 565	...	...	...	...	...	...	...	...
Liabilities to direct investors	4 570	...	...	...	...	...	...	...	...
Reinvested earnings	4 575	1,410	144	–189	148	476	621	1,215	2,215
Other capital	4 580	61	87	1,595	411	582	818	188	–10
Claims on direct investors	4 585	...	...	...	...	...	...	...	...
Liabilities to direct investors	4 590	...	...	...	...	...	...	...	...
B. PORTFOLIO INVESTMENT	4 600	...	30	171	–151	369	2,148	1,532	297
Assets	4 602	**...**	**–40**	**–111**	**–68**	**–14**	**–286**	**75**	**63**
Equity securities	4 610	...	–50	–97	–53	–11	–185	–4	22
Monetary authorities	4 611	...	...	...	...	...	...	...	...
General government	4 612	...	...	...	...	...	...	...	...
Banks	4 613	...	...	...	...	...	...	...	...
Other sectors	4 614	...	...	...	...	...	...	...	...
Debt securities	4 619	...	10	–14	–15	–2	–101	79	41
Bonds and notes	4 620	...	10	–14	–15	–2	–101	79	41
Monetary authorities	4 621	...	...	...	...	...	...	...	...
General government	4 622	...	...	...	...	...	...	...	...
Banks	4 623	...	...	...	...	...	...	...	...
Other sectors	4 624	...	...	...	...	...	...	...	...
Money market instruments	4 630	...	...	...	...	...	...	...	...
Monetary authorities	4 631	...	...	...	...	...	...	...	...
General government	4 632	...	...	...	...	...	...	...	...
Banks	4 633	...	...	...	...	...	...	...	...
Other sectors	4 634	...	...	...	...	...	...	...	...
Financial derivatives	4 640	...	...	...	...	...	...	...	...
Monetary authorities	4 641	...	...	...	...	...	...	...	...
General government	4 642	...	...	...	...	...	...	...	...
Banks	4 643	...	...	...	...	...	...	...	...
Other sectors	4 644	...	...	...	...	...	...	...	...
Liabilities	4 652	**...**	**70**	**282**	**–83**	**382**	**2,435**	**1,457**	**234**
Equity securities	4 660	...	12	146	129	52	116	21	–6
Banks	4 663	...	...	...	...	...	...	...	...
Other sectors	4 664	...	...	...	...	...	...	...	...
Debt securities	4 669	...	58	136	–212	331	2,319	1,436	241
Bonds and notes	4 670	...	58	136	–212	331	2,319	1,436	241
Monetary authorities	4 671	...	...	...	...	...	...	...	...
General government	4 672	...	–100	–34	...	...	...	...	...
Banks	4 673	...	...	...	...	...	...	...	...
Other sectors	4 674	...	158	170	–212	331	2,319	1,436	241
Money market instruments	4 680	...	...	...	...	...	...	...	...
Monetary authorities	4 681	...	...	...	...	...	...	...	...
General government	4 682	...	...	...	...	...	...	...	...
Banks	4 683	...	...	...	...	...	...	...	...
Other sectors	4 684	...	...	...	...	...	...	...	...
Financial derivatives	4 690	...	...	...	...	...	...	...	...
Monetary authorities	4 691	...	...	...	...	...	...	...	...
General government	4 692	...	...	...	...	...	...	...	...
Banks	4 693	...	...	...	...	...	...	...	...
Other sectors	4 694	...	...	...	...	...	...	...	...

Table 2 (Concluded). STANDARD PRESENTATION, 1988–95
(Millions of U.S. dollars)

	Code	1988	1989	1990	1991	1992	1993	1994	1995
C. OTHER INVESTMENT	4 700	–948	965	1,398	–966	–937	–2,139	290	–1,304
Assets	4 703	**628**	**–254**	**–81**	**–207**	**113**	**–618**	**261**	**174**
Trade credits	4 706	...	...	...	...	...	...	...	...
General government: long-term	4 708	...	...	...	...	...	...	...	...
General government: short-term	4 709	...	...	...	...	...	...	...	...
Other sectors: long-term	4 711	...	...	...	...	...	...	...	...
Other sectors: short-term	4 712	...	...	...	...	...	...	...	...
Loans	4 714	...	...	...	...	...	...	...	...
Monetary authorities: long-term	4 717	...	...	...	...	...	...	...	...
Monetary authorities: short-term	4 718	...	...	...	...	...	...	...	...
General government: long-term	4 720	...	...	...	...	...	...	...	...
General government: short-term	4 721	...	...	...	...	...	...	...	...
Banks: long-term	4 723	...	...	...	...	...	...	...	...
Banks: short-term	4 724	...	...	...	...	...	...	...	...
Other sectors: long-term	4 726	...	...	...	...	...	...	...	...
Other sectors: short-term	4 727	...	...	...	...	...	...	...	...
Currency and deposits	4 730	628	–69	94	–75	152	–560	352	201
Monetary authorities	4 731	...	...	...	...	...	...	...	...
General government	4 732	...	...	...	...	...	...	...	...
Banks	4 733	628	–411	–42	31	7	86	–41	–26
Other sectors	4 734	...	342	135	–106	145	–645	393	226
Other assets	4 736	...	–185	–174	–132	–39	–58	–90	–26
Monetary authorities: long-term	4 738	...	...	...	...	...	...	...	...
Monetary authorities: short-term	4 739	...	...	...	...	...	...	...	...
General government: long-term	4 741	...	–24	–45	–47	–47	–62	–81	–23
General government: short-term	4 742	...	...	...	...	...	...	...	...
Banks: long-term	4 744	...	...	...	...	...	...	...	...
Banks: short-term	4 745	...	...	...	...	...	...	...	...
Other sectors: long-term	4 747	...	–161	–129	–86	8	3	–9	–3
Other sectors: short-term	4 748	...	...	...	...	...	...	...	...
Liabilities	4 753	**–1,576**	**1,219**	**1,479**	**–759**	**–1,050**	**–1,520**	**28**	**–1,478**
Trade credits	4 756	...	...	...	...	...	...	...	...
General government: long-term	4 758	...	...	...	...	...	...	...	...
General government: short-term	4 759	...	...	...	...	...	...	...	...
Other sectors: long-term	4 761	...	...	...	...	...	...	...	...
Other sectors: short-term	4 762	...	...	...	...	...	...	...	...
Loans	4 764	–452	234	3	–1,046	–743	–1,075	–989	–1,883
Use of Fund credit and loans from the Fund	4 766	...	...	...	...	...	...	...	...
Monetary authorities: other long-term	4 767	...	...	...	...	...	...	...	...
Monetary authorities: short-term	4 768	...	...	...	...	...	...	...	...
General government: long-term	4 770	–533	–53	23	–984	–748	–1,046	–401	–1,681
General government: short-term	4 771	81	288	–20	–63	5	–29	–588	–202
Banks: long-term	4 773	...	...	...	...	...	...	...	...
Banks: short-term	4 774	...	...	...	...	...	...	...	...
Other sectors: long-term	4 776	...	...	...	...	...	...	...	...
Other sectors: short-term	4 777	...	...	...	...	...	...	...	...
Currency and deposits	4 780	95	–397	–58	–23	19	–85	75	38
Monetary authorities	4 781	...	...	...	...	...	...	...	...
General government	4 782	...	...	...	...	...	...	...	...
Banks	4 783	95	–397	–58	–23	19	–85	75	38
Other sectors	4 784	...	...	...	...	...	...	...	...
Other liabilities	4 786	–1,219	1,382	1,534	310	–326	–360	942	366
Monetary authorities: long-term	4 788	...	...	...	...	...	...	...	...
Monetary authorities: short-term	4 789	...	...	...	...	...	...	...	...
General government: long-term	4 791	–35	...	...	...	...	...	...	...
General government: short-term	4 792	...	...	...	...	...	...	...	...
Banks: long-term	4 794	...	...	...	...	...	...	...	...
Banks: short-term	4 795	...	...	...	...	...	...	...	...
Other sectors: long-term	4 797	–1,183	81	–202	–167	–1,181	–739	–336	–75
Other sectors: short-term	4 798	...	1,301	1,737	478	855	379	1,279	441
D. RESERVE ASSETS	4 800	735	–248	–1,014	1,319	–131	74	–422	–384
Monetary gold	4 810	...	...	...	...	...	...	...	...
Special drawing rights	4 820	...	...	...	...	...	...	...	–1
Reserve position in the Fund	4 830	–11	–40	...	–19	–77	8	4	–14
Foreign exchange	4 840	746	–209	–1,014	1,338	–55	67	–425	–369
Other claims	4 880	...	...	...	...	...	...	...	...
NET ERRORS AND OMISSIONS	4 998	**782**	**1,000**	**544**	**104**	**–1,101**	**–725**	**–788**	**2,345**

Part 3 of the *Yearbook* contains descriptions of the methodologies, compilation practices, and sources used to compile these data.

Table 3. INTERNATIONAL INVESTMENT POSITION (End–March stocks), 1988–95
(Millions of U.S. dollars)

	Code	1988	1989	1990	1991	1992	1993	1994	1995
ASSETS	8 995 C.	...	...	8,814	12,255	12,204	10,037	13,251	15,367
Direct investment abroad	8 505 . .	...	...	**3,269**	**5,951**	**6,302**	**4,221**	**5,458**	**7,497**
Equity capital and reinvested earnings	8 506 . .	...	...	4,389	7,687	7,845	7,547	8,371	9,623
Claims on affiliated enterprises	8 507 . .	...	...	...	...	...	...	...	...
Liabilities to affiliated enterprises	8 508 . .	...	...	...	...	...	...	...	...
Other capital	8 530 . .	...	...	–1,120	–1,735	–1,543	–3,327	–2,913	–2,126
Claims on affiliated enterprises	8 535 . .	...	...	1,898	1,870	2,075	995	780	1,092
Liabilities to affiliated enterprises	8 540 . .	...	...	–3,019	–3,605	–3,618	–4,321	–3,692	–3,218
Portfolio investment	8 602 . .	...	...	**148**	**298**	**731**	**835**	**1,193**	**1,348**
Equity securities	8 610 . .	...	...	143	270	503	603	808	1,077
Monetary authorities	8 611 . .	...	...	...	...	...	...	...	...
General government	8 612 . .	...	...	...	...	...	...	...	...
Banks	8 613 . .	...	...	...	...	...	...	...	...
Other sectors	8 614 . .	...	...	...	...	...	...	...	...
Debt securities	8 619 . .	...	...	5	28	228	232	385	271
Bonds and notes	8 620 . .	...	...	...	...	...	...	...	...
Monetary authorities	8 621 . .	...	...	...	...	...	...	...	...
General government	8 622 . .	...	...	...	...	...	...	...	...
Banks	8 623 . .	...	...	...	...	...	...	...	...
Other sectors	8 624 . .	...	...	...	...	...	...	...	...
Money market instruments	8 630 . .	...	...	...	...	...	...	...	...
Monetary authorities	8 631 . .	...	...	...	...	...	...	...	...
General government	8 632 . .	...	...	...	...	...	...	...	...
Banks	8 633 . .	...	...	...	...	...	...	...	...
Other sectors	8 634 . .	...	...	...	...	...	...	...	...
Financial derivatives	8 640 . .	...	...	...	...	...	...	...	...
Monetary authorities	8 641 . .	...	...	...	...	...	...	...	...
General government	8 642 . .	...	...	...	...	...	...	...	...
Banks	8 643 . .	...	...	...	...	...	...	...	...
Other sectors	8 644 . .	...	...	...	...	...	...	...	...
Other investment	8 703 . .	...	...	**2,149**	**2,130**	**2,001**	**1,687**	**2,715**	**2,422**
Trade credits	8 706 . .	...	...	576	689	583	812	805	986
General government: long-term	8 708 . .	...	...	...	...	...	...	...	...
General government: short-term	8 709 . .	...	...	...	...	...	...	...	...
Other sectors: long-term	8 711 . .	...	...	...	...	...	...	...	...
Other sectors: short-term	8 712 . .	...	...	...	...	...	...	...	...
Loans	8 714 . .	...	...	636	379	237	92	1,218	420
Monetary authorities: long-term	8 717 . .	...	...	...	...	...	...	...	...
Monetary authorities: short-term	8 718 . .	...	...	...	...	...	...	...	...
General government: long-term	8 720 . .	...	...	...	...	...	...	...	...
General government: short-term	8 721 . .	...	...	...	...	...	...	...	...
Banks: long-term	8 723 . .	...	...	...	...	...	...	...	...
Banks: short-term	8 724 . .	...	...	...	...	...	...	...	...
Other sectors: long-term	8 726 . .	...	...	...	...	...	...	...	...
Other sectors: short-term	8 727 . .	...	...	...	...	...	...	...	...
Currency and deposits	8 730 . .	...	...	566	557	754	460	388	466
Monetary authorities	8 731 . .	...	...	...	...	...	...	...	...
General government	8 732 . .	...	...	...	...	...	...	...	...
Banks	8 733 . .	...	...	...	...	...	...	...	...
Other sectors	8 734 . .	...	...	...	...	...	...	...	...
Other assets	8 736 . .	...	...	370	505	426	322	305	551
Monetary authorities: long-term	8 738 . .	...	...	...	...	...	...	...	...
Monetary authorities: short-term	8 739 . .	...	...	...	...	...	...	...	...
General government: long-term	8 741 . .	...	...	...	...	...	...	...	...
General government: short-term	8 742 . .	...	...	...	...	...	...	...	...
Banks: long-term	8 744 . .	...	...	...	...	...	...	...	...
Banks: short-term	8 745 . .	...	...	...	...	...	...	...	...
Other sectors: long-term	8 747 . .	...	...	...	...	...	...	...	...
Other sectors: short-term	8 748 . .	...	...	...	...	...	...	...	...
Reserve assets	8 800 . .	...	...	**3,248**	**3,876**	**3,171**	**3,294**	**3,885**	**4,100**
Monetary gold	8 810 . .	...	...	...	...	...	...	...	...
Special drawing rights	8 820 . .	10	...	...	...	1	...	...	...
Reserve position in the Fund	8 830 . .	...	11	57	62	82	149	146	158
Foreign exchange	8 840 . .	...	...	3,190	3,814	3,089	3,146	3,741	3,942
Other claims	8 880 . .	...	...	...	...	...	...	...	...

Table 3 (Continued). INTERNATIONAL INVESTMENT POSITION (End–March stocks), 1988–95
(Millions of U.S. dollars)

	Code		1988	1989	1990	1991	1992	1993	1994	1995
LIABILITIES	8 995	D.	...	...	34,995	40,085	40,835	44,140	51,811	62,814
Direct investment in New Zealand	8 555	..	...	...	**7,938**	**10,760**	**12,456**	**14,852**	**20,228**	**26,166**
Equity capital and reinvested earnings	8 556	..	...	...	7,113	7,796	9,722	11,407	15,689	21,020
Claims on direct investors	8 557	..	...	...	...	...	...	...	...	...
Liabilities to direct investors	8 558	..	...	...	...	...	...	...	...	...
Other capital	8 580	..	...	...	826	2,965	2,735	3,445	4,539	5,146
Claims on direct investors	8 585	..	...	...	–800	–1,359	–836	–923	–862	–944
Liabilities to direct investors	8 590	..	...	...	1,625	4,324	3,570	4,368	5,401	6,090
Portfolio investment	8 652	..	...	...	**11,941**	**12,642**	**12,802**	**14,049**	**16,016**	**17,519**
Equity securities	8 660	..	...	...	903	1,036	466	1,318	889	1,119
Banks	8 663	..	...	...	...	...	...	...	...	...
Other sectors	8 664	..	...	...	...	...	...	...	...	...
Debt securities	8 669	..	...	...	11,037	11,607	12,336	12,731	15,127	16,400
Bonds and notes	8 670	..	...	...	...	...	...	...	...	...
Monetary authorities	8 671	..	...	...	...	...	...	...	...	...
General government	8 672	..	...	...	...	...	...	...	...	...
Banks	8 673	..	...	...	...	...	...	...	...	...
Other sectors	8 674	..	...	...	...	...	...	...	...	...
Money market instruments	8 680	..	...	...	...	...	...	...	...	...
Monetary authorities	8 681	..	...	...	...	...	...	...	...	...
General government	8 682	..	...	...	...	...	...	...	...	...
Banks	8 683	..	...	...	...	...	...	...	...	...
Other sectors	8 684	..	...	...	...	...	...	...	...	...
Financial derivatives	8 690	..	...	...	...	...	...	...	...	...
Monetary authorities	8 691	..	...	...	...	...	...	...	...	...
General government	8 692	..	...	...	...	...	...	...	...	...
Banks	8 692	..	...	...	...	...	...	...	...	...
Other sectors	8 694	..	...	...	...	...	...	...	...	...
Other investment	8 753	..	...	...	**15,117**	**16,683**	**15,577**	**15,238**	**15,567**	**19,129**
Trade credits	8 756	..	...	...	371	450	180	487	546	730
General government: long-term	8 758	..	...	...	...	...	...	...	...	...
General government: short-term	8 759	..	...	...	...	...	...	...	...	...
Other sectors: long-term	8 761	..	...	...	...	...	...	...	...	...
Other sectors: short-term	8 762	..	...	...	...	...	...	...	...	...
Loans	8 764	..	...	...	10,496	9,533	8,518	6,217	5,844	6,392
Use of Fund credit and loans from the Fund	8 766	..	...	...	...	...	...	...	...	...
Monetary authorities: other long-term	8 767	..	...	...	...	...	...	...	...	...
Monetary authorities: short-term	8 768	..	...	...	...	...	...	...	...	...
General government: long-term	8 770	..	...	...	...	...	...	...	...	...
General government: short-term	8 771	..	...	...	...	...	...	...	...	...
Banks: long-term	8 773	..	...	...	...	...	...	...	...	...
Banks: short-term	8 774	..	...	...	...	...	...	...	...	...
Other sectors: long-term	8 776	..	...	...	...	...	...	...	...	...
Other sectors: short-term	8 777	..	...	...	...	...	...	...	...	...
Currency and deposits	8 780	..	...	...	2,609	4,762	4,772	6,886	7,232	9,540
Monetary authorities	8 781	..	...	...	...	...	...	...	...	...
General government	8 782	..	...	...	...	...	...	...	...	...
Banks	8 783	..	...	...	...	...	...	...	...	...
Other sectors	8 784	..	...	...	...	...	...	...	...	...
Other liabilities	8 786	..	...	...	1,640	1,938	2,108	1,648	1,945	2,468
Monetary authorities: long-term	8 788	..	...	...	...	...	...	...	...	...
Monetary authorities: short-term	8 789	..	...	...	...	...	...	...	...	...
General government: long-term	8 791	..	...	...	...	...	...	...	...	...
General government: short-term	8 792	..	...	...	...	...	...	...	...	...
Banks: long-term	8 794	..	...	...	...	...	...	...	...	...
Banks: short-term	8 795	..	...	...	...	...	...	...	...	...
Other sectors: long-term	8 797	..	...	...	...	...	...	...	...	...
Other sectors: short-term	8 798	..	...	...	...	...	...	...	...	...
NET INTERNATIONAL INVESTMENT POSITION	8 995	..	...	...	**–26,182**	**–27,830**	**–28,630**	**–34,102**	**–38,559**	**–47,447**
Conversion rates: New Zealand dollars per U.S. dollar (end of period)	0 102	..	**1.5106**	**1.6239**	**1.7283**	**1.7053**	**1.8258**	**1.8728**	**1.7778**	**1.5399**

Table 1. ANALYTIC PRESENTATION, 1988–95
(Millions of U.S. dollars)

	Code	1988	1989	1990	1991	1992	1993	1994	1995
A. Current Account[1]	4 993 Y.	**–715.4**	**–361.7**	**–305.2**	**–4.8**	**–834.0**	**–644.3**	**–728.9**	**–706.0**
Goods: exports f.o.b	2 100 ..	235.7	318.7	332.4	268.1	223.1	267.0	351.2	528.6
Goods: imports f.o.b	3 100 ..	–718.3	–547.3	–569.7	–688.0	–770.8	–659.4	–784.7	–852.1
Balance on Goods	4 100 ..	*–482.6*	*–228.6*	*–237.3*	*–419.9*	*–547.7*	*–392.4*	*–433.5*	*–323.5*
Services: credit	2 200 ..	37.4	22.0	59.8	70.2	86.2	100.2	101.4	118.9
Services: debit	3 200 ..	–138.1	–119.2	–112.3	–136.2	–148.3	–156.6	–172.2	–217.9
Balance on Goods and Services	4 991 ..	*–583.3*	*–325.8*	*–289.8*	*–485.9*	*–609.8*	*–448.8*	*–504.3*	*–422.5*
Income: credit	2 300 ..	2.1	6.8	11.8	9.7	7.5	5.4	6.7	7.2
Income: debit	3 300 ..	–264.2	–211.6	–228.8	–373.0	–502.3	–434.5	–472.2	–365.7
Balance on Goods, Services, and Income	4 992 ..	*–845.4*	*–530.6*	*–506.8*	*–849.2*	*–1,104.6*	*–877.9*	*–969.8*	*–781.0*
Current transfers: credit	2 379 Y.	130.0	168.9	201.6	844.4	270.6	233.6	240.9	75.0
Current transfers: debit	3 379 ..	...	...	...	...	...	...	...	...
B. Capital Account[1]	4 994 Y.	**...**	**...**	**...**	**...**	**...**	**...**	**...**	**...**
Capital account: credit	2 994 Y.	...	...	...	...	...	...	...	...
Capital account: debit	3 994 ..	...	...	...	...	...	...	...	...
Total, Groups A Plus B	4 010 ..	*–715.4*	*–361.7*	*–305.2*	*–4.8*	*–834.0*	*–644.3*	*–728.9*	*–706.0*
C. Financial Account[1]	4 995 X.	**303.5**	**–89.3**	**–161.1**	**–543.6**	**–538.3**	**–502.8**	**–209.1**	**–560.5**
Direct investment abroad	4 505 ..	...	...	...	...	...	...	...	...
Direct investment in Nicaragua	4 555 Y.	...	...	...	...	15.0	38.8	40.0	70.4
Portfolio investment assets	4 602 ..	...	...	...	...	...	...	...	...
Equity securities	4 610 ..	...	...	...	...	...	...	...	...
Debt securities	4 619 ..	...	...	...	...	...	...	...	...
Portfolio investment liabilities	4 652 Y.	...	...	...	...	...	...	...	...
Equity securities	4 660 Y.	...	...	...	...	...	...	...	...
Debt securities	4 669 Y.	...	...	...	...	...	...	...	...
Other investment assets	4 703 ..	...	...	...	–21.1	–5.9	–10.1	–8.8	8.4
Monetary authorities	4 703 .A	...	...	...	...	...	...	...	...
General government	4 703 .B	...	...	...	–8.0	...	...	2.6	...
Banks	4 703 .C	...	...	...	–13.1	–6.4	–10.1	–11.4	8.4
Other sectors	4 703 .D	...	...	...	...	.5	...	...	...
Other investment liabilities	4 753 X.	303.5	–89.3	–161.1	–522.5	–547.4	–531.5	–240.3	–639.3
Monetary authorities	4 753 XA	191.9	–20.1	–78.4	–59.3	–88.0	–94.9	–199.1	–210.1
General government	4 753 YB	132.9	–67.2	–57.9	–380.6	–459.7	–390.7	–96.6	–439.4
Banks	4 753 YC	–10.2	–5.3	–16.9	4.2	–1.7	–16.6	14.2	...
Other sectors	4 753 YD	–11.1	3.3	–7.9	–86.8	2.0	–29.3	41.2	10.2
Total, Groups A Through C	4 020 ..	*–411.9*	*–451.0*	*–466.3*	*–548.4*	*–1,372.3*	*–1,147.1*	*–938.0*	*–1,266.5*
D. Net Errors and Omissions	4 998 ..	**51.9**	**–69.2**	**–181.2**	**84.7**	**60.2**	**128.1**	**154.3**	**64.5**
Total, Groups A Through D	4 030 ..	*–360.0*	*–520.2*	*–647.5*	*–463.7*	*–1,312.0*	*–1,019.0*	*–783.7*	*–1,202.0*
E. Reserves and Related Items	4 040 ..	**360.0**	**520.2**	**647.5**	**463.7**	**1,312.0**	**1,019.0**	**783.7**	**1,202.0**
Reserve assets	4 800 ..	–43.9	–64.1	39.3	–109.2	–.5	79.4	–80.8	–3.7
Use of Fund credit and loans	4 766 ..	...	...	...	23.1	...	...	26.1	–12.9
Liabilities constituting foreign authorities' reserves	4 900 ..	–60.5	...	...	...	...	...	...	...
Exceptional financing	4 920 ..	464.4	584.3	608.2	549.8	1,312.5	939.6	838.4	1,218.6
Conversion rates: córdobas per U.S. dollar	0 101 ..	**.0001**	**.0031**	**.1409**	**4.2708**	**5.0000**	**5.6204**	**6.7229**	**7.5456**

[1] Excludes components that have been classified in the categories of Group E.

Table 2. STANDARD PRESENTATION, 1988–95

(Millions of U.S. dollars)

	Code			1988	1989	1990	1991	1992	1993	1994	1995
CURRENT ACCOUNT	4	993	. .	**–715.4**	**–361.7**	**–305.2**	**–4.8**	**–769.0**	**–604.3**	**–694.4**	**–462.1**
A. GOODS	4	100	. .	–482.6	–228.6	–237.3	–419.9	–547.7	–392.4	–433.5	–323.5
Credit	2	100	. .	**235.7**	**318.7**	**332.4**	**268.1**	**223.1**	**267.0**	**351.2**	**528.6**
General merchandise: exports f.o.b.	2	110	. .	235.7	318.7	332.4	268.1	223.1	267.0	351.2	524.8
Goods for processing: exports f.o.b.	2	150	. .	...	...	...	...	...	...	...	...
Repairs on goods	2	160	. .	...	...	...	...	...	...	...	...
Goods procured in ports by carriers	2	170	. .	...	...	...	...	...	...	...	3.8
Nonmonetary gold	2	180	. .	...	...	...	...	...	...	...	...
Debit	3	100	. .	**–718.3**	**–547.3**	**–569.7**	**–688.0**	**–770.8**	**–659.4**	**–784.7**	**–852.1**
General merchandise: imports f.o.b.	3	110	. .	–718.3	–547.3	–569.7	–688.0	–770.8	–659.4	–784.7	–852.1
Goods for processing: imports f.o.b.	3	150	. .	...	...	...	...	...	...	...	...
Repairs on goods	3	160	. .	...	...	...	...	...	...	...	...
Goods procured in ports by carriers	3	170	. .	...	...	...	...	...	...	...	...
Nonmonetary gold	3	180	. .	...	...	...	...	...	...	...	...
B. SERVICES	4	200	. .	–100.7	–97.2	–52.5	–66.0	–62.1	–56.4	–70.8	–99.0
Total credit	2	200	. .	*37.4*	*22.0*	*59.8*	*70.2*	*86.2*	*100.2*	*101.4*	*118.9*
Total debit	3	200	. .	*–138.1*	*–119.2*	*–112.3*	*–136.2*	*–148.3*	*–156.6*	*–172.2*	*–217.9*
Transportation services, credit	2	205	. .	**5.0**	**6.2**	**6.6**	**11.7**	**11.7**	**12.2**	**14.2**	**14.2**
Passenger	2	205	BA	...	...	...	...	...	...	...	...
Freight	2	205	BB	*5.0*	*6.2*	*6.6*	*5.3*	*4.5*	*5.4*	*7.0*	*8.5*
Other	2	205	BC	...	...	...	*6.4*	*7.2*	*6.8*	*7.2*	*5.7*
Sea transport, passenger	2	207	. .	...	...	...	...	...	...	...	...
Sea transport, freight	2	208	. .	...	...	...	...	...	...	...	...
Sea transport, other	2	209	. .	...	...	...	...	...	...	...	...
Air transport, passenger	2	211	. .	...	...	...	...	...	...	...	...
Air transport, freight	2	212	. .	...	...	...	...	...	...	...	1.7
Air transport, other	2	213	. .	...	...	...	...	...	...	...	...
Other transport, passenger	2	215	. .	...	...	...	...	...	...	...	...
Other transport, freight	2	216	. .	...	...	...	...	...	...	...	6.8
Other transport, other	2	217	. .	...	...	...	...	...	...	...	5.7
Transportation services, debit	3	205	. .	**–72.1**	**–49.8**	**–51.8**	**–41.3**	**–76.7**	**–65.0**	**–76.4**	**–81.8**
Passenger	3	205	BA	...	...	...	...	*–15.5*	*–15.4*	*–15.5*	*–16.0*
Freight	3	205	BB	*–72.1*	*–49.8*	*–51.8*	*–41.3*	*–61.2*	*–49.6*	*–60.9*	*–65.8*
Other	3	205	BC	...	...	...	...	...	...	...	...
Sea transport, passenger	3	207	. .	...	...	...	...	...	...	...	...
Sea transport, freight	3	208	. .	...	...	...	...	...	...	...	–27.7
Sea transport, other	3	209	. .	...	...	...	...	...	...	...	...
Air transport, passenger	3	211	. .	...	...	...	...	...	...	...	–16.0
Air transport, freight	3	212	. .	...	...	...	...	...	...	...	–13.2
Air transport, other	3	213	. .	...	...	...	...	...	...	...	...
Other transport, passenger	3	215	. .	...	...	...	...	...	...	...	...
Other transport, freight	3	216	. .	...	...	...	...	...	...	...	–24.9
Other transport, other	3	217	. .	...	...	...	...	...	...	...	...
Travel, credit	2	236	. .	**5.4**	**4.3**	**12.2**	**16.7**	**23.3**	**41.1**	**40.2**	**54.6**
Business travel	2	237	. .	...	...	...	...	...	...	...	...
Personal travel	2	240	. .	...	4.3	12.2	16.7	23.3	41.1	40.2	54.6
Travel, debit	3	236	. .	**–1.8**	**–1.1**	**–14.7**	**–28.1**	**–30.2**	**–30.9**	**–30.1**	**–40.0**
Business travel	3	237	. .	...	...	...	...	...	...	...	...
Personal travel	3	240	. .	...	–1.1	–14.7	–28.1	–30.2	–30.9	–30.1	–40.0
Other services, credit	2	200	BA	**27.0**	**11.5**	**41.0**	**41.8**	**51.2**	**46.9**	**47.0**	**50.1**
Communications	2	245	. .	...	...	...	...	...	...	...	25.8
Construction	2	249	. .	...	...	...	...	...	...	...	...
Insurance	2	253	. .	...	...	...	...	...	...	...	2.0
Financial	2	260	. .	...	...	...	...	...	...	...	...
Computer and information	2	262	. .	...	...	...	...	...	...	...	...
Royalties and licence fees	2	266	. .	...	...	...	...	...	...	...	...
Other business services	2	268	. .	27.0	6.0	15.6	21.8	15.6	18.3	25.9	...
Personal, cultural, and recreational	2	287	. .	...	...	...	...	...	...	...	...
Government, n.i.e.	2	291	. .	...	5.5	25.4	20.0	35.6	28.6	21.1	22.3
Other services, debit	3	200	BA	**–64.2**	**–68.3**	**–45.8**	**–66.8**	**–41.4**	**–60.7**	**–65.7**	**–96.1**
Communications	3	245	. .	...	...	...	...	...	...	...	–5.1
Construction	3	249	. .	...	...	...	...	...	...	...	...
Insurance	3	253	. .	–8.0	–5.5	–5.8	–5.6	–6.1	–4.9	–11.1	–6.9
Financial	3	260	. .	...	...	...	...	...	...	...	...
Computer and information	3	262	. .	...	...	...	...	...	...	...	...
Royalties and licence fees	3	266	. .	...	...	...	...	...	...	...	...
Other business services	3	268	. .	–56.2	–1.6	–1.0	–1.6	–2.6	–5.4	–4.3	–74.3
Personal, cultural, and recreational	3	287	. .	...	...	...	...	...	...	...	...
Government, n.i.e.	3	291	. .	...	–61.2	–39.0	–59.6	–32.7	–50.4	–50.3	–9.8

Table 2 (Continued). STANDARD PRESENTATION, 1988–95
(Millions of U.S. dollars)

	Code	1988	1989	1990	1991	1992	1993	1994	1995
C. INCOME	4 300	–262.1	–204.8	–217.0	–363.3	–494.8	–429.1	–465.5	–358.5
Total credit	2 300	*2.1*	*6.8*	*11.8*	*9.7*	*7.5*	*5.4*	*6.7*	*7.2*
Total debit	3 300	*–264.2*	*–211.6*	*–228.8*	*–373.0*	*–502.3*	*–434.5*	*–472.2*	*–365.7*
Compensation of employees, credit	2 310	...	...	...	...	...	...	...	...
Compensation of employees, debit	3 310	...	...	...	...	...	...	...	...
Investment income, credit	2 320	**2.1**	**6.8**	**11.8**	**9.7**	**7.5**	**5.4**	**6.7**	**7.2**
Direct investment income	2 330	...	...	...	...	...	...	...	...
Dividends and distributed branch profits	2 332	...	...	...	...	...	...	...	...
Reinvested earnings and undistributed branch profits	2 333	...	...	...	...	...	...	...	...
Income on debt (interest)	2 334	...	...	...	...	...	...	...	...
Portfolio investment income	2 339	...	...	...	...	...	...	...	...
Income on equity	2 340	...	...	...	...	...	...	...	...
Income on bonds and notes	2 350	...	...	...	...	...	...	...	...
Income on money market instruments and financial derivatives	2 360	...	...	...	...	...	...	...	...
Other investment income	2 370	2.1	6.8	11.8	9.7	7.5	5.4	6.7	7.2
Investment income, debit	3 320	**–264.2**	**–211.6**	**–228.8**	**–373.0**	**–502.3**	**–434.5**	**–472.2**	**–365.7**
Direct investment income	3 330	...	...	...	...	–12.0	–10.0	–10.0	–15.0
Dividends and distributed branch profits	3 332	...	...	...	...	...	...	...	...
Reinvested earnings and undistributed branch profits	3 333	...	...	...	...	–12.0	–10.0	–10.0	–15.0
Income on debt (interest)	3 334	...	...	...	...	...	...	...	...
Portfolio investment income	3 339	...	...	...	...	...	...	...	...
Income on equity	3 340	...	...	...	...	...	...	...	...
Income on bonds and notes	3 350	...	...	...	...	...	...	...	...
Income on money market instruments and financial derivatives	3 360	...	...	...	...	...	...	...	...
Other investment income	3 370	–264.2	–211.6	–228.8	–373.0	–490.3	–424.5	–462.2	–350.7
D. CURRENT TRANSFERS	4 379	130.0	168.9	201.6	844.4	335.6	273.6	275.4	318.9
Credit	2 379	**130.0**	**168.9**	**201.6**	**844.4**	**335.6**	**273.6**	**275.4**	**318.9**
General government	2 380	130.0	168.9	201.6	184.6	257.8	185.6	193.1	243.9
Other sectors	2 390	...	...	...	659.8	77.8	88.0	82.3	75.0
Workers' remittances	2 391	...	...	...	...	10.0	25.0	30.0	75.0
Other current transfers	2 392	...	...	...	659.8	67.8	63.0	52.3	...
Debit	3 379	...	...	...	...	...	...	...	...
General government	3 380	...	...	...	...	...	...	...	...
Other sectors	3 390	...	...	...	...	...	...	...	...
Workers' remittances	3 391	...	...	...	...	...	...	...	...
Other current transfers	3 392	...	...	...	...	...	...	...	...
CAPITAL AND FINANCIAL ACCOUNT	4 996	**663.5**	**430.9**	**486.4**	**–79.9**	**708.8**	**476.2**	**540.1**	**397.6**
CAPITAL ACCOUNT	4 994	...	...	...	...	**53.0**	**147.7**	**141.5**	**1,452.7**
Total credit	2 994	...	...	...	...	*53.0*	*147.7*	*141.5*	*1,452.7*
Total debit	3 994	...	...	...	...	...	...	...	...
Capital transfers, credit	2 400	...	...	...	...	**53.0**	**147.7**	**141.5**	**1,452.7**
General government	2 401	...	...	...	...	53.0	147.7	141.5	1,452.7
Debt forgiveness	2 402	...	...	...	...	53.0	147.7	141.5	1,452.7
Other capital transfers	2 410	...	...	...	...	...	...	...	...
Other sectors	2 430	...	...	...	...	...	...	...	...
Migrants' transfers	2 431	...	...	...	...	...	...	...	...
Debt forgiveness	2 432	...	...	...	...	...	...	...	...
Other capital transfers	2 440	...	...	...	...	...	...	...	...
Capital transfers, debit	3 400	...	...	...	...	...	...	...	...
General government	3 401	...	...	...	...	...	...	...	...
Debt forgiveness	3 402	...	...	...	...	...	...	...	...
Other capital transfers	3 410	...	...	...	...	...	...	...	...
Other sectors	3 430	...	...	...	...	...	...	...	...
Migrants' transfers	3 431	...	...	...	...	...	...	...	...
Debt forgiveness	3 432	...	...	...	...	...	...	...	...
Other capital transfers	3 440	...	...	...	...	...	...	...	...
Nonproduced nonfinancial assets, credit	2 480	...	...	...	...	...	...	...	...
Nonproduced nonfinancial assets, debit	3 480	...	...	...	...	...	...	...	...

Table 2 (Continued). STANDARD PRESENTATION, 1988–95
(Millions of U.S. dollars)

	Code	1988	1989	1990	1991	1992	1993	1994	1995
FINANCIAL ACCOUNT	4 995 . .	**663.5**	**430.9**	**486.4**	**–79.9**	**655.8**	**328.5**	**398.6**	**–1,055.1**
A. DIRECT INVESTMENT	4 500 . .	. . .	. . .	. . .	. . .	15.0	38.8	40.0	70.4
Direct investment abroad	4 505 . .	**. . .**	**. . .**	**. . .**	**. . .**	**. . .**	**. . .**	**. . .**	**. . .**
Equity capital	4 510 . .	. . .	. . .	. . .	. . .	. . .	. . .	. . .	. . .
Claims on affiliated enterprises	4 515 . .	. . .	. . .	. . .	. . .	. . .	. . .	. . .	. . .
Liabilities to affiliated enterprises	4 520 . .	. . .	. . .	. . .	. . .	. . .	. . .	. . .	. . .
Reinvested earnings	4 525 . .	. . .	. . .	. . .	. . .	. . .	. . .	. . .	. . .
Other capital	4 530 . .	. . .	. . .	. . .	. . .	. . .	. . .	. . .	. . .
Claims on affiliated enterprises	4 535 . .	. . .	. . .	. . .	. . .	. . .	. . .	. . .	. . .
Liabilities to affiliated enterprises	4 540 . .	. . .	. . .	. . .	. . .	. . .	. . .	. . .	. . .
Direct investment in Nicaragua	4 555 . .	**. . .**	**. . .**	**. . .**	**. . .**	**15.0**	**38.8**	**40.0**	**70.4**
Equity capital	4 560 . .	. . .	. . .	. . .	. . .	3.0	28.8	30.0	55.4
Claims on direct investors	4 565 . .	. . .	. . .	. . .	. . .	. . .	. . .	. . .	. . .
Liabilities to direct investors	4 570 . .	. . .	. . .	. . .	. . .	. . .	. . .	. . .	55.4
Reinvested earnings	4 575 . .	. . .	. . .	. . .	. . .	12.0	10.0	10.0	15.0
Other capital	4 580 . .	. . .	. . .	. . .	. . .	. . .	. . .	. . .	. . .
Claims on direct investors	4 585 . .	. . .	. . .	. . .	. . .	. . .	. . .	. . .	. . .
Liabilities to direct investors	4 590 . .	. . .	. . .	. . .	. . .	. . .	. . .	. . .	. . .
B. PORTFOLIO INVESTMENT	4 600 . .	. . .	. . .	. . .	. . .	. . .	. . .	. . .	. . .
Assets	4 602 . .	**. . .**	**. . .**	**. . .**	**. . .**	**. . .**	**. . .**	**. . .**	**. . .**
Equity securities	4 610 . .	. . .	. . .	. . .	. . .	. . .	. . .	. . .	. . .
Monetary authorities	4 611 . .	. . .	. . .	. . .	. . .	. . .	. . .	. . .	. . .
General government	4 612 . .	. . .	. . .	. . .	. . .	. . .	. . .	. . .	. . .
Banks	4 613 . .	. . .	. . .	. . .	. . .	. . .	. . .	. . .	. . .
Other sectors	4 614 . .	. . .	. . .	. . .	. . .	. . .	. . .	. . .	. . .
Debt securities	4 619 . .	. . .	. . .	. . .	. . .	. . .	. . .	. . .	. . .
Bonds and notes	4 620 . .	. . .	. . .	. . .	. . .	. . .	. . .	. . .	. . .
Monetary authorities	4 621 . .	. . .	. . .	. . .	. . .	. . .	. . .	. . .	. . .
General government	4 622 . .	. . .	. . .	. . .	. . .	. . .	. . .	. . .	. . .
Banks	4 623 . .	. . .	. . .	. . .	. . .	. . .	. . .	. . .	. . .
Other sectors	4 624 . .	. . .	. . .	. . .	. . .	. . .	. . .	. . .	. . .
Money market instruments	4 630 . .	. . .	. . .	. . .	. . .	. . .	. . .	. . .	. . .
Monetary authorities	4 631 . .	. . .	. . .	. . .	. . .	. . .	. . .	. . .	. . .
General government	4 632 . .	. . .	. . .	. . .	. . .	. . .	. . .	. . .	. . .
Banks	4 633 . .	. . .	. . .	. . .	. . .	. . .	. . .	. . .	. . .
Other sectors	4 634 . .	. . .	. . .	. . .	. . .	. . .	. . .	. . .	. . .
Financial derivatives	4 640 . .	. . .	. . .	. . .	. . .	. . .	. . .	. . .	. . .
Monetary authorities	4 641 . .	. . .	. . .	. . .	. . .	. . .	. . .	. . .	. . .
General government	4 642 . .	. . .	. . .	. . .	. . .	. . .	. . .	. . .	. . .
Banks	4 643 . .	. . .	. . .	. . .	. . .	. . .	. . .	. . .	. . .
Other sectors	4 644 . .	. . .	. . .	. . .	. . .	. . .	. . .	. . .	. . .
Liabilities	4 652 . .	**. . .**	**. . .**	**. . .**	**. . .**	**. . .**	**. . .**	**. . .**	**. . .**
Equity securities	4 660 . .	. . .	. . .	. . .	. . .	. . .	. . .	. . .	. . .
Banks	4 663 . .	. . .	. . .	. . .	. . .	. . .	. . .	. . .	. . .
Other sectors	4 664 . .	. . .	. . .	. . .	. . .	. . .	. . .	. . .	. . .
Debt securities	4 669 . .	. . .	. . .	. . .	. . .	. . .	. . .	. . .	. . .
Bonds and notes	4 670 . .	. . .	. . .	. . .	. . .	. . .	. . .	. . .	. . .
Monetary authorities	4 671 . .	. . .	. . .	. . .	. . .	. . .	. . .	. . .	. . .
General government	4 672 . .	. . .	. . .	. . .	. . .	. . .	. . .	. . .	. . .
Banks	4 673 . .	. . .	. . .	. . .	. . .	. . .	. . .	. . .	. . .
Other sectors	4 674 . .	. . .	. . .	. . .	. . .	. . .	. . .	. . .	. . .
Money market instruments	4 680 . .	. . .	. . .	. . .	. . .	. . .	. . .	. . .	. . .
Monetary authorities	4 681 . .	. . .	. . .	. . .	. . .	. . .	. . .	. . .	. . .
General government	4 682 . .	. . .	. . .	. . .	. . .	. . .	. . .	. . .	. . .
Banks	4 683 . .	. . .	. . .	. . .	. . .	. . .	. . .	. . .	. . .
Other sectors	4 684 . .	. . .	. . .	. . .	. . .	. . .	. . .	. . .	. . .
Financial derivatives	4 690 . .	. . .	. . .	. . .	. . .	. . .	. . .	. . .	. . .
Monetary authorities	4 691 . .	. . .	. . .	. . .	. . .	. . .	. . .	. . .	. . .
General government	4 692 . .	. . .	. . .	. . .	. . .	. . .	. . .	. . .	. . .
Banks	4 693 . .	. . .	. . .	. . .	. . .	. . .	. . .	. . .	. . .
Other sectors	4 694 . .	. . .	. . .	. . .	. . .	. . .	. . .	. . .	. . .

Table 2 (Concluded). STANDARD PRESENTATION, 1988–95
(Millions of U.S. dollars)

	Code	1988	1989	1990	1991	1992	1993	1994	1995
C. OTHER INVESTMENT	4 700 . .	707.4	495.0	447.1	29.3	641.2	210.3	439.4	–1,121.8
Assets	4 703 . .	**. . .**	**. . .**	**. . .**	**–21.1**	**–5.9**	**–10.1**	**–8.8**	**8.4**
Trade credits	4 706 . .	. . .	. . .	. . .	. . .	. . .	. . .	. . .	. . .
General government: long-term	4 708 . .	. . .	. . .	. . .	. . .	. . .	. . .	. . .	. . .
General government: short-term	4 709 . .	. . .	. . .	. . .	. . .	. . .	. . .	. . .	. . .
Other sectors: long-term	4 711 . .	. . .	. . .	. . .	. . .	. . .	. . .	. . .	. . .
Other sectors: short-term	4 712 . .	. . .	. . .	. . .	. . .	. . .	. . .	. . .	. . .
Loans	4 714 . .	. . .	. . .	. . .	. . .	. . .	. . .	. . .	. . .
Monetary authorities: long-term	4 717 . .	. . .	. . .	. . .	. . .	. . .	. . .	. . .	. . .
Monetary authorities: short-term	4 718 . .	. . .	. . .	. . .	. . .	. . .	. . .	. . .	. . .
General government: long-term	4 720 . .	. . .	. . .	. . .	. . .	. . .	. . .	. . .	. . .
General government: short-term	4 721 . .	. . .	. . .	. . .	. . .	. . .	. . .	. . .	. . .
Banks: long-term	4 723 . .	. . .	. . .	. . .	. . .	. . .	. . .	. . .	. . .
Banks: short-term	4 724 . .	. . .	. . .	. . .	. . .	. . .	. . .	. . .	. . .
Other sectors: long-term	4 726 . .	. . .	. . .	. . .	. . .	. . .	. . .	. . .	. . .
Other sectors: short-term	4 727 . .	. . .	. . .	. . .	. . .	. . .	. . .	. . .	. . .
Currency and deposits	4 730 . .	. . .	. . .	. . .	–13.1	–5.9	–10.1	–8.8	8.4
Monetary authorities	4 731 . .	. . .	. . .	. . .	. . .	. . .	. . .	. . .	. . .
General government	4 732 . .	. . .	. . .	. . .	. . .	. . .	. . .	2.6	. . .
Banks	4 733 . .	. . .	. . .	. . .	–13.1	–6.4	–10.1	–11.4	8.4
Other sectors	4 734 . .	. . .	. . .	. . .	. . .	.5	. . .	. . .	. . .
Other assets	4 736 . .	. . .	. . .	. . .	–8.0	. . .	. . .	. . .	. . .
Monetary authorities: long-term	4 738 . .	. . .	. . .	. . .	. . .	. . .	. . .	. . .	. . .
Monetary authorities: short-term	4 739 . .	. . .	. . .	. . .	. . .	. . .	. . .	. . .	. . .
General government: long-term	4 741 . .	. . .	. . .	. . .	–8.0	. . .	. . .	. . .	. . .
General government: short-term	4 742 . .	. . .	. . .	. . .	. . .	. . .	. . .	. . .	. . .
Banks: long-term	4 744 . .	. . .	. . .	. . .	. . .	. . .	. . .	. . .	. . .
Banks: short-term	4 745 . .	. . .	. . .	. . .	. . .	. . .	. . .	. . .	. . .
Other sectors: long-term	4 747 . .	. . .	. . .	. . .	. . .	. . .	. . .	. . .	. . .
Other sectors: short-term	4 748 . .	. . .	. . .	. . .	. . .	. . .	. . .	. . .	. . .
Liabilities	4 753 . .	**707.4**	**495.0**	**447.1**	**50.4**	**647.1**	**220.4**	**448.2**	**–1,130.2**
Trade credits	4 756 . .	. . .	. . .	. . .	. . .	. . .	. . .	. . .	31.3
General government: long-term	4 758 . .	. . .	. . .	. . .	. . .	. . .	. . .	. . .	. . .
General government: short-term	4 759 . .	. . .	. . .	. . .	. . .	. . .	. . .	. . .	. . .
Other sectors: long-term	4 761 . .	. . .	. . .	. . .	. . .	. . .	. . .	. . .	. . .
Other sectors: short-term	4 762 . .	. . .	. . .	. . .	. . .	. . .	. . .	. . .	31.3
Loans	4 764 . .	115.4	–90.4	–159.7	229.0	–472.1	–400.5	–284.9	–90.1
Use of Fund credit and loans from the Fund	4 766 . .	. . .	. . .	. . .	23.1	. . .	. . .	26.1	–12.9
Monetary authorities: other long-term	4 767 . .	–16.6	–21.2	–77.0	297.6	–46.5	–2.6	–469.5	–178.0
Monetary authorities: short-term	4 768 . .	–87.8	. . .	. . .	. . .	. . .	. . .	314.9	. . .
General government: long-term	4 770 . .	218.3	–67.2	–57.9	–49.3	–423.4	–360.3	–197.6	80.8
General government: short-term	4 771 . .	. . .	. . .	. . .	. . .	. . .	. . .	. . .	. . .
Banks: long-term	4 773 . .	. . .	–5.3	–16.9	–13.4	–4.2	–8.3	. . .	6.3
Banks: short-term	4 774 . .	. . .	. . .	. . .	. . .	. . .	. . .	. . .	. . .
Other sectors: long-term	4 776 . .	1.5	–4.9	–16.1	–37.2	2.0	–57.9	41.2	13.7
Other sectors: short-term	4 777 . .	. . .	8.2	8.2	8.2	. . .	28.6	. . .	. . .
Currency and deposits	4 780 . .	–70.7	. . .	. . .	17.6	2.5	–8.3	14.2	. . .
Monetary authorities	4 781 . .	–60.5	. . .	. . .	. . .	. . .	. . .	. . .	. . .
General government	4 782 . .	. . .	. . .	. . .	. . .	. . .	. . .	. . .	. . .
Banks	4 783 . .	–10.2	. . .	. . .	17.6	2.5	–8.3	14.2	. . .
Other sectors	4 784 . .	. . .	. . .	. . .	. . .	. . .	. . .	. . .	. . .
Other liabilities	4 786 . .	662.7	585.4	606.8	–196.2	1,116.7	629.2	718.9	–1,071.4
Monetary authorities: long-term	4 788 . .	. . .	. . .	. . .	. . .	. . .	. . .	. . .	. . .
Monetary authorities: short-term	4 789 . .	243.7	60.3	151.3	–94.1	164.6	–41.6	616.0	145.9
General government: long-term	4 791 . .	. . .	. . .	. . .	. . .	. . .	. . .	. . .	. . .
General government: short-term	4 792 . .	431.6	497.0	405.4	15.8	944.4	631.1	108.8	–1,217.3
Banks: long-term	4 794 . .	. . .	. . .	. . .	. . .	. . .	. . .	. . .	. . .
Banks: short-term	4 795 . .	. . .	6.6	22.4	5.6	7.4	11.5	3.8	. . .
Other sectors: long-term	4 797 . .	. . .	. . .	. . .	. . .	. . .	. . .	. . .	. . .
Other sectors: short-term	4 798 . .	–12.6	21.5	27.7	–123.5	.3	28.2	–9.7	. . .
D. RESERVE ASSETS	4 800 . .	–43.9	–64.1	39.3	–109.2	–.5	79.4	–80.8	–3.7
Monetary gold	4 810 . .	–1.6	. . .	. . .	. . .	. . .	. . .	. . .	–.6
Special drawing rights	4 820 . .	. . .	. . .	. . .	. . .	–.1	. . .	. . .	. . .
Reserve position in the Fund	4 830 . .	. . .	. . .	. . .	. . .	. . .	. . .	. . .	. . .
Foreign exchange	4 840 . .	–51.6	–63.2	41.2	–95.0	3.7	75.4	–86.0	–10.4
Other claims	4 880 . .	9.3	–.9	–1.9	–14.2	–4.1	4.0	5.2	7.3
NET ERRORS AND OMISSIONS	4 998 . .	**51.9**	**–69.2**	**–181.2**	**84.7**	**60.2**	**128.1**	**154.3**	**64.5**

Part 3 of the *Yearbook* contains descriptions of the methodologies, compilation practices, and sources used to compile these data.

Table 1. ANALYTIC PRESENTATION, 1988–95
(Millions of U.S. dollars)

	Code	1988	1989	1990	1991	1992	1993	1994	1995
A. Current Account [1]	4 993 Y.	**–230.5**	**–256.9**	**–235.9**	**–176.2**	**–159.2**	**–97.2**	**–126.1**	**...**
Goods: exports f.o.b	2 100 . .	426.3	390.8	488.4	351.5	347.3	300.4	226.8	...
Goods: imports f.o.b	3 100 . .	–459.3	–414.8	–501.7	–417.9	–396.5	–312.1	–271.3	...
Balance on Goods	4 100 . .	*–33.0*	*–24.0*	*–13.3*	*–66.3*	*–49.2*	*–11.7*	*–44.5*	...
Services: credit	2 200 . .	40.7	31.7	44.4	49.6	57.7	36.5	30.4	...
Services: debit	3 200 . .	–208.0	–202.2	–226.8	–203.2	–201.0	–185.6	–149.1	...
Balance on Goods and Services	4 991 . .	*–200.2*	*–194.5*	*–195.7*	*–220.0*	*–192.6*	*–160.9*	*–163.2*	...
Income: credit	2 300 . .	16.7	18.0	20.4	20.1	19.7	19.3	15.6	...
Income: debit	3 300 . .	–82.4	–59.0	–74.4	–33.7	–54.1	–30.2	–45.2	...
Balance on Goods, Services, and Income	4 992 . .	*–265.9*	*–235.5*	*–249.7*	*–233.6*	*–227.0*	*–171.7*	*–192.8*	...
Current transfers: credit	2 379 Y.	103.3	37.2	81.4	122.2	133.6	139.5	115.1	...
Current transfers: debit	3 379 . .	–67.9	–58.6	–67.6	–64.8	–65.7	–65.0	–48.5	...
B. Capital Account [1]	4 994 Y.	**116.4**	**149.1**	**117.4**	**103.5**	**109.0**	**109.3**	**88.2**	**...**
Capital account: credit	2 994 Y.	116.4	149.1	117.4	103.5	109.0	109.3	88.2	...
Capital account: debit	3 994 . .	...	...	...	...	...	...	...	...
Total, Groups A Plus B	4 010 . .	*–114.1*	*–107.8*	*–118.4*	*–72.7*	*–50.2*	*12.2*	*–37.9*	...
C. Financial Account [1]	4 995 X.	**40.3**	**9.2**	**54.9**	**–120.9**	**3.9**	**–131.4**	**34.7**	**...**
Direct investment abroad	4 505 . .	–4.7	–1.6	...	–2.6	–40.7	–5.8	1.8	...
Direct investment in Niger	4 555 Y.	6.9	.8	40.8	15.2	56.4	–34.4	–11.3	...
Portfolio investment assets	4 602 . .	...	...	...	...	...	...	...	...
Equity securities	4 610 . .	...	...	...	...	...	...	...	...
Debt securities	4 619 . .	...	...	...	...	...	...	...	...
Portfolio investment liabilities	4 652 Y.	...	...	...	...	...	...	...	...
Equity securities	4 660 Y.	...	...	...	...	...	...	...	...
Debt securities	4 669 Y.	...	...	...	...	...	...	...	...
Other investment assets	4 703 . .	–35.7	–13.7	–1.8	–43.0	10.4	11.2	22.3	...
Monetary authorities	4 703 .A	...	...	...	...	...	...	...	...
General government	4 703 .B	.7	1.2	.6	.7	.1	.1	.3	...
Banks	4 703 .C	...	...	...	...	...	...	...	...
Other sectors	4 703 .D	–36.4	–14.9	–2.4	–43.7	10.2	11.1	22.0	...
Other investment liabilities	4 753 X.	73.8	23.7	15.9	–90.4	–22.1	–102.5	21.8	...
Monetary authorities	4 753 XA	...	...	...	...	...	...	...	...
General government	4 753 YB	60.1	31.1	28.6	–18.5	31.4	–10.8	6.7	...
Banks	4 753 YC	–8.9	–5.2	–.3	17.7	–6.1	–65.4	1.9	...
Other sectors	4 753 YD	22.6	–2.2	–12.3	–89.7	–47.4	–26.3	13.3	...
Total, Groups A Through C	4 020 . .	*–73.7*	*–98.6*	*–63.5*	*–193.6*	*–46.2*	*–119.3*	*–3.2*	...
D. Net Errors and Omissions	4 998 . .	**11.2**	**86.6**	**–18.4**	**174.7**	**–95.5**	**87.2**	**–67.8**	**...**
Total, Groups A Through D	4 030 . .	*–62.5*	*–12.0*	*–81.9*	*–18.9*	*–141.7*	*–32.0*	*–71.0*	...
E. Reserves and Related Items	4 040 . .	**62.5**	**12.0**	**81.9**	**18.9**	**141.7**	**32.0**	**71.0**	**...**
Reserve assets	4 800 . .	27.5	–29.2	–10.1	–6.4	31.0	–19.9	28.7	...
Use of Fund credit and loans	4 766 . .	–21.5	–7.8	–6.1	–11.4	–9.4	–9.6	5.4	...
Liabilities constituting foreign authorities' reserves	4 900 . .	–4.5	1.1	–8.4	–2.0	46.9	8.2	–4.7	...
Exceptional financing	4 920 . .	61.0	47.9	106.5	38.7	73.3	53.3	41.7	...
Conversion rates: CFA francs per U.S. dollar	0 101 . .	**297.85**	**319.01**	**272.26**	**282.11**	**264.69**	**283.16**	**555.20**	**499.15**

[1] Excludes components that have been classified in the categories of Group E.

Table 2. STANDARD PRESENTATION, 1988–95
(Millions of U.S. dollars)

	Code	1988	1989	1990	1991	1992	1993	1994	1995
CURRENT ACCOUNT	4 993 . .	**–230.5**	**–256.9**	**–235.9**	**–176.2**	**–159.2**	**–97.2**	**–126.1**	. . .
A. GOODS	4 100 . .	–33.0	–24.0	–13.3	–66.3	–49.2	–11.7	–44.5	. . .
Credit	2 100 . .	**426.3**	**390.8**	**488.4**	**351.5**	**347.3**	**300.4**	**226.8**	. . .
General merchandise: exports f.o.b.	2 110 . .	412.3	376.6	469.5	338.0	333.2	286.8	225.4	. . .
Goods for processing: exports f.o.b.	2 150 . .	. . .	. . .	. . .	. . .	. . .	. . .	. . .	. . .
Repairs on goods	2 160 . .	. . .	. . .	. . .	. . .	. . .	. . .	. . .	. . .
Goods procured in ports by carriers	2 170 . .	14.1	14.2	18.8	13.6	14.0	13.6	1.4	. . .
Nonmonetary gold	2 180 . .	. . .	. . .	. . .	. . .	. . .	. . .	. . .	. . .
Debit	3 100 . .	**–459.3**	**–414.8**	**–501.7**	**–417.9**	**–396.5**	**–312.1**	**–271.3**	. . .
General merchandise: imports f.o.b.	3 110 . .	–448.8	–404.3	–486.2	–403.0	–381.9	–299.1	–262.9	. . .
Goods for processing: imports f.o.b.	3 150 . .	. . .	. . .	. . .	. . .	. . .	. . .	. . .	. . .
Repairs on goods	3 160 . .	. . .	. . .	. . .	. . .	. . .	. . .	. . .	. . .
Goods procured in ports by carriers	3 170 . .	–9.7	–9.3	–14.6	–14.2	–13.9	–12.7	–8.1	. . .
Nonmonetary gold	3 180 . .	–.7	–1.2	–.9	–.7	–.6	–.3	–.3	. . .
B. SERVICES	4 200 . .	–167.3	–170.5	–182.3	–153.7	–143.3	–149.1	–118.8	. . .
Total credit	2 200 . .	*40.7*	*31.7*	*44.4*	*49.6*	*57.7*	*36.5*	*30.4*	. . .
Total debit	3 200 . .	*–208.0*	*–202.2*	*–226.8*	*–203.2*	*–201.0*	*–185.6*	*–149.1*	. . .
Transportation services, credit	2 205 . .	**.7**	**.9**	**1.1**	**.8**	**.6**	**.6**	**.4**	. . .
Passenger	2 205 BA	. . .	. . .	*.1*	*.1*	. . .	. . .	. . .	. . .
Freight	2 205 BB	*.6*	*.5*	*.7*	*.5*	*.5*	*.4*	*.4*	. . .
Other	2 205 BC	*.2*	*.3*	*.4*	*.1*	*.2*	*.1*	. . .	. . .
Sea transport, passenger	2 207 . .	. . .	. . .	. . .	. . .	. . .	. . .	. . .	. . .
Sea transport, freight	2 208 . .	. . .	. . .	. . .	. . .	. . .	. . .	. . .	. . .
Sea transport, other	2 209 . .	. . .	. . .	. . .	. . .	. . .	. . .	. . .	. . .
Air transport, passenger	2 211 . .	. . .	. . .	.1	.1	. . .	. . .	. . .	. . .
Air transport, freight	2 212 . .	. . .	. . .	. . .	. . .	. . .	. . .	. . .	. . .
Air transport, other	2 213 . .	.1	.2	.2	. . .	. . .	. . .	. . .	. . .
Other transport, passenger	2 215 . .	. . .	. . .	. . .	. . .	. . .	. . .	. . .	. . .
Other transport, freight	2 216 . .	.6	.5	.7	.5	.5	.4	.4	. . .
Other transport, other	2 217 . .	.1	.1	.1	.1	.2	.1	. . .	. . .
Transportation services, debit	3 205 . .	**–126.2**	**–116.3**	**–142.5**	**–106.2**	**–111.1**	**–87.9**	**–77.3**	. . .
Passenger	3 205 BA	*–17.3*	*–15.7*	*–19.4*	*–13.3*	*–14.4*	*–12.2*	*–12.2*	. . .
Freight	3 205 BB	*–108.9*	*–100.6*	*–123.0*	*–92.9*	*–96.7*	*–75.7*	*–65.1*	. . .
Other	3 205 BC	. . .	. . .	. . .	. . .	. . .	. . .	. . .	. . .
Sea transport, passenger	3 207 . .	. . .	. . .	. . .	. . .	. . .	. . .	. . .	. . .
Sea transport, freight	3 208 . .	. . .	. . .	. . .	. . .	. . .	. . .	. . .	. . .
Sea transport, other	3 209 . .	. . .	. . .	. . .	. . .	. . .	. . .	. . .	. . .
Air transport, passenger	3 211 . .	–16.4	–14.6	–17.7	–11.5	–12.6	–10.6	–10.5	. . .
Air transport, freight	3 212 . .	. . .	. . .	. . .	. . .	. . .	. . .	. . .	. . .
Air transport, other	3 213 . .	. . .	. . .	. . .	. . .	. . .	. . .	. . .	. . .
Other transport, passenger	3 215 . .	–.9	–1.0	–1.8	–1.8	–1.8	–1.6	–1.7	. . .
Other transport, freight	3 216 . .	–108.9	–100.6	–123.0	–92.9	–96.7	–75.7	–65.1	. . .
Other transport, other	3 217 . .	. . .	. . .	. . .	. . .	. . .	. . .	. . .	. . .
Travel, credit	2 236 . .	**11.1**	**10.4**	**13.1**	**12.7**	**12.1**	**9.7**	**4.6**	. . .
Business travel	2 237 . .	. . .	. . .	. . .	. . .	. . .	. . .	. . .	. . .
Personal travel	2 240 . .	11.1	10.4	13.1	12.7	12.1	9.7	4.6	. . .
Travel, debit	3 236 . .	**–20.3**	**–17.8**	**–21.6**	**–20.7**	**–19.7**	**–17.4**	**–19.6**	. . .
Business travel	3 237 . .	–1.9	–1.8	–2.3	–1.9	–1.9	–1.8	–.8	. . .
Personal travel	3 240 . .	–18.4	–16.0	–19.4	–18.9	–17.9	–15.6	–18.7	. . .
Other services, credit	2 200 BA	**28.9**	**20.4**	**30.2**	**36.1**	**45.0**	**26.2**	**25.4**	. . .
Communications	2 245 . .	.2	.2	.2	. . .	. . .	.2	.1	. . .
Construction	2 249 . .	. . .	. . .	. . .	. . .	. . .	. . .	. . .	. . .
Insurance	2 253 . .	1.7	4.0	3.0	3.2	1.3	1.7	. . .	. . .
Financial	2 260 . .	. . .	. . .	. . .	. . .	. . .	. . .	. . .	. . .
Computer and information	2 262 . .	. . .	. . .	. . .	. . .	. . .	. . .	. . .	. . .
Royalties and licence fees	2 266 . .	. . .	. . .	. . .	. . .	. . .	. . .	. . .	. . .
Other business services	2 268 . .	8.4	6.6	4.6	8.8	2.8	2.4	2.6	. . .
Personal, cultural, and recreational	2 287 . .	. . .	. . .	. . .	. . .	. . .	. . .	. . .	. . .
Government, n.i.e.	2 291 . .	18.6	9.6	22.4	24.1	40.9	22.0	22.7	. . .
Other services, debit	3 200 BA	**–61.5**	**–68.2**	**–62.6**	**–76.3**	**–70.2**	**–80.3**	**–52.2**	. . .
Communications	3 245 . .	. . .	. . .	. . .	. . .	. . .	. . .	. . .	. . .
Construction	3 249 . .	. . .	. . .	. . .	. . .	. . .	. . .	. . .	. . .
Insurance	3 253 . .	–10.6	–11.5	–8.9	–7.9	–7.8	–8.2	–2.3	. . .
Financial	3 260 . .	. . .	. . .	. . .	. . .	. . .	. . .	. . .	. . .
Computer and information	3 262 . .	–.2	–.2	–.2	–.2	–.2	–.2	–.1	. . .
Royalties and licence fees	3 266 . .	–.9	–.9	. . .	. . .	–1.8	–1.9	–.5	. . .
Other business services	3 268 . .	–31.2	–34.4	–35.5	–35.7	–25.3	–25.7	–14.6	. . .
Personal, cultural, and recreational	3 287 . .	. . .	. . .	. . .	. . .	. . .	. . .	. . .	. . .
Government, n.i.e.	3 291 . .	–18.7	–21.2	–18.0	–32.5	–35.1	–44.4	–34.7	. . .

Table 2 (Continued). STANDARD PRESENTATION, 1988–95
(Millions of U.S. dollars)

	Code	1988	1989	1990	1991	1992	1993	1994	1995
C. INCOME	4 300 . .	–65.7	–41.0	–54.1	–13.5	–34.4	–10.9	–29.6	. . .
Total credit	2 300 . .	*16.7*	*18.0*	*20.4*	*20.1*	*19.7*	*19.3*	*15.6*	. . .
Total debit	3 300 . .	*–82.4*	*–59.0*	*–74.4*	*–33.7*	*–54.1*	*–30.2*	*–45.2*	. . .
Compensation of employees, credit	2 310 . .	**.6**	**.7**	**.8**	**.1**	**.2**	**2.0**	**1.2**	**. . .**
Compensation of employees, debit	3 310 . .	**–4.8**	**–1.1**	**–2.7**	**–1.0**	**–1.1**	**. . .**	**. . .**	**. . .**
Investment income, credit	2 320 . .	**16.1**	**17.3**	**19.5**	**20.0**	**19.5**	**17.3**	**14.4**	**. . .**
Direct investment income	2 330 . .	.5	.7	.1	.1	. . .	.3	11.0	. . .
Dividends and distributed branch profits	2 332 . .	. . .	. . .	. . .	. . .	. . .	. . .	.3	. . .
Reinvested earnings and undistributed branch profits	2 333 . .	. . .	. . .	. . .	. . .	. . .	. . .	9.8	. . .
Income on debt (interest)	2 334 . .	.5	.7	.1	.1	. . .	.3	.9	. . .
Portfolio investment income	2 339 . .	. . .	. . .	. . .	. . .	. . .	. . .	. . .	. . .
Income on equity	2 340 . .	. . .	. . .	. . .	. . .	. . .	. . .	. . .	. . .
Income on bonds and notes	2 350 . .	. . .	. . .	. . .	. . .	. . .	. . .	. . .	. . .
Income on money market instruments and financial derivatives	2 360 . .	. . .	. . .	. . .	. . .	. . .	. . .	. . .	. . .
Other investment income	2 370 . .	15.7	16.6	19.4	19.9	19.5	17.1	3.4	. . .
Investment income, debit	3 320 . .	**–77.6**	**–57.8**	**–71.8**	**–32.7**	**–53.0**	**–30.2**	**–45.2**	**. . .**
Direct investment income	3 330 . .	–1.5	2.4	–22.6	3.6	–15.4	6.2	–7.8	. . .
Dividends and distributed branch profits	3 332 . .	10.3	10.5	–2.3	–10.9	–6.9	–7.2	–7.4	. . .
Reinvested earnings and undistributed branch profits	3 333 . .	–1.3	.5	. . .	25.2	–4.3	19.5	4.2	. . .
Income on debt (interest)	3 334 . .	–10.4	–8.6	–20.3	–10.7	–4.3	–6.1	–4.6	. . .
Portfolio investment income	3 339 . .	–58.1	–45.3	–30.4	–34.7	–35.1	–33.9	–33.3	. . .
Income on equity	3 340 . .	. . .	. . .	. . .	. . .	. . .	. . .	. . .	. . .
Income on bonds and notes	3 350 . .	–58.1	–45.3	–30.4	–34.7	–35.1	–33.9	–33.3	. . .
Income on money market instruments and financial derivatives	3 360 . .	. . .	. . .	. . .	. . .	. . .	. . .	. . .	. . .
Other investment income	3 370 . .	–18.0	–14.9	–18.8	–1.5	–2.5	–2.5	–4.0	. . .
D. CURRENT TRANSFERS	4 379 . .	35.4	–21.4	13.8	57.4	67.8	74.6	66.7	. . .
Credit	2 379 . .	**103.3**	**37.2**	**81.4**	**122.2**	**133.6**	**139.5**	**115.1**	**. . .**
General government	2 380 . .	88.2	24.6	68.3	109.3	115.6	125.7	109.5	. . .
Other sectors	2 390 . .	15.1	12.6	13.1	12.9	18.0	13.9	5.7	. . .
Workers' remittances	2 391 . .	15.1	12.6	13.1	12.9	18.0	13.9	5.7	. . .
Other current transfers	2 392 . .	. . .	. . .	. . .	. . .	. . .	. . .	. . .	. . .
Debit	3 379 . .	**–67.9**	**–58.6**	**–67.6**	**–64.8**	**–65.7**	**–65.0**	**–48.5**	**. . .**
General government	3 380 . .	–3.8	–3.4	–3.7	–.4	–1.9	–3.7	–1.9	. . .
Other sectors	3 390 . .	–64.1	–55.2	–63.8	–64.4	–63.8	–61.3	–46.5	. . .
Workers' remittances	3 391 . .	–64.1	–55.2	–63.8	–64.4	–63.8	–61.3	–46.5	. . .
Other current transfers	3 392 . .	. . .	. . .	. . .	. . .	. . .	. . .	. . .	. . .
CAPITAL AND FINANCIAL ACCOUNT	4 996 . .	**219.3**	**170.3**	**254.3**	**1.5**	**254.7**	**9.9**	**194.0**	**. . .**
CAPITAL ACCOUNT	4 994 . .	**116.4**	**149.1**	**201.9**	**103.5**	**109.0**	**109.3**	**158.9**	**. . .**
Total credit	2 994 . .	*116.4*	*149.1*	*201.9*	*103.5*	*109.0*	*109.3*	*158.9*	. . .
Total debit	3 994 . .	. . .	. . .	. . .	. . .	. . .	. . .	. . .	. . .
Capital transfers, credit	2 400 . .	**116.4**	**149.1**	**201.9**	**103.5**	**109.0**	**109.3**	**158.9**	**. . .**
General government	2 401 . .	116.4	149.1	201.9	103.5	109.0	109.3	158.9	. . .
Debt forgiveness	2 402 . .	. . .	. . .	84.5	. . .	. . .	. . .	70.7	. . .
Other capital transfers	2 410 . .	116.4	149.1	117.4	103.5	109.0	109.3	88.2	. . .
Other sectors	2 430 . .	. . .	. . .	. . .	. . .	. . .	. . .	. . .	. . .
Migrants' transfers	2 431 . .	. . .	. . .	. . .	. . .	. . .	. . .	. . .	. . .
Debt forgiveness	2 432 . .	. . .	. . .	. . .	. . .	. . .	. . .	. . .	. . .
Other capital transfers	2 440 . .	. . .	. . .	. . .	. . .	. . .	. . .	. . .	. . .
Capital transfers, debit	3 400 . .	**. . .**	**. . .**	**. . .**	**. . .**	**. . .**	**. . .**	**. . .**	**. . .**
General government	3 401 . .	. . .	. . .	. . .	. . .	. . .	. . .	. . .	. . .
Debt forgiveness	3 402 . .	. . .	. . .	. . .	. . .	. . .	. . .	. . .	. . .
Other capital transfers	3 410 . .	. . .	. . .	. . .	. . .	. . .	. . .	. . .	. . .
Other sectors	3 430 . .	. . .	. . .	. . .	. . .	. . .	. . .	. . .	. . .
Migrants' transfers	3 431 . .	. . .	. . .	. . .	. . .	. . .	. . .	. . .	. . .
Debt forgiveness	3 432 . .	. . .	. . .	. . .	. . .	. . .	. . .	. . .	. . .
Other capital transfers	3 440 . .	. . .	. . .	. . .	. . .	. . .	. . .	. . .	. . .
Nonproduced nonfinancial assets, credit	2 480 . .	**. . .**	**. . .**	**. . .**	**. . .**	**. . .**	**. . .**	**. . .**	**. . .**
Nonproduced nonfinancial assets, debit	3 480 . .	**. . .**	**. . .**	**. . .**	**. . .**	**. . .**	**. . .**	**. . .**	**. . .**

Table 2 (Continued). STANDARD PRESENTATION, 1988–95

(Millions of U.S. dollars)

	Code	1988	1989	1990	1991	1992	1993	1994	1995
FINANCIAL ACCOUNT	4 995	**102.9**	**21.2**	**52.4**	**–102.0**	**145.7**	**–99.4**	**35.0**	**. . .**
A. DIRECT INVESTMENT	4 500	2.2	–.8	40.8	12.5	15.7	–40.1	–9.5	. . .
Direct investment abroad	4 505	**–4.7**	**–1.6**	**. . .**	**–2.6**	**–40.7**	**–5.8**	**1.8**	**. . .**
Equity capital	4 510	. . .	. . .	. . .	. . .	. . .	. . .	. . .	. . .
Claims on affiliated enterprises	4 515	. . .	. . .	. . .	. . .	. . .	. . .	. . .	. . .
Liabilities to affiliated enterprises	4 520	. . .	. . .	. . .	. . .	. . .	. . .	. . .	. . .
Reinvested earnings	4 525	. . .	. . .	. . .	. . .	. . .	. . .	–9.8	. . .
Other capital	4 530	–4.7	–1.6	. . .	–2.6	–40.7	–5.8	11.6	. . .
Claims on affiliated enterprises	4 535	. . .	. . .	. . .	. . .	–40.7	–5.8	–2.3	. . .
Liabilities to affiliated enterprises	4 540	–4.7	–1.6	. . .	–2.6	. . .	. . .	14.0	. . .
Direct investment in Niger	4 555	**6.9**	**.8**	**40.8**	**15.2**	**56.4**	**–34.4**	**–11.3**	**. . .**
Equity capital	4 560	. . .	. . .	. . .	. . .	. . .	. . .	. . .	. . .
Claims on direct investors	4 565	. . .	. . .	. . .	. . .	. . .	. . .	. . .	. . .
Liabilities to direct investors	4 570	. . .	. . .	. . .	. . .	. . .	. . .	. . .	. . .
Reinvested earnings	4 575	1.3	–.5	. . .	–25.2	4.3	–19.5	–4.2	. . .
Other capital	4 580	5.6	1.2	40.8	40.4	52.1	–14.8	–7.0	. . .
Claims on direct investors	4 585	.1	.8	. . .	1.3	. . .	–.2	–1.4	. . .
Liabilities to direct investors	4 590	5.5	.5	40.8	39.1	52.1	–14.7	–5.7	. . .
B. PORTFOLIO INVESTMENT	4 600	. . .	. . .	. . .	. . .	. . .	. . .	. . .	. . .
Assets	4 602	**. . .**	**. . .**	**. . .**	**. . .**	**. . .**	**. . .**	**. . .**	**. . .**
Equity securities	4 610	. . .	. . .	. . .	. . .	. . .	. . .	. . .	. . .
Monetary authorities	4 611	. . .	. . .	. . .	. . .	. . .	. . .	. . .	. . .
General government	4 612	. . .	. . .	. . .	. . .	. . .	. . .	. . .	. . .
Banks	4 613	. . .	. . .	. . .	. . .	. . .	. . .	. . .	. . .
Other sectors	4 614	. . .	. . .	. . .	. . .	. . .	. . .	. . .	. . .
Debt securities	4 619	. . .	. . .	. . .	. . .	. . .	. . .	. . .	. . .
Bonds and notes	4 620	. . .	. . .	. . .	. . .	. . .	. . .	. . .	. . .
Monetary authorities	4 621	. . .	. . .	. . .	. . .	. . .	. . .	. . .	. . .
General government	4 622	. . .	. . .	. . .	. . .	. . .	. . .	. . .	. . .
Banks	4 623	. . .	. . .	. . .	. . .	. . .	. . .	. . .	. . .
Other sectors	4 624	. . .	. . .	. . .	. . .	. . .	. . .	. . .	. . .
Money market instruments	4 630	. . .	. . .	. . .	. . .	. . .	. . .	. . .	. . .
Monetary authorities	4 631	. . .	. . .	. . .	. . .	. . .	. . .	. . .	. . .
General government	4 632	. . .	. . .	. . .	. . .	. . .	. . .	. . .	. . .
Banks	4 633	. . .	. . .	. . .	. . .	. . .	. . .	. . .	. . .
Other sectors	4 634	. . .	. . .	. . .	. . .	. . .	. . .	. . .	. . .
Financial derivatives	4 640	. . .	. . .	. . .	. . .	. . .	. . .	. . .	. . .
Monetary authorities	4 641	. . .	. . .	. . .	. . .	. . .	. . .	. . .	. . .
General government	4 642	. . .	. . .	. . .	. . .	. . .	. . .	. . .	. . .
Banks	4 643	. . .	. . .	. . .	. . .	. . .	. . .	. . .	. . .
Other sectors	4 644	. . .	. . .	. . .	. . .	. . .	. . .	. . .	. . .
Liabilities	4 652	**. . .**	**. . .**	**. . .**	**. . .**	**. . .**	**. . .**	**. . .**	**. . .**
Equity securities	4 660	. . .	. . .	. . .	. . .	. . .	. . .	. . .	. . .
Banks	4 663	. . .	. . .	. . .	. . .	. . .	. . .	. . .	. . .
Other sectors	4 664	. . .	. . .	. . .	. . .	. . .	. . .	. . .	. . .
Debt securities	4 669	. . .	. . .	. . .	. . .	. . .	. . .	. . .	. . .
Bonds and notes	4 670	. . .	. . .	. . .	. . .	. . .	. . .	. . .	. . .
Monetary authorities	4 671	. . .	. . .	. . .	. . .	. . .	. . .	. . .	. . .
General government	4 672	. . .	. . .	. . .	. . .	. . .	. . .	. . .	. . .
Banks	4 673	. . .	. . .	. . .	. . .	. . .	. . .	. . .	. . .
Other sectors	4 674	. . .	. . .	. . .	. . .	. . .	. . .	. . .	. . .
Money market instruments	4 680	. . .	. . .	. . .	. . .	. . .	. . .	. . .	. . .
Monetary authorities	4 681	. . .	. . .	. . .	. . .	. . .	. . .	. . .	. . .
General government	4 682	. . .	. . .	. . .	. . .	. . .	. . .	. . .	. . .
Banks	4 683	. . .	. . .	. . .	. . .	. . .	. . .	. . .	. . .
Other sectors	4 684	. . .	. . .	. . .	. . .	. . .	. . .	. . .	. . .
Financial derivatives	4 690	. . .	. . .	. . .	. . .	. . .	. . .	. . .	. . .
Monetary authorities	4 691	. . .	. . .	. . .	. . .	. . .	. . .	. . .	. . .
General government	4 692	. . .	. . .	. . .	. . .	. . .	. . .	. . .	. . .
Banks	4 693	. . .	. . .	. . .	. . .	. . .	. . .	. . .	. . .
Other sectors	4 694	. . .	. . .	. . .	. . .	. . .	. . .	. . .	. . .

Table 2 (Concluded). STANDARD PRESENTATION, 1988–95
(Millions of U.S. dollars)

	Code	1988	1989	1990	1991	1992	1993	1994	1995
C. OTHER INVESTMENT	4 700 . .	73.2	51.2	21.7	–108.2	99.0	–39.4	15.8	. . .
Assets	4 703 . .	**–35.7**	**–13.7**	**–1.8**	**–43.0**	**10.4**	**11.2**	**22.3**	. . .
Trade credits	4 706 . .	–37.7	–17.0	–6.8	–43.0	9.8	11.2	22.2	. . .
General government: long-term	4 708 . .	. . .	. . .	. . .	. . .	. . .	. . .	. . .	. . .
General government: short-term	4 709 . .	. . .	. . .	. . .	. . .	. . .	. . .	. . .	. . .
Other sectors: long-term	4 711 . .	. . .	. . .	. . .	. . .	. . .	. . .	. . .	. . .
Other sectors: short-term	4 712 . .	–37.7	–17.0	–6.8	–43.0	9.8	11.2	22.2	. . .
Loans	4 714 . .	. . .	. . .	. . .	. . .	. . .	. . .	. . .	. . .
Monetary authorities: long-term	4 717 . .	. . .	. . .	. . .	. . .	. . .	. . .	. . .	. . .
Monetary authorities: short-term	4 718 . .	. . .	. . .	. . .	. . .	. . .	. . .	. . .	. . .
General government: long-term	4 720 . .	. . .	. . .	. . .	. . .	. . .	. . .	. . .	. . .
General government: short-term	4 721 . .	. . .	. . .	. . .	. . .	. . .	. . .	. . .	. . .
Banks: long-term	4 723 . .	. . .	. . .	. . .	. . .	. . .	. . .	. . .	. . .
Banks: short-term	4 724 . .	. . .	. . .	. . .	. . .	. . .	. . .	. . .	. . .
Other sectors: long-term	4 726 . .	. . .	. . .	. . .	. . .	. . .	. . .	. . .	. . .
Other sectors: short-term	4 727 . .	. . .	. . .	. . .	. . .	. . .	. . .	. . .	. . .
Currency and deposits	4 730 . .	1.7	.1	1.2	. . .	. . .	. . .	. . .	. . .
Monetary authorities	4 731 . .	. . .	. . .	. . .	. . .	. . .	. . .	. . .	. . .
General government	4 732 . .	. . .	. . .	. . .	. . .	. . .	. . .	. . .	. . .
Banks	4 733 . .	. . .	. . .	. . .	. . .	. . .	. . .	. . .	. . .
Other sectors	4 734 . .	1.7	.1	1.2	. . .	. . .	. . .	. . .	. . .
Other assets	4 736 . .	.3	3.2	3.8	. . .	.6	. . .	.1	. . .
Monetary authorities: long-term	4 738 . .	. . .	. . .	. . .	. . .	. . .	. . .	. . .	. . .
Monetary authorities: short-term	4 739 . .	. . .	. . .	. . .	. . .	. . .	. . .	. . .	. . .
General government: long-term	4 741 . .	.7	1.2	.7	.7	. . .	. . .	.3	. . .
General government: short-term	4 742 . .	. . .	–.1	–.1	. . .	.1	.1	. . .	. . .
Banks: long-term	4 744 . .	. . .	. . .	. . .	. . .	. . .	. . .	. . .	. . .
Banks: short-term	4 745 . .	. . .	. . .	. . .	. . .	. . .	. . .	. . .	. . .
Other sectors: long-term	4 747 . .	–.4	2.0	2.3	–.6	1.6	–.4	. . .	. . .
Other sectors: short-term	4 748 . .	. . .	. . .	.9	–.1	–1.2	.2	–.2	. . .
Liabilities	4 753 . .	**108.9**	**64.9**	**23.5**	**–65.2**	**88.7**	**–50.6**	**–6.5**	. . .
Trade credits	4 756 . .	9.6	15.9	–5.4	–18.9	–5.5	.1	15.3	. . .
General government: long-term	4 758 . .	. . .	. . .	. . .	. . .	. . .	. . .	. . .	. . .
General government: short-term	4 759 . .	. . .	. . .	. . .	. . .	. . .	. . .	. . .	. . .
Other sectors: long-term	4 761 . .	. . .	. . .	. . .	. . .	. . .	. . .	. . .	. . .
Other sectors: short-term	4 762 . .	9.6	15.9	–5.4	–18.9	–5.5	.1	15.3	. . .
Loans	4 764 . .	99.3	26.9	47.3	–59.2	14.8	3.0	106.3	. . .
Use of Fund credit and loans from the Fund	4 766 . .	–21.5	–7.8	–6.1	–11.4	–9.4	–9.6	5.4	. . .
Monetary authorities: other long-term	4 767 . .	. . .	. . .	. . .	. . .	. . .	. . .	. . .	. . .
Monetary authorities: short-term	4 768 . .	. . .	. . .	. . .	. . .	. . .	. . .	. . .	. . .
General government: long-term	4 770 . .	107.7	52.8	60.6	15.9	47.3	–1.6	97.5	. . .
General government: short-term	4 771 . .	. . .	. . .	. . .	. . .	. . .	. . .	. . .	. . .
Banks: long-term	4 773 . .	. . .	. . .	. . .	. . .	. . .	. . .	. . .	. . .
Banks: short-term	4 774 . .	. . .	. . .	. . .	. . .	. . .	. . .	. . .	. . .
Other sectors: long-term	4 776 . .	13.0	–18.1	–7.2	–63.7	–23.0	14.2	3.4	. . .
Other sectors: short-term	4 777 . .	. . .	. . .	. . .	. . .	. . .	. . .	. . .	. . .
Currency and deposits	4 780 . .	–4.5	1.1	–8.4	–2.0	46.9	8.2	–4.7	. . .
Monetary authorities	4 781 . .	1.4	1.2	–4.3	–1.3	34.6	7.7	–22.3	. . .
General government	4 782 . .	. . .	. . .	. . .	. . .	. . .	. . .	. . .	. . .
Banks	4 783 . .	–5.9	–.1	–4.1	–.7	12.3	.5	17.5	. . .
Other sectors	4 784 . .	. . .	. . .	. . .	. . .	. . .	. . .	. . .	. . .
Other liabilities	4 786 . .	4.5	21.0	–10.1	15.0	32.5	–61.9	–123.3	. . .
Monetary authorities: long-term	4 788 . .	. . .	. . .	. . .	. . .	. . .	. . .	. . .	. . .
Monetary authorities: short-term	4 789 . .	. . .	. . .	. . .	. . .	. . .	. . .	. . .	. . .
General government: long-term	4 791 . .	. . .	. . .	. . .	. . .	. . .	. . .	. . .	. . .
General government: short-term	4 792 . .	13.3	26.2	–9.9	4.3	57.4	44.1	–119.8	. . .
Banks: long-term	4 794 . .	. . .	. . .	. . .	. . .	. . .	. . .	. . .	. . .
Banks: short-term	4 795 . .	–8.9	–5.2	–.3	17.7	–6.1	–65.4	1.9	. . .
Other sectors: long-term	4 797 . .	. . .	. . .	. . .	. . .	. . .	. . .	. . .	. . .
Other sectors: short-term	4 798 . .	. . .	. . .	.2	–7.1	–18.9	–40.6	–5.4	. . .
D. RESERVE ASSETS	4 800 . .	27.5	–29.2	–10.1	–6.4	31.0	–19.9	28.7	. . .
Monetary gold	4 810 . .	. . .	. . .	. . .	. . .	. . .	. . .	. . .	. . .
Special drawing rights	4 820 . .	. . .	–1.1	1.2	–.4	.4	–.6	.1	. . .
Reserve position in the Fund	4 830 . .	. . .	. . .	. . .	. . .	. . .	. . .	. . .	. . .
Foreign exchange	4 840 . .	21.0	–31.8	–24.3	–20.0	50.1	–29.3	12.5	. . .
Other claims	4 880 . .	6.4	3.7	13.0	14.0	–19.5	9.9	16.1	. . .
NET ERRORS AND OMISSIONS	4 998 . .	**11.2**	**86.6**	**–18.4**	**174.7**	**–95.5**	**87.2**	**–67.8**	. . .

Part 3 of the *Yearbook* contains descriptions of the methodologies, compilation practices, and sources used to compile these data.

Table 1. ANALYTIC PRESENTATION, 1988–95
(Millions of U.S. dollars)

	Code	1988	1989	1990	1991	1992	1993	1994	1995
A. Current Account[1]	4 993 Y.	**–296**	**1,090**	**4,988**	**1,203**	**2,268**	**–780**	**–2,128**	. . .
Goods: exports f.o.b	2 100 . .	6,875	7,871	13,585	12,254	11,791	9,910	9,459	. . .
Goods: imports f.o.b	3 100 . .	–4,355	–3,693	–4,932	–7,813	–7,181	–6,662	–6,511	. . .
Balance on Goods	4 100 . .	*2,520*	*4,178*	*8,653*	*4,441*	*4,611*	*3,248*	*2,948*	. . .
Services: credit	2 200 . .	364	552	965	886	1,053	1,163	371	. . .
Services: debit	3 200 . .	–804	–1,375	–1,976	–2,448	–1,810	–2,726	–3,007	. . .
Balance on Goods and Services	4 991 . .	*2,080*	*3,355*	*7,642*	*2,879*	*3,853*	*1,685*	*312*	. . .
Income: credit	2 300 . .	41	152	211	211	156	58	49	. . .
Income: debit	3 300 . .	–2,405	–2,544	–2,949	–2,631	–2,494	–3,335	–2,986	. . .
Balance on Goods, Services, and Income	4 992 . .	*–285*	*963*	*4,904*	*458*	*1,515*	*–1,593*	*–2,626*	. . .
Current transfers: credit	2 379 Y.	28	157	167	877	817	857	550	. . .
Current transfers: debit	3 379 . .	–40	–31	–82	–132	–64	–44	–52	. . .
B. Capital Account[1]	4 994 Y.	**. . .**	**. . .**	**. . .**	**. . .**	**. . .**	**. . .**	**. . .**	. . .
Capital account: credit	2 994 Y.	. . .	. . .	. . .	. . .	. . .	. . .	. . .	. . .
Capital account: debit	3 994 . .	. . .	. . .	. . .	. . .	. . .	. . .	. . .	. . .
Total, Groups A Plus B	4 010 . .	*–296*	*1,090*	*4,988*	*1,203*	*2,268*	*–780*	*–2,128*	. . .
C. Financial Account[1]	4 995 X.	**–4,611**	**–3,649**	**–4,182**	**–2,633**	**–7,784**	**–1,043**	**329**	. . .
Direct investment abroad	4 505 . .	. . .	. . .	. . .	. . .	. . .	. . .	. . .	. . .
Direct investment in Nigeria	4 555 Y.	379	1,884	588	712	897	1,345	1,959	. . .
Portfolio investment assets	4 602 . .	. . .	. . .	. . .	. . .	. . .	. . .	. . .	. . .
Equity securities	4 610 . .	. . .	. . .	. . .	. . .	. . .	. . .	. . .	. . .
Debt securities	4 619 . .	. . .	. . .	. . .	. . .	. . .	. . .	. . .	. . .
Portfolio investment liabilities	4 652 Y.	–69	–220	–197	–61	1,884	–18	–27	. . .
Equity securities	4 660 Y.	. . .	. . .	. . .	. . .	. . .	. . .	. . .	. . .
Debt securities	4 669 Y.	–69	–220	–197	–61	1,884	–18	–27	. . .
Other investment assets	4 703 . .	–1,121	–2,534	–2,886	–2,487	–5,840	–1,345	–1,286	. . .
Monetary authorities	4 703 . A	. . .	. . .	. . .	. . .	. . .	. . .	. . .	. . .
General government	4 703 . B	–174	–2,397	–2,086	–771	–2,168	–1,087	–969	. . .
Banks	4 703 . C	–187	–123	–3	–171	–746	–249	320	. . .
Other sectors	4 703 . D	–760	–15	–797	–1,545	–2,926	–8	–637	. . .
Other investment liabilities	4 753 X.	–3,799	–2,779	–1,687	–797	–4,725	–1,026	–317	. . .
Monetary authorities	4 753 XA	–113	. . .	49	. . .	. . .	. . .	. . .	. . .
General government	4 753 YB	–3,448	–2,817	–1,644	–3,088	–5,180	–1,736	–1,885	. . .
Banks	4 753 YC	–148	36	–79	53	33	–28	–1	. . .
Other sectors	4 753 YD	–90	2	–13	2,238	423	738	1,570	. . .
Total, Groups A Through C	4 020 . .	*–4,908*	*–2,559*	*806*	*–1,430*	*–5,516*	*–1,823*	*–1,799*	. . .
D. Net Errors and Omissions	4 998 . .	**–221**	**–107**	**235**	**–93**	**–122**	**–88**	**–139**	. . .
Total, Groups A Through D	4 030 . .	*–5,129*	*–2,667*	*1,041*	*–1,523*	*–5,638*	*–1,911*	*–1,938*	. . .
E. Reserves and Related Items	4 040 . .	**5,129**	**2,667**	**–1,041**	**1,523**	**5,638**	**1,911**	**1,938**	. . .
Reserve assets	4 800 . .	506	–1,186	–2,478	–640	3,727	–611	–327	. . .
Use of Fund credit and loans	4 766 . .	. . .	. . .	. . .	. . .	. . .	. . .	. . .	. . .
Liabilities constituting foreign authorities' reserves	4 900 . .	. . .	. . .	. . .	. . .	. . .	. . .	. . .	. . .
Exceptional financing	4 920 . .	4,623	3,853	1,437	2,163	1,911	2,522	2,265	. . .
Conversion rates: naira per U.S. dollar	0 101 . .	**4.537**	**7.365**	**8.038**	**9.909**	**17.298**	**22.065**	**21.996**	. . .

[1] Excludes components that have been classified in the categories of Group E.

Table 2. STANDARD PRESENTATION, 1988–95
(Millions of U.S. dollars)

	Code	1988	1989	1990	1991	1992	1993	1994	1995
CURRENT ACCOUNT	4 993 . .	**–296**	**1,090**	**4,988**	**1,203**	**2,268**	**–780**	**–2,128**	. . .
A. GOODS	4 100 . .	2,520	4,178	8,653	4,441	4,611	3,248	2,948	. . .
Credit	2 100 . .	**6,875**	**7,871**	**13,585**	**12,254**	**11,791**	**9,910**	**9,459**	. . .
General merchandise: exports f.o.b.	2 110 . .	6,875	7,871	13,585	12,254	11,791	9,910	9,459	. . .
Goods for processing: exports f.o.b.	2 150 . .	. . .	. . .	. . .	. . .	. . .	. . .	. . .	. . .
Repairs on goods	2 160 . .	. . .	. . .	. . .	. . .	. . .	. . .	. . .	. . .
Goods procured in ports by carriers	2 170 . .	. . .	. . .	. . .	. . .	. . .	. . .	. . .	. . .
Nonmonetary gold	2 180 . .	. . .	. . .	. . .	. . .	. . .	. . .	. . .	. . .
Debit	3 100 . .	**–4,355**	**–3,693**	**–4,932**	**–7,813**	**–7,181**	**–6,662**	**–6,511**	. . .
General merchandise: imports f.o.b.	3 110 . .	–4,355	–3,693	–4,932	–7,813	–7,181	–6,662	–6,511	. . .
Goods for processing: imports f.o.b.	3 150 . .	. . .	. . .	. . .	. . .	. . .	. . .	. . .	. . .
Repairs on goods	3 160 . .	. . .	. . .	. . .	. . .	. . .	. . .	. . .	. . .
Goods procured in ports by carriers	3 170 . .	. . .	. . .	. . .	. . .	. . .	. . .	. . .	. . .
Nonmonetary gold	3 180 . .	. . .	. . .	. . .	. . .	. . .	. . .	. . .	. . .
B. SERVICES	4 200 . .	–440	–823	–1,011	–1,562	–757	–1,563	–2,636	. . .
Total credit	2 200 . .	*364*	*552*	*965*	*886*	*1,053*	*1,163*	*371*	. . .
Total debit	3 200 . .	*–804*	*–1,375*	*–1,976*	*–2,448*	*–1,810*	*–2,726*	*–3,007*	. . .
Transportation services, credit	2 205 . .	**132**	**16**	**37**	**100**	**154**	**200**	**51**	. . .
Passenger	2 205 BA	*10*	*1*	*5*	*19*	*22*	*46*	*15*	. . .
Freight	2 205 BB	*84*	*11*	*25*	*59*	*106*	*99*	*14*	. . .
Other	2 205 BC	*38*	*3*	*7*	*22*	*26*	*55*	*21*	. . .
Sea transport, passenger	2 207 . .	. . .	. . .	. . .	. . .	. . .	. . .	. . .	. . .
Sea transport, freight	2 208 . .	. . .	. . .	. . .	. . .	. . .	. . .	. . .	. . .
Sea transport, other	2 209 . .	. . .	. . .	. . .	. . .	. . .	. . .	. . .	. . .
Air transport, passenger	2 211 . .	. . .	. . .	. . .	. . .	. . .	. . .	. . .	. . .
Air transport, freight	2 212 . .	. . .	. . .	. . .	. . .	. . .	. . .	. . .	. . .
Air transport, other	2 213 . .	. . .	. . .	. . .	. . .	. . .	. . .	. . .	. . .
Other transport, passenger	2 215 . .	. . .	. . .	. . .	. . .	. . .	. . .	. . .	. . .
Other transport, freight	2 216 . .	. . .	. . .	. . .	. . .	. . .	. . .	. . .	. . .
Other transport, other	2 217 . .	. . .	. . .	. . .	. . .	. . .	. . .	. . .	. . .
Transportation services, debit	3 205 . .	**–428**	**–579**	**–639**	**–1,079**	**–921**	**–853**	**–754**	. . .
Passenger	3 205 BA	*–67*	*–123*	*–34*	*–44*	*–70*	*–56*	*–24*	. . .
Freight	3 205 BB	*–335*	*–428*	*–535*	*–981*	*–774*	*–724*	*–692*	. . .
Other	3 205 BC	*–26*	*–28*	*–71*	*–54*	*–77*	*–73*	*–38*	. . .
Sea transport, passenger	3 207 . .	. . .	. . .	. . .	. . .	. . .	. . .	. . .	. . .
Sea transport, freight	3 208 . .	. . .	. . .	. . .	. . .	. . .	. . .	. . .	. . .
Sea transport, other	3 209 . .	. . .	. . .	. . .	. . .	. . .	. . .	. . .	. . .
Air transport, passenger	3 211 . .	. . .	. . .	. . .	. . .	. . .	. . .	. . .	. . .
Air transport, freight	3 212 . .	. . .	. . .	. . .	. . .	. . .	. . .	. . .	. . .
Air transport, other	3 213 . .	. . .	. . .	. . .	. . .	. . .	. . .	. . .	. . .
Other transport, passenger	3 215 . .	. . .	. . .	. . .	. . .	. . .	. . .	. . .	. . .
Other transport, freight	3 216 . .	. . .	. . .	. . .	. . .	. . .	. . .	. . .	. . .
Other transport, other	3 217 . .	. . .	. . .	. . .	. . .	. . .	. . .	. . .	. . .
Travel, credit	2 236 . .	**54**	**5**	**25**	**39**	**29**	**33**	**10**	. . .
Business travel	2 237 . .	. . .	. . .	. . .	. . .	. . .	. . .	. . .	. . .
Personal travel	2 240 . .	. . .	. . .	. . .	. . .	. . .	. . .	. . .	. . .
Travel, debit	3 236 . .	**–42**	**–417**	**–576**	**–839**	**–348**	**–298**	**–858**	. . .
Business travel	3 237 . .	. . .	. . .	. . .	. . .	. . .	. . .	. . .	. . .
Personal travel	3 240 . .	. . .	. . .	. . .	. . .	. . .	. . .	. . .	. . .
Other services, credit	2 200 BA	**177**	**531**	**903**	**747**	**870**	**930**	**310**	. . .
Communications	2 245 . .	. . .	. . .	. . .	. . .	. . .	. . .	. . .	. . .
Construction	2 249 . .	. . .	. . .	. . .	. . .	. . .	. . .	. . .	. . .
Insurance	2 253 . .	9	1	3	7	12	11	2	. . .
Financial	2 260 . .	. . .	. . .	. . .	. . .	. . .	. . .	. . .	. . .
Computer and information	2 262 . .	. . .	. . .	. . .	. . .	. . .	. . .	. . .	. . .
Royalties and licence fees	2 266 . .	. . .	. . .	. . .	. . .	. . .	. . .	. . .	. . .
Other business services	2 268 . .	168	530	901	741	858	918	309	. . .
Personal, cultural, and recreational	2 287 . .	. . .	. . .	. . .	. . .	. . .	. . .	. . .	. . .
Government, n.i.e.	2 291 . .	. . .	. . .	. . .	. . .	. . .	. . .	. . .	. . .
Other services, debit	3 200 BA	**–335**	**–379**	**–760**	**–531**	**–541**	**–1,575**	**–1,395**	. . .
Communications	3 245 . .	. . .	. . .	. . .	. . .	. . .	. . .	. . .	. . .
Construction	3 249 . .	. . .	. . .	. . .	. . .	. . .	. . .	. . .	. . .
Insurance	3 253 . .	–37	–48	–59	–109	–86	–80	–77	. . .
Financial	3 260 . .	. . .	. . .	. . .	. . .	. . .	. . .	. . .	. . .
Computer and information	3 262 . .	. . .	. . .	. . .	. . .	. . .	. . .	. . .	. . .
Royalties and licence fees	3 266 . .	. . .	. . .	. . .	. . .	. . .	. . .	. . .	. . .
Other business services	3 268 . .	–297	–282	–626	–360	–383	–1,450	–1,292	. . .
Personal, cultural, and recreational	3 287 . .	. . .	. . .	. . .	. . .	. . .	. . .	. . .	. . .
Government, n.i.e.	3 291 . .	. . .	–50	–75	–62	–71	–45	–26	. . .

Table 2 (Continued). STANDARD PRESENTATION, 1988–95
(Millions of U.S. dollars)

	Code	1988	1989	1990	1991	1992	1993	1994	1995
C. INCOME	4 300	–2,364	–2,392	–2,738	–2,420	–2,338	–3,278	–2,938	...
Total credit	2 300	*41*	*152*	*211*	*211*	*156*	*58*	*49*	...
Total debit	3 300	*–2,405*	*–2,544*	*–2,949*	*–2,631*	*–2,494*	*–3,335*	*–2,986*	...
Compensation of employees, credit	2 310	...	...	...	...	...	...	...	...
Compensation of employees, debit	3 310	...	...	...	...	...	...	...	...
Investment income, credit	2 320	**41**	**152**	**211**	**211**	**156**	**58**	**49**	...
Direct investment income	2 330	...	...	...	...	...	...	...	...
Dividends and distributed branch profits	2 332	...	...	...	...	...	...	...	...
Reinvested earnings and undistributed branch profits	2 333	...	...	...	...	...	...	...	...
Income on debt (interest)	2 334	...	...	...	...	...	...	...	...
Portfolio investment income	2 339	...	...	...	...	...	...	...	...
Income on equity	2 340	...	...	...	...	...	...	...	...
Income on bonds and notes	2 350	...	...	...	...	...	...	...	...
Income on money market instruments and financial derivatives	2 360	...	...	...	...	...	...	...	...
Other investment income	2 370	41	152	211	211	156	58	49	...
Investment income, debit	3 320	**–2,405**	**–2,544**	**–2,949**	**–2,631**	**–2,494**	**–3,335**	**–2,986**	...
Direct investment income	3 330	–360	–97	–135	–186	–116	–1,326	–1,334	...
Dividends and distributed branch profits	3 332	–360	–97	–135	–186	–116	–1,326	–1,334	...
Reinvested earnings and undistributed branch profits	3 333	...	...	...	...	...	...	...	...
Income on debt (interest)	3 334	...	...	...	...	...	...	...	...
Portfolio investment income	3 339	...	...	...	...	...	...	...	...
Income on equity	3 340	...	...	...	...	...	...	...	...
Income on bonds and notes	3 350	...	...	...	...	...	...	...	...
Income on money market instruments and financial derivatives	3 360	...	...	...	...	...	...	...	...
Other investment income	3 370	–2,045	–2,447	–2,814	–2,445	–2,378	–2,009	–1,653	...
D. CURRENT TRANSFERS	4 379	–12	127	85	744	753	812	498	...
Credit	2 379	**28**	**157**	**167**	**877**	**817**	**857**	**550**	...
General government	2 380	25	147	157	811	760	63	...	...
Other sectors	2 390	2	10	10	66	56	793	550	...
Workers' remittances	2 391	2	10	10	66	56	793	550	...
Other current transfers	2 392	...	...	...	...	...	...	...	...
Debit	3 379	**–40**	**–31**	**–82**	**–132**	**–64**	**–44**	**–52**	...
General government	3 380	–3	–2	–74	–79	–29	–42	–48	...
Other sectors	3 390	–37	–29	–9	–54	–35	–2	–4	...
Workers' remittances	3 391	–37	–29	–9	–54	–35	–2	–4	...
Other current transfers	3 392	...	...	...	...	...	...	...	...
CAPITAL AND FINANCIAL ACCOUNT	4 996	**518**	**–982**	**–5,223**	**–1,110**	**–2,146**	**868**	**2,267**	...
CAPITAL ACCOUNT	4 994	...	...	...	...	...	...	...	...
Total credit	2 994	...	...	...	...	...	...	...	...
Total debit	3 994	...	...	...	...	...	...	...	...
Capital transfers, credit	2 400	...	...	...	...	...	...	...	...
General government	2 401	...	...	...	...	...	...	...	...
Debt forgiveness	2 402	...	...	...	...	...	...	...	...
Other capital transfers	2 410	...	...	...	...	...	...	...	...
Other sectors	2 430	...	...	...	...	...	...	...	...
Migrants' transfers	2 431	...	...	...	...	...	...	...	...
Debt forgiveness	2 432	...	...	...	...	...	...	...	...
Other capital transfers	2 440	...	...	...	...	...	...	...	...
Capital transfers, debit	3 400	...	...	...	...	...	...	...	...
General government	3 401	...	...	...	...	...	...	...	...
Debt forgiveness	3 402	...	...	...	...	...	...	...	...
Other capital transfers	3 410	...	...	...	...	...	...	...	...
Other sectors	3 430	...	...	...	...	...	...	...	...
Migrants' transfers	3 431	...	...	...	...	...	...	...	...
Debt forgiveness	3 432	...	...	...	...	...	...	...	...
Other capital transfers	3 440	...	...	...	...	...	...	...	...
Nonproduced nonfinancial assets, credit	2 480	...	...	...	...	...	...	...	...
Nonproduced nonfinancial assets, debit	3 480	...	...	...	...	...	...	...	...

Table 2 (Continued). STANDARD PRESENTATION, 1988–95
(Millions of U.S. dollars)

	Code	1988	1989	1990	1991	1992	1993	1994	1995
FINANCIAL ACCOUNT	4 995 . .	**518**	**–982**	**–5,223**	**–1,110**	**–2,146**	**868**	**2,267**	. . .
A. DIRECT INVESTMENT	4 500 . .	379	1,884	588	712	897	1,345	1,959	. . .
Direct investment abroad	4 505 . .	. . .	. . .	. . .	. . .	. . .	. . .	. . .	. . .
Equity capital	4 510 . .	. . .	. . .	. . .	. . .	. . .	. . .	. . .	. . .
Claims on affiliated enterprises	4 515 . .	. . .	. . .	. . .	. . .	. . .	. . .	. . .	. . .
Liabilities to affiliated enterprises	4 520 . .	. . .	. . .	. . .	. . .	. . .	. . .	. . .	. . .
Reinvested earnings	4 525 . .	. . .	. . .	. . .	. . .	. . .	. . .	. . .	. . .
Other capital	4 530 . .	. . .	. . .	. . .	. . .	. . .	. . .	. . .	. . .
Claims on affiliated enterprises	4 535 . .	. . .	. . .	. . .	. . .	. . .	. . .	. . .	. . .
Liabilities to affiliated enterprises	4 540 . .	. . .	. . .	. . .	. . .	. . .	. . .	. . .	. . .
Direct investment in Nigeria	4 555 . .	**379**	**1,884**	**588**	**712**	**897**	**1,345**	**1,959**	. . .
Equity capital	4 560 . .	. . .	. . .	. . .	. . .	. . .	. . .	. . .	. . .
Claims on direct investors	4 565 . .	. . .	. . .	. . .	. . .	. . .	. . .	. . .	. . .
Liabilities to direct investors	4 570 . .	. . .	. . .	. . .	. . .	. . .	. . .	. . .	. . .
Reinvested earnings	4 575 . .	. . .	. . .	. . .	. . .	. . .	. . .	. . .	. . .
Other capital	4 580 . .	379	1,884	588	712	897	1,345	1,959	. . .
Claims on direct investors	4 585 . .	. . .	. . .	. . .	. . .	. . .	. . .	. . .	. . .
Liabilities to direct investors	4 590 . .	. . .	. . .	. . .	. . .	. . .	. . .	. . .	. . .
B. PORTFOLIO INVESTMENT	4 600 . .	576	–220	–197	–61	1,884	–18	–27	. . .
Assets	4 602 . .	. . .	. . .	. . .	. . .	. . .	. . .	. . .	. . .
Equity securities	4 610 . .	. . .	. . .	. . .	. . .	. . .	. . .	. . .	. . .
Monetary authorities	4 611 . .	. . .	. . .	. . .	. . .	. . .	. . .	. . .	. . .
General government	4 612 . .	. . .	. . .	. . .	. . .	. . .	. . .	. . .	. . .
Banks	4 613 . .	. . .	. . .	. . .	. . .	. . .	. . .	. . .	. . .
Other sectors	4 614 . .	. . .	. . .	. . .	. . .	. . .	. . .	. . .	. . .
Debt securities	4 619 . .	. . .	. . .	. . .	. . .	. . .	. . .	. . .	. . .
Bonds and notes	4 620 . .	. . .	. . .	. . .	. . .	. . .	. . .	. . .	. . .
Monetary authorities	4 621 . .	. . .	. . .	. . .	. . .	. . .	. . .	. . .	. . .
General government	4 622 . .	. . .	. . .	. . .	. . .	. . .	. . .	. . .	. . .
Banks	4 623 . .	. . .	. . .	. . .	. . .	. . .	. . .	. . .	. . .
Other sectors	4 624 . .	. . .	. . .	. . .	. . .	. . .	. . .	. . .	. . .
Money market instruments	4 630 . .	. . .	. . .	. . .	. . .	. . .	. . .	. . .	. . .
Monetary authorities	4 631 . .	. . .	. . .	. . .	. . .	. . .	. . .	. . .	. . .
General government	4 632 . .	. . .	. . .	. . .	. . .	. . .	. . .	. . .	. . .
Banks	4 633 . .	. . .	. . .	. . .	. . .	. . .	. . .	. . .	. . .
Other sectors	4 634 . .	. . .	. . .	. . .	. . .	. . .	. . .	. . .	. . .
Financial derivatives	4 640 . .	. . .	. . .	. . .	. . .	. . .	. . .	. . .	. . .
Monetary authorities	4 641 . .	. . .	. . .	. . .	. . .	. . .	. . .	. . .	. . .
General government	4 642 . .	. . .	. . .	. . .	. . .	. . .	. . .	. . .	. . .
Banks	4 643 . .	. . .	. . .	. . .	. . .	. . .	. . .	. . .	. . .
Other sectors	4 644 . .	. . .	. . .	. . .	. . .	. . .	. . .	. . .	. . .
Liabilities	4 652 . .	**576**	**–220**	**–197**	**–61**	**1,884**	**–18**	**–27**	. . .
Equity securities	4 660 . .	. . .	. . .	. . .	. . .	. . .	. . .	. . .	. . .
Banks	4 663 . .	. . .	. . .	. . .	. . .	. . .	. . .	. . .	. . .
Other sectors	4 664 . .	. . .	. . .	. . .	. . .	. . .	. . .	. . .	. . .
Debt securities	4 669 . .	576	–220	–197	–61	1,884	–18	–27	. . .
Bonds and notes	4 670 . .	576	–220	–197	–61	1,884	–18	–27	. . .
Monetary authorities	4 671 . .	. . .	. . .	. . .	. . .	. . .	. . .	. . .	. . .
General government	4 672 . .	576	–220	–197	–61	1,884	–18	–27	. . .
Banks	4 673 . .	. . .	. . .	. . .	. . .	. . .	. . .	. . .	. . .
Other sectors	4 674 . .	. . .	. . .	. . .	. . .	. . .	. . .	. . .	. . .
Money market instruments	4 680 . .	. . .	. . .	. . .	. . .	. . .	. . .	. . .	. . .
Monetary authorities	4 681 . .	. . .	. . .	. . .	. . .	. . .	. . .	. . .	. . .
General government	4 682 . .	. . .	. . .	. . .	. . .	. . .	. . .	. . .	. . .
Banks	4 683 . .	. . .	. . .	. . .	. . .	. . .	. . .	. . .	. . .
Other sectors	4 684 . .	. . .	. . .	. . .	. . .	. . .	. . .	. . .	. . .
Financial derivatives	4 690 . .	. . .	. . .	. . .	. . .	. . .	. . .	. . .	. . .
Monetary authorities	4 691 . .	. . .	. . .	. . .	. . .	. . .	. . .	. . .	. . .
General government	4 692 . .	. . .	. . .	. . .	. . .	. . .	. . .	. . .	. . .
Banks	4 693 . .	. . .	. . .	. . .	. . .	. . .	. . .	. . .	. . .
Other sectors	4 694 . .	. . .	. . .	. . .	. . .	. . .	. . .	. . .	. . .

Table 2 (Concluded). STANDARD PRESENTATION, 1988–95
(Millions of U.S. dollars)

	Code	1988	1989	1990	1991	1992	1993	1994	1995
C. OTHER INVESTMENT	4 700 . .	–942	–1,461	–3,136	–1,121	–8,654	151	662	. . .
Assets	4 703 . .	**–1,121**	**–2,534**	**–2,886**	**–2,487**	**–5,840**	**–1,345**	**–1,286**	**. . .**
Trade credits	4 706 . .	. . .	. . .	. . .	. . .	. . .	. . .	. . .	. . .
General government: long-term	4 708 . .	. . .	. . .	. . .	. . .	. . .	. . .	. . .	. . .
General government: short-term	4 709 . .	. . .	. . .	. . .	. . .	. . .	. . .	. . .	. . .
Other sectors: long-term	4 711 . .	. . .	. . .	. . .	. . .	. . .	. . .	. . .	. . .
Other sectors: short-term	4 712 . .	. . .	. . .	. . .	. . .	. . .	. . .	. . .	. . .
Loans	4 714 . .	. . .	. . .	. . .	. . .	. . .	. . .	. . .	. . .
Monetary authorities: long-term	4 717 . .	. . .	. . .	. . .	. . .	. . .	. . .	. . .	. . .
Monetary authorities: short-term	4 718 . .	. . .	. . .	. . .	. . .	. . .	. . .	. . .	. . .
General government: long-term	4 720 . .	. . .	. . .	. . .	. . .	. . .	. . .	. . .	. . .
General government: short-term	4 721 . .	. . .	. . .	. . .	. . .	. . .	. . .	. . .	. . .
Banks: long-term	4 723 . .	. . .	. . .	. . .	. . .	. . .	. . .	. . .	. . .
Banks: short-term	4 724 . .	. . .	. . .	. . .	. . .	. . .	. . .	. . .	. . .
Other sectors: long-term	4 726 . .	. . .	. . .	. . .	. . .	. . .	. . .	. . .	. . .
Other sectors: short-term	4 727 . .	. . .	. . .	. . .	. . .	. . .	. . .	. . .	. . .
Currency and deposits	4 730 . .	–1,121	–2,534	–2,886	–2,487	–5,840	–1,345	–1,286	. . .
Monetary authorities	4 731 . .	. . .	. . .	. . .	. . .	. . .	. . .	. . .	. . .
General government	4 732 . .	–174	–2,397	–2,086	–771	–2,168	–1,087	–969	. . .
Banks	4 733 . .	–187	–123	–3	–171	–746	–249	320	. . .
Other sectors	4 734 . .	–760	–15	–797	–1,545	–2,926	–8	–637	. . .
Other assets	4 736 . .	. . .	. . .	. . .	. . .	. . .	. . .	. . .	. . .
Monetary authorities: long-term	4 738 . .	. . .	. . .	. . .	. . .	. . .	. . .	. . .	. . .
Monetary authorities: short-term	4 739 . .	. . .	. . .	. . .	. . .	. . .	. . .	. . .	. . .
General government: long-term	4 741 . .	. . .	. . .	. . .	. . .	. . .	. . .	. . .	. . .
General government: short-term	4 742 . .	. . .	. . .	. . .	. . .	. . .	. . .	. . .	. . .
Banks: long-term	4 744 . .	. . .	. . .	. . .	. . .	. . .	. . .	. . .	. . .
Banks: short-term	4 745 . .	. . .	. . .	. . .	. . .	. . .	. . .	. . .	. . .
Other sectors: long-term	4 747 . .	. . .	. . .	. . .	. . .	. . .	. . .	. . .	. . .
Other sectors: short-term	4 748 . .	. . .	. . .	. . .	. . .	. . .	. . .	. . .	. . .
Liabilities	4 753 . .	**179**	**1,073**	**–250**	**1,366**	**–2,814**	**1,496**	**1,948**	**. . .**
Trade credits	4 756 . .	–104	–15	. . .	. . .	. . .	. . .	. . .	. . .
General government: long-term	4 758 . .	. . .	. . .	. . .	. . .	. . .	. . .	. . .	. . .
General government: short-term	4 759 . .	. . .	. . .	. . .	. . .	. . .	. . .	. . .	. . .
Other sectors: long-term	4 761 . .	. . .	. . .	. . .	. . .	. . .	. . .	. . .	. . .
Other sectors: short-term	4 762 . .	–104	–15	. . .	. . .	. . .	. . .	. . .	. . .
Loans	4 764 . .	–3,473	–2,835	–1,639	–3,088	–5,180	–1,736	–1,885	. . .
Use of Fund credit and loans from the Fund	4 766 . .	. . .	. . .	. . .	. . .	. . .	. . .	. . .	. . .
Monetary authorities: other long-term	4 767 . .	. . .	. . .	. . .	. . .	. . .	. . .	. . .	. . .
Monetary authorities: short-term	4 768 . .	. . .	. . .	. . .	. . .	. . .	. . .	. . .	. . .
General government: long-term	4 770 . .	–3,448	–2,817	–1,644	–3,088	–5,180	–1,736	–1,885	. . .
General government: short-term	4 771 . .	. . .	. . .	. . .	. . .	. . .	. . .	. . .	. . .
Banks: long-term	4 773 . .	. . .	. . .	. . .	. . .	. . .	. . .	. . .	. . .
Banks: short-term	4 774 . .	. . .	. . .	. . .	. . .	. . .	. . .	. . .	. . .
Other sectors: long-term	4 776 . .	–25	–18	5	. . .	. . .	. . .	. . .	. . .
Other sectors: short-term	4 777 . .	. . .	. . .	. . .	. . .	. . .	. . .	. . .	. . .
Currency and deposits	4 780 . .	–148	36	–79	53	33	–28	–1	. . .
Monetary authorities	4 781 . .	. . .	. . .	. . .	. . .	. . .	. . .	. . .	. . .
General government	4 782 . .	. . .	. . .	. . .	. . .	. . .	. . .	. . .	. . .
Banks	4 783 . .	–148	36	–79	53	33	–28	–1	. . .
Other sectors	4 784 . .	. . .	. . .	. . .	. . .	. . .	. . .	. . .	. . .
Other liabilities	4 786 . .	3,904	3,887	1,467	4,401	2,334	3,260	3,835	. . .
Monetary authorities: long-term	4 788 . .	. . .	. . .	. . .	. . .	. . .	. . .	. . .	. . .
Monetary authorities: short-term	4 789 . .	3,865	3,853	1,486	2,163	1,911	2,522	2,265	. . .
General government: long-term	4 791 . .	. . .	. . .	. . .	. . .	. . .	. . .	. . .	. . .
General government: short-term	4 792 . .	. . .	. . .	. . .	. . .	. . .	. . .	. . .	. . .
Banks: long-term	4 794 . .	. . .	. . .	. . .	. . .	. . .	. . .	. . .	. . .
Banks: short-term	4 795 . .	. . .	. . .	. . .	. . .	. . .	. . .	. . .	. . .
Other sectors: long-term	4 797 . .	. . .	. . .	. . .	. . .	. . .	. . .	. . .	. . .
Other sectors: short-term	4 798 . .	39	35	–19	2,238	423	738	1,570	. . .
D. RESERVE ASSETS	4 800 . .	506	–1,186	–2,478	–640	3,727	–611	–327	. . .
Monetary gold	4 810 . .	. . .	. . .	. . .	. . .	. . .	. . .	. . .	. . .
Special drawing rights	4 820 . .	. . .	–1	. . .	1	. . .	. . .	. . .	. . .
Reserve position in the Fund	4 830 . .	. . .	. . .	. . .	. . .	. . .	. . .	. . .	. . .
Foreign exchange	4 840 . .	506	–1,185	–2,477	–641	3,727	–611	–327	. . .
Other claims	4 880 . .	. . .	. . .	. . .	. . .	. . .	. . .	. . .	. . .
NET ERRORS AND OMISSIONS	4 998 . .	**–221**	**–107**	**235**	**–93**	**–122**	**–88**	**–139**	**. . .**

Part 3 of the *Yearbook* contains descriptions of the methodologies, compilation practices, and sources used to compile these data.

Table 1. ANALYTIC PRESENTATION, 1988–95
(Millions of U.S. dollars)

	Code	1988	1989	1990	1991	1992	1993	1994	1995
A. Current Account [1]	4 993 Y.	**–3,896**	**212**	**3,992**	**5,032**	**2,982**	**2,152**	**3,645**	**. . .**
Goods: exports f.o.b	2 100 . .	23,075	27,171	34,313	34,212	35,162	31,989	34,922	. . .
Goods: imports f.o.b	3 100 . .	–23,284	–23,401	–26,552	–25,516	–25,860	–23,995	–26,601	. . .
Balance on Goods	4 100 . .	*–209*	*3,770*	*7,761*	*8,696*	*9,303*	*7,995*	*8,321*	. . .
Services: credit	2 200 . .	9,729	10,770	12,765	13,330	13,642	12,744	13,105	. . .
Services: debit	3 200 . .	–10,270	–10,623	–12,358	–12,701	–14,789	–13,848	–14,392	. . .
Balance on Goods and Services	4 991 . .	*–750*	*3,916*	*8,168*	*9,326*	*8,156*	*6,890*	*7,034*	. . .
Income: credit	2 300 . .	3,265	3,425	3,896	3,540	3,040	2,448	2,810	. . .
Income: debit	3 300 . .	–5,274	–5,995	–6,596	–6,293	–6,457	–5,785	–4,579	. . .
Balance on Goods, Services, and Income	4 992 . .	*–2,759*	*1,346*	*5,468*	*6,573*	*4,739*	*3,553*	*5,265*	. . .
Current transfers: credit	2 379 Y.	168	164	217	239	287	319	266	. . .
Current transfers: debit	3 379 . .	–1,305	–1,299	–1,693	–1,780	–2,044	–1,720	–1,886	. . .
B. Capital Account [1]	4 994 Y.	**8**	**2**	**31**	**17**	**–21**	**14**	**–19**	**. . .**
Capital account: credit	2 994 Y.	107	101	109	118	143	180	76	. . .
Capital account: debit	3 994 . .	–99	–99	–78	–101	–164	–165	–94	. . .
Total, Groups A Plus B	4 010 . .	*–3,889*	*214*	*4,023*	*5,049*	*2,961*	*2,167*	*3,626*	. . .
C. Financial Account [1]	4 995 X.	**4,900**	**2,056**	**–761**	**–7,581**	**–375**	**3,280**	**–1,321**	**. . .**
Direct investment abroad	4 505 . .	–978	–1,358	–1,470	–1,782	–411	–877	–1,628	. . .
Direct investment in Norway	4 555 Y.	279	1,519	1,003	–398	716	2,003	623	. . .
Portfolio investment assets	4 602 . .	–392	–563	–987	–2,523	–192	853	750	. . .
Equity securities	4 610 . .	28	–310	–569	–298	–467	–252	160	. . .
Debt securities	4 619 . .	–420	–252	–418	–2,224	275	1,105	590	. . .
Portfolio investment liabilities	4 652 Y.	4,618	3,606	1,548	–585	1,054	–1,188	–599	. . .
Equity securities	4 660 Y.	336	1,035	644	159	872	228	821	. . .
Debt securities	4 669 Y.	4,282	2,571	904	–743	182	–1,416	–1,420	. . .
Other investment assets	4 703 . .	643	–274	–1,502	–326	–1,068	2,146	1,501	. . .
Monetary authorities	4 703 . A	. . .	. . .	. . .	. . .	. . .	. . .	. . .	. . .
General government	4 703 . B	–159	76	170	207	–478	–4,485	1,159	. . .
Banks	4 703 . C	1,343	–222	–223	–1,549	–2,695	5,152	–317	. . .
Other sectors	4 703 . D	–542	–129	–1,448	1,016	2,106	1,479	658	. . .
Other investment liabilities	4 753 X.	730	–874	648	–1,968	–474	344	–1,968	. . .
Monetary authorities	4 753 XA	124	–58	3	56	1,233	–458	–69	. . .
General government	4 753 YB	–93	–2	35	3	–15	648	70	. . .
Banks	4 753 YC	–1,101	–817	–740	–4,174	–3,985	–4	–880	. . .
Other sectors	4 753 YD	1,801	3	1,350	2,147	2,293	158	–1,089	. . .
Total, Groups A Through C	4 020 . .	*1,011*	*2,270*	*3,262*	*–2,532*	*2,587*	*5,447*	*2,305*	. . .
D. Net Errors and Omissions	4 998 . .	**–1,149**	**–1,305**	**–2,848**	**–219**	**–3,442**	**–1,309**	**–854**	**. . .**
Total, Groups A Through D	4 030 . .	*–138*	*965*	*414*	*–2,751*	*–855*	*4,138*	*1,451*	. . .
E. Reserves and Related Items	4 040 . .	**138**	**–965**	**–414**	**2,751**	**855**	**–4,138**	**–1,451**	**. . .**
Reserve assets	4 800 . .	138	–965	–414	2,751	855	–4,138	–1,451	. . .
Use of Fund credit and loans	4 766 . .	. . .	. . .	. . .	. . .	. . .	. . .	. . .	. . .
Liabilities constituting foreign authorities' reserves	4 900 . .	. . .	. . .	. . .	. . .	. . .	. . .	. . .	. . .
Exceptional financing	4 920 . .	. . .	. . .	. . .	. . .	. . .	. . .	. . .	. . .
Conversion rates: Norwegian kroner per U.S. dollar	0 101 . .	**6.5170**	**6.9045**	**6.2597**	**6.4829**	**6.2145**	**7.0941**	**7.0576**	**6.3352**

[1] Excludes components that have been classified in the categories of Group E.

Table 2. STANDARD PRESENTATION, 1988–95
(Millions of U.S. dollars)

	Code	1988	1989	1990	1991	1992	1993	1994	1995
CURRENT ACCOUNT	4 993 . .	**–3,896**	**212**	**3,992**	**5,032**	**2,982**	**2,152**	**3,645**	**. . .**
A. GOODS	4 100 . .	–209	3,770	7,761	8,696	9,303	7,995	8,321	. . .
Credit	2 100 . .	**23,075**	**27,171**	**34,313**	**34,212**	**35,162**	**31,989**	**34,922**	**. . .**
General merchandise: exports f.o.b.	2 110 . .	23,075	27,171	34,313	34,212	35,162	31,989	34,922	. . .
Goods for processing: exports f.o.b.	2 150 . .	. . .	. . .	. . .	. . .	. . .	. . .	. . .	. . .
Repairs on goods	2 160 . .	. . .	. . .	. . .	. . .	. . .	. . .	. . .	. . .
Goods procured in ports by carriers	2 170 . .	. . .	. . .	. . .	. . .	. . .	. . .	. . .	. . .
Nonmonetary gold	2 180 . .	. . .	. . .	. . .	. . .	. . .	. . .	. . .	. . .
Debit	3 100 . .	**–23,284**	**–23,401**	**–26,552**	**–25,516**	**–25,860**	**–23,995**	**–26,601**	**. . .**
General merchandise: imports f.o.b.	3 110 . .	–23,284	–23,401	–26,552	–25,516	–25,860	–23,995	–26,601	. . .
Goods for processing: imports f.o.b.	3 150 . .	. . .	. . .	. . .	. . .	. . .	. . .	. . .	. . .
Repairs on goods	3 160 . .	. . .	. . .	. . .	. . .	. . .	. . .	. . .	. . .
Goods procured in ports by carriers	3 170 . .	. . .	. . .	. . .	. . .	. . .	. . .	. . .	. . .
Nonmonetary gold	3 180 . .	. . .	. . .	. . .	. . .	. . .	. . .	. . .	. . .
B. SERVICES	4 200 . .	–541	147	407	630	–1,147	–1,104	–1,287	. . .
Total credit	2 200 . .	*9,729*	*10,770*	*12,765*	*13,330*	*13,642*	*12,744*	*13,105*	. . .
Total debit	3 200 . .	*–10,270*	*–10,623*	*–12,358*	*–12,701*	*–14,789*	*–13,848*	*–14,392*	. . .
Transportation services, credit	2 205 . .	**6,151**	**7,248**	**8,555**	**8,998**	**7,980**	**7,463**	**7,459**	**. . .**
Passenger	2 205 BA	*580*	*520*	*597*	*495*	*516*	*487*	*540*	. . .
Freight	2 205 BB	*4,971*	*6,143*	*7,352*	*7,883*	*6,877*	*6,461*	*6,283*	. . .
Other	2 205 BC	*600*	*586*	*606*	*620*	*587*	*515*	*636*	. . .
Sea transport, passenger	2 207 . .	. . .	. . .	. . .	. . .	. . .	. . .	. . .	. . .
Sea transport, freight	2 208 . .	. . .	. . .	. . .	. . .	. . .	. . .	. . .	. . .
Sea transport, other	2 209 . .	. . .	. . .	. . .	. . .	. . .	. . .	. . .	. . .
Air transport, passenger	2 211 . .	. . .	. . .	. . .	. . .	. . .	. . .	. . .	. . .
Air transport, freight	2 212 . .	. . .	. . .	. . .	. . .	. . .	. . .	. . .	. . .
Air transport, other	2 213 . .	. . .	. . .	. . .	. . .	. . .	. . .	. . .	. . .
Other transport, passenger	2 215 . .	. . .	. . .	. . .	. . .	. . .	. . .	. . .	. . .
Other transport, freight	2 216 . .	. . .	. . .	. . .	. . .	. . .	. . .	. . .	. . .
Other transport, other	2 217 . .	. . .	. . .	. . .	. . .	. . .	. . .	. . .	. . .
Transportation services, debit	3 205 . .	**–4,094**	**–4,741**	**–5,464**	**–5,527**	**–5,588**	**–4,938**	**–5,541**	**. . .**
Passenger	3 205 BA	. . .	. . .	. . .	. . .	. . .	. . .	. . .	. . .
Freight	3 205 BB	*–389*	*–518*	*–683*	*–573*	*–635*	*–662*	*–828*	. . .
Other	3 205 BC	*–3,705*	*–4,223*	*–4,782*	*–4,955*	*–4,953*	*–4,276*	*–4,713*	. . .
Sea transport, passenger	3 207 . .	. . .	. . .	. . .	. . .	. . .	. . .	. . .	. . .
Sea transport, freight	3 208 . .	. . .	. . .	. . .	. . .	. . .	. . .	. . .	. . .
Sea transport, other	3 209 . .	. . .	. . .	. . .	. . .	. . .	. . .	. . .	. . .
Air transport, passenger	3 211 . .	. . .	. . .	. . .	. . .	. . .	. . .	. . .	. . .
Air transport, freight	3 212 . .	. . .	. . .	. . .	. . .	. . .	. . .	. . .	. . .
Air transport, other	3 213 . .	. . .	. . .	. . .	. . .	. . .	. . .	. . .	. . .
Other transport, passenger	3 215 . .	. . .	. . .	. . .	. . .	. . .	. . .	. . .	. . .
Other transport, freight	3 216 . .	. . .	. . .	. . .	. . .	. . .	. . .	. . .	. . .
Other transport, other	3 217 . .	. . .	. . .	. . .	. . .	. . .	. . .	. . .	. . .
Travel, credit	2 236 . .	**1,479**	**1,347**	**1,570**	**1,646**	**2,016**	**1,851**	**2,194**	**. . .**
Business travel	2 237 . .	. . .	. . .	. . .	. . .	. . .	. . .	. . .	. . .
Personal travel	2 240 . .	. . .	. . .	. . .	. . .	. . .	. . .	. . .	. . .
Travel, debit	3 236 . .	**–3,532**	**–2,986**	**–3,679**	**–3,413**	**–4,075**	**–3,686**	**–4,106**	**. . .**
Business travel	3 237 . .	. . .	. . .	. . .	. . .	. . .	. . .	. . .	. . .
Personal travel	3 240 . .	. . .	. . .	. . .	. . .	. . .	. . .	. . .	. . .
Other services, credit	2 200 BA	**2,099**	**2,175**	**2,640**	**2,687**	**3,646**	**3,430**	**3,452**	**. . .**
Communications	2 245 . .	. . .	. . .	. . .	. . .	. . .	. . .	. . .	. . .
Construction	2 249 . .	. . .	. . .	. . .	. . .	. . .	. . .	. . .	. . .
Insurance	2 253 . .	44	42	51	54	1,303	1,118	967	. . .
Financial	2 260 . .	. . .	. . .	. . .	. . .	. . .	. . .	. . .	. . .
Computer and information	2 262 . .	. . .	. . .	. . .	. . .	. . .	. . .	. . .	. . .
Royalties and licence fees	2 266 . .	81	107	133	116	121	143	287	. . .
Other business services	2 268 . .	1,739	1,820	2,143	2,169	2,000	1,922	2,053	. . .
Personal, cultural, and recreational	2 287 . .	. . .	. . .	. . .	. . .	. . .	. . .	. . .	. . .
Government, n.i.e.	2 291 . .	235	206	313	348	222	247	144	. . .
Other services, debit	3 200 BA	**–2,644**	**–2,896**	**–3,214**	**–3,760**	**–5,126**	**–5,225**	**–4,745**	**. . .**
Communications	3 245 . .	. . .	. . .	. . .	. . .	. . .	. . .	. . .	. . .
Construction	3 249 . .	. . .	. . .	. . .	. . .	. . .	. . .	. . .	. . .
Insurance	3 253 . .	–134	–123	–207	–140	–1,528	–1,530	–1,447	. . .
Financial	3 260 . .	. . .	. . .	. . .	. . .	. . .	. . .	. . .	. . .
Computer and information	3 262 . .	. . .	. . .	. . .	. . .	. . .	. . .	. . .	. . .
Royalties and licence fees	3 266 . .	–161	–133	–148	–168	–184	–267	–231	. . .
Other business services	3 268 . .	–2,237	–2,540	–2,748	–3,280	–3,307	–3,344	–3,009	. . .
Personal, cultural, and recreational	3 287 . .	. . .	. . .	. . .	. . .	. . .	. . .	. . .	. . .
Government, n.i.e.	3 291 . .	–111	–101	–111	–173	–106	–83	–57	. . .

Table 2 (Continued). STANDARD PRESENTATION, 1988–95
(Millions of U.S. dollars)

	Code	1988	1989	1990	1991	1992	1993	1994	1995
C. INCOME	4 300	–2,009	–2,570	–2,700	–2,753	–3,416	–3,337	–1,769	...
Total credit	2 300	*3,265*	*3,425*	*3,896*	*3,540*	*3,040*	*2,448*	*2,810*	...
Total debit	3 300	*–5,274*	*–5,995*	*–6,596*	*–6,293*	*–6,457*	*–5,785*	*–4,579*	...
Compensation of employees, credit	2 310	**22**	**23**	**27**	**28**	**29**	**25**	**27**	...
Compensation of employees, debit	3 310	**–68**	**–68**	**–81**	**–78**	**–81**	**–89**	**–93**	...
Investment income, credit	2 320	**3,243**	**3,403**	**3,870**	**3,513**	**3,011**	**2,422**	**2,783**	...
Direct investment income	2 330	82	57	86	169	99	103	67	...
Dividends and distributed branch profits	2 332	82	57	86	169	99	103	67	...
Reinvested earnings and undistributed branch profits	2 333	...	...	...	...	...	...	...	...
Income on debt (interest)	2 334	...	...	...	...	...	...	...	...
Portfolio investment income	2 339	...	...	...	...	...	...	...	...
Income on equity	2 340	...	...	...	...	...	...	...	...
Income on bonds and notes	2 350	...	...	...	...	...	...	...	...
Income on money market instruments and financial derivatives	2 360	...	...	...	...	...	...	...	...
Other investment income	2 370	3,161	3,346	3,784	3,344	2,913	2,319	2,716	...
Investment income, debit	3 320	**–5,206**	**–5,927**	**–6,515**	**–6,215**	**–6,375**	**–5,695**	**–4,486**	...
Direct investment income	3 330	–518	–676	–798	–1,241	–2,260	–2,091	–941	...
Dividends and distributed branch profits	3 332	–518	–676	–798	–1,241	–2,260	–2,091	–941	...
Reinvested earnings and undistributed branch profits	3 333	...	...	...	...	...	...	...	...
Income on debt (interest)	3 334	...	...	...	...	...	...	...	...
Portfolio investment income	3 339	...	...	...	...	...	...	...	...
Income on equity	3 340	...	...	...	...	...	...	...	...
Income on bonds and notes	3 350	...	...	...	...	...	...	...	...
Income on money market instruments and financial derivatives	3 360	...	...	...	...	...	...	...	...
Other investment income	3 370	–4,688	–5,251	–5,717	–4,974	–4,115	–3,604	–3,545	...
D. CURRENT TRANSFERS	4 379	–1,137	–1,135	–1,476	–1,541	–1,757	–1,401	–1,620	...
Credit	2 379	**168**	**164**	**217**	**239**	**287**	**319**	**266**	...
General government	2 380	...	...	...	...	...	...	...	...
Other sectors	2 390	168	164	217	239	287	319	266	...
Workers' remittances	2 391	9	17	22	28	20	21	23	...
Other current transfers	2 392	159	147	195	211	267	298	243	...
Debit	3 379	**–1,305**	**–1,299**	**–1,693**	**–1,780**	**–2,044**	**–1,720**	**–1,886**	...
General government	3 380	–962	–910	–1,208	–1,185	–1,288	–1,082	–1,187	...
Other sectors	3 390	–343	–389	–485	–595	–756	–638	–699	...
Workers' remittances	3 391	–59	–84	–136	–231	–277	–249	–259	...
Other current transfers	3 392	–284	–305	–349	–363	–479	–389	–439	...
CAPITAL AND FINANCIAL ACCOUNT	4 996	**5,046**	**1,093**	**–1,144**	**–4,813**	**459**	**–843**	**–2,791**	...
CAPITAL ACCOUNT	4 994	**8**	**2**	**31**	**17**	**–21**	**14**	**–19**	...
Total credit	2 994	*107*	*101*	*109*	*118*	*143*	*180*	*76*	...
Total debit	3 994	*–99*	*–99*	*–78*	*–101*	*–164*	*–165*	*–94*	...
Capital transfers, credit	2 400	**107**	**101**	**109**	**118**	**143**	**180**	**76**	...
General government	2 401	...	...	...	...	...	...	...	...
Debt forgiveness	2 402	...	...	...	...	...	...	...	...
Other capital transfers	2 410	...	...	...	...	...	...	...	...
Other sectors	2 430	107	101	109	118	143	180	76	...
Migrants' transfers	2 431	107	101	109	118	143	180	76	...
Debt forgiveness	2 432	...	...	...	...	...	...	...	...
Other capital transfers	2 440	...	...	...	...	...	...	...	...
Capital transfers, debit	3 400	**–99**	**–99**	**–78**	**–101**	**–164**	**–165**	**–94**	...
General government	3 401	...	...	...	...	...	...	...	...
Debt forgiveness	3 402	...	...	...	...	...	...	...	...
Other capital transfers	3 410	...	...	...	...	...	...	...	...
Other sectors	3 430	–99	–99	–78	–101	–164	–165	–94	...
Migrants' transfers	3 431	–99	–99	–78	–101	–164	–165	–94	...
Debt forgiveness	3 432	...	...	...	...	...	...	...	...
Other capital transfers	3 440	...	...	...	...	...	...	...	...
Nonproduced nonfinancial assets, credit	2 480	...	...	...	...	...	...	...	...
Nonproduced nonfinancial assets, debit	3 480	...	...	...	...	...	...	...	...

Table 2 (Continued). STANDARD PRESENTATION, 1988–95
(Millions of U.S. dollars)

	Code	1988	1989	1990	1991	1992	1993	1994	1995
FINANCIAL ACCOUNT	4 995	**5,038**	**1,091**	**–1,175**	**–4,831**	**480**	**–857**	**–2,772**	...
A. DIRECT INVESTMENT	4 500	–699	161	–467	–2,180	305	1,126	–1,005	...
Direct investment abroad	4 505	**–978**	**–1,358**	**–1,470**	**–1,782**	**–411**	**–877**	**–1,628**	...
Equity capital	4 510	–769	–1,174	–700	–1,371	–118	–762	–915	...
Claims on affiliated enterprises	4 515	...	...	...	...	...	...	...	...
Liabilities to affiliated enterprises	4 520	...	...	...	...	...	...	...	...
Reinvested earnings	4 525	...	...	...	...	...	...	...	...
Other capital	4 530	–209	–184	–771	–411	–293	–115	–714	...
Claims on affiliated enterprises	4 535	...	...	...	...	...	...	...	...
Liabilities to affiliated enterprises	4 540	...	...	...	...	...	...	...	...
Direct investment in Norway	4 555	**279**	**1,519**	**1,003**	**–398**	**716**	**2,003**	**623**	...
Equity capital	4 560	87	845	356	689	431	1,715	168	...
Claims on direct investors	4 565	...	...	...	...	...	...	...	...
Liabilities to direct investors	4 570	...	...	...	...	...	...	...	...
Reinvested earnings	4 575	...	...	...	...	...	...	...	...
Other capital	4 580	192	674	647	–1,086	285	288	455	...
Claims on direct investors	4 585	...	...	...	...	...	...	...	...
Liabilities to direct investors	4 590	...	...	...	...	...	...	...	...
B. PORTFOLIO INVESTMENT	4 600	4,226	3,043	561	–3,107	862	–335	151	...
Assets	4 602	**–392**	**–563**	**–987**	**–2,523**	**–192**	**853**	**750**	...
Equity securities	4 610	28	–310	–569	–298	–467	–252	160	...
Monetary authorities	4 611	...	...	...	...	...	...	...	...
General government	4 612	...	...	...	...	...	...	...	...
Banks	4 613	...	...	...	...	...	...	...	...
Other sectors	4 614	...	...	...	...	...	...	...	...
Debt securities	4 619	–420	–252	–418	–2,224	275	1,105	590	...
Bonds and notes	4 620	–420	–252	–418	–2,224	275	1,105	590	...
Monetary authorities	4 621	...	...	...	...	...	...	...	...
General government	4 622	...	...	...	...	...	...	...	...
Banks	4 623	...	...	...	...	...	...	...	...
Other sectors	4 624	...	...	...	...	...	...	...	...
Money market instruments	4 630	...	...	...	...	...	...	...	...
Monetary authorities	4 631	...	...	...	...	...	...	...	...
General government	4 632	...	...	...	...	...	...	...	...
Banks	4 633	...	...	...	...	...	...	...	...
Other sectors	4 634	...	...	...	...	...	...	...	...
Financial derivatives	4 640	...	...	...	...	...	...	...	...
Monetary authorities	4 641	...	...	...	...	...	...	...	...
General government	4 642	...	...	...	...	...	...	...	...
Banks	4 643	...	...	...	...	...	...	...	...
Other sectors	4 644	...	...	...	...	...	...	...	...
Liabilities	4 652	**4,618**	**3,606**	**1,548**	**–585**	**1,054**	**–1,188**	**–599**	...
Equity securities	4 660	336	1,035	644	159	872	228	821	...
Banks	4 663	...	...	...	...	...	...	...	...
Other sectors	4 664	...	...	...	...	...	...	...	...
Debt securities	4 669	4,282	2,571	904	–743	182	–1,416	–1,420	...
Bonds and notes	4 670	4,282	2,571	904	–743	182	–1,416	–1,420	...
Monetary authorities	4 671	...	...	...	...	...	...	...	...
General government	4 672	2,219	349	–1,065	580	3,269	1,167	–1,080	...
Banks	4 673	...	...	...	...	...	...	...	...
Other sectors	4 674	2,063	2,222	1,969	–1,323	–3,087	–2,583	–340	...
Money market instruments	4 680	...	...	...	...	...	...	...	...
Monetary authorities	4 681	...	...	...	...	...	...	...	...
General government	4 682	...	...	...	...	...	...	...	...
Banks	4 683	...	...	...	...	...	...	...	...
Other sectors	4 684	...	...	...	...	...	...	...	...
Financial derivatives	4 690	...	...	...	...	...	...	...	...
Monetary authorities	4 691	...	...	...	...	...	...	...	...
General government	4 692	...	...	...	...	...	...	...	...
Banks	4 693	...	...	...	...	...	...	...	...
Other sectors	4 694	...	...	...	...	...	...	...	...

Table 2 (Concluded). STANDARD PRESENTATION, 1988–95
(Millions of U.S. dollars)

	Code	1988	1989	1990	1991	1992	1993	1994	1995
C. OTHER INVESTMENT	4 700 . .	1,373	–1,148	–854	–2,294	–1,542	2,489	–467	. . .
Assets	4 703 . .	**643**	**–274**	**–1,502**	**–326**	**–1,068**	**2,146**	**1,501**	**. . .**
Trade credits	4 706 . .	–206	199	–109	576	1,728	989	1,263	. . .
General government: long-term	4 708 . .	. . .	. . .	. . .	. . .	. . .	. . .	. . .	. . .
General government: short-term	4 709 . .	. . .	. . .	. . .	. . .	. . .	. . .	. . .	. . .
Other sectors: long-term	4 711 . .	. . .	. . .	. . .	. . .	. . .	. . .	. . .	. . .
Other sectors: short-term	4 712 . .	–206	199	–109	576	1,728	989	1,263	. . .
Loans	4 714 . .	–305	–1,392	–1,551	–50	46	–3,918	792	. . .
Monetary authorities: long-term	4 717 . .	. . .	. . .	. . .	. . .	. . .	. . .	. . .	. . .
Monetary authorities: short-term	4 718 . .	. . .	. . .	. . .	. . .	. . .	. . .	. . .	. . .
General government: long-term	4 720 . .	1	1	2	. . .	. . .	. . .	. . .	. . .
General government: short-term	4 721 . .	. . .	. . .	. . .	. . .	. . .	–4,346	1,156	. . .
Banks: long-term	4 723 . .	–205	–775	–1,091	–122	37	514	–70	. . .
Banks: short-term	4 724 . .	. . .	. . .	. . .	. . .	. . .	. . .	. . .	. . .
Other sectors: long-term	4 726 . .	–26	–554	–386	–89	149	–78	. . .	. . .
Other sectors: short-term	4 727 . .	–75	–65	–75	161	–139	–8	–294	. . .
Currency and deposits	4 730 . .	1,187	686	418	–1,045	–3,023	5,072	–290	. . .
Monetary authorities	4 731 . .	. . .	. . .	. . .	. . .	. . .	. . .	. . .	. . .
General government	4 732 . .	–54	77	–13	12	–568	–90	38	. . .
Banks	4 733 . .	1,545	576	887	–1,419	–2,725	4,673	–234	. . .
Other sectors	4 734 . .	–305	32	–456	362	269	489	–94	. . .
Other assets	4 736 . .	–33	233	–260	194	181	3	–264	. . .
Monetary authorities: long-term	4 738 . .	. . .	. . .	. . .	. . .	. . .	. . .	. . .	. . .
Monetary authorities: short-term	4 739 . .	. . .	. . .	. . .	. . .	. . .	. . .	. . .	. . .
General government: long-term	4 741 . .	–106	–2	181	195	89	–49	–35	. . .
General government: short-term	4 742 . .	. . .	. . .	. . .	. . .	. . .	. . .	. . .	. . .
Banks: long-term	4 744 . .	3	–23	–19	–7	–8	–35	–13	. . .
Banks: short-term	4 745 . .	. . .	. . .	. . .	. . .	. . .	. . .	. . .	. . .
Other sectors: long-term	4 747 . .	70	258	–422	6	100	87	–216	. . .
Other sectors: short-term	4 748 . .	. . .	. . .	. . .	. . .	. . .	. . .	. . .	. . .
Liabilities	4 753 . .	**730**	**–874**	**648**	**–1,968**	**–474**	**344**	**–1,968**	**. . .**
Trade credits	4 756 . .	54	–131	–112	113	499	256	60	. . .
General government: long-term	4 758 . .	. . .	. . .	. . .	. . .	. . .	. . .	. . .	. . .
General government: short-term	4 759 . .	. . .	. . .	. . .	. . .	. . .	. . .	. . .	. . .
Other sectors: long-term	4 761 . .	. . .	. . .	. . .	. . .	. . .	. . .	. . .	. . .
Other sectors: short-term	4 762 . .	54	–131	–112	113	499	256	60	. . .
Loans	4 764 . .	1,944	182	1,920	2,514	2,481	679	–603	. . .
Use of Fund credit and loans from the Fund	4 766 . .	. . .	. . .	. . .	. . .	. . .	. . .	. . .	. . .
Monetary authorities: other long-term	4 767 . .	. . .	. . .	. . .	. . .	. . .	. . .	. . .	. . .
Monetary authorities: short-term	4 768 . .	. . .	. . .	. . .	. . .	. . .	. . .	. . .	. . .
General government: long-term	4 770 . .	–28	–2	35	2	–15	–10	–143	. . .
General government: short-term	4 771 . .	–65	. . .	. . .	1	. . .	658	209	. . .
Banks: long-term	4 773 . .	358	61	–2	–74	–59	–140	–135	. . .
Banks: short-term	4 774 . .	. . .	. . .	. . .	. . .	. . .	. . .	. . .	. . .
Other sectors: long-term	4 776 . .	952	763	650	2,863	1,712	241	–1,013	. . .
Other sectors: short-term	4 777 . .	727	–640	1,237	–278	843	–69	480	. . .
Currency and deposits	4 780 . .	–1,463	–912	–762	–4,126	–3,936	–72	–872	. . .
Monetary authorities	4 781 . .	. . .	. . .	. . .	. . .	. . .	. . .	. . .	. . .
General government	4 782 . .	. . .	. . .	. . .	. . .	. . .	. . .	. . .	. . .
Banks	4 783 . .	–1,463	–912	–762	–4,126	–3,936	–72	–872	. . .
Other sectors	4 784 . .	. . .	. . .	. . .	. . .	. . .	. . .	. . .	. . .
Other liabilities	4 786 . .	195	–14	–398	–469	482	–519	–553	. . .
Monetary authorities: long-term	4 788 . .	. . .	. . .	. . .	. . .	. . .	. . .	. . .	. . .
Monetary authorities: short-term	4 789 . .	124	–58	3	56	1,233	–458	–69	. . .
General government: long-term	4 791 . .	. . .	. . .	. . .	. . .	. . .	. . .	5	. . .
General government: short-term	4 792 . .	. . .	. . .	. . .	. . .	. . .	. . .	. . .	. . .
Banks: long-term	4 794 . .	3	33	24	27	10	208	126	. . .
Banks: short-term	4 795 . .	. . .	. . .	. . .	. . .	. . .	. . .	. . .	. . .
Other sectors: long-term	4 797 . .	105	57	–330	–461	–737	–222	–40	. . .
Other sectors: short-term	4 798 . .	–37	–46	–95	–91	–24	–47	–576	. . .
D. RESERVE ASSETS	4 800 . .	138	–965	–414	2,751	855	–4,138	–1,451	. . .
Monetary gold	4 810 . .	. . .	. . .	. . .	. . .	. . .	. . .	. . .	. . .
Special drawing rights	4 820 . .	–71	24	39	. . .	247	–208	29	. . .
Reserve position in the Fund	4 830 . .	64	12	44	10	–100	63	–22	. . .
Foreign exchange	4 840 . .	145	–1,001	–498	2,740	708	–3,993	–1,458	. . .
Other claims	4 880 . .	. . .	. . .	. . .	. . .	. . .	. . .	. . .	. . .
NET ERRORS AND OMISSIONS	4 998 . .	**–1,149**	**–1,305**	**–2,848**	**–219**	**–3,442**	**–1,309**	**–854**	**. . .**

Part 3 of the *Yearbook* contains descriptions of the methodologies, compilation practices, and sources used to compile these data.

Table 3. INTERNATIONAL INVESTMENT POSITION (End–period stocks), 1988–95

(Millions of U.S. dollars)

	Code	1988	1989	1990	1991	1992	1993	1994	1995
ASSETS	8 995 C.	38,309	40,826	49,691	50,170	48,393	46,433	...	...
Direct investment abroad	8 505 . .	**2,757**	**3,506**	**4,403**	**5,170**	**4,234**	**5,080**	...	...
Equity capital and reinvested earnings	8 506 . .	2,757	3,506	4,403	5,170	4,234	5,080	...	...
Claims on affiliated enterprises	8 507 . .	...	...	...	...	...	...	...	...
Liabilities to affiliated enterprises	8 508 . .	...	...	...	...	...	...	...	...
Other capital	8 530 . .	...	...	...	...	...	...	...	...
Claims on affiliated enterprises	8 535 . .	...	...	...	...	...	...	...	...
Liabilities to affiliated enterprises	8 540 . .	...	...	...	...	...	...	...	...
Portfolio investment	8 602 . .	**1,626**	**1,565**	**2,320**	**3,403**	**5,607**	**5,762**	...	...
Equity securities	8 610 . .	...	...	...	...	...	...	...	...
Monetary authorities	8 611 . .	...	...	...	...	...	...	...	...
General government	8 612 . .	...	...	...	...	...	...	...	...
Banks	8 613 . .	...	...	...	...	...	...	...	...
Other sectors	8 614 . .	...	...	...	...	...	...	...	...
Debt securities	8 619 . .	1,626	1,565	2,320	3,403	5,607	5,762	...	...
Bonds and notes	8 620 . .	1,626	1,565	2,320	3,403	5,607	5,762	...	...
Monetary authorities	8 621 . .	...	...	...	...	...	...	...	...
General government	8 622 . .	...	...	...	...	...	...	...	...
Banks	8 623 . .	...	...	...	...	...	...	...	...
Other sectors	8 624 . .	...	...	...	...	...	...	...	...
Money market instruments	8 630 . .	...	...	...	...	...	...	...	...
Monetary authorities	8 631 . .	...	...	...	...	...	...	...	...
General government	8 632 . .	...	...	...	...	...	...	...	...
Banks	8 633 . .	...	...	...	...	...	...	...	...
Other sectors	8 634 . .	...	...	...	...	...	...	...	...
Financial derivatives	8 640 . .	...	...	...	...	...	...	...	...
Monetary authorities	8 641 . .	...	...	...	...	...	...	...	...
General government	8 642 . .	...	...	...	...	...	...	...	...
Banks	8 643 . .	...	...	...	...	...	...	...	...
Other sectors	8 644 . .	...	...	...	...	...	...	...	...
Other investment	8 703 . .	**20,733**	**21,785**	**27,426**	**28,420**	**26,673**	**19,910**	...	...
Trade credits	8 706 . .	...	...	...	...	...	...	...	...
General government: long-term	8 708 . .	...	...	...	...	...	...	...	...
General government: short-term	8 709 . .	...	...	...	...	...	...	...	...
Other sectors: long-term	8 711 . .	...	...	...	...	...	...	...	...
Other sectors: short-term	8 712 . .	...	...	...	...	...	...	...	...
Loans	8 714 . .	10,128	10,233	12,405	12,428	11,231	8,769	...	...
Monetary authorities: long-term	8 717 . .	...	...	...	...	...	...	...	...
Monetary authorities: short-term	8 718 . .	...	...	...	...	...	...	...	...
General government: long-term	8 720 . .	39	34	34	31	33	103	...	...
General government: short-term	8 721 . .	...	...	...	...	...	...	...	...
Banks: long-term	8 723 . .	2,803	3,086	4,523	4,284	3,886	3,261	...	...
Banks: short-term	8 724 . .	...	...	...	...	...	...	...	...
Other sectors: long-term	8 726 . .	7,287	7,112	7,849	8,112	7,312	5,405	...	...
Other sectors: short-term	8 727 . .	...	...	...	...	...	...	...	...
Currency and deposits	8 730 . .	2,452	1,921	2,598	4,129	5,313	2,473	...	...
Monetary authorities	8 731 . .	...	...	...	...	...	...	...	...
General government	8 732 . .	31	32	315	153	24	81	...	...
Banks	8 733 . .	2,421	1,888	2,284	3,976	5,290	2,392	...	...
Other sectors	8 734 . .	...	...	...	...	...	...	...	...
Other assets	8 736 . .	8,152	9,631	12,423	11,863	10,128	8,668	...	...
Monetary authorities: long-term	8 738 . .	...	...	...	...	...	...	...	...
Monetary authorities: short-term	8 739 . .	...	...	...	...	...	...	...	...
General government: long-term	8 741 . .	1,526	1,533	1,564	1,357	1,640	1,684	...	...
General government: short-term	8 742 . .	...	...	...	...	...	...	...	...
Banks: long-term	8 744 . .	76	519	51	98	149	161	...	...
Banks: short-term	8 745 . .	...	...	...	...	...	...	...	...
Other sectors: long-term	8 747 . .	5,231	6,128	8,969	8,735	6,672	5,592	...	...
Other sectors: short-term	8 748 . .	1,319	1,451	1,839	1,673	1,668	1,232	...	...
Reserve assets	8 800 . .	**13,193**	**13,971**	**15,541**	**13,177**	**11,880**	**15,680**	...	...
Monetary gold	8 810 . .	43	43	48	48	41	38	...	...
Special drawing rights	8 820 . .	487	454	449	452	191	396	389	463
Reserve position in the Fund	8 830 . .	607	581	580	571	648	584	644	946
Foreign exchange	8 840 . .	12,054	12,894	14,464	12,106	11,000	14,662	...	...
Other claims	8 880 . .	...	...	...	...	...	...	...	...

Table 3 (Continued). INTERNATIONAL INVESTMENT POSITION (End–period stocks), 1988–95
(Millions of U.S. dollars)

	Code		1988	1989	1990	1991	1992	1993	1994	1995
LIABILITIES	8 995	D.	57,367	61,414	67,329	63,639	58,399	57,536	...	...
Direct investment in Norway	8 555	..	**2,450**	**3,157**	**4,066**	**4,570**	**3,969**	**3,880**	...	...
Equity capital and reinvested earnings	8 556	..	2,450	3,157	4,066	4,570	3,969	3,880	...	...
Claims on direct investors	8 557	..	...	...	...	...	...	...	...	...
Liabilities to direct investors	8 558	..	...	...	...	...	...	...	...	...
Other capital	8 580	..	...	...	...	...	...	...	...	...
Claims on direct investors	8 585	..	...	...	...	...	...	...	...	...
Liabilities to direct investors	8 590	..	...	...	...	...	...	...	...	...
Portfolio investment	8 652	..	**21,620**	**24,031**	**26,722**	**26,176**	**24,400**	**22,449**	...	...
Equity securities	8 660	..	...	...	...	...	...	...	...	...
Banks	8 663	..	...	...	...	...	...	...	...	...
Other sectors	8 664	..	...	...	...	...	...	...	...	...
Debt securities	8 669	..	21,620	24,031	26,722	26,176	24,400	22,449	...	...
Bonds and notes	8 670	..	21,620	24,031	26,722	26,176	24,400	22,449	...	...
Monetary authorities	8 671	..	...	...	...	...	...	...	...	...
General government	8 672	..	...	...	...	...	...	...	...	...
Banks	8 673	..	...	...	...	...	...	...	...	...
Other sectors	8 674	..	...	...	...	...	...	...	...	...
Money market instruments	8 680	..	...	...	...	...	...	...	...	...
Monetary authorities	8 681	..	...	...	...	...	...	...	...	...
General government	8 682	..	...	...	...	...	...	...	...	...
Banks	8 683	..	...	...	...	...	...	...	...	...
Other sectors	8 684	..	...	...	...	...	...	...	...	...
Financial derivatives	8 690	..	...	...	...	...	...	...	...	...
Monetary authorities	8 691	..	...	...	...	...	...	...	...	...
General government	8 692	..	...	...	...	...	...	...	...	...
Banks	8 692	..	...	...	...	...	...	...	...	...
Other sectors	8 694	..	...	...	...	...	...	...	...	...
Other investment	8 753	..	**33,297**	**34,226**	**36,541**	**32,893**	**30,030**	**31,207**	...	...
Trade credits	8 756	..	...	...	...	...	...	...	...	...
General government: long-term	8 758	..	...	...	...	...	...	...	...	...
General government: short-term	8 759	..	...	...	...	...	...	...	...	...
Other sectors: long-term	8 761	..	...	...	...	...	...	...	...	...
Other sectors: short-term	8 762	..	...	...	...	...	...	...	...	...
Loans	8 764	..	16,357	16,117	17,702	17,519	18,223	19,706	...	...
Use of Fund credit and loans from the Fund	8 766	..	...	...	...	...	...	...	...	...
Monetary authorities: other long-term	8 767	..	...	...	...	...	...	...	...	...
Monetary authorities: short-term	8 768	..	...	...	...	...	...	...	...	...
General government: long-term	8 770	..	102	89	175	187	353	335	...	...
General government: short-term	8 771	..	...	...	...	...	...	...	...	...
Banks: long-term	8 773	..	1,359	1,081	786	605	491	547	...	...
Banks: short-term	8 774	..	...	...	...	...	...	...	...	...
Other sectors: long-term	8 776	..	14,896	14,946	16,741	16,728	17,379	18,824	...	...
Other sectors: short-term	8 777	..	...	...	...	...	...	...	...	...
Currency and deposits	8 780	..	11,643	11,521	12,553	8,869	5,349	5,576	...	...
Monetary authorities	8 781	..	...	...	...	...	...	...	...	...
General government	8 782	..	...	...	...	...	...	...	...	...
Banks	8 783	..	11,643	11,521	12,553	8,869	5,349	5,576	...	...
Other sectors	8 784	..	...	...	...	...	...	...	...	...
Other liabilities	8 786	..	5,297	6,588	6,286	6,505	6,458	5,925	...	...
Monetary authorities: long-term	8 788	..	...	...	...	...	...	...	...	...
Monetary authorities: short-term	8 789	..	125	61	29	72	705	101	...	...
General government: long-term	8 791	..	588	614	820	860	1,339	1,904	...	...
General government: short-term	8 792	..	...	...	...	...	...	...	...	...
Banks: long-term	8 794	..	79	270	170	108	61	57	...	...
Banks: short-term	8 795	..	...	...	...	...	...	...	...	...
Other sectors: long-term	8 797	..	4,504	5,644	5,266	5,465	4,353	3,864	...	...
Other sectors: short-term	8 798	..	...	...	...	...	...	...	...	...
NET INTERNATIONAL INVESTMENT POSITION	8 995	..	**–19,058**	**–20,588**	**–17,639**	**–13,469**	**–10,006**	**–11,103**	...	...
Conversion rates: Norwegian kroner per U.S. dollar (end of period)	0 102	..	**6.5700**	**6.6150**	**5.9075**	**5.9730**	**6.9245**	**7.5180**	**6.7620**	**6.3190**

Oman
449

Table 1. ANALYTIC PRESENTATION, 1988–95
(Millions of U.S. dollars)

	Code	1988	1989	1990	1991	1992	1993	1994	1995
A. Current Account [1]	4 993 Y.	**–309**	**305**	**1,106**	**–245**	**–592**	**–1,191**	**–984**	**–979**
Goods: exports f.o.b	2 100 ..	3,342	4,068	5,508	4,871	5,555	5,365	5,542	6,065
Goods: imports f.o.b	3 100 ..	–2,107	–2,225	–2,623	–3,112	–3,627	–4,030	–3,693	–4,050
Balance on Goods	4 100 ..	*1,235*	*1,842*	*2,885*	*1,759*	*1,928*	*1,336*	*1,849*	*2,015*
Services: credit	2 200 ..	13	59	68	61	13	13	13	13
Services: debit	3 200 ..	–523	–570	–719	–961	–932	–906	–895	–964
Balance on Goods and Services	4 991 ..	*726*	*1,331*	*2,235*	*860*	*1,009*	*442*	*967*	*1,064*
Income: credit	2 300 ..	257	338	375	359	328	421	257	325
Income: debit	3 300 ..	–572	–588	–629	–590	–733	–689	–695	–657
Balance on Goods, Services, and Income	4 992 ..	*411*	*1,080*	*1,980*	*629*	*604*	*174*	*530*	*732*
Current transfers: credit	2 379 Y.	81	55	39	39	39	57	65	68
Current transfers: debit	3 379 ..	–801	–830	–913	–913	–1,235	–1,423	–1,579	–1,779
B. Capital Account [1]	4 994 Y.	**...**	**...**	**...**	**...**	**...**	**...**	**...**	**...**
Capital account: credit	2 994 Y.	...	...	...	...	...	...	...	...
Capital account: debit	3 994 ..	...	...	...	...	...	...	...	...
Total, Groups A Plus B	4 010 ..	*–309*	*305*	*1,106*	*–245*	*–592*	*–1,191*	*–984*	*–979*
C. Financial Account [1]	4 995 X.	**221**	**–15**	**–498**	**506**	**493**	**–74**	**213**	**–9**
Direct investment abroad	4 505 ..	...	...	...	...	...	...	...	...
Direct investment in Oman	4 555 Y.	92	112	142	132	101	147	62	35
Portfolio investment assets	4 602 ..	...	...	...	...	...	...	...	...
Equity securities	4 610 ..	...	...	...	...	...	...	...	...
Debt securities	4 619 ..	...	...	...	...	...	...	...	...
Portfolio investment liabilities	4 652 Y.	...	...	...	...	...	...	...	...
Equity securities	4 660 Y.	...	...	...	...	...	...	...	...
Debt securities	4 669 Y.	...	...	...	...	...	...	...	...
Other investment assets	4 703 ..	–88	–179	–270	146	120	–187	–174	–52
Monetary authorities	4 703 .A	...	...	...	...	...	...	...	...
General government	4 703 .B	–5	–39	–10	...	...	–31	–104	–88
Banks	4 703 .C	–117	–75	–49	–55	169	–187	–10	62
Other sectors	4 703 .D	34	–65	–211	200	–49	31	–60	–26
Other investment liabilities	4 753 X.	217	52	–369	229	273	–34	325	8
Monetary authorities	4 753 XA	...	...	...	...	...	...	...	...
General government	4 753 YB	186	52	–372	226	260	–91	325	5
Banks	4 753 YC	31	...	3	3	13	57	...	3
Other sectors	4 753 YD	...	...	...	...	...	...	...	...
Total, Groups A Through C	4 020 ..	*–88*	*290*	*609*	*261*	*–99*	*–1,265*	*–771*	*–989*
D. Net Errors and Omissions	4 998 ..	**–379**	**33**	**–474**	**282**	**399**	**207**	**110**	**557**
Total, Groups A Through D	4 030 ..	*–467*	*324*	*135*	*543*	*300*	*–1,058*	*–661*	*–432*
E. Reserves and Related Items	4 040 ..	**467**	**–324**	**–135**	**–543**	**–300**	**1,058**	**661**	**432**
Reserve assets	4 800 ..	467	–324	–135	–543	–300	1,058	661	432
Use of Fund credit and loans	4 766 ..	...	...	...	...	...	...	...	...
Liabilities constituting foreign authorities' reserves	4 900 ..	...	...	...	...	...	...	...	...
Exceptional financing	4 920 ..	...	...	...	...	...	...	...	...
Conversion rates: rial Omani per U.S. dollar	0 101 ..	**.38450**	**.38450**	**.38450**	**.38450**	**.38450**	**.38450**	**.38450**	**.38450**

[1] Excludes components that have been classified in the categories of Group E.

Table 2. STANDARD PRESENTATION, 1988–95
(Millions of U.S. dollars)

	Code	1988	1989	1990	1991	1992	1993	1994	1995
CURRENT ACCOUNT	4 993 . .	**–309**	**305**	**1,106**	**–245**	**–592**	**–1,191**	**–984**	**–979**
A. GOODS	4 100 . .	1,235	1,842	2,885	1,759	1,928	1,336	1,849	2,015
Credit	2 100 . .	**3,342**	**4,068**	**5,508**	**4,871**	**5,555**	**5,365**	**5,542**	**6,065**
General merchandise: exports f.o.b.	2 110 . .	3,342	4,068	5,508	4,871	5,555	5,365	5,542	6,065
Goods for processing: exports f.o.b.	2 150 . .	...	...	...	...	...	...	...	...
Repairs on goods	2 160 . .	...	...	...	...	...	...	...	...
Goods procured in ports by carriers	2 170 . .	...	...	...	...	...	...	...	...
Nonmonetary gold	2 180 . .	...	...	...	...	...	...	...	...
Debit	3 100 . .	**–2,107**	**–2,225**	**–2,623**	**–3,112**	**–3,627**	**–4,030**	**–3,693**	**–4,050**
General merchandise: imports f.o.b.	3 110 . .	–2,107	–2,225	–2,623	–3,112	–3,627	–4,030	–3,693	–4,050
Goods for processing: imports f.o.b.	3 150 . .	...	...	...	...	...	...	...	...
Repairs on goods	3 160 . .	...	...	...	...	...	...	...	...
Goods procured in ports by carriers	3 170 . .	...	...	...	...	...	...	...	...
Nonmonetary gold	3 180 . .	...	...	...	...	...	...	...	...
B. SERVICES	4 200 . .	–510	–512	–650	–900	–919	–893	–882	–951
Total credit	2 200 . .	*13*	*59*	*68*	*61*	*13*	*13*	*13*	*13*
Total debit	3 200 . .	*–523*	*–570*	*–719*	*–961*	*–932*	*–906*	*–895*	*–964*
Transportation services, credit	2 205 . .	**13**	**10**	**10**	**13**	**13**	**13**	**13**	**13**
Passenger	2 205 BA	...	...	...	...	...	...	...	...
Freight	2 205 BB	...	...	...	...	...	...	...	...
Other	2 205 BC	*13*	*10*	*10*	*13*	*13*	*13*	*13*	*13*
Sea transport, passenger	2 207 . .	...	...	...	...	...	...	...	...
Sea transport, freight	2 208 . .	...	...	...	...	...	...	...	...
Sea transport, other	2 209 . .	...	...	...	...	...	...	...	...
Air transport, passenger	2 211 . .	...	...	...	...	...	...	...	...
Air transport, freight	2 212 . .	...	...	...	...	...	...	...	...
Air transport, other	2 213 . .	...	...	...	...	...	...	...	...
Other transport, passenger	2 215 . .	...	...	...	...	...	...	...	...
Other transport, freight	2 216 . .	...	...	...	...	...	...	...	...
Other transport, other	2 217 . .	...	...	...	...	...	...	...	...
Transportation services, debit	3 205 . .	**–211**	**–223**	**–263**	**–312**	**–366**	**–404**	**–377**	**–411**
Passenger	3 205 BA	...	...	...	...	...	...	...	...
Freight	3 205 BB	*–211*	*–223*	*–263*	*–312*	*–366*	*–404*	*–377*	*–411*
Other	3 205 BC	...	...	...	...	...	...	...	...
Sea transport, passenger	3 207 . .	...	...	...	...	...	...	...	...
Sea transport, freight	3 208 . .	...	...	...	...	...	...	...	...
Sea transport, other	3 209 . .	...	...	...	...	...	...	...	...
Air transport, passenger	3 211 . .	...	...	...	...	...	...	...	...
Air transport, freight	3 212 . .	...	...	...	...	...	...	...	...
Air transport, other	3 213 . .	...	...	...	...	...	...	...	...
Other transport, passenger	3 215 . .	...	...	...	...	...	...	...	...
Other transport, freight	3 216 . .	...	...	...	...	...	...	...	...
Other transport, other	3 217 . .	...	...	...	...	...	...	...	...
Travel, credit	2 236 . .	**...**	**48**	**58**	**48**	**...**	**...**	**...**	**...**
Business travel	2 237 . .	...	...	...	...	...	...	...	...
Personal travel	2 240 . .	...	...	...	...	...	...	...	...
Travel, debit	3 236 . .	**–47**	**–47**	**–47**	**–47**	**–47**	**–47**	**–47**	**–47**
Business travel	3 237 . .	...	...	...	...	...	...	...	...
Personal travel	3 240 . .	...	...	...	...	...	...	...	...
Other services, credit	2 200 BA	**...**	**...**	**...**	**...**	**...**	**...**	**...**	**...**
Communications	2 245 . .	...	...	...	...	...	...	...	...
Construction	2 249 . .	...	...	...	...	...	...	...	...
Insurance	2 253 . .	...	...	...	...	...	...	...	...
Financial	2 260 . .	...	...	...	...	...	...	...	...
Computer and information	2 262 . .	...	...	...	...	...	...	...	...
Royalties and licence fees	2 266 . .	...	...	...	...	...	...	...	...
Other business services	2 268 . .	...	...	...	...	...	...	...	...
Personal, cultural, and recreational	2 287 . .	...	...	...	...	...	...	...	...
Government, n.i.e.	2 291 . .	...	...	...	...	...	...	...	...
Other services, debit	3 200 BA	**–265**	**–300**	**–409**	**–602**	**–519**	**–456**	**–471**	**–506**
Communications	3 245 . .	...	...	...	...	...	...	...	...
Construction	3 249 . .	...	...	...	...	...	...	...	...
Insurance	3 253 . .	–23	–25	–29	–35	–41	–45	–42	–46
Financial	3 260 . .	...	...	...	...	...	...	...	...
Computer and information	3 262 . .	...	...	...	...	...	...	...	...
Royalties and licence fees	3 266 . .	...	...	...	...	...	...	...	...
Other business services	3 268 . .	–242	–276	–380	–567	–479	–411	–429	–460
Personal, cultural, and recreational	3 287 . .	...	...	...	...	...	...	...	...
Government, n.i.e.	3 291 . .	...	...	...	...	...	...	...	...

Table 2 (Continued). STANDARD PRESENTATION, 1988–95
(Millions of U.S. dollars)

	Code	1988	1989	1990	1991	1992	1993	1994	1995
C. INCOME	4 300	–315	–250	–254	–231	–405	–268	–437	–332
Total credit	2 300	*257*	*338*	*375*	*359*	*328*	*421*	*257*	*325*
Total debit	3 300	*–572*	*–588*	*–629*	*–590*	*–733*	*–689*	*–695*	*–657*
Compensation of employees, credit	2 310	...	...	...	...	...	...	...	...
Compensation of employees, debit	3 310	...	...	...	...	...	...	...	...
Investment income, credit	2 320	**257**	**338**	**375**	**359**	**328**	**421**	**257**	**325**
Direct investment income	2 330	...	...	...	...	...	...	...	...
Dividends and distributed branch profits	2 332	...	...	...	...	...	...	...	...
Reinvested earnings and undistributed branch profits	2 333	...	...	...	...	...	...	...	...
Income on debt (interest)	2 334	...	...	...	...	...	...	...	...
Portfolio investment income	2 339	...	...	...	...	...	...	...	...
Income on equity	2 340	...	...	...	...	...	...	...	...
Income on bonds and notes	2 350	...	...	...	...	...	...	...	...
Income on money market instruments and financial derivatives	2 360	...	...	...	...	...	...	...	...
Other investment income	2 370	257	338	375	359	328	421	257	325
Investment income, debit	3 320	**–572**	**–588**	**–629**	**–590**	**–733**	**–689**	**–695**	**–657**
Direct investment income	3 330	–354	–341	–390	–408	–535	–515	–495	–464
Dividends and distributed branch profits	3 332	–353	–341	–388	–404	–531	–508	–493	–458
Reinvested earnings and undistributed branch profits	3 333	–1	–1	–2	–4	–4	–7	–2	–6
Income on debt (interest)	3 334	...	...	...	...	...	...	...	...
Portfolio investment income	3 339	...	...	...	...	...	...	...	...
Income on equity	3 340	...	...	...	...	...	...	...	...
Income on bonds and notes	3 350	...	...	...	...	...	...	...	...
Income on money market instruments and financial derivatives	3 360	...	...	...	...	...	...	...	...
Other investment income	3 370	–218	–247	–239	–182	–198	–174	–200	–192
D. CURRENT TRANSFERS	4 379	–720	–775	–874	–874	–1,196	–1,365	–1,514	–1,711
Credit	2 379	**81**	**55**	**39**	**39**	**39**	**57**	**65**	**68**
General government	2 380	42	16	...	...	...	18	26	29
Other sectors	2 390	39	39	39	39	39	39	39	39
Workers' remittances	2 391	39	39	39	39	39	39	39	39
Other current transfers	2 392	...	...	...	...	...	...	...	...
Debit	3 379	**–801**	**–830**	**–913**	**–913**	**–1,235**	**–1,423**	**–1,579**	**–1,779**
General government	3 380	...	...	–57	–3	–16	...	...	...
Other sectors	3 390	–801	–830	–856	–910	–1,220	–1,423	–1,579	–1,779
Workers' remittances	3 391	–801	–830	–856	–910	–1,220	–1,423	–1,579	–1,779
Other current transfers	3 392	...	...	...	...	...	...	...	...
CAPITAL AND FINANCIAL ACCOUNT	4 996	**688**	**–339**	**–633**	**–37**	**193**	**984**	**874**	**422**
CAPITAL ACCOUNT	4 994	...	...	...	...	...	...	...	...
Total credit	2 994	...	...	...	...	...	...	...	...
Total debit	3 994	...	...	...	...	...	...	...	...
Capital transfers, credit	2 400	...	...	...	...	...	...	...	...
General government	2 401	...	...	...	...	...	...	...	...
Debt forgiveness	2 402	...	...	...	...	...	...	...	...
Other capital transfers	2 410	...	...	...	...	...	...	...	...
Other sectors	2 430	...	...	...	...	...	...	...	...
Migrants' transfers	2 431	...	...	...	...	...	...	...	...
Debt forgiveness	2 432	...	...	...	...	...	...	...	...
Other capital transfers	2 440	...	...	...	...	...	...	...	...
Capital transfers, debit	3 400	...	...	...	...	...	...	...	...
General government	3 401	...	...	...	...	...	...	...	...
Debt forgiveness	3 402	...	...	...	...	...	...	...	...
Other capital transfers	3 410	...	...	...	...	...	...	...	...
Other sectors	3 430	...	...	...	...	...	...	...	...
Migrants' transfers	3 431	...	...	...	...	...	...	...	...
Debt forgiveness	3 432	...	...	...	...	...	...	...	...
Other capital transfers	3 440	...	...	...	...	...	...	...	...
Nonproduced nonfinancial assets, credit	2 480	...	...	...	...	...	...	...	...
Nonproduced nonfinancial assets, debit	3 480	...	...	...	...	...	...	...	...

Table 2 (Continued). STANDARD PRESENTATION, 1988–95
(Millions of U.S. dollars)

	Code		1988	1989	1990	1991	1992	1993	1994	1995
FINANCIAL ACCOUNT	4 995	. .	**688**	**–339**	**–633**	**–37**	**193**	**984**	**874**	**422**
A. DIRECT INVESTMENT	4 500	. .	92	112	142	132	101	147	62	35
Direct investment abroad	4 505	. .	...	...	...	...	...	...	...	...
Equity capital	4 510	. .	...	...	...	...	...	...	...	...
Claims on affiliated enterprises	4 515	. .	...	...	...	...	...	...	...	...
Liabilities to affiliated enterprises	4 520	. .	...	...	...	...	...	...	...	...
Reinvested earnings	4 525	. .	...	...	...	...	...	...	...	...
Other capital	4 530	. .	...	...	...	...	...	...	...	...
Claims on affiliated enterprises	4 535	. .	...	...	...	...	...	...	...	...
Liabilities to affiliated enterprises	4 540	. .	...	...	...	...	...	...	...	...
Direct investment in Oman	4 555	. .	**92**	**112**	**142**	**132**	**101**	**147**	**62**	**35**
Equity capital	4 560	. .	91	112	140	127	96	140	60	29
Claims on direct investors	4 565	. .	...	...	...	...	...	...	...	...
Liabilities to direct investors	4 570	. .	...	...	...	...	...	...	...	...
Reinvested earnings	4 575	. .	1	1	2	4	4	7	2	6
Other capital	4 580	. .	...	...	...	...	...	...	...	...
Claims on direct investors	4 585	. .	...	...	...	...	...	...	...	...
Liabilities to direct investors	4 590	. .	...	...	...	...	...	...	...	...
B. PORTFOLIO INVESTMENT	4 600	. .	...	...	...	...	...	...	...	...
Assets	4 602	. .	...	...	...	...	...	...	...	...
Equity securities	4 610	. .	...	...	...	...	...	...	...	...
Monetary authorities	4 611	. .	...	...	...	...	...	...	...	...
General government	4 612	. .	...	...	...	...	...	...	...	...
Banks	4 613	. .	...	...	...	...	...	...	...	...
Other sectors	4 614	. .	...	...	...	...	...	...	...	...
Debt securities	4 619	. .	...	...	...	...	...	...	...	...
Bonds and notes	4 620	. .	...	...	...	...	...	...	...	...
Monetary authorities	4 621	. .	...	...	...	...	...	...	...	...
General government	4 622	. .	...	...	...	...	...	...	...	...
Banks	4 623	. .	...	...	...	...	...	...	...	...
Other sectors	4 624	. .	...	...	...	...	...	...	...	...
Money market instruments	4 630	. .	...	...	...	...	...	...	...	...
Monetary authorities	4 631	. .	...	...	...	...	...	...	...	...
General government	4 632	. .	...	...	...	...	...	...	...	...
Banks	4 633	. .	...	...	...	...	...	...	...	...
Other sectors	4 634	. .	...	...	...	...	...	...	...	...
Financial derivatives	4 640	. .	...	...	...	...	...	...	...	...
Monetary authorities	4 641	. .	...	...	...	...	...	...	...	...
General government	4 642	. .	...	...	...	...	...	...	...	...
Banks	4 643	. .	...	...	...	...	...	...	...	...
Other sectors	4 644	. .	...	...	...	...	...	...	...	...
Liabilities	4 652	. .	...	...	...	...	...	...	...	...
Equity securities	4 660	. .	...	...	...	...	...	...	...	...
Banks	4 663	. .	...	...	...	...	...	...	...	...
Other sectors	4 664	. .	...	...	...	...	...	...	...	...
Debt securities	4 669	. .	...	...	...	...	...	...	...	...
Bonds and notes	4 670	. .	...	...	...	...	...	...	...	...
Monetary authorities	4 671	. .	...	...	...	...	...	...	...	...
General government	4 672	. .	...	...	...	...	...	...	...	...
Banks	4 673	. .	...	...	...	...	...	...	...	...
Other sectors	4 674	. .	...	...	...	...	...	...	...	...
Money market instruments	4 680	. .	...	...	...	...	...	...	...	...
Monetary authorities	4 681	. .	...	...	...	...	...	...	...	...
General government	4 682	. .	...	...	...	...	...	...	...	...
Banks	4 683	. .	...	...	...	...	...	...	...	...
Other sectors	4 684	. .	...	...	...	...	...	...	...	...
Financial derivatives	4 690	. .	...	...	...	...	...	...	...	...
Monetary authorities	4 691	. .	...	...	...	...	...	...	...	...
General government	4 692	. .	...	...	...	...	...	...	...	...
Banks	4 693	. .	...	...	...	...	...	...	...	...
Other sectors	4 694	. .	...	...	...	...	...	...	...	...

Table 2 (Concluded). STANDARD PRESENTATION, 1988–95
(Millions of U.S. dollars)

	Code	1988	1989	1990	1991	1992	1993	1994	1995
C. OTHER INVESTMENT	4 700 . .	130	–127	–640	375	393	–221	151	–44
Assets	4 703 . .	**–88**	**–179**	**–270**	**146**	**120**	**–187**	**–174**	**–52**
Trade credits	4 706 . .	. . .	. . .	. . .	. . .	. . .	. . .	. . .	. . .
General government: long-term	4 708 . .	. . .	. . .	. . .	. . .	. . .	. . .	. . .	. . .
General government: short-term	4 709 . .	. . .	. . .	. . .	. . .	. . .	. . .	. . .	. . .
Other sectors: long-term	4 711 . .	. . .	. . .	. . .	. . .	. . .	. . .	. . .	. . .
Other sectors: short-term	4 712 . .	. . .	. . .	. . .	. . .	. . .	. . .	. . .	. . .
Loans	4 714 . .	34	–65	–211	200	–49	31	–60	–26
Monetary authorities: long-term	4 717 . .	. . .	. . .	. . .	. . .	. . .	. . .	. . .	. . .
Monetary authorities: short-term	4 718 . .	. . .	. . .	. . .	. . .	. . .	. . .	. . .	. . .
General government: long-term	4 720 . .	. . .	. . .	. . .	. . .	. . .	. . .	. . .	. . .
General government: short-term	4 721 . .	. . .	. . .	. . .	. . .	. . .	. . .	. . .	. . .
Banks: long-term	4 723 . .	. . .	. . .	. . .	. . .	. . .	. . .	. . .	. . .
Banks: short-term	4 724 . .	. . .	. . .	. . .	. . .	. . .	. . .	. . .	. . .
Other sectors: long-term	4 726 . .	. . .	. . .	. . .	. . .	. . .	. . .	. . .	. . .
Other sectors: short-term	4 727 . .	34	–65	–211	200	–49	31	–60	–26
Currency and deposits	4 730 . .	–117	–75	–49	–55	169	–187	–10	62
Monetary authorities	4 731 . .	. . .	. . .	. . .	. . .	. . .	. . .	. . .	. . .
General government	4 732 . .	. . .	. . .	. . .	. . .	. . .	. . .	. . .	. . .
Banks	4 733 . .	–117	–75	–49	–55	169	–187	–10	62
Other sectors	4 734 . .	. . .	. . .	. . .	. . .	. . .	. . .	. . .	. . .
Other assets	4 736 . .	–5	–39	–10	. . .	. . .	–31	–104	–88
Monetary authorities: long-term	4 738 . .	. . .	. . .	. . .	. . .	. . .	. . .	. . .	. . .
Monetary authorities: short-term	4 739 . .	. . .	. . .	. . .	. . .	. . .	. . .	. . .	. . .
General government: long-term	4 741 . .	–5	–39	–10	. . .	. . .	–31	–104	–88
General government: short-term	4 742 . .	. . .	. . .	. . .	. . .	. . .	. . .	. . .	. . .
Banks: long-term	4 744 . .	. . .	. . .	. . .	. . .	. . .	. . .	. . .	. . .
Banks: short-term	4 745 . .	. . .	. . .	. . .	. . .	. . .	. . .	. . .	. . .
Other sectors: long-term	4 747 . .	. . .	. . .	. . .	. . .	. . .	. . .	. . .	. . .
Other sectors: short-term	4 748 . .	. . .	. . .	. . .	. . .	. . .	. . .	. . .	. . .
Liabilities	4 753 . .	**217**	**52**	**–369**	**229**	**273**	**–34**	**325**	**8**
Trade credits	4 756 . .	. . .	. . .	. . .	. . .	. . .	. . .	. . .	. . .
General government: long-term	4 758 . .	. . .	. . .	. . .	. . .	. . .	. . .	. . .	. . .
General government: short-term	4 759 . .	. . .	. . .	. . .	. . .	. . .	. . .	. . .	. . .
Other sectors: long-term	4 761 . .	. . .	. . .	. . .	. . .	. . .	. . .	. . .	. . .
Other sectors: short-term	4 762 . .	. . .	. . .	. . .	. . .	. . .	. . .	. . .	. . .
Loans	4 764 . .	187	91	–382	221	104	–211	421	–133
Use of Fund credit and loans from the Fund	4 766 . .	. . .	. . .	. . .	. . .	. . .	. . .	. . .	. . .
Monetary authorities: other long-term	4 767 . .	. . .	. . .	. . .	. . .	. . .	. . .	. . .	. . .
Monetary authorities: short-term	4 768 . .	. . .	. . .	. . .	. . .	. . .	. . .	. . .	. . .
General government: long-term	4 770 . .	187	91	–382	221	–60	–68	286	21
General government: short-term	4 771 . .	. . .	. . .	. . .	. . .	164	–143	135	–153
Banks: long-term	4 773 . .	. . .	. . .	. . .	. . .	. . .	. . .	. . .	. . .
Banks: short-term	4 774 . .	. . .	. . .	. . .	. . .	. . .	. . .	. . .	. . .
Other sectors: long-term	4 776 . .	. . .	. . .	. . .	. . .	. . .	. . .	. . .	. . .
Other sectors: short-term	4 777 . .	. . .	. . .	. . .	. . .	. . .	. . .	. . .	. . .
Currency and deposits	4 780 . .	31	. . .	3	3	13	57	. . .	3
Monetary authorities	4 781 . .	. . .	. . .	. . .	. . .	. . .	. . .	. . .	. . .
General government	4 782 . .	. . .	. . .	. . .	. . .	. . .	. . .	. . .	. . .
Banks	4 783 . .	31	. . .	3	3	13	57	. . .	3
Other sectors	4 784 . .	. . .	. . .	. . .	. . .	. . .	. . .	. . .	. . .
Other liabilities	4 786 . .	–1	–39	10	5	156	120	–96	138
Monetary authorities: long-term	4 788 . .	. . .	. . .	. . .	. . .	. . .	. . .	. . .	. . .
Monetary authorities: short-term	4 789 . .	. . .	. . .	. . .	. . .	. . .	. . .	. . .	. . .
General government: long-term	4 791 . .	–1	–39	10	5	156	120	–96	138
General government: short-term	4 792 . .	. . .	. . .	. . .	. . .	. . .	. . .	. . .	. . .
Banks: long-term	4 794 . .	. . .	. . .	. . .	. . .	. . .	. . .	. . .	. . .
Banks: short-term	4 795 . .	. . .	. . .	. . .	. . .	. . .	. . .	. . .	. . .
Other sectors: long-term	4 797 . .	. . .	. . .	. . .	. . .	. . .	. . .	. . .	. . .
Other sectors: short-term	4 798 . .	. . .	. . .	. . .	. . .	. . .	. . .	. . .	. . .
D. RESERVE ASSETS	4 800 . .	467	–324	–135	–543	–300	1,058	661	432
Monetary gold	4 810 . .	. . .	. . .	. . .	. . .	. . .	. . .	. . .	. . .
Special drawing rights	4 820 . .	–2	–3	–3	–3	17	–2	–2	–2
Reserve position in the Fund	4 830 . .	4	1	3	3	–23	2	3	2
Foreign exchange	4 840 . .	260	–386	–205	–374	193	533	236	–157
Other claims	4 880 . .	205	63	70	–169	–486	525	424	588
NET ERRORS AND OMISSIONS	4 998 . .	**–379**	**33**	**–474**	**282**	**399**	**207**	**110**	**557**

Part 3 of the *Yearbook* contains descriptions of the methodologies, compilation practices, and sources used to compile these data.

Table 1. ANALYTIC PRESENTATION, 1988–95
(Millions of U.S. dollars)

	Code	1988	1989	1990	1991	1992	1993	1994	1995
A. Current Account[1]	4 993 Y .	**–1,423**	**–1,334**	**–1,654**	**–1,396**	**–1,868**	**–2,887**	**–1,804**	**. . .**
Goods: exports f.o.b	2 100 . .	4,405	4,796	5,380	6,381	6,881	6,761	7,083	. . .
Goods: imports f.o.b	3 100 . .	–7,097	–7,366	–8,094	–8,642	–9,671	–9,336	–9,311	. . .
Balance on Goods	4 100 . .	*–2,693*	*–2,571*	*–2,714*	*–2,262*	*–2,790*	*–2,574*	*–2,228*	. . .
Services: credit	2 200 . .	853	1,182	1,423	1,524	1,552	1,566	1,744	. . .
Services: debit	3 200 . .	–1,486	–1,704	–2,063	–2,303	–2,671	–2,626	–2,518	. . .
Balance on Goods and Services	4 991 . .	*–3,326*	*–3,093*	*–3,355*	*–3,041*	*–3,909*	*–3,635*	*–3,001*	. . .
Income: credit	2 300 . .	94	141	96	73	73	62	149	. . .
Income: debit	3 300 . .	–907	–1,104	–1,175	–1,256	–1,478	–1,602	–1,821	. . .
Balance on Goods, Services, and Income	4 992 . .	*–4,140*	*–4,055*	*–4,434*	*–4,224*	*–5,313*	*–5,175*	*–4,673*	. . .
Current transfers: credit	2 379 Y .	2,747	2,757	2,820	2,877	3,485	2,326	2,905	. . .
Current transfers: debit	3 379 . .	–30	–36	–40	–49	–40	–38	–35	. . .
B. Capital Account[1]	4 994 Y .	**–1**	**–1**	**–1**	**–1**	**–1**	**. . .**	**. . .**	**. . .**
Capital account: credit	2 994 Y .	. . .	. . .	. . .	. . .	. . .	. . .	. . .	. . .
Capital account: debit	3 994 . .	–1	–1	–1	–1	–1	. . .	. . .	. . .
Total, Groups A Plus B	4 010 . .	*–1,424*	*–1,335*	*–1,654*	*–1,397*	*–1,868*	*–2,887*	*–1,804*	. . .
C. Financial Account[1]	4 995 X .	**1,662**	**1,382**	**1,446**	**1,320**	**2,137**	**3,318**	**2,963**	**. . .**
Direct investment abroad	4 505 . .	–13	–43	–2	4	12	2	–1	. . .
Direct investment in Pakistan	4 555 Y .	186	210	244	257	335	347	419	. . .
Portfolio investment assets	4 602 . .	. . .	. . .	. . .	. . .	. . .	. . .	. . .	. . .
Equity securities	4 610 . .	. . .	. . .	. . .	. . .	. . .	. . .	. . .	. . .
Debt securities	4 619 . .	. . .	. . .	. . .	. . .	. . .	. . .	. . .	. . .
Portfolio investment liabilities	4 652 Y .	126	15	87	92	370	292	1,464	. . .
Equity securities	4 660 Y .	6	–1	. . .	42	240	224	1,248	. . .
Debt securities	4 669 Y .	120	17	87	50	130	67	216	. . .
Other investment assets	4 703 . .	–188	–199	–363	–309	–565	–285	–282	. . .
Monetary authorities	4 703 . A	. . .	. . .	. . .	. . .	. . .	. . .	. . .	. . .
General government	4 703 . B	–26	1	–11	–13	–454	46	–19	. . .
Banks	4 703 . C	–61	–124	–606	–302	172	–85	–107	. . .
Other sectors	4 703 . D	–100	–76	254	6	–283	–245	–156	. . .
Other investment liabilities	4 753 X .	1,550	1,399	1,479	1,276	1,986	2,962	1,363	. . .
Monetary authorities	4 753 XA	256	73	49	–61	382	–140	–280	. . .
General government	4 753 YB	1,002	974	951	499	1,286	1,254	1,127	. . .
Banks	4 753 YC	195	320	339	498	–358	610	312	. . .
Other sectors	4 753 YD	96	33	141	340	677	1,238	205	. . .
Total, Groups A Through C	4 020 . .	*238*	*48*	*–209*	*–77*	*269*	*431*	*1,160*	. . .
D. Net Errors and Omissions	4 998 . .	**23**	**–242**	**–103**	**–78**	**120**	**–6**	**175**	**. . .**
Total, Groups A Through D	4 030 . .	*261*	*–195*	*–312*	*–155*	*389*	*426*	*1,335*	. . .
E. Reserves and Related Items	4 040 . .	**–261**	**195**	**312**	**155**	**–389**	**–426**	**–1,335**	**. . .**
Reserve assets	4 800 . .	40	–214	469	–216	–494	–424	–1,736	. . .
Use of Fund credit and loans	4 766 . .	–317	398	–165	227	100	–4	401	. . .
Liabilities constituting foreign authorities' reserves	4 900 . .	. . .	. . .	. . .	. . .	. . .	. . .	. . .	. . .
Exceptional financing	4 920 . .	16	11	9	144	5	2	. . .	. . .
Conversion rates: Pakistan rupees per U.S. dollar	0 101 . .	**18.003**	**20.541**	**21.707**	**23.801**	**25.083**	**28.107**	**30.567**	**31.643**

[1] Excludes components that have been classified in the categories of Group E.

Table 2. STANDARD PRESENTATION, 1988–95
(Millions of U.S. dollars)

	Code	1988	1989	1990	1991	1992	1993	1994	1995
CURRENT ACCOUNT	4 993 . .	**–1,416**	**–1,332**	**–1,654**	**–1,260**	**–1,867**	**–2,887**	**–1,804**	. . .
A. GOODS	4 100 . .	–2,693	–2,571	–2,714	–2,262	–2,790	–2,574	–2,228	. . .
Credit	2 100 . .	**4,405**	**4,796**	**5,380**	**6,381**	**6,881**	**6,761**	**7,083**	. . .
General merchandise: exports f.o.b.	2 110 . .	4,405	4,796	5,380	6,381	6,881	6,761	7,083	. . .
Goods for processing: exports f.o.b.	2 150 . .	. . .	. . .	. . .	. . .	. . .	. . .	. . .	. . .
Repairs on goods	2 160 . .	. . .	. . .	. . .	. . .	. . .	. . .	. . .	. . .
Goods procured in ports by carriers	2 170 . .	. . .	. . .	. . .	. . .	. . .	. . .	. . .	. . .
Nonmonetary gold	2 180 . .	. . .	. . .	. . .	. . .	. . .	. . .	. . .	. . .
Debit	3 100 . .	**–7,097**	**–7,366**	**–8,094**	**–8,642**	**–9,671**	**–9,336**	**–9,311**	. . .
General merchandise: imports f.o.b.	3 110 . .	–7,097	–7,366	–8,094	–8,642	–9,671	–9,336	–9,311	. . .
Goods for processing: imports f.o.b.	3 150 . .	. . .	. . .	. . .	. . .	. . .	. . .	. . .	. . .
Repairs on goods	3 160 . .	. . .	. . .	. . .	. . .	. . .	. . .	. . .	. . .
Goods procured in ports by carriers	3 170 . .	. . .	. . .	. . .	. . .	. . .	. . .	. . .	. . .
Nonmonetary gold	3 180 . .	. . .	. . .	. . .	. . .	. . .	. . .	. . .	. . .
B. SERVICES	4 200 . .	–633	–522	–641	–780	–1,119	–1,061	–773	. . .
Total credit	2 200 . .	*853*	*1,182*	*1,423*	*1,524*	*1,552*	*1,566*	*1,744*	. . .
Total debit	3 200 . .	*–1,486*	*–1,704*	*–2,063*	*–2,303*	*–2,671*	*–2,626*	*–2,518*	. . .
Transportation services, credit	2 205 . .	**319**	**503**	**719**	**786**	**854**	**763**	**865**	. . .
Passenger	2 205 BA	*57*	*260*	*468*	*478*	*526*	*422*	*521*	. . .
Freight	2 205 BB	*48*	*46*	*46*	*59*	*55*	*60*	*60*	. . .
Other	2 205 BC	*214*	*197*	*205*	*250*	*274*	*281*	*283*	. . .
Sea transport, passenger	2 207 . .	. . .	. . .	. . .	. . .	. . .	. . .	. . .	. . .
Sea transport, freight	2 208 . .	. . .	. . .	. . .	. . .	. . .	22	16	. . .
Sea transport, other	2 209 . .	. . .	. . .	. . .	. . .	. . .	143	154	. . .
Air transport, passenger	2 211 . .	. . .	. . .	. . .	. . .	. . .	422	521	. . .
Air transport, freight	2 212 . .	. . .	. . .	. . .	. . .	. . .	38	45	. . .
Air transport, other	2 213 . .	4	4	9	9	7	138	129	. . .
Other transport, passenger	2 215 . .	. . .	. . .	. . .	. . .	. . .	. . .	. . .	. . .
Other transport, freight	2 216 . .	. . .	. . .	. . .	. . .	. . .	. . .	. . .	. . .
Other transport, other	2 217 . .	210	193	196	240	267	. . .	. . .	. . .
Transportation services, debit	3 205 . .	**–789**	**–1,001**	**–1,242**	**–1,287**	**–1,475**	**–1,450**	**–1,482**	. . .
Passenger	3 205 BA	*–126*	*–132*	*–116*	*–169*	*–232*	*–206*	*–192*	. . .
Freight	3 205 BB	*–602*	*–625*	*–683*	*–650*	*–798*	*–809*	*–811*	. . .
Other	3 205 BC	*–61*	*–244*	*–443*	*–468*	*–445*	*–435*	*–478*	. . .
Sea transport, passenger	3 207 . .	. . .	. . .	. . .	. . .	. . .	. . .	. . .	. . .
Sea transport, freight	3 208 . .	. . .	. . .	. . .	. . .	. . .	–809	–811	. . .
Sea transport, other	3 209 . .	. . .	. . .	. . .	. . .	. . .	–52	–85	. . .
Air transport, passenger	3 211 . .	. . .	. . .	. . .	. . .	. . .	–206	–192	. . .
Air transport, freight	3 212 . .	. . .	. . .	. . .	. . .	. . .	. . .	. . .	. . .
Air transport, other	3 213 . .	–20	–186	–408	–460	–441	–383	–393	. . .
Other transport, passenger	3 215 . .	. . .	. . .	. . .	. . .	. . .	. . .	. . .	. . .
Other transport, freight	3 216 . .	. . .	. . .	. . .	. . .	. . .	. . .	. . .	. . .
Other transport, other	3 217 . .	–41	–58	–35	–8	–4	. . .	. . .	. . .
Travel, credit	2 236 . .	**147**	**169**	**146**	**157**	**111**	**103**	**123**	. . .
Business travel	2 237 . .	. . .	. . .	. . .	. . .	. . .	. . .	1	. . .
Personal travel	2 240 . .	. . .	. . .	. . .	. . .	. . .	103	122	. . .
Travel, debit	3 236 . .	**–334**	**–326**	**–429**	**–549**	**–679**	**–636**	**–410**	. . .
Business travel	3 237 . .	. . .	. . .	. . .	. . .	. . .	–31	–12	. . .
Personal travel	3 240 . .	. . .	. . .	. . .	. . .	. . .	–604	–398	. . .
Other services, credit	2 200 BA	**386**	**510**	**558**	**580**	**587**	**700**	**756**	. . .
Communications	2 245 . .	. . .	. . .	. . .	. . .	. . .	230	248	. . .
Construction	2 249 . .	. . .	. . .	. . .	. . .	. . .	. . .	. . .	. . .
Insurance	2 253 . .	4	6	17	11	5	6	6	. . .
Financial	2 260 . .	. . .	. . .	. . .	. . .	. . .	14	14	. . .
Computer and information	2 262 . .	. . .	. . .	. . .	. . .	. . .	. . .	. . .	. . .
Royalties and licence fees	2 266 . .	. . .	. . .	. . .	. . .	. . .	1	2	. . .
Other business services	2 268 . .	244	297	331	306	317	176	157	. . .
Personal, cultural, and recreational	2 287 . .	. . .	. . .	. . .	. . .	. . .	31	22	. . .
Government, n.i.e.	2 291 . .	137	207	210	264	265	242	308	. . .
Other services, debit	3 200 BA	**–363**	**–377**	**–393**	**–467**	**–517**	**–541**	**–626**	. . .
Communications	3 245 . .	. . .	. . .	. . .	. . .	. . .	–3	–6	. . .
Construction	3 249 . .	. . .	. . .	. . .	. . .	. . .	. . .	. . .	. . .
Insurance	3 253 . .	–31	–28	–25	–63	–37	–41	–43	. . .
Financial	3 260 . .	. . .	. . .	. . .	. . .	. . .	–39	–52	. . .
Computer and information	3 262 . .	. . .	. . .	. . .	. . .	. . .	. . .	. . .	. . .
Royalties and licence fees	3 266 . .	. . .	. . .	. . .	. . .	. . .	–6	–12	. . .
Other business services	3 268 . .	–136	–154	–159	–175	–221	–180	–158	. . .
Personal, cultural, and recreational	3 287 . .	. . .	. . .	. . .	. . .	. . .	–10	–10	. . .
Government, n.i.e.	3 291 . .	–196	–194	–209	–229	–260	–261	–346	. . .

Table 2 (Continued). STANDARD PRESENTATION, 1988–95
(Millions of U.S. dollars)

	Code	1988	1989	1990	1991	1992	1993	1994	1995
C. INCOME	4 300	–814	–963	–1,079	–1,183	–1,405	–1,540	–1,672	...
Total credit	2 300	*94*	*141*	*96*	*73*	*73*	*62*	*149*	...
Total debit	3 300	*–907*	*–1,104*	*–1,175*	*–1,256*	*–1,478*	*–1,602*	*–1,821*	...
Compensation of employees, credit	2 310	...	...	...	...	...	...	...	...
Compensation of employees, debit	3 310	...	...	...	...	...	...	...	...
Investment income, credit	2 320	**94**	**141**	**96**	**73**	**73**	**62**	**149**	...
Direct investment income	2 330	...	1	...	...	...	10	30	...
Dividends and distributed branch profits	2 332	...	1	...	...	...	10	30	...
Reinvested earnings and undistributed branch profits	2 333	...	...	...	...	...	...	...	...
Income on debt (interest)	2 334	...	...	...	...	...	...	...	...
Portfolio investment income	2 339	...	...	...	...	...	...	...	...
Income on equity	2 340	...	...	...	...	...	...	...	...
Income on bonds and notes	2 350	...	...	...	...	...	...	...	...
Income on money market instruments and financial derivatives	2 360	...	...	...	...	...	...	...	...
Other investment income	2 370	94	140	96	73	73	52	119	...
Investment income, debit	3 320	**–907**	**–1,104**	**–1,175**	**–1,256**	**–1,478**	**–1,602**	**–1,821**	...
Direct investment income	3 330	–56	–45	–53	–42	–54	–205	–247	...
Dividends and distributed branch profits	3 332	–56	–45	–53	–42	–54	–136	–169	...
Reinvested earnings and undistributed branch profits	3 333	...	...	...	...	...	–69	–78	...
Income on debt (interest)	3 334	...	...	...	...	...	...	...	...
Portfolio investment income	3 339	...	...	...	...	...	–41	–34	...
Income on equity	3 340	...	...	...	...	...	...	...	...
Income on bonds and notes	3 350	...	...	...	...	...	...	...	...
Income on money market instruments and financial derivatives	3 360	...	...	...	...	...	–41	–34	...
Other investment income	3 370	–852	–1,059	–1,122	–1,213	–1,424	–1,357	–1,540	...
D. CURRENT TRANSFERS	4 379	2,724	2,724	2,780	2,964	3,446	2,288	2,870	...
Credit	2 379	**2,754**	**2,760**	**2,820**	**3,013**	**3,486**	**2,326**	**2,905**	...
General government	2 380	644	536	530	652	403	344	367	...
Other sectors	2 390	2,110	2,223	2,290	2,361	3,083	1,981	2,538	...
Workers' remittances	2 391	1,863	2,008	1,997	1,541	1,566	1,439	1,741	...
Other current transfers	2 392	247	216	294	819	1,517	542	797	...
Debit	3 379	**–30**	**–36**	**–40**	**–49**	**–40**	**–38**	**–35**	...
General government	3 380	–22	–21	–26	–33	–25	–11	–12	...
Other sectors	3 390	–9	–15	–14	–16	–15	–27	–23	...
Workers' remittances	3 391	...	...	...	...	...	–1	–2	...
Other current transfers	3 392	–9	–15	–14	–16	–15	–26	–22	...
CAPITAL AND FINANCIAL ACCOUNT	4 996	**1,392**	**1,574**	**1,757**	**1,339**	**1,747**	**2,892**	**1,629**	...
CAPITAL ACCOUNT	4 994	**8**	**8**	**8**	**8**	**3**	**2**	...	...
Total credit	2 994	*9*	*9*	*8*	*8*	*4*	*2*	...	...
Total debit	3 994	*–1*	*–1*	*–1*	*–1*	*–1*	...	...	...
Capital transfers, credit	2 400	**9**	**9**	**8**	**8**	**4**	**2**	...	...
General government	2 401	9	9	8	8	4	2	...	...
Debt forgiveness	2 402	9	9	8	8	4	2	...	...
Other capital transfers	2 410	...	...	...	...	...	...	...	...
Other sectors	2 430	...	...	...	...	...	...	...	...
Migrants' transfers	2 431	...	...	...	...	...	...	...	...
Debt forgiveness	2 432	...	...	...	...	...	...	...	...
Other capital transfers	2 440	...	...	...	...	...	...	...	...
Capital transfers, debit	3 400	**–1**	**–1**	**–1**	**–1**	**–1**	...	...	...
General government	3 401	...	...	...	...	...	...	...	...
Debt forgiveness	3 402	...	...	...	...	...	...	...	...
Other capital transfers	3 410	...	...	...	...	...	...	...	...
Other sectors	3 430	–1	–1	–1	–1	–1	...	...	...
Migrants' transfers	3 431	–1	–1	–1	–1	–1	...	...	...
Debt forgiveness	3 432	...	...	...	...	...	...	...	...
Other capital transfers	3 440	...	...	...	...	...	...	...	...
Nonproduced nonfinancial assets, credit	2 480	...	...	...	...	...	...	...	...
Nonproduced nonfinancial assets, debit	3 480	...	...	...	...	...	...	...	...

Table 2 (Continued). STANDARD PRESENTATION, 1988–95
(Millions of U.S. dollars)

	Code	1988	1989	1990	1991	1992	1993	1994	1995
FINANCIAL ACCOUNT	4 995	**1,384**	**1,566**	**1,749**	**1,331**	**1,743**	**2,890**	**1,629**	...
A. DIRECT INVESTMENT	4 500	173	167	242	261	346	349	418	...
Direct investment abroad	4 505	**–13**	**–43**	**–2**	**4**	**12**	**2**	**–1**	...
Equity capital	4 510	–13	–43	–2	4	12	2	–1	...
Claims on affiliated enterprises	4 515	...	...	...	...	...	...	...	...
Liabilities to affiliated enterprises	4 520	...	...	...	...	...	...	...	...
Reinvested earnings	4 525	...	...	...	...	...	...	...	...
Other capital	4 530	...	...	...	...	...	...	...	...
Claims on affiliated enterprises	4 535	...	...	...	...	...	...	...	...
Liabilities to affiliated enterprises	4 540	...	...	...	...	...	...	...	...
Direct investment in Pakistan	4 555	**186**	**210**	**244**	**257**	**335**	**347**	**419**	...
Equity capital	4 560	186	210	244	257	335	221	273	...
Claims on direct investors	4 565	...	...	...	...	...	...	...	...
Liabilities to direct investors	4 570	...	...	...	...	...	...	...	...
Reinvested earnings	4 575	...	...	...	...	...	69	78	...
Other capital	4 580	...	...	...	...	...	57	68	...
Claims on direct investors	4 585	...	...	...	...	...	...	...	...
Liabilities to direct investors	4 590	...	...	...	...	...	...	...	...
B. PORTFOLIO INVESTMENT	4 600	126	15	87	92	370	292	1,464	...
Assets	4 602	...	...	...	...	...	...	...	...
Equity securities	4 610	...	...	...	...	...	...	...	...
Monetary authorities	4 611	...	...	...	...	...	...	...	...
General government	4 612	...	...	...	...	...	...	...	...
Banks	4 613	...	...	...	...	...	...	...	...
Other sectors	4 614	...	...	...	...	...	...	...	...
Debt securities	4 619	...	...	...	...	...	...	...	...
Bonds and notes	4 620	...	...	...	...	...	...	...	...
Monetary authorities	4 621	...	...	...	...	...	...	...	...
General government	4 622	...	...	...	...	...	...	...	...
Banks	4 623	...	...	...	...	...	...	...	...
Other sectors	4 624	...	...	...	...	...	...	...	...
Money market instruments	4 630	...	...	...	...	...	...	...	...
Monetary authorities	4 631	...	...	...	...	...	...	...	...
General government	4 632	...	...	...	...	...	...	...	...
Banks	4 633	...	...	...	...	...	...	...	...
Other sectors	4 634	...	...	...	...	...	...	...	...
Financial derivatives	4 640	...	...	...	...	...	...	...	...
Monetary authorities	4 641	...	...	...	...	...	...	...	...
General government	4 642	...	...	...	...	...	...	...	...
Banks	4 643	...	...	...	...	...	...	...	...
Other sectors	4 644	...	...	...	...	...	...	...	...
Liabilities	4 652	**126**	**15**	**87**	**92**	**370**	**292**	**1,464**	...
Equity securities	4 660	6	–1	...	42	240	224	1,248	...
Banks	4 663	...	...	...	...	...	...	...	...
Other sectors	4 664	...	...	...	...	...	...	...	...
Debt securities	4 669	120	17	87	50	130	67	216	...
Bonds and notes	4 670	120	17	87	50	130	67	216	...
Monetary authorities	4 671	...	...	...	...	...	...	...	...
General government	4 672	120	17	87	50	130	67	216	...
Banks	4 673	...	...	...	...	...	...	...	...
Other sectors	4 674	...	...	...	...	...	...	...	...
Money market instruments	4 680	...	...	...	...	...	...	...	...
Monetary authorities	4 681	...	...	...	...	...	...	...	...
General government	4 682	...	...	...	...	...	...	...	...
Banks	4 683	...	...	...	...	...	...	...	...
Other sectors	4 684	...	...	...	...	...	...	...	...
Financial derivatives	4 690	...	...	...	...	...	...	...	...
Monetary authorities	4 691	...	...	...	...	...	...	...	...
General government	4 692	...	...	...	...	...	...	...	...
Banks	4 693	...	...	...	...	...	...	...	...
Other sectors	4 694	...	...	...	...	...	...	...	...

Table 2 (Concluded). STANDARD PRESENTATION, 1988–95
(Millions of U.S. dollars)

	Code	1988	1989	1990	1991	1992	1993	1994	1995
C. OTHER INVESTMENT	4 700 . .	1,045	1,598	951	1,194	1,521	2,674	1,482	. . .
Assets	4 703 . .	**–188**	**–199**	**–363**	**–309**	**–565**	**–285**	**–282**	. . .
Trade credits	4 706 . .	. . .	. . .	. . .	. . .	. . .	–12	–15	. . .
General government: long-term	4 708 . .	. . .	. . .	. . .	. . .	. . .	–12	–15	. . .
General government: short-term	4 709 . .	. . .	. . .	. . .	. . .	. . .	. . .	. . .	. . .
Other sectors: long-term	4 711 . .	. . .	. . .	. . .	. . .	. . .	. . .	. . .	. . .
Other sectors: short-term	4 712 . .	. . .	. . .	. . .	. . .	. . .	. . .	. . .	. . .
Loans	4 714 . .	. . .	. . .	. . .	. . .	–62	. . .	. . .	. . .
Monetary authorities: long-term	4 717 . .	. . .	. . .	. . .	. . .	. . .	. . .	. . .	. . .
Monetary authorities: short-term	4 718 . .	. . .	. . .	. . .	. . .	. . .	. . .	. . .	. . .
General government: long-term	4 720 . .	. . .	. . .	. . .	. . .	–62	. . .	. . .	. . .
General government: short-term	4 721 . .	. . .	. . .	. . .	. . .	. . .	. . .	. . .	. . .
Banks: long-term	4 723 . .	. . .	. . .	. . .	. . .	. . .	. . .	. . .	. . .
Banks: short-term	4 724 . .	. . .	. . .	. . .	. . .	. . .	. . .	. . .	. . .
Other sectors: long-term	4 726 . .	. . .	. . .	. . .	. . .	. . .	. . .	. . .	. . .
Other sectors: short-term	4 727 . .	. . .	. . .	. . .	. . .	. . .	. . .	. . .	. . .
Currency and deposits	4 730 . .	–163	–198	–354	–321	–210	. . .	. . .	. . .
Monetary authorities	4 731 . .	. . .	. . .	. . .	. . .	. . .	. . .	. . .	. . .
General government	4 732 . .	–2	2	–3	–25	–99	. . .	. . .	. . .
Banks	4 733 . .	–61	–124	–606	–302	172	. . .	. . .	. . .
Other sectors	4 734 . .	–100	–76	254	6	–283	. . .	. . .	. . .
Other assets	4 736 . .	–25	–1	–9	12	–293	–273	–267	. . .
Monetary authorities: long-term	4 738 . .	. . .	. . .	. . .	. . .	. . .	. . .	. . .	. . .
Monetary authorities: short-term	4 739 . .	. . .	. . .	. . .	. . .	. . .	. . .	. . .	. . .
General government: long-term	4 741 . .	–25	–1	–9	12	–293	. . .	–5	. . .
General government: short-term	4 742 . .	. . .	. . .	. . .	. . .	. . .	58	1	. . .
Banks: long-term	4 744 . .	. . .	. . .	. . .	. . .	. . .	. . .	. . .	. . .
Banks: short-term	4 745 . .	. . .	. . .	. . .	. . .	. . .	–85	–107	. . .
Other sectors: long-term	4 747 . .	. . .	. . .	. . .	. . .	. . .	. . .	. . .	. . .
Other sectors: short-term	4 748 . .	. . .	. . .	. . .	. . .	. . .	–245	–156	. . .
Liabilities	4 753 . .	**1,233**	**1,797**	**1,314**	**1,503**	**2,086**	**2,959**	**1,764**	. . .
Trade credits	4 756 . .	. . .	. . .	. . .	. . .	. . .	. . .	. . .	. . .
General government: long-term	4 758 . .	. . .	. . .	. . .	. . .	. . .	. . .	. . .	. . .
General government: short-term	4 759 . .	. . .	. . .	. . .	. . .	. . .	. . .	. . .	. . .
Other sectors: long-term	4 761 . .	. . .	. . .	. . .	. . .	. . .	. . .	. . .	. . .
Other sectors: short-term	4 762 . .	. . .	. . .	. . .	. . .	. . .	. . .	. . .	. . .
Loans	4 764 . .	1,020	1,772	1,256	1,573	1,225	1,543	1,652	. . .
Use of Fund credit and loans from the Fund	4 766 . .	–317	398	–165	227	100	–4	401	. . .
Monetary authorities: other long-term	4 767 . .	. . .	. . .	. . .	. . .	. . .	. . .	. . .	. . .
Monetary authorities: short-term	4 768 . .	. . .	. . .	. . .	. . .	. . .	. . .	. . .	. . .
General government: long-term	4 770 . .	795	1,218	859	744	807	854	1,041	. . .
General government: short-term	4 771 . .	241	–219	93	–224	216	425	104	. . .
Banks: long-term	4 773 . .	116	80	67	59	59	97	36	. . .
Banks: short-term	4 774 . .	114	244	273	429	–419	9	2	. . .
Other sectors: long-term	4 776 . .	71	51	128	338	462	163	68	. . .
Other sectors: short-term	4 777 . .	. . .	. . .	. . .	. . .	. . .	. . .	. . .	. . .
Currency and deposits	4 780 . .	–36	–6	–2	12	–3	. . .	. . .	. . .
Monetary authorities	4 781 . .	. . .	. . .	. . .	. . .	. . .	. . .	. . .	. . .
General government	4 782 . .	. . .	. . .	. . .	. . .	. . .	. . .	. . .	. . .
Banks	4 783 . .	–36	–6	–2	12	–3	. . .	. . .	. . .
Other sectors	4 784 . .	. . .	. . .	. . .	. . .	. . .	. . .	. . .	. . .
Other liabilities	4 786 . .	249	32	60	–82	864	1,415	112	. . .
Monetary authorities: long-term	4 788 . .	. . .	. . .	. . .	. . .	. . .	. . .	. . .	. . .
Monetary authorities: short-term	4 789 . .	256	73	49	–61	382	–140	–280	. . .
General government: long-term	4 791 . .	–34	–26	–2	–21	263	–25	–17	. . .
General government: short-term	4 792 . .	. . .	. . .	. . .	. . .	. . .	. . .	. . .	. . .
Banks: long-term	4 794 . .	1	2	. . .	–3	4	–4	11	. . .
Banks: short-term	4 795 . .	. . .	. . .	. . .	. . .	. . .	509	263	. . .
Other sectors: long-term	4 797 . .	21	–19	10	–4	205	621	–13	. . .
Other sectors: short-term	4 798 . .	4	1	2	7	10	454	150	. . .
D. RESERVE ASSETS	4 800 . .	40	–214	469	–216	–494	–424	–1,736	. . .
Monetary gold	4 810 . .	. . .	. . .	. . .	. . .	. . .	. . .	. . .	. . .
Special drawing rights	4 820 . .	9	4	2	–6	7	–1	1	. . .
Reserve position in the Fund	4 830 . .	. . .	. . .	. . .	. . .	. . .	. . .	. . .	. . .
Foreign exchange	4 840 . .	49	–231	481	–214	–474	–338	–1,747	. . .
Other claims	4 880 . .	–18	13	–14	3	–27	–85	10	. . .
NET ERRORS AND OMISSIONS	4 998 . .	**23**	**–242**	**–103**	**–78**	**120**	**–6**	**175**	. . .

Table 1. ANALYTIC PRESENTATION, 1988–95

(Millions of U.S. dollars)

	Code	1988	1989	1990	1991	1992	1993	1994	1995
A. Current Account[1]	4 993 Y.	**720.9**	**110.9**	**206.5**	**–216.1**	**–278.8**	**–141.3**	**. . .**	**. . .**
Goods: exports f.o.b	2 100 . .	2,506.0	2,742.1	3,346.3	4,192.0	5,103.5	5,416.9	. . .	. . .
Goods: imports f.o.b	3 100 . .	–2,349.2	–2,865.9	–3,503.8	–4,591.3	–5,479.9	–5,751.1	. . .	. . .
Balance on Goods	4 100 . .	*156.8*	*–123.8*	*–157.5*	*–399.3*	*–376.4*	*–334.2*	. . .	. . .
Services: credit	2 200 . .	1,062.4	981.1	1,091.7	1,196.0	1,213.9	1,271.8	. . .	. . .
Services: debit	3 200 . .	–518.1	–575.2	–682.8	–847.3	–919.6	–970.1	. . .	. . .
Balance on Goods and Services	4 991 . .	*701.1*	*282.1*	*251.4*	*–50.6*	*–82.1*	*–32.5*	. . .	. . .
Income: credit	2 300 . .	976.2	976.0	1,139.1	1,078.9	1,139.0	1,301.7	. . .	. . .
Income: debit	3 300 . .	–1,064.8	–1,242.7	–1,403.4	–1,466.9	–1,536.6	–1,613.5	. . .	. . .
Balance on Goods, Services, and Income	4 992 . .	*612.5*	*15.4*	*–12.9*	*–438.6*	*–479.7*	*–344.3*	. . .	. . .
Current transfers: credit	2 379 Y.	153.6	139.7	248.8	249.8	229.9	236.4	. . .	. . .
Current transfers: debit	3 379 . .	–45.2	–44.2	–29.4	–27.3	–29.0	–33.4	. . .	. . .
B. Capital Account[1]	4 994 Y.	**. . .**	**. . .**	**. . .**	**. . .**	**. . .**	**. . .**	**. . .**	**. . .**
Capital account: credit	2 994 Y.	. . .	. . .	. . .	. . .	. . .	. . .	. . .	. . .
Capital account: debit	3 994 . .	. . .	. . .	. . .	. . .	. . .	. . .	. . .	. . .
Total, Groups A Plus B	4 010 . .	*720.9*	*110.9*	*206.5*	*–216.1*	*–278.8*	*–141.3*	. . .	. . .
C. Financial Account[1]	4 995 X.	**–933.5**	**–678.6**	**–191.1**	**–721.7**	**–425.9**	**–414.4**	**. . .**	**. . .**
Direct investment abroad	4 505 . .	. . .	. . .	. . .	. . .	. . .	. . .	. . .	. . .
Direct investment in Panama	4 555 Y.	–595.1	51.5	132.1	41.3	138.7	155.6	. . .	. . .
Portfolio investment assets	4 602 . .	2,216.4	–439.0	–203.4	–230.9	–49.4	–792.5	. . .	. . .
Equity securities	4 610 . .	.7	. . .	–1.0	1.8	–1.5	–.1	. . .	. . .
Debt securities	4 619 . .	2,215.7	–439.0	–202.4	–232.7	–47.9	–792.4	. . .	. . .
Portfolio investment liabilities	4 652 Y.	–17.8	–1.5	–1.5	–1.6	–1.7	–1.3	. . .	. . .
Equity securities	4 660 Y.	. . .	. . .	. . .	. . .	. . .	. . .	. . .	. . .
Debt securities	4 669 Y.	–17.8	–1.5	–1.5	–1.6	–1.7	–1.3	. . .	. . .
Other investment assets	4 703 . .	12,830.5	–433.8	–1,405.7	–1,353.7	–1,492.9	–1,176.0	. . .	. . .
Monetary authorities	4 703 .A	. . .	. . .	. . .	. . .	. . .	. . .	. . .	. . .
General government	4 703 .B	–164.8	–135.2	299.1	–.9	–.9	–.9	. . .	. . .
Banks	4 703 .C	13,170.3	–153.0	–1,923.3	–1,259.5	–1,442.9	–1,140.9	. . .	. . .
Other sectors	4 703 .D	–175.0	–145.6	218.5	–93.3	–49.1	–34.2	. . .	. . .
Other investment liabilities	4 753 X.	–15,367.5	144.2	1,287.4	823.2	979.4	1,399.8	. . .	. . .
Monetary authorities	4 753 XA	–92.9	–53.6	–24.5	1.2	14.5	–3.2	. . .	. . .
General government	4 753 YB	–350.0	–270.4	–148.1	–179.8	–156.2	–117.8	. . .	. . .
Banks	4 753 YC	–14,840.3	541.6	1,516.1	945.7	1,179.7	1,606.7	. . .	. . .
Other sectors	4 753 YD	–84.3	–73.4	–56.1	56.1	–58.6	–85.9	. . .	. . .
Total, Groups A Through C	4 020 . .	*–212.6*	*–567.7*	*15.4*	*–937.8*	*–704.7*	*–555.7*	. . .	. . .
D. Net Errors and Omissions	4 998 . .	**–744.3**	**–236.1**	**–134.5**	**633.8**	**455.4**	**301.0**	**. . .**	**. . .**
Total, Groups A Through D	4 030 . .	*–956.9*	*–803.8*	*–119.1*	*–304.0*	*–249.3*	*–254.7*	. . .	. . .
E. Reserves and Related Items	4 040 . .	**956.9**	**803.8**	**119.1**	**304.0**	**249.3**	**254.7**	**. . .**	**. . .**
Reserve assets	4 800 . .	5.5	–47.9	–355.8	–148.3	116.2	–93.0	. . .	. . .
Use of Fund credit and loans	4 766 . .	–.1	–.8	–70.7	–55.7	–98.6	3.4	. . .	. . .
Liabilities constituting foreign authorities' reserves	4 900 . .	. . .	. . .	. . .	. . .	. . .	. . .	. . .	. . .
Exceptional financing	4 920 . .	951.5	852.5	545.6	508.1	231.7	344.3	. . .	. . .
Conversion rates: balboa per U.S. dollar	0 101 . .	**1.0000**	**1.0000**	**1.0000**	**1.0000**	**1.0000**	**1.0000**	**1.0000**	**1.0000**

[1] Excludes components that have been classified in the categories of Group E.

Table 2. STANDARD PRESENTATION, 1988–95
(Millions of U.S. dollars)

	Code	1988	1989	1990	1991	1992	1993	1994	1995
CURRENT ACCOUNT	4 993 . .	**720.9**	**110.9**	**206.5**	**–216.1**	**–145.8**	**–141.3**	. . .	. . .
A. GOODS	4 100 . .	156.8	–123.8	–157.5	–399.3	–376.4	–334.2	. . .	. . .
Credit	2 100 . .	**2,506.0**	**2,742.1**	**3,346.3**	**4,192.0**	**5,103.5**	**5,416.9**	. . .	. . .
General merchandise: exports f.o.b.	2 110 . .	2,452.3	2,680.8	3,269.0	4,129.5	4,998.4	5,321.6	. . .	. . .
Goods for processing: exports f.o.b.	2 150 . .	. . .	. . .	. . .	. . .	. . .	. . .	. . .	. . .
Repairs on goods	2 160 . .	.8	.7	.6	1.3	.4	.3	. . .	. . .
Goods procured in ports by carriers	2 170 . .	52.9	60.6	76.7	61.2	104.7	95.0	. . .	. . .
Nonmonetary gold	2 180 . .	. . .	. . .	. . .	. . .	. . .	. . .	. . .	. . .
Debit	3 100 . .	**–2,349.2**	**–2,865.9**	**–3,503.8**	**–4,591.3**	**–5,479.9**	**–5,751.1**	. . .	. . .
General merchandise: imports f.o.b.	3 110 . .	–2,343.3	–2,860.3	–3,501.7	–4,587.9	–5,474.3	–5,743.1	. . .	. . .
Goods for processing: imports f.o.b.	3 150 . .	. . .	. . .	. . .	. . .	. . .	. . .	. . .	. . .
Repairs on goods	3 160 . .	–.9	–.7	–.7	–.9	–.9	–1.2	. . .	. . .
Goods procured in ports by carriers	3 170 . .	–5.0	–4.9	–1.4	–2.5	–4.7	–6.8	. . .	. . .
Nonmonetary gold	3 180 . .	. . .	. . .	. . .	. . .	. . .	. . .	. . .	. . .
B. SERVICES	4 200 . .	544.3	405.9	408.9	348.7	294.3	301.7	. . .	. . .
Total credit	2 200 . .	*1,062.4*	*981.1*	*1,091.7*	*1,196.0*	*1,213.9*	*1,271.8*	. . .	. . .
Total debit	3 200 . .	*–518.1*	*–575.2*	*–682.8*	*–847.3*	*–919.6*	*–970.1*	. . .	. . .
Transportation services, credit	2 205 . .	**594.5**	**541.4**	**588.4**	**641.1**	**630.2**	**649.4**	. . .	. . .
Passenger	2 205 BA	*17.0*	*16.8*	*6.8*	*8.5*	*13.3*	*20.8*	. . .	. . .
Freight	2 205 BB	*117.4*	*78.0*	*66.4*	*66.0*	*52.8*	*27.8*	. . .	. . .
Other	2 205 BC	*460.1*	*446.6*	*515.2*	*566.6*	*564.1*	*600.8*	. . .	. . .
Sea transport, passenger	2 207 . .	. . .	. . .	. . .	. . .	. . .	. . .	. . .	. . .
Sea transport, freight	2 208 . .	. . .	. . .	. . .	. . .	. . .	. . .	. . .	. . .
Sea transport, other	2 209 . .	. . .	. . .	. . .	. . .	. . .	. . .	. . .	. . .
Air transport, passenger	2 211 . .	. . .	. . .	. . .	. . .	. . .	. . .	. . .	. . .
Air transport, freight	2 212 . .	. . .	. . .	. . .	. . .	. . .	. . .	. . .	. . .
Air transport, other	2 213 . .	. . .	. . .	. . .	. . .	. . .	. . .	. . .	. . .
Other transport, passenger	2 215 . .	. . .	. . .	. . .	. . .	. . .	. . .	. . .	. . .
Other transport, freight	2 216 . .	. . .	. . .	. . .	. . .	. . .	. . .	. . .	. . .
Other transport, other	2 217 . .	. . .	. . .	. . .	. . .	. . .	. . .	. . .	. . .
Transportation services, debit	3 205 . .	**–311.9**	**–368.9**	**–444.2**	**–576.2**	**–653.5**	**–674.5**	. . .	. . .
Passenger	3 205 BA	*–39.3*	*–41.7*	*–35.6*	*–41.7*	*–53.9*	*–54.2*	. . .	. . .
Freight	3 205 BB	*–265.4*	*–314.0*	*–405.7*	*–529.8*	*–593.3*	*–614.2*	. . .	. . .
Other	3 205 BC	*–7.2*	*–13.2*	*–2.9*	*–4.7*	*–6.3*	*–6.1*	. . .	. . .
Sea transport, passenger	3 207 . .	. . .	. . .	. . .	. . .	. . .	. . .	. . .	. . .
Sea transport, freight	3 208 . .	. . .	. . .	. . .	. . .	. . .	. . .	. . .	. . .
Sea transport, other	3 209 . .	. . .	. . .	. . .	. . .	. . .	. . .	. . .	. . .
Air transport, passenger	3 211 . .	. . .	. . .	. . .	. . .	. . .	. . .	. . .	. . .
Air transport, freight	3 212 . .	. . .	. . .	. . .	. . .	. . .	. . .	. . .	. . .
Air transport, other	3 213 . .	. . .	. . .	. . .	. . .	. . .	. . .	. . .	. . .
Other transport, passenger	3 215 . .	. . .	. . .	. . .	. . .	. . .	. . .	. . .	. . .
Other transport, freight	3 216 . .	. . .	. . .	. . .	. . .	. . .	. . .	. . .	. . .
Other transport, other	3 217 . .	. . .	. . .	. . .	. . .	. . .	. . .	. . .	. . .
Travel, credit	2 236 . .	**166.3**	**160.9**	**171.7**	**203.4**	**215.0**	**225.7**	. . .	. . .
Business travel	2 237 . .	34.1	35.3	42.2	54.2	59.6	63.3	. . .	. . .
Personal travel	2 240 . .	132.2	125.6	129.5	149.2	155.4	162.4	. . .	. . .
Travel, debit	3 236 . .	**–88.6**	**–86.3**	**–98.6**	**–109.0**	**–120.0**	**–122.5**	. . .	. . .
Business travel	3 237 . .	–8.0	–8.3	–9.5	–11.4	–13.2	–13.2	. . .	. . .
Personal travel	3 240 . .	–80.6	–78.0	–89.1	–97.6	–106.8	–109.3	. . .	. . .
Other services, credit	2 200 BA	**301.6**	**278.8**	**331.6**	**351.5**	**368.7**	**396.7**	. . .	. . .
Communications	2 245 . .	3.5	. . .	. . .	. . .	. . .	. . .	. . .	. . .
Construction	2 249 . .	. . .	. . .	. . .	. . .	. . .	. . .	. . .	. . .
Insurance	2 253 . .	7.9	11.8	10.7	11.2	20.9	16.6	. . .	. . .
Financial	2 260 . .	35.0	30.3	23.3	44.3	45.9	37.4	. . .	. . .
Computer and information	2 262 . .	. . .	. . .	. . .	. . .	. . .	. . .	. . .	. . .
Royalties and licence fees	2 266 . .	. . .	. . .	. . .	. . .	. . .	. . .	. . .	. . .
Other business services	2 268 . .	72.0	59.8	85.2	74.2	79.8	88.2	. . .	. . .
Personal, cultural, and recreational	2 287 . .	. . .	. . .	. . .	. . .	. . .	. . .	. . .	. . .
Government, n.i.e.	2 291 . .	183.2	176.9	212.4	221.8	222.1	254.5	. . .	. . .
Other services, debit	3 200 BA	**–117.6**	**–120.0**	**–140.0**	**–162.1**	**–146.1**	**–173.1**	. . .	. . .
Communications	3 245 . .	–2.7	. . .	. . .	. . .	. . .	. . .	. . .	. . .
Construction	3 249 . .	. . .	. . .	. . .	. . .	. . .	. . .	. . .	. . .
Insurance	3 253 . .	–30.8	–32.6	–49.0	–54.1	–39.3	–64.9	. . .	. . .
Financial	3 260 . .	–15.6	–14.7	–10.6	–10.3	–12.3	–13.8	. . .	. . .
Computer and information	3 262 . .	. . .	. . .	. . .	. . .	. . .	. . .	. . .	. . .
Royalties and licence fees	3 266 . .	–9.9	–9.0	–9.3	–9.1	–10.1	–10.6	. . .	. . .
Other business services	3 268 . .	–36.5	–42.3	–46.2	–59.4	–52.4	–45.2	. . .	. . .
Personal, cultural, and recreational	3 287 . .	. . .	. . .	. . .	. . .	. . .	. . .	. . .	. . .
Government, n.i.e.	3 291 . .	–22.1	–21.4	–24.9	–29.2	–32.0	–38.6	. . .	. . .

Table 2 (Continued). STANDARD PRESENTATION, 1988–95

(Millions of U.S. dollars)

	Code	1988	1989	1990	1991	1992	1993	1994	1995
C. INCOME	4 300 . .	-88.6	-266.7	-264.3	-388.0	-397.6	-311.8	. . .	. . .
Total credit	2 300 . .	*976.2*	*976.0*	*1,139.1*	*1,078.9*	*1,139.0*	*1,301.7*	. . .	. . .
Total debit	3 300 . .	*-1,064.8*	*-1,242.7*	*-1,403.4*	*-1,466.9*	*-1,536.6*	*-1,613.5*	. . .	. . .
Compensation of employees, credit	2 310 . .	**82.7**	**88.2**	**92.0**	**93.9**	**89.0**	**92.0**	. . .	. . .
Compensation of employees, debit	3 310 . .	. . .	. . .	. . .	. . .	. . .	. . .	. . .	. . .
Investment income, credit	2 320 . .	**893.5**	**887.8**	**1,047.1**	**985.0**	**1,050.0**	**1,209.7**	. . .	. . .
Direct investment income	2 330 . .	. . .	. . .	. . .	. . .	. . .	. . .	. . .	. . .
Dividends and distributed branch profits	2 332 . .	. . .	. . .	. . .	. . .	. . .	. . .	. . .	. . .
Reinvested earnings and undistributed branch profits	2 333 . .	. . .	. . .	. . .	. . .	. . .	. . .	. . .	. . .
Income on debt (interest)	2 334 . .	. . .	. . .	. . .	. . .	. . .	. . .	. . .	. . .
Portfolio investment income	2 339 . .	. . .	. . .	. . .	. . .	. . .	. . .	. . .	. . .
Income on equity	2 340 . .	. . .	. . .	. . .	. . .	. . .	. . .	. . .	. . .
Income on bonds and notes	2 350 . .	. . .	. . .	. . .	. . .	. . .	. . .	. . .	. . .
Income on money market instruments and financial derivatives	2 360 . .	. . .	. . .	. . .	. . .	. . .	. . .	. . .	. . .
Other investment income	2 370 . .	893.5	887.8	1,047.1	985.0	1,050.0	1,209.7	. . .	. . .
Investment income, debit	3 320 . .	**-1,064.8**	**-1,242.7**	**-1,403.4**	**-1,466.9**	**-1,536.6**	**-1,613.5**	. . .	. . .
Direct investment income	3 330 . .	62.1	-103.7	-203.1	-226.7	-325.3	-317.8	. . .	. . .
Dividends and distributed branch profits	3 332 . .	-459.8	-155.3	-174.6	-150.4	-204.5	-168.9	. . .	. . .
Reinvested earnings and undistributed branch profits	3 333 . .	521.9	51.6	-28.5	-76.3	-120.8	-148.9	. . .	. . .
Income on debt (interest)	3 334 . .	. . .	. . .	. . .	. . .	. . .	. . .	. . .	. . .
Portfolio investment income	3 339 . .	-3.1	-3.1	-1.0	-.6	-.7	-.8	. . .	. . .
Income on equity	3 340 . .	-3.1	-3.1	-1.0	-.6	-.7	-.8	. . .	. . .
Income on bonds and notes	3 350 . .	. . .	. . .	. . .	. . .	. . .	. . .	. . .	. . .
Income on money market instruments and financial derivatives	3 360 . .	. . .	. . .	. . .	. . .	. . .	. . .	. . .	. . .
Other investment income	3 370 . .	-1,123.8	-1,135.9	-1,199.3	-1,239.6	-1,210.6	-1,294.9	. . .	. . .
D. CURRENT TRANSFERS	4 379 . .	108.4	95.5	219.4	222.5	333.9	203.0	. . .	. . .
Credit	2 379 . .	**153.6**	**139.7**	**248.8**	**249.8**	**362.9**	**236.4**	. . .	. . .
General government	2 380 . .	61.8	50.4	152.5	149.8	258.2	129.4	. . .	. . .
Other sectors	2 390 . .	91.8	89.3	96.3	100.0	104.7	107.0	. . .	. . .
Workers' remittances	2 391 . .	19.4	13.8	17.7	14.2	13.3	16.7	. . .	. . .
Other current transfers	2 392 . .	72.4	75.5	78.6	85.8	91.4	90.3	. . .	. . .
Debit	3 379 . .	**-45.2**	**-44.2**	**-29.4**	**-27.3**	**-29.0**	**-33.4**	. . .	. . .
General government	3 380 . .	-1.0	-5.1	-4.9	-8.4	-6.0	-6.5	. . .	. . .
Other sectors	3 390 . .	-44.2	-39.1	-24.5	-18.9	-23.0	-26.9	. . .	. . .
Workers' remittances	3 391 . .	-40.5	-35.9	-21.8	-16.1	-20.0	-23.7	. . .	. . .
Other current transfers	3 392 . .	-3.7	-3.2	-2.7	-2.8	-3.0	-3.2	. . .	. . .
CAPITAL AND FINANCIAL ACCOUNT	4 996 . .	**23.4**	**125.2**	**-72.0**	**-417.7**	**-309.6**	**-159.7**	. . .	. . .
CAPITAL ACCOUNT	4 994 . .	. . .	. . .	. . .	. . .	. . .	. . .	. . .	. . .
Total credit	2 994 . .	. . .	. . .	. . .	. . .	. . .	. . .	. . .	. . .
Total debit	3 994 . .	. . .	. . .	. . .	. . .	. . .	. . .	. . .	. . .
Capital transfers, credit	2 400 . .	. . .	. . .	. . .	. . .	. . .	. . .	. . .	. . .
General government	2 401 . .	. . .	. . .	. . .	. . .	. . .	. . .	. . .	. . .
Debt forgiveness	2 402 . .	. . .	. . .	. . .	. . .	. . .	. . .	. . .	. . .
Other capital transfers	2 410 . .	. . .	. . .	. . .	. . .	. . .	. . .	. . .	. . .
Other sectors	2 430 . .	. . .	. . .	. . .	. . .	. . .	. . .	. . .	. . .
Migrants' transfers	2 431 . .	. . .	. . .	. . .	. . .	. . .	. . .	. . .	. . .
Debt forgiveness	2 432 . .	. . .	. . .	. . .	. . .	. . .	. . .	. . .	. . .
Other capital transfers	2 440 . .	. . .	. . .	. . .	. . .	. . .	. . .	. . .	. . .
Capital transfers, debit	3 400 . .	. . .	. . .	. . .	. . .	. . .	. . .	. . .	. . .
General government	3 401 . .	. . .	. . .	. . .	. . .	. . .	. . .	. . .	. . .
Debt forgiveness	3 402 . .	. . .	. . .	. . .	. . .	. . .	. . .	. . .	. . .
Other capital transfers	3 410 . .	. . .	. . .	. . .	. . .	. . .	. . .	. . .	. . .
Other sectors	3 430 . .	. . .	. . .	. . .	. . .	. . .	. . .	. . .	. . .
Migrants' transfers	3 431 . .	. . .	. . .	. . .	. . .	. . .	. . .	. . .	. . .
Debt forgiveness	3 432 . .	. . .	. . .	. . .	. . .	. . .	. . .	. . .	. . .
Other capital transfers	3 440 . .	. . .	. . .	. . .	. . .	. . .	. . .	. . .	. . .
Nonproduced nonfinancial assets, credit	2 480 . .	. . .	. . .	. . .	. . .	. . .	. . .	. . .	. . .
Nonproduced nonfinancial assets, debit	3 480 . .	. . .	. . .	. . .	. . .	. . .	. . .	. . .	. . .

Table 2 (Continued). STANDARD PRESENTATION, 1988–95
(Millions of U.S. dollars)

	Code	1988	1989	1990	1991	1992	1993	1994	1995
FINANCIAL ACCOUNT	4 995	**23.4**	**125.2**	**–72.0**	**–417.7**	**–309.6**	**–159.7**	...	...
A. DIRECT INVESTMENT	4 500	–595.1	51.5	132.1	41.3	138.7	155.6	...	...
Direct investment abroad	4 505	...	...	...	...	...	...	...	...
Equity capital	4 510	...	...	...	...	...	...	...	...
Claims on affiliated enterprises	4 515	...	...	...	...	...	...	...	...
Liabilities to affiliated enterprises	4 520	...	...	...	...	...	...	...	...
Reinvested earnings	4 525	...	...	...	...	...	...	...	...
Other capital	4 530	...	...	...	...	...	...	...	...
Claims on affiliated enterprises	4 535	...	...	...	...	...	...	...	...
Liabilities to affiliated enterprises	4 540	...	...	...	...	...	...	...	...
Direct investment in Panama	4 555	**–595.1**	**51.5**	**132.1**	**41.3**	**138.7**	**155.6**	...	...
Equity capital	4 560	–134.6	60.9	66.6	–21.2	–3.5	–29.2	...	...
Claims on direct investors	4 565	...	...	...	...	...	...	...	...
Liabilities to direct investors	4 570	–134.6	60.9	66.6	–21.2	–3.5	–29.2	...	...
Reinvested earnings	4 575	–521.9	–51.6	28.6	76.4	120.8	148.9	...	...
Other capital	4 580	61.4	42.2	36.9	–13.9	21.4	35.9	...	...
Claims on direct investors	4 585	...	...	...	...	...	...	...	...
Liabilities to direct investors	4 590	...	...	...	...	...	...	...	...
B. PORTFOLIO INVESTMENT	4 600	2,151.6	–468.9	–238.2	–256.8	–119.1	–847.2	...	...
Assets	4 602	**2,216.4**	**–439.0**	**–203.4**	**–230.9**	**–49.4**	**–792.5**	...	...
Equity securities	4 610	.7	...	–1.0	1.8	–1.5	–.1	...	...
Monetary authorities	4 611	...	...	...	...	...	...	...	...
General government	4 612	...	...	...	...	...	...	...	...
Banks	4 613	...	...	...	...	...	...	...	...
Other sectors	4 614	.7	...	–1.0	1.8	–1.5	–.1	...	...
Debt securities	4 619	2,215.7	–439.0	–202.4	–232.7	–47.9	–792.4	...	...
Bonds and notes	4 620	2,215.7	–439.0	–202.4	–232.7	–47.9	–792.4	...	...
Monetary authorities	4 621	...	...	...	...	...	...	...	...
General government	4 622	...	...	...	...	...	...	...	...
Banks	4 623	2,218.3	–438.2	–200.0	–222.6	–46.3	–754.6	...	...
Other sectors	4 624	–2.6	–.8	–2.4	–10.1	–1.6	–37.8	...	...
Money market instruments	4 630	...	...	...	...	...	...	...	...
Monetary authorities	4 631	...	...	...	...	...	...	...	...
General government	4 632	...	...	...	...	...	...	...	...
Banks	4 633	...	...	...	...	...	...	...	...
Other sectors	4 634	...	...	...	...	...	...	...	...
Financial derivatives	4 640	...	...	...	...	...	...	...	...
Monetary authorities	4 641	...	...	...	...	...	...	...	...
General government	4 642	...	...	...	...	...	...	...	...
Banks	4 643	...	...	...	...	...	...	...	...
Other sectors	4 644	...	...	...	...	...	...	...	...
Liabilities	4 652	**–64.8**	**–29.9**	**–34.8**	**–25.9**	**–69.7**	**–54.7**	...	...
Equity securities	4 660	...	...	...	...	...	...	...	...
Banks	4 663	...	...	...	...	...	...	...	...
Other sectors	4 664	...	...	...	...	...	...	...	...
Debt securities	4 669	–64.8	–29.9	–34.8	–25.9	–69.7	–54.7	...	...
Bonds and notes	4 670	–64.8	–29.9	–34.8	–25.9	–69.7	–54.7	...	...
Monetary authorities	4 671	...	...	...	...	...	...	...	...
General government	4 672	–64.8	–29.9	–34.8	–25.9	–69.7	–54.7	...	...
Banks	4 673	...	...	...	...	...	...	...	...
Other sectors	4 674	...	...	...	...	...	...	...	...
Money market instruments	4 680	...	...	...	...	...	...	...	...
Monetary authorities	4 681	...	...	...	...	...	...	...	...
General government	4 682	...	...	...	...	...	...	...	...
Banks	4 683	...	...	...	...	...	...	...	...
Other sectors	4 684	...	...	...	...	...	...	...	...
Financial derivatives	4 690	...	...	...	...	...	...	...	...
Monetary authorities	4 691	...	...	...	...	...	...	...	...
General government	4 692	...	...	...	...	...	...	...	...
Banks	4 693	...	...	...	...	...	...	...	...
Other sectors	4 694	...	...	...	...	...	...	...	...

Table 2 (Concluded). STANDARD PRESENTATION, 1988–95
(Millions of U.S. dollars)

	Code	1988	1989	1990	1991	1992	1993	1994	1995
C. OTHER INVESTMENT	4 700	–1,538.6	590.5	389.9	–53.8	–445.4	624.9	. . .	. . .
Assets	4 703	**12,830.5**	**–433.8**	**–1,405.7**	**–1,353.7**	**–1,492.9**	**–1,176.0**	**. . .**	**. . .**
Trade credits	4 706	–88.1	–41.6	21.9	–86.1	–35.0	–27.3	. . .	. . .
General government: long-term	4 708	. . .	. . .	. . .	. . .	. . .	. . .	. . .	. . .
General government: short-term	4 709	. . .	. . .	. . .	. . .	. . .	. . .	. . .	. . .
Other sectors: long-term	4 711	–.4	–118.5	30.0	–33.6	–25.4	–7.1	. . .	. . .
Other sectors: short-term	4 712	–87.7	76.9	–8.1	–52.5	–9.6	–20.2	. . .	. . .
Loans	4 714	7,570.1	–167.9	–882.6	–202.5	–1,194.0	–1,480.3	. . .	. . .
Monetary authorities: long-term	4 717	. . .	. . .	. . .	. . .	. . .	. . .	. . .	. . .
Monetary authorities: short-term	4 718	. . .	. . .	. . .	. . .	. . .	. . .	. . .	. . .
General government: long-term	4 720	. . .	. . .	. . .	. . .	. . .	. . .	. . .	. . .
General government: short-term	4 721	. . .	. . .	. . .	. . .	. . .	. . .	. . .	. . .
Banks: long-term	4 723	. . .	. . .	. . .	. . .	. . .	. . .	. . .	. . .
Banks: short-term	4 724	7,570.1	–167.9	–882.6	–202.5	–1,194.0	–1,480.3	. . .	. . .
Other sectors: long-term	4 726	. . .	. . .	. . .	. . .	. . .	. . .	. . .	. . .
Other sectors: short-term	4 727	. . .	. . .	. . .	. . .	. . .	. . .	. . .	. . .
Currency and deposits	4 730	3,880.2	385.7	–267.8	–1,223.8	–53.2	–301.5	. . .	. . .
Monetary authorities	4 731	. . .	. . .	. . .	. . .	. . .	. . .	. . .	. . .
General government	4 732	. . .	. . .	. . .	. . .	. . .	. . .	. . .	. . .
Banks	4 733	3,880.2	385.7	–267.8	–1,223.8	–53.2	–301.5	. . .	. . .
Other sectors	4 734	. . .	. . .	. . .	. . .	. . .	. . .	. . .	. . .
Other assets	4 736	1,468.3	–610.0	–277.2	158.7	–210.7	633.1	. . .	. . .
Monetary authorities: long-term	4 738	. . .	. . .	. . .	. . .	. . .	. . .	. . .	. . .
Monetary authorities: short-term	4 739	. . .	. . .	. . .	. . .	. . .	. . .	. . .	. . .
General government: long-term	4 741	–164.8	–135.2	299.1	–.9	–.9	–.9	. . .	. . .
General government: short-term	4 742	. . .	. . .	. . .	. . .	. . .	. . .	. . .	. . .
Banks: long-term	4 744	. . .	. . .	. . .	. . .	. . .	. . .	. . .	. . .
Banks: short-term	4 745	1,720.0	–370.8	–772.9	166.8	–195.7	640.9	. . .	. . .
Other sectors: long-term	4 747	–.5	. . .	–2.8	. . .	–1.4	–.4	. . .	. . .
Other sectors: short-term	4 748	–86.4	–104.0	199.4	–7.2	–12.7	–6.5	. . .	. . .
Liabilities	4 753	**–14,369.1**	**1,024.3**	**1,795.6**	**1,299.9**	**1,047.5**	**1,800.9**	**. . .**	**. . .**
Trade credits	4 756	. . .	. . .	. . .	. . .	. . .	. . .	. . .	. . .
General government: long-term	4 758	. . .	. . .	. . .	. . .	. . .	. . .	. . .	. . .
General government: short-term	4 759	. . .	. . .	. . .	. . .	. . .	. . .	. . .	. . .
Other sectors: long-term	4 761	. . .	. . .	. . .	. . .	. . .	. . .	. . .	. . .
Other sectors: short-term	4 762	. . .	. . .	. . .	. . .	. . .	. . .	. . .	. . .
Loans	4 764	–2,434.3	–307.9	–283.1	70.2	110.3	376.1	. . .	. . .
Use of Fund credit and loans from the Fund	4 766	–.1	–.8	–70.7	–55.7	–98.6	3.4	. . .	. . .
Monetary authorities: other long-term	4 767	–1.5	6.6	2.8	–1.6	–17.2	–4.4	. . .	. . .
Monetary authorities: short-term	4 768	. . .	. . .	. . .	. . .	. . .	. . .	. . .	. . .
General government: long-term	4 770	–345.9	–279.5	–128.5	–174.0	188.4	–117.8	. . .	. . .
General government: short-term	4 771	–3.4	9.1	–3.2	–4.8	–.4	–.3	. . .	. . .
Banks: long-term	4 773	–102.0	47.8	–29.4	257.4	167.3	577.4	. . .	. . .
Banks: short-term	4 774	–1,870.4	–18.9	–.6	39.5	–45.6	–29.6	. . .	. . .
Other sectors: long-term	4 776	–151.4	–100.9	–70.5	–52.8	–127.6	–46.9	. . .	. . .
Other sectors: short-term	4 777	40.4	28.7	17.0	62.2	44.0	–5.7	. . .	. . .
Currency and deposits	4 780	–9,161.3	–453.9	62.9	1,048.6	512.4	2,219.1	. . .	. . .
Monetary authorities	4 781	. . .	. . .	. . .	. . .	20.0	. . .	. . .	. . .
General government	4 782	. . .	. . .	. . .	. . .	. . .	. . .	. . .	. . .
Banks	4 783	–9,161.3	–453.9	62.9	1,048.6	492.4	2,219.1	. . .	. . .
Other sectors	4 784	. . .	. . .	. . .	. . .	. . .	. . .	. . .	. . .
Other liabilities	4 786	–2,773.5	1,786.1	2,015.8	181.1	424.8	–794.3	. . .	. . .
Monetary authorities: long-term	4 788	–90.3	–58.8	–27.0	. . .	. . .	. . .	. . .	. . .
Monetary authorities: short-term	4 789	116.0	88.6	35.9	2.8	–58.8	1.2	. . .	. . .
General government: long-term	4 791	. . .	. . .	. . .	. . .	. . .	. . .	. . .	. . .
General government: short-term	4 792	671.4	593.8	406.0	444.8	51.2	369.1	. . .	. . .
Banks: long-term	4 794	. . .	. . .	. . .	. . .	. . .	. . .	. . .	. . .
Banks: short-term	4 795	–3,706.6	966.6	1,483.2	–399.8	565.6	–1,160.2	. . .	. . .
Other sectors: long-term	4 797	.6	.5	–5.0	.5	1.4	2.1	. . .	. . .
Other sectors: short-term	4 798	235.4	195.4	122.7	132.8	–134.6	–6.5	. . .	. . .
D. RESERVE ASSETS	4 800	5.5	–47.9	–355.8	–148.3	116.2	–93.0	. . .	. . .
Monetary gold	4 810	. . .	. . .	. . .	. . .	. . .	. . .	. . .	. . .
Special drawing rights	4 820	. . .	. . .	–27.7	16.1	6.8	4.5	. . .	. . .
Reserve position in the Fund	4 830	. . .	. . .	. . .	. . .	–16.4	. . .	. . .	. . .
Foreign exchange	4 840	5.5	–47.9	–199.3	–159.2	–8.2	–97.5	. . .	. . .
Other claims	4 880	. . .	. . .	–128.8	–5.2	134.0	. . .	. . .	. . .
NET ERRORS AND OMISSIONS	4 998	**–744.3**	**–236.1**	**–134.5**	**633.8**	**455.4**	**301.0**	**. . .**	**. . .**

Part 3 of the *Yearbook* contains descriptions of the methodologies, compilation practices, and sources used to compile these data.

Table 1. ANALYTIC PRESENTATION, 1988–95
(Millions of U.S. dollars)

	Code	1988	1989	1990	1991	1992	1993	1994	1995
A. Current Account[1]	4 993 Y.	**–296.4**	**–312.7**	**–75.7**	**–156.5**	**95.1**	**646.0**	**569.3**	**673.9**
Goods: exports f.o.b.	2 100 . .	1,475.3	1,318.5	1,175.2	1,482.1	1,947.7	2,604.4	2,651.0	2,670.4
Goods: imports f.o.b.	3 100 . .	–1,384.5	–1,341.3	–1,105.9	–1,403.9	–1,322.9	–1,134.7	–1,324.9	–1,262.4
Balance on Goods	4 100 . .	*90.8*	*–22.8*	*69.2*	*78.1*	*624.9*	*1,469.7*	*1,326.1*	*1,408.0*
Services: credit	2 200 . .	122.3	167.9	205.7	303.3	349.6	316.9	246.1	309.4
Services: debit	3 200 . .	–435.1	–408.8	–402.9	–543.0	–685.8	–806.7	–609.2	–613.4
Balance on Goods and Services	4 991 . .	*–222.0*	*–263.7*	*–128.0*	*–161.6*	*288.7*	*979.9*	*963.0*	*1,104.1*
Income: credit	2 300 . .	118.6	87.0	106.6	70.6	39.3	23.4	11.7	34.4
Income: debit	3 300 . .	–326.2	–265.2	–209.9	–320.4	–425.3	–400.2	–421.9	–539.5
Balance on Goods, Services, and Income	4 992 . .	*–429.6*	*–441.9*	*–231.2*	*–411.4*	*–97.4*	*603.1*	*552.9*	*599.0*
Current transfers: credit	2 379 Y.	249.4	256.3	273.7	361.0	303.6	220.8	225.7	248.8
Current transfers: debit	3 379 . .	–116.2	–127.2	–118.1	–106.2	–111.1	–178.0	–209.3	–173.9
B. Capital Account[1]	4 994 Y.	**–40.1**	**–42.6**	**–37.3**	**. . .**	**. . .**	**. . .**	**. . .**	**. . .**
Capital account: credit	2 994 Y.	10.0	7.2	5.4	21.0	20.7	20.4	19.9	15.7
Capital account: debit	3 994 . .	–50.1	–49.8	–42.7	–21.0	–20.7	–20.4	–19.9	–15.7
Total, Groups A Plus B	4 010 . .	*–336.5*	*–355.3*	*–113.0*	*–156.5*	*95.1*	*646.0*	*569.3*	*673.9*
C. Financial Account[1]	4 995 X.	**245.1**	**265.0**	**214.4**	**64.5**	**–148.3**	**–715.4**	**–600.1**	**–478.6**
Direct investment abroad	4 505 . .	–33.8	17.9	. . .	. . .	. . .	. . .	. . .	. . .
Direct investment in Papua New Guinea	4 555 Y.	153.5	203.4	155.4	202.5	293.6	–1.7	–4.9	453.4
Portfolio investment assets	4 602 . .	. . .	. . .	. . .	. . .	. . .	. . .	. . .	–1,373.0
Equity securities	4 610 . .	. . .	. . .	. . .	. . .	. . .	. . .	. . .	. . .
Debt securities	4 619 . .	. . .	. . .	. . .	. . .	. . .	. . .	. . .	–1,373.0
Portfolio investment liabilities	4 652 Y.	. . .	. . .	. . .	. . .	. . .	. . .	. . .	1,066.2
Equity securities	4 660 Y.	. . .	. . .	. . .	. . .	. . .	. . .	. . .	. . .
Debt securities	4 669 Y.	. . .	. . .	. . .	. . .	. . .	. . .	. . .	1,066.2
Other investment assets	4 703 . .	. . .	. . .	. . .	. . .	. . .	. . .	. . .	–283.8
Monetary authorities	4 703 . A	. . .	. . .	. . .	. . .	. . .	. . .	. . .	. . .
General government	4 703 . B	. . .	. . .	. . .	. . .	. . .	. . .	. . .	. . .
Banks	4 703 . C	. . .	. . .	. . .	. . .	. . .	. . .	. . .	. . .
Other sectors	4 703 . D	. . .	. . .	. . .	. . .	. . .	. . .	. . .	–283.8
Other investment liabilities	4 753 X.	125.4	43.7	59.0	–138.0	–441.9	–713.7	–595.2	–341.4
Monetary authorities	4 753 XA	. . .	. . .	. . .	. . .	. . .	. . .	. . .	. . .
General government	4 753 YB	27.2	–18.4	88.1	–38.6	59.6	66.5	–102.1	–23.5
Banks	4 753 YC	34.6	13.0	–23.4	. . .	–36.1	–110.3	–7.9	–6.5
Other sectors	4 753 YD	63.6	49.1	–5.6	–99.5	–465.5	–670.0	–485.2	–311.5
Total, Groups A Through C	4 020 . .	*–91.4*	*–90.3*	*101.5*	*–92.0*	*–53.2*	*–69.4*	*–30.9*	*195.3*
D. Net Errors and Omissions	4 998 . .	**37.9**	**31.6**	**–79.7**	**6.8**	**–18.0**	**–12.2**	**28.3**	**–53.3**
Total, Groups A Through D	4 030 . .	*–53.5*	*–58.7*	*21.7*	*–85.2*	*–71.2*	*–81.6*	*–2.5*	*142.1*
E. Reserves and Related Items	4 040 . .	**53.5**	**58.7**	**–21.7**	**85.2**	**71.2**	**81.6**	**2.5**	**–142.1**
Reserve assets	4 800 . .	58.7	61.6	–75.2	85.3	71.2	96.6	33.1	–177.1
Use of Fund credit and loans	4 766 . .	–5.2	–2.9	53.5	–.1	. . .	–15.0	–30.6	35.0
Liabilities constituting foreign authorities' reserves	4 900 . .	. . .	. . .	. . .	. . .	. . .	. . .	. . .	. . .
Exceptional financing	4 920 . .	. . .	. . .	. . .	. . .	. . .	. . .	. . .	. . .
Conversion rates: kina per U.S. dollar	0 101 . .	**.8671**	**.8588**	**.9550**	**.9517**	**.9647**	**.9782**	**1.0113**	**1.2798**

[1] Excludes components that have been classified in the categories of Group E.

Table 2. STANDARD PRESENTATION, 1988–95
(Millions of U.S. dollars)

	Code	1988	1989	1990	1991	1992	1993	1994	1995
CURRENT ACCOUNT	4 993 . .	**-296.4**	**-312.7**	**-75.7**	**-156.5**	**95.1**	**646.0**	**569.3**	**673.9**
A. GOODS	4 100 . .	90.8	-22.8	69.2	78.1	624.9	1,469.7	1,326.1	1,408.0
Credit	2 100 . .	**1,475.3**	**1,318.5**	**1,175.2**	**1,482.1**	**1,947.7**	**2,604.4**	**2,651.0**	**2,670.4**
General merchandise: exports f.o.b.	2 110 . .	1,475.3	1,318.5	1,175.2	1,482.1	1,947.7	2,604.4	2,651.0	2,670.4
Goods for processing: exports f.o.b.	2 150 . .	. . .	. . .	. . .	. . .	. . .	. . .	. . .	. . .
Repairs on goods	2 160 . .	. . .	. . .	. . .	. . .	. . .	. . .	. . .	. . .
Goods procured in ports by carriers	2 170 . .	. . .	. . .	. . .	. . .	. . .	. . .	. . .	. . .
Nonmonetary gold	2 180 . .	. . .	. . .	. . .	. . .	. . .	. . .	. . .	. . .
Debit	3 100 . .	**-1,384.5**	**-1,341.3**	**-1,105.9**	**-1,403.9**	**-1,322.9**	**-1,134.7**	**-1,324.9**	**-1,262.4**
General merchandise: imports f.o.b.	3 110 . .	-1,384.5	-1,341.3	-1,105.9	-1,403.9	-1,322.9	-1,134.7	-1,324.9	-1,262.4
Goods for processing: imports f.o.b.	3 150 . .	. . .	. . .	. . .	. . .	. . .	. . .	. . .	. . .
Repairs on goods	3 160 . .	. . .	. . .	. . .	. . .	. . .	. . .	. . .	. . .
Goods procured in ports by carriers	3 170 . .	. . .	. . .	. . .	. . .	. . .	. . .	. . .	. . .
Nonmonetary gold	3 180 . .	. . .	. . .	. . .	. . .	. . .	. . .	. . .	. . .
B. SERVICES	4 200 . .	-312.8	-240.9	-197.2	-239.8	-336.2	-489.8	-363.1	-303.9
Total credit	2 200 . .	*122.3*	*167.9*	*205.7*	*303.3*	*349.6*	*316.9*	*246.1*	*309.4*
Total debit	3 200 . .	*-435.1*	*-408.8*	*-402.9*	*-543.0*	*-685.8*	*-806.7*	*-609.2*	*-613.4*
Transportation services, credit	2 205 . .	**21.4**	**30.0**	**22.2**	**14.4**	**23.4**	**25.4**	**37.4**	**38.6**
Passenger	2 205 BA	*11.8*	*20.3*	*13.7*	. . .	. . .	. . .	. . .	. . .
Freight	2 205 BB	*9.6*	*9.6*	*8.5*	*14.4*	*23.4*	*25.4*	*37.4*	*38.6*
Other	2 205 BC	. . .	. . .	. . .	. . .	. . .	. . .	. . .	. . .
Sea transport, passenger	2 207 . .	. . .	. . .	. . .	. . .	. . .	. . .	. . .	. . .
Sea transport, freight	2 208 . .	. . .	. . .	. . .	. . .	. . .	. . .	. . .	. . .
Sea transport, other	2 209 . .	. . .	. . .	. . .	. . .	. . .	. . .	. . .	. . .
Air transport, passenger	2 211 . .	. . .	. . .	. . .	. . .	. . .	. . .	. . .	. . .
Air transport, freight	2 212 . .	. . .	. . .	. . .	. . .	. . .	. . .	. . .	. . .
Air transport, other	2 213 . .	. . .	. . .	. . .	. . .	. . .	. . .	. . .	. . .
Other transport, passenger	2 215 . .	. . .	. . .	. . .	. . .	. . .	. . .	. . .	. . .
Other transport, freight	2 216 . .	. . .	. . .	. . .	. . .	. . .	. . .	. . .	. . .
Other transport, other	2 217 . .	. . .	. . .	. . .	. . .	. . .	. . .	. . .	. . .
Transportation services, debit	3 205 . .	**-198.7**	**-170.1**	**-140.1**	**-139.0**	**-125.0**	**-132.4**	**-174.3**	**-179.7**
Passenger	3 205 BA	*-54.9*	. . .	. . .	. . .	. . .	. . .	. . .	. . .
Freight	3 205 BB	*-143.8*	*-170.1*	*-140.1*	*-139.0*	*-125.0*	*-132.4*	*-174.3*	*-179.7*
Other	3 205 BC	. . .	. . .	. . .	. . .	. . .	. . .	. . .	. . .
Sea transport, passenger	3 207 . .	. . .	. . .	. . .	. . .	. . .	. . .	. . .	. . .
Sea transport, freight	3 208 . .	. . .	. . .	. . .	. . .	. . .	. . .	. . .	. . .
Sea transport, other	3 209 . .	. . .	. . .	. . .	. . .	. . .	. . .	. . .	. . .
Air transport, passenger	3 211 . .	. . .	. . .	. . .	. . .	. . .	. . .	. . .	. . .
Air transport, freight	3 212 . .	. . .	. . .	. . .	. . .	. . .	. . .	. . .	. . .
Air transport, other	3 213 . .	. . .	. . .	. . .	. . .	. . .	. . .	. . .	. . .
Other transport, passenger	3 215 . .	. . .	. . .	. . .	. . .	. . .	. . .	. . .	. . .
Other transport, freight	3 216 . .	. . .	. . .	. . .	. . .	. . .	. . .	. . .	. . .
Other transport, other	3 217 . .	. . .	. . .	. . .	. . .	. . .	. . .	. . .	. . .
Travel, credit	2 236 . .	**17.0**	**20.8**	**23.8**	**25.2**	**20.8**	**21.8**	**30.0**	**25.2**
Business travel	2 237 . .	. . .	. . .	. . .	. . .	. . .	. . .	. . .	. . .
Personal travel	2 240 . .	. . .	. . .	. . .	. . .	. . .	. . .	. . .	. . .
Travel, debit	3 236 . .	**-47.9**	**-42.2**	**-50.5**	**-56.5**	**-56.6**	**-68.9**	**-70.5**	**-58.2**
Business travel	3 237 . .	. . .	. . .	. . .	. . .	. . .	. . .	. . .	. . .
Personal travel	3 240 . .	. . .	. . .	. . .	. . .	. . .	. . .	. . .	. . .
Other services, credit	2 200 BA	**83.9**	**117.1**	**159.7**	**263.7**	**305.3**	**269.8**	**178.8**	**245.7**
Communications	2 245 . .	. . .	. . .	. . .	. . .	. . .	. . .	. . .	. . .
Construction	2 249 . .	. . .	. . .	. . .	. . .	. . .	. . .	. . .	. . .
Insurance	2 253 . .	1.1	1.1	.9	1.6	2.6	2.8	4.2	. . .
Financial	2 260 . .	. . .	. . .	. . .	. . .	. . .	. . .	. . .	. . .
Computer and information	2 262 . .	. . .	. . .	. . .	. . .	. . .	. . .	. . .	. . .
Royalties and licence fees	2 266 . .	. . .	. . .	. . .	. . .	. . .	. . .	. . .	. . .
Other business services	2 268 . .	59.6	96.1	151.2	262.1	302.7	267.0	174.6	245.7
Personal, cultural, and recreational	2 287 . .	. . .	. . .	. . .	. . .	. . .	. . .	. . .	. . .
Government, n.i.e.	2 291 . .	23.3	20.0	7.6	. . .	. . .	. . .	. . .	. . .
Other services, debit	3 200 BA	**-188.5**	**-196.6**	**-212.4**	**-347.5**	**-504.2**	**-605.4**	**-364.3**	**-375.4**
Communications	3 245 . .	. . .	. . .	. . .	. . .	. . .	. . .	. . .	. . .
Construction	3 249 . .	. . .	. . .	. . .	. . .	. . .	. . .	. . .	. . .
Insurance	3 253 . .	-16.0	-18.9	-15.6	-15.4	-13.9	-14.7	-19.4	. . .
Financial	3 260 . .	. . .	. . .	. . .	. . .	. . .	. . .	. . .	. . .
Computer and information	3 262 . .	. . .	. . .	. . .	. . .	. . .	. . .	. . .	. . .
Royalties and licence fees	3 266 . .	. . .	. . .	. . .	. . .	. . .	. . .	. . .	. . .
Other business services	3 268 . .	-154.4	-158.8	-187.1	-332.1	-490.3	-590.7	-345.0	-375.4
Personal, cultural, and recreational	3 287 . .	. . .	. . .	. . .	. . .	. . .	. . .	. . .	. . .
Government, n.i.e.	3 291 . .	-18.1	-18.9	-9.7	. . .	. . .	. . .	. . .	. . .

Table 2 (Continued). STANDARD PRESENTATION, 1988–95
(Millions of U.S. dollars)

	Code	1988	1989	1990	1991	1992	1993	1994	1995
C. INCOME	4 300 . .	–207.6	–178.2	–103.3	–249.7	–386.0	–376.8	–410.1	–505.1
Total credit	2 300 . .	*118.6*	*87.0*	*106.6*	*70.6*	*39.3*	*23.4*	*11.7*	*34.4*
Total debit	3 300 . .	*–326.2*	*–265.2*	*–209.9*	*–320.4*	*–425.3*	*–400.2*	*–421.9*	*–539.5*
Compensation of employees, credit	2 310 . .	...	...	...	...	...	...	...	...
Compensation of employees, debit	3 310 . .	...	...	...	...	...	...	...	...
Investment income, credit	2 320 . .	**118.6**	**87.0**	**106.6**	**70.6**	**39.3**	**23.4**	**11.7**	**34.4**
Direct investment income	2 330 . .	...	...	...	23.1	1.5	10.3	.1	3.9
Dividends and distributed branch profits	2 332 . .	...	...	...	23.1	1.5	10.3	.1	3.9
Reinvested earnings and undistributed branch profits	2 333 . .	...	...	...	...	...	...	...	...
Income on debt (interest)	2 334 . .	...	...	...	...	...	...	...	...
Portfolio investment income	2 339 . .	...	...	...	...	...	...	...	...
Income on equity	2 340 . .	...	...	...	...	...	...	...	...
Income on bonds and notes	2 350 . .	...	...	...	...	...	...	...	...
Income on money market instruments and financial derivatives	2 360 . .	...	...	...	...	...	...	...	...
Other investment income	2 370 . .	118.6	87.0	106.6	47.5	37.8	13.1	11.7	30.5
Investment income, debit	3 320 . .	**–326.2**	**–265.2**	**–209.9**	**–320.4**	**–425.3**	**–400.2**	**–421.9**	**–539.5**
Direct investment income	3 330 . .	–244.3	–209.4	–157.7	–190.4	–267.9	–251.0	–247.7	–408.9
Dividends and distributed branch profits	3 332 . .	–175.0	–139.6	–94.9	–127.4	–205.7	–189.6	–188.0	–361.9
Reinvested earnings and undistributed branch profits	3 333 . .	–69.2	–69.9	–62.8	–63.0	–62.2	–61.3	–59.7	–47.0
Income on debt (interest)	3 334 . .	...	...	...	...	...	...	...	...
Portfolio investment income	3 339 . .	...	...	...	...	...	...	...	...
Income on equity	3 340 . .	...	...	...	...	...	...	...	...
Income on bonds and notes	3 350 . .	...	...	...	...	...	...	...	...
Income on money market instruments and financial derivatives	3 360 . .	...	...	...	...	...	...	...	...
Other investment income	3 370 . .	–81.9	–55.7	–52.2	–129.9	–157.4	–149.2	–174.1	–130.6
D. CURRENT TRANSFERS	4 379 . .	133.2	129.2	155.6	254.9	192.5	42.9	16.4	74.9
Credit	2 379 . .	**249.4**	**256.3**	**273.7**	**361.0**	**303.6**	**220.8**	**225.7**	**248.8**
General government	2 380 . .	217.7	217.3	225.4	324.2	255.0	171.8	166.8	181.9
Other sectors	2 390 . .	31.7	39.1	48.3	36.9	48.6	49.0	58.8	66.9
Workers' remittances	2 391 . .	...	...	...	...	...	...	...	...
Other current transfers	2 392 . .	31.7	39.1	48.3	36.9	48.6	49.0	58.8	66.9
Debit	3 379 . .	**–116.2**	**–127.2**	**–118.1**	**–106.2**	**–111.1**	**–178.0**	**–209.3**	**–173.9**
General government	3 380 . .	...	...	...	...	...	...	...	...
Other sectors	3 390 . .	–116.2	–127.2	–118.1	–106.2	–111.1	–178.0	–209.3	–173.9
Workers' remittances	3 391 . .	...	...	...	...	...	...	...	...
Other current transfers	3 392 . .	–116.2	–127.2	–118.1	–106.2	–111.1	–178.0	–209.3	–173.9
CAPITAL AND FINANCIAL ACCOUNT	4 996 . .	**258.5**	**281.1**	**155.4**	**149.7**	**–77.1**	**–633.7**	**–597.6**	**–620.7**
CAPITAL ACCOUNT	4 994 . .	**–40.1**	**–42.6**	**–37.3**	...	...	...	...	...
Total credit	2 994 . .	*10.0*	*7.2*	*5.4*	*21.0*	*20.7*	*20.4*	*19.9*	*15.7*
Total debit	3 994 . .	*–50.1*	*–49.8*	*–42.7*	*–21.0*	*–20.7*	*–20.4*	*–19.9*	*–15.7*
Capital transfers, credit	2 400 . .	**10.0**	**7.2**	**5.4**	**21.0**	**20.7**	**20.4**	**19.9**	**15.7**
General government	2 401 . .	...	...	...	...	...	...	...	...
Debt forgiveness	2 402 . .	...	...	...	...	...	...	...	...
Other capital transfers	2 410 . .	...	...	...	...	...	...	...	...
Other sectors	2 430 . .	10.0	7.2	5.4	21.0	20.7	20.4	19.9	15.7
Migrants' transfers	2 431 . .	10.0	7.2	5.4	21.0	20.7	20.4	19.9	15.7
Debt forgiveness	2 432 . .	...	...	...	...	...	...	...	...
Other capital transfers	2 440 . .	...	...	...	...	...	...	...	...
Capital transfers, debit	3 400 . .	**–50.1**	**–49.8**	**–42.7**	**–21.0**	**–20.7**	**–20.4**	**–19.9**	**–15.7**
General government	3 401 . .	...	...	...	...	...	...	...	...
Debt forgiveness	3 402 . .	...	...	...	...	...	...	...	...
Other capital transfers	3 410 . .	...	...	...	...	...	...	...	...
Other sectors	3 430 . .	–50.1	–49.8	–42.7	–21.0	–20.7	–20.4	–19.9	–15.7
Migrants' transfers	3 431 . .	–50.1	–49.8	–42.7	–21.0	–20.7	–20.4	–19.9	–15.7
Debt forgiveness	3 432 . .	...	...	...	...	...	...	...	...
Other capital transfers	3 440 . .	...	...	...	...	...	...	...	...
Nonproduced nonfinancial assets, credit	2 480 . .	...	...	...	...	...	...	...	...
Nonproduced nonfinancial assets, debit	3 480 . .	...	...	...	...	...	...	...	...

Table 2 (Continued). STANDARD PRESENTATION, 1988–95
(Millions of U.S. dollars)

	Code	1988	1989	1990	1991	1992	1993	1994	1995
FINANCIAL ACCOUNT	4 995	**298.5**	**323.7**	**192.7**	**149.7**	**–77.1**	**–633.7**	**–597.6**	**–620.7**
A. DIRECT INVESTMENT	4 500	119.7	221.3	155.4	202.5	293.6	–1.7	–4.9	453.4
Direct investment abroad	4 505	**–33.8**	**17.9**	**. . .**	**. . .**	**. . .**	**. . .**	**. . .**	**. . .**
Equity capital	4 510	. . .	. . .	. . .	. . .	. . .	. . .	. . .	. . .
Claims on affiliated enterprises	4 515	. . .	. . .	. . .	. . .	. . .	. . .	. . .	. . .
Liabilities to affiliated enterprises	4 520	. . .	. . .	. . .	. . .	. . .	. . .	. . .	. . .
Reinvested earnings	4 525	. . .	. . .	. . .	. . .	. . .	. . .	. . .	. . .
Other capital	4 530	–33.8	17.9	. . .	. . .	. . .	. . .	. . .	. . .
Claims on affiliated enterprises	4 535	. . .	. . .	. . .	. . .	. . .	. . .	. . .	. . .
Liabilities to affiliated enterprises	4 540	. . .	. . .	. . .	. . .	. . .	. . .	. . .	. . .
Direct investment in Papua New Guinea	4 555	**153.5**	**203.4**	**155.4**	**202.5**	**293.6**	**–1.7**	**–4.9**	**453.4**
Equity capital	4 560	. . .	. . .	. . .	53.7	42.1	.7	. . .	406.4
Claims on direct investors	4 565	. . .	. . .	. . .	. . .	. . .	. . .	. . .	407.6
Liabilities to direct investors	4 570	. . .	. . .	. . .	. . .	. . .	. . .	. . .	–1.1
Reinvested earnings	4 575	69.2	69.9	62.8	63.0	62.2	61.3	59.7	47.0
Other capital	4 580	84.3	133.5	92.6	85.8	189.3	–63.7	–64.7	. . .
Claims on direct investors	4 585	. . .	. . .	. . .	. . .	. . .	. . .	. . .	. . .
Liabilities to direct investors	4 590	. . .	. . .	. . .	. . .	. . .	. . .	. . .	. . .
B. PORTFOLIO INVESTMENT	4 600	. . .	. . .	. . .	. . .	. . .	. . .	. . .	–306.8
Assets	4 602	**. . .**	**. . .**	**. . .**	**. . .**	**. . .**	**. . .**	**. . .**	**–1,373.0**
Equity securities	4 610	. . .	. . .	. . .	. . .	. . .	. . .	. . .	. . .
Monetary authorities	4 611	. . .	. . .	. . .	. . .	. . .	. . .	. . .	. . .
General government	4 612	. . .	. . .	. . .	. . .	. . .	. . .	. . .	. . .
Banks	4 613	. . .	. . .	. . .	. . .	. . .	. . .	. . .	. . .
Other sectors	4 614	. . .	. . .	. . .	. . .	. . .	. . .	. . .	. . .
Debt securities	4 619	. . .	. . .	. . .	. . .	. . .	. . .	. . .	–1,373.0
Bonds and notes	4 620	. . .	. . .	. . .	. . .	. . .	. . .	. . .	. . .
Monetary authorities	4 621	. . .	. . .	. . .	. . .	. . .	. . .	. . .	. . .
General government	4 622	. . .	. . .	. . .	. . .	. . .	. . .	. . .	. . .
Banks	4 623	. . .	. . .	. . .	. . .	. . .	. . .	. . .	. . .
Other sectors	4 624	. . .	. . .	. . .	. . .	. . .	. . .	. . .	. . .
Money market instruments	4 630	. . .	. . .	. . .	. . .	. . .	. . .	. . .	–1,373.0
Monetary authorities	4 631	. . .	. . .	. . .	. . .	. . .	. . .	. . .	. . .
General government	4 632	. . .	. . .	. . .	. . .	. . .	. . .	. . .	. . .
Banks	4 633	. . .	. . .	. . .	. . .	. . .	. . .	. . .	–258.1
Other sectors	4 634	. . .	. . .	. . .	. . .	. . .	. . .	. . .	–1,114.9
Financial derivatives	4 640	. . .	. . .	. . .	. . .	. . .	. . .	. . .	. . .
Monetary authorities	4 641	. . .	. . .	. . .	. . .	. . .	. . .	. . .	. . .
General government	4 642	. . .	. . .	. . .	. . .	. . .	. . .	. . .	. . .
Banks	4 643	. . .	. . .	. . .	. . .	. . .	. . .	. . .	. . .
Other sectors	4 644	. . .	. . .	. . .	. . .	. . .	. . .	. . .	. . .
Liabilities	4 652	**. . .**	**. . .**	**. . .**	**. . .**	**. . .**	**. . .**	**. . .**	**1,066.2**
Equity securities	4 660	. . .	. . .	. . .	. . .	. . .	. . .	. . .	. . .
Banks	4 663	. . .	. . .	. . .	. . .	. . .	. . .	. . .	. . .
Other sectors	4 664	. . .	. . .	. . .	. . .	. . .	. . .	. . .	. . .
Debt securities	4 669	. . .	. . .	. . .	. . .	. . .	. . .	. . .	1,066.2
Bonds and notes	4 670	. . .	. . .	. . .	. . .	. . .	. . .	. . .	. . .
Monetary authorities	4 671	. . .	. . .	. . .	. . .	. . .	. . .	. . .	. . .
General government	4 672	. . .	. . .	. . .	. . .	. . .	. . .	. . .	. . .
Banks	4 673	. . .	. . .	. . .	. . .	. . .	. . .	. . .	. . .
Other sectors	4 674	. . .	. . .	. . .	. . .	. . .	. . .	. . .	. . .
Money market instruments	4 680	. . .	. . .	. . .	. . .	. . .	. . .	. . .	1,066.2
Monetary authorities	4 681	. . .	. . .	. . .	. . .	. . .	. . .	. . .	. . .
General government	4 682	. . .	. . .	. . .	. . .	. . .	. . .	. . .	. . .
Banks	4 683	. . .	. . .	. . .	. . .	. . .	. . .	. . .	. . .
Other sectors	4 684	. . .	. . .	. . .	. . .	. . .	. . .	. . .	1,066.2
Financial derivatives	4 690	. . .	. . .	. . .	. . .	. . .	. . .	. . .	. . .
Monetary authorities	4 691	. . .	. . .	. . .	. . .	. . .	. . .	. . .	. . .
General government	4 692	. . .	. . .	. . .	. . .	. . .	. . .	. . .	. . .
Banks	4 693	. . .	. . .	. . .	. . .	. . .	. . .	. . .	. . .
Other sectors	4 694	. . .	. . .	. . .	. . .	. . .	. . .	. . .	. . .

Table 2 (Concluded). STANDARD PRESENTATION, 1988–95
(Millions of U.S. dollars)

	Code	1988	1989	1990	1991	1992	1993	1994	1995
C. OTHER INVESTMENT	4 700	120.2	40.8	112.5	–138.1	–441.9	–728.7	–625.7	–590.2
Assets	4 703	**. . .**	**. . .**	**. . .**	**. . .**	**. . .**	**. . .**	**. . .**	**–283.8**
Trade credits	4 706	. . .	. . .	. . .	. . .	. . .	. . .	. . .	. . .
General government: long-term	4 708	. . .	. . .	. . .	. . .	. . .	. . .	. . .	. . .
General government: short-term	4 709	. . .	. . .	. . .	. . .	. . .	. . .	. . .	. . .
Other sectors: long-term	4 711	. . .	. . .	. . .	. . .	. . .	. . .	. . .	. . .
Other sectors: short-term	4 712	. . .	. . .	. . .	. . .	. . .	. . .	. . .	. . .
Loans	4 714	. . .	. . .	. . .	. . .	. . .	. . .	. . .	. . .
Monetary authorities: long-term	4 717	. . .	. . .	. . .	. . .	. . .	. . .	. . .	. . .
Monetary authorities: short-term	4 718	. . .	. . .	. . .	. . .	. . .	. . .	. . .	. . .
General government: long-term	4 720	. . .	. . .	. . .	. . .	. . .	. . .	. . .	. . .
General government: short-term	4 721	. . .	. . .	. . .	. . .	. . .	. . .	. . .	. . .
Banks: long-term	4 723	. . .	. . .	. . .	. . .	. . .	. . .	. . .	. . .
Banks: short-term	4 724	. . .	. . .	. . .	. . .	. . .	. . .	. . .	. . .
Other sectors: long-term	4 726	. . .	. . .	. . .	. . .	. . .	. . .	. . .	. . .
Other sectors: short-term	4 727	. . .	. . .	. . .	. . .	. . .	. . .	. . .	. . .
Currency and deposits	4 730	. . .	. . .	. . .	. . .	. . .	. . .	. . .	–283.8
Monetary authorities	4 731	. . .	. . .	. . .	. . .	. . .	. . .	. . .	. . .
General government	4 732	. . .	. . .	. . .	. . .	. . .	. . .	. . .	. . .
Banks	4 733	. . .	. . .	. . .	. . .	. . .	. . .	. . .	. . .
Other sectors	4 734	. . .	. . .	. . .	. . .	. . .	. . .	. . .	–283.8
Other assets	4 736	. . .	. . .	. . .	. . .	. . .	. . .	. . .	. . .
Monetary authorities: long-term	4 738	. . .	. . .	. . .	. . .	. . .	. . .	. . .	. . .
Monetary authorities: short-term	4 739	. . .	. . .	. . .	. . .	. . .	. . .	. . .	. . .
General government: long-term	4 741	. . .	. . .	. . .	. . .	. . .	. . .	. . .	. . .
General government: short-term	4 742	. . .	. . .	. . .	. . .	. . .	. . .	. . .	. . .
Banks: long-term	4 744	. . .	. . .	. . .	. . .	. . .	. . .	. . .	. . .
Banks: short-term	4 745	. . .	. . .	. . .	. . .	. . .	. . .	. . .	. . .
Other sectors: long-term	4 747	. . .	. . .	. . .	. . .	. . .	. . .	. . .	. . .
Other sectors: short-term	4 748	. . .	. . .	. . .	. . .	. . .	. . .	. . .	. . .
Liabilities	4 753	**120.2**	**40.8**	**112.5**	**–138.1**	**–441.9**	**–728.7**	**–625.7**	**–306.4**
Trade credits	4 756	. . .	. . .	. . .	. . .	. . .	. . .	. . .	. . .
General government: long-term	4 758	. . .	. . .	. . .	. . .	. . .	. . .	. . .	. . .
General government: short-term	4 759	. . .	. . .	. . .	. . .	. . .	. . .	. . .	. . .
Other sectors: long-term	4 761	. . .	. . .	. . .	. . .	. . .	. . .	. . .	. . .
Other sectors: short-term	4 762	. . .	. . .	. . .	. . .	. . .	. . .	. . .	. . .
Loans	4 764	85.6	27.8	135.9	–138.2	–405.8	–618.4	–617.8	–300.0
Use of Fund credit and loans from the Fund	4 766	–5.2	–2.9	53.5	–.1	. . .	–15.0	–30.6	35.0
Monetary authorities: other long-term	4 767	. . .	. . .	. . .	. . .	. . .	. . .	. . .	. . .
Monetary authorities: short-term	4 768	. . .	. . .	. . .	. . .	. . .	. . .	. . .	. . .
General government: long-term	4 770	27.2	–18.4	88.1	–38.6	59.6	66.5	–102.1	–23.5
General government: short-term	4 771	. . .	. . .	. . .	. . .	. . .	. . .	. . .	. . .
Banks: long-term	4 773	. . .	. . .	. . .	. . .	. . .	. . .	. . .	. . .
Banks: short-term	4 774	. . .	. . .	. . .	. . .	. . .	. . .	. . .	. . .
Other sectors: long-term	4 776	63.6	49.1	–5.6	–99.5	–465.5	–670.0	–485.2	–311.5
Other sectors: short-term	4 777	. . .	. . .	. . .	. . .	. . .	. . .	. . .	. . .
Currency and deposits	4 780	34.6	13.0	–23.4	. . .	–36.1	–110.3	–7.9	–6.5
Monetary authorities	4 781	. . .	. . .	. . .	. . .	. . .	. . .	. . .	. . .
General government	4 782	. . .	. . .	. . .	. . .	. . .	. . .	. . .	. . .
Banks	4 783	34.6	13.0	–23.4	. . .	–36.1	–110.3	–7.9	–6.5
Other sectors	4 784	. . .	. . .	. . .	. . .	. . .	. . .	. . .	. . .
Other liabilities	4 786	. . .	. . .	. . .	. . .	. . .	. . .	. . .	. . .
Monetary authorities: long-term	4 788	. . .	. . .	. . .	. . .	. . .	. . .	. . .	. . .
Monetary authorities: short-term	4 789	. . .	. . .	. . .	. . .	. . .	. . .	. . .	. . .
General government: long-term	4 791	. . .	. . .	. . .	. . .	. . .	. . .	. . .	. . .
General government: short-term	4 792	. . .	. . .	. . .	. . .	. . .	. . .	. . .	. . .
Banks: long-term	4 794	. . .	. . .	. . .	. . .	. . .	. . .	. . .	. . .
Banks: short-term	4 795	. . .	. . .	. . .	. . .	. . .	. . .	. . .	. . .
Other sectors: long-term	4 797	. . .	. . .	. . .	. . .	. . .	. . .	. . .	. . .
Other sectors: short-term	4 798	. . .	. . .	. . .	. . .	. . .	. . .	. . .	. . .
D. RESERVE ASSETS	4 800	58.7	61.6	–75.2	85.3	71.2	96.6	33.1	–177.1
Monetary gold	4 810	. . .	. . .	. . .	. . .	. . .	. . .	. . .	. . .
Special drawing rights	4 820	.4	.5	3.7	. . .	–.1	.1	. . .	–.6
Reserve position in the Fund	4 830	. . .	. . .	9.1	. . .	–.1	. . .	. . .	. . .
Foreign exchange	4 840	58.3	61.2	–88.0	85.3	71.4	96.5	33.2	–176.5
Other claims	4 880	. . .	. . .	. . .	. . .	. . .	. . .	. . .	. . .
NET ERRORS AND OMISSIONS	4 998	**37.9**	**31.6**	**–79.7**	**6.8**	**–18.0**	**–12.2**	**28.3**	**–53.3**

Table 1. ANALYTIC PRESENTATION, 1988–95
(Millions of U.S. dollars)

	Code	1988	1989	1990	1991	1992	1993	1994	1995
A. Current Account [1]	4 993 Y.	**–210.2**	**255.6**	**–172.3**	**–324.1**	**–600.1**	**–834.0**	**–748.8**	**. . .**
Goods: exports f.o.b	2 100 . .	871.0	1,180.0	1,382.3	1,120.8	1,081.5	1,500.0	1,871.3	. . .
Goods: imports f.o.b	3 100 . .	–1,030.1	–1,015.9	–1,635.8	–1,867.6	–1,950.6	–2,710.7	–3,148.0	. . .
Balance on Goods	4 100 . .	*–159.1*	*164.1*	*–253.5*	*–746.8*	*–869.1*	*–1,210.7*	*–1,276.7*	. . .
Services: credit	2 200 . .	295.9	394.9	497.5	903.6	825.6	987.4	1,266.7	. . .
Services: debit	3 200 . .	–300.8	–303.5	–457.6	–546.9	–541.9	–608.8	–747.0	. . .
Balance on Goods and Services	4 991 . .	*–164.0*	*255.5*	*–213.6*	*–390.1*	*–585.4*	*–832.1*	*–757.0*	. . .
Income: credit	2 300 . .	56.7	88.7	106.8	108.6	129.6	86.9	90.9	. . .
Income: debit	3 300 . .	–138.0	–112.1	–121.1	–114.9	–178.2	–130.8	–124.7	. . .
Balance on Goods, Services, and Income	4 992 . .	*–245.3*	*232.1*	*–227.9*	*–396.4*	*–634.0*	*–876.0*	*–790.8*	. . .
Current transfers: credit	2 379 Y.	37.7	24.3	55.9	73.7	34.2	42.4	42.4	. . .
Current transfers: debit	3 379 . .	–2.6	–.8	–.3	–1.4	–.3	–.4	–.4	. . .
B. Capital Account [1]	4 994 Y.	**.1**	**.4**	**. . .**	**. . .**	**. . .**	**. . .**	**. . .**	**. . .**
Capital account: credit	2 994 Y.	.2	.4	. . .	. . .	. . .	. . .	. . .	. . .
Capital account: debit	3 994 . .	–.1	. . .	. . .	. . .	. . .	. . .	. . .	. . .
Total, Groups A Plus B	4 010 . .	*–210.1*	*256.0*	*–172.3*	*–324.1*	*–600.1*	*–834.0*	*–748.8*	. . .
C. Financial Account [1]	4 995 X.	**–199.3**	**–173.9**	**–75.8**	**215.0**	**192.0**	**323.0**	**456.6**	**. . .**
Direct investment abroad	4 505 . .	. . .	. . .	. . .	. . .	. . .	. . .	. . .	. . .
Direct investment in Paraguay	4 555 Y.	8.4	12.8	76.3	83.5	136.6	110.8	179.8	. . .
Portfolio investment assets	4 602 . .	. . .	. . .	. . .	. . .	. . .	. . .	. . .	. . .
Equity securities	4 610 . .	. . .	. . .	. . .	. . .	. . .	. . .	. . .	. . .
Debt securities	4 619 . .	. . .	. . .	. . .	. . .	. . .	. . .	. . .	. . .
Portfolio investment liabilities	4 652 Y.	. . .	. . .	. . .	. . .	. . .	. . .	. . .	. . .
Equity securities	4 660 Y.	. . .	. . .	. . .	. . .	. . .	. . .	. . .	. . .
Debt securities	4 669 Y.	. . .	. . .	. . .	. . .	. . .	. . .	. . .	. . .
Other investment assets	4 703 . .	–49.0	–63.5	–70.3	–38.4	–16.6	64.9	145.9	. . .
Monetary authorities	4 703 .A	. . .	. . .	. . .	. . .	. . .	. . .	. . .	. . .
General government	4 703 .B	–52.4	–54.8	–45.0	–35.1	57.9	125.7	158.3	. . .
Banks	4 703 .C	3.4	–8.7	–25.3	4.3	–82.1	–57.2	–1.3	. . .
Other sectors	4 703 .D	. . .	. . .	. . .	–7.6	7.6	–3.6	–11.1	. . .
Other investment liabilities	4 753 X.	–158.7	–123.2	–81.8	169.9	72.0	147.3	130.9	. . .
Monetary authorities	4 753 XA	–36.1	6.1	–8.8	–4.1	2.2	2.6	1.8	. . .
General government	4 753 YB	–11.5	–71.9	–120.1	29.1	7.1	5.4	37.7	. . .
Banks	4 753 YC	–5.4	–10.9	–3.4	43.3	59.1	33.9	73.2	. . .
Other sectors	4 753 YD	–105.7	–46.5	50.5	101.6	3.6	105.4	18.2	. . .
Total, Groups A Through C	4 020 . .	*–409.4*	*82.1*	*–248.1*	*–109.1*	*–408.1*	*–511.0*	*–292.2*	. . .
D. Net Errors and Omissions	4 998 . .	**198.3**	**–90.6**	**362.4**	**472.0**	**457.7**	**700.4**	**686.5**	**. . .**
Total, Groups A Through D	4 030 . .	*–211.1*	*–8.5*	*114.3*	*362.9*	*49.6*	*189.4*	*394.3*	. . .
E. Reserves and Related Items	4 040 . .	**211.1**	**8.5**	**–114.3**	**–362.9**	**–49.6**	**–189.4**	**–394.3**	**. . .**
Reserve assets	4 800 . .	168.2	–145.2	–219.3	–298.9	346.9	–86.3	–338.3	. . .
Use of Fund credit and loans	4 766 . .	. . .	. . .	. . .	. . .	. . .	. . .	. . .	. . .
Liabilities constituting foreign authorities' reserves	4 900 . .	–17.2	. . .	. . .	. . .	. . .	. . .	. . .	. . .
Exceptional financing	4 920 . .	60.1	153.7	105.0	–64.0	–396.5	–103.1	–56.0	. . .
Conversion rates: guaraníes per U.S. dollar	0 101 . .	**550.0**	**1,056.2**	**1,229.8**	**1,325.2**	**1,500.3**	**1,744.3**	**1,911.5**	**1,970.4**

[1] Excludes components that have been classified in the categories of Group E.

Table 2. STANDARD PRESENTATION, 1988–95
(Millions of U.S. dollars)

	Code	1988	1989	1990	1991	1992	1993	1994	1995
CURRENT ACCOUNT	4 993 . .	**–210.2**	**255.6**	**–172.3**	**–324.1**	**–600.1**	**–834.0**	**–748.8**	...
A. GOODS	4 100 . .	–159.1	164.1	–253.5	–746.8	–869.1	–1,210.7	–1,276.7	...
Credit	2 100 . .	**871.0**	**1,180.0**	**1,382.3**	**1,120.8**	**1,081.5**	**1,500.0**	**1,871.3**	...
General merchandise: exports f.o.b.	2 110 . .	871.0	1,180.0	1,382.3	1,120.8	1,081.5	1,500.0	1,871.3	...
Goods for processing: exports f.o.b.	2 150 . .	...	...	...	...	...	...	...	...
Repairs on goods	2 160 . .	...	...	...	...	...	...	...	...
Goods procured in ports by carriers	2 170 . .	...	...	...	...	...	...	...	...
Nonmonetary gold	2 180 . .	...	...	...	...	...	...	...	...
Debit	3 100 . .	**–1,030.1**	**–1,015.9**	**–1,635.8**	**–1,867.6**	**–1,950.6**	**–2,710.7**	**–3,148.0**	...
General merchandise: imports f.o.b.	3 110 . .	–1,030.1	–1,015.9	–1,635.8	–1,867.6	–1,950.6	–2,710.7	–3,148.0	...
Goods for processing: imports f.o.b.	3 150 . .	...	...	...	...	...	...	...	...
Repairs on goods	3 160 . .	...	...	...	...	...	...	...	...
Goods procured in ports by carriers	3 170 . .	...	...	...	...	...	...	...	...
Nonmonetary gold	3 180 . .	...	...	...	...	...	...	...	...
B. SERVICES	4 200 . .	–4.9	91.4	39.9	356.7	283.7	378.6	519.7	...
Total credit	2 200 . .	*295.9*	*394.9*	*497.5*	*903.6*	*825.6*	*987.4*	*1,266.7*	...
Total debit	3 200 . .	*–300.8*	*–303.5*	*–457.6*	*–546.9*	*–541.9*	*–608.8*	*–747.0*	...
Transportation services, credit	2 205 . .	**23.2**	**29.4**	**61.2**	**71.9**	**76.7**	**75.8**	**37.1**	...
Passenger	2 205 BA	*15.6*	*17.2*	*40.7*	*58.8*	*59.3*	*49.8*	*12.6*	...
Freight	2 205 BB	*7.6*	*12.2*	*14.6*	*11.9*	*16.0*	*26.0*	*24.5*	...
Other	2 205 BC	...	...	*5.9*	*1.2*	*1.4*	...	...	...
Sea transport, passenger	2 207 . .	...	...	...	...	...	...	...	...
Sea transport, freight	2 208 . .	...	...	...	...	...	...	...	...
Sea transport, other	2 209 . .	...	...	...	...	...	...	...	...
Air transport, passenger	2 211 . .	...	...	...	...	...	...	...	...
Air transport, freight	2 212 . .	...	...	...	...	...	...	...	...
Air transport, other	2 213 . .	...	...	...	...	...	...	...	...
Other transport, passenger	2 215 . .	...	...	...	...	...	...	...	...
Other transport, freight	2 216 . .	...	...	...	...	...	...	...	...
Other transport, other	2 217 . .	...	...	...	...	...	...	...	...
Transportation services, debit	3 205 . .	**–173.9**	**–166.3**	**–245.9**	**–259.5**	**–285.3**	**–321.9**	**–402.0**	...
Passenger	3 205 BA	*–16.5*	*–18.1*	*–19.2*	*–10.9*	*–15.9*	*–15.6*	*–19.7*	...
Freight	3 205 BB	*–126.7*	*–121.9*	*–183.3*	*–220.9*	*–235.4*	*–272.7*	*–339.8*	...
Other	3 205 BC	*–30.7*	*–26.3*	*–43.4*	*–27.7*	*–34.0*	*–33.6*	*–42.5*	...
Sea transport, passenger	3 207 . .	...	...	...	...	...	...	...	...
Sea transport, freight	3 208 . .	...	...	...	...	...	...	...	...
Sea transport, other	3 209 . .	...	...	...	...	...	...	...	...
Air transport, passenger	3 211 . .	...	...	...	...	...	...	...	...
Air transport, freight	3 212 . .	...	...	...	...	...	...	...	...
Air transport, other	3 213 . .	...	...	...	...	...	...	...	...
Other transport, passenger	3 215 . .	...	...	...	...	...	...	...	...
Other transport, freight	3 216 . .	...	...	...	...	...	...	...	...
Other transport, other	3 217 . .	...	...	...	...	...	...	...	...
Travel, credit	2 236 . .	**113.7**	**127.2**	**127.9**	**483.5**	**472.6**	**550.4**	**716.0**	...
Business travel	2 237 . .	...	...	...	...	...	...	...	...
Personal travel	2 240 . .	...	...	...	...	...	...	...	...
Travel, debit	3 236 . .	**–58.9**	**–75.0**	**–103.0**	**–117.9**	**–134.9**	**–138.0**	**–176.5**	...
Business travel	3 237 . .	...	...	...	...	...	...	...	...
Personal travel	3 240 . .	...	...	...	...	...	...	...	...
Other services, credit	2 200 BA	**159.0**	**238.3**	**308.4**	**348.2**	**276.3**	**361.2**	**513.6**	...
Communications	2 245 . .	...	...	...	...	...	...	...	...
Construction	2 249 . .	...	...	...	...	...	...	...	...
Insurance	2 253 . .	.2	.3	1.3	...	...	...	...	...
Financial	2 260 . .	...	...	...	...	...	...	...	...
Computer and information	2 262 . .	...	...	...	...	...	...	...	...
Royalties and licence fees	2 266 . .	64.9	...	...	...	...	...	...	...
Other business services	2 268 . .	83.9	227.0	292.6	333.7	261.4	346.2	498.6	...
Personal, cultural, and recreational	2 287 . .	...	...	...	...	...	...	...	...
Government, n.i.e.	2 291 . .	10.0	11.0	14.5	14.5	14.9	15.0	15.0	...
Other services, debit	3 200 BA	**–68.0**	**–62.2**	**–108.7**	**–169.5**	**–121.7**	**–148.9**	**–168.5**	...
Communications	3 245 . .	...	...	...	...	...	...	...	...
Construction	3 249 . .	...	...	...	...	...	...	...	...
Insurance	3 253 . .	–31.7	–30.2	–41.7	–42.5	–52.0	–75.6	–75.4	...
Financial	3 260 . .	...	...	...	...	...	...	...	...
Computer and information	3 262 . .	...	...	...	...	...	...	...	...
Royalties and licence fees	3 266 . .	...	...	–.1	...	–.1	...	...	...
Other business services	3 268 . .	–2.1	–1.3	–19.2	–51.8	–29.5	–39.0	–56.9	...
Personal, cultural, and recreational	3 287 . .	...	...	...	...	...	...	...	...
Government, n.i.e.	3 291 . .	–34.2	–30.7	–47.7	–75.2	–40.1	–34.3	–36.2	...

Table 2 (Continued). STANDARD PRESENTATION, 1988–95
(Millions of U.S. dollars)

	Code	1988	1989	1990	1991	1992	1993	1994	1995
C. INCOME	4 300	–81.3	–23.4	–14.3	–6.3	–48.6	–43.9	–33.8	...
Total credit	2 300	*56.7*	*88.7*	*106.8*	*108.6*	*129.6*	*86.9*	*90.9*	...
Total debit	3 300	*–138.0*	*–112.1*	*–121.1*	*–114.9*	*–178.2*	*–130.8*	*–124.7*	...
Compensation of employees, credit	2 310	**23.7**	**39.1**	**33.8**	**42.4**	**63.9**	**47.7**	**47.7**	...
Compensation of employees, debit	3 310	...	...	...	...	...	...	...	...
Investment income, credit	2 320	**33.0**	**49.6**	**73.0**	**66.2**	**65.7**	**39.2**	**43.2**	...
Direct investment income	2 330	...	...	...	.1	...	...	...	...
Dividends and distributed branch profits	2 332	...	...	...	.1	...	...	...	...
Reinvested earnings and undistributed branch profits	2 333	...	...	...	...	...	...	...	...
Income on debt (interest)	2 334	...	...	...	...	...	...	...	...
Portfolio investment income	2 339	...	...	...	...	...	...	...	...
Income on equity	2 340	...	...	...	...	...	...	...	...
Income on bonds and notes	2 350	...	...	...	...	...	...	...	...
Income on money market instruments and financial derivatives	2 360	...	...	...	...	...	...	...	...
Other investment income	2 370	33.0	49.6	73.0	66.1	65.7	39.2	43.2	...
Investment income, debit	3 320	**–138.0**	**–112.1**	**–121.1**	**–114.9**	**–178.2**	**–130.8**	**–124.7**	...
Direct investment income	3 330	...	...	–22.2	–19.5	–19.5	–40.1	–40.1	...
Dividends and distributed branch profits	3 332	...	...	–9.6	–3.6	–2.9	–17.5	–17.5	...
Reinvested earnings and undistributed branch profits	3 333	...	...	–12.6	–13.3	–14.1	–18.6	–18.6	...
Income on debt (interest)	3 334	...	...	...	–2.6	–2.5	–4.0	–4.0	...
Portfolio investment income	3 339	...	...	...	...	...	...	...	...
Income on equity	3 340	...	...	...	...	...	...	...	...
Income on bonds and notes	3 350	...	...	...	...	...	...	...	...
Income on money market instruments and financial derivatives	3 360	...	...	...	...	...	...	...	...
Other investment income	3 370	–138.0	–112.1	–98.9	–95.4	–158.7	–90.7	–84.6	...
D. CURRENT TRANSFERS	4 379	35.1	23.5	55.6	72.3	33.9	42.0	42.0	...
Credit	2 379	**37.7**	**24.3**	**55.9**	**73.7**	**34.2**	**42.4**	**42.4**	...
General government	2 380	34.3	23.1	44.2	60.2	27.5	35.0	35.0	...
Other sectors	2 390	3.4	1.2	11.7	13.5	6.7	7.4	7.4	...
Workers' remittances	2 391	...	...	...	...	...	...	...	...
Other current transfers	2 392	3.4	1.2	11.7	13.5	6.7	7.4	7.4	...
Debit	3 379	**–2.6**	**–.8**	**–.3**	**–1.4**	**–.3**	**–.4**	**–.4**	...
General government	3 380	–2.4	–.6	–.3	–1.4	–.3	–.4	–.4	...
Other sectors	3 390	–.2	–.2	...	...	...	...	...	...
Workers' remittances	3 391	...	...	...	...	...	...	...	...
Other current transfers	3 392	–.2	–.2	...	...	...	...	...	...
CAPITAL AND FINANCIAL ACCOUNT	4 996	**11.9**	**–165.0**	**–190.1**	**–147.9**	**142.4**	**133.6**	**62.3**	...
CAPITAL ACCOUNT	4 994	**.1**	**.4**	...	...	...	...	...	...
Total credit	2 994	*.2*	*.4*	...	...	...	...	...	...
Total debit	3 994	*–.1*	...	...	...	...	...	...	...
Capital transfers, credit	2 400	**.2**	**.4**	...	...	...	...	...	...
General government	2 401	...	...	...	...	...	...	...	...
Debt forgiveness	2 402	...	...	...	...	...	...	...	...
Other capital transfers	2 410	...	...	...	...	...	...	...	...
Other sectors	2 430	.2	.4	...	...	...	...	...	...
Migrants' transfers	2 431	.2	.4	...	...	...	...	...	...
Debt forgiveness	2 432	...	...	...	...	...	...	...	...
Other capital transfers	2 440	...	...	...	...	...	...	...	...
Capital transfers, debit	3 400	**–.1**	...	...	...	...	...	...	...
General government	3 401	...	...	...	...	...	...	...	...
Debt forgiveness	3 402	...	...	...	...	...	...	...	...
Other capital transfers	3 410	...	...	...	...	...	...	...	...
Other sectors	3 430	–.1	...	...	...	...	...	...	...
Migrants' transfers	3 431	–.1	...	...	...	...	...	...	...
Debt forgiveness	3 432	...	...	...	...	...	...	...	...
Other capital transfers	3 440	...	...	...	...	...	...	...	...
Nonproduced nonfinancial assets, credit	2 480	...	...	...	...	...	...	...	...
Nonproduced nonfinancial assets, debit	3 480	...	...	...	...	...	...	...	...

Table 2 (Continued). STANDARD PRESENTATION, 1988–95
(Millions of U.S. dollars)

	Code	1988	1989	1990	1991	1992	1993	1994	1995
FINANCIAL ACCOUNT	4 995 . .	**11.8**	**−165.4**	**−190.1**	**−147.9**	**142.4**	**133.6**	**62.3**	**. . .**
A. DIRECT INVESTMENT	4 500 . .	8.4	12.8	76.3	83.5	136.6	110.8	179.8	. . .
Direct investment abroad	4 505 . .	**. . .**	**. . .**	**. . .**	**. . .**	**. . .**	**. . .**	**. . .**	**. . .**
Equity capital	4 510 . .	. . .	. . .	. . .	. . .	. . .	. . .	. . .	. . .
Claims on affiliated enterprises	4 515 . .	. . .	. . .	. . .	. . .	. . .	. . .	. . .	. . .
Liabilities to affiliated enterprises	4 520 . .	. . .	. . .	. . .	. . .	. . .	. . .	. . .	. . .
Reinvested earnings	4 525 . .	. . .	. . .	. . .	. . .	. . .	. . .	. . .	. . .
Other capital	4 530 . .	. . .	. . .	. . .	. . .	. . .	. . .	. . .	. . .
Claims on affiliated enterprises	4 535 . .	. . .	. . .	. . .	. . .	. . .	. . .	. . .	. . .
Liabilities to affiliated enterprises	4 540 . .	. . .	. . .	. . .	. . .	. . .	. . .	. . .	. . .
Direct investment in Paraguay	4 555 . .	**8.4**	**12.8**	**76.3**	**83.5**	**136.6**	**110.8**	**179.8**	**. . .**
Equity capital	4 560 . .	. . .	12.8	33.7	49.4	99.9	41.6	79.1	. . .
Claims on direct investors	4 565 . .	. . .	. . .	. . .	. . .	. . .	. . .	. . .	. . .
Liabilities to direct investors	4 570 . .	. . .	. . .	. . .	. . .	. . .	. . .	. . .	. . .
Reinvested earnings	4 575 . .	. . .	. . .	12.6	13.3	14.1	18.6	18.6	. . .
Other capital	4 580 . .	8.4	. . .	30.0	20.8	22.6	50.6	82.1	. . .
Claims on direct investors	4 585 . .	. . .	. . .	. . .	. . .	. . .	. . .	. . .	. . .
Liabilities to direct investors	4 590 . .	. . .	. . .	. . .	. . .	. . .	. . .	. . .	. . .
B. PORTFOLIO INVESTMENT	4 600 . .	. . .	. . .	. . .	. . .	. . .	. . .	. . .	. . .
Assets	4 602 . .	**. . .**	**. . .**	**. . .**	**. . .**	**. . .**	**. . .**	**. . .**	**. . .**
Equity securities	4 610 . .	. . .	. . .	. . .	. . .	. . .	. . .	. . .	. . .
Monetary authorities	4 611 . .	. . .	. . .	. . .	. . .	. . .	. . .	. . .	. . .
General government	4 612 . .	. . .	. . .	. . .	. . .	. . .	. . .	. . .	. . .
Banks	4 613 . .	. . .	. . .	. . .	. . .	. . .	. . .	. . .	. . .
Other sectors	4 614 . .	. . .	. . .	. . .	. . .	. . .	. . .	. . .	. . .
Debt securities	4 619 . .	. . .	. . .	. . .	. . .	. . .	. . .	. . .	. . .
Bonds and notes	4 620 . .	. . .	. . .	. . .	. . .	. . .	. . .	. . .	. . .
Monetary authorities	4 621 . .	. . .	. . .	. . .	. . .	. . .	. . .	. . .	. . .
General government	4 622 . .	. . .	. . .	. . .	. . .	. . .	. . .	. . .	. . .
Banks	4 623 . .	. . .	. . .	. . .	. . .	. . .	. . .	. . .	. . .
Other sectors	4 624 . .	. . .	. . .	. . .	. . .	. . .	. . .	. . .	. . .
Money market instruments	4 630 . .	. . .	. . .	. . .	. . .	. . .	. . .	. . .	. . .
Monetary authorities	4 631 . .	. . .	. . .	. . .	. . .	. . .	. . .	. . .	. . .
General government	4 632 . .	. . .	. . .	. . .	. . .	. . .	. . .	. . .	. . .
Banks	4 633 . .	. . .	. . .	. . .	. . .	. . .	. . .	. . .	. . .
Other sectors	4 634 . .	. . .	. . .	. . .	. . .	. . .	. . .	. . .	. . .
Financial derivatives	4 640 . .	. . .	. . .	. . .	. . .	. . .	. . .	. . .	. . .
Monetary authorities	4 641 . .	. . .	. . .	. . .	. . .	. . .	. . .	. . .	. . .
General government	4 642 . .	. . .	. . .	. . .	. . .	. . .	. . .	. . .	. . .
Banks	4 643 . .	. . .	. . .	. . .	. . .	. . .	. . .	. . .	. . .
Other sectors	4 644 . .	. . .	. . .	. . .	. . .	. . .	. . .	. . .	. . .
Liabilities	4 652 . .	**. . .**	**. . .**	**. . .**	**. . .**	**. . .**	**. . .**	**. . .**	**. . .**
Equity securities	4 660 . .	. . .	. . .	. . .	. . .	. . .	. . .	. . .	. . .
Banks	4 663 . .	. . .	. . .	. . .	. . .	. . .	. . .	. . .	. . .
Other sectors	4 664 . .	. . .	. . .	. . .	. . .	. . .	. . .	. . .	. . .
Debt securities	4 669 . .	. . .	. . .	. . .	. . .	. . .	. . .	. . .	. . .
Bonds and notes	4 670 . .	. . .	. . .	. . .	. . .	. . .	. . .	. . .	. . .
Monetary authorities	4 671 . .	. . .	. . .	. . .	. . .	. . .	. . .	. . .	. . .
General government	4 672 . .	. . .	. . .	. . .	. . .	. . .	. . .	. . .	. . .
Banks	4 673 . .	. . .	. . .	. . .	. . .	. . .	. . .	. . .	. . .
Other sectors	4 674 . .	. . .	. . .	. . .	. . .	. . .	. . .	. . .	. . .
Money market instruments	4 680 . .	. . .	. . .	. . .	. . .	. . .	. . .	. . .	. . .
Monetary authorities	4 681 . .	. . .	. . .	. . .	. . .	. . .	. . .	. . .	. . .
General government	4 682 . .	. . .	. . .	. . .	. . .	. . .	. . .	. . .	. . .
Banks	4 683 . .	. . .	. . .	. . .	. . .	. . .	. . .	. . .	. . .
Other sectors	4 684 . .	. . .	. . .	. . .	. . .	. . .	. . .	. . .	. . .
Financial derivatives	4 690 . .	. . .	. . .	. . .	. . .	. . .	. . .	. . .	. . .
Monetary authorities	4 691 . .	. . .	. . .	. . .	. . .	. . .	. . .	. . .	. . .
General government	4 692 . .	. . .	. . .	. . .	. . .	. . .	. . .	. . .	. . .
Banks	4 693 . .	. . .	. . .	. . .	. . .	. . .	. . .	. . .	. . .
Other sectors	4 694 . .	. . .	. . .	. . .	. . .	. . .	. . .	. . .	. . .

Table 2 (Concluded). STANDARD PRESENTATION, 1988–95
(Millions of U.S. dollars)

	Code	1988	1989	1990	1991	1992	1993	1994	1995
C. OTHER INVESTMENT	4 700	–164.8	–33.0	–47.1	67.5	–341.1	109.1	220.8	...
Assets	4 703	**–49.0**	**–63.5**	**–70.3**	**–38.4**	**–16.6**	**64.9**	**145.9**	...
Trade credits	4 706	...	...	...	...	...	...	...	...
General government: long-term	4 708	...	...	...	...	...	...	...	...
General government: short-term	4 709	...	...	...	...	...	...	...	...
Other sectors: long-term	4 711	...	...	...	...	...	...	...	...
Other sectors: short-term	4 712	...	...	...	...	...	...	...	...
Loans	4 714	...	...	...	...	...	...	...	...
Monetary authorities: long-term	4 717	...	...	...	...	...	...	...	...
Monetary authorities: short-term	4 718	...	...	...	...	...	...	...	...
General government: long-term	4 720	...	...	...	...	...	...	...	...
General government: short-term	4 721	...	...	...	...	...	...	...	...
Banks: long-term	4 723	...	...	...	...	...	...	...	...
Banks: short-term	4 724	...	...	...	...	...	...	...	...
Other sectors: long-term	4 726	...	...	...	...	...	...	...	...
Other sectors: short-term	4 727	...	...	...	...	...	...	...	...
Currency and deposits	4 730	–19.6	–33.5	–50.2	–25.8	62.3	–24.8	29.7	...
Monetary authorities	4 731	...	...	...	...	...	...	...	...
General government	4 732	–23.0	–24.8	–24.9	–22.5	136.8	36.0	42.1	...
Banks	4 733	3.4	–8.7	–25.3	4.3	–82.1	–57.2	–1.3	...
Other sectors	4 734	...	...	...	–7.6	7.6	–3.6	–11.1	...
Other assets	4 736	–29.4	–30.0	–20.1	–12.6	–78.9	89.7	116.2	...
Monetary authorities: long-term	4 738	...	...	...	...	...	...	...	...
Monetary authorities: short-term	4 739	...	...	...	...	...	...	...	...
General government: long-term	4 741	–29.4	–30.0	–20.1	–12.6	–78.9	89.7	116.2	...
General government: short-term	4 742	...	...	...	...	...	...	...	...
Banks: long-term	4 744	...	...	...	...	...	...	...	...
Banks: short-term	4 745	...	...	...	...	...	...	...	...
Other sectors: long-term	4 747	...	...	...	...	...	...	...	...
Other sectors: short-term	4 748	...	...	...	...	...	...	...	...
Liabilities	4 753	**–115.8**	**30.5**	**23.2**	**105.9**	**–324.5**	**44.2**	**74.9**	...
Trade credits	4 756	–52.5	–10.7	42.8	59.2	43.2	116.9	35.7	...
General government: long-term	4 758	...	...	...	...	...	...	...	...
General government: short-term	4 759	...	...	...	...	...	...	...	...
Other sectors: long-term	4 761	...	...	...	...	...	...	...	...
Other sectors: short-term	4 762	–52.5	–10.7	42.8	59.2	43.2	116.9	35.7	...
Loans	4 764	–77.3	47.7	–118.7	63.6	–17.5	–5.2	18.1	...
Use of Fund credit and loans from the Fund	4 766	...	...	...	...	...	...	...	...
Monetary authorities: other long-term	4 767	...	...	...	...	...	...	...	...
Monetary authorities: short-term	4 768	...	...	...	...	...	...	...	...
General government: long-term	4 770	–11.5	89.0	–120.1	29.2	25.5	8.6	41.0	...
General government: short-term	4 771	...	...	...	...	...	...	...	...
Banks: long-term	4 773	–12.6	–5.5	–6.3	–.7	–3.4	3.9	–5.4	...
Banks: short-term	4 774	...	...	...	...	...	...	...	...
Other sectors: long-term	4 776	–53.2	–35.8	7.7	–50.3	–60.7	–35.5	–33.6	...
Other sectors: short-term	4 777	...	...	...	85.4	21.1	17.8	16.1	...
Currency and deposits	4 780	–10.0	–5.4	6.6	44.0	62.5	30.0	78.6	...
Monetary authorities	4 781	–17.2	...	...	...	...	...	...	...
General government	4 782	...	...	...	...	...	...	...	...
Banks	4 783	7.2	–5.4	6.6	44.0	62.5	30.0	78.6	...
Other sectors	4 784	...	...	...	...	...	...	...	...
Other liabilities	4 786	24.0	–1.1	92.5	–60.9	–412.7	–97.5	–57.5	...
Monetary authorities: long-term	4 788	...	...	...	...	...	...	...	...
Monetary authorities: short-term	4 789	–36.1	6.1	–8.8	–4.1	2.2	2.6	1.8	...
General government: long-term	4 791	...	...	...	–.1	–.4	–3.2	–3.3	...
General government: short-term	4 792	64.1	–102.0	51.8	37.6	–146.5	–.5	1.9	...
Banks: long-term	4 794	...	...	–3.7	...	...	...	...	...
Banks: short-term	4 795	–1.5	–.6	–.9	...	...	...	...	...
Other sectors: long-term	4 797	...	...	...	...	...	...	...	...
Other sectors: short-term	4 798	–2.5	95.4	54.1	–94.3	–268.0	–96.4	–57.9	...
D. RESERVE ASSETS	4 800	168.2	–145.2	–219.3	–298.9	346.9	–86.3	–338.3	...
Monetary gold	4 810	...	...	...	...	...	...	...	...
Special drawing rights	4 820	–3.5	–4.4	–5.6	–5.3	–4.7	–4.1	–3.7	...
Reserve position in the Fund	4 830	6.2	3.2	2.0	...	–8.2	.6	2.8	...
Foreign exchange	4 840	165.5	–144.0	–215.7	–293.6	359.8	–82.8	–337.4	...
Other claims	4 880	...	...	...	...	...	...	...	...
NET ERRORS AND OMISSIONS	4 998	**198.3**	**–90.6**	**362.4**	**472.0**	**457.7**	**700.4**	**686.5**	...

Table 1. ANALYTIC PRESENTATION, 1988–95
(Millions of U.S. dollars)

	Code	1988	1989	1990	1991	1992	1993	1994	1995
A. Current Account [1]	4 993 Y.	**–1,657**	**–240**	**–1,066**	**–1,368**	**–1,922**	**–2,170**	**–2,544**	**–4,223**
Goods: exports f.o.b.	2 100 . .	2,731	3,533	3,321	3,406	3,661	3,523	4,574	5,576
Goods: imports f.o.b.	3 100 . .	–2,865	–2,286	–2,922	–3,595	–4,001	–4,123	–5,545	–7,687
Balance on Goods	4 100 . .	*–134*	*1,246*	*399*	*–189*	*–340*	*–599*	*–972*	*–2,111*
Services: credit	2 200 . .	831	836	841	869	869	902	1,144	1,234
Services: debit	3 200 . .	–1,164	–1,143	–1,173	–1,251	–1,425	–1,436	–1,624	–2,015
Balance on Goods and Services	4 991 . .	*–466*	*939*	*67*	*–571*	*–897*	*–1,134*	*–1,452*	*–2,892*
Income: credit	2 300 . .	123	196	195	224	204	209	332	573
Income: debit	3 300 . .	–1,476	–1,551	–1,644	–1,433	–1,661	–1,715	–2,025	–2,395
Balance on Goods, Services, and Income	4 992 . .	*–1,819*	*–416*	*–1,382*	*–1,779*	*–2,354*	*–2,640*	*–3,145*	*–4,714*
Current transfers: credit	2 379 Y.	163	176	316	411	440	476	607	496
Current transfers: debit	3 379 . .	. . .	. . .	. . .	. . .	–8	–6	–7	–5
B. Capital Account [1]	4 994 Y.	**4**	**–20**	**–25**	**–52**	**–50**	**–78**	**–78**	**10**
Capital account: credit	2 994 Y.	50	39	50	56	40	47	31	63
Capital account: debit	3 994 . .	–46	–59	–75	–108	–90	–125	–109	–53
Total, Groups A Plus B	4 010 . .	*–1,653*	*–260*	*–1,091*	*–1,420*	*–1,973*	*–2,247*	*–2,622*	*–4,213*
C. Financial Account [1]	4 995 X.	**–1,613**	**–1,798**	**–765**	**–872**	**443**	**–245**	**3,292**	**1,933**
Direct investment abroad	4 505 . .	. . .	. . .	. . .	. . .	. . .	. . .	. . .	. . .
Direct investment in Peru	4 555 Y.	26	59	41	–7	136	670	2,860	1,895
Portfolio investment assets	4 602 . .	. . .	. . .	. . .	. . .	. . .	. . .	. . .	. . .
Equity securities	4 610 . .	. . .	. . .	. . .	. . .	. . .	. . .	. . .	. . .
Debt securities	4 619 . .	. . .	. . .	. . .	. . .	. . .	. . .	. . .	. . .
Portfolio investment liabilities	4 652 Y.	. . .	. . .	. . .	. . .	. . .	228	584	151
Equity securities	4 660 Y.	. . .	. . .	. . .	. . .	. . .	222	465	171
Debt securities	4 669 Y.	. . .	. . .	. . .	. . .	. . .	6	120	–20
Other investment assets	4 703 . .	–461	–666	432	–289	318	269	–250	–576
Monetary authorities	4 703 . A	. . .	. . .	. . .	. . .	. . .	. . .	. . .	. . .
General government	4 703 . B	. . .	. . .	. . .	. . .	. . .	. . .	. . .	. . .
Banks	4 703 . C	–13	–181	63	–476	84	119	–265	–455
Other sectors	4 703 . D	–448	–485	369	187	234	150	15	–121
Other investment liabilities	4 753 X.	–1,178	–1,191	–1,238	–576	–11	–1,412	98	464
Monetary authorities	4 753 XA	523	–204	109	68	–65	–670	38	–24
General government	4 753 YB	–1,477	–1,139	–1,197	–1,026	–791	–963	–1,009	–912
Banks	4 753 YC	8	6	–88	22	174	196	–268	840
Other sectors	4 753 YD	–232	146	–62	361	671	25	1,337	560
Total, Groups A Through C	4 020 . .	*–3,266*	*–2,058*	*–1,857*	*–2,292*	*–1,530*	*–2,493*	*670*	*–2,281*
D. Net Errors and Omissions	4 998 . .	**297**	**–157**	**–257**	**1,073**	**383**	**1,178**	**290**	**1,145**
Total, Groups A Through D	4 030 . .	*–2,969*	*–2,215*	*–2,114*	*–1,219*	*–1,147*	*–1,314*	*959*	*–1,136*
E. Reserves and Related Items	4 040 . .	**2,969**	**2,215**	**2,114**	**1,219**	**1,147**	**1,314**	**–959**	**1,136**
Reserve assets	4 800 . .	149	–242	–212	–899	–554	–667	–3,070	–916
Use of Fund credit and loans	4 766 . .	. . .	–24	–63	–51	–49	254	. . .	. . .
Liabilities constituting foreign authorities' reserves	4 900 . .	. . .	. . .	. . .	. . .	. . .	. . .	. . .	. . .
Exceptional financing	4 920 . .	2,820	2,481	2,390	2,169	1,749	1,727	2,111	2,051
Conversion rates: nuevos soles per U.S. dollar	0 101 . .	**.0001**	**.0027**	**.1879**	**.7725**	**1.2458**	**1.9883**	**2.1950**	**2.2533**

[1] Excludes components that have been classified in the categories of Group E.

Table 2. STANDARD PRESENTATION, 1988–95
(Millions of U.S. dollars)

	Code	1988	1989	1990	1991	1992	1993	1994	1995
CURRENT ACCOUNT	4 993 . .	**–1,657**	**–240**	**–1,066**	**–1,320**	**–1,907**	**–2,145**	**–2,539**	**–4,223**
A. GOODS	4 100 . .	–134	1,246	399	–189	–340	–599	–972	–2,111
Credit	2 100 . .	**2,731**	**3,533**	**3,321**	**3,406**	**3,661**	**3,523**	**4,574**	**5,576**
General merchandise: exports f.o.b.	2 110 . .	2,705	3,505	3,279	3,222	3,212	3,248	4,188	5,053
Goods for processing: exports f.o.b.	2 150 . .	. . .	. . .	. . .	. . .	. . .	. . .	. . .	. . .
Repairs on goods	2 160 . .	. . .	. . .	1	1	1	1	1	1
Goods procured in ports by carriers	2 170 . .	24	25	32	40	49	50	46	59
Nonmonetary gold	2 180 . .	3	2	9	145	399	225	338	463
Debit	3 100 . .	**–2,865**	**–2,286**	**–2,922**	**–3,595**	**–4,001**	**–4,123**	**–5,545**	**–7,687**
General merchandise: imports f.o.b.	3 110 . .	–2,822	–2,202	–2,856	–3,530	–3,817	–3,920	–5,256	–7,340
Goods for processing: imports f.o.b.	3 150 . .	–11	–53	–28	–30	–93	–132	–242	–306
Repairs on goods	3 160 . .	. . .	. . .	–6	–5	–8	–5	–8	–11
Goods procured in ports by carriers	3 170 . .	–32	–31	–33	–30	–31	–30	–26	–30
Nonmonetary gold	3 180 . .	. . .	. . .	. . .	. . .	–52	–36	–14	. . .
B. SERVICES	4 200 . .	–333	–307	–332	–382	–556	–534	–480	–781
Total credit	2 200 . .	*831*	*836*	*841*	*869*	*869*	*902*	*1,144*	*1,234*
Total debit	3 200 . .	*–1,164*	*–1,143*	*–1,173*	*–1,251*	*–1,425*	*–1,436*	*–1,624*	*–2,015*
Transportation services, credit	2 205 . .	**304**	**298**	**310**	**304**	**317**	**293**	**307**	**338**
Passenger	2 205 BA	*46*	*49*	*45*	*43*	*39*	*48*	*79*	*93*
Freight	2 205 BB	*127*	*115*	*98*	*74*	*84*	*91*	*55*	*54*
Other	2 205 BC	*131*	*135*	*167*	*186*	*193*	*154*	*173*	*191*
Sea transport, passenger	2 207 . .	. . .	. . .	. . .	. . .	. . .	. . .	. . .	. . .
Sea transport, freight	2 208 . .	123	111	95	72	80	84	49	48
Sea transport, other	2 209 . .	42	49	60	68	92	63	77	86
Air transport, passenger	2 211 . .	46	49	45	43	39	48	79	93
Air transport, freight	2 212 . .	4	3	3	2	4	7	6	6
Air transport, other	2 213 . .	89	86	108	118	101	91	95	105
Other transport, passenger	2 215 . .	. . .	. . .	. . .	. . .	. . .	. . .	. . .	. . .
Other transport, freight	2 216 . .	. . .	. . .	. . .	. . .	. . .	. . .	. . .	. . .
Other transport, other	2 217 . .	. . .	. . .	. . .	. . .	. . .	. . .	. . .	. . .
Transportation services, debit	3 205 . .	**–473**	**–393**	**–465**	**–601**	**–608**	**–626**	**–732**	**–905**
Passenger	3 205 BA	*–110*	*–98*	*–116*	*–153*	*–141*	*–115*	*–113*	*–131*
Freight	3 205 BB	*–185*	*–125*	*–218*	*–328*	*–342*	*–388*	*–499*	*–625*
Other	3 205 BC	*–178*	*–170*	*–131*	*–119*	*–125*	*–124*	*–120*	*–149*
Sea transport, passenger	3 207 . .	. . .	. . .	. . .	. . .	. . .	. . .	. . .	. . .
Sea transport, freight	3 208 . .	–170	–105	–202	–301	–318	–359	–454	–563
Sea transport, other	3 209 . .	–138	–130	–89	–81	–90	–78	–58	–64
Air transport, passenger	3 211 . .	–110	–98	–116	–153	–141	–115	–113	–131
Air transport, freight	3 212 . .	–15	–20	–16	–27	–25	–28	–44	–63
Air transport, other	3 213 . .	–40	–40	–42	–39	–34	–46	–63	–85
Other transport, passenger	3 215 . .	. . .	. . .	. . .	. . .	. . .	. . .	. . .	. . .
Other transport, freight	3 216 . .	. . .	. . .	. . .	. . .	. . .	. . .	. . .	. . .
Other transport, other	3 217 . .	. . .	. . .	. . .	. . .	. . .	. . .	. . .	. . .
Travel, credit	2 236 . .	**252**	**247**	**259**	**268**	**188**	**265**	**401**	**516**
Business travel	2 237 . .	. . .	. . .	. . .	. . .	. . .	. . .	. . .	. . .
Personal travel	2 240 . .	. . .	. . .	. . .	. . .	. . .	. . .	. . .	. . .
Travel, debit	3 236 . .	**–222**	**–263**	**–296**	**–264**	**–256**	**–269**	**–288**	**–302**
Business travel	3 237 . .	. . .	. . .	. . .	. . .	. . .	. . .	. . .	. . .
Personal travel	3 240 . .	. . .	. . .	. . .	. . .	. . .	. . .	. . .	. . .
Other services, credit	2 200 BA	**276**	**291**	**272**	**297**	**364**	**344**	**436**	**380**
Communications	2 245 . .	55	73	95	126	134	146	164	174
Construction	2 249 . .	. . .	. . .	. . .	. . .	. . .	. . .	. . .	. . .
Insurance	2 253 . .	139	135	80	72	125	67	117	75
Financial	2 260 . .	. . .	. . .	. . .	. . .	. . .	. . .	. . .	. . .
Computer and information	2 262 . .	. . .	. . .	. . .	. . .	. . .	. . .	. . .	. . .
Royalties and licence fees	2 266 . .	. . .	. . .	. . .	. . .	. . .	. . .	1	1
Other business services	2 268 . .	. . .	. . .	12	16	20	36	41	42
Personal, cultural, and recreational	2 287 . .	. . .	. . .	. . .	. . .	. . .	. . .	. . .	. . .
Government, n.i.e.	2 291 . .	81	83	84	84	85	96	113	89
Other services, debit	3 200 BA	**–469**	**–487**	**–413**	**–387**	**–561**	**–542**	**–605**	**–808**
Communications	3 245 . .	–29	–36	–36	–42	–42	–57	–67	–79
Construction	3 249 . .	. . .	. . .	. . .	. . .	. . .	. . .	. . .	. . .
Insurance	3 253 . .	–147	–134	–111	–110	–171	–141	–147	–129
Financial	3 260 . .	–9	–14	–6	–13	–19	–25	–37	–53
Computer and information	3 262 . .	. . .	. . .	. . .	. . .	. . .	. . .	. . .	. . .
Royalties and licence fees	3 266 . .	–4	–2	–5	–9	–12	–26	–47	–60
Other business services	3 268 . .	–183	–208	–152	–118	–223	–200	–212	–381
Personal, cultural, and recreational	3 287 . .	. . .	. . .	. . .	. . .	. . .	. . .	. . .	. . .
Government, n.i.e.	3 291 . .	–97	–95	–103	–94	–94	–93	–95	–106

Table 2 (Continued). STANDARD PRESENTATION, 1988–95
(Millions of U.S. dollars)

	Code	1988	1989	1990	1991	1992	1993	1994	1995
C. INCOME	4 300	–1,353	–1,355	–1,449	–1,208	–1,457	–1,506	–1,693	–1,823
Total credit	2 300	*123*	*196*	*195*	*224*	*204*	*209*	*332*	*573*
Total debit	3 300	*–1,476*	*–1,551*	*–1,644*	*–1,433*	*–1,661*	*–1,715*	*–2,025*	*–2,395*
Compensation of employees, credit	2 310	...	...	...	...	...	...	...	...
Compensation of employees, debit	3 310	...	...	...	...	...	...	...	...
Investment income, credit	2 320	**123**	**196**	**195**	**224**	**204**	**209**	**332**	**573**
Direct investment income	2 330	...	...	...	...	...	...	...	...
Dividends and distributed branch profits	2 332	...	...	...	...	...	...	...	...
Reinvested earnings and undistributed branch profits	2 333	...	...	...	...	...	...	...	...
Income on debt (interest)	2 334	...	...	...	...	...	...	...	...
Portfolio investment income	2 339	...	...	...	...	...	...	...	...
Income on equity	2 340	...	...	...	...	...	...	...	...
Income on bonds and notes	2 350	...	...	...	...	...	...	...	...
Income on money market instruments and financial derivatives	2 360	...	...	...	...	...	...	...	...
Other investment income	2 370	123	196	195	224	204	209	332	573
Investment income, debit	3 320	**–1,476**	**–1,551**	**–1,644**	**–1,433**	**–1,661**	**–1,715**	**–2,025**	**–2,395**
Direct investment income	3 330	–40	–21	–15	–36	–159	–132	–187	–202
Dividends and distributed branch profits	3 332	–4	–4	–7	–32	–141	–109	–135	–102
Reinvested earnings and undistributed branch profits	3 333	–36	–17	–8	–4	–18	–23	–52	–100
Income on debt (interest)	3 334	...	...	...	...	...	...	...	...
Portfolio investment income	3 339	...	...	...	...	...	...	–6	–65
Income on equity	3 340	...	...	...	...	...	...	...	–60
Income on bonds and notes	3 350	...	...	...	...	...	...	–6	–6
Income on money market instruments and financial derivatives	3 360	...	...	...	...	...	...	...	...
Other investment income	3 370	–1,436	–1,530	–1,629	–1,397	–1,502	–1,583	–1,832	–2,128
D. CURRENT TRANSFERS	4 379	163	176	316	459	446	495	606	491
Credit	2 379	**163**	**176**	**316**	**459**	**455**	**501**	**612**	**496**
General government	2 380	84	99	126	198	82	71	68	30
Other sectors	2 390	79	77	190	261	372	431	544	466
Workers' remittances	2 391	...	...	122	186	244	276	366	334
Other current transfers	2 392	79	77	68	75	128	154	178	132
Debit	3 379	...	...	...	...	**–8**	**–6**	**–7**	**–5**
General government	3 380	...	...	...	...	–8	–6	–7	–5
Other sectors	3 390	...	...	...	...	...	...	...	...
Workers' remittances	3 391	...	...	...	...	...	...	...	...
Other current transfers	3 392	...	...	...	...	...	...	...	...
CAPITAL AND FINANCIAL ACCOUNT	4 996	**1,360**	**397**	**1,324**	**248**	**1,524**	**966**	**2,250**	**3,078**
CAPITAL ACCOUNT	4 994	**4**	**–20**	**–25**	**–40**	**3**	**–71**	**60**	**30**
Total credit	2 994	*50*	*39*	*50*	*68*	*93*	*54*	*169*	*83*
Total debit	3 994	*–46*	*–59*	*–75*	*–108*	*–90*	*–125*	*–109*	*–53*
Capital transfers, credit	2 400	**50**	**39**	**50**	**68**	**93**	**54**	**169**	**83**
General government	2 401	50	39	50	68	89	46	163	77
Debt forgiveness	2 402	...	...	...	12	53	7	138	20
Other capital transfers	2 410	50	39	50	56	36	39	25	57
Other sectors	2 430	...	...	...	...	4	8	6	5
Migrants' transfers	2 431	...	...	...	...	...	...	...	...
Debt forgiveness	2 432	...	...	...	...	...	...	...	...
Other capital transfers	2 440	...	...	...	...	4	8	6	5
Capital transfers, debit	3 400	**–46**	**–59**	**–75**	**–108**	**–90**	**–125**	**–109**	**–53**
General government	3 401	...	...	...	...	...	...	...	...
Debt forgiveness	3 402	...	...	...	...	...	...	...	...
Other capital transfers	3 410	...	...	...	...	...	...	...	...
Other sectors	3 430	–46	–59	–75	–108	–90	–125	–109	–53
Migrants' transfers	3 431	–46	–59	–75	–108	–90	–125	–109	–53
Debt forgiveness	3 432	...	...	...	...	...	...	...	...
Other capital transfers	3 440	...	...	...	...	...	...	...	...
Nonproduced nonfinancial assets, credit	2 480	...	...	...	...	...	...	...	...
Nonproduced nonfinancial assets, debit	3 480	...	...	...	...	...	...	...	...

Table 2 (Continued). STANDARD PRESENTATION, 1988–95
(Millions of U.S. dollars)

	Code	1988	1989	1990	1991	1992	1993	1994	1995
FINANCIAL ACCOUNT	4 995	**1,356**	**417**	**1,349**	**287**	**1,522**	**1,037**	**2,189**	**3,048**
A. DIRECT INVESTMENT	4 500	26	59	41	–7	136	670	2,860	1,895
Direct investment abroad	4 505	**. . .**	**. . .**	**. . .**	**. . .**	**. . .**	**. . .**	**. . .**	**. . .**
Equity capital	4 510	. . .	. . .	. . .	. . .	. . .	. . .	. . .	. . .
Claims on affiliated enterprises	4 515	. . .	. . .	. . .	. . .	. . .	. . .	. . .	. . .
Liabilities to affiliated enterprises	4 520	. . .	. . .	. . .	. . .	. . .	. . .	. . .	. . .
Reinvested earnings	4 525	. . .	. . .	. . .	. . .	. . .	. . .	. . .	. . .
Other capital	4 530	. . .	. . .	. . .	. . .	. . .	. . .	. . .	. . .
Claims on affiliated enterprises	4 535	. . .	. . .	. . .	. . .	. . .	. . .	. . .	. . .
Liabilities to affiliated enterprises	4 540	. . .	. . .	. . .	. . .	. . .	. . .	. . .	. . .
Direct investment in Peru	4 555	**26**	**59**	**41**	**–7**	**136**	**670**	**2,860**	**1,895**
Equity capital	4 560	–10	42	33	–11	118	647	2,808	1,795
Claims on direct investors	4 565	. . .	. . .	. . .	. . .	. . .	. . .	. . .	. . .
Liabilities to direct investors	4 570	. . .	. . .	. . .	. . .	. . .	. . .	. . .	. . .
Reinvested earnings	4 575	36	17	8	4	18	23	52	100
Other capital	4 580	. . .	. . .	. . .	. . .	. . .	. . .	. . .	. . .
Claims on direct investors	4 585	. . .	. . .	. . .	. . .	. . .	. . .	. . .	. . .
Liabilities to direct investors	4 590	. . .	. . .	. . .	. . .	. . .	. . .	. . .	. . .
B. PORTFOLIO INVESTMENT	4 600	. . .	. . .	. . .	. . .	. . .	228	584	151
Assets	4 602	**. . .**	**. . .**	**. . .**	**. . .**	**. . .**	**. . .**	**. . .**	**. . .**
Equity securities	4 610	. . .	. . .	. . .	. . .	. . .	. . .	. . .	. . .
Monetary authorities	4 611	. . .	. . .	. . .	. . .	. . .	. . .	. . .	. . .
General government	4 612	. . .	. . .	. . .	. . .	. . .	. . .	. . .	. . .
Banks	4 613	. . .	. . .	. . .	. . .	. . .	. . .	. . .	. . .
Other sectors	4 614	. . .	. . .	. . .	. . .	. . .	. . .	. . .	. . .
Debt securities	4 619	. . .	. . .	. . .	. . .	. . .	. . .	. . .	. . .
Bonds and notes	4 620	. . .	. . .	. . .	. . .	. . .	. . .	. . .	. . .
Monetary authorities	4 621	. . .	. . .	. . .	. . .	. . .	. . .	. . .	. . .
General government	4 622	. . .	. . .	. . .	. . .	. . .	. . .	. . .	. . .
Banks	4 623	. . .	. . .	. . .	. . .	. . .	. . .	. . .	. . .
Other sectors	4 624	. . .	. . .	. . .	. . .	. . .	. . .	. . .	. . .
Money market instruments	4 630	. . .	. . .	. . .	. . .	. . .	. . .	. . .	. . .
Monetary authorities	4 631	. . .	. . .	. . .	. . .	. . .	. . .	. . .	. . .
General government	4 632	. . .	. . .	. . .	. . .	. . .	. . .	. . .	. . .
Banks	4 633	. . .	. . .	. . .	. . .	. . .	. . .	. . .	. . .
Other sectors	4 634	. . .	. . .	. . .	. . .	. . .	. . .	. . .	. . .
Financial derivatives	4 640	. . .	. . .	. . .	. . .	. . .	. . .	. . .	. . .
Monetary authorities	4 641	. . .	. . .	. . .	. . .	. . .	. . .	. . .	. . .
General government	4 642	. . .	. . .	. . .	. . .	. . .	. . .	. . .	. . .
Banks	4 643	. . .	. . .	. . .	. . .	. . .	. . .	. . .	. . .
Other sectors	4 644	. . .	. . .	. . .	. . .	. . .	. . .	. . .	. . .
Liabilities	4 652	**. . .**	**. . .**	**. . .**	**. . .**	**. . .**	**228**	**584**	**151**
Equity securities	4 660	. . .	. . .	. . .	. . .	. . .	222	465	171
Banks	4 663	. . .	. . .	. . .	. . .	. . .	. . .	. . .	. . .
Other sectors	4 664	. . .	. . .	. . .	. . .	. . .	222	465	171
Debt securities	4 669	. . .	. . .	. . .	. . .	. . .	6	120	–20
Bonds and notes	4 670	. . .	. . .	. . .	. . .	. . .	6	120	–20
Monetary authorities	4 671	. . .	. . .	. . .	. . .	. . .	. . .	. . .	. . .
General government	4 672	. . .	. . .	. . .	. . .	. . .	. . .	. . .	. . .
Banks	4 673	. . .	. . .	. . .	. . .	. . .	. . .	. . .	. . .
Other sectors	4 674	. . .	. . .	. . .	. . .	. . .	6	120	–20
Money market instruments	4 680	. . .	. . .	. . .	. . .	. . .	. . .	. . .	. . .
Monetary authorities	4 681	. . .	. . .	. . .	. . .	. . .	. . .	. . .	. . .
General government	4 682	. . .	. . .	. . .	. . .	. . .	. . .	. . .	. . .
Banks	4 683	. . .	. . .	. . .	. . .	. . .	. . .	. . .	. . .
Other sectors	4 684	. . .	. . .	. . .	. . .	. . .	. . .	. . .	. . .
Financial derivatives	4 690	. . .	. . .	. . .	. . .	. . .	. . .	. . .	. . .
Monetary authorities	4 691	. . .	. . .	. . .	. . .	. . .	. . .	. . .	. . .
General government	4 692	. . .	. . .	. . .	. . .	. . .	. . .	. . .	. . .
Banks	4 693	. . .	. . .	. . .	. . .	. . .	. . .	. . .	. . .
Other sectors	4 694	. . .	. . .	. . .	. . .	. . .	. . .	. . .	. . .

Table 2 (Concluded). STANDARD PRESENTATION, 1988–95
(Millions of U.S. dollars)

	Code	1988	1989	1990	1991	1992	1993	1994	1995
C. OTHER INVESTMENT	4 700 . .	1,181	600	1,520	1,193	1,939	806	1,816	1,919
Assets	4 703 . .	**–461**	**–666**	**432**	**–289**	**318**	**269**	**–250**	**–576**
Trade credits	4 706 . .	. . .	. . .	. . .	. . .	. . .	. . .	. . .	. . .
General government: long-term	4 708 . .	. . .	. . .	. . .	. . .	. . .	. . .	. . .	. . .
General government: short-term	4 709 . .	. . .	. . .	. . .	. . .	. . .	. . .	. . .	. . .
Other sectors: long-term	4 711 . .	. . .	. . .	. . .	. . .	. . .	. . .	. . .	. . .
Other sectors: short-term	4 712 . .	. . .	. . .	. . .	. . .	. . .	. . .	. . .	. . .
Loans	4 714 . .	. . .	. . .	. . .	. . .	. . .	. . .	. . .	. . .
Monetary authorities: long-term	4 717 . .	. . .	. . .	. . .	. . .	. . .	. . .	. . .	. . .
Monetary authorities: short-term	4 718 . .	. . .	. . .	. . .	. . .	. . .	. . .	. . .	. . .
General government: long-term	4 720 . .	. . .	. . .	. . .	. . .	. . .	. . .	. . .	. . .
General government: short-term	4 721 . .	. . .	. . .	. . .	. . .	. . .	. . .	. . .	. . .
Banks: long-term	4 723 . .	. . .	. . .	. . .	. . .	. . .	. . .	. . .	. . .
Banks: short-term	4 724 . .	. . .	. . .	. . .	. . .	. . .	. . .	. . .	. . .
Other sectors: long-term	4 726 . .	. . .	. . .	. . .	. . .	. . .	. . .	. . .	. . .
Other sectors: short-term	4 727 . .	. . .	. . .	. . .	. . .	. . .	. . .	. . .	. . .
Currency and deposits	4 730 . .	–461	–666	432	–289	318	269	–250	–576
Monetary authorities	4 731 . .	. . .	. . .	. . .	. . .	. . .	. . .	. . .	. . .
General government	4 732 . .	. . .	. . .	. . .	. . .	. . .	. . .	. . .	. . .
Banks	4 733 . .	–13	–181	63	–476	84	119	–265	–455
Other sectors	4 734 . .	–448	–485	369	187	234	150	15	–121
Other assets	4 736 . .	. . .	. . .	. . .	. . .	. . .	. . .	. . .	. . .
Monetary authorities: long-term	4 738 . .	. . .	. . .	. . .	. . .	. . .	. . .	. . .	. . .
Monetary authorities: short-term	4 739 . .	. . .	. . .	. . .	. . .	. . .	. . .	. . .	. . .
General government: long-term	4 741 . .	. . .	. . .	. . .	. . .	. . .	. . .	. . .	. . .
General government: short-term	4 742 . .	. . .	. . .	. . .	. . .	. . .	. . .	. . .	. . .
Banks: long-term	4 744 . .	. . .	. . .	. . .	. . .	. . .	. . .	. . .	. . .
Banks: short-term	4 745 . .	. . .	. . .	. . .	. . .	. . .	. . .	. . .	. . .
Other sectors: long-term	4 747 . .	. . .	. . .	. . .	. . .	. . .	. . .	. . .	. . .
Other sectors: short-term	4 748 . .	. . .	. . .	. . .	. . .	. . .	. . .	. . .	. . .
Liabilities	4 753 . .	**1,642**	**1,266**	**1,088**	**1,483**	**1,621**	**537**	**2,066**	**2,495**
Trade credits	4 756 . .	. . .	. . .	. . .	. . .	. . .	. . .	. . .	. . .
General government: long-term	4 758 . .	. . .	. . .	. . .	. . .	. . .	. . .	. . .	. . .
General government: short-term	4 759 . .	. . .	. . .	. . .	. . .	. . .	. . .	. . .	. . .
Other sectors: long-term	4 761 . .	. . .	. . .	. . .	. . .	. . .	. . .	. . .	. . .
Other sectors: short-term	4 762 . .	. . .	. . .	. . .	. . .	. . .	. . .	. . .	. . .
Loans	4 764 . .	–991	–206	–1,037	5,811	1,008	2,196	1,428	1,711
Use of Fund credit and loans from the Fund	4 766 . .	. . .	–24	–63	–51	–49	254	. . .	. . .
Monetary authorities: other long-term	4 767 . .	. . .	. . .	. . .	. . .	. . .	. . .	. . .	. . .
Monetary authorities: short-term	4 768 . .	332	–331	109	68	–65	–83	38	–24
General government: long-term	4 770 . .	–1,099	–3	–932	5,412	277	1,804	321	335
General government: short-term	4 771 . .	. . .	. . .	. . .	. . .	. . .	. . .	. . .	. . .
Banks: long-term	4 773 . .	. . .	. . .	–4	–2	28	36	25	85
Banks: short-term	4 774 . .	8	6	–84	24	146	160	–293	755
Other sectors: long-term	4 776 . .	–22	–10	4	117	42	270	357	118
Other sectors: short-term	4 777 . .	–210	156	–66	244	629	–245	980	442
Currency and deposits	4 780 . .	. . .	. . .	. . .	. . .	. . .	. . .	. . .	. . .
Monetary authorities	4 781 . .	. . .	. . .	. . .	. . .	. . .	. . .	. . .	. . .
General government	4 782 . .	. . .	. . .	. . .	. . .	. . .	. . .	. . .	. . .
Banks	4 783 . .	. . .	. . .	. . .	. . .	. . .	. . .	. . .	. . .
Other sectors	4 784 . .	. . .	. . .	. . .	. . .	. . .	. . .	. . .	. . .
Other liabilities	4 786 . .	2,633	1,472	2,125	–4,329	613	–1,659	638	784
Monetary authorities: long-term	4 788 . .	191	127	. . .	. . .	. . .	–587	. . .	. . .
Monetary authorities: short-term	4 789 . .	28	. . .	. . .	. . .	. . .	–263	. . .	. . .
General government: long-term	4 791 . .	. . .	. . .	. . .	. . .	. . .	. . .	. . .	. . .
General government: short-term	4 792 . .	2,393	1,337	2,204	–4,319	614	–808	638	784
Banks: long-term	4 794 . .	. . .	. . .	. . .	. . .	. . .	. . .	. . .	. . .
Banks: short-term	4 795 . .	. . .	. . .	. . .	. . .	. . .	. . .	. . .	. . .
Other sectors: long-term	4 797 . .	. . .	. . .	. . .	. . .	. . .	. . .	. . .	. . .
Other sectors: short-term	4 798 . .	21	8	–79	–10	–1	–1	. . .	. . .
D. RESERVE ASSETS	4 800 . .	149	–242	–212	–899	–554	–667	–3,070	–916
Monetary gold	4 810 . .	73	62	16	116	–1	78	63	. . .
Special drawing rights	4 820 . .	. . .	. . .	. . .	. . .	. . .	–1	1	. . .
Reserve position in the Fund	4 830 . .	. . .	. . .	. . .	. . .	. . .	. . .	. . .	. . .
Foreign exchange	4 840 . .	180	–292	–191	–966	–524	–850	–3,085	–916
Other claims	4 880 . .	–104	–11	–37	–49	–29	106	–49	1
NET ERRORS AND OMISSIONS	4 998 . .	**297**	**–157**	**–257**	**1,073**	**383**	**1,178**	**290**	**1,145**

Part 3 of the *Yearbook* contains descriptions of the methodologies, compilation practices, and sources used to compile these data.

Table 3. INTERNATIONAL INVESTMENT POSITION (End–period stocks), 1988–95
(Millions of U.S. dollars)

	Code	1988	1989	1990	1991	1992	1993	1994	1995
ASSETS	8 995 C.	4,168	5,279	5,123	6,235	6,432	6,814	10,409	11,599
Direct investment abroad	8 505 . .	...	...	...	...	...	...	...	...
Equity capital and reinvested earnings	8 506 . .	...	...	...	...	...	...	...	...
Claims on affiliated enterprises	8 507 . .	...	...	...	...	...	...	...	...
Liabilities to affiliated enterprises	8 508 . .	...	...	...	...	...	...	...	...
Other capital	8 530 . .	...	...	...	...	...	...	...	...
Claims on affiliated enterprises	8 535 . .	...	...	...	...	...	...	...	...
Liabilities to affiliated enterprises	8 540 . .	...	...	...	...	...	...	...	...
Portfolio investment	8 602 . .	...	...	...	...	...	...	...	...
Equity securities	8 610 . .	...	...	...	...	...	...	...	...
Monetary authorities	8 611 . .	...	...	...	...	...	...	...	...
General government	8 612 . .	...	...	...	...	...	...	...	...
Banks	8 613 . .	...	...	...	...	...	...	...	...
Other sectors	8 614 . .	...	...	...	...	...	...	...	...
Debt securities	8 619 . .	...	...	...	...	...	...	...	...
Bonds and notes	8 620 . .	...	...	...	...	...	...	...	...
Monetary authorities	8 621 . .	...	...	...	...	...	...	...	...
General government	8 622 . .	...	...	...	...	...	...	...	...
Banks	8 623 . .	...	...	...	...	...	...	...	...
Other sectors	8 624 . .	...	...	...	...	...	...	...	...
Money market instruments	8 630 . .	...	...	...	...	...	...	...	...
Monetary authorities	8 631 . .	...	...	...	...	...	...	...	...
General government	8 632 . .	...	...	...	...	...	...	...	...
Banks	8 633 . .	...	...	...	...	...	...	...	...
Other sectors	8 634 . .	...	...	...	...	...	...	...	...
Financial derivatives	8 640 . .	...	...	...	...	...	...	...	...
Monetary authorities	8 641 . .	...	...	...	...	...	...	...	...
General government	8 642 . .	...	...	...	...	...	...	...	...
Banks	8 643 . .	...	...	...	...	...	...	...	...
Other sectors	8 644 . .	...	...	...	...	...	...	...	...
Other investment	8 703 . .	**3,105**	**3,826**	**3,385**	**3,662**	**3,339**	**3,061**	**3,592**	**3,863**
Trade credits	8 706 . .	...	...	...	...	...	...	...	...
General government: long-term	8 708 . .	...	...	...	...	...	...	...	...
General government: short-term	8 709 . .	...	...	...	...	...	...	...	...
Other sectors: long-term	8 711 . .	...	...	...	...	...	...	...	...
Other sectors: short-term	8 712 . .	...	...	...	...	...	...	...	...
Loans	8 714 . .	...	...	...	...	...	...	...	...
Monetary authorities: long-term	8 717 . .	...	...	...	...	...	...	...	...
Monetary authorities: short-term	8 718 . .	...	...	...	...	...	...	...	...
General government: long-term	8 720 . .	...	...	...	...	...	...	...	...
General government: short-term	8 721 . .	...	...	...	...	...	...	...	...
Banks: long-term	8 723 . .	...	...	...	...	...	...	...	...
Banks: short-term	8 724 . .	...	...	...	...	...	...	...	...
Other sectors: long-term	8 726 . .	...	...	...	...	...	...	...	...
Other sectors: short-term	8 727 . .	...	...	...	...	...	...	...	...
Currency and deposits	8 730 . .	3,105	3,826	3,385	3,662	3,339	3,061	3,592	3,863
Monetary authorities	8 731 . .	...	...	...	...	...	...	...	...
General government	8 732 . .	...	...	...	...	...	...	...	...
Banks	8 733 . .	354	535	472	948	864	745	1,010	1,465
Other sectors	8 734 . .	2,751	3,291	2,913	2,714	2,475	2,316	2,582	2,398
Other assets	8 736 . .	...	...	...	...	...	...	...	...
Monetary authorities: long-term	8 738 . .	...	...	...	...	...	...	...	...
Monetary authorities: short-term	8 739 . .	...	...	...	...	...	...	...	...
General government: long-term	8 741 . .	...	...	...	...	...	...	...	...
General government: short-term	8 742 . .	...	...	...	...	...	...	...	...
Banks: long-term	8 744 . .	...	...	...	...	...	...	...	...
Banks: short-term	8 745 . .	...	...	...	...	...	...	...	...
Other sectors: long-term	8 747 . .	...	...	...	...	...	...	...	...
Other sectors: short-term	8 748 . .	...	...	...	...	...	...	...	...
Reserve assets	8 800 . .	**1,063**	**1,453**	**1,738**	**2,573**	**3,093**	**3,753**	**6,816**	**7,736**
Monetary gold	8 810 . .	619	704	761	582	548	466	395	399
Special drawing rights	8 820 . .	...	...	...	...	...	1	...	1
Reserve position in the Fund	8 830 . .	...	...	...	...	...	...	...	...
Foreign exchange	8 840 . .	163	457	648	1,613	2,138	2,985	6,071	6,987
Other claims	8 880 . .	281	292	329	378	407	301	350	349

Table 3 (Continued). INTERNATIONAL INVESTMENT POSITION (End–period stocks), 1988–95
(Millions of U.S. dollars)

	Code		1988	1989	1990	1991	1992	1993	1994	1995
LIABILITIES	8 995	D.	21,238	22,052	23,450	25,851	27,007	28,651	35,340	39,162
Direct investment in Peru	8 555	. .	**1,258**	**1,287**	**1,330**	**1,370**	**1,501**	**1,663**	**4,462**	**5,466**
Equity capital and reinvested earnings	8 556	. .	1,258	1,287	1,330	1,370	1,501	1,663	4,462	5,466
Claims on direct investors	8 557	. .	...	...	...	...	...	...	...	...
Liabilities to direct investors	8 558	. .	...	...	...	...	...	...	...	...
Other capital	8 580	. .	...	...	...	...	...	...	...	...
Claims on direct investors	8 585	. .	...	...	...	...	...	...	...	...
Liabilities to direct investors	8 590	. .	...	...	...	...	...	...	...	...
Portfolio investment	8 652	. .	**...**	**...**	**...**	**...**	**27**	**695**	**1,673**	**1,717**
Equity securities	8 660	. .	...	...	...	...	27	689	1,547	1,611
Banks	8 663	. .	...	...	...	...	...	...	...	...
Other sectors	8 664	. .	...	...	...	...	27	689	1,547	1,611
Debt securities	8 669	. .	...	...	...	...	...	6	126	106
Bonds and notes	8 670	. .	...	...	...	...	...	6	126	106
Monetary authorities	8 671	. .	...	...	...	...	...	...	...	...
General government	8 672	. .	...	...	...	...	...	...	...	...
Banks	8 673	. .	...	...	...	...	...	...	...	...
Other sectors	8 674	. .	...	...	...	...	...	6	126	106
Money market instruments	8 680	. .	...	...	...	...	...	...	...	...
Monetary authorities	8 681	. .	...	...	...	...	...	...	...	...
General government	8 682	. .	...	...	...	...	...	...	...	...
Banks	8 683	. .	...	...	...	...	...	...	...	...
Other sectors	8 684	. .	...	...	...	...	...	...	...	...
Financial derivatives	8 690	. .	...	...	...	...	...	...	...	...
Monetary authorities	8 691	. .	...	...	...	...	...	...	...	...
General government	8 692	. .	...	...	...	...	...	...	...	...
Banks	8 692	. .	...	...	...	...	...	...	...	...
Other sectors	8 694	. .	...	...	...	...	...	...	...	...
Other investment	8 753	. .	**19,980**	**20,765**	**22,120**	**24,481**	**25,479**	**26,293**	**29,204**	**31,979**
Trade credits	8 756	. .	...	...	...	...	...	...	...	...
General government: long-term	8 758	. .	...	...	...	...	...	...	...	...
General government: short-term	8 759	. .	...	...	...	...	...	...	...	...
Other sectors: long-term	8 761	. .	...	...	...	...	...	...	...	...
Other sectors: short-term	8 762	. .	...	...	...	...	...	...	...	...
Loans	8 764	. .	19,980	20,765	22,120	24,481	25,479	26,293	29,204	31,979
Use of Fund credit and loans from the Fund	8 766	. .	801	758	755	706	631	883	938	955
Monetary authorities: other long-term	8 767	. .	...	...	...	...	...	...	...	...
Monetary authorities: short-term	8 768	. .	650	363	494	599	493	162	200	176
General government: long-term	8 770	. .	16,002	16,904	18,289	20,180	20,476	21,126	22,942	24,295
General government: short-term	8 771	. .	853	906	978	1,020	1,058	1,081	1,008	1,070
Banks: long-term	8 773	. .	...	...	10	8	36	72	97	182
Banks: short-term	8 774	. .	757	763	679	703	848	1,008	715	1,470
Other sectors: long-term	8 776	. .	386	384	295	401	443	712	1,075	1,195
Other sectors: short-term	8 777	. .	531	687	621	864	1,494	1,249	2,229	2,636
Currency and deposits	8 780	. .	...	...	...	...	...	...	...	...
Monetary authorities	8 781	. .	...	...	...	...	...	...	...	...
General government	8 782	. .	...	...	...	...	...	...	...	...
Banks	8 783	. .	...	...	...	...	...	...	...	...
Other sectors	8 784	. .	...	...	...	...	...	...	...	...
Other liabilities	8 786	. .	...	...	...	...	...	...	...	...
Monetary authorities: long-term	8 788	. .	...	...	...	...	...	...	...	...
Monetary authorities: short-term	8 789	. .	...	...	...	...	...	...	...	...
General government: long-term	8 791	. .	...	...	...	...	...	...	...	...
General government: short-term	8 792	. .	...	...	...	...	...	...	...	...
Banks: long-term	8 794	. .	...	...	...	...	...	...	...	...
Banks: short-term	8 795	. .	...	...	...	...	...	...	...	...
Other sectors: long-term	8 797	. .	...	...	...	...	...	...	...	...
Other sectors: short-term	8 798	. .	...	...	...	...	...	...	...	...
NET INTERNATIONAL INVESTMENT POSITION	8 995	. .	**–17,070**	**–16,774**	**–18,327**	**–19,616**	**–20,575**	**–21,838**	**–24,931**	**–27,563**
Conversion rates: nuevos soles per U.S. dollar (end of period)	0 102	. .	**.0005**	**.0053**	**.5169**	**.9600**	**1.6300**	**2.1600**	**2.1800**	**2.3100**

Table 1. ANALYTIC PRESENTATION, 1988–95
(Millions of U.S. dollars)

	Code	1988	1989	1990	1991	1992	1993	1994	1995
A. Current Account [1]	4 993 Y.	**–390**	**–1,456**	**–2,695**	**–1,034**	**–1,000**	**–3,016**	**–2,950**	**–1,980**
Goods: exports f.o.b.	2 100 . .	7,074	7,821	8,186	8,840	9,824	11,375	13,483	17,447
Goods: imports f.o.b.	3 100 . .	–8,159	–10,419	–12,206	–12,051	–14,519	–17,597	–21,333	–26,391
Balance on Goods	4 100 . .	*–1,085*	*–2,598*	*–4,020*	*–3,211*	*–4,695*	*–6,222*	*–7,850*	*–8,944*
Services: credit	2 200 . .	2,413	3,225	3,244	3,654	4,742	4,673	6,768	9,348
Services: debit	3 200 . .	–1,308	–1,564	–1,761	–1,804	–2,308	–3,090	–4,654	–6,926
Balance on Goods and Services	4 991 . .	*20*	*–937*	*–2,537*	*–1,361*	*–2,261*	*–4,639*	*–5,736*	*–6,522*
Income: credit	2 300 . .	1,179	1,361	1,598	1,969	2,755	2,824	3,782	6,067
Income: debit	3 300 . .	–2,364	–2,710	–2,470	–2,469	–2,310	–1,900	–1,932	–2,405
Balance on Goods, Services, and Income	4 992 . .	*–1,165*	*–2,286*	*–3,409*	*–1,861*	*–1,816*	*–3,715*	*–3,886*	*–2,860*
Current transfers: credit	2 379 Y.	778	832	717	828	825	746	1,041	1,147
Current transfers: debit	3 379 . .	–3	–2	–3	–1	–9	–47	–105	–267
B. Capital Account [1]	4 994 Y.	**. . .**	**. . .**	**. . .**	**. . .**	**1**	**. . .**	**. . .**	**. . .**
Capital account: credit	2 994 Y.	. . .	. . .	. . .	. . .	1	. . .	. . .	. . .
Capital account: debit	3 994 . .	. . .	. . .	. . .	. . .	. . .	. . .	. . .	. . .
Total, Groups A Plus B	4 010 . .	*–390*	*–1,456*	*–2,695*	*–1,034*	*–999*	*–3,016*	*–2,950*	*–1,980*
C. Financial Account [1]	4 995 X.	**571**	**1,354**	**2,057**	**2,927**	**3,208**	**3,267**	**5,120**	**5,309**
Direct investment abroad	4 505 . .	. . .	. . .	. . .	. . .	. . .	–374	–302	–399
Direct investment in Philippines	4 555 Y.	936	563	530	544	228	1,238	1,591	1,478
Portfolio investment assets	4 602 . .	–1	–14	. . .	–15	–115	–949	–632	–1,429
Equity securities	4 610 . .	. . .	. . .	. . .	. . .	. . .	. . .	. . .	. . .
Debt securities	4 619 . .	–1	–14	. . .	–15	–115	–949	–632	–1,429
Portfolio investment liabilities	4 652 Y.	51	294	–50	125	155	897	901	2,619
Equity securities	4 660 Y.	. . .	. . .	. . .	. . .	. . .	. . .	. . .	. . .
Debt securities	4 669 Y.	51	294	–50	125	155	897	901	2,619
Other investment assets	4 703 . .	. . .	. . .	. . .	. . .	. . .	. . .	. . .	. . .
Monetary authorities	4 703 . A	. . .	. . .	. . .	. . .	. . .	. . .	. . .	. . .
General government	4 703 . B	. . .	. . .	. . .	. . .	. . .	. . .	. . .	. . .
Banks	4 703 . C	. . .	. . .	. . .	. . .	. . .	. . .	. . .	. . .
Other sectors	4 703 . D	. . .	. . .	. . .	. . .	. . .	. . .	. . .	. . .
Other investment liabilities	4 753 X.	–415	511	1,577	2,273	2,940	2,455	3,562	3,040
Monetary authorities	4 753 XA	. . .	. . .	. . .	. . .	. . .	. . .	. . .	. . .
General government	4 753 YB	–68	108	875	375	2,731	1,065	–1,121	–408
Banks	4 753 YC	321	370	307	473	1,921	–229	1,694	1,648
Other sectors	4 753 YD	–668	33	395	1,425	–1,712	1,619	2,989	1,800
Total, Groups A Through C	4 020 . .	*181*	*–102*	*–638*	*1,893*	*2,209*	*251*	*2,170*	*3,329*
D. Net Errors and Omissions	4 998 . .	**493**	**402**	**593**	**–138**	**–520**	**85**	**157**	**–2,094**
Total, Groups A Through D	4 030 . .	*674*	*300*	*–45*	*1,755*	*1,689*	*336*	*2,327*	*1,235*
E. Reserves and Related Items	4 040 . .	**–674**	**–300**	**45**	**–1,755**	**–1,689**	**–336**	**–2,327**	**–1,235**
Reserve assets	4 800 . .	–570	–408	388	–1,937	–1,746	–447	–2,107	–873
Use of Fund credit and loans	4 766 . .	–104	108	–343	182	58	111	–220	–362
Liabilities constituting foreign authorities' reserves	4 900 . .	. . .	. . .	. . .	. . .	. . .	. . .	. . .	. . .
Exceptional financing	4 920 . .	. . .	. . .	. . .	. . .	. . .	. . .	. . .	. . .
Conversion rates: Philippine pesos per U.S. dollar	0 101 . .	**21.095**	**21.737**	**24.311**	**27.479**	**25.512**	**27.120**	**26.417**	**25.714**

[1] Excludes components that have been classified in the categories of Group E.

Table 2. STANDARD PRESENTATION, 1988–95
(Millions of U.S. dollars)

	Code	1988	1989	1990	1991	1992	1993	1994	1995
CURRENT ACCOUNT	4 993 . .	**–390**	**–1,456**	**–2,695**	**–1,034**	**–1,000**	**–3,016**	**–2,950**	**–1,980**
A. GOODS	4 100 . .	–1,085	–2,598	–4,020	–3,211	–4,695	–6,222	–7,850	–8,944
Credit	2 100 . .	**7,074**	**7,821**	**8,186**	**8,840**	**9,824**	**11,375**	**13,483**	**17,447**
General merchandise: exports f.o.b.	2 110 . .	6,956	7,712	8,096	8,775	9,668	11,324	13,418	17,381
Goods for processing: exports f.o.b.	2 150 . .	...	...	...	...	...	...	...	...
Repairs on goods	2 160 . .	...	...	...	...	...	...	...	...
Goods procured in ports by carriers	2 170 . .	...	...	...	...	...	...	...	...
Nonmonetary gold	2 180 . .	118	109	90	65	156	51	65	66
Debit	3 100 . .	**–8,159**	**–10,419**	**–12,206**	**–12,051**	**–14,519**	**–17,597**	**–21,333**	**–26,391**
General merchandise: imports f.o.b.	3 110 . .	–8,159	–10,419	–12,206	–12,051	–14,519	–17,597	–21,333	–26,391
Goods for processing: imports f.o.b.	3 150 . .	...	...	...	...	...	...	...	...
Repairs on goods	3 160 . .	...	...	...	...	...	...	...	...
Goods procured in ports by carriers	3 170 . .	...	...	...	...	...	...	...	...
Nonmonetary gold	3 180 . .	...	...	...	...	...	...	...	...
B. SERVICES	4 200 . .	1,105	1,661	1,483	1,850	2,434	1,583	2,114	2,422
Total credit	2 200 . .	*2,413*	*3,225*	*3,244*	*3,654*	*4,742*	*4,673*	*6,768*	*9,348*
Total debit	3 200 . .	*–1,308*	*–1,564*	*–1,761*	*–1,804*	*–2,308*	*–3,090*	*–4,654*	*–6,926*
Transportation services, credit	2 205 . .	**220**	**235**	**246**	**242**	**273**	**218**	**233**	**274**
Passenger	2 205 BA	*50*	*39*	*40*	*38*	*83*	*43*	*29*	*5*
Freight	2 205 BB	*131*	*151*	*163*	*160*	*145*	*147*	*179*	*242*
Other	2 205 BC	*39*	*45*	*43*	*44*	*45*	*28*	*25*	*27*
Sea transport, passenger	2 207 . .	...	...	...	...	...	...	...	...
Sea transport, freight	2 208 . .	...	...	...	...	...	...	...	...
Sea transport, other	2 209 . .	...	...	...	...	...	...	...	...
Air transport, passenger	2 211 . .	...	...	...	...	...	...	...	...
Air transport, freight	2 212 . .	...	...	...	...	...	...	...	...
Air transport, other	2 213 . .	...	...	...	...	...	...	...	...
Other transport, passenger	2 215 . .	...	...	...	...	...	...	...	...
Other transport, freight	2 216 . .	...	...	...	...	...	...	...	...
Other transport, other	2 217 . .	...	...	...	...	...	...	...	...
Transportation services, debit	3 205 . .	**–726**	**–887**	**–980**	**–1,062**	**–1,199**	**–1,425**	**–1,457**	**–2,051**
Passenger	3 205 BA	*–156*	*–137*	*–149*	*–237*	*–235*	*–235*	*–176*	*–129*
Freight	3 205 BB	*–560*	*–730*	*–800*	*–782*	*–916*	*–1,147*	*–1,276*	*–1,917*
Other	3 205 BC	*–10*	*–20*	*–31*	*–43*	*–48*	*–43*	*–5*	*–5*
Sea transport, passenger	3 207 . .	...	...	...	...	...	...	...	...
Sea transport, freight	3 208 . .	...	...	...	...	...	...	...	...
Sea transport, other	3 209 . .	...	...	...	...	...	...	...	...
Air transport, passenger	3 211 . .	...	...	...	...	...	...	...	...
Air transport, freight	3 212 . .	...	...	...	...	...	...	...	...
Air transport, other	3 213 . .	...	...	...	...	...	...	...	...
Other transport, passenger	3 215 . .	...	...	...	...	...	...	...	...
Other transport, freight	3 216 . .	...	...	...	...	...	...	...	...
Other transport, other	3 217 . .	...	...	...	...	...	...	...	...
Travel, credit	2 236 . .	**405**	**469**	**466**	**570**	**944**	**1,178**	**973**	**1,136**
Business travel	2 237 . .	...	...	...	...	...	...	...	...
Personal travel	2 240 . .	...	...	...	...	...	...	...	...
Travel, debit	3 236 . .	**–76**	**–77**	**–111**	**–61**	**–102**	**–130**	**–196**	**–422**
Business travel	3 237 . .	...	...	...	...	...	...	...	...
Personal travel	3 240 . .	...	...	...	...	...	...	...	...
Other services, credit	2 200 BA	**1,788**	**2,521**	**2,532**	**2,842**	**3,525**	**3,277**	**5,562**	**7,938**
Communications	2 245 . .	...	...	...	...	...	...	...	...
Construction	2 249 . .	9	11	3	2	4	10	6	10
Insurance	2 253 . .	13	17	14	20	23	21	10	62
Financial	2 260 . .	...	...	...	...	...	...	...	...
Computer and information	2 262 . .	...	...	...	...	...	...	...	...
Royalties and licence fees	2 266 . .	...	...	1	...	...	...	...	2
Other business services	2 268 . .	1,377	1,950	2,167	2,479	3,321	3,190	5,527	7,839
Personal, cultural, and recreational	2 287 . .	...	...	...	...	...	...	...	...
Government, n.i.e.	2 291 . .	389	543	347	341	177	56	19	25
Other services, debit	3 200 BA	**–506**	**–600**	**–670**	**–681**	**–1,007**	**–1,535**	**–3,001**	**–4,453**
Communications	3 245 . .	...	...	...	...	...	...	...	...
Construction	3 249 . .	–18	–6	–5	–28	–25	–23	–23	–58
Insurance	3 253 . .	–40	–50	–59	–47	–74	–93	–101	–109
Financial	3 260 . .	...	...	...	...	...	...	...	...
Computer and information	3 262 . .	...	...	...	...	...	...	...	...
Royalties and licence fees	3 266 . .	–27	–37	–38	–56	–55	–60	–95	–99
Other business services	3 268 . .	–414	–479	–528	–529	–850	–1,341	–2,767	–4,167
Personal, cultural, and recreational	3 287 . .	...	...	...	...	...	...	...	...
Government, n.i.e.	3 291 . .	–7	–28	–40	–21	–3	–18	–15	–20

Table 2 (Continued). STANDARD PRESENTATION, 1988–95

(Millions of U.S. dollars)

	Code	1988	1989	1990	1991	1992	1993	1994	1995
C. INCOME	4 300	–1,185	–1,349	–872	–500	445	924	1,850	3,662
Total credit	2 300	*1,179*	*1,361*	*1,598*	*1,969*	*2,755*	*2,824*	*3,782*	*6,067*
Total debit	3 300	*–2,364*	*–2,710*	*–2,470*	*–2,469*	*–2,310*	*–1,900*	*–1,932*	*–2,405*
Compensation of employees, credit	2 310	**874**	**1,002**	**1,203**	**1,521**	**2,222**	**2,276**	**3,009**	**4,928**
Compensation of employees, debit	3 310	**–10**	**–4**	**–5**	**–9**	**–7**	**–13**	**–13**	**–15**
Investment income, credit	2 320	**305**	**359**	**395**	**448**	**533**	**548**	**773**	**1,139**
Direct investment income	2 330	8	11	17	50	110	70	116	342
Dividends and distributed branch profits	2 332	8	11	17	50	110	70	116	342
Reinvested earnings and undistributed branch profits	2 333	...	...	...	...	...	...	...	...
Income on debt (interest)	2 334	...	...	...	...	...	...	...	...
Portfolio investment income	2 339	...	...	...	...	...	...	...	...
Income on equity	2 340	...	...	...	...	...	...	...	...
Income on bonds and notes	2 350	...	...	...	...	...	...	...	...
Income on money market instruments and financial derivatives	2 360	...	...	...	...	...	...	...	...
Other investment income	2 370	297	348	378	398	423	478	657	797
Investment income, debit	3 320	**–2,354**	**–2,706**	**–2,465**	**–2,460**	**–2,303**	**–1,887**	**–1,919**	**–2,390**
Direct investment income	3 330	–195	–295	–311	–303	–405	–369	–340	–515
Dividends and distributed branch profits	3 332	–178	–239	–283	–269	–363	–326	–311	–492
Reinvested earnings and undistributed branch profits	3 333	–17	–56	–28	–34	–42	–43	–29	–23
Income on debt (interest)	3 334	...	...	...	...	...	...	...	...
Portfolio investment income	3 339	...	...	...	...	...	...	...	...
Income on equity	3 340	...	...	...	...	...	...	...	...
Income on bonds and notes	3 350	...	...	...	...	...	...	...	...
Income on money market instruments and financial derivatives	3 360	...	...	...	...	...	...	...	...
Other investment income	3 370	–2,159	–2,411	–2,154	–2,157	–1,898	–1,518	–1,579	–1,875
D. CURRENT TRANSFERS	4 379	775	830	714	827	816	699	936	880
Credit	2 379	**778**	**832**	**717**	**828**	**825**	**746**	**1,041**	**1,147**
General government	2 380	81	59	91	150	200	139	72	77
Other sectors	2 390	697	773	626	678	625	607	969	1,070
Workers' remittances	2 391	388	360	262	329	315	311	443	432
Other current transfers	2 392	309	413	364	349	310	296	526	638
Debit	3 379	**–3**	**–2**	**–3**	**–1**	**–9**	**–47**	**–105**	**–267**
General government	3 380	...	...	...	...	...	...	...	...
Other sectors	3 390	–3	–2	–3	–1	–9	–47	–105	–267
Workers' remittances	3 391	...	...	...	...	–1	–32	–76	–136
Other current transfers	3 392	–3	–2	–3	–1	–8	–15	–29	–131
CAPITAL AND FINANCIAL ACCOUNT	4 996	**–103**	**1,054**	**2,102**	**1,172**	**1,520**	**2,931**	**2,793**	**4,074**
CAPITAL ACCOUNT	4 994	**...**	**...**	**...**	**...**	**1**	**...**	**...**	**...**
Total credit	2 994	...	...	...	...	*1*	...	...	...
Total debit	3 994	...	...	...	...	...	...	...	...
Capital transfers, credit	2 400	**...**	**...**	**...**	**...**	**1**	**...**	**...**	**...**
General government	2 401	...	...	...	...	...	...	...	...
Debt forgiveness	2 402	...	...	...	...	...	...	...	...
Other capital transfers	2 410	...	...	...	...	...	...	...	...
Other sectors	2 430	...	...	...	...	1	...	...	...
Migrants' transfers	2 431	...	...	...	...	1	...	...	...
Debt forgiveness	2 432	...	...	...	...	...	...	...	...
Other capital transfers	2 440	...	...	...	...	...	...	...	...
Capital transfers, debit	3 400	**...**	**...**	**...**	**...**	**...**	**...**	**...**	**...**
General government	3 401	...	...	...	...	...	...	...	...
Debt forgiveness	3 402	...	...	...	...	...	...	...	...
Other capital transfers	3 410	...	...	...	...	...	...	...	...
Other sectors	3 430	...	...	...	...	...	...	...	...
Migrants' transfers	3 431	...	...	...	...	...	...	...	...
Debt forgiveness	3 432	...	...	...	...	...	...	...	...
Other capital transfers	3 440	...	...	...	...	...	...	...	...
Nonproduced nonfinancial assets, credit	2 480	**...**	**...**	**...**	**...**	**...**	**...**	**...**	**...**
Nonproduced nonfinancial assets, debit	3 480	**...**	**...**	**...**	**...**	**...**	**...**	**...**	**...**

Table 2 (Continued). STANDARD PRESENTATION, 1988–95

(Millions of U.S. dollars)

	Code	1988	1989	1990	1991	1992	1993	1994	1995
FINANCIAL ACCOUNT	4 995	**–103**	**1,054**	**2,102**	**1,172**	**1,519**	**2,931**	**2,793**	**4,074**
A. DIRECT INVESTMENT	4 500	936	563	530	544	228	864	1,289	1,079
Direct investment abroad	4 505	**. . .**	**. . .**	**. . .**	**. . .**	**. . .**	**–374**	**–302**	**–399**
Equity capital	4 510	. . .	. . .	. . .	. . .	. . .	–374	–302	–399
Claims on affiliated enterprises	4 515	. . .	. . .	. . .	. . .	. . .	–374	–302	–399
Liabilities to affiliated enterprises	4 520	. . .	. . .	. . .	. . .	. . .	. . .	. . .	. . .
Reinvested earnings	4 525	. . .	. . .	. . .	. . .	. . .	. . .	. . .	. . .
Other capital	4 530	. . .	. . .	. . .	. . .	. . .	. . .	. . .	. . .
Claims on affiliated enterprises	4 535	. . .	. . .	. . .	. . .	. . .	. . .	. . .	. . .
Liabilities to affiliated enterprises	4 540	. . .	. . .	. . .	. . .	. . .	. . .	. . .	. . .
Direct investment in Philippines	4 555	**936**	**563**	**530**	**544**	**228**	**1,238**	**1,591**	**1,478**
Equity capital	4 560	. . .	. . .	. . .	. . .	. . .	. . .	. . .	. . .
Claims on direct investors	4 565	. . .	. . .	. . .	. . .	. . .	. . .	. . .	. . .
Liabilities to direct investors	4 570	. . .	. . .	. . .	. . .	. . .	. . .	. . .	. . .
Reinvested earnings	4 575	17	56	28	34	42	43	29	23
Other capital	4 580	919	507	502	510	186	1,195	1,562	1,455
Claims on direct investors	4 585	. . .	. . .	. . .	. . .	. . .	. . .	. . .	. . .
Liabilities to direct investors	4 590	. . .	. . .	. . .	. . .	. . .	1,195	1,562	1,455
B. PORTFOLIO INVESTMENT	4 600	50	280	–50	110	40	–52	269	1,190
Assets	4 602	**–1**	**–14**	**. . .**	**–15**	**–115**	**–949**	**–632**	**–1,429**
Equity securities	4 610	. . .	. . .	. . .	. . .	. . .	. . .	. . .	. . .
Monetary authorities	4 611	. . .	. . .	. . .	. . .	. . .	. . .	. . .	. . .
General government	4 612	. . .	. . .	. . .	. . .	. . .	. . .	. . .	. . .
Banks	4 613	. . .	. . .	. . .	. . .	. . .	. . .	. . .	. . .
Other sectors	4 614	. . .	. . .	. . .	. . .	. . .	. . .	. . .	. . .
Debt securities	4 619	–1	–14	. . .	–15	–115	–949	–632	–1,429
Bonds and notes	4 620	–1	–14	. . .	–15	–115	–949	–632	–1,429
Monetary authorities	4 621	. . .	. . .	. . .	. . .	. . .	. . .	. . .	. . .
General government	4 622	. . .	. . .	. . .	. . .	. . .	. . .	. . .	. . .
Banks	4 623	. . .	. . .	. . .	. . .	. . .	. . .	. . .	. . .
Other sectors	4 624	. . .	. . .	. . .	. . .	. . .	. . .	. . .	. . .
Money market instruments	4 630	. . .	. . .	. . .	. . .	. . .	. . .	. . .	. . .
Monetary authorities	4 631	. . .	. . .	. . .	. . .	. . .	. . .	. . .	. . .
General government	4 632	. . .	. . .	. . .	. . .	. . .	. . .	. . .	. . .
Banks	4 633	. . .	. . .	. . .	. . .	. . .	. . .	. . .	. . .
Other sectors	4 634	. . .	. . .	. . .	. . .	. . .	. . .	. . .	. . .
Financial derivatives	4 640	. . .	. . .	. . .	. . .	. . .	. . .	. . .	. . .
Monetary authorities	4 641	. . .	. . .	. . .	. . .	. . .	. . .	. . .	. . .
General government	4 642	. . .	. . .	. . .	. . .	. . .	. . .	. . .	. . .
Banks	4 643	. . .	. . .	. . .	. . .	. . .	. . .	. . .	. . .
Other sectors	4 644	. . .	. . .	. . .	. . .	. . .	. . .	. . .	. . .
Liabilities	4 652	**51**	**294**	**–50**	**125**	**155**	**897**	**901**	**2,619**
Equity securities	4 660	. . .	. . .	. . .	. . .	. . .	. . .	. . .	. . .
Banks	4 663	. . .	. . .	. . .	. . .	. . .	. . .	. . .	. . .
Other sectors	4 664	. . .	. . .	. . .	. . .	. . .	. . .	. . .	. . .
Debt securities	4 669	51	294	–50	125	155	897	901	2,619
Bonds and notes	4 670	51	294	–50	125	155	897	901	2,619
Monetary authorities	4 671	. . .	. . .	. . .	. . .	. . .	. . .	. . .	. . .
General government	4 672	. . .	. . .	. . .	. . .	. . .	. . .	. . .	. . .
Banks	4 673	. . .	. . .	. . .	. . .	. . .	. . .	. . .	. . .
Other sectors	4 674	51	294	–50	125	155	897	901	2,619
Money market instruments	4 680	. . .	. . .	. . .	. . .	. . .	. . .	. . .	. . .
Monetary authorities	4 681	. . .	. . .	. . .	. . .	. . .	. . .	. . .	. . .
General government	4 682	. . .	. . .	. . .	. . .	. . .	. . .	. . .	. . .
Banks	4 683	. . .	. . .	. . .	. . .	. . .	. . .	. . .	. . .
Other sectors	4 684	. . .	. . .	. . .	. . .	. . .	. . .	. . .	. . .
Financial derivatives	4 690	. . .	. . .	. . .	. . .	. . .	. . .	. . .	. . .
Monetary authorities	4 691	. . .	. . .	. . .	. . .	. . .	. . .	. . .	. . .
General government	4 692	. . .	. . .	. . .	. . .	. . .	. . .	. . .	. . .
Banks	4 693	. . .	. . .	. . .	. . .	. . .	. . .	. . .	. . .
Other sectors	4 694	. . .	. . .	. . .	. . .	. . .	. . .	. . .	. . .

Table 2 (Concluded). STANDARD PRESENTATION, 1988–95
(Millions of U.S. dollars)

	Code	1988	1989	1990	1991	1992	1993	1994	1995
C. OTHER INVESTMENT	4 700 . .	–519	619	1,234	2,455	2,998	2,566	3,342	2,678
Assets	4 703 . .	...	...	...	...	...	...	...	...
Trade credits	4 706 . .	...	...	...	...	...	...	...	...
General government: long-term	4 708 . .	...	...	...	...	...	...	...	...
General government: short-term	4 709 . .	...	...	...	...	...	...	...	...
Other sectors: long-term	4 711 . .	...	...	...	...	...	...	...	...
Other sectors: short-term	4 712 . .	...	...	...	...	...	...	...	...
Loans	4 714 . .	...	...	...	...	...	...	...	...
Monetary authorities: long-term	4 717 . .	...	...	...	...	...	...	...	...
Monetary authorities: short-term	4 718 . .	...	...	...	...	...	...	...	...
General government: long-term	4 720 . .	...	...	...	...	...	...	...	...
General government: short-term	4 721 . .	...	...	...	...	...	...	...	...
Banks: long-term	4 723 . .	...	...	...	...	...	...	...	...
Banks: short-term	4 724 . .	...	...	...	...	...	...	...	...
Other sectors: long-term	4 726 . .	...	...	...	...	...	...	...	...
Other sectors: short-term	4 727 . .	...	...	...	...	...	...	...	...
Currency and deposits	4 730 . .	...	...	...	...	...	...	...	...
Monetary authorities	4 731 . .	...	...	...	...	...	...	...	...
General government	4 732 . .	...	...	...	...	...	...	...	...
Banks	4 733 . .	...	...	...	...	...	...	...	...
Other sectors	4 734 . .	...	...	...	...	...	...	...	...
Other assets	4 736 . .	...	...	...	...	...	...	...	...
Monetary authorities: long-term	4 738 . .	...	...	...	...	...	...	...	...
Monetary authorities: short-term	4 739 . .	...	...	...	...	...	...	...	...
General government: long-term	4 741 . .	...	...	...	...	...	...	...	...
General government: short-term	4 742 . .	...	...	...	...	...	...	...	...
Banks: long-term	4 744 . .	...	...	...	...	...	...	...	...
Banks: short-term	4 745 . .	...	...	...	...	...	...	...	...
Other sectors: long-term	4 747 . .	...	...	...	...	...	...	...	...
Other sectors: short-term	4 748 . .	...	...	...	...	...	...	...	...
Liabilities	4 753 . .	**–519**	**619**	**1,234**	**2,455**	**2,998**	**2,566**	**3,342**	**2,678**
Trade credits	4 756 . .	...	...	...	...	...	...	...	...
General government: long-term	4 758 . .	...	...	...	...	...	...	...	...
General government: short-term	4 759 . .	...	...	...	...	...	...	...	...
Other sectors: long-term	4 761 . .	...	...	...	...	...	...	...	...
Other sectors: short-term	4 762 . .	...	...	...	...	...	...	...	...
Loans	4 764 . .	–673	526	1,076	1,910	869	2,715	1,610	1,030
Use of Fund credit and loans from the Fund	4 766 . .	–104	108	–343	182	58	111	–220	–362
Monetary authorities: other long-term	4 767 . .	...	...	...	...	...	...	...	...
Monetary authorities: short-term	4 768 . .	...	...	...	...	...	...	...	...
General government: long-term	4 770 . .	–19	443	837	164	3,424	435	–675	–752
General government: short-term	4 771 . .	–52	–351	24	197	–693	630	–446	344
Banks: long-term	4 773 . .	...	...	...	...	...	...	...	...
Banks: short-term	4 774 . .	...	...	...	...	...	...	...	...
Other sectors: long-term	4 776 . .	–513	–49	199	765	–2,430	1,687	1,949	1,856
Other sectors: short-term	4 777 . .	15	375	359	602	510	–148	1,002	–56
Currency and deposits	4 780 . .	321	370	307	473	1,921	–229	1,694	1,648
Monetary authorities	4 781 . .	...	...	...	...	...	...	...	...
General government	4 782 . .	...	...	...	...	...	...	...	...
Banks	4 783 . .	321	370	307	473	1,921	–229	1,694	1,648
Other sectors	4 784 . .	...	...	...	...	...	...	...	...
Other liabilities	4 786 . .	–167	–277	–149	72	208	80	38	...
Monetary authorities: long-term	4 788 . .	...	...	...	...	...	...	...	...
Monetary authorities: short-term	4 789 . .	...	...	...	...	...	...	...	...
General government: long-term	4 791 . .	3	16	14	14	...	...	...	...
General government: short-term	4 792 . .	...	...	...	...	...	...	...	...
Banks: long-term	4 794 . .	...	...	...	...	...	...	...	...
Banks: short-term	4 795 . .	...	...	...	...	...	...	...	...
Other sectors: long-term	4 797 . .	148	171	177	291	368	...	38	...
Other sectors: short-term	4 798 . .	–318	–464	–340	–233	–160	80	...	...
D. RESERVE ASSETS	4 800 . .	–570	–408	388	–1,937	–1,746	–447	–2,107	–873
Monetary gold	4 810 . .	252	442	48	90	475	–197	295	–109
Special drawing rights	4 820 . .	...	–1	...	–3	4	–10	–14	17
Reserve position in the Fund	4 830 . .	...	...	...	...	–67	...	...	...
Foreign exchange	4 840 . .	–72	–564	565	–2,249	–1,316	–240	–2,388	–781
Other claims	4 880 . .	–750	–285	–225	225	–842	...	...	...
NET ERRORS AND OMISSIONS	4 998 . .	**493**	**402**	**593**	**–138**	**–520**	**85**	**157**	**–2,094**

Part 3 of the *Yearbook* contains descriptions of the methodologies, compilation practices, and sources used to compile these data.

Table 1. ANALYTIC PRESENTATION, 1988–95
(Millions of U.S. dollars)

	Code	1988	1989	1990	1991	1992	1993	1994	1995
A. Current Account [1]	4 993 Y.	**–107**	**–1,409**	**3,067**	**–2,146**	**–3,104**	**–5,788**	**–2,590**	**–4,245**
Goods: exports f.o.b	2 100 . .	13,846	12,869	15,837	14,393	13,929	13,582	17,121	23,463
Goods: imports f.o.b	3 100 . .	–12,757	–12,822	–12,248	–15,104	–14,060	–17,087	–18,930	–26,687
Balance on Goods	4 100 . .	*1,089*	*47*	*3,589*	*–711*	*–131*	*–3,505*	*–1,809*	*–3,224*
Services: credit	2 200 . .	2,472	3,201	3,200	3,687	4,773	4,201	4,522	8,617
Services: debit	3 200 . .	–2,404	–3,053	–2,847	–2,994	–4,045	–3,631	–3,859	–7,158
Balance on Goods and Services	4 991 . .	*1,157*	*195*	*3,942*	*–18*	*597*	*–2,935*	*–1,146*	*–1,765*
Income: credit	2 300 . .	271	410	603	573	728	579	546	1,089
Income: debit	3 300 . .	–3,226	–3,623	–3,989	–3,469	–4,895	–4,192	–3,109	–3,084
Balance on Goods, Services, and Income	4 992 . .	*–1,798*	*–3,018*	*556*	*–2,914*	*–3,570*	*–6,548*	*–3,709*	*–3,760*
Current transfers: credit	2 379 Y.	2,777	4,246	6,865	6,707	6,214	5,840	6,464	6,022
Current transfers: debit	3 379 . .	–1,086	–2,637	–4,354	–5,939	–5,748	–5,080	–5,345	–6,507
B. Capital Account [1]	4 994 Y.	**. . .**	**. . .**	**. . .**	**. . .**	**. . .**	**. . .**	**. . .**	**. . .**
Capital account: credit	2 994 Y.	. . .	. . .	. . .	. . .	. . .	. . .	. . .	. . .
Capital account: debit	3 994 . .	. . .	. . .	. . .	. . .	. . .	. . .	. . .	. . .
Total, Groups A Plus B	4 010 . .	*–107*	*–1,409*	*3,067*	*–2,146*	*–3,104*	*–5,788*	*–2,590*	*–4,245*
C. Financial Account [1]	4 995 X.	**–10,661**	**–1,796**	**–8,731**	**–4,183**	**–1,045**	**2,341**	**2,356**	**14,240**
Direct investment abroad	4 505 . .	–22	–18	. . .	7	–13	–18	–29	–42
Direct investment in Poland	4 555 Y.	15	11	89	291	678	1,715	1,875	3,659
Portfolio investment assets	4 602 . .	. . .	. . .	. . .	. . .	. . .	. . .	–624	–128
Equity securities	4 610 . .	. . .	. . .	. . .	. . .	. . .	. . .	. . .	–2
Debt securities	4 619 . .	. . .	. . .	. . .	. . .	. . .	. . .	–624	–126
Portfolio investment liabilities	4 652 Y.	. . .	. . .	. . .	. . .	. . .	. . .	. . .	1,299
Equity securities	4 660 Y.	. . .	. . .	. . .	. . .	. . .	. . .	. . .	234
Debt securities	4 669 Y.	. . .	. . .	. . .	. . .	. . .	. . .	. . .	1,065
Other investment assets	4 703 . .	–1,226	–155	–4,504	–1,497	–958	848	1,787	8,483
Monetary authorities	4 703 . A	. . .	. . .	. . .	. . .	. . .	. . .	. . .	. . .
General government	4 703 . B	–161	–137	46	27	26	16	18	44
Banks	4 703 . C	–26	111	–4,096	–980	–823	649	1,682	8,708
Other sectors	4 703 . D	–1,039	–129	–454	–544	–161	183	87	–269
Other investment liabilities	4 753 X.	–9,428	–1,634	–4,316	–2,984	–752	–204	–653	969
Monetary authorities	4 753 XA	. . .	. . .	. . .	. . .	. . .	. . .	. . .	. . .
General government	4 753 YB	–285	–1,034	–3,936	–3,418	–1,439	–570	–974	205
Banks	4 753 YC	–9,744	–601	–827	–227	437	114	242	240
Other sectors	4 753 YD	601	1	447	661	250	252	79	524
Total, Groups A Through C	4 020 . .	*–10,768*	*–3,205*	*–5,664*	*–6,329*	*–4,149*	*–3,447*	*–234*	*9,995*
D. Net Errors and Omissions	4 998 . .	**–267**	**–110**	**162**	**–745**	**–181**	**219**	**–325**	**–244**
Total, Groups A Through D	4 030 . .	*–11,035*	*–3,315*	*–5,502*	*–7,074*	*–4,330*	*–3,228*	*–559*	*9,751*
E. Reserves and Related Items	4 040 . .	**11,035**	**3,315**	**5,502**	**7,074**	**4,330**	**3,228**	**559**	**–9,751**
Reserve assets	4 800 . .	–561	–259	–2,418	830	–616	–100	–1,514	–8,431
Use of Fund credit and loans	4 766 . .	. . .	. . .	479	323	. . .	–138	603	–1,408
Liabilities constituting foreign authorities' reserves	4 900 . .	. . .	. . .	. . .	. . .	. . .	. . .	. . .	. . .
Exceptional financing	4 920 . .	11,596	3,574	7,440	5,921	4,946	3,466	1,469	88
Conversion rates: zlotys per U.S. dollar	0 101 . .	**.0431**	**.1439**	**.9500**	**1.0576**	**1.3626**	**1.8115**	**2.2723**	**2.4250**

[1] Excludes components that have been classified in the categories of Group E.

Table 2. STANDARD PRESENTATION, 1988–95
(Millions of U.S. dollars)

	Code	1988	1989	1990	1991	1992	1993	1994	1995
CURRENT ACCOUNT	4 993 . .	**–107**	**–1,409**	**3,067**	**–2,146**	**–3,104**	**–5,788**	**–2,590**	**–4,245**
A. GOODS	4 100 . .	1,089	47	3,589	–711	–131	–3,505	–1,809	–3,224
Credit	2 100 . .	**13,846**	**12,869**	**15,837**	**14,393**	**13,929**	**13,582**	**17,121**	**23,463**
General merchandise: exports f.o.b.	2 110 . .	13,846	12,869	15,837	14,393	13,929	13,582	17,121	23,463
Goods for processing: exports f.o.b.	2 150 . .	. . .	. . .	. . .	. . .	. . .	. . .	. . .	. . .
Repairs on goods	2 160 . .	. . .	. . .	. . .	. . .	. . .	. . .	. . .	. . .
Goods procured in ports by carriers	2 170 . .	. . .	. . .	. . .	. . .	. . .	. . .	. . .	. . .
Nonmonetary gold	2 180 . .	. . .	. . .	. . .	. . .	. . .	. . .	. . .	. . .
Debit	3 100 . .	**–12,757**	**–12,822**	**–12,248**	**–15,104**	**–14,060**	**–17,087**	**–18,930**	**–26,687**
General merchandise: imports f.o.b.	3 110 . .	–12,757	–12,822	–12,248	–15,104	–14,060	–17,087	–18,930	–26,687
Goods for processing: imports f.o.b.	3 150 . .	. . .	. . .	. . .	. . .	. . .	. . .	. . .	. . .
Repairs on goods	3 160 . .	. . .	. . .	. . .	. . .	. . .	. . .	. . .	. . .
Goods procured in ports by carriers	3 170 . .	. . .	. . .	. . .	. . .	. . .	. . .	. . .	. . .
Nonmonetary gold	3 180 . .	. . .	. . .	. . .	. . .	. . .	. . .	. . .	. . .
B. SERVICES	4 200 . .	68	148	353	693	728	570	663	1,459
Total credit	2 200 . .	*2,472*	*3,201*	*3,200*	*3,687*	*4,773*	*4,201*	*4,522*	*8,617*
Total debit	3 200 . .	*–2,404*	*–3,053*	*–2,847*	*–2,994*	*–4,045*	*–3,631*	*–3,859*	*–7,158*
Transportation services, credit	2 205 . .	**1,314**	**1,979**	**1,833**	**1,970**	**1,993**	**2,052**	**2,438**	**3,041**
Passenger	2 205 BA	*144*	*300*	*334*	*207*	*173*	*270*	*282*	*313*
Freight	2 205 BB	*883*	*1,231*	*1,138*	*1,303*	*1,360*	*1,356*	*1,705*	*2,093*
Other	2 205 BC	*287*	*448*	*361*	*460*	*460*	*426*	*451*	*635*
Sea transport, passenger	2 207 . .	. . .	. . .	. . .	. . .	. . .	. . .	13	12
Sea transport, freight	2 208 . .	. . .	. . .	. . .	. . .	. . .	. . .	1,101	1,331
Sea transport, other	2 209 . .	. . .	. . .	. . .	. . .	. . .	. . .	231	259
Air transport, passenger	2 211 . .	. . .	. . .	. . .	. . .	. . .	. . .	233	247
Air transport, freight	2 212 . .	. . .	. . .	. . .	. . .	. . .	. . .	18	22
Air transport, other	2 213 . .	. . .	. . .	. . .	. . .	. . .	. . .	82	91
Other transport, passenger	2 215 . .	. . .	. . .	. . .	. . .	. . .	. . .	36	54
Other transport, freight	2 216 . .	. . .	. . .	. . .	. . .	. . .	. . .	586	740
Other transport, other	2 217 . .	. . .	. . .	. . .	. . .	. . .	. . .	138	285
Transportation services, debit	3 205 . .	**–1,246**	**–1,843**	**–1,492**	**–1,525**	**–1,452**	**–1,340**	**–1,365**	**–1,768**
Passenger	3 205 BA	*–104*	*–179*	*–177*	*–103*	*–85*	*–107*	*–109*	*–365*
Freight	3 205 BB	*–339*	*–415*	*–248*	*–440*	*–254*	*–338*	*–345*	*–488*
Other	3 205 BC	*–803*	*–1,249*	*–1,067*	*–982*	*–1,113*	*–895*	*–911*	*–915*
Sea transport, passenger	3 207 . .	. . .	. . .	. . .	. . .	. . .	. . .	–3	–3
Sea transport, freight	3 208 . .	. . .	. . .	. . .	. . .	. . .	. . .	–124	–152
Sea transport, other	3 209 . .	. . .	. . .	. . .	. . .	. . .	. . .	–717	–609
Air transport, passenger	3 211 . .	. . .	. . .	. . .	. . .	. . .	. . .	–88	–342
Air transport, freight	3 212 . .	. . .	. . .	. . .	. . .	. . .	. . .	–10	–13
Air transport, other	3 213 . .	. . .	. . .	. . .	. . .	. . .	. . .	–108	–65
Other transport, passenger	3 215 . .	. . .	. . .	. . .	. . .	. . .	. . .	–18	–20
Other transport, freight	3 216 . .	. . .	. . .	. . .	. . .	. . .	. . .	–211	–323
Other transport, other	3 217 . .	. . .	. . .	. . .	. . .	. . .	. . .	–86	–241
Travel, credit	2 236 . .	**206**	**202**	**358**	**149**	**183**	**147**	**148**	**246**
Business travel	2 237 . .	. . .	. . .	. . .	. . .	. . .	. . .	65	67
Personal travel	2 240 . .	. . .	. . .	. . .	. . .	. . .	. . .	83	179
Travel, debit	3 236 . .	**–251**	**–215**	**–423**	**–143**	**–134**	**–189**	**–320**	**–430**
Business travel	3 237 . .	. . .	. . .	. . .	. . .	. . .	. . .	–253	–359
Personal travel	3 240 . .	. . .	. . .	. . .	. . .	. . .	. . .	–67	–71
Other services, credit	2 200 BA	**952**	**1,020**	**1,009**	**1,568**	**2,597**	**2,002**	**1,936**	**5,330**
Communications	2 245 . .	. . .	. . .	. . .	. . .	. . .	. . .	209	302
Construction	2 249 . .	. . .	. . .	. . .	. . .	. . .	. . .	618	2,799
Insurance	2 253 . .	98	137	126	145	151	151	152	738
Financial	2 260 . .	. . .	. . .	. . .	. . .	. . .	. . .	69	145
Computer and information	2 262 . .	. . .	. . .	. . .	. . .	. . .	. . .	2	12
Royalties and licence fees	2 266 . .	. . .	. . .	. . .	. . .	. . .	. . .	1	4
Other business services	2 268 . .	854	883	883	1,423	2,446	1,851	827	1,265
Personal, cultural, and recreational	2 287 . .	. . .	. . .	. . .	. . .	. . .	. . .	14	27
Government, n.i.e.	2 291 . .	. . .	. . .	. . .	. . .	. . .	. . .	44	38
Other services, debit	3 200 BA	**–907**	**–995**	**–933**	**–1,326**	**–2,459**	**–2,103**	**–2,174**	**–4,960**
Communications	3 245 . .	. . .	. . .	. . .	. . .	. . .	. . .	–160	–195
Construction	3 249 . .	. . .	. . .	. . .	. . .	. . .	. . .	–406	–2,056
Insurance	3 253 . .	–38	–46	–28	–49	–28	–38	–236	–727
Financial	3 260 . .	. . .	. . .	. . .	. . .	. . .	. . .	–127	–228
Computer and information	3 262 . .	. . .	. . .	. . .	. . .	. . .	. . .	–35	–58
Royalties and licence fees	3 266 . .	. . .	. . .	. . .	. . .	. . .	. . .	–18	–44
Other business services	3 268 . .	–869	–949	–905	–1,277	–2,431	–2,065	–1,066	–1,496
Personal, cultural, and recreational	3 287 . .	. . .	. . .	. . .	. . .	. . .	. . .	–13	–26
Government, n.i.e.	3 291 . .	. . .	. . .	. . .	. . .	. . .	. . .	–113	–130

Table 2 (Continued). STANDARD PRESENTATION, 1988–95
(Millions of U.S. dollars)

	Code		1988	1989	1990	1991	1992	1993	1994	1995
C. INCOME	4 300	. .	–2,955	–3,213	–3,386	–2,896	–4,167	–3,613	–2,563	–1,995
Total credit	2 300	. .	*271*	*410*	*603*	*573*	*728*	*579*	*546*	*1,089*
Total debit	3 300	. .	*–3,226*	*–3,623*	*–3,989*	*–3,469*	*–4,895*	*–4,192*	*–3,109*	*–3,084*
Compensation of employees, credit	2 310	. .	...	...	...	...	...	...	**23**	**28**
Compensation of employees, debit	3 310	. .	...	...	...	...	...	...	**–130**	**–251**
Investment income, credit	2 320	. .	**271**	**410**	**603**	**573**	**728**	**579**	**523**	**1,061**
Direct investment income	2 330	. .	...	...	...	2	3	3	12	20
Dividends and distributed branch profits	2 332	. .	...	...	...	...	...	...	2	7
Reinvested earnings and undistributed branch profits	2 333	. .	...	...	...	2	3	3	10	13
Income on debt (interest)	2 334	. .	...	...	...	...	...	...	...	...
Portfolio investment income	2 339	. .	...	...	...	...	...	...	191	516
Income on equity	2 340	. .	...	...	...	...	...	...	...	6
Income on bonds and notes	2 350	. .	...	...	...	...	...	...	171	372
Income on money market instruments and financial derivatives	2 360	. .	...	...	...	...	...	...	20	138
Other investment income	2 370	. .	271	410	603	571	725	576	320	525
Investment income, debit	3 320	. .	**–3,226**	**–3,623**	**–3,989**	**–3,469**	**–4,895**	**–4,192**	**–2,979**	**–2,833**
Direct investment income	3 330	. .	...	...	–20	–50	–154	–199	–389	–1,048
Dividends and distributed branch profits	3 332	. .	...	...	...	...	...	...	–7	–155
Reinvested earnings and undistributed branch profits	3 333	. .	...	...	–20	–50	–154	–199	–382	–888
Income on debt (interest)	3 334	. .	...	...	...	...	...	...	...	–5
Portfolio investment income	3 339	. .	...	...	...	...	...	...	–18	–391
Income on equity	3 340	. .	...	...	...	...	...	...	...	–2
Income on bonds and notes	3 350	. .	...	...	...	...	...	...	–18	–363
Income on money market instruments and financial derivatives	3 360	. .	...	...	...	...	...	...	...	–26
Other investment income	3 370	. .	–3,226	–3,623	–3,969	–3,419	–4,741	–3,993	–2,572	–1,394
D. CURRENT TRANSFERS	4 379	. .	1,691	1,609	2,511	768	466	760	1,119	–485
Credit	2 379	. .	**2,777**	**4,246**	**6,865**	**6,707**	**6,214**	**5,840**	**6,464**	**6,022**
General government	2 380	. .	...	88	305	45	253	139	128	244
Other sectors	2 390	. .	2,777	4,158	6,560	6,662	5,961	5,701	6,336	5,778
Workers' remittances	2 391	. .	...	...	...	...	...	...	58	46
Other current transfers	2 392	. .	2,777	4,158	6,560	6,662	5,961	5,701	6,278	5,732
Debit	3 379	. .	**–1,086**	**–2,637**	**–4,354**	**–5,939**	**–5,748**	**–5,080**	**–5,345**	**–6,507**
General government	3 380	. .	...	...	...	...	...	...	...	...
Other sectors	3 390	. .	–1,086	–2,637	–4,354	–5,939	–5,748	–5,080	–5,345	–6,507
Workers' remittances	3 391	. .	...	...	...	...	...	...	–25	–11
Other current transfers	3 392	. .	–1,086	–2,637	–4,354	–5,939	–5,748	–5,080	–5,320	–6,496
CAPITAL AND FINANCIAL ACCOUNT	4 996	. .	**374**	**1,519**	**–3,229**	**2,891**	**3,285**	**5,569**	**2,915**	**4,489**
CAPITAL ACCOUNT	4 994	. .	...	**424**	...	**864**	**2,446**	**2,090**	**779**	**71**
Total credit	2 994	. .	...	*424*	...	*864*	*2,446*	*2,090*	*779*	*71*
Total debit	3 994	. .	...	...	...	...	...	...	...	...
Capital transfers, credit	2 400	. .	...	**424**	...	**864**	**2,446**	**2,090**	**779**	**71**
General government	2 401	. .	...	424	...	864	2,446	2,090	779	71
Debt forgiveness	2 402	. .	...	424	...	864	2,446	2,090	779	71
Other capital transfers	2 410	. .	...	...	...	...	...	...	...	...
Other sectors	2 430	. .	...	...	...	...	...	...	...	...
Migrants' transfers	2 431	. .	...	...	...	...	...	...	...	...
Debt forgiveness	2 432	. .	...	...	...	...	...	...	...	...
Other capital transfers	2 440	. .	...	...	...	...	...	...	...	...
Capital transfers, debit	3 400	. .	...	...	...	...	...	...	...	...
General government	3 401	. .	...	...	...	...	...	...	...	...
Debt forgiveness	3 402	. .	...	...	...	...	...	...	...	...
Other capital transfers	3 410	. .	...	...	...	...	...	...	...	...
Other sectors	3 430	. .	...	...	...	...	...	...	...	...
Migrants' transfers	3 431	. .	...	...	...	...	...	...	...	...
Debt forgiveness	3 432	. .	...	...	...	...	...	...	...	...
Other capital transfers	3 440	. .	...	...	...	...	...	...	...	...
Nonproduced nonfinancial assets, credit	2 480	. .	...	...	...	...	...	...	...	...
Nonproduced nonfinancial assets, debit	3 480	. .	...	...	...	...	...	...	...	...

Table 2 (Continued). STANDARD PRESENTATION, 1988–95
(Millions of U.S. dollars)

	Code	1988	1989	1990	1991	1992	1993	1994	1995
FINANCIAL ACCOUNT	4 995	**374**	**1,095**	**–3,229**	**2,027**	**839**	**3,479**	**2,136**	**4,418**
A. DIRECT INVESTMENT	4 500	–7	–7	89	298	665	1,697	1,846	3,617
Direct investment abroad	4 505	**–22**	**–18**	**. . .**	**7**	**–13**	**–18**	**–29**	**–42**
Equity capital	4 510	–22	–18	. . .	9	–10	–15	–19	–29
Claims on affiliated enterprises	4 515	. . .	. . .	. . .	. . .	. . .	. . .	–19	–29
Liabilities to affiliated enterprises	4 520	. . .	. . .	. . .	. . .	. . .	. . .	. . .	. . .
Reinvested earnings	4 525	. . .	. . .	. . .	–2	–3	–3	–10	–13
Other capital	4 530	. . .	. . .	. . .	. . .	. . .	. . .	. . .	. . .
Claims on affiliated enterprises	4 535	. . .	. . .	. . .	. . .	. . .	. . .	. . .	. . .
Liabilities to affiliated enterprises	4 540	. . .	. . .	. . .	. . .	. . .	. . .	. . .	. . .
Direct investment in Poland	4 555	**15**	**11**	**89**	**291**	**678**	**1,715**	**1,875**	**3,659**
Equity capital	4 560	15	11	69	216	433	1,109	1,096	2,105
Claims on direct investors	4 565	. . .	. . .	. . .	. . .	. . .	. . .	1,096	2,105
Liabilities to direct investors	4 570	. . .	. . .	. . .	. . .	. . .	. . .	. . .	. . .
Reinvested earnings	4 575	. . .	. . .	20	50	154	199	382	888
Other capital	4 580	. . .	. . .	. . .	25	91	407	397	666
Claims on direct investors	4 585	. . .	. . .	. . .	. . .	. . .	. . .	397	666
Liabilities to direct investors	4 590	. . .	. . .	. . .	. . .	. . .	. . .	. . .	. . .
B. PORTFOLIO INVESTMENT	4 600	. . .	. . .	. . .	. . .	. . .	. . .	–624	1,171
Assets	4 602	**. . .**	**. . .**	**. . .**	**. . .**	**. . .**	**. . .**	**–624**	**–128**
Equity securities	4 610	. . .	. . .	. . .	. . .	. . .	. . .	. . .	–2
Monetary authorities	4 611	. . .	. . .	. . .	. . .	. . .	. . .	. . .	. . .
General government	4 612	. . .	. . .	. . .	. . .	. . .	. . .	. . .	. . .
Banks	4 613	. . .	. . .	. . .	. . .	. . .	. . .	. . .	–2
Other sectors	4 614	. . .	. . .	. . .	. . .	. . .	. . .	. . .	. . .
Debt securities	4 619	. . .	. . .	. . .	. . .	. . .	. . .	–624	–126
Bonds and notes	4 620	. . .	. . .	. . .	. . .	. . .	. . .	–624	–86
Monetary authorities	4 621	. . .	. . .	. . .	. . .	. . .	. . .	. . .	. . .
General government	4 622	. . .	. . .	. . .	. . .	. . .	. . .	–624	45
Banks	4 623	. . .	. . .	. . .	. . .	. . .	. . .	. . .	–131
Other sectors	4 624	. . .	. . .	. . .	. . .	. . .	. . .	. . .	. . .
Money market instruments	4 630	. . .	. . .	. . .	. . .	. . .	. . .	. . .	–40
Monetary authorities	4 631	. . .	. . .	. . .	. . .	. . .	. . .	. . .	. . .
General government	4 632	. . .	. . .	. . .	. . .	. . .	. . .	. . .	. . .
Banks	4 633	. . .	. . .	. . .	. . .	. . .	. . .	. . .	–40
Other sectors	4 634	. . .	. . .	. . .	. . .	. . .	. . .	. . .	. . .
Financial derivatives	4 640	. . .	. . .	. . .	. . .	. . .	. . .	. . .	. . .
Monetary authorities	4 641	. . .	. . .	. . .	. . .	. . .	. . .	. . .	. . .
General government	4 642	. . .	. . .	. . .	. . .	. . .	. . .	. . .	. . .
Banks	4 643	. . .	. . .	. . .	. . .	. . .	. . .	. . .	. . .
Other sectors	4 644	. . .	. . .	. . .	. . .	. . .	. . .	. . .	. . .
Liabilities	4 652	**. . .**	**. . .**	**. . .**	**. . .**	**. . .**	**. . .**	**. . .**	**1,299**
Equity securities	4 660	. . .	. . .	. . .	. . .	. . .	. . .	. . .	234
Banks	4 663	. . .	. . .	. . .	. . .	. . .	. . .	. . .	25
Other sectors	4 664	. . .	. . .	. . .	. . .	. . .	. . .	. . .	209
Debt securities	4 669	. . .	. . .	. . .	. . .	. . .	. . .	. . .	1,065
Bonds and notes	4 670	. . .	. . .	. . .	. . .	. . .	. . .	. . .	176
Monetary authorities	4 671	. . .	. . .	. . .	. . .	. . .	. . .	. . .	. . .
General government	4 672	. . .	. . .	. . .	. . .	. . .	. . .	. . .	182
Banks	4 673	. . .	. . .	. . .	. . .	. . .	. . .	. . .	–5
Other sectors	4 674	. . .	. . .	. . .	. . .	. . .	. . .	. . .	–1
Money market instruments	4 680	. . .	. . .	. . .	. . .	. . .	. . .	. . .	891
Monetary authorities	4 681	. . .	. . .	. . .	. . .	. . .	. . .	. . .	. . .
General government	4 682	. . .	. . .	. . .	. . .	. . .	. . .	. . .	807
Banks	4 683	. . .	. . .	. . .	. . .	. . .	. . .	. . .	84
Other sectors	4 684	. . .	. . .	. . .	. . .	. . .	. . .	. . .	. . .
Financial derivatives	4 690	. . .	. . .	. . .	. . .	. . .	. . .	. . .	–2
Monetary authorities	4 691	. . .	. . .	. . .	. . .	. . .	. . .	. . .	. . .
General government	4 692	. . .	. . .	. . .	. . .	. . .	. . .	. . .	. . .
Banks	4 693	. . .	. . .	. . .	. . .	. . .	. . .	. . .	. . .
Other sectors	4 694	. . .	. . .	. . .	. . .	. . .	. . .	. . .	–2

Table 2 (Concluded). STANDARD PRESENTATION, 1988–95
(Millions of U.S. dollars)

	Code	1988	1989	1990	1991	1992	1993	1994	1995
C. OTHER INVESTMENT	4 700 . .	942	1,361	–901	899	790	1,882	2,427	8,061
Assets	4 703 . .	**–1,226**	**–155**	**–4,504**	**–1,497**	**–958**	**848**	**1,787**	**8,483**
Trade credits	4 706 . .	. . .	. . .	. . .	. . .	. . .	. . .	. . .	. . .
General government: long-term	4 708 . .	. . .	. . .	. . .	. . .	. . .	. . .	. . .	. . .
General government: short-term	4 709 . .	. . .	. . .	. . .	. . .	. . .	. . .	. . .	. . .
Other sectors: long-term	4 711 . .	. . .	. . .	. . .	. . .	. . .	. . .	. . .	. . .
Other sectors: short-term	4 712 . .	. . .	. . .	. . .	. . .	. . .	. . .	. . .	. . .
Loans	4 714 . .	–1,127	–119	–318	–162	–130	273	105	–178
Monetary authorities: long-term	4 717 . .	. . .	. . .	. . .	. . .	. . .	. . .	. . .	. . .
Monetary authorities: short-term	4 718 . .	. . .	. . .	. . .	. . .	. . .	. . .	. . .	. . .
General government: long-term	4 720 . .	–161	–137	46	27	26	16	18	44
General government: short-term	4 721 . .	. . .	. . .	. . .	. . .	. . .	. . .	. . .	. . .
Banks: long-term	4 723 . .	73	147	20	–3	. . .	54	. . .	21
Banks: short-term	4 724 . .	. . .	. . .	. . .	. . .	. . .	. . .	. . .	26
Other sectors: long-term	4 726 . .	–30	38	29	3	33	5	–39	2
Other sectors: short-term	4 727 . .	–1,009	–167	–413	–189	–189	198	126	–271
Currency and deposits	4 730 . .	–99	–36	–4,186	–1,335	–828	575	–1,610	1,176
Monetary authorities	4 731 . .	. . .	. . .	. . .	. . .	. . .	. . .	. . .	. . .
General government	4 732 . .	. . .	. . .	. . .	. . .	. . .	. . .	. . .	. . .
Banks	4 733 . .	–99	–36	–4,116	–977	–823	595	–1,610	1,176
Other sectors	4 734 . .	. . .	. . .	–70	–358	–5	–20	. . .	. . .
Other assets	4 736 . .	. . .	. . .	. . .	. . .	. . .	. . .	3,292	7,485
Monetary authorities: long-term	4 738 . .	. . .	. . .	. . .	. . .	. . .	. . .	. . .	. . .
Monetary authorities: short-term	4 739 . .	. . .	. . .	. . .	. . .	. . .	. . .	. . .	. . .
General government: long-term	4 741 . .	. . .	. . .	. . .	. . .	. . .	. . .	. . .	. . .
General government: short-term	4 742 . .	. . .	. . .	. . .	. . .	. . .	. . .	. . .	. . .
Banks: long-term	4 744 . .	. . .	. . .	. . .	. . .	. . .	. . .	. . .	. . .
Banks: short-term	4 745 . .	. . .	. . .	. . .	. . .	. . .	. . .	3,292	7,485
Other sectors: long-term	4 747 . .	. . .	. . .	. . .	. . .	. . .	. . .	. . .	. . .
Other sectors: short-term	4 748 . .	. . .	. . .	. . .	. . .	. . .	. . .	. . .	. . .
Liabilities	4 753 . .	**2,168**	**1,516**	**3,603**	**2,396**	**1,748**	**1,034**	**640**	**–422**
Trade credits	4 756 . .	. . .	. . .	. . .	. . .	. . .	. . .	. . .	. . .
General government: long-term	4 758 . .	. . .	. . .	. . .	. . .	. . .	. . .	. . .	. . .
General government: short-term	4 759 . .	. . .	. . .	. . .	. . .	. . .	. . .	. . .	. . .
Other sectors: long-term	4 761 . .	. . .	. . .	. . .	. . .	. . .	. . .	. . .	. . .
Other sectors: short-term	4 762 . .	. . .	. . .	. . .	. . .	. . .	. . .	. . .	. . .
Loans	4 764 . .	1,557	–1,257	6,910	–1,772	–998	–555	–319	–599
Use of Fund credit and loans from the Fund	4 766 . .	. . .	. . .	479	323	. . .	–138	603	–1,408
Monetary authorities: other long term	4 767 . .	. . .	. . .	. . .	. . .	. . .	. . .	. . .	. . .
Monetary authorities: short-term	4 768 . .	. . .	. . .	. . .	. . .	. . .	. . .	. . .	. . .
General government: long-term	4 770 . .	–285	–1,249	6,649	–2,819	–1,388	–490	–924	205
General government: short-term	4 771 . .	. . .	215	–215	–20	–51	–80	–50	. . .
Banks: long-term	4 773 . .	1,241	–224	–468	1	133	–104	–25	80
Banks: short-term	4 774 . .	. . .	. . .	. . .	. . .	. . .	. . .	–2	. . .
Other sectors: long-term	4 776 . .	62	6	123	200	319	510	252	309
Other sectors: short-term	4 777 . .	539	–5	342	543	–11	–253	–173	215
Currency and deposits	4 780 . .	. . .	. . .	. . .	. . .	. . .	. . .	720	597
Monetary authorities	4 781 . .	. . .	. . .	. . .	. . .	. . .	. . .	. . .	. . .
General government	4 782 . .	. . .	. . .	. . .	. . .	. . .	. . .	. . .	. . .
Banks	4 783 . .	. . .	. . .	. . .	. . .	. . .	. . .	720	597
Other sectors	4 784 . .	. . .	. . .	. . .	. . .	. . .	. . .	. . .	. . .
Other liabilities	4 786 . .	611	2,773	–3,307	4,168	2,746	1,589	239	–420
Monetary authorities: long-term	4 788 . .	. . .	. . .	. . .	. . .	. . .	. . .	. . .	. . .
Monetary authorities: short-term	4 789 . .	. . .	. . .	. . .	. . .	. . .	. . .	. . .	. . .
General government: long-term	4 791 . .	. . .	. . .	. . .	. . .	. . .	. . .	. . .	. . .
General government: short-term	4 792 . .	554	2,913	–4,113	4,478	2,500	1,376	690	17
Banks: long-term	4 794 . .	. . .	. . .	. . .	. . .	. . .	. . .	. . .	. . .
Banks: short-term	4 795 . .	57	–140	824	–228	304	218	–451	–437
Other sectors: long-term	4 797 . .	. . .	. . .	–18	–25	–58	–5	. . .	. . .
Other sectors: short-term	4 798 . .	. . .	. . .	. . .	–57	. . .	. . .	. . .	. . .
D. RESERVE ASSETS	4 800 . .	–561	–259	–2,418	830	–616	–100	–1,514	–8,431
Monetary gold	4 810 . .	. . .	. . .	. . .	. . .	. . .	. . .	. . .	. . .
Special drawing rights	4 820 . .	. . .	. . .	–1	–7	7	. . .	–1	–1
Reserve position in the Fund	4 830 . .	. . .	. . .	. . .	. . .	–107	. . .	. . .	. . .
Foreign exchange	4 840 . .	–561	–259	–2,417	837	–516	–100	–1,513	–8,430
Other claims	4 880 . .	. . .	. . .	. . .	. . .	. . .	. . .	. . .	. . .
NET ERRORS AND OMISSIONS	4 998 . .	**–267**	**–110**	**162**	**–745**	**–181**	**219**	**–325**	**–244**

Part 3 of the *Yearbook* contains descriptions of the methodologies, compilation practices, and sources used to compile these data.

Table 1. ANALYTIC PRESENTATION, 1988–95
(Millions of U.S. dollars)

	Code	1988	1989	1990	1991	1992	1993	1994	1995
A. Current Account [1]	4 993 Y.	**–1,066**	**153**	**–181**	**–716**	**–184**	**233**	**–1,505**	**–229**
Goods: exports f.o.b	2 100 . .	11,015	12,843	16,458	16,391	18,348	15,931	18,635	23,928
Goods: imports f.o.b	3 100 . .	–16,392	–17,585	–23,141	–24,079	–27,735	–23,981	–26,713	–32,413
Balance on Goods	4 100 . .	*–5,377*	*–4,742*	*–6,684*	*–7,688*	*–9,387*	*–8,050*	*–8,078*	*–8,484*
Services: credit	2 200 . .	3,418	3,789	5,096	5,231	5,497	6,846	6,761	8,173
Services: debit	3 200 . .	–2,668	–2,830	–4,005	–4,420	–4,732	–5,481	–5,472	–6,536
Balance on Goods and Services	4 991 . .	*–4,627*	*–3,784*	*–5,592*	*–6,877*	*–8,621*	*–6,685*	*–6,789*	*–6,847*
Income: credit	2 300 . .	477	719	1,360	1,550	2,067	2,455	2,232	3,564
Income: debit	3 300 . .	–1,238	–1,322	–1,457	–1,364	–1,456	–2,236	–2,369	–4,078
Balance on Goods, Services, and Income	4 992 . .	*–5,388*	*–4,387*	*–5,689*	*–6,691*	*–8,010*	*–6,466*	*–6,926*	*–7,360*
Current transfers: credit	2 379 Y.	4,946	5,227	6,433	7,237	9,344	8,395	7,410	9,048
Current transfers: debit	3 379 . .	–624	–687	–926	–1,263	–1,518	–1,696	–1,989	–1,917
B. Capital Account [1]	4 994 Y.	**. . .**	**. . .**	**. . .**	**. . .**	**. . .**	**. . .**	**. . .**	**. . .**
Capital account: credit	2 994 Y.	. . .	. . .	. . .	. . .	. . .	. . .	. . .	. . .
Capital account: debit	3 994 . .	. . .	. . .	. . .	. . .	. . .	. . .	. . .	. . .
Total, Groups A Plus B	4 010 . .	*–1,066*	*153*	*–181*	*–716*	*–184*	*233*	*–1,505*	*–229*
C. Financial Account [1]	4 995 X.	**293**	**4,005**	**2,563**	**4,537**	**–950**	**–3,033**	**625**	**3,226**
Direct investment abroad	4 505 . .	–80	–84	–163	–463	–687	–148	–287	–685
Direct investment in Portugal	4 555 Y.	922	1,737	2,610	2,448	1,873	1,534	1,270	653
Portfolio investment assets	4 602 . .	–27	. . .	. . .	. . .	–379	–2,387	–3,456	–2,657
Equity securities	4 610 . .	–1	. . .	. . .	. . .	–9	–168	–66	–138
Debt securities	4 619 . .	–27	. . .	. . .	. . .	–370	–2,218	–3,390	–2,519
Portfolio investment liabilities	4 652 Y.	1,841	1,050	961	1,895	–2,685	4,214	3,507	1,072
Equity securities	4 660 Y.	220	605	508	215	570	579	507	–208
Debt securities	4 669 Y.	1,622	445	453	1,681	–3,255	3,634	3,000	1,280
Other investment assets	4 703 . .	–1,145	–7	–2,442	–1,511	–1,923	–8,424	–7,098	–6,910
Monetary authorities	4 703 .A	. . .	. . .	. . .	. . .	. . .	9	. . .	–26
General government	4 703 .B	–108	–114	–137	–98	–40	. . .	. . .	. . .
Banks	4 703 .C	–1,256	–584	–1,786	–1,250	–2,207	–7,024	–4,738	–6,209
Other sectors	4 703 .D	219	690	–520	–163	324	–1,409	–2,360	–674
Other investment liabilities	4 753 X.	–1,218	1,310	1,598	2,168	2,851	2,178	6,689	11,753
Monetary authorities	4 753 XA	–1,402	–470	–518	–385	–24	–32	299	–99
General government	4 753 YB	. . .	. . .	. . .	. . .	. . .	–146	–139	102
Banks	4 753 YC	233	1,241	1,329	2,376	1,757	1,327	7,069	11,725
Other sectors	4 753 YD	–49	538	786	176	1,117	1,028	–540	25
Total, Groups A Through C	4 020 . .	*–773*	*4,158*	*2,382*	*3,820*	*–1,134*	*–2,800*	*–880*	*2,997*
D. Net Errors and Omissions	4 998 . .	**1,640**	**497**	**1,160**	**1,893**	**978**	**–48**	**–550**	**–3,296**
Total, Groups A Through D	4 030 . .	*867*	*4,654*	*3,542*	*5,713*	*–156*	*–2,848*	*–1,430*	*–299*
E. Reserves and Related Items	4 040 . .	**–867**	**–4,654**	**–3,542**	**–5,713**	**156**	**2,848**	**1,430**	**299**
Reserve assets	4 800 . .	–365	–4,654	–3,542	–5,713	156	2,848	1,430	299
Use of Fund credit and loans	4 766 . .	–502	. . .	. . .	. . .	. . .	. . .	. . .	. . .
Liabilities constituting foreign authorities' reserves	4 900 . .	. . .	. . .	. . .	. . .	. . .	. . .	. . .	. . .
Exceptional financing	4 920 . .	. . .	. . .	. . .	. . .	. . .	. . .	. . .	. . .
Conversion rates: Portuguese escudos per U.S. dollar	0 101 . .	**143.95**	**157.46**	**142.55**	**144.48**	**135.00**	**160.80**	**165.99**	**151.11**

[1] Excludes components that have been classified in the categories of Group E.

Table 2. STANDARD PRESENTATION, 1988–95
(Millions of U.S. dollars)

	Code	1988	1989	1990	1991	1992	1993	1994	1995
CURRENT ACCOUNT	4 993 . .	**–1,066**	**153**	**–181**	**–716**	**–184**	**233**	**–1,505**	**–229**
A. GOODS	4 100 . .	–5,377	–4,742	–6,684	–7,688	–9,387	–8,050	–8,078	–8,484
Credit	2 100 . .	**11,015**	**12,843**	**16,458**	**16,391**	**18,348**	**15,931**	**18,635**	**23,928**
General merchandise: exports f.o.b.	2 110 . .	10,874	12,720	16,311	16,231	18,195	15,526	18,334	23,639
Goods for processing: exports f.o.b.	2 150 . .	. . .	. . .	. . .	. . .	. . .	33	52	40
Repairs on goods	2 160 . .	. . .	. . .	. . .	. . .	. . .	114	145	149
Goods procured in ports by carriers	2 170 . .	141	122	147	159	153	258	102	100
Nonmonetary gold	2 180 . .	. . .	. . .	. . .	. . .	. . .	1	2	. . .
Debit	3 100 . .	**–16,392**	**–17,585**	**–23,141**	**–24,079**	**–27,735**	**–23,981**	**–26,713**	**–32,413**
General merchandise: imports f.o.b.	3 110 . .	–16,392	–17,585	–23,141	–24,079	–27,735	–23,758	–26,554	–32,240
Goods for processing: imports f.o.b.	3 150 . .	. . .	. . .	. . .	. . .	. . .	–10	–11	–6
Repairs on goods	3 160 . .	. . .	. . .	. . .	. . .	. . .	–19	–10	–10
Goods procured in ports by carriers	3 170 . .	. . .	. . .	. . .	. . .	. . .	–95	–63	–70
Nonmonetary gold	3 180 . .	. . .	. . .	. . .	. . .	. . .	–98	–76	–86
B. SERVICES	4 200 . .	750	958	1,091	812	766	1,365	1,289	1,637
Total credit	2 200 . .	*3,418*	*3,789*	*5,096*	*5,231*	*5,497*	*6,846*	*6,761*	*8,173*
Total debit	3 200 . .	*–2,668*	*–2,830*	*–4,005*	*–4,420*	*–4,732*	*–5,481*	*–5,472*	*–6,536*
Transportation services, credit	2 205 . .	**517**	**537**	**791**	**741**	**793**	**1,160**	**1,028**	**1,464**
Passenger	2 205 BA	*113*	*106*	*96*	*156*	*170*	*632*	*482*	*764*
Freight	2 205 BB	*126*	*134*	*142*	*139*	*135*	*271*	*277*	*325*
Other	2 205 BC	*278*	*297*	*553*	*447*	*488*	*257*	*269*	*375*
Sea transport, passenger	2 207 . .	. . .	. . .	. . .	. . .	. . .	. . .	2	. . .
Sea transport, freight	2 208 . .	. . .	. . .	. . .	. . .	. . .	116	107	113
Sea transport, other	2 209 . .	. . .	. . .	. . .	. . .	. . .	105	106	129
Air transport, passenger	2 211 . .	. . .	. . .	. . .	. . .	. . .	620	472	759
Air transport, freight	2 212 . .	. . .	. . .	. . .	. . .	. . .	36	45	50
Air transport, other	2 213 . .	. . .	. . .	. . .	. . .	. . .	125	146	216
Other transport, passenger	2 215 . .	. . .	. . .	. . .	. . .	. . .	12	7	5
Other transport, freight	2 216 . .	. . .	. . .	. . .	. . .	. . .	119	125	161
Other transport, other	2 217 . .	. . .	. . .	. . .	. . .	. . .	26	18	31
Transportation services, debit	3 205 . .	**–1,246**	**–1,323**	**–1,828**	**–1,923**	**–2,017**	**–1,335**	**–1,426**	**–1,679**
Passenger	3 205 BA	*–28*	*–32*	*–55*	*–36*	*–26*	*–292*	*–341*	*–436*
Freight	3 205 BB	*–1,008*	*–1,079*	*–1,426*	*–1,491*	*–1,670*	*–842*	*–925*	*–1,123*
Other	3 205 BC	*–211*	*–212*	*–347*	*–395*	*–321*	*–202*	*–159*	*–119*
Sea transport, passenger	3 207 . .	. . .	. . .	. . .	. . .	. . .	–1	–2	–3
Sea transport, freight	3 208 . .	. . .	. . .	. . .	. . .	. . .	–539	–583	–707
Sea transport, other	3 209 . .	. . .	. . .	. . .	. . .	. . .	–75	–74	–63
Air transport, passenger	3 211 . .	. . .	. . .	. . .	. . .	. . .	–267	–331	–424
Air transport, freight	3 212 . .	. . .	. . .	. . .	. . .	. . .	–71	–85	–103
Air transport, other	3 213 . .	. . .	. . .	. . .	. . .	. . .	–110	–78	–49
Other transport, passenger	3 215 . .	. . .	. . .	. . .	. . .	. . .	–24	–9	–9
Other transport, freight	3 216 . .	. . .	. . .	. . .	. . .	. . .	–231	–258	–313
Other transport, other	3 217 . .	. . .	. . .	. . .	. . .	. . .	–17	–8	–8
Travel, credit	2 236 . .	**2,403**	**2,684**	**3,556**	**3,712**	**3,721**	**4,052**	**4,148**	**4,841**
Business travel	2 237 . .	. . .	. . .	. . .	. . .	. . .	. . .	. . .	. . .
Personal travel	2 240 . .	. . .	. . .	. . .	. . .	. . .	. . .	. . .	. . .
Travel, debit	3 236 . .	**–532**	**–584**	**–867**	**–1,023**	**–1,166**	**–1,899**	**–1,707**	**–2,121**
Business travel	3 237 . .	. . .	. . .	. . .	. . .	. . .	. . .	. . .	. . .
Personal travel	3 240 . .	. . .	. . .	. . .	. . .	. . .	. . .	. . .	. . .
Other services, credit	2 200 BA	**499**	**568**	**749**	**778**	**983**	**1,634**	**1,585**	**1,868**
Communications	2 245 . .	. . .	. . .	. . .	. . .	. . .	358	336	320
Construction	2 249 . .	. . .	. . .	. . .	. . .	. . .	107	153	233
Insurance	2 253 . .	29	29	35	56	29	70	92	110
Financial	2 260 . .	. . .	. . .	. . .	. . .	. . .	127	116	248
Computer and information	2 262 . .	. . .	. . .	. . .	. . .	. . .	14	22	41
Royalties and licence fees	2 266 . .	8	8	14	15	13	36	29	20
Other business services	2 268 . .	413	447	659	645	877	730	667	701
Personal, cultural, and recreational	2 287 . .	. . .	. . .	. . .	. . .	. . .	141	117	120
Government, n.i.e.	2 291 . .	49	83	42	61	65	50	54	75
Other services, debit	3 200 BA	**–890**	**–923**	**–1,310**	**–1,474**	**–1,549**	**–2,247**	**–2,339**	**–2,736**
Communications	3 245 . .	. . .	. . .	. . .	. . .	. . .	–161	–165	–175
Construction	3 249 . .	. . .	. . .	. . .	. . .	. . .	–117	–81	–206
Insurance	3 253 . .	–142	–143	–193	–223	–227	–170	–247	–317
Financial	3 260 . .	. . .	. . .	. . .	. . .	. . .	–247	–162	–247
Computer and information	3 262 . .	. . .	. . .	. . .	. . .	. . .	–41	–49	–64
Royalties and licence fees	3 266 . .	–77	–69	–117	–114	–75	–174	–206	–217
Other business services	3 268 . .	–451	–494	–768	–876	–1,001	–963	–1,069	–1,072
Personal, cultural, and recreational	3 287 . .	. . .	. . .	. . .	. . .	. . .	–150	–128	–165
Government, n.i.e.	3 291 . .	–221	–217	–232	–261	–246	–223	–231	–272

Table 2 (Continued). STANDARD PRESENTATION, 1988–95

(Millions of U.S. dollars)

	Code	1988	1989	1990	1991	1992	1993	1994	1995
C. INCOME	4 300	–761	–603	–96	186	611	220	–137	–513
Total credit	2 300	*477*	*719*	*1,360*	*1,550*	*2,067*	*2,455*	*2,232*	*3,564*
Total debit	3 300	*–1,238*	*–1,322*	*–1,457*	*–1,364*	*–1,456*	*–2,236*	*–2,369*	*–4,078*
Compensation of employees, credit	2 310	**147**	**144**	**216**	**200**	**112**	**136**	**137**	**153**
Compensation of employees, debit	3 310	**–29**	**–28**	**–77**	**–94**	**–109**	**–51**	**–66**	**–87**
Investment income, credit	2 320	**330**	**575**	**1,144**	**1,350**	**1,956**	**2,320**	**2,096**	**3,411**
Direct investment income	2 330	4	...	1	...	...	44	62	43
Dividends and distributed branch profits	2 332	...	...	...	...	...	33	62	42
Reinvested earnings and undistributed branch profits	2 333	4	...	1	...	...	11	...	1
Income on debt (interest)	2 334	...	...	...	...	...	...	...	...
Portfolio investment income	2 339	...	...	...	...	...	1,202	599	898
Income on equity	2 340	...	...	...	...	...	...	...	...
Income on bonds and notes	2 350	...	...	...	...	...	...	...	...
Income on money market instruments and financial derivatives	2 360	...	...	...	...	...	...	...	...
Other investment income	2 370	327	575	1,143	1,350	1,956	1,073	1,435	2,470
Investment income, debit	3 320	**–1,208**	**–1,294**	**–1,380**	**–1,270**	**–1,348**	**–2,185**	**–2,304**	**–3,991**
Direct investment income	3 330	–46	–69	–102	–63	–47	–171	–231	–300
Dividends and distributed branch profits	3 332	...	...	...	...	...	–173	–231	–300
Reinvested earnings and undistributed branch profits	3 333	–46	–69	–102	–63	–47	2	...	...
Income on debt (interest)	3 334	...	...	...	...	...	...	...	...
Portfolio investment income	3 339	...	...	...	...	...	–195	–299	–726
Income on equity	3 340	...	...	...	...	...	...	...	...
Income on bonds and notes	3 350	...	...	...	...	...	...	...	...
Income on money market instruments and financial derivatives	3 360	...	...	...	...	...	...	...	...
Other investment income	3 370	–1,162	–1,224	–1,277	–1,208	–1,301	–1,819	–1,774	–2,965
D. CURRENT TRANSFERS	4 379	4,322	4,540	5,507	5,975	7,826	6,699	5,421	7,131
Credit	2 379	**4,946**	**5,227**	**6,433**	**7,237**	**9,344**	**8,395**	**7,410**	**9,048**
General government	2 380	1,207	1,328	1,665	2,279	4,139	4,067	3,511	5,171
Other sectors	2 390	3,739	3,899	4,769	4,958	5,205	4,328	3,899	3,877
Workers' remittances	2 391	3,378	3,562	4,263	4,517	4,650	4,179	3,669	3,791
Other current transfers	2 392	362	338	506	441	555	149	230	86
Debit	3 379	**–624**	**–687**	**–926**	**–1,263**	**–1,518**	**–1,696**	**–1,989**	**–1,917**
General government	3 380	–482	–514	–666	–898	–1,107	–1,187	–1,569	–1,423
Other sectors	3 390	–142	–174	–260	–365	–411	–509	–420	–494
Workers' remittances	3 391	...	...	...	...	...	–408	–321	–443
Other current transfers	3 392	–142	–174	–260	–365	–411	–101	–100	–51
CAPITAL AND FINANCIAL ACCOUNT	4 996	**–574**	**–650**	**–979**	**–1,177**	**–794**	**–185**	**2,055**	**3,525**
CAPITAL ACCOUNT	4 994	...	...	...	...	...	...	...	...
Total credit	2 994	...	...	...	...	...	...	...	...
Total debit	3 994	...	...	...	...	...	...	...	...
Capital transfers, credit	2 400	...	...	...	...	...	...	...	...
General government	2 401	...	...	...	...	...	...	...	...
Debt forgiveness	2 402	...	...	...	...	...	...	...	...
Other capital transfers	2 410	...	...	...	...	...	...	...	...
Other sectors	2 430	...	...	...	...	...	...	...	...
Migrants' transfers	2 431	...	...	...	...	...	...	...	...
Debt forgiveness	2 432	...	...	...	...	...	...	...	...
Other capital transfers	2 440	...	...	...	...	...	...	...	...
Capital transfers, debit	3 400	...	...	...	...	...	...	...	...
General government	3 401	...	...	...	...	...	...	...	...
Debt forgiveness	3 402	...	...	...	...	...	...	...	...
Other capital transfers	3 410	...	...	...	...	...	...	...	...
Other sectors	3 430	...	...	...	...	...	...	...	...
Migrants' transfers	3 431	...	...	...	...	...	...	...	...
Debt forgiveness	3 432	...	...	...	...	...	...	...	...
Other capital transfers	3 440	...	...	...	...	...	...	...	...
Nonproduced nonfinancial assets, credit	2 480	...	...	...	...	...	...	...	...
Nonproduced nonfinancial assets, debit	3 480	...	...	...	...	...	...	...	...

Table 2 (Continued). STANDARD PRESENTATION, 1988–95
(Millions of U.S. dollars)

	Code	1988	1989	1990	1991	1992	1993	1994	1995
FINANCIAL ACCOUNT	4 995 . .	**–574**	**–650**	**–979**	**–1,177**	**–794**	**–185**	**2,055**	**3,525**
A. DIRECT INVESTMENT	4 500 . .	842	1,653	2,447	1,985	1,186	1,386	983	–32
Direct investment abroad	4 505 . .	**–80**	**–84**	**–163**	**–463**	**–687**	**–148**	**–287**	**–685**
Equity capital	4 510 . .	–39	–75	–106	–310	–614	–50	–185	–512
Claims on affiliated enterprises	4 515 . .	...	...	...	...	...	...	...	...
Liabilities to affiliated enterprises	4 520 . .	...	...	...	...	...	...	...	...
Reinvested earnings	4 525 . .	–4	...	–1	...	...	–11	...	–1
Other capital	4 530 . .	–37	–9	–56	–153	–73	–87	–102	–171
Claims on affiliated enterprises	4 535 . .	...	...	...	...	...	...	...	...
Liabilities to affiliated enterprises	4 540 . .	...	...	...	...	...	...	...	...
Direct investment in Portugal	4 555 . .	**922**	**1,737**	**2,610**	**2,448**	**1,873**	**1,534**	**1,270**	**653**
Equity capital	4 560 . .	855	1,579	2,503	2,370	1,825	1,067	989	165
Claims on direct investors	4 565 . .	...	...	...	...	...	...	...	...
Liabilities to direct investors	4 570 . .	...	...	...	...	...	...	...	...
Reinvested earnings	4 575 . .	46	69	102	63	47	–2	...	...
Other capital	4 580 . .	21	88	4	16	2	469	281	488
Claims on direct investors	4 585 . .	...	...	...	...	...	...	...	...
Liabilities to direct investors	4 590 . .	...	...	...	...	...	...	...	...
B. PORTFOLIO INVESTMENT	4 600 . .	1,814	1,050	961	1,895	–3,064	1,827	51	–1,585
Assets	4 602 . .	**–27**	**...**	**...**	**...**	**–379**	**–2,387**	**–3,456**	**–2,657**
Equity securities	4 610 . .	–1	...	...	...	–9	–168	–66	–138
Monetary authorities	4 611 . .	...	...	...	...	...	...	...	...
General government	4 612 . .	...	...	...	...	...	...	...	...
Banks	4 613 . .	...	...	...	...	...	–49	–23	–77
Other sectors	4 614 . .	...	...	...	...	...	–119	–43	–61
Debt securities	4 619 . .	–27	...	...	...	–370	–2,218	–3,390	–2,519
Bonds and notes	4 620 . .	–27	...	...	...	–370	–568	–1,607	–4,413
Monetary authorities	4 621 . .	...	...	...	...	...	...	...	...
General government	4 622 . .	...	...	...	...	...	...	...	...
Banks	4 623 . .	...	...	...	...	...	–228	–827	–2,096
Other sectors	4 624 . .	...	...	...	...	...	–339	–780	–2,316
Money market instruments	4 630 . .	...	...	...	...	...	–1,646	–1,784	1,893
Monetary authorities	4 631 . .	...	...	...	...	...	...	...	...
General government	4 632 . .	...	...	...	...	...	...	...	...
Banks	4 633 . .	...	...	...	...	...	...	...	68
Other sectors	4 634 . .	...	...	...	...	...	–1,646	–1,784	1,826
Financial derivatives	4 640 . .	...	...	...	...	...	–5	...	...
Monetary authorities	4 641 . .	...	...	...	...	...	...	...	...
General government	4 642 . .	...	...	...	...	...	...	...	...
Banks	4 643 . .	...	...	...	...	...	–5	...	...
Other sectors	4 644 . .	...	...	...	...	...	...	...	...
Liabilities	4 652 . .	**1,841**	**1,050**	**961**	**1,895**	**–2,685**	**4,214**	**3,507**	**1,072**
Equity securities	4 660 . .	220	605	508	215	570	579	507	–208
Banks	4 663 . .	220	605	508	215	570	...	...	...
Other sectors	4 664 . .	...	...	...	...	...	...	...	...
Debt securities	4 669 . .	1,622	445	453	1,681	–3,255	3,634	3,000	1,280
Bonds and notes	4 670 . .	1,622	445	453	1,681	–3,255	3,634	3,000	623
Monetary authorities	4 671 . .	...	...	...	...	...	...	...	...
General government	4 672 . .	1,486	64	383	1,602	–3,467	...	...	...
Banks	4 673 . .	...	...	...	...	...	...	...	...
Other sectors	4 674 . .	135	380	69	79	212	...	...	...
Money market instruments	4 680 . .	...	...	...	...	...	...	...	657
Monetary authorities	4 681 . .	...	...	...	...	...	...	...	...
General government	4 682 . .	...	...	...	...	...	...	...	...
Banks	4 683 . .	...	...	...	...	...	...	...	...
Other sectors	4 684 . .	...	...	...	...	...	...	...	...
Financial derivatives	4 690 . .	...	...	...	...	...	...	...	...
Monetary authorities	4 691 . .	...	...	...	...	...	...	...	...
General government	4 692 . .	...	...	...	...	...	...	...	...
Banks	4 693 . .	...	...	...	...	...	...	...	...
Other sectors	4 694 . .	...	...	...	...	...	...	...	...

Table 2 (Concluded). STANDARD PRESENTATION, 1988–95
(Millions of U.S. dollars)

	Code	1988	1989	1990	1991	1992	1993	1994	1995
C. OTHER INVESTMENT	4 700 . .	–2,865	1,302	–845	656	928	–6,246	–409	4,843
Assets	4 703 . .	**–1,145**	**–7**	**–2,442**	**–1,511**	**–1,923**	**–8,424**	**–7,098**	**–6,910**
Trade credits	4 706 . .	–538	661	–384	–29	106	. . .	. . .	. . .
General government: long-term	4 708 . .	. . .	. . .	. . .	. . .	. . .	. . .	. . .	. . .
General government: short-term	4 709 . .	. . .	. . .	. . .	. . .	. . .	. . .	. . .	. . .
Other sectors: long-term	4 711 . .	42	13	–13	–26	–87	. . .	. . .	. . .
Other sectors: short-term	4 712 . .	–580	647	–371	–3	194	. . .	. . .	. . .
Loans	4 714 . .	654	–73	–258	–233	193	–171	–51	–307
Monetary authorities: long-term	4 717 . .	. . .	. . .	. . .	. . .	. . .	. . .	. . .	. . .
Monetary authorities: short-term	4 718 . .	. . .	. . .	. . .	. . .	. . .	. . .	. . .	. . .
General government: long-term	4 720 . .	–108	–114	–137	–98	–40	. . .	. . .	. . .
General government: short-term	4 721 . .	. . .	. . .	. . .	. . .	. . .	. . .	. . .	. . .
Banks: long-term	4 723 . .	. . .	. . .	. . .	. . .	. . .	38	9	–75
Banks: short-term	4 724 . .	. . .	. . .	. . .	. . .	. . .	. . .	. . .	. . .
Other sectors: long-term	4 726 . .	. . .	1	. . .	–2	–10	–96	–23	–8
Other sectors: short-term	4 727 . .	763	40	–121	–133	243	–113	–37	–224
Currency and deposits	4 730 . .	–1,204	–507	–1,729	–1,227	–2,103	–7,925	–6,684	–6,536
Monetary authorities	4 731 . .	. . .	. . .	. . .	. . .	. . .	. . .	. . .	. . .
General government	4 732 . .	. . .	. . .	. . .	. . .	. . .	. . .	. . .	. . .
Banks	4 733 . .	–1,204	–507	–1,729	–1,227	–2,103	–7,062	–4,747	–6,134
Other sectors	4 734 . .	. . .	. . .	. . .	. . .	. . .	–863	–1,937	–402
Other assets	4 736 . .	–57	–88	–71	–23	–119	–327	–363	–67
Monetary authorities: long-term	4 738 . .	. . .	. . .	. . .	. . .	. . .	. . .	. . .	–14
Monetary authorities: short-term	4 739 . .	. . .	. . .	. . .	. . .	. . .	9	. . .	–12
General government: long-term	4 741 . .	. . .	. . .	. . .	. . .	. . .	. . .	. . .	. . .
General government: short-term	4 742 . .	. . .	. . .	. . .	. . .	. . .	. . .	. . .	. . .
Banks: long-term	4 744 . .	–52	–77	–56	–23	–104	. . .	. . .	. . .
Banks: short-term	4 745 . .	. . .	. . .	. . .	. . .	. . .	. . .	. . .	. . .
Other sectors: long-term	4 747 . .	–5	–11	–14	. . .	–15	. . .	. . .	. . .
Other sectors: short-term	4 748 . .	. . .	. . .	. . .	. . .	. . .	–336	–363	–41
Liabilities	4 753 . .	**–1,720**	**1,310**	**1,598**	**2,168**	**2,851**	**2,178**	**6,689**	**11,753**
Trade credits	4 756 . .	–148	–68	124	248	359	. . .	. . .	. . .
General government: long-term	4 758 . .	. . .	. . .	. . .	. . .	. . .	. . .	. . .	. . .
General government: short-term	4 759 . .	. . .	. . .	. . .	. . .	. . .	. . .	. . .	. . .
Other sectors: long-term	4 761 . .	–148	–68	124	248	359	. . .	. . .	. . .
Other sectors: short-term	4 762 . .	. . .	. . .	. . .	. . .	. . .	. . .	. . .	. . .
Loans	4 764 . .	–2,195	37	–35	16	698	496	–834	–49
Use of Fund credit and loans from the Fund	4 766 . .	–502	. . .	. . .	. . .	. . .	. . .	. . .	. . .
Monetary authorities: other long-term	4 767 . .	–1,392	–348	–437	–293	–36	. . .	. . .	. . .
Monetary authorities: short-term	4 768 . .	. . .	–211	–104	. . .	. . .	. . .	. . .	. . .
General government: long-term	4 770 . .	. . .	. . .	. . .	. . .	. . .	–146	–139	102
General government: short-term	4 771 . .	. . .	. . .	. . .	. . .	. . .	. . .	. . .	. . .
Banks: long-term	4 773 . .	–310	91	38	383	189	–237	–136	–202
Banks: short-term	4 774 . .	. . .	. . .	. . .	. . .	. . .	. . .	. . .	. . .
Other sectors: long-term	4 776 . .	10	505	469	–75	544	507	–480	–320
Other sectors: short-term	4 777 . .	. . .	. . .	. . .	. . .	. . .	372	–79	372
Currency and deposits	4 780 . .	543	1,150	1,292	1,994	1,568	1,564	7,205	11,928
Monetary authorities	4 781 . .	. . .	. . .	. . .	. . .	. . .	. . .	. . .	. . .
General government	4 782 . .	. . .	. . .	. . .	. . .	. . .	. . .	. . .	. . .
Banks	4 783 . .	543	1,150	1,292	1,994	1,568	1,564	7,205	11,928
Other sectors	4 784 . .	. . .	. . .	. . .	. . .	. . .	. . .	. . .	. . .
Other liabilities	4 786 . .	80	191	217	–90	226	118	319	–126
Monetary authorities: long-term	4 788 . .	. . .	. . .	. . .	. . .	. . .	. . .	. . .	. . .
Monetary authorities: short-term	4 789 . .	–10	90	24	–92	12	–32	299	–99
General government: long-term	4 791 . .	. . .	. . .	. . .	. . .	. . .	. . .	. . .	. . .
General government: short-term	4 792 . .	. . .	. . .	. . .	. . .	. . .	. . .	. . .	. . .
Banks: long-term	4 794 . .	. . .	. . .	. . .	. . .	. . .	. . .	. . .	. . .
Banks: short-term	4 795 . .	. . .	. . .	. . .	. . .	. . .	. . .	. . .	. . .
Other sectors: long-term	4 797 . .	90	101	194	2	214	. . .	. . .	. . .
Other sectors: short-term	4 798 . .	. . .	. . .	. . .	. . .	. . .	150	19	–27
D. RESERVE ASSETS	4 800 . .	–365	–4,654	–3,542	–5,713	156	2,848	1,430	299
Monetary gold	4 810 . .	1,740	–138	–209	–67	–68	–1	–1	. . .
Special drawing rights	4 820 . .	74	2	–52	–38	48	–12	–9	–13
Reserve position in the Fund	4 830 . .	. . .	–83	–39	–92	–54	12	–16	–110
Foreign exchange	4 840 . .	–2,158	–4,452	–3,241	–5,516	230	2,848	1,456	422
Other claims	4 880 . .	–20	16	. . .	. . .	. . .	. . .	. . .	. . .
NET ERRORS AND OMISSIONS	4 998 . .	**1,640**	**497**	**1,160**	**1,893**	**978**	**–48**	**–550**	**–3,296**

Part 3 of the *Yearbook* contains descriptions of the methodologies, compilation practices, and sources used to compile these data.

Table 1. ANALYTIC PRESENTATION, 1988–95
(Millions of U.S. dollars)

	Code	1988	1989	1990	1991	1992	1993	1994	1995
A. Current Account [1]	4 993 Y.	**3,922**	**2,514**	**–3,254**	**–1,012**	**–1,506**	**–1,231**	**–455**	**–1,342**
Goods: exports f.o.b	2 100 . .	11,392	10,487	5,770	4,266	4,364	4,892	6,151	7,519
Goods: imports f.o.b	3 100 . .	–7,642	–8,437	–9,114	–5,372	–5,558	–6,020	–6,562	–8,750
Balance on Goods	4 100 . .	*3,750*	*2,050*	*–3,344*	*–1,106*	*–1,194*	*–1,128*	*–411*	*–1,231*
Services: credit	2 200 . .	850	834	610	680	659	799	1,044	1,494
Services: debit	3 200 . .	–480	–450	–787	–819	–946	–914	–1,215	–1,727
Balance on Goods and Services	4 991 . .	*4,120*	*2,434*	*–3,521*	*–1,245*	*–1,481*	*–1,243*	*–582*	*–1,464*
Income: credit	2 300 . .	173	181	175	104	54	63	116	81
Income: debit	3 300 . .	–371	–101	–14	–89	–144	–208	–245	–322
Balance on Goods, Services, and Income	4 992 . .	*3,922*	*2,514*	*–3,360*	*–1,230*	*–1,571*	*–1,388*	*–711*	*–1,705*
Current transfers: credit	2 379 Y.	. . .	. . .	138	277	136	174	317	473
Current transfers: debit	3 379 . .	. . .	. . .	–32	–59	–71	–17	–61	–110
B. Capital Account [1]	4 994 Y.	**. . .**	**. . .**	**. . .**	**. . .**	**. . .**	**. . .**	**. . .**	**32**
Capital account: credit	2 994 Y.	. . .	. . .	. . .	. . .	. . .	. . .	. . .	32
Capital account: debit	3 994 . .	. . .	. . .	. . .	. . .	. . .	. . .	. . .	. . .
Total, Groups A Plus B	4 010 . .	*3,922*	*2,514*	*–3,254*	*–1,012*	*–1,506*	*–1,231*	*–455*	*–1,310*
C. Financial Account [1]	4 995 X.	**–4,223**	**–1,376**	**1,613**	**320**	**1,380**	**640**	**535**	**992**
Direct investment abroad	4 505 . .	. . .	. . .	–18	–3	–4	–7	. . .	–2
Direct investment in Romania	4 555 Y.	. . .	. . .	. . .	40	77	94	341	419
Portfolio investment assets	4 602 . .	. . .	. . .	. . .	. . .	. . .	–73	75	–22
Equity securities	4 610 . .	. . .	. . .	. . .	. . .	. . .	. . .	. . .	–4
Debt securities	4 619 . .	. . .	. . .	. . .	. . .	. . .	–73	75	–18
Portfolio investment liabilities	4 652 Y.	. . .	. . .	. . .	. . .	. . .	. . .	. . .	1
Equity securities	4 660 Y.	. . .	. . .	. . .	. . .	. . .	. . .	. . .	. . .
Debt securities	4 669 Y.	. . .	. . .	. . .	. . .	. . .	. . .	. . .	1
Other investment assets	4 703 . .	–765	98	562	–86	94	–45	–671	186
Monetary authorities	4 703 . A	. . .	. . .	. . .	. . .	. . .	. . .	. . .	. . .
General government	4 703 . B	–400	169	529	162	112	–49	–24	–62
Banks	4 703 . C	–365	–71	33	–37	. . .	–168	–621	256
Other sectors	4 703 . D	. . .	. . .	. . .	–211	–18	172	–26	–8
Other investment liabilities	4 753 X.	–3,458	–1,474	1,069	369	1,213	671	790	410
Monetary authorities	4 753 XA	. . .	. . .	. . .	–533	–159	. . .	. . .	. . .
General government	4 753 YB	. . .	. . .	. . .	. . .	812	68	75	–107
Banks	4 753 YC	–3,458	–1,474	1,069	149	–73	19	190	–5
Other sectors	4 753 YD	. . .	. . .	. . .	753	633	584	525	522
Total, Groups A Through C	4 020 . .	*–301*	*1,138*	*–1,641*	*–692*	*–126*	*–591*	*80*	*–318*
D. Net Errors and Omissions	4 998 . .	**16**	**114**	**147**	**15**	**–12**	**152**	**91**	**–182**
Total, Groups A Through D	4 030 . .	*–285*	*1,252*	*–1,494*	*–677*	*–138*	*–439*	*171*	*–500*
E. Reserves and Related Items	4 040 . .	**285**	**–1,252**	**1,494**	**677**	**138**	**439**	**–171**	**500**
Reserve assets	4 800 . .	622	–1,111	1,494	–93	–124	54	–616	259
Use of Fund credit and loans	4 766 . .	–337	–141	. . .	770	262	. . .	217	–316
Liabilities constituting foreign authorities' reserves	4 900 . .	. . .	. . .	. . .	. . .	. . .	. . .	. . .	. . .
Exceptional financing	4 920 . .	. . .	. . .	. . .	. . .	. . .	385	228	556
Conversion rates: lei per U.S. dollar	0 101 . .	**14.3**	**14.9**	**22.4**	**76.4**	**308.0**	**760.1**	**1,655.1**	**2,033.3**

[1] Excludes components that have been classified in the categories of Group E.

Table 2. STANDARD PRESENTATION, 1988–95

(Millions of U.S. dollars)

	Code	1988	1989	1990	1991	1992	1993	1994	1995
CURRENT ACCOUNT	4 993 . .	**3,922**	**2,514**	**–3,254**	**–1,012**	**–1,506**	**–1,174**	**–428**	**–1,336**
A. GOODS	4 100 . .	3,750	2,050	–3,344	–1,106	–1,194	–1,128	–411	–1,231
Credit	2 100 . .	**11,392**	**10,487**	**5,770**	**4,266**	**4,364**	**4,892**	**6,151**	**7,519**
General merchandise: exports f.o.b.	2 110 . .	11,392	10,487	5,770	4,266	4,364	4,892	6,146	7,509
Goods for processing: exports f.o.b.	2 150 . .	. . .	. . .	. . .	. . .	. . .	. . .	. . .	. . .
Repairs on goods	2 160 . .	. . .	. . .	. . .	. . .	. . .	. . .	5	10
Goods procured in ports by carriers	2 170 . .	. . .	. . .	. . .	. . .	. . .	. . .	. . .	. . .
Nonmonetary gold	2 180 . .	. . .	. . .	. . .	. . .	. . .	. . .	. . .	. . .
Debit	3 100 . .	**–7,642**	**–8,437**	**–9,114**	**–5,372**	**–5,558**	**–6,020**	**–6,562**	**–8,750**
General merchandise: imports f.o.b.	3 110 . .	–7,642	–8,437	–9,114	–5,372	–5,558	–6,020	–6,544	–8,718
Goods for processing: imports f.o.b.	3 150 . .	. . .	. . .	. . .	. . .	. . .	. . .	–2	–3
Repairs on goods	3 160 . .	. . .	. . .	. . .	. . .	. . .	. . .	–5	–8
Goods procured in ports by carriers	3 170 . .	. . .	. . .	. . .	. . .	. . .	. . .	–11	–21
Nonmonetary gold	3 180 . .	. . .	. . .	. . .	. . .	. . .	. . .	. . .	. . .
B. SERVICES	4 200 . .	370	384	–177	–139	–287	–115	–171	–233
Total credit	2 200 . .	*850*	*834*	*610*	*680*	*659*	*799*	*1,044*	*1,494*
Total debit	3 200 . .	*–480*	*–450*	*–787*	*–819*	*–946*	*–914*	*–1,215*	*–1,727*
Transportation services, credit	2 205 . .	**426**	**417**	**308**	**223**	**136**	**291**	**381**	**471**
Passenger	2 205 BA	. . .	. . .	. . .	. . .	. . .	. . .	*114*	*99*
Freight	2 205 BB	*426*	*417*	*308*	*223*	*136*	*291*	*200*	*264*
Other	2 205 BC	. . .	. . .	. . .	. . .	. . .	. . .	*67*	*108*
Sea transport, passenger	2 207 . .	. . .	. . .	. . .	. . .	. . .	. . .	. . .	. . .
Sea transport, freight	2 208 . .	. . .	. . .	. . .	. . .	. . .	. . .	67	95
Sea transport, other	2 209 . .	. . .	. . .	. . .	. . .	. . .	. . .	6	16
Air transport, passenger	2 211 . .	. . .	. . .	. . .	. . .	. . .	. . .	113	96
Air transport, freight	2 212 . .	. . .	. . .	. . .	. . .	. . .	. . .	. . .	4
Air transport, other	2 213 . .	. . .	. . .	. . .	. . .	. . .	. . .	52	76
Other transport, passenger	2 215 . .	. . .	. . .	. . .	. . .	. . .	. . .	1	3
Other transport, freight	2 216 . .	. . .	. . .	. . .	. . .	. . .	. . .	133	165
Other transport, other	2 217 . .	. . .	. . .	. . .	. . .	. . .	. . .	9	16
Transportation services, debit	3 205 . .	**–343**	**–353**	**–516**	**–374**	**–377**	**–341**	**–403**	**–512**
Passenger	3 205 BA	. . .	. . .	. . .	. . .	. . .	. . .	*–52*	*–52*
Freight	3 205 BB	*–343*	*–353*	*–516*	*–374*	*–377*	*–341*	*–324*	*–432*
Other	3 205 BC	. . .	. . .	. . .	. . .	. . .	. . .	*–27*	*–28*
Sea transport, passenger	3 207 . .	. . .	. . .	. . .	. . .	. . .	. . .	. . .	. . .
Sea transport, freight	3 208 . .	. . .	. . .	. . .	. . .	. . .	. . .	–78	–176
Sea transport, other	3 209 . .	. . .	. . .	. . .	. . .	. . .	. . .	–9	–6
Air transport, passenger	3 211 . .	. . .	. . .	. . .	. . .	. . .	. . .	–48	–44
Air transport, freight	3 212 . .	. . .	. . .	. . .	. . .	. . .	. . .	. . .	–11
Air transport, other	3 213 . .	. . .	. . .	. . .	. . .	. . .	. . .	–7	–9
Other transport, passenger	3 215 . .	. . .	. . .	. . .	. . .	. . .	. . .	–4	–8
Other transport, freight	3 216 . .	. . .	. . .	. . .	. . .	. . .	. . .	–246	–245
Other transport, other	3 217 . .	. . .	. . .	. . .	. . .	. . .	. . .	–11	–13
Travel, credit	2 236 . .	**171**	**167**	**106**	**145**	**262**	**197**	**414**	**590**
Business travel	2 237 . .	. . .	. . .	. . .	. . .	. . .	. . .	. . .	. . .
Personal travel	2 240 . .	. . .	. . .	. . .	. . .	. . .	. . .	414	590
Travel, debit	3 236 . .	**–33**	**–35**	**–103**	**–143**	**–260**	**–195**	**–449**	**–697**
Business travel	3 237 . .	. . .	. . .	. . .	. . .	. . .	. . .	–134	–175
Personal travel	3 240 . .	. . .	. . .	. . .	. . .	. . .	. . .	–315	–522
Other services, credit	2 200 BA	**253**	**250**	**196**	**312**	**261**	**311**	**249**	**433**
Communications	2 245 . .	. . .	. . .	. . .	. . .	. . .	. . .	44	66
Construction	2 249 . .	. . .	. . .	. . .	. . .	. . .	. . .	28	137
Insurance	2 253 . .	47	46	34	25	15	29	17	30
Financial	2 260 . .	. . .	. . .	. . .	. . .	. . .	. . .	52	50
Computer and information	2 262 . .	. . .	. . .	. . .	. . .	. . .	. . .	2	2
Royalties and licence fees	2 266 . .	. . .	. . .	. . .	. . .	. . .	. . .	2	3
Other business services	2 268 . .	206	204	162	287	246	282	54	87
Personal, cultural, and recreational	2 287 . .	. . .	. . .	. . .	. . .	. . .	. . .	29	40
Government, n.i.e.	2 291 . .	. . .	. . .	. . .	. . .	. . .	. . .	21	18
Other services, debit	3 200 BA	**–104**	**–62**	**–168**	**–303**	**–309**	**–378**	**–363**	**–518**
Communications	3 245 . .	. . .	. . .	. . .	. . .	. . .	. . .	–11	–28
Construction	3 249 . .	. . .	. . .	. . .	. . .	. . .	. . .	–3	–20
Insurance	3 253 . .	–38	–39	–57	–42	–42	–34	–20	–24
Financial	3 260 . .	. . .	. . .	. . .	. . .	. . .	. . .	–46	–72
Computer and information	3 262 . .	. . .	. . .	. . .	. . .	. . .	. . .	–5	–2
Royalties and licence fees	3 266 . .	. . .	. . .	. . .	. . .	. . .	. . .	–3	–8
Other business services	3 268 . .	–66	–23	–111	–261	–267	–344	–212	–321
Personal, cultural, and recreational	3 287 . .	. . .	. . .	. . .	. . .	. . .	. . .	–14	–25
Government, n.i.e.	3 291 . .	. . .	. . .	. . .	. . .	. . .	. . .	–49	–18

Table 2 (Continued). STANDARD PRESENTATION, 1988–95
(Millions of U.S. dollars)

	Code	1988	1989	1990	1991	1992	1993	1994	1995
C. INCOME	4 300	–198	80	161	15	–90	–145	–129	–241
Total credit	2 300	*173*	*181*	*175*	*104*	*54*	*63*	*116*	*81*
Total debit	3 300	*–371*	*–101*	*–14*	*–89*	*–144*	*–208*	*–245*	*–322*
Compensation of employees, credit	2 310	...	...	...	...	...	...	**7**	**5**
Compensation of employees, debit	3 310	...	...	...	...	...	...	...	**–1**
Investment income, credit	2 320	**173**	**181**	**175**	**104**	**54**	**63**	**109**	**76**
Direct investment income	2 330	15	10	1	18	1	2	2	6
Dividends and distributed branch profits	2 332	15	10	1	18	1	2	2	6
Reinvested earnings and undistributed branch profits	2 333	...	...	...	...	...	...	...	...
Income on debt (interest)	2 334	...	...	...	...	...	...	...	...
Portfolio investment income	2 339	...	...	...	...	...	...	...	6
Income on equity	2 340	...	...	...	...	...	...	...	...
Income on bonds and notes	2 350	...	...	...	...	...	...	...	6
Income on money market instruments and financial derivatives	2 360	...	...	...	...	...	...	...	...
Other investment income	2 370	158	171	174	86	53	61	107	64
Investment income, debit	3 320	**–371**	**–101**	**–14**	**–89**	**–144**	**–208**	**–245**	**–321**
Direct investment income	3 330	...	...	...	...	...	–4	–12	–28
Dividends and distributed branch profits	3 332	...	...	...	...	...	–4	–12	–28
Reinvested earnings and undistributed branch profits	3 333	...	...	...	...	...	...	...	...
Income on debt (interest)	3 334	...	...	...	...	...	...	...	...
Portfolio investment income	3 339	...	...	...	...	...	...	...	...
Income on equity	3 340	...	...	...	...	...	...	...	...
Income on bonds and notes	3 350	...	...	...	...	...	...	...	...
Income on money market instruments and financial derivatives	3 360	...	...	...	...	...	...	...	...
Other investment income	3 370	–371	–101	–14	–89	–144	–204	–233	–293
D. CURRENT TRANSFERS	4 379	...	...	106	218	65	214	283	369
Credit	2 379	...	...	**138**	**277**	**136**	**231**	**344**	**479**
General government	2 380	...	...	138	208	56	115	117	92
Other sectors	2 390	...	...	...	69	80	116	227	387
Workers' remittances	2 391	...	...	...	...	...	...	4	4
Other current transfers	2 392	...	...	...	69	80	...	223	383
Debit	3 379	...	...	**–32**	**–59**	**–71**	**–17**	**–61**	**–110**
General government	3 380	...	...	–32	–10	–10	–4	–16	–29
Other sectors	3 390	...	...	...	–49	–61	–13	–45	–81
Workers' remittances	3 391	...	...	...	...	...	...	–5	–1
Other current transfers	3 392	...	...	...	–49	–61	...	–40	–80
CAPITAL AND FINANCIAL ACCOUNT	4 996	**–3,938**	**–2,628**	**3,107**	**997**	**1,518**	**1,022**	**337**	**1,518**
CAPITAL ACCOUNT	4 994	...	...	...	...	...	**8**	**12**	**242**
Total credit	2 994	...	...	...	...	...	*8*	*12*	*242*
Total debit	3 994	...	...	...	...	...	...	...	...
Capital transfers, credit	2 400	...	...	...	...	...	**8**	**12**	**242**
General government	2 401	...	...	...	...	...	8	12	228
Debt forgiveness	2 402	...	...	...	...	...	8	12	210
Other capital transfers	2 410	...	...	...	...	...	...	...	18
Other sectors	2 430	...	...	...	...	...	...	...	14
Migrants' transfers	2 431	...	...	...	...	...	...	...	...
Debt forgiveness	2 432	...	...	...	...	...	...	...	...
Other capital transfers	2 440	...	...	...	...	...	...	...	14
Capital transfers, debit	3 400	...	...	...	...	...	...	...	...
General government	3 401	...	...	...	...	...	...	...	...
Debt forgiveness	3 402	...	...	...	...	...	...	...	...
Other capital transfers	3 410	...	...	...	...	...	...	...	...
Other sectors	3 430	...	...	...	...	...	...	...	...
Migrants' transfers	3 431	...	...	...	...	...	...	...	...
Debt forgiveness	3 432	...	...	...	...	...	...	...	...
Other capital transfers	3 440	...	...	...	...	...	...	...	...
Nonproduced nonfinancial assets, credit	2 480	...	...	...	...	...	...	...	...
Nonproduced nonfinancial assets, debit	3 480	...	...	...	...	...	...	...	...

Table 2 (Continued). STANDARD PRESENTATION, 1988–95

(Millions of U.S. dollars)

	Code	1988	1989	1990	1991	1992	1993	1994	1995
FINANCIAL ACCOUNT	4 995	**–3,938**	**–2,628**	**3,107**	**997**	**1,518**	**1,014**	**325**	**1,276**
A. DIRECT INVESTMENT	4 500	...	...	–18	37	73	87	341	417
Direct investment abroad	4 505	**...**	**...**	**–18**	**–3**	**–4**	**–7**	**...**	**–2**
Equity capital	4 510	...	...	–18	–3	–4	–7	...	–2
Claims on affiliated enterprises	4 515	...	...	...	...	...	–7	...	–2
Liabilities to affiliated enterprises	4 520	...	...	...	...	...	...	...	...
Reinvested earnings	4 525	...	...	...	...	...	...	...	...
Other capital	4 530	...	...	...	...	...	...	...	...
Claims on affiliated enterprises	4 535	...	...	...	...	...	...	...	...
Liabilities to affiliated enterprises	4 540	...	...	...	...	...	...	...	...
Direct investment in Romania	4 555	**...**	**...**	**...**	**40**	**77**	**94**	**341**	**419**
Equity capital	4 560	...	...	...	40	77	94	341	419
Claims on direct investors	4 565	...	...	...	...	...	...	...	...
Liabilities to direct investors	4 570	...	...	...	...	...	94	341	419
Reinvested earnings	4 575	...	...	...	...	...	...	...	...
Other capital	4 580	...	...	...	...	...	...	...	...
Claims on direct investors	4 585	...	...	...	...	...	...	...	...
Liabilities to direct investors	4 590	...	...	...	...	...	...	...	...
B. PORTFOLIO INVESTMENT	4 600	...	...	...	...	...	–73	75	–21
Assets	4 602	**...**	**...**	**...**	**...**	**...**	**–73**	**75**	**–22**
Equity securities	4 610	...	...	...	...	...	...	...	–4
Monetary authorities	4 611	...	...	...	...	...	...	...	...
General government	4 612	...	...	...	...	...	...	...	–4
Banks	4 613	...	...	...	...	...	...	...	...
Other sectors	4 614	...	...	...	...	...	...	...	...
Debt securities	4 619	...	...	...	...	...	–73	75	–18
Bonds and notes	4 620	...	...	...	...	...	–73	75	–18
Monetary authorities	4 621	...	...	...	...	...	...	...	...
General government	4 622	...	...	...	...	...	...	...	...
Banks	4 623	...	...	...	...	...	–73	81	–7
Other sectors	4 624	...	...	...	...	...	...	–6	–11
Money market instruments	4 630	...	...	...	...	...	...	...	...
Monetary authorities	4 631	...	...	...	...	...	...	...	...
General government	4 632	...	...	...	...	...	...	...	...
Banks	4 633	...	...	...	...	...	...	...	...
Other sectors	4 634	...	...	...	...	...	...	...	...
Financial derivatives	4 640	...	...	...	...	...	...	...	...
Monetary authorities	4 641	...	...	...	...	...	...	...	...
General government	4 642	...	...	...	...	...	...	...	...
Banks	4 643	...	...	...	...	...	...	...	...
Other sectors	4 644	...	...	...	...	...	...	...	...
Liabilities	4 652	**...**	**...**	**...**	**...**	**...**	**...**	**...**	**1**
Equity securities	4 660	...	...	...	...	...	...	...	...
Banks	4 663	...	...	...	...	...	...	...	...
Other sectors	4 664	...	...	...	...	...	...	...	...
Debt securities	4 669	...	...	...	...	...	...	...	1
Bonds and notes	4 670	...	...	...	...	...	...	...	1
Monetary authorities	4 671	...	...	...	...	...	...	...	...
General government	4 672	...	...	...	...	...	...	...	...
Banks	4 673	...	...	...	...	...	...	...	1
Other sectors	4 674	...	...	...	...	...	...	...	...
Money market instruments	4 680	...	...	...	...	...	...	...	...
Monetary authorities	4 681	...	...	...	...	...	...	...	...
General government	4 682	...	...	...	...	...	...	...	...
Banks	4 683	...	...	...	...	...	...	...	...
Other sectors	4 684	...	...	...	...	...	...	...	...
Financial derivatives	4 690	...	...	...	...	...	...	...	...
Monetary authorities	4 691	...	...	...	...	...	...	...	...
General government	4 692	...	...	...	...	...	...	...	...
Banks	4 693	...	...	...	...	...	...	...	...
Other sectors	4 694	...	...	...	...	...	...	...	...

Table 2 (Concluded). STANDARD PRESENTATION, 1988–95
(Millions of U.S. dollars)

	Code		1988	1989	1990	1991	1992	1993	1994	1995
C. OTHER INVESTMENT	4 700	. .	–4,560	–1,517	1,631	1,053	1,569	946	525	620
Assets	4 703	. .	**–765**	**98**	**562**	**–86**	**94**	**–45**	**–671**	**186**
Trade credits	4 706	. .	...	...	...	...	...	...	...	...
General government: long-term	4 708	. .	...	...	...	...	...	...	...	...
General government: short-term	4 709	. .	...	...	...	...	...	...	...	...
Other sectors: long-term	4 711	. .	...	...	...	...	...	...	...	...
Other sectors: short-term	4 712	. .	...	...	...	...	...	...	...	...
Loans	4 714	. .	–231	–87	29	–78	94	123	–103	–113
Monetary authorities: long-term	4 717	. .	...	...	...	...	...	...	...	...
Monetary authorities: short-term	4 718	. .	...	...	...	...	...	...	...	...
General government: long-term	4 720	. .	...	...	...	133	112	–49	–24	–63
General government: short-term	4 721	. .	...	...	...	...	...	...	...	...
Banks: long-term	4 723	. .	–231	–87	29	...	...	...	...	8
Banks: short-term	4 724	. .	...	...	...	...	...	...	...	–9
Other sectors: long-term	4 726	. .	...	...	...	...	...	–26	21	57
Other sectors: short-term	4 727	. .	...	...	...	–211	–18	198	–100	–106
Currency and deposits	4 730	. .	–534	185	533	–8	...	–163	–500	274
Monetary authorities	4 731	. .	...	...	...	...	...	...	...	...
General government	4 732	. .	–400	169	529	29	...	...	...	...
Banks	4 733	. .	–134	16	4	–37	...	–163	–500	274
Other sectors	4 734	. .	...	...	...	...	...	...	...	...
Other assets	4 736	. .	...	...	...	...	...	–5	–68	25
Monetary authorities: long-term	4 738	. .	...	...	...	...	...	...	...	...
Monetary authorities: short-term	4 739	. .	...	...	...	...	...	...	...	...
General government: long-term	4 741	. .	...	...	...	...	...	...	...	...
General government: short-term	4 742	. .	...	...	...	...	...	...	...	1
Banks: long-term	4 744	. .	...	...	...	...	...	...	...	...
Banks: short-term	4 745	. .	...	...	...	...	...	–5	–121	–17
Other sectors: long-term	4 747	. .	...	...	...	...	...	...	...	...
Other sectors: short-term	4 748	. .	...	...	...	...	...	...	53	41
Liabilities	4 753	. .	**–3,795**	**–1,615**	**1,069**	**1,139**	**1,475**	**991**	**1,196**	**434**
Trade credits	4 756	. .	...	...	...	...	...	...	...	...
General government: long-term	4 758	. .	...	...	...	...	...	...	...	...
General government: short-term	4 759	. .	...	...	...	...	...	...	...	...
Other sectors: long-term	4 761	. .	...	...	...	...	...	...	...	...
Other sectors: short-term	4 762	. .	...	...	...	...	...	...	...	...
Loans	4 764	. .	–3,725	–1,761	29	1,523	1,707	1,092	1,204	1,068
Use of Fund credit and loans from the Fund	4 766	. .	–337	–141	...	770	262	...	217	–316
Monetary authorities: other long-term	4 767	. .	...	...	...	...	...	...	...	170
Monetary authorities: short-term	4 768	. .	...	...	...	...	...	...	...	90
General government: long-term	4 770	. .	...	...	...	...	812	388	264	479
General government: short-term	4 771	. .	...	...	...	...	...	...	...	...
Banks: long-term	4 773	. .	–3,388	–1,620	29	...	...	43	38	54
Banks: short-term	4 774	. .	...	...	...	...	...	–13	48	16
Other sectors: long-term	4 776	. .	...	...	...	112	210	469	610	344
Other sectors: short-term	4 777	. .	...	...	...	641	423	205	27	231
Currency and deposits	4 780	. .	–70	146	1,040	149	–73	–11	104	–75
Monetary authorities	4 781	. .	...	...	...	...	...	...	...	...
General government	4 782	. .	...	...	...	...	...	...	...	...
Banks	4 783	. .	–70	146	1,040	149	–73	–11	104	–75
Other sectors	4 784	. .	...	...	...	...	...	...	...	...
Other liabilities	4 786	. .	...	...	...	–533	–159	–90	–112	–559
Monetary authorities: long-term	4 788	. .	...	...	...	...	...	...	...	...
Monetary authorities: short-term	4 789	. .	...	...	...	–533	–159	...	...	...
General government: long-term	4 791	. .	...	...	...	...	...	...	...	...
General government: short-term	4 792	. .	...	...	...	...	...	...	...	–506
Banks: long-term	4 794	. .	...	...	...	...	...	...	...	...
Banks: short-term	4 795	. .	...	...	...	...	...	...	...	...
Other sectors: long-term	4 797	. .	...	...	...	...	...	...	...	...
Other sectors: short-term	4 798	. .	...	...	...	...	...	–90	–112	–53
D. RESERVE ASSETS	4 800	. .	622	–1,111	1,494	–93	–124	54	–616	259
Monetary gold	4 810	. .	...	–32	...	...	...	...	–69	...
Special drawing rights	4 820	. .	...	–100	108	–55	45	9	–51	1
Reserve position in the Fund	4 830	. .	...	...	...	...	...	...	...	...
Foreign exchange	4 840	. .	622	–979	1,386	–38	–169	45	–496	258
Other claims	4 880	. .	...	...	...	...	...	...	...	...
NET ERRORS AND OMISSIONS	4 998	. .	**16**	**114**	**147**	**15**	**–12**	**152**	**91**	**–182**

Part 3 of the *Yearbook* contains descriptions of the methodologies, compilation practices, and sources used to compile these data.

Table 3. INTERNATIONAL INVESTMENT POSITION (End–period stocks), 1988–95
(Millions of U.S. dollars)

	Code	1988	1989	1990	1991	1992	1993	1994	1995
ASSETS	8 995 C	...	...	6,254	6,355	7,249	7,483	8,847	8,611
Direct investment abroad	8 505	**...**	**...**	**874**	**904**	**1,192**	**1,227**	**1,282**	**1,331**
Equity capital and reinvested earnings	8 506	...	...	874	904	1,192	1,227	1,282	1,331
Claims on affiliated enterprises	8 507	...	...	874	904	1,192	1,227	1,282	1,331
Liabilities to affiliated enterprises	8 508	...	...	...	...	...	...	...	...
Other capital	8 530	...	...	...	...	...	...	...	...
Claims on affiliated enterprises	8 535	...	...	...	...	...	...	...	...
Liabilities to affiliated enterprises	8 540	...	...	...	...	...	...	...	...
Portfolio investment	8 602	**...**	**...**	**...**	**...**	**11**	**84**	**3**	**13**
Equity securities	8 610	...	...	...	...	...	...	...	...
Monetary authorities	8 611	...	...	...	...	...	...	...	...
General government	8 612	...	...	...	...	...	...	...	...
Banks	8 613	...	...	...	...	...	...	...	...
Other sectors	8 614	...	...	...	...	...	...	...	...
Debt securities	8 619	...	...	...	...	11	84	3	13
Bonds and notes	8 620	...	...	...	...	11	84	3	11
Monetary authorities	8 621	...	...	...	...	...	...	...	...
General government	8 622	...	...	...	...	...	...	...	...
Banks	8 623	...	...	...	...	11	84	3	11
Other sectors	8 624	...	...	...	...	...	...	...	...
Money market instruments	8 630	...	...	...	...	...	...	...	2
Monetary authorities	8 631	...	...	...	...	...	...	...	...
General government	8 632	...	...	...	...	...	...	...	...
Banks	8 633	...	...	...	...	...	...	...	...
Other sectors	8 634	...	...	...	...	...	...	...	2
Financial derivatives	8 640	...	...	...	...	...	...	...	...
Monetary authorities	8 641	...	...	...	...	...	...	...	...
General government	8 642	...	...	...	...	...	...	...	...
Banks	8 643	...	...	...	...	...	...	...	...
Other sectors	8 644	...	...	...	...	...	...	...	...
Other investment	8 703	**...**	**...**	**4,002**	**3,951**	**4,458**	**4,345**	**4,473**	**4,527**
Trade credits	8 706	...	...	290	405	594	396	501	629
General government: long-term	8 708	...	...	...	...	...	...	...	...
General government: short-term	8 709	...	...	...	...	...	...	...	...
Other sectors: long-term	8 711	...	...	...	...	...	...	...	22
Other sectors: short-term	8 712	...	...	290	405	594	396	501	607
Loans	8 714	...	...	3,508	3,350	3,551	3,611	3,619	3,559
Monetary authorities: long-term	8 717	...	...	...	...	...	...	...	...
Monetary authorities: short-term	8 718	...	...	...	...	...	...	...	...
General government: long-term	8 720	...	...	2,195	2,274	2,644	2,692	2,720	2,723
General government: short-term	8 721	...	...	...	...	...	...	...	...
Banks: long-term	8 723	...	...	...	...	...	...	...	...
Banks: short-term	8 724	...	...	...	...	...	...	1	10
Other sectors: long-term	8 726	...	...	1,313	1,076	907	919	898	826
Other sectors: short-term	8 727	...	...	...	...	...	...	...	...
Currency and deposits	8 730	...	...	...	...	33	40	51	31
Monetary authorities	8 731	...	...	...	...	...	...	...	...
General government	8 732	...	...	...	...	22	18	7	4
Banks	8 733	...	...	...	...	...	...	...	...
Other sectors	8 734	...	...	...	...	11	23	44	26
Other assets	8 736	...	...	204	197	280	297	302	308
Monetary authorities: long-term	8 738	...	...	...	...	...	...	...	...
Monetary authorities: short-term	8 739	...	...	...	...	...	...	...	...
General government: long-term	8 741	...	...	...	...	99	101	101	104
General government: short-term	8 742	...	...	204	197	164	179	176	177
Banks: long-term	8 744	...	...	...	...	...	...	...	...
Banks: short-term	8 745	...	...	...	...	...	...	...	...
Other sectors: long-term	8 747	...	...	...	...	...	...	...	...
Other sectors: short-term	8 748	...	...	...	...	17	17	25	26
Reserve assets	8 800	**...**	**...**	**1,378**	**1,500**	**1,588**	**1,827**	**3,089**	**2,740**
Monetary gold	8 810	...	...	850	795	762	914	1,006	1,046
Special drawing rights	8 820	...	100	...	58	11	2	56	56
Reserve position in the Fund	8 830	...	...	...	...	...	...	...	...
Foreign exchange	8 840	...	...	528	647	815	911	2,027	1,637
Other claims	8 880	...	...	...	...	...	...	...	...

Table 3 (Continued). INTERNATIONAL INVESTMENT POSITION (End–period stocks), 1988–95
(Millions of U.S. dollars)

	Code	1988	1989	1990	1991	1992	1993	1994	1995
LIABILITIES	8 995 D.	...	...	3,499	4,018	5,398	6,412	7,901	9,002
Direct investment in Romania	8 555 . .	**...**	**...**	**766**	**815**	**1,186**	**1,289**	**1,521**	**1,968**
Equity capital and reinvested earnings	8 556 . .	...	...	766	815	1,186	1,289	1,521	1,968
Claims on direct investors	8 557 . .	...	...	766	815	1,186	1,289	1,521	1,968
Liabilities to direct investors	8 558 . .	...	...	...	...	...	...	...	...
Other capital	8 580 . .	...	...	...	...	...	...	...	...
Claims on direct investors	8 585 . .	...	...	...	...	...	...	...	...
Liabilities to direct investors	8 590 . .	...	...	...	...	...	...	...	...
Portfolio investment	8 652 . .	**...**	**...**	**...**	**...**	**...**	**...**	**...**	**1**
Equity securities	8 660 . .	...	...	...	...	...	...	...	...
Banks	8 663 . .	...	...	...	...	...	...	...	...
Other sectors	8 664 . .	...	...	...	...	...	...	...	...
Debt securities	8 669 . .	...	...	...	...	...	...	...	1
Bonds and notes	8 670 . .	...	...	...	...	...	...	...	1
Monetary authorities	8 671 . .	...	...	...	...	...	...	...	...
General government	8 672 . .	...	...	...	...	...	...	...	...
Banks	8 673 . .	...	...	...	...	...	...	...	...
Other sectors	8 674 . .	...	...	...	...	...	...	...	1
Money market instruments	8 680 . .	...	...	...	...	...	...	...	...
Monetary authorities	8 681 . .	...	...	...	...	...	...	...	...
General government	8 682 . .	...	...	...	...	...	...	...	...
Banks	8 683 . .	...	...	...	...	...	...	...	...
Other sectors	8 684 . .	...	...	...	...	...	...	...	...
Financial derivatives	8 690 . .	...	...	...	...	...	...	...	...
Monetary authorities	8 691 . .	...	...	...	...	...	...	...	...
General government	8 692 . .	...	...	...	...	...	...	...	...
Banks	8 692 . .	...	...	...	...	...	...	...	...
Other sectors	8 694 . .	...	...	...	...	...	...	...	...
Other investment	8 753 . .	**...**	**...**	**2,733**	**3,203**	**4,212**	**5,123**	**6,380**	**7,033**
Trade credits	8 756 . .	...	...	817	892	574	799	891	1,204
General government: long-term	8 758 . .	...	...	...	...	...	...	...	...
General government: short-term	8 759 . .	...	...	...	...	...	...	...	...
Other sectors: long-term	8 761 . .	...	...	...	...	...	...	6	86
Other sectors: short-term	8 762 . .	...	...	817	892	574	799	885	1,118
Loans	8 764 . .	...	...	323	1,238	2,614	3,440	4,638	5,556
Use of Fund credit and loans from the Fund	8 766 . .	144	...	...	809	1,032	1,031	1,323	1,038
Monetary authorities: other long-term	8 767 . .	...	...	...	...	...	...	...	170
Monetary authorities: short-term	8 768 . .	...	...	...	...	...	...	60	150
General government: long-term	8 770 . .	...	...	223	218	1,112	1,685	1,704	2,234
General government: short-term	8 771 . .	...	...	...	...	...	...	...	...
Banks: long-term	8 773 . .	...	...	7	92	143	256	409	483
Banks: short-term	8 774 . .	...	...	93	95	137	92	22	35
Other sectors: long-term	8 776 . .	...	...	...	24	190	375	1,120	1,446
Other sectors: short-term	8 777 . .	...	...	...	...	...	...	...	...
Currency and deposits	8 780 . .	...	...	63	53	168	156	251	177
Monetary authorities	8 781 . .	...	...	...	...	...	...	...	...
General government	8 782 . .	...	...	...	...	...	...	...	...
Banks	8 783 . .	...	...	63	53	168	156	251	177
Other sectors	8 784 . .	...	...	...	...	...	...	...	...
Other liabilities	8 786 . .	...	...	1,531	1,019	857	729	601	96
Monetary authorities: long-term	8 788 . .	...	...	...	...	...	...	...	...
Monetary authorities: short-term	8 789 . .	...	...	...	...	...	...	...	...
General government: long-term	8 791 . .	...	...	...	...	...	...	...	...
General government: short-term	8 792 . .	...	...	1,531	1,019	832	703	594	91
Banks: long-term	8 794 . .	...	...	...	...	...	...	...	...
Banks: short-term	8 795 . .	...	...	...	...	...	...	...	...
Other sectors: long-term	8 797 . .	...	...	...	...	...	...	...	...
Other sectors: short-term	8 798 . .	...	...	...	...	25	25	7	4
NET INTERNATIONAL INVESTMENT POSITION	8 995 . .	**...**	**...**	**2,755**	**2,337**	**1,851**	**1,071**	**946**	**–391**
Conversion rates: lei per U.S. dollar (end of period)	0 102 . .	**14.37**	**14.44**	**34.71**	**189.00**	**460.00**	**1,276.00**	**1,767.00**	**2,578.00**

Table 1. ANALYTIC PRESENTATION, 1988–95
(Millions of U.S. dollars)

	Code	1988	1989	1990	1991	1992	1993	1994	1995
A. Current Account [1]	4 993 Y.	...	...	...	...	...	...	**11,381**	**11,288**
Goods: exports f.o.b	2 100 ..	...	...	...	...	...	...	67,716	81,453
Goods: imports f.o.b	3 100 ..	...	...	...	...	...	...	–48,005	–58,967
Balance on Goods	4 100 ..	...	...	...	...	...	...	*19,711*	*22,486*
Services: credit	2 200 ..	...	...	...	...	...	...	8,951	12,445
Services: debit	3 200 ..	...	...	...	...	...	...	–15,443	–20,538
Balance on Goods and Services	4 991 ..	...	...	...	...	...	...	*13,219*	*14,393*
Income: credit	2 300 ..	...	...	...	...	...	...	3,502	4,293
Income: debit	3 300 ..	...	...	...	...	...	...	–5,282	–7,566
Balance on Goods, Services, and Income	4 992 ..	...	...	...	...	...	...	*11,439*	*11,120*
Current transfers: credit	2 379 Y.	...	...	...	...	...	...	449	764
Current transfers: debit	3 379 ..	...	...	...	...	...	...	–507	–596
B. Capital Account [1]	4 994 Y.	...	...	...	...	...	...	**840**	**–348**
Capital account: credit	2 994 Y.	...	...	...	...	...	...	4,310	3,122
Capital account: debit	3 994 ..	...	...	...	...	...	...	–3,470	–3,470
Total, Groups A Plus B	4 010 ..	...	...	...	...	...	...	*12,221*	*10,940*
C. Financial Account [1]	4 995 X.	...	...	...	...	...	...	**–31,728**	**–12,589**
Direct investment abroad	4 505 ..	...	...	...	...	...	...	–1	–62
Direct investment in Russia	4 555 Y.	...	...	...	...	...	...	637	2,017
Portfolio investment assets	4 602 ..	...	...	...	...	...	...	113	–1,525
Equity securities	4 610 ..	...	...	...	...	...	...	...	...
Debt securities	4 619 ..	...	...	...	...	...	...	113	–1,525
Portfolio investment liabilities	4 652 Y.	...	...	...	...	...	...	–26	90
Equity securities	4 660 Y.	...	...	...	...	...	...	...	...
Debt securities	4 669 Y.	...	...	...	...	...	...	–26	90
Other investment assets	4 703 ..	...	...	...	...	...	...	–17,167	5,315
Monetary authorities	4 703 .A	...	...	...	...	...	...	–9	6
General government	4 703 .B	...	...	...	...	...	...	–15	–252
Banks	4 703 .C	...	...	...	...	...	...	–1,863	4,798
Other sectors	4 703 .D	...	...	...	...	...	...	–15,280	763
Other investment liabilities	4 753 X.	...	...	...	...	...	...	–15,284	–18,424
Monetary authorities	4 753 XA	...	...	...	...	...	...	–838	188
General government	4 753 YB	...	...	...	...	...	...	–15,318	–13,614
Banks	4 753 YC	...	...	...	...	...	...	1,032	2,482
Other sectors	4 753 YD	...	...	...	...	...	...	–160	–7,480
Total, Groups A Through C	4 020 ..	...	...	...	...	...	...	*–19,507*	*–1,649*
D. Net Errors and Omissions	4 998 ..	...	...	...	...	...	...	**–2,152**	**–9,454**
Total, Groups A Through D	4 030 ..	...	...	...	...	...	...	*–21,659*	*–11,103*
E. Reserves and Related Items	4 040 ..	...	...	...	...	...	...	**21,659**	**11,103**
Reserve assets	4 800 ..	...	...	...	...	...	...	1,934	–10,382
Use of Fund credit and loans	4 766 ..	...	...	...	...	...	...	1,514	5,473
Liabilities constituting foreign authorities' reserves	4 900 ..	...	...	...	...	...	...	...	...
Exceptional financing	4 920 ..	...	...	...	...	...	...	18,211	16,012
Conversion rates: rubles per U.S. dollar	0 101 ..	...	...	...	...	...	**991.7**	**2,190.8**	**4,559.2**

[1] Excludes components that have been classified in the categories of Group E.

Table 2. STANDARD PRESENTATION, 1988–95
(Millions of U.S. dollars)

	Code		1988	1989	1990	1991	1992	1993	1994	1995
CURRENT ACCOUNT	4 993	. .	...	...	...	...	...	...	**11,381**	**11,288**
A. GOODS	4 100	. .	...	...	...	...	...	...	19,711	22,486
Credit	2 100	. .	...	...	...	...	...	...	**67,716**	**81,453**
General merchandise: exports f.o.b.	2 110	. .	...	...	...	...	...	...	67,716	81,453
Goods for processing: exports f.o.b.	2 150	. .	...	...	...	...	...	...	...	...
Repairs on goods	2 160	. .	...	...	...	...	...	...	...	...
Goods procured in ports by carriers	2 170	. .	...	...	...	...	...	...	...	...
Nonmonetary gold	2 180	. .	...	...	...	...	...	...	...	...
Debit	3 100	. .	...	...	...	...	...	...	**–48,005**	**–58,967**
General merchandise: imports f.o.b.	3 110	. .	...	...	...	...	...	...	–48,005	–58,967
Goods for processing: imports f.o.b.	3 150	. .	...	...	...	...	...	...	...	...
Repairs on goods	3 160	. .	...	...	...	...	...	...	...	...
Goods procured in ports by carriers	3 170	. .	...	...	...	...	...	...	...	...
Nonmonetary gold	3 180	. .	...	...	...	...	...	...	...	...
B. SERVICES	4 200	. .	...	...	...	...	...	...	–6,492	–8,093
Total credit	2 200	. .	...	...	...	...	...	...	*8,951*	*12,445*
Total debit	3 200	. .	...	...	...	...	...	...	*–15,443*	*–20,538*
Transportation services, credit	2 205	. .	...	...	...	...	...	...	**4,745**	**6,154**
Passenger	2 205	BA	...	...	...	...	...	...	...	...
Freight	2 205	BB	...	...	...	...	...	...	...	...
Other	2 205	BC	...	...	...	...	...	...	...	...
Sea transport, passenger	2 207	. .	...	...	...	...	...	...	...	...
Sea transport, freight	2 208	. .	...	...	...	...	...	...	...	...
Sea transport, other	2 209	. .	...	...	...	...	...	...	...	...
Air transport, passenger	2 211	. .	...	...	...	...	...	...	...	...
Air transport, freight	2 212	. .	...	...	...	...	...	...	...	...
Air transport, other	2 213	. .	...	...	...	...	...	...	...	...
Other transport, passenger	2 215	. .	...	...	...	...	...	...	...	...
Other transport, freight	2 216	. .	...	...	...	...	...	...	...	...
Other transport, other	2 217	. .	...	...	...	...	...	...	...	...
Transportation services, debit	3 205	. .	...	...	...	...	...	...	**–3,812**	**–4,115**
Passenger	3 205	BA	...	...	...	...	...	...	...	...
Freight	3 205	BB	...	...	...	...	...	...	...	...
Other	3 205	BC	...	...	...	...	...	...	...	...
Sea transport, passenger	3 207	. .	...	...	...	...	...	...	...	...
Sea transport, freight	3 208	. .	...	...	...	...	...	...	...	...
Sea transport, other	3 209	. .	...	...	...	...	...	...	...	...
Air transport, passenger	3 211	. .	...	...	...	...	...	...	...	...
Air transport, freight	3 212	. .	...	...	...	...	...	...	...	...
Air transport, other	3 213	. .	...	...	...	...	...	...	...	...
Other transport, passenger	3 215	. .	...	...	...	...	...	...	...	...
Other transport, freight	3 216	. .	...	...	...	...	...	...	...	...
Other transport, other	3 217	. .	...	...	...	...	...	...	...	...
Travel, credit	2 236	. .	...	...	...	...	...	...	**2,412**	**4,312**
Business travel	2 237	. .	...	...	...	...	...	...	...	...
Personal travel	2 240	. .	...	...	...	...	...	...	...	...
Travel, debit	3 236	. .	...	...	...	...	...	...	**–7,092**	**–11,599**
Business travel	3 237	. .	...	...	...	...	...	...	...	...
Personal travel	3 240	. .	...	...	...	...	...	...	...	...
Other services, credit	2 200	BA	...	...	...	...	...	...	**1,794**	**1,979**
Communications	2 245	. .	...	...	...	...	...	...	...	...
Construction	2 249	. .	...	...	...	...	...	...	131	103
Insurance	2 253	. .	...	...	...	...	...	...	...	...
Financial	2 260	. .	...	...	...	...	...	...	92	67
Computer and information	2 262	. .	...	...	...	...	...	...	...	...
Royalties and licence fees	2 266	. .	...	...	...	...	...	...	...	...
Other business services	2 268	. .	...	...	...	...	...	...	1,571	1,809
Personal, cultural, and recreational	2 287	. .	...	...	...	...	...	...	...	...
Government, n.i.e.	2 291	. .	...	...	...	...	...	...	...	...
Other services, debit	3 200	BA	...	...	...	...	...	...	**–4,539**	**–4,824**
Communications	3 245	. .	...	...	...	...	...	...	...	...
Construction	3 249	. .	...	...	...	...	...	...	–1,860	–1,671
Insurance	3 253	. .	...	...	...	...	...	...	...	...
Financial	3 260	. .	...	...	...	...	...	...	–63	–71
Computer and information	3 262	. .	...	...	...	...	...	...	...	...
Royalties and licence fees	3 266	. .	...	...	...	...	...	...	...	...
Other business services	3 268	. .	...	...	...	...	...	...	–2,616	–3,082
Personal, cultural, and recreational	3 287	. .	...	...	...	...	...	...	...	...
Government, n.i.e.	3 291	. .	...	...	...	...	...	...	...	...

Table 2 (Continued). STANDARD PRESENTATION, 1988–95
(Millions of U.S. dollars)

	Code	1988	1989	1990	1991	1992	1993	1994	1995
C. INCOME	4 300 . .	...	...	...	...	...	...	–1,780	–3,273
Total credit	2 300 . .	...	...	...	...	...	...	*3,502*	*4,293*
Total debit	3 300 . .	...	...	...	...	...	...	*–5,282*	*–7,566*
Compensation of employees, credit	2 310 . .	**...**	**...**	**...**	**...**	**...**	**...**	**108**	**167**
Compensation of employees, debit	3 310 . .	**...**	**...**	**...**	**...**	**...**	**...**	**–221**	**–469**
Investment income, credit	2 320 . .	**...**	**...**	**...**	**...**	**...**	**...**	**3,394**	**4,126**
Direct investment income	2 330 . .	...	...	...	...	...	...	125	138
Dividends and distributed branch profits	2 332 . .	...	...	...	...	...	...	...	...
Reinvested earnings and undistributed branch profits	2 333 . .	...	...	...	...	...	...	...	...
Income on debt (interest)	2 334 . .	...	...	...	...	...	...	...	...
Portfolio investment income	2 339 . .	...	...	...	...	...	...	...	...
Income on equity	2 340 . .	...	...	...	...	...	...	...	...
Income on bonds and notes	2 350 . .	...	...	...	...	...	...	...	...
Income on money market instruments and financial derivatives	2 360 . .	...	...	...	...	...	...	...	...
Other investment income	2 370 . .	...	...	...	...	...	...	3,269	3,988
Investment income, debit	3 320 . .	**...**	**...**	**...**	**...**	**...**	**...**	**–5,061**	**–7,097**
Direct investment income	3 330 . .	...	...	...	...	...	...	–93	–206
Dividends and distributed branch profits	3 332 . .	...	...	...	...	...	...	...	...
Reinvested earnings and undistributed branch profits	3 333 . .	...	...	...	...	...	...	...	...
Income on debt (interest)	3 334 . .	...	...	...	...	...	...	...	...
Portfolio investment income	3 339 . .	...	...	...	...	...	...	...	...
Income on equity	3 340 . .	...	...	...	...	...	...	...	...
Income on bonds and notes	3 350 . .	...	...	...	...	...	...	...	...
Income on money market instruments and financial derivatives	3 360 . .	...	...	...	...	...	...	...	...
Other investment income	3 370 . .	...	...	...	...	...	...	–4,968	–6,891
D. CURRENT TRANSFERS	4 379 . .	...	...	...	...	...	...	–58	168
Credit	2 379 . .	**...**	**...**	**...**	**...**	**...**	**...**	**449**	**764**
General government	2 380 . .	...	...	...	...	...	...	449	764
Other sectors	2 390 . .	...	...	...	...	...	...	...	...
Workers' remittances	2 391 . .	...	...	...	...	...	...	...	...
Other current transfers	2 392 . .	...	...	...	...	...	...	...	...
Debit	3 379 . .	**...**	**...**	**...**	**...**	**...**	**...**	**–507**	**–596**
General government	3 380 . .	...	...	...	...	...	...	–495	–576
Other sectors	3 390 . .	...	...	...	...	...	...	–12	–20
Workers' remittances	3 391 . .	...	...	...	...	...	...	...	...
Other current transfers	3 392 . .	...	...	...	...	...	...	–12	–20
CAPITAL AND FINANCIAL ACCOUNT	4 996 . .	**...**	**...**	**...**	**...**	**...**	**...**	**–9,229**	**–1,834**
CAPITAL ACCOUNT	4 994 . .	**...**	**...**	**...**	**...**	**...**	**...**	**840**	**–348**
Total credit	2 994 . .	...	...	...	...	...	...	*4,310*	*3,122*
Total debit	3 994 . .	...	...	...	...	...	...	*–3,470*	*–3,470*
Capital transfers, credit	2 400 . .	**...**	**...**	**...**	**...**	**...**	**...**	**4,310**	**3,122**
General government	2 401 . .	...	...	...	...	...	...	1,068	786
Debt forgiveness	2 402 . .	...	...	...	...	...	...	...	...
Other capital transfers	2 410 . .	...	...	...	...	...	...	1,068	786
Other sectors	2 430 . .	...	...	...	...	...	...	3,242	2,336
Migrants' transfers	2 431 . .	...	...	...	...	...	...	3,242	2,336
Debt forgiveness	2 432 . .	...	...	...	...	...	...	...	...
Other capital transfers	2 440 . .	...	...	...	...	...	...	...	...
Capital transfers, debit	3 400 . .	**...**	**...**	**...**	**...**	**...**	**...**	**–3,470**	**–3,470**
General government	3 401 . .	...	...	...	...	...	...	...	...
Debt forgiveness	3 402 . .	...	...	...	...	...	...	...	...
Other capital transfers	3 410 . .	...	...	...	...	...	...	...	...
Other sectors	3 430 . .	...	...	...	...	...	...	–3,470	–3,470
Migrants' transfers	3 431 . .	...	...	...	...	...	...	–3,470	–3,470
Debt forgiveness	3 432 . .	...	...	...	...	...	...	...	...
Other capital transfers	3 440 . .	...	...	...	...	...	...	...	...
Nonproduced nonfinancial assets, credit	2 480 . .	**...**	**...**	**...**	**...**	**...**	**...**	**...**	**...**
Nonproduced nonfinancial assets, debit	3 480 . .	**...**	**...**	**...**	**...**	**...**	**...**	**...**	**...**

Table 2 (Continued). STANDARD PRESENTATION, 1988–95
(Millions of U.S. dollars)

	Code	1988	1989	1990	1991	1992	1993	1994	1995
FINANCIAL ACCOUNT	4 995	...	...	...	...	...	...	**–10,069**	**–1,486**
A. DIRECT INVESTMENT	4 500	...	...	...	...	...	...	636	1,955
Direct investment abroad	4 505	...	...	...	...	...	...	**–1**	**–62**
Equity capital	4 510	...	...	...	...	...	...	...	...
Claims on affiliated enterprises	4 515	...	...	...	...	...	...	...	...
Liabilities to affiliated enterprises	4 520	...	...	...	...	...	...	...	...
Reinvested earnings	4 525	...	...	...	...	...	...	...	...
Other capital	4 530	...	...	...	...	...	...	...	...
Claims on affiliated enterprises	4 535	...	...	...	...	...	...	...	...
Liabilities to affiliated enterprises	4 540	...	...	...	...	...	...	...	...
Direct investment in Russia	4 555	...	...	...	...	...	...	**637**	**2,017**
Equity capital	4 560	...	...	...	...	...	...	...	...
Claims on direct investors	4 565	...	...	...	...	...	...	...	...
Liabilities to direct investors	4 570	...	...	...	...	...	...	...	...
Reinvested earnings	4 575	...	...	...	...	...	...	...	...
Other capital	4 580	...	...	...	...	...	...	...	...
Claims on direct investors	4 585	...	...	...	...	...	...	...	...
Liabilities to direct investors	4 590	...	...	...	...	...	...	...	...
B. PORTFOLIO INVESTMENT	4 600	...	...	...	...	...	...	87	–1,435
Assets	4 602	...	...	...	...	...	...	**113**	**–1,525**
Equity securities	4 610	...	...	...	...	...	...	...	...
Monetary authorities	4 611	...	...	...	...	...	...	...	...
General government	4 612	...	...	...	...	...	...	...	...
Banks	4 613	...	...	...	...	...	...	...	...
Other sectors	4 614	...	...	...	...	...	...	...	...
Debt securities	4 619	...	...	...	...	...	...	113	–1,525
Bonds and notes	4 620	...	...	...	...	...	...	113	–1,525
Monetary authorities	4 621	...	...	...	...	...	...	...	...
General government	4 622	...	...	...	...	...	...	...	...
Banks	4 623	...	...	...	...	...	...	113	–125
Other sectors	4 624	...	...	...	...	...	...	...	–1,400
Money market instruments	4 630	...	...	...	...	...	...	...	...
Monetary authorities	4 631	...	...	...	...	...	...	...	...
General government	4 632	...	...	...	...	...	...	...	...
Banks	4 633	...	...	...	...	...	...	...	...
Other sectors	4 634	...	...	...	...	...	...	...	...
Financial derivatives	4 640	...	...	...	...	...	...	...	...
Monetary authorities	4 641	...	...	...	...	...	...	...	...
General government	4 642	...	...	...	...	...	...	...	...
Banks	4 643	...	...	...	...	...	...	...	...
Other sectors	4 644	...	...	...	...	...	...	...	...
Liabilities	4 652	...	...	...	...	...	...	**–26**	**90**
Equity securities	4 660	...	...	...	...	...	...	...	...
Banks	4 663	...	...	...	...	...	...	...	...
Other sectors	4 664	...	...	...	...	...	...	...	...
Debt securities	4 669	...	...	...	...	...	...	–26	90
Bonds and notes	4 670	...	...	...	...	...	...	–26	90
Monetary authorities	4 671	...	...	...	...	...	...	...	...
General government	4 672	...	...	...	...	...	...	...	...
Banks	4 673	...	...	...	...	...	...	–26	50
Other sectors	4 674	...	...	...	...	...	...	...	40
Money market instruments	4 680	...	...	...	...	...	...	...	...
Monetary authorities	4 681	...	...	...	...	...	...	...	...
General government	4 682	...	...	...	...	...	...	...	...
Banks	4 683	...	...	...	...	...	...	...	...
Other sectors	4 684	...	...	...	...	...	...	...	...
Financial derivatives	4 690	...	...	...	...	...	...	...	...
Monetary authorities	4 691	...	...	...	...	...	...	...	...
General government	4 692	...	...	...	...	...	...	...	...
Banks	4 693	...	...	...	...	...	...	...	...
Other sectors	4 694	...	...	...	...	...	...	...	...

Table 2 (Concluded). STANDARD PRESENTATION, 1988–95
(Millions of U.S. dollars)

	Code	1988	1989	1990	1991	1992	1993	1994	1995
C. OTHER INVESTMENT	4 700	...	...	...	...	...	...	–12,726	8,376
Assets	4 703	**...**	**...**	**...**	**...**	**...**	**...**	**–17,167**	**5,315**
Trade credits	4 706	...	...	...	...	...	...	...	...
General government: long-term	4 708	...	...	...	...	...	...	...	...
General government: short-term	4 709	...	...	...	...	...	...	...	...
Other sectors: long-term	4 711	...	...	...	...	...	...	...	...
Other sectors: short-term	4 712	...	...	...	...	...	...	...	...
Loans	4 714	...	...	...	...	...	...	5,879	16,602
Monetary authorities: long-term	4 717	...	...	...	...	...	...	...	...
Monetary authorities: short-term	4 718	...	...	...	...	...	...	...	...
General government: long-term	4 720	...	...	...	...	...	...	...	...
General government: short-term	4 721	...	...	...	...	...	...	...	...
Banks: long-term	4 723	...	...	...	...	...	...	...	...
Banks: short-term	4 724	...	...	...	...	...	...	...	...
Other sectors: long-term	4 726	...	...	...	...	...	...	...	...
Other sectors: short-term	4 727	...	...	...	...	...	...	...	...
Currency and deposits	4 730	...	...	...	...	...	...	–4,262	6,512
Monetary authorities	4 731	...	...	...	...	...	...	–9	6
General government	4 732	...	...	...	...	...	...	1,997	1,370
Banks	4 733	...	...	...	...	...	...	–871	4,808
Other sectors	4 734	...	...	...	...	...	...	–5,379	328
Other assets	4 736	...	...	...	...	...	...	–18,784	–17,799
Monetary authorities: long-term	4 738	...	...	...	...	...	...	...	...
Monetary authorities: short-term	4 739	...	...	...	...	...	...	...	...
General government: long-term	4 741	...	...	...	...	...	...	...	...
General government: short-term	4 742	...	...	...	...	...	...	...	...
Banks: long-term	4 744	...	...	...	...	...	...	...	...
Banks: short-term	4 745	...	...	...	...	...	...	...	...
Other sectors: long-term	4 747	...	...	...	...	...	...	...	...
Other sectors: short-term	4 748	...	...	...	...	...	...	...	...
Liabilities	4 753	**...**	**...**	**...**	**...**	**...**	**...**	**4,441**	**3,061**
Trade credits	4 756	...	...	...	...	...	...	...	...
General government: long-term	4 758	...	...	...	...	...	...	...	...
General government: short-term	4 759	...	...	...	...	...	...	...	...
Other sectors: long-term	4 761	...	...	...	...	...	...	...	...
Other sectors: short-term	4 762	...	...	...	...	...	...	...	...
Loans	4 764	...	...	...	...	...	...	1,254	–604
Use of Fund credit and loans from the Fund	4 766	...	...	...	...	...	...	1,514	5,473
Monetary authorities: other long term	4 767	...	...	...	...	...	...	...	...
Monetary authorities: short-term	4 768	...	...	...	...	...	...	...	...
General government: long-term	4 770	...	...	...	...	...	...	–267	1,267
General government: short-term	4 771	...	...	...	...	...	...	...	...
Banks: long-term	4 773	...	...	...	...	...	...	...	...
Banks: short-term	4 774	...	...	...	...	...	...	...	...
Other sectors: long-term	4 776	...	...	...	...	...	...	...	...
Other sectors: short-term	4 777	...	...	...	...	...	...	...	...
Currency and deposits	4 780	...	...	...	...	...	...	–125	1,554
Monetary authorities	4 781	...	...	...	...	...	...	–838	188
General government	4 782	...	...	...	...	...	...	...	...
Banks	4 783	...	...	...	...	...	...	713	1,366
Other sectors	4 784	...	...	...	...	...	...	...	...
Other liabilities	4 786	...	...	...	...	...	...	3,312	2,111
Monetary authorities: long-term	4 788	...	...	...	...	...	...	...	...
Monetary authorities: short-term	4 789	...	...	...	...	...	...	...	...
General government: long-term	4 791	...	...	...	...	...	...	...	...
General government: short-term	4 792	...	...	...	...	...	...	3,160	1,131
Banks: long-term	4 794	...	...	...	...	...	...	...	...
Banks: short-term	4 795	...	...	...	...	...	...	–108	438
Other sectors: long-term	4 797	...	...	...	...	...	...	...	...
Other sectors: short-term	4 798	...	...	...	...	...	...	...	...
D. RESERVE ASSETS	4 800	...	...	...	...	...	...	1,934	–10,382
Monetary gold	4 810	...	...	...	...	...	...	...	...
Special drawing rights	4 820	...	...	...	...	...	...	41	–118
Reserve position in the Fund	4 830	...	...	...	...	...	...	...	...
Foreign exchange	4 840	...	...	...	...	...	...	1,893	–10,264
Other claims	4 880	...	...	...	...	...	...	...	...
NET ERRORS AND OMISSIONS	4 998	**...**	**...**	**...**	**...**	**...**	**...**	**–2,152**	**–9,454**

Part 3 of the *Yearbook* contains descriptions of the methodologies, compilation practices, and sources used to compile these data.

Table 3. INTERNATIONAL INVESTMENT POSITION (End–period stocks), 1988–95
(Millions of U.S. dollars)

	Code	1988	1989	1990	1991	1992	1993	1994	1995
ASSETS	8 995 C.	...	...	...	...	...	...	21,737	27,908
Direct investment abroad	8 505 . .	...	...	...	...	...	...	**54**	**34**
Equity capital and reinvested earnings	8 506 . .	...	...	...	...	...	...	54	34
Claims on affiliated enterprises	8 507 . .	...	...	...	...	...	...	54	34
Liabilities to affiliated enterprises	8 508 . .	...	...	...	...	...	...	...	...
Other capital	8 530 . .	...	...	...	...	...	...	...	...
Claims on affiliated enterprises	8 535 . .	...	...	...	...	...	...	...	...
Liabilities to affiliated enterprises	8 540 . .	...	...	...	...	...	...	...	...
Portfolio investment	8 602 . .	...	...	...	...	...	...	**194**	**224**
Equity securities	8 610 . .	...	...	...	...	...	...	...	...
Monetary authorities	8 611 . .	...	...	...	...	...	...	...	...
General government	8 612 . .	...	...	...	...	...	...	...	...
Banks	8 613 . .	...	...	...	...	...	...	...	...
Other sectors	8 614 . .	...	...	...	...	...	...	...	...
Debt securities	8 619 . .	...	...	...	...	...	...	...	...
Bonds and notes	8 620 . .	...	...	...	...	...	...	...	...
Monetary authorities	8 621 . .	...	...	...	...	...	...	...	...
General government	8 622 . .	...	...	...	...	...	...	...	...
Banks	8 623 . .	...	...	...	...	...	...	...	...
Other sectors	8 624 . .	...	...	...	...	...	...	...	...
Money market instruments	8 630 . .	...	...	...	...	...	...	...	...
Monetary authorities	8 631 . .	...	...	...	...	...	...	...	...
General government	8 632 . .	...	...	...	...	...	...	...	...
Banks	8 633 . .	...	...	...	...	...	...	...	...
Other sectors	8 634 . .	...	...	...	...	...	...	...	...
Financial derivatives	8 640 . .	...	...	...	...	...	...	...	...
Monetary authorities	8 641 . .	...	...	...	...	...	...	...	...
General government	8 642 . .	...	...	...	...	...	...	...	...
Banks	8 643 . .	...	...	...	...	...	...	...	...
Other sectors	8 644 . .	...	...	...	...	...	...	...	...
Other investment	8 703 . .	...	...	...	...	...	...	**14,983**	**10,443**
Trade credits	8 706 . .	...	...	...	...	...	...	...	...
General government: long-term	8 708 . .	...	...	...	...	...	...	...	...
General government: short-term	8 709 . .	...	...	...	...	...	...	...	...
Other sectors: long-term	8 711 . .	...	...	...	...	...	...	...	...
Other sectors: short-term	8 712 . .	...	...	...	...	...	...	...	...
Loans	8 714 . .	...	...	...	...	...	...	652	1,047
Monetary authorities: long-term	8 717 . .	...	...	...	...	...	...	...	...
Monetary authorities: short-term	8 718 . .	...	...	...	...	...	...	...	...
General government: long-term	8 720 . .	...	...	...	...	...	...	...	...
General government: short-term	8 721 . .	...	...	...	...	...	...	...	...
Banks: long-term	8 723 . .	...	...	...	...	...	...	131	154
Banks: short-term	8 724 . .	...	...	...	...	...	...	522	893
Other sectors: long-term	8 726 . .	...	...	...	...	...	...	...	...
Other sectors: short-term	8 727 . .	...	...	...	...	...	...	...	...
Currency and deposits	8 730 . .	...	...	...	...	...	...	9,492	4,666
Monetary authorities	8 731 . .	...	...	...	...	...	...	...	...
General government	8 732 . .	...	...	...	...	...	...	...	...
Banks	8 733 . .	...	...	...	...	...	...	9,492	4,666
Other sectors	8 734 . .	...	...	...	...	...	...	...	...
Other assets	8 736 . .	...	...	...	...	...	...	4,839	4,730
Monetary authorities: long-term	8 738 . .	...	...	...	...	...	...	...	...
Monetary authorities: short-term	8 739 . .	...	...	...	...	...	...	...	...
General government: long-term	8 741 . .	...	...	...	...	...	...	...	...
General government: short-term	8 742 . .	...	...	...	...	...	...	...	...
Banks: long-term	8 744 . .	...	...	...	...	...	...	67	129
Banks: short-term	8 745 . .	...	...	...	...	...	...	1,293	1,136
Other sectors: long-term	8 747 . .	...	...	...	...	...	...	...	...
Other sectors: short-term	8 748 . .	...	...	...	...	...	...	...	...
Reserve assets	8 800 . .	...	...	...	...	...	...	**6,505**	**17,207**
Monetary gold	8 810 . .	...	...	...	...	...	...	2,525	2,824
Special drawing rights	8 820 . .	...	...	...	...	1	5	3	117
Reserve position in the Fund	8 830 . .	...	...	...	...	1	1	1	1
Foreign exchange	8 840 . .	...	...	...	...	...	...	3,976	14,265
Other claims	8 880 . .	...	...	...	...	...	...	...	...

Table 3 (Continued). INTERNATIONAL INVESTMENT POSITION (End–period stocks), 1988–95
(Millions of U.S. dollars)

	Code	1988	1989	1990	1991	1992	1993	1994	1995
LIABILITIES	8 995 D.	...	...	...	...	...	...	2,979	5,429
Direct investment in Russia	8 555 . .	**...**	**...**	**...**	**...**	**...**	**...**	**166**	**172**
Equity capital and reinvested earnings	8 556 . .	...	...	...	...	...	...	166	172
Claims on direct investors	8 557 . .	...	...	...	...	...	...	...	...
Liabilities to direct investors	8 558 . .	...	...	...	...	...	...	...	...
Other capital	8 580 . .	...	...	...	...	...	...	...	...
Claims on direct investors	8 585 . .	...	...	...	...	...	...	...	...
Liabilities to direct investors	8 590 . .	...	...	...	...	...	...	...	...
Portfolio investment	8 652 . .	**...**	**...**	**...**	**...**	**...**	**...**	**245**	**304**
Equity securities	8 660 . .	...	...	...	...	...	...	245	304
Banks	8 663 . .	...	...	...	...	...	...	245	304
Other sectors	8 664 . .	...	...	...	...	...	...	...	...
Debt securities	8 669 . .	...	...	...	...	...	...	...	...
Bonds and notes	8 670 . .	...	...	...	...	...	...	...	...
Monetary authorities	8 671 . .	...	...	...	...	...	...	...	...
General government	8 672 . .	...	...	...	...	...	...	...	...
Banks	8 673 . .	...	...	...	...	...	...	...	...
Other sectors	8 674 . .	...	...	...	...	...	...	...	...
Money market instruments	8 680 . .	...	...	...	...	...	...	...	...
Monetary authorities	8 681 . .	...	...	...	...	...	...	...	...
General government	8 682 . .	...	...	...	...	...	...	...	...
Banks	8 683 . .	...	...	...	...	...	...	...	...
Other sectors	8 684 . .	...	...	...	...	...	...	...	...
Financial derivatives	8 690 . .	...	...	...	...	...	...	...	...
Monetary authorities	8 691 . .	...	...	...	...	...	...	...	...
General government	8 692 . .	...	...	...	...	...	...	...	...
Banks	8 692 . .	...	...	...	...	...	...	...	...
Other sectors	8 694 . .	...	...	...	...	...	...	...	...
Other investment	8 753 . .	**...**	**...**	**...**	**...**	**...**	**...**	**2,568**	**4,953**
Trade credits	8 756 . .	...	...	...	...	...	...	...	...
General government: long-term	8 758 . .	...	...	...	...	...	...	...	...
General government: short-term	8 759 . .	...	...	...	...	...	...	...	...
Other sectors: long-term	8 761 . .	...	...	...	...	...	...	...	...
Other sectors: short-term	8 762 . .	...	...	...	...	...	...	...	...
Loans	8 764 . .	...	...	...	...	...	...	451	1,130
Use of Fund credit and loans from the Fund	8 766 . .	...	...	...	...	989	2,469	4,198	9,617
Monetary authorities: other long-term	8 767 . .	...	...	...	...	...	...	...	...
Monetary authorities: short-term	8 768 . .	...	...	...	...	...	...	...	...
General government: long-term	8 770 . .	...	...	...	...	...	...	...	...
General government: short-term	8 771 . .	...	...	...	...	...	...	...	...
Banks: long-term	8 773 . .	...	...	...	...	...	...	97	300
Banks: short-term	8 774 . .	...	...	...	...	...	...	354	830
Other sectors: long-term	8 776 . .	...	...	...	...	...	...	...	...
Other sectors: short-term	8 777 . .	...	...	...	...	...	...	...	...
Currency and deposits	8 780 . .	...	...	...	...	...	...	1,109	2,417
Monetary authorities	8 781 . .	...	...	...	...	...	...	...	...
General government	8 782 . .	...	...	...	...	...	...	...	...
Banks	8 783 . .	...	...	...	...	...	...	1,109	2,417
Other sectors	8 784 . .	...	...	...	...	...	...	...	...
Other liabilities	8 786 . .	...	...	...	...	...	...	1,009	1,406
Monetary authorities: long-term	8 788 . .	...	...	...	...	...	...	...	...
Monetary authorities: short-term	8 789 . .	...	...	...	...	...	...	...	...
General government: long-term	8 791 . .	...	...	...	...	...	...	...	...
General government: short-term	8 792 . .	...	...	...	...	...	...	...	...
Banks: long-term	8 794 . .	...	...	...	...	...	...	2	4
Banks: short-term	8 795 . .	...	...	...	...	...	...	694	1,100
Other sectors: long-term	8 797 . .	...	...	...	...	...	...	...	...
Other sectors: short-term	8 798 . .	...	...	...	...	...	...	...	...
NET INTERNATIONAL INVESTMENT POSITION	8 995 . .	**...**	**...**	**...**	**...**	**...**	**...**	**18,757**	**22,478**
Conversion rates: rubles per U.S. dollar (end of period)	0 102 . .	**...**	**...**	**...**	**...**	**415.0**	**1,247.0**	**3,550.0**	**4,640.0**

Table 1. ANALYTIC PRESENTATION, 1988–95
(Millions of U.S. dollars)

	Code	1988	1989	1990	1991	1992	1993	1994	1995
A. Current Account[1]	4 993 Y.	**–144.9**	**–123.0**	**–108.1**	**–33.8**	**–83.3**	**–128.9**	**. . .**	**. . .**
Goods: exports f.o.b	2 100 . .	117.9	104.7	102.6	95.6	68.5	67.7	. . .	. . .
Goods: imports f.o.b	3 100 . .	–278.6	–254.1	–227.7	–228.1	–240.4	–267.7	. . .	. . .
Balance on Goods	4 100 . .	*–160.7*	*–149.4*	*–125.0*	*–132.5*	*–171.9*	*–200.0*	. . .	. . .
Services: credit	2 200 . .	48.2	43.0	42.2	43.0	31.4	34.3	. . .	. . .
Services: debit	3 200 . .	–134.3	–118.6	–131.1	–111.6	–114.6	–136.4	. . .	. . .
Balance on Goods and Services	4 991 . .	*–246.8*	*–225.0*	*–213.9*	*–201.1*	*–255.1*	*–302.1*	. . .	. . .
Income: credit	2 300 . .	8.7	9.3	4.4	3.5	4.7	3.0	. . .	. . .
Income: debit	3 300 . .	–30.7	–23.4	–20.9	–17.2	–16.1	–18.2	. . .	. . .
Balance on Goods, Services, and Income	4 992 . .	*–268.9*	*–239.1*	*–230.4*	*–214.8*	*–266.5*	*–317.3*	. . .	. . .
Current transfers: credit	2 379 Y.	153.0	141.6	147.4	209.3	213.6	208.5	. . .	. . .
Current transfers: debit	3 379 . .	–29.0	–25.5	–25.1	–28.3	–30.4	–20.1	. . .	. . .
B. Capital Account[1]	4 994 Y.	**.4**	**.5**	**–.6**	**–.3**	**.1**	**–1.3**	**. . .**	**. . .**
Capital account: credit	2 994 Y.	2.4	2.7	1.7	2.6	1.9	1.0	. . .	. . .
Capital account: debit	3 994 . .	–2.0	–2.2	–2.4	–2.9	–1.7	–2.4	. . .	. . .
Total, Groups A Plus B	4 010 . .	*–144.5*	*–122.6*	*–108.8*	*–34.1*	*–83.1*	*–130.2*	. . .	. . .
C. Financial Account[1]	4 995 X.	**93.7**	**53.9**	**55.7**	**99.1**	**62.4**	**88.5**	**. . .**	**. . .**
Direct investment abroad	4 505 . .	. . .	. . .	. . .	. . .	. . .	. . .	. . .	. . .
Direct investment in Rwanda	4 555 Y.	21.0	15.5	7.7	4.6	2.2	5.8	. . .	. . .
Portfolio investment assets	4 602 . .	. . .	. . .	–.3	–.1	. . .	. . .	. . .	. . .
Equity securities	4 610 . .	. . .	. . .	–.3	–.1	. . .	. . .	. . .	. . .
Debt securities	4 619 . .	. . .	. . .	. . .	. . .	. . .	. . .	. . .	. . .
Portfolio investment liabilities	4 652 Y.	. . .	. . .	. . .	. . .	. . .	. . .	. . .	. . .
Equity securities	4 660 Y.	. . .	. . .	. . .	. . .	. . .	. . .	. . .	. . .
Debt securities	4 669 Y.	. . .	. . .	. . .	. . .	. . .	. . .	. . .	. . .
Other investment assets	4 703 . .	17.7	8.8	8.3	23.8	19.2	. . .	. . .	. . .
Monetary authorities	4 703 .A	. . .	. . .	. . .	. . .	. . .	. . .	. . .	. . .
General government	4 703 .B	. . .	. . .	–.6	–.2	. . .	. . .	. . .	. . .
Banks	4 703 .C	. . .	. . .	. . .	. . .	. . .	. . .	. . .	. . .
Other sectors	4 703 .D	17.7	8.8	8.9	24.0	19.2	. . .	. . .	. . .
Other investment liabilities	4 753 X.	55.0	29.6	40.0	70.8	41.0	82.7	. . .	. . .
Monetary authorities	4 753 XA	4.2	–5.7	27.9	–13.6	4.5	3.9	. . .	. . .
General government	4 753 YB	66.6	44.7	39.3	75.3	34.6	61.8	. . .	. . .
Banks	4 753 YC	4.1	–5.8	.5	1.0	1.9	7.4	. . .	. . .
Other sectors	4 753 YD	–19.9	–3.5	–27.6	8.0	. . .	9.6	. . .	. . .
Total, Groups A Through C	4 020 . .	*–50.8*	*–68.6*	*–53.1*	*65.0*	*–20.7*	*–41.7*	. . .	. . .
D. Net Errors and Omissions	4 998 . .	**.4**	**1.9**	**30.3**	**.2**	**16.7**	**–9.5**	**. . .**	**. . .**
Total, Groups A Through D	4 030 . .	*–50.4*	*–66.7*	*–22.9*	*65.2*	*–4.0*	*–51.2*	. . .	. . .
E. Reserves and Related Items	4 040 . .	**50.4**	**66.7**	**22.9**	**–65.2**	**4.0**	**51.2**	**. . .**	**. . .**
Reserve assets	4 800 . .	27.8	48.9	1.2	–77.0	4.0	26.7	. . .	. . .
Use of Fund credit and loans	4 766 . .	–2.9	–2.7	–.8	11.7	. . .	. . .	. . .	. . .
Liabilities constituting foreign authorities' reserves	4 900 . .	. . .	. . .	. . .	. . .	. . .	. . .	. . .	. . .
Exceptional financing	4 920 . .	25.5	20.5	22.4	. . .	. . .	24.5	. . .	. . .
Conversion rates: Rwanda francs per U.S. dollar	0 101 . .	**76.45**	**79.98**	**82.60**	**125.14**	**133.35**	**144.31**	**168.20**	**168.20**

[1] Excludes components that have been classified in the categories of Group E.

Table 2. STANDARD PRESENTATION, 1988–95

(Millions of U.S. dollars)

	Code			1988	1989	1990	1991	1992	1993	1994	1995
CURRENT ACCOUNT	4	993	. .	**–119.4**	**–102.5**	**–85.8**	**–33.8**	**–83.3**	**–128.9**	**. . .**	**. . .**
A. GOODS	4	100	. .	–160.7	–149.4	–125.0	–132.5	–171.9	–200.0	. . .	. . .
Credit	2	100	. .	**117.9**	**104.7**	**102.6**	**95.6**	**68.5**	**67.7**	**. . .**	**. . .**
General merchandise: exports f.o.b.	2	110	. .	117.9	104.7	102.6	95.6	68.5	67.7	. . .	. . .
Goods for processing: exports f.o.b.	2	150	. .	. . .	. . .	. . .	. . .	. . .	. . .	. . .	. . .
Repairs on goods	2	160	. .	. . .	. . .	. . .	. . .	. . .	. . .	. . .	. . .
Goods procured in ports by carriers	2	170	. .	. . .	. . .	. . .	. . .	. . .	. . .	. . .	. . .
Nonmonetary gold	2	180	. .	. . .	. . .	. . .	. . .	. . .	. . .	. . .	. . .
Debit	3	100	. .	**–278.6**	**–254.1**	**–227.7**	**–228.1**	**–240.4**	**–267.7**	**. . .**	**. . .**
General merchandise: imports f.o.b.	3	110	. .	–278.6	–254.1	–227.7	–228.1	–240.4	–267.7	. . .	. . .
Goods for processing: imports f.o.b.	3	150	. .	. . .	. . .	. . .	. . .	. . .	. . .	. . .	. . .
Repairs on goods	3	160	. .	. . .	. . .	. . .	. . .	. . .	. . .	. . .	. . .
Goods procured in ports by carriers	3	170	. .	. . .	. . .	. . .	. . .	. . .	. . .	. . .	. . .
Nonmonetary gold	3	180	. .	. . .	. . .	. . .	. . .	. . .	. . .	. . .	. . .
B. SERVICES	4	200	. .	–86.1	–75.7	–88.9	–68.6	–83.2	–102.1	. . .	. . .
Total credit	2	200	. .	*48.2*	*43.0*	*42.2*	*43.0*	*31.4*	*34.3*	. . .	. . .
Total debit	3	200	. .	*–134.3*	*–118.6*	*–131.1*	*–111.6*	*–114.6*	*–136.4*	. . .	. . .
Transportation services, credit	2	205	. .	**22.4**	**19.8**	**17.5**	**13.4**	**12.3**	**11.6**	**. . .**	**. . .**
Passenger	2	205	BA	*.2*	*.2*	. . .	. . .	. . .	*.2*	. . .	. . .
Freight	2	205	BB	*10.0*	*9.3*	*8.2*	*6.7*	*5.7*	*4.8*	. . .	. . .
Other	2	205	BC	*12.2*	*10.4*	*9.3*	*6.7*	*6.6*	*6.6*	. . .	. . .
Sea transport, passenger	2	207	. .	. . .	. . .	. . .	. . .	. . .	. . .	. . .	. . .
Sea transport, freight	2	208	. .	. . .	. . .	. . .	. . .	. . .	. . .	. . .	. . .
Sea transport, other	2	209	. .	. . .	. . .	. . .	. . .	. . .	. . .	. . .	. . .
Air transport, passenger	2	211	. .	. . .	. . .	. . .	. . .	. . .	. . .	. . .	. . .
Air transport, freight	2	212	. .	. . .	. . .	. . .	. . .	. . .	. . .	. . .	. . .
Air transport, other	2	213	. .	. . .	. . .	. . .	. . .	. . .	. . .	. . .	. . .
Other transport, passenger	2	215	. .	. . .	. . .	. . .	. . .	. . .	. . .	. . .	. . .
Other transport, freight	2	216	. .	. . .	. . .	. . .	. . .	. . .	. . .	. . .	. . .
Other transport, other	2	217	. .	. . .	. . .	. . .	. . .	. . .	. . .	. . .	. . .
Transportation services, debit	3	205	. .	**–69.4**	**–59.3**	**–66.0**	**–55.4**	**–64.3**	**–68.6**	**. . .**	**. . .**
Passenger	3	205	BA	*–8.6*	*–8.4*	*–10.7*	*–7.6*	. . .	*–7.8*	. . .	. . .
Freight	3	205	BB	*–52.7*	*–44.1*	*–48.6*	*–42.7*	*–50.9*	*–55.3*	. . .	. . .
Other	3	205	BC	*–8.1*	*–6.9*	*–6.6*	*–5.2*	*–13.4*	*–5.5*	. . .	. . .
Sea transport, passenger	3	207	. .	. . .	. . .	. . .	. . .	. . .	. . .	. . .	. . .
Sea transport, freight	3	208	. .	. . .	. . .	. . .	. . .	. . .	. . .	. . .	. . .
Sea transport, other	3	209	. .	. . .	. . .	. . .	. . .	. . .	. . .	. . .	. . .
Air transport, passenger	3	211	. .	. . .	. . .	. . .	. . .	. . .	. . .	. . .	. . .
Air transport, freight	3	212	. .	. . .	. . .	. . .	. . .	. . .	. . .	. . .	. . .
Air transport, other	3	213	. .	. . .	. . .	. . .	. . .	. . .	. . .	. . .	. . .
Other transport, passenger	3	215	. .	. . .	. . .	. . .	. . .	. . .	. . .	. . .	. . .
Other transport, freight	3	216	. .	. . .	. . .	. . .	. . .	. . .	. . .	. . .	. . .
Other transport, other	3	217	. .	. . .	. . .	. . .	. . .	. . .	. . .	. . .	. . .
Travel, credit	2	236	. .	**7.4**	**10.0**	**10.3**	**4.3**	**4.4**	**6.2**	**. . .**	**. . .**
Business travel	2	237	. .	. . .	. . .	. . .	. . .	. . .	. . .	. . .	. . .
Personal travel	2	240	. .	. . .	. . .	. . .	. . .	. . .	. . .	. . .	. . .
Travel, debit	3	236	. .	**–16.3**	**–17.4**	**–22.7**	**–17.2**	**–16.6**	**–17.9**	**. . .**	**. . .**
Business travel	3	237	. .	. . .	. . .	. . .	. . .	. . .	. . .	. . .	. . .
Personal travel	3	240	. .	. . .	. . .	. . .	. . .	. . .	. . .	. . .	. . .
Other services, credit	2	200	BA	**18.4**	**13.2**	**14.4**	**25.3**	**14.7**	**16.5**	**. . .**	**. . .**
Communications	2	245	. .	. . .	. . .	. . .	. . .	. . .	. . .	. . .	. . .
Construction	2	249	. .	. . .	. . .	. . .	. . .	. . .	. . .	. . .	. . .
Insurance	2	253	. .	.4	.3	.3	.2	.2	. . .	. . .	. . .
Financial	2	260	. .	. . .	. . .	. . .	. . .	. . .	. . .	. . .	. . .
Computer and information	2	262	. .	. . .	. . .	. . .	. . .	. . .	. . .	. . .	. . .
Royalties and licence fees	2	266	. .	. . .	. . .	. . .	. . .	. . .	. . .	. . .	. . .
Other business services	2	268	. .	2.7	3.1	3.1	9.8	3.1	3.4	. . .	. . .
Personal, cultural, and recreational	2	287	. .	. . .	. . .	. . .	. . .	. . .	. . .	. . .	. . .
Government, n.i.e.	2	291	. .	15.4	9.8	11.0	15.2	11.4	13.1	. . .	. . .
Other services, debit	3	200	BA	**–48.6**	**–41.9**	**–42.5**	**–38.9**	**–33.6**	**–49.9**	**. . .**	**. . .**
Communications	3	245	. .	. . .	. . .	. . .	. . .	. . .	. . .	. . .	. . .
Construction	3	249	. .	. . .	. . .	. . .	. . .	. . .	. . .	. . .	. . .
Insurance	3	253	. .	–.6	–.4	. . .	–.7	–.7	. . .	. . .	. . .
Financial	3	260	. .	. . .	. . .	. . .	. . .	. . .	. . .	. . .	. . .
Computer and information	3	262	. .	. . .	. . .	. . .	. . .	. . .	. . .	. . .	. . .
Royalties and licence fees	3	266	. .	. . .	–.1	–.2	–.1	. . .	. . .	. . .	. . .
Other business services	3	268	. .	–8.4	–5.7	–6.7	–4.1	–7.1	–10.5	. . .	. . .
Personal, cultural, and recreational	3	287	. .	. . .	. . .	. . .	. . .	. . .	. . .	. . .	. . .
Government, n.i.e.	3	291	. .	–39.5	–35.7	–35.5	–34.1	–25.8	–39.4	. . .	. . .

Table 2 (Continued). STANDARD PRESENTATION, 1988–95
(Millions of U.S. dollars)

	Code	1988	1989	1990	1991	1992	1993	1994	1995
C. INCOME	4 300 . .	–22.0	–14.1	–16.5	–13.7	–11.4	–15.2	. . .	. . .
Total credit	2 300 . .	*8.7*	*9.3*	*4.4*	*3.5*	*4.7*	*3.0*	. . .	. . .
Total debit	3 300 . .	*–30.7*	*–23.4*	*–20.9*	*–17.2*	*–16.1*	*–18.2*	. . .	. . .
Compensation of employees, credit	2 310 . .	**.3**	**.4**	**.3**	**.3**	. . .	. . .	. . .	. . .
Compensation of employees, debit	3 310 . .	**–8.2**	**–4.6**	**–4.8**	**–3.1**	. . .	. . .	. . .	. . .
Investment income, credit	2 320 . .	**8.3**	**8.9**	**4.1**	**3.1**	**4.7**	**3.0**	. . .	. . .
Direct investment income	2 330 . .	. . .	. . .	. . .	. . .	. . .	. . .	. . .	. . .
Dividends and distributed branch profits	2 332 . .	. . .	. . .	. . .	. . .	. . .	. . .	. . .	. . .
Reinvested earnings and undistributed branch profits	2 333 . .	. . .	. . .	. . .	. . .	. . .	. . .	. . .	. . .
Income on debt (interest)	2 334 . .	. . .	. . .	. . .	. . .	. . .	. . .	. . .	. . .
Portfolio investment income	2 339 . .	. . .	. . .	. . .	. . .	. . .	. . .	. . .	. . .
Income on equity	2 340 . .	. . .	. . .	. . .	. . .	. . .	. . .	. . .	. . .
Income on bonds and notes	2 350 . .	. . .	. . .	. . .	. . .	. . .	. . .	. . .	. . .
Income on money market instruments and financial derivatives	2 360 . .	. . .	. . .	. . .	. . .	. . .	. . .	. . .	. . .
Other investment income	2 370 . .	8.3	8.9	4.1	3.1	4.7	3.0	. . .	. . .
Investment income, debit	3 320 . .	**–22.5**	**–18.8**	**–16.1**	**–14.1**	**–16.1**	**–18.2**	. . .	. . .
Direct investment income	3 330 . .	–11.2	–8.9	–6.1	–5.4	–3.9	–3.2	. . .	. . .
Dividends and distributed branch profits	3 332 . .	–2.4	–1.3	–.6	–1.8	. . .	. . .	. . .	. . .
Reinvested earnings and undistributed branch profits	3 333 . .	–8.8	–7.6	–5.5	–3.6	. . .	. . .	. . .	. . .
Income on debt (interest)	3 334 . .	. . .	. . .	. . .	. . .	. . .	. . .	. . .	. . .
Portfolio investment income	3 339 . .	. . .	. . .	. . .	. . .	. . .	. . .	. . .	. . .
Income on equity	3 340 . .	. . .	. . .	. . .	. . .	. . .	. . .	. . .	. . .
Income on bonds and notes	3 350 . .	. . .	. . .	. . .	. . .	. . .	. . .	. . .	. . .
Income on money market instruments and financial derivatives	3 360 . .	. . .	. . .	. . .	. . .	. . .	. . .	. . .	. . .
Other investment income	3 370 . .	–11.3	–10.0	–10.0	–8.7	–12.2	–15.0	. . .	. . .
D. CURRENT TRANSFERS	4 379 . .	149.5	136.6	144.7	181.0	183.2	188.4	. . .	. . .
Credit	2 379 . .	**178.5**	**162.2**	**169.8**	**209.3**	**213.6**	**208.5**	. . .	. . .
General government	2 380 . .	143.4	131.3	143.4	170.7	173.8	171.5	. . .	. . .
Other sectors	2 390 . .	35.0	30.9	26.4	38.7	39.8	37.0	. . .	. . .
Workers' remittances	2 391 . .	1.1	.9	.7	.6	. . .	2.9	. . .	. . .
Other current transfers	2 392 . .	33.9	30.0	25.7	38.0	39.8	34.1	. . .	. . .
Debit	3 379 . .	**–29.0**	**–25.5**	**–25.1**	**–28.3**	**–30.4**	**–20.1**	. . .	. . .
General government	3 380 . .	–1.0	–1.1	–1.9	–9.2	–12.7	–6.5	. . .	. . .
Other sectors	3 390 . .	–28.0	–24.5	–23.2	–19.1	–17.7	–13.6	. . .	. . .
Workers' remittances	3 391 . .	–18.1	–16.5	–14.6	–12.0	. . .	–10.3	. . .	. . .
Other current transfers	3 392 . .	–9.9	–8.0	–8.6	–7.0	–17.7	–3.2	. . .	. . .
CAPITAL AND FINANCIAL ACCOUNT	4 996 . .	**119.0**	**100.6**	**55.5**	**33.6**	**66.5**	**138.4**	. . .	. . .
CAPITAL ACCOUNT	4 994 . .	**.4**	**.5**	**–.6**	**–.3**	**.1**	**–1.3**	. . .	. . .
Total credit	2 994 . .	*2.4*	*2.7*	*1.7*	*2.6*	*1.9*	*1.0*	. . .	. . .
Total debit	3 994 . .	*–2.0*	*–2.2*	*–2.4*	*–2.9*	*–1.7*	*–2.4*	. . .	. . .
Capital transfers, credit	2 400 . .	**2.4**	**2.7**	**1.7**	**2.6**	**1.9**	**1.0**	. . .	. . .
General government	2 401 . .	. . .	. . .	. . .	. . .	. . .	. . .	. . .	. . .
Debt forgiveness	2 402 . .	. . .	. . .	. . .	. . .	. . .	. . .	. . .	. . .
Other capital transfers	2 410 . .	. . .	. . .	. . .	. . .	. . .	. . .	. . .	. . .
Other sectors	2 430 . .	2.4	2.7	1.7	2.6	1.9	1.0	. . .	. . .
Migrants' transfers	2 431 . .	2.4	2.7	1.7	2.6	1.9	1.0	. . .	. . .
Debt forgiveness	2 432 . .	. . .	. . .	. . .	. . .	. . .	. . .	. . .	. . .
Other capital transfers	2 440 . .	. . .	. . .	. . .	. . .	. . .	. . .	. . .	. . .
Capital transfers, debit	3 400 . .	**–2.0**	**–2.2**	**–2.4**	**–2.9**	**–1.7**	**–2.4**	. . .	. . .
General government	3 401 . .	. . .	. . .	. . .	. . .	. . .	. . .	. . .	. . .
Debt forgiveness	3 402 . .	. . .	. . .	. . .	. . .	. . .	. . .	. . .	. . .
Other capital transfers	3 410 . .	. . .	. . .	. . .	. . .	. . .	. . .	. . .	. . .
Other sectors	3 430 . .	–2.0	–2.2	–2.4	–2.9	–1.7	–2.4	. . .	. . .
Migrants' transfers	3 431 . .	–2.0	–2.2	–2.4	–2.9	–1.7	–2.4	. . .	. . .
Debt forgiveness	3 432 . .	. . .	. . .	. . .	. . .	. . .	. . .	. . .	. . .
Other capital transfers	3 440 . .	. . .	. . .	. . .	. . .	. . .	. . .	. . .	. . .
Nonproduced nonfinancial assets, credit	2 480 . .	. . .	. . .	. . .	. . .	. . .	. . .	. . .	. . .
Nonproduced nonfinancial assets, debit	3 480 . .	. . .	. . .	. . .	. . .	. . .	. . .	. . .	. . .

Table 2 (Continued). STANDARD PRESENTATION, 1988–95
(Millions of U.S. dollars)

	Code	1988	1989	1990	1991	1992	1993	1994	1995
FINANCIAL ACCOUNT	4 995	**118.6**	**100.1**	**56.1**	**33.8**	**66.4**	**139.8**	**...**	**...**
A. DIRECT INVESTMENT	4 500	21.0	15.5	7.7	4.6	2.2	5.8	...	...
Direct investment abroad	4 505	**...**	**...**	**...**	**...**	**...**	**...**	**...**	**...**
Equity capital	4 510	...	...	...	...	...	...	...	...
Claims on affiliated enterprises	4 515	...	...	...	...	...	...	...	...
Liabilities to affiliated enterprises	4 520	...	...	...	...	...	...	...	...
Reinvested earnings	4 525	...	...	...	...	...	...	...	...
Other capital	4 530	...	...	...	...	...	...	...	...
Claims on affiliated enterprises	4 535	...	...	...	...	...	...	...	...
Liabilities to affiliated enterprises	4 540	...	...	...	...	...	...	...	...
Direct investment in Rwanda	4 555	**21.0**	**15.5**	**7.7**	**4.6**	**2.2**	**5.8**	**...**	**...**
Equity capital	4 560	3.8	.6	.2	...	...	...	...	...
Claims on direct investors	4 565	...	...	...	...	...	...	...	...
Liabilities to direct investors	4 570	...	...	...	...	...	...	...	...
Reinvested earnings	4 575	8.8	7.6	5.5	3.6	...	...	...	...
Other capital	4 580	8.5	7.4	1.9	.9	2.2	...	...	...
Claims on direct investors	4 585	...	...	...	...	...	...	...	...
Liabilities to direct investors	4 590	...	...	...	...	...	...	...	...
B. PORTFOLIO INVESTMENT	4 600	...	...	–.3	–.1	...	...	...	...
Assets	4 602	**...**	**...**	**–.3**	**–.1**	**...**	**...**	**...**	**...**
Equity securities	4 610	...	...	–.3	–.1	...	...	...	...
Monetary authorities	4 611	...	...	...	...	...	...	...	...
General government	4 612	...	...	...	...	...	...	...	...
Banks	4 613	...	...	...	...	...	...	...	...
Other sectors	4 614	...	...	...	...	...	...	...	...
Debt securities	4 619	...	...	...	...	...	...	...	...
Bonds and notes	4 620	...	...	...	...	...	...	...	...
Monetary authorities	4 621	...	...	...	...	...	...	...	...
General government	4 622	...	...	...	...	...	...	...	...
Banks	4 623	...	...	...	...	...	...	...	...
Other sectors	4 624	...	...	...	...	...	...	...	...
Money market instruments	4 630	...	...	...	...	...	...	...	...
Monetary authorities	4 631	...	...	...	...	...	...	...	...
General government	4 632	...	...	...	...	...	...	...	...
Banks	4 633	...	...	...	...	...	...	...	...
Other sectors	4 634	...	...	...	...	...	...	...	...
Financial derivatives	4 640	...	...	...	...	...	...	...	...
Monetary authorities	4 641	...	...	...	...	...	...	...	...
General government	4 642	...	...	...	...	...	...	...	...
Banks	4 643	...	...	...	...	...	...	...	...
Other sectors	4 644	...	...	...	...	...	...	...	...
Liabilities	4 652	**...**	**...**	**...**	**...**	**...**	**...**	**...**	**...**
Equity securities	4 660	...	...	...	...	...	...	...	...
Banks	4 663	...	...	...	...	...	...	...	...
Other sectors	4 664	...	...	...	...	...	...	...	...
Debt securities	4 669	...	...	...	...	...	...	...	...
Bonds and notes	4 670	...	...	...	...	...	...	...	...
Monetary authorities	4 671	...	...	...	...	...	...	...	...
General government	4 672	...	...	...	...	...	...	...	...
Banks	4 673	...	...	...	...	...	...	...	...
Other sectors	4 674	...	...	...	...	...	...	...	...
Money market instruments	4 680	...	...	...	...	...	...	...	...
Monetary authorities	4 681	...	...	...	...	...	...	...	...
General government	4 682	...	...	...	...	...	...	...	...
Banks	4 683	...	...	...	...	...	...	...	...
Other sectors	4 684	...	...	...	...	...	...	...	...
Financial derivatives	4 690	...	...	...	...	...	...	...	...
Monetary authorities	4 691	...	...	...	...	...	...	...	...
General government	4 692	...	...	...	...	...	...	...	...
Banks	4 693	...	...	...	...	...	...	...	...
Other sectors	4 694	...	...	...	...	...	...	...	...

Table 2 (Concluded). STANDARD PRESENTATION, 1988–95
(Millions of U.S. dollars)

	Code	1988	1989	1990	1991	1992	1993	1994	1995
C. OTHER INVESTMENT	4 700 . .	69.8	35.7	47.6	106.3	60.2	107.2	. . .	. . .
Assets	4 703 . .	**17.7**	**8.8**	**8.3**	**23.8**	**19.2**	**. . .**	**. . .**	**. . .**
Trade credits	4 706 . .	7.1	1.5	–3.3	4.6	. . .	. . .	. . .	. . .
General government: long-term	4 708 . .	. . .	. . .	. . .	. . .	. . .	. . .	. . .	. . .
General government: short-term	4 709 . .	. . .	. . .	. . .	. . .	. . .	. . .	. . .	. . .
Other sectors: long-term	4 711 . .	. . .	. . .	. . .	. . .	. . .	. . .	. . .	. . .
Other sectors: short-term	4 712 . .	7.1	1.5	–3.3	4.6	. . .	. . .	. . .	. . .
Loans	4 714 . .	. . .	. . .	. . .	. . .	. . .	. . .	. . .	. . .
Monetary authorities: long-term	4 717 . .	. . .	. . .	. . .	. . .	. . .	. . .	. . .	. . .
Monetary authorities: short-term	4 718 . .	. . .	. . .	. . .	. . .	. . .	. . .	. . .	. . .
General government: long-term	4 720 . .	. . .	. . .	. . .	. . .	. . .	. . .	. . .	. . .
General government: short-term	4 721 . .	. . .	. . .	. . .	. . .	. . .	. . .	. . .	. . .
Banks: long-term	4 723 . .	. . .	. . .	. . .	. . .	. . .	. . .	. . .	. . .
Banks: short-term	4 724 . .	. . .	. . .	. . .	. . .	. . .	. . .	. . .	. . .
Other sectors: long-term	4 726 . .	. . .	. . .	. . .	. . .	. . .	. . .	. . .	. . .
Other sectors: short-term	4 727 . .	. . .	. . .	. . .	. . .	. . .	. . .	. . .	. . .
Currency and deposits	4 730 . .	10.6	7.3	12.3	19.4	19.2	. . .	. . .	. . .
Monetary authorities	4 731 . .	. . .	. . .	. . .	. . .	. . .	. . .	. . .	. . .
General government	4 732 . .	. . .	. . .	. . .	. . .	. . .	. . .	. . .	. . .
Banks	4 733 . .	. . .	. . .	. . .	. . .	. . .	. . .	. . .	. . .
Other sectors	4 734 . .	10.6	7.3	12.3	19.4	19.2	. . .	. . .	. . .
Other assets	4 736 . .	. . .	. . .	–.6	–.2	. . .	. . .	. . .	. . .
Monetary authorities: long-term	4 738 . .	. . .	. . .	. . .	. . .	. . .	. . .	. . .	. . .
Monetary authorities: short-term	4 739 . .	. . .	. . .	. . .	. . .	. . .	. . .	. . .	. . .
General government: long-term	4 741 . .	. . .	. . .	–.6	–.2	. . .	. . .	. . .	. . .
General government: short-term	4 742 . .	. . .	. . .	. . .	. . .	. . .	. . .	. . .	. . .
Banks: long-term	4 744 . .	. . .	. . .	. . .	. . .	. . .	. . .	. . .	. . .
Banks: short-term	4 745 . .	. . .	. . .	. . .	. . .	. . .	. . .	. . .	. . .
Other sectors: long-term	4 747 . .	. . .	. . .	. . .	. . .	. . .	. . .	. . .	. . .
Other sectors: short-term	4 748 . .	. . .	. . .	. . .	. . .	. . .	. . .	. . .	. . .
Liabilities	4 753 . .	**52.1**	**26.9**	**39.2**	**82.5**	**41.0**	**107.2**	**. . .**	**. . .**
Trade credits	4 756 . .	–19.9	–2.9	–38.3	.8	. . .	9.6	. . .	. . .
General government: long-term	4 758 . .	. . .	. . .	. . .	. . .	. . .	. . .	. . .	. . .
General government: short-term	4 759 . .	. . .	. . .	. . .	. . .	. . .	. . .	. . .	. . .
Other sectors: long-term	4 761 . .	. . .	. . .	. . .	. . .	. . .	. . .	. . .	. . .
Other sectors: short-term	4 762 . .	–19.9	–2.9	–38.3	.8	. . .	9.6	. . .	. . .
Loans	4 764 . .	63.0	44.1	48.9	94.3	34.6	61.8	. . .	. . .
Use of Fund credit and loans from the Fund	4 766 . .	–2.9	–2.7	–.8	11.7	. . .	. . .	. . .	. . .
Monetary authorities: other long-term	4 767 . .	. . .	. . .	. . .	. . .	. . .	. . .	. . .	. . .
Monetary authorities: short-term	4 768 . .	. . .	. . .	. . .	. . .	. . .	. . .	. . .	. . .
General government: long-term	4 770 . .	65.9	47.4	39.3	75.3	34.6	61.8	. . .	. . .
General government: short-term	4 771 . .	. . .	. . .	. . .	. . .	. . .	. . .	. . .	. . .
Banks: long-term	4 773 . .	. . .	. . .	. . .	. . .	. . .	. . .	. . .	. . .
Banks: short-term	4 774 . .	. . .	. . .	. . .	. . .	. . .	. . .	. . .	. . .
Other sectors: long-term	4 776 . .	. . .	–.6	.8	.2	. . .	. . .	. . .	. . .
Other sectors: short-term	4 777 . .	. . .	. . .	9.6	7.1	. . .	. . .	. . .	. . .
Currency and deposits	4 780 . .	4.1	–5.8	.5	1.0	1.9	7.4	. . .	. . .
Monetary authorities	4 781 . .	. . .	. . .	. . .	. . .	. . .	. . .	. . .	. . .
General government	4 782 . .	. . .	. . .	. . .	. . .	. . .	. . .	. . .	. . .
Banks	4 783 . .	4.1	–5.8	.5	1.0	1.9	7.4	. . .	. . .
Other sectors	4 784 . .	. . .	. . .	. . .	. . .	. . .	. . .	. . .	. . .
Other liabilities	4 786 . .	4.8	–8.5	28.1	–13.6	4.5	28.4	. . .	. . .
Monetary authorities: long-term	4 788 . .	. . .	. . .	. . .	. . .	. . .	. . .	. . .	. . .
Monetary authorities: short-term	4 789 . .	4.2	–5.7	27.9	–13.6	4.5	3.9	. . .	. . .
General government: long-term	4 791 . .	.7	–2.7	. . .	. . .	. . .	. . .	. . .	. . .
General government: short-term	4 792 . .	. . .	. . .	. . .	. . .	. . .	24.5	. . .	. . .
Banks: long-term	4 794 . .	. . .	. . .	. . .	. . .	. . .	. . .	. . .	. . .
Banks: short-term	4 795 . .	. . .	. . .	. . .	. . .	. . .	. . .	. . .	. . .
Other sectors: long-term	4 797 . .	. . .	. . .	.2	. . .	. . .	. . .	. . .	. . .
Other sectors: short-term	4 798 . .	. . .	. . .	. . .	. . .	. . .	. . .	. . .	. . .
D. RESERVE ASSETS	4 800 . .	27.8	48.9	1.2	–77.0	4.0	26.7	. . .	. . .
Monetary gold	4 810 . .	. . .	. . .	. . .	. . .	. . .	. . .	. . .	. . .
Special drawing rights	4 820 . .	.2	.4	.5	.6	6.0	.4	. . .	. . .
Reserve position in the Fund	4 830 . .	3.1	. . .	.9	. . .	–5.5	.8	. . .	. . .
Foreign exchange	4 840 . .	32.4	43.4	8.2	–65.3	15.0	25.4	. . .	. . .
Other claims	4 880 . .	–7.9	5.1	–8.5	–12.2	–11.5	. . .	. . .	. . .
NET ERRORS AND OMISSIONS	4 998 . .	**.4**	**1.9**	**30.3**	**.2**	**16.7**	**–9.5**	**. . .**	**. . .**

Table 1. ANALYTIC PRESENTATION, 1988–95
(Millions of U.S. dollars)

	Code	1988	1989	1990	1991	1992	1993	1994	1995
A. Current Account [1]	4 993 Y.	**-27.53**	**-38.37**	**-46.97**	**-34.90**	**-15.77**	**-30.07**	**-26.44**	**...**
Goods: exports f.o.b	2 100 ..	28.41	29.20	28.32	28.58	33.00	31.93	29.29	...
Goods: imports f.o.b	3 100 ..	-81.96	-90.19	-97.44	-97.05	-84.15	-94.57	-98.27	...
Balance on Goods	4 100 ..	*-53.56*	*-60.98*	*-69.12*	*-68.47*	*-51.16*	*-62.64*	*-68.98*	...
Services: credit	2 200 ..	46.75	50.00	54.06	68.39	79.11	83.72	91.67	...
Services: debit	3 200 ..	-24.90	-29.22	-34.93	-35.35	-41.26	-46.46	-45.57	...
Balance on Goods and Services	4 991 ..	*-31.70*	*-40.20*	*-49.98*	*-35.43*	*-13.31*	*-25.38*	*-22.89*	...
Income: credit	2 300 ..	4.51	3.54	3.31	2.65	2.51	2.14	2.86	...
Income: debit	3 300 ..	-8.63	-12.71	-7.77	-9.87	-12.99	-14.81	-15.90	...
Balance on Goods, Services, and Income	4 992 ..	*-35.83*	*-49.36*	*-54.44*	*-42.66*	*-23.79*	*-38.05*	*-35.92*	...
Current transfers: credit	2 379 Y.	11.80	17.68	17.17	13.94	13.74	14.16	15.15	...
Current transfers: debit	3 379 ..	-3.50	-6.69	-9.70	-6.18	-5.72	-6.18	-5.67	...
B. Capital Account [1]	4 994 Y.	**7.60**	**5.14**	**2.43**	**3.84**	**3.67**	**3.33**	**1.73**	**...**
Capital account: credit	2 994 Y.	7.80	5.34	3.05	3.84	3.83	3.53	2.61	...
Capital account: debit	3 994 ..	-.20	-.20	-.62	...	-.17	-.20	-.88	...
Total, Groups A Plus B	4 010 ..	*-19.92*	*-33.24*	*-44.54*	*-31.06*	*-12.10*	*-26.74*	*-24.71*	...
C. Financial Account [1]	4 995 X.	**18.78**	**51.16**	**51.06**	**25.23**	**23.56**	**15.22**	**26.05**	**...**
Direct investment abroad	4 505 ..	...	...	...	...	...	...	...	...
Direct investment in St. Kitts and Nevis	4 555 Y.	13.13	40.80	48.79	21.44	12.51	13.71	15.34	...
Portfolio investment assets	4 602 ..	...	...	...	-.07	...	2.22	...	...
Equity securities	4 610 ..	...	...	...	-.07	...	2.22	...	...
Debt securities	4 619 ..	...	...	...	...	...	...	...	...
Portfolio investment liabilities	4 652 Y.	...	...	...	...	...	2.22	...	...
Equity securities	4 660 Y.	...	...	...	...	...	...	...	...
Debt securities	4 669 Y.	...	...	...	...	...	2.22	...	...
Other investment assets	4 703 ..	-.40	4.80	-1.05	3.66	5.95	-.20	3.43	...
Monetary authorities	4 703 .A	...	...	...	...	...	...	...	...
General government	4 703 .B	...	...	...	...	...	...	...	...
Banks	4 703 .C	-.40	4.80	-1.05	3.66	5.95	-.20	3.43	...
Other sectors	4 703 .D	...	...	...	...	...	...	...	...
Other investment liabilities	4 753 X.	6.04	5.56	3.33	.20	5.10	-2.73	7.28	...
Monetary authorities	4 753 XA	...	...	...	...	...	...	...	...
General government	4 753 YB	5.85	5.99	3.38	.41	1.28	2.02	3.65	...
Banks	4 753 YC	...	...	...	...	...	...	...	...
Other sectors	4 753 YD	.19	-.43	-.05	-.21	3.82	-4.75	3.63	...
Total, Groups A Through C	4 020 ..	*-1.14*	*17.92*	*6.52*	*-5.83*	*11.46*	*-11.52*	*1.34*	...
D. Net Errors and Omissions	4 998 ..	**1.07**	**-11.59**	**-6.43**	**6.48**	**-1.65**	**14.89**	**.98**	**...**
Total, Groups A Through D	4 030 ..	*-.08*	*6.33*	*.09*	*.65*	*9.81*	*3.37*	*2.32*	...
E. Reserves and Related Items	4 040 ..	**.08**	**-6.33**	**-.09**	**-.65**	**-9.81**	**-3.37**	**-2.32**	**...**
Reserve assets	4 800 ..	.08	-6.33	-.09	-.65	-9.81	-3.37	-2.32	...
Use of Fund credit and loans	4 766 ..	...	...	...	...	...	...	...	...
Liabilities constituting foreign authorities' reserves	4 900 ..	...	...	...	...	...	...	...	...
Exceptional financing	4 920 ..	...	...	...	...	...	...	...	...
Conversion rates: Eastern Caribbean dollars per U.S. dollar	0 101 ..	**2.7000**	**2.7000**	**2.7000**	**2.7000**	**2.7000**	**2.7000**	**2.7000**	**2.7000**

[1] Excludes components that have been classified in the categories of Group E.

Table 2. STANDARD PRESENTATION, 1988–95
(Millions of U.S. dollars)

	Code	1988	1989	1990	1991	1992	1993	1994	1995
CURRENT ACCOUNT	4 993 . .	**–27.53**	**–38.37**	**–46.97**	**–34.90**	**–15.77**	**–30.07**	**–26.44**	. . .
A. GOODS	4 100 . .	–53.56	–60.98	–69.12	–68.47	–51.16	–62.64	–68.98	. . .
Credit	2 100 . .	**28.41**	**29.20**	**28.32**	**28.58**	**33.00**	**31.93**	**29.29**	. . .
General merchandise: exports f.o.b.	2 110 . .	27.44	28.61	27.65	27.89	32.33	31.31	28.57	. . .
Goods for processing: exports f.o.b.	2 150 . .	. . .	. . .	. . .	. . .	. . .	. . .	. . .	. . .
Repairs on goods	2 160 . .	. . .	. . .	. . .	. . .	. . .	. . .	. . .	. . .
Goods procured in ports by carriers	2 170 . .	.96	.60	.67	.69	.67	.62	.72	. . .
Nonmonetary gold	2 180 . .	. . .	. . .	. . .	. . .	. . .	. . .	. . .	. . .
Debit	3 100 . .	**–81.96**	**–90.19**	**–97.44**	**–97.05**	**–84.15**	**–94.57**	**–98.27**	. . .
General merchandise: imports f.o.b.	3 110 . .	–81.96	–90.19	–97.44	–97.05	–84.15	–94.57	–98.27	. . .
Goods for processing: imports f.o.b.	3 150 . .	. . .	. . .	. . .	. . .	. . .	. . .	. . .	. . .
Repairs on goods	3 160 . .	. . .	. . .	. . .	. . .	. . .	. . .	. . .	. . .
Goods procured in ports by carriers	3 170 . .	. . .	. . .	. . .	. . .	. . .	. . .	. . .	. . .
Nonmonetary gold	3 180 . .	. . .	. . .	. . .	. . .	. . .	. . .	. . .	. . .
B. SERVICES	4 200 . .	21.85	20.79	19.14	33.04	37.84	37.26	46.09	. . .
Total credit	2 200 . .	*46.75*	*50.00*	*54.06*	*68.39*	*79.11*	*83.72*	*91.67*	. . .
Total debit	3 200 . .	*–24.90*	*–29.22*	*–34.93*	*–35.35*	*–41.26*	*–46.46*	*–45.57*	. . .
Transportation services, credit	2 205 . .	**3.33**	**3.73**	**4.03**	**3.92**	**3.70**	**4.03**	**4.74**	. . .
Passenger	2 205 BA	. . .	. . .	. . .	. . .	. . .	. . .	. . .	. . .
Freight	2 205 BB	. . .	. . .	. . .	. . .	. . .	. . .	. . .	. . .
Other	2 205 BC	*3.33*	*3.73*	*4.03*	*3.92*	*3.70*	*4.03*	*4.74*	. . .
Sea transport, passenger	2 207 . .	. . .	. . .	. . .	. . .	. . .	. . .	. . .	. . .
Sea transport, freight	2 208 . .	. . .	. . .	. . .	. . .	. . .	. . .	. . .	. . .
Sea transport, other	2 209 . .	. . .	. . .	. . .	. . .	. . .	. . .	. . .	. . .
Air transport, passenger	2 211 . .	. . .	. . .	. . .	. . .	. . .	. . .	. . .	. . .
Air transport, freight	2 212 . .	. . .	. . .	. . .	. . .	. . .	. . .	. . .	. . .
Air transport, other	2 213 . .	. . .	. . .	. . .	. . .	. . .	. . .	. . .	. . .
Other transport, passenger	2 215 . .	. . .	. . .	. . .	. . .	. . .	. . .	. . .	. . .
Other transport, freight	2 216 . .	. . .	. . .	. . .	. . .	. . .	. . .	. . .	. . .
Other transport, other	2 217 . .	. . .	. . .	. . .	. . .	. . .	. . .	. . .	. . .
Transportation services, debit	3 205 . .	**–13.43**	**–15.33**	**–16.93**	**–17.44**	**–16.44**	**–17.16**	**–16.06**	. . .
Passenger	3 205 BA	*–4.06*	*–4.74*	*–5.59*	*–6.27*	*–6.37*	*–5.91*	*–4.69*	. . .
Freight	3 205 BB	*–9.37*	*–10.59*	*–11.34*	*–11.17*	*–10.07*	*–11.25*	*–11.37*	. . .
Other	3 205 BC	. . .	. . .	. . .	. . .	. . .	. . .	. . .	. . .
Sea transport, passenger	3 207 . .	. . .	. . .	. . .	. . .	. . .	. . .	. . .	. . .
Sea transport, freight	3 208 . .	. . .	. . .	. . .	. . .	. . .	. . .	. . .	. . .
Sea transport, other	3 209 . .	. . .	. . .	. . .	. . .	. . .	. . .	. . .	. . .
Air transport, passenger	3 211 . .	. . .	. . .	. . .	. . .	. . .	. . .	. . .	. . .
Air transport, freight	3 212 . .	. . .	. . .	. . .	. . .	. . .	. . .	. . .	. . .
Air transport, other	3 213 . .	. . .	. . .	. . .	. . .	. . .	. . .	. . .	. . .
Other transport, passenger	3 215 . .	. . .	. . .	. . .	. . .	. . .	. . .	. . .	. . .
Other transport, freight	3 216 . .	. . .	. . .	. . .	. . .	. . .	. . .	. . .	. . .
Other transport, other	3 217 . .	. . .	. . .	. . .	. . .	. . .	. . .	. . .	. . .
Travel, credit	2 236 . .	**37.77**	**39.95**	**43.57**	**55.82**	**67.41**	**69.79**	**76.86**	. . .
Business travel	2 237 . .	. . .	. . .	. . .	. . .	. . .	. . .	. . .	. . .
Personal travel	2 240 . .	. . .	. . .	. . .	. . .	. . .	. . .	. . .	. . .
Travel, debit	3 236 . .	**–3.00**	**–3.39**	**–4.43**	**–4.50**	**–4.96**	**–5.27**	**–5.79**	. . .
Business travel	3 237 . .	. . .	. . .	. . .	. . .	. . .	. . .	. . .	. . .
Personal travel	3 240 . .	. . .	. . .	. . .	. . .	. . .	. . .	. . .	. . .
Other services, credit	2 200 BA	**5.65**	**6.33**	**6.46**	**8.65**	**8.00**	**9.90**	**10.07**	. . .
Communications	2 245 . .	. . .	. . .	. . .	. . .	. . .	. . .	. . .	. . .
Construction	2 249 . .	. . .	. . .	. . .	. . .	. . .	. . .	. . .	. . .
Insurance	2 253 . .	.27	.28	.65	.41	.51	.98	.92	. . .
Financial	2 260 . .	. . .	. . .	. . .	. . .	. . .	. . .	. . .	. . .
Computer and information	2 262 . .	. . .	. . .	. . .	. . .	. . .	. . .	. . .	. . .
Royalties and licence fees	2 266 . .	. . .	. . .	. . .	. . .	. . .	. . .	. . .	. . .
Other business services	2 268 . .	4.90	5.73	5.51	7.93	7.09	8.07	8.47	. . .
Personal, cultural, and recreational	2 287 . .	. . .	. . .	. . .	. . .	. . .	. . .	. . .	. . .
Government, n.i.e.	2 291 . .	.48	.32	.30	.30	.40	.85	.68	. . .
Other services, debit	3 200 BA	**–8.47**	**–10.50**	**–13.56**	**–13.40**	**–19.86**	**–24.03**	**–23.73**	. . .
Communications	3 245 . .	. . .	. . .	. . .	. . .	. . .	. . .	. . .	. . .
Construction	3 249 . .	. . .	. . .	. . .	. . .	. . .	. . .	. . .	. . .
Insurance	3 253 . .	–1.94	–2.11	–2.33	–2.89	–3.07	–3.89	–5.79	. . .
Financial	3 260 . .	. . .	. . .	. . .	. . .	. . .	. . .	. . .	. . .
Computer and information	3 262 . .	. . .	. . .	. . .	. . .	. . .	. . .	. . .	. . .
Royalties and licence fees	3 266 . .	. . .	. . .	–.13	–.16	–.11	–.05	–.01	. . .
Other business services	3 268 . .	–3.86	–6.85	–10.17	–9.09	–13.90	–18.20	–15.65	. . .
Personal, cultural, and recreational	3 287 . .	. . .	. . .	. . .	. . .	. . .	. . .	. . .	. . .
Government, n.i.e.	3 291 . .	–2.67	–1.53	–.93	–1.27	–2.79	–1.90	–2.28	. . .

Table 2 (Continued). STANDARD PRESENTATION, 1988–95

(Millions of U.S. dollars)

	Code	1988	1989	1990	1991	1992	1993	1994	1995
C. INCOME	4 300	-4.12	-9.17	-4.46	-7.22	-10.48	-12.67	-13.03	...
Total credit	2 300	*4.51*	*3.54*	*3.31*	*2.65*	*2.51*	*2.14*	*2.86*	...
Total debit	3 300	*-8.63*	*-12.71*	*-7.77*	*-9.87*	*-12.99*	*-14.81*	*-15.90*	...
Compensation of employees, credit	2 310	**.22**	**.18**	**.22**	**.16**	**.12**	**.13**	**.11**	...
Compensation of employees, debit	3 310	**-.40**	**-3.12**	**-.12**	**-.38**	**-.37**	**-.87**	**-.87**	...
Investment income, credit	2 320	**4.29**	**3.37**	**3.09**	**2.49**	**2.39**	**2.01**	**2.75**	...
Direct investment income	2 330	...	...	...	.03	...	...	...	...
Dividends and distributed branch profits	2 332	...	...	...	...	...	...	...	...
Reinvested earnings and undistributed branch profits	2 333	...	...	...	...	...	...	...	...
Income on debt (interest)	2 334	...	...	...	.03	...	...	...	...
Portfolio investment income	2 339	...	...	...	...	...	...	...	...
Income on equity	2 340	...	...	...	...	...	...	...	...
Income on bonds and notes	2 350	...	...	...	...	...	...	...	...
Income on money market instruments and financial derivatives	2 360	...	...	...	...	...	...	...	...
Other investment income	2 370	4.29	3.37	3.09	2.46	2.39	2.01	2.75	...
Investment income, debit	3 320	**-8.23**	**-9.59**	**-7.64**	**-9.49**	**-12.61**	**-13.94**	**-15.03**	...
Direct investment income	3 330	-6.69	-7.84	-4.96	-6.96	-10.53	-11.93	-12.60	...
Dividends and distributed branch profits	3 332	-2.16	-3.39	-3.21	-2.17	-2.57	-3.65	-4.20	...
Reinvested earnings and undistributed branch profits	3 333	-3.77	-3.47	-.81	-.30	-2.51	-2.89	-3.25	...
Income on debt (interest)	3 334	-.75	-.99	-.94	-4.49	-5.45	-5.39	-5.16	...
Portfolio investment income	3 339	...	...	...	...	...	...	...	...
Income on equity	3 340	...	...	...	...	...	...	...	...
Income on bonds and notes	3 350	...	...	...	...	...	...	...	...
Income on money market instruments and financial derivatives	3 360	...	...	...	...	...	...	...	...
Other investment income	3 370	-1.54	-1.75	-2.68	-2.53	-2.08	-2.01	-2.42	...
D. CURRENT TRANSFERS	4 379	8.30	10.99	7.47	7.76	8.02	7.98	9.48	...
Credit	2 379	**11.80**	**17.68**	**17.17**	**13.94**	**13.74**	**14.16**	**15.15**	...
General government	2 380	.23	.29	.02	.53	.47	.54	1.03	...
Other sectors	2 390	11.57	17.39	17.16	13.41	13.27	13.61	14.12	...
Workers' remittances	2 391	10.67	17.13	17.16	13.41	13.27	13.61	14.07	...
Other current transfers	2 392	.90	.26	...	...	...	...	.04	...
Debit	3 379	**-3.50**	**-6.69**	**-9.70**	**-6.18**	**-5.72**	**-6.18**	**-5.67**	...
General government	3 380	-1.70	-1.53	-1.68	-2.05	-2.51	-2.17	-3.97	...
Other sectors	3 390	-1.80	-5.16	-8.03	-4.13	-3.21	-4.00	-1.70	...
Workers' remittances	3 391	-1.80	-4.32	-6.23	-2.47	-1.66	-1.76	-.93	...
Other current transfers	3 392	...	-.84	-1.80	-1.66	-1.56	-2.25	-.78	...
CAPITAL AND FINANCIAL ACCOUNT	4 996	**26.46**	**49.96**	**53.40**	**28.41**	**17.41**	**15.18**	**25.46**	...
CAPITAL ACCOUNT	4 994	**7.60**	**5.14**	**2.43**	**3.84**	**3.67**	**3.33**	**1.73**	...
Total credit	2 994	*7.80*	*5.34*	*3.05*	*3.84*	*3.83*	*3.53*	*2.61*	...
Total debit	3 994	*-.20*	*-.20*	*-.62*	...	*-.17*	*-.20*	*-.88*	...
Capital transfers, credit	2 400	**7.80**	**5.34**	**3.05**	**3.84**	**3.83**	**3.53**	**2.61**	...
General government	2 401	6.53	3.44	1.14	2.35	2.36	2.02	.62	...
Debt forgiveness	2 402	...	...	...	...	...	...	...	...
Other capital transfers	2 410	6.53	3.44	1.14	2.35	2.36	2.02	.62	...
Other sectors	2 430	1.27	1.90	1.91	1.49	1.47	1.51	1.99	...
Migrants' transfers	2 431	1.27	1.90	1.91	1.49	1.47	1.51	1.99	...
Debt forgiveness	2 432	...	...	...	...	...	...	...	...
Other capital transfers	2 440	...	...	...	...	...	...	...	...
Capital transfers, debit	3 400	**-.20**	**-.20**	**-.62**	...	**-.17**	**-.20**	**-.29**	...
General government	3 401	...	...	...	...	...	...	...	...
Debt forgiveness	3 402	...	...	...	...	...	...	...	...
Other capital transfers	3 410	...	...	...	...	...	...	...	...
Other sectors	3 430	-.20	-.20	-.62	...	-.17	-.20	-.29	...
Migrants' transfers	3 431	-.20	-.20	-.62	...	-.17	-.20	-.29	...
Debt forgiveness	3 432	...	...	...	...	...	...	...	...
Other capital transfers	3 440	...	...	...	...	...	...	...	...
Nonproduced nonfinancial assets, credit	2 480	...	...	...	...	...	...	...	...
Nonproduced nonfinancial assets, debit	3 480	...	...	...	...	...	...	**-.59**	...

Table 2 (Continued). STANDARD PRESENTATION, 1988–95
(Millions of U.S. dollars)

	Code	1988	1989	1990	1991	1992	1993	1994	1995
FINANCIAL ACCOUNT	4 995	**18.86**	**44.83**	**50.97**	**24.58**	**13.75**	**11.85**	**23.73**	...
A. DIRECT INVESTMENT	4 500	13.13	40.80	48.79	21.44	12.51	13.71	15.34	...
Direct investment abroad	4 505	...	...	...	...	...	...	...	...
Equity capital	4 510	...	...	...	...	...	...	...	...
Claims on affiliated enterprises	4 515	...	...	...	...	...	...	...	...
Liabilities to affiliated enterprises	4 520	...	...	...	...	...	...	...	...
Reinvested earnings	4 525	...	...	...	...	...	...	...	...
Other capital	4 530	...	...	...	...	...	...	...	...
Claims on affiliated enterprises	4 535	...	...	...	...	...	...	...	...
Liabilities to affiliated enterprises	4 540	...	...	...	...	...	...	...	...
Direct investment in St. Kitts and Nevis	4 555	**13.13**	**40.80**	**48.79**	**21.44**	**12.51**	**13.71**	**15.34**	...
Equity capital	4 560	2.22	5.52	1.27	.09	.61	1.09	...	...
Claims on direct investors	4 565	...	...	...	...	...	...	...	...
Liabilities to direct investors	4 570	...	...	...	...	...	...	...	...
Reinvested earnings	4 575	3.77	3.47	.81	.30	2.50	2.89	3.25	...
Other capital	4 580	7.14	31.81	46.70	21.05	9.39	9.74	12.10	...
Claims on direct investors	4 585	...	...	...	...	...	...	...	...
Liabilities to direct investors	4 590	...	...	...	...	...	...	...	...
B. PORTFOLIO INVESTMENT	4 600	...	...	...	–.07	...	4.44	...	...
Assets	4 602	...	...	...	**–.07**	...	**2.22**	...	...
Equity securities	4 610	...	...	...	–.07	...	2.22	...	...
Monetary authorities	4 611	...	...	...	...	...	...	...	...
General government	4 612	...	...	...	...	...	...	...	...
Banks	4 613	...	...	...	...	...	...	...	...
Other sectors	4 614	...	...	...	...	...	...	...	...
Debt securities	4 619	...	...	...	...	...	...	...	...
Bonds and notes	4 620	...	...	...	...	...	...	...	...
Monetary authorities	4 621	...	...	...	...	...	...	...	...
General government	4 622	...	...	...	...	...	...	...	...
Banks	4 623	...	...	...	...	...	...	...	...
Other sectors	4 624	...	...	...	...	...	...	...	...
Money market instruments	4 630	...	...	...	...	...	...	...	...
Monetary authorities	4 631	...	...	...	...	...	...	...	...
General government	4 632	...	...	...	...	...	...	...	...
Banks	4 633	...	...	...	...	...	...	...	...
Other sectors	4 634	...	...	...	...	...	...	...	...
Financial derivatives	4 640	...	...	...	...	...	...	...	...
Monetary authorities	4 641	...	...	...	...	...	...	...	...
General government	4 642	...	...	...	...	...	...	...	...
Banks	4 643	...	...	...	...	...	...	...	...
Other sectors	4 644	...	...	...	...	...	...	...	...
Liabilities	4 652	...	...	...	...	...	**2.22**	...	...
Equity securities	4 660	...	...	...	...	...	...	...	...
Banks	4 663	...	...	...	...	...	...	...	...
Other sectors	4 664	...	...	...	...	...	...	...	...
Debt securities	4 669	...	...	...	...	...	2.22	...	...
Bonds and notes	4 670	...	...	...	...	...	2.22	...	...
Monetary authorities	4 671	...	...	...	...	...	...	...	...
General government	4 672	...	...	...	...	...	...	...	...
Banks	4 673	...	...	...	...	...	...	...	...
Other sectors	4 674	...	...	...	...	...	2.22	...	...
Money market instruments	4 680	...	...	...	...	...	...	...	...
Monetary authorities	4 681	...	...	...	...	...	...	...	...
General government	4 682	...	...	...	...	...	...	...	...
Banks	4 683	...	...	...	...	...	...	...	...
Other sectors	4 684	...	...	...	...	...	...	...	...
Financial derivatives	4 690	...	...	...	...	...	...	...	...
Monetary authorities	4 691	...	...	...	...	...	...	...	...
General government	4 692	...	...	...	...	...	...	...	...
Banks	4 693	...	...	...	...	...	...	...	...
Other sectors	4 694	...	...	...	...	...	...	...	...

Table 2 (Concluded). STANDARD PRESENTATION, 1988–95

(Millions of U.S. dollars)

	Code	1988	1989	1990	1991	1992	1993	1994	1995
C. OTHER INVESTMENT	4 700	5.64	10.36	2.28	3.86	11.05	–2.94	10.70	...
Assets	4 703	**–.40**	**4.80**	**–1.05**	**3.66**	**5.95**	**–.20**	**3.43**	**...**
Trade credits	4 706	...	...	...	...	...	...	...	...
General government: long-term	4 708	...	...	...	...	...	...	...	...
General government: short-term	4 709	...	...	...	...	...	...	...	...
Other sectors: long-term	4 711	...	...	...	...	...	...	...	...
Other sectors: short-term	4 712	...	...	...	...	...	...	...	...
Loans	4 714	...	...	...	...	...	...	...	...
Monetary authorities: long-term	4 717	...	...	...	...	...	...	...	...
Monetary authorities: short-term	4 718	...	...	...	...	...	...	...	...
General government: long-term	4 720	...	...	...	...	...	...	...	...
General government: short-term	4 721	...	...	...	...	...	...	...	...
Banks: long-term	4 723	...	...	...	...	...	...	...	...
Banks: short-term	4 724	...	...	...	...	...	...	...	...
Other sectors: long-term	4 726	...	...	...	...	...	...	...	...
Other sectors: short-term	4 727	...	...	...	...	...	...	...	...
Currency and deposits	4 730	–.40	4.80	–1.05	3.66	5.95	–.20	3.43	...
Monetary authorities	4 731	...	...	...	...	...	...	...	...
General government	4 732	...	...	...	...	...	...	...	...
Banks	4 733	–.40	4.80	–1.05	3.66	5.95	–.20	3.43	...
Other sectors	4 734	...	...	...	...	...	...	...	...
Other assets	4 736	...	...	...	...	...	...	...	...
Monetary authorities: long-term	4 738	...	...	...	...	...	...	...	...
Monetary authorities: short-term	4 739	...	...	...	...	...	...	...	...
General government: long-term	4 741	...	...	...	...	...	...	...	...
General government: short-term	4 742	...	...	...	...	...	...	...	...
Banks: long-term	4 744	...	...	...	...	...	...	...	...
Banks: short-term	4 745	...	...	...	...	...	...	...	...
Other sectors: long-term	4 747	...	...	...	...	...	...	...	...
Other sectors: short-term	4 748	...	...	...	...	...	...	...	...
Liabilities	4 753	**6.04**	**5.56**	**3.33**	**.20**	**5.10**	**–2.73**	**7.28**	**...**
Trade credits	4 756	...	...	...	...	...	...	...	...
General government: long-term	4 758	...	...	...	...	...	...	...	...
General government: short-term	4 759	...	...	...	...	...	...	...	...
Other sectors: long-term	4 761	...	...	...	...	...	...	...	...
Other sectors: short-term	4 762	...	...	...	...	...	...	...	...
Loans	4 764	6.04	5.56	3.33	.20	5.10	–2.73	7.28	...
Use of Fund credit and loans from the Fund	4 766	...	...	...	...	...	...	...	...
Monetary authorities: other long-term	4 767	...	...	...	...	...	...	...	...
Monetary authorities: short-term	4 768	...	...	...	...	...	...	...	...
General government: long-term	4 770	5.85	5.99	3.38	.41	1.28	2.02	3.65	...
General government: short-term	4 771	...	...	...	...	...	...	...	...
Banks: long-term	4 773	...	...	...	...	...	...	...	...
Banks: short-term	4 774	...	...	...	...	...	...	...	...
Other sectors: long-term	4 776	.19	–.43	–.05	–.21	3.82	–4.75	3.63	...
Other sectors: short-term	4 777	...	...	...	...	...	...	...	...
Currency and deposits	4 780	...	...	...	...	...	...	...	...
Monetary authorities	4 781	...	...	...	...	...	...	...	...
General government	4 782	...	...	...	...	...	...	...	...
Banks	4 783	...	...	...	...	...	...	...	...
Other sectors	4 784	...	...	...	...	...	...	...	...
Other liabilities	4 786	...	...	...	...	...	...	...	...
Monetary authorities: long-term	4 788	...	...	...	...	...	...	...	...
Monetary authorities: short-term	4 789	...	...	...	...	...	...	...	...
General government: long-term	4 791	...	...	...	...	...	...	...	...
General government: short-term	4 792	...	...	...	...	...	...	...	...
Banks: long-term	4 794	...	...	...	...	...	...	...	...
Banks: short-term	4 795	...	...	...	...	...	...	...	...
Other sectors: long-term	4 797	...	...	...	...	...	...	...	...
Other sectors: short-term	4 798	...	...	...	...	...	...	...	...
D. RESERVE ASSETS	4 800	.08	–6.33	–.09	–.65	–9.81	–3.37	–2.32	...
Monetary gold	4 810	...	...	...	...	...	...	...	...
Special drawing rights	4 820	...	...	...	...	...	...	...	...
Reserve position in the Fund	4 830	...	...	...	...	...	–.01	...	...
Foreign exchange	4 840	.26	–6.07	.11	–.34	–9.64	–3.22	–2.32	...
Other claims	4 880	–.18	–.27	–.20	–.30	–.17	–.15	...	...
NET ERRORS AND OMISSIONS	4 998	**1.07**	**–11.59**	**–6.43**	**6.48**	**–1.65**	**14.89**	**.98**	**...**

Part 3 of the *Yearbook* contains descriptions of the methodologies, compilation practices, and sources used to compile these data.

Table 1. ANALYTIC PRESENTATION, 1988–95
(Millions of U.S. dollars)

	Code	1988	1989	1990	1991	1992	1993	1994	1995
A. Current Account[1]	4 993 Y.	**–17.97**	**–63.26**	**–45.49**	**–72.07**	**–54.82**	**–41.24**	**–64.95**	. . .
Goods: exports f.o.b	2 100 . .	122.26	116.04	130.95	113.89	127.16	123.52	99.90	. . .
Goods: imports f.o.b	3 100 . .	–194.48	–240.89	–238.77	–261.39	–270.84	–264.00	–265.62	. . .
Balance on Goods	4 100 . .	*–72.22*	*–124.85*	*–107.82*	*–147.51*	*–143.67*	*–140.48*	*–165.72*	. . .
Services: credit	2 200 . .	117.19	136.43	150.60	172.19	194.94	204.67	225.89	. . .
Services: debit	3 200 . .	–59.70	–71.32	–69.66	–80.55	–86.34	–89.01	–103.90	. . .
Balance on Goods and Services	4 991 . .	*–14.73*	*–59.74*	*–26.88*	*–55.87*	*–35.07*	*–24.83*	*–43.73*	. . .
Income: credit	2 300 . .	6.41	5.85	5.94	4.63	5.46	4.36	4.97	. . .
Income: debit	3 300 . .	–17.22	–16.44	–32.13	–34.28	–34.23	–30.02	–38.33	. . .
Balance on Goods, Services, and Income	4 992 . .	*–25.55*	*–70.33*	*–53.07*	*–85.52*	*–63.84*	*–50.49*	*–77.10*	. . .
Current transfers: credit	2 379 Y.	12.73	12.30	13.86	16.90	16.38	21.87	20.45	. . .
Current transfers: debit	3 379 . .	–5.15	–5.23	–6.28	–3.45	–7.36	–12.63	–8.30	. . .
B. Capital Account[1]	4 994 Y.	**7.86**	**8.48**	**3.85**	**6.57**	**8.95**	**3.84**	**7.43**	. . .
Capital account: credit	2 994 Y.	7.86	8.48	3.85	6.57	9.13	4.18	8.54	. . .
Capital account: debit	3 994 . .	. . .	. . .	. . .	. . .	–.19	–.34	–1.12	. . .
Total, Groups A Plus B	4 010 . .	*–10.11*	*–54.78*	*–41.63*	*–65.50*	*–45.87*	*–37.40*	*–57.52*	. . .
C. Financial Account[1]	4 995 X.	**7.60**	**52.20**	**51.40**	**59.34**	**59.79**	**56.08**	**46.33**	. . .
Direct investment abroad	4 505 . .	. . .	. . .	. . .	. . .	. . .	. . .	. . .	. . .
Direct investment in St. Lucia	4 555 Y.	16.44	26.63	44.79	57.74	40.89	34.09	32.41	. . .
Portfolio investment assets	4 602 . .	. . .	. . .	–.14	. . .	. . .	. . .	. . .	. . .
Equity securities	4 610 . .	. . .	. . .	–.14	. . .	. . .	. . .	. . .	. . .
Debt securities	4 619 . .	. . .	. . .	. . .	. . .	. . .	. . .	. . .	. . .
Portfolio investment liabilities	4 652 Y.	. . .	. . .	.18	. . .	–.51	. . .	–.47	. . .
Equity securities	4 660 Y.	. . .	. . .	.18	. . .	–.51	. . .	–.47	. . .
Debt securities	4 669 Y.	. . .	. . .	. . .	. . .	. . .	. . .	. . .	. . .
Other investment assets	4 703 . .	–11.52	18.15	1.96	–.48	.79	17.00	17.11	. . .
Monetary authorities	4 703 .A	. . .	. . .	. . .	. . .	. . .	. . .	. . .	. . .
General government	4 703 .B	. . .	. . .	. . .	. . .	. . .	. . .	. . .	. . .
Banks	4 703 .C	–11.52	18.15	1.96	–.48	.79	17.00	17.11	. . .
Other sectors	4 703 .D	. . .	. . .	. . .	. . .	. . .	. . .	. . .	. . .
Other investment liabilities	4 753 X.	2.68	7.42	4.61	2.07	18.62	4.99	–2.72	. . .
Monetary authorities	4 753 XA	. . .	. . .	. . .	. . .	. . .	. . .	. . .	. . .
General government	4 753 YB	7.41	11.74	4.38	3.12	21.03	5.81	3.62	. . .
Banks	4 753 YC	. . .	. . .	. . .	. . .	. . .	. . .	. . .	. . .
Other sectors	4 753 YD	–4.73	–4.32	.23	–1.05	–2.41	–.81	–6.34	. . .
Total, Groups A Through C	4 020 . .	*–2.50*	*–2.59*	*9.76*	*–6.16*	*13.92*	*18.67*	*–11.20*	. . .
D. Net Errors and Omissions	4 998 . .	**4.36**	**8.18**	**–3.46**	**13.90**	**–7.14**	**–14.19**	**15.42**	. . .
Total, Groups A Through D	4 030 . .	*1.85*	*5.59*	*6.30*	*7.74*	*6.78*	*4.49*	*4.22*	. . .
E. Reserves and Related Items	4 040 . .	**–1.85**	**–5.59**	**–6.30**	**–7.74**	**–6.78**	**–4.49**	**–4.22**	. . .
Reserve assets	4 800 . .	–1.85	–5.59	–6.30	–7.74	–6.78	–4.49	–4.22	. . .
Use of Fund credit and loans	4 766 . .	. . .	. . .	. . .	. . .	. . .	. . .	. . .	. . .
Liabilities constituting foreign authorities' reserves	4 900 . .	. . .	. . .	. . .	. . .	. . .	. . .	. . .	. . .
Exceptional financing	4 920 . .	. . .	. . .	. . .	. . .	. . .	. . .	. . .	. . .
Conversion rates: Eastern Caribbean dollars per U.S. dollar	0 101 . .	**2.7000**	**2.7000**	**2.7000**	**2.7000**	**2.7000**	**2.7000**	**2.7000**	**2.7000**

[1] Excludes components that have been classified in the categories of Group E.

Table 2. STANDARD PRESENTATION, 1988–95
(Millions of U.S. dollars)

	Code	1988	1989	1990	1991	1992	1993	1994	1995
CURRENT ACCOUNT	4 993 . .	**–17.97**	**–63.26**	**–45.49**	**–72.07**	**–54.82**	**–41.24**	**–64.95**	. . .
A. GOODS	4 100 . .	–72.22	–124.85	–107.82	–147.51	–143.67	–140.48	–165.72	. . .
Credit	2 100 . .	**122.26**	**116.04**	**130.95**	**113.89**	**127.16**	**123.52**	**99.90**	. . .
General merchandise: exports f.o.b.	2 110 . .	119.11	111.96	127.30	110.30	122.78	119.74	94.85	. . .
Goods for processing: exports f.o.b.	2 150 . .	. . .	. . .	. . .	. . .	. . .	. . .	. . .	. . .
Repairs on goods	2 160 . .	. . .	. . .	. . .	. . .	. . .	. . .	. . .	. . .
Goods procured in ports by carriers	2 170 . .	3.15	4.07	3.66	3.59	4.39	3.78	5.05	. . .
Nonmonetary gold	2 180 . .	. . .	. . .	. . .	. . .	. . .	. . .	. . .	. . .
Debit	3 100 . .	**–194.48**	**–240.89**	**–238.77**	**–261.39**	**–270.84**	**–264.00**	**–265.62**	. . .
General merchandise: imports f.o.b.	3 110 . .	–194.48	–240.89	–238.71	–261.39	–270.84	–264.00	–265.56	. . .
Goods for processing: imports f.o.b.	3 150 . .	. . .	. . .	. . .	. . .	. . .	. . .	. . .	. . .
Repairs on goods	3 160 . .	. . .	. . .	. . .	. . .	. . .	. . .	. . .	. . .
Goods procured in ports by carriers	3 170 . .	. . .	. . .	–.06	. . .	. . .	. . .	–.06	. . .
Nonmonetary gold	3 180 . .	. . .	. . .	. . .	. . .	. . .	. . .	. . .	. . .
B. SERVICES	4 200 . .	57.49	65.11	80.94	91.64	108.61	115.66	121.99	. . .
Total credit	2 200 . .	*117.19*	*136.43*	*150.60*	*172.19*	*194.94*	*204.67*	*225.89*	. . .
Total debit	3 200 . .	*–59.70*	*–71.32*	*–69.66*	*–80.55*	*–86.34*	*–89.01*	*–103.90*	. . .
Transportation services, credit	2 205 . .	**11.37**	**12.84**	**14.44**	**16.45**	**15.14**	**14.55**	**13.58**	. . .
Passenger	2 205 BA	*1.11*	*1.30*	*.01*	. . .	. . .	. . .	*.01*	. . .
Freight	2 205 BB	. . .	. . .	*.17*	*2.42*	*.06*	*.08*	. . .	. . .
Other	2 205 BC	*10.26*	*11.54*	*14.26*	*14.03*	*15.08*	*14.47*	*13.57*	. . .
Sea transport, passenger	2 207 . .	. . .	. . .	. . .	. . .	. . .	. . .	. . .	. . .
Sea transport, freight	2 208 . .	. . .	. . .	. . .	. . .	. . .	. . .	. . .	. . .
Sea transport, other	2 209 . .	. . .	. . .	. . .	. . .	. . .	. . .	. . .	. . .
Air transport, passenger	2 211 . .	. . .	. . .	. . .	. . .	. . .	. . .	. . .	. . .
Air transport, freight	2 212 . .	. . .	. . .	. . .	. . .	. . .	. . .	. . .	. . .
Air transport, other	2 213 . .	. . .	. . .	. . .	. . .	. . .	. . .	. . .	. . .
Other transport, passenger	2 215 . .	. . .	. . .	. . .	. . .	. . .	. . .	. . .	. . .
Other transport, freight	2 216 . .	. . .	. . .	. . .	. . .	. . .	. . .	. . .	. . .
Other transport, other	2 217 . .	. . .	. . .	. . .	. . .	. . .	. . .	. . .	. . .
Transportation services, debit	3 205 . .	**–32.06**	**–37.56**	**–41.17**	**–40.79**	**–43.86**	**–42.15**	**–42.02**	. . .
Passenger	3 205 BA	*–7.89*	*–8.56*	*–12.07*	*–10.87*	*–13.08*	*–12.14*	*–11.28*	. . .
Freight	3 205 BB	*–22.47*	*–27.38*	*–27.36*	*–29.91*	*–30.78*	*–30.00*	*–30.54*	. . .
Other	3 205 BC	*–1.70*	*–1.63*	*–1.74*	. . .	. . .	. . .	*–.20*	. . .
Sea transport, passenger	3 207 . .	. . .	. . .	. . .	. . .	. . .	. . .	. . .	. . .
Sea transport, freight	3 208 . .	. . .	. . .	. . .	. . .	. . .	. . .	. . .	. . .
Sea transport, other	3 209 . .	. . .	. . .	. . .	. . .	. . .	. . .	. . .	. . .
Air transport, passenger	3 211 . .	. . .	. . .	. . .	. . .	. . .	. . .	. . .	. . .
Air transport, freight	3 212 . .	. . .	. . .	. . .	. . .	. . .	. . .	. . .	. . .
Air transport, other	3 213 . .	. . .	. . .	. . .	. . .	. . .	. . .	. . .	. . .
Other transport, passenger	3 215 . .	. . .	. . .	. . .	. . .	. . .	. . .	. . .	. . .
Other transport, freight	3 216 . .	. . .	. . .	. . .	. . .	. . .	. . .	. . .	. . .
Other transport, other	3 217 . .	. . .	. . .	. . .	. . .	. . .	. . .	. . .	. . .
Travel, credit	2 236 . .	**95.59**	**111.85**	**120.97**	**144.14**	**165.63**	**177.58**	**207.15**	. . .
Business travel	2 237 . .	. . .	. . .	. . .	. . .	. . .	. . .	. . .	. . .
Personal travel	2 240 . .	. . .	. . .	. . .	. . .	. . .	. . .	. . .	. . .
Travel, debit	3 236 . .	**–11.83**	**–12.83**	**–16.88**	**–17.83**	**–20.91**	**–19.63**	**–22.51**	. . .
Business travel	3 237 . .	. . .	. . .	. . .	. . .	. . .	. . .	. . .	. . .
Personal travel	3 240 . .	. . .	. . .	. . .	. . .	. . .	. . .	. . .	. . .
Other services, credit	2 200 BA	**10.22**	**11.74**	**15.19**	**11.60**	**14.17**	**12.54**	**5.16**	. . .
Communications	2 245 . .	. . .	. . .	. . .	. . .	. . .	. . .	. . .	. . .
Construction	2 249 . .	. . .	. . .	. . .	. . .	. . .	. . .	. . .	. . .
Insurance	2 253 . .	1.59	1.15	2.81	2.57	2.41	2.54	2.94	. . .
Financial	2 260 . .	. . .	. . .	. . .	. . .	. . .	. . .	. . .	. . .
Computer and information	2 262 . .	. . .	. . .	. . .	. . .	. . .	. . .	. . .	. . .
Royalties and licence fees	2 266 . .	. . .	. . .	. . .	. . .	. . .	. . .	. . .	. . .
Other business services	2 268 . .	7.00	8.48	11.11	7.71	7.70	10.01	1.18	. . .
Personal, cultural, and recreational	2 287 . .	. . .	. . .	. . .	. . .	. . .	. . .	. . .	. . .
Government, n.i.e.	2 291 . .	1.63	2.11	1.27	1.32	4.06	. . .	1.05	. . .
Other services, debit	3 200 BA	**–15.80**	**–20.93**	**–11.61**	**–21.94**	**–21.57**	**–27.24**	**–39.37**	. . .
Communications	3 245 . .	. . .	. . .	. . .	. . .	. . .	. . .	. . .	. . .
Construction	3 249 . .	. . .	. . .	. . .	. . .	. . .	. . .	. . .	. . .
Insurance	3 253 . .	–4.76	–5.74	–5.83	–6.29	–6.78	–6.78	–7.31	. . .
Financial	3 260 . .	. . .	. . .	. . .	. . .	. . .	. . .	. . .	. . .
Computer and information	3 262 . .	. . .	. . .	. . .	. . .	. . .	. . .	. . .	. . .
Royalties and licence fees	3 266 . .	. . .	. . .	. . .	–.57	. . .	. . .	. . .	. . .
Other business services	3 268 . .	–10.26	–14.52	–2.36	–10.39	–10.28	–15.47	–26.19	. . .
Personal, cultural, and recreational	3 287 . .	. . .	. . .	. . .	. . .	. . .	. . .	. . .	. . .
Government, n.i.e.	3 291 . .	–.78	–.67	–3.43	–4.70	–4.51	–4.99	–5.86	. . .

Table 2 (Continued). STANDARD PRESENTATION, 1988–95
(Millions of U.S. dollars)

	Code		1988	1989	1990	1991	1992	1993	1994	1995
C. INCOME	4 300	. .	–10.81	–10.59	–26.19	–29.65	–28.77	–25.66	–33.37	. . .
Total credit	2 300	. .	*6.41*	*5.85*	*5.94*	*4.63*	*5.46*	*4.36*	*4.97*	. . .
Total debit	3 300	. .	*–17.22*	*–16.44*	*–32.13*	*–34.28*	*–34.23*	*–30.02*	*–38.33*	. . .
Compensation of employees, credit	2 310	. .	**1.70**	**1.70**	**.93**	**.44**	**.27**	**.29**	**.37**	. . .
Compensation of employees, debit	3 310	. .	. . .	. . .	**–.37**	**–.21**	. . .	. . .	. . .	. . .
Investment income, credit	2 320	. .	**4.70**	**4.15**	**5.01**	**4.19**	**5.19**	**4.07**	**4.60**	. . .
Direct investment income	2 330	. .	. . .	. . .	. . .	. . .	. . .	. . .	. . .	. . .
Dividends and distributed branch profits	2 332	. .	. . .	. . .	. . .	. . .	. . .	. . .	. . .	. . .
Reinvested earnings and undistributed branch profits	2 333	. .	. . .	. . .	. . .	. . .	. . .	. . .	. . .	. . .
Income on debt (interest)	2 334	. .	. . .	. . .	. . .	. . .	. . .	. . .	. . .	. . .
Portfolio investment income	2 339	. .	. . .	. . .	. . .	. . .	. . .	. . .	. . .	. . .
Income on equity	2 340	. .	. . .	. . .	. . .	. . .	. . .	. . .	. . .	. . .
Income on bonds and notes	2 350	. .	. . .	. . .	. . .	. . .	. . .	. . .	. . .	. . .
Income on money market instruments and financial derivatives	2 360	. .	. . .	. . .	. . .	. . .	. . .	. . .	. . .	. . .
Other investment income	2 370	. .	4.70	4.15	5.01	4.19	5.19	4.07	4.60	. . .
Investment income, debit	3 320	. .	**–17.22**	**–16.44**	**–31.76**	**–34.07**	**–34.23**	**–30.02**	**–38.33**	. . .
Direct investment income	3 330	. .	–14.70	–13.48	–26.49	–29.06	–29.14	–31.57	–29.35	. . .
Dividends and distributed branch profits	3 332	. .	–10.85	–8.26	–15.63	–10.96	–13.73	–17.98	–12.24	. . .
Reinvested earnings and undistributed branch profits	3 333	. .	–3.33	–3.78	–7.70	–14.75	–15.24	–12.89	–16.01	. . .
Income on debt (interest)	3 334	. .	–.52	–1.44	–3.16	–3.34	–.17	–.70	–1.10	. . .
Portfolio investment income	3 339	. .	. . .	. . .	. . .	. . .	. . .	. . .	. . .	. . .
Income on equity	3 340	. .	. . .	. . .	. . .	. . .	. . .	. . .	. . .	. . .
Income on bonds and notes	3 350	. .	. . .	. . .	. . .	. . .	. . .	. . .	. . .	. . .
Income on money market instruments and financial derivatives	3 360	. .	. . .	. . .	. . .	. . .	. . .	. . .	. . .	. . .
Other investment income	3 370	. .	–2.52	–2.96	–5.27	–5.01	–5.09	1.55	–8.98	. . .
D. CURRENT TRANSFERS	4 379	. .	7.58	7.07	7.59	13.45	9.02	9.24	12.15	. . .
Credit	2 379	. .	**12.73**	**12.30**	**13.86**	**16.90**	**16.38**	**21.87**	**20.45**	. . .
General government	2 380	. .	. . .	. . .	.20	1.33	.25	8.25	1.85	. . .
Other sectors	2 390	. .	12.73	12.30	13.67	15.57	16.13	13.62	18.60	. . .
Workers' remittances	2 391	. .	12.73	12.30	13.67	15.57	16.13	13.62	14.00	. . .
Other current transfers	2 392	. .	. . .	. . .	. . .	. . .	. . .	. . .	4.60	. . .
Debit	3 379	. .	**–5.15**	**–5.23**	**–6.28**	**–3.45**	**–7.36**	**–12.63**	**–8.30**	. . .
General government	3 380	. .	–1.00	–1.85	–2.19	–1.68	–1.22	–2.44	–1.58	. . .
Other sectors	3 390	. .	–4.15	–3.38	–4.09	–1.77	–6.14	–10.20	–6.72	. . .
Workers' remittances	3 391	. .	. . .	. . .	. . .	. . .	–1.67	–3.04	–1.85	. . .
Other current transfers	3 392	. .	–4.15	–3.38	–4.09	–1.77	–4.47	–7.16	–4.87	. . .
CAPITAL AND FINANCIAL ACCOUNT	4 996	. .	**13.61**	**55.08**	**48.95**	**58.17**	**61.96**	**55.43**	**49.53**	. . .
CAPITAL ACCOUNT	4 994	. .	**7.86**	**8.48**	**3.85**	**6.57**	**8.95**	**3.84**	**7.43**	. . .
Total credit	2 994	. .	*7.86*	*8.48*	*3.85*	*6.57*	*9.13*	*4.18*	*8.54*	. . .
Total debit	3 994	. .	. . .	. . .	. . .	. . .	*–.19*	*–.34*	*–1.12*	. . .
Capital transfers, credit	2 400	. .	**7.86**	**8.48**	**3.85**	**6.57**	**9.13**	**4.18**	**8.54**	. . .
General government	2 401	. .	6.44	7.11	2.33	4.84	7.34	2.66	6.69	. . .
Debt forgiveness	2 402	. .	. . .	. . .	. . .	. . .	. . .	. . .	. . .	. . .
Other capital transfers	2 410	. .	6.44	7.11	2.33	4.84	7.34	2.66	6.69	. . .
Other sectors	2 430	. .	1.41	1.37	1.52	1.73	1.79	1.51	1.86	. . .
Migrants' transfers	2 431	. .	1.41	1.37	1.52	1.73	1.79	1.51	1.86	. . .
Debt forgiveness	2 432	. .	. . .	. . .	. . .	. . .	. . .	. . .	. . .	. . .
Other capital transfers	2 440	. .	. . .	. . .	. . .	. . .	. . .	. . .	. . .	. . .
Capital transfers, debit	3 400	. .	. . .	. . .	. . .	. . .	**–.19**	**–.34**	**–.38**	. . .
General government	3 401	. .	. . .	. . .	. . .	. . .	. . .	. . .	. . .	. . .
Debt forgiveness	3 402	. .	. . .	. . .	. . .	. . .	. . .	. . .	. . .	. . .
Other capital transfers	3 410	. .	. . .	. . .	. . .	. . .	. . .	. . .	. . .	. . .
Other sectors	3 430	. .	. . .	. . .	. . .	. . .	–.19	–.34	–.38	. . .
Migrants' transfers	3 431	. .	. . .	. . .	. . .	. . .	–.19	–.34	–.38	. . .
Debt forgiveness	3 432	. .	. . .	. . .	. . .	. . .	. . .	. . .	. . .	. . .
Other capital transfers	3 440	. .	. . .	. . .	. . .	. . .	. . .	. . .	. . .	. . .
Nonproduced nonfinancial assets, credit	2 480	. .	. . .	. . .	. . .	. . .	. . .	. . .	. . .	. . .
Nonproduced nonfinancial assets, debit	3 480	. .	. . .	. . .	. . .	. . .	. . .	. . .	**–.74**	. . .

Table 2 (Continued). STANDARD PRESENTATION, 1988–95
(Millions of U.S. dollars)

	Code	1988	1989	1990	1991	1992	1993	1994	1995
FINANCIAL ACCOUNT	4 995	**5.75**	**46.60**	**45.10**	**51.60**	**53.01**	**51.59**	**42.10**	**. . .**
A. DIRECT INVESTMENT	4 500	16.44	26.63	44.79	57.74	40.89	34.09	32.41	. . .
Direct investment abroad	4 505	**. . .**	**. . .**	**. . .**	**. . .**	**. . .**	**. . .**	**. . .**	**. . .**
Equity capital	4 510	. . .	. . .	. . .	. . .	. . .	. . .	. . .	. . .
Claims on affiliated enterprises	4 515	. . .	. . .	. . .	. . .	. . .	. . .	. . .	. . .
Liabilities to affiliated enterprises	4 520	. . .	. . .	. . .	. . .	. . .	. . .	. . .	. . .
Reinvested earnings	4 525	. . .	. . .	. . .	. . .	. . .	. . .	. . .	. . .
Other capital	4 530	. . .	. . .	. . .	. . .	. . .	. . .	. . .	. . .
Claims on affiliated enterprises	4 535	. . .	. . .	. . .	. . .	. . .	. . .	. . .	. . .
Liabilities to affiliated enterprises	4 540	. . .	. . .	. . .	. . .	. . .	. . .	. . .	. . .
Direct investment in St. Lucia	4 555	**16.44**	**26.63**	**44.79**	**57.74**	**40.89**	**34.09**	**32.41**	**. . .**
Equity capital	4 560	5.70	10.59	. . .	2.77	1.14	5.49	. . .	. . .
Claims on direct investors	4 565	. . .	. . .	. . .	. . .	. . .	. . .	. . .	. . .
Liabilities to direct investors	4 570	. . .	. . .	. . .	. . .	. . .	. . .	. . .	. . .
Reinvested earnings	4 575	3.33	3.78	7.70	14.75	15.24	12.89	16.01	. . .
Other capital	4 580	7.41	12.26	37.08	40.22	24.51	15.71	16.40	. . .
Claims on direct investors	4 585	. . .	. . .	. . .	. . .	. . .	. . .	. . .	. . .
Liabilities to direct investors	4 590	. . .	. . .	. . .	. . .	. . .	. . .	. . .	. . .
B. PORTFOLIO INVESTMENT	4 600	. . .	. . .	.04	. . .	–.51	. . .	–.47	. . .
Assets	4 602	**. . .**	**. . .**	**–.14**	**. . .**	**. . .**	**. . .**	**. . .**	**. . .**
Equity securities	4 610	. . .	. . .	–.14	. . .	. . .	. . .	. . .	. . .
Monetary authorities	4 611	. . .	. . .	. . .	. . .	. . .	. . .	. . .	. . .
General government	4 612	. . .	. . .	. . .	. . .	. . .	. . .	. . .	. . .
Banks	4 613	. . .	. . .	. . .	. . .	. . .	. . .	. . .	. . .
Other sectors	4 614	. . .	. . .	. . .	. . .	. . .	. . .	. . .	. . .
Debt securities	4 619	. . .	. . .	. . .	. . .	. . .	. . .	. . .	. . .
Bonds and notes	4 620	. . .	. . .	. . .	. . .	. . .	. . .	. . .	. . .
Monetary authorities	4 621	. . .	. . .	. . .	. . .	. . .	. . .	. . .	. . .
General government	4 622	. . .	. . .	. . .	. . .	. . .	. . .	. . .	. . .
Banks	4 623	. . .	. . .	. . .	. . .	. . .	. . .	. . .	. . .
Other sectors	4 624	. . .	. . .	. . .	. . .	. . .	. . .	. . .	. . .
Money market instruments	4 630	. . .	. . .	. . .	. . .	. . .	. . .	. . .	. . .
Monetary authorities	4 631	. . .	. . .	. . .	. . .	. . .	. . .	. . .	. . .
General government	4 632	. . .	. . .	. . .	. . .	. . .	. . .	. . .	. . .
Banks	4 633	. . .	. . .	. . .	. . .	. . .	. . .	. . .	. . .
Other sectors	4 634	. . .	. . .	. . .	. . .	. . .	. . .	. . .	. . .
Financial derivatives	4 640	. . .	. . .	. . .	. . .	. . .	. . .	. . .	. . .
Monetary authorities	4 641	. . .	. . .	. . .	. . .	. . .	. . .	. . .	. . .
General government	4 642	. . .	. . .	. . .	. . .	. . .	. . .	. . .	. . .
Banks	4 643	. . .	. . .	. . .	. . .	. . .	. . .	. . .	. . .
Other sectors	4 644	. . .	. . .	. . .	. . .	. . .	. . .	. . .	. . .
Liabilities	4 652	**. . .**	**. . .**	**.18**	**. . .**	**–.51**	**. . .**	**–.47**	**. . .**
Equity securities	4 660	. . .	. . .	.18	. . .	–.51	. . .	–.47	. . .
Banks	4 663	. . .	. . .	. . .	. . .	. . .	. . .	. . .	. . .
Other sectors	4 664	. . .	. . .	. . .	. . .	. . .	. . .	. . .	. . .
Debt securities	4 669	. . .	. . .	. . .	. . .	. . .	. . .	. . .	. . .
Bonds and notes	4 670	. . .	. . .	. . .	. . .	. . .	. . .	. . .	. . .
Monetary authorities	4 671	. . .	. . .	. . .	. . .	. . .	. . .	. . .	. . .
General government	4 672	. . .	. . .	. . .	. . .	. . .	. . .	. . .	. . .
Banks	4 673	. . .	. . .	. . .	. . .	. . .	. . .	. . .	. . .
Other sectors	4 674	. . .	. . .	. . .	. . .	. . .	. . .	. . .	. . .
Money market instruments	4 680	. . .	. . .	. . .	. . .	. . .	. . .	. . .	. . .
Monetary authorities	4 681	. . .	. . .	. . .	. . .	. . .	. . .	. . .	. . .
General government	4 682	. . .	. . .	. . .	. . .	. . .	. . .	. . .	. . .
Banks	4 683	. . .	. . .	. . .	. . .	. . .	. . .	. . .	. . .
Other sectors	4 684	. . .	. . .	. . .	. . .	. . .	. . .	. . .	. . .
Financial derivatives	4 690	. . .	. . .	. . .	. . .	. . .	. . .	. . .	. . .
Monetary authorities	4 691	. . .	. . .	. . .	. . .	. . .	. . .	. . .	. . .
General government	4 692	. . .	. . .	. . .	. . .	. . .	. . .	. . .	. . .
Banks	4 693	. . .	. . .	. . .	. . .	. . .	. . .	. . .	. . .
Other sectors	4 694	. . .	. . .	. . .	. . .	. . .	. . .	. . .	. . .

Table 2 (Concluded). STANDARD PRESENTATION, 1988–95
(Millions of U.S. dollars)

	Code	1988	1989	1990	1991	1992	1993	1994	1995
C. OTHER INVESTMENT	4 700	−8.84	25.57	6.57	1.59	19.41	21.99	14.39	...
Assets	4 703	**−11.52**	**18.15**	**1.96**	**−.48**	**.79**	**17.00**	**17.11**	...
Trade credits	4 706	...	...	...	...	...	...	...	...
General government: long-term	4 708	...	...	...	...	...	...	...	...
General government: short-term	4 709	...	...	...	...	...	...	...	...
Other sectors: long-term	4 711	...	...	...	...	...	...	...	...
Other sectors: short-term	4 712	...	...	...	...	...	...	...	...
Loans	4 714	...	...	...	...	...	...	...	...
Monetary authorities: long-term	4 717	...	...	...	...	...	...	...	...
Monetary authorities: short-term	4 718	...	...	...	...	...	...	...	...
General government: long-term	4 720	...	...	...	...	...	...	...	...
General government: short-term	4 721	...	...	...	...	...	...	...	...
Banks: long-term	4 723	...	...	...	...	...	...	...	...
Banks: short-term	4 724	...	...	...	...	...	...	...	...
Other sectors: long-term	4 726	...	...	...	...	...	...	...	...
Other sectors: short-term	4 727	...	...	...	...	...	...	...	...
Currency and deposits	4 730	−11.52	18.15	1.96	−.48	.79	17.00	17.11	...
Monetary authorities	4 731	...	...	...	...	...	...	...	...
General government	4 732	...	...	...	...	...	...	...	...
Banks	4 733	−11.52	18.15	1.96	−.48	.79	17.00	17.11	...
Other sectors	4 734	...	...	...	...	...	...	...	...
Other assets	4 736	...	...	...	...	...	...	...	...
Monetary authorities: long-term	4 738	...	...	...	...	...	...	...	...
Monetary authorities: short-term	4 739	...	...	...	...	...	...	...	...
General government: long-term	4 741	...	...	...	...	...	...	...	...
General government: short-term	4 742	...	...	...	...	...	...	...	...
Banks: long-term	4 744	...	...	...	...	...	...	...	...
Banks: short-term	4 745	...	...	...	...	...	...	...	...
Other sectors: long-term	4 747	...	...	...	...	...	...	...	...
Other sectors: short-term	4 748	...	...	...	...	...	...	...	...
Liabilities	4 753	**2.68**	**7.42**	**4.61**	**2.07**	**18.62**	**4.99**	**−2.72**	...
Trade credits	4 756	...	...	...	...	...	...	...	...
General government: long-term	4 758	...	...	...	...	...	...	...	...
General government: short-term	4 759	...	...	...	...	...	...	...	...
Other sectors: long-term	4 761	...	...	...	...	...	...	...	...
Other sectors: short-term	4 762	...	...	...	...	...	...	...	...
Loans	4 764	2.68	7.42	4.61	2.07	18.62	4.99	−2.72	...
Use of Fund credit and loans from the Fund	4 766	...	...	...	...	...	...	...	...
Monetary authorities: other long-term	4 767	...	...	...	...	...	...	...	...
Monetary authorities: short-term	4 768	...	...	...	...	...	...	...	...
General government: long-term	4 770	7.41	11.74	4.38	3.12	21.03	5.81	3.62	...
General government: short-term	4 771	...	...	...	...	...	...	...	...
Banks: long-term	4 773	...	...	...	...	...	...	...	...
Banks: short-term	4 774	...	...	...	...	...	...	...	...
Other sectors: long-term	4 776	−4.73	−4.32	.23	−1.05	−2.41	−.81	−6.34	...
Other sectors: short-term	4 777	...	...	...	...	...	...	...	...
Currency and deposits	4 780	...	...	...	...	...	...	...	...
Monetary authorities	4 781	...	...	...	...	...	...	...	...
General government	4 782	...	...	...	...	...	...	...	...
Banks	4 783	...	...	...	...	...	...	...	...
Other sectors	4 784	...	...	...	...	...	...	...	...
Other liabilities	4 786	...	...	...	...	...	...	...	...
Monetary authorities: long-term	4 788	...	...	...	...	...	...	...	...
Monetary authorities: short-term	4 789	...	...	...	...	...	...	...	...
General government: long-term	4 791	...	...	...	...	...	...	...	...
General government: short-term	4 792	...	...	...	...	...	...	...	...
Banks: long-term	4 794	...	...	...	...	...	...	...	...
Banks: short-term	4 795	...	...	...	...	...	...	...	...
Other sectors: long-term	4 797	...	...	...	...	...	...	...	...
Other sectors: short-term	4 798	...	...	...	...	...	...	...	...
D. RESERVE ASSETS	4 800	−1.85	−5.59	−6.30	−7.74	−6.78	−4.49	−4.22	...
Monetary gold	4 810	...	...	...	...	...	...	...	...
Special drawing rights	4 820	...	...	−1.67	−.06	−.06	−.04	−.04	...
Reserve position in the Fund	4 830	...	...	...	...	...	...	...	...
Foreign exchange	4 840	−1.81	−5.59	−4.63	−7.68	−6.73	−4.45	−4.19	...
Other claims	4 880	−.04	...	...	...	...	...	...	...
NET ERRORS AND OMISSIONS	4 998	**4.36**	**8.18**	**−3.46**	**13.90**	**−7.14**	**−14.19**	**15.42**	...

Part 3 of the *Yearbook* contains descriptions of the methodologies, compilation practices, and sources used to compile these data.

Table 1. ANALYTIC PRESENTATION, 1988–95
(Millions of U.S. dollars)

	Code	1988	1989	1990	1991	1992	1993	1994	1995
A. Current Account[1]	4 993 Y.	**–16.79**	**–29.66**	**–26.89**	**–44.03**	**–25.86**	**–47.45**	**–61.27**	**–36.00**
Goods: exports f.o.b	2 100 . .	87.41	77.37	85.41	67.41	79.01	57.11	45.69	57.05
Goods: imports f.o.b	3 100 . .	–107.59	–112.56	–120.41	–120.35	–116.87	–118.11	–119.36	–120.54
Balance on Goods	4 100 . .	*–20.19*	*–35.19*	*–35.00*	*–52.94*	*–37.86*	*–61.00*	*–73.67*	*–63.49*
Services: credit	2 200 . .	37.10	38.14	44.76	45.94	49.50	48.71	48.04	68.53
Services: debit	3 200 . .	–28.69	–34.05	–35.19	–33.01	–35.96	–33.10	–38.30	–38.33
Balance on Goods and Services	4 991 . .	*–11.78*	*–31.10*	*–25.43*	*–40.01*	*–24.33*	*–45.40*	*–63.94*	*–33.28*
Income: credit	2 300 . .	4.48	4.63	4.62	5.10	4.82	2.89	3.70	3.60
Income: debit	3 300 . .	–15.74	–11.48	–15.67	–16.30	–11.77	–11.11	–14.33	–14.19
Balance on Goods, Services, and Income	4 992 . .	*–23.04*	*–37.95*	*–36.48*	*–51.21*	*–31.27*	*–53.62*	*–74.57*	*–43.87*
Current transfers: credit	2 379 Y.	12.33	13.00	14.46	13.80	14.17	14.76	21.27	16.25
Current transfers: debit	3 379 . .	–6.08	–4.71	–4.87	–6.62	–8.76	–8.59	–7.98	–8.37
B. Capital Account[1]	4 994 Y.	**9.89**	**11.96**	**18.64**	**21.40**	**14.45**	**6.70**	**5.00**	**3.26**
Capital account: credit	2 994 Y.	10.15	12.15	18.88	21.65	14.70	7.00	5.37	3.26
Capital account: debit	3 994 . .	–.26	–.19	–.23	–.25	–.25	–.30	–.37	. . .
Total, Groups A Plus B	4 010 . .	*–6.90*	*–17.70*	*–8.24*	*–22.63*	*–11.41*	*–40.74*	*–56.27*	*–32.73*
C. Financial Account[1]	4 995 X.	**3.51**	**17.52**	**1.99**	**20.63**	**25.22**	**32.78**	**57.03**	**35.18**
Direct investment abroad	4 505 . .	. . .	. . .	. . .	. . .	. . .	. . .	. . .	. . .
Direct investment in St. Vincent and the Grenadines	4 555 Y.	9.11	10.59	7.67	8.83	18.84	31.36	50.61	31.38
Portfolio investment assets	4 602 . .	. . .	. . .	. . .	. . .	. . .	. . .	. . .	. . .
Equity securities	4 610 . .	. . .	. . .	. . .	. . .	. . .	. . .	. . .	. . .
Debt securities	4 619 . .	. . .	. . .	. . .	. . .	. . .	. . .	. . .	. . .
Portfolio investment liabilities	4 652 Y.	. . .	. . .	. . .	. . .	. . .	.03	.45	. . .
Equity securities	4 660 Y.	. . .	. . .	. . .	. . .	. . .	. . .	. . .	. . .
Debt securities	4 669 Y.	. . .	. . .	. . .	. . .	. . .	.03	.45	. . .
Other investment assets	4 703 . .	–12.04	1.96	–10.78	5.68	2.96	–4.53	.73	9.13
Monetary authorities	4 703 .A	. . .	. . .	. . .	. . .	. . .	. . .	. . .	. . .
General government	4 703 .B	. . .	. . .	. . .	. . .	. . .	. . .	. . .	. . .
Banks	4 703 .C	–12.04	1.96	–10.78	5.68	2.96	–4.53	.73	9.13
Other sectors	4 703 .D	. . .	. . .	. . .	. . .	. . .	. . .	. . .	. . .
Other investment liabilities	4 753 X.	6.44	4.96	5.10	6.12	3.42	5.91	5.23	–5.34
Monetary authorities	4 753 XA	. . .	. . .	. . .	. . .	. . .	. . .	. . .	. . .
General government	4 753 YB	6.59	4.93	6.44	6.33	3.43	3.67	1.68	–3.70
Banks	4 753 YC	. . .	. . .	. . .	. . .	. . .	. . .	. . .	. . .
Other sectors	4 753 YD	–.15	.04	–1.34	–.20	–.01	2.25	3.56	–1.64
Total, Groups A Through C	4 020 . .	*–3.39*	*–.18*	*–6.25*	*–2.00*	*13.81*	*–7.97*	*.76*	*2.44*
D. Net Errors and Omissions	4 998 . .	**5.31**	**1.61**	**11.69**	**–1.52**	**–4.26**	**6.67**	**–.50**	**–3.03**
Total, Groups A Through D	4 030 . .	*1.93*	*1.43*	*5.44*	*–3.51*	*9.55*	*–1.29*	*.26*	*–.59*
E. Reserves and Related Items	4 040 . .	**–1.93**	**–1.43**	**–5.44**	**3.51**	**–9.55**	**1.29**	**–.26**	**.59**
Reserve assets	4 800 . .	–1.93	–1.43	–5.44	3.51	–9.55	1.29	–.26	.59
Use of Fund credit and loans	4 766 . .	. . .	. . .	. . .	. . .	. . .	. . .	. . .	. . .
Liabilities constituting foreign authorities' reserves	4 900 . .	. . .	. . .	. . .	. . .	. . .	. . .	. . .	. . .
Exceptional financing	4 920 . .	. . .	. . .	. . .	. . .	. . .	. . .	. . .	. . .
Conversion rates: Eastern Caribbean dollars per U.S. dollar	0 101 . .	**2.7000**	**2.7000**	**2.7000**	**2.7000**	**2.7000**	**2.7000**	**2.7000**	**2.7000**

[1] Excludes components that have been classified in the categories of Group E.

Table 2. STANDARD PRESENTATION, 1988–95
(Millions of U.S. dollars)

	Code	1988	1989	1990	1991	1992	1993	1994	1995
CURRENT ACCOUNT	4 993 . .	**–16.79**	**–29.66**	**–26.89**	**–44.03**	**–25.86**	**–47.45**	**–61.27**	**–36.00**
A. GOODS	4 100 . .	–20.19	–35.19	–35.00	–52.94	–37.86	–61.00	–73.67	–63.49
Credit	2 100 . .	**87.41**	**77.37**	**85.41**	**67.41**	**79.01**	**57.11**	**45.69**	**57.05**
General merchandise: exports f.o.b.	2 110 . .	85.30	74.70	82.74	67.25	78.87	57.06	43.03	54.52
Goods for processing: exports f.o.b.	2 150 . .	. . .	. . .	. . .	. . .	. . .	. . .	. . .	. . .
Repairs on goods	2 160 . .	. . .	. . .	. . .	. . .	. . .	. . .	. . .	. . .
Goods procured in ports by carriers	2 170 . .	2.11	2.67	2.67	.16	.13	.06	2.66	2.53
Nonmonetary gold	2 180 . .	. . .	. . .	. . .	. . .	. . .	. . .	. . .	. . .
Debit	3 100 . .	**–107.59**	**–112.56**	**–120.41**	**–120.35**	**–116.87**	**–118.11**	**–119.36**	**–120.54**
General merchandise: imports f.o.b.	3 110 . .	–107.59	–112.19	–119.78	–119.71	–116.23	–117.35	–118.34	–119.53
Goods for processing: imports f.o.b.	3 150 . .	. . .	. . .	. . .	. . .	. . .	. . .	. . .	. . .
Repairs on goods	3 160 . .	. . .	. . .	. . .	. . .	. . .	. . .	. . .	. . .
Goods procured in ports by carriers	3 170 . .	. . .	–.37	–.63	–.64	–.64	–.77	–1.03	–1.01
Nonmonetary gold	3 180 . .	. . .	. . .	. . .	. . .	. . .	. . .	. . .	. . .
B. SERVICES	4 200 . .	8.40	4.09	9.57	12.93	13.54	15.60	9.74	30.21
Total credit	2 200 . .	*37.10*	*38.14*	*44.76*	*45.94*	*49.50*	*48.71*	*48.04*	*68.53*
Total debit	3 200 . .	*–28.69*	*–34.05*	*–35.19*	*–33.01*	*–35.96*	*–33.10*	*–38.30*	*–38.33*
Transportation services, credit	2 205 . .	**3.00**	**3.00**	**3.70**	**4.44**	**4.06**	**4.36**	**4.36**	**5.14**
Passenger	2 205 BA	*.67*	*.67*	*1.19*	*1.19*	*1.74*	*1.98*	*2.26*	*2.94*
Freight	2 205 BB	. . .	. . .	. . .	*.14*	*.01*	. . .	. . .	. . .
Other	2 205 BC	*2.33*	*2.33*	*2.52*	*3.11*	*2.31*	*2.38*	*2.10*	*2.21*
Sea transport, passenger	2 207 . .	. . .	. . .	. . .	. . .	. . .	. . .	. . .	. . .
Sea transport, freight	2 208 . .	. . .	. . .	. . .	. . .	. . .	. . .	. . .	. . .
Sea transport, other	2 209 . .	. . .	. . .	. . .	. . .	. . .	. . .	. . .	. . .
Air transport, passenger	2 211 . .	. . .	. . .	. . .	. . .	. . .	. . .	. . .	. . .
Air transport, freight	2 212 . .	. . .	. . .	. . .	. . .	. . .	. . .	. . .	. . .
Air transport, other	2 213 . .	. . .	. . .	. . .	. . .	. . .	. . .	. . .	. . .
Other transport, passenger	2 215 . .	. . .	. . .	. . .	. . .	. . .	. . .	. . .	. . .
Other transport, freight	2 216 . .	. . .	. . .	. . .	. . .	. . .	. . .	. . .	. . .
Other transport, other	2 217 . .	. . .	. . .	. . .	. . .	. . .	. . .	. . .	. . .
Transportation services, debit	3 205 . .	**–16.89**	**–18.27**	**–17.99**	**–18.27**	**–17.65**	**–18.46**	**–19.39**	**–19.16**
Passenger	3 205 BA	*–3.89*	*–5.41*	*–4.19*	*–4.49*	*–4.29*	*–4.84*	*–5.89*	*–5.44*
Freight	3 205 BB	*–12.59*	*–12.75*	*–13.58*	*–13.63*	*–13.21*	*–13.41*	*–13.45*	*–13.61*
Other	3 205 BC	*–.41*	*–.11*	*–.22*	*–.16*	*–.15*	*–.21*	*–.05*	*–.11*
Sea transport, passenger	3 207 . .	. . .	. . .	. . .	. . .	. . .	. . .	. . .	. . .
Sea transport, freight	3 208 . .	. . .	. . .	. . .	. . .	. . .	. . .	. . .	. . .
Sea transport, other	3 209 . .	. . .	. . .	. . .	. . .	. . .	. . .	. . .	. . .
Air transport, passenger	3 211 . .	. . .	. . .	. . .	. . .	. . .	. . .	. . .	. . .
Air transport, freight	3 212 . .	. . .	. . .	. . .	. . .	. . .	. . .	. . .	. . .
Air transport, other	3 213 . .	. . .	. . .	. . .	. . .	. . .	. . .	. . .	. . .
Other transport, passenger	3 215 . .	. . .	. . .	. . .	. . .	. . .	. . .	. . .	. . .
Other transport, freight	3 216 . .	. . .	. . .	. . .	. . .	. . .	. . .	. . .	. . .
Other transport, other	3 217 . .	. . .	. . .	. . .	. . .	. . .	. . .	. . .	. . .
Travel, credit	2 236 . .	**26.82**	**27.30**	**29.37**	**28.92**	**29.02**	**30.49**	**28.78**	**46.71**
Business travel	2 237 . .	. . .	. . .	. . .	. . .	. . .	. . .	. . .	. . .
Personal travel	2 240 . .	. . .	. . .	. . .	. . .	. . .	. . .	. . .	. . .
Travel, debit	3 236 . .	**–4.44**	**–5.10**	**–4.19**	**–3.77**	**–3.60**	**–2.90**	**–3.38**	**–3.93**
Business travel	3 237 . .	. . .	. . .	. . .	. . .	. . .	. . .	. . .	. . .
Personal travel	3 240 . .	. . .	. . .	. . .	. . .	. . .	. . .	. . .	. . .
Other services, credit	2 200 BA	**7.27**	**7.84**	**11.69**	**12.59**	**16.41**	**13.86**	**14.90**	**16.68**
Communications	2 245 . .	. . .	. . .	. . .	. . .	. . .	. . .	. . .	. . .
Construction	2 249 . .	. . .	. . .	. . .	. . .	. . .	. . .	. . .	. . .
Insurance	2 253 . .	.52	.33	.30	1.07	3.11	1.76	.94	1.01
Financial	2 260 . .	. . .	. . .	. . .	. . .	. . .	. . .	. . .	. . .
Computer and information	2 262 . .	. . .	. . .	. . .	. . .	. . .	. . .	. . .	. . .
Royalties and licence fees	2 266 . .	. . .	. . .	. . .	. . .	. . .	. . .	. . .	. . .
Other business services	2 268 . .	5.01	5.99	7.72	9.37	10.27	10.37	11.37	15.20
Personal, cultural, and recreational	2 287 . .	. . .	. . .	. . .	. . .	. . .	. . .	. . .	. . .
Government, n.i.e.	2 291 . .	1.74	1.52	3.67	2.14	3.03	1.72	2.60	.47
Other services, debit	3 200 BA	**–7.36**	**–10.69**	**–13.02**	**–10.97**	**–14.71**	**–11.75**	**–15.54**	**–15.23**
Communications	3 245 . .	. . .	. . .	. . .	. . .	. . .	. . .	. . .	. . .
Construction	3 249 . .	. . .	. . .	. . .	. . .	. . .	. . .	. . .	. . .
Insurance	3 253 . .	–2.54	–2.65	–2.80	–3.04	–3.99	–3.23	–3.03	–3.99
Financial	3 260 . .	. . .	. . .	. . .	. . .	. . .	. . .	. . .	. . .
Computer and information	3 262 . .	. . .	. . .	. . .	. . .	. . .	. . .	. . .	. . .
Royalties and licence fees	3 266 . .	. . .	. . .	. . .	–.17	. . .	. . .	–.28	. . .
Other business services	3 268 . .	–3.59	–6.33	–8.11	–6.01	–7.23	–7.03	–6.81	–9.40
Personal, cultural, and recreational	3 287 . .	. . .	. . .	. . .	. . .	. . .	. . .	. . .	. . .
Government, n.i.e.	3 291 . .	–1.22	–1.70	–2.11	–1.74	–3.49	–1.49	–5.41	–1.85

Table 2 (Continued). STANDARD PRESENTATION, 1988–95
(Millions of U.S. dollars)

	Code		1988	1989	1990	1991	1992	1993	1994	1995
C. INCOME	4 300	. .	−11.26	−6.85	−11.04	−11.20	−6.94	−8.22	−10.63	−10.60
Total credit	2 300	. .	*4.48*	*4.63*	*4.62*	*5.10*	*4.82*	*2.89*	*3.70*	*3.60*
Total debit	3 300	. .	*−15.74*	*−11.48*	*−15.67*	*−16.30*	*−11.77*	*−11.11*	*−14.33*	*−14.19*
Compensation of employees, credit	2 310	. .	**1.26**	**.93**	**.19**	**.92**	**.87**	**.22**	**.31**	**.31**
Compensation of employees, debit	3 310	. .	**. . .**	**. . .**	**. . .**	**−.80**	**. . .**	**. . .**	**−.03**	**. . .**
Investment income, credit	2 320	. .	**3.22**	**3.70**	**4.44**	**4.18**	**3.96**	**2.67**	**3.39**	**3.28**
Direct investment income	2 330	. .	. . .	. . .	.11	.03	.06	.01	.01	.04
Dividends and distributed branch profits	2 332	. .	. . .	. . .	. . .	. . .	. . .	. . .	. . .	. . .
Reinvested earnings and undistributed branch profits	2 333	. .	. . .	. . .	. . .	. . .	. . .	. . .	. . .	. . .
Income on debt (interest)	2 334	. .	. . .	. . .	.11	.03	.06	.01	.01	.04
Portfolio investment income	2 339	. .	. . .	. . .	. . .	. . .	. . .	. . .	. . .	. . .
Income on equity	2 340	. .	. . .	. . .	. . .	. . .	. . .	. . .	. . .	. . .
Income on bonds and notes	2 350	. .	. . .	. . .	. . .	. . .	. . .	. . .	. . .	. . .
Income on money market instruments and financial derivatives	2 360	. .	. . .	. . .	. . .	. . .	. . .	. . .	. . .	. . .
Other investment income	2 370	. .	3.22	3.70	4.33	4.14	3.90	2.66	3.38	3.24
Investment income, debit	3 320	. .	**−15.74**	**−11.48**	**−15.67**	**−15.50**	**−11.77**	**−11.11**	**−14.30**	**−14.19**
Direct investment income	3 330	. .	−10.56	−8.30	−13.26	−12.26	−9.17	−7.37	−10.45	−9.57
Dividends and distributed branch profits	3 332	. .	−6.37	−4.63	−10.07	−4.39	−4.98	−2.70	−4.51	−2.91
Reinvested earnings and undistributed branch profits	3 333	. .	−4.19	−3.67	−3.15	−7.81	−4.12	−4.67	−5.90	−6.66
Income on debt (interest)	3 334	. .	. . .	. . .	−.04	−.05	−.07	. . .	−.04	. . .
Portfolio investment income	3 339	. .	. . .	. . .	. . .	. . .	. . .	. . .	. . .	. . .
Income on equity	3 340	. .	. . .	. . .	. . .	. . .	. . .	. . .	. . .	. . .
Income on bonds and notes	3 350	. .	. . .	. . .	. . .	. . .	. . .	. . .	. . .	. . .
Income on money market instruments and financial derivatives	3 360	. .	. . .	. . .	. . .	. . .	. . .	. . .	. . .	. . .
Other investment income	3 370	. .	−5.19	−3.19	−2.41	−3.24	−2.60	−3.74	−3.85	−4.62
D. CURRENT TRANSFERS	4 379	. .	6.25	8.29	9.59	7.18	5.41	6.17	13.30	7.88
Credit	2 379	. .	**12.33**	**13.00**	**14.46**	**13.80**	**14.17**	**14.76**	**21.27**	**16.25**
General government	2 380	. .	. . .	. . .	.56	.08	.31	.22	3.81	1.11
Other sectors	2 390	. .	12.33	13.00	13.90	13.72	13.86	14.53	17.46	15.14
Workers' remittances	2 391	. .	12.33	13.00	13.90	13.72	13.86	14.53	16.67	14.81
Other current transfers	2 392	. .	. . .	. . .	. . .	. . .	. . .	. . .	.79	.33
Debit	3 379	. .	**−6.08**	**−4.71**	**−4.87**	**−6.62**	**−8.76**	**−8.59**	**−7.98**	**−8.37**
General government	3 380	. .	−2.48	−1.85	−1.81	−1.91	−2.42	−1.80	−2.47	−3.19
Other sectors	3 390	. .	−3.60	−2.86	−3.05	−4.71	−6.34	−6.79	−5.50	−5.18
Workers' remittances	3 391	. .	−2.33	−1.67	−2.10	−2.23	−2.23	−2.67	−3.33	−3.33
Other current transfers	3 392	. .	−1.27	−1.20	−.95	−2.48	−4.10	−4.12	−2.17	−1.85
CAPITAL AND FINANCIAL ACCOUNT	4 996	. .	**11.48**	**28.05**	**15.20**	**45.55**	**30.12**	**40.77**	**61.77**	**39.03**
CAPITAL ACCOUNT	4 994	. .	**9.89**	**11.96**	**18.64**	**21.40**	**14.45**	**6.70**	**5.00**	**3.26**
Total credit	2 994	. .	*10.15*	*12.15*	*18.88*	*21.65*	*14.70*	*7.00*	*5.37*	*3.26*
Total debit	3 994	. .	*−.26*	*−.19*	*−.23*	*−.25*	*−.25*	*−.30*	*−.37*	. . .
Capital transfers, credit	2 400	. .	**10.15**	**12.15**	**18.88**	**21.65**	**14.70**	**7.00**	**5.37**	**3.26**
General government	2 401	. .	8.78	10.70	17.33	20.12	13.16	5.39	3.52	. . .
Debt forgiveness	2 402	. .	. . .	. . .	. . .	. . .	. . .	. . .	. . .	. . .
Other capital transfers	2 410	. .	8.78	10.70	17.33	20.12	13.16	5.39	3.52	. . .
Other sectors	2 430	. .	1.37	1.44	1.54	1.53	1.54	1.61	1.85	. . .
Migrants' transfers	2 431	. .	1.37	1.44	1.54	1.53	1.54	1.61	1.85	. . .
Debt forgiveness	2 432	. .	. . .	. . .	. . .	. . .	. . .	. . .	. . .	. . .
Other capital transfers	2 440	. .	. . .	. . .	. . .	. . .	. . .	. . .	. . .	. . .
Capital transfers, debit	3 400	. .	**−.26**	**−.19**	**−.23**	**−.25**	**−.25**	**−.30**	**−.37**	**. . .**
General government	3 401	. .	. . .	. . .	. . .	. . .	. . .	. . .	. . .	. . .
Debt forgiveness	3 402	. .	. . .	. . .	. . .	. . .	. . .	. . .	. . .	. . .
Other capital transfers	3 410	. .	. . .	. . .	. . .	. . .	. . .	. . .	. . .	. . .
Other sectors	3 430	. .	−.26	−.19	−.23	−.25	−.25	−.30	−.37	. . .
Migrants' transfers	3 431	. .	−.26	−.19	−.23	−.25	−.25	−.30	−.37	. . .
Debt forgiveness	3 432	. .	. . .	. . .	. . .	. . .	. . .	. . .	. . .	. . .
Other capital transfers	3 440	. .	. . .	. . .	. . .	. . .	. . .	. . .	. . .	. . .
Nonproduced nonfinancial assets, credit	2 480	. .	**. . .**	**. . .**	**. . .**	**. . .**	**. . .**	**. . .**	**. . .**	**. . .**
Nonproduced nonfinancial assets, debit	3 480	. .	**. . .**	**. . .**	**. . .**	**. . .**	**. . .**	**. . .**	**. . .**	**. . .**

Table 2 (Continued). STANDARD PRESENTATION, 1988–95
(Millions of U.S. dollars)

	Code	1988	1989	1990	1991	1992	1993	1994	1995
FINANCIAL ACCOUNT	4 995	**1.59**	**16.09**	**–3.44**	**24.15**	**15.67**	**34.07**	**56.77**	**35.76**
A. DIRECT INVESTMENT	4 500	9.11	10.59	7.67	8.83	18.84	31.36	50.61	31.38
Direct investment abroad	4 505	...	...	...	...	...	...	...	...
Equity capital	4 510	...	...	...	...	...	...	...	...
Claims on affiliated enterprises	4 515	...	...	...	...	...	...	...	...
Liabilities to affiliated enterprises	4 520	...	...	...	...	...	...	...	...
Reinvested earnings	4 525	...	...	...	...	...	...	...	...
Other capital	4 530	...	...	...	...	...	...	...	...
Claims on affiliated enterprises	4 535	...	...	...	...	...	...	...	...
Liabilities to affiliated enterprises	4 540	...	...	...	...	...	...	...	...
Direct investment in St. Vincent and the Grenadines	4 555	**9.11**	**10.59**	**7.67**	**8.83**	**18.84**	**31.36**	**50.61**	**31.38**
Equity capital	4 560	1.11	.74	.74	...	...	...	6.19	...
Claims on direct investors	4 565	...	...	...	...	...	...	...	...
Liabilities to direct investors	4 570	...	...	...	...	...	...	...	...
Reinvested earnings	4 575	4.19	3.67	3.15	7.81	4.12	4.67	5.90	6.66
Other capital	4 580	3.81	6.19	3.78	1.02	14.73	26.68	38.53	24.72
Claims on direct investors	4 585	...	...	...	...	...	...	...	...
Liabilities to direct investors	4 590	...	...	...	...	...	...	...	...
B. PORTFOLIO INVESTMENT	4 600	...	...	...	...	...	.03	.45	...
Assets	4 602	...	...	...	...	...	...	...	...
Equity securities	4 610	...	...	...	...	...	...	...	...
Monetary authorities	4 611	...	...	...	...	...	...	...	...
General government	4 612	...	...	...	...	...	...	...	...
Banks	4 613	...	...	...	...	...	...	...	...
Other sectors	4 614	...	...	...	...	...	...	...	...
Debt securities	4 619	...	...	...	...	...	...	...	...
Bonds and notes	4 620	...	...	...	...	...	...	...	...
Monetary authorities	4 621	...	...	...	...	...	...	...	...
General government	4 622	...	...	...	...	...	...	...	...
Banks	4 623	...	...	...	...	...	...	...	...
Other sectors	4 624	...	...	...	...	...	...	...	...
Money market instruments	4 630	...	...	...	...	...	...	...	...
Monetary authorities	4 631	...	...	...	...	...	...	...	...
General government	4 632	...	...	...	...	...	...	...	...
Banks	4 633	...	...	...	...	...	...	...	...
Other sectors	4 634	...	...	...	...	...	...	...	...
Financial derivatives	4 640	...	...	...	...	...	...	...	...
Monetary authorities	4 641	...	...	...	...	...	...	...	...
General government	4 642	...	...	...	...	...	...	...	...
Banks	4 643	...	...	...	...	...	...	...	...
Other sectors	4 644	...	...	...	...	...	...	...	...
Liabilities	4 652	...	...	...	...	...	**.03**	**.45**	...
Equity securities	4 660	...	...	...	...	...	...	...	...
Banks	4 663	...	...	...	...	...	...	...	...
Other sectors	4 664	...	...	...	...	...	...	...	...
Debt securities	4 669	...	...	...	...	...	.03	.45	...
Bonds and notes	4 670	...	...	...	...	...	.03	.45	...
Monetary authorities	4 671	...	...	...	...	...	...	...	...
General government	4 672	...	...	...	...	...	.03	.45	...
Banks	4 673	...	...	...	...	...	...	...	...
Other sectors	4 674	...	...	...	...	...	...	...	...
Money market instruments	4 680	...	...	...	...	...	...	...	...
Monetary authorities	4 681	...	...	...	...	...	...	...	...
General government	4 682	...	...	...	...	...	...	...	...
Banks	4 683	...	...	...	...	...	...	...	...
Other sectors	4 684	...	...	...	...	...	...	...	...
Financial derivatives	4 690	...	...	...	...	...	...	...	...
Monetary authorities	4 691	...	...	...	...	...	...	...	...
General government	4 692	...	...	...	...	...	...	...	...
Banks	4 693	...	...	...	...	...	...	...	...
Other sectors	4 694	...	...	...	...	...	...	...	...

Table 2 (Concluded). STANDARD PRESENTATION, 1988–95
(Millions of U.S. dollars)

	Code	1988	1989	1990	1991	1992	1993	1994	1995
C. OTHER INVESTMENT	4 700	–5.60	6.93	–5.67	11.80	6.37	1.39	5.96	3.80
Assets	4 703	**–12.04**	**1.96**	**–10.78**	**5.68**	**2.96**	**–4.53**	**.73**	**9.13**
Trade credits	4 706	...	...	...	...	...	...	...	...
General government: long-term	4 708	...	...	...	...	...	...	...	...
General government: short-term	4 709	...	...	...	...	...	...	...	...
Other sectors: long-term	4 711	...	...	...	...	...	...	...	...
Other sectors: short-term	4 712	...	...	...	...	...	...	...	...
Loans	4 714	...	...	...	...	...	...	...	...
Monetary authorities: long-term	4 717	...	...	...	...	...	...	...	...
Monetary authorities: short-term	4 718	...	...	...	...	...	...	...	...
General government: long-term	4 720	...	...	...	...	...	...	...	...
General government: short-term	4 721	...	...	...	...	...	...	...	...
Banks: long-term	4 723	...	...	...	...	...	...	...	...
Banks: short-term	4 724	...	...	...	...	...	...	...	...
Other sectors: long-term	4 726	...	...	...	...	...	...	...	...
Other sectors: short-term	4 727	...	...	...	...	...	...	...	...
Currency and deposits	4 730	–12.04	1.96	–10.78	5.68	2.96	–4.53	.73	9.13
Monetary authorities	4 731	...	...	...	...	...	...	...	...
General government	4 732	...	...	...	...	...	...	...	...
Banks	4 733	–12.04	1.96	–10.78	5.68	2.96	–4.53	.73	9.13
Other sectors	4 734	...	...	...	...	...	...	...	...
Other assets	4 736	...	...	...	...	...	...	...	...
Monetary authorities: long-term	4 738	...	...	...	...	...	...	...	...
Monetary authorities: short-term	4 739	...	...	...	...	...	...	...	...
General government: long-term	4 741	...	...	...	...	...	...	...	...
General government: short-term	4 742	...	...	...	...	...	...	...	...
Banks: long-term	4 744	...	...	...	...	...	...	...	...
Banks: short-term	4 745	...	...	...	...	...	...	...	...
Other sectors: long-term	4 747	...	...	...	...	...	...	...	...
Other sectors: short-term	4 748	...	...	...	...	...	...	...	...
Liabilities	4 753	**6.44**	**4.96**	**5.10**	**6.12**	**3.42**	**5.91**	**5.23**	**–5.34**
Trade credits	4 756	...	...	...	...	...	...	...	...
General government: long-term	4 758	...	...	...	...	...	...	...	...
General government: short-term	4 759	...	...	...	...	...	...	...	...
Other sectors: long-term	4 761	...	...	...	...	...	...	...	...
Other sectors: short-term	4 762	...	...	...	...	...	...	...	...
Loans	4 764	6.44	4.96	5.10	6.12	3.42	5.91	5.23	–5.34
Use of Fund credit and loans from the Fund	4 766	...	...	...	...	...	...	...	...
Monetary authorities: other long term	4 767	...	...	...	...	...	...	...	...
Monetary authorities: short-term	4 768	...	...	...	...	...	...	...	...
General government: long-term	4 770	6.59	4.93	6.44	6.33	3.43	3.67	1.68	–3.70
General government: short-term	4 771	...	...	...	...	...	...	...	...
Banks: long-term	4 773	...	...	...	...	...	...	...	...
Banks: short-term	4 774	...	...	...	...	...	...	...	...
Other sectors: long-term	4 776	–.15	.04	–1.34	–.20	–.01	2.25	3.56	–1.64
Other sectors: short-term	4 777	...	...	...	...	...	...	...	...
Currency and deposits	4 780	...	...	...	...	...	...	...	...
Monetary authorities	4 781	...	...	...	...	...	...	...	...
General government	4 782	...	...	...	...	...	...	...	...
Banks	4 783	...	...	...	...	...	...	...	...
Other sectors	4 784	...	...	...	...	...	...	...	...
Other liabilities	4 786	...	...	...	...	...	...	...	...
Monetary authorities: long-term	4 788	...	...	...	...	...	...	...	...
Monetary authorities: short-term	4 789	...	...	...	...	...	...	...	...
General government: long-term	4 791	...	...	...	...	...	...	...	...
General government: short-term	4 792	...	...	...	...	...	...	...	...
Banks: long-term	4 794	...	...	...	...	...	...	...	...
Banks: short-term	4 795	...	...	...	...	...	...	...	...
Other sectors: long-term	4 797	...	...	...	...	...	...	...	...
Other sectors: short-term	4 798	...	...	...	...	...	...	...	...
D. RESERVE ASSETS	4 800	–1.93	–1.43	–5.44	3.51	–9.55	1.29	–.26	.59
Monetary gold	4 810	...	...	...	...	...	...	...	...
Special drawing rights	4 820	...	...	...	–.02	–.11	...	.01	.01
Reserve position in the Fund	4 830	...	...	...	...	–.69	...	...	...
Foreign exchange	4 840	–1.59	–.95	–5.14	3.53	–8.11	1.83	.27	1.43
Other claims	4 880	–.33	–.48	–.30	...	–.63	–.54	–.54	–.85
NET ERRORS AND OMISSIONS	4 998	**5.31**	**1.61**	**11.69**	**–1.52**	**–4.26**	**6.67**	**–.50**	**–3.03**

Part 3 of the *Yearbook* contains descriptions of the methodologies, compilation practices, and sources used to compile these data.

Table 1. ANALYTIC PRESENTATION, 1988–95
(Millions of U.S. dollars)

	Code	1988	1989	1990	1991	1992	1993	1994	1995
A. Current Account [1]	4 993 Y .	**-10.77**	**-11.37**	**-14.33**	**. . .**	**. . .**	**. . .**	**. . .**	**. . .**
Goods: exports f.o.b	2 100 . .	9.51	4.91	4.22	. . .	. . .	. . .	. . .	. . .
Goods: imports f.o.b	3 100 . .	-14.13	-13.31	-13.02	. . .	. . .	. . .	. . .	. . .
Balance on Goods	4 100 . .	*-4.62*	*-8.40*	*-8.80*	. . .	. . .	. . .	. . .	. . .
Services: credit	2 200 . .	1.55	4.48	3.66	. . .	. . .	. . .	. . .	. . .
Services: debit	3 200 . .	-8.39	-8.51	-9.02	. . .	. . .	. . .	. . .	. . .
Balance on Goods and Services	4 991 . .	*-11.47*	*-12.43*	*-14.16*	. . .	. . .	. . .	. . .	. . .
Income: credit	2 300 . .	.43	.11	.26	. . .	. . .	. . .	. . .	. . .
Income: debit	3 300 . .	-.60	-.33	-.31	. . .	. . .	. . .	. . .	. . .
Balance on Goods, Services, and Income	4 992 . .	*-11.64*	*-12.65*	*-14.21*	. . .	. . .	. . .	. . .	. . .
Current transfers: credit	2 379 Y .	1.66	2.42	.67	. . .	. . .	. . .	. . .	. . .
Current transfers: debit	3 379 . .	-.80	-1.14	-.79	. . .	. . .	. . .	. . .	. . .
B. Capital Account [1]	4 994 Y .	**. . .**	**. . .**	**. . .**	**. . .**	**. . .**	**. . .**	**. . .**	**. . .**
Capital account: credit	2 994 Y .	. . .	. . .	. . .	. . .	. . .	. . .	. . .	. . .
Capital account: debit	3 994 . .	. . .	. . .	. . .	. . .	. . .	. . .	. . .	. . .
Total, Groups A Plus B	4 010 . .	*-10.77*	*-11.37*	*-14.33*	. . .	. . .	. . .	. . .	. . .
C. Financial Account [1]	4 995 X .	**6.34**	**6.73**	**7.58**	**. . .**	**. . .**	**. . .**	**. . .**	**. . .**
Direct investment abroad	4 505 . .	.20	. . .	. . .	. . .	. . .	. . .	. . .	. . .
Direct investment in São Tomé and Príncipe	4 555 Y .	. . .	. . .	. . .	. . .	. . .	. . .	. . .	. . .
Portfolio investment assets	4 602 . .	. . .	. . .	. . .	. . .	. . .	. . .	. . .	. . .
Equity securities	4 610 . .	. . .	. . .	. . .	. . .	. . .	. . .	. . .	. . .
Debt securities	4 619 . .	. . .	. . .	. . .	. . .	. . .	. . .	. . .	. . .
Portfolio investment liabilities	4 652 Y .	. . .	. . .	. . .	. . .	. . .	. . .	. . .	. . .
Equity securities	4 660 Y .	. . .	. . .	. . .	. . .	. . .	. . .	. . .	. . .
Debt securities	4 669 Y .	. . .	. . .	. . .	. . .	. . .	. . .	. . .	. . .
Other investment assets	4 703 . .	. . .	. . .	. . .	. . .	. . .	. . .	. . .	. . .
Monetary authorities	4 703 . A	. . .	. . .	. . .	. . .	. . .	. . .	. . .	. . .
General government	4 703 . B	. . .	. . .	. . .	. . .	. . .	. . .	. . .	. . .
Banks	4 703 . C	. . .	. . .	. . .	. . .	. . .	. . .	. . .	. . .
Other sectors	4 703 . D	. . .	. . .	. . .	. . .	. . .	. . .	. . .	. . .
Other investment liabilities	4 753 X .	6.14	6.73	7.58	. . .	. . .	. . .	. . .	. . .
Monetary authorities	4 753 XA	.06	. . .	. . .	. . .	. . .	. . .	. . .	. . .
General government	4 753 YB	1.77	3.90	11.23	. . .	. . .	. . .	. . .	. . .
Banks	4 753 YC	. . .	. . .	. . .	. . .	. . .	. . .	. . .	. . .
Other sectors	4 753 YD	4.32	2.83	-3.65	. . .	. . .	. . .	. . .	. . .
Total, Groups A Through C	4 020 . .	*-4.44*	*-4.64*	*-6.75*	. . .	. . .	. . .	. . .	. . .
D. Net Errors and Omissions	4 998 . .	**. . .**	**-.98**	**-2.66**	**. . .**	**. . .**	**. . .**	**. . .**	**. . .**
Total, Groups A Through D	4 030 . .	*-4.44*	*-5.62*	*-9.41*	. . .	. . .	. . .	. . .	. . .
E. Reserves and Related Items	4 040 . .	**4.44**	**5.62**	**9.41**	**. . .**	**. . .**	**. . .**	**. . .**	**. . .**
Reserve assets	4 800 . .	4.44	4.62	.52	. . .	. . .	. . .	. . .	. . .
Use of Fund credit and loans	4 766 . .	. . .	.99	. . .	. . .	. . .	. . .	. . .	. . .
Liabilities constituting foreign authorities' reserves	4 900 . .	. . .	. . .	. . .	. . .	. . .	. . .	. . .	. . .
Exceptional financing	4 920 . .	. . .	. . .	8.89	. . .	. . .	. . .	. . .	. . .
Conversion rates: dobras per U.S. dollar	0 101 . .	**86.34**	**124.67**	**143.33**	**201.82**	**321.34**	**429.85**	**732.63**	**1,420.34**

[1] Excludes components that have been classified in the categories of Group E.

Table 2. STANDARD PRESENTATION, 1988–95
(Millions of U.S. dollars)

	Code	1988	1989	1990	1991	1992	1993	1994	1995
CURRENT ACCOUNT	4 993 . .	**–10.77**	**–11.37**	**–12.04**	**. . .**	**. . .**	**. . .**	**. . .**	**. . .**
A. GOODS	4 100 . .	–4.62	–8.40	–8.80	. . .	. . .	. . .	. . .	. . .
Credit	2 100 . .	**9.51**	**4.91**	**4.22**	**. . .**	**. . .**	**. . .**	**. . .**	**. . .**
General merchandise: exports f.o.b.	2 110 . .	9.51	4.91	4.22	. . .	. . .	. . .	. . .	. . .
Goods for processing: exports f.o.b.	2 150 . .	. . .	. . .	. . .	. . .	. . .	. . .	. . .	. . .
Repairs on goods	2 160 . .	. . .	. . .	. . .	. . .	. . .	. . .	. . .	. . .
Goods procured in ports by carriers	2 170 . .	. . .	. . .	. . .	. . .	. . .	. . .	. . .	. . .
Nonmonetary gold	2 180 . .	. . .	. . .	. . .	. . .	. . .	. . .	. . .	. . .
Debit	3 100 . .	**–14.13**	**–13.31**	**–13.02**	**. . .**	**. . .**	**. . .**	**. . .**	**. . .**
General merchandise: imports f.o.b.	3 110 . .	–14.13	–13.31	–13.02	. . .	. . .	. . .	. . .	. . .
Goods for processing: imports f.o.b.	3 150 . .	. . .	. . .	. . .	. . .	. . .	. . .	. . .	. . .
Repairs on goods	3 160 . .	. . .	. . .	. . .	. . .	. . .	. . .	. . .	. . .
Goods procured in ports by carriers	3 170 . .	. . .	. . .	. . .	. . .	. . .	. . .	. . .	. . .
Nonmonetary gold	3 180 . .	. . .	. . .	. . .	. . .	. . .	. . .	. . .	. . .
B. SERVICES	4 200 . .	–6.84	–4.03	–5.36	. . .	. . .	. . .	. . .	. . .
Total credit	2 200 . .	*1.55*	*4.48*	*3.66*	. . .	. . .	. . .	. . .	. . .
Total debit	3 200 . .	*–8.39*	*–8.51*	*–9.02*	. . .	. . .	. . .	. . .	. . .
Transportation services, credit	2 205 . .	**.39**	**.81**	**.45**	**. . .**	**. . .**	**. . .**	**. . .**	**. . .**
Passenger	2 205 BA	. . .	*.01*	*.01*	. . .	. . .	. . .	. . .	. . .
Freight	2 205 BB	*.01*	. . .	*.02*	. . .	. . .	. . .	. . .	. . .
Other	2 205 BC	*.38*	*.80*	*.42*	. . .	. . .	. . .	. . .	. . .
Sea transport, passenger	2 207 . .	. . .	. . .	. . .	. . .	. . .	. . .	. . .	. . .
Sea transport, freight	2 208 . .	.01	. . .	.02	. . .	. . .	. . .	. . .	. . .
Sea transport, other	2 209 . .	.38	.80	.42	. . .	. . .	. . .	. . .	. . .
Air transport, passenger	2 211 . .	. . .	. . .	. . .	. . .	. . .	. . .	. . .	. . .
Air transport, freight	2 212 . .	. . .	. . .	. . .	. . .	. . .	. . .	. . .	. . .
Air transport, other	2 213 . .	. . .	. . .	. . .	. . .	. . .	. . .	. . .	. . .
Other transport, passenger	2 215 . .	. . .	.01	.01	. . .	. . .	. . .	. . .	. . .
Other transport, freight	2 216 . .	. . .	. . .	. . .	. . .	. . .	. . .	. . .	. . .
Other transport, other	2 217 . .	. . .	. . .	. . .	. . .	. . .	. . .	. . .	. . .
Transportation services, debit	3 205 . .	**–5.62**	**–5.23**	**–5.42**	**. . .**	**. . .**	**. . .**	**. . .**	**. . .**
Passenger	3 205 BA	*–2.69*	*–2.78*	*–2.57*	. . .	. . .	. . .	. . .	. . .
Freight	3 205 BB	*–2.78*	*–2.45*	*–2.76*	. . .	. . .	. . .	. . .	. . .
Other	3 205 BC	*–.15*	. . .	*–.09*	. . .	. . .	. . .	. . .	. . .
Sea transport, passenger	3 207 . .	. . .	. . .	. . .	. . .	. . .	. . .	. . .	. . .
Sea transport, freight	3 208 . .	–2.78	–2.45	–2.76	. . .	. . .	. . .	. . .	. . .
Sea transport, other	3 209 . .	–.15	. . .	–.09	. . .	. . .	. . .	. . .	. . .
Air transport, passenger	3 211 . .	–2.69	–2.78	–2.57	. . .	. . .	. . .	. . .	. . .
Air transport, freight	3 212 . .	. . .	. . .	. . .	. . .	. . .	. . .	. . .	. . .
Air transport, other	3 213 . .	. . .	. . .	. . .	. . .	. . .	. . .	. . .	. . .
Other transport, passenger	3 215 . .	. . .	. . .	. . .	. . .	. . .	. . .	. . .	. . .
Other transport, freight	3 216 . .	. . .	. . .	. . .	. . .	. . .	. . .	. . .	. . .
Other transport, other	3 217 . .	. . .	. . .	. . .	. . .	. . .	. . .	. . .	. . .
Travel, credit	2 236 . .	**.92**	**1.32**	**1.67**	**. . .**	**. . .**	**. . .**	**. . .**	**. . .**
Business travel	2 237 . .	.31	.55	.48	. . .	. . .	. . .	. . .	. . .
Personal travel	2 240 . .	.61	.77	1.19	. . .	. . .	. . .	. . .	. . .
Travel, debit	3 236 . .	**–.96**	**–1.51**	**–1.92**	**. . .**	**. . .**	**. . .**	**. . .**	**. . .**
Business travel	3 237 . .	–.55	–1.12	–1.28	. . .	. . .	. . .	. . .	. . .
Personal travel	3 240 . .	–.40	–.39	–.64	. . .	. . .	. . .	. . .	. . .
Other services, credit	2 200 BA	**.24**	**2.35**	**1.54**	**. . .**	**. . .**	**. . .**	**. . .**	**. . .**
Communications	2 245 . .	.13	.13	.12	. . .	. . .	. . .	. . .	. . .
Construction	2 249 . .	. . .	. . .	. . .	. . .	. . .	. . .	. . .	. . .
Insurance	2 253 . .	. . .	. . .	. . .	. . .	. . .	. . .	. . .	. . .
Financial	2 260 . .	. . .	. . .	. . .	. . .	. . .	. . .	. . .	. . .
Computer and information	2 262 . .	. . .	. . .	. . .	. . .	. . .	. . .	. . .	. . .
Royalties and licence fees	2 266 . .	. . .	. . .	. . .	. . .	. . .	. . .	. . .	. . .
Other business services	2 268 . .	.02	.15	.65	. . .	. . .	. . .	. . .	. . .
Personal, cultural, and recreational	2 287 . .	. . .	. . .	. . .	. . .	. . .	. . .	. . .	. . .
Government, n.i.e.	2 291 . .	.09	2.07	.77	. . .	. . .	. . .	. . .	. . .
Other services, debit	3 200 BA	**–1.82**	**–1.77**	**–1.68**	**. . .**	**. . .**	**. . .**	**. . .**	**. . .**
Communications	3 245 . .	–.03	. . .	–.03	. . .	. . .	. . .	. . .	. . .
Construction	3 249 . .	. . .	. . .	. . .	. . .	. . .	. . .	. . .	. . .
Insurance	3 253 . .	–.31	–.27	–.31	. . .	. . .	. . .	. . .	. . .
Financial	3 260 . .	. . .	. . .	. . .	. . .	. . .	. . .	. . .	. . .
Computer and information	3 262 . .	. . .	. . .	. . .	. . .	. . .	. . .	. . .	. . .
Royalties and licence fees	3 266 . .	. . .	. . .	. . .	. . .	. . .	. . .	. . .	. . .
Other business services	3 268 . .	–.21	–.39	–.30	. . .	. . .	. . .	. . .	. . .
Personal, cultural, and recreational	3 287 . .	. . .	. . .	. . .	. . .	. . .	. . .	. . .	. . .
Government, n.i.e.	3 291 . .	–1.26	–1.11	–1.04	. . .	. . .	. . .	. . .	. . .

Table 2 (Continued). STANDARD PRESENTATION, 1988–95
(Millions of U.S. dollars)

	Code	1988	1989	1990	1991	1992	1993	1994	1995
C. INCOME	4 300	–.17	–.22	–.05	...	...	...	...	...
Total credit	2 300	*.43*	*.11*	*.26*	...	...	...	...	...
Total debit	3 300	*–.60*	*–.33*	*–.31*	...	...	...	...	...
Compensation of employees, credit	2 310	**.05**	**.06**	**.21**	...	...	...	...	...
Compensation of employees, debit	3 310	...	**–.01**	**–.03**	...	...	...	...	...
Investment income, credit	2 320	**.38**	**.05**	**.05**	...	...	...	...	...
Direct investment income	2 330	...	...	...	...	...	...	...	...
Dividends and distributed branch profits	2 332	...	...	...	...	...	...	...	...
Reinvested earnings and undistributed branch profits	2 333	...	...	...	...	...	...	...	...
Income on debt (interest)	2 334	...	...	...	...	...	...	...	...
Portfolio investment income	2 339	...	...	...	...	...	...	...	...
Income on equity	2 340	...	...	...	...	...	...	...	...
Income on bonds and notes	2 350	...	...	...	...	...	...	...	...
Income on money market instruments and financial derivatives	2 360	...	...	...	...	...	...	...	...
Other investment income	2 370	.38	.05	.05	...	...	...	...	...
Investment income, debit	3 320	**–.60**	**–.32**	**–.28**	...	...	...	...	...
Direct investment income	3 330	...	...	...	...	...	...	...	...
Dividends and distributed branch profits	3 332	...	...	...	...	...	...	...	...
Reinvested earnings and undistributed branch profits	3 333	...	...	...	...	...	...	...	...
Income on debt (interest)	3 334	...	...	...	...	...	...	...	...
Portfolio investment income	3 339	...	...	...	...	...	...	...	...
Income on equity	3 340	...	...	...	...	...	...	...	...
Income on bonds and notes	3 350	...	...	...	...	...	...	...	...
Income on money market instruments and financial derivatives	3 360	...	...	...	...	...	...	...	...
Other investment income	3 370	–.60	–.32	–.28	...	...	...	...	...
D. CURRENT TRANSFERS	4 379	.87	1.28	2.17	...	...	...	...	...
Credit	2 379	**1.66**	**2.42**	**2.96**	...	...	...	...	...
General government	2 380	1.35	2.29	2.55	...	...	...	...	...
Other sectors	2 390	.31	.13	.41	...	...	...	...	...
Workers' remittances	2 391	.01	.10	.10	...	...	...	...	...
Other current transfers	2 392	.29	.03	.31	...	...	...	...	...
Debit	3 379	**–.80**	**–1.14**	**–.79**	...	...	...	...	...
General government	3 380	–.50	–.77	–.45	...	...	...	...	...
Other sectors	3 390	–.29	–.37	–.34	...	...	...	...	...
Workers' remittances	3 391	–.18	–.08	–.06	...	...	...	...	...
Other current transfers	3 392	–.11	–.29	–.28	...	...	...	...	...
CAPITAL AND FINANCIAL ACCOUNT	4 996	**10.77**	**12.35**	**14.70**	...	...	...	...	...
CAPITAL ACCOUNT	4 994	...	...	...	...	...	...	...	...
Total credit	2 994	...	...	...	...	...	...	...	...
Total debit	3 994	...	...	...	...	...	...	...	...
Capital transfers, credit	2 400	...	...	...	...	...	...	...	...
General government	2 401	...	...	...	...	...	...	...	...
Debt forgiveness	2 402	...	...	...	...	...	...	...	...
Other capital transfers	2 410	...	...	...	...	...	...	...	...
Other sectors	2 430	...	...	...	...	...	...	...	...
Migrants' transfers	2 431	...	...	...	...	...	...	...	...
Debt forgiveness	2 432	...	...	...	...	...	...	...	...
Other capital transfers	2 440	...	...	...	...	...	...	...	...
Capital transfers, debit	3 400	...	...	...	...	...	...	...	...
General government	3 401	...	...	...	...	...	...	...	...
Debt forgiveness	3 402	...	...	...	...	...	...	...	...
Other capital transfers	3 410	...	...	...	...	...	...	...	...
Other sectors	3 430	...	...	...	...	...	...	...	...
Migrants' transfers	3 431	...	...	...	...	...	...	...	...
Debt forgiveness	3 432	...	...	...	...	...	...	...	...
Other capital transfers	3 440	...	...	...	...	...	...	...	...
Nonproduced nonfinancial assets, credit	2 480	...	...	...	...	...	...	...	...
Nonproduced nonfinancial assets, debit	3 480	...	...	...	...	...	...	...	...

Table 2 (Continued). STANDARD PRESENTATION, 1988–95
(Millions of U.S. dollars)

	Code	1988	1989	1990	1991	1992	1993	1994	1995
FINANCIAL ACCOUNT	4 995 . .	**10.77**	**12.35**	**14.70**	...	...	...	...	...
A. DIRECT INVESTMENT	4 500 . .	.20	...	...	...	...	...	...	...
Direct investment abroad	4 505 . .	**.20**	...	...	...	...	...	...	...
Equity capital	4 510 . .	.20	...	...	...	...	...	...	...
Claims on affiliated enterprises	4 515 . .	...	...	...	...	...	...	...	...
Liabilities to affiliated enterprises	4 520 . .	...	...	...	...	...	...	...	...
Reinvested earnings	4 525 . .	...	...	...	...	...	...	...	...
Other capital	4 530 . .	...	...	...	...	...	...	...	...
Claims on affiliated enterprises	4 535 . .	...	...	...	...	...	...	...	...
Liabilities to affiliated enterprises	4 540 . .	...	...	...	...	...	...	...	...
Direct investment in São Tomé and Príncipe	4 555 . .	...	...	...	...	...	...	...	...
Equity capital	4 560 . .	...	...	...	...	...	...	...	...
Claims on direct investors	4 565 . .	...	...	...	...	...	...	...	...
Liabilities to direct investors	4 570 . .	...	...	...	...	...	...	...	...
Reinvested earnings	4 575 . .	...	...	...	...	...	...	...	...
Other capital	4 580 . .	...	...	...	...	...	...	...	...
Claims on direct investors	4 585 . .	...	...	...	...	...	...	...	...
Liabilities to direct investors	4 590 . .	...	...	...	...	...	...	...	...
B. PORTFOLIO INVESTMENT	4 600 . .	...	...	...	...	...	...	...	...
Assets	4 602 . .	...	...	...	...	...	...	...	...
Equity securities	4 610 . .	...	...	...	...	...	...	...	...
Monetary authorities	4 611 . .	...	...	...	...	...	...	...	...
General government	4 612 . .	...	...	...	...	...	...	...	...
Banks	4 613 . .	...	...	...	...	...	...	...	...
Other sectors	4 614 . .	...	...	...	...	...	...	...	...
Debt securities	4 619 . .	...	...	...	...	...	...	...	...
Bonds and notes	4 620 . .	...	...	...	...	...	...	...	...
Monetary authorities	4 621 . .	...	...	...	...	...	...	...	...
General government	4 622 . .	...	...	...	...	...	...	...	...
Banks	4 623 . .	...	...	...	...	...	...	...	...
Other sectors	4 624 . .	...	...	...	...	...	...	...	...
Money market instruments	4 630 . .	...	...	...	...	...	...	...	...
Monetary authorities	4 631 . .	...	...	...	...	...	...	...	...
General government	4 632 . .	...	...	...	...	...	...	...	...
Banks	4 633 . .	...	...	...	...	...	...	...	...
Other sectors	4 634 . .	...	...	...	...	...	...	...	...
Financial derivatives	4 640 . .	...	...	...	...	...	...	...	...
Monetary authorities	4 641 . .	...	...	...	...	...	...	...	...
General government	4 642 . .	...	...	...	...	...	...	...	...
Banks	4 643 . .	...	...	...	...	...	...	...	...
Other sectors	4 644 . .	...	...	...	...	...	...	...	...
Liabilities	4 652 . .	...	...	...	...	...	...	...	...
Equity securities	4 660 . .	...	...	...	...	...	...	...	...
Banks	4 663 . .	...	...	...	...	...	...	...	...
Other sectors	4 664 . .	...	...	...	...	...	...	...	...
Debt securities	4 669 . .	...	...	...	...	...	...	...	...
Bonds and notes	4 670 . .	...	...	...	...	...	...	...	...
Monetary authorities	4 671 . .	...	...	...	...	...	...	...	...
General government	4 672 . .	...	...	...	...	...	...	...	...
Banks	4 673 . .	...	...	...	...	...	...	...	...
Other sectors	4 674 . .	...	...	...	...	...	...	...	...
Money market instruments	4 680 . .	...	...	...	...	...	...	...	...
Monetary authorities	4 681 . .	...	...	...	...	...	...	...	...
General government	4 682 . .	...	...	...	...	...	...	...	...
Banks	4 683 . .	...	...	...	...	...	...	...	...
Other sectors	4 684 . .	...	...	...	...	...	...	...	...
Financial derivatives	4 690 . .	...	...	...	...	...	...	...	...
Monetary authorities	4 691 . .	...	...	...	...	...	...	...	...
General government	4 692 . .	...	...	...	...	...	...	...	...
Banks	4 693 . .	...	...	...	...	...	...	...	...
Other sectors	4 694 . .	...	...	...	...	...	...	...	...

Table 2 (Concluded). STANDARD PRESENTATION, 1988–95
(Millions of U.S. dollars)

	Code	1988	1989	1990	1991	1992	1993	1994	1995
C. OTHER INVESTMENT	4 700	6.14	7.73	14.18	...	...	...	...	...
Assets	4 703	...	...	...	...	...	...	...	...
Trade credits	4 706	...	...	...	...	...	...	...	...
General government: long-term	4 708	...	...	...	...	...	...	...	...
General government: short-term	4 709	...	...	...	...	...	...	...	...
Other sectors: long-term	4 711	...	...	...	...	...	...	...	...
Other sectors: short-term	4 712	...	...	...	...	...	...	...	...
Loans	4 714	...	...	...	...	...	...	...	...
Monetary authorities: long-term	4 717	...	...	...	...	...	...	...	...
Monetary authorities: short-term	4 718	...	...	...	...	...	...	...	...
General government: long-term	4 720	...	...	...	...	...	...	...	...
General government: short-term	4 721	...	...	...	...	...	...	...	...
Banks: long-term	4 723	...	...	...	...	...	...	...	...
Banks: short-term	4 724	...	...	...	...	...	...	...	...
Other sectors: long-term	4 726	...	...	...	...	...	...	...	...
Other sectors: short-term	4 727	...	...	...	...	...	...	...	...
Currency and deposits	4 730	...	...	...	...	...	...	...	...
Monetary authorities	4 731	...	...	...	...	...	...	...	...
General government	4 732	...	...	...	...	...	...	...	...
Banks	4 733	...	...	...	...	...	...	...	...
Other sectors	4 734	...	...	...	...	...	...	...	...
Other assets	4 736	...	...	...	...	...	...	...	...
Monetary authorities: long-term	4 738	...	...	...	...	...	...	...	...
Monetary authorities: short-term	4 739	...	...	...	...	...	...	...	...
General government: long-term	4 741	...	...	...	...	...	...	...	...
General government: short-term	4 742	...	...	...	...	...	...	...	...
Banks: long-term	4 744	...	...	...	...	...	...	...	...
Banks: short-term	4 745	...	...	...	...	...	...	...	...
Other sectors: long-term	4 747	...	...	...	...	...	...	...	...
Other sectors: short-term	4 748	...	...	...	...	...	...	...	...
Liabilities	4 753	**6.14**	**7.73**	**14.18**	...	...	...	...	...
Trade credits	4 756	...	2.83	–3.65	...	...	...	...	...
General government: long-term	4 758	...	...	...	...	...	...	...	...
General government: short-term	4 759	...	...	...	...	...	...	...	...
Other sectors: long-term	4 761	...	...	...	...	...	...	...	...
Other sectors: short-term	4 762	...	2.83	–3.65	...	...	...	...	...
Loans	4 764	6.08	4.89	10.86	...	...	...	...	...
Use of Fund credit and loans from the Fund	4 766	...	.99	...	...	...	...	...	...
Monetary authorities: other long-term	4 767	...	...	...	...	...	...	...	...
Monetary authorities: short-term	4 768	...	...	...	...	...	...	...	...
General government: long-term	4 770	1.77	3.90	10.86	...	...	...	...	...
General government: short-term	4 771	...	...	...	...	...	...	...	...
Banks: long-term	4 773	...	...	...	...	...	...	...	...
Banks: short-term	4 774	...	...	...	...	...	...	...	...
Other sectors: long-term	4 776	...	...	...	...	...	...	...	...
Other sectors: short-term	4 777	4.32	...	...	...	...	...	...	...
Currency and deposits	4 780	...	...	...	...	...	...	...	...
Monetary authorities	4 781	...	...	...	...	...	...	...	...
General government	4 782	...	...	...	...	...	...	...	...
Banks	4 783	...	...	...	...	...	...	...	...
Other sectors	4 784	...	...	...	...	...	...	...	...
Other liabilities	4 786	.06	...	6.97	...	...	...	...	...
Monetary authorities: long-term	4 788	...	...	...	...	...	...	...	...
Monetary authorities: short-term	4 789	.06	...	6.60	...	...	...	...	...
General government: long-term	4 791	...	...	.37	...	...	...	...	...
General government: short-term	4 792	...	...	...	...	...	...	...	...
Banks: long-term	4 794	...	...	...	...	...	...	...	...
Banks: short-term	4 795	...	...	...	...	...	...	...	...
Other sectors: long-term	4 797	...	...	...	...	...	...	...	...
Other sectors: short-term	4 798	...	...	...	...	...	...	...	...
D. RESERVE ASSETS	4 800	4.44	4.62	.52	...	...	...	...	...
Monetary gold	4 810	...	...	...	...	...	...	...	...
Special drawing rights	4 820	...	–.01	.02	...	...	...	...	...
Reserve position in the Fund	4 830	...	...	...	...	...	...	...	...
Foreign exchange	4 840	4.44	4.64	.50	...	...	...	...	...
Other claims	4 880	...	...	...	...	...	...	...	...
NET ERRORS AND OMISSIONS	4 998	...	**–.98**	**–2.66**	...	...	...	...	...

Table 1. ANALYTIC PRESENTATION, 1988–95
(Millions of U.S. dollars)

	Code	1988	1989	1990	1991	1992	1993	1994	1995
A. Current Account [1]	4 993 Y.	**-7,340**	**-9,538**	**-4,152**	**-27,546**	**-17,740**	**-17,268**	**-10,480**	**-8,108**
Goods: exports f.o.b	2 100 . .	24,377	28,385	44,414	47,789	50,287	42,395	42,614	46,624
Goods: imports f.o.b	3 100 . .	-19,805	-19,231	-21,525	-25,971	-30,248	-25,873	-21,318	-25,071
Balance on Goods	4 100 . .	*4,571*	*9,154*	*22,889*	*21,818*	*20,039*	*16,522*	*21,296*	*21,553*
Services: credit	2 200 . .	2,294	2,510	3,031	2,908	3,466	3,283	3,347	3,480
Services: debit	3 200 . .	-14,935	-19,874	-22,414	-38,804	-31,782	-24,325	-17,892	-18,328
Balance on Goods and Services	4 991 . .	*-8,069*	*-8,211*	*3,506*	*-14,077*	*-8,276*	*-4,520*	*6,751*	*6,705*
Income: credit	2 300 . .	10,454	10,433	9,199	8,700	7,378	6,208	4,032	4,987
Income: debit	3 300 . .	-716	-1,017	-1,220	-1,933	-1,944	-2,300	-2,560	-2,184
Balance on Goods, Services, and Income	4 992 . .	*1,669*	*1,204*	*11,485*	*-7,311*	*-2,842*	*-611*	*8,223*	*9,508*
Current transfers: credit	2 379 Y.	...	...	...	...	...	...	...	...
Current transfers: debit	3 379 . .	-9,009	-10,742	-15,637	-20,235	-14,898	-16,657	-18,703	-17,616
B. Capital Account [1]	4 994 Y.	...	...	...	...	...	...	...	...
Capital account: credit	2 994 Y.	...	...	...	...	...	...	...	...
Capital account: debit	3 994 . .	...	...	...	...	...	...	...	...
Total, Groups A Plus B	4 010 . .	*-7,340*	*-9,538*	*-4,152*	*-27,546*	*-17,740*	*-17,268*	*-10,480*	*-8,108*
C. Financial Account [1]	4 995 X.	**5,821**	**6,030**	**-1,224**	**27,595**	**12,075**	**18,763**	**10,334**	**9,325**
Direct investment abroad	4 505 . .	...	...	...	...	...	...	...	...
Direct investment in Saudi Arabia	4 555 Y.	-328	-654	1,864	160	-79	1,369	350	-1,877
Portfolio investment assets	4 602 . .	3,060	-1,786	-3,342	471	-6,527	7,195	-1,509	4,025
Equity securities	4 610 . .	...	...	...	...	...	...	...	...
Debt securities	4 619 . .	3,060	-1,786	-3,342	471	-6,527	7,195	-1,509	4,025
Portfolio investment liabilities	4 652 Y.	...	...	...	...	...	...	...	...
Equity securities	4 660 Y.	...	...	...	...	...	...	...	...
Debt securities	4 669 Y.	...	...	...	...	...	...	...	...
Other investment assets	4 703 . .	1,957	6,903	1,437	27,562	18,473	7,903	10,997	7,035
Monetary authorities	4 703 .A	...	...	...	...	...	...	...	...
General government	4 703 .B	...	...	...	...	...	...	...	...
Banks	4 703 .C	-3,348	-1,095	-1,234	1,207	4,372	-2,259	3,704	94
Other sectors	4 703 .D	5,306	7,997	2,670	26,355	14,101	10,162	7,293	6,941
Other investment liabilities	4 753 X.	1,132	1,567	-1,183	-598	208	2,296	497	142
Monetary authorities	4 753 XA	...	...	...	...	...	...	...	...
General government	4 753 YB	...	...	...	...	...	...	...	...
Banks	4 753 YC	1,132	1,567	-1,183	-598	208	2,296	497	142
Other sectors	4 753 YD	...	...	...	...	...	...	...	...
Total, Groups A Through C	4 020 . .	*-1,519*	*-3,508*	*-5,377*	*49*	*-5,665*	*1,495*	*-146*	*1,217*
D. Net Errors and Omissions	4 998 . .	...	...	...	...	...	...	...	...
Total, Groups A Through D	4 030 . .	*-1,519*	*-3,508*	*-5,376*	*49*	*-5,664*	*1,495*	*-146*	*1,217*
E. Reserves and Related Items	4 040 . .	**1,519**	**3,508**	**5,376**	**-49**	**5,664**	**-1,495**	**146**	**-1,217**
Reserve assets	4 800 . .	1,519	3,508	5,376	-49	5,664	-1,495	146	-1,217
Use of Fund credit and loans	4 766 . .	...	...	...	...	...	...	...	...
Liabilities constituting foreign authorities' reserves	4 900 . .	...	...	...	...	...	...	...	...
Exceptional financing	4 920 . .	...	...	...	...	...	...	...	...
Conversion rates: riyals per U.S. dollar	0 101 . .	**3.7450**	**3.7450**	**3.7450**	**3.7450**	**3.7450**	**3.7450**	**3.7450**	**3.7450**

[1] Excludes components that have been classified in the categories of Group E.

Table 2. STANDARD PRESENTATION, 1988–95
(Millions of U.S. dollars)

	Code	1988	1989	1990	1991	1992	1993	1994	1995
CURRENT ACCOUNT	4 993 . .	**–7,340**	**–9,538**	**–4,152**	**–27,546**	**–17,740**	**–17,268**	**–10,480**	**–8,108**
A. GOODS	4 100 . .	4,571	9,154	22,889	21,818	20,039	16,522	21,296	21,553
Credit	2 100 . .	**24,377**	**28,385**	**44,414**	**47,789**	**50,287**	**42,395**	**42,614**	**46,624**
General merchandise: exports f.o.b.	2 110 . .	24,315	28,312	44,246	47,669	50,156	42,279	42,500	46,503
Goods for processing: exports f.o.b.	2 150 . .	. . .	. . .	. . .	. . .	. . .	. . .	. . .	. . .
Repairs on goods	2 160 . .	. . .	. . .	. . .	. . .	. . .	. . .	. . .	. . .
Goods procured in ports by carriers	2 170 . .	61	72	168	120	131	116	114	120
Nonmonetary gold	2 180 . .	. . .	. . .	. . .	. . .	. . .	. . .	. . .	. . .
Debit	3 100 . .	**–19,805**	**–19,231**	**–21,525**	**–25,971**	**–30,248**	**–25,873**	**–21,318**	**–25,071**
General merchandise: imports f.o.b.	3 110 . .	–19,805	–19,231	–21,525	–25,971	–30,248	–25,873	–21,318	–25,071
Goods for processing: imports f.o.b.	3 150 . .	. . .	. . .	. . .	. . .	. . .	. . .	. . .	. . .
Repairs on goods	3 160 . .	. . .	. . .	. . .	. . .	. . .	. . .	. . .	. . .
Goods procured in ports by carriers	3 170 . .	. . .	. . .	. . .	. . .	. . .	. . .	. . .	. . .
Nonmonetary gold	3 180 . .	. . .	. . .	. . .	. . .	. . .	. . .	. . .	. . .
B. SERVICES	4 200 . .	–12,641	–17,364	–19,383	–35,896	–28,315	–21,042	–14,545	–14,848
Total credit	2 200 . .	*2,294*	*2,510*	*3,031*	*2,908*	*3,466*	*3,283*	*3,347*	*3,480*
Total debit	3 200 . .	*–14,935*	*–19,874*	*–22,414*	*–38,804*	*–31,782*	*–24,325*	*–17,892*	*–18,328*
Transportation services, credit	2 205 . .	. . .	. . .	. . .	. . .	. . .	. . .	. . .	. . .
Passenger	2 205 BA	. . .	. . .	. . .	. . .	. . .	. . .	. . .	. . .
Freight	2 205 BB	. . .	. . .	. . .	. . .	. . .	. . .	. . .	. . .
Other	2 205 BC	. . .	. . .	. . .	. . .	. . .	. . .	. . .	. . .
Sea transport, passenger	2 207 . .	. . .	. . .	. . .	. . .	. . .	. . .	. . .	. . .
Sea transport, freight	2 208 . .	. . .	. . .	. . .	. . .	. . .	. . .	. . .	. . .
Sea transport, other	2 209 . .	. . .	. . .	. . .	. . .	. . .	. . .	. . .	. . .
Air transport, passenger	2 211 . .	. . .	. . .	. . .	. . .	. . .	. . .	. . .	. . .
Air transport, freight	2 212 . .	. . .	. . .	. . .	. . .	. . .	. . .	. . .	. . .
Air transport, other	2 213 . .	. . .	. . .	. . .	. . .	. . .	. . .	. . .	. . .
Other transport, passenger	2 215 . .	. . .	. . .	. . .	. . .	. . .	. . .	. . .	. . .
Other transport, freight	2 216 . .	. . .	. . .	. . .	. . .	. . .	. . .	. . .	. . .
Other transport, other	2 217 . .	. . .	. . .	. . .	. . .	. . .	. . .	. . .	. . .
Transportation services, debit	3 205 . .	**–1,760**	**–1,712**	**–2,296**	**–2,774**	**–2,722**	**–2,096**	**–1,823**	**–2,144**
Passenger	3 205 BA	. . .	. . .	. . .	. . .	. . .	. . .	. . .	. . .
Freight	3 205 BB	*–1,760*	*–1,712*	*–2,296*	*–2,774*	*–2,722*	*–2,096*	*–1,823*	*–2,144*
Other	3 205 BC	. . .	. . .	. . .	. . .	. . .	. . .	. . .	. . .
Sea transport, passenger	3 207 . .	. . .	. . .	. . .	. . .	. . .	. . .	. . .	. . .
Sea transport, freight	3 208 . .	–1,760	–1,712	–2,296	–2,774	–2,722	–2,096	–1,823	–2,144
Sea transport, other	3 209 . .	. . .	. . .	. . .	. . .	. . .	. . .	. . .	. . .
Air transport, passenger	3 211 . .	. . .	. . .	. . .	. . .	. . .	. . .	. . .	. . .
Air transport, freight	3 212 . .	. . .	. . .	. . .	. . .	. . .	. . .	. . .	. . .
Air transport, other	3 213 . .	. . .	. . .	. . .	. . .	. . .	. . .	. . .	. . .
Other transport, passenger	3 215 . .	. . .	. . .	. . .	. . .	. . .	. . .	. . .	. . .
Other transport, freight	3 216 . .	. . .	. . .	. . .	. . .	. . .	. . .	. . .	. . .
Other transport, other	3 217 . .	. . .	. . .	. . .	. . .	. . .	. . .	. . .	. . .
Travel, credit	2 236 . .	. . .	. . .	. . .	. . .	. . .	. . .	. . .	. . .
Business travel	2 237 . .	. . .	. . .	. . .	. . .	. . .	. . .	. . .	. . .
Personal travel	2 240 . .	. . .	. . .	. . .	. . .	. . .	. . .	. . .	. . .
Travel, debit	3 236 . .	. . .	. . .	. . .	. . .	. . .	. . .	. . .	. . .
Business travel	3 237 . .	. . .	. . .	. . .	. . .	. . .	. . .	. . .	. . .
Personal travel	3 240 . .	. . .	. . .	. . .	. . .	. . .	. . .	. . .	. . .
Other services, credit	2 200 BA	**2,294**	**2,510**	**3,031**	**2,908**	**3,466**	**3,283**	**3,347**	**3,480**
Communications	2 245 . .	. . .	. . .	. . .	. . .	. . .	. . .	. . .	. . .
Construction	2 249 . .	. . .	. . .	. . .	. . .	. . .	. . .	. . .	. . .
Insurance	2 253 . .	. . .	. . .	. . .	. . .	. . .	. . .	. . .	. . .
Financial	2 260 . .	. . .	. . .	. . .	. . .	. . .	. . .	. . .	. . .
Computer and information	2 262 . .	. . .	. . .	. . .	. . .	. . .	. . .	. . .	. . .
Royalties and licence fees	2 266 . .	. . .	. . .	. . .	. . .	. . .	. . .	. . .	. . .
Other business services	2 268 . .	2,294	2,510	3,031	2,908	3,466	3,283	3,347	3,480
Personal, cultural, and recreational	2 287 . .	. . .	. . .	. . .	. . .	. . .	. . .	. . .	. . .
Government, n.i.e.	2 291 . .	. . .	. . .	. . .	. . .	. . .	. . .	. . .	. . .
Other services, debit	3 200 BA	**–13,175**	**–18,163**	**–20,117**	**–36,029**	**–29,059**	**–22,229**	**–16,069**	**–16,185**
Communications	3 245 . .	. . .	. . .	. . .	. . .	. . .	. . .	. . .	. . .
Construction	3 249 . .	. . .	. . .	. . .	. . .	. . .	. . .	. . .	. . .
Insurance	3 253 . .	–222	–211	–283	–342	–302	–233	–203	–238
Financial	3 260 . .	. . .	. . .	. . .	. . .	. . .	. . .	. . .	. . .
Computer and information	3 262 . .	. . .	. . .	. . .	. . .	. . .	. . .	. . .	. . .
Royalties and licence fees	3 266 . .	. . .	. . .	. . .	. . .	. . .	. . .	. . .	. . .
Other business services	3 268 . .	–5,570	–7,231	–10,115	–11,239	–12,152	–11,599	–6,902	–6,244
Personal, cultural, and recreational	3 287 . .	. . .	. . .	. . .	. . .	. . .	. . .	. . .	. . .
Government, n.i.e.	3 291 . .	–7,383	–10,721	–9,720	–24,449	–16,604	–10,397	–8,964	–9,702

Table 2 (Continued). STANDARD PRESENTATION, 1988–95
(Millions of U.S. dollars)

	Code		1988	1989	1990	1991	1992	1993	1994	1995
C. INCOME	4 300	. .	9,738	9,415	7,979	6,766	5,433	3,908	1,472	2,803
Total credit	2 300	. .	*10,454*	*10,433*	*9,199*	*8,700*	*7,378*	*6,208*	*4,032*	*4,987*
Total debit	3 300	. .	*–716*	*–1,017*	*–1,220*	*–1,933*	*–1,944*	*–2,300*	*–2,560*	*–2,184*
Compensation of employees, credit	2 310	. .	**. . .**	**. . .**	**. . .**	**. . .**	**. . .**	**. . .**	**. . .**	**. . .**
Compensation of employees, debit	3 310	. .	**. . .**	**. . .**	**. . .**	**. . .**	**. . .**	**. . .**	**. . .**	**. . .**
Investment income, credit	2 320	. .	**10,454**	**10,433**	**9,199**	**8,700**	**7,378**	**6,208**	**4,032**	**4,987**
Direct investment income	2 330	. .	. . .	. . .	. . .	. . .	. . .	. . .	. . .	. . .
Dividends and distributed branch profits	2 332	. .	. . .	. . .	. . .	. . .	. . .	. . .	. . .	. . .
Reinvested earnings and undistributed branch profits	2 333	. .	. . .	. . .	. . .	. . .	. . .	. . .	. . .	. . .
Income on debt (interest)	2 334	. .	. . .	. . .	. . .	. . .	. . .	. . .	. . .	. . .
Portfolio investment income	2 339	. .	. . .	. . .	. . .	. . .	. . .	. . .	. . .	. . .
Income on equity	2 340	. .	. . .	. . .	. . .	. . .	. . .	. . .	. . .	. . .
Income on bonds and notes	2 350	. .	. . .	. . .	. . .	. . .	. . .	. . .	. . .	. . .
Income on money market instruments and financial derivatives	2 360	. .	. . .	. . .	. . .	. . .	. . .	. . .	. . .	. . .
Other investment income	2 370	. .	10,454	10,433	9,199	8,700	7,378	6,208	4,032	4,987
Investment income, debit	3 320	. .	**–716**	**–1,017**	**–1,220**	**–1,933**	**–1,944**	**–2,300**	**–2,560**	**–2,184**
Direct investment income	3 330	. .	–716	–1,017	–1,220	–1,933	–1,944	–2,300	–2,560	–2,184
Dividends and distributed branch profits	3 332	. .	–716	–1,017	–1,220	–1,933	–1,944	–2,300	–2,560	–2,184
Reinvested earnings and undistributed branch profits	3 333	. .	. . .	. . .	. . .	. . .	. . .	. . .	. . .	. . .
Income on debt (interest)	3 334	. .	. . .	. . .	. . .	. . .	. . .	. . .	. . .	. . .
Portfolio investment income	3 339	. .	. . .	. . .	. . .	. . .	. . .	. . .	. . .	. . .
Income on equity	3 340	. .	. . .	. . .	. . .	. . .	. . .	. . .	. . .	. . .
Income on bonds and notes	3 350	. .	. . .	. . .	. . .	. . .	. . .	. . .	. . .	. . .
Income on money market instruments and financial derivatives	3 360	. .	. . .	. . .	. . .	. . .	. . .	. . .	. . .	. . .
Other investment income	3 370	. .	. . .	. . .	. . .	. . .	. . .	. . .	. . .	. . .
D. CURRENT TRANSFERS	4 379	. .	–9,009	–10,742	–15,637	–20,235	–14,898	–16,657	–18,703	–17,616
Credit	2 379	. .	**. . .**	**. . .**	**. . .**	**. . .**	**. . .**	**. . .**	**. . .**	**. . .**
General government	2 380	. .	. . .	. . .	. . .	. . .	. . .	. . .	. . .	. . .
Other sectors	2 390	. .	. . .	. . .	. . .	. . .	. . .	. . .	. . .	. . .
Workers' remittances	2 391	. .	. . .	. . .	. . .	. . .	. . .	. . .	. . .	. . .
Other current transfers	2 392	. .	. . .	. . .	. . .	. . .	. . .	. . .	. . .	. . .
Debit	3 379	. .	**–9,009**	**–10,742**	**–15,637**	**–20,235**	**–14,898**	**–16,657**	**–18,703**	**–17,616**
General government	3 380	. .	–2,499	–2,200	–4,401	–6,489	–1,501	–940	–601	–1,000
Other sectors	3 390	. .	–6,510	–8,542	–11,236	–13,746	–13,397	–15,717	–18,102	–16,616
Workers' remittances	3 391	. .	–6,510	–8,542	–11,236	–13,746	–13,397	–15,717	–18,102	–16,616
Other current transfers	3 392	. .	. . .	. . .	. . .	. . .	. . .	. . .	. . .	. . .
CAPITAL AND FINANCIAL ACCOUNT	4 996	. .	**7,340**	**9,538**	**4,152**	**27,546**	**17,740**	**17,268**	**10,480**	**8,108**
CAPITAL ACCOUNT	4 994	. .	**. . .**	**. . .**	**. . .**	**. . .**	**. . .**	**. . .**	**. . .**	**. . .**
Total credit	2 994	. .	. . .	. . .	. . .	. . .	. . .	. . .	. . .	. . .
Total debit	3 994	. .	. . .	. . .	. . .	. . .	. . .	. . .	. . .	. . .
Capital transfers, credit	2 400	. .	**. . .**	**. . .**	**. . .**	**. . .**	**. . .**	**. . .**	**. . .**	**. . .**
General government	2 401	. .	. . .	. . .	. . .	. . .	. . .	. . .	. . .	. . .
Debt forgiveness	2 402	. .	. . .	. . .	. . .	. . .	. . .	. . .	. . .	. . .
Other capital transfers	2 410	. .	. . .	. . .	. . .	. . .	. . .	. . .	. . .	. . .
Other sectors	2 430	. .	. . .	. . .	. . .	. . .	. . .	. . .	. . .	. . .
Migrants' transfers	2 431	. .	. . .	. . .	. . .	. . .	. . .	. . .	. . .	. . .
Debt forgiveness	2 432	. .	. . .	. . .	. . .	. . .	. . .	. . .	. . .	. . .
Other capital transfers	2 440	. .	. . .	. . .	. . .	. . .	. . .	. . .	. . .	. . .
Capital transfers, debit	3 400	. .	**. . .**	**. . .**	**. . .**	**. . .**	**. . .**	**. . .**	**. . .**	**. . .**
General government	3 401	. .	. . .	. . .	. . .	. . .	. . .	. . .	. . .	. . .
Debt forgiveness	3 402	. .	. . .	. . .	. . .	. . .	. . .	. . .	. . .	. . .
Other capital transfers	3 410	. .	. . .	. . .	. . .	. . .	. . .	. . .	. . .	. . .
Other sectors	3 430	. .	. . .	. . .	. . .	. . .	. . .	. . .	. . .	. . .
Migrants' transfers	3 431	. .	. . .	. . .	. . .	. . .	. . .	. . .	. . .	. . .
Debt forgiveness	3 432	. .	. . .	. . .	. . .	. . .	. . .	. . .	. . .	. . .
Other capital transfers	3 440	. .	. . .	. . .	. . .	. . .	. . .	. . .	. . .	. . .
Nonproduced nonfinancial assets, credit	2 480	. .	**. . .**	**. . .**	**. . .**	**. . .**	**. . .**	**. . .**	**. . .**	**. . .**
Nonproduced nonfinancial assets, debit	3 480	. .	**. . .**	**. . .**	**. . .**	**. . .**	**. . .**	**. . .**	**. . .**	**. . .**

Table 2 (Continued). STANDARD PRESENTATION, 1988–95
(Millions of U.S. dollars)

	Code		1988	1989	1990	1991	1992	1993	1994	1995
FINANCIAL ACCOUNT	4 995	. .	**7,340**	**9,538**	**4,152**	**27,546**	**17,740**	**17,268**	**10,480**	**8,108**
A. DIRECT INVESTMENT	4 500	. .	–328	–654	1,864	160	–79	1,369	350	–1,877
Direct investment abroad	4 505	. .	**. . .**	**. . .**	**. . .**	**. . .**	**. . .**	**. . .**	**. . .**	**. . .**
Equity capital	4 510	. .	. . .	. . .	. . .	. . .	. . .	. . .	. . .	. . .
Claims on affiliated enterprises	4 515	. .	. . .	. . .	. . .	. . .	. . .	. . .	. . .	. . .
Liabilities to affiliated enterprises	4 520	. .	. . .	. . .	. . .	. . .	. . .	. . .	. . .	. . .
Reinvested earnings	4 525	. .	. . .	. . .	. . .	. . .	. . .	. . .	. . .	. . .
Other capital	4 530	. .	. . .	. . .	. . .	. . .	. . .	. . .	. . .	. . .
Claims on affiliated enterprises	4 535	. .	. . .	. . .	. . .	. . .	. . .	. . .	. . .	. . .
Liabilities to affiliated enterprises	4 540	. .	. . .	. . .	. . .	. . .	. . .	. . .	. . .	. . .
Direct investment in Saudi Arabia	4 555	. .	**–328**	**–654**	**1,864**	**160**	**–79**	**1,369**	**350**	**–1,877**
Equity capital	4 560	. .	. . .	. . .	. . .	. . .	. . .	. . .	. . .	. . .
Claims on direct investors	4 565	. .	. . .	. . .	. . .	. . .	. . .	. . .	. . .	. . .
Liabilities to direct investors	4 570	. .	. . .	. . .	. . .	. . .	. . .	. . .	. . .	. . .
Reinvested earnings	4 575	. .	. . .	. . .	. . .	. . .	. . .	. . .	. . .	. . .
Other capital	4 580	. .	–328	–654	1,864	160	–79	1,369	350	–1,877
Claims on direct investors	4 585	. .	. . .	. . .	. . .	. . .	. . .	. . .	. . .	. . .
Liabilities to direct investors	4 590	. .	. . .	. . .	. . .	. . .	. . .	. . .	. . .	. . .
B. PORTFOLIO INVESTMENT	4 600	. .	3,060	–1,786	–3,342	471	–6,527	7,195	–1,509	4,025
Assets	4 602	. .	**3,060**	**–1,786**	**–3,342**	**471**	**–6,527**	**7,195**	**–1,509**	**4,025**
Equity securities	4 610	. .	. . .	. . .	. . .	. . .	. . .	. . .	. . .	. . .
Monetary authorities	4 611	. .	. . .	. . .	. . .	. . .	. . .	. . .	. . .	. . .
General government	4 612	. .	. . .	. . .	. . .	. . .	. . .	. . .	. . .	. . .
Banks	4 613	. .	. . .	. . .	. . .	. . .	. . .	. . .	. . .	. . .
Other sectors	4 614	. .	. . .	. . .	. . .	. . .	. . .	. . .	. . .	. . .
Debt securities	4 619	. .	3,060	–1,786	–3,342	471	–6,527	7,195	–1,509	4,025
Bonds and notes	4 620	. .	3,060	–1,786	–3,342	471	–6,527	7,195	–1,509	4,025
Monetary authorities	4 621	. .	. . .	. . .	. . .	. . .	. . .	. . .	. . .	. . .
General government	4 622	. .	3,060	–1,786	–3,342	471	–6,527	7,195	–1,509	4,025
Banks	4 623	. .	. . .	. . .	. . .	. . .	. . .	. . .	. . .	. . .
Other sectors	4 624	. .	. . .	. . .	. . .	. . .	. . .	. . .	. . .	. . .
Money market instruments	4 630	. .	. . .	. . .	. . .	. . .	. . .	. . .	. . .	. . .
Monetary authorities	4 631	. .	. . .	. . .	. . .	. . .	. . .	. . .	. . .	. . .
General government	4 632	. .	. . .	. . .	. . .	. . .	. . .	. . .	. . .	. . .
Banks	4 633	. .	. . .	. . .	. . .	. . .	. . .	. . .	. . .	. . .
Other sectors	4 634	. .	. . .	. . .	. . .	. . .	. . .	. . .	. . .	. . .
Financial derivatives	4 640	. .	. . .	. . .	. . .	. . .	. . .	. . .	. . .	. . .
Monetary authorities	4 641	. .	. . .	. . .	. . .	. . .	. . .	. . .	. . .	. . .
General government	4 642	. .	. . .	. . .	. . .	. . .	. . .	. . .	. . .	. . .
Banks	4 643	. .	. . .	. . .	. . .	. . .	. . .	. . .	. . .	. . .
Other sectors	4 644	. .	. . .	. . .	. . .	. . .	. . .	. . .	. . .	. . .
Liabilities	4 652	. .	**. . .**	**. . .**	**. . .**	**. . .**	**. . .**	**. . .**	**. . .**	**. . .**
Equity securities	4 660	. .	. . .	. . .	. . .	. . .	. . .	. . .	. . .	. . .
Banks	4 663	. .	. . .	. . .	. . .	. . .	. . .	. . .	. . .	. . .
Other sectors	4 664	. .	. . .	. . .	. . .	. . .	. . .	. . .	. . .	. . .
Debt securities	4 669	. .	. . .	. . .	. . .	. . .	. . .	. . .	. . .	. . .
Bonds and notes	4 670	. .	. . .	. . .	. . .	. . .	. . .	. . .	. . .	. . .
Monetary authorities	4 671	. .	. . .	. . .	. . .	. . .	. . .	. . .	. . .	. . .
General government	4 672	. .	. . .	. . .	. . .	. . .	. . .	. . .	. . .	. . .
Banks	4 673	. .	. . .	. . .	. . .	. . .	. . .	. . .	. . .	. . .
Other sectors	4 674	. .	. . .	. . .	. . .	. . .	. . .	. . .	. . .	. . .
Money market instruments	4 680	. .	. . .	. . .	. . .	. . .	. . .	. . .	. . .	. . .
Monetary authorities	4 681	. .	. . .	. . .	. . .	. . .	. . .	. . .	. . .	. . .
General government	4 682	. .	. . .	. . .	. . .	. . .	. . .	. . .	. . .	. . .
Banks	4 683	. .	. . .	. . .	. . .	. . .	. . .	. . .	. . .	. . .
Other sectors	4 684	. .	. . .	. . .	. . .	. . .	. . .	. . .	. . .	. . .
Financial derivatives	4 690	. .	. . .	. . .	. . .	. . .	. . .	. . .	. . .	. . .
Monetary authorities	4 691	. .	. . .	. . .	. . .	. . .	. . .	. . .	. . .	. . .
General government	4 692	. .	. . .	. . .	. . .	. . .	. . .	. . .	. . .	. . .
Banks	4 693	. .	. . .	. . .	. . .	. . .	. . .	. . .	. . .	. . .
Other sectors	4 694	. .	. . .	. . .	. . .	. . .	. . .	. . .	. . .	. . .

Table 2 (Concluded). STANDARD PRESENTATION, 1988–95
(Millions of U.S. dollars)

	Code	1988	1989	1990	1991	1992	1993	1994	1995
C. OTHER INVESTMENT	4 700 . .	3,089	8,470	254	26,964	18,681	10,199	11,493	7,177
Assets	4 703 . .	**1,957**	**6,903**	**1,437**	**27,562**	**18,473**	**7,903**	**10,997**	**7,035**
Trade credits	4 706 . .	...	...	...	...	...	...	...	...
General government: long-term	4 708 . .	...	...	...	...	...	...	...	...
General government: short-term	4 709 . .	...	...	...	...	...	...	...	...
Other sectors: long-term	4 711 . .	...	...	...	...	...	...	...	...
Other sectors: short-term	4 712 . .	...	...	...	...	...	...	...	...
Loans	4 714 . .	...	...	...	...	...	...	...	...
Monetary authorities: long-term	4 717 . .	...	...	...	...	...	...	...	...
Monetary authorities: short-term	4 718 . .	...	...	...	...	...	...	...	...
General government: long-term	4 720 . .	...	...	...	...	...	...	...	...
General government: short-term	4 721 . .	...	...	...	...	...	...	...	...
Banks: long-term	4 723 . .	...	...	...	...	...	...	...	...
Banks: short-term	4 724 . .	...	...	...	...	...	...	...	...
Other sectors: long-term	4 726 . .	...	...	...	...	...	...	...	...
Other sectors: short-term	4 727 . .	...	...	...	...	...	...	...	...
Currency and deposits	4 730 . .	1,957	6,903	1,437	27,562	18,473	7,903	10,997	7,035
Monetary authorities	4 731 . .	...	...	...	...	...	...	...	...
General government	4 732 . .	...	...	...	...	...	...	...	...
Banks	4 733 . .	–3,348	–1,095	–1,234	1,207	4,372	–2,259	3,704	94
Other sectors	4 734 . .	5,306	7,997	2,670	26,355	14,101	10,162	7,293	6,941
Other assets	4 736 . .	...	...	...	...	...	...	...	...
Monetary authorities: long-term	4 738 . .	...	...	...	...	...	...	...	...
Monetary authorities: short-term	4 739 . .	...	...	...	...	...	...	...	...
General government: long-term	4 741 . .	...	...	...	...	...	...	...	...
General government: short-term	4 742 . .	...	...	...	...	...	...	...	...
Banks: long-term	4 744 . .	...	...	...	...	...	...	...	...
Banks: short-term	4 745 . .	...	...	...	...	...	...	...	...
Other sectors: long-term	4 747 . .	...	...	...	...	...	...	...	...
Other sectors: short-term	4 748 . .	...	...	...	...	...	...	...	...
Liabilities	4 753 . .	**1,132**	**1,567**	**–1,183**	**–598**	**208**	**2,296**	**497**	**142**
Trade credits	4 756 . .	...	...	...	...	...	...	...	...
General government: long-term	4 758 . .	...	...	...	...	...	...	...	...
General government: short-term	4 759 . .	...	...	...	...	...	...	...	...
Other sectors: long-term	4 761 . .	...	...	...	...	...	...	...	...
Other sectors: short-term	4 762 . .	...	...	...	...	...	...	...	...
Loans	4 764 . .	...	...	...	...	...	...	...	...
Use of Fund credit and loans from the Fund	4 766 . .	...	...	...	...	...	...	...	...
Monetary authorities: other long-term	4 767 . .	...	...	...	...	...	...	...	...
Monetary authorities: short-term	4 768 . .	...	...	...	...	...	...	...	...
General government: long-term	4 770 . .	...	...	...	...	...	...	...	...
General government: short-term	4 771 . .	...	...	...	...	...	...	...	...
Banks: long-term	4 773 . .	...	...	...	...	...	...	...	...
Banks: short-term	4 774 . .	...	...	...	...	...	...	...	...
Other sectors: long-term	4 776 . .	...	...	...	...	...	...	...	...
Other sectors: short-term	4 777 . .	...	...	...	...	...	...	...	...
Currency and deposits	4 780 . .	1,132	1,567	–1,183	–598	208	2,296	497	142
Monetary authorities	4 781 . .	...	...	...	...	...	...	...	...
General government	4 782 . .	...	...	...	...	...	...	...	...
Banks	4 783 . .	1,132	1,567	–1,183	–598	208	2,296	497	142
Other sectors	4 784 . .	...	...	...	...	...	...	...	...
Other liabilities	4 786 . .	...	...	...	...	...	...	...	...
Monetary authorities: long-term	4 788 . .	...	...	...	...	...	...	...	...
Monetary authorities: short-term	4 789 . .	...	...	...	...	...	...	...	...
General government: long-term	4 791 . .	...	...	...	...	...	...	...	...
General government: short-term	4 792 . .	...	...	...	...	...	...	...	...
Banks: long-term	4 794 . .	...	...	...	...	...	...	...	...
Banks: short-term	4 795 . .	...	...	...	...	...	...	...	...
Other sectors: long-term	4 797 . .	...	...	...	...	...	...	...	...
Other sectors: short-term	4 798 . .	...	...	...	...	...	...	...	...
D. RESERVE ASSETS	4 800 . .	1,519	3,508	5,376	–49	5,664	–1,495	146	–1,217
Monetary gold	4 810 . .	...	...	...	...	...	...	...	...
Special drawing rights	4 820 . .	–51	–91	541	–5	–197	–285	–21	–49
Reserve position in the Fund	4 830 . .	2,003	3,666	2,131	1,111	687	–90	373	45
Foreign exchange	4 840 . .	–433	–67	2,705	–1,156	5,175	–1,121	–206	–1,213
Other claims	4 880 . .	...	...	...	...	...	...	...	...
NET ERRORS AND OMISSIONS	4 998 . .	...	...	...	...	...	...	...	...

Table 1: ANALYTIC PRESENTATION, 1988–95
(Millions of U.S. dollars)

	Code	1988	1989	1990	1991	1992	1993	1994	1995
A. Current Account [1]	4 993 Y.	**–257.5**	**–199.8**	**–191.6**	**–200.0**	**–218.5**	**–279.2**	**3.2**	**...**
Goods: exports f.o.b.	2 100 . .	713.2	804.1	937.9	848.5	860.6	736.8	818.8	...
Goods: imports f.o.b.	3 100 . .	–956.0	–1,004.1	–1,164.3	–1,114.0	–1,191.8	–1,086.7	–1,022.0	...
Balance on Goods	4 100 . .	*–242.8*	*–199.9*	*–226.4*	*–265.5*	*–331.1*	*–349.9*	*–203.2*	...
Services: credit	2 200 . .	434.1	433.7	561.3	500.8	532.8	462.1	439.0	...
Services: debit	3 200 . .	–519.3	–514.5	–675.6	–622.6	–654.2	–581.3	–492.7	...
Balance on Goods and Services	4 991 . .	*–328.0*	*–280.7*	*–340.7*	*–387.3*	*–452.5*	*–469.1*	*–256.9*	...
Income: credit	2 300 . .	14.5	21.0	37.8	33.1	45.1	34.6	36.7	...
Income: debit	3 300 . .	–222.3	–219.5	–213.2	–175.9	–173.0	–162.3	–164.5	...
Balance on Goods, Services, and Income	4 992 . .	*–535.8*	*–479.1*	*–516.2*	*–530.1*	*–580.4*	*–596.8*	*–384.7*	...
Current transfers: credit	2 379 Y.	387.7	385.0	454.5	462.7	489.0	432.9	467.5	...
Current transfers: debit	3 379 . .	–109.5	–105.7	–129.9	–132.6	–127.1	–115.4	–79.6	...
B. Capital Account [1]	4 994 Y.	**...**	**...**	**...**	**...**	**...**	**...**	**...**	**...**
Capital account: credit	2 994 Y.	...	...	...	...	...	...	...	...
Capital account: debit	3 994 . .	...	...	...	...	...	...	...	...
Total, Groups A Plus B	4 010 . .	*–257.5*	*–199.8*	*–191.6*	*–200.0*	*–218.5*	*–279.2*	*3.2*	...
C. Financial Account [1]	4 995 X.	**163.7**	**24.2**	**55.6**	**16.7**	**113.4**	**129.4**	**27.9**	**...**
Direct investment abroad	4 505 . .	–13.8	–8.6	9.5	19.1	–51.3	–.3	–17.4	...
Direct investment in Senegal	4 555 Y.	14.9	26.8	56.9	–7.6	21.4	–.8	66.9	...
Portfolio investment assets	4 602 . .	–.1	...	–1.0	...	...	...	–1.5	...
Equity securities	4 610 . .	–.1	...	–1.0	...	...	...	–1.5	...
Debt securities	4 619 . .	...	...	...	...	...	...	...	...
Portfolio investment liabilities	4 652 Y.	1.2	.1	1.6	6.5	.7	5.8	.5	...
Equity securities	4 660 Y.	1.2	–.7	1.3	–.2	.9	6.1	.5	...
Debt securities	4 669 Y.	...	.8	.3	6.7	–.2	–.3	...	...
Other investment assets	4 703 . .	–41.8	–15.1	57.8	–34.2	–24.9	4.1	–92.5	...
Monetary authorities	4 703 .A	...	...	...	...	...	...	...	...
General government	4 703 .B	.1	...	.3	...	–.7	–.6	...	...
Banks	4 703 .C	–28.9	–15.4	56.7	–31.1	–24.4	–2.6	–108.8	...
Other sectors	4 703 .D	–13.1	.3	.8	–3.1	.2	7.4	16.3	...
Other investment liabilities	4 753 X.	203.2	20.9	–69.3	32.9	167.6	120.7	72.0	...
Monetary authorities	4 753 XA	121.1	–100.6	–12.2	–42.7	34.4	135.3	–125.0	...
General government	4 753 YB	96.9	106.8	82.9	87.3	173.0	69.0	118.9	...
Banks	4 753 YC	47.2	32.4	–94.9	13.4	–23.4	–6.6	9.8	...
Other sectors	4 753 YD	–61.9	–17.6	–45.2	–25.1	–16.5	–77.0	68.3	...
Total, Groups A Through C	4 020 . .	*–93.8*	*–175.6*	*–136.0*	*–183.3*	*–105.1*	*–149.8*	*31.1*	...
D. Net Errors and Omissions	4 998 . .	**–21.0**	**12.3**	**–1.3**	**3.1**	**–19.6**	**8.4**	**–57.2**	**...**
Total, Groups A Through D	4 030 . .	*–114.8*	*–163.3*	*–137.3*	*–180.2*	*–124.7*	*–141.5*	*–26.0*	...
E. Reserves and Related Items	4 040 . .	**114.8**	**163.3**	**137.3**	**180.2**	**124.7**	**141.5**	**26.0**	**...**
Reserve assets	4 800 . .	–2.3	–7.8	9.8	–2.1	.1	8.5	–170.1	...
Use of Fund credit and loans	4 766 . .	–6.5	6.2	–27.7	10.6	–44.2	–27.4	38.9	...
Liabilities constituting foreign authorities' reserves	4 900 . .	9.3	–9.8	–.2	.1	–.2	...	48.8	...
Exceptional financing	4 920 . .	114.3	174.8	155.4	171.6	169.0	160.3	108.4	...
Conversion rates: CFA francs per U.S. dollar	0 101 . .	**297.85**	**319.01**	**272.26**	**282.11**	**264.69**	**283.16**	**555.20**	**499.15**

[1] Excludes components that have been classified in the categories of Group E.

Table 2. STANDARD PRESENTATION, 1988–95
(Millions of U.S. dollars)

	Code	1988	1989	1990	1991	1992	1993	1994	1995
CURRENT ACCOUNT	4 993 . .	**–257.0**	**–199.6**	**–191.6**	**–200.0**	**–218.5**	**–279.2**	**3.2**	**. . .**
A. GOODS	4 100 . .	–242.8	–199.9	–226.4	–265.5	–331.1	–349.9	–203.2	. . .
Credit	2 100 . .	**713.2**	**804.1**	**937.9**	**848.5**	**860.6**	**736.8**	**818.8**	**. . .**
General merchandise: exports f.o.b.	2 110 . .	678.6	764.0	893.6	802.9	827.3	707.2	790.9	. . .
Goods for processing: exports f.o.b.	2 150 . .	. . .	. . .	. . .	. . .	. . .	. . .	. . .	. . .
Repairs on goods	2 160 . .	. . .	. . .	. . .	. . .	. . .	. . .	. . .	. . .
Goods procured in ports by carriers	2 170 . .	34.6	40.2	44.3	45.7	33.4	29.6	27.9	. . .
Nonmonetary gold	2 180 . .	. . .	. . .	. . .	. . .	. . .	. . .	. . .	. . .
Debit	3 100 . .	**–956.0**	**–1,004.1**	**–1,164.3**	**–1,114.0**	**–1,191.8**	**–1,086.7**	**–1,022.0**	**. . .**
General merchandise: imports f.o.b.	3 110 . .	–956.0	–1,004.1	–1,164.3	–1,114.0	–1,191.8	–1,086.7	–1,022.0	. . .
Goods for processing: imports f.o.b.	3 150 . .	. . .	. . .	. . .	. . .	. . .	. . .	. . .	. . .
Repairs on goods	3 160 . .	. . .	. . .	. . .	. . .	. . .	. . .	. . .	. . .
Goods procured in ports by carriers	3 170 . .	. . .	. . .	. . .	. . .	. . .	. . .	. . .	. . .
Nonmonetary gold	3 180 . .	. . .	. . .	. . .	. . .	. . .	. . .	. . .	. . .
B. SERVICES	4 200 . .	–85.2	–80.8	–114.3	–121.8	–121.3	–119.2	–53.7	. . .
Total credit	2 200 . .	*434.1*	*433.7*	*561.3*	*500.8*	*532.8*	*462.1*	*439.0*	. . .
Total debit	3 200 . .	*–519.3*	*–514.5*	*–675.6*	*–622.6*	*–654.2*	*–581.3*	*–492.7*	. . .
Transportation services, credit	2 205 . .	**55.0**	**53.9**	**68.2**	**56.8**	**60.0**	**50.0**	**41.8**	**. . .**
Passenger	2 205 BA	*.5*	*.2*	*1.2*	*.1*	*1.2*	*1.2*	*.2*	. . .
Freight	2 205 BB	*14.1*	*15.8*	*17.3*	*17.8*	*19.8*	*20.3*	*15.4*	. . .
Other	2 205 BC	*40.5*	*37.8*	*49.7*	*38.9*	*39.1*	*28.5*	*26.3*	. . .
Sea transport, passenger	2 207 . .	. . .	. . .	. . .	. . .	. . .	. . .	. . .	. . .
Sea transport, freight	2 208 . .	. . .	. . .	. . .	. . .	. . .	. . .	. . .	. . .
Sea transport, other	2 209 . .	. . .	. . .	. . .	. . .	. . .	. . .	. . .	. . .
Air transport, passenger	2 211 . .	. . .	. . .	. . .	. . .	. . .	. . .	. . .	. . .
Air transport, freight	2 212 . .	. . .	. . .	. . .	. . .	. . .	. . .	. . .	. . .
Air transport, other	2 213 . .	. . .	. . .	. . .	. . .	. . .	. . .	. . .	. . .
Other transport, passenger	2 215 . .	. . .	. . .	. . .	. . .	. . .	. . .	. . .	. . .
Other transport, freight	2 216 . .	. . .	. . .	. . .	. . .	. . .	. . .	. . .	. . .
Other transport, other	2 217 . .	. . .	. . .	. . .	. . .	. . .	. . .	. . .	. . .
Transportation services, debit	3 205 . .	**–163.4**	**–179.4**	**–221.1**	**–219.5**	**–242.4**	**–215.4**	**–181.0**	**. . .**
Passenger	3 205 BA	*–50.8*	*–58.7*	*–75.8*	*–80.0*	*–97.7*	*–84.1*	*–57.9*	. . .
Freight	3 205 BB	*–108.6*	*–114.1*	*–132.3*	*–126.6*	*–135.4*	*–123.5*	*–116.1*	. . .
Other	3 205 BC	*–3.9*	*–6.6*	*–13.1*	*–12.9*	*–9.3*	*–7.8*	*–6.9*	. . .
Sea transport, passenger	3 207 . .	. . .	. . .	. . .	. . .	. . .	. . .	. . .	. . .
Sea transport, freight	3 208 . .	. . .	. . .	. . .	. . .	. . .	. . .	. . .	. . .
Sea transport, other	3 209 . .	. . .	. . .	. . .	. . .	. . .	. . .	. . .	. . .
Air transport, passenger	3 211 . .	. . .	. . .	. . .	. . .	. . .	. . .	. . .	. . .
Air transport, freight	3 212 . .	. . .	. . .	. . .	. . .	. . .	. . .	. . .	. . .
Air transport, other	3 213 . .	. . .	. . .	. . .	. . .	. . .	. . .	. . .	. . .
Other transport, passenger	3 215 . .	. . .	. . .	. . .	. . .	. . .	. . .	. . .	. . .
Other transport, freight	3 216 . .	. . .	. . .	. . .	. . .	. . .	. . .	. . .	. . .
Other transport, other	3 217 . .	. . .	. . .	. . .	. . .	. . .	. . .	. . .	. . .
Travel, credit	2 236 . .	**147.4**	**143.2**	**152.4**	**170.3**	**184.7**	**128.7**	**129.6**	**. . .**
Business travel	2 237 . .	. . .	. . .	. . .	. . .	. . .	. . .	. . .	. . .
Personal travel	2 240 . .	. . .	. . .	. . .	. . .	. . .	. . .	. . .	. . .
Travel, debit	3 236 . .	**–75.7**	**–39.4**	**–45.8**	**–45.5**	**–52.9**	**–49.9**	**–47.7**	**. . .**
Business travel	3 237 . .	. . .	. . .	. . .	. . .	. . .	. . .	. . .	. . .
Personal travel	3 240 . .	. . .	. . .	. . .	. . .	. . .	. . .	. . .	. . .
Other services, credit	2 200 BA	**231.7**	**236.6**	**340.7**	**273.7**	**288.1**	**283.4**	**267.5**	**. . .**
Communications	2 245 . .	. . .	. . .	. . .	. . .	. . .	. . .	. . .	. . .
Construction	2 249 . .	. . .	. . .	. . .	. . .	. . .	. . .	. . .	. . .
Insurance	2 253 . .	1.6	1.8	1.9	2.0	2.2	2.3	1.7	. . .
Financial	2 260 . .	. . .	. . .	. . .	. . .	. . .	. . .	. . .	. . .
Computer and information	2 262 . .	. . .	. . .	. . .	. . .	. . .	. . .	. . .	. . .
Royalties and licence fees	2 266 . .	.9	.8	1.2	1.2	1.1	1.0	.7	. . .
Other business services	2 268 . .	72.3	72.7	132.7	66.1	87.9	85.9	135.6	. . .
Personal, cultural, and recreational	2 287 . .	. . .	. . .	. . .	. . .	. . .	. . .	. . .	. . .
Government, n.i.e.	2 291 . .	156.9	161.4	204.9	204.4	196.9	194.3	129.6	. . .
Other services, debit	3 200 BA	**–280.2**	**–295.7**	**–408.6**	**–357.7**	**–358.9**	**–316.0**	**–264.0**	**. . .**
Communications	3 245 . .	. . .	. . .	. . .	. . .	. . .	. . .	. . .	. . .
Construction	3 249 . .	. . .	. . .	. . .	. . .	. . .	. . .	. . .	. . .
Insurance	3 253 . .	–28.6	–28.2	–32.5	–29.2	–31.0	–24.8	–23.3	. . .
Financial	3 260 . .	. . .	. . .	. . .	. . .	. . .	. . .	. . .	. . .
Computer and information	3 262 . .	. . .	. . .	. . .	. . .	. . .	. . .	. . .	. . .
Royalties and licence fees	3 266 . .	–.1	–.1	–.3	–.3	–.5	–.1	–.1	. . .
Other business services	3 268 . .	–50.9	–24.9	–68.4	–63.9	–76.4	–62.9	–80.7	. . .
Personal, cultural, and recreational	3 287 . .	. . .	. . .	. . .	. . .	. . .	. . .	. . .	. . .
Government, n.i.e.	3 291 . .	–200.5	–242.5	–307.5	–264.2	–251.0	–228.3	–159.8	. . .

Table 2 (Continued). STANDARD PRESENTATION, 1988–95
(Millions of U.S. dollars)

	Code		1988	1989	1990	1991	1992	1993	1994	1995
C. INCOME	4 300	. .	–207.8	–198.5	–175.5	–142.8	–127.9	–127.7	–127.8	. . .
Total credit	2 300	. .	*14.5*	*21.0*	*37.8*	*33.1*	*45.1*	*34.6*	*36.7*	. . .
Total debit	3 300	. .	*–222.3*	*–219.5*	*–213.2*	*–175.9*	*–173.0*	*–162.3*	*–164.5*	. . .
Compensation of employees, credit	2 310	. .	**4.4**	**4.0**	**4.7**	**5.0**	**4.8**	**4.5**	**14.1**	. . .
Compensation of employees, debit	3 310	. .	. . .	. . .	. . .	. . .	. . .	. . .	. . .	. . .
Investment income, credit	2 320	. .	**10.2**	**17.1**	**33.0**	**28.0**	**40.3**	**30.1**	**22.6**	. . .
Direct investment income	2 330	. .	9.4	16.0	31.4	26.8	37.6	27.5	3.6	. . .
Dividends and distributed branch profits	2 332	. .	9.4	16.0	31.4	26.8	37.6	27.5	3.6	. . .
Reinvested earnings and undistributed branch profits	2 333	. .	. . .	. . .	. . .	. . .	. . .	. . .	. . .	. . .
Income on debt (interest)	2 334	. .	. . .	. . .	. . .	. . .	. . .	. . .	. . .	. . .
Portfolio investment income	2 339	. .	. . .	. . .	. . .	. . .	. . .	. . .	. . .	. . .
Income on equity	2 340	. .	. . .	. . .	. . .	. . .	. . .	. . .	. . .	. . .
Income on bonds and notes	2 350	. .	. . .	. . .	. . .	. . .	. . .	. . .	. . .	. . .
Income on money market instruments and financial derivatives	2 360	. .	. . .	. . .	. . .	. . .	. . .	. . .	. . .	. . .
Other investment income	2 370	. .	.7	1.0	1.6	1.2	2.6	2.6	19.0	. . .
Investment income, debit	3 320	. .	**–222.3**	**–219.5**	**–213.2**	**–175.9**	**–173.0**	**–162.3**	**–164.5**	. . .
Direct investment income	3 330	. .	–29.8	–34.2	–60.4	–26.8	–29.4	–24.5	–34.4	. . .
Dividends and distributed branch profits	3 332	. .	–17.9	–19.9	–17.0	–37.1	–42.2	–26.6	–15.3	. . .
Reinvested earnings and undistributed branch profits	3 333	. .	–12.0	–14.3	–43.4	10.4	12.8	2.0	–19.1	. . .
Income on debt (interest)	3 334	. .	. . .	. . .	. . .	. . .	. . .	. . .	. . .	. . .
Portfolio investment income	3 339	. .	. . .	. . .	. . .	. . .	. . .	. . .	. . .	. . .
Income on equity	3 340	. .	. . .	. . .	. . .	. . .	. . .	. . .	. . .	. . .
Income on bonds and notes	3 350	. .	. . .	. . .	. . .	. . .	. . .	. . .	. . .	. . .
Income on money market instruments and financial derivatives	3 360	. .	. . .	. . .	. . .	. . .	. . .	. . .	. . .	. . .
Other investment income	3 370	. .	–192.5	–185.3	–152.9	–149.1	–143.6	–137.7	–130.1	. . .
D. CURRENT TRANSFERS	4 379	. .	278.8	279.5	324.6	330.1	361.9	317.5	387.9	. . .
Credit	2 379	. .	**388.2**	**385.2**	**454.5**	**462.7**	**489.0**	**432.9**	**467.5**	. . .
General government	2 380	. .	294.8	295.1	347.2	335.8	343.0	283.8	359.8	. . .
Other sectors	2 390	. .	93.5	90.1	107.2	127.0	146.1	149.2	107.7	. . .
Workers' remittances	2 391	. .	77.2	72.8	90.8	105.3	119.5	117.3	73.1	. . .
Other current transfers	2 392	. .	16.3	17.2	16.4	21.7	26.6	31.9	34.6	. . .
Debit	3 379	. .	**–109.5**	**–105.7**	**–129.9**	**–132.6**	**–127.1**	**–115.4**	**–79.6**	. . .
General government	3 380	. .	–20.8	–19.3	–21.7	–14.2	–14.2	–9.1	–6.8	. . .
Other sectors	3 390	. .	–88.6	–86.4	–108.2	–118.5	–112.9	–106.3	–72.8	. . .
Workers' remittances	3 391	. .	–67.2	–65.6	–79.4	–89.4	–96.0	–94.1	–59.9	. . .
Other current transfers	3 392	. .	–21.4	–20.8	–28.8	–29.0	–16.9	–12.2	–12.9	. . .
CAPITAL AND FINANCIAL ACCOUNT	4 996	. .	**278.0**	**187.3**	**192.9**	**196.9**	**238.1**	**270.9**	**54.0**	. . .
CAPITAL ACCOUNT	4 994	. .	. . .	. . .	. . .	. . .	. . .	. . .	**28.3**	. . .
Total credit	2 994	. .	. . .	. . .	. . .	. . .	. . .	. . .	*28.3*	. . .
Total debit	3 994	. .	. . .	. . .	. . .	. . .	. . .	. . .	. . .	. . .
Capital transfers, credit	2 400	. .	. . .	. . .	. . .	. . .	. . .	. . .	**28.3**	. . .
General government	2 401	. .	. . .	. . .	. . .	. . .	. . .	. . .	28.3	. . .
Debt forgiveness	2 402	. .	. . .	. . .	. . .	. . .	. . .	. . .	28.3	. . .
Other capital transfers	2 410	. .	. . .	. . .	. . .	. . .	. . .	. . .	. . .	. . .
Other sectors	2 430	. .	. . .	. . .	. . .	. . .	. . .	. . .	. . .	. . .
Migrants' transfers	2 431	. .	. . .	. . .	. . .	. . .	. . .	. . .	. . .	. . .
Debt forgiveness	2 432	. .	. . .	. . .	. . .	. . .	. . .	. . .	. . .	. . .
Other capital transfers	2 440	. .	. . .	. . .	. . .	. . .	. . .	. . .	. . .	. . .
Capital transfers, debit	3 400	. .	. . .	. . .	. . .	. . .	. . .	. . .	. . .	. . .
General government	3 401	. .	. . .	. . .	. . .	. . .	. . .	. . .	. . .	. . .
Debt forgiveness	3 402	. .	. . .	. . .	. . .	. . .	. . .	. . .	. . .	. . .
Other capital transfers	3 410	. .	. . .	. . .	. . .	. . .	. . .	. . .	. . .	. . .
Other sectors	3 430	. .	. . .	. . .	. . .	. . .	. . .	. . .	. . .	. . .
Migrants' transfers	3 431	. .	. . .	. . .	. . .	. . .	. . .	. . .	. . .	. . .
Debt forgiveness	3 432	. .	. . .	. . .	. . .	. . .	. . .	. . .	. . .	. . .
Other capital transfers	3 440	. .	. . .	. . .	. . .	. . .	. . .	. . .	. . .	. . .
Nonproduced nonfinancial assets, credit	2 480	. .	. . .	. . .	. . .	. . .	. . .	. . .	. . .	. . .
Nonproduced nonfinancial assets, debit	3 480	. .	. . .	. . .	. . .	. . .	. . .	. . .	. . .	. . .

Table 2 (Continued). STANDARD PRESENTATION, 1988–95

(Millions of U.S. dollars)

	Code	1988	1989	1990	1991	1992	1993	1994	1995
FINANCIAL ACCOUNT	4 995 . .	**278.0**	**187.3**	**192.9**	**196.9**	**238.1**	**270.9**	**25.7**	**. . .**
A. DIRECT INVESTMENT	4 500 . .	1.2	18.2	66.4	11.6	–30.0	–1.1	49.5	. . .
Direct investment abroad	4 505 . .	**–13.8**	**–8.6**	**9.5**	**19.1**	**–51.3**	**–.3**	**–17.4**	**. . .**
Equity capital	4 510 . .	–1.3	–8.9	–3.2	8.9	–12.1	.1	–5.9	. . .
Claims on affiliated enterprises	4 515 . .	. . .	. . .	. . .	. . .	. . .	. . .	. . .	. . .
Liabilities to affiliated enterprises	4 520 . .	. . .	. . .	. . .	. . .	. . .	. . .	. . .	. . .
Reinvested earnings	4 525 . .	. . .	. . .	. . .	. . .	. . .	. . .	. . .	. . .
Other capital	4 530 . .	–12.4	.3	12.7	10.2	–39.3	–.4	–11.5	. . .
Claims on affiliated enterprises	4 535 . .	. . .	. . .	. . .	. . .	. . .	. . .	. . .	. . .
Liabilities to affiliated enterprises	4 540 . .	. . .	. . .	. . .	. . .	. . .	. . .	. . .	. . .
Direct investment in Senegal	4 555 . .	**14.9**	**26.8**	**56.9**	**–7.6**	**21.4**	**–.8**	**66.9**	**. . .**
Equity capital	4 560 . .	1.7	2.8	5.4	4.0	2.1	2.4	–.4	. . .
Claims on direct investors	4 565 . .	. . .	. . .	. . .	. . .	. . .	. . .	. . .	. . .
Liabilities to direct investors	4 570 . .	. . .	. . .	. . .	. . .	. . .	. . .	. . .	. . .
Reinvested earnings	4 575 . .	12.0	14.3	43.4	–10.4	–12.8	–2.0	19.1	. . .
Other capital	4 580 . .	1.3	9.7	8.0	–1.2	32.1	–1.2	48.3	. . .
Claims on direct investors	4 585 . .	. . .	. . .	. . .	. . .	. . .	. . .	. . .	. . .
Liabilities to direct investors	4 590 . .	. . .	. . .	. . .	. . .	. . .	. . .	. . .	. . .
B. PORTFOLIO INVESTMENT	4 600 . .	1.1	.1	.6	6.5	.7	5.8	–1.1	. . .
Assets	4 602 . .	**–.1**	**. . .**	**–1.0**	**. . .**	**. . .**	**. . .**	**–1.5**	**. . .**
Equity securities	4 610 . .	–.1	. . .	–1.0	. . .	. . .	. . .	–1.5	. . .
Monetary authorities	4 611 . .	. . .	. . .	. . .	. . .	. . .	. . .	. . .	. . .
General government	4 612 . .	. . .	. . .	. . .	. . .	. . .	. . .	. . .	. . .
Banks	4 613 . .	. . .	. . .	. . .	. . .	. . .	. . .	. . .	. . .
Other sectors	4 614 . .	. . .	. . .	. . .	. . .	. . .	. . .	. . .	. . .
Debt securities	4 619 . .	. . .	. . .	. . .	. . .	. . .	. . .	. . .	. . .
Bonds and notes	4 620 . .	. . .	. . .	. . .	. . .	. . .	. . .	. . .	. . .
Monetary authorities	4 621 . .	. . .	. . .	. . .	. . .	. . .	. . .	. . .	. . .
General government	4 622 . .	. . .	. . .	. . .	. . .	. . .	. . .	. . .	. . .
Banks	4 623 . .	. . .	. . .	. . .	. . .	. . .	. . .	. . .	. . .
Other sectors	4 624 . .	. . .	. . .	. . .	. . .	. . .	. . .	. . .	. . .
Money market instruments	4 630 . .	. . .	. . .	. . .	. . .	. . .	. . .	. . .	. . .
Monetary authorities	4 631 . .	. . .	. . .	. . .	. . .	. . .	. . .	. . .	. . .
General government	4 632 . .	. . .	. . .	. . .	. . .	. . .	. . .	. . .	. . .
Banks	4 633 . .	. . .	. . .	. . .	. . .	. . .	. . .	. . .	. . .
Other sectors	4 634 . .	. . .	. . .	. . .	. . .	. . .	. . .	. . .	. . .
Financial derivatives	4 640 . .	. . .	. . .	. . .	. . .	. . .	. . .	. . .	. . .
Monetary authorities	4 641 . .	. . .	. . .	. . .	. . .	. . .	. . .	. . .	. . .
General government	4 642 . .	. . .	. . .	. . .	. . .	. . .	. . .	. . .	. . .
Banks	4 643 . .	. . .	. . .	. . .	. . .	. . .	. . .	. . .	. . .
Other sectors	4 644 . .	. . .	. . .	. . .	. . .	. . .	. . .	. . .	. . .
Liabilities	4 652 . .	**1.2**	**.1**	**1.6**	**6.5**	**.7**	**5.8**	**.5**	**. . .**
Equity securities	4 660 . .	1.2	–.7	1.3	–.2	.9	6.1	.5	. . .
Banks	4 663 . .	. . .	. . .	. . .	. . .	. . .	. . .	. . .	. . .
Other sectors	4 664 . .	. . .	. . .	. . .	. . .	. . .	. . .	. . .	. . .
Debt securities	4 669 . .	. . .	.8	.3	6.7	–.2	–.3	. . .	. . .
Bonds and notes	4 670 . .	. . .	.8	.3	6.7	–.2	–.3	. . .	. . .
Monetary authorities	4 671 . .	. . .	. . .	. . .	. . .	. . .	. . .	. . .	. . .
General government	4 672 . .	. . .	.8	.3	6.6	–.3	–.2	. . .	. . .
Banks	4 673 . .	. . .	. . .	. . .	. . .	. . .	. . .	. . .	. . .
Other sectors	4 674 . .	. . .	–.1	. . .	.1	.1	–.1	. . .	. . .
Money market instruments	4 680 . .	. . .	. . .	. . .	. . .	. . .	. . .	. . .	. . .
Monetary authorities	4 681 . .	. . .	. . .	. . .	. . .	. . .	. . .	. . .	. . .
General government	4 682 . .	. . .	. . .	. . .	. . .	. . .	. . .	. . .	. . .
Banks	4 683 . .	. . .	. . .	. . .	. . .	. . .	. . .	. . .	. . .
Other sectors	4 684 . .	. . .	. . .	. . .	. . .	. . .	. . .	. . .	. . .
Financial derivatives	4 690 . .	. . .	. . .	. . .	. . .	. . .	. . .	. . .	. . .
Monetary authorities	4 691 . .	. . .	. . .	. . .	. . .	. . .	. . .	. . .	. . .
General government	4 692 . .	. . .	. . .	. . .	. . .	. . .	. . .	. . .	. . .
Banks	4 693 . .	. . .	. . .	. . .	. . .	. . .	. . .	. . .	. . .
Other sectors	4 694 . .	. . .	. . .	. . .	. . .	. . .	. . .	. . .	. . .

Table 2 (Concluded). STANDARD PRESENTATION, 1988–95
(Millions of U.S. dollars)

	Code	1988	1989	1990	1991	1992	1993	1994	1995
C. OTHER INVESTMENT	4 700 . .	278.0	176.8	116.0	181.0	267.3	257.7	147.4	...
Assets	4 703 . .	**–41.8**	**–15.1**	**57.8**	**–34.2**	**–24.9**	**4.1**	**–92.5**	**...**
Trade credits	4 706 . .	...	...	...	...	...	...	...	...
General government: long-term	4 708 . .	...	...	...	...	...	...	...	...
General government: short-term	4 709 . .	...	...	...	...	...	...	...	...
Other sectors: long-term	4 711 . .	...	...	...	...	...	...	...	...
Other sectors: short-term	4 712 . .	...	...	...	...	...	...	...	...
Loans	4 714 . .	5.6	–9.8	1.3	–4.4	1.4	7.6	–24.3	...
Monetary authorities: long-term	4 717 . .	...	...	...	...	...	...	...	...
Monetary authorities: short-term	4 718 . .	...	...	...	...	...	...	...	...
General government: long-term	4 720 . .	...	...	...	...	...	...	...	...
General government: short-term	4 721 . .	...	...	...	...	...	...	...	...
Banks: long-term	4 723 . .	...	...	...	...	...	...	...	...
Banks: short-term	4 724 . .	...	...	...	...	...	...	...	...
Other sectors: long-term	4 726 . .	...	...	...	...	...	...	...	...
Other sectors: short-term	4 727 . .	5.6	–9.8	1.3	–4.4	1.4	7.6	–24.3	...
Currency and deposits	4 730 . .	–41.2	18.8	31.4	–23.5	–21.3	–10.7	–48.6	...
Monetary authorities	4 731 . .	...	...	...	...	...	...	...	...
General government	4 732 . .	.1	...	.3	...	–.7	–.6	...	...
Banks	4 733 . .	–27.5	11.9	31.3	–24.7	–20.2	–10.6	–88.5	...
Other sectors	4 734 . .	–13.9	7.0	–.2	1.1	–.4	.6	39.9	...
Other assets	4 736 . .	–6.2	–24.1	25.0	–6.2	–5.0	7.2	–19.6	...
Monetary authorities: long-term	4 738 . .	...	...	...	...	...	...	...	...
Monetary authorities: short-term	4 739 . .	...	...	...	...	...	...	...	...
General government: long-term	4 741 . .	...	...	...	...	...	...	...	...
General government: short-term	4 742 . .	...	...	...	...	...	...	...	...
Banks: long-term	4 744 . .	–1.4	–27.3	25.4	–6.4	–4.1	8.0	–20.3	...
Banks: short-term	4 745 . .	...	...	...	...	...	...	...	...
Other sectors: long-term	4 747 . .	–4.8	3.2	–.3	.1	–.9	–.7	.6	...
Other sectors: short-term	4 748 . .	...	...	...	...	...	...	...	...
Liabilities	4 753 . .	**319.9**	**191.9**	**58.2**	**215.1**	**292.2**	**253.6**	**239.9**	**...**
Trade credits	4 756 . .	...	...	...	...	...	...	...	...
General government: long-term	4 758 . .	...	...	...	...	...	...	...	...
General government: short-term	4 759 . .	...	...	...	...	...	...	...	...
Other sectors: long-term	4 761 . .	...	...	...	...	...	...	...	...
Other sectors: short-term	4 762 . .	...	...	...	...	...	...	...	...
Loans	4 764 . .	243.5	260.1	211.6	226.5	173.7	29.9	471.3	...
Use of Fund credit and loans from the Fund	4 766 . .	–6.5	6.2	–27.7	10.6	–44.2	–27.4	38.9	...
Monetary authorities: other long-term	4 767 . .	...	...	...	...	...	...	...	...
Monetary authorities: short-term	4 768 . .	...	...	...	...	...	...	...	...
General government: long-term	4 770 . .	212.6	242.9	271.9	236.7	220.6	97.2	430.5	...
General government: short-term	4 771 . .	–1.9	2.7	–6.0	2.7	–.2	.4	.4	...
Banks: long-term	4 773 . .	11.0	–9.3	–15.4	10.5	9.6	–14.5	8.2	...
Banks: short-term	4 774 . .	...	...	...	...	...	...	...	...
Other sectors: long-term	4 776 . .	16.1	23.4	–11.6	–26.7	–29.2	–28.9	–27.9	...
Other sectors: short-term	4 777 . .	12.3	–5.8	.4	–7.2	17.2	3.2	21.1	...
Currency and deposits	4 780 . .	20.8	77.9	–57.7	–21.4	–13.1	–14.8	37.2	...
Monetary authorities	4 781 . .	9.3	–9.8	–.2	.1	–.2	...	48.8	...
General government	4 782 . .	...	...	...	...	...	...	...	...
Banks	4 783 . .	11.5	87.7	–57.6	–21.5	–13.0	–14.8	–11.6	...
Other sectors	4 784 . .	...	...	...	...	...	...	...	...
Other liabilities	4 786 . .	55.5	–146.1	–95.6	10.0	131.5	238.5	–268.5	...
Monetary authorities: long-term	4 788 . .	...	...	...	...	...	...	...	...
Monetary authorities: short-term	4 789 . .	121.1	–100.6	–12.2	–42.7	34.4	135.3	–125.0	...
General government: long-term	4 791 . .	...	...	...	...	...	...	...	...
General government: short-term	4 792 . .	...	35.7	–27.5	19.5	121.7	131.7	–231.8	...
Banks: long-term	4 794 . .	24.6	–46.0	–22.0	24.4	–20.1	22.7	13.3	...
Banks: short-term	4 795 . .	...	...	...	...	...	...	...	...
Other sectors: long-term	4 797 . .	3.6	–3.9	–1.3	–17.2	–4.2	7.4	70.6	...
Other sectors: short-term	4 798 . .	–93.9	–31.4	–32.7	26.0	–.3	–58.6	4.5	...
D. RESERVE ASSETS	4 800 . .	–2.3	–7.8	9.8	–2.1	.1	8.5	–170.1	...
Monetary gold	4 810 . .	...	...	...	...	...	...	...	...
Special drawing rights	4 820 . .	...	–4.6	4.7	–.1	.4	–.5	–.6	...
Reserve position in the Fund	4 830 . .	...	...	...	...	...	–.1	–.1	...
Foreign exchange	4 840 . .	–2.3	–3.1	5.1	–1.9	–.3	9.1	–169.5	...
Other claims	4 880 . .	...	...	...	...	...	...	...	...
NET ERRORS AND OMISSIONS	4 998 . .	**–21.0**	**12.3**	**–1.3**	**3.1**	**–19.6**	**8.4**	**–57.2**	**...**

Part 3 of the *Yearbook* contains descriptions of the methodologies, compilation practices, and sources used to compile these data.

Table 1. ANALYTIC PRESENTATION, 1988–95
(Millions of U.S. dollars)

	Code	1988	1989	1990	1991	1992	1993	1994	1995
A. Current Account [1]	4 993 Y.	**-28.41**	**-39.65**	**-12.98**	**-8.17**	**-6.90**	**-38.82**	**-14.72**	**-33.13**
Goods: exports f.o.b	2 100 ..	17.26	34.36	57.15	49.33	48.07	51.30	52.14	55.45
Goods: imports f.o.b	3 100 ..	-134.96	-154.16	-166.38	-162.84	-180.50	-216.30	-188.64	-218.29
Balance on Goods	4 100 ..	*-117.70*	*-119.80*	*-109.23*	*-113.51*	*-132.42*	*-165.00*	*-136.50*	*-162.83*
Services: credit	2 200 ..	164.42	144.22	171.78	167.49	194.07	213.41	204.73	224.05
Services: debit	3 200 ..	-81.61	-65.55	-80.48	-67.80	-76.59	-93.03	-79.76	-86.78
Balance on Goods and Services	4 991 ..	*-34.89*	*-41.12*	*-17.94*	*-13.82*	*-14.94*	*-44.62*	*-11.53*	*-25.56*
Income: credit	2 300 ..	3.09	3.91	4.50	5.03	5.24	5.04	5.54	6.49
Income: debit	3 300 ..	-20.53	-14.86	-17.77	-15.84	-14.46	-15.96	-16.68	-22.40
Balance on Goods, Services, and Income	4 992 ..	*-52.33*	*-52.07*	*-31.20*	*-24.62*	*-24.16*	*-55.54*	*-22.67*	*-41.48*
Current transfers: credit	2 379 Y.	34.00	22.16	28.55	26.31	31.10	31.83	21.32	19.55
Current transfers: debit	3 379 ..	-10.08	-9.74	-10.32	-9.86	-13.84	-15.11	-13.37	-11.21
B. Capital Account [1]	4 994 Y.	...	...	...	...	...	...	...	...
Capital account: credit	2 994 Y.	...	...	...	...	...	...	...	...
Capital account: debit	3 994 ..	...	...	...	...	...	...	...	...
Total, Groups A Plus B	4 010 ..	*-28.41*	*-39.65*	*-12.98*	*-8.17*	*-6.90*	*-38.82*	*-14.72*	*-33.13*
C. Financial Account [1]	4 995 X.	**21.33**	**44.30**	**22.94**	**30.72**	**-2.49**	**25.59**	**22.40**	**33.03**
Direct investment abroad	4 505 ..	-4.29	-.92	-1.13	-1.14	-1.17	-1.16	-1.27	-1.51
Direct investment in Seychelles	4 555 Y.	23.20	22.43	20.24	19.58	9.01	18.64	29.78	40.31
Portfolio investment assets	4 602 ..	...	.80	1.53	-.42	-.14	-.34	-.88	-2.67
Equity securities	4 610 ..	...	...	...	...	...	...	...	...
Debt securities	4 619 ..	...	.80	1.53	-.42	-.14	-.34	-.88	-2.67
Portfolio investment liabilities	4 652 Y.	...	...	...	...	-.02	.04	.16	-.18
Equity securities	4 660 Y.	...	...	...	...	...	...	...	...
Debt securities	4 669 Y.	...	...	...	...	-.02	.04	.16	-.18
Other investment assets	4 703 ..	-.93	.45	-2.84	-6.24	.13	-1.56	-2.26	-4.36
Monetary authorities	4 703 .A	...	...	...	...	...	...	...	...
General government	4 703 .B	.04	...	...	...	...	...	...	...
Banks	4 703 .C	-.97	.45	-.96	-4.35	2.09	1.34	1.70	-1.16
Other sectors	4 703 .D	...	...	-1.88	-1.89	-1.95	-2.89	-3.96	-3.19
Other investment liabilities	4 753 X.	3.35	21.55	5.14	18.93	-10.31	9.97	-3.14	1.44
Monetary authorities	4 753 XA	...	4.37	.09	-1.05	-.86	.82	-1.89	2.86
General government	4 753 YB	3.35	8.95	-4.40	14.49	-6.48	4.28	-3.77	-10.81
Banks	4 753 YC	...	3.19	3.20	2.32	-7.10	.53	-1.52	5.75
Other sectors	4 753 YD	...	5.04	6.25	3.17	4.13	4.34	4.03	3.64
Total, Groups A Through C	4 020 ..	*-7.08*	*4.65*	*9.97*	*22.56*	*-9.39*	*-13.23*	*7.68*	*-.11*
D. Net Errors and Omissions	4 998 ..	**2.82**	**-5.53**	**-5.71**	**-20.75**	**5.44**	**3.17**	**-19.38**	**-13.93**
Total, Groups A Through D	4 030 ..	*-4.26*	*-.88*	*4.26*	*1.81*	*-3.95*	*-10.06*	*-11.70*	*-14.03*
E. Reserves and Related Items	4 040 ..	**4.26**	**.88**	**-4.26**	**-1.81**	**3.95**	**10.06**	**11.70**	**14.03**
Reserve assets	4 800 ..	4.26	.88	-4.26	-11.65	-5.43	-3.45	6.08	1.43
Use of Fund credit and loans	4 766 ..	...	...	...	...	...	...	...	...
Liabilities constituting foreign authorities' reserves	4 900 ..	...	...	...	...	...	...	...	...
Exceptional financing	4 920 ..	...	...	...	9.84	9.38	13.51	5.62	12.60
Conversion rates: Seychelles rupees per U.S. dollar	0 101 ..	**5.3836**	**5.6457**	**5.3369**	**5.2893**	**5.1220**	**5.1815**	**5.0559**	**4.7620**

[1] Excludes components that have been classified in the categories of Group E.

Table 2. STANDARD PRESENTATION, 1988–95
(Millions of U.S. dollars)

	Code	1988	1989	1990	1991	1992	1993	1994	1995
CURRENT ACCOUNT	4 993 . .	**–28.41**	**–39.65**	**–12.98**	**–8.17**	**–6.90**	**–38.82**	**–14.72**	**–33.13**
A. GOODS	4 100 . .	–117.70	–119.80	–109.23	–113.51	–132.42	–165.00	–136.50	–162.83
Credit	2 100 . .	**17.26**	**34.36**	**57.15**	**49.33**	**48.07**	**51.30**	**52.14**	**55.45**
General merchandise: exports f.o.b.	2 110 . .	17.26	14.34	28.40	19.10	19.75	22.37	27.28	29.16
Goods for processing: exports f.o.b.	2 150 . .	. . .	. . .	. . .	. . .	. . .	. . .	. . .	. . .
Repairs on goods	2 160 . .	. . .	.14	.15	.15	.16	.23	.16	.25
Goods procured in ports by carriers	2 170 . .	. . .	19.88	28.60	30.08	28.17	28.69	24.70	26.04
Nonmonetary gold	2 180 . .	. . .	. . .	. . .	. . .	. . .	. . .	. . .	. . .
Debit	3 100 . .	**–134.96**	**–154.16**	**–166.38**	**–162.84**	**–180.50**	**–216.30**	**–188.64**	**–218.29**
General merchandise: imports f.o.b.	3 110 . .	–134.96	–139.97	–158.84	–146.64	–162.70	–202.64	–175.58	–202.01
Goods for processing: imports f.o.b.	3 150 . .	. . .	. . .	. . .	. . .	. . .	. . .	. . .	. . .
Repairs on goods	3 160 . .	. . .	–2.34	–2.55	–11.65	–13.44	–7.18	–7.76	–6.12
Goods procured in ports by carriers	3 170 . .	. . .	–11.86	–4.99	–4.54	–4.36	–6.47	–5.30	–10.15
Nonmonetary gold	3 180 . .	. . .	. . .	. . .	. . .	. . .	. . .	. . .	. . .
B. SERVICES	4 200 . .	82.81	78.68	91.30	99.69	117.48	120.38	124.97	137.27
Total credit	2 200 . .	*164.42*	*144.22*	*171.78*	*167.49*	*194.07*	*213.41*	*204.73*	*224.05*
Total debit	3 200 . .	*–81.61*	*–65.55*	*–80.48*	*–67.80*	*–76.59*	*–93.03*	*–79.76*	*–86.78*
Transportation services, credit	2 205 . .	**48.48**	**40.69**	**40.03**	**56.26**	**61.97**	**66.73**	**66.26**	**74.18**
Passenger	2 205 BA	*15.74*	*21.20*	*19.16*	*33.41*	*37.26*	*43.23*	*43.76*	*47.44*
Freight	2 205 BB	. . .	*1.15*	*2.01*	*2.10*	*2.79*	*2.53*	*2.55*	*3.13*
Other	2 205 BC	*32.74*	*18.34*	*18.85*	*20.76*	*21.92*	*20.98*	*19.94*	*23.61*
Sea transport, passenger	2 207 . .	. . .	. . .	. . .	. . .	. . .	. . .	. . .	. . .
Sea transport, freight	2 208 . .	. . .	. . .	. . .	. . .	. . .	. . .	. . .	. . .
Sea transport, other	2 209 . .	. . .	. . .	. . .	. . .	. . .	. . .	. . .	. . .
Air transport, passenger	2 211 . .	. . .	21.20	19.16	33.41	37.26	43.23	43.76	47.44
Air transport, freight	2 212 . .	. . .	. . .	. . .	. . .	. . .	. . .	. . .	. . .
Air transport, other	2 213 . .	. . .	. . .	. . .	. . .	. . .	. . .	. . .	. . .
Other transport, passenger	2 215 . .	. . .	. . .	. . .	. . .	. . .	. . .	. . .	. . .
Other transport, freight	2 216 . .	. . .	. . .	. . .	. . .	. . .	. . .	. . .	. . .
Other transport, other	2 217 . .	. . .	18.34	18.85	20.76	21.92	20.98	19.94	23.61
Transportation services, debit	3 205 . .	**–39.25**	**–26.41**	**–29.94**	**–28.32**	**–31.76**	**–38.25**	**–32.05**	**–38.52**
Passenger	3 205 BA	*–5.67*	*–5.66*	*–6.38*	*–6.40*	*–7.31*	*–8.17*	*–6.31*	*–8.01*
Freight	3 205 BB	*–21.50*	*–19.75*	*–22.43*	*–20.71*	*–22.97*	*–28.61*	*–24.79*	*–28.49*
Other	3 205 BC	*–12.08*	*–.99*	*–1.13*	*–1.21*	*–1.48*	*–1.47*	*–.95*	*–2.02*
Sea transport, passenger	3 207 . .	. . .	. . .	. . .	. . .	. . .	. . .	. . .	. . .
Sea transport, freight	3 208 . .	. . .	. . .	. . .	. . .	. . .	. . .	. . .	. . .
Sea transport, other	3 209 . .	. . .	. . .	. . .	. . .	. . .	. . .	. . .	. . .
Air transport, passenger	3 211 . .	. . .	–5.66	–6.38	–6.40	–7.31	–8.17	–6.31	–8.01
Air transport, freight	3 212 . .	. . .	. . .	. . .	. . .	. . .	. . .	. . .	. . .
Air transport, other	3 213 . .	. . .	. . .	. . .	. . .	. . .	. . .	. . .	. . .
Other transport, passenger	3 215 . .	. . .	. . .	. . .	. . .	. . .	. . .	. . .	. . .
Other transport, freight	3 216 . .	. . .	. . .	. . .	. . .	. . .	. . .	. . .	. . .
Other transport, other	3 217 . .	. . .	–.99	–1.13	–1.21	–1.48	–1.47	–.95	–2.02
Travel, credit	2 236 . .	**80.57**	**93.63**	**121.94**	**100.14**	**120.34**	**133.79**	**126.30**	**134.77**
Business travel	2 237 . .	. . .	. . .	. . .	. . .	. . .	. . .	. . .	. . .
Personal travel	2 240 . .	. . .	. . .	. . .	. . .	. . .	. . .	. . .	. . .
Travel, debit	3 236 . .	**–13.10**	**–29.35**	**–33.99**	**–23.74**	**–28.33**	**–34.60**	**–26.43**	**–23.95**
Business travel	3 237 . .	. . .	. . .	. . .	. . .	. . .	. . .	. . .	. . .
Personal travel	3 240 . .	. . .	. . .	. . .	. . .	. . .	. . .	. . .	. . .
Other services, credit	2 200 BA	**35.38**	**9.90**	**9.81**	**11.09**	**11.76**	**12.89**	**12.18**	**15.10**
Communications	2 245 . .	. . .	. . .	. . .	. . .	. . .	. . .	. . .	. . .
Construction	2 249 . .	. . .	. . .	. . .	. . .	. . .	. . .	. . .	. . .
Insurance	2 253 . .	. . .	. . .	. . .	. . .	. . .	. . .	. . .	. . .
Financial	2 260 . .	. . .	. . .	. . .	. . .	. . .	. . .	. . .	. . .
Computer and information	2 262 . .	. . .	. . .	. . .	. . .	. . .	. . .	. . .	. . .
Royalties and licence fees	2 266 . .	. . .	. . .	. . .	. . .	. . .	. . .	. . .	. . .
Other business services	2 268 . .	22.88	. . .	. . .	. . .	. . .	. . .	. . .	. . .
Personal, cultural, and recreational	2 287 . .	. . .	. . .	. . .	. . .	. . .	. . .	. . .	. . .
Government, n.i.e.	2 291 . .	12.50	9.90	9.81	11.09	11.76	12.89	12.18	15.10
Other services, debit	3 200 BA	**–29.27**	**–9.79**	**–16.55**	**–15.74**	**–16.49**	**–20.18**	**–21.28**	**–24.32**
Communications	3 245 . .	. . .	. . .	. . .	. . .	. . .	. . .	. . .	. . .
Construction	3 249 . .	. . .	. . .	. . .	. . .	. . .	. . .	. . .	. . .
Insurance	3 253 . .	–2.39	–5.20	–5.79	–6.76	–7.12	–7.74	–6.33	–8.29
Financial	3 260 . .	. . .	. . .	. . .	. . .	. . .	. . .	. . .	. . .
Computer and information	3 262 . .	. . .	. . .	. . .	. . .	. . .	. . .	. . .	. . .
Royalties and licence fees	3 266 . .	–.43	–.35	–.38	–.38	–.39	–.39	–.40	–.42
Other business services	3 268 . .	–17.03	–2.81	–8.58	–6.64	–6.64	–9.66	–11.80	–12.45
Personal, cultural, and recreational	3 287 . .	. . .	. . .	. . .	. . .	. . .	. . .	. . .	. . .
Government, n.i.e.	3 291 . .	–9.42	–1.42	–1.80	–1.97	–2.34	–2.39	–2.75	–3.15

Table 2 (Continued). STANDARD PRESENTATION, 1988–95
(Millions of U.S. dollars)

	Code	1988	1989	1990	1991	1992	1993	1994	1995
C. INCOME	4 300	-17.44	-10.95	-13.27	-10.80	-9.22	-10.92	-11.14	-15.91
Total credit	2 300	*3.09*	*3.91*	*4.50*	*5.03*	*5.24*	*5.04*	*5.54*	*6.49*
Total debit	3 300	*-20.53*	*-14.86*	*-17.77*	*-15.84*	*-14.46*	*-15.96*	*-16.68*	*-22.40*
Compensation of employees, credit	2 310	**...**	**.35**	**.38**	**.38**	**.39**	**.39**	**.40**	**.50**
Compensation of employees, debit	3 310	**...**	**-.14**	**-.15**	**-.15**	**-.16**	**-.15**	**-.16**	**-.25**
Investment income, credit	2 320	**3.09**	**3.56**	**4.13**	**4.65**	**4.84**	**4.65**	**5.15**	**5.99**
Direct investment income	2 330	.74	.92	1.13	1.14	1.17	1.16	1.27	1.51
Dividends and distributed branch profits	2 332	...	...	...	...	...	...	...	...
Reinvested earnings and undistributed branch profits	2 333	.74	.92	1.13	1.14	1.17	1.16	1.27	1.51
Income on debt (interest)	2 334	...	...	...	...	...	...	...	...
Portfolio investment income	2 339	...	2.64	3.00	3.52	3.67	3.49	3.88	4.47
Income on equity	2 340	...	...	...	...	...	...	...	...
Income on bonds and notes	2 350	...	2.64	3.00	3.52	3.67	3.49	3.88	4.47
Income on money market instruments and financial derivatives	2 360	...	...	...	...	...	...	...	...
Other investment income	2 370	2.34	...	...	...	...	...	...	...
Investment income, debit	3 320	**-20.53**	**-14.72**	**-17.62**	**-15.69**	**-14.30**	**-15.81**	**-16.52**	**-22.15**
Direct investment income	3 330	-11.74	-6.59	-8.26	-7.34	-6.41	-7.72	-8.19	-12.59
Dividends and distributed branch profits	3 332	-5.37	-1.98	-1.43	-.68	-.55	-.46	-1.15	-1.09
Reinvested earnings and undistributed branch profits	3 333	-6.36	-4.61	-6.83	-6.66	-5.86	-7.26	-7.04	-11.50
Income on debt (interest)	3 334	...	...	...	...	...	...	...	...
Portfolio investment income	3 339	...	-8.13	-9.37	-8.35	-7.89	-8.09	-8.33	-9.56
Income on equity	3 340	...	...	...	...	...	...	...	...
Income on bonds and notes	3 350	...	-8.13	-9.37	-8.35	-7.89	-8.09	-8.33	-9.56
Income on money market instruments and financial derivatives	3 360	...	...	...	...	...	...	...	...
Other investment income	3 370	-8.79	...	...	...	...	...	...	...
D. CURRENT TRANSFERS	4 379	23.92	12.42	18.23	16.45	17.26	16.72	7.95	8.34
Credit	2 379	**34.00**	**22.16**	**28.55**	**26.31**	**31.10**	**31.83**	**21.32**	**19.55**
General government	2 380	29.52	18.25	21.42	19.37	20.73	23.02	15.32	13.65
Other sectors	2 390	4.48	3.91	7.13	6.94	10.37	8.82	6.00	5.89
Workers' remittances	2 391	...	3.91	7.13	6.94	10.37	8.82	6.00	5.89
Other current transfers	2 392	4.48	...	...	...	...	...	...	...
Debit	3 379	**-10.08**	**-9.74**	**-10.32**	**-9.86**	**-13.84**	**-15.11**	**-13.37**	**-11.21**
General government	3 380	-.67	-.64	-.68	-.45	-.70	-.54	-.40	-.31
Other sectors	3 390	-9.41	-9.10	-9.64	-9.41	-13.14	-14.57	-12.98	-10.90
Workers' remittances	3 391	...	-9.10	-9.64	-9.41	-13.14	-14.57	-12.98	-10.90
Other current transfers	3 392	-9.41	...	...	...	...	...	...	...
CAPITAL AND FINANCIAL ACCOUNT	4 996	**25.59**	**45.19**	**18.69**	**28.92**	**1.46**	**35.65**	**34.10**	**47.06**
CAPITAL ACCOUNT	4 994	**...**	**...**	**...**	**...**	**...**	**...**	**...**	**...**
Total credit	2 994	...	...	...	...	...	...	...	...
Total debit	3 994	...	...	...	...	...	...	...	...
Capital transfers, credit	2 400	**...**	**...**	**...**	**...**	**...**	**...**	**...**	**...**
General government	2 401	...	...	...	...	...	...	...	...
Debt forgiveness	2 402	...	...	...	...	...	...	...	...
Other capital transfers	2 410	...	...	...	...	...	...	...	...
Other sectors	2 430	...	...	...	...	...	...	...	...
Migrants' transfers	2 431	...	...	...	...	...	...	...	...
Debt forgiveness	2 432	...	...	...	...	...	...	...	...
Other capital transfers	2 440	...	...	...	...	...	...	...	...
Capital transfers, debit	3 400	**...**	**...**	**...**	**...**	**...**	**...**	**...**	**...**
General government	3 401	...	...	...	...	...	...	...	...
Debt forgiveness	3 402	...	...	...	...	...	...	...	...
Other capital transfers	3 410	...	...	...	...	...	...	...	...
Other sectors	3 430	...	...	...	...	...	...	...	...
Migrants' transfers	3 431	...	...	...	...	...	...	...	...
Debt forgiveness	3 432	...	...	...	...	...	...	...	...
Other capital transfers	3 440	...	...	...	...	...	...	...	...
Nonproduced nonfinancial assets, credit	2 480	**...**	**...**	**...**	**...**	**...**	**...**	**...**	**...**
Nonproduced nonfinancial assets, debit	3 480	**...**	**...**	**...**	**...**	**...**	**...**	**...**	**...**

Table 2 (Continued). STANDARD PRESENTATION, 1988–95

(Millions of U.S. dollars)

	Code	1988	1989	1990	1991	1992	1993	1994	1995
FINANCIAL ACCOUNT	4 995 ..	**25.59**	**45.19**	**18.69**	**28.92**	**1.46**	**35.65**	**34.10**	**47.06**
A. DIRECT INVESTMENT	4 500 ..	18.92	21.51	19.11	18.45	7.84	17.48	28.51	38.79
Direct investment abroad	4 505 ..	**–4.29**	**–.92**	**–1.13**	**–1.14**	**–1.17**	**–1.16**	**–1.27**	**–1.51**
Equity capital	4 510 ..	...	...	...	...	...	...	...	...
Claims on affiliated enterprises	4 515 ..	...	...	...	...	...	...	...	...
Liabilities to affiliated enterprises	4 520 ..	...	...	...	...	...	...	...	...
Reinvested earnings	4 525 ..	–.74	–.92	–1.13	–1.14	–1.17	–1.16	–1.27	–1.51
Other capital	4 530 ..	–3.54	...	...	...	...	...	...	...
Claims on affiliated enterprises	4 535 ..	...	...	...	...	...	...	...	...
Liabilities to affiliated enterprises	4 540 ..	...	...	...	...	...	...	...	...
Direct investment in Seychelles	4 555 ..	**23.20**	**22.43**	**20.24**	**19.58**	**9.01**	**18.64**	**29.78**	**40.31**
Equity capital	4 560 ..	...	17.82	13.41	12.92	3.15	11.38	22.73	28.81
Claims on direct investors	4 565 ..	...	...	...	...	...	...	...	...
Liabilities to direct investors	4 570 ..	...	...	...	...	...	...	...	...
Reinvested earnings	4 575 ..	6.36	4.61	6.83	6.66	5.86	7.26	7.04	11.50
Other capital	4 580 ..	16.84	...	...	...	...	...	...	...
Claims on direct investors	4 585 ..	...	...	...	...	...	...	...	...
Liabilities to direct investors	4 590 ..	...	...	...	...	...	...	...	...
B. PORTFOLIO INVESTMENT	4 600 ..	...	.80	1.53	–.42	–.15	–.30	–.72	–2.85
Assets	4 602 ..	**...**	**.80**	**1.53**	**–.42**	**–.14**	**–.34**	**–.88**	**–2.67**
Equity securities	4 610 ..	...	...	...	...	...	...	...	...
Monetary authorities	4 611 ..	...	...	...	...	...	...	...	...
General government	4 612 ..	...	...	...	...	...	...	...	...
Banks	4 613 ..	...	...	...	...	...	...	...	...
Other sectors	4 614 ..	...	...	...	...	...	...	...	...
Debt securities	4 619 ..	...	.80	1.53	–.42	–.14	–.34	–.88	–2.67
Bonds and notes	4 620 ..	...	...	...	...	...	...	...	...
Monetary authorities	4 621 ..	...	...	...	...	...	...	...	...
General government	4 622 ..	...	...	...	...	...	...	...	...
Banks	4 623 ..	...	...	...	...	...	...	...	...
Other sectors	4 624 ..	...	...	...	...	...	...	...	...
Money market instruments	4 630 ..	...	.80	1.53	–.42	–.14	–.34	–.88	–2.67
Monetary authorities	4 631 ..	...	...	...	...	...	...	...	...
General government	4 632 ..	...	...	...	...	...	...	...	...
Banks	4 633 ..	...	.80	1.53	–.42	–.14	–.34	–.88	–2.67
Other sectors	4 634 ..	...	...	...	...	...	...	...	...
Financial derivatives	4 640 ..	...	...	...	...	...	...	...	...
Monetary authorities	4 641 ..	...	...	...	...	...	...	...	...
General government	4 642 ..	...	...	...	...	...	...	...	...
Banks	4 643 ..	...	...	...	...	...	...	...	...
Other sectors	4 644 ..	...	...	...	...	...	...	...	...
Liabilities	4 652 ..	**...**	**...**	**...**	**...**	**–.02**	**.04**	**.16**	**–.18**
Equity securities	4 660 ..	...	...	...	...	...	...	...	...
Banks	4 663 ..	...	...	...	...	...	...	...	...
Other sectors	4 664 ..	...	...	...	...	...	...	...	...
Debt securities	4 669 ..	...	...	...	...	–.02	.04	.16	–.18
Bonds and notes	4 670 ..	...	...	...	...	...	...	...	...
Monetary authorities	4 671 ..	...	...	...	...	...	...	...	...
General government	4 672 ..	...	...	...	...	...	...	...	...
Banks	4 673 ..	...	...	...	...	...	...	...	...
Other sectors	4 674 ..	...	...	...	...	...	...	...	...
Money market instruments	4 680 ..	...	...	...	...	–.02	.04	.16	–.18
Monetary authorities	4 681 ..	...	...	...	...	...	...	...	...
General government	4 682 ..	...	...	...	...	...	...	...	...
Banks	4 683 ..	...	...	...	...	–.02	.04	.16	–.18
Other sectors	4 684 ..	...	...	...	...	...	...	...	...
Financial derivatives	4 690 ..	...	...	...	...	...	...	...	...
Monetary authorities	4 691 ..	...	...	...	...	...	...	...	...
General government	4 692 ..	...	...	...	...	...	...	...	...
Banks	4 693 ..	...	...	...	...	...	...	...	...
Other sectors	4 694 ..	...	...	...	...	...	...	...	...

Table 2 (Concluded). STANDARD PRESENTATION, 1988–95
(Millions of U.S. dollars)

	Code	1988	1989	1990	1991	1992	1993	1994	1995
C. OTHER INVESTMENT	4 700	2.41	22.00	2.30	22.53	–.80	21.93	.22	9.69
Assets	4 703	**–.93**	**.45**	**–2.84**	**–6.24**	**.13**	**–1.56**	**–2.26**	**–4.36**
Trade credits	4 706	...	...	...	...	...	...	...	...
General government: long-term	4 708	...	...	...	...	...	...	...	...
General government: short-term	4 709	...	...	...	...	...	...	...	...
Other sectors: long-term	4 711	...	...	...	...	...	...	...	...
Other sectors: short-term	4 712	...	...	...	...	...	...	...	...
Loans	4 714	...	...	...	...	...	...	...	...
Monetary authorities: long-term	4 717	...	...	...	...	...	...	...	...
Monetary authorities: short-term	4 718	...	...	...	...	...	...	...	...
General government: long-term	4 720	...	...	...	...	...	...	...	...
General government: short-term	4 721	...	...	...	...	...	...	...	...
Banks: long-term	4 723	...	...	...	...	...	...	...	...
Banks: short-term	4 724	...	...	...	...	...	...	...	...
Other sectors: long-term	4 726	...	...	...	...	...	...	...	...
Other sectors: short-term	4 727	...	...	...	...	...	...	...	...
Currency and deposits	4 730	–.93	.45	–2.84	–6.24	.13	–1.56	–2.26	–4.36
Monetary authorities	4 731	...	...	...	...	...	...	...	...
General government	4 732	.04	...	...	...	...	...	...	...
Banks	4 733	–.97	.45	–.96	–4.35	2.09	1.34	1.70	–1.16
Other sectors	4 734	...	...	–1.88	–1.89	–1.95	–2.89	–3.96	–3.19
Other assets	4 736	...	...	...	...	...	...	...	...
Monetary authorities: long-term	4 738	...	...	...	...	...	...	...	...
Monetary authorities: short-term	4 739	...	...	...	...	...	...	...	...
General government: long-term	4 741	...	...	...	...	...	...	...	...
General government: short-term	4 742	...	...	...	...	...	...	...	...
Banks: long-term	4 744	...	...	...	...	...	...	...	...
Banks: short-term	4 745	...	...	...	...	...	...	...	...
Other sectors: long-term	4 747	...	...	...	...	...	...	...	...
Other sectors: short-term	4 748	...	...	...	...	...	...	...	...
Liabilities	4 753	**3.35**	**21.55**	**5.14**	**28.77**	**–.94**	**23.48**	**2.48**	**14.04**
Trade credits	4 756	...	...	...	...	...	–.12	2.77	...
General government: long-term	4 758	...	...	...	...	...	...	...	...
General government: short-term	4 759	...	...	...	...	...	–.12	2.77	...
Other sectors: long-term	4 761	...	...	...	...	...	...	...	...
Other sectors: short-term	4 762	...	...	...	...	...	...	...	...
Loans	4 764	3.35	16.51	–1.11	15.76	–14.44	5.75	–9.94	–2.20
Use of Fund credit and loans from the Fund	4 766	...	...	...	...	...	...	...	...
Monetary authorities: other long-term	4 767	...	4.37	.09	–1.05	–.86	.82	–1.89	2.86
Monetary authorities: short-term	4 768	...	...	...	...	...	...	...	...
General government: long-term	4 770	3.35	8.95	–4.40	14.49	–6.48	4.40	–6.53	–10.81
General government: short-term	4 771	...	...	...	...	...	...	...	...
Banks: long-term	4 773	...	...	...	...	...	...	...	...
Banks: short-term	4 774	...	3.19	3.20	2.32	–7.10	.53	–1.52	5.75
Other sectors: long-term	4 776	...	...	...	...	...	...	...	...
Other sectors: short-term	4 777	...	...	...	...	...	...	...	...
Currency and deposits	4 780	...	...	...	...	...	...	...	...
Monetary authorities	4 781	...	...	...	...	...	...	...	...
General government	4 782	...	...	...	...	...	...	...	...
Banks	4 783	...	...	...	...	...	...	...	...
Other sectors	4 784	...	...	...	...	...	...	...	...
Other liabilities	4 786	...	5.04	6.25	13.01	13.50	17.85	9.65	16.25
Monetary authorities: long-term	4 788	...	...	...	...	...	...	...	...
Monetary authorities: short-term	4 789	...	...	...	...	...	...	...	...
General government: long-term	4 791	...	...	...	...	...	...	...	...
General government: short-term	4 792	...	...	...	...	...	...	...	...
Banks: long-term	4 794	...	...	...	...	...	...	...	...
Banks: short-term	4 795	...	...	...	...	...	...	...	...
Other sectors: long-term	4 797	...	...	...	...	...	...	...	...
Other sectors: short-term	4 798	...	5.04	6.25	13.01	13.50	17.85	9.65	16.25
D. RESERVE ASSETS	4 800	4.26	.88	–4.26	–11.65	–5.43	–3.45	6.08	1.43
Monetary gold	4 810	...	...	...	...	...	...	...	...
Special drawing rights	4 820	–.01	...	...	–.04	.04	–.01	...	...
Reserve position in the Fund	4 830	–.01	–.01	...	...	–1.04	–.01	...	...
Foreign exchange	4 840	4.29	.90	–4.26	–11.61	–4.43	–3.44	6.09	1.43
Other claims	4 880	...	...	...	...	...	...	...	...
NET ERRORS AND OMISSIONS	4 998	**2.82**	**–5.53**	**–5.71**	**–20.75**	**5.44**	**3.17**	**–19.38**	**–13.93**

Part 3 of the *Yearbook* contains descriptions of the methodologies, compilation practices, and sources used to compile these data.

Table 1. ANALYTIC PRESENTATION, 1988–95
(Millions of U.S. dollars)

	Code	1988	1989	1990	1991	1992	1993	1994	1995
A. Current Account [1]	4 993 Y.	**–2.8**	**–59.7**	**–69.4**	**15.3**	**–5.5**	**–57.8**	**–89.1**	**. . .**
Goods: exports f.o.b	2 100 . .	107.9	142.0	148.5	149.5	150.4	118.3	116.0	. . .
Goods: imports f.o.b	3 100 . .	–138.2	–160.4	–140.4	–138.6	–139.0	–187.1	–188.7	. . .
Balance on Goods	4 100 . .	*–30.3*	*–18.3*	*8.1*	*11.0*	*11.4*	*–68.8*	*–72.7*	. . .
Services: credit	2 200 . .	48.6	35.8	61.1	67.6	47.0	58.5	100.2	. . .
Services: debit	3 200 . .	–34.6	–44.8	–74.4	–63.8	–62.9	–61.5	–107.6	. . .
Balance on Goods and Services	4 991 . .	*–16.3*	*–27.3*	*–5.2*	*14.7*	*–4.5*	*–71.9*	*–80.1*	. . .
Income: credit	2 300 . .	.2	.2	.7	7.9	6.8	2.3	1.5	. . .
Income: debit	3 300 . .	4.6	–39.9	–71.8	–17.1	–15.1	–5.6	–57.0	. . .
Balance on Goods, Services, and Income	4 992 . .	*–11.5*	*–67.0*	*–76.3*	*5.5*	*–12.8*	*–75.2*	*–135.7*	. . .
Current transfers: credit	2 379 Y.	9.3	7.9	7.1	10.0	8.2	19.1	47.5	. . .
Current transfers: debit	3 379 . .	–.6	–.7	–.2	–.2	–.8	–1.7	–.9	. . .
B. Capital Account [1]	4 994 Y.	**.1**	**.1**	**. . .**	**. . .**	**.1**	**.1**	**.1**	**. . .**
Capital account: credit	2 994 Y.	.1	.1	. . .	. . .	.1	.1	.1	. . .
Capital account: debit	3 994 . .	. . .	. . .	. . .	. . .	. . .	. . .	. . .	. . .
Total, Groups A Plus B	4 010 . .	*–2.8*	*–59.7*	*–69.4*	*15.4*	*–5.4*	*–57.7*	*–89.1*	. . .
C. Financial Account [1]	4 995 X.	**–6.7**	**–17.9**	**–.8**	**–1.4**	**–18.2**	**49.1**	**–26.8**	**. . .**
Direct investment abroad	4 505 . .	. . .	. . .	. . .	. . .	. . .	. . .	. . .	. . .
Direct investment in Sierra Leone	4 555 Y.	–23.1	22.4	32.4	7.5	–5.6	–7.5	–4.2	. . .
Portfolio investment assets	4 602 . .	. . .	. . .	. . .	. . .	. . .	. . .	. . .	. . .
Equity securities	4 610 . .	. . .	. . .	. . .	. . .	. . .	. . .	. . .	. . .
Debt securities	4 619 . .	. . .	. . .	. . .	. . .	. . .	. . .	. . .	. . .
Portfolio investment liabilities	4 652 Y.	. . .	. . .	. . .	. . .	. . .	. . .	. . .	. . .
Equity securities	4 660 Y.	. . .	. . .	. . .	. . .	. . .	. . .	. . .	. . .
Debt securities	4 669 Y.	. . .	. . .	. . .	. . .	. . .	. . .	. . .	. . .
Other investment assets	4 703 . .	32.0	23.4	–20.1	–9.5	–31.2	–14.6	–.8	. . .
Monetary authorities	4 703 . A	. . .	. . .	. . .	. . .	. . .	. . .	. . .	. . .
General government	4 703 . B	. . .	. . .	. . .	. . .	. . .	. . .	. . .	. . .
Banks	4 703 . C	–4.8	–6.3	–5.1	–5.6	–7.8	–10.0	4.4	. . .
Other sectors	4 703 . D	36.8	29.7	–15.0	–3.9	–23.4	–4.6	–5.2	. . .
Other investment liabilities	4 753 X.	–15.6	–63.7	–13.1	.7	18.6	71.2	–21.8	. . .
Monetary authorities	4 753 XA	26.9	5.6	19.8	19.4	. . .	44.5	. . .	. . .
General government	4 753 YB	–36.2	–68.3	–33.3	–25.3	16.6	31.1	–15.2	. . .
Banks	4 753 YC	.2	–.6	. . .	. . .	3.1	–2.6	2.8	. . .
Other sectors	4 753 YD	–6.5	–.4	.3	6.5	–1.1	–1.8	–9.5	. . .
Total, Groups A Through C	4 020 . .	*–9.5*	*–77.6*	*–70.2*	*14.0*	*–23.6*	*–8.6*	*–115.9*	. . .
D. Net Errors and Omissions	4 998 . .	**–62.5**	**29.2**	**49.2**	**–28.9**	**39.8**	**16.1**	**56.4**	**. . .**
Total, Groups A Through D	4 030 . .	*–71.9*	*–48.4*	*–20.9*	*–14.9*	*16.2*	*7.5*	*–59.5*	. . .
E. Reserves and Related Items	4 040 . .	**71.9**	**48.4**	**20.9**	**14.9**	**–16.2**	**–7.5**	**59.5**	**. . .**
Reserve assets	4 800 . .	–6.7	9.3	–5.1	–10.7	–14.0	–13.6	–18.6	. . .
Use of Fund credit and loans	4 766 . .	–1.0	–1.6	–4.5	–7.5	–5.2	–8.4	55.1	. . .
Liabilities constituting foreign authorities' reserves	4 900 . .	. . .	. . .	. . .	. . .	. . .	. . .	. . .	. . .
Exceptional financing	4 920 . .	79.6	40.7	30.6	33.0	3.0	14.4	22.9	. . .
Conversion rates: leones per U.S. dollar	0 101 . .	**32.51**	**59.81**	**151.45**	**295.34**	**499.44**	**567.46**	**586.74**	**755.22**

[1] Excludes components that have been classified in the categories of Group E.

Table 2. STANDARD PRESENTATION, 1988–95

(Millions of U.S. dollars)

	Code	1988	1989	1990	1991	1992	1993	1994	1995
CURRENT ACCOUNT	4 993 . .	**–2.8**	**–59.7**	**–69.4**	**15.3**	**–5.5**	**–57.8**	**–89.1**	. . .
A. GOODS	4 100 . .	–30.3	–18.3	8.1	11.0	11.4	–68.8	–72.7	. . .
Credit	2 100 . .	**107.9**	**142.0**	**148.5**	**149.5**	**150.4**	**118.3**	**116.0**	. . .
General merchandise: exports f.o.b.	2 110 . .	104.5	139.5	139.8	143.9	147.4	115.6	112.6	. . .
Goods for processing: exports f.o.b.	2 150 . .	. . .	. . .	. . .	. . .	. . .	. . .	. . .	. . .
Repairs on goods	2 160 . .	. . .	. . .	. . .	. . .	. . .	. . .	. . .	. . .
Goods procured in ports by carriers	2 170 . .	3.4	2.5	8.7	5.6	3.0	2.7	3.4	. . .
Nonmonetary gold	2 180 . .	. . .	. . .	. . .	. . .	. . .	. . .	. . .	. . .
Debit	3 100 . .	**–138.2**	**–160.4**	**–140.4**	**–138.6**	**–139.0**	**–187.1**	**–188.7**	. . .
General merchandise: imports f.o.b.	3 110 . .	–138.2	–160.4	–140.4	–138.6	–139.0	–187.1	–188.7	. . .
Goods for processing: imports f.o.b.	3 150 . .	. . .	. . .	. . .	. . .	. . .	. . .	. . .	. . .
Repairs on goods	3 160 . .	. . .	. . .	. . .	. . .	. . .	. . .	. . .	. . .
Goods procured in ports by carriers	3 170 . .	. . .	. . .	. . .	. . .	. . .	. . .	. . .	. . .
Nonmonetary gold	3 180 . .	. . .	. . .	. . .	. . .	. . .	. . .	. . .	. . .
B. SERVICES	4 200 . .	14.0	–9.0	–13.3	3.8	–15.8	–3.0	–7.4	. . .
Total credit	2 200 . .	*48.6*	*35.8*	*61.1*	*67.6*	*47.0*	*58.5*	*100.2*	. . .
Total debit	3 200 . .	*–34.6*	*–44.8*	*–74.4*	*–63.8*	*–62.9*	*–61.5*	*–107.6*	. . .
Transportation services, credit	2 205 . .	**4.4**	**8.3**	**4.4**	**9.8**	**4.7**	**11.9**	**12.4**	. . .
Passenger	2 205 BA	. . .	. . .	. . .	. . .	. . .	. . .	. . .	. . .
Freight	2 205 BB	. . .	. . .	. . .	. . .	. . .	. . .	. . .	. . .
Other	2 205 BC	*4.4*	*8.3*	*4.4*	*9.8*	*4.7*	*11.9*	*12.4*	. . .
Sea transport, passenger	2 207 . .	. . .	. . .	. . .	. . .	. . .	. . .	. . .	. . .
Sea transport, freight	2 208 . .	. . .	. . .	. . .	. . .	. . .	. . .	. . .	. . .
Sea transport, other	2 209 . .	. . .	. . .	. . .	. . .	. . .	. . .	. . .	. . .
Air transport, passenger	2 211 . .	. . .	. . .	. . .	. . .	. . .	. . .	. . .	. . .
Air transport, freight	2 212 . .	. . .	. . .	. . .	. . .	. . .	. . .	. . .	. . .
Air transport, other	2 213 . .	. . .	. . .	. . .	. . .	. . .	. . .	. . .	. . .
Other transport, passenger	2 215 . .	. . .	. . .	. . .	. . .	. . .	. . .	. . .	. . .
Other transport, freight	2 216 . .	. . .	. . .	. . .	. . .	. . .	. . .	. . .	. . .
Other transport, other	2 217 . .	. . .	. . .	. . .	. . .	. . .	. . .	. . .	. . .
Transportation services, debit	3 205 . .	**–16.5**	**–19.2**	**–19.8**	**–16.1**	**–16.4**	**–15.3**	**–15.6**	. . .
Passenger	3 205 BA	*–.4*	*–.9*	*–4.1*	*–.7*	*–.8*	*–.6*	*–.6*	. . .
Freight	3 205 BB	*–16.0*	*–18.2*	*–15.7*	*–15.4*	*–15.6*	*–14.7*	*–15.1*	. . .
Other	3 205 BC	. . .	. . .	. . .	. . .	. . .	. . .	. . .	. . .
Sea transport, passenger	3 207 . .	. . .	. . .	. . .	. . .	. . .	. . .	. . .	. . .
Sea transport, freight	3 208 . .	. . .	. . .	. . .	. . .	. . .	. . .	. . .	. . .
Sea transport, other	3 209 . .	. . .	. . .	. . .	. . .	. . .	. . .	. . .	. . .
Air transport, passenger	3 211 . .	. . .	. . .	. . .	. . .	. . .	. . .	. . .	. . .
Air transport, freight	3 212 . .	. . .	. . .	. . .	. . .	. . .	. . .	. . .	. . .
Air transport, other	3 213 . .	. . .	. . .	. . .	. . .	. . .	. . .	. . .	. . .
Other transport, passenger	3 215 . .	. . .	. . .	. . .	. . .	. . .	. . .	. . .	. . .
Other transport, freight	3 216 . .	. . .	. . .	. . .	. . .	. . .	. . .	. . .	. . .
Other transport, other	3 217 . .	. . .	. . .	. . .	. . .	. . .	. . .	. . .	. . .
Travel, credit	2 236 . .	**10.0**	**4.5**	**34.5**	**40.3**	**30.7**	**32.2**	**69.1**	. . .
Business travel	2 237 . .	. . .	. . .	. . .	. . .	. . .	. . .	. . .	. . .
Personal travel	2 240 . .	. . .	. . .	. . .	. . .	. . .	. . .	. . .	. . .
Travel, debit	3 236 . .	**–6.7**	**–3.4**	**–22.0**	**–22.9**	**–22.7**	**–27.9**	**–61.8**	. . .
Business travel	3 237 . .	. . .	. . .	. . .	. . .	. . .	. . .	. . .	. . .
Personal travel	3 240 . .	. . .	. . .	. . .	. . .	. . .	. . .	. . .	. . .
Other services, credit	2 200 BA	**34.2**	**23.0**	**22.3**	**17.5**	**11.6**	**14.4**	**18.7**	. . .
Communications	2 245 . .	. . .	. . .	. . .	. . .	. . .	. . .	. . .	. . .
Construction	2 249 . .	. . .	. . .	. . .	. . .	. . .	. . .	. . .	. . .
Insurance	2 253 . .	. . .	. . .	. . .	.1	. . .	. . .	.2	. . .
Financial	2 260 . .	. . .	. . .	. . .	. . .	. . .	. . .	. . .	. . .
Computer and information	2 262 . .	. . .	. . .	. . .	. . .	. . .	. . .	. . .	. . .
Royalties and licence fees	2 266 . .	. . .	. . .	. . .	. . .	. . .	. . .	. . .	. . .
Other business services	2 268 . .	.3	.6	6.4	.5	.4	.8	4.3	. . .
Personal, cultural, and recreational	2 287 . .	. . .	. . .	. . .	. . .	. . .	. . .	. . .	. . .
Government, n.i.e.	2 291 . .	33.9	22.4	15.9	16.9	11.2	13.6	14.2	. . .
Other services, debit	3 200 BA	**–11.4**	**–22.2**	**–32.6**	**–24.9**	**–23.8**	**–18.4**	**–30.1**	. . .
Communications	3 245 . .	. . .	. . .	. . .	. . .	. . .	. . .	. . .	. . .
Construction	3 249 . .	. . .	. . .	. . .	. . .	. . .	. . .	. . .	. . .
Insurance	3 253 . .	–3.4	–3.9	–3.2	–3.4	–3.2	–3.0	–3.4	. . .
Financial	3 260 . .	. . .	. . .	. . .	. . .	. . .	. . .	. . .	. . .
Computer and information	3 262 . .	. . .	. . .	. . .	. . .	. . .	. . .	. . .	. . .
Royalties and licence fees	3 266 . .	. . .	. . .	. . .	. . .	. . .	. . .	. . .	. . .
Other business services	3 268 . .	–6.0	–16.0	–22.2	–20.3	–16.6	–14.3	–12.5	. . .
Personal, cultural, and recreational	3 287 . .	. . .	. . .	. . .	. . .	. . .	. . .	. . .	. . .
Government, n.i.e.	3 291 . .	–2.0	–2.3	–7.3	–1.2	–4.0	–1.0	–14.2	. . .

Table 2 (Continued). STANDARD PRESENTATION, 1988–95
(Millions of U.S. dollars)

	Code	1988	1989	1990	1991	1992	1993	1994	1995
C. INCOME	4 300 . .	4.8	–39.7	–71.1	–9.2	–8.3	–3.3	–55.6	. . .
Total credit	2 300 . .	*.2*	*.2*	*.7*	*7.9*	*6.8*	*2.3*	*1.5*	. . .
Total debit	3 300 . .	*4.6*	*–39.9*	*–71.8*	*–17.1*	*–15.1*	*–5.6*	*–57.0*	. . .
Compensation of employees, credit	2 310 . .	. . .	. . .	. . .	. . .	. . .	. . .	. . .	. . .
Compensation of employees, debit	3 310 . .	. . .	. . .	. . .	. . .	. . .	. . .	. . .	. . .
Investment income, credit	2 320 . .	**.2**	**.2**	**.7**	**7.9**	**6.8**	**2.3**	**1.5**	. . .
Direct investment income	2 330 . .	.2	.2	.7	.9	.1	.1	.3	. . .
Dividends and distributed branch profits	2 332 . .	.2	.2	.7	.9	.1	.1	.3	. . .
Reinvested earnings and undistributed branch profits	2 333 . .	. . .	. . .	. . .	. . .	. . .	. . .	. . .	. . .
Income on debt (interest)	2 334 . .	. . .	. . .	. . .	. . .	. . .	. . .	. . .	. . .
Portfolio investment income	2 339 . .	. . .	. . .	. . .	. . .	. . .	. . .	. . .	. . .
Income on equity	2 340 . .	. . .	. . .	. . .	. . .	. . .	. . .	. . .	. . .
Income on bonds and notes	2 350 . .	. . .	. . .	. . .	. . .	. . .	. . .	. . .	. . .
Income on money market instruments and financial derivatives	2 360 . .	. . .	. . .	. . .	. . .	. . .	. . .	. . .	. . .
Other investment income	2 370 . .	. . .	. . .	. . .	7.1	6.8	2.2	1.1	. . .
Investment income, debit	3 320 . .	**4.6**	**–39.9**	**–71.8**	**–17.1**	**–15.1**	**–5.6**	**–57.0**	. . .
Direct investment income	3 330 . .	12.4	–29.9	–50.7	–15.9	–1.3	.8	.2	. . .
Dividends and distributed branch profits	3 332 . .	–7.9	–8.8	–18.2	–4.5	–6.7	–6.6	–2.9	. . .
Reinvested earnings and undistributed branch profits	3 333 . .	20.3	–21.1	–32.5	–11.4	5.4	7.4	3.2	. . .
Income on debt (interest)	3 334 . .	. . .	. . .	. . .	. . .	. . .	. . .	. . .	. . .
Portfolio investment income	3 339 . .	. . .	. . .	. . .	. . .	. . .	. . .	. . .	. . .
Income on equity	3 340 . .	. . .	. . .	. . .	. . .	. . .	. . .	. . .	. . .
Income on bonds and notes	3 350 . .	. . .	. . .	. . .	. . .	. . .	. . .	. . .	. . .
Income on money market instruments and financial derivatives	3 360 . .	. . .	. . .	. . .	. . .	. . .	. . .	. . .	. . .
Other investment income	3 370 . .	–7.8	–10.0	–21.1	–1.2	–13.9	–6.4	–57.3	. . .
D. CURRENT TRANSFERS	4 379 . .	8.7	7.2	6.9	9.8	7.3	17.4	46.6	. . .
Credit	2 379 . .	**9.3**	**7.9**	**7.1**	**10.0**	**8.2**	**19.1**	**47.5**	. . .
General government	2 380 . .	8.8	7.5	7.0	7.3	4.1	16.0	46.3	. . .
Other sectors	2 390 . .	.5	.4	.1	2.8	4.0	3.1	1.1	. . .
Workers' remittances	2 391 . .	. . .	. . .	. . .	. . .	. . .	. . .	. . .	. . .
Other current transfers	2 392 . .	.5	.4	.1	2.8	4.0	3.1	1.1	. . .
Debit	3 379 . .	**–.6**	**–.7**	**–.2**	**–.2**	**–.8**	**–1.7**	**–.9**	. . .
General government	3 380 . .	–.3	–.3	–.2	–.1	–.8	–1.7	–.8	. . .
Other sectors	3 390 . .	–.3	–.4	–.1	–.1	–.1	. . .	–.1	. . .
Workers' remittances	3 391 . .	–.3	–.1	–.1	. . .	. . .	. . .	. . .	. . .
Other current transfers	3 392 . .	. . .	–.3	. . .	–.1	–.1	. . .	–.1	. . .
CAPITAL AND FINANCIAL ACCOUNT	4 996 . .	**65.3**	**30.5**	**20.2**	**13.6**	**–34.3**	**41.7**	**32.7**	. . .
CAPITAL ACCOUNT	4 994 . .	**.1**	**.1**	. . .	. . .	**.1**	**.1**	**.1**	. . .
Total credit	2 994 . .	*.1*	*.1*	. . .	. . .	*.1*	*.1*	*.1*	. . .
Total debit	3 994 . .	. . .	. . .	. . .	. . .	. . .	. . .	. . .	. . .
Capital transfers, credit	2 400 . .	**.1**	**.1**	. . .	. . .	**.1**	**.1**	**.1**	. . .
General government	2 401 . .	. . .	. . .	. . .	. . .	. . .	. . .	. . .	. . .
Debt forgiveness	2 402 . .	. . .	. . .	. . .	. . .	. . .	. . .	. . .	. . .
Other capital transfers	2 410 . .	. . .	. . .	. . .	. . .	. . .	. . .	. . .	. . .
Other sectors	2 430 . .	.1	.1	. . .	. . .	.1	.1	.1	. . .
Migrants' transfers	2 431 . .	.1	.1	. . .	. . .	.1	.1	.1	. . .
Debt forgiveness	2 432 . .	. . .	. . .	. . .	. . .	. . .	. . .	. . .	. . .
Other capital transfers	2 440 . .	. . .	. . .	. . .	. . .	. . .	. . .	. . .	. . .
Capital transfers, debit	3 400 . .	. . .	. . .	. . .	. . .	. . .	. . .	. . .	. . .
General government	3 401 . .	. . .	. . .	. . .	. . .	. . .	. . .	. . .	. . .
Debt forgiveness	3 402 . .	. . .	. . .	. . .	. . .	. . .	. . .	. . .	. . .
Other capital transfers	3 410 . .	. . .	. . .	. . .	. . .	. . .	. . .	. . .	. . .
Other sectors	3 430 . .	. . .	. . .	. . .	. . .	. . .	. . .	. . .	. . .
Migrants' transfers	3 431 . .	. . .	. . .	. . .	. . .	. . .	. . .	. . .	. . .
Debt forgiveness	3 432 . .	. . .	. . .	. . .	. . .	. . .	. . .	. . .	. . .
Other capital transfers	3 440 . .	. . .	. . .	. . .	. . .	. . .	. . .	. . .	. . .
Nonproduced nonfinancial assets, credit	2 480 . .	. . .	. . .	. . .	. . .	. . .	. . .	. . .	. . .
Nonproduced nonfinancial assets, debit	3 480 . .	. . .	. . .	. . .	. . .	. . .	. . .	. . .	. . .

Table 2 (Continued). STANDARD PRESENTATION, 1988–95
(Millions of U.S. dollars)

	Code		1988	1989	1990	1991	1992	1993	1994	1995
FINANCIAL ACCOUNT	4 995	. .	**65.2**	**30.5**	**20.1**	**13.5**	**–34.4**	**41.6**	**32.7**	**. . .**
A. DIRECT INVESTMENT	4 500	. .	–23.1	22.4	32.4	7.5	–5.6	–7.5	–4.2	. . .
Direct investment abroad	4 505	. .	**. . .**	**. . .**	**. . .**	**. . .**	**. . .**	**. . .**	**. . .**	**. . .**
Equity capital	4 510	. .	. . .	. . .	. . .	. . .	. . .	. . .	. . .	. . .
Claims on affiliated enterprises	4 515	. .	. . .	. . .	. . .	. . .	. . .	. . .	. . .	. . .
Liabilities to affiliated enterprises	4 520	. .	. . .	. . .	. . .	. . .	. . .	. . .	. . .	. . .
Reinvested earnings	4 525	. .	. . .	. . .	. . .	. . .	. . .	. . .	. . .	. . .
Other capital	4 530	. .	. . .	. . .	. . .	. . .	. . .	. . .	. . .	. . .
Claims on affiliated enterprises	4 535	. .	. . .	. . .	. . .	. . .	. . .	. . .	. . .	. . .
Liabilities to affiliated enterprises	4 540	. .	. . .	. . .	. . .	. . .	. . .	. . .	. . .	. . .
Direct investment in Sierra Leone	4 555	. .	**–23.1**	**22.4**	**32.4**	**7.5**	**–5.6**	**–7.5**	**–4.2**	**. . .**
Equity capital	4 560	. .	. . .	. . .	. . .	. . .	. . .	. . .	. . .	. . .
Claims on direct investors	4 565	. .	. . .	. . .	. . .	. . .	. . .	. . .	. . .	. . .
Liabilities to direct investors	4 570	. .	. . .	. . .	. . .	. . .	. . .	. . .	. . .	. . .
Reinvested earnings	4 575	. .	–20.3	21.1	32.5	11.4	–5.4	–7.4	–3.2	. . .
Other capital	4 580	. .	–2.7	1.3	. . .	–3.9	–.2	. . .	–1.0	. . .
Claims on direct investors	4 585	. .	. . .	. . .	. . .	. . .	. . .	. . .	. . .	. . .
Liabilities to direct investors	4 590	. .	. . .	. . .	. . .	. . .	. . .	. . .	. . .	. . .
B. PORTFOLIO INVESTMENT	4 600	. .	. . .	. . .	. . .	. . .	. . .	. . .	. . .	. . .
Assets	4 602	. .	**. . .**	**. . .**	**. . .**	**. . .**	**. . .**	**. . .**	**. . .**	**. . .**
Equity securities	4 610	. .	. . .	. . .	. . .	. . .	. . .	. . .	. . .	. . .
Monetary authorities	4 611	. .	. . .	. . .	. . .	. . .	. . .	. . .	. . .	. . .
General government	4 612	. .	. . .	. . .	. . .	. . .	. . .	. . .	. . .	. . .
Banks	4 613	. .	. . .	. . .	. . .	. . .	. . .	. . .	. . .	. . .
Other sectors	4 614	. .	. . .	. . .	. . .	. . .	. . .	. . .	. . .	. . .
Debt securities	4 619	. .	. . .	. . .	. . .	. . .	. . .	. . .	. . .	. . .
Bonds and notes	4 620	. .	. . .	. . .	. . .	. . .	. . .	. . .	. . .	. . .
Monetary authorities	4 621	. .	. . .	. . .	. . .	. . .	. . .	. . .	. . .	. . .
General government	4 622	. .	. . .	. . .	. . .	. . .	. . .	. . .	. . .	. . .
Banks	4 623	. .	. . .	. . .	. . .	. . .	. . .	. . .	. . .	. . .
Other sectors	4 624	. .	. . .	. . .	. . .	. . .	. . .	. . .	. . .	. . .
Money market instruments	4 630	. .	. . .	. . .	. . .	. . .	. . .	. . .	. . .	. . .
Monetary authorities	4 631	. .	. . .	. . .	. . .	. . .	. . .	. . .	. . .	. . .
General government	4 632	. .	. . .	. . .	. . .	. . .	. . .	. . .	. . .	. . .
Banks	4 633	. .	. . .	. . .	. . .	. . .	. . .	. . .	. . .	. . .
Other sectors	4 634	. .	. . .	. . .	. . .	. . .	. . .	. . .	. . .	. . .
Financial derivatives	4 640	. .	. . .	. . .	. . .	. . .	. . .	. . .	. . .	. . .
Monetary authorities	4 641	. .	. . .	. . .	. . .	. . .	. . .	. . .	. . .	. . .
General government	4 642	. .	. . .	. . .	. . .	. . .	. . .	. . .	. . .	. . .
Banks	4 643	. .	. . .	. . .	. . .	. . .	. . .	. . .	. . .	. . .
Other sectors	4 644	. .	. . .	. . .	. . .	. . .	. . .	. . .	. . .	. . .
Liabilities	4 652	. .	**. . .**	**. . .**	**. . .**	**. . .**	**. . .**	**. . .**	**. . .**	**. . .**
Equity securities	4 660	. .	. . .	. . .	. . .	. . .	. . .	. . .	. . .	. . .
Banks	4 663	. .	. . .	. . .	. . .	. . .	. . .	. . .	. . .	. . .
Other sectors	4 664	. .	. . .	. . .	. . .	. . .	. . .	. . .	. . .	. . .
Debt securities	4 669	. .	. . .	. . .	. . .	. . .	. . .	. . .	. . .	. . .
Bonds and notes	4 670	. .	. . .	. . .	. . .	. . .	. . .	. . .	. . .	. . .
Monetary authorities	4 671	. .	. . .	. . .	. . .	. . .	. . .	. . .	. . .	. . .
General government	4 672	. .	. . .	. . .	. . .	. . .	. . .	. . .	. . .	. . .
Banks	4 673	. .	. . .	. . .	. . .	. . .	. . .	. . .	. . .	. . .
Other sectors	4 674	. .	. . .	. . .	. . .	. . .	. . .	. . .	. . .	. . .
Money market instruments	4 680	. .	. . .	. . .	. . .	. . .	. . .	. . .	. . .	. . .
Monetary authorities	4 681	. .	. . .	. . .	. . .	. . .	. . .	. . .	. . .	. . .
General government	4 682	. .	. . .	. . .	. . .	. . .	. . .	. . .	. . .	. . .
Banks	4 683	. .	. . .	. . .	. . .	. . .	. . .	. . .	. . .	. . .
Other sectors	4 684	. .	. . .	. . .	. . .	. . .	. . .	. . .	. . .	. . .
Financial derivatives	4 690	. .	. . .	. . .	. . .	. . .	. . .	. . .	. . .	. . .
Monetary authorities	4 691	. .	. . .	. . .	. . .	. . .	. . .	. . .	. . .	. . .
General government	4 692	. .	. . .	. . .	. . .	. . .	. . .	. . .	. . .	. . .
Banks	4 693	. .	. . .	. . .	. . .	. . .	. . .	. . .	. . .	. . .
Other sectors	4 694	. .	. . .	. . .	. . .	. . .	. . .	. . .	. . .	. . .

Table 2 (Concluded). STANDARD PRESENTATION, 1988–95
(Millions of U.S. dollars)

	Code	1988	1989	1990	1991	1992	1993	1994	1995
C. OTHER INVESTMENT	4 700 . .	95.0	–1.2	–7.2	16.7	–14.8	62.6	55.4	. . .
Assets	4 703 . .	**32.0**	**23.4**	**–20.1**	**–9.5**	**–31.2**	**–14.6**	**–.8**	**. . .**
Trade credits	4 706 . .	. . .	12.0	7.5	6.3	–.8	2.4	1.0	. . .
General government: long-term	4 708 . .	. . .	. . .	. . .	. . .	. . .	. . .	. . .	. . .
General government: short-term	4 709 . .	. . .	. . .	. . .	. . .	. . .	. . .	. . .	. . .
Other sectors: long-term	4 711 . .	. . .	. . .	. . .	. . .	. . .	. . .	. . .	. . .
Other sectors: short-term	4 712 . .	. . .	12.0	7.5	6.3	–.8	2.4	1.0	. . .
Loans	4 714 . .	. . .	. . .	. . .	. . .	. . .	. . .	. . .	. . .
Monetary authorities: long-term	4 717 . .	. . .	. . .	. . .	. . .	. . .	. . .	. . .	. . .
Monetary authorities: short-term	4 718 . .	. . .	. . .	. . .	. . .	. . .	. . .	. . .	. . .
General government: long-term	4 720 . .	. . .	. . .	. . .	. . .	. . .	. . .	. . .	. . .
General government: short-term	4 721 . .	. . .	. . .	. . .	. . .	. . .	. . .	. . .	. . .
Banks: long-term	4 723 . .	. . .	. . .	. . .	. . .	. . .	. . .	. . .	. . .
Banks: short-term	4 724 . .	. . .	. . .	. . .	. . .	. . .	. . .	. . .	. . .
Other sectors: long-term	4 726 . .	. . .	. . .	. . .	. . .	. . .	. . .	. . .	. . .
Other sectors: short-term	4 727 . .	. . .	. . .	. . .	. . .	. . .	. . .	. . .	. . .
Currency and deposits	4 730 . .	32.0	11.4	–27.6	–15.8	–30.4	–17.0	–1.8	. . .
Monetary authorities	4 731 . .	. . .	. . .	. . .	. . .	. . .	. . .	. . .	. . .
General government	4 732 . .	. . .	. . .	. . .	. . .	. . .	. . .	. . .	. . .
Banks	4 733 . .	–4.8	–6.3	–5.1	–5.6	–7.8	–10.0	4.4	. . .
Other sectors	4 734 . .	36.8	17.8	–22.5	–10.2	–22.6	–6.9	–6.1	. . .
Other assets	4 736 . .	. . .	. . .	. . .	. . .	. . .	. . .	. . .	. . .
Monetary authorities: long-term	4 738 . .	. . .	. . .	. . .	. . .	. . .	. . .	. . .	. . .
Monetary authorities: short-term	4 739 . .	. . .	. . .	. . .	. . .	. . .	. . .	. . .	. . .
General government: long-term	4 741 . .	. . .	. . .	. . .	. . .	. . .	. . .	. . .	. . .
General government: short-term	4 742 . .	. . .	. . .	. . .	. . .	. . .	. . .	. . .	. . .
Banks: long-term	4 744 . .	. . .	. . .	. . .	. . .	. . .	. . .	. . .	. . .
Banks: short-term	4 745 . .	. . .	. . .	. . .	. . .	. . .	. . .	. . .	. . .
Other sectors: long-term	4 747 . .	. . .	. . .	. . .	. . .	. . .	. . .	. . .	. . .
Other sectors: short-term	4 748 . .	. . .	. . .	. . .	. . .	. . .	. . .	. . .	. . .
Liabilities	4 753 . .	**63.0**	**–24.6**	**12.9**	**26.2**	**16.4**	**77.2**	**56.2**	**. . .**
Trade credits	4 756 . .	.3	4.3	1.3	–2.1	3.6	–1.1	.2	. . .
General government: long-term	4 758 . .	. . .	. . .	. . .	. . .	. . .	. . .	. . .	. . .
General government: short-term	4 759 . .	. . .	. . .	. . .	. . .	. . .	. . .	. . .	. . .
Other sectors: long-term	4 761 . .	. . .	. . .	. . .	. . .	. . .	. . .	. . .	. . .
Other sectors: short-term	4 762 . .	.3	4.3	1.3	–2.1	3.6	–1.1	.2	. . .
Loans	4 764 . .	–.8	–31.8	3.4	–6.4	–13.8	35.6	96.4	. . .
Use of Fund credit and loans from the Fund	4 766 . .	–1.0	–1.6	–4.5	–7.5	–5.2	–8.4	55.1	. . .
Monetary authorities: other long-term	4 767 . .	. . .	. . .	. . .	. . .	. . .	. . .	. . .	. . .
Monetary authorities: short-term	4 768 . .	. . .	. . .	. . .	. . .	. . .	. . .	. . .	. . .
General government: long-term	4 770 . .	13.3	–17.8	8.5	–4.4	–4.3	47.5	40.6	. . .
General government: short-term	4 771 . .	–5.1	–7.9	1.3	–3.6	. . .	–3.3	. . .	. . .
Banks: long-term	4 773 . .	. . .	. . .	. . .	. . .	. . .	. . .	. . .	. . .
Banks: short-term	4 774 . .	. . .	. . .	. . .	. . .	. . .	. . .	. . .	. . .
Other sectors: long-term	4 776 . .	–7.7	–4.6	–1.7	–1.5	–1.2	–.8	. . .	. . .
Other sectors: short-term	4 777 . .	–.3	. . .	. . .	10.5	–3.1	.6	.7	. . .
Currency and deposits	4 780 . .	.2	–.6	. . .	. . .	3.1	–2.6	2.8	. . .
Monetary authorities	4 781 . .	. . .	. . .	. . .	. . .	. . .	. . .	. . .	. . .
General government	4 782 . .	. . .	. . .	. . .	. . .	. . .	. . .	. . .	. . .
Banks	4 783 . .	.2	–.6	. . .	. . .	3.1	–2.6	2.8	. . .
Other sectors	4 784 . .	. . .	. . .	. . .	. . .	. . .	. . .	. . .	. . .
Other liabilities	4 786 . .	63.3	3.5	8.1	34.6	23.5	45.3	–43.3	. . .
Monetary authorities: long-term	4 788 . .	–26.5	–11.6	–13.0	–6.1	. . .	. . .	. . .	. . .
Monetary authorities: short-term	4 789 . .	87.4	39.7	55.2	31.6	. . .	44.5	. . .	. . .
General government: long-term	4 791 . .	–20.8	–25.6	–43.0	–20.9	–3.0	–25.1	–71.2	. . .
General government: short-term	4 792 . .	22.0	1.2	8.2	30.4	26.9	26.4	38.3	. . .
Banks: long-term	4 794 . .	. . .	. . .	. . .	. . .	. . .	. . .	. . .	. . .
Banks: short-term	4 795 . .	. . .	. . .	. . .	. . .	. . .	. . .	. . .	. . .
Other sectors: long-term	4 797 . .	1.2	–.2	.7	–.4	–.4	–.4	–10.4	. . .
Other sectors: short-term	4 798 . .	. . .	. . .	. . .	. . .	. . .	. . .	. . .	. . .
D. RESERVE ASSETS	4 800 . .	–6.7	9.3	–5.1	–10.7	–14.0	–13.6	–18.6	. . .
Monetary gold	4 810 . .	. . .	. . .	. . .	. . .	. . .	. . .	. . .	. . .
Special drawing rights	4 820 . .	. . .	. . .	. . .	. . .	–1.8	–2.2	–4.6	. . .
Reserve position in the Fund	4 830 . .	. . .	. . .	. . .	. . .	. . .	. . .	. . .	. . .
Foreign exchange	4 840 . .	–6.7	9.3	–5.1	–10.7	–12.2	–11.4	–13.9	. . .
Other claims	4 880 . .	. . .	. . .	. . .	. . .	. . .	. . .	. . .	. . .
NET ERRORS AND OMISSIONS	4 998 . .	**–62.5**	**29.2**	**49.2**	**–28.9**	**39.8**	**16.1**	**56.4**	**. . .**

Part 3 of the *Yearbook* contains descriptions of the methodologies, compilation practices, and sources used to compile these data.

Table 1. ANALYTIC PRESENTATION, 1988–95
(Millions of U.S. dollars)

	Code	1988	1989	1990	1991	1992	1993	1994	1995
A. Current Account[1]	4 993 Y.	**1,882**	**2,923**	**3,097**	**4,884**	**5,615**	**4,205**	**11,284**	**15,093**
Goods: exports f.o.b	2 100 . .	40,703	45,700	54,678	61,333	66,565	77,858	97,918	119,019
Goods: imports f.o.b	3 100 . .	–40,675	–46,012	–56,311	–61,443	–68,388	–80,582	–96,567	–117,394
Balance on Goods	4 100 . .	*28*	*–312*	*–1,633*	*–111*	*–1,823*	*–2,724*	*1,351*	*1,625*
Services: credit	2 200 . .	7,563	9,658	12,811	13,821	15,938	18,514	23,366	29,375
Services: debit	3 200 . .	–5,791	–6,849	–8,645	–9,085	–9,497	–11,196	–13,556	–16,634
Balance on Goods and Services	4 991 . .	*1,800*	*2,497*	*2,533*	*4,626*	*4,618*	*4,593*	*11,161*	*14,366*
Income: credit	2 300 . .	3,882	4,752	6,509	7,558	8,214	8,085	8,803	11,043
Income: debit	3 300 . .	–3,501	–3,959	–5,502	–6,801	–6,678	–7,874	–7,945	–9,428
Balance on Goods, Services, and Income	4 992 . .	*2,181*	*3,289*	*3,540*	*5,383*	*6,154*	*4,805*	*12,019*	*15,981*
Current transfers: credit	2 379 Y.	132	156	187	186	197	176	193	253
Current transfers: debit	3 379 . .	–431	–523	–630	–685	–736	–775	–928	–1,142
B. Capital Account[1]	4 994 Y.	. . .	. . .	. . .	. . .	. . .	. . .	. . .	. . .
Capital account: credit	2 994 Y.	. . .	. . .	. . .	. . .	. . .	. . .	. . .	. . .
Capital account: debit	3 994 . .	. . .	. . .	. . .	. . .	. . .	. . .	. . .	. . .
Total, Groups A Plus B	4 010 . .	*1,882*	*2,923*	*3,097*	*4,884*	*5,615*	*4,205*	*11,284*	*15,093*
C. Financial Account[1]	4 995 X.	**988**	**1,251**	**3,948**	**2,345**	**1,793**	**–1,081**	**–9,068**	**–6,870**
Direct investment abroad	4 505 . .	–118	–882	–2,034	–526	–1,317	–2,021	–3,104	–3,906
Direct investment in Singapore	4 555 Y.	3,655	2,887	5,575	4,887	2,204	4,686	5,480	6,912
Portfolio investment assets	4 602 . .	–329	–450	–1,610	–666	1,091	–7,833	–7,766	–7,469
Equity securities	4 610 . .	–260	–358	–468	–524	–481	–7,588	–7,147	–7,095
Debt securities	4 619 . .	–69	–92	–1,142	–141	1,573	–246	–619	–375
Portfolio investment liabilities	4 652 Y.	36	375	573	–242	1,398	2,867	238	342
Equity securities	4 660 Y.	36	400	573	–242	1,398	2,759	293	394
Debt securities	4 669 Y.	. . .	–25	. . .	. . .	. . .	108	–55	–52
Other investment assets	4 703 . .	–2,625	–7,032	3,924	142	–4,729	–1,716	–8,283	–34
Monetary authorities	4 703 .A	. . .	. . .	. . .	. . .	. . .	. . .	. . .	. . .
General government	4 703 .B	. . .	–1	–1	–1	–1	–1	. . .	. . .
Banks	4 703 .C	–2,520	–7,280	2,708	1,025	–5,866	769	–4,291	1,147
Other sectors	4 703 .D	–105	249	1,216	–883	1,138	–2,484	–3,992	–1,181
Other investment liabilities	4 753 X.	369	6,354	–2,480	–1,250	3,144	2,935	4,367	–2,716
Monetary authorities	4 753 XA	. . .	. . .	. . .	. . .	. . .	. . .	. . .	. . .
General government	4 753 YB	–20	–17	–37	–14	–9	–9	–4	–4
Banks	4 753 YC	1,529	5,938	–1,028	–1,992	5,146	1,949	5,408	4,495
Other sectors	4 753 YD	–1,139	433	–1,415	757	–1,993	996	–1,038	–7,207
Total, Groups A Through C	4 020 . .	*2,870*	*4,173*	*7,044*	*7,229*	*7,408*	*3,125*	*2,216*	*8,222*
D. Net Errors and Omissions	4 998 . .	**–1,211**	**–1,436**	**–1,613**	**–3,031**	**–1,308**	**4,453**	**2,520**	**377**
Total, Groups A Through D	4 030 . .	*1,659*	*2,738*	*5,431*	*4,198*	*6,100*	*7,578*	*4,736*	*8,599*
E. Reserves and Related Items	4 040 . .	**–1,659**	**–2,738**	**–5,431**	**–4,198**	**–6,100**	**–7,578**	**–4,736**	**–8,599**
Reserve assets	4 800 . .	–1,659	–2,738	–5,431	–4,198	–6,100	–7,578	–4,736	–8,599
Use of Fund credit and loans	4 766 . .	. . .	. . .	. . .	. . .	. . .	. . .	. . .	. . .
Liabilities constituting foreign authorities' reserves	4 900 . .	. . .	. . .	. . .	. . .	. . .	. . .	. . .	. . .
Exceptional financing	4 920 . .	. . .	. . .	. . .	. . .	. . .	. . .	. . .	. . .
Conversion rates: Singapore dollars per U.S. dollar	0 101 . .	**2.0124**	**1.9503**	**1.8125**	**1.7276**	**1.6290**	**1.6158**	**1.5274**	**1.4174**

[1] Excludes components that have been classified in the categories of Group E.

Table 2. STANDARD PRESENTATION, 1988–95
(Millions of U.S. dollars)

	Code	1988	1989	1990	1991	1992	1993	1994	1995
CURRENT ACCOUNT	4 993 . .	**1,882**	**2,923**	**3,097**	**4,884**	**5,615**	**4,205**	**11,284**	**15,093**
A. GOODS	4 100 . .	28	–312	–1,633	–111	–1,823	–2,724	1,351	1,625
Credit	2 100 . .	**40,703**	**45,700**	**54,678**	**61,333**	**66,565**	**77,858**	**97,918**	**119,019**
General merchandise: exports f.o.b.	2 110 . .	39,574	44,443	53,059	59,494	65,106	76,209	96,236	117,258
Goods for processing: exports f.o.b.	2 150 . .	. . .	. . .	. . .	. . .	. . .	. . .	. . .	. . .
Repairs on goods	2 160 . .	. . .	. . .	. . .	. . .	. . .	. . .	. . .	. . .
Goods procured in ports by carriers	2 170 . .	1,129	1,257	1,619	1,839	1,459	1,649	1,683	1,761
Nonmonetary gold	2 180 . .	. . .	. . .	. . .	. . .	. . .	. . .	. . .	. . .
Debit	3 100 . .	**–40,675**	**–46,012**	**–56,311**	**–61,443**	**–68,388**	**–80,582**	**–96,567**	**–117,394**
General merchandise: imports f.o.b.	3 110 . .	–40,675	–46,012	–56,311	–61,443	–68,388	–80,582	–96,567	–117,394
Goods for processing: imports f.o.b.	3 150 . .	. . .	. . .	. . .	. . .	. . .	. . .	. . .	. . .
Repairs on goods	3 160 . .	. . .	. . .	. . .	. . .	. . .	. . .	. . .	. . .
Goods procured in ports by carriers	3 170 . .	. . .	. . .	. . .	. . .	. . .	. . .	. . .	. . .
Nonmonetary gold	3 180 . .	. . .	. . .	. . .	. . .	. . .	. . .	. . .	. . .
B. SERVICES	4 200 . .	1,772	2,809	4,166	4,737	6,441	7,318	9,810	12,741
Total credit	2 200 . .	*7,563*	*9,658*	*12,811*	*13,821*	*15,938*	*18,514*	*23,366*	*29,375*
Total debit	3 200 . .	*–5,791*	*–6,849*	*–8,645*	*–9,085*	*–9,497*	*–11,196*	*–13,556*	*–16,634*
Transportation services, credit	2 205 . .	**1,571**	**1,810**	**2,191**	**2,506**	**2,750**	**3,160**	**4,028**	**4,932**
Passenger	2 205 BA	. . .	. . .	. . .	. . .	. . .	. . .	. . .	. . .
Freight	2 205 BB	*1,178*	*1,340*	*1,576*	*1,769*	*1,904*	*2,218*	*2,894*	*3,545*
Other	2 205 BC	*393*	*470*	*615*	*737*	*847*	*942*	*1,134*	*1,387*
Sea transport, passenger	2 207 . .	. . .	. . .	. . .	. . .	. . .	. . .	. . .	. . .
Sea transport, freight	2 208 . .	. . .	. . .	. . .	. . .	. . .	. . .	. . .	. . .
Sea transport, other	2 209 . .	. . .	. . .	. . .	. . .	. . .	. . .	. . .	. . .
Air transport, passenger	2 211 . .	. . .	. . .	. . .	. . .	. . .	. . .	. . .	. . .
Air transport, freight	2 212 . .	. . .	. . .	. . .	. . .	. . .	. . .	. . .	. . .
Air transport, other	2 213 . .	. . .	. . .	. . .	. . .	. . .	. . .	. . .	. . .
Other transport, passenger	2 215 . .	. . .	. . .	. . .	. . .	. . .	. . .	. . .	. . .
Other transport, freight	2 216 . .	. . .	. . .	. . .	. . .	. . .	. . .	. . .	. . .
Other transport, other	2 217 . .	. . .	. . .	. . .	. . .	. . .	. . .	. . .	. . .
Transportation services, debit	3 205 . .	**–2,037**	**–2,356**	**–2,964**	**–3,204**	**–2,786**	**–3,231**	**–3,880**	**–4,888**
Passenger	3 205 BA	. . .	. . .	. . .	. . .	. . .	. . .	. . .	. . .
Freight	3 205 BB	*–2,037*	*–2,356*	*–2,964*	*–3,204*	*–2,786*	*–3,231*	*–3,880*	*–4,888*
Other	3 205 BC	. . .	. . .	. . .	. . .	. . .	. . .	. . .	. . .
Sea transport, passenger	3 207 . .	. . .	. . .	. . .	. . .	. . .	. . .	. . .	. . .
Sea transport, freight	3 208 . .	. . .	. . .	. . .	. . .	. . .	. . .	. . .	. . .
Sea transport, other	3 209 . .	. . .	. . .	. . .	. . .	. . .	. . .	. . .	. . .
Air transport, passenger	3 211 . .	. . .	. . .	. . .	. . .	. . .	. . .	. . .	. . .
Air transport, freight	3 212 . .	. . .	. . .	. . .	. . .	. . .	. . .	. . .	. . .
Air transport, other	3 213 . .	. . .	. . .	. . .	. . .	. . .	. . .	. . .	. . .
Other transport, passenger	3 215 . .	. . .	. . .	. . .	. . .	. . .	. . .	. . .	. . .
Other transport, freight	3 216 . .	. . .	. . .	. . .	. . .	. . .	. . .	. . .	. . .
Other transport, other	3 217 . .	. . .	. . .	. . .	. . .	. . .	. . .	. . .	. . .
Travel, credit	2 236 . .	**2,672**	**3,359**	**4,649**	**4,616**	**5,616**	**6,327**	**7,223**	**8,294**
Business travel	2 237 . .	. . .	. . .	. . .	. . .	. . .	. . .	. . .	. . .
Personal travel	2 240 . .	. . .	. . .	. . .	. . .	. . .	. . .	. . .	. . .
Travel, debit	3 236 . .	**–930**	**–1,334**	**–1,803**	**–1,844**	**–2,514**	**–3,145**	**–3,960**	**–5,140**
Business travel	3 237 . .	. . .	. . .	. . .	. . .	. . .	. . .	. . .	. . .
Personal travel	3 240 . .	. . .	. . .	. . .	. . .	. . .	. . .	. . .	. . .
Other services, credit	2 200 BA	**3,319**	**4,489**	**5,971**	**6,700**	**7,572**	**9,027**	**12,116**	**16,149**
Communications	2 245 . .	. . .	. . .	. . .	. . .	. . .	. . .	. . .	. . .
Construction	2 249 . .	. . .	. . .	. . .	. . .	. . .	. . .	. . .	. . .
Insurance	2 253 . .	98	95	88	115	168	262	338	390
Financial	2 260 . .	. . .	. . .	. . .	. . .	. . .	. . .	. . .	. . .
Computer and information	2 262 . .	. . .	. . .	. . .	. . .	. . .	. . .	. . .	. . .
Royalties and licence fees	2 266 . .	. . .	. . .	. . .	. . .	. . .	. . .	. . .	. . .
Other business services	2 268 . .	3,125	4,305	5,790	6,491	7,306	8,664	11,672	15,644
Personal, cultural, and recreational	2 287 . .	. . .	. . .	. . .	. . .	. . .	. . .	. . .	. . .
Government, n.i.e.	2 291 . .	96	89	92	94	98	101	105	115
Other services, debit	3 200 BA	**–2,824**	**–3,160**	**–3,877**	**–4,037**	**–4,197**	**–4,821**	**–5,715**	**–6,605**
Communications	3 245 . .	. . .	. . .	. . .	. . .	. . .	. . .	. . .	. . .
Construction	3 249 . .	. . .	. . .	. . .	. . .	. . .	. . .	. . .	. . .
Insurance	3 253 . .	–557	–631	–779	–832	–533	–633	–770	–972
Financial	3 260 . .	. . .	. . .	. . .	. . .	. . .	. . .	. . .	. . .
Computer and information	3 262 . .	. . .	. . .	. . .	. . .	. . .	. . .	. . .	. . .
Royalties and licence fees	3 266 . .	. . .	. . .	. . .	. . .	. . .	. . .	. . .	. . .
Other business services	3 268 . .	–2,203	–2,477	–3,032	–3,134	–3,562	–4,083	–4,847	–5,530
Personal, cultural, and recreational	3 287 . .	. . .	. . .	. . .	. . .	. . .	. . .	. . .	. . .
Government, n.i.e.	3 291 . .	–65	–52	–66	–71	–102	–105	–98	–104

Table 2 (Continued). STANDARD PRESENTATION, 1988–95
(Millions of U.S. dollars)

	Code		1988	1989	1990	1991	1992	1993	1994	1995
C. INCOME	4 300	. .	382	793	1,007	757	1,536	212	858	1,615
Total credit	2 300	. .	*3,882*	*4,752*	*6,509*	*7,558*	*8,214*	*8,085*	*8,803*	*11,043*
Total debit	3 300	. .	*–3,501*	*–3,959*	*–5,502*	*–6,801*	*–6,678*	*–7,874*	*–7,945*	*–9,428*
Compensation of employees, credit	2 310	. .	...	...	...	...	...	...	...	...
Compensation of employees, debit	3 310	. .	...	...	...	...	...	...	...	...
Investment income, credit	2 320	. .	**3,882**	**4,752**	**6,509**	**7,558**	**8,214**	**8,085**	**8,803**	**11,043**
Direct investment income	2 330	. .	...	...	...	...	...	...	...	...
Dividends and distributed branch profits	2 332	. .	...	...	...	...	...	...	...	...
Reinvested earnings and undistributed branch profits	2 333	. .	...	...	...	...	...	...	...	...
Income on debt (interest)	2 334	. .	...	...	...	...	...	...	...	...
Portfolio investment income	2 339	. .	...	...	...	...	...	...	...	...
Income on equity	2 340	. .	...	...	...	...	...	...	...	...
Income on bonds and notes	2 350	. .	...	...	...	...	...	...	...	...
Income on money market instruments and financial derivatives	2 360	. .	...	...	...	...	...	...	...	...
Other investment income	2 370	. .	3,882	4,752	6,509	7,558	8,214	8,085	8,803	11,043
Investment income, debit	3 320	. .	**–3,501**	**–3,959**	**–5,502**	**–6,801**	**–6,678**	**–7,874**	**–7,945**	**–9,428**
Direct investment income	3 330	. .	...	...	...	...	...	...	...	...
Dividends and distributed branch profits	3 332	. .	...	...	...	...	...	...	...	...
Reinvested earnings and undistributed branch profits	3 333	. .	...	...	...	...	...	...	...	...
Income on debt (interest)	3 334	. .	...	...	...	...	...	...	...	...
Portfolio investment income	3 339	. .	...	...	...	...	...	...	...	...
Income on equity	3 340	. .	...	...	...	...	...	...	...	...
Income on bonds and notes	3 350	. .	...	...	...	...	...	...	...	...
Income on money market instruments and financial derivatives	3 360	. .	...	...	...	...	...	...	...	...
Other investment income	3 370	. .	–3,501	–3,959	–5,502	–6,801	–6,678	–7,874	–7,945	–9,428
D. CURRENT TRANSFERS	4 379	. .	–299	–367	–443	–500	–539	–600	–735	–888
Credit	2 379	. .	**132**	**156**	**187**	**186**	**197**	**176**	**193**	**253**
General government	2 380	. .	4	5	5	6	6	6	7	7
Other sectors	2 390	. .	127	151	182	180	191	170	187	246
Workers' remittances	2 391	. .	...	...	...	...	...	...	...	...
Other current transfers	2 392	. .	127	151	182	180	191	170	187	246
Debit	3 379	. .	**–431**	**–523**	**–630**	**–685**	**–736**	**–775**	**–928**	**–1,142**
General government	3 380	. .	–10	–9	–9	–11	–14	–16	–18	–20
Other sectors	3 390	. .	–421	–514	–621	–674	–723	–759	–909	–1,122
Workers' remittances	3 391	. .	...	...	...	...	...	...	...	...
Other current transfers	3 392	. .	–421	–514	–621	–674	–723	–759	–909	–1,122
CAPITAL AND FINANCIAL ACCOUNT	4 996	. .	**–671**	**–1,487**	**–1,483**	**–1,853**	**–4,307**	**–8,658**	**–13,804**	**–15,470**
CAPITAL ACCOUNT	4 994	. .	...	...	...	...	...	...	...	...
Total credit	2 994	. .	...	...	...	...	...	...	...	...
Total debit	3 994	. .	...	...	...	...	...	...	...	...
Capital transfers, credit	2 400	. .	...	...	...	...	...	...	...	...
General government	2 401	. .	...	...	...	...	...	...	...	...
Debt forgiveness	2 402	. .	...	...	...	...	...	...	...	...
Other capital transfers	2 410	. .	...	...	...	...	...	...	...	...
Other sectors	2 430	. .	...	...	...	...	...	...	...	...
Migrants' transfers	2 431	. .	...	...	...	...	...	...	...	...
Debt forgiveness	2 432	. .	...	...	...	...	...	...	...	...
Other capital transfers	2 440	. .	...	...	...	...	...	...	...	...
Capital transfers, debit	3 400	. .	...	...	...	...	...	...	...	...
General government	3 401	. .	...	...	...	...	...	...	...	...
Debt forgiveness	3 402	. .	...	...	...	...	...	...	...	...
Other capital transfers	3 410	. .	...	...	...	...	...	...	...	...
Other sectors	3 430	. .	...	...	...	...	...	...	...	...
Migrants' transfers	3 431	. .	...	...	...	...	...	...	...	...
Debt forgiveness	3 432	. .	...	...	...	...	...	...	...	...
Other capital transfers	3 440	. .	...	...	...	...	...	...	...	...
Nonproduced nonfinancial assets, credit	2 480	. .	...	...	...	...	...	...	...	...
Nonproduced nonfinancial assets, debit	3 480	. .	...	...	...	...	...	...	...	...

Table 2 (Continued). STANDARD PRESENTATION, 1988–95
(Millions of U.S. dollars)

	Code	1988	1989	1990	1991	1992	1993	1994	1995
FINANCIAL ACCOUNT	4 995 . .	**–671**	**–1,487**	**–1,483**	**–1,853**	**–4,307**	**–8,658**	**–13,804**	**–15,470**
A. DIRECT INVESTMENT	4 500 . .	3,537	2,004	3,541	4,361	888	2,666	2,377	3,006
Direct investment abroad	4 505 . .	**–118**	**–882**	**–2,034**	**–526**	**–1,317**	**–2,021**	**–3,104**	**–3,906**
Equity capital	4 510 . .	–118	–882	–2,034	–526	–1,317	–2,021	–3,104	–3,906
Claims on affiliated enterprises	4 515 . .	...	...	...	...	...	...	...	...
Liabilities to affiliated enterprises	4 520 . .	...	...	...	...	...	...	...	...
Reinvested earnings	4 525 . .	...	...	...	...	...	...	...	...
Other capital	4 530 . .	...	...	...	...	...	...	...	...
Claims on affiliated enterprises	4 535 . .	...	...	...	...	...	...	...	...
Liabilities to affiliated enterprises	4 540 . .	...	...	...	...	...	...	...	...
Direct investment in Singapore	4 555 . .	**3,655**	**2,887**	**5,575**	**4,887**	**2,204**	**4,686**	**5,480**	**6,912**
Equity capital	4 560 . .	3,655	2,887	5,575	4,887	2,204	4,686	5,480	6,912
Claims on direct investors	4 565 . .	...	...	...	...	...	...	...	...
Liabilities to direct investors	4 570 . .	...	...	...	...	...	...	...	...
Reinvested earnings	4 575 . .	...	...	...	...	...	...	...	...
Other capital	4 580 . .	...	...	...	...	...	...	...	...
Claims on direct investors	4 585 . .	...	...	...	...	...	...	...	...
Liabilities to direct investors	4 590 . .	...	...	...	...	...	...	...	...
B. PORTFOLIO INVESTMENT	4 600 . .	–293	–75	–1,037	–908	2,490	–4,966	–7,528	–7,127
Assets	4 602 . .	**–329**	**–450**	**–1,610**	**–666**	**1,091**	**–7,833**	**–7,766**	**–7,469**
Equity securities	4 610 . .	–260	–358	–468	–524	–481	–7,588	–7,147	–7,095
Monetary authorities	4 611 . .	...	...	...	...	...	...	...	...
General government	4 612 . .	...	...	...	...	...	...	...	...
Banks	4 613 . .	...	...	...	...	...	...	...	...
Other sectors	4 614 . .	–260	–358	–468	–524	–481	–7,588	–7,147	–7,095
Debt securities	4 619 . .	–69	–92	–1,142	–141	1,573	–246	–619	–375
Bonds and notes	4 620 . .	–69	–92	–1,142	–141	1,573	–246	–619	–375
Monetary authorities	4 621 . .	...	...	...	...	...	...	...	...
General government	4 622 . .	...	...	...	...	...	...	...	...
Banks	4 623 . .	...	...	...	...	...	...	...	...
Other sectors	4 624 . .	–69	–92	–1,142	–141	1,573	–246	–619	–375
Money market instruments	4 630 . .	...	...	...	...	...	...	...	...
Monetary authorities	4 631 . .	...	...	...	...	...	...	...	...
General government	4 632 . .	...	...	...	...	...	...	...	...
Banks	4 633 . .	...	...	...	...	...	...	...	...
Other sectors	4 634 . .	...	...	...	...	...	...	...	...
Financial derivatives	4 640 . .	...	...	...	...	...	...	...	...
Monetary authorities	4 641 . .	...	...	...	...	...	...	...	...
General government	4 642 . .	...	...	...	...	...	...	...	...
Banks	4 643 . .	...	...	...	...	...	...	...	...
Other sectors	4 644 . .	...	...	...	...	...	...	...	...
Liabilities	4 652 . .	**36**	**375**	**573**	**–242**	**1,398**	**2,867**	**238**	**342**
Equity securities	4 660 . .	36	400	573	–242	1,398	2,759	293	394
Banks	4 663 . .	...	...	...	...	...	...	...	...
Other sectors	4 664 . .	36	400	573	–242	1,398	2,759	293	394
Debt securities	4 669 . .	...	–25	...	...	...	108	–55	–52
Bonds and notes	4 670 . .	...	–25	...	...	...	108	–55	–52
Monetary authorities	4 671 . .	...	...	...	...	...	...	...	...
General government	4 672 . .	...	–25	...	...	...	108	–55	–52
Banks	4 673 . .	...	...	...	...	...	...	...	...
Other sectors	4 674 . .	...	...	...	...	...	...	...	...
Money market instruments	4 680 . .	...	...	...	...	...	...	...	...
Monetary authorities	4 681 . .	...	...	...	...	...	...	...	...
General government	4 682 . .	...	...	...	...	...	...	...	...
Banks	4 683 . .	...	...	...	...	...	...	...	...
Other sectors	4 684 . .	...	...	...	...	...	...	...	...
Financial derivatives	4 690 . .	...	...	...	...	...	...	...	...
Monetary authorities	4 691 . .	...	...	...	...	...	...	...	...
General government	4 692 . .	...	...	...	...	...	...	...	...
Banks	4 693 . .	...	...	...	...	...	...	...	...
Other sectors	4 694 . .	...	...	...	...	...	...	...	...

Table 2 (Concluded). STANDARD PRESENTATION, 1988–95

(Millions of U.S. dollars)

	Code	1988	1989	1990	1991	1992	1993	1994	1995
C. OTHER INVESTMENT	4 700	–2,256	–678	1,444	–1,109	–1,584	1,220	–3,916	–2,749
Assets	4 703	**–2,625**	**–7,032**	**3,924**	**142**	**–4,729**	**–1,716**	**–8,283**	**–34**
Trade credits	4 706	...	...	...	...	...	...	...	...
General government: long-term	4 708	...	...	...	...	...	...	...	...
General government: short-term	4 709	...	...	...	...	...	...	...	...
Other sectors: long-term	4 711	...	...	...	...	...	...	...	...
Other sectors: short-term	4 712	...	...	...	...	...	...	...	...
Loans	4 714	–188	–333	–844	–467	–273	–563	–870	–1,302
Monetary authorities: long-term	4 717	...	...	...	...	...	...	...	...
Monetary authorities: short-term	4 718	...	...	...	...	...	...	...	...
General government: long-term	4 720	...	...	...	...	...	...	...	...
General government: short-term	4 721	...	...	...	...	...	...	...	...
Banks: long-term	4 723	...	...	...	...	...	...	...	...
Banks: short-term	4 724	...	...	...	...	...	...	...	...
Other sectors: long-term	4 726	–188	–333	–844	–467	–273	–563	–870	–1,302
Other sectors: short-term	4 727	...	...	...	...	...	...	...	...
Currency and deposits	4 730	–2,429	–6,573	4,947	842	–3,272	3,314	–2,262	5,099
Monetary authorities	4 731	...	...	...	...	...	...	...	...
General government	4 732	...	...	...	...	...	...	...	...
Banks	4 733	–2,460	–6,962	3,099	1,192	–5,514	1,401	–3,295	1,907
Other sectors	4 734	31	389	1,848	–351	2,242	1,913	1,033	3,192
Other assets	4 736	–8	–126	–179	–233	–1,184	–4,466	–5,151	–3,830
Monetary authorities: long-term	4 738	...	...	...	...	...	...	...	...
Monetary authorities: short-term	4 739	...	...	...	...	...	...	...	...
General government: long-term	4 741	...	–1	–1	–1	–1	–1	...	...
General government: short-term	4 742	...	...	...	...	...	...	...	...
Banks: long-term	4 744	–60	–318	–391	–167	–352	–632	–996	–760
Banks: short-term	4 745	...	...	...	...	...	...	...	...
Other sectors: long-term	4 747	52	193	212	–65	–831	–3,833	–4,155	–3,070
Other sectors: short-term	4 748	...	...	...	...	...	...	...	...
Liabilities	4 753	**369**	**6,354**	**–2,480**	**–1,250**	**3,144**	**2,935**	**4,367**	**–2,716**
Trade credits	4 756	–51	–30	–26	–25	–25	–35	–12	–11
General government: long-term	4 758	...	...	...	...	...	...	...	...
General government: short-term	4 759	...	...	...	...	...	...	...	...
Other sectors: long-term	4 761	–51	–30	–26	–25	–25	–35	–12	–11
Other sectors: short-term	4 762	...	...	...	...	...	...	...	...
Loans	4 764	–36	–301	–83	–32	–303	–59	–4	–4
Use of Fund credit and loans from the Fund	4 766	...	...	...	...	...	...	...	...
Monetary authorities: other long-term	4 767	...	...	...	...	...	...	...	...
Monetary authorities: short-term	4 768	...	...	...	...	...	...	...	...
General government: long-term	4 770	–20	–17	–37	–14	–9	–9	–4	–4
General government: short-term	4 771	...	...	...	...	...	...	...	...
Banks: long-term	4 773	...	...	...	...	...	...	...	...
Banks: short-term	4 774	...	...	...	...	...	...	...	...
Other sectors: long-term	4 776	–16	–284	–46	–18	–294	–50	...	...
Other sectors: short-term	4 777	...	...	...	...	...	...	...	...
Currency and deposits	4 780	1,460	5,716	–809	–1,984	4,983	2,306	5,454	4,034
Monetary authorities	4 781	...	...	...	...	...	...	...	...
General government	4 782	...	...	...	...	...	...	...	...
Banks	4 783	1,460	5,716	–809	–1,984	4,983	2,306	5,454	4,034
Other sectors	4 784	...	...	...	...	...	...	...	...
Other liabilities	4 786	–1,004	969	–1,561	792	–1,511	723	–1,071	–6,736
Monetary authorities: long-term	4 788	...	...	...	...	...	...	...	...
Monetary authorities: short-term	4 789	...	...	...	...	...	...	...	...
General government: long-term	4 791	...	...	...	...	...	...	...	...
General government: short-term	4 792	...	...	...	...	...	...	...	...
Banks: long-term	4 794	68	222	–219	–8	163	–357	–46	461
Banks: short-term	4 795	...	...	...	...	...	...	...	...
Other sectors: long-term	4 797	10	573	94	–2	262	157	154	–1,100
Other sectors: short-term	4 798	–1,082	174	–1,437	802	–1,936	924	–1,179	–6,096
D. RESERVE ASSETS	4 800	–1,659	–2,738	–5,431	–4,198	–6,100	–7,578	–4,736	–8,599
Monetary gold	4 810	...	...	...	...	...	...	...	...
Special drawing rights	4 820	3	–1	–3	...	44	–10	46	–14
Reserve position in the Fund	4 830	2	–3	16	12	–74	–62	–22	–42
Foreign exchange	4 840	–1,664	–2,735	–5,444	–4,209	–6,070	–7,505	–4,761	–8,544
Other claims	4 880	...	...	...	...	...	...	...	...
NET ERRORS AND OMISSIONS	4 998	**–1,211**	**–1,436**	**–1,613**	**–3,031**	**–1,308**	**4,453**	**2,520**	**377**

Part 3 of the *Yearbook* contains descriptions of the methodologies, compilation practices, and sources used to compile these data.

Table 1. ANALYTIC PRESENTATION, 1988–95
(Millions of U.S. dollars)

	Code	1988	1989	1990	1991	1992	1993	1994	1995
A. Current Account [1]	4 993 Y.	...	...	...	...	...	**–580**	**719**	**648**
Goods: exports f.o.b.	2 100 ..	...	...	...	...	...	5,452	6,743	8,557
Goods: imports f.o.b.	3 100 ..	...	...	...	...	...	–6,365	–6,634	–8,534
Balance on Goods	4 100 ..	...	...	...	...	...	*–912*	*109*	*23*
Services: credit	2 200 ..	...	...	...	...	...	1,939	2,261	2,378
Services: debit	3 200 ..	...	...	...	...	...	–1,666	–1,600	–1,832
Balance on Goods and Services	4 991 ..	...	...	...	...	...	*–640*	*770*	*569*
Income: credit	2 300 ..	...	...	...	...	...	185	155	250
Income: debit	3 300 ..	...	...	...	...	...	–224	–275	–263
Balance on Goods, Services, and Income	4 992 ..	...	...	...	...	...	*–678*	*650*	*555*
Current transfers: credit	2 379 Y.	...	...	...	...	...	216	166	243
Current transfers: debit	3 379 ..	...	...	...	...	...	–118	–98	–150
B. Capital Account [1]	4 994 Y.	...	...	...	...	...	**564**	**84**	**46**
Capital account: credit	2 994 Y.	...	...	...	...	...	771	84	46
Capital account: debit	3 994 ..	...	...	...	...	...	–208	...	...
Total, Groups A Plus B	4 010 ..	...	...	...	...	...	*–16*	*803*	*694*
C. Financial Account [1]	4 995 X.	...	...	...	...	...	**–153**	**4**	**1,158**
Direct investment abroad	4 505 ..	...	...	...	...	...	–61	–14	–10
Direct investment in Slovak Republic	4 555 Y.	...	...	...	...	...	199	203	183
Portfolio investment assets	4 602 ..	...	...	...	...	...	–774	–26	157
Equity securities	4 610 ..	...	...	...	...	...	–774	–26	174
Debt securities	4 619 ..	...	...	...	...	...	...	...	–17
Portfolio investment liabilities	4 652 Y.	...	...	...	...	...	465	304	53
Equity securities	4 660 Y.	...	...	...	...	...	465	111	–16
Debt securities	4 669 Y.	...	...	...	...	...	...	193	69
Other investment assets	4 703 ..	...	...	...	...	...	–412	–548	–116
Monetary authorities	4 703 .A	...	...	...	...	...	...	...	...
General government	4 703 .B	...	...	...	...	...	232	–211	140
Banks	4 703 .C	...	...	...	...	...	–530	–344	–248
Other sectors	4 703 .D	...	...	...	...	...	–114	7	–8
Other investment liabilities	4 753 X.	...	...	...	...	...	430	84	891
Monetary authorities	4 753 XA	...	...	...	...	...	...	38	42
General government	4 753 YB	...	...	...	...	...	145	–52	–173
Banks	4 753 YC	...	...	...	...	...	99	38	463
Other sectors	4 753 YD	...	...	...	...	...	186	60	559
Total, Groups A Through C	4 020 ..	...	...	...	...	...	*–169*	*807*	*1,851*
D. Net Errors and Omissions	4 998 ..	...	...	...	...	...	**183**	**398**	**–60**
Total, Groups A Through D	4 030 ..	...	...	...	...	...	*14*	*1,205*	*1,791*
E. Reserves and Related Items	4 040 ..	...	...	...	...	...	**–14**	**–1,205**	**–1,791**
Reserve assets	4 800 ..	...	...	...	...	...	–104	–1,256	–1,590
Use of Fund credit and loans	4 766 ..	...	...	...	...	...	89	51	–201
Liabilities constituting foreign authorities' reserves	4 900 ..	...	...	...	...	...	...	...	...
Exceptional financing	4 920 ..	...	...	...	...	...	...	...	...
Conversion rates: Slovak koruny per U.S. dollar	0 101 ..	...	...	...	...	...	**30.770**	**32.045**	**29.713**

[1] Excludes components that have been classified in the categories of Group E.

Table 2. STANDARD PRESENTATION, 1988–95
(Millions of U.S. dollars)

	Code	1988	1989	1990	1991	1992	1993	1994	1995
CURRENT ACCOUNT	4 993 . .	...	...	...	...	...	**–580**	**719**	**648**
A. GOODS	4 100 . .	...	...	...	...	...	–912	109	23
Credit	2 100 . .	...	...	...	...	...	**5,452**	**6,743**	**8,557**
General merchandise: exports f.o.b.	2 110 . .	...	...	...	...	...	...	...	...
Goods for processing: exports f.o.b.	2 150 . .	...	...	...	...	...	...	...	...
Repairs on goods	2 160 . .	...	...	...	...	...	...	...	...
Goods procured in ports by carriers	2 170 . .	...	...	...	...	...	...	...	...
Nonmonetary gold	2 180 . .	...	...	...	...	...	...	...	...
Debit	3 100 . .	...	...	...	...	...	**–6,365**	**–6,634**	**–8,534**
General merchandise: imports f.o.b.	3 110 . .	...	...	...	...	...	...	...	...
Goods for processing: imports f.o.b.	3 150 . .	...	...	...	...	...	...	...	...
Repairs on goods	3 160 . .	...	...	...	...	...	...	...	...
Goods procured in ports by carriers	3 170 . .	...	...	...	...	...	...	...	...
Nonmonetary gold	3 180 . .	...	...	...	...	...	...	...	...
B. SERVICES	4 200 . .	...	...	...	...	...	272	662	546
Total credit	2 200 . .	...	...	...	...	...	*1,939*	*2,261*	*2,378*
Total debit	3 200 . .	...	...	...	...	...	*–1,666*	*–1,600*	*–1,832*
Transportation services, credit	2 205 . .	...	...	...	...	...	**460**	**539**	**616**
Passenger	2 205 BA	...	...	...	...	...	...	*7*	*7*
Freight	2 205 BB	...	...	...	...	...	...	*523*	*605*
Other	2 205 BC	...	...	...	...	...	...	*9*	*4*
Sea transport, passenger	2 207 . .	...	...	...	...	...	...	...	...
Sea transport, freight	2 208 . .	...	...	...	...	...	...	6	1
Sea transport, other	2 209 . .	...	...	...	...	...	...	...	...
Air transport, passenger	2 211 . .	...	...	...	...	...	...	3	5
Air transport, freight	2 212 . .	...	...	...	...	...	...	...	2
Air transport, other	2 213 . .	...	...	...	...	...	...	...	...
Other transport, passenger	2 215 . .	...	...	...	...	...	...	4	2
Other transport, freight	2 216 . .	...	...	...	...	...	...	517	601
Other transport, other	2 217 . .	...	...	...	...	...	...	9	4
Transportation services, debit	3 205 . .	...	...	...	...	...	**–289**	**–162**	**–301**
Passenger	3 205 BA	...	...	...	...	...	...	*–12*	*–17*
Freight	3 205 BB	...	...	...	...	...	...	*–143*	*–272*
Other	3 205 BC	...	...	...	...	...	...	*–8*	*–11*
Sea transport, passenger	3 207 . .	...	...	...	...	...	...	...	...
Sea transport, freight	3 208 . .	...	...	...	...	...	...	–10	–13
Sea transport, other	3 209 . .	...	...	...	...	...	...	...	...
Air transport, passenger	3 211 . .	...	...	...	...	...	...	–9	–15
Air transport, freight	3 212 . .	...	...	...	...	...	...	–2	–5
Air transport, other	3 213 . .	...	...	...	...	...	...	...	...
Other transport, passenger	3 215 . .	...	...	...	...	...	...	–2	–1
Other transport, freight	3 216 . .	...	...	...	...	...	...	–131	–254
Other transport, other	3 217 . .	...	...	...	...	...	...	–8	–11
Travel, credit	2 236 . .	...	...	...	...	...	**383**	**568**	**623**
Business travel	2 237 . .	...	...	...	...	...	...	...	...
Personal travel	2 240 . .	...	...	...	...	...	...	568	623
Travel, debit	3 236 . .	...	...	...	...	...	**–217**	**–282**	**–321**
Business travel	3 237 . .	...	...	...	...	...	...	–88	–173
Personal travel	3 240 . .	...	...	...	...	...	...	–194	–148
Other services, credit	2 200 BA	...	...	...	...	...	**1,096**	**1,154**	**1,140**
Communications	2 245 . .	...	...	...	...	...	...	274	265
Construction	2 249 . .	...	...	...	...	...	...	74	109
Insurance	2 253 . .	...	...	...	...	...	...	16	2
Financial	2 260 . .	...	...	...	...	...	...	64	114
Computer and information	2 262 . .	...	...	...	...	...	...	...	...
Royalties and licence fees	2 266 . .	...	...	...	...	...	...	7	11
Other business services	2 268 . .	...	...	...	...	...	1,096	679	638
Personal, cultural, and recreational	2 287 . .	...	...	...	...	...	...	...	...
Government, n.i.e.	2 291 . .	...	...	...	...	...	...	40	...
Other services, debit	3 200 BA	...	...	...	...	...	**–1,160**	**–1,156**	**–1,210**
Communications	3 245 . .	...	...	...	...	...	...	–304	–279
Construction	3 249 . .	...	...	...	...	...	...	–24	–31
Insurance	3 253 . .	...	...	...	...	...	...	–33	–24
Financial	3 260 . .	...	...	...	...	...	...	–38	–65
Computer and information	3 262 . .	...	...	...	...	...	...	...	...
Royalties and licence fees	3 266 . .	...	...	...	...	...	...	–64	–79
Other business services	3 268 . .	...	...	...	...	...	–1,160	–642	–695
Personal, cultural, and recreational	3 287 . .	...	...	...	...	...	...	...	...
Government, n.i.e.	3 291 . .	...	...	...	...	...	...	–51	–38

Table 2 (Continued). STANDARD PRESENTATION, 1988–95
(Millions of U.S. dollars)

	Code	1988	1989	1990	1991	1992	1993	1994	1995
C. INCOME	4 300 . .	...	...	...	...	...	–38	–120	–14
Total credit	2 300 . .	...	...	...	...	...	*185*	*155*	*250*
Total debit	3 300 . .	...	...	...	...	...	*–224*	*–275*	*–263*
Compensation of employees, credit	2 310 . .	**...**	**...**	**...**	**...**	**...**	**79**	**48**	**26**
Compensation of employees, debit	3 310 . .	**...**	**...**	**...**	**...**	**...**	**–2**	**–6**	**–3**
Investment income, credit	2 320 . .	**...**	**...**	**...**	**...**	**...**	**107**	**107**	**224**
Direct investment income	2 330 . .	...	...	...	...	...	...	...	...
Dividends and distributed branch profits	2 332 . .	...	...	...	...	...	...	...	...
Reinvested earnings and undistributed branch profits	2 333 . .	...	...	...	...	...	...	...	...
Income on debt (interest)	2 334 . .	...	...	...	...	...	...	...	...
Portfolio investment income	2 339 . .	...	...	...	...	...	...	27	46
Income on equity	2 340 . .	...	...	...	...	...	...	27	10
Income on bonds and notes	2 350 . .	...	...	...	...	...	...	...	18
Income on money market instruments and financial derivatives	2 360 . .	...	...	...	...	...	...	...	18
Other investment income	2 370 . .	...	...	...	...	...	...	80	178
Investment income, debit	3 320 . .	**...**	**...**	**...**	**...**	**...**	**–222**	**–269**	**–261**
Direct investment income	3 330 . .	...	...	...	...	...	...	...	...
Dividends and distributed branch profits	3 332 . .	...	...	...	...	...	...	...	...
Reinvested earnings and undistributed branch profits	3 333 . .	...	...	...	...	...	...	...	...
Income on debt (interest)	3 334 . .	...	...	...	...	...	...	...	...
Portfolio investment income	3 339 . .	...	...	...	...	...	...	–33	–75
Income on equity	3 340 . .	...	...	...	...	...	...	–33	–18
Income on bonds and notes	3 350 . .	...	...	...	...	...	...	...	–58
Income on money market instruments and financial derivatives	3 360 . .	...	...	...	...	...	...	...	...
Other investment income	3 370 . .	...	...	...	...	...	...	–236	–186
D. CURRENT TRANSFERS	4 379 . .	...	...	...	...	...	98	68	93
Credit	2 379 . .	**...**	**...**	**...**	**...**	**...**	**216**	**166**	**243**
General government	2 380 . .	...	...	...	...	...	14	14	43
Other sectors	2 390 . .	...	...	...	...	...	202	151	199
Workers' remittances	2 391 . .	...	...	...	...	...	...	...	...
Other current transfers	2 392 . .	...	...	...	...	...	202	151	199
Debit	3 379 . .	**...**	**...**	**...**	**...**	**...**	**–118**	**–98**	**–150**
General government	3 380 . .	...	...	...	...	...	–11	–8	–27
Other sectors	3 390 . .	...	...	...	...	...	–107	–89	–123
Workers' remittances	3 391 . .	...	...	...	...	...	...	...	...
Other current transfers	3 392 . .	...	...	...	...	...	–107	–89	–123
CAPITAL AND FINANCIAL ACCOUNT	4 996 . .	**...**	**...**	**...**	**...**	**...**	**396**	**–1,117**	**–588**
CAPITAL ACCOUNT	4 994 . .	**...**	**...**	**...**	**...**	**...**	**564**	**84**	**46**
Total credit	2 994 . .	...	...	...	...	...	*771*	*84*	*46*
Total debit	3 994 . .	...	...	...	...	...	*–208*	...	...
Capital transfers, credit	2 400 . .	**...**	**...**	**...**	**...**	**...**	**771**	**84**	**46**
General government	2 401 . .	...	...	...	...	...	...	...	...
Debt forgiveness	2 402 . .	...	...	...	...	...	...	...	...
Other capital transfers	2 410 . .	...	...	...	...	...	...	...	...
Other sectors	2 430 . .	...	...	...	...	...	771	84	46
Migrants' transfers	2 431 . .	...	...	...	...	...	...	...	...
Debt forgiveness	2 432 . .	...	...	...	...	...	...	84	46
Other capital transfers	2 440 . .	...	...	...	...	...	771	...	...
Capital transfers, debit	3 400 . .	**...**	**...**	**...**	**...**	**...**	**–208**	**...**	**...**
General government	3 401 . .	...	...	...	...	...	...	...	...
Debt forgiveness	3 402 . .	...	...	...	...	...	...	...	...
Other capital transfers	3 410 . .	...	...	...	...	...	...	...	...
Other sectors	3 430 . .	...	...	...	...	...	–208	...	...
Migrants' transfers	3 431 . .	...	...	...	...	...	...	...	...
Debt forgiveness	3 432 . .	...	...	...	...	...	...	...	...
Other capital transfers	3 440 . .	...	...	...	...	...	–208	...	...
Nonproduced nonfinancial assets, credit	2 480 . .	**...**	**...**	**...**	**...**	**...**	**...**	**...**	**...**
Nonproduced nonfinancial assets, debit	3 480 . .	**...**	**...**	**...**	**...**	**...**	**...**	**...**	**...**

Table 2 (Continued). STANDARD PRESENTATION, 1988–95
(Millions of U.S. dollars)

	Code	1988	1989	1990	1991	1992	1993	1994	1995
FINANCIAL ACCOUNT	4 995	...	...	...	...	...	**–167**	**–1,201**	**–634**
A. DIRECT INVESTMENT	4 500	...	...	...	...	...	138	190	173
Direct investment abroad	4 505	...	...	...	...	...	**–61**	**–14**	**–10**
Equity capital	4 510	...	...	...	...	...	...	–14	–9
Claims on affiliated enterprises	4 515	...	...	...	...	...	...	–14	–9
Liabilities to affiliated enterprises	4 520	...	...	...	...	...	...	...	...
Reinvested earnings	4 525	...	...	...	...	...	...	...	...
Other capital	4 530	...	...	...	...	...	...	...	–1
Claims on affiliated enterprises	4 535	...	...	...	...	...	...	...	...
Liabilities to affiliated enterprises	4 540	...	...	...	...	...	...	...	...
Direct investment in Slovak Republic	4 555	...	...	...	...	...	**199**	**203**	**183**
Equity capital	4 560	...	...	...	...	...	...	203	171
Claims on direct investors	4 565	...	...	...	...	...	...	...	...
Liabilities to direct investors	4 570	...	...	...	...	...	...	203	171
Reinvested earnings	4 575	...	...	...	...	...	...	...	...
Other capital	4 580	...	...	...	...	...	...	...	11
Claims on direct investors	4 585	...	...	...	...	...	...	...	...
Liabilities to direct investors	4 590	...	...	...	...	...	...	...	...
B. PORTFOLIO INVESTMENT	4 600	...	...	...	...	...	–309	278	210
Assets	4 602	...	...	...	...	...	**–774**	**–26**	**157**
Equity securities	4 610	...	...	...	...	...	–774	–26	174
Monetary authorities	4 611	...	...	...	...	...	...	...	...
General government	4 612	...	...	...	...	...	...	...	...
Banks	4 613	...	...	...	...	...	...	3	...
Other sectors	4 614	...	...	...	...	...	–774	–29	174
Debt securities	4 619	...	...	...	...	...	...	...	–17
Bonds and notes	4 620	...	...	...	...	...	...	...	–17
Monetary authorities	4 621	...	...	...	...	...	...	...	...
General government	4 622	...	...	...	...	...	...	...	...
Banks	4 623	...	...	...	...	...	...	...	–17
Other sectors	4 624	...	...	...	...	...	...	...	...
Money market instruments	4 630	...	...	...	...	...	...	...	...
Monetary authorities	4 631	...	...	...	...	...	...	...	...
General government	4 632	...	...	...	...	...	...	...	...
Banks	4 633	...	...	...	...	...	...	...	...
Other sectors	4 634	...	...	...	...	...	...	...	...
Financial derivatives	4 640	...	...	...	...	...	...	...	...
Monetary authorities	4 641	...	...	...	...	...	...	...	...
General government	4 642	...	...	...	...	...	...	...	...
Banks	4 643	...	...	...	...	...	...	...	...
Other sectors	4 644	...	...	...	...	...	...	...	...
Liabilities	4 652	...	...	...	...	...	**465**	**304**	**53**
Equity securities	4 660	...	...	...	...	...	465	111	–16
Banks	4 663	...	...	...	...	...	...	...	...
Other sectors	4 664	...	...	...	...	...	465	111	–16
Debt securities	4 669	...	...	...	...	...	...	193	69
Bonds and notes	4 670	...	...	...	...	...	...	193	70
Monetary authorities	4 671	...	...	...	...	...	...	193	...
General government	4 672	...	...	...	...	...	...	...	...
Banks	4 673	...	...	...	...	...	...	...	...
Other sectors	4 674	...	...	...	...	...	...	...	70
Money market instruments	4 680	...	...	...	...	...	...	...	...
Monetary authorities	4 681	...	...	...	...	...	...	...	...
General government	4 682	...	...	...	...	...	...	...	...
Banks	4 683	...	...	...	...	...	...	...	...
Other sectors	4 684	...	...	...	...	...	...	...	...
Financial derivatives	4 690	...	...	...	...	...	...	...	...
Monetary authorities	4 691	...	...	...	...	...	...	...	...
General government	4 692	...	...	...	...	...	...	...	...
Banks	4 693	...	...	...	...	...	...	...	...
Other sectors	4 694	...	...	...	...	...	...	...	...

Table 2 (Concluded). STANDARD PRESENTATION, 1988–95
(Millions of U.S. dollars)

	Code	1988	1989	1990	1991	1992	1993	1994	1995
C. OTHER INVESTMENT	4 700	...	...	...	...	...	107	–412	574
Assets	4 703	...	...	...	...	...	**–412**	**–548**	**–116**
Trade credits	4 706	...	...	...	...	...	...	–10	60
General government: long-term	4 708	...	...	...	...	...	...	...	...
General government: short-term	4 709	...	...	...	...	...	...	...	...
Other sectors: long-term	4 711	...	...	...	...	...	...	24	59
Other sectors: short-term	4 712	...	...	...	...	...	...	–34	2
Loans	4 714	...	...	...	...	...	241	76	46
Monetary authorities: long-term	4 717	...	...	...	...	...	...	...	...
Monetary authorities: short-term	4 718	...	...	...	...	...	...	...	...
General government: long-term	4 720	...	...	...	...	...	232	159	57
General government: short-term	4 721	...	...	...	...	...	...	...	...
Banks: long-term	4 723	...	...	...	...	...	–9	–6	–10
Banks: short-term	4 724	...	...	...	...	...	...	–77	51
Other sectors: long-term	4 726	...	...	...	...	...	18	...	–52
Other sectors: short-term	4 727	...	...	...	...	...	...	...	...
Currency and deposits	4 730	...	...	...	...	...	–521	–226	–291
Monetary authorities	4 731	...	...	...	...	...	...	...	...
General government	4 732	...	...	...	...	...	...	...	...
Banks	4 733	...	...	...	...	...	–521	–244	–275
Other sectors	4 734	...	...	...	...	...	...	17	–17
Other assets	4 736	...	...	...	...	...	–132	–387	69
Monetary authorities: long-term	4 738	...	...	...	...	...	...	...	...
Monetary authorities: short-term	4 739	...	...	...	...	...	...	...	...
General government: long-term	4 741	...	...	...	...	...	...	...	...
General government: short-term	4 742	...	...	...	...	...	...	–370	84
Banks: long-term	4 744	...	...	...	...	...	...	–2	12
Banks: short-term	4 745	...	...	...	...	...	...	–15	–26
Other sectors: long-term	4 747	...	...	...	...	...	–132	...	...
Other sectors: short-term	4 748	...	...	...	...	...	...	...	...
Liabilities	4 753	...	...	...	...	...	**519**	**135**	**689**
Trade credits	4 756	...	...	...	...	...	...	–92	–16
General government: long-term	4 758	...	...	...	...	...	...	...	...
General government: short-term	4 759	...	...	...	...	...	...	...	...
Other sectors: long-term	4 761	...	...	...	...	...	...	–8	–100
Other sectors: short-term	4 762	...	...	...	...	...	...	–84	84
Loans	4 764	...	...	...	...	...	151	331	482
Use of Fund credit and loans from the Fund	4 766	...	...	...	...	...	89	51	–201
Monetary authorities: other long-term	4 767	...	...	...	...	...	...	36	42
Monetary authorities: short-term	4 768	...	...	...	...	...	...	...	...
General government: long-term	4 770	...	...	...	...	...	–20	–15	–173
General government: short-term	4 771	...	...	...	...	...	...	...	...
Banks: long-term	4 773	...	...	...	...	...	–16	92	210
Banks: short-term	4 774	...	...	...	...	...	...	16	30
Other sectors: long-term	4 776	...	...	...	...	...	97	170	519
Other sectors: short-term	4 777	...	...	...	...	...	...	–19	56
Currency and deposits	4 780	...	...	...	...	...	115	–43	161
Monetary authorities	4 781	...	...	...	...	...	...	3	...
General government	4 782	...	...	...	...	...	...	...	...
Banks	4 783	...	...	...	...	...	115	–46	162
Other sectors	4 784	...	...	...	...	...	...	...	...
Other liabilities	4 786	...	...	...	...	...	254	–61	61
Monetary authorities: long-term	4 788	...	...	...	...	...	...	...	...
Monetary authorities: short-term	4 789	...	...	...	...	...	...	...	...
General government: long-term	4 791	...	...	...	...	...	...	...	...
General government: short-term	4 792	...	...	...	...	...	165	–37	...
Banks: long-term	4 794	...	...	...	...	...	...	–24	45
Banks: short-term	4 795	...	...	...	...	...	...	...	16
Other sectors: long-term	4 797	...	...	...	...	...	...	...	...
Other sectors: short-term	4 798	...	...	...	...	...	89	...	...
D. RESERVE ASSETS	4 800	...	...	...	...	...	–104	–1,256	–1,590
Monetary gold	4 810	...	...	...	...	...	–6	94	–2
Special drawing rights	4 820	...	...	...	...	...	9	–85	33
Reserve position in the Fund	4 830	...	...	...	...	...	...	...	...
Foreign exchange	4 840	...	...	...	...	...	–106	–1,265	–1,621
Other claims	4 880	...	...	...	...	...	...	...	...
NET ERRORS AND OMISSIONS	4 998	...	...	...	...	...	**183**	**398**	**–60**

Table 3. INTERNATIONAL INVESTMENT POSITION (End–period stocks), 1988–95
(Millions of U.S. dollars)

	Code	1988	1989	1990	1991	1992	1993	1994	1995
ASSETS	8 995 C.	...	...	...	...	...	...	5,541	7,319
Direct investment abroad	8 505 . .	...	...	...	...	...	...	**77**	**92**
Equity capital and reinvested earnings	8 506 . .	...	...	...	...	...	...	...	...
Claims on affiliated enterprises	8 507 . .	...	...	...	...	...	...	...	...
Liabilities to affiliated enterprises	8 508 . .	...	...	...	...	...	...	...	...
Other capital	8 530 . .	...	...	...	...	...	...	24	27
Claims on affiliated enterprises	8 535 . .	...	...	...	...	...	...	...	...
Liabilities to affiliated enterprises	8 540 . .	...	...	...	...	...	...	...	...
Portfolio investment	8 602 . .	...	...	...	...	...	...	**433**	**231**
Equity securities	8 610 . .	...	...	...	...	...	...	427	208
Monetary authorities	8 611 . .	...	...	...	...	...	...	...	...
General government	8 612 . .	...	...	...	...	...	...	...	...
Banks	8 613 . .	...	...	...	...	...	...	3	3
Other sectors	8 614 . .	...	...	...	...	...	...	424	205
Debt securities	8 619 . .	...	...	...	...	...	...	6	23
Bonds and notes	8 620 . .	...	...	...	...	...	...	5	23
Monetary authorities	8 621 . .	...	...	...	...	...	...	...	...
General government	8 622 . .	...	...	...	...	...	...	...	...
Banks	8 623 . .	...	...	...	...	...	...	...	18
Other sectors	8 624 . .	...	...	...	...	...	...	5	5
Money market instruments	8 630 . .	...	...	...	...	...	...	1	1
Monetary authorities	8 631 . .	...	...	...	...	...	...	...	...
General government	8 632 . .	...	...	...	...	...	...	...	...
Banks	8 633 . .	...	...	...	...	...	...	...	...
Other sectors	8 634 . .	...	...	...	...	...	...	1	1
Financial derivatives	8 640 . .	...	...	...	...	...	...	...	...
Monetary authorities	8 641 . .	...	...	...	...	...	...	...	...
General government	8 642 . .	...	...	...	...	...	...	...	...
Banks	8 643 . .	...	...	...	...	...	...	...	...
Other sectors	8 644 . .	...	...	...	...	...	...	...	...
Other investment	8 703 . .	...	...	...	...	...	...	**2,838**	**3,133**
Trade credits	8 706 . .	...	...	...	...	...	...	1,212	1,215
General government: long-term	8 708 . .	...	...	...	...	...	...	...	...
General government: short-term	8 709 . .	...	...	...	...	...	...	...	...
Other sectors: long-term	8 711 . .	...	...	...	...	...	...	114	60
Other sectors: short-term	8 712 . .	...	...	...	...	...	...	1,098	1,155
Loans	8 714 . .	...	...	...	...	...	...	126	83
Monetary authorities: long-term	8 717 . .	...	...	...	...	...	...	...	...
Monetary authorities: short-term	8 718 . .	...	...	...	...	...	...	...	...
General government: long-term	8 720 . .	...	...	...	...	...	...	...	...
General government: short-term	8 721 . .	...	...	...	...	...	...	...	...
Banks: long-term	8 723 . .	...	...	...	...	...	...	32	44
Banks: short-term	8 724 . .	...	...	...	...	...	...	94	44
Other sectors: long-term	8 726 . .	...	...	...	...	...	...	...	...
Other sectors: short-term	8 727 . .	...	...	...	...	...	...	...	...
Currency and deposits	8 730 . .	...	...	...	...	...	...	1,191	1,573
Monetary authorities	8 731 . .	...	...	...	...	...	...	...	...
General government	8 732 . .	...	...	...	...	...	...	...	...
Banks	8 733 . .	...	...	...	...	...	...	1,184	1,541
Other sectors	8 734 . .	...	...	...	...	...	...	7	32
Other assets	8 736 . .	...	...	...	...	...	...	309	262
Monetary authorities: long-term	8 738 . .	...	...	...	...	...	...	...	...
Monetary authorities: short-term	8 739 . .	...	...	...	...	...	...	...	...
General government: long-term	8 741 . .	...	...	...	...	...	...	...	...
General government: short-term	8 742 . .	...	...	...	...	...	...	168	45
Banks: long-term	8 744 . .	...	...	...	...	...	...	11	...
Banks: short-term	8 745 . .	...	...	...	...	...	...	130	164
Other sectors: long-term	8 747 . .	...	...	...	...	...	...	...	...
Other sectors: short-term	8 748 . .	...	...	...	...	...	...	...	...
Reserve assets	8 800 . .	...	...	...	...	...	...	**2,192**	**3,863**
Monetary gold	8 810 . .	...	...	...	...	...	...	379	379
Special drawing rights	8 820 . .	...	...	...	...	...	...	86	58
Reserve position in the Fund	8 830 . .	...	...	...	...	...	...	...	...
Foreign exchange	8 840 . .	...	...	...	...	...	...	1,727	3,426
Other claims	8 880 . .	...	...	...	...	...	...	...	...

Table 3 (Continued). INTERNATIONAL INVESTMENT POSITION (End-period stocks), 1988–95
(Millions of U.S. dollars)

	Code	1988	1989	1990	1991	1992	1993	1994	1995
LIABILITIES	8 995 D.	...	...	...	...	...	...	5,458	6,676
Direct investment in Slovak Republic	8 555 . .	**...**	**...**	**...**	**...**	**...**	**...**	**796**	**1,060**
Equity capital and reinvested earnings	8 556 . .	...	...	...	...	...	...	...	...
Claims on direct investors	8 557 . .	...	...	...	...	...	...	...	...
Liabilities to direct investors	8 558 . .	...	...	...	...	...	...	...	...
Other capital	8 580 . .	...	...	...	...	...	...	108	124
Claims on direct investors	8 585 . .	...	...	...	...	...	...	...	...
Liabilities to direct investors	8 590 . .	...	...	...	...	...	...	...	...
Portfolio investment	8 652 . .	**...**	**...**	**...**	**...**	**...**	**...**	**78**	**134**
Equity securities	8 660 . .	...	...	...	...	...	...	55	43
Banks	8 663 . .	...	...	...	...	...	...	...	...
Other sectors	8 664 . .	...	...	...	...	...	...	55	43
Debt securities	8 669 . .	...	...	...	...	...	...	22	91
Bonds and notes	8 670 . .	...	...	...	...	...	...	22	91
Monetary authorities	8 671 . .	...	...	...	...	...	...	...	...
General government	8 672 . .	...	...	...	...	...	...	...	...
Banks	8 673 . .	...	...	...	...	...	...	...	...
Other sectors	8 674 . .	...	...	...	...	...	...	22	91
Money market instruments	8 680 . .	...	...	...	...	...	...	...	...
Monetary authorities	8 681 . .	...	...	...	...	...	...	...	...
General government	8 682 . .	...	...	...	...	...	...	...	...
Banks	8 683 . .	...	...	...	...	...	...	...	...
Other sectors	8 684 . .	...	...	...	...	...	...	...	...
Financial derivatives	8 690 . .	...	...	...	...	...	...	...	...
Monetary authorities	8 691 . .	...	...	...	...	...	...	...	...
General government	8 692 . .	...	...	...	...	...	...	...	...
Banks	8 692 . .	...	...	...	...	...	...	...	...
Other sectors	8 694 . .	...	...	...	...	...	...	...	...
Other investment	8 753 . .	**...**	**...**	**...**	**...**	**...**	**...**	**4,585**	**5,482**
Trade credits	8 756 . .	...	...	...	...	...	...	1,603	1,675
General government: long-term	8 758 . .	...	...	...	...	...	...	...	...
General government: short-term	8 759 . .	...	...	...	...	...	...	...	...
Other sectors: long-term	8 761 . .	...	...	...	...	...	...	399	321
Other sectors: short-term	8 762 . .	...	...	...	...	...	...	1,205	1,354
Loans	8 764 . .	...	...	...	...	...	...	2,775	3,366
Use of Fund credit and loans from the Fund	8 766 . .	...	...	...	...	...	557	642	457
Monetary authorities: other long-term	8 767 . .	...	...	...	...	...	...	37	76
Monetary authorities: short-term	8 768 . .	...	...	...	...	...	...	...	...
General government: long-term	8 770 . .	...	...	...	...	...	...	1,101	958
General government: short-term	8 771 . .	...	...	...	...	...	...	...	...
Banks: long-term	8 773 . .	...	...	...	...	...	...	222	445
Banks: short-term	8 774 . .	...	...	...	...	...	...	111	150
Other sectors: long-term	8 776 . .	...	...	...	...	...	...	642	1,198
Other sectors: short-term	8 777 . .	...	...	...	...	...	...	25	83
Currency and deposits	8 780 . .	...	...	...	...	...	...	132	301
Monetary authorities	8 781 . .	...	...	...	...	...	...	3	4
General government	8 782 . .	...	...	...	...	...	...	...	...
Banks	8 783 . .	...	...	...	...	...	...	129	298
Other sectors	8 784 . .	...	...	...	...	...	...	...	...
Other liabilities	8 786 . .	...	...	...	...	...	...	74	140
Monetary authorities: long-term	8 788 . .	...	...	...	...	...	...	...	...
Monetary authorities: short-term	8 789 . .	...	...	...	...	...	...	...	...
General government: long-term	8 791 . .	...	...	...	...	...	...	...	...
General government: short-term	8 792 . .	...	...	...	...	...	...	...	...
Banks: long-term	8 794 . .	...	...	...	...	...	...	68	117
Banks: short-term	8 795 . .	...	...	...	...	...	...	7	24
Other sectors: long-term	8 797 . .	...	...	...	...	...	...	...	...
Other sectors: short-term	8 798 . .	...	...	...	...	...	...	...	...
NET INTERNATIONAL INVESTMENT POSITION	8 995 . .	**...**	**...**	**...**	**...**	**...**	**...**	**82**	**643**
Conversion rates: Slovak koruny per U.S. dollar (end of period)	0 102 . .	**...**	**...**	**...**	**...**	**...**	**33.202**	**31.277**	**29.569**

Table 1. ANALYTIC PRESENTATION, 1988–95
(Millions of U.S. dollars)

	Code		1988	1989	1990	1991	1992	1993	1994	1995
A. Current Account [1]	4 993	Y.	...	...	...	...	**978.3**	**187.5**	**547.4**	**–36.5**
Goods: exports f.o.b	2 100	..	...	...	...	...	6,680.9	6,082.9	6,829.9	8,344.8
Goods: imports f.o.b	3 100	..	...	...	...	...	–5,891.8	–6,237.1	–7,168.0	–9,298.3
Balance on Goods	4 100	..	...	...	...	...	*789.1*	*–154.2*	*–338.1*	*–953.5*
Services: credit	2 200	..	...	...	...	...	1,219.3	1,392.7	1,851.0	2,017.6
Services: debit	3 200	..	...	...	...	...	–1,037.8	–1,019.0	–1,128.0	–1,292.5
Balance on Goods and Services	4 991	..	...	...	...	...	*970.6*	*219.5*	*384.9*	*–228.4*
Income: credit	2 300	..	...	...	...	...	111.7	114.8	287.6	368.4
Income: debit	3 300	..	...	...	...	...	–150.1	–166.6	–174.1	–221.3
Balance on Goods, Services, and Income	4 992	..	...	...	...	...	*932.2*	*167.7*	*498.4*	*–81.3*
Current transfers: credit	2 379	Y.	...	...	...	...	93.0	158.5	194.0	205.4
Current transfers: debit	3 379	..	...	...	...	...	–46.9	–138.7	–145.0	–160.6
B. Capital Account [1]	4 994	Y.	...	...	...	...	...	**4.1**	**–4.2**	**–14.4**
Capital account: credit	2 994	Y.	...	...	...	...	...	6.7	2.7	3.0
Capital account: debit	3 994	..	...	...	...	...	...	–2.6	–6.9	–17.4
Total, Groups A Plus B	4 010	..	...	...	...	...	*978.3*	*191.6*	*543.2*	*–50.9*
C. Financial Account [1]	4 995	X.	...	...	...	...	**–13.3**	**–63.9**	**–53.8**	**394.5**
Direct investment abroad	4 505	..	...	...	...	...	1.8	–1.3	3.1	–5.9
Direct investment in Slovenia	4 555	Y.	...	...	...	...	111.0	113.4	128.1	176.1
Portfolio investment assets	4 602	..	...	...	...	...	–8.9	–1.4	–84.1	–31.1
Equity securities	4 610	..	...	...	...	...	...	...	...	...
Debt securities	4 619	..	...	...	...	...	–8.9	–1.4	–84.1	–31.1
Portfolio investment liabilities	4 652	Y.	...	...	...	...	...	4.5	22.1	20.9
Equity securities	4 660	Y.	...	...	...	...	...	...	...	...
Debt securities	4 669	Y.	...	...	...	...	...	4.5	22.1	20.9
Other investment assets	4 703	..	...	...	...	...	–157.6	–297.4	–273.8	–372.6
Monetary authorities	4 703	.A	...	...	...	...	.5	...	–98.2	–66.8
General government	4 703	.B	...	...	...	...	–.1	–.3	–.4	–2.2
Banks	4 703	.C	...	...	...	...	–173.8	–473.6	–386.6	–294.6
Other sectors	4 703	.D	...	...	...	...	15.8	176.5	211.4	–9.0
Other investment liabilities	4 753	X.	...	...	...	...	40.4	118.3	150.8	607.1
Monetary authorities	4 753	XA	...	...	...	...	...	...	...	...
General government	4 753	YB	...	...	...	...	–18.3	80.2	64.5	127.4
Banks	4 753	YC	...	...	...	...	11.3	–41.9	–53.8	257.5
Other sectors	4 753	YD	...	...	...	...	47.4	80.0	140.1	222.2
Total, Groups A Through C	4 020	..	...	...	...	...	*965.0*	*127.7*	*489.4*	*343.6*
D. Net Errors and Omissions	4 998	..	...	...	...	...	**–332.4**	**–2.8**	**158.1**	**–119.8**
Total, Groups A Through D	4 030	..	...	...	...	...	*632.6*	*124.9*	*647.5*	*223.8*
E. Reserves and Related Items	4 040	..	...	...	...	...	**–632.6**	**–124.9**	**–647.5**	**–223.8**
Reserve assets	4 800	..	...	...	...	...	–632.6	–111.0	–642.3	–220.3
Use of Fund credit and loans	4 766	..	...	...	...	...	...	–13.8	–5.2	–3.4
Liabilities constituting foreign authorities' reserves	4 900	..	...	...	...	...	...	...	...	...
Exceptional financing	4 920	..	...	...	...	...	...	...	...	...
Conversion rates: tolars per U.S. dollar	0 101	..	...	...	...	**27.57**	**81.29**	**113.24**	**128.81**	**118.52**

[1] Excludes components that have been classified in the categories of Group E.

Table 2. STANDARD PRESENTATION, 1988–95
(Millions of U.S. dollars)

	Code	1988	1989	1990	1991	1992	1993	1994	1995
CURRENT ACCOUNT	4 993 . .	...	...	...	...	**978.3**	**187.5**	**547.4**	**–36.5**
A. GOODS	4 100 . .	...	...	...	...	789.1	–154.2	–338.1	–953.5
Credit	2 100 . .	...	...	...	...	**6,680.9**	**6,082.9**	**6,829.9**	**8,344.8**
General merchandise: exports f.o.b.	2 110 . .	...	...	...	...	5,611.7	4,918.3	5,917.4	7,331.5
Goods for processing: exports f.o.b.	2 150 . .	...	...	...	...	1,069.2	1,164.6	912.5	1,013.3
Repairs on goods	2 160 . .	...	...	...	...	...	...	...	...
Goods procured in ports by carriers	2 170 . .	...	...	...	...	...	...	...	...
Nonmonetary gold	2 180 . .	...	...	...	...	...	...	...	...
Debit	3 100 . .	...	...	...	...	**–5,891.8**	**–6,237.1**	**–7,168.0**	**–9,298.3**
General merchandise: imports f.o.b.	3 110 . .	...	...	...	...	–5,024.3	–5,374.7	–6,524.7	–8,577.7
Goods for processing: imports f.o.b.	3 150 . .	...	...	...	...	–867.5	–862.4	–643.3	–720.6
Repairs on goods	3 160 . .	...	...	...	...	...	...	...	...
Goods procured in ports by carriers	3 170 . .	...	...	...	...	...	...	...	...
Nonmonetary gold	3 180 . .	...	...	...	...	...	...	...	...
B. SERVICES	4 200 . .	...	...	...	...	181.5	373.7	723.0	725.1
Total credit	2 200 . .	...	...	...	...	*1,219.3*	*1,392.7*	*1,851.0*	*2,017.6*
Total debit	3 200 . .	...	...	...	...	*–1,037.8*	*–1,019.0*	*–1,128.0*	*–1,292.5*
Transportation services, credit	2 205 . .	...	...	...	...	**275.6**	**446.2**	**485.6**	**504.2**
Passenger	2 205 BA	...	...	...	...	...	*32.6*	*42.3*	*43.6*
Freight	2 205 BB	...	...	...	...	...	*258.8*	*273.2*	*262.0*
Other	2 205 BC	...	...	...	...	...	*154.8*	*170.1*	*198.6*
Sea transport, passenger	2 207 . .	...	...	...	...	...	...	...	...
Sea transport, freight	2 208 . .	...	...	...	...	...	71.6	55.5	56.6
Sea transport, other	2 209 . .	...	...	...	...	...	.5	.4	24.8
Air transport, passenger	2 211 . .	...	...	...	...	...	26.1	35.4	37.1
Air transport, freight	2 212 . .	...	...	...	...	...	1.6	2.4	2.5
Air transport, other	2 213 . .	...	...	...	...	...	.4	.2	1.6
Other transport, passenger	2 215 . .	...	...	...	...	...	6.5	6.9	6.5
Other transport, freight	2 216 . .	...	...	...	...	...	185.6	215.3	202.9
Other transport, other	2 217 . .	...	...	...	...	...	153.9	169.5	172.2
Transportation services, debit	3 205 . .	...	...	...	...	**–439.4**	**–390.1**	**–417.9**	**–434.9**
Passenger	3 205 BA	...	...	...	...	...	*–11.4*	*–21.0*	*–29.2*
Freight	3 205 BB	...	...	...	...	...	*–177.3*	*–208.7*	*–203.9*
Other	3 205 BC	...	...	...	...	...	*–201.4*	*–188.2*	*–201.8*
Sea transport, passenger	3 207 . .	...	...	...	...	...	...	–.6	–1.0
Sea transport, freight	3 208 . .	...	...	...	...	...	–25.4	–27.5	–27.9
Sea transport, other	3 209 . .	...	...	...	...	...	–.5	–.5	–15.8
Air transport, passenger	3 211 . .	...	...	...	...	...	–7.0	–15.1	–22.8
Air transport, freight	3 212 . .	...	...	...	...	...	–3.2	–4.2	–4.1
Air transport, other	3 213 . .	...	...	...	...	...	–.7	–.2	–.8
Other transport, passenger	3 215 . .	...	...	...	...	...	–4.4	–5.3	–5.4
Other transport, freight	3 216 . .	...	...	...	...	...	–148.7	–177.0	–171.9
Other transport, other	3 217 . .	...	...	...	...	...	–200.2	–187.5	–185.2
Travel, credit	2 236 . .	...	...	...	...	**671.0**	**734.0**	**958.7**	**1,078.9**
Business travel	2 237 . .	...	...	...	...	...	...	...	...
Personal travel	2 240 . .	...	...	...	...	671.0	734.0	958.7	1,078.9
Travel, debit	3 236 . .	...	...	...	...	**–281.9**	**–305.5**	**–369.0**	**–413.1**
Business travel	3 237 . .	...	...	...	...	–45.6	–60.3	–59.6	–63.1
Personal travel	3 240 . .	...	...	...	...	–236.3	–245.2	–309.4	–350.0
Other services, credit	2 200 BA	...	...	...	...	**272.7**	**212.5**	**406.7**	**434.5**
Communications	2 245 . .	...	...	...	...	...	5.3	12.6	11.8
Construction	2 249 . .	...	...	...	...	...	...	125.3	135.1
Insurance	2 253 . .	...	...	...	...	13.8	.5	.6	.6
Financial	2 260 . .	...	...	...	...	.4	6.5	6.4	8.1
Computer and information	2 262 . .	...	...	...	...	1.2	4.4	5.3	11.9
Royalties and licence fees	2 266 . .	...	...	...	...	3.9	3.5	3.3	4.0
Other business services	2 268 . .	...	...	...	...	252.1	185.7	244.2	246.4
Personal, cultural, and recreational	2 287 . .	...	...	...	...	1.3	5.7	6.4	5.4
Government, n.i.e.	2 291 . .	...	...	...	...	...	.9	2.6	11.2
Other services, debit	3 200 BA	...	...	...	...	**–316.5**	**–323.4**	**–341.1**	**–444.5**
Communications	3 245 . .	...	...	...	...	–.1	–1.9	–5.5	–10.2
Construction	3 249 . .	...	...	...	...	...	...	–3.3	–23.3
Insurance	3 253 . .	...	...	...	...	–15.7	–1.6	–1.4	–1.9
Financial	3 260 . .	...	...	...	...	–10.0	–14.5	–12.4	–16.9
Computer and information	3 262 . .	...	...	...	...	–9.4	–17.6	–19.0	–27.1
Royalties and licence fees	3 266 . .	...	...	...	...	–4.9	–12.8	–16.2	–22.7
Other business services	3 268 . .	...	...	...	...	–260.2	–257.5	–253.5	–301.3
Personal, cultural, and recreational	3 287 . .	...	...	...	...	–12.6	–10.3	–13.5	–19.2
Government, n.i.e.	3 291 . .	...	...	...	...	–3.6	–7.2	–16.3	–21.9

Table 2 (Continued). STANDARD PRESENTATION, 1988–95
(Millions of U.S. dollars)

	Code	1988	1989	1990	1991	1992	1993	1994	1995
C. INCOME	4 300 . .	...	...	...	...	–38.4	–51.8	113.5	147.1
Total credit	2 300 . .	...	...	...	...	*111.7*	*114.8*	*287.6*	*368.4*
Total debit	3 300 . .	...	...	...	...	*–150.1*	*–166.6*	*–174.1*	*–221.3*
Compensation of employees, credit	2 310 . .	**...**	**...**	**...**	**...**	**...**	**7.9**	**153.3**	**165.8**
Compensation of employees, debit	3 310 . .	**...**	**...**	**...**	**...**	**–1.6**	**–16.2**	**–12.9**	**–12.7**
Investment income, credit	2 320 . .	**...**	**...**	**...**	**...**	**111.7**	**106.9**	**134.3**	**202.6**
Direct investment income	2 330 . .	...	...	...	...	7.7	2.9	7.9	13.7
Dividends and distributed branch profits	2 332 . .	...	...	...	...	7.7	2.9	7.9	13.7
Reinvested earnings and undistributed branch profits	2 333 . .	...	...	...	...	...	...	...	...
Income on debt (interest)	2 334 . .	...	...	...	...	...	...	...	...
Portfolio investment income	2 339 . .	...	...	...	...	...	...	17.2	17.4
Income on equity	2 340 . .	...	...	...	...	...	...	...	...
Income on bonds and notes	2 350 . .	...	...	...	...	...	...	17.1	17.0
Income on money market instruments and financial derivatives	2 360 . .	...	...	...	...	...	...	.1	.4
Other investment income	2 370 . .	...	...	...	...	104.0	104.0	109.2	171.5
Investment income, debit	3 320 . .	**...**	**...**	**...**	**...**	**–148.5**	**–150.4**	**–161.2**	**–208.6**
Direct investment income	3 330 . .	...	...	...	...	–1.5	–3.4	–6.5	–21.3
Dividends and distributed branch profits	3 332 . .	...	...	...	...	–1.5	–3.4	–6.5	–21.3
Reinvested earnings and undistributed branch profits	3 333 . .	...	...	...	...	...	...	...	...
Income on debt (interest)	3 334 . .	...	...	...	...	...	...	...	...
Portfolio investment income	3 339 . .	...	...	...	...	...	...	–11.5	–11.5
Income on equity	3 340 . .	...	...	...	...	...	...	...	...
Income on bonds and notes	3 350 . .	...	...	...	...	...	...	–11.5	–11.5
Income on money market instruments and financial derivatives	3 360 . .	...	...	...	...	...	...	...	...
Other investment income	3 370 . .	...	...	...	...	–147.0	–147.0	–143.2	–175.8
D. CURRENT TRANSFERS	4 379 . .	...	...	...	...	46.1	19.8	49.0	44.8
Credit	2 379 . .	**...**	**...**	**...**	**...**	**93.0**	**158.5**	**194.0**	**205.4**
General government	2 380 . .	...	...	...	...	13.3	62.1	49.0	21.5
Other sectors	2 390 . .	...	...	...	...	79.7	96.4	145.0	183.9
Workers' remittances	2 391 . .	...	...	...	...	38.3	44.3	55.6	54.2
Other current transfers	2 392 . .	...	...	...	...	41.4	52.1	89.4	129.7
Debit	3 379 . .	**...**	**...**	**...**	**...**	**–46.9**	**–138.7**	**–145.0**	**–160.6**
General government	3 380 . .	...	...	...	...	–43.9	–122.1	–118.5	–101.8
Other sectors	3 390 . .	...	...	...	...	–3.0	–16.6	–26.5	–58.8
Workers' remittances	3 391 . .	...	...	...	...	...	...	...	–1.7
Other current transfers	3 392 . .	...	...	...	...	–3.0	–16.6	–26.5	–57.1
CAPITAL AND FINANCIAL ACCOUNT	4 996 . .	**...**	**...**	**...**	**...**	**–645.9**	**–184.7**	**–705.5**	**156.3**
CAPITAL ACCOUNT	4 994 . .	**...**	**...**	**...**	**...**	**...**	**4.1**	**–4.2**	**–14.4**
Total credit	2 994 . .	...	...	...	...	...	*6.7*	*2.7*	*3.0*
Total debit	3 994 . .	...	...	...	...	...	*–2.6*	*–6.9*	*–17.4*
Capital transfers, credit	2 400 . .	**...**	**...**	**...**	**...**	**...**	**5.5**	**2.2**	**2.8**
General government	2 401 . .	...	...	...	...	...	...	...	.9
Debt forgiveness	2 402 . .	...	...	...	...	...	...	...	...
Other capital transfers	2 410 . .	...	...	...	...	...	...	...	.9
Other sectors	2 430 . .	...	...	...	...	...	5.5	2.2	1.9
Migrants' transfers	2 431 . .	...	...	...	...	...	...	.5	1.9
Debt forgiveness	2 432 . .	...	...	...	...	...	...	...	...
Other capital transfers	2 440 . .	...	...	...	...	...	5.5	1.7	...
Capital transfers, debit	3 400 . .	**...**	**...**	**...**	**...**	**...**	**–.8**	**–4.8**	**–14.9**
General government	3 401 . .	...	...	...	...	...	...	...	–4.0
Debt forgiveness	3 402 . .	...	...	...	...	...	...	...	...
Other capital transfers	3 410 . .	...	...	...	...	...	...	...	–4.0
Other sectors	3 430 . .	...	...	...	...	...	–.8	–4.8	–10.9
Migrants' transfers	3 431 . .	...	...	...	...	...	–.8	–3.7	–3.6
Debt forgiveness	3 432 . .	...	...	...	...	...	...	–1.1	–7.3
Other capital transfers	3 440 . .	...	...	...	...	...	...	...	...
Nonproduced nonfinancial assets, credit	2 480 . .	**...**	**...**	**...**	**...**	**...**	**1.2**	**.5**	**.2**
Nonproduced nonfinancial assets, debit	3 480 . .	**...**	**...**	**...**	**...**	**...**	**–1.8**	**–2.1**	**–2.5**

Table 2 (Continued). STANDARD PRESENTATION, 1988–95
(Millions of U.S. dollars)

	Code	1988	1989	1990	1991	1992	1993	1994	1995
FINANCIAL ACCOUNT	4 995 . .	**. . .**	**. . .**	**. . .**	**. . .**	**–645.9**	**–188.8**	**–701.3**	**170.7**
A. DIRECT INVESTMENT	4 500 . .	. . .	. . .	. . .	. . .	112.8	112.1	131.2	170.2
Direct investment abroad	4 505 . .	**. . .**	**. . .**	**. . .**	**. . .**	**1.8**	**–1.3**	**3.1**	**–5.9**
Equity capital	4 510 . .	. . .	. . .	. . .	. . .	1.8	–1.3	3.1	–5.9
Claims on affiliated enterprises	4 515 . .	. . .	. . .	. . .	. . .	. . .	. . .	. . .	. . .
Liabilities to affiliated enterprises	4 520 . .	. . .	. . .	. . .	. . .	. . .	. . .	. . .	. . .
Reinvested earnings	4 525 . .	. . .	. . .	. . .	. . .	. . .	. . .	. . .	. . .
Other capital	4 530 . .	. . .	. . .	. . .	. . .	. . .	. . .	. . .	. . .
Claims on affiliated enterprises	4 535 . .	. . .	. . .	. . .	. . .	. . .	. . .	. . .	. . .
Liabilities to affiliated enterprises	4 540 . .	. . .	. . .	. . .	. . .	. . .	. . .	. . .	. . .
Direct investment in Slovenia	4 555 . .	**. . .**	**. . .**	**. . .**	**. . .**	**111.0**	**113.4**	**128.1**	**176.1**
Equity capital	4 560 . .	. . .	. . .	. . .	. . .	111.0	113.4	128.1	176.1
Claims on direct investors	4 565 . .	. . .	. . .	. . .	. . .	. . .	. . .	. . .	. . .
Liabilities to direct investors	4 570 . .	. . .	. . .	. . .	. . .	. . .	. . .	. . .	. . .
Reinvested earnings	4 575 . .	. . .	. . .	. . .	. . .	. . .	. . .	. . .	. . .
Other capital	4 580 . .	. . .	. . .	. . .	. . .	. . .	. . .	. . .	. . .
Claims on direct investors	4 585 . .	. . .	. . .	. . .	. . .	. . .	. . .	. . .	. . .
Liabilities to direct investors	4 590 . .	. . .	. . .	. . .	. . .	. . .	. . .	. . .	. . .
B. PORTFOLIO INVESTMENT	4 600 . .	. . .	. . .	. . .	. . .	–8.9	3.1	–62.0	–10.2
Assets	4 602 . .	**. . .**	**. . .**	**. . .**	**. . .**	**–8.9**	**–1.4**	**–84.1**	**–31.1**
Equity securities	4 610 . .	. . .	. . .	. . .	. . .	. . .	. . .	. . .	. . .
Monetary authorities	4 611 . .	. . .	. . .	. . .	. . .	. . .	. . .	. . .	. . .
General government	4 612 . .	. . .	. . .	. . .	. . .	. . .	. . .	. . .	. . .
Banks	4 613 . .	. . .	. . .	. . .	. . .	. . .	. . .	. . .	. . .
Other sectors	4 614 . .	. . .	. . .	. . .	. . .	. . .	. . .	. . .	. . .
Debt securities	4 619 . .	. . .	. . .	. . .	. . .	–8.9	–1.4	–84.1	–31.1
Bonds and notes	4 620 . .	. . .	. . .	. . .	. . .	–8.9	–1.4	–84.1	–35.9
Monetary authorities	4 621 . .	. . .	. . .	. . .	. . .	. . .	. . .	. . .	. . .
General government	4 622 . .	. . .	. . .	. . .	. . .	. . .	. . .	–.1	. . .
Banks	4 623 . .	. . .	. . .	. . .	. . .	–8.9	–1.3	–83.1	9.2
Other sectors	4 624 . .	. . .	. . .	. . .	. . .	. . .	–.1	–.9	–45.1
Money market instruments	4 630 . .	. . .	. . .	. . .	. . .	. . .	. . .	. . .	4.8
Monetary authorities	4 631 . .	. . .	. . .	. . .	. . .	. . .	. . .	. . .	. . .
General government	4 632 . .	. . .	. . .	. . .	. . .	. . .	. . .	. . .	. . .
Banks	4 633 . .	. . .	. . .	. . .	. . .	. . .	. . .	. . .	9.2
Other sectors	4 634 . .	. . .	. . .	. . .	. . .	. . .	. . .	. . .	–4.4
Financial derivatives	4 640 . .	. . .	. . .	. . .	. . .	. . .	. . .	. . .	. . .
Monetary authorities	4 641 . .	. . .	. . .	. . .	. . .	. . .	. . .	. . .	. . .
General government	4 642 . .	. . .	. . .	. . .	. . .	. . .	. . .	. . .	. . .
Banks	4 643 . .	. . .	. . .	. . .	. . .	. . .	. . .	. . .	. . .
Other sectors	4 644 . .	. . .	. . .	. . .	. . .	. . .	. . .	. . .	. . .
Liabilities	4 652 . .	**. . .**	**. . .**	**. . .**	**. . .**	**. . .**	**4.5**	**22.1**	**20.9**
Equity securities	4 660 . .	. . .	. . .	. . .	. . .	. . .	. . .	. . .	. . .
Banks	4 663 . .	. . .	. . .	. . .	. . .	. . .	. . .	. . .	. . .
Other sectors	4 664 . .	. . .	. . .	. . .	. . .	. . .	. . .	. . .	. . .
Debt securities	4 669 . .	. . .	. . .	. . .	. . .	. . .	4.5	22.1	20.9
Bonds and notes	4 670 . .	. . .	. . .	. . .	. . .	. . .	4.5	18.4	17.2
Monetary authorities	4 671 . .	. . .	. . .	. . .	. . .	. . .	. . .	. . .	. . .
General government	4 672 . .	. . .	. . .	. . .	. . .	. . .	. . .	. . .	. . .
Banks	4 673 . .	. . .	. . .	. . .	. . .	. . .	2.2	16.4	. . .
Other sectors	4 674 . .	. . .	. . .	. . .	. . .	. . .	2.3	2.0	17.2
Money market instruments	4 680 . .	. . .	. . .	. . .	. . .	. . .	. . .	3.7	3.7
Monetary authorities	4 681 . .	. . .	. . .	. . .	. . .	. . .	. . .	. . .	. . .
General government	4 682 . .	. . .	. . .	. . .	. . .	. . .	. . .	. . .	. . .
Banks	4 683 . .	. . .	. . .	. . .	. . .	. . .	. . .	–.3	. . .
Other sectors	4 684 . .	. . .	. . .	. . .	. . .	. . .	. . .	4.0	3.7
Financial derivatives	4 690 . .	. . .	. . .	. . .	. . .	. . .	. . .	. . .	. . .
Monetary authorities	4 691 . .	. . .	. . .	. . .	. . .	. . .	. . .	. . .	. . .
General government	4 692 . .	. . .	. . .	. . .	. . .	. . .	. . .	. . .	. . .
Banks	4 693 . .	. . .	. . .	. . .	. . .	. . .	. . .	. . .	. . .
Other sectors	4 694 . .	. . .	. . .	. . .	. . .	. . .	. . .	. . .	. . .

Table 2 (Concluded). STANDARD PRESENTATION, 1988–95
(Millions of U.S. dollars)

	Code	1988	1989	1990	1991	1992	1993	1994	1995
C. OTHER INVESTMENT	4 700 . .	...	...	...	...	–117.2	–192.9	–128.2	231.1
Assets	4 703 . .	**...**	**...**	**...**	**...**	**–157.6**	**–297.4**	**–273.8**	**–372.6**
Trade credits	4 706 . .	...	...	...	...	6.6	109.7	18.8	–38.3
General government: long-term	4 708 . .	...	...	...	...	...	...	...	...
General government: short-term	4 709 . .	...	...	...	...	...	...	...	...
Other sectors: long-term	4 711 . .	...	...	...	...	...	5.3	–1.3	9.2
Other sectors: short-term	4 712 . .	...	...	...	...	...	104.4	20.1	–47.5
Loans	4 714 . .	...	...	...	...	–30.7	11.5	–18.2	–15.7
Monetary authorities: long-term	4 717 . .	...	...	...	...	...	...	...	...
Monetary authorities: short-term	4 718 . .	...	...	...	...	...	...	...	...
General government: long-term	4 720 . .	...	...	...	...	...	...	...	...
General government: short-term	4 721 . .	...	...	...	...	...	...	...	...
Banks: long-term	4 723 . .	...	...	...	...	–36.8	21.7	–13.2	–5.9
Banks: short-term	4 724 . .	...	...	...	...	6.1	–10.2	–5.5	–6.9
Other sectors: long-term	4 726 . .	...	...	...	...	...	...	.8	–2.9
Other sectors: short-term	4 727 . .	...	...	...	...	...	...	–.3	...
Currency and deposits	4 730 . .	...	...	...	...	–139.5	–384.0	–163.1	–169.5
Monetary authorities	4 731 . .	...	...	...	...	...	...	...	...
General government	4 732 . .	...	...	...	...	...	...	...	...
Banks	4 733 . .	...	...	...	...	–148.7	–450.8	–354.9	–201.4
Other sectors	4 734 . .	...	...	...	...	9.2	66.8	191.8	31.9
Other assets	4 736 . .	...	...	...	...	6.0	–34.6	–111.3	–149.1
Monetary authorities: long-term	4 738 . .	...	...	...	...	...	...	...	...
Monetary authorities: short-term	4 739 . .	...	...	...	...	.5	...	–98.2	–66.8
General government: long-term	4 741 . .	...	...	...	...	–.1	–.3	–.4	–2.2
General government: short-term	4 742 . .	...	...	...	...	...	...	...	...
Banks: long-term	4 744 . .	...	...	...	...	1.0	.1	–8.3	–.7
Banks: short-term	4 745 . .	...	...	...	...	4.6	–34.4	–4.7	–79.7
Other sectors: long-term	4 747 . .	...	...	...	...	...	...	.3	.3
Other sectors: short-term	4 748 . .	...	...	...	...	...	...	...	...
Liabilities	4 753 . .	**...**	**...**	**...**	**...**	**40.4**	**104.5**	**145.6**	**603.7**
Trade credits	4 756 . .	...	...	...	...	–13.0	–13.0	–8.0	–7.3
General government: long-term	4 758 . .	...	...	...	...	–1.5	1.6	–2.8	–3.1
General government: short-term	4 759 . .	...	...	...	...	...	...	...	...
Other sectors: long-term	4 761 . .	...	...	...	...	–11.5	–14.6	–5.2	–4.2
Other sectors: short-term	4 762 . .	...	...	...	...	...	...	...	...
Loans	4 764 . .	...	...	...	...	32.8	161.3	303.2	585.8
Use of Fund credit and loans from the Fund	4 766 . .	...	...	...	...	...	–13.8	–5.2	–3.4
Monetary authorities: other long term	4 767 . .	...	...	...	...	...	...	...	...
Monetary authorities: short-term	4 768 . .	...	...	...	...	...	...	...	...
General government: long-term	4 770 . .	...	...	...	...	–16.8	78.6	67.3	130.5
General government: short-term	4 771 . .	...	...	...	...	...	...	...	...
Banks: long-term	4 773 . .	...	...	...	...	–6.9	–2.2	97.3	222.9
Banks: short-term	4 774 . .	...	...	...	...	–2.4	4.1	–3.2	2.9
Other sectors: long-term	4 776 . .	...	...	...	...	52.2	27.2	129.7	274.3
Other sectors: short-term	4 777 . .	...	...	...	...	6.7	67.4	17.3	–41.4
Currency and deposits	4 780 . .	...	...	...	...	13.8	–40.3	19.3	14.1
Monetary authorities	4 781 . .	...	...	...	...	...	...	...	...
General government	4 782 . .	...	...	...	...	...	...	...	...
Banks	4 783 . .	...	...	...	...	13.8	–40.3	19.3	14.1
Other sectors	4 784 . .	...	...	...	...	...	...	...	...
Other liabilities	4 786 . .	...	...	...	...	6.8	–3.5	–168.9	11.1
Monetary authorities: long-term	4 788 . .	...	...	...	...	...	...	...	...
Monetary authorities: short-term	4 789 . .	...	...	...	...	...	...	...	...
General government: long-term	4 791 . .	...	...	...	...	...	...	...	...
General government: short-term	4 792 . .	...	...	...	...	...	...	...	...
Banks: long-term	4 794 . .	...	...	...	...	...	...	...	...
Banks: short-term	4 795 . .	...	...	...	...	6.8	–3.5	–167.2	17.6
Other sectors: long-term	4 797 . .	...	...	...	...	...	...	–1.7	–6.5
Other sectors: short-term	4 798 . .	...	...	...	...	...	...	...	...
D. RESERVE ASSETS	4 800 . .	...	...	...	...	–632.6	–111.0	–642.3	–220.3
Monetary gold	4 810 . .	...	...	...	...	...	...	...	...
Special drawing rights	4 820 . .	...	...	...	...	...	–.1	...	...
Reserve position in the Fund	4 830 . .	...	...	...	...	...	–17.8	...	...
Foreign exchange	4 840 . .	...	...	...	...	–632.6	–93.2	–642.3	–220.3
Other claims	4 880 . .	...	...	...	...	...	...	...	...
NET ERRORS AND OMISSIONS	4 998 . .	**...**	**...**	**...**	**...**	**–332.4**	**–2.8**	**158.1**	**–119.8**

Part 3 of the *Yearbook* contains descriptions of the methodologies, compilation practices, and sources used to compile these data.

Table 3. INTERNATIONAL INVESTMENT POSITION (End–period stocks), 1988–95
(Millions of U.S. dollars)

	Code	1988	1989	1990	1991	1992	1993	1994	1995
ASSETS	8 995 C.	...	...	...	...	...	...	5,214.5	6,150.5
Direct investment abroad	8 505 ..	**...**	**...**	**...**	**...**	**...**	**...**	**246.6**	**403.5**
Equity capital and reinvested earnings	8 506 ..	...	...	...	...	...	...	235.8	255.2
Claims on affiliated enterprises	8 507 ..	...	...	...	...	...	...	...	...
Liabilities to affiliated enterprises	8 508 ..	...	...	...	...	...	...	...	...
Other capital	8 530 ..	...	...	...	...	...	...	10.8	148.3
Claims on affiliated enterprises	8 535 ..	...	...	...	...	...	...	251.3	382.8
Liabilities to affiliated enterprises	8 540 ..	...	...	...	...	...	...	–240.5	–234.5
Portfolio investment	8 602 ..	**...**	**...**	**...**	**...**	**...**	**...**	**58.1**	**107.8**
Equity securities	8 610 ..	...	...	...	...	...	...	12.5	18.5
Monetary authorities	8 611 ..	...	...	...	...	...	...	...	...
General government	8 612 ..	...	...	...	...	...	...	...	...
Banks	8 613 ..	...	...	...	...	...	...	4.8	6.9
Other sectors	8 614 ..	...	...	...	...	...	...	7.7	11.6
Debt securities	8 619 ..	...	...	...	...	...	...	45.6	89.3
Bonds and notes	8 620 ..	...	...	...	...	...	...	45.6	89.3
Monetary authorities	8 621 ..	...	...	...	...	...	...	...	...
General government	8 622 ..	...	...	...	...	...	...	...	...
Banks	8 623 ..	...	...	...	...	...	...	45.6	89.3
Other sectors	8 624 ..	...	...	...	...	...	...	...	...
Money market instruments	8 630 ..	...	...	...	...	...	...	...	...
Monetary authorities	8 631 ..	...	...	...	...	...	...	...	...
General government	8 632 ..	...	...	...	...	...	...	...	...
Banks	8 633 ..	...	...	...	...	...	...	...	...
Other sectors	8 634 ..	...	...	...	...	...	...	...	...
Financial derivatives	8 640 ..	...	...	...	...	...	...	...	...
Monetary authorities	8 641 ..	...	...	...	...	...	...	...	...
General government	8 642 ..	...	...	...	...	...	...	...	...
Banks	8 643 ..	...	...	...	...	...	...	...	...
Other sectors	8 644 ..	...	...	...	...	...	...	...	...
Other investment	8 703 ..	**...**	**...**	**...**	**...**	**...**	**...**	**3,410.7**	**3,820.7**
Trade credits	8 706 ..	...	...	...	...	...	...	1,524.4	1,674.0
General government: long-term	8 708 ..	...	...	...	...	...	...	...	...
General government: short-term	8 709 ..	...	...	...	...	...	...	...	...
Other sectors: long-term	8 711 ..	...	...	...	...	...	...	186.5	184.7
Other sectors: short-term	8 712 ..	...	...	...	...	...	...	1,337.9	1,489.3
Loans	8 714 ..	...	...	...	...	...	...	25.4	39.5
Monetary authorities: long-term	8 717 ..	...	...	...	...	...	...	...	...
Monetary authorities: short-term	8 718 ..	...	...	...	...	...	...	...	...
General government: long-term	8 720 ..	...	...	...	...	...	...	...	...
General government: short-term	8 721 ..	...	...	...	...	...	...	...	...
Banks: long-term	8 723 ..	...	...	...	...	...	...	10.4	17.2
Banks: short-term	8 724 ..	...	...	...	...	...	...	12.9	20.5
Other sectors: long-term	8 726 ..	...	...	...	...	...	...	2.1	1.8
Other sectors: short-term	8 727 ..	...	...	...	...	...	...	...	...
Currency and deposits	8 730 ..	...	...	...	...	...	...	1,347.1	1,625.4
Monetary authorities	8 731 ..	...	...	...	...	...	...	...	...
General government	8 732 ..	...	...	...	...	...	...	...	...
Banks	8 733 ..	...	...	...	...	...	...	1,274.6	1,561.5
Other sectors	8 734 ..	...	...	...	...	...	...	72.5	63.9
Other assets	8 736 ..	...	...	...	...	...	...	513.8	481.8
Monetary authorities: long-term	8 738 ..	...	...	...	...	...	...	...	...
Monetary authorities: short-term	8 739 ..	...	...	...	...	...	...	103.3	170.1
General government: long-term	8 741 ..	...	...	...	...	...	...	...	...
General government: short-term	8 742 ..	...	...	...	...	...	...	...	...
Banks: long-term	8 744 ..	...	...	...	...	...	...	...	...
Banks: short-term	8 745 ..	...	...	...	...	...	...	410.5	311.7
Other sectors: long-term	8 747 ..	...	...	...	...	...	...	...	...
Other sectors: short-term	8 748 ..	...	...	...	...	...	...	...	...
Reserve assets	8 800 ..	**...**	**...**	**...**	**...**	**...**	**...**	**1,499.1**	**1,818.5**
Monetary gold	8 810 ..	...	...	...	...	...	...	.1	.1
Special drawing rights	8 820 ..	...	...	...	...	...	...	.1	.1
Reserve position in the Fund	8 830 ..	...	...	...	...	...	17.7	18.8	19.1
Foreign exchange	8 840 ..	...	...	...	...	...	...	1,480.1	1,799.2
Other claims	8 880 ..	...	...	...	...	...	...	...	...

Table 3 (Continued). INTERNATIONAL INVESTMENT POSITION (End–period stocks), 1988–95

(Millions of U.S. dollars)

	Code	1988	1989	1990	1991	1992	1993	1994	1995
LIABILITIES	8 995 D.	...	...	...	...	...	...	4,689.4	5,805.9
Direct investment in Slovenia	8 555 . .	**...**	**...**	**...**	**...**	**...**	**...**	**1,274.8**	**1,642.9**
Equity capital and reinvested earnings	8 556 . .	...	...	...	...	...	...	919.1	1,133.1
Claims on direct investors	8 557 . .	...	...	...	...	...	...	...	...
Liabilities to direct investors	8 558 . .	...	...	...	...	...	...	...	...
Other capital	8 580 . .	...	...	...	...	...	...	355.7	509.8
Claims on direct investors	8 585 . .	...	...	...	...	...	...	–116.5	–136.5
Liabilities to direct investors	8 590 . .	...	...	...	...	...	...	472.2	646.3
Portfolio investment	8 652 . .	**...**	**...**	**...**	**...**	**...**	**...**	**47.7**	**50.5**
Equity securities	8 660 . .	...	...	...	...	...	...	47.7	50.5
Banks	8 663 . .	...	...	...	...	...	...	15.2	23.8
Other sectors	8 664 . .	...	...	...	...	...	...	32.5	26.7
Debt securities	8 669 . .	...	...	...	...	...	...	...	...
Bonds and notes	8 670 . .	...	...	...	...	...	...	...	...
Monetary authorities	8 671 . .	...	...	...	...	...	...	...	...
General government	8 672 . .	...	...	...	...	...	...	...	...
Banks	8 673 . .	...	...	...	...	...	...	...	...
Other sectors	8 674 . .	...	...	...	...	...	...	...	...
Money market instruments	8 680 . .	...	...	...	...	...	...	...	...
Monetary authorities	8 681 . .	...	...	...	...	...	...	...	...
General government	8 682 . .	...	...	...	...	...	...	...	...
Banks	8 683 . .	...	...	...	...	...	...	...	...
Other sectors	8 684 . .	...	...	...	...	...	...	...	...
Financial derivatives	8 690 . .	...	...	...	...	...	...	...	...
Monetary authorities	8 691 . .	...	...	...	...	...	...	...	...
General government	8 692 . .	...	...	...	...	...	...	...	...
Banks	8 692 . .	...	...	...	...	...	...	...	...
Other sectors	8 694 . .	...	...	...	...	...	...	...	...
Other investment	8 753 . .	**...**	**...**	**...**	**...**	**...**	**...**	**3,366.9**	**4,112.5**
Trade credits	8 756 . .	...	...	...	...	...	...	1,240.9	1,448.1
General government: long-term	8 758 . .	...	...	...	...	...	...	...	...
General government: short-term	8 759 . .	...	...	...	...	...	...	...	...
Other sectors: long-term	8 761 . .	...	...	...	...	...	...	68.7	55.5
Other sectors: short-term	8 762 . .	...	...	...	...	...	...	1,172.2	1,392.6
Loans	8 764 . .	...	...	...	...	...	...	1,731.4	2,193.4
Use of Fund credit and loans from the Fund	8 766 . .	...	...	...	...	...	11.7	7.2	4.0
Monetary authorities: other long-term	8 767 . .	...	...	...	...	...	...	...	...
Monetary authorities: short-term	8 768 . .	...	...	...	...	...	...	...	...
General government: long-term	8 770 . .	...	...	...	...	...	...	382.2	570.8
General government: short-term	8 771 . .	...	...	...	...	...	...	...	...
Banks: long-term	8 773 . .	...	...	...	...	...	...	866.2	1,001.9
Banks: short-term	8 774 . .	...	...	...	...	...	...	1.4	3.4
Other sectors: long-term	8 776 . .	...	...	...	...	...	...	457.9	606.9
Other sectors: short-term	8 777 . .	...	...	...	...	...	...	16.5	6.4
Currency and deposits	8 780 . .	...	...	...	...	...	...	171.4	218.9
Monetary authorities	8 781 . .	...	...	...	...	...	...	.1	.1
General government	8 782 . .	...	...	...	...	...	...	...	...
Banks	8 783 . .	...	...	...	...	...	...	171.3	218.8
Other sectors	8 784 . .	...	...	...	...	...	...	...	...
Other liabilities	8 786 . .	...	...	...	...	...	...	223.2	252.1
Monetary authorities: long-term	8 788 . .	...	...	...	...	...	...	...	...
Monetary authorities: short-term	8 789 . .	...	...	...	...	...	...	...	...
General government: long-term	8 791 . .	...	...	...	...	...	...	...	...
General government: short-term	8 792 . .	...	...	...	...	...	...	...	...
Banks: long-term	8 794 . .	...	...	...	...	...	...	65.5	78.1
Banks: short-term	8 795 . .	...	...	...	...	...	...	22.3	51.6
Other sectors: long-term	8 797 . .	...	...	...	...	...	...	135.4	122.4
Other sectors: short-term	8 798 . .	...	...	...	...	...	...	...	...
NET INTERNATIONAL INVESTMENT POSITION	8 995 . .	**...**	**...**	**...**	**...**	**...**	**...**	**525.1**	**344.6**
Conversion rates: tolars per U.S. dollar (end of period)	0 102 . .	**...**	**...**	**...**	**56.69**	**98.70**	**131.84**	**126.46**	**125.99**

Table 1. ANALYTIC PRESENTATION, 1988–95
(Millions of U.S. dollars)

	Code		1988	1989	1990	1991	1992	1993	1994	1995
A. Current Account [1]	4 993	Y .	**–37.65**	**–33.23**	**–27.76**	**–35.84**	**–1.43**	**. . .**	**. . .**	**. . .**
Goods: exports f.o.b	2 100	. .	81.92	74.70	70.11	83.43	101.74	. . .	. . .	. . .
Goods: imports f.o.b	3 100	. .	–104.63	–94.28	–77.35	–91.98	–87.43	. . .	. . .	. . .
Balance on Goods	4 100	. .	*–22.71*	*–19.58*	*–7.24*	*–8.55*	*14.31*	. . .	. . .	. . .
Services: credit	2 200	. .	21.99	26.51	25.35	31.61	36.03	. . .	. . .	. . .
Services: debit	3 200	. .	–66.22	–75.26	–78.69	–88.26	–78.04	. . .	. . .	. . .
Balance on Goods and Services	4 991	. .	*–66.94*	*–68.33*	*–60.58*	*–65.20*	*–27.70*	. . .	. . .	. . .
Income: credit	2 300	. .	3.55	3.88	2.33	1.36	.99	. . .	. . .	. . .
Income: debit	3 300	. .	–12.10	–11.77	–7.59	–10.39	–10.89	. . .	. . .	. . .
Balance on Goods, Services, and Income	4 992	. .	*–75.49*	*–76.22*	*–65.84*	*–74.22*	*–37.60*	. . .	. . .	. . .
Current transfers: credit	2 379	Y .	42.93	47.14	43.66	46.82	43.78	. . .	. . .	. . .
Current transfers: debit	3 379	. .	–5.09	–4.14	–5.58	–8.44	–7.62	. . .	. . .	. . .
B. Capital Account [1]	4 994	Y .	**–.38**	**–.17**	**–.16**	**–.26**	**–.44**	**. . .**	**. . .**	**. . .**
Capital account: credit	2 994	Y .	. . .	. . .	. . .	. . .	. . .	. . .	. . .	. . .
Capital account: debit	3 994	. .	–.38	–.17	–.16	–.26	–.44	. . .	. . .	. . .
Total, Groups A Plus B	4 010	. .	*–38.03*	*–33.40*	*–27.92*	*–36.10*	*–1.88*	. . .	. . .	. . .
C. Financial Account [1]	4 995	X .	**43.79**	**25.12**	**22.86**	**15.10**	**22.44**	**. . .**	**. . .**	**. . .**
Direct investment abroad	4 505	. .	. . .	. . .	. . .	. . .	. . .	. . .	. . .	. . .
Direct investment in Solomon Islands	4 555	Y .	1.68	11.60	10.44	14.51	14.17	. . .	. . .	. . .
Portfolio investment assets	4 602	. .	. . .	. . .	. . .	. . .	. . .	. . .	. . .	. . .
Equity securities	4 610	. .	. . .	. . .	. . .	. . .	. . .	. . .	. . .	. . .
Debt securities	4 619	. .	. . .	. . .	. . .	. . .	. . .	. . .	. . .	. . .
Portfolio investment liabilities	4 652	Y .	. . .	. . .	. . .	. . .	. . .	. . .	. . .	. . .
Equity securities	4 660	Y .	. . .	. . .	. . .	. . .	. . .	. . .	. . .	. . .
Debt securities	4 669	Y .	. . .	. . .	. . .	. . .	. . .	. . .	. . .	. . .
Other investment assets	4 703	. .	18.82	–.74	–.75	–1.25	–.07	. . .	. . .	. . .
Monetary authorities	4 703	. A	. . .	. . .	. . .	. . .	. . .	. . .	. . .	. . .
General government	4 703	. B	19.74	. . .	. . .	. . .	. . .	. . .	. . .	. . .
Banks	4 703	. C	–.91	–.74	–.75	–1.25	–.07	. . .	. . .	. . .
Other sectors	4 703	. D	. . .	. . .	. . .	. . .	. . .	. . .	. . .	. . .
Other investment liabilities	4 753	X .	23.29	14.26	13.17	1.84	8.33	. . .	. . .	. . .
Monetary authorities	4 753	XA	. . .	2.22	1.07	. . .	.41	. . .	. . .	. . .
General government	4 753	YB	8.50	–1.74	–5.97	–5.01	1.57	. . .	. . .	. . .
Banks	4 753	YC	.05	–1.35	2.77	–.85	–.82	. . .	. . .	. . .
Other sectors	4 753	YD	14.74	15.13	15.30	7.70	7.17	. . .	. . .	. . .
Total, Groups A Through C	4 020	. .	*5.76*	*–8.29*	*–5.06*	*–21.00*	*20.56*	. . .	. . .	. . .
D. Net Errors and Omissions	4 998	. .	**–10.87**	**–5.21**	**–8.60**	**8.36**	**–6.16**	**. . .**	**. . .**	**. . .**
Total, Groups A Through D	4 030	. .	*–5.10*	*–13.49*	*–13.67*	*–12.64*	*14.40*	. . .	. . .	. . .
E. Reserves and Related Items	4 040	. .	**5.10**	**13.49**	**13.67**	**12.64**	**–14.40**	**. . .**	**. . .**	**. . .**
Reserve assets	4 800	. .	–4.28	11.61	8.58	8.34	–17.14	. . .	. . .	. . .
Use of Fund credit and loans	4 766	. .	–.41	–.21	–.84	–.64	. . .	. . .	. . .	. . .
Liabilities constituting foreign authorities' reserves	4 900	. .	. . .	. . .	. . .	. . .	. . .	. . .	. . .	. . .
Exceptional financing	4 920	. .	9.80	2.09	5.93	4.94	2.73	. . .	. . .	. . .
Conversion rates: Solomon Islands dollars per U.S. dollar	0 101	. .	**2.0825**	**2.2932**	**2.5288**	**2.7148**	**2.9281**	**3.1877**	**3.2914**	**3.4059**

[1] Excludes components that have been classified in the categories of Group E.

Table 2. STANDARD PRESENTATION, 1988–95
(Millions of U.S. dollars)

	Code	1988	1989	1990	1991	1992	1993	1994	1995
CURRENT ACCOUNT	4 993 . .	**–27.85**	**–33.23**	**–27.76**	**–35.84**	**1.30**	**. . .**	**. . .**	**. . .**
A. GOODS	4 100 . .	–22.71	–19.58	–7.24	–8.55	14.31	. . .	. . .	. . .
Credit	2 100 . .	**81.92**	**74.70**	**70.11**	**83.43**	**101.74**	**. . .**	**. . .**	**. . .**
General merchandise: exports f.o.b.	2 110 . .	81.92	74.70	70.11	83.43	101.74	. . .	. . .	. . .
Goods for processing: exports f.o.b.	2 150 . .	. . .	. . .	. . .	. . .	. . .	. . .	. . .	. . .
Repairs on goods	2 160 . .	. . .	. . .	. . .	. . .	. . .	. . .	. . .	. . .
Goods procured in ports by carriers	2 170 . .	. . .	. . .	. . .	. . .	. . .	. . .	. . .	. . .
Nonmonetary gold	2 180 . .	. . .	. . .	. . .	. . .	. . .	. . .	. . .	. . .
Debit	3 100 . .	**–104.63**	**–94.28**	**–77.35**	**–91.98**	**–87.43**	**. . .**	**. . .**	**. . .**
General merchandise: imports f.o.b.	3 110 . .	–104.63	–94.28	–77.35	–91.98	–87.43	. . .	. . .	. . .
Goods for processing: imports f.o.b.	3 150 . .	. . .	. . .	. . .	. . .	. . .	. . .	. . .	. . .
Repairs on goods	3 160 . .	. . .	. . .	. . .	. . .	. . .	. . .	. . .	. . .
Goods procured in ports by carriers	3 170 . .	. . .	. . .	. . .	. . .	. . .	. . .	. . .	. . .
Nonmonetary gold	3 180 . .	. . .	. . .	. . .	. . .	. . .	. . .	. . .	. . .
B. SERVICES	4 200 . .	–44.23	–48.75	–53.35	–56.65	–42.01	. . .	. . .	. . .
Total credit	2 200 . .	*21.99*	*26.51*	*25.35*	*31.61*	*36.03*	. . .	. . .	. . .
Total debit	3 200 . .	*–66.22*	*–75.26*	*–78.69*	*–88.26*	*–78.04*	. . .	. . .	. . .
Transportation services, credit	2 205 . .	**1.54**	**1.88**	**2.49**	**3.87**	**3.62**	**. . .**	**. . .**	**. . .**
Passenger	2 205 BA	*.58*	*.78*	*1.11*	*2.58*	*2.42*	. . .	. . .	. . .
Freight	2 205 BB	. . .	. . .	. . .	. . .	. . .	. . .	. . .	. . .
Other	2 205 BC	*.96*	*1.09*	*1.38*	*1.29*	*1.20*	. . .	. . .	. . .
Sea transport, passenger	2 207 . .	. . .	. . .	. . .	. . .	. . .	. . .	. . .	. . .
Sea transport, freight	2 208 . .	. . .	. . .	. . .	. . .	. . .	. . .	. . .	. . .
Sea transport, other	2 209 . .	. . .	. . .	. . .	. . .	. . .	. . .	. . .	. . .
Air transport, passenger	2 211 . .	. . .	. . .	. . .	. . .	. . .	. . .	. . .	. . .
Air transport, freight	2 212 . .	. . .	. . .	. . .	. . .	. . .	. . .	. . .	. . .
Air transport, other	2 213 . .	. . .	. . .	. . .	. . .	. . .	. . .	. . .	. . .
Other transport, passenger	2 215 . .	. . .	. . .	. . .	. . .	. . .	. . .	. . .	. . .
Other transport, freight	2 216 . .	. . .	. . .	. . .	. . .	. . .	. . .	. . .	. . .
Other transport, other	2 217 . .	. . .	. . .	. . .	. . .	. . .	. . .	. . .	. . .
Transportation services, debit	3 205 . .	**–19.40**	**–22.14**	**–19.97**	**–22.77**	**–18.44**	**. . .**	**. . .**	**. . .**
Passenger	3 205 BA	*–4.75*	*–5.15*	*–5.46*	*–3.90*	*–2.70*	. . .	. . .	. . .
Freight	3 205 BB	*–14.65*	*–16.99*	*–13.92*	*–16.54*	*–15.74*	. . .	. . .	. . .
Other	3 205 BC	. . .	. . .	*–.59*	*–2.32*	. . .	. . .	. . .	. . .
Sea transport, passenger	3 207 . .	. . .	. . .	. . .	. . .	. . .	. . .	. . .	. . .
Sea transport, freight	3 208 . .	. . .	. . .	. . .	. . .	. . .	. . .	. . .	. . .
Sea transport, other	3 209 . .	. . .	. . .	. . .	. . .	. . .	. . .	. . .	. . .
Air transport, passenger	3 211 . .	. . .	. . .	. . .	. . .	. . .	. . .	. . .	. . .
Air transport, freight	3 212 . .	. . .	. . .	. . .	. . .	. . .	. . .	. . .	. . .
Air transport, other	3 213 . .	. . .	. . .	. . .	. . .	. . .	. . .	. . .	. . .
Other transport, passenger	3 215 . .	. . .	. . .	. . .	. . .	. . .	. . .	. . .	. . .
Other transport, freight	3 216 . .	. . .	. . .	. . .	. . .	. . .	. . .	. . .	. . .
Other transport, other	3 217 . .	. . .	. . .	. . .	. . .	. . .	. . .	. . .	. . .
Travel, credit	2 236 . .	**5.57**	**6.50**	**7.08**	**9.28**	**10.83**	**. . .**	**. . .**	**. . .**
Business travel	2 237 . .	. . .	. . .	. . .	. . .	. . .	. . .	. . .	. . .
Personal travel	2 240 . .	. . .	. . .	. . .	. . .	. . .	. . .	. . .	. . .
Travel, debit	3 236 . .	**–8.07**	**–9.64**	**–10.60**	**–12.16**	**–11.10**	**. . .**	**. . .**	**. . .**
Business travel	3 237 . .	. . .	. . .	. . .	. . .	. . .	. . .	. . .	. . .
Personal travel	3 240 . .	–8.07	–9.64	–10.60	–12.16	–11.10	. . .	. . .	. . .
Other services, credit	2 200 BA	**14.89**	**18.14**	**15.78**	**18.45**	**21.58**	**. . .**	**. . .**	**. . .**
Communications	2 245 . .	. . .	. . .	. . .	. . .	. . .	. . .	. . .	. . .
Construction	2 249 . .	. . .	. . .	. . .	. . .	. . .	. . .	. . .	. . .
Insurance	2 253 . .	. . .	. . .	. . .	. . .	. . .	. . .	. . .	. . .
Financial	2 260 . .	. . .	. . .	. . .	. . .	. . .	. . .	. . .	. . .
Computer and information	2 262 . .	. . .	. . .	. . .	. . .	. . .	. . .	. . .	. . .
Royalties and licence fees	2 266 . .	. . .	. . .	. . .	. . .	. . .	. . .	. . .	. . .
Other business services	2 268 . .	9.89	11.47	9.29	10.54	14.79	. . .	. . .	. . .
Personal, cultural, and recreational	2 287 . .	. . .	. . .	. . .	. . .	. . .	. . .	. . .	. . .
Government, n.i.e.	2 291 . .	4.99	6.67	6.49	7.92	6.80	. . .	. . .	. . .
Other services, debit	3 200 BA	**–38.75**	**–43.49**	**–48.13**	**–53.33**	**–48.50**	**. . .**	**. . .**	**. . .**
Communications	3 245 . .	. . .	. . .	. . .	. . .	. . .	. . .	. . .	. . .
Construction	3 249 . .	. . .	. . .	. . .	. . .	. . .	. . .	. . .	. . .
Insurance	3 253 . .	–1.63	–1.89	–1.55	–1.84	–1.75	. . .	. . .	. . .
Financial	3 260 . .	. . .	. . .	. . .	. . .	. . .	. . .	. . .	. . .
Computer and information	3 262 . .	. . .	. . .	. . .	. . .	. . .	. . .	. . .	. . .
Royalties and licence fees	3 266 . .	. . .	. . .	. . .	. . .	. . .	. . .	. . .	. . .
Other business services	3 268 . .	–14.79	–16.22	–23.45	–28.51	–29.23	. . .	. . .	. . .
Personal, cultural, and recreational	3 287 . .	. . .	. . .	. . .	. . .	. . .	. . .	. . .	. . .
Government, n.i.e.	3 291 . .	–22.33	–25.38	–23.13	–22.99	–17.52	. . .	. . .	. . .

Table 2 (Continued). STANDARD PRESENTATION, 1988–95

(Millions of U.S. dollars)

	Code	1988	1989	1990	1991	1992	1993	1994	1995
C. INCOME	4 300 . .	−8.55	−7.89	−5.26	−9.02	−9.90	. . .	. . .	. . .
Total credit	2 300 . .	*3.55*	*3.88*	*2.33*	*1.36*	*.99*	. . .	. . .	. . .
Total debit	3 300 . .	*−12.10*	*−11.77*	*−7.59*	*−10.39*	*−10.89*	. . .	. . .	. . .
Compensation of employees, credit	2 310 . .	**. . .**	**. . .**	**. . .**	**. . .**	**. . .**	**. . .**	**. . .**	**. . .**
Compensation of employees, debit	3 310 . .	**−2.54**	**−2.09**	**−1.07**	**−1.47**	**−1.71**	**. . .**	**. . .**	**. . .**
Investment income, credit	2 320 . .	**3.55**	**3.88**	**2.33**	**1.36**	**.99**	**. . .**	**. . .**	**. . .**
Direct investment income	2 330 . .	. . .	. . .	. . .	. . .	. . .	. . .	. . .	. . .
Dividends and distributed branch profits	2 332 . .	. . .	. . .	. . .	. . .	. . .	. . .	. . .	. . .
Reinvested earnings and undistributed branch profits	2 333 . .	. . .	. . .	. . .	. . .	. . .	. . .	. . .	. . .
Income on debt (interest)	2 334 . .	. . .	. . .	. . .	. . .	. . .	. . .	. . .	. . .
Portfolio investment income	2 339 . .	. . .	. . .	. . .	. . .	. . .	. . .	. . .	. . .
Income on equity	2 340 . .	. . .	. . .	. . .	. . .	. . .	. . .	. . .	. . .
Income on bonds and notes	2 350 . .	. . .	. . .	. . .	. . .	. . .	. . .	. . .	. . .
Income on money market instruments and financial derivatives	2 360 . .	. . .	. . .	. . .	. . .	. . .	. . .	. . .	. . .
Other investment income	2 370 . .	3.55	3.88	2.33	1.36	.99	. . .	. . .	. . .
Investment income, debit	3 320 . .	**−9.56**	**−9.68**	**−6.52**	**−8.91**	**−9.19**	**. . .**	**. . .**	**. . .**
Direct investment income	3 330 . .	−5.33	−5.93	−2.02	−3.83	−4.00	. . .	. . .	. . .
Dividends and distributed branch profits	3 332 . .	−5.33	−5.93	−2.02	−3.83	−4.00	. . .	. . .	. . .
Reinvested earnings and undistributed branch profits	3 333 . .	. . .	. . .	. . .	. . .	. . .	. . .	. . .	. . .
Income on debt (interest)	3 334 . .	. . .	. . .	. . .	. . .	. . .	. . .	. . .	. . .
Portfolio investment income	3 339 . .	. . .	. . .	. . .	. . .	. . .	. . .	. . .	. . .
Income on equity	3 340 . .	. . .	. . .	. . .	. . .	. . .	. . .	. . .	. . .
Income on bonds and notes	3 350 . .	. . .	. . .	. . .	. . .	. . .	. . .	. . .	. . .
Income on money market instruments and financial derivatives	3 360 . .	. . .	. . .	. . .	. . .	. . .	. . .	. . .	. . .
Other investment income	3 370 . .	−4.23	−3.75	−4.51	−5.08	−5.19	. . .	. . .	. . .
D. CURRENT TRANSFERS	4 379 . .	47.63	43.00	38.08	38.38	38.90	. . .	. . .	. . .
Credit	2 379 . .	**52.72**	**47.14**	**43.66**	**46.82**	**46.51**	**. . .**	**. . .**	**. . .**
General government	2 380 . .	42.02	36.76	33.26	36.25	36.68	. . .	. . .	. . .
Other sectors	2 390 . .	10.71	10.38	10.40	10.57	9.84	. . .	. . .	. . .
Workers' remittances	2 391 . .	. . .	. . .	. . .	. . .	. . .	. . .	. . .	. . .
Other current transfers	2 392 . .	10.71	10.38	10.40	10.57	9.84	. . .	. . .	. . .
Debit	3 379 . .	**−5.09**	**−4.14**	**−5.58**	**−8.44**	**−7.62**	**. . .**	**. . .**	**. . .**
General government	3 380 . .	. . .	. . .	. . .	. . .	. . .	. . .	. . .	. . .
Other sectors	3 390 . .	−5.09	−4.14	−5.58	−8.44	−7.62	. . .	. . .	. . .
Workers' remittances	3 391 . .	−2.79	−2.49	−4.55	−5.30	−3.89	. . .	. . .	. . .
Other current transfers	3 392 . .	−2.30	−1.66	−1.03	−3.13	−3.72	. . .	. . .	. . .
CAPITAL AND FINANCIAL ACCOUNT	4 996 . .	**38.72**	**38.43**	**36.36**	**27.49**	**4.86**	**. . .**	**. . .**	**. . .**
CAPITAL ACCOUNT	4 994 . .	**−.38**	**−.17**	**−.16**	**−.26**	**−.44**	**. . .**	**. . .**	**. . .**
Total credit	2 994 . .	. . .	. . .	. . .	. . .	. . .	. . .	. . .	. . .
Total debit	3 994 . .	*−.38*	*−.17*	*−.16*	*−.26*	*−.44*	. . .	. . .	. . .
Capital transfers, credit	2 400 . .	**. . .**	**. . .**	**. . .**	**. . .**	**. . .**	**. . .**	**. . .**	**. . .**
General government	2 401 . .	. . .	. . .	. . .	. . .	. . .	. . .	. . .	. . .
Debt forgiveness	2 402 . .	. . .	. . .	. . .	. . .	. . .	. . .	. . .	. . .
Other capital transfers	2 410 . .	. . .	. . .	. . .	. . .	. . .	. . .	. . .	. . .
Other sectors	2 430 . .	. . .	. . .	. . .	. . .	. . .	. . .	. . .	. . .
Migrants' transfers	2 431 . .	. . .	. . .	. . .	. . .	. . .	. . .	. . .	. . .
Debt forgiveness	2 432 . .	. . .	. . .	. . .	. . .	. . .	. . .	. . .	. . .
Other capital transfers	2 440 . .	. . .	. . .	. . .	. . .	. . .	. . .	. . .	. . .
Capital transfers, debit	3 400 . .	**−.38**	**−.17**	**−.16**	**−.26**	**−.44**	**. . .**	**. . .**	**. . .**
General government	3 401 . .	. . .	. . .	. . .	. . .	. . .	. . .	. . .	. . .
Debt forgiveness	3 402 . .	. . .	. . .	. . .	. . .	. . .	. . .	. . .	. . .
Other capital transfers	3 410 . .	. . .	. . .	. . .	. . .	. . .	. . .	. . .	. . .
Other sectors	3 430 . .	−.38	−.17	−.16	−.26	−.44	. . .	. . .	. . .
Migrants' transfers	3 431 . .	−.38	−.17	−.16	−.26	−.44	. . .	. . .	. . .
Debt forgiveness	3 432 . .	. . .	. . .	. . .	. . .	. . .	. . .	. . .	. . .
Other capital transfers	3 440 . .	. . .	. . .	. . .	. . .	. . .	. . .	. . .	. . .
Nonproduced nonfinancial assets, credit	2 480 . .	**. . .**	**. . .**	**. . .**	**. . .**	**. . .**	**. . .**	**. . .**	**. . .**
Nonproduced nonfinancial assets, debit	3 480 . .	**. . .**	**. . .**	**. . .**	**. . .**	**. . .**	**. . .**	**. . .**	**. . .**

Table 2 (Continued). STANDARD PRESENTATION, 1988–95
(Millions of U.S. dollars)

	Code	1988	1989	1990	1991	1992	1993	1994	1995
FINANCIAL ACCOUNT	4 995	**39.10**	**38.61**	**36.52**	**27.74**	**5.30**	...	...	...
A. DIRECT INVESTMENT	4 500	1.68	11.60	10.44	14.51	14.17	...	...	...
Direct investment abroad	4 505	...	...	...	...	...	...	...	...
Equity capital	4 510	...	...	...	...	...	...	...	...
Claims on affiliated enterprises	4 515	...	...	...	...	...	...	...	...
Liabilities to affiliated enterprises	4 520	...	...	...	...	...	...	...	...
Reinvested earnings	4 525	...	...	...	...	...	...	...	...
Other capital	4 530	...	...	...	...	...	...	...	...
Claims on affiliated enterprises	4 535	...	...	...	...	...	...	...	...
Liabilities to affiliated enterprises	4 540	...	...	...	...	...	...	...	...
Direct investment in Solomon Islands	4 555	**1.68**	**11.60**	**10.44**	**14.51**	**14.17**	...	...	...
Equity capital	4 560	1.68	11.60	10.44	14.51	6.25	...	...	...
Claims on direct investors	4 565	...	...	...	...	...	...	...	...
Liabilities to direct investors	4 570	...	...	...	...	...	...	...	...
Reinvested earnings	4 575	...	...	...	...	...	...	...	...
Other capital	4 580	...	...	...	...	7.92	...	...	...
Claims on direct investors	4 585	...	...	...	...	...	...	...	...
Liabilities to direct investors	4 590	...	...	...	...	...	...	...	...
B. PORTFOLIO INVESTMENT	4 600	...	...	...	...	...	...	...	...
Assets	4 602	...	...	...	...	...	...	...	...
Equity securities	4 610	...	...	...	...	...	...	...	...
Monetary authorities	4 611	...	...	...	...	...	...	...	...
General government	4 612	...	...	...	...	...	...	...	...
Banks	4 613	...	...	...	...	...	...	...	...
Other sectors	4 614	...	...	...	...	...	...	...	...
Debt securities	4 619	...	...	...	...	...	...	...	...
Bonds and notes	4 620	...	...	...	...	...	...	...	...
Monetary authorities	4 621	...	...	...	...	...	...	...	...
General government	4 622	...	...	...	...	...	...	...	...
Banks	4 623	...	...	...	...	...	...	...	...
Other sectors	4 624	...	...	...	...	...	...	...	...
Money market instruments	4 630	...	...	...	...	...	...	...	...
Monetary authorities	4 631	...	...	...	...	...	...	...	...
General government	4 632	...	...	...	...	...	...	...	...
Banks	4 633	...	...	...	...	...	...	...	...
Other sectors	4 634	...	...	...	...	...	...	...	...
Financial derivatives	4 640	...	...	...	...	...	...	...	...
Monetary authorities	4 641	...	...	...	...	...	...	...	...
General government	4 642	...	...	...	...	...	...	...	...
Banks	4 643	...	...	...	...	...	...	...	...
Other sectors	4 644	...	...	...	...	...	...	...	...
Liabilities	4 652	...	...	...	...	...	...	...	...
Equity securities	4 660	...	...	...	...	...	...	...	...
Banks	4 663	...	...	...	...	...	...	...	...
Other sectors	4 664	...	...	...	...	...	...	...	...
Debt securities	4 669	...	...	...	...	...	...	...	...
Bonds and notes	4 670	...	...	...	...	...	...	...	...
Monetary authorities	4 671	...	...	...	...	...	...	...	...
General government	4 672	...	...	...	...	...	...	...	...
Banks	4 673	...	...	...	...	...	...	...	...
Other sectors	4 674	...	...	...	...	...	...	...	...
Money market instruments	4 680	...	...	...	...	...	...	...	...
Monetary authorities	4 681	...	...	...	...	...	...	...	...
General government	4 682	...	...	...	...	...	...	...	...
Banks	4 683	...	...	...	...	...	...	...	...
Other sectors	4 684	...	...	...	...	...	...	...	...
Financial derivatives	4 690	...	...	...	...	...	...	...	...
Monetary authorities	4 691	...	...	...	...	...	...	...	...
General government	4 692	...	...	...	...	...	...	...	...
Banks	4 693	...	...	...	...	...	...	...	...
Other sectors	4 694	...	...	...	...	...	...	...	...

Table 2 (Concluded). STANDARD PRESENTATION, 1988–95
(Millions of U.S. dollars)

	Code	1988	1989	1990	1991	1992	1993	1994	1995
C. OTHER INVESTMENT	4 700 . .	41.71	15.40	17.51	4.89	8.26	. . .	. . .	. . .
Assets	4 703 . .	**18.82**	**–.74**	**–.75**	**–1.25**	**–.07**	**. . .**	**. . .**	**. . .**
Trade credits	4 706 . .	. . .	. . .	. . .	. . .	. . .	. . .	. . .	. . .
General government: long-term	4 708 . .	. . .	. . .	. . .	. . .	. . .	. . .	. . .	. . .
General government: short-term	4 709 . .	. . .	. . .	. . .	. . .	. . .	. . .	. . .	. . .
Other sectors: long-term	4 711 . .	. . .	. . .	. . .	. . .	. . .	. . .	. . .	. . .
Other sectors: short-term	4 712 . .	. . .	. . .	. . .	. . .	. . .	. . .	. . .	. . .
Loans	4 714 . .	. . .	. . .	. . .	. . .	. . .	. . .	. . .	. . .
Monetary authorities: long-term	4 717 . .	. . .	. . .	. . .	. . .	. . .	. . .	. . .	. . .
Monetary authorities: short-term	4 718 . .	. . .	. . .	. . .	. . .	. . .	. . .	. . .	. . .
General government: long-term	4 720 . .	. . .	. . .	. . .	. . .	. . .	. . .	. . .	. . .
General government: short-term	4 721 . .	. . .	. . .	. . .	. . .	. . .	. . .	. . .	. . .
Banks: long-term	4 723 . .	. . .	. . .	. . .	. . .	. . .	. . .	. . .	. . .
Banks: short-term	4 724 . .	. . .	. . .	. . .	. . .	. . .	. . .	. . .	. . .
Other sectors: long-term	4 726 . .	. . .	. . .	. . .	. . .	. . .	. . .	. . .	. . .
Other sectors: short-term	4 727 . .	. . .	. . .	. . .	. . .	. . .	. . .	. . .	. . .
Currency and deposits	4 730 . .	18.82	–.74	–.75	–1.25	–.07	. . .	. . .	. . .
Monetary authorities	4 731 . .	. . .	. . .	. . .	. . .	. . .	. . .	. . .	. . .
General government	4 732 . .	19.74	. . .	. . .	. . .	. . .	. . .	. . .	. . .
Banks	4 733 . .	–.91	–.74	–.75	–1.25	–.07	. . .	. . .	. . .
Other sectors	4 734 . .	. . .	. . .	. . .	. . .	. . .	. . .	. . .	. . .
Other assets	4 736 . .	. . .	. . .	. . .	. . .	. . .	. . .	. . .	. . .
Monetary authorities: long-term	4 738 . .	. . .	. . .	. . .	. . .	. . .	. . .	. . .	. . .
Monetary authorities: short-term	4 739 . .	. . .	. . .	. . .	. . .	. . .	. . .	. . .	. . .
General government: long-term	4 741 . .	. . .	. . .	. . .	. . .	. . .	. . .	. . .	. . .
General government: short-term	4 742 . .	. . .	. . .	. . .	. . .	. . .	. . .	. . .	. . .
Banks: long-term	4 744 . .	. . .	. . .	. . .	. . .	. . .	. . .	. . .	. . .
Banks: short-term	4 745 . .	. . .	. . .	. . .	. . .	. . .	. . .	. . .	. . .
Other sectors: long-term	4 747 . .	. . .	. . .	. . .	. . .	. . .	. . .	. . .	. . .
Other sectors: short-term	4 748 . .	. . .	. . .	. . .	. . .	. . .	. . .	. . .	. . .
Liabilities	4 753 . .	**22.88**	**16.14**	**18.26**	**6.14**	**8.33**	**. . .**	**. . .**	**. . .**
Trade credits	4 756 . .	. . .	. . .	. . .	. . .	. . .	. . .	. . .	. . .
General government: long-term	4 758 . .	. . .	. . .	. . .	. . .	. . .	. . .	. . .	. . .
General government: short-term	4 759 . .	. . .	. . .	. . .	. . .	. . .	. . .	. . .	. . .
Other sectors: long-term	4 761 . .	. . .	. . .	. . .	. . .	. . .	. . .	. . .	. . .
Other sectors: short-term	4 762 . .	. . .	. . .	. . .	. . .	. . .	. . .	. . .	. . .
Loans	4 764 . .	21.20	16.75	12.09	7.17	8.81	. . .	. . .	. . .
Use of Fund credit and loans from the Fund	4 766 . .	–.41	–.21	–.84	–.64	. . .	. . .	. . .	. . .
Monetary authorities: other long-term	4 767 . .	. . .	. . .	. . .	. . .	. . .	. . .	. . .	. . .
Monetary authorities: short-term	4 768 . .	. . .	. . .	. . .	. . .	. . .	. . .	. . .	. . .
General government: long-term	4 770 . .	8.50	.35	–.04	–.07	1.57	. . .	. . .	. . .
General government: short-term	4 771 . .	. . .	. . .	. . .	. . .	. . .	. . .	. . .	. . .
Banks: long-term	4 773 . .	. . .	. . .	. . .	. . .	. . .	. . .	. . .	. . .
Banks: short-term	4 774 . .	. . .	. . .	. . .	. . .	. . .	. . .	. . .	. . .
Other sectors: long-term	4 776 . .	11.76	14.52	12.50	5.93	5.43	. . .	. . .	. . .
Other sectors: short-term	4 777 . .	1.34	2.09	.47	1.95	1.81	. . .	. . .	. . .
Currency and deposits	4 780 . .	–.05	–1.44	2.69	–.88	–.85	. . .	. . .	. . .
Monetary authorities	4 781 . .	. . .	. . .	. . .	. . .	. . .	. . .	. . .	. . .
General government	4 782 . .	. . .	. . .	. . .	. . .	. . .	. . .	. . .	. . .
Banks	4 783 . .	–.05	–1.44	2.69	–.88	–.85	. . .	. . .	. . .
Other sectors	4 784 . .	. . .	. . .	. . .	. . .	. . .	. . .	. . .	. . .
Other liabilities	4 786 . .	1.73	.83	3.48	–.15	.38	. . .	. . .	. . .
Monetary authorities: long-term	4 788 . .	. . .	. . .	. . .	. . .	. . .	. . .	. . .	. . .
Monetary authorities: short-term	4 789 . .	. . .	2.22	1.07	. . .	.41	. . .	. . .	. . .
General government: long-term	4 791 . .	. . .	. . .	. . .	. . .	. . .	. . .	. . .	. . .
General government: short-term	4 792 . .	. . .	. . .	. . .	. . .	. . .	. . .	. . .	. . .
Banks: long-term	4 794 . .	.10	.09	.08	.04	.03	. . .	. . .	. . .
Banks: short-term	4 795 . .	. . .	. . .	. . .	. . .	. . .	. . .	. . .	. . .
Other sectors: long-term	4 797 . .	. . .	–1.48	–.16	–.18	–.07	. . .	. . .	. . .
Other sectors: short-term	4 798 . .	1.63	. . .	2.49	. . .	. . .	. . .	. . .	. . .
D. RESERVE ASSETS	4 800 . .	–4.28	11.61	8.58	8.34	–17.14	. . .	. . .	. . .
Monetary gold	4 810 . .	. . .	. . .	. . .	. . .	. . .	. . .	. . .	. . .
Special drawing rights	4 820 . .	.23	–.07	–.28	.25	.04	. . .	. . .	. . .
Reserve position in the Fund	4 830 . .	. . .	–.01	. . .	–.01	. . .	. . .	. . .	. . .
Foreign exchange	4 840 . .	–4.51	11.69	8.86	8.10	–17.18	. . .	. . .	. . .
Other claims	4 880 . .	. . .	. . .	. . .	. . .	. . .	. . .	. . .	. . .
NET ERRORS AND OMISSIONS	4 998 . .	**–10.87**	**–5.21**	**–8.60**	**8.36**	**–6.16**	**. . .**	**. . .**	**. . .**

South Africa
199

Table 1. ANALYTIC PRESENTATION, 1988–95
(Millions of U.S. dollars)

	Code	1988	1989	1990	1991	1992	1993	1994	1995
A. Current Account[1]	4 993 Y.	**1,204**	**1,564**	**2,065**	**2,243**	**1,376**	**1,804**	**–611**	**–3,500**
Goods: exports f.o.b	2 100 . .	22,432	22,399	23,560	23,289	23,645	24,068	24,654	27,879
Goods: imports f.o.b	3 100 . .	–17,210	–16,810	–16,778	–17,156	–18,216	–18,287	–21,452	–27,132
Balance on Goods	4 100 . .	*5,222*	*5,589*	*6,783*	*6,134*	*5,429*	*5,781*	*3,202*	*746*
Services: credit	2 200 . .	2,585	2,729	3,559	3,474	3,611	3,571	3,989	4,516
Services: debit	3 200 . .	–3,484	–3,655	–4,239	–4,238	–4,833	–5,101	–5,483	–5,970
Balance on Goods and Services	4 991 . .	*4,323*	*4,664*	*6,102*	*5,370*	*4,207*	*4,251*	*1,708*	*–708*
Income: credit	2 300 . .	659	815	833	1,012	1,058	872	1,075	1,077
Income: debit	3 300 . .	–3,940	–4,101	–4,929	–4,195	–3,983	–3,449	–3,444	–3,891
Balance on Goods, Services, and Income	4 992 . .	*1,043*	*1,378*	*2,006*	*2,187*	*1,282*	*1,675*	*–662*	*–3,522*
Current transfers: credit	2 379 Y.	309	325	298	242	215	262	246	240
Current transfers: debit	3 379 . .	–148	–139	–238	–186	–121	–132	–196	–218
B. Capital Account[1]	4 994 Y.	**14**	**15**	**12**	**16**	**11**	**1**	**–5**	**15**
Capital account: credit	2 994 Y.	29	23	23	27	25	24	18	38
Capital account: debit	3 994 . .	–15	–8	–12	–12	–14	–23	–23	–23
Total, Groups A Plus B	4 010 . .	*1,218*	*1,579*	*2,077*	*2,258*	*1,388*	*1,805*	*–617*	*–3,485*
C. Financial Account[1]	4 995 X.	**–1,640**	**–1,117**	**344**	**64**	**383**	**–1,664**	**2,364**	**5,252**
Direct investment abroad	4 505 . .	–18	2	. . .	226	–25	–27	327	139
Direct investment in South Africa	4 555 Y.	116	8	–5	–215	–753	–285	–143	3
Portfolio investment assets	4 602 . .	. . .	. . .	. . .	. . .	. . .	. . .	. . .	. . .
Equity securities	4 610 . .	. . .	. . .	. . .	. . .	. . .	. . .	. . .	. . .
Debt securities	4 619 . .	. . .	. . .	. . .	. . .	. . .	. . .	. . .	. . .
Portfolio investment liabilities	4 652 Y.	–54	–138	–50	–264	–106	1,097	2,133	1,702
Equity securities	4 660 Y.	. . .	. . .	. . .	–849	–806	877	133	1,342
Debt securities	4 669 Y.	–54	–138	–50	586	700	221	1,999	360
Other investment assets	4 703 . .	–175	–742	–97	–241	–299	–284	–243	15
Monetary authorities	4 703 . A	34	. . .	–99	–17	–266	–24	43	75
General government	4 703 . B	–31	–44	–26	–82	–2	. . .	–1	–4
Banks	4 703 . C	–2	–10	113	–62	. . .	3	–24	–76
Other sectors	4 703 . D	–176	–687	–85	–80	–30	–262	–260	20
Other investment liabilities	4 753 X.	–1,507	–248	495	558	1,565	–2,166	290	3,393
Monetary authorities	4 753 XA	–3	59	32	. . .	. . .	. . .	. . .	. . .
General government	4 753 YB	–169	–141	–193	329	644	–84	–8	–9
Banks	4 753 YC	233	488	258	1,000	1,170	–1,042	556	2,842
Other sectors	4 753 YD	–1,568	–654	399	–771	–249	–1,040	–259	560
Total, Groups A Through C	4 020 . .	*–421*	*462*	*2,421*	*2,322*	*1,771*	*141*	*1,747*	*1,767*
D. Net Errors and Omissions	4 998 . .	**–965**	**–575**	**–1,016**	**–815**	**–1,640**	**–2,968**	**–879**	**741**
Total, Groups A Through D	4 030 . .	*–1,386*	*–113*	*1,405*	*1,506*	*131*	*–2,828*	*868*	*2,508*
E. Reserves and Related Items	4 040 . .	**1,386**	**113**	**–1,405**	**–1,506**	**–131**	**2,828**	**–868**	**–2,508**
Reserve assets	4 800 . .	766	–527	–356	–1,111	–402	575	–868	–1,131
Use of Fund credit and loans	4 766 . .	. . .	. . .	. . .	. . .	. . .	850	. . .	. . .
Liabilities constituting foreign authorities' reserves	4 900 . .	8	27	11	–7	–11	90	41	24
Exceptional financing	4 920 . .	612	613	–1,060	–389	282	1,313	–41	–1,401
Conversion rates: rand per U.S. dollar	0 101 . .	**2.2735**	**2.6227**	**2.5873**	**2.7613**	**2.8520**	**3.2677**	**3.5508**	**3.6271**

[1] Excludes components that have been classified in the categories of Group E.

Table 2. STANDARD PRESENTATION, 1988–95
(Millions of U.S. dollars)

	Code	1988	1989	1990	1991	1992	1993	1994	1995
CURRENT ACCOUNT	4 993 . .	**1,204**	**1,564**	**2,065**	**2,243**	**1,376**	**1,804**	**–611**	**–3,500**
A. GOODS	4 100 . .	5,222	5,589	6,783	6,134	5,429	5,781	3,202	746
Credit	2 100 . .	**22,432**	**22,399**	**23,560**	**23,289**	**23,645**	**24,068**	**24,654**	**27,879**
General merchandise: exports f.o.b.	2 110 . .	13,792	15,058	16,534	16,202	17,200	17,265	18,277	22,322
Goods for processing: exports f.o.b.	2 150 . .	. . .	. . .	. . .	. . .	. . .	. . .	. . .	. . .
Repairs on goods	2 160 . .	. . .	. . .	. . .	. . .	. . .	. . .	. . .	. . .
Goods procured in ports by carriers	2 170 . .	. . .	. . .	. . .	. . .	. . .	. . .	. . .	. . .
Nonmonetary gold	2 180 . .	8,640	7,341	7,026	7,087	6,445	6,803	6,377	5,557
Debit	3 100 . .	**–17,210**	**–16,810**	**–16,778**	**–17,156**	**–18,216**	**–18,287**	**–21,452**	**–27,132**
General merchandise: imports f.o.b.	3 110 . .	–17,210	–16,810	–16,778	–17,156	–18,216	–18,287	–21,452	–27,132
Goods for processing: imports f.o.b.	3 150 . .	. . .	. . .	. . .	. . .	. . .	. . .	. . .	. . .
Repairs on goods	3 160 . .	. . .	. . .	. . .	. . .	. . .	. . .	. . .	. . .
Goods procured in ports by carriers	3 170 . .	. . .	. . .	. . .	. . .	. . .	. . .	. . .	. . .
Nonmonetary gold	3 180 . .	. . .	. . .	. . .	. . .	. . .	. . .	. . .	. . .
B. SERVICES	4 200 . .	–899	–925	–681	–764	–1,222	–1,530	–1,494	–1,454
Total credit	2 200 . .	*2,585*	*2,729*	*3,559*	*3,474*	*3,611*	*3,571*	*3,989*	*4,516*
Total debit	3 200 . .	*–3,484*	*–3,655*	*–4,239*	*–4,238*	*–4,833*	*–5,101*	*–5,483*	*–5,970*
Transportation services, credit	2 205 . .	**851**	**909**	**1,161**	**1,151**	**1,308**	**1,287**	**1,314**	**1,329**
Passenger	2 205 BA	*211*	*245*	*331*	*305*	*362*	*316*	*362*	*528*
Freight	2 205 BB	*214*	*231*	*265*	*221*	*328*	*318*	*343*	*383*
Other	2 205 BC	*426*	*434*	*564*	*625*	*617*	*654*	*609*	*418*
Sea transport, passenger	2 207 . .	. . .	. . .	. . .	. . .	. . .	. . .	. . .	. . .
Sea transport, freight	2 208 . .	. . .	. . .	. . .	. . .	. . .	. . .	. . .	. . .
Sea transport, other	2 209 . .	. . .	. . .	. . .	. . .	. . .	. . .	. . .	. . .
Air transport, passenger	2 211 . .	. . .	. . .	. . .	. . .	. . .	. . .	. . .	. . .
Air transport, freight	2 212 . .	. . .	. . .	. . .	. . .	. . .	. . .	. . .	. . .
Air transport, other	2 213 . .	. . .	. . .	. . .	. . .	. . .	. . .	. . .	. . .
Other transport, passenger	2 215 . .	. . .	. . .	. . .	. . .	. . .	. . .	. . .	. . .
Other transport, freight	2 216 . .	. . .	. . .	. . .	. . .	. . .	. . .	. . .	. . .
Other transport, other	2 217 . .	. . .	. . .	. . .	. . .	. . .	. . .	. . .	. . .
Transportation services, debit	3 205 . .	**–1,637**	**–1,838**	**–2,018**	**–2,047**	**–2,179**	**–2,127**	**–2,391**	**–2,850**
Passenger	3 205 BA	*–216*	*–290*	*–410*	*–508*	*–494*	*–454*	*–585*	*–674*
Freight	3 205 BB	*–1,025*	*–1,075*	*–914*	*–955*	*–1,085*	*–1,118*	*–1,226*	*–1,575*
Other	3 205 BC	*–396*	*–474*	*–694*	*–584*	*–600*	*–555*	*–580*	*–601*
Sea transport, passenger	3 207 . .	. . .	. . .	. . .	. . .	. . .	. . .	. . .	. . .
Sea transport, freight	3 208 . .	. . .	. . .	. . .	. . .	. . .	. . .	. . .	. . .
Sea transport, other	3 209 . .	. . .	. . .	. . .	. . .	. . .	. . .	. . .	. . .
Air transport, passenger	3 211 . .	. . .	. . .	. . .	. . .	. . .	. . .	. . .	. . .
Air transport, freight	3 212 . .	. . .	. . .	. . .	. . .	. . .	. . .	. . .	. . .
Air transport, other	3 213 . .	. . .	. . .	. . .	. . .	. . .	. . .	. . .	. . .
Other transport, passenger	3 215 . .	. . .	. . .	. . .	. . .	. . .	. . .	. . .	. . .
Other transport, freight	3 216 . .	. . .	. . .	. . .	. . .	. . .	. . .	. . .	. . .
Other transport, other	3 217 . .	. . .	. . .	. . .	. . .	. . .	. . .	. . .	. . .
Travel, credit	2 236 . .	**1,446**	**1,522**	**1,835**	**1,849**	**1,810**	**1,786**	**2,064**	**2,378**
Business travel	2 237 . .	. . .	. . .	. . .	. . .	. . .	. . .	493	538
Personal travel	2 240 . .	. . .	. . .	. . .	. . .	. . .	. . .	1,571	1,840
Travel, debit	3 236 . .	**–971**	**–949**	**–1,132**	**–1,164**	**–1,554**	**–1,868**	**–1,861**	**–1,758**
Business travel	3 237 . .	. . .	. . .	. . .	. . .	. . .	. . .	–15	–28
Personal travel	3 240 . .	. . .	. . .	. . .	. . .	. . .	. . .	–1,847	–1,730
Other services, credit	2 200 BA	**288**	**298**	**563**	**474**	**493**	**497**	**611**	**809**
Communications	2 245 . .	. . .	. . .	. . .	. . .	. . .	. . .	. . .	. . .
Construction	2 249 . .	. . .	. . .	. . .	. . .	. . .	. . .	. . .	. . .
Insurance	2 253 . .	198	187	354	181	236	197	282	390
Financial	2 260 . .	. . .	. . .	. . .	. . .	. . .	. . .	. . .	. . .
Computer and information	2 262 . .	. . .	. . .	. . .	. . .	. . .	. . .	. . .	. . .
Royalties and licence fees	2 266 . .	14	12	54	43	27	50	51	66
Other business services	2 268 . .	59	68	38	111	89	94	83	103
Personal, cultural, and recreational	2 287 . .	. . .	. . .	. . .	. . .	. . .	. . .	. . .	. . .
Government, n.i.e.	2 291 . .	16	30	116	139	141	156	194	251
Other services, debit	3 200 BA	**–877**	**–867**	**–1,089**	**–1,027**	**–1,100**	**–1,105**	**–1,231**	**–1,362**
Communications	3 245 . .	. . .	. . .	. . .	. . .	. . .	. . .	. . .	. . .
Construction	3 249 . .	. . .	. . .	. . .	. . .	. . .	. . .	. . .	. . .
Insurance	3 253 . .	–338	–302	–421	–314	–371	–380	–438	–488
Financial	3 260 . .	. . .	. . .	. . .	. . .	. . .	. . .	. . .	. . .
Computer and information	3 262 . .	. . .	. . .	. . .	. . .	. . .	. . .	. . .	. . .
Royalties and licence fees	3 266 . .	–166	–144	–130	–139	–137	–124	–119	–102
Other business services	3 268 . .	–336	–375	–396	–418	–436	–424	–474	–508
Personal, cultural, and recreational	3 287 . .	. . .	. . .	. . .	. . .	. . .	. . .	. . .	. . .
Government, n.i.e.	3 291 . .	–36	–46	–144	–157	–156	–178	–200	–264

Table 2 (Continued). STANDARD PRESENTATION, 1988–95
(Millions of U.S. dollars)

	Code	1988	1989	1990	1991	1992	1993	1994	1995
C. INCOME	4 300	–3,280	–3,286	–4,096	–3,183	–2,925	–2,577	–2,369	–2,814
Total credit	2 300	*659*	*815*	*833*	*1,012*	*1,058*	*872*	*1,075*	*1,077*
Total debit	3 300	*–3,940*	*–4,101*	*–4,929*	*–4,195*	*–3,983*	*–3,449*	*–3,444*	*–3,891*
Compensation of employees, credit	2 310	**55**	**208**	**284**	**237**	**219**	**161**	**184**	**205**
Compensation of employees, debit	3 310	**–1,011**	**–1,043**	**–1,116**	**–915**	**–851**	**–630**	**–621**	**–622**
Investment income, credit	2 320	**605**	**606**	**549**	**775**	**840**	**711**	**891**	**872**
Direct investment income	2 330	373	523	484	681	763	681	588	510
Dividends and distributed branch profits	2 332	363	223	386	571	659	583	566	485
Reinvested earnings and undistributed branch profits	2 333	...	...	...	...	...	...	...	...
Income on debt (interest)	2 334	10	300	98	110	104	97	22	26
Portfolio investment income	2 339	21	...	...	...	...	...	249	261
Income on equity	2 340	21	...	...	...	...	...	69	53
Income on bonds and notes	2 350	...	...	...	...	...	...	...	...
Income on money market instruments and financial derivatives	2 360	...	...	...	...	...	...	...	...
Other investment income	2 370	211	83	65	93	77	31	54	101
Investment income, debit	3 320	**–2,928**	**–3,058**	**–3,813**	**–3,280**	**–3,132**	**–2,819**	**–2,823**	**–3,269**
Direct investment income	3 330	–671	–2,657	–3,235	–2,988	–2,860	–2,669	–620	–645
Dividends and distributed branch profits	3 332	–612	–1,297	–1,346	–1,203	–1,244	–922	–584	–599
Reinvested earnings and undistributed branch profits	3 333	...	...	...	...	...	...	...	...
Income on debt (interest)	3 334	–59	–1,361	–1,889	–1,784	–1,616	–1,748	–37	–46
Portfolio investment income	3 339	–631	...	...	...	...	...	–2,026	–2,465
Income on equity	3 340	–631	...	...	...	...	...	–243	–226
Income on bonds and notes	3 350	...	...	...	...	...	...	...	...
Income on money market instruments and financial derivatives	3 360	...	...	...	...	...	...	...	...
Other investment income	3 370	–1,626	–400	–578	–293	–272	–149	–176	–159
D. CURRENT TRANSFERS	4 379	161	186	60	56	94	130	50	23
Credit	2 379	**309**	**325**	**298**	**242**	**215**	**262**	**246**	**240**
General government	2 380	181	176	167	119	99	101	120	120
Other sectors	2 390	128	149	131	123	117	161	126	120
Workers' remittances	2 391	...	...	...	...	...	...	...	...
Other current transfers	2 392	128	149	131	123	117	161	126	120
Debit	3 379	**–148**	**–139**	**–238**	**–186**	**–121**	**–132**	**–196**	**–218**
General government	3 380	...	...	...	...	...	...	–46	–51
Other sectors	3 390	–148	–139	–238	–186	–121	–132	–150	–167
Workers' remittances	3 391	...	...	...	...	...	...	...	...
Other current transfers	3 392	–148	–139	–238	–186	–121	–132	–150	–167
CAPITAL AND FINANCIAL ACCOUNT	4 996	**–239**	**–989**	**–1,050**	**–1,427**	**263**	**1,164**	**1,491**	**2,759**
CAPITAL ACCOUNT	4 994	**14**	**15**	**12**	**16**	**11**	**1**	**–5**	**15**
Total credit	2 994	*29*	*23*	*23*	*27*	*25*	*24*	*18*	*38*
Total debit	3 994	*–15*	*–8*	*–12*	*–12*	*–14*	*–23*	*–23*	*–23*
Capital transfers, credit	2 400	**29**	**23**	**23**	**27**	**25**	**24**	**18**	**38**
General government	2 401	...	...	...	...	...	...	...	...
Debt forgiveness	2 402	...	...	...	...	...	...	...	...
Other capital transfers	2 410	...	...	...	...	...	...	...	...
Other sectors	2 430	29	23	23	27	25	24	18	38
Migrants' transfers	2 431	29	23	23	27	25	24	18	38
Debt forgiveness	2 432	...	...	...	...	...	...	...	...
Other capital transfers	2 440	...	...	...	...	...	...	...	...
Capital transfers, debit	3 400	**–15**	**–8**	**–12**	**–12**	**–14**	**–23**	**–23**	**–23**
General government	3 401	...	...	...	...	...	...	...	...
Debt forgiveness	3 402	...	...	...	...	...	...	...	...
Other capital transfers	3 410	...	...	...	...	...	...	...	...
Other sectors	3 430	–15	–8	–12	–12	–14	–23	–23	–23
Migrants' transfers	3 431	–15	–8	–12	–12	–14	–23	–23	–23
Debt forgiveness	3 432	...	...	...	...	...	...	...	...
Other capital transfers	3 440	...	...	...	...	...	...	...	...
Nonproduced nonfinancial assets, credit	2 480	...	...	...	...	...	...	...	...
Nonproduced nonfinancial assets, debit	3 480	...	...	...	...	...	...	...	...

Table 2 (Continued). STANDARD PRESENTATION, 1988–95
(Millions of U.S. dollars)

	Code	1988	1989	1990	1991	1992	1993	1994	1995
FINANCIAL ACCOUNT	4 995	**–254**	**–1,004**	**–1,061**	**–1,443**	**252**	**1,164**	**1,496**	**2,744**
A. DIRECT INVESTMENT	4 500	98	10	–5	11	–777	–311	184	142
Direct investment abroad	4 505	**–18**	**2**	**...**	**226**	**–25**	**–27**	**327**	**139**
Equity capital	4 510	...	2	...	84	40	48	10	486
Claims on affiliated enterprises	4 515	...	...	...	...	...	...	...	...
Liabilities to affiliated enterprises	4 520	...	...	...	...	...	...	...	...
Reinvested earnings	4 525	...	...	...	...	...	...	...	...
Other capital	4 530	–19	...	...	142	–65	–75	317	–347
Claims on affiliated enterprises	4 535	...	...	...	...	...	...	...	...
Liabilities to affiliated enterprises	4 540	...	...	...	...	...	...	...	...
Direct investment in South Africa	4 555	**116**	**8**	**–5**	**–215**	**–753**	**–285**	**–143**	**3**
Equity capital	4 560	4	8	–5	–280	–638	–243	–112	3
Claims on direct investors	4 565	...	...	...	...	...	...	...	...
Liabilities to direct investors	4 570	...	...	...	...	...	...	...	...
Reinvested earnings	4 575	...	...	...	...	...	...	...	...
Other capital	4 580	111	...	...	65	–115	–42	–31	...
Claims on direct investors	4 585	...	...	...	...	...	...	...	...
Liabilities to direct investors	4 590	...	...	...	...	...	...	...	...
B. PORTFOLIO INVESTMENT	4 600	–54	–138	–50	–264	–106	1,097	2,133	1,702
Assets	4 602	**...**	**...**	**...**	**...**	**...**	**...**	**...**	**...**
Equity securities	4 610	...	...	...	...	...	...	...	...
Monetary authorities	4 611	...	...	...	...	...	...	...	...
General government	4 612	...	...	...	...	...	...	...	...
Banks	4 613	...	...	...	...	...	...	...	...
Other sectors	4 614	...	...	...	...	...	...	...	...
Debt securities	4 619	...	...	...	...	...	...	...	...
Bonds and notes	4 620	...	...	...	...	...	...	...	...
Monetary authorities	4 621	...	...	...	...	...	...	...	...
General government	4 622	...	...	...	...	...	...	...	...
Banks	4 623	...	...	...	...	...	...	...	...
Other sectors	4 624	...	...	...	...	...	...	...	...
Money market instruments	4 630	...	...	...	...	...	...	...	...
Monetary authorities	4 631	...	...	...	...	...	...	...	...
General government	4 632	...	...	...	...	...	...	...	...
Banks	4 633	...	...	...	...	...	...	...	...
Other sectors	4 634	...	...	...	...	...	...	...	...
Financial derivatives	4 640	...	...	...	...	...	...	...	...
Monetary authorities	4 641	...	...	...	...	...	...	...	...
General government	4 642	...	...	...	...	...	...	...	...
Banks	4 643	...	...	...	...	...	...	...	...
Other sectors	4 644	...	...	...	...	...	...	...	...
Liabilities	4 652	**–54**	**–138**	**–50**	**–264**	**–106**	**1,097**	**2,133**	**1,702**
Equity securities	4 660	...	...	...	–849	–806	877	133	1,342
Banks	4 663	...	...	...	...	...	...	...	...
Other sectors	4 664	...	...	...	–849	–806	877	133	1,342
Debt securities	4 669	–54	–138	–50	586	700	221	1,999	360
Bonds and notes	4 670	–54	–138	–50	586	700	221	1,514	832
Monetary authorities	4 671	...	...	...	...	...	...	...	...
General government	4 672	–54	–138	–50	167	117	136	997	454
Banks	4 673	...	...	...	...	...	...	...	...
Other sectors	4 674	...	...	...	419	583	85	517	378
Money market instruments	4 680	...	...	...	...	...	...	486	–472
Monetary authorities	4 681	...	...	...	...	...	...	...	...
General government	4 682	...	...	...	...	...	...	486	–472
Banks	4 683	...	...	...	...	...	...	...	...
Other sectors	4 684	...	...	...	...	...	...	...	...
Financial derivatives	4 690	...	...	...	...	...	...	...	...
Monetary authorities	4 691	...	...	...	...	...	...	...	...
General government	4 692	...	...	...	...	...	...	...	...
Banks	4 693	...	...	...	...	...	...	...	...
Other sectors	4 694	...	...	...	...	...	...	...	...

Table 2 (Concluded). STANDARD PRESENTATION, 1988–95
(Millions of U.S. dollars)

	Code	1988	1989	1990	1991	1992	1993	1994	1995
C. OTHER INVESTMENT	4 700 . .	–1,063	–349	–651	–79	1,538	–198	47	2,032
Assets	4 703 . .	**–175**	**–742**	**–97**	**–241**	**–299**	**–284**	**–243**	**15**
Trade credits	4 706 . .	. . .	. . .	. . .	. . .	. . .	. . .	. . .	. . .
General government: long-term	4 708 . .	. . .	. . .	. . .	. . .	. . .	. . .	. . .	. . .
General government: short-term	4 709 . .	. . .	. . .	. . .	. . .	. . .	. . .	. . .	. . .
Other sectors: long-term	4 711 . .	. . .	. . .	. . .	. . .	. . .	. . .	. . .	. . .
Other sectors: short-term	4 712 . .	. . .	. . .	. . .	. . .	. . .	. . .	. . .	. . .
Loans	4 714 . .	36	–10	14	–79	–267	–22	19	–1
Monetary authorities: long-term	4 717 . .	34	. . .	–99	–17	–266	–24	43	75
Monetary authorities: short-term	4 718 . .	. . .	. . .	. . .	. . .	. . .	. . .	. . .	. . .
General government: long-term	4 720 . .	. . .	. . .	. . .	. . .	. . .	. . .	. . .	. . .
General government: short-term	4 721 . .	. . .	. . .	. . .	. . .	. . .	. . .	. . .	. . .
Banks: long-term	4 723 . .	–2	–10	113	–62	. . .	3	–24	–76
Banks: short-term	4 724 . .	. . .	. . .	. . .	. . .	. . .	. . .	. . .	. . .
Other sectors: long-term	4 726 . .	4	. . .	. . .	. . .	. . .	. . .	. . .	. . .
Other sectors: short-term	4 727 . .	. . .	. . .	. . .	. . .	. . .	. . .	. . .	. . .
Currency and deposits	4 730 . .	–197	–538	227	. . .	. . .	. . .	. . .	. . .
Monetary authorities	4 731 . .	. . .	. . .	. . .	. . .	. . .	. . .	. . .	. . .
General government	4 732 . .	–25	–43	–19	. . .	. . .	. . .	. . .	. . .
Banks	4 733 . .	. . .	. . .	. . .	. . .	. . .	. . .	. . .	. . .
Other sectors	4 734 . .	–172	–495	246	. . .	. . .	. . .	. . .	. . .
Other assets	4 736 . .	–14	–193	–338	–162	–32	–262	–261	16
Monetary authorities: long-term	4 738 . .	. . .	. . .	. . .	. . .	. . .	. . .	. . .	. . .
Monetary authorities: short-term	4 739 . .	. . .	. . .	. . .	. . .	. . .	. . .	. . .	. . .
General government: long-term	4 741 . .	–6	–1	–7	–82	–2	. . .	–1	–4
General government: short-term	4 742 . .	. . .	. . .	. . .	. . .	. . .	. . .	. . .	. . .
Banks: long-term	4 744 . .	. . .	. . .	. . .	. . .	. . .	. . .	. . .	. . .
Banks: short-term	4 745 . .	. . .	. . .	. . .	. . .	. . .	. . .	. . .	. . .
Other sectors: long-term	4 747 . .	–8	–192	–331	–112	–25	–1	–1	–14
Other sectors: short-term	4 748 . .	. . .	. . .	. . .	32	–5	–261	–260	34
Liabilities	4 753 . .	**–888**	**393**	**–554**	**162**	**1,836**	**86**	**289**	**2,017**
Trade credits	4 756 . .	. . .	. . .	. . .	. . .	. . .	. . .	. . .	. . .
General government: long-term	4 758 . .	. . .	. . .	. . .	. . .	. . .	. . .	. . .	. . .
General government: short-term	4 759 . .	. . .	. . .	. . .	. . .	. . .	. . .	. . .	. . .
Other sectors: long-term	4 761 . .	. . .	. . .	. . .	. . .	. . .	. . .	. . .	. . .
Other sectors: short-term	4 762 . .	. . .	. . .	. . .	. . .	. . .	. . .	. . .	. . .
Loans	4 764 . .	293	474	–1,253	–25	951	2,080	–456	–1,342
Use of Fund credit and loans from the Fund	4 766 . .	. . .	. . .	. . .	. . .	. . .	850	. . .	. . .
Monetary authorities: other long-term	4 767 . .	. . .	. . .	. . .	. . .	. . .	. . .	. . .	. . .
Monetary authorities: short-term	4 768 . .	612	613	–1,060	–389	282	1,313	–41	–1,401
General government: long-term	4 770 . .	–169	–141	–193	329	644	–84	–8	–9
General government: short-term	4 771 . .	. . .	. . .	. . .	. . .	. . .	. . .	. . .	. . .
Banks: long-term	4 773 . .	–5	2	. . .	34	25	2	–407	67
Banks: short-term	4 774 . .	. . .	. . .	. . .	. . .	. . .	. . .	. . .	. . .
Other sectors: long-term	4 776 . .	–145	. . .	. . .	. . .	. . .	. . .	. . .	. . .
Other sectors: short-term	4 777 . .	. . .	. . .	. . .	. . .	. . .	. . .	. . .	. . .
Currency and deposits	4 780 . .	246	513	269	959	1,134	–954	1,004	2,503
Monetary authorities	4 781 . .	8	27	11	–7	–11	90	41	24
General government	4 782 . .	. . .	. . .	. . .	. . .	. . .	. . .	. . .	. . .
Banks	4 783 . .	238	486	258	966	1,145	–1,044	963	2,479
Other sectors	4 784 . .	. . .	. . .	. . .	. . .	. . .	. . .	. . .	. . .
Other liabilities	4 786 . .	–1,426	–595	430	–771	–249	–1,040	–259	856
Monetary authorities: long-term	4 788 . .	. . .	. . .	. . .	. . .	. . .	. . .	. . .	. . .
Monetary authorities: short-term	4 789 . .	–3	59	32	. . .	. . .	. . .	. . .	. . .
General government: long-term	4 791 . .	. . .	. . .	. . .	. . .	. . .	. . .	. . .	. . .
General government: short-term	4 792 . .	. . .	. . .	. . .	. . .	. . .	. . .	. . .	. . .
Banks: long-term	4 794 . .	. . .	. . .	. . .	. . .	. . .	. . .	. . .	296
Banks: short-term	4 795 . .	. . .	. . .	. . .	. . .	. . .	. . .	. . .	. . .
Other sectors: long-term	4 797 . .	–133	–20	532	–265	–176	–872	–166	437
Other sectors: short-term	4 798 . .	–1,290	–634	–133	–506	–73	–169	–93	123
D. RESERVE ASSETS	4 800 . .	766	–527	–356	–1,111	–402	575	–868	–1,131
Monetary gold	4 810 . .	813	–445	–589	–1,019	–213	560	191	–31
Special drawing rights	4 820 . .	1	–1	. . .	1	1	–12	11	–5
Reserve position in the Fund	4 830 . .	. . .	. . .	. . .	. . .	. . .	. . .	. . .	. . .
Foreign exchange	4 840 . .	–187	–147	–7	87	–21	–102	–773	–1,251
Other claims	4 880 . .	140	65	240	–179	–170	130	–297	155
NET ERRORS AND OMISSIONS	4 998 . .	**–965**	**–575**	**–1,016**	**–815**	**–1,640**	**–2,968**	**–879**	**741**

Part 3 of the *Yearbook* contains descriptions of the methodologies, compilation practices, and sources used to compile these data.

Table 3. INTERNATIONAL INVESTMENT POSITION (End–period stocks), 1988–95
(Millions of U.S. dollars)

	Code	1988	1989	1990	1991	1992	1993	1994	1995
ASSETS	8 995 C.	13,765	18,901	20,107	21,930	23,959	23,606	27,930	...
Direct investment abroad	8 505 . .	**7,630**	**13,143**	**14,772**	**15,813**	**17,621**	**17,485**	**21,128**	...
Equity capital and reinvested earnings	8 506 . .	6,113	12,621	14,268	15,286	16,502	16,292	19,785	...
Claims on affiliated enterprises	8 507 . .	...	...	...	...	...	...	...	...
Liabilities to affiliated enterprises	8 508 . .	...	...	...	...	...	...	...	...
Other capital	8 530 . .	1,517	522	503	528	1,119	1,193	1,342	...
Claims on affiliated enterprises	8 535 . .	...	...	...	...	...	...	...	...
Liabilities to affiliated enterprises	8 540 . .	...	...	...	...	...	...	...	...
Portfolio investment	8 602 . .	**570**	**297**	**322**	**416**	**319**	**437**	**124**	...
Equity securities	8 610 . .	570	263	288	369	280	401	89	...
Monetary authorities	8 611 . .	...	...	...	...	...	...	...	...
General government	8 612 . .	...	...	...	...	...	...	...	...
Banks	8 613 . .	...	...	...	...	...	...	...	...
Other sectors	8 614 . .	...	...	...	...	...	...	...	...
Debt securities	8 619 . .	...	34	34	47	39	36	34	...
Bonds and notes	8 620 . .	...	34	34	47	39	36	34	...
Monetary authorities	8 621 . .	...	...	...	...	...	...	...	...
General government	8 622 . .	...	...	...	...	...	...	...	...
Banks	8 623 . .	...	...	...	...	...	...	...	...
Other sectors	8 624 . .	...	34	34	47	39	36	34	...
Money market instruments	8 630 . .	...	...	...	...	...	...	...	...
Monetary authorities	8 631 . .	...	...	...	...	...	...	...	...
General government	8 632 . .	...	...	...	...	...	...	...	...
Banks	8 633 . .	...	...	...	...	...	...	...	...
Other sectors	8 634 . .	...	...	...	...	...	...	...	...
Financial derivatives	8 640 . .	...	...	...	...	...	...	...	...
Monetary authorities	8 641 . .	...	...	...	...	...	...	...	...
General government	8 642 . .	...	...	...	...	...	...	...	...
Banks	8 643 . .	...	...	...	...	...	...	...	...
Other sectors	8 644 . .	...	...	...	...	...	...	...	...
Other investment	8 703 . .	**2,927**	**2,861**	**2,370**	**2,257**	**2,293**	**2,419**	**2,726**	...
Trade credits	8 706 . .	...	...	...	...	...	...	...	...
General government: long-term	8 708 . .	...	...	...	...	...	...	...	...
General government: short-term	8 709 . .	...	...	...	...	...	...	...	...
Other sectors: long-term	8 711 . .	...	...	...	...	...	...	...	...
Other sectors: short-term	8 712 . .	...	...	...	...	...	...	...	...
Loans	8 714 . .	483	787	584	585	868	789	815	...
Monetary authorities: long-term	8 717 . .	...	...	...	...	...	...	...	...
Monetary authorities: short-term	8 718 . .	...	...	...	...	...	...	...	...
General government: long-term	8 720 . .	296	213	226	230	227	221	207	...
General government: short-term	8 721 . .	...	218	9	106	106	154	344	...
Banks: long-term	8 723 . .	...	267	302	212	399	323	219	...
Banks: short-term	8 724 . .	...	...	...	...	...	...	...	...
Other sectors: long-term	8 726 . .	188	89	46	37	136	91	45	...
Other sectors: short-term	8 727 . .	...	...	...	...	...	...	...	...
Currency and deposits	8 730 . .	74	...	...	...	...	...	...	...
Monetary authorities	8 731 . .	...	...	...	...	...	...	...	...
General government	8 732 . .	74	...	...	...	...	...	...	...
Banks	8 733 . .	...	...	...	...	...	...	...	...
Other sectors	8 734 . .	...	...	...	...	...	...	...	...
Other assets	8 736 . .	2,369	2,074	1,824	1,672	1,425	1,630	1,911	...
Monetary authorities: long-term	8 738 . .	...	...	...	...	...	...	...	...
Monetary authorities: short-term	8 739 . .	...	...	...	...	...	...	...	...
General government: long-term	8 741 . .	78	...	...	...	...	...	...	...
General government: short-term	8 742 . .	...	...	...	...	...	...	...	...
Banks: long-term	8 744 . .	11	...	...	...	...	...	...	...
Banks: short-term	8 745 . .	...	...	...	...	...	...	...	...
Other sectors: long-term	8 747 . .	39	...	...	...	...	...	...	...
Other sectors: short-term	8 748 . .	2,240	2,074	1,824	1,672	1,425	1,630	1,911	...
Reserve assets	8 800 . .	**2,638**	**2,599**	**2,643**	**3,444**	**3,726**	**3,265**	**3,953**	...
Monetary gold	8 810 . .	1,295	1,137	1,415	2,074	1,992	1,659	1,445	...
Special drawing rights	8 820 . .	1	2	2	2	...	12	1	5
Reserve position in the Fund	8 830 . .	...	...	...	...	...	...	...	...
Foreign exchange	8 840 . .	779	958	989	896	990	1,006	1,683	...
Other claims	8 880 . .	562	502	236	472	744	588	824	...

Table 3 (Continued). INTERNATIONAL INVESTMENT POSITION (End–period stocks), 1988–95

(Millions of U.S. dollars)

	Code	1988	1989	1990	1991	1992	1993	1994	1995
LIABILITIES	8 995 D.	28,352	32,578	33,823	34,690	36,827	36,996	43,129	...
Direct investment in South Africa	8 555 . .	**11,057**	**8,067**	**8,503**	**9,100**	**8,754**	**8,583**	**10,166**	...
Equity capital and reinvested earnings	8 556 . .	6,875	6,433	7,043	7,475	7,356	6,744	7,635	...
Claims on direct investors	8 557 . .	...	...	...	...	...	...	...	...
Liabilities to direct investors	8 558 . .	...	...	...	...	...	...	...	...
Other capital	8 580 . .	4,182	1,634	1,461	1,625	1,398	1,839	2,532	...
Claims on direct investors	8 585 . .	...	...	...	...	...	...	...	...
Liabilities to direct investors	8 590 . .	...	...	...	...	...	...	...	...
Portfolio investment	8 652 . .	**4,667**	**6,778**	**8,524**	**8,463**	**10,279**	**10,294**	**13,372**	...
Equity securities	8 660 . .	1,750	2,788	3,366	3,464	4,054	3,283	3,968	...
Banks	8 663 . .	...	...	...	...	...	...	...	...
Other sectors	8 664 . .	...	2,788	3,366	3,464	4,054	3,283	3,968	...
Debt securities	8 669 . .	2,917	3,990	5,158	4,998	6,225	7,011	9,404	...
Bonds and notes	8 670 . .	2,917	3,990	5,158	4,998	6,225	7,011	9,404	...
Monetary authorities	8 671 . .	...	...	...	...	...	...	...	...
General government	8 672 . .	...	3,979	4,960	4,756	6,002	6,835	8,854	...
Banks	8 673 . .	...	...	...	...	...	...	...	...
Other sectors	8 674 . .	...	11	198	242	222	176	551	...
Money market instruments	8 680 . .	...	...	...	...	...	...	...	...
Monetary authorities	8 681 . .	...	...	...	...	...	...	...	...
General government	8 682 . .	...	...	...	...	...	...	...	...
Banks	8 683 . .	...	...	...	...	...	...	...	...
Other sectors	8 684 . .	...	...	...	...	...	...	...	...
Financial derivatives	8 690 . .	...	...	...	...	...	...	...	...
Monetary authorities	8 691 . .	...	...	...	...	...	...	...	...
General government	8 692 . .	...	...	...	...	...	...	...	...
Banks	8 692 . .	...	...	...	...	...	...	...	...
Other sectors	8 694 . .	...	...	...	...	...	...	...	...
Other investment	8 753 . .	**12,628**	**17,733**	**16,796**	**17,127**	**17,794**	**18,118**	**19,591**	...
Trade credits	8 756 . .	...	...	...	...	...	...	...	...
General government: long-term	8 758 . .	...	...	...	...	...	...	...	...
General government: short-term	8 759 . .	...	...	...	...	...	...	...	...
Other sectors: long-term	8 761 . .	...	...	...	...	...	...	...	...
Other sectors: short-term	8 762 . .	...	...	...	...	...	...	...	...
Loans	8 764 . .	6,757	10,946	10,285	10,135	10,072	11,497	12,068	...
Use of Fund credit and loans from the Fund	8 766 . .	...	...	...	...	...	844	897	913
Monetary authorities: other long-term	8 767 . .	...	...	...	...	...	829	565	...
Monetary authorities: short-term	8 768 . .	...	...	...	...	...	...	...	...
General government: long-term	8 770 . .	1,819	7,351	6,438	6,214	5,548	4,206	4,775	...
General government: short-term	8 771 . .	521	2,382	2,415	2,177	2,823	3,925	4,064	...
Banks: long-term	8 773 . .	7	39	39	36	33	29	28	...
Banks: short-term	8 774 . .	...	...	...	...	...	...	...	...
Other sectors: long-term	8 776 . .	4,411	1,173	1,393	1,708	1,668	1,664	1,738	...
Other sectors: short-term	8 777 . .	...	...	...	...	...	...	...	...
Currency and deposits	8 780 . .	1,972	1,272	1,873	2,819	3,993	2,711	3,469	...
Monetary authorities	8 781 . .	...	...	...	...	...	...	...	...
General government	8 782 . .	...	...	...	...	...	...	...	...
Banks	8 783 . .	1,972	1,272	1,873	2,819	3,993	2,711	3,469	...
Other sectors	8 784 . .	...	...	...	...	...	...	...	...
Other liabilities	8 786 . .	3,899	5,514	4,638	4,173	3,729	3,910	4,054	...
Monetary authorities: long-term	8 788 . .	...	...	...	...	...	...	...	...
Monetary authorities: short-term	8 789 . .	41	...	...	...	...	...	...	...
General government: long-term	8 791 . .	...	...	...	...	...	...	...	...
General government: short-term	8 792 . .	...	...	...	...	...	...	...	...
Banks: long-term	8 794 . .	...	...	...	...	...	...	...	...
Banks: short-term	8 795 . .	...	...	...	...	...	...	...	...
Other sectors: long-term	8 797 . .	65	...	...	...	...	...	...	...
Other sectors: short-term	8 798 . .	3,793	5,514	4,638	4,173	3,729	3,910	4,054	...
NET INTERNATIONAL INVESTMENT POSITION	8 995 . .	**–14,587**	**–13,678**	**–13,717**	**–12,760**	**–12,868**	**–13,390**	**–15,199**	...
Conversion rates: rand per U.S. dollar (end of period)	0 102 . .	**2.3777**	**2.5360**	**2.5625**	**2.7430**	**3.0530**	**3.3975**	**3.5435**	**3.6475**

Table 1. ANALYTIC PRESENTATION, 1988–95
(Millions of U.S. dollars)

	Code	1988	1989	1990	1991	1992	1993	1994	1995
A. Current Account [1]	4 993 Y.	**–3,795**	**–10,924**	**–18,010**	**–19,798**	**–21,287**	**–5,767**	**–6,817**	**1,280**
Goods: exports f.o.b	2 100 . .	40,692	44,945	55,658	60,167	65,826	62,019	73,924	92,626
Goods: imports f.o.b	3 100 . .	–59,396	–70,351	–84,815	–90,501	–96,247	–76,965	–88,757	–110,346
Balance on Goods	4 100 . .	*–18,703*	*–25,406*	*–29,158*	*–30,335*	*–30,420*	*–14,946*	*–14,833*	*–17,721*
Services: credit	2 200 . .	24,457	24,618	27,937	29,171	33,952	30,764	34,149	40,027
Services: debit	3 200 . .	–10,732	–11,983	–16,054	–17,263	–21,423	–19,657	–19,437	–22,161
Balance on Goods and Services	4 991 . .	*–4,979*	*–12,772*	*–17,275*	*–18,426*	*–17,891*	*–3,838*	*–121*	*145*
Income: credit	2 300 . .	2,690	3,775	7,817	10,923	14,084	11,811	8,676	13,389
Income: debit	3 300 . .	–5,999	–6,544	–11,350	–15,193	–19,874	–15,384	–16,869	–17,356
Balance on Goods, Services, and Income	4 992 . .	*–8,287*	*–15,540*	*–20,808*	*–22,696*	*–23,681*	*–7,411*	*–8,314*	*–3,822*
Current transfers: credit	2 379 Y.	7,478	8,496	7,849	9,767	11,410	9,150	9,387	12,430
Current transfers: debit	3 379 . .	–2,986	–3,880	–5,050	–6,870	–9,015	–7,506	–7,890	–7,328
B. Capital Account [1]	4 994 Y.	**11**	**–9**	**1,451**	**3,166**	**3,484**	**2,918**	**2,612**	**5,942**
Capital account: credit	2 994 Y.	48	50	1,753	3,535	3,978	3,366	3,134	6,423
Capital account: debit	3 994 . .	–37	–59	–302	–370	–493	–449	–522	–481
Total, Groups A Plus B	4 010 . .	*–3,784*	*–10,933*	*–16,559*	*–16,632*	*–17,802*	*–2,849*	*–4,205*	*7,221*
C. Financial Account [1]	4 995 X.	**14,615**	**18,342**	**22,970**	**32,015**	**5,959**	**–279**	**5,468**	**–7,533**
Direct investment abroad	4 505 . .	–1,235	–1,473	–3,522	–4,442	–2,192	–2,652	–3,831	–3,574
Direct investment in Spain	4 555 Y.	7,021	8,428	13,984	12,493	13,276	8,144	9,359	6,250
Portfolio investment assets	4 602 . .	–136	–166	–1,367	–2,410	–2,811	–6,772	–1,837	–619
Equity securities	4 610 . .	–136	–166	–329	–327	–145	–764	–1,047	–534
Debt securities	4 619 . .	. . .	. . .	–1,038	–2,083	–2,666	–6,008	–790	–85
Portfolio investment liabilities	4 652 Y.	2,427	8,155	10,385	22,489	12,169	56,125	–19,310	21,307
Equity securities	4 660 Y.	2,100	6,387	4,309	2,772	3,648	6,491	1,154	4,346
Debt securities	4 669 Y.	327	1,768	6,077	19,717	8,521	49,633	–20,464	16,961
Other investment assets	4 703 . .	–596	–108	–13,175	–7,740	–40,442	–75,296	9,149	–37,481
Monetary authorities	4 703 . A	. . .	. . .	. . .	. . .	. . .	. . .	. . .	. . .
General government	4 703 . B	–785	–737	–532	–635	–823	–641	–733	–353
Banks	4 703 . C	1,315	1,336	–7,520	–3,215	–28,758	–66,398	14,791	–27,075
Other sectors	4 703 . D	–1,127	–708	–4,704	–3,849	–10,786	–8,256	–4,909	–10,053
Other investment liabilities	4 753 X.	7,134	3,506	16,665	11,624	25,958	20,172	11,940	6,583
Monetary authorities	4 753 XA	–303	643	. . .	. . .	. . .	. . .	. . .	. . .
General government	4 753 YB	670	1,364	1,274	–271	3,418	152	1,495	1,783
Banks	4 753 YC	2,643	1,547	14,402	8,169	13,609	13,615	10,637	4,046
Other sectors	4 753 YD	4,125	–47	988	3,725	8,932	6,405	–192	755
Total, Groups A Through C	4 020 . .	*10,831*	*7,408*	*6,411*	*15,382*	*–11,844*	*–3,128*	*1,264*	*–312*
D. Net Errors and Omissions	4 998 . .	**–2,414**	**–2,693**	**777**	**–1,075**	**–5,965**	**–1,680**	**–1,214**	**–6,179**
Total, Groups A Through D	4 030 . .	*8,416*	*4,716*	*7,188*	*14,307*	*–17,809*	*–4,808*	*50*	*–6,491*
E. Reserves and Related Items	4 040 . .	**–8,416**	**–4,716**	**–7,188**	**–14,307**	**17,809**	**4,808**	**–50**	**6,491**
Reserve assets	4 800 . .	–8,416	–4,716	–7,188	–14,307	17,809	4,808	–50	6,491
Use of Fund credit and loans	4 766 . .	. . .	. . .	. . .	. . .	. . .	. . .	. . .	. . .
Liabilities constituting foreign authorities' reserves	4 900 . .	. . .	. . .	. . .	. . .	. . .	. . .	. . .	. . .
Exceptional financing	4 920 . .	. . .	. . .	. . .	. . .	. . .	. . .	. . .	. . .
Conversion rates: pesetas per U.S. dollar	0 101 . .	**116.49**	**118.38**	**101.93**	**103.91**	**102.38**	**127.26**	**133.96**	**124.69**

[1] Excludes components that have been classified in the categories of Group E.

Table 2. STANDARD PRESENTATION, 1988–95
(Millions of U.S. dollars)

	Code		1988	1989	1990	1991	1992	1993	1994	1995
CURRENT ACCOUNT	4 993	. .	**–3,795**	**–10,924**	**–18,010**	**–19,798**	**–21,287**	**–5,767**	**–6,817**	**1,280**
A. GOODS	4 100	. .	–18,703	–25,406	–29,158	–30,335	–30,420	–14,946	–14,833	–17,721
Credit	2 100	. .	**40,692**	**44,945**	**55,658**	**60,167**	**65,826**	**62,019**	**73,924**	**92,626**
General merchandise: exports f.o.b.	2 110	. .	39,652	43,301	. . .	. . .	. . .	. . .	. . .	. . .
Goods for processing: exports f.o.b.	2 150	. .	747	1,162	. . .	. . .	. . .	. . .	. . .	. . .
Repairs on goods	2 160	. .	. . .	. . .	. . .	. . .	. . .	. . .	. . .	. . .
Goods procured in ports by carriers	2 170	. .	293	482	. . .	. . .	. . .	. . .	. . .	. . .
Nonmonetary gold	2 180	. .	. . .	. . .	. . .	. . .	. . .	. . .	. . .	. . .
Debit	3 100	. .	**–59,396**	**–70,351**	**–84,815**	**–90,501**	**–96,247**	**–76,965**	**–88,757**	**–110,346**
General merchandise: imports f.o.b.	3 110	. .	–57,650	–67,797	. . .	. . .	. . .	. . .	. . .	. . .
Goods for processing: imports f.o.b.	3 150	. .	–1,745	–2,554	. . .	. . .	. . .	. . .	. . .	. . .
Repairs on goods	3 160	. .	. . .	. . .	. . .	. . .	. . .	. . .	. . .	. . .
Goods procured in ports by carriers	3 170	. .	. . .	. . .	. . .	. . .	. . .	. . .	. . .	. . .
Nonmonetary gold	3 180	. .	. . .	. . .	. . .	. . .	. . .	. . .	. . .	. . .
B. SERVICES	4 200	. .	13,725	12,635	11,882	11,908	12,529	11,108	14,713	17,866
Total credit	2 200	. .	*24,457*	*24,618*	*27,937*	*29,171*	*33,952*	*30,764*	*34,149*	*40,027*
Total debit	3 200	. .	*–10,732*	*–11,983*	*–16,054*	*–17,263*	*–21,423*	*–19,657*	*–19,437*	*–22,161*
Transportation services, credit	2 205	. .	**4,712**	**4,706**	**4,752**	**4,732**	**4,777**	**4,194**	**5,043**	**5,884**
Passenger	2 205	BA	*1,733*	*1,717*	. . .	. . .	. . .	*1,168*	*1,505*	*1,996*
Freight	2 205	BB	*1,314*	*1,486*	. . .	. . .	. . .	*1,819*	*2,169*	*2,256*
Other	2 205	BC	*1,665*	*1,502*	. . .	. . .	. . .	*1,208*	*1,369*	*1,632*
Sea transport, passenger	2 207	. .	. . .	. . .	. . .	. . .	. . .	24	29	21
Sea transport, freight	2 208	. .	644	709	. . .	. . .	. . .	672	802	1,009
Sea transport, other	2 209	. .	694	661	. . .	. . .	. . .	420	493	329
Air transport, passenger	2 211	. .	. . .	. . .	. . .	. . .	. . .	1,122	1,455	1,952
Air transport, freight	2 212	. .	34	51	. . .	. . .	. . .	384	458	101
Air transport, other	2 213	. .	765	566	. . .	. . .	. . .	703	778	1,220
Other transport, passenger	2 215	. .	. . .	. . .	. . .	. . .	. . .	22	22	22
Other transport, freight	2 216	. .	636	726	. . .	. . .	. . .	764	910	1,146
Other transport, other	2 217	. .	205	275	. . .	. . .	. . .	84	99	83
Transportation services, debit	3 205	. .	**–3,936**	**–4,301**	**–4,688**	**–4,795**	**–5,060**	**–4,495**	**–5,175**	**–6,391**
Passenger	3 205	BA	*–587*	*–604*	. . .	. . .	. . .	*–870*	*–945*	*–1,276*
Freight	3 205	BB	*–2,006*	*–2,239*	. . .	. . .	. . .	*–2,472*	*–2,826*	*–3,494*
Other	3 205	BC	*–1,343*	*–1,458*	. . .	. . .	. . .	*–1,153*	*–1,405*	*–1,621*
Sea transport, passenger	3 207	. .	. . .	. . .	. . .	. . .	. . .	–25	–22	–29
Sea transport, freight	3 208	. .	–1,193	–1,252	. . .	. . .	. . .	–1,596	–1,843	–2,300
Sea transport, other	3 209	. .	–255	–267	. . .	. . .	. . .	–240	–272	–224
Air transport, passenger	3 211	. .	. . .	. . .	. . .	. . .	. . .	–830	–885	–1,240
Air transport, freight	3 212	. .	. . .	. . .	. . .	. . .	. . .	–126	–110	–115
Air transport, other	3 213	. .	–949	–1,045	. . .	. . .	. . .	–744	–942	–1,338
Other transport, passenger	3 215	. .	. . .	. . .	. . .	. . .	. . .	–15	–38	–7
Other transport, freight	3 216	. .	–813	–987	. . .	. . .	. . .	–750	–873	–1,080
Other transport, other	3 217	. .	–139	–146	. . .	. . .	. . .	–169	–191	–58
Travel, credit	2 236	. .	**16,570**	**16,200**	**18,581**	**19,010**	**22,363**	**19,603**	**21,629**	**25,455**
Business travel	2 237	. .	. . .	. . .	. . .	. . .	. . .	. . .	. . .	. . .
Personal travel	2 240	. .	. . .	. . .	. . .	. . .	. . .	. . .	. . .	. . .
Travel, debit	3 236	. .	**–2,444**	**–3,079**	**–4,254**	**–4,532**	**–5,570**	**–4,734**	**–4,155**	**–4,465**
Business travel	3 237	. .	. . .	. . .	. . .	. . .	. . .	. . .	. . .	. . .
Personal travel	3 240	. .	. . .	. . .	. . .	. . .	. . .	. . .	. . .	. . .
Other services, credit	2 200	BA	**3,175**	**3,711**	**4,604**	**5,428**	**6,812**	**6,966**	**7,477**	**8,689**
Communications	2 245	. .	. . .	. . .	113	124	170	458	474	539
Construction	2 249	. .	. . .	. . .	150	268	431	443	417	455
Insurance	2 253	. .	328	469	462	576	971	900	945	936
Financial	2 260	. .	. . .	. . .	730	822	1,021	633	625	612
Computer and information	2 262	. .	. . .	. . .	104	169	239	587	606	1,029
Royalties and licence fees	2 266	. .	40	52	90	84	133	150	220	196
Other business services	2 268	. .	2,549	2,942	2,435	2,732	3,063	3,326	3,594	4,247
Personal, cultural, and recreational	2 287	. .	. . .	. . .	232	293	398	186	202	216
Government, n.i.e.	2 291	. .	259	248	288	361	386	282	394	459
Other services, debit	3 200	BA	**–4,353**	**–4,603**	**–7,112**	**–7,936**	**–10,793**	**–10,428**	**–10,107**	**–11,306**
Communications	3 245	. .	. . .	. . .	–84	–114	–249	–305	–328	–397
Construction	3 249	. .	. . .	. . .	–139	–209	–375	–293	–135	–264
Insurance	3 253	. .	–553	–651	–596	–583	–854	–863	–954	–1,125
Financial	3 260	. .	. . .	. . .	–360	–380	–469	–739	–585	–561
Computer and information	3 262	. .	. . .	. . .	–442	–473	–832	–686	–636	–728
Royalties and licence fees	3 266	. .	–647	–702	–1,022	–1,021	–1,180	–982	–1,061	–1,269
Other business services	3 268	. .	–2,475	–2,684	–3,105	–3,549	–4,837	–4,574	–4,844	–5,654
Personal, cultural, and recreational	3 287	. .	. . .	. . .	–506	–730	–933	–678	–597	–767
Government, n.i.e.	3 291	. .	–678	–565	–858	–877	–1,064	–1,308	–966	–540

Table 2 (Continued). STANDARD PRESENTATION, 1988–95
(Millions of U.S. dollars)

	Code	1988	1989	1990	1991	1992	1993	1994	1995
C. INCOME	4 300	–3,308	–2,768	–3,533	–4,269	–5,790	–3,573	–8,194	–3,967
Total credit	2 300	*2,690*	*3,775*	*7,817*	*10,923*	*14,084*	*11,811*	*8,676*	*13,389*
Total debit	3 300	*–5,999*	*–6,544*	*–11,350*	*–15,193*	*–19,874*	*–15,384*	*–16,869*	*–17,356*
Compensation of employees, credit	2 310	**212**	**210**	**229**	**228**	**242**	**112**	**104**	**156**
Compensation of employees, debit	3 310	**–9**	**–11**	**–11**	**–12**	**–21**	**–115**	**–98**	**–162**
Investment income, credit	2 320	**2,478**	**3,566**	**7,588**	**10,695**	**13,843**	**11,700**	**8,571**	**13,232**
Direct investment income	2 330	296	371	357	525	576	406	475	346
Dividends and distributed branch profits	2 332	296	371	...	...	...	...	...	...
Reinvested earnings and undistributed branch profits	2 333	...	...	...	...	...	...	...	...
Income on debt (interest)	2 334	...	...	5	30	15	94	32	–59
Portfolio investment income	2 339	...	...	309	517	326	884	842	1,070
Income on equity	2 340	...	...	56	89	83	72	56	121
Income on bonds and notes	2 350	...	...	...	...	...	...	...	...
Income on money market instruments and financial derivatives	2 360	...	...	...	...	...	...	...	...
Other investment income	2 370	2,182	3,194	6,922	9,653	12,940	10,409	7,254	11,816
Investment income, debit	3 320	**–5,990**	**–6,533**	**–11,339**	**–15,181**	**–19,853**	**–15,270**	**–16,771**	**–17,193**
Direct investment income	3 330	–2,215	–1,929	–2,455	–3,591	–3,106	–1,393	–2,329	–1,525
Dividends and distributed branch profits	3 332	–2,215	–1,929	...	...	...	...	...	...
Reinvested earnings and undistributed branch profits	3 333	...	...	...	...	...	...	...	...
Income on debt (interest)	3 334	...	...	–435	–552	–858	–310	–344	–401
Portfolio investment income	3 339	...	...	–2,045	–3,001	–5,712	–5,441	–6,928	–6,814
Income on equity	3 340	...	...	–1,135	–1,182	–1,385	–1,029	–1,109	–1,352
Income on bonds and notes	3 350	...	...	...	...	...	...	...	...
Income on money market instruments and financial derivatives	3 360	...	...	...	...	...	...	...	...
Other investment income	3 370	–3,775	–4,604	–6,838	–8,589	–11,035	–8,436	–7,514	–8,854
D. CURRENT TRANSFERS	4 379	4,492	4,616	2,799	2,898	2,395	1,644	1,498	5,102
Credit	2 379	**7,478**	**8,496**	**7,849**	**9,767**	**11,410**	**9,150**	**9,387**	**12,430**
General government	2 380	3,600	4,193	3,914	6,258	6,425	5,975	6,117	8,684
Other sectors	2 390	3,877	4,303	3,935	3,510	4,985	3,176	3,271	3,746
Workers' remittances	2 391	1,530	1,601	1,886	1,792	2,562	1,926	2,167	2,588
Other current transfers	2 392	2,347	2,701	2,049	1,718	2,423	1,249	1,103	1,157
Debit	3 379	**–2,986**	**–3,880**	**–5,050**	**–6,870**	**–9,015**	**–7,506**	**–7,890**	**–7,328**
General government	3 380	–2,115	–2,749	–3,749	–5,328	–6,510	–5,902	–6,346	–5,753
Other sectors	3 390	–871	–1,131	–1,301	–1,542	–2,506	–1,604	–1,543	–1,575
Workers' remittances	3 391	–117	–177	–148	–195	–682	–382	–387	–470
Other current transfers	3 392	–754	–954	–1,153	–1,347	–1,824	–1,222	–1,156	–1,105
CAPITAL AND FINANCIAL ACCOUNT	4 996	**6,210**	**13,617**	**17,232**	**20,873**	**27,252**	**7,447**	**8,030**	**4,899**
CAPITAL ACCOUNT	4 994	**11**	**–9**	**1,451**	**3,166**	**3,484**	**2,918**	**2,612**	**5,942**
Total credit	2 994	*48*	*50*	*1,753*	*3,535*	*3,978*	*3,366*	*3,134*	*6,423*
Total debit	3 994	*–37*	*–59*	*–302*	*–370*	*–493*	*–449*	*–522*	*–481*
Capital transfers, credit	2 400	**48**	**50**	**1,749**	**3,530**	**3,946**	**3,260**	**3,071**	**6,352**
General government	2 401	...	...	1,654	3,325	3,577	2,916	2,658	5,778
Debt forgiveness	2 402	...	...	...	...	...	...	...	...
Other capital transfers	2 410	...	...	1,654	3,325	3,577	2,916	2,658	5,778
Other sectors	2 430	48	50	95	205	369	345	414	574
Migrants' transfers	2 431	48	50	71	116	220	273	348	472
Debt forgiveness	2 432	...	...	...	...	...	...	...	5
Other capital transfers	2 440	...	...	23	89	149	72	66	96
Capital transfers, debit	3 400	**–37**	**–59**	**–220**	**–319**	**–384**	**–340**	**–432**	**–377**
General government	3 401	...	...	–104	–126	–145	–131	–145	–131
Debt forgiveness	3 402	...	...	...	...	...	...	...	...
Other capital transfers	3 410	...	...	–104	–126	–145	–131	–145	–131
Other sectors	3 430	–37	–59	–116	–193	–239	–209	–287	–246
Migrants' transfers	3 431	–37	–59	–95	–179	–168	–167	–224	–215
Debt forgiveness	3 432	...	...	...	...	...	...	...	...
Other capital transfers	3 440	...	...	–21	–14	–70	–43	–62	–31
Nonproduced nonfinancial assets, credit	2 480	**...**	**...**	**4**	**5**	**31**	**106**	**63**	**72**
Nonproduced nonfinancial assets, debit	3 480	**...**	**...**	**–82**	**–51**	**–110**	**–109**	**–90**	**–104**

Table 2 (Continued). STANDARD PRESENTATION, 1988–95
(Millions of U.S. dollars)

	Code	1988	1989	1990	1991	1992	1993	1994	1995
FINANCIAL ACCOUNT	4 995	**6,199**	**13,626**	**15,782**	**17,707**	**23,768**	**4,530**	**5,418**	**–1,043**
A. DIRECT INVESTMENT	4 500	5,786	6,955	10,461	8,051	11,084	5,492	5,528	2,676
Direct investment abroad	4 505	**–1,235**	**–1,473**	**–3,522**	**–4,442**	**–2,192**	**–2,652**	**–3,831**	**–3,574**
Equity capital	4 510	–1,235	–1,473	–3,225	–4,343	–2,078	–2,521	–3,729	–3,370
Claims on affiliated enterprises	4 515	...	...	...	...	...	...	...	...
Liabilities to affiliated enterprises	4 520	...	...	...	...	...	...	...	...
Reinvested earnings	4 525	...	...	...	...	...	...	...	...
Other capital	4 530	...	...	–297	–99	–114	–131	–103	–205
Claims on affiliated enterprises	4 535	...	...	...	...	...	–307	–92	–248
Liabilities to affiliated enterprises	4 540	...	...	...	...	...	176	–10	43
Direct investment in Spain	4 555	**7,021**	**8,428**	**13,984**	**12,493**	**13,276**	**8,144**	**9,359**	**6,250**
Equity capital	4 560	7,021	8,428	11,246	10,571	8,879	6,734	8,453	5,439
Claims on direct investors	4 565	...	...	...	...	...	...	...	...
Liabilities to direct investors	4 570	...	...	...	...	...	...	...	...
Reinvested earnings	4 575	...	...	...	...	...	...	...	...
Other capital	4 580	...	...	2,737	1,922	4,397	1,410	906	812
Claims on direct investors	4 585	...	...	...	...	...	–974	691	–153
Liabilities to direct investors	4 590	...	...	...	...	...	2,384	215	965
B. PORTFOLIO INVESTMENT	4 600	2,291	7,989	9,018	20,080	9,358	49,353	–21,148	20,689
Assets	4 602	**–136**	**–166**	**–1,367**	**–2,410**	**–2,811**	**–6,772**	**–1,837**	**–619**
Equity securities	4 610	–136	–166	–329	–327	–145	–764	–1,047	–534
Monetary authorities	4 611	...	...	...	...	...	...	...	...
General government	4 612	...	...	...	...	...	...	...	...
Banks	4 613	...	...	–66	–187	16	–48	–150	–233
Other sectors	4 614	...	...	–263	–139	–161	–715	–897	–300
Debt securities	4 619	...	...	–1,038	–2,083	–2,666	–6,008	–790	–85
Bonds and notes	4 620	...	...	–1,028	–1,947	–2,684	–5,869	–447	–154
Monetary authorities	4 621	...	...	...	...	...	...	...	...
General government	4 622	...	...	...	...	...	...	...	...
Banks	4 623	...	...	–1,301	–1,975	–2,041	–3,706	–574	–532
Other sectors	4 624	...	...	273	28	–643	–2,162	127	378
Money market instruments	4 630	...	...	...	–85	...	–59	–6	206
Monetary authorities	4 631	...	...	...	...	...	...	...	...
General government	4 632	...	...	...	...	...	...	...	...
Banks	4 633	...	...	...	–69	10	–142	–37	269
Other sectors	4 634	...	...	...	–16	–10	84	31	–63
Financial derivatives	4 640	...	...	–10	–50	18	–80	–337	–138
Monetary authorities	4 641	...	...	...	...	...	...	...	...
General government	4 642	...	...	...	...	...	...	...	...
Banks	4 643	...	...	–4	–28	–22	23	–197	–66
Other sectors	4 644	...	...	–6	–22	40	–103	–140	–72
Liabilities	4 652	**2,427**	**8,155**	**10,385**	**22,489**	**12,169**	**56,125**	**–19,310**	**21,307**
Equity securities	4 660	2,100	6,387	4,309	2,772	3,648	6,491	1,154	4,346
Banks	4 663	...	...	1,183	737	1,018	...	...	...
Other sectors	4 664	...	...	3,125	2,035	2,630	...	...	...
Debt securities	4 669	327	1,768	6,077	19,717	8,521	49,633	–20,464	16,961
Bonds and notes	4 670	327	1,768	5,394	18,813	8,360	49,399	–19,962	15,795
Monetary authorities	4 671	...	...	...	...	...	...	...	...
General government	4 672	327	1,768	2,716	15,881	8,968	49,193	–21,880	15,945
Banks	4 673	...	...	2,659	1,099	328	368	1,008	–568
Other sectors	4 674	...	...	19	1,832	–937	–161	910	418
Money market instruments	4 680	...	...	679	932	90	523	–913	1,129
Monetary authorities	4 681	...	...	...	...	...	...	...	...
General government	4 682	...	...	874	373	185	589	–915	1,154
Banks	4 683	...	...	77	60	88	23	–10	...
Other sectors	4 684	...	...	–272	499	–183	–89	11	–25
Financial derivatives	4 690	...	...	3	–28	71	–289	411	38
Monetary authorities	4 691	...	...	...	...	...	...	...	...
General government	4 692	...	...	...	...	...	...	...	...
Banks	4 693	...	...	–1	–22	53	78	79	60
Other sectors	4 694	...	...	4	–6	18	–367	333	–22

Table 2 (Concluded). STANDARD PRESENTATION, 1988–95
(Millions of U.S. dollars)

	Code	1988	1989	1990	1991	1992	1993	1994	1995
C. OTHER INVESTMENT	4 700	6,538	3,398	3,490	3,884	−14,483	−55,124	21,088	−30,898
Assets	4 703	**−596**	**−108**	**−13,175**	**−7,740**	**−40,442**	**−75,296**	**9,149**	**−37,481**
Trade credits	4 706	−437	−21	...	...	...	7	−9	−21
General government: long-term	4 708	...	...	...	...	...	...	...	...
General government: short-term	4 709	...	...	...	...	...	...	...	...
Other sectors: long-term	4 711	87	241	...	...	...	7	−9	−21
Other sectors: short-term	4 712	−524	−263	...	...	...	...	...	...
Loans	4 714	−1,873	−830	−2,533	−1,551	−13,267	−29,667	9,804	−10,220
Monetary authorities: long-term	4 717	...	...	...	...	...	...	...	...
Monetary authorities: short-term	4 718	...	...	...	...	...	...	...	...
General government: long-term	4 720	−669	−660	−532	−539	−783	−598	−699	−230
General government: short-term	4 721	...	...	...	−96	...	...	...	...
Banks: long-term	4 723	−515	517	−644	−497	−570	−525	−654	239
Banks: short-term	4 724	...	...	−279	−645	−11,019	−28,198	11,239	−9,944
Other sectors: long-term	4 726	−673	−146	−351	16	−321	−52	−162	−293
Other sectors: short-term	4 727	−17	−540	−727	210	−574	−295	79	9
Currency and deposits	4 730	1,829	822	−10,223	−6,147	−27,100	−45,514	−463	−26,866
Monetary authorities	4 731	...	...	...	...	...	...	...	...
General government	4 732	−2	3	...	...	−40	11	4	−5
Banks	4 733	1,830	819	−6,596	−2,073	−17,170	−37,666	4,206	−17,302
Other sectors	4 734	...	...	−3,626	−4,074	−9,891	−7,859	−4,673	−9,558
Other assets	4 736	−115	−79	−419	−41	−74	−121	−183	−375
Monetary authorities: long-term	4 738	...	...	...	...	...	...	...	...
Monetary authorities: short-term	4 739	...	...	...	...	...	...	...	...
General government: long-term	4 741	−115	−79	...	...	...	−54	−38	−117
General government: short-term	4 742	...	...	...	...	...	...	...	...
Banks: long-term	4 744	...	...	...	...	...	−10	−1	−68
Banks: short-term	4 745	...	...	...	...	...	...	...	...
Other sectors: long-term	4 747	...	...	...	...	...	−58	−144	−190
Other sectors: short-term	4 748	...	...	...	...	...	...	...	...
Liabilities	4 753	**7,134**	**3,506**	**16,665**	**11,624**	**25,958**	**20,172**	**11,940**	**6,583**
Trade credits	4 756	407	−1,020	...	...	...	−56	29	−88
General government: long-term	4 758	...	...	...	...	...	...	...	...
General government: short-term	4 759	...	...	...	...	...	...	...	...
Other sectors: long-term	4 761	−158	−149	...	...	...	−56	29	−88
Other sectors: short-term	4 762	566	−871	...	...	...	...	...	...
Loans	4 764	4,387	2,337	2,952	4,313	14,870	7,863	10,859	−338
Use of Fund credit and loans from the Fund	4 766	...	...	...	...	...	...	...	...
Monetary authorities: other long-term	4 767	...	...	...	...	...	...	...	...
Monetary authorities: short-term	4 768	...	...	...	...	...	...	...	...
General government: long-term	4 770	−89	1,226	794	63	3,269	935	375	832
General government: short-term	4 771	759	138	480	−334	148	−783	1,120	951
Banks: long-term	4 773	...	...	689	826	1,584	−91	−226	58
Banks: short-term	4 774	...	...	...	32	937	1,341	9,811	−3,022
Other sectors: long-term	4 776	3,665	986	966	3,415	6,409	5,121	−29	−251
Other sectors: short-term	4 777	52	−12	22	310	2,523	1,340	−192	1,094
Currency and deposits	4 780	1,352	1,547	13,713	7,311	11,088	12,365	1,052	7,010
Monetary authorities	4 781	...	...	...	...	...	...	...	...
General government	4 782	...	...	...	...	...	...	...	...
Banks	4 783	1,352	1,547	13,713	7,311	11,088	12,365	1,052	7,010
Other sectors	4 784	...	...	...	...	...	...	...	...
Other liabilities	4 786	988	643	...	...	...	...	...	...
Monetary authorities: long-term	4 788	...	...	...	...	...	...	...	...
Monetary authorities: short-term	4 789	−303	643	...	...	...	...	...	...
General government: long-term	4 791	...	...	...	...	...	...	...	...
General government: short-term	4 792	...	...	...	...	...	...	...	...
Banks: long-term	4 794	...	...	...	...	...	...	...	...
Banks: short-term	4 795	1,291	...	...	...	...	...	...	...
Other sectors: long-term	4 797	...	...	...	...	...	...	...	...
Other sectors: short-term	4 798	...	...	...	...	...	...	...	...
D. RESERVE ASSETS	4 800	−8,416	−4,716	−7,188	−14,307	17,809	4,808	−50	6,491
Monetary gold	4 810	−721	−579	...	...	...	...	...	−4
Special drawing rights	4 820	−49	−85	53	227	258	−33	−25	−152
Reserve position in the Fund	4 830	−312	−183	181	64	−111	113	−13	−462
Foreign exchange	4 840	−7,334	−3,869	−7,422	−14,598	17,663	4,728	−13	7,109
Other claims	4 880	...	...	...	...	...	...	...	...
NET ERRORS AND OMISSIONS	4 998	**−2,414**	**−2,693**	**777**	**−1,075**	**−5,965**	**−1,680**	**−1,214**	**−6,179**

Part 3 of the *Yearbook* contains descriptions of the methodologies, compilation practices, and sources used to compile these data.

Table 3. INTERNATIONAL INVESTMENT POSITION (End–period stocks), 1988–95
(Millions of U.S. dollars)

	Code	1988	1989	1990	1991	1992	1993	1994	1995
ASSETS	8 995 C.	86,418	102,968	135,315	164,422	170,863	217,435	225,782	270,276
Direct investment abroad	8 505 . .	**9,434**	**11,372**	**16,128**	**21,140**	**21,292**	**22,283**	**28,203**	**33,540**
Equity capital and reinvested earnings	8 506 . .	9,434	11,269	15,720	20,641	20,772	21,743	27,521	32,603
Claims on affiliated enterprises	8 507 . .	...	...	...	...	...	...	...	...
Liabilities to affiliated enterprises	8 508 . .	...	...	...	...	...	...	...	...
Other capital	8 530 . .	...	103	408	500	520	540	682	937
Claims on affiliated enterprises	8 535 . .	...	...	...	...	...	...	...	...
Liabilities to affiliated enterprises	8 540 . .	...	...	...	...	...	...	...	...
Portfolio investment	8 602 . .	**2,848**	**3,860**	**5,917**	**8,880**	**10,509**	**15,806**	**18,720**	**20,470**
Equity securities	8 610 . .	987	1,267	1,788	2,154	1,939	2,266	3,540	4,384
Monetary authorities	8 611 . .	...	...	...	...	...	...	...	...
General government	8 612 . .	...	...	...	...	...	...	...	...
Banks	8 613 . .	...	...	278	485	392	358	538	823
Other sectors	8 614 . .	...	...	1,511	1,669	1,548	1,908	3,001	3,562
Debt securities	8 619 . .	1,861	2,593	4,129	6,726	8,570	13,539	15,181	16,085
Bonds and notes	8 620 . .	1,861	2,593	3,540	6,043	7,977	13,005	14,589	15,649
Monetary authorities	8 621 . .	...	...	...	...	...	...	...	...
General government	8 622 . .	...	...	...	...	...	...	...	...
Banks	8 623 . .	...	...	1,356	2,778	3,929	7,132	7,791	8,224
Other sectors	8 624 . .	...	...	2,185	3,265	4,047	5,874	6,798	7,424
Money market instruments	8 630 . .	...	...	588	683	593	534	592	437
Monetary authorities	8 631 . .	...	...	...	...	...	...	...	...
General government	8 632 . .	...	...	...	...	...	...	...	...
Banks	8 633 . .	...	...	351	424	349	415	493	264
Other sectors	8 634 . .	...	...	237	259	244	120	99	173
Financial derivatives	8 640 . .	...	...	...	...	...	...	...	...
Monetary authorities	8 641 . .	...	...	...	...	...	...	...	...
General government	8 642 . .	...	...	...	...	...	...	...	...
Banks	8 643 . .	...	...	...	...	...	...	...	...
Other sectors	8 644 . .	...	...	...	...	...	...	...	...
Other investment	8 703 . .	**33,572**	**42,794**	**58,261**	**64,955**	**90,340**	**136,243**	**135,024**	**178,903**
Trade credits	8 706 . .	...	...	...	...	...	...	...	...
General government: long-term	8 708 . .	...	...	...	...	...	...	...	...
General government: short-term	8 709 . .	...	...	...	...	...	...	...	...
Other sectors: long-term	8 711 . .	...	...	...	...	...	...	...	...
Other sectors: short-term	8 712 . .	...	...	...	...	...	...	...	...
Loans	8 714 . .	10,356	12,429	16,640	18,083	19,347	24,670	26,105	31,956
Monetary authorities: long-term	8 717 . .	...	...	...	...	...	...	...	...
Monetary authorities: short-term	8 718 . .	...	...	...	...	...	...	...	...
General government: long-term	8 720 . .	1,983	2,475	...	...	...	...	...	...
General government: short-term	8 721 . .	...	...	...	...	...	...	...	...
Banks: long-term	8 723 . .	6,621	7,453	...	...	...	...	...	...
Banks: short-term	8 724 . .	...	...	...	...	...	...	...	...
Other sectors: long-term	8 726 . .	1,752	2,501	...	...	...	...	...	...
Other sectors: short-term	8 727 . .	...	...	...	...	...	...	...	...
Currency and deposits	8 730 . .	152	183	38,688	43,777	68,093	108,809	105,782	143,137
Monetary authorities	8 731 . .	...	...	184	173	168	151	161	247
General government	8 732 . .	...	...	...	...	...	...	...	...
Banks	8 733 . .	152	183	24,813	28,591	49,991	89,486	82,085	111,260
Other sectors	8 734 . .	...	...	13,691	15,013	17,934	19,172	23,536	31,629
Other assets	8 736 . .	23,064	30,182	2,933	3,096	2,900	2,765	3,137	3,810
Monetary authorities: long-term	8 738 . .	...	...	...	...	...	...	...	...
Monetary authorities: short-term	8 739 . .	...	...	...	...	...	...	...	...
General government: long-term	8 741 . .	347	285	...	...	...	...	...	...
General government: short-term	8 742 . .	...	...	...	...	...	...	...	...
Banks: long-term	8 744 . .	15,754	16,910	...	...	...	...	...	...
Banks: short-term	8 745 . .	...	...	...	...	...	...	...	...
Other sectors: long-term	8 747 . .	5,664	11,190	...	...	...	...	...	...
Other sectors: short-term	8 748 . .	1,298	1,796	...	...	...	...	...	...
Reserve assets	8 800 . .	**40,565**	**44,942**	**55,010**	**69,447**	**48,721**	**43,103**	**43,835**	**37,363**
Monetary gold	8 810 . .	3,218	3,462	3,944	3,721	2,943	2,372	2,560	2,782
Special drawing rights	8 820 . .	615	687	696	456	184	216	255	411
Reserve position in the Fund	8 830 . .	1,058	1,222	1,134	1,071	1,144	1,031	1,109	1,583
Foreign exchange	8 840 . .	31,569	35,170	44,218	56,149	36,084	32,340	32,567	26,800
Other claims	8 880 . .	4,105	4,402	5,018	8,050	8,367	7,144	7,345	5,787

Table 3 (Continued). INTERNATIONAL INVESTMENT POSITION (End–period stocks), 1988–95
(Millions of U.S. dollars)

	Code		1988	1989	1990	1991	1992	1993	1994	1995
LIABILITIES	8 995	D.	109,765	138,975	193,803	245,893	256,663	295,365	319,930	375,333
Direct investment in Spain	8 555	. .	**21,427**	**28,893**	**65,234**	**78,146**	**77,662**	**69,788**	**84,923**	**98,580**
Equity capital and reinvested earnings	8 556	. .	21,375	28,119	61,506	72,280	68,773	61,431	74,929	86,879
Claims on direct investors	8 557	. .	...	...	...	...	...	...	...	...
Liabilities to direct investors	8 558	. .	...	...	...	...	...	...	...	...
Other capital	8 580	. .	52	774	3,728	5,866	8,888	8,358	9,994	11,701
Claims on direct investors	8 585	. .	...	...	...	...	...	...	...	...
Liabilities to direct investors	8 590	. .	...	...	...	...	...	...	...	...
Portfolio investment	8 652	. .	**10,757**	**20,350**	**35,683**	**59,651**	**56,981**	**95,335**	**84,359**	**111,335**
Equity securities	8 660	. .	7,893	14,067	20,343	23,275	22,809	24,164	27,216	33,922
Banks	8 663	. .	...	...	3,980	4,765	4,953	7,107	8,097	9,741
Other sectors	8 664	. .	...	...	16,363	18,510	17,856	17,057	19,119	24,180
Debt securities	8 669	. .	2,864	6,283	15,340	36,376	34,172	71,172	57,143	77,414
Bonds and notes	8 670	. .	2,864	6,283	13,456	34,040	31,900	68,281	55,409	75,544
Monetary authorities	8 671	. .	...	...	...	...	...	...	...	...
General government	8 672	. .	...	...	9,518	28,258	27,574	64,255	49,113	68,885
Banks	8 673	. .	...	...	1,338	1,307	1,088	1,202	2,292	1,851
Other sectors	8 674	. .	...	...	2,599	4,475	3,238	2,823	4,003	4,808
Money market instruments	8 680	. .	...	...	1,884	2,335	2,272	2,891	1,734	1,870
Monetary authorities	8 681	. .	...	...	...	...	...	...	...	...
General government	8 682	. .	...	...	1,755	1,606	1,753	2,536	1,351	1,475
Banks	8 683	. .	...	...	111	174	216	195	203	224
Other sectors	8 684	. .	...	...	18	555	303	160	180	170
Financial derivatives	8 690	. .	...	...	...	...	...	...	...	...
Monetary authorities	8 691	. .	...	...	...	...	...	...	...	...
General government	8 692	. .	...	...	...	...	...	...	...	...
Banks	8 692	. .	...	...	...	...	...	...	...	...
Other sectors	8 694	. .	...	...	...	...	...	...	...	...
Other investment	8 753	. .	**77,580**	**89,732**	**92,886**	**108,096**	**122,021**	**130,242**	**150,648**	**165,418**
Trade credits	8 756	. .	...	...	...	...	...	...	...	...
General government: long-term	8 758	. .	...	...	...	...	...	...	...	...
General government: short-term	8 759	. .	...	...	...	...	...	...	...	...
Other sectors: long-term	8 761	. .	...	...	...	...	...	...	...	...
Other sectors: short-term	8 762	. .	...	...	...	...	...	...	...	...
Loans	8 764	. .	39,609	45,079	27,053	31,307	36,094	42,700	48,053	53,630
Use of Fund credit and loans from the Fund	8 766	. .	...	...	...	...	...	...	...	...
Monetary authorities: other long-term	8 767	. .	...	...	...	...	...	...	...	...
Monetary authorities: short-term	8 768	. .	...	...	...	...	...	...	...	...
General government: long-term	8 770	. .	5,659	6,980	...	...	...	...	...	...
General government: short-term	8 771	. .	...	...	...	...	...	...	...	...
Banks: long-term	8 773	. .	...	...	...	...	...	...	...	...
Banks: short-term	8 774	. .	...	...	...	...	...	...	...	...
Other sectors: long-term	8 776	. .	33,950	38,100	...	...	...	...	...	...
Other sectors: short-term	8 777	. .	...	...	...	...	...	...	...	...
Currency and deposits	8 780	. .	4,324	4,499	65,411	76,362	85,515	87,130	102,159	111,343
Monetary authorities	8 781	. .	...	...	101	56	45	51	79	107
General government	8 782	. .	...	...	...	...	...	...	...	...
Banks	8 783	. .	4,324	4,499	64,752	75,914	84,936	86,676	101,560	110,707
Other sectors	8 784	. .	...	...	557	392	534	402	520	530
Other liabilities	8 786	. .	33,647	40,154	422	427	412	411	436	444
Monetary authorities: long-term	8 788	. .	...	...	422	427	412	411	436	444
Monetary authorities: short-term	8 789	. .	415	406	...	...	...	...	...	...
General government: long-term	8 791	. .	54	82	...	...	...	...	...	...
General government: short-term	8 792	. .	...	...	...	...	...	...	...	...
Banks: long-term	8 794	. .	32,677	39,129	...	...	...	...	...	...
Banks: short-term	8 795	. .	...	...	...	...	...	...	...	...
Other sectors: long-term	8 797	. .	502	538	...	...	...	...	...	...
Other sectors: short-term	8 798	. .	...	...	...	...	...	...	...	...
NET INTERNATIONAL INVESTMENT POSITION	8 995	. .	**–23,346**	**–36,007**	**–58,489**	**–81,471**	**–85,800**	**–77,931**	**–94,148**	**–105,057**
Conversion rates: pesetas per U.S. dollar (end of period)	0 102	. .	**113.45**	**109.72**	**96.91**	**96.69**	**114.62**	**142.21**	**131.74**	**121.41**

Table 1. ANALYTIC PRESENTATION, 1988–95
(Millions of U.S. dollars)

	Code			1988	1989	1990	1991	1992	1993	1994	1995
A. Current Account[1]	4	993	Y.	**–394.5**	**–413.7**	**–298.3**	**–594.8**	**–450.7**	**–382.2**	**–546.0**	**. . .**
Goods: exports f.o.b	2	100	. .	1,477.1	1,505.1	1,853.0	2,003.3	2,301.4	2,785.7	3,201.8	. . .
Goods: imports f.o.b	3	100	. .	–2,017.5	–2,055.1	–2,325.6	–2,808.0	–3,016.5	–3,527.8	–4,072.5	. . .
Balance on Goods	4	100	. .	*–540.5*	*–550.1*	*–472.5*	*–804.7*	*–715.1*	*–742.1*	*–870.7*	. . .
Services: credit	2	200	. .	339.2	345.6	439.6	546.6	621.4	634.4	753.9	. . .
Services: debit	3	200	. .	–547.1	–565.8	–639.2	–762.5	–823.2	–874.3	–1,053.2	. . .
Balance on Goods and Services	4	991	. .	*–748.4*	*–770.3*	*–672.0*	*–1,020.6*	*–916.9*	*–982.1*	*–1,170.0*	. . .
Income: credit	2	300	. .	68.7	58.6	93.0	54.5	68.1	111.4	143.9	. . .
Income: debit	3	300	. .	–240.8	–221.3	–259.8	–232.5	–246.2	–234.3	–310.3	. . .
Balance on Goods, Services, and Income	4	992	. .	*–920.5*	*–933.0*	*–838.8*	*–1,198.5*	*–1,094.9*	*–1,105.0*	*–1,336.4*	. . .
Current transfers: credit	2	379	Y.	563.7	546.6	578.8	644.5	730.4	795.4	878.5	. . .
Current transfers: debit	3	379	. .	–37.7	–27.3	–38.3	–40.8	–86.1	–72.6	–88.1	. . .
B. Capital Account[1]	4	994	Y.	**. . .**	**. . .**	**. . .**	**. . .**	**. . .**	**. . .**	**. . .**	**. . .**
Capital account: credit	2	994	Y.	. . .	. . .	. . .	. . .	. . .	. . .	. . .	. . .
Capital account: debit	3	994	. .	. . .	. . .	. . .	. . .	. . .	. . .	. . .	. . .
Total, Groups A Plus B	4	010	. .	*–394.5*	*–413.7*	*–298.3*	*–594.8*	*–450.7*	*–382.2*	*–546.0*	. . .
C. Financial Account[1]	4	995	X.	**256.0**	**577.0**	**478.1**	**689.0**	**501.3**	**994.2**	**911.7**	**. . .**
Direct investment abroad	4	505	. .	–2.1	–2.0	–.8	–4.5	–1.6	–6.9	–8.3	. . .
Direct investment in Sri Lanka	4	555	Y.	45.7	19.7	43.4	48.4	122.6	194.5	166.4	. . .
Portfolio investment assets	4	602	. .	. . .	. . .	. . .	32.1	25.7	65.2	27.0	. . .
Equity securities	4	610	. .	. . .	. . .	. . .	. . .	. . .	. . .	. . .	. . .
Debt securities	4	619	. .	. . .	. . .	. . .	32.1	25.7	65.2	27.0	. . .
Portfolio investment liabilities	4	652	Y.	. . .	. . .	. . .	. . .	. . .	. . .	. . .	. . .
Equity securities	4	660	Y.	. . .	. . .	. . .	. . .	. . .	. . .	. . .	. . .
Debt securities	4	669	Y.	. . .	. . .	. . .	. . .	. . .	. . .	. . .	. . .
Other investment assets	4	703	. .	–15.8	–11.3	–115.8	–51.6	–100.3	16.4	–134.0	. . .
Monetary authorities	4	703	. A	. . .	. . .	. . .	. . .	. . .	. . .	. . .	. . .
General government	4	703	. B	.7	–27.5	14.8	–13.0	3.3	–2.4	9.4	. . .
Banks	4	703	. C	–16.6	16.2	–130.6	–38.6	–103.6	18.8	–143.4	. . .
Other sectors	4	703	. D	. . .	. . .	. . .	. . .	. . .	. . .	. . .	. . .
Other investment liabilities	4	753	X.	228.2	570.6	551.4	664.8	454.9	725.0	860.5	. . .
Monetary authorities	4	753	XA	–40.2	247.8	65.8	. . .	. . .	. . .	. . .	. . .
General government	4	753	YB	277.2	217.2	408.9	532.5	233.3	262.6	209.4	. . .
Banks	4	753	YC	28.9	63.1	55.5	106.2	108.3	128.2	73.4	. . .
Other sectors	4	753	YD	–37.7	42.4	21.2	26.1	113.3	334.3	577.8	. . .
Total, Groups A Through C	4	020	. .	*–138.5*	*163.3*	*179.8*	*94.3*	*50.6*	*611.9*	*365.7*	. . .
D. Net Errors and Omissions	4	998	. .	**37.3**	**–115.0**	**–115.1**	**225.6**	**173.3**	**130.1**	**–67.6**	**. . .**
Total, Groups A Through D	4	030	. .	*–101.2*	*48.3*	*64.8*	*319.9*	*223.9*	*742.0*	*298.1*	. . .
E. Reserves and Related Items	4	040	. .	**101.2**	**–48.3**	**–64.8**	**–319.9**	**–223.9**	**–742.0**	**–298.1**	**. . .**
Reserve assets	4	800	. .	3.2	–65.1	–132.3	–312.5	–284.6	–820.7	–373.5	. . .
Use of Fund credit and loans	4	766	. .	100.7	13.6	16.5	–11.2	82.9	52.8	65.9	. . .
Liabilities constituting foreign authorities' reserves	4	900	. .	–2.7	3.3	51.0	3.8	–22.2	25.9	9.6	. . .
Exceptional financing	4	920	. .	. . .	. . .	. . .	. . .	. . .	. . .	. . .	. . .
Conversion rates: Sri Lanka rupees per U.S. dollar	0	101	. .	**31.807**	**36.047**	**40.063**	**41.372**	**43.830**	**48.322**	**49.415**	**51.252**

[1] Excludes components that have been classified in the categories of Group E.

Table 2. STANDARD PRESENTATION, 1988–95
(Millions of U.S. dollars)

	Code	1988	1989	1990	1991	1992	1993	1994	1995
CURRENT ACCOUNT	4 993 . .	**–394.5**	**–413.7**	**–298.3**	**–594.8**	**–450.7**	**–382.2**	**–546.0**	. . .
A. GOODS	4 100 . .	–540.5	–550.1	–472.5	–804.7	–715.1	–742.1	–870.7	. . .
Credit	2 100 . .	**1,477.1**	**1,505.1**	**1,853.0**	**2,003.3**	**2,301.4**	**2,785.7**	**3,201.8**	. . .
General merchandise: exports f.o.b.	2 110 . .	1,477.1	1,505.1	1,853.0	2,003.3	2,301.4	2,785.7	3,201.8	. . .
Goods for processing: exports f.o.b.	2 150 . .	. . .	. . .	. . .	. . .	. . .	. . .	. . .	. . .
Repairs on goods	2 160 . .	. . .	. . .	. . .	. . .	. . .	. . .	. . .	. . .
Goods procured in ports by carriers	2 170 . .	. . .	. . .	. . .	. . .	. . .	. . .	. . .	. . .
Nonmonetary gold	2 180 . .	. . .	. . .	. . .	. . .	. . .	. . .	. . .	. . .
Debit	3 100 . .	**–2,017.5**	**–2,055.1**	**–2,325.6**	**–2,808.0**	**–3,016.5**	**–3,527.8**	**–4,072.5**	. . .
General merchandise: imports f.o.b.	3 110 . .	–2,017.5	–2,055.1	–2,325.6	–2,808.0	–3,016.5	–3,527.8	–4,072.5	. . .
Goods for processing: imports f.o.b.	3 150 . .	. . .	. . .	. . .	. . .	. . .	. . .	. . .	. . .
Repairs on goods	3 160 . .	. . .	. . .	. . .	. . .	. . .	. . .	. . .	. . .
Goods procured in ports by carriers	3 170 . .	. . .	. . .	. . .	. . .	. . .	. . .	. . .	. . .
Nonmonetary gold	3 180 . .	. . .	. . .	. . .	. . .	. . .	. . .	. . .	. . .
B. SERVICES	4 200 . .	–207.9	–220.2	–199.5	–215.9	–201.8	–240.0	–299.3	. . .
Total credit	2 200 . .	*339.2*	*345.6*	*439.6*	*546.6*	*621.4*	*634.4*	*753.9*	. . .
Total debit	3 200 . .	*–547.1*	*–565.8*	*–639.2*	*–762.5*	*–823.2*	*–874.3*	*–1,053.2*	. . .
Transportation services, credit	2 205 . .	**122.3**	**129.2**	**168.7**	**203.9**	**219.6**	**235.9**	**293.1**	. . .
Passenger	2 205 BA	*36.4*	*42.9*	*95.7*	*109.7*	*112.0*	*113.1*	*124.4*	. . .
Freight	2 205 BB	*11.4*	*12.0*	*8.4*	*12.4*	*13.8*	*20.7*	*26.1*	. . .
Other	2 205 BC	*74.6*	*74.3*	*64.6*	*81.8*	*93.8*	*102.1*	*142.6*	. . .
Sea transport, passenger	2 207 . .	. . .	. . .	. . .	. . .	. . .	. . .	. . .	. . .
Sea transport, freight	2 208 . .	. . .	. . .	. . .	. . .	. . .	. . .	. . .	. . .
Sea transport, other	2 209 . .	. . .	. . .	. . .	. . .	. . .	. . .	. . .	. . .
Air transport, passenger	2 211 . .	. . .	. . .	. . .	. . .	. . .	. . .	. . .	. . .
Air transport, freight	2 212 . .	. . .	. . .	. . .	. . .	. . .	. . .	. . .	. . .
Air transport, other	2 213 . .	. . .	. . .	. . .	. . .	. . .	. . .	. . .	. . .
Other transport, passenger	2 215 . .	. . .	. . .	. . .	. . .	. . .	. . .	. . .	. . .
Other transport, freight	2 216 . .	. . .	. . .	. . .	. . .	. . .	. . .	. . .	. . .
Other transport, other	2 217 . .	. . .	. . .	. . .	. . .	. . .	. . .	. . .	. . .
Transportation services, debit	3 205 . .	**–314.7**	**–339.2**	**–398.1**	**–439.0**	**–487.4**	**–493.3**	**–584.1**	. . .
Passenger	3 205 BA	*–41.7*	*–46.7*	*–51.3*	*–51.0*	*–42.2*	*–25.1*	*–62.0*	. . .
Freight	3 205 BB	*–207.0*	*–204.8*	*–246.6*	*–281.7*	*–328.8*	*–391.9*	*–466.0*	. . .
Other	3 205 BC	*–66.0*	*–87.6*	*–100.2*	*–106.3*	*–116.4*	*–76.3*	*–56.0*	. . .
Sea transport, passenger	3 207 . .	. . .	. . .	. . .	. . .	. . .	. . .	. . .	. . .
Sea transport, freight	3 208 . .	. . .	. . .	. . .	. . .	. . .	. . .	. . .	. . .
Sea transport, other	3 209 . .	. . .	. . .	. . .	. . .	. . .	. . .	. . .	. . .
Air transport, passenger	3 211 . .	. . .	. . .	. . .	. . .	. . .	. . .	. . .	. . .
Air transport, freight	3 212 . .	. . .	. . .	. . .	. . .	. . .	. . .	. . .	. . .
Air transport, other	3 213 . .	. . .	. . .	. . .	. . .	. . .	. . .	. . .	. . .
Other transport, passenger	3 215 . .	. . .	. . .	. . .	. . .	. . .	. . .	. . .	. . .
Other transport, freight	3 216 . .	. . .	. . .	. . .	. . .	. . .	. . .	. . .	. . .
Other transport, other	3 217 . .	. . .	. . .	. . .	. . .	. . .	. . .	. . .	. . .
Travel, credit	2 236 . .	**65.6**	**76.0**	**128.3**	**158.4**	**195.3**	**203.0**	**230.2**	. . .
Business travel	2 237 . .	. . .	. . .	. . .	. . .	. . .	. . .	. . .	. . .
Personal travel	2 240 . .	. . .	. . .	. . .	. . .	. . .	. . .	. . .	. . .
Travel, debit	3 236 . .	**–67.8**	**–68.9**	**–73.7**	**–97.2**	**–110.9**	**–120.3**	**–169.6**	. . .
Business travel	3 237 . .	. . .	. . .	. . .	. . .	. . .	. . .	. . .	. . .
Personal travel	3 240 . .	. . .	. . .	. . .	. . .	. . .	. . .	. . .	. . .
Other services, credit	2 200 BA	**151.2**	**140.4**	**142.6**	**184.4**	**206.5**	**195.5**	**230.6**	. . .
Communications	2 245 . .	. . .	. . .	. . .	. . .	. . .	. . .	. . .	. . .
Construction	2 249 . .	. . .	. . .	. . .	. . .	. . .	. . .	. . .	. . .
Insurance	2 253 . .	11.8	11.6	17.9	29.4	29.2	17.4	20.4	. . .
Financial	2 260 . .	. . .	. . .	. . .	. . .	. . .	. . .	. . .	. . .
Computer and information	2 262 . .	. . .	. . .	. . .	. . .	. . .	. . .	. . .	. . .
Royalties and licence fees	2 266 . .	. . .	. . .	. . .	. . .	. . .	. . .	. . .	. . .
Other business services	2 268 . .	116.2	107.0	110.1	131.9	158.4	162.9	185.4	. . .
Personal, cultural, and recreational	2 287 . .	. . .	. . .	. . .	. . .	. . .	. . .	. . .	. . .
Government, n.i.e.	2 291 . .	23.2	21.8	14.6	23.1	18.9	15.2	24.8	. . .
Other services, debit	3 200 BA	**–164.7**	**–157.7**	**–167.4**	**–226.3**	**–224.9**	**–260.8**	**–299.5**	. . .
Communications	3 245 . .	. . .	. . .	. . .	. . .	. . .	. . .	. . .	. . .
Construction	3 249 . .	. . .	. . .	. . .	. . .	. . .	. . .	. . .	. . .
Insurance	3 253 . .	–40.0	–37.8	–42.1	–40.9	–44.1	–48.4	–60.1	. . .
Financial	3 260 . .	. . .	. . .	. . .	. . .	. . .	. . .	. . .	. . .
Computer and information	3 262 . .	. . .	. . .	. . .	. . .	. . .	. . .	. . .	. . .
Royalties and licence fees	3 266 . .	. . .	. . .	. . .	. . .	. . .	. . .	. . .	. . .
Other business services	3 268 . .	–103.7	–100.2	–105.8	–158.3	–158.0	–182.4	–201.3	. . .
Personal, cultural, and recreational	3 287 . .	. . .	. . .	. . .	. . .	. . .	. . .	. . .	. . .
Government, n.i.e.	3 291 . .	–20.9	–19.7	–19.5	–27.0	–22.8	–30.0	–38.1	. . .

Table 2 (Continued). STANDARD PRESENTATION, 1988–95
(Millions of U.S. dollars)

	Code		1988	1989	1990	1991	1992	1993	1994	1995
C. INCOME	4 300	..	-172.1	-162.6	-166.8	-177.9	-178.0	-123.0	-166.3	...
Total credit	2 300	..	*68.7*	*58.6*	*93.0*	*54.5*	*68.1*	*111.4*	*143.9*	...
Total debit	3 300	..	*-240.8*	*-221.3*	*-259.8*	*-232.5*	*-246.2*	*-234.3*	*-310.3*	...
Compensation of employees, credit	2 310	..	...	...	...	...	...	...	...	...
Compensation of employees, debit	3 310	..	...	...	...	...	...	...	...	...
Investment income, credit	2 320	..	**68.7**	**58.6**	**93.0**	**54.5**	**68.1**	**111.4**	**143.9**	...
Direct investment income	2 330	..	.4	.5	.3	2.2	1.9	5.8	.7	...
Dividends and distributed branch profits	2 332	..	.4	.5	.3	2.2	1.9	5.8	.7	...
Reinvested earnings and undistributed branch profits	2 333	..	...	...	...	...	...	...	...	...
Income on debt (interest)	2 334	..	...	...	...	...	...	...	...	...
Portfolio investment income	2 339	..	...	...	...	...	...	...	...	...
Income on equity	2 340	..	...	...	...	...	...	...	...	...
Income on bonds and notes	2 350	..	...	...	...	...	...	...	...	...
Income on money market instruments and financial derivatives	2 360	..	...	...	...	...	...	...	...	...
Other investment income	2 370	..	68.3	58.1	92.7	52.4	66.2	105.6	143.2	...
Investment income, debit	3 320	..	**-240.8**	**-221.3**	**-259.8**	**-232.5**	**-246.2**	**-234.3**	**-310.3**	...
Direct investment income	3 330	..	-19.8	-21.1	-25.4	-19.5	-33.4	-32.8	-74.8	...
Dividends and distributed branch profits	3 332	..	-13.2	-18.2	-23.5	-16.8	-15.1	-27.9	-67.3	...
Reinvested earnings and undistributed branch profits	3 333	..	-6.7	-2.9	-1.9	-2.7	-18.3	-4.9	-7.5	...
Income on debt (interest)	3 334	..	...	...	...	...	...	...	...	...
Portfolio investment income	3 339	..	...	...	...	...	...	...	...	...
Income on equity	3 340	..	...	...	...	...	...	...	...	...
Income on bonds and notes	3 350	..	...	...	...	...	...	...	...	...
Income on money market instruments and financial derivatives	3 360	..	...	...	...	...	...	...	...	...
Other investment income	3 370	..	-221.0	-200.2	-234.4	-213.0	-212.8	-201.5	-235.4	...
D. CURRENT TRANSFERS	4 379	..	526.0	519.3	540.5	603.7	644.2	722.8	790.3	...
Credit	2 379	..	**563.7**	**546.6**	**578.8**	**644.5**	**730.4**	**795.4**	**878.5**	...
General government	2 380	..	206.1	188.6	178.1	202.4	182.6	163.0	163.3	...
Other sectors	2 390	..	357.7	358.0	400.8	442.1	547.8	632.4	715.2	...
Workers' remittances	2 391	..	357.7	358.0	400.8	442.1	547.8	632.4	715.2	...
Other current transfers	2 392	..	...	...	...	...	...	...	...	...
Debit	3 379	..	**-37.7**	**-27.3**	**-38.3**	**-40.8**	**-86.1**	**-72.6**	**-88.1**	...
General government	3 380	..	...	...	...	...	...	...	...	...
Other sectors	3 390	..	-37.7	-27.3	-38.3	-40.8	-86.1	-72.6	-88.1	...
Workers' remittances	3 391	..	...	...	...	...	...	...	...	...
Other current transfers	3 392	..	-37.7	-27.3	-38.3	-40.8	-86.1	-72.6	-88.1	...
CAPITAL AND FINANCIAL ACCOUNT	4 996	..	**357.1**	**528.7**	**413.4**	**369.2**	**277.3**	**252.2**	**613.6**	...
CAPITAL ACCOUNT	4 994	..	...	...	...	...	...	...	...	...
Total credit	2 994	..	...	...	...	...	...	...	...	...
Total debit	3 994	..	...	...	...	...	...	...	...	...
Capital transfers, credit	2 400	..	...	...	...	...	...	...	...	...
General government	2 401	..	...	...	...	...	...	...	...	...
Debt forgiveness	2 402	..	...	...	...	...	...	...	...	...
Other capital transfers	2 410	..	...	...	...	...	...	...	...	...
Other sectors	2 430	..	...	...	...	...	...	...	...	...
Migrants' transfers	2 431	..	...	...	...	...	...	...	...	...
Debt forgiveness	2 432	..	...	...	...	...	...	...	...	...
Other capital transfers	2 440	..	...	...	...	...	...	...	...	...
Capital transfers, debit	3 400	..	...	...	...	...	...	...	...	...
General government	3 401	..	...	...	...	...	...	...	...	...
Debt forgiveness	3 402	..	...	...	...	...	...	...	...	...
Other capital transfers	3 410	..	...	...	...	...	...	...	...	...
Other sectors	3 430	..	...	...	...	...	...	...	...	...
Migrants' transfers	3 431	..	...	...	...	...	...	...	...	...
Debt forgiveness	3 432	..	...	...	...	...	...	...	...	...
Other capital transfers	3 440	..	...	...	...	...	...	...	...	...
Nonproduced nonfinancial assets, credit	2 480	..	...	...	...	...	...	...	...	...
Nonproduced nonfinancial assets, debit	3 480	..	...	...	...	...	...	...	...	...

Table 2 (Continued). STANDARD PRESENTATION, 1988–95
(Millions of U.S. dollars)

	Code	1988	1989	1990	1991	1992	1993	1994	1995
FINANCIAL ACCOUNT	4 995 . .	**357.1**	**528.7**	**413.4**	**369.2**	**277.3**	**252.2**	**613.6**	**. . .**
A. DIRECT INVESTMENT	4 500 . .	43.6	17.7	42.5	43.8	121.0	187.6	158.2	. . .
Direct investment abroad	4 505 . .	**–2.1**	**–2.0**	**–.8**	**–4.5**	**–1.6**	**–6.9**	**–8.3**	**. . .**
Equity capital	4 510 . .	–2.1	–2.0	–.8	–4.5	–1.6	–6.9	–8.3	. . .
Claims on affiliated enterprises	4 515 . .	. . .	. . .	. . .	. . .	. . .	. . .	. . .	. . .
Liabilities to affiliated enterprises	4 520 . .	. . .	. . .	. . .	. . .	. . .	. . .	. . .	. . .
Reinvested earnings	4 525 . .	. . .	. . .	. . .	. . .	. . .	. . .	. . .	. . .
Other capital	4 530 . .	. . .	. . .	. . .	. . .	. . .	. . .	. . .	. . .
Claims on affiliated enterprises	4 535 . .	. . .	. . .	. . .	. . .	. . .	. . .	. . .	. . .
Liabilities to affiliated enterprises	4 540 . .	. . .	. . .	. . .	. . .	. . .	. . .	. . .	. . .
Direct investment in Sri Lanka	4 555 . .	**45.7**	**19.7**	**43.4**	**48.4**	**122.6**	**194.5**	**166.4**	**. . .**
Equity capital	4 560 . .	39.1	16.9	41.5	45.7	104.3	189.6	158.9	. . .
Claims on direct investors	4 565 . .	. . .	. . .	. . .	. . .	. . .	. . .	. . .	. . .
Liabilities to direct investors	4 570 . .	. . .	. . .	. . .	. . .	. . .	. . .	. . .	. . .
Reinvested earnings	4 575 . .	6.7	2.9	1.9	2.7	18.3	4.9	7.5	. . .
Other capital	4 580 . .	. . .	. . .	. . .	. . .	. . .	. . .	. . .	. . .
Claims on direct investors	4 585 . .	. . .	. . .	. . .	. . .	. . .	. . .	. . .	. . .
Liabilities to direct investors	4 590 . .	. . .	. . .	. . .	. . .	. . .	. . .	. . .	. . .
B. PORTFOLIO INVESTMENT	4 600 . .	. . .	. . .	. . .	32.1	25.7	65.2	27.0	. . .
Assets	4 602 . .	**. . .**	**. . .**	**. . .**	**32.1**	**25.7**	**65.2**	**27.0**	**. . .**
Equity securities	4 610 . .	. . .	. . .	. . .	. . .	. . .	. . .	. . .	. . .
Monetary authorities	4 611 . .	. . .	. . .	. . .	. . .	. . .	. . .	. . .	. . .
General government	4 612 . .	. . .	. . .	. . .	. . .	. . .	. . .	. . .	. . .
Banks	4 613 . .	. . .	. . .	. . .	. . .	. . .	. . .	. . .	. . .
Other sectors	4 614 . .	. . .	. . .	. . .	. . .	. . .	. . .	. . .	. . .
Debt securities	4 619 . .	. . .	. . .	. . .	32.1	25.7	65.2	27.0	. . .
Bonds and notes	4 620 . .	. . .	. . .	. . .	32.1	25.7	65.2	27.0	. . .
Monetary authorities	4 621 . .	. . .	. . .	. . .	. . .	. . .	. . .	. . .	. . .
General government	4 622 . .	. . .	. . .	. . .	. . .	. . .	. . .	. . .	. . .
Banks	4 623 . .	. . .	. . .	. . .	. . .	. . .	. . .	. . .	. . .
Other sectors	4 624 . .	. . .	. . .	. . .	. . .	. . .	. . .	. . .	. . .
Money market instruments	4 630 . .	. . .	. . .	. . .	. . .	. . .	. . .	. . .	. . .
Monetary authorities	4 631 . .	. . .	. . .	. . .	. . .	. . .	. . .	. . .	. . .
General government	4 632 . .	. . .	. . .	. . .	. . .	. . .	. . .	. . .	. . .
Banks	4 633 . .	. . .	. . .	. . .	. . .	. . .	. . .	. . .	. . .
Other sectors	4 634 . .	. . .	. . .	. . .	. . .	. . .	. . .	. . .	. . .
Financial derivatives	4 640 . .	. . .	. . .	. . .	. . .	. . .	. . .	. . .	. . .
Monetary authorities	4 641 . .	. . .	. . .	. . .	. . .	. . .	. . .	. . .	. . .
General government	4 642 . .	. . .	. . .	. . .	. . .	. . .	. . .	. . .	. . .
Banks	4 643 . .	. . .	. . .	. . .	. . .	. . .	. . .	. . .	. . .
Other sectors	4 644 . .	. . .	. . .	. . .	. . .	. . .	. . .	. . .	. . .
Liabilities	4 652 . .	**. . .**	**. . .**	**. . .**	**. . .**	**. . .**	**. . .**	**. . .**	**. . .**
Equity securities	4 660 . .	. . .	. . .	. . .	. . .	. . .	. . .	. . .	. . .
Banks	4 663 . .	. . .	. . .	. . .	. . .	. . .	. . .	. . .	. . .
Other sectors	4 664 . .	. . .	. . .	. . .	. . .	. . .	. . .	. . .	. . .
Debt securities	4 669 . .	. . .	. . .	. . .	. . .	. . .	. . .	. . .	. . .
Bonds and notes	4 670 . .	. . .	. . .	. . .	. . .	. . .	. . .	. . .	. . .
Monetary authorities	4 671 . .	. . .	. . .	. . .	. . .	. . .	. . .	. . .	. . .
General government	4 672 . .	. . .	. . .	. . .	. . .	. . .	. . .	. . .	. . .
Banks	4 673 . .	. . .	. . .	. . .	. . .	. . .	. . .	. . .	. . .
Other sectors	4 674 . .	. . .	. . .	. . .	. . .	. . .	. . .	. . .	. . .
Money market instruments	4 680 . .	. . .	. . .	. . .	. . .	. . .	. . .	. . .	. . .
Monetary authorities	4 681 . .	. . .	. . .	. . .	. . .	. . .	. . .	. . .	. . .
General government	4 682 . .	. . .	. . .	. . .	. . .	. . .	. . .	. . .	. . .
Banks	4 683 . .	. . .	. . .	. . .	. . .	. . .	. . .	. . .	. . .
Other sectors	4 684 . .	. . .	. . .	. . .	. . .	. . .	. . .	. . .	. . .
Financial derivatives	4 690 . .	. . .	. . .	. . .	. . .	. . .	. . .	. . .	. . .
Monetary authorities	4 691 . .	. . .	. . .	. . .	. . .	. . .	. . .	. . .	. . .
General government	4 692 . .	. . .	. . .	. . .	. . .	. . .	. . .	. . .	. . .
Banks	4 693 . .	. . .	. . .	. . .	. . .	. . .	. . .	. . .	. . .
Other sectors	4 694 . .	. . .	. . .	. . .	. . .	. . .	. . .	. . .	. . .

Table 2 (Concluded). STANDARD PRESENTATION, 1988–95
(Millions of U.S. dollars)

	Code	1988	1989	1990	1991	1992	1993	1994	1995
C. OTHER INVESTMENT	4 700 . .	310.3	576.2	503.1	605.8	415.3	820.1	801.9	. . .
Assets	4 703 . .	**–15.8**	**–11.3**	**–115.8**	**–51.6**	**–100.3**	**16.4**	**–134.0**	**. . .**
Trade credits	4 706 . .	. . .	. . .	. . .	. . .	. . .	. . .	. . .	. . .
General government: long-term	4 708 . .	. . .	. . .	. . .	. . .	. . .	. . .	. . .	. . .
General government: short-term	4 709 . .	. . .	. . .	. . .	. . .	. . .	. . .	. . .	. . .
Other sectors: long-term	4 711 . .	. . .	. . .	. . .	. . .	. . .	. . .	. . .	. . .
Other sectors: short-term	4 712 . .	. . .	. . .	. . .	. . .	. . .	. . .	. . .	. . .
Loans	4 714 . .	. . .	. . .	. . .	. . .	. . .	. . .	. . .	. . .
Monetary authorities: long-term	4 717 . .	. . .	. . .	. . .	. . .	. . .	. . .	. . .	. . .
Monetary authorities: short-term	4 718 . .	. . .	. . .	. . .	. . .	. . .	. . .	. . .	. . .
General government: long-term	4 720 . .	. . .	. . .	. . .	. . .	. . .	. . .	. . .	. . .
General government: short-term	4 721 . .	. . .	. . .	. . .	. . .	. . .	. . .	. . .	. . .
Banks: long-term	4 723 . .	. . .	. . .	. . .	. . .	. . .	. . .	. . .	. . .
Banks: short-term	4 724 . .	. . .	. . .	. . .	. . .	. . .	. . .	. . .	. . .
Other sectors: long-term	4 726 . .	. . .	. . .	. . .	. . .	. . .	. . .	. . .	. . .
Other sectors: short-term	4 727 . .	. . .	. . .	. . .	. . .	. . .	. . .	. . .	. . .
Currency and deposits	4 730 . .	–15.8	–11.3	–115.8	–51.6	–100.3	16.4	–134.0	. . .
Monetary authorities	4 731 . .	. . .	. . .	. . .	. . .	. . .	. . .	. . .	. . .
General government	4 732 . .	.7	–27.5	14.8	–13.0	3.3	–2.4	9.4	. . .
Banks	4 733 . .	–16.6	16.2	–130.6	–38.6	–103.6	18.8	–143.4	. . .
Other sectors	4 734 . .	. . .	. . .	. . .	. . .	. . .	. . .	. . .	. . .
Other assets	4 736 . .	. . .	. . .	. . .	. . .	. . .	. . .	. . .	. . .
Monetary authorities: long-term	4 738 . .	. . .	. . .	. . .	. . .	. . .	. . .	. . .	. . .
Monetary authorities: short-term	4 739 . .	. . .	. . .	. . .	. . .	. . .	. . .	. . .	. . .
General government: long-term	4 741 . .	. . .	. . .	. . .	. . .	. . .	. . .	. . .	. . .
General government: short-term	4 742 . .	. . .	. . .	. . .	. . .	. . .	. . .	. . .	. . .
Banks: long-term	4 744 . .	. . .	. . .	. . .	. . .	. . .	. . .	. . .	. . .
Banks: short-term	4 745 . .	. . .	. . .	. . .	. . .	. . .	. . .	. . .	. . .
Other sectors: long-term	4 747 . .	. . .	. . .	. . .	. . .	. . .	. . .	. . .	. . .
Other sectors: short-term	4 748 . .	. . .	. . .	. . .	. . .	. . .	. . .	. . .	. . .
Liabilities	4 753 . .	**326.2**	**587.4**	**618.9**	**657.4**	**515.6**	**803.7**	**936.0**	**. . .**
Trade credits	4 756 . .	. . .	. . .	. . .	. . .	. . .	. . .	. . .	. . .
General government: long-term	4 758 . .	. . .	. . .	. . .	. . .	. . .	. . .	. . .	. . .
General government: short-term	4 759 . .	. . .	. . .	. . .	. . .	. . .	. . .	. . .	. . .
Other sectors: long-term	4 761 . .	. . .	. . .	. . .	. . .	. . .	. . .	. . .	. . .
Other sectors: short-term	4 762 . .	. . .	. . .	. . .	. . .	. . .	. . .	. . .	. . .
Loans	4 764 . .	582.2	516.6	801.9	1,042.4	822.0	1,037.7	1,161.6	. . .
Use of Fund credit and loans from the Fund	4 766 . .	100.7	13.6	16.5	–11.2	82.9	52.8	65.9	. . .
Monetary authorities: other long-term	4 767 . .	. . .	. . .	. . .	. . .	. . .	. . .	. . .	. . .
Monetary authorities: short-term	4 768 . .	. . .	. . .	. . .	. . .	. . .	. . .	. . .	. . .
General government: long-term	4 770 . .	277.2	217.2	408.9	532.5	233.3	262.6	209.4	. . .
General government: short-term	4 771 . .	. . .	. . .	. . .	. . .	. . .	. . .	. . .	. . .
Banks: long-term	4 773 . .	. . .	. . .	. . .	. . .	. . .	. . .	. . .	. . .
Banks: short-term	4 774 . .	. . .	. . .	. . .	. . .	. . .	. . .	. . .	. . .
Other sectors: long-term	4 776 . .	–51.6	–50.2	–45.7	–24.4	26.0	187.7	316.1	. . .
Other sectors: short-term	4 777 . .	255.9	335.9	422.2	545.6	479.8	534.7	570.3	. . .
Currency and deposits	4 780 . .	26.2	66.4	106.5	110.0	86.1	154.1	83.0	. . .
Monetary authorities	4 781 . .	–2.7	3.3	51.0	3.8	–22.2	25.9	9.6	. . .
General government	4 782 . .	. . .	. . .	. . .	. . .	. . .	. . .	. . .	. . .
Banks	4 783 . .	28.9	63.1	55.5	106.2	108.3	128.2	73.4	. . .
Other sectors	4 784 . .	. . .	. . .	. . .	. . .	. . .	. . .	. . .	. . .
Other liabilities	4 786 . .	–282.3	4.5	–289.5	–495.1	–392.5	–388.1	–308.6	. . .
Monetary authorities: long-term	4 788 . .	. . .	. . .	. . .	. . .	. . .	. . .	. . .	. . .
Monetary authorities: short-term	4 789 . .	–40.2	247.8	65.8	. . .	. . .	. . .	. . .	. . .
General government: long-term	4 791 . .	. . .	. . .	. . .	. . .	. . .	. . .	. . .	. . .
General government: short-term	4 792 . .	. . .	. . .	. . .	. . .	. . .	. . .	. . .	. . .
Banks: long-term	4 794 . .	. . .	. . .	. . .	. . .	. . .	. . .	. . .	. . .
Banks: short-term	4 795 . .	. . .	. . .	. . .	. . .	. . .	. . .	. . .	. . .
Other sectors: long-term	4 797 . .	. . .	. . .	. . .	. . .	. . .	. . .	. . .	. . .
Other sectors: short-term	4 798 . .	–242.0	–243.3	–355.3	–495.1	–392.5	–388.1	–308.6	. . .
D. RESERVE ASSETS	4 800 . .	3.2	–65.1	–132.3	–312.5	–284.6	–820.7	–373.5	. . .
Monetary gold	4 810 . .	. . .	. . .	. . .	. . .	. . .	. . .	. . .	. . .
Special drawing rights	4 820 . .	.1	–12.8	13.2	.2	.1	–.3	.1	. . .
Reserve position in the Fund	4 830 . .	. . .	. . .	. . .	. . .	–27.9	. . .	–.1	. . .
Foreign exchange	4 840 . .	3.1	–52.4	–145.5	–312.6	–256.8	–820.3	–373.6	. . .
Other claims	4 880 . .	. . .	. . .	. . .	. . .	. . .	. . .	. . .	. . .
NET ERRORS AND OMISSIONS	4 998 . .	**37.3**	**–115.0**	**–115.1**	**225.6**	**173.3**	**130.1**	**–67.6**	**. . .**

Part 3 of the *Yearbook* contains descriptions of the methodologies, compilation practices, and sources used to compile these data.

Table 1. ANALYTIC PRESENTATION, 1988–95
(Millions of U.S. dollars)

	Code	1988	1989	1990	1991	1992	1993	1994	1995
A. Current Account [1]	4 993 Y.	**–358.0**	**–150.3**	**–372.2**	**–954.7**	**–506.2**	**–202.2**	**–601.7**	**–499.9**
Goods: exports f.o.b	2 100 . .	427.0	544.4	326.5	302.5	213.4	306.3	523.9	555.7
Goods: imports f.o.b	3 100 . .	–948.5	–1,051.0	–648.8	–1,138.2	–810.2	–532.8	–1,045.4	–1,066.0
Balance on Goods	4 100 . .	*–521.5*	*–506.6*	*–322.3*	*–835.7*	*–596.8*	*–226.5*	*–521.5*	*–510.3*
Services: credit	2 200 . .	161.7	272.6	172.5	77.0	155.5	69.4	76.2	125.3
Services: debit	3 200 . .	–244.6	–378.2	–228.0	–197.3	–204.1	–109.8	–223.7	–172.3
Balance on Goods and Services	4 991 . .	*–604.4*	*–612.2*	*–377.8*	*–956.0*	*–645.4*	*–266.9*	*–669.0*	*–557.3*
Income: credit	2 300 . .	9.9	7.0	12.4	2.7	. . .	.7	1.6	1.9
Income: debit	3 300 . .	–96.7	–117.5	–148.0	–129.1	–93.5	–20.9	–15.9	–4.9
Balance on Goods, Services, and Income	4 992 . .	*–691.2*	*–722.6*	*–513.4*	*–1,082.4*	*–738.9*	*–287.1*	*–683.3*	*–560.3*
Current transfers: credit	2 379 Y.	334.4	576.7	143.3	127.9	232.7	84.9	120.1	346.2
Current transfers: debit	3 379 . .	–1.1	–4.4	–2.1	–.2	. . .	. . .	–38.5	–285.8
B. Capital Account [1]	4 994 Y.	**. . .**	**. . .**	**. . .**	**. . .**	**. . .**	**. . .**	**. . .**	**. . .**
Capital account: credit	2 994 Y.	. . .	. . .	. . .	. . .	. . .	. . .	. . .	. . .
Capital account: debit	3 994 . .	. . .	. . .	. . .	. . .	. . .	. . .	. . .	. . .
Total, Groups A Plus B	4 010 . .	*–358.0*	*–150.3*	*–372.2*	*–954.7*	*–506.2*	*–202.2*	*–601.7*	*–499.9*
C. Financial Account [1]	4 995 X.	**67.5**	**117.8**	**116.9**	**584.1**	**316.4**	**326.6**	**276.0**	**473.7**
Direct investment abroad	4 505 . .	. . .	. . .	. . .	. . .	. . .	. . .	. . .	. . .
Direct investment in Sudan	4 555 Y.	. . .	3.5	. . .	. . .	. . .	. . .	. . .	. . .
Portfolio investment assets	4 602 . .	. . .	. . .	. . .	. . .	. . .	. . .	. . .	. . .
Equity securities	4 610 . .	. . .	. . .	. . .	. . .	. . .	. . .	. . .	. . .
Debt securities	4 619 . .	. . .	. . .	. . .	. . .	. . .	. . .	. . .	. . .
Portfolio investment liabilities	4 652 Y.	. . .	. . .	. . .	. . .	. . .	. . .	. . .	. . .
Equity securities	4 660 Y.	. . .	. . .	. . .	. . .	. . .	. . .	. . .	. . .
Debt securities	4 669 Y.	. . .	. . .	. . .	. . .	. . .	. . .	. . .	. . .
Other investment assets	4 703 . .	–65.3	–39.6	–28.5	–74.0	–82.8	. . .	. . .	. . .
Monetary authorities	4 703 .A	. . .	. . .	. . .	. . .	. . .	. . .	. . .	. . .
General government	4 703 .B	80.5	. . .	. . .	. . .	. . .	. . .	. . .	. . .
Banks	4 703 .C	–145.8	–39.6	–28.5	–74.0	–82.8	. . .	. . .	. . .
Other sectors	4 703 .D	. . .	. . .	. . .	. . .	. . .	. . .	. . .	. . .
Other investment liabilities	4 753 X.	132.8	153.9	145.4	658.1	399.2	326.6	276.0	473.7
Monetary authorities	4 753 XA	75.9	44.8	30.6	155.6	110.4	163.3	28.3	73.6
General government	4 753 YB	63.1	111.4	102.7	486.3	268.5	200.8	–3.1	9.8
Banks	4 753 YC	–6.3	–2.3	12.1	16.1	20.3	–37.5	250.8	390.3
Other sectors	4 753 YD	. . .	. . .	. . .	. . .	. . .	. . .	. . .	. . .
Total, Groups A Through C	4 020 . .	*–290.5*	*–32.4*	*–255.3*	*–370.7*	*–189.8*	*124.4*	*–325.7*	*–26.2*
D. Net Errors and Omissions	4 998 . .	**3.1**	**–160.3**	**10.9**	**97.9**	**31.0**	**–82.6**	**344.8**	**89.3**
Total, Groups A Through D	4 030 . .	*–287.4*	*–192.8*	*–244.4*	*–272.8*	*–158.8*	*41.8*	*19.1*	*63.1*
E. Reserves and Related Items	4 040 . .	**287.4**	**192.8**	**244.4**	**272.8**	**158.8**	**–41.8**	**–19.1**	**–63.1**
Reserve assets	4 800 . .	–.4	–3.8	4.5	3.8	29.3	–41.8	–19.1	–23.6
Use of Fund credit and loans	4 766 . .	. . .	. . .	–1.4	. . .	. . .	. . .	. . .	–39.5
Liabilities constituting foreign authorities' reserves	4 900 . .	. . .	. . .	. . .	. . .	. . .	. . .	. . .	. . .
Exceptional financing	4 920 . .	287.8	196.6	241.3	269.0	129.5	. . .	. . .	. . .
Conversion rates: Sudanese pounds per U.S. dollar	0 101 . .	**4.50**	**4.50**	**4.50**	**6.96**	**97.43**	**159.31**	**289.61**	**. . .**

[1] Excludes components that have been classified in the categories of Group E.

Table 2. STANDARD PRESENTATION, 1988–95
(Millions of U.S. dollars)

	Code	1988	1989	1990	1991	1992	1993	1994	1995
CURRENT ACCOUNT	4 993 . .	**–358.0**	**–149.0**	**–372.2**	**–954.7**	**–506.2**	**–202.2**	**–601.7**	**–499.9**
A. GOODS	4 100 . .	–521.5	–506.6	–322.3	–835.7	–596.8	–226.5	–521.5	–510.3
Credit	2 100 . .	**427.0**	**544.4**	**326.5**	**302.5**	**213.4**	**306.3**	**523.9**	**555.7**
General merchandise: exports f.o.b.	2 110 . .	427.0	544.4	326.5	302.5	213.4	306.3	523.9	555.7
Goods for processing: exports f.o.b.	2 150 . .	. . .	. . .	. . .	. . .	. . .	. . .	. . .	. . .
Repairs on goods	2 160 . .	. . .	. . .	. . .	. . .	. . .	. . .	. . .	. . .
Goods procured in ports by carriers	2 170 . .	. . .	. . .	. . .	. . .	. . .	. . .	. . .	. . .
Nonmonetary gold	2 180 . .	. . .	. . .	. . .	. . .	. . .	. . .	. . .	. . .
Debit	3 100 . .	**–948.5**	**–1,051.0**	**–648.8**	**–1,138.2**	**–810.2**	**–532.8**	**–1,045.4**	**–1,066.0**
General merchandise: imports f.o.b.	3 110 . .	–948.5	–1,051.0	–648.8	–1,138.2	–810.2	–532.8	–1,045.4	–1,066.0
Goods for processing: imports f.o.b.	3 150 . .	. . .	. . .	. . .	. . .	. . .	. . .	. . .	. . .
Repairs on goods	3 160 . .	. . .	. . .	. . .	. . .	. . .	. . .	. . .	. . .
Goods procured in ports by carriers	3 170 . .	. . .	. . .	. . .	. . .	. . .	. . .	. . .	. . .
Nonmonetary gold	3 180 . .	. . .	. . .	. . .	. . .	. . .	. . .	. . .	. . .
B. SERVICES	4 200 . .	–82.9	–105.5	–55.5	–120.3	–48.6	–40.4	–147.5	–47.0
Total credit	2 200 . .	*161.7*	*272.6*	*172.5*	*77.0*	*155.5*	*69.4*	*76.2*	*125.3*
Total debit	3 200 . .	*–244.6*	*–378.2*	*–228.0*	*–197.3*	*–204.1*	*–109.8*	*–223.7*	*–172.3*
Transportation services, credit	2 205 . .	**22.1**	**45.5**	**18.9**	**14.4**	**13.7**	**.6**	**.6**	**.7**
Passenger	2 205 BA	. . .	*35.6*	*13.0*	*8.8*	*9.7*	. . .	. . .	. . .
Freight	2 205 BB	*22.1*	*10.0*	*5.9*	*5.6*	*4.0*	. . .	. . .	. . .
Other	2 205 BC	. . .	. . .	. . .	. . .	. . .	*.6*	*.6*	*.7*
Sea transport, passenger	2 207 . .	. . .	. . .	. . .	. . .	. . .	. . .	. . .	. . .
Sea transport, freight	2 208 . .	. . .	. . .	. . .	. . .	. . .	. . .	. . .	. . .
Sea transport, other	2 209 . .	. . .	. . .	. . .	. . .	. . .	. . .	. . .	. . .
Air transport, passenger	2 211 . .	. . .	. . .	. . .	. . .	. . .	. . .	. . .	. . .
Air transport, freight	2 212 . .	. . .	. . .	. . .	. . .	. . .	. . .	. . .	. . .
Air transport, other	2 213 . .	. . .	. . .	. . .	. . .	. . .	. . .	. . .	. . .
Other transport, passenger	2 215 . .	. . .	. . .	. . .	. . .	. . .	. . .	. . .	. . .
Other transport, freight	2 216 . .	. . .	. . .	. . .	. . .	. . .	. . .	. . .	. . .
Other transport, other	2 217 . .	. . .	. . .	. . .	. . .	. . .	.6	.6	.7
Transportation services, debit	3 205 . .	**–63.8**	**–104.1**	**–64.5**	**–111.9**	**–75.8**	**–50.9**	**–97.9**	**–40.8**
Passenger	3 205 BA	. . .	*–10.6*	*–6.8*	*–10.6*	*–3.8*	. . .	. . .	. . .
Freight	3 205 BB	*–63.8*	*–93.5*	*–57.7*	*–101.3*	*–72.0*	*–47.4*	*–92.9*	*–36.5*
Other	3 205 BC	. . .	. . .	. . .	. . .	. . .	*–3.5*	*–5.0*	*–4.3*
Sea transport, passenger	3 207 . .	. . .	. . .	. . .	. . .	. . .	. . .	. . .	. . .
Sea transport, freight	3 208 . .	. . .	. . .	. . .	. . .	. . .	. . .	. . .	. . .
Sea transport, other	3 209 . .	. . .	. . .	. . .	. . .	. . .	. . .	. . .	. . .
Air transport, passenger	3 211 . .	. . .	. . .	. . .	. . .	. . .	. . .	. . .	. . .
Air transport, freight	3 212 . .	. . .	. . .	. . .	. . .	. . .	. . .	. . .	. . .
Air transport, other	3 213 . .	. . .	. . .	. . .	. . .	. . .	. . .	. . .	. . .
Other transport, passenger	3 215 . .	. . .	. . .	. . .	. . .	. . .	. . .	. . .	. . .
Other transport, freight	3 216 . .	. . .	. . .	. . .	. . .	. . .	. . .	. . .	. . .
Other transport, other	3 217 . .	. . .	. . .	. . .	. . .	. . .	–3.5	–5.0	–4.3
Travel, credit	2 236 . .	**29.4**	**45.2**	**21.0**	**8.0**	**5.0**	**5.9**	**4.4**	**7.9**
Business travel	2 237 . .	. . .	. . .	. . .	. . .	. . .	. . .	. . .	. . .
Personal travel	2 240 . .	. . .	. . .	. . .	. . .	. . .	. . .	. . .	. . .
Travel, debit	3 236 . .	**–98.6**	**–143.8**	**–51.4**	**–11.9**	**–33.3**	**–14.9**	**–46.9**	**–42.9**
Business travel	3 237 . .	. . .	. . .	. . .	. . .	. . .	. . .	. . .	. . .
Personal travel	3 240 . .	. . .	. . .	. . .	. . .	. . .	–14.9	–46.9	–42.9
Other services, credit	2 200 BA	**110.1**	**181.9**	**132.6**	**54.6**	**136.8**	**62.9**	**71.2**	**116.7**
Communications	2 245 . .	. . .	. . .	. . .	. . .	. . .	. . .	. . .	. . .
Construction	2 249 . .	. . .	. . .	. . .	. . .	. . .	. . .	. . .	. . .
Insurance	2 253 . .	2.5	1.1	.7	.6	.4	1.0	.7	3.0
Financial	2 260 . .	. . .	. . .	. . .	. . .	. . .	. . .	. . .	. . .
Computer and information	2 262 . .	. . .	. . .	. . .	. . .	. . .	. . .	. . .	. . .
Royalties and licence fees	2 266 . .	. . .	. . .	. . .	. . .	. . .	. . .	. . .	. . .
Other business services	2 268 . .	58.4	71.0	93.5	14.1	115.9	31.0	38.3	70.2
Personal, cultural, and recreational	2 287 . .	. . .	. . .	. . .	. . .	. . .	. . .	. . .	. . .
Government, n.i.e.	2 291 . .	49.2	109.8	38.4	39.9	20.5	30.9	32.2	43.5
Other services, debit	3 200 BA	**–82.3**	**–130.3**	**–112.1**	**–73.5**	**–95.0**	**–44.0**	**–78.9**	**–88.6**
Communications	3 245 . .	. . .	. . .	. . .	. . .	. . .	. . .	. . .	. . .
Construction	3 249 . .	. . .	. . .	. . .	. . .	. . .	–.9	–4.2	–.2
Insurance	3 253 . .	–7.1	–21.2	–9.9	–12.8	–9.4	–.2	–6.5	–.5
Financial	3 260 . .	. . .	. . .	. . .	. . .	. . .	. . .	. . .	. . .
Computer and information	3 262 . .	. . .	. . .	. . .	. . .	. . .	. . .	. . .	. . .
Royalties and licence fees	3 266 . .	. . .	. . .	. . .	. . .	. . .	. . .	. . .	. . .
Other business services	3 268 . .	–47.8	–78.1	–76.4	–47.8	–78.5	–32.8	–43.7	–65.1
Personal, cultural, and recreational	3 287 . .	. . .	. . .	. . .	. . .	. . .	. . .	. . .	. . .
Government, n.i.e.	3 291 . .	–27.4	–31.0	–25.8	–12.9	–7.1	–10.1	–24.5	–22.8

Table 2 (Continued). STANDARD PRESENTATION, 1988–95
(Millions of U.S. dollars)

	Code	1988	1989	1990	1991	1992	1993	1994	1995
C. INCOME	4 300	–86.8	–110.5	–135.6	–126.4	–93.5	–20.2	–14.3	–3.0
Total credit	2 300	*9.9*	*7.0*	*12.4*	*2.7*	. . .	*.7*	*1.6*	*1.9*
Total debit	3 300	*–96.7*	*–117.5*	*–148.0*	*–129.1*	*–93.5*	*–20.9*	*–15.9*	*–4.9*
Compensation of employees, credit	2 310	. . .	. . .	. . .	. . .	. . .	. . .	. . .	. . .
Compensation of employees, debit	3 310	. . .	. . .	. . .	. . .	. . .	. . .	**–.2**	**–.9**
Investment income, credit	2 320	**9.9**	**7.0**	**12.4**	**2.7**	. . .	**.7**	**1.6**	**1.9**
Direct investment income	2 330	. . .	. . .	. . .	. . .	. . .	. . .	. . .	. . .
Dividends and distributed branch profits	2 332	. . .	. . .	. . .	. . .	. . .	. . .	. . .	. . .
Reinvested earnings and undistributed branch profits	2 333	. . .	. . .	. . .	. . .	. . .	. . .	. . .	. . .
Income on debt (interest)	2 334	. . .	. . .	. . .	. . .	. . .	. . .	. . .	. . .
Portfolio investment income	2 339	. . .	. . .	. . .	. . .	. . .	. . .	. . .	. . .
Income on equity	2 340	. . .	. . .	. . .	. . .	. . .	. . .	. . .	. . .
Income on bonds and notes	2 350	. . .	. . .	. . .	. . .	. . .	. . .	. . .	. . .
Income on money market instruments and financial derivatives	2 360	. . .	. . .	. . .	. . .	. . .	. . .	. . .	. . .
Other investment income	2 370	9.9	7.0	12.4	2.7	. . .	.7	1.6	1.9
Investment income, debit	3 320	**–96.7**	**–117.5**	**–148.0**	**–129.1**	**–93.5**	**–20.9**	**–15.7**	**–4.0**
Direct investment income	3 330	. . .	. . .	. . .	. . .	. . .	. . .	. . .	. . .
Dividends and distributed branch profits	3 332	. . .	. . .	. . .	. . .	. . .	. . .	. . .	. . .
Reinvested earnings and undistributed branch profits	3 333	. . .	. . .	. . .	. . .	. . .	. . .	. . .	. . .
Income on debt (interest)	3 334	. . .	. . .	. . .	. . .	. . .	. . .	. . .	. . .
Portfolio investment income	3 339	. . .	. . .	. . .	. . .	. . .	. . .	. . .	. . .
Income on equity	3 340	. . .	. . .	. . .	. . .	. . .	. . .	. . .	. . .
Income on bonds and notes	3 350	. . .	. . .	. . .	. . .	. . .	. . .	. . .	. . .
Income on money market instruments and financial derivatives	3 360	. . .	. . .	. . .	. . .	. . .	. . .	. . .	. . .
Other investment income	3 370	–96.7	–117.5	–148.0	–129.1	–93.5	–20.9	–15.7	–4.0
D. CURRENT TRANSFERS	4 379	333.3	573.6	141.2	127.7	232.7	84.9	81.6	60.4
Credit	2 379	**334.4**	**578.0**	**143.3**	**127.9**	**232.7**	**84.9**	**120.1**	**346.2**
General government	2 380	117.0	161.3	81.4	82.5	109.0	9.7	12.6	. . .
Other sectors	2 390	217.4	416.7	61.9	45.4	123.7	75.2	107.5	346.2
Workers' remittances	2 391	217.4	416.7	61.9	45.4	123.7	75.2	107.2	346.2
Other current transfers	2 392	. . .	. . .	. . .	. . .	. . .	. . .	.3	. . .
Debit	3 379	**–1.1**	**–4.4**	**–2.1**	**–.2**	. . .	. . .	**–38.5**	**–285.8**
General government	3 380	. . .	. . .	. . .	. . .	. . .	. . .	. . .	. . .
Other sectors	3 390	–1.1	–4.4	–2.1	–.2	. . .	. . .	–38.5	–285.8
Workers' remittances	3 391	–1.1	–4.4	–2.1	–.2	. . .	. . .	. . .	. . .
Other current transfers	3 392	. . .	. . .	. . .	. . .	. . .	. . .	–38.5	–285.8
CAPITAL AND FINANCIAL ACCOUNT	4 996	**354.8**	**309.3**	**361.3**	**856.8**	**475.2**	**284.8**	**256.9**	**410.6**
CAPITAL ACCOUNT	4 994	. . .	. . .	. . .	. . .	. . .	. . .	. . .	. . .
Total credit	2 994	. . .	. . .	. . .	. . .	. . .	. . .	. . .	. . .
Total debit	3 994	. . .	. . .	. . .	. . .	. . .	. . .	. . .	. . .
Capital transfers, credit	2 400	. . .	. . .	. . .	. . .	. . .	. . .	. . .	. . .
General government	2 401	. . .	. . .	. . .	. . .	. . .	. . .	. . .	. . .
Debt forgiveness	2 402	. . .	. . .	. . .	. . .	. . .	. . .	. . .	. . .
Other capital transfers	2 410	. . .	. . .	. . .	. . .	. . .	. . .	. . .	. . .
Other sectors	2 430	. . .	. . .	. . .	. . .	. . .	. . .	. . .	. . .
Migrants' transfers	2 431	. . .	. . .	. . .	. . .	. . .	. . .	. . .	. . .
Debt forgiveness	2 432	. . .	. . .	. . .	. . .	. . .	. . .	. . .	. . .
Other capital transfers	2 440	. . .	. . .	. . .	. . .	. . .	. . .	. . .	. . .
Capital transfers, debit	3 400	. . .	. . .	. . .	. . .	. . .	. . .	. . .	. . .
General government	3 401	. . .	. . .	. . .	. . .	. . .	. . .	. . .	. . .
Debt forgiveness	3 402	. . .	. . .	. . .	. . .	. . .	. . .	. . .	. . .
Other capital transfers	3 410	. . .	. . .	. . .	. . .	. . .	. . .	. . .	. . .
Other sectors	3 430	. . .	. . .	. . .	. . .	. . .	. . .	. . .	. . .
Migrants' transfers	3 431	. . .	. . .	. . .	. . .	. . .	. . .	. . .	. . .
Debt forgiveness	3 432	. . .	. . .	. . .	. . .	. . .	. . .	. . .	. . .
Other capital transfers	3 440	. . .	. . .	. . .	. . .	. . .	. . .	. . .	. . .
Nonproduced nonfinancial assets, credit	2 480	. . .	. . .	. . .	. . .	. . .	. . .	. . .	. . .
Nonproduced nonfinancial assets, debit	3 480	. . .	. . .	. . .	. . .	. . .	. . .	. . .	. . .

Table 2 (Continued). STANDARD PRESENTATION, 1988–95
(Millions of U.S. dollars)

	Code	1988	1989	1990	1991	1992	1993	1994	1995
FINANCIAL ACCOUNT	4 995	**354.8**	**309.3**	**361.3**	**856.8**	**475.2**	**284.8**	**256.9**	**410.6**
A. DIRECT INVESTMENT	4 500	...	3.5	...	...	...	...	...	...
Direct investment abroad	4 505	...	...	...	...	...	...	...	...
Equity capital	4 510	...	...	...	...	...	...	...	...
Claims on affiliated enterprises	4 515	...	...	...	...	...	...	...	...
Liabilities to affiliated enterprises	4 520	...	...	...	...	...	...	...	...
Reinvested earnings	4 525	...	...	...	...	...	...	...	...
Other capital	4 530	...	...	...	...	...	...	...	...
Claims on affiliated enterprises	4 535	...	...	...	...	...	...	...	...
Liabilities to affiliated enterprises	4 540	...	...	...	...	...	...	...	...
Direct investment in Sudan	4 555	...	**3.5**	...	...	...	...	...	...
Equity capital	4 560	...	3.5	...	...	...	...	...	...
Claims on direct investors	4 565	...	...	...	...	...	...	...	...
Liabilities to direct investors	4 570	...	...	...	...	...	...	...	...
Reinvested earnings	4 575	...	...	...	...	...	...	...	...
Other capital	4 580	...	...	...	...	...	...	...	...
Claims on direct investors	4 585	...	...	...	...	...	...	...	...
Liabilities to direct investors	4 590	...	...	...	...	...	...	...	...
B. PORTFOLIO INVESTMENT	4 600	...	...	...	...	...	...	...	...
Assets	4 602	...	...	...	...	...	...	...	...
Equity securities	4 610	...	...	...	...	...	...	...	...
Monetary authorities	4 611	...	...	...	...	...	...	...	...
General government	4 612	...	...	...	...	...	...	...	...
Banks	4 613	...	...	...	...	...	...	...	...
Other sectors	4 614	...	...	...	...	...	...	...	...
Debt securities	4 619	...	...	...	...	...	...	...	...
Bonds and notes	4 620	...	...	...	...	...	...	...	...
Monetary authorities	4 621	...	...	...	...	...	...	...	...
General government	4 622	...	...	...	...	...	...	...	...
Banks	4 623	...	...	...	...	...	...	...	...
Other sectors	4 624	...	...	...	...	...	...	...	...
Money market instruments	4 630	...	...	...	...	...	...	...	...
Monetary authorities	4 631	...	...	...	...	...	...	...	...
General government	4 632	...	...	...	...	...	...	...	...
Banks	4 633	...	...	...	...	...	...	...	...
Other sectors	4 634	...	...	...	...	...	...	...	...
Financial derivatives	4 640	...	...	...	...	...	...	...	...
Monetary authorities	4 641	...	...	...	...	...	...	...	...
General government	4 642	...	...	...	...	...	...	...	...
Banks	4 643	...	...	...	...	...	...	...	...
Other sectors	4 644	...	...	...	...	...	...	...	...
Liabilities	4 652	...	...	...	...	...	...	...	...
Equity securities	4 660	...	...	...	...	...	...	...	...
Banks	4 663	...	...	...	...	...	...	...	...
Other sectors	4 664	...	...	...	...	...	...	...	...
Debt securities	4 669	...	...	...	...	...	...	...	...
Bonds and notes	4 670	...	...	...	...	...	...	...	...
Monetary authorities	4 671	...	...	...	...	...	...	...	...
General government	4 672	...	...	...	...	...	...	...	...
Banks	4 673	...	...	...	...	...	...	...	...
Other sectors	4 674	...	...	...	...	...	...	...	...
Money market instruments	4 680	...	...	...	...	...	...	...	...
Monetary authorities	4 681	...	...	...	...	...	...	...	...
General government	4 682	...	...	...	...	...	...	...	...
Banks	4 683	...	...	...	...	...	...	...	...
Other sectors	4 684	...	...	...	...	...	...	...	...
Financial derivatives	4 690	...	...	...	...	...	...	...	...
Monetary authorities	4 691	...	...	...	...	...	...	...	...
General government	4 692	...	...	...	...	...	...	...	...
Banks	4 693	...	...	...	...	...	...	...	...
Other sectors	4 694	...	...	...	...	...	...	...	...

Table 2 (Concluded). STANDARD PRESENTATION, 1988–95
(Millions of U.S. dollars)

	Code	1988	1989	1990	1991	1992	1993	1994	1995
C. OTHER INVESTMENT	4 700 . .	355.2	309.7	356.8	853.0	445.9	326.6	276.0	434.2
Assets	4 703 . .	**–65.3**	**–39.6**	**–28.5**	**–74.0**	**–82.8**	**...**	**...**	**...**
Trade credits	4 706 . .	...	...	...	...	...	...	...	...
General government: long-term	4 708 . .	...	...	...	...	...	...	...	...
General government: short-term	4 709 . .	...	...	...	...	...	...	...	...
Other sectors: long-term	4 711 . .	...	...	...	...	...	...	...	...
Other sectors: short-term	4 712 . .	...	...	...	...	...	...	...	...
Loans	4 714 . .	...	...	...	...	...	...	...	...
Monetary authorities: long-term	4 717 . .	...	...	...	...	...	...	...	...
Monetary authorities: short-term	4 718 . .	...	...	...	...	...	...	...	...
General government: long-term	4 720 . .	...	...	...	...	...	...	...	...
General government: short-term	4 721 . .	...	...	...	...	...	...	...	...
Banks: long-term	4 723 . .	...	...	...	...	...	...	...	...
Banks: short-term	4 724 . .	...	...	...	...	...	...	...	...
Other sectors: long-term	4 726 . .	...	...	...	...	...	...	...	...
Other sectors: short-term	4 727 . .	...	...	...	...	...	...	...	...
Currency and deposits	4 730 . .	–65.3	–39.6	–28.5	–74.0	–82.8	...	...	...
Monetary authorities	4 731 . .	...	...	...	...	...	...	...	...
General government	4 732 . .	80.5	...	...	...	...	...	...	...
Banks	4 733 . .	–145.8	–39.6	–28.5	–74.0	–82.8	...	...	...
Other sectors	4 734 . .	...	...	...	...	...	...	...	...
Other assets	4 736 . .	...	...	...	...	...	...	...	...
Monetary authorities: long-term	4 738 . .	...	...	...	...	...	...	...	...
Monetary authorities: short-term	4 739 . .	...	...	...	...	...	...	...	...
General government: long-term	4 741 . .	...	...	...	...	...	...	...	...
General government: short-term	4 742 . .	...	...	...	...	...	...	...	...
Banks: long-term	4 744 . .	...	...	...	...	...	...	...	...
Banks: short-term	4 745 . .	...	...	...	...	...	...	...	...
Other sectors: long-term	4 747 . .	...	...	...	...	...	...	...	...
Other sectors: short-term	4 748 . .	...	...	...	...	...	...	...	...
Liabilities	4 753 . .	**420.6**	**349.2**	**385.3**	**927.0**	**528.7**	**326.6**	**276.0**	**434.2**
Trade credits	4 756 . .	...	...	...	...	...	–7.6	–11.8	–.1
General government: long-term	4 758 . .	...	...	...	...	...	–7.6	–11.8	–.1
General government: short-term	4 759 . .	...	...	...	...	...	...	...	...
Other sectors: long-term	4 761 . .	...	...	...	...	...	...	...	...
Other sectors: short-term	4 762 . .	...	...	...	...	...	...	...	...
Loans	4 764 . .	228.4	200.1	167.4	735.6	354.3	289.4	198.0	361.9
Use of Fund credit and loans from the Fund	4 766 . .	...	...	–1.4	...	...	...	...	–39.5
Monetary authorities: other long-term	4 767 . .	...	...	...	...	...	...	...	...
Monetary authorities: short-term	4 768 . .	23.6	–5.4	1.7	236.2	65.8	102.8	–11.9	61.0
General government: long-term	4 770 . .	204.8	205.5	167.1	499.4	288.5	208.4	8.7	9.9
General government: short-term	4 771 . .	...	...	...	...	...	...	...	...
Banks: long-term	4 773 . .	...	...	...	...	...	–37.8	...	–.2
Banks: short-term	4 774 . .	...	...	...	...	...	16.0	201.2	330.7
Other sectors: long-term	4 776 . .	...	...	...	...	...	...	...	...
Other sectors: short-term	4 777 . .	...	...	...	...	...	...	...	...
Currency and deposits	4 780 . .	–6.3	–2.3	12.1	16.1	20.3	–15.7	49.6	21.7
Monetary authorities	4 781 . .	...	...	...	...	...	...	...	...
General government	4 782 . .	...	...	...	...	...	...	...	...
Banks	4 783 . .	–6.3	–2.3	12.1	16.1	20.3	–15.7	49.6	21.7
Other sectors	4 784 . .	...	...	...	...	...	...	...	...
Other liabilities	4 786 . .	198.4	151.4	205.8	175.3	154.1	60.5	40.2	50.7
Monetary authorities: long-term	4 788 . .	...	...	...	...	...	...	...	...
Monetary authorities: short-term	4 789 . .	340.1	245.5	270.2	188.4	174.1	60.5	40.2	12.6
General government: long-term	4 791 . .	–141.7	–94.1	–64.4	–13.1	–20.0	...	...	...
General government: short-term	4 792 . .	...	...	...	...	...	...	...	...
Banks: long-term	4 794 . .	...	...	...	...	...	...	...	...
Banks: short-term	4 795 . .	...	...	...	...	...	...	...	38.1
Other sectors: long-term	4 797 . .	...	...	...	...	...	...	...	...
Other sectors: short-term	4 798 . .	...	...	...	...	...	...	...	...
D. RESERVE ASSETS	4 800 . .	–.4	–3.8	4.5	3.8	29.3	–41.8	–19.1	–23.6
Monetary gold	4 810 . .	...	...	...	...	...	...	...	...
Special drawing rights	4 820 . .	...	...	...	...	...	...	...	...
Reserve position in the Fund	4 830 . .	...	...	...	...	...	...	...	...
Foreign exchange	4 840 . .	–.4	–3.8	4.5	3.8	29.3	–41.8	–19.1	–23.6
Other claims	4 880 . .	...	...	...	...	...	...	...	...
NET ERRORS AND OMISSIONS	4 998 . .	**3.1**	**–160.3**	**10.9**	**97.9**	**31.0**	**–82.6**	**344.8**	**89.3**

Part 3 of the *Yearbook* contains descriptions of the methodologies, compilation practices, and sources used to compile these data.

Table 1. ANALYTIC PRESENTATION, 1988–95
(*Millions of U.S. dollars*)

	Code		1988	1989	1990	1991	1992	1993	1994	1995
A. Current Account [1]	4 993	Y.	**64.0**	**164.4**	**37.4**	**–74.7**	**14.2**	**44.0**	**58.6**	...
Goods: exports f.o.b	2 100	..	358.4	549.2	465.9	345.9	341.0	298.3	293.6	...
Goods: imports f.o.b	3 100	..	–239.4	–330.9	–374.4	–347.1	–272.5	–213.9	–194.3	...
Balance on Goods	4 100	..	*118.9*	*218.3*	*91.5*	*–1.1*	*68.4*	*84.4*	*99.3*	...
Services: credit	2 200	..	22.7	23.7	20.7	22.3	22.6	46.5	72.6	...
Services: debit	3 200	..	–76.3	–90.7	–96.0	–97.7	–98.7	–101.6	–113.5	...
Balance on Goods and Services	4 991	..	*65.3*	*151.3*	*16.2*	*–76.5*	*–7.6*	*29.3*	*58.4*	...
Income: credit	2 300	..	1.3	1.0	2.2	1.4	.7	.2	.9	...
Income: debit	3 300	..	–9.8	–7.3	–10.8	–12.6	–8.2	–6.4	–4.7	...
Balance on Goods, Services, and Income	4 992	..	*56.9*	*145.0*	*7.7*	*–87.7*	*–15.1*	*23.1*	*54.6*	...
Current transfers: credit	2 379	Y.	11.3	24.1	35.5	20.4	37.9	26.7	6.2	...
Current transfers: debit	3 379	..	–4.1	–4.6	–5.8	–7.5	–8.6	–5.8	–2.2	...
B. Capital Account [1]	4 994	Y.	**–1.5**	**–1.6**	**–2.8**	**–1.1**	**–3.2**	**.5**	**–.2**	...
Capital account: credit	2 994	Y.	1.5	1.1	.3	2.3	2.6	3.5	.2	...
Capital account: debit	3 994	..	–3.0	–2.7	–3.1	–3.4	–5.8	–3.0	–.4	...
Total, Groups A Plus B	4 010	..	*62.5*	*162.9*	*34.6*	*–75.8*	*11.0*	*44.5*	*58.4*	...
C. Financial Account [1]	4 995	X.	**–65.9**	**–172.9**	**–15.0**	**32.4**	**–48.5**	**–73.1**	**–84.1**	...
Direct investment abroad	4 505	..	...	...	...	...	...	...	...	...
Direct investment in Suriname	4 555	Y.	–95.8	–167.9	–43.0	10.4	–30.4	–46.6	–30.2	...
Portfolio investment assets	4 602	..	...	...	...	...	...	...	...	...
Equity securities	4 610	..	...	...	...	...	...	...	...	...
Debt securities	4 619	..	...	...	...	...	...	...	...	...
Portfolio investment liabilities	4 652	Y.	...	...	.5	–2.3	1.5	...	...	...
Equity securities	4 660	Y.	...	...	...	...	...	...	...	...
Debt securities	4 669	Y.	...	...	.5	–2.3	1.5	...	...	...
Other investment assets	4 703	..	–.5	–13.3	15.6	2.7	–.1	–4.4	–19.1	...
Monetary authorities	4 703	.A	...	...	...	...	...	...	...	...
General government	4 703	.B	...	...	...	...	...	...	...	...
Banks	4 703	.C	...	1.0	.1	–.2	–3.7	–14.5	–31.3	...
Other sectors	4 703	.D	–.5	–14.3	15.5	3.0	3.6	10.1	12.2	...
Other investment liabilities	4 753	X.	30.4	8.3	12.0	21.6	–19.5	–22.1	–34.8	...
Monetary authorities	4 753	XA	.4	.1	.1	.1	.3	...	...	...
General government	4 753	YB	7.1	6.4	–1.8	5.0	5.9	2.0	2.1	...
Banks	4 753	YC	20.8	11.0	5.2	.1	–23.4	–23.7	–29.6	...
Other sectors	4 753	YD	2.1	–9.2	8.6	16.4	–2.4	–.4	–7.3	...
Total, Groups A Through C	4 020	..	*–3.4*	*–10.0*	*19.7*	*–43.4*	*–37.5*	*–28.6*	*–25.7*	...
D. Net Errors and Omissions	4 998	..	**–1.8**	**9.9**	**–9.4**	**–.5**	**25.4**	**41.3**	**60.0**	...
Total, Groups A Through D	4 030	..	*–5.2*	*–.1*	*10.3*	*–43.9*	*–12.0*	*12.7*	*34.3*	...
E. Reserves and Related Items	4 040	..	**5.2**	**.1**	**–10.3**	**43.9**	**12.0**	**–12.7**	**–34.3**	...
Reserve assets	4 800	..	5.2	.1	–10.3	43.9	12.0	–12.7	–34.3	...
Use of Fund credit and loans	4 766	..	...	...	...	...	...	...	...	...
Liabilities constituting foreign authorities' reserves	4 900	..	...	...	...	...	...	...	...	...
Exceptional financing	4 920	..	...	...	...	...	...	...	...	...
Conversion rates: Suriname guilders per U.S. dollar	0 101	..	**1.78500**	**1.78500**	**1.78500**	**1.78500**	**1.78500**	**1.00000**	**1.00000**	...

[1] Excludes components that have been classified in the categories of Group E.

Table 2. STANDARD PRESENTATION, 1988–95
(Millions of U.S. dollars)

	Code	1988	1989	1990	1991	1992	1993	1994	1995
CURRENT ACCOUNT	4 993 . .	**64.0**	**164.4**	**37.4**	**–74.7**	**14.2**	**44.0**	**58.6**	**. . .**
A. GOODS	4 100 . .	118.9	218.3	91.5	–1.1	68.4	84.4	99.3	. . .
Credit	2 100 . .	**358.4**	**549.2**	**465.9**	**345.9**	**341.0**	**298.3**	**293.6**	**. . .**
General merchandise: exports f.o.b.	2 110 . .	358.4	549.2	465.9	345.9	341.0	298.3	293.6	. . .
Goods for processing: exports f.o.b.	2 150 . .	. . .	. . .	. . .	. . .	. . .	. . .	. . .	. . .
Repairs on goods	2 160 . .	. . .	. . .	. . .	. . .	. . .	. . .	. . .	. . .
Goods procured in ports by carriers	2 170 . .	. . .	. . .	. . .	. . .	. . .	. . .	. . .	. . .
Nonmonetary gold	2 180 . .	. . .	. . .	. . .	. . .	. . .	. . .	. . .	. . .
Debit	3 100 . .	**–239.4**	**–330.9**	**–374.4**	**–347.1**	**–272.5**	**–213.9**	**–194.3**	**. . .**
General merchandise: imports f.o.b.	3 110 . .	–239.4	–330.9	–374.4	–347.1	–272.5	–213.9	–194.3	. . .
Goods for processing: imports f.o.b.	3 150 . .	. . .	. . .	. . .	. . .	. . .	. . .	. . .	. . .
Repairs on goods	3 160 . .	. . .	. . .	. . .	. . .	. . .	. . .	. . .	. . .
Goods procured in ports by carriers	3 170 . .	. . .	. . .	. . .	. . .	. . .	. . .	. . .	. . .
Nonmonetary gold	3 180 . .	. . .	. . .	. . .	. . .	. . .	. . .	. . .	. . .
B. SERVICES	4 200 . .	–53.6	–67.0	–75.2	–75.4	–76.0	–55.1	–40.9	. . .
Total credit	2 200 . .	*22.7*	*23.7*	*20.7*	*22.3*	*22.6*	*46.5*	*72.6*	. . .
Total debit	3 200 . .	*–76.3*	*–90.7*	*–96.0*	*–97.7*	*–98.7*	*–101.6*	*–113.5*	. . .
Transportation services, credit	2 205 . .	**3.6**	**3.8**	**3.5**	**4.6**	**2.7**	**18.5**	**35.2**	**. . .**
Passenger	2 205 BA	*2.5*	*2.0*	*1.5*	*1.7*	*1.8*	*13.4*	*25.2*	. . .
Freight	2 205 BB	*.5*	*.7*	*.4*	*1.5*	*.4*	*4.5*	*4.9*	. . .
Other	2 205 BC	*.7*	*1.2*	*1.7*	*1.4*	*.6*	*.6*	*5.1*	. . .
Sea transport, passenger	2 207 . .	. . .	. . .	. . .	. . .	. . .	. . .	. . .	. . .
Sea transport, freight	2 208 . .	. . .	. . .	. . .	. . .	. . .	. . .	. . .	. . .
Sea transport, other	2 209 . .	. . .	. . .	. . .	. . .	. . .	. . .	. . .	. . .
Air transport, passenger	2 211 . .	. . .	. . .	. . .	. . .	. . .	. . .	. . .	. . .
Air transport, freight	2 212 . .	. . .	. . .	. . .	. . .	. . .	. . .	. . .	. . .
Air transport, other	2 213 . .	. . .	. . .	. . .	. . .	. . .	. . .	. . .	. . .
Other transport, passenger	2 215 . .	. . .	. . .	. . .	. . .	. . .	. . .	. . .	. . .
Other transport, freight	2 216 . .	. . .	. . .	. . .	. . .	. . .	. . .	. . .	. . .
Other transport, other	2 217 . .	. . .	. . .	. . .	. . .	. . .	. . .	. . .	. . .
Transportation services, debit	3 205 . .	**–31.3**	**–36.5**	**–38.6**	**–35.5**	**–30.4**	**–49.0**	**–56.9**	**. . .**
Passenger	3 205 BA	*–2.4*	*–5.5*	*–6.1*	*–6.9*	*–3.9*	*–16.7*	*–21.6*	. . .
Freight	3 205 BB	*–19.7*	*–22.1*	*–20.4*	*–16.4*	*–18.5*	*–25.1*	*–17.8*	. . .
Other	3 205 BC	*–9.2*	*–8.9*	*–12.0*	*–12.2*	*–8.0*	*–7.2*	*–17.5*	. . .
Sea transport, passenger	3 207 . .	. . .	. . .	. . .	. . .	. . .	. . .	. . .	. . .
Sea transport, freight	3 208 . .	. . .	. . .	. . .	. . .	. . .	. . .	. . .	. . .
Sea transport, other	3 209 . .	. . .	. . .	. . .	. . .	. . .	. . .	. . .	. . .
Air transport, passenger	3 211 . .	. . .	. . .	. . .	. . .	. . .	. . .	. . .	. . .
Air transport, freight	3 212 . .	. . .	. . .	. . .	. . .	. . .	. . .	. . .	. . .
Air transport, other	3 213 . .	. . .	. . .	. . .	. . .	. . .	. . .	. . .	. . .
Other transport, passenger	3 215 . .	. . .	. . .	. . .	. . .	. . .	. . .	. . .	. . .
Other transport, freight	3 216 . .	. . .	. . .	. . .	. . .	. . .	. . .	. . .	. . .
Other transport, other	3 217 . .	. . .	. . .	. . .	. . .	. . .	. . .	. . .	. . .
Travel, credit	2 236 . .	**5.7**	**4.4**	**.6**	**.9**	**2.1**	**8.0**	**11.2**	**. . .**
Business travel	2 237 . .	. . .	. . .	. . .	. . .	. . .	. . .	. . .	. . .
Personal travel	2 240 . .	. . .	. . .	. . .	. . .	. . .	. . .	. . .	. . .
Travel, debit	3 236 . .	**–9.5**	**–10.0**	**–12.3**	**–16.2**	**–11.5**	**–2.9**	**–3.1**	**. . .**
Business travel	3 237 . .	. . .	. . .	. . .	. . .	. . .	. . .	. . .	. . .
Personal travel	3 240 . .	. . .	. . .	. . .	. . .	. . .	. . .	. . .	. . .
Other services, credit	2 200 BA	**13.3**	**15.4**	**16.7**	**16.8**	**17.8**	**20.0**	**26.2**	**. . .**
Communications	2 245 . .	. . .	. . .	. . .	. . .	. . .	. . .	. . .	. . .
Construction	2 249 . .	. . .	. . .	. . .	. . .	. . .	. . .	. . .	. . .
Insurance	2 253 . .	.1	.1	. . .	.2	. . .	.5	.5	. . .
Financial	2 260 . .	. . .	. . .	. . .	. . .	. . .	. . .	. . .	. . .
Computer and information	2 262 . .	. . .	. . .	. . .	. . .	. . .	. . .	. . .	. . .
Royalties and licence fees	2 266 . .	. . .	. . .	. . .	. . .	. . .	. . .	. . .	. . .
Other business services	2 268 . .	10.0	11.1	13.1	12.7	15.1	17.6	22.6	. . .
Personal, cultural, and recreational	2 287 . .	. . .	. . .	. . .	. . .	. . .	. . .	. . .	. . .
Government, n.i.e.	2 291 . .	3.3	4.2	3.5	4.0	2.7	1.9	3.1	. . .
Other services, debit	3 200 BA	**–35.5**	**–44.2**	**–45.1**	**–45.9**	**–56.8**	**–49.7**	**–53.5**	**. . .**
Communications	3 245 . .	. . .	. . .	. . .	. . .	. . .	. . .	. . .	. . .
Construction	3 249 . .	. . .	. . .	. . .	. . .	. . .	. . .	. . .	. . .
Insurance	3 253 . .	–2.2	–2.5	–2.3	–1.8	–2.1	–2.8	–2.0	. . .
Financial	3 260 . .	. . .	. . .	. . .	. . .	. . .	. . .	. . .	. . .
Computer and information	3 262 . .	. . .	. . .	. . .	. . .	. . .	. . .	. . .	. . .
Royalties and licence fees	3 266 . .	. . .	. . .	. . .	. . .	. . .	. . .	. . .	. . .
Other business services	3 268 . .	–23.2	–27.5	–31.0	–29.0	–42.2	–37.6	–36.6	. . .
Personal, cultural, and recreational	3 287 . .	. . .	. . .	. . .	. . .	. . .	. . .	. . .	. . .
Government, n.i.e.	3 291 . .	–10.1	–14.2	–11.8	–15.1	–12.5	–9.3	–14.9	. . .

Table 2 (Continued). STANDARD PRESENTATION, 1988–95
(Millions of U.S. dollars)

	Code	1988	1989	1990	1991	1992	1993	1994	1995
C. INCOME	4 300 . .	–8.5	–6.3	–8.5	–11.2	–7.5	–6.2	–3.8	. . .
Total credit	2 300 . .	*1.3*	*1.0*	*2.2*	*1.4*	*.7*	*.2*	*.9*	. . .
Total debit	3 300 . .	*–9.8*	*–7.3*	*–10.8*	*–12.6*	*–8.2*	*–6.4*	*–4.7*	. . .
Compensation of employees, credit	2 310 . .	**.1**	. . .	. . .	. . .	. . .	. . .	. . .	. . .
Compensation of employees, debit	3 310 . .	**–1.7**	**–1.0**	**–1.2**	**–1.7**	**–1.6**	**–1.6**	**–1.0**	. . .
Investment income, credit	2 320 . .	**1.3**	**1.0**	**2.2**	**1.4**	**.7**	**.2**	**.9**	. . .
Direct investment income	2 330 . .	. . .	. . .	. . .	. . .	. . .	. . .	. . .	. . .
Dividends and distributed branch profits	2 332 . .	. . .	. . .	. . .	. . .	. . .	. . .	. . .	. . .
Reinvested earnings and undistributed branch profits	2 333 . .	. . .	. . .	. . .	. . .	. . .	. . .	. . .	. . .
Income on debt (interest)	2 334 . .	. . .	. . .	. . .	. . .	. . .	. . .	. . .	. . .
Portfolio investment income	2 339 . .	. . .	. . .	. . .	. . .	. . .	. . .	. . .	. . .
Income on equity	2 340 . .	. . .	. . .	. . .	. . .	. . .	. . .	. . .	. . .
Income on bonds and notes	2 350 . .	. . .	. . .	. . .	. . .	. . .	. . .	. . .	. . .
Income on money market instruments and financial derivatives	2 360 . .	. . .	. . .	. . .	. . .	. . .	. . .	. . .	. . .
Other investment income	2 370 . .	1.3	1.0	2.2	1.4	.7	.2	.9	. . .
Investment income, debit	3 320 . .	**–8.1**	**–6.3**	**–9.5**	**–10.9**	**–6.6**	**–4.8**	**–3.7**	. . .
Direct investment income	3 330 . .	–5.3	–2.6	–1.6	–3.4	–1.1	–.3	. . .	. . .
Dividends and distributed branch profits	3 332 . .	–5.3	–2.6	–1.6	–3.4	–1.1	–.3	. . .	. . .
Reinvested earnings and undistributed branch profits	3 333 . .	. . .	. . .	. . .	. . .	. . .	. . .	. . .	. . .
Income on debt (interest)	3 334 . .	. . .	. . .	. . .	. . .	. . .	. . .	. . .	. . .
Portfolio investment income	3 339 . .	. . .	. . .	. . .	. . .	. . .	. . .	. . .	. . .
Income on equity	3 340 . .	. . .	. . .	. . .	. . .	. . .	. . .	. . .	. . .
Income on bonds and notes	3 350 . .	. . .	. . .	. . .	. . .	. . .	. . .	. . .	. . .
Income on money market instruments and financial derivatives	3 360 . .	. . .	. . .	. . .	. . .	. . .	. . .	. . .	. . .
Other investment income	3 370 . .	–2.8	–3.7	–7.9	–7.5	–5.4	–4.5	–3.7	. . .
D. CURRENT TRANSFERS	4 379 . .	7.2	19.4	29.7	13.0	29.3	20.9	4.0	. . .
Credit	2 379 . .	**11.3**	**24.1**	**35.5**	**20.4**	**37.9**	**26.7**	**6.2**	. . .
General government	2 380 . .	10.3	23.5	34.4	19.3	33.4	23.5	5.7	. . .
Other sectors	2 390 . .	1.1	.6	1.1	1.2	4.5	3.2	.5	. . .
Workers' remittances	2 391 . .	. . .	. . .	. . .	. . .	. . .	. . .	. . .	. . .
Other current transfers	2 392 . .	1.1	.6	1.1	1.2	4.5	3.2	.5	. . .
Debit	3 379 . .	**–4.1**	**–4.6**	**–5.8**	**–7.5**	**–8.6**	**–5.8**	**–2.2**	. . .
General government	3 380 . .	. . .	. . .	. . .	. . .	. . .	. . .	. . .	. . .
Other sectors	3 390 . .	–4.1	–4.6	–5.8	–7.5	–8.6	–5.8	–2.2	. . .
Workers' remittances	3 391 . .	–.4	–.4	–.4	–1.0	–.8	–1.0	–1.1	. . .
Other current transfers	3 392 . .	–3.8	–4.3	–5.4	–6.5	–7.8	–4.8	–1.1	. . .
CAPITAL AND FINANCIAL ACCOUNT	4 996 . .	**–62.2**	**–174.3**	**–28.0**	**75.2**	**–39.7**	**–85.3**	**–118.6**	. . .
CAPITAL ACCOUNT	4 994 . .	**–1.5**	**–1.6**	**–2.8**	**–1.1**	**–3.2**	**.5**	**–.2**	. . .
Total credit	2 994 . .	*1.5*	*1.1*	*.3*	*2.3*	*2.6*	*3.5*	*.2*	. . .
Total debit	3 994 . .	*–3.0*	*–2.7*	*–3.1*	*–3.4*	*–5.8*	*–3.0*	*–.4*	. . .
Capital transfers, credit	2 400 . .	**1.5**	**1.1**	**.3**	**2.3**	**2.6**	**3.5**	**.2**	. . .
General government	2 401 . .	. . .	. . .	. . .	. . .	. . .	. . .	. . .	. . .
Debt forgiveness	2 402 . .	. . .	. . .	. . .	. . .	. . .	. . .	. . .	. . .
Other capital transfers	2 410 . .	. . .	. . .	. . .	. . .	. . .	. . .	. . .	. . .
Other sectors	2 430 . .	1.5	1.1	.3	2.3	2.6	3.5	.2	. . .
Migrants' transfers	2 431 . .	1.5	1.1	.3	2.3	2.6	3.5	.2	. . .
Debt forgiveness	2 432 . .	. . .	. . .	. . .	. . .	. . .	. . .	. . .	. . .
Other capital transfers	2 440 . .	. . .	. . .	. . .	. . .	. . .	. . .	. . .	. . .
Capital transfers, debit	3 400 . .	**–3.0**	**–2.7**	**–3.1**	**–3.4**	**–5.8**	**–3.0**	**–.4**	. . .
General government	3 401 . .	. . .	. . .	. . .	. . .	. . .	. . .	. . .	. . .
Debt forgiveness	3 402 . .	. . .	. . .	. . .	. . .	. . .	. . .	. . .	. . .
Other capital transfers	3 410 . .	. . .	. . .	. . .	. . .	. . .	. . .	. . .	. . .
Other sectors	3 430 . .	–3.0	–2.7	–3.1	–3.4	–5.8	–3.0	–.4	. . .
Migrants' transfers	3 431 . .	–3.0	–2.7	–3.1	–3.4	–5.8	–3.0	–.4	. . .
Debt forgiveness	3 432 . .	. . .	. . .	. . .	. . .	. . .	. . .	. . .	. . .
Other capital transfers	3 440 . .	. . .	. . .	. . .	. . .	. . .	. . .	. . .	. . .
Nonproduced nonfinancial assets, credit	2 480 . .	. . .	. . .	. . .	. . .	. . .	. . .	. . .	. . .
Nonproduced nonfinancial assets, debit	3 480 . .	. . .	. . .	. . .	. . .	. . .	. . .	. . .	. . .

Table 2 (Continued). STANDARD PRESENTATION, 1988–95
(Millions of U.S. dollars)

	Code	1988	1989	1990	1991	1992	1993	1994	1995
FINANCIAL ACCOUNT	4 995	**–60.7**	**–172.8**	**–25.2**	**76.3**	**–36.5**	**–85.8**	**–118.4**	**. . .**
A. DIRECT INVESTMENT	4 500	–95.8	–167.9	–43.0	10.4	–30.4	–46.6	–30.2	. . .
Direct investment abroad	4 505	**. . .**	**. . .**	**. . .**	**. . .**	**. . .**	**. . .**	**. . .**	**. . .**
Equity capital	4 510	. . .	. . .	. . .	. . .	. . .	. . .	. . .	. . .
Claims on affiliated enterprises	4 515	. . .	. . .	. . .	. . .	. . .	. . .	. . .	. . .
Liabilities to affiliated enterprises	4 520	. . .	. . .	. . .	. . .	. . .	. . .	. . .	. . .
Reinvested earnings	4 525	. . .	. . .	. . .	. . .	. . .	. . .	. . .	. . .
Other capital	4 530	. . .	. . .	. . .	. . .	. . .	. . .	. . .	. . .
Claims on affiliated enterprises	4 535	. . .	. . .	. . .	. . .	. . .	. . .	. . .	. . .
Liabilities to affiliated enterprises	4 540	. . .	. . .	. . .	. . .	. . .	. . .	. . .	. . .
Direct investment in Suriname	4 555	**–95.8**	**–167.9**	**–43.0**	**10.4**	**–30.4**	**–46.6**	**–30.2**	**. . .**
Equity capital	4 560	.2	–.4	–.7	–.7	–3.1	–3.6	–.1	. . .
Claims on direct investors	4 565	. . .	. . .	. . .	. . .	. . .	. . .	. . .	. . .
Liabilities to direct investors	4 570	. . .	. . .	. . .	. . .	. . .	. . .	. . .	. . .
Reinvested earnings	4 575	. . .	. . .	. . .	. . .	. . .	. . .	. . .	. . .
Other capital	4 580	–96.0	–167.5	–42.4	11.0	–27.3	–43.0	–30.1	. . .
Claims on direct investors	4 585	. . .	. . .	. . .	. . .	. . .	. . .	. . .	. . .
Liabilities to direct investors	4 590	. . .	. . .	. . .	. . .	. . .	. . .	. . .	. . .
B. PORTFOLIO INVESTMENT	4 600	. . .	. . .	.5	–2.3	1.5	. . .	. . .	. . .
Assets	4 602	**. . .**	**. . .**	**. . .**	**. . .**	**. . .**	**. . .**	**. . .**	**. . .**
Equity securities	4 610	. . .	. . .	. . .	. . .	. . .	. . .	. . .	. . .
Monetary authorities	4 611	. . .	. . .	. . .	. . .	. . .	. . .	. . .	. . .
General government	4 612	. . .	. . .	. . .	. . .	. . .	. . .	. . .	. . .
Banks	4 613	. . .	. . .	. . .	. . .	. . .	. . .	. . .	. . .
Other sectors	4 614	. . .	. . .	. . .	. . .	. . .	. . .	. . .	. . .
Debt securities	4 619	. . .	. . .	. . .	. . .	. . .	. . .	. . .	. . .
Bonds and notes	4 620	. . .	. . .	. . .	. . .	. . .	. . .	. . .	. . .
Monetary authorities	4 621	. . .	. . .	. . .	. . .	. . .	. . .	. . .	. . .
General government	4 622	. . .	. . .	. . .	. . .	. . .	. . .	. . .	. . .
Banks	4 623	. . .	. . .	. . .	. . .	. . .	. . .	. . .	. . .
Other sectors	4 624	. . .	. . .	. . .	. . .	. . .	. . .	. . .	. . .
Money market instruments	4 630	. . .	. . .	. . .	. . .	. . .	. . .	. . .	. . .
Monetary authorities	4 631	. . .	. . .	. . .	. . .	. . .	. . .	. . .	. . .
General government	4 632	. . .	. . .	. . .	. . .	. . .	. . .	. . .	. . .
Banks	4 633	. . .	. . .	. . .	. . .	. . .	. . .	. . .	. . .
Other sectors	4 634	. . .	. . .	. . .	. . .	. . .	. . .	. . .	. . .
Financial derivatives	4 640	. . .	. . .	. . .	. . .	. . .	. . .	. . .	. . .
Monetary authorities	4 641	. . .	. . .	. . .	. . .	. . .	. . .	. . .	. . .
General government	4 642	. . .	. . .	. . .	. . .	. . .	. . .	. . .	. . .
Banks	4 643	. . .	. . .	. . .	. . .	. . .	. . .	. . .	. . .
Other sectors	4 644	. . .	. . .	. . .	. . .	. . .	. . .	. . .	. . .
Liabilities	4 652	**. . .**	**. . .**	**.5**	**–2.3**	**1.5**	**. . .**	**. . .**	**. . .**
Equity securities	4 660	. . .	. . .	. . .	. . .	. . .	. . .	. . .	. . .
Banks	4 663	. . .	. . .	. . .	. . .	. . .	. . .	. . .	. . .
Other sectors	4 664	. . .	. . .	. . .	. . .	. . .	. . .	. . .	. . .
Debt securities	4 669	. . .	. . .	.5	–2.3	1.5	. . .	. . .	. . .
Bonds and notes	4 670	. . .	. . .	.5	–2.3	1.5	. . .	. . .	. . .
Monetary authorities	4 671	. . .	. . .	. . .	. . .	. . .	. . .	. . .	. . .
General government	4 672	. . .	. . .	.5	–2.3	1.5	. . .	. . .	. . .
Banks	4 673	. . .	. . .	. . .	. . .	. . .	. . .	. . .	. . .
Other sectors	4 674	. . .	. . .	. . .	. . .	. . .	. . .	. . .	. . .
Money market instruments	4 680	. . .	. . .	. . .	. . .	. . .	. . .	. . .	. . .
Monetary authorities	4 681	. . .	. . .	. . .	. . .	. . .	. . .	. . .	. . .
General government	4 682	. . .	. . .	. . .	. . .	. . .	. . .	. . .	. . .
Banks	4 683	. . .	. . .	. . .	. . .	. . .	. . .	. . .	. . .
Other sectors	4 684	. . .	. . .	. . .	. . .	. . .	. . .	. . .	. . .
Financial derivatives	4 690	. . .	. . .	. . .	. . .	. . .	. . .	. . .	. . .
Monetary authorities	4 691	. . .	. . .	. . .	. . .	. . .	. . .	. . .	. . .
General government	4 692	. . .	. . .	. . .	. . .	. . .	. . .	. . .	. . .
Banks	4 693	. . .	. . .	. . .	. . .	. . .	. . .	. . .	. . .
Other sectors	4 694	. . .	. . .	. . .	. . .	. . .	. . .	. . .	. . .

Table 2 (Concluded). STANDARD PRESENTATION, 1988–95
(Millions of U.S. dollars)

	Code	1988	1989	1990	1991	1992	1993	1994	1995
C. OTHER INVESTMENT	4 700 . .	29.9	–5.0	27.6	24.4	–19.6	–26.5	–53.9	. . .
Assets	4 703 . .	**–.5**	**–13.3**	**15.6**	**2.7**	**–.1**	**–4.4**	**–19.1**	**. . .**
Trade credits	4 706 . .	. . .	. . .	. . .	. . .	. . .	. . .	. . .	. . .
General government: long-term	4 708 . .	. . .	. . .	. . .	. . .	. . .	. . .	. . .	. . .
General government: short-term	4 709 . .	. . .	. . .	. . .	. . .	. . .	. . .	. . .	. . .
Other sectors: long-term	4 711 . .	. . .	. . .	. . .	. . .	. . .	. . .	. . .	. . .
Other sectors: short-term	4 712 . .	. . .	. . .	. . .	. . .	. . .	. . .	. . .	. . .
Loans	4 714 . .	. . .	. . .	. . .	. . .	. . .	. . .	. . .	. . .
Monetary authorities: long-term	4 717 . .	. . .	. . .	. . .	. . .	. . .	. . .	. . .	. . .
Monetary authorities: short-term	4 718 . .	. . .	. . .	. . .	. . .	. . .	. . .	. . .	. . .
General government: long-term	4 720 . .	. . .	. . .	. . .	. . .	. . .	. . .	. . .	. . .
General government: short-term	4 721 . .	. . .	. . .	. . .	. . .	. . .	. . .	. . .	. . .
Banks: long-term	4 723 . .	. . .	. . .	. . .	. . .	. . .	. . .	. . .	. . .
Banks: short-term	4 724 . .	. . .	. . .	. . .	. . .	. . .	. . .	. . .	. . .
Other sectors: long-term	4 726 . .	. . .	. . .	. . .	. . .	. . .	. . .	. . .	. . .
Other sectors: short-term	4 727 . .	. . .	. . .	. . .	. . .	. . .	. . .	. . .	. . .
Currency and deposits	4 730 . .	–.5	–13.3	15.6	2.7	–.1	–4.4	–19.1	. . .
Monetary authorities	4 731 . .	. . .	. . .	. . .	. . .	. . .	. . .	. . .	. . .
General government	4 732 . .	. . .	. . .	. . .	. . .	. . .	. . .	. . .	. . .
Banks	4 733 . .	. . .	1.0	.1	–.2	–3.7	–14.5	–31.3	. . .
Other sectors	4 734 . .	–.5	–14.3	15.5	3.0	3.6	10.1	12.2	. . .
Other assets	4 736 . .	. . .	. . .	. . .	. . .	. . .	. . .	. . .	. . .
Monetary authorities: long-term	4 738 . .	. . .	. . .	. . .	. . .	. . .	. . .	. . .	. . .
Monetary authorities: short-term	4 739 . .	. . .	. . .	. . .	. . .	. . .	. . .	. . .	. . .
General government: long-term	4 741 . .	. . .	. . .	. . .	. . .	. . .	. . .	. . .	. . .
General government: short-term	4 742 . .	. . .	. . .	. . .	. . .	. . .	. . .	. . .	. . .
Banks: long-term	4 744 . .	. . .	. . .	. . .	. . .	. . .	. . .	. . .	. . .
Banks: short-term	4 745 . .	. . .	. . .	. . .	. . .	. . .	. . .	. . .	. . .
Other sectors: long-term	4 747 . .	. . .	. . .	. . .	. . .	. . .	. . .	. . .	. . .
Other sectors: short-term	4 748 . .	. . .	. . .	. . .	. . .	. . .	. . .	. . .	. . .
Liabilities	4 753 . .	**30.4**	**8.3**	**12.0**	**21.6**	**–19.5**	**–22.1**	**–34.8**	**. . .**
Trade credits	4 756 . .	. . .	. . .	. . .	. . .	. . .	. . .	. . .	. . .
General government: long-term	4 758 . .	. . .	. . .	. . .	. . .	. . .	. . .	. . .	. . .
General government: short-term	4 759 . .	. . .	. . .	. . .	. . .	. . .	. . .	. . .	. . .
Other sectors: long-term	4 761 . .	. . .	. . .	. . .	. . .	. . .	. . .	. . .	. . .
Other sectors: short-term	4 762 . .	. . .	. . .	. . .	. . .	. . .	. . .	. . .	. . .
Loans	4 764 . .	2.2	19.6	7.6	21.5	3.6	2.4	–5.2	. . .
Use of Fund credit and loans from the Fund	4 766 . .	. . .	. . .	. . .	. . .	. . .	. . .	. . .	. . .
Monetary authorities: other long-term	4 767 . .	. . .	. . .	. . .	. . .	. . .	. . .	. . .	. . .
Monetary authorities: short-term	4 768 . .	. . .	. . .	. . .	. . .	. . .	. . .	. . .	. . .
General government: long-term	4 770 . .	4.0	6.7	–1.8	5.0	5.9	2.0	2.1	. . .
General government: short-term	4 771 . .	. . .	. . .	. . .	. . .	. . .	. . .	. . .	. . .
Banks: long-term	4 773 . .	. . .	. . .	. . .	. . .	. . .	. . .	. . .	. . .
Banks: short-term	4 774 . .	. . .	. . .	. . .	. . .	. . .	. . .	. . .	. . .
Other sectors: long-term	4 776 . .	–1.7	9.5	8.7	16.4	–2.4	.4	–7.3	. . .
Other sectors: short-term	4 777 . .	. . .	3.4	.8	. . .	. . .	. . .	. . .	. . .
Currency and deposits	4 780 . .	20.8	11.0	5.2	.1	–23.4	–23.7	–29.6	. . .
Monetary authorities	4 781 . .	. . .	. . .	. . .	. . .	. . .	. . .	. . .	. . .
General government	4 782 . .	. . .	. . .	. . .	. . .	. . .	. . .	. . .	. . .
Banks	4 783 . .	20.8	11.0	5.2	.1	–23.4	–23.7	–29.6	. . .
Other sectors	4 784 . .	. . .	. . .	. . .	. . .	. . .	. . .	. . .	. . .
Other liabilities	4 786 . .	7.4	–22.3	–.8	.1	.3	–.8	. . .	. . .
Monetary authorities: long-term	4 788 . .	. . .	. . .	. . .	. . .	. . .	. . .	. . .	. . .
Monetary authorities: short-term	4 789 . .	.4	.1	.1	.1	.3	. . .	. . .	. . .
General government: long-term	4 791 . .	3.1	–.3	. . .	. . .	. . .	. . .	. . .	. . .
General government: short-term	4 792 . .	. . .	. . .	. . .	. . .	. . .	. . .	. . .	. . .
Banks: long-term	4 794 . .	. . .	. . .	. . .	. . .	. . .	. . .	. . .	. . .
Banks: short-term	4 795 . .	. . .	. . .	. . .	. . .	. . .	. . .	. . .	. . .
Other sectors: long-term	4 797 . .	. . .	. . .	. . .	. . .	. . .	. . .	. . .	. . .
Other sectors: short-term	4 798 . .	3.9	–22.1	–.8	. . .	. . .	–.8	. . .	. . .
D. RESERVE ASSETS	4 800 . .	5.2	.1	–10.3	43.9	12.0	–12.7	–34.3	. . .
Monetary gold	4 810 . .	. . .	. . .	. . .	. . .	. . .	. . .	. . .	. . .
Special drawing rights	4 820 . .	. . .	. . .	. . .	. . .	. . .	. . .	. . .	. . .
Reserve position in the Fund	4 830 . .	. . .	. . .	. . .	. . .	. . .	. . .	. . .	. . .
Foreign exchange	4 840 . .	2.2	3.3	–10.9	36.3	1.0	–6.6	–31.2	. . .
Other claims	4 880 . .	3.0	–3.2	.6	7.6	11.0	–6.1	–3.1	. . .
NET ERRORS AND OMISSIONS	4 998 . .	**–1.8**	**9.9**	**–9.4**	**–.5**	**25.4**	**41.3**	**60.0**	**. . .**

Table 1. ANALYTIC PRESENTATION, 1988–95
(Millions of U.S. dollars)

	Code			1988	1989	1990	1991	1992	1993	1994	1995
A. Current Account [1]	4	993	Y.	**65.7**	**17.2**	**65.9**	**28.3**	**23.4**	**–41.3**	**–41.4**	**–51.1**
Goods: exports f.o.b	2	100	. .	466.6	494.1	550.3	593.8	639.0	674.3	745.4	798.3
Goods: imports f.o.b	3	100	. .	–441.5	–518.5	–588.9	–635.0	–767.2	–773.6	–818.7	–898.4
Balance on Goods	4	100	. .	*25.1*	*–24.4*	*–38.7*	*–41.2*	*–128.2*	*–99.3*	*–73.3*	*–100.1*
Services: credit	2	200	. .	61.0	88.4	110.1	96.3	96.5	99.6	97.6	102.2
Services: debit	3	200	. .	–119.7	–98.3	–143.3	–161.7	–121.7	–135.8	–120.0	–161.0
Balance on Goods and Services	4	991	. .	*–33.5*	*–34.3*	*–71.8*	*–106.6*	*–153.4*	*–135.4*	*–95.6*	*–158.8*
Income: credit	2	300	. .	123.5	125.1	165.1	170.5	184.8	140.0	137.4	137.9
Income: debit	3	300	. .	–97.0	–160.9	–123.4	–134.0	–131.7	–144.5	–171.4	–128.0
Balance on Goods, Services, and Income	4	992	. .	*–7.1*	*–70.1*	*–30.2*	*–70.0*	*–100.3*	*–140.0*	*–129.6*	*–149.0*
Current transfers: credit	2	379	Y.	129.2	142.0	169.7	178.6	219.0	190.7	186.0	201.7
Current transfers: debit	3	379	. .	–56.5	–54.8	–73.7	–80.3	–95.3	–92.0	–97.8	–103.8
B. Capital Account [1]	4	994	Y.	**.1**	**.6**	**2.2**	**.1**	**.2**	**.3**	**–.2**	**–.2**
Capital account: credit	2	994	Y.	.3	.7	2.3	.3	.4	.3	.1	.2
Capital account: debit	3	994	. .	–.2	–.1	. . .	–.3	–.1	. . .	–.3	–.4
Total, Groups A Plus B	4	010	. .	*65.8*	*17.8*	*68.1*	*28.4*	*23.6*	*–41.0*	*–41.6*	*–51.3*
C. Financial Account [1]	4	995	X.	**–60.3**	**–10.2**	**–38.4**	**19.3**	**38.6**	**–45.3**	**–33.9**	**–7.1**
Direct investment abroad	4	505	. .	–12.3	–15.6	–7.6	–25.0	–31.0	–29.1	–57.7	–17.4
Direct investment in Swaziland	4	555	Y.	50.6	67.2	36.9	79.3	81.2	60.1	81.2	57.7
Portfolio investment assets	4	602	. .	–.2	–.5	–.5	–.6	–1.0	–.1	–3.9	–1.8
Equity securities	4	610	. .	. . .	. . .	. . .	. . .	–.9	. . .	. . .	–1.6
Debt securities	4	619	. .	–.2	–.5	–.5	–.5	–.1	–.1	–3.9	–.3
Portfolio investment liabilities	4	652	Y.	6.3	7.4	–8.4	.1	4.0	–1.3	.1	–.1
Equity securities	4	660	Y.	6.3	7.4	–8.4	.1	4.0	–1.3	.1	–.1
Debt securities	4	669	Y.	. . .	. . .	. . .	. . .	. . .	. . .	. . .	. . .
Other investment assets	4	703	. .	–110.3	–81.0	–39.0	–41.5	–41.7	–96.4	–38.5	–46.5
Monetary authorities	4	703	. A	. . .	. . .	. . .	. . .	. . .	. . .	. . .	. . .
General government	4	703	. B	–24.6	–35.3	–14.7	.4	–.7	–25.3	–16.1	18.5
Banks	4	703	. C	–52.9	–3.9	4.3	12.8	–15.4	–6.9	5.7	–5.3
Other sectors	4	703	. D	–32.8	–41.9	–28.5	–54.6	–25.6	–64.3	–28.1	–59.7
Other investment liabilities	4	753	X.	5.6	12.4	–19.8	7.1	27.0	21.5	–15.0	1.0
Monetary authorities	4	753	XA	. . .	. . .	. . .	. . .	. . .	. . .	. . .	. . .
General government	4	753	YB	–4.7	–1.9	–20.8	–8.4	–10.7	–10.8	–15.0	–7.7
Banks	4	753	YC	14.1	–1.1	.5	–1.3	12.5	–.3	.7	.4
Other sectors	4	753	YD	–3.8	15.4	.5	16.8	25.2	32.7	–.8	8.3
Total, Groups A Through C	4	020	. .	*5.5*	*7.6*	*29.7*	*47.7*	*62.2*	*–86.3*	*–75.4*	*–58.4*
D. Net Errors and Omissions	4	998	. .	**7.2**	**42.4**	**–19.5**	**–34.2**	**30.5**	**22.4**	**63.5**	**88.8**
Total, Groups A Through D	4	030	. .	*12.7*	*50.0*	*10.2*	*13.4*	*92.7*	*–63.9*	*–11.9*	*30.5*
E. Reserves and Related Items	4	040	. .	**–12.7**	**–50.0**	**–10.2**	**–13.4**	**–92.7**	**63.9**	**11.9**	**–30.5**
Reserve assets	4	800	. .	–10.6	–50.0	–10.7	–13.7	–91.7	63.8	12.5	–29.9
Use of Fund credit and loans	4	766	. .	–4.2	–1.2	–.3	. . .	. . .	. . .	. . .	. . .
Liabilities constituting foreign authorities' reserves	4	900	. .	2.2	1.1	.9	.3	–1.1	.1	–.6	–.6
Exceptional financing	4	920	. .	. . .	. . .	. . .	. . .	. . .	. . .	. . .	. . .
Conversion rates: emalangeni per U.S. dollar	0	101	. .	**2.2735**	**2.6227**	**2.5873**	**2.7613**	**2.8520**	**3.2677**	**3.5508**	**3.6271**

[1] Excludes components that have been classified in the categories of Group E.

Table 2. STANDARD PRESENTATION, 1988–95
(Millions of U.S. dollars)

	Code			1988	1989	1990	1991	1992	1993	1994	1995
CURRENT ACCOUNT	4	993	. .	**65.7**	**17.2**	**65.9**	**28.3**	**23.4**	**–41.3**	**–41.4**	**–51.1**
A. GOODS	4	100	. .	25.1	–24.4	–38.7	–41.2	–128.2	–99.3	–73.3	–100.1
Credit	2	100	. .	**466.6**	**494.1**	**550.3**	**593.8**	**639.0**	**674.3**	**745.4**	**798.3**
General merchandise: exports f.o.b.	2	110	. .	466.2	493.8	549.6	593.6	638.7	674.0	745.2	797.9
Goods for processing: exports f.o.b.	2	150	. .	. . .	. . .	. . .	. . .	. . .	. . .	. . .	. . .
Repairs on goods	2	160	. .	. . .	. . .	. . .	. . .	. . .	. . .	. . .	. . .
Goods procured in ports by carriers	2	170	. .	.4	.3	.7	.2	.2	.3	.3	.4
Nonmonetary gold	2	180	. .	. . .	. . .	. . .	. . .	. . .	. . .	. . .	. . .
Debit	3	100	. .	**–441.5**	**–518.5**	**–588.9**	**–635.0**	**–767.2**	**–773.6**	**–818.7**	**–898.4**
General merchandise: imports f.o.b.	3	110	. .	–441.0	–515.4	–586.5	–632.2	–764.8	–770.9	–815.4	–894.0
Goods for processing: imports f.o.b.	3	150	. .	. . .	. . .	. . .	. . .	. . .	. . .	. . .	. . .
Repairs on goods	3	160	. .	. . .	. . .	. . .	. . .	. . .	. . .	–1.2	–1.3
Goods procured in ports by carriers	3	170	. .	–.5	–3.1	–2.4	–2.7	–2.3	–2.7	–2.1	–3.1
Nonmonetary gold	3	180	. .	. . .	. . .	. . .	. . .	. . .	. . .	. . .	. . .
B. SERVICES	4	200	. .	–58.7	–9.9	–33.2	–65.4	–25.2	–36.1	–22.4	–58.8
Total credit	2	200	. .	*61.0*	*88.4*	*110.1*	*96.3*	*96.5*	*99.6*	*97.6*	*102.2*
Total debit	3	200	. .	*–119.7*	*–98.3*	*–143.3*	*–161.7*	*–121.7*	*–135.8*	*–120.0*	*–161.0*
Transportation services, credit	2	205	. .	**18.4**	**27.2**	**25.3**	**20.4**	**24.7**	**23.1**	**24.5**	**25.7**
Passenger	2	205	BA	*3.7*	*3.8*	*4.8*	*6.1*	*5.8*	*4.9*	*5.7*	*6.5*
Freight	2	205	BB	*14.3*	*23.1*	*19.9*	*14.0*	*18.7*	*18.0*	*18.8*	*19.2*
Other	2	205	BC	*.4*	*.3*	*.7*	*.2*	*.2*	*.3*	. . .	. . .
Sea transport, passenger	2	207	. .	. . .	. . .	. . .	. . .	. . .	. . .	. . .	. . .
Sea transport, freight	2	208	. .	.7	1.7	2.5	3.6	3.9	4.1	. . .	. . .
Sea transport, other	2	209	. .	.4	.3	.7	.2	.2	.3	. . .	. . .
Air transport, passenger	2	211	. .	3.7	3.8	4.8	6.1	5.8	4.9	5.7	6.5
Air transport, freight	2	212	. .	. . .	. . .	. . .	. . .	. . .	. . .	. . .	. . .
Air transport, other	2	213	. .	. . .	. . .	. . .	. . .	. . .	. . .	. . .	. . .
Other transport, passenger	2	215	. .	. . .	. . .	. . .	. . .	. . .	. . .	. . .	. . .
Other transport, freight	2	216	. .	13.6	21.4	17.4	10.4	14.8	13.9	18.8	19.2
Other transport, other	2	217	. .	. . .	. . .	. . .	. . .	. . .	. . .	. . .	. . .
Transportation services, debit	3	205	. .	**–15.3**	**–16.3**	**–11.3**	**–9.0**	**–10.4**	**–13.4**	**–23.0**	**–26.9**
Passenger	3	205	BA	*–4.0*	*–4.2*	*–4.6*	*–4.5*	*–3.1*	*–2.6*	*–2.4*	*–2.4*
Freight	3	205	BB	*–7.2*	*–9.4*	*–5.3*	*–2.5*	*–5.5*	*–8.7*	. . .	. . .
Other	3	205	BC	*–4.0*	*–2.7*	*–1.4*	*–2.0*	*–1.9*	*–2.1*	*–20.6*	*–24.5*
Sea transport, passenger	3	207	. .	. . .	. . .	. . .	. . .	. . .	. . .	. . .	. . .
Sea transport, freight	3	208	. .	–7.2	–9.4	–5.3	–2.5	–5.5	–8.7	. . .	. . .
Sea transport, other	3	209	. .	–4.0	–2.7	–1.4	–2.0	–1.9	–2.1	. . .	. . .
Air transport, passenger	3	211	. .	4.0	–4.2	–4.6	–4.5	–3.1	–2.6	–2.4	–2.4
Air transport, freight	3	212	. .	. . .	. . .	. . .	. . .	. . .	. . .	. . .	. . .
Air transport, other	3	213	. .	. . .	. . .	. . .	. . .	. . .	. . .	–20.6	–24.5
Other transport, passenger	3	215	. .	. . .	. . .	. . .	. . .	. . .	. . .	. . .	. . .
Other transport, freight	3	216	. .	. . .	. . .	. . .	. . .	. . .	. . .	. . .	. . .
Other transport, other	3	217	. .	. . .	. . .	. . .	. . .	. . .	. . .	. . .	. . .
Travel, credit	2	236	. .	**22.2**	**24.9**	**27.2**	**26.3**	**31.0**	**29.6**	**30.0**	**35.4**
Business travel	2	237	. .	22.2	24.9	27.2	26.3	31.0	29.6	30.0	35.4
Personal travel	2	240	. .	. . .	. . .	. . .	. . .	. . .	. . .	. . .	. . .
Travel, debit	3	236	. .	**–18.4**	**–10.0**	**–14.0**	**–20.0**	**–17.5**	**–27.1**	**–35.4**	**–37.1**
Business travel	3	237	. .	. . .	. . .	. . .	. . .	. . .	. . .	–11.3	–11.8
Personal travel	3	240	. .	–18.4	–10.0	–14.0	–20.0	–17.5	–27.1	–24.1	–25.3
Other services, credit	2	200	BA	**20.5**	**36.3**	**57.6**	**49.6**	**40.7**	**46.9**	**43.2**	**41.2**
Communications	2	245	. .	. . .	. . .	. . .	. . .	. . .	. . .	. . .	. . .
Construction	2	249	. .	. . .	. . .	. . .	. . .	. . .	. . .	. . .	. . .
Insurance	2	253	. .	. . .	. . .	. . .	. . .	. . .	. . .	. . .	. . .
Financial	2	260	. .	. . .	. . .	. . .	. . .	. . .	. . .	. . .	. . .
Computer and information	2	262	. .	. . .	. . .	. . .	. . .	. . .	. . .	. . .	. . .
Royalties and licence fees	2	266	. .	.1	. . .	. . .	.1	.2	.3	.3	.1
Other business services	2	268	. .	15.7	31.7	51.8	43.6	36.6	40.0	39.7	38.8
Personal, cultural, and recreational	2	287	. .	. . .	. . .	. . .	. . .	. . .	. . .	. . .	. . .
Government, n.i.e.	2	291	. .	4.7	4.6	5.8	5.9	4.0	6.6	3.2	2.2
Other services, debit	3	200	BA	**–86.0**	**–72.0**	**–118.0**	**–132.7**	**–93.8**	**–95.2**	**–61.6**	**–97.0**
Communications	3	245	. .	–7.2	–3.1	–6.1	–.3	–2.2	–2.8	. . .	. . .
Construction	3	249	. .	. . .	. . .	. . .	. . .	. . .	. . .	–1.1	–1.2
Insurance	3	253	. .	–12.2	–11.3	–20.6	–24.4	–13.4	–14.1	–1.2	–1.4
Financial	3	260	. .	. . .	. . .	. . .	. . .	. . .	. . .	. . .	. . .
Computer and information	3	262	. .	. . .	. . .	. . .	. . .	. . .	. . .	–.1	–.1
Royalties and licence fees	3	266	. .	–6.1	–6.7	–9.3	–10.0	–11.9	–11.5	–12.7	–14.5
Other business services	3	268	. .	–29.1	–21.2	–41.2	–57.9	–28.4	–28.6	–34.8	–76.4
Personal, cultural, and recreational	3	287	. .	. . .	. . .	. . .	. . .	. . .	. . .	. . .	. . .
Government, n.i.e.	3	291	. .	–31.4	–29.6	–40.9	–40.1	–37.8	–38.2	–11.8	–3.4

Table 2 (Continued). STANDARD PRESENTATION, 1988–95
(Millions of U.S. dollars)

	Code	1988	1989	1990	1991	1992	1993	1994	1995
C. INCOME	4 300 . .	26.5	–35.8	41.7	36.6	53.1	–4.6	–34.0	9.9
Total credit	2 300 . .	*123.5*	*125.1*	*165.1*	*170.5*	*184.8*	*140.0*	*137.4*	*137.9*
Total debit	3 300 . .	*–97.0*	*–160.9*	*–123.4*	*–134.0*	*–131.7*	*–144.5*	*–171.4*	*–128.0*
Compensation of employees, credit	2 310 . .	**94.5**	**88.1**	**110.5**	**108.3**	**110.3**	**82.4**	**76.9**	**82.2**
Compensation of employees, debit	3 310 . .	**–19.8**	**–17.6**	**–21.2**	**–20.8**	**–21.2**	**–15.7**	**. . .**	**. . .**
Investment income, credit	2 320 . .	**28.9**	**37.0**	**54.6**	**62.2**	**74.5**	**57.6**	**60.5**	**55.7**
Direct investment income	2 330 . .	8.4	4.5	8.7	13.0	34.9	23.3	9.0	9.3
Dividends and distributed branch profits	2 332 . .	3.8	2.9	4.3	3.8	4.8	4.2	2.6	2.6
Reinvested earnings and undistributed branch profits	2 333 . .	4.6	1.6	4.4	9.3	30.1	19.1	6.4	6.6
Income on debt (interest)	2 334 . .	. . .	. . .	. . .	. . .	. . .	. . .	. . .	. . .
Portfolio investment income	2 339 . .	. . .	. . .	. . .	. . .	. . .	. . .	. . .	. . .
Income on equity	2 340 . .	. . .	. . .	. . .	. . .	. . .	. . .	. . .	. . .
Income on bonds and notes	2 350 . .	. . .	. . .	. . .	. . .	. . .	. . .	. . .	. . .
Income on money market instruments and financial derivatives	2 360 . .	. . .	. . .	. . .	. . .	. . .	. . .	. . .	. . .
Other investment income	2 370 . .	20.5	32.5	45.9	49.2	39.6	34.3	51.4	46.4
Investment income, debit	3 320 . .	**–77.2**	**–143.3**	**–102.3**	**–113.2**	**–110.4**	**–128.8**	**–171.4**	**–128.0**
Direct investment income	3 330 . .	–57.5	–122.1	–85.0	–94.8	–95.8	–114.1	–155.6	–113.8
Dividends and distributed branch profits	3 332 . .	–50.4	–72.1	–52.1	–61.1	–67.5	–72.4	–78.2	–60.7
Reinvested earnings and undistributed branch profits	3 333 . .	–7.2	–50.0	–32.9	–33.7	–28.2	–41.7	–77.3	–53.0
Income on debt (interest)	3 334 . .	. . .	. . .	. . .	. . .	. . .	. . .	. . .	. . .
Portfolio investment income	3 339 . .	. . .	. . .	. . .	. . .	. . .	. . .	. . .	. . .
Income on equity	3 340 . .	. . .	. . .	. . .	. . .	. . .	. . .	. . .	. . .
Income on bonds and notes	3 350 . .	. . .	. . .	. . .	. . .	. . .	. . .	. . .	. . .
Income on money market instruments and financial derivatives	3 360 . .	. . .	. . .	. . .	. . .	. . .	. . .	. . .	. . .
Other investment income	3 370 . .	–19.7	–21.2	–17.3	–18.3	–14.7	–14.7	–15.8	–14.2
D. CURRENT TRANSFERS	4 379 . .	72.8	87.2	96.0	98.3	123.7	98.7	88.2	97.9
Credit	2 379 . .	**129.2**	**142.0**	**169.7**	**178.6**	**219.0**	**190.7**	**186.0**	**201.7**
General government	2 380 . .	120.3	135.3	163.0	173.8	210.1	183.4	179.5	196.2
Other sectors	2 390 . .	9.0	6.7	6.7	4.8	8.9	7.3	6.5	5.4
Workers' remittances	2 391 . .	. . .	. . .	. . .	. . .	. . .	. . .	. . .	. . .
Other current transfers	2 392 . .	9.0	6.7	6.7	4.8	8.9	7.3	6.5	5.4
Debit	3 379 . .	**–56.5**	**–54.8**	**–73.7**	**–80.3**	**–95.3**	**–92.0**	**–97.8**	**–103.8**
General government	3 380 . .	–51.6	–49.8	–63.3	–74.1	–86.7	–84.7	–90.8	–100.1
Other sectors	3 390 . .	–4.8	–4.9	–10.4	–6.2	–8.7	–7.3	–7.0	–3.7
Workers' remittances	3 391 . .	–4.4	–4.3	–4.1	–5.1	–7.6	–6.6	–5.9	–3.4
Other current transfers	3 392 . .	–.4	–.6	–6.3	–1.1	–1.1	–.6	–1.1	–.2
CAPITAL AND FINANCIAL ACCOUNT	4 996 . .	**–72.9**	**–59.6**	**–46.3**	**5.9**	**–53.9**	**18.9**	**–22.1**	**–37.8**
CAPITAL ACCOUNT	4 994 . .	**.1**	**.6**	**2.2**	**.1**	**.2**	**.3**	**–.2**	**–.2**
Total credit	2 994 . .	*.3*	*.7*	*2.3*	*.3*	*.4*	*.3*	*.1*	*.2*
Total debit	3 994 . .	*–.2*	*–.1*	. . .	*–.3*	*–.1*	. . .	*–.3*	*–.4*
Capital transfers, credit	2 400 . .	**.3**	**.7**	**2.3**	**.3**	**.4**	**.3**	**.1**	**.2**
General government	2 401 . .	. . .	. . .	. . .	. . .	. . .	. . .	. . .	. . .
Debt forgiveness	2 402 . .	. . .	. . .	. . .	. . .	. . .	. . .	. . .	. . .
Other capital transfers	2 410 . .	. . .	. . .	. . .	. . .	. . .	. . .	. . .	. . .
Other sectors	2 430 . .	.3	.7	2.3	.3	.4	.3	.1	.2
Migrants' transfers	2 431 . .	.3	.7	2.3	.3	.4	.3	.1	.2
Debt forgiveness	2 432 . .	. . .	. . .	. . .	. . .	. . .	. . .	. . .	. . .
Other capital transfers	2 440 . .	. . .	. . .	. . .	. . .	. . .	. . .	. . .	. . .
Capital transfers, debit	3 400 . .	**–.2**	**–.1**	**. . .**	**–.3**	**–.1**	**. . .**	**–.3**	**–.4**
General government	3 401 . .	. . .	. . .	. . .	. . .	. . .	. . .	–.3	–.2
Debt forgiveness	3 402 . .	. . .	. . .	. . .	. . .	. . .	. . .	. . .	. . .
Other capital transfers	3 410 . .	. . .	. . .	. . .	. . .	. . .	. . .	–.3	–.2
Other sectors	3 430 . .	–.2	–.1	. . .	–.3	–.1	. . .	. . .	–.1
Migrants' transfers	3 431 . .	–.2	–.1	. . .	–.3	–.1	. . .	. . .	–.1
Debt forgiveness	3 432 . .	. . .	. . .	. . .	. . .	. . .	. . .	. . .	. . .
Other capital transfers	3 440 . .	. . .	. . .	. . .	. . .	. . .	. . .	. . .	. . .
Nonproduced nonfinancial assets, credit	2 480 . .	**. . .**	**. . .**	**. . .**	**. . .**	**. . .**	**. . .**	**. . .**	**. . .**
Nonproduced nonfinancial assets, debit	3 480 . .	**. . .**	**. . .**	**. . .**	**. . .**	**. . .**	**. . .**	**. . .**	**. . .**

Table 2 (Continued). STANDARD PRESENTATION, 1988–95
(Millions of U.S. dollars)

	Code	1988	1989	1990	1991	1992	1993	1994	1995
FINANCIAL ACCOUNT	4 995 ..	**-73.0**	**-60.2**	**-48.6**	**5.9**	**-54.1**	**18.6**	**-22.0**	**-37.6**
A. DIRECT INVESTMENT	4 500 ..	38.3	51.6	29.3	54.2	50.2	31.0	23.5	40.3
Direct investment abroad	4 505 ..	**-12.3**	**-15.6**	**-7.6**	**-25.0**	**-31.0**	**-29.1**	**-57.7**	**-17.4**
Equity capital	4 510 ..	-2.4	-2.8	...	-.2	.7	...	-.9	...
Claims on affiliated enterprises	4 515 ..	-2.4	-2.8	...	-.2	.7	...	-.9	...
Liabilities to affiliated enterprises	4 520 ..	...	...	...	...	...	...	...	...
Reinvested earnings	4 525 ..	-4.6	-1.6	-4.4	-9.3	-30.1	-19.1	-6.4	-6.6
Other capital	4 530 ..	-5.2	-11.2	-3.2	-15.5	-1.6	-10.0	-50.4	-10.7
Claims on affiliated enterprises	4 535 ..	-5.2	-11.2	-3.2	-15.5	-1.6	-10.0	-50.4	-10.7
Liabilities to affiliated enterprises	4 540 ..	...	...	...	...	...	...	...	...
Direct investment in Swaziland	4 555 ..	**50.6**	**67.2**	**36.9**	**79.3**	**81.2**	**60.1**	**81.2**	**57.7**
Equity capital	4 560 ..	9.9	14.0	7.0	14.4	3.5	9.8	5.6	.6
Claims on direct investors	4 565 ..	...	...	...	...	...	...	...	...
Liabilities to direct investors	4 570 ..	9.9	14.0	7.0	14.4	3.5	9.8	5.6	.6
Reinvested earnings	4 575 ..	7.2	50.0	32.9	33.7	28.2	41.7	77.3	53.0
Other capital	4 580 ..	33.6	3.2	-3.0	31.1	49.5	8.6	-1.7	4.0
Claims on direct investors	4 585 ..	...	...	...	...	...	...	...	...
Liabilities to direct investors	4 590 ..	33.6	3.2	-3.0	31.1	49.5	8.6	-1.7	4.0
B. PORTFOLIO INVESTMENT	4 600 ..	6.1	6.9	-8.9	-.5	3.1	-1.3	-3.8	-1.9
Assets	4 602 ..	**-.2**	**-.5**	**-.5**	**-.6**	**-1.0**	**-.1**	**-3.9**	**-1.8**
Equity securities	4 610 ..	...	...	...	...	-.9	...	...	-1.6
Monetary authorities	4 611 ..	...	...	...	...	...	...	...	...
General government	4 612 ..	...	...	...	...	...	...	...	...
Banks	4 613 ..	...	...	...	...	...	...	...	...
Other sectors	4 614 ..	...	...	...	...	-.9	...	...	-1.6
Debt securities	4 619 ..	-.2	-.5	-.5	-.5	-.1	-.1	-3.9	-.3
Bonds and notes	4 620 ..	...	-.2	...	...	.1	...	...	...
Monetary authorities	4 621 ..	...	...	...	...	...	...	...	...
General government	4 622 ..	...	...	...	...	...	...	...	...
Banks	4 623 ..	...	...	...	...	...	...	...	...
Other sectors	4 624 ..	...	-.2	...	...	.1	...	...	...
Money market instruments	4 630 ..	-.2	-.4	-.5	-.5	-.2	-.1	-3.9	-.3
Monetary authorities	4 631 ..	...	...	...	...	...	...	...	...
General government	4 632 ..	...	...	...	...	...	...	...	...
Banks	4 633 ..	...	...	...	...	...	...	...	...
Other sectors	4 634 ..	-.2	-.4	-.5	-.5	-.2	-.1	-3.9	-.3
Financial derivatives	4 640 ..	...	...	...	...	...	...	...	...
Monetary authorities	4 641 ..	...	...	...	...	...	...	...	...
General government	4 642 ..	...	...	...	...	...	...	...	...
Banks	4 643 ..	...	...	...	...	...	...	...	...
Other sectors	4 644 ..	...	...	...	...	...	...	...	...
Liabilities	4 652 ..	**6.3**	**7.4**	**-8.4**	**.1**	**4.0**	**-1.3**	**.1**	**-.1**
Equity securities	4 660 ..	6.3	7.4	-8.4	.1	4.0	-1.3	.1	-.1
Banks	4 663 ..	...	...	...	...	...	...	...	...
Other sectors	4 664 ..	6.3	7.4	-8.4	.1	4.0	-1.3	.1	-.1
Debt securities	4 669 ..	...	...	...	...	...	...	...	...
Bonds and notes	4 670 ..	...	...	...	...	...	...	...	...
Monetary authorities	4 671 ..	...	...	...	...	...	...	...	...
General government	4 672 ..	...	...	...	...	...	...	...	...
Banks	4 673 ..	...	...	...	...	...	...	...	...
Other sectors	4 674 ..	...	...	...	...	...	...	...	...
Money market instruments	4 680 ..	...	...	...	...	...	...	...	...
Monetary authorities	4 681 ..	...	...	...	...	...	...	...	...
General government	4 682 ..	...	...	...	...	...	...	...	...
Banks	4 683 ..	...	...	...	...	...	...	...	...
Other sectors	4 684 ..	...	...	...	...	...	...	...	...
Financial derivatives	4 690 ..	...	...	...	...	...	...	...	...
Monetary authorities	4 691 ..	...	...	...	...	...	...	...	...
General government	4 692 ..	...	...	...	...	...	...	...	...
Banks	4 693 ..	...	...	...	...	...	...	...	...
Other sectors	4 694 ..	...	...	...	...	...	...	...	...

Table 2 (Concluded). STANDARD PRESENTATION, 1988–95
(Millions of U.S. dollars)

	Code		1988	1989	1990	1991	1992	1993	1994	1995
C. OTHER INVESTMENT	4 700	. .	–106.8	–68.6	–58.2	–34.2	–15.7	–74.9	–54.2	–46.1
Assets	4 703	. .	**–110.3**	**–81.0**	**–39.0**	**–41.5**	**–41.7**	**–96.4**	**–38.5**	**–46.5**
Trade credits	4 706	. .	–13.0	–16.9	–12.8	–9.6	–27.3	–17.4	13.9	–13.0
General government: long-term	4 708	. .	. . .	. . .	. . .	. . .	. . .	. . .	. . .	. . .
General government: short-term	4 709	. .	. . .	. . .	. . .	. . .	. . .	. . .	. . .	. . .
Other sectors: long-term	4 711	. .	. . .	. . .	. . .	. . .	. . .	. . .	. . .	. . .
Other sectors: short-term	4 712	. .	–13.0	–16.9	–12.8	–9.6	–27.3	–17.4	13.9	–13.0
Loans	4 714	. .	–1.7	–.2	–1.2	–1.4	–.3	.4	1.2	.2
Monetary authorities: long-term	4 717	. .	. . .	. . .	. . .	. . .	. . .	. . .	. . .	. . .
Monetary authorities: short-term	4 718	. .	. . .	. . .	. . .	. . .	. . .	. . .	. . .	. . .
General government: long-term	4 720	. .	. . .	. . .	. . .	. . .	. . .	. . .	. . .	. . .
General government: short-term	4 721	. .	. . .	. . .	. . .	. . .	. . .	. . .	. . .	. . .
Banks: long-term	4 723	. .	. . .	. . .	. . .	. . .	. . .	. . .	. . .	. . .
Banks: short-term	4 724	. .	. . .	. . .	. . .	. . .	. . .	. . .	. . .	. . .
Other sectors: long-term	4 726	. .	–1.7	–.2	–1.2	–1.4	–.3	.4	1.2	.2
Other sectors: short-term	4 727	. .	. . .	. . .	. . .	. . .	. . .	. . .	. . .	. . .
Currency and deposits	4 730	. .	–70.4	–22.2	–1.2	–7.4	5.4	–20.0	8.2	–18.8
Monetary authorities	4 731	. .	. . .	. . .	. . .	. . .	. . .	. . .	. . .	. . .
General government	4 732	. .	. . .	. . .	. . .	. . .	. . .	. . .	. . .	. . .
Banks	4 733	. .	–52.9	–3.9	4.3	12.8	–15.4	–6.9	5.7	–5.3
Other sectors	4 734	. .	–17.5	–18.3	–5.4	–20.1	20.8	–13.1	2.5	–13.5
Other assets	4 736	. .	–25.2	–41.9	–23.8	–23.1	–19.4	–59.5	–61.7	–14.9
Monetary authorities: long-term	4 738	. .	. . .	. . .	. . .	. . .	. . .	. . .	. . .	. . .
Monetary authorities: short-term	4 739	. .	. . .	. . .	. . .	. . .	. . .	. . .	. . .	. . .
General government: long-term	4 741	. .	–2.6	–3.1	–3.5	–3.5	21.0	–1.4	–2.3	10.8
General government: short-term	4 742	. .	–21.9	–32.2	–11.2	3.9	–21.7	–23.9	–13.9	7.8
Banks: long-term	4 744	. .	. . .	. . .	. . .	. . .	. . .	. . .	. . .	. . .
Banks: short-term	4 745	. .	. . .	. . .	. . .	. . .	. . .	. . .	. . .	. . .
Other sectors: long-term	4 747	. .	–.6	–6.6	–9.1	–23.5	–18.8	–34.2	–45.6	–33.5
Other sectors: short-term	4 748	. .	. . .	. . .	. . .	. . .	. . .	. . .	. . .	. . .
Liabilities	4 753	. .	**3.5**	**12.4**	**–19.3**	**7.4**	**26.0**	**21.6**	**–15.6**	**.4**
Trade credits	4 756	. .	8.9	12.3	5.0	1.3	24.4	29.3	–17.5	–5.5
General government: long-term	4 758	. .	. . .	. . .	. . .	. . .	. . .	. . .	. . .	. . .
General government: short-term	4 759	. .	. . .	. . .	. . .	. . .	. . .	. . .	. . .	. . .
Other sectors: long-term	4 761	. .	. . .	. . .	. . .	. . .	. . .	. . .	. . .	. . .
Other sectors: short-term	4 762	. .	8.9	12.3	5.0	1.3	24.4	29.3	–17.5	–5.5
Loans	4 764	. .	–16.2	7.7	–27.9	1.6	–13.6	–5.0	–5.9	11.4
Use of Fund credit and loans from the Fund	4 766	. .	–4.2	–1.2	–.3	. . .	. . .	. . .	. . .	. . .
Monetary authorities: other long-term	4 767	. .	. . .	. . .	. . .	. . .	. . .	. . .	. . .	. . .
Monetary authorities: short-term	4 768	. .	. . .	. . .	. . .	. . .	. . .	. . .	. . .	. . .
General government: long-term	4 770	. .	–4.7	–1.9	–20.8	–8.4	–10.7	–10.8	–15.0	–7.7
General government: short-term	4 771	. .	. . .	. . .	. . .	. . .	. . .	. . .	. . .	. . .
Banks: long-term	4 773	. .	. . .	. . .	. . .	. . .	. . .	. . .	. . .	. . .
Banks: short-term	4 774	. .	. . .	. . .	. . .	. . .	. . .	. . .	. . .	. . .
Other sectors: long-term	4 776	. .	–7.2	10.8	–6.7	10.0	–2.9	5.9	9.2	19.1
Other sectors: short-term	4 777	. .	. . .	. . .	. . .	. . .	. . .	. . .	. . .	. . .
Currency and deposits	4 780	. .	2.2	1.1	.9	.3	–1.1	.1	–.6	–.6
Monetary authorities	4 781	. .	2.2	1.1	.9	.3	–1.1	.1	–.6	–.6
General government	4 782	. .	. . .	. . .	. . .	. . .	. . .	. . .	. . .	. . .
Banks	4 783	. .	. . .	. . .	. . .	. . .	. . .	. . .	. . .	. . .
Other sectors	4 784	. .	. . .	. . .	. . .	. . .	. . .	. . .	. . .	. . .
Other liabilities	4 786	. .	8.7	–8.8	2.7	4.2	16.3	–2.8	8.4	–5.0
Monetary authorities: long-term	4 788	. .	. . .	. . .	. . .	. . .	. . .	. . .	. . .	. . .
Monetary authorities: short-term	4 789	. .	. . .	. . .	. . .	. . .	. . .	. . .	. . .	. . .
General government: long-term	4 791	. .	. . .	. . .	. . .	. . .	. . .	. . .	. . .	. . .
General government: short-term	4 792	. .	. . .	. . .	. . .	. . .	. . .	. . .	. . .	. . .
Banks: long-term	4 794	. .	. . .	. . .	. . .	. . .	. . .	. . .	. . .	. . .
Banks: short-term	4 795	. .	14.1	–1.1	.5	–1.3	12.5	–.3	.7	.4
Other sectors: long-term	4 797	. .	. . .	. . .	. . .	. . .	. . .	. . .	. . .	. . .
Other sectors: short-term	4 798	. .	–5.5	–7.7	2.2	5.4	3.8	–2.5	7.6	–5.4
D. RESERVE ASSETS	4 800	. .	–10.6	–50.0	–10.7	–13.7	–91.7	63.8	12.5	–29.9
Monetary gold	4 810	. .	. . .	. . .	. . .	. . .	. . .	. . .	. . .	. . .
Special drawing rights	4 820	. .	2.1	.6	–10.5	–.2	3.9	–.1	. . .	. . .
Reserve position in the Fund	4 830	. .	. . .	. . .	. . .	. . .	–4.1	. . .	. . .	. . .
Foreign exchange	4 840	. .	–12.8	–50.5	–.2	–13.5	–91.4	63.9	12.5	–29.9
Other claims	4 880	. .	. . .	. . .	. . .	. . .	. . .	. . .	. . .	. . .
NET ERRORS AND OMISSIONS	4 998	. .	**7.2**	**42.4**	**–19.5**	**–34.2**	**30.5**	**22.4**	**63.5**	**88.8**

Part 3 of the *Yearbook* contains descriptions of the methodologies, compilation practices, and sources used to compile these data.

Table 3. INTERNATIONAL INVESTMENT POSITION (End–period stocks), 1988–95
(Millions of U.S. dollars)

	Code	1988	1989	1990	1991	1992	1993	1994	1995
ASSETS	8 995 C.	331.1	433.2	487.3	546.3	615.3	605.8	678.1	774.6
Direct investment abroad	8 505 . .	**18.7**	**31.0**	**40.4**	**53.5**	**49.0**	**54.7**	**103.9**	**111.6**
Equity capital and reinvested earnings	8 506 . .	7.9	10.3	10.2	9.8	8.1	6.3	6.9	6.7
Claims on affiliated enterprises	8 507 . .	. . .	. . .	. . .	. . .	. . .	. . .	. . .	. . .
Liabilities to affiliated enterprises	8 508 . .	. . .	. . .	. . .	. . .	. . .	. . .	. . .	. . .
Other capital	8 530 . .	10.8	20.7	30.2	43.7	40.9	48.4	97.0	104.9
Claims on affiliated enterprises	8 535 . .	. . .	. . .	. . .	. . .	. . .	. . .	. . .	. . .
Liabilities to affiliated enterprises	8 540 . .	. . .	. . .	. . .	. . .	. . .	. . .	. . .	. . .
Portfolio investment	8 602 . .	**2.0**	**2.5**	**2.9**	**3.4**	**3.9**	**3.6**	**7.3**	**9.0**
Equity securities	8 610 . .	. . .	. . .	. . .	.1	.9	.8	.8	2.3
Monetary authorities	8 611 . .	. . .	. . .	. . .	. . .	. . .	. . .	. . .	. . .
General government	8 612 . .	. . .	. . .	. . .	. . .	. . .	. . .	. . .	. . .
Banks	8 613 . .	. . .	. . .	. . .	. . .	. . .	. . .	. . .	. . .
Other sectors	8 614 . .	. . .	. . .	. . .	. . .	. . .	. . .	. . .	. . .
Debt securities	8 619 . .	2.0	2.5	2.9	3.3	3.0	2.8	6.6	6.7
Bonds and notes	8 620 . .	2.0	2.5	2.9	3.3	3.0	2.8	6.6	6.7
Monetary authorities	8 621 . .	. . .	. . .	. . .	. . .	. . .	. . .	. . .	. . .
General government	8 622 . .	. . .	. . .	. . .	. . .	. . .	. . .	. . .	. . .
Banks	8 623 . .	. . .	. . .	. . .	. . .	. . .	. . .	. . .	. . .
Other sectors	8 624 . .	. . .	. . .	. . .	. . .	. . .	. . .	. . .	. . .
Money market instruments	8 630 . .	. . .	. . .	. . .	. . .	. . .	. . .	. . .	. . .
Monetary authorities	8 631 . .	. . .	. . .	. . .	. . .	. . .	. . .	. . .	. . .
General government	8 632 . .	. . .	. . .	. . .	. . .	. . .	. . .	. . .	. . .
Banks	8 633 . .	. . .	. . .	. . .	. . .	. . .	. . .	. . .	. . .
Other sectors	8 634 . .	. . .	. . .	. . .	. . .	. . .	. . .	. . .	. . .
Financial derivatives	8 640 . .	. . .	. . .	. . .	. . .	. . .	. . .	. . .	. . .
Monetary authorities	8 641 . .	. . .	. . .	. . .	. . .	. . .	. . .	. . .	. . .
General government	8 642 . .	. . .	. . .	. . .	. . .	. . .	. . .	. . .	. . .
Banks	8 643 . .	. . .	. . .	. . .	. . .	. . .	. . .	. . .	. . .
Other sectors	8 644 . .	. . .	. . .	. . .	. . .	. . .	. . .	. . .	. . .
Other investment	8 703 . .	**176.9**	**217.1**	**236.4**	**266.4**	**259.4**	**308.1**	**323.9**	**376.6**
Trade credits	8 706 . .	51.6	65.9	78.0	82.6	99.7	106.3	88.0	98.5
General government: long-term	8 708 . .	. . .	. . .	. . .	. . .	. . .	. . .	. . .	. . .
General government: short-term	8 709 . .	. . .	. . .	. . .	. . .	. . .	. . .	. . .	. . .
Other sectors: long-term	8 711 . .	. . .	. . .	. . .	. . .	. . .	. . .	. . .	. . .
Other sectors: short-term	8 712 . .	51.6	65.9	78.0	82.6	99.7	106.3	88.0	98.5
Loans	8 714 . .	7.7	8.0	2.7	3.7	3.3	3.2	1.9	1.7
Monetary authorities: long-term	8 717 . .	. . .	. . .	. . .	. . .	. . .	. . .	. . .	. . .
Monetary authorities: short-term	8 718 . .	. . .	. . .	. . .	. . .	. . .	. . .	. . .	. . .
General government: long-term	8 720 . .	. . .	. . .	. . .	. . .	. . .	. . .	. . .	. . .
General government: short-term	8 721 . .	. . .	. . .	. . .	. . .	. . .	. . .	. . .	. . .
Banks: long-term	8 723 . .	. . .	. . .	. . .	. . .	. . .	. . .	. . .	. . .
Banks: short-term	8 724 . .	. . .	. . .	. . .	. . .	. . .	. . .	. . .	. . .
Other sectors: long-term	8 726 . .	7.7	8.0	2.7	3.7	3.3	3.2	1.9	1.7
Other sectors: short-term	8 727 . .	. . .	. . .	. . .	. . .	. . .	. . .	. . .	. . .
Currency and deposits	8 730 . .	65.6	65.5	60.5	43.7	53.7	54.8	46.9	50.8
Monetary authorities	8 731 . .	. . .	. . .	. . .	. . .	. . .	. . .	. . .	. . .
General government	8 732 . .	. . .	. . .	. . .	. . .	. . .	. . .	. . .	. . .
Banks	8 733 . .	65.6	65.5	60.5	43.7	53.7	54.8	46.9	50.8
Other sectors	8 734 . .	. . .	. . .	. . .	. . .	. . .	. . .	. . .	. . .
Other assets	8 736 . .	52.1	77.7	95.1	136.4	102.7	143.8	187.1	225.6
Monetary authorities: long-term	8 738 . .	. . .	. . .	. . .	. . .	. . .	. . .	. . .	. . .
Monetary authorities: short-term	8 739 . .	. . .	. . .	. . .	. . .	. . .	. . .	. . .	. . .
General government: long-term	8 741 . .	11.7	14.2	17.5	20.0	. . .	1.9	3.0	. . .
General government: short-term	8 742 . .	. . .	. . .	. . .	. . .	. . .	. . .	. . .	. . .
Banks: long-term	8 744 . .	. . .	. . .	. . .	. . .	. . .	. . .	. . .	. . .
Banks: short-term	8 745 . .	. . .	. . .	. . .	. . .	. . .	. . .	. . .	. . .
Other sectors: long-term	8 747 . .	25.5	30.8	39.6	60.7	72.1	97.6	139.3	168.6
Other sectors: short-term	8 748 . .	14.8	32.8	37.9	55.7	30.6	44.2	44.9	57.0
Reserve assets	8 800 . .	**133.6**	**182.6**	**207.6**	**223.1**	**303.0**	**239.3**	**243.0**	**277.4**
Monetary gold	8 810 . .	.1	.1	.1	.1	.1	.1	.1	.1
Special drawing rights	8 820 . .	1.7	1.1	12.1	12.4	8.0	8.1	8.6	8.8
Reserve position in the Fund	8 830 . .	. . .	. . .	. . .	. . .	4.1	4.1	4.4	4.5
Foreign exchange	8 840 . .	131.8	181.4	195.4	210.6	290.8	227.0	229.9	264.1
Other claims	8 880 . .	. . .	. . .	. . .	. . .	. . .	. . .	. . .	. . .

Table 3 (Continued). INTERNATIONAL INVESTMENT POSITION (End–period stocks), 1988–95
(Millions of U.S. dollars)

	Code		1988	1989	1990	1991	1992	1993	1994	1995
LIABILITIES	8 995	D.	584.1	650.7	682.8	735.5	775.2	807.2	850.8	900.2
Direct investment in Swaziland	8 555	. .	**238.6**	**295.3**	**331.4**	**389.7**	**424.0**	**434.2**	**497.6**	**535.3**
Equity capital and reinvested earnings	8 556	. .	167.0	224.5	264.3	295.8	293.4	306.3	376.8	419.4
Claims on direct investors	8 557	. .	...	...	...	...	...	...	...	...
Liabilities to direct investors	8 558	. .	...	...	...	...	...	...	...	...
Other capital	8 580	. .	71.7	70.8	67.0	93.9	130.6	127.9	120.9	115.9
Claims on direct investors	8 585	. .	...	...	...	...	...	...	...	...
Liabilities to direct investors	8 590	. .	...	...	...	...	...	...	...	...
Portfolio investment	8 652	. .	**15.7**	**22.3**	**9.4**	**8.8**	**11.7**	**9.0**	**8.7**	**8.5**
Equity securities	8 660	. .	15.7	22.3	9.4	8.8	11.7	9.0	8.7	8.5
Banks	8 663	. .	...	...	...	...	...	...	...	...
Other sectors	8 664	. .	...	...	...	...	...	...	...	...
Debt securities	8 669	. .	...	...	...	...	...	...	...	...
Bonds and notes	8 670	. .	...	...	...	...	...	...	...	...
Monetary authorities	8 671	. .	...	...	...	...	...	...	...	...
General government	8 672	. .	...	...	...	...	...	...	...	...
Banks	8 673	. .	...	...	...	...	...	...	...	...
Other sectors	8 674	. .	...	...	...	...	...	...	...	...
Money market instruments	8 680	. .	...	...	...	...	...	...	...	...
Monetary authorities	8 681	. .	...	...	...	...	...	...	...	...
General government	8 682	. .	...	...	...	...	...	...	...	...
Banks	8 683	. .	...	...	...	...	...	...	...	...
Other sectors	8 684	. .	...	...	...	...	...	...	...	...
Financial derivatives	8 690	. .	...	...	...	...	...	...	...	...
Monetary authorities	8 691	. .	...	...	...	...	...	...	...	...
General government	8 692	. .	...	...	...	...	...	...	...	...
Banks	8 692	. .	...	...	...	...	...	...	...	...
Other sectors	8 694	. .	...	...	...	...	...	...	...	...
Other investment	8 753	. .	**329.8**	**333.0**	**342.0**	**337.0**	**339.5**	**364.0**	**344.4**	**356.5**
Trade credits	8 756	. .	22.2	33.3	38.2	37.0	56.1	78.7	57.9	50.8
General government: long-term	8 758	. .	...	...	...	...	...	...	...	...
General government: short-term	8 759	. .	...	...	...	...	...	...	...	...
Other sectors: long-term	8 761	. .	...	...	...	...	...	...	...	...
Other sectors: short-term	8 762	. .	22.2	33.3	38.2	37.0	56.1	78.7	57.9	50.8
Loans	8 764	. .	253.8	253.2	255.5	252.8	228.0	239.5	229.1	255.7
Use of Fund credit and loans from the Fund	8 766	. .	1.6	.3	...	...	...	...	...	...
Monetary authorities: other long-term	8 767	. .	...	...	...	...	...	...	...	...
Monetary authorities: short-term	8 768	. .	...	...	...	...	...	...	...	...
General government: long-term	8 770	. .	227.9	225.1	227.4	214.0	194.7	202.5	190.3	203.8
General government: short-term	8 771	. .	...	...	...	...	...	...	...	...
Banks: long-term	8 773	. .	...	...	...	...	...	...	...	...
Banks: short-term	8 774	. .	...	...	...	...	...	...	...	...
Other sectors: long-term	8 776	. .	24.4	27.8	28.1	38.9	33.3	36.9	38.7	51.9
Other sectors: short-term	8 777	. .	...	...	...	...	...	...	...	...
Currency and deposits	8 780	. .	...	...	...	...	...	...	...	...
Monetary authorities	8 781	. .	...	...	...	...	...	...	...	...
General government	8 782	. .	...	...	...	...	...	...	...	...
Banks	8 783	. .	...	...	...	...	...	...	...	...
Other sectors	8 784	. .	...	...	...	...	...	...	...	...
Other liabilities	8 786	. .	53.9	46.5	48.3	47.1	55.4	45.8	57.4	50.0
Monetary authorities: long-term	8 788	. .	...	...	...	...	...	...	...	...
Monetary authorities: short-term	8 789	. .	4.0	2.6	2.7	2.8	1.5	1.5	.8	.6
General government: long-term	8 791	. .	...	...	...	...	...	...	...	...
General government: short-term	8 792	. .	...	...	...	...	...	...	...	...
Banks: long-term	8 794	. .	...	...	...	...	...	...	...	...
Banks: short-term	8 795	. .	18.9	16.6	16.9	14.5	24.7	21.9	21.7	21.5
Other sectors: long-term	8 797	. .	8.9	14.5	13.7	10.4	8.2	6.0	11.5	10.4
Other sectors: short-term	8 798	. .	22.1	12.8	14.9	19.4	21.0	16.4	23.4	17.4
NET INTERNATIONAL INVESTMENT POSITION	8 995	. .	**–253.0**	**–217.5**	**–195.5**	**–189.1**	**–159.9**	**–201.5**	**–172.7**	**–125.7**
Conversion rates: emalangeni per U.S. dollar (end of period)	0 102	. .	**2.3777**	**2.5360**	**2.5625**	**2.7430**	**3.0531**	**3.3975**	**3.5435**	**3.6475**

Table 1. ANALYTIC PRESENTATION, 1988–95
(Millions of U.S. dollars)

	Code	1988	1989	1990	1991	1992	1993	1994	1995
A. Current Account [1]	4 993 Y .	**–534**	**–3,101**	**–6,338**	**–4,652**	**–8,829**	**–4,161**	**807**	**4,633**
Goods: exports f.o.b	2 100 . .	49,367	51,071	56,835	54,542	55,363	49,348	60,197	79,183
Goods: imports f.o.b	3 100 . .	–44,487	–47,054	–53,433	–48,185	–48,642	–41,801	–50,636	–63,210
Balance on Goods	4 100 . .	*4,880*	*4,017*	*3,402*	*6,357*	*6,720*	*7,548*	*9,561*	*15,973*
Services: credit	2 200 . .	10,420	11,355	13,724	14,725	16,194	12,587	13,669	15,444
Services: debit	3 200 . .	–12,662	–14,389	–17,056	–17,352	–19,090	–13,354	–14,675	–17,206
Balance on Goods and Services	4 991 . .	*2,637*	*983*	*71*	*3,731*	*3,824*	*6,781*	*8,556*	*14,211*
Income: credit	2 300 . .	5,277	6,968	9,691	9,435	8,142	7,127	9,609	14,437
Income: debit	3 300 . .	–7,070	–9,302	–14,164	–15,833	–18,181	–16,261	–15,479	–21,023
Balance on Goods, Services, and Income	4 992 . .	*844*	*–1,350*	*–4,402*	*–2,668*	*–6,215*	*–2,353*	*2,686*	*7,624*
Current transfers: credit	2 379 Y .	382	298	386	393	405	456	545	1,544
Current transfers: debit	3 379 . .	–1,760	–2,049	–2,321	–2,378	–3,019	–2,263	–2,424	–4,535
B. Capital Account [1]	4 994 Y .	**–234**	**–296**	**–353**	**–63**	**6**	**23**	**23**	**15**
Capital account: credit	2 994 Y .	29	38	38	38	37	37	37	33
Capital account: debit	3 994 . .	–263	–334	–391	–101	–31	–15	–14	–17
Total, Groups A Plus B	4 010 . .	*–768*	*–3,397*	*–6,691*	*–4,715*	*–8,823*	*–4,138*	*830*	*4,648*
C. Financial Account [1]	4 995 X .	**2,897**	**9,837**	**19,278**	**–1,336**	**10,214**	**11,518**	**6,438**	**–2,752**
Direct investment abroad	4 505 . .	–7,471	–10,296	–14,629	–7,262	–419	–1,471	–6,596	–10,733
Direct investment in Sweden	4 555 Y .	1,673	1,812	1,982	6,351	–5	3,705	6,241	14,273
Portfolio investment assets	4 602 . .	–686	–4,475	–3,644	–2,313	–1,578	–94	–1,933	–8,881
Equity securities	4 610 . .	–509	–4,324	–3,271	–2,350	–505	–76	–1,983	–7,495
Debt securities	4 619 . .	–177	–150	–373	37	–1,073	–18	50	–1,386
Portfolio investment liabilities	4 652 Y .	–673	3,227	6,112	8,859	2,563	1,472	719	8,136
Equity securities	4 660 Y .	–446	–290	192	1,817	2,257	4,212	6,794	1,789
Debt securities	4 669 Y .	–227	3,517	5,920	7,042	306	–2,741	–6,075	6,347
Other investment assets	4 703 . .	–2,133	–5,074	–9,618	–946	1,633	1,159	–3,507	–11,775
Monetary authorities	4 703 . A	. . .	. . .	. . .	. . .	. . .	. . .	. . .	. . .
General government	4 703 . B	–160	–384	–559	–350	–337	–144	–292	–478
Banks	4 703 . C	–479	–2,010	–6,597	342	1,083	4,682	2,900	–7,931
Other sectors	4 703 . D	–1,494	–2,681	–2,462	–938	887	–3,379	–6,114	–3,366
Other investment liabilities	4 753 X .	12,187	24,643	39,074	–6,025	8,020	6,748	11,514	6,228
Monetary authorities	4 753 XA	. . .	. . .	. . .	. . .	. . .	. . .	. . .	. . .
General government	4 753 YB	–1,924	–1,933	–2,216	–2,780	28,567	11,723	5,091	8,849
Banks	4 753 YC	8,171	16,626	27,867	–8,276	–26,461	–10,851	–1,957	–1,074
Other sectors	4 753 YD	5,940	9,950	13,423	5,031	5,914	5,876	8,381	–1,546
Total, Groups A Through C	4 020 . .	*2,129*	*6,439*	*12,586*	*–6,052*	*1,391*	*7,380*	*7,268*	*1,896*
D. Net Errors and Omissions	4 998 . .	**–1,190**	**–5,185**	**–5,035**	**5,988**	**5,561**	**–4,851**	**–4,937**	**–3,061**
Total, Groups A Through D	4 030 . .	*938*	*1,254*	*7,552*	*–63*	*6,953*	*2,530*	*2,331*	*–1,165*
E. Reserves and Related Items	4 040 . .	**–938**	**–1,254**	**–7,552**	**63**	**–6,953**	**–2,530**	**–2,331**	**1,165**
Reserve assets	4 800 . .	–938	–1,254	–7,552	63	–6,953	–2,530	–2,331	1,165
Use of Fund credit and loans	4 766 . .	. . .	. . .	. . .	. . .	. . .	. . .	. . .	. . .
Liabilities constituting foreign authorities' reserves	4 900 . .	. . .	. . .	. . .	. . .	. . .	. . .	. . .	. . .
Exceptional financing	4 920 . .	. . .	. . .	. . .	. . .	. . .	. . .	. . .	. . .
Conversion rates: kronor per U.S. dollar	0 101 . .	**6.1272**	**6.4469**	**5.9188**	**6.0475**	**5.8238**	**7.7834**	**7.7160**	**7.1333**

[1] Excludes components that have been classified in the categories of Group E.

Table 2. STANDARD PRESENTATION, 1988–95
(Millions of U.S. dollars)

	Code	1988	1989	1990	1991	1992	1993	1994	1995
CURRENT ACCOUNT	4 993 . .	**–534**	**–3,101**	**–6,338**	**–4,652**	**–8,829**	**–4,161**	**807**	**4,633**
A. GOODS	4 100 . .	4,880	4,017	3,402	6,357	6,720	7,548	9,561	15,973
Credit	2 100 . .	**49,367**	**51,071**	**56,835**	**54,542**	**55,363**	**49,348**	**60,197**	**79,183**
General merchandise: exports f.o.b.	2 110 . .	49,256	50,974	56,728	54,361	55,282	49,111	60,079	79,183
Goods for processing: exports f.o.b.	2 150 . .	...	...	...	...	...	...	...	...
Repairs on goods	2 160 . .	...	...	...	...	...	...	...	...
Goods procured in ports by carriers	2 170 . .	...	...	...	...	...	...	...	...
Nonmonetary gold	2 180 . .	112	96	107	182	81	238	118	...
Debit	3 100 . .	**–44,487**	**–47,054**	**–53,433**	**–48,185**	**–48,642**	**–41,801**	**–50,636**	**–63,210**
General merchandise: imports f.o.b.	3 110 . .	–44,460	–47,029	–53,402	–48,140	–48,622	–41,783	–50,617	–63,210
Goods for processing: imports f.o.b.	3 150 . .	...	...	...	...	...	...	...	...
Repairs on goods	3 160 . .	...	...	...	...	...	...	...	...
Goods procured in ports by carriers	3 170 . .	...	...	...	...	...	...	...	...
Nonmonetary gold	3 180 . .	–28	–25	–30	–46	–20	–18	–19	...
B. SERVICES	4 200 . .	–2,242	–3,034	–3,331	–2,627	–2,896	–767	–1,005	–1,762
Total credit	2 200 . .	*10,420*	*11,355*	*13,724*	*14,725*	*16,194*	*12,587*	*13,669*	*15,444*
Total debit	3 200 . .	*–12,662*	*–14,389*	*–17,056*	*–17,352*	*–19,090*	*–13,354*	*–14,675*	*–17,206*
Transportation services, credit	2 205 . .	**3,698**	**3,862**	**4,812**	**4,781**	**5,108**	**4,289**	**4,391**	**4,984**
Passenger	2 205 BA	*847*	*872*	*985*	*990*	*1,110*	*793*	*821*	*980*
Freight	2 205 BB	*2,031*	*2,144*	*2,898*	*2,606*	*2,598*	*2,325*	*2,457*	*2,840*
Other	2 205 BC	*820*	*846*	*929*	*1,185*	*1,399*	*1,172*	*1,113*	*1,165*
Sea transport, passenger	2 207 . .	...	...	...	...	...	...	...	...
Sea transport, freight	2 208 . .	...	...	...	...	...	...	...	...
Sea transport, other	2 209 . .	...	...	...	...	...	...	...	...
Air transport, passenger	2 211 . .	...	...	...	...	...	...	...	...
Air transport, freight	2 212 . .	...	...	...	...	...	...	...	...
Air transport, other	2 213 . .	...	...	...	...	...	...	...	...
Other transport, passenger	2 215 . .	...	...	...	...	...	...	...	...
Other transport, freight	2 216 . .	...	...	...	...	...	...	...	...
Other transport, other	2 217 . .	...	...	...	...	...	...	...	...
Transportation services, debit	3 205 . .	**–3,020**	**–3,778**	**–3,932**	**–4,113**	**–4,408**	**–3,796**	**–4,039**	**–4,859**
Passenger	3 205 BA	*–731*	*–774*	*–968*	*–950*	*–1,027*	*–802*	*–1,069*	*–1,374*
Freight	3 205 BB	*–715*	*–1,273*	*–709*	*–914*	*–680*	*–648*	*–726*	*–928*
Other	3 205 BC	*–1,574*	*–1,730*	*–2,256*	*–2,249*	*–2,702*	*–2,346*	*–2,244*	*–2,557*
Sea transport, passenger	3 207 . .	...	...	...	...	...	...	...	...
Sea transport, freight	3 208 . .	...	...	...	...	...	...	...	...
Sea transport, other	3 209 . .	...	...	...	...	...	...	...	...
Air transport, passenger	3 211 . .	...	...	...	...	...	...	...	...
Air transport, freight	3 212 . .	...	...	...	...	...	...	...	...
Air transport, other	3 213 . .	...	...	...	...	...	...	...	...
Other transport, passenger	3 215 . .	...	...	...	...	...	...	...	...
Other transport, freight	3 216 . .	...	...	...	...	...	...	...	...
Other transport, other	3 217 . .	...	...	...	...	...	...	...	...
Travel, credit	2 236 . .	**2,334**	**2,536**	**2,915**	**2,685**	**3,087**	**2,652**	**2,822**	**3,452**
Business travel	2 237 . .	...	...	...	...	...	...	...	...
Personal travel	2 240 . .	...	...	...	...	...	...	...	...
Travel, debit	3 236 . .	**–4,635**	**–5,065**	**–6,297**	**–6,262**	**–7,059**	**–4,483**	**–4,872**	**–5,434**
Business travel	3 237 . .	...	...	...	...	...	...	...	...
Personal travel	3 240 . .	...	...	...	...	...	...	...	...
Other services, credit	2 200 BA	**4,387**	**4,956**	**5,997**	**7,259**	**7,999**	**5,646**	**6,456**	**7,007**
Communications	2 245 . .	276	300	337	366	267	481	589	762
Construction	2 249 . .	1,475	1,509	1,804	2,094	2,311	1,922	1,968	2,318
Insurance	2 253 . .	871	1,056	1,225	1,792	1,962	421	384	184
Financial	2 260 . .	...	...	...	...	...	...	...	...
Computer and information	2 262 . .	...	...	...	...	...	...	...	...
Royalties and licence fees	2 266 . .	364	438	563	697	641	748	1,153	876
Other business services	2 268 . .	1,179	1,427	1,795	1,968	2,501	1,784	2,070	2,587
Personal, cultural, and recreational	2 287 . .	...	...	...	...	...	...	...	...
Government, n.i.e.	2 291 . .	222	226	273	342	317	291	292	280
Other services, debit	3 200 BA	**–5,008**	**–5,547**	**–6,826**	**–6,977**	**–7,623**	**–5,074**	**–5,763**	**–6,914**
Communications	3 245 . .	–271	–313	–317	–346	–222	–364	–440	–584
Construction	3 249 . .	–1,416	–1,649	–2,041	–1,952	–2,031	–1,791	–1,969	–2,435
Insurance	3 253 . .	–894	–942	–1,347	–1,721	–1,994	–350	–365	–236
Financial	3 260 . .	...	...	...	...	...	...	...	...
Computer and information	3 262 . .	...	...	...	...	...	...	...	...
Royalties and licence fees	3 266 . .	–594	–673	–743	–691	–717	–590	–762	–999
Other business services	3 268 . .	–1,737	–1,878	–2,279	–2,154	–2,544	–1,880	–2,131	–2,555
Personal, cultural, and recreational	3 287 . .	...	...	...	...	...	...	...	...
Government, n.i.e.	3 291 . .	–95	–92	–99	–113	–114	–100	–95	–105

Table 2 (Continued). STANDARD PRESENTATION, 1988–95
(Millions of U.S. dollars)

	Code	1988	1989	1990	1991	1992	1993	1994	1995
C. INCOME	4 300	-1,793	-2,334	-4,473	-6,399	-10,039	-9,134	-5,870	-6,586
Total credit	2 300	*5,277*	*6,968*	*9,691*	*9,435*	*8,142*	*7,127*	*9,609*	*14,437*
Total debit	3 300	*-7,070*	*-9,302*	*-14,164*	*-15,833*	*-18,181*	*-16,261*	*-15,479*	*-21,023*
Compensation of employees, credit	2 310	**52**	**56**	**82**	**128**	**115**	**93**	**105**	**128**
Compensation of employees, debit	3 310	**-189**	**-214**	**-249**	**-338**	**-297**	**-234**	**-203**	**-289**
Investment income, credit	2 320	**5,225**	**6,913**	**9,608**	**9,307**	**8,027**	**7,034**	**9,504**	**14,309**
Direct investment income	2 330	2,998	3,276	3,690	2,546	1,101	1,597	4,472	6,820
Dividends and distributed branch profits	2 332	813	845	1,685	1,754	1,620	1,803	1,252	1,803
Reinvested earnings and undistributed branch profits	2 333	2,185	2,432	2,005	792	-518	-206	3,220	5,017
Income on debt (interest)	2 334	...	...	...	...	...	...	...	...
Portfolio investment income	2 339	...	...	...	...	...	...	...	...
Income on equity	2 340	...	...	...	...	...	...	...	...
Income on bonds and notes	2 350	...	...	...	...	...	...	...	...
Income on money market instruments and financial derivatives	2 360	...	...	...	...	...	...	...	...
Other investment income	2 370	2,227	3,636	5,918	6,761	6,926	5,438	5,032	7,489
Investment income, debit	3 320	**-6,881**	**-9,087**	**-13,915**	**-15,496**	**-17,884**	**-16,027**	**-15,277**	**-20,734**
Direct investment income	3 330	-1,050	-1,032	-473	-536	568	-1,409	-2,199	-3,944
Dividends and distributed branch profits	3 332	-317	-414	-539	-497	-383	-409	-789	-1,665
Reinvested earnings and undistributed branch profits	3 333	-733	-617	66	-39	952	-1,000	-1,410	-2,279
Income on debt (interest)	3 334	...	...	...	...	...	...	...	...
Portfolio investment income	3 339	...	...	...	...	...	...	...	...
Income on equity	3 340	...	...	...	...	...	...	...	...
Income on bonds and notes	3 350	...	...	...	...	...	...	...	...
Income on money market instruments and financial derivatives	3 360	...	...	...	...	...	...	...	...
Other investment income	3 370	-5,830	-8,056	-13,443	-14,959	-18,452	-14,618	-13,077	-16,790
D. CURRENT TRANSFERS	4 379	-1,378	-1,751	-1,936	-1,984	-2,614	-1,807	-1,879	-2,992
Credit	2 379	**382**	**298**	**386**	**393**	**405**	**456**	**545**	**1,544**
General government	2 380	41	34	57	84	52	70	117	224
Other sectors	2 390	341	264	329	310	353	385	429	1,320
Workers' remittances	2 391	23	34	32	41	80	101	106	122
Other current transfers	2 392	318	230	297	269	273	284	322	1,198
Debit	3 379	**-1,760**	**-2,049**	**-2,321**	**-2,378**	**-3,019**	**-2,263**	**-2,424**	**-4,535**
General government	3 380	-1,181	-1,372	-1,702	-1,736	-2,226	-1,696	-1,790	-1,758
Other sectors	3 390	-579	-677	-620	-642	-793	-567	-634	-2,778
Workers' remittances	3 391	-33	-6	-14	-22	-22	-11	-15	-16
Other current transfers	3 392	-547	-671	-606	-620	-771	-556	-619	-2,762
CAPITAL AND FINANCIAL ACCOUNT	4 996	**1,724**	**8,286**	**11,373**	**-1,336**	**3,268**	**9,011**	**4,130**	**-1,572**
CAPITAL ACCOUNT	4 994	**-234**	**-296**	**-353**	**-63**	**6**	**23**	**23**	**15**
Total credit	2 994	*29*	*38*	*38*	*38*	*37*	*37*	*37*	*33*
Total debit	3 994	*-263*	*-334*	*-391*	*-101*	*-31*	*-15*	*-14*	*-17*
Capital transfers, credit	2 400	**29**	**38**	**38**	**38**	**37**	**37**	**37**	**33**
General government	2 401	...	...	...	...	...	...	...	...
Debt forgiveness	2 402	...	...	...	...	...	...	...	...
Other capital transfers	2 410	...	...	...	...	...	...	...	...
Other sectors	2 430	29	38	38	38	37	37	37	33
Migrants' transfers	2 431	29	38	38	38	37	37	37	33
Debt forgiveness	2 432	...	...	...	...	...	...	...	...
Other capital transfers	2 440	...	...	...	...	...	...	...	...
Capital transfers, debit	3 400	**-263**	**-334**	**-391**	**-101**	**-31**	**-15**	**-14**	**-17**
General government	3 401	...	...	...	...	...	...	...	...
Debt forgiveness	3 402	...	...	...	...	...	...	...	...
Other capital transfers	3 410	...	...	...	...	...	...	...	...
Other sectors	3 430	-263	-334	-391	-101	-31	-15	-14	-17
Migrants' transfers	3 431	-263	-334	-391	-101	-31	-15	-14	-17
Debt forgiveness	3 432	...	...	...	...	...	...	...	...
Other capital transfers	3 440	...	...	...	...	...	...	...	...
Nonproduced nonfinancial assets, credit	2 480	...	...	...	...	...	...	...	...
Nonproduced nonfinancial assets, debit	3 480	...	...	...	...	...	...	...	...

Table 2 (Continued). STANDARD PRESENTATION, 1988–95
(Millions of U.S. dollars)

	Code	1988	1989	1990	1991	1992	1993	1994	1995
FINANCIAL ACCOUNT	4 995	**1,958**	**8,583**	**11,726**	**–1,273**	**3,262**	**8,989**	**4,107**	**–1,587**
A. DIRECT INVESTMENT	4 500	–5,798	–8,484	–12,647	–912	–424	2,234	–355	3,539
Direct investment abroad	4 505	**–7,471**	**–10,296**	**–14,629**	**–7,262**	**–419**	**–1,471**	**–6,596**	**–10,733**
Equity capital	4 510	...	...	...	...	...	...	...	...
Claims on affiliated enterprises	4 515	...	...	...	...	...	...	...	...
Liabilities to affiliated enterprises	4 520	...	...	...	...	...	...	...	...
Reinvested earnings	4 525	–2,185	–2,432	–2,005	–792	518	206	–3,220	–5,017
Other capital	4 530	–5,286	–7,864	–12,624	–6,470	–937	–1,677	–3,377	–5,717
Claims on affiliated enterprises	4 535	...	...	...	...	...	...	...	...
Liabilities to affiliated enterprises	4 540	...	...	...	...	...	...	...	...
Direct investment in Sweden	4 555	**1,673**	**1,812**	**1,982**	**6,351**	**–5**	**3,705**	**6,241**	**14,273**
Equity capital	4 560	...	...	...	...	...	...	...	...
Claims on direct investors	4 565	...	...	...	...	...	...	...	...
Liabilities to direct investors	4 570	...	...	...	...	...	...	...	...
Reinvested earnings	4 575	733	617	–66	39	–952	1,000	1,410	2,279
Other capital	4 580	941	1,195	2,049	6,312	946	2,705	4,831	11,994
Claims on direct investors	4 585	...	...	...	...	...	...	...	...
Liabilities to direct investors	4 590	...	...	...	...	...	...	...	...
B. PORTFOLIO INVESTMENT	4 600	–1,359	–1,248	2,467	6,546	985	1,377	–1,214	–745
Assets	4 602	**–686**	**–4,475**	**–3,644**	**–2,313**	**–1,578**	**–94**	**–1,933**	**–8,881**
Equity securities	4 610	–509	–4,324	–3,271	–2,350	–505	–76	–1,983	–7,495
Monetary authorities	4 611	...	...	...	...	...	...	...	...
General government	4 612	...	...	...	...	...	...	...	...
Banks	4 613	...	...	...	...	...	...	...	...
Other sectors	4 614	...	...	...	...	...	...	...	...
Debt securities	4 619	–177	–150	–373	37	–1,073	–18	50	–1,386
Bonds and notes	4 620	–177	–150	–373	37	–1,073	–18	50	–1,386
Monetary authorities	4 621	...	...	...	...	...	...	...	...
General government	4 622	...	...	...	...	...	...	...	...
Banks	4 623	...	...	...	...	...	...	...	...
Other sectors	4 624	...	...	...	...	...	...	...	...
Money market instruments	4 630	...	...	...	...	...	...	...	...
Monetary authorities	4 631	...	...	...	...	...	...	...	...
General government	4 632	...	...	...	...	...	...	...	...
Banks	4 633	...	...	...	...	...	...	...	...
Other sectors	4 634	...	...	...	...	...	...	...	...
Financial derivatives	4 640	...	...	...	...	...	...	...	...
Monetary authorities	4 641	...	...	...	...	...	...	...	...
General government	4 642	...	...	...	...	...	...	...	...
Banks	4 643	...	...	...	...	...	...	...	...
Other sectors	4 644	...	...	...	...	...	...	...	...
Liabilities	4 652	**–673**	**3,227**	**6,112**	**8,859**	**2,563**	**1,472**	**719**	**8,136**
Equity securities	4 660	–446	–290	192	1,817	2,257	4,212	6,794	1,789
Banks	4 663	...	...	...	...	...	...	...	...
Other sectors	4 664	...	...	...	...	...	...	...	...
Debt securities	4 669	–227	3,517	5,920	7,042	306	–2,741	–6,075	6,347
Bonds and notes	4 670	–227	3,517	5,920	7,042	306	–2,741	–6,075	6,347
Monetary authorities	4 671	...	...	...	...	...	...	...	...
General government	4 672	2	1,773	4,104	7,041	4,789	1,385	–21	7,872
Banks	4 673	...	...	...	...	...	...	...	...
Other sectors	4 674	–229	1,743	1,816	1	–4,484	–4,125	–6,054	–1,525
Money market instruments	4 680	...	...	...	...	...	...	...	...
Monetary authorities	4 681	...	...	...	...	...	...	...	...
General government	4 682	...	...	...	...	...	...	...	...
Banks	4 683	...	...	...	...	...	...	...	...
Other sectors	4 684	...	...	...	...	...	...	...	...
Financial derivatives	4 690	...	...	...	...	...	...	...	...
Monetary authorities	4 691	...	...	...	...	...	...	...	...
General government	4 692	...	...	...	...	...	...	...	...
Banks	4 693	...	...	...	...	...	...	...	...
Other sectors	4 694	...	...	...	...	...	...	...	...

Table 2 (Concluded). STANDARD PRESENTATION, 1988–95
(Millions of U.S. dollars)

	Code	1988	1989	1990	1991	1992	1993	1994	1995
C. OTHER INVESTMENT	4 700	10,054	19,569	29,457	–6,971	9,653	7,907	8,008	–5,546
Assets	4 703	**–2,133**	**–5,074**	**–9,618**	**–946**	**1,633**	**1,159**	**–3,507**	**–11,775**
Trade credits	4 706	–640	261	–137	135	–242	–1,193	–2,002	–1,388
General government: long-term	4 708	...	...	...	...	...	...	...	...
General government: short-term	4 709	...	...	...	...	...	...	...	...
Other sectors: long-term	4 711	...	...	...	...	...	...	...	...
Other sectors: short-term	4 712	–640	261	–137	135	–242	–1,193	–2,002	–1,388
Loans	4 714	–1,392	–3,702	–5,414	982	560	–72	–616	–1,707
Monetary authorities: long-term	4 717	...	...	...	...	...	...	...	...
Monetary authorities: short-term	4 718	...	...	...	...	...	...	...	...
General government: long-term	4 720	–67	–123	–145	–162	–62	–92	–102	22
General government: short-term	4 721	...	...	...	...	...	...	...	...
Banks: long-term	4 723	–479	–1,287	–4,614	1,080	259	1,964	679	838
Banks: short-term	4 724	...	...	...	...	...	...	...	...
Other sectors: long-term	4 726	–628	–693	–112	140	737	–156	–275	–397
Other sectors: short-term	4 727	–219	–1,599	–544	–76	–374	–1,789	–918	–2,169
Currency and deposits	4 730	...	–722	–1,983	–738	823	2,718	2,221	–8,769
Monetary authorities	4 731	...	...	...	...	...	...	...	...
General government	4 732	...	...	...	...	...	...	...	...
Banks	4 733	...	–722	–1,983	–738	823	2,718	2,221	–8,769
Other sectors	4 734	...	...	...	...	...	...	...	...
Other assets	4 736	–102	–911	–2,084	–1,325	492	–294	–3,109	89
Monetary authorities: long-term	4 738	...	...	...	...	...	...	...	...
Monetary authorities: short-term	4 739	...	...	...	...	...	...	...	...
General government: long-term	4 741	–100	–268	–418	–188	–279	–51	–199	–498
General government: short-term	4 742	6	6	3	...	4	–1	9	–2
Banks: long-term	4 744	...	...	...	...	...	...	...	...
Banks: short-term	4 745	...	...	...	...	...	...	...	...
Other sectors: long-term	4 747	–67	–395	–708	–218	–952	–555	–1,331	–300
Other sectors: short-term	4 748	59	–254	–962	–919	1,719	313	–1,588	889
Liabilities	4 753	**12,187**	**24,643**	**39,074**	**–6,025**	**8,020**	**6,748**	**11,514**	**6,228**
Trade credits	4 756	612	670	–572	–440	717	–80	1,470	–121
General government: long-term	4 758	...	...	...	...	...	...	...	...
General government: short-term	4 759	...	...	...	...	...	...	...	...
Other sectors: long-term	4 761	...	...	...	...	...	...	...	...
Other sectors: short-term	4 762	612	670	–572	–440	717	–80	1,470	–121
Loans	4 764	8,043	9,440	9,876	7,601	25,655	13,044	10,120	6,135
Use of Fund credit and loans from the Fund	4 766	...	...	...	...	...	...	...	...
Monetary authorities: other long-term	4 767	...	...	...	...	...	...	...	...
Monetary authorities: short-term	4 768	...	...	...	...	...	...	...	...
General government: long-term	4 770	–1,151	–1,686	–3,143	–1,955	19,216	9,548	6,135	7,806
General government: short-term	4 771	–805	–271	727	–722	9,064	1,930	–700	187
Banks: long-term	4 773	4,700	2,117	–1,711	4,830	–7,301	–4,418	–2,293	–390
Banks: short-term	4 774	...	...	...	...	...	...	...	...
Other sectors: long-term	4 776	3,932	3,649	3,962	8,756	5,743	8,485	4,868	–3,392
Other sectors: short-term	4 777	1,367	5,632	10,041	–3,308	–1,066	–2,501	2,110	1,924
Currency and deposits	4 780	3,472	14,510	29,578	–13,106	–19,160	–6,433	335	–684
Monetary authorities	4 781	...	...	...	...	...	...	...	...
General government	4 782	...	...	...	...	...	...	...	...
Banks	4 783	3,472	14,510	29,578	–13,106	–19,160	–6,433	335	–684
Other sectors	4 784	...	...	...	...	...	...	...	...
Other liabilities	4 786	60	24	192	–80	808	217	–411	898
Monetary authorities: long-term	4 788	...	...	...	...	...	...	...	...
Monetary authorities: short-term	4 789	...	...	...	...	...	...	...	...
General government: long-term	4 791	...	...	...	...	...	...	...	...
General government: short-term	4 792	32	24	200	–103	288	245	–344	856
Banks: long-term	4 794	...	...	...	...	...	...	...	...
Banks: short-term	4 795	...	...	...	...	...	...	...	...
Other sectors: long-term	4 797	...	...	...	...	...	...	...	...
Other sectors: short-term	4 798	29	–1	–8	22	521	–28	–67	42
D. RESERVE ASSETS	4 800	–938	–1,254	–7,552	63	–6,953	–2,530	–2,331	1,165
Monetary gold	4 810	...	...	...	...	...	...	...	...
Special drawing rights	4 820	–128	56	73	–122	360	–13	–6	–367
Reserve position in the Fund	4 830	36	–3	28	–105	–201	...	...	...
Foreign exchange	4 840	–847	–1,308	–7,652	290	–7,111	–2,516	–2,325	1,532
Other claims	4 880	...	...	...	...	...	...	...	...
NET ERRORS AND OMISSIONS	4 998	**–1,190**	**–5,185**	**–5,035**	**5,988**	**5,561**	**–4,851**	**–4,937**	**–3,061**

Part 3 of the *Yearbook* contains descriptions of the methodologies, compilation practices, and sources used to compile these data.

Table 3. INTERNATIONAL INVESTMENT POSITION (End–period stocks), 1988–95
(Millions of U.S. dollars)

	Code	1988	1989	1990	1991	1992	1993	1994	1995
ASSETS	8 995 C.	74,387	101,012	141,102	150,827	148,658	135,124	165,516	227,990
Direct investment abroad	8 505 . .	**28,423**	**38,221**	**49,491**	**53,531**	**47,707**	**44,560**	**59,237**	**69,088**
Equity capital and reinvested earnings	8 506 . .	28,423	38,221	49,491	53,531	47,707	44,560	59,237	69,088
Claims on affiliated enterprises	8 507 . .	...	...	...	...	...	...	...	...
Liabilities to affiliated enterprises	8 508 . .	...	...	...	...	...	...	...	...
Other capital	8 530 . .	...	...	...	...	...	...	...	...
Claims on affiliated enterprises	8 535 . .	...	...	...	...	...	...	...	...
Liabilities to affiliated enterprises	8 540 . .	...	...	...	...	...	...	...	...
Portfolio investment	8 602 . .	**2,924**	**8,833**	**12,110**	**17,000**	**14,057**	**17,583**	**22,114**	**52,867**
Equity securities	8 610 . .	1,787	7,548	10,355	14,830	11,217	15,054	18,227	29,738
Monetary authorities	8 611 . .	...	...	...	...	...	...	...	...
General government	8 612 . .	...	...	...	...	...	...	...	...
Banks	8 613 . .	...	...	...	...	...	...	...	...
Other sectors	8 614 . .	1,787	7,548	10,355	14,830	11,217	15,054	18,227	29,738
Debt securities	8 619 . .	1,137	1,285	1,755	2,170	2,840	2,529	3,887	23,129
Bonds and notes	8 620 . .	...	...	...	...	...	...	...	7,209
Monetary authorities	8 621 . .	...	...	...	...	...	...	...	...
General government	8 622 . .	...	...	...	...	...	...	...	...
Banks	8 623 . .	...	...	...	...	...	...	...	...
Other sectors	8 624 . .	...	...	...	...	...	...	...	...
Money market instruments	8 630 . .	...	...	...	...	...	...	...	...
Monetary authorities	8 631 . .	...	...	...	...	...	...	...	...
General government	8 632 . .	...	...	...	...	...	...	...	...
Banks	8 633 . .	...	...	...	...	...	...	...	...
Other sectors	8 634 . .	...	...	...	...	...	...	...	...
Financial derivatives	8 640 . .	...	...	...	...	...	...	...	15,920
Monetary authorities	8 641 . .	...	...	...	...	...	...	...	...
General government	8 642 . .	...	...	...	...	...	...	...	1,502
Banks	8 643 . .	...	...	...	...	...	...	...	11,565
Other sectors	8 644 . .	...	...	...	...	...	...	...	2,854
Other investment	8 703 . .	**34,270**	**44,163**	**61,250**	**62,212**	**63,609**	**51,785**	**60,310**	**80,352**
Trade credits	8 706 . .	10,070	9,796	10,004	10,670	8,377	8,069	11,794	14,869
General government: long-term	8 708 . .	...	...	...	...	...	...	...	...
General government: short-term	8 709 . .	...	...	...	...	...	...	...	...
Other sectors: long-term	8 711 . .	...	...	...	...	...	...	...	...
Other sectors: short-term	8 712 . .	...	...	...	...	...	...	...	...
Loans	8 714 . .	6,497	18,147	27,027	26,404	22,434	21,316	23,722	27,785
Monetary authorities: long-term	8 717 . .	...	...	...	...	...	...	...	...
Monetary authorities: short-term	8 718 . .	...	...	...	...	...	...	...	...
General government: long-term	8 720 . .	487	1,445	1,755	1,808	1,704	1,806	2,010	2,103
General government: short-term	8 721 . .	...	...	...	...	...	...	...	...
Banks: long-term	8 723 . .	162	5,139	10,355	9,223	8,519	6,262	5,763	5,106
Banks: short-term	8 724 . .	...	3,051	5,441	6,149	3,834	2,409	1,876	1,952
Other sectors: long-term	8 726 . .	4,873	4,818	5,265	5,064	4,118	4,817	5,629	6,759
Other sectors: short-term	8 727 . .	975	3,694	4,212	4,160	4,260	6,022	8,443	11,865
Currency and deposits	8 730 . .	15,105	13,650	21,060	21,702	21,582	19,751	21,577	33,643
Monetary authorities	8 731 . .	...	...	...	...	...	...	...	...
General government	8 732 . .	...	...	...	...	...	...	...	...
Banks	8 733 . .	14,618	12,847	19,130	18,808	19,878	17,583	17,021	29,287
Other sectors	8 734 . .	487	803	1,931	2,894	1,704	2,168	4,557	4,356
Other assets	8 736 . .	2,599	2,569	3,159	3,436	11,217	2,649	3,217	4,055
Monetary authorities: long-term	8 738 . .	...	...	...	...	...	...	...	...
Monetary authorities: short-term	8 739 . .	...	...	...	...	...	...	...	...
General government: long-term	8 741 . .	2,599	2,569	3,159	3,436	2,982	2,649	3,217	4,055
General government: short-term	8 742 . .	...	...	...	...	8,235	...	...	...
Banks: long-term	8 744 . .	...	...	...	...	...	...	...	...
Banks: short-term	8 745 . .	...	...	...	...	...	...	...	...
Other sectors: long-term	8 747 . .	...	...	...	...	...	...	...	...
Other sectors: short-term	8 748 . .	...	...	...	...	...	...	...	...
Reserve assets	8 800 . .	**8,771**	**9,796**	**18,252**	**18,085**	**23,286**	**21,196**	**23,856**	**25,683**
Monetary gold	8 810 . .	286	279	302	304	292	291	310	249
Special drawing rights	8 820 . .	402	341	290	414	45	58	68	441
Reserve position in the Fund	8 830 . .	337	333	333	441	621	620	659	671
Foreign exchange	8 840 . .	7,746	8,844	17,327	16,926	22,327	20,226	22,818	24,320
Other claims	8 880 . .	...	...	...	...	...	...	...	...

Table 3 (Continued). INTERNATIONAL INVESTMENT POSITION (End–period stocks), 1988–95
(Millions of U.S. dollars)

	Code	1988	1989	1990	1991	1992	1993	1994	1995
LIABILITIES	8 995 D.	108,332	141,802	202,176	219,007	208,434	215,813	261,074	324,863
Direct investment in Sweden	8 555 . .	**9,907**	**10,920**	**12,461**	**17,904**	**13,773**	**12,886**	**23,454**	**33,042**
Equity capital and reinvested earnings	8 556 . .	9,907	10,920	12,461	17,904	13,773	12,886	23,454	33,042
Claims on direct investors	8 557 . .	...	...	...	...	...	...	...	...
Liabilities to direct investors	8 558 . .	...	...	...	...	...	...	...	...
Other capital	8 580 . .	...	...	...	...	...	...	...	...
Claims on direct investors	8 585 . .	...	...	...	...	...	...	...	...
Liabilities to direct investors	8 590 . .	...	...	...	...	...	...	...	...
Portfolio investment	8 652 . .	**5,035**	**10,760**	**18,252**	**28,755**	**30,953**	**47,089**	**57,897**	**94,170**
Equity securities	8 660 . .	5,685	6,905	6,669	10,489	13,063	21,798	35,918	48,061
Banks	8 663 . .	...	...	...	...	...	...	...	...
Other sectors	8 664 . .	5,685	6,905	6,669	10,489	13,063	21,798	35,918	48,061
Debt securities	8 669 . .	–650	3,854	11,583	18,266	17,890	25,291	21,979	46,109
Bonds and notes	8 670 . .	...	...	...	...	...	...	...	29,287
Monetary authorities	8 671 . .	...	...	...	...	...	...	...	...
General government	8 672 . .	...	...	...	...	...	...	...	...
Banks	8 673 . .	...	...	...	...	...	...	...	...
Other sectors	8 674 . .	...	...	...	...	...	...	...	...
Money market instruments	8 680 . .	...	...	...	...	...	...	...	...
Monetary authorities	8 681 . .	...	...	...	...	...	...	...	...
General government	8 682 . .	...	...	...	...	...	...	...	...
Banks	8 683 . .	...	...	...	...	...	...	...	...
Other sectors	8 684 . .	...	...	...	...	...	...	...	...
Financial derivatives	8 690 . .	...	...	...	...	...	...	...	16,821
Monetary authorities	8 691 . .	...	...	...	...	...	...	...	...
General government	8 692 . .	...	...	...	...	...	...	...	3,304
Banks	8 692 . .	...	...	...	...	...	...	...	3,304
Other sectors	8 694 . .	...	...	...	...	...	...	...	3,454
Other investment	8 753 . .	**93,390**	**120,122**	**171,464**	**172,348**	**163,709**	**155,838**	**179,723**	**197,651**
Trade credits	8 756 . .	6,659	7,227	7,371	8,319	6,105	5,901	8,175	9,913
General government: long-term	8 758 . .	...	...	...	...	...	...	...	...
General government: short-term	8 759 . .	...	...	...	...	...	...	...	...
Other sectors: long-term	8 761 . .	...	...	...	...	...	...	...	...
Other sectors: short-term	8 762 . .	...	...	...	...	...	...	...	...
Loans	8 764 . .	67,078	92,019	132,678	135,274	130,342	120,672	135,093	144,784
Use of Fund credit and loans from the Fund	8 766 . .	...	...	...	...	...	...	...	...
Monetary authorities: other long-term	8 767 . .	...	...	...	...	...	...	...	...
Monetary authorities: short-term	8 768 . .	...	...	...	...	1,704	...	...	...
General government: long-term	8 770 . .	17,054	15,096	13,338	11,574	29,249	37,093	46,237	54,369
General government: short-term	8 771 . .	975	803	1,580	1,085	7,241	9,394	10,186	10,664
Banks: long-term	8 773 . .	14,293	17,023	16,497	21,340	13,773	9,032	7,103	7,209
Banks: short-term	8 774 . .	10,557	25,695	51,948	43,223	22,434	12,645	8,175	6,008
Other sectors: long-term	8 776 . .	19,490	17,986	23,342	34,361	35,354	35,527	42,217	40,852
Other sectors: short-term	8 777 . .	4,710	15,417	25,974	23,691	20,588	16,981	21,175	25,683
Currency and deposits	8 780 . .	33,295	37,418	47,561	49,552	40,324	37,695	42,753	49,263
Monetary authorities	8 781 . .	...	...	...	...	...	...	...	...
General government	8 782 . .	...	...	...	...	...	...	...	...
Banks	8 783 . .	33,295	37,418	47,561	49,552	40,324	37,695	42,753	49,263
Other sectors	8 784 . .	...	...	...	...	...	...	...	...
Other liabilities	8 786 . .	–13,643	–16,541	–16,146	–20,798	–13,063	–8,430	–6,299	–6,308
Monetary authorities: long-term	8 788 . .	...	...	...	...	...	...	...	...
Monetary authorities: short-term	8 789 . .	...	...	...	...	...	...	...	...
General government: long-term	8 791 . .	650	482	351	543	710	602	804	901
General government: short-term	8 792 . .	...	...	...	...	...	...	...	...
Banks: long-term	8 794 . .	–14,293	–17,023	–16,497	–21,340	–13,773	–9,032	–7,103	–7,209
Banks: short-term	8 795 . .	...	...	...	...	...	...	...	...
Other sectors: long-term	8 797 . .	...	...	...	...	...	...	...	...
Other sectors: short-term	8 798 . .	...	...	...	...	...	...	...	...
NET INTERNATIONAL INVESTMENT POSITION	8 995 . .	**–33,945**	**–40,790**	**–61,074**	**–68,180**	**–59,776**	**–80,689**	**–95,557**	**–96,873**
Conversion rates: kronor per U.S. dollar (end of period)	0 102 . .	**6.1570**	**6.2270**	**5.6980**	**5.5295**	**7.0430**	**8.3035**	**7.4615**	**6.6582**

Table 1. ANALYTIC PRESENTATION, 1988–95
(Millions of U.S. dollars)

	Code	1988	1989	1990	1991	1992	1993	1994	1995
A. Current Account [1]	4 993 Y.	**8,846**	**8,043**	**6,941**	**10,374**	**14,235**	**17,908**	**17,984**	**21,622**
Goods: exports f.o.b	2 100 . .	63,164	65,811	78,033	74,256	79,870	75,424	82,625	97,139
Goods: imports f.o.b	3 100 . .	–68,359	–70,769	–85,207	–78,853	–80,155	–73,853	–79,295	–93,902
Balance on Goods	4 100 . .	*–5,194*	*–4,958*	*–7,174*	*–4,597*	*–285*	*1,571*	*3,330*	*3,237*
Services: credit	2 200 . .	16,114	15,811	18,893	19,785	21,065	21,476	22,962	26,095
Services: debit	3 200 . .	–9,226	–9,183	–11,195	–11,096	–11,928	–11,544	–12,784	–15,402
Balance on Goods and Services	4 991 . .	*1,693*	*1,669*	*524*	*4,092*	*8,852*	*11,503*	*13,508*	*13,930*
Income: credit	2 300 . .	20,057	22,697	28,686	27,518	26,238	25,019	26,836	31,606
Income: debit	3 300 . .	–11,191	–14,640	–19,939	–18,663	–17,902	–15,874	–18,932	–19,809
Balance on Goods, Services, and Income	4 992 . .	*10,559*	*9,726*	*9,270*	*12,946*	*17,189*	*20,648*	*21,413*	*25,727*
Current transfers: credit	2 379 Y.	2,054	1,919	2,357	2,367	2,531	2,484	2,527	2,991
Current transfers: debit	3 379 . .	–3,768	–3,602	–4,686	–4,939	–5,484	–5,225	–5,955	–7,096
B. Capital Account [1]	4 994 Y.	**. . .**	**. . .**	**. . .**	**–48**	**–43**	**–133**	**–146**	**–132**
Capital account: credit	2 994 Y.	. . .	. . .	. . .	. . .	. . .	. . .	. . .	. . .
Capital account: debit	3 994 . .	. . .	. . .	. . .	–48	–43	–133	–146	–132
Total, Groups A Plus B	4 010 . .	*8,846*	*8,043*	*6,941*	*10,326*	*14,192*	*17,775*	*17,838*	*21,490*
C. Financial Account [1]	4 995 X.	**–14,742**	**–7,618**	**–11,459**	**–11,678**	**–15,370**	**–19,065**	**–16,548**	**–18,357**
Direct investment abroad	4 505 . .	–8,695	–7,850	–6,370	–6,541	–5,671	–8,763	–10,839	–11,851
Direct investment in Switzerland	4 555 Y.	405	2,827	4,961	3,178	1,249	899	4,104	2,600
Portfolio investment assets	4 602 . .	–13,837	–9,394	–577	–17,549	–9,698	–30,337	–19,058	–9,326
Equity securities	4 610 . .	3,358	958	679	–4,531	–6,464	–16,650	–8,073	–3,032
Debt securities	4 619 . .	–17,195	–10,352	–1,255	–13,018	–3,234	–13,687	–10,986	–6,294
Portfolio investment liabilities	4 652 Y.	6,421	6,371	–551	5,570	3,571	12,501	912	4,960
Equity securities	4 660 Y.	4,255	5,310	–1,579	2,951	1,810	7,923	–1,572	5,851
Debt securities	4 669 Y.	2,166	1,062	1,028	2,619	1,761	4,578	2,484	–891
Other investment assets	4 703 . .	–7,641	–14,202	–28,846	2,828	–8,496	7,405	–31,086	–7,915
Monetary authorities	4 703 . A	. . .	. . .	. . .	. . .	. . .	. . .	. . .	. . .
General government	4 703 . B	–215	–156	–184	–246	–250	–173	–115	–67
Banks	4 703 . C	–297	6,832	–6,008	1,778	–4,811	–2,449	–19,220	–9,451
Other sectors	4 703 . D	–7,129	–20,879	–22,654	1,296	–3,434	10,026	–11,751	1,603
Other investment liabilities	4 753 X.	8,604	14,631	19,924	836	3,675	–769	39,420	3,175
Monetary authorities	4 753 XA	–40	21	–40	16	–20	9	–6	1
General government	4 753 YB	–42	–185	–53	–1	84	79	40	266
Banks	4 753 YC	3,314	8,285	12,056	1,896	–732	4,074	30,262	1,609
Other sectors	4 753 YD	5,372	6,509	7,962	–1,075	4,344	–4,932	9,123	1,298
Total, Groups A Through C	4 020 . .	*–5,896*	*425*	*–4,518*	*–1,352*	*–1,178*	*–1,291*	*1,290*	*3,133*
D. Net Errors and Omissions	4 998 . .	**3,470**	**995**	**5,686**	**2,325**	**5,560**	**1,692**	**–129**	**–3,076**
Total, Groups A Through D	4 030 . .	*–2,426*	*1,419*	*1,168*	*973*	*4,383*	*401*	*1,160*	*57*
E. Reserves and Related Items	4 040 . .	**2,426**	**–1,419**	**–1,168**	**–973**	**–4,383**	**–401**	**–1,160**	**–57**
Reserve assets	4 800 . .	2,382	–1,369	–1,165	–995	–4,360	–483	–1,062	–53
Use of Fund credit and loans	4 766 . .	. . .	. . .	. . .	. . .	. . .	. . .	. . .	. . .
Liabilities constituting foreign authorities' reserves	4 900 . .	44	–51	–3	22	–23	82	–98	–4
Exceptional financing	4 920 . .	. . .	. . .	. . .	. . .	. . .	. . .	. . .	. . .
Conversion rates: Swiss francs per U.S. dollar	0 101 . .	**1.4633**	**1.6359**	**1.3892**	**1.4340**	**1.4062**	**1.4776**	**1.3677**	**1.1825**

[1] Excludes components that have been classified in the categories of Group E.

Table 2. STANDARD PRESENTATION, 1988–95
(Millions of U.S. dollars)

	Code	1988	1989	1990	1991	1992	1993	1994	1995
CURRENT ACCOUNT	4 993 . .	**8,846**	**8,043**	**6,941**	**10,374**	**14,235**	**17,908**	**17,984**	**21,622**
A. GOODS	4 100 . .	-5,194	-4,958	-7,174	-4,597	-285	1,571	3,330	3,237
Credit	2 100 . .	**63,164**	**65,811**	**78,033**	**74,256**	**79,870**	**75,424**	**82,625**	**97,139**
General merchandise: exports f.o.b.	2 110 . .	50,983	51,864	63,995	62,138	66,532	64,288	71,309	82,822
Goods for processing: exports f.o.b.	2 150 . .	...	...	...	...	...	...	...	...
Repairs on goods	2 160 . .	...	...	...	...	...	...	...	...
Goods procured in ports by carriers	2 170 . .	...	...	...	...	...	...	...	...
Nonmonetary gold	2 180 . .	12,181	13,947	14,038	12,117	13,338	11,136	11,315	14,317
Debit	3 100 . .	**-68,359**	**-70,769**	**-85,207**	**-78,853**	**-80,155**	**-73,853**	**-79,295**	**-93,902**
General merchandise: imports f.o.b.	3 110 . .	-55,524	-57,400	-68,862	-66,090	-65,546	-60,738	-67,615	-79,410
Goods for processing: imports f.o.b.	3 150 . .	...	...	...	...	...	...	...	...
Repairs on goods	3 160 . .	...	...	...	...	...	...	...	...
Goods procured in ports by carriers	3 170 . .	...	...	...	...	...	...	...	...
Nonmonetary gold	3 180 . .	-12,834	-13,369	-16,345	-12,762	-14,609	-13,114	-11,680	-14,492
B. SERVICES	4 200 . .	6,887	6,627	7,698	8,689	9,137	9,932	10,178	10,693
Total credit	2 200 . .	*16,114*	*15,811*	*18,893*	*19,785*	*21,065*	*21,476*	*22,962*	*26,095*
Total debit	3 200 . .	*-9,226*	*-9,183*	*-11,195*	*-11,096*	*-11,928*	*-11,544*	*-12,784*	*-15,402*
Transportation services, credit	2 205 . .	**1,849**	**1,847**	**2,160**	**2,277**	**2,281**	**2,141**	**2,207**	**2,521**
Passenger	2 205 BA	*1,398*	*1,395*	*1,630*	*1,702*	*1,686*	*1,606*	*1,667*	*1,895*
Freight	2 205 BB	*451*	*452*	*530*	*575*	*595*	*535*	*540*	*626*
Other	2 205 BC	...	...	...	...	...	...	...	...
Sea transport, passenger	2 207 . .	...	...	...	...	...	...	...	...
Sea transport, freight	2 208 . .	...	...	...	...	...	...	...	...
Sea transport, other	2 209 . .	...	...	...	...	...	...	...	...
Air transport, passenger	2 211 . .	...	...	...	...	...	...	...	...
Air transport, freight	2 212 . .	...	...	...	...	...	...	...	...
Air transport, other	2 213 . .	...	...	...	...	...	...	...	...
Other transport, passenger	2 215 . .	...	...	...	...	...	...	...	...
Other transport, freight	2 216 . .	...	...	...	...	...	...	...	...
Other transport, other	2 217 . .	...	...	...	...	...	...	...	...
Transportation services, debit	3 205 . .	**-1,903**	**-2,168**	**-2,676**	**-2,563**	**-2,709**	**-2,690**	**-3,112**	**-3,792**
Passenger	3 205 BA	*-640*	*-862*	*-1,110*	*-1,115*	*-1,237*	*-1,331*	*-1,647*	*-2,058*
Freight	3 205 BB	*-1,263*	*-1,306*	*-1,566*	*-1,448*	*-1,472*	*-1,359*	*-1,465*	*-1,735*
Other	3 205 BC	...	...	...	...	...	...	...	...
Sea transport, passenger	3 207 . .	...	...	...	...	...	...	...	...
Sea transport, freight	3 208 . .	...	...	...	...	...	...	...	...
Sea transport, other	3 209 . .	...	...	...	...	...	...	...	...
Air transport, passenger	3 211 . .	...	...	...	...	...	...	...	...
Air transport, freight	3 212 . .	...	...	...	...	...	...	...	...
Air transport, other	3 213 . .	...	...	...	...	...	...	...	...
Other transport, passenger	3 215 . .	...	...	...	...	...	...	...	...
Other transport, freight	3 216 . .	...	...	...	...	...	...	...	...
Other transport, other	3 217 . .	...	...	...	...	...	...	...	...
Travel, credit	2 236 . .	**6,166**	**6,041**	**7,411**	**7,684**	**8,173**	**7,623**	**8,359**	**9,459**
Business travel	2 237 . .	...	...	...	...	...	...	...	...
Personal travel	2 240 . .	...	...	...	...	...	...	...	...
Travel, debit	3 236 . .	**-5,059**	**-4,978**	**-5,873**	**-5,735**	**-6,154**	**-5,972**	**-6,417**	**-7,714**
Business travel	3 237 . .	...	...	...	...	...	...	...	...
Personal travel	3 240 . .	...	...	...	...	...	...	...	...
Other services, credit	2 200 BA	**8,100**	**7,923**	**9,322**	**9,824**	**10,611**	**11,712**	**12,396**	**14,115**
Communications	2 245 . .	401	346	423	406	481	454	466	515
Construction	2 249 . .	...	...	...	...	...	...	...	...
Insurance	2 253 . .	793	762	1,002	1,036	1,205	1,285	1,474	1,307
Financial	2 260 . .	3,069	2,974	3,241	3,608	3,974	4,768	4,796	5,627
Computer and information	2 262 . .	...	...	...	...	...	...	...	...
Royalties and licence fees	2 266 . .	...	...	...	...	...	...	...	...
Other business services	2 268 . .	3,836	3,841	4,656	4,775	4,950	5,205	5,660	6,666
Personal, cultural, and recreational	2 287 . .	...	...	...	...	...	...	...	...
Government, n.i.e.	2 291 . .	...	...	...	...	...	...	...	...
Other services, debit	3 200 BA	**-2,264**	**-2,037**	**-2,645**	**-2,798**	**-3,065**	**-2,882**	**-3,254**	**-3,896**
Communications	3 245 . .	-459	-424	-549	-592	-649	-606	-585	-681
Construction	3 249 . .	...	...	...	...	...	...	...	...
Insurance	3 253 . .	-118	-123	-150	-137	-138	-130	-140	-165
Financial	3 260 . .	...	...	...	...	...	...	...	...
Computer and information	3 262 . .	...	...	...	...	...	...	...	...
Royalties and licence fees	3 266 . .	...	...	...	...	...	...	...	...
Other business services	3 268 . .	-1,687	-1,490	-1,947	-2,068	-2,278	-2,147	-2,529	-3,050
Personal, cultural, and recreational	3 287 . .	...	...	...	...	...	...	...	...
Government, n.i.e.	3 291 . .	...	...	...	...	...	...	...	...

Table 2 (Continued). STANDARD PRESENTATION, 1988–95

(Millions of U.S. dollars)

	Code	1988	1989	1990	1991	1992	1993	1994	1995
C. INCOME	4 300 . .	8,866	8,057	8,746	8,854	8,337	9,145	7,905	11,797
Total credit	2 300 . .	*20,057*	*22,697*	*28,686*	*27,518*	*26,238*	*25,019*	*26,836*	*31,606*
Total debit	3 300 . .	*–11,191*	*–14,640*	*–19,939*	*–18,663*	*–17,902*	*–15,874*	*–18,932*	*–19,809*
Compensation of employees, credit	2 310 . .	**696**	**639**	**787**	**848**	**902**	**914**	**1,060**	**1,233**
Compensation of employees, debit	3 310 . .	**–4,102**	**–4,272**	**–5,752**	**–6,146**	**–6,241**	**–5,776**	**–6,078**	**–7,054**
Investment income, credit	2 320 . .	**19,361**	**22,058**	**27,899**	**26,670**	**25,336**	**24,104**	**25,776**	**30,373**
Direct investment income	2 330 . .	3,219	3,058	2,829	2,388	2,104	4,961	5,468	6,009
Dividends and distributed branch profits	2 332 . .	683	611	1,080	1,046	1,422	1,625	2,852	2,452
Reinvested earnings and undistributed branch profits	2 333 . .	2,536	2,446	1,749	1,342	682	3,336	2,617	3,557
Income on debt (interest)	2 334 . .	...	...	...	...	...	...	...	...
Portfolio investment income	2 339 . .	6,092	6,678	9,236	9,707	9,806	8,507	9,798	11,394
Income on equity	2 340 . .	...	...	...	...	...	...	...	...
Income on bonds and notes	2 350 . .	...	...	...	...	...	...	...	...
Income on money market instruments and financial derivatives	2 360 . .	...	...	...	...	...	...	...	...
Other investment income	2 370 . .	10,049	12,323	15,834	14,574	13,425	10,636	10,510	12,969
Investment income, debit	3 320 . .	**–7,089**	**–10,368**	**–14,188**	**–12,517**	**–11,661**	**–10,097**	**–12,854**	**–12,756**
Direct investment income	3 330 . .	–27	–1,249	–1,286	–827	–204	–654	–2,764	–821
Dividends and distributed branch profits	3 332 . .	...	...	...	...	...	...	...	...
Reinvested earnings and undistributed branch profits	3 333 . .	–27	–1,249	–1,286	–827	–204	–654	–2,764	–821
Income on debt (interest)	3 334 . .	...	...	...	...	...	...	...	...
Portfolio investment income	3 339 . .	–2,048	–2,042	–2,720	–2,750	–2,855	–2,976	–3,191	–3,759
Income on equity	3 340 . .	...	...	...	...	...	...	...	...
Income on bonds and notes	3 350 . .	...	...	...	...	...	...	...	...
Income on money market instruments and financial derivatives	3 360 . .	...	...	...	...	...	...	...	...
Other investment income	3 370 . .	–5,013	–7,077	–10,182	–8,939	–8,602	–6,466	–6,899	–8,175
D. CURRENT TRANSFERS	4 379 . .	–1,713	–1,683	–2,329	–2,573	–2,953	–2,740	–3,428	–4,105
Credit	2 379 . .	**2,054**	**1,919**	**2,357**	**2,367**	**2,531**	**2,484**	**2,527**	**2,991**
General government	2 380 . .	1,790	1,691	2,088	2,093	2,251	2,216	2,232	2,648
Other sectors	2 390 . .	264	228	269	274	279	269	295	343
Workers' remittances	2 391 . .	130	116	137	132	135	129	139	161
Other current transfers	2 392 . .	134	112	132	142	144	140	156	183
Debit	3 379 . .	**–3,768**	**–3,602**	**–4,686**	**–4,939**	**–5,484**	**–5,225**	**–5,955**	**–7,096**
General government	3 380 . .	–1,793	–1,709	–2,234	–2,391	–2,832	–2,727	–3,250	–3,969
Other sectors	3 390 . .	–1,975	–1,893	–2,452	–2,549	–2,653	–2,498	–2,705	–3,127
Workers' remittances	3 391 . .	–1,663	–1,605	–2,116	–2,195	–2,276	–2,135	–2,311	–2,680
Other current transfers	3 392 . .	–312	–289	–335	–354	–376	–363	–394	–447
CAPITAL AND FINANCIAL ACCOUNT	4 996 . .	**–12,316**	**–9,037**	**–12,627**	**–12,699**	**–19,796**	**–19,600**	**–17,855**	**–18,545**
CAPITAL ACCOUNT	4 994 . .	**...**	**...**	**...**	**–48**	**–43**	**–133**	**–146**	**–132**
Total credit	2 994 . .	...	...	...	...	...	...	...	...
Total debit	3 994 . .	...	...	...	*–48*	*–43*	*–133*	*–146*	*–132*
Capital transfers, credit	2 400 . .	**...**	**...**	**...**	**...**	**...**	**...**	**...**	**...**
General government	2 401 . .	...	...	...	...	...	...	...	...
Debt forgiveness	2 402 . .	...	...	...	...	...	...	...	...
Other capital transfers	2 410 . .	...	...	...	...	...	...	...	...
Other sectors	2 430 . .	...	...	...	...	...	...	...	...
Migrants' transfers	2 431 . .	...	...	...	...	...	...	...	...
Debt forgiveness	2 432 . .	...	...	...	...	...	...	...	...
Other capital transfers	2 440 . .	...	...	...	...	...	...	...	...
Capital transfers, debit	3 400 . .	**...**	**...**	**...**	**–48**	**–43**	**–133**	**–146**	**–132**
General government	3 401 . .	...	...	...	–48	–43	–133	–146	–132
Debt forgiveness	3 402 . .	...	...	...	–48	–43	–133	–146	–132
Other capital transfers	3 410 . .	...	...	...	...	...	...	...	...
Other sectors	3 430 . .	...	...	...	...	...	...	...	...
Migrants' transfers	3 431 . .	...	...	...	...	...	...	...	...
Debt forgiveness	3 432 . .	...	...	...	...	...	...	...	...
Other capital transfers	3 440 . .	...	...	...	...	...	...	...	...
Nonproduced nonfinancial assets, credit	2 480 . .	**...**	**...**	**...**	**...**	**...**	**...**	**...**	**...**
Nonproduced nonfinancial assets, debit	3 480 . .	**...**	**...**	**...**	**...**	**...**	**...**	**...**	**...**

Table 2 (Continued). STANDARD PRESENTATION, 1988–95

(Millions of U.S. dollars)

	Code	1988	1989	1990	1991	1992	1993	1994	1995
FINANCIAL ACCOUNT	4 995	**–12,316**	**–9,037**	**–12,627**	**–12,650**	**–19,752**	**–19,466**	**–17,709**	**–18,413**
A. DIRECT INVESTMENT	4 500	–8,289	–5,023	–1,409	–3,363	–4,422	–7,865	–6,735	–9,250
Direct investment abroad	4 505	**–8,695**	**–7,850**	**–6,370**	**–6,541**	**–5,671**	**–8,763**	**–10,839**	**–11,851**
Equity capital	4 510	–4,158	–6,690	–3,442	–4,113	–4,686	–4,811	–8,179	–7,922
Claims on affiliated enterprises	4 515	–4,158	–6,690	–3,442	–4,113	–4,686	–4,811	–8,179	–7,922
Liabilities to affiliated enterprises	4 520	...	...	...	...	...	...	...	...
Reinvested earnings	4 525	–2,536	–2,446	–1,749	–1,342	–682	–3,336	–2,617	–3,557
Other capital	4 530	–2,000	1,286	–1,178	–1,086	–303	–616	–43	–372
Claims on affiliated enterprises	4 535	–2,000	1,286	–1,178	–1,086	–303	–616	–43	–372
Liabilities to affiliated enterprises	4 540	...	...	...	...	...	...	...	...
Direct investment in Switzerland	4 555	**405**	**2,827**	**4,961**	**3,178**	**1,249**	**899**	**4,104**	**2,600**
Equity capital	4 560	1,318	1,114	4,128	1,982	924	1,199	919	2,351
Claims on direct investors	4 565	...	...	...	...	...	...	...	...
Liabilities to direct investors	4 570	1,318	1,114	4,128	1,982	924	1,199	919	2,351
Reinvested earnings	4 575	27	1,249	1,286	827	204	654	2,764	821
Other capital	4 580	–940	463	–453	369	120	–955	421	–572
Claims on direct investors	4 585	...	...	...	...	...	...	...	...
Liabilities to direct investors	4 590	–940	463	–453	369	120	–955	421	–572
B. PORTFOLIO INVESTMENT	4 600	–7,415	–3,023	–1,127	–11,978	–6,127	–17,836	–18,147	–4,366
Assets	4 602	**–13,837**	**–9,394**	**–577**	**–17,549**	**–9,698**	**–30,337**	**–19,058**	**–9,326**
Equity securities	4 610	3,358	958	679	–4,531	–6,464	–16,650	–8,073	–3,032
Monetary authorities	4 611	...	...	...	...	...	...	...	...
General government	4 612	...	...	...	...	...	...	...	...
Banks	4 613	...	...	...	...	...	...	...	...
Other sectors	4 614	...	...	...	...	...	...	...	...
Debt securities	4 619	–17,195	–10,352	–1,255	–13,018	–3,234	–13,687	–10,986	–6,294
Bonds and notes	4 620	–17,195	–10,352	–1,255	–13,018	–3,234	–13,687	–10,986	–6,294
Monetary authorities	4 621	...	...	...	...	...	...	...	...
General government	4 622	...	...	...	...	...	...	...	...
Banks	4 623	...	...	...	...	...	...	...	...
Other sectors	4 624	...	...	...	...	...	...	...	...
Money market instruments	4 630	...	...	...	...	...	...	...	...
Monetary authorities	4 631	...	...	...	...	...	...	...	...
General government	4 632	...	...	...	...	...	...	...	...
Banks	4 633	...	...	...	...	...	...	...	...
Other sectors	4 634	...	...	...	...	...	...	...	...
Financial derivatives	4 640	...	...	...	...	...	...	...	...
Monetary authorities	4 641	...	...	...	...	...	...	...	...
General government	4 642	...	...	...	...	...	...	...	...
Banks	4 643	...	...	...	...	...	...	...	...
Other sectors	4 644	...	...	...	...	...	...	...	...
Liabilities	4 652	**6,421**	**6,371**	**–551**	**5,570**	**3,571**	**12,501**	**912**	**4,960**
Equity securities	4 660	4,255	5,310	–1,579	2,951	1,810	7,923	–1,572	5,851
Banks	4 663	...	...	...	...	...	...	...	...
Other sectors	4 664	...	...	...	...	...	...	...	...
Debt securities	4 669	2,166	1,062	1,028	2,619	1,761	4,578	2,484	–891
Bonds and notes	4 670	2,166	1,062	1,028	2,619	1,761	4,578	2,484	–891
Monetary authorities	4 671	...	...	...	...	...	...	...	...
General government	4 672	–170	–119	73	–37	508	416	533	596
Banks	4 673	...	...	...	...	...	...	...	...
Other sectors	4 674	2,336	1,180	955	2,656	1,253	4,163	1,951	–1,488
Money market instruments	4 680	...	...	...	...	...	...	...	...
Monetary authorities	4 681	...	...	...	...	...	...	...	...
General government	4 682	...	...	...	...	...	...	...	...
Banks	4 683	...	...	...	...	...	...	...	...
Other sectors	4 684	...	...	...	...	...	...	...	...
Financial derivatives	4 690	...	...	...	...	...	...	...	...
Monetary authorities	4 691	...	...	...	...	...	...	...	...
General government	4 692	...	...	...	...	...	...	...	...
Banks	4 693	...	...	...	...	...	...	...	...
Other sectors	4 694	...	...	...	...	...	...	...	...

Table 2 (Concluded). STANDARD PRESENTATION, 1988–95
(Millions of U.S. dollars)

	Code	1988	1989	1990	1991	1992	1993	1994	1995
C. OTHER INVESTMENT	4 700	1,007	378	–8,925	3,686	–4,843	6,718	8,236	–4,744
Assets	4 703	**–7,641**	**–14,202**	**–28,846**	**2,828**	**–8,496**	**7,405**	**–31,086**	**–7,915**
Trade credits	4 706	. . .	. . .	. . .	. . .	. . .	. . .	. . .	. . .
General government: long-term	4 708	. . .	. . .	. . .	. . .	. . .	. . .	. . .	. . .
General government: short-term	4 709	. . .	. . .	. . .	. . .	. . .	. . .	. . .	. . .
Other sectors: long-term	4 711	. . .	. . .	. . .	. . .	. . .	. . .	. . .	. . .
Other sectors: short-term	4 712	. . .	. . .	. . .	. . .	. . .	. . .	. . .	. . .
Loans	4 714	–3,366	–2,043	–4,041	–427	–64	54	–4,785	–2,852
Monetary authorities: long-term	4 717	. . .	. . .	. . .	. . .	. . .	. . .	. . .	. . .
Monetary authorities: short-term	4 718	. . .	. . .	. . .	. . .	. . .	. . .	. . .	. . .
General government: long-term	4 720	–350	–172	–160	–255	–233	–166	–89	–15
General government: short-term	4 721	. . .	. . .	. . .	. . .	. . .	. . .	. . .	. . .
Banks: long-term	4 723	–3,016	–1,872	–3,881	–172	169	220	–4,696	–2,836
Banks: short-term	4 724	. . .	. . .	. . .	. . .	. . .	. . .	. . .	. . .
Other sectors: long-term	4 726	. . .	. . .	. . .	. . .	. . .	. . .	. . .	. . .
Other sectors: short-term	4 727	. . .	. . .	. . .	. . .	. . .	. . .	. . .	. . .
Currency and deposits	4 730	1,344	10,092	–2,134	911	–5,183	–2,078	–15,096	–6,058
Monetary authorities	4 731	. . .	. . .	. . .	. . .	. . .	. . .	. . .	. . .
General government	4 732	. . .	. . .	. . .	. . .	. . .	. . .	. . .	. . .
Banks	4 733	1,344	10,092	–2,134	911	–5,183	–2,078	–15,096	–6,058
Other sectors	4 734	. . .	. . .	. . .	. . .	. . .	. . .	. . .	. . .
Other assets	4 736	–5,619	–22,251	–22,671	2,345	–3,249	9,429	–11,204	995
Monetary authorities: long-term	4 738	. . .	. . .	. . .	. . .	. . .	. . .	. . .	. . .
Monetary authorities: short-term	4 739	. . .	. . .	. . .	. . .	. . .	. . .	. . .	. . .
General government: long-term	4 741	–7	–3	–5	–3	–73	–39	–45	–52
General government: short-term	4 742	141	19	–19	13	55	32	19	. . .
Banks: long-term	4 744	. . .	. . .	. . .	. . .	. . .	. . .	. . .	. . .
Banks: short-term	4 745	1,376	–1,388	8	1,039	203	–591	572	–557
Other sectors: long-term	4 747	. . .	. . .	. . .	. . .	. . .	. . .	. . .	. . .
Other sectors: short-term	4 748	. . .	. . .	. . .	. . .	. . .	. . .	. . .	. . .
Liabilities	4 753	**8,648**	**14,580**	**19,921**	**858**	**3,652**	**–688**	**39,322**	**3,170**
Trade credits	4 756	. . .	. . .	. . .	. . .	. . .	. . .	. . .	. . .
General government: long-term	4 758	. . .	. . .	. . .	. . .	. . .	. . .	. . .	. . .
General government: short-term	4 759	. . .	. . .	. . .	. . .	. . .	. . .	. . .	. . .
Other sectors: long-term	4 761	. . .	. . .	. . .	. . .	. . .	. . .	. . .	. . .
Other sectors: short-term	4 762	. . .	. . .	. . .	. . .	. . .	. . .	. . .	. . .
Loans	4 764	788	42	571	–478	–254	399	5,203	5,225
Use of Fund credit and loans from the Fund	4 766	. . .	. . .	. . .	. . .	. . .	. . .	. . .	. . .
Monetary authorities: other long-term	4 767	. . .	. . .	. . .	. . .	. . .	. . .	. . .	. . .
Monetary authorities: short-term	4 768	. . .	. . .	. . .	. . .	. . .	. . .	. . .	. . .
General government: long-term	4 770	. . .	. . .	. . .	. . .	. . .	. . .	. . .	. . .
General government: short-term	4 771	. . .	. . .	. . .	. . .	. . .	. . .	. . .	. . .
Banks: long-term	4 773	788	42	571	–478	–254	399	5,203	5,225
Banks: short-term	4 774	. . .	. . .	. . .	. . .	. . .	. . .	. . .	. . .
Other sectors: long-term	4 776	. . .	. . .	. . .	. . .	. . .	. . .	. . .	. . .
Other sectors: short-term	4 777	. . .	. . .	. . .	. . .	. . .	. . .	. . .	. . .
Currency and deposits	4 780	3,828	8,536	11,796	2,789	–390	3,091	25,485	–4,002
Monetary authorities	4 781	. . .	. . .	. . .	. . .	. . .	. . .	. . .	. . .
General government	4 782	. . .	. . .	. . .	. . .	. . .	. . .	. . .	. . .
Banks	4 783	3,828	8,536	11,796	2,789	–390	3,091	25,485	–4,002
Other sectors	4 784	. . .	. . .	. . .	. . .	. . .	. . .	. . .	. . .
Other liabilities	4 786	4,031	6,002	7,555	–1,453	4,297	–4,178	8,634	1,948
Monetary authorities: long-term	4 788	. . .	. . .	. . .	. . .	. . .	. . .	. . .	. . .
Monetary authorities: short-term	4 789	3	–30	–42	38	–43	91	–104	–3
General government: long-term	4 791	. . .	. . .	. . .	. . .	. . .	. . .	. . .	. . .
General government: short-term	4 792	. . .	. . .	. . .	. . .	. . .	. . .	. . .	. . .
Banks: long-term	4 794	. . .	. . .	. . .	. . .	. . .	. . .	. . .	. . .
Banks: short-term	4 795	. . .	. . .	. . .	. . .	. . .	. . .	. . .	. . .
Other sectors: long-term	4 797	. . .	. . .	. . .	. . .	. . .	. . .	. . .	. . .
Other sectors: short-term	4 798	. . .	. . .	. . .	. . .	. . .	. . .	. . .	. . .
D. RESERVE ASSETS	4 800	2,382	–1,369	–1,165	–995	–4,360	–483	–1,062	–53
Monetary gold	4 810	. . .	. . .	. . .	. . .	. . .	. . .	. . .	. . .
Special drawing rights	4 820	–7	15	3	. . .	–14	–134	–76	–16
Reserve position in the Fund	4 830	148	91	42	. . .	–833	–33	–56	–512
Foreign exchange	4 840	2,231	–1,487	–1,227	–927	–3,471	–274	–947	455
Other claims	4 880	10	12	17	–68	–42	–42	17	20
NET ERRORS AND OMISSIONS	4 998	**3,470**	**995**	**5,686**	**2,325**	**5,560**	**1,692**	**–129**	**–3,076**

Table 3. INTERNATIONAL INVESTMENT POSITION (End-period stocks), 1988–95
(Millions of U.S. dollars)

	Code		1988	1989	1990	1991	1992	1993	1994	1995
ASSETS	8 995	C.	436,493	475,781	564,737	589,065	586,035	632,383	...	...
Direct investment abroad	8 505	..	**47,148**	**52,613**	**65,730**	**75,335**	**73,817**	**84,632**	...	...
Equity capital and reinvested earnings	8 506	..	38,356	45,745	55,568	65,344	62,464	70,793	...	...
Claims on affiliated enterprises	8 507	..	...	...	...	...	...	...	...	...
Liabilities to affiliated enterprises	8 508	..	...	...	...	...	...	...	...	...
Other capital	8 530	..	8,792	6,868	10,162	9,991	11,353	13,839	...	...
Claims on affiliated enterprises	8 535	..	...	...	...	...	...	...	...	...
Liabilities to affiliated enterprises	8 540	..	...	...	...	...	...	...	...	...
Portfolio investment	8 602	..	**175,095**	**184,836**	**189,535**	**213,622**	**218,271**	**266,260**	...	...
Equity securities	8 610	..	36,888	46,083	41,552	51,635	56,416	88,065	...	...
Monetary authorities	8 611	..	...	...	...	...	...	...	...	...
General government	8 612	..	...	...	...	...	...	...	...	...
Banks	8 613	..	...	...	...	...	...	...	...	...
Other sectors	8 614	..	...	...	...	...	...	...	...	...
Debt securities	8 619	..	138,207	138,753	147,983	161,987	161,856	178,195	...	...
Bonds and notes	8 620	..	138,207	138,753	147,983	161,987	161,856	178,195	...	...
Monetary authorities	8 621	..	...	...	...	...	...	...	...	...
General government	8 622	..	...	...	...	...	...	...	...	...
Banks	8 623	..	...	...	...	...	...	...	...	...
Other sectors	8 624	..	...	...	...	...	...	...	...	...
Money market instruments	8 630	..	...	...	...	...	...	...	...	...
Monetary authorities	8 631	..	...	...	...	...	...	...	...	...
General government	8 632	..	...	...	...	...	...	...	...	...
Banks	8 633	..	...	...	...	...	...	...	...	...
Other sectors	8 634	..	...	...	...	...	...	...	...	...
Financial derivatives	8 640	..	...	...	...	...	...	...	...	...
Monetary authorities	8 641	..	...	...	...	...	...	...	...	...
General government	8 642	..	...	...	...	...	...	...	...	...
Banks	8 643	..	...	...	...	...	...	...	...	...
Other sectors	8 644	..	...	...	...	...	...	...	...	...
Other investment	8 703	..	**182,412**	**204,954**	**271,560**	**261,571**	**253,353**	**240,524**	...	...
Trade credits	8 706	..	...	...	...	...	...	...	...	...
General government: long-term	8 708	..	...	...	...	...	...	...	...	...
General government: short-term	8 709	..	...	...	...	...	...	...	...	...
Other sectors: long-term	8 711	..	...	...	...	...	...	...	...	...
Other sectors: short-term	8 712	..	...	...	...	...	...	...	...	...
Loans	8 714	..	38,533	39,974	49,596	48,101	45,659	44,690	...	...
Monetary authorities: long-term	8 717	..	...	...	...	...	...	...	...	...
Monetary authorities: short-term	8 718	..	...	...	...	...	...	...	...	...
General government: long-term	8 720	..	852	881	1,109	972	835	864	...	...
General government: short-term	8 721	..	...	...	...	...	...	...	...	...
Banks: long-term	8 723	..	37,680	39,093	48,486	47,129	44,823	43,826	...	...
Banks: short-term	8 724	..	...	...	...	...	...	...	...	...
Other sectors: long-term	8 726	..	...	...	...	...	...	...	...	...
Other sectors: short-term	8 727	..	...	...	...	...	...	...	...	...
Currency and deposits	8 730	..	86,519	76,404	86,631	82,773	84,302	85,682	...	...
Monetary authorities	8 731	..	...	...	...	...	...	...	...	...
General government	8 732	..	118	94	134	114	54	20	...	...
Banks	8 733	..	86,401	76,310	86,497	82,659	84,249	85,662	...	...
Other sectors	8 734	..	...	...	...	...	...	...	...	...
Other assets	8 736	..	57,360	88,576	135,334	130,697	123,392	110,152	...	...
Monetary authorities: long-term	8 738	..	...	...	...	...	...	...	...	...
Monetary authorities: short-term	8 739	..	...	...	...	...	...	...	...	...
General government: long-term	8 741	..	...	...	...	...	...	...	...	...
General government: short-term	8 742	..	...	...	...	...	...	...	...	...
Banks: long-term	8 744	..	...	...	...	...	...	...	...	...
Banks: short-term	8 745	..	...	...	...	...	...	...	...	...
Other sectors: long-term	8 747	..	9,860	11,798	15,016	15,272	16,622	17,286	...	...
Other sectors: short-term	8 748	..	47,501	76,778	120,318	115,425	106,771	92,867	...	...
Reserve assets	8 800	..	**31,838**	**33,378**	**37,913**	**38,536**	**40,594**	**40,967**	...	...
Monetary gold	8 810	..	7,915	7,697	9,189	8,782	8,176	8,046	...	...
Special drawing rights	8 820	..	20	5	2	2	16	155	236	269
Reserve position in the Fund	8 830	..	137	42	...	...	799	830	939	1,459
Foreign exchange	8 840	..	23,765	25,634	28,723	29,752	31,603	31,936	...	...
Other claims	8 880	..	...	...	...	...	...	...	...	...

Table 3 (Continued). INTERNATIONAL INVESTMENT POSITION (End-period stocks), 1988–95
(Millions of U.S. dollars)

	Code		1988	1989	1990	1991	1992	1993	1994	1995
LIABILITIES	8 995	D.	249,766	290,253	347,211	353,457	350,909	393,358	...	...
Direct investment in Switzerland	8 555	..	**32,566**	**32,891**	**43,393**	**45,016**	**42,551**	**47,311**	...	...
Equity capital and reinvested earnings	8 556	..	31,954	33,395	43,986	44,705	42,531	50,851	...	...
Claims on direct investors	8 557	..	...	...	...	...	...	...	...	...
Liabilities to direct investors	8 558	..	...	...	...	...	...	...	...	...
Other capital	8 580	..	612	–504	–594	311	20	–3,540	...	...
Claims on direct investors	8 585	..	...	...	...	...	...	...	...	...
Liabilities to direct investors	8 590	..	...	...	...	...	...	...	...	...
Portfolio investment	8 652	..	**76,228**	**93,655**	**93,784**	**103,124**	**109,190**	**153,500**	...	...
Equity securities	8 660	..	65,761	81,930	78,971	85,946	90,876	131,380	...	...
Banks	8 663	..	...	...	...	...	...	...	...	...
Other sectors	8 664	..	...	...	...	...	...	...	...	...
Debt securities	8 669	..	10,467	11,725	14,813	17,177	18,314	22,120	...	...
Bonds and notes	8 670	..	10,467	11,725	14,813	17,177	18,314	22,120	...	...
Monetary authorities	8 671	..	...	...	...	...	...	...	...	...
General government	8 672	..	...	...	...	...	...	...	...	...
Banks	8 673	..	...	...	...	...	...	...	...	...
Other sectors	8 674	..	...	...	...	...	...	...	...	...
Money market instruments	8 680	..	...	...	...	...	...	...	...	...
Monetary authorities	8 681	..	...	...	...	...	...	...	...	...
General government	8 682	..	...	...	...	...	...	...	...	...
Banks	8 683	..	...	...	...	...	...	...	...	...
Other sectors	8 684	..	...	...	...	...	...	...	...	...
Financial derivatives	8 690	..	...	...	...	...	...	...	...	...
Monetary authorities	8 691	..	...	...	...	...	...	...	...	...
General government	8 692	..	...	...	...	...	...	...	...	...
Banks	8 692	..	...	...	...	...	...	...	...	...
Other sectors	8 694	..	...	...	...	...	...	...	...	...
Other investment	8 753	..	**140,971**	**163,708**	**210,035**	**205,318**	**199,168**	**192,547**	...	...
Trade credits	8 756	..	...	...	...	...	...	...	...	...
General government: long-term	8 758	..	...	...	...	...	...	...	...	...
General government: short-term	8 759	..	...	...	...	...	...	...	...	...
Other sectors: long-term	8 761	..	...	...	...	...	...	...	...	...
Other sectors: short-term	8 762	..	...	...	...	...	...	...	...	...
Loans	8 764	..	12,251	10,926	12,753	11,430	9,938	10,998	...	...
Use of Fund credit and loans from the Fund	8 766	..	...	...	...	...	...	...	...	...
Monetary authorities: other long-term	8 767	..	...	...	...	...	...	...	...	...
Monetary authorities: short-term	8 768	..	...	...	...	...	...	...	...	...
General government: long-term	8 770	..	...	...	...	...	...	...	...	...
General government: short-term	8 771	..	...	...	...	...	...	...	...	...
Banks: long-term	8 773	..	12,251	10,926	12,753	11,430	9,938	10,998	...	...
Banks: short-term	8 774	..	...	...	...	...	...	...	...	...
Other sectors: long-term	8 776	..	...	...	...	...	...	...	...	...
Other sectors: short-term	8 777	..	...	...	...	...	...	...	...	...
Currency and deposits	8 780	..	89,979	98,867	120,188	119,711	114,658	116,432	...	...
Monetary authorities	8 781	..	...	...	...	...	...	...	...	...
General government	8 782	..	...	...	...	...	...	...	...	...
Banks	8 783	..	89,979	98,867	120,188	119,711	114,658	116,432	...	...
Other sectors	8 784	..	...	...	...	...	...	...	...	...
Other liabilities	8 786	..	38,741	53,915	77,095	74,176	74,573	65,117	...	...
Monetary authorities: long-term	8 788	..	...	...	...	...	...	...	...	...
Monetary authorities: short-term	8 789	..	396	158	86	121	152	320	...	...
General government: long-term	8 791	..	...	...	...	...	...	...	...	...
General government: short-term	8 792	..	...	...	...	...	...	...	...	...
Banks: long-term	8 794	..	...	...	...	...	...	...	...	...
Banks: short-term	8 795	..	...	...	...	...	...	...	...	...
Other sectors: long-term	8 797	..	9,232	11,084	13,159	13,563	15,435	15,141	...	...
Other sectors: short-term	8 798	..	29,114	42,672	63,850	60,492	58,986	49,657	...	...
NET INTERNATIONAL INVESTMENT POSITION	8 995	..	**186,727**	**185,528**	**217,526**	**235,608**	**235,125**	**239,025**	...	...
Conversion rates: Swiss francs per U.S. dollar (end of period)	0 102	..	**1.5040**	**1.5465**	**1.2955**	**1.3555**	**1.4560**	**1.4795**	**1.3115**	**1.1505**

Table 1. ANALYTIC PRESENTATION, 1988–95
(Millions of U.S. dollars)

	Code		1988	1989	1990	1991	1992	1993	1994	1995
A. Current Account[1]	4 993	Y.	**–151**	**1,222**	**1,762**	**699**	**55**	**–493**	**–922**	**440**
Goods: exports f.o.b	2 100	..	1,348	3,013	4,156	3,438	3,100	3,203	3,329	3,858
Goods: imports f.o.b	3 100	..	–1,986	–1,821	–2,062	–2,354	–2,941	–3,476	–4,604	–4,001
Balance on Goods	4 100	..	*–639*	*1,192*	*2,094*	*1,084*	*159*	*–273*	*–1,275*	*–143*
Services: credit	2 200	..	667	893	874	1,065	1,281	1,531	1,847	1,966
Services: debit	3 200	..	–636	–792	–892	–1,002	–1,102	–1,265	–1,489	–1,437
Balance on Goods and Services	4 991	..	*–608*	*1,293*	*2,075*	*1,146*	*338*	*–7*	*–917*	*386*
Income: credit	2 300	..	22	22	45	65	69	80	103	105
Income: debit	3 300	..	–461	–745	–831	–1,096	–1,214	–1,052	–986	–968
Balance on Goods, Services, and Income	4 992	..	*–1,047*	*570*	*1,289*	*115*	*–808*	*–979*	*–1,800*	*–477*
Current transfers: credit	2 379	Y.	897	657	476	588	871	494	895	935
Current transfers: debit	3 379	..	–1	–5	–3	–4	–8	–8	–17	–18
B. Capital Account[1]	4 994	Y.	**...**	**...**	**...**	**...**	**...**	**...**	**102**	**20**
Capital account: credit	2 994	Y.	...	...	...	...	...	...	102	20
Capital account: debit	3 994	..	...	...	...	...	...	...	...	...
Total, Groups A Plus B	4 010	..	*–151*	*1,222*	*1,762*	*699*	*55*	*–493*	*–820*	*460*
C. Financial Account[1]	4 995	X.	**85**	**–1,708**	**–1,836**	**–515**	**–50**	**599**	**2,498**	**1,705**
Direct investment abroad	4 505	..	...	...	...	...	...	...	...	...
Direct investment in Syrian Arab Republic	4 555	Y.	...	...	...	...	...	176	143	65
Portfolio investment assets	4 602	..	...	...	...	...	...	...	...	...
Equity securities	4 610	..	...	...	...	...	...	...	...	...
Debt securities	4 619	..	...	...	...	...	...	...	...	...
Portfolio investment liabilities	4 652	Y.	...	...	...	...	...	...	...	...
Equity securities	4 660	Y.	...	...	...	...	...	...	...	...
Debt securities	4 669	Y.	...	...	...	...	...	...	...	...
Other investment assets	4 703	..	–256	–1,580	–2,008	–1,294	–1,175	–116	...	...
Monetary authorities	4 703	.A	...	...	...	...	...	–116	...	...
General government	4 703	.B	–196	–977	–831	–194	–74	...	...	...
Banks	4 703	.C	–60	–198	–493	–313	–241	...	...	...
Other sectors	4 703	.D	...	–405	–684	–787	–860	...	...	...
Other investment liabilities	4 753	X.	341	–128	172	779	1,126	539	2,355	1,640
Monetary authorities	4 753	XA	–69	103	154	7	28	11	51	–13
General government	4 753	YB	297	–757	–731	–35	173	656	1,809	771
Banks	4 753	YC	45	–64	–143	–190	–226	–128	–147	–112
Other sectors	4 753	YD	68	590	892	997	1,151	...	642	994
Total, Groups A Through C	4 020	..	*–66*	*–486*	*–74*	*184*	*6*	*106*	*1,678*	*2,165*
D. Net Errors and Omissions	4 998	..	**34**	**420**	**110**	**–112**	**70**	**170**	**–906**	**–1,385**
Total, Groups A Through D	4 030	..	*–32*	*–66*	*36*	*72*	*76*	*276*	*772*	*780*
E. Reserves and Related Items	4 040	..	**32**	**66**	**–36**	**–72**	**–76**	**–276**	**–772**	**–780**
Reserve assets	4 800	..	32	66	–36	–72	–76	–276	–772	–780
Use of Fund credit and loans	4 766	..	...	...	...	...	...	...	...	...
Liabilities constituting foreign authorities' reserves	4 900	..	...	...	...	...	...	...	...	...
Exceptional financing	4 920	..	...	...	...	...	...	...	...	...
Conversion rates: Syrian pounds per U.S. dollar	0 101	..	**11.225**	**11.225**	**11.225**	**11.225**	**11.225**	**11.225**	**11.225**	**11.225**

[1] Excludes components that have been classified in the categories of Group E.

Table 2. STANDARD PRESENTATION, 1988–95
(Millions of U.S. dollars)

	Code	1988	1989	1990	1991	1992	1993	1994	1995
CURRENT ACCOUNT	4 993 . .	**–151**	**1,222**	**1,762**	**699**	**55**	**–493**	**–922**	**440**
A. GOODS	4 100 . .	–639	1,192	2,094	1,084	159	–273	–1,275	–143
Credit	2 100 . .	**1,348**	**3,013**	**4,156**	**3,438**	**3,100**	**3,203**	**3,329**	**3,858**
General merchandise: exports f.o.b.	2 110 . .	1,348	3,013	4,156	3,438	3,100	3,203	3,329	3,858
Goods for processing: exports f.o.b.	2 150 . .	...	...	...	...	...	...	...	...
Repairs on goods	2 160 . .	...	...	...	...	...	...	...	...
Goods procured in ports by carriers	2 170 . .	...	...	...	...	...	...	...	...
Nonmonetary gold	2 180 . .	...	...	...	...	...	...	...	...
Debit	3 100 . .	**–1,986**	**–1,821**	**–2,062**	**–2,354**	**–2,941**	**–3,476**	**–4,604**	**–4,001**
General merchandise: imports f.o.b.	3 110 . .	–1,986	–1,821	–2,062	–2,354	–2,941	–3,476	–4,604	–4,001
Goods for processing: imports f.o.b.	3 150 . .	...	...	...	...	...	...	...	...
Repairs on goods	3 160 . .	...	...	...	...	...	...	...	...
Goods procured in ports by carriers	3 170 . .	...	...	...	...	...	...	...	...
Nonmonetary gold	3 180 . .	...	...	...	...	...	...	...	...
B. SERVICES	4 200 . .	31	101	–19	62	179	266	358	529
Total credit	2 200 . .	*667*	*893*	*874*	*1,065*	*1,281*	*1,531*	*1,847*	*1,966*
Total debit	3 200 . .	*–636*	*–792*	*–892*	*–1,002*	*–1,102*	*–1,265*	*–1,489*	*–1,437*
Transportation services, credit	2 205 . .	**187**	**215**	**220**	**245**	**260**	**285**	**342**	**237**
Passenger	2 205 BA	...	...	...	...	...	...	...	...
Freight	2 205 BB	*46*	*32*	*39*	*54*	*29*	*24*	*342*	*237*
Other	2 205 BC	*142*	*184*	*182*	*191*	*231*	*261*	...	...
Sea transport, passenger	2 207 . .	...	...	...	...	...	...	...	...
Sea transport, freight	2 208 . .	...	...	...	...	...	...	...	...
Sea transport, other	2 209 . .	...	...	...	...	...	...	...	...
Air transport, passenger	2 211 . .	...	...	...	...	...	...	...	...
Air transport, freight	2 212 . .	...	...	...	...	...	...	...	...
Air transport, other	2 213 . .	...	...	...	...	...	...	...	...
Other transport, passenger	2 215 . .	...	...	...	...	...	...	...	...
Other transport, freight	2 216 . .	...	...	...	...	...	...	...	...
Other transport, other	2 217 . .	...	...	...	...	...	...	...	...
Transportation services, debit	3 205 . .	**–281**	**–301**	**–382**	**–457**	**–584**	**–725**	**–879**	**–777**
Passenger	3 205 BA	...	...	...	...	...	...	...	...
Freight	3 205 BB	*–222*	*–226*	*–277*	*–345*	*–459*	*–570*	*–879*	*–777*
Other	3 205 BC	*–59*	*–75*	*–105*	*–112*	*–125*	*–155*	...	...
Sea transport, passenger	3 207 . .	...	...	...	...	...	...	...	...
Sea transport, freight	3 208 . .	...	...	...	...	...	...	...	...
Sea transport, other	3 209 . .	...	...	...	...	...	...	...	...
Air transport, passenger	3 211 . .	...	...	...	...	...	...	...	...
Air transport, freight	3 212 . .	...	...	...	...	...	...	...	...
Air transport, other	3 213 . .	...	...	...	...	...	...	...	...
Other transport, passenger	3 215 . .	...	...	...	...	...	...	...	...
Other transport, freight	3 216 . .	...	...	...	...	...	...	...	...
Other transport, other	3 217 . .	...	...	...	...	...	...	...	...
Travel, credit	2 236 . .	**266**	**374**	**320**	**410**	**600**	**758**	**1,130**	**1,325**
Business travel	2 237 . .	...	...	...	...	...	...	...	...
Personal travel	2 240 . .	...	...	...	...	...	...	...	...
Travel, debit	3 236 . .	**–170**	**–246**	**–249**	**–256**	**–260**	**–300**	**–390**	**–398**
Business travel	3 237 . .	...	...	...	...	...	...	...	...
Personal travel	3 240 . .	...	...	...	...	...	...	...	...
Other services, credit	2 200 BA	**214**	**305**	**334**	**410**	**421**	**488**	**375**	**404**
Communications	2 245 . .	...	...	...	...	...	...	...	...
Construction	2 249 . .	...	...	...	...	...	...	...	...
Insurance	2 253 . .	...	...	...	...	...	...	...	...
Financial	2 260 . .	...	...	...	...	...	...	...	...
Computer and information	2 262 . .	...	...	...	...	...	...	...	...
Royalties and licence fees	2 266 . .	...	...	...	...	...	...	...	...
Other business services	2 268 . .	75	167	200	211	225	268	128	137
Personal, cultural, and recreational	2 287 . .	...	...	...	...	...	...	...	...
Government, n.i.e.	2 291 . .	139	137	134	199	196	220	247	267
Other services, debit	3 200 BA	**–185**	**–246**	**–261**	**–289**	**–258**	**–240**	**–220**	**–262**
Communications	3 245 . .	...	...	...	...	...	...	...	...
Construction	3 249 . .	...	...	...	...	...	...	...	...
Insurance	3 253 . .	–25	–25	–31	–38	–51	...	...	...
Financial	3 260 . .	...	...	...	...	...	...	...	...
Computer and information	3 262 . .	...	...	...	...	...	...	...	...
Royalties and licence fees	3 266 . .	...	...	...	...	...	...	...	...
Other business services	3 268 . .	–19	–31	–40	–41	–16	–22	–59	–83
Personal, cultural, and recreational	3 287 . .	...	...	...	...	...	...	...	...
Government, n.i.e.	3 291 . .	–142	–189	–190	–210	–191	–218	–161	–179

Table 2 (Continued). STANDARD PRESENTATION, 1988–95

(Millions of U.S. dollars)

	Code	1988	1989	1990	1991	1992	1993	1994	1995
C. INCOME	4 300 . .	–439	–723	–786	–1,031	–1,146	–972	–883	–863
Total credit	2 300 . .	*22*	*22*	*45*	*65*	*69*	*80*	*103*	*105*
Total debit	3 300 . .	*–461*	*–745*	*–831*	*–1,096*	*–1,214*	*–1,052*	*–986*	*–968*
Compensation of employees, credit	2 310 . .	**. . .**	**. . .**	**. . .**	**. . .**	**. . .**	**. . .**	**. . .**	**. . .**
Compensation of employees, debit	3 310 . .	**. . .**	**. . .**	**. . .**	**. . .**	**. . .**	**. . .**	**. . .**	**. . .**
Investment income, credit	2 320 . .	**22**	**22**	**45**	**65**	**69**	**80**	**103**	**105**
Direct investment income	2 330 . .	. . .	. . .	. . .	. . .	. . .	. . .	. . .	. . .
Dividends and distributed branch profits	2 332 . .	. . .	. . .	. . .	. . .	. . .	. . .	. . .	. . .
Reinvested earnings and undistributed branch profits	2 333 . .	. . .	. . .	. . .	. . .	. . .	. . .	. . .	. . .
Income on debt (interest)	2 334 . .	. . .	. . .	. . .	. . .	. . .	. . .	. . .	. . .
Portfolio investment income	2 339 . .	. . .	. . .	. . .	. . .	. . .	. . .	. . .	. . .
Income on equity	2 340 . .	. . .	. . .	. . .	. . .	. . .	. . .	. . .	. . .
Income on bonds and notes	2 350 . .	. . .	. . .	. . .	. . .	. . .	. . .	. . .	. . .
Income on money market instruments and financial derivatives	2 360 . .	. . .	. . .	. . .	. . .	. . .	. . .	. . .	. . .
Other investment income	2 370 . .	22	22	45	65	69	80	103	105
Investment income, debit	3 320 . .	**–461**	**–745**	**–831**	**–1,096**	**–1,214**	**–1,052**	**–986**	**–968**
Direct investment income	3 330 . .	. . .	. . .	. . .	. . .	. . .	. . .	–828	–857
Dividends and distributed branch profits	3 332 . .	. . .	. . .	. . .	. . .	. . .	. . .	–828	–857
Reinvested earnings and undistributed branch profits	3 333 . .	. . .	. . .	. . .	. . .	. . .	. . .	. . .	. . .
Income on debt (interest)	3 334 . .	. . .	. . .	. . .	. . .	. . .	. . .	. . .	. . .
Portfolio investment income	3 339 . .	. . .	. . .	. . .	. . .	. . .	. . .	. . .	. . .
Income on equity	3 340 . .	. . .	. . .	. . .	. . .	. . .	. . .	. . .	. . .
Income on bonds and notes	3 350 . .	. . .	. . .	. . .	. . .	. . .	. . .	. . .	. . .
Income on money market instruments and financial derivatives	3 360 . .	. . .	. . .	. . .	. . .	. . .	. . .	. . .	. . .
Other investment income	3 370 . .	–461	–745	–831	–1,096	–1,214	–1,052	–158	–111
D. CURRENT TRANSFERS	4 379 . .	896	653	473	584	863	486	878	917
Credit	2 379 . .	**897**	**657**	**476**	**588**	**871**	**494**	**895**	**935**
General government	2 380 . .	537	227	91	238	321	68	27	12
Other sectors	2 390 . .	360	430	385	350	550	426	868	923
Workers' remittances	2 391 . .	360	430	385	350	550	426	370	400
Other current transfers	2 392 . .	. . .	. . .	. . .	. . .	. . .	. . .	498	523
Debit	3 379 . .	**–1**	**–5**	**–3**	**–4**	**–8**	**–8**	**–17**	**–18**
General government	3 380 . .	–1	–5	–3	–4	–8	–8	–6	–3
Other sectors	3 390 . .	. . .	. . .	. . .	. . .	. . .	. . .	–11	–15
Workers' remittances	3 391 . .	. . .	. . .	. . .	. . .	. . .	. . .	–11	–15
Other current transfers	3 392 . .	. . .	. . .	. . .	. . .	. . .	. . .	. . .	. . .
CAPITAL AND FINANCIAL ACCOUNT	4 996 . .	**117**	**–1,642**	**–1,872**	**–587**	**–125**	**323**	**1,828**	**945**
CAPITAL ACCOUNT	4 994 . .	**. . .**	**. . .**	**. . .**	**. . .**	**. . .**	**. . .**	**102**	**20**
Total credit	2 994 . .	. . .	. . .	. . .	. . .	. . .	. . .	*102*	*20*
Total debit	3 994 . .	. . .	. . .	. . .	. . .	. . .	. . .	. . .	. . .
Capital transfers, credit	2 400 . .	**. . .**	**. . .**	**. . .**	**. . .**	**. . .**	**. . .**	**102**	**20**
General government	2 401 . .	. . .	. . .	. . .	. . .	. . .	. . .	. . .	. . .
Debt forgiveness	2 402 . .	. . .	. . .	. . .	. . .	. . .	. . .	. . .	. . .
Other capital transfers	2 410 . .	. . .	. . .	. . .	. . .	. . .	. . .	. . .	. . .
Other sectors	2 430 . .	. . .	. . .	. . .	. . .	. . .	. . .	102	20
Migrants' transfers	2 431 . .	. . .	. . .	. . .	. . .	. . .	. . .	. . .	. . .
Debt forgiveness	2 432 . .	. . .	. . .	. . .	. . .	. . .	. . .	. . .	. . .
Other capital transfers	2 440 . .	. . .	. . .	. . .	. . .	. . .	. . .	102	20
Capital transfers, debit	3 400 . .	**. . .**	**. . .**	**. . .**	**. . .**	**. . .**	**. . .**	**. . .**	**. . .**
General government	3 401 . .	. . .	. . .	. . .	. . .	. . .	. . .	. . .	. . .
Debt forgiveness	3 402 . .	. . .	. . .	. . .	. . .	. . .	. . .	. . .	. . .
Other capital transfers	3 410 . .	. . .	. . .	. . .	. . .	. . .	. . .	. . .	. . .
Other sectors	3 430 . .	. . .	. . .	. . .	. . .	. . .	. . .	. . .	. . .
Migrants' transfers	3 431 . .	. . .	. . .	. . .	. . .	. . .	. . .	. . .	. . .
Debt forgiveness	3 432 . .	. . .	. . .	. . .	. . .	. . .	. . .	. . .	. . .
Other capital transfers	3 440 . .	. . .	. . .	. . .	. . .	. . .	. . .	. . .	. . .
Nonproduced nonfinancial assets, credit	2 480 . .	**. . .**	**. . .**	**. . .**	**. . .**	**. . .**	**. . .**	**. . .**	**. . .**
Nonproduced nonfinancial assets, debit	3 480 . .	**. . .**	**. . .**	**. . .**	**. . .**	**. . .**	**. . .**	**. . .**	**. . .**

Table 2 (Continued). STANDARD PRESENTATION, 1988–95
(Millions of U.S. dollars)

	Code		1988	1989	1990	1991	1992	1993	1994	1995
FINANCIAL ACCOUNT	4 995	. .	**117**	**–1,642**	**–1,872**	**–587**	**–125**	**323**	**1,726**	**925**
A. DIRECT INVESTMENT	4 500	. .	. . .	. . .	. . .	. . .	. . .	176	143	65
Direct investment abroad	4 505	. .	. . .	. . .	. . .	. . .	. . .	. . .	. . .	. . .
Equity capital	4 510	. .	. . .	. . .	. . .	. . .	. . .	. . .	. . .	. . .
Claims on affiliated enterprises	4 515	. .	. . .	. . .	. . .	. . .	. . .	. . .	. . .	. . .
Liabilities to affiliated enterprises	4 520	. .	. . .	. . .	. . .	. . .	. . .	. . .	. . .	. . .
Reinvested earnings	4 525	. .	. . .	. . .	. . .	. . .	. . .	. . .	. . .	. . .
Other capital	4 530	. .	. . .	. . .	. . .	. . .	. . .	. . .	. . .	. . .
Claims on affiliated enterprises	4 535	. .	. . .	. . .	. . .	. . .	. . .	. . .	. . .	. . .
Liabilities to affiliated enterprises	4 540	. .	. . .	. . .	. . .	. . .	. . .	. . .	. . .	. . .
Direct investment in Syrian Arab Republic	4 555	. .	. . .	. . .	. . .	. . .	. . .	**176**	**143**	**65**
Equity capital	4 560	. .	. . .	. . .	. . .	. . .	. . .	176	143	65
Claims on direct investors	4 565	. .	. . .	. . .	. . .	. . .	. . .	. . .	. . .	. . .
Liabilities to direct investors	4 570	. .	. . .	. . .	. . .	. . .	. . .	. . .	143	65
Reinvested earnings	4 575	. .	. . .	. . .	. . .	. . .	. . .	. . .	. . .	. . .
Other capital	4 580	. .	. . .	. . .	. . .	. . .	. . .	. . .	. . .	. . .
Claims on direct investors	4 585	. .	. . .	. . .	. . .	. . .	. . .	. . .	. . .	. . .
Liabilities to direct investors	4 590	. .	. . .	. . .	. . .	. . .	. . .	. . .	. . .	. . .
B. PORTFOLIO INVESTMENT	4 600	. .	. . .	. . .	. . .	. . .	. . .	. . .	. . .	. . .
Assets	4 602	. .	. . .	. . .	. . .	. . .	. . .	. . .	. . .	. . .
Equity securities	4 610	. .	. . .	. . .	. . .	. . .	. . .	. . .	. . .	. . .
Monetary authorities	4 611	. .	. . .	. . .	. . .	. . .	. . .	. . .	. . .	. . .
General government	4 612	. .	. . .	. . .	. . .	. . .	. . .	. . .	. . .	. . .
Banks	4 613	. .	. . .	. . .	. . .	. . .	. . .	. . .	. . .	. . .
Other sectors	4 614	. .	. . .	. . .	. . .	. . .	. . .	. . .	. . .	. . .
Debt securities	4 619	. .	. . .	. . .	. . .	. . .	. . .	. . .	. . .	. . .
Bonds and notes	4 620	. .	. . .	. . .	. . .	. . .	. . .	. . .	. . .	. . .
Monetary authorities	4 621	. .	. . .	. . .	. . .	. . .	. . .	. . .	. . .	. . .
General government	4 622	. .	. . .	. . .	. . .	. . .	. . .	. . .	. . .	. . .
Banks	4 623	. .	. . .	. . .	. . .	. . .	. . .	. . .	. . .	. . .
Other sectors	4 624	. .	. . .	. . .	. . .	. . .	. . .	. . .	. . .	. . .
Money market instruments	4 630	. .	. . .	. . .	. . .	. . .	. . .	. . .	. . .	. . .
Monetary authorities	4 631	. .	. . .	. . .	. . .	. . .	. . .	. . .	. . .	. . .
General government	4 632	. .	. . .	. . .	. . .	. . .	. . .	. . .	. . .	. . .
Banks	4 633	. .	. . .	. . .	. . .	. . .	. . .	. . .	. . .	. . .
Other sectors	4 634	. .	. . .	. . .	. . .	. . .	. . .	. . .	. . .	. . .
Financial derivatives	4 640	. .	. . .	. . .	. . .	. . .	. . .	. . .	. . .	. . .
Monetary authorities	4 641	. .	. . .	. . .	. . .	. . .	. . .	. . .	. . .	. . .
General government	4 642	. .	. . .	. . .	. . .	. . .	. . .	. . .	. . .	. . .
Banks	4 643	. .	. . .	. . .	. . .	. . .	. . .	. . .	. . .	. . .
Other sectors	4 644	. .	. . .	. . .	. . .	. . .	. . .	. . .	. . .	. . .
Liabilities	4 652	. .	. . .	. . .	. . .	. . .	. . .	. . .	. . .	. . .
Equity securities	4 660	. .	. . .	. . .	. . .	. . .	. . .	. . .	. . .	. . .
Banks	4 663	. .	. . .	. . .	. . .	. . .	. . .	. . .	. . .	. . .
Other sectors	4 664	. .	. . .	. . .	. . .	. . .	. . .	. . .	. . .	. . .
Debt securities	4 669	. .	. . .	. . .	. . .	. . .	. . .	. . .	. . .	. . .
Bonds and notes	4 670	. .	. . .	. . .	. . .	. . .	. . .	. . .	. . .	. . .
Monetary authorities	4 671	. .	. . .	. . .	. . .	. . .	. . .	. . .	. . .	. . .
General government	4 672	. .	. . .	. . .	. . .	. . .	. . .	. . .	. . .	. . .
Banks	4 673	. .	. . .	. . .	. . .	. . .	. . .	. . .	. . .	. . .
Other sectors	4 674	. .	. . .	. . .	. . .	. . .	. . .	. . .	. . .	. . .
Money market instruments	4 680	. .	. . .	. . .	. . .	. . .	. . .	. . .	. . .	. . .
Monetary authorities	4 681	. .	. . .	. . .	. . .	. . .	. . .	. . .	. . .	. . .
General government	4 682	. .	. . .	. . .	. . .	. . .	. . .	. . .	. . .	. . .
Banks	4 683	. .	. . .	. . .	. . .	. . .	. . .	. . .	. . .	. . .
Other sectors	4 684	. .	. . .	. . .	. . .	. . .	. . .	. . .	. . .	. . .
Financial derivatives	4 690	. .	. . .	. . .	. . .	. . .	. . .	. . .	. . .	. . .
Monetary authorities	4 691	. .	. . .	. . .	. . .	. . .	. . .	. . .	. . .	. . .
General government	4 692	. .	. . .	. . .	. . .	. . .	. . .	. . .	. . .	. . .
Banks	4 693	. .	. . .	. . .	. . .	. . .	. . .	. . .	. . .	. . .
Other sectors	4 694	. .	. . .	. . .	. . .	. . .	. . .	. . .	. . .	. . .

Table 2 (Concluded). STANDARD PRESENTATION, 1988–95
(Millions of U.S. dollars)

	Code	1988	1989	1990	1991	1992	1993	1994	1995
C. OTHER INVESTMENT	4 700	85	–1,708	–1,836	–515	–50	423	2,355	1,640
Assets	4 703	**–256**	**–1,580**	**–2,008**	**–1,294**	**–1,175**	**–116**	**. . .**	**. . .**
Trade credits	4 706	. . .	. . .	. . .	. . .	. . .	. . .	. . .	. . .
General government: long-term	4 708	. . .	. . .	. . .	. . .	. . .	. . .	. . .	. . .
General government: short-term	4 709	. . .	. . .	. . .	. . .	. . .	. . .	. . .	. . .
Other sectors: long-term	4 711	. . .	. . .	. . .	. . .	. . .	. . .	. . .	. . .
Other sectors: short-term	4 712	. . .	. . .	. . .	. . .	. . .	. . .	. . .	. . .
Loans	4 714	. . .	. . .	. . .	. . .	. . .	. . .	. . .	. . .
Monetary authorities: long-term	4 717	. . .	. . .	. . .	. . .	. . .	. . .	. . .	. . .
Monetary authorities: short-term	4 718	. . .	. . .	. . .	. . .	. . .	. . .	. . .	. . .
General government: long-term	4 720	. . .	. . .	. . .	. . .	. . .	. . .	. . .	. . .
General government: short-term	4 721	. . .	. . .	. . .	. . .	. . .	. . .	. . .	. . .
Banks: long-term	4 723	. . .	. . .	. . .	. . .	. . .	. . .	. . .	. . .
Banks: short-term	4 724	. . .	. . .	. . .	. . .	. . .	. . .	. . .	. . .
Other sectors: long-term	4 726	. . .	. . .	. . .	. . .	. . .	. . .	. . .	. . .
Other sectors: short-term	4 727	. . .	. . .	. . .	. . .	. . .	. . .	. . .	. . .
Currency and deposits	4 730	–256	–1,175	–1,324	–507	–315	. . .	. . .	. . .
Monetary authorities	4 731	. . .	. . .	. . .	. . .	. . .	. . .	. . .	. . .
General government	4 732	–196	–977	–831	–194	–74	. . .	. . .	. . .
Banks	4 733	–60	–198	–493	–313	–241	. . .	. . .	. . .
Other sectors	4 734	. . .	. . .	. . .	. . .	. . .	. . .	. . .	. . .
Other assets	4 736	. . .	–405	–684	–787	–860	–116	. . .	. . .
Monetary authorities: long-term	4 738	. . .	. . .	. . .	. . .	. . .	. . .	. . .	. . .
Monetary authorities: short-term	4 739	. . .	. . .	. . .	. . .	. . .	–116	. . .	. . .
General government: long-term	4 741	. . .	. . .	. . .	. . .	. . .	. . .	. . .	. . .
General government: short-term	4 742	. . .	. . .	. . .	. . .	. . .	. . .	. . .	. . .
Banks: long-term	4 744	. . .	. . .	. . .	. . .	. . .	. . .	. . .	. . .
Banks: short-term	4 745	. . .	. . .	. . .	. . .	. . .	. . .	. . .	. . .
Other sectors: long-term	4 747	. . .	. . .	. . .	. . .	. . .	. . .	. . .	. . .
Other sectors: short-term	4 748	. . .	–405	–684	–787	–860	. . .	. . .	. . .
Liabilities	4 753	**341**	**–128**	**172**	**779**	**1,126**	**539**	**2,355**	**1,640**
Trade credits	4 756	. . .	. . .	. . .	. . .	. . .	. . .	. . .	. . .
General government: long-term	4 758	. . .	. . .	. . .	. . .	. . .	. . .	. . .	. . .
General government: short-term	4 759	. . .	. . .	. . .	. . .	. . .	. . .	. . .	. . .
Other sectors: long-term	4 761	. . .	. . .	. . .	. . .	. . .	. . .	. . .	. . .
Other sectors: short-term	4 762	. . .	. . .	. . .	. . .	. . .	. . .	. . .	. . .
Loans	4 764	297	–167	161	962	1,324	–121	2,451	1,765
Use of Fund credit and loans from the Fund	4 766	. . .	. . .	. . .	. . .	. . .	. . .	. . .	. . .
Monetary authorities: other long-term	4 767	. . .	. . .	. . .	. . .	. . .	. . .	. . .	. . .
Monetary authorities: short-term	4 768	. . .	. . .	. . .	. . .	. . .	. . .	. . .	. . .
General government: long-term	4 770	297	–757	–731	–35	173	–121	245	–404
General government: short-term	4 771	. . .	. . .	. . .	. . .	. . .	. . .	1,564	1,175
Banks: long-term	4 773	. . .	. . .	. . .	. . .	. . .	. . .	. . .	. . .
Banks: short-term	4 774	. . .	. . .	. . .	. . .	. . .	. . .	. . .	. . .
Other sectors: long-term	4 776	. . .	. . .	. . .	. . .	. . .	. . .	. . .	. . .
Other sectors: short-term	4 777	. . .	590	892	997	1,151	. . .	642	994
Currency and deposits	4 780	45	–64	–143	–190	–226	. . .	. . .	. . .
Monetary authorities	4 781	. . .	. . .	. . .	. . .	. . .	. . .	. . .	. . .
General government	4 782	. . .	. . .	. . .	. . .	. . .	. . .	. . .	. . .
Banks	4 783	45	–64	–143	–190	–226	. . .	. . .	. . .
Other sectors	4 784	. . .	. . .	. . .	. . .	. . .	. . .	. . .	. . .
Other liabilities	4 786	–1	103	154	7	28	660	–96	–125
Monetary authorities: long-term	4 788	. . .	. . .	. . .	. . .	. . .	. . .	. . .	. . .
Monetary authorities: short-term	4 789	–69	103	154	7	28	11	51	–13
General government: long-term	4 791	. . .	. . .	. . .	. . .	. . .	. . .	. . .	. . .
General government: short-term	4 792	. . .	. . .	. . .	. . .	. . .	777	. . .	. . .
Banks: long-term	4 794	. . .	. . .	. . .	. . .	. . .	. . .	. . .	. . .
Banks: short-term	4 795	. . .	. . .	. . .	. . .	. . .	–128	–147	–112
Other sectors: long-term	4 797	. . .	. . .	. . .	. . .	. . .	. . .	. . .	. . .
Other sectors: short-term	4 798	68	. . .	. . .	. . .	. . .	. . .	. . .	. . .
D. RESERVE ASSETS	4 800	32	66	–36	–72	–76	–276	–772	–780
Monetary gold	4 810	. . .	. . .	. . .	. . .	. . .	. . .	. . .	. . .
Special drawing rights	4 820	. . .	. . .	. . .	. . .	. . .	. . .	. . .	. . .
Reserve position in the Fund	4 830	. . .	. . .	. . .	. . .	. . .	. . .	. . .	. . .
Foreign exchange	4 840	32	66	–36	–72	–76	–276	–772	–780
Other claims	4 880	. . .	. . .	. . .	. . .	. . .	. . .	. . .	. . .
NET ERRORS AND OMISSIONS	4 998	**34**	**420**	**110**	**–112**	**70**	**170**	**–906**	**–1,385**

Part 3 of the *Yearbook* contains descriptions of the methodologies, compilation practices, and sources used to compile these data.

Table 1. ANALYTIC PRESENTATION, 1988–95
(Millions of U.S. dollars)

	Code	1988	1989	1990	1991	1992	1993	1994	1995
A. Current Account [1]	4 993 Y .	**–356.6**	**–335.1**	**–558.9**	**–737.5**	**–704.3**	**–770.0**	**–680.7**	**–629.2**
Goods: exports f.o.b	2 100 . .	386.5	415.1	407.8	363.0	400.7	444.6	519.4	682.9
Goods: imports f.o.b	3 100 . .	–1,033.0	–1,070.1	–1,186.3	–1,229.9	–1,316.6	–1,288.6	–1,309.3	–1,340.4
Balance on Goods	4 100 . .	*–646.5*	*–655.0*	*–778.5*	*–867.0*	*–915.9*	*–844.0*	*–790.0*	*–657.5*
Services: credit	2 200 . .	117.4	117.3	130.6	142.3	167.5	312.6	410.5	566.4
Services: debit	3 200 . .	–263.4	–272.5	–287.7	–300.1	–336.6	–595.8	–538.9	–754.5
Balance on Goods and Services	4 991 . .	*–792.5*	*–810.2*	*–935.6*	*–1,024.7*	*–1,084.9*	*–1,127.2*	*–918.3*	*–845.5*
Income: credit	2 300 . .	3.2	5.4	5.9	7.9	8.1	21.6	30.9	3.9
Income: debit	3 300 . .	–188.4	–182.5	–190.9	–192.5	–233.5	–170.8	–153.4	–141.2
Balance on Goods, Services, and Income	4 992 . .	*–977.8*	*–987.3*	*–1,120.6*	*–1,209.3*	*–1,310.4*	*–1,276.4*	*–1,040.8*	*–982.8*
Current transfers: credit	2 379 Y .	642.9	682.0	592.8	504.5	641.1	536.7	385.1	385.9
Current transfers: debit	3 379 . .	–21.7	–29.8	–31.0	–32.7	–35.0	–30.3	–25.0	–32.3
B. Capital Account [1]	4 994 Y .	**. . .**	**. . .**	**327.2**	**353.7**	**298.2**	**202.8**	**262.6**	**236.7**
Capital account: credit	2 994 Y .	. . .	. . .	327.2	353.7	298.2	202.8	262.6	236.7
Capital account: debit	3 994 . .	. . .	. . .	. . .	. . .	. . .	. . .	. . .	. . .
Total, Groups A Plus B	4 010 . .	*–356.6*	*–335.1*	*–231.7*	*–383.8*	*–406.1*	*–567.3*	*–418.1*	*–392.5*
C. Financial Account [1]	4 995 X .	**33.9**	**21.8**	**42.3**	**118.2**	**107.3**	**106.9**	**73.8**	**154.2**
Direct investment abroad	4 505 . .	. . .	. . .	. . .	. . .	. . .	. . .	. . .	. . .
Direct investment in Tanzania	4 555 Y .	. . .	. . .	. . .	. . .	12.0	20.2	50.0	150.0
Portfolio investment assets	4 602 . .	. . .	. . .	. . .	. . .	. . .	. . .	. . .	. . .
Equity securities	4 610 . .	. . .	. . .	. . .	. . .	. . .	. . .	. . .	. . .
Debt securities	4 619 . .	. . .	. . .	. . .	. . .	. . .	. . .	. . .	. . .
Portfolio investment liabilities	4 652 Y .	. . .	. . .	. . .	. . .	. . .	. . .	. . .	. . .
Equity securities	4 660 Y .	. . .	. . .	. . .	. . .	. . .	. . .	. . .	. . .
Debt securities	4 669 Y .	. . .	. . .	. . .	. . .	. . .	. . .	. . .	. . .
Other investment assets	4 703 . .	. . .	. . .	–25.8	–1.8	6.5	–68.6	–75.6	–162.5
Monetary authorities	4 703 . A	. . .	. . .	. . .	. . .	. . .	. . .	. . .	. . .
General government	4 703 . B	. . .	. . .	. . .	. . .	. . .	. . .	. . .	. . .
Banks	4 703 . C	. . .	. . .	–25.8	–1.8	6.5	–68.6	–75.6	–162.5
Other sectors	4 703 . D	. . .	. . .	. . .	. . .	. . .	. . .	. . .	. . .
Other investment liabilities	4 753 X .	33.9	21.8	68.1	120.0	88.8	155.3	99.4	166.7
Monetary authorities	4 753 XA	–1.6	–3.1	4.4	–5.5	8.7	.2	22.1	15.2
General government	4 753 YB	30.7	26.2	54.7	115.0	30.9	34.8	45.3	95.2
Banks	4 753 YC	. . .	. . .	1.9	1.4	31.7	–1.4	–11.7	22.9
Other sectors	4 753 YD	4.8	–1.3	7.2	9.1	17.5	121.7	43.6	33.3
Total, Groups A Through C	4 020 . .	*–322.6*	*–313.3*	*–189.4*	*–265.6*	*–298.8*	*–460.3*	*–344.3*	*–238.3*
D. Net Errors and Omissions	4 998 . .	**–61.3**	**–13.5**	**63.2**	**3.5**	**96.7**	**13.4**	**–5.0**	**–53.5**
Total, Groups A Through D	4 030 . .	*–383.9*	*–326.8*	*–126.2*	*–262.1*	*–202.0*	*–447.0*	*–349.3*	*–291.8*
E. Reserves and Related Items	4 040 . .	**383.9**	**326.8**	**126.2**	**262.1**	**202.0**	**447.0**	**349.3**	**291.8**
Reserve assets	4 800 . .	–45.9	23.5	–140.8	–85.3	–252.0	60.5	–122.8	43.3
Use of Fund credit and loans	4 766 . .	34.2	–9.3	. . .	2.1	83.7	–6.0	–15.4	–19.6
Liabilities constituting foreign authorities' reserves	4 900 . .	. . .	. . .	. . .	. . .	. . .	. . .	. . .	. . .
Exceptional financing	4 920 . .	395.6	312.6	267.0	345.4	370.4	392.5	487.6	268.2
Conversion rates: Tanzania shillings per U.S. dollar	0 101 . .	**99.29**	**143.38**	**195.06**	**219.16**	**297.71**	**405.27**	**509.63**	**574.76**

[1] Excludes components that have been classified in the categories of Group E.

Table 2. STANDARD PRESENTATION, 1988–95
(Millions of U.S. dollars)

	Code	1988	1989	1990	1991	1992	1993	1994	1995
CURRENT ACCOUNT	4 993 . .	**–356.5**	**–335.1**	**–558.9**	**–737.5**	**–704.3**	**–770.0**	**–680.7**	**–629.2**
A. GOODS	4 100 . .	–646.5	–655.0	–778.5	–867.0	–915.9	–844.0	–790.0	–657.5
Credit	2 100 . .	**386.5**	**415.1**	**407.8**	**363.0**	**400.7**	**444.6**	**519.4**	**682.9**
General merchandise: exports f.o.b.	2 110 . .	386.5	415.1	407.8	363.0	400.7	444.6	519.4	682.9
Goods for processing: exports f.o.b.	2 150 . .	. . .	. . .	. . .	. . .	. . .	. . .	. . .	. . .
Repairs on goods	2 160 . .	. . .	. . .	. . .	. . .	. . .	. . .	. . .	. . .
Goods procured in ports by carriers	2 170 . .	. . .	. . .	. . .	. . .	. . .	. . .	. . .	. . .
Nonmonetary gold	2 180 . .	. . .	. . .	. . .	. . .	. . .	. . .	. . .	. . .
Debit	3 100 . .	**–1,033.0**	**–1,070.1**	**–1,186.3**	**–1,229.9**	**–1,316.6**	**–1,288.6**	**–1,309.3**	**–1,340.4**
General merchandise: imports f.o.b.	3 110 . .	–1,033.0	–1,070.1	–1,186.3	–1,229.9	–1,316.6	–1,288.6	–1,309.3	–1,340.4
Goods for processing: imports f.o.b.	3 150 . .	. . .	. . .	. . .	. . .	. . .	. . .	. . .	. . .
Repairs on goods	3 160 . .	. . .	. . .	. . .	. . .	. . .	. . .	. . .	. . .
Goods procured in ports by carriers	3 170 . .	. . .	. . .	. . .	. . .	. . .	. . .	. . .	. . .
Nonmonetary gold	3 180 . .	. . .	. . .	. . .	. . .	. . .	. . .	. . .	. . .
B. SERVICES	4 200 . .	–146.1	–155.2	–157.1	–157.8	–169.0	–283.2	–128.3	–188.0
Total credit	2 200 . .	*117.4*	*117.3*	*130.6*	*142.3*	*167.5*	*312.6*	*410.5*	*566.4*
Total debit	3 200 . .	*–263.4*	*–272.5*	*–287.7*	*–300.1*	*–336.6*	*–595.8*	*–538.9*	*–754.5*
Transportation services, credit	2 205 . .	**26.9**	**23.3**	**26.0**	**39.6**	**. . .**	**19.6**	**6.7**	**1.7**
Passenger	2 205 BA	. . .	. . .	. . .	. . .	. . .	. . .	. . .	*.8*
Freight	2 205 BB	*6.8*	*5.5*	*6.1*	*10.5*	. . .	*6.1*	*6.7*	*.9*
Other	2 205 BC	*20.2*	*17.8*	*19.9*	*29.1*	. . .	*13.5*	. . .	. . .
Sea transport, passenger	2 207 . .	. . .	. . .	. . .	. . .	. . .	. . .	. . .	. . .
Sea transport, freight	2 208 . .	. . .	. . .	. . .	. . .	. . .	. . .	. . .	. . .
Sea transport, other	2 209 . .	. . .	. . .	. . .	. . .	. . .	. . .	. . .	. . .
Air transport, passenger	2 211 . .	. . .	. . .	. . .	. . .	. . .	. . .	. . .	. . .
Air transport, freight	2 212 . .	. . .	. . .	. . .	. . .	. . .	. . .	. . .	. . .
Air transport, other	2 213 . .	. . .	. . .	. . .	. . .	. . .	. . .	. . .	. . .
Other transport, passenger	2 215 . .	. . .	. . .	. . .	. . .	. . .	. . .	. . .	. . .
Other transport, freight	2 216 . .	. . .	. . .	. . .	. . .	. . .	. . .	. . .	. . .
Other transport, other	2 217 . .	. . .	. . .	. . .	. . .	. . .	. . .	. . .	. . .
Transportation services, debit	3 205 . .	**–146.1**	**–151.4**	**–166.9**	**–166.4**	**–177.1**	**–278.6**	**–176.1**	**–217.1**
Passenger	3 205 BA	. . .	. . .	. . .	. . .	. . .	. . .	. . .	*–36.6*
Freight	3 205 BB	*–138.9*	*–143.9*	*–159.5*	*–165.4*	*–177.1*	*–173.3*	*–176.1*	*–180.3*
Other	3 205 BC	*–7.2*	*–7.5*	*–7.4*	*–1.0*	. . .	*–105.3*	. . .	*–.2*
Sea transport, passenger	3 207 . .	. . .	. . .	. . .	. . .	. . .	. . .	. . .	. . .
Sea transport, freight	3 208 . .	. . .	. . .	. . .	. . .	. . .	. . .	. . .	. . .
Sea transport, other	3 209 . .	. . .	. . .	. . .	. . .	. . .	. . .	. . .	. . .
Air transport, passenger	3 211 . .	. . .	. . .	. . .	. . .	. . .	. . .	. . .	. . .
Air transport, freight	3 212 . .	. . .	. . .	. . .	. . .	. . .	. . .	. . .	. . .
Air transport, other	3 213 . .	. . .	. . .	. . .	. . .	. . .	. . .	. . .	. . .
Other transport, passenger	3 215 . .	. . .	. . .	. . .	. . .	. . .	. . .	. . .	. . .
Other transport, freight	3 216 . .	. . .	. . .	. . .	. . .	. . .	. . .	. . .	. . .
Other transport, other	3 217 . .	. . .	. . .	. . .	. . .	. . .	. . .	. . .	. . .
Travel, credit	2 236 . .	**33.7**	**42.8**	**47.6**	**46.6**	**68.8**	**132.1**	**183.1**	**501.8**
Business travel	2 237 . .	. . .	. . .	. . .	. . .	. . .	. . .	. . .	. . .
Personal travel	2 240 . .	. . .	. . .	. . .	. . .	. . .	. . .	. . .	. . .
Travel, debit	3 236 . .	**–22.5**	**–23.2**	**–22.8**	**–60.4**	**–71.6**	**–177.6**	**–206.3**	**–360.5**
Business travel	3 237 . .	. . .	. . .	. . .	. . .	. . .	. . .	. . .	. . .
Personal travel	3 240 . .	. . .	. . .	. . .	. . .	. . .	. . .	. . .	. . .
Other services, credit	2 200 BA	**56.7**	**51.1**	**57.0**	**56.1**	**98.7**	**160.9**	**220.7**	**62.9**
Communications	2 245 . .	. . .	. . .	. . .	. . .	. . .	. . .	. . .	.1
Construction	2 249 . .	. . .	. . .	. . .	. . .	. . .	. . .	. . .	2.0
Insurance	2 253 . .	.8	.6	.7	. . .	. . .	.7	.8	.1
Financial	2 260 . .	. . .	. . .	. . .	. . .	. . .	. . .	. . .	. . .
Computer and information	2 262 . .	. . .	. . .	. . .	. . .	. . .	. . .	. . .	. . .
Royalties and licence fees	2 266 . .	. . .	. . .	. . .	. . .	. . .	. . .	. . .	.2
Other business services	2 268 . .	56.0	50.5	56.3	56.1	98.7	160.2	219.9	44.3
Personal, cultural, and recreational	2 287 . .	. . .	. . .	. . .	. . .	. . .	. . .	. . .	. . .
Government, n.i.e.	2 291 . .	. . .	. . .	. . .	. . .	. . .	. . .	. . .	16.3
Other services, debit	3 200 BA	**–94.8**	**–97.8**	**–98.0**	**–73.3**	**–87.9**	**–139.6**	**–156.5**	**–176.9**
Communications	3 245 . .	. . .	. . .	. . .	. . .	. . .	. . .	. . .	–2.1
Construction	3 249 . .	. . .	. . .	. . .	. . .	. . .	. . .	. . .	–3.1
Insurance	3 253 . .	–15.4	–16.0	–17.7	–18.4	–19.7	–19.3	–19.6	–20.0
Financial	3 260 . .	. . .	. . .	. . .	. . .	. . .	. . .	. . .	. . .
Computer and information	3 262 . .	. . .	. . .	. . .	. . .	. . .	. . .	. . .	. . .
Royalties and licence fees	3 266 . .	. . .	. . .	. . .	. . .	. . .	. . .	. . .	. . .
Other business services	3 268 . .	–79.4	–81.8	–80.3	–54.9	–68.3	–120.4	–137.0	–110.7
Personal, cultural, and recreational	3 287 . .	. . .	. . .	. . .	. . .	. . .	. . .	. . .	. . .
Government, n.i.e.	3 291 . .	. . .	. . .	. . .	. . .	. . .	. . .	. . .	–40.9

Table 2 (Continued). STANDARD PRESENTATION, 1988–95
(Millions of U.S. dollars)

	Code	1988	1989	1990	1991	1992	1993	1994	1995
C. INCOME	4 300 . .	–185.2	–177.1	–185.0	–184.5	–225.4	–149.2	–122.5	–137.2
Total credit	2 300 . .	*3.2*	*5.4*	*5.9*	*7.9*	*8.1*	*21.6*	*30.9*	*3.9*
Total debit	3 300 . .	*–188.4*	*–182.5*	*–190.9*	*–192.5*	*–233.5*	*–170.8*	*–153.4*	*–141.2*
Compensation of employees, credit	2 310 . .	**...**	**...**	**...**	**...**	**...**	**...**	**...**	**.8**
Compensation of employees, debit	3 310 . .	**...**	**...**	**...**	**...**	**...**	**...**	**...**	**–.5**
Investment income, credit	2 320 . .	**3.2**	**5.4**	**5.9**	**7.9**	**8.1**	**21.6**	**30.9**	**3.1**
Direct investment income	2 330 . .	...	...	...	...	...	...	...	.5
Dividends and distributed branch profits	2 332 . .	...	...	...	...	...	...	...	.5
Reinvested earnings and undistributed branch profits	2 333 . .	...	...	...	...	...	...	...	...
Income on debt (interest)	2 334 . .	...	...	...	...	...	...	...	...
Portfolio investment income	2 339 . .	...	...	...	...	...	...	...	...
Income on equity	2 340 . .	...	...	...	...	...	...	...	...
Income on bonds and notes	2 350 . .	...	...	...	...	...	...	...	...
Income on money market instruments and financial derivatives	2 360 . .	...	...	...	...	...	...	...	...
Other investment income	2 370 . .	3.2	5.4	5.9	7.9	8.1	21.6	30.9	2.5
Investment income, debit	3 320 . .	**–188.4**	**–182.5**	**–190.9**	**–192.5**	**–233.5**	**–170.8**	**–153.4**	**–140.6**
Direct investment income	3 330 . .	...	...	...	...	...	...	...	–.5
Dividends and distributed branch profits	3 332 . .	...	...	...	...	...	...	...	–.5
Reinvested earnings and undistributed branch profits	3 333 . .	...	...	...	...	...	...	...	...
Income on debt (interest)	3 334 . .	...	...	...	...	...	...	...	...
Portfolio investment income	3 339 . .	...	...	...	...	...	...	...	–.2
Income on equity	3 340 . .	...	...	...	...	...	...	...	...
Income on bonds and notes	3 350 . .	...	...	...	...	...	...	...	...
Income on money market instruments and financial derivatives	3 360 . .	...	...	...	...	...	...	...	...
Other investment income	3 370 . .	–188.4	–182.5	–190.9	–192.5	–233.5	–170.8	–153.4	–140.0
D. CURRENT TRANSFERS	4 379 . .	621.2	652.2	561.8	471.8	606.1	506.4	360.1	353.6
Credit	2 379 . .	**642.9**	**682.0**	**592.8**	**504.5**	**641.1**	**536.7**	**385.1**	**385.9**
General government	2 380 . .	392.7	480.0	538.4	481.2	506.2	526.4	288.6	242.0
Other sectors	2 390 . .	250.3	202.0	54.3	23.2	134.8	10.3	96.5	143.9
Workers' remittances	2 391 . .	...	...	...	...	...	...	...	...
Other current transfers	2 392 . .	250.3	202.0	54.3	23.2	134.8	10.3	96.5	143.9
Debit	3 379 . .	**–21.7**	**–29.8**	**–31.0**	**–32.7**	**–35.0**	**–30.3**	**–25.0**	**–32.3**
General government	3 380 . .	–3.4	–10.2	–24.8	–26.1	–28.0	–10.1	–10.0	–10.0
Other sectors	3 390 . .	–18.3	–19.6	–6.2	–6.5	–7.0	–20.2	–15.0	–22.3
Workers' remittances	3 391 . .	...	...	...	...	...	...	...	...
Other current transfers	3 392 . .	–18.3	–19.6	–6.2	–6.5	–7.0	–20.2	–15.0	–22.3
CAPITAL AND FINANCIAL ACCOUNT	4 996 . .	**417.8**	**348.5**	**495.6**	**734.0**	**607.6**	**756.7**	**685.8**	**682.7**
CAPITAL ACCOUNT	4 994 . .	**...**	**...**	**338.2**	**353.7**	**323.2**	**226.6**	**286.4**	**236.7**
Total credit	2 994 . .	...	...	*338.2*	*353.7*	*323.2*	*226.6*	*286.4*	*236.7*
Total debit	3 994 . .	...	...	...	...	...	...	...	...
Capital transfers, credit	2 400 . .	**...**	**...**	**338.2**	**353.7**	**323.2**	**226.6**	**286.4**	**236.7**
General government	2 401 . .	...	...	323.1	341.9	314.6	226.5	280.8	231.9
Debt forgiveness	2 402 . .	...	...	11.0	...	25.0	23.8	23.8	...
Other capital transfers	2 410 . .	...	...	312.0	341.9	289.6	202.7	257.0	231.9
Other sectors	2 430 . .	...	...	15.1	11.8	8.6	...	5.6	4.8
Migrants' transfers	2 431 . .	...	...	...	...	...	...	...	...
Debt forgiveness	2 432 . .	...	...	...	...	...	...	...	...
Other capital transfers	2 440 . .	...	...	15.1	11.8	8.6	...	5.6	4.8
Capital transfers, debit	3 400 . .	**...**	**...**	**...**	**...**	**...**	**...**	**...**	**...**
General government	3 401 . .	...	...	...	...	...	...	...	...
Debt forgiveness	3 402 . .	...	...	...	...	...	...	...	...
Other capital transfers	3 410 . .	...	...	...	...	...	...	...	...
Other sectors	3 430 . .	...	...	...	...	...	...	...	...
Migrants' transfers	3 431 . .	...	...	...	...	...	...	...	...
Debt forgiveness	3 432 . .	...	...	...	...	...	...	...	...
Other capital transfers	3 440 . .	...	...	...	...	...	...	...	...
Nonproduced nonfinancial assets, credit	2 480 . .	**...**	**...**	**...**	**...**	**...**	**...**	**...**	**...**
Nonproduced nonfinancial assets, debit	3 480 . .	**...**	**...**	**...**	**...**	**...**	**...**	**...**	**...**

Table 2 (Continued). STANDARD PRESENTATION, 1988–95
(Millions of U.S. dollars)

	Code	1988	1989	1990	1991	1992	1993	1994	1995
FINANCIAL ACCOUNT	4 995	**417.8**	**348.5**	**157.4**	**380.3**	**284.4**	**530.1**	**399.3**	**446.0**
A. DIRECT INVESTMENT	4 500	...	...	...	...	12.0	20.2	50.0	150.0
Direct investment abroad	4 505	...	...	...	...	...	...	...	...
Equity capital	4 510	...	...	...	...	...	...	...	...
Claims on affiliated enterprises	4 515	...	...	...	...	...	...	...	...
Liabilities to affiliated enterprises	4 520	...	...	...	...	...	...	...	...
Reinvested earnings	4 525	...	...	...	...	...	...	...	...
Other capital	4 530	...	...	...	...	...	...	...	...
Claims on affiliated enterprises	4 535	...	...	...	...	...	...	...	...
Liabilities to affiliated enterprises	4 540	...	...	...	...	...	...	...	...
Direct investment in Tanzania	4 555	...	...	...	...	**12.0**	**20.2**	**50.0**	**150.0**
Equity capital	4 560	...	...	...	...	12.0	20.2	50.0	150.0
Claims on direct investors	4 565	...	...	...	...	...	...	...	...
Liabilities to direct investors	4 570	...	...	...	...	...	...	...	...
Reinvested earnings	4 575	...	...	...	...	...	...	...	...
Other capital	4 580	...	...	...	...	...	...	...	...
Claims on direct investors	4 585	...	...	...	...	...	...	...	...
Liabilities to direct investors	4 590	...	...	...	...	...	...	...	...
B. PORTFOLIO INVESTMENT	4 600	...	...	...	...	...	...	...	...
Assets	4 602	...	...	...	...	...	...	...	...
Equity securities	4 610	...	...	...	...	...	...	...	...
Monetary authorities	4 611	...	...	...	...	...	...	...	...
General government	4 612	...	...	...	...	...	...	...	...
Banks	4 613	...	...	...	...	...	...	...	...
Other sectors	4 614	...	...	...	...	...	...	...	...
Debt securities	4 619	...	...	...	...	...	...	...	...
Bonds and notes	4 620	...	...	...	...	...	...	...	...
Monetary authorities	4 621	...	...	...	...	...	...	...	...
General government	4 622	...	...	...	...	...	...	...	...
Banks	4 623	...	...	...	...	...	...	...	...
Other sectors	4 624	...	...	...	...	...	...	...	...
Money market instruments	4 630	...	...	...	...	...	...	...	...
Monetary authorities	4 631	...	...	...	...	...	...	...	...
General government	4 632	...	...	...	...	...	...	...	...
Banks	4 633	...	...	...	...	...	...	...	...
Other sectors	4 634	...	...	...	...	...	...	...	...
Financial derivatives	4 640	...	...	...	...	...	...	...	...
Monetary authorities	4 641	...	...	...	...	...	...	...	...
General government	4 642	...	...	...	...	...	...	...	...
Banks	4 643	...	...	...	...	...	...	...	...
Other sectors	4 644	...	...	...	...	...	...	...	...
Liabilities	4 652	...	...	...	...	...	...	...	...
Equity securities	4 660	...	...	...	...	...	...	...	...
Banks	4 663	...	...	...	...	...	...	...	...
Other sectors	4 664	...	...	...	...	...	...	...	...
Debt securities	4 669	...	...	...	...	...	...	...	...
Bonds and notes	4 670	...	...	...	...	...	...	...	...
Monetary authorities	4 671	...	...	...	...	...	...	...	...
General government	4 672	...	...	...	...	...	...	...	...
Banks	4 673	...	...	...	...	...	...	...	...
Other sectors	4 674	...	...	...	...	...	...	...	...
Money market instruments	4 680	...	...	...	...	...	...	...	...
Monetary authorities	4 681	...	...	...	...	...	...	...	...
General government	4 682	...	...	...	...	...	...	...	...
Banks	4 683	...	...	...	...	...	...	...	...
Other sectors	4 684	...	...	...	...	...	...	...	...
Financial derivatives	4 690	...	...	...	...	...	...	...	...
Monetary authorities	4 691	...	...	...	...	...	...	...	...
General government	4 692	...	...	...	...	...	...	...	...
Banks	4 693	...	...	...	...	...	...	...	...
Other sectors	4 694	...	...	...	...	...	...	...	...

Table 2 (Concluded). STANDARD PRESENTATION, 1988–95
(Millions of U.S. dollars)

	Code	1988	1989	1990	1991	1992	1993	1994	1995
C. OTHER INVESTMENT	4 700 . .	463.7	325.0	298.2	465.6	524.4	449.4	472.2	252.8
Assets	4 703 . .	**. . .**	**. . .**	**–25.8**	**–1.8**	**6.5**	**–68.6**	**–75.6**	**–162.5**
Trade credits	4 706 . .	. . .	. . .	. . .	. . .	. . .	. . .	. . .	. . .
General government: long-term	4 708 . .	. . .	. . .	. . .	. . .	. . .	. . .	. . .	. . .
General government: short-term	4 709 . .	. . .	. . .	. . .	. . .	. . .	. . .	. . .	. . .
Other sectors: long-term	4 711 . .	. . .	. . .	. . .	. . .	. . .	. . .	. . .	. . .
Other sectors: short-term	4 712 . .	. . .	. . .	. . .	. . .	. . .	. . .	. . .	. . .
Loans	4 714 . .	. . .	. . .	. . .	. . .	. . .	. . .	. . .	. . .
Monetary authorities: long-term	4 717 . .	. . .	. . .	. . .	. . .	. . .	. . .	. . .	. . .
Monetary authorities: short-term	4 718 . .	. . .	. . .	. . .	. . .	. . .	. . .	. . .	. . .
General government: long-term	4 720 . .	. . .	. . .	. . .	. . .	. . .	. . .	. . .	. . .
General government: short-term	4 721 . .	. . .	. . .	. . .	. . .	. . .	. . .	. . .	. . .
Banks: long-term	4 723 . .	. . .	. . .	. . .	. . .	. . .	. . .	. . .	. . .
Banks: short-term	4 724 . .	. . .	. . .	. . .	. . .	. . .	. . .	. . .	. . .
Other sectors: long-term	4 726 . .	. . .	. . .	. . .	. . .	. . .	. . .	. . .	. . .
Other sectors: short-term	4 727 . .	. . .	. . .	. . .	. . .	. . .	. . .	. . .	. . .
Currency and deposits	4 730 . .	. . .	. . .	–25.8	–1.8	6.5	–68.6	–75.6	–162.5
Monetary authorities	4 731 . .	. . .	. . .	. . .	. . .	. . .	. . .	. . .	. . .
General government	4 732 . .	. . .	. . .	. . .	. . .	. . .	. . .	. . .	. . .
Banks	4 733 . .	. . .	. . .	–25.8	–1.8	6.5	–68.6	–75.6	–162.5
Other sectors	4 734 . .	. . .	. . .	. . .	. . .	. . .	. . .	. . .	. . .
Other assets	4 736 . .	. . .	. . .	. . .	. . .	. . .	. . .	. . .	. . .
Monetary authorities: long-term	4 738 . .	. . .	. . .	. . .	. . .	. . .	. . .	. . .	. . .
Monetary authorities: short-term	4 739 . .	. . .	. . .	. . .	. . .	. . .	. . .	. . .	. . .
General government: long-term	4 741 . .	. . .	. . .	. . .	. . .	. . .	. . .	. . .	. . .
General government: short-term	4 742 . .	. . .	. . .	. . .	. . .	. . .	. . .	. . .	. . .
Banks: long-term	4 744 . .	. . .	. . .	. . .	. . .	. . .	. . .	. . .	. . .
Banks: short-term	4 745 . .	. . .	. . .	. . .	. . .	. . .	. . .	. . .	. . .
Other sectors: long-term	4 747 . .	. . .	. . .	. . .	. . .	. . .	. . .	. . .	. . .
Other sectors: short-term	4 748 . .	. . .	. . .	. . .	. . .	. . .	. . .	. . .	. . .
Liabilities	4 753 . .	**463.7**	**325.0**	**324.0**	**467.4**	**517.8**	**518.0**	**547.8**	**415.3**
Trade credits	4 756 . .	. . .	. . .	7.2	9.1	17.5	20.8	16.1	25.6
General government: long-term	4 758 . .	. . .	. . .	. . .	. . .	. . .	. . .	. . .	. . .
General government: short-term	4 759 . .	. . .	. . .	. . .	. . .	. . .	. . .	. . .	. . .
Other sectors: long-term	4 761 . .	. . .	. . .	. . .	. . .	. . .	. . .	. . .	. . .
Other sectors: short-term	4 762 . .	. . .	. . .	7.2	9.1	17.5	20.8	16.1	25.6
Loans	4 764 . .	308.9	282.0	310.6	357.7	460.0	486.3	496.9	341.3
Use of Fund credit and loans from the Fund	4 766 . .	34.2	–9.3	. . .	2.1	83.7	–6.0	–15.4	–19.6
Monetary authorities: other long-term	4 767 . .	. . .	. . .	. . .	. . .	. . .	. . .	. . .	. . .
Monetary authorities: short-term	4 768 . .	. . .	. . .	. . .	. . .	. . .	. . .	. . .	. . .
General government: long-term	4 770 . .	269.9	292.7	310.6	355.7	376.3	391.5	484.7	353.2
General government: short-term	4 771 . .	. . .	. . .	. . .	. . .	. . .	. . .	. . .	. . .
Banks: long-term	4 773 . .	. . .	. . .	. . .	. . .	. . .	. . .	. . .	. . .
Banks: short-term	4 774 . .	. . .	. . .	. . .	. . .	. . .	. . .	. . .	. . .
Other sectors: long-term	4 776 . .	. . .	. . .	. . .	. . .	. . .	100.9	27.5	7.7
Other sectors: short-term	4 777 . .	4.8	–1.3	. . .	. . .	. . .	. . .	. . .	. . .
Currency and deposits	4 780 . .	. . .	. . .	6.2	–4.2	8.9	–1.2	37.2	17.0
Monetary authorities	4 781 . .	. . .	. . .	4.4	–5.5	8.7	.2	30.5	15.2
General government	4 782 . .	. . .	. . .	. . .	. . .	. . .	. . .	. . .	. . .
Banks	4 783 . .	. . .	. . .	1.9	1.4	.2	–1.4	6.7	1.8
Other sectors	4 784 . .	. . .	. . .	. . .	. . .	. . .	. . .	. . .	. . .
Other liabilities	4 786 . .	154.8	43.0	. . .	104.7	31.5	12.0	–2.4	31.3
Monetary authorities: long-term	4 788 . .	. . .	. . .	. . .	. . .	. . .	. . .	. . .	. . .
Monetary authorities: short-term	4 789 . .	163.7	49.1	. . .	. . .	. . .	. . .	–8.4	. . .
General government: long-term	4 791 . .	–8.9	–6.1	. . .	. . .	. . .	. . .	. . .	. . .
General government: short-term	4 792 . .	. . .	. . .	. . .	. . .	. . .	. . .	. . .	. . .
Banks: long-term	4 794 . .	. . .	. . .	. . .	. . .	31.5	. . .	–18.4	21.1
Banks: short-term	4 795 . .	. . .	. . .	. . .	. . .	. . .	. . .	. . .	. . .
Other sectors: long-term	4 797 . .	. . .	. . .	. . .	. . .	. . .	. . .	. . .	. . .
Other sectors: short-term	4 798 . .	. . .	. . .	. . .	104.7	. . .	12.0	24.4	10.2
D. RESERVE ASSETS	4 800 . .	–45.9	23.5	–140.8	–85.3	–252.0	60.5	–122.8	43.3
Monetary gold	4 810 . .	. . .	. . .	–11.9	–21.6	–65.2	7.5	7.7	7.0
Special drawing rights	4 820 . .	.1	. . .	.1	. . .	. . .	. . .	. . .	–.1
Reserve position in the Fund	4 830 . .	. . .	. . .	. . .	. . .	–13.8	. . .	. . .	. . .
Foreign exchange	4 840 . .	–46.0	23.5	–128.9	–63.7	–173.0	57.2	–133.4	36.6
Other claims	4 880 . .	. . .	. . .	. . .	. . .	. . .	–4.2	2.8	–.3
NET ERRORS AND OMISSIONS	4 998 . .	**–61.3**	**–13.5**	**63.2**	**3.5**	**96.7**	**13.4**	**–5.0**	**–53.5**

Part 3 of the *Yearbook* contains descriptions of the methodologies, compilation practices, and sources used to compile these data.

Table 1. ANALYTIC PRESENTATION, 1988–95
(Millions of U.S. dollars)

	Code	1988	1989	1990	1991	1992	1993	1994	1995
A. Current Account [1]	4 993 Y.	**–1,654**	**–2,498**	**–7,281**	**–7,571**	**–6,303**	**–6,364**	**–8,085**	**–13,554**
Goods: exports f.o.b	2 100 . .	15,781	19,834	22,811	28,232	32,100	36,398	44,478	55,447
Goods: imports f.o.b	3 100 . .	–17,856	–22,750	–29,561	–34,222	–36,261	–40,695	–48,204	–63,415
Balance on Goods	4 100 . .	*–2,074*	*–2,916*	*–6,751*	*–5,989*	*–4,161*	*–4,297*	*–3,726*	*–7,968*
Services: credit	2 200 . .	4,648	5,457	6,419	7,272	9,288	11,059	11,640	14,845
Services: debit	3 200 . .	–3,569	–4,505	–6,309	–8,040	–10,368	–12,469	–15,396	–18,804
Balance on Goods and Services	4 991 . .	*–996*	*–1,964*	*–6,641*	*–6,757*	*–5,241*	*–5,707*	*–7,482*	*–11,927*
Income: credit	2 300 . .	1,297	1,589	2,059	2,254	1,532	2,140	2,562	3,801
Income: debit	3 300 . .	–2,191	–2,369	–2,913	–3,329	–3,240	–3,546	–4,293	–5,915
Balance on Goods, Services, and Income	4 992 . .	*–1,891*	*–2,744*	*–7,494*	*–7,832*	*–6,949*	*–7,113*	*–9,213*	*–14,041*
Current transfers: credit	2 379 Y.	268	281	278	411	1,000	1,222	1,901	1,190
Current transfers: debit	3 379 . .	–31	–34	–65	–150	–355	–473	–774	–704
B. Capital Account [1]	4 994 Y.	**. . .**	**. . .**	**–1**	**. . .**	**. . .**	**. . .**	**. . .**	**. . .**
Capital account: credit	2 994 Y.	. . .	. . .	. . .	. . .	. . .	. . .	. . .	. . .
Capital account: debit	3 994 . .	. . .	. . .	–1	. . .	. . .	. . .	. . .	. . .
Total, Groups A Plus B	4 010 . .	*–1,655*	*–2,498*	*–7,282*	*–7,571*	*–6,303*	*–6,364*	*–8,085*	*–13,554*
C. Financial Account [1]	4 995 X.	**3,840**	**6,599**	**9,098**	**11,759**	**9,475**	**10,500**	**12,167**	**21,909**
Direct investment abroad	4 505 . .	–24	–50	–140	–167	–147	–233	–493	–886
Direct investment in Thailand	4 555 Y.	1,105	1,775	2,444	2,014	2,113	1,804	1,366	2,068
Portfolio investment assets	4 602 . .	. . .	. . .	. . .	. . .	. . .	. . .	–5	–2
Equity securities	4 610 . .	. . .	. . .	. . .	. . .	. . .	. . .	–5	–2
Debt securities	4 619 . .	. . .	. . .	. . .	. . .	. . .	. . .	. . .	. . .
Portfolio investment liabilities	4 652 Y.	530	1,486	–38	–81	924	5,455	2,486	4,083
Equity securities	4 660 Y.	444	1,424	440	37	455	2,679	–389	2,123
Debt securities	4 669 Y.	86	63	–478	–118	469	2,776	2,875	1,960
Other investment assets	4 703 . .	269	–313	–164	352	104	–3,265	–1,027	–2,738
Monetary authorities	4 703 .A	. . .	. . .	. . .	. . .	. . .	. . .	. . .	. . .
General government	4 703 .B	250	–337	–220	247	. . .	. . .	. . .	. . .
Banks	4 703 .C	. . .	. . .	. . .	. . .	104	–3,265	–1,027	–2,738
Other sectors	4 703 .D	19	23	57	105	. . .	. . .	. . .	. . .
Other investment liabilities	4 753 X.	1,960	3,700	6,996	9,642	6,479	6,739	9,839	19,383
Monetary authorities	4 753 XA	. . .	. . .	. . .	. . .	. . .	. . .	. . .	. . .
General government	4 753 YB	–51	–206	–999	9	–611	–464	–705	46
Banks	4 753 YC	984	700	1,027	213	1,758	6,589	14,295	13,218
Other sectors	4 753 YD	1,027	3,207	6,969	9,420	5,333	614	–3,751	6,118
Total, Groups A Through C	4 020 . .	*2,185*	*4,101*	*1,816*	*4,188*	*3,171*	*4,136*	*4,082*	*8,355*
D. Net Errors and Omissions	4 998 . .	**411**	**928**	**1,419**	**431**	**–142**	**–230**	**87**	**–1,196**
Total, Groups A Through D	4 030 . .	*2,596*	*5,029*	*3,235*	*4,618*	*3,029*	*3,907*	*4,169*	*7,159*
E. Reserves and Related Items	4 040 . .	**–2,596**	**–5,029**	**–3,235**	**–4,618**	**–3,029**	**–3,907**	**–4,169**	**–7,159**
Reserve assets	4 800 . .	–2,336	–4,667	–2,961	–4,618	–3,029	–3,907	–4,169	–7,159
Use of Fund credit and loans	4 766 . .	–260	–363	–274	–1	. . .	. . .	. . .	. . .
Liabilities constituting foreign authorities' reserves	4 900 . .	. . .	. . .	. . .	. . .	. . .	. . .	. . .	. . .
Exceptional financing	4 920 . .	. . .	. . .	. . .	. . .	. . .	. . .	. . .	. . .
Conversion rates: baht per U.S. dollar	0 101 . .	**25.294**	**25.702**	**25.585**	**25.517**	**25.400**	**25.319**	**25.150**	**24.915**

[1] Excludes components that have been classified in the categories of Group E.

Table 2. STANDARD PRESENTATION, 1988–95
(Millions of U.S. dollars)

	Code	1988	1989	1990	1991	1992	1993	1994	1995
CURRENT ACCOUNT	4 993 . .	**–1,654**	**–2,498**	**–7,281**	**–7,571**	**–6,303**	**–6,364**	**–8,085**	**–13,554**
A. GOODS	4 100 . .	–2,074	–2,916	–6,751	–5,989	–4,161	–4,297	–3,726	–7,968
Credit	2 100 . .	**15,781**	**19,834**	**22,811**	**28,232**	**32,100**	**36,398**	**44,478**	**55,447**
General merchandise: exports f.o.b.	2 110 . .	15,781	19,834	22,811	28,232	32,100	36,398	44,478	55,447
Goods for processing: exports f.o.b.	2 150 . .	. . .	. . .	. . .	. . .	. . .	. . .	. . .	. . .
Repairs on goods	2 160 . .	. . .	. . .	. . .	. . .	. . .	. . .	. . .	. . .
Goods procured in ports by carriers	2 170 . .	. . .	. . .	. . .	. . .	. . .	. . .	. . .	. . .
Nonmonetary gold	2 180 . .	. . .	. . .	. . .	. . .	. . .	. . .	. . .	. . .
Debit	3 100 . .	**–17,856**	**–22,750**	**–29,561**	**–34,222**	**–36,261**	**–40,695**	**–48,204**	**–63,415**
General merchandise: imports f.o.b.	3 110 . .	–17,856	–22,660	–29,338	–34,053	–36,060	–40,433	–47,874	–63,045
Goods for processing: imports f.o.b.	3 150 . .	. . .	. . .	. . .	. . .	. . .	. . .	. . .	. . .
Repairs on goods	3 160 . .	. . .	. . .	. . .	. . .	. . .	. . .	. . .	. . .
Goods procured in ports by carriers	3 170 . .	. . .	. . .	. . .	. . .	. . .	. . .	. . .	. . .
Nonmonetary gold	3 180 . .	. . .	–89	–224	–168	–200	–261	–330	–371
B. SERVICES	4 200 . .	1,078	952	110	–768	–1,080	–1,410	–3,756	–3,959
Total credit	2 200 . .	*4,648*	*5,457*	*6,419*	*7,272*	*9,288*	*11,059*	*11,640*	*14,845*
Total debit	3 200 . .	*–3,569*	*–4,505*	*–6,309*	*–8,040*	*–10,368*	*–12,469*	*–15,396*	*–18,804*
Transportation services, credit	2 205 . .	**989**	**1,071**	**1,327**	**1,484**	**1,526**	**1,964**	**1,842**	**2,455**
Passenger	2 205 BA	*401*	*416*	*663*	*487*	*847*	*1,364*	*1,153*	*1,222*
Freight	2 205 BB	*453*	*443*	*455*	*584*	*329*	*423*	*448*	*584*
Other	2 205 BC	*136*	*212*	*210*	*413*	*350*	*177*	*241*	*649*
Sea transport, passenger	2 207 . .	. . .	. . .	. . .	. . .	. . .	. . .	. . .	. . .
Sea transport, freight	2 208 . .	. . .	. . .	. . .	. . .	. . .	. . .	. . .	. . .
Sea transport, other	2 209 . .	. . .	. . .	. . .	. . .	. . .	. . .	. . .	. . .
Air transport, passenger	2 211 . .	. . .	. . .	. . .	. . .	. . .	. . .	. . .	. . .
Air transport, freight	2 212 . .	. . .	. . .	. . .	. . .	. . .	. . .	. . .	. . .
Air transport, other	2 213 . .	. . .	. . .	. . .	. . .	. . .	. . .	. . .	. . .
Other transport, passenger	2 215 . .	. . .	. . .	. . .	. . .	. . .	. . .	. . .	. . .
Other transport, freight	2 216 . .	. . .	. . .	. . .	. . .	. . .	. . .	. . .	. . .
Other transport, other	2 217 . .	. . .	. . .	. . .	. . .	. . .	. . .	. . .	. . .
Transportation services, debit	3 205 . .	**–2,235**	**–2,864**	**–3,576**	**–4,185**	**–4,539**	**–5,005**	**–5,862**	**–7,780**
Passenger	3 205 BA	*–161*	*–196*	*–252*	*–228*	*–316*	*–307*	*–384*	*–520*
Freight	3 205 BB	*–2,049*	*–2,628*	*–3,255*	*–3,802*	*–4,088*	*–4,596*	*–5,375*	*–7,125*
Other	3 205 BC	*–25*	*–41*	*–69*	*–155*	*–135*	*–103*	*–103*	*–135*
Sea transport, passenger	3 207 . .	. . .	. . .	. . .	. . .	. . .	. . .	. . .	. . .
Sea transport, freight	3 208 . .	. . .	. . .	. . .	. . .	. . .	. . .	. . .	. . .
Sea transport, other	3 209 . .	. . .	. . .	. . .	. . .	. . .	. . .	. . .	. . .
Air transport, passenger	3 211 . .	. . .	. . .	. . .	. . .	. . .	. . .	. . .	. . .
Air transport, freight	3 212 . .	. . .	. . .	. . .	. . .	. . .	. . .	. . .	. . .
Air transport, other	3 213 . .	. . .	. . .	. . .	. . .	. . .	. . .	. . .	. . .
Other transport, passenger	3 215 . .	. . .	. . .	. . .	. . .	. . .	. . .	. . .	. . .
Other transport, freight	3 216 . .	. . .	. . .	. . .	. . .	. . .	. . .	. . .	. . .
Other transport, other	3 217 . .	. . .	. . .	. . .	. . .	. . .	. . .	. . .	. . .
Travel, credit	2 236 . .	**3,118**	**3,754**	**4,325**	**4,537**	**5,092**	**5,638**	**6,063**	**8,035**
Business travel	2 237 . .	. . .	. . .	. . .	. . .	. . .	. . .	. . .	. . .
Personal travel	2 240 . .	. . .	. . .	. . .	. . .	. . .	. . .	. . .	. . .
Travel, debit	3 236 . .	**–603**	**–746**	**–1,432**	**–1,900**	**–2,461**	**–3,040**	**–4,065**	**–3,780**
Business travel	3 237 . .	. . .	. . .	. . .	. . .	. . .	. . .	. . .	. . .
Personal travel	3 240 . .	. . .	. . .	. . .	. . .	. . .	. . .	. . .	. . .
Other services, credit	2 200 BA	**540**	**632**	**767**	**1,251**	**2,670**	**3,457**	**3,735**	**4,356**
Communications	2 245 . .	. . .	. . .	. . .	. . .	. . .	. . .	. . .	. . .
Construction	2 249 . .	. . .	. . .	. . .	. . .	. . .	. . .	. . .	. . .
Insurance	2 253 . .	6	7	10	12	44	55	55	99
Financial	2 260 . .	. . .	. . .	. . .	. . .	. . .	. . .	. . .	. . .
Computer and information	2 262 . .	. . .	. . .	. . .	. . .	. . .	. . .	. . .	. . .
Royalties and licence fees	2 266 . .	. . .	. . .	. . .	2	9	3	4	1
Other business services	2 268 . .	404	486	630	1,097	2,490	3,217	3,461	4,063
Personal, cultural, and recreational	2 287 . .	. . .	. . .	. . .	. . .	. . .	. . .	. . .	. . .
Government, n.i.e.	2 291 . .	130	139	128	140	126	182	215	194
Other services, debit	3 200 BA	**–731**	**–894**	**–1,301**	**–1,955**	**–3,369**	**–4,424**	**–5,469**	**–7,244**
Communications	3 245 . .	. . .	. . .	. . .	. . .	. . .	. . .	. . .	. . .
Construction	3 249 . .	. . .	. . .	. . .	. . .	. . .	. . .	. . .	. . .
Insurance	3 253 . .	–205	–259	–336	–389	–569	–614	–756	–961
Financial	3 260 . .	. . .	. . .	. . .	. . .	. . .	. . .	. . .	. . .
Computer and information	3 262 . .	. . .	. . .	. . .	. . .	. . .	. . .	. . .	. . .
Royalties and licence fees	3 266 . .	–88	–128	–170	–206	–281	–427	–452	–630
Other business services	3 268 . .	–333	–386	–646	–1,174	–2,405	–3,221	–4,096	–5,450
Personal, cultural, and recreational	3 287 . .	. . .	. . .	. . .	. . .	. . .	. . .	. . .	. . .
Government, n.i.e.	3 291 . .	–105	–121	–149	–186	–114	–162	–165	–203

Table 2 (Continued). STANDARD PRESENTATION, 1988–95
(Millions of U.S. dollars)

	Code	1988	1989	1990	1991	1992	1993	1994	1995
C. INCOME	4 300	–894	–781	–853	–1,075	–1,708	–1,406	–1,731	–2,114
Total credit	2 300	*1,297*	*1,589*	*2,059*	*2,254*	*1,532*	*2,140*	*2,562*	*3,801*
Total debit	3 300	*–2,191*	*–2,369*	*–2,913*	*–3,329*	*–3,240*	*–3,546*	*–4,293*	*–5,915*
Compensation of employees, credit	2 310	**927**	**943**	**973**	**1,019**	**445**	**1,112**	**1,281**	**1,695**
Compensation of employees, debit	3 310	**–91**	**–122**	**–198**	**–53**	**. . .**	**. . .**	**. . .**	**. . .**
Investment income, credit	2 320	**370**	**645**	**1,086**	**1,235**	**1,087**	**1,028**	**1,281**	**2,106**
Direct investment income	2 330	12	5	1	1	. . .	. . .	. . .	. . .
Dividends and distributed branch profits	2 332	12	5	1	1	. . .	. . .	. . .	. . .
Reinvested earnings and undistributed branch profits	2 333	. . .	. . .	. . .	. . .	. . .	. . .	. . .	. . .
Income on debt (interest)	2 334	. . .	. . .	. . .	. . .	. . .	. . .	. . .	. . .
Portfolio investment income	2 339	. . .	. . .	. . .	. . .	. . .	. . .	. . .	. . .
Income on equity	2 340	. . .	. . .	. . .	. . .	. . .	. . .	. . .	. . .
Income on bonds and notes	2 350	. . .	. . .	. . .	. . .	. . .	. . .	. . .	. . .
Income on money market instruments and financial derivatives	2 360	. . .	. . .	. . .	. . .	. . .	. . .	. . .	. . .
Other investment income	2 370	358	640	1,085	1,233	1,087	1,028	1,281	2,106
Investment income, debit	3 320	**–2,100**	**–2,247**	**–2,715**	**–3,276**	**–3,240**	**–3,546**	**–4,293**	**–5,915**
Direct investment income	3 330	–215	–329	–312	–56	. . .	. . .	. . .	. . .
Dividends and distributed branch profits	3 332	–215	–329	–312	–56	. . .	. . .	. . .	. . .
Reinvested earnings and undistributed branch profits	3 333	. . .	. . .	. . .	. . .	. . .	. . .	. . .	. . .
Income on debt (interest)	3 334	. . .	. . .	. . .	. . .	. . .	. . .	. . .	. . .
Portfolio investment income	3 339	. . .	. . .	. . .	. . .	. . .	. . .	. . .	. . .
Income on equity	3 340	. . .	. . .	. . .	. . .	. . .	. . .	. . .	. . .
Income on bonds and notes	3 350	. . .	. . .	. . .	. . .	. . .	. . .	. . .	. . .
Income on money market instruments and financial derivatives	3 360	. . .	. . .	. . .	. . .	. . .	. . .	. . .	. . .
Other investment income	3 370	–1,885	–1,918	–2,403	–3,220	–3,240	–3,546	–4,293	–5,915
D. CURRENT TRANSFERS	4 379	236	246	213	261	646	750	1,128	487
Credit	2 379	**268**	**281**	**278**	**411**	**1,000**	**1,222**	**1,901**	**1,190**
General government	2 380	180	186	176	83	59	53	75	57
Other sectors	2 390	87	95	102	328	941	1,170	1,826	1,133
Workers' remittances	2 391	. . .	. . .	. . .	. . .	. . .	. . .	. . .	. . .
Other current transfers	2 392	87	95	102	328	941	1,170	1,826	1,133
Debit	3 379	**–31**	**–34**	**–65**	**–150**	**–355**	**–473**	**–774**	**–704**
General government	3 380	–1	–1	–1	–6	–17	–20	–14	–15
Other sectors	3 390	–30	–33	–64	–144	–337	–453	–760	–688
Workers' remittances	3 391	. . .	. . .	. . .	. . .	. . .	. . .	. . .	. . .
Other current transfers	3 392	–30	–33	–64	–144	–337	–453	–760	–688
CAPITAL AND FINANCIAL ACCOUNT	4 996	**1,243**	**1,569**	**5,862**	**7,141**	**6,445**	**6,593**	**7,998**	**14,750**
CAPITAL ACCOUNT	4 994	**. . .**	**. . .**	**–1**	**. . .**	**. . .**	**. . .**	**. . .**	**. . .**
Total credit	2 994	. . .	. . .	. . .	. . .	. . .	. . .	. . .	. . .
Total debit	3 994	. . .	. . .	*–1*	. . .	. . .	. . .	. . .	. . .
Capital transfers, credit	2 400	**. . .**	**. . .**	**. . .**	**. . .**	**. . .**	**. . .**	**. . .**	**. . .**
General government	2 401	. . .	. . .	. . .	. . .	. . .	. . .	. . .	. . .
Debt forgiveness	2 402	. . .	. . .	. . .	. . .	. . .	. . .	. . .	. . .
Other capital transfers	2 410	. . .	. . .	. . .	. . .	. . .	. . .	. . .	. . .
Other sectors	2 430	. . .	. . .	. . .	. . .	. . .	. . .	. . .	. . .
Migrants' transfers	2 431	. . .	. . .	. . .	. . .	. . .	. . .	. . .	. . .
Debt forgiveness	2 432	. . .	. . .	. . .	. . .	. . .	. . .	. . .	. . .
Other capital transfers	2 440	. . .	. . .	. . .	. . .	. . .	. . .	. . .	. . .
Capital transfers, debit	3 400	**. . .**	**. . .**	**–1**	**. . .**	**. . .**	**. . .**	**. . .**	**. . .**
General government	3 401	. . .	. . .	. . .	. . .	. . .	. . .	. . .	. . .
Debt forgiveness	3 402	. . .	. . .	. . .	. . .	. . .	. . .	. . .	. . .
Other capital transfers	3 410	. . .	. . .	. . .	. . .	. . .	. . .	. . .	. . .
Other sectors	3 430	. . .	. . .	–1	. . .	. . .	. . .	. . .	. . .
Migrants' transfers	3 431	. . .	. . .	–1	. . .	. . .	. . .	. . .	. . .
Debt forgiveness	3 432	. . .	. . .	. . .	. . .	. . .	. . .	. . .	. . .
Other capital transfers	3 440	. . .	. . .	. . .	. . .	. . .	. . .	. . .	. . .
Nonproduced nonfinancial assets, credit	2 480	**. . .**	**. . .**	**. . .**	**. . .**	**. . .**	**. . .**	**. . .**	**. . .**
Nonproduced nonfinancial assets, debit	3 480	**. . .**	**. . .**	**. . .**	**. . .**	**. . .**	**. . .**	**. . .**	**. . .**

Table 2 (Continued). STANDARD PRESENTATION, 1988–95
(Millions of U.S. dollars)

	Code	1988	1989	1990	1991	1992	1993	1994	1995
FINANCIAL ACCOUNT	4 995 . .	**1,244**	**1,570**	**5,863**	**7,141**	**6,445**	**6,593**	**7,998**	**14,750**
A. DIRECT INVESTMENT	4 500 . .	1,081	1,726	2,303	1,847	1,966	1,571	873	1,182
Direct investment abroad	4 505 . .	**–24**	**–50**	**–140**	**–167**	**–147**	**–233**	**–493**	**–886**
Equity capital	4 510 . .	–24	–50	–140	–167	–147	–233	–493	–886
Claims on affiliated enterprises	4 515 . .	. . .	. . .	. . .	. . .	. . .	. . .	. . .	. . .
Liabilities to affiliated enterprises	4 520 . .	. . .	. . .	. . .	. . .	. . .	. . .	. . .	. . .
Reinvested earnings	4 525 . .	. . .	. . .	. . .	. . .	. . .	. . .	. . .	. . .
Other capital	4 530 . .	. . .	. . .	. . .	. . .	. . .	. . .	. . .	. . .
Claims on affiliated enterprises	4 535 . .	. . .	. . .	. . .	. . .	. . .	. . .	. . .	. . .
Liabilities to affiliated enterprises	4 540 . .	. . .	. . .	. . .	. . .	. . .	. . .	. . .	. . .
Direct investment in Thailand	4 555 . .	**1,105**	**1,775**	**2,444**	**2,014**	**2,113**	**1,804**	**1,366**	**2,068**
Equity capital	4 560 . .	901	1,454	1,681	1,392	1,681	1,453	1,290	1,959
Claims on direct investors	4 565 . .	. . .	. . .	. . .	. . .	. . .	. . .	. . .	. . .
Liabilities to direct investors	4 570 . .	. . .	. . .	. . .	. . .	. . .	. . .	. . .	. . .
Reinvested earnings	4 575 . .	. . .	. . .	. . .	. . .	. . .	. . .	. . .	. . .
Other capital	4 580 . .	205	322	762	622	432	351	76	109
Claims on direct investors	4 585 . .	. . .	. . .	. . .	. . .	. . .	. . .	. . .	. . .
Liabilities to direct investors	4 590 . .	. . .	. . .	. . .	. . .	. . .	. . .	. . .	. . .
B. PORTFOLIO INVESTMENT	4 600 . .	530	1,486	–38	–81	924	5,455	2,482	4,081
Assets	4 602 . .	**. . .**	**. . .**	**. . .**	**. . .**	**. . .**	**. . .**	**–5**	**–2**
Equity securities	4 610 . .	. . .	. . .	. . .	. . .	. . .	. . .	–5	–2
Monetary authorities	4 611 . .	. . .	. . .	. . .	. . .	. . .	. . .	. . .	. . .
General government	4 612 . .	. . .	. . .	. . .	. . .	. . .	. . .	. . .	. . .
Banks	4 613 . .	. . .	. . .	. . .	. . .	. . .	. . .	. . .	. . .
Other sectors	4 614 . .	. . .	. . .	. . .	. . .	. . .	. . .	–5	–2
Debt securities	4 619 . .	. . .	. . .	. . .	. . .	. . .	. . .	. . .	. . .
Bonds and notes	4 620 . .	. . .	. . .	. . .	. . .	. . .	. . .	. . .	. . .
Monetary authorities	4 621 . .	. . .	. . .	. . .	. . .	. . .	. . .	. . .	. . .
General government	4 622 . .	. . .	. . .	. . .	. . .	. . .	. . .	. . .	. . .
Banks	4 623 . .	. . .	. . .	. . .	. . .	. . .	. . .	. . .	. . .
Other sectors	4 624 . .	. . .	. . .	. . .	. . .	. . .	. . .	. . .	. . .
Money market instruments	4 630 . .	. . .	. . .	. . .	. . .	. . .	. . .	. . .	. . .
Monetary authorities	4 631 . .	. . .	. . .	. . .	. . .	. . .	. . .	. . .	. . .
General government	4 632 . .	. . .	. . .	. . .	. . .	. . .	. . .	. . .	. . .
Banks	4 633 . .	. . .	. . .	. . .	. . .	. . .	. . .	. . .	. . .
Other sectors	4 634 . .	. . .	. . .	. . .	. . .	. . .	. . .	. . .	. . .
Financial derivatives	4 640 . .	. . .	. . .	. . .	. . .	. . .	. . .	. . .	. . .
Monetary authorities	4 641 . .	. . .	. . .	. . .	. . .	. . .	. . .	. . .	. . .
General government	4 642 . .	. . .	. . .	. . .	. . .	. . .	. . .	. . .	. . .
Banks	4 643 . .	. . .	. . .	. . .	. . .	. . .	. . .	. . .	. . .
Other sectors	4 644 . .	. . .	. . .	. . .	. . .	. . .	. . .	. . .	. . .
Liabilities	4 652 . .	**530**	**1,486**	**–38**	**–81**	**924**	**5,455**	**2,486**	**4,083**
Equity securities	4 660 . .	444	1,424	440	37	455	2,679	–389	2,123
Banks	4 663 . .	. . .	. . .	. . .	. . .	. . .	. . .	. . .	. . .
Other sectors	4 664 . .	444	1,424	440	37	455	2,679	–389	2,123
Debt securities	4 669 . .	86	63	–478	–118	469	2,776	2,875	1,960
Bonds and notes	4 670 . .	86	63	–478	–118	469	2,776	2,875	1,960
Monetary authorities	4 671 . .	. . .	. . .	. . .	. . .	. . .	. . .	. . .	. . .
General government	4 672 . .	182	72	–445	. . .	298	299	672	246
Banks	4 673 . .	. . .	. . .	. . .	. . .	75	144	574	745
Other sectors	4 674 . .	–95	–9	–33	–118	96	2,333	1,629	969
Money market instruments	4 680 . .	. . .	. . .	. . .	. . .	. . .	. . .	. . .	. . .
Monetary authorities	4 681 . .	. . .	. . .	. . .	. . .	. . .	. . .	. . .	. . .
General government	4 682 . .	. . .	. . .	. . .	. . .	. . .	. . .	. . .	. . .
Banks	4 683 . .	. . .	. . .	. . .	. . .	. . .	. . .	. . .	. . .
Other sectors	4 684 . .	. . .	. . .	. . .	. . .	. . .	. . .	. . .	. . .
Financial derivatives	4 690 . .	. . .	. . .	. . .	. . .	. . .	. . .	. . .	. . .
Monetary authorities	4 691 . .	. . .	. . .	. . .	. . .	. . .	. . .	. . .	. . .
General government	4 692 . .	. . .	. . .	. . .	. . .	. . .	. . .	. . .	. . .
Banks	4 693 . .	. . .	. . .	. . .	. . .	. . .	. . .	. . .	. . .
Other sectors	4 694 . .	. . .	. . .	. . .	. . .	. . .	. . .	. . .	. . .

Table 2 (Concluded). STANDARD PRESENTATION, 1988–95
(Millions of U.S. dollars)

	Code	1988	1989	1990	1991	1992	1993	1994	1995
C. OTHER INVESTMENT	4 700 . .	1,968	3,025	6,559	9,993	6,584	3,474	8,812	16,645
Assets	4 703 . .	**269**	**–313**	**–164**	**352**	**104**	**–3,265**	**–1,027**	**–2,738**
Trade credits	4 706 . .	. . .	. . .	. . .	. . .	. . .	. . .	. . .	. . .
General government: long-term	4 708 . .	. . .	. . .	. . .	. . .	. . .	. . .	. . .	. . .
General government: short-term	4 709 . .	. . .	. . .	. . .	. . .	. . .	. . .	. . .	. . .
Other sectors: long-term	4 711 . .	. . .	. . .	. . .	. . .	. . .	. . .	. . .	. . .
Other sectors: short-term	4 712 . .	. . .	. . .	. . .	. . .	. . .	. . .	. . .	. . .
Loans	4 714 . .	. . .	. . .	. . .	. . .	. . .	–3	–68	–1
Monetary authorities: long-term	4 717 . .	. . .	. . .	. . .	. . .	. . .	. . .	. . .	. . .
Monetary authorities: short-term	4 718 . .	. . .	. . .	. . .	. . .	. . .	. . .	. . .	. . .
General government: long-term	4 720 . .	. . .	. . .	. . .	. . .	. . .	. . .	. . .	. . .
General government: short-term	4 721 . .	. . .	. . .	. . .	. . .	. . .	. . .	. . .	. . .
Banks: long-term	4 723 . .	. . .	. . .	. . .	. . .	. . .	. . .	. . .	. . .
Banks: short-term	4 724 . .	. . .	. . .	. . .	. . .	. . .	–3	–68	–1
Other sectors: long-term	4 726 . .	. . .	. . .	. . .	. . .	. . .	. . .	. . .	. . .
Other sectors: short-term	4 727 . .	. . .	. . .	. . .	. . .	. . .	. . .	. . .	. . .
Currency and deposits	4 730 . .	195	–82	86	138	104	–3,262	–959	–2,737
Monetary authorities	4 731 . .	. . .	. . .	. . .	. . .	. . .	. . .	. . .	. . .
General government	4 732 . .	195	–82	86	138	. . .	. . .	. . .	. . .
Banks	4 733 . .	. . .	. . .	. . .	. . .	104	–3,262	–959	–2,737
Other sectors	4 734 . .	. . .	. . .	. . .	. . .	. . .	. . .	. . .	. . .
Other assets	4 736 . .	73	–231	–250	214	. . .	. . .	. . .	. . .
Monetary authorities: long-term	4 738 . .	. . .	. . .	. . .	. . .	. . .	. . .	. . .	. . .
Monetary authorities: short-term	4 739 . .	. . .	. . .	. . .	. . .	. . .	. . .	. . .	. . .
General government: long-term	4 741 . .	54	–255	–306	109	. . .	. . .	. . .	. . .
General government: short-term	4 742 . .	. . .	. . .	. . .	. . .	. . .	. . .	. . .	. . .
Banks: long-term	4 744 . .	. . .	. . .	. . .	. . .	. . .	. . .	. . .	. . .
Banks: short-term	4 745 . .	. . .	. . .	. . .	. . .	. . .	. . .	. . .	. . .
Other sectors: long-term	4 747 . .	19	23	57	105	. . .	. . .	. . .	. . .
Other sectors: short-term	4 748 . .	. . .	. . .	. . .	. . .	. . .	. . .	. . .	. . .
Liabilities	4 753 . .	**1,700**	**3,338**	**6,722**	**9,641**	**6,479**	**6,739**	**9,839**	**19,383**
Trade credits	4 756 . .	309	110	659	735	280	502	256	207
General government: long-term	4 758 . .	. . .	. . .	. . .	. . .	–12	. . .	. . .	. . .
General government: short-term	4 759 . .	. . .	. . .	. . .	. . .	. . .	. . .	. . .	. . .
Other sectors: long-term	4 761 . .	93	8	224	75	162	–158	–439	–198
Other sectors: short-term	4 762 . .	215	102	435	660	130	660	695	405
Loans	4 764 . .	406	2,524	5,031	8,578	4,465	4,128	8,371	15,725
Use of Fund credit and loans from the Fund	4 766 . .	–260	–363	–274	–1	. . .	. . .	. . .	. . .
Monetary authorities: other long-term	4 767 . .	. . .	. . .	. . .	. . .	. . .	. . .	. . .	. . .
Monetary authorities: short-term	4 768 . .	. . .	. . .	. . .	. . .	. . .	. . .	. . .	. . .
General government: long-term	4 770 . .	–51	–206	–999	9	–328	40	–666	–63
General government: short-term	4 771 . .	. . .	. . .	. . .	. . .	–105	–290	180	–92
Banks: long-term	4 773 . .	. . .	. . .	. . .	. . .	. . .	. . .	. . .	. . .
Banks: short-term	4 774 . .	. . .	. . .	. . .	. . .	. . .	. . .	. . .	. . .
Other sectors: long-term	4 776 . .	–386	1,485	2,362	3,030	1,715	502	496	4,025
Other sectors: short-term	4 777 . .	1,103	1,608	3,942	5,540	1,426	–2,714	–5,934	–1,363
Currency and deposits	4 780 . .	984	700	1,027	213	1,754	2,680	2,061	3,396
Monetary authorities	4 781 . .	. . .	. . .	. . .	. . .	. . .	. . .	. . .	. . .
General government	4 782 . .	. . .	. . .	. . .	. . .	. . .	. . .	. . .	. . .
Banks	4 783 . .	984	700	1,027	213	. . .	. . .	. . .	. . .
Other sectors	4 784 . .	. . .	. . .	. . .	. . .	1,754	2,680	2,061	3,396
Other liabilities	4 786 . .	1	4	6	115	–20	–571	–849	55
Monetary authorities: long-term	4 788 . .	. . .	. . .	. . .	. . .	. . .	. . .	. . .	. . .
Monetary authorities: short-term	4 789 . .	. . .	. . .	. . .	. . .	. . .	. . .	. . .	. . .
General government: long-term	4 791 . .	. . .	. . .	. . .	. . .	. . .	. . .	. . .	. . .
General government: short-term	4 792 . .	. . .	. . .	. . .	. . .	–165	–214	–220	201
Banks: long-term	4 794 . .	. . .	. . .	. . .	. . .	. . .	. . .	. . .	. . .
Banks: short-term	4 795 . .	. . .	. . .	. . .	. . .	. . .	. . .	. . .	. . .
Other sectors: long-term	4 797 . .	1	4	. . .	. . .	. . .	. . .	. . .	. . .
Other sectors: short-term	4 798 . .	. . .	. . .	6	115	146	–357	–629	–146
D. RESERVE ASSETS	4 800 . .	–2,336	–4,667	–2,961	–4,618	–3,029	–3,907	–4,169	–7,159
Monetary gold	4 810 . .	. . .	. . .	. . .	. . .	. . .	. . .	. . .	. . .
Special drawing rights	4 820 . .	–6	42	6	5	–4	–10	–8	–13
Reserve position in the Fund	4 830 . .	. . .	. . .	–4	–170	–124	–40	–20	–52
Foreign exchange	4 840 . .	–2,197	–3,655	–3,517	–3,978	–2,901	–3,857	–4,141	–7,094
Other claims	4 880 . .	–133	–1,054	554	–474	. . .	. . .	. . .	. . .
NET ERRORS AND OMISSIONS	4 998 . .	**411**	**928**	**1,419**	**431**	**–142**	**–230**	**87**	**–1,196**

Part 3 of the *Yearbook* contains descriptions of the methodologies, compilation practices, and sources used to compile these data.

Table 1. ANALYTIC PRESENTATION, 1988–95
(Millions of U.S. dollars)

	Code	1988	1989	1990	1991	1992	1993	1994	1995
A. Current Account[1]	4 993 Y.	**–87.2**	**–50.8**	**–99.8**	**–146.9**	**–140.6**	**–173.7**	**–56.8**	**. . .**
Goods: exports f.o.b	2 100 . .	435.3	411.7	513.8	514.4	419.7	264.0	328.4	. . .
Goods: imports f.o.b	3 100 . .	–504.5	–470.1	–602.7	–567.0	–547.4	–375.3	–365.5	. . .
Balance on Goods	4 100 . .	*–69.1*	*–58.4*	*–88.9*	*–52.6*	*–127.7*	*–111.3*	*–37.1*	. . .
Services: credit	2 200 . .	105.1	128.0	149.1	116.4	129.2	71.5	73.5	. . .
Services: debit	3 200 . .	–200.2	–195.8	–244.1	–286.3	–203.3	–142.0	–78.3	. . .
Balance on Goods and Services	4 991 . .	*–164.1*	*–126.2*	*–183.9*	*–222.4*	*–201.8*	*–181.8*	*–42.0*	. . .
Income: credit	2 300 . .	20.8	24.0	32.8	29.7	31.4	16.2	5.2	. . .
Income: debit	3 300 . .	–70.5	–63.8	–65.3	–58.7	–58.6	–48.7	–50.3	. . .
Balance on Goods, Services, and Income	4 992 . .	*–213.8*	*–166.0*	*–216.4*	*–251.4*	*–229.0*	*–214.3*	*–87.0*	. . .
Current transfers: credit	2 379 Y.	148.4	134.0	145.6	128.7	111.1	54.0	35.1	. . .
Current transfers: debit	3 379 . .	–21.8	–18.8	–29.1	–24.2	–22.7	–13.4	–4.9	. . .
B. Capital Account[1]	4 994 Y.	**. . .**	**. . .**	**. . .**	**. . .**	**. . .**	**. . .**	**. . .**	**. . .**
Capital account: credit	2 994 Y.	. . .	. . .	. . .	. . .	. . .	. . .	. . .	. . .
Capital account: debit	3 994 . .	. . .	. . .	. . .	. . .	. . .	. . .	. . .	. . .
Total, Groups A Plus B	4 010 . .	*–87.2*	*–50.8*	*–99.8*	*–146.9*	*–140.6*	*–173.7*	*–56.8*	. . .
C. Financial Account[1]	4 995 X.	**29.9**	**–2.8**	**75.2**	**67.8**	**–23.8**	**–55.1**	**–16.0**	**. . .**
Direct investment abroad	4 505 . .	. . .	. . .	. . .	. . .	. . .	. . .	. . .	. . .
Direct investment in Togo	4 555 Y.	13.0	9.2	18.2	6.5	. . .	. . .	. . .	. . .
Portfolio investment assets	4 602 . .	–.3	–1.1	–1.8	1.1	. . .	. . .	. . .	. . .
Equity securities	4 610 . .	.4	–.4	–1.0	1.1	. . .	. . .	. . .	. . .
Debt securities	4 619 . .	–.7	–.6	–.7	. . .	. . .	. . .	. . .	. . .
Portfolio investment liabilities	4 652 Y.	1.0	1.3	4.4	2.6	. . .	. . .	. . .	. . .
Equity securities	4 660 Y.	1.0	1.3	4.4	2.6	. . .	. . .	. . .	. . .
Debt securities	4 669 Y.	. . .	. . .	. . .	. . .	. . .	. . .	. . .	. . .
Other investment assets	4 703 . .	–15.6	–72.3	25.2	7.5	.2	24.7	. . .	. . .
Monetary authorities	4 703 .A	. . .	. . .	. . .	. . .	. . .	. . .	. . .	. . .
General government	4 703 .B	–.5	–.3	–.2	–.1	. . .	. . .	. . .	. . .
Banks	4 703 .C	–20.4	–49.9	38.6	11.8	.2	24.7	. . .	. . .
Other sectors	4 703 .D	5.3	–22.1	–13.2	–4.1	. . .	. . .	. . .	. . .
Other investment liabilities	4 753 X.	31.8	60.1	29.1	50.1	–24.0	–79.7	–16.0	. . .
Monetary authorities	4 753 XA	. . .	. . .	. . .	. . .	. . .	. . .	. . .	. . .
General government	4 753 YB	8.5	.2	–28.4	21.3	–53.3	–56.5	–22.3	. . .
Banks	4 753 YC	–.3	–2.8	–11.3	2.4	10.4	–25.0	. . .	. . .
Other sectors	4 753 YD	23.6	62.7	68.8	26.5	18.9	1.8	6.3	. . .
Total, Groups A Through C	4 020 . .	*–57.3*	*–53.7*	*–24.6*	*–79.1*	*–164.4*	*–228.7*	*–72.8*	. . .
D. Net Errors and Omissions	4 998 . .	**9.4**	**26.1**	**–19.3**	**31.0**	**4.0**	**41.2**	**–24.3**	**. . .**
Total, Groups A Through D	4 030 . .	*–47.9*	*–27.6*	*–43.9*	*–48.1*	*–160.3*	*–187.5*	*–97.1*	. . .
E. Reserves and Related Items	4 040 . .	**47.9**	**27.6**	**43.9**	**48.1**	**160.3**	**187.5**	**97.1**	**. . .**
Reserve assets	4 800 . .	3.5	–38.6	–29.5	–13.9	73.6	102.2	–7.7	. . .
Use of Fund credit and loans	4 766 . .	–2.8	–.7	5.3	–7.9	.6	–8.3	9.3	. . .
Liabilities constituting foreign authorities' reserves	4 900 . .	. . .	. . .	. . .	. . .	. . .	. . .	. . .	. . .
Exceptional financing	4 920 . .	47.1	66.9	68.1	69.9	86.1	93.6	95.5	. . .
Conversion rates: CFA francs per U.S. dollar	0 101 . .	**297.85**	**319.01**	**272.26**	**282.11**	**264.69**	**283.16**	**555.20**	**499.15**

[1] Excludes components that have been classified in the categories of Group E.

Table 2. STANDARD PRESENTATION, 1988–95
(Millions of U.S. dollars)

	Code	1988	1989	1990	1991	1992	1993	1994	1995
CURRENT ACCOUNT	4 993 . .	**–87.2**	**–50.8**	**–84.2**	**–140.8**	**–138.7**	**–173.7**	**–56.8**	**. . .**
A. GOODS	4 100 . .	–69.1	–58.4	–88.9	–52.6	–127.7	–111.3	–37.1	. . .
Credit	2 100 . .	**435.3**	**411.7**	**513.8**	**514.4**	**419.7**	**264.0**	**328.4**	**. . .**
General merchandise: exports f.o.b.	2 110 . .	435.3	411.7	513.8	514.4	419.7	264.0	328.4	. . .
Goods for processing: exports f.o.b.	2 150 . .	. . .	. . .	. . .	. . .	. . .	. . .	. . .	. . .
Repairs on goods	2 160 . .	. . .	. . .	. . .	. . .	. . .	. . .	. . .	. . .
Goods procured in ports by carriers	2 170 . .	. . .	. . .	. . .	. . .	. . .	. . .	. . .	. . .
Nonmonetary gold	2 180 . .	. . .	. . .	. . .	. . .	. . .	. . .	. . .	. . .
Debit	3 100 . .	**–504.5**	**–470.1**	**–602.7**	**–567.0**	**–547.4**	**–375.3**	**–365.5**	**. . .**
General merchandise: imports f.o.b.	3 110 . .	–504.5	–470.1	–602.7	–567.0	–547.4	–375.3	–365.5	. . .
Goods for processing: imports f.o.b.	3 150 . .	. . .	. . .	. . .	. . .	. . .	. . .	. . .	. . .
Repairs on goods	3 160 . .	. . .	. . .	. . .	. . .	. . .	. . .	. . .	. . .
Goods procured in ports by carriers	3 170 . .	. . .	. . .	. . .	. . .	. . .	. . .	. . .	. . .
Nonmonetary gold	3 180 . .	. . .	. . .	. . .	. . .	. . .	. . .	. . .	. . .
B. SERVICES	4 200 . .	–95.0	–67.8	–95.0	–169.8	–74.0	–70.5	–4.9	. . .
Total credit	2 200 . .	*105.1*	*128.0*	*149.1*	*116.4*	*129.2*	*71.5*	*73.5*	. . .
Total debit	3 200 . .	*–200.2*	*–195.8*	*–244.1*	*–286.3*	*–203.3*	*–142.0*	*–78.3*	. . .
Transportation services, credit	2 205 . .	**24.5**	**21.7**	**30.7**	**26.1**	**27.8**	**17.3**	**10.4**	**. . .**
Passenger	2 205 BA	*1.1*	. . .	. . .	. . .	. . .	. . .	. . .	. . .
Freight	2 205 BB	*3.5*	*3.6*	*6.0*	*4.5*	*4.8*	*3.2*	*3.2*	. . .
Other	2 205 BC	*19.8*	*18.0*	*24.8*	*21.6*	*23.0*	*14.1*	*7.2*	. . .
Sea transport, passenger	2 207 . .	. . .	. . .	. . .	. . .	. . .	. . .	. . .	. . .
Sea transport, freight	2 208 . .	3.5	3.6	6.0	4.5	4.8	3.2	3.2	. . .
Sea transport, other	2 209 . .	19.8	18.0	24.8	21.6	23.0	14.1	7.2	. . .
Air transport, passenger	2 211 . .	. . .	. . .	. . .	. . .	. . .	. . .	. . .	. . .
Air transport, freight	2 212 . .	. . .	. . .	. . .	. . .	. . .	. . .	. . .	. . .
Air transport, other	2 213 . .	. . .	. . .	. . .	. . .	. . .	. . .	. . .	. . .
Other transport, passenger	2 215 . .	. . .	. . .	. . .	. . .	. . .	. . .	. . .	. . .
Other transport, freight	2 216 . .	. . .	. . .	. . .	. . .	. . .	. . .	. . .	. . .
Other transport, other	2 217 . .	. . .	. . .	. . .	. . .	. . .	. . .	. . .	. . .
Transportation services, debit	3 205 . .	**–104.1**	**–96.6**	**–123.3**	**–110.3**	**–86.8**	**–55.3**	**–37.9**	**. . .**
Passenger	3 205 BA	*–21.0*	*–22.5*	*–39.8*	*–32.6*	*–20.8*	*–15.5*	*–7.9*	. . .
Freight	3 205 BB	*–72.2*	*–65.9*	*–72.7*	*–64.6*	*–58.5*	*–34.8*	*–28.2*	. . .
Other	3 205 BC	*–10.8*	*–8.3*	*–10.8*	*–13.1*	*–7.6*	*–4.9*	*–1.8*	. . .
Sea transport, passenger	3 207 . .	. . .	. . .	. . .	. . .	. . .	. . .	. . .	. . .
Sea transport, freight	3 208 . .	–72.2	–65.9	–72.7	–64.6	–58.5	–34.8	–28.2	. . .
Sea transport, other	3 209 . .	–10.8	–8.3	–10.8	–13.1	–7.6	–4.9	–1.8	. . .
Air transport, passenger	3 211 . .	–21.0	–22.5	–39.8	–32.6	–20.8	–15.5	–7.9	. . .
Air transport, freight	3 212 . .	. . .	. . .	. . .	. . .	. . .	. . .	. . .	. . .
Air transport, other	3 213 . .	. . .	. . .	. . .	. . .	. . .	. . .	. . .	. . .
Other transport, passenger	3 215 . .	. . .	. . .	. . .	. . .	. . .	. . .	. . .	. . .
Other transport, freight	3 216 . .	. . .	. . .	. . .	. . .	. . .	. . .	. . .	. . .
Other transport, other	3 217 . .	. . .	. . .	. . .	. . .	. . .	. . .	. . .	. . .
Travel, credit	2 236 . .	**36.4**	**49.8**	**57.9**	**48.6**	**38.9**	**18.7**	**24.0**	**. . .**
Business travel	2 237 . .	. . .	. . .	. . .	. . .	. . .	. . .	. . .	. . .
Personal travel	2 240 . .	36.4	49.8	57.9	48.6	38.9	18.7	24.0	. . .
Travel, debit	3 236 . .	**–33.7**	**–34.2**	**–39.9**	**–55.7**	**–48.0**	**–45.9**	**–23.2**	**. . .**
Business travel	3 237 . .	. . .	. . .	. . .	. . .	. . .	. . .	. . .	. . .
Personal travel	3 240 . .	–33.7	–34.2	–39.9	–55.7	–48.0	–45.9	–23.2	. . .
Other services, credit	2 200 BA	**44.3**	**56.5**	**60.4**	**41.8**	**62.5**	**35.4**	**39.1**	**. . .**
Communications	2 245 . .	. . .	. . .	. . .	. . .	. . .	. . .	. . .	. . .
Construction	2 249 . .	. . .	. . .	. . .	. . .	. . .	. . .	. . .	. . .
Insurance	2 253 . .	.4	6.0	15.7	4.7	.5	.4	.4	. . .
Financial	2 260 . .	. . .	. . .	. . .	. . .	. . .	. . .	. . .	. . .
Computer and information	2 262 . .	. . .	. . .	. . .	. . .	. . .	. . .	. . .	. . .
Royalties and licence fees	2 266 . .	. . .	. . .	. . .	. . .	. . .	. . .	. . .	. . .
Other business services	2 268 . .	17.7	20.9	9.8	8.0	26.1	9.0	26.1	. . .
Personal, cultural, and recreational	2 287 . .	. . .	. . .	. . .	. . .	. . .	. . .	. . .	. . .
Government, n.i.e.	2 291 . .	26.1	29.6	34.9	29.1	35.9	26.1	12.6	. . .
Other services, debit	3 200 BA	**–62.4**	**–65.0**	**–80.9**	**–120.3**	**–68.4**	**–40.8**	**–17.2**	**. . .**
Communications	3 245 . .	. . .	. . .	. . .	. . .	. . .	. . .	. . .	. . .
Construction	3 249 . .	. . .	. . .	. . .	. . .	. . .	. . .	. . .	. . .
Insurance	3 253 . .	–13.4	–9.0	–19.8	–19.6	–20.8	–15.7	–8.2	. . .
Financial	3 260 . .	. . .	. . .	. . .	. . .	. . .	. . .	. . .	. . .
Computer and information	3 262 . .	. . .	. . .	. . .	. . .	. . .	. . .	. . .	. . .
Royalties and licence fees	3 266 . .	. . .	. . .	. . .	. . .	. . .	. . .	. . .	. . .
Other business services	3 268 . .	–31.9	–34.2	–33.7	–69.0	–25.7	–14.5	–3.6	. . .
Personal, cultural, and recreational	3 287 . .	. . .	. . .	. . .	. . .	. . .	. . .	. . .	. . .
Government, n.i.e.	3 291 . .	–17.1	–21.8	–27.4	–31.7	–21.9	–10.6	–5.4	. . .

Table 2 (Continued). STANDARD PRESENTATION, 1988–95
(Millions of U.S. dollars)

	Code	1988	1989	1990	1991	1992	1993	1994	1995
C. INCOME	4 300	–49.6	–39.8	–32.5	–29.0	–27.2	–32.5	–45.0	...
Total credit	2 300	*20.8*	*24.0*	*32.8*	*29.7*	*31.4*	*16.2*	*5.2*	...
Total debit	3 300	*–70.5*	*–63.8*	*–65.3*	*–58.7*	*–58.6*	*–48.7*	*–50.3*	...
Compensation of employees, credit	2 310	...	...	...	...	...	...	...	...
Compensation of employees, debit	3 310	...	...	...	...	...	...	...	...
Investment income, credit	2 320	**20.8**	**24.0**	**32.8**	**29.7**	**31.4**	**16.2**	**5.2**	...
Direct investment income	2 330	...	...	...	...	...	...	...	...
Dividends and distributed branch profits	2 332	...	...	...	...	...	...	...	...
Reinvested earnings and undistributed branch profits	2 333	...	...	...	...	...	...	...	...
Income on debt (interest)	2 334	...	...	...	...	...	...	...	...
Portfolio investment income	2 339	...	...	...	...	...	...	...	...
Income on equity	2 340	...	...	...	...	...	...	...	...
Income on bonds and notes	2 350	...	...	...	...	...	...	...	...
Income on money market instruments and financial derivatives	2 360	...	...	...	...	...	...	...	...
Other investment income	2 370	20.8	24.0	32.8	29.7	31.4	16.2	5.2	...
Investment income, debit	3 320	**–70.5**	**–63.8**	**–65.3**	**–58.7**	**–58.6**	**–48.7**	**–50.3**	...
Direct investment income	3 330	–7.0	–9.6	–15.3	–11.5	–13.6	...	...	...
Dividends and distributed branch profits	3 332	–8.3	–8.9	–10.6	–11.5	–13.6	...	...	...
Reinvested earnings and undistributed branch profits	3 333	1.3	–.7	–4.8	...	...	...	...	...
Income on debt (interest)	3 334	...	...	...	...	...	...	...	...
Portfolio investment income	3 339	...	...	...	...	...	...	...	...
Income on equity	3 340	...	...	...	...	...	...	...	...
Income on bonds and notes	3 350	...	...	...	...	...	...	...	...
Income on money market instruments and financial derivatives	3 360	...	...	...	...	...	...	...	...
Other investment income	3 370	–63.5	–54.3	–49.9	–47.1	–45.0	–48.7	–50.3	...
D. CURRENT TRANSFERS	4 379	126.6	115.2	132.1	110.6	90.3	40.6	30.3	...
Credit	2 379	**148.4**	**134.0**	**161.2**	**134.8**	**113.0**	**54.0**	**35.1**	...
General government	2 380	114.9	104.1	126.5	99.5	96.7	45.2	25.4	...
Other sectors	2 390	33.5	29.8	34.7	35.2	16.2	8.8	9.7	...
Workers' remittances	2 391	21.2	22.9	26.9	29.0	16.2	8.8	9.7	...
Other current transfers	2 392	12.3	7.0	7.8	6.3	...	...	...	...
Debit	3 379	**–21.8**	**–18.8**	**–29.1**	**–24.2**	**–22.7**	**–13.4**	**–4.9**	...
General government	3 380	–5.9	–3.8	–13.2	–8.6	–6.0	–5.7	...	...
Other sectors	3 390	–15.9	–15.0	–15.8	–15.6	–16.6	–7.8	–4.9	...
Workers' remittances	3 391	–13.6	–12.8	–13.4	–12.7	–16.2	–7.4	–4.5	...
Other current transfers	3 392	–2.2	–2.2	–2.4	–3.0	–.4	–.4	–.4	...
CAPITAL AND FINANCIAL ACCOUNT	4 996	**77.7**	**24.7**	**103.6**	**109.8**	**134.6**	**132.4**	**81.1**	...
CAPITAL ACCOUNT	4 994	**4.4**	**20.7**	...	...	...	...	**5.8**	...
Total credit	2 994	*4.4*	*20.7*	...	...	...	...	*5.8*	...
Total debit	3 994	...	...	...	...	...	...	...	...
Capital transfers, credit	2 400	**4.4**	**20.7**	...	...	...	...	**5.8**	...
General government	2 401	4.4	20.7	...	...	...	...	5.8	...
Debt forgiveness	2 402	4.4	20.7	...	...	...	...	5.8	...
Other capital transfers	2 410	...	...	...	...	...	...	...	...
Other sectors	2 430	...	...	...	...	...	...	...	...
Migrants' transfers	2 431	...	...	...	...	...	...	...	...
Debt forgiveness	2 432	...	...	...	...	...	...	...	...
Other capital transfers	2 440	...	...	...	...	...	...	...	...
Capital transfers, debit	3 400	...	...	...	...	...	...	...	...
General government	3 401	...	...	...	...	...	...	...	...
Debt forgiveness	3 402	...	...	...	...	...	...	...	...
Other capital transfers	3 410	...	...	...	...	...	...	...	...
Other sectors	3 430	...	...	...	...	...	...	...	...
Migrants' transfers	3 431	...	...	...	...	...	...	...	...
Debt forgiveness	3 432	...	...	...	...	...	...	...	...
Other capital transfers	3 440	...	...	...	...	...	...	...	...
Nonproduced nonfinancial assets, credit	2 480	...	...	...	...	...	...	...	...
Nonproduced nonfinancial assets, debit	3 480	...	...	...	...	...	...	...	...

Table 2 (Continued). STANDARD PRESENTATION, 1988–95
(Millions of U.S. dollars)

	Code		1988	1989	1990	1991	1992	1993	1994	1995
FINANCIAL ACCOUNT	4 995	. .	**73.4**	**4.0**	**103.6**	**109.8**	**134.6**	**132.4**	**75.3**	**. . .**
A. DIRECT INVESTMENT	4 500	. .	13.0	9.2	18.2	6.5	. . .	. . .	. . .	. . .
Direct investment abroad	4 505	. .	**. . .**	**. . .**	**. . .**	**. . .**	**. . .**	**. . .**	**. . .**	**. . .**
Equity capital	4 510	. .	. . .	. . .	. . .	. . .	. . .	. . .	. . .	. . .
Claims on affiliated enterprises	4 515	. .	. . .	. . .	. . .	. . .	. . .	. . .	. . .	. . .
Liabilities to affiliated enterprises	4 520	. .	. . .	. . .	. . .	. . .	. . .	. . .	. . .	. . .
Reinvested earnings	4 525	. .	. . .	. . .	. . .	. . .	. . .	. . .	. . .	. . .
Other capital	4 530	. .	. . .	. . .	. . .	. . .	. . .	. . .	. . .	. . .
Claims on affiliated enterprises	4 535	. .	. . .	. . .	. . .	. . .	. . .	. . .	. . .	. . .
Liabilities to affiliated enterprises	4 540	. .	. . .	. . .	. . .	. . .	. . .	. . .	. . .	. . .
Direct investment in Togo	4 555	. .	**13.0**	**9.2**	**18.2**	**6.5**	**. . .**	**. . .**	**. . .**	**. . .**
Equity capital	4 560	. .	9.4	5.1	10.2	5.5	. . .	. . .	. . .	. . .
Claims on direct investors	4 565	. .	. . .	. . .	. . .	. . .	. . .	. . .	. . .	. . .
Liabilities to direct investors	4 570	. .	. . .	. . .	. . .	. . .	. . .	. . .	. . .	. . .
Reinvested earnings	4 575	. .	−1.3	.7	4.8	. . .	. . .	. . .		. . .
Other capital	4 580	. .	4.9	3.3	3.3	1.0	. . .	. . .	. . .	. . .
Claims on direct investors	4 585	. .	. . .	. . .	. . .	. . .	. . .	. . .	. . .	. . .
Liabilities to direct investors	4 590	. .	. . .	. . .	. . .	. . .	. . .	. . .	. . .	. . .
B. PORTFOLIO INVESTMENT	4 600	. .	.7	.2	2.7	3.7	. . .	. . .	. . .	. . .
Assets	4 602	. .	**−.3**	**−1.1**	**−1.8**	**1.1**	**. . .**	**. . .**	**. . .**	**. . .**
Equity securities	4 610	. .	.4	−.4	−1.0	1.1	. . .	. . .	. . .	. . .
Monetary authorities	4 611	. .	. . .	. . .	. . .	. . .	. . .	. . .	. . .	. . .
General government	4 612	. .	. . .	. . .	. . .	. . .	. . .	. . .	. . .	. . .
Banks	4 613	. .	. . .	. . .	. . .	. . .	. . .	. . .	. . .	. . .
Other sectors	4 614	. .	. . .	. . .	. . .	. . .	. . .	. . .	. . .	. . .
Debt securities	4 619	. .	−.7	−.6	−.7		. . .	. . .	. . .	. . .
Bonds and notes	4 620	. .	−.7	−.6	−.7	. . .	. . .	. . .	. . .	. . .
Monetary authorities	4 621	. .	. . .	. . .	. . .	. . .	. . .	. . .	. . .	. . .
General government	4 622	. .	. . .	. . .	. . .	. . .	. . .	. . .	. . .	. . .
Banks	4 623	. .	. . .	. . .	. . .	. . .	. . .	. . .	. . .	. . .
Other sectors	4 624	. .	. . .	. . .	. . .	. . .	. . .	. . .	. . .	. . .
Money market instruments	4 630	. .	. . .	. . .	. . .	. . .	. . .	. . .	. . .	. . .
Monetary authorities	4 631	. .	. . .	. . .	. . .	. . .	. . .	. . .	. . .	. . .
General government	4 632	. .	. . .	. . .	. . .	. . .	. . .	. . .	. . .	. . .
Banks	4 633	. .	. . .	. . .	. . .	. . .	. . .	. . .	. . .	. . .
Other sectors	4 634	. .	. . .	. . .	. . .	. . .	. . .	. . .	. . .	. . .
Financial derivatives	4 640	. .	. . .	. . .	. . .	. . .	. . .	. . .	. . .	. . .
Monetary authorities	4 641	. .	. . .	. . .	. . .	. . .	. . .	. . .	. . .	. . .
General government	4 642	. .	. . .	. . .	. . .	. . .	. . .	. . .	. . .	. . .
Banks	4 643	. .	. . .	. . .	. . .	. . .	. . .	. . .	. . .	. . .
Other sectors	4 644	. .	. . .	. . .	. . .	. . .	. . .	. . .	. . .	. . .
Liabilities	4 652	. .	**1.0**	**1.3**	**4.4**	**2.6**	**. . .**	**. . .**	**. . .**	**. . .**
Equity securities	4 660	. .	1.0	1.3	4.4	2.6	. . .	. . .	. . .	. . .
Banks	4 663	. .	. . .	. . .	. . .	. . .	. . .	. . .	. . .	. . .
Other sectors	4 664	. .	. . .	. . .	. . .	. . .	. . .	. . .	. . .	. . .
Debt securities	4 669	. .	. . .	. . .	. . .	. . .	. . .	. . .	. . .	. . .
Bonds and notes	4 670	. .	. . .	. . .	. . .	. . .	. . .	. . .	. . .	. . .
Monetary authorities	4 671	. .	. . .	. . .	. . .	. . .	. . .	. . .	. . .	. . .
General government	4 672	. .	. . .	. . .	. . .	. . .	. . .	. . .	. . .	. . .
Banks	4 673	. .	. . .	. . .	. . .	. . .	. . .	. . .	. . .	. . .
Other sectors	4 674	. .	. . .	. . .	. . .	. . .	. . .	. . .	. . .	. . .
Money market instruments	4 680	. .	. . .	. . .	. . .	. . .	. . .	. . .	. . .	. . .
Monetary authorities	4 681	. .	. . .	. . .	. . .	. . .	. . .	. . .	. . .	. . .
General government	4 682	. .	. . .	. . .	. . .	. . .	. . .	. . .	. . .	. . .
Banks	4 683	. .	. . .	. . .	. . .	. . .	. . .	. . .	. . .	. . .
Other sectors	4 684	. .	. . .	. . .	. . .	. . .	. . .	. . .	. . .	. . .
Financial derivatives	4 690	. .	. . .	. . .	. . .	. . .	. . .	. . .	. . .	. . .
Monetary authorities	4 691	. .	. . .	. . .	. . .	. . .	. . .	. . .	. . .	. . .
General government	4 692	. .	. . .	. . .	. . .	. . .	. . .	. . .	. . .	. . .
Banks	4 693	. .	. . .	. . .	. . .	. . .	. . .	. . .	. . .	. . .
Other sectors	4 694	. .	. . .	. . .	. . .	. . .	. . .	. . .	. . .	. . .

Table 2 (Concluded). STANDARD PRESENTATION, 1988–95
(Millions of U.S. dollars)

	Code		1988	1989	1990	1991	1992	1993	1994	1995
C. OTHER INVESTMENT	4 700	. .	56.2	33.2	112.2	113.5	61.0	30.2	83.0	. . .
Assets	4 703	. .	**–15.6**	**–72.3**	**25.2**	**7.5**	**.2**	**24.7**	**. . .**	**. . .**
Trade credits	4 706	. .	. . .	. . .	. . .	. . .	. . .	. . .	. . .	. . .
General government: long-term	4 708	. .	. . .	. . .	. . .	. . .	. . .	. . .	. . .	. . .
General government: short-term	4 709	. .	. . .	. . .	. . .	. . .	. . .	. . .	. . .	. . .
Other sectors: long-term	4 711	. .	. . .	. . .	. . .	. . .	. . .	. . .	. . .	. . .
Other sectors: short-term	4 712	. .	. . .	. . .	. . .	. . .	. . .	. . .	. . .	. . .
Loans	4 714	. .	4.8	–35.7	–1.0	17.9	. . .	. . .	. . .	. . .
Monetary authorities: long-term	4 717	. .	. . .	. . .	. . .	. . .	. . .	. . .	. . .	. . .
Monetary authorities: short-term	4 718	. .	. . .	. . .	. . .	. . .	. . .	. . .	. . .	. . .
General government: long-term	4 720	. .	. . .	. . .	. . .	. . .	. . .	. . .	. . .	. . .
General government: short-term	4 721	. .	. . .	. . .	. . .	. . .	. . .	. . .	. . .	. . .
Banks: long-term	4 723	. .	–2.7	–19.6	3.5	11.6	. . .	. . .	. . .	. . .
Banks: short-term	4 724	. .	. . .	. . .	. . .	. . .	. . .	. . .	. . .	. . .
Other sectors: long-term	4 726	. .	. . .	. . .	. . .	. . .	. . .	. . .	. . .	. . .
Other sectors: short-term	4 727	. .	7.5	–16.1	–4.5	6.4	. . .	. . .	. . .	. . .
Currency and deposits	4 730	. .	–29.2	–38.5	26.3	–10.3	.2	24.7	. . .	. . .
Monetary authorities	4 731	. .	. . .	. . .	. . .	. . .	. . .	. . .	. . .	. . .
General government	4 732	. .	–.1	. . .	. . .	. . .	. . .	. . .	. . .	. . .
Banks	4 733	. .	–17.6	–30.2	35.0	.2	.2	24.7	. . .	. . .
Other sectors	4 734	. .	–11.4	–8.3	–8.8	–10.5	. . .	. . .	. . .	. . .
Other assets	4 736	. .	8.8	2.0	–.2	–.1	. . .	. . .	. . .	. . .
Monetary authorities: long-term	4 738	. .	. . .	. . .	. . .	. . .	. . .	. . .	. . .	. . .
Monetary authorities: short-term	4 739	. .	. . .	. . .	. . .	. . .	. . .	. . .	. . .	. . .
General government: long-term	4 741	. .	–.4	–.3	–.2	–.1	. . .	. . .	. . .	. . .
General government: short-term	4 742	. .	. . .	. . .	. . .	. . .	. . .	. . .	. . .	. . .
Banks: long-term	4 744	. .	. . .	. . .	. . .	. . .	. . .	. . .	. . .	. . .
Banks: short-term	4 745	. .	. . .	. . .	. . .	. . .	. . .	. . .	. . .	. . .
Other sectors: long-term	4 747	. .	9.2	2.3	. . .	. . .	. . .	. . .	. . .	. . .
Other sectors: short-term	4 748	. .	. . .	. . .	. . .	. . .	. . .	. . .	. . .	. . .
Liabilities	4 753	. .	**71.8**	**105.5**	**87.0**	**106.0**	**60.9**	**5.5**	**83.0**	**. . .**
Trade credits	4 756	. .	–.2	. . .	. . .	.1	. . .	. . .	. . .	. . .
General government: long-term	4 758	. .	. . .	. . .	. . .	. . .	. . .	. . .	. . .	. . .
General government: short-term	4 759	. .	–.2	. . .	. . .	.1	. . .	. . .	. . .	. . .
Other sectors: long-term	4 761	. .	. . .	. . .	. . .	. . .	. . .	. . .	. . .	. . .
Other sectors: short-term	4 762	. .	. . .	. . .	. . .	. . .	. . .	. . .	. . .	. . .
Loans	4 764	. .	151.3	80.6	38.9	49.5	8.5	–39.8	–13.0	. . .
Use of Fund credit and loans from the Fund	4 766	. .	–2.8	–.7	5.3	–7.9	.6	–8.3	9.3	. . .
Monetary authorities: other long-term	4 767	. .	. . .	. . .	. . .	. . .	. . .	. . .	. . .	. . .
Monetary authorities: short-term	4 768	. .	. . .	. . .	. . .	. . .	. . .	. . .	. . .	. . .
General government: long-term	4 770	. .	149.2	50.6	27.0	66.9	7.9	–31.4	–22.3	. . .
General government: short-term	4 771	. .	. . .	. . .	. . .	. . .	. . .	. . .	. . .	. . .
Banks: long-term	4 773	. .	1.4	–1.4	–2.7	–.7	. . .	. . .	. . .	. . .
Banks: short-term	4 774	. .	. . .	. . .	. . .	. . .	. . .	. . .	. . .	. . .
Other sectors: long-term	4 776	. .	.4	11.3	. . .	. . .	. . .	. . .	. . .	. . .
Other sectors: short-term	4 777	. .	3.1	20.8	9.3	–8.8	. . .	. . .	. . .	. . .
Currency and deposits	4 780	. .	–1.6	–1.4	–8.6	3.1	10.4	–25.0	. . .	. . .
Monetary authorities	4 781	. .	. . .	. . .	. . .	. . .	. . .	. . .	. . .	. . .
General government	4 782	. .	. . .	. . .	. . .	. . .	. . .	. . .	. . .	. . .
Banks	4 783	. .	–1.6	–1.4	–8.6	3.1	10.4	–25.0	. . .	. . .
Other sectors	4 784	. .	. . .	. . .	. . .	. . .	. . .	. . .	. . .	. . .
Other liabilities	4 786	. .	–77.7	26.3	56.7	53.4	41.9	70.3	96.0	. . .
Monetary authorities: long-term	4 788	. .	. . .	. . .	. . .	. . .	. . .	. . .	. . .	. . .
Monetary authorities: short-term	4 789	. .	. . .	. . .	. . .	. . .	. . .	. . .	. . .	. . .
General government: long-term	4 791	. .	–4.4	. . .	. . .	. . .	. . .	. . .	. . .	. . .
General government: short-term	4 792	. .	–93.3	–4.3	–2.8	18.1	23.0	68.5	89.7	. . .
Banks: long-term	4 794	. .	. . .	. . .	. . .	. . .	. . .	. . .	. . .	. . .
Banks: short-term	4 795	. .	. . .	. . .	. . .	. . .	. . .	. . .	. . .	. . .
Other sectors: long-term	4 797	. .	6.8	8.3	29.8	11.7	18.9	1.8	6.3	. . .
Other sectors: short-term	4 798	. .	13.3	22.3	29.8	23.6	. . .	. . .	. . .	. . .
D. RESERVE ASSETS	4 800	. .	3.5	–38.6	–29.5	–13.9	73.6	102.2	–7.7	. . .
Monetary gold	4 810	. .	. . .	. . .	. . .	. . .	. . .	. . .	. . .	. . .
Special drawing rights	4 820	. .	. . .	–1.6	1.6	–.2	.1	.2	. . .	. . .
Reserve position in the Fund	4 830	. .	. . .	. . .	. . .	. . .	. . .	. . .	. . .	. . .
Foreign exchange	4 840	. .	43.8	–37.0	–31.1	–13.7	73.5	102.1	–7.7	. . .
Other claims	4 880	. .	–40.3	. . .	. . .	. . .	. . .	. . .	. . .	. . .
NET ERRORS AND OMISSIONS	4 998	. .	**9.4**	**26.1**	**–19.3**	**31.0**	**4.0**	**41.2**	**–24.3**	**. . .**

Table 1. ANALYTIC PRESENTATION, 1988–95
(Thousands of U.S. dollars)

	Code	1988	1989	1990	1991	1992	1993	1994	1995
A. Current Account[1]	4 993 Y.	**–12,743**	**7,435**	**5,795**	**–74**	**–468**	**–5,928**	...	...
Goods: exports f.o.b	2 100 ..	8,722	9,395	11,912	13,437	12,306	16,082	...	...
Goods: imports f.o.b	3 100 ..	–48,592	–49,728	–50,769	–49,452	–51,301	–56,606	...	...
Balance on Goods	4 100 ..	*–39,870*	*–40,333*	*–38,857*	*–36,015*	*–38,995*	*–40,524*	...	...
Services: credit	2 200 ..	17,192	27,067	26,363	20,370	16,623	15,953	...	...
Services: debit	3 200 ..	–25,719	–21,037	–23,351	–22,445	–22,246	–21,145	...	...
Balance on Goods and Services	4 991 ..	*–48,397*	*–34,304*	*–35,845*	*–38,089*	*–44,619*	*–45,716*	...	...
Income: credit	2 300 ..	4,876	3,911	5,180	3,560	4,244	5,557	...	...
Income: debit	3 300 ..	–1,275	–1,145	–893	–1,059	–1,211	–2,383	...	...
Balance on Goods, Services, and Income	4 992 ..	*–44,795*	*–31,538*	*–31,558*	*–35,588*	*–41,586*	*–42,542*	...	...
Current transfers: credit	2 379 Y.	36,930	44,063	43,528	41,774	50,552	49,740	...	...
Current transfers: debit	3 379 ..	–4,877	–5,089	–6,176	–6,259	–9,434	–13,125	...	...
B. Capital Account[1]	4 994 Y.	**34**	**–238**	**–115**	**127**	**557**	**605**	...	...
Capital account: credit	2 994 Y.	124	138	241	485	732	1,340	...	...
Capital account: debit	3 994 ..	–90	–376	–356	–358	–176	–735	...	...
Total, Groups A Plus B	4 010 ..	*–12,709*	*7,197*	*5,680*	*53*	*88*	*–5,323*	...	...
C. Financial Account[1]	4 995 X.	**4,405**	**–8,203**	**–1,733**	**2,984**	**4,421**	**3,189**	...	...
Direct investment abroad	4 505 ..	...	...	–1	–24	–2	–1	...	...
Direct investment in Tonga	4 555 Y.	29	174	198	359	1,224	2,178	...	...
Portfolio investment assets	4 602 ..	...	1	32	128	...	...	...	...
Equity securities	4 610 ..	...	...	...	...	...	...	...	...
Debt securities	4 619 ..	...	1	32	128	...	...	...	...
Portfolio investment liabilities	4 652 Y.	–82	–9,392	–8,162	–2,381	–141	–64	...	...
Equity securities	4 660 Y.	–82	–8	–89	–19	–33	...	...	...
Debt securities	4 669 Y.	...	–9,384	–8,073	–2,361	–109	–64	...	...
Other investment assets	4 703 ..	755	727	4,787	4,768	815	...	...	...
Monetary authorities	4 703 .A	...	...	...	...	...	...	...	...
General government	4 703 .B	755	723	3,611	1,235	812	...	...	...
Banks	4 703 .C	...	...	...	62	...	...	...	...
Other sectors	4 703 .D	...	4	1,176	3,471	4	...	...	...
Other investment liabilities	4 753 X.	3,703	287	1,412	134	2,525	1,076	...	...
Monetary authorities	4 753 XA	–285	...	–363	–80	–68	–14	...	...
General government	4 753 YB	2,625	1,612	248	–725	3,095	1,095	...	...
Banks	4 753 YC	511	411	1,750	134	–208	...	...	...
Other sectors	4 753 YD	851	–1,735	–222	805	–294	–4	...	...
Total, Groups A Through C	4 020 ..	*–8,304*	*–1,006*	*3,947*	*3,037*	*4,509*	*–2,133*	...	...
D. Net Errors and Omissions	4 998 ..	**9,992**	**–4,628**	**2,443**	**–2,144**	**–3,437**	**–260**	...	...
Total, Groups A Through D	4 030 ..	*1,688*	*–5,634*	*6,390*	*893*	*1,072*	*–2,393*	...	...
E. Reserves and Related Items	4 040 ..	**–1,688**	**5,634**	**–6,390**	**–893**	**–1,072**	**2,393**	...	...
Reserve assets	4 800 ..	–1,688	5,634	–6,390	–893	–1,072	2,393	...	...
Use of Fund credit and loans	4 766 ..	...	...	...	...	...	...	...	...
Liabilities constituting foreign authorities' reserves	4 900 ..	...	...	...	...	...	...	...	...
Exceptional financing	4 920 ..	...	...	...	...	...	...	...	...
Conversion rates: pa'anga per U.S. dollar	0 101 ..	**1.2797**	**1.2637**	**1.2809**	**1.2961**	**1.3471**	**1.3841**	**1.3202**	**1.2709**

[1] Excludes components that have been classified in the categories of Group E.

Table 2. STANDARD PRESENTATION, 1988–95
(Thousands of U.S. dollars)

	Code			1988	1989	1990	1991	1992	1993	1994	1995
CURRENT ACCOUNT	4	993	. .	**–12,743**	**7,435**	**5,795**	**–74**	**–468**	**–5,928**	**. . .**	**. . .**
A. GOODS	4	100	. .	–39,870	–40,333	–38,857	–36,015	–38,995	–40,524	. . .	. . .
Credit	2	100	. .	**8,722**	**9,395**	**11,912**	**13,437**	**12,306**	**16,082**	**. . .**	**. . .**
General merchandise: exports f.o.b.	2	110	. .	8,722	9,395	11,912	13,437	12,306	16,082	. . .	. . .
Goods for processing: exports f.o.b.	2	150	. .	. . .	. . .	. . .	. . .	. . .	. . .	. . .	. . .
Repairs on goods	2	160	. .	. . .	. . .	. . .	. . .	. . .	. . .	. . .	. . .
Goods procured in ports by carriers	2	170	. .	. . .	. . .	. . .	. . .	. . .	. . .	. . .	. . .
Nonmonetary gold	2	180	. .	. . .	. . .	. . .	. . .	. . .	. . .	. . .	. . .
Debit	3	100	. .	**–48,592**	**–49,728**	**–50,769**	**–49,452**	**–51,301**	**–56,606**	**. . .**	**. . .**
General merchandise: imports f.o.b.	3	110	. .	–48,592	–49,728	–50,769	–49,452	–51,301	–56,606	. . .	. . .
Goods for processing: imports f.o.b.	3	150	. .	. . .	. . .	. . .	. . .	. . .	. . .	. . .	. . .
Repairs on goods	3	160	. .	. . .	. . .	. . .	. . .	. . .	. . .	. . .	. . .
Goods procured in ports by carriers	3	170	. .	. . .	. . .	. . .	. . .	. . .	. . .	. . .	. . .
Nonmonetary gold	3	180	. .	. . .	. . .	. . .	. . .	. . .	. . .	. . .	. . .
B. SERVICES	4	200	. .	–8,526	6,029	3,012	–2,074	–5,624	–5,192	. . .	. . .
Total credit	2	200	. .	*17,192*	*27,067*	*26,363*	*20,370*	*16,623*	*15,953*	. . .	. . .
Total debit	3	200	. .	*–25,719*	*–21,037*	*–23,351*	*–22,445*	*–22,246*	*–21,145*	. . .	. . .
Transportation services, credit	2	205	. .	**2,579**	**2,870**	**3,089**	**3,273**	**3,971**	**2,994**	**. . .**	**. . .**
Passenger	2	205	BA	*99*	*100*	*172*	*112*	*306*	*66*	. . .	. . .
Freight	2	205	BB	*282*	*199*	*156*	*267*	*542*	*182*	. . .	. . .
Other	2	205	BC	*2,198*	*2,571*	*2,761*	*2,894*	*3,122*	*2,746*	. . .	. . .
Sea transport, passenger	2	207	. .	. . .	. . .	. . .	. . .	. . .	. . .	. . .	. . .
Sea transport, freight	2	208	. .	. . .	. . .	. . .	. . .	. . .	. . .	. . .	. . .
Sea transport, other	2	209	. .	. . .	. . .	. . .	. . .	. . .	. . .	. . .	. . .
Air transport, passenger	2	211	. .	. . .	. . .	. . .	. . .	. . .	. . .	. . .	. . .
Air transport, freight	2	212	. .	. . .	. . .	. . .	. . .	. . .	. . .	. . .	. . .
Air transport, other	2	213	. .	. . .	. . .	. . .	. . .	. . .	. . .	. . .	. . .
Other transport, passenger	2	215	. .	. . .	. . .	. . .	. . .	. . .	. . .	. . .	. . .
Other transport, freight	2	216	. .	. . .	. . .	. . .	. . .	. . .	. . .	. . .	. . .
Other transport, other	2	217	. .	. . .	. . .	. . .	. . .	. . .	. . .	. . .	. . .
Transportation services, debit	3	205	. .	**–18,478**	**–14,209**	**–16,155**	**–16,024**	**–15,179**	**–14,571**	**. . .**	**. . .**
Passenger	3	205	BA	*–6,199*	*–3,485*	*–4,324*	*–3,811*	*–3,219*	*–2,870*	. . .	. . .
Freight	3	205	BB	*–8,986*	*–8,745*	*–10,007*	*–9,599*	*–10,134*	*–9,976*	. . .	. . .
Other	3	205	BC	*–3,293*	*–1,980*	*–1,823*	*–2,614*	*–1,825*	*–1,725*	. . .	. . .
Sea transport, passenger	3	207	. .	. . .	. . .	. . .	. . .	. . .	. . .	. . .	. . .
Sea transport, freight	3	208	. .	. . .	. . .	. . .	. . .	. . .	. . .	. . .	. . .
Sea transport, other	3	209	. .	. . .	. . .	. . .	. . .	. . .	. . .	. . .	. . .
Air transport, passenger	3	211	. .	. . .	. . .	. . .	. . .	. . .	. . .	. . .	. . .
Air transport, freight	3	212	. .	. . .	. . .	. . .	. . .	. . .	. . .	. . .	. . .
Air transport, other	3	213	. .	. . .	. . .	. . .	. . .	. . .	. . .	. . .	. . .
Other transport, passenger	3	215	. .	. . .	. . .	. . .	. . .	. . .	. . .	. . .	. . .
Other transport, freight	3	216	. .	. . .	. . .	. . .	. . .	. . .	. . .	. . .	. . .
Other transport, other	3	217	. .	. . .	. . .	. . .	. . .	. . .	. . .	. . .	. . .
Travel, credit	2	236	. .	**7,348**	**6,785**	**7,161**	**8,305**	**8,393**	**9,104**	**. . .**	**. . .**
Business travel	2	237	. .	. . .	. . .	. . .	. . .	. . .	. . .	. . .	. . .
Personal travel	2	240	. .	. . .	. . .	. . .	. . .	. . .	. . .	. . .	. . .
Travel, debit	3	236	. .	**–2,705**	**–2,057**	**–1,399**	**–1,308**	**–1,051**	**–925**	**. . .**	**. . .**
Business travel	3	237	. .	. . .	. . .	. . .	. . .	. . .	. . .	. . .	. . .
Personal travel	3	240	. .	. . .	. . .	. . .	. . .	. . .	. . .	. . .	. . .
Other services, credit	2	200	BA	**7,265**	**17,411**	**16,113**	**8,792**	**4,259**	**3,855**	**. . .**	**. . .**
Communications	2	245	. .	. . .	. . .	. . .	. . .	. . .	. . .	. . .	. . .
Construction	2	249	. .	. . .	. . .	. . .	. . .	. . .	. . .	. . .	. . .
Insurance	2	253	. .	31	22	17	30	60	20	. . .	. . .
Financial	2	260	. .	. . .	. . .	. . .	. . .	. . .	. . .	. . .	. . .
Computer and information	2	262	. .	. . .	. . .	. . .	. . .	. . .	. . .	. . .	. . .
Royalties and licence fees	2	266	. .	. . .	. . .	. . .	. . .	. . .	. . .	. . .	. . .
Other business services	2	268	. .	878	413	458	1,033	718	141	. . .	. . .
Personal, cultural, and recreational	2	287	. .	. . .	. . .	. . .	. . .	. . .	. . .	. . .	. . .
Government, n.i.e.	2	291	. .	6,356	16,976	15,637	7,729	3,481	3,694	. . .	. . .
Other services, debit	3	200	BA	**–4,536**	**–4,771**	**–5,797**	**–5,113**	**–6,017**	**–5,649**	**. . .**	**. . .**
Communications	3	245	. .	. . .	. . .	. . .	. . .	. . .	. . .	. . .	. . .
Construction	3	249	. .	. . .	. . .	. . .	. . .	. . .	. . .	. . .	. . .
Insurance	3	253	. .	–998	–972	–1,112	–1,067	–1,126	–1,108	. . .	. . .
Financial	3	260	. .	. . .	. . .	. . .	. . .	. . .	. . .	. . .	. . .
Computer and information	3	262	. .	. . .	. . .	. . .	. . .	. . .	. . .	. . .	. . .
Royalties and licence fees	3	266	. .	. . .	. . .	–12	. . .	–125	. . .	. . .	. . .
Other business services	3	268	. .	–1,214	–1,329	–1,711	–1,937	–2,590	–1,444	. . .	. . .
Personal, cultural, and recreational	3	287	. .	. . .	. . .	. . .	. . .	. . .	. . .	. . .	. . .
Government, n.i.e.	3	291	. .	–2,324	–2,470	–2,961	–2,109	–2,176	–3,097	. . .	. . .

Table 2 (Continued). STANDARD PRESENTATION, 1988–95

(Thousands of U.S. dollars)

	Code	1988	1989	1990	1991	1992	1993	1994	1995
C. INCOME	4 300 . .	3,601	2,766	4,287	2,501	3,033	3,174	. . .	. . .
Total credit	2 300 . .	*4,876*	*3,911*	*5,180*	*3,560*	*4,244*	*5,557*	. . .	. . .
Total debit	3 300 . .	*–1,275*	*–1,145*	*–893*	*–1,059*	*–1,211*	*–2,383*	. . .	. . .
Compensation of employees, credit	2 310 . .	**831**	**693**	**712**	**449**	**544**	**824**	**. . .**	**. . .**
Compensation of employees, debit	3 310 . .	**–2**	**. . .**	**. . .**	**. . .**	**. . .**	**–211**	**. . .**	**. . .**
Investment income, credit	2 320 . .	**4,045**	**3,218**	**4,467**	**3,111**	**3,700**	**4,733**	**. . .**	**. . .**
Direct investment income	2 330 . .	. . .	19	1	24	2	1	. . .	. . .
Dividends and distributed branch profits	2 332 . .	. . .	19	. . .	. . .	. . .	. . .	. . .	. . .
Reinvested earnings and undistributed branch profits	2 333 . .	. . .	. . .	1	24	2	1	. . .	. . .
Income on debt (interest)	2 334 . .	. . .	. . .	. . .	. . .	. . .	. . .	. . .	. . .
Portfolio investment income	2 339 . .	. . .	. . .	. . .	. . .	. . .	. . .	. . .	. . .
Income on equity	2 340 . .	. . .	. . .	. . .	. . .	. . .	. . .	. . .	. . .
Income on bonds and notes	2 350 . .	. . .	. . .	. . .	. . .	. . .	. . .	. . .	. . .
Income on money market instruments and financial derivatives	2 360 . .	. . .	. . .	. . .	. . .	. . .	. . .	. . .	. . .
Other investment income	2 370 . .	4,045	3,199	4,467	3,087	3,698	4,732	. . .	. . .
Investment income, debit	3 320 . .	**–1,273**	**–1,145**	**–893**	**–1,059**	**–1,211**	**–2,172**	**. . .**	**. . .**
Direct investment income	3 330 . .	–651	–602	–296	–35	–7	–4	. . .	. . .
Dividends and distributed branch profits	3 332 . .	–651	–602	–296	–35	–7	–4	. . .	. . .
Reinvested earnings and undistributed branch profits	3 333 . .	. . .	. . .	. . .	. . .	. . .	. . .	. . .	. . .
Income on debt (interest)	3 334 . .	. . .	. . .	. . .	. . .	. . .	. . .	. . .	. . .
Portfolio investment income	3 339 . .	. . .	. . .	. . .	. . .	. . .	. . .	. . .	. . .
Income on equity	3 340 . .	. . .	. . .	. . .	. . .	. . .	. . .	. . .	. . .
Income on bonds and notes	3 350 . .	. . .	. . .	. . .	. . .	. . .	. . .	. . .	. . .
Income on money market instruments and financial derivatives	3 360 . .	. . .	. . .	. . .	. . .	. . .	. . .	. . .	. . .
Other investment income	3 370 . .	–622	–543	–598	–1,025	–1,203	–2,168	. . .	. . .
D. CURRENT TRANSFERS	4 379 . .	32,052	38,974	37,353	35,515	41,117	36,614	. . .	. . .
Credit	2 379 . .	**36,930**	**44,063**	**43,528**	**41,774**	**50,552**	**49,740**	**. . .**	**. . .**
General government	2 380 . .	9,662	12,011	6,087	11,259	12,538	8,768	. . .	. . .
Other sectors	2 390 . .	27,267	32,052	37,442	30,515	38,013	40,971	. . .	. . .
Workers' remittances	2 391 . .	15,658	14,037	23,005	17,831	20,059	18,798	. . .	. . .
Other current transfers	2 392 . .	11,609	18,015	14,437	12,684	17,954	22,173	. . .	. . .
Debit	3 379 . .	**–4,877**	**–5,089**	**–6,176**	**–6,259**	**–9,434**	**–13,125**	**. . .**	**. . .**
General government	3 380 . .	–880	–494	–1,290	–1,988	–3,326	–4,252	. . .	. . .
Other sectors	3 390 . .	–3,997	–4,595	–4,886	–4,272	–6,109	–8,873	. . .	. . .
Workers' remittances	3 391 . .	–891	–1,436	–861	–774	–1,039	–1,508	. . .	. . .
Other current transfers	3 392 . .	–3,106	–3,159	–4,025	–3,498	–5,070	–7,366	. . .	. . .
CAPITAL AND FINANCIAL ACCOUNT	4 996 . .	**2,751**	**–2,807**	**–8,238**	**2,218**	**3,906**	**6,188**	**. . .**	**. . .**
CAPITAL ACCOUNT	4 994 . .	**34**	**–238**	**–115**	**127**	**557**	**605**	**. . .**	**. . .**
Total credit	2 994 . .	*124*	*138*	*241*	*485*	*732*	*1,340*	. . .	. . .
Total debit	3 994 . .	*–90*	*–376*	*–356*	*–358*	*–176*	*–735*	. . .	. . .
Capital transfers, credit	2 400 . .	**124**	**138**	**241**	**485**	**732**	**1,340**	**. . .**	**. . .**
General government	2 401 . .	. . .	. . .	. . .	. . .	. . .	. . .	. . .	. . .
Debt forgiveness	2 402 . .	. . .	. . .	. . .	. . .	. . .	. . .	. . .	. . .
Other capital transfers	2 410 . .	. . .	. . .	. . .	. . .	. . .	. . .	. . .	. . .
Other sectors	2 430 . .	124	138	241	485	732	1,340	. . .	. . .
Migrants' transfers	2 431 . .	124	138	241	485	732	1,340	. . .	. . .
Debt forgiveness	2 432 . .	. . .	. . .	. . .	. . .	. . .	. . .	. . .	. . .
Other capital transfers	2 440 . .	. . .	. . .	. . .	. . .	. . .	. . .	. . .	. . .
Capital transfers, debit	3 400 . .	**–90**	**–376**	**–356**	**–358**	**–176**	**–735**	**. . .**	**. . .**
General government	3 401 . .	. . .	. . .	. . .	. . .	. . .	. . .	. . .	. . .
Debt forgiveness	3 402 . .	. . .	. . .	. . .	. . .	. . .	. . .	. . .	. . .
Other capital transfers	3 410 . .	. . .	. . .	. . .	. . .	. . .	. . .	. . .	. . .
Other sectors	3 430 . .	–90	–376	–356	–358	–176	–735	. . .	. . .
Migrants' transfers	3 431 . .	–90	–376	–356	–358	–176	–735	. . .	. . .
Debt forgiveness	3 432 . .	. . .	. . .	. . .	. . .	. . .	. . .	. . .	. . .
Other capital transfers	3 440 . .	. . .	. . .	. . .	. . .	. . .	. . .	. . .	. . .
Nonproduced nonfinancial assets, credit	2 480 . .	**. . .**	**. . .**	**. . .**	**. . .**	**. . .**	**. . .**	**. . .**	**. . .**
Nonproduced nonfinancial assets, debit	3 480 . .	**. . .**	**. . .**	**. . .**	**. . .**	**. . .**	**. . .**	**. . .**	**. . .**

Table 2 (Continued). STANDARD PRESENTATION, 1988–95
(Thousands of U.S. dollars)

	Code	1988	1989	1990	1991	1992	1993	1994	1995
FINANCIAL ACCOUNT	4 995 . .	**2,717**	**–2,569**	**–8,123**	**2,092**	**3,349**	**5,583**	. . .	. . .
A. DIRECT INVESTMENT	4 500 . .	29	174	197	335	1,222	2,177	. . .	. . .
Direct investment abroad	4 505 . .	. . .	. . .	**–1**	**–24**	**–2**	**–1**	. . .	. . .
Equity capital	4 510 . .	. . .	. . .	. . .	. . .	. . .	. . .	. . .	. . .
Claims on affiliated enterprises	4 515 . .	. . .	. . .	. . .	. . .	. . .	. . .	. . .	. . .
Liabilities to affiliated enterprises	4 520 . .	. . .	. . .	. . .	. . .	. . .	. . .	. . .	. . .
Reinvested earnings	4 525 . .	. . .	. . .	–1	–24	–2	–1	. . .	. . .
Other capital	4 530 . .	. . .	. . .	. . .	. . .	. . .	. . .	. . .	. . .
Claims on affiliated enterprises	4 535 . .	. . .	. . .	. . .	. . .	. . .	. . .	. . .	. . .
Liabilities to affiliated enterprises	4 540 . .	. . .	. . .	. . .	. . .	. . .	. . .	. . .	. . .
Direct investment in Tonga	4 555 . .	**29**	**174**	**198**	**359**	**1,224**	**2,178**	. . .	. . .
Equity capital	4 560 . .	9	. . .	190	359	1,224	2,178	. . .	. . .
Claims on direct investors	4 565 . .	. . .	. . .	. . .	. . .	. . .	. . .	. . .	. . .
Liabilities to direct investors	4 570 . .	. . .	. . .	. . .	. . .	. . .	. . .	. . .	. . .
Reinvested earnings	4 575 . .	. . .	. . .	. . .	. . .	. . .	. . .	. . .	. . .
Other capital	4 580 . .	20	174	8	. . .	. . .	. . .	. . .	. . .
Claims on direct investors	4 585 . .	. . .	. . .	. . .	. . .	. . .	. . .	. . .	. . .
Liabilities to direct investors	4 590 . .	. . .	. . .	. . .	. . .	. . .	. . .	. . .	. . .
B. PORTFOLIO INVESTMENT	4 600 . .	–82	–9,391	–8,129	–2,253	–141	–64	. . .	. . .
Assets	4 602 . .	. . .	**1**	**32**	**128**	. . .	. . .	. . .	. . .
Equity securities	4 610 . .	. . .	. . .	. . .	. . .	. . .	. . .	. . .	. . .
Monetary authorities	4 611 . .	. . .	. . .	. . .	. . .	. . .	. . .	. . .	. . .
General government	4 612 . .	. . .	. . .	. . .	. . .	. . .	. . .	. . .	. . .
Banks	4 613 . .	. . .	. . .	. . .	. . .	. . .	. . .	. . .	. . .
Other sectors	4 614 . .	. . .	. . .	. . .	. . .	. . .	. . .	. . .	. . .
Debt securities	4 619 . .	. . .	1	32	128	. . .	. . .	. . .	. . .
Bonds and notes	4 620 . .	. . .	1	32	128	. . .	. . .	. . .	. . .
Monetary authorities	4 621 . .	. . .	. . .	. . .	. . .	. . .	. . .	. . .	. . .
General government	4 622 . .	. . .	. . .	. . .	. . .	. . .	. . .	. . .	. . .
Banks	4 623 . .	. . .	. . .	. . .	. . .	. . .	. . .	. . .	. . .
Other sectors	4 624 . .	. . .	. . .	. . .	. . .	. . .	. . .	. . .	. . .
Money market instruments	4 630 . .	. . .	. . .	. . .	. . .	. . .	. . .	. . .	. . .
Monetary authorities	4 631 . .	. . .	. . .	. . .	. . .	. . .	. . .	. . .	. . .
General government	4 632 . .	. . .	. . .	. . .	. . .	. . .	. . .	. . .	. . .
Banks	4 633 . .	. . .	. . .	. . .	. . .	. . .	. . .	. . .	. . .
Other sectors	4 634 . .	. . .	. . .	. . .	. . .	. . .	. . .	. . .	. . .
Financial derivatives	4 640 . .	. . .	. . .	. . .	. . .	. . .	. . .	. . .	. . .
Monetary authorities	4 641 . .	. . .	. . .	. . .	. . .	. . .	. . .	. . .	. . .
General government	4 642 . .	. . .	. . .	. . .	. . .	. . .	. . .	. . .	. . .
Banks	4 643 . .	. . .	. . .	. . .	. . .	. . .	. . .	. . .	. . .
Other sectors	4 644 . .	. . .	. . .	. . .	. . .	. . .	. . .	. . .	. . .
Liabilities	4 652 . .	**–82**	**–9,392**	**–8,162**	**–2,381**	**–141**	**–64**	. . .	. . .
Equity securities	4 660 . .	–82	–8	–89	–19	–33	. . .	. . .	. . .
Banks	4 663 . .	. . .	. . .	. . .	. . .	. . .	. . .	. . .	. . .
Other sectors	4 664 . .	. . .	. . .	. . .	. . .	. . .	. . .	. . .	. . .
Debt securities	4 669 . .	. . .	–9,384	–8,073	–2,361	–109	–64	. . .	. . .
Bonds and notes	4 670 . .	. . .	–9,384	–8,073	–2,361	–109	–64	. . .	. . .
Monetary authorities	4 671 . .	. . .	. . .	. . .	. . .	. . .	. . .	. . .	. . .
General government	4 672 . .	. . .	–9,384	–8,073	–2,361	–109	–64	. . .	. . .
Banks	4 673 . .	. . .	. . .	. . .	. . .	. . .	. . .	. . .	. . .
Other sectors	4 674 . .	. . .	. . .	. . .	. . .	. . .	. . .	. . .	. . .
Money market instruments	4 680 . .	. . .	. . .	. . .	. . .	. . .	. . .	. . .	. . .
Monetary authorities	4 681 . .	. . .	. . .	. . .	. . .	. . .	. . .	. . .	. . .
General government	4 682 . .	. . .	. . .	. . .	. . .	. . .	. . .	. . .	. . .
Banks	4 683 . .	. . .	. . .	. . .	. . .	. . .	. . .	. . .	. . .
Other sectors	4 684 . .	. . .	. . .	. . .	. . .	. . .	. . .	. . .	. . .
Financial derivatives	4 690 . .	. . .	. . .	. . .	. . .	. . .	. . .	. . .	. . .
Monetary authorities	4 691 . .	. . .	. . .	. . .	. . .	. . .	. . .	. . .	. . .
General government	4 692 . .	. . .	. . .	. . .	. . .	. . .	. . .	. . .	. . .
Banks	4 693 . .	. . .	. . .	. . .	. . .	. . .	. . .	. . .	. . .
Other sectors	4 694 . .	. . .	. . .	. . .	. . .	. . .	. . .	. . .	. . .

Table 2 (Concluded). STANDARD PRESENTATION, 1988–95

(Thousands of U.S. dollars)

	Code	1988	1989	1990	1991	1992	1993	1994	1995
C. OTHER INVESTMENT	4 700 . .	4,458	1,015	6,199	4,902	3,340	1,076	. . .	. . .
Assets	4 703 . .	**755**	**727**	**4,787**	**4,768**	**815**	**. . .**	**. . .**	**. . .**
Trade credits	4 706 . .	. . .	. . .	. . .	. . .	. . .	. . .	. . .	. . .
General government: long-term	4 708 . .	. . .	. . .	. . .	. . .	. . .	. . .	. . .	. . .
General government: short-term	4 709 . .	. . .	. . .	. . .	. . .	. . .	. . .	. . .	. . .
Other sectors: long-term	4 711 . .	. . .	. . .	. . .	. . .	. . .	. . .	. . .	. . .
Other sectors: short-term	4 712 . .	. . .	. . .	. . .	. . .	. . .	. . .	. . .	. . .
Loans	4 714 . .	755	723	3,611	1,235	812	. . .	. . .	. . .
Monetary authorities: long-term	4 717 . .	. . .	. . .	. . .	. . .	. . .	. . .	. . .	. . .
Monetary authorities: short-term	4 718 . .	. . .	. . .	. . .	. . .	. . .	. . .	. . .	. . .
General government: long-term	4 720 . .	. . .	. . .	. . .	. . .	. . .	. . .	. . .	. . .
General government: short-term	4 721 . .	755	723	3,611	1,235	812	. . .	. . .	. . .
Banks: long-term	4 723 . .	. . .	. . .	. . .	. . .	. . .	. . .	. . .	. . .
Banks: short-term	4 724 . .	. . .	. . .	. . .	. . .	. . .	. . .	. . .	. . .
Other sectors: long-term	4 726 . .	. . .	. . .	. . .	. . .	. . .	. . .	. . .	. . .
Other sectors: short-term	4 727 . .	. . .	. . .	. . .	. . .	. . .	. . .	. . .	. . .
Currency and deposits	4 730 . .	. . .	4	1,176	3,533	4	. . .	. . .	. . .
Monetary authorities	4 731 . .	. . .	. . .	. . .	. . .	. . .	. . .	. . .	. . .
General government	4 732 . .	. . .	. . .	. . .	. . .	. . .	. . .	. . .	. . .
Banks	4 733 . .	. . .	. . .	. . .	62	. . .	. . .	. . .	. . .
Other sectors	4 734 . .	. . .	4	1,176	3,471	4	. . .	. . .	. . .
Other assets	4 736 . .	. . .	. . .	. . .	. . .	. . .	. . .	. . .	. . .
Monetary authorities: long-term	4 738 . .	. . .	. . .	. . .	. . .	. . .	. . .	. . .	. . .
Monetary authorities: short-term	4 739 . .	. . .	. . .	. . .	. . .	. . .	. . .	. . .	. . .
General government: long-term	4 741 . .	. . .	. . .	. . .	. . .	. . .	. . .	. . .	. . .
General government: short-term	4 742 . .	. . .	. . .	. . .	. . .	. . .	. . .	. . .	. . .
Banks: long-term	4 744 . .	. . .	. . .	. . .	. . .	. . .	. . .	. . .	. . .
Banks: short-term	4 745 . .	. . .	. . .	. . .	. . .	. . .	. . .	. . .	. . .
Other sectors: long-term	4 747 . .	. . .	. . .	. . .	. . .	. . .	. . .	. . .	. . .
Other sectors: short-term	4 748 . .	. . .	. . .	. . .	. . .	. . .	. . .	. . .	. . .
Liabilities	4 753 . .	**3,703**	**287**	**1,412**	**134**	**2,525**	**1,076**	**. . .**	**. . .**
Trade credits	4 756 . .	. . .	. . .	. . .	. . .	. . .	. . .	. . .	. . .
General government: long-term	4 758 . .	. . .	. . .	. . .	. . .	. . .	. . .	. . .	. . .
General government: short-term	4 759 . .	. . .	. . .	. . .	. . .	. . .	. . .	. . .	. . .
Other sectors: long-term	4 761 . .	. . .	. . .	. . .	. . .	. . .	. . .	. . .	. . .
Other sectors: short-term	4 762 . .	. . .	. . .	. . .	. . .	. . .	. . .	. . .	. . .
Loans	4 764 . .	3,590	287	1,787	333	2,832	1,096	. . .	. . .
Use of Fund credit and loans from the Fund	4 766 . .	. . .	. . .	. . .	. . .	. . .	. . .	. . .	. . .
Monetary authorities: other long term	4 767 . .	. . .	. . .	. . .	. . .	. . .	. . .	. . .	. . .
Monetary authorities: short-term	4 768 . .	. . .	. . .	. . .	. . .	. . .	. . .	. . .	. . .
General government: long-term	4 770 . .	2,625	1,612	248	–725	3,095	1,094	. . .	. . .
General government: short-term	4 771 . .	. . .	. . .	. . .	. . .	. . .	1	. . .	. . .
Banks: long-term	4 773 . .	48	411	1,751	154	–143	. . .	. . .	. . .
Banks: short-term	4 774 . .	. . .	. . .	. . .	. . .	. . .	. . .	. . .	. . .
Other sectors: long-term	4 776 . .	917	–1,735	–212	904	–120	. . .	. . .	. . .
Other sectors: short-term	4 777 . .	. . .	. . .	. . .	. . .	. . .	1	. . .	. . .
Currency and deposits	4 780 . .	464	. . .	–2	–20	–65	. . .	. . .	. . .
Monetary authorities	4 781 . .	. . .	. . .	. . .	. . .	. . .	. . .	. . .	. . .
General government	4 782 . .	. . .	. . .	. . .	. . .	. . .	. . .	. . .	. . .
Banks	4 783 . .	464	. . .	–2	–20	–65	. . .	. . .	. . .
Other sectors	4 784 . .	. . .	. . .	. . .	. . .	. . .	. . .	. . .	. . .
Other liabilities	4 786 . .	–350	. . .	–373	–179	–242	–20	. . .	. . .
Monetary authorities: long-term	4 788 . .	. . .	. . .	. . .	. . .	. . .	. . .	. . .	. . .
Monetary authorities: short-term	4 789 . .	–285	. . .	–363	–80	–68	–14	. . .	. . .
General government: long-term	4 791 . .	. . .	. . .	. . .	. . .	. . .	. . .	. . .	. . .
General government: short-term	4 792 . .	. . .	. . .	. . .	. . .	. . .	. . .	. . .	. . .
Banks: long-term	4 794 . .	. . .	. . .	. . .	. . .	. . .	. . .	. . .	. . .
Banks: short-term	4 795 . .	. . .	. . .	. . .	. . .	. . .	. . .	. . .	. . .
Other sectors: long-term	4 797 . .	. . .	. . .	. . .	. . .	. . .	. . .	. . .	. . .
Other sectors: short-term	4 798 . .	–66	. . .	–10	–99	–174	–5	. . .	. . .
D. RESERVE ASSETS	4 800 . .	–1,688	5,634	–6,390	–893	–1,072	2,393	. . .	. . .
Monetary gold	4 810 . .	. . .	. . .	. . .	. . .	. . .	3,171	. . .	. . .
Special drawing rights	4 820 . .	–41	–51	–68	–772	498	–81	. . .	. . .
Reserve position in the Fund	4 830 . .	. . .	. . .	. . .	. . .	–610	–17	. . .	. . .
Foreign exchange	4 840 . .	–1,647	5,685	–6,322	–120	–959	–680	. . .	. . .
Other claims	4 880 . .	. . .	. . .	. . .	. . .	. . .	. . .	. . .	. . .
NET ERRORS AND OMISSIONS	4 998 . .	**9,992**	**–4,628**	**2,443**	**–2,144**	**–3,437**	**–260**	**. . .**	**. . .**

Table 1. ANALYTIC PRESENTATION, 1988–95
(Millions of U.S. dollars)

	Code	1988	1989	1990	1991	1992	1993	1994	1995
A. Current Account [1]	4 993 Y .	**-88.6**	**-38.5**	**459.0**	**-4.7**	**138.9**	**113.1**	**217.8**	**293.8**
Goods: exports f.o.b	2 100 . .	1,469.5	1,550.8	1,960.1	1,774.5	1,691.4	1,500.1	1,777.6	2,456.1
Goods: imports f.o.b	3 100 . .	-1,064.2	-1,045.2	-947.6	-1,210.3	-995.6	-952.9	-1,036.6	-1,868.5
Balance on Goods	4 100 . .	*405.3*	*505.5*	*1,012.5*	*564.2*	*695.7*	*547.2*	*741.1*	*587.7*
Services: credit	2 200 . .	271.3	280.8	328.5	405.3	452.7	353.4	326.6	342.6
Services: debit	3 200 . .	-453.9	-439.8	-479.2	-534.4	-561.9	-466.4	-438.1	-241.9
Balance on Goods and Services	4 991 . .	*222.6*	*346.6*	*861.9*	*435.1*	*586.6*	*434.2*	*629.5*	*688.4*
Income: credit	2 300 . .	20.3	32.4	39.6	48.6	29.8	40.2	56.7	76.6
Income: debit	3 300 . .	-322.3	-410.1	-436.4	-490.7	-477.9	-366.0	-468.7	-466.7
Balance on Goods, Services, and Income	4 992 . .	*-79.4*	*-31.1*	*465.2*	*-7.0*	*138.5*	*108.4*	*217.5*	*298.3*
Current transfers: credit	2 379 Y .	3.5	5.2	7.8	15.6	11.1	23.7	28.3	34.0
Current transfers: debit	3 379 . .	-12.7	-12.7	-13.9	-13.3	-10.7	-19.0	-27.9	-38.5
B. Capital Account [1]	4 994 Y .	**-20.4**	**-17.2**	**-19.2**	**-16.1**	**-16.5**	**-11.5**	**-6.4**	**-11.9**
Capital account: credit	2 994 Y .	. . .	.4	.4	.4	.4	1.3	1.1	1.1
Capital account: debit	3 994 . .	-20.4	-17.5	-19.6	-16.5	-16.9	-12.8	-7.5	-13.0
Total, Groups A Plus B	4 010 . .	*-109.0*	*-55.7*	*439.8*	*-20.8*	*122.4*	*101.6*	*211.4*	*281.9*
C. Financial Account [1]	4 995 X .	**-141.5**	**-166.5**	**-506.3**	**-226.8**	**-154.2**	**98.8**	**-32.2**	**-279.5**
Direct investment abroad	4 505 . .	. . .	. . .	. . .	. . .	. . .	. . .	. . .	. . .
Direct investment in Trinidad and Tobago	4 555 Y .	62.9	148.9	109.4	169.3	177.9	379.2	516.2	298.9
Portfolio investment assets	4 602 . .	. . .	. . .	. . .	. . .	. . .	. . .	. . .	-7.9
Equity securities	4 610 . .	. . .	. . .	. . .	. . .	. . .	. . .	. . .	-7.9
Debt securities	4 619 . .	. . .	. . .	. . .	. . .	. . .	. . .	. . .	. . .
Portfolio investment liabilities	4 652 Y .	. . .	. . .	. . .	. . .	. . .	. . .	. . .	16.7
Equity securities	4 660 Y .	. . .	. . .	. . .	. . .	. . .	. . .	. . .	16.7
Debt securities	4 669 Y .	. . .	. . .	. . .	. . .	. . .	. . .	. . .	. . .
Other investment assets	4 703 . .	60.9	44.5	63.0	4.4	-31.3	-76.2	-233.5	-122.1
Monetary authorities	4 703 .A	. . .	. . .	. . .	. . .	. . .	. . .	. . .	-32.4
General government	4 703 .B	88.2	8.1	.9	-5.2	. . .	. . .	-56.1	. . .
Banks	4 703 .C	-51.9	-20.3	17.1	16.2	-5.3	-105.6	-109.3	-23.7
Other sectors	4 703 .D	24.6	56.7	45.0	-6.6	-26.0	29.3	-68.2	-66.0
Other investment liabilities	4 753 X .	-265.4	-359.8	-678.8	-400.5	-300.8	-204.2	-314.9	-465.1
Monetary authorities	4 753 XA	. . .	-47.3	. . .	. . .	. . .	. . .	. . .	. . .
General government	4 753 YB	3.8	-153.8	-244.5	-166.1	-101.9	19.9	-7.2	-116.8
Banks	4 753 YC	-24.7	-2.3	-2.8	-6.4	16.5	20.4	-10.2	-51.3
Other sectors	4 753 YD	-244.4	-156.4	-431.4	-228.1	-215.4	-244.4	-297.4	-297.0
Total, Groups A Through C	4 020 . .	*-250.5*	*-222.2*	*-66.5*	*-247.6*	*-31.8*	*200.4*	*179.2*	*2.4*
D. Net Errors and Omissions	4 998 . .	**21.1**	**45.4**	**-112.0**	**-29.0**	**-72.6**	**-41.8**	**6.3**	**81.4**
Total, Groups A Through D	4 030 . .	*-229.4*	*-176.8*	*-178.5*	*-276.5*	*-104.4*	*158.6*	*185.5*	*83.7*
E. Reserves and Related Items	4 040 . .	**229.4**	**176.8**	**178.5**	**276.5**	**104.4**	**-158.6**	**-185.5**	**-83.7**
Reserve assets	4 800 . .	27.4	-158.5	-197.7	102.7	124.4	-29.4	-113.6	-40.1
Use of Fund credit and loans	4 766 . .	115.4	91.4	100.9	50.7	-89.8	-129.2	-71.9	-43.6
Liabilities constituting foreign authorities' reserves	4 900 . .	. . .	. . .	. . .	. . .	. . .	. . .	. . .	. . .
Exceptional financing	4 920 . .	86.6	243.8	275.3	123.1	69.8	. . .	. . .	. . .
Conversion rates: Trinidad and Tobago dollars per U.S. dollar	0 101 . .	**3.8438**	**4.2500**	**4.2500**	**4.2500**	**4.2500**	**5.3511**	**5.9249**	**5.9478**

[1] Excludes components that have been classified in the categories of Group E.

Table 2. STANDARD PRESENTATION, 1988–95
(Millions of U.S. dollars)

	Code	1988	1989	1990	1991	1992	1993	1994	1995
CURRENT ACCOUNT	4 993 . .	**–88.6**	**–38.5**	**459.0**	**–4.7**	**138.9**	**113.1**	**217.8**	**293.8**
A. GOODS	4 100 . .	405.3	505.5	1,012.5	564.2	695.7	547.2	741.1	587.7
Credit	2 100 . .	**1,469.5**	**1,550.8**	**1,960.1**	**1,774.5**	**1,691.4**	**1,500.1**	**1,777.6**	**2,456.1**
General merchandise: exports f.o.b.	2 110 . .	1,453.3	1,534.6	1,935.2	1,751.3	1,661.9	1,477.2	1,760.0	2,436.2
Goods for processing: exports f.o.b.	2 150 . .	. . .	. . .	. . .	. . .	. . .	. . .	. . .	. . .
Repairs on goods	2 160 . .	. . .	. . .	. . .	. . .	. . .	. . .	. . .	. . .
Goods procured in ports by carriers	2 170 . .	16.1	16.2	24.9	23.2	29.5	22.9	17.6	19.9
Nonmonetary gold	2 180 . .	. . .	. . .	. . .	. . .	. . .	. . .	. . .	. . .
Debit	3 100 . .	**–1,064.2**	**–1,045.2**	**–947.6**	**–1,210.3**	**–995.6**	**–952.9**	**–1,036.6**	**–1,868.5**
General merchandise: imports f.o.b.	3 110 . .	–1,064.2	–1,045.2	–947.6	–1,210.3	–995.6	–952.9	–1,036.6	–1,868.5
Goods for processing: imports f.o.b.	3 150 . .	. . .	. . .	. . .	. . .	. . .	. . .	. . .	. . .
Repairs on goods	3 160 . .	. . .	. . .	. . .	. . .	. . .	. . .	. . .	. . .
Goods procured in ports by carriers	3 170 . .	. . .	. . .	. . .	. . .	. . .	. . .	. . .	. . .
Nonmonetary gold	3 180 . .	. . .	. . .	. . .	. . .	. . .	. . .	. . .	. . .
B. SERVICES	4 200 . .	–182.7	–158.9	–150.6	–129.1	–109.1	–112.9	–111.5	100.7
Total credit	2 200 . .	*271.3*	*280.8*	*328.5*	*405.3*	*452.7*	*353.4*	*326.6*	*342.6*
Total debit	3 200 . .	*–453.9*	*–439.8*	*–479.2*	*–534.4*	*–561.9*	*–466.4*	*–438.1*	*–241.9*
Transportation services, credit	2 205 . .	**115.9**	**129.0**	**163.1**	**171.7**	**207.3**	**197.6**	**176.4**	**193.8**
Passenger	2 205 BA	*87.4*	*87.9*	*126.7*	*142.3*	*173.3*	*168.8*	*145.5*	*155.2*
Freight	2 205 BB	*8.7*	*10.8*	*9.8*	*7.8*	*10.5*	*9.4*	*9.8*	*9.7*
Other	2 205 BC	*19.8*	*30.4*	*26.6*	*21.6*	*23.5*	*19.4*	*21.1*	*28.9*
Sea transport, passenger	2 207 . .	. . .	. . .	. . .	. . .	. . .	. . .	. . .	. . .
Sea transport, freight	2 208 . .	. . .	. . .	. . .	. . .	. . .	. . .	. . .	. . .
Sea transport, other	2 209 . .	. . .	. . .	. . .	. . .	. . .	. . .	. . .	. . .
Air transport, passenger	2 211 . .	. . .	. . .	. . .	. . .	. . .	. . .	. . .	. . .
Air transport, freight	2 212 . .	. . .	. . .	. . .	. . .	. . .	. . .	. . .	. . .
Air transport, other	2 213 . .	. . .	. . .	. . .	. . .	. . .	. . .	. . .	. . .
Other transport, passenger	2 215 . .	. . .	. . .	. . .	. . .	. . .	. . .	. . .	. . .
Other transport, freight	2 216 . .	. . .	. . .	. . .	. . .	. . .	. . .	. . .	. . .
Other transport, other	2 217 . .	. . .	. . .	. . .	. . .	. . .	. . .	. . .	. . .
Transportation services, debit	3 205 . .	**–173.8**	**–219.9**	**–237.8**	**–278.0**	**–269.2**	**–242.1**	**–235.2**	**–94.2**
Passenger	3 205 BA	*–24.5*	*–20.0*	*–25.6*	*–20.3*	*–19.5*	*–15.7*	*–22.0*	*–22.2*
Freight	3 205 BB	*–79.8*	*–122.1*	*–126.2*	*–166.7*	*–143.6*	*–146.1*	*–130.3*	*–47.2*
Other	3 205 BC	*–69.4*	*–77.8*	*–86.1*	*–91.1*	*–106.2*	*–80.3*	*–82.9*	*–24.7*
Sea transport, passenger	3 207 . .	. . .	. . .	. . .	. . .	. . .	. . .	. . .	. . .
Sea transport, freight	3 208 . .	. . .	. . .	. . .	. . .	. . .	. . .	. . .	. . .
Sea transport, other	3 209 . .	. . .	. . .	. . .	. . .	. . .	. . .	. . .	. . .
Air transport, passenger	3 211 . .	. . .	. . .	. . .	. . .	. . .	. . .	. . .	. . .
Air transport, freight	3 212 . .	. . .	. . .	. . .	. . .	. . .	. . .	. . .	. . .
Air transport, other	3 213 . .	. . .	. . .	. . .	. . .	. . .	. . .	. . .	. . .
Other transport, passenger	3 215 . .	. . .	. . .	. . .	. . .	. . .	. . .	. . .	. . .
Other transport, freight	3 216 . .	. . .	. . .	. . .	. . .	. . .	. . .	. . .	. . .
Other transport, other	3 217 . .	. . .	. . .	. . .	. . .	. . .	. . .	. . .	. . .
Travel, credit	2 236 . .	**91.9**	**84.5**	**94.7**	**103.6**	**111.2**	**80.9**	**86.5**	**77.4**
Business travel	2 237 . .	28.4	23.7	24.4	25.1	27.1	18.6	27.5	25.4
Personal travel	2 240 . .	63.5	60.8	70.3	78.4	84.1	62.4	59.0	52.0
Travel, debit	3 236 . .	**–168.4**	**–118.7**	**–122.3**	**–112.8**	**–115.0**	**–106.4**	**–89.5**	**–69.3**
Business travel	3 237 . .	–17.3	–16.4	–19.8	–20.4	–31.3	–11.4	–11.4	–1.8
Personal travel	3 240 . .	–151.1	–102.3	–102.5	–92.4	–83.7	–95.0	–78.1	–67.5
Other services, credit	2 200 BA	**63.6**	**67.3**	**70.7**	**130.0**	**134.2**	**74.9**	**63.7**	**71.4**
Communications	2 245 . .	. . .	. . .	. . .	. . .	. . .	. . .	. . .	. . .
Construction	2 249 . .	. . .	. . .	. . .	. . .	. . .	. . .	. . .	. . .
Insurance	2 253 . .	. . .	. . .	. . .	. . .	. . .	. . .	. . .	30.4
Financial	2 260 . .	. . .	. . .	. . .	. . .	. . .	. . .	. . .	. . .
Computer and information	2 262 . .	. . .	. . .	. . .	. . .	. . .	. . .	. . .	. . .
Royalties and licence fees	2 266 . .	. . .	. . .	. . .	. . .	. . .	. . .	. . .	. . .
Other business services	2 268 . .	52.2	54.0	64.0	121.8	125.7	64.7	54.4	29.1
Personal, cultural, and recreational	2 287 . .	. . .	. . .	. . .	. . .	. . .	. . .	. . .	. . .
Government, n.i.e.	2 291 . .	11.4	13.3	6.7	8.2	8.5	10.3	9.3	11.9
Other services, debit	3 200 BA	**–111.7**	**–101.2**	**–119.1**	**–143.6**	**–177.6**	**–117.9**	**–113.4**	**–78.4**
Communications	3 245 . .	. . .	. . .	. . .	. . .	. . .	. . .	. . .	. . .
Construction	3 249 . .	. . .	. . .	. . .	. . .	. . .	. . .	. . .	. . .
Insurance	3 253 . .	–53.0	–43.2	–45.5	–73.2	–79.2	–55.2	–43.8	–17.7
Financial	3 260 . .	. . .	. . .	. . .	. . .	. . .	. . .	. . .	. . .
Computer and information	3 262 . .	. . .	. . .	. . .	. . .	. . .	. . .	. . .	. . .
Royalties and licence fees	3 266 . .	–6.3	–6.2	–6.5	–8.0	–10.7	–4.4	–1.0	–.4
Other business services	3 268 . .	–43.2	–34.8	–48.2	–39.7	–70.6	–46.6	–54.3	–41.6
Personal, cultural, and recreational	3 287 . .	. . .	. . .	. . .	. . .	. . .	. . .	. . .	. . .
Government, n.i.e.	3 291 . .	–9.2	–16.8	–18.9	–22.7	–17.1	–11.8	–14.3	–18.6

Table 2 (Continued). STANDARD PRESENTATION, 1988–95
(Millions of U.S. dollars)

	Code	1988	1989	1990	1991	1992	1993	1994	1995
C. INCOME	4 300	–302.0	–377.6	–396.8	–442.1	–448.1	–325.8	–412.1	–390.1
Total credit	2 300	*20.3*	*32.4*	*39.6*	*48.6*	*29.8*	*40.2*	*56.7*	*76.6*
Total debit	3 300	*–322.3*	*–410.1*	*–436.4*	*–490.7*	*–477.9*	*–366.0*	*–468.7*	*–466.7*
Compensation of employees, credit	2 310	**. . .**	**. . .**	**. . .**	**. . .**	**. . .**	**. . .**	**. . .**	**. . .**
Compensation of employees, debit	3 310	**–4.1**	**–2.0**	**–2.0**	**–2.8**	**–3.8**	**–1.5**	**–1.3**	**–1.3**
Investment income, credit	2 320	**20.3**	**32.4**	**39.6**	**48.6**	**29.8**	**40.2**	**56.7**	**76.6**
Direct investment income	2 330	. . .	. . .	. . .	. . .	. . .	. . .	. . .	. . .
Dividends and distributed branch profits	2 332	. . .	. . .	. . .	. . .	. . .	. . .	. . .	. . .
Reinvested earnings and undistributed branch profits	2 333	. . .	. . .	. . .	. . .	. . .	. . .	. . .	. . .
Income on debt (interest)	2 334	. . .	. . .	. . .	. . .	. . .	. . .	. . .	. . .
Portfolio investment income	2 339	. . .	. . .	. . .	. . .	. . .	. . .	. . .	. . .
Income on equity	2 340	. . .	. . .	. . .	. . .	. . .	. . .	. . .	. . .
Income on bonds and notes	2 350	. . .	. . .	. . .	. . .	. . .	. . .	. . .	. . .
Income on money market instruments and financial derivatives	2 360	. . .	. . .	. . .	. . .	. . .	. . .	. . .	. . .
Other investment income	2 370	20.3	32.4	39.6	48.6	29.8	40.2	56.7	76.6
Investment income, debit	3 320	**–318.2**	**–408.1**	**–434.4**	**–487.9**	**–474.1**	**–364.5**	**–467.4**	**–465.4**
Direct investment income	3 330	–130.6	–176.1	–197.2	–236.0	–250.8	–153.6	–269.6	–186.8
Dividends and distributed branch profits	3 332	–55.6	–84.8	–122.5	–118.9	–114.7	–62.3	–80.5	–27.7
Reinvested earnings and undistributed branch profits	3 333	–75.0	–91.3	–74.6	–117.1	–136.1	–91.3	–189.0	–159.1
Income on debt (interest)	3 334	. . .	. . .	. . .	. . .	. . .	. . .	. . .	. . .
Portfolio investment income	3 339	. . .	. . .	. . .	. . .	. . .	. . .	. . .	. . .
Income on equity	3 340	. . .	. . .	. . .	. . .	. . .	. . .	. . .	. . .
Income on bonds and notes	3 350	. . .	. . .	. . .	. . .	. . .	. . .	. . .	. . .
Income on money market instruments and financial derivatives	3 360	. . .	. . .	. . .	. . .	. . .	. . .	. . .	. . .
Other investment income	3 370	–187.6	–232.0	–237.2	–251.9	–223.3	–211.0	–197.8	–278.6
D. CURRENT TRANSFERS	4 379	–9.2	–7.5	–6.2	2.4	.4	4.7	.3	–4.5
Credit	2 379	**3.5**	**5.2**	**7.8**	**15.6**	**11.1**	**23.7**	**28.3**	**34.0**
General government	2 380	1.2	1.7	4.0	10.4	4.4	4.4	2.2	3.2
Other sectors	2 390	2.3	3.5	3.8	5.3	6.7	19.3	26.1	30.8
Workers' remittances	2 391	1.7	2.9	3.0	4.8	6.2	18.3	25.7	30.4
Other current transfers	2 392	.5	.6	.8	.5	.5	1.0	.4	.4
Debit	3 379	**–12.7**	**–12.7**	**–13.9**	**–13.3**	**–10.7**	**–19.0**	**–27.9**	**–38.5**
General government	3 380	–7.6	–7.2	–8.5	–8.0	–4.9	–4.2	–4.1	–6.3
Other sectors	3 390	–5.0	–5.5	–5.5	–5.3	–5.8	–14.8	–23.9	–32.2
Workers' remittances	3 391	. . .	. . .	. . .	. . .	. . .	. . .	. . .	. . .
Other current transfers	3 392	–5.0	–5.5	–5.5	–5.3	–5.8	–14.8	–23.9	–32.2
CAPITAL AND FINANCIAL ACCOUNT	4 996	**67.4**	**–6.9**	**–347.0**	**33.6**	**–66.3**	**–71.3**	**–224.1**	**–375.2**
CAPITAL ACCOUNT	4 994	**–20.4**	**–17.2**	**–19.2**	**–16.1**	**–16.5**	**–11.5**	**–6.4**	**–11.9**
Total credit	2 994	. . .	*.4*	*.4*	*.4*	*.4*	*1.3*	*1.1*	*1.1*
Total debit	3 994	*–20.4*	*–17.5*	*–19.6*	*–16.5*	*–16.9*	*–12.8*	*–7.5*	*–13.0*
Capital transfers, credit	2 400	**. . .**	**.4**	**.4**	**.4**	**.4**	**1.3**	**1.1**	**1.1**
General government	2 401	. . .	. . .	. . .	. . .	. . .	. . .	. . .	. . .
Debt forgiveness	2 402	. . .	. . .	. . .	. . .	. . .	. . .	. . .	. . .
Other capital transfers	2 410	. . .	. . .	. . .	. . .	. . .	. . .	. . .	. . .
Other sectors	2 430	. . .	.4	.4	.4	.4	1.3	1.1	1.1
Migrants' transfers	2 431	. . .	.4	.4	.4	.4	1.3	1.1	1.1
Debt forgiveness	2 432	. . .	. . .	. . .	. . .	. . .	. . .	. . .	. . .
Other capital transfers	2 440	. . .	. . .	. . .	. . .	. . .	. . .	. . .	. . .
Capital transfers, debit	3 400	**–20.4**	**–17.5**	**–19.6**	**–16.5**	**–16.9**	**–12.8**	**–7.5**	**–13.0**
General government	3 401	. . .	. . .	. . .	. . .	. . .	. . .	. . .	. . .
Debt forgiveness	3 402	. . .	. . .	. . .	. . .	. . .	. . .	. . .	. . .
Other capital transfers	3 410	. . .	. . .	. . .	. . .	. . .	. . .	. . .	. . .
Other sectors	3 430	–20.4	–17.5	–19.6	–16.5	–16.9	–12.8	–7.5	–13.0
Migrants' transfers	3 431	–20.4	–17.5	–19.6	–16.5	–16.9	–12.8	–7.5	–13.0
Debt forgiveness	3 432	. . .	. . .	. . .	. . .	. . .	. . .	. . .	. . .
Other capital transfers	3 440	. . .	. . .	. . .	. . .	. . .	. . .	. . .	. . .
Nonproduced nonfinancial assets, credit	2 480	**. . .**	**. . .**	**. . .**	**. . .**	**. . .**	**. . .**	**. . .**	**. . .**
Nonproduced nonfinancial assets, debit	3 480	**. . .**	**. . .**	**. . .**	**. . .**	**. . .**	**. . .**	**. . .**	**. . .**

Table 2 (Continued). STANDARD PRESENTATION, 1988–95

(Millions of U.S. dollars)

	Code	1988	1989	1990	1991	1992	1993	1994	1995
FINANCIAL ACCOUNT	4 995 . .	**87.9**	**10.3**	**–327.8**	**49.7**	**–49.8**	**–59.8**	**–217.7**	**–363.3**
A. DIRECT INVESTMENT	4 500 . .	62.9	148.9	109.4	169.3	177.9	379.2	516.2	298.9
Direct investment abroad	4 505 . .	**. . .**	**. . .**	**. . .**	**. . .**	**. . .**	**. . .**	**. . .**	**. . .**
Equity capital	4 510 . .	. . .	. . .	. . .	. . .	. . .	. . .	. . .	. . .
Claims on affiliated enterprises	4 515 . .	. . .	. . .	. . .	. . .	. . .	. . .	. . .	. . .
Liabilities to affiliated enterprises	4 520 . .	. . .	. . .	. . .	. . .	. . .	. . .	. . .	. . .
Reinvested earnings	4 525 . .	. . .	. . .	. . .	. . .	. . .	. . .	. . .	. . .
Other capital	4 530 . .	. . .	. . .	. . .	. . .	. . .	. . .	. . .	. . .
Claims on affiliated enterprises	4 535 . .	. . .	. . .	. . .	. . .	. . .	. . .	. . .	. . .
Liabilities to affiliated enterprises	4 540 . .	. . .	. . .	. . .	. . .	. . .	. . .	. . .	. . .
Direct investment in Trinidad and Tobago	4 555 . .	**62.9**	**148.9**	**109.4**	**169.3**	**177.9**	**379.2**	**516.2**	**298.9**
Equity capital	4 560 . .	.9	50.0	58.4	30.6	20.9	258.2	378.0	137.3
Claims on direct investors	4 565 . .	. . .	. . .	. . .	. . .	. . .	. . .	. . .	. . .
Liabilities to direct investors	4 570 . .	. . .	. . .	. . .	. . .	. . .	. . .	. . .	. . .
Reinvested earnings	4 575 . .	75.0	91.3	74.6	117.1	136.1	91.3	189.0	159.1
Other capital	4 580 . .	–13.0	7.6	–23.7	21.6	20.9	29.7	–50.9	2.5
Claims on direct investors	4 585 . .	. . .	. . .	. . .	. . .	. . .	. . .	. . .	. . .
Liabilities to direct investors	4 590 . .	. . .	. . .	. . .	. . .	. . .	. . .	. . .	. . .
B. PORTFOLIO INVESTMENT	4 600 . .	. . .	. . .	. . .	. . .	. . .	. . .	. . .	8.8
Assets	4 602 . .	**. . .**	**. . .**	**. . .**	**. . .**	**. . .**	**. . .**	**. . .**	**–7.9**
Equity securities	4 610 . .	. . .	. . .	. . .	. . .	. . .	. . .	. . .	–7.9
Monetary authorities	4 611 . .	. . .	. . .	. . .	. . .	. . .	. . .	. . .	. . .
General government	4 612 . .	. . .	. . .	. . .	. . .	. . .	. . .	. . .	. . .
Banks	4 613 . .	. . .	. . .	. . .	. . .	. . .	. . .	. . .	. . .
Other sectors	4 614 . .	. . .	. . .	. . .	. . .	. . .	. . .	. . .	–7.9
Debt securities	4 619 . .	. . .	. . .	. . .	. . .	. . .	. . .	. . .	. . .
Bonds and notes	4 620 . .	. . .	. . .	. . .	. . .	. . .	. . .	. . .	. . .
Monetary authorities	4 621 . .	. . .	. . .	. . .	. . .	. . .	. . .	. . .	. . .
General government	4 622 . .	. . .	. . .	. . .	. . .	. . .	. . .	. . .	. . .
Banks	4 623 . .	. . .	. . .	. . .	. . .	. . .	. . .	. . .	. . .
Other sectors	4 624 . .	. . .	. . .	. . .	. . .	. . .	. . .	. . .	. . .
Money market instruments	4 630 . .	. . .	. . .	. . .	. . .	. . .	. . .	. . .	. . .
Monetary authorities	4 631 . .	. . .	. . .	. . .	. . .	. . .	. . .	. . .	. . .
General government	4 632 . .	. . .	. . .	. . .	. . .	. . .	. . .	. . .	. . .
Banks	4 633 . .	. . .	. . .	. . .	. . .	. . .	. . .	. . .	. . .
Other sectors	4 634 . .	. . .	. . .	. . .	. . .	. . .	. . .	. . .	. . .
Financial derivatives	4 640 . .	. . .	. . .	. . .	. . .	. . .	. . .	. . .	. . .
Monetary authorities	4 641 . .	. . .	. . .	. . .	. . .	. . .	. . .	. . .	. . .
General government	4 642 . .	. . .	. . .	. . .	. . .	. . .	. . .	. . .	. . .
Banks	4 643 . .	. . .	. . .	. . .	. . .	. . .	. . .	. . .	. . .
Other sectors	4 644 . .	. . .	. . .	. . .	. . .	. . .	. . .	. . .	. . .
Liabilities	4 652 . .	**. . .**	**. . .**	**. . .**	**. . .**	**. . .**	**. . .**	**. . .**	**16.7**
Equity securities	4 660 . .	. . .	. . .	. . .	. . .	. . .	. . .	. . .	16.7
Banks	4 663 . .	. . .	. . .	. . .	. . .	. . .	. . .	. . .	16.7
Other sectors	4 664 . .	. . .	. . .	. . .	. . .	. . .	. . .	. . .	. . .
Debt securities	4 669 . .	. . .	. . .	. . .	. . .	. . .	. . .	. . .	. . .
Bonds and notes	4 670 . .	. . .	. . .	. . .	. . .	. . .	. . .	. . .	. . .
Monetary authorities	4 671 . .	. . .	. . .	. . .	. . .	. . .	. . .	. . .	. . .
General government	4 672 . .	. . .	. . .	. . .	. . .	. . .	. . .	. . .	. . .
Banks	4 673 . .	. . .	. . .	. . .	. . .	. . .	. . .	. . .	. . .
Other sectors	4 674 . .	. . .	. . .	. . .	. . .	. . .	. . .	. . .	. . .
Money market instruments	4 680 . .	. . .	. . .	. . .	. . .	. . .	. . .	. . .	. . .
Monetary authorities	4 681 . .	. . .	. . .	. . .	. . .	. . .	. . .	. . .	. . .
General government	4 682 . .	. . .	. . .	. . .	. . .	. . .	. . .	. . .	. . .
Banks	4 683 . .	. . .	. . .	. . .	. . .	. . .	. . .	. . .	. . .
Other sectors	4 684 . .	. . .	. . .	. . .	. . .	. . .	. . .	. . .	. . .
Financial derivatives	4 690 . .	. . .	. . .	. . .	. . .	. . .	. . .	. . .	. . .
Monetary authorities	4 691 . .	. . .	. . .	. . .	. . .	. . .	. . .	. . .	. . .
General government	4 692 . .	. . .	. . .	. . .	. . .	. . .	. . .	. . .	. . .
Banks	4 693 . .	. . .	. . .	. . .	. . .	. . .	. . .	. . .	. . .
Other sectors	4 694 . .	. . .	. . .	. . .	. . .	. . .	. . .	. . .	. . .

Table 2 (Concluded). STANDARD PRESENTATION, 1988–95
(Millions of U.S. dollars)

	Code	1988	1989	1990	1991	1992	1993	1994	1995
C. OTHER INVESTMENT	4 700	–2.5	19.8	–239.5	–222.4	–352.1	–409.6	–620.3	–630.8
Assets	4 703	**60.9**	**44.5**	**63.0**	**4.4**	**–31.3**	**–76.2**	**–233.5**	**–122.1**
Trade credits	4 706	...	...	...	...	...	...	...	–26.0
General government: long-term	4 708	...	...	...	...	...	...	...	...
General government: short-term	4 709	...	...	...	...	...	...	...	...
Other sectors: long-term	4 711	...	...	...	...	...	...	...	...
Other sectors: short-term	4 712	...	...	...	...	...	...	...	–26.0
Loans	4 714	27.3	8.1	.9	–5.2	...	...	...	–32.4
Monetary authorities: long-term	4 717	...	...	...	...	...	...	...	–32.4
Monetary authorities: short-term	4 718	...	...	...	...	...	...	...	...
General government: long-term	4 720	27.3	8.1	.9	–5.2	...	...	...	...
General government: short-term	4 721	...	...	...	...	...	...	...	...
Banks: long-term	4 723	...	...	...	...	...	...	...	...
Banks: short-term	4 724	...	...	...	...	...	...	...	...
Other sectors: long-term	4 726	...	...	...	...	...	...	...	...
Other sectors: short-term	4 727	...	...	...	...	...	...	...	...
Currency and deposits	4 730	–51.9	–20.3	17.1	16.2	–5.3	–105.6	–109.3	–23.7
Monetary authorities	4 731	...	...	...	...	...	...	...	...
General government	4 732	...	...	...	...	...	...	...	...
Banks	4 733	–51.9	–20.3	17.1	16.2	–5.3	–105.6	–109.3	–23.7
Other sectors	4 734	...	...	...	...	...	...	...	...
Other assets	4 736	85.6	56.7	45.0	–6.6	–26.0	29.3	–124.2	–40.1
Monetary authorities: long-term	4 738	...	...	...	...	...	...	...	...
Monetary authorities: short-term	4 739	...	...	...	...	...	...	...	...
General government: long-term	4 741	61.0	...	...	...	...	...	–56.1	...
General government: short-term	4 742	...	...	...	...	...	...	...	...
Banks: long-term	4 744	...	...	...	...	...	...	...	...
Banks: short-term	4 745	...	...	...	...	...	...	...	...
Other sectors: long-term	4 747	24.6	56.7	45.0	–6.6	–26.0	29.3	–68.2	–40.1
Other sectors: short-term	4 748	...	...	...	...	...	...	...	...
Liabilities	4 753	**–63.4**	**–24.6**	**–302.5**	**–226.7**	**–320.8**	**–333.3**	**–386.8**	**–508.7**
Trade credits	4 756	...	...	...	...	...	...	...	–133.1
General government: long-term	4 758	...	...	...	...	...	...	...	...
General government: short-term	4 759	...	...	...	...	...	...	...	...
Other sectors: long-term	4 761	...	...	...	...	...	...	...	...
Other sectors: short-term	4 762	...	...	...	...	...	...	...	–133.1
Loans	4 764	62.8	165.4	42.6	–105.7	–194.1	–185.1	–117.6	–200.8
Use of Fund credit and loans from the Fund	4 766	115.4	91.4	100.9	50.7	–89.8	–129.2	–71.9	–43.6
Monetary authorities: other long-term	4 767	...	...	...	...	...	...	...	...
Monetary authorities: short-term	4 768	...	...	...	...	...	...	...	...
General government: long-term	4 770	51.6	–6.2	–74.0	–68.0	–32.2	27.2	–7.2	–116.8
General government: short-term	4 771	...	...	...	...	...	...	...	...
Banks: long-term	4 773	...	...	...	...	...	...	...	...
Banks: short-term	4 774	...	...	...	...	...	...	...	...
Other sectors: long-term	4 776	–104.1	80.2	15.7	–88.4	–72.0	–83.1	–38.4	–40.4
Other sectors: short-term	4 777	...	...	...	...	...	...	...	...
Currency and deposits	4 780	–24.7	–2.3	–2.8	–6.4	16.5	20.4	–10.2	–51.3
Monetary authorities	4 781	...	...	...	...	...	...	...	...
General government	4 782	...	...	...	...	...	...	...	...
Banks	4 783	–24.7	–2.3	–2.8	–6.4	16.5	20.4	–10.2	–51.3
Other sectors	4 784	...	...	...	...	...	...	...	...
Other liabilities	4 786	–101.5	–187.8	–342.3	–114.7	–143.2	–168.6	–259.0	–123.5
Monetary authorities: long-term	4 788	...	...	...	...	...	...	...	...
Monetary authorities: short-term	4 789	...	–47.3	...	...	...	...	...	...
General government: long-term	4 791	...	...	...	–25.2	–6.9	–7.4	...	...
General government: short-term	4 792	...	...	...	...	...	...	...	...
Banks: long-term	4 794	...	...	...	...	...	...	...	...
Banks: short-term	4 795	...	...	...	...	...	...	...	...
Other sectors: long-term	4 797	–101.5	–140.5	–342.3	–89.4	–136.3	–161.3	–259.0	...
Other sectors: short-term	4 798	...	...	...	...	...	...	...	–123.5
D. RESERVE ASSETS	4 800	27.4	–158.5	–197.7	102.7	124.4	–29.4	–113.6	–40.1
Monetary gold	4 810	...	...	...	...	...	...	...	...
Special drawing rights	4 820	...	–9.7	8.2	–.8	1.6	...	.2	–.2
Reserve position in the Fund	4 830	72.5	...	...	...	...	...	...	...
Foreign exchange	4 840	–61.5	–148.4	–205.9	103.8	123.7	–31.0	–113.6	–40.0
Other claims	4 880	16.4	–.3	–.1	–.3	–.8	1.6	–.2	...
NET ERRORS AND OMISSIONS	4 998	**21.1**	**45.4**	**–112.0**	**–29.0**	**–72.6**	**–41.8**	**6.3**	**81.4**

Part 3 of the *Yearbook* contains descriptions of the methodologies, compilation practices, and sources used to compile these data.

Table 1. ANALYTIC PRESENTATION, 1988–95
(Millions of U.S. dollars)

	Code	1988	1989	1990	1991	1992	1993	1994	1995
A. Current Account [1]	4 993 Y.	**210**	**–218**	**–463**	**–469**	**–1,104**	**–1,323**	**–539**	**–737**
Goods: exports f.o.b	2 100 . .	2,399	2,931	3,515	3,696	4,041	3,746	4,643	5,470
Goods: imports f.o.b	3 100 . .	–3,496	–4,138	–5,193	–4,895	–6,078	–5,810	–6,210	–7,459
Balance on Goods	4 100 . .	*–1,097*	*–1,207*	*–1,678*	*–1,199*	*–2,037*	*–2,064*	*–1,567*	*–1,989*
Services: credit	2 200 . .	1,854	1,446	1,688	1,410	1,972	2,040	2,267	2,509
Services: debit	3 200 . .	–750	–716	–846	–841	–1,158	–1,356	–1,363	–1,352
Balance on Goods and Services	4 991 . .	*7*	*–477*	*–836*	*–631*	*–1,223*	*–1,380*	*–663*	*–832*
Income: credit	2 300 . .	48	70	97	56	101	73	71	119
Income: debit	3 300 . .	–513	–518	–552	–609	–646	–629	–745	–835
Balance on Goods, Services, and Income	4 992 . .	*–458*	*–926*	*–1,291*	*–1,183*	*–1,768*	*–1,936*	*–1,338*	*–1,548*
Current transfers: credit	2 379 Y.	678	719	847	728	682	629	816	843
Current transfers: debit	3 379 . .	–10	–12	–19	–14	–17	–16	–17	–32
B. Capital Account [1]	4 994 Y.	**–3**	**–7**	**–7**	**–5**	**–5**	**–2**	**–3**	**–7**
Capital account: credit	2 994 Y.	. . .	. . .	. . .	. . .	. . .	5	5	7
Capital account: debit	3 994 . .	–3	–7	–7	–5	–5	–7	–8	–15
Total, Groups A Plus B	4 010 . .	*206*	*–225*	*–470*	*–475*	*–1,108*	*–1,325*	*–542*	*–744*
C. Financial Account [1]	4 995 X.	**323**	**132**	**326**	**401**	**957**	**1,272**	**1,144**	**958**
Direct investment abroad	4 505 . .	–1	–4	1	–3	–5	. . .	–6	5
Direct investment in Tunisia	4 555 Y.	61	78	76	125	526	562	432	264
Portfolio investment assets	4 602 . .	–5	–1	–1	–2	–3	–6	–1	2
Equity securities	4 610 . .	–2	. . .	–3	–1	–3	. . .	1	. . .
Debt securities	4 619 . .	–2	–1	2	–1	. . .	–6	–2	2
Portfolio investment liabilities	4 652 Y.	8	19	3	36	50	24	16	23
Equity securities	4 660 Y.	9	16	5	34	47	20	6	12
Debt securities	4 669 Y.	–1	3	–1	2	2	4	10	12
Other investment assets	4 703 . .	59	–124	–343	–261	–369	–143	–326	–327
Monetary authorities	4 703 . A	–44	–4	–82	–43	35	15	86	88
General government	4 703 . B	. . .	. . .	. . .	. . .	. . .	. . .	. . .	. . .
Banks	4 703 . C	166	–90	–17	61	–320	–12	67	150
Other sectors	4 703 . D	–62	–31	–244	–278	–84	–146	–479	–565
Other investment liabilities	4 753 X.	201	164	589	506	758	836	1,029	990
Monetary authorities	4 753 XA	–1	–1	–2	11	11	5	. . .	–1
General government	4 753 YB	169	218	57	294	166	234	411	546
Banks	4 753 YC	30	27	57	34	122	75	168	44
Other sectors	4 753 YD	2	–80	477	168	458	522	450	401
Total, Groups A Through C	4 020 . .	*529*	*–94*	*–145*	*–74*	*–152*	*–53*	*602*	*214*
D. Net Errors and Omissions	4 998 . .	**144**	**185**	**98**	**96**	**–28**	**122**	**–76**	**–117**
Total, Groups A Through D	4 030 . .	*673*	*92*	*–47*	*23*	*–180*	*70*	*527*	*97*
E. Reserves and Related Items	4 040 . .	**–673**	**–92**	**47**	**–23**	**180**	**–70**	**–527**	**–97**
Reserve assets	4 800 . .	–694	–92	159	–97	134	–64	–527	–82
Use of Fund credit and loans	4 766 . .	21	. . .	–112	74	45	–5	. . .	–15
Liabilities constituting foreign authorities' reserves	4 900 . .	. . .	. . .	. . .	. . .	. . .	. . .	. . .	. . .
Exceptional financing	4 920 . .	. . .	. . .	. . .	. . .	. . .	. . .	. . .	. . .
Conversion rates: Tunisian dinar per U.S. dollar	0 101 . .	**.8578**	**.9493**	**.8783**	**.9246**	**.8844**	**1.0037**	**1.0116**	**.9458**

[1] Excludes components that have been classified in the categories of Group E.

Table 2. STANDARD PRESENTATION, 1988–95
(Millions of U.S. dollars)

	Code	1988	1989	1990	1991	1992	1993	1994	1995
CURRENT ACCOUNT	4 993 . .	**210**	**–218**	**–463**	**–469**	**–1,104**	**–1,323**	**–539**	**–737**
A. GOODS	4 100 . .	–1,097	–1,207	–1,678	–1,199	–2,037	–2,064	–1,567	–1,989
Credit	2 100 . .	**2,399**	**2,931**	**3,515**	**3,696**	**4,041**	**3,746**	**4,643**	**5,470**
General merchandise: exports f.o.b.	2 110 . .	2,399	2,931	3,515	3,696	4,041	3,746	4,643	5,470
Goods for processing: exports f.o.b.	2 150 . .	. . .	. . .	. . .	. . .	. . .	. . .	. . .	. . .
Repairs on goods	2 160 . .	. . .	. . .	. . .	. . .	. . .	. . .	. . .	. . .
Goods procured in ports by carriers	2 170 . .	. . .	. . .	. . .	. . .	. . .	. . .	. . .	. . .
Nonmonetary gold	2 180 . .	. . .	. . .	. . .	. . .	. . .	. . .	. . .	. . .
Debit	3 100 . .	**–3,496**	**–4,138**	**–5,193**	**–4,895**	**–6,078**	**–5,810**	**–6,210**	**–7,459**
General merchandise: imports f.o.b.	3 110 . .	–3,496	–4,138	–5,193	–4,895	–6,078	–5,810	–6,210	–7,459
Goods for processing: imports f.o.b.	3 150 . .	. . .	. . .	. . .	. . .	. . .	. . .	. . .	. . .
Repairs on goods	3 160 . .	. . .	. . .	. . .	. . .	. . .	. . .	. . .	. . .
Goods procured in ports by carriers	3 170 . .	. . .	. . .	. . .	. . .	. . .	. . .	. . .	. . .
Nonmonetary gold	3 180 . .	. . .	. . .	. . .	. . .	. . .	. . .	. . .	. . .
B. SERVICES	4 200 . .	1,104	730	843	569	814	684	904	1,157
Total credit	2 200 . .	*1,854*	*1,446*	*1,688*	*1,410*	*1,972*	*2,040*	*2,267*	*2,509*
Total debit	3 200 . .	*–750*	*–716*	*–846*	*–841*	*–1,158*	*–1,356*	*–1,363*	*–1,352*
Transportation services, credit	2 205 . .	**302**	**293**	**362**	**361**	**491**	**521**	**508**	**598**
Passenger	2 205 BA	*149*	*150*	*176*	*172*	*266*	*280*	*271*	*308*
Freight	2 205 BB	*87*	*85*	*115*	*122*	*130*	*129*	*116*	*153*
Other	2 205 BC	*65*	*58*	*71*	*67*	*95*	*113*	*122*	*137*
Sea transport, passenger	2 207 . .	. . .	. . .	. . .	. . .	. . .	. . .	. . .	. . .
Sea transport, freight	2 208 . .	. . .	. . .	. . .	. . .	. . .	. . .	. . .	. . .
Sea transport, other	2 209 . .	. . .	. . .	. . .	. . .	. . .	. . .	. . .	. . .
Air transport, passenger	2 211 . .	. . .	. . .	. . .	. . .	. . .	. . .	. . .	. . .
Air transport, freight	2 212 . .	. . .	. . .	. . .	. . .	. . .	. . .	. . .	. . .
Air transport, other	2 213 . .	. . .	. . .	. . .	. . .	. . .	. . .	. . .	. . .
Other transport, passenger	2 215 . .	. . .	. . .	. . .	. . .	. . .	. . .	. . .	. . .
Other transport, freight	2 216 . .	. . .	. . .	. . .	. . .	. . .	. . .	. . .	. . .
Other transport, other	2 217 . .	. . .	. . .	. . .	. . .	. . .	. . .	. . .	. . .
Transportation services, debit	3 205 . .	**–302**	**–309**	**–351**	**–347**	**–425**	**–429**	**–464**	**–564**
Passenger	3 205 BA	*–20*	*–24*	*–32*	*–25*	*–41*	*–34*	*–38*	*–43*
Freight	3 205 BB	*–213*	*–197*	*–220*	*–229*	*–267*	*–273*	*–293*	*–364*
Other	3 205 BC	*–69*	*–87*	*–99*	*–93*	*–118*	*–123*	*–133*	*–156*
Sea transport, passenger	3 207 . .	. . .	. . .	. . .	. . .	. . .	. . .	. . .	. . .
Sea transport, freight	3 208 . .	. . .	. . .	. . .	. . .	. . .	. . .	. . .	. . .
Sea transport, other	3 209 . .	. . .	. . .	. . .	. . .	. . .	. . .	. . .	. . .
Air transport, passenger	3 211 . .	. . .	. . .	. . .	. . .	. . .	. . .	. . .	. . .
Air transport, freight	3 212 . .	. . .	. . .	. . .	. . .	. . .	. . .	. . .	. . .
Air transport, other	3 213 . .	. . .	. . .	. . .	. . .	. . .	. . .	. . .	. . .
Other transport, passenger	3 215 . .	. . .	. . .	. . .	. . .	. . .	. . .	. . .	. . .
Other transport, freight	3 216 . .	. . .	. . .	. . .	. . .	. . .	. . .	. . .	. . .
Other transport, other	3 217 . .	. . .	. . .	. . .	. . .	. . .	. . .	. . .	. . .
Travel, credit	2 236 . .	**1,337**	**873**	**1,020**	**765**	**1,174**	**1,225**	**1,417**	**1,530**
Business travel	2 237 . .	68	47	74	78	99	107	104	119
Personal travel	2 240 . .	1,270	826	946	687	1,074	1,119	1,313	1,411
Travel, debit	3 236 . .	**–120**	**–134**	**–179**	**–128**	**–167**	**–203**	**–216**	**–251**
Business travel	3 237 . .	–6	–6	–8	–10	–12	–17	–18	–19
Personal travel	3 240 . .	–114	–127	–171	–118	–155	–186	–198	–232
Other services, credit	2 200 BA	**215**	**280**	**306**	**284**	**308**	**294**	**342**	**381**
Communications	2 245 . .	8	14	19	10	10	16	18	26
Construction	2 249 . .	. . .	. . .	. . .	. . .	. . .	. . .	. . .	. . .
Insurance	2 253 . .	16	13	15	23	24	14	14	16
Financial	2 260 . .	8	6	9	11	16	17	22	21
Computer and information	2 262 . .	. . .	. . .	. . .	. . .	. . .	. . .	. . .	. . .
Royalties and licence fees	2 266 . .	. . .	3	1	. . .	. . .	. . .	1	1
Other business services	2 268 . .	94	124	146	138	171	158	192	206
Personal, cultural, and recreational	2 287 . .	1	2	2	. . .	2	1	3	2
Government, n.i.e.	2 291 . .	86	118	114	103	85	88	93	108
Other services, debit	3 200 BA	**–328**	**–274**	**–317**	**–367**	**–565**	**–723**	**–684**	**–538**
Communications	3 245 . .	–5	–2	–6	–4	–7	–3	–5	–7
Construction	3 249 . .	. . .	. . .	. . .	. . .	. . .	. . .	. . .	. . .
Insurance	3 253 . .	–40	–35	–38	–43	–47	–52	–53	–61
Financial	3 260 . .	–7	–7	–13	–12	–14	–15	–15	–19
Computer and information	3 262 . .	. . .	. . .	. . .	. . .	. . .	. . .	. . .	. . .
Royalties and licence fees	3 266 . .	. . .	–1	–1	–1	–1	–1	–2	–2
Other business services	3 268 . .	–101	–81	–94	–127	–306	–485	–441	–336
Personal, cultural, and recreational	3 287 . .	–2	–2	–1	–2	–2	–6	–5	–4
Government, n.i.e.	3 291 . .	–173	–145	–164	–177	–188	–161	–163	–108

Table 2 (Continued). STANDARD PRESENTATION, 1988–95
(Millions of U.S. dollars)

	Code	1988	1989	1990	1991	1992	1993	1994	1995
C. INCOME	4 300 . .	–465	–449	–455	–553	–545	–556	–674	–716
Total credit	2 300 . .	*48*	*70*	*97*	*56*	*101*	*73*	*71*	*119*
Total debit	3 300 . .	*–513*	*–518*	*–552*	*–609*	*–646*	*–629*	*–745*	*–835*
Compensation of employees, credit	2 310 . .	**. . .**	**. . .**	**. . .**	**. . .**	**. . .**	**. . .**	**. . .**	**. . .**
Compensation of employees, debit	3 310 . .	**. . .**	**. . .**	**. . .**	**. . .**	**. . .**	**. . .**	**. . .**	**. . .**
Investment income, credit	2 320 . .	**48**	**70**	**97**	**56**	**101**	**73**	**71**	**119**
Direct investment income	2 330 . .	. . .	. . .	1	5	11	1	1	1
Dividends and distributed branch profits	2 332 . .	. . .	. . .	1	5	11	1	1	1
Reinvested earnings and undistributed branch profits	2 333 . .	. . .	. . .	. . .	. . .	. . .	. . .	. . .	. . .
Income on debt (interest)	2 334 . .	. . .	. . .	. . .	. . .	. . .	. . .	. . .	. . .
Portfolio investment income	2 339 . .	2	2	1	3	1	2	2	3
Income on equity	2 340 . .	2	2	1	3	1	2	2	3
Income on bonds and notes	2 350 . .	. . .	. . .	. . .	. . .	. . .	. . .	. . .	. . .
Income on money market instruments and financial derivatives	2 360 . .	. . .	. . .	. . .	. . .	. . .	. . .	. . .	. . .
Other investment income	2 370 . .	45	67	94	48	88	70	68	115
Investment income, debit	3 320 . .	**–513**	**–518**	**–552**	**–609**	**–646**	**–629**	**–745**	**–835**
Direct investment income	3 330 . .	–61	–68	–97	–190	–182	–122	–187	–174
Dividends and distributed branch profits	3 332 . .	–61	–68	–97	–190	–182	–122	–187	–174
Reinvested earnings and undistributed branch profits	3 333 . .	. . .	. . .	. . .	. . .	. . .	. . .	. . .	. . .
Income on debt (interest)	3 334 . .	. . .	. . .	. . .	. . .	. . .	. . .	. . .	. . .
Portfolio investment income	3 339 . .	–41	–37	–33	–16	–23	–40	–42	–54
Income on equity	3 340 . .	–41	–37	–33	–16	–23	–40	–42	–54
Income on bonds and notes	3 350 . .	. . .	. . .	. . .	. . .	. . .	. . .	. . .	. . .
Income on money market instruments and financial derivatives	3 360 . .	. . .	. . .	. . .	. . .	. . .	. . .	. . .	. . .
Other investment income	3 370 . .	–412	–413	–422	–402	–441	–467	–517	–607
D. CURRENT TRANSFERS	4 379 . .	668	708	828	714	665	613	799	811
Credit	2 379 . .	**678**	**719**	**847**	**728**	**682**	**629**	**816**	**843**
General government	2 380 . .	110	208	221	122	83	105	104	63
Other sectors	2 390 . .	569	512	626	606	599	524	712	779
Workers' remittances	2 391 . .	498	450	551	525	531	446	629	680
Other current transfers	2 392 . .	71	62	75	81	68	78	83	99
Debit	3 379 . .	**–10**	**–12**	**–19**	**–14**	**–17**	**–16**	**–17**	**–32**
General government	3 380 . .	–6	–6	–9	–3	–3	–5	–2	–4
Other sectors	3 390 . .	–5	–5	–10	–11	–14	–11	–15	–27
Workers' remittances	3 391 . .	–2	–2	–6	–5	–8	–7	–11	–21
Other current transfers	3 392 . .	–2	–3	–5	–5	–6	–4	–4	–6
CAPITAL AND FINANCIAL ACCOUNT	4 996 . .	**–354**	**33**	**365**	**373**	**1,132**	**1,201**	**614**	**854**
CAPITAL ACCOUNT	4 994 . .	**–3**	**–7**	**–7**	**–5**	**–5**	**–2**	**–3**	**–7**
Total credit	2 994 . .	. . .	. . .	. . .	. . .	. . .	*5*	*5*	*7*
Total debit	3 994 . .	*–3*	*–7*	*–7*	*–5*	*–5*	*–7*	*–8*	*–15*
Capital transfers, credit	2 400 . .	**. . .**	**. . .**	**. . .**	**. . .**	**. . .**	**5**	**5**	**7**
General government	2 401 . .	. . .	. . .	. . .	. . .	. . .	5	5	7
Debt forgiveness	2 402 . .	. . .	. . .	. . .	. . .	. . .	5	5	7
Other capital transfers	2 410 . .	. . .	. . .	. . .	. . .	. . .	. . .	. . .	. . .
Other sectors	2 430 . .	. . .	. . .	. . .	. . .	. . .	. . .	. . .	. . .
Migrants' transfers	2 431 . .	. . .	. . .	. . .	. . .	. . .	. . .	. . .	. . .
Debt forgiveness	2 432 . .	. . .	. . .	. . .	. . .	. . .	. . .	. . .	. . .
Other capital transfers	2 440 . .	. . .	. . .	. . .	. . .	. . .	. . .	. . .	. . .
Capital transfers, debit	3 400 . .	**–3**	**–7**	**–7**	**–5**	**–5**	**–7**	**–8**	**–15**
General government	3 401 . .	. . .	. . .	. . .	. . .	. . .	. . .	. . .	. . .
Debt forgiveness	3 402 . .	. . .	. . .	. . .	. . .	. . .	. . .	. . .	. . .
Other capital transfers	3 410 . .	. . .	. . .	. . .	. . .	. . .	. . .	. . .	. . .
Other sectors	3 430 . .	–3	–7	–7	–5	–5	–7	–8	–15
Migrants' transfers	3 431 . .	–3	–7	–7	–5	–5	–7	–8	–15
Debt forgiveness	3 432 . .	. . .	. . .	. . .	. . .	. . .	. . .	. . .	. . .
Other capital transfers	3 440 . .	. . .	. . .	. . .	. . .	. . .	. . .	. . .	. . .
Nonproduced nonfinancial assets, credit	2 480 . .	**. . .**	**. . .**	**. . .**	**. . .**	**. . .**	**. . .**	**. . .**	**. . .**
Nonproduced nonfinancial assets, debit	3 480 . .	**. . .**	**. . .**	**. . .**	**. . .**	**. . .**	**. . .**	**. . .**	**. . .**

Table 2 (Continued). STANDARD PRESENTATION, 1988–95
(Millions of U.S. dollars)

	Code	1988	1989	1990	1991	1992	1993	1994	1995
FINANCIAL ACCOUNT	4 995	**–350**	**40**	**372**	**378**	**1,136**	**1,203**	**617**	**861**
A. DIRECT INVESTMENT	4 500	59	74	77	122	521	562	426	270
Direct investment abroad	4 505	**–1**	**–4**	**1**	**–3**	**–5**	**. . .**	**–6**	**5**
Equity capital	4 510	–1	–4	1	–3	–5	. . .	–6	5
Claims on affiliated enterprises	4 515	–1	–4	1	–3	–5	. . .	–6	5
Liabilities to affiliated enterprises	4 520	. . .	. . .	. . .	. . .	. . .	. . .	. . .	. . .
Reinvested earnings	4 525	. . .	. . .	. . .	. . .	. . .	. . .	. . .	. . .
Other capital	4 530	. . .	. . .	. . .	. . .	. . .	. . .	. . .	. . .
Claims on affiliated enterprises	4 535	. . .	. . .	. . .	. . .	. . .	. . .	. . .	. . .
Liabilities to affiliated enterprises	4 540	. . .	. . .	. . .	. . .	. . .	. . .	. . .	. . .
Direct investment in Tunisia	4 555	**61**	**78**	**76**	**125**	**526**	**562**	**432**	**264**
Equity capital	4 560	58	75	72	121	523	562	430	271
Claims on direct investors	4 565	. . .	. . .	. . .	. . .	. . .	. . .	. . .	. . .
Liabilities to direct investors	4 570	58	75	72	121	523	562	430	271
Reinvested earnings	4 575	. . .	. . .	. . .	. . .	. . .	. . .	. . .	. . .
Other capital	4 580	2	3	5	4	2	. . .	2	–6
Claims on direct investors	4 585	. . .	. . .	. . .	. . .	. . .	. . .	. . .	. . .
Liabilities to direct investors	4 590	2	3	5	4	2	. . .	2	–6
B. PORTFOLIO INVESTMENT	4 600	3	18	2	34	46	18	15	25
Assets	4 602	**–5**	**–1**	**–1**	**–2**	**–3**	**–6**	**–1**	**2**
Equity securities	4 610	–2	. . .	–3	–1	–3	. . .	1	. . .
Monetary authorities	4 611	. . .	. . .	. . .	. . .	. . .	. . .	. . .	. . .
General government	4 612	. . .	. . .	. . .	. . .	. . .	. . .	. . .	. . .
Banks	4 613	. . .	. . .	. . .	. . .	. . .	. . .	. . .	. . .
Other sectors	4 614	–2	. . .	–3	. . .	–3	. . .	1	. . .
Debt securities	4 619	–2	–1	2	–1	. . .	–6	–2	2
Bonds and notes	4 620	–2	–1	2	–1	. . .	–6	–2	2
Monetary authorities	4 621	. . .	. . .	. . .	. . .	. . .	. . .	. . .	. . .
General government	4 622	–2	–1	2	–1	. . .	–6	–2	2
Banks	4 623	. . .	. . .	. . .	. . .	. . .	. . .	. . .	. . .
Other sectors	4 624	. . .	. . .	. . .	. . .	. . .	. . .	. . .	. . .
Money market instruments	4 630	. . .	. . .	. . .	. . .	. . .	. . .	. . .	. . .
Monetary authorities	4 631	. . .	. . .	. . .	. . .	. . .	. . .	. . .	. . .
General government	4 632	. . .	. . .	. . .	. . .	. . .	. . .	. . .	. . .
Banks	4 633	. . .	. . .	. . .	. . .	. . .	. . .	. . .	. . .
Other sectors	4 634	. . .	. . .	. . .	. . .	. . .	. . .	. . .	. . .
Financial derivatives	4 640	. . .	. . .	. . .	. . .	. . .	. . .	. . .	. . .
Monetary authorities	4 641	. . .	. . .	. . .	. . .	. . .	. . .	. . .	. . .
General government	4 642	. . .	. . .	. . .	. . .	. . .	. . .	. . .	. . .
Banks	4 643	. . .	. . .	. . .	. . .	. . .	. . .	. . .	. . .
Other sectors	4 644	. . .	. . .	. . .	. . .	. . .	. . .	. . .	. . .
Liabilities	4 652	**8**	**19**	**3**	**36**	**50**	**24**	**16**	**23**
Equity securities	4 660	9	16	5	34	47	20	6	12
Banks	4 663	. . .	. . .	. . .	. . .	. . .	. . .	. . .	. . .
Other sectors	4 664	9	16	5	34	47	20	6	12
Debt securities	4 669	–1	3	–1	2	2	4	10	12
Bonds and notes	4 670	–1	3	–1	2	2	. . .	. . .	. . .
Monetary authorities	4 671	. . .	. . .	. . .	. . .	. . .	. . .	. . .	. . .
General government	4 672	–1	3	–1	2	2	. . .	. . .	. . .
Banks	4 673	. . .	. . .	. . .	. . .	. . .	. . .	. . .	. . .
Other sectors	4 674	. . .	. . .	. . .	. . .	. . .	. . .	. . .	. . .
Money market instruments	4 680	. . .	. . .	. . .	. . .	. . .	4	10	12
Monetary authorities	4 681	. . .	. . .	. . .	. . .	. . .	. . .	. . .	. . .
General government	4 682	. . .	. . .	. . .	. . .	. . .	4	10	12
Banks	4 683	. . .	. . .	. . .	. . .	. . .	. . .	. . .	. . .
Other sectors	4 684	. . .	. . .	. . .	. . .	. . .	. . .	. . .	. . .
Financial derivatives	4 690	. . .	. . .	. . .	. . .	. . .	. . .	. . .	. . .
Monetary authorities	4 691	. . .	. . .	. . .	. . .	. . .	. . .	. . .	. . .
General government	4 692	. . .	. . .	. . .	. . .	. . .	. . .	. . .	. . .
Banks	4 693	. . .	. . .	. . .	. . .	. . .	. . .	. . .	. . .
Other sectors	4 694	. . .	. . .	. . .	. . .	. . .	. . .	. . .	. . .

Table 2 (Concluded). STANDARD PRESENTATION, 1988–95
(Millions of U.S. dollars)

	Code	1988	1989	1990	1991	1992	1993	1994	1995
C. OTHER INVESTMENT	4 700	281	40	134	320	434	687	703	648
Assets	4 703	**59**	**–124**	**–343**	**–261**	**–369**	**–143**	**–326**	**–327**
Trade credits	4 706	–62	–31	–244	–278	–84	–146	–479	–565
General government: long-term	4 708	...	...	...	...	...	...	...	...
General government: short-term	4 709	...	...	...	...	...	...	...	...
Other sectors: long-term	4 711	...	...	...	...	...	...	...	...
Other sectors: short-term	4 712	–62	–31	–244	–278	–84	–146	–479	–565
Loans	4 714	–8	20	11	11	31	39	35	43
Monetary authorities: long-term	4 717	...	...	...	...	...	...	...	...
Monetary authorities: short-term	4 718	...	...	...	...	...	...	...	...
General government: long-term	4 720	...	...	...	...	...	...	...	...
General government: short-term	4 721	...	...	...	...	...	...	...	...
Banks: long-term	4 723	–8	20	11	11	31	39	35	43
Banks: short-term	4 724	...	...	...	...	...	...	...	...
Other sectors: long-term	4 726	...	...	...	...	...	...	...	...
Other sectors: short-term	4 727	...	...	...	...	...	...	...	...
Currency and deposits	4 730	–29	–22	–59	48	26	–22	–26	...
Monetary authorities	4 731	...	...	...	...	...	...	...	...
General government	4 732	...	...	...	...	...	...	...	...
Banks	4 733	–29	–22	–59	48	26	–22	–26	...
Other sectors	4 734	...	...	...	...	...	...	...	...
Other assets	4 736	159	–92	–51	–41	–341	–14	144	195
Monetary authorities: long-term	4 738	...	...	...	...	...	...	...	...
Monetary authorities: short-term	4 739	–44	–4	–82	–43	35	15	86	88
General government: long-term	4 741	...	...	...	...	...	...	...	...
General government: short-term	4 742	...	...	...	...	...	...	...	...
Banks: long-term	4 744	...	...	...	...	...	...	...	...
Banks: short-term	4 745	203	–87	31	2	–377	–29	58	107
Other sectors: long-term	4 747	...	...	...	...	...	...	...	...
Other sectors: short-term	4 748	...	...	...	...	...	...	...	...
Liabilities	4 753	**221**	**164**	**476**	**580**	**803**	**831**	**1,029**	**974**
Trade credits	4 756	162	117	578	263	445	437	284	394
General government: long-term	4 758	...	...	...	...	...	...	...	...
General government: short-term	4 759	...	...	...	...	...	...	...	...
Other sectors: long-term	4 761	...	...	...	...	...	...	...	...
Other sectors: short-term	4 762	162	117	578	263	445	437	284	394
Loans	4 764	30	21	–157	273	224	314	577	537
Use of Fund credit and loans from the Fund	4 766	21	...	–112	74	45	–5	...	–15
Monetary authorities: other long-term	4 767	...	...	...	...	...	...	...	...
Monetary authorities: short-term	4 768	...	...	...	...	...	...	...	...
General government: long-term	4 770	169	218	57	294	166	234	411	546
General government: short-term	4 771	...	...	...	...	...	...	...	...
Banks: long-term	4 773	...	...	...	...	...	...	...	...
Banks: short-term	4 774	...	...	...	...	...	...	...	...
Other sectors: long-term	4 776	–160	–197	–101	–95	12	85	166	6
Other sectors: short-term	4 777	...	...	...	...	...	...	...	...
Currency and deposits	4 780	29	26	55	44	133	80	168	43
Monetary authorities	4 781	–1	–1	–2	11	11	5	...	–1
General government	4 782	...	...	...	...	...	...	...	...
Banks	4 783	30	27	57	34	122	75	168	44
Other sectors	4 784	...	...	...	...	...	...	...	...
Other liabilities	4 786	...	...	...	...	...	...	...	...
Monetary authorities: long-term	4 788	...	...	...	...	...	...	...	...
Monetary authorities: short-term	4 789	...	...	...	...	...	...	...	...
General government: long-term	4 791	...	...	...	...	...	...	...	...
General government: short-term	4 792	...	...	...	...	...	...	...	...
Banks: long-term	4 794	...	...	...	...	...	...	...	...
Banks: short-term	4 795	...	...	...	...	...	...	...	...
Other sectors: long-term	4 797	...	...	...	...	...	...	...	...
Other sectors: short-term	4 798	...	...	...	...	...	...	...	...
D. RESERVE ASSETS	4 800	–694	–92	159	–97	134	–64	–527	–82
Monetary gold	4 810	...	...	...	...	...	...	...	–1
Special drawing rights	4 820	23	19	9	–29	20	10	–1	–5
Reserve position in the Fund	4 830	...	...	...	...	...	...	...	...
Foreign exchange	4 840	–717	–111	150	–68	114	–75	–526	–75
Other claims	4 880	...	...	...	...	...	...	...	...
NET ERRORS AND OMISSIONS	4 998	**144**	**185**	**98**	**96**	**–28**	**122**	**–76**	**–117**

Part 3 of the *Yearbook* contains descriptions of the methodologies, compilation practices, and sources used to compile these data.

Table 1. ANALYTIC PRESENTATION, 1988–95
(Millions of U.S. dollars)

	Code	1988	1989	1990	1991	1992	1993	1994	1995
A. Current Account[1]	4 993 Y.	**1,596**	**938**	**–2,625**	**250**	**–974**	**–6,433**	**2,631**	**–2,339**
Goods: exports f.o.b	2 100 . .	11,929	11,780	13,026	13,667	14,891	15,611	18,390	21,975
Goods: imports f.o.b	3 100 . .	–13,706	–15,999	–22,581	–21,007	–23,081	–29,771	–22,606	–35,187
Balance on Goods	4 100 . .	*–1,777*	*–4,219*	*–9,555*	*–7,340*	*–8,190*	*–14,160*	*–4,216*	*–13,212*
Services: credit	2 200 . .	5,652	6,414	8,016	8,372	9,407	10,652	10,801	14,606
Services: debit	3 200 . .	–1,925	–2,465	–3,071	–3,218	–3,625	–3,948	–3,782	–5,024
Balance on Goods and Services	4 991 . .	*1,950*	*–270*	*–4,610*	*–2,186*	*–2,408*	*–7,456*	*2,803*	*–3,630*
Income: credit	2 300 . .	374	684	917	935	1,012	1,135	890	1,488
Income: debit	3 300 . .	–2,887	–3,011	–3,425	–3,598	–3,637	–3,880	–4,154	–4,693
Balance on Goods, Services, and Income	4 992 . .	*–563*	*–2,597*	*–7,118*	*–4,849*	*–5,033*	*–10,201*	*–461*	*–6,835*
Current transfers: credit	2 379 Y.	2,220	3,574	4,525	5,131	4,075	3,800	3,113	4,512
Current transfers: debit	3 379 . .	–61	–39	–32	–32	–16	–32	–21	–16
B. Capital Account[1]	4 994 Y.	**. . .**	**23**	**. . .**	**. . .**	**. . .**	**. . .**	**. . .**	**. . .**
Capital account: credit	2 994 Y.	. . .	23	. . .	. . .	. . .	. . .	. . .	. . .
Capital account: debit	3 994 . .	. . .	. . .	. . .	. . .	. . .	. . .	. . .	. . .
Total, Groups A Plus B	4 010 . .	*1,596*	*961*	*–2,625*	*250*	*–974*	*–6,433*	*2,631*	*–2,339*
C. Financial Account[1]	4 995 X.	**–958**	**780**	**4,037**	**–2,397**	**3,648**	**8,963**	**–4,194**	**4,722**
Direct investment abroad	4 505 . .	. . .	. . .	16	–27	–65	–14	–49	–113
Direct investment in Turkey	4 555 Y.	354	663	684	810	844	636	608	885
Portfolio investment assets	4 602 . .	–6	–59	–134	–91	–754	–563	35	1,021
Equity securities	4 610 . .	–6	–59	–134	–91	–50	–139	5	1,412
Debt securities	4 619 . .	. . .	. . .	. . .	. . .	–704	–424	30	–391
Portfolio investment liabilities	4 652 Y.	1,184	1,445	681	714	3,165	4,480	1,123	703
Equity securities	4 660 Y.	. . .	17	89	147	350	570	989	195
Debt securities	4 669 Y.	1,184	1,428	592	567	2,815	3,910	134	508
Other investment assets	4 703 . .	–1,428	371	–409	–2,563	–2,438	–3,291	2,423	–1,791
Monetary authorities	4 703 . A	–381	712	361	29	36	–61	–18	–102
General government	4 703 . B	. . .	. . .	. . .	. . .	. . .	. . .	. . .	. . .
Banks	4 703 . C	–1,046	–370	–769	–2,595	–2,474	–3,230	2,441	–1,689
Other sectors	4 703 . D	–1	29	–1	3	. . .	. . .	. . .	. . .
Other investment liabilities	4 753 X.	–1,062	–1,640	3,199	–1,240	2,896	7,715	–8,334	4,017
Monetary authorities	4 753 XA	–697	–13	–419	–1,089	300	1,085	1,415	1,734
General government	4 753 YB	610	–1,089	503	330	–1,310	–1,953	–2,516	–1,991
Banks	4 753 YC	–144	240	2,279	396	2,100	4,495	–7,053	1,973
Other sectors	4 753 YD	–831	–778	836	–877	1,806	4,088	–180	2,301
Total, Groups A Through C	4 020 . .	*638*	*1,741*	*1,412*	*–2,147*	*2,674*	*2,530*	*–1,563*	*2,383*
D. Net Errors and Omissions	4 998 . .	**515**	**969**	**–469**	**948**	**–1,190**	**–2,222**	**1,766**	**2,277**
Total, Groups A Through D	4 030 . .	*1,153*	*2,710*	*943*	*–1,199*	*1,484*	*308*	*203*	*4,660*
E. Reserves and Related Items	4 040 . .	**–1,153**	**–2,710**	**–943**	**1,199**	**–1,484**	**–308**	**–203**	**–4,660**
Reserve assets	4 800 . .	–721	–2,471	–895	1,199	–1,484	–308	–547	–5,007
Use of Fund credit and loans	4 766 . .	–432	–239	–48	. . .	. . .	. . .	344	347
Liabilities constituting foreign authorities' reserves	4 900 . .	. . .	. . .	. . .	. . .	. . .	. . .	. . .	. . .
Exceptional financing	4 920 . .	. . .	. . .	. . .	. . .	. . .	. . .	. . .	. . .
Conversion rates: liras per U.S. dollar	0 101 . .	**1,422**	**2,122**	**2,609**	**4,172**	**6,872**	**10,985**	**29,609**	**45,845**

[1] Excludes components that have been classified in the categories of Group E.

Table 2. STANDARD PRESENTATION, 1988–95

(Millions of U.S. dollars)

	Code	1988	1989	1990	1991	1992	1993	1994	1995
CURRENT ACCOUNT	4 993 . .	**1,596**	**938**	**–2,625**	**250**	**–974**	**–6,433**	**2,631**	**–2,339**
A. GOODS	4 100 . .	–1,777	–4,219	–9,555	–7,340	–8,190	–14,160	–4,216	–13,212
Credit	2 100 . .	**11,929**	**11,780**	**13,026**	**13,667**	**14,891**	**15,611**	**18,390**	**21,975**
General merchandise: exports f.o.b.	2 110 . .	11,929	11,780	13,026	13,667	14,891	15,611	18,390	21,975
Goods for processing: exports f.o.b.	2 150 . .	. . .	. . .	. . .	. . .	. . .	. . .	. . .	. . .
Repairs on goods	2 160 . .	. . .	. . .	. . .	. . .	. . .	. . .	. . .	. . .
Goods procured in ports by carriers	2 170 . .	. . .	. . .	. . .	. . .	. . .	. . .	. . .	. . .
Nonmonetary gold	2 180 . .	. . .	. . .	. . .	. . .	. . .	. . .	. . .	. . .
Debit	3 100 . .	**–13,706**	**–15,999**	**–22,581**	**–21,007**	**–23,081**	**–29,771**	**–22,606**	**–35,187**
General merchandise: imports f.o.b.	3 110 . .	–13,674	–14,941	–21,049	–19,846	–21,651	–27,890	–22,126	–33,865
Goods for processing: imports f.o.b.	3 150 . .	. . .	. . .	. . .	. . .	. . .	. . .	. . .	. . .
Repairs on goods	3 160 . .	. . .	. . .	. . .	. . .	. . .	. . .	. . .	. . .
Goods procured in ports by carriers	3 170 . .	. . .	. . .	. . .	. . .	. . .	. . .	. . .	. . .
Nonmonetary gold	3 180 . .	–32	–1,058	–1,532	–1,161	–1,430	–1,881	–480	–1,322
B. SERVICES	4 200 . .	3,727	3,949	4,945	5,154	5,782	6,704	7,019	9,582
Total credit	2 200 . .	*5,652*	*6,414*	*8,016*	*8,372*	*9,407*	*10,652*	*10,801*	*14,606*
Total debit	3 200 . .	*–1,925*	*–2,465*	*–3,071*	*–3,218*	*–3,625*	*–3,948*	*–3,782*	*–5,024*
Transportation services, credit	2 205 . .	**837**	**967**	**920**	**1,098**	**1,136**	**1,241**	**1,221**	**1,712**
Passenger	2 205 BA	. . .	. . .	. . .	. . .	. . .	. . .	. . .	. . .
Freight	2 205 BB	*777*	*771*	*833*	*936*	*924*	*999*	*1,037*	*1,426*
Other	2 205 BC	*60*	*196*	*87*	*162*	*212*	*242*	*184*	*286*
Sea transport, passenger	2 207 . .	. . .	. . .	. . .	. . .	. . .	. . .	. . .	. . .
Sea transport, freight	2 208 . .	. . .	. . .	. . .	. . .	. . .	. . .	. . .	. . .
Sea transport, other	2 209 . .	. . .	. . .	. . .	. . .	. . .	. . .	. . .	. . .
Air transport, passenger	2 211 . .	. . .	. . .	. . .	. . .	. . .	. . .	. . .	. . .
Air transport, freight	2 212 . .	. . .	. . .	. . .	. . .	. . .	. . .	. . .	. . .
Air transport, other	2 213 . .	. . .	. . .	. . .	. . .	. . .	. . .	. . .	. . .
Other transport, passenger	2 215 . .	. . .	. . .	. . .	. . .	. . .	. . .	. . .	. . .
Other transport, freight	2 216 . .	. . .	. . .	. . .	. . .	. . .	. . .	. . .	. . .
Other transport, other	2 217 . .	. . .	. . .	. . .	. . .	. . .	. . .	. . .	. . .
Transportation services, debit	3 205 . .	**–573**	**–668**	**–900**	**–863**	**–975**	**–1,194**	**–953**	**–1,412**
Passenger	3 205 BA	. . .	. . .	. . .	. . .	. . .	. . .	. . .	. . .
Freight	3 205 BB	*–399*	*–471*	*–677*	*–654*	*–716*	*–912*	*–717*	*–1,106*
Other	3 205 BC	*–174*	*–197*	*–223*	*–209*	*–259*	*–282*	*–236*	*–306*
Sea transport, passenger	3 207 . .	. . .	. . .	. . .	. . .	. . .	. . .	. . .	. . .
Sea transport, freight	3 208 . .	. . .	. . .	. . .	. . .	. . .	. . .	. . .	. . .
Sea transport, other	3 209 . .	. . .	. . .	. . .	. . .	. . .	. . .	. . .	. . .
Air transport, passenger	3 211 . .	. . .	. . .	. . .	. . .	. . .	. . .	. . .	. . .
Air transport, freight	3 212 . .	. . .	. . .	. . .	. . .	. . .	. . .	. . .	. . .
Air transport, other	3 213 . .	. . .	. . .	. . .	. . .	. . .	. . .	. . .	. . .
Other transport, passenger	3 215 . .	. . .	. . .	. . .	. . .	. . .	. . .	. . .	. . .
Other transport, freight	3 216 . .	. . .	. . .	. . .	. . .	. . .	. . .	. . .	. . .
Other transport, other	3 217 . .	. . .	. . .	. . .	. . .	. . .	. . .	. . .	. . .
Travel, credit	2 236 . .	**2,355**	**2,557**	**3,225**	**2,654**	**3,639**	**3,959**	**4,321**	**4,957**
Business travel	2 237 . .	. . .	. . .	. . .	. . .	323	317	258	203
Personal travel	2 240 . .	. . .	. . .	. . .	. . .	3,316	3,642	4,063	4,754
Travel, debit	3 236 . .	**–358**	**–565**	**–520**	**–592**	**–776**	**–934**	**–866**	**–911**
Business travel	3 237 . .	. . .	. . .	. . .	. . .	–274	–315	–209	–227
Personal travel	3 240 . .	. . .	. . .	. . .	. . .	–502	–619	–657	–684
Other services, credit	2 200 BA	**2,460**	**2,890**	**3,871**	**4,620**	**4,632**	**5,452**	**5,259**	**7,937**
Communications	2 245 . .	. . .	. . .	. . .	. . .	. . .	. . .	. . .	. . .
Construction	2 249 . .	476	582	741	713	955	1,142	1,263	1,863
Insurance	2 253 . .	. . .	. . .	. . .	. . .	. . .	3	9	20
Financial	2 260 . .	. . .	. . .	. . .	. . .	153	171	123	201
Computer and information	2 262 . .	. . .	. . .	. . .	. . .	. . .	. . .	. . .	. . .
Royalties and licence fees	2 266 . .	. . .	. . .	. . .	. . .	. . .	. . .	. . .	. . .
Other business services	2 268 . .	1,885	2,185	2,996	3,698	1,685	1,850	2,152	3,440
Personal, cultural, and recreational	2 287 . .	. . .	. . .	. . .	. . .	1,694	2,152	1,634	2,282
Government, n.i.e.	2 291 . .	99	123	134	209	145	134	78	131
Other services, debit	3 200 BA	**–994**	**–1,232**	**–1,651**	**–1,763**	**–1,874**	**–1,820**	**–1,963**	**–2,701**
Communications	3 245 . .	. . .	. . .	. . .	. . .	. . .	. . .	. . .	. . .
Construction	3 249 . .	. . .	. . .	. . .	. . .	–10	. . .	–7	–4
Insurance	3 253 . .	. . .	. . .	. . .	. . .	–22	–38	–34	–42
Financial	3 260 . .	. . .	. . .	. . .	. . .	–294	–337	–288	–350
Computer and information	3 262 . .	. . .	. . .	. . .	. . .	. . .	. . .	. . .	. . .
Royalties and licence fees	3 266 . .	. . .	. . .	. . .	. . .	. . .	. . .	. . .	. . .
Other business services	3 268 . .	–770	–975	–1,374	–1,476	–573	–599	–500	–557
Personal, cultural, and recreational	3 287 . .	. . .	. . .	. . .	. . .	–627	–489	–770	–1,378
Government, n.i.e.	3 291 . .	–224	–257	–277	–287	–348	–357	–364	–370

Table 2 (Continued). STANDARD PRESENTATION, 1988–95
(Millions of U.S. dollars)

	Code		1988	1989	1990	1991	1992	1993	1994	1995
C. INCOME	4 300	. .	–2,513	–2,327	–2,508	–2,663	–2,625	–2,745	–3,264	–3,205
Total credit	2 300	. .	*374*	*684*	*917*	*935*	*1,012*	*1,135*	*890*	*1,488*
Total debit	3 300	. .	*–2,887*	*–3,011*	*–3,425*	*–3,598*	*–3,637*	*–3,880*	*–4,154*	*–4,693*
Compensation of employees, credit	2 310	. .	**. . .**	**. . .**	**. . .**	**. . .**	**. . .**	**. . .**	**. . .**	**. . .**
Compensation of employees, debit	3 310	. .	**. . .**	**. . .**	**. . .**	**. . .**	**. . .**	**. . .**	**. . .**	**. . .**
Investment income, credit	2 320	. .	**374**	**684**	**917**	**935**	**1,012**	**1,135**	**890**	**1,488**
Direct investment income	2 330	. .	. . .	. . .	. . .	. . .	10	10	10	40
Dividends and distributed branch profits	2 332	. .	. . .	. . .	. . .	. . .	10	10	10	40
Reinvested earnings and undistributed branch profits	2 333	. .	. . .	. . .	. . .	. . .	. . .	. . .	. . .	. . .
Income on debt (interest)	2 334	. .	. . .	. . .	. . .	. . .	. . .	. . .	. . .	. . .
Portfolio investment income	2 339	. .	. . .	. . .	. . .	. . .	231	428	189	240
Income on equity	2 340	. .	. . .	. . .	. . .	. . .	2	1	2	9
Income on bonds and notes	2 350	. .	. . .	. . .	. . .	. . .	229	427	187	231
Income on money market instruments and financial derivatives	2 360	. .	. . .	. . .	. . .	. . .	. . .	. . .	. . .	. . .
Other investment income	2 370	. .	374	684	917	935	771	697	691	1,208
Investment income, debit	3 320	. .	**–2,887**	**–3,011**	**–3,425**	**–3,598**	**–3,637**	**–3,880**	**–4,154**	**–4,693**
Direct investment income	3 330	. .	–88	–104	–161	–158	–155	–253	–112	–312
Dividends and distributed branch profits	3 332	. .	–88	–104	–161	–158	–155	–253	–112	–262
Reinvested earnings and undistributed branch profits	3 333	. .	. . .	. . .	. . .	. . .	. . .	. . .	. . .	–50
Income on debt (interest)	3 334	. .	. . .	. . .	. . .	. . .	. . .	. . .	. . .	. . .
Portfolio investment income	3 339	. .	. . .	. . .	. . .	. . .	–267	–164	–731	–981
Income on equity	3 340	. .	. . .	. . .	. . .	. . .	–20	–17	–91	–48
Income on bonds and notes	3 350	. .	. . .	. . .	. . .	. . .	–247	–147	–640	–933
Income on money market instruments and financial derivatives	3 360	. .	. . .	. . .	. . .	. . .	. . .	. . .	. . .	. . .
Other investment income	3 370	. .	–2,799	–2,907	–3,264	–3,440	–3,215	–3,463	–3,311	–3,400
D. CURRENT TRANSFERS	4 379	. .	2,159	3,535	4,493	5,099	4,059	3,768	3,092	4,496
Credit	2 379	. .	**2,220**	**3,574**	**4,525**	**5,131**	**4,075**	**3,800**	**3,113**	**4,512**
General government	2 380	. .	374	426	1,151	2,252	928	765	404	1,087
Other sectors	2 390	. .	1,846	3,148	3,374	2,879	3,147	3,035	2,709	3,425
Workers' remittances	2 391	. .	1,776	3,040	3,246	2,819	3,008	2,919	2,627	3,327
Other current transfers	2 392	. .	70	108	128	60	139	116	82	98
Debit	3 379	. .	**–61**	**–39**	**–32**	**–32**	**–16**	**–32**	**–21**	**–16**
General government	3 380	. .	–42	–3	–7	–7	–16	–32	–21	–16
Other sectors	3 390	. .	–19	–36	–25	–25	. . .	. . .	. . .	. . .
Workers' remittances	3 391	. .	. . .	. . .	. . .	. . .	. . .	. . .	. . .	. . .
Other current transfers	3 392	. .	–19	–36	–25	–25	. . .	. . .	. . .	. . .
CAPITAL AND FINANCIAL ACCOUNT	4 996	. .	**–2,111**	**–1,907**	**3,094**	**–1,198**	**2,164**	**8,655**	**–4,397**	**62**
CAPITAL ACCOUNT	4 994	. .	**. . .**	**23**	**. . .**	**. . .**	**. . .**	**. . .**	**. . .**	**. . .**
Total credit	2 994	. .	. . .	*23*	. . .	. . .	. . .	. . .	. . .	. . .
Total debit	3 994	. .	. . .	. . .	. . .	. . .	. . .	. . .	. . .	. . .
Capital transfers, credit	2 400	. .	**. . .**	**23**	**. . .**	**. . .**	**. . .**	**. . .**	**. . .**	**. . .**
General government	2 401	. .	. . .	. . .	. . .	. . .	. . .	. . .	. . .	. . .
Debt forgiveness	2 402	. .	. . .	. . .	. . .	. . .	. . .	. . .	. . .	. . .
Other capital transfers	2 410	. .	. . .	. . .	. . .	. . .	. . .	. . .	. . .	. . .
Other sectors	2 430	. .	. . .	23	. . .	. . .	. . .	. . .	. . .	. . .
Migrants' transfers	2 431	. .	. . .	23	. . .	. . .	. . .	. . .	. . .	. . .
Debt forgiveness	2 432	. .	. . .	. . .	. . .	. . .	. . .	. . .	. . .	. . .
Other capital transfers	2 440	. .	. . .	. . .	. . .	. . .	. . .	. . .	. . .	. . .
Capital transfers, debit	3 400	. .	**. . .**	**. . .**	**. . .**	**. . .**	**. . .**	**. . .**	**. . .**	**. . .**
General government	3 401	. .	. . .	. . .	. . .	. . .	. . .	. . .	. . .	. . .
Debt forgiveness	3 402	. .	. . .	. . .	. . .	. . .	. . .	. . .	. . .	. . .
Other capital transfers	3 410	. .	. . .	. . .	. . .	. . .	. . .	. . .	. . .	. . .
Other sectors	3 430	. .	. . .	. . .	. . .	. . .	. . .	. . .	. . .	. . .
Migrants' transfers	3 431	. .	. . .	. . .	. . .	. . .	. . .	. . .	. . .	. . .
Debt forgiveness	3 432	. .	. . .	. . .	. . .	. . .	. . .	. . .	. . .	. . .
Other capital transfers	3 440	. .	. . .	. . .	. . .	. . .	. . .	. . .	. . .	. . .
Nonproduced nonfinancial assets, credit	2 480	. .	**. . .**	**. . .**	**. . .**	**. . .**	**. . .**	**. . .**	**. . .**	**. . .**
Nonproduced nonfinancial assets, debit	3 480	. .	**. . .**	**. . .**	**. . .**	**. . .**	**. . .**	**. . .**	**. . .**	**. . .**

Table 2 (Continued). STANDARD PRESENTATION, 1988–95
(Millions of U.S. dollars)

	Code	1988	1989	1990	1991	1992	1993	1994	1995
FINANCIAL ACCOUNT	4 995	**–2,111**	**–1,930**	**3,094**	**–1,198**	**2,164**	**8,655**	**–4,397**	**62**
A. DIRECT INVESTMENT	4 500	354	663	700	783	779	622	559	772
Direct investment abroad	4 505	**...**	**...**	**16**	**–27**	**–65**	**–14**	**–49**	**–113**
Equity capital	4 510	...	...	16	–27	–65	–14	–49	–113
Claims on affiliated enterprises	4 515	...	...	16	–27	–65	–14	–49	–113
Liabilities to affiliated enterprises	4 520	...	...	...	...	...	...	...	...
Reinvested earnings	4 525	...	...	...	...	...	...	...	...
Other capital	4 530	...	...	...	...	...	...	...	...
Claims on affiliated enterprises	4 535	...	...	...	...	...	...	...	...
Liabilities to affiliated enterprises	4 540	...	...	...	...	...	...	...	...
Direct investment in Turkey	4 555	**354**	**663**	**684**	**810**	**844**	**636**	**608**	**885**
Equity capital	4 560	354	663	684	810	844	636	608	835
Claims on direct investors	4 565	...	...	...	...	...	...	...	...
Liabilities to direct investors	4 570	354	663	684	810	844	636	608	835
Reinvested earnings	4 575	...	...	...	...	...	...	...	50
Other capital	4 580	...	...	...	...	...	...	...	...
Claims on direct investors	4 585	...	...	...	...	...	...	...	...
Liabilities to direct investors	4 590	...	...	...	...	...	...	...	...
B. PORTFOLIO INVESTMENT	4 600	1,178	1,386	547	623	2,411	3,917	1,158	1,724
Assets	4 602	**–6**	**–59**	**–134**	**–91**	**–754**	**–563**	**35**	**1,021**
Equity securities	4 610	–6	–59	–134	–91	–50	–139	5	1,412
Monetary authorities	4 611	...	...	...	...	...	...	...	...
General government	4 612	...	...	...	...	–3	...	–15	–33
Banks	4 613	...	...	...	...	...	...	...	...
Other sectors	4 614	...	...	...	...	–47	–139	20	1,445
Debt securities	4 619	...	...	...	...	–704	–424	30	–391
Bonds and notes	4 620	...	...	...	...	–704	–424	30	–391
Monetary authorities	4 621	...	...	...	...	...	...	...	...
General government	4 622	...	...	...	...	–345	330	67	...
Banks	4 623	...	...	...	...	–359	–754	–37	–391
Other sectors	4 624	...	...	...	...	...	...	...	...
Money market instruments	4 630	...	...	...	...	...	...	...	...
Monetary authorities	4 631	...	...	...	...	...	...	...	...
General government	4 632	...	...	...	...	...	...	...	...
Banks	4 633	...	...	...	...	...	...	...	...
Other sectors	4 634	...	...	...	...	...	...	...	...
Financial derivatives	4 640	...	...	...	...	...	...	...	...
Monetary authorities	4 641	...	...	...	...	...	...	...	...
General government	4 642	...	...	...	...	...	...	...	...
Banks	4 643	...	...	...	...	...	...	...	...
Other sectors	4 644	...	...	...	...	...	...	...	...
Liabilities	4 652	**1,184**	**1,445**	**681**	**714**	**3,165**	**4,480**	**1,123**	**703**
Equity securities	4 660	...	17	89	147	350	570	989	195
Banks	4 663	...	...	...	...	...	...	...	...
Other sectors	4 664	...	17	89	147	350	570	989	195
Debt securities	4 669	1,184	1,428	592	567	2,815	3,910	134	508
Bonds and notes	4 670	1,184	1,428	592	567	2,815	3,910	134	508
Monetary authorities	4 671	179	...	...	...	–216	...	...	–213
General government	4 672	618	1,043	572	593	2,988	3,903	446	933
Banks	4 673	387	385	20	–26	43	7	–312	–212
Other sectors	4 674	...	...	...	...	...	...	...	...
Money market instruments	4 680	...	...	...	...	...	...	...	...
Monetary authorities	4 681	...	...	...	...	...	...	...	...
General government	4 682	...	...	...	...	...	...	...	...
Banks	4 683	...	...	...	...	...	...	...	...
Other sectors	4 684	...	...	...	...	...	...	...	...
Financial derivatives	4 690	...	...	...	...	...	...	...	...
Monetary authorities	4 691	...	...	...	...	...	...	...	...
General government	4 692	...	...	...	...	...	...	...	...
Banks	4 693	...	...	...	...	...	...	...	...
Other sectors	4 694	...	...	...	...	...	...	...	...

Table 2 (Concluded). STANDARD PRESENTATION, 1988–95
(Millions of U.S. dollars)

	Code	1988	1989	1990	1991	1992	1993	1994	1995
C. OTHER INVESTMENT	4 700	–2,922	–1,508	2,742	–3,803	458	4,424	–5,567	2,573
Assets	4 703	**–1,428**	**371**	**–409**	**–2,563**	**–2,438**	**–3,291**	**2,423**	**–1,791**
Trade credits	4 706	...	...	...	...	...	...	...	...
General government: long-term	4 708	...	...	...	...	...	...	...	...
General government: short-term	4 709	...	...	...	...	...	...	...	...
Other sectors: long-term	4 711	...	...	...	...	...	...	...	...
Other sectors: short-term	4 712	...	...	...	...	...	...	...	...
Loans	4 714	–607	390	156	–811	–327	–289	–38	293
Monetary authorities: long-term	4 717	–381	573	358	24	5	47	–28	–48
Monetary authorities: short-term	4 718	...	...	...	...	...	...	...	...
General government: long-term	4 720	...	...	...	...	...	...	...	...
General government: short-term	4 721	...	...	...	...	...	...	...	...
Banks: long-term	4 723	...	...	...	...	–7	–127	...	–279
Banks: short-term	4 724	–226	–183	–202	–835	–325	–209	–10	620
Other sectors: long-term	4 726	...	...	...	...	...	...	...	...
Other sectors: short-term	4 727	...	...	...	...	...	...	...	...
Currency and deposits	4 730	–820	–187	–567	–1,760	–2,142	–2,894	2,451	–2,030
Monetary authorities	4 731	...	...	...	...	...	...	...	...
General government	4 732	...	...	...	...	...	...	...	...
Banks	4 733	–820	–187	–567	–1,760	–2,142	–2,894	2,451	–2,030
Other sectors	4 734	...	...	...	...	...	...	...	...
Other assets	4 736	–1	168	2	8	31	–108	10	–54
Monetary authorities: long-term	4 738	...	...	...	...	...	...	...	...
Monetary authorities: short-term	4 739	...	139	3	5	31	–108	10	–54
General government: long-term	4 741	...	...	...	...	...	...	...	...
General government: short-term	4 742	...	...	...	...	...	...	...	...
Banks: long-term	4 744	...	...	...	...	...	...	...	...
Banks: short-term	4 745	...	...	...	...	...	...	...	...
Other sectors: long-term	4 747	...	...	...	...	...	...	...	...
Other sectors: short-term	4 748	–1	29	–1	3	...	...	...	...
Liabilities	4 753	**–1,494**	**–1,879**	**3,151**	**–1,240**	**2,896**	**7,715**	**–7,990**	**4,364**
Trade credits	4 756	–213	67	361	433	1,645	2,244	–816	1,671
General government: long-term	4 758	...	...	...	...	...	...	...	...
General government: short-term	4 759	...	...	...	...	...	...	...	...
Other sectors: long-term	4 761	...	...	...	...	...	...	...	...
Other sectors: short-term	4 762	–213	67	361	433	1,645	2,244	–816	1,671
Loans	4 764	–1,979	–2,573	1,714	–91	1,052	3,833	–8,487	53
Use of Fund credit and loans from the Fund	4 766	–432	–239	–48	...	...	...	344	347
Monetary authorities: other long-term	4 767	–777	–322	–466	–241	–210	–33	–68	–7
Monetary authorities: short-term	4 768	–564	...	5	–69	...	...	...	...
General government: long-term	4 770	610	–60	503	330	–1,310	–1,953	–2,516	–1,991
General government: short-term	4 771	...	–1,029	...	...	...	...	...	...
Banks: long-term	4 773	–155	–49	231	536	7	193	–282	273
Banks: short-term	4 774	–43	–29	1,014	663	2,404	3,782	–6,601	801
Other sectors: long-term	4 776	–481	–772	–527	–911	165	2,238	767	184
Other sectors: short-term	4 777	–137	–73	1,002	–399	–4	–394	–131	446
Currency and deposits	4 780	686	790	938	–1,544	153	1,589	1,260	2,462
Monetary authorities	4 781	632	472	–96	–741	464	1,069	1,430	1,563
General government	4 782	...	...	...	...	...	...	...	...
Banks	4 783	54	318	1,034	–803	–311	520	–170	899
Other sectors	4 784	...	...	...	...	...	...	...	...
Other liabilities	4 786	12	–163	138	–38	46	49	53	178
Monetary authorities: long-term	4 788	...	...	...	...	...	...	...	...
Monetary authorities: short-term	4 789	12	–163	138	–38	46	49	53	178
General government: long-term	4 791	...	...	...	...	...	...	...	...
General government: short-term	4 792	...	...	...	...	...	...	...	...
Banks: long-term	4 794	...	...	...	...	...	...	...	...
Banks: short-term	4 795	...	...	...	...	...	...	...	...
Other sectors: long-term	4 797	...	...	...	...	...	...	...	...
Other sectors: short-term	4 798	...	...	...	...	...	...	...	...
D. RESERVE ASSETS	4 800	–721	–2,471	–895	1,199	–1,484	–308	–547	–5,007
Monetary gold	4 810	...	14	–114	–25	...	6	79	27
Special drawing rights	4 820	...	...	...	1	...	...	–1	–2
Reserve position in the Fund	4 830	...	...	...	...	...	...	...	...
Foreign exchange	4 840	–721	–2,485	–781	1,223	–1,484	–314	–625	–5,032
Other claims	4 880	...	...	...	...	...	...	...	...
NET ERRORS AND OMISSIONS	4 998	**515**	**969**	**–469**	**948**	**–1,190**	**–2,222**	**1,766**	**2,277**

Part 3 of the *Yearbook* contains descriptions of the methodologies, compilation practices, and sources used to compile these data.

Table 3. INTERNATIONAL INVESTMENT POSITION (End–period stocks), 1988–95
(Millions of U.S. dollars)

	Code		1988	1989	1990	1991	1992	1993	1994	1995
ASSETS	8 995	C.	9,466	11,688	13,686	15,319	18,555	21,291	20,194	27,396
Direct investment abroad	8 505	. .	...	...	...	...	...	...	...	...
Equity capital and reinvested earnings	8 506	. .	...	...	...	...	...	...	...	...
Claims on affiliated enterprises	8 507	. .	...	...	...	...	...	...	...	...
Liabilities to affiliated enterprises	8 508	. .	...	...	...	...	...	...	...	...
Other capital	8 530	. .	...	...	...	...	...	...	...	...
Claims on affiliated enterprises	8 535	. .	...	...	...	...	...	...	...	...
Liabilities to affiliated enterprises	8 540	. .	...	...	...	...	...	...	...	...
Portfolio investment	8 602	. .	...	...	...	...	...	...	...	...
Equity securities	8 610	. .	...	...	...	...	...	...	...	...
Monetary authorities	8 611	. .	...	...	...	...	...	...	...	...
General government	8 612	. .	...	...	...	...	...	...	...	...
Banks	8 613	. .	...	...	...	...	...	...	...	...
Other sectors	8 614	. .	...	...	...	...	...	...	...	...
Debt securities	8 619	. .	...	...	...	...	...	...	...	...
Bonds and notes	8 620	. .	...	...	...	...	...	...	...	...
Monetary authorities	8 621	. .	...	...	...	...	...	...	...	...
General government	8 622	. .	...	...	...	...	...	...	...	...
Banks	8 623	. .	...	...	...	...	...	...	...	...
Other sectors	8 624	. .	...	...	...	...	...	...	...	...
Money market instruments	8 630	. .	...	...	...	...	...	...	...	...
Monetary authorities	8 631	. .	...	...	...	...	...	...	...	...
General government	8 632	. .	...	...	...	...	...	...	...	...
Banks	8 633	. .	...	...	...	...	...	...	...	...
Other sectors	8 634	. .	...	...	...	...	...	...	...	...
Financial derivatives	8 640	. .	...	...	...	...	...	...	...	...
Monetary authorities	8 641	. .	...	...	...	...	...	...	...	...
General government	8 642	. .	...	...	...	...	...	...	...	...
Banks	8 643	. .	...	...	...	...	...	...	...	...
Other sectors	8 644	. .	...	...	...	...	...	...	...	...
Other investment	8 703	. .	**5,748**	**5,461**	**6,199**	**8,862**	**10,901**	**13,545**	**11,624**	**13,571**
Trade credits	8 706	. .	...	...	...	...	...	...	...	...
General government: long-term	8 708	. .	...	...	...	...	...	...	...	...
General government: short-term	8 709	. .	...	...	...	...	...	...	...	...
Other sectors: long-term	8 711	. .	...	...	...	...	...	...	...	...
Other sectors: short-term	8 712	. .	...	...	...	...	...	...	...	...
Loans	8 714	. .	2,675	2,320	2,216	3,013	3,257	3,484	3,627	3,402
Monetary authorities: long-term	8 717	. .	2,049	1,476	1,118	1,094	1,088	1,034	1,061	1,103
Monetary authorities: short-term	8 718	. .	...	...	...	...	...	...	...	...
General government: long-term	8 720	. .	...	...	...	...	...	...	...	...
General government: short-term	8 721	. .	...	...	...	...	...	...	...	...
Banks: long-term	8 723	. .	152	193	422	706	704	818	824	1,106
Banks: short-term	8 724	. .	474	651	676	1,213	1,465	1,632	1,742	1,193
Other sectors: long-term	8 726	. .	...	...	...	...	...	...	...	...
Other sectors: short-term	8 727	. .	...	...	...	...	...	...	...	...
Currency and deposits	8 730	. .	2,921	3,128	3,971	5,842	7,644	10,061	7,997	10,169
Monetary authorities	8 731	. .	...	...	...	...	...	...	...	...
General government	8 732	. .	...	...	...	...	...	...	...	...
Banks	8 733	. .	2,921	3,128	3,971	5,842	7,644	10,061	7,997	10,169
Other sectors	8 734	. .	...	...	...	...	...	...	...	...
Other assets	8 736	. .	152	13	12	7	...	...	...	...
Monetary authorities: long-term	8 738	. .	...	...	...	...	...	...	...	...
Monetary authorities: short-term	8 739	. .	152	13	12	7	...	...	...	...
General government: long-term	8 741	. .	...	...	...	...	...	...	...	...
General government: short-term	8 742	. .	...	...	...	...	...	...	...	...
Banks: long-term	8 744	. .	...	...	...	...	...	...	...	...
Banks: short-term	8 745	. .	...	...	...	...	...	...	...	...
Other sectors: long-term	8 747	. .	...	...	...	...	...	...	...	...
Other sectors: short-term	8 748	. .	...	...	...	...	...	...	...	...
Reserve assets	8 800	. .	**3,718**	**6,227**	**7,487**	**6,457**	**7,654**	**7,746**	**8,570**	**13,825**
Monetary gold	8 810	. .	1,368	1,354	1,468	1,493	1,494	1,488	1,410	1,383
Special drawing rights	8 820	. .	...	...	1	...	...	...	1	3
Reserve position in the Fund	8 830	. .	43	42	46	46	44	44	47	48
Foreign exchange	8 840	. .	2,307	4,831	5,972	4,918	6,116	6,213	7,112	12,391
Other claims	8 880	. .	...	...	...	...	...	...	...	...

Table 3 (Continued). INTERNATIONAL INVESTMENT POSITION (End–period stocks), 1988–95

(Millions of U.S. dollars)

	Code	1988	1989	1990	1991	1992	1993	1994	1995
LIABILITIES	8 995 D.	39,939	42,064	50,285	50,578	55,736	67,452	66,027	74,015
Direct investment in Turkey	8 555 . .	...	...	...	...	...	...	...	...
Equity capital and reinvested earnings	8 556 . .	...	...	...	...	...	...	...	...
Claims on direct investors	8 557 . .	...	...	...	...	...	...	...	...
Liabilities to direct investors	8 558 . .	...	...	...	...	...	...	...	...
Other capital	8 580 . .	...	...	...	...	...	...	...	...
Claims on direct investors	8 585 . .	...	...	...	...	...	...	...	...
Liabilities to direct investors	8 590 . .	...	...	...	...	...	...	...	...
Portfolio investment	8 652 . .	**3,321**	**5,226**	**5,877**	**6,683**	**9,316**	**12,623**	**13,788**	**14,186**
Equity securities	8 660 . .	...	...	...	...	...	...	...	...
Banks	8 663 . .	...	...	...	...	...	...	...	...
Other sectors	8 664 . .	...	...	...	...	...	...	...	...
Debt securities	8 669 . .	3,321	5,226	5,877	6,683	9,316	12,623	13,788	14,186
Bonds and notes	8 670 . .	3,321	5,226	5,877	6,683	9,316	12,623	13,788	14,186
Monetary authorities	8 671 . .	353	369	416	411	186	173	193	...
General government	8 672 . .	2,124	3,711	4,224	5,012	7,828	11,065	12,407	13,234
Banks	8 673 . .	844	1,146	1,237	1,260	1,302	1,385	1,188	952
Other sectors	8 674 . .	...	...	...	...	...	...	...	...
Money market instruments	8 680 . .	...	...	...	...	...	...	...	...
Monetary authorities	8 681 . .	...	...	...	...	...	...	...	...
General government	8 682 . .	...	...	...	...	...	...	...	...
Banks	8 683 . .	...	...	...	...	...	...	...	...
Other sectors	8 684 . .	...	...	...	...	...	...	...	...
Financial derivatives	8 690 . .	...	...	...	...	...	...	...	...
Monetary authorities	8 691 . .	...	...	...	...	...	...	...	...
General government	8 692 . .	...	...	...	...	...	...	...	...
Banks	8 692 . .	...	...	...	...	...	...	...	...
Other sectors	8 694 . .	...	...	...	...	...	...	...	...
Other investment	8 753 . .	**36,618**	**36,838**	**44,408**	**43,895**	**46,420**	**54,829**	**52,239**	**59,829**
Trade credits	8 756 . .	4,778	5,453	7,099	6,656	8,118	10,586	11,049	13,486
General government: long-term	8 758 . .	513	999	933	964	1,079	976	1,876	1,641
General government: short-term	8 759 . .	...	...	...	...	...	...	...	...
Other sectors: long-term	8 761 . .	3,231	3,345	3,634	3,702	3,464	3,700	4,030	4,878
Other sectors: short-term	8 762 . .	1,034	1,109	2,532	1,990	3,575	5,910	5,143	6,967
Loans	8 764 . .	24,684	22,760	26,669	28,451	29,790	34,767	29,529	31,403
Use of Fund credit and loans from the Fund	8 766 . .	299	48	...	...	...	...	344	685
Monetary authorities: other long-term	8 767 . .	1,470	1,106	650	406	193	163	96	89
Monetary authorities: short-term	8 768 . .	...	...	...	...	...	...	...	...
General government: long-term	8 770 . .	19,609	18,323	20,474	21,429	19,556	18,757	19,784	19,787
General government: short-term	8 771 . .	...	...	...	...	...	...	...	...
Banks: long-term	8 773 . .	1,008	301	496	1,404	1,105	1,334	1,130	1,366
Banks: short-term	8 774 . .	1,082	1,057	2,093	2,787	5,132	8,696	2,241	3,161
Other sectors: long-term	8 776 . .	430	1,206	1,216	1,071	2,448	4,988	5,279	5,233
Other sectors: short-term	8 777 . .	786	719	1,740	1,354	1,356	829	655	1,082
Currency and deposits	8 780 . .	7,155	8,429	10,343	8,696	8,365	9,379	11,574	14,868
Monetary authorities	8 781 . .	5,470	6,368	7,063	6,267	6,340	6,948	9,131	11,370
General government	8 782 . .	...	...	...	...	...	...	...	...
Banks	8 783 . .	1,685	2,061	3,280	2,429	2,025	2,431	2,443	3,498
Other sectors	8 784 . .	...	...	...	...	...	...	...	...
Other liabilities	8 786 . .	1	196	297	92	147	97	87	72
Monetary authorities: long-term	8 788 . .	...	...	...	...	...	...	...	...
Monetary authorities: short-term	8 789 . .	1	196	297	92	147	97	87	72
General government: long-term	8 791 . .	...	...	...	...	...	...	...	...
General government: short-term	8 792 . .	...	...	...	...	...	...	...	...
Banks: long-term	8 794 . .	...	...	...	...	...	...	...	...
Banks: short-term	8 795 . .	...	...	...	...	...	...	...	...
Other sectors: long-term	8 797 . .	...	...	...	...	...	...	...	...
Other sectors: short-term	8 798 . .	...	...	...	...	...	...	...	...
NET INTERNATIONAL INVESTMENT POSITION	8 995 . .	**–30,472**	**–30,375**	**–36,599**	**–35,259**	**–37,181**	**–46,161**	**–45,832**	**–46,619**
Conversion rates: liras per U.S. dollar (end of period)	0 102 . .	**1,815**	**2,314**	**2,930**	**5,080**	**8,564**	**14,473**	**38,726**	**59,650**

Table 1. ANALYTIC PRESENTATION, 1988–95
(Millions of U.S. dollars)

	Code	1988	1989	1990	1991	1992	1993	1994	1995
A. Current Account[1]	4 993 Y.	**–195.2**	**–259.5**	**–263.3**	**–169.8**	**–99.6**	**–170.8**	**–157.7**	**–275.7**
Goods: exports f.o.b	2 100 . .	266.3	277.7	177.8	173.2	151.2	200.0	440.9	548.9
Goods: imports f.o.b	3 100 . .	–523.5	–588.3	–491.0	–377.1	–421.9	–441.7	–672.2	–866.7
Balance on Goods	4 100 . .	*–257.2*	*–310.6*	*–313.2*	*–203.9*	*–270.7*	*–241.7*	*–231.3*	*–317.8*
Services: credit	2 200 . .	. . .	. . .	. . .	20.8	34.5	93.6	64.1	99.4
Services: debit	3 200 . .	–235.2	–237.2	–195.3	–241.8	–247.7	–269.8	–409.5	–528.0
Balance on Goods and Services	4 991 . .	*–492.4*	*–547.8*	*–508.5*	*–424.9*	*–483.9*	*–417.9*	*–576.7*	*–746.4*
Income: credit	2 300 . .	. . .	. . .	. . .	2.8	4.1	6.4	13.8	17.7
Income: debit	3 300 . .	–25.2	–23.3	–47.8	–76.7	–88.3	–65.3	–71.0	–113.3
Balance on Goods, Services, and Income	4 992 . .	*–517.6*	*–571.1*	*–556.3*	*–498.8*	*–568.1*	*–476.8*	*–633.9*	*–842.0*
Current transfers: credit	2 379 Y.	322.4	311.6	293.0	329.0	468.5	306.0	476.2	566.3
Current transfers: debit	3 379 . .	. . .	. . .	. . .	. . .	. . .	. . .	. . .	. . .
B. Capital Account[1]	4 994 Y.	**. . .**	**. . .**	**. . .**	**. . .**	**. . .**	**42.4**	**36.1**	**48.3**
Capital account: credit	2 994 Y.	. . .	. . .	. . .	. . .	. . .	42.4	36.1	48.3
Capital account: debit	3 994 . .	. . .	. . .	. . .	. . .	. . .	. . .	. . .	. . .
Total, Groups A Plus B	4 010 . .	*–195.2*	*–259.5*	*–263.3*	*–169.8*	*–99.6*	*–128.4*	*–121.6*	*–227.4*
C. Financial Account[1]	4 995 X.	**3.6**	**213.0**	**211.8**	**137.6**	**114.8**	**–12.2**	**–4.1**	**115.1**
Direct investment abroad	4 505 . .	. . .	. . .	. . .	. . .	. . .	. . .	. . .	. . .
Direct investment in Uganda	4 555 Y.	. . .	. . .	. . .	1.0	3.0	54.6	88.2	121.2
Portfolio investment assets	4 602 . .	. . .	. . .	. . .	. . .	. . .	. . .	. . .	. . .
Equity securities	4 610 . .	. . .	. . .	. . .	. . .	. . .	. . .	. . .	. . .
Debt securities	4 619 . .	. . .	. . .	. . .	. . .	. . .	. . .	. . .	. . .
Portfolio investment liabilities	4 652 Y.	. . .	. . .	. . .	. . .	. . .	. . .	. . .	. . .
Equity securities	4 660 Y.	. . .	. . .	. . .	. . .	. . .	. . .	. . .	. . .
Debt securities	4 669 Y.	. . .	. . .	. . .	. . .	. . .	. . .	. . .	. . .
Other investment assets	4 703 . .	. . .	. . .	. . .	.4	1.8	–5.0	–40.3	–9.9
Monetary authorities	4 703 . A	. . .	. . .	. . .	. . .	. . .	. . .	. . .	. . .
General government	4 703 . B	. . .	. . .	. . .	. . .	. . .	. . .	. . .	. . .
Banks	4 703 . C	. . .	. . .	. . .	. . .	. . .	–8.7	–53.0	12.7
Other sectors	4 703 . D	. . .	. . .	. . .	.4	1.8	3.7	12.7	–22.6
Other investment liabilities	4 753 X.	3.6	213.0	211.8	136.2	110.0	–61.8	–52.0	3.8
Monetary authorities	4 753 XA	–42.1	–19.5	–.3	–.2	–6.6	. . .	.9	1.7
General government	4 753 YB	75.6	233.3	257.9	167.8	150.7	–10.3	–30.7	16.1
Banks	4 753 YC	. . .	40.6	–26.3	–9.6	–22.8	. . .	. . .	. . .
Other sectors	4 753 YD	–29.9	–41.4	–19.5	–21.8	–11.3	–51.5	–22.2	–14.0
Total, Groups A Through C	4 020 . .	*–191.6*	*–46.5*	*–51.5*	*–32.2*	*15.2*	*–140.6*	*–125.7*	*–112.3*
D. Net Errors and Omissions	4 998 . .	**154.9**	**–38.0**	**9.5**	**.6**	**9.0**	**–11.1**	**52.5**	**47.5**
Total, Groups A Through D	4 030 . .	*–36.7*	*–84.5*	*–41.9*	*–31.7*	*24.2*	*–151.7*	*–73.2*	*–64.8*
E. Reserves and Related Items	4 040 . .	**36.7**	**84.5**	**41.9**	**31.7**	**–24.2**	**151.7**	**73.2**	**64.8**
Reserve assets	4 800 . .	2.4	1.8	5.2	–12.7	–50.6	–51.8	–175.0	–137.4
Use of Fund credit and loans	4 766 . .	–7.8	–20.7	36.5	44.4	26.4	–9.8	27.1	27.5
Liabilities constituting foreign authorities' reserves	4 900 . .	. . .	. . .	. . .	. . .	. . .	. . .	. . .	. . .
Exceptional financing	4 920 . .	42.1	103.4	.3	. . .	. . .	213.4	221.1	174.6
Conversion rates: Uganda shillings per U.S. dollar	0 101 . .	**106.14**	**223.09**	**428.85**	**734.01**	**1,133.83**	**1,195.02**	**979.45**	**968.92**

[1] Excludes components that have been classified in the categories of Group E.

Table 2. STANDARD PRESENTATION, 1988–95

(Millions of U.S. dollars)

	Code	1988	1989	1990	1991	1992	1993	1994	1995
CURRENT ACCOUNT	4 993 . .	**–195.2**	**–259.5**	**–263.3**	**–169.8**	**–99.6**	**–117.6**	**–124.4**	**–218.3**
A. GOODS	4 100 . .	–257.2	–310.6	–313.2	–203.9	–270.7	–241.7	–231.3	–317.8
Credit	2 100 . .	**266.3**	**277.7**	**177.8**	**173.2**	**151.2**	**200.0**	**440.9**	**548.9**
General merchandise: exports f.o.b.	2 110 . .	266.3	277.7	177.8	173.2	151.2	194.6	436.5	543.5
Goods for processing: exports f.o.b.	2 150 . .	...	...	...	...	...	...	...	...
Repairs on goods	2 160 . .	...	...	...	...	...	...	...	...
Goods procured in ports by carriers	2 170 . .	...	...	...	...	...	5.4	4.4	5.4
Nonmonetary gold	2 180 . .	...	...	...	...	...	...	...	...
Debit	3 100 . .	**–523.5**	**–588.3**	**–491.0**	**–377.1**	**–421.9**	**–441.7**	**–672.2**	**–866.7**
General merchandise: imports f.o.b.	3 110 . .	–523.5	–588.3	–491.0	–377.1	–421.9	–441.7	–672.2	–866.7
Goods for processing: imports f.o.b.	3 150 . .	...	...	...	...	...	...	...	...
Repairs on goods	3 160 . .	...	...	...	...	...	...	...	...
Goods procured in ports by carriers	3 170 . .	...	...	...	...	...	...	...	...
Nonmonetary gold	3 180 . .	...	...	...	...	...	...	...	...
B. SERVICES	4 200 . .	–235.2	–237.2	–195.3	–221.0	–213.2	–176.2	–345.4	–428.6
Total credit	2 200 . .	...	...	...	*20.8*	*34.5*	*93.6*	*64.1*	*99.4*
Total debit	3 200 . .	*–235.2*	*–237.2*	*–195.3*	*–241.8*	*–247.7*	*–269.8*	*–409.5*	*–528.0*
Transportation services, credit	2 205 . .	**...**	**...**	**...**	**...**	**...**	**11.8**	**16.8**	**18.6**
Passenger	2 205 BA	...	...	...	...	...	...	...	...
Freight	2 205 BB	...	...	...	...	...	*11.8*	*16.8*	*18.6*
Other	2 205 BC	...	...	...	...	...	...	...	...
Sea transport, passenger	2 207 . .	...	...	...	...	...	...	...	...
Sea transport, freight	2 208 . .	...	...	...	...	...	...	...	...
Sea transport, other	2 209 . .	...	...	...	...	...	...	...	...
Air transport, passenger	2 211 . .	...	...	...	...	...	...	...	...
Air transport, freight	2 212 . .	...	...	...	...	...	9.1	11.2	12.4
Air transport, other	2 213 . .	...	...	...	...	...	...	...	...
Other transport, passenger	2 215 . .	...	...	...	...	...	...	...	...
Other transport, freight	2 216 . .	...	...	...	...	...	2.7	5.6	6.2
Other transport, other	2 217 . .	...	...	...	...	...	...	...	...
Transportation services, debit	3 205 . .	**–121.4**	**–136.5**	**–113.9**	**–87.6**	**–97.9**	**–102.5**	**–156.0**	**–201.2**
Passenger	3 205 BA	...	...	...	...	...	...	...	...
Freight	3 205 BB	*–121.4*	*–136.5*	*–113.9*	*–87.6*	*–97.9*	*–102.5*	*–156.0*	*–201.2*
Other	3 205 BC	...	...	...	...	...	...	...	...
Sea transport, passenger	3 207 . .	...	...	...	...	...	...	...	...
Sea transport, freight	3 208 . .	...	...	...	...	...	...	...	...
Sea transport, other	3 209 . .	...	...	...	...	...	...	...	...
Air transport, passenger	3 211 . .	...	...	...	...	...	...	...	...
Air transport, freight	3 212 . .	...	...	...	...	...	...	...	...
Air transport, other	3 213 . .	...	...	...	...	...	...	...	...
Other transport, passenger	3 215 . .	...	...	...	...	...	...	...	...
Other transport, freight	3 216 . .	...	...	...	...	...	...	...	...
Other transport, other	3 217 . .	...	...	...	...	...	...	...	...
Travel, credit	2 236 . .	**...**	**...**	**...**	**...**	**...**	**29.6**	**40.2**	**73.5**
Business travel	2 237 . .	...	...	...	...	...	...	...	...
Personal travel	2 240 . .	...	...	...	...	...	...	...	...
Travel, debit	3 236 . .	**...**	**...**	**...**	**...**	**...**	**–39.7**	**–77.6**	**–80.2**
Business travel	3 237 . .	...	...	...	...	...	...	...	...
Personal travel	3 240 . .	...	...	...	...	...	...	...	...
Other services, credit	2 200 BA	**...**	**...**	**...**	**20.8**	**34.5**	**52.2**	**7.1**	**7.3**
Communications	2 245 . .	...	...	...	...	...	...	...	...
Construction	2 249 . .	...	...	...	...	...	...	...	...
Insurance	2 253 . .	...	...	...	...	...	...	...	...
Financial	2 260 . .	...	...	...	...	...	...	...	...
Computer and information	2 262 . .	...	...	...	...	...	...	...	...
Royalties and licence fees	2 266 . .	...	...	...	...	...	...	...	...
Other business services	2 268 . .	...	...	...	20.8	34.5	52.2	7.1	7.3
Personal, cultural, and recreational	2 287 . .	...	...	...	...	...	...	...	...
Government, n.i.e.	2 291 . .	...	...	...	...	...	...	...	...
Other services, debit	3 200 BA	**–113.8**	**–100.7**	**–81.4**	**–154.2**	**–149.8**	**–127.6**	**–175.9**	**–246.6**
Communications	3 245 . .	...	...	...	...	...	...	...	...
Construction	3 249 . .	...	...	...	...	...	...	...	...
Insurance	3 253 . .	–13.5	–15.2	–12.7	–9.7	–10.9	–11.4	–17.3	–22.3
Financial	3 260 . .	...	...	...	...	...	...	...	...
Computer and information	3 262 . .	...	...	...	...	...	...	...	...
Royalties and licence fees	3 266 . .	...	...	...	...	...	...	...	...
Other business services	3 268 . .	–100.3	–85.5	–68.7	–144.5	–138.9	–116.2	–158.6	–224.3
Personal, cultural, and recreational	3 287 . .	...	...	...	...	...	...	...	...
Government, n.i.e.	3 291 . .	...	...	...	...	...	...	...	...

Table 2 (Continued). STANDARD PRESENTATION, 1988–95
(Millions of U.S. dollars)

	Code	1988	1989	1990	1991	1992	1993	1994	1995
C. INCOME	4 300	–25.2	–23.3	–47.8	–73.9	–84.2	–58.9	–57.2	–95.6
Total credit	2 300	*. . .*	*. . .*	*. . .*	*2.8*	*4.1*	*6.4*	*13.8*	*17.7*
Total debit	3 300	*–25.2*	*–23.3*	*–47.8*	*–76.7*	*–88.3*	*–65.3*	*–71.0*	*–113.3*
Compensation of employees, credit	2 310	**. . .**	**. . .**	**. . .**	**. . .**	**. . .**	**. . .**	**. . .**	**. . .**
Compensation of employees, debit	3 310	**. . .**	**. . .**	**. . .**	**. . .**	**. . .**	**. . .**	**. . .**	**. . .**
Investment income, credit	2 320	**. . .**	**. . .**	**. . .**	**2.8**	**4.1**	**6.4**	**13.8**	**17.7**
Direct investment income	2 330	. . .	. . .	. . .	. . .	. . .	. . .	. . .	. . .
Dividends and distributed branch profits	2 332	. . .	. . .	. . .	. . .	. . .	. . .	. . .	. . .
Reinvested earnings and undistributed branch profits	2 333	. . .	. . .	. . .	. . .	. . .	. . .	. . .	. . .
Income on debt (interest)	2 334	. . .	. . .	. . .	. . .	. . .	. . .	. . .	. . .
Portfolio investment income	2 339	. . .	. . .	. . .	. . .	. . .	. . .	. . .	. . .
Income on equity	2 340	. . .	. . .	. . .	. . .	. . .	. . .	. . .	. . .
Income on bonds and notes	2 350	. . .	. . .	. . .	. . .	. . .	. . .	. . .	. . .
Income on money market instruments and financial derivatives	2 360	. . .	. . .	. . .	. . .	. . .	. . .	. . .	. . .
Other investment income	2 370	. . .	. . .	. . .	2.8	4.1	6.4	13.8	17.7
Investment income, debit	3 320	**–25.2**	**–23.3**	**–47.8**	**–76.7**	**–88.3**	**–65.3**	**–71.0**	**–113.3**
Direct investment income	3 330	. . .	. . .	. . .	. . .	. . .	–17.9	–20.5	–59.6
Dividends and distributed branch profits	3 332	. . .	. . .	. . .	. . .	. . .	–12.9	–10.5	–24.6
Reinvested earnings and undistributed branch profits	3 333	. . .	. . .	. . .	. . .	. . .	–5.0	–10.0	–35.0
Income on debt (interest)	3 334	. . .	. . .	. . .	. . .	. . .	. . .	. . .	. . .
Portfolio investment income	3 339	. . .	. . .	. . .	. . .	. . .	. . .	. . .	. . .
Income on equity	3 340	. . .	. . .	. . .	. . .	. . .	. . .	. . .	. . .
Income on bonds and notes	3 350	. . .	. . .	. . .	. . .	. . .	. . .	. . .	. . .
Income on money market instruments and financial derivatives	3 360	. . .	. . .	. . .	. . .	. . .	. . .	. . .	. . .
Other investment income	3 370	–25.2	–23.3	–47.8	–76.7	–88.3	–47.4	–50.5	–53.7
D. CURRENT TRANSFERS	4 379	322.4	311.6	293.0	329.0	468.5	359.2	509.5	623.7
Credit	2 379	**322.4**	**311.6**	**293.0**	**329.0**	**468.5**	**359.2**	**509.5**	**623.7**
General government	2 380	322.4	311.6	293.0	225.6	261.2	242.8	196.3	245.9
Other sectors	2 390	. . .	. . .	. . .	103.4	207.3	116.4	313.2	377.8
Workers' remittances	2 391	. . .	. . .	. . .	. . .	. . .	. . .	. . .	. . .
Other current transfers	2 392	. . .	. . .	. . .	103.4	207.3	116.4	313.2	377.8
Debit	3 379	**. . .**	**. . .**	**. . .**	**. . .**	**. . .**	**. . .**	**. . .**	**. . .**
General government	3 380	. . .	. . .	. . .	. . .	. . .	. . .	. . .	. . .
Other sectors	3 390	. . .	. . .	. . .	. . .	. . .	. . .	. . .	. . .
Workers' remittances	3 391	. . .	. . .	. . .	. . .	. . .	. . .	. . .	. . .
Other current transfers	3 392	. . .	. . .	. . .	. . .	. . .	. . .	. . .	. . .
CAPITAL AND FINANCIAL ACCOUNT	4 996	**40.3**	**297.6**	**253.8**	**169.2**	**90.6**	**128.7**	**71.9**	**170.8**
CAPITAL ACCOUNT	4 994	**. . .**	**. . .**	**. . .**	**. . .**	**. . .**	**219.6**	**40.0**	**48.3**
Total credit	2 994	*. . .*	*. . .*	*. . .*	*. . .*	*. . .*	*219.6*	*40.0*	*48.3*
Total debit	3 994	*. . .*	*. . .*	*. . .*	*. . .*	*. . .*	*. . .*	*. . .*	*. . .*
Capital transfers, credit	2 400	**. . .**	**. . .**	**. . .**	**. . .**	**. . .**	**219.6**	**40.0**	**48.3**
General government	2 401	. . .	. . .	. . .	. . .	. . .	219.6	34.0	48.3
Debt forgiveness	2 402	. . .	. . .	. . .	. . .	. . .	177.2	3.9	. . .
Other capital transfers	2 410	. . .	. . .	. . .	. . .	. . .	42.4	30.1	48.3
Other sectors	2 430	. . .	. . .	. . .	. . .	. . .	. . .	6.0	. . .
Migrants' transfers	2 431	. . .	. . .	. . .	. . .	. . .	. . .	. . .	. . .
Debt forgiveness	2 432	. . .	. . .	. . .	. . .	. . .	. . .	. . .	. . .
Other capital transfers	2 440	. . .	. . .	. . .	. . .	. . .	. . .	. . .	. . .
Capital transfers, debit	3 400	**. . .**	**. . .**	**. . .**	**. . .**	**. . .**	**. . .**	**. . .**	**. . .**
General government	3 401	. . .	. . .	. . .	. . .	. . .	. . .	. . .	. . .
Debt forgiveness	3 402	. . .	. . .	. . .	. . .	. . .	. . .	. . .	. . .
Other capital transfers	3 410	. . .	. . .	. . .	. . .	. . .	. . .	. . .	. . .
Other sectors	3 430	. . .	. . .	. . .	. . .	. . .	. . .	. . .	. . .
Migrants' transfers	3 431	. . .	. . .	. . .	. . .	. . .	. . .	. . .	. . .
Debt forgiveness	3 432	. . .	. . .	. . .	. . .	. . .	. . .	. . .	. . .
Other capital transfers	3 440	. . .	. . .	. . .	. . .	. . .	. . .	. . .	. . .
Nonproduced nonfinancial assets, credit	2 480	**. . .**	**. . .**	**. . .**	**. . .**	**. . .**	**. . .**	**. . .**	**. . .**
Nonproduced nonfinancial assets, debit	3 480	**. . .**	**. . .**	**. . .**	**. . .**	**. . .**	**. . .**	**. . .**	**. . .**

Table 2 (Continued). STANDARD PRESENTATION, 1988–95
(Millions of U.S. dollars)

	Code	1988	1989	1990	1991	1992	1993	1994	1995
FINANCIAL ACCOUNT	4 995	**40.3**	**297.6**	**253.8**	**169.2**	**90.6**	**–90.9**	**31.9**	**122.5**
A. DIRECT INVESTMENT	4 500	...	...	...	1.0	3.0	54.6	88.2	121.2
Direct investment abroad	4 505	...	...	...	...	...	...	...	...
Equity capital	4 510	...	...	...	...	...	...	...	...
Claims on affiliated enterprises	4 515	...	...	...	...	...	...	...	...
Liabilities to affiliated enterprises	4 520	...	...	...	...	...	...	...	...
Reinvested earnings	4 525	...	...	...	...	...	...	...	...
Other capital	4 530	...	...	...	...	...	...	...	...
Claims on affiliated enterprises	4 535	...	...	...	...	...	...	...	...
Liabilities to affiliated enterprises	4 540	...	...	...	...	...	...	...	...
Direct investment in Uganda	4 555	...	...	...	**1.0**	**3.0**	**54.6**	**88.2**	**121.2**
Equity capital	4 560	...	...	...	...	...	49.6	78.2	86.2
Claims on direct investors	4 565	...	...	...	...	...	...	...	...
Liabilities to direct investors	4 570	...	...	...	...	...	...	...	...
Reinvested earnings	4 575	...	...	...	...	...	5.0	10.0	35.0
Other capital	4 580	...	...	...	1.0	3.0	...	...	...
Claims on direct investors	4 585	...	...	...	...	...	...	...	...
Liabilities to direct investors	4 590	...	...	...	...	...	...	...	...
B. PORTFOLIO INVESTMENT	4 600	...	...	...	...	...	...	...	...
Assets	4 602	...	...	...	...	...	...	...	...
Equity securities	4 610	...	...	...	...	...	...	...	...
Monetary authorities	4 611	...	...	...	...	...	...	...	...
General government	4 612	...	...	...	...	...	...	...	...
Banks	4 613	...	...	...	...	...	...	...	...
Other sectors	4 614	...	...	...	...	...	...	...	...
Debt securities	4 619	...	...	...	...	...	...	...	...
Bonds and notes	4 620	...	...	...	...	...	...	...	...
Monetary authorities	4 621	...	...	...	...	...	...	...	...
General government	4 622	...	...	...	...	...	...	...	...
Banks	4 623	...	...	...	...	...	...	...	...
Other sectors	4 624	...	...	...	...	...	...	...	...
Money market instruments	4 630	...	...	...	...	...	...	...	...
Monetary authorities	4 631	...	...	...	...	...	...	...	...
General government	4 632	...	...	...	...	...	...	...	...
Banks	4 633	...	...	...	...	...	...	...	...
Other sectors	4 634	...	...	...	...	...	...	...	...
Financial derivatives	4 640	...	...	...	...	...	...	...	...
Monetary authorities	4 641	...	...	...	...	...	...	...	...
General government	4 642	...	...	...	...	...	...	...	...
Banks	4 643	...	...	...	...	...	...	...	...
Other sectors	4 644	...	...	...	...	...	...	...	...
Liabilities	4 652	...	...	...	...	...	...	...	...
Equity securities	4 660	...	...	...	...	...	...	...	...
Banks	4 663	...	...	...	...	...	...	...	...
Other sectors	4 664	...	...	...	...	...	...	...	...
Debt securities	4 669	...	...	...	...	...	...	...	...
Bonds and notes	4 670	...	...	...	...	...	...	...	...
Monetary authorities	4 671	...	...	...	...	...	...	...	...
General government	4 672	...	...	...	...	...	...	...	...
Banks	4 673	...	...	...	...	...	...	...	...
Other sectors	4 674	...	...	...	...	...	...	...	...
Money market instruments	4 680	...	...	...	...	...	...	...	...
Monetary authorities	4 681	...	...	...	...	...	...	...	...
General government	4 682	...	...	...	...	...	...	...	...
Banks	4 683	...	...	...	...	...	...	...	...
Other sectors	4 684	...	...	...	...	...	...	...	...
Financial derivatives	4 690	...	...	...	...	...	...	...	...
Monetary authorities	4 691	...	...	...	...	...	...	...	...
General government	4 692	...	...	...	...	...	...	...	...
Banks	4 693	...	...	...	...	...	...	...	...
Other sectors	4 694	...	...	...	...	...	...	...	...

Table 2 (Concluded). STANDARD PRESENTATION, 1988–95
(Millions of U.S. dollars)

	Code	1988	1989	1990	1991	1992	1993	1994	1995
C. OTHER INVESTMENT	4 700	37.9	295.7	248.6	181.0	138.2	–93.6	118.7	138.6
Assets	4 703	**. . .**	**. . .**	**. . .**	**.4**	**1.8**	**–5.0**	**–40.3**	**–9.9**
Trade credits	4 706	. . .	. . .	. . .	. . .	. . .	12.7	4.5	. . .
General government: long-term	4 708	. . .	. . .	. . .	. . .	. . .	. . .	. . .	. . .
General government: short-term	4 709	. . .	. . .	. . .	. . .	. . .	. . .	. . .	. . .
Other sectors: long-term	4 711	. . .	. . .	. . .	. . .	. . .	. . .	. . .	. . .
Other sectors: short-term	4 712	. . .	. . .	. . .	. . .	. . .	12.7	4.5	. . .
Loans	4 714	. . .	. . .	. . .	. . .	. . .	. . .	. . .	. . .
Monetary authorities: long-term	4 717	. . .	. . .	. . .	. . .	. . .	. . .	. . .	. . .
Monetary authorities: short-term	4 718	. . .	. . .	. . .	. . .	. . .	. . .	. . .	. . .
General government: long-term	4 720	. . .	. . .	. . .	. . .	. . .	. . .	. . .	. . .
General government: short-term	4 721	. . .	. . .	. . .	. . .	. . .	. . .	. . .	. . .
Banks: long-term	4 723	. . .	. . .	. . .	. . .	. . .	. . .	. . .	. . .
Banks: short-term	4 724	. . .	. . .	. . .	. . .	. . .	. . .	. . .	. . .
Other sectors: long-term	4 726	. . .	. . .	. . .	. . .	. . .	. . .	. . .	. . .
Other sectors: short-term	4 727	. . .	. . .	. . .	. . .	. . .	. . .	. . .	. . .
Currency and deposits	4 730	. . .	. . .	. . .	.4	1.8	–17.7	–44.8	–9.9
Monetary authorities	4 731	. . .	. . .	. . .	. . .	. . .	. . .	. . .	. . .
General government	4 732	. . .	. . .	. . .	. . .	. . .	. . .	. . .	. . .
Banks	4 733	. . .	. . .	. . .	. . .	. . .	–8.7	–53.0	12.7
Other sectors	4 734	. . .	. . .	. . .	.4	1.8	–9.0	8.2	–22.6
Other assets	4 736	. . .	. . .	. . .	. . .	. . .	. . .	. . .	. . .
Monetary authorities: long-term	4 738	. . .	. . .	. . .	. . .	. . .	. . .	. . .	. . .
Monetary authorities: short-term	4 739	. . .	. . .	. . .	. . .	. . .	. . .	. . .	. . .
General government: long-term	4 741	. . .	. . .	. . .	. . .	. . .	. . .	. . .	. . .
General government: short-term	4 742	. . .	. . .	. . .	. . .	. . .	. . .	. . .	. . .
Banks: long-term	4 744	. . .	. . .	. . .	. . .	. . .	. . .	. . .	. . .
Banks: short-term	4 745	. . .	. . .	. . .	. . .	. . .	. . .	. . .	. . .
Other sectors: long-term	4 747	. . .	. . .	. . .	. . .	. . .	. . .	. . .	. . .
Other sectors: short-term	4 748	. . .	. . .	. . .	. . .	. . .	. . .	. . .	. . .
Liabilities	4 753	**37.9**	**295.7**	**248.6**	**180.5**	**136.4**	**–88.6**	**159.0**	**148.5**
Trade credits	4 756	. . .	. . .	. . .	. . .	. . .	–13.8	.5	–11.5
General government: long-term	4 758	. . .	. . .	. . .	. . .	. . .	. . .	. . .	. . .
General government: short-term	4 759	. . .	. . .	. . .	. . .	. . .	. . .	. . .	. . .
Other sectors: long-term	4 761	. . .	. . .	. . .	. . .	. . .	. . .	. . .	. . .
Other sectors: short-term	4 762	. . .	. . .	. . .	. . .	. . .	–13.8	.5	–11.5
Loans	4 764	67.8	297.6	294.4	212.1	177.1	118.4	144.1	160.6
Use of Fund credit and loans from the Fund	4 766	–7.8	–20.7	36.5	44.4	26.4	–9.8	27.1	27.5
Monetary authorities: other long-term	4 767	. . .	. . .	. . .	. . .	. . .	. . .	. . .	. . .
Monetary authorities: short-term	4 768	. . .	. . .	. . .	. . .	. . .	. . .	–.5	. . .
General government: long-term	4 770	61.3	340.1	252.2	167.8	150.7	166.4	141.9	135.6
General government: short-term	4 771	14.3	–21.8	5.7	. . .	. . .	–.5	–1.7	. . .
Banks: long-term	4 773	. . .	. . .	. . .	. . .	. . .	. . .	. . .	. . .
Banks: short-term	4 774	. . .	. . .	. . .	. . .	. . .	. . .	. . .	. . .
Other sectors: long-term	4 776	. . .	. . .	. . .	. . .	. . .	–37.7	–22.7	–2.5
Other sectors: short-term	4 777	. . .	. . .	. . .	. . .	. . .	. . .	. . .	. . .
Currency and deposits	4 780	. . .	40.6	–26.3	–9.6	–22.8	. . .	. . .	. . .
Monetary authorities	4 781	. . .	. . .	. . .	. . .	. . .	. . .	. . .	. . .
General government	4 782	. . .	. . .	. . .	. . .	. . .	. . .	. . .	. . .
Banks	4 783	. . .	40.6	–26.3	–9.6	–22.8	. . .	. . .	. . .
Other sectors	4 784	. . .	. . .	. . .	. . .	. . .	. . .	. . .	. . .
Other liabilities	4 786	–29.9	–42.5	–19.5	–22.0	–17.9	–193.2	14.4	–.6
Monetary authorities: long-term	4 788	–42.1	–19.5	–.3	. . .	. . .	. . .	. . .	. . .
Monetary authorities: short-term	4 789	. . .	. . .	. . .	–.2	–6.6	. . .	1.4	1.7
General government: long-term	4 791	. . .	. . .	. . .	. . .	. . .	. . .	. . .	. . .
General government: short-term	4 792	42.1	18.4	.3	. . .	. . .	–193.2	13.0	–2.3
Banks: long-term	4 794	. . .	. . .	. . .	. . .	. . .	. . .	. . .	. . .
Banks: short-term	4 795	. . .	. . .	. . .	. . .	. . .	. . .	. . .	. . .
Other sectors: long-term	4 797	. . .	. . .	. . .	. . .	. . .	. . .	. . .	. . .
Other sectors: short-term	4 798	–29.9	–41.4	–19.5	–21.8	–11.3	. . .	. . .	. . .
D. RESERVE ASSETS	4 800	2.4	1.8	5.2	–12.7	–50.6	–51.8	–175.0	–137.4
Monetary gold	4 810	. . .	. . .	. . .	. . .	. . .	. . .	. . .	. . .
Special drawing rights	4 820	.1	–.5	–6.4	–3.2	1.2	9.1	–3.0	2.7
Reserve position in the Fund	4 830	. . .	. . .	. . .	. . .	. . .	. . .	. . .	. . .
Foreign exchange	4 840	2.3	2.3	11.6	–9.5	–51.8	–60.9	–172.0	–140.1
Other claims	4 880	. . .	. . .	. . .	. . .	. . .	. . .	. . .	. . .
NET ERRORS AND OMISSIONS	4 998	**154.9**	**–38.0**	**9.5**	**.6**	**9.0**	**–11.1**	**52.5**	**47.5**

Table 1. ANALYTIC PRESENTATION, 1988–95
(Millions of U.S. dollars)

	Code	1988	1989	1990	1991	1992	1993	1994	1995
A. Current Account [1]	4 993 Y .	**. . .**	**. . .**	**. . .**	**. . .**	**. . .**	**. . .**	**–1,163.0**	**–1,152.0**
Goods: exports f.o.b	2 100 . .	. . .	. . .	. . .	. . .	. . .	. . .	13,894.0	14,244.0
Goods: imports f.o.b	3 100 . .	. . .	. . .	. . .	. . .	. . .	. . .	–16,469.0	–16,946.0
Balance on Goods	4 100 . .	. . .	. . .	. . .	. . .	. . .	. . .	*–2,575.0*	*–2,702.0*
Services: credit	2 200 . .	. . .	. . .	. . .	. . .	. . .	. . .	2,747.0	2,846.0
Services: debit	3 200 . .	. . .	. . .	. . .	. . .	. . .	. . .	–1,538.0	–1,334.0
Balance on Goods and Services	4 991 . .	. . .	. . .	. . .	. . .	. . .	. . .	*–1,366.0*	*–1,190.0*
Income: credit	2 300 . .	. . .	. . .	. . .	. . .	. . .	. . .	56.0	247.0
Income: debit	3 300 . .	. . .	. . .	. . .	. . .	. . .	. . .	–400.0	–681.0
Balance on Goods, Services, and Income	4 992 . .	. . .	. . .	. . .	. . .	. . .	. . .	*–1,710.0*	*–1,624.0*
Current transfers: credit	2 379 Y .	. . .	. . .	. . .	. . .	. . .	. . .	583.0	557.0
Current transfers: debit	3 379 . .	. . .	. . .	. . .	. . .	. . .	. . .	–36.0	–85.0
B. Capital Account [1]	4 994 Y .	**. . .**	**. . .**	**. . .**	**. . .**	**. . .**	**. . .**	**97.0**	**6.0**
Capital account: credit	2 994 Y .	. . .	. . .	. . .	. . .	. . .	. . .	106.0	6.0
Capital account: debit	3 994 . .	. . .	. . .	. . .	. . .	. . .	. . .	–9.0	. . .
Total, Groups A Plus B	4 010 . .	. . .	. . .	. . .	. . .	. . .	. . .	*–1,066.0*	*–1,146.0*
C. Financial Account [1]	4 995 X .	**. . .**	**. . .**	**. . .**	**. . .**	**. . .**	**. . .**	**–557.0**	**–526.0**
Direct investment abroad	4 505 . .	. . .	. . .	. . .	. . .	. . .	. . .	–8.0	–10.0
Direct investment in Ukraine	4 555 Y .	. . .	. . .	. . .	. . .	. . .	. . .	159.0	267.0
Portfolio investment assets	4 602 . .	. . .	. . .	. . .	. . .	. . .	. . .	. . .	–12.0
Equity securities	4 610 . .	. . .	. . .	. . .	. . .	. . .	. . .	. . .	. . .
Debt securities	4 619 . .	. . .	. . .	. . .	. . .	. . .	. . .	. . .	. . .
Portfolio investment liabilities	4 652 Y .	. . .	. . .	. . .	. . .	. . .	. . .	. . .	16.0
Equity securities	4 660 Y .	. . .	. . .	. . .	. . .	. . .	. . .	. . .	. . .
Debt securities	4 669 Y .	. . .	. . .	. . .	. . .	. . .	. . .	. . .	16.0
Other investment assets	4 703 . .	. . .	. . .	. . .	. . .	. . .	. . .	–3,026.0	–1,574.0
Monetary authorities	4 703 . A	. . .	. . .	. . .	. . .	. . .	. . .	. . .	. . .
General government	4 703 . B	. . .	. . .	. . .	. . .	. . .	. . .	. . .	. . .
Banks	4 703 . C	. . .	. . .	. . .	. . .	. . .	. . .	. . .	12.0
Other sectors	4 703 . D	. . .	. . .	. . .	. . .	. . .	. . .	–2,247.0	–1,246.0
Other investment liabilities	4 753 X .	. . .	. . .	. . .	. . .	. . .	. . .	2,318.0	787.0
Monetary authorities	4 753 XA	. . .	. . .	. . .	. . .	. . .	. . .	. . .	. . .
General government	4 753 YB	. . .	. . .	. . .	. . .	. . .	. . .	–1,097.0	–583.0
Banks	4 753 YC	. . .	. . .	. . .	. . .	. . .	. . .	577.0	724.0
Other sectors	4 753 YD	. . .	. . .	. . .	. . .	. . .	. . .	2,838.0	646.0
Total, Groups A Through C	4 020 . .	. . .	. . .	. . .	. . .	. . .	. . .	*–1,623.0*	*–1,672.0*
D. Net Errors and Omissions	4 998 . .	**. . .**	**. . .**	**. . .**	**. . .**	**. . .**	**. . .**	**423.5**	**48.2**
Total, Groups A Through D	4 030 . .	. . .	. . .	. . .	. . .	. . .	. . .	*–1,199.5*	*–1,623.8*
E. Reserves and Related Items	4 040 . .	**. . .**	**. . .**	**. . .**	**. . .**	**. . .**	**. . .**	**1,199.5**	**1,623.8**
Reserve assets	4 800 . .	. . .	. . .	. . .	. . .	. . .	. . .	–548.8	–468.5
Use of Fund credit and loans	4 766 . .	. . .	. . .	. . .	. . .	. . .	. . .	368.3	1,221.3
Liabilities constituting foreign authorities' reserves	4 900 . .	. . .	. . .	. . .	. . .	. . .	. . .	. . .	. . .
Exceptional financing	4 920 . .	. . .	. . .	. . .	. . .	. . .	. . .	1,380.0	871.0
Conversion rates: hryvnias per U.S. dollar	0 101 . .	**. . .**	**. . .**	**. . .**	**. . .**	**. . .**	**.05**	**.33**	**1.47**

[1] Excludes components that have been classified in the categories of Group E.

Table 2. STANDARD PRESENTATION, 1988–95

(Millions of U.S. dollars)

	Code	1988	1989	1990	1991	1992	1993	1994	1995
CURRENT ACCOUNT	4 993 . .	**...**	**...**	**...**	**...**	**...**	**...**	**–1,163.0**	**–1,152.0**
A. GOODS	4 100 . .	...	...	...	...	...	...	–2,575.0	–2,702.0
Credit	2 100 . .	**...**	**...**	**...**	**...**	**...**	**...**	**13,894.0**	**14,244.0**
General merchandise: exports f.o.b.	2 110 . .	...	...	...	...	...	...	13,221.0	13,149.0
Goods for processing: exports f.o.b.	2 150 . .	...	...	...	...	...	...	598.0	1,046.0
Repairs on goods	2 160 . .	...	...	...	...	...	...	75.0	49.0
Goods procured in ports by carriers	2 170 . .	...	...	...	...	...	...	...	...
Nonmonetary gold	2 180 . .	...	...	...	...	...	...	...	...
Debit	3 100 . .	**...**	**...**	**...**	**...**	**...**	**...**	**–16,469.0**	**–16,946.0**
General merchandise: imports f.o.b.	3 110 . .	...	...	...	...	...	...	–15,705.0	–15,480.0
Goods for processing: imports f.o.b.	3 150 . .	...	...	...	...	...	...	–756.0	–1,376.0
Repairs on goods	3 160 . .	...	...	...	...	...	...	–8.0	–61.0
Goods procured in ports by carriers	3 170 . .	...	...	...	...	...	...	...	–29.0
Nonmonetary gold	3 180 . .	...	...	...	...	...	...	...	...
B. SERVICES	4 200 . .	...	...	...	...	...	...	1,209.0	1,512.0
Total credit	2 200 . .	...	...	...	...	...	...	*2,747.0*	*2,846.0*
Total debit	3 200 . .	...	...	...	...	...	...	*–1,538.0*	*–1,334.0*
Transportation services, credit	2 205 . .	**...**	**...**	**...**	**...**	**...**	**...**	**1,894.0**	**2,152.0**
Passenger	2 205 BA	...	...	...	...	...	...	...	...
Freight	2 205 BB	...	...	...	...	...	...	...	...
Other	2 205 BC	...	...	...	...	...	...	...	...
Sea transport, passenger	2 207 . .	...	...	...	...	...	...	...	...
Sea transport, freight	2 208 . .	...	...	...	...	...	...	...	...
Sea transport, other	2 209 . .	...	...	...	...	...	...	...	...
Air transport, passenger	2 211 . .	...	...	...	...	...	...	...	...
Air transport, freight	2 212 . .	...	...	...	...	...	...	...	...
Air transport, other	2 213 . .	...	...	...	...	...	...	...	...
Other transport, passenger	2 215 . .	...	...	...	...	...	...	...	...
Other transport, freight	2 216 . .	...	...	...	...	...	...	...	...
Other transport, other	2 217 . .	...	...	...	...	...	...	...	...
Transportation services, debit	3 205 . .	**...**	**...**	**...**	**...**	**...**	**...**	**–244.0**	**–454.0**
Passenger	3 205 BA	...	...	...	...	...	...	...	...
Freight	3 205 BB	...	...	...	...	...	...	...	...
Other	3 205 BC	...	...	...	...	...	...	...	...
Sea transport, passenger	3 207 . .	...	...	...	...	...	...	...	...
Sea transport, freight	3 208 . .	...	...	...	...	...	...	...	...
Sea transport, other	3 209 . .	...	...	...	...	...	...	...	...
Air transport, passenger	3 211 . .	...	...	...	...	...	...	...	...
Air transport, freight	3 212 . .	...	...	...	...	...	...	...	...
Air transport, other	3 213 . .	...	...	...	...	...	...	...	...
Other transport, passenger	3 215 . .	...	...	...	...	...	...	...	...
Other transport, freight	3 216 . .	...	...	...	...	...	...	...	...
Other transport, other	3 217 . .	...	...	...	...	...	...	...	...
Travel, credit	2 236 . .	**...**	**...**	**...**	**...**	**...**	**...**	**175.0**	**191.0**
Business travel	2 237 . .	...	...	...	...	...	...	...	...
Personal travel	2 240 . .	...	...	...	...	...	...	...	...
Travel, debit	3 236 . .	**...**	**...**	**...**	**...**	**...**	**...**	**–141.0**	**–210.0**
Business travel	3 237 . .	...	...	...	...	...	...	...	...
Personal travel	3 240 . .	...	...	...	...	...	...	...	...
Other services, credit	2 200 BA	**...**	**...**	**...**	**...**	**...**	**...**	**678.0**	**503.0**
Communications	2 245 . .	...	...	...	...	...	...	74.0	176.0
Construction	2 249 . .	...	...	...	...	...	...	26.0	31.0
Insurance	2 253 . .	...	...	...	...	...	...	...	...
Financial	2 260 . .	...	...	...	...	...	...	186.0	76.0
Computer and information	2 262 . .	...	...	...	...	...	...	...	...
Royalties and licence fees	2 266 . .	...	...	...	...	...	...	...	...
Other business services	2 268 . .	...	...	...	...	...	...	392.0	220.0
Personal, cultural, and recreational	2 287 . .	...	...	...	...	...	...	...	...
Government, n.i.e.	2 291 . .	...	...	...	...	...	...	...	...
Other services, debit	3 200 BA	**...**	**...**	**...**	**...**	**...**	**...**	**–1,153.0**	**–670.0**
Communications	3 245 . .	...	...	...	...	...	...	–76.0	–212.0
Construction	3 249 . .	...	...	...	...	...	...	–163.0	–36.0
Insurance	3 253 . .	...	...	...	...	...	...	...	...
Financial	3 260 . .	...	...	...	...	...	...	–215.0	–98.0
Computer and information	3 262 . .	...	...	...	...	...	...	...	...
Royalties and licence fees	3 266 . .	...	...	...	...	...	...	...	...
Other business services	3 268 . .	...	...	...	...	...	...	–699.0	–324.0
Personal, cultural, and recreational	3 287 . .	...	...	...	...	...	...	...	...
Government, n.i.e.	3 291 . .	...	...	...	...	...	...	...	...

Table 2 (Continued). STANDARD PRESENTATION, 1988–95
(Millions of U.S. dollars)

	Code	1988	1989	1990	1991	1992	1993	1994	1995
C. INCOME	4 300	...	...	...	...	...	...	–344.0	–434.0
Total credit	2 300	...	...	...	...	...	...	*56.0*	*247.0*
Total debit	3 300	...	...	...	...	...	...	*–400.0*	*–681.0*
Compensation of employees, credit	2 310	...	...	...	...	...	...	...	...
Compensation of employees, debit	3 310	...	...	...	...	...	...	...	...
Investment income, credit	2 320	...	...	...	...	...	...	...	...
Direct investment income	2 330	...	...	...	...	...	...	...	...
Dividends and distributed branch profits	2 332	...	...	...	...	...	...	...	...
Reinvested earnings and undistributed branch profits	2 333	...	...	...	...	...	...	...	...
Income on debt (interest)	2 334	...	...	...	...	...	...	...	...
Portfolio investment income	2 339	...	...	...	...	...	...	...	...
Income on equity	2 340	...	...	...	...	...	...	...	...
Income on bonds and notes	2 350	...	...	...	...	...	...	...	...
Income on money market instruments and financial derivatives	2 360	...	...	...	...	...	...	...	...
Other investment income	2 370	...	...	...	...	...	...	...	...
Investment income, debit	3 320	...	...	...	...	...	...	...	...
Direct investment income	3 330	...	...	...	...	...	...	...	...
Dividends and distributed branch profits	3 332	...	...	...	...	...	...	...	...
Reinvested earnings and undistributed branch profits	3 333	...	...	...	...	...	...	...	...
Income on debt (interest)	3 334	...	...	...	...	...	...	...	...
Portfolio investment income	3 339	...	...	...	...	...	...	...	...
Income on equity	3 340	...	...	...	...	...	...	...	...
Income on bonds and notes	3 350	...	...	...	...	...	...	...	...
Income on money market instruments and financial derivatives	3 360	...	...	...	...	...	...	...	...
Other investment income	3 370	...	...	...	...	...	...	...	...
D. CURRENT TRANSFERS	4 379	...	...	...	...	...	...	547.0	472.0
Credit	2 379	...	...	...	...	...	...	**583.0**	**557.0**
General government	2 380	...	...	...	...	...	...	...	...
Other sectors	2 390	...	...	...	...	...	...	...	...
Workers' remittances	2 391	...	...	...	...	...	...	...	...
Other current transfers	2 392	...	...	...	...	...	...	...	...
Debit	3 379	...	...	...	...	...	...	**–36.0**	**–85.0**
General government	3 380	...	...	...	...	...	...	...	...
Other sectors	3 390	...	...	...	...	...	...	...	...
Workers' remittances	3 391	...	...	...	...	...	...	...	...
Other current transfers	3 392	...	...	...	...	...	...	...	...
CAPITAL AND FINANCIAL ACCOUNT	4 996	...	...	...	...	...	...	**739.5**	**1,103.8**
CAPITAL ACCOUNT	4 994	...	...	...	...	...	...	**97.0**	**6.0**
Total credit	2 994	...	...	...	...	...	...	*106.0*	*6.0*
Total debit	3 994	...	...	...	...	...	...	*–9.0*	...
Capital transfers, credit	2 400	...	...	...	...	...	...	**106.0**	**6.0**
General government	2 401	...	...	...	...	...	...	...	6.0
Debt forgiveness	2 402	...	...	...	...	...	...	...	6.0
Other capital transfers	2 410	...	...	...	...	...	...	...	...
Other sectors	2 430	...	...	...	...	...	...	...	...
Migrants' transfers	2 431	...	...	...	...	...	...	...	...
Debt forgiveness	2 432	...	...	...	...	...	...	...	...
Other capital transfers	2 440	...	...	...	...	...	...	...	...
Capital transfers, debit	3 400	...	...	...	...	...	...	**–9.0**	...
General government	3 401	...	...	...	...	...	...	...	...
Debt forgiveness	3 402	...	...	...	...	...	...	...	...
Other capital transfers	3 410	...	...	...	...	...	...	...	...
Other sectors	3 430	...	...	...	...	...	...	...	...
Migrants' transfers	3 431	...	...	...	...	...	...	...	...
Debt forgiveness	3 432	...	...	...	...	...	...	...	...
Other capital transfers	3 440	...	...	...	...	...	...	...	...
Nonproduced nonfinancial assets, credit	2 480	...	...	...	...	...	...	...	...
Nonproduced nonfinancial assets, debit	3 480	...	...	...	...	...	...	...	...

Table 2 (Continued). STANDARD PRESENTATION, 1988–95
(Millions of U.S. dollars)

	Code	1988	1989	1990	1991	1992	1993	1994	1995
FINANCIAL ACCOUNT	4 995	**...**	**...**	**...**	**...**	**...**	**...**	**642.5**	**1,097.8**
A. DIRECT INVESTMENT	4 500	...	...	...	...	...	...	151.0	257.0
Direct investment abroad	4 505	**...**	**...**	**...**	**...**	**...**	**...**	**–8.0**	**–10.0**
Equity capital	4 510	...	...	...	...	...	...	...	...
Claims on affiliated enterprises	4 515	...	...	...	...	...	...	...	...
Liabilities to affiliated enterprises	4 520	...	...	...	...	...	...	...	...
Reinvested earnings	4 525	...	...	...	...	...	...	...	...
Other capital	4 530	...	...	...	...	...	...	...	...
Claims on affiliated enterprises	4 535	...	...	...	...	...	...	...	...
Liabilities to affiliated enterprises	4 540	...	...	...	...	...	...	...	...
Direct investment in Ukraine	4 555	**...**	**...**	**...**	**...**	**...**	**...**	**159.0**	**267.0**
Equity capital	4 560	...	...	...	...	...	...	...	...
Claims on direct investors	4 565	...	...	...	...	...	...	...	...
Liabilities to direct investors	4 570	...	...	...	...	...	...	...	...
Reinvested earnings	4 575	...	...	...	...	...	...	...	...
Other capital	4 580	...	...	...	...	...	...	...	...
Claims on direct investors	4 585	...	...	...	...	...	...	...	...
Liabilities to direct investors	4 590	...	...	...	...	...	...	...	...
B. PORTFOLIO INVESTMENT	4 600	...	...	...	...	...	...	...	4.0
Assets	4 602	**...**	**...**	**...**	**...**	**...**	**...**	**...**	**–12.0**
Equity securities	4 610	...	...	...	...	...	...	...	...
Monetary authorities	4 611	...	...	...	...	...	...	...	...
General government	4 612	...	...	...	...	...	...	...	...
Banks	4 613	...	...	...	...	...	...	...	...
Other sectors	4 614	...	...	...	...	...	...	...	...
Debt securities	4 619	...	...	...	...	...	...	...	...
Bonds and notes	4 620	...	...	...	...	...	...	...	...
Monetary authorities	4 621	...	...	...	...	...	...	...	...
General government	4 622	...	...	...	...	...	...	...	...
Banks	4 623	...	...	...	...	...	...	...	...
Other sectors	4 624	...	...	...	...	...	...	...	...
Money market instruments	4 630	...	...	...	...	...	...	...	...
Monetary authorities	4 631	...	...	...	...	...	...	...	...
General government	4 632	...	...	...	...	...	...	...	...
Banks	4 633	...	...	...	...	...	...	...	...
Other sectors	4 634	...	...	...	...	...	...	...	...
Financial derivatives	4 640	...	...	...	...	...	...	...	...
Monetary authorities	4 641	...	...	...	...	...	...	...	...
General government	4 642	...	...	...	...	...	...	...	...
Banks	4 643	...	...	...	...	...	...	...	...
Other sectors	4 644	...	...	...	...	...	...	...	...
Liabilities	4 652	**...**	**...**	**...**	**...**	**...**	**...**	**...**	**16.0**
Equity securities	4 660	...	...	...	...	...	...	...	...
Banks	4 663	...	...	...	...	...	...	...	...
Other sectors	4 664	...	...	...	...	...	...	...	...
Debt securities	4 669	...	...	...	...	...	...	...	16.0
Bonds and notes	4 670	...	...	...	...	...	...	...	16.0
Monetary authorities	4 671	...	...	...	...	...	...	...	...
General government	4 672	...	...	...	...	...	...	...	16.0
Banks	4 673	...	...	...	...	...	...	...	...
Other sectors	4 674	...	...	...	...	...	...	...	...
Money market instruments	4 680	...	...	...	...	...	...	...	...
Monetary authorities	4 681	...	...	...	...	...	...	...	...
General government	4 682	...	...	...	...	...	...	...	...
Banks	4 683	...	...	...	...	...	...	...	...
Other sectors	4 684	...	...	...	...	...	...	...	...
Financial derivatives	4 690	...	...	...	...	...	...	...	...
Monetary authorities	4 691	...	...	...	...	...	...	...	...
General government	4 692	...	...	...	...	...	...	...	...
Banks	4 693	...	...	...	...	...	...	...	...
Other sectors	4 694	...	...	...	...	...	...	...	...

Table 2 (Concluded). STANDARD PRESENTATION, 1988–95
(Millions of U.S. dollars)

	Code	1988	1989	1990	1991	1992	1993	1994	1995
C. OTHER INVESTMENT	4 700	...	...	...	...	...	...	1,040.3	1,305.3
Assets	4 703	**...**	**...**	**...**	**...**	**...**	**...**	**–3,026.0**	**–1,574.0**
Trade credits	4 706	...	...	...	...	...	...	...	...
General government: long-term	4 708	...	...	...	...	...	...	...	...
General government: short-term	4 709	...	...	...	...	...	...	...	...
Other sectors: long-term	4 711	...	...	...	...	...	...	...	...
Other sectors: short-term	4 712	...	...	...	...	...	...	...	...
Loans	4 714	...	...	...	...	...	...	...	12.0
Monetary authorities: long-term	4 717	...	...	...	...	...	...	...	...
Monetary authorities: short-term	4 718	...	...	...	...	...	...	...	...
General government: long-term	4 720	...	...	...	...	...	...	...	...
General government: short-term	4 721	...	...	...	...	...	...	...	...
Banks: long-term	4 723	...	...	...	...	...	...	...	...
Banks: short-term	4 724	...	...	...	...	...	...	...	12.0
Other sectors: long-term	4 726	...	...	...	...	...	...	...	...
Other sectors: short-term	4 727	...	...	...	...	...	...	...	...
Currency and deposits	4 730	...	...	...	...	...	...	–779.0	–340.0
Monetary authorities	4 731	...	...	...	...	...	...	...	...
General government	4 732	...	...	...	...	...	...	...	...
Banks	4 733	...	...	...	...	...	...	...	...
Other sectors	4 734	...	...	...	...	...	...	...	...
Other assets	4 736	...	...	...	...	...	...	–2,247.0	–1,246.0
Monetary authorities: long-term	4 738	...	...	...	...	...	...	...	...
Monetary authorities: short-term	4 739	...	...	...	...	...	...	...	...
General government: long-term	4 741	...	...	...	...	...	...	...	...
General government: short-term	4 742	...	...	...	...	...	...	...	...
Banks: long-term	4 744	...	...	...	...	...	...	...	...
Banks: short-term	4 745	...	...	...	...	...	...	...	...
Other sectors: long-term	4 747	...	...	...	...	...	...	–2,247.0	...
Other sectors: short-term	4 748	...	...	...	...	...	...	...	–1,246.0
Liabilities	4 753	**...**	**...**	**...**	**...**	**...**	**...**	**4,066.3**	**2,879.3**
Trade credits	4 756	...	...	...	...	...	...	...	...
General government: long-term	4 758	...	...	...	...	...	...	...	...
General government: short-term	4 759	...	...	...	...	...	...	...	...
Other sectors: long-term	4 761	...	...	...	...	...	...	...	...
Other sectors: short-term	4 762	...	...	...	...	...	...	...	...
Loans	4 764	...	...	...	...	...	...	28.3	3,932.3
Use of Fund credit and loans from the Fund	4 766	...	...	...	...	...	...	368.3	1,221.3
Monetary authorities: other long term	4 767	...	...	...	...	...	...	...	...
Monetary authorities: short-term	4 768	...	...	...	...	...	...	...	...
General government: long-term	4 770	...	...	...	...	...	...	–374.0	2,459.0
General government: short-term	4 771	...	...	...	...	...	...	...	...
Banks: long-term	4 773	...	...	...	...	...	...	...	...
Banks: short-term	4 774	...	...	...	...	...	...	...	220.0
Other sectors: long-term	4 776	...	...	...	...	...	...	34.0	32.0
Other sectors: short-term	4 777	...	...	...	...	...	...	...	...
Currency and deposits	4 780	...	...	...	...	...	...	577.0	504.0
Monetary authorities	4 781	...	...	...	...	...	...	...	...
General government	4 782	...	...	...	...	...	...	...	...
Banks	4 783	...	...	...	...	...	...	577.0	504.0
Other sectors	4 784	...	...	...	...	...	...	...	...
Other liabilities	4 786	...	...	...	...	...	...	3,461.0	–1,557.0
Monetary authorities: long-term	4 788	...	...	...	...	...	...	...	...
Monetary authorities: short-term	4 789	...	...	...	...	...	...	...	...
General government: long-term	4 791	...	...	...	...	...	...	...	...
General government: short-term	4 792	...	...	...	...	...	...	658.0	–2,169.0
Banks: long-term	4 794	...	...	...	...	...	...	...	...
Banks: short-term	4 795	...	...	...	...	...	...	...	...
Other sectors: long-term	4 797	...	...	...	...	...	...	...	...
Other sectors: short-term	4 798	...	...	...	...	...	...	2,803.0	612.0
D. RESERVE ASSETS	4 800	...	...	...	...	...	...	–548.8	–468.5
Monetary gold	4 810	...	...	...	...	...	...	–7.0	...
Special drawing rights	4 820	...	...	...	...	...	...	–182.8	36.5
Reserve position in the Fund	4 830	...	...	...	...	...	...	...	...
Foreign exchange	4 840	...	...	...	...	...	...	–359.0	–505.0
Other claims	4 880	...	...	...	...	...	...	...	...
NET ERRORS AND OMISSIONS	4 998	**...**	**...**	**...**	**...**	**...**	**...**	**423.5**	**48.2**

Part 3 of the *Yearbook* contains descriptions of the methodologies, compilation practices, and sources used to compile these data.

Table 1. ANALYTIC PRESENTATION, 1988–95
(Billions of U.S. dollars)

	Code	1988	1989	1990	1991	1992	1993	1994	1995
A. Current Account[1]	4 993 Y.	**–29.32**	**–36.66**	**–32.50**	**–14.26**	**–18.35**	**–16.21**	**–3.50**	**–4.63**
Goods: exports f.o.b	2 100 ..	143.08	150.70	181.73	182.58	188.45	182.06	206.46	240.38
Goods: imports f.o.b	3 100 ..	–181.24	–191.24	–214.47	–200.85	–211.88	–202.30	–222.94	–258.77
Balance on Goods	4 100 ..	*–38.16*	*–40.54*	*–32.74*	*–18.27*	*–23.43*	*–20.24*	*–16.49*	*–18.39*
Services: credit	2 200 ..	47.82	47.93	56.23	54.32	61.50	57.91	63.47	71.40
Services: debit	3 200 ..	–40.76	–42.40	–49.67	–47.99	–52.86	–49.68	–56.20	–61.72
Balance on Goods and Services	4 991 ..	*–31.10*	*–35.02*	*–26.18*	*–11.94*	*–14.79*	*–12.00*	*–9.22*	*–8.70*
Income: credit	2 300 ..	100.59	121.00	141.44	136.07	120.51	111.19	119.43	146.94
Income: debit	3 300 ..	–92.48	–115.19	–139.02	–135.93	–114.98	–107.89	–106.07	–131.87
Balance on Goods, Services, and Income	4 992 ..	*–22.99*	*–29.21*	*–23.76*	*–11.80*	*–9.25*	*–8.71*	*4.13*	*6.37*
Current transfers: credit	2 379 Y.	6.82	6.42	7.22	12.06	8.52	8.31	8.57	9.68
Current transfers: debit	3 379 ..	–13.15	–13.88	–15.96	–14.52	–17.62	–15.81	–16.20	–20.69
B. Capital Account[1]	4 994 Y.	**. . .**	**. . .**	**. . .**	**. . .**	**. . .**	**. . .**	**. . .**	**. . .**
Capital account: credit	2 994 Y.	. . .	. . .	. . .	. . .	. . .	. . .	. . .	. . .
Capital account: debit	3 994 ..	. . .	. . .	. . .	. . .	. . .	. . .	. . .	. . .
Total, Groups A Plus B	4 010 ..	*–29.32*	*–36.66*	*–32.50*	*–14.26*	*–18.35*	*–16.21*	*–3.50*	*–4.63*
C. Financial Account[1]	4 995 X.	**25.11**	**15.30**	**26.64**	**27.06**	**.31**	**13.43**	**–23.32**	**.18**
Direct investment abroad	4 505 ..	–37.29	–35.48	–19.32	–16.31	–18.99	–25.52	–28.28	–40.33
Direct investment in United Kingdom	4 555 Y.	21.41	30.55	32.43	16.21	16.14	15.54	10.30	32.21
Portfolio investment assets	4 602 ..	–19.62	–63.02	–32.63	–55.56	–50.85	–131.01	31.83	–67.50
Equity securities	4 610 ..	–9.98	–25.71	–1.02	–24.45	7.60	–13.60	–.69	–15.96
Debt securities	4 619 ..	–9.64	–37.31	–31.62	–31.11	–58.45	–117.41	32.52	–51.54
Portfolio investment liabilities	4 652 Y.	51.49	28.73	24.89	12.42	22.94	41.02	52.25	57.92
Equity securities	4 660 Y.	9.35	9.87	2.81	4.41	18.04	25.70	5.81	5.07
Debt securities	4 669 Y.	42.14	18.86	22.07	8.00	4.90	15.32	46.44	52.85
Other investment assets	4 703 ..	–40.02	–59.60	–94.58	43.10	–79.18	–75.48	–57.92	–87.90
Monetary authorities	4 703 .A	. . .	. . .	. . .	. . .	. . .	. . .	. . .	. . .
General government	4 703 .B	–1.58	–1.43	–1.83	–1.58	–1.19	–.91	–.95	–1.01
Banks	4 703 .C	–33.48	–48.86	–68.86	59.45	–44.93	6.07	–82.32	–38.15
Other sectors	4 703 .D	–4.97	–9.32	–23.89	–14.77	–33.06	–80.64	25.36	–48.75
Other investment liabilities	4 753 X.	49.12	114.12	115.86	27.20	110.24	188.87	–31.50	105.78
Monetary authorities	4 753 XA	.08	.09	–.07	.07	.13	.08	.13	.07
General government	4 753 YB	.19	–.30	–.11	–1.49	–.69	–.36	1.03	.34
Banks	4 753 YC	42.64	72.60	88.69	–6.87	52.32	50.47	55.10	34.93
Other sectors	4 753 YD	6.21	41.73	27.35	35.50	58.49	138.68	–87.76	70.43
Total, Groups A Through C	4 020 ..	*–4.22*	*–21.36*	*–5.86*	*12.80*	*–18.04*	*–2.79*	*–26.82*	*–4.46*
D. Net Errors and Omissions	4 998 ..	**2.72**	**5.77**	**3.33**	**.45**	**10.60**	**–3.60**	**7.64**	**3.49**
Total, Groups A Through D	4 030 ..	*–1.49*	*–15.60*	*–2.53*	*13.25*	*–7.44*	*–6.38*	*–19.18*	*–.96*
E. Reserves and Related Items	4 040 ..	**1.49**	**15.60**	**2.53**	**–13.25**	**7.44**	**6.38**	**19.18**	**.96**
Reserve assets	4 800 ..	–4.89	8.80	–.12	–4.66	2.43	–1.26	–1.48	.90
Use of Fund credit and loans	4 766 ..	. . .	. . .	. . .	. . .	. . .	. . .	. . .	. . .
Liabilities constituting foreign authorities' reserves	4 900 ..	6.43	7.78	2.56	–8.55	.55	11.49	20.56	–.08
Exceptional financing	4 920 ..	–.05	–.99	.09	–.04	4.46	–3.85	.10	.15
Conversion rates: pound sterling per U.S. dollar	0 101 ..	**.56217**	**.61117**	**.56318**	**.56702**	**.56977**	**.66676**	**.65343**	**.63367**

[1] Excludes components that have been classified in the categories of Group E.

Table 2. STANDARD PRESENTATION, 1988–95
(Billions of U.S. dollars)

	Code	1988	1989	1990	1991	1992	1993	1994	1995
CURRENT ACCOUNT	4 993 . .	**–29.32**	**–36.66**	**–32.50**	**–14.26**	**–18.35**	**–16.21**	**–3.50**	**–4.63**
A. GOODS	4 100 . .	–38.16	–40.54	–32.74	–18.27	–23.43	–20.24	–16.49	–18.39
Credit	2 100 . .	**143.08**	**150.70**	**181.73**	**182.58**	**188.45**	**182.06**	**206.46**	**240.38**
General merchandise: exports f.o.b.	2 110 . .	143.08	150.70	181.73	182.58	188.45	182.06	206.46	240.38
Goods for processing: exports f.o.b.	2 150 . .	. . .	. . .	. . .	. . .	. . .	. . .	. . .	. . .
Repairs on goods	2 160 . .	. . .	. . .	. . .	. . .	. . .	. . .	. . .	. . .
Goods procured in ports by carriers	2 170 . .	. . .	. . .	. . .	. . .	. . .	. . .	. . .	. . .
Nonmonetary gold	2 180 . .	. . .	. . .	. . .	. . .	. . .	. . .	. . .	. . .
Debit	3 100 . .	**–181.24**	**–191.24**	**–214.47**	**–200.85**	**–211.88**	**–202.30**	**–222.94**	**–258.77**
General merchandise: imports f.o.b.	3 110 . .	–181.24	–191.24	–214.47	–200.85	–211.88	–202.30	–222.94	–258.77
Goods for processing: imports f.o.b.	3 150 . .	. . .	. . .	. . .	. . .	. . .	. . .	. . .	. . .
Repairs on goods	3 160 . .	. . .	. . .	. . .	. . .	. . .	. . .	. . .	. . .
Goods procured in ports by carriers	3 170 . .	. . .	. . .	. . .	. . .	. . .	. . .	. . .	. . .
Nonmonetary gold	3 180 . .	. . .	. . .	. . .	. . .	. . .	. . .	. . .	. . .
B. SERVICES	4 200 . .	7.06	5.53	6.56	6.33	8.64	8.24	7.27	9.68
Total credit	2 200 . .	*47.82*	*47.93*	*56.23*	*54.32*	*61.50*	*57.91*	*63.47*	*71.40*
Total debit	3 200 . .	*–40.76*	*–42.40*	*–49.67*	*–47.99*	*–52.86*	*–49.68*	*–56.20*	*–61.72*
Transportation services, credit	2 205 . .	**11.54**	**11.98**	**14.19**	**13.18**	**14.51**	**13.86**	**15.27**	**17.03**
Passenger	2 205 BA	*4.31*	*4.55*	*5.66*	*4.97*	*5.94*	*5.63*	*6.11*	*7.06*
Freight	2 205 BB	*3.79*	*3.84*	*3.98*	*3.80*	*3.71*	*3.64*	*4.22*	*4.48*
Other	2 205 BC	*3.45*	*3.59*	*4.55*	*4.41*	*4.86*	*4.59*	*4.94*	*5.49*
Sea transport, passenger	2 207 . .	.88	.79	.91	.84	1.04	.88	.91	1.14
Sea transport, freight	2 208 . .	3.12	3.12	3.14	3.11	2.98	2.96	3.44	3.63
Sea transport, other	2 209 . .	1.35	1.35	1.54	1.54	1.76	1.61	1.70	1.84
Air transport, passenger	2 211 . .	3.43	3.75	4.76	4.13	4.89	4.75	5.20	5.92
Air transport, freight	2 212 . .	.67	.72	.83	.69	.73	.68	.79	.85
Air transport, other	2 213 . .	1.74	1.83	2.44	2.24	2.37	2.30	2.39	2.59
Other transport, passenger	2 215 . .	. . .	. . .	. . .	. . .	. . .	. . .	. . .	. . .
Other transport, freight	2 216 . .	. . .	. . .	. . .	. . .	. . .	. . .	. . .	. . .
Other transport, other	2 217 . .	.36	.42	.57	.63	.73	.69	.84	1.06
Transportation services, debit	3 205 . .	**–13.66**	**–13.30**	**–15.07**	**–13.96**	**–15.40**	**–14.23**	**–16.16**	**–17.24**
Passenger	3 205 BA	*–4.63*	*–4.32*	*–5.17*	*–4.76*	*–5.69*	*–5.01*	*–5.70*	*–5.81*
Freight	3 205 BB	*–3.63*	*–3.41*	*–3.90*	*–3.58*	*–3.80*	*–3.58*	*–3.76*	*–3.93*
Other	3 205 BC	*–5.40*	*–5.56*	*–6.00*	*–5.62*	*–5.91*	*–5.64*	*–6.70*	*–7.50*
Sea transport, passenger	3 207 . .	–.44	–.46	–.61	–.62	–.78	–.67	–.80	–.87
Sea transport, freight	3 208 . .	–3.02	–2.84	–3.29	–3.04	–3.17	–3.03	–3.18	–3.29
Sea transport, other	3 209 . .	–2.21	–2.26	–2.03	–1.95	–1.94	–1.88	–2.20	–2.45
Air transport, passenger	3 211 . .	–4.19	–3.86	–4.56	–4.15	–4.91	–4.34	–4.90	–4.94
Air transport, freight	3 212 . .	–.61	–.57	–.60	–.54	–.63	–.55	–.58	–.65
Air transport, other	3 213 . .	–2.67	–2.74	–3.36	–3.10	–3.37	–3.23	–3.91	–4.31
Other transport, passenger	3 215 . .	. . .	. . .	. . .	. . .	. . .	. . .	. . .	. . .
Other transport, freight	3 216 . .	. . .	. . .	. . .	. . .	. . .	. . .	. . .	. . .
Other transport, other	3 217 . .	–.52	–.56	–.60	–.56	–.60	–.53	–.58	–.74
Travel, credit	2 236 . .	**10.94**	**11.29**	**14.00**	**12.52**	**14.39**	**14.25**	**15.23**	**18.78**
Business travel	2 237 . .	3.29	3.31	3.93	3.56	3.87	3.63	3.97	5.12
Personal travel	2 240 . .	7.65	7.98	10.08	8.96	10.52	10.62	11.26	13.66
Travel, debit	3 236 . .	**–14.51**	**–15.22**	**–17.79**	**–17.15**	**–20.18**	**–19.50**	**–22.25**	**–24.63**
Business travel	3 237 . .	–2.58	–2.64	–3.32	–3.16	–3.39	–3.43	–4.00	–4.80
Personal travel	3 240 . .	–11.93	–12.58	–14.47	–13.99	–16.79	–16.07	–18.25	–19.83
Other services, credit	2 200 BA	**25.34**	**24.66**	**28.04**	**28.62**	**32.60**	**29.80**	**32.96**	**35.59**
Communications	2 245 . .	1.23	1.29	1.63	1.77	1.55	1.57	1.52	1.57
Construction	2 249 . .	. . .	. . .	. . .	. . .	. . .	. . .	. . .	. . .
Insurance	2 253 . .	3.33	1.64	.71	1.79	1.97	2.46	2.70	2.89
Financial	2 260 . .	4.50	4.67	5.37	4.41	5.35	4.58	4.64	5.26
Computer and information	2 262 . .	. . .	. . .	. . .	. . .	1.09	1.18	1.80	1.58
Royalties and licence fees	2 266 . .	2.01	2.13	2.54	2.80	3.54	3.40	3.98	4.57
Other business services	2 268 . .	9.61	10.35	12.57	12.36	13.61	11.70	13.32	14.36
Personal, cultural, and recreational	2 287 . .	1.88	2.03	2.52	2.66	2.84	2.64	2.99	3.33
Government, n.i.e.	2 291 . .	2.78	2.56	2.72	2.84	2.65	2.26	2.03	2.03
Other services, debit	3 200 BA	**–12.59**	**–13.88**	**–16.81**	**–16.88**	**–17.28**	**–15.95**	**–17.79**	**–19.84**
Communications	3 245 . .	–1.37	–1.42	–1.71	–2.02	–1.67	–1.82	–1.84	–2.01
Construction	3 249 . .	. . .	. . .	. . .	. . .	. . .	. . .	. . .	. . .
Insurance	3 253 . .	–.59	–.63	–.72	–.71	–.73	–.61	–.68	–.80
Financial	3 260 . .	. . .	. . .	. . .	. . .	. . .	. . .	. . .	. . .
Computer and information	3 262 . .	. . .	. . .	. . .	. . .	–.96	–.97	–1.39	–1.52
Royalties and licence fees	3 266 . .	–1.96	–2.17	–2.99	–2.56	–2.26	–2.16	–2.61	–2.86
Other business services	3 268 . .	–3.95	–4.65	–5.56	–5.73	–6.27	–6.02	–6.27	–7.20
Personal, cultural, and recreational	3 287 . .	–.52	–.60	–.85	–.90	–.91	–.87	–1.14	–1.50
Government, n.i.e.	3 291 . .	–4.19	–4.42	–4.98	–4.96	–4.49	–3.50	–3.86	–3.95

Table 2 (Continued). STANDARD PRESENTATION, 1988–95
(Billions of U.S. dollars)

	Code	1988	1989	1990	1991	1992	1993	1994	1995
C. INCOME	4 300	8.11	5.81	2.42	.14	5.53	3.30	13.35	15.07
Total credit	2 300	*100.59*	*121.00*	*141.44*	*136.07*	*120.51*	*111.19*	*119.43*	*146.94*
Total debit	3 300	*–92.48*	*–115.19*	*–139.02*	*–135.93*	*–114.98*	*–107.89*	*–106.07*	*–131.87*
Compensation of employees, credit	2 310	...	...	...	...	...	...	...	...
Compensation of employees, debit	3 310	...	...	...	...	...	...	...	...
Investment income, credit	2 320	**100.59**	**121.00**	**141.44**	**136.07**	**120.51**	**111.19**	**119.43**	**146.94**
Direct investment income	2 330	24.65	27.29	28.06	22.54	23.54	25.30	32.06	39.15
Dividends and distributed branch profits	2 332	8.93	10.98	12.66	11.46	14.85	10.46	12.04	12.49
Reinvested earnings and undistributed branch profits	2 333	14.61	14.81	14.70	10.52	8.89	14.62	20.07	25.31
Income on debt (interest)	2 334	1.11	1.51	.70	.55	–.20	.21	–.04	1.35
Portfolio investment income	2 339	10.31	11.99	14.21	16.62	21.40	24.52	24.54	30.63
Income on equity	2 340	2.50	2.90	3.44	3.12	4.32	4.27	3.80	4.81
Income on bonds and notes	2 350	7.55	8.88	10.34	12.99	16.57	19.82	20.39	25.44
Income on money market instruments and financial derivatives	2 360	.26	.22	.43	.51	.51	.43	.36	.38
Other investment income	2 370	65.63	81.71	99.16	96.91	75.57	61.37	62.82	77.16
Investment income, debit	3 320	**–92.48**	**–115.19**	**–139.02**	**–135.93**	**–114.98**	**–107.89**	**–106.07**	**–131.87**
Direct investment income	3 330	–15.43	–15.11	–12.60	–8.05	–9.19	–15.70	–14.57	–18.88
Dividends and distributed branch profits	3 332	–10.06	–6.83	–5.40	–2.56	–5.13	–7.06	–7.79	–7.09
Reinvested earnings and undistributed branch profits	3 333	–4.01	–6.14	–3.27	–.95	–.52	–6.08	–5.38	–9.70
Income on debt (interest)	3 334	–1.36	–2.15	–3.92	–4.53	–3.55	–2.55	–1.40	–2.09
Portfolio investment income	3 339	–8.86	–12.09	–16.18	–17.30	–19.32	–18.17	–22.40	–26.99
Income on equity	3 340	–2.99	–3.76	–4.88	–5.71	–6.12	–6.26	–6.50	–8.15
Income on bonds and notes	3 350	–5.24	–7.02	–9.00	–9.62	–11.76	–11.10	–14.86	–17.28
Income on money market instruments and financial derivatives	3 360	–.63	–1.30	–2.29	–1.97	–1.45	–.81	–1.04	–1.56
Other investment income	3 370	–68.20	–87.99	–110.24	–110.58	–86.47	–74.02	–69.10	–86.00
D. CURRENT TRANSFERS	4 379	–6.34	–7.46	–8.74	–2.46	–9.09	–7.50	–7.63	–11.00
Credit	2 379	**6.82**	**6.42**	**7.22**	**12.06**	**8.52**	**8.31**	**8.57**	**9.68**
General government	2 380	3.76	3.56	4.00	8.70	5.08	4.99	5.01	5.84
Other sectors	2 390	3.05	2.87	3.21	3.36	3.45	3.32	3.56	3.85
Workers' remittances	2 391	...	...	...	...	...	...	...	...
Other current transfers	2 392	3.05	2.87	3.21	...	...	...	...	...
Debit	3 379	**–13.15**	**–13.88**	**–15.96**	**–14.52**	**–17.62**	**–15.81**	**–16.20**	**–20.69**
General government	3 380	–9.62	–10.52	–12.21	–10.63	–13.70	–12.44	–12.81	–17.16
Other sectors	3 390	–3.53	–3.36	–3.75	–3.89	–3.92	–3.37	–3.39	–3.53
Workers' remittances	3 391	...	...	...	...	...	...	...	...
Other current transfers	3 392	–3.53	–3.36	–3.75	...	...	...	...	...
CAPITAL AND FINANCIAL ACCOUNT	4 996	**26.60**	**30.90**	**29.17**	**13.81**	**7.75**	**19.81**	**–4.15**	**1.14**
CAPITAL ACCOUNT	4 994	...	...	...	...	...	...	...	...
Total credit	2 994	...	...	...	...	...	...	...	...
Total debit	3 994	...	...	...	...	...	...	...	...
Capital transfers, credit	2 400	...	...	...	...	...	...	...	...
General government	2 401	...	...	...	...	...	...	...	...
Debt forgiveness	2 402	...	...	...	...	...	...	...	...
Other capital transfers	2 410	...	...	...	...	...	...	...	...
Other sectors	2 430	...	...	...	...	...	...	...	...
Migrants' transfers	2 431	...	...	...	...	...	...	...	...
Debt forgiveness	2 432	...	...	...	...	...	...	...	...
Other capital transfers	2 440	...	...	...	...	...	...	...	...
Capital transfers, debit	3 400	...	...	...	...	...	...	...	...
General government	3 401	...	...	...	...	...	...	...	...
Debt forgiveness	3 402	...	...	...	...	...	...	...	...
Other capital transfers	3 410	...	...	...	...	...	...	...	...
Other sectors	3 430	...	...	...	...	...	...	...	...
Migrants' transfers	3 431	...	...	...	...	...	...	...	...
Debt forgiveness	3 432	...	...	...	...	...	...	...	...
Other capital transfers	3 440	...	...	...	...	...	...	...	...
Nonproduced nonfinancial assets, credit	2 480	...	...	...	...	...	...	...	...
Nonproduced nonfinancial assets, debit	3 480	...	...	...	...	...	...	...	...

Table 2 (Continued). STANDARD PRESENTATION, 1988–95

(Billions of U.S. dollars)

	Code	1988	1989	1990	1991	1992	1993	1994	1995
FINANCIAL ACCOUNT	4 995 . .	**26.60**	**30.90**	**29.17**	**13.81**	**7.75**	**19.81**	**–4.15**	**1.14**
A. DIRECT INVESTMENT	4 500 . .	–15.87	–4.93	13.10	–.09	–2.86	–9.97	–17.99	–8.12
Direct investment abroad	4 505 . .	**–37.29**	**–35.48**	**–19.32**	**–16.31**	**–18.99**	**–25.52**	**–28.28**	**–40.33**
Equity capital	4 510 . .	–13.75	–15.59	–13.20	–8.24	–8.84	–5.51	–10.35	–9.77
Claims on affiliated enterprises	4 515 . .	...	...	...	...	...	...	...	...
Liabilities to affiliated enterprises	4 520 . .	...	...	...	...	...	...	...	...
Reinvested earnings	4 525 . .	–14.61	–14.81	–14.70	–10.52	–8.89	–14.62	–20.07	–25.31
Other capital	4 530 . .	–8.93	–5.09	8.57	2.46	–1.27	–5.39	2.13	–5.24
Claims on affiliated enterprises	4 535 . .	...	...	...	...	...	...	...	...
Liabilities to affiliated enterprises	4 540 . .	...	...	...	...	...	...	...	...
Direct investment in United Kingdom	4 555 . .	**21.41**	**30.55**	**32.43**	**16.21**	**16.14**	**15.54**	**10.30**	**32.21**
Equity capital	4 560 . .	6.12	8.84	18.10	7.43	10.87	7.90	4.55	19.62
Claims on direct investors	4 565 . .	...	...	...	...	...	...	...	...
Liabilities to direct investors	4 570 . .	...	...	...	...	...	...	...	...
Reinvested earnings	4 575 . .	4.01	6.14	3.27	.95	.52	6.08	5.38	9.70
Other capital	4 580 . .	11.28	15.58	11.05	7.83	4.75	1.56	.36	2.89
Claims on direct investors	4 585 . .	...	...	...	...	...	...	...	...
Liabilities to direct investors	4 590 . .	...	...	...	...	...	...	...	...
B. PORTFOLIO INVESTMENT	4 600 . .	32.50	–34.31	–7.72	–40.78	–24.96	–88.45	87.17	–10.74
Assets	4 602 . .	**–19.62**	**–63.02**	**–32.63**	**–55.56**	**–50.85**	**–131.01**	**31.83**	**–67.50**
Equity securities	4 610 . .	–9.98	–25.71	–1.02	–24.45	7.60	–13.60	–.69	–15.96
Monetary authorities	4 611 . .	...	...	...	...	...	...	...	...
General government	4 612 . .	...	...	...	...	...	...	...	...
Banks	4 613 . .	–1.12	–1.10	1.17	.22	1.11	–1.82	–2.58	–.20
Other sectors	4 614 . .	–8.86	–24.61	–2.19	–24.67	6.49	–11.78	1.89	–15.76
Debt securities	4 619 . .	–9.64	–37.31	–31.62	–31.11	–58.45	–117.41	32.52	–51.54
Bonds and notes	4 620 . .	–10.17	–33.56	–30.80	–26.97	–53.78	–112.97	26.49	–47.48
Monetary authorities	4 621 . .	...	...	...	...	...	...	...	...
General government	4 622 . .	...	...	...	...	...	...	...	...
Banks	4 623 . .	–1.07	–9.37	–12.20	–15.23	–23.40	–51.50	–20.36	–38.01
Other sectors	4 624 . .	–9.10	–24.18	–18.59	–11.74	–30.38	–61.47	46.85	–9.47
Money market instruments	4 630 . .	.53	–3.75	–.82	–4.14	–4.66	–4.44	6.02	–4.06
Monetary authorities	4 631 . .	.33	.66	–.35	–.51	–3.67	.83	1.55	.51
General government	4 632 . .	...	...	...	...	...	...	...	...
Banks	4 633 . .	–.24	–1.34	–3.94	–2.99	–4.10	–.98	4.45	–3.30
Other sectors	4 634 . .	.44	–3.08	3.47	–.65	3.10	–4.28	.02	–1.27
Financial derivatives	4 640 . .	...	...	...	...	...	...	...	...
Monetary authorities	4 641 . .	...	...	...	...	...	...	...	...
General government	4 642 . .	...	...	...	...	...	...	...	...
Banks	4 643 . .	...	...	...	...	...	...	...	...
Other sectors	4 644 . .	...	...	...	...	...	...	...	...
Liabilities	4 652 . .	**52.11**	**28.71**	**24.91**	**14.78**	**25.88**	**42.56**	**55.34**	**56.76**
Equity securities	4 660 . .	9.35	9.87	2.81	4.41	18.04	25.70	5.81	5.07
Banks	4 663 . .	...	...	...	...	...	...	...	...
Other sectors	4 664 . .	...	...	...	...	...	...	...	...
Debt securities	4 669 . .	42.76	18.84	22.10	10.36	7.84	16.86	49.53	51.69
Bonds and notes	4 670 . .	26.95	13.00	17.48	25.69	24.38	42.52	42.08	19.83
Monetary authorities	4 671 . .	...	...	...	...	...	...	...	...
General government	4 672 . .	2.07	–3.46	.17	13.17	14.11	24.59	8.69	–.46
Banks	4 673 . .	...	...	...	...	...	...	...	...
Other sectors	4 674 . .	24.89	16.46	17.31	12.52	10.27	17.94	33.40	20.29
Money market instruments	4 680 . .	15.81	5.84	4.62	–15.32	–16.54	–25.67	7.45	31.86
Monetary authorities	4 681 . .	...	...	...	...	...	...	...	...
General government	4 682 . .	1.45	3.30	1.51	–2.99	–3.88	–.46	–.25	2.06
Banks	4 683 . .	11.23	–.76	–2.54	–18.74	–11.54	–27.10	1.95	26.23
Other sectors	4 684 . .	3.12	3.30	5.64	6.40	–1.12	1.89	5.74	3.57
Financial derivatives	4 690 . .	...	...	...	...	...	...	...	...
Monetary authorities	4 691 . .	...	...	...	...	...	...	...	...
General government	4 692 . .	...	...	...	...	...	...	...	...
Banks	4 693 . .	...	...	...	...	...	...	...	...
Other sectors	4 694 . .	...	...	...	...	...	...	...	...

Table 2 (Concluded). STANDARD PRESENTATION, 1988–95
(Billions of U.S. dollars)

	Code	1988	1989	1990	1991	1992	1993	1994	1995
C. OTHER INVESTMENT	4 700	14.86	61.33	23.90	59.34	33.14	119.50	–71.85	19.10
Assets	4 703	**–40.02**	**–59.60**	**–94.58**	**43.10**	**–79.18**	**–75.48**	**–57.92**	**–87.90**
Trade credits	4 706	–.79	–.63	–1.91	–.24	.46	.05	–.61	–1.83
General government: long-term	4 708	–1.25	–.98	–1.55	–1.11	–.60	–.60	–.61	–.63
General government: short-term	4 709	...	...	...	...	...	...	...	...
Other sectors: long-term	4 711	.42	.87	–.21	.98	.91	.72	–.29	–1.10
Other sectors: short-term	4 712	.04	–.52	–.14	–.11	.15	–.07	.29	–.10
Loans	4 714	–31.92	–47.81	–69.25	59.20	–47.57	3.28	–84.12	–40.16
Monetary authorities: long-term	4 717	...	...	...	...	...	...	...	...
Monetary authorities: short-term	4 718	...	...	...	...	...	...	...	...
General government: long-term	4 720	.12	.08	.09	.08	.06	.09	.08	.09
General government: short-term	4 721	...	...	...	...	...	...	...	...
Banks: long-term	4 723	...	...	...	...	...	...	...	...
Banks: short-term	4 724	–33.48	–48.86	–68.86	59.45	–44.93	6.07	–82.32	–38.15
Other sectors: long-term	4 726	–.09	–.10	–.09	–.08	–.13	–.11	–.09	–.23
Other sectors: short-term	4 727	1.52	1.07	–.39	–.26	–2.57	–2.76	–1.79	–1.88
Currency and deposits	4 730	–7.24	–12.56	–18.53	–7.84	–11.99	–13.15	–17.31	–17.10
Monetary authorities	4 731	...	...	...	...	...	...	...	...
General government	4 732	...	...	...	...	...	...	...	...
Banks	4 733	...	...	...	...	...	...	...	...
Other sectors	4 734	–7.24	–12.56	–18.53	–7.84	–11.99	–13.15	–17.31	–17.10
Other assets	4 736	–.07	1.40	–4.90	–8.02	–20.07	–65.67	44.13	–28.81
Monetary authorities: long-term	4 738	...	...	...	...	...	...	...	...
Monetary authorities: short-term	4 739	...	...	...	...	...	...	...	...
General government: long-term	4 741	–.45	–.52	–.37	–.56	–.65	–.40	–.42	–.47
General government: short-term	4 742	...	...	...	...	...	...	...	...
Banks: long-term	4 744	...	...	...	...	...	...	...	...
Banks: short-term	4 745	...	...	...	...	...	...	...	...
Other sectors: long-term	4 747	.10	.04	.12	.10	.02	.04	.03	.04
Other sectors: short-term	4 748	.28	1.89	–4.65	–7.56	–19.45	–65.30	44.51	–28.38
Liabilities	4 753	**54.88**	**120.94**	**118.48**	**16.24**	**112.32**	**194.98**	**–13.93**	**107.00**
Trade credits	4 756	.37	.47	...	.12	.30	.49	.55	.34
General government: long-term	4 758	...	...	...	...	...	...	...	...
General government: short-term	4 759	...	...	...	...	...	...	...	...
Other sectors: long-term	4 761	.11	–.07	–.04	.13	.35	.50	.53	.35
Other sectors: short-term	4 762	.26	.54	.04	–.01	–.05	...	.01	...
Loans	4 764	5.04	39.90	25.62	34.19	61.49	133.61	–89.10	69.57
Use of Fund credit and loans from the Fund	4 766	...	...	...	...	...	...	...	...
Monetary authorities: other long-term	4 767	...	...	...	...	...	...	...	...
Monetary authorities: short-term	4 768	...	...	...	...	4.42	–4.17	...	...
General government: long-term	4 770	–.11	.63	–1.06	–.31	–.14	–.07	–.34	–.25
General government: short-term	4 771	...	...	...	...	...	...	...	...
Banks: long-term	4 773	...	...	...	...	...	...	...	...
Banks: short-term	4 774	...	...	...	...	...	...	...	...
Other sectors: long-term	4 776	–.63	–2.95	–.32	–.16	–1.11	–.12	–.18	–.24
Other sectors: short-term	4 777	5.78	42.22	27.00	34.66	58.32	137.98	–88.58	70.06
Currency and deposits	4 780	48.61	79.55	91.58	–17.85	50.12	60.15	73.00	36.03
Monetary authorities	4 781	.08	.09	–.07	.07	.13	.08	.13	.07
General government	4 782	.01	.01	–.01	.01	.01	.01	.01	.01
Banks	4 783	48.52	79.45	91.66	–17.92	49.98	60.07	72.86	35.95
Other sectors	4 784	...	...	...	...	...	...	...	...
Other liabilities	4 786	.86	1.02	1.28	–.22	.40	.72	1.62	1.05
Monetary authorities: long-term	4 788	...	...	...	...	...	...	...	...
Monetary authorities: short-term	4 789	...	...	...	...	...	...	...	...
General government: long-term	4 791	...	...	...	...	...	...	...	...
General government: short-term	4 792	.32	.33	.61	–1.05	–.32	.40	1.17	.81
Banks: long-term	4 794	...	...	...	...	...	...	...	...
Banks: short-term	4 795	...	...	...	...	...	...	...	...
Other sectors: long-term	4 797	...	...	...	...	...	...	...	...
Other sectors: short-term	4 798	.55	.68	.67	.83	.72	.32	.45	.24
D. RESERVE ASSETS	4 800	–4.89	8.80	–.12	–4.66	2.43	–1.26	–1.48	.90
Monetary gold	4 810	...	.01	.02	.37	.48	.31	–1.12	.11
Special drawing rights	4 820	–.01	.15	–.01	–.07	.73	.26	–.18	.09
Reserve position in the Fund	4 830	.02	–.01	.09	–.16	–.24	.15	–.02	–.40
Foreign exchange	4 840	–4.89	8.65	–.21	–4.81	1.46	–1.99	–.16	1.09
Other claims	4 880	...	...	...	...	...	...	...	...
NET ERRORS AND OMISSIONS	4 998	**2.72**	**5.77**	**3.33**	**.45**	**10.60**	**–3.60**	**7.64**	**3.49**

Part 3 of the *Yearbook* contains descriptions of the methodologies, compilation practices, and sources used to compile these data.

Table 3. INTERNATIONAL INVESTMENT POSITION (End-period stocks), 1988–95
(Billions of U.S. dollars)

	Code	1988	1989	1990	1991	1992	1993	1994	1995
ASSETS	8 995 C.	1,401.68	1,536.52	1,756.95	1,775.80	1,779.35	2,055.91	2,170.18	2,506.22
Direct investment abroad	8 505 . .	**187.57**	**196.57**	**230.82**	**234.31**	**224.45**	**250.65**	**280.49**	**331.35**
Equity capital and reinvested earnings	8 506 . .	...	...	...	...	...	...	...	...
Claims on affiliated enterprises	8 507 . .	...	...	...	...	...	...	...	...
Liabilities to affiliated enterprises	8 508 . .	...	...	...	...	...	...	...	...
Other capital	8 530 . .	...	...	...	...	...	...	...	...
Claims on affiliated enterprises	8 535 . .	...	...	...	...	...	...	...	...
Liabilities to affiliated enterprises	8 540 . .	...	...	...	...	...	...	...	...
Portfolio investment	8 602 . .	**273.43**	**362.68**	**385.10**	**474.28**	**481.70**	**675.33**	**649.40**	**772.96**
Equity securities	8 610 . .	165.88	221.43	193.10	237.39	207.86	284.29	287.87	340.23
Monetary authorities	8 611 . .	...	...	...	...	...	...	...	...
General government	8 612 . .	...	...	...	...	...	...	...	...
Banks	8 613 . .	7.60	10.27	9.02	8.67	5.50	2.89	5.49	7.36
Other sectors	8 614 . .	158.28	211.16	184.08	228.71	202.36	281.41	282.38	332.87
Debt securities	8 619 . .	107.55	141.25	191.99	236.90	273.84	391.04	361.53	432.72
Bonds and notes	8 620 . .	97.57	124.14	172.39	213.31	250.26	365.04	339.58	406.71
Monetary authorities	8 621 . .	...	...	...	...	...	...	...	...
General government	8 622 . .	...	...	...	...	...	...	...	...
Banks	8 623 . .	48.91	57.01	76.43	91.44	108.97	163.76	188.22	227.06
Other sectors	8 624 . .	48.66	67.13	95.97	121.86	141.29	201.28	151.36	179.65
Money market instruments	8 630 . .	9.98	17.11	19.60	23.59	23.58	26.00	21.95	26.01
Monetary authorities	8 631 . .	1.22	.48	.95	1.35	3.90	2.97	1.50	1.00
General government	8 632 . .	...	...	...	...	...	...	...	...
Banks	8 633 . .	7.91	8.98	14.11	16.89	17.88	17.00	14.20	17.40
Other sectors	8 634 . .	.85	7.65	4.54	5.34	1.80	6.03	6.25	7.61
Financial derivatives	8 640 . .	...	...	...	...	...	...	...	...
Monetary authorities	8 641 . .	...	...	...	...	...	...	...	...
General government	8 642 . .	...	...	...	...	...	...	...	...
Banks	8 643 . .	...	...	...	...	...	...	...	...
Other sectors	8 644 . .	...	...	...	...	...	...	...	...
Other investment	8 703 . .	**888.74**	**935.06**	**1,097.75**	**1,018.59**	**1,030.42**	**1,085.88**	**1,192.36**	**1,352.76**
Trade credits	8 706 . .	24.08	22.46	28.18	27.61	22.55	21.82	23.53	25.08
General government: long-term	8 708 . .	7.79	7.77	10.87	11.65	9.98	10.37	11.56	12.09
General government: short-term	8 709 . .	...	...	...	...	...	...	...	...
Other sectors: long-term	8 711 . .	14.24	12.18	14.50	13.06	10.02	8.85	9.63	10.54
Other sectors: short-term	8 712 . .	2.05	2.51	2.81	2.90	2.55	2.60	2.34	2.44
Loans	8 714 . .	797.85	823.92	943.91	842.76	839.75	821.95	938.43	1,045.95
Monetary authorities: long-term	8 717 . .	...	...	...	...	...	...	...	...
Monetary authorities: short-term	8 718 . .	...	...	...	...	...	...	...	...
General government: long-term	8 720 . .	1.65	1.39	1.57	1.44	1.11	1.01	.98	.88
General government: short-term	8 721 . .	...	...	...	...	...	...	...	...
Banks: long-term	8 723 . .	...	...	...	...	...	...	...	...
Banks: short-term	8 724 . .	789.23	816.88	934.57	833.23	827.75	806.92	921.03	1,029.31
Other sectors: long-term	8 726 . .	1.29	1.25	1.60	1.63	1.43	1.52	1.69	1.91
Other sectors: short-term	8 727 . .	5.67	4.40	6.17	6.47	9.45	12.51	14.72	13.85
Currency and deposits	8 730 . .	59.72	74.57	103.25	108.18	112.72	126.61	148.67	167.94
Monetary authorities	8 731 . .	...	...	...	...	...	...	...	...
General government	8 732 . .	...	...	...	...	...	...	...	...
Banks	8 733 . .	...	...	...	...	...	...	...	...
Other sectors	8 734 . .	59.72	74.57	103.25	108.18	112.72	126.61	148.67	167.94
Other assets	8 736 . .	7.08	14.11	22.41	40.04	55.40	115.51	81.73	113.80
Monetary authorities: long-term	8 738 . .	...	...	...	...	...	...	...	...
Monetary authorities: short-term	8 739 . .	...	...	...	...	...	...	...	...
General government: long-term	8 741 . .	6.16	5.97	7.58	7.93	6.98	7.23	8.05	8.45
General government: short-term	8 742 . .	...	...	...	...	...	...	...	...
Banks: long-term	8 744 . .	...	...	...	...	...	...	...	...
Banks: short-term	8 745 . .	...	...	...	...	...	...	...	...
Other sectors: long-term	8 747 . .	.49	.41	.26	.39	.89	.62	.86	1.12
Other sectors: short-term	8 748 . .	.43	7.73	14.57	31.72	47.53	107.66	72.81	104.23
Reserve assets	8 800 . .	**51.95**	**42.21**	**43.28**	**48.61**	**42.78**	**44.04**	**47.93**	**49.15**
Monetary gold	8 810 . .	7.81	7.58	7.42	6.69	6.19	7.23	7.05	7.15
Special drawing rights	8 820 . .	1.32	1.14	1.25	1.31	.54	.29	.49	.41
Reserve position in the Fund	8 830 . .	1.67	1.64	1.68	1.85	2.01	1.86	1.99	2.42
Foreign exchange	8 840 . .	41.15	31.85	32.94	38.76	34.04	34.67	38.40	39.17
Other claims	8 880 . .	...	...	...	...	...	...	...	...

Table 3 (Continued). INTERNATIONAL INVESTMENT POSITION (End–period stocks), 1988–95

(Billions of U.S. dollars)

	Code	1988	1989	1990	1991	1992	1993	1994	1995
LIABILITIES	8 995 D.	1,286.90	1,438.76	1,743.63	1,755.38	1,745.65	2,000.71	2,117.28	2,429.02
Direct investment in United Kingdom	8 555	**139.02**	**160.28**	**218.21**	**225.80**	**185.59**	**189.41**	**202.43**	**233.08**
Equity capital and reinvested earnings	8 556	...	...	...	...	...	...	...	...
Claims on direct investors	8 557	...	...	...	...	...	...	...	...
Liabilities to direct investors	8 558	...	...	...	...	...	...	...	...
Other capital	8 580	...	...	...	...	...	...	...	...
Claims on direct investors	8 585	...	...	...	...	...	...	...	...
Liabilities to direct investors	8 590	...	...	...	...	...	...	...	...
Portfolio investment	8 652	**283.46**	**308.85**	**344.69**	**366.82**	**372.22**	**451.15**	**494.19**	**585.60**
Equity securities	8 660	78.97	101.92	111.50	129.05	137.92	195.28	192.53	231.85
Banks	8 663	...	...	...	...	...	...	...	...
Other sectors	8 664	...	...	...	...	...	...	...	...
Debt securities	8 669	204.49	206.93	233.19	237.77	234.30	255.86	301.66	353.75
Bonds and notes	8 670	77.28	74.27	97.19	120.81	134.73	181.57	219.93	240.73
Monetary authorities	8 671	...	...	...	...	...	...	...	...
General government	8 672	...	...	...	...	...	...	...	...
Banks	8 673	...	...	...	...	...	...	...	...
Other sectors	8 674	...	...	...	...	...	...	...	...
Money market instruments	8 680	127.21	132.67	136.00	116.96	99.57	74.29	81.73	113.02
Monetary authorities	8 681	...	...	...	...	...	...	...	...
General government	8 682	5.24	8.23	11.56	8.18	3.70	2.75	2.79	4.91
Banks	8 683	117.36	117.18	114.76	95.80	83.15	57.21	59.37	84.70
Other sectors	8 684	4.61	7.26	9.67	12.99	12.72	14.33	19.57	23.41
Financial derivatives	8 690	...	...	...	...	...	...	...	...
Monetary authorities	8 691	...	...	...	...	...	...	...	...
General government	8 692	...	...	...	...	...	...	...	...
Banks	8 692	...	...	...	...	...	...	...	...
Other sectors	8 694	...	...	...	...	...	...	...	...
Other investment	8 753	**864.42**	**969.63**	**1,180.72**	**1,162.76**	**1,187.84**	**1,360.15**	**1,420.66**	**1,610.34**
Trade credits	8 756	2.14	2.49	2.65	2.75	2.75	3.20	3.85	4.25
General government: long-term	8 758	...	...	...	...	...	...	...	...
General government: short-term	8 759	...	...	...	...	...	...	...	...
Other sectors: long-term	8 761	.64	.50	.53	.65	.80	1.25	1.88	2.27
Other sectors: short-term	8 762	1.50	1.99	2.11	2.10	1.96	1.95	1.98	1.97
Loans	8 764	57.41	102.22	146.41	192.75	234.07	370.27	300.90	367.04
Use of Fund credit and loans from the Fund	8 766	...	...	...	...	...	...	...	...
Monetary authorities: other long-term	8 767	...	...	...	...	...	...	...	...
Monetary authorities: short-term	8 768	...	...	...	...	4.19	...	...	...
General government: long-term	8 770	4.75	5.31	4.85	4.44	3.89	3.75	3.53	3.35
General government: short-term	8 771	...	...	...	...	...	...	...	...
Banks: long-term	8 773	...	...	...	...	...	...	...	...
Banks: short-term	8 774	...	...	...	...	...	...	...	...
Other sectors: long-term	8 776	4.86	2.38	2.06	1.89	.90	.78	.49	.25
Other sectors: short-term	8 777	47.81	94.52	139.49	186.42	225.10	365.74	296.88	363.44
Currency and deposits	8 780	798.34	858.11	1,022.18	958.17	943.32	978.46	1,105.59	1,227.79
Monetary authorities	8 781	.68	.69	.79	.85	.78	.84	1.03	1.09
General government	8 782	.08	.08	.09	.10	.09	.09	.11	.12
Banks	8 783	797.58	857.34	1,021.30	957.23	942.45	977.53	1,104.44	1,226.58
Other sectors	8 784	...	...	...	...	...	...	...	...
Other liabilities	8 786	6.53	6.81	9.48	9.10	7.70	8.22	10.32	11.27
Monetary authorities: long-term	8 788	...	...	...	...	...	...	...	...
Monetary authorities: short-term	8 789	...	...	...	...	...	...	...	...
General government: long-term	8 791	...	...	...	...	...	...	...	...
General government: short-term	8 792	2.14	2.26	3.30	2.13	1.38	1.74	3.03	3.82
Banks: long-term	8 794	...	...	...	...	...	...	...	...
Banks: short-term	8 795	...	...	...	...	...	...	...	...
Other sectors: long-term	8 797	...	...	...	...	...	...	...	...
Other sectors: short-term	8 798	4.40	4.55	6.18	6.96	6.32	6.48	7.28	7.45
NET INTERNATIONAL INVESTMENT POSITION	8 995	**114.78**	**97.76**	**13.32**	**20.42**	**33.69**	**55.21**	**52.90**	**77.20**
Conversion rates: pound sterling per U.S. dollar (end of period)	0 102	**.55264**	**.62286**	**.51867**	**.53456**	**.66138**	**.67513**	**.64000**	**.64516**

Table 1. ANALYTIC PRESENTATION, 1988–95
(Billions of U.S. dollars)

	Code	1988	1989	1990	1991	1992	1993	1994	1995
A. Current Account [1]	4 993 Y.	**-127.71**	**-104.26**	**-94.26**	**-9.26**	**-61.36**	**-99.72**	**-147.77**	**-148.23**
Goods: exports f.o.b	2 100 . .	320.23	362.16	389.31	416.91	440.35	458.73	504.55	577.82
Goods: imports f.o.b	3 100 . .	-447.19	-477.30	-498.34	-490.98	-536.45	-590.10	-669.15	-749.81
Balance on Goods	4 100 . .	*-126.96*	*-115.14*	*-109.03*	*-74.07*	*-96.10*	*-131.37*	*-164.60*	*-171.99*
Services: credit	2 200 . .	111.16	127.72	147.35	163.67	177.14	184.09	193.62	208.55
Services: debit	3 200 . .	-98.53	-102.54	-117.64	-118.46	-118.29	-123.62	-132.23	-140.43
Balance on Goods and Services	4 991 . .	*-114.33*	*-89.96*	*-79.32*	*-28.86*	*-37.25*	*-70.91*	*-103.21*	*-103.87*
Income: credit	2 300 . .	129.20	152.65	160.42	137.14	119.21	120.05	141.87	182.85
Income: debit	3 300 . .	-116.69	-139.68	-140.54	-122.33	-109.04	-111.42	-147.17	-192.02
Balance on Goods, Services, and Income	4 992 . .	*-101.82*	*-76.99*	*-59.44*	*-14.05*	*-27.09*	*-62.27*	*-108.51*	*-113.04*
Current transfers: credit	2 379 Y.	3.66	4.09	8.79	46.84	6.50	5.20	5.22	5.65
Current transfers: debit	3 379 . .	-29.55	-31.37	-43.61	-42.05	-40.77	-42.65	-44.48	-40.84
B. Capital Account [1]	4 994 Y.	**.23**	**.24**	**.26**	**.28**	**.43**	**-.20**	**-.61**	**.10**
Capital account: credit	2 994 Y.	.23	.24	.26	.28	.43	.47	.47	.53
Capital account: debit	3 994 . .	...	...	...	...	...	-.67	-1.08	-.43
Total, Groups A Plus B	4 010 . .	*-127.48*	*-104.02*	*-94.00*	*-8.98*	*-60.93*	*-99.92*	*-148.38*	*-148.13*
C. Financial Account [1]	4 995 X.	**103.38**	**63.44**	**13.75**	**13.74**	**35.34**	**-10.73**	**88.96**	**20.70**
Direct investment abroad	4 505 . .	-16.18	-36.83	-29.95	-31.38	-42.66	-78.17	-54.47	-95.53
Direct investment in United States	4 555 Y.	57.27	67.73	47.92	22.01	17.58	43.01	49.76	60.23
Portfolio investment assets	4 602 . .	-7.88	-22.10	-28.80	-45.69	-49.17	-146.26	-60.29	-98.96
Equity securities	4 610 . .	-.92	-17.22	-7.41	-30.64	-32.40	-63.38	-48.09	-50.70
Debt securities	4 619 . .	-6.96	-4.88	-21.39	-15.05	-16.77	-82.88	-12.20	-48.26
Portfolio investment liabilities	4 652 Y.	48.18	65.60	-4.20	53.29	62.20	103.83	91.11	192.38
Equity securities	4 660 Y.	-.48	6.96	-14.52	9.47	-4.17	20.92	.91	16.41
Debt securities	4 669 Y.	48.66	58.64	10.32	43.83	66.37	82.91	90.20	175.97
Other investment assets	4 703 . .	-73.28	-83.40	-13.73	13.81	17.79	31.18	-41.31	-103.63
Monetary authorities	4 703 . A	...	...	...	...	...	...	...	...
General government	4 703 . B	1.84	2.39	1.71	3.32	-3.16	-.34	-.35	-.28
Banks	4 703 . C	-46.74	-40.12	15.53	-15.08	23.82	29.95	-8.16	-69.14
Other sectors	4 703 . D	-28.38	-45.67	-30.97	25.58	-2.87	1.58	-32.80	-34.21
Other investment liabilities	4 753 X.	95.27	72.44	42.52	1.69	29.59	35.68	104.15	66.21
Monetary authorities	4 753 XA	...	...	...	...	...	2.59	-2.35	5.28
General government	4 753 YB	-.47	.16	1.87	1.36	2.19	1.71	2.34	1.08
Banks	4 753 YC	61.92	50.25	-2.04	2.75	10.30	20.92	111.54	25.28
Other sectors	4 753 YD	33.82	22.03	42.69	-2.42	17.10	10.46	-7.38	34.57
Total, Groups A Through C	4 020 . .	*-24.10*	*-40.58*	*-80.25*	*4.76*	*-25.59*	*-110.65*	*-59.43*	*-127.43*
D. Net Errors and Omissions	4 998 . .	**-11.73**	**55.83**	**46.54**	**-26.83**	**-23.11**	**43.55**	**13.71**	**31.54**
Total, Groups A Through D	4 030 . .	*-35.83*	*15.25*	*-33.71*	*-22.07*	*-48.70*	*-67.11*	*-45.72*	*-95.89*
E. Reserves and Related Items	4 040 . .	**35.83**	**-15.25**	**33.71**	**22.07**	**48.70**	**67.11**	**45.72**	**95.89**
Reserve assets	4 800 . .	-3.92	-25.27	-2.23	5.76	3.92	-1.38	5.34	-9.74
Use of Fund credit and loans	4 766 . .	...	...	...	...	...	...	...	...
Liabilities constituting foreign authorities' reserves	4 900 . .	39.75	10.02	35.94	16.31	44.77	68.49	40.38	105.63
Exceptional financing	4 920 . .	...	...	...	...	...	...	...	...

[1] Excludes components that have been classified in the categories of Group E.

Table 2. STANDARD PRESENTATION, 1988–95

(Billions of U.S. dollars)

	Code	1988	1989	1990	1991	1992	1993	1994	1995
CURRENT ACCOUNT	4 993 . .	**–127.71**	**–104.26**	**–94.26**	**–9.26**	**–61.36**	**–99.72**	**–147.77**	**–148.23**
A. GOODS	4 100 . .	–126.96	–115.14	–109.03	–74.07	–96.10	–131.37	–164.60	–171.99
Credit	2 100 . .	**320.23**	**362.16**	**389.31**	**416.91**	**440.35**	**458.73**	**504.55**	**577.82**
General merchandise: exports f.o.b.	2 110 . .	319.63	361.62	388.56	416.69	439.94	456.83	502.39	575.91
Goods for processing: exports f.o.b.	2 150 . .	. . .	. . .	. . .	. . .	. . .	. . .	. . .	. . .
Repairs on goods	2 160 . .	. . .	. . .	. . .	. . .	. . .	1.90	2.06	1.87
Goods procured in ports by carriers	2 170 . .	. . .	. . .	. . .	. . .	. . .	. . .	. . .	. . .
Nonmonetary gold	2 180 . .	.60	.54	.75	.22	.41	. . .	.10	.04
Debit	3 100 . .	**–447.19**	**–477.30**	**–498.34**	**–490.98**	**–536.45**	**–590.10**	**–669.15**	**–749.81**
General merchandise: imports f.o.b.	3 110 . .	–443.62	–475.17	–496.99	–490.04	–534.57	–582.66	–665.84	–746.30
Goods for processing: imports f.o.b.	3 150 . .	. . .	. . .	. . .	. . .	. . .	. . .	. . .	. . .
Repairs on goods	3 160 . .	. . .	. . .	. . .	. . .	. . .	–.66	–.56	–.43
Goods procured in ports by carriers	3 170 . .	. . .	. . .	. . .	. . .	. . .	. . .	. . .	. . .
Nonmonetary gold	3 180 . .	–3.57	–2.13	–1.35	–.94	–1.88	–6.78	–2.75	–3.08
B. SERVICES	4 200 . .	12.63	25.18	29.72	45.21	58.85	60.46	61.39	68.12
Total credit	2 200 . .	*111.16*	*127.72*	*147.35*	*163.67*	*177.14*	*184.09*	*193.62*	*208.55*
Total debit	3 200 . .	*–98.53*	*–102.54*	*–117.64*	*–118.46*	*–118.29*	*–123.62*	*–132.23*	*–140.43*
Transportation services, credit	2 205 . .	**28.76**	**31.77**	**38.04**	**39.18**	**40.29**	**40.50**	**42.94**	**46.59**
Passenger	2 205 BA	*8.96*	*10.66*	*15.30*	*15.86*	*16.61*	*16.61*	*17.06*	*18.53*
Freight	2 205 BB	*6.25*	*6.92*	*8.06*	*8.34*	*8.44*	*8.66*	*9.72*	*10.78*
Other	2 205 BC	*13.55*	*14.19*	*14.68*	*14.98*	*15.24*	*15.23*	*16.16*	*17.28*
Sea transport, passenger	2 207 . .	.11	.13	.15	.16	.18	.24	.28	.28
Sea transport, freight	2 208 . .	3.74	3.90	4.10	4.01	3.97	3.95	4.46	5.20
Sea transport, other	2 209 . .	. . .	. . .	. . .	. . .	. . .	. . .	. . .	. . .
Air transport, passenger	2 211 . .	8.85	10.53	15.15	15.70	16.43	16.38	16.78	18.25
Air transport, freight	2 212 . .	1.38	1.72	2.43	2.72	2.59	2.81	3.18	3.47
Air transport, other	2 213 . .	. . .	. . .	. . .	. . .	. . .	. . .	. . .	. . .
Other transport, passenger	2 215 . .	. . .	. . .	. . .	. . .	. . .	. . .	. . .	. . .
Other transport, freight	2 216 . .	1.13	1.30	1.53	1.61	1.88	1.90	2.08	2.11
Other transport, other	2 217 . .	13.55	14.19	14.68	14.98	15.24	15.23	16.16	17.28
Transportation services, debit	3 205 . .	**–28.70**	**–30.48**	**–35.69**	**–35.21**	**–36.00**	**–37.63**	**–40.88**	**–43.53**
Passenger	3 205 BA	*–7.73*	*–8.25*	*–10.52*	*–10.01*	*–10.56*	*–11.31*	*–12.89*	*–14.31*
Freight	3 205 BB	*–13.14*	*–13.29*	*–14.36*	*–13.88*	*–13.77*	*–14.85*	*–16.45*	*–17.10*
Other	3 205 BC	*–7.83*	*–8.94*	*–10.81*	*–11.32*	*–11.67*	*–11.48*	*–11.54*	*–12.12*
Sea transport, passenger	3 207 . .	–.17	–.19	–.24	–.29	–.31	–.34	–.35	–.35
Sea transport, freight	3 208 . .	–9.37	–9.39	–10.29	–9.59	–9.26	–10.05	–10.99	–11.17
Sea transport, other	3 209 . .	. . .	. . .	. . .	. . .	. . .	. . .	. . .	. . .
Air transport, passenger	3 211 . .	–7.56	–8.06	–10.28	–9.72	–10.25	–10.97	–12.54	–13.96
Air transport, freight	3 212 . .	–2.22	–2.19	–2.21	–2.26	–2.37	–2.58	–2.92	–3.21
Air transport, other	3 213 . .	. . .	. . .	. . .	. . .	. . .	. . .	. . .	. . .
Other transport, passenger	3 215 . .	. . .	. . .	. . .	. . .	. . .	. . .	. . .	. . .
Other transport, freight	3 216 . .	–1.55	–1.71	–1.86	–2.03	–2.14	–2.21	–2.54	–2.72
Other transport, other	3 217 . .	–7.83	–8.94	–10.81	–11.32	–11.67	–11.48	–11.54	–12.12
Travel, credit	2 236 . .	**33.57**	**40.78**	**48.14**	**54.06**	**60.92**	**65.67**	**66.74**	**69.84**
Business travel	2 237 . .	. . .	. . .	. . .	. . .	. . .	.31	.33	.34
Personal travel	2 240 . .	. . .	. . .	. . .	. . .	. . .	65.37	66.41	69.50
Travel, debit	3 236 . .	**–32.67**	**–34.01**	**–38.01**	**–36.02**	**–39.26**	**–41.63**	**–44.75**	**–46.90**
Business travel	3 237 . .	. . .	. . .	. . .	. . .	. . .	–.14	–.15	–.17
Personal travel	3 240 . .	. . .	. . .	. . .	. . .	. . .	–41.49	–44.60	–46.73
Other services, credit	2 200 BA	**48.83**	**55.17**	**61.17**	**70.43**	**75.93**	**77.91**	**83.94**	**92.12**
Communications	2 245 . .	2.20	2.52	2.73	3.29	2.89	2.94	3.08	3.14
Construction	2 249 . .	. . .	. . .	. . .	. . .	. . .	2.41	2.45	2.63
Insurance	2 253 . .	1.04	.47	.58	.95	1.22	1.03	1.50	1.39
Financial	2 260 . .	3.83	5.04	4.42	5.00	3.35	5.00	5.63	6.10
Computer and information	2 262 . .	. . .	. . .	. . .	. . .	. . .	. . .	. . .	. . .
Royalties and licence fees	2 266 . .	12.15	13.82	16.64	17.82	19.72	20.33	22.27	26.96
Other business services	2 268 . .	19.65	24.17	26.21	31.54	35.50	25.14	28.76	30.55
Personal, cultural, and recreational	2 287 . .	. . .	. . .	. . .	. . .	. . .	2.16	2.24	2.26
Government, n.i.e.	2 291 . .	9.96	9.16	10.60	11.82	13.25	18.91	18.01	19.09
Other services, debit	3 200 BA	**–37.16**	**–38.05**	**–43.94**	**–47.23**	**–43.03**	**–44.36**	**–46.60**	**–50.00**
Communications	3 245 . .	–4.58	–5.18	–5.58	–6.61	–6.06	–6.72	–7.41	–7.28
Construction	3 249 . .	. . .	. . .	. . .	. . .	. . .	–.31	–.31	–.32
Insurance	3 253 . .	–2.66	–.82	–1.91	–2.47	–1.33	–3.09	–3.78	–4.47
Financial	3 260 . .	–1.66	–2.05	–2.48	–2.67	–2.46	–1.37	–1.60	–1.71
Computer and information	3 262 . .	. . .	. . .	. . .	. . .	. . .	. . .	. . .	. . .
Royalties and licence fees	3 266 . .	–2.59	–2.53	–3.14	–4.04	–5.07	–4.77	–5.52	–6.30
Other business services	3 268 . .	–8.15	–10.28	–11.40	–12.92	–11.98	–13.86	–15.37	–17.68
Personal, cultural, and recreational	3 287 . .	. . .	. . .	. . .	. . .	. . .	–.06	–.14	–.16
Government, n.i.e.	3 291 . .	–17.53	–17.19	–19.43	–18.53	–16.14	–14.18	–12.47	–12.08

Table 2 (Continued). STANDARD PRESENTATION, 1988–95

(Billions of U.S. dollars)

	Code	1988	1989	1990	1991	1992	1993	1994	1995
C. INCOME	4 300 . .	12.51	12.97	19.88	14.81	10.16	8.64	–5.30	–9.17
Total credit	2 300 . .	*129.20*	*152.65*	*160.42*	*137.14*	*119.21*	*120.05*	*141.87*	*182.85*
Total debit	3 300 . .	*–116.69*	*–139.68*	*–140.54*	*–122.33*	*–109.04*	*–111.42*	*–147.17*	*–192.02*
Compensation of employees, credit	2 310 . .	**.13**	**.12**	**.12**	**.13**	**.16**	**.16**	**.16**	**.16**
Compensation of employees, debit	3 310 . .	**–.96**	**–1.03**	**–1.13**	**–1.16**	**–1.18**	**–1.26**	**–1.33**	**–1.36**
Investment income, credit	2 320 . .	**129.07**	**152.53**	**160.30**	**137.01**	**119.05**	**119.90**	**141.71**	**182.69**
Direct investment income	2 330 . .	52.08	55.37	58.74	52.21	51.91	61.47	68.66	88.88
Dividends and distributed branch profits	2 332 . .	40.44	43.44	38.33	35.20	35.61	28.84	33.07	31.95
Reinvested earnings and undistributed branch profits	2 333 . .	11.64	11.93	20.41	17.01	16.30	30.94	33.46	54.47
Income on debt (interest)	2 334 . .	. . .	. . .	. . .	. . .	. . .	1.69	2.13	2.46
Portfolio investment income	2 339 . .	. . .	. . .	. . .	. . .	. . .	23.59	30.06	33.23
Income on equity	2 340 . .	. . .	. . .	. . .	. . .	. . .	6.38	8.10	9.75
Income on bonds and notes	2 350 . .	. . .	. . .	. . .	. . .	. . .	17.21	21.96	23.48
Income on money market instruments and financial derivatives	2 360 . .	. . .	. . .	. . .	. . .	. . .	. . .	. . .	. . .
Other investment income	2 370 . .	76.99	97.16	101.56	84.81	67.13	34.84	42.99	60.58
Investment income, debit	3 320 . .	**–115.73**	**–138.65**	**–139.41**	**–121.17**	**–107.86**	**–110.16**	**–145.84**	**–190.66**
Direct investment income	3 330 . .	–11.70	–6.52	–2.87	3.42	–.33	–5.56	–21.23	–31.40
Dividends and distributed branch profits	3 332 . .	–11.03	–15.18	–17.54	–16.06	–13.72	–8.81	–9.10	–9.82
Reinvested earnings and undistributed branch profits	3 333 . .	–.67	8.67	14.66	19.48	13.39	9.19	–4.52	–13.28
Income on debt (interest)	3 334 . .	. . .	. . .	. . .	. . .	. . .	–5.93	–7.61	–8.30
Portfolio investment income	3 339 . .	. . .	. . .	. . .	. . .	. . .	–70.00	–76.13	–91.10
Income on equity	3 340 . .	. . .	. . .	. . .	. . .	. . .	–9.76	–10.46	–11.19
Income on bonds and notes	3 350 . .	. . .	. . .	. . .	. . .	. . .	–60.24	–65.67	–79.91
Income on money market instruments and financial derivatives	3 360 . .	. . .	. . .	. . .	. . .	. . .	. . .	. . .	. . .
Other investment income	3 370 . .	–104.03	–132.13	–136.53	–124.59	–107.53	–34.61	–48.48	–68.16
D. CURRENT TRANSFERS	4 379 . .	–25.89	–27.28	–34.82	4.79	–34.27	–37.45	–39.26	–35.19
Credit	2 379 . .	**3.66**	**4.09**	**8.79**	**46.84**	**6.50**	**5.20**	**5.22**	**5.65**
General government	2 380 . .	.05	.08	4.30	42.57	1.32	. . .	. . .	. . .
Other sectors	2 390 . .	3.61	4.01	4.49	4.27	5.18	5.20	5.22	5.65
Workers' remittances	2 391 . .	. . .	. . .	. . .	. . .	. . .	. . .	. . .	. . .
Other current transfers	2 392 . .	3.61	4.01	4.49	4.27	5.18	5.20	5.22	5.65
Debit	3 379 . .	**–29.55**	**–31.37**	**–43.61**	**–42.05**	**–40.77**	**–42.65**	**–44.48**	**–40.84**
General government	3 380 . .	–13.24	–13.64	–24.84	–22.14	–19.95	–20.24	–19.27	–13.96
Other sectors	3 390 . .	–16.31	–17.73	–18.78	–19.91	–20.82	–22.42	–25.21	–26.88
Workers' remittances	3 391 . .	–7.16	–7.93	–8.40	–9.05	–9.44	–10.61	–11.35	–12.23
Other current transfers	3 392 . .	–9.15	–9.80	–10.38	–10.86	–11.38	–11.80	–13.86	–14.65
CAPITAL AND FINANCIAL ACCOUNT	4 996 . .	**139.44**	**48.43**	**47.72**	**36.09**	**84.46**	**56.17**	**134.06**	**116.69**
CAPITAL ACCOUNT	4 994 . .	**.23**	**.24**	**.26**	**.28**	**.43**	**–.20**	**–.61**	**.10**
Total credit	2 994 . .	*.23*	*.24*	*.26*	*.28*	*.43*	*.47*	*.47*	*.53*
Total debit	3 994 . .	. . .	. . .	. . .	. . .	. . .	*–.67*	*–1.08*	*–.43*
Capital transfers, credit	2 400 . .	**.23**	**.24**	**.26**	**.28**	**.43**	**.47**	**.47**	**.53**
General government	2 401 . .	. . .	. . .	. . .	. . .	. . .	. . .	. . .	. . .
Debt forgiveness	2 402 . .	. . .	. . .	. . .	. . .	. . .	. . .	. . .	. . .
Other capital transfers	2 410 . .	. . .	. . .	. . .	. . .	. . .	. . .	. . .	. . .
Other sectors	2 430 . .	.23	.24	.26	.28	.43	.47	.47	.53
Migrants' transfers	2 431 . .	.23	.24	.26	.28	.43	.47	.47	.53
Debt forgiveness	2 432 . .	. . .	. . .	. . .	. . .	. . .	. . .	. . .	. . .
Other capital transfers	2 440 . .	. . .	. . .	. . .	. . .	. . .	. . .	. . .	. . .
Capital transfers, debit	3 400 . .	**. . .**	**. . .**	**. . .**	**. . .**	**. . .**	**–.67**	**–1.08**	**–.43**
General government	3 401 . .	. . .	. . .	. . .	. . .	. . .	–.67	–1.08	–.43
Debt forgiveness	3 402 . .	. . .	. . .	. . .	. . .	. . .	–.67	–1.08	–.43
Other capital transfers	3 410 . .	. . .	. . .	. . .	. . .	. . .	. . .	. . .	. . .
Other sectors	3 430 . .	. . .	. . .	. . .	. . .	. . .	. . .	. . .	. . .
Migrants' transfers	3 431 . .	. . .	. . .	. . .	. . .	. . .	. . .	. . .	. . .
Debt forgiveness	3 432 . .	. . .	. . .	. . .	. . .	. . .	. . .	. . .	. . .
Other capital transfers	3 440 . .	. . .	. . .	. . .	. . .	. . .	. . .	. . .	. . .
Nonproduced nonfinancial assets, credit	2 480 . .	**. . .**	**. . .**	**. . .**	**. . .**	**. . .**	**. . .**	**. . .**	**. . .**
Nonproduced nonfinancial assets, debit	3 480 . .	**. . .**	**. . .**	**. . .**	**. . .**	**. . .**	**. . .**	**. . .**	**. . .**

Table 2 (Continued). STANDARD PRESENTATION, 1988–95

(Billions of U.S. dollars)

	Code	1988	1989	1990	1991	1992	1993	1994	1995
FINANCIAL ACCOUNT	4 995	**139.21**	**48.19**	**47.46**	**35.81**	**84.03**	**56.38**	**134.67**	**116.59**
A. DIRECT INVESTMENT	4 500	41.09	30.90	17.97	–9.37	–25.08	–35.16	–4.71	–35.30
Direct investment abroad	4 505	**–16.18**	**–36.83**	**–29.95**	**–31.38**	**–42.66**	**–78.17**	**–54.47**	**–95.53**
Equity capital	4 510	6.65	–6.39	–8.74	–17.68	–14.65	–24.57	–12.75	–36.30
Claims on affiliated enterprises	4 515	...	...	...	...	...	...	...	...
Liabilities to affiliated enterprises	4 520	...	...	...	...	...	...	...	...
Reinvested earnings	4 525	–11.64	–11.93	–20.41	–17.01	–16.30	–30.94	–33.46	–54.47
Other capital	4 530	–11.19	–18.51	–.81	3.31	–11.71	–22.67	–8.26	–4.76
Claims on affiliated enterprises	4 535	–4.15	–24.55	–9.39	1.77	–10.95	–26.51	–14.23	–23.64
Liabilities to affiliated enterprises	4 540	–7.04	6.03	8.58	1.55	–.76	3.85	5.97	18.88
Direct investment in United States	4 555	**57.27**	**67.73**	**47.92**	**22.01**	**17.58**	**43.01**	**49.76**	**60.23**
Equity capital	4 560	45.04	51.77	56.24	45.82	31.58	28.10	34.50	39.54
Claims on direct investors	4 565	...	...	...	...	...	...	...	...
Liabilities to direct investors	4 570	...	...	...	...	...	...	...	...
Reinvested earnings	4 575	.67	–8.67	–14.66	–19.48	–13.39	–9.19	4.52	13.28
Other capital	4 580	11.56	24.63	6.34	–4.33	–.61	24.10	10.74	7.41
Claims on direct investors	4 585	17.77	26.12	20.51	5.49	9.02	–1.29	4.65	–8.03
Liabilities to direct investors	4 590	–6.21	–1.49	–14.17	–9.82	–9.63	25.38	6.09	15.44
B. PORTFOLIO INVESTMENT	4 600	65.97	73.60	–6.78	11.84	22.83	–35.29	79.16	137.22
Assets	4 602	**–7.88**	**–22.10**	**–28.80**	**–45.69**	**–49.17**	**–146.26**	**–60.29**	**–98.96**
Equity securities	4 610	–.92	–17.22	–7.41	–30.64	–32.40	–63.38	–48.09	–50.70
Monetary authorities	4 611	...	...	...	...	...	...	...	...
General government	4 612	...	...	...	...	...	...	...	...
Banks	4 613	...	...	...	...	...	...	...	...
Other sectors	4 614	–.92	–17.22	–7.41	–30.64	–32.40	–63.38	–48.09	–50.70
Debt securities	4 619	–6.96	–4.88	–21.39	–15.05	–16.77	–82.88	–12.20	–48.26
Bonds and notes	4 620	–6.96	–4.88	–21.39	–15.05	–16.77	–82.88	–12.20	–48.26
Monetary authorities	4 621	...	...	...	...	...	...	...	...
General government	4 622	...	...	...	...	...	...	...	...
Banks	4 623	...	...	...	...	...	...	...	...
Other sectors	4 624	–6.96	–4.88	–21.39	–15.05	–16.77	–82.88	–12.20	–48.26
Money market instruments	4 630	...	...	...	...	...	...	...	...
Monetary authorities	4 631	...	...	...	...	...	...	...	...
General government	4 632	...	...	...	...	...	...	...	...
Banks	4 633	...	...	...	...	...	...	...	...
Other sectors	4 634	...	...	...	...	...	...	...	...
Financial derivatives	4 640	...	...	...	...	...	...	...	...
Monetary authorities	4 641	...	...	...	...	...	...	...	...
General government	4 642	...	...	...	...	...	...	...	...
Banks	4 643	...	...	...	...	...	...	...	...
Other sectors	4 644	...	...	...	...	...	...	...	...
Liabilities	4 652	**73.85**	**95.70**	**22.02**	**57.53**	**72.00**	**110.97**	**139.45**	**236.18**
Equity securities	4 660	–.48	6.96	–14.52	9.47	–4.17	20.92	.91	16.41
Banks	4 663	...	...	...	...	...	...	...	...
Other sectors	4 664	...	...	...	...	...	...	...	...
Debt securities	4 669	74.33	88.74	36.54	48.06	76.17	90.05	138.54	219.77
Bonds and notes	4 670	74.33	88.74	36.54	48.06	76.17	90.05	138.54	219.77
Monetary authorities	4 671	...	...	...	...	...	...	...	...
General government	4 672	52.91	70.63	26.01	31.31	56.24	60.27	100.49	162.83
Banks	4 673	...	...	...	...	...	...	...	...
Other sectors	4 674	21.42	18.11	10.53	16.75	19.93	29.78	38.05	56.94
Money market instruments	4 680	...	...	...	...	...	...	...	...
Monetary authorities	4 681	...	...	...	...	...	...	...	...
General government	4 682	...	...	...	...	...	...	...	...
Banks	4 683	...	...	...	...	...	...	...	...
Other sectors	4 684	...	...	...	...	...	...	...	...
Financial derivatives	4 690	...	...	...	...	...	...	...	...
Monetary authorities	4 691	...	...	...	...	...	...	...	...
General government	4 692	...	...	...	...	...	...	...	...
Banks	4 693	...	...	...	...	...	...	...	...
Other sectors	4 694	...	...	...	...	...	...	...	...

Table 2 (Concluded). STANDARD PRESENTATION, 1988–95
(Billions of U.S. dollars)

	Code	1988	1989	1990	1991	1992	1993	1994	1995
C. OTHER INVESTMENT	4 700	36.07	−31.04	38.50	27.58	82.36	128.20	54.88	24.41
Assets	4 703	**−73.28**	**−83.40**	**−13.73**	**13.81**	**17.79**	**31.18**	**−41.31**	**−103.63**
Trade credits	4 706	−1.55	−1.16	−1.40	−.81	−1.34	−1.65	−2.73	−1.81
General government: long-term	4 708	...	...	...	...	...	...	...	...
General government: short-term	4 709	...	...	...	...	...	...	...	...
Other sectors: long-term	4 711	...	...	...	...	...	...	...	...
Other sectors: short-term	4 712	−1.55	−1.16	−1.40	−.81	−1.34	−1.65	−2.73	−1.81
Loans	4 714	4.02	2.35	3.72	5.41	−.19	−.06	−.19	−.42
Monetary authorities: long-term	4 717	...	...	...	...	...	...	...	...
Monetary authorities: short-term	4 718	...	...	...	...	...	...	...	...
General government: long-term	4 720	4.02	2.35	3.72	5.41	−.19	−.06	−.19	−.42
General government: short-term	4 721	...	...	...	...	...	...	...	...
Banks: long-term	4 723	...	...	...	...	...	...	...	...
Banks: short-term	4 724	...	...	...	...	...	...	...	...
Other sectors: long-term	4 726	...	...	...	...	...	...	...	...
Other sectors: short-term	4 727	...	...	...	...	...	...	...	...
Currency and deposits	4 730	−83.85	−85.29	−29.36	7.49	22.69	32.86	−38.41	−101.44
Monetary authorities	4 731	...	...	...	...	...	...	...	...
General government	4 732	.29	.12	−.13	−1.00	−.07	−.31	−.18	.10
Banks	4 733	−57.32	−40.90	.34	−17.90	24.29	29.95	−8.16	−69.14
Other sectors	4 734	−26.82	−44.51	−29.57	26.39	−1.53	3.22	−30.07	−32.40
Other assets	4 736	8.11	.70	13.31	1.73	−3.37	.03	.02	.04
Monetary authorities: long-term	4 738	...	...	...	...	...	...	...	...
Monetary authorities: short-term	4 739	...	...	...	...	...	...	...	...
General government: long-term	4 741	−2.47	−.08	−1.88	−1.10	−2.90	.03	.02	.04
General government: short-term	4 742	...	...	...	...	...	...	...	...
Banks: long-term	4 744	10.58	.78	15.19	2.82	−.47	...	...	...
Banks: short-term	4 745	...	...	...	...	...	...	...	...
Other sectors: long-term	4 747	...	...	...	...	...	...	...	...
Other sectors: short-term	4 748	...	...	...	...	...	...	...	...
Liabilities	4 753	**109.35**	**52.36**	**52.24**	**13.77**	**64.56**	**97.02**	**96.19**	**128.04**
Trade credits	4 756	−.84	1.57	2.62	−1.43	.63	−.75	1.21	1.00
General government: long-term	4 758	...	...	...	...	...	...	...	...
General government: short-term	4 759	...	...	...	...	...	...	...	...
Other sectors: long-term	4 761	...	...	...	...	...	...	...	...
Other sectors: short-term	4 762	−.84	1.57	2.62	−1.43	.63	−.75	1.21	1.00
Loans	4 764	...	...	...	...	...	...	...	...
Use of Fund credit and loans from the Fund	4 766	...	...	...	...	...	...	...	...
Monetary authorities: other long-term	4 767	...	...	...	...	...	...	...	...
Monetary authorities: short-term	4 768	...	...	...	...	...	...	...	...
General government: long-term	4 770	...	...	...	...	...	...	...	...
General government: short-term	4 771	...	...	...	...	...	...	...	...
Banks: long-term	4 773	...	...	...	...	...	...	...	...
Banks: short-term	4 774	...	...	...	...	...	...	...	...
Other sectors: long-term	4 776	...	...	...	...	...	...	...	...
Other sectors: short-term	4 777	...	...	...	...	...	...	...	...
Currency and deposits	4 780	61.19	55.82	2.43	2.80	28.74	35.70	115.41	58.15
Monetary authorities	4 781	...	...	...	...	...	...	...	...
General government	4 782	...	...	...	...	...	...	...	...
Banks	4 783	61.19	55.82	2.43	2.80	28.74	35.70	115.41	58.15
Other sectors	4 784	...	...	...	...	...	...	...	...
Other liabilities	4 786	49.00	−5.03	47.19	12.40	35.19	62.07	−20.43	68.89
Monetary authorities: long-term	4 788	...	...	...	...	...	...	...	...
Monetary authorities: short-term	4 789	14.43	−25.07	6.34	13.56	18.41	49.09	−13.88	34.25
General government: long-term	4 791	−.47	.16	1.87	1.36	2.19	1.71	2.34	1.08
General government: short-term	4 792	...	...	...	...	...	...	...	...
Banks: long-term	4 794	−.89	−1.56	−.67	−.55	−1.65	.06	−.30	−.01
Banks: short-term	4 795	...	...	...	...	...	...	...	...
Other sectors: long-term	4 797	...	...	...	...	...	−.04	.32	...
Other sectors: short-term	4 798	35.93	21.44	39.65	−1.97	16.24	11.24	−8.91	33.57
D. RESERVE ASSETS	4 800	−3.92	−25.27	−2.23	5.76	3.92	−1.38	5.34	−9.74
Monetary gold	4 810	...	.01	...	...	...	...	...	...
Special drawing rights	4 820	.13	−.53	−.20	−.18	2.32	−.54	−.44	−.81
Reserve position in the Fund	4 830	1.02	.47	.66	−.37	−2.66	−.04	.50	−2.47
Foreign exchange	4 840	−5.07	−25.22	−2.70	6.31	4.27	−.80	5.28	−6.46
Other claims	4 880	...	...	...	...	...	...	...	...
NET ERRORS AND OMISSIONS	4 998	**−11.73**	**55.83**	**46.54**	**−26.83**	**−23.11**	**43.55**	**13.71**	**31.54**

Part 3 of the *Yearbook* contains descriptions of the methodologies, compilation practices, and sources used to compile these data.

Table 3. INTERNATIONAL INVESTMENT POSITION (End–period stocks), 1988–95

(Billions of U.S. dollars)

	Code	1988	1989	1990	1991	1992	1993	1994	1995
ASSETS	8 995 C.	1,949.72	2,251.40	2,178.11	2,314.96	2,285.59	2,750.28	2,825.83	3,352.91
Direct investment abroad	8 505 . .	**692.46**	**832.46**	**731.76**	**827.54**	**798.63**	**1,027.55**	**1,058.94**	**1,301.13**
Equity capital and reinvested earnings	8 506 . .	...	...	...	...	...	...	...	...
Claims on affiliated enterprises	8 507 . .	...	...	...	...	...	...	...	...
Liabilities to affiliated enterprises	8 508 . .	...	...	...	...	...	...	...	...
Other capital	8 530 . .	...	...	...	...	...	...	...	...
Claims on affiliated enterprises	8 535 . .	...	...	...	...	...	...	...	...
Liabilities to affiliated enterprises	8 540 . .	...	...	...	...	...	...	...	...
Portfolio investment	8 602 . .	**175.98**	**217.61**	**228.69**	**302.43**	**336.55**	**550.63**	**556.24**	**721.75**
Equity securities	8 610 . .	85.99	119.86	110.03	158.81	179.71	302.79	323.98	411.08
Monetary authorities	8 611 . .	...	...	...	...	...	...	...	...
General government	8 612 . .	...	...	...	...	...	...	...	...
Banks	8 613 . .	...	...	...	...	...	...	...	...
Other sectors	8 614 . .	...	...	...	...	...	...	...	...
Debt securities	8 619 . .	89.99	97.75	118.66	143.62	156.83	247.84	232.27	310.67
Bonds and notes	8 620 . .	89.99	97.75	118.66	143.62	156.83	247.84	232.27	310.67
Monetary authorities	8 621 . .	...	...	...	...	...	...	...	...
General government	8 622 . .	...	...	...	...	...	...	...	...
Banks	8 623 . .	...	...	...	...	...	...	...	...
Other sectors	8 624 . .	...	...	...	...	...	...	...	...
Money market instruments	8 630 . .	...	...	...	...	...	...	...	...
Monetary authorities	8 631 . .	...	...	...	...	...	...	...	...
General government	8 632 . .	...	...	...	...	...	...	...	...
Banks	8 633 . .	...	...	...	...	...	...	...	...
Other sectors	8 634 . .	...	...	...	...	...	...	...	...
Financial derivatives	8 640 . .	...	...	...	...	...	...	...	...
Monetary authorities	8 641 . .	...	...	...	...	...	...	...	...
General government	8 642 . .	...	...	...	...	...	...	...	...
Banks	8 643 . .	...	...	...	...	...	...	...	...
Other sectors	8 644 . .	...	...	...	...	...	...	...	...
Other investment	8 703 . .	**937.10**	**1,032.61**	**1,043.00**	**1,025.78**	**1,002.98**	**1,007.19**	**1,047.25**	**1,153.97**
Trade credits	8 706 . .	11.09	12.25	13.66	14.47	15.80	18.43	21.16	22.97
General government: long-term	8 708 . .	...	...	...	...	...	...	...	...
General government: short-term	8 709 . .	...	...	...	...	...	...	...	...
Other sectors: long-term	8 711 . .	...	...	...	...	...	...	...	...
Other sectors: short-term	8 712 . .	...	...	...	...	...	...	...	...
Loans	8 714 . .	86.12	84.49	81.99	79.08	80.66	80.95	81.27	81.55
Monetary authorities: long-term	8 717 . .	...	...	...	...	...	...	...	...
Monetary authorities: short-term	8 718 . .	...	...	...	...	...	...	...	...
General government: long-term	8 720 . .	...	...	...	...	...	...	...	...
General government: short-term	8 721 . .	...	...	...	...	...	...	...	...
Banks: long-term	8 723 . .	...	...	...	...	...	...	...	...
Banks: short-term	8 724 . .	...	...	...	...	...	...	...	...
Other sectors: long-term	8 726 . .	...	...	...	...	...	...	...	...
Other sectors: short-term	8 727 . .	...	...	...	...	...	...	...	...
Currency and deposits	8 730 . .	...	...	...	...	...	...	...	...
Monetary authorities	8 731 . .	...	...	...	...	...	...	...	...
General government	8 732 . .	...	...	...	...	...	...	...	...
Banks	8 733 . .	...	...	...	...	...	...	...	...
Other sectors	8 734 . .	...	...	...	...	...	...	...	...
Other assets	8 736 . .	839.89	935.87	947.35	932.23	906.52	907.82	944.82	1,049.45
Monetary authorities: long-term	8 738 . .	...	...	...	...	...	...	...	...
Monetary authorities: short-term	8 739 . .	...	...	...	...	...	...	...	...
General government: long-term	8 741 . .	...	...	...	...	...	...	...	...
General government: short-term	8 742 . .	...	...	...	...	...	...	...	...
Banks: long-term	8 744 . .	...	...	...	...	...	...	...	...
Banks: short-term	8 745 . .	...	...	...	...	...	...	...	...
Other sectors: long-term	8 747 . .	...	...	...	...	...	...	...	...
Other sectors: short-term	8 748 . .	...	...	...	...	...	...	...	...
Reserve assets	8 800 . .	**144.18**	**168.71**	**174.66**	**159.22**	**147.44**	**164.91**	**163.39**	**176.06**
Monetary gold	8 810 . .	107.43	105.16	102.41	92.56	87.17	102.56	100.11	101.28
Special drawing rights	8 820 . .	9.64	9.95	10.99	11.24	8.50	9.02	10.04	11.04
Reserve position in the Fund	8 830 . .	9.75	9.05	9.08	9.49	11.76	11.80	12.03	14.65
Foreign exchange	8 840 . .	17.36	44.55	52.19	45.93	40.01	41.53	41.22	49.10
Other claims	8 880 . .	...	...	...	...	...	...	...	...

Table 3 (Continued). INTERNATIONAL INVESTMENT POSITION (End–period stocks), 1988–95

(Billions of U.S. dollars)

	Code	1988	1989	1990	1991	1992	1993	1994	1995
LIABILITIES	8 995 D.	1,934.96	2,328.51	2,389.78	2,663.98	2,853.99	3,162.86	3,318.31	4,126.56
Direct investment in United States	8 555 ..	**391.53**	**534.73**	**539.60**	**669.14**	**694.21**	**760.86**	**771.85**	**1,019.20**
Equity capital and reinvested earnings	8 556 ..	...	...	...	...	...	...	...	...
Claims on direct investors	8 557 ..	...	...	...	...	...	...	...	...
Liabilities to direct investors	8 558 ..	...	...	...	...	...	...	...	...
Other capital	8 580 ..	...	...	...	...	...	...	...	...
Claims on direct investors	8 585 ..	...	...	...	...	...	...	...	...
Liabilities to direct investors	8 590 ..	...	...	...	...	...	...	...	...
Portfolio investment	8 652 ..	**768.49**	**939.34**	**948.06**	**1,093.36**	**1,212.31**	**1,408.84**	**1,467.26**	**1,933.37**
Equity securities	8 660 ..	213.81	276.10	243.79	298.96	329.22	373.52	368.90	509.00
Banks	8 663 ..	...	...	...	...	...	...	...	...
Other sectors	8 664 ..	...	...	...	...	...	...	...	...
Debt securities	8 669 ..	554.67	663.24	704.27	794.40	883.09	1,035.32	1,098.36	1,424.37
Bonds and notes	8 670 ..	554.67	663.24	704.27	794.40	883.09	1,035.32	1,098.36	1,424.37
Monetary authorities	8 671 ..	353.84	423.80	450.29	496.60	548.08	625.07	660.03	860.45
General government	8 672 ..	7.97	6.41	7.12	8.84	12.73	17.15	21.57	27.40
Banks	8 673 ..	...	...	...	...	...	...	...	...
Other sectors	8 674 ..	192.86	233.03	246.86	288.96	322.29	393.11	416.76	536.52
Money market instruments	8 680 ..	...	...	...	...	...	...	...	...
Monetary authorities	8 681 ..	...	...	...	...	...	...	...	...
General government	8 682 ..	...	...	...	...	...	...	...	...
Banks	8 683 ..	...	...	...	...	...	...	...	...
Other sectors	8 684 ..	...	...	...	...	...	...	...	...
Financial derivatives	8 690 ..	...	...	...	...	...	...	...	...
Monetary authorities	8 691 ..	...	...	...	...	...	...	...	...
General government	8 692 ..	...	...	...	...	...	...	...	...
Banks	8 692 ..	...	...	...	...	...	...	...	...
Other sectors	8 694 ..	...	...	...	...	...	...	...	...
Other investment	8 753 ..	**774.95**	**854.43**	**902.13**	**901.49**	**947.47**	**993.16**	**1,079.20**	**1,173.99**
Trade credits	8 756 ..	6.50	8.07	10.68	9.25	9.89	8.80	10.01	11.01
General government: long-term	8 758 ..	...	...	...	...	...	...	...	...
General government: short-term	8 759 ..	...	...	...	...	...	...	...	...
Other sectors: long-term	8 761 ..	...	...	...	...	...	...	...	...
Other sectors: short-term	8 762 ..	...	...	...	...	...	...	...	...
Loans	8 764 ..	...	...	...	...	...	...	...	...
Use of Fund credit and loans from the Fund	8 766 ..	...	...	...	...	...	...	...	...
Monetary authorities: other long-term	8 767 ..	...	...	...	...	...	...	...	...
Monetary authorities: short-term	8 768 ..	...	...	...	...	...	...	...	...
General government: long-term	8 770 ..	...	...	...	...	...	...	...	...
General government: short-term	8 771 ..	...	...	...	...	...	...	...	...
Banks: long-term	8 773 ..	...	...	...	...	...	...	...	...
Banks: short-term	8 774 ..	...	...	...	...	...	...	...	...
Other sectors: long-term	8 776 ..	...	...	...	...	...	...	...	...
Other sectors: short-term	8 777 ..	...	...	...	...	...	...	...	...
Currency and deposits	8 780 ..	...	...	...	...	...	...	...	...
Monetary authorities	8 781 ..	...	...	...	...	...	...	...	...
General government	8 782 ..	...	...	...	...	...	...	...	...
Banks	8 783 ..	...	...	...	...	...	...	...	...
Other sectors	8 784 ..	...	...	...	...	...	...	...	...
Other liabilities	8 786 ..	768.44	846.36	891.44	892.23	937.58	984.36	1,069.19	1,162.98
Monetary authorities: long-term	8 788 ..	...	...	...	...	...	...	...	...
Monetary authorities: short-term	8 789 ..	...	...	...	...	...	...	...	...
General government: long-term	8 791 ..	...	...	...	...	...	...	...	...
General government: short-term	8 792 ..	...	...	...	...	...	...	...	...
Banks: long-term	8 794 ..	...	...	...	...	...	...	...	...
Banks: short-term	8 795 ..	...	...	...	...	...	...	...	...
Other sectors: long-term	8 797 ..	...	...	...	...	...	...	...	...
Other sectors: short-term	8 798 ..	...	...	...	...	...	...	...	...
NET INTERNATIONAL INVESTMENT POSITION	8 995 ..	**14.76**	**–77.11**	**–211.67**	**–349.02**	**–568.40**	**–412.58**	**–492.48**	**–773.65**

Table 1. ANALYTIC PRESENTATION, 1988–95
(Millions of U.S. dollars)

	Code	1988	1989	1990	1991	1992	1993	1994	1995
A. Current Account [1]	4 993 Y.	**22.1**	**133.5**	**185.9**	**42.4**	**–8.8**	**–243.8**	**–438.3**	**–358.4**
Goods: exports f.o.b	2 100 . .	1,404.5	1,599.0	1,692.9	1,604.7	1,801.4	1,731.6	1,917.6	2,106.0
Goods: imports f.o.b	3 100 . .	–1,112.2	–1,136.2	–1,266.9	–1,543.7	–1,923.2	–2,118.3	–2,623.6	–2,682.2
Balance on Goods	4 100 . .	*292.3*	*462.8*	*426.0*	*61.0*	*–121.8*	*–386.7*	*–706.0*	*–576.2*
Services: credit	2 200 . .	348.3	433.3	465.6	596.2	830.3	1,028.4	1,330.7	1,171.3
Services: debit	3 200 . .	–315.4	–421.7	–392.5	–422.5	–558.8	–746.5	–861.6	–813.0
Balance on Goods and Services	4 991 . .	*325.1*	*474.4*	*499.1*	*234.7*	*149.7*	*–104.8*	*–236.9*	*–217.9*
Income: credit	2 300 . .	114.7	203.2	258.3	234.7	225.0	250.1	282.5	401.2
Income: debit	3 300 . .	–439.0	–552.1	–579.6	–467.1	–412.1	–442.5	–525.1	–573.7
Balance on Goods, Services, and Income	4 992 . .	*.8*	*125.5*	*177.8*	*2.3*	*–37.4*	*–297.2*	*–479.5*	*–390.4*
Current transfers: credit	2 379 Y.	26.0	15.0	15.8	50.1	36.0	61.2	49.2	40.0
Current transfers: debit	3 379 . .	–4.7	–7.0	–7.7	–10.0	–7.4	–7.8	–8.0	–8.0
B. Capital Account [1]	4 994 Y.	**. . .**	**. . .**	**. . .**	**. . .**	**. . .**	**. . .**	**. . .**	**. . .**
Capital account: credit	2 994 Y.	. . .	. . .	. . .	. . .	. . .	. . .	. . .	. . .
Capital account: debit	3 994 . .	. . .	. . .	. . .	. . .	. . .	. . .	. . .	. . .
Total, Groups A Plus B	4 010 . .	*22.1*	*133.5*	*185.9*	*42.4*	*–8.8*	*–243.8*	*–438.3*	*–358.4*
C. Financial Account [1]	4 995 X.	**186.5**	**–5.9**	**–85.9**	**–429.2**	**–91.5**	**223.6**	**537.2**	**390.3**
Direct investment abroad	4 505 . .	–2.3	. . .	. . .	. . .	. . .	. . .	. . .	. . .
Direct investment in Uruguay	4 555 Y.	46.8	. . .	. . .	. . .	. . .	101.5	154.5	123.5
Portfolio investment assets	4 602 . .	–60.1	. . .	. . .	. . .	. . .	. . .	. . .	. . .
Equity securities	4 610 . .	–24.9	. . .	. . .	. . .	. . .	. . .	. . .	. . .
Debt securities	4 619 . .	–35.2	. . .	. . .	. . .	. . .	. . .	. . .	. . .
Portfolio investment liabilities	4 652 Y.	224.3	129.8	107.8	47.4	83.4	29.3	158.1	288.9
Equity securities	4 660 Y.	. . .	. . .	. . .	. . .	. . .	. . .	. . .	. . .
Debt securities	4 669 Y.	224.3	129.8	107.8	47.4	83.4	29.3	158.1	288.9
Other investment assets	4 703 . .	–390.4	–764.3	–632.0	–399.0	–589.8	–19.3	–71.8	–413.1
Monetary authorities	4 703 .A	. . .	. . .	. . .	. . .	. . .	. . .	–10.1	. . .
General government	4 703 .B	–.6	. . .	. . .	. . .	. . .	. . .	. . .	. . .
Banks	4 703 .C	–290.1	–586.6	–441.5	–387.2	–589.8	–18.6	–44.0	–412.5
Other sectors	4 703 .D	–99.7	–177.7	–190.5	–11.8	. . .	–.7	–17.7	–.6
Other investment liabilities	4 753 X.	368.2	628.6	438.3	–77.6	414.9	112.1	296.4	391.0
Monetary authorities	4 753 XA	–67.0	–76.2	–17.8	–279.2	–139.2	–28.1	5.7	–62.5
General government	4 753 YB	–12.2	11.0	15.6	111.1	104.9	120.3	134.0	61.1
Banks	4 753 YC	464.7	641.2	393.0	234.7	434.2	16.0	99.8	466.4
Other sectors	4 753 YD	–17.3	52.6	47.5	–144.2	15.0	3.9	56.9	–74.0
Total, Groups A Through C	4 020 . .	*208.6*	*127.6*	*100.0*	*–386.8*	*–100.3*	*–20.2*	*98.9*	*31.9*
D. Net Errors and Omissions	4 998 . .	**–247.0**	**–62.6**	**35.7**	**468.8**	**238.3**	**208.7**	**10.2**	**195.9**
Total, Groups A Through D	4 030 . .	*–38.4*	*65.0*	*135.7*	*82.0*	*138.0*	*188.5*	*109.1*	*227.8*
E. Reserves and Related Items	4 040 . .	**38.4**	**–65.0**	**–135.7**	**–82.0**	**–138.0**	**–188.5**	**–109.1**	**–227.8**
Reserve assets	4 800 . .	46.8	3.2	–40.2	–113.5	–186.2	–178.6	–98.5	–218.0
Use of Fund credit and loans	4 766 . .	–63.3	–98.0	–111.5	–41.3	–2.5	–14.4	–10.6	–9.8
Liabilities constituting foreign authorities' reserves	4 900 . .	14.9	–5.2	–3.8	–2.2	. . .	4.4	. . .	. . .
Exceptional financing	4 920 . .	40.0	35.0	19.8	75.0	50.7	. . .	. . .	. . .
Conversion rates: Uruguayan pesos per U.S. dollar	0 101 . .	**.3594**	**.6055**	**1.1710**	**2.0188**	**3.0270**	**3.9484**	**5.0529**	**6.3491**

[1] Excludes components that have been classified in the categories of Group E.

Table 2. STANDARD PRESENTATION, 1988–95
(Millions of U.S. dollars)

	Code	1988	1989	1990	1991	1992	1993	1994	1995
CURRENT ACCOUNT	4 993 . .	**22.1**	**133.5**	**185.9**	**42.4**	**–8.8**	**–243.8**	**–438.3**	**–358.4**
A. GOODS	4 100 . .	292.3	462.8	426.0	61.0	–121.8	–386.7	–706.0	–576.2
Credit	2 100 . .	**1,404.5**	**1,599.0**	**1,692.9**	**1,604.7**	**1,801.4**	**1,731.6**	**1,917.6**	**2,106.0**
General merchandise: exports f.o.b.	2 110 . .	1,404.5	1,599.0	1,692.9	1,604.7	1,702.5	1,645.3	1,913.4	2,106.0
Goods for processing: exports f.o.b.	2 150 . .	. . .	. . .	. . .	. . .	. . .	. . .	. . .	. . .
Repairs on goods	2 160 . .	. . .	. . .	. . .	. . .	. . .	. . .	. . .	. . .
Goods procured in ports by carriers	2 170 . .	. . .	. . .	. . .	. . .	. . .	. . .	4.2	. . .
Nonmonetary gold	2 180 . .	. . .	. . .	. . .	. . .	98.9	86.3	. . .	. . .
Debit	3 100 . .	**–1,112.2**	**–1,136.2**	**–1,266.9**	**–1,543.7**	**–1,923.2**	**–2,118.3**	**–2,623.6**	**–2,682.2**
General merchandise: imports f.o.b.	3 110 . .	–1,112.2	–1,136.2	–1,266.9	–1,543.7	–1,923.2	–2,118.3	–2,599.6	–2,682.2
Goods for processing: imports f.o.b.	3 150 . .	. . .	. . .	. . .	. . .	. . .	. . .	. . .	. . .
Repairs on goods	3 160 . .	. . .	. . .	. . .	. . .	. . .	. . .	. . .	. . .
Goods procured in ports by carriers	3 170 . .	. . .	. . .	. . .	. . .	. . .	. . .	–24.0	. . .
Nonmonetary gold	3 180 . .	. . .	. . .	. . .	. . .	. . .	. . .	. . .	. . .
B. SERVICES	4 200 . .	32.8	11.6	73.1	173.7	271.5	281.9	469.1	358.3
Total credit	2 200 . .	*348.3*	*433.3*	*465.6*	*596.2*	*830.3*	*1,028.4*	*1,330.7*	*1,171.3*
Total debit	3 200 . .	*–315.4*	*–421.7*	*–392.5*	*–422.5*	*–558.8*	*–746.5*	*–861.6*	*–813.0*
Transportation services, credit	2 205 . .	**73.5**	**145.2**	**169.7**	**198.9**	**334.6**	**351.4**	**392.7**	**270.6**
Passenger	2 205 BA	*20.8*	*45.0*	*64.3*	*44.9*	*78.3*	*113.9*	*88.7*	. . .
Freight	2 205 BB	*24.0*	*26.9*	*41.3*	*80.3*	*119.2*	*142.7*	*205.4*	*169.6*
Other	2 205 BC	*28.7*	*73.3*	*64.1*	*73.7*	*137.1*	*94.8*	*98.6*	*101.0*
Sea transport, passenger	2 207 . .	. . .	. . .	. . .	. . .	. . .	. . .	. . .	. . .
Sea transport, freight	2 208 . .	24.0	26.9	41.3	80.3	119.2	142.7	205.4	169.6
Sea transport, other	2 209 . .	28.7	73.3	64.1	73.7	137.1	94.8	98.6	101.0
Air transport, passenger	2 211 . .	9.8	21.1	30.2	21.1	36.8	53.5	43.6	. . .
Air transport, freight	2 212 . .	. . .	. . .	. . .	. . .	. . .	. . .	. . .	. . .
Air transport, other	2 213 . .	. . .	. . .	. . .	. . .	. . .	. . .	. . .	. . .
Other transport, passenger	2 215 . .	11.0	23.9	34.1	23.8	41.5	60.4	45.1	. . .
Other transport, freight	2 216 . .	. . .	. . .	. . .	. . .	. . .	. . .	. . .	. . .
Other transport, other	2 217 . .	. . .	. . .	. . .	. . .	. . .	. . .	. . .	. . .
Transportation services, debit	3 205 . .	**–88.6**	**–145.7**	**–175.0**	**–218.4**	**–284.5**	**–361.7**	**–376.2**	**–357.0**
Passenger	3 205 BA	*–37.7*	*–63.8*	*–72.9*	*–60.5*	*–91.0*	*–77.7*	*–87.0*	. . .
Freight	3 205 BB	*–42.6*	*–48.8*	*–48.6*	*–62.0*	*–79.4*	*–122.9*	*–130.7*	*–120.2*
Other	3 205 BC	*–8.3*	*–33.1*	*–53.5*	*–95.9*	*–114.1*	*–161.1*	*–158.5*	*–236.8*
Sea transport, passenger	3 207 . .	. . .	. . .	. . .	. . .	. . .	. . .	. . .	. . .
Sea transport, freight	3 208 . .	–42.6	–48.8	–48.6	–62.0	–79.4	–122.9	–130.7	–120.2
Sea transport, other	3 209 . .	–8.3	–33.1	–53.5	–95.9	–114.1	–161.1	–158.5	–236.8
Air transport, passenger	3 211 . .	–36.5	–61.8	–70.6	–58.6	–88.1	–75.2	–84.2	. . .
Air transport, freight	3 212 . .	. . .	. . .	. . .	. . .	. . .	. . .	. . .	. . .
Air transport, other	3 213 . .	. . .	. . .	. . .	. . .	. . .	. . .	. . .	. . .
Other transport, passenger	3 215 . .	–1.2	–2.0	–2.3	–1.9	–2.9	–2.5	–2.8	. . .
Other transport, freight	3 216 . .	. . .	. . .	. . .	. . .	. . .	. . .	. . .	. . .
Other transport, other	3 217 . .	. . .	. . .	. . .	. . .	. . .	. . .	. . .	. . .
Travel, credit	2 236 . .	**202.8**	**227.9**	**238.2**	**332.5**	**381.3**	**446.8**	**632.0**	**610.9**
Business travel	2 237 . .	. . .	. . .	. . .	. . .	. . .	. . .	. . .	. . .
Personal travel	2 240 . .	202.8	227.9	238.2	332.5	381.3	446.8	632.0	610.9
Travel, debit	3 236 . .	**–138.5**	**–166.5**	**–111.4**	**–99.7**	**–104.3**	**–128.7**	**–234.0**	**–236.0**
Business travel	3 237 . .	. . .	. . .	. . .	. . .	. . .	. . .	. . .	. . .
Personal travel	3 240 . .	–138.5	–166.5	–111.4	–99.7	–104.3	–128.7	–234.0	–236.0
Other services, credit	2 200 BA	**72.0**	**60.2**	**57.7**	**64.8**	**114.4**	**230.2**	**306.0**	**289.8**
Communications	2 245 . .	. . .	. . .	. . .	. . .	. . .	. . .	. . .	. . .
Construction	2 249 . .	. . .	. . .	. . .	. . .	. . .	. . .	. . .	. . .
Insurance	2 253 . .	2.7	3.0	4.6	8.9	13.2	15.9	16.0	. . .
Financial	2 260 . .	. . .	. . .	. . .	. . .	. . .	. . .	. . .	. . .
Computer and information	2 262 . .	. . .	. . .	. . .	. . .	. . .	. . .	. . .	. . .
Royalties and licence fees	2 266 . .	. . .	. . .	. . .	. . .	. . .	.4	.5	. . .
Other business services	2 268 . .	59.7	49.4	47.4	49.8	92.7	205.4	282.7	289.8
Personal, cultural, and recreational	2 287 . .	. . .	. . .	. . .	. . .	. . .	. . .	. . .	. . .
Government, n.i.e.	2 291 . .	9.6	7.8	5.7	6.1	8.5	8.5	6.8	. . .
Other services, debit	3 200 BA	**–88.3**	**–109.5**	**–106.1**	**–104.4**	**–170.0**	**–256.1**	**–251.4**	**–220.0**
Communications	3 245 . .	. . .	. . .	. . .	. . .	. . .	. . .	. . .	. . .
Construction	3 249 . .	. . .	. . .	. . .	. . .	. . .	. . .	. . .	. . .
Insurance	3 253 . .	–4.7	–5.4	–5.4	–6.9	–8.8	–13.7	–12.9	. . .
Financial	3 260 . .	. . .	. . .	. . .	. . .	. . .	. . .	. . .	. . .
Computer and information	3 262 . .	. . .	. . .	. . .	. . .	. . .	. . .	. . .	. . .
Royalties and licence fees	3 266 . .	–6.3	. . .	. . .	. . .	. . .	–5.7	–5.0	. . .
Other business services	3 268 . .	–52.5	–75.1	–71.3	–63.4	–118.8	–201.5	–192.6	–220.0
Personal, cultural, and recreational	3 287 . .	. . .	. . .	. . .	. . .	. . .	. . .	. . .	. . .
Government, n.i.e.	3 291 . .	–24.8	–29.0	–29.4	–34.1	–42.4	–35.2	–40.9	. . .

Table 2 (Continued). STANDARD PRESENTATION, 1988–95
(Millions of U.S. dollars)

	Code		1988	1989	1990	1991	1992	1993	1994	1995
C. INCOME	4 300	. .	–324.3	–348.9	–321.3	–232.4	–187.1	–192.4	–242.6	–172.5
Total credit	2 300	. .	*114.7*	*203.2*	*258.3*	*234.7*	*225.0*	*250.1*	*282.5*	*401.2*
Total debit	3 300	. .	*–439.0*	*–552.1*	*–579.6*	*–467.1*	*–412.1*	*–442.5*	*–525.1*	*–573.7*
Compensation of employees, credit	2 310	. .	**. . .**	**. . .**	**. . .**	**. . .**	**. . .**	**. . .**	**. . .**	**. . .**
Compensation of employees, debit	3 310	. .	**. . .**	**. . .**	**. . .**	**. . .**	**. . .**	**. . .**	**. . .**	**. . .**
Investment income, credit	2 320	. .	**114.7**	**203.2**	**258.3**	**234.7**	**225.0**	**250.1**	**282.5**	**401.2**
Direct investment income	2 330	. .	. . .	. . .	. . .	. . .	. . .	.2	.5	. . .
Dividends and distributed branch profits	2 332	. .	. . .	. . .	. . .	. . .	. . .	.2	.5	. . .
Reinvested earnings and undistributed branch profits	2 333	. .	. . .	. . .	. . .	. . .	. . .	. . .	. . .	. . .
Income on debt (interest)	2 334	. .	. . .	. . .	. . .	. . .	. . .	. . .	. . .	. . .
Portfolio investment income	2 339	. .	. . .	. . .	. . .	. . .	. . .	. . .	. . .	. . .
Income on equity	2 340	. .	. . .	. . .	. . .	. . .	. . .	. . .	. . .	. . .
Income on bonds and notes	2 350	. .	. . .	. . .	. . .	. . .	. . .	. . .	. . .	. . .
Income on money market instruments and financial derivatives	2 360	. .	. . .	. . .	. . .	. . .	. . .	. . .	. . .	. . .
Other investment income	2 370	. .	114.7	203.2	258.3	234.7	225.0	249.9	282.0	401.2
Investment income, debit	3 320	. .	**–439.0**	**–552.1**	**–579.6**	**–467.1**	**–412.1**	**–442.5**	**–525.1**	**–573.7**
Direct investment income	3 330	. .	–18.6	. . .	. . .	. . .	. . .	–45.9	–40.7	. . .
Dividends and distributed branch profits	3 332	. .	. . .	. . .	. . .	. . .	. . .	–30.5	–22.3	. . .
Reinvested earnings and undistributed branch profits	3 333	. .	–18.6	. . .	. . .	. . .	. . .	–15.4	–18.4	. . .
Income on debt (interest)	3 334	. .	. . .	. . .	. . .	. . .	. . .	. . .	. . .	. . .
Portfolio investment income	3 339	. .	–91.0	–128.0	–121.0	–110.0	–102.0	–94.0	–90.0	–129.5
Income on equity	3 340	. .	. . .	. . .	. . .	. . .	. . .	. . .	. . .	. . .
Income on bonds and notes	3 350	. .	–91.0	–128.0	–121.0	–110.0	–102.0	–94.0	–90.0	–129.5
Income on money market instruments and financial derivatives	3 360	. .	. . .	. . .	. . .	. . .	. . .	. . .	. . .	. . .
Other investment income	3 370	. .	–329.4	–424.1	–458.6	–357.1	–310.1	–302.6	–394.4	–444.2
D. CURRENT TRANSFERS	4 379	. .	21.3	8.0	8.1	40.1	28.6	53.4	41.2	32.0
Credit	2 379	. .	**26.0**	**15.0**	**15.8**	**50.1**	**36.0**	**61.2**	**49.2**	**40.0**
General government	2 380	. .	26.0	15.0	15.8	50.1	36.0	29.5	16.4	7.0
Other sectors	2 390	. .	. . .	. . .	. . .	. . .	. . .	31.7	32.8	33.0
Workers' remittances	2 391	. .	. . .	. . .	. . .	. . .	. . .	. . .	. . .	. . .
Other current transfers	2 392	. .	. . .	. . .	. . .	. . .	. . .	31.7	32.8	33.0
Debit	3 379	. .	**–4.7**	**–7.0**	**–7.7**	**–10.0**	**–7.4**	**–7.8**	**–8.0**	**–8.0**
General government	3 380	. .	–4.7	–7.0	–7.7	–10.0	–7.4	–7.8	–8.0	–8.0
Other sectors	3 390	. .	. . .	. . .	. . .	. . .	. . .	. . .	. . .	. . .
Workers' remittances	3 391	. .	. . .	. . .	. . .	. . .	. . .	. . .	. . .	. . .
Other current transfers	3 392	. .	. . .	. . .	. . .	. . .	. . .	. . .	. . .	. . .
CAPITAL AND FINANCIAL ACCOUNT	4 996	. .	**224.9**	**–70.9**	**–221.6**	**–511.2**	**–229.5**	**35.1**	**428.1**	**162.5**
CAPITAL ACCOUNT	4 994	. .	**. . .**	**. . .**	**. . .**	**. . .**	**. . .**	**. . .**	**. . .**	**. . .**
Total credit	2 994	. .	. . .	. . .	. . .	. . .	. . .	. . .	. . .	. . .
Total debit	3 994	. .	. . .	. . .	. . .	. . .	. . .	. . .	. . .	. . .
Capital transfers, credit	2 400	. .	**. . .**	**. . .**	**. . .**	**. . .**	**. . .**	**. . .**	**. . .**	**. . .**
General government	2 401	. .	. . .	. . .	. . .	. . .	. . .	. . .	. . .	. . .
Debt forgiveness	2 402	. .	. . .	. . .	. . .	. . .	. . .	. . .	. . .	. . .
Other capital transfers	2 410	. .	. . .	. . .	. . .	. . .	. . .	. . .	. . .	. . .
Other sectors	2 430	. .	. . .	. . .	. . .	. . .	. . .	. . .	. . .	. . .
Migrants' transfers	2 431	. .	. . .	. . .	. . .	. . .	. . .	. . .	. . .	. . .
Debt forgiveness	2 432	. .	. . .	. . .	. . .	. . .	. . .	. . .	. . .	. . .
Other capital transfers	2 440	. .	. . .	. . .	. . .	. . .	. . .	. . .	. . .	. . .
Capital transfers, debit	3 400	. .	**. . .**	**. . .**	**. . .**	**. . .**	**. . .**	**. . .**	**. . .**	**. . .**
General government	3 401	. .	. . .	. . .	. . .	. . .	. . .	. . .	. . .	. . .
Debt forgiveness	3 402	. .	. . .	. . .	. . .	. . .	. . .	. . .	. . .	. . .
Other capital transfers	3 410	. .	. . .	. . .	. . .	. . .	. . .	. . .	. . .	. . .
Other sectors	3 430	. .	. . .	. . .	. . .	. . .	. . .	. . .	. . .	. . .
Migrants' transfers	3 431	. .	. . .	. . .	. . .	. . .	. . .	. . .	. . .	. . .
Debt forgiveness	3 432	. .	. . .	. . .	. . .	. . .	. . .	. . .	. . .	. . .
Other capital transfers	3 440	. .	. . .	. . .	. . .	. . .	. . .	. . .	. . .	. . .
Nonproduced nonfinancial assets, credit	2 480	. .	**. . .**	**. . .**	**. . .**	**. . .**	**. . .**	**. . .**	**. . .**	**. . .**
Nonproduced nonfinancial assets, debit	3 480	. .	**. . .**	**. . .**	**. . .**	**. . .**	**. . .**	**. . .**	**. . .**	**. . .**

Table 2 (Continued). STANDARD PRESENTATION, 1988–95
(Millions of U.S. dollars)

	Code	1988	1989	1990	1991	1992	1993	1994	1995
FINANCIAL ACCOUNT	4 995 . .	**224.9**	**–70.9**	**–221.6**	**–511.2**	**–229.5**	**35.1**	**428.1**	**162.5**
A. DIRECT INVESTMENT	4 500 . .	44.5	. . .	. . .	. . .	. . .	101.5	154.5	123.5
Direct investment abroad	4 505 . .	**–2.3**	**. . .**	**. . .**	**. . .**	**. . .**	**. . .**	**. . .**	**. . .**
Equity capital	4 510 . .	–2.3	. . .	. . .	. . .	. . .	. . .	. . .	. . .
Claims on affiliated enterprises	4 515 . .	. . .	. . .	. . .	. . .	. . .	. . .	. . .	. . .
Liabilities to affiliated enterprises	4 520 . .	. . .	. . .	. . .	. . .	. . .	. . .	. . .	. . .
Reinvested earnings	4 525 . .	. . .	. . .	. . .	. . .	. . .	. . .	. . .	. . .
Other capital	4 530 . .	. . .	. . .	. . .	. . .	. . .	. . .	. . .	. . .
Claims on affiliated enterprises	4 535 . .	. . .	. . .	. . .	. . .	. . .	. . .	. . .	. . .
Liabilities to affiliated enterprises	4 540 . .	. . .	. . .	. . .	. . .	. . .	. . .	. . .	. . .
Direct investment in Uruguay	4 555 . .	**46.8**	**. . .**	**. . .**	**. . .**	**. . .**	**101.5**	**154.5**	**123.5**
Equity capital	4 560 . .	10.0	. . .	. . .	. . .	. . .	86.1	136.1	123.5
Claims on direct investors	4 565 . .	. . .	. . .	. . .	. . .	. . .	. . .	. . .	. . .
Liabilities to direct investors	4 570 . .	. . .	. . .	. . .	. . .	. . .	. . .	. . .	. . .
Reinvested earnings	4 575 . .	18.6	. . .	. . .	. . .	. . .	15.4	18.4	. . .
Other capital	4 580 . .	18.2	. . .	. . .	. . .	. . .	. . .	. . .	. . .
Claims on direct investors	4 585 . .	. . .	. . .	. . .	. . .	. . .	. . .	. . .	. . .
Liabilities to direct investors	4 590 . .	. . .	. . .	. . .	. . .	. . .	. . .	. . .	. . .
B. PORTFOLIO INVESTMENT	4 600 . .	164.2	129.8	107.8	47.4	83.4	29.3	158.1	288.9
Assets	4 602 . .	**–60.1**	**. . .**	**. . .**	**. . .**	**. . .**	**. . .**	**. . .**	**. . .**
Equity securities	4 610 . .	–24.9	. . .	. . .	. . .	. . .	. . .	. . .	. . .
Monetary authorities	4 611 . .	. . .	. . .	. . .	. . .	. . .	. . .	. . .	. . .
General government	4 612 . .	. . .	. . .	. . .	. . .	. . .	. . .	. . .	. . .
Banks	4 613 . .	. . .	. . .	. . .	. . .	. . .	. . .	. . .	. . .
Other sectors	4 614 . .	. . .	. . .	. . .	. . .	. . .	. . .	. . .	. . .
Debt securities	4 619 . .	–35.2	. . .	. . .	. . .	. . .	. . .	. . .	. . .
Bonds and notes	4 620 . .	–35.2	. . .	. . .	. . .	. . .	. . .	. . .	. . .
Monetary authorities	4 621 . .	. . .	. . .	. . .	. . .	. . .	. . .	. . .	. . .
General government	4 622 . .	. . .	. . .	. . .	. . .	. . .	. . .	. . .	. . .
Banks	4 623 . .	. . .	. . .	. . .	. . .	. . .	. . .	. . .	. . .
Other sectors	4 624 . .	. . .	. . .	. . .	. . .	. . .	. . .	. . .	. . .
Money market instruments	4 630 . .	. . .	. . .	. . .	. . .	. . .	. . .	. . .	. . .
Monetary authorities	4 631 . .	. . .	. . .	. . .	. . .	. . .	. . .	. . .	. . .
General government	4 632 . .	. . .	. . .	. . .	. . .	. . .	. . .	. . .	. . .
Banks	4 633 . .	. . .	. . .	. . .	. . .	. . .	. . .	. . .	. . .
Other sectors	4 634 . .	. . .	. . .	. . .	. . .	. . .	. . .	. . .	. . .
Financial derivatives	4 640 . .	. . .	. . .	. . .	. . .	. . .	. . .	. . .	. . .
Monetary authorities	4 641 . .	. . .	. . .	. . .	. . .	. . .	. . .	. . .	. . .
General government	4 642 . .	. . .	. . .	. . .	. . .	. . .	. . .	. . .	. . .
Banks	4 643 . .	. . .	. . .	. . .	. . .	. . .	. . .	. . .	. . .
Other sectors	4 644 . .	. . .	. . .	. . .	. . .	. . .	. . .	. . .	. . .
Liabilities	4 652 . .	**224.3**	**129.8**	**107.8**	**47.4**	**83.4**	**29.3**	**158.1**	**288.9**
Equity securities	4 660 . .	. . .	. . .	. . .	. . .	. . .	. . .	. . .	. . .
Banks	4 663 . .	. . .	. . .	. . .	. . .	. . .	. . .	. . .	. . .
Other sectors	4 664 . .	. . .	. . .	. . .	. . .	. . .	. . .	. . .	. . .
Debt securities	4 669 . .	224.3	129.8	107.8	47.4	83.4	29.3	158.1	288.9
Bonds and notes	4 670 . .	97.5	49.9	17.5	109.4	229.1	158.3	178.0	183.1
Monetary authorities	4 671 . .	. . .	. . .	. . .	. . .	. . .	. . .	. . .	. . .
General government	4 672 . .	97.5	49.9	17.5	109.4	229.1	158.3	178.0	183.1
Banks	4 673 . .	. . .	. . .	. . .	. . .	. . .	. . .	. . .	. . .
Other sectors	4 674 . .	. . .	. . .	. . .	. . .	. . .	. . .	. . .	. . .
Money market instruments	4 680 . .	126.8	79.9	90.3	–62.0	–145.7	–129.0	–19.9	105.8
Monetary authorities	4 681 . .	. . .	. . .	. . .	. . .	. . .	. . .	. . .	. . .
General government	4 682 . .	126.8	79.9	90.3	–62.0	–145.7	–129.0	–19.9	105.8
Banks	4 683 . .	. . .	. . .	. . .	. . .	. . .	. . .	. . .	. . .
Other sectors	4 684 . .	. . .	. . .	. . .	. . .	. . .	. . .	. . .	. . .
Financial derivatives	4 690 . .	. . .	. . .	. . .	. . .	. . .	. . .	. . .	. . .
Monetary authorities	4 691 . .	. . .	. . .	. . .	. . .	. . .	. . .	. . .	. . .
General government	4 692 . .	. . .	. . .	. . .	. . .	. . .	. . .	. . .	. . .
Banks	4 693 . .	. . .	. . .	. . .	. . .	. . .	. . .	. . .	. . .
Other sectors	4 694 . .	. . .	. . .	. . .	. . .	. . .	. . .	. . .	. . .

Table 2 (Concluded). STANDARD PRESENTATION, 1988–95
(Millions of U.S. dollars)

	Code		1988	1989	1990	1991	1992	1993	1994	1995
C. OTHER INVESTMENT	4 700	. .	–30.6	–203.9	–289.2	–445.1	–126.7	82.8	214.0	–31.9
Assets	4 703	. .	**–390.4**	**–764.3**	**–632.0**	**–399.0**	**–589.8**	**–19.3**	**–71.8**	**–413.1**
Trade credits	4 706	. .	–99.7	–177.7	–190.5	–11.8	. . .	. . .	–17.7	–.6
General government: long-term	4 708	. .	. . .	. . .	. . .	. . .	. . .	. . .	. . .	. . .
General government: short-term	4 709	. .	. . .	. . .	. . .	. . .	. . .	. . .	. . .	. . .
Other sectors: long-term	4 711	. .	. . .	. . .	. . .	. . .	. . .	. . .	. . .	. . .
Other sectors: short-term	4 712	. .	–99.7	–177.7	–190.5	–11.8	. . .	. . .	–17.7	–.6
Loans	4 714	. .	. . .	. . .	. . .	. . .	. . .	. . .	. . .	. . .
Monetary authorities: long-term	4 717	. .	. . .	. . .	. . .	. . .	. . .	. . .	. . .	. . .
Monetary authorities: short-term	4 718	. .	. . .	. . .	. . .	. . .	. . .	. . .	. . .	. . .
General government: long-term	4 720	. .	. . .	. . .	. . .	. . .	. . .	. . .	. . .	. . .
General government: short-term	4 721	. .	. . .	. . .	. . .	. . .	. . .	. . .	. . .	. . .
Banks: long-term	4 723	. .	. . .	. . .	. . .	. . .	. . .	. . .	. . .	. . .
Banks: short-term	4 724	. .	. . .	. . .	. . .	. . .	. . .	. . .	. . .	. . .
Other sectors: long-term	4 726	. .	. . .	. . .	. . .	. . .	. . .	. . .	. . .	. . .
Other sectors: short-term	4 727	. .	. . .	. . .	. . .	. . .	. . .	. . .	. . .	. . .
Currency and deposits	4 730	. .	–290.1	–586.6	–441.5	–387.2	–589.8	–18.6	–54.1	–412.5
Monetary authorities	4 731	. .	. . .	. . .	. . .	. . .	. . .	. . .	–10.1	. . .
General government	4 732	. .	. . .	. . .	. . .	. . .	. . .	. . .	. . .	. . .
Banks	4 733	. .	–290.1	–586.6	–441.5	–387.2	–589.8	–18.6	–44.0	–412.5
Other sectors	4 734	. .	. . .	. . .	. . .	. . .	. . .	. . .	. . .	. . .
Other assets	4 736	. .	–.6	. . .	. . .	. . .	. . .	–.7	. . .	. . .
Monetary authorities: long-term	4 738	. .	. . .	. . .	. . .	. . .	. . .	. . .	. . .	. . .
Monetary authorities: short-term	4 739	. .	. . .	. . .	. . .	. . .	. . .	. . .	. . .	. . .
General government: long-term	4 741	. .	–.6	. . .	. . .	. . .	. . .	. . .	. . .	. . .
General government: short-term	4 742	. .	. . .	. . .	. . .	. . .	. . .	. . .	. . .	. . .
Banks: long-term	4 744	. .	. . .	. . .	. . .	. . .	. . .	. . .	. . .	. . .
Banks: short-term	4 745	. .	. . .	. . .	. . .	. . .	. . .	. . .	. . .	. . .
Other sectors: long-term	4 747	. .	. . .	. . .	. . .	. . .	. . .	–.7	. . .	. . .
Other sectors: short-term	4 748	. .	. . .	. . .	. . .	. . .	. . .	. . .	. . .	. . .
Liabilities	4 753	. .	**359.8**	**560.4**	**342.8**	**–46.1**	**463.1**	**102.1**	**285.8**	**381.2**
Trade credits	4 756	. .	. . .	. . .	. . .	. . .	. . .	. . .	92.4	–37.1
General government: long-term	4 758	. .	. . .	. . .	. . .	. . .	. . .	. . .	. . .	. . .
General government: short-term	4 759	. .	. . .	. . .	. . .	. . .	. . .	. . .	. . .	. . .
Other sectors: long-term	4 761	. .	. . .	. . .	. . .	. . .	. . .	. . .	92.4	–37.1
Other sectors: short-term	4 762	. .	. . .	. . .	. . .	. . .	. . .	. . .	. . .	. . .
Loans	4 764	. .	–118.9	–67.8	–81.2	–310.6	102.5	96.4	7.1	375.7
Use of Fund credit and loans from the Fund	4 766	. .	–63.3	–98.0	–111.5	–41.3	–2.5	–14.4	–10.6	–9.8
Monetary authorities: other long-term	4 767	. .	–67.0	–76.2	–98.2	–287.9	–27.7	–16.3	4.0	–24.6
Monetary authorities: short-term	4 768	. .	. . .	. . .	. . .	40.0	–40.0	. . .	. . .	–37.9
General government: long-term	4 770	. .	27.8	46.0	35.4	146.1	155.6	120.3	134.0	61.1
General government: short-term	4 771	. .	. . .	. . .	. . .	. . .	. . .	. . .	. . .	. . .
Banks: long-term	4 773	. .	.9	7.8	45.6	–23.3	2.1	2.9	34.5	303.0
Banks: short-term	4 774	. .	. . .	. . .	. . .	. . .	. . .	. . .	–119.3	120.8
Other sectors: long-term	4 776	. .	–20.9	19.7	9.3	–92.5	–34.5	4.9	–35.5	–36.9
Other sectors: short-term	4 777	. .	3.6	32.9	38.2	–51.7	49.5	–1.0	. . .	. . .
Currency and deposits	4 780	. .	478.7	628.2	343.6	255.8	432.1	17.5	184.6	42.6
Monetary authorities	4 781	. .	14.9	–5.2	–3.8	–2.2	. . .	4.4	. . .	. . .
General government	4 782	. .	. . .	. . .	. . .	. . .	. . .	. . .	. . .	. . .
Banks	4 783	. .	463.8	633.4	347.4	258.0	432.1	13.1	184.6	42.6
Other sectors	4 784	. .	. . .	. . .	. . .	. . .	. . .	. . .	. . .	. . .
Other liabilities	4 786	. .	. . .	. . .	80.4	8.7	–71.5	–11.8	1.7	. . .
Monetary authorities: long-term	4 788	. .	. . .	. . .	. . .	. . .	. . .	. . .	–25.3	. . .
Monetary authorities: short-term	4 789	. .	. . .	. . .	80.4	8.7	–71.5	–11.8	27.0	. . .
General government: long-term	4 791	. .	. . .	. . .	. . .	. . .	. . .	. . .	. . .	. . .
General government: short-term	4 792	. .	. . .	. . .	. . .	. . .	. . .	. . .	. . .	. . .
Banks: long-term	4 794	. .	. . .	. . .	. . .	. . .	. . .	. . .	. . .	. . .
Banks: short-term	4 795	. .	. . .	. . .	. . .	. . .	. . .	. . .	. . .	. . .
Other sectors: long-term	4 797	. .	. . .	. . .	. . .	. . .	. . .	. . .	. . .	. . .
Other sectors: short-term	4 798	. .	. . .	. . .	. . .	. . .	. . .	. . .	. . .	. . .
D. RESERVE ASSETS	4 800	. .	46.8	3.2	–40.2	–113.5	–186.2	–178.6	–98.5	–218.0
Monetary gold	4 810	. .	. . .	. . .	64.1	54.5	. . .	. . .	. . .	–3.4
Special drawing rights	4 820	. .	35.2	6.2	12.8	6.0	4.7	–.5	.4	–3.5
Reserve position in the Fund	4 830	. .	. . .	. . .	. . .	. . .	–21.3	. . .	. . .	. . .
Foreign exchange	4 840	. .	–42.3	25.8	–32.5	182.8	–154.9	–253.1	–228.5	–155.1
Other claims	4 880	. .	53.9	–28.8	–84.6	–356.8	–14.7	75.0	129.6	–56.0
NET ERRORS AND OMISSIONS	4 998	. .	**–247.0**	**–62.6**	**35.7**	**468.8**	**238.3**	**208.7**	**10.2**	**195.9**

Part 3 of the *Yearbook* contains descriptions of the methodologies, compilation practices, and sources used to compile these data.

Table 1. ANALYTIC PRESENTATION, 1988–95
(Millions of U.S. dollars)

	Code	1988	1989	1990	1991	1992	1993	1994	1995
A. Current Account [1]	4 993 Y.	**–15.19**	**–12.25**	**–6.18**	**–13.71**	**–13.07**	**–14.93**	**–19.78**	**–18.25**
Goods: exports f.o.b	2 100 . .	15.39	13.74	13.73	14.86	17.80	17.43	25.11	28.28
Goods: imports f.o.b	3 100 . .	–57.89	–57.92	–79.34	–74.01	–66.79	–64.71	–74.68	–79.44
Balance on Goods	4 100 . .	*–42.50*	*–44.18*	*–65.61*	*–59.15*	*–48.99*	*–47.28*	*–49.58*	*–51.16*
Services: credit	2 200 . .	39.97	40.29	60.17	66.09	69.93	68.88	78.14	81.65
Services: debit	3 200 . .	–17.79	–19.11	–23.86	–26.95	–26.79	–29.97	–33.44	–35.27
Balance on Goods and Services	4 991 . .	*–20.32*	*–23.01*	*–29.30*	*–20.01*	*–5.85*	*–8.36*	*–4.88*	*–4.78*
Income: credit	2 300 . .	23.38	23.42	31.92	24.88	17.60	14.95	9.94	13.07
Income: debit	3 300 . .	–40.99	–29.18	–33.32	–49.18	–47.55	–43.48	–47.36	–49.79
Balance on Goods, Services, and Income	4 992 . .	*–37.93*	*–28.76*	*–30.70*	*–44.31*	*–35.80*	*–36.89*	*–42.30*	*–41.49*
Current transfers: credit	2 379 Y.	26.28	20.42	25.01	31.10	23.28	22.54	23.24	23.81
Current transfers: debit	3 379 . .	–3.54	–3.90	–.50	–.50	–.55	–.58	–.72	–.56
B. Capital Account [1]	4 994 Y.	**17.87**	**8.78**	**16.47**	**19.14**	**17.22**	**26.30**	**37.28**	**31.62**
Capital account: credit	2 994 Y.	17.96	8.91	16.51	19.34	26.59	32.04	41.45	38.33
Capital account: debit	3 994 . .	–.10	–.13	–.04	–.20	–9.37	–5.74	–4.17	–6.71
Total, Groups A Plus B	4 010 . .	*2.68*	*–3.46*	*10.29*	*5.43*	*4.15*	*11.36*	*17.50*	*13.38*
C. Financial Account [1]	4 995 X.	**9.95**	**24.19**	**13.79**	**–27.79**	**23.71**	**14.53**	**–13.41**	**25.30**
Direct investment abroad	4 505 . .	. . .	. . .	. . .	. . .	. . .	. . .	. . .	. . .
Direct investment in Vanuatu	4 555 Y.	10.81	9.17	13.11	25.47	26.45	25.97	29.79	31.04
Portfolio investment assets	4 602 . .	. . .	. . .	. . .	. . .	. . .	. . .	. . .	. . .
Equity securities	4 610 . .	. . .	. . .	. . .	. . .	. . .	. . .	. . .	. . .
Debt securities	4 619 . .	. . .	. . .	. . .	. . .	. . .	. . .	. . .	. . .
Portfolio investment liabilities	4 652 Y.	. . .	. . .	. . .	. . .	. . .	. . .	. . .	. . .
Equity securities	4 660 Y.	. . .	. . .	. . .	. . .	. . .	. . .	. . .	. . .
Debt securities	4 669 Y.	. . .	. . .	. . .	. . .	. . .	. . .	. . .	. . .
Other investment assets	4 703 . .	145.38	–.79	–.93	15.28	–8.57	–27.50	–45.47	–1.59
Monetary authorities	4 703 . A	. . .	. . .	. . .	. . .	. . .	. . .	. . .	. . .
General government	4 703 . B	–.22	–.13	–.34	–.39	–.38	–.43	–.45	–.30
Banks	4 703 . C	145.60	–.66	3.88	52.40	21.22	–10.76	10.60	–2.18
Other sectors	4 703 . D	. . .	. . .	–4.46	–36.74	–29.42	–16.31	–55.62	.89
Other investment liabilities	4 753 X.	–146.25	15.81	1.60	–68.55	5.83	16.05	2.27	–4.15
Monetary authorities	4 753 XA	.18	–.14	.34	. . .	–.36	.16	–.05	.18
General government	4 753 YB	.87	1.51	7.56	12.48	7.03	6.60	2.17	2.21
Banks	4 753 YC	–147.29	14.44	–6.30	–81.03	–.84	9.29	.16	–6.54
Other sectors	4 753 YD	. . .	. . .	. . .	. . .	. . .	. . .	. . .	. . .
Total, Groups A Through C	4 020 . .	*12.63*	*20.73*	*24.07*	*–22.36*	*27.86*	*25.89*	*4.09*	*38.68*
D. Net Errors and Omissions	4 998 . .	**–17.30**	**–12.96**	**–19.38**	**19.31**	**–27.10**	**–22.44**	**–10.21**	**–33.38**
Total, Groups A Through D	4 030 . .	*–4.67*	*7.77*	*4.69*	*–3.05*	*.75*	*3.45*	*–6.12*	*5.30*
E. Reserves and Related Items	4 040 . .	**4.67**	**–7.77**	**–4.69**	**3.05**	**–.75**	**–3.45**	**6.12**	**–5.30**
Reserve assets	4 800 . .	–.68	–7.77	–4.69	–.40	–4.16	–6.70	4.86	–5.30
Use of Fund credit and loans	4 766 . .	. . .	. . .	. . .	. . .	. . .	. . .	. . .	. . .
Liabilities constituting foreign authorities' reserves	4 900 . .	. . .	. . .	. . .	. . .	. . .	. . .	. . .	. . .
Exceptional financing	4 920 . .	5.36	. . .	. . .	3.45	3.41	3.26	1.26	. . .
Conversion rates: vatu per U.S. dollar	0 101 . .	**104.43**	**116.04**	**117.06**	**111.68**	**113.39**	**121.58**	**116.41**	**112.11**

[1] Excludes components that have been classified in the categories of Group E.

Table 2. STANDARD PRESENTATION, 1988–95
(Millions of U.S. dollars)

	Code	1988	1989	1990	1991	1992	1993	1994	1995
CURRENT ACCOUNT	4 993 . .	**–9.83**	**–12.25**	**–6.18**	**–10.26**	**–9.67**	**–11.68**	**–18.52**	**–18.25**
A. GOODS	4 100 . .	–42.50	–44.18	–65.61	–59.15	–48.99	–47.28	–49.58	–51.16
Credit	2 100 . .	**15.39**	**13.74**	**13.73**	**14.86**	**17.80**	**17.43**	**25.11**	**28.28**
General merchandise: exports f.o.b.	2 110 . .	15.39	13.74	13.73	14.86	17.80	17.43	25.11	28.28
Goods for processing: exports f.o.b.	2 150 . .	. . .	. . .	. . .	. . .	. . .	. . .	. . .	. . .
Repairs on goods	2 160 . .	. . .	. . .	. . .	. . .	. . .	. . .	. . .	. . .
Goods procured in ports by carriers	2 170 . .	. . .	. . .	. . .	. . .	. . .	. . .	. . .	. . .
Nonmonetary gold	2 180 . .	. . .	. . .	. . .	. . .	. . .	. . .	. . .	. . .
Debit	3 100 . .	**–57.89**	**–57.92**	**–79.34**	**–74.01**	**–66.79**	**–64.71**	**–74.68**	**–79.44**
General merchandise: imports f.o.b.	3 110 . .	–57.89	–57.92	–79.34	–74.01	–66.79	–64.71	–74.68	–79.44
Goods for processing: imports f.o.b.	3 150 . .	. . .	. . .	. . .	. . .	. . .	. . .	. . .	. . .
Repairs on goods	3 160 . .	. . .	. . .	. . .	. . .	. . .	. . .	. . .	. . .
Goods procured in ports by carriers	3 170 . .	. . .	. . .	. . .	. . .	. . .	. . .	. . .	. . .
Nonmonetary gold	3 180 . .	. . .	. . .	. . .	. . .	. . .	. . .	. . .	. . .
B. SERVICES	4 200 . .	22.18	21.17	36.31	39.14	43.14	38.91	44.70	46.38
Total credit	2 200 . .	*39.97*	*40.29*	*60.17*	*66.09*	*69.93*	*68.88*	*78.14*	*81.65*
Total debit	3 200 . .	*–17.79*	*–19.11*	*–23.86*	*–26.95*	*–26.79*	*–29.97*	*–33.44*	*–35.27*
Transportation services, credit	2 205 . .	**4.47**	**3.90**	**5.82**	**7.22**	**7.64**	**8.78**	**10.13**	**11.09**
Passenger	2 205 BA	. . .	. . .	. . .	. . .	. . .	. . .	. . .	. . .
Freight	2 205 BB	. . .	. . .	. . .	. . .	. . .	. . .	. . .	. . .
Other	2 205 BC	*4.47*	*3.90*	*5.82*	*7.22*	*7.64*	*8.78*	*10.13*	*11.09*
Sea transport, passenger	2 207 . .	. . .	. . .	. . .	. . .	. . .	. . .	. . .	. . .
Sea transport, freight	2 208 . .	. . .	. . .	. . .	. . .	. . .	. . .	. . .	. . .
Sea transport, other	2 209 . .	2.24	1.95	2.91	3.61	3.82	4.39	5.06	5.55
Air transport, passenger	2 211 . .	. . .	. . .	. . .	. . .	. . .	. . .	. . .	. . .
Air transport, freight	2 212 . .	. . .	. . .	. . .	. . .	. . .	. . .	. . .	. . .
Air transport, other	2 213 . .	2.24	1.95	2.91	3.61	3.82	4.39	5.06	5.55
Other transport, passenger	2 215 . .	. . .	. . .	. . .	. . .	. . .	. . .	. . .	. . .
Other transport, freight	2 216 . .	. . .	. . .	. . .	. . .	. . .	. . .	. . .	. . .
Other transport, other	2 217 . .	. . .	. . .	. . .	. . .	. . .	. . .	. . .	. . .
Transportation services, debit	3 205 . .	**–11.51**	**–13.57**	**–18.46**	**–17.35**	**–16.09**	**–16.11**	**–18.28**	**–19.40**
Passenger	3 205 BA	*–1.16*	*–3.28*	*–4.36*	*–4.18*	*–4.21*	*–4.37*	*–5.22*	*–5.42*
Freight	3 205 BB	*–10.35*	*–10.29*	*–14.10*	*–13.16*	*–11.88*	*–11.75*	*–13.06*	*–13.97*
Other	3 205 BC	. . .	. . .	. . .	. . .	. . .	. . .	. . .	. . .
Sea transport, passenger	3 207 . .	. . .	. . .	. . .	. . .	. . .	. . .	. . .	. . .
Sea transport, freight	3 208 . .	–10.35	–10.29	–14.10	–13.16	–11.88	–11.75	–13.06	–13.97
Sea transport, other	3 209 . .	. . .	. . .	. . .	. . .	. . .	. . .	. . .	. . .
Air transport, passenger	3 211 . .	–1.16	–3.28	–4.36	–4.18	–4.21	–4.37	–5.22	–5.42
Air transport, freight	3 212 . .	. . .	. . .	. . .	. . .	. . .	. . .	. . .	. . .
Air transport, other	3 213 . .	. . .	. . .	. . .	. . .	. . .	. . .	. . .	. . .
Other transport, passenger	3 215 . .	. . .	. . .	. . .	. . .	. . .	. . .	. . .	. . .
Other transport, freight	3 216 . .	. . .	. . .	. . .	. . .	. . .	. . .	. . .	. . .
Other transport, other	3 217 . .	. . .	. . .	. . .	. . .	. . .	. . .	. . .	. . .
Travel, credit	2 236 . .	**17.72**	**22.72**	**38.56**	**34.76**	**38.63**	**38.65**	**40.51**	**45.39**
Business travel	2 237 . .	. . .	. . .	. . .	. . .	. . .	. . .	. . .	. . .
Personal travel	2 240 . .	17.72	22.72	38.56	34.76	38.63	38.65	40.51	45.39
Travel, debit	3 236 . .	**–1.85**	**–1.49**	**–1.07**	**–.76**	**–.86**	**–3.96**	**–4.34**	**–4.61**
Business travel	3 237 . .	. . .	. . .	. . .	. . .	. . .	. . .	. . .	. . .
Personal travel	3 240 . .	–1.85	–1.49	–1.07	–.76	–.86	–3.96	–4.34	–4.61
Other services, credit	2 200 BA	**17.77**	**13.67**	**15.79**	**24.12**	**23.66**	**21.45**	**27.50**	**25.16**
Communications	2 245 . .	. . .	. . .	. . .	. . .	. . .	. . .	. . .	. . .
Construction	2 249 . .	. . .	. . .	. . .	. . .	. . .	. . .	. . .	. . .
Insurance	2 253 . .	. . .	. . .	. . .	. . .	. . .	. . .	. . .	. . .
Financial	2 260 . .	. . .	. . .	. . .	. . .	. . .	. . .	. . .	. . .
Computer and information	2 262 . .	. . .	. . .	. . .	. . .	. . .	. . .	. . .	. . .
Royalties and licence fees	2 266 . .	. . .	. . .	. . .	. . .	. . .	. . .	. . .	. . .
Other business services	2 268 . .	13.29	12.09	12.11	18.12	19.14	16.83	19.03	18.69
Personal, cultural, and recreational	2 287 . .	. . .	. . .	. . .	. . .	. . .	. . .	. . .	. . .
Government, n.i.e.	2 291 . .	4.48	1.58	3.68	5.99	4.52	4.61	8.47	6.47
Other services, debit	3 200 BA	**–4.42**	**–4.06**	**–4.33**	**–8.84**	**–9.84**	**–9.90**	**–10.82**	**–11.27**
Communications	3 245 . .	. . .	. . .	. . .	. . .	. . .	. . .	. . .	. . .
Construction	3 249 . .	. . .	. . .	. . .	. . .	. . .	. . .	. . .	. . .
Insurance	3 253 . .	–1.15	–1.14	–1.57	–1.46	–1.32	–1.31	–1.61	–1.67
Financial	3 260 . .	. . .	. . .	. . .	. . .	. . .	. . .	. . .	. . .
Computer and information	3 262 . .	. . .	. . .	. . .	. . .	. . .	. . .	. . .	. . .
Royalties and licence fees	3 266 . .	. . .	. . .	. . .	. . .	. . .	. . .	. . .	. . .
Other business services	3 268 . .	–3.20	–2.75	–2.63	–7.23	–8.30	–8.13	–8.71	–9.03
Personal, cultural, and recreational	3 287 . .	. . .	. . .	. . .	. . .	. . .	. . .	. . .	. . .
Government, n.i.e.	3 291 . .	–.08	–.16	–.13	–.14	–.22	–.46	–.50	–.57

Table 2 (Continued). STANDARD PRESENTATION, 1988–95
(Millions of U.S. dollars)

	Code	1988	1989	1990	1991	1992	1993	1994	1995
C. INCOME	4 300 . .	-17.61	-5.76	-1.40	-24.30	-29.95	-28.53	-37.42	-36.71
Total credit	2 300 . .	*23.38*	*23.42*	*31.92*	*24.88*	*17.60*	*14.95*	*9.94*	*13.07*
Total debit	3 300 . .	*-40.99*	*-29.18*	*-33.32*	*-49.18*	*-47.55*	*-43.48*	*-47.36*	*-49.79*
Compensation of employees, credit	2 310 . .	**. . .**	**. . .**	**. . .**	**. . .**	**. . .**	**. . .**	**. . .**	**. . .**
Compensation of employees, debit	3 310 . .	**-13.12**	**-12.09**	**-12.39**	**-12.99**	**-12.78**	**-9.23**	**-10.73**	**-11.45**
Investment income, credit	2 320 . .	**23.38**	**23.42**	**31.92**	**24.88**	**17.60**	**14.95**	**9.94**	**13.07**
Direct investment income	2 330 . .	. . .	. . .	. . .	. . .	. . .	. . .	. . .	. . .
Dividends and distributed branch profits	2 332 . .	. . .	. . .	. . .	. . .	. . .	. . .	. . .	. . .
Reinvested earnings and undistributed branch profits	2 333 . .	. . .	. . .	. . .	. . .	. . .	. . .	. . .	. . .
Income on debt (interest)	2 334 . .	. . .	. . .	. . .	. . .	. . .	. . .	. . .	. . .
Portfolio investment income	2 339 . .	. . .	. . .	. . .	. . .	. . .	. . .	. . .	. . .
Income on equity	2 340 . .	. . .	. . .	. . .	. . .	. . .	. . .	. . .	. . .
Income on bonds and notes	2 350 . .	. . .	. . .	. . .	. . .	. . .	. . .	. . .	. . .
Income on money market instruments and financial derivatives	2 360 . .	. . .	. . .	. . .	. . .	. . .	. . .	. . .	. . .
Other investment income	2 370 . .	23.38	23.42	31.92	24.88	17.60	14.95	9.94	13.07
Investment income, debit	3 320 . .	**-27.87**	**-17.09**	**-20.93**	**-36.20**	**-34.77**	**-34.25**	**-36.63**	**-38.33**
Direct investment income	3 330 . .	-15.30	-11.94	-15.25	-29.18	-30.19	-30.32	-34.67	-35.58
Dividends and distributed branch profits	3 332 . .	-4.48	-3.27	-2.91	-4.45	-4.46	-4.35	-5.59	-5.42
Reinvested earnings and undistributed branch profits	3 333 . .	-10.81	-8.67	-12.34	-24.73	-25.73	-25.97	-29.07	-30.15
Income on debt (interest)	3 334 . .	. . .	. . .	. . .	. . .	. . .	. . .	. . .	. . .
Portfolio investment income	3 339 . .	. . .	. . .	. . .	. . .	. . .	. . .	. . .	. . .
Income on equity	3 340 . .	. . .	. . .	. . .	. . .	. . .	. . .	. . .	. . .
Income on bonds and notes	3 350 . .	. . .	. . .	. . .	. . .	. . .	. . .	. . .	. . .
Income on money market instruments and financial derivatives	3 360 . .	. . .	. . .	. . .	. . .	. . .	. . .	. . .	. . .
Other investment income	3 370 . .	-12.57	-5.15	-5.68	-7.02	-4.58	-3.93	-1.96	-2.76
D. CURRENT TRANSFERS	4 379 . .	28.10	16.52	24.51	34.05	26.14	25.21	23.78	23.25
Credit	2 379 . .	**31.63**	**20.42**	**25.01**	**34.55**	**26.68**	**25.80**	**24.50**	**23.81**
General government	2 380 . .	19.75	13.14	15.17	18.74	17.53	17.10	12.22	13.70
Other sectors	2 390 . .	11.88	7.28	9.84	15.80	9.15	8.70	12.28	10.11
Workers' remittances	2 391 . .	7.02	6.48	6.89	6.97	6.81	4.94	5.76	6.13
Other current transfers	2 392 . .	4.86	.80	2.95	8.84	2.34	3.75	6.52	3.98
Debit	3 379 . .	**-3.54**	**-3.90**	**-.50**	**-.50**	**-.55**	**-.58**	**-.72**	**-.56**
General government	3 380 . .	-.54	-.50	-.50	-.50	-.55	-.58	-.72	-.56
Other sectors	3 390 . .	-3.00	-3.39	. . .	. . .	. . .	. . .	. . .	. . .
Workers' remittances	3 391 . .	-3.00	-3.39	. . .	. . .	. . .	. . .	. . .	. . .
Other current transfers	3 392 . .	. . .	. . .	. . .	. . .	. . .	. . .	. . .	. . .
CAPITAL AND FINANCIAL ACCOUNT	4 996 . .	**27.13**	**25.21**	**25.57**	**-9.05**	**36.77**	**34.12**	**28.72**	**51.63**
CAPITAL ACCOUNT	4 994 . .	**17.87**	**8.78**	**16.47**	**19.14**	**17.22**	**26.30**	**37.28**	**31.62**
Total credit	2 994 . .	*17.96*	*8.91*	*16.51*	*19.34*	*26.59*	*32.04*	*41.45*	*38.33*
Total debit	3 994 . .	*-.10*	*-.13*	*-.04*	*-.20*	*-9.37*	*-5.74*	*-4.17*	*-6.71*
Capital transfers, credit	2 400 . .	**17.96**	**8.91**	**16.51**	**19.34**	**26.59**	**32.04**	**41.45**	**38.33**
General government	2 401 . .	16.97	8.07	15.19	17.25	19.31	24.94	29.09	30.95
Debt forgiveness	2 402 . .	. . .	. . .	. . .	. . .	. . .	. . .	. . .	. . .
Other capital transfers	2 410 . .	16.97	8.07	15.19	17.25	19.31	24.94	29.09	30.95
Other sectors	2 430 . .	.99	.84	1.32	2.09	7.28	7.10	12.36	7.38
Migrants' transfers	2 431 . .	.99	.84	1.32	2.09	7.28	7.10	12.36	7.38
Debt forgiveness	2 432 . .	. . .	. . .	. . .	. . .	. . .	. . .	. . .	. . .
Other capital transfers	2 440 . .	. . .	. . .	. . .	. . .	. . .	. . .	. . .	. . .
Capital transfers, debit	3 400 . .	**-.10**	**-.13**	**-.04**	**-.20**	**-9.37**	**-5.74**	**-4.17**	**-6.71**
General government	3 401 . .	. . .	. . .	. . .	. . .	. . .	. . .	. . .	. . .
Debt forgiveness	3 402 . .	. . .	. . .	. . .	. . .	. . .	. . .	. . .	. . .
Other capital transfers	3 410 . .	. . .	. . .	. . .	. . .	. . .	. . .	. . .	. . .
Other sectors	3 430 . .	-.10	-.13	-.04	-.20	-9.37	-5.74	-4.17	-6.71
Migrants' transfers	3 431 . .	-.10	-.13	-.04	-.20	-9.37	-5.74	-4.17	-6.71
Debt forgiveness	3 432 . .	. . .	. . .	. . .	. . .	. . .	. . .	. . .	. . .
Other capital transfers	3 440 . .	. . .	. . .	. . .	. . .	. . .	. . .	. . .	. . .
Nonproduced nonfinancial assets, credit	2 480 . .	**. . .**	**. . .**	**. . .**	**. . .**	**. . .**	**. . .**	**. . .**	**. . .**
Nonproduced nonfinancial assets, debit	3 480 . .	**. . .**	**. . .**	**. . .**	**. . .**	**. . .**	**. . .**	**. . .**	**. . .**

Table 2 (Continued). STANDARD PRESENTATION, 1988–95

(Millions of U.S. dollars)

	Code	1988	1989	1990	1991	1992	1993	1994	1995
FINANCIAL ACCOUNT	4 995	**9.26**	**16.42**	**9.10**	**-28.19**	**19.55**	**7.82**	**-8.55**	**20.01**
A. DIRECT INVESTMENT	4 500	10.81	9.17	13.11	25.47	26.45	25.97	29.79	31.04
Direct investment abroad	4 505	**. . .**	**. . .**	**. . .**	**. . .**	**. . .**	**. . .**	**. . .**	**. . .**
Equity capital	4 510	. . .	. . .	. . .	. . .	. . .	. . .	. . .	. . .
Claims on affiliated enterprises	4 515	. . .	. . .	. . .	. . .	. . .	. . .	. . .	. . .
Liabilities to affiliated enterprises	4 520	. . .	. . .	. . .	. . .	. . .	. . .	. . .	. . .
Reinvested earnings	4 525	. . .	. . .	. . .	. . .	. . .	. . .	. . .	. . .
Other capital	4 530	. . .	. . .	. . .	. . .	. . .	. . .	. . .	. . .
Claims on affiliated enterprises	4 535	. . .	. . .	. . .	. . .	. . .	. . .	. . .	. . .
Liabilities to affiliated enterprises	4 540	. . .	. . .	. . .	. . .	. . .	. . .	. . .	. . .
Direct investment in Vanuatu	4 555	**10.81**	**9.17**	**13.11**	**25.47**	**26.45**	**25.97**	**29.79**	**31.04**
Equity capital	4 560	. . .	. . .	.07	. . .	. . .	. . .	. . .	. . .
Claims on direct investors	4 565	. . .	. . .	. . .	. . .	. . .	. . .	. . .	. . .
Liabilities to direct investors	4 570	. . .	. . .	. . .	. . .	. . .	. . .	. . .	. . .
Reinvested earnings	4 575	10.81	8.67	12.34	24.73	25.73	25.97	29.07	30.15
Other capital	4 580	. . .	.49	.70	.74	.72	. . .	.71	.89
Claims on direct investors	4 585	. . .	. . .	. . .	. . .	. . .	. . .	. . .	. . .
Liabilities to direct investors	4 590	. . .	. . .	. . .	. . .	. . .	. . .	. . .	. . .
B. PORTFOLIO INVESTMENT	4 600	. . .	. . .	. . .	. . .	. . .	. . .	. . .	. . .
Assets	4 602	**. . .**	**. . .**	**. . .**	**. . .**	**. . .**	**. . .**	**. . .**	**. . .**
Equity securities	4 610	. . .	. . .	. . .	. . .	. . .	. . .	. . .	. . .
Monetary authorities	4 611	. . .	. . .	. . .	. . .	. . .	. . .	. . .	. . .
General government	4 612	. . .	. . .	. . .	. . .	. . .	. . .	. . .	. . .
Banks	4 613	. . .	. . .	. . .	. . .	. . .	. . .	. . .	. . .
Other sectors	4 614	. . .	. . .	. . .	. . .	. . .	. . .	. . .	. . .
Debt securities	4 619	. . .	. . .	. . .	. . .	. . .	. . .	. . .	. . .
Bonds and notes	4 620	. . .	. . .	. . .	. . .	. . .	. . .	. . .	. . .
Monetary authorities	4 621	. . .	. . .	. . .	. . .	. . .	. . .	. . .	. . .
General government	4 622	. . .	. . .	. . .	. . .	. . .	. . .	. . .	. . .
Banks	4 623	. . .	. . .	. . .	. . .	. . .	. . .	. . .	. . .
Other sectors	4 624	. . .	. . .	. . .	. . .	. . .	. . .	. . .	. . .
Money market instruments	4 630	. . .	. . .	. . .	. . .	. . .	. . .	. . .	. . .
Monetary authorities	4 631	. . .	. . .	. . .	. . .	. . .	. . .	. . .	. . .
General government	4 632	. . .	. . .	. . .	. . .	. . .	. . .	. . .	. . .
Banks	4 633	. . .	. . .	. . .	. . .	. . .	. . .	. . .	. . .
Other sectors	4 634	. . .	. . .	. . .	. . .	. . .	. . .	. . .	. . .
Financial derivatives	4 640	. . .	. . .	. . .	. . .	. . .	. . .	. . .	. . .
Monetary authorities	4 641	. . .	. . .	. . .	. . .	. . .	. . .	. . .	. . .
General government	4 642	. . .	. . .	. . .	. . .	. . .	. . .	. . .	. . .
Banks	4 643	. . .	. . .	. . .	. . .	. . .	. . .	. . .	. . .
Other sectors	4 644	. . .	. . .	. . .	. . .	. . .	. . .	. . .	. . .
Liabilities	4 652	**. . .**	**. . .**	**. . .**	**. . .**	**. . .**	**. . .**	**. . .**	**. . .**
Equity securities	4 660	. . .	. . .	. . .	. . .	. . .	. . .	. . .	. . .
Banks	4 663	. . .	. . .	. . .	. . .	. . .	. . .	. . .	. . .
Other sectors	4 664	. . .	. . .	. . .	. . .	. . .	. . .	. . .	. . .
Debt securities	4 669	. . .	. . .	. . .	. . .	. . .	. . .	. . .	. . .
Bonds and notes	4 670	. . .	. . .	. . .	. . .	. . .	. . .	. . .	. . .
Monetary authorities	4 671	. . .	. . .	. . .	. . .	. . .	. . .	. . .	. . .
General government	4 672	. . .	. . .	. . .	. . .	. . .	. . .	. . .	. . .
Banks	4 673	. . .	. . .	. . .	. . .	. . .	. . .	. . .	. . .
Other sectors	4 674	. . .	. . .	. . .	. . .	. . .	. . .	. . .	. . .
Money market instruments	4 680	. . .	. . .	. . .	. . .	. . .	. . .	. . .	. . .
Monetary authorities	4 681	. . .	. . .	. . .	. . .	. . .	. . .	. . .	. . .
General government	4 682	. . .	. . .	. . .	. . .	. . .	. . .	. . .	. . .
Banks	4 683	. . .	. . .	. . .	. . .	. . .	. . .	. . .	. . .
Other sectors	4 684	. . .	. . .	. . .	. . .	. . .	. . .	. . .	. . .
Financial derivatives	4 690	. . .	. . .	. . .	. . .	. . .	. . .	. . .	. . .
Monetary authorities	4 691	. . .	. . .	. . .	. . .	. . .	. . .	. . .	. . .
General government	4 692	. . .	. . .	. . .	. . .	. . .	. . .	. . .	. . .
Banks	4 693	. . .	. . .	. . .	. . .	. . .	. . .	. . .	. . .
Other sectors	4 694	. . .	. . .	. . .	. . .	. . .	. . .	. . .	. . .

Table 2 (Concluded). STANDARD PRESENTATION, 1988–95
(Millions of U.S. dollars)

	Code	1988	1989	1990	1991	1992	1993	1994	1995
C. OTHER INVESTMENT	4 700 . .	–.87	15.02	.68	–53.27	–2.75	–11.44	–43.20	–5.74
Assets	4 703 . .	**145.38**	**–.79**	**–.93**	**15.28**	**–8.57**	**–27.50**	**–45.47**	**–1.59**
Trade credits	4 706 . .	. . .	. . .	. . .	. . .	. . .	. . .	. . .	. . .
General government: long-term	4 708 . .	. . .	. . .	. . .	. . .	. . .	. . .	. . .	. . .
General government: short-term	4 709 . .	. . .	. . .	. . .	. . .	. . .	. . .	. . .	. . .
Other sectors: long-term	4 711 . .	. . .	. . .	. . .	. . .	. . .	. . .	. . .	. . .
Other sectors: short-term	4 712 . .	. . .	. . .	. . .	. . .	. . .	. . .	. . .	. . .
Loans	4 714 . .	117.85	–.33	1.32	.75	.72	–.29	2.18	.62
Monetary authorities: long-term	4 717 . .	. . .	. . .	. . .	. . .	. . .	. . .	. . .	. . .
Monetary authorities: short-term	4 718 . .	. . .	. . .	. . .	. . .	. . .	. . .	. . .	. . .
General government: long-term	4 720 . .	. . .	. . .	. . .	. . .	. . .	. . .	. . .	. . .
General government: short-term	4 721 . .	. . .	. . .	. . .	. . .	. . .	. . .	. . .	. . .
Banks: long-term	4 723 . .	117.85	–.33	1.32	.75	. . .	–.97	1.46	–.27
Banks: short-term	4 724 . .	. . .	. . .	. . .	. . .	. . .	. . .	. . .	. . .
Other sectors: long-term	4 726 . .	. . .	. . .	. . .	. . .	.72	.68	.71	.89
Other sectors: short-term	4 727 . .	. . .	. . .	. . .	. . .	. . .	. . .	. . .	. . .
Currency and deposits	4 730 . .	27.56	–.16	–1.90	14.92	–8.92	–26.78	–47.20	–1.90
Monetary authorities	4 731 . .	. . .	. . .	. . .	. . .	. . .	. . .	. . .	. . .
General government	4 732 . .	–.19	.17	. . .	. . .	. . .	. . .	. . .	. . .
Banks	4 733 . .	27.74	–.33	2.56	51.66	21.22	–9.79	9.13	–1.90
Other sectors	4 734 . .	. . .	. . .	–4.46	–36.74	–30.14	–16.99	–56.33	. . .
Other assets	4 736 . .	–.03	–.30	–.34	–.39	–.38	–.43	–.45	–.30
Monetary authorities: long-term	4 738 . .	. . .	. . .	. . .	. . .	. . .	. . .	. . .	. . .
Monetary authorities: short-term	4 739 . .	. . .	. . .	. . .	. . .	. . .	. . .	. . .	. . .
General government: long-term	4 741 . .	–.03	–.30	–.34	–.39	–.38	–.43	–.45	–.30
General government: short-term	4 742 . .	. . .	. . .	. . .	. . .	. . .	. . .	. . .	. . .
Banks: long-term	4 744 . .	. . .	. . .	. . .	. . .	. . .	. . .	. . .	. . .
Banks: short-term	4 745 . .	. . .	. . .	. . .	. . .	. . .	. . .	. . .	. . .
Other sectors: long-term	4 747 . .	. . .	. . .	. . .	. . .	. . .	. . .	. . .	. . .
Other sectors: short-term	4 748 . .	. . .	. . .	. . .	. . .	. . .	. . .	. . .	. . .
Liabilities	4 753 . .	**–146.25**	**15.81**	**1.60**	**–68.55**	**5.83**	**16.05**	**2.27**	**–4.15**
Trade credits	4 756 . .	. . .	. . .	. . .	. . .	. . .	. . .	. . .	. . .
General government: long-term	4 758 . .	. . .	. . .	. . .	. . .	. . .	. . .	. . .	. . .
General government: short-term	4 759 . .	. . .	. . .	. . .	. . .	. . .	. . .	. . .	. . .
Other sectors: long-term	4 761 . .	. . .	. . .	. . .	. . .	. . .	. . .	. . .	. . .
Other sectors: short-term	4 762 . .	. . .	. . .	. . .	. . .	. . .	. . .	. . .	. . .
Loans	4 764 . .	–101.46	1.51	7.56	12.48	7.03	6.60	2.17	2.21
Use of Fund credit and loans from the Fund	4 766 . .	. . .	. . .	. . .	. . .	. . .	. . .	. . .	. . .
Monetary authorities: other long-term	4 767 . .	. . .	. . .	. . .	. . .	. . .	. . .	. . .	. . .
Monetary authorities: short-term	4 768 . .	. . .	. . .	. . .	. . .	. . .	. . .	. . .	. . .
General government: long-term	4 770 . .	.87	1.51	7.56	12.48	7.03	6.60	2.17	2.21
General government: short-term	4 771 . .	. . .	. . .	. . .	. . .	. . .	. . .	. . .	. . .
Banks: long-term	4 773 . .	–102.32	. . .	. . .	. . .	. . .	. . .	. . .	. . .
Banks: short-term	4 774 . .	. . .	. . .	. . .	. . .	. . .	. . .	. . .	. . .
Other sectors: long-term	4 776 . .	. . .	. . .	. . .	. . .	. . .	. . .	. . .	. . .
Other sectors: short-term	4 777 . .	. . .	. . .	. . .	. . .	. . .	. . .	. . .	. . .
Currency and deposits	4 780 . .	–44.79	14.30	–5.96	–81.03	–1.20	9.46	.10	–6.36
Monetary authorities	4 781 . .	.18	–.14	.34	. . .	–.36	.16	–.05	.18
General government	4 782 . .	. . .	. . .	. . .	. . .	. . .	. . .	. . .	. . .
Banks	4 783 . .	–44.97	14.44	–6.30	–81.03	–.84	9.29	.16	–6.54
Other sectors	4 784 . .	. . .	. . .	. . .	. . .	. . .	. . .	. . .	. . .
Other liabilities	4 786 . .	. . .	. . .	. . .	. . .	. . .	. . .	. . .	. . .
Monetary authorities: long-term	4 788 . .	. . .	. . .	. . .	. . .	. . .	. . .	. . .	. . .
Monetary authorities: short-term	4 789 . .	. . .	. . .	. . .	. . .	. . .	. . .	. . .	. . .
General government: long-term	4 791 . .	. . .	. . .	. . .	. . .	. . .	. . .	. . .	. . .
General government: short-term	4 792 . .	. . .	. . .	. . .	. . .	. . .	. . .	. . .	. . .
Banks: long-term	4 794 . .	. . .	. . .	. . .	. . .	. . .	. . .	. . .	. . .
Banks: short-term	4 795 . .	. . .	. . .	. . .	. . .	. . .	. . .	. . .	. . .
Other sectors: long-term	4 797 . .	. . .	. . .	. . .	. . .	. . .	. . .	. . .	. . .
Other sectors: short-term	4 798 . .	. . .	. . .	. . .	. . .	. . .	. . .	. . .	. . .
D. RESERVE ASSETS	4 800 . .	–.68	–7.77	–4.69	–.40	–4.16	–6.70	4.86	–5.30
Monetary gold	4 810 . .	. . .	. . .	. . .	. . .	. . .	. . .	. . .	. . .
Special drawing rights	4 820 . .	–.07	–.12	–.14	–.12	–.13	.72	–.09	–.11
Reserve position in the Fund	4 830 . .	–.01	–.01	. . .	. . .	. . .	–1.20	. . .	. . .
Foreign exchange	4 840 . .	–.60	–7.64	–4.55	–.28	–4.03	–6.22	4.95	–5.18
Other claims	4 880 . .	. . .	. . .	. . .	. . .	. . .	. . .	. . .	. . .
NET ERRORS AND OMISSIONS	4 998 . .	**–17.30**	**–12.96**	**–19.38**	**19.31**	**–27.10**	**–22.44**	**–10.21**	**–33.38**

Part 3 of the *Yearbook* contains descriptions of the methodologies, compilation practices, and sources used to compile these data.

Table 1. ANALYTIC PRESENTATION, 1988–95
(Millions of U.S. dollars)

	Code	1988	1989	1990	1991	1992	1993	1994	1995
A. Current Account[1]	4 993 Y.	**–5,809**	**2,161**	**8,279**	**1,736**	**–3,749**	**–1,993**	**2,541**	**2,255**
Goods: exports f.o.b	2 100 . .	10,217	13,059	17,623	15,159	14,202	14,779	16,110	18,870
Goods: imports f.o.b	3 100 . .	–12,080	–7,365	–6,917	–10,259	–12,880	–11,504	–8,504	–11,580
Balance on Goods	4 100 . .	*–1,863*	*5,694*	*10,706*	*4,900*	*1,322*	*3,275*	*7,606*	*7,290*
Services: credit	2 200 . .	835	929	1,183	1,229	1,312	1,340	1,569	1,487
Services: debit	3 200 . .	–2,863	–1,911	–2,534	–3,431	–4,263	–4,525	–4,655	–4,887
Balance on Goods and Services	4 991 . .	*–3,891*	*4,712*	*9,355*	*2,698*	*–1,629*	*90*	*4,520*	*3,890*
Income: credit	2 300 . .	1,653	1,582	2,658	2,168	1,607	1,599	1,626	2,049
Income: debit	3 300 . .	–3,424	–3,950	–3,432	–2,766	–3,353	–3,314	–3,522	–3,795
Balance on Goods, Services, and Income	4 992 . .	*–5,662*	*2,344*	*8,581*	*2,100*	*–3,375*	*–1,625*	*2,624*	*2,144*
Current transfers: credit	2 379 Y.	87	237	444	370	533	452	608	415
Current transfers: debit	3 379 . .	–234	–420	–746	–734	–907	–820	–691	–304
B. Capital Account[1]	4 994 Y.	**. . .**	**. . .**	**. . .**	**. . .**	**. . .**	**. . .**	**. . .**	**. . .**
Capital account: credit	2 994 Y.	. . .	. . .	. . .	. . .	. . .	. . .	. . .	. . .
Capital account: debit	3 994 . .	. . .	. . .	. . .	. . .	. . .	. . .	. . .	. . .
Total, Groups A Plus B	4 010 . .	*–5,809*	*2,161*	*8,279*	*1,736*	*–3,749*	*–1,993*	*2,541*	*2,255*
C. Financial Account[1]	4 995 X.	**–2,043**	**–5,432**	**–5,023**	**1,741**	**2,700**	**2,002**	**–3,561**	**–2,696**
Direct investment abroad	4 505 . .	–68	–179	–375	–188	–156	–886	–677	–303
Direct investment in Venezuela	4 555 Y.	89	213	451	1,916	629	372	813	900
Portfolio investment assets	4 602 . .	. . .	–8	–1,952	17	2	79	–14	241
Equity securities	4 610 . .	. . .	–8	–2	–8	–44	–1	10	. . .
Debt securities	4 619 . .	. . .	. . .	–1,950	25	46	80	–24	241
Portfolio investment liabilities	4 652 Y.	. . .	–526	14,974	39	705	542	275	106
Equity securities	4 660 Y.	. . .	. . .	. . .	. . .	165	48	585	270
Debt securities	4 669 Y.	. . .	–526	14,974	39	540	494	–310	–164
Other investment assets	4 703 . .	–1,595	–369	–2,305	–925	–590	615	–3,860	–1,380
Monetary authorities	4 703 .A	. . .	. . .	. . .	. . .	. . .	. . .	. . .	. . .
General government	4 703 .B	–51	–58	–46	–12	–45	–16	–30	–32
Banks	4 703 .C	–379	767	–899	–147	–58	–538	–1,028	198
Other sectors	4 703 .D	–1,165	–1,078	–1,360	–766	–487	1,169	–2,802	–1,546
Other investment liabilities	4 753 X.	–469	–4,563	–15,816	882	2,110	1,280	–98	–2,260
Monetary authorities	4 753 XA	–32	81	619	–668	–16	–21	–20	–17
General government	4 753 YB	227	–962	–16,652	328	501	–65	–260	–106
Banks	4 753 YC	–726	–411	16	308	86	113	–70	52
Other sectors	4 753 YD	62	–3,271	201	914	1,539	1,253	252	–2,189
Total, Groups A Through C	4 020 . .	*–7,852*	*–3,271*	*3,256*	*3,477*	*–1,049*	*9*	*–1,020*	*–441*
D. Net Errors and Omissions	4 998 . .	**3,117**	**1,603**	**–1,742**	**–1,516**	**–299**	**–539**	**–310**	**–574**
Total, Groups A Through D	4 030 . .	*–4,735*	*–1,668*	*1,514*	*1,961*	*–1,348*	*–530*	*–1,330*	*–1,015*
E. Reserves and Related Items	4 040 . .	**4,735**	**1,668**	**–1,514**	**–1,961**	**1,348**	**530**	**1,330**	**1,015**
Reserve assets	4 800 . .	3,872	–1,077	–4,376	–2,645	845	144	1,173	1,906
Use of Fund credit and loans	4 766 . .	. . .	964	1,900	221	–183	–268	–201	–463
Liabilities constituting foreign authorities' reserves	4 900 . .	863	–70	–473	–90	298	799	–30	–300
Exceptional financing	4 920 . .	. . .	1,852	1,435	553	388	–145	388	–128
Conversion rates: bolívares per U.S. dollar	0 101 . .	**14.50**	**34.68**	**46.90**	**56.82**	**68.38**	**90.83**	**148.50**	**176.84**

[1] Excludes components that have been classified in the categories of Group E.

Table 2. STANDARD PRESENTATION, 1988–95
(Millions of U.S. dollars)

	Code	1988	1989	1990	1991	1992	1993	1994	1995
CURRENT ACCOUNT	4 993 . .	**–5,809**	**2,161**	**8,279**	**1,736**	**–3,749**	**–1,993**	**2,541**	**2,255**
A. GOODS	4 100 . .	–1,863	5,694	10,706	4,900	1,322	3,275	7,606	7,290
Credit	2 100 . .	**10,217**	**13,059**	**17,623**	**15,159**	**14,202**	**14,779**	**16,110**	**18,870**
General merchandise: exports f.o.b.	2 110 . .	10,082	12,892	17,437	14,962	13,978	14,401	15,632	18,530
Goods for processing: exports f.o.b.	2 150 . .	. . .	. . .	. . .	. . .	. . .	. . .	. . .	. . .
Repairs on goods	2 160 . .	. . .	3	3	4	15	14	17	14
Goods procured in ports by carriers	2 170 . .	135	141	176	187	199	179	188	226
Nonmonetary gold	2 180 . .	. . .	23	7	6	10	185	273	100
Debit	3 100 . .	**–12,080**	**–7,365**	**–6,917**	**–10,259**	**–12,880**	**–11,504**	**–8,504**	**–11,580**
General merchandise: imports f.o.b.	3 110 . .	–12,080	–7,283	–6,807	–10,131	–12,714	–11,390	–8,346	–11,447
Goods for processing: imports f.o.b.	3 150 . .	. . .	. . .	. . .	. . .	. . .	. . .	. . .	. . .
Repairs on goods	3 160 . .	. . .	–32	–55	–64	–73	–44	–72	–63
Goods procured in ports by carriers	3 170 . .	. . .	–50	–55	–64	–93	–70	–86	–70
Nonmonetary gold	3 180 . .	. . .	. . .	. . .	. . .	. . .	. . .	. . .	. . .
B. SERVICES	4 200 . .	–2,028	–982	–1,351	–2,202	–2,951	–3,185	–3,086	–3,400
Total credit	2 200 . .	*835*	*929*	*1,183*	*1,229*	*1,312*	*1,340*	*1,569*	*1,487*
Total debit	3 200 . .	*–2,863*	*–1,911*	*–2,534*	*–3,431*	*–4,263*	*–4,525*	*–4,655*	*–4,887*
Transportation services, credit	2 205 . .	**414**	**403**	**458**	**532**	**634**	**515**	**589**	**574**
Passenger	2 205 BA	*160*	*159*	*153*	*195*	*121*	*110*	*134*	*141*
Freight	2 205 BB	*86*	*154*	*220*	*233*	*406*	*304*	*229*	*145*
Other	2 205 BC	*168*	*90*	*85*	*104*	*107*	*101*	*226*	*288*
Sea transport, passenger	2 207 . .	. . .	. . .	. . .	. . .	. . .	. . .	. . .	. . .
Sea transport, freight	2 208 . .	. . .	136	204	214	381	281	201	115
Sea transport, other	2 209 . .	. . .	77	73	101	99	92	218	281
Air transport, passenger	2 211 . .	. . .	159	153	195	121	110	134	141
Air transport, freight	2 212 . .	. . .	18	16	19	25	23	28	30
Air transport, other	2 213 . .	. . .	13	12	3	8	9	8	7
Other transport, passenger	2 215 . .	. . .	. . .	. . .	. . .	. . .	. . .	. . .	. . .
Other transport, freight	2 216 . .	. . .	. . .	. . .	. . .	. . .	. . .	. . .	. . .
Other transport, other	2 217 . .	. . .	. . .	. . .	. . .	. . .	. . .	. . .	. . .
Transportation services, debit	3 205 . .	**–1,603**	**–658**	**–801**	**–1,404**	**–1,768**	**–1,488**	**–1,059**	**–1,366**
Passenger	3 205 BA	*–124*	*–92*	*–98*	*–143*	*–151*	*–110*	*–108*	*–116*
Freight	3 205 BB	*–1,040*	*–499*	*–616*	*–1,140*	*–1,487*	*–1,293*	*–848*	*–1,151*
Other	3 205 BC	*–439*	*–67*	*–87*	*–121*	*–130*	*–85*	*–103*	*–99*
Sea transport, passenger	3 207 . .	. . .	–6	–7	–10	–11	–11	–11	–13
Sea transport, freight	3 208 . .	. . .	–499	–616	–1,140	–1,487	–1,293	–848	–1,151
Sea transport, other	3 209 . .	. . .	–59	–12	–20	–15	–14	–8	–10
Air transport, passenger	3 211 . .	. . .	–86	–91	–133	–140	–99	–97	–103
Air transport, freight	3 212 . .	. . .	. . .	. . .	. . .	. . .	. . .	. . .	. . .
Air transport, other	3 213 . .	. . .	–8	–75	–101	–115	–71	–95	–89
Other transport, passenger	3 215 . .	. . .	. . .	. . .	. . .	. . .	. . .	. . .	. . .
Other transport, freight	3 216 . .	. . .	. . .	. . .	. . .	. . .	. . .	. . .	. . .
Other transport, other	3 217 . .	. . .	. . .	. . .	. . .	. . .	. . .	. . .	. . .
Travel, credit	2 236 . .	**291**	**389**	**496**	**510**	**444**	**562**	**787**	**679**
Business travel	2 237 . .	. . .	. . .	. . .	. . .	. . .	. . .	. . .	. . .
Personal travel	2 240 . .	. . .	389	496	510	444	562	787	679
Travel, debit	3 236 . .	**–509**	**–640**	**–1,023**	**–1,227**	**–1,428**	**–2,083**	**–1,950**	**–1,713**
Business travel	3 237 . .	. . .	–118	–182	–223	–257	–322	–353	–294
Personal travel	3 240 . .	. . .	–522	–841	–1,004	–1,171	–1,761	–1,597	–1,419
Other services, credit	2 200 BA	**131**	**137**	**229**	**187**	**234**	**263**	**193**	**234**
Communications	2 245 . .	. . .	9	9	13	31	31	29	30
Construction	2 249 . .	. . .	. . .	. . .	. . .	. . .	. . .	. . .	. . .
Insurance	2 253 . .	38	14	2	1	2	6	3	3
Financial	2 260 . .	. . .	. . .	. . .	. . .	. . .	. . .	. . .	. . .
Computer and information	2 262 . .	. . .	. . .	. . .	. . .	. . .	. . .	. . .	. . .
Royalties and licence fees	2 266 . .	. . .	. . .	. . .	. . .	. . .	. . .	. . .	. . .
Other business services	2 268 . .	73	83	156	92	95	116	49	59
Personal, cultural, and recreational	2 287 . .	. . .	. . .	. . .	. . .	. . .	. . .	. . .	. . .
Government, n.i.e.	2 291 . .	20	31	62	81	106	110	112	142
Other services, debit	3 200 BA	**–751**	**–613**	**–710**	**–800**	**–1,067**	**–954**	**–1,646**	**–1,808**
Communications	3 245 . .	. . .	–23	–6	–10	–11	–16	–19	–23
Construction	3 249 . .	. . .	. . .	. . .	. . .	. . .	. . .	. . .	. . .
Insurance	3 253 . .	–162	–37	–29	–31	–29	–45	–68	–85
Financial	3 260 . .	. . .	. . .	–74	–42	–43	–43	–37	–23
Computer and information	3 262 . .	. . .	. . .	. . .	. . .	. . .	. . .	. . .	. . .
Royalties and licence fees	3 266 . .	. . .	. . .	. . .	. . .	. . .	. . .	. . .	. . .
Other business services	3 268 . .	–539	–502	–441	–542	–811	–670	–1,353	–1,478
Personal, cultural, and recreational	3 287 . .	. . .	–13	–16	–16	–16	–16	–16	–16
Government, n.i.e.	3 291 . .	–50	–38	–144	–159	–157	–164	–153	–183

Table 2 (Continued). STANDARD PRESENTATION, 1988–95
(Millions of U.S. dollars)

	Code	1988	1989	1990	1991	1992	1993	1994	1995
C. INCOME	4 300	–1,771	–2,368	–774	–598	–1,746	–1,715	–1,896	–1,746
Total credit	2 300	*1,653*	*1,582*	*2,658*	*2,168*	*1,607*	*1,599*	*1,626*	*2,049*
Total debit	3 300	*–3,424*	*–3,950*	*–3,432*	*–2,766*	*–3,353*	*–3,314*	*–3,522*	*–3,795*
Compensation of employees, credit	2 310	**. . .**	**. . .**	**1**	**2**	**2**	**2**	**2**	**2**
Compensation of employees, debit	3 310	**–8**	**. . .**	**–10**	**–8**	**–3**	**–3**	**–3**	**–11**
Investment income, credit	2 320	**1,653**	**1,582**	**2,657**	**2,166**	**1,605**	**1,597**	**1,624**	**2,047**
Direct investment income	2 330	68	146	231	161	185	347	285	262
Dividends and distributed branch profits	2 332	. . .	12	9	14	101	77	29	71
Reinvested earnings and undistributed branch profits	2 333	68	134	222	147	84	270	256	191
Income on debt (interest)	2 334	. . .	. . .	. . .	. . .	. . .	. . .	. . .	. . .
Portfolio investment income	2 339	. . .	272	483	805	644	631	415	575
Income on equity	2 340	. . .	. . .	. . .	. . .	. . .	. . .	. . .	. . .
Income on bonds and notes	2 350	. . .	. . .	. . .	189	46	16	. . .	50
Income on money market instruments and financial derivatives	2 360	. . .	272	483	616	598	615	415	525
Other investment income	2 370	1,585	1,164	1,943	1,200	776	619	924	1,210
Investment income, debit	3 320	**–3,416**	**–3,950**	**–3,422**	**–2,758**	**–3,350**	**–3,311**	**–3,519**	**–3,784**
Direct investment income	3 330	–210	–225	–224	–228	–507	–574	–514	–429
Dividends and distributed branch profits	3 332	–210	–225	–224	–228	–507	–574	–514	–429
Reinvested earnings and undistributed branch profits	3 333	. . .	. . .	. . .	. . .	. . .	. . .	. . .	. . .
Income on debt (interest)	3 334	. . .	. . .	. . .	. . .	. . .	. . .	. . .	. . .
Portfolio investment income	3 339	. . .	–246	–137	–1,364	–1,232	–1,117	–1,398	–1,610
Income on equity	3 340	. . .	. . .	. . .	. . .	. . .	. . .	–175	–188
Income on bonds and notes	3 350	. . .	–246	–137	–1,364	–1,232	–1,117	–1,223	–1,422
Income on money market instruments and financial derivatives	3 360	. . .	. . .	. . .	. . .	. . .	. . .	. . .	. . .
Other investment income	3 370	–3,206	–3,479	–3,061	–1,166	–1,611	–1,620	–1,607	–1,745
D. CURRENT TRANSFERS	4 379	–147	–183	–302	–364	–374	–368	–83	111
Credit	2 379	**87**	**237**	**444**	**370**	**533**	**452**	**608**	**415**
General government	2 380	7	. . .	. . .	. . .	9	12	12	13
Other sectors	2 390	80	237	444	370	524	440	596	402
Workers' remittances	2 391	. . .	. . .	. . .	. . .	. . .	. . .	. . .	. . .
Other current transfers	2 392	80	237	444	370	524	440	596	402
Debit	3 379	**–234**	**–420**	**–746**	**–734**	**–907**	**–820**	**–691**	**–304**
General government	3 380	–31	–16	–24	–33	–15	–49	–25	–46
Other sectors	3 390	–203	–404	–722	–701	–892	–771	–666	–258
Workers' remittances	3 391	–203	–368	–691	–669	–855	–726	–598	–173
Other current transfers	3 392	. . .	–36	–31	–32	–37	–45	–68	–85
CAPITAL AND FINANCIAL ACCOUNT	4 996	**2,692**	**–3,764**	**–6,537**	**–220**	**4,048**	**2,532**	**–2,231**	**–1,681**
CAPITAL ACCOUNT	4 994	**. . .**	**. . .**	**. . .**	**. . .**	**. . .**	**. . .**	**. . .**	**. . .**
Total credit	2 994	. . .	. . .	. . .	. . .	. . .	. . .	. . .	. . .
Total debit	3 994	. . .	. . .	. . .	. . .	. . .	. . .	. . .	. . .
Capital transfers, credit	2 400	**. . .**	**. . .**	**. . .**	**. . .**	**. . .**	**. . .**	**. . .**	**. . .**
General government	2 401	. . .	. . .	. . .	. . .	. . .	. . .	. . .	. . .
Debt forgiveness	2 402	. . .	. . .	. . .	. . .	. . .	. . .	. . .	. . .
Other capital transfers	2 410	. . .	. . .	. . .	. . .	. . .	. . .	. . .	. . .
Other sectors	2 430	. . .	. . .	. . .	. . .	. . .	. . .	. . .	. . .
Migrants' transfers	2 431	. . .	. . .	. . .	. . .	. . .	. . .	. . .	. . .
Debt forgiveness	2 432	. . .	. . .	. . .	. . .	. . .	. . .	. . .	. . .
Other capital transfers	2 440	. . .	. . .	. . .	. . .	. . .	. . .	. . .	. . .
Capital transfers, debit	3 400	**. . .**	**. . .**	**. . .**	**. . .**	**. . .**	**. . .**	**. . .**	**. . .**
General government	3 401	. . .	. . .	. . .	. . .	. . .	. . .	. . .	. . .
Debt forgiveness	3 402	. . .	. . .	. . .	. . .	. . .	. . .	. . .	. . .
Other capital transfers	3 410	. . .	. . .	. . .	. . .	. . .	. . .	. . .	. . .
Other sectors	3 430	. . .	. . .	. . .	. . .	. . .	. . .	. . .	. . .
Migrants' transfers	3 431	. . .	. . .	. . .	. . .	. . .	. . .	. . .	. . .
Debt forgiveness	3 432	. . .	. . .	. . .	. . .	. . .	. . .	. . .	. . .
Other capital transfers	3 440	. . .	. . .	. . .	. . .	. . .	. . .	. . .	. . .
Nonproduced nonfinancial assets, credit	2 480	**. . .**	**. . .**	**. . .**	**. . .**	**. . .**	**. . .**	**. . .**	**. . .**
Nonproduced nonfinancial assets, debit	3 480	**. . .**	**. . .**	**. . .**	**. . .**	**. . .**	**. . .**	**. . .**	**. . .**

Table 2 (Continued). STANDARD PRESENTATION, 1988–95
(Millions of U.S. dollars)

	Code	1988	1989	1990	1991	1992	1993	1994	1995
FINANCIAL ACCOUNT	4 995	**2,692**	**–3,764**	**–6,537**	**–220**	**4,048**	**2,532**	**–2,231**	**–1,681**
A. DIRECT INVESTMENT	4 500	21	34	76	1,728	473	–514	136	597
Direct investment abroad	4 505	**–68**	**–179**	**–375**	**–188**	**–156**	**–886**	**–677**	**–303**
Equity capital	4 510	...	–45	–153	–41	–72	–616	–421	–112
Claims on affiliated enterprises	4 515	...	–45	–153	–41	–72	–616	–421	–112
Liabilities to affiliated enterprises	4 520	...	...	...	...	...	...	...	...
Reinvested earnings	4 525	–68	–134	–222	–147	–84	–270	–256	–191
Other capital	4 530	...	...	...	...	...	...	...	...
Claims on affiliated enterprises	4 535	...	...	...	...	...	...	...	...
Liabilities to affiliated enterprises	4 540	...	...	...	...	...	...	...	...
Direct investment in Venezuela	4 555	**89**	**213**	**451**	**1,916**	**629**	**372**	**813**	**900**
Equity capital	4 560	89	213	451	1,916	629	372	813	900
Claims on direct investors	4 565	...	...	...	...	...	...	...	...
Liabilities to direct investors	4 570	...	213	451	1,916	629	372	813	900
Reinvested earnings	4 575	...	...	...	...	...	...	...	...
Other capital	4 580	...	...	...	...	...	...	...	...
Claims on direct investors	4 585	...	...	...	...	...	...	...	...
Liabilities to direct investors	4 590	...	...	...	...	...	...	...	...
B. PORTFOLIO INVESTMENT	4 600	...	–534	15,976	351	1,003	621	261	347
Assets	4 602	**...**	**–8**	**–1,952**	**17**	**2**	**79**	**–14**	**241**
Equity securities	4 610	...	–8	–2	–8	–44	–1	10	...
Monetary authorities	4 611	...	...	...	...	...	...	...	...
General government	4 612	...	...	...	...	...	...	...	...
Banks	4 613	...	–8	–2	–7	–36	7	...	...
Other sectors	4 614	...	...	...	–1	–8	–8	10	...
Debt securities	4 619	...	...	–1,950	25	46	80	–24	241
Bonds and notes	4 620	...	...	–1,071	...	43	35	–27	12
Monetary authorities	4 621	...	...	...	...	...	...	...	...
General government	4 622	...	...	–1,071	...	43	35	...	37
Banks	4 623	...	...	...	...	...	...	–27	–25
Other sectors	4 624	...	...	...	...	...	...	...	...
Money market instruments	4 630	...	...	–879	25	3	45	3	229
Monetary authorities	4 631	...	...	...	...	...	...	...	...
General government	4 632	...	...	–879	25	3	45	3	229
Banks	4 633	...	...	...	...	...	...	...	...
Other sectors	4 634	...	...	...	...	...	...	...	...
Financial derivatives	4 640	...	...	...	...	...	...	...	...
Monetary authorities	4 641	...	...	...	...	...	...	...	...
General government	4 642	...	...	...	...	...	...	...	...
Banks	4 643	...	...	...	...	...	...	...	...
Other sectors	4 644	...	...	...	...	...	...	...	...
Liabilities	4 652	**...**	**–526**	**17,928**	**334**	**1,001**	**542**	**275**	**106**
Equity securities	4 660	...	...	...	...	165	48	585	270
Banks	4 663	...	...	...	...	...	...	8	10
Other sectors	4 664	...	...	...	...	165	48	577	260
Debt securities	4 669	...	–526	17,928	334	836	494	–310	–164
Bonds and notes	4 670	...	–526	17,928	334	836	494	–266	–165
Monetary authorities	4 671	...	...	400	177	168	–32	–18	–27
General government	4 672	...	–526	17,528	–73	–109	526	–248	–138
Banks	4 673	...	...	...	...	...	...	...	...
Other sectors	4 674	...	...	...	230	777	...	...	...
Money market instruments	4 680	...	...	...	...	...	...	–44	1
Monetary authorities	4 681	...	...	...	...	...	...	–44	1
General government	4 682	...	...	...	...	...	...	...	...
Banks	4 683	...	...	...	...	...	...	...	...
Other sectors	4 684	...	...	...	...	...	...	...	...
Financial derivatives	4 690	...	...	...	...	...	...	...	...
Monetary authorities	4 691	...	...	...	...	...	...	...	...
General government	4 692	...	...	...	...	...	...	...	...
Banks	4 693	...	...	...	...	...	...	...	...
Other sectors	4 694	...	...	...	...	...	...	...	...

Table 2 (Concluded). STANDARD PRESENTATION, 1988–95
(Millions of U.S. dollars)

	Code	1988	1989	1990	1991	1992	1993	1994	1995
C. OTHER INVESTMENT	4 700	–1,201	–2,186	–18,213	346	1,727	2,281	–3,801	–4,531
Assets	4 703	**–1,595**	**–369**	**–2,305**	**–925**	**–590**	**615**	**–3,860**	**–1,380**
Trade credits	4 706	...	16	–562	176	247	185	–428	3
General government: long-term	4 708	...	...	...	...	...	...	...	...
General government: short-term	4 709	...	...	...	...	...	...	...	...
Other sectors: long-term	4 711	...	...	...	...	...	...	...	...
Other sectors: short-term	4 712	...	16	–562	176	247	185	–428	3
Loans	4 714	...	–5	–30	81	–1	110	49	100
Monetary authorities: long-term	4 717	...	...	...	...	...	...	...	...
Monetary authorities: short-term	4 718	...	...	...	...	...	...	...	...
General government: long-term	4 720	...	...	...	...	...	...	...	...
General government: short-term	4 721	...	...	...	...	...	...	...	...
Banks: long-term	4 723	...	...	...	...	...	...	...	–15
Banks: short-term	4 724	...	...	...	...	...	...	...	–11
Other sectors: long-term	4 726	...	11	–17	58	–6	138	63	115
Other sectors: short-term	4 727	...	–16	–13	23	5	–28	–14	11
Currency and deposits	4 730	–1,581	–322	–1,546	–1,122	–682	456	–3,472	–1,476
Monetary authorities	4 731	...	...	...	...	...	...	...	...
General government	4 732	...	...	...	...	...	...	...	...
Banks	4 733	–379	767	–899	–147	–58	–538	–1,028	224
Other sectors	4 734	–1,202	–1,089	–647	–975	–624	994	–2,444	–1,700
Other assets	4 736	–14	–58	–167	–60	–154	–136	–9	–7
Monetary authorities: long-term	4 738	...	...	...	...	...	...	...	...
Monetary authorities: short-term	4 739	...	...	...	...	...	...	...	...
General government: long-term	4 741	–51	–58	–46	–12	–45	–16	–30	–32
General government: short-term	4 742	...	...	...	...	...	...	...	...
Banks: long-term	4 744	...	...	...	...	...	...	...	...
Banks: short-term	4 745	...	...	...	...	...	...	...	...
Other sectors: long-term	4 747	37	...	...	...	–109	–131	–13	4
Other sectors: short-term	4 748	...	...	–121	–48	...	11	34	21
Liabilities	4 753	**394**	**–1,817**	**–15,908**	**1,271**	**2,317**	**1,666**	**59**	**–3,151**
Trade credits	4 756	...	–3,327	–708	–114	–162	72	458	–1,086
General government: long-term	4 758	...	1	–220	–422	–163	–185	–421	–200
General government: short-term	4 759	...	...	...	...	...	...	...	...
Other sectors: long-term	4 761	...	...	...	46	13	2	–16	–9
Other sectors: short-term	4 762	...	–3,328	–488	262	–12	255	895	–877
Loans	4 764	208	1,677	–15,413	1,882	2,185	580	–283	–1,677
Use of Fund credit and loans from the Fund	4 766	...	964	1,900	221	–183	–268	–201	–463
Monetary authorities: other long-term	4 767	...	...	...	...	...	...	...	...
Monetary authorities: short-term	4 768	...	...	...	...	...	...	...	...
General government: long-term	4 770	225	–911	–16,119	750	648	122	170	79
General government: short-term	4 771	...	1,852	–1,832	258	92	–145	388	–128
Banks: long-term	4 773	...	...	...	...	...	...	–17	–5
Banks: short-term	4 774	...	–284	–49	45	71	3	15	33
Other sectors: long-term	4 776	–723	6	447	–7	1,088	1,731	–997	–1,276
Other sectors: short-term	4 777	706	50	240	615	469	–863	359	83
Currency and deposits	4 780	137	–126	67	261	–4	117	–75	24
Monetary authorities	4 781	863	...	...	...	...	...	...	...
General government	4 782	...	...	...	...	...	...	...	...
Banks	4 783	–726	–127	65	263	15	110	–68	24
Other sectors	4 784	...	1	2	–2	–19	7	–7	...
Other liabilities	4 786	49	–41	146	–758	298	897	–41	–412
Monetary authorities: long-term	4 788	...	...	...	...	...	...	...	...
Monetary authorities: short-term	4 789	–32	11	146	–758	282	778	–50	–317
General government: long-term	4 791	...	...	...	...	...	...	...	...
General government: short-term	4 792	2	–52	...	...	16	–2	–9	15
Banks: long-term	4 794	...	...	...	...	...	...	...	...
Banks: short-term	4 795	...	...	...	...	...	...	...	...
Other sectors: long-term	4 797	...	...	...	...	...	121	13	–105
Other sectors: short-term	4 798	79	...	...	...	...	...	5	–5
D. RESERVE ASSETS	4 800	3,872	–1,077	–4,376	–2,645	845	144	1,173	1,906
Monetary gold	4 810	...	...	...	...	...	...	...	...
Special drawing rights	4 820	616	26	39	–240	189	–411	51	88
Reserve position in the Fund	4 830	598	35	4	...	–201	...	...	...
Foreign exchange	4 840	1,441	–1,002	–4,260	–2,054	796	708	1,225	1,740
Other claims	4 880	1,217	–136	–159	–351	61	–153	–103	78
NET ERRORS AND OMISSIONS	4 998	**3,117**	**1,603**	**–1,742**	**–1,516**	**–299**	**–539**	**–310**	**–574**

Part 3 of the *Yearbook* contains descriptions of the methodologies, compilation practices, and sources used to compile these data.

Table 3. INTERNATIONAL INVESTMENT POSITION (End–period stocks), 1988–95
(Millions of U.S. dollars)

	Code	1988	1989	1990	1991	1992	1993	1994	1995
ASSETS	8 995 C.	27,731	29,488	38,443	42,227	41,806	43,156	46,634	45,944
Direct investment abroad	8 505 . .	**730**	**866**	**1,221**	**1,368**	**1,568**	**2,447**	**3,124**	**3,427**
Equity capital and reinvested earnings	8 506 . .	730	866	1,221	1,368	1,568	2,447	3,124	3,427
Claims on affiliated enterprises	8 507 . .	...	...	...	...	...	...	...	...
Liabilities to affiliated enterprises	8 508 . .	...	...	...	...	...	...	...	...
Other capital	8 530 . .	...	...	...	...	...	...	...	...
Claims on affiliated enterprises	8 535 . .	...	...	...	...	...	...	...	...
Liabilities to affiliated enterprises	8 540 . .	...	...	...	...	...	...	...	...
Portfolio investment	8 602 . .	**...**	**...**	**1,950**	**1,925**	**1,879**	**1,799**	**1,796**	**1,530**
Equity securities	8 610 . .	...	...	...	...	...	...	...	...
Monetary authorities	8 611 . .	...	...	...	...	...	...	...	...
General government	8 612 . .	...	...	...	...	...	...	...	...
Banks	8 613 . .	...	...	...	...	...	...	...	...
Other sectors	8 614 . .	...	...	...	...	...	...	...	...
Debt securities	8 619 . .	...	...	1,950	1,925	1,879	1,799	1,796	1,530
Bonds and notes	8 620 . .	...	...	1,950	1,925	1,879	1,799	1,796	1,530
Monetary authorities	8 621 . .	...	...	...	...	...	...	...	...
General government	8 622 . .	...	...	...	...	...	...	...	...
Banks	8 623 . .	...	...	...	...	...	...	...	...
Other sectors	8 624 . .	...	...	...	...	...	...	...	...
Money market instruments	8 630 . .	...	...	...	...	...	...	...	...
Monetary authorities	8 631 . .	...	...	...	...	...	...	...	...
General government	8 632 . .	...	...	...	...	...	...	...	...
Banks	8 633 . .	...	...	...	...	...	...	...	...
Other sectors	8 634 . .	...	...	...	...	...	...	...	...
Financial derivatives	8 640 . .	...	...	...	...	...	...	...	...
Monetary authorities	8 641 . .	...	...	...	...	...	...	...	...
General government	8 642 . .	...	...	...	...	...	...	...	...
Banks	8 643 . .	...	...	...	...	...	...	...	...
Other sectors	8 644 . .	...	...	...	...	...	...	...	...
Other investment	8 703 . .	**19,983**	**20,529**	**22,806**	**23,773**	**24,363**	**25,106**	**28,955**	**30,391**
Trade credits	8 706 . .	...	...	...	...	...	...	...	...
General government: long-term	8 708 . .	...	...	...	...	...	...	...	...
General government: short-term	8 709 . .	...	...	...	...	...	...	...	...
Other sectors: long-term	8 711 . .	...	...	...	...	...	...	...	...
Other sectors: short-term	8 712 . .	...	...	...	...	...	...	...	...
Loans	8 714 . .	...	...	...	...	...	...	...	...
Monetary authorities: long-term	8 717 . .	...	...	...	...	...	...	...	...
Monetary authorities: short-term	8 718 . .	...	...	...	...	...	...	...	...
General government: long-term	8 720 . .	...	...	...	...	...	...	...	...
General government: short-term	8 721 . .	...	...	...	...	...	...	...	...
Banks: long-term	8 723 . .	...	...	...	...	...	...	...	...
Banks: short-term	8 724 . .	...	...	...	...	...	...	...	...
Other sectors: long-term	8 726 . .	...	...	...	...	...	...	...	...
Other sectors: short-term	8 727 . .	...	...	...	...	...	...	...	...
Currency and deposits	8 730 . .	18,147	18,749	20,946	21,901	22,331	23,069	26,978	28,452
Monetary authorities	8 731 . .	...	...	...	...	...	...	...	...
General government	8 732 . .	...	...	...	...	...	...	...	...
Banks	8 733 . .	1,579	1,111	1,978	2,123	2,181	2,719	3,774	3,586
Other sectors	8 734 . .	16,568	17,638	18,968	19,778	20,150	20,350	23,204	24,866
Other assets	8 736 . .	1,836	1,780	1,860	1,872	2,032	2,037	1,977	1,939
Monetary authorities: long-term	8 738 . .	...	...	...	...	...	...	...	...
Monetary authorities: short-term	8 739 . .	...	...	...	...	...	...	...	...
General government: long-term	8 741 . .	635	693	739	751	796	812	812	874
General government: short-term	8 742 . .	...	...	...	...	...	...	...	...
Banks: long-term	8 744 . .	...	...	...	...	...	...	...	...
Banks: short-term	8 745 . .	...	...	...	...	...	...	...	...
Other sectors: long-term	8 747 . .	1,201	1,087	1,121	1,121	1,236	1,225	1,165	1,065
Other sectors: short-term	8 748 . .	...	...	...	...	...	...	...	...
Reserve assets	8 800 . .	**7,018**	**8,093**	**12,466**	**15,161**	**13,996**	**13,804**	**12,759**	**10,596**
Monetary gold	8 810 . .	3,439	3,439	3,439	3,439	3,439	3,439	3,439	3,439
Special drawing rights	8 820 . .	76	47	10	269	75	486	463	380
Reserve position in the Fund	8 830 . .	41	4	...	...	199	199	212	215
Foreign exchange	8 840 . .	3,051	4,056	8,311	10,396	9,287	8,531	7,394	5,388
Other claims	8 880 . .	411	547	706	1,057	996	1,149	1,252	1,174

Table 3 (Continued). INTERNATIONAL INVESTMENT POSITION (End–period stocks), 1988–95
(Millions of U.S. dollars)

	Code		1988	1989	1990	1991	1992	1993	1994	1995
LIABILITIES	8 995	D.	38,729	37,102	39,689	42,988	47,046	50,713	51,730	49,250
Direct investment in Venezuela	8 555	. .	**1,478**	**1,691**	**2,142**	**4,058**	**4,687**	**5,059**	**5,872**	**6,772**
Equity capital and reinvested earnings	8 556	. .	1,478	1,691	2,142	4,058	4,687	5,059	5,872	6,772
Claims on direct investors	8 557	. .	...	...	...	...	...	...	...	...
Liabilities to direct investors	8 558	. .	...	...	...	...	...	...	...	...
Other capital	8 580	. .	...	...	...	...	...	...	...	...
Claims on direct investors	8 585	. .	...	...	...	...	...	...	...	...
Liabilities to direct investors	8 590	. .	...	...	...	...	...	...	...	...
Portfolio investment	8 652	. .	**...**	**...**	**18,483**	**18,945**	**20,241**	**22,816**	**22,844**	**22,555**
Equity securities	8 660	. .	...	...	...	...	...	917	1,184	1,060
Banks	8 663	. .	...	...	...	...	...	...	...	...
Other sectors	8 664	. .	...	...	...	...	...	...	...	...
Debt securities	8 669	. .	...	...	18,483	18,945	20,241	21,899	21,660	21,495
Bonds and notes	8 670	. .	...	...	18,483	18,945	20,241	21,899	21,660	21,495
Monetary authorities	8 671	. .	...	...	...	...	...	...	...	...
General government	8 672	. .	...	...	18,348	18,735	19,956	21,534	21,295	21,130
Banks	8 673	. .	...	...	...	...	...	...	...	...
Other sectors	8 674	. .	...	...	135	210	285	365	365	365
Money market instruments	8 680	. .	...	...	...	...	...	...	...	...
Monetary authorities	8 681	. .	...	...	...	...	...	...	...	...
General government	8 682	. .	...	...	...	...	...	...	...	...
Banks	8 683	. .	...	...	...	...	...	...	...	...
Other sectors	8 684	. .	...	...	...	...	...	...	...	...
Financial derivatives	8 690	. .	...	...	...	...	...	...	...	...
Monetary authorities	8 691	. .	...	...	...	...	...	...	...	...
General government	8 692	. .	...	...	...	...	...	...	...	...
Banks	8 692	. .	...	...	...	...	...	...	...	...
Other sectors	8 694	. .	...	...	...	...	...	...	...	...
Other investment	8 753	. .	**37,251**	**35,411**	**19,064**	**19,985**	**22,118**	**22,838**	**23,014**	**19,923**
Trade credits	8 756	. .	...	...	...	...	...	...	...	...
General government: long-term	8 758	. .	...	...	...	...	...	...	...	...
General government: short-term	8 759	. .	...	...	...	...	...	...	...	...
Other sectors: long-term	8 761	. .	...	...	...	...	...	...	...	...
Other sectors: short-term	8 762	. .	...	...	...	...	...	...	...	...
Loans	8 764	. .	34,478	31,019	15,852	16,085	16,266	16,452	16,377	13,559
Use of Fund credit and loans from the Fund	8 766	. .	...	998	3,012	3,249	2,946	2,679	2,643	2,239
Monetary authorities: other long-term	8 767	. .	...	...	...	...	...	...	...	...
Monetary authorities: short-term	8 768	. .	...	...	...	...	...	...	...	...
General government: long-term	8 770	. .	26,158	24,880	8,121	8,147	8,372	8,003	7,465	7,040
General government: short-term	8 771	. .	...	...	...	...	...	...	...	...
Banks: long-term	8 773	. .	...	...	...	...	...	...	...	...
Banks: short-term	8 774	. .	...	...	...	...	...	...	...	...
Other sectors: long-term	8 776	. .	3,690	3,675	3,872	3,423	3,657	3,898	3,291	2,540
Other sectors: short-term	8 777	. .	4,630	1,466	847	1,266	1,291	1,872	2,978	1,740
Currency and deposits	8 780	. .	1,124	981	940	1,248	1,335	1,447	1,394	1,451
Monetary authorities	8 781	. .	...	...	...	...	...	...	...	...
General government	8 782	. .	...	...	...	...	...	...	...	...
Banks	8 783	. .	1,124	981	940	1,248	1,335	1,447	1,394	1,451
Other sectors	8 784	. .	...	...	...	...	...	...	...	...
Other liabilities	8 786	. .	1,649	3,411	2,272	2,652	4,517	4,939	5,243	4,913
Monetary authorities: long-term	8 788	. .	...	...	...	...	...	...	...	...
Monetary authorities: short-term	8 789	. .	1,142	1,153	1,351	592	875	1,697	1,603	1,286
General government: long-term	8 791	. .	...	...	...	...	...	...	...	...
General government: short-term	8 792	. .	269	2,069	237	495	603	456	989	969
Banks: long-term	8 794	. .	...	...	...	...	...	...	...	...
Banks: short-term	8 795	. .	...	...	...	...	...	...	...	...
Other sectors: long-term	8 797	. .	...	...	121	560	1,622	2,366	2,237	1,901
Other sectors: short-term	8 798	. .	238	189	563	1,005	1,417	420	414	757
NET INTERNATIONAL INVESTMENT POSITION	8 995	. .	**–10,998**	**–7,614**	**–1,246**	**–761**	**–5,240**	**–7,558**	**–5,095**	**–3,306**
Conversion rates: bolívares per U.S. dollar (end of period)	0 102	. .	**14.50**	**43.08**	**50.38**	**61.55**	**79.45**	**105.64**	**170.00**	**290.00**

Table 1. ANALYTIC PRESENTATION, 1988–95
(Millions of U.S. dollars)

	Code	1988	1989	1990	1991	1992	1993	1994	1995
A. Current Account [1]	4 993 Y.	**7.95**	**12.81**	**7.26**	**–28.66**	**–52.50**	**–38.68**	**5.78**	**9.78**
Goods: exports f.o.b	2 100 . .	15.09	12.87	8.85	6.48	5.82	6.43	3.53	8.75
Goods: imports f.o.b	3 100 . .	–66.57	–66.99	–70.00	–77.62	–89.90	–87.37	–69.01	–80.22
Balance on Goods	4 100 . .	*–51.47*	*–54.12*	*–61.15*	*–71.15*	*–84.07*	*–80.94*	*–65.49*	*–71.46*
Services: credit	2 200 . .	26.89	30.90	35.58	30.75	36.65	35.78	43.12	55.33
Services: debit	3 200 . .	–18.25	–18.80	–24.72	–34.64	–43.43	–38.22	–28.25	–34.73
Balance on Goods and Services	4 991 . .	*–42.83*	*–42.02*	*–50.29*	*–75.04*	*–90.85*	*–83.38*	*–50.61*	*–50.86*
Income: credit	2 300 . .	2.89	4.48	6.68	7.21	6.15	4.33	4.04	4.65
Income: debit	3 300 . .	–2.12	–2.39	–1.53	–2.39	–2.55	–4.42	–4.46	–4.22
Balance on Goods, Services, and Income	4 992 . .	*–42.07*	*–39.94*	*–45.14*	*–70.22*	*–87.25*	*–83.47*	*–51.03*	*–50.43*
Current transfers: credit	2 379 Y.	52.95	56.29	56.54	44.66	39.07	49.91	62.93	66.83
Current transfers: debit	3 379 . .	–2.93	–3.54	–4.15	–3.09	–4.32	–5.11	–6.12	–6.62
B. Capital Account [1]	4 994 Y.	**. . .**	**. . .**	**. . .**	**. . .**	**. . .**	**. . .**	**. . .**	**. . .**
Capital account: credit	2 994 Y.	. . .	. . .	. . .	. . .	. . .	. . .	. . .	. . .
Capital account: debit	3 994 . .	. . .	. . .	. . .	. . .	. . .	. . .	. . .	. . .
Total, Groups A Plus B	4 010 . .	*7.95*	*12.81*	*7.26*	*–28.66*	*–52.50*	*–38.68*	*5.78*	*9.78*
C. Financial Account [1]	4 995 X.	**.49**	**.48**	**9.40**	**21.69**	**15.94**	**15.55**	**–5.47**	**–5.79**
Direct investment abroad	4 505 . .	. . .	. . .	. . .	. . .	. . .	. . .	. . .	. . .
Direct investment in Western Samoa	4 555 Y.	. . .	. . .	. . .	. . .	. . .	. . .	. . .	. . .
Portfolio investment assets	4 602 . .	. . .	. . .	. . .	. . .	. . .	. . .	. . .	. . .
Equity securities	4 610 . .	. . .	. . .	. . .	. . .	. . .	. . .	. . .	. . .
Debt securities	4 619 . .	. . .	. . .	. . .	. . .	. . .	. . .	. . .	. . .
Portfolio investment liabilities	4 652 Y.	. . .	. . .	. . .	. . .	. . .	. . .	. . .	. . .
Equity securities	4 660 Y.	. . .	. . .	. . .	. . .	. . .	. . .	. . .	. . .
Debt securities	4 669 Y.	. . .	. . .	. . .	. . .	. . .	. . .	. . .	. . .
Other investment assets	4 703 . .	–.31	–.08	–.03	–.22	. . .	. . .	. . .	. . .
Monetary authorities	4 703 .A	. . .	. . .	. . .	. . .	. . .	. . .	. . .	. . .
General government	4 703 .B	. . .	. . .	. . .	. . .	. . .	. . .	. . .	. . .
Banks	4 703 .C	. . .	. . .	. . .	. . .	. . .	. . .	. . .	. . .
Other sectors	4 703 .D	–.31	–.08	–.03	–.22	. . .	. . .	. . .	. . .
Other investment liabilities	4 753 X.	.80	.56	9.43	21.91	15.94	15.55	–5.47	–5.79
Monetary authorities	4 753 XA	–.04	. . .	. . .	. . .	. . .	. . .	–.13	.01
General government	4 753 YB	1.12	1.54	9.71	21.56	16.54	15.25	6.84	2.54
Banks	4 753 YC	.25	–.37	.16	.68	–.24	.56	.03	.82
Other sectors	4 753 YD	–.53	–.61	–.44	–.33	–.36	–.27	–12.22	–9.17
Total, Groups A Through C	4 020 . .	*8.43*	*13.29*	*16.66*	*–6.97*	*–36.56*	*–23.13*	*.31*	*3.99*
D. Net Errors and Omissions	4 998 . .	**1.67**	**–2.61**	**–5.66**	**4.89**	**23.83**	**13.82**	**–4.18**	**–1.95**
Total, Groups A Through D	4 030 . .	*10.10*	*10.68*	*11.00*	*–2.08*	*–12.72*	*–9.31*	*–3.87*	*2.04*
E. Reserves and Related Items	4 040 . .	**–10.10**	**–10.68**	**–11.00**	**2.08**	**12.72**	**9.31**	**3.87**	**–2.04**
Reserve assets	4 800 . .	–8.42	–10.66	–11.49	–.42	12.95	8.29	3.87	–2.04
Use of Fund credit and loans	4 766 . .	–3.96	–2.09	–.86	–.59	–.22	. . .	. . .	. . .
Liabilities constituting foreign authorities' reserves	4 900 . .	. . .	. . .	. . .	. . .	. . .	. . .	. . .	. . .
Exceptional financing	4 920 . .	2.28	2.07	1.34	3.09	. . .	1.01	. . .	. . .
Conversion rates: tala per U.S. dollar	0 101 . .	**2.0804**	**2.2702**	**2.3152**	**2.3983**	**2.4663**	**2.5699**	**2.5276**	**2.4757**

[1] Excludes components that have been classified in the categories of Group E.

Table 2. STANDARD PRESENTATION, 1988–95

(Millions of U.S. dollars)

	Code	1988	1989	1990	1991	1992	1993	1994	1995
CURRENT ACCOUNT	4 993 . .	**10.23**	**14.88**	**8.60**	**–25.57**	**–52.50**	**–37.66**	**5.78**	**9.78**
A. GOODS	4 100 . .	–51.47	–54.12	–61.15	–71.15	–84.07	–80.94	–65.49	–71.46
Credit	2 100 . .	**15.09**	**12.87**	**8.85**	**6.48**	**5.82**	**6.43**	**3.53**	**8.75**
General merchandise: exports f.o.b.	2 110 . .	15.09	12.87	8.85	6.48	5.82	6.43	3.53	8.75
Goods for processing: exports f.o.b.	2 150 . .	. . .	. . .	. . .	. . .	. . .	. . .	. . .	. . .
Repairs on goods	2 160 . .	. . .	. . .	. . .	. . .	. . .	. . .	. . .	. . .
Goods procured in ports by carriers	2 170 . .	. . .	. . .	. . .	. . .	. . .	. . .	. . .	. . .
Nonmonetary gold	2 180 . .	. . .	. . .	. . .	. . .	. . .	. . .	. . .	. . .
Debit	3 100 . .	**–66.57**	**–66.99**	**–70.00**	**–77.62**	**–89.90**	**–87.37**	**–69.01**	**–80.22**
General merchandise: imports f.o.b.	3 110 . .	–66.57	–66.99	–70.00	–77.62	–89.90	–87.37	–69.01	–80.22
Goods for processing: imports f.o.b.	3 150 . .	. . .	. . .	. . .	. . .	. . .	. . .	. . .	. . .
Repairs on goods	3 160 . .	. . .	. . .	. . .	. . .	. . .	. . .	. . .	. . .
Goods procured in ports by carriers	3 170 . .	. . .	. . .	. . .	. . .	. . .	. . .	. . .	. . .
Nonmonetary gold	3 180 . .	. . .	. . .	. . .	. . .	. . .	. . .	. . .	. . .
B. SERVICES	4 200 . .	8.64	12.10	10.86	–3.89	–6.78	–2.44	14.88	20.60
Total credit	2 200 . .	*26.89*	*30.90*	*35.58*	*30.75*	*36.65*	*35.78*	*43.12*	*55.33*
Total debit	3 200 . .	*–18.25*	*–18.80*	*–24.72*	*–34.64*	*–43.43*	*–38.22*	*–28.25*	*–34.73*
Transportation services, credit	2 205 . .	**3.63**	**3.23**	**5.16**	**5.34**	**3.44**	**2.50**	**2.18**	**1.69**
Passenger	2 205 BA	*1.10*	*1.27*	*1.65*	*1.71*	*1.01*	*1.47*	*.98*	*.70*
Freight	2 205 BB	*.07*	. . .	*.95*	*.98*	*.24*	*.19*	*.35*	*.42*
Other	2 205 BC	*2.45*	*1.96*	*2.55*	*2.65*	*2.19*	*.84*	*.84*	*.57*
Sea transport, passenger	2 207 . .	. . .	. . .	. . .	. . .	. . .	. . .	. . .	. . .
Sea transport, freight	2 208 . .	. . .	. . .	. . .	. . .	. . .	. . .	. . .	. . .
Sea transport, other	2 209 . .	. . .	. . .	. . .	. . .	. . .	. . .	. . .	. . .
Air transport, passenger	2 211 . .	. . .	. . .	. . .	. . .	. . .	. . .	. . .	. . .
Air transport, freight	2 212 . .	. . .	. . .	. . .	. . .	. . .	. . .	. . .	. . .
Air transport, other	2 213 . .	. . .	. . .	. . .	. . .	. . .	. . .	. . .	. . .
Other transport, passenger	2 215 . .	. . .	. . .	. . .	. . .	. . .	. . .	. . .	. . .
Other transport, freight	2 216 . .	. . .	. . .	. . .	. . .	. . .	. . .	. . .	. . .
Other transport, other	2 217 . .	. . .	. . .	. . .	. . .	. . .	. . .	. . .	. . .
Transportation services, debit	3 205 . .	**–9.04**	**–8.98**	**–8.59**	**–15.38**	**–17.92**	**–16.62**	**–14.71**	**–15.47**
Passenger	3 205 BA	*–2.02*	*–1.85*	*–2.16*	*–2.60*	*–3.10*	*–2.35*	*–3.43*	*–3.57*
Freight	3 205 BB	*–6.02*	*–6.15*	*–6.43*	*–12.78*	*–14.30*	*–13.26*	*–11.28*	*–11.90*
Other	3 205 BC	*–.99*	*–.98*	. . .	. . .	*–.51*	*–1.01*	. . .	. . .
Sea transport, passenger	3 207 . .	. . .	. . .	. . .	. . .	. . .	. . .	. . .	. . .
Sea transport, freight	3 208 . .	. . .	. . .	. . .	. . .	. . .	. . .	. . .	. . .
Sea transport, other	3 209 . .	. . .	. . .	. . .	. . .	. . .	. . .	. . .	. . .
Air transport, passenger	3 211 . .	. . .	. . .	. . .	. . .	. . .	. . .	. . .	. . .
Air transport, freight	3 212 . .	. . .	. . .	. . .	. . .	. . .	. . .	. . .	. . .
Air transport, other	3 213 . .	. . .	. . .	. . .	. . .	. . .	. . .	. . .	. . .
Other transport, passenger	3 215 . .	. . .	. . .	. . .	. . .	. . .	. . .	. . .	. . .
Other transport, freight	3 216 . .	. . .	. . .	. . .	. . .	. . .	. . .	. . .	. . .
Other transport, other	3 217 . .	. . .	. . .	. . .	. . .	. . .	. . .	. . .	. . .
Travel, credit	2 236 . .	**17.20**	**20.15**	**20.54**	**15.79**	**15.66**	**18.93**	**24.77**	**34.75**
Business travel	2 237 . .	. . .	. . .	. . .	. . .	. . .	. . .	. . .	. . .
Personal travel	2 240 . .	. . .	. . .	. . .	. . .	. . .	. . .	. . .	. . .
Travel, debit	3 236 . .	**–1.43**	**–1.65**	**–1.97**	**–1.76**	**–1.91**	**–2.37**	**–3.72**	**–3.13**
Business travel	3 237 . .	. . .	. . .	. . .	. . .	. . .	. . .	. . .	. . .
Personal travel	3 240 . .	. . .	. . .	. . .	. . .	. . .	. . .	. . .	. . .
Other services, credit	2 200 BA	**6.06**	**7.51**	**9.88**	**9.62**	**17.55**	**14.35**	**16.18**	**18.89**
Communications	2 245 . .	. . .	. . .	. . .	. . .	. . .	. . .	. . .	. . .
Construction	2 249 . .	. . .	. . .	. . .	. . .	. . .	. . .	. . .	. . .
Insurance	2 253 . .	.01	. . .	.11	.11	.03	.02	1.06	.13
Financial	2 260 . .	. . .	. . .	. . .	. . .	. . .	. . .	. . .	. . .
Computer and information	2 262 . .	. . .	. . .	. . .	. . .	. . .	. . .	. . .	. . .
Royalties and licence fees	2 266 . .	. . .	. . .	. . .	.26	.16	.17	.15	.41
Other business services	2 268 . .	5.08	6.13	8.06	5.27	14.03	10.97	5.22	5.68
Personal, cultural, and recreational	2 287 . .	. . .	. . .	. . .	. . .	. . .	. . .	6.39	9.18
Government, n.i.e.	2 291 . .	.98	1.39	1.71	3.98	3.33	3.19	3.35	3.49
Other services, debit	3 200 BA	**–7.78**	**–8.17**	**–14.17**	**–17.50**	**–23.60**	**–19.23**	**–9.82**	**–16.13**
Communications	3 245 . .	. . .	. . .	. . .	. . .	. . .	. . .	. . .	. . .
Construction	3 249 . .	. . .	. . .	. . .	. . .	. . .	. . .	. . .	. . .
Insurance	3 253 . .	–.75	–.77	–.80	–1.58	–2.20	–1.98	–1.21	–1.41
Financial	3 260 . .	. . .	. . .	. . .	. . .	. . .	. . .	. . .	. . .
Computer and information	3 262 . .	. . .	. . .	. . .	. . .	. . .	. . .	. . .	. . .
Royalties and licence fees	3 266 . .	. . .	. . .	. . .	. . .	. . .	. . .	. . .	. . .
Other business services	3 268 . .	–4.17	–3.92	–9.29	–11.80	–18.34	–14.06	–7.95	–12.55
Personal, cultural, and recreational	3 287 . .	. . .	. . .	. . .	. . .	. . .	. . .	. . .	. . .
Government, n.i.e.	3 291 . .	–2.86	–3.47	–4.08	–4.11	–3.06	–3.19	–.65	–2.16

Table 2 (Continued). STANDARD PRESENTATION, 1988–95
(Millions of U.S. dollars)

	Code	1988	1989	1990	1991	1992	1993	1994	1995
C. INCOME	4 300 . .	.76	2.08	5.15	4.82	3.60	–.09	–.42	.44
Total credit	2 300 . .	*2.89*	*4.48*	*6.68*	*7.21*	*6.15*	*4.33*	*4.04*	*4.65*
Total debit	3 300 . .	*–2.12*	*–2.39*	*–1.53*	*–2.39*	*–2.55*	*–4.42*	*–4.46*	*–4.22*
Compensation of employees, credit	2 310 . .	**. . .**	**. . .**	**. . .**	**.73**	**.97**	**.95**	**1.09**	**1.27**
Compensation of employees, debit	3 310 . .	**. . .**	**. . .**	**. . .**	**. . .**	**. . .**	**. . .**	**–.06**	**–.18**
Investment income, credit	2 320 . .	**2.89**	**4.48**	**6.68**	**6.48**	**5.19**	**3.37**	**2.96**	**3.38**
Direct investment income	2 330 . .	. . .	. . .	. . .	. . .	. . .	. . .	. . .	. . .
Dividends and distributed branch profits	2 332 . .	. . .	. . .	. . .	. . .	. . .	. . .	. . .	. . .
Reinvested earnings and undistributed branch profits	2 333 . .	. . .	. . .	. . .	. . .	. . .	. . .	. . .	. . .
Income on debt (interest)	2 334 . .	. . .	. . .	. . .	. . .	. . .	. . .	. . .	. . .
Portfolio investment income	2 339 . .	. . .	. . .	. . .	. . .	. . .	. . .	. . .	. . .
Income on equity	2 340 . .	. . .	. . .	. . .	. . .	. . .	. . .	. . .	. . .
Income on bonds and notes	2 350 . .	. . .	. . .	. . .	. . .	. . .	. . .	. . .	. . .
Income on money market instruments and financial derivatives	2 360 . .	. . .	. . .	. . .	. . .	. . .	. . .	. . .	. . .
Other investment income	2 370 . .	2.89	4.48	6.68	6.48	5.19	3.37	2.96	3.38
Investment income, debit	3 320 . .	**–2.12**	**–2.39**	**–1.53**	**–2.39**	**–2.55**	**–4.42**	**–4.41**	**–4.04**
Direct investment income	3 330 . .	–.43	–.90	. . .	. . .	. . .	. . .	. . .	. . .
Dividends and distributed branch profits	3 332 . .	–.43	–.90	. . .	. . .	. . .	. . .	. . .	. . .
Reinvested earnings and undistributed branch profits	3 333 . .	. . .	. . .	. . .	. . .	. . .	. . .	. . .	. . .
Income on debt (interest)	3 334 . .	. . .	. . .	. . .	. . .	. . .	. . .	. . .	. . .
Portfolio investment income	3 339 . .	. . .	. . .	. . .	. . .	. . .	. . .	. . .	. . .
Income on equity	3 340 . .	. . .	. . .	. . .	. . .	. . .	. . .	. . .	. . .
Income on bonds and notes	3 350 . .	. . .	. . .	. . .	. . .	. . .	. . .	. . .	. . .
Income on money market instruments and financial derivatives	3 360 . .	. . .	. . .	. . .	. . .	. . .	. . .	. . .	. . .
Other investment income	3 370 . .	–1.69	–1.49	–1.53	–2.39	–2.55	–4.42	–4.41	–4.04
D. CURRENT TRANSFERS	4 379 . .	52.30	54.82	53.74	44.65	34.75	45.81	56.81	60.21
Credit	2 379 . .	**55.23**	**58.36**	**57.88**	**47.75**	**39.07**	**50.92**	**62.93**	**66.83**
General government	2 380 . .	17.52	17.49	15.12	13.65	. . .	19.61	26.43	27.47
Other sectors	2 390 . .	37.71	40.87	42.77	34.09	39.07	31.31	36.51	39.36
Workers' remittances	2 391 . .	37.71	40.87	42.77	34.09	39.07	31.31	36.51	39.36
Other current transfers	2 392 . .	. . .	. . .	. . .	. . .	. . .	. . .	. . .	. . .
Debit	3 379 . .	**–2.93**	**–3.54**	**–4.15**	**–3.09**	**–4.32**	**–5.11**	**–6.12**	**–6.62**
General government	3 380 . .	–.70	–.82	–1.10	. . .	. . .	–2.18	–2.61	–2.50
Other sectors	3 390 . .	–2.24	–2.72	–3.05	–3.09	–4.32	–2.93	–3.51	–4.11
Workers' remittances	3 391 . .	–2.24	–2.72	–3.05	–3.09	–4.32	–2.93	–3.51	–4.11
Other current transfers	3 392 . .	. . .	. . .	. . .	. . .	. . .	. . .	. . .	. . .
CAPITAL AND FINANCIAL ACCOUNT	4 996 . .	**–11.90**	**–12.27**	**–2.94**	**20.68**	**28.66**	**23.84**	**–1.60**	**–7.83**
CAPITAL ACCOUNT	4 994 . .	**. . .**	**. . .**	**. . .**	**. . .**	**. . .**	**. . .**	**. . .**	**. . .**
Total credit	2 994 . .	. . .	. . .	. . .	. . .	. . .	. . .	. . .	. . .
Total debit	3 994 . .	. . .	. . .	. . .	. . .	. . .	. . .	. . .	. . .
Capital transfers, credit	2 400 . .	**. . .**	**. . .**	**. . .**	**. . .**	**. . .**	**. . .**	**. . .**	**. . .**
General government	2 401 . .	. . .	. . .	. . .	. . .	. . .	. . .	. . .	. . .
Debt forgiveness	2 402 . .	. . .	. . .	. . .	. . .	. . .	. . .	. . .	. . .
Other capital transfers	2 410 . .	. . .	. . .	. . .	. . .	. . .	. . .	. . .	. . .
Other sectors	2 430 . .	. . .	. . .	. . .	. . .	. . .	. . .	. . .	. . .
Migrants' transfers	2 431 . .	. . .	. . .	. . .	. . .	. . .	. . .	. . .	. . .
Debt forgiveness	2 432 . .	. . .	. . .	. . .	. . .	. . .	. . .	. . .	. . .
Other capital transfers	2 440 . .	. . .	. . .	. . .	. . .	. . .	. . .	. . .	. . .
Capital transfers, debit	3 400 . .	**. . .**	**. . .**	**. . .**	**. . .**	**. . .**	**. . .**	**. . .**	**. . .**
General government	3 401 . .	. . .	. . .	. . .	. . .	. . .	. . .	. . .	. . .
Debt forgiveness	3 402 . .	. . .	. . .	. . .	. . .	. . .	. . .	. . .	. . .
Other capital transfers	3 410 . .	. . .	. . .	. . .	. . .	. . .	. . .	. . .	. . .
Other sectors	3 430 . .	. . .	. . .	. . .	. . .	. . .	. . .	. . .	. . .
Migrants' transfers	3 431 . .	. . .	. . .	. . .	. . .	. . .	. . .	. . .	. . .
Debt forgiveness	3 432 . .	. . .	. . .	. . .	. . .	. . .	. . .	. . .	. . .
Other capital transfers	3 440 . .	. . .	. . .	. . .	. . .	. . .	. . .	. . .	. . .
Nonproduced nonfinancial assets, credit	2 480 . .	**. . .**	**. . .**	**. . .**	**. . .**	**. . .**	**. . .**	**. . .**	**. . .**
Nonproduced nonfinancial assets, debit	3 480 . .	**. . .**	**. . .**	**. . .**	**. . .**	**. . .**	**. . .**	**. . .**	**. . .**

Table 2 (Continued). STANDARD PRESENTATION, 1988–95
(Millions of U.S. dollars)

	Code		1988	1989	1990	1991	1992	1993	1994	1995
FINANCIAL ACCOUNT	4 995	. .	**–11.90**	**–12.27**	**–2.94**	**20.68**	**28.66**	**23.84**	**–1.60**	**–7.83**
A. DIRECT INVESTMENT	4 500	. .	...	...	...	...	...	...	...	...
Direct investment abroad	4 505	. .	...	...	...	...	...	...	...	...
Equity capital	4 510	. .	...	...	...	...	...	...	...	...
Claims on affiliated enterprises	4 515	. .	...	...	...	...	...	...	...	...
Liabilities to affiliated enterprises	4 520	. .	...	...	...	...	...	...	...	...
Reinvested earnings	4 525	. .	...	...	...	...	...	...	...	...
Other capital	4 530	. .	...	...	...	...	...	...	...	...
Claims on affiliated enterprises	4 535	. .	...	...	...	...	...	...	...	...
Liabilities to affiliated enterprises	4 540	. .	...	...	...	...	...	...	...	...
Direct investment in Western Samoa	4 555	. .	...	...	...	...	...	...	...	...
Equity capital	4 560	. .	...	...	...	...	...	...	...	...
Claims on direct investors	4 565	. .	...	...	...	...	...	...	...	...
Liabilities to direct investors	4 570	. .	...	...	...	...	...	...	...	...
Reinvested earnings	4 575	. .	...	...	...	...	...	...	...	...
Other capital	4 580	. .	...	...	...	...	...	...	...	...
Claims on direct investors	4 585	. .	...	...	...	...	...	...	...	...
Liabilities to direct investors	4 590	. .	...	...	...	...	...	...	...	...
B. PORTFOLIO INVESTMENT	4 600	. .	...	...	...	...	...	...	...	...
Assets	4 602	. .	...	...	...	...	...	...	...	...
Equity securities	4 610	. .	...	...	...	...	...	...	...	...
Monetary authorities	4 611	. .	...	...	...	...	...	...	...	...
General government	4 612	. .	...	...	...	...	...	...	...	...
Banks	4 613	. .	...	...	...	...	...	...	...	...
Other sectors	4 614	. .	...	...	...	...	...	...	...	...
Debt securities	4 619	. .	...	...	...	...	...	...	...	...
Bonds and notes	4 620	. .	...	...	...	...	...	...	...	...
Monetary authorities	4 621	. .	...	...	...	...	...	...	...	...
General government	4 622	. .	...	...	...	...	...	...	...	...
Banks	4 623	. .	...	...	...	...	...	...	...	...
Other sectors	4 624	. .	...	...	...	...	...	...	...	...
Money market instruments	4 630	. .	...	...	...	...	...	...	...	...
Monetary authorities	4 631	. .	...	...	...	...	...	...	...	...
General government	4 632	. .	...	...	...	...	...	...	...	...
Banks	4 633	. .	...	...	...	...	...	...	...	...
Other sectors	4 634	. .	...	...	...	...	...	...	...	...
Financial derivatives	4 640	. .	...	...	...	...	...	...	...	...
Monetary authorities	4 641	. .	...	...	...	...	...	...	...	...
General government	4 642	. .	...	...	...	...	...	...	...	...
Banks	4 643	. .	...	...	...	...	...	...	...	...
Other sectors	4 644	. .	...	...	...	...	...	...	...	...
Liabilities	4 652	. .	...	...	...	...	...	...	...	...
Equity securities	4 660	. .	...	...	...	...	...	...	...	...
Banks	4 663	. .	...	...	...	...	...	...	...	...
Other sectors	4 664	. .	...	...	...	...	...	...	...	...
Debt securities	4 669	. .	...	...	...	...	...	...	...	...
Bonds and notes	4 670	. .	...	...	...	...	...	...	...	...
Monetary authorities	4 671	. .	...	...	...	...	...	...	...	...
General government	4 672	. .	...	...	...	...	...	...	...	...
Banks	4 673	. .	...	...	...	...	...	...	...	...
Other sectors	4 674	. .	...	...	...	...	...	...	...	...
Money market instruments	4 680	. .	...	...	...	...	...	...	...	...
Monetary authorities	4 681	. .	...	...	...	...	...	...	...	...
General government	4 682	. .	...	...	...	...	...	...	...	...
Banks	4 683	. .	...	...	...	...	...	...	...	...
Other sectors	4 684	. .	...	...	...	...	...	...	...	...
Financial derivatives	4 690	. .	...	...	...	...	...	...	...	...
Monetary authorities	4 691	. .	...	...	...	...	...	...	...	...
General government	4 692	. .	...	...	...	...	...	...	...	...
Banks	4 693	. .	...	...	...	...	...	...	...	...
Other sectors	4 694	. .	...	...	...	...	...	...	...	...

Table 2 (Concluded). STANDARD PRESENTATION, 1988–95
(Millions of U.S. dollars)

	Code	1988	1989	1990	1991	1992	1993	1994	1995
C. OTHER INVESTMENT	4 700 . .	–3.47	–1.61	8.55	21.10	15.71	15.55	–5.47	–5.79
Assets	4 703 . .	**–.31**	**–.08**	**–.03**	**–.22**	**. . .**	**. . .**	**. . .**	**. . .**
Trade credits	4 706 . .	. . .	. . .	. . .	. . .	. . .	. . .	. . .	. . .
General government: long-term	4 708 . .	. . .	. . .	. . .	. . .	. . .	. . .	. . .	. . .
General government: short-term	4 709 . .	. . .	. . .	. . .	. . .	. . .	. . .	. . .	. . .
Other sectors: long-term	4 711 . .	. . .	. . .	. . .	. . .	. . .	. . .	. . .	. . .
Other sectors: short-term	4 712 . .	. . .	. . .	. . .	. . .	. . .	. . .	. . .	. . .
Loans	4 714 . .	. . .	. . .	. . .	. . .	. . .	. . .	. . .	. . .
Monetary authorities: long-term	4 717 . .	. . .	. . .	. . .	. . .	. . .	. . .	. . .	. . .
Monetary authorities: short-term	4 718 . .	. . .	. . .	. . .	. . .	. . .	. . .	. . .	. . .
General government: long-term	4 720 . .	. . .	. . .	. . .	. . .	. . .	. . .	. . .	. . .
General government: short-term	4 721 . .	. . .	. . .	. . .	. . .	. . .	. . .	. . .	. . .
Banks: long-term	4 723 . .	. . .	. . .	. . .	. . .	. . .	. . .	. . .	. . .
Banks: short-term	4 724 . .	. . .	. . .	. . .	. . .	. . .	. . .	. . .	. . .
Other sectors: long-term	4 726 . .	. . .	. . .	. . .	. . .	. . .	. . .	. . .	. . .
Other sectors: short-term	4 727 . .	. . .	. . .	. . .	. . .	. . .	. . .	. . .	. . .
Currency and deposits	4 730 . .	–.31	–.08	–.03	–.22	. . .	. . .	. . .	. . .
Monetary authorities	4 731 . .	. . .	. . .	. . .	. . .	. . .	. . .	. . .	. . .
General government	4 732 . .	. . .	. . .	. . .	. . .	. . .	. . .	. . .	. . .
Banks	4 733 . .	. . .	. . .	. . .	. . .	. . .	. . .	. . .	. . .
Other sectors	4 734 . .	–.31	–.08	–.03	–.22	. . .	. . .	. . .	. . .
Other assets	4 736 . .	. . .	. . .	. . .	. . .	. . .	. . .	. . .	. . .
Monetary authorities: long-term	4 738 . .	. . .	. . .	. . .	. . .	. . .	. . .	. . .	. . .
Monetary authorities: short-term	4 739 . .	. . .	. . .	. . .	. . .	. . .	. . .	. . .	. . .
General government: long-term	4 741 . .	. . .	. . .	. . .	. . .	. . .	. . .	. . .	. . .
General government: short-term	4 742 . .	. . .	. . .	. . .	. . .	. . .	. . .	. . .	. . .
Banks: long-term	4 744 . .	. . .	. . .	. . .	. . .	. . .	. . .	. . .	. . .
Banks: short-term	4 745 . .	. . .	. . .	. . .	. . .	. . .	. . .	. . .	. . .
Other sectors: long-term	4 747 . .	. . .	. . .	. . .	. . .	. . .	. . .	. . .	. . .
Other sectors: short-term	4 748 . .	. . .	. . .	. . .	. . .	. . .	. . .	. . .	. . .
Liabilities	4 753 . .	**–3.16**	**–1.53**	**8.57**	**21.32**	**15.71**	**15.55**	**–5.47**	**–5.79**
Trade credits	4 756 . .	. . .	. . .	. . .	. . .	. . .	. . .	. . .	. . .
General government: long-term	4 758 . .	. . .	. . .	. . .	. . .	. . .	. . .	. . .	. . .
General government: short-term	4 759 . .	. . .	. . .	. . .	. . .	. . .	. . .	. . .	. . .
Other sectors: long-term	4 761 . .	. . .	. . .	. . .	. . .	. . .	. . .	. . .	. . .
Other sectors: short-term	4 762 . .	. . .	. . .	. . .	. . .	. . .	. . .	. . .	. . .
Loans	4 764 . .	–3.36	–1.16	8.42	20.63	15.95	14.98	–7.60	–4.69
Use of Fund credit and loans from the Fund	4 766 . .	–3.96	–2.09	–.86	–.59	–.22	. . .	. . .	. . .
Monetary authorities: other long-term	4 767 . .	. . .	. . .	. . .	. . .	. . .	. . .	. . .	. . .
Monetary authorities: short-term	4 768 . .	. . .	. . .	. . .	. . .	. . .	. . .	. . .	. . .
General government: long-term	4 770 . .	1.12	1.54	9.71	21.56	16.54	15.25	6.84	2.54
General government: short-term	4 771 . .	. . .	. . .	. . .	. . .	. . .	. . .	. . .	. . .
Banks: long-term	4 773 . .	. . .	. . .	. . .	. . .	. . .	. . .	. . .	. . .
Banks: short-term	4 774 . .	. . .	. . .	. . .	. . .	. . .	. . .	. . .	. . .
Other sectors: long-term	4 776 . .	–.53	–.61	–.44	–.33	–.36	–.27	–14.44	–7.23
Other sectors: short-term	4 777 . .	. . .	. . .	. . .	. . .	. . .	. . .	. . .	. . .
Currency and deposits	4 780 . .	.25	–.37	.16	.68	–.24	.56	1.72	–.89
Monetary authorities	4 781 . .	. . .	. . .	. . .	. . .	. . .	. . .	–.13	.01
General government	4 782 . .	. . .	. . .	. . .	. . .	. . .	. . .	. . .	. . .
Banks	4 783 . .	.25	–.37	.16	.68	–.24	.56	.03	.82
Other sectors	4 784 . .	. . .	. . .	. . .	. . .	. . .	. . .	1.82	–1.72
Other liabilities	4 786 . .	–.04	. . .	. . .	. . .	. . .	. . .	.40	–.21
Monetary authorities: long-term	4 788 . .	. . .	. . .	. . .	. . .	. . .	. . .	. . .	. . .
Monetary authorities: short-term	4 789 . .	–.04	. . .	. . .	. . .	. . .	. . .	. . .	. . .
General government: long-term	4 791 . .	. . .	. . .	. . .	. . .	. . .	. . .	. . .	. . .
General government: short-term	4 792 . .	. . .	. . .	. . .	. . .	. . .	. . .	. . .	. . .
Banks: long-term	4 794 . .	. . .	. . .	. . .	. . .	. . .	. . .	. . .	. . .
Banks: short-term	4 795 . .	. . .	. . .	. . .	. . .	. . .	. . .	. . .	. . .
Other sectors: long-term	4 797 . .	. . .	. . .	. . .	. . .	. . .	. . .	. . .	. . .
Other sectors: short-term	4 798 . .	. . .	. . .	. . .	. . .	. . .	. . .	.40	–.21
D. RESERVE ASSETS	4 800 . .	–8.42	–10.66	–11.49	–.42	12.95	8.29	3.87	–2.04
Monetary gold	4 810 . .	. . .	. . .	. . .	. . .	. . .	. . .	. . .	. . .
Special drawing rights	4 820 . .	–1.45	2.26	–3.03	.48	.97	–.09	–.06	–.07
Reserve position in the Fund	4 830 . .	–.01	–.02	. . .	. . .	–.87	–.01	. . .	–.01
Foreign exchange	4 840 . .	–6.96	–12.89	–8.45	–.90	12.85	8.39	3.93	–1.96
Other claims	4 880 . .	. . .	. . .	. . .	. . .	. . .	. . .	. . .	. . .
NET ERRORS AND OMISSIONS	4 998 . .	**1.67**	**–2.61**	**–5.66**	**4.89**	**23.83**	**13.82**	**–4.18**	**–1.95**

Part 3 of the *Yearbook* contains descriptions of the methodologies, compilation practices, and sources used to compile these data.

Table 1. ANALYTIC PRESENTATION, 1988–95
(Millions of U.S. dollars)

	Code	1988	1989	1990	1991	1992	1993	1994	1995
A. Current Account [1]	4 993 Y.	...	...	**738.7**	**–663.2**	**–1,091.3**	**–1,247.6**	**365.9**	**182.7**
Goods: exports f.o.b	2 100 . .	...	...	1,384.4	1,196.6	1,094.9	1,166.9	1,824.0	1,937.2
Goods: imports f.o.b	3 100 . .	...	...	–1,475.6	–1,896.8	–1,891.1	–2,086.9	–1,521.9	–1,948.2
Balance on Goods	4 100 . .	...	...	*–91.2*	*–700.2*	*–796.2*	*–920.0*	*302.1*	*–11.0*
Services: credit	2 200 . .	...	...	105.6	114.0	161.9	177.2	148.0	179.4
Services: debit	3 200 . .	...	...	–694.4	–775.0	–1,013.8	–1,094.6	–622.6	–590.5
Balance on Goods and Services	4 991 . .	...	...	*–680.0*	*–1,361.2*	*–1,648.1*	*–1,837.4*	*–172.5*	*–422.1*
Income: credit	2 300 . .	...	...	37.9	43.3	38.1	22.0	22.0	37.4
Income: debit	3 300 . .	...	...	–491.6	–609.5	–552.5	–499.5	–600.6	–536.5
Balance on Goods, Services, and Income	4 992 . .	...	...	*–1,133.7*	*–1,927.4*	*–2,162.5*	*–2,314.9*	*–751.1*	*–921.2*
Current transfers: credit	2 379 Y.	...	...	1,896.8	1,309.1	1,100.2	1,092.8	1,133.6	1,120.5
Current transfers: debit	3 379 . .	...	...	–24.4	–44.9	–29.0	–25.5	–16.6	–16.6
B. Capital Account [1]	4 994 Y.	...	...	...	...	...	...	...	...
Capital account: credit	2 994 Y.	...	...	...	...	...	...	...	...
Capital account: debit	3 994 . .	...	...	...	...	...	...	...	...
Total, Groups A Plus B	4 010 . .	...	...	*738.7*	*–663.2*	*–1,091.3*	*–1,247.6*	*365.9*	*182.7*
C. Financial Account [1]	4 995 X.	...	...	**–284.2**	**237.7**	**91.8**	**–87.9**	**–837.5**	**–819.0**
Direct investment abroad	4 505 . .	...	...	...	...	...	...	...	...
Direct investment in Yemen	4 555 Y.	...	...	–130.9	582.5	713.6	897.1	10.5	–217.7
Portfolio investment assets	4 602 . .	...	...	...	...	...	...	...	...
Equity securities	4 610 . .	...	...	...	...	...	...	...	...
Debt securities	4 619 . .	...	...	...	...	...	...	...	...
Portfolio investment liabilities	4 652 Y.	...	...	...	...	...	...	...	...
Equity securities	4 660 Y.	...	...	...	...	...	...	...	...
Debt securities	4 669 Y.	...	...	...	...	...	...	...	...
Other investment assets	4 703 . .	...	...	–348.5	–57.1	32.3	–53.7	71.8	105.7
Monetary authorities	4 703 .A	...	...	...	...	...	...	...	...
General government	4 703 .B	...	...	...	...	...	...	...	...
Banks	4 703 .C	...	...	–348.5	–45.0	20.2	–2.4	70.5	138.2
Other sectors	4 703 .D	...	...	...	–12.1	12.1	–51.3	1.3	–32.5
Other investment liabilities	4 753 X.	...	...	195.2	–287.7	–654.1	–931.3	–919.8	–707.0
Monetary authorities	4 753 XA	...	...	46.1	13.6	–43.2	–31.0	57.0	3.4
General government	4 753 YB	...	...	83.8	–660.2	–737.6	–774.5	–682.3	–678.9
Banks	4 753 YC	...	...	65.3	158.9	26.7	–225.8	–94.5	–81.5
Other sectors	4 753 YD	...	...	...	200.0	100.0	100.0	–200.0	50.0
Total, Groups A Through C	4 020 . .	...	...	*454.5*	*–425.5*	*–999.5*	*–1,335.5*	*–471.6*	*–636.3*
D. Net Errors and Omissions	4 998 . .	...	...	**–711.4**	**–268.0**	**–248.5**	**222.4**	**–181.0**	**161.8**
Total, Groups A Through D	4 030 . .	...	...	*–256.9*	*–693.5*	*–1,248.0*	*–1,113.1*	*–652.6*	*–474.5*
E. Reserves and Related Items	4 040 . .	...	...	**256.9**	**693.5**	**1,248.0**	**1,113.1**	**652.6**	**474.5**
Reserve assets	4 800 . .	...	...	–14.0	–254.6	343.8	174.8	–204.2	–263.2
Use of Fund credit and loans	4 766 . .	...	...	.1	–.2	...	...	...	...
Liabilities constituting foreign authorities' reserves	4 900 . .	...	...	...	...	...	...	...	...
Exceptional financing	4 920 . .	...	...	270.8	948.3	904.2	938.3	856.8	737.7
Conversion rates: Yemeni rials per U.S. dollar	0 101 . .	...	...	...	**12.010**	**12.010**	**12.010**	**12.010**	**40.839**

[1] Excludes components that have been classified in the categories of Group E.

Table 2. STANDARD PRESENTATION, 1988–95
(Millions of U.S. dollars)

	Code	1988	1989	1990	1991	1992	1993	1994	1995
CURRENT ACCOUNT	4 993 . .	**...**	**...**	**738.7**	**–663.2**	**–1,091.3**	**–1,247.6**	**365.9**	**182.7**
A. GOODS	4 100 . .	...	...	–91.2	–700.2	–796.2	–920.0	302.1	–11.0
Credit	2 100 . .	**...**	**...**	**1,384.4**	**1,196.6**	**1,094.9**	**1,166.9**	**1,824.0**	**1,937.2**
General merchandise: exports f.o.b.	2 110 . .	...	...	1,384.4	1,196.6	1,094.9	1,166.9	1,824.0	1,937.2
Goods for processing: exports f.o.b.	2 150 . .	...	...	...	...	...	...	...	...
Repairs on goods	2 160 . .	...	...	...	...	...	...	...	...
Goods procured in ports by carriers	2 170 . .	...	...	...	...	...	...	...	...
Nonmonetary gold	2 180 . .	...	...	...	...	...	...	...	...
Debit	3 100 . .	**...**	**...**	**–1,475.6**	**–1,896.8**	**–1,891.1**	**–2,086.9**	**–1,521.9**	**–1,948.2**
General merchandise: imports f.o.b.	3 110 . .	...	...	–1,475.6	–1,896.8	–1,891.1	–2,086.9	–1,521.9	–1,948.2
Goods for processing: imports f.o.b.	3 150 . .	...	...	...	...	...	...	...	...
Repairs on goods	3 160 . .	...	...	...	...	...	...	...	...
Goods procured in ports by carriers	3 170 . .	...	...	...	...	...	...	...	...
Nonmonetary gold	3 180 . .	...	...	...	...	...	...	...	...
B. SERVICES	4 200 . .	...	...	–588.8	–661.0	–851.9	–917.4	–474.6	–411.1
Total credit	2 200 . .	...	...	*105.6*	*114.0*	*161.9*	*177.2*	*148.0*	*179.4*
Total debit	3 200 . .	...	...	*–694.4*	*–775.0*	*–1,013.8*	*–1,094.6*	*–622.6*	*–590.5*
Transportation services, credit	2 205 . .	**...**	**...**	**22.3**	**22.0**	**30.0**	**30.0**	**27.0**	**31.0**
Passenger	2 205 BA	...	...	...	...	...	...	...	...
Freight	2 205 BB	...	...	*22.3*	*22.0*	*30.0*	*30.0*	*27.0*	*31.0*
Other	2 205 BC	...	...	...	...	...	...	...	...
Sea transport, passenger	2 207 . .	...	...	...	...	...	...	...	...
Sea transport, freight	2 208 . .	...	...	...	...	...	...	...	...
Sea transport, other	2 209 . .	...	...	...	...	...	...	...	...
Air transport, passenger	2 211 . .	...	...	...	...	...	...	...	...
Air transport, freight	2 212 . .	...	...	...	...	...	...	...	...
Air transport, other	2 213 . .	...	...	...	...	...	...	...	...
Other transport, passenger	2 215 . .	...	...	...	...	...	...	...	...
Other transport, freight	2 216 . .	...	...	...	...	...	...	...	...
Other transport, other	2 217 . .	...	...	...	...	...	...	...	...
Transportation services, debit	3 205 . .	**...**	**...**	**–222.7**	**–260.6**	**–259.8**	**–286.6**	**–209.3**	**–267.8**
Passenger	3 205 BA	...	...	*–2.1*	*–2.0*	*–2.0*	*–2.0*	*–1.8*	*–2.2*
Freight	3 205 BB	...	...	*–220.6*	*–258.6*	*–257.8*	*–284.6*	*–207.5*	*–265.6*
Other	3 205 BC	...	...	...	...	...	...	...	...
Sea transport, passenger	3 207 . .	...	...	–2.1	–2.0	–2.0	–2.0	–1.8	–2.2
Sea transport, freight	3 208 . .	...	...	–220.6	–258.6	–257.8	–284.6	–207.5	–265.6
Sea transport, other	3 209 . .	...	...	...	...	...	...	...	...
Air transport, passenger	3 211 . .	...	...	...	...	...	...	...	...
Air transport, freight	3 212 . .	...	...	...	...	...	...	...	...
Air transport, other	3 213 . .	...	...	...	...	...	...	...	...
Other transport, passenger	3 215 . .	...	...	...	...	...	...	...	...
Other transport, freight	3 216 . .	...	...	...	...	...	...	...	...
Other transport, other	3 217 . .	...	...	...	...	...	...	...	...
Travel, credit	2 236 . .	**...**	**...**	**40.0**	**21.0**	**46.9**	**45.4**	**18.5**	**49.9**
Business travel	2 237 . .	...	...	...	...	...	...	...	...
Personal travel	2 240 . .	...	...	...	...	...	...	...	...
Travel, debit	3 236 . .	**...**	**...**	**–63.5**	**–70.0**	**–100.6**	**–79.7**	**–77.7**	**–75.7**
Business travel	3 237 . .	...	...	...	...	...	...	...	...
Personal travel	3 240 . .	...	...	...	...	...	...	...	...
Other services, credit	2 200 BA	**...**	**...**	**43.3**	**71.0**	**85.0**	**101.8**	**102.5**	**98.5**
Communications	2 245 . .	...	...	...	...	...	...	...	...
Construction	2 249 . .	...	...	...	...	...	...	...	...
Insurance	2 253 . .	...	...	...	...	...	...	...	...
Financial	2 260 . .	...	...	...	...	...	...	...	...
Computer and information	2 262 . .	...	...	...	...	...	...	...	...
Royalties and licence fees	2 266 . .	...	...	...	...	...	...	...	...
Other business services	2 268 . .	...	...	19.7	45.5	42.8	59.4	58.9	60.5
Personal, cultural, and recreational	2 287 . .	...	...	...	...	...	...	...	...
Government, n.i.e.	2 291 . .	...	...	23.6	25.5	42.2	42.4	43.6	38.0
Other services, debit	3 200 BA	**...**	**...**	**–408.2**	**–444.4**	**–653.4**	**–728.3**	**–335.6**	**–247.0**
Communications	3 245 . .	...	...	...	...	...	...	...	...
Construction	3 249 . .	...	...	...	...	...	...	...	...
Insurance	3 253 . .	...	...	...	...	...	...	...	...
Financial	3 260 . .	...	...	...	...	...	...	...	...
Computer and information	3 262 . .	...	...	...	...	...	...	...	...
Royalties and licence fees	3 266 . .	...	...	...	...	...	...	...	...
Other business services	3 268 . .	...	...	–206.9	–299.2	–592.9	–671.4	–280.6	–201.8
Personal, cultural, and recreational	3 287 . .	...	...	...	...	...	...	...	...
Government, n.i.e.	3 291 . .	...	...	–201.3	–145.2	–60.5	–56.9	–55.0	–45.2

Table 2 (Continued). STANDARD PRESENTATION, 1988–95
(Millions of U.S. dollars)

	Code	1988	1989	1990	1991	1992	1993	1994	1995
C. INCOME	4 300	...	...	–453.7	–566.2	–514.4	–477.5	–578.6	–499.1
Total credit	2 300	...	...	*37.9*	*43.3*	*38.1*	*22.0*	*22.0*	*37.4*
Total debit	3 300	...	...	*–491.6*	*–609.5*	*–552.5*	*–499.5*	*–600.6*	*–536.5*
Compensation of employees, credit	2 310	**...**	**...**	**...**	**...**	**...**	**...**	**...**	**...**
Compensation of employees, debit	3 310	**...**	**...**	**–82.0**	**–80.5**	**–68.5**	**–69.3**	**–53.4**	**–47.9**
Investment income, credit	2 320	**...**	**...**	**37.9**	**43.3**	**38.1**	**22.0**	**22.0**	**37.4**
Direct investment income	2 330	...	...	...	...	...	...	...	...
Dividends and distributed branch profits	2 332	...	...	...	...	...	...	...	...
Reinvested earnings and undistributed branch profits	2 333	...	...	...	...	...	...	...	...
Income on debt (interest)	2 334	...	...	...	...	...	...	...	...
Portfolio investment income	2 339	...	...	...	...	...	...	...	...
Income on equity	2 340	...	...	...	...	...	...	...	...
Income on bonds and notes	2 350	...	...	...	...	...	...	...	...
Income on money market instruments and financial derivatives	2 360	...	...	...	...	...	...	...	...
Other investment income	2 370	...	...	37.9	43.3	38.1	22.0	22.0	37.4
Investment income, debit	3 320	**...**	**...**	**–409.6**	**–529.0**	**–484.0**	**–430.2**	**–547.2**	**–488.6**
Direct investment income	3 330	...	...	–283.5	–290.3	–264.9	–243.9	–371.8	–322.2
Dividends and distributed branch profits	3 332	...	...	–283.5	–290.3	–264.9	–243.9	–371.8	–322.2
Reinvested earnings and undistributed branch profits	3 333	...	...	...	...	...	...	...	...
Income on debt (interest)	3 334	...	...	...	...	...	...	...	...
Portfolio investment income	3 339	...	...	...	...	...	...	...	...
Income on equity	3 340	...	...	...	...	...	...	...	...
Income on bonds and notes	3 350	...	...	...	...	...	...	...	...
Income on money market instruments and financial derivatives	3 360	...	...	...	...	...	...	...	...
Other investment income	3 370	...	...	–126.1	–238.7	–219.1	–186.3	–175.4	–166.4
D. CURRENT TRANSFERS	4 379	...	...	1,872.4	1,264.2	1,071.2	1,067.3	1,117.0	1,103.9
Credit	2 379	**...**	**...**	**1,896.8**	**1,309.1**	**1,100.2**	**1,092.8**	**1,133.6**	**1,120.5**
General government	2 380	...	...	398.6	310.8	82.0	54.2	74.3	40.0
Other sectors	2 390	...	...	1,498.2	998.3	1,018.2	1,038.6	1,059.3	1,080.5
Workers' remittances	2 391	...	...	1,498.2	998.3	1,018.2	1,038.6	1,059.3	1,080.5
Other current transfers	2 392	...	...	...	...	...	...	...	...
Debit	3 379	**...**	**...**	**–24.4**	**–44.9**	**–29.0**	**–25.5**	**–16.6**	**–16.6**
General government	3 380	...	...	...	...	–3.7	–.5	–1.6	–3.3
Other sectors	3 390	...	...	–24.4	–44.9	–25.3	–25.0	–15.0	–13.3
Workers' remittances	3 391	...	...	...	...	...	...	...	...
Other current transfers	3 392	...	...	–24.4	–44.9	–25.3	–25.0	–15.0	–13.3
CAPITAL AND FINANCIAL ACCOUNT	4 996	**...**	**...**	**–27.3**	**931.2**	**1,339.8**	**1,025.2**	**–184.9**	**–344.5**
CAPITAL ACCOUNT	4 994	**...**	**...**	**...**	**...**	**...**	**...**	**...**	**...**
Total credit	2 994	...	...	...	...	...	...	...	...
Total debit	3 994	...	...	...	...	...	...	...	...
Capital transfers, credit	2 400	**...**	**...**	**...**	**...**	**...**	**...**	**...**	**...**
General government	2 401	...	...	...	...	...	...	...	...
Debt forgiveness	2 402	...	...	...	...	...	...	...	...
Other capital transfers	2 410	...	...	...	...	...	...	...	...
Other sectors	2 430	...	...	...	...	...	...	...	...
Migrants' transfers	2 431	...	...	...	...	...	...	...	...
Debt forgiveness	2 432	...	...	...	...	...	...	...	...
Other capital transfers	2 440	...	...	...	...	...	...	...	...
Capital transfers, debit	3 400	**...**	**...**	**...**	**...**	**...**	**...**	**...**	**...**
General government	3 401	...	...	...	...	...	...	...	...
Debt forgiveness	3 402	...	...	...	...	...	...	...	...
Other capital transfers	3 410	...	...	...	...	...	...	...	...
Other sectors	3 430	...	...	...	...	...	...	...	...
Migrants' transfers	3 431	...	...	...	...	...	...	...	...
Debt forgiveness	3 432	...	...	...	...	...	...	...	...
Other capital transfers	3 440	...	...	...	...	...	...	...	...
Nonproduced nonfinancial assets, credit	2 480	**...**	**...**	**...**	**...**	**...**	**...**	**...**	**...**
Nonproduced nonfinancial assets, debit	3 480	**...**	**...**	**...**	**...**	**...**	**...**	**...**	**...**

Table 2 (Continued). STANDARD PRESENTATION, 1988–95
(Millions of U.S. dollars)

	Code	1988	1989	1990	1991	1992	1993	1994	1995
FINANCIAL ACCOUNT	4 995 . .	**. . .**	**. . .**	**–27.3**	**931.2**	**1,339.8**	**1,025.2**	**–184.9**	**–344.5**
A. DIRECT INVESTMENT	4 500 . .	. . .	. . .	–130.9	582.5	713.6	897.1	10.5	–217.7
Direct investment abroad	4 505 . .	**. . .**	**. . .**	**. . .**	**. . .**	**. . .**	**. . .**	**. . .**	**. . .**
Equity capital	4 510 . .	. . .	. . .	. . .	. . .	. . .	. . .	. . .	. . .
Claims on affiliated enterprises	4 515 . .	. . .	. . .	. . .	. . .	. . .	. . .	. . .	. . .
Liabilities to affiliated enterprises	4 520 . .	. . .	. . .	. . .	. . .	. . .	. . .	. . .	. . .
Reinvested earnings	4 525 . .	. . .	. . .	. . .	. . .	. . .	. . .	. . .	. . .
Other capital	4 530 . .	. . .	. . .	. . .	. . .	. . .	. . .	. . .	. . .
Claims on affiliated enterprises	4 535 . .	. . .	. . .	. . .	. . .	. . .	. . .	. . .	. . .
Liabilities to affiliated enterprises	4 540 . .	. . .	. . .	. . .	. . .	. . .	. . .	. . .	. . .
Direct investment in Yemen	4 555 . .	**. . .**	**. . .**	**–130.9**	**582.5**	**713.6**	**897.1**	**10.5**	**–217.7**
Equity capital	4 560 . .	. . .	. . .	–130.9	282.5	718.0	903.0	12.0	–217.7
Claims on direct investors	4 565 . .	. . .	. . .	. . .	. . .	. . .	. . .	. . .	. . .
Liabilities to direct investors	4 570 . .	. . .	. . .	. . .	. . .	. . .	. . .	. . .	. . .
Reinvested earnings	4 575 . .	. . .	. . .	. . .	. . .	. . .	. . .	. . .	. . .
Other capital	4 580 . .	. . .	. . .	. . .	300.0	–4.4	–5.9	–1.5	. . .
Claims on direct investors	4 585 . .	. . .	. . .	. . .	. . .	. . .	. . .	. . .	. . .
Liabilities to direct investors	4 590 . .	. . .	. . .	. . .	. . .	. . .	. . .	. . .	. . .
B. PORTFOLIO INVESTMENT	4 600 . .	. . .	. . .	. . .	. . .	. . .	. . .	. . .	. . .
Assets	4 602 . .	**. . .**	**. . .**	**. . .**	**. . .**	**. . .**	**. . .**	**. . .**	**. . .**
Equity securities	4 610 . .	. . .	. . .	. . .	. . .	. . .	. . .	. . .	. . .
Monetary authorities	4 611 . .	. . .	. . .	. . .	. . .	. . .	. . .	. . .	. . .
General government	4 612 . .	. . .	. . .	. . .	. . .	. . .	. . .	. . .	. . .
Banks	4 613 . .	. . .	. . .	. . .	. . .	. . .	. . .	. . .	. . .
Other sectors	4 614 . .	. . .	. . .	. . .	. . .	. . .	. . .	. . .	. . .
Debt securities	4 619 . .	. . .	. . .	. . .	. . .	. . .	. . .	. . .	. . .
Bonds and notes	4 620 . .	. . .	. . .	. . .	. . .	. . .	. . .	. . .	. . .
Monetary authorities	4 621 . .	. . .	. . .	. . .	. . .	. . .	. . .	. . .	. . .
General government	4 622 . .	. . .	. . .	. . .	. . .	. . .	. . .	. . .	. . .
Banks	4 623 . .	. . .	. . .	. . .	. . .	. . .	. . .	. . .	. . .
Other sectors	4 624 . .	. . .	. . .	. . .	. . .	. . .	. . .	. . .	. . .
Money market instruments	4 630 . .	. . .	. . .	. . .	. . .	. . .	. . .	. . .	. . .
Monetary authorities	4 631 . .	. . .	. . .	. . .	. . .	. . .	. . .	. . .	. . .
General government	4 632 . .	. . .	. . .	. . .	. . .	. . .	. . .	. . .	. . .
Banks	4 633 . .	. . .	. . .	. . .	. . .	. . .	. . .	. . .	. . .
Other sectors	4 634 . .	. . .	. . .	. . .	. . .	. . .	. . .	. . .	. . .
Financial derivatives	4 640 . .	. . .	. . .	. . .	. . .	. . .	. . .	. . .	. . .
Monetary authorities	4 641 . .	. . .	. . .	. . .	. . .	. . .	. . .	. . .	. . .
General government	4 642 . .	. . .	. . .	. . .	. . .	. . .	. . .	. . .	. . .
Banks	4 643 . .	. . .	. . .	. . .	. . .	. . .	. . .	. . .	. . .
Other sectors	4 644 . .	. . .	. . .	. . .	. . .	. . .	. . .	. . .	. . .
Liabilities	4 652 . .	**. . .**	**. . .**	**. . .**	**. . .**	**. . .**	**. . .**	**. . .**	**. . .**
Equity securities	4 660 . .	. . .	. . .	. . .	. . .	. . .	. . .	. . .	. . .
Banks	4 663 . .	. . .	. . .	. . .	. . .	. . .	. . .	. . .	. . .
Other sectors	4 664 . .	. . .	. . .	. . .	. . .	. . .	. . .	. . .	. . .
Debt securities	4 669 . .	. . .	. . .	. . .	. . .	. . .	. . .	. . .	. . .
Bonds and notes	4 670 . .	. . .	. . .	. . .	. . .	. . .	. . .	. . .	. . .
Monetary authorities	4 671 . .	. . .	. . .	. . .	. . .	. . .	. . .	. . .	. . .
General government	4 672 . .	. . .	. . .	. . .	. . .	. . .	. . .	. . .	. . .
Banks	4 673 . .	. . .	. . .	. . .	. . .	. . .	. . .	. . .	. . .
Other sectors	4 674 . .	. . .	. . .	. . .	. . .	. . .	. . .	. . .	. . .
Money market instruments	4 680 . .	. . .	. . .	. . .	. . .	. . .	. . .	. . .	. . .
Monetary authorities	4 681 . .	. . .	. . .	. . .	. . .	. . .	. . .	. . .	. . .
General government	4 682 . .	. . .	. . .	. . .	. . .	. . .	. . .	. . .	. . .
Banks	4 683 . .	. . .	. . .	. . .	. . .	. . .	. . .	. . .	. . .
Other sectors	4 684 . .	. . .	. . .	. . .	. . .	. . .	. . .	. . .	. . .
Financial derivatives	4 690 . .	. . .	. . .	. . .	. . .	. . .	. . .	. . .	. . .
Monetary authorities	4 691 . .	. . .	. . .	. . .	. . .	. . .	. . .	. . .	. . .
General government	4 692 . .	. . .	. . .	. . .	. . .	. . .	. . .	. . .	. . .
Banks	4 693 . .	. . .	. . .	. . .	. . .	. . .	. . .	. . .	. . .
Other sectors	4 694 . .	. . .	. . .	. . .	. . .	. . .	. . .	. . .	. . .

Table 2 (Concluded). STANDARD PRESENTATION, 1988–95
(Millions of U.S. dollars)

	Code	1988	1989	1990	1991	1992	1993	1994	1995
C. OTHER INVESTMENT	4 700	...	...	117.6	603.3	282.4	–46.7	8.8	136.4
Assets	4 703	**...**	**...**	**–348.5**	**–57.1**	**32.3**	**–53.7**	**71.8**	**105.7**
Trade credits	4 706	...	...	...	–12.1	12.1	–51.3	1.3	–32.5
General government: long-term	4 708	...	...	...	...	...	...	...	...
General government: short-term	4 709	...	...	...	...	...	...	...	...
Other sectors: long-term	4 711	...	...	...	...	...	...	...	...
Other sectors: short-term	4 712	...	...	...	–12.1	12.1	–51.3	1.3	–32.5
Loans	4 714	...	...	...	...	...	...	...	...
Monetary authorities: long-term	4 717	...	...	...	...	...	...	...	...
Monetary authorities: short-term	4 718	...	...	...	...	...	...	...	...
General government: long-term	4 720	...	...	...	...	...	...	...	...
General government: short-term	4 721	...	...	...	...	...	...	...	...
Banks: long-term	4 723	...	...	...	...	...	...	...	...
Banks: short-term	4 724	...	...	...	...	...	...	...	...
Other sectors: long-term	4 726	...	...	...	...	...	...	...	...
Other sectors: short-term	4 727	...	...	...	...	...	...	...	...
Currency and deposits	4 730	...	...	–348.5	–45.0	20.2	–2.4	70.5	138.2
Monetary authorities	4 731	...	...	...	...	...	...	...	...
General government	4 732	...	...	...	...	...	...	...	...
Banks	4 733	...	...	–348.5	–45.0	20.2	–2.4	70.5	138.2
Other sectors	4 734	...	...	...	...	...	...	...	...
Other assets	4 736	...	...	...	...	...	...	...	...
Monetary authorities: long-term	4 738	...	...	...	...	...	...	...	...
Monetary authorities: short-term	4 739	...	...	...	...	...	...	...	...
General government: long-term	4 741	...	...	...	...	...	...	...	...
General government: short-term	4 742	...	...	...	...	...	...	...	...
Banks: long-term	4 744	...	...	...	...	...	...	...	...
Banks: short-term	4 745	...	...	...	...	...	...	...	...
Other sectors: long-term	4 747	...	...	...	...	...	...	...	...
Other sectors: short-term	4 748	...	...	...	...	...	...	...	...
Liabilities	4 753	**...**	**...**	**466.1**	**660.4**	**250.1**	**7.0**	**–63.0**	**30.7**
Trade credits	4 756	...	...	–113.2	–127.3	–54.7	–54.5	–64.4	–56.4
General government: long-term	4 758	...	...	–113.2	–127.3	–54.7	–54.5	–64.4	–56.4
General government: short-term	4 759	...	...	...	...	...	...	...	...
Other sectors: long-term	4 761	...	...	...	...	...	...	...	...
Other sectors: short-term	4 762	...	...	...	...	...	...	...	...
Loans	4 764	...	...	197.1	–533.1	–682.9	–720.0	–617.9	–622.5
Use of Fund credit and loans from the Fund	4 766	...	...	.1	–.2	...	...	...	...
Monetary authorities: other long term	4 767	...	...	...	...	...	...	...	...
Monetary authorities: short-term	4 768	...	...	...	...	...	...	...	...
General government: long-term	4 770	...	...	197.0	–532.9	–682.9	–720.0	–617.9	–622.5
General government: short-term	4 771	...	...	...	...	...	...	...	...
Banks: long-term	4 773	...	...	...	...	...	...	...	...
Banks: short-term	4 774	...	...	...	...	...	...	...	...
Other sectors: long-term	4 776	...	...	...	...	...	...	...	...
Other sectors: short-term	4 777	...	...	...	...	...	...	...	...
Currency and deposits	4 780	...	...	111.4	372.5	83.5	–156.8	–237.5	–28.1
Monetary authorities	4 781	...	...	46.1	13.6	–43.2	–31.0	57.0	3.4
General government	4 782	...	...	...	...	...	...	...	...
Banks	4 783	...	...	65.3	158.9	26.7	–225.8	–94.5	–81.5
Other sectors	4 784	...	...	...	200.0	100.0	100.0	–200.0	50.0
Other liabilities	4 786	...	...	270.8	948.3	904.2	938.3	856.8	737.7
Monetary authorities: long-term	4 788	...	...	...	...	...	...	...	...
Monetary authorities: short-term	4 789	...	...	...	...	...	...	...	...
General government: long-term	4 791	...	...	...	...	...	...	...	...
General government: short-term	4 792	...	...	270.8	948.3	904.2	938.3	856.8	737.7
Banks: long-term	4 794	...	...	...	...	...	...	...	...
Banks: short-term	4 795	...	...	...	...	...	...	...	...
Other sectors: long-term	4 797	...	...	...	...	...	...	...	...
Other sectors: short-term	4 798	...	...	...	...	...	...	...	...
D. RESERVE ASSETS	4 800	...	...	–14.0	–254.6	343.8	174.8	–204.2	–263.2
Monetary gold	4 810	...	...	...	–.3	.1	...	...	...
Special drawing rights	4 820	...	...	25.4	–3.5	12.8	3.4	–46.8	–4.6
Reserve position in the Fund	4 830	...	...	...	...	...	...	...	...
Foreign exchange	4 840	...	...	–21.7	–241.8	318.1	171.7	–152.0	–246.3
Other claims	4 880	...	...	–17.7	–9.0	12.8	–.3	–5.4	–12.3
NET ERRORS AND OMISSIONS	4 998	**...**	**...**	**–711.4**	**–268.0**	**–248.5**	**222.4**	**–181.0**	**161.8**

Table 1. ANALYTIC PRESENTATION, 1988–95
(Millions of U.S. dollars)

	Code		1988	1989	1990	1991	1992	1993	1994	1995
A. Current Account [1]	4 993	Y.	**–293**	**–219**	**–594**	**–306**	...	...	...	...
Goods: exports f.o.b	2 100	..	1,189	1,340	1,254	1,172	...	...	...	...
Goods: imports f.o.b	3 100	..	–687	–774	–1,511	–752	...	...	...	...
Balance on Goods	4 100	..	*502*	*566*	*–257*	*420*	...	...	...	...
Services: credit	2 200	..	58	85	107	83	...	...	...	...
Services: debit	3 200	..	–289	–444	–386	–363	...	...	...	...
Balance on Goods and Services	4 991	..	*271*	*208*	*–537*	*140*	...	...	...	...
Income: credit	2 300	..	3	1	2	10	...	...	...	...
Income: debit	3 300	..	–604	–509	–439	–696	...	...	...	...
Balance on Goods, Services, and Income	4 992	..	*–330*	*–300*	*–974*	*–546*	...	...	...	...
Current transfers: credit	2 379	Y.	64	114	398	262	...	...	...	...
Current transfers: debit	3 379	..	–27	–32	–18	–22	...	...	...	...
B. Capital Account [1]	4 994	Y.	**–2**	**–3**	**–3**	**–1**	...	...	...	...
Capital account: credit	2 994	Y.	...	...	...	...	...	...	...	...
Capital account: debit	3 994	..	–2	–3	–3	–1	...	...	...	...
Total, Groups A Plus B	4 010	..	*–295*	*–222*	*–597*	*–307*	...	...	...	...
C. Financial Account [1]	4 995	X.	**23**	**1,827**	**497**	**18**	...	...	...	...
Direct investment abroad	4 505	..	...	...	...	...	...	...	...	...
Direct investment in Zambia	4 555	Y.	93	164	203	34	...	...	...	...
Portfolio investment assets	4 602	..	...	...	...	...	...	...	...	...
Equity securities	4 610	..	...	...	...	...	...	...	...	...
Debt securities	4 619	..	...	...	...	...	...	...	...	...
Portfolio investment liabilities	4 652	Y.	...	...	...	...	...	...	...	...
Equity securities	4 660	Y.	...	...	...	...	...	...	...	...
Debt securities	4 669	Y.	...	...	...	...	...	...	...	...
Other investment assets	4 703	..	–347	26	–275	–125	...	...	...	...
Monetary authorities	4 703	.A	...	...	...	...	...	...	...	...
General government	4 703	.B	1	...	–7	–54	...	...	...	...
Banks	4 703	.C	–56	–172	–109	–76	...	...	...	...
Other sectors	4 703	.D	–292	197	–159	6	...	...	...	...
Other investment liabilities	4 753	X.	277	1,637	569	108	...	...	...	...
Monetary authorities	4 753	XA	–4	–3	23	5	...	...	...	...
General government	4 753	YB	24	–241	11	38	...	...	...	...
Banks	4 753	YC	1	50	30	14	...	...	...	...
Other sectors	4 753	YD	256	1,831	504	51	...	...	...	...
Total, Groups A Through C	4 020	..	*–272*	*1,605*	*–100*	*–289*	...	...	...	...
D. Net Errors and Omissions	4 998	..	**40**	**–1,712**	**322**	**110**	...	...	...	...
Total, Groups A Through D	4 030	..	*–232*	*–106*	*222*	*–179*	...	...	...	...
E. Reserves and Related Items	4 040	..	**232**	**106**	**–222**	**179**	...	...	...	...
Reserve assets	4 800	..	–51	–82	–119	–26	...	...	...	...
Use of Fund credit and loans	4 766	..	...	–17	–25	–35	...	...	...	...
Liabilities constituting foreign authorities' reserves	4 900	..	...	...	...	...	...	...	...	...
Exceptional financing	4 920	..	284	205	–77	241	...	...	...	...
Conversion rates: Zambian kwacha per U.S. dollar	0 101	..	**8.27**	**13.81**	**30.29**	**64.64**	**172.21**	**452.76**	**669.37**	**857.23**

[1] Excludes components that have been classified in the categories of Group E.

Table 2. STANDARD PRESENTATION, 1988–95
(Millions of U.S. dollars)

	Code	1988	1989	1990	1991	1992	1993	1994	1995
CURRENT ACCOUNT	4 993 ..	**–293**	**–219**	**–594**	**–306**	...	...	...	...
A. GOODS	4 100 ..	502	566	–257	420	...	...	...	...
Credit	2 100 ..	**1,189**	**1,340**	**1,254**	**1,172**	...	...	...	...
General merchandise: exports f.o.b.	2 110 ..	1,189	1,340	1,254	1,172	...	...	...	...
Goods for processing: exports f.o.b.	2 150 ..	...	...	...	...	...	...	...	...
Repairs on goods	2 160 ..	...	...	...	...	...	...	...	...
Goods procured in ports by carriers	2 170 ..	...	...	...	...	...	...	...	...
Nonmonetary gold	2 180 ..	...	...	...	...	...	...	...	...
Debit	3 100 ..	**–687**	**–774**	**–1,511**	**–752**	...	...	...	...
General merchandise: imports f.o.b.	3 110 ..	–687	–774	–1,511	–752	...	...	...	...
Goods for processing: imports f.o.b.	3 150 ..	...	...	...	...	...	...	...	...
Repairs on goods	3 160 ..	...	...	...	...	...	...	...	...
Goods procured in ports by carriers	3 170 ..	...	...	...	...	...	...	...	...
Nonmonetary gold	3 180 ..	...	...	...	...	...	...	...	...
B. SERVICES	4 200 ..	–231	–359	–279	–280	...	...	...	...
Total credit	2 200 ..	*58*	*85*	*107*	*83*	...	...	...	...
Total debit	3 200 ..	*–289*	*–444*	*–386*	*–363*	...	...	...	...
Transportation services, credit	2 205 ..	**43**	**61**	**65**	**49**	...	...	...	...
Passenger	2 205 BA	*11*	*25*	*28*	*21*	...	...	...	...
Freight	2 205 BB	*32*	*36*	*35*	*28*	...	...	...	...
Other	2 205 BC	...	...	*2*	...	...	...	...	...
Sea transport, passenger	2 207 ..	...	...	...	...	...	...	...	...
Sea transport, freight	2 208 ..	...	...	...	...	...	...	...	...
Sea transport, other	2 209 ..	...	...	...	...	...	...	...	...
Air transport, passenger	2 211 ..	...	...	...	...	...	...	...	...
Air transport, freight	2 212 ..	...	...	...	...	...	...	...	...
Air transport, other	2 213 ..	...	...	...	...	...	...	...	...
Other transport, passenger	2 215 ..	...	...	...	...	...	...	...	...
Other transport, freight	2 216 ..	...	...	...	...	...	...	...	...
Other transport, other	2 217 ..	...	...	...	...	...	...	...	...
Transportation services, debit	3 205 ..	**–164**	**–281**	**–284**	**–203**	...	...	...	...
Passenger	3 205 BA	*–30*	*–100*	*–88*	*–77*	...	...	...	...
Freight	3 205 BB	*–133*	*–181*	*–176*	*–110*	...	...	...	...
Other	3 205 BC	...	...	*–20*	*–16*	...	...	...	...
Sea transport, passenger	3 207 ..	...	...	...	...	...	...	...	...
Sea transport, freight	3 208 ..	...	...	...	...	...	...	...	...
Sea transport, other	3 209 ..	...	...	...	...	...	...	...	...
Air transport, passenger	3 211 ..	...	...	...	...	...	...	...	...
Air transport, freight	3 212 ..	...	...	...	...	...	...	...	...
Air transport, other	3 213 ..	...	...	...	...	...	...	...	...
Other transport, passenger	3 215 ..	...	...	...	...	...	...	...	...
Other transport, freight	3 216 ..	...	...	...	...	...	...	...	...
Other transport, other	3 217 ..	...	...	...	...	...	...	...	...
Travel, credit	2 236 ..	**5**	**12**	**13**	**10**	...	...	...	...
Business travel	2 237 ..	...	...	...	...	...	...	...	...
Personal travel	2 240 ..	...	...	...	...	...	...	...	...
Travel, debit	3 236 ..	**–49**	**–98**	**–54**	**–87**	...	...	...	...
Business travel	3 237 ..	...	...	...	...	...	...	...	...
Personal travel	3 240 ..	...	...	...	...	...	...	...	...
Other services, credit	2 200 BA	**10**	**12**	**29**	**24**	...	...	...	...
Communications	2 245 ..	...	...	...	...	...	...	...	...
Construction	2 249 ..	...	...	...	...	...	...	...	...
Insurance	2 253 ..	4	4	4	3	...	...	...	...
Financial	2 260 ..	...	...	...	...	...	...	...	...
Computer and information	2 262 ..	...	...	...	...	...	...	...	...
Royalties and licence fees	2 266 ..	...	...	...	...	...	...	...	...
Other business services	2 268 ..	1	...	13	6	...	...	...	...
Personal, cultural, and recreational	2 287 ..	...	...	...	...	...	...	...	...
Government, n.i.e.	2 291 ..	6	7	12	14	...	...	...	...
Other services, debit	3 200 BA	**–77**	**–65**	**–48**	**–73**	...	...	...	...
Communications	3 245 ..	...	...	...	...	...	...	...	...
Construction	3 249 ..	...	...	...	...	...	...	...	...
Insurance	3 253 ..	–15	–20	–20	–12	...	...	...	...
Financial	3 260 ..	...	...	...	...	...	...	...	...
Computer and information	3 262 ..	...	...	...	...	...	...	...	...
Royalties and licence fees	3 266 ..	...	...	...	...	...	...	...	...
Other business services	3 268 ..	–33	–9	–12	–50	...	...	...	...
Personal, cultural, and recreational	3 287 ..	...	...	...	...	...	...	...	...
Government, n.i.e.	3 291 ..	–29	–36	–16	–11	...	...	...	...

Table 2 (Continued). STANDARD PRESENTATION, 1988–95
(Millions of U.S. dollars)

	Code	1988	1989	1990	1991	1992	1993	1994	1995
C. INCOME	4 300 . .	–601	–508	–437	–686	...	...	...	...
Total credit	2 300 . .	*3*	*1*	*2*	*10*	...	...	...	...
Total debit	3 300 . .	*–604*	*–509*	*–439*	*–696*	...	...	...	...
Compensation of employees, credit	2 310 . .	...	...	...	...	...	...	...	...
Compensation of employees, debit	3 310 . .	...	...	...	...	...	...	...	...
Investment income, credit	2 320 . .	**3**	**1**	**2**	**10**	...	...	...	...
Direct investment income	2 330 . .	...	...	...	...	...	...	...	...
Dividends and distributed branch profits	2 332 . .	...	...	...	...	...	...	...	...
Reinvested earnings and undistributed branch profits	2 333 . .	...	...	...	...	...	...	...	...
Income on debt (interest)	2 334 . .	...	...	...	...	...	...	...	...
Portfolio investment income	2 339 . .	...	...	...	...	...	...	...	...
Income on equity	2 340 . .	...	...	...	...	...	...	...	...
Income on bonds and notes	2 350 . .	...	...	...	...	...	...	...	...
Income on money market instruments and financial derivatives	2 360 . .	...	...	...	...	...	...	...	...
Other investment income	2 370 . .	3	1	2	10	...	...	...	...
Investment income, debit	3 320 . .	**–604**	**–509**	**–439**	**–696**	...	...	...	...
Direct investment income	3 330 . .	–106	–38	–115	–28	...	...	...	...
Dividends and distributed branch profits	3 332 . .	–13	–23	–12	–8	...	...	...	...
Reinvested earnings and undistributed branch profits	3 333 . .	–93	–15	–103	–20	...	...	...	...
Income on debt (interest)	3 334 . .	...	...	...	...	...	...	...	...
Portfolio investment income	3 339 . .	...	...	...	...	...	...	...	...
Income on equity	3 340 . .	...	...	...	...	...	...	...	...
Income on bonds and notes	3 350 . .	...	...	...	...	...	...	...	...
Income on money market instruments and financial derivatives	3 360 . .	...	...	...	...	...	...	...	...
Other investment income	3 370 . .	–498	–471	–324	–668	...	...	...	...
D. CURRENT TRANSFERS	4 379 . .	36	81	380	240	...	...	...	...
Credit	2 379 . .	**64**	**114**	**398**	**262**	...	...	...	...
General government	2 380 . .	63	113	398	262	...	...	...	...
Other sectors	2 390 . .	1	...	...	...	...	...	...	...
Workers' remittances	2 391 . .	...	...	...	...	...	...	...	...
Other current transfers	2 392 . .	1	...	...	...	...	...	...	...
Debit	3 379 . .	**–27**	**–32**	**–18**	**–22**	...	...	...	...
General government	3 380 . .	–4	–5	–2	–1	...	...	...	...
Other sectors	3 390 . .	–24	–28	–16	–21	...	...	...	...
Workers' remittances	3 391 . .	–21	–23	–15	–19	...	...	...	...
Other current transfers	3 392 . .	–2	–5	–1	–2	...	...	...	...
CAPITAL AND FINANCIAL ACCOUNT	4 996 . .	**253**	**1,930**	**272**	**196**	...	...	...	...
CAPITAL ACCOUNT	4 994 . .	**–2**	**–3**	**–3**	**–1**	...	...	...	...
Total credit	2 994 . .	...	...	...	...	...	...	...	...
Total debit	3 994 . .	*–2*	*–3*	*–3*	*–1*	...	...	...	...
Capital transfers, credit	2 400 . .	...	...	...	...	...	...	...	...
General government	2 401 . .	...	...	...	...	...	...	...	...
Debt forgiveness	2 402 . .	...	...	...	...	...	...	...	...
Other capital transfers	2 410 . .	...	...	...	...	...	...	...	...
Other sectors	2 430 . .	...	...	...	...	...	...	...	...
Migrants' transfers	2 431 . .	...	...	...	...	...	...	...	...
Debt forgiveness	2 432 . .	...	...	...	...	...	...	...	...
Other capital transfers	2 440 . .	...	...	...	...	...	...	...	...
Capital transfers, debit	3 400 . .	**–2**	**–3**	**–3**	**–1**	...	...	...	...
General government	3 401 . .	...	...	...	...	...	...	...	...
Debt forgiveness	3 402 . .	...	...	...	...	...	...	...	...
Other capital transfers	3 410 . .	...	...	...	...	...	...	...	...
Other sectors	3 430 . .	–2	–3	–3	–1	...	...	...	...
Migrants' transfers	3 431 . .	–2	–3	–3	–1	...	...	...	...
Debt forgiveness	3 432 . .	...	...	...	...	...	...	...	...
Other capital transfers	3 440 . .	...	...	...	...	...	...	...	...
Nonproduced nonfinancial assets, credit	2 480 . .	...	...	...	...	...	...	...	...
Nonproduced nonfinancial assets, debit	3 480 . .	...	...	...	...	...	...	...	...

Table 2 (Continued). STANDARD PRESENTATION, 1988–95
(Millions of U.S. dollars)

	Code	1988	1989	1990	1991	1992	1993	1994	1995
FINANCIAL ACCOUNT	4 995 . .	**255**	**1,933**	**275**	**197**	**. . .**	**. . .**	**. . .**	**. . .**
A. DIRECT INVESTMENT	4 500 . .	93	164	203	34	. . .	. . .	. . .	. . .
Direct investment abroad	4 505 . .	**. . .**	**. . .**	**. . .**	**. . .**	**. . .**	**. . .**	**. . .**	**. . .**
Equity capital	4 510 . .	. . .	. . .	. . .	. . .	. . .	. . .	. . .	. . .
Claims on affiliated enterprises	4 515 . .	. . .	. . .	. . .	. . .	. . .	. . .	. . .	. . .
Liabilities to affiliated enterprises	4 520 . .	. . .	. . .	. . .	. . .	. . .	. . .	. . .	. . .
Reinvested earnings	4 525 . .	. . .	. . .	. . .	. . .	. . .	. . .	. . .	. . .
Other capital	4 530 . .	. . .	. . .	. . .	. . .	. . .	. . .	. . .	. . .
Claims on affiliated enterprises	4 535 . .	. . .	. . .	. . .	. . .	. . .	. . .	. . .	. . .
Liabilities to affiliated enterprises	4 540 . .	. . .	. . .	. . .	. . .	. . .	. . .	. . .	. . .
Direct investment in Zambia	4 555 . .	**93**	**164**	**203**	**34**	**. . .**	**. . .**	**. . .**	**. . .**
Equity capital	4 560 . .	. . .	13	12	11	. . .	. . .	. . .	. . .
Claims on direct investors	4 565 . .	. . .	. . .	. . .	. . .	. . .	. . .	. . .	. . .
Liabilities to direct investors	4 570 . .	. . .	. . .	. . .	. . .	. . .	. . .	. . .	. . .
Reinvested earnings	4 575 . .	93	15	103	20	. . .	. . .	. . .	. . .
Other capital	4 580 . .	. . .	135	88	3	. . .	. . .	. . .	. . .
Claims on direct investors	4 585 . .	. . .	. . .	. . .	. . .	. . .	. . .	. . .	. . .
Liabilities to direct investors	4 590 . .	. . .	. . .	. . .	. . .	. . .	. . .	. . .	. . .
B. PORTFOLIO INVESTMENT	4 600 . .	. . .	. . .	. . .	. . .	. . .	. . .	. . .	. . .
Assets	4 602 . .	**. . .**	**. . .**	**. . .**	**. . .**	**. . .**	**. . .**	**. . .**	**. . .**
Equity securities	4 610 . .	. . .	. . .	. . .	. . .	. . .	. . .	. . .	. . .
Monetary authorities	4 611 . .	. . .	. . .	. . .	. . .	. . .	. . .	. . .	. . .
General government	4 612 . .	. . .	. . .	. . .	. . .	. . .	. . .	. . .	. . .
Banks	4 613 . .	. . .	. . .	. . .	. . .	. . .	. . .	. . .	. . .
Other sectors	4 614 . .	. . .	. . .	. . .	. . .	. . .	. . .	. . .	. . .
Debt securities	4 619 . .	. . .	. . .	. . .	. . .	. . .	. . .	. . .	. . .
Bonds and notes	4 620 . .	. . .	. . .	. . .	. . .	. . .	. . .	. . .	. . .
Monetary authorities	4 621 . .	. . .	. . .	. . .	. . .	. . .	. . .	. . .	. . .
General government	4 622 . .	. . .	. . .	. . .	. . .	. . .	. . .	. . .	. . .
Banks	4 623 . .	. . .	. . .	. . .	. . .	. . .	. . .	. . .	. . .
Other sectors	4 624 . .	. . .	. . .	. . .	. . .	. . .	. . .	. . .	. . .
Money market instruments	4 630 . .	. . .	. . .	. . .	. . .	. . .	. . .	. . .	. . .
Monetary authorities	4 631 . .	. . .	. . .	. . .	. . .	. . .	. . .	. . .	. . .
General government	4 632 . .	. . .	. . .	. . .	. . .	. . .	. . .	. . .	. . .
Banks	4 633 . .	. . .	. . .	. . .	. . .	. . .	. . .	. . .	. . .
Other sectors	4 634 . .	. . .	. . .	. . .	. . .	. . .	. . .	. . .	. . .
Financial derivatives	4 640 . .	. . .	. . .	. . .	. . .	. . .	. . .	. . .	. . .
Monetary authorities	4 641 . .	. . .	. . .	. . .	. . .	. . .	. . .	. . .	. . .
General government	4 642 . .	. . .	. . .	. . .	. . .	. . .	. . .	. . .	. . .
Banks	4 643 . .	. . .	. . .	. . .	. . .	. . .	. . .	. . .	. . .
Other sectors	4 644 . .	. . .	. . .	. . .	. . .	. . .	. . .	. . .	. . .
Liabilities	4 652 . .	**. . .**	**. . .**	**. . .**	**. . .**	**. . .**	**. . .**	**. . .**	**. . .**
Equity securities	4 660 . .	. . .	. . .	. . .	. . .	. . .	. . .	. . .	. . .
Banks	4 663 . .	. . .	. . .	. . .	. . .	. . .	. . .	. . .	. . .
Other sectors	4 664 . .	. . .	. . .	. . .	. . .	. . .	. . .	. . .	. . .
Debt securities	4 669 . .	. . .	. . .	. . .	. . .	. . .	. . .	. . .	. . .
Bonds and notes	4 670 . .	. . .	. . .	. . .	. . .	. . .	. . .	. . .	. . .
Monetary authorities	4 671 . .	. . .	. . .	. . .	. . .	. . .	. . .	. . .	. . .
General government	4 672 . .	. . .	. . .	. . .	. . .	. . .	. . .	. . .	. . .
Banks	4 673 . .	. . .	. . .	. . .	. . .	. . .	. . .	. . .	. . .
Other sectors	4 674 . .	. . .	. . .	. . .	. . .	. . .	. . .	. . .	. . .
Money market instruments	4 680 . .	. . .	. . .	. . .	. . .	. . .	. . .	. . .	. . .
Monetary authorities	4 681 . .	. . .	. . .	. . .	. . .	. . .	. . .	. . .	. . .
General government	4 682 . .	. . .	. . .	. . .	. . .	. . .	. . .	. . .	. . .
Banks	4 683 . .	. . .	. . .	. . .	. . .	. . .	. . .	. . .	. . .
Other sectors	4 684 . .	. . .	. . .	. . .	. . .	. . .	. . .	. . .	. . .
Financial derivatives	4 690 . .	. . .	. . .	. . .	. . .	. . .	. . .	. . .	. . .
Monetary authorities	4 691 . .	. . .	. . .	. . .	. . .	. . .	. . .	. . .	. . .
General government	4 692 . .	. . .	. . .	. . .	. . .	. . .	. . .	. . .	. . .
Banks	4 693 . .	. . .	. . .	. . .	. . .	. . .	. . .	. . .	. . .
Other sectors	4 694 . .	. . .	. . .	. . .	. . .	. . .	. . .	. . .	. . .

Table 2 (Concluded). STANDARD PRESENTATION, 1988–95
(Millions of U.S. dollars)

	Code	1988	1989	1990	1991	1992	1993	1994	1995
C. OTHER INVESTMENT	4 700 . .	213	1,851	191	189	. . .	. . .	. . .	. . .
Assets	4 703 . .	**–347**	**26**	**–275**	**–125**	**. . .**	**. . .**	**. . .**	**. . .**
Trade credits	4 706 . .	–171	162	–119	. . .	. . .	. . .	. . .	. . .
General government: long-term	4 708 . .	. . .	. . .	. . .	. . .	. . .	. . .	. . .	. . .
General government: short-term	4 709 . .	. . .	. . .	. . .	. . .	. . .	. . .	. . .	. . .
Other sectors: long-term	4 711 . .	. . .	. . .	. . .	. . .	. . .	. . .	. . .	. . .
Other sectors: short-term	4 712 . .	–171	162	–119	. . .	. . .	. . .	. . .	. . .
Loans	4 714 . .	. . .	. . .	. . .	. . .	. . .	. . .	. . .	. . .
Monetary authorities: long-term	4 717 . .	. . .	. . .	. . .	. . .	. . .	. . .	. . .	. . .
Monetary authorities: short-term	4 718 . .	. . .	. . .	. . .	. . .	. . .	. . .	. . .	. . .
General government: long-term	4 720 . .	. . .	. . .	. . .	. . .	. . .	. . .	. . .	. . .
General government: short-term	4 721 . .	. . .	. . .	. . .	. . .	. . .	. . .	. . .	. . .
Banks: long-term	4 723 . .	. . .	. . .	. . .	. . .	. . .	. . .	. . .	. . .
Banks: short-term	4 724 . .	. . .	. . .	. . .	. . .	. . .	. . .	. . .	. . .
Other sectors: long-term	4 726 . .	. . .	. . .	. . .	. . .	. . .	. . .	. . .	. . .
Other sectors: short-term	4 727 . .	. . .	. . .	. . .	. . .	. . .	. . .	. . .	. . .
Currency and deposits	4 730 . .	–159	–134	–151	–71	. . .	. . .	. . .	. . .
Monetary authorities	4 731 . .	. . .	. . .	. . .	. . .	. . .	. . .	. . .	. . .
General government	4 732 . .	. . .	. . .	. . .	. . .	. . .	. . .	. . .	. . .
Banks	4 733 . .	–56	–172	–109	–76	. . .	. . .	. . .	. . .
Other sectors	4 734 . .	–103	38	–42	6	. . .	. . .	. . .	. . .
Other assets	4 736 . .	–18	–2	–5	–54	. . .	. . .	. . .	. . .
Monetary authorities: long-term	4 738 . .	. . .	. . .	. . .	. . .	. . .	. . .	. . .	. . .
Monetary authorities: short-term	4 739 . .	. . .	. . .	. . .	. . .	. . .	. . .	. . .	. . .
General government: long-term	4 741 . .	1	. . .	–7	–54	. . .	. . .	. . .	. . .
General government: short-term	4 742 . .	. . .	. . .	. . .	. . .	. . .	. . .	. . .	. . .
Banks: long-term	4 744 . .	. . .	. . .	. . .	. . .	. . .	. . .	. . .	. . .
Banks: short-term	4 745 . .	. . .	. . .	. . .	. . .	. . .	. . .	. . .	. . .
Other sectors: long-term	4 747 . .	–18	–3	2	. . .	. . .	. . .	. . .	. . .
Other sectors: short-term	4 748 . .	. . .	. . .	. . .	. . .	. . .	. . .	. . .	. . .
Liabilities	4 753 . .	**561**	**1,825**	**467**	**314**	**. . .**	**. . .**	**. . .**	**. . .**
Trade credits	4 756 . .	73	19	42	7	. . .	. . .	. . .	. . .
General government: long-term	4 758 . .	. . .	. . .	. . .	. . .	. . .	. . .	. . .	. . .
General government: short-term	4 759 . .	. . .	. . .	. . .	. . .	. . .	. . .	. . .	. . .
Other sectors: long-term	4 761 . .	. . .	. . .	. . .	. . .	. . .	. . .	. . .	. . .
Other sectors: short-term	4 762 . .	73	19	42	7	. . .	. . .	. . .	. . .
Loans	4 764 . .	238	22	667	81	. . .	. . .	. . .	. . .
Use of Fund credit and loans from the Fund	4 766 . .	. . .	–17	–25	–35	. . .	. . .	. . .	. . .
Monetary authorities: other long-term	4 767 . .	. . .	. . .	. . .	. . .	. . .	. . .	. . .	. . .
Monetary authorities: short-term	4 768 . .	37	–59	–13	37	. . .	. . .	. . .	. . .
General government: long-term	4 770 . .	243	–104	125	76	. . .	. . .	. . .	. . .
General government: short-term	4 771 . .	. . .	. . .	. . .	. . .	. . .	. . .	. . .	. . .
Banks: long-term	4 773 . .	. . .	. . .	. . .	. . .	. . .	. . .	. . .	. . .
Banks: short-term	4 774 . .	. . .	. . .	. . .	. . .	. . .	. . .	. . .	. . .
Other sectors: long-term	4 776 . .	–77	37	193	3	. . .	. . .	. . .	. . .
Other sectors: short-term	4 777 . .	36	164	387	. . .	. . .	. . .	. . .	. . .
Currency and deposits	4 780 . .	1	50	30	14	. . .	. . .	. . .	. . .
Monetary authorities	4 781 . .	. . .	. . .	. . .	. . .	. . .	. . .	. . .	. . .
General government	4 782 . .	. . .	. . .	. . .	. . .	. . .	. . .	. . .	. . .
Banks	4 783 . .	1	50	30	14	. . .	. . .	. . .	. . .
Other sectors	4 784 . .	. . .	. . .	. . .	. . .	. . .	. . .	. . .	. . .
Other liabilities	4 786 . .	248	1,735	–273	212	. . .	. . .	. . .	. . .
Monetary authorities: long-term	4 788 . .	. . .	. . .	. . .	. . .	. . .	. . .	. . .	. . .
Monetary authorities: short-term	4 789 . .	291	230	225	44	. . .	. . .	. . .	. . .
General government: long-term	4 791 . .	. . .	. . .	. . .	. . .	. . .	. . .	. . .	. . .
General government: short-term	4 792 . .	–218	–137	–114	–38	. . .	. . .	. . .	. . .
Banks: long-term	4 794 . .	. . .	. . .	. . .	. . .	. . .	. . .	. . .	. . .
Banks: short-term	4 795 . .	. . .	. . .	. . .	. . .	. . .	. . .	. . .	. . .
Other sectors: long-term	4 797 . .	74	202	308	34	. . .	. . .	. . .	. . .
Other sectors: short-term	4 798 . .	101	1,441	–692	172	. . .	. . .	. . .	. . .
D. RESERVE ASSETS	4 800 . .	–51	–82	–119	–26	. . .	. . .	. . .	. . .
Monetary gold	4 810 . .	–3	–1	–2	–1	. . .	. . .	. . .	. . .
Special drawing rights	4 820 . .	. . .	. . .	. . .	. . .	. . .	. . .	. . .	. . .
Reserve position in the Fund	4 830 . .	. . .	. . .	. . .	. . .	. . .	. . .	. . .	. . .
Foreign exchange	4 840 . .	–48	–81	–117	–25	. . .	. . .	. . .	. . .
Other claims	4 880 . .	. . .	. . .	. . .	. . .	. . .	. . .	. . .	. . .
NET ERRORS AND OMISSIONS	4 998 . .	**40**	**–1,712**	**322**	**110**	**. . .**	**. . .**	**. . .**	**. . .**

Table 1. ANALYTIC PRESENTATION, 1988–95
(Millions of U.S. dollars)

	Code	1988	1989	1990	1991	1992	1993	1994	1995
A. Current Account [1]	4 993 Y.	**125.3**	**17.0**	**–139.8**	**–457.0**	**–603.7**	**–115.7**	**–424.9**	**. . .**
Goods: exports f.o.b	2 100 . .	1,664.9	1,693.5	1,747.9	1,693.8	1,527.6	1,609.1	1,961.1	. . .
Goods: imports f.o.b	3 100 . .	–1,163.6	–1,318.3	–1,505.2	–1,645.7	–1,782.1	–1,487.0	–1,803.5	. . .
Balance on Goods	4 100 . .	*501.3*	*375.2*	*242.7*	*48.1*	*–254.5*	*122.1*	*157.6*	. . .
Services: credit	2 200 . .	190.3	241.8	264.2	273.5	305.1	372.1	383.2	. . .
Services: debit	3 200 . .	–410.9	–457.0	–495.5	–627.4	–660.9	–563.8	–711.7	. . .
Balance on Goods and Services	4 991 . .	*280.7*	*160.0*	*11.3*	*–305.9*	*–610.3*	*–69.6*	*–170.9*	. . .
Income: credit	2 300 . .	17.4	26.0	22.9	26.1	26.0	35.0	27.5	. . .
Income: debit	3 300 . .	–234.0	–236.1	–286.3	–278.0	–302.3	–287.1	–321.2	. . .
Balance on Goods, Services, and Income	4 992 . .	*64.1*	*–50.0*	*–252.0*	*–557.8*	*–886.6*	*–321.6*	*–464.5*	. . .
Current transfers: credit	2 379 Y.	211.2	211.4	204.0	191.7	347.3	270.6	69.4	. . .
Current transfers: debit	3 379 . .	–150.1	–144.3	–91.8	–90.9	–64.4	–64.7	–29.8	. . .
B. Capital Account [1]	4 994 Y.	**–8.6**	**–7.6**	**–7.0**	**–2.8**	**–1.4**	**–.4**	**284.4**	**. . .**
Capital account: credit	2 994 Y.	.3	.2	.4	.1	.2	.6	285.4	. . .
Capital account: debit	3 994 . .	–9.0	–7.9	–7.4	–2.9	–1.6	–1.0	–1.0	. . .
Total, Groups A Plus B	4 010 . .	*116.6*	*9.3*	*–146.8*	*–459.8*	*–605.1*	*–116.1*	*–140.5*	. . .
C. Financial Account [1]	4 995 X.	**48.0**	**47.8**	**242.6**	**536.5**	**373.4**	**327.2**	**–25.5**	**. . .**
Direct investment abroad	4 505 . .	22.2	. . .	. . .	. . .	. . .	. . .	–4.7	. . .
Direct investment in Zimbabwe	4 555 Y.	–18.1	–10.2	–12.2	2.8	15.0	28.0	34.7	. . .
Portfolio investment assets	4 602 . .	. . .	. . .	10.4	41.8	27.6	. . .	. . .	. . .
Equity securities	4 610 . .	. . .	. . .	. . .	. . .	. . .	. . .	. . .	. . .
Debt securities	4 619 . .	. . .	. . .	10.4	41.8	27.6	. . .	. . .	. . .
Portfolio investment liabilities	4 652 Y.	–60.9	–36.7	–32.1	–34.6	–37.1	–5.1	50.2	. . .
Equity securities	4 660 Y.	. . .	. . .	. . .	. . .	. . .	. . .	56.9	. . .
Debt securities	4 669 Y.	–60.9	–36.7	–32.1	–34.6	–37.1	–5.1	–6.7	. . .
Other investment assets	4 703 . .	4.9	. . .	. . .	38.0	15.9	99.9	–260.3	. . .
Monetary authorities	4 703 . A	. . .	. . .	. . .	. . .	. . .	. . .	. . .	. . .
General government	4 703 . B	. . .	. . .	. . .	. . .	. . .	. . .	. . .	. . .
Banks	4 703 . C	4.9	. . .	. . .	38.0	15.9	99.9	–260.3	. . .
Other sectors	4 703 . D	. . .	. . .	. . .	. . .	. . .	. . .	. . .	. . .
Other investment liabilities	4 753 X.	99.9	94.7	276.5	488.4	352.0	204.4	154.7	. . .
Monetary authorities	4 753 XA	. . .	3.0	97.6	128.7	–78.2	–7.8	–109.9	. . .
General government	4 753 YB	70.4	67.6	88.6	275.0	407.9	191.0	62.0	. . .
Banks	4 753 YC	. . .	3.1	14.6	. . .	. . .	. . .	. . .	. . .
Other sectors	4 753 YD	29.4	21.0	75.8	84.7	22.3	21.2	202.6	. . .
Total, Groups A Through C	4 020 . .	*164.6*	*57.1*	*95.7*	*76.7*	*–231.7*	*211.0*	*–166.0*	. . .
D. Net Errors and Omissions	4 998 . .	**–63.0**	**–103.8**	**–9.9**	**–31.4**	**37.2**	**14.9**	**80.2**	**. . .**
Total, Groups A Through D	4 030 . .	*101.6*	*–46.8*	*85.8*	*45.2*	*–194.6*	*225.9*	*–85.8*	. . .
E. Reserves and Related Items	4 040 . .	**–101.6**	**46.8**	**–85.8**	**–45.2**	**194.6**	**–225.9**	**85.8**	**. . .**
Reserve assets	4 800 . .	–23.0	85.5	–62.8	–38.4	–31.1	–293.6	12.9	. . .
Use of Fund credit and loans	4 766 . .	–78.6	–38.8	–23.0	–6.9	225.7	67.7	72.8	. . .
Liabilities constituting foreign authorities' reserves	4 900 . .	. . .	. . .	. . .	. . .	. . .	. . .	. . .	. . .
Exceptional financing	4 920 . .	. . .	. . .	. . .	. . .	. . .	. . .	. . .	. . .
Conversion rates: Zimbabwe dollars per U.S. dollar	0 101 . .	**1.8057**	**2.1189**	**2.4517**	**3.6214**	**5.0985**	**6.4831**	**8.1515**	**8.6654**

[1] Excludes components that have been classified in the categories of Group E.

Table 2. STANDARD PRESENTATION, 1988–95
(Millions of U.S. dollars)

	Code		1988	1989	1990	1991	1992	1993	1994	1995
CURRENT ACCOUNT	4 993	. .	**125.3**	**17.0**	**–139.8**	**–457.0**	**–603.7**	**–115.7**	**–424.9**	. . .
A. GOODS	4 100	. .	501.3	375.2	242.7	48.1	–254.5	122.1	157.6	. . .
Credit	2 100	. .	**1,664.9**	**1,693.5**	**1,747.9**	**1,693.8**	**1,527.6**	**1,609.1**	**1,961.1**	. . .
General merchandise: exports f.o.b.	2 110	. .	1,664.9	1,693.5	1,747.9	1,693.8	1,527.6	1,609.1	1,961.0	. . .
Goods for processing: exports f.o.b.	2 150	. .	. . .	. . .	. . .	. . .	. . .	. . .	. . .	. . .
Repairs on goods	2 160	. .	. . .	. . .	. . .	. . .	. . .	. . .	. . .	. . .
Goods procured in ports by carriers	2 170	. .	. . .	. . .	. . .	. . .	. . .	. . .	. . .	. . .
Nonmonetary gold	2 180	. .	. . .	. . .	. . .	. . .	. . .	. . .	. . .	. . .
Debit	3 100	. .	**–1,163.6**	**–1,318.3**	**–1,505.2**	**–1,645.7**	**–1,782.1**	**–1,487.0**	**–1,803.5**	. . .
General merchandise: imports f.o.b.	3 110	. .	–1,163.6	–1,318.3	–1,505.2	–1,645.7	–1,782.1	–1,487.0	–1,791.8	. . .
Goods for processing: imports f.o.b.	3 150	. .	. . .	. . .	. . .	. . .	. . .	. . .	. . .	. . .
Repairs on goods	3 160	. .	. . .	. . .	. . .	. . .	. . .	. . .	–6.2	. . .
Goods procured in ports by carriers	3 170	. .	. . .	. . .	. . .	. . .	. . .	. . .	–5.5	. . .
Nonmonetary gold	3 180	. .	. . .	. . .	. . .	. . .	. . .	. . .	. . .	. . .
B. SERVICES	4 200	. .	–220.6	–215.2	–231.4	–353.9	–355.8	–191.7	–328.5	. . .
Total credit	2 200	. .	*190.3*	*241.8*	*264.2*	*273.5*	*305.1*	*372.1*	*383.2*	. . .
Total debit	3 200	. .	*–410.9*	*–457.0*	*–495.5*	*–627.4*	*–660.9*	*–563.8*	*–711.7*	. . .
Transportation services, credit	2 205	. .	**83.1**	**101.1**	**112.1**	**105.5**	**94.7**	**94.5**	**93.2**	. . .
Passenger	2 205	BA	*35.2*	*45.1*	*47.4*	*42.3*	*40.6*	*31.9*	*28.0*	. . .
Freight	2 205	BB	*19.0*	*19.8*	*27.1*	*28.4*	*24.8*	*25.6*	*28.2*	. . .
Other	2 205	BC	*28.9*	*36.2*	*37.6*	*34.8*	*29.4*	*37.0*	*37.0*	. . .
Sea transport, passenger	2 207	. .	. . .	. . .	. . .	. . .	. . .	. . .	. . .	. . .
Sea transport, freight	2 208	. .	. . .	. . .	. . .	. . .	. . .	. . .	. . .	. . .
Sea transport, other	2 209	. .	. . .	. . .	. . .	. . .	. . .	. . .	9.3	. . .
Air transport, passenger	2 211	. .	. . .	. . .	. . .	. . .	. . .	. . .	28.0	. . .
Air transport, freight	2 212	. .	. . .	. . .	. . .	. . .	. . .	. . .	9.3	. . .
Air transport, other	2 213	. .	. . .	. . .	. . .	. . .	. . .	. . .	7.2	. . .
Other transport, passenger	2 215	. .	. . .	. . .	. . .	. . .	. . .	. . .	. . .	. . .
Other transport, freight	2 216	. .	. . .	. . .	. . .	. . .	. . .	. . .	18.9	. . .
Other transport, other	2 217	. .	. . .	. . .	. . .	. . .	. . .	. . .	20.6	. . .
Transportation services, debit	3 205	. .	**–184.6**	**–214.5**	**–238.2**	**–283.5**	**–367.5**	**–291.0**	**–360.8**	. . .
Passenger	3 205	BA	*–29.4*	*–35.0*	*–38.4*	*–36.0*	*–40.8*	*–34.0*	*–40.1*	. . .
Freight	3 205	BB	*–111.3*	*–129.5*	*–138.9*	*–187.3*	*–247.3*	*–181.5*	*–240.0*	. . .
Other	3 205	BC	*–43.9*	*–50.0*	*–60.9*	*–60.2*	*–79.4*	*–75.5*	*–80.8*	. . .
Sea transport, passenger	3 207	. .	. . .	. . .	. . .	. . .	. . .	. . .	. . .	. . .
Sea transport, freight	3 208	. .	. . .	. . .	. . .	. . .	. . .	. . .	–156.8	. . .
Sea transport, other	3 209	. .	. . .	. . .	. . .	. . .	. . .	. . .	–28.5	. . .
Air transport, passenger	3 211	. .	. . .	. . .	. . .	. . .	. . .	. . .	–38.6	. . .
Air transport, freight	3 212	. .	. . .	. . .	. . .	. . .	. . .	. . .	–2.2	. . .
Air transport, other	3 213	. .	. . .	. . .	. . .	. . .	. . .	. . .	–36.4	. . .
Other transport, passenger	3 215	. .	. . .	. . .	. . .	. . .	. . .	. . .	–1.5	. . .
Other transport, freight	3 216	. .	. . .	. . .	. . .	. . .	. . .	. . .	–81.0	. . .
Other transport, other	3 217	. .	. . .	. . .	. . .	. . .	. . .	. . .	–15.9	. . .
Travel, credit	2 236	. .	**53.6**	**54.9**	**64.2**	**74.8**	**107.9**	**137.7**	**178.9**	. . .
Business travel	2 237	. .	. . .	. . .	. . .	. . .	. . .	. . .	23.3	. . .
Personal travel	2 240	. .	. . .	. . .	. . .	. . .	. . .	. . .	155.6	. . .
Travel, debit	3 236	. .	**–58.4**	**–63.0**	**–66.3**	**–70.0**	**–54.5**	**–43.9**	**–120.2**	. . .
Business travel	3 237	. .	. . .	. . .	. . .	. . .	. . .	. . .	–33.6	. . .
Personal travel	3 240	. .	. . .	. . .	. . .	. . .	. . .	. . .	–86.7	. . .
Other services, credit	2 200	BA	**53.6**	**85.8**	**87.9**	**93.2**	**102.5**	**139.9**	**111.1**	. . .
Communications	2 245	. .	. . .	. . .	. . .	. . .	. . .	. . .	8.1	. . .
Construction	2 249	. .	. . .	. . .	. . .	. . .	. . .	. . .	. . .	. . .
Insurance	2 253	. .	2.1	2.2	3.0	3.2	2.8	2.8	1.2	. . .
Financial	2 260	. .	. . .	. . .	. . .	. . .	. . .	. . .	. . .	. . .
Computer and information	2 262	. .	. . .	. . .	. . .	. . .	. . .	. . .	.1	. . .
Royalties and licence fees	2 266	. .	.6	17.8	.8	1.6	1.0	.8	.6	. . .
Other business services	2 268	. .	42.3	50.1	73.3	74.2	70.3	109.1	71.4	. . .
Personal, cultural, and recreational	2 287	. .	. . .	. . .	. . .	. . .	. . .	. . .	. . .	. . .
Government, n.i.e.	2 291	. .	8.7	15.7	10.8	14.2	28.4	27.2	29.7	. . .
Other services, debit	3 200	BA	**–168.0**	**–179.6**	**–191.0**	**–273.9**	**–239.0**	**–228.9**	**–230.6**	. . .
Communications	3 245	. .	. . .	. . .	. . .	. . .	. . .	. . .	–8.9	. . .
Construction	3 249	. .	. . .	. . .	. . .	. . .	. . .	. . .	. . .	. . .
Insurance	3 253	. .	–12.4	–14.4	–15.4	–20.8	–27.5	–20.2	–18.5	. . .
Financial	3 260	. .	. . .	. . .	. . .	. . .	. . .	. . .	. . .	. . .
Computer and information	3 262	. .	. . .	. . .	. . .	. . .	. . .	. . .	–3.6	. . .
Royalties and licence fees	3 266	. .	–5.9	–5.3	–8.2	–40.0	–5.8	–5.3	–6.0	. . .
Other business services	3 268	. .	–123.7	–131.9	–131.9	–170.4	–166.4	–156.5	–126.4	. . .
Personal, cultural, and recreational	3 287	. .	. . .	. . .	. . .	. . .	. . .	. . .	–.2	. . .
Government, n.i.e.	3 291	. .	–26.0	–28.0	–35.5	–42.7	–39.3	–46.9	–67.1	. . .

Table 2 (Continued). STANDARD PRESENTATION, 1988–95
(Millions of U.S. dollars)

	Code	1988	1989	1990	1991	1992	1993	1994	1995
C. INCOME	4 300	–216.5	–210.1	–263.3	–251.9	–276.3	–252.0	–293.7	...
Total credit	2 300	*17.4*	*26.0*	*22.9*	*26.1*	*26.0*	*35.0*	*27.5*	...
Total debit	3 300	*–234.0*	*–236.1*	*–286.3*	*–278.0*	*–302.3*	*–287.1*	*–321.2*	...
Compensation of employees, credit	2 310	**1.1**	**.5**	**.5**	**.3**	**.4**	**.5**	**.6**	...
Compensation of employees, debit	3 310	**–6.5**	**–6.3**	**–7.7**	**–7.2**	**–9.1**	**–6.7**	**–4.5**	...
Investment income, credit	2 320	**16.4**	**25.6**	**22.4**	**25.8**	**25.6**	**34.5**	**26.9**	...
Direct investment income	2 330	.1	.7	.9	.1	.6	.9	2.7	...
Dividends and distributed branch profits	2 332	.1	.7	.9	.1	.6	.9	2.7	...
Reinvested earnings and undistributed branch profits	2 333	...	...	...	...	...	...	...	...
Income on debt (interest)	2 334	...	...	...	...	...	...	...	...
Portfolio investment income	2 339	...	...	...	...	...	...	.2	...
Income on equity	2 340	...	...	...	...	...	...	.2	...
Income on bonds and notes	2 350	...	...	...	...	...	...	...	...
Income on money market instruments and financial derivatives	2 360	...	...	...	...	...	...	...	...
Other investment income	2 370	16.3	24.9	21.6	25.8	25.0	33.6	24.1	...
Investment income, debit	3 320	**–227.4**	**–229.8**	**–278.5**	**–270.8**	**–293.2**	**–280.4**	**–316.7**	...
Direct investment income	3 330	–61.6	–69.6	–92.3	–71.4	–73.6	–60.8	–110.5	...
Dividends and distributed branch profits	3 332	–61.6	–69.6	–92.3	–71.4	–73.6	–60.8	–110.5	...
Reinvested earnings and undistributed branch profits	3 333	...	...	...	...	...	...	...	...
Income on debt (interest)	3 334	...	...	...	...	...	...	...	...
Portfolio investment income	3 339	...	...	...	...	...	...	–1.8	...
Income on equity	3 340	...	...	...	...	...	...	...	...
Income on bonds and notes	3 350	...	...	...	...	...	...	–1.8	...
Income on money market instruments and financial derivatives	3 360	...	...	...	...	...	...	...	...
Other investment income	3 370	–165.8	–160.2	–186.2	–199.4	–219.6	–219.6	–204.4	...
D. CURRENT TRANSFERS	4 379	61.1	67.0	112.2	100.8	282.9	205.9	39.6	...
Credit	2 379	**211.2**	**211.4**	**204.0**	**191.7**	**347.3**	**270.6**	**69.4**	...
General government	2 380	65.7	78.6	108.3	94.7	241.9	179.2	...	...
Other sectors	2 390	145.5	132.8	95.7	97.1	105.4	91.4	69.4	...
Workers' remittances	2 391	...	...	...	...	...	...	...	...
Other current transfers	2 392	145.5	132.8	95.7	97.1	105.4	91.4	69.4	...
Debit	3 379	**–150.1**	**–144.3**	**–91.8**	**–90.9**	**–64.4**	**–64.7**	**–29.8**	...
General government	3 380	...	–.1	–.1	–.1	–.1	–.2	...	...
Other sectors	3 390	–150.1	–144.3	–91.7	–90.8	–64.3	–64.5	–29.8	...
Workers' remittances	3 391	...	–1.7	–1.4	...	...	...	–1.7	...
Other current transfers	3 392	–150.1	–142.6	–90.3	–90.8	–64.3	–64.5	–28.1	...
CAPITAL AND FINANCIAL ACCOUNT	4 996	**–62.3**	**86.9**	**149.8**	**488.4**	**566.5**	**100.8**	**344.7**	...
CAPITAL ACCOUNT	4 994	**–8.6**	**–7.6**	**–7.0**	**–2.8**	**–1.4**	**–.4**	**284.4**	...
Total credit	2 994	*.3*	*.2*	*.4*	*.1*	*.2*	*.6*	*285.4*	...
Total debit	3 994	*–9.0*	*–7.9*	*–7.4*	*–2.9*	*–1.6*	*–1.0*	*–1.0*	...
Capital transfers, credit	2 400	**.3**	**.2**	**.4**	**.1**	**.2**	**.6**	**285.4**	...
General government	2 401	...	...	...	...	...	...	183.2	...
Debt forgiveness	2 402	...	...	...	...	...	...	...	...
Other capital transfers	2 410	...	...	...	...	...	...	183.2	...
Other sectors	2 430	.3	.2	.4	.1	.2	.6	102.3	...
Migrants' transfers	2 431	.3	.2	.4	.1	.2	.6	43.1	...
Debt forgiveness	2 432	...	...	...	...	...	...	...	...
Other capital transfers	2 440	...	...	...	...	...	...	59.1	...
Capital transfers, debit	3 400	**–9.0**	**–7.9**	**–7.4**	**–2.9**	**–1.6**	**–1.0**	**–1.0**	...
General government	3 401	...	...	...	...	...	...	...	...
Debt forgiveness	3 402	...	...	...	...	...	...	...	...
Other capital transfers	3 410	...	...	...	...	...	...	...	...
Other sectors	3 430	–9.0	–7.9	–7.4	–2.9	–1.6	–1.0	–1.0	...
Migrants' transfers	3 431	–9.0	–7.9	–7.4	–2.9	–1.6	–1.0	–1.0	...
Debt forgiveness	3 432	...	...	...	...	...	...	...	...
Other capital transfers	3 440	...	...	...	...	...	...	...	...
Nonproduced nonfinancial assets, credit	2 480	...	...	...	...	...	...	...	...
Nonproduced nonfinancial assets, debit	3 480	...	...	...	...	...	...	...	...

Table 2 (Continued). STANDARD PRESENTATION, 1988–95
(Millions of U.S. dollars)

	Code	1988	1989	1990	1991	1992	1993	1994	1995
FINANCIAL ACCOUNT	4 995 . .	**–53.6**	**94.5**	**156.8**	**491.2**	**568.0**	**101.2**	**60.3**	**. . .**
A. DIRECT INVESTMENT	4 500 . .	4.1	–10.2	–12.2	2.8	15.0	28.0	30.0	. . .
Direct investment abroad	4 505 . .	**22.2**	**. . .**	**. . .**	**. . .**	**. . .**	**. . .**	**–4.7**	**. . .**
Equity capital	4 510 . .	22.2	. . .	. . .	. . .	. . .	. . .	–4.7	. . .
Claims on affiliated enterprises	4 515 . .	. . .	. . .	. . .	. . .	. . .	. . .	–4.7	. . .
Liabilities to affiliated enterprises	4 520 . .	. . .	. . .	. . .	. . .	. . .	. . .	. . .	. . .
Reinvested earnings	4 525 . .	. . .	. . .	. . .	. . .	. . .	. . .	. . .	. . .
Other capital	4 530 . .	. . .	. . .	. . .	. . .	. . .	. . .	. . .	. . .
Claims on affiliated enterprises	4 535 . .	. . .	. . .	. . .	. . .	. . .	. . .	. . .	. . .
Liabilities to affiliated enterprises	4 540 . .	. . .	. . .	. . .	. . .	. . .	. . .	. . .	. . .
Direct investment in Zimbabwe	4 555 . .	**–18.1**	**–10.2**	**–12.2**	**2.8**	**15.0**	**28.0**	**34.7**	**. . .**
Equity capital	4 560 . .	–18.1	–10.2	–12.2	2.8	15.0	28.0	34.7	. . .
Claims on direct investors	4 565 . .	. . .	. . .	. . .	. . .	. . .	. . .	. . .	. . .
Liabilities to direct investors	4 570 . .	. . .	. . .	. . .	. . .	. . .	. . .	34.7	. . .
Reinvested earnings	4 575 . .	. . .	. . .	. . .	. . .	. . .	. . .	. . .	. . .
Other capital	4 580 . .	. . .	. . .	. . .	. . .	. . .	. . .	. . .	. . .
Claims on direct investors	4 585 . .	. . .	. . .	. . .	. . .	. . .	. . .	. . .	. . .
Liabilities to direct investors	4 590 . .	. . .	. . .	. . .	. . .	. . .	. . .	. . .	. . .
B. PORTFOLIO INVESTMENT	4 600 . .	–60.9	–36.7	–21.7	7.3	–9.5	–5.1	50.2	. . .
Assets	4 602 . .	**. . .**	**. . .**	**10.4**	**41.8**	**27.6**	**. . .**	**. . .**	**. . .**
Equity securities	4 610 . .	. . .	. . .	. . .	. . .	. . .	. . .	. . .	. . .
Monetary authorities	4 611 . .	. . .	. . .	. . .	. . .	. . .	. . .	. . .	. . .
General government	4 612 . .	. . .	. . .	. . .	. . .	. . .	. . .	. . .	. . .
Banks	4 613 . .	. . .	. . .	. . .	. . .	. . .	. . .	. . .	. . .
Other sectors	4 614 . .	. . .	. . .	. . .	. . .	. . .	. . .	. . .	. . .
Debt securities	4 619 . .	. . .	. . .	10.4	41.8	27.6	. . .	. . .	. . .
Bonds and notes	4 620 . .	. . .	. . .	10.4	41.8	27.6	. . .	. . .	. . .
Monetary authorities	4 621 . .	. . .	. . .	. . .	. . .	. . .	. . .	. . .	. . .
General government	4 622 . .	. . .	. . .	. . .	. . .	. . .	. . .	. . .	. . .
Banks	4 623 . .	. . .	. . .	. . .	. . .	. . .	. . .	. . .	. . .
Other sectors	4 624 . .	. . .	. . .	. . .	. . .	. . .	. . .	. . .	. . .
Money market instruments	4 630 . .	. . .	. . .	. . .	. . .	. . .	. . .	. . .	. . .
Monetary authorities	4 631 . .	. . .	. . .	. . .	. . .	. . .	. . .	. . .	. . .
General government	4 632 . .	. . .	. . .	. . .	. . .	. . .	. . .	. . .	. . .
Banks	4 633 . .	. . .	. . .	. . .	. . .	. . .	. . .	. . .	. . .
Other sectors	4 634 . .	. . .	. . .	. . .	. . .	. . .	. . .	. . .	. . .
Financial derivatives	4 640 . .	. . .	. . .	. . .	. . .	. . .	. . .	. . .	. . .
Monetary authorities	4 641 . .	. . .	. . .	. . .	. . .	. . .	. . .	. . .	. . .
General government	4 642 . .	. . .	. . .	. . .	. . .	. . .	. . .	. . .	. . .
Banks	4 643 . .	. . .	. . .	. . .	. . .	. . .	. . .	. . .	. . .
Other sectors	4 644 . .	. . .	. . .	. . .	. . .	. . .	. . .	. . .	. . .
Liabilities	4 652 . .	**–60.9**	**–36.7**	**–32.1**	**–34.6**	**–37.1**	**–5.1**	**50.2**	**. . .**
Equity securities	4 660 . .	. . .	. . .	. . .	. . .	. . .	. . .	56.9	. . .
Banks	4 663 . .	. . .	. . .	. . .	. . .	. . .	. . .	. . .	. . .
Other sectors	4 664 . .	. . .	. . .	. . .	. . .	. . .	. . .	56.9	. . .
Debt securities	4 669 . .	–60.9	–36.7	–32.1	–34.6	–37.1	–5.1	–6.7	. . .
Bonds and notes	4 670 . .	–60.9	–36.7	–32.1	–34.6	–37.1	–5.1	–6.7	. . .
Monetary authorities	4 671 . .	. . .	. . .	. . .	. . .	. . .	. . .	. . .	. . .
General government	4 672 . .	–60.9	–36.7	–32.1	–34.6	–37.1	–5.1	–6.7	. . .
Banks	4 673 . .	. . .	. . .	. . .	. . .	. . .	. . .	. . .	. . .
Other sectors	4 674 . .	. . .	. . .	. . .	. . .	. . .	. . .	. . .	. . .
Money market instruments	4 680 . .	. . .	. . .	. . .	. . .	. . .	. . .	. . .	. . .
Monetary authorities	4 681 . .	. . .	. . .	. . .	. . .	. . .	. . .	. . .	. . .
General government	4 682 . .	. . .	. . .	. . .	. . .	. . .	. . .	. . .	. . .
Banks	4 683 . .	. . .	. . .	. . .	. . .	. . .	. . .	. . .	. . .
Other sectors	4 684 . .	. . .	. . .	. . .	. . .	. . .	. . .	. . .	. . .
Financial derivatives	4 690 . .	. . .	. . .	. . .	. . .	. . .	. . .	. . .	. . .
Monetary authorities	4 691 . .	. . .	. . .	. . .	. . .	. . .	. . .	. . .	. . .
General government	4 692 . .	. . .	. . .	. . .	. . .	. . .	. . .	. . .	. . .
Banks	4 693 . .	. . .	. . .	. . .	. . .	. . .	. . .	. . .	. . .
Other sectors	4 694 . .	. . .	. . .	. . .	. . .	. . .	. . .	. . .	. . .

Table 2 (Concluded). STANDARD PRESENTATION, 1988–95
(Millions of U.S. dollars)

	Code	1988	1989	1990	1991	1992	1993	1994	1995
C. OTHER INVESTMENT	4 700 . .	26.2	55.9	253.5	519.5	593.6	371.9	–32.8	. . .
Assets	4 703 . .	**4.9**	**. . .**	**. . .**	**38.0**	**15.9**	**99.9**	**–260.3**	**. . .**
Trade credits	4 706 . .	. . .	. . .	. . .	. . .	. . .	. . .	. . .	. . .
General government: long-term	4 708 . .	. . .	. . .	. . .	. . .	. . .	. . .	. . .	. . .
General government: short-term	4 709 . .	. . .	. . .	. . .	. . .	. . .	. . .	. . .	. . .
Other sectors: long-term	4 711 . .	. . .	. . .	. . .	. . .	. . .	. . .	. . .	. . .
Other sectors: short-term	4 712 . .	. . .	. . .	. . .	. . .	. . .	. . .	. . .	. . .
Loans	4 714 . .	. . .	. . .	. . .	. . .	. . .	. . .	. . .	. . .
Monetary authorities: long-term	4 717 . .	. . .	. . .	. . .	. . .	. . .	. . .	. . .	. . .
Monetary authorities: short-term	4 718 . .	. . .	. . .	. . .	. . .	. . .	. . .	. . .	. . .
General government: long-term	4 720 . .	. . .	. . .	. . .	. . .	. . .	. . .	. . .	. . .
General government: short-term	4 721 . .	. . .	. . .	. . .	. . .	. . .	. . .	. . .	. . .
Banks: long-term	4 723 . .	. . .	. . .	. . .	. . .	. . .	. . .	. . .	. . .
Banks: short-term	4 724 . .	. . .	. . .	. . .	. . .	. . .	. . .	. . .	. . .
Other sectors: long-term	4 726 . .	. . .	. . .	. . .	. . .	. . .	. . .	. . .	. . .
Other sectors: short-term	4 727 . .	. . .	. . .	. . .	. . .	. . .	. . .	. . .	. . .
Currency and deposits	4 730 . .	4.9	. . .	. . .	38.0	15.9	99.9	–260.3	. . .
Monetary authorities	4 731 . .	. . .	. . .	. . .	. . .	. . .	. . .	. . .	. . .
General government	4 732 . .	. . .	. . .	. . .	. . .	. . .	. . .	. . .	. . .
Banks	4 733 . .	4.9	. . .	. . .	38.0	15.9	99.9	–260.3	. . .
Other sectors	4 734 . .	. . .	. . .	. . .	. . .	. . .	. . .	. . .	. . .
Other assets	4 736 . .	. . .	. . .	. . .	. . .	. . .	. . .	. . .	. . .
Monetary authorities: long-term	4 738 . .	. . .	. . .	. . .	. . .	. . .	. . .	. . .	. . .
Monetary authorities: short-term	4 739 . .	. . .	. . .	. . .	. . .	. . .	. . .	. . .	. . .
General government: long-term	4 741 . .	. . .	. . .	. . .	. . .	. . .	. . .	. . .	. . .
General government: short-term	4 742 . .	. . .	. . .	. . .	. . .	. . .	. . .	. . .	. . .
Banks: long-term	4 744 . .	. . .	. . .	. . .	. . .	. . .	. . .	. . .	. . .
Banks: short-term	4 745 . .	. . .	. . .	. . .	. . .	. . .	. . .	. . .	. . .
Other sectors: long-term	4 747 . .	. . .	. . .	. . .	. . .	. . .	. . .	. . .	. . .
Other sectors: short-term	4 748 . .	. . .	. . .	. . .	. . .	. . .	. . .	. . .	. . .
Liabilities	4 753 . .	**21.2**	**55.9**	**253.5**	**481.5**	**577.7**	**272.0**	**227.5**	**. . .**
Trade credits	4 756 . .	. . .	. . .	. . .	. . .	. . .	. . .	219.5	. . .
General government: long-term	4 758 . .	. . .	. . .	. . .	. . .	. . .	. . .	. . .	. . .
General government: short-term	4 759 . .	. . .	. . .	. . .	. . .	. . .	. . .	. . .	. . .
Other sectors: long-term	4 761 . .	. . .	. . .	. . .	. . .	. . .	. . .	. . .	. . .
Other sectors: short-term	4 762 . .	. . .	. . .	. . .	. . .	. . .	. . .	219.5	. . .
Loans	4 764 . .	21.2	49.8	141.4	352.8	656.0	279.9	117.9	. . .
Use of Fund credit and loans from the Fund	4 766 . .	–78.6	–38.8	–23.0	–6.9	225.7	67.7	72.8	. . .
Monetary authorities: other long-term	4 767 . .	. . .	. . .	. . .	. . .	. . .	. . .	. . .	. . .
Monetary authorities: short-term	4 768 . .	. . .	. . .	. . .	. . .	. . .	. . .	. . .	. . .
General government: long-term	4 770 . .	72.2	67.6	88.6	187.3	450.1	228.7	86.6	. . .
General government: short-term	4 771 . .	–1.8	. . .	. . .	87.7	–42.1	–37.7	–24.6	. . .
Banks: long-term	4 773 . .	. . .	. . .	. . .	. . .	. . .	. . .	. . .	. . .
Banks: short-term	4 774 . .	. . .	. . .	. . .	. . .	. . .	. . .	. . .	. . .
Other sectors: long-term	4 776 . .	20.5	21.0	75.8	84.7	22.3	21.2	–16.9	. . .
Other sectors: short-term	4 777 . .	8.9	. . .	. . .	. . .	. . .	. . .	. . .	. . .
Currency and deposits	4 780 . .	. . .	3.1	14.6	. . .	. . .	. . .	. . .	. . .
Monetary authorities	4 781 . .	. . .	. . .	. . .	. . .	. . .	. . .	. . .	. . .
General government	4 782 . .	. . .	. . .	. . .	. . .	. . .	. . .	. . .	. . .
Banks	4 783 . .	. . .	3.1	14.6	. . .	. . .	. . .	. . .	. . .
Other sectors	4 784 . .	. . .	. . .	. . .	. . .	. . .	. . .	. . .	. . .
Other liabilities	4 786 . .	. . .	3.0	97.6	128.7	–78.2	–7.8	–109.9	. . .
Monetary authorities: long-term	4 788 . .	. . .	. . .	. . .	. . .	. . .	. . .	. . .	. . .
Monetary authorities: short-term	4 789 . .	. . .	3.0	97.6	128.7	–78.2	–7.8	–109.9	. . .
General government: long-term	4 791 . .	. . .	. . .	. . .	. . .	. . .	. . .	. . .	. . .
General government: short-term	4 792 . .	. . .	. . .	. . .	. . .	. . .	. . .	. . .	. . .
Banks: long-term	4 794 . .	. . .	. . .	. . .	. . .	. . .	. . .	. . .	. . .
Banks: short-term	4 795 . .	. . .	. . .	. . .	. . .	. . .	. . .	. . .	. . .
Other sectors: long-term	4 797 . .	. . .	. . .	. . .	. . .	. . .	. . .	. . .	. . .
Other sectors: short-term	4 798 . .	. . .	. . .	. . .	. . .	. . .	. . .	. . .	. . .
D. RESERVE ASSETS	4 800 . .	–23.0	85.5	–62.8	–38.4	–31.1	–293.6	12.9	. . .
Monetary gold	4 810 . .	. . .	. . .	. . .	–38.5	–19.7	–16.8	–7.8	. . .
Special drawing rights	4 820 . .	21.9	–.1	.5	.1	–.3	–.5	.9	. . .
Reserve position in the Fund	4 830 . .	. . .	. . .	. . .	. . .	. . .	. . .	. . .	. . .
Foreign exchange	4 840 . .	–44.9	85.6	–63.3	. . .	–11.2	–276.3	19.9	. . .
Other claims	4 880 . .	. . .	. . .	. . .	. . .	. . .	. . .	. . .	. . .
NET ERRORS AND OMISSIONS	4 998 . .	**–63.0**	**–103.8**	**–9.9**	**–31.4**	**37.2**	**14.9**	**80.2**	**. . .**

Part 3 of the *Yearbook* contains descriptions of the methodologies, compilation practices, and sources used to compile these data.